Best Books for
Middle School and
Junior High Readers

Recent Titles in the
Children's and Young Adult Literature Reference Series
Catherine Barr, Series Editor

War and Peace: A Guide to Literature and New Media, Grades 4–8
Virginia A. Walter

Across Cultures: A Guide to Multicultural Literature for Children
Kathy East and Rebecca L. Thomas

Best Books for Children, Supplement to the 8th Edition: Preschool
through Grade 6
Catherine Barr and John T. Gillespie

Best Books for Boys: A Resource for Educators
Matthew D. Zbaracki

Beyond Picture Books: Subject Access to Best Books for
Beginning Readers
Barbara Barstow, Judith Riggle, and Leslie Molnar

A to Zoo: Subject Access to Children's Picture Books. Supplement to the
7th Edition
Carolyn W. Lima and Rebecca L. Thomas

Gentle Reads: Great Books to Warm Hearts and Lift Spirits, Grades 5–9
Deanna J. McDaniel

Best New Media, K–12: A Guide to Movies, Subscription Web Sites, and
Educational Software and Games
Catherine Barr

Historical Fiction for Young Readers (Grades 4–8): An Introduction
John T. Gillespie

Twice Upon a Time: A Guide to Fractured, Altered, and Retold Folk and
Fairy Tales
Catharine Bomhold and Terri E. Elder

Popular Series Fiction for K–6 Readers: A Reading and Selection Guide.
2nd Edition
Rebecca L. Thomas and Catherine Barr

Popular Series Fiction for Middle School and Teen Readers: A Reading
and Selection Guide. 2nd Edition
Rebecca L. Thomas and Catherine Barr

Best Books for Middle School and Junior High Readers

GRADES 6–9

2nd edition

Catherine Barr and John T. Gillespie

Children's and Young Adult Literature Reference

Catherine Barr, Series Editor

A Member of the Greenwood Publishing Group

Westport, Connecticut • London

Library of Congress Cataloging-in-Publication Data

Barr, Catherine, 1951–
    Best books for middle school and junior high readers : grades 6–9 / Catherine Barr and John T. Gillespie.
— 2nd ed.
        p. cm. — (Children's and young adult literature reference)
    Gillespie's name appears first on the earlier edition.
    Includes bibliographical references and indexes.
    ISBN 978-1-59158-573-2 (alk. paper)
    1. Middle school students—Books and reading—United States. 2. Junior high school students—Books
and reading—United States. 3. Preteens—Books and reading—United States. 4. Teenagers—Books and
reading—United States. 5. Children's literature—Bibliography. 6. Young adult literature—Bibliography.
7. Middle school libraries—United States—Book lists. 8. Junior high school libraries—United States—
Book lists. I. Gillespie, John Thomas, 1928– II. Title.
    Z1037.G482   2009
    028.5'35--dc22   2008050755

British Library Cataloguing in Publication Data is available.

Library of Congress Catalog Card Number: 2008050755
ISBN: 978-1-59158-573-2

First published in 2009

Libraries Unlimited, 88 Post Road West, Westport, CT 06881
A Member of the Greenwood Publishing Group, Inc.
www.lu.com

Printed in the United States of America

The paper used in this book complies with the
Permanent Paper Standard issued by the National
Information Standards Organization (Z39.48–1984).

10   9   8   7   6   5   4   3   2   1

Contents

Literary Forms

Literary History and Criticism

Language and Communication

Biography, Memoirs, Etc.

The Arts and Entertainment

History and Geography

Philosophy and Religion

Society and the Individual

Guidance and Personal Development

Physical and Applied Sciences

Contents

Recreation and Sports

Major Subjects Arranged Alphabetically

Preface

Librarians and other specialists in children's literature have available, through print and online sources, a large number of bibliographies that recommend books suitable for young people. Unfortunately, these sources vary widely in quality and usefulness. The Best Books series was created to furnish authoritative, reliable, and comprehensive bibliographies for use in libraries that collect materials for readers from preschool through grade 12. The series now consists of three volumes: *Best Books for Children, Best Books for Middle School and Junior High Readers*, and *Best Books for High School Readers*. A companion volume is *Best New Media* (Libraries Unlimited, 2008).

Best Books for Middle School and Junior High Readers, Second Edition is a continuation of *Best Books for Children, Eighth Edition* (Libraries Unlimited, 2006) and its two-year supplement (Libraries Unlimited, 2007). *Best Books for Middle School and Junior High Readers* supplies information on books recommended for readers in grades 6 through 9 or roughly ages 11 through 15. *Best Books for Children* contains books recommended for preschool through grade 6 readers and *Best Books for High School Readers, Second Edition* (Libraries Unlimited, 2009) covers grades 9 through 12.

As every librarian knows, reading levels are elastic. There is no such thing, for example, as a seventh-grade book. Instead there are only seventh-grade readers who, in their diversity, can represent a wide range of reading abilities and interests. This bibliography contains a liberal selection of entries that, one hopes, will accommodate readers in these grades and make allowance for their great range of tastes and reading competencies. By the ninth grade, a percentage of the books read should be at the adult level. Keeping this in mind, about one fifth of the entries in this volume are adult books suitable for young adult readers (they are designated by reading level grades of 6–12, 7–12, and 8–12 within the entries). At the other end of the spectrum, there are also many titles that are suitable for readers below the sixth grade (indicated by grade level designations such as 4–7, 4–8, 4–9,

5–7, and 5–8 within the entries). This has resulted in a slight duplication of titles in this book with those in *Best Books for Children*. Similarly, there is a slight overlap with *Best Books for High School Readers*.

In selecting books for inclusion, deciding on their arrangement, and collecting the information supplied on each, it was the editors' intention to reflect the current needs and interests of young readers while keeping in mind the latest trends and curricular emphases in today's schools.

General Scope and Criteria for Inclusion

Of the 14,588 titles listed in *Best Books for Middle School and Junior High Readers*, 13,793 are individually numbered entries and 795 are cited within the annotations as additional recommended titles by the same author (often these are titles that are part of an extensive series). It should be noted that some series are so extensive that, because of space limitations, only representative titles are included.

Excluded from this bibliography are general reference works, such as dictionaries and encyclopedias, except for a few single-volume works that are so heavily illustrated and attractive that they can also be used in the general circulation collection. Also excluded are professional books for librarians and teachers and mass market series books.

For most fiction and nonfiction, a minimum of two recommendations were required from the current reviewing sources consulted for a title to be considered for listing. However, there were a number of necessary exceptions. For example, in some reviewing journals only a few representative titles from extensive nonfiction series are reviewed even though others in the series will also be recommended. In such cases a single favorable review was enough for inclusion. This also held true for some of the adult titles suitable for young adult readers where, it has been found, reviewing journals tend to be less inclusive than with juvenile titles. Again, depending on the strength of the review, a single positive one was sufficient for inclusion. As well as favorable reviews, additional criteria such as availability, currency, accuracy, usefulness, and relevance were considered. All titles were in print as of the end of October 2008.

Sources Used

A number of current and retrospective sources were used in compiling this bibliography. Book reviewing journals consulted were *Booklist*, *Library Media Connection* (formerly *Book Report*), *School Library Journal*, and *VOYA (Voice of Youth Advocates)*. Other sources used include *Bulletin of the Center for Children's Books*, *Horn Book*, and *Horn Book Guide*. Reviews in issues of these journals were read and evaluated from January 2004 through July 2008, when this book's coverage ends.

Uses of This Book

Best Books for Middle School and Junior High Readers was designed to help librarians and media specialists with four vital tasks: (1) evaluating the adequacy of existing collections; (2) building new collections or strengthening existing holdings; (3) providing reading guidance to young adults; and (4) preparing bibliographies and reading lists. To increase the book's usefulness, particularly in preparation of bibliographies or suggested reading lists, titles are arranged under broad areas of interest or, in the case of nonfiction works, by curriculum-oriented subjects rather than the Dewey Decimal classification (suggested Dewey classification numbers are nevertheless provided within nonfiction entries). The subject arrangement corresponds roughly to the one used in *Best Books for Children*, minus its large section on picture books.

Some arbitrary decisions were made concerning placement of books under specific subjects. For example, books of experiments and projects in general science are placed under "Physical and Applied Sciences—Experiments and Projects," whereas books of experiments and projects on a specific branch of science (e.g., physics) appear under that branch. It is hoped that use of the many "see" and "see also" references in the Subject/Grade Level Index will help guide the user in this regard.

With this edition, we have added a symbol ⑨ to indicate that an audio version of the book is available; we expect to see increasing use of this symbol with each new edition.

Arrangement

In the Table of Contents, subjects are arranged by the order in which they appear in the book. Following the Table of Contents is a listing of Major Subjects Arranged Alphabetically, which provides entry numbers as well as page numbers for easy access. Following the main body of the text, there are three indexes. The Author Index cites authors and editors, titles, and entry numbers (joint authors and editors are listed separately). The Title Index gives the book's entry number. Works of fiction in both of these indexes are indicated by (F) following the entry number. Finally, an extensive Subject/Grade Level Index lists entry numbers under hundreds of subject headings with specific grade-level suitability given for each entry. The following codes are used to identify general grade levels:

IJ (Intermediate–Junior High) suitable for upper elementary and lower middle school

J   (Junior High) suitable for middle school and junior high

JS (Junior–Senior High) suitable for junior high and senior high

Entries

A typical entry contains the following information where applicable: (1) author, joint author, or editor; (2) title and subtitle; (3) specific grade levels given in parentheses; (4) adapter or translator; (5) indication of illustrations; (6) publication date; (7) publisher and price of hardbound edition (LB = library binding); (8) International Standard Book Number (ISBN) of hardbound edition; (9) paperback publisher (paper) and price (if no publisher is listed it is the same as the hardbound edition); (10) ISBN of paperback edition; (11) annotation; (12) review citations; (13) Dewey Decimal classification number; (14) indication that an audio version is available.

Review Citations

Review citations are given for books published and reviewed from 1985 through July 2008. These citations can be used to find more detailed information about each of the books listed. The periodical sources identified are:

Booklist (BL)
Bulletin of the Center for Children's Books (BCCB)
Book Report (BR)
Horn Book (HB)
Horn Book Guide (HBG)
Library Media Connection (LMC)
School Library Journal (SLJ)
VOYA (Voice of Youth Advocates) (VOYA)

Additional Pointers for Users

For series that contain an extensive number of titles — numbered graphic novel series, for example — only a representative number of books are listed. For more complete listings of titles, it is suggested that the user consult Books in Print (Bowker), book jobbers' catalogs (print or online), author or publisher Web sites, or the Web sites of such online booksellers as Amazon (amazon.com) and Barnes and Noble (bn.com).

All graphic novels are collected in one section, which includes graphic adaptations of classics such as *Moby Dick*.

Anthologies of short stories on a single subject are found under that subject (an anthology of science fiction short stories will be listed under "Science Fiction," for example), but general anthologies or collections by a single author on diverse subjects are listed in the "Short Stories and General Anthologies" section.

Similarly, books of experiments and projects on a specific subject in science are placed under that subject, but general science project books are in the section "Physical and Applied Sciences — Experiments and Projects."

Books of criticism about individual authors, even though they contain some biographical information, are placed in the "Literary History and Criticism" section.

Books on World War II are found in the "World War II and Holocaust" section but books on internal conditions in the United States during this period are found in the United States history section under "World War II."

Books on the history of specific ethnic groups (for example, books that are historical accounts of African American slavery) are generally found in the "Ethnic Groups and Prejudice" section.

Acknowledgments

Many people were involved in the preparation of this bibliography. In particular, we are grateful to Barbara Ittner of Libraries Unlimited and to Julie Miller and Christine McNaull, who make production of this book possible. Thanks are also due to Susan Olmstead, Janell Cipriano, and Kris Aparicio for their contributions.

Catherine Barr
John Gillespie

Literary Forms

Fiction

Adventure and Survival Stories

1 Aaron, Chester. *Lackawanna* (6–9). 1986, Harper-Collins LB $11.89 (978-0-397-32058-5). In Depression New York, the youthful Lackawanna gang sets out to find a member who has been kidnapped. (Rev: BL 2/15/86; SLJ 4/86; VOYA 6/86)

2 Aaron, Chester. *Out of Sight, Out of Mind* (6–9). 1985, HarperCollins LB $11.89 (978-0-397-32101-8). Twins with psychic powers are pursued by foreign agents who want their secret. (Rev: VOYA 12/85)

3 Adams, W. Royce. *Me and Jay* (5–8). 2001, Rairarubia paper $10.99 (978-1-58832-021-6). Two 13-year-olds meet with trouble at every turn when they venture into forbidden territory in search of a hidden pond. (Rev: BL 1/1–15/02)

4 Aiken, Joan. *Midnight Is a Place* (7–10). Series: Wolves Chronicles. 1974, Scholastic paper $2.95 (978-0-590-45496-4). In Victorian England, two young waifs are cast adrift in a hostile town when their guardian's house burns.

5 Aiken, Joan. *Midwinter Nightingale* (5–8). Series: Wolves Chronicles. 2003, Delacorte $15.95 (978-0-385-73081-5). Dido Twite and Simon, Duke of Battersea, continue their adventures in this eighth installment in the series, protecting a dying king, searching for a missing coronet, and defeating an evil baron. (Rev: BL 6/1–15/03; HBG 10/03; SLJ 6/03)

6 Alexander, Lloyd. *The Golden Dreams of Carlo Chuchio* (5–8). 2007, Holt $17.95 (978-0-8050-8333-0). The final book by the late Alexander takes Carlo along the Road of Golden Dreams in search of treasure. (Rev: BCCB 10/07; BL 7/07; HB 9–10/07; LMC 2/08; SLJ 8/07)

7 Alexander, Lloyd. *The Xanadu Adventure* (5–8). 2005, Button $16.99 (978-0-525-47371-8). Vesper Holly, accompanied by friends and guardians, sets off for Asia Minor to search for an artifact in the ancient city of Troy but soon finds herself in the clutches of her nemesis, Dr. Desmond Helvitius. (Rev: BL 2/1/05*; SLJ 2/05)

8 Allende, Isabel. *Kingdom of the Golden Dragon* (7–12). 2004, HarperCollins $19.99 (978-0-06-058942-4). Yetis, high in the Himalayas, help 16-year-old Alexander in his fight against American corporate villains in this sequel to *City of the Beasts*. (Rev: BL 2/15/04; SLJ 4/04)

9 Allison, Jennifer. *Gilda Joyce: The Ladies of the Lake* (5–8). 2006, Dutton $16.99 (978-0-525-47693-1). Thirteen-year-old Gilda Joyce — introduced in *Gilda Joyce: Psychic Investigator* (2005) — uses all her psychic abilities to unravel the mystery surrounding a drowning death at her school. (Rev: BL 10/15/06; HBG 4/07; SLJ 9/06)

10 Anderson, M. T. *Whales on Stilts!* (5–7). 2005, Harcourt $15.00 (978-0-15-205340-6). Twelve-year-old Lily Gefelty enlists the help of two friends to foil a plan to take over the world using an army of mind-controlled whales on stilts; a fast-paced adventure full of tongue-in-cheek fun. (Rev: BL 2/15/05*; SLJ 5/05)

11 Anderson, Scott. *Unknown Rider* (6–9). 1995, Dennoch Pr. paper $12.50 (978-0-9644521-0-7). Combining fact and fiction, this is the story of fighter pilot Rick Wedon — his training, experiences in officer school, and his missions. (Rev: VOYA 8/96)

12 Asai, Carrie. *The Book of the Sword* (6–12). Series: Samurai Girl. 2003, Simon & Schuster paper

$6.99 (978-0-689-85948-9). Heaven abandons her adoptive family when her brother is murdered in the middle of her arranged wedding and devotes herself to studying to be a samurai and avenging her brother. (Rev: SLJ 8/03)

13 Ashby, John. *Sea Gift* (6–8). 2003, Clarion $15.00 (978-0-395-77603-2). Lauchie and his friends set off on an exciting treasure hunt on the coast of Cape Breton Island after they discover a pistol and letter dating to 1632. (Rev: BL 9/15/03; SLJ 12/03)

14 Ashley, Bernard. *Break in the Sun* (6–9). Illus. 1980, Phillips $26.95 (978-0-87599-230-3). Patsy Bleigh runs away on a ship belonging to a theatrical company.

15 Ashley, Bernard. *A Kind of Wild Justice* (6–9). Illus. 1978, Phillips $26.95 (978-0-87599-229-7). Ronnie is threatened by the same gang that made his father a criminal.

16 Avi. *Captain Grey* (5–8). 1993, Morrow paper $4.95 (978-0-688-12234-8). In 1783, young Kevin is captured by pirates. A reissue.

17 Avi. *Windcatcher* (4–7). 1991, Avon paper $4.99 (978-0-380-71805-4). Eleven-year-old Tony dreads a summer by the sea, but ends up finding a sailing adventure. (Rev: BCCB 5/91; BL 3/1/91; HB 5–6/91; SLJ 4/91)

18 Baird, Thomas. *Finding Fever* (6–8). 1982, HarperCollins $12.95 (978-0-06-020353-5). Kidnappers make off with Benny's sister's dog, and Benny sets out to investigate.

19 Bawden, Nina. *Rebel on a Rock* (6–8). 1978, HarperCollins LB $13.89 (978-0-397-32140-7). Jo reluctantly believes that her stepfather is a spy for a cruel dictator.

20 Bernardo, Anilú. *Jumping Off to Freedom* (7–10). 1996, Arte Publico paper $9.95 (978-1-55885-088-0). The story of four refugees, including teenage David, on a harrowing voyage from Cuba to Florida on a raft. (Rev: BL 5/1/96; SLJ 7/96; VOYA 6/96)

21 Blades, Ann. *A Boy of Tache* (6–9). 1995, Tundra paper $5.95 (978-0-88776-350-2). A Canadian novel of a boy's trek through the wilderness to save his grandfather's life.

22 Bledsoe, Lucy Jane. *The Antarctic Scoop* (4–7). 2003, Holiday House $16.95 (978-0-8234-1792-6). In this fast-paced adventure story, 12-year-old Victoria, a shy girl with ambitious dreams, wins a trip to Antarctica but discovers during her travels that the real goal of the contest sponsor is to develop and exploit the icy continent. (Rev: BL 1/1–15/04; SLJ 1/04)

23 Bodeen, S. A. *The Compound* (7–12). 2008, Feiwel and Friends $16.95 (978-0-312-37015-2). Eli and members of his family have lived in an elaborate underground shelter for years, believing that the world as they knew it was destroyed. But was it? Or did Eli's wealthy father have other reasons for building the compound? (Rev: BL 4/15/08; SLJ 7/08)

24 Bodett, Tom. *Williwaw* (5–8). 1999, Random paper $5.50 (978-0-375-80687-2). The story of two youngsters — 13-year-old September Crane and her 12-year-old brother Ivan — and their life in the wilds of Alaska, where they are often left alone by their fisherman father. (Rev: BCCB 6/99; BL 4/1/99; HBG 10/99; SLJ 5/99)

25 Bondoux, Anne-Laure. *The Princetta* (6–9). 2006, Bloomsbury $17.95 (978-1-58234-924-4). Malva, the Princetta of Galnicia, flees the strictness of her parents and her arranged marriage and boards a ship, hoping to find freedom in a new land. (Rev: BL 9/1/06; SLJ 12/06)

26 Brand, Max. *Dan Barry's Daughter* (7–12). 1976, Amereon LB $25.95 (978-0-88411-516-8). Harry is an accused murderer who, though innocent, is forced to hide. One of many recommended westerns by this prolific author.

27 Bruchac, Joseph. *Bearwalker* (5–8). Illus. by Sally Wern Comport. 2007, HarperCollins $15.99 (978-0-06-112309-2). Thirteen-year-old Baron, Native American and not as tall as he would like, comes into his own on a class trip to the Adirondacks as he draws on strengths that were not apparent to his classmates. (Rev: BL 9/15/07; SLJ 8/07)

28 Bruchac, Joseph. *The Return of Skeleton Man* (5–8). Illus. by Sally Wern Comport. 2006, HarperCollins $15.99 (978-0-06-058090-2). Molly, the Mohawk teen who survived a terrifying kidnapping in *Skeleton Man* (2001), discovers her nemesis is back. (Rev: BL 9/15/06; SLJ 8/06)

29 Bunting, Eve. *Someone Is Hiding on Alcatraz Island* (5–8). 1986, Berkley paper $5.99 (978-0-425-10294-7). A boy and a young woman ranger are trapped by a gang of thugs on Alcatraz. (Rev: BL 7/88)

30 Bunting, Eve. *SOS Titanic* (6–9). 1996, Harcourt paper $6.00 (978-0-15-201305-9). During his voyage on the *Titanic*, 15-year-old Barry O'Neill learns about the inequities of the class system and the true meaning of heroism. (Rev: BL 3/15/96; SLJ 4/96; VOYA 6/96)

31 Butler, Geoff. *The Hangashore* (6–8). Illus. 1998, Tundra $15.95 (978-0-88776-444-8). A picture book for older children about a stubborn, self-righteous magistrate from England who changes his mind about a slow-witted local boy and his own role in the Newfoundland community after the boy saves his life. (Rev: HBG 3/99; SLJ 2/99)

32 Butler, William. *The Butterfly Revolution* (7–12). 1961, Ballantine paper $6.50 (978-0-345-33182-3).

A frightening story of problems in a boys' camp told in diary form by one of the campers.

33 Campbell, Eric. *The Place of Lions* (6–9). 1991, Harcourt $17.00 (978-0-15-262408-8). When their plane crashes over the Serengeti, Chris and his injured father must learn a lesson in survival while surrounded by poachers and a pride of lions. (Rev: BL 11/15/91; SLJ 11/91)

34 Cavanagh, Helen. *Panther Glade* (5–8). 1993, Simon & Schuster paper $16.00 (978-0-671-75617-8). Bill spends a summer in Florida with his great-aunt Cait. He's afraid of the Everglades and alligators, but he comes to appreciate Indian history and crafts. (Rev: BL 6/1–15/93; SLJ 6/93; VOYA 10/93)

35 Cole, Stephen. *Thieves till We Die* (8–11). 2007, Bloomsbury $16.95 (978-1-59990-082-7). Nathaniel Coldhart sends his band of teen outlaws on another action-packed adventure (after 2006's *Thieves Like Us*), this time to steal a priceless sword. (Rev: BL 5/1/07; SLJ 5/07)

36 Cooney, Caroline B. *Flash Fire* (7–10). 1995, Scholastic paper $14.95 (978-0-590-25253-9). A girl's wish for a more exciting life comes true when a fire sweeps the wealthy Los Angeles neighborhood where she lives. (Rev: BL 11/1/95; SLJ 12/95; VOYA 12/95)

37 Cooney, Caroline B. *Flight No. 116 Is Down* (7–10). 1992, Scholastic paper $14.95 (978-0-590-44465-1). With a lightning pace, the author depicts the drama and human interest inherent in disaster. (Rev: BL 1/15/92; SLJ 2/92)

38 Couloumbis, Audrey. *Maude March on the Run! or, Trouble Is Her Middle Name* (5–7). 2007, Random $15.99 (978-0-375-83246-8). In this action-packed sequel to *The Misadventures of Maude March*, 16-year-old Maude and her 12-year-old sister, both orphans, are pursued by the law after Maude is unjustly accused of multiple crimes. (Rev: SLJ 1/07)

39 Creech, Sharon. *The Wanderer* (5–9). Illus. by David Diaz. 2000, HarperCollins LB $17.89 (978-0-06-027731-4). In this Newbery Honor Book, 13-year-old Sophie, her two cousins, and three uncles sail across the Atlantic to England in a 45-foot yacht. (Rev: BCCB 4/00*; BL 4/1/00; HB 5–6/00; HBG 10/00; SLJ 4/00*)

40 DeFelice, Cynthia. *Lostman's River* (5–7). 1994, Macmillan LB $15.00 (978-0-02-726466-1). Tyler's trust is betrayed when he takes an eccentric scientist to a secret rookery in the Everglades and the man reveals himself to be an unscrupulous plume hunter. (Rev: BCCB 6/94; BL 5/15/94; HB 9–10/94; SLJ 7/94)

41 Demers, Barbara. *Willa's New World* (5–8). 2000, Coteau paper $6.95 (978-1-55050-150-6). An adventure story set in Canada around 1800 in which 15-year-old Willa is sent to a trading post on Hudson's Bay. (Rev: BL 9/15/00; SLJ 9/00)

42 Docherty, Jimmy. *The Ice Cream Con* (6–10). 2008, Scholastic $16.99 (978-0-545-02885-1). Jake, who lives in a bad section of Glasgow, is tired of getting mugged and spreads a rumor about a bodyguard called the Big Baresi in this fun, vulgar, action-packed story. (Rev: BL 5/1/08; SLJ 6/08)

43 Doder, Joshua. *A Dog Called Grk* (5–8). 2007, Delacorte $14.99 (978-0-385-73359-5). In this fast-paced adventure, 12-year-old Londoner Tim, trying to help the Stanislavian ambassador's family — and dog — becomes enmeshed in international political intrigue. A sequel is *Grk and the Pelotti Gang* (2007). (Rev: BL 1/1–15/07; SLJ 3/07)

44 Dowd, John. *Rare and Endangered: A Caribbean Island Eco-Adventure* (6–8). 2000, Peachtree paper $5.95 (978-1-56145-217-0). While tagging turtles on an exotic island, Jim and Julia must save themselves and their friend Miles from evil poachers. (Rev: SLJ 7/00; VOYA 6/00)

45 Dowswell, Paul. *Battle Fleet* (5–8). 2008, Bloomsbury $16.95 (978-1-59990-080-3). Young Sam is again on the high seas, this time on Lord Nelson's ship for the battle of Trafalgar. A follow-up to *Powder Monkey* and *Prison Ship*. (Rev: BL 4/15/08; SLJ 9/08)

46 Doyle, Roddy. *Wilderness* (5–7). 2007, Scholastic $16.99 (978-0-439-02356-6). Johnny and Tom must find their mother in frozen Lapland when her dogsled team is lost; meanwhile the boys' half sister is reunited with her own mother, who left her family long ago. (Rev: BL 11/15/07; HB 1–2/08; SLJ 11/07)

47 Draper, Penny. *Terror at Turtle Mountain* (4–7). 2006, Coteau paper $7.95 (978-1-55050-343-2). In Canada's Northwest Territory in 1903, a 13-year-old girl participates in frantic efforts to rescue victims of a rock slide; an action-packed novel based on a real-life incident. (Rev: SLJ 10/06)

48 Easton, Kelly. *Aftershock* (7–10). 2006, Simon & Schuster $16.95 (978-1-4169-0052-8). Mute and in shock after seeing his parents die in a car crash, Adam hitchhikes from Idaho to Rhode Island, his life flashing through his mind as he makes his way home. (Rev: BL 12/15/06; SLJ 12/06)

49 Ernst, Kathleen. *Secrets in the Hills: A Josefina Mystery* (4–7). Series: American Girl Mystery. 2006, Pleasant paper $6.95 (978-1-59369-097-7). In 1820s New Mexico, Josefina decides to investigate the possibility that there is treasure buried near her home. (Rev: BL 5/15/06; SLJ 4/06)

50 Ewing, Lynne. *Drive-By* (5–8). 1996, HarperCollins paper $4.99 (978-0-06-440649-9). When Tito's brother is killed in a gang-related shooting, he is bullied and threatened by the gang to reveal where his brother hid a cache of stolen money. (Rev: SLJ 8/96)

51 Fama, Elizabeth. *Overboard* (4–8). 2002, Cricket $15.95 (978-0-8126-2652-0). Fourteen-year-old Emily struggles to save her own life and that of a boy named Isman when a ferry sinks off the coast of Sumatra. (Rev: BCCB 6/02; BL 7/02; HBG 10/02; SLJ 7/02)

52 Fardell, John. *The Flight of the Silver Turtle* (5–8). 2006, Putnam $15.99 (978-0-399-24382-0). The same crew from *The 7 Professors of the Far North* (2005) must find an antigravity machine before the villains discover it, in an exciting chase around Europe. (Rev: BL 12/15/06; SLJ 10/06)

53 Ferris, Jean. *Song of the Sea* (7–9). Series: American Dreams. 1996, Avon paper $3.99 (978-0-380-78199-7). In the second title of this adventure series, set on the sea and in the Yucatan in 1814, privateer Raider Lyons lies near death as a result of wounds inflicted by the evil Captain Lawrence of the British navy and longs for the love of Rosie. (Rev: VOYA 10/96)

54 Fields, T. S. *Danger in the Desert* (5–7). 1997, Rising Moon $12.95 (978-0-87358-666-5); paper $6.95 (978-0-87358-664-1). A survival story about two boys who endure great hardships when they are left without food or supplies in the desert. (Rev: HBG 3/98; SLJ 11/97)

55 Fleck, Earl. *Chasing Bears: A Canoe-Country Adventure* (5–8). Illus. by author. 1999, Holy Cow paper $12.95 (978-0-930100-90-2). An adventure story set near the Minnesota-Canada border that involves Danny, a 12-year-old who is on a canoe trip with his father and older brother. (Rev: SLJ 12/99)

56 Fleischman, Paul. *The Half-a-Moon Inn* (5–7). Illus. by Kathryn Jacobi. 1991, HarperCollins paper $5.99 (978-0-06-440364-1). A young mute boy sets out to find his mother in a violent snowstorm.

57 Fleischman, Sid. *The Ghost in the Noonday Sun* (5–7). Illus. by Warren Chappell. 1989, Scholastic paper $3.50 (978-0-590-43662-5). This pirate story features all the standard ingredients — a shanghaied boy, a villainous captain, and buried treasure. (Rev: VOYA 8/89)

58 Fleischman, Sid. *The Whipping Boy* (5–7). Illus. 1986, Greenwillow $16.99 (978-0-688-06216-3). Prince Brat and his whipping boy, Jemmy, who takes the blame for all the bad things the prince does, find their roles reversed when they meet up with CutWater and Hold-Your-Nose Billy. Newbery Medal winner, 1987. (Rev: BCCB 3/86; BL 3/1/86; SLJ 5/86)

59 Flores-Galbis, Enrique. *Raining Sardines* (6–9). 2007, Roaring Brook $16.95 (978-1-59643-166-9).

A dramatic, operatic adventure set in pre-revolutionary Cuba, where young Ernestina and Enriquito ultimately triumph over an evil landowner after encountering much danger and magic. (Rev: BCCB 6/07; BL 4/1/07; SLJ 4/07)

60 Freedman, Benedict, and Nancy Freedman. *Mrs. Mike* (7–12). 1968, Berkley paper $5.99 (978-0-425-10328-9). Based on a true story, this tells of Kathy, her love for her Mountie husband Mike, and her hard life in the Canadian Northwest.

61 Frost, Helen. *Diamond Willow* (6–9). 2008, Farrar $16.00 (978-0-374-31776-8). A survival story in diamond-shaped poems about 12-year-old Diamond Willow, a part-Athabascan girl caught with her blind dog in a blizzard in Alaska; she's saved with the help of her ancestral spirits. (Rev: BL 6/1–15/08; SLJ 6/08)

62 Garland, Sherry. *The Silent Storm* (4–7). 1993, Harcourt $14.95 (978-0-15-274170-9). Alyssa, who has lost both of her parents in a violent storm and has become mute because of the trauma, hears that another hurricane is approaching. (Rev: BCCB 4/93; BL 6/1–15/93; SLJ 7/04)

63 George, Jean Craighead. *Julie of the Wolves* (5–8). Illus. by John Schoenherr. 1974, HarperCollins LB $16.89 (978-0-06-021944-4); paper $5.99 (978-0-06-440058-9). Julie (Inuit name, Miyax) begins a trek across frozen Alaska and is saved only by the friendship of a pack of wolves. Newbery Medal winner, 1973.

64 George, Jean Craighead. *Julie's Wolf Pack* (5–7). Illus. Series: Julie of the Wolves. 1997, HarperCollins LB $18.89 (978-0-06-027407-8). Kapu, leader of the pack, is captured by researchers in this continuing story of Julie and her wolf friends. (Rev: BL 9/1/97; HBG 3/98; SLJ 9/97; VOYA 6/98)

65 George, Jean Craighead. *Shark Beneath the Reef* (7–9). 1989, HarperCollins $13.95 (978-0-06-021992-5); paper $5.99 (978-0-06-440308-5). The story of a young Mexican boy who is torn between becoming a shark fisherman like his father or going to college to be a marine biologist. (Rev: BL 6/1/89; SLJ 6/89; VOYA 6/89)

66 George, Jean Craighead. *The Talking Earth* (6–8). 1983, HarperCollins paper $5.99 (978-0-06-440212-5). A young Seminole girl spends three months in the Everglades alone. (Rev: BL 11/1/88)

67 George, Jean Craighead. *Water Sky* (6–8). 1987, HarperCollins paper $6.99 (978-0-06-440202-6). A boy is sent by his father to an Eskimo whaling camp to learn survival techniques. (Rev: BL 2/1/87)

68 Golding, William. *Lord of the Flies* (8–12). 1999, Viking paper $15.00 (978-0-14-028333-4). When they are marooned on a deserted island, a group of English schoolboys soon lose their civilized ways.

69 Goodman, Joan Elizabeth. *Paradise* (7–12). 2002, Houghton $16.00 (978-0-618-11450-4). The fictionalized story of Marguerite de la Rocque, who in 1536, after being left on Canada's Isle of Demons by her explorer uncle, struggled to survive along with her maid and the young man she loved. (Rev: BL 11/15/02; HBG 3/03; SLJ 12/02; VOYA 12/02)

70 Gordon, Amy. *Return to Gill Park* (5–8). Series: Gill Park. 2006, Holiday $16.95 (978-0-8234-1998-2). This oddball sequel to *The Gorillas of Gill Park* (2006) finds Willy Wilson on the trail of vandals determined to destroy the beauty of the park he now owns. (Rev: BL 5/15/06; SLJ 4/06)

71 Gourley, Catherine, ed. *Read for Your Life: Tales of Survival from the Editors of Read Magazine* (5–8). Series: Best of Read. 1998, Millbrook paper $5.95 (978-0-7613-0344-2). This is a collection of excellent survival stories from 50 years of *Read*, a literary magazine for middle and high school students. (Rev: BL 8/98)

72 Graf, Mike. *Bryce and Zion: Danger in the Narrows* (5–8). Illus. by Marjorie Leggitt. Series: Adventures with the Parkers. 2006, Fulcrum paper $9.95 (978-1-55591-532-2). On a vacation in the national parks of southern Utah, 10-year-old twins James and Morgan Parker learn about the delicate ecology of the area, rescue an injured hiker, and come to the aid of their father when he slips and falls in the Narrows; a fact-filled adventure story with full-color photographs and nature sketches. (Rev: SLJ 12/06)

73 Greenburg, Dan. *Claws* (6–9). 2006, Random $15.95 (978-0-375-83410-3). A fast-paced story about 14-year-old Cody, on the run from an abusive mother and finding new challenges at a tiger ranch in Texas. (Rev: BL 6/1–15/06; LMC 8-9/06; SLJ 7/06)

74 Gross, Philip. *The Lastling* (8–12). 2006, Clarion $16 (978-0-618-65998-2). Melding themes of the environment, adventure, and personal growth, this exciting story is about Paris — a privileged 14-year-old on a hunting expedition in the Himalayas with her uncle — who befriends a 12-year-old monk-to-be named Tahr and sets in motion a horrifying episode with a young yeti. (Rev: LMC 2/07*; SLJ 12/06)

75 Gutman, Dan. *Getting Air* (5–8). 2007, Simon & Schuster $15.99 (978-0-689-87680-6). Thirteen-year-old Jimmy and five others prevent a hijacking, survive a plane crash, and find themselves faced with surviving in a Canadian forest; girl scout lore comes to their aid and they even find time to build a half-pipe for skateboarding. (Rev: BL 7/07; SLJ 6/07)

76 Harlow, Joan Hiatt. *Star in the Storm* (4–7). Illus. 2000, Simon & Schuster $16.00 (978-0-689-82905-5). This novel, set in Newfoundland in 1912, tells how a girl and her dog save a ship full of stranded passengers. (Rev: BCCB 3/00; BL 1/1–15/00; HB 3–4/00; HBG 10/00; SLJ 4/00)

77 Harper, Jo. *Delfino's Journey* (6–12). 2001, Texas Tech Univ. $15.95 (978-0-89672-437-2). Delfino and Salvador travel from Mexico to the United States in search of a new life but face many difficult challenges in this novel that interweaves Aztec folklore and information on illegal immigration. (Rev: BL 4/15/01; HBG 10/01)

78 Harrison, Michael. *It's My Life* (6–8). 1998, Holiday $15.95 (978-0-8234-1363-8). Martin's mother and her lover conspire to "kidnap" Martin to collect a ransom in this British thriller that is told alternately by Martin and his friend, Hannah. (Rev: BCCB 3/98; BL 3/1/98; HB 5–6/98; HBG 9/98; SLJ 4/98; VOYA 8/98)

79 Haugaard, Erik C. *Under the Black Flag* (5–7). 1994, Roberts Rinehart paper $8.95 (978-1-879373-63-1). Fourteen-year-old William is captured by the pirate Blackbeard and held for ransom in this 18th-century yarn. (Rev: BL 4/1/94; HB 9–10/94; SLJ 5/94)

80 Hausman, Gerald. *Tom Cringle: Battle on the High Seas* (6–8). Illus. by Tad Hills. 2000, Simon & Schuster $16.95 (978-0-689-82810-2). This action novel set in the Caribbean in 1812 tells how an English boy becomes involved in battles, mutinies, an earthquake, and a shipwreck. (Rev: BCCB 7–8/00; BL 11/1/00; HBG 3/01; SLJ 11/00; VOYA 12/00)

81 Hausman, Gerald. *Tom Cringle: The Pirate and the Patriot* (6–8). Illus. by Tad Hills. 2001, Simon & Schuster $16.00 (978-0-689-82811-9). Tom Cringle, a 14-year-old lieutenant in the Royal Navy, fights pirates, braves storms, and conquers slave traders in this sequel to *Tom Cringle: Battle on the High Seas* (2000). (Rev: BL 9/15/01; HBG 3/02; SLJ 10/01)

82 Hawks, Robert. *The Richest Kid in the World* (4–8). 1992, Avon paper $2.99 (978-0-380-76241-5). Josh is kidnapped and taken to the estate of billionaire Grizzle Welch. (Rev: SLJ 5/92)

83 Hesse, Karen. *Stowaway* (5–8). Illus. 2000, Simon & Schuster $17.95 (978-0-689-83987-0). Told by an 11-year-old stowaway, this adventurous sea story tells of Captain Cook's two-and-a-half-year voyage around the world beginning in 1768. (Rev: BL 12/15/00; HB 1–2/01; HBG 3/01; SLJ 11/00; VOYA 4/01)

84 Higgins, F. E. *The Black Book of Secrets* (5–7). 2007, Feiwel and Friends $14.95 (978-0-312-36844-9). Joe Zabbidou takes the confessions of everyone in the remote village of Pagus Parvus, collecting them in a black book. Ludlow Fitch, a desperate boy on the run from cruel parents, acts as Joe's scribe, a dangerous position in a dangerous world. (Rev: BL 10/15/07; HB 1–2/08; LMC 4-5/08; SLJ 4/08)

85 Higgins, Jack, and Justin Richards. *Sure Fire* (6–9). 2007, Putnam $16.99 (978-0-399-24784-2). When their mother dies suddenly, 15-year-old twins Rich and Jane move to London with their long-absent, secret-agent father, and they soon get caught up in his life of nonstop action. (Rev: BL 10/1/07; SLJ 2/08)

86 Higson, Charlie. *Blood Fever: A James Bond Adventure* (5–8). Series: Young Bond. 2006, Hyperion $16.95 (978-0-7868-3662-8). Even at 13, Bond is having adventures: this one finds him on the island of Sardinia, caught up in an art-theft mystery and rescuing a girl in peril. (Rev: SLJ 6/06)

87 Hilgartner, Beth. *A Murder for Her Majesty* (5–8). 1986, Houghton paper $6.95 (978-0-395-61619-2). Alice disguises herself as a boy to escape her father's murderers. (Rev: BCCB 9/86; SLJ 10/86)

88 Hill, David. *Running Hot* (5–8). 2007, Simply Read paper $9.95 (978-1-894965-52-1). A group of students clearing forest trees in rural New Zealand suddenly find themselves threatened by a raging fire. (Rev: SLJ 4/07)

89 Hinton, S. E. *The Outsiders* (7–10). 1967, Viking $17.99 (978-0-670-53257-5). Two rival gangs — the "haves" and "have-nots" — fight it out on the streets of an Oklahoma city. (Rev: BL 11/15/97)

90 Hinton, S. E. *Rumble Fish* (7–10). 1975, Dell paper $5.99 (978-0-440-97534-2). Rusty-James loses everything he loves most — including his brother.

91 Hinton, S. E. *Tex* (7–10). 1979, Dell paper $5.50 (978-0-440-97850-3). Tex and his 17-year-old older brother encounter problems with family, sex, and drugs.

92 Hinton, S. E. *That Was Then, This Is Now* (7–10). 1971, Viking $17.99 (978-0-670-69798-4). Bryon discovers that his "brother" Mark is a drug pusher.

93 Hobbs, Will. *The Big Wander* (7–10). 1992, Avon paper $5.95 (978-0-380-72140-5). Clay Lancaster, 14, and his brother Mike are on a "big wander," their last trip together before Mike goes away to college. (Rev: BL 10/15/92*; SLJ 11/92)

94 Hobbs, Will. *Far North* (7–12). 1996, Morrow $17.99 (978-0-688-14192-9). Fifteen-year old Gabe, his school roommate, and an elderly Native American are stranded in the Canadian wilderness. The boys survive even after the death of the wise old man. (Rev: BL 7/96; SLJ 9/96; VOYA 2/97)

95 Hobbs, Will. *Ghost Canoe* (6–8). 1997, Morrow $16.99 (978-0-688-14193-6); Avon paper $5.99 (978-0-380-72537-3). Mystery, plenty of action, murder, Spanish treasure, and a dangerous villain are some of the elements in this historical adventure

set on the northwest coast of Washington state. (Rev: BL 5/1/97; SLJ 4/97; VOYA 8/97)

96 Hobbs, Will. *Jackie's Wild Seattle* (5–8). 2003, HarperCollins LB $16.89 (978-0-06-051631-4). In the aftermath of September 11, 2001, Shannon, 14, and her younger brother spend an exciting and healing summer in Seattle with their animal rescuer uncle. (Rev: BL 6/1–15/03; HBG 4/04; SLJ 5/03; VOYA 8/03)

97 Hobbs, Will. *Jason's Gold* (5–9). 1999, Morrow $17.99 (978-0-688-15093-8). In this sharply realistic novel, 15-year-old Jason leaves Seattle in 1897 and, with a dog he has saved, heads for the Klondike and gold. (Rev: BL 8/99; HB 9–10/99; HBG 3/00; SLJ 11/99)

98 Hobbs, Will. *Leaving Protection* (7–12). 2004, HarperCollins $19.99 (978-0-688-17475-0). An exciting novel about a 16-year-old boy, his work on an Alaskan salmon trawler, and the secret plans of its skipper. (Rev: BL 3/1/04; SLJ 4/04)

99 Hobbs, Will. *The Maze* (6–12). 1998, Morrow $19.99 (978-0-688-15092-1). After living in a series of foster homes and detention centers, Rick escapes to Canyonlands National Park in Utah where he is befriended by a loner who helps him find himself. (Rev: BL 9/1/98; HBG 3/99; SLJ 10/98; VOYA 2/99)

100 Hobbs, Will. *Wild Man Island* (7–10). 2002, HarperCollins LB $16.89 (978-0-06-029810-4); HarperTrophy paper $5.99 (978-0-380-73310-1). An adventure story in which 14-year-old Andy becomes stranded on a remote Alaska island, faces many dangers, and tests his dead archaeologist father's theories about the earliest prehistoric immigrants to America. (Rev: BL 4/15/02; HB 7–8/02; HBG 10/02; SLJ 5/02; VOYA 6/02)

101 Hokenson, Terry. *The Winter Road* (6–9). 2006, Front St. $16.95 (978-1-932425-45-1). In this survival story, licensed pilot Willa, 17, flies her uncle's plane without permission and crash-lands in the freezing Canadian wilderness. (Rev: BL 6/1–15/06; HB 5–6/06; LMC 11-12/06; SLJ 5/06)

102 Holman, Felice. *Slake's Limbo* (5–9). 1974, Macmillan paper $4.99 (978-0-689-71066-7). Thirteen-year-old Artemis Slake finds an ideal hideaway for four months in the labyrinth of the New York City subway. (Rev: BL 6/1/88)

103 Horowitz, Anthony. *Snakehead: An Alex Rider Adventure* (6–8). Series: Alex Rider. 2007, Philomel $17.99 (978-0-399-24161-1). This seventh title in the series follows Alex as he's reunited with his godfather, Ash, and goes on a mission for the Australian Secret Intelligence Service that brings him face to face with a terrorist organization. (Rev: BL 9/15/07; SLJ 1/08)

104 Houston, James. *Frozen Fire* (6–8). Illus. by author. 1977, Macmillan paper $4.95 (978-0-689-71612-6). An Eskimo boy, Kayak, and his white friend set out to find Kayak's father, a prospector who has disappeared. A sequel is *Black Diamond*.

105 Hunt, L. J. *The Abernathy Boys* (5–7). 2004, HarperCollins LB $16.89 (978-0-06-029259-1). Young Bud and Temple Abernathy survive an eventful journey through the desert in this fictionalized version of a real expedition in the early 20th century. (Rev: BL 1/1–15/04; SLJ 3/04)

106 Hyde, Dayton O. *Mr. Beans* (5–7). 2000, Boyds Mills $14.95 (978-1-56397-866-1). In a small town in Oregon in the early 1940s, bully Mugsy wrongfully accuses a tame bear of attacking him, and timid Chirp frees the bear and takes off with him on a wilderness journey. (Rev: BL 11/15/00; HBG 10/01; SLJ 1/01; VOYA 4/01)

107 Hyland, Hilary. *The Wreck of the Ethie* (4–7). Illus. by Paul Bachem. 1999, Peachtree paper $7.95 (978-1-56145-198-2). Told through the eyes of two youngsters, this is a novelization of a true incident in which a dog saved passengers after their ship sank off the coast of Newfoundland. (Rev: SLJ 4/00)

108 Jaramillo, Ann. *La Línea* (5–8). 2006, Roaring Brook $16.95 (978-1-59643-154-6). Miguel, 15, and his sister Elena, 13, survive a terrifying journey across the border (la linea) from Mexico to California to join their parents. (Rev: BCCB 5/06; BL 3/15/06*; HBG 10/06; LMC 10/06; SLJ 4/06; VOYA 4/06)

109 Jennings, Richard W. *The Pirates of Turtle Rock* (5–8). 2008, Houghton $16.00 (978-0-618-98793-1). A modern-day Florida girl falls for a young pirate and the two embark on a treasure hunt for an ancient Caribbean artifact; a novel full of humor and adventure. (Rev: BL 4/15/08; SLJ 8/08)

110 Jinks, Catherine. *Evil Genius* (7–10). 2007, Harcourt $17.00 (978-0-15-205988-0). By age 13, Cadel's illegal computer hacking skills have landed him in the secretive Axis Institute for World Domination, where he's surrounded by aspiring villains but questions his own commitment to the cause. (Rev: BL 5/15/07; SLJ 7/07)

111 Jinks, Catherine. *Genius Squad* (7–10). 2008, Harcourt $17.00 (978-0-15-205985-9). In this fast-paced sequel to *Evil Genius* (2007), 15-year-old Cadel and his friend Sonja join teen computer hackers enlisted to expose an evil corporation. (Rev: BL 6/1–15/08; SLJ 6/08)

112 Johns, Linda. *Hannah West in Deep Water* (5–8). 2006, Puffin paper $5.99 (978-0-14-240700-4). Hannah investigates environmental shenanigans while she and her mother are house-sitting a houseboat and a dog. (Rev: BL 12/15/06)

113 Johns, Linda. *Hannah West in the Belltown Towers: A Mystery* (5–8). 2006, Sleuth paper $5.99 (978-0-14-240637-3). Hannah, an adopted Chinese girl with lots of nerve and curiosity, moves with her mother to Seattle and soon finds herself embroiled in an art theft. (Rev: BL 5/1/06)

114 Johnson, Annabel, and Edgar Johnson. *The Grizzly* (5–7). Illus. by Gilbert Riswold. 1964, HarperCollins paper $4.95 (978-0-06-440036-7). A perceptive story of a father-son relationship in which David, on a camping trip, saves his father's life when a grizzly bear attacks.

115 Johnson, Maureen. *Girl at Sea* (8–11). 2007, HarperTeen $15.99 (978-0-06-054144-6). Clio, 17, is crushed to learn she must spend the summer with her father and his girlfriend sailing on the Mediterranean, but soon discovers that she's part of a treasure hunt. (Rev: BCCB 10/07; BL 7/07; SLJ 6/07)

116 Karr, Kathleen. *Born for Adventure* (6–9). 2007, Marshall Cavendish $16.99 (978-0-7614-5348-2). While accompanying explorer Henry Morton Stanley on a trip to Africa in 1887, young Tom encounters disease, danger, and disaster. (Rev: BCCB 6/07; BL 4/1/07; LMC 10/07; SLJ 7/07)

117 Kehret, Peg. *Earthquake Terror* (4–7). 1998, Puffin paper $5.99 (978-0-14-038343-0). A violent earthquake strikes the small island on which 12-year-old Jonathan is alone with his younger sister, Abby. (Rev: BCCB 3/96; BL 1/1–15/96; SLJ 2/96)

118 Konigsburg, E. L. *From the Mixed-Up Files of Mrs. Basil E. Frankweiler* (5–7). Illus. by author. 1967, Macmillan $17.00 (978-0-689-20586-6). Adventure, suspense, detection, and humor are involved when 12-year-old Claudia and her younger brother elude the security guards and live for a week in New York's Metropolitan Museum of Art. Newbery Medal winner, 1968.

119 Korman, Gordon. *The Abduction* (4–7). Series: Kidnapped. 2006, Scholastic paper $4.99 (978-0-439-84777-3). A fast-paced thriller, the opening volume of a new series, in which 15-year-old Aiden works with the FBI to rescue his 11-year-old sister Meg, who was abducted while on her way home from school and is meanwhile resisting her captors. The second volume is *The Search* (2006). (Rev: BL 8/06; SLJ 9/06)

120 Korman, Gordon. *Chasing the Falconers* (4–7). 2005, Scholastic paper $4.99 (978-0-439-65136-3). In this fast-paced adventure, Aiden and Meg Falconer must evade pursuers as they work to gather evidence that will prove their parents' innocence of treason. (Rev: BL 5/15/05; SLJ 8/05)

121 Lamensdorf, Len. *The Crouching Dragon* (6–9). 1999, Seascape $19.95 (978-0-9669741-5-7). In this novel set in a French coastal town in 1959, 14-year-old William and his friends secretly renovate a crumbling castle called the Crouching Dragon. (Rev: BL 9/1/99; VOYA 12/99)

122 Lamensdorf, Len. *The Raging Dragon* (6–9). Series: Will to Conquer. 2002, Seascape $22.95 (978-0-9669741-7-1). William and Louise become embroiled in exciting events in 1960s Paris, including an effort to counter Algerian terrorists, in this sequel to *The Crouching Dragon* (1999). (Rev: BL 10/1/02; SLJ 10/02)

123 Lee, Norman. *Camel Rider* (5–7). 2007, Charlesbridge $15.95 (978-1-58089-314-5). Two boys — a 12-year-old Australian named Adam and Walid, a camel driver from Bangladesh — find themselves alone in the desert during a Middle Eastern war and must struggle to survive; told in alternating first-person narratives, this is an exciting story that also shows how people with no common language can learn to communicate. (Rev: BL 9/1/07; SLJ 7/07)

124 Lee, Tanith. *Piratica II: Return to Parrot Island* (7–10). Series: Piratica. 2006, Dutton $17.99 (978-0-525-47769-3). The second action-packed installment in the series finds Art the pirate queen leaving her husband behind on dry land as she sails the seas on behalf of the government — and perhaps with the opportunity to vanquish old enemies. (Rev: BL 12/15/06; SLJ 4/07)

125 Lester, Alison. *The Snow Pony* (6–12). 2003, Houghton $15.00 (978-0-618-25404-0). Fourteen-year-old Dusty's love for Snow Pony lightens the problems of her life in this novel set on an Australian cattle ranch. (Rev: BL 3/15/03; HBG 10/03; SLJ 4/03; VOYA 6/03)

126 Little, Kimberly Griffiths. *Enchanted Runner* (5–7). 1999, Avon $15.00 (978-0-380-97623-2). Twelve-year-old Kendall, who is half Native American, hopes to excel in running as his ancestors did, and is given an unusual opportunity to test himself. (Rev: BCCB 9/99; BL 9/1/99; HBG 3/00; SLJ 12/99)

127 Lourie, Peter. *The Lost Treasure of Captain Kidd* (5–8). Illus. 1996, Shawangunk Pr. paper $10.95 (978-1-885482-03-7). Friends Killian and Alex set out to discover Captain Kidd's treasure buried on the banks of the Hudson River centuries ago. (Rev: BL 2/15/96; SLJ 6/96)

128 McCaughrean, Geraldine. *The White Darkness* (7–10). 2007, HarperCollins $16.99 (978-0-06-089035-3). Symone is thrilled when her uncle Victor offers to take her on a trip to the South Pole, since her "hero" is Captain Laurence "Titus" Oates, who traveled there in 1911 as part of Robert Scott's expedition. But the trip — and her uncle's obsession — turn out to be more than she bargained for. (Rev: BL 12/1/06; HB 3–4/07; SLJ 4/07) ✇

129 McFadden, Deanna. *Robinson Crusoe: Retold from the Daniel Defoe Original* (4–7). Illus. by Jamel Akib. Series: Classic Starts. 2006, Sterling $4.95 (978-1-4027-2664-4). The 1719 original text is retold in brief, accessible sentences that portray Crusoe and Friday as equals. (Rev: BL 2/15/06)

130 Mack, Tracy, and Michael Citrin. *The Fall of the Amazing Zalindas* (4–7). Illus. by Greg Ruth. Series: Sherlock Holmes and the Baker Street Irregulars. 2006, Scholastic $16.99 (978-0-439-82836-9). Sherlock Holmes calls on a gang of street children to help him investigate the mysterious deaths of a family of trapeze artists. (Rev: BL 11/1/06; SLJ 1/07)

131 McNicoll, Sylvia. *Last Chance for Paris* (6–9). 2008, Fitzhenry & Whiteside paper $11.95 (978-1-55455-061-6). Zanna, 14, who had hoped to be in Paris with her mom, ends up instead in the Canadian wilderness searching for her lost twin brother with the help of a wolf puppy. (Rev: BL 3/1/08; SLJ 5/08)

132 MacPhail, Catherine. *Underworld* (7–10). 2005, Bloomsbury $16.95 (978-1-58234-997-8). Five British teens with very different personalities find themselves trapped in a cave on a remote Scottish island; adding to their predicament is their fear of a giant worm reputed to inhabit the caves. (Rev: BL 7/05; SLJ 7/05; VOYA 8/05)

133 Marsden, John. *The Dead of Night* (6–10). Series: Tomorrow. 1997, Houghton $16.00 (978-0-395-83734-4). In this sequel to *Tomorrow, When the War Began* (1996), the teenage group continues its guerrilla activities against their enemy, a country that has invaded their homeland, Australia. (Rev: HBG 3/98; SLJ 11/97; VOYA 2/98)

134 Marsden, John. *A Killing Frost* (7–12). Series: Tomorrow. 1998, Houghton $17.00 (978-0-395-83735-1). In this third episode of an adventure series about a group of Australian teens who fight an enemy that has occupied their country, five young people carry out a plan to sink a container ship. (Rev: BCCB 4/98; BL 5/15/98; HB 7–8/98; HBG 9/98; SLJ 6/98; VOYA 6/98)

135 Marsden, John. *The Other Side of Dawn* (8–12). Series: Tomorrow. 2002, Houghton $16.00 (978-0-618-07028-2). Ellie's exploits are at the center of this action-packed seventh and final installment in the Tomorrow series, which leaves Ellie back home after peace has been declared, trying to adjust to postwar life. (Rev: BCCB 10/02; BL 10/15/02; HB 11/02; HBG 3/03; SLJ 10/02; VOYA 2/03)

136 Marsden, John. *Tomorrow, When the War Began* (8–12). 1995, Houghton $16.00 (978-0-395-70673-2). A girl and her friends return from a camping trip in the bush to find that Australia has been invaded and their families taken prisoner. (Rev: BL 4/15/95; SLJ 6/95)

137 Marsden, John. *While I Live* (8–12). Series: Ellie Chronicles. 2007, Scholastic $16.99 (978-0-439-78318-7). Ellie is back on her farm after the upheavals of the Tomorrow series, but new violence soon disrupts her life again; knowledge of the previous series will enhance understanding of this new story arc. (Rev: BCCB 6/07; HB 5–6/07; LMC 10/07; SLJ 5/07)

138 Mass, Wendy. *Jeremy Fink and the Meaning of Life* (5–8). 2006, Little, Brown $15.99 (978-0-316-05829-2). Just before his 13th birthday, Jeremy Fink receives a package from his dead father containing a locked box but no keys; Jeremy and Liz set off on a tour of New York City in search of the keys and meet a number of characters with different views on the meaning of life. (Rev: BL 12/15/06; SLJ 12/06)

139 Mazer, Harry. *Snow Bound* (5–7). 1987, Dell $21.50 (978-0-8446-6240-4); paper $5.50 (978-0-440-96134-5). Tony and Cindy survive for several days after being trapped in a snow storm. (Rev: BL 9/1/89)

140 Meyer, L. A. *In the Belly of the Bloodhound: Being an Account of a Particularly Peculiar Adventure in the Life of Jacky Faber* (8–11). Series: Bloody Jack. 2006, Harcourt $17.00 (978-0-15-205557-8). Jacky Faber, girl pirate, is kidnapped along with her classmates from the Lawson Peabody School for Young Girls in Boston; they find themselves on a slave ship bound for North Africa and Jacky must devise an escape plan. (Rev: BL 11/1/06; SLJ 1/07)

141 Meyer, L. A. *Mississippi Jack: Being an Account of the Further Waterborne Adventures of Jacky Faber, Midshipman, Fine Lady, and the Lily of the West* (8–11). Series: Bloody Jack. 2007, Harcourt $17.00 (978-0-15-206003-9). Jacky has plenty of outsized adventures as she travels down the Mississippi in search of her true love in this latest installment. (Rev: BL 11/1/07; SLJ 12/07)

142 Meyer, L. A. *Under the Jolly Roger: Being an Account of the Further Nautical Adventures of Jacky Faber* (7–10). Series: Bloody Jack. 2005, Harcourt $17.00 (978-0-15-205345-1). In this volume full of adventure, plucky 15-year-old Jacky Faber — last seen in *Bloody Jack* (2002) and *Curse of the Blue Tattoo* (2004) — travels from Boston to England in 1804 in search of her true love but ends up taking control of a British warship. (Rev: BL 8/05; SLJ 9/05; VOYA 8/05)

143 Miklowitz, Gloria D. *After the Bomb* (7–12). 1987, Scholastic paper $2.50 (978-0-590-40568-3). This novel describes the experiences of a group of young people after an atomic bomb falls on Los Angeles. (Rev: BL 6/15/86; SLJ 9/85; VOYA 8/85)

144 Miklowitz, Gloria D. *Camouflage* (8–10). 1998, Harcourt $16.00 (978-0-15-201467-4). When 14-year-old Kyle visits northern Michigan to spend a summer with his father, he becomes involved in a government-hating militia movement in which his

father is a general. (Rev: BCCB 5/98; HBG 9/98; SLJ 4/98; VOYA 10/98)

145 Miller, Kirsten. *Kiki Strike: Inside the Shadow City* (5–8). 2006, Bloomsbury $16.95 (978-1-58234-960-2). A complex story featuring adventurous and multitalented 12-year-old girls exploring the subterranean levels of New York City. (Rev: BL 7/06; HBG 10/06; LMC 10/06; SLJ 6/06; VOYA 8/06)

146 Mitchell, Nancy. *Global Warning: Attack on the Pacific Rim!* (5–8). Illus. by Darren Wiebe and Ryan T. Fong. Series: The Changing Earth Trilogy. 1999, Lightstream paper $5.95 (978-1-892713-02-5). A thrilling adventure story about Jenny Powers, a wheelchair-bound youngster, who must warn the authorities of an impending biological disaster at her school. (Rev: SLJ 10/99)

147 Morey, Walt. *Angry Waters* (6–9). 1990, Blue Heron paper $7.95 (978-0-936085-10-4). A hostile 15-year-old boy is unwillingly paroled to a family farm, where he comes to terms with himself. (Rev: VOYA 8/90)

148 Morey, Walt. *Death Walk* (6–10). 1991, Blue Heron $13.95 (978-0-936085-18-0). After being stranded in the Alaskan wilderness, a teenage boy must learn to survive in the harsh climate while on the run from killers. (Rev: BL 6/1/91; SLJ 6/91)

149 Morpurgo, Michael. *Kensuke's Kingdom* (4–7). 2003, Scholastic paper $16.95 (978-0-439-38202-1). A boy washed onto a seemingly deserted island finds a friend in a Japanese soldier who has lived there since World War II. (Rev: BL 2/15/03; HB 5–6/03; HBG 10/03; SLJ 3/03; VOYA 6/03)

150 Morris, Deborah. *Teens 911: Snowbound, Helicopter Crash and Other True Survival Stories* (7–12). 2002, Health Communications paper $12.95 (978-0-7573-0039-4). Five stories that portray teens facing emergencies (being stranded, in helicopter crashes, rescuing residents of burning houses, and so forth) are followed by postscripts and survival quizzes. (Rev: SLJ 2/03; VOYA 2/03)

151 Mowat, Farley. *Lost in the Barrens* (7–9). 1985, Bantam paper $5.50 (978-0-553-27525-4). Two boys lost in the wilderness of northern Canada must fight for survival.

152 Mowll, Joshua. *Operation Red Jericho* (8–11). Illus. Series: Guild Trilogy. 2005, Candlewick $15.99 (978-0-7636-2634-1). In this first volume of a graphic novel trilogy set in the early 20th century, teens Becca and Doug MacKenzie search for their parents, who disappeared in China, and document their exciting adventures. (Rev: BL 11/15/05; SLJ 12/05)

153 Mowll, Joshua. *Operation Typhoon Shore* (8–12). Illus. by Joshua Mowll, et al. Series: The Guild of Specialists. 2006, Candlewick $15.99

(978-0-7636-3122-2). In 1920, siblings Doug and Becca sail through a typhoon on their uncle's ship while seeking the gyrolabe that may offer a clue to their parents' disappearance; the second installment in the series. (Rev: BL 1/1–15/07; SLJ 3/07)

154 Myers, Edward. *Survival of the Fittest* (6–9). 2000, Montemayor paper $11.95 (978-0-9674477-2-8). Rus and his cousins survive a plane crash in the Peruvian rainforest and set off through the dangerous terrain in search of help. (Rev: SLJ 1/01)

155 Napoli, Donna Jo. *North* (4–7). 2004, Greenwillow $16.99 (978-0-06-057987-6). Twelve-year-old Alvin, an African American boy fascinated by explorer Matthew Henson, sets off for the Arctic and, with the help of several adults along the way, makes the long and complex journey safely. (Rev: BL 3/1/04; SLJ 5/04)

156 Nolan, Peggy. *The Spy Who Came in from the Sea* (4–8). 1999, Pineapple $14.95 (978-1-56164-186-4). In this adventure story set in World War II Florida, 14-year-old Frank, who has a reputation for lying, is not believed when he claims to have seen a German sub off the coast. (Rev: HBG 3/00; SLJ 1/00)

157 Nordin, Sofia. *In the Wild* (4–7). Trans. from Swedish by Maria Lundin. 2005, Groundwood $15.95 (978-0-88899-648-0). Set in Sweden, this is an adventure story featuring 6th-grade outcast Amanda and bully Philip, who become lost and must rely on their own resources to survive. (Rev: SLJ 10/05)

158 O'Dell, Scott. *The Black Pearl* (7–9). 1967, Houghton $17.00 (978-0-395-06961-5). Young Ramon dives into a forbidden cave to collect a fabulous black pearl that in time seems to bring a curse to his family.

159 O'Dell, Scott. *Black Star, Bright Dawn* (5–8). 1988, Houghton $18.00 (978-0-395-47778-6). An Inuit girl decides to run the 1,197-mile sled dog race called the Iditarod. (Rev: BCCB 6/88; BL 4/1/88; SLJ 5/88; VOYA 6/88)

160 O'Dell, Scott. *Island of the Blue Dolphins* (5–8). 1960, Houghton $16.00 (978-0-395-06962-2); Dell paper $6.50 (978-0-440-43988-2). An Indian girl spends 18 years alone on an island off the coast of California in the 1800s. Newbery Medal winner, 1961. A sequel is *Zia* (1976). (Rev: BL 3/1/88)

161 Olshan, Matthew. *Finn* (8–12). 2001, Bancrof $19.95 (978-1-890862-13-8); paper $14.95 (978-1-890862-14-5). Teenage Chloe, who has suffered an abusive childhood, and a pregnant Hispanic girl set off to find new lives in a Huck Finn-like adventure full of insight and social commentary. (Rev: BL 4/1/01; SLJ 4/01; VOYA 4/01)

162 Parkinson, Curtis. *Storm-Blast* (4–8). 2003, Tundra paper $7.95 (978-0-88776-630-5). On a sail-ing trip in the Caribbean, three teens become stranded in a small dinghy and must use their resources to survive. (Rev: SLJ 10/03; VOYA 8/03)

163 Patneaude, David. *The Last Man's Reward* (5–8). 1996, Albert Whitman LB $15.99 (978-0-8075-4370-2). In this adventure, a group of boys agree to a pact rewarding the last to leave the neighborhood. (Rev: BL 6/1–15/96; SLJ 7/96)

164 Patneaude, David. *A Piece of the Sky* (5–8). 2007, Albert Whitman $15.95 (978-0-8075-6536-0). In Oregon to help his grandfather settle into an assisted-living residence, 14-year-old Russell and his new friend Phoebe, pursued by a sinister character, set off on an unexpectedly dangerous meteorite search. (Rev: SLJ 5/07)

165 Paulsen, Gary. *Brian's Hunt* (6–9). 2003, Random $14.95 (978-0-385-74647-2). This story of Brian's return to the wilderness at the age of 16, his care for a wounded dog, and his distress over the fate of his Cree friends will please Hatchet fans. (Rev: BCCB 2/04; BL 1/1–15/04; SLJ 12/03)

166 Paulsen, Gary. *Brian's Winter* (5–9). 1996, Delacorte $15.95 (978-0-385-32198-3). In a reworking of the ending of *Hatchet,* in which Brian Robeson is rescued after surviving a plane crash, this novel tells what would have happened had Brian had to survive a harsh winter in the wilderness. (Rev: BL 12/15/95; SLJ 2/96; VOYA 2/97)

167 Paulsen, Gary. *Canyons* (7–10). 1991, Dell paper $5.99 (978-0-440-21023-8). Blennan becomes obsessed with the story of a young Indian boy murdered by white men 100 years before. (Rev: SLJ 9/90)

168 Paulsen, Gary. *The Haymeadow* (6–9). Illus. 1992, Dell paper $4.99 (978-0-440-40923-6). A 14-year-old boy takes sheep out to pasture for the summer in this story about a boy who is trying to gain acceptance by his father. (Rev: BL 5/15/92*; SLJ 6/92)

169 Paulsen, Gary. *The River* (5–10). 1991, Delacorte $15.95 (978-0-385-30388-0). In this sequel to *Hatchet,* Paulsen takes the wilderness adventure beyond self-preservation and makes teen Brian responsible for saving someone else. (Rev: BL 5/15/91)

170 Paulsen, Gary. *The Voyage of the Frog* (6–8). 1989, Orchard $16.95 (978-0-531-05805-3). Alone on a 22-foot sailboat, a 14-year-old boy survives a 9-day sea ordeal. (Rev: BL 3/1/89; SLJ 1/89; VOYA 2/89)

171 Peck, Robert Newton. *Arly's Run* (6–9). 1991, Walker $16.95 (978-0-8027-8120-8). Orphaned Arly escapes from an early 19th-century Florida work farm and journeys to Moore Haven, where shelter has been arranged for him. (Rev: BL 12/15/91; SLJ 2/92)

172 Petrucha, Stefan. *Teen, Inc.* (8–10). 2007, Walker $16.95 (978-0-8027-9650-9). Jaiden, 14, is being raised by a corporation after being orphaned as a baby, and he's coming to discover that his "parent" is harming his community in this action-packed eco-thriller. (Rev: BL 12/1/07; SLJ 12/07)

173 Pfeffer, Susan Beth. *The Dead and the Gone* (8–12). 2008, Harcourt $17.00 (978-0-15-206311-5). A tilt in the moon's orbit sends Earth into environmental and social chaos, and Alex, Bri, and Julie must fend for themselves and find food, safety, and shelter when their parents disappear. (Rev: BL 5/15/08; SLJ 8/08)

174 Philbrick, Rodman. *Max the Mighty* (6–9). 1998, Scholastic $16.95 (978-0-590-18892-0); paper $6.99 (978-0-590-57964-3). Maxwell Kane and his new friend Worm, who is being abused by her stepfather, run away in a cross-country search for Worm's real father. (Rev: BL 6/1–15/98; HB 7–8/98; HBG 9/98; SLJ 4/98; VOYA 6/98)

175 Pilling, Ann. *The Year of the Worm* (5–7). 2000, Lion paper $7.50 (978-0-7459-4294-0). Lonely Peter Wrigley, who is mourning his father's death, gets his chance to become a hero when he uncovers a group of birds'-nest poachers in this English novel set in the Lake District. (Rev: SLJ 3/01)

176 Pratchett, Terry. *Nation* (7–10). 2008, HarperCollins $16.99 (978-0-06-143301-6). In this survival tale, a tidal wave leaves survivors of very different backgrounds to re-create civilization and consider what it is they treasure and why. (Rev: BL 8/08)

177 Ransome, Arthur. *Swallows and Amazons* (4–7). Illus. by author. 1985, Godine paper $14.95 (978-0-87923-573-4). These adventures of the four Walker children have been read for many years. A reissue. Others in the series *Swallowdale* (1985); *Peter Duck* (1987).

178 Ransome, Arthur. *Winter Holiday* (4–7). Illus. by author. 1989, Godine paper $14.95 (978-0-87923-661-8). Further adventures of the Swallows and Amazons. A reissue. A sequel is *Coot Club*.

179 Rees, Celia. *Pirates!* (7–10). 2003, Bloomsbury $17.95 (978-1-58234-816-2). Horrified by the prospect of an arranged marriage to a plantation owner, teenage Nancy and a close slave friend run off and join a pirate crew in this swashbuckling adventure set in the 18th century. (Rev: BCCB 1/04; BL 12/15/03*; HBG 4/04; SLJ 10/03*)

180 Repp, Gloria. *Mik-Shrok* (4–8). Illus. by Jim Brooks. 1998, Bob Jones Univ. paper $7.49 (978-1-57924-069-1). A married missionary couple journey to a remote Alaska village in 1950, where they begin their work and, in time, acquire a dog team led by Mik-Shrok. (Rev: BL 3/1/99)

181 Richards, Justin. *The Chaos Code* (7–10). 2007, Bloomsbury $16.95 (978-1-59990-124-4). Matt's father is missing, and Matt must travel through time and kingdoms to find him in this fast-paced tale. (Rev: BL 10/15/07) ⑨

182 Richardson, V. A. *The Moneylender's Daughter* (5–8). 2006, Bloomsbury $17.95 (978-1-58234-885-8). In this exciting sequel to *The House of Windjammer* (2003), Adam Windjammer sets sail for America, finds himself burdened with more responsibility on the death of his uncle, and is preoccupied with thoughts of Jade van Helsen, daughter of the man who brought his family to the brink of ruin. (Rev: BL 6/1–15/06; SLJ 9/06)

183 Rochman, Hazel, and Darlene Z. McCampbell, eds. *Leaving Home* (7–12). 1997, HarperCollins LB $16.89 (978-0-06-024874-1). These 16 stories by well-known writers describe various forms of leaving home, from immigration to a new country to running away or taking a trip. (Rev: BL 1/1–15/97; SLJ 3/97*)

184 Rossell, Judith. *Jack Jones and the Pirate Curse* (4–7). 2007, Walker $15.95 (978-0-8027-9661-5). Jack inherits the family curse and finds himself suddenly facing a band of vengeful pirates he knows he must fight with brain rather than brawn. (Rev: BL 4/1/07; SLJ 6/07)

185 Ruckman, Ivy. *Night of the Twisters* (6–8). 1984, HarperCollins paper $5.99 (978-0-06-440176-0). An account based on actual events about children who survive a devastating series of tornadoes.

186 Salisbury, Graham. *Night of the Howling Dogs* (5–8). 2007, Random $16.99 (978-0-385-73122-5). Dylan, an 8th-grader from Hilo, Hawaii, goes on a trip to the coast with his scout troop to camp in the shadow of a volcano and faces a bully and natural disasters. (Rev: BL 8/07; HB 9–10/07; SLJ 8/07) ⑨

187 Scrimger, Richard. *Into the Ravine* (6–9). 2007, Tundra paper $9.95 (978-0-88776-822-4). Jules, Chris, and Cory build a raft and float down the town creek in this adventure that has all the elements boys could want — including bullies, cute girls, and jewel thieves; the action will appeal to reluctant readers. (Rev: BL 11/1/07; SLJ 1/08)

188 Selznick, Brian. *The Invention of Hugo Cabret* (4–9). Illus. by author. 2007, Scholastic $22.99 (978-0-439-81378-5). In 1930s Paris a young apprentice clock keeper, an orphan who struggles to make his way in life, finds himself drawn into a complex mystery that threatens the anonymity he treasures; part graphic novel, part flip book, the design is as compelling as the story. (Rev: BL 1/1–15/07; SLJ 3/07*)

189 Shahan, Sherry. *Death Mountain* (5–8). 2005, Peachtree $15.95 (978-1-56145-353-5). In this gripping thriller, 14-year-old Erin uses her survival skills to rescue her new friend Mae and navigate their way through a mountain wilderness to safety. (Rev: SLJ 11/05; VOYA 2/06)

190 Shusterman, Neal. *Dissidents* (7–10). 1989, Little, Brown $13.95 (978-0-316-78904-2). A teenage boy joins his mother, the American ambassador in Moscow, and becomes involved in a spy caper. (Rev: BL 8/89; SLJ 10/89)

191 Skurzynski, Gloria, and Alane Ferguson. *Cliff-Hanger* (4–7). Series: Mysteries in Our National Parks. 1999, National Geographic $15.95 (978-0-7922-7036-2). In Mesa Verde National Park, the Landon family encounters two problems — a foster care girl named Lucky, who is deceitful, and a rampaging cougar. (Rev: BL 4/15/99; HBG 10/99; SLJ 5/99)

192 Smelcer, John. *The Trap* (6–9). 2006, Holt $15.95 (978-0-8050-7939-5). Johnny, a young Native American, sets out to find his grandfather, who is caught in an animal trap in the Alaskan wilderness. (Rev: HB 11-12/06; SLJ 10/06)

193 Smith, Cotton. *Dark Trail to Dodge* (7–10). 1997, Walker $20.95 (978-0-8027-4158-5). Eighteen-year-old Tyrel Bannon faces unusual problems on his first cattle drive when rustlers attack and plan on taking no prisoners. (Rev: BL 6/1–15/97; VOYA 8/97)

194 Smith, Roland. *Cryptid Hunters* (5–8). 2005, Hyperion $15.99 (978-0-7868-5161-4). Thirteen-year-old twins Marty and Grace find themselves in an action-packed adventure in the Congo. (Rev: BL 2/1/05; SLJ 5/05)

195 Smith, Roland. *Peak* (8–11). 2007, Harcourt $17.00 (978-0-15-202417-8). Aptly named Peak joins his father in Tibet, where he may become the youngest person (at 14) to climb Mount Everest; this is an exciting, multilayered adventure story. (Rev: BL 4/1/07; HB 5–6/07; SLJ 6/07) ⊘

196 Soto, Gary. *Crazy Weekend* (4–7). 1994, Scholastic paper $13.95 (978-0-590-47814-4). Two boys are being pursued by some crooks in this fast-moving adventure story. (Rev: BCCB 7–8/94; SLJ 3/94)

197 Sperry, Armstrong. *Call It Courage* (5–8). Illus. by author. 1968, Macmillan $16.95 (978-0-02-786030-6); paper $4.99 (978-0-689-71391-0). The "Crusoe" theme is interwoven with this story of a Polynesian boy's courage in facing the sea he feared. Newbery Medal winner, 1941.

198 Springer, Nancy. *Lionclaw* (5–8). Series: Tales of Rowan Hood. 2002, Putnam $16.99 (978-0-399-23716-4). Gentle, music-loving Lionel abandons his timidity when Rowan Hood is captured, but, despite his newfound courage, his father still refuses to accept him in this sequel to *Rowan Hood: Outlaw Girl of Sherwood Forest* (2001). (Rev: BL 10/1/02; HBG 10/03; SLJ 10/02; VOYA 12/02)

199 Springer, Nancy. *Outlaw Princess of Sherwood* (4–7). Series: Tales of Rowan Hood. 2003, Putnam $16.99 (978-0-399-23721-8). The third installment of this series features Princess Ettarde, whose father has hatched a dastardly plot to lure Etty away from Sherwood Forest. (Rev: BL 12/1/03; HBG 4/04; SLJ 9/03)

200 Steer, Dugald, ed. *Pirateology: The Sea Journal of Captain William Lubber* (4–7). Illus. by Yvonne Gilbert. 2006, Candlewick $19.99 (978-0-7636-3143-7). An authentic-looking large-format scrapbook chronicling the pirate-chasing adventures of a sea captain of old, complete with treasure maps and a working compass. (Rev: BL 7/06; SLJ 12/06)

201 Stenhouse, Ted. *Murder on the Ridge* (5–8). 2006, Kids Can $16.95 (978-1-55337-892-1); paper $6.95 (978-1-55337-893-8). Will and Arthur, a white boy and an Indian boy who are friends despite the prejudices of 1950s Canada, investigate a World War I mystery in the latest installment in the series that started with *Across the Steel River* (2001) and *A Dirty Deed* (2003). (Rev: BL 5/15/06)

202 Stevenson, Robin. *Dead in the Water* (5–8). Series: Orca Sports. 2008, Orca paper $9.95 (978-1-55143-962-4). While at sea as part of a sailing camp, Simon ends up a captive on a boat full of poachers in this thriller for reluctant readers. (Rev: BL 3/15/08)

203 Stewart, A. C. *Ossian House* (6–8). 1976, Phillips LB $26.95 (978-0-87599-219-8). An 11-year-old boy inherits a mansion in Scotland and sets out alone to live there for the summer.

204 Stewart, Trenton Lee. *The Mysterious Benedict Society and the Perilous Journey* (4–7). Illus. by Diana Sudyka. Series: The Mysterious Benedict Society. 2008, Little, Brown $16.99 (978-0-316-05780-6). Reynie, Kate, Sticky, and Constance have many adventures as they travel to rescue Mr. Benedict from the evil Mr. Curtain in this action-packed sequel to *The Mysterious Benedict Society* (2007). (Rev: BL 3/15/08; SLJ 5/08)

205 Strickland, Brad. *The House Where Nobody Lived* (5–8). Series: Lewis Barnavelt. 2006, Dial $16.99 (978-0-8037-3148-6). Lewis befriends David, whose family has moved into a creepy, long-abandoned house, which may be haunted; with help from Uncle Jonathan and a neighborhood witch, Lewis confronts magic and danger. (Rev: BL 1/1–15/07; SLJ 1/07)

206 Sullivan, Paul. *The Unforgiving Land* (7–10). 1996, Royal Fireworks paper $9.99 (978-0-88092-256-2). A white trader gives guns and bullets to a group of Inuit, causing a breakdown in the delicate harmony between nature and humankind and destruction of the Inuit way of life. (Rev: VOYA 8/96)

207 Swarthout, Glendon, and Kathryn Swarthout. *Whichaway* (7–10). 1997, Rising Moon paper $6.95 (978-0-87358-676-4). A reissue of an exciting story about a boy whose character is tested when he is trapped with two broken legs on top of a windmill in an isolated area of Texas. (Rev: HBG 3/98; VOYA 2/98)

208 Taylor, Theodore. *The Cay* (5–8). 1987, Doubleday $16.95 (978-0-385-07906-8); Avon paper $4.95 (978-0-380-00142-2). A blind boy and an old black sailor are shipwrecked on a coral island. (Rev: BL 9/1/89)

209 Taylor, Theodore. *Ice Drift* (4–7). 2005, Harcourt $16.00 (978-0-15-205081-8). Inuit brothers Alika, 14, and Sulu, 10, struggle to survive over the months that they are trapped on an ice floe that is slowly floating south in the Greenland Strait. (Rev: BL 2/1/05; SLJ 1/05)

210 Taylor, Theodore. *The Odyssey of Ben O'Neal* (6–8). Illus. by Richard Cuffari. 1991, Avon paper $3.99 (978-0-380-71026-3). Action and humor are skillfully combined in this story of a trip by Ben and his friend Tee to England at the turn of the 20th century. Two others in the series *Teetoncey; Teetoncey and Ben O'Neal* (both 1981).

211 Thomas, Jane Resh. *Blind Mountain* (4–7). 2006, Clarion $15.00 (978-0-618-64872-6). Forced to go on a hiking trip with his bossy father in the mountainous Montana wilderness, 12-year-old Sam finds himself in charge of their survival when his father is temporarily blinded by a branch. (Rev: BL 12/1/06; SLJ 12/06)

212 Thomas, Jane Resh. *Courage at Indian Deep* (5–7). 1984, Houghton paper $6.95 (978-0-395-55699-3). A young boy must help save a ship caught in a sudden storm.

213 Thompson, Julian. *The Grounding of Group Six* (8–12). 1983, Avon paper $3.99 (978-0-380-83386-3). Five 16-year-olds think they are being sent to an exclusive school but actually they have been slated for murder.

214 Tomlinson, Theresa. *Voyage of the Snake Lady* (6–9). 2007, Eos $16.99 (978-0-06-084739-5). Myrina and her fellow women warriors must come to the aid of Iphigenia, the daughter of Agamemnon, in this sequel to *The Moon Riders* that draws on ancient Greek mythology. (Rev: BL 11/15/07; SLJ 3/08)

215 Torrey, Michele. *Voyage of Ice* (4–7). Series: Chronicle of Courage. 2004, Knopf LB $17.99 (978-0-375-92381-4). In 1851, 15-year-old Nick signs on as a hand aboard the whaler *Sea Hawk* and soon discovers unexpected hardships, including struggling to survive in the Arctic. (Rev: BL 5/15/04; SLJ 7/04)

216 Townsend, John Rowe. *The Islanders* (7–10). 1981, HarperCollins $11.95 (978-0-397-31940-4). Two strangers washed up on a remote island are regarded as enemies by the inhabitants.

217 Townsend, John Rowe. *Kate and the Revolution* (7–10). 1983, HarperCollins LB $12.89 (978-0-397-32016-5). A 17-year-old girl is attracted to a visiting prince and then the adventure begins.

218 Trueman, Terry. *Hurricane* (5–7). 2008, HarperCollins $15.99 (978-0-06-000018-9). José is 13 when Hurricane Mitch hits his village in Honduras and he must deal with the death and destruction left behind. (Rev: BL 12/1/07; SLJ 3/08)

219 Ullman, James R. *Banner in the Sky* (7–9). 1988, HarperCollins LB $12.89 (978-0-397-30264-2); paper $6.99 (978-0-06-447048-3). The thrilling story of a boy's determination to conquer a challenging Swiss mountain. (Rev: SLJ 2/88)

220 Umansky, Kaye. *Solomon Snow and the Stolen Jewel* (4–7). 2007, Candlewick $12.99 (978-0-7636-2793-5). In this sequel to *Solomon Snow and the Silver Spoon* (2005), Solomon and Prudence set out to help Prudence's father escape from a prison ship and become caught up in a plot to steal a cursed ruby. (Rev: BL 4/15/07; SLJ 7/07)

221 Volponi, Paul. *Hurricane Song* (7–12). 2008, Viking $15.99 (978-0-670-06160-0). Miles and his father find themselves in the middle of the chaos following Hurricane Katrina when they head to the New Orleans Superdome for shelter. (Rev: BL 5/1/08; SLJ 8/08)

222 Wallace, Bill. *Danger in Quicksand Swamp* (4–7). 1989, Holiday $16.95 (978-0-8234-0786-6). While searching for buried treasure, Ben and Jake become stranded on an island near Quicksand Swamp. (Rev: BL 1/1/90; SLJ 10/89)

223 Wallace, Bill. *Trapped in Death Cave* (5–8). 1984, Holiday $16.95 (978-0-8234-0516-9). Gary is convinced his grandpa was murdered to secure a map indicating where gold is buried.

224 Whittaker, Dorothy Raymond. *Angels of the Swamp* (6–8). 1991, Walker $17.95 (978-0-8027-8129-1). Two teenage orphans who manage to survive on an island off the Florida coast discover they're not alone. (Rev: BL 1/15/92; SLJ 4/92)

225 Williams, Michael. *The Genuine Half-Moon Kid* (7–10). 1994, Dutton $15.99 (978-0-525-67479-5). Like questing Jason in Greek mythology, 18-year-old South African Jay Watson sets out with some friends to find a yellow wood box left him by his grandfather. (Rev: BL 6/1–15/94)

226 Wilson, N. D. *Leepike Ridge* (4–7). 2007, Random $15.99 (978-0-375-83873-6). Eleven-year-old Tom must use his survival skills when he finds himself trapped in a series of caves where he meets Reg, who's been trapped for three years, and discovers mysterious carvings on the wall. (Rev: BL 5/15/07; HB 5–6/07; LMC 10/07; SLJ 5/07)

227 Withers, Pam. *Camp Wild* (7–9). Series: Orca Currents. 2005, Orca paper $7.95 (978-1-55143-361-5). For reluctant readers, this is the story of 14-year-old Wilf, who must learn to work with others to succeed in his escape from summer camp. (Rev: SLJ 10/05; VOYA 10/05)

228 Wynne-Jones, Tim. *The Maestro* (6–8). 1996, Orchard LB $17.99 (978-0-531-08894-4). This moving novel describes a boy's maturation in the wilderness of northern Ontario and his friendship with a gifted musician. (Rev: BL 12/15/96*; SLJ 1/97; VOYA 4/97)

229 Yolen, Jane, and Robert J. Harris. *The Rogues* (6–10). Series: Scottish Quartet. 2007, Philomel $18.99 (978-0-399-23898-7). In the late 18th century, Roddy Macallan's family is forced to leave its Scottish tenant farm; Roddy goes back to retrieve a treasure and finds himself in big trouble, from which he is saved by a rogue named Alan Dunbar; historical facts are found throughout the adventure, which ends in North America. (Rev: BL 9/15/07; SLJ 9/07)

230 Zindel, Paul. *Reef of Death* (7–12). 1998, HarperCollins $15.95 (978-0-06-024728-7). A tale of terror about two teens, a monster creature that lives on an Australian reef, and a mad geologist who has a torture chamber on her freighter. (Rev: BL 3/1/98; HBG 9/98; SLJ 3/98; VOYA 4/98)

Animal Stories

231 Adler, C. S. *More Than a Horse* (5–7). 1997, Clarion $15.00 (978-0-395-79769-3). Leeann and her mother move to a dude ranch in Arizona, where the young girl develops a love of horses. (Rev: BCCB 3/97; BL 3/15/97; SLJ 4/97)

232 Adler, C. S. *One Unhappy Horse* (5–7). 2001, Clarion $16.00 (978-0-618-04912-7). Set on a small ranch near Tucson, this novel features 12-year-old Jan, her horse, Dove, an old lady in a retirement home, and Jan's new friend, Lisa. (Rev: BL 3/1/01; HBG 10/01; SLJ 4/01)

233 Adler, C. S. *That Horse Whiskey!* (6–8). 1996, Avon paper $3.99 (978-0-380-72601-1). Lainey, 13, disappointed that she didn't get a horse for her birthday, works at a stable training a stubborn horse and falls for a city boy. (Rev: BL 11/1/94; SLJ 11/94; VOYA 12/94)

234 Alter, Judith. *Callie Shaw, Stable Boy* (5–8). 1996, Eakin $16.95 (978-1-57168-092-1). During the Great Depression, Callie, disguised as a boy, works in a stable and uncovers a race-fixing racket. (Rev: BL 2/1/97; SLJ 8/97)

235 Alter, Judith. *Maggie and a Horse Named Devildust* (5–7). 1989, Ellen C. Temple paper $5.95 (978-0-936650-08-1). Maggie is determined to ride her spirited horse in the Wild West show in this historical horse story. (Rev: BL 4/15/89)

236 Alter, Judith. *Maggie and the Search for Devildust* (5–7). 1989, Ellen C. Temple paper $5.95 (978-0-936650-09-8). Maggie, a gorgeous girl of the Old West, sets out to find her horse, which has been stolen. (Rev: BL 10/1/89)

237 Appelt, Kathi. *The Underneath* (4–8). Illus. by David Small. 2008, Atheneum $16.99 (978-1-4169-5058-5). Newborn kittens, a bloodhound named Ranger, and a water snake find safety together in this story set in the mysterious bayous of East Texas. Newbery Honor Book, 2009. (Rev: BL 5/15/08; SLJ 6/08)

238 Armstrong, William H. *Sounder* (6–10). Illus. 1969, HarperCollins LB $17.89 (978-0-06-020144-9); paper $5.99 (978-0-06-440020-6). The moving story of an African American sharecropper, his family, and his devoted coon dog, Sounder. Newbery Medal winner, 1970. A sequel is *Sour Land* (1971).

239 Bagnold, Enid. *National Velvet* (5–8). Illus. by Ted Lewin. 1985, Avon paper $4.99 (978-0-380-71235-9). The now-classic story of Heather Brown and her struggle to ride in the Grand National. A reissue. (Rev: BL 12/15/85)

240 Bastedo, Jamie. *Tracking Triple Seven* (5–7). 2001, Red Deer paper $9.95 (978-0-88995-238-6). Benji, a teenage boy grieving his mother's death, becomes involved with biologists tracking grizzly bears near his father's mine in Canada. (Rev: BL 2/1/02)

241 Benchley, Peter. *Jaws* (8–12). 1974, Doubleday paper $6.99 (978-0-449-21963-8). The best-selling novel about a small Long Island town and the creature that became a threat to its beaches.

242 Brooke, Lauren. *Heartland: Coming Home* (4–7). 2000, Scholastic paper $4.99 (978-0-439-13020-2). When her mother dies, Amy works through her grief by helping horses with behavioral problems in this novel set on a Virginia horse farm. (Rev: BL 9/15/00)

243 Burgess, Melvin. *The Cry of the Wolf* (5–8). 1994, Morrow $17.99 (978-0-397-30693-0). Young Ben Tilley insists that wolves run past his farm in rural Surrey, even though they have supposedly been gone from England for 500 years. (Rev: BL 10/15/92; SLJ 9/92)

244 Burnford, Sheila. *Bel Ria* (7–12). 2006, Random $17.95 (978-1-59017-211-7). Set in France during World War II, this is a novel about a poodle's amazing adventures.

245 Carlson, Nolan. *Summer and Shiner* (5–8). 1992, Hearth paper $6.95 (978-0-9627947-4-2). In a small Kansas town in the 1940s, 12-year-old Carley adopts a raccoon called Shiner. (Rev: BL 9/15/92)

246 Cleary, Beverly. *Strider* (5–9). Illus. 1991, Morrow LB $17.89 (978-0-688-09901-5). In this sequel to the 1984 Newbery winner *Dear Mr. Henshaw,* Leigh Botts is beginning high school and still writing in his diary, with his beloved dog, Strider, by his side. (Rev: BCCB 10/91; BL 7/91*; HB 9–10/91; SLJ 9/91)

247 DeJong, Meindert. *Along Came a Dog* (4–7). Illus. by Maurice Sendak. 1958, HarperCollins paper $5.95 (978-0-06-440114-2). The friendship of a timid, lonely dog and a toeless little red hen is the basis for a very moving story, full of suspense.

248 Eckert, Allan W. *Incident at Hawk's Hill* (6–8). Illus. by John Schoenherr. 1995, Bantam paper $6.99 (978-0-316-20948-9). A 6-year-old boy wanders away from home and is nurtured and protected by a badger.

249 Gallico, Paul. *The Snow Goose* (7–12). Illus. 1941, Knopf $15.00 (978-0-394-44593-9); Tundra paper $9.99 (978-0-7710-3250-9). A hunchbacked artist and a young child nurse a wounded snow goose back to health, and it later returns to protect them in this large, illustrated 50th anniversary edition of the classic tale. (Rev: BL 9/15/92)

250 George, Jean Craighead. *The Cry of the Crow* (5–7). 1980, HarperCollins paper $5.99 (978-0-06-440131-9). Mandy finds a helpless baby crow in the woods and tames it.

251 George, Jean Craighead. *Frightful's Mountain* (5–8). 1999, Dutton $18.99 (978-0-525-46166-1). Frightful, the falcon in *My Side of the Mountain,* is the central character in this novel in which she has difficult and enjoyable adventures in the wild. (Rev: BL 9/1/99; HBG 3/00; SLJ 9/99; VOYA 6/00)

252 Ghent, Natale. *No Small Thing* (5–8). 2005, Candlewick $15.00 (978-0-7636-2422-4). Nathaniel and his siblings struggle to keep their horse while their single mother struggles to keep her family afloat. (Rev: BL 3/1/05; SLJ 4/05)

253 Ghent, Natale. *Piper* (5–7). 2001, Orca paper $6.95 (978-1-55143-167-3). The love and attention young Wesley showers on a tiny Australian shepherd puppy helps her recover from the death of her father. (Rev: BL 3/1/01)

254 Gipson, Fred. *Old Yeller* (6–9). Illus. by Carl Burger. 1956, HarperCollins $23.00 (978-0-06-011545-6); paper $5.99 (978-0-06-440382-5). A powerful story set in the Texas hill country about a 14-year-old boy and the ugly stray dog he comes to love. Also use *Savage Sam* (1976).

255 Graeber, Charlotte. *Grey Cloud* (6–8). Illus. 1979, Macmillan $8.95 (978-0-02-736690-7). Tom and Orville become friends when they train pigeons for a big race.

256 Hall, Elizabeth. *Child of the Wolves* (4–7). 1996, Houghton $16.00 (978-0-395-76502-9). Granite, a Siberian husky pup, must survive in the wilderness when he is separated from his family. (Rev: BCCB 3/96; BL 4/1/96; VOYA 6/96)

257 Hall, Lynn. *The Soul of the Silver Dog* (5–8). 1992, Harcourt $16.95 (978-0-15-277196-6). A handicapped dog bonds with his new teenage owner living in a troubled family. (Rev: BL 4/15/92; SLJ 6/92)

258 Heinz, Brian. *Cheyenne Medicine Hat* (4–8). Illus. by Gregory Manchess. 2006, Creative Editions $18.95 (978-1-56846-181-6). The story of a summer in the life of a wild mustang mare as she tries to keep her band safe from predators — both animal and human. (Rev: SLJ 11/06)

259 Henkes, Kevin. *Protecting Marie* (5–7). 1995, Greenwillow $19.99 (978-0-688-13958-2). Fanny is afraid that she will lose her pet dog if her temperamental father decides the dog must go. (Rev: BCCB 3/95; BL 3/15/95; HB 7–8/95; SLJ 5/95*)

260 Henry, Marguerite. *King of the Wind* (5–8). Illus. by Wesley Dennis. 1990, Macmillan $17.95 (978-0-02-743629-7). The story of the famous stallion Godolphin Arabian, ancestor of Man O'War and founder of the Thoroughbred breed. Newbery Medal winner, 1949. Also use *Black Gold* and *Born to Trot* (both 1987).

261 Henry, Marguerite. *Mustang, Wild Spirit of the West* (6–8). Illus. by Robert Lougheed. 1992, Macmillan paper $4.99 (978-0-689-71601-0). An excellent horse story written by a master.

262 High, Linda O. *Hound Heaven* (5–8). 1995, Holiday $15.95 (978-0-8234-1195-5). More than anything in the world, Silver Iris wants a dog, but her grandfather won't allow it. (Rev: BCCB 12/95; SLJ 11/95; VOYA 2/96)

263 Holland, Isabelle. *Toby the Splendid* (6–8). 1987, Walker $13.95 (978-0-8027-6674-8). An intense argument arises between mother and daughter when young Janet buys a horse and wants to start riding. (Rev: BL 4/1/87; SLJ 4/87; VOYA 8/89)

264 Howard, Jean G. *Half a Cage* (6–8). Illus. 1978, Tidal Pr. $5.50 (978-0-930954-07-9). Ann's pet monkey causes so many problems she wonders if she should give it away.

265 Hunter, Erin. *Seekers: The Quest Begins* (5–8). Series: Seekers. 2008, HarperCollins $16.99 (978-0-06-087122-2). Readers are introduced to three bear cubs — a polar bear, a black bear, and a grizzly — in this first installment in a series about survival and the realities of bear life in the wild and in captivity. (Rev: BL 5/15/08)

266 Jimenez, Juan Ramon. *Platero y Yo / Platero and I* (5–7). Trans. by Myra Cohn Livingston and Joseph F. Dominguez. Illus. by Antonio Frasconi.

1994, Clarion $16.00 (978-0-395-62365-7). Using both Spanish and English texts, this book contains excerpts from the prose poem about a writer and his donkey. (Rev: BL 6/1–15/94) [863]

267 Jones, Adrienne. *The Hawks of Chelney* (7–9). Illus. 1978, HarperCollins $13.95 (978-0-06-023057-9). A young outcast and his girlfriend try to understand the hawks and their habits.

268 Kipling, Rudyard. *The Jungle Book: The Mowgli Stories* (4–7). Illus. by Jerry Pinkney. 1995, Morrow $25.99 (978-0-688-09979-4). Eight stories about Mowgli are reprinted with 18 handsome watercolors. (Rev: BCCB 6/96; BL 10/15/95; SLJ 11/95)

269 Kjelgaard, James A. *Big Red* (6–9). 1956, Holiday $17.95 (978-0-8234-0007-2); Bantam paper $5.50 (978-0-553-15434-4). This is the perennial favorite about Danny and his Irish setter. Continued in *Irish Red* and *Outlaw Red*. (Rev: BL 9/1/89)

270 Kjelgaard, James A. *Snow Dog* (6–8). 1983, Bantam paper $4.99 (978-0-553-15560-0). In the wilderness, a snow dog fights for survival. A sequel is *Wild Trek*.

271 Kjelgaard, James A. *Stormy* (6–8). 1983, Bantam paper $5.50 (978-0-553-15468-9). Alan is helped to accept his father's being sent to prison through love for a retriever named Stormy.

272 Levin, Betty. *Look Back, Moss* (5–8). 1998, Greenwillow $15.00 (978-0-688-15696-1). Young Moss, disturbed by his mother's lack of attention and his own weight problems, welcomes an injured sheepdog into the family. (Rev: BCCB 10/98; BL 8/98; HB 1–2/99; HBG 3/99; SLJ 11/98)

273 Lippincott, Joseph W. *Wilderness Champion* (7–9). 1944, HarperCollins $11.95 (978-0-397-30099-0). This novel, now almost 50 years old, tells about a most unusual hound dog.

274 Lowry, Lois. *Stay! Keeper's Story* (5–8). Illus. 1997, Houghton $16.00 (978-0-395-87048-8). A dog named Keeper narrates this story about his puppyhood and the three different masters he has had. (Rev: BL 11/1/97; HBG 3/98; SLJ 10/97)

275 Malterre, Elona. *The Last Wolf of Ireland* (5–7). 1990, Houghton $15.00 (978-0-395-54381-8). Devin and his friend Katey hide wolf pups when the pups are threatened. (Rev: BCCB 10/90; BL 9/15/90*; SLJ 10/90)

276 Morey, Walt. *Gentle Ben* (5–8). Illus. 1991, Puffin paper $6.99 (978-0-14-036035-6). A warm story of deep trust and friendship between a boy and an Alaskan bear.

277 Morey, Walt. *Scrub Dog of Alaska* (4–8). 1989, Blue Heron paper $7.95 (978-0-936085-13-5). A pup, abandoned because of its small size, turns out to be a winner. Also use *Kavik the Wolf Dog* (1977, Dutton).

278 Morey, Walt. *Year of the Black Pony* (5–8). Illus. by Fredrika Spillman. 1989, Blue Heron paper $6.95 (978-0-936085-14-2). A family story about a boy's love for his pony in rural Oregon at the turn of the 20th century.

279 Morgan, Clay. *The Boy Who Spoke Dog* (5–8). 2003, Dutton $15.99 (978-0-525-47159-2). Marooned on an island dominated by two warring dog packs, Jack, a young cabin boy, feels very much alone until he develops a friendship with a border collie named Moxie. (Rev: BL 1/1–15/04; SLJ 1/04; VOYA 6/04)

280 Mowat, Farley. *The Dog Who Wouldn't Be* (4–7). Illus. by Paul Galdone. 1957, Bantam paper $4.99 (978-0-553-27928-3). The humorous story of Mutt, a dog of character and personality, and his boy.

281 Mukerji, Dhan Gopal. *Gay-Neck: The Story of a Pigeon* (4–8). Illus. by Boris Artzybasheff. 1968, Dutton $16.99 (978-0-525-30400-5). A boy from India's brave carrier pigeon is selected to perform dangerous missions during World War I. Newbery Medal winner, 1928.

282 Myers, Anna. *Red-Dirt Jessie* (4–7). 1992, Walker $13.95 (978-0-8027-8172-7). In this tale of the Depression era in Oklahoma, 12-year-old Jessie helps keep her family together. (Rev: BCCB 10/92; BL 1/15/93; HB 1–2/93; SLJ 11/92*)

283 Naylor, Phyllis Reynolds. *Saving Shiloh* (4–7). 1997, Simon & Schuster $15.00 (978-0-689-81460-0). In this sequel to the Newbery Medal–winning *Shiloh* and *Shiloh Season*, Marty again encounters the evil Judd Travers, who has been accused of murder. (Rev: BL 9/1/97*; HB 9–10/97; HBG 3/98; SLJ 9/97)

284 Naylor, Phyllis Reynolds. *Shiloh* (4–8). 1991, Macmillan $16.00 (978-0-689-31614-2). When a beagle follows him home, Marty, from a West Virginia family with a strict code of honor, learns a painful lesson about right and wrong. Newbery Medal winner, 1992. (Rev: BCCB 10/91; BL 12/1/91*; HB 1–2/92; SLJ 9/91)

285 Naylor, Phyllis Reynolds. *Shiloh Season* (4–8). 1996, Simon & Schuster $15.00 (978-0-689-80647-6). The evil Judd Travers wants his dog back from the Prestons in this sequel to *Shiloh* (1991). (Rev: BCCB 12/96; BL 11/15/96*; HB 11–12/96; SLJ 11/96)

286 O'Hara, Mary. *My Friend Flicka* (7–12). 1988, HarperCollins paper $6.00 (978-0-06-080902-7). This story about Ken McLaughlin and the filly named Flicka is continued in *Thunderhead, Son of Flicka*.

287 Oppel, Kenneth. *Darkwing* (6–9). 2007, Eos $16.99 (978-0-06-085054-8). In this story set 65 million years ago, Dusk is different from the rest of his colony of chiropters — he's the first bat with the ability to fly and use echo vision — and he uses his abilities to save the colony from other changing species. (Rev: BL 9/1/07; SLJ 9/07)

288 Parker, Cam. *A Horse in New York* (4–8). 1989, Avon paper $2.75 (978-0-380-75704-6). To save Blue, the horse she rode at summer camp, from destruction, Tiffin has to convince her parents to board him for the winter. (Rev: BL 12/15/89)

289 Peterson, Shelley. *Sundancer* (6–9). 2007, Key Porter paper $7.95 (978-1-55263-842-2). Bird is the only one at Saddle Creek Farm who can handle the new horse, Sundancer, and her work with him helps her through her own personal and family problems. (Rev: BL 8/07)

290 Peyton, K. M. *The Team* (7–9). Illus. 1976, HarperCollins $12.95 (978-0-690-01083-1). Ruth is determined to own the special show pony that is for sale.

291 Platt, Chris. *Moon Shadow* (4–7). 2006, Peachtree $14.95 (978-1-56145-382-5). When a wild mustang mare dies giving birth near her Nevada home, 13-year-old Callie vows to raise and train the foal. (Rev: BL 11/1/06; SLJ 1/07)

292 Rawlings, Marjorie Kinnan. *The Yearling* (6–9). Illus. 1983, Macmillan paper $5.95 (978-0-02-044931-7). The classic story of Joss and the orphaned fawn he adopts. Illus. by N. C. Wyeth. (Rev: BL 9/1/89)

293 Salten, Felix. *Bambi: A Life in the Woods* (5–8). 1926, Pocket paper $4.99 (978-0-671-66607-1). The growing to maturity of an Austrian deer.

294 Sewell, Anna. *Black Beauty* (7–9). 1974, Airmont paper $1.50 (978-0-8049-0023-2). The classic sentimental story about the cruelty and kindness experienced by a horse in Victorian England.

295 Sherlock, Patti. *Four of a Kind* (5–9). 1991, Holiday $13.95 (978-0-8234-0913-6). Andy's grandfather agrees to lend him money to buy a pair of horses, and he sets his sights on winning the horse-pulling contest at a state fair. (Rev: BL 12/1/91; SLJ 10/91)

296 Snelling, Lauraine. *The Winner's Circle* (5–8). Series: Golden Filly. 1995, Bethany House paper $5.99 (978-1-55661-533-7). In this horse story, Trish Evanston, a high school senior who is also a jockey and Triple Crown winner, is being stalked by a mystery man who sends her threatening notes. (Rev: SLJ 10/95; VOYA 4/96)

297 Springer, Nancy. *A Horse to Love* (4–8). 1987, HarperCollins $11.95 (978-0-06-025824-5). Erin's parents buy her a horse hoping that this will help cure her shyness. (Rev: BL 3/87; SLJ 3/87)

298 Sullivan, Paul. *Legend of the North* (7–12). 1995, Royal Fireworks paper $9.99 (978-0-88092-308-8). Set in northern Canada, this novel contains two narratives, the first about a young wolf's strug-

gle for dominance within the pack, and the second about an elderly Inuit and his survival in the harsh tundra regions. (Rev: BL 1/1–15/96; VOYA 4/96)

299 Taylor, Theodore. *Tuck Triumphant* (4–7). 1991, Avon paper $5.99 (978-0-380-71323-3). A 1950s novel about a blind dog in a loving family and the deaf Korean boy they adopt. (Rev: BL 2/1/91)

300 Terhune, Albert Payson. *Lad: A Dog* (7–9). 1993, Puffin paper $7.99 (978-0-14-036474-3). The classic story of a beautiful collie. The beginning of a lengthy series now all out of print.

301 Wilbur, Frances. *The Dog with Golden Eyes* (4–7). Illus. 1998, Milkweed paper $6.95 (978-1-57131-615-8). Cassie befriends a white dog that turns out to be an arctic wolf, and she must find his owners before he becomes a target for the police or hunters. (Rev: BCCB 9/98; BL 9/1/98; HBG 3/99; SLJ 7/98; VOYA 8/98)

Classics

Europe

GENERAL AND MISCELLANEOUS

302 Dumas, Alexandre. *The Count of Monte Cristo* (8–12). Illus. 1996, Random $25.95 (978-0-679-60199-9). The classic French novel about false imprisonment, escape, and revenge.

303 Dumas, Alexandre. *The Three Musketeers* (8–12). 1984, Dodd paper $5.95 (978-0-553-21337-9). A novel of daring and intrigue in France. Sequels are *The Man in the Iron Mask* and *Twenty Years After* (available in various editions).

304 Maupassant, Guy de. *The Best Short Stories of Guy de Maupassant* (7–12). 1968, Amereon $26.95 (978-0-88411-589-2). The French master is represented by 19 tales including "The Diamond Necklace."

305 Verne, Jules. *Around the World in Eighty Days* (7–12). 1996, Puffin paper $4.99 (978-0-14-036711-9). Phileas Fogg and servant Passepartout leave on a world trip in this 1873 classic adventure. (Rev: SLJ 7/96)

306 Verne, Jules. *A Journey to the Center of the Earth* (7–12). Illus. 1984, Penguin paper $7.00 (978-0-14-002265-0). A group of adventurers enter the earth through a volcano in Iceland. First published in French in 1864.

307 Verne, Jules. *Twenty Thousand Leagues Under the Sea* (7–12). 1990, Viking paper $5.99 (978-0-14-036721-8). Evil Captain Nemo captures a group of underwater explorers. First published in 1869. A sequel is *The Mysterious Island* (1988 Macmillan).

308 Wyss, Johann. *The Swiss Family Robinson* (6–9). 1999, Bantam paper $4.99 (978-0-440-41594-7). One of many editions of the classic survival story, first published in 1814, of a family marooned on a deserted island.

GREAT BRITAIN AND IRELAND

309 Barrie, J. M. *Peter Pan* (5–8). Illus. 1995, NAL paper $4.95 (978-0-451-52088-3). The classic tale of the boy who wouldn't grow up and of his adventures with the Darling children. (Rev: BL 12/15/87)

310 Barrie, J. M. *Peter Pan* (5–7). Illus. 2000, Chronicle $19.95 (978-0-8118-2297-8). Using illustrations from 15 different artists, this is an unusual, unabridged edition of Barrie's classic fantasy. (Rev: BL 11/1/00; HBG 3/01; SLJ 12/00)

311 Brontë, Charlotte. *Jane Eyre* (6–12). Illus. by Kathy Mitchell. Series: Illustrated Junior Library. 1983, Putnam $19.99 (978-0-448-06031-6); Bantam paper $4.95 (978-0-553-21140-5). The immortal love story of Jane and Mr. Rochester.

312 Burnett, Frances Hodgson. *The Secret Garden* (5–8). 1999, Scholastic paper $4.99 (978-0-439-09939-4). An easily read classic about a spoiled girl relocated to England and the unusual friendship she finds there.

313 Carroll, Lewis. *Alice's Adventures in Wonderland* (5–12). Illus. by Iassen Ghiuselev. 2003, Simply Read $29.95 (978-1-894965-00-2). Interesting illustrations by Ghiuselev that interpret incidents and characters in a different way highlight this new edition of an old classic. (Rev: BL 2/1/04; SLJ 6/04)

314 Carroll, Lewis. *Alice in Wonderland and Through the Looking Glass* (4–7). Illus. by John Tenniel. 1963, Putnam $18.99 (978-0-448-06004-0). One of many recommended editions of these enduring fantasies.

315 Carroll, Lewis. *Alice Through the Looking-Glass* (4–7). Illus. by Helen Oxenbury. 2005, Candlewick $24.99 (978-0-7636-2892-5). Faithful to the original text, Oxenbury's inviting artwork will draw young readers; a companion to her award-winning *Alice's Adventures in Wonderland* (1999). (Rev: BL 12/15/05*; HBG 4/06; SLJ 12/05)

316 Carroll, Lewis. *Alice's Adventures in Wonderland* (5–7). Illus. 2000, Chronicle $19.95 (978-0-8118-2274-9). This oversize edition of the complete text of Carroll's classic features illustrations from 29 artists. (Rev: BL 11/1/00; HBG 3/01; SLJ 11/00)

317 Carroll, Lewis. *Through the Looking Glass, and What Alice Found There* (4–7). Illus. by John Tenniel. 1977, St. Martin's $14.95 (978-0-312-80374-2). The sequel to *Alice's Adventures in Wonderland*. One of many editions.

318 Chaucer, Geoffrey. *Canterbury Tales* (4–8). Adapted by Barbara Cohen. Illus. by Trina S. Hyman. 1988, Lothrop $26.99 (978-0-688-06201-9). Several of the popular stories are retold with handsome illustrations by Trina Schart Hyman. (Rev: BL 9/1/88; SLJ 8/88)

319 Dickens, Charles. *A Christmas Carol* (6–8). Illus. by Trina S. Hyman. 1983, Holiday $18.95 (978-0-8234-0486-5). A handsome edition of this classic illustrated by Trina S. Hyman.

320 Dickens, Charles. *Great Expectations* (8–12). 1998, NAL paper $4.95 (978-0-451-52671-7). The story of Pip and his slow journey to maturity and fortune.

321 Doyle, Arthur Conan. *The Adventures of Sherlock Holmes* (7–12). 1981, Avon paper $2.95 (978-0-380-78105-8). A collection of 12 of the most famous stories about this famous sleuth.

322 Doyle, Arthur Conan. *The Complete Sherlock Holmes: All 4 Novels and 56 Stories* (7–12). 1998, Bantam paper $13.90 (978-0-553-32825-7). In two volumes, all the stories and novels involving Holmes and his foil Watson.

323 Doyle, Arthur Conan. *Sherlock Holmes: The Complete Novels and Stories* (8–12). 1986, Bantam paper $6.95 (978-0-553-21241-9). A handy collection in two volumes of all the writings about Holmes and Watson. (Rev: BL 3/15/87)

324 Grahame, Kenneth. *The Wind in the Willows* (4–7). Illus. by E. H. Shepard. 1983, Macmillan $19.95 (978-0-684-17957-5). The classic that introduced Mole, Ratty, and Mr. Toad. Two of many other editions are: illus. by Michael Hague (1980, Henry Holt); illus. by John Burningham (1983, Viking).

325 Kipling, Rudyard. *Captains Courageous* (7–10). 1964, Amereon LB $20.95 (978-0-88411-818-3). The story of a spoiled teenager who learns about life from common fishermen who save him when he falls overboard from an ocean liner.

326 Stevenson, Robert Louis. *The Black Arrow* (7–12). 1998, Tor paper $3.99 (978-0-8125-6562-1). Set against the War of the Roses, this is an adventure story involving a young hero, Dick Shelton. First published in 1888.

327 Stevenson, Robert Louis. *Dr. Jekyll and Mr. Hyde* (7–12). 1990, Buccaneer LB $16.95 (978-0-89968-552-6). This 1886 horror classic involves a drug-induced change of personality. One of several editions.

328 Stevenson, Robert Louis. *The Strange Case of Dr. Jekyll and Mr. Hyde* (5–8). Illus. Series: Whole Story. 2003, Barnes & Noble paper $3.95 (978-1-59308-054-9). Using lively ink-and-watercolor illustrations, this book offers the complete text of the classic in an attractive format. (Rev: BL 5/1/00; HBG 10/00)

329 Stevenson, Robert Louis. *Treasure Island* (5–9). Illus. by N. C. Wyeth. Series: Scribner Storybook Classic. 2003, Simon & Schuster $18.95 (978-0-689-85468-2). This picture-book adaptation of the classic story features beautiful paintings by N. C. Wyeth. (Rev: BL 8/03; HBG 4/04)

330 Wilde, Oscar. *The Picture of Dorian Gray* (6–12). Illus. 2001, Viking $25.99 (978-0-670-89494-9). Informative sidebars and bright illustrations amplify many of the more esoteric aspects of Wilde's classic story about the young man who never ages. (Rev: BL 5/15/01; HBG 10/01; SLJ 8/01; VOYA 8/01)

United States

331 Alcott, Louisa May. *Little Women* (5–9). 1947, Putnam $21.99 (978-0-448-06019-4). One of the many fine editions of this enduring story. Two sequels are *Little Men* and *Jo's Boys*.

332 Camfield, Gregg, ed. *Mark Twain* (6–9). Illus. by Sally Wern Comport. Series: Stories for Young People. 2005, Sterling LB $14.95 (978-1-4027-1178-7). A collection of five stories by Mark Twain, plus a brief biography and glossary notes. (Rev: SLJ 10/05)

333 Cooper, James Fenimore. *The Last of the Mohicans* (8–12). 1986, Macmillan paper $4.95 (978-0-553-21329-4). This is the second of the classic Leatherstocking Tales. The others are *The Pioneers, The Prairie, The Pathfinder,* and *The Deerslayer* (all available in various editions). (Rev: BL 1/87)

334 Crane, Stephen. *The Red Badge of Courage* (8–12). 1991, Airmont paper $2.50 (978-0-8049-0003-4). The classic novel of a young man who explored the meanings of courage during the Civil War.

335 Henry, O. *The Gift of the Magi* (5–8). Illus. by Carol Heyer. 1994, Ideals $14.95 (978-1-57102-003-1). The classic story of unselfish love at Christmas gets some handsome illustrations. Another fine edition is illustrated by Kevin King (1988, Simon & Schuster). (Rev: BL 8/94)

336 London, Jack. *The Sea-Wolf* (7–12). 1958, Macmillan $15.95 (978-0-02-574630-5). Wolf Larsen helps a ne'er-do-well and a female poet find their destinies in the classic that was originally published in 1904.

337 Needle, Jan. *Moby Dick* (6–9). Illus. by Patrick Benson. 2006, Candlewick $21.99 (978-0-7636-3018-8). Commentary and illustrations enhance this adaptation of Melville's classic sea story. (Rev: BL 11/1/06; LMC 4-5/07; SLJ 4/07)

338 Poe, Edgar Allan. *Edgar Allan Poe* (6–9). Ed. by Andrew Delbanco. Illus. by Gerard DuBois. 2006, Sterling $14.95 (978-1-4027-1515-0). This collection of five well-known stories by Poe, including "The Fall of the House of Usher" and "The Cask of Amontillado," is enhanced by general information about Poe and his writing, an introduction to each tale, and a glossary. (Rev: BL 11/1/06; SLJ 2/07)

339 Poe, Edgar Allan. *Edgar Allan Poe's Tales of Mystery and Madness* (7–12). Trans. by Stephen Soenkson. Illus. by Gris Grimly. 2004, Simon & Schuster $17.95 (978-0-689-84837-7). Striking artwork brings to life four of Edgar Allan Poe's classic mystery tales, presented here in abridged form. (Rev: BL 10/15/04*; SLJ 10/04)

340 Schmidt, Gary D. *Pilgrim's Progress* (4–7). Illus. by Barry Moser. 1994, Eerdmans $22.00 (978-0-8028-5080-5). A simple retelling of the classic in which Christian leaves his home to find the Celestial City. (Rev: BL 11/1/94; SLJ 12/94)

341 Twain, Mark. *The Adventures of Huckleberry Finn* (7–12). 1993, Random $16.50 (978-0-679-42470-3). One of many editions of this classic.

342 Twain, Mark. *A Connecticut Yankee in King Arthur's Court* (7–12). 1988, Morrow $25.99 (978-0-688-06346-7); Bantam paper $4.95 (978-0-553-21143-6). Through a time-travel fantasy, a swaggering Yankee is plummeted into the age of chivalry. First published in 1889. (Rev: BL 2/15/89)

343 Twain, Mark. *The Prince and the Pauper* (7–12). 1996, Andre Deutsch $9.95 (978-0-233-99081-1); Airmont paper $2.50 (978-0-8049-0032-4). A king and a poor boy switch places in 16th-century England. First published in 1881.

344 Twain, Mark. *Pudd'nhead Wilson* (7–12). 1966, Airmont paper $2.50 (978-0-8049-0124-6). In the Midwest of over 100 years ago, a black servant switches her baby with a white couple's child to ensure that he gets a fair chance at life.

345 Twain, Mark. *Tom Sawyer Abroad [and] Tom Sawyer, Detective* (7–12). 1981, Univ. of California $50.00 (978-0-520-04560-6). Two sequels to *The Adventures of Tom Sawyer,* both involving Tom and Huck.

Contemporary Life and Problems

General and Miscellaneous

346 Adler, C. S. *Always and Forever Friends* (5–7). 1990, Avon paper $3.99 (978-0-380-70687-7). Wendy, at 11, is having a painful struggle making new friends after Meg moves away until she meets Honor, who is African American and very hesitant about accepting Wendy. (Rev: BCCB 4/88; BL 4/1/88; SLJ 4/88)

347 Adler, C. S. *The Magic of the Glits* (5–7). Illus. by Ati Forberg. 1987, Avon paper $2.50 (978-0-380-70403-3). Jeremy, age 12, takes care of 7-year-old Lynette for the summer. A reissue of the 1979 edition. Also use *Some Other Summer* (1988).

348 Almond, David. *Click* (7–10). 2007, Scholastic $16.99 (978-0-439-41138-7). Ten well-known authors collaborate to form this compelling well-crafted novel (written to support Amnesty International) about a character named George "Gee" Keane — a famous photojournalist but something of a mystery man. (Rev: BL 9/15/07; SLJ 10/07)

349 Anderson, Jodi Lynn. *Peaches* (8–11). 2005, HarperCollins LB $16.89 (978-0-06-073306-3). Three teenage girls from diverse backgrounds forge lasting bonds during a summer picking peaches in a Georgia orchard. (Rev: BL 10/1/05; SLJ 8/05; VOYA 2/06)

350 Anderson, Mary. *The Unsinkable Molly Malone* (7–10). 1991, Harcourt $16.95 (978-0-15-213801-1). Molly, 16, sells her collages outside New York's Metropolitan Museum, starts an art class for kids on welfare, and learns that her boyfriend is rich. (Rev: BL 11/15/91; SLJ 12/91)

351 Applegate, Katherine. *Home of the Brave* (5–8). 2007, Feiwel and Friends $16.95 (978-0-312-36765-7). Young refugee Kek, who barely escaped death in Sudan, where his brother and father were murdered, finds a new home — and culture shock — in Minnesota. (Rev: BCCB 2/08; BL 7/07; HB 11-12/07; SLJ 10/07) 🖊

352 Archer, Lily. *The Poison Apples* (7–10). 2007, Feiwel and Friends $16.95 (978-0-312-36762-6). Three 15-year-old girls — Molly, Reena, and Alice — who have been shipped off to boarding school are united in their hatred for their new stepmothers in this funny novel full of pop-culture references. (Rev: BL 10/15/07; SLJ 9/07)

353 Ashton, Victoria. *Confessions of a Teen Nanny* (8–12). 2005, HarperCollins LB $16.89 (978-0-06-077524-7). Hired as a temporary nanny for an 8-year-old child prodigy, 16-year-old Adrienne finds herself being manipulated by her charge's older sister. (Rev: BL 8/05; SLJ 7/05)

354 Banks, Kate. *Friends of the Heart/Amici del Cuore* (6–9). 2005, Farrar $16.00 (978-0-374-32455-1). Lucrezia looks back a few years to the idyllic summer she and her childhood friend spent an idyllic summer in a seaside Italian village until tragedy struck. (Rev: BL 12/1/05)

355 Barkley, Brad, and Heather Hepler. *Scrambled Eggs at Midnight* (7–10). 2006, Dutton $16.99 (978-0-525-47760-0). Unhappy with the nomadic life she lives with her mother, 15-year-old Calliope finds friendship and romance and learns about herself in the process. (Rev: BL 6/1–15/06; LMC 1/07; SLJ 5/06)

356 Bateson, Catherine. *Stranded in Boringsville* (5–8). 2005, Holiday House $16.95 (978-0-8234-1969-2). Twelve-year-old Rain's life is turned upside down when she and her mother move from cosmopolitan Melbourne to a small Australian town in the middle of nowhere; but she finds a good friend in her neighbor Daniel. (Rev: BL 12/1/05; SLJ 2/06; VOYA 2/06)

357 Bauer, Joan. *Best Foot Forward* (6–9). 2005, Penguin $16.99 (978-0-399-23474-3). In this funny sequel to *Rules of the Road* (1998), 17-year-old Jenna finds it difficult to juggle her high school studies, her alcoholic father, her declining grandmother, and her part-time job at the shoe store, where she has been appointed a supervisor. (Rev: BCCB 6/05; BL 5/1/05; HB 5–6/05; SLJ 6/05; VOYA 6/05)

358 Bauer, Joan. *Hope Was Here* (7–9). 2000, Putnam $16.99 (978-0-399-23142-1). When she and her aunt move to Wisconsin, 16-year-old Hope is pleasantly surprised and becomes involved in politics while working in a diner. (Rev: BL 9/15/00; HB 9–10/00; HBG 3/01; SLJ 11/00*; VOYA 2/01)

359 Bauer, Marion Dane. *On My Honor* (5–7). 1986, Houghton $15.00 (978-0-89919-439-4); Dell paper $4.99 (978-0-440-46633-8). A powerful story in which 12-year-old Joel faces telling his parents that his friend Tony has drowned in the river they promised never to swim. (Rev: BCCB 10/86; BL 9/1/86; SLJ 11/86)

360 Bell, Joanne. *Breaking Trail* (5–7). 2005, Groundwood $15.95 (978-0-88899-630-5); paper $6.95 (978-0-88899-662-6). Becky's dreams of training a dog team to participate in the Junior Quest fade when her father grows increasingly depressed, but a sled trip back to the family's cabin offers a chance to make those dreams come true. (Rev: SLJ 10/05)

361 Bernard, Virginia. *Eliza Down Under: Going to Sydney* (5–8). Series: Going To. 2000, Four Corners paper $7.95 (978-1-893577-02-2). This novel deals with Eliza's adventures in Australia when she accompanies her mother to the 2000 Olympic Games in Sydney. (Rev: SLJ 3/00)

362 Blacker, Terence. *Boy2Girl* (6–9). 2005, Farrar $16.00 (978-0-374-30926-8). After the death of his mother, American-born Sam is sent to London to live with relatives; on a dare from his cousin, Sam shows up for his first day of school dressed as a girl. (Rev: BCCB 3/05; BL 3/1/05; SLJ 3/05; VOYA 4/05)

363 Blatchford, Claire H. *Nick's Secret* (5–7). 2000, Lerner LB $14.95 (978-0-8225-0743-7). When 13-year-old Nick, who is deaf, is summoned to a motel by Darryl Smythe and his gang of vandals, the boy knows he is in for trouble. (Rev: BL 9/15/00; HBG 3/01; SLJ 12/00; VOYA 2/01)

364 Bodett, Tom. *Norman Tuttle on the Last Frontier: A Novel in Stories* (8–10). 2004, Knopf LB $17.99 (978-0-679-99031-4). In this coming-of-age story presented in interconnected episodes, klutzy Alaskan teenager Norman Tuttle experiences many firsts — first job, first date, first hunting expedition — and his relationship with his father evolves. (Rev: BL 12/1/04; SLJ 12/04; VOYA 12/04)

365 Boles, Philana Marie. *Little Divas* (5–8). 2006, HarperCollins LB $16.89 (978-0-06-073300-1). Twelve-year-old Cass is facing a lot of change in her life: her parents' divorce, living with her father, a new friend, a first kiss, and perhaps a new school. (Rev: BL 4/1/06; SLJ 1/06)

366 Brande, Robin. *Evolution, Me and Other Freaks of Nature* (6–9). 2007, Knopf $15.99 (978-0-375-84349-5). Mena's views on evolution, gays, and other topics are challenged by her peers, parents, and church. (Rev: BL 6/1–15/07; HB 9–10/07; SLJ 10/07)

367 Brashares, Ann. *Forever in Blue: The Fourth Summer of the Sisterhood* (8–11). Series: The Sisterhood of the Traveling Pants. 2007, Delacorte $18.99 (978-0-385-72936-9). The four girls of *The Sisterhood of the Traveling Pants* are growing up, exploring love and life, and recognizing their ability to succeed without the pants in this final book in the series. (Rev: BL 12/15/06; SLJ 2/07) ⑨

368 Brashares, Ann. *The Sisterhood of the Traveling Pants* (6–9). 2001, Delacorte $14.95 (978-0-385-72933-8). Four teenage girls who are spending the summer apart pin their hopes on a pair of jeans that seems to magically fit and flatter them all. (Rev: BCCB 12/01; BL 8/01; HB 11–12/01; HBG 3/02; SLJ 8/01*; VOYA 10/01)

369 Brian, Kate. *Megan Meade's Guide to the McGowan Boys* (8–11). 2005, Simon & Schuster $14.95 (978-1-4169-0030-6). Megan does not want to move to South Korea with her military parents and chooses instead to stay with the McGowans, a family with seven sons, requiring adjustments all round. (Rev: BL 9/15/05; SLJ 11/05; VOYA 12/05)

370 Brinkerhoff, Shirley. *Second Choices* (6–8). Series: Nikki Sheridan. 2000, Bethany paper $5.99 (978-1-56179-880-3). Nikki Sheridan finds comfort in her Christian values as she faces her parents' divorce, telling the father of her child about his paternity, and an incident of school violence in this sixth and final installment in the series. (Rev: BL 3/1/01)

371 Brooks, Bruce. *Everywhere* (5–8). 1990, HarperCollins LB $16.89 (978-0-06-020729-8). Eleven-year-old Dooley, who is African American, helps a 10-year-old white boy live through the emotional trauma of waiting to see if his beloved grandfather will recover from a heart attack. (Rev: BCCB 10/90; BL 10/15/90*; SLJ 9/90*)

372 Brugman, Alyssa. *Finding Grace* (6–12). 2004, Dell LB $17.99 (978-0-385-90142-0). College-bound Rachel is hired to care for a brain-injured woman named Grace and in the process learns some valuable lessons about both Grace and herself. (Rev: BL 9/15/04; SLJ 11/04; VOYA 12/04)

373 Buckley, Kristen. *Thirteen Reasons Why* (8–11). 2007, Penguin $16.99 (978-1-59514-171-2). Clay Jenson describes his thoughts as he listens to cassette tapes bearing the voice of his dead classmate, Hannah, who describes events and circumstances that led to her suicide. (Rev: BL 9/1/07; SLJ 11/07) ⑨

374 Burch, Christian. *The Manny Files* (6–9). 2006, Simon & Schuster $15.95 (978-1-4169-0039-9). A fun, creative male nanny, or "manny," takes charge of the Dalinger children and bonds with 3rd-grader Keats, while older sister Lulu is unimpressed and puts the manny on mock trial. (Rev: BL 5/1/06; LMC 11-12/06; SLJ 7/06) ⑨

375 Burton, Rebecca. *Leaving Jetty Road* (8–11). 2006, Knopf $15.95 (978-0-375-83488-2). Three Australian high school girls decide to become vegetarians, a choice that affects each in a different way and becomes more critical as Lise suffers serious anorexia. (Rev: BL 6/1–15/06; LMC 10/06; SLJ 8/06)

376 Butcher, Kristin. *The Runaways* (5–8). 1998, Kids Can $16.95 (978-1-55074-413-2). During an unsuccessful attempt to run away from home, young Nick Battle meets Luther, a homeless man, and through this friendship gains insights into poverty in America. (Rev: BL 4/15/98; HBG 10/98; SLJ 4/98)

377 Butler, Dori Hillestad. *The Truth about Truman School* (5–8). 2008, Albert Whitman $15.95 (978-0-8075-8095-0). Zebby and Amr start an alternative, online school newspaper and soon learn that not all postings are fit to print in this story told from many characters' points of view. (Rev: BL 3/15/08; SLJ 5/08)

378 Byars, Betsy. *The Pinballs* (5–7). 1977, HarperCollins LB $16.89 (978-0-06-020918-6). Three misfits in a foster home band together to help lessen their problems.

379 Byrd, Sandra. *Island Girl* (5–8). Series: Friends for a Season. 2005, Bethany House paper $9.99 (978-0-7642-0020-5). Confused by changes in her family situation, 13-year-old Meg spends a summer with her grandparents on an Oregon island where she meets and befriends Tia. (Rev: BL 10/1/05)

380 Cabot, Meg. *How to Be Popular* (6–9). 2006, HarperTempest $16.99 (978-0-06-088012-5). Steph is determined no longer to be the class klutz and studies a book she finds titled *How to Be Popular,* surprising everyone with the results. (Rev: BL 9/15/06)

381 Caletti, Deb. *Wild Roses* (7–10). 2005, Simon & Schuster $15.95 (978-0-689-86766-8). Seventeen-year-old Cassie finds life with her stepfather — an unstable violinist and composer — difficult at the best of times, but things go from bad to worse when she falls for one of his music students. (Rev: BCCB 10/05; BL 10/1/05; SLJ 11/05*; VOYA 12/05)

382 Calonita, Jen. *Secrets of My Hollywood Life: On Location* (7–12). 2007, Little, Brown $16.99 (978-0-316-15439-0). Kaitlin is a likable Hollywood starlet whose life gets tricky when she has to make a movie co-starring her ex-boyfriend and her biggest enemy. (Rev: SLJ 7/07)

383 Carlson, Ron. *The Speed of Light* (4–7). 2003, HarperTempest LB $16.89 (978-0-06-029825-8). Baseball, science experiments, and the mysteries of the universe occupy Larry and his two best friends during the summer before junior high. (Rev: BL 8/03; HBG 4/04; SLJ 7/03; VOYA 10/03)

384 Carlyle, Carolyn. *Mercy Hospital: Crisis!* (5–8). 1993, Avon paper $3.50 (978-0-380-76846-2). Three friends volunteer at a local hospital. (Rev: SLJ 7/93)

385 Caseley, Judith. *The Kissing Diary* (5–8). 2007, Farrar $16.00 (978-0-374-36346-8). After her parents' divorce, 12-year-old Rosie keeps a diary in which she describes problems at home and at school and her crush on Robbie Romano. (Rev: BL 8/07; SLJ 11/07)

386 Chase, Paula. *Don't Get It Twisted* (7–10). Series: Del Rio Bay Clique. 2007, Dafina paper $9.95 (978-0-7582-1861-2). Friends (and enemies) gossiping, IM-ing, and flirting fill the pages of this second novel about freshman Mina and her friends, full of slick, slangy dialogue and pop-culture references. (Rev: BL 1/1–15/08) ⑨

387 Cheripko, Jan. *Rat* (7–12). 2002, Boyds Mills $16.95 (978-1-59078-034-3). Fifteen-year-old Jeremy faces difficult choices in this novel that looks at moral questions against a backdrop of basketball. (Rev: HBG 10/03; SLJ 8/02)

388 Chocolate, Deborah M. *NEATE to the Rescue!* (4–7). 1992, Just Us Bks. paper $3.95 (978-0-940975-42-2). A 13-year-old African American girl and her friends help out when her mother's seat on the local council is put in doubt by a racist. (Rev: BCCB 3/93; BL 3/15/93)

389 Cirrone, Dorian. *Prom Kings and Drama Queens* (6–9). 2008, HarperTeen $16.99 (978-0-06-114372-4). Emily writes for the school newspaper but is still a social outcast; this begins to change as she starts to date her popular next-door neighbor. (Rev: SLJ 3/08)

390 Clark, Catherine. *Frozen Rodeo* (8–12). 2003, HarperCollins LB $16.89 (978-0-06-623008-5). What starts out as a dull summer has its high points

for P.F. (Peggy Fleming) Farrell as she enjoys a teen romance, foils a robbery, and even finds time to help deliver her mother's baby. (Rev: BL 2/15/03; HBG 10/03; SLJ 3/03; VOYA 4/03)

391 Clements, Andrew. *The Report Card* (4–7). 2004, Simon & Schuster $15.95 (978-0-689-84515-4). Nora, a bright 5th-grader, deliberately gets low grades in a bid to boost her friend Stephen's self-esteem, but her plans backfire. (Rev: BL 2/15/04; SLJ 3/04)

392 Clements, Andrew. *The School Story* (4–7). Illus. 2001, Simon & Schuster $16.00 (978-0-689-82594-1). Two 12-year-old girls tackle the task of getting a book by a new author published. (Rev: BCCB 7–8/01; BL 6/1–15/01; HB 7–8/01; HBG 10/01; SLJ 6/01)

393 Clements, Andrew. *A Week in the Woods* (4–8). 2002, Simon & Schuster $16.95 (978-0-689-82596-5). Mark, a lonely 5th-grader, and a forceful teacher test each other — and Mark's survival skills — on a weeklong camping trip. (Rev: BCCB 1/03; BL 10/1/02; HBG 3/03; SLJ 11/02)

394 Cobb, Katie. *Happenings* (6–10). 2002, Harper-Collins LB $15.89 (978-0-06-028928-7). Kelsey and her classmates start a protest against their AP English teacher that spirals out of control, causing conflict between Kelsey and her guardian brother. (Rev: BL 3/1/02; HBG 10/02; SLJ 3/02; VOYA 2/02)

395 Cohen, Tish. *The Invisible Rules of the Zoe Lama* (4–7). 2007, Dutton $15.99 (978-0-525-47810-2). This playfully illustrated story about 7th-grader Zoë describes her busy life at home and at school, offering advice and organizing projects and lives. (Rev: BL 10/1/07; SLJ 8/07)

396 Cole, Stephen. *Thieves Like Us* (8–11). 2006, Bloomsbury $16.95 (978-1-58234-653-3). Jonah Wish, a member of a gang of teenage thieves, finds himself questioning the morality of certain activities. (Rev: BL 4/1/06)

397 Colfer, Eoin. *Benny and Babe* (6–8). 2001, O'Brien paper $7.95 (978-0-86278-603-8). On a visit to his grandfather, Benny, 13, makes a new friend, and he and Babe have money-making and other, more dangerous adventures. (Rev: SLJ 3/02)

398 Colfer, Eoin. *Benny and Omar* (5–8). 2001, O'Brien paper $7.95 (978-0-86278-567-3). Benny, a young Irish lad, has trouble adjusting to his new life in Tunisia until he befriends Omar, a local orphan without a home, and the two have some exciting and amusing adventures. (Rev: BL 8/01; SLJ 12/01)

399 Collard, Sneed B., III. *Flash Point* (7–10). 2006, . Luther, a high school sophomore, has turned away from sports and is now interested in birds of prey and the environment but this new focus threatens to alienate many in his logging community; when his girlfriend's beloved falcon is shot, this fast-paced story becomes even more exciting. (Rev: SLJ 12/06)

400 Collins, Yvonne, and Sandy Rideout. *Introducing Vivien Leigh Reid: Daughter of the Diva* (7–10). 2005, St. Martin's $11.95 (978-0-312-33837-4). Sent to Ireland to spend the summer on the set of her actress mother's latest film, 15-year-old Leigh Reid wins a bit part in the movie, develops a crush on a costar, and finally begins to build a meaningful relationship with her mom. (Rev: BL 6/1–15/05; SLJ 9/05)

401 Collins, Yvonne, and Sandy Rideout. *The New and Improved Vivien Leigh Reid: Diva in Control* (7–10). 2007, Griffin paper $9.95 (978-0-312-35828-0). Despite her determination to make her life better, Leigh continues to face challenges in both her personal and professional lives in this third book in the series. (Rev: SLJ 3/07)

402 Collins, Yvonne, and Sandy Rideout. *Now Starring Vivien Leigh Reid: Diva in Training* (8–12). 2006, Griffin paper $9.95 (978-0-312-33839-8). In this sequel to the witty *Introducing Vivien Leigh Reid: Daughter of the Diva* (2005), 16-year-old Leigh lands a role in a soap opera and initially adopts a prima donna attitude that threatens her friendships and her job. (Rev: SLJ 1/06; VOYA 4/06)

403 Coman, Carolyn. *Many Stones* (7–12). 2000, Front St. $15.95 (978-1-886910-55-3). A year after her sister was murdered there, Berry reluctantly travels with her father to South Africa to attend her memorial in this novel set during the proceedings of the Truth and Reconciliation Commission. (Rev: BL 11/1/00; HB 1–2/01; HBG 3/01; SLJ 11/00*; VOYA 2/01)

404 Conrad, Pam. *Our House: The Stories of Levittown* (4–7). Illus. by Brian Selznick. 1995, Scholastic paper $14.95 (978-0-590-46523-6). A series of fictional vignettes trace the history of the middle-class community of Levittown, New York. (Rev: BCCB 12/95; BL 1/1–15/96; HB 11–12/95; SLJ 11/95)

405 Cooney, Caroline B. *Hit the Road* (6–9). 2006, Delacorte LB $17.99 (978-0-385-90174-1). When Brit's parents leave the 16-year-old with her grandmother, they have no idea the brand-new driver will be setting off on a road trip to get the elderly woman and her two friends to their 65th college reunion. (Rev: BL 3/15/06*; SLJ 5/06)

406 Craven, Margaret. *I Heard the Owl Call My Name* (7–12). 1973, Dell paper $6.99 (978-0-440-34369-1). A terminally ill Anglican priest and his assignment in a coastal Indian community in British Columbia. The nonfiction story behind this book is told in *Again Calls the Owl*.

407 Crew, Linda. *Brides of Eden: A True Story Imagined* (7–12). 2001, HarperCollins LB $15.89

(978-0-06-028751-1). Teenage Eva Mae Hurt describes the influence that magnetic preacher Joshua Creffield has on a group of women, who renounce their families and their everyday lives to follow his lead in this book based on fact, set in early 20th-century Oregon. (Rev: BCCB 2/01; BL 12/15/00; HB 3–4/01; HBG 10/01; SLJ 2/01; VOYA 6/01)

408 Crutcher, Chris. *Athletic Shorts: 6 Short Stories* (8–12). 1991, Greenwillow $18.99 (978-0-688-10816-8). These short stories focus on themes important to teens, such as sports, father–son friction, insecurity, and friendship. (Rev: BL 10/15/91; SLJ 9/91*)

409 Cummings, Priscilla. *Red Kayak* (6–9). 2004, Penguin $15.99 (978-0-525-47317-6). Brady's long-time friendship with J.T. and Digger is tested after a childish prank results in the death of a neighbor's child. (Rev: BL 9/1/04; SLJ 9/04; VOYA 10/04)

410 Cummings, Priscilla. *What Mr. Mattero Did* (6–9). 2005, Dutton $16.99 (978-0-525-47621-4). Three 7th-grade girls thoughtlessly accuse their music teacher of inappropriate behavior and are overwhelmed by the consequences. (Rev: BL 7/05; SLJ 8/05)

411 Dahl, Lesley. *The Problem with Paradise* (6–9). 2006, Delacorte $15.95 (978-0-385-73335-9). Fourteen-year-old Casey isn't excited about spending the summer on a small tropical island with her naturalist father and new stepfamily but storms, an interesting boy, and mild adventure await her there. (Rev: BL 11/15/06; SLJ 1/07)

412 Danziger, Paula, and Ann M. Martin. *P. S. Longer Letter Later* (5–8). 1998, Scholastic paper $16.95 (978-0-590-21310-3). This novel consists of letters between two recently separated girlfriends — one who is adjusting well and the other who is facing family problems after her father loses his job and the family must change its lifestyle. (Rev: BL 6/1–15/98; HBG 10/98; SLJ 5/98; VOYA 8/98)

413 Deaver, Julie Reece. *Say Goodnight Gracie* (8–10). 1988, HarperCollins $15.00 (978-0-06-021418-0); paper $6.99 (978-0-06-447007-0). When her best friend Jimmy dies in an accident, Morgan struggles with her grief. (Rev: SLJ 2/88)

414 DeFelice, Cynthia. *The Light on Hogback Hill* (4–8). 1993, Macmillan paper $15.00 (978-0-02-726453-1). When 11-year-olds Hadley and Josh discover that the Witch Woman of Hogback Hill is really a shy, deformed woman, they help her find the courage to return to town. (Rev: BCCB 12/93; BL 11/1/93; SLJ 11/93)

415 Denman, K. L. *Mirror Image* (5–8). Series: Currents. 2007, Orca $14.95 (978-1-55143-667-8); paper $8.95 (978-1-55143-667-4). Popular Lacey and Sable, an immigrant to Canada from Bosnia who is a loner, could not be more different, and the girls are initially disappointed to be paired for an art project. (Rev: BL 3/15/07)

416 Draper, Sharon M. *The Battle of Jericho* (7–10). 2003, Simon & Schuster $16.95 (978-0-689-84232-0). Sixteen-year-old Jericho is initially thrilled when he's asked to pledge for membership in the Warriors of Distinction club, but subsequent events turn chilling. (Rev: BL 6/1–15/03; HBG 4/04; SLJ 6/03; VOYA 8/03)

417 Draper, Sharon M. *Darkness Before Dawn* (8–12). Series: Hazelwood High. 2001, Simon & Schuster $16.95 (978-0-689-83080-8). Keisha Montgomery copes with many issues — the suicide of her ex-boyfriend, a new relationship, date rape, and more in this novel set at Hazelwood High. (Rev: BCCB 3/01; BL 1/1–15/01; HBG 10/01; SLJ 2/01; VOYA 8/01)

418 Draper, Sharon M. *Double Dutch* (7–10). 2002, Simon & Schuster $16.00 (978-0-689-84230-6). Eighth-graders Delia and Randy both have secrets — Delia can't read and Randy's father has disappeared, leaving him on his own. (Rev: BCCB 10/02; BL 9/1/02; HBG 10/02; SLJ 6/02; VOYA 8/02)

419 Dunlop, Eileen. *Finn's Search* (4–7). 1994, Holiday $14.95 (978-0-8234-1099-6). Two Scottish boys try to save a gravel pit from local developers. (Rev: BCCB 12/94; BL 10/1/94; SLJ 10/94)

420 DuPrau, Jeanne. *Car Trouble* (7–10). 2005, Greenwillow LB $16.89 (978-0-06-073674-3). Seventeen-year-old Duff Pringle has various car and people adventures on the road from Virginia to a promised job in California. (Rev: BL 8/05; SLJ 10/05; VOYA 10/05)

421 Easton, Kelly. *White Magic: Spells to Hold You* (8–11). 2007, Random $15.99 (978-0-375-83769-2). After moving to Los Angeles, Chrissie befriends Yvonne (a self-proclaimed witch) and Karen, who welcome her to their coven in this book that is more about friendship than magic. (Rev: BL 6/1–15/07; HB 9–10/07; SLJ 12/07)

422 Ehrenberg, Pamela. *Ethan, Suspended* (7–10). 2007, Eerdmans $16.00 (978-0-8028-5324-0). After being suspended from school, Ethan is sent to live with his grandparents in inner-city Washington, D.C., where he's one of the very few white students and learns about segregation, poverty, making new friends, and falling in love. (Rev: BL 5/15/07; SLJ 7/07)

423 Elkeles, Simone. *How to Ruin My Teenage Life* (7–10). Series: How to Ruin a Summer Vacation. 2007, Flux paper $8.95 (978-0-7387-1019-8). In this followup to *How to Ruin a Summer Vacation* (2006), Amy's life in Chicago with her Israeli father is full of irritating people, including her dad — who badly needs a girlfriend, her mother and her new husband and forthcoming baby, and a nerdy new guy in her apartment building. (Rev: SLJ 7/07)

424 Ellerbee, Linda. *Girl Reporter Blows Lid Off Town!* (4–7). Series: Get Real. 2000, HarperCollins LB $14.89 (978-0-06-028245-5). Casey Smith, a 6th-grade reporter, discovers the thrill of tracking down stories and getting at the truth in this light-hearted story set in a small town in the Berkshires. Also use *Girl Reporter Sinks School!* (Rev: BL 3/1/00; HBG 10/00; SLJ 6/00)

425 Feldman, Jody. *The Gollywhopper Games* (4–7). Illus. by Victoria Jamieson. 2008, Greenwillow $16.99 (978-0-06-121450-9). Gil Goodson is determined to win the Gollywhopper Games, sponsored by the Golly Toy and Game Company, in this engaging novel that includes the puzzles that Gil must solve to be victorious. (Rev: BL 12/1/07; SLJ 3/08)

426 Finch, Susan. *The Intimacy of Indiana* (8–12). 2001, Tudor $5.95 (978-0-936389-79-0). Readers follow three teens through the trials of their senior year in high school in small-town Indiana — SATs, college finance, romance, drugs, and of course parents. (Rev: BL 7/01)

427 Fleischman, Paul. *Seek* (7–12). 2001, Cricket $16.95 (978-0-8126-4900-0). For a school autobiography project, 17-year-old Rob makes a recording of important sounds in his life, including the voice of the father he never knew. (Rev: BCCB 11/01; BL 12/15/01; HB 11–12/01; HBG 3/02; SLJ 9/01*; VOYA 12/01)

428 Fletcher, Ralph. *Flying Solo* (5–8). 1998, Clarion $16.00 (978-0-395-87323-6). This novel answers the question, "What would a 6th-grade class do if their substitute teacher fails to appear and they are left alone for a whole day?" (Rev: BCCB 9/98; BL 8/98*; HB 11–12/98; HBG 3/99; SLJ 10/98)

429 Fletcher, Ralph. *One O'Clock Chop* (8–10). 2007, Holt $16.95 (978-0-8050-8143-5). In 1973, 14-year-old Matt falls for his gorgeous first cousin Jazzy, who ends up breaking his heart. (Rev: BL 9/15/07; SLJ 10/07)

430 Flinn, Alex. *Diva* (8–11). 2006, HarperTempest $15.99 (978-0-06-056843-6). Caitlin (last seen in the 2005 *Breathing Underwater*) deals with her past abusive relationship, weight issues, troubles with her mom, and her dream of attending a performing arts school for opera. (Rev: BL 10/1/06; SLJ 11/06)

431 Fogelin, Adrian. *The Big Nothing* (7–9). 2004, Peachtree $14.95 (978-1-56145-326-9). Thirteen-year-old Justin has a miserable home life and generally feels abandoned until neighbor Jemmie starts paying attention to him and he discovers he has a talent for playing the piano; this novel shares a setting and some with characters with *Crossing Jordan* (2000) and *My Brother's Hero* (2002). (Rev: BL 12/15/04; SLJ 12/04)

432 Fogelin, Adrian. *The Real Question* (7–10). 2006, Peachtree $15.95 (978-1-56145-383-2). Fisher Brown, 16, is just under too much pressure — from his counselor dad, academic stress, a sick dog, and so forth — and on an impulse he sets off to do an out-of-town roofing job with a carefree guy named Lonny. (Rev: LMC 3/07; SLJ 11/06)

433 Frank, Lucy. *Lucky Stars* (4–7). 2005, Simon & Schuster $16.95 (978-0-689-85933-5). Kira, a talented singer with a feisty character, arrives in New York City to find that her father has plans that don't fit in with her own. (Rev: BL 5/15/05; SLJ 7/05)

434 Frederick, Heather Vogel. *The Mother-Daughter Book Club* (4–7). 2007, Simon & Schuster $15.99 (978-0-689-86412-4). Four very different 6th-grade girls join a book club where they will read *Little Women* with their mothers. (Rev: BL 6/1–15/07; SLJ 8/07)

435 Fredericks, Mariah. *Crunch Time* (8–11). 2006, Simon & Schuster $15.95 (978-0-689-86938-9). Four members of a private SAT study group — who have formed emotional attachments as they study — find themselves under suspicion of cheating. (Rev: BL 1/1–15/06; SLJ 1/06; VOYA 12/05)

436 Fredericks, Mariah. *Fame* (5–8). Illus. by Liselotte Watkins. Series: In the Cards. 2008, Atheneum $15.99 (978-0-689-87656-1). Eve tries out for the 8th-grade play only after the tarot cards tell her it could lead to fame in this sequel to *In the Cards: Love* (2007). (Rev: BL 1/1–15/08; SLJ 8/08)

437 Freymann-Weyr, Garret. *The Kings Are Already Here* (7–10). 2003, Houghton $15.00 (978-0-618-26363-9). Phebe's love of ballet dominates her life until she travels to Geneva to visit her father and meets Nikolai, a 16-year-old refugee who is obsessed with chess. (Rev: BL 2/15/03; HB 3–4/03; HBG 10/03; SLJ 4/03; VOYA 4/03)

438 Friedman, Aimee. *The Year My Sister Got Lucky* (7–10). 2008, Scholastic $16.99 (978-0-439-92227-2). When Katie and Michaela's parents move them from New York City to the Adirondacks, Katie is crushed and angry, while Michaela adapts and thrives. (Rev: BL 12/1/07; SLJ 3/08)

439 Friesen, Gayle. *The Isabel Factor* (7–10). 2005, Kids Can $16.95 (978-1-55337-737-5). Anna's best friend Zoe breaks her arm and, for the first time in years, Anna finds herself running her own life. (Rev: BL 9/1/05; SLJ 11/05)

440 Funke, Cornelia. *The Thief Lord* (6–9). 2002, Scholastic $19.99 (978-0-439-40437-2). Inspired by their dead mother's stories of the wonders of Venice, two boys run away from Hamburg and find an unusual home under the protection of a young Venetian thief. (Rev: BCCB 11/02; BL 10/15/02; HB 11–12/02; HBG 3/03; SLJ 10/02*; VOYA 4/03)

441 Gallagher, Diana G. *Guilty! The Complicated Life of Claudia Cristina Cortez* (4–7). Illus. by Brann Garvey. Series: Claudia Cristina Cortez.

2008, Stone Arch LB $23.93 (978-1-59889-838-5); paper $5.95 (978-1-59889-881-1). Claudia and are friend Monica are accused of stealing $10 in this novel that will attract reluctant readers. Also use *Whatever!* (2008), in which the girls in Claudia's club must decide whether a boy can join and *Camp Can't* (2008), about Claudia's efforts to become a junior counselor. (Rev: SLJ 1/08)

442 Gantos, Jack. *Heads or Tails: Stories from the Sixth Grade* (5–8). 1994, Farrar $16.00 (978-0-374-32909-9). A collection of eight unusual short stories about 6th-grader Jack, a born survivor who overcomes amazing obstacles in this book set in Fort Lauderdale. (Rev: BCCB 7–8/94; HB 7–8/94; SLJ 6/94*)

443 Gantos, Jack. *Jack on the Tracks: Four Seasons of Fifth Grade* (5–7). 1999, Farrar $16.00 (978-0-374-33665-3). An episodic novel (the fourth about Jack Henry) in which Jack, a preadolescent, has several innocent adventures while growing up. (Rev: BCCB 9/99; BL 9/1/99; HB 11–12/99; HBG 3/00; SLJ 10/99; VOYA 2/00)

444 German, Carol. *A Midsummer Night's Dork* (4–7). 2004, HarperCollins $15.99 (978-0-06-050718-3). In this sequel to *Dork on the Run* (2002), 6th-grader Jerry's class puts on an Elizabethan fair and Jerry has to stand up to another bully, even if it means making a fool of himself. (Rev: BL 2/1/04; SLJ 3/04)

445 Gilbert, Barbara Snow. *Paper Trail* (7–10). 2000, Front St. $16.95 (978-1-886910-44-7). A thought-provoking story of a boy torn between family loyalties and connections to a cult known as the Soldiers of God. (Rev: BL 7/00; HB 7–8/00; HBG 9/00; SLJ 8/00)

446 Gilson, Jamie. *Thirteen Ways to Sink a Sub* (4–7). Illus. by Linda Strauss Edwards. 1982, Lothrop $15.95 (978-0-688-01304-2). The girls in Room 4A challenge the boys to see who can first make their substitute teacher cry. A sequel is *4B Goes Wild* (1983).

447 Givner, Joan. *Ellen Fremedon* (5–7). 2004, Groundwood $15.95 (978-0-88899-557-5). When her family seeks to block a proposed housing development, 12-year-old Ellen Fremedon, an aspiring novelist, must set aside her summer project to cope with the repercussions. (Rev: BL 11/15/04)

448 Givner, Joan. *Ellen Fremedon, Journalist* (5–7). 2005, Groundwood $15.95 (978-0-88899-668-8). In this appealing sequel to *Ellen Fremedon* (2004), young Ellen uncovers some shocking stories when she starts a newspaper in quiet Partridge Cove. (Rev: BL 11/1/05; SLJ 2/06)

449 Goldschmidt, Judy. *The Secret Blog of Raisin Rodriguez* (6–9). 2005, Penguin $12.99 (978-1-59514-018-0). Uprooted from her familiar life in California and trying to adjust to her new digs in

Philadelphia, 13-year-old Raisin Rodriguez keeps old friends up to date on what's happening in her life through a frank blog that she does not intend to become public. (Rev: BCCB 5/05; BL 3/1/05; SLJ 5/05)

450 Goldschmidt, Judy. *Will the Real Raisin Rodriguez Please Stand Up?* (6–8). 2007, Penguin $12.99 (978-1-59514-058-6). Raisin, still in 7th grade, travels back home to visit her dad in Berkeley and is jealous to see that her two best friends have made a friendship with another girl; this third installment in the humorous series is also delivered in blogging/texting format. (Rev: SLJ 7/07)

451 Gonzalez, Julie. *Wings* (8–11). 2005, Delacorte LB $17.99 (978-0-385-90253-3). A suspenseful story in which Ben is convinced he will someday sprout wings and take to the sky despite evidence to the contrary. (Rev: BCCB 4/05; BL 3/15/05; SLJ 8/05; VOYA 4/05)

452 Goobie, Beth. *Before Wings* (7–10). 2001, Orca $16.95 (978-1-55143-161-1). An absorbing story that centers on the counselors at a summer camp and on 15-year-old Adrien's past illness and present mystical experiences. (Rev: BL 3/15/01; HB 3–4/01; HBG 10/01; SLJ 4/01; VOYA 4/01)

453 Goobie, Beth. *The Lottery* (7–12). 2002, Orca $15.95 (978-1-55143-238-0). As the lottery winner, 15-year-old Sal must spend the year doing the bidding of a sinister student group, the Shadow Council. (Rev: BL 1/1–15/03; HBG 10/03; SLJ 3/03; VOYA 2/03)

454 Greene, Constance C. *A Girl Called Al* (5–7). Illus. by Byron Barton. 1991, Puffin paper $5.99 (978-0-14-034786-9). The friendship between two 7th-graders and their apartment building superintendent is humorously and deftly recounted.

455 Gregory, Deborah. *Wishing on a Star* (5–8). Series: The Cheetah Girls. 1999, Hyperion paper $3.99 (978-0-7868-1384-1). A light novel about five girls in New York City who form a singing group, the Cheetah Girls, and are soon signed up for an important gig. (Rev: SLJ 1/00)

456 Grunwell, Jeanne Marie. *Mind Games* (5–8). 2003, Houghton $15.00 (978-0-618-17672-4). Six very different 7th-graders get to know each other as they collaborate on a science fair project in this inventive novel sprinkled with press clippings and project notes. (Rev: BL 5/15/03; HB 5–6/03; HBG 10/03; LMC 10/03; SLJ 5/03)

457 Gutman, Dan. *The Million Dollar Putt* (6–8). 2006, . Birdie, a 12-year-old loner with asthma, is the perfect coach for Bogie, a blind golfer who hopes to win a tournament with a $1 million prize. (Rev: SLJ 9/06)

458 Haber, Melissa Glenn. *The Pluto Project* (7–10). 2006, Dutton $17.99 (978-0-525-47721-1). Alan

Green acts cool and indifferent to cover up his emotions after his mother's death, but a new love interest and a spy game that turns realistic force him to confront his feelings. (Rev: BL 7/06; SLJ 7/06)

459 Haddix, Margaret P. *Leaving Fishers* (6–9). 2008, Paw Prints $14.99 (978-1-4395-2932-4). High-schooler Dorrie becomes innocently involved in a religious cult called Fishers of Men and soon finds that getting out is difficult; first published in 1997. (Rev: BL 12/15/97; BR 5–6/98; SLJ 10/97; VOYA 2/98)

460 Hahn, Mary D. *Daphne's Book* (6–8). 1983, Houghton $15.00 (978-0-89919-183-6). The story of a friendship between two very different girls.

461 Hall, Katy, and Lisa Eisenberg. *The Paxton Cheerleaders: Go for It, Patti!* (4–7). 1994, Simon & Schuster paper $3.50 (978-0-671-89490-0). Four 7th-grade girls from different backgrounds make the cheerleading team in their junior high school. (Rev: BL 2/1/95)

462 Han, Jenny. *Shug* (5–8). 2006, Simon & Schuster $14.95 (978-1-4169-0942-2). Annemarie Wilcox, a 7th-grader better known as Shug, faces numerous challenges in addition to the usual middle-school problems: a gorgeous older sister, squabbling parents, a fight with her best friend, and a crush on Mark that doesn't seem to be reciprocated. (Rev: BL 2/15/06; SLJ 5/06)

463 Harper, Suzanne. *The Juliet Club* (8–12). 2008, Greenwillow $16.99 (978-0-06-136691-8). High school junior Kate wins a writing contest and gets to attend a summer program in Verona, Italy, studying Shakespeare's *Romeo and Juliet*, volunteering at the Juliet Club, and finding romance of her own; a light novel suitable for summer reading. (Rev: BL 8/08; SLJ 7/08)

464 Harrington, Jane. *Four Things My Geeky-Jock-of-a-Best-Friend Must Do in Europe* (5–8). 2006, Darby Creek LB $15.95 (978-1-58196-041-9). From the European cruise she is taking with her mother, 13-year-old Brady reports via letter on her progress in meeting her must-dos — which include wearing a revealing bikini and meeting a "code-red Euro-hottie." (Rev: SLJ 6/06)

465 Hautman, Pete. *All-In* (7–10). 2007, Simon & Schuster $15.99 (978-1-4169-1325-2). Seventeen-year-old Denn, the poker prodigy last seen in *Stone Cold* (1998), finds his luck deserting him in this fast-action story. (Rev: BL 5/1/07; HB 7–8/07; SLJ 7/07)

466 Hazuka, Tom. *Last Chance for First* (8–11). 2008, Brown Barn paper $8.95 (978-0-9798824-0-1). Robby, a high school junior, faces a lot of challenges: unfavorable comparisons with his older brother, an attraction to an unpopular girl, problems with his coach and a soccer teammate. . . . (Rev: BL 6/1–15/08; SLJ 9/08)

467 Headley, Justina Chen. *Girl Overboard* (7–11). 2008, Little, Brown $16.99 (978-0-316-01130-3). Super-rich Chinese American Syrah learns more about her family's heritage and about the satisfaction in helping others when she uses her family's power to help a sick friend. (Rev: BL 1/1–15/08; SLJ 2/08)

468 Heneghan, James. *Payback* (6–9). 2007, Groundwood $16.95 (978-0-88899-701-2). When fellow new student Benny commits suicide because of the torment he was subjected to by bullies, Charley blames himself for not helping and feels he has to make amends. (Rev: BL 5/1/07; SLJ 9/07)

469 Henkes, Kevin. *Bird Lake Moon* (5–7). 2008, Greenwillow $15.99 (978-0-06-147076-9). Unsettled because his parents are divorcing, Mitch hopes to move into the empty house next door and is annoyed when the family who owns it turns up; he decides to trick them into thinking their dead son is haunting them, a choice that has consequences when he becomes friends with the son. (Rev: BL 3/15/08; SLJ 3/08) 🍂

470 Henkes, Kevin. *Olive's Ocean* (5–8). 2003, Greenwillow LB $16.89 (978-0-06-053544-5). During a summer at the beach, Martha, an aspiring writer, wrestles with a classmate's sudden death, has her first whiff of romance, and gets to know her family and herself better. Newbery Honor Book, 2004. (Rev: BL 9/1/03*; HB 11–12/03*; HBG 4/04; SLJ 8/03*)

471 Herrera, Juan Felipe. *Cinnamon Girl: Letters Found Inside a Cereal Box* (6–9). 2005, HarperCollins LB $16.89 (978-0-06-057985-2). In free verse, 13-year-old Yolanda struggles to cope with the impact of 9/11 and the uncertainties in her life that this shock has revived. (Rev: BL 8/05; SLJ 11/05)

472 Hershey, Mary. *The One Where the Kid Nearly Jumps to His Death and Lands in California* (7–10). 2007, Penguin $15.99 (978-1-59514-150-7). Thirteen-year-old Stump, so named because one of his legs was amputated below the knee after a skiing accident, expects a difficult summer with his father and his new wife but in addition to dealing with his dad, he falls for a soap opera star and learns to swim. (Rev: BL 5/1/07; SLJ 3/07)

473 Hiaasen, Carl. *Flush* (5–8). 2005, Knopf LB $18.99 (978-0-375-92182-7). Noah Underwood and his younger sister Abbey set out to prove their father was justified in sinking a floating casino because it was polluting. (Rev: BL 8/05; SLJ 9/05)

474 High, Linda Oatman. *Sister Slam and the Poetic Motormouth Road Trip* (8–12). 2004, Bloomsbury $16.95 (978-1-58234-948-0). Laüra Rose Crapper, a.k.a. Sister Slam, and her friend Twig head for New York, where they meet a handsome boy named Jake. (Rev: BL 5/1/04; SLJ 5/04)

475 Hobbs, Valerie. *Defiance* (4–7). 2005, Farrar $16.00 (978-0-374-30847-6). An elderly neighbor named Pearl — and her cow — become valuable friends to 11-year-old Toby, who does not want to tell his parents that his cancer is back. (Rev: BL 8/05; SLJ 9/05)

476 Holm, Jennifer. *Middle School Is Worse Than Meatloaf: A Year Told through Stuff* (5–8). Illus. by Elicia Castaldi. 2007, Atheneum $12.99 (978-0-689-85281-7). Receipts, notes, cards, magazine clippings, and other "stuff" tell of an eventful year in Ginny's life that includes bad hair days, iffy report cards, her mother's remarriage, and other tragedies. (Rev: BL 10/15/07; SLJ 9/07)

477 Holt, Kimberly Willis. *When Zachary Beaver Came to Town* (5–9). 1999, Holt $16.95 (978-0-8050-6116-1). Thirteen-year-old Toby Wilson learns the value of love and friendship when he gets to know Zachary Beaver, a 643-pound teen who has been abandoned by his guardian. (Rev: BCCB 12/99; BL 9/15/99; HB 11–12/99; HBG 3/00; SLJ 11/99*; VOYA 12/99)

478 Holtwijk, Ineke. *Asphalt Angels* (8–12). Trans. by Wanda Boeke. 1999, Front St. $15.95 (978-1-886910-24-9). When a homeless boy in the slums of Rio de Janeiro joins a street gang, the Asphalt Angels, for protection from corrupt police officers, pedophiles, and other homeless people, he finds himself being drawn into a life of crime. (Rev: BL 8/99; HBG 4/00; SLJ 9/99; VOYA 12/99)

479 Honeycutt, Natalie. *Josie's Beau* (5–7). 1988, Avon paper $2.95 (978-0-380-70524-5). Beau's mother doesn't want him fighting, so Josie offers to say she's the one who fights — but the lie backfires. (Rev: BCCB 12/87; BL 12/1/87; SLJ 12/87)

480 Hossack, Sylvie. *Green Mango Magic* (4–7). 1999, Avon $14.00 (978-0-380-97613-3). Maile, who lives alone with her grandmother in Hawaii since her father abandoned her, finds a friend in Brooke, from Seattle, who is a recovering cancer patient. (Rev: BCCB 12/98; BL 5/1/99; HBG 10/99; SLJ 2/99; VOYA 8/99)

481 Howe, James. *The Misfits* (5–8). 2001, Simon & Schuster $16.00 (978-0-689-83955-9). A group of 7th-grade social misfits challenge the so-called norms at their school by running for student council and instituting a no-names-calling day. (Rev: BCCB 1/02; BL 11/15/01; HB 11–12/01; HBG 3/02; SLJ 11/01; VOYA 12/01)

482 Hudson, Wade. *Anthony's Big Surprise* (5–7). Series: NEATE. 1998, Just Us Bks. paper $3.95 (978-0-940975-42-2). Interracial tensions erupt in junior high school when some African American students are suspended and Anthony, who is also trying to cope with a family crisis, must deal with both problems. (Rev: SLJ 6/99)

483 Hughes, Mark Peter. *Lemonade Mouth* (8–11). 2007, Delacorte $15.99 (978-0-385-73392-2). Five teens in the band Lemonade Mouth take turns — tied together by a fan's comments — telling the story of their rise to fame (and their various stumbles) at Opoquonsett High in Rhode Island. (Rev: BCCB 6/07; BL 2/15/07; SLJ 5/07)

484 Ingold, Jeanette. *Mountain Solo* (6–9). 2003, Harcourt $17.00 (978-0-15-202670-7). After an unsuccessful violin concert, 16-year-old Tess flees to her father's home in Montana where she meets Frederick, another violinist, and reviews her love of music, her past life, and her goals for the future. (Rev: BL 12/1/03; SLJ 11/03)

485 Ishizaki, Hiroshi. *Chain Mail: Addicted to You* (6–9). Trans. from Japanese by Richard Kim. 2007, TokyoPop paper $7.99 (978-1-59816-581-4). This is the story of Sawako, a lonely and troubled Japanese teen who collaborates with strangers on the Internet to write a story about a girl in danger. (Rev: SLJ 7/07)

486 Jenkins, A. M. *Out of Order* (8–10). 2003, HarperCollins LB $16.89 (978-0-06-623969-9). Sophomore Colt relies on his good looks and athletic prowess to pull him through, but failing grades place him in the company of a brainy girl and his attitudes begin to change. (Rev: BL 9/1/03; HB 11–12/03; HBG 4/04; SLJ 9/03*; VOYA 10/03)

487 Jennings, Patrick. *The Beastly Arms* (5–7). 2001, Scholastic paper $16.95 (978-0-439-16589-1). A dreamy 6th-grader who pictures animals in everything he sees, discovers a world of real beasts when he and his mother move to the Beastly Arms. (Rev: BCCB 10/01; BL 5/1/01; HB 7–8/01; HBG 10/01; SLJ 4/01)

488 Jennings, Richard W. *The Great Whale of Kansas* (5–9). 2001, Houghton $15.00 (978-0-618-10228-0). When a boy finds a prehistoric whale fossil in his backyard, the discovery brings unexpected consequences. (Rev: HB 9–10/01; HBG 3/02; SLJ 8/01; VOYA 2/02)

489 Johnson, Angela. *Bird* (6–10). 2004, Penguin $16.99 (978-0-8037-2847-9). Heartbroken when her stepfather abandons the family, 13-year-old Bird travels from Cleveland to Alabama to find him and bring him home and instead finds unexpected friendship. (Rev: BL 9/1/04; SLJ 9/04; VOYA 2/05)

490 Johnson, Maureen. *Suite Scarlett* (7–12). 2008, Scholastic $16.99 (978-0-439-89927-7). When Scarlett turns 15, she's "given" the Empire Suite in the family's rundown hotel to care for; the suite comes with Mrs. Amberson, an unusual long-term guest, and here this zany adventure involving four siblings begins. (Rev: BL 6/1–15/08)

491 Johnson, Maureen. *13 Little Blue Envelopes* (8–11). 2005, HarperCollins LB $17.89 (978-0-06-054142-2). On a trip through Europe following

instructions left to her in 13 letters written by her Aunt Peg before her death, 17-year-old Ginny learns about Peg's past and about herself. (Rev: BL 9/15/05; SLJ 10/05; VOYA 10/05)

492 Jordan, Rosa. *The Goatnappers* (6–9). 2007, Peachtree $14.95 (978-1-56145-400-6). Justin is thrilled to be the first freshman picked for the varsity baseball team, but must also cope with his newly reappeared father and with the goat he and others have liberated from its abuser; a sequel to *Lost Goat Lane* (2004). (Rev: BL 5/1/07; SLJ 9/07)

493 Juby, Susan. *Another Kind of Cowboy* (8–11). 2007, HarperTeen $16.99 (978-0-06-076517-0). A horse story with a male protagonist, this novel set in Vancouver centers on Alex, who is 16 and questioning his sexuality, and on Cleo, a fellow dressage student who needs a friend. (Rev: BL 12/1/07; HB 1–2/08; SLJ 2/08)

494 Jukes, Mavis. *Getting Even* (5–7). 1988, Knopf paper $4.50 (978-0-679-86570-4). Maggie seems unable to stop the nasty pranks of classmate Corky, and receives differing advice from her divorced parents. (Rev: BCCB 5/88; BL 4/1/88; SLJ 5/88)

495 Kantor, Melissa. *The Breakup Bible* (8–10). 2007, Hyperion $15.99 (978-0-7868-0962-2). Jen turns to a book called *The Breakup Bible* after Max, the editor at her school's newspaper, dumps her for another girl. (Rev: BL 7/07)

496 Karasyov, Carrie, and Jill Kargman. *Bittersweet Sixteen* (7–10). 2006, HarperCollins $15.99 (978-0-06-077844-6). Laura learns who her true friends are when new girl Sophie starts at her school and everyone starts planning their 16th-birthday parties. (Rev: SLJ 10/06)

497 Karasyov, Carrie, and Jill Kargman. *Summer Intern* (7–12). 2007, HarperCollins $16.99 (978-0-06-115375-4). In this entertaining novel, hardworking Kira gets a summer internship at a national fashion magazine in New York City and learns about both fashion and office politics. (Rev: SLJ 6/07)

498 Kaye, Amy. *The Real Deal: Unscripted* (7–12). 2004, Dorchester paper $5.99 (978-0-8439-5315-2). Claire juggles a potential Broadway career, a romance with a teen star, and the needs of her new-found half-sister, all under the glare of reality TV cameras. (Rev: SLJ 5/04)

499 Kephart, Beth. *Undercover* (7–10). 2007, HarperCollins $16.99 (978-0-06-123893-2). Sensitive soul Elisa writes love letters for boys to give to their girlfriends as she deals with problems at home and tries to find solace in nature and her love of ice skating; her growing friendship with Theo gives her hope. (Rev: BL 10/15/07; SLJ 10/07) ♪

500 Key, Watt. *Alabama Moon* (6–9). 2006, Farrar $17.00 (978-0-374-30184-2). Moon, 10, is raised in the forest by a Vietnam vet father who trusts nobody; when his father dies, Moon's life changes dramatically — he is taken into custody and repeatedly escapes before he finally finds friends. (Rev: BL 11/1/06; HB 9–10/06; SLJ 9/06) 🔊

501 Kherdian, David. *The Revelations of Alvin Toliver* (5–7). 2001, Hampton Roads paper $7.95 (978-1-57174-255-1). Twelve-year-old Alvin is fascinated with nature and the great outdoors, and finds some unusual adult friends who introduce him to nature's charms. (Rev: BL 12/1/01; SLJ 3/02)

502 Kimmel, Elizabeth Cody. *Lily B. on the Brink of Paris* (5–8). 2006, HarperCollins $16.99 (978-0-06-083948-2). Lily B.'s latest diary entries record the cultural sights of Paris, where the 13-year-old travels with her French class. (Rev: BL 1/1–15/07; SLJ 1/07)

503 Klass, David. *Dark Angel* (8–11). 2005, Farrar $17.00 (978-0-374-39950-4). Seventeen-year-old Jeff's family has hidden the existence of his older brother, a murderer who has been in jail; when Troy is released and comes home to live, Jeff's life is turned upside down. (Rev: BL 9/15/05; SLJ 10/05; VOYA 10/05)

504 Kline, Lisa Williams. *The Princesses of Atlantis* (5–7). 2002, Cricket $16.95 (978-0-8126-2855-5). Twelve-year-old Arlene experiences ups and downs in her friendship with Carly, with whom she is writing a novel about two princesses. (Rev: BL 4/15/02; HBG 10/02; SLJ 7/02)

505 Klinger, Shula. *The Kingdom of Strange* (6–9). 2008, Marshall Cavendish $16.99 (978-0-7614-5395-6). Fourteen-year-old Thisbe works on her writing skills by recording her thoughts — on life and on writing — in a journal. (Rev: BL 5/1/08; LMC 10/08)

506 Kluger, Steve. *My Most Excellent Year: A Novel of Love, Mary Poppins, and Fenway Park* (8–12). 2008, Dial $16.99 (978-0-8037-3227-8). The freshman year of three diverse Boston-area teenagers is filled with romance, good works, sexual awakenings, sports, and more, as revealed in this collection of entries that includes letters, poems, e-mails, and other artifacts. (Rev: BL 3/15/08; SLJ 4/08)

507 Koertge, Ron. *The Heart of the City* (5–7). 1998, Orchard LB $16.99 (978-0-531-33078-4). Apprehensive about moving to the big city of Los Angeles, 10-year-old Joy soon finds a friend in a young African American girl and together they fight the takeover of an abandoned house by hoods. (Rev: BCCB 4/98; BL 4/1/98; HBG 10/98)

508 Konigsburg, E. L. *The Mysterious Edge of the Heroic World* (5–7). 2007, Simon & Schuster $16.99 (978-1-4169-4972-5). Amedeo Kaplan hopes to make a name for himself by discovering something important; could he have the opportunity as he and his new friend William help to clean out

the home of Mrs. Aida Zender, a former opera singer? Blending humor and mystery, this story has an added layer of Holocaust history. (Rev: BL 9/15/07; SLJ 9/07) 🔊

509 Konigsburg, E. L. *The Outcasts of 19 Schuyler Place* (4–8). 2004, Simon & Schuster $16.95 (978-0-689-86636-4). Rescued from summer camp by aging uncles, Margaret is dismayed to find that their prized garden sculptures are endangered in this absorbing, amusing, and thought-provoking novel. (Rev: BL 12/15/03*; HB 3–4/04; SLJ 1/04*)

510 Konigsburg, E. L. *The View from Saturday* (5–7). 1996, Simon & Schuster $16.00 (978-0-689-80993-4). A complicated tale about four 6th-graders who are contestants in an Academic Bowl competition. Newbery Medal winner, 1997. (Rev: BCCB 11/96; BL 10/15/96; SLJ 9/96*)

511 Korman, Gordon. *Schooled* (6–9). 2007, Hyperion $15.99 (978-0-7868-5692-3). When his grandmother becomes ill, 13-year-old Cap is removed from the farm commune where he has grown up and been homeschooled, and must deal with a whole new world at the local junior high; the often-funny story is told from various perspectives. (Rev: BL 8/07*; LMC 11/07; SLJ 8/07)

512 Korman, Gordon. *The Twinkie Squad* (5–7). 1992, Scholastic paper $13.95 (978-0-590-45249-6). A bossy, insecure 6th-grader and a defender of weaker kids are sentenced to the school's Special Discussion Group. (Rev: BCCB 11/92; BL 9/15/92; SLJ 9/92)

513 Koss, Amy Goldman. *Poison Ivy* (7–10). 2006, Roaring Brook $16.95 (978-1-59643-118-8). Multiple voices tell the story of the mock trial of the three bullies who have been making unpopular Ivy's life a misery. (Rev: BL 2/15/06; SLJ 3/06; VOYA 4/06)

514 Kraft, Erik P. *Miracle Wimp* (8–11). Illus. by author. 2007, Little, Brown $16.99 (978-0-316-01165-5). In often humorous anecdotes with accompanying drawings, Tom Mayo describes a year of his high school life as he deals with school and bullies, makes friends, gets his license, and finds a girlfriend. (Rev: BL 6/1–15/07; SLJ 10/07)

515 Kropp, Paul. *The Countess and Me* (6–9). 2002, Fitzhenry & Whiteside $14.95 (978-1-55041-680-0). Young Jordan, eager to fit in at his new school, must decide whether to betray his eccentric neighbor to a group of delinquent boys. (Rev: BL 10/1/02; SLJ 11/02)

516 Lamm, Drew. *Bittersweet* (8–11). 2003, Clarion $15.00 (978-0-618-16443-1). When Taylor's grandmother, who has essentially raised her, falls ill, artist Taylor suddenly finds she lacks creativity and is unsure of her other relationships. (Rev: BCCB 2/04; BL 11/15/03; HBG 4/04; SLJ 12/03; VOYA 12/03)

31

517 Langan, John. *Search for Safety* (7–12). Series: Bluford. 2006, Townsend paper $4.95 (978-1-59194-070-8). Sophomore Ben is new at Bluford High and must find someone to talk to about his abusive home life before it is too late; suitable for reluctant readers. (Rev: SLJ 7/07)

518 Langan, Paul. *The Fallen* (7–12). Series: Bluford. 2006, Townsend paper $4.95 (978-1-59194-066-1). Martin Luna starts his sophomore year at Bluford High with the goal of avoiding the gang conflicts that took his brother's life; suitable for reluctant readers. (Rev: SLJ 7/07)

519 Langan, Paul. *Shattered* (7–12). Series: Bluford. 2006, Townsend paper $4.95 (978-1-59194-069-2). When Darcy's ex-boyfriend returns to town, the 11th-grader must come to terms with her past; suitable for reluctant readers. (Rev: SLJ 7/07)

520 Larson, Kirby. *Hattie Big Sky* (7–10). 2006, Delacorte $17.99 (978-0-385-73313-7). Hattie Brooks, a 16-year-old orphan, inherits a Montana homestead from her uncle, and learns to farm the land and make a home for herself despite the many difficulties she faces. Newbery Honor Book, 2007. (Rev: BL 9/1/06; SLJ 11/06*)

521 Lecesne, James. *Absolute Brightness* (8–12). 2008, HarperTeen $17.99 (978-0-06-125627-1). A gay teenager disappears from a small New Jersey town in this multilayered, well-written novel. (Rev: SLJ 3/08; VOYA 4/08)

522 Lenhard, Elizabeth. *It's a Purl Thing* (6–9). Series: Chicks with Sticks. 2005, Dutton $16.99 (978-0-525-47622-1). Four Chicago high school girls from diverse backgrounds become friends when they join a class at KnitWit, a local yarn shop. (Rev: BL 10/15/05; SLJ 2/06)

523 Levithan, David. *Wide Awake* (8–11). 2006, Knopf $16.95 (978-0-375-83466-0). When a recount is demanded after a gay Jewish man is elected president, Duncan — with his boyfriend Jimmy — joins the millions who protest and learns a lot about himself, his beliefs and feelings. (Rev: BL 9/15/06; SLJ 9/06)

524 Lewis, J. Patrick. *The Last Resort* (6–9). Illus. by Roberto Innocenti. 2002, Creative $17.95 (978-1-56846-172-4). Noted poet J. Patrick Lewis uses word play and inventive characters to tell the story of an artist looking for inspiration, in this picture book for older readers full of thought-provoking images. (Rev: BL 2/1/03; HBG 3/03)

525 Lewis, Wendy. *Graveyard Girl* (7–10). 2000, Red Deer paper $7.95 (978-0-88995-202-7). While looking back at her high school yearbook, Ginger reminisces about her classmates and vignettes reveal their stories of marriage, achievement, and lost romance. (Rev: BL 1/1–15/01; SLJ 5/01; VOYA 6/01)

526 Lichtman, Wendy. *Do the Math: Secrets, Lies, and Algebra* (5–9). 2007, HarperCollins $16.99 (978-0-06-122955-8). Tess, 13, applies mathematical principles to all situations in her life including a cheating classmate, untrustworthy friends, and a potential murder. (Rev: BCCB 9/07; SLJ 12/07)

527 Lockhart, E. *The Disreputable History of Frankie Landau-Banks* (7–12). 2008, Hyperion $16.99 (978-0-7868-3818-9). In her sophomore year at Alabaster Prep, Frankie shakes up her boyfriend's all-male secret club, the Loyal Order of the Basset Hounds, and brings much-needed change to her elite boarding school; combining humor and social commentary, this is an appealing book full of wordplay. (Rev: BL 1/1–15/08; HB 5–6/08; LMC 10/08; SLJ 3/08) 📖

528 Lord, Cynthia. *Rules* (4–7). 2006, Scholastic $15.99 (978-0-439-44382-1). Catherine is a likable 12-year-old struggling to cope with the family challenges posed by her younger autistic brother. Newbery Honor Book, 2007. (Rev: BL 2/15/06; SLJ 4/06)

529 Lowry, Brigid. *Guitar Highway Rose* (8–12). 2003, Holiday $16.95 (978-0-8234-1790-2). Set in Australia, this story of two teens who run away from home presents the voices of various characters including teachers, family, and friends. (Rev: BL 2/15/04; HBG 4/04; SLJ 12/03; VOYA 4/04)

530 Lubar, David. *Hidden Talents* (5–9). 1999, Tor $16.95 (978-0-312-86646-4). Five misfits, who are attending the last-resort Edgeview Alternative School, become friends and discover extrasensory talents they can use against the school bully. (Rev: BL 9/15/99; HBG 10/99; SLJ 11/99; VOYA 10/99)

531 Luddy, Karon. *Spelldown: The Big-Time Dreams of a Small-Town Word Whiz* (5–8). 2007, Simon & Schuster $15.99 (978-1-4169-1610-9). Mentored by her Latin teacher, 13-year-old Karlene manages to win the spelling championship in her rural South Carolina county and moves on to competitions at the state and national levels. (Rev: BL 1/1–15/07; LMC 8-9/07; SLJ 2/07)

532 Lurie, April. *The Latent Powers of Dylan Fontaine* (8–12). 2008, Delacorte $15.99 (978-0-385-73125-6). Sixteen-year-old Dylan's problems include separated parents, a brother doing drugs, his own arrest for shoplifting, and his best friend Angie appearing unaware of his romantic interest; humor adds to the appeal of this story. (Rev: BL 4/1/08; SLJ 9/08)

533 Lyga, Barry. *The Astonishing Adventures of Fanboy and Goth Girl* (8–11). 2006, Houghton $16.95 (978-0-618-72392-8). Fanboy confides in his friend Goth girl and creates his own comic book as a way of escaping the violence he experiences at school. (Rev: BL 9/1/06; SLJ 11/06)

534 Lyons, Kelly Starling. *Eddie's Ordeal* (5–8). Illus. 2004, Just Us Bks. paper $3.95 (978-0-940975-16-3). When Eddie's grades slip, his father makes him quit baseball. (Rev: BL 2/1/05)

535 McNeal, Laura, and Tom McNeal. *The Decoding of Lana Morris* (8–11). 2007, Knopf $15.99 (978-0-375-83106-5). Lana suffers through the circumstances of her foster home — four special needs kids, a foster father who behaves inappropriately — until she gets an art kit that appears to have magical powers. (Rev: BCCB 7–8/07; BL 4/1/07; SLJ 6/07)

536 McNicoll, Sylvia. *A Different Kind of Beauty* (7–10). 2004, Fitzhenry & Whiteside $15.95 (978-1-55005-059-2); paper $8.95 (978-1-55005-060-8). Elizabeth, who is training a puppy as a guide dog, and Kyle, whose diabetes has left him blind, attend the same high school without knowing each other. (Rev: SLJ 8/04; VOYA 8/04)

537 Mankell, Henning. *A Bridge to the Stars* (6–9). 2007, Delacorte $15.99 (978-0-385-73495-0). Set in Sweden in the 1950s, this novel centers on Joel and his single father; their shaky relationship is cemented one night when Joel risks his life on a dare. (Rev: BL 12/1/07; HB 1–2/08; LMC 1/08; SLJ 1/08)

538 Marks, Graham. *Radio Radio* (8–11). 2004, Bloomsbury paper $11.99 (978-0-7475-5939-9). A group of London club kids goes up against both the government and some unsavory competitors when they set up a pirate radio station. (Rev: BL 1/1–15/05; SLJ 1/05)

539 Martineau, Diane. *The Wall on 7th Street* (6–8). 2005, Llewellyn paper $7.95 (978-0-7387-0715-0). An unlikely friendship between a 12-year-old boy and a homeless man helps the boy deal with his parents' divorce and results in a plan to save 7th Street from the gang that has ruled there. (Rev: SLJ 1/06)

540 Mass, Wendy. *Heaven Looks a Lot like the Mall* (7–10). 2007, Little, Brown $16.99 (978-0-316-05851-3). Thanks to a poorly aimed dodge ball, 16-year-old Tessa has a near-death experience and looks back on her life in free verse. (Rev: BL 10/15/07; SLJ 9/07)

541 Maude, Rachel. *Poseur* (8–12). Illus. Series: Poseur. 2008, Little, Brown paper $9.99 (978-0-316-06583-2). Charlotte, Janie, Petra, and Melissa — who attend an expensive private school in Los Angeles — are assigned to work together on creating their own clothing line. (Rev: BL 3/3/08; SLJ 3/08)

542 Maynard, Joyce. *The Cloud Chamber* (6–9). 2005, Simon & Schuster $16.95 (978-0-689-87152-8). In 1950s Montana, 14-year-old Nate finds a friend in his science project partner Naomi as he struggles to cope with his father's apparent suicide attempt and subsequent hospitalization, his mother's withdrawal, and the needs of his younger sister. (Rev: BL 7/05; SLJ 7/05; VOYA 2/06)

543 Mazer, Norma Fox. *Mrs. Fish, Ape, and Me, the Dump Queen* (6–9). 1981, Avon paper $3.50 (978-0-380-69153-1). Joyce has been hurt by supposed friends but somehow she trusts the school custodian, Mrs. Fish.

544 Mechling, Lauren, and Laura Moser. *Foreign Exposure: The Social Climber Abroad* (7–10). 2007, Houghton paper $8.99 (978-0-618-66379-8). Sixteen-year-old Mimi visits a friend in London and soon finds herself immersed in the celebrity gossip scene. (Rev: SLJ 6/07)

545 Mendle, Jane. *Better Off Famous?* (7–12). 2007, St. Martin's paper $8.95 (978-0-312-36903-3). On a visit to New York from Alabama, 16-year-old Annie, a talented violinist, unexpectedly wins a part on a TV series and becomes an instant celebrity — and an instant brat. (Rev: SLJ 2/08)

546 Mikaelsen, Ben. *Ghost of Spirit Bear* (6–9). 2008, HarperCollins $16.99 (978-0-06-009007-4). In this sequel to *Touching Spirit Bear* (2001), Peter and Cole are back from exile on an Alaskan island and now face the rigors of high school life. (Rev: BL 6/1–15/08; SLJ 8/08) 🐾

547 Mikaelsen, Ben. *Touching Spirit Bear* (6–9). 2001, HarperCollins $16.99 (978-0-380-97744-4). Cole, an angry and violent 15-year-old, is sentenced according to Native American tradition to a year of solitude on an island in Alaska. (Rev: BCCB 5/01; BL 1/1–15/01; HBG 10/01; SLJ 2/01; VOYA 6/01)

548 Minter, J. *Inside Girl* (8–12). 2007, Bloomsbury paper $8.95 (978-1-59990-086-5). Flan, younger sister of popular Patch Flood of the Insiders series, tries to escape her high-society world by transferring to a public school, but soon her ultra-rich friends show up to blow her cover. (Rev: BL 7/07; SLJ 7/07)

549 Moeyaert, Bart. *Hornet's Nest* (8–10). Trans. from Dutch by David Colmer. 2000, Front St. $15.95 (978-1-886910-48-5). Translated from Dutch, this is a fablelike story of Susanna's efforts to solve some of the problems in her life and her village. (Rev: BL 9/15/00; HB 11–12/00; HBG 3/01; SLJ 11/00)

550 Moriarty, Jaclyn. *The Murder of Bindy Mackenzie* (8–11). 2006, Scholastic $16.99 (978-0-439-74051-7). Humor and mystery are combined in this story about the precocious Bindy, whose perfectionism has lost her many friends; her growth through this story is shown in diary entries, assignments, and other documents. (Rev: BL 10/15/06; HB 1–2/07*; SLJ 1/07)

551 Morris, Taylor. *Class Favorite* (5–8). 2007, Simon & Schuster paper $5.99 (978-1-4169-3598-8). It's hard enough being an 8th-grader, but Sara has to endure countless public embarrassments at her school — still, this hilarious book shows how this unflappable girl keeps trying to climb the social ladder in spite of it all. (Rev: SLJ 3/08)

552 Moss, Marissa. *Vote 4 Amelia* (4–7). Illus. by author. 2007, Simon & Schuster $9.99 (978-1-4169-2789-1). Amelia is running for secretary and her friend Carly for president; they didn't expect the campaign to be so intense and Amelia's diary entries are — as always — humorous and revealing. (Rev: SLJ 9/07)

553 Murdock, Catherine Gilbert. *Dairy Queen* (6–9). 2006, Houghton $16.00 (978-0-618-68307-9). Fifteen-year-old D.J., who comes from an uncommunicative family, has quietly taken over the work of the family dairy farm, but when she decides to try out for the football team she suddenly becomes the focus of attention. (Rev: BL 4/1/06; SLJ 4/06)

554 Murphy, Pat. *The Wild Girls* (5–8). 2007, Viking $16.99 (978-0-670-06226-3). Joan and best friend Sarah (who calls herself Fox) love to explore in the woods and to write — a pastime that wins them spots at a writing camp and an outlet for their frustrations with their family lives. (Rev: BL 10/1/07; SLJ 11/07) ⊘

555 Myracle, Lauren. *Eleven* (4–7). 2004, Dutton $16.99 (978-0-525-47165-3). Covering Winnie's life from her 11th birthday to her 12th, this novel reveals typical friendship and family tensions. (Rev: BL 4/15/04; SLJ 2/04)

556 Myracle, Lauren. *The Fashion Disaster That Changed My Life* (5–8). 2005, Dutton $15.99 (978-0-525-47222-3). Through her diary and instant messages, Allison relates the turmoil of 7th grade, from her humiliating first-day arrival with her mother's underwear clinging to her pants to her problems making and keeping friends. (Rev: BL 9/15/05; SLJ 7/05)

557 Myracle, Lauren. *Thirteen* (6–9). 2008, Dutton $15.99 (978-0-525-47896-6). In this installment — following *Eleven* (2004) and *Twelve* (2007) — Winnie is 13 and busy with friends, boys, and family (including a new baby sister — and an older sister leaving for college). (Rev: BL 1/1–15/08; SLJ 7/08)

558 Na, An. *Wait for Me* (8–11). 2006, Penguin $15.99 (978-0-399-24275-5). Unable to meet her mother's expectations, Korean American high school senior Mina resorts to lies and plans for escape, but when Ysrael, with whom she has fallen in love, is blamed for Mina's actions she must make a difficult choice. (Rev: BL 3/15/06*; SLJ 7/06)

559 Nash, Naomi. *I Am So Jinxed!* (8–12). 2006, Dorchester paper $5.99 (978-0-8439-5405-0). Vick Marotti gives up her Goth girl ways and gets in a relationship with a cute senior guy, but things are still far from perfect in her life; a sequel to *You Are So Cursed!* (2004). (Rev: SLJ 5/06)

560 Nelson, Blake. *Paranoid Park* (8–11). 2006, Viking $15.99 (978-0-670-06118-1). The narrator of this title, a 16-year-old skateboarder, is involved in the death of security officer and must deal with his feelings of confusion, fear, and the decision to confess or not. (Rev: BL 9/1/06; SLJ 11/06)

561 Nields, Nerissa. *Plastic Angel* (7–10). 2005, Scholastic $17.95 (978-0-439-70913-2). Thirteen-year-olds Randi and Gellie become friends despite their differences and form a band called Plastic Angel. (Rev: BL 8/05; SLJ 9/05; VOYA 2/06)

562 Noël, Alyson. *Saving Zoë* (7–10). 2007, St. Martin's paper $8.95 (978-0-312-35510-4). Fifteen-year-old Echo's world fell apart when her older sister Zoë was murdered; when she gets Zoë's diaries, however, she discovers just how many risks her sister had been taking and is able to start healing herself and her family. (Rev: SLJ 12/07; VOYA date)

563 Nolan, Han. *When We Were Saints* (7–10). 2003, Harcourt $17.00 (978-0-15-216371-6). After his grandfather's death, Archie, 14, is overwhelmed by a need to find God and, with his religious friend Clare, sets off on a pilgrimage to the Cloisters in New York. (Rev: BL 10/1/03; HBG 4/04; SLJ 11/03; VOYA 12/03)

564 O'Connell, Tyne. *Pulling Princes* (7–10). 2004, Bloomsbury $16.95 (978-1-58234-957-2). Calypso Kelly, a 15-year-old from LA, finds it difficult to fit in at her posh English boarding school. (Rev: SLJ 12/04; VOYA 4/05)

565 O'Keefe, Susan Heyboer. *My Life and Death by Alexandra Canarsie* (7–10). 2002, Peachtree $14.95 (978-1-56145-264-4). Allie, a lonely teenager, finds a friend and a mystery when she starts going to strangers' funerals. (Rev: HBG 10/02; SLJ 9/02; VOYA 4/02)

566 Ostow, Micol. *Gettin' Lucky* (6–9). 2007, Simon & Schuster paper $5.99 (978-1-4169-3536-0). A breezy book about Cass, a girl who has it all until her best friend kisses her boyfriend, forcing her to make new friends. (Rev: SLJ 7/07)

567 Ostow, Micol. *Westminster Abby* (6–9). Series: Students Across the Seven Seas. 2005, Penguin paper $6.99 (978-0-14-240413-3). Sent to study in London for the summer, Abby has a great time and learns a lot about herself. (Rev: BL 8/05; SLJ 6/05)

568 Padian, Maria. *Brett McCarthy: Work in Progress* (6–9). 2008, Knopf $15.99 (978-0-375-84675-5). In 8th grade, Brett's life changes; although she's still good at soccer and her studies, her friendship with Diane is disrupted and her beloved grandmother has cancer. (Rev: SLJ 2/08)

569 Paratore, Coleen Murtagh. *The Cupid Chronicles* (5–9). 2006, Simon & Schuster $15.95 (978-1-4169-0867-8). Now that her mother is married, Willa puts her considerable energies into the campaign to save the town library, and somehow romance keeps intruding; a sequel to *The Wedding Planner's Daughter* (2005). (Rev: SLJ 4/07) ☺

570 Parkinson, Siobhan. *Something Invisible* (4–7). 2006, Roaring Brook $16.95 (978-1-59643-123-2). Jake, a self-absorbed 11-year-old, learns a lot about family and friendship over a summer that involves tragedy. (Rev: BL 3/1/06; SLJ 4/06; VOYA 6/06)

571 Paterson, Katherine. *Bridge to Terabithia* (6–8). Illus. by Donna Diamond. 1977, HarperCollins LB $16.89 (978-0-690-04635-9); paper $6.99 (978-0-06-440184-5). Jess becomes a close friend of Leslie, a new girl in his school, and suffers agony after her accidental death. Newbery Medal winner, 1978. (Rev: SLJ 1/00)

572 Paulsen, Gary. *The Glass Cafe* (6–8). 2003, Random $12.95 (978-0-385-32499-1). Tony, 12, has an unusual mother who allows him to draw the women at the Kitty Kat Club, a situation that does not please social services. (Rev: BL 9/1/03; HBG 10/03; SLJ 6/03; VOYA 8/03)

573 Pavlcin, Karen. *Perch, Mrs. Sackets, and Crow's Nest* (4–7). 2007, Alma Little $16.95 (978-1-934617-00-7). Ten-year-old Andy Parker dreads the idea of a summer in the country but in the end finds he really enjoys it. (Rev: SLJ 12/07)

574 Pearsall, Shelley. *All of the Above* (5–8). 2006, Little, Brown $15.99 (978-0-316-11524-7). In this inspiring, fact-based novel, a 7th-grade math teacher challenges his students to build the world's largest tetrahedron and ends up involving the whole community; alternating chapters are narrated by the teacher and four of the students. (Rev: BL 9/1/06; SLJ 9/06)

575 Perkins, Lynne Rae. *All Alone in the Universe* (5–8). 1999, Greenwillow $16.99 (978-0-688-16881-0). Debbie is crushed when her friend of many years drops her for another, but she has the courage to adjust and reach out to others. (Rev: BCCB 10/99; BL 9/1/99*; HB 9–10/99; HBG 3/00; SLJ 10/99)

576 Perkins, Mitali. *Extreme American Makeover* (7–10). Series: First Daughter. 2007, Dutton $16.99 (978-0-525-47800-3). Sixteen-year-old Sameera is the adopted Pakistani daughter of the Republican candidate for president and finds herself half enjoying and half hating efforts to make her over for public scrutiny. (Rev: BL 5/15/07; SLJ 6/07)

577 Perkins, Mitali. *White House Rules* (7–10). Series: First Daughter. 2008, Dutton $16.99 (978-0-525-47951-2). Sameera, the adopted Pakistani daughter of President Righton, lives up the White House with a blog (that readers can actually access), parties for her friends, and her thoughts on politics; the sequel to *Extreme American Makeover* (2007). (Rev: BL 2/1/08; SLJ 2/08)

578 Peters, Kimberly Joy. *Painting Caitlyn* (8–11). 2006, Lobster paper $9.95 (978-1-897073-40-7). Fourteen-year-old Caitlyn feels alone and depressed about her life until she starts dating an older boy named Tyler. But when Tyler starts controlling her and the relationship becomes abusive, Caitlyn must make a choice. (Rev: BL 9/15/06; SLJ 9/06)

579 Pixley, Marcella. *Freak* (6–9). 2007, Farrar $16.00 (978-0-374-32453-7). Miriam — already a talented poet in 7th grade but unpopular because of her social awkwardness — eventually lashes out at her bullies. (Rev: BL 9/15/07; SLJ 11/07)

580 Pollack, Jenny. *Klepto: Best Friends, First Love, and Shoplifting* (8–11). 2006, Viking $16.99 (978-0-670-06061-0). In the early 1980s, Julie Prodsky, a 14-year-old drama major at New York's High School of Performing Arts, meets cool Julie Braverman and sets out on a career of "getting" rather than buying. (Rev: BL 2/15/06; SLJ 4/06)

581 Rallison, Janette. *How to Take the Ex Out of Ex-boyfriend* (7–10). 2007, Putnam $15.99 (978-0-399-24617-3). This funny novel follows Giovanna as she is torn between being loyal to her brother, who is running for student body president, and her boyfriend, the other candidate's campaign manager. (Rev: SLJ 7/07)

582 Rallison, Janette. *Revenge of the Cheerleaders* (7–9). 2007, Walker $16.95 (978-0-8027-8999-0). Chelsea's cheerleader persona is resented by her younger sister, a sullen 15-year-old Goth, and her sister's boyfriend, a singer with a heavy-metal group. (Rev: BL 1/15/08; SLJ 3/08)

583 Randle, Kristen D. *Slumming* (8–11). 2003, HarperTempest LB $16.89 (978-0-06-001023-2). Three Mormon high school seniors decide to befriend the friendless and invite them to the school prom. (Rev: BCCB 9/03; BL 8/03; HB 7–8/03; HBG 4/04; SLJ 8/03; VOYA 8/03)

584 Rayban, Chloe. *Hollywood Bliss: My Life So Far* (5–8). Series: Hollywood Bliss. 2007, Bloomsbury $16.95 (978-1-59990-093-3). Hollywood's famous and super-rich mom is getting married in an over-the-top ceremony — and Hollywood is gaining a new stepbrother in this glamorous and funny sequel to *Hollywood Bliss: My Life Starring Mum* (2006). (Rev: BL 7/07; SLJ 2/08)

585 Rayburn, Tricia. *The Melting of Maggie Bean* (6–8). 2007, Simon & Schuster paper $5.99 (978-1-4169-3348-9). Maggie discovers her inner strength and gains confidence as she loses unwanted pounds with the goal of joining her school's synchronized swim team. (Rev: SLJ 7/07)

586 Resau, Laura. *Red Glass* (7–10). 2007, Delacorte $15.99 (978-0-385-73466-0). Sixteen-year-old Sophie, a girl beset by trepidations, befriends 6-year-old Pablo, whose parents died trying to cross the border illegally, and decides to take him back to see his relatives in Mexico with life-changing results. (Rev: BL 9/15/07; SLJ 10/07)

587 Rettig, Liz. *My Desperate Love Diary* (8–12). 2007, Holiday House $16.95 (978-0-8234-2033-9). Wittily written in diary format, this book tells the story of Kelly Ann, a 15-year-old British girl with family problems who finds herself obsessed with a boy who doesn't return her feelings, while a caring boy waits on the sidelines. (Rev: SLJ 7/07)

588 Reynolds, Marilyn. *Love Rules: True-to-Life Stories from Hamilton High* (8–12). Series: True-to-Life. 2001, Morning Glory $18.95 (978-1-885356-75-8); paper $9.95 (978-1-885356-76-5). Lynn, a white high school senior, learns about prejudice as she dates an African American football player and supports her lesbian friend Kit. (Rev: BL 8/01; HBG 3/02; SLJ 9/01; VOYA 10/01)

589 Ritter, John H. *Under the Baseball Moon* (7–10). 2006, Philomel $16.99 (978-0-399-23623-5). Andy and his friend Glory lean on each other for support as they both pursue their dreams; he wants to be a famous musician and she wants to be a professional softball player. (Rev: BL 8/06*; SLJ 10/06) ⚘

590 Robinson, Sharon. *Safe at Home* (4–7). 2006, Scholastic $16.99 (978-0-439-67197-2). Still shaken by the sudden death of his father, 10-year-old Elijah Breeze must cope with culture shock when his mother moves him from suburban Connecticut to New York City's Harlem and he attends a coed summer baseball camp. (Rev: SLJ 10/06)

591 Romain, Trevor. *Under the Big Sky* (4–7). Illus. 2001, HarperCollins LB $14.89 (978-0-06-029495-3). Encouraged by his grandfather, a young boy searches far and wide for the secret of life. (Rev: BL 8/01; HBG 10/01; SLJ 8/01)

592 Roter, Jordan. *Camp Rules* (7–9). 2007, Dutton $15.99 (978-0-525-47803-4). Penny can't crack the cliques at all-girls Fern Lake Camp, which she attends for the first time as a 16-year-old. (Rev: BL 7/07; SLJ 6/07)

593 Ruditis, Paul. *Everyone's a Critic (Drama!)* (6–9). Series: Drama! 2007, Simon & Schuster paper $8.99 (978-1-4169-3392-2). The students we met in *The Four Dorothys* (2007) now eagerly await the arrival at Orion Academy's summer drama camp of Hartley Blackstone, a famous director; narrator Bryan enjoys watching all the behind-the-scenes drama. (Rev: BL 1/1–15/08; SLJ 12/07)

594 Rushton, Rosie. *Friends, Enemies* (6–8). 2004, Hyperion $15.74 (978-0-7868-5177-5). Four teenage girls, longtime friends, begin to have doubts about each other after a newcomer named Hannah is reluctantly accepted into their circle in this fast-paced novel set in Britain. (Rev: BL 12/15/04; SLJ 2/05)

595 Ryan, Darlene. *Saving Grace* (7–12). 2006, Orca $14.95 (978-1-55143-668-5). Evie, 15, soon regrets that she gave up her baby and persuades the child's father to help her kidnap Brianna (now named Grace) and head for a new life in Montreal. (Rev: SLJ 4/07)

596 Rylant, Cynthia. *God Went to Beauty School* (4–8). 2003, HarperCollins LB $15.89 (978-0-06-009434-8). God indulges in a lot of mortal activities, some fairly wacky, in this collection of thought-provoking poems. (Rev: BL 8/03; HB 7–8/03*; HBG 10/03; SLJ 6/03; VOYA 8/03)

597 Sachs, Marilyn. *The Bears' House* (4–7). Illus. by Louis Glanzman. 1987, Avon paper $2.99 (978-0-380-70582-5). A poor girl escapes from reality by living in a fantasy in her classroom. A reissue of the 1971 edition.

598 Schwartz, Ellen. *Stealing Home* (4–7). 2006, Tundra $8.95 (978-0-88776-765-4). Joey, a biracial 9-year-old baseball fan living in the Bronx, is orphaned with his mother's death and moved to live with his Jewish maternal grandparents in Brooklyn, where he must cope with a startlingly different world. (Rev: BL 9/1/06; SLJ 10/06)

599 Selzer, Adam. *How to Get Suspended and Influence People* (6–9). 2007, Delacorte $15.99 (978-0-385-73369-4). Gifted student Leon, 13, makes an "artistic and frank" sex education video that includes artistic nudes and poems about masturbation — and that gets him suspended before "free speech" prevails. (Rev: BCCB 5/07; BL 1/1–15/07; SLJ 3/07)

600 Senate, Melissa. *Theodora Twist* (8–11). 2006, Delacorte $15.95 (978-0-385-73301-4). Dora, a teen star with a wild past, moves in with average teen Emily and her family, with a reality show TV crew monitoring their every move. (Rev: BL 5/15/06; SLJ 2/07)

601 Shaw, Susan. *The Boy in the Basement* (6–9). 2004, Penguin $16.99 (978-0-525-47223-0). Locked in the basement for years by his abusive father, 12-year-old Charlie one day escapes his domestic prison but finds himself totally unequipped to deal with his newfound freedom. (Rev: BL 11/15/04; SLJ 11/04; VOYA 12/04)

602 Shulman, Polly. *Enthusiasm* (7–10). 2006, Penguin $15.99 (978-0-399-24389-9). A romantic comedy of errors featuring Jane and Ashleigh, both fans of Jane Austen, who get roles in a play at the local boys' prep school. (Rev: BL 1/1–15/06*; SLJ 3/06; VOYA 4/06)

603 Shura, Mary Francis. *The Josie Gambit* (5–7). 1986, Avon paper $2.50 (978-0-380-70497-2). Josie's friend Tory behaves in an inexplicable way to his new friend Greg. (Rev: BCCB 5/86; SLJ 9/86)

604 Smith, Sherri L. *Sparrow* (7–10). 2006, Delacorte $15.95 (978-0-385-73324-3). Orphaned when she was little, African American teen Kendall searches for an estranged aunt after her grandmother dies but her search does not progress as she hoped. (Rev: BL 6/1–15/06; SLJ 10/06)

605 Snyder, Zilpha Keatley. *The Egypt Game* (5–7). Illus. by Alton Raible. 1967, Dell paper $5.99 (978-0-440-42225-9). Humor and suspense mark an outstanding story of city children whose safety, while playing at an unsupervised re-creation of an Egyptian ritual, is threatened by a violent lunatic.

606 Sonnenblick, Jordan. *Drums, Girls and Dangerous Pie* (6–9). 2004, Turning Tide $15.95 (978-0-9761030-1-1). A moving, often funny story about 8th-grader Steven and the impact on his life and his family of his younger brother's leukemia. (Rev: BL 9/15/05; SLJ 10/04)

607 Sonnenblick, Jordan. *Zen and the Art of Faking It* (5–8). 2007, Scholastic $16.99 (978-0-439-83707-1). Adopted from China as a child and tired of moving to new schools, 8th-grader San Lee decides to play the role of a Zen master when he arrives in Pennsylvania. (Rev: BL 10/1/07; HB 11–12/07; LMC 1/08; SLJ 10/07)

608 Spinelli, Jerry. *Smiles to Go* (6–10). 2008, HarperCollins $16.99 (978-0-06-028133-5). The discovery that protons decay unsettles high school freshman Will Tuppence, causing him to take a new look at all sorts of things, including his little sister Tabby and his best friends Mi-Su and BT. (Rev: BL 2/15/08; SLJ 5/08)

609 Springer, Nancy. *Blood Trail* (6–8). 2003, Holiday $16.95 (978-0-8234-1723-0). A suspenseful story about a boy afraid to reveal what he knows about his friend's murder. (Rev: BL 5/1/03; HBG 10/03; SLJ 5/03; VOYA 8/03)

610 Staples, Suzanne Fisher. *Under the Persimmon Tree* (7–10). 2005, Farrar $17.00 (978-0-374-38025-0). The stories of Najmal, a brave young Afghani refugee, and Nusrat, an American woman helping with a refugee school, intersect as they wait for news of their loved ones in the chaos of the 2001 Afghan War. (Rev: BL 7/05*; SLJ 7/05; VOYA 10/05)

611 Steele, J. M. *The Taker* (8–11). 2006, Hyperion $15.99 (978-0-7868-4930-7). Carly's SAT scores are not good enough to get her into Princeton as her family expects, so she accepts an offer to cheat next time she takes the test, a decision that has wide-ranging repercussions. (Rev: BL 10/1/06; SLJ 12/06)

612 Stolz, Mary. *The Bully of Barkham Street* (4–8). Illus. by Leonard Shortall. 1963, HarperCollins paper $6.99 (978-0-06-440159-3). Eleven-year-old Martin goes through a typical phase of growing up — feeling misunderstood. Also use *A Dog on Barkham Street* (1960).

613 Strong, Jeremy. *Stuff: The Life of a Cool Demented Dude* (6–8). Illus. by Matthew S. Armstrong. 2007, HarperTempest $15.99 (978-0-06-084105-8). This entertaining story about a British teen nicknamed "Stuff" who has a chaotic home life and an equally complicated love life; the only thing that keeps him sane is the anonymous weekly comic strip he writes for a school publication. (Rev: SLJ 7/07)

614 Sutherland, Tui T. *This Must Be Love* (7–10). 2004, HarperCollins LB $16.89 (978-0-06-056476-6). Shakespearean plots are interwoven in this tale of Helena and Hermia, best friends in a modern New Jersey high school, and the comedy of errors that is their romantic life. (Rev: BCCB 1/05; SLJ 9/04)

615 Tashjian, Janet. *The Gospel According to Larry* (7–10). 2001, Holt $16.95 (978-0-8050-6378-3). When Josh (a.k.a. "Larry") publishes his anticonsumerism worldview on the Web, he develops a cult following and discovers the dark side of fame. (Rev: BCCB 1/02; BL 11/1/01; HB 1–2/02*; HBG 3/02; SLJ 10/01; VOYA 12/01)

616 Tashjian, Janet. *Vote for Larry* (7–10). 2004, Holt $16.95 (978-0-8050-7201-3). In this sequel to *The Gospel According to Larry* (2001), our young hero decides to run for president of the United States. (Rev: BL 5/1/04; HB 7–8/04; SLJ 5/04; VOYA 6/04)

617 Thesman, Jean. *In the House of the Queen's Beasts* (6–8). 2001, Viking $11.99 (978-0-670-89288-4). Two diffident 14-year-old girls, Emily and Rowan, share their secrets and develop a tentative friendship in a secluded tree house. (Rev: BCCB 6/01; BL 2/15/01; SLJ 3/01; VOYA 4/01)

618 Tigelaar, Liz. *Pretty Tough* (7–12). 2007, Penguin paper $8.99 (978-1-59514-112-5). Krista and Charlie Brown are sisters but very different — one popular, one solitary; when they are both chosen for the soccer team they must work together. (Rev: BCCB 2/08; SLJ 9/07)

619 Timberlake, Amy. *That Girl Lucy Moon* (5–8). 2006, Hyperio $15.99 (978-0-7868-5298-7). When her mother takes off on an extended photography assignment, Lucy Moon is left without her biggest ally in her campaigns for animal rights, social justice, and, now, for the liberation of a sledding hill. (Rev: SLJ 9/06)

620 Townsend, Wendy. *Lizard Love* (6–12). 2008, Front St. $17.95 (978-1-932425-34-5). Grace, a country girl living in Manhattan, is thrilled to discover a city pet store that is stocked with reptiles and that becomes a refuge from the pressures of school and life. (Rev: BL 5/1/08; SLJ 8/08)

621 Tracey, Rhian. *When Isla Meets Luke Meets Isla* (8–10). 2004, Bloomsbury paper $9.95 (978-0-7475-6344-0). Told from alternating points of view, this is the story of troubled teens Isla and Luke — a Scottish girl who has just moved to England and a son of a newly divorced, obsessive mother — and the support and affection they give to each other. (Rev: SLJ 2/04)

622 Trueit, Trudi. *Julep O'Toole: What I Really Want to Do Is Direct* (5–7). 2007, Dutton $16.99 (978-0-525-47781-5). Julep auditions for the school play to earn extra English credit but ends up as assistant director in this enjoyable third installment in the series. (Rev: SLJ 6/07)

623 Tulloch, Richard. *Freaky Stuff* (5–8). Illus. by Shane Nagle. 2007, Walker $16.95 (978-0-8027-9623-3). Funny illustrations are included in this sequel to *Weird Stuff* (2006), in which Brian is unhappy with a TV series based on his favorite books and the effect the show has on his little brother. (Rev: SLJ 6/07)

624 Vail, Rachel. *If You Only Knew* (4–7). Series: Friendship Ring. 1998, Scholastic paper $14.95 (978-0-590-03370-1). In this book shaped like a CD, Zoe Grandon, a 7th grader, gives up a boy she likes to pursue a friendship. (Rev: BCCB 10/98; BL 10/15/98; HBG 3/99; SLJ 10/98; VOYA 6/99)

625 Vail, Rachel. *Not That I Care* (4–7). Series: Friendship Ring. 1998, Scholastic paper $14.95 (978-0-590-03476-0). For a classroom presentation on 10 items that reveal who you are, Morgan Miller remembers crucial incidents in her life but, in her final report, glosses over the truth. (Rev: BCCB 12/98; BL 11/15/98; HBG 3/99; SLJ 12/98; VOYA 6/99)

626 Vail, Rachel. *Please, Please, Please* (4–7). Series: Friendship Ring. 1998, Scholastic paper $14.95 (978-0-590-00327-8). CJ Hurley has to overcome a controlling mother in order to hang out with her friends in this book shaped like a CD. (Rev: BCCB 10/98; BL 10/15/98; HBG 3/99; SLJ 12/98; VOYA 6/99)

627 Vande Velde, Vivian. *Remembering Raquel* (8–11). 2007, Harcourt $16.00 (978-0-15-205976-7). In text, emails, and blogs, classmates and others remember Raquel, a high-school freshman who died in a car accident, and learn that there was more to her than met the eye; this will appeal to reluctant readers. (Rev: BL 11/15/07; HB 1–2/08; LMC 2/08; SLJ 12/07)

628 van de Ruit, John. *Spud* (8–12). 2007, Penguin paper $16.99 (978-1-59514-170-5). Attending an elite boys boarding school in Australia in 1990, 13-year-old Spud describes in diary form his problems with his classmates and his family as well as his thoughts on Mandela's release from prison; the fast-paced humor of this novel will get readers past the unfamiliar vocabulary and sports. (Rev: BL 9/15/07; SLJ 12/07)

629 Van Draanen, Wendelin. *Flipped* (5–8). 2001, Knopf $14.95 (978-0-375-81174-6). In 2nd grade Julianna was infatuated with Bryce, but now, six years later, the situation is reversed in this story told from each viewpoint in alternating chapters. (Rev: BCCB 1/02; BL 12/15/01; HBG 3/02; SLJ 11/01*; VOYA 12/01)

630 Vaupel, Robin. *My Contract with Henry* (5–8). 2003, Holiday $16.95 (978-0-8234-1701-8). An 8th-grade Thoreau project brings a group of outsider students together as they learn about the environment, the simple life, and each other. (Rev: BL 7/03; HBG 10/03; SLJ 7/03; VOYA 10/03)

631 Velasquez, Gloria. *Ankiza* (7–12). Series: Roosevelt High School. 2000, Piñata $16.95 (978-1-55885-308-9); paper $9.95 (978-1-55885-309-6). African American Ankiza learns about prejudice when she starts dating a white boy. (Rev: SLJ 4/01; VOYA 8/01)

632 Vivian, Siobhan. *A Little Friendly Advice* (7–9). 2008, Scholastic $16.99 (978-0-545-00404-6). Ruby, 16, has been a quiet girl, prepared to accept advice from her friends no matter how self-serving or ill-advised; the gift of a Polaroid camera gives Ruby the chance to look at things differently and she learns a lot about her family and friends. (Rev: BL 6/1–15/08; SLJ 2/08)

633 Volponi, Paul. *The Hand You're Dealt* (8–11). 2008, Atheneum $16.99 (978-1-4169-6935-8). A raw and gritty coming-of-age page-turner about grief, family, and Texas Hold 'Em poker, featuring Huck Porter, a young man determined to avenge his father. (Rev: BL 8/08)

634 Vrettos, Adrienne Maria. *Skin* (8–11). 2006, Simon & Schuster $16.95 (978-1-4169-0655-1). Fourteen-year-old Donnie tells the story of his parents' unhappy marriage and his older sister's death from anorexia. (Rev: BL 3/1/06; SLJ 6/06)

635 Waite, Judy. *Forbidden* (8–11). 2006, Simon & Schuster $16.95 (978-0-689-87642-4). As one of the Chosen girls in the True Cause cult led by Howard, 16-year-old Elinor does not question her life until Outsider Jaime appears. (Rev: BCCB 2/06; BL 4/15/06; SLJ 3/06)

636 Walters, Eric. *Stuffed* (8–12). Series: Orca Soundings. 2006, Orca $14.95 (978-1-55143-519-0). Ian gets even more of a reaction than he bargained for when he and his friends boycott a fast-food restaurant. (Rev: SLJ 10/06)

637 Warner, Sally. *It's Only Temporary* (5–7). Illus. by author. 2008, Viking $15.99 (978-0-670-06111-2). With sketches and lists, 12-year-old Skye reviews her problems in her journal when she is sent to live with her grandmother after her brother has a bad accident. (Rev: BL 6/1–15/08; SLJ 8/08)

638 Wasserman, Robin. *Hacking Harvard* (8–11). 2007, Simon & Schuster paper $8.99 (978-1-4169-3633-6). Eric, Max, and Schwarz set out to hack into Harvard's admissions computer system and get their classmate Clay (who is definitely not Harvard material) admitted to the university. (Rev: BL 1/1–15/08; SLJ 1/08)

639 Waysman, Dvora. *Back of Beyond: A Bar Mitzvah Journey* (5–7). Illus. 1996, Pitspopany paper $4.95 (978-0-943706-54-2). On a trip to Australia, a 12-year-old Jewish boy becomes involved in the Aborigine culture and witnesses a ritual of manhood similar to a bar mitzvah. (Rev: SLJ 5/96)

640 Wedekind, Annie. *A Horse of Her Own* (5–7). 2008, Feiwel and Friends $16.95 (978-0-312-36927-9). At horse camp, Jane is surrounded by girls who come from wealthy families and who have horses of their own, a fact that bothers her until she wins an important competition. (Rev: BL 5/15/08; SLJ 8/08)

641 Wilson, Jacqueline. *Candyfloss* (4–7). Illus. by Nick Sharratt. 2007, Roaring Brook $14.95 (978-1-59643-241-3). Flossie, busy helping her divorced dad at his restaurant while her mother and stepfather are in Australia, must also deal with old and new friends at school in this story set in England. (Rev: BL 10/1/07; HB 9–10/07; LMC 11/07; SLJ 9/07)

642 Winerip, Michael. *Adam Canfield of the Slash* (4–7). 2005, Candlewick $15.99 (978-0-7636-2340-1). As editors of the *Slash*, the Harris Elementary/Middle School student newspaper, Adam and Jennifer chase scoops and tackle ethical questions. (Rev: BL 5/1/05; SLJ 3/05)

643 Winerip, Michael. *Adam Canfield, Watch Your Back!* (5–8). Series: Adam Canfield. 2007, Candlewick $15.99 (978-0-7636-2341-8). Adam of *Adam Canfield of the Slash* has even more on his plate in this sequel: writing for the school newspaper, exposing an unfair science fair, and even facing down high school muggers. (Rev: BL 4/1/08; SLJ 12/07)

644 Wittlinger, Ellen. *Blind Faith* (7–10). 2006, Simon & Schuster $15.95 (978-1-4169-0273-7). Her mother's grief following the death of her grandmother causes 15-year-old Elizabeth to struggle with questions of faith even as she finds some solace in the new boy across the street. (Rev: BL 6/1–15/06; HB 7–8/06; SLJ 9/06)

645 Wittlinger, Ellen. *Gracie's Girl* (4–7). 2000, Simon & Schuster $16.95 (978-0-689-82249-0). Bess and her best friend Ethan, both middle schoolers, get involved with a homeless old lady. (Rev: BCCB 2/01; BL 9/15/00; HBG 3/01; SLJ 11/00; VOYA 10/01)

646 Wittlinger, Ellen. *Razzle* (7–12). 2001, Simon & Schuster $17.00 (978-0-689-83565-0). New on Cape Cod, Kenyon becomes friends with an offbeat girl named Razzle — until he falls for beautiful Harley — in this mutilayered and appealing novel. (Rev: BCCB 10/01; BL 11/1/01; HB 11–12/01; HBG 3/02; SLJ 9/01; VOYA 10/01)

647 Wolff, Virginia Euwer. *True Believer* (7–12). 2001, Simon & Schuster $17.00 (978-0-689-82827-0). Poverty and violence are continuing forces in this sequel to *Make Lemonade*, in which LaVaughn fosters her college ambitions and finds romance. (Rev: BL 6/1–15/02; HB 1–2/01; HBG 10/01; SLJ 1/01; VOYA 4/01)

648 Wood, Maryrose. *My Life the Musical* (8–12). 2008, Delacorte $15.99 (978-0-385-73278-9). Emily and Philip, both 16, have seen the musical "Aurora" umpteen times; what will they do if the show closes? (Rev: BL 2/20/08; SLJ 5/08)

649 Woodson, Jacqueline. *After Tupac and D Foster* (6–9). 2008, Putnam $16.99 (978-0-399-24654-8). In Queens, New York, in the mid-1990s three tween girls — one of them foster child D — enjoy the music of Tupac Shakur and try to cope with the puzzles of a gritty urban life. Newbery Honor Book, 2009. (Rev: BL 2/1/08; SLJ 4/08)

650 Wynne-Jones, Tim. *A Thief in the House of Memory* (7–10). 2005, Farrar $17.00 (978-0-374-37478-5). Sixteen-year-old Dec can barely recall the events surrounding his mother's sudden disappearance six years earlier until the death of an intruder in the family home reawakens forgotten memories. (Rev: BCCB 5/05; BL 3/1/05; HB 5–6/05; SLJ 4/05; VOYA 6/05)

651 Zindel, Lizabeth. *Girl of the Moment* (7–10). 2007, Viking $16.99 (978-0-670-06210-2). Being a celebrity's assistant isn't all it's cracked up to be, as Lily learns when she takes a job working for the ultra-famous, ultra-rich Sabrina Snow. (Rev: BL 3/15/07; SLJ 6/07)

Ethnic Groups and Problems

652 Abdel-Fattah, Randa. *Does My Head Look Big in This?* (7–10). 2007, Scholastic $16.99 (978-0-439-91947-0). Amal is a Muslim Palestinian growing up in Australia, where family, friends, and strangers all react in different ways to her decision to veil herself in the traditional hijab. (Rev: BCCB 9/07; BL 7/07; LMC 11–12/07; SLJ 6/07)

653 Abraham, Susan Gonzales, and Denise Gonzales Abraham. *Cecilia's Year* (4–7). 2004, Cinco Puntos $16.95 (978-0-938317-87-6). Inspired by the real-life story of the authors' mother, this is the story of a 14-year-old Hispanic American girl's determination to defy cultural tradition and continue her schooling in Depression-era New Mexico. (Rev: BL 1/1–15/05; SLJ 4/05)

654 Abraham, Susan Gonzales, and Denise Gonzales Abraham. *Surprising Cecilia* (6–9). Series: Latino Fiction for Young Adults. 2005, Cinco Puntos $16.95 (978-0-938317-96-8). In this appealing sequel to *Cecilia's Year*, set in the Rio Grande Valley during the Depression, the title character gets a chance to move to El Paso to further her education but is given little encouragement at home to do so. (Rev: BL 11/15/05; SLJ 1/06)

655 Alegría, Malín. *Estrella's Quinceañera* (7–10). 2006, Simon & Schuster $14.95 (978-0-689-87809-1). Planning for her 15th birthday celebration, Mexican American Estrella finds herself balancing her hopes against reality. (Rev: BL 2/15/06; SLJ 4/06)

656 Alvarez, Julia. *Finding Miracles* (8–11). 2004, Knopf LB $17.99 (978-0-375-82760-0). Sixteen-year-old Milly Kaufman, rescued as a child from a strife-torn Latin American nation, is encouraged to return to her native country and learn more about her family roots. (Rev: BL 10/15/04; SLJ 10/04; VOYA 12/04)

657 Angell, Judie. *One-Way to Ansonia* (7–10). 2001, iUniverse paper $12.95 (978-0-595-15830-0). In novel format this is the story of a young Russian girl's experience in this country around the turn of the century; originally published in 1985. (Rev: BL 1/1/86; SLJ 12/85; VOYA 2/86)

658 Bailey-Williams, Nicole. *A Little Piece of Sky* (7–12). 2002, Broadway paper $9.95 (978-0-7679-1216-7). Song Byrd is an African American girl who rises above her very difficult circumstances in this realistic and compelling novel. (Rev: VOYA 4/03)

659 Barrett, William E. *The Lilies of the Field* (8–12). Illus. 1988, Warner paper $5.99 (978-0-446-31500-5). A young black man, Homer Smith, helps a group of German nuns to achieve their dream.

660 Barth-Grozinger, Inge. *Something Remains* (8–11). Trans. by Anthea Bell. 2006, Hyperion $16.99 (978-0-7868-3880-6). This book is based on the true story of a 12-year-old Jewish boy named Erich Levi and what life was like for him and his family, dealing with prejudice and persecution, during Hitler's first years in power. (Rev: BL 9/1/06; SLJ 12/06)

661 Baskin, Nora Raleigh. *The Truth about My Bat Mitzvah* (5–8). 2008, Simon & Schuster $15.99 (978-1-4169-3558-2). Caroline, daughter of a Jewish mother and Christian father, has never been a practicing Jew but when her grandmother dies and leaves her a Star of David necklace — and her best friend Rachel is preparing for her bat mitzvah at the same time — she begins to acknowledge this part of her identity. (Rev: BL 3/15/08; SLJ 4/08)

662 Bernier-Grand, Carmen T. *In the Shade of the Nispero Tree* (4–7). 1999, Orchard LB $16.99 (978-0-531-33154-5). Prejudice and racism separate two friends in this story set in Ponce, Puerto Rico, during 1961. (Rev: BCCB 3/99; BL 4/1/99; HBG 10/99; SLJ 3/99)

663 Bertrand, Diane Gonzales. *Sweet Fifteen* (8–12). 1995, Arte Publico paper $9.95 (978-1-55885-133-7). While making a party dress for Stefanie Bonilla, age 14, Rita Navarro falls in love with her uncle and befriends her widowed mother, maturing in the process. (Rev: BL 6/1–15/95; SLJ 9/95)

664 Blume, Judy. *Iggie's House* (4–7). 1970, Dell paper $4.99 (978-0-440-44062-8). An African American family moves into Iggie's old house.

665 Bosse, Malcolm. *Ganesh* (7–9). 1981, Harper-Collins LB $11.89 (978-0-690-04103-3). A young boy from India has difficulty fitting into the American Midwest and its ways.

666 Bush, Lawrence. *Rooftop Secrets: And Other Stories of Anti-Semitism* (6–9). Illus. 1986, American Hebrew Cong. paper $9.95 (978-0-8074-0314-3). In each of these eight short stories, some form of anti-Semitism is encountered by a young person. (Rev: SLJ 11/86)

667 Canales, Viola. *Orange Candy Slices and Other Secret Tales* (6–12). 2001, Arte Publico paper $9.95 (978-1-55885-332-4). Life on the Texas-Mexico border is the focus of this collection of coming-of-age short stories. (Rev: VOYA 6/02)

668 Carlson, Lori M., ed. *American Eyes: New Asian-American Short Stories for Young Adults* (8–12). 1994, Holt $15.95 (978-0-8050-3544-5). These stories present widely varied answers to the question, What does it mean to Asian American adolescents to grow up in a country that views them as aliens? (Rev: BL 1/1/95; SLJ 1/95; VOYA 5/95)

669 Chambers, Veronica. *Quinceañera Means Sweet 15* (6–9). 2001, Hyperion LB $16.49 (978-0-7868-2426-7). Fourteen-year-old Brooklyn friends Marisol and Magdalena look ahead to their quinceanera coming-of-age parties with anticipation and some frustration. (Rev: BCCB 5/01; HBG 10/01; SLJ 6/01)

670 Chase, Paula. *So Not the Drama* (7–10). Series: Del Rio Bay Clique . 2007, Kensington paper $9.95 (978-0-7582-1859-9). Mina deals with issues of popularity and prejudice at her high school, where students of all races and many backgrounds intermingle but don't always get along. (Rev: BL 2/1/07)

671 Cheng, Andrea. *Honeysuckle House* (4–7). 2004, Front St. $16.95 (978-1-886910-99-7). The problems of immigration and adjustment to new cultures are shown in this story of two girls of Chinese heritage, told in the girls' alternating voices. (Rev: BL 4/1/04; HB 7–8/04; SLJ 6/04)

672 Childress, Alice. *A Hero Ain't Nothin' but a Sandwich* (7–10). 2000, Putnam paper $5.99 (978-0-698-11854-6). Benjie's life in Harlem, told from many viewpoints, involves drugs and rejection. (Rev: BL 10/15/88)

673 Cofer, Judith Ortiz. *Call Me María* (6–10). 2004, Scholastic $16.95 (978-0-439-38577-0). Initially María mourns the loss of her island landscape when she moves from Puerto Rico to the mainland, but gradually she adapts, makes new friends, and writes new poetry; the appealing format includes poems and letters. (Rev: BL 12/1/04; HB 1–2/05; LMC 3/05; SLJ 11/04)

674 Cofer, Judith Ortiz. *An Island Like You* (7–12). 2008, Paw Prints paper $15.99 (978-1-4395-0880-0). Stories of Puerto Rican immigrant children experiencing the tensions between two cultures. (Rev: BL 2/15/95*; SLJ 7/95)

675 Cruz, Maria Colleen. *Border Crossing* (4–8). 2003, Arte Publico paper $9.95 (978-1-55885-405-5). Ceci, 12, can't understand why her Mexican father won't speak Spanish or talk about his home, so she decides to go and investigate. (Rev: BL 11/15/03; SLJ 2/04)

676 Curtis, Christopher Paul. *The Watsons Go to Birmingham — 1963* (4–8). 1995, Delacorte $16.95 (978-0-385-32175-4); Dell paper $6.50 (978-0-440-41412-4). An African American family returns to Alabama from Michigan to place their troubled son with his grandmother in this novel set in the 1960s. (Rev: BL 8/95; SLJ 10/95*; VOYA 12/95)

677 Daswani, Kavita. *Indie Girl* (7–10). 2007, Simon & Schuster paper $8.99 (978-1-4169-4892-6). Indira, who lives in Los Angeles, is thrilled to get a job for a fashion editor (even if she's only babysitting) until she discovers the woman is prejudiced against Indians. (Rev: BL 10/15/07; SLJ 12/07)

678 Easton, Kelly. *Hiroshima Dreams* (7–10). 2007, Dutton $16.99 (978-0-525-47821-8). Lin's Japanese mother wants their family to be more American but when her grandmother, Obaachan, arrives from Japan, she reminds them of their heritage. (Rev: BL 9/15/07; SLJ 12/07)

679 Ellison, James W. *Finding Forrester* (7–12). 2000, Newmarket paper $9.95 (978-1-55704-479-2). This inspiring novel tells how a reclusive author helps a promising inner-city African American youth to develop his writing skills. (Rev: SLJ 9/01; VOYA 6/01)

680 English, Karen. *Francie* (5–8). 1999, Farrar $17.00 (978-0-374-32456-8). Francie, a black girl growing up in segregated Alabama, places her family in danger when she helps a friend who is escaping a racist employer. (Rev: BCCB 10/99; BL 10/15/99; HB 9–10/99; HBG 3/00; SLJ 9/99; VOYA 2/00)

681 Felin, M. Sindy. *Touching Snow* (8–10). 2007, Atheneum $16.99 (978-1-4169-1795-3). Karina, 13, and her two Haitian sisters are referred to social services when their stepfather brutally beats Enid, the oldest sister, in this novel that shows the tensions in an immigrant family and the often unfulfilled aspirations. (Rev: BL 5/15/07; HB 7–8/07; SLJ 9/07)

682 Flake, Sharon G. *Who Am I Without Him?* (6–12). 2004, Hyperion $15.99 (978-0-7868-0693-5). Funny, moving, and truthful, these 10 short stories deal with growing up black in today's society. (Rev: BL 4/15/04*; HB 7–8/04; SLJ 5/04; VOYA 6/04)

683 Fleischman, Paul. *Seedfolks* (4–8). Illus. 1997, HarperCollins LB $15.89 (978-0-06-027472-6). Thirteen people from many cultures explain why they have planted gardens in a vacant lot in Cleveland, Ohio. (Rev: BCCB 7–8/97; BL 5/15/97; HB 5–6/97; SLJ 5/97*; VOYA 6/97)

684 Flores, Bettina R. *Chiquita's Diary* (6–9). Illus. 1995, Pepper Vine paper $13.50 (978-0-9625777-7-2). Twelve-year-old Chiquita is determined to break out of the poverty that her widowed Mexican American mother endures, and she makes a start by becoming a mother's helper. (Rev: BL 2/15/96)

685 Fogelin, Adrian. *Crossing Jordan* (5–8). Illus. by Suzy Schultz. 2000, Peachtree $14.95 (978-1-56145-215-6). Set in contemporary Florida, this novel tells how 12-year-old Cass must keep her friendship with African American Jemmie a secret from her racist father. (Rev: BCCB 4/00; HBG 10/00; SLJ 6/00)

686 Gallo, Donald R., ed. *Join In: Multiethnic Short Stories by Outstanding Writers for Young Adults* (7–12). 1995, Bantam paper $5.99 (978-0-440-21957-6). Seventeen stories concerning the problems teenagers of various ethnic backgrounds have living in the United States. (Rev: BL 1/15/94; SLJ 11/93; VOYA 10/93)

687 Garland, Sherry. *Shadow of the Dragon* (6–12). 1993, Harcourt $10.95 (978-0-15-273530-2); paper $6.00 (978-0-15-273532-6). Danny Vo has grown up American since he emigrated from Vietnam as a child. Now traditional Vietnamese ways, the new American culture, and skinhead prejudice clash, resulting in his cousin's death. (Rev: BL 11/15/93*; SLJ 11/93; VOYA 12/93)

688 Green, Richard G. *Sing, Like a Hermit Thrush* (6–9). 1995, Ricara paper $12.95 (978-0-911737-01-1). A young Native American teenager growing up on the Six Nations Reserve is confused by his gift of seeing events before they happen. (Rev: BL 4/15/96)

689 Griffis, Molly Levite. *Simon Says* (6–12). 2004, Eakin $22.95 (978-1-57168-836-1). It's 1942, and 11-year-old Jewish refugee Simon, shipped from

Poland to live with an American family five years earlier, is remembering his past amid signs of rising anti-Semitism in his adopted Oklahoma home; a sequel to *The Rachel Resistance* (2001) and *The Feester Filibuster* (2002). (Rev: BL 11/1/04; SLJ 1/05)

690 Grimes, Nikki. *Jazmin's Notebook* (6–10). 1998, Dial $15.99 (978-0-8037-2224-8). The journal of 14-year-old Jazmin, who writes about her tough, tender, and angry life in Harlem in the 1960s, living with her sister after her mother is hospitalized with a breakdown and her father has died. (Rev: BL 9/15/98; HBG 9/98; SLJ 7/98; VOYA 10/98)

691 Guy, Rosa. *The Friends* (7–10). 1995, Random paper $5.99 (978-0-440-22667-3). Phyllisia, a new-comer to Harlem, finds a friend in the unusual Edith Jackson; first published in 1973.

692 Hamilton, Virginia. *A White Romance* (8–12). 1987, Scholastic paper $4.50 (978-0-590-13005-9). A formerly all-black high school becomes integrated and social values and relationships change. (Rev: SLJ 1/88; VOYA 2/88)

693 Hayes, Rosemary. *Mixing It* (7–12). 2007, Frances Lincoln paper $7.95 (978-1-84507-495-1). Fatimah, a Muslim, rescues a boy from a church bombing and exposes her family to unwanted attention in this novel set in England. (Rev: BL 1/1–15/08)

694 Hernandez, Irene B. *Across the Great River* (7–10). 1989, Arte Publico paper $9.95 (978-0-934770-96-5). The harrowing story of a young Mexican girl and her family, who enter the United States illegally. (Rev: BL 8/89; SLJ 8/89)

695 Hernandez, Irene B. *The Secret of Two Brothers* (7–10). 1995, Arte Publico paper $9.95 (978-1-55885-142-9). An action-packed story about two Mexican American boys who meet many challenges. Especially appealing to those whose first language is Spanish or for reluctant readers. (Rev: BL 10/1/95; SLJ 11/95)

696 Hernandez, Jo Ann Y. *White Bread Competition* (7–12). 1997, Arte Publico paper $9.95 (978-1-55885-210-5). The effects of winning a spelling bee on Luz Rios and her Hispanic American family in San Antonio are explored in a series of vignettes. (Rev: BL 1/1–15/98; SLJ 8/98; VOYA 4/98)

697 Herrera, Juan Felipe. *Downtown Boy* (5–8). 2005, Scholastic $16.99 (978-0-439-64489-1). This poignant free-verse novel, narrated by 10-year-old Juanito, offers an unflinching look at what life was like for Chicano migrant workers and their families in 1950s California. (Rev: BL 12/15/05; SLJ 1/06; VOYA 4/06)

698 Hirsch, Odo. *Have Courage, Hazel Green!* (4–7). 2006, Bloomsbury $15.95 (978-1-58234-659-5). Independent-minded Hazel Green and her friends must mend some fences when her plan to

shame a neighbor into apologizing for a blatant act of ethnic prejudice backfires. (Rev: BL 6/1–15/06; SLJ 8/06)

699 Irwin, Hadley. *Kim / Kimi* (7–10). 1987, Penguin paper $5.99 (978-0-14-032593-5). A half-Japanese teenager brought up in an all-white small town sets out to explore her Asian roots. (Rev: BL 3/15/87; SLJ 5/87; VOYA 6/87)

700 Jimenez, Francisco. *The Circuit: Stories from the Life of a Migrant Child* (5–10). 1997, Univ. of New Mexico paper $11.95 (978-0-8263-1797-1). Eleven moving stories about the lives, fears, hopes, and problems of children in Mexican migrant worker families. (Rev: BL 12/1/97)

701 Johnson, Angela. *Toning the Sweep* (7–12). 1993, Scholastic paper $6.99 (978-0-590-48142-7). This novel captures the innocence, vulnerability, and love of human interaction, as well as the melancholy, self-discovery, and introspection of an African American adolescent. (Rev: BL 4/1/93*; SLJ 4/93*)

702 Johnston, Tony. *Any Small Goodness: A Novel of the Barrio* (4–7). Illus. by Raul Colon. 2001, Scholastic paper $16.95 (978-0-439-18936-1). Eleven-year-old Arturo Rodriguez, whose Mexican family is new to Los Angeles, describes family life, school, celebrations, and dangers. (Rev: BL 9/15/01; HBG 3/02; SLJ 9/01; VOYA 10/01)

703 Johnston, Tony. *Bone by Bone by Bone* (6–9). 2007, Roaring Brook $16.95 (978-1-59643-113-3). David, a 9-year-old white boy, and Malcolm, an 8-year-old black boy, are best friends in a small town in Tennessee in the 1950s, but David's father forbids the relationship. (Rev: BL 8/07; LMC 11/07; SLJ 10/07)

704 Jones, Traci L. *Standing against the Wind* (6–9). 2006, Farrar $16.00 (978-0-374-37174-6). Being raised by her aunt in an impoverished city neighborhood, African American Patrice struggles to overcome her environment in order to succeed. (Rev: BL 7/06; SLJ 11/06)

705 Krech, Bob. *Rebound* (8–11). 2006, Marshall Cavendish $16.99 (978-0-7614-5319-2). In a school where Polish kids wrestle and African American kids play basketball, a student named Ray Wisniewski challenges the status quo and tries out for basketball, dealing with racism on and off the court. (Rev: BL 9/1/06; LMC 2/07; SLJ 12/06)

706 Laird, Elizabeth. *Kiss the Dust* (6–10). 1992, Penguin $6.99 (978-0-14-036855-0). A docunovel about a refugee Kurdish teen caught up in the 1984 Iran-Iraq War. (Rev: BL 6/15/92)

707 Lamba, Marie. *What I Meant . . .* (6–9). 2007, Random $16.99 (978-0-375-84091-3). Sangeet's strict Indian father and crazy aunt make her life in an American suburb very complicated, especially when Sangeet gets caught going out on a date. (Rev: BL 7/07; SLJ 11/07)

708 Lee, Harper. *To Kill a Mockingbird* (8–12). 1977, HarperCollins $23.00 (978-0-397-00151-4). A lawyer in a small Southern town defends an African American man wrongfully accused of rape.

709 Lee, Lauren. *Stella: On the Edge of Popularity* (5–7). 1994, Polychrome $10.95 (978-1-879965-08-9). A Korean American girl has to choose between being popular and being loyal to her Korean culture. (Rev: BCCB 7–8/94; SLJ 9/94)

710 Lee, Marie G. *F Is for Fabuloso* (6–9). 1999, Avon $15.95 (978-0-380-97648-5). A sensitive story about Jin-Ha, a Korean girl, and the troubles she and her parents face in the United States. (Rev: BL 9/15/99; HBG 4/00)

711 Lee, Marie G. *Necessary Roughness* (7–12). 1996, HarperCollins LB $14.89 (978-0-06-025130-7). Chan, a Korean American football enthusiast, and his twin sister, Young, encounter prejudice when their family moves to a small Minnesota community. (Rev: BL 1/1–15/97; SLJ 1/97; VOYA 6/97)

712 Lester, Julius. *Long Journey Home* (6–8). 1998, Viking paper $6.99 (978-0-14-038981-4). Six based-on-fact stories concerning slaves, ex-slaves, and their lives in a hostile America.

713 Lester, Julius. *This Strange New Feeling* (7–9). 2006, Penguin $16.99 (978-0-8037-3172-1). Three stories about black couples and the meaning of freedom; originally published in 1982.

714 Levitin, Sonia. *Strange Relations* (8–11). 2007, Knopf $15.99 (978-0-375-83751-7). Fifteen-year-old Marne, from a secular Jewish family, visits her conservative Jewish relatives in Hawaii and comes to appreciate their differences. (Rev: BL 6/1–15/07; SLJ 5/07)

715 Lipsyte, Robert. *The Brave* (8–12). 1991, HarperCollins paper $5.99 (978-0-06-447079-7). A Native American heavyweight boxer is rescued from drugs, pimps, and hookers by a tough but tender ex-boxer/New York City cop. (Rev: BL 10/15/91; SLJ 10/91*)

716 Lipsyte, Robert. *The Chief* (7–10). 1995, HarperCollins paper $6.50 (978-0-06-447097-1). Sonny Bear can't decide whether to go back to the reservation, continue boxing, or become Hollywood's new Native American darling. Sequel to *The Brave*. (Rev: BL 6/1–15/93; VOYA 12/93)

717 López, Lorraine M. *Call Me Henri* (6–9). 2006, Curbstone $17.95 (978-1-931896-27-6). Enrique, a Latino middle-school student, does his best to juggle all the responsibilities on his plate — including school and caring for baby triplets — and does so with very little help until a medical emergency rais-

es him to hero status; but just when things are looking promising, more troubles loom. (Rev: SLJ 8/06)

718 Lord, Bette Bao. *In the Year of the Boar and Jackie Robinson* (6–8). Illus. 1984, HarperCollins paper $5.99 (978-0-06-440175-3). A young Chinese girl finds that the world of baseball helps her adjust to her new home in America.

719 Ly, Many. *Roots and Wings* (6–10). 2008, Delacorte $15.99 (978-0-385-73500-1). Fourteen-year-old Grace learns about her Cambodian heritage when she and her mother travel to Florida for her grandmother's funeral. (Rev: BL 3/15/08; SLJ 7/08)

720 McDonald, Janet. *Brother Hood* (7–12). 2004, Farrar $16.00 (978-0-374-30995-4). Nate Whitely, a 16-year-old student at a prestigious boarding school, finds himself straddling two very different cultures as he seeks to remain loyal to his Harlem roots. (Rev: BL 9/1/04; SLJ 11/04; VOYA 2/05)

721 Marino, Jan. *The Day That Elvis Came to Town* (7–10). 1993, Avon paper $3.50 (978-0-380-71672-2). In this tale of southern blacks, Wanda is thrilled when a room in her parents' boarding house is rented to Mercedes, who makes her feel pretty and smart — and who once went to school with Elvis Presley. (Rev: BL 12/15/90*; SLJ 1/91*)

722 Markle, Sandra. *The Fledglings* (6–9). 1998, Boyds Mills paper $9.95 (978-1-56397-696-4). With her parents dead, Kate, 14, runs away to live with her Cherokee grandfather and immerses herself happily in his world. (Rev: BL 6/15/92)

723 Martinez, Victor. *Parrot in the Oven: Mi Vida* (7–10). 1996, HarperCollins LB $16.89 (978-0-06-026706-3). Through a series of vignettes, the story of Manuel, a teenage Mexican American, unfolds as he grows up in the city projects with an abusive father and a loving mother. (Rev: BL 10/15/96; SLJ 11/96)

724 Meriwether, Louise. *Daddy Was a Number Runner* (7–12). 1986, Feminist paper $16.59 (978-1-55861-442-0). The story of Frances, a black girl, growing up in Harlem during the Depression.

725 Miklowitz, Gloria D. *The War Between the Classes* (7–10). 1986, Dell paper $4.99 (978-0-440-99406-0). A Japanese American girl finds that hidden prejudices and bigotry emerge when students in school are divided into four socioeconomic groups. (Rev: BL 4/15/85; SLJ 8/85; VOYA 6/85)

726 Mobin-Uddi, Asma. *My Name Is Bilal* (4–7). Illus. by Barbara Kiawk. 2005, Boyds Mills $15.95 (978-1-59078-175-3). When they start at a new school, Muslim Bilal and his sister Ayesha balance pride in their own heritage and their desire to blend in. (Rev: BL 8/05; SLJ 8/05)

727 Mohr, Nicholasa. *El Bronx Remembered: A Novella and Stories* (7–9). 1993, HarperCollins paper $5.99 (978-0-06-447100-8). These 12 stories set in the Bronx reflect the general Puerto Rican experience in New York.

728 Mohr, Nicholasa. *Going Home* (6–8). 1986, Puffin paper $6.99 (978-0-14-130644-5). The young heroine finds a boyfriend and spends a summer in her family's home in Puerto Rico in this sequel to *Felita*. (Rev: BL 7/86; SLJ 8/86)

729 Mohr, Nicholasa. *Nilda* (7–9). 1986, Publico paper $11.95 (978-0-934770-61-3). The story of a 12-year-old Puerto Rican girl growing up in the New York barrio.

730 Moodley, Ermila. *Path to My African Eyes* (6–9). 2007, Just Us Bks. $15.95 (978-1-933491-09-7). Thandi, 14, and her family move from South Africa to California, and she finds that her classmates' misconceptions about her background — as well as the natural culture shock — make it hard for her to adjust to her new home. (Rev: BL 11/15/07; SLJ 12/07)

731 Moore, Yvette. *Freedom Songs* (6–12). 1991, Penguin paper $5.99 (978-0-14-036017-2). In 1968, Sheryl, 14, witnesses and then experiences acts of prejudice while visiting relatives in North Carolina. (Rev: BL 4/15/91; SLJ 3/91)

732 Myers, Walter Dean. *Autobiography of My Dead Brother* (8–11). Illus. by Christopher Myers. 2005, HarperCollins LB $16.89 (978-0-06-058292-0). In this compelling novel of teenage life in contemporary Harlem, Jessie watches helplessly as his friend Rise drifts away from him, dragged down in a whirlpool of drugs and crime. (Rev: BL 6/1–15/05; SLJ 8/05; VOYA 10/05)

733 Myers, Walter Dean. *The Dream Bearer* (5–8). 2003, HarperCollins LB $24.00 (978-0-06-054277-1). David, 12 and living in Harlem, gains valuable insights about his heritage and his ambitions when he gets to know an old man who calls himself a "dream bearer." (Rev: BL 7/03; HBG 4/04; SLJ 6/03; VOYA 6/03)

734 Myers, Walter Dean. *Fast Sam, Cool Clyde, and Stuff* (7–10). 1995, Peter Smith $20.75 (978-0-8446-6798-0); Puffin paper $6.99 (978-0-14-032613-0). Three male friends in Harlem join forces to found the 116th Street Good People.

735 Myers, Walter Dean. *145th Street: Stories* (5–9). 2000, Delacorte $15.95 (978-0-385-32137-2). A Harlem neighborhood is the setting for this collection of short stories dealing with a wide range of human emotions. (Rev: BL 12/15/99; HB 3–4/00; HBG 10/00; SLJ 4/00)

736 Myers, Walter Dean. *Scorpions* (7–9). 1988, HarperCollins LB $18.89 (978-0-06-024365-4). Gang warfare, death, and despair are the elements of this story set in present-day Harlem. (Rev: BL 9/1/88; SLJ 9/88; VOYA 8/88)

737 Myers, Walter Dean. *Slam!* (8–12). 1996, Scholastic paper $15.95 (978-0-590-48667-5). Although Slam is successful on the school's basketball court, his personal life has problems caused by difficulties fitting into an all-white school, a very sick grandmother, and a friend who is involved in drugs. (Rev: BL 11/15/96; SLJ 11/96; VOYA 2/97)

738 Myers, Walter Dean. *The Young Landlords* (7–10). 1979, Penguin paper $6.99 (978-0-14-034244-4). A group of African American teenagers take over a slum building in Harlem.

739 Na, An. *The Fold* (6–10). 2008, Putnam $16.99 (978-0-399-24276-2). Sixteen-year-old Korean American Joyce Park longs to be beautiful like her gorgeous older sister, but when her aunt offers to pay for eyelid surgery that will make her look more Western, Joyce finds the decision very difficult. (Rev: BL 3/15/08; SLJ 3/08) ⊘

740 Namioka, Lensey. *April and the Dragon Lady* (7–12). 1994, Harcourt $10.95 (978-0-15-276644-3). A Chinese American high school junior must relinquish important activities to care for her ailing grandmother and struggles with the constraints of a traditional female role. (Rev: BL 3/1/94; SLJ 4/94; VOYA 6/94)

741 Namioka, Lensey. *Yang the Third and Her Impossible Family* (4–7). Illus. by Kees de Kiefte. 1996, Bantam paper $4.50 (978-0-440-41231-1). Mary, part of a Chinese family newly arrived in Seattle, is embarrassed by her parents' old-country ways in this humorous story. (Rev: BCCB 5/95; BL 4/15/95; SLJ 8/95)

742 Neufeld, John. *Edgar Allan* (6–8). 1968, Phillips $26.95 (978-0-87599-149-8). Michael's family adopts a 3-year-old African American boy and the signs of bigotry begin.

743 Nislick, June Levitt. *Zayda Was a Cowboy* (4–7). 2005, Jewish Publication Soc. paper $9.95 (978-0-8276-0817-7). A Jewish grandfather tells his grandchildren about his exploits as a cowboy when he first arrived in America from Eastern Europe; an epilogue gives background and there is a glossary and a bibliography. (Rev: BL 8/05*)

744 Okimoto, Jean D. *Talent Night* (6–10). 1995, Scholastic paper $14.95 (978-0-590-47809-0). In this story, Rodney Suyama, 17, wants to be the first Japanese American rapper and to date beautiful Ivy Ramos. (Rev: BL 6/1–15/95; SLJ 5/95)

745 Olsen, Sylvia. *The Girl with a Baby* (6–10). 2004, Sono Nis paper $7.95 (978-1-55039-142-8). A biracial girl of white and Indian parents wants to stay in school and raise her baby but finds it difficult. (Rev: BL 3/15/04; SLJ 7/04)

746 Olsen, Sylvia. *White Girl* (7–10). 2005, Sono Nis paper $8.95 (978-1-55039-147-3). When her mother marries a native Canadian, 15-year-old Josie feels anger at being moved to a reservation where she is taunted for being different, but she eventually works past her resentment and begins to appreciate the larger family of which she is now a part. (Rev: BCCB 9/05; BL 4/15/05*; SLJ 7/05; VOYA 6/05)

747 Osa, Nancy. *Cuba 15* (6–10). 2003, Delacorte $15.95 (978-0-385-72021-2). Violet Paz, who considers herself totally American, is surprised when her grandmother insists that she celebrate a traditional coming-of-age ceremony. (Rev: BL 7/03*)

748 Ostow, Micol. *Emily Goldberg Learns to Salsa* (8–11). 2006, Penguin $16.99 (978-1-59514-081-4). When Emily's grandmother dies, Emily visits Puerto Rico — where her mother grew up — for the first time, and is amazed by a culture so foreign to her yet part of her heritage. (Rev: BL 12/15/06; SLJ 1/07)

749 Pagliarulo, Antonio. *A Different Kind of Heat* (7–10). 2006, Delacorte LB $9.99 (978-0-385-90319-6). Luz Cordero's anger about life in general and her brother's violent death in particular begins to abate when she finds friendship at the St. Therese Home for Boys and Girls and faces the truth. (Rev: BL 4/1/06; SLJ 12/06)

750 Park, Linda Sue. *Project Mulberry* (5–8). 2005, Clarion $16.00 (978-0-618-47786-9). Working on a silkworm project with her friend Patrick, Korean American Julia also learns about prejudices and friendship. (Rev: BL 8/05; SLJ 5/05)

751 Pinkney, Andrea D. *Hold Fast to Dreams* (5–8). 1995, Morrow $16.00 (978-0-688-12832-6). A bright, resourceful African American girl faces problems when she finds she is the only black student in her new middle school. (Rev: BCCB 5/95; BL 2/15/95; HB 9–10/95; SLJ 4/95)

752 Pitts, Paul. *Racing the Sun* (5–7). 1988, Avon paper $6.99 (978-0-380-75496-0). Brandon begins to understand his Navajo heritage after his grandfather comes to live with him. (Rev: BL 9/15/88; SLJ 2/89)

753 Porte, Barbara Ann. *Something Terrible Happened* (6–10). 1994, Orchard LB $17.99 (978-0-531-08719-0). Part white, part West Indian, Gillian, 12, must adjust to living with her deceased father's "plain white" relatives when her mother contracts AIDS. (Rev: BL 9/15/94; SLJ 10/94; VOYA 10/94)

754 Roseman, Kenneth. *The Other Side of the Hudson: A Jewish Immigrant Adventure* (5–8). Illus. Series: Do-It-Yourself Adventure. 1993, UAHC paper $11.95 (978-0-8074-0506-2). Using an interactive format, readers can choose various destinations for a young male Jewish immigrant after he arrives in New York City from Germany in 1851. (Rev: SLJ 6/94)

755 Savage, Deborah. *Kotuku* (7–12). 2002, Houghton $16.00 (978-0-618-07456-3). Struggling to recover from the death of her best friend, 17-year-old Wim throws herself into her job at a Cape Cod riding stable, but visitors from afar prompt her to delve into the mystery surrounding her Maori heritage. (Rev: BL 5/15/02; HBG 10/02; SLJ 3/02; VOYA 4/02)

756 Schorr, Melissa. *Goy Crazy* (8–11). 2006, Hyperion $15.99 (978-0-7868-3852-3). Rachel, a 15-year-old Jewish girl facing typical teen challenges, dates a popular basketball player from a Catholic school and hides this from her parents while at the same time questioning her own beliefs. (Rev: BL 10/1/06; SLJ 10/06)

757 Sebestyen, Ouida. *On Fire* (7–12). 1985, Little, Brown $12.95 (978-0-87113-010-5). Tater leaves home with his brother Sammy and takes a mining job where he confronts labor problems in this sequel to the author's powerful *Words by Heart*. (Rev: BL 5/15/85; SLJ 4/85; VOYA 8/85)

758 Sebestyen, Ouida. *Words by Heart* (5–7). 1979, Little, Brown $15.95 (978-0-316-77931-9). Race relations are explored when an African American family moves to an all-white community during the Reconstruction era. (Rev: BL 6/1/88)

759 Shea, Pegi Deitz. *Tangled Threads: A Hmong Girl's Story* (6–8). 2003, Clarion $15.00 (978-0-618-24748-6). Mai, a Hmong refugee newly arrived in the United States, is initially overwhelmed by her Americanized cousins and her new surroundings in this novel that conveys much information about Hmong culture. (Rev: BL 9/15/03; SLJ 11/03)

760 Singer, Isaac Bashevis. *The Power of Light: Eight Stories for Hanukkah* (7–10). Illus. 1980, Avon paper $2.50 (978-0-380-60103-5). Eight stories of the Festival of Lights that span centuries of Jewish history.

761 Singer, Marilyn, ed. *Face Relations: 11 Stories About Seeing Beyond Color* (7–12). 2004, Simon & Schuster $17.95 (978-0-689-85637-2). This collection of 11 original short stories by well-known authors explores the issues of racial identity and race relations in American high schools. (Rev: BL 8/04*; SLJ 6/04; VOYA 8/04)

762 Smith, Sherri L. *Hot, Sour, Salty, Sweet* (5–7). 2008, Delacorte $15.99 (978-0-385-73417-2). As her grandmothers, one Chinese American and one African American, argue over food and family, Ana's junior high graduation party gets more and more complicated. (Rev: BL 2/1/08; SLJ 4/08)

763 Son, John. *Finding My Hat* (4–8). Series: First Person Fiction. 2003, Scholastic $16.95 (978-0-439-43538-3). Autobiography plays a large part in this frank, often funny novel about the son of Korean immigrants growing up in America in the 1970s and 1980s. (Rev: BL 11/15/03; HBG 4/04; LMC 11–12/03; SLJ 10/03)

764 Soto, Gary. *Facts of Life* (5–8). 2008, Harcourt $16.00 (978-0-15-206181-4). Soto offers 10 new stories about important events in the lives of Latino tweens and teens living in California. (Rev: BL 3/1/08; SLJ 7/08)

765 Soto, Gary. *Local News* (4–7). 1993, Harcourt $14.00 (978-0-15-248117-9). This collection of 13 short stories deals with a number of Mexican American youngsters at home, school, and play. (Rev: BL 4/15/93; HB 7–8/93*)

766 Soto, Gary. *Petty Crimes* (5–8). 1998, Harcourt $17.00 (978-0-15-201658-6). Ten short stories about Mexican American teenagers in California's Central Valley deal with some humorous situations but more often with gangs, violence, and poverty. (Rev: BL 3/15/98; HBG 10/98; SLJ 5/98)

767 Soto, Gary. *Taking Sides* (6–9). 1991, Harcourt $17.00 (978-0-15-284076-1). Lincoln Mendoza moves from his inner-city San Francisco neighborhood to a middle-class suburb and must adjust to life in a new high school. (Rev: BL 12/1/91; SLJ 11/91)

768 Spinelli, Jerry. *Maniac Magee* (5–7). 1990, Little, Brown $15.95 (978-0-316-80722-7). This thought-provoking Newbery Medal winner (1991) tells the story of an amazing white boy who runs away from home and suddenly becomes aware of the racism in his town. (Rev: BL 6/1/90*; SLJ 6/90)

769 Stepto, Michele, ed. *African-American Voices* (7–12). Series: Writers of America. 1995, Millbrook LB $23.90 (978-1-56294-474-2). Selections by W. E. B. Du Bois, Toni Morrison, Ralph Ellison, and others, plus traditional chants, speeches, and poetry. (Rev: BL 5/15/95; SLJ 3/95)

770 Stering, Shirley. *My Name Is Seepeetza* (5–10). 1997, Douglas & McIntyre paper $5.95 (978-0-88899-165-2). Told in diary form, this autobiographical novel about a 6th-grade Native American girl tells of her heartbreak at the terrible conditions at her school, where she is persecuted because of her race. (Rev: BL 3/1/97)

771 Taylor, Mildred D. *The Road to Memphis* (7–12). 1990, Dial $18.99 (978-0-8037-0340-7). Set in 1941, this is a continuation of the story of the Logans, a poor black southern family who were previously featured in *Roll of Thunder, Hear My Cry* and *Let the Circle Be Unbroken*. (Rev: BL 5/15/90; SLJ 1/90; VOYA 8/90)

772 Uchida, Yoshiko. *Journey Home* (7–9). Illus. 1978, Macmillan paper $4.99 (978-0-689-71641-6). A Japanese American family return to their ordinary life after being relocated during World War II.

773 Vaught, Susan. *Stormwitch* (7–10). 2005, Bloomsbury $16.95 (978-1-58234-952-7). Sixteen-year-old Ruba Cleo, transplanted in 1969 to a Mississippi Gulf Coast town from Haiti, wants to strike back at the racism and hostility she encounters by calling on the voodoo skills she learned in her native land. (Rev: BCCB 3/05; BL 2/15/05; SLJ 5/05; VOYA 2/05)

774 Veciana-Suarez, Ana. *Flight to Freedom* (6–9). 2002, Scholastic $16.95 (978-0-439-38199-4). In her diary, Yara describes her old life in Cuba and her new life in 1960s Miami with all the attendant problems of new immigrants and teen development. (Rev: BCCB 2/03; BL 11/15/02; HB 1–2/03; HBG 3/03; SLJ 10/02; VOYA 2/03)

775 Vogiel, Eva. *Invisible Chains* (5–8). 2000, Judaica $19.95 (978-1-880582-57-2). In 1948, 14-year-old Frumie is sent with her crippled younger sister, Judy, to a boarding school for religiously observant Jewish girls. (Rev: BL 7/00; HBG 10/00)

776 Volponi, Paul. *Rooftop* (8–11). 2006, Viking $15.99 (978-0-670-06069-6). As teen cousins Clay and Addison struggle to overcome their drug problems, Addison is shot dead by a white police officer and Clay must cope with the aftermath of the shooting. (Rev: BL 4/15/06*; SLJ 8/06)

777 Walters, Eric. *War of the Eagles* (5–7). 1998, Orca $14.00 (978-1-55143-118-5); paper $7.95 (978-1-55143-099-7). During the opening months of the war against Japan, a West Coast Canadian boy witnesses the growing prejudice against Japanese Canadians and also becomes aware of his own Indian heritage. (Rev: BL 12/15/98; HBG 3/99; SLJ 12/98)

778 Winston, Sherri. *The Kayla Chronicles* (5–9). 2008, Little, Brown $16.99 (978-0-316-11430-1). African American Kayla alienates her friend Rosalie when she joins her Florida high school's hip-hop dance team. (Rev: BL 2/1/08; SLJ 4/08)

779 Wiseman, Eva. *No One Must Know* (4–7). 2004, Tundra paper $8.95 (978-0-88776-680-0). Thirteen-year-old Alexandra, who's been raised as a Catholic in Canada, learns that her parents are really Jewish Holocaust survivors. (Rev: BL 1/1–15/05; SLJ 6/05)

780 Wishinsky, Frieda. *Queen of the Toilet Bowl* (7–9). Series: Orca Currents. 2005, Orca paper $7.95 (978-1-55143-364-6). For reluctant readers, this is the story of high school student Renata, who immigrated to the United States from Brazil with her mother and now faces — and conquers — bullying by a classmate. (Rev: SLJ 10/05; VOYA 10/05)

781 Woodson, Jacqueline. *Behind You* (7–12). 2004, Putnam $15.99 (978-0-399-23988-5). In this sequel to *If You Come Softly* (1998), Jeremiah, though dead from a policeman's bullet, watches over the people he left behind. (Rev: BL 2/15/04; HB 5–6/04; SLJ 6/04; VOYA 6/04)

782 Woodson, Jacqueline. *From the Notebooks of Melanin Sun* (6–10). 1995, Scholastic paper $5.99 (978-0-590-45881-8). A 13-year-old African American boy's mother announces that she loves a fellow student, a white woman. (Rev: BL 4/15/95; SLJ 8/95)

783 Wright, Bil. *When the Black Girl Sings* (7–10). 2008, Simon & Schuster $16.99 (978-1-4169-3995-5). When adopted Lahni (who has grown up in a white family and attended a mostly white private school) discovers gospel music, she also finds a new pride in her identity. (Rev: BL 2/1/08; SLJ 1/08)

784 Wright, Richard. *Rite of Passage* (7–12). 1994, HarperCollins paper $6.99 (978-0-06-447111-4). This newly discovered novella, written in the 1940s, concerns a gifted 15-year-old who runs away from his loving Harlem home and survives on the streets with a violent gang. (Rev: BL 1/1/94; SLJ 2/94; VOYA 4/94)

785 Yep, Laurence, ed. *American Dragons: Twenty-Five Asian American Voices* (7–12). 1995, HarperCollins paper $7.99 (978-0-06-440603-1). Autobiographical stories, poems, and essays about children whose parents come from China, Japan, Korea, and Tibet, struggling to find "an identity that isn't generic." (Rev: BL 5/15/93; SLJ 7/93; VOYA 10/93)

786 Yep, Laurence. *Dragonwings* (7–9). 1975, HarperCollins LB $16.89 (978-0-06-026738-4); paper $6.99 (978-0-06-440085-5). At the turn of the 20th century, a young Chinese boy in San Francisco becomes an aviation pioneer. (Rev: BL 3/1/88)

787 Yep, Laurence. *Dream Soul* (5–8). 2000, HarperCollins LB $14.89 (978-0-06-028309-4). In this sequel to *Star Fisher* (1991), the Lees, a family of Chinese immigrants who live in Clarksburg, West Virginia, in 1927, face conflicts when the children want to celebrate Christmas. (Rev: BCCB 12/00; BL 12/1/00)

788 Yoo, Paula. *Good Enough* (7–10). 2008, HarperTeen $16.99 (978-0-06-079085-1). In her senior year of high school, Patti must juggle pressure to be the "Perfect Korean Daughter" with college applications, a crush on a musician, and racist comments from school bullies; reluctant readers will enjoy the humor. (Rev: BL 11/15/07; SLJ 2/08)

Family Life and Problems

789 Abbott, Hailey. *The Bridesmaid* (6–9). 2005, Delacorte $7.95 (978-0-385-73220-8). Abby Beaumont, 15-year-old daughter of parents who run a wedding planning service and jaundiced by the whole idea, watches with wry amusement as her older sister falls into the trap. (Rev: BCCB 9/05; BL 4/15/05; SLJ 4/05)

790 Aciman, André. *Baby* (8–11). 2007, Front St. $16.95 (978-1-59078-502-7). After her alcoholic mother disappears again, 15-year-old Baby finds herself in another foster home; this time, though, it turns out to be a real refuge, with an older couple who race sled dogs. (Rev: BL 9/1/07; SLJ 11/07)

791 Ackermann, Joan. *In the Space Left Behind* (7–10). 2007, HarperCollins $16.99 (978-0-06-072255-5). Fifteen-year-old Colm's mother has married for the third time and is threatening to sell the family home when Colm's long-lost father shows up and offers to pay $70,000 if Colm will accompany him on a cross-country road trip. (Rev: BL 10/1/07; SLJ 12/07)

792 Adler, C. S. *Ghost Brother* (5–8). 1990, Houghton $15.00 (978-0-395-52592-0). After his older brother dies in an accident, 11-year-old Wally finds comfort in his ghost. (Rev: BCCB 5/90; BL 5/15/90; SLJ 5/90; VOYA 8/90)

793 Adler, C. S. *The Lump in the Middle* (6–10). 1991, Avon paper $3.50 (978-0-380-71176-5). Kelsey, the middle child, struggles for her identity after Dad loses his job. (Rev: BL 10/1/89; SLJ 10/89; VOYA 2/90)

794 Adler, C. S. *The No Place Cat* (5–8). 2002, Clarion $15.00 (978-0-618-09644-2). Twelve-year-old Tess runs away from home only to find that life with her father and new stepfamily had its good side after all. (Rev: BCCB 4/02; HBG 10/02; SLJ 3/02)

795 Adler, C. S. *One Sister Too Many* (5–7). 1989, Macmillan paper $3.95 (978-0-689-71521-1). Casey and her reunited family are being driven crazy by the newest addition — a colicky baby. (Rev: BCCB 3/89; BL 3/15/89; SLJ 4/89)

796 Adler, C. S. *The Shell Lady's Daughter* (7–10). 2004, iUniverse paper $10.95 (978-0-595-33912-9). Kelly's mother has emotional problems and attempts suicide; first published in 1983.

797 Adoff, Jaime. *Jimi and Me* (8–11). 2005, Hyperion $15.99 (978-0-7868-5214-7). Struggling to recover from the shock of his father's brutal murder, Keith, a biracial teen who loves the music of Hendrix, moves from Brooklyn to Ohio and discovers that his father had another son, named Jimi. (Rev: BL 10/1/05; SLJ 9/05)

798 Alphin, Elaine Marie. *Picture Perfect* (6–9). 2003, Carolrhoda $15.95 (978-0-8225-0535-8). When his friend Teddy disappears, Ian, son of the principal, wonders if his father might be involved. (Rev: BL 8/03; SLJ 10/03)

799 Alvarez, Julia. *How Tia Lola Came to Visit Stay* (4–7). 2001, Knopf $15.95 (978-0-375-80215-7). Aunt Lola from the Dominican Republic comes to visit 10-year-old Miguel and his family in Vermont and everywhere she goes she spreads friendliness, enthusiasm, stories, and surprise parties. (Rev: BCCB 4/01; BL 2/15/01; HBG 10/01; SLJ 3/01)

800 Amateau, Gigi. *Claiming Georgia Tate* (8–12). 2005, Candlewick $15.99 (978-0-7636-2339-5). When her beloved and protective grandmother dies,

12-year-old Georgia Tate finds herself at the mercy of her sexually abusive father in this novel set in the 1970s. (Rev: SLJ 6/05; VOYA 6/05)

801 Amato, Mary. *The Naked Mole Rat Letters* (4–7). 2005, Holiday $16.95 (978-0-8234-1927-2). Through emails and diary entries, readers learn about Frankie's fear that her father is becoming involved in a new romance. (Rev: BL 6/1–15/05; SLJ 8/05)

802 Anfousse, Ginette. *A Terrible Secret* (7–12). Trans. from French by Jennifer Hutchison. 2001, Lorimer paper $4.99 (978-1-55028-704-2). A new neighbor, Ben, helps Maggie to recover from the death of her Down syndrome brother. (Rev: SLJ 9/01)

803 Banks, Kate. *Walk Softly, Rachel* (7–10). 2003, Farrar $16.00 (978-0-374-38230-8). When Rachel, 14, reads her dead brother's diary she discovers that his life was not the ideal she had thought. (Rev: BL 10/15/03; HBG 4/04; SLJ 9/03*; VOYA 2/04)

804 Baptiste, Tracey. *Angel's Grace* (5–8). Illus. 2005, Simon & Schuster $15.95 (978-0-689-86773-6). Thirteen-year-old Grace, who has always felt different, embarks on a search for the man she believes is her biological father. (Rev: BL 2/1/05; SLJ 3/05)

805 Barwin, Gary. *Seeing Stars* (6–12). 2002, Stoddart paper $7.95 (978-0-7737-6227-5). A quirky story about a boy who has been brought up in strange circumstances and who now wants the truth about his father and his family. (Rev: BL 7/02; SLJ 5/02)

806 Bauer, Cat. *Harley, Like a Person* (7–10). 2000, Winslow $16.95 (978-1-890817-48-0); paper $6.95 (978-1-890817-49-7). Unhappy with her distant mother and an alcoholic father, Harley Columba becomes convinced that she is an adopted child. (Rev: BL 6/1–15/00; HB 5–6/00; HBG 9/00; SLJ 5/00)

807 Bauer, Joan. *Backwater* (7–10). 1999, Putnam $18.99 (978-0-399-23141-4). When 16-year-old Ivy Breedlove begins working on her family history, the trail leads to the New York State Adirondacks and eccentric, talented Aunt Jo. (Rev: BL 5/15/99; HB 7–8/99; HBG 9/99; SLJ 6/99; VOYA 8/99)

808 Bauer, Joan. *Rules of the Road* (6–10). 1998, Putnam $20.99 (978-0-399-23140-7). Jenna Boller is the confident, smart, and moral heroine of this novel that deals with the effects of alcoholism on a family and a girl's growing friendship with a wealthy, elderly woman. (Rev: BL 2/1/98; HB 5–6/98; HBG 9/98; SLJ 3/98*; VOYA 6/98)

809 Bauer, Joan. *Stand Tall* (5–7). 2002, Putnam $16.99 (978-0-399-23473-6). Tree, a tall 7th grader, has a lot of challenges in this nonetheless humorous novel: his height, his lack of athletic ability, shuf-

fling between his divorced parents' homes, and his veteran grandfather's ailments, to name just a few. (Rev: BCCB 10/02; BL 9/15/02; HB 11–12/02; HBG 3/03; SLJ 8/02)

810 Bawden, Nina. *Granny the Pag* (5–8). 1996, Clarion $16.00 (978-0-395-77604-9). Catriona is embarrassed by her grandmother's eccentric ways, such as riding motorbikes and wearing leather jackets, but that doesn't mean she wants to live with her parents instead. (Rev: BCCB 3/96; BL 4/1/96; HB 9–10/96; SLJ 4/96*; VOYA 6/96)

811 Belton, Sandra. *Store-Bought Baby* (7–10). 2006, Greenwillow $15.99 (978-0-06-085086-9). The death of her adopted older brother forces Leah to face issues of love, jealousy, and what it means to truly be a family. (Rev: BL 5/1/06; HB 5–6/06; LMC 3/07; SLJ 6/06)

812 Benedict, Helen. *The Opposite of Love* (7–12). 2007, Viking $16.99 (978-0-670-06135-8). Seventeen-year-old Madge, who never knew her Jamaican dad and has an irresponsible illegal-alien British mom, faces prejudice in her Pennsylvania town but helps an abandoned black foster kid. (Rev: BL 9/1/07; SLJ 3/08)

813 Berry, James. *A Thief in the Village and Other Stories* (7–12). 1988, Penguin paper $5.99 (978-0-14-034357-1). Nine stories about a teenager in Jamaica and everyday life on the Caribbean island. (Rev: BL 4/15/88)

814 Birdsall, Jeanne. *The Penderwicks on Gardam Street* (4–7). Series: The Penderwicks. 2008, Knopf $15.99 (978-0-375-84090-6). The loving, close Penderwick sisters, who were introduced in *The Penderwicks*, are loath to see their widower father start dating again and come up with a plan to discourage him. (Rev: BL 5/1/08; SLJ 3/08)

815 Birdsall, Olivia. *Notes on a Near-Life Experience* (6–12). 2007, Delacorte $15.99 (978-0-385-73370-0). Mia is 15 when her parents separate and her life changes dramatically; although she finds it hard to cope at first, she does — with some help — adapt and is happy to spark some interest in her brother's friend Julian. (Rev: BCCB 3/07; SLJ 3/07)

816 Birdseye, Tom. *Tucker* (5–8). 1990, Holiday $16.95 (978-0-8234-0813-9). A story set in rural Kentucky of a young boy reunited with his younger sister after seven years of separation caused by divorce. (Rev: BL 7/90; SLJ 6/90)

817 Blacker, Terence. *Parent Swap* (6–9). 2006, Farrar $16 (978-0-374-35752-8). Thirteen-year-old Danny is fed up with his ex-rocker dad and absent mother, so he answers an ad for "ParentSwap," a secret London agency promising kids a better life with a new set of parents; eventually Danny catches on to the true nature of this business and his role in it — an unknowing star of a new reality TV show. (Rev: SLJ 8/06)

818 Blume, Judy. *It's Not the End of the World* (5–8). 1972, Dell paper $5.50 (978-0-440-44158-8). Twelve-year-old Karen's world seems to end when her parents are divorced and her older brother runs away.

819 Bond, Nancy. *Truth to Tell* (6–8). 1994, Macmillan $17.95 (978-0-689-50601-7). A 14-year-old girl finds herself on her way to New Zealand with her mother and not really understanding the reason for the relocation. (Rev: BL 4/15/94; SLJ 6/94; VOYA 8/94)

820 Bondoux, Anne-Laure. *Life as It Comes* (7–10). Trans. by Y. Mauder. 2007, Delacorte $15.99 (978-0-385-90390-5). After their parents are killed in a car crash, two French sisters — 15-year-old Mado and 20-year-old Patty — find adapting to a new life difficult, especially when Patty becomes pregnant. (Rev: BCCB 4/07; BL 3/1/07; SLJ 3/07)

821 Bowers, Laura. *Beauty Shop for Rent: . . . Fully Equipped, Inquire Within* (6–9). 2007, Harcourt $17.00 (978-0-15-205764-0). Fifteen-year-old Abbey's life changes dramatically when strong, smart Gena takes over Abbey's grandmother's beauty shop. (Rev: BL 9/15/07; SLJ 4/07)

822 Brandis, Marianne. *The Tinderbox* (6–8). 2003, Tundra paper $9.95 (978-0-88776-626-8). In Canada in 1830, 14-year-old Emma and her younger brother, recently orphaned in a fire, must decide whether to trust a woman who claims a family relationship. (Rev: BL 9/1/03; SLJ 2/04)

823 Bridgers, Sue Ellen. *Home Before Dark* (7–10). 1998, Replica LB $29.95 (978-0-7351-0053-4). A migrant worker and his family settle down in a permanent home.

824 Bridgers, Sue Ellen. *Notes for Another Life* (7–12). 1981, Replica $29.95 (978-0-7351-0044-2). A brother and sister cope with a frequently absent mother and a mentally ill father. (Rev: BL 9/1/85; SLJ 10/85; VOYA 4/86)

825 Brokaw, Nancy Steele. *Leaving Emma* (4–7). 1999, Clarion $15.00 (978-0-395-90699-6). When Emma's best friend moves away and her father is sent to work overseas, the young girl is left with a mother who suffers from bouts of depression. (Rev: BCCB 3/99; BL 3/1/99; HBG 10/99; SLJ 5/99)

826 Brooks, Kevin. *Martyn Pig* (7–10). 2002, Scholastic $16.95 (978-0-439-29595-6). When Martyn's abusive father dies during a drunken argument, Martyn and a friend dispose of the body, setting off a complicated, suspenseful, and often amusing string of events. (Rev: BCCB 9/02; BL 5/1/02; HBG 10/02; SLJ 5/02*)

827 Brown, Susan Taylor. *Hugging the Rock* (5–8). 2006, Tricycle $15.95 (978-1-58246-180-9). In this poignant novel told in free-verse poetry, Rachel describes the difficulties she and her dad have in coping after her mother's departure. (Rev: SLJ 9/06)

828 Bryant, Ann. *One Mom Too Many! Book No. 1* (4–7). Series: Step-Chain. 2003, Lobster paper $3.95 (978-1-894222-78-5). Sarah, 12, is not pleased to discover that both her divorced parents have found new romantic interests. (Rev: SLJ 5/04)

829 Bryant, Ann. *You Can't Fall for Your Stepsister* (4–7). Series: Step-Chain. 2003, Lobster paper $3.95 (978-1-894222-77-8). Ollie, 13, thinks he may be falling in love with his stepsister Frankie, but she ends up becoming his new best friend. (Rev: SLJ 5/04)

830 Buffie, Margaret. *Out of Focus* (7–10). 2006, Kids Can $16.95 (978-1-55337-955-3); paper $6.95 (978-1-55337-956-0). Sixteen-year-old Bernie moves his alcoholic mother and younger siblings into a lake cabin in hopes of keeping the family together. (Rev: LMC 3/07; SLJ 10/06)

831 Bunting, Eve. *Is Anybody There?* (4–7). 1990, HarperCollins paper $6.99 (978-0-06-440347-4). Marcus is both scared and angry after his latchkey disappears and things are stolen. (Rev: BCCB 10/88; BL 12/15/88; SLJ 12/88)

832 Bunting, Eve. *Surrogate Sister* (7–10). 1984, HarperCollins LB $13.89 (978-0-397-32099-8). A 16-year-old girl copes with a pregnant mother who has offered to be a surrogate mother for a childless couple.

833 Burch, Robert. *Ida Early Comes over the Mountain* (4–8). 1990, Puffin paper $5.99 (978-0-14-034534-6). The four motherless Sutton children find a new and most unusual housekeeper in Ida.

834 Burtinshaw, Julie. *Adrift* (6–8). 2002, Raincoast paper $7.95 (978-1-55192-469-4). David, 14, and his younger sister Laura have exciting adventures when they rebel against the adults' plans for their future after their mother is hospitalized for depression. (Rev: SLJ 1/03; VOYA 12/02)

835 Byalick, Marcia. *It's a Matter of Trust* (7–9). 1995, Browndeer paper $5.00 (978-0-15-200240-4). Erika's father confesses to a white-collar crime, and this novel traces the effects of this confession on the family, particularly on 16-year-old Erika and her relations with boyfriend Greg. (Rev: SLJ 12/95; VOYA 2/96)

836 Cardenas, Teresa. *Letters to My Mother* (5–8). Trans. by David Unger. 2006, Groundwood paper $6.95 (978-0-88899-721-0). In unhappy letters to her dead mother, a 10-year-old Cuban girl describes cruelty and prejudice at the hands of her relatives. (Rev: BL 5/1/06; SLJ 8/06)

837 Carlson, Melody. *Just Ask* (8–12). Series: Diary of a Teenage Girl. 2005, Multnomah paper $12.99 (978-1-59052-321-6). A family tragedy shakes the faith of 16-year-old Kim, who's been struggling to live a Christian life. (Rev: SLJ 12/05)

838 Cassidy, Cathy. *Indigo Blue* (5–8). 2005, Viking $15.99 (978-0-670-05927-0). As her family life slowly disintegrates, 11-year-old Indigo tries her best to conceal the truth from her friends at school in this realistic story set in Britain. (Rev: BL 10/1/05; SLJ 11/05)

839 Chambers, Veronica. *Marisol and Magdalena: The Sound of Our Sisterhood* (5–9). 1998, Hyperion LB $15.49 (978-0-7868-2385-7). Hispanic American Marisol is sent to live with her grandmother in Panama for a year, and hopes to track down her absent father. (Rev: BL 10/1/98; SLJ 12/98)

840 Charlton-Trujillo, E. E. *Feels Like Home* (8–10). 2007, Delacorte $15.99 (978-0-385-73332-8). Two siblings in South Texas — 17-year-old Michelle (Mickey) and her older brother — come together after their father's death and, after some false starts, find a way to heal. (Rev: SLJ 7/07)

841 Cheaney, J. B. *The Middle of Somewhere* (5–8). 2007, Knopf $15.99 (978-0-375-83790-6). Put in charge of her learning disabled brother while her mother recovers from knee surgery, 12-year-old Ronnie Sparks comes under even greater pressure when she and her brother accompany their grandfather on a trip to Kansas. (Rev: BL 3/15/07; SLJ 7/07)

842 Christian, Mary Blount. *Growin' Pains* (6–8). 1985, Penguin paper $3.95 (978-0-317-63785-4). With the help of a disabled neighbor, Ginny Ruth continues to develop her writing talent in spite of her mother's objections. (Rev: BL 2/1/86)

843 Clarke, Judith. *One Whole and Perfect Day* (8–10). 2007, Front St. $16.95 (978-1-932425-95-6). Lily, 16, finally gets what she longs for — a single day when her irritating and eccentric family comes together happily — in this gentle novel set in Australia. (Rev: BL 5/1/07; HB 5–6/07; SLJ 8/07)

844 Cleary, Beverly. *Sister of the Bride* (6–9). 1963, Morrow $19.89 (978-0-688-31742-3); Avon paper $6.99 (978-0-380-72807-7). A young girl becomes too involved with the plans for her sister's wedding.

845 Cleaver, Vera. *Sweetly Sings the Donkey* (6–9). Illus. 1985, HarperCollins LB $12.89 (978-0-397-32157-5). Fourteen-year-old Lily Snow and her family hope that their inheritance in Florida will help them financially but this is not to be. (Rev: BL 10/1/85)

846 Cleaver, Vera, and Bill Cleaver. *Dust of the Earth* (7–9). 1975, HarperCollins $13.95 (978-0-397-31650-2). Fern and her family face problems when they move to a farm in South Dakota. (Rev: BL 3/1/89)

847 Cleaver, Vera, and Bill Cleaver. *Queen of Hearts* (7–9). 1978, HarperCollins $14.00 (978-0-

397-31771-4). Wilma must take care of her grandmother whom she really dislikes.

848 Clements, Andrew. *Things Hoped For* (8–11). 2006, Philomel $16.99 (978-0-399-24350-9). Gwen lives with her grandfather in New York City and studies violin at the Manhattan School of Music; when her grandfather disappears, Gwen teams up with Robert, a fellow music student, to solve the mystery. A sequel to *Things Not Seen* (2002). (Rev: BL 8/06; SLJ 11/06) 🐝

849 Cohn, Rachel. *The Steps* (4–7). 2003, Simon & Schuster $16.95 (978-0-689-84549-9). Annabel resents the complexity of her family life as she reluctantly sets out to visit her father and his new wife, baby, and stepchildren in Australia, but she gradually learns to accept the situation in this humorous portrayal. (Rev: BCCB 2/03; BL 1/1–15/03; HB 5–6/03; HBG 10/03; SLJ 2/03*)

850 Cohn, Rachel. *Two Steps Forward* (6–8). 2006, Simon & Schuster $15.95 (978-0-689-86614-2). In this sequel to *The Steps,* 14-year-old stepsisters Annabel and Lucy, as well as their stepbrothers Ben and Wheaties, provide alternate views of their four blended families and the tensions, humor, and feelings that arise. (Rev: SLJ 5/06)

851 Cohn, Rachel. *You Know Where to Find Me* (8–11). 2008, Simon & Schuster $15.99 (978-0-689-87859-6). Miles turns to drugs following her cousin Laura's suicide in this story full of complicated families and relationships. (Rev: BL 4/1/08; SLJ 3/08)

852 Collier, James Lincoln. *Outside Looking In* (6–8). 1990, Avon paper $2.95 (978-0-380-70961-8). Fergie and his sister hate the nomadic life their parents lead and long to settle down. (Rev: BL 4/1/87; SLJ 5/87; VOYA 10/87)

853 Collins, Yvonne, and Sandy Rideout. *The Black Sheep* (8–12). 2007, Hyperion $15.99 (978-1-4231-0156-7). Sick of her boring Manhattan lifestyle, 15-year-old Kendra agrees to be on a reality show where she switches lives with Maya, who comes from a hippie family that's all about saving otters. (Rev: BL 5/15/07; SLJ 9/07)

854 Colman, Hila. *Rich and Famous Like My Mom* (6–9). 1988, Bantam paper $5.50 (978-0-5175-6836-1). Cassandra is growing up in the shadow of her mother, a world-famous rock star. (Rev: BL 6/15/88)

855 Coman, Carolyn. *What Jamie Saw* (5–8). 1995, Front St. $15.95 (978-1-886910-02-7). In this novel seen through the eyes of a young boy, a mother and her family flee her physically abusive husband. (Rev: BCCB 12/95; BL 12/15/95*; SLJ 12/95*)

856 Connor, Leslie. *Waiting for Normal* (5–7). 2008, HarperCollins $15.99 (978-0-06-089088-9). Addie lives in a trailer with her mother and looks forward to visits with her stepfather and half sisters, whose life is far more "normal." (Rev: BL 4/1/08; SLJ 2/08)

857 Cooley, Beth. *Shelter* (7–10). 2006, Delacorte $15.95 (978-0-385-73330-4). Lucy and her mother and little brother go from affluence to a homeless shelter after Lucy's father dies, and Lucy must learn to adjust to new circumstances and improve her life. (Rev: BCCB 1/07; BL 1/1–15/07; SLJ 12/06)

858 Cooney, Caroline B. *A Friend at Midnight* (6–9). 2006, Delacorte $15.95 (978-0-385-73326-7). Despite her Christian beliefs, Lily has a hard time forgiving her father for his neglect of herself and her siblings, and her resentment grows when her big sister wants him to be a part of her wedding. (Rev: BL 12/15/06; LMC 2/07; SLJ 11/06)

859 Cooney, Caroline B. *Whatever Happened to Janie?* (6–10). 1993, Dell paper $5.50 (978-0-440-21924-8). Janie, 15, after discovering she's a missing child on a milk carton, returns to her birth family, which has been searching for her since her kidnapping at age three. Sequel to *The Face on the Milk Carton*. (Rev: BL 6/1–15/93; SLJ 6/93; VOYA 8/93)

860 Corcoran, Barbara. *I Am the Universe* (6–8). 1993, Harcourt paper $23.40 (978-0-15-300366-0). With an indifferent father at home and her mother seriously ill in the hospital, Katherine and her older brother take care of the house. (Rev: BL 10/1/86; SLJ 10/86; VOYA 12/86)

861 Corcoran, Barbara. *The Potato Kid* (5–8). 1993, Avon paper $3.50 (978-0-380-71213-7). In spite of her protests, Ellis must look after an underprivileged girl her mother takes in for the summer. (Rev: BCCB 11/89; BL 11/15/89; HB 1–2/90; SLJ 10/89; VOYA 2/90)

862 Cotten, Cynthia. *Fair Has Nothing to Do with It* (4–7). 2007, Farrar $16.00 (978-0-374-39935-1). Upset by the death of his grandfather, 12-year-old Michael focuses his energies on an art project to honor his memory. (Rev: BL 4/1/07; SLJ 6/07)

863 Couloumbis, Audrey. *Getting Near to Baby* (5–9). 1999, Putnam $17.99 (978-0-399-23389-0). When their baby sister dies and their mother sinks into a depression, 12-year-old Willa Jo and Little Sister go to live with a bossy aunt in this story set in North Carolina. (Rev: BCCB 11/99; BL 11/1/99; HB 11–12/99; HBG 3/00; SLJ 10/99; VOYA 2/00)

864 Couloumbis, Audrey. *Love Me Tender* (5–8). 2008, Random $16.99 (978-0-375-83839-2). Thirteen-year-old Elvira initially questions her future when after a fight, her father leaves for Vegas to compete in an Elvis-impersonation contest and her pregnant mother takes Elvira and her younger sister to Memphis to reunite with her family. (Rev: BL 2/15/08; SLJ 4/08)

865 Couvillon, Jacques. *The Chicken Dance* (6–9). 2007, Bloomsbury $16.95 (978-1-59990-043-8). In this poignantly funny story set in the late 1970s, 11-year-old Don's skill at judging chickens brings him welcome acceptance but also triggers some unhappy discoveries. (Rev: BCCB 11/07; SLJ 11/07) 🔖

866 Creech, Sharon. *Replay* (4–7). 2005, HarperCollins LB $16.89 (978-0-06-054020-3). Twelve-year-old Leo untangles some of the secrets of his boisterous Italian American family when he finds his father's boyhood journal. (Rev: BCCB 11/05; BL 9/1/05*; HBG 4/06; LMC 3–4/06; SLJ 9/05; VOYA 12/05)

867 Creech, Sharon. *Walk Two Moons* (7–9). 1994, HarperCollins LB $17.89 (978-0-06-023337-2). The story of Sal, 13, who goes to Idaho with her grandparents to be with her mother, who has been killed in a bus accident. (Rev: BL 11/15/94; SLJ 10/94*; VOYA 2/95)

868 Dalton, Annie, and Maria Dalton. *Invisible Threads* (8–11). 2006, Delacorte LB $17.99 (978-0-385-90303-5). In alternating chapters, Carrie Ann describes her need to find her birth mother and Naomi, the birth mother, talks about her pregnancy and the decision to give up her baby. (Rev: BL 4/1/06; SLJ 4/06)

869 Darrow, Sharon. *Trash* (8–11). 2006, Candlewick $16.99 (978-0-7636-2624-2). The sad story of two abandoned siblings—Sissy Lexie and Boy—who suffer through abuse, poverty, depression, and death; written in rhythmic prose and free verse. (Rev: BL 12/1/06; SLJ 10/06)

870 Day, Karen. *Tall Tales* (5–8). 2007, Random $15.99 (978-0-375-83773-9). As she starts school in yet another new town, 12-year-old Meg conceals her father's alcoholism and abuse, afraid it will frighten off potential friends. (Rev: BL 4/1/07; SLJ 6/07)

871 Deaver, Julie Reece. *Chicago Blues* (6–10). 1995, HarperCollins $15.95 (978-0-06-024675-4). Two sisters are forced to make it on their own because of an alcoholic mother and experience struggle, success, and eventual forgiveness. (Rev: BL 9/1/95; SLJ 8/95; VOYA 12/95)

872 Deedy, Carmen A. *The Last Dance* (7–10). Illus. 1995, Peachtree $16.95 (978-1-56145-109-8). A picture book for young adults that tells of the abiding love through the years of husband and wife Ninny and Bessie. (Rev: BL 1/1–15/96; SLJ 1/96)

873 Delacre, Lulu. *Salsa Stories* (4–7). Illus. 2000, Scholastic paper $16.99 (978-0-590-63118-1). After each of her relatives tells a childhood story about a favorite food, Carmen Teresa records them and supplies appropriate recipes. (Rev: BCCB 5/00; BL 5/1/00; HBG 10/00; SLJ 3/00; VOYA 6/00)

874 Deuker, Carl. *High Heat* (5–8). 2003, Houghton $16.00 (978-0-618-31117-0). Even his baseball prowess seems to desert Shane when his father commits suicide and he must move to a tough new neighborhood and school. (Rev: BL 8/03; HBG 10/03; SLJ 7/03; VOYA 8/03)

875 Deuker, Carl. *Runner* (7–10). 2005, Houghton $16.00 (978-0-618-54298-7). Living on a weather-beaten sailboat on Puget Sound with his alcoholic father, high school senior Chance Taylor gets mixed up in some shady dealings to help pay the family bills. (Rev: BL 6/1–15/05; SLJ 6/05; VOYA 8/05)

876 Doherty, Berlie. *Holly Starcross* (6–10). 2002, HarperCollins LB $17.89 (978-0-06-001342-4). Holly is forced to choose between her mother's new family and her long-lost father in this dramatic British novel. (Rev: BCCB 12/02; BL 11/1/02; HB 9–10/02; HBG 3/03; SLJ 8/02)

877 Doody, Margaret Anne, et al., ed. *The Annotated Anne of Green Gables* (7–12). 1997, Oxford $49.95 (978-0-19-510428-8). A biography of Lucy Maud Montgomery and notes and annotations explaining references to the places, people, and settings add to this edition of Montgomery's novel. (Rev: SLJ 3/98; VOYA 6/98)

878 Doucet, Sharon Arms. *Fiddle Fever* (4–7). 2000, Clarion $15.00 (978-0-618-04324-8). Felix disobeys his mother, who hates fiddle playing, and builds one out of a cigar box and practices in secret. (Rev: BL 9/1/00; HB 9–10/00; HBG 3/01; SLJ 10/00)

879 Dowell, Frances O'Roark. *Chicken Boy* (4–7). 2005, Simon & Schuster $15.95 (978-0-689-85816-1). A new friend called Henry brings some comfort into Tobin's sad life. (Rev: BL 5/15/05*; SLJ 7/05*)

880 Dowell, Frances O'Roark. *Dovey Coe* (4–7). 2000, Simon & Schuster $16.00 (978-0-689-83174-4). The mountain country of North Carolina in 1928 is the setting of this story of a plucky girl who cares for her siblings and who gets involved in a murder trial. (Rev: BL 4/15/00; HBG 10/00; SLJ 5/00; VOYA 6/00)

881 Doyle, Eugenie. *Stray Voltage* (5–7). 2002, Front St. $16.95 (978-1-886910-86-7). The electrical problems in Ian's family barn reflect the flickering, unpredictable relationships at home, but a wise teacher helps Ian to cope with his circumstances. (Rev: BCCB 1/03; BL 1/1–15/03*; HBG 3/03; SLJ 10/02*; VOYA 2/03)

882 Draper, Sharon M. *Forged by Fire* (7–10). 1997, Simon & Schuster $16.95 (978-0-689-80699-5). Nine-year-old African American Gerald Nickelby must leave the comfort of his aunt's home to live with a neglectful mother, her daughter Angel, and husband Jordan, who is secretly sexually abusing young Angel. A companion volume to *Tears of a Tiger*. (Rev: BL 2/15/97; SLJ 3/97; VOYA 6/97)

883 Duble, Kathleen Benner. *Bravo Zulu, Samantha!* (5–8). 2007, Peachtree $14.95 (978-1-56145-401-3). Twelve-year-old Samantha unwillingly spends the summer with her grandparents but her retired Air Force grandfather turns out to have an exciting secret. (Rev: BL 6/1–15/07; SLJ 6/07)

884 Dunmore, Helen. *Brother Brother, Sister Sister* (5–8). 2000, Scholastic paper $4.50 (978-0-439-11322-9). Written in diary format, this is the story of Tanya, once an only child and now surrounded by babies after her mother has quadruplets. (Rev: SLJ 8/00)

885 Durrant, Sabine. *Cross Your Heart, Connie Pickles* (6–9). 2007, HarperTempest $16.99 (978-0-06-085479-9). This engaging story of Connie's quest to find a husband for her widowed mother is written in appealing diary format. (Rev: SLJ 6/07)

886 Elkeles, Simone. *How to Ruin a Summer Vacation* (8–10). 2006, Flux paper $8.95 (978-0-7387-0961-1). Amy, 16, enters a whole new world when she goes to Israel for the summer with her father and must share a room with a cousin she's neverr met. (Rev: SLJ 12/06)

887 Ellis, Sarah. *Out of the Blue* (5–7). Illus. 1995, Simon & Schuster paper $15.00 (978-0-689-80025-2). Twelve-year-old Megan discovers that she has a 24-year-old half-sister whom her mother gave up for adoption years ago. (Rev: BCCB 4/95; BL 5/1/95; HB 7–8/95; SLJ 5/95)

888 Ephron, Delia. *Frannie in Pieces* (7–10). 2007, HarperCollins $16.99 (978-0-06-074716-9). Frannie, devastated by her father's death, discovers a magical jigsaw puzzle that he made before his death and that allows Frannie to see him again. (Rev: BL 11/1/07; SLJ 10/07) ◈

889 Ernst, Kathleen. *Highland Fling* (6–9). 2006, Cricket $15.95 (978-0-8126-2742-8). Tanya, a budding documentary filmmaker, must overcome her negativity as she attends a Scottish heritage festival with her recently divorced mom. (Rev: BL 4/15/06; SLJ 6/06)

890 Erskine, Kathryn. *Quaking* (8–10). 2007, Philomel $16.99 (978-0-399-24774-3). Fourteen-year-old Matilda's resistance gradually breaks down as she settles into her new, Quaker foster home; community differences over antiwar protests threaten this new ease. (Rev: BL 5/1/07; HB 7–8/07; SLJ 7/07)

891 Eulo, Elena Yates. *Mixed-Up Doubles* (8–11). 2003, Holiday $16.95 (978-0-8234-1706-3). In this poignant yet funny story of a tennis-playing family hit by divorce, middle child Hank, 14, narrates the effects on the children. (Rev: BCCB 7–8/03; BL 5/15/03; HBG 4/04; SLJ 7/03; VOYA 6/03)

892 Ferber, Brenda. *Julia's Kitchen* (5–8). 2006, Farrar $16.00 (978-0-374-39932-0). Eleven-year-old Cara Segal's faith is tested when her mother and sister die in a house fire while Cara is sleeping over at a friend's home. (Rev: BL 2/1/06; SLJ 4/06)

893 Fine, Anne. *The Book of the Banshee* (6–9). 1992, Little, Brown $13.95 (978-0-316-28315-1). English teenager Will Flowers's younger sister, Estelle, has become a banshee, and he decides his family life is like an account of World War I he is reading. (Rev: BL 12/1/91*)

894 Flake, Sharon G. *Begging for Change* (7–12). 2003, Hyperion $15.99 (978-0-7868-0601-0). Raspberry resorts to stealing from a friend when her mother is hospitalized after being hit in the head and her addicted father reappears on the scene in this sequel to *Money Hungry* (2001). (Rev: BL 8/03*; HBG 4/04; SLJ 7/03; VOYA 6/03)

895 Fleischman, Paul. *Rear-View Mirrors* (7–10). 1986, HarperCollins $12.95 (978-0-06-021866-9). After her father's death, Olivia relives through memory a summer when she and her estranged father reconciled. (Rev: BL 3/1/86; SLJ 5/86; VOYA 8/86)

896 Fleischman, Sid. *Bo and Mzzz Mad* (5–7). 2001, Greenwillow LB $15.89 (978-0-06-029398-7). When his father dies, 12-year-old Bo accepts an invitation from relatives despite a longstanding family feud. (Rev: BL 5/15/01*; HB 5–6/01; HBG 10/01; SLJ 5/01)

897 Fletcher, Ralph. *Fig Pudding* (5–7). 1995, Clarion $15.00 (978-0-395-71125-5). A year that brings both tragedy and hilarity in the life of a family of six children. (Rev: BCCB 5/95; BL 5/15/95; SLJ 7/95)

898 Flinn, Alex. *Nothing to Lose* (7–12). 2004, HarperCollins $16.99 (978-0-06-051750-2). At age 17, Michael returns home after being a runaway for a year to find that his mother is on trial for the murder of his abusive father. (Rev: BL 3/15/04; HB 5–6/04; SLJ 3/04; VOYA 6/04)

899 Fogelin, Adrian. *Anna Casey's Place in the World* (6–8). 2001, Peachtree $14.95 (978-1-56145-249-1). Twelve-year-old orphan Anna must adjust to her new foster home and begin to make friends. (Rev: BL 10/15/01; HBG 3/02; SLJ 12/01; VOYA 12/01)

900 Fogelin, Adrian. *My Brother's Hero* (5–8). 2002, Peachtree $14.95 (978-1-56145-274-3). When Ben and his family travel to Florida for a vacation, Ben meets a girl named Mica, whose life he finds exciting and mysterious. (Rev: BL 2/1/03; HBG 10/03; SLJ 2/03)

901 Fogelin, Adrian. *Sister Spider Knows All* (6–9). 2003, Peachtree $14.95 (978-1-56145-290-3). A sensitive and humorous novel narrated by Rox, 12,

who is doing OK being brought up by her financially strapped grandmother and cousin John until John brings home a rich girlfriend who sees things differently. (Rev: BCCB 2/04; BL 12/15/03; SLJ 12/03)

902 Foggo, Cheryl. *One Thing That's True* (5–8). 1998, Kids Can $16.95 (978-1-55074-411-8). Roxanne is heartbroken when her older brother runs away after learning that he is adopted. (Rev: BCCB 5/98; BL 2/15/98; HBG 10/98; SLJ 4/98)

903 Forbes, Kathryn. *Mama's Bank Account* (7–10). 1968, Harcourt paper $11.00 (978-0-15-656377-2). The story, told in vignettes, of a loving Norwegian family and of Mama's mythical bank account.

904 Fox, Paula. *The Eagle Kite* (6–10). 1995, Orchard LB $16.99 (978-0-531-08742-8). Liam goes through a tangle of denial, anger, shame, grief, and empathy after learning that his father is dying of AIDS. His mother says he got it from a blood transfusion, but Liam remembers seeing his father embrace a young man two years before. (Rev: BL 2/1/95*; SLJ 4/95*; VOYA 5/95)

905 Fox, Paula. *The Village by the Sea* (5–8). 1988, Orchard $15.95 (978-0-531-05788-9). Emma is staying with an aunt and uncle while her father has heart surgery, and the three interact in complex ways. Also use the reissued *A Likely Place* (1997). (Rev: BCCB 7–8/88; BL 9/1/88; HB 9–10/88; SLJ 8/88; VOYA 10/88)

906 Frechette, Carole. *In the Key of Do* (6–9). 2003, Red Deer paper $9.95 (978-0-88995-254-6). Past and present are interwoven in this story of two girls in Montreal whose family circumstances bring them together. (Rev: BL 6/1–15/03; SLJ 6/03; VOYA 10/03)

907 French, Simon. *Where in the World* (5–8). 2003, Peachtree $14.95 (978-1-56145-292-7). A move from Germany to Australia is difficult for Ari, a talented young violinist who spends time living in the past while trying to find ways to cope with the present. (Rev: BL 12/1/03; HBG 4/04; SLJ 12/03*)

908 Friend, Natasha. *Bounce* (6–9). 2007, Scholastic $16.99 (978-0-439-85350-7). Thirteen-year-old Evyn has a hard time adjusting to six new stepsiblings, a pregnant stepmother, and a new home and school — until she decides to let things bounce. (Rev: BL 11/1/07; SLJ 9/07)

909 Friend, Natasha. *Lush* (7–10). 2006, Scholastic $16.99 (978-0-439-85346-0). Thirteen-year-old Sam writes anonymous letters to an older student at school, sharing the truth about her family life and her father's alcoholism, and asking for advice. (Rev: BL 11/1/06; SLJ 12/06)

910 Friesen, Gayle. *Janey's Girl* (6–9). 1998, Kids Can $16.95 (978-1-55074-461-3). When Claire and her mother visit her mother's hometown in rural British Columbia, the young girl meets her father for the first time and begins to find out truths about her family's past. (Rev: HBG 3/99; SLJ 11/98)

911 Friesen, Gayle. *Losing Forever* (7–10). 2002, Kids Can $16.95 (978-1-55337-031-4). As her mother prepares to remarry, 9th-grader Jes is still coping with her parents' divorce, her changing relationships with her friends, and her beautiful soon-to-be stepsister. (Rev: BCCB 11/02; BL 1/1–15/03; HBG 3/03; SLJ 11/02; VOYA 2/03)

912 Gantos, Jack. *I Am Not Joey Pigza* (5–8). 2007, Farrar $16.00 (978-0-374-39941-2). Joey's father returns to the Pigza family with lottery winnings, a new name, and promises of a new future based on a diner. (Rev: BL 8/07; SLJ 9/07) ❷

913 Gantos, Jack. *Jack Adrift: Fourth Grade Without a Clue* (4–7). 2003, Farrar $16.00 (978-0-374-39987-0). In this prequel to the four previous books, Jack Henry is 9 and has just moved to Cape Hatteras where he has comic experiences and more serious conversations with his dad. (Rev: BL 8/03; HB 11–12/03; HBG 4/04; SLJ 9/03)

914 Garland, Sherry. *Rainmaker's Dream* (6–9). 1997, Harcourt paper $6.00 (978-0-15-200652-5). After her family falls apart, 13-year-old Caroline runs away to a Wild West show where she discovers a secret about her mother's identity. (Rev: BL 4/1/97; SLJ 6/97; VOYA 8/97)

915 Garsee, Jeannine. *Before, After, and Somebody in Between* (8–11). 2007, Bloomsbury $16.95 (978-1-59990-022-3). This is a problem novel in which 14-year-old Martha — smart, sensitive, and musically gifted — copes with an alcoholic mother, poverty and violence, foster care, and ill-advised sex but finds hope at the end of it all. (Rev: BL 8/07; SLJ 10/07)

916 Gates, Doris. *Blue Willow* (5–8). 1940, Penguin paper $6.99 (978-0-14-030924-9). An easily read novel about a poor girl and the china plate that belonged to her mother. (Rev: BCCB 12/99)

917 Gates, Susan. *Beyond the Billboard* (5–8). 2007, Harcourt $16.00 (978-0-15-205983-5). Ford and Firebird, 13-year-old twins, have grown up secluded from the modern world but their lives are about to change as secrets are revealed. (Rev: BL 6/1–15/07; SLJ 8/07)

918 Giff, Patricia Reilly. *Pictures of Hollis Woods* (5–7). 2002, Random $15.95 (978-0-385-32655-1). Twelve-year-old Hollis Woods has finally found a foster home where she feels safe, but when the artist who takes her in begins to suffer from dementia, Hollis finds herself in the position of caregiver. Newbery Honor Book, 2003. (Rev: BCCB 12/02; BL 10/15/02; HB 1–2/03; HBG 3/03; SLJ 9/02)

919 Gilliland, Hap, and William Walters. *Flint's Rock* (5–7). 1996, Roberts Rinehart paper $8.95 (978-1-879373-82-2). Flint, a young Cheyenne, faces problems when he moves with his parents from the reservation to Butte, Montana. (Rev: BCCB 5/96; BL 5/1/96)

920 Gilmore, Rachna. *Mina's Spring of Colors* (4–7). 2000, Fitzhenry & Whiteside $14.95 (978-1-55041-549-0); paper $8.95 (978-1-55041-534-6). Mina is happy when her grandfather comes from India, but with his arrival comes a culture clash that troubles the girl. (Rev: BL 6/1–15/00; SLJ 9/00; VOYA 12/00)

921 Going, K. L. *Saint Iggy* (8–11). 2006, Harcourt $17.00 (978-0-15-205795-4). Sixteen-year-old Iggy Corso, who lives in public housing with his drug-addicted parents, faces expulsion from school and decides to make something of himself. (Rev: BL 9/15/06; HB 11–12/06; SLJ 9/06) ❷

922 Golding, Theresa Martin. *The Secret Within* (5–8). 2002, Boyds Mills $16.95 (978-1-56397-995-8). Eighth-grader Carly's secret is that her father is abusive and a criminal; the neighbors in the family's new town help her and her mother to finally escape his grip. (Rev: BL 9/15/02; HBG 3/03; SLJ 8/02; VOYA 2/03)

923 Goobie, Beth. *Something Girl* (5–8). 2005, Orca paper $7.95 (978-1-55143-347-9). Fifteen-year-old Sophie tries to hide the fact that her mother is an alcoholic and her father abusive in this book for reluctant readers. (Rev: BL 7/05; SLJ 12/05)

924 Goobie, Beth. *Who Owns Kelly Paddik?* (7–10). Series: Orca Soundings. 2003, Orca paper $7.95 (978-1-55143-239-7). Kelly, 15, slowly comes to realize that she is not alone as she recovers from the sexual abuse inflicted by her father. (Rev: SLJ 11/03)

925 Goodman, Joan E. *Songs from Home* (5–7). Illus. 1994, Harcourt paper $4.95 (978-0-15-203591-4). Anna discovers the truth about her father, who has become a drifter in Italy singing for tips in restaurants. (Rev: BCCB 12/94; BL 9/1/94; SLJ 10/94)

926 Greenfield, Eloise. *Sister* (5–7). Illus. by Moneta Barnett. 1974, HarperCollins $15.99 (978-0-690-00497-7); paper $5.99 (978-0-06-440199-9). Four years in an African American girl's life, as revealed through scattered diary entries, during which she shows maturation, particularly in her attitude toward her sister.

927 Gregory, Nan. *I'll Sing You One-O* (5–8). 2006, Clarion $16.00 (978-0-618-60708-2). Twelve-year-old Gemma is overwhelmed when relatives — including a twin brother — turn up to take her from the foster home she's come to love, and she becomes convinced that an angel will save the day. (Rev: BL 8/06; SLJ 10/06*)

928 Grimes, Nikki. *Dark Sons* (5–8). 2005, Hyperion $15.99 (978-0-7868-1888-4). Alternating between biblical times and contemporary New York, free-verse narratives express the frustrations of Ishmael — son of Abraham, who must wander the desert with his rejected mother -- and of Sam, whose father has left his mother for a young white woman. (Rev: BL 8/05*; SLJ 11/05; VOYA 10/05)

929 Grimes, Nikki. *The Road to Paris* (4–7). 2006, Putnam $15.99 (978-0-399-24537-4). Half-white and half-black, 9-year-old Paris suddenly finds herself separated from her older brother Malcolm and living with a foster family in a mostly white neighborhood. Coretta Scott King Author Honor Book, 2007. (Rev: BL 8/06; SLJ 12/06) ❂

930 Hahn, Mary D. *As Ever, Gordy* (5–8). 1998, Houghton $15.00 (978-0-395-83627-9). After his grandmother's death, 13-year-old Gordy must move back to his hometown to live with his older brother, and there he finds himself in a downward spiral. A sequel to *Stepping on Cracks* and *Following My Own Footsteps*. (Rev: BCCB 6/98; BL 5/1/98; HBG 10/98; SLJ 7/98; VOYA 4/99)

931 Hall, Barbara. *Dixie Storms* (7–12). 1990, Harcourt $15.95 (978-0-15-223825-4). Dutch's troubled relationships within her family worsen when cousin Norma comes to stay. (Rev: BL 5/1/90; SLJ 9/90)

932 Hall, Barbara. *The Noah Confessions* (8–12). 2007, Random $15.99 (978-0-385-73328-1). The compelling story of Lynnie, a 16-year-old girl who comes to terms with her family's secret past when she reads a letter written by her deceased mother. (Rev: SLJ 6/07)

933 Hamilton, Virginia. *Plain City* (5–7). 1993, Scholastic paper $13.95 (978-0-590-47364-4). Buhlaire's life changes dramatically when the father she believed to be dead unexpectedly arrives in town. (Rev: BCCB 11/93; BL 9/15/93*; SLJ 11/93*)

934 Hamilton, Virginia. *Second Cousins* (5–8). 1998, Scholastic paper $14.95 (978-0-590-47368-2). In this sequel to *Cousins*, 12-year-old Cammy learns a secret during a family reunion in her small Ohio town. (Rev: BCCB 11/98; BL 8/98; HB 1–2/99; HBG 3/99; SLJ 11/98; VOYA 2/99)

935 Hansen, Joyce. *One True Friend* (4–7). 2001, Clarion $14.00 (978-0-395-84983-5). Amir's correspondence with his friend Doris comforts him as he tries to fulfill a deathbed promise to his mother to keep his family together. (Rev: BCCB 12/01; BL 12/15/01; HBG 3/02; SLJ 12/01; VOYA 10/01)

936 Harmon, Michael. *Skate* (7–10). 2006, Knopf $15.95 (978-0-375-87516-8). Facing foster care and separation from his younger brother Sammy, Ian takes Sammy and the two run away, heading across Washington State to find their long-absent father. (Rev: BL 11/15/06; SLJ 12/06)

937 Harness, Cheryl. *Just for You to Know* (5–8). 2006, HarperCollins $17.99 (978-0-06-078313-6).

Life is turned upside down for 13-year-old Carmen Cathcart, an aspiring artist, when her mother dies during childbirth. (Rev: SLJ 9/06)

938 Harrar, George. *Parents Wanted* (6–9). 2001, Milkweed $17.95 (978-1-57131-632-5); paper $6.95 (978-1-57131-633-2). Andy Fleck, a foster child with ADD, sabotages his own adoption by accusing his prospective father of abuse. (Rev: BL 12/15/01; HBG 3/02; SLJ 11/01)

939 Harrison, Mette Ivie. *The Monster in Me* (5–8). 2003, Holiday $16.95 (978-0-8234-1713-1). A caring foster family and her growing enjoyment in running make Natalie, 13, more optimistic about life. (Rev: BL 4/1/03; HBG 10/03; SLJ 6/03; VOYA 10/03)

940 Harrison, Troon. *Goodbye to Atlantis* (7–10). 2002, Stoddart paper $7.95 (978-0-7737-6229-9). Stella, 14, whose mother died of cancer, initially resents being stuck with her father's girlfriend as a traveling companion. (Rev: BL 9/1/02; SLJ 4/02)

941 Hartnett, Sonya. *What the Birds See* (7–12). 2003, Candlewick $15.99 (978-0-7636-2092-9). A beautifully written complex story featuring three missing children and a lonely and fearful boy who is fascinated by three children who move in next door. (Rev: BCCB 3/03; BL 4/15/03; HB 5–6/03; HBG 10/03; SLJ 5/03; VOYA 6/03)

942 Hathorn, Libby. *Thunderwith* (7–10). 1991, Little, Brown $15.95 (978-0-316-35034-1). This story of an unhappy 15-year-old girl and a beautiful dingolike dog she finds is set in the Australian rain forest. (Rev: BL 9/1/91; SLJ 5/91*)

943 Hausman, Gerald, and Uton Hinds. *The Jacob Ladder* (5–8). 2001, Orchard paper $15.95 (978-0-531-30331-3). This story of a young Jamaican who struggles valiantly to cope with poverty, a charismatic but neglectful father, and the problems of growing up is based on the youth of coauthor Uton Hinds. (Rev: BL 5/1/01; HBG 3/02; SLJ 4/01; VOYA 6/01)

944 Henkes, Kevin. *The Birthday Room* (5–7). 1999, Greenwillow $19.99 (978-0-688-16733-2). Ben travels to Oregon with his mother to visit Uncle Ian who was responsible for Ben's losing his little finger in an accident. (Rev: BCCB 9/99; BL 7/99; HB 9–10/99; HBG 3/00; SLJ 10/99)

945 Hermes, Patricia. *You Shouldn't Have to Say Good-bye* (5–8). 1982, Scholastic paper $3.25 (978-0-590-43174-3). A moving novel about a girl whose mother is dying of cancer.

946 Herschler, Mildred Barger. *The Darkest Corner* (5–9). 2000, Front St. $17.95 (978-1-886910-54-6). In this novel set in the Deep South of the 1960s, 10-year-old Teddy is shocked to discover that her beloved dad participated in the lynching of her best friend's father. (Rev: BL 1/1–15/01; HBG 3/01; SLJ 2/01; VOYA 2/01)

947 Hicks, Betty. *Get Real* (6–9). 2006, Roaring Brook $16.95 (978-1-59643-089-1). Best friends Destiny and Jil come from very different families and Dez is puzzled but supporting when Jil fixates on her birth mother. (Rev: BL 10/15/06; SLJ 1/07)

948 Hicks, Betty. *Out of Order* (4–7). 2005, Roaring Brook $15.95 (978-1-59643-061-7). In alternating chapters, four new stepsiblings relate the problems — and the fun — they have had adjusting to life together. (Rev: BL 9/15/05; SLJ 10/05; VOYA 12/05)

949 High, Linda O. *Maizie* (4–8). 1995, Holiday $14.95 (978-0-8234-1161-0). Maizie, a survivor, succeeds in spite of being abandoned by her mother and left with an alcoholic father. (Rev: BCCB 4/95; BL 4/15/95; HB 5–6/95; SLJ 4/95)

950 Hill, Kirkpatrick. *Do Not Pass Go* (6–9). 2007, Simon & Schuster $15.99 (978-1-4169-1400-6). Deet must deal with new family pressures when his stepfather is sent to jail for drug possession. (Rev: BL 12/15/06; SLJ 3/07)

951 Hinton, S. E. *Taming the Star Runner* (7–12). 1989, Bantam paper $5.50 (978-0-440-20479-4). A tough delinquent is sent to his uncle's ranch to be straightened out and there he falls in love with Casey, who is trying to tame a wild horse named Star Runner. (Rev: BL 10/15/88; SLJ 10/88; VOYA 12/88)

952 Hirahara, Naomi. *1001 Cranes* (4–7). 2008, Delacorte $15.99 (978-0-385-73556-8). Twelve-year-old Angela reluctantly spends the summer with her Japanese American grandparents, where she learns to cope with her parents' separation while creating origami for the family business. (Rev: BL 8/08; SLJ 8/08)

953 Hite, Sid. *The King of Slippery Falls* (6–9). 2004, Scholastic $16.95 (978-0-439-34257-5). Sixteen-year-old adoptee Lewis Hinton believes he may be a descendant of French royalty, and the whole town of Slippery Falls follows the story. (Rev: BCCB 7–8/04; BL 4/15/04; SLJ 5/04; VOYA 8/04)

954 Hoffman, Alice. *Green Angel* (6–12). 2003, Scholastic $16.95 (978-0-439-44384-5). Fifteen-year-old Green, so-called for her gardening skills, is the only member of her family to survive a major disaster. (Rev: BL 4/15/03; HB 3–4/03; HBG 10/03; SLJ 3/03*; VOYA 4/03)

955 Holcomb, Jerry Kimble. *The Chinquapin Tree* (5–9). 1998, Marshall Cavendish $14.95 (978-0-7614-5028-3). Faced with being sent back to their abusive mother, three youngsters head for the wilderness in this survival story set in Oregon. (Rev: BL 5/1/98; HBG 10/98; SLJ 5/98)

956 Holeman, Linda. *Raspberry House Blues* (6–10). 2000, Tundra paper $6.95 (978-0-88776-493-6). Poppy's search for her birth mother looks hopeful for a while when she spends a summer in Winnipeg. (Rev: SLJ 12/00; VOYA 2/01)

957 Holt, Kimberly Willis. *Keeper of the Night* (6–10). 2003, Holt $16.95 (978-0-8050-6361-5). Isabel, a 13-year-old who lives on Guam, tells the story of her mother's suicide and the family's subsequent grief. (Rev: BL 4/15/03; HB 5–6/03; HBG 10/03; SLJ 5/03*; VOYA 6/03)

958 Holt, Kimberly Willis. *My Louisiana Sky* (6–9). 1998, Holt $16.95 (978-0-8050-5251-0). When Tiger Ann's caring grandmother dies, the young girl is tempted to leave her retarded parents and relocate to Baton Rouge to live with an aunt. (Rev: BCCB 6/98; BL 4/15/98; HB 7–8/98*; HBG 9/98; SLJ 7/98; VOYA 8/98)

959 Honeycutt, Natalie. *Twilight in Grace Falls* (5–9). 1997, Orchard LB $17.99 (978-0-531-33007-4). A moving novel about the closing of a lumber mill that brings unemployment to 11-year-old Dasie Jenson's father. (Rev: BCCB 6/97; BL 3/15/97*; HB 7–8/97; SLJ 5/97; VOYA 8/97)

960 Hood, Ann. *How I Saved My Father's Life (And Ruined Everything Else)* (6–8). 2008, Scholastic $16.99 (978-0-439-92819-9). Twelve-year-old Madeline knows that it was her prayers that saved her father from a terrible accident, so she goes to work on becoming religious enough to pray her parents back together. (Rev: BL 12/15/07; SLJ 7/08)

961 Horrocks, Anita. *What They Don't Know* (7–9). 1999, Stoddart paper $8.95 (978-0-7737-6001-1). After Hannah discovers a family secret that involves her identity, she heads down a path of self-destruction that her older sister tries to stop. (Rev: BL 11/1/99; SLJ 8/99; VOYA 10/99)

962 Horvath, Polly. *The Canning Season* (6–9). 2003, Farrar $16.00 (978-0-374-39956-6). Thirteen-year-old Ratchet is sent to live with twin great aunts in Maine in this complex and dark tale that includes some strong language and will appeal to readers interested in adult characters. (Rev: BL 4/1/03; HB 5–6/03*; HBG 10/03; SLJ 5/03*; VOYA 8/03)

963 Horvath, Polly. *The Corps of the Bare-Boned Plane* (6–9). 2007, Farrar $17.00 (978-0-374-31553-5). Teen cousins Jocelyn and Meline move to British Columbia to live with their wealthy uncle after the deaths of their parents, where they try to cope with their grief. (Rev: BL 6/1–15/07; HB 9–10/07; LMC 1/08; SLJ 9/07)

964 Hunter, Evan. *Me and Mr. Stenner* (5–8). 1976, HarperCollins $11.95 (978-0-397-31689-2). Abby's attitudes toward her new stepfather gradually change from resentment to love.

965 Hyde, Catherine Ryan. *The Year of My Miraculous Reappearance* (7–10). 2007, Knopf $15.99 (978-0-375-83257-4). In the void created by her alcoholic mother with her constantly changing boyfriends, Cynnie, 13, treasures her relationship with her young brother; when he is taken away, Cynnie sinks into alcoholism herself. (Rev: BCCB 7–8/07; BL 3/1/07; LMC 4–5/07; SLJ 4/07)

966 Jarrow, Gail. *If Phyllis Were Here* (5–7). 1989, Avon paper $2.75 (978-0-380-70634-1). Libby, age 11, has to learn to adjust to living without her best friend — her grandmother who moves to Florida. (Rev: BL 10/15/87; SLJ 9/87)

967 Johnson, Angela. *Heaven* (6–10). 1998, Simon & Schuster $16.00 (978-0-689-82229-2). Marley, a 14-year-old African American girl, is devastated when she learns that she is adopted and that the couple she has regarded as her mother and father are really her aunt and uncle. (Rev: BCCB 12/98; BL 9/15/98; HBG 3/99; SLJ 10/98; VOYA 2/99)

968 Johnson, Angela. *Songs of Faith* (5–8). 1998, Orchard LB $16.99 (978-0-531-33023-4). Doreen is a child of divorce who is particularly upset by her younger brother's problems adjusting after their father moves away. (Rev: BCCB 6/98; BL 2/15/98; HBG 10/98; SLJ 3/98; VOYA 6/98)

969 Johnson, Peter. *What Happened* (7–12). 2007, Front St. $16.95 (978-1-932425-67-3). A hit-and-run accident reveals long-concealed relationships between the parents of Duane on one side and Kyle and the unnamed narrator on the other side in this novel about troubled young people facing difficult choices. (Rev: BL 5/1/07; SLJ 6/07)

970 Johnston, Lindsay Lee. *Soul Moon Soup* (5–7). 2002, Front St. $15.95 (978-1-886910-87-4). When homeless Phoebe and her mother hit bottom, Phoebe goes to live with her grandmother and slowly learns to value her own resources in this story told in verse. (Rev: BCCB 2/03; BL 11/15/02; HB 1–2/03; HBG 3/03; SLJ 11/02)

971 Jones, Kimberly K. *Sand Dollar Summer* (5–8). 2006, Simon & Schuster $15.95 (978-1-4169-0362-8). Annalise's summer in Maine with her mother and younger, often-mute brother Free takes a dramatic turn when a hurricane hits their island. (Rev: BL 5/15/06; HBG 10/06; LMC 1/07; SLJ 6/06*)

972 Jongman, Mariken. *Rits* (7–9). Trans. by Wanda Boeke. 2008, Front St. $17.95 (978-1-59078-545-4). Rits befriends a neighbor named Rita when family circumstances force him to move in with his unemployed uncle in this novel translated from the Dutch. (Rev: BL 4/15/08; SLJ 5/08)

973 Joosse, Barbara M. *Pieces of the Picture* (5–8). 1989, HarperCollins LB $12.89 (978-0-397-32343-2); paper $3.50 (978-0-06-440310-8). Emily is not happy when she and her mother move to Wisconsin

after her father's death to earn a livelihood running an inn. (Rev: BL 6/1/89; SLJ 4/89)

974 Kadohata, Cynthia. *Outside Beauty* (6–9). 2008, Atheneum $16.99 (978-0-689-86575-6). Four sisters — Shelby, Maddie, Lakey, and Marilyn — are sent to live with their respective fathers after their beautiful mother is in an accident; but the girls need each other and go to great lengths to get back together. (Rev: BL 6/1–15/08; SLJ 7/08)

975 Kearney, Meg. *The Secret of Me* (7–10). 2005, Persea $17.95 (978-0-89255-322-8). Lizzie, 14, is disappointed that her family won't discuss her adoption with her and her obsession with this secret affects her whole life; a novel told in verse. (Rev: BCCB 1/06; SLJ 1/06)

976 Kehret, Peg. *Sisters Long Ago* (5–8). 1992, Pocket paper $3.99 (978-0-671-78433-1). While surviving a near drowning, Willow has a glimpse of herself living another life in ancient Egypt. (Rev: SLJ 3/90)

977 Kelly, Tom. *Finn's Going* (6–9). 2007, Greenwillow $16.99 (978-0-06-121453-0). When his identical twin brother dies, 10-year-old Danny feels that his very existence reminds others of their loss, and he runs away to the island where the family last vacationed together and there finally starts to overcome his grief. (Rev: BL 5/1/07; SLJ 6/07)

978 Kephart, Beth. *House of Dance* (7–10). 2008, HarperTeen $16.99 (978-0-06-142928-6). Fifteen-year-old Rosie's grandfather is dying, and she decides to bring back his youth by throwing a party with ballroom dancing. (Rev: BL 6/1–15/08; SLJ 7/08)

979 Klass, David. *You Don't Know Me* (6–9). 2001, Farrar $17.00 (978-0-374-38706-8). John, 14, retreats into his own world when faced with abuse from his mother's boyfriend. (Rev: BCCB 2/01; BL 3/1/01; HB 7–8/01; HBG 10/01; SLJ 3/01; VOYA 6/01)

980 Klein, Norma. *Breaking Up* (7–10). 1981, Avon paper $2.50 (978-0-380-55830-8). While visiting her divorced father in California, Alison falls in love with her best friend's brother.

981 Klein, Norma. *Mom, the Wolfman and Me* (5–8). 1972, Avon paper $3.50 (978-0-380-00791-2). Brett's mother is single but the Wolfman is becoming more than a steady boyfriend.

982 Klise, Kate. *Deliver Us from Normal* (5–8). 2005, Scholastic $16.95 (978-0-439-52322-6). Charles Harrisong, 11, is embarrassed by his abnormal family life in Normal, Illinois, and horrified when his parents decide to move them all to a houseboat off the Alabama coast. (Rev: BL 3/1/05; SLJ 5/05)

983 Klise, Kate. *Far from Normal* (5–8). 2006, Scholastic $16.99 (978-0-439-79447-3). In this sequel to *Deliver Us from Normal* (2005), the Harrisong family makes a deal with the devil when a retailing giant threatens to sue over disparaging remarks made about the chain in a book written by Charles. (Rev: BL 10/15/06; VOYA 4/07)

984 Koertge, Ron. *Strays* (7–10). 2007, Candlewick $16.99 (978-0-7636-2705-8). After the death of his parents, 16-year-old Ted is placed in foster care and initially finds comfort in talking to animals but gradually learns to trust his roommates and other human beings. (Rev: BL 5/1/07; HB 7–8/07; SLJ 7/07)

985 Kogler, Jennifer Anne. *Ruby Tuesday* (8–10). 2005, HarperCollins LB $16.89 (978-0-06-073957-7). The world of 13-year-old Ruby Tuesday Sweet is turned upside down when her father is arrested for the murder of a bookie. (Rev: BCCB 5/05; SLJ 4/05; VOYA 8/05)

986 Krishnaswami, Uma. *Naming Maya* (5–8). 2004, Farrar $16.00 (978-0-374-35485-5). On a trip to India with her mother, 12-year-old Maya learns some important lessons about herself and the real reasons for the breakup of her parents' marriage. (Rev: BL 4/1/04; HB 7–8/04; SLJ 6/04; VOYA 6/04)

987 Lantz, Francess. *Someone to Love* (7–10). 1997, Avon $14.00 (978-0-380-97477-1). Sara's secure family life changes when her parents decide to adopt the yet-unborn child of Iris, an unmarried teen. (Rev: BL 4/15/97)

988 Leavitt, Martine. *Heck, Superhero!* (7–9). 2004, Front St. $16.95 (978-1-886910-94-2). In this surprisingly upbeat tale, 13-year-old talented artist Heck, left homeless after the sudden disappearance of his mentally ill mother, wanders the streets in search of her. (Rev: BL 10/1/04; SLJ 10/04)

989 Les Becquets, Diane. *Season of Ice* (8–12). 2008, Bloomsbury $16.95 (978-1-59990-063-6). When her father disappears one day, 17-year-old Genesis must deal not only with grief but also with helping to support her stepbrothers in this novel set in wintry northern Maine. (Rev: BL 1/1–15/08; HB 5–6/08; SLJ 4/08)

990 Levoy, Myron. *The Witch of Fourth Street and Other Stories* (4–7). Illus. 1991, Peter Smith $19.75 (978-0-8446-6450-7); HarperCollins paper $5.99 (978-0-06-440059-6). Eight stories about growing up poor on the Lower East Side of New York City.

991 Lewis, Beverly. *Whispers down the Lane* (5–8). Series: Summerhill Secrets. 1995, Bethany paper $5.99 (978-1-55661-476-7). An Amish girl agrees to hide Lissa, who has run away from her father's abusive treatment. (Rev: BL 9/1/95; SLJ 2/96)

992 Lindbergh, Anne. *The Worry Week* (5–7). Illus. by Kathryn Hewitt. 1985, Harcourt $12.95 (978-0-15-299675-8); Avon paper $2.95 (978-0-380-

70394-4). Left alone with her sisters for a week in Maine, 11-year-old "Legs" spends most of her time tending to and worrying about her siblings. (Rev: BL 6/1/85; HB 9–10/85; SLJ 8/85)

993 Love, D. Anne. *Picture Perfect* (6–9). 2007, Simon & Schuster $16.99 (978-0-689-87390-4). When Phoebe's mother decides to leave Texas and take a job in Nevada, Phoebe's life begins to change; she must deal with her dad befriending an attractive widow, her brother getting in trouble with the law, and her first love. (Rev: BL 5/1/07; SLJ 6/07)

994 Lowenstein, Sallie. *Waiting for Eugene* (6–9). Illus. 2005, Lion Stone $19.00 (978-0-9658486-5-7). Twelve-year-old Sara Goldman's father suffers from mental illness and often retreats into memories of his nightmarish experiences in France during World War II. (Rev: BL 12/1/05; SLJ 11/05)

995 Lowry, Lois. *Autumn Street* (7–9). 1980, Houghton $16.00 (978-0-395-27812-3); Dell paper $5.50 (978-0-440-40344-9). With her father away, Elizabeth and her mother and older sister move in with her grandmother. (Rev: BL 12/15/89)

996 Lowry, Lois. *Find a Stranger, Say Goodbye* (7–10). 1978, Houghton $18.00 (978-0-395-26459-1). A college-bound girl decides to find her natural mother.

997 Lowry, Lois. *Rabble Starkey* (6–9). 1987, Houghton $16.00 (978-0-395-43607-3). The story of a friendship between two girls (Rabble and Veronica), their 6th-grade year, and their many experiences with family and friends. (Rev: BL 3/15/87; SLJ 4/87; VOYA 4/87)

998 Lowry, Lois. *Us and Uncle Fraud* (6–9). 1984, Houghton $16.00 (978-0-395-36633-2). Uncle Claude visits his sister and her four children and an experience in human relations begins.

999 Luger, Harriett. *Bye, Bye, Bali Kai* (5–7). 1996, Harcourt paper $5.00 (978-0-15-200863-5). Suzie's family hits rock bottom when they are evicted and forced to live in an abandoned building. (Rev: BCCB 3/96; BL 6/1–15/96; SLJ 6/96; VOYA 6/96)

1000 Lupica, Mike. *Miracle on 49th Street* (5–8). 2006, Philomel $17.99 (978-0-399-24488-9). The life of pro basketball star Josh Cameron is turned upside down when 12-year-old Molly Parker turns up claiming to be his daughter. (Rev: BL 9/1/06; SLJ 11/06) 🌣

1001 Lurie, April. *Dancing in the Streets of Brooklyn* (5–9). 2002, Delacorte LB $17.99 (978-0-385-90066-9). Judy, from a Norwegian immigrant family, is devastated to learn that the man she knows as "Pa" is not her birth father in this novel set in 1944. (Rev: BCCB 12/02; BL 11/15/02; HBG 3/03; SLJ 9/02)

1002 Lyon, Annabel. *All-Season Edie* (5–7). 2008, Orca paper $8.95 (978-1-55143-713-2). Edie, 11, flirts with witchcraft as a solution to her family's problems and to aid her in her quest for coolness; this is a fast-paced first-person narrative full of humor. (Rev: BL 3/1/08)

1003 McCord, Patricia. *Pictures in the Dark* (7–10). 2004, Bloomsbury $16.95 (978-1-58234-848-3). Set in the 1950s, this is the story of two sisters, one 12 and the other 15, and how their mother gradually sank into insanity. (Rev: BL 5/15/04; HB 7–8/04; SLJ 5/04)

1004 MacCullough, Carolyn. *Drawing the Ocean* (8–11). 2006, Roaring Brook $16.95 (978-1-59643-092-1). Sadie, a gifted 16-year-old artist, wants to fit in and be popular at her new school but finds it hard when her dead twin brother still haunts her and she's drawn to an outcast poet named Ryan. (Rev: BL 11/15/06; LMC 2/07; SLJ 2/07)

1005 McDonald, Janet. *Off-Color* (7–12). 2007, Farrar $16.00 (978-0-374-37196-8). When her single mother gets a job on the other side of Brooklyn, 15-year-old Cameron has to leave her white neighborhood and move to the projects, where she learns about diversity and a secret about her absentee father. (Rev: BL 8/07; SLJ 3/08)

1006 McDonald, Janet. *Spellbound* (7–12). 2001, Farrar $16.00 (978-0-374-37140-1). Despite enormous obstacles, 16-year-old African American mother Raven decides to enter a spelling bee in hopes of going to college. (Rev: BCCB 10/01; BL 11/1/01; HB 1–2/02; HBG 3/02; SLJ 9/01; VOYA 10/01)

1007 Mack, Tracy. *Birdland* (7–10). 2003, Scholastic $16.95 (978-0-439-53590-8). Jed's family has not recovered from the death of his brother Zeke, and Jed finds some comfort in videotaping their neighborhood and finding links to Zeke through the poems and journal he left. (Rev: BL 10/15/03*; SLJ 10/03)

1008 McKay, Hilary. *Caddy Ever After* (6–9). 2006, Simon & Schuster $15.95 (978-1-4169-0930-9). The youngest members of the Casson family narrate this funny, moving fourth installment in the series, which focuses on Caddy's proposed marriage to someone other than Darling Michael. (Rev: BL 6/1–15/06; HB 7–8/06; SLJ 7/06)

1009 McKay, Hilary. *Forever Rose* (4–7). 2008, Simon & Schuster $16.99 (978-1-4169-5486-6). Rose, part of the flighty and dramatic Casson family, gets her own book in the series, in which she and her friends cook up a dangerous adventure and her family unveils a series of surprises. (Rev: BL 4/1/08; SLJ 5/08)

1010 McKay, Hilary. *Indigo's Star* (5–8). 2004, Simon & Schuster $15.95 (978-0-689-86563-3). In this sequel to *Saffy's Angel* (2002), Saffy's younger siblings — 12-year-old Indigo and 8-year-old Rose — take a stand against school bullies with the help of a lonely young American called Tom. (Rev: BL 9/15/04; SLJ 9/04*)

1011 McKay, Hilary. *Permanent Rose* (6–9). 2005, Simon & Schuster $15.95 (978-1-4169-0372-7). This third volume of a fast-paced series about the eccentric and colorful Casson family finds all four children — Cadmium, Indigo, Saffron, and Rose — struggling with their individual crises during a hot summer in England. (Rev: BCCB 6/05; BL 5/15/05; HB 7–8/05; SLJ 6/05; VOYA 12/05)

1012 McKay, Hilary. *Saffy's Angel* (4–7). 2002, Simon & Schuster $16.00 (978-0-689-84933-6). Saffron learns she was adopted into her artistic family and travels to Italy in search of her roots. (Rev: BCCB 5/02; BL 5/15/02; HB 7–8/02*; HBG 10/02; SLJ 5/02)

1013 MacLachlan, Patricia. *All the Places to Love* (5–8). Illus. 1994, HarperCollins LB $18.89 (978-0-06-021099-1). This picture book celebrates the love found in an extended rural family and the joy that a new arrival brings. (Rev: BCCB 7–8/94; BL 6/1–15/94*; SLJ 6/94)

1014 MacLachlan, Patricia. *Cassie Binegar* (4–7). 1982, HarperCollins paper $5.99 (978-0-06-440195-1). Cassie is not happy with the disorder in her family situation.

1015 Mansfield, Creina. *Cherokee* (5–8). 2001, O'Brien paper $7.95 (978-0-86278-368-6). Gene's wonderful life with his jazz musician grandfather, Cherokee, comes to an end when his aunt decides he needs a home and an education. (Rev: SLJ 11/01)

1016 Marchetta, Melina. *Saving Francesca* (8–10). 2004, Knopf LB $17.99 (978-0-375-92982-3). Unhappy with life at her new Australian high school, Francesca desperately needs the help and support of her mother, who is struggling with her own battle against depression. (Rev: BL 10/1/04; SLJ 9/04; VOYA 10/04)

1017 Marino, Jan. *For the Love of Pete* (5–8). 1994, Avon paper $3.50 (978-0-380-72281-5). Three devoted servants take Phoebe on a journey to find the father she has never met. (Rev: BCCB 7–8/93; BL 6/1–15/93; SLJ 5/93*)

1018 Martin, Nora. *The Eagle's Shadow* (6–9). Illus. 1997, Scholastic paper $15.95 (978-0-590-36087-6). Twelve-year-old Clearie is sent to live with Tlingit relatives in Alaska and comes to accept the desertion by her mother. (Rev: BL 8/97; HBG 3/98; SLJ 10/97; VOYA 4/98)

1019 Martin, Patricia A. *Travels with Rainie Marie* (5–7). 1997, Hyperion LB $16.49 (978-0-7868-2212-6). When there is no one to care for her and her five brothers and sisters, Rainie Marie is afraid that her bossy aunt will try to split up the family among various relatives. (Rev: BL 5/15/97; SLJ 7/97)

1020 Martinez, Arturo O. *Pedrito's World* (5–7). 2007, Texas Tech Univ. $16.95 (978-0-89672-600-0). In rural south Texas in 1941, 6-year-old Pedrito describes the important things in his life — his first day of school, the death of a friend, a Christmas celebration, his first words of English. (Rev: BL 5/1/07)

1021 Masterman-Smith, Virginia. *First Mate Tate* (7–9). 2000, Marshall Cavendish $14.95 (978-0-7614-5075-7). When her father's gambling brings the family close to financial ruin, First Mate Tate thinks up daring schemes to keep her family afloat. (Rev: BL 10/15/00; HBG 3/01; SLJ 9/00)

1022 Matas, Carol. *Sparks Fly Upward* (4–8). 2002, Clarion $15.00 (978-0-618-15964-2). Set in Manitoba in the early 20th century, this is the story of 12-year-old Rebecca, a Jewish girl, and her life with a Ukrainian foster family. (Rev: BCCB 7–8/02; BL 4/1/02; HBG 10/02; SLJ 3/02)

1023 Matthews, Kezi. *Flying Lessons* (5–7). 2002, Cricket $16.95 (978-0-8126-2671-1). A girl in a small southern town bonds with an eclectic bunch of adults after the airplane in which her mother was traveling disappears. (Rev: BL 12/15/02; HB 1–2/03; HBG 3/03; SLJ 12/02; VOYA 6/03)

1024 Matthews, Kezi. *John Riley's Daughter* (6–9). 2000, Front St. $15.95 (978-0-8126-2775-6). Memphis feels responsible when her mentally disabled aunt, Clover, runs off in this story of tangled family ties. (Rev: BCCB 6/00; HB 7–8/00; HBG 9/00; SLJ 7/00)

1025 Mazer, Norma Fox. *After the Rain* (7–10). 1987, Avon paper $5.99 (978-0-380-75025-2). Rachel gradually develops a warm relationship with her terminally ill grandfather who is noted for his bad temper. (Rev: BL 5/1/87; SLJ 5/87; VOYA 6/87)

1026 Mazer, Norma Fox. *D, My Name Is Danita* (6–8). 1991, Scholastic $13.95 (978-0-590-43655-7). The latest in this light series presents an interesting premise: Girl meets boy who turns out to be her older half-brother. (Rev: BL 4/1/91; SLJ 3/91)

1027 Mazer, Norma Fox. *Downtown* (7–10). 1984, Avon paper $4.95 (978-0-380-88534-3). Pete, 15, the son of anti-war demonstrators who are in hiding, faces problems when his mother reappears and wants to be part of his life.

1028 Mazer, Norma Fox. *Missing Pieces* (7–10). 1995, Morrow $16.00 (978-0-688-13349-8). A 14-year-old seeks a missing part of her life by looking for a father who abandoned her. (Rev: BL 4/1/95; SLJ 4/95*; VOYA 5/95)

1029 Mazer, Norma Fox. *What I Believe* (5–8). 2005, Harcourt $16.00 (978-0-15-201462-9). When

Vicki's father loses his job and the family's fortunes go into free fall, Vicki finds the resulting changes hard to accept and reveals in her poems and journal her coping strategies. (Rev: BL 9/15/05; SLJ 10/05)

1030 Mead, Alice. *Junebug in Trouble* (5–8). 2002, Farrar $16.00 (978-0-374-33969-2). Young Junebug and his mother move out of the housing projects, but Junebug continues to get into the trouble his mother was hoping to avoid. (Rev: BCCB 6/02; BL 4/15/02; HB 5–6/02; HBG 10/02; SLJ 3/02)

1031 Mead, Alice. *Madame Squidley and Beanie* (4–7). 2004, Farrar $16.00 (978-0-374-34688-1). Ten-year-old Beanie's mother has chronic fatigue syndrome and her illness is affecting the 5th-grader's life. (Rev: BL 4/15/04; SLJ 6/04)

1032 Miles, Betty. *Just the Beginning* (6–8). 1978, Avon paper $2.50 (978-0-380-01913-7). Being relatively poor in an upper-class neighborhood causes problems for 13-year-old Catherine Myers.

1033 Modiano, Patrick. *Catherine Certitude* (4–7). Trans. by William Rodarmor. Illus. by Jean-Jacques Sempé. 2001, Godine $17.95 (978-0-87923-959-6). An adult Catherine reminisces about her life as a youngster in Paris — living with her father, puzzling over his job, going to ballet classes, eating in restaurants — in this stylishly illustrated chapter book delivered in picture-book format. (Rev: BL 12/15/01; HBG 3/02; SLJ 2/02)

1034 Montgomery, L. M. *Anne of Green Gables* (7–9). 1995, Puffin paper $4.99 (978-0-14-036741-6). This is a reissue of the classic Canadian story of Anne and how she was gradually accepted in a foster home. Her story continued in *Anne of Avonlea, Anne of the Island, Anne of Windy Poplars, Anne's House of Dreams,* and *Anne of Ingleside.*

1035 Montgomery, L. M. *Christmas with Anne and Other Holiday Stories* (4–7). 1996, McClelland & Stewart $12.95 (978-0-7710-6204-9). A collection of 16 short pieces and stories (two from the Anne of Green Gables books) that deal with Christmas. (Rev: BL 9/1/96)

1036 Montgomery, L. M. *Emily of New Moon* (7–9). 1986, Bantam paper $4.99 (978-0-553-23370-4). Beginning when Emily is only 11, this trilogy continues in *Emily Climbs* and *Emily's Quest* and tells about the making of a writer. These are reissues.

1037 Monthei, Betty. *Looking for Normal* (5–8). 2005, HarperCollins LB $16.89 (978-0-06-072506-8). Annie, 12, and her younger brother are sent to live with their grandparents after their father kills their mother and then himself; unfortunately, life does not improve as they must cope with Grandma's drinking and abuse and Grandpa's indifference. (Rev: BL 6/1–15/05; SLJ 4/05)

1038 Moore, Ishbel. *Daughter* (6–12). 1999, Kids Can $16.95 (978-1-55074-535-1). Sylvie struggles to cope with her parents' divorce and her mother's Alzheimer's disease in this moving story. (Rev: BCCB 12/99; BL 11/15/99; HBG 4/00; SLJ 11/99)

1039 Mori, Kyoko. *One Bird* (8–12). 1996, Fawcett paper $6.50 (978-0-449-70453-0). A coming-of-age story set in Japan about 15-year-old girl Megumi, who loses her mother yet finds people who understand and love her. (Rev: BL 10/15/95; SLJ 11/95; VOYA 2/96)

1040 Mourlevat, Jean-Claude. *The Pull of the Ocean* (5–8). Trans. by Y. Mauder. 2006, Delacorte $15.95 (978-0-385-73348-9). In this modern version of "Tom Thumb," Yann — the smallest and youngest of seven — leads his six older brothers (three sets of twins) away from their dismal home to the ocean that's far to the west, meeting many characters along the way. (Rev: BL 12/1/06; SLJ 1/07*)

1041 Nelson, Theresa. *Earthshine* (5–9). 1994, Orchard LB $17.99 (978-0-531-08717-6). "Slim" decides to live with her father and his lover, who is dying of AIDS. At a support group, she meets Isaiah, whose pregnant mother also has AIDS. (Rev: BL 9/1/94; SLJ 9/94*; VOYA 10/94)

1042 Nelson, Theresa. *Ruby Electric* (5–8). 2003, Simon & Schuster $16.95 (978-0-689-83852-1). The movie script she is writing brings 12-year-old Ruby needed relief from the realities of her life. (Rev: BL 7/03; HB 7–8/03; HBG 10/03; SLJ 6/03*; VOYA 10/03)

1043 Nixon, Joan Lowery. *Maggie Forevermore* (5–8). 1987, Harcourt $13.95 (978-0-15-250345-1). In this sequel to *Maggie, Too* and *And Maggie Makes Three* (both o.p.), 13-year-old Maggie resents spending Christmas with her father and his new wife in California. (Rev: BCCB 4/87; BL 3/1/87; SLJ 3/87)

1044 Nuzum, K. A. *A Small White Scar* (6–9). 2006, HarperCollins $15.99 (978-0-06-075639-0). Will, 15, tries to leave home to become a cowboy, but things get complicated when his brother Denny, who has Down syndrome, follows him. (Rev: BL 8/06; SLJ 8/06*)

1045 Oates, Joyce Carol. *Freaky Green Eyes* (7–10). 2003, HarperCollins LB $17.89 (978-0-06-623757-2). Franky, 15, recounts the tensions between her artist mother and her abusive, controlling father and the buildup to her mother's eventual disappearance. (Rev: BL 12/1/03; HB 11–12/03; HBG 4/04; SLJ 10/03; VOYA 10/03)

1046 Olson, Gretchen. *Call Me Hope* (4–7). 2007, Little, Brown $15.99 (978-0-316-01236-2). Beaten down by her mother's verbal abuse, 11-year-old Hope screws up the courage to confront her mother and tell her how badly she has been hurt by the name calling. (Rev: BL 3/15/07; SLJ 5/07)

1047 Oughton, Jerrie. *Perfect Family* (6–9). 2000, Houghton $15.00 (978-0-395-98668-4). Set in a small town in North Carolina in the 1950s, this is the story of a girl named Welcome, an unwanted pregnancy, and the family that loves and supports her. (Rev: BL 4/15/00; HBG 9/00; SLJ 4/00; VOYA 6/00)

1048 Paratore, Coleen Murtagh. *Willa by Heart* (6–9). Series: Wedding Planner's Daughter. 2008, Simon & Schuster $15.99 (978-1-4169-4076-0). In this third installment in the series, Willa has a busy summer helping to plan two weddings, preparing to become a big sister, and worrying about a beautiful new girl in town. (Rev: BL 2/1/08; SLJ 4/08)

1049 Park, Barbara. *The Graduation of Jake Moon* (5–8). 2000, Simon & Schuster $15.00 (978-0-689-83912-2). Jake Moon finds it impossible to cope with his grandfather's gradual disintegration from Alzheimer's disease. (Rev: BCCB 12/00; BL 6/1–15/00; HB 9–10/00; HBG 3/01; SLJ 9/00)

1050 Parkinson, Siobhan. *Blue like Friday* (4–7). 2008, Roaring Brook $16.95 (978-1-59643-340-3). In Ireland, tweens Olivia and Hal are unlikely friends but Olivia helps Hal to accept his mother's fiancé. (Rev: BL 3/1/08; SLJ 6/08)

1051 Paterson, Katherine. *Come Sing, Jimmy Jo* (6–10). 1985, Avon paper $3.99 (978-0-380-70052-3). The family decides it's time to include James in their singing group. (Rev: BL 9/1/87; SLJ 4/85)

1052 Paterson, Katherine. *Jacob Have I Loved* (6–10). 1980, HarperCollins LB $17.89 (978-0-690-04079-1); paper $6.99 (978-0-06-440368-9). A story set in the Chesapeake Bay region about the rivalry between two sisters. Newbery Medal winner, 1981.

1053 Paterson, Katherine. *Park's Quest* (4–7). 1989, Puffin paper $5.99 (978-0-14-034262-8). A boy searches for the cause of his father's death in Vietnam. (Rev: BCCB 4/88; HB 7–8/88; SLJ 5/88)

1054 Paterson, Katherine. *The Same Stuff as Stars* (5–7). 2002, Clarion $15.00 (978-0-618-24744-8). An unhappy 11-year-old Angel and her younger brother Bernie are sent to live with their father's grandmother, where Angel finds comfort in a mysterious man who introduces her to astronomy. (Rev: BCCB 10/02; BL 9/15/02; HB 9–10/02; HBG 3/03; SLJ 8/02*)

1055 Patneaude, David. *Framed in Fire* (6–9). 1999, Albert Whitman LB $15.99 (978-0-8075-9098-0). Peter Larson, who lives with his mother and verbally abusive stepfather, discovers that his mother has lied to him about the death of his real father and sets out to find the truth. (Rev: BCCB 5/99; HBG 9/99; SLJ 4/99)

1056 Paul, Dominique. *The Possibility of Fireflies* (7–10). 2006, Simon & Schuster $15.95 (978-1-

4169-1310-8). Ellie, 14, lives with an abusive, alcoholic mother and a rebellious older sister but tries to make right choices and looks for support from a neighbor named Leo. (Rev: BL 11/15/06; SLJ 11/06)

1057 Paulsen, Gary. *The Winter Room* (6–8). 1989, Watts LB $16.99 (978-0-531-08439-7). A quiet novel about an 11-year-old boy growing up on a farm in Minnesota. (Rev: BL 11/1/89; SLJ 10/89; VOYA 12/89)

1058 Pearsall, Shelley. *All Shook Up* (5–8). 2008, Knopf $15.99 (978-0-375-83698-5). Josh's divorced dad has a new girlfriend and a new job as an Elvis impersonator, much to Josh's horror. (Rev: BL 5/1/08; SLJ 7/08)

1059 Peck, Richard. *Father Figure* (7–10). 1996, Puffin paper $6.99 (978-0-14-037969-3). Jim and his younger brother are sent to live in Florida with a father they scarcely know.

1060 Peck, Robert Newton. *Bro* (7–9). 2004, HarperCollins $16.99 (978-0-06-052974-1). When his parents' sudden death forces 9-year-old Tug to return to his grandfather's ranch, the scene of an earlier trauma, the boy's older brother, Bro, escapes from a prison labor camp to rescue him; a compelling story set in 1930s Florida. (Rev: BL 3/15/04; SLJ 8/04; VOYA 6/04)

1061 Peck, Robert Newton. *A Day No Pigs Would Die* (7–9). 1973, Knopf $25.00 (978-0-394-48235-4); Random paper $5.50 (978-0-679-85306-0). A Shaker farm boy in Vermont must give up his pet pig to help his family. (Rev: BL 3/1/89)

1062 Pfeffer, Susan Beth. *Devil's Den* (4–7). 1998, Walker $15.95 (978-0-8027-8650-0). Joey faces the pain of rejection when he seeks out his real father, discovers he is not wanted by him, and must accept living permanently with his mom and loving stepfather. (Rev: BCCB 5/98; BL 5/15/98; HBG 10/98; SLJ 6/98)

1063 Prose, Francine. *Bullyville* (7–9). 2007, HarperTeen $16.99 (978-0-06-057497-0). Eighth-grader Bart faces extreme bullying when he gets a scholarship to Bailywell prep school not long after his father dies in the September 11 attacks. (Rev: BL 9/1/07; SLJ 8/07)

1064 Provoost, Anne. *My Aunt Is a Pilot Whale* (6–9). Trans. by Ria Bleumer. 1995, Women's Pr. paper $12.95 (978-0-88961-202-0). A story of family relationships and friendship but also of incest. (Rev: BL 3/1/95)

1065 Resau, Laura. *What the Moon Saw* (6–9). 2006, Delacorte $15.95 (978-0-385-73343-4). Fourteen-year-old Clara travels from Maryland to a remote part of Mexico to visit her father's parents for the first time and learns a lot about her family

and herself while there. (Rev: BL 10/15/06; LMC 2/07; SLJ 9/06)

1066 Reynolds, Marilyn. *Baby Help: True-to-Life Series from Hamilton High* (8–12). Series: Hamilton High. 1998, Morning Glory $15.95 (978-1-885356-26-0); paper $8.95 (978-1-885356-27-7). Partner-abuse is explored in this novel about a teenage mother who is living with a difficult boyfriend and his unsympathetic mother. (Rev: BL 2/1/98; HBG 9/98; SLJ 3/98; VOYA 6/98)

1067 Rinn, Miriam. *The Saturday Secret* (4–7). Illus. 1998, Alef Design Group paper $7.95 (978-1-881283-26-3). Jason's resentment and anger at having to obey the strict rules imposed by his devout Orthodox Jewish stepfather are made more intense because of his grief at the death of his beloved father. (Rev: BL 10/1/98; SLJ 2/99)

1068 Rodowsky, Colby. *That Fernhill Summer* (5–8). 2006, Farrar $16.00 (978-0-374-37442-6). When her grandmother becomes ill, biracial teen Kiara confronts family problems and develops relationships with two white cousins she didn't know existed. (Rev: BL 4/15/06; SLJ 6/06)

1069 Rottman, S. L. *Shadow of a Doubt* (7–10). Illus. 2003, Peachtree $14.95 (978-1-56145-291-0). Shadow is newly 15 and entering high school when his brother Daniel, who has been missing for years, reappears on the scene, suspected of murder. (Rev: BCCB 1/04; BL 11/15/03; HBG 4/04; SLJ 1/04; VOYA 12/03)

1070 Russo, Marisabina. *A Portrait of Pia* (5–8). 2007, Harcourt $17.00 (978-0-15-205577-6). Overwhelmed by her brother's schizophrenia and her mother's new boyfriend, 12-year-old Pia, already a talented artist, travels to Italy to meet her long-absent father and learns how to love her family despite its flaws. (Rev: BL 4/1/07; SLJ 8/07)

1071 Ryan, Darlene. *Rules for Life* (7–12). 2004, Orca paper $7.95 (978-1-55143-350-9). Sixteen-year-old Izzy, whose mother died two years earlier, has difficulty coming to terms with her father's decision to remarry; suitable for reluctant readers. (Rev: BCCB 2/05; SLJ 3/05; VOYA 6/05)

1072 Ryan, Pam Muñoz. *Paint the Wind* (4–7). 2007, Scholastic $16.99 (978-0-439-87362-8). On the death of her grandmother — who has been a distant and strict guardian — orphaned 11-year-old Maya is sent to relatives in Wyoming, where she learns about the love of horses and family. (Rev: BL 11/15/07; LMC 1/08; SLJ 11/07)

1073 Sachs, Marilyn. *Baby Sister* (7–10). 1986, Avon paper $3.50 (978-0-380-70358-6). Penny is torn between her admiration for her older sister and the realization that she is really selfish. (Rev: BL 2/15/86; SLJ 8/86; VOYA 8/86)

1074 Sachs, Marilyn. *Just Like a Friend* (6–9). 1990, Avon paper $2.95 (978-0-380-70964-9). The friendship between a mother and a daughter falls apart when father has a heart attack. (Rev: BL 10/15/89; SLJ 12/89; VOYA 12/89)

1075 St. Anthony, Jane. *Grace above All* (5–7). 2007, Farrar $16.00 (978-0-374-39940-5). In this gentle story set in the 1960s, 13-year-old Grace expects to have a boring summer watching over her siblings but a neighboring boy and Great Aunt Hilda provide unexpected interest. (Rev: BL 5/15/07; SLJ 7/07)

1076 Salmansohn, Karen. *Wherever I Go, There I Am* (4–7). Illus. by author. Series: Alexandra Rambles On! 2002, Tricycle $12.95 (978-1-58246-079-6). Alexandra's journal reveals her angst about issues such as scary movies and becoming a teenager. (Rev: HBG 3/03; SLJ 2/03)

1077 Savage, Deborah. *Summer Hawk* (7–10). 1999, Houghton $16.00 (978-0-395-91163-1). In this coming-of-age story, 15-year-old Taylor has trouble relating to her mother and father, shuns the company of Rail Bogart, the other smart kid in her school, and showers her attention and affection on a young hawk she rescues. (Rev: BCCB 6/99; BL 3/1/99; HBG 9/99; SLJ 4/99; VOYA 4/99)

1078 Sebestyen, Ouida. *Far from Home* (7–10). 1980, Little, Brown $15.95 (978-0-316-77932-6). An orphaned boy is taken in by a couple who run a boardinghouse and there he uncovers secrets about his family's past.

1079 Seidler, Tor. *Brothers Below Zero* (5–8). 2002, HarperCollins LB $15.89 (978-0-06-029180-8). Artistic Tim, overwhelmed by his athletic younger brother, eventually runs away to the place he has felt most valued. (Rev: BCCB 3/02; BL 1/1–15/02; HBG 10/02; SLJ 4/02)

1080 Shafer, Audrey. *The Mailbox* (5–7). 2006, Delacorte $15.95 (978-0-385-73344-1). Twelve-year-old Gabe, who has been happy with Uncle Vernon after years in foster care, is shocked when he comes home to find Uncle Vernon dead. (Rev: SLJ 11/06) ⏚

1081 Shearer, Alex. *The Great Blue Yonder* (5–8). 2002, Clarion $15.00 (978-0-618-21257-6). Twelve-year-old Harry, who has died in an accident, experiences afterlife on the Other Side and has the opportunity to review his relations with other family members. (Rev: BCCB 6/02; HBG 10/02; SLJ 4/02; VOYA 6/02)

1082 Shimko, Bonnie. *Letters in the Attic* (7–12). 2002, Academy Chicago $23.50 (978-0-89733-511-9). Twelve-year-old Lizzie and her mother move to upstate New York after her father leaves home, and there Lizzie finds new attachments and a new understanding of her mother's behavior. (Rev: VOYA 4/03)

1083 Shusterman, Neal. *What Daddy Did* (7–10). 1991, Little, Brown paper $15.95 (978-0-316-78906-6). A young boy recounts the story of how his father murdered his mother and how he ultimately comes to understand and forgive him. (Rev: BL 7/91; SLJ 6/91)

1084 Simmons, Michael. *Vandal* (7–10). 2006, Roaring Brook $16.95 (978-1-59643-070-9). In a story laced with tragedy, 16-year-old guitar player Will struggles to forge a relationship with his destructive older brother. (Rev: BL 7/06; HB 7–8/06; LMC 11–12/06; SLJ 6/06)

1085 Slate, Joseph. *Crossing the Trestle* (5–8). 1999, Marshall Cavendish $14.95 (978-0-7614-5053-5). Set in West Virginia in 1944, this novel centers on 11-year-old Petey and the problems he and his family face after their father is killed in an accident. (Rev: BCCB 12/99; BL 1/1–15/00; HBG 3/00; SLJ 10/99)

1086 Smith, Anne Warren. *Sister in the Shadow* (7–10). 1986, Avon paper $2.75 (978-0-380-70378-4). In competition with her successful younger sister, Sharon becomes a live-in baby-sitter, with unhappy results. (Rev: BL 5/1/86; SLJ 5/86; VOYA 8/86)

1087 Sones, Sonya. *One of Those Hideous Books Where the Mother Dies* (7–12). 2004, Simon & Schuster $15.95 (978-0-689-85820-8). In this free-verse novel, a high schooler, after the death of her mother, is sent to live with her father, a famous movie actor whom she detests. (Rev: BL 5/1/04*; SLJ 8/04)

1088 Sonnenblick, Jordan. *Notes from the Midnight Driver* (8–11). 2006, Scholastic $16.99 (978-0-439-75779-9). Unhappy about his parents' separation, 16-year-old Alex drives drunk and ends up with a sentence of 100 hours of community service at a nursing home, during which he ends up learning some very valuable life lessons from an older man named Solomon. (Rev: BL 10/1/06; SLJ 10/06)

1089 Sparks, Beatrice, ed. *Finding Katie: The Diary of Anonymous, a Teenager in Foster Care* (7–10). 2005, Avon paper $5.99 (978-0-06-050721-3). In this angst-filled fictional diary, Katie, a teenager living on a California estate, makes it clear that money and privilege do nothing to ensure a happy life. (Rev: SLJ 10/05)

1090 Spollen, Anne. *The Shape of Water* (7–10). 2008, Flux paper $9.95 (978-0-7387-1101-0). Fifteen-year-old Magda initially grieves her artistic mother's death by committing arson and imagining talking fish. (Rev: BLO 6/17/08; SLJ 6/08)

1091 Springer, Nancy. *Separate Sisters* (5–7). 2001, Holiday $16.95 (978-0-8234-1544-1). Two teenage girls deal with the divorce of their parents in different ways. (Rev: BCCB 2/02; BL 2/1/02; HB 3–4/02; HBG 10/02; SLJ 2/02; VOYA 4/02)

1092 Stacey, Cherylyn. *How Do You Spell Abducted?* (4–8). 1996, Red Deer paper $7.95 (978-0-88995-148-8). When their divorced father abducts Deb, Paige, and Cory, the three youngsters must escape from his home in the U.S. and make their way back to their mother in Canada. (Rev: SLJ 12/96)

1093 Stauffacher, Sue. *Harry Sue* (5–8). 2005, Knopf LB $17.99 (978-0-375-93274-8). Both her parents are in prison and 11-year-old Harry Sue Clotkin acts as tough as she can in the face of a difficult life with her grandmother. (Rev: BL 5/1/05; SLJ 8/05)

1094 Strauss, Linda Leopold. *Really, Truly, Everything's Fine* (5–8). 2004, Marshall Cavendish $15.95 (978-0-7614-5163-1). Life changes dramatically for 14-year-old Jill Rider when her father is arrested for jewelry theft. (Rev: BL 5/15/04; SLJ 7/04)

1095 Swanson, Julie A. *Going for the Record* (7–12). 2004, Eerdmans paper $8.00 (978-0-8028-5273-1). High school soccer star Leah Weiczynkowski finds herself torn between family responsibilities and her sports aspirations when her father is diagnosed with terminal cancer. (Rev: BL 9/1/04*; SLJ 8/04; VOYA 10/04)

1096 Sweeney, Joyce. *Headlock: A Novel* (8–10). 2006, Holt $16.95 (978-0-8050-8018-6). Kyle, 18, wants to become a professional wrestler but must put his dream aside when his grandmother becomes ill. (Rev: BL 11/1/06; SLJ 11/06)

1097 Talbert, Marc. *The Purple Heart* (5–8). 1992, HarperCollins $14.95 (978-0-06-020428-0); Avon paper $3.50 (978-0-380-71985-3). Luke's father has returned from Vietnam an anguished, brooding war hero, and Luke loses his father's Purple Heart, leading to confrontation and reconciliation. (Rev: BL 12/15/91*; SLJ 2/92)

1098 Thesman, Jean. *The Last April Dancers* (7–10). 1987, Avon paper $2.75 (978-0-380-70614-3). Catherine tries to recover from the guilt caused by her father's suicide through friendship and love of a neighboring boy. (Rev: BL 9/15/87; SLJ 10/87; VOYA 10/87)

1099 Thomson, John. *A Small Boat at the Bottom of the Sea* (5–7). 2005, Milkweed $16.95 (978-1-57131-657-8); paper $6.95 (978-1-57131-656-1). Upset and angry when he's sent to spend the summer with his ex-con uncle and dying aunt on Puget Sound, 12-year-old Donovan begins to develop a closer relationship with his uncle as his vacation progresses. (Rev: SLJ 10/05; VOYA 4/06)

1100 Tilly, Meg. *Porcupine* (5–8). 2007, Tundra $15.95 (978-0-88776-810-1). Jacqueline and her younger brother and sister go to Canada to live with a great-grandmother after their father dies in Afghanistan. (Rev: BL 11/15/07; SLJ 12/07)

1101 Torres, Laura. *Crossing Montana* (7–10). 2002, Holiday $16.95 (978-0-8234-1643-1). Callie sets off on a journey across Montana in search of her missing grandfather, and in the process finds out the truth about her father's death. (Rev: BCCB 10/02; BL 8/02; HBG 10/02; SLJ 7/02; VOYA 8/02)

1102 Trembath, Don. *The Popsicle Journal* (7–12). 2001, Orca paper $6.95 (978-1-55143-185-7). Fledgling journalist Harper Winslow finds himself torn between professional responsibility and family loyalty when his sister is involved in a DUI auto accident while his father is running for mayor. (Rev: SLJ 7/02; VOYA 4/02)

1103 Trueman, Terry. *Cruise Control* (7–10). 2004, HarperCollins LB $16.89 (978-0-06-623961-3). High school senior Paul McDaniel is a star athlete, but he's filled with rage over his brother's disabilities and his father's desertion; a companion to *Stuck in Neutral* (2000). (Rev: BCCB 11/04; BL 3/15/05; SLJ 1/05; VOYA 10/04)

1104 Underdahl, S. T. *The Other Sister* (7–12). 2007, Flux paper $8.95 (978-0-7387-0933-8). The happy, secure life of 15-year-old Josey Muller is turned upside down when her parents tell her that she has an older sister, conceived when they were in high school and given up for adoption. (Rev: SLJ 3/07)

1105 Valgardson, W. D. *Frances* (6–10). 2000, Groundwood $15.95 (978-0-88899-386-1); paper $5.95 (978-0-88899-397-7). Growing up in Manitoba, young Frances probes into her Icelandic background and uncovers many family secrets, past and present. (Rev: BL 9/1/00; HBG 3/01; SLJ 9/00; VOYA 2/01)

1106 Van Draanen, Wendelin. *Runaway* (6–9). 2006, Knopf $15.95 (978-0-375-83522-3). After Holly's mother dies of a drug overdose, Holly initially goes to foster homes but decides that being on her own is better; she keeps a journal as she makes her way to Los Angeles, struggling to find food, shelter, and warmth. (Rev: BL 9/1/06; SLJ 9/06)

1107 Van Steenwyk, Elizabeth. *Three Dog Winter* (5–8). 1987, Walker $13.95 (978-0-8027-6718-9). A story of dog racing, this family tale tells of 12-year-old Scott and his Malamute, Kaylah. (Rev: BL 2/1/88; SLJ 12/87)

1108 Velasquez, Gloria. *Rina's Family Secret* (8–12). Series: Roosevelt High School. 1998, Arte Publico paper $9.95 (978-1-55885-233-4). Puerto Rican teenager Rina cannot endure life with her alcoholic stepfather, and so moves in with her grandmother. Also use *Tyrone's Betrayal* (2006). (Rev: BL 8/98; SLJ 10/98)

1109 Viglucci, Patricia C. *Sun Dance at Turtle Rock* (5–7). 1996, Patri paper $4.95 (978-0-9645914-9-3). The child of a racially mixed marriage feels uncomfortable when he visits his white grandfather. (Rev: BL 4/15/96)

1110 Villareal, Ray. *My Father, the Angel of Death* (5–8). 2006, Piñata paper $9.95 (978-1-55885-466-6). Newly relocated to Texas and unhappy with his home life, Jesse Baron wonders what life would be like if his dad were not the well-known wrestler called the Angel of Death; suitable for reluctant readers. (Rev: SLJ 10/06)

1111 Vincent, Zu. *The Lucky Place* (7–10). 2008, Front St. $17.95 (978-1-932425-70-3). Cassie struggles with the reality of having a stepfather as well as an "Old Daddy," especially when her stepfather becomes ill. (Rev: BL 5/1/08; SLJ 5/08)

1112 Voigt, Cynthia. *Dicey's Song* (5–9). 1982, Macmillan $17.95 (978-0-689-30944-1). This story of Dicey's life with her "Gram" in Maryland won a Newbery Medal (1983). Preceding it was *Homecoming* (1981) and a sequel is *A Solitary Blue* (1983). (Rev: BL 12/15/89)

1113 Waldorf, Heather. *Grist* (7–10). 2006, Red Deer paper $9.95 (978-0-88995-347-5). Sixteen-year-old Charlie decides to spend the summer with her grandmother at Lake Ringrose, Ontario, and discovers some secrets about her past while there. (Rev: BL 11/1/06; SLJ 1/07)

1114 Walker, Pamela. *Pray Hard* (5–8). 2001, Scholastic paper $15.95 (978-0-439-21586-2). After Amelia Forest's father dies in an airplane accident for which she feels responsible, her life and that of her family fall apart. (Rev: BL 3/1/01; HBG 10/01; SLJ 7/01; VOYA 8/01)

1115 Wallace, Bill. *Beauty* (5–7). 1988, Holiday $16.95 (978-0-8234-0715-6). Luke finds the adjustment difficult when he and his mother go to live on his grandfather's Oklahoma farm. (Rev: BCCB 11/88; BL 2/1/89; SLJ 10/88)

1116 Wallace, Bill. *True Friends* (4–7). 1994, Holiday $15.95 (978-0-8234-1141-2). Everything in Courtney's life becomes a shambles and she must rely on her new friend Judy to help her. (Rev: BCCB 11/94; BL 10/15/94; SLJ 10/94)

1117 Walsh, Marissa. *A Field Guide to High School* (7–9). 2007, Delacorte $14.99 (978-0-385-73410-3). When Andie's perfect sister Claire leaves for college she gives Andie a field guide, full of advice on how to navigate the world of private high school. (Rev: BL 6/1–15/07; SLJ 9/07)

1118 Weeks, Sarah. *My Guy* (4–7). 2001, HarperCollins LB $14.89 (978-0-06-028370-4). Guy and Lana agree on only one thing — they don't want to become part of a blended family — and they set out to make sure it won't happen. (Rev: BCCB 6/01; BL 8/01; HB 7–8/01; HBG 10/01; SLJ 5/01)

1119 Weissenberg, Fran. *The Streets Are Paved with Gold* (7–9). 1990, Harbinger paper $6.95 (978-0-943173-51-1). Debbie is from a poor immigrant Jewish family and she is ashamed to bring her friends home. (Rev: BL 8/90; SLJ 8/90)

1120 Werlin, Nancy. *The Rules of Survival* (7–10). 2006, Dial $16.99 (978-0-8037-3001-4). Written as a letter to his younger sister Emmy, Matt tells the story of their abusive mother, their everyday struggles to stay safe, and their search for an adult who is willing to help free them from the situation. (Rev: BL 8/06; SLJ 9/06)

1121 White, Ellen Emerson. *The President's Daughter* (7–10). 2008, Feiwel and Friends paper $8.99 (978-0-312-37488-4). Meg Powers, 16, is not pleased when her mother runs for and wins the presidency; an update of a book first published in 1984. (Rev: BL 8/08)

1122 White, Ellen Emerson. *White House Autumn* (7–10). 1985, Avon paper $2.95 (978-0-380-89780-3). The daughter of the first female president of the United States feels her family is coming apart after an assassination attempt on her mother. (Rev: BL 11/1/85; SLJ 2/86; VOYA 4/86)

1123 White, Ruth. *Belle Prater's Boy* (5–9). 1996, Farrar $17.00 (978-0-374-30668-7). Set in Appalachia in the 1950s, this moving, often humorous story tells about Gypsy and her unusual cousin Woodrow, who hides a secret involving his mother's disappearance. (Rev: BL 4/15/96; SLJ 4/96*)

1124 White, Ruth. *Tadpole* (5–8). 2003, Farrar $16.00 (978-0-374-31002-8). In this novel set in 1950s Appalachia, uncertain 10-year-old Carolina finds her own strengths when her 13-year-old cousin Tadpole arrives, running away from an abusive uncle. (Rev: BL 5/1/03; HB 5–6/03; HBG 10/03; SLJ 3/03*)

1125 Wilder, Laura Ingalls. *Little House in the Big Woods* (4–7). Illus. by Garth Williams. 1953, HarperCollins LB $17.89 (978-0-06-026431-4); paper $6.99 (978-0-06-440001-5). Outstanding story of a log-cabin family in Wisconsin in the late 1800s. Also use *By the Shores of Silver Lake; Farmer Boy; Little House on the Prairie; Long Winter; On the Banks of Plum Creek; These Happy Golden Years* (all 1953); *Little Town on the Prairie* (1961); *The First Four Years* (1971).

1126 Willis, Patricia. *The Barn Burner* (5–8). 2000, Clarion $15.00 (978-0-395-98409-3). In 1933, 14-year-old Ross, a runaway, becomes involved with the Warfield family whose father is away looking for work. (Rev: BCCB 5/00; BL 4/15/00; HBG 10/00; SLJ 7/00)

1127 Wilson, Nancy Hope. *Mountain Pose* (5–7). 2001, Farrar $17.00 (978-0-374-35078-9). Ellie is surprised to inherit her grandmother's farm, but when she reads the diaries left for her she begins to understand more about her family. (Rev: BCCB

6/01; BL 8/01; HB 7–8/01; HBG 10/01; SLJ 4/01*; VOYA 6/01)

1128 Wolff, Virginia E. *Make Lemonade* (7–12). 1993, Holt $17.95 (978-0-8050-2228-5). Rooted in the community of poverty, this story offers a penetrating view of the conditions that foster ignorance, destroy self-esteem, and challenge strength. (Rev: BL 6/1–15/93*; SLJ 7/93*; VOYA 10/93)

1129 Woodson, Jacqueline. *Hush* (5–9). 2002, Putnam $15.99 (978-0-399-23114-8). A girl and her family are relocated in the witness protection program after her father, a police officer, testifies against fellow cops in a case that involves racial prejudice. (Rev: BCCB 3/02; BL 1/1–15/02; HB 1–2/02; HBG 10/02; SLJ 2/02*; VOYA 2/02)

1130 Woodson, Jacqueline. *Miracle's Boys* (6–10). 2000, Putnam $15.99 (978-0-399-23113-1). Twelve-year-old African American LaFayette, growing up in a poor inner-city environment, is cared for by his oldest brother who is also responsible for the troubled middle brother, Charlie. (Rev: BL 2/15/00; HB 3–4/00; HBG 9/00; SLJ 5/00; VOYA 4/00)

1131 Woodworth, Chris. *When Ratboy Lived Next Door* (4–8). 2005, Farrar $16.00 (978-0-374-34677-5). Twelve-year-old Lydia takes an instant dislike to her new neighbor Willis and his pet raccoon, but as she gains a better understanding of the family dynamics that make the boy who he is, she also gains valuable insights into her strained relationship with her mother. (Rev: BCCB 2/05; BL 1/1–15/05; SLJ 3/05)

Physical and Emotional Problems

1132 Abbott, Tony. *Firegirl* (5–8). 2006, Little, Brown $15.99 (978-0-316-01171-6). Tom, already an outsider at his Catholic school, bravely befriends a girl scarred by burns even when his classmates ostracize and ridicule her. (Rev: BL 7/06; SLJ 7/06)

1133 Bingham, Kelly. *Shark Girl* (7–10). 2007, Candlewick $16.99 (978-0-7636-3207-6). When she's attacked by a shark and loses an arm, 15-year-old Jane feels divorced from her former popular self and has trouble adjusting to her new life. (Rev: BL 5/1/07; SLJ 6/07)

1134 Blume, Judy. *Deenie* (5–8). 1982, Dell paper $5.50 (978-0-440-93259-8). Instead of becoming a model, Deenie must cope with scoliosis and wearing a back brace.

1135 Brooks, Bruce. *Vanishing* (5–8). 1999, HarperCollins LB $14.89 (978-0-06-028237-0). A challenging novel about a hospitalized girl who gives up eating so she can't be sent home to her dysfunctional family, and the boy she meets who is in remission from a fatal disease. (Rev: BL 5/15/99; HB 5–6/99; HBG 10/99; SLJ 6/99; VOYA 10/99)

1136 Brothers, Meagan. *Debbie Harry Sings in French* (8–12). 2008, Holt $16.95 (978-0-8050-8080-3). Johnny, who has struggled with alcohol and bullies who think he is gay, is encouraged by his girlfriend to pursue his passion and sing in drag. (Rev: BL 4/1/08; SLJ 9/08)

1137 Brown, Kay. *Willy's Summer Dream* (6–9). 1989, Harcourt $13.95 (978-0-15-200645-7). Willy lacks confidence because he is a slow learner. (Rev: BL 2/1/90; SLJ 12/89)

1138 Bryson, Bill. *Choices* (7–10). 2007, Roaring Brook $16.95 (978-1-59643-217-8). Kathleen finds herself switching between realities after her brother is killed on his way to pick her up; when she meets Luke, this "phase shifting" takes on more meaning. (Rev: BL 9/1/07; SLJ 10/07)

1139 Buchanan, Dawna Lisa. *The Falcon's Wing* (6–9). 1992, Orchard paper $16.99 (978-0-531-08586-8). A teenage girl learns to understand and defend her retarded cousin. (Rev: BL 2/1/92; SLJ 4/92)

1140 Buckley, James. *The Very Ordered Existence of Merilee Marvelous* (5–8). 2007, Greenwillow $16.99 (978-0-06-123197-1). Marilee, a bright young girl with Asperger's syndrome, enjoys order in her life until a new boy in town — Biswick, who has fetal alcohol syndrome — decides to attach himself to her. (Rev: BL 9/1/07; SLJ 10/07)

1141 Butts, Nancy. *Cheshire Moon* (5–7). 1996, Front St. $14.95 (978-1-886910-08-9). A friendless deaf girl grieves for a cousin who has drowned at sea in this novel in an island setting. (Rev: BL 10/15/96; SLJ 11/96; VOYA 4/97)

1142 Byars, Betsy. *The Summer of the Swans* (5–7). Illus. by Ted Coconis. 1970, Puffin paper $5.99 (978-0-14-031420-5). The story of a 14-year-old named Sara — moody, unpredictable, and on the brink of womanhood — and how her life changes when her younger, mentally retarded brother disappears. Newbery Medal winner, 1971.

1143 Carter, Anne Laurel. *In the Clear* (4–7). 2001, Orca paper $6.95 (978-1-55143-192-5). A 12-year-old Canadian polio survivor in the 1950s works through her fears and struggles to recapture her lost childhood. (Rev: BL 11/15/01; SLJ 1/02)

1144 Chappell, Crissa-Jean. *Total Constant Order* (7–10). 2007, HarperTeen $16.99 (978-0-06-088605-9). Plagued by obsessive-compulsive behavior, 9th-grader Frances (called Fin) finds some relief when she meets Thayer, who has ADD, and starts seeing a new therapist. (Rev: BL 11/15/07; SLJ 1/08)

1145 Cleaver, Vera, and Bill Cleaver. *Me Too* (7–9). 1973, HarperCollins $13.95 (978-0-397-31485-0); paper $2.95 (978-0-06-440161-6). Linda is convinced that she can make her slightly retarded sister normal.

1146 Cole, Barbara. *Alex the Great* (8–12). 1989, Rosen LB $12.95 (978-0-8239-0941-4). The events leading up to Alex's drug overdose are told first by Alex and then by her friend, Deonna. (Rev: VOYA 8/89)

1147 Cormier, Robert. *The Bumblebee Flies Anyway* (7–12). 1983, Dell paper $4.99 (978-0-440-90871-5). A terminally ill boy and his gradual realization of his situation.

1148 Crane, E. M. *Skin Deep* (7–10). 2008, Delacorte $16.99 (978-0-385-73479-0). Andrea, 16, befriends a woman named Honora, who is dying of cancer but teaches the unhappy girl a lot about life. (Rev: BL 1/1–15/08; SLJ 5/08)

1149 Davis, Rebecca Fjelland. *Jake Riley: Irreparably Damaged* (7–10). 2003, HarperCollins LB $16.89 (978-0-06-051838-7). Lainey, a farm girl, struggles to cope with her friend Jake, a 15-year-old with frightening emotional problems. (Rev: BL 9/1/03; HBG 10/03; SLJ 7/03; VOYA 10/03)

1150 Denenberg, Barry. *Mirror, Mirror on the Wall: The Diary of Bess Brennan* (4–8). Series: Dear America. 2002, Scholastic paper $10.95 (978-0-439-19446-4). When she comes home at weekends, 12-year-old Bess, who has lost her sight, shares her new life and school experiences with her twin sister, in this novel set in the Depression that includes many details of how the blind cope. (Rev: BL 10/1/02; HBG 3/03; SLJ 10/02)

1151 Dewey, Jennifer Owlings. *Borderlands* (7–12). 2002, Marshall Cavendish $14.95 (978-0-7614-5114-3). When Jamie, an unhappy 17-year-old, is hospitalized after a suicide attempt she finds new friends and slowly comes to terms with her difficult relationship with her parents. (Rev: BL 9/1/02; HBG 10/02; SLJ 7/02)

1152 Diersch, Sandra. *Ceiling Stars* (7–12). Series: SideStreets. 2004, Lorimer paper $4.99 (978-1-55028-834-6). The close friendship of two high school girls is put to the test when one falls victim to mental illness and begins acting strangely; suitable for reluctant readers. (Rev: SLJ 1/05)

1153 Diezeno, Patricia. *Why Me? The Story of Jenny* (7–10). 1976, Avon paper $3.50 (978-0-380-00563-5). A young rape victim doesn't know how to cope.

1154 Doyle, Malachy. *Georgie* (6–10). 2002, Bloomsbury $13.95 (978-1-58234-753-0). Georgie, 14, who has buried horrible memories under a cloak of isolation, slowly learns to trust his teacher and recovers his sanity. (Rev: BCCB 11/02; BL 9/1/02; SLJ 7/02; VOYA 12/03)

1155 Draper, Sharon M. *Tears of a Tiger* (7–10). 1994, Atheneum $16.95 (978-0-689-31878-8). A star basketball player is killed in an accident after he and his friends drink and drive. The driver, who survives, is depressed and ultimately commits suicide. (Rev: BL 11/1/94; SLJ 2/95)

1156 Dreyer, Ellen. *The Glow Stone* (8–12). 2006, Peachtree $15.95 (978-1-56145-370-2). When 15-year-old Phoebe begins to suspect that her uncle's death was not an accident, she journeys into a metaphorical and actual cave. (Rev: SLJ 7/06)

1157 Edwards, Johanna. *The Next Big Thing* (8–12). 2005, Berkley paper $14.00 (978-0-425-20028-5). Kat, determined to lose weight to win the heart of her online boyfriend, lands a spot on a reality TV makeover show but finds in the end that she likes herself just the way she is. (Rev: SLJ 11/05)

1158 Ellis, Ann Dee. *This Is What I Did* (6–9). 2007, Little, Brown $16.99 (978-0-316-01363-5). After witnessing a violent encounter between his best friend Zyler and Zyler's abusive father, Logan struggles to cope and finds comfort in a new friendship, help from a counselor, and a part in the school play; this novel will appeal to reluctant readers. (Rev: BL 5/15/07; SLJ 10/07)

1159 Farnes, Catherine. *Snow* (5–9). 1999, Bob Jones Univ. $6.49 (978-1-57924-199-5). A thoughtful novel about an albino girl's problems being accepted, even among students who profess to have Christian charity. (Rev: BL 7/99)

1160 Fensham, Elizabeth. *Helicopter Man* (6–9). 2005, Bloomsbury $15.95 (978-1-58234-981-7). Twelve-year-old Peter's journal entries reveal the difficulties of living with a single parent who is schizophrenic; set in Australia. (Rev: BL 8/05; SLJ 6/05; VOYA 6/05)

1161 Fields, Terri. *After the Death of Anna Gonzales* (7–12). 2002, Holt $16.95 (978-0-8050-7127-6). A collection of poems written by her friends reveals the terrible aftermath of a teenager's suicide. (Rev: BL 12/15/02; HBG 3/03; SLJ 11/02; VOYA 12/02)

1162 Fraustino, Lisa Rowe, ed. *Don't Cramp My Style: Stories About That Time of the Month* (8–12). 2004, Simon & Schuster $15.95 (978-0-689-85882-6). This collection of stories about girls' menstrual periods includes fiction about different places, cultures, and times. (Rev: BL 3/1/04; HB 3–4/04; SLJ 4/04; VOYA 4/04)

1163 Friend, Natasha. *Perfect* (6–9). 2004, Milkweed $16.95 (978-1-57131-652-3); paper $6.95 (978-1-57131-651-6). Thirteen-year-old Isabelle Lee struggles to recover from an eating disorder that began shortly after the death of her father. (Rev: BL 1/1–15/05; SLJ 12/04)

1164 Galante, Cecilia. *Hershey Herself* (5–8). 2008, Aladdin paper $5.99 (978-1-4169-5463-7). While living at a shelter for battered women with her mother and younger sister, Hershey discovers real friends and a real talent. (Rev: BL 5/15/08)

1165 Gantos, Jack. *Joey Pigza Loses Control* (4–7). 2000, Farrar $16.00 (978-0-374-39989-4). Joey, a hyperactive kid, tries to please his father but goes haywire when his father destroys his medication in this Newbery Honor Book. (Rev: BCCB 9/00*; BL 9/1/00*; HB 9–10/00; HBG 3/01; SLJ 9/00; VOYA 2/01)

1166 Gantos, Jack. *Joey Pigza Swallowed the Key* (4–8). 1998, Farrar $16.00 (978-0-374-33664-6). Joey, who suffers from attention deficit disorder, causes so much trouble that he is sent to a special education center, where he learns to cope with his problem. (Rev: BCCB 11/98; BL 12/15/98; HB 11–12/98; HBG 3/99; SLJ 12/98*; VOYA 2/99)

1167 Gantos, Jack. *What Would Joey Do?* (5–8). 2002, Farrar $16.00 (978-0-374-39986-3). Hyperactive Joey is nearly overwhelmed by the antics of his parents, his dying grandmother, and the needs of his blind homeschool partner, but manages to cope in his own unusual way in this final installment in the Joey Pigza trilogy. (Rev: BCCB 11/02; BL 10/1/02*; HB 11–12/02; HBG 3/03; SLJ 9/02*; VOYA 12/02)

1168 Garden, Nancy. *Endgame* (8–12). 2006, Harcourt $16 (978-0-15-205416-8). While awaiting his murder trial, 15-year-old Gray Wilton reveals in a series of interviews with his lawyer the extreme bullying, both physical and emotional, that finally drove him to take a gun to school. (Rev: SLJ 5/06*)

1169 Going, K. L. *Fat Kid Rules the World* (8–12). 2003, Putnam $17.99 (978-0-399-23990-8). An unlikely but beneficial friendship develops between suicidal, 300-pound Troy and dropout punk rock guitarist Curt. (Rev: BCCB 6/03*; BL 5/15/03*; HB 7–8/03; HBG 10/03; SLJ 5/03*; VOYA 6/03)

1170 Goobie, Beth. *The Dream Where the Losers Go* (7–12). 2006, Orca paper $8.95 (978-1-55143-455-1). Skey finds herself institutionalized after a suicide attempt, but she doesn't know what caused her actions, just that she travels in tunnels in both her sleep and waking hours; a disturbing but compelling book about the ways in which we survive traumas. (Rev: SLJ 6/06)

1171 Gould, Marilyn. *Golden Daffodils* (5–7). 1991, Allied Crafts paper $10.95 (978-0-9632305-1-5). Janis adjusts to her handicap resulting from cerebral palsy.

1172 Gould, Marilyn. *The Twelfth of June* (5–8). 1994, Allied Crafts LB $12.95 (978-0-9632305-4-6). Janis, who suffers from cerebral palsy, is suffering the first pangs of adolescence and is still fighting the battle to be treated like other girls her age, in this sequel to *Golden Daffodils* (1982). (Rev: SLJ 11/86; VOYA 12/86)

1173 Greene, Shep. *The Boy Who Drank Too Much* (7–9). 1979, Dell paper $5.50 (978-0-440-90493-9). At one time Buff's main concern was sports, now it's alcohol.

1174 Griffin, Adele. *Where I Want to Be* (7–10). 2005, Penguin $15.99 (978-0-399-23783-6). In alternating chapters, teenage sisters Lily and Jane tell about their relationship and the mental illness that led to Jane's tragic death. (Rev: BCCB 3/05; BL 2/15/05*; HB 3–4/05; SLJ 4/05; VOYA 4/05)

1175 Hall, Liza F. *Perk! The Story of a Teenager with Bulimia* (6–9). 1997, Gurze paper $10.95 (978-0-936077-27-7). The story of Priscilla, who binges on food then vomits, her disapproving parents, and her crush on an unsuitable boy. (Rev: BL 9/15/97; SLJ 4/98; VOYA 4/98)

1176 Halpern, Julie. *Get Well Soon* (8–12). 2007, Feiwel and Friends $16.95 (978-0-312-36795-4). Anna is sent to a psychiatric hospital for her depression and anxiety, and in letters to her best friend— full of profanity, sarcasm, and humor—she describes her experiences there. (Rev: BL 10/15/07; LMC 4–5/08; SLJ 10/07)

1177 Hamilton, Virginia. *The Planet of Junior Brown* (7–9). 1971, Macmillan paper $4.99 (978-0-02-043540-2). A 300-pound misfit is taken care of by his friends.

1178 Harrar, George. *Not as Crazy as I Seem* (7–10). 2003, Houghton $15.00 (978-0-618-26365-3). Devon, 15, is frustrated by his obsessive-compulsive disorder and the different responses of his peers, his parents, and his doctor. (Rev: BL 2/15/03; HBG 10/03; SLJ 4/03; VOYA 6/03)

1179 Hautman, Pete. *Invisible* (7–10). 2005, Simon & Schuster $15.95 (978-0-689-86800-9). It's clear to the reader from the beginning that there's something odd about the friendship between 17-year-old Doug Hanson and his only friend Andy, and the mystery unravels as Doug's state of mind deteriorates through the course of the book. (Rev: BL 6/1–15/05; SLJ 6/05; VOYA 8/05)

1180 Hautman, Pete. *Sweetblood* (8–12). 2003, Simon & Schuster $16.95 (978-0-689-85048-6). Sixteen-year-old Lucy, an insulin-dependent diabetic, links her condition with her interest in vampires. (Rev: BL 5/1/03*; HB 7–8/03; HBG 10/03; SLJ 7/03; VOYA 10/03)

1181 Helfman, Elizabeth. *On Being Sarah* (7–9). Illus. 1992, Albert Whitman LB $14.99 (978-0-8075-6068-6). Based on the life of a real person, this is the story of wheelchair-bound Sarah, 12, who has cerebral palsy, cannot vocalize, and communicates through Blissymbols. (Rev: BL 12/15/92; SLJ 1/93)

1182 Hesse, Karen. *The Music of Dolphins* (6–9). 1996, Scholastic paper $5.99 (978-0-590-89798-3). An intriguing novel about a young girl who has been raised by dolphins and, after being returned to the world of humans, longs for her life in the sea. (Rev: BL 10/15/96; SLJ 11/96*; VOYA 2/97)

1183 Heuston, Kimberley. *The Book of Jude* (6–9). 2008, Front St. $17.95 (978-1-932425-26-0). While living with her family in Prague in 1989, Jude suffers a breakdown triggered in part by the political unrest she sees around her. (Rev: BL 4/15/08; SLJ 8/08)

1184 Hoekstra, Molly. *Upstream: A Novel* (7–12). 2001, Tudor paper $15.95 (978-0-936389-86-8). This story of a 16-year-old girl's struggle with anorexia gives a clear idea of the psychological problems associated with this illness. (Rev: SLJ 12/01)

1185 Howe, James. *A Night Without Stars* (5–7). 1983, Avon paper $2.95 (978-0-380-69877-6). A novel about a young girl's hospitalization and serious operation.

1186 Howe, James. *The Watcher* (8–12). 1997, Simon & Schuster $16.00 (978-0-689-80186-0). The lives of three troubled teens converge in a horrific climax in this novel of child abuse. (Rev: BL 6/1–15/97; SLJ 5/97; VOYA 8/97)

1187 Hughes, Monica. *The King's Shadow* (7–10). 2003, Fitzhenry & Whiteside paper $9.95 (978-1-55005-056-1). In spite of his leukemia, Mike goes on a secret hunting trip; originally published in 1983.

1188 Hurwin, Davida Wills. *A Time for Dancing* (7–12). 1995, Puffin paper $6.99 (978-0-14-038618-9). A powerful story of two friends, one of whom is diagnosed with lymphoma. Their friendship becomes a story of saying good-bye and death. (Rev: BL 11/1/95*; SLJ 10/95; VOYA 12/95)

1189 Johnson, Angela. *Humming Whispers* (8–12). 1995, Orchard LB $16.99 (978-0-531-08748-0). Sophy, 14, reveals the impact of her 24-year-old sister Nicole's schizophrenia on the lives of those who love her. (Rev: BL 2/15/95; SLJ 4/95; VOYA 5/95)

1190 Johnson, Harriet McBryde. *Accidents of Nature* (8–11). 2006, Holt $16.95 (978-0-8050-7634-9). Set in 1970, this is the story of Jean, a teen with cerebral palsy who attends a camp for the disabled and discovers new possibilities for living her life. (Rev: BL 7/06; LMC 1/07; SLJ 5/06*) ⚫

1191 Jonsberg, Barry. *Dreamrider* (8–11). 2008, Knopf $15.99 (978-0-375-84457-7). Overweight Michael, starting at a new school yet again, is bullied and miserable; the only respite he finds is in his "lucid dreams," which he can control — can he use his dreams to control life too? (Rev: BL 2/15/08; SLJ 7/08)

1192 Jung, Reinhardt. *Dreaming in Black and White* (5–8). Trans. from German by Anthea Bell. 2003, Penguin $15.99 (978-0-8037-2811-0). A boy with disabilities has waking dreams in which he travels back to Nazi Germany and suffers at the hands of his classmates, teachers, and eventually his father,

in this compelling novel translated from German. (Rev: BCCB 9/03; BL 5/15/03; HB 9–10/03*; HBG 4/04; SLJ 8/03)

1193 Kachur, Wanda G. *The Nautilus* (5–7). 1997, Peytral paper $7.95 (978-0-9644271-5-0). A compassionate novel about a girl's rehabilitation after receiving spinal cord injuries in an automobile accident. (Rev: SLJ 9/97)

1194 Knowles, Jo. *Lessons from a Dead Girl* (8–11). 2007, Candlewick $16.99 (978-0-7636-3279-3). When Leah dies in an accident, Laine recalls their complicated relationship, including Leah's blackmail, threatening to reveal their "practice" sexual encounters. (Rev: BL 12/1/07; LMC 1/08; SLJ 12/07)

1195 Koertge, Ron. *Stoner and Spaz* (8–12). 2002, Candlewick $15.99 (978-0-7636-1608-3). An unlikely romance between a 16-year-old boy with cerebral palsy and a girl who is constantly stoned brings benefits to both of them. (Rev: BCCB 3/02; BL 5/1/02*; SLJ 4/02)

1196 Koss, Amy Goldman. *Side Effects* (8–11). 2006, Roaring Brook $16.95 (978-1-59643-167-6). Isabelle, 15, is diagnosed with lymphoma and is scared that she might miss out on all the things she wants to do but she makes it through. (Rev: BL 9/15/06; SLJ 9/06)

1197 Kwasney, Michelle D. *Itch* (5–8). 2008, Holt $16.95 (978-0-8050-8083-4). When Itch and her grandmother move from Florida to Ohio, Itch makes friends with a popular girl who has a sad secret. (Rev: BL 4/15/08; SLJ 9/08)

1198 Lachtman, Ofelia Dumas. *Leticia's Secret* (5–8). 1997, Arte Publico $14.95 (978-1-55885-205-1); paper $7.95 (978-1-55885-209-9). Rosario, from a Mexican American family, shares many adventures with her cousin, the pretty Leticia, and is devastated to learn that she has a fatal disease. (Rev: SLJ 1/98)

1199 Levoy, Myron. *Alan and Naomi* (7–9). 1977, HarperCollins paper $5.99 (978-0-06-440209-5). Alan tries to reach Naomi, whose mind has been warped by memories of the Holocaust. (Rev: BL 10/1/97)

1200 Lipsyte, Robert. *One Fat Summer* (7–12). 1991, HarperCollins paper $5.99 (978-0-06-447073-5). Bobby Marks is 14, fat, and unhappy in this first novel of three that traces Bobby's career through his first year of college. (Rev: BL 1/1–15/98)

1201 McBay, Bruce, and James Heneghan. *Waiting for Sarah* (7–10). 2003, Orca paper $7.95 (978-1-55143-270-0). Crippled in a car accident, Mike suffers from depression and withdrawal until he gets to know 8th-grader Sarah. (Rev: BL 9/15/03; SLJ 10/03; VOYA 12/03)

1202 McCormick, Patricia. *Cut* (7–10). 2000, Front St. $16.95 (978-1-886910-61-4). In a hospital that treats teens with serious issues, including drugs and anorexia, Callie participates in group therapy and tries to face her own self-mutilation. (Rev: BL 1/1–15/01; HB 11–12/00; HBG 3/01; SLJ 12/00; VOYA 2/01)

1203 McDaniel, Lurlene. *How Do I Love Thee? Three Stories* (6–10). 2001, Bantam $9.95 (978-0-553-57154-7). Three dramatic stories combine young romance and critical illness with clever twists of plot. (Rev: BL 10/15/01; HBG 3/02; SLJ 11/01; VOYA 12/01)

1204 McDaniel, Lurlene. *Saving Jessica* (7–10). 1996, Bantam paper $4.99 (978-0-553-56721-2). When Jessica is stricken with kidney failure, her boyfriend, Jeremy, volunteers to donate one of his but his parents, fearful that he will die, refuse permission. (Rev: VOYA 4/96)

1205 McDaniel, Lurlene. *To Live Again* (5–9). 2001, Bantam paper $4.99 (978-0-553-57151-6). After three years of remission from leukemia, 16-year-old Dawn suffers a stroke that produces a terrible bout of depression. (Rev: BL 3/1/01)

1206 Maclean, John. *Mac* (8–12). 1987, Avon paper $2.95 (978-0-380-70700-3). A high school sophomore's life falls apart after he is sexually assaulted by a doctor during a physical exam. (Rev: BL 10/1/87; SLJ 11/87)

1207 Marino, Jan. *Eighty-Eight Steps to September* (5–7). 1989, Avon paper $2.95 (978-0-380-71001-0). Amy and Robbie have the usual sibling rivalry, until Robbie develops leukemia. (Rev: BCCB 5/89; BL 8/89)

1208 Martin, Ann M. *A Corner of the Universe* (6–8). 2002, Scholastic paper $15.95 (978-0-439-38880-1). Hattie recalls the summer she became 12, when a mentally disabled uncle came to stay with her family. Newbery Honor Book, 2003. (Rev: BCCB 2/03; BL 12/1/02; HB 1–2/03*; HBG 3/03; SLJ 9/02*; VOYA 12/02)

1209 Mathis, Sharon. *Teacup Full of Roses* (7–12). 1987, Puffin paper $5.99 (978-0-14-032328-3). For mature teens, a novel about the devastating effects of drugs on an African American family.

1210 Miller, Sarah. *Miss Spitfire: Reaching Helen Keller* (8–11). 2007, Atheneum $16.99 (978-1-4169-2542-2). A fictionalized account of Annie Sullivan's first experiences and struggles with her famous student. (Rev: BL 8/07; LMC 11/07; SLJ 7/07) ❂

1211 Mitchard, Jacquelyn. *All We Know of Heaven* (8–12). 2008, HarperTeen $16.99 (978-0-06-134578-4). Inspired by a true but almost unbelievable story, this novel centers on a girl who is mistaken for her dead best friend after a terrible car accident; Maureen has to deal not only with learning to walk and talk again, but also with her guilt about her friend Bridget's death. (Rev: BL 3/15/08; SLJ 6/08)

1212 Morgenroth, Kate. *Echo* (7–10). 2007, Simon & Schuster $15.99 (978-1-4169-1438-9). Justin finds it hard to cope with his brother's accidental death and on the one-year anniversary of the tragedy he relives the day — again and again. (Rev: BL 11/15/06; LMC 4–5/07; SLJ 2/07)

1213 Neufeld, John. *Lisa, Bright and Dark* (7–9). 1969, Phillips $26.95 (978-0-87599-153-5). Her friend notices that Lisa is gradually sinking into mental illness but her parents seem indifferent.

1214 Oates, Joyce Carol. *After the Wreck I Picked Myself Up, Spread My Wings, and Flew Away* (7–10). 2006, HarperCollins $16.99 (978-0-06-073525-8). After her mother dies in a car crash, 15-year-old Jenna moves in with her aunt's family and struggles to cope with feelings of guilt and loss. (Rev: BL 7/06; LMC 4–5/07; SLJ 10/06) ❂

1215 Oke, Janette, and Laurel Oke Logan. *Dana's Valley* (7–12). 2001, Bethany House paper $11.95 (978-0-7642-2451-5). Erin, 10 years old and part of a happy Christian family, has her faith tested when her beloved older sister is diagnosed with leukemia. (Rev: VOYA 2/02)

1216 Orr, Wendy. *Peeling the Onion* (8–12). 1997, Holiday $16.95 (978-0-8234-1289-1); Bantam paper $4.99 (978-0-440-22773-1). An automobile accident leaves Anna with a broken back, debilitating pain, physical and mental handicaps, and questions about what to do with her life. (Rev: BL 4/1/97; SLJ 5/97*; VOYA 10/97)

1217 Page, Katherine Hall. *Club Meds* (6–10). 2006, Simon & Schuster paper $6.99 (978-1-4169-0903-3). Jack has ADHD and depends on the drug Ritalin to function, but as he enters 9th grade he is forced by bully Chuck Williams to hand over a quota of the drug each week; Jack teams up with fellow ADHD sufferer and "Club Meds" (kids who have to take medications) member Mary to deal with this problem. (Rev: BL 8/06; SLJ 8/06)

1218 Paley, Sasha. *Huge* (7–9). 2007, Simon & Schuster $15.99 (978-1-4169-3517-9). Wil and April, both overweight teenage girls, meet as roommates at Wellness Canyon Camp, and change in ways they didn't expect. (Rev: BL 5/15/07; SLJ 12/07)

1219 Paulsen, Gary. *The Monument* (6–9). 1991, Delacorte $15.00 (978-0-385-30518-1). A 13-year-old girl's friendship with an artist who is hired to create a monument in her small town transforms her. (Rev: BL 9/15/91; SLJ 10/91*)

1220 Peck, Richard. *Remembering the Good Times* (7–10). 1986, Bantam paper $5.50 (978-0-440-

97339-3). A strong friendship between two boys and a girl is destroyed when one of them commits suicide. (Rev: BL 3/1/85)

1221 Platt, Kin. *The Ape Inside Me* (6–8). 1979, HarperCollins LB $11.89 (978-0-397-31863-6). Eddie and Debbie work together to try and curb their terrible tempers.

1222 Ruckman, Ivy. *The Hunger Scream* (7–10). 1983, Walker $14.95 (978-0-8027-6514-7). Lily starves herself to become a popular member of the in-crowd.

1223 Scoppettone, Sandra. *Long Time Between Kisses* (7–10). 1982, HarperCollins $12.95 (978-0-06-025229-8). A 16-year-old brings together a victim of multiple sclerosis and his fiance.

1224 Seidler, Tor. *The Silent Spillbills* (5–8). 1998, HarperCollins LB $14.89 (978-0-06-205181-3). Katrina faces problems trying to overcome her stuttering but stands up to her tyrannical grandfather to help save from extinction a rare bird known as the silent spillbill. (Rev: BCCB 1/99; BL 12/15/98; HBG 3/99; SLJ 4/99)

1225 Shaw, Susan. *Black-Eyed Suzie* (7–9). 2002, Boyds Mills $15.95 (978-1-56397-729-9); paper $4.95 (978-1-56397-701-5). In the pages of her diary and with the help of hospital staff, Suzie struggles to recover emotionally from her mother's physical abuse. (Rev: BCCB 9/02; BL 5/15/02; HBG 10/02; VOYA 8/02)

1226 Shyer, Marlene Fanta. *Welcome Home, Jellybean* (5–8). 1978, Macmillan paper $4.99 (978-0-689-71213-5). Twelve-year-old Neil encounters a near-tragic situation when his older retarded sister comes home to stay.

1227 Smith, Jennifer E. *The Comeback Season* (6–9). 2008, Simon & Schuster $15.99 (978-1-4169-5213-8). Two friends with painful problems (a deceased parent and a cancer diagnosis) help each other through compassion and a love of baseball. (Rev: BL 3/1/08)

1228 Snyder, Zilpha Keatley. *The Witches of Worm* (5–8). Illus. by Alton Raible. 1972, Dell paper $5.50 (978-0-440-49727-1). A deeply disturbed girl believes that her selfish and destructive acts are caused by bewitchment.

1229 Spencer, Katherine. *Saving Grace* (8–11). 2006, Harcourt $15.00 (978-0-15-205740-4). Grace is emotionally lost and heading down a dangerous path after her brother, Matt, dies in a car accident. Help comes in the form of a girl named Philomena who guides her back to God. (Rev: BCCB 11/06; BL 1/1–15/07; SLJ 10/06)

1230 Strachan, Ian. *The Flawed Glass* (5–8). 1990, Little, Brown $14.95 (978-0-316-81813-1). Physically disabled Shona makes friends with an Ameri-

can boy on an island off the Scottish coast. (Rev: BCCB 11/90; BL 12/1/90; SLJ 1/91)

1231 Stratton, Allan. *Leslie's Journal* (8–12). 2000, Annick $19.95 (978-1-55037-665-4); paper $8.95 (978-1-55037-664-7). A new teacher reads Leslie's journal and learns about her boyfriend's abusive behavior. (Rev: HBG 10/01; SLJ 4/01; VOYA 2/01)

1232 Striegel, Jana. *Homeroom Exercise* (4–7). 2002, Holiday $16.95 (978-0-8234-1579-3). A 12-year-old who dreams of becoming a professional dancer is diagnosed with juvenile rheumatoid arthritis. (Rev: BL 3/1/02; HBG 10/02; SLJ 6/02; VOYA 8/02)

1233 Tan, Shaun. *The Red Tree* (6–12). Illus. 2003, Simply Read $15.95 (978-0-9688767-3-2). This arresting picture book for older readers portrays a girl searching for meaning in a frightening world, with a glimmer of hope that grows as the book reaches its conclusion. (Rev: BL 5/1/03)

1234 Tashjian, Janet. *Fault Line* (8–12). 2003, Holt $16.95 (978-0-8050-7200-6). Becky, 17, happy and enjoying doing comedy routines, finds her life changing when she falls for Kip, whose apparent self-confidence hides his abusive nature. (Rev: BL 9/1/03; HB 9–10/03; HBG 4/04; SLJ 10/03; VOYA 10/03)

1235 Taylor, Michelle A. *The Angel of Barbican High* (7–12). 2002, Univ. of Queensland paper $15.95 (978-0-7022-3251-0). Jez feels responsible for the death of her boyfriend and pours out her guilt in her poems, which reveal that she is close to suicide. (Rev: SLJ 8/02)

1236 Tokio, Mamelle. *More Than You Can Chew* (8–10). 2003, Tundra paper $9.95 (978-0-88776-639-8). Anorexic 17-year-old Marty Black faces an uphill struggle as she begins treatment for her eating disorder but tackles it with some humor. (Rev: BL 1/1–15/04; SLJ 6/04; VOYA 8/04)

1237 Toten, Teresa. *The Game* (7–12). 2001, Red Deer paper $7.95 (978-0-88995-232-4). A dramatic story about Dani, a suicidal girl who finds friendship and succor at a clinic for troubled adolescents. (Rev: BL 2/15/02; VOYA 4/02)

1238 Trembath, Don. *Lefty Carmichael Has a Fit* (8–12). 2000, Orca paper $6.95 (978-1-55143-166-6). When 15-year-old Lefty discovers that he is an epileptic, he develops a fearful, cautious lifestyle that his friends and family try to change. (Rev: BL 1/1–15/00; SLJ 2/00; VOYA 4/00)

1239 Trueman, Terry. *Inside Out* (7–10). 2003, HarperCollins LB $16.89 (978-0-06-623963-7). An absorbing story about a schizophrenic teenager who is held hostage in a robbery attempt. (Rev: BL 9/1/03; HBG 4/04; SLJ 9/03; VOYA 10/03)

1240 Trueman, Terry. *Stuck in Neutral* (6–10). 2000, HarperCollins LB $16.89 (978-0-06-028518-

0). Fourteen-year-old Shawn, whose severe cerebral palsy does not hamper his great intelligence, fears that his father may be planning to put him out of his misery. (Rev: BL 7/00*; HB 5–6/00; HBG 10/00; SLJ 7/00; VOYA 12/00)

1241 Tullson, Diane. *Zero* (8–11). 2007, Fitzhenry & Whiteside paper $9.95 (978-1-55041-950-4). While at a boarding school for the arts, Kas becomes anorexic and manages to hide her problem from everyone until she nearly dies. (Rev: BL 4/15/07; SLJ 6/07)

1242 Waite, Judy. *Shopaholic* (6–10). 2003, Simon & Schuster $16.95 (978-0-689-85138-4). Unhappy Taylor, a British 14-year-old, allows herself to fall in with glamorous Kat's plans despite her reservations. (Rev: BL 5/1/03; HBG 10/03; SLJ 7/03; VOYA 8/03)

1243 Weatherly, Lee. *Kat Got Your Tongue* (8–10). 2007, Random $15.99 (978-0-385-75117-9). After being hit by a car, Kat doesn't remember who she is and struggles with her new identity and relationships with her mother and friends. (Rev: BL 8/07; SLJ 9/07)

1244 Wersba, Barbara. *Fat: A Love Story* (8–12). 1987, HarperCollins $11.95 (978-0-06-026400-0). Rita Formica, fat and unhappy, falls for rich, attractive Robert. (Rev: BL 6/1/87; SLJ 8/87; VOYA 6/87)

1245 White, Ruth. *Memories of Summer* (7–12). 2000, Farrar $16.00 (978-0-374-34945-5). Lyric is devastated when her older sister, Summer, must be hospitalized for her schizophrenia in this novel set in 1955. (Rev: BL 9/1/00; HB 9–10/00; HBG 3/01; SLJ 8/00*; VOYA 12/00)

1246 White, Ruth. *Weeping Willow* (7–10). 1992, Farrar paper $5.95 (978-0-374-48280-0). This uplifting novel conveying hill country life is about a girl who overcomes abuse to make her own way. (Rev: BL 6/15/92; SLJ 7/92)

1247 Wilson, Dawn. *Saint Jude* (8–12). 2001, Tudor $15.95 (978-0-936389-68-4). Taylor, who is bipolar, makes friends and learns to cope with her illness while in an outpatient program at St. Jude Hospital. (Rev: BL 11/1/01; SLJ 11/01)

1248 Wolff, Virginia E. *Probably Still Nick Swansen* (7–12). 1988, Holt $14.95 (978-0-8050-0701-5). Nick, a 16-year-old victim of slight brain dysfunction, tells his story of rejection and separation. (Rev: BL 11/15/88; SLJ 12/88; VOYA 6/89)

1249 Woodruff, Joan L. *The Shiloh Renewal* (7–10). 1998, Black Heron $22.95 (978-0-930773-50-2). Sandy, who has been mentally and physically disabled since an automobile accident, tries to regain basic skills, recover from the brain trauma, and straighten out her life in this novel that takes place on a small farm near Shiloh National Park in Tennessee. (Rev: VOYA 12/98)

1250 Yeomans, Ellen. *Rubber Houses* (6–12). 2007, Little, Brown $15.99 (978-0-316-10647-X). This novel in verse follows Kit's grief when her younger brother, with whom she shared a love of baseball, is diagnosed with and then dies of cancer. (Rev: BCCB 2/07; BL 1/1–15/07; SLJ 3/07)

1251 Zarr, Sara. *Sweethearts* (8–12). 2008, Little, Brown $16.99 (978-0-316-01455-7). Jenna has remade herself in an attempt to forget her troubled childhood, but when Cameron — who suffered abuse along with Jenna long ago — reappears in her life, her past seems to come back with him. (Rev: BL 1/1–15/08; HB 5–6/08; SLJ 4/08) ⚐

1252 Zevin, Gabrielle. *Memoirs of a Teenage Amnesiac* (6–10). 2007, Farrar $17.00 (978-0-374-34946-2). After a head injury, Naomi, a high school junior, can't remember anything that's happened since 6th grade and struggles with her present and past life, a new romance, and her parents' separation. (Rev: BL 9/1/07; SLJ 10/07)

1253 Zimmer, Tracie Vaughn. *Reaching for the Sun* (5–8). 2007, Bloomsbury $14.95 (978-1-59990-037-7). Seventh-grader Josie faces daunting troubles: school, loneliness, cerebral palsy, and her rural area's development; a new, science-loving neighbor becomes a friend and Josie redefines her relationship with her mother in this appealing verse novel. (Rev: BL 1/1–15/07; SLJ 3/07)

Personal Problems and Growing into Maturity

1254 Adams, Lenora. *Baby Girl* (7–10). 2007, Simon & Schuster paper $6.99 (978-1-4169-2512-5). Sheree, a pregnant runaway, exchanges letters with her mother expressing anguish over her life, which has included neglect, drugs, and disappointment. (Rev: BL 3/1/07)

1255 Adler, C. S. *Willie, the Frog Prince* (4–7). 1994, Clarion $15.00 (978-0-395-65615-0). Willie's inability to accept responsibility almost causes the loss of his dog, Booboo. (Rev: BL 4/15/94; SLJ 6/94)

1256 Aker, Don. *Stranger at Bay* (6–9). 1998, Stoddart paper $5.95 (978-0-7736-7468-4). Set in a town on the Bay of Fundy in Canada, this novel tells about Randy Forsythe's adjustment to a new home and stepmother while coping with a gang of bullies who want him to steal drugs from his father, who is a pharmaceutical salesman. (Rev: SLJ 7/98)

1257 Alexie, Sherman. *The Absolutely True Diary of a Part-Time Indian* (7–10). 2007, Little, Brown $16.99 (978-0-316-01368-0). Arnold Spirit, a teenager on the Spokane Indian reservation, expects obstacles when he switches to a privileged white school but finds there are challenges at home too. (Rev: BL 8/07; HB 1–2/08; LMC 1/08; SLJ 9/07)

1258 Allen, M. E. *Gotta Get Some Bish Bash Bosh* (7–10). 2005, HarperCollins LB $16.89 (978-0-06-073201-1). When he's dumped by his girlfriend Sandi, the 14-year-old narrator resolves to cultivate a brand-new image in this entertaining novel set in Britain. (Rev: BL 1/1–15/05; SLJ 4/05; VOYA 2/05)

1259 Almond, David. *The Fire-Eaters* (6–8). 2004, Delacorte $15.95 (978-0-385-73170-6). In 1962, 12-year-old Bobby Burns grows increasingly troubled by his father's deteriorating health, the growing threat of another world war, and his clashes at school with a cruel teacher. (Rev: BCCB 5/04; BL 3/15/04; HB 5–6/04; SLJ 5/04; VOYA 10/04)

1260 Alphin, Elaine Marie. *Simon Says* (8–12). 2002, Harcourt $17.00 (978-0-15-216355-6). Charles, a brooding 16-year-old artist, is determined to remain nonconformist when he starts attending a boarding school for the arts in this thoughtful novel. (Rev: BCCB 6/02; BL 4/15/02; HBG 10/02; SLJ 6/02)

1261 Anderson, Laurie Halse. *Speak* (8–12). 1999, Farrar $16.00 (978-0-374-37152-4). A victim of rape, high school freshman Mellinda Sordino finds that her attacker is again threatening her. (Rev: BL 9/15/99; HB 9–10/99; HBG 4/00; SLJ 10/99; VOYA 12/99)

1262 Anderson, Mary. *Tune in Tomorrow* (7–9). 1985, Avon paper $2.50 (978-0-380-69870-7). Jo is fixated on two soap opera characters whom she later meets in real life.

1263 *Annie's Baby: The Diary of Anonymous, a Pregnant Teenager* (6–10). 1998, Avon paper $5.99 (978-0-380-79141-5). In diary format, this is the story of 14-year-old Annie, her love for an abusive rich boyfriend, and her rape and subsequent pregnancy. (Rev: SLJ 7/98; VOYA 6/98)

1264 Ashley, Bernard. *All My Men* (7–9). 1978, Phillips $26.95 (978-0-87599-228-0). In this English story, Paul pays a heavy price to be part of the "in" crowd.

1265 Ashley, Bernard. *Little Soldier* (8–12). 2002, Scholastic $16.95 (978-0-439-22424-6). Young Kaninda Bulumba is rescued from the incredible violence taking place in his native country only to find himself confronting gang violence in his new neighborhood in London. (Rev: BCCB 7–8/02; BL 5/1/02; HBG 10/02; SLJ 6/02*; VOYA 8/02)

1266 Ashley, Bernard. *Terry on the Fence* (6–8). Illus. 1977, Phillips $26.95 (978-0-87599-222-8). Unhappy at home, Terry unwillingly becomes a member of a street gang.

1267 Atkinson, Elizabeth. *From Alice to Zen and Everyone in Between* (5–7). 2008, Carolrhoda $16.95 (978-0-8225-7271-8). Alice moves to a new suburb with her dad and quickly becomes friends with Zen, but when school starts she realizes he's part of the wrong crowd. (Rev: BL 5/1/08; SLJ 9/08)

1268 Auch, Mary Jane. *Seven Long Years Until College* (4–7). 1991, Holiday $13.95 (978-0-8234-0901-3). Natalie runs away from home to join her older sister at college. (Rev: BCCB 1/92; SLJ 10/91)

1269 Avi. *A Place Called Ugly* (6–9). 1995, Avon paper $6.99 (978-0-380-72423-9). A 14-year-old boy protests the tearing down of a beach cottage to build a hotel.

1270 Bagert, Brod. *Hormone Jungle: Coming of Age in Middle School* (5–8). Illus. 2006, Maupin House $23.95 (978-0-929895-87-1). The scrapbook of Christina Curtis's middle-school years tells the story of the poetry war that erupted in sixth grade and of the changing relationships between the young people as they learned more about each other. (Rev: SLJ 6/06)

1271 Barnholdt, Lauren. *The Secret Identity of Devon Delaney* (4–7). 2007, Aladdin Mix paper $5.99 (978-1-4169-3503-2). The lies that Devon tells while spending the summer at her grandmother's house come back to bite her when her new friend Lexi moves to Devon's town and attends Devon's middle school. (Rev: BL 8/07; SLJ 8/07)

1272 Bartek, Mary. *Funerals and Fly Fishing* (4–7). 2004, Holt $16.95 (978-0-8050-7409-3). A visit to the grandfather he has never met gives Brad Stanislawski new confidence to deal with the classmates at his new school. (Rev: SLJ 8/04)

1273 Bateson, Catherine. *The Boyfriend Rules of Good Behavior* (6–8). 2006, Holiday House $16.95 (978-0-8234-2026-1). Millie learns to make adjustments as her mother finds a new boyfriend and circumstances alter yet again in this Australian import full of Down Under flavor. (Rev: SLJ 11/06)

1274 Bauer, A. C. E. *No Castles Here* (4–7). 2007, Random $15.99 (978-0-375-83921-4). A magical book, a Big Brother, and a school chorus rescue 11-year-old Augie Boretski from feeling completely lost in his life of poverty and loneliness in Camden, New Jersey. (Rev: BL 12/1/07; SLJ 10/07)

1275 Bawden, Nina. *The Peppermint Pig* (6–8). 1975, HarperCollins LB $13.89 (978-0-397-31618-2). A brother and sister save a pig that they soon regard as a pet but they find something terrible is going to happen to it.

1276 Beaudoin, Sean. *Going Nowhere Faster* (8–12). 2007, Little, Brown $16.99 (978-0-316-01415-1). Stan Smith, 17, has a high IQ and showed promise when he was younger but now spends his time working in a video store, inventing dreadful screenplay scenarios, avoiding his embarrassing hippie parents, and worrying about a stalker; a darkly comic story with a satisfying resolution. (Rev: BCCB 5/07; HB 5–6/07; SLJ 4/07)

1277 Bell, William. *Death Wind* (7–12). 2002, Orca paper $7.95 (978-1-55143-215-1). After running away from her unhappy home when she thinks she may be pregnant, Allie returns to find that a tornado has devastated her town. (Rev: SLJ 10/02; VOYA 12/02)

1278 Benjamin, Carol Lea. *The Wicked Stepdog* (4–7). Illus. by author. 1982, Avon paper $2.50 (978-0-380-70089-9). Louise is in the midst of puberty problems and her father's remarriage.

1279 Benway, Robin. *Audrey, Wait!* (8–11). 2008, Penguin $16.99 (978-1-59514-191-0). Sixteen-year-old Audrey gains instant fame when her ex-boyfriend writes a hit song about their breakup. (Rev: BL 8/08; SLJ 8/08)

1280 Bertrand, Diane Gonzales. *Trino's Choice* (6–9). 1999, Arte Publico $16.95 (978-1-55885-279-2); paper $9.95 (978-1-55885-268-6). A Latino boy growing up in a Texas trailer park succumbs to the offer of a hood who offers him chance at quick cash, but in time it leads to tragedy. (Rev: BL 6/1–15/99; VOYA 4/00)

1281 Bertrand, Diane Gonzales. *Trino's Time* (6–12). 2001, Arte Publico $14.95 (978-1-55885-316-4); paper $14.95 (978-1-55885-317-1). In this sequel to *Trino's Choice* (1999), things begin to look better for Trino's family as Trino gets a job and starts enjoying school. (Rev: BL 11/1/01; SLJ 7/01; VOYA 12/01)

1282 Betancourt, Jeanne. *Kate's Turn* (5–8). 1992, Scholastic $13.95 (978-0-590-43103-3). This story of the young ballerina Kate, who decides the price of fame is too high, shows the grueling, often painful life of a dancer. (Rev: BL 1/1/92; SLJ 2/92)

1283 Billingsley, ReShonda Tate. *With Friends Like These* (7–12). Series: African American Christian Teen Fiction. 2007, Pocket paper $9.95 (978-1-4165-2562-2). The four girls we first met in *Nothing but Drama* (2006) now become enemies in their efforts to get on a TV show. (Rev: BL 4/1/07)

1284 Block, Francesca L. *Echo* (8–12). 2001, HarperCollins LB $14.89 (978-0-06-028128-1). A series of interconnected stories set in glamorous Los Angeles follows the maturing of an unhappy young girl called Echo, who feels neglected by her talented parents and seeks attention where she can find it. (Rev: BCCB 10/01; BL 8/01; HB 9–10/01; HBG 3/02; SLJ 8/01; VOYA 10/01)

1285 Bloor, Edward. *Tangerine* (7–10). 1997, Harcourt $17.00 (978-0-15-201246-5); Scholastic paper $4.99 (978-0-590-43277-1). Although he wears thick glasses, Paul is able to see clearly the people around him, their problems and their mistakes, as he adjusts to his new home in Tangerine County, Florida. (Rev: BL 5/15/97; SLJ 4/97; VOYA 8/97)

1286 Blume, Judy. *Here's to You, Rachel Robinson* (6–8). 1993, Dell paper $5.50 (978-0-440-40946-5). This sequel to *Just As Long As We're Together* is full of multidimensional characters. (Rev: BL 9/1/93; SLJ 11/93; VOYA 12/93)

1287 Blume, Judy. *Just as Long as We're Together* (6–8). 1987, Dell paper $5.50 (978-0-440-40075-2). A student entering junior high faces problems involving weight, friendships, and a family that is disintegrating. (Rev: BL 8/87; VOYA 2/88)

1288 Blume, Judy. *Then Again, Maybe I Won't* (5–8). 1971, Dell paper $4.99 (978-0-440-48659-6). Thirteen-year-old Tony faces many problems when his family relocates to suburban Long Island.

1289 Blume, Judy. *Tiger Eyes* (7–10). 1981, Dell paper $5.99 (978-0-440-98469-6). A girl struggles to cope with her father's violent death. (Rev: BL 7/88)

1290 Boock, Paula. *Dare Truth or Promise* (8–12). 1999, Houghton $15.00 (978-0-395-97117-8). Two girls, Willa and Louise, attend a New Zealand high school and, though they are opposites in many ways, they fall in love. (Rev: BL 9/15/99; HB 9–10/99; HBG 4/00; SLJ 11/99; VOYA 10/99)

1291 Book, Rick. *Necking With Louise* (7–12). 1999, Red Deer paper $7.95 (978-0-88995-194-5). Set in Saskatchewan in 1965, this is a book of stories about Eric Anderson's 16th year, when he has his first date, plays in a championship hockey game, has a summer job, and reacts to his family and the land on which he lives. (Rev: BL 10/15/99*; SLJ 3/00)

1292 Borntrager, Mary Christner. *Rebecca* (7–12). 1989, Herald paper $8.99 (978-0-8361-3500-8). A coming-of-age novel about an Amish girl and her attraction to a Mennonite young man. (Rev: SLJ 11/89)

1293 Bottner, Barbara. *Nothing in Common* (7–10). 1986, HarperCollins $12.95 (978-0-06-020604-8). When Mrs. Gregori dies, both her daughter and Melissa Warren, a teenager in the household where Mrs. Gregori worked, enter a period of grief. (Rev: VOYA 2/87)

1294 Bradley, Kimberly Brubaker. *Leap of Faith* (4–7). 2007, Dial $16.99 (978-0-8037-3127-1). Abigail finds herself attracted to the new ideas she's learning at the Catholic school where she ended up after being expelled from public school. (Rev: BCCB 9/07; BL 7/07; SLJ 8/07)

1295 Branscum, Robbie. *Johnny May Grows Up* (6–8). Illus. 1987, HarperCollins $11.95 (978-0-06-

020606-2). Johnny May, a spunky mountain girl, has no money to continue her schooling after 8th grade. (Rev: BL 10/1/87; SLJ 12/87)

1296 Brashares, Ann. *Girls in Pants: The Third Summer of the Sisterhood* (8–12). Series: Sisterhood of the Traveling Pants. 2005, Delacorte LB $18.99 (978-0-385-90919-8). It's summer again for the four friends and they manage to get together for a weekend before they leave for separate colleges; the pants continue their travels. (Rev: BL 12/15/04*; SLJ 1/05; VOYA 2/05)

1297 Brian, Kate. *Fake Boyfriend* (7–10). 2007, Simon & Schuster $16.99 (978-1-4169-1367-2). A fast-paced, humorous read about Vivi and Lane's efforts to help their friend Izzy, whose boyfriend has turned undependable just before the senior prom; they naturally turn to the Internet and MySpace. (Rev: SLJ 1/08)

1298 Bridgers, Sue Ellen. *Keeping Christina* (7–10). 1998, Replica LB $29.95 (978-0-7351-0042-8). Annie takes sad newcomer Christina under her wing, but she turns out to be a liar and troublemaker, which creates conflicts with Annie's family, friends, and boyfriend. (Rev: BL 7/93; SLJ 7/93)

1299 Bridgers, Sue Ellen. *Permanent Connections* (8–12). 1998, Replica LB $29.95 (978-0-7351-0043-5). When Rob's behavior gets out of control, the teenager is sent to his uncle's farm to cool off. (Rev: BL 2/15/87; SLJ 3/87; VOYA 4/87)

1300 Brooks, Martha. *Traveling On into the Light* (7–12). 1994, Orchard LB $16.99 (978-0-531-08713-8). Stories about runaways, suicide, and desertion, featuring romantic, sensitive, and smart teenage outsiders. (Rev: BL 8/94; SLJ 8/94*; VOYA 10/94)

1301 Bruchac, Joseph. *The Way* (6–8). 2007, Darby Creek $16.95 (978-1-58196-062-4). Cody, a Native American teenager who is used to being bullied, feels empowered when his uncle teaches him about his ancestors' traditions and the art of self-defense. (Rev: BL 10/1/07; SLJ 11/07)

1302 Brugman, Alyssa. *Walking Naked* (7–12). 2002, Allen & Unwin $17.95 (978-1-86508-822-8). A tragic tale in which a member of a 10th-grade elite group finds peer pressure more important than her growing friendship with the class outcast. (Rev: BCCB 4/04; BL 2/1/04; HB 7–8/04; SLJ 7/04; VOYA 4/03)

1303 Bulion, Leslie. *Uncharted Waters* (4–8). 2006, Peachtree $14.95 (978-1-56145-365-8). Jonah's summer of self-discovery following a dismal school year includes a heroic rescue at sea and excelling at his true talent. (Rev: SLJ 6/06)

1304 Bunting, Eve. *Doll Baby* (5–10). Illus. by Catherine Stock. 2000, Clarion $15.00 (978-0-395-93094-6). A simple, direct narrative in which 15-year-old Ellie explains how being pregnant and having a baby radically changed her life. (Rev: BL 11/1/00; HB 9–10/00; HBG 3/01; SLJ 10/00)

1305 Bunting, Eve. *If I Asked You, Would You Stay?* (8–10). 1984, HarperCollins LB $12.89 (978-0-397-32066-0). Two lonely people find comfort in love for each other.

1306 Burch, Robert. *Queenie Peavy* (5–7). 1987, Penguin paper $5.99 (978-0-14-032305-4). Queenie, whose father is in prison, is growing up a defiant, disobedient girl in rural Georgia in the 1930s.

1307 Cabot, Meg. *Pants on Fire* (8–12). 2007, HarperTempest $16.99 (978-0-06-088015-6). Katie, 16, is a bit loose with the truth, and a bit loose with the guys; when her former best friend Tommy — who exposed some cheaters in the past — returns to town she finds herself reviewing her behavior. (Rev: BL 5/1/07; SLJ 8/07) ⑨

1308 Caldwell, V. M. *The Ocean Within* (5–7). 1999, Milkweed paper $6.95 (978-1-57131-624-0). Elizabeth, who is on her third set of foster parents since she was orphaned five years before, has built walls of silence around herself that are impossible to penetrate. (Rev: BCCB 1/00; BL 9/1/99; HBG 3/00; SLJ 11/99; VOYA 4/00)

1309 Caldwell, V. M. *Runt* (5–7). 2006, Milkweed $16.95 (978-1-57131-662-2); paper $6.95 (978-1-57131-661-5). Runt, a 13-year-old who is trying to cope with his mother's death and his new living arrangements, becomes close to Mitch, who is dying of cancer. (Rev: SLJ 7/06)

1310 Caletti, Deb. *The Queen of Everything* (8–12). 2002, Simon & Schuster paper $5.99 (978-0-7434-3684-7). Jordan's life is turned upside-down by her grandmother's death, her father's new romance, and her own sexual experimentation. (Rev: BCCB 1/03; BL 11/15/02; SLJ 11/02; VOYA 2/03)

1311 Calonita, Jen. *Secrets of My Hollywood Life: A Novel* (6–12). 2006, Little, Brown $16.99 (978-0-316-15442-0). Kaitlin needs a break from celebrity and enrolls, incognito, at a friend's high school where she establishes a new persona — complete with new boyfriend — until a coincidental visit from her costar blows her cover. (Rev: SLJ 6/06)

1312 Cameron, Ann. *Colibri* (5–8). 2003, Farrar $17.00 (978-0-374-31519-1). Twelve-year-old Rosa, who was kidnapped from her Mayan village when she was four, seeks to escape from the abusive "uncle" who is exploiting her. (Rev: BCCB 10/03; BL 10/1/03*; HB 9–10/03; HBG 4/04; SLJ 10/03*)

1313 Carr, Dennis, and Elise Carr. *Welcome to Wahoo* (8–11). 2006, Bloomsbury $16.95 (978-1-58234-696-0). Snooty socialite Victoria gets a taste of what it means to be an outsider when she is forced to transfer to a small-town high school in Nebraska. (Rev: BL 7/06; SLJ 6/06)

1314 Carter, Alden R. *Dogwolf* (7–10). 1994, Scholastic paper $13.95 (978-0-590-46741-4). In this coming-of-age novel, Pete realizes that a dog-wolf that he's set free must be found and killed before it harms a human. (Rev: BL 1/1/95; SLJ 4/95; VOYA 2/95)

1315 Caseley, Judith. *Praying to A. L.* (5–8). 2000, Greenwillow $15.95 (978-0-688-15934-4). After her father dies, 12-year-old Sierra transfers all her love to a portrait of Abraham Lincoln given to her by her father. (Rev: BL 5/15/00; HBG 10/00; SLJ 6/00)

1316 Cassidy, Anne. *Looking for JJ* (8–11). 2007, Harcourt $17.00 (978-0-15-206190-6). Alice was called Jennifer Jones during the disturbed childhood that came to an abrupt end when she murdered another child; now Alice, released from prison, hopes to lead a new life. (Rev: BL 10/1/07; LMC 1/08; SLJ 10/07) ⑨

1317 Castellucci, Cecil. *Boy Proof* (7–10). 2005, Candlewick $15.99 (978-0-7636-2333-3). Sixteen-year-old Victoria, who prefers to be known as Egg, is smart, cool, and totally in control until Max Carter enters her life and breaks the shell. (Rev: BCCB 2/05; BL 2/15/05; HB 5–6/05; SLJ 4/05; VOYA 4/05)

1318 Chan, Gillian. *Glory Days and Other Stories* (7–10). 1997, Kids Can $16.95 (978-1-55074-381-4). Five stories about young people at Elmwood High School, each of whom faces problems because of decisions that have been made. (Rev: BL 1/1–15/98; SLJ 10/97)

1319 Chan, Gillian. *Golden Girl and Other Stories* (7–10). 1997, Kids Can $14.95 (978-1-55074-385-2). Short stories about students in a high school, with details of their pleasures, pains, and concerns. (Rev: BL 9/15/97; SLJ 11/97)

1320 Chin, Michael. *Free Throw* (7–12). 2001, PublishAmerica paper $24.95 (978-1-58851-166-9). Basketball and romance play major roles in the life of high school sophomore Mike Weaver. (Rev: VOYA 4/02)

1321 Choldenko, Gennifer. *If a Tree Falls at Lunch Period* (6–8). 2007, Harcourt $17.00 (978-0-15-205753-4). The mean girls at Kirsten's private school are making her life miserable, but things start to look up when Walk, a new kid from the inner city, enrolls in her class; chapters alternate between Kirsten's and Walk's points of view. (Rev: BL 10/1/07; HB 9–10/07; LMC 1/08; SLJ 8/07) ⑨

1322 Clairday, Robynn. *Confessions of a Boyfriend Stealer* (8–11). 2005, Delacorte paper $7.95 (978-0-385-73242-0). In entries from a blog, 16-year-old Gen, high school junior and aspiring documentary filmmaker, describes her growing disillusion with her best friends CJ and Tasha. (Rev: BL 9/15/05; SLJ 9/05)

1323 Clark, Catherine. *The Alison Rules* (7–12). 2004, HarperCollins LB $16.89 (978-0-06-055981-6). Reeling from her mother's death, high school sophomore Alison retreats into herself and creates sets of rules to help her cope; the arrival of a new student called Patrick finally brings her out of her shell. (Rev: BL 10/15/04; SLJ 8/04; VOYA 12/04)

1324 Clarke, Judith. *Night Train* (8–11). 2000, Holt $16.95 (978-0-8050-6151-2). Luke Leman, an Australian teenager, finds that he is cracking under scholastic and family pressures and thinks he might be going insane. (Rev: BCCB 5/00; BL 6/1–15/00; HBG 9/00; SLJ 5/00)

1325 Clarke, Nicole. *Spin City* (6–9). 2006, Grosset & Dunlap paper $6.99 (978-0-448-44123-8). Kiyoka, a nonconformist / go-getter / pop-culture-loving teen, has taken an internship at *Flirt* fashion magazine in New York City where she works hard but hasn't gotten the big break assignment she is anticipating, so she decides to try her hand at music composition — a true passion — which produces both disappointing and triumphant results. (Rev: SLJ 8/06)

1326 Cleary, Beverly. *Dear Mr. Henshaw* (4–7). Illus. by Paul O. Zelinsky. 1983, Morrow LB $16.89 (978-0-688-02406-2). A Newbery Medal winner (1984) about a boy who pours out his problems in letters to a writer he greatly admires.

1327 Cleaver, Vera, and Bill Cleaver. *Ellen Grae* (6–8). 1967, HarperCollins LB $12.89 (978-0-397-30938-2). Ellen Grae, an imaginative girl, finds it impossible to assimilate the story of the death of her friend Ira's parents. Included in this volume is the sequel *Lady Ellen Grae*.

1328 Cleaver, Vera, and Bill Cleaver. *Grover* (6–9). 1987, HarperCollins $13.95 (978-0-397-31118-7). The death of his beloved mother seems more than Grover can handle. A reissue.

1329 Cleaver, Vera, and Bill Cleaver. *Hazel Rye* (6–9). 1983, HarperCollins LB $13.89 (978-0-397-31952-7); paper $3.95 (978-0-06-440156-2). Eleven-year-old Hazel rents the Poole family a small house in a citrus grove.

1330 Cohen, Miriam. *Robert and Dawn Marie 4Ever* (6–9). 1986, HarperCollins $11.95 (978-0-06-021396-1). Robert, a street waif, finds a new home and forms a friendship with Dawn Marie, a young girl whose mother disapproves of Robert. (Rev: BL 11/1/86; SLJ 12/86; VOYA 12/86)

1331 Cohn, Rachel. *Pop Princess* (8–12). 2004, Simon & Schuster $15.95 (978-0-689-85205-3). Sixteen-year-old Wonder Blake has a wry understanding of the changes affecting her life when she is offered a recording contract. (Rev: BCCB 4/04; BL 1/1–15/04; SLJ 3/04; VOYA 8/04)

1332 Colasanti, Susane. *Take Me There* (7–10). 2008, Viking $17.99 (978-0-670-06333-8). Three high school students in New York — Rhiannon, James, and Nicole — deal with family problems, school, and romantic entanglements in this compelling story told in three alternating narratives. (Rev: BL 8/08; SLJ 9/08)

1333 Cole, Brock. *The Goats* (6–9). 1987, Farrar paper $5.95 (978-0-374-42575-3). Two misfits at summer camp find inner strength and self-knowledge when they are cruelly marooned on an island by fellow campers. (Rev: BL 11/15/87; SLJ 11/87; VOYA 4/88)

1334 Coleman, Rowan. *Ruby Parker Hits the Small Time* (6–9). 2007, HarperCollins $15.99 (978-0-06-077628-2). Ruby, 13, a child star on a British soap opera, must deal with jealous peers, divorcing parents, and fans who look to her for advice in this appealing, fast-paced novel. (Rev: BCCB 3/07; BL 2/1/07; SLJ 4/07)

1335 Collard, Sneed B., III. *Dog Sense* (5–8). 2005, Peachtree $14.95 (978-1-56145-351-1). Unhappy after moving from sunny California to a small town in Montana, 13-year-old Guy Martinez finds solace in time spent with his dog, Streak, and a newfound friend named Luke. (Rev: BL 10/15/05; SLJ 11/05)

1336 Collier, Kristi. *Throwing Stones* (7–10). 2006, Holt $16.95 (978-0-8050-7614-1). In the year 1923, Andy begins high school and dreams of being a basketball star like his late brother, hoping that it will help his parents cope with his death, but a bet could ruin his plan. (Rev: BL 9/1/06; SLJ 11/06)

1337 Conford, Ellen. *Hail, Hail Camp Timberwood* (5–7). Illus. by Gail Owens. 1978, Little, Brown $14.95 (978-0-316-15291-4). Thirteen-year-old Melanie's first summer at camp.

1338 Conford, Ellen. *You Never Can Tell* (7–9). 1984, Little, Brown $14.95 (978-0-316-15267-9). Katie's soap opera heartthrob enters her high school.

1339 Conly, Jane L. *Crazy Lady!* (5–8). 1993, HarperCollins LB $18.89 (978-0-06-021360-2). In a city slum, Vernon forms a friendship with an eccentric woman and helps her care for her disabled teenage son. (Rev: BCCB 7–8/93; BL 5/15/93*; SLJ 4/93*)

1340 Cooney, Caroline B. *Summer Nights* (7–12). 1992, Scholastic paper $3.25 (978-0-590-45786-6). At a farewell party, five high school girls look back on their school years and their friendship. (Rev: SLJ 1/89)

1341 Corcoran, Barbara. *You Put Up with Me, I'll Put Up with You* (6–8). 1989, Avon paper $2.50 (978-0-380-70558-0). A somewhat self-centered girl moves with her mother to a new community and

has problems adjusting. (Rev: BL 3/15/87; SLJ 3/87; VOYA 4/87)

1342 Cormier, Robert. *The Chocolate War* (7–12). 1993, Dell paper $3.99 (978-0-440-90032-0). A chocolate sale in a boys' private school creates power struggles. Followed by *Beyond the Chocolate War*.

1343 Cormier, Robert. *The Rag and Bone Shop* (8–10). 2001, Delacorte $15.95 (978-0-385-72962-8). Shy, introverted 13-year-old Jason is a suspect in the murder of a 7-year-old girl in this dark and suspenseful story that features an ambitious and ruthless detective. (Rev: BCCB 12/01; BL 7/01; HB 11–12/01; HBG 3/02; SLJ 9/01; VOYA 10/01)

1344 Cormier, Robert. *Tunes for Bears to Dance To* (6–12). 1992, Dell paper $5.50 (978-0-440-21903-3). In a stark morality tale set in a Massachusetts town after World War II, Henry, 11, is tempted, corrupted, and redeemed. (Rev: BL 6/15/92; SLJ 9/92)

1345 Cormier, Robert. *We All Fall Down* (8–12). 1991, Dell paper $5.50 (978-0-440-21556-1). Random violence committed by four high school seniors is observed by the Avenger, who also witnesses the budding love affair of one of the victims of the attack. (Rev: BL 9/15/91*; SLJ 9/91*)

1346 Coryell, Susan. *Eaglebait* (6–9). 1989, Harcourt $14.95 (978-0-15-200442-2). An unpopular teenage nerd thinks he has found a friend in a new science teacher. (Rev: BL 11/1/89; SLJ 6/90)

1347 Cossi, Olga. *The Magic Box* (7–9). 1990, Pelican $14.95 (978-0-88289-748-6). Mara cannot seem to give up smoking until her mother, a former smoker, develops throat cancer. (Rev: BL 10/15/90; SLJ 8/90; VOYA 8/90)

1348 Crocker, Nancy. *Billie Standish Was Here* (6–9). 2007, Simon & Schuster $16.99 (978-1-4169-2423-4). Billie, an unhappy 11-year-old, befriends her elderly neighbor Miss Lydia, and they rely on each other as they navigate some major personal and natural upheavals. (Rev: BL 6/1–15/07; SLJ 7/07)

1349 Cross, Gillian. *Tightrope* (7–12). 1999, Holiday $16.95 (978-0-8234-1512-0). To take her mind off the hours she spends caring for her invalid mother, Ashley begins to hang out with a local street gang. (Rev: BCCB 12/99; BL 9/15/99; HBG 4/00; SLJ 10/99; VOYA 4/00)

1350 Crowe, Carole. *Waiting for Dolphins* (6–12). 2000, Boyds Mills $16.95 (978-1-56397-847-0). Still recovering from her father's death in a boating incident, Molly must also adjust to her mother's new love interest. (Rev: BL 3/1/00; HBG 9/00; SLJ 4/00; VOYA 6/00)

1351 Crutcher, Chris. *The Sledding Hill* (8–11). 2005, HarperCollins LB $17.89 (978-0-06-050244-7). Not even death can separate teenage friends

Billy Bartholomew and Eddie Proffit in this thought-provoking novel that not only features author Crutcher but also a controversial novel called *Warren Peace*. (Rev: BL 5/1/05; SLJ 6/05; VOYA 6/05)

1352 Cumbie, Patricia. *Where People like Us Live* (7–12). 2008, HarperCollins $16.99 (978-0-06-137597-2). When her family moves to a depressed town in Wisconsin, Libby makes friends with a girl named Angie and soon discovers that Angie is being sexually abused by her stepfather. (Rev: BL 4/1/08; SLJ 6/08)

1353 Danziger, Paula. *Can You Sue Your Parents for Malpractice?* (6–9). 1998, Putnam paper $4.99 (978-0-698-11688-7). Lauren, 14 years old, faces a variety of problems both at home and at school.

1354 Danziger, Paula. *Remember Me to Harold Square* (6–9). Illus. 1999, Putnam paper $5.99 (978-0-698-11694-8). Kendra gets to know attractive Frank when they participate in scavenger hunts in New York City. (Rev: BL 10/1/87; SLJ 11/87; VOYA 12/87)

1355 Daoust, Jerry. *Waking Up Bees: Stories of Living Life's Questions* (7–12). 1999, Saint Mary's paper $6.95 (978-0-88489-527-5). In this collection of 10 short stories, young Christians find answers to life's dilemmas in their faith. (Rev: VOYA 4/00)

1356 Davis, Tanita S. *A La Carte* (7–10). 2008, Knopf $15.99 (978-0-375-84815-5). African American high school senior Lainey hopes to become a celebrity vegetarian chef; when her best friend Simeon disappears with $500 of her money, Lainey is alone in the kitchen and with her thoughts. (Rev: BL 8/08)

1357 Dean, Carolee. *Comfort* (7–10). 2002, Houghton $15.00 (978-0-618-13846-3). Fourteen-year-old Kenny persists in his dreams of making something of himself in spite of his mother's conflicting desires. (Rev: HBG 10/02; SLJ 3/02*; VOYA 4/02)

1358 Deckers, Amber. *Ella Mental: And the Good Sense Guide* (6–9). 2006, Simon & Schuster paper $5.99 (978-1-4169-1322-1). Fourteen-year-old Ella brings her high standards of morality and her off-beat sense of humor to bear as she attempts to help her British mates deal with very serious problems while struggling with her own interest in Toby. (Rev: SLJ 7/06)

1359 Dee, Barbara. *Just Another Day in My Insanely Real Life* (4–7). 2006, Simon & Schuster $15.95 (978-1-4169-0861-6). Cassie must deal with the fallout from her parents' divorce, with her irresponsible older sister and demanding little brother, and with her former best friends in this novel about an all-too-real situation. (Rev: BL 5/15/06; SLJ 8/06)

1360 de Guzman, Michael. *Finding Stinko* (5–8). 2007, Farrar $16.00 (978-0-374-32305-9). On the run from his latest and worst set of foster parents, Newboy, an elective mute, finds new voice with a ventriloquist's dummy; a compelling book of survival on the streets. (Rev: BL 4/15/07; SLJ 6/07)

1361 DeKeyser, Stacy. *Jump the Cracks* (5–8). 2008, Flux paper $9.95 (978-0-7387-1274-1). Victoria, 15, sees a little boy being mistreated at a train station and ends up taking him to Georgia — an originally compassionate act that she soon finds will have huge complications. (Rev: BL 3/1/08; SLJ 9/08)

1362 Delaney, Mark. *Pepperland* (8–12). 2004, Peachtree $14.95 (978-1-56145-317-7). In this poignant coming-of-age novel set in 1980, 16-year-old Pamela Jean tries to cope with the pain of her mother's death from cancer. (Rev: BL 12/1/04; SLJ 11/04; VOYA 10/04)

1363 De Palma, Toni. *Under the Banyan Tree* (6–9). 2007, Holiday $16.95 (978-0-8234-1965-4). Irena, 15 but seeming younger, runs away from home after her mother leaves and tries to make a better life for herself working at the Banyan Tree Motel in Key West. (Rev: BL 8/07; SLJ 7/07)

1364 Deriso, Christine Hurley. *Do-Over* (5–8). 2006, Delacorte LB $17.99 (978-0-385-90350-9). Between the recent death of her mother and the move to a new school, 7th-grader Elsa is having a hard time of it, but things look up when her mother mysteriously appears one night and grants her do-over power. (Rev: SLJ 8/06)

1365 Dessen, Sarah. *Dreamland* (8–10). 2000, Viking $16.99 (978-0-670-89122-1). After her sister runs away, Caitlin's life comes apart and she descends into drugs and sex. (Rev: BL 11/1/00*; HB 9–10/00; HBG 3/01; SLJ 9/00)

1366 Dessen, Sarah. *Just Listen* (8–11). 2006, Viking $17.99 (978-0-670-06105-1). Annabel is shunned by her friends after being seen in a compromising situation with her best friend's boyfriend. (Rev: BL 3/15/06; SLJ 5/06; VOYA 4/06)

1367 Dessen, Sarah. *Keeping the Moon* (6–10). 1999, Viking $17.99 (978-0-670-88549-7). Colie, a 15-year-old girl with little self-esteem, spends a summer with an eccentric aunt and finds a kind of salvation in a friendship with two waitresses and the love of a shy teenage artist. (Rev: BL 9/1/99; HBG 4/00; SLJ 9/99; VOYA 12/99)

1368 Dessen, Sarah. *Lock and Key* (8–12). 2008, Viking $18.99 (978-0-670-01088-2). After a life of experiencing abandonment, 17-year-old Ruby moves in with her older sister Cora and her husband, starts attending a private school, and slowly learns to trust others and make friends. (Rev: BL 2/1/08; SLJ 5/08)

1369 Dessen, Sarah. *Someone Like You* (7–12). 1998, Viking $17.99 (978-0-670-87778-2). Young Halley discovers that her best friend Scarlett is pregnant and Scarlett's boyfriend has been killed in an accident. (Rev: BL 5/15/98; HB 7–8/98; HBG 9/98; SLJ 6/98; VOYA 8/98)

1370 Dessen, Sarah. *That Summer* (7–12). 1996, Orchard LB $17.99 (978-0-531-08888-3). Haven is 15 and 5 feet 11, and to make matters worse, she has to be bridesmaid at her picture-perfect sister's wedding. (Rev: BL 10/15/96*; SLJ 10/96; VOYA 12/96)

1371 De Vries, Anke. *Bruises* (6–10). Trans. by Stacey Knecht. 1996, Front St. $15.95 (978-1-886910-03-4). This novel, set in Holland, tells of the friendship between a sympathetic boy, Michael, and Judith, a disturbed, abused young girl. (Rev: BL 4/1/96; SLJ 6/96; VOYA 6/96)

1372 Douglas, Lola. *True Confessions of a Hollywood Starlet* (8–10). 2005, Penguin $16.99 (978-1-59514-035-7). Teen movie star Morgan Carter, on the mend from a drug overdose in Hollywood, adopts a new identity when she is sent to a midwestern high school in this credible and amusing novel. (Rev: BCCB 2/06; SLJ 12/05; VOYA 4/06)

1373 Doyle, Malachy. *Who Is Jesse Flood?* (6–9). 2002, Bloomsbury $14.95 (978-1-58234-776-9). Unhappy 14-year-old Jesse struggles to cope with his parents and his loneliness in his Northern Ireland hometown. (Rev: BCCB 12/02; BL 10/1/02; SLJ 10/02*)

1374 Draper, Sharon M. *Romiette and Julio* (6–10). 1999, Simon & Schuster $16.00 (978-0-689-82180-6). An updated version of Romeo and Juliet set in contemporary Cincinnati involving a Hispanic American boy, an African American girl, street gangs, and, in this case, a happy ending. (Rev: BL 9/15/99; HBG 4/00; SLJ 9/99; VOYA 12/99)

1375 Dreyer, Ellen. *Speechless in New York: Going to New York* (5–8). Series: Going To. 2000, Four Corners paper $7.95 (978-1-893577-01-5). Jessie is beset with personal problems when she flies to New York from Minnesota with the Prairie Youth Chorale. (Rev: SLJ 3/00)

1376 Ellis, Deborah. *Looking for X* (6–9). 2000, Douglas & McIntyre paper $7.95 (978-0-88899-382-3). Khyber, a waif who is considered a loner by her classmates, is wrongfully accused of vandalism. (Rev: BCCB 9/00; BL 5/15/00; HB 7–8/00; HBG 9/00; SLJ 7/00)

1377 Ellis, Sarah. *Pick-Up Sticks* (5–8). 1992, Macmillan LB $15.00 (978-0-689-50550-8). A disgruntled teen learns a lesson in life after being sent to live with relatives. (Rev: BL 1/15/92; SLJ 3/92*)

1378 Erlings, Fridrik. *Benjamin Dove* (5–8). 2007, North-South $15.95 (978-0-7358-2150-7); paper $7.95 (978-0-7358-2149-1). Set in Iceland, this story of four boys' friendship ends in violence when

some of the friends take tragically wrong turns in their lives. (Rev: BL 2/1/08; SLJ 12/07)

1379 Esckilsen, Erik E. *The Last Mall Rat* (7–10). 2003, Houghton $15.00 (978-0-618-23417-2). Bored and penniless, 15-year-old Mitch agrees to harass rude shoppers. (Rev: BL 4/1/03; HBG 4/04; SLJ 6/03; VOYA 6/03)

1380 Evangelista, Beth. *Gifted* (5–8). 2005, Walker $16.95 (978-0-8027-8994-5). George R. Clark is gifted and colossally unpopular with most of his classmates, so he is uneasy about going on his 8th-grade science field trip without his principal-father to protect him from the bullies; funny and real. (Rev: BL 12/15/05*; HBG 4/06; LMC 11–12/05; SLJ 1/06; VOYA 10/05)

1381 Evans, Douglas. *So What Do You Do?* (5–8). 1997, Front St. $14.95 (978-1-886910-20-1). Two middle-schoolers help their beloved former teacher who has become a homeless drunk. (Rev: BCCB 3/98; BL 11/1/97; HBG 3/98; SLJ 1/98; VOYA 2/98)

1382 Evans, Mari. *I'm Late: The Story of LaNeese and Moonlight and Alisha Who Didn't Have Anyone of Her Own* (7–12). Illus. by Varnette Honeywood. 2006, Just Us Bks. $14.95 (978-1-933491-00-4). Using an authentic voice and effective line drawings, Evans interweaves stories about pregnancy, loneliness, and bad decisions as experienced by three African American teenagers and shows their growth as they learn to make better choices. (Rev: SLJ 7/06)

1383 Eyerly, Jeannette. *Someone to Love Me* (7–10). 1987, HarperCollins LB $11.89 (978-0-397-32206-0). An unpopular high school girl is seduced by the school's glamour boy and decides, when she finds she is pregnant, to keep the child. (Rev: BL 2/1/87; SLJ 4/87; VOYA 4/87)

1384 Facklam, Margery. *The Trouble with Mothers* (6–8). 1991, Avon paper $2.95 (978-0-380-71139-0). Troy is angered when the town censors target his mother's historical novel. (Rev: BL 3/1/89; SLJ 5/89; VOYA 6/89)

1385 Fergus, Maureen. *Exploits of a Reluctant (but Extremely Goodlooking) Hero* (8–10). 2007, Kids Can $16.95 (978-1-55453-024-3). A nameless 13-year-old narrator records his comments on life on a tape recorder; this is a funny story about a self-centered kid who eventually learns a little about sensitivity. (Rev: HB 5–6/07; LMC 10/07; SLJ 4/07)

1386 Ferris, Jean. *Across the Grain* (8–12). 1993, Topeka LB $16.35 (978-0-7857-0723-3). Paige and his elder sister head to a community in the desert where they take jobs in a restaurant. (Rev: BL 11/15/90)

1387 Ferris, Jean. *Bad* (7–10). 1998, Farrar paper $4.95 (978-0-374-40475-8). Dallas gains self knowledge when she is sent to a women's correctional center for six months and meets gang members, drug dealers, a 14-year-old prostitute, and other unfortunates. (Rev: BL 10/1/98; SLJ 12/98; VOYA 2/99)

1388 Ferris, Jean. *Of Sound Mind* (6–9). 2001, Farrar $16.00 (978-0-374-35580-7). High school senior Theo, who is the only hearing member of his demanding family, finds support and romance when he meets Ivy, who also can both hear and sign. (Rev: BCCB 10/01; BL 9/15/01; HB 11–12/01; HBG 3/02; SLJ 9/01; VOYA 10/01)

1389 Ferry, Charles. *A Fresh Start* (7–10). 1996, Proctor paper $8.95 (978-1-882792-18-4). This novel explores the problems of troubled teens in a summer-school program for young alcoholics. (Rev: SLJ 5/96; VOYA 10/96)

1390 Filichia, Peter. *What's in a Name?* (7–12). 1988, Avon paper $2.75 (978-0-380-75536-3). Rose is so unhappy with her foreign-sounding last name that she decides to change it. (Rev: BL 3/1/89; VOYA 4/89)

1391 Fitzhugh, Louise. *Harriet the Spy* (6–8). 2001, Random paper $5.99 (978-0-440-41679-1). The story of a girl whose passion for honesty gets her into trouble. Followed by *The Long Secret*.

1392 Flake, Sharon G. *A Freak Like Me* (5–9). 1999, Hyperion paper $5.99 (978-0-7868-1307-0). In her inner-city middle school, Maleeka Madison is picked on by classmates because she is poorly dressed, darker than the others, and gets good grades. (Rev: BL 9/1/98; SLJ 11/98)

1393 Fletcher, Christine. *Tallulah Falls* (8–11). 2006, Bloomsbury $16.95 (978-1-58234-662-5). At the age of 17, unhappy Tallulah (formerly known as Debbie) runs away from home looking for her older friend Maeve, who has bipolar disease and has left Oregon for Florida; on the way, Tallulah becomes stranded in Tennessee and finds a haven working in a veterinary clinic. (Rev: BL 4/1/06; SLJ 6/06)

1394 Fletcher, Ralph J. *Spider Boy* (5–8). 1997, Houghton $16.00 (978-0-395-77606-3). Bobby — nicknamed Spider Boy because he knows so much about spiders — has trouble adjusting to his new life in the town of New Paltz, New York. (Rev: BCCB 4/97; BL 6/1–15/97; HB 7–8/97; SLJ 7/97)

1395 Flinn, Alex. *Breathing Underwater* (7–12). 2001, HarperCollins $18.99 (978-0-06-029198-3). In this harrowing account of domestic violence, the sins of the father are reflected in troubled teen Nick Andreas's savage treatment of his girlfriend, Caitlin. (Rev: BCCB 7–8/01; BL 8/01; HBG 10/01; SLJ 5/01; VOYA 6/01)

1396 Fogelin, Adrian. *The Sorta Sisters* (5–8). Illus. by author. 2007, Peachtree $14.95 (978-1-56145-424-2). Anna, a foster child who lives in Tallahas-

see, Florida, corresponds with Mica, who lives with her alcoholic father on a boat in the Florida Keys, and their friendship brings them both solace. (Rev: BL 1/1–15/08; SLJ 12/07)

1397 Foon, Dennis. *Double or Nothing* (6–12). 2000, Annick $17.95 (978-1-55037-627-2); paper $6.95 (978-1-55037-626-5). High school senior Kip feels secure that he has saved enough money for college until he meets King, a magician and con artist who takes advantage of Kip's love of gambling. (Rev: BL 8/00; HBG 9/00; SLJ 9/00)

1398 Fox, Paula. *Monkey Island* (5–8). 1991, Watts LB $16.99 (978-0-531-08562-2). A homeless, abandoned 11-year-old boy in New York City contracts pneumonia and is cared for by a homeless African American teenager and retired teacher, who share their place in the park with him. (Rev: BCCB 10/91*; BL 9/1/91*; HB 9–10/91*; SLJ 8/91)

1399 Fox, Paula. *Western Wind* (5–9). 1993, Orchard LB $17.99 (978-0-531-08652-0). At first resentful of being sent to spend a summer with her grandmother on a Maine island, Elizabeth gradually adjusts and learns a great deal about herself. (Rev: BCCB 9/93; BL 10/15/93; SLJ 12/93*; VOYA 12/93)

1400 Franco, Betsy, ed. *Things I Have to Tell You: Poems and Writing by Teenage Girls* (7–12). Photos by Nina Nickles. 2001, Candlewick paper $8.99 (978-0-7636-1035-7). Teen girls reveal their aspirations, fears, and frustrations in this appealing collection of poems, stories, and essays. (Rev: BL 3/15/01; HB 5–6/01; HBG 10/01; SLJ 5/01; VOYA 10/01)

1401 Fredericks, Mariah. *The True Meaning of Cleavage* (7–10). 2003, Simon & Schuster $15.95 (978-0-689-85092-9). High school freshman Jess describes her friend Sari's obsession with an older student in this novel of sexuality, betrayal, and self-image. (Rev: BCCB 3/03; BL 3/15/03*; HB 7–8/03; HBG 10/03; SLJ 2/03; VOYA 4/03)

1402 Freeman, Martha. *1,000 Reasons Never to Kiss a Boy* (7–10). 2007, Holiday $16.95 (978-0-8234-2044-5). Sixteen-year-old Jane actually comes up with only 40+ reasons not to kiss boys before she gets over her first boyfriend and finds reasons to love and kiss again; a funny, light novel. (Rev: BL 8/07; SLJ 10/07)

1403 Freeman, Martha. *The Year My Parents Ruined My Life* (6–9). 1997, Holiday $15.95 (978-0-8234-1324-9). Twelve-year-old Kate has many problems adjusting to her new home in a small Pennsylvania town and longs to return to the suburbs of Los Angeles, her friends, and dreamy boyfriend. (Rev: BL 12/1/97; HBG 3/98; SLJ 12/97)

1404 Freymann-Weyr, Garret. *My Heartbeat* (8–12). 2002, Houghton $15.00 (978-0-618-14181-4). Fourteen-year-old Ellen is in love with James, but James and her older brother Link are also involved. (Rev: BCCB 5/02; BL 6/1–15/02; HB 5–6/02*; HBG 10/02; SLJ 4/02; VOYA 4/02)

1405 Friel, Maeve. *Charlie's Story* (8–10). 1997, Peachtree $14.95 (978-0-561-45167-1). Charlie, who was abandoned by her mother as a child, now lives with her father in Ireland and, at age 14, is facing a group of bullies at school who accuse her of a theft and cause a terrible field hockey incident. (Rev: BL 1/1–15/98; VOYA 2/98)

1406 Friesen, Gayle. *Men of Stone* (5–8). 2000, Kids Can $16.95 (978-1-55074-781-2). While Ben Conrad traces his own family roots, he confronts a local bully in this story of a boy's journey to maturity. (Rev: HBG 3/01; SLJ 10/00; VOYA 2/01)

1407 Frizzell, Colin. *Chill* (7–10). 2006, Orca paper $8.95 (978-1-55143-507-7). Chill, a talented artist with a crippled leg, has a very low opinion of the new English teacher, Mr. Sfinkter, and shows this in a mural he paints at the front of the school; suitable for reluctant readers. (Rev: SLJ 3/07)

1408 Froese, Deborah. *Out of the Fire* (8–11). 2002, Sumach paper $7.95 (978-1-894549-09-7). Sixteen-year-old Dayle is badly burned at a riotous bonfire party and spends the painful months that follow reassessing her feelings about friends and family. (Rev: BL 7/02; SLJ 8/02)

1409 Frost, Helen. *Keesha's House* (6–10). 2003, Farrar $16.00 (978-0-374-34064-3). Keesha reaches out to other teens in trouble as they describe their problems in brief, poetic vignettes. (Rev: BL 3/1/03; HBG 10/03; SLJ 3/03*; VOYA 4/03)

1410 Gabhart, Ann. *Bridge to Courage* (6–8). 1993, Avon paper $3.50 (978-0-380-76051-0). Luke is afraid of bridges and walks away from the initiation rites of the elite Truelanders, who then shun him. Luke finally learns self-confidence in this deftly plotted tale. (Rev: BL 5/15/93; VOYA 10/93)

1411 Galante, Cecilia. *The Patron Saint of Butterflies* (6–10). 2008, Bloomsbury $16.95 (978-1-59990-249-4). Honey and Agnes are whisked away from the religious commune in which they have grown up and are amazed to discover the world that has always existed around them. (Rev: BL 4/15/08; SLJ 6/08)

1412 Gallagher, Liz. *The Opposite of Invisible* (8–10). 2008, Random $15.99 (978-0-375-84152-1). Should Alice return the affections of popular, football-playing Simon or remain true to her friend Julian (Jewel), an artistic loner who also has feelings for her? (Rev: BL 11/15/07; LMC 4–5/08; SLJ 5/08) 🏵

1413 Garcia, Cristina. *I Wanna Be Your Shoebox* (5–8). 2008, Simon & Schuster $16.99 (978-1-4169-6229-8). Thirteen-year-old Yumi is part Cuban, part Japanese, and part Jewish, and it is only

when her terminally ill grandfather, a Russian Jew, tells her his life story that she begins to understand her own identity. (Rev: BL 8/08)

1414 Garden, Nancy. *The Year They Burned the Books* (7–12). 1999, Farrar $17.00 (978-0-374-38667-2). High school senior Jamie Crawford's problems as editor of the school newspaper under attack by a right-wing group are compounded when she realizes that she is a lesbian and falling in love with Tessa, a new girl in school. (Rev: BL 8/99; HBG 4/00; SLJ 9/99; VOYA 12/99)

1415 Gardner, Graham. *Inventing Elliot* (5–9). 2004, Dial $16.99 (978-0-8037-2964-3). Despite efforts to avoid bullies at his new high school, 14-year-old Elliot Sutton finds himself embroiled with the Guardians, a group that metes out punishment to those it deems "losers." (Rev: BL 5/15/04; SLJ 3/04; VOYA 4/04)

1416 Garfinkle, D. L. *Storky: How I Lost My Nickname and Won the Girl* (8–11). 2005, Penguin $16.99 (978-0-399-24284-7). In journal entries, 14-year-old Mike Pomerantz chronicles the troubles and unexpected joys of his first year in high school. (Rev: BCCB 5/05; BL 3/15/05; SLJ 3/05)

1417 Gauthier, Gail. *Happy Kid!* (6–9). 2006, Penguin $16.99 (978-0-399-24266-3). Kyle starts 7th grade with a negative attitude that is sometimes lightened and sometimes reinforced by the advice in a book his mother gives him called *Happy Kid!* (Rev: BL 4/1/06; SLJ 7/06)

1418 Gilbert, Barbara Snow. *Broken Chords* (8–12). 1998, Front St. $15.95 (978-1-886910-23-2). As she prepares for the piano competition that could lead to a place at Juilliard, Clara has doubts about the lifetime of sacrifice that a career in music would require. (Rev: BL 12/15/98; HB 11–12/98; HBG 3/99; SLJ 12/98; VOYA 2/99)

1419 Gilbert, Barbara Snow. *Stone Water* (5–9). 1996, Front St. $15.95 (978-1-886910-11-9). Fourteen-year-old Grant must decide if he will honor his ailing grandfather's wish to help him commit suicide. (Rev: BL 12/15/96; SLJ 12/96*; VOYA 4/97)

1420 Giles, Gail. *Right Behind You* (8–11). 2007, Little, Brown $15.99 (978-0-316-16636-2). Four years after killing a child by setting him on fire, 14-year-old Kip is released from a juvenile mental facility and must try to start over in a new place with a new name. (Rev: BL 10/15/07; LMC 1/08; SLJ 9/07)

1421 Godden, Rumer. *An Episode of Sparrows* (7–10). 1993, Pan Books paper $16.95 (978-0-330-32779-4). In postwar London two waifs try to grow a secret garden. (Rev: SLJ 6/89)

1422 Golding, Theresa Martin. *Kat's Surrender* (5–8). 1999, Boyds Mills $16.95 (978-1-56397-755-8). Thirteen-year-old Kat misses her deceased moth-

81

er terribly, but she tries to hide it in her friendships for an old man and a wacky girl. (Rev: BL 10/15/99; HBG 3/00; SLJ 11/99; VOYA 4/00)

1423 Gonzalez, Gabriela, and Gaby Triana. *Backstage Pass* (6–12). 2004, HarperCollins LB $16.89 (978-0-06-056018-8). Desert McGraw, 16-year-old daughter of an aging rock star, moves to Miami and longs more than anything for normalcy in her life. (Rev: BL 7/04; SLJ 8/04)

1424 Gonzalez, Julie. *Ricochet* (7–9). 2007, Delacorte $17.99 (978-0-385-73228-4). While playing a game of Russian roulette, Connor's best friend Daniel is killed, and Connor, who was a part of the game, must deal with guilt and grief. (Rev: BL 4/1/07; LMC 4-5/07; SLJ 4/07)

1425 Gordon, Amy. *The Gorillas of Gill Park* (4–7). Illus. 2003, Holiday $16.95 (978-0-8234-1751-3). Shy, lonely Willie comes into his own when he spends the summer with his eccentric Aunt Bridget and meets her zany neighbors. (Rev: BL 6/1–15/03; HBG 10/03; SLJ 5/03)

1426 Gordon, Amy. *The Secret Life of a Boarding School Brat* (5–7). 2004, Holiday House $16.95 (978-0-8234-1779-7). Lydia, already unhappy about her parents' divorce and her grandmother's death, becomes even more miserable at her new boarding school and chronicles her woes in her diary. (Rev: HB 7–8/04; SLJ 8/04)

1427 Gorman, Carol. *Games: A Tale of Two Bullies* (4–7). 2007, HarperCollins $16.99 (978-0-06-057027-9). Instead of suspending Mick and Boot for fighting, their principal requires them to play board games together; after a rocky start punctuated with petty crimes, the boys explore a hidden tunnel together, discovering that they both cope with alcoholic, abusive fathers. (Rev: BL 1/1–15/07; SLJ 1/07)

1428 Grab, Daphne. *Alive and Well in Prague, New York* (7–10). 2008, HarperCollins $16.99 (978-0-06-125670-7). Matisse's father becomes ill and the family moves from Manhattan to a tiny town in upstate New York, resulting in culture shock and resentment until Matisse learns to appreciate her new school and surroundings. (Rev: BL 5/15/08; SLJ 6/08)

1429 Grant, Vicki. *Dead-End Job* (7–12). 2005, Orca paper $7.95 (978-1-55143-378-3). Frances finds her life coming apart at the seams after she meets an emotionally disturbed loner named Devin; suitable for reluctant readers. (Rev: SLJ 11/05)

1430 Grant, Vicki. *Pigboy* (5–9). Series: Orca Currents. 2006, Orca $14.95 (978-1-55143-666-1); paper $8.95 (978-1-5314-3643-8). Certain that his classmates' teasing will reach a new high, Dan Hogg dreads the field trip to a pig farm, but he deals well with the challenges that await him as he faces off with an escaped convict; suitable for reluctant

readers and gripping enough for others. (Rev: SLJ 12/06)

1431 Gray, Dianne E. *Holding Up the Earth* (5–8). 2000, Houghton $15.00 (978-0-618-00703-5). Sarah, a foster child now living on a Nebraska farm, does some research and uncovers stories of the many generations of women who preceded her on the farm and their struggles and problems. (Rev: BL 1/1–15/01; HB 9–10/00; HBG 3/01; SLJ 10/00)

1432 Greene, Bette. *I've Already Forgotten Your Name, Philip Hall!* (4–7). Illus. by Leonard Jenkins. 2004, HarperCollins $15.99 (978-0-06-051835-6). A little white lie that strains her relationship with her best friend, Philip Hall, is only one of the dramas Beth Lambert must deal with in this story set in small-town Arkansas. (Rev: BL 5/1/04; HB 3–4/04; SLJ 3/04; VOYA 6/04)

1433 Greene, Constance C. *Monday I Love You* (7–10). 1988, HarperCollins $11.95 (978-0-06-022183-6). An overdeveloped bust is just one of the problems 15-year-old Grace faces. (Rev: BL 7/88; VOYA 8/88)

1434 Griffin, Adele. *My Almost Epic Summer* (7–10). 2006, Penguin $15.99 (978-0-399-23784-3). Irene, 14, who is spending the summer babysitting, learns about friendship when she takes up with the beautiful and manipulative Starla. (Rev: BL 2/15/06; SLJ 4/06; VOYA 4/06)

1435 Grimes, Nikki. *Bronx Masquerade* (7–12). 2002, Dial $16.99 (978-0-8037-2569-0). Eighteen high school English students enjoy the weekly open-mike opportunity to express themselves in poetry and prose, revealing much about their lives and their maturing selves. (Rev: BCCB 3/02; BL 2/15/02; HB 3–4/02; HBG 10/02; SLJ 1/02; VOYA 2/02)

1436 Grove, Vicki. *Reaching Dustin* (5–8). 1998, Putnam paper $6.99 (978-0-698-11839-3). As part of a 6th-grade assignment, Carly must get to know Dustin Groat, the class outcast, and as she learns more about him and his family, she realizes that her attitudes toward him in the past have helped create his problems. (Rev: BCCB 3/98; BL 5/1/98; SLJ 5/98)

1437 Haas, Jessie. *Will You, Won't You?* (5–8). 2000, Greenwillow LB $15.89 (978-0-06-029197-6). Mad (short for Madison) is a shy middle-schooler who comes out of her shell during a summer she spends with her wise grandmother in the country. (Rev: BCCB 10/00; BL 2/1/01; HBG 3/01; SLJ 10/00)

1438 Haddix, Margaret P. *Just Ella* (7–12). 2008, Paw Prints $14.99 (978-1-4352-7937-7). The story of Cinderella after the ball, when she finds out that castle life with Prince Charming isn't all it's cut out to be, meets a social activist tutor, and rethinks her priorities in life; first published in 1999. (Rev: BL 9/1/99; SLJ 9/99; VOYA 12/99)

1439 Haines, J. D. *Vision Quest: Journey to Manhood* (6–9). 1999, Arrowsmith paper $11.95 (978-0-9653119-0-8). A 13-year-old boy is mentored by his Native American grandfather when he and his mother move from gang-ridden Chicago to the wilderness of Oklahoma. (Rev: BL 9/1/99)

1440 Halpin, Brendan. *How Ya Like Me Now* (7–10). 2007, Farrar $16.00 (978-0-374-33495-6). After his mom finally checks into rehab, Eddie moves to Boston to live with his aunt, uncle, and cousin Alex; there he deals with a totally new school and social environment and begins to blossom. (Rev: BL 5/1/07; SLJ 7/07)

1441 Hantz, Sara. *The Second Virginity of Suzy Green* (8–10). 2007, Llewellyn paper $9.95 (978-0-7387-1139-3). Suzy decides to turn over a new leaf when her sister dies and her family moves to a new town in Australia, even joining her school's virginity club and befriending the good students. (Rev: BL 10/1/07; SLJ 12/07)

1442 Hartinger, Brent. *The Order of the Poison Oak* (7–10). 2005, HarperCollins LB $16.89 (978-0-06-056731-6). Anxious to escape the "gay kid" label, 16-year-old Russel Middlebrook and two of his friends sign up to be counselors at a summer camp for young burn victims; a sequel to *Geography Club* (2003). (Rev: BCCB 3/05; BL 1/1–15/05; SLJ 4/05; VOYA 4/05)

1443 Harvey-Fitzhenry, Alyxandra. *Waking* (7–10). 2006, Orca paper $8.95 (978-1-55143-489-6). Since her mother's suicide, 16-year old Beauty has withdrawn into herself, but a new classmate, Luna, manages to reach her and Beauty soon finds the confidence to paint again and to take hesitant steps toward love. (Rev: SLJ 7/06)

1444 Hawks, Robert. *The Twenty-Six Minutes* (6–10). 1988, Square One paper $4.95 (978-0-938961-03-1). Two teenage misfits join an anti-nuclear protest group. (Rev: SLJ 11/88; VOYA 4/89)

1445 Haworth-Attard, Barbara. *Theories of Relativity* (8–11). 2005, Holt $16.95 (978-0-8050-7790-2). When his mother sends him packing to make room for her latest boyfriend, 16-year-old Dylan Wallace struggles to survive on the streets without resorting to a life of crime. (Rev: BL 11/1/05; SLJ 11/05; VOYA 2/06)

1446 Head, Ann. *Mr. and Mrs. Bo Jo Jones* (7–12). 1973, Signet paper $4.99 (978-0-451-16319-6). The perennial favorite about two teenagers madly in love but unprepared for the responsibilities of parenthood.

1447 Heide, Florence Parry. *Growing Anyway Up* (6–8). 1976, HarperCollins $12.95 (978-0-397-

31657-1). Florence is shy when confronted with new situations but an aunt helps her conquer her fears.

1448 Hemphill, Stephanie. *Things Left Unsaid* (8–12). 2005, Hyperion $16.99 (978-0-7868-1850-1). In this powerful free-verse novel, good girl Sarah Lewis becomes bored with her predictable life and adopts defiant Robin's bad habits, until Robin attempts suicide and Sarah must review her priorities. (Rev: BCCB 7–8/05; BL 5/1/05; HB 5–6/05; SLJ 2/05; VOYA 10/04)

1449 Henderson, Aileen K. *Treasure of Panther Peak* (4–7). Illus. 1998, Milkweed paper $6.95 (978-1-57131-619-6). Twelve-year-old Ellie Williams gradually adjusts to her new home when her mother, fleeing an abusive husband, moves to Big Bend National Park to teach in a one-room school. (Rev: BL 12/1/98; HBG 3/99; VOYA 8/99)

1450 Herrick, Steven. *The Wolf* (7–10). 2007, Front St. $17.95 (978-1-932425-75-8). Sixteen-year-old Lucy, who lives in the shadow of her abusive father, and 15-year-old Jake, who comes from a loving household, find romance when they set out to discover whether the howling heard at night is a wolf or a dog. (Rev: BL 5/1/07; HB 5–6/07; SLJ 4/07*)

1451 High, Linda O. *The Summer of the Great Divide* (5–8). 1996, Holiday $15.95 (978-0-8234-1228-0). With the political events of 1969 as a backdrop, 13-year-old Wheezie sorts herself out at her relatives' farm. (Rev: BCCB 7–8/96; BL 6/1–15/96; SLJ 4/96)

1452 High, Linda Oatman. *Planet Pregnancy* (7–12). 2008, Front St. $16.95 (978-1-59078-584-3). Written in free verse, this is the story of 16-year-old Sahara, a teen from a small Texas town coping with pregnancy, her emotions, and the difficult decision she must make. (Rev: BL 8/08)

1453 Hill, David. *Time Out* (6–9). 2001, Cricket $15.95 (978-0-8126-2899-9). Kit is training for a race when a serious accident seems to send him into a parallel universe, where people and circumstances are eerily familiar. (Rev: BCCB 11/01; HBG 3/02; SLJ 10/01; VOYA 2/02)

1454 Hite, Sid. *A Hole in the World* (7–9). 2001, Scholastic $16.95 (978-0-439-09830-4). When Paul spends the summer on a Virginia farm, he is introduced to hard work and to the memory of a man who committed suicide the year before. (Rev: BCCB 11/01; BL 11/15/01; HBG 3/02; SLJ 10/01; VOYA 10/01)

1455 Hite, Sid. *I'm Exploding Now* (8–12). 2007, Hyperion $16.99 (978-0-7868-3757-1). Sixteen-year-old Max Whooten is disgruntled with life until he travels from Manhattan to Woodstock to bury his cat on his aunt's property and there finds some interest in life; Max's diary entries are intense and often funny. (Rev: SLJ 11/07)

1456 Holeman, Linda. *Mercy's Birds* (6–10). 1998, Tundra paper $5.95 (978-0-88776-463-9). Fifteen-year-old Mercy lives a life of loneliness and hurt as she cares for a depressed mother and an alcoholic aunt while working after school in a flower shop. (Rev: BL 12/15/98; SLJ 3/99; VOYA 12/98)

1457 Holland, Isabelle. *The Man Without a Face* (7–10). 1972, HarperCollins paper $5.99 (978-0-06-447028-5). Charles's close relations with his reclusive tutor lead to a physical experience.

1458 Holmes, Sara. *Letters from Rapunzel* (5–8). 2007, HarperCollins $15.99 (978-0-06-078073-9). In letters to an unknown correspondent, Cadence — who calls herself Rapunzel — describes her father's depression and her sense of being alone. (Rev: SLJ 2/07)

1459 Hopkins, Cathy. *Mates, Dates, and Cosmic Kisses* (6–10). 2003, Simon & Schuster paper $5.99 (978-0-689-85545-0). Teen anxieties about dating, friendship, and making decisions fill this funny novel about Izzy's attraction to a boy — and how her friends help her cope. (Rev: BL 2/1/03; SLJ 4/03)

1460 Hopkins, Cathy. *Mates, Dates, and Inflatable Bras* (6–10). 2003, Simon & Schuster paper $4.99 (978-0-689-85544-3). Lucy, 14, is concerned about her lack of development but, with the help of her friends, she is able to accept herself and even attract a cute boy. Other titles in this series include *Mates, Dates, and Designer Divas* (2003). (Rev: BL 2/1/03; SLJ 4/03)

1461 Hopkins, Cathy. *Mates, Dates, and Mad Mistakes* (6–9). 2004, Simon & Schuster paper $5.99 (978-0-689-86722-4). Izzie is ready for some rebellion anyway, but when Josh turns up her infatuation leads her into embarrassing territory. (Rev: SLJ 10/04)

1462 Hopkins, Cathy. *Mates, Dates, and Sequin Smiles* (6–9). 2004, Simon & Schuster paper $5.99 (978-0-689-86723-1). The prospect of braces sends Nesta into a funk, so she joins an acting class and there meets a cute guy named Luke. (Rev: SLJ 9/04)

1463 Horrocks, Anita. *Almost Eden* (5–8). 2006, Tundra paper $9.95 (978-0-88776-742-5). Elsie is a Mennonite girl who must deal with her mother's depression, the onset of puberty, and religious doubts in this story set in Canada in the 1960s. (Rev: BL 5/15/06)

1464 Horvath, Penny. *Everything on a Waffle* (5–7). 2001, Farrar $16.00 (978-0-374-32236-6). Eleven-year-old Primrose Squarp does not believe her parents drowned during a storm. In the meantime she is moved from pillar to post, ending up as a foster child to an elderly couple. (Rev: BCCB 3/01*; BL 2/15/01; HB 5–6/01*; HBG 10/01; SLJ 4/01; VOYA 6/01)

1465 Horvath, Polly. *The Vacation* (5–7). 2005, Farrar $16.00 (978-0-374-30870-4). When his parents go to Africa as missionaries, 12-year-old Henry is taken on an eye-opening, cross-country trip by his eccentric maiden aunts, Magnolia and Pigg; comedy and weirdness ensue. (Rev: BCCB 10/05; BL 6/05; HB 7–8/05; SLJ 8/05*)

1466 Howe, James. *Totally Joe* (6–9). 2005, Simon & Schuster $15.95 (978-0-689-83957-3). At the age of 12, Joe knows he is gay and this is reflected in his "alphabiography" (in which he must present his life from A to Z), which shows him to be a generally happy person despite some bullying. (Rev: BL 8/05; SLJ 11/05; VOYA 12/05)

1467 Howe, Norma. *Blue Avenger and the Theory of Everything* (8–10). Series: Blue Avenger. 2002, Cricket $17.95 (978-0-8126-2654-4). David Schumacher (a.k.a. Blue Avenger) faces a dilemma as he seeks to save his girlfriend from eviction. (Rev: BCCB 7–8/02; BL 5/15/02; HBG 3/03; SLJ 7/02; VOYA 12/02)

1468 Howe, Norma. *God, the Universe, and Hot Fudge Sundaes* (7–10). 1986, Avon paper $2.50 (978-0-380-70074-5). A 16-year-old girl would like to share her mother's born-again faith but can't.

1469 Howell, Simmone. *Notes from the Teenage Underground* (8–11). 2007, Bloomsbury $16.95 (978-1-58234-835-3). Gem, 17, sets out to make an original film but has problems with her friends and makes discoveries about herself along the way. (Rev: BL 6/1–15/07; SLJ 4/07)

1470 Hrdlitschka, Shelley. *Dancing Naked* (7–12). 2001, Orca $6.95 (978-1-55143-210-6). Finding herself pregnant after her first sexual encounter, 16-year-old Kia walks away from an abortion at the last minute and must draw on her inner strength to deal with the consequences of that decision. (Rev: BL 3/15/02; SLJ 3/02*)

1471 Hrdlitschka, Shelley. *Disconnected* (7–12). 1999, Orca paper $6.95 (978-1-55143-105-5). The lives of Tanner, a hockey-playing teen who has recurring dreams of trying to escape an underwater attacker, and Alex, a boy escaping his father's abuse, connect in a most unusual way. (Rev: BL 4/1/99; SLJ 6/99; VOYA 6/99)

1472 Hughes, Mark Peter. *I Am the Wallpaper* (6–9). 2005, Delacorte LB $17.99 (978-0-385-90265-6). Tired of being overshadowed by her older and prettier sister, 13-year-old Floey Packer decides it's time to give herself a radical makeover. (Rev: BCCB 9/05; BL 3/1/05; SLJ 5/05; VOYA 8/05)

1473 Huser, Glen. *Stitches* (7–10). 2003, Groundwood paper $9.95 (978-0-88899-578-0). Disfigured Chantelle and much-bullied Travis support each other through the difficult years of junior high school. (Rev: BCCB 2/04; HB 11–12/03*; HBG 4/04; SLJ 12/03; VOYA 4/04)

1474 Huser, Glen. *Touch of the Clown* (7–10). 1999, Groundwood $15.95 (978-0-88899-343-4). Neglected sisters Barbara and Livvy get a new lease on life when they meet the eccentric Cosmo, who runs a teen clown workshop. (Rev: SLJ 11/99; VOYA 10/99)

1475 Ingold, Jeanette. *Pictures, 1918* (6–9). 1998, Harcourt $16.00 (978-0-15-201802-3). In this novel set in the final days of World War I, 16-year-old Asa faces many personal problems but finds release when she becomes an apprentice to the local portrait photographer. (Rev: BCCB 10/98; VOYA 2/99)

1476 Irwin, Hadley. *The Lilith Summer* (6–8). 1979, Feminist paper $8.95 (978-0-912670-52-2). Twelve-year-old Ellen learns about old age when she "lady sits" with 77-year-old Lilith Adams.

1477 Jahn-Clough, Lisa. *Me, Penelope* (8–10). 2007, Houghton $16.00 (978-0-618-77366-4). Penelope (called Lopi) is trying to lose her virginity, and her good friend Toad helps her out while also helping Lopi make sense of her difficult past. (Rev: BL 4/1/07; HB 5–6/07; SLJ 7/07)

1478 James, Brian. *A Perfect World* (7–10). 2004, Scholastic $16.95 (978-0-439-67364-8). Haunted by the suicide of her father, Lacie Johnson follows mindlessly in the footsteps of her best friend Jenna, but when she meets Benji and falls in love, she realizes that Jenna is not a real friend at all. (Rev: BL 1/1–15/05; SLJ 1/05)

1479 Jellen, Michelle. *Spain or Shine* (6–9). Series: Students Across the Seven Seas. 2005, Penguin paper $6.99 (978-0-14-240368-6). A semester in Spain helps to bring 16-year-old Elena Holloway out of her shell. (Rev: BL 12/1/05; SLJ 1/06)

1480 Jimenez, Francisco. *Breaking Through* (6–12). 2001, Houghton $16.00 (978-0-618-01173-5). In this sequel to *The Circuit: Stories from the Life of a Migrant Child* (2001), 14-year-old Francisco recounts his efforts to improve his lot in life and describes his school and romantic experiences. (Rev: BCCB 1/02; BL 9/1/01; HB 11–12/01; HBG 3/02; SLJ 9/01; VOYA 12/01)

1481 Jimenez, Francisco. *Reaching Out* (7–12). 2008, Houghton $16.00 (978-0-618-03851-0). This sequel to the fictionalized autobiographies *The Circuit* (1997) and *Breaking Through* (2001) describes the author's time in college while his Mexican American migrant family struggles to make it in America. (Rev: BL 8/08)

1482 Johnson, Angela. *The First Part Last* (6–12). 2003, Simon & Schuster $15.95 (978-0-689-84922-0). Sixteen-year-old single-parent Bobby is overwhelmed and exhausted, but he loves his baby daughter. (Rev: BL 9/1/03*; HB 7–8/03; HBG 10/03; SLJ 6/03*; VOYA 6/03)

1483 Johnson, Lissa Halls. *Fast Forward to Normal* (6–10). Series: Brio Girls. 2001, Bethany paper $5.99 (978-1-56179-952-7). Becca, one of a quartet of high school juniors who call themselves the Brio Girls, isn't happy with her parents' idea of adopting the Guatemalan boy they have been fostering. Also in this series is *Stuck in the Sky* (2001). (Rev: BL 10/15/01)

1484 Jones, Patrick. *Cheated* (7–12). 2008, Walker $16.95 (978-0-8027-9699-8). This disturbing story about a teenager surrounded by people who cheat — and worse— spirals downward into drunken violence. (Rev: BL 3/15/08; SLJ 4/08)

1485 Jones, Patrick. *Things Change* (8–11). 2004, Walker $16.95 (978-0-8027-8901-3). Johanna, age 16, has her first boyfriend, Paul, a disturbed boy, in this novel about dating, violence, and the problems of falling in love. (Rev: BL 5/1/04; SLJ 5/04; VOYA 6/04)

1486 Jonsberg, Barry. *Am I Right or Am I Right?* (7–10). 2007, Knopf $15.99 (978-0-375-83637-4). Calma, 16, has a lot to cope with: her friend Vanessa, who is being abused; her long-absent father's return; her mother's behavior; and her crush on the gorgeous Jason. The interesting format and Calma's humor lighten the drama. (Rev: BL 1/1–15/07; SLJ 2/07)

1487 Joyce, Graham. *TWOC* (8–12). 2007, Viking $16.99 (978-0-670-06090-0). Matt's brother, who taught Matt how to steal cars (TWOC equals "take without consent"), dies in a car accident. When he appears as a ghost to Matt, Matt becomes so difficult that he is sent to a camp for troubled teens for a life-changing weekend. (Rev: BL 4/1/07; SLJ 3/07)

1488 Juby, Susan. *Alice, I Think* (8–12). 2003, HarperTempest LB $16.89 (978-0-06-051544-7). Alice, a quirky 15-year-old who has been home-schooled, enters public school and narrates in her diary all her new experiences. (Rev: BCCB 9/03; BL 8/03; HB 7–8/03; HBG 10/03; SLJ 7/03; VOYA 8/03)

1489 Juby, Susan. *Alice MacLeod, Realist at Last* (8–11). 2005, HarperCollins LB $16.89 (978-0-06-051550-8). It's an eventful summer for unconventional 16-year-old Alice McLeod, who breaks up with her boyfriend, gets and loses jobs, attracts three new male admirers, and sees her activist mom packed off to jail — all with dark good humor. (Rev: BL 4/15/05; HB 9–10/05; SLJ 9/05)

1490 Kaplow, Robert. *Alessandra in Between* (8–12). 1992, HarperCollins LB $13.89 (978-0-06-023298-6). A young heroine has a lot on her mind, including her grandfather's deteriorating health, her friendships, and an unrequited love. (Rev: BL 9/15/92; SLJ 9/92)

1491 Kassem, Lou. *Secret Wishes* (6–8). 1989, Avon paper $2.95 (978-0-380-75544-8). A girl summons up her resources to try to lose weight to be a cheerleader. (Rev: BL 4/15/89; SLJ 4/89)

1492 Katcher, Brian. *Playing with Matches* (8–11). 2008, Delacorte $15.99 (978-0-385-73544-5). Katcher combines humor and a serious teen dilemma in this story of geeky 17-year-old Leon who gets involved with Melody, who bears facial scars resulting from an accident, but then drops her to date the popular Amy. (Rev: BL 8/08)

1493 Kaye, Marilyn. *The Atonement of Mindy Wise* (6–9). 1991, Harcourt $15.95 (978-0-15-200402-6). A Jewish girl reviews a year's worth of sins on Yom Kippur and realizes she isn't as bad as she thought. (Rev: BL 6/15/91)

1494 Kaye, Marilyn. *Cassie* (6–9). 1987, Harcourt paper $4.95 (978-0-15-200422-4). A shoplifting incident forces Cassie to examine her values. A companion volume is *Lydia*, about Cassie's older sister. (Rev: SLJ 12/87)

1495 Kaye, Marilyn. *Real Heroes* (5–7). 1993, Avon paper $3.50 (978-0-380-72283-9). Kevin finds he is in the middle of a situation involving quarrels between parents and between best friends, and a controversy about a teacher who is HIV positive. (Rev: BCCB 5/93; BL 4/1/93)

1496 Keene, Carolyn. *Love Times Three* (5–8). Series: River Heights. 1991, Pocket paper $3.50 (978-0-671-96703-1). Nikki has a crush on Tim, but Brittany wants him too. (Rev: BL 12/15/89)

1497 Kennen, Ally. *Beast* (8–12). 2006, Scholastic $16.99 (978-0-439-86549-4). Stephen, 17, has faced many challenges — a criminal father, a series of foster families, arrest for theft and arson — and now he must rid himself of the huge crocodile his father gave him; this suspenseful novel full of dark humor is set in Britain. (Rev: LMC 2/07; SLJ 11/06)

1498 Kerr, Dan. *Candy on the Edge* (5–8). 2002, Coteau paper $8.95 (978-1-55050-189-6). Candy, an 8th grader, finds herself drawn into a world of crime as she makes new friends and falls for Ramon. (Rev: SLJ 5/02)

1499 Kerr, M. E. *Dinky Hocker Shoots Smack!* (6–9). 1989, HarperCollins paper $6.99 (978-0-06-447006-3). Overweight and underloved Dinky finds a unique way to gain her parents' attention in this humorous novel.

1500 Kerr, M. E. *Gentlehands* (7–12). 1990, HarperCollins paper $5.99 (978-0-06-447067-4). Buddy Boyle wonders if the grandfather he has recently grown to love is really a Nazi war criminal in this novel set on the eastern tip of Long Island.

1501 Kerr, M. E. *The Son of Someone Famous* (7–10). 1991, HarperCollins paper $3.95 (978-0-06-447069-8). In chapters alternately written by each, two teenagers in rural Vermont write about their friendship and their problems.

1502 Kerr, M. E. *What I Really Think of You* (7–10). 1982, HarperCollins $13.00 (978-0-06-023188-0); paper $3.50 (978-0-06-447062-9). The meeting of two teenagers who represent two kinds of religion — the evangelical mission and the TV pulpit. (Rev: BL 9/1/95)

1503 Ketchum, Liza. *Blue Coyote* (7–12). 1997, Simon & Schuster $16.00 (978-0-689-80790-9). High school junior Alex Beekman denies that he is gay, but, in time, he realizes the truth about himself. (Rev: BL 6/1–15/97; SLJ 5/97; VOYA 8/97)

1504 Killien, Christi. *Artie's Brief: The Whole Truth, and Nothing But* (5–7). 1989, Avon paper $2.95 (978-0-380-71108-6). Sixth-grader Artie deals with the suicide of his older brother. (Rev: BL 5/15/89)

1505 Kimmel, Elizabeth Cody. *Lily B. on the Brink of Love* (5–8). 2005, HarperCollins LB $16.89 (978-0-06-075543-0). In this charming sequel to *Lily B. on the Brink of Cool* (2003), the title character, an aspiring writer and advice columnist for her school paper, needs counsel herself when she falls in love. (Rev: BL 10/1/05; SLJ 7/05)

1506 Kimmel, Elizabeth Cody. *Spin the Bottle* (5–7). 2008, Dial $16.99 (978-0-8037-3191-2). Phoebe gets a small part in a middle-school play and must deal with spin-the-bottle games, the popular crowd, and changing friendships. (Rev: BL 5/1/08; SLJ 6/08)

1507 Kinney, Jeff. *Diary of a Wimpy Kid* (5–8). 2007, Abrams $14.95 (978-0-8109-9313-6). Greg Heffley writes in his very funny journal about the highlights — and the frequent low moments — of his first year in middle school. (Rev: BL 4/1/07; SLJ 4/07; VOYA 4/07)

1508 Klass, David. *Home of the Braves* (8–12). 2002, Farrar $18.00 (978-0-374-39963-4). Joe's plans for his senior year in high school are changed by the arrival of a Brazilian student who threatens Joe's position as soccer star and steals his would-be girlfriend too. (Rev: BCCB 12/02; BL 9/1/02; HB 1–2/03; HBG 3/03; SLJ 9/02)

1509 Klass, Sheila S. *The Uncivil War* (6–9). 1997, Holiday $15.95 (978-0-8234-1329-4). An engaging novel about a 6th-grade girl who wants to get control of her life, which includes dealing with a lifelong weight problem and the pending birth of a sibling. (Rev: BL 2/15/98; HBG 9/98; SLJ 4/98)

1510 Koertge, Ron. *The Arizona Kid* (8–12). 1989, Avon paper $3.99 (978-0-380-70776-8). Teenage Billy discovers that his uncle Wes is gay and learns about rodeos as well as the nature of love when he meets an outspoken girl named Cara. (Rev: BL 5/1/88; SLJ 6/88; VOYA 10/88)

1511 Koertge, Ron. *Boy Girl Boy* (8–11). 2005, Harcourt $16.00 (978-0-15-205325-3). Longtime friends Elliot, Teresa, and Larry find that their lives and their relationships change dramatically with high school graduation. (Rev: BL 9/1/05*; VOYA 12/05)

1512 Koertge, Ron. *Confess-O-Rama* (7–9). 1996, Orchard LB $17.99 (978-0-531-08865-4). Beset with problems about his mother and his new school, Tony unburdens himself on Confess-O-Rama, a telephone hot line, only to discover he has told all to the school's weirdo, who then makes Tony her new project. (Rev: BL 10/1/96; SLJ 9/96*; VOYA 12/96)

1513 Koertge, Ron. *The Harmony Arms* (7–9). 1992, Avon paper $3.99 (978-0-380-72188-7). Gabriel and his father have gone to Los Angeles to break into the movies. By summer's end, Gabriel has embarked on his first romance and confronted death for the first time. (Rev: BL 10/15/92; SLJ 8/92*)

1514 Koja, Kathe. *Buddha Boy* (6–10). 2003, Farrar $16.00 (978-0-374-30998-5). Justin is intrigued by "Buddha Boy," a new student whose appearance and beliefs make him the target of bullies. (Rev: BL 2/15/03; HB 5–6/03; HBG 10/03; SLJ 2/03; VOYA 4/03)

1515 Koja, Kathe. *Straydog* (7–10). 2002, Farrar $16.00 (978-0-374-37278-1). Rachel, a lonely teenager who enjoys writing, is devastated when her favorite dog at the animal shelter is put to sleep, and her anger affects the people closest to her. (Rev: BL 4/15/02; HB 5–6/02; HBG 10/02; SLJ 4/02; VOYA 6/02)

1516 Konigsburg, E. L. *Jennifer, Hecate, Macbeth, William McKinley, and Me, Elizabeth* (6–8). 1967, Macmillan $16.00 (978-0-689-30007-3). Elizabeth finds a new friend in Jennifer, an unusual girl who is interested in witchcraft.

1517 Kornblatt, Marc. *Izzy's Place* (4–7). 2003, Simon & Schuster $16.95 (978-0-689-84639-7). Summer with his grandmother proves more rewarding than 10-year-old Henry anticipated as he makes friends and gains a new outlook on life. (Rev: BL 6/1–15/03; HBG 10/03; SLJ 7/03)

1518 Koss, Amy Goldman. *The Girls* (5–9). 2000, Dial $17.99 (978-0-8037-2494-5). In chapters narrated by different protagonists, this book tells of Maya who has been dropped for no apparent reason from a clique of five popular girls in the middle school she attends. (Rev: BCCB 6/00; BL 8/00; HB 7–8/00; HBG 10/00; SLJ 6/00)

1519 Krantz, Hazel. *Walks in Beauty* (6–9). 1997, Northland paper $6.95 (978-0-87358-671-9). The story of a 15-year-old Navajo girl and how she copes with such adolescent woes as popularity, boyfriends, prom dates, and family problems. (Rev: BL 8/97; HBG 3/98; SLJ 10/97)

1520 Kropp, Paul. *Moonkid and Liberty* (6–9). 1990, Little, Brown $13.95 (978-0-316-50485-0). The teenage son and daughter of two hippies try to sort out their lives and plan for their future. (Rev: BL 6/15/90; SLJ 4/90; VOYA 6/90)

1521 Kropp, Paul. *Moonkid and Prometheus* (6–8). 1998, Stoddart paper $5.95 (978-0-7736-7465-3). In this sequel to *Moonkid and Liberty,* Moonkid takes on the job of tutoring a black student, Prometheus, in reading and Pro in turn teaches Moonkid techniques in basketball. (Rev: BL 6/1–15/98; SLJ 10/98)

1522 Krumgold, Joseph. *Onion John* (5–8). Illus. by Symeon Shimin. 1959, HarperCollins LB $17.89 (978-0-690-04698-4); paper $5.99 (978-0-06-440144-9). A Newbery Medal winner (1960) about a boy's friendship with an old man. Also use the Newbery winner . . . *And Now Miguel* (1954).

1523 Kurland, Morton L. *Our Sacred Honor* (7–12). 1987, Rosen LB $12.95 (978-0-8239-0692-5). A story from two points of view about a pregnant teenage girl, her boyfriend, and their decision for abortion. (Rev: SLJ 6/87)

1524 Kyi, Tanya L. *My Time as Caz Hazard* (8–12). 2004, Orca paper $7.95 (978-1-55143-319-6). Caz Hazard — who faces problems at home and at school — strikes up a friendship with Amanda and is drawn into a series of antisocial activities, one of which leads to the suicide of a classmate. (Rev: SLJ 3/05; VOYA 2/05)

1525 Larimer, Tamela. *Buck* (7–10). 1986, Avon paper $2.50 (978-0-380-75172-3). The friendship between runaway Buck and Rich is threatened when Buck becomes friendly with Rich's girlfriend. (Rev: BL 4/87; SLJ 6/87; VOYA 4/87)

1526 LaRochelle, David. *Absolutely, Positively Not* (7–10). 2005, Scholastic $16.95 (978-0-439-59109-6). A funny and sensitive first-person portrayal of a 16-year-old's efforts to deny his homosexuality. (Rev: BL 7/05*; SLJ 9/05; VOYA 10/05)

1527 Laser, Michael. *Cheater* (7–10). 2008, Dutton $16.99 (978-0-525-47826-3). When Karl is drawn into a secret cheating ring at his high school, he is found out by the evil assistant principal and faces challenges to his morality from all sides. (Rev: BL 3/1/08; SLJ 5/08)

1528 Lawson, Julie. *Turns on a Dime* (5–8). 1999, Stoddart paper $7.95 (978-0-7737-5942-8). In this sequel to *Goldstone* (1998), set in British Columbia, 11-year-old Jo faces many new situations, including finding a boyfriend, discovering that she is adopted, and learning that her beloved babysitter is pregnant. (Rev: SLJ 6/99)

1529 Le Guin, Ursula K. *Very Far Away from Anywhere Else* (7–10). 2004, Harcourt paper $6.95 (978-0-15-205208-9). In his friendship for Natalie,

Owen finds the fulfillment he seeks; first published in 1976.

1530 Lekich, John. *King of the Lost and Found* (6–9). 2007, Raincoast paper $9.95 (978-1-55192-802-9). Wimpy Raymond, a 10th-grader with embarrassing health problems, finds that his social status changes when he is put in charge of the school's lost-and-found and becomes business partners with popular Jack. (Rev: BL 11/15/07; SLJ 11/07)

1531 Lemieux, Michele. *Stormy Night* (4–8). Illus. by author. 1999, Kids Can $15.95 (978-1-55074-692-1). A long picture book in which a young girl who can't sleep ponders questions that are common to preteen girls. (Rev: BL 12/1/99; HBG 3/00; SLJ 12/99)

1532 Lenhard, Elizabeth. *Chicks with Sticks (Knitwise)* (7–10). Series: Chicks with Sticks. 2007, Dutton $16.99 (978-0-525-47838-6). Now in their final year of high school (and in the final book of the series), the knitting friends must deal with family problems and plans for the future; includes four knitting projects. (Rev: BL 11/1/07; SLJ 12/07)

1533 Les Becquets, Diane. *Love, Cajun Style* (8–11). 2005, Bloomsbury $16.95 (978-1-58234-674-8). Romance seems to be in the air in Lucy Beauregard's Louisiana town, spicing her interest in Dewey, son of the artist who has just opened an art gallery. (Rev: BL 9/15/05*; SLJ 10/05; VOYA 10/05)

1534 Lester, Alison. *The Quicksand Pony* (5–8). 1998, Houghton $15.00 (978-0-395-93749-5). In this novel set in Australia, 17-year-old Joycie fakes a drowning and seeks a new life in the bush with her infant son, but two young girls stumble on the truth nine years later. (Rev: BCCB 10/98; BL 12/15/98; HB 1–2/99; HBG 3/99; SLJ 10/98; VOYA 2/99)

1535 Levoy, Myron. *A Shadow Like a Leopard* (7–9). 2000, iUniverse paper $12.95 (978-0-595-09355-7). The story of an unlikely friendship between a streetwise Puerto Rican punk and a wheelchair-ridden artist, this was first published in 1981.

1536 Levy, Elizabeth. *Cheater, Cheater* (5–8). 1994, Scholastic paper $3.50 (978-0-590-45866-5). Lucy Lovello has been labeled a cheater and even her teachers don't trust her. When she finds her best friend cheating, she faces a moral dilemma. (Rev: BL 10/1/93; SLJ 10/93; VOYA 12/93)

1537 Lewis, Beverly. *Catch a Falling Star* (5–8). Series: Summerhill Secrets. 1995, Bethany paper $5.99 (978-1-55661-478-1). An Amish boy faces excommunication when he begins paying too much attention to a non-Amish girl. (Rev: BL 3/15/96)

1538 Lewis, Beverly. *Night of the Fireflies* (5–8). Series: Summerhill Secrets. 1995, Bethany House

paper $5.99 (978-1-55661-479-8). In this sequel to *Catch a Falling Star* (1995), Levi, an Amish boy, tries to save his young sister, who has been struck by a car. (Rev: BL 3/15/96)

1539 Linker, Julie. *Disenchanted Princess* (8–10). 2007, Simon & Schuster paper $8.99 (978-1-4169-3472-1). West's father is in prison and West is sent from her ritzy life in Beverly Hills to remote Possum Grape, Arkansas, to live with her aunt's family. (Rev: BL 7/07; SLJ 8/07)

1540 Lisle, Janet Taylor. *Sirens and Spies* (7–10). 2003, Aladdin paper $4.99 (978-0-689-84457-7). Elsie discovers that her beloved music teacher, originally from France, was an accused collaborator who had a child by a German soldier; originally published in 1985. (Rev: BL 5/15/85; SLJ 8/85; VOYA 12/85)

1541 Littke, Lael. *Loydene in Love* (8–10). 1986, Harcourt $13.95 (978-0-15-249888-7). A high school junior from a small town gets a different view of life when she visits Los Angeles for the summer. (Rev: BL 2/15/87; SLJ 3/87)

1542 Littke, Lael. *Shanny on Her Own* (6–9). 1985, Harcourt $12.95 (978-0-15-273531-9). Shanny is sent to live with an aunt in rural Idaho to counteract her developing punkiness. (Rev: BL 1/1/86; SLJ 12/85; VOYA 4/86)

1543 Littman, Sarah Darer. *Confessions of a Closet Catholic* (4–7). 2005, Dutton $15.99 (978-0-525-47365-7). Since she made friends with Mac, a Catholic girl, 11-year-old Justine has been questioning her Jewish faith. (Rev: SLJ 1/05)

1544 Lockhart, E. *The Boyfriend List* (8–11). 2005, Delacorte LB $17.99 (978-0-385-90238-0). After her disastrous social life triggers a series of panic attacks, 15-year-old Ruby consults a psychiatrist. (Rev: BCCB 3/05; BL 4/1/05; SLJ 4/05)

1545 Lockhart, E. *Dramarama* (8–12). 2007, Hyperion $15.99 (978-0-7868-3815-8). Sarah and her gay friend Demi find their true selves and the fun of musical theater at drama camp. (Rev: BL 4/1/07; SLJ 7/07)

1546 Love, D. Anne. *Defying the Diva* (7–10). 2008, Simon & Schuster $16.99 (978-1-4169-5209-1). When Haley publishes a piece about diva Camilla in the school newspaper's gossip column, Camilla retaliates with force, leaving Haley friendless. (Rev: BL 3/15/08; SLJ 5/08)

1547 Lowry, Brigid. *Things You Either Hate or Love* (8–11). 2006, Holiday $16.95 (978-0-8234-2004-9). The funny, compelling story of 15-year-old Georgia, a creative misfit whose quest to earn enough money for a concert ticket leads to valuable learning experiences in life and love; set in Australia, this novel includes journal entries that discuss

Georgia's weight problems. (Rev: BL 4/15/06; SLJ 4/06)

1548 Lowry, Lois. *A Summer to Die* (7–10). Illus. 1977, Houghton $16.00 (978-0-395-25338-0). Meg is confused and dismayed by her older sister's death. (Rev: BL 7/88)

1549 Lowry, Lois. *Taking Care of Terrific* (7–9). 1983, Houghton $16.00 (978-0-395-34070-7). A baby-sitting job leads to all sorts of hectic adventures for 14-year-old Enid.

1550 Lubar, David. *Dunk* (8–12). 2002, Clarion $15.00 (978-0-618-19455-1). Over the course of a summer, troubled young Chad learns a lot about himself and his anger. (Rev: BCCB 12/02; BL 9/1/02; HB 11–12/02; HBG 3/03; SLJ 8/02*)

1551 Lubar, David. *Sleeping Freshmen Never Lie* (8–11). 2005, Dutton $16.99 (978-0-525-47311-4). Aspiring writer Scott Hudson chronicles the highs and lows of his freshman year in high school. (Rev: BCCB 10/05; BL 5/15/05; SLJ 7/05*; VOYA 6/05)

1552 Lynch, Chris. *Who the Man* (6–9). 2002, HarperCollins $15.99 (978-0-06-623938-5). Thirteen-year-old Earl Pryor's ideas about manhood are turned upside-down when he sees how his father reacts to problems in his marriage. (Rev: BCCB 1/03; BL 11/15/02; HBG 10/03; SLJ 12/02; VOYA 2/03)

1553 Mac, Carrie. *Crush* (8–12). 2006, Orca $14.95 (978-1-55143-521-3); paper $7.95 (978-1-55143-526-8). While spending the summer with her older sister Joy in New York City, Hope discovers some surprises about both Joy (drug use and a live-in boyfriend) and herself (an apparent crush on a lesbian babysitting client); for reluctant readers. (Rev: SLJ 8/06)

1554 McCall, Edith. *Better Than a Brother* (6–9). 1988, Walker $14.85 (978-0-8027-6783-7). Hughie turns to her friend Jerry for help when she loses her new gold locket. (Rev: SLJ 5/88)

1555 McDaniel, Lurlene. *The Girl Death Left Behind* (6–9). 1999, Bantam paper $4.99 (978-0-553-57091-5). A touching story of a girl's adjustment to the sudden death of her parents and starting a new life living with relatives. (Rev: SLJ 3/99; VOYA 4/99)

1556 McDaniel, Lurlene. *I'll Be Seeing You* (6–9). 1996, Bantam paper $4.99 (978-0-553-56718-2). Carley's face has been disfigured by the removal of a tumor and she tries to keep this secret from a blind boy with whom she has fallen in love. (Rev: BL 7/96; SLJ 12/96)

1557 McDaniel, Lurlene. *Telling Christina Goodbye* (6–10). 2002, Bantam paper $4.99 (978-0-533-57087-4). Tucker, who had been driving recklessly, is the only person uninjured in the accident that kills Christina. (Rev: BL 3/15/02; SLJ 7/02)

1558 MacDonald, Caroline. *Speaking to Miranda* (7–10). 1992, HarperCollins LB $13.89 (978-0-06-021103-5). Set in Australia and New Zealand, Ruby, 18, leaves her boyfriend, travels with her father, and gradually decides to explore the mysteries of her life: Who was her mother? Who is her family? Who is she? (Rev: BL 12/15/92*; SLJ 10/92)

1559 McDonald, Janet. *Harlem Hustle* (8–11). 2006, Farrar $16.00 (978-0-374-37184-5). When he raps, Eric is known as "Hustle" (and he hustles on the street, too, stealing), in this novel about a young man struggling to make it against tough odds. (Rev: BL 12/1/06; HB 9–10/06; SLJ 10/06*)

1560 McDonald, Joyce. *Swallowing Stones* (7–10). 1997, Bantam paper $4.99 (978-0-440-22672-7). When Michael accidentally kills a man with his rifle, he and his friend decide to hide the gun and feign ignorance. (Rev: BL 10/15/97; SLJ 9/97; VOYA 12/97)

1561 MacKall, Dandi Daley. *Crazy in Love* (8–12). 2007, Dutton $16.99 (978-0-525-47780-8). Seventeen-year-old Mary Jane finally gets together with Jackson House and the two become an item; soon, however, Mary-Jane must decide whether to have sex with Jackson, recognizing that saying no might jeopardize their relationship. (Rev: SLJ 2/07)

1562 Mackey, Weezie Kerr. *Throwing Like a Girl* (7–10). 2007, Marshall Cavendish $16.99 (978-0-7614-5342-0). Ella adjusts to her new home in Dallas by playing on a softball team and dating a senior named Nate. (Rev: BL 3/15/07; SLJ 5/07)

1563 Mackler, Carolyn. *The Earth, My Butt, and Other Big Round Things* (7–10). 2003, Candlewick $15.99 (978-0-7636-1958-9). Virginia, a privileged New York 15-year-old, struggles with her weight, her lack of self confidence, her family, the absence of her best friend, and her aspiring boyfriend. (Rev: BL 9/1/03; HB 9–10/03; HBG 4/04; SLJ 9/03)

1564 Mackler, Carolyn. *Vegan Virgin Valentine* (8–12). 2004, Candlewick $16.99 (978-0-7636-2155-1). High school senior Mara Valentine, a classic overachiever, is right on schedule with her short-term goals for her future when Vivian comes to live with Mara's family. (Rev: BL 6/1–15/04; SLJ 8/04; VOYA 10/04)

1565 MacLachlan, Patricia. *The Facts and Fictions of Minna Pratt* (5–7). 1988, HarperCollins paper $6.99 (978-0-06-440265-1). A budding young cellist on the verge of adolescence experiences her first boyfriend. (Rev: BCCB 4/88; BL 6/15/88; SLJ 6–7/88)

1566 MacLachlan, Patricia. *Unclaimed Treasures* (5–8). 1984, HarperCollins paper $6.99 (978-0-06-440189-0). A romantic story of a young girl finding herself.

1567 McNaughton, Janet. *To Dance at the Palais Royale* (7–10). 1999, Stoddart paper $5.95 (978-0-7736-7473-8). The story of the loneliness and growing maturity of Aggie Maxwell who leaves her home in Scotland at age 17 to become a domestic servant with her sister in Toronto. (Rev: SLJ 5/99; VOYA 10/99)

1568 McVeity, Jen. *On Different Shores* (6–10). 1998, Orchard LB $17.99 (978-0-531-33115-6). The problems of a teenage Australian girl surface when the guerrilla environmental group to which she belongs is caught and a crisis develops over a beached whale. (Rev: BCCB 11/98; BL 11/15/98; HBG 3/99; SLJ 3/99; VOYA 10/98)

1569 Maguire, Gregory. *Oasis* (7–10). 1996, Clarion $15.00 (978-0-395-67019-4). This story of grief and guilt involves 13-year-old Hand, his adjustment to his father's sudden death, and his mother's efforts to save the motel her husband had managed. (Rev: BL 9/15/96; SLJ 11/96; VOYA 2/97)

1570 Mahy, Margaret. *The Catalogue of the Universe* (8–12). 1987, Scholastic paper $2.75 (978-0-590-42318-2). Through their friendship, Angela, who longs to meet her absent father, and Tycho, who believes he is physically ugly, find tenderness and compassion. (Rev: BL 3/15/86; SLJ 4/86; VOYA 12/86)

1571 Makris, Kathryn. *A Different Way* (7–10). 1989, Avon paper $2.95 (978-0-380-75728-2). A newcomer in a Texas high school wonders if acceptance by the in-crowd is worth the effort. (Rev: BL 10/15/89)

1572 Malloy, Brian. *Twelve Long Months* (8–12). 2008, Scholastic $17.99 (978-0-439-87761-9). Molly meets many challenges when she moves from a Minnesota high school to Columbia University, including finding out that the boy she loves is gay. (Rev: BL 8/08; SLJ 8/08)

1573 Mandabach, Brian. . . . *Or Not?* (7–10). 2007, Llewellyn $16.95 (978-0-7387-1100-3). From her 8th-grade classmates' point of view, Cassie is a contrarian — she rejects cell phones but loves vinyl records, she won't shave her legs, nor will she stand for the Pledge of Allegiance, and above all she's against the U.S. reaction to 9/11. (Rev: BL 9/15/07; SLJ 3/08)

1574 Manning, Sara. *French Kiss* (8–11). Series: Diary of a Crush. 2006, Penguin paper $6.99 (978-0-14-240632-8). Edie, a 16-year-old English teen, falls in love with Dylan, a brooding art student, in this first volume in a trilogy. (Rev: BL 7/06)

1575 Margolis, Leslie. *Fix* (7–12). 2006, Simon & Schuster paper $6.99 (978-1-4169-2456-2). Two sisters take different stands when their mother wants them to get nose jobs. (Rev: SLJ 10/06)

1576 Marineau, Michele. *Lean Mean Machines* (7–12). 2001, Red Deer paper $7.95 (978-0-88995-230-0). Canadian teen Jeremy Martucci befriends Laure, the new girl at his high school, but senses she's keeping a painful secret. (Rev: SLJ 11/01; VOYA 8/01)

1577 Marino, Peter. *Dough Boy* (7–10). 2005, Holiday House $16.95 (978-0-8234-1873-2). Fifteen-year-old Tristan, a child of divorce, is unfazed by his weight until Kelly, the health-obsessed daughter of his mother's boyfriend, starts picking on him. (Rev: BL 11/15/05; SLJ 11/05; VOYA 2/06)

1578 Matthews, Phoebe. *Switchstance* (7–10). 1989, Avon paper $2.95 (978-0-380-75729-9). After her parents' divorce, Elvy moves in with her grandmother and forms friendships with two very different boys. (Rev: VOYA 2/90)

1579 Mazer, Anne, ed. *Working Days: Stories About Teenagers and Work* (6–12). 1997, Persea paper $9.95 (978-0-89255-224-5). An anthology of 15 varied, multicultural short stories about teenagers at their jobs. (Rev: BL 7/97; HBG 3/98; SLJ 9/97; VOYA 12/97)

1580 Mazer, Harry. *Hey, Kid! Does She Love Me?* (7–12). 1986, Avon paper $2.95 (978-0-380-70025-7). Stage-struck Jeff falls in love with a woman who was once an aspiring actress in this romance that contains some sexually explicit language.

1581 Mazer, Norma Fox, and Harry Mazer. *Bright Days, Stupid Nights* (7–10). 1993, Bantam paper $3.50 (978-0-553-56253-8). Charts the course of four youths who are brought together for a summer newspaper internship. (Rev: BL 6/15/92; SLJ 7/92)

1582 Miles, Betty. *The Real Me* (6–8). 1975, Avon paper $2.75 (978-0-380-00347-1). Barbara rebels against all the restrictions placed on her life because she is a girl.

1583 Miller-Lachmann, Lyn. *Hiding Places* (8–12). 1987, Square One paper $4.95 (978-0-938961-00-0). Mark runs away from his suburban home and ends up in a shelter in New York City. (Rev: SLJ 5/87)

1584 Mills, Claudia. *Makeovers by Marcia* (4–7). Series: West Creek Middle School. 2005, Farrar $16.00 (978-0-374-34654-6). Marcia learns that beauty is more than skin deep — and that there are more important things than the school dance — when she gives makeovers to the women in a nursing home. (Rev: BL 3/1/05; SLJ 2/05)

1585 Moiles, Steven. *The Summer of My First Pediddle* (7–9). 1995, Royal Fireworks paper $9.99 (978-0-88092-122-0). Set in a small Illinois town during 1953, this is 14-year-old Brad Thatcher's story of how he weathered two firsts in his life — first love and his first encounter with prejudice after his father is investigated during the McCarthy hearings. (Rev: VOYA 2/96)

1586 Moore, Peter. *Caught in the Act* (8–11). 2005, Viking $16.99 (978-0-670-05990-4). Honor student Ethan Lederer is having trouble keeping his grades up and his problems multiply when he falls for Lydia, a Goth-type who turns out to be alarmingly manipulative. (Rev: BCCB 6/05; BL 3/1/05; HB 3–4/05; SLJ 5/05; VOYA 4/05)

1587 Moranville, Sharelle Byars. *The Snows* (7–10). 2007, Holt $16.95 (978-0-8050-7469-7). The stories of four 16-year-old characters in the Snow family (Jim, Cathy, Jim's daughter Jill, and Jill's daughter Mona), spanning the years 1931 to 2006 and describing key events in their adolescent lives, come together at a funeral. (Rev: BL 8/07; LMC 2/08; SLJ 9/07)

1588 Morgan, Nicola. *Chicken Friend* (5–7). 2005, Candlewick $15.99 (978-0-7636-2735-5). When her family moves to the country, Becca tries too hard to be cool and winds up in trouble in this story told from a believable pre-teen point of view. (Rev: BL 3/1/05; SLJ 4/05)

1589 Moriarty, Jaclyn. *The Year of Secret Assignments* (8–12). 2004, Scholastic $16.95 (978-0-439-49881-4). A rollicking year in the lives of three Australian high school girls — Lydia, Emily, and Cassie — is chronicled in their correspondence with male pen pals at a rival school. (Rev: BCCB 4/04; BL 1/1–15/04; HB 3–4/04; SLJ 3/04; VOYA 6/04)

1590 Morris, Winifred. *Liar* (7–10). 1996, Walker $15.95 (978-0-8027-8461-2). Fourteen-year-old Alex starts life over on his grandparents' farm in Oregon, but there are many obstacles, including school bullies, a hostile principal, and an unloving grandfather. (Rev: BL 12/1/96; SLJ 1/97; VOYA 12/96)

1591 Murdoch, Patricia. *Exposure* (8–12). Series: Orca Soundings. 2006, Orca $14.95 (978-1-55143-523-7). Revenge is the theme of this story about a girl who uses incriminating photographs to get back at a classmate who has been tormenting her; for reluctant readers. (Rev: SLJ 10/06)

1592 Murdock, Catherine Gilbert. *The Off Season* (7–10). 2007, Houghton $16.00 (978-0-618-68695-7). The unconventional D.J., first introduced to readers in 2006's *Diary Queen,* is now a junior in high school and must juggle work on her family's diary farm, playing on her school football team, and her first boyfriend. (Rev: BCCB 9/07; BL 4/15/07; HB 7–8/07; SLJ 4/07*) ⚐

1593 Murphy, Claire Rudolf. *Free Radical* (7–10). 2002, Clarion $15.00 (978-0-618-11134-3). Luke, a baseball star in Fairbanks, Alaska, is stunned when his mother turns herself in for her role in a fatal bombing more than 30 years before. (Rev: BCCB 6/02; BL 3/15/02; HBG 10/02; SLJ 3/02; VOYA 6/02)

1594 Myers, Walter Dean. *Shooter* (7–12). 2004, HarperCollins $15.99 (978-0-06-029519-6). Told from many viewpoints, this is the story of a high school senior who commits suicide after shooting a star football player and injuring several others. (Rev: BL 2/15/04*; HB 5–6/04; SLJ 5/04; VOYA 6/04)

1595 Myers, Walter Dean. *Won't Know Till I Get There* (7–10). 1982, Penguin paper $5.99 (978-0-14-032612-3). A young subway graffiti artist is sentenced to help out in a senior citizens' home.

1596 Myracle, Lauren. *ttyl* (6–10). 2004, Abrams $15.95 (978-0-8109-4821-1). This story of three 10th-graders and their lives is told through instant messages. (Rev: BL 5/15/04; SLJ 4/04; VOYA 6/04)

1597 Naylor, Phyllis Reynolds. *Alice in the Know* (7–10). 2006, Simon & Schuster $15.95 (978-0-689-87092-7). Alice, now 16, must find work for the summer, longs for more family contact, and copes with the often embarrassing teen rites of passage. (Rev: BL 5/1/06; HB 7–8/06; SLJ 8/06)

1598 Naylor, Phyllis Reynolds. *Alice on Her Way* (7–10). 2005, Simon & Schuster $15.95 (978-0-689-87090-3). Alice, now almost 16 and hoping to get her driver's license, protests the idea of attending a sex class at church, but finds to her surprise that it's interesting and informative. (Rev: BL 7/05; SLJ 5/05; VOYA 8/05)

1599 Naylor, Phyllis Reynolds. *Cricket Man* (7–9). 2008, Atheneum $16.99 (978-1-4169-4981-7). Thirteen-year-old Kenny spends his summer saving crickets from his family's pool, building his self-confidence, and nursing a desire to save his depressed 16-year-old neighbor in a story that combines humor with the heavier issues of depression and teen pregnancy. (Rev: BL 8/08)

1600 Naylor, Phyllis Reynolds. *Dangerously Alice* (7–11). Series: Alice. 2007, Simon & Schuster $15.99 (978-0-689-87094-1). Alice is worried that she's being labeled a prude at school but is reluctant to "go all the way" with her boyfriend Tony in this installment in the Alice series. (Rev: BL 4/1/07; HB 7–8/07; SLJ 8/07; VOYA 4/07)

1601 Nelson, Suzanne. *The Sound of Munich* (6–10). 2006, Penguin paper $6.99 (978-0-14-240576-5). While Siena studies in Munich, she looks for the individual who enabled her father to escape from East Germany. (Rev: SLJ 6/06)

1602 Nelson, Theresa. *The Beggar's Ride* (6–8). 1992, Orchard LB $17.99 (978-0-531-08496-0). A compelling chronicle of a runaway's time on the tawdry boardwalks of Atlantic City. (Rev: BL 11/1/92; SLJ 11/92*)

1603 Neri, G. *Chess Rumble* (5–8). Illus. by Jesse Joshua Watson. 2007, Lee & Low $18.95 (978-1-58430-279-7). Marcus learns to channel his anger — over his sister's death and his father's absence — into chess, and tells about it in free verse. (Rev: BL 1/1–15/08; SLJ 11/07)

1604 Neville, Emily C. *It's Like This, Cat* (7–9). Illus. 1963, HarperCollins LB $17.89 (978-0-06-024391-3); paper $5.99 (978-0-06-440073-2). A New York City 14-year-old boy has more in common with his cat than his father. Newbery Medal, 1964.

1605 Newbery, Linda. *Sisterland* (8–12). 2004, Random $15.95 (978-0-385-75026-4). This powerful story of love, anger, and guilt includes many generations and countries and revolves around Hilly, a contemporary British teen who is love with a Palestinian. (Rev: BL 3/1/04; HB 3–4/04; SLJ 4/04; VOYA 4/04)

1606 Noël, Alyson. *Kiss and Blog* (7–9). 2007, St. Martin's paper $8.95 (978-0-312-35509-8). Friends Winter and Sloane have a pact and when Sloane reneges, Winter gets revenge through her blog. (Rev: SLJ 6/07)

1607 Norris, Shana. *Something to Blog About* (7–10). 2008, Abrams $15.95 (978-0-8109-9474-4). Libby is horrified when her 10th-grade classmate Angel posts Libby's diary entries on the Web for all to see, and it's all made worse by the fact that her mother is dating Angel's father. (Rev: BL 2/8/08; SLJ 5/08)

1608 Paratore, Coleen Murtagh. *Mack McGinn's Big Win* (4–7). 2007, Simon & Schuster $15.99 (978-1-4169-1613-0). Mack is unhappy about his family's move to a new neighborhood and jealous of the attention his older brother gets for his athletic abilities, until a heroic act on Mack's part changes perceptions. (Rev: BL 7/07; SLJ 8/07)

1609 Park, Barbara. *Beanpole* (7–9). 1983, Avon paper $2.95 (978-0-380-69840-0). On her 13th birthday Lillian, who is extra tall for her age, makes three wishes and they seem to be coming true.

1610 Parkinson, Siobhan. *Second Fiddle* (4–7). 2007, Roaring Brook $16.95 (978-1-59643-122-5). Mags and Gillian attempt to track down Gillian's father in the hopes that he will help finance her education at a music school in England. (Rev: BCCB 6/07; BL 2/15/07; HB 3-4/07; SLJ 6/07)

1611 Pascal, Francine. *The Ruling Class* (8–11). 2004, Simon & Schuster $14.95 (978-0-689-87332-4). Brutally harassed by bullies at her new high school in Dallas, 16-year-old Twyla Gay briefly considers dropping out but decides instead to seek revenge. (Rev: BCCB 12/04; BL 1/1–15/05; SLJ 12/04)

1612 Paulsen, Gary. *The Amazing Life of Birds: (The Twenty-Day Puberty Journal of Duane Homer Leech)* (5–7). 2006, Random $13.95 (978-0-385-74660-1). Having a bad time with the onset of puberty and its accompanying embarrassments — amusingly confided in his journal — 12-year-old Duane identifies with a baby bird developing in a nest outside his window. (Rev: SLJ 10/06)

1613 Paulsen, Gary. *The Boy Who Owned the School* (6–9). 1990, Orchard paper $15.95 (978-0-531-05865-7). Jacob's main object in life is to be as invisible as possible and to avoid trouble. (Rev: BL 4/1/90; SLJ 4/90; VOYA 6/90)

1614 Paulsen, Gary. *Brian's Return* (5–8). 1999, Delacorte $15.95 (978-0-385-32500-4). Brian, the hero of *Brian's Winter,* becomes so disheartened with life at school away from the wilderness that he decides to leave society behind forever. (Rev: BL 2/1/99; HB 1–2/99; HBG 10/99; SLJ 2/99)

1615 Paulsen, Gary. *The Car* (6–9). 1994, Harcourt $17.00 (978-0-15-292878-0). The cross-country adventures of Terry, 14, and Waylon, a 45-year-old Vietnam vet who sometimes suffers flashback memories and becomes violent. (Rev: BL 4/1/94; SLJ 5/94; VOYA 6/94)

1616 Paulsen, Gary. *The Cookcamp* (5–7). 1991, Orchard paper $15.95 (978-0-531-05927-2). After a 5-year-old boy discovers his mother is having an affair, he is sent off to northern Minnesota in this World War II story. (Rev: BCCB 3/91; BL 3/1/91; HB 3–4/91; SLJ 2/91*)

1617 Paulsen, Gary. *Dancing Carl* (7–9). 1987, Puffin paper $3.95 (978-0-685-19101-9). A young boy recalls his friendship with Carl, a troubled man who is an expert ice skater.

1618 Paulsen, Gary. *The Island* (7–10). 1988, Orchard paper $17.95 (978-0-531-05749-0). A 15-year-old boy finds peace and a meaning to life when he explores his own private island. (Rev: BL 3/15/88; SLJ 5/88; VOYA 6/88)

1619 Paulsen, Gary. *Popcorn Days and Buttermilk Nights* (8–12). 1989, Penguin paper $4.99 (978-0-14-034204-8). Carley finds adventure after he is sent to his Uncle David's farm in Minnesota to sort himself out.

1620 Paulsen, Gary. *Sisters / Hermanas* (8–10). Trans. by Gloria de Aragón Andújar. 1993, Harcourt $10.95 (978-0-15-275323-8); paper $6.00 (978-0-15-275324-5). The bilingual story of two girls, age 14, in a Texas town, one an illegal Mexican immigrant prostitute, the other a superficial blond cheerleader. (Rev: BL 1/1/94; SLJ 1/94; VOYA 12/93)

1621 Paulsen, Gary. *Tracker* (7–9). 1984, Bradbury paper $3.95 (978-0-317-62280-5). John's encounters with nature help him accept the approaching death of his grandfather.

1622 Perkins, Lynne Rae. *Criss Cross* (6–9). 2005, Greenwillow LB $17.89 (978-0-06-009273-3). In a series of intersecting vignettes, a group of young teenage friends tell about their experiences on the difficult road to adulthood in this sequel to *All Alone in the Universe* (1999). Newbery Medal, 2006. (Rev: BL 10/15/05*; SLJ 9/05; VOYA 10/05)

1623 Peterseil, Tehila. *The Safe Place* (5–8). 1996, Pitspopany $16.95 (978-0-943706-71-9); paper $12.95 (978-0-943706-72-6). A moving story of an Israeli girl and the problems she faces at school because of a learning disability. (Rev: SLJ 12/96)

1624 Pfeffer, Susan Beth. *Kid Power* (6–9). Illus. 1988, Scholastic paper $2.99 (978-0-590-42607-7). A group of youngsters join together to do jobs for money.

1625 Philbrick, Rodman. *The Fire Pony* (5–8). 1996, Scholastic paper $14.95 (978-0-590-55251-6). Rescued from a foster home by his half-brother Joe, Roy hopes that life will be better on the ranch where Joe finds work. (Rev: BCCB 7–8/96; BL 5/1/96; HB 7–8/96; SLJ 9/96; VOYA 10/96)

1626 Philbrick, Rodman. *Freak the Mighty* (7–10). 1993, Scholastic paper $16.95 (978-0-590-47412-2). When Maxwell Kane, the son of Killer Kane, becomes friends with Kevin, a new boy with a birth defect, he gains a new interest in school and learning. (Rev: BL 12/15/93; SLJ 12/93*; VOYA 4/94)

1627 Plaisted, Caroline. *10 Things to Do Before You're 16* (7–9). 2006, Simon & Schuster paper $5.99 (978-1-4169-2460-9). London teens Beth and Anna aim to become gorgeous goddesses for their 16th birthdays and create a list of key tasks, which don't all go smoothly. (Rev: SLJ 8/06)

1628 Platt, Kin. *Crocker* (7–10). 1983, Harper-Collins $11.95 (978-0-397-32025-7). Dorothy is attracted to a new boy in school.

1629 Platt, Randall B. *The Cornerstone* (8–12). 1998, Catbird Pr. $21.95 (978-0-945774-40-2). Using flashbacks, this novel tells about the growth of a tough 15-year-old charity case at summer camp on a scholarship in 1944, where he meets a Navy man on medical leave who changes his life. (Rev: VOYA 2/99)

1630 Plum-Ucci, Carol. *What Happened to Lani Garver* (8–12). 2002, Harcourt $17.00 (978-0-15-216813-1). Claire, a popular 16-year-old who is battling private demons, finds support and a cause in a newly arrived, curiously androgynous student who disturbs her friends. (Rev: BCCB 11/02; BL 8/02; HBG 10/03; SLJ 10/02*; VOYA 12/02)

1631 Polikoff, Barbara Garland. *Why Does the Coqui Sing?* (5–8). 2004, Holiday $16.95 (978-0-8234-1817-6). Thirteen-year-old Luz and her broth-

er Rome have trouble adjusting when they move from Chicago to Puerto Rico with their mother and stepfather. (Rev: BL 5/15/04; SLJ 6/04)

1632 Porter, Tracey. *A Dance of Sisters* (5–8). 2002, HarperCollins LB $17.89 (978-0-06-029239-3). When a young ballet dancer's dreams are dashed, she is comforted by her sister. (Rev: BCCB 1/03; BL 2/15/03; HBG 3/03; SLJ 1/03)

1633 Prosek, James. *The Day My Mother Left* (6–12). Illus. 2007, Simon & Schuster $15.99 (978-1-4169-0770-1). Jeremy's mother leaves his family to be with another man, and over the next few difficult years Jeremy finds some comfort being outside and sketching birds. (Rev: BCCB 2/07; BL 4/15/07; LMC 8–9/07; SLJ 3/07) ⑨

1634 Prue, Sally. *The Devil's Toenail* (7–10). 2004, Scholastic $16.95 (978-0-439-48634-7). Thirteen-year-old Stevie Saunders, still trying to recover from a brutal bullying incident that left him scarred, enters a new school determined to endear himself. (Rev: BCCB 9/04; BL 4/15/04; SLJ 8/04)

1635 Rayburn, Tricia. *Maggie Bean Stays Afloat* (6–9). 2008, Aladdin Mix paper $5.99 (978-1-4169-6264-9). Now that Maggie has lost all her excess weight (in *The Melting of Maggie Bean*), things change, including her friends and her confidence. (Rev: BL 4/15/08)

1636 Reed, Don C. *The Kraken* (6–10). 1997, Boyds Mills paper $7.95 (978-1-56397-693-3). In Newfoundland in the late 1800s, a boy struggles to survive against the impersonal rich and the harsh environment. (Rev: BL 3/15/95; SLJ 2/95)

1637 Reinhardt, Dana. *Harmless* (7–12). 2007, Random $15.99 (978-0-385-74699-1). Anna and Emma have been friends forever when Mariah enters the picture and widens their horizons, leading them, however, into a lie that has wide repercussions. (Rev: BCCB 2/07; BL 12/1/06; LMC 4–5/07; SLJ 3/07) ⑨

1638 Reynolds, Marilyn. *Detour for Emmy* (8–12). 1993, Morning Glory paper $8.95 (978-0-930934-76-7). Emmy is a good student and a hunk's girlfriend, but her home life includes a deserter father and an alcoholic mother. Emmy's pregnancy causes more hardship when she keeps the baby. (Rev: BL 10/1/93; SLJ 7/93; VOYA 12/93)

1639 Reynolds, Marilyn. *If You Loved Me: True-to-Life Series from Hamilton High* (8–12). 1999, Morning Glory paper $8.95 (978-1-885356-55-0). Seventeen-year-old Lauren, born to a drug-addicted mother now deceased, vows to abstain from drugs and sex, but the latter is particularly difficult because of an insistent boyfriend. (Rev: BL 9/1/99; HBG 4/00; VOYA 2/00)

1640 Reynolds, Marilyn. *Telling: True-to-Life Series from Hamilton High* (7–10). 1996, Morning

Glory paper $8.95 (978-1-885356-03-1). Twelve-year-old Cassie is confused and embarrassed when her adult neighbor makes sexual advances towards her. (Rev: BL 4/1/96; SLJ 5/96; VOYA 6/96)

1641 Reynolds, Marilyn. *Too Soon for Jeff* (8–12). 1994, Morning Glory $15.95 (978-0-930934-90-3); paper $8.95 (978-0-930934-91-0). Jeff's hopes of going to college on a debate scholarship are put in jeopardy when his girlfriend happily announces she's pregnant. Jeff reluctantly prepares for father-hood. (Rev: BL 9/15/94; SLJ 9/94; VOYA 12/94)

1642 Rhue, Morton. *The Wave* (7–10). 1981, Dell paper $5.50 (978-0-440-99371-1). A high school experiment to test social interaction backfires when an elitist group is formed.

1643 Rosenberg, Liz. *Heart and Soul* (8–12). 1996, Harcourt $11.00 (978-0-15-200942-7). It is only when Willie helps a troubled Jewish classmate that she is able to straighten out her own problems. (Rev: BL 6/1–15/96; VOYA 8/96)

1644 Rottman, S. L. *Head Above Water* (6–9). 1999, Peachtree $14.95 (978-1-56145-185-2). Skye's efforts to care for her mentally disabled brother, to work toward a swimming scholarship, and to deal with a violent boyfriend threaten to overwhelm her in this arresting novel. (Rev: BL 11/15/99; HBG 4/00)

1645 Rottman, S. L. *Hero* (5–8). 1997, Peachtree $14.95 (978-1-56145-159-3). When his home life becomes unbearable, Sean is sent to Carbondale Ranch, where his sense of self-worth gradually grows. (Rev: BL 12/1/97; HBG 3/98; SLJ 12/97; VOYA 12/97)

1646 Rottman, S. L. *Rough Waters* (7–12). 1998, Peachtree $14.95 (978-1-56145-172-2). After the deaths of their parents, teenage brothers Gregg and Scott move to Colorado to live with an uncle who runs a white-water rafting business. (Rev: BL 5/1/98; HBG 9/98; SLJ 8/98; VOYA 8/98)

1647 Ryan, Mary C. *The Voice from the Mendelsohns' Maple* (5–7). Illus. by Irena Roman. 1990, Little, Brown $13.95 (978-0-316-76360-8). Penny tries to cope with many problems, including finding out the identity of the woman who is hiding in the neighbor's maple tree. (Rev: SLJ 12/89)

1648 Ryan, P. E. *Saints of Augustine* (8–11). 2007, HarperTempest $16.99 (978-0-06-085810-0). Charlie and Sam's close friendship was abruptly severed a year ago but their respective problems — including Charlie's use of drugs and Sam's worries about his sexuality — finally bring them together again. (Rev: BL 7/07; SLJ 10/07)

1649 Rylant, Cynthia. *Missing May* (5–8). 1992, Orchard LB $15.99 (978-0-531-08596-7). Caring about each other is the tender message in this story of 12-year-old Summer, who, along with her uncle,

must cope with the death of her beloved aunt. New-bery Medal winner, 1993. (Rev: BCCB 3/92*; BL 2/15/92*; HB 3–4/92; SLJ 3/92*)

1650 Sachar, Louis. *Small Steps* (5–8). 2006, Dela-corte LB $18.99 (978-0-385-90333-2). Two years after being released from Camp Green Lake, African American 17-year-old Armpit is home in Texas and trying to find good work, which is hard when you have a record, when X-Ray turns up with an interesting proposal; a sequel to *Holes* (1998). (Rev: BL 1/1–15/06*; SLJ 1/06; VOYA 2/06)

1651 Sachs, Marilyn. *Almost Fifteen* (6–8). 1988, Avon paper $2.95 (978-0-380-70357-9). A light story of a practical girl, her boyfriends, and her impractical parents. (Rev: BL 6/15/87; SLJ 5/87)

1652 Sachs, Marilyn. *Class Pictures* (7–9). 1980, Avon paper $2.95 (978-0-380-61408-0). The friend-ship from kindergarten through high school between two girls is recalled through old class pictures.

1653 Sachs, Marilyn. *Fourteen* (7–9). 1983, Avon paper $2.95 (978-0-380-69842-4). First love comes to Rebecca by way of a new neighbor.

1654 Saenz, Benjamin Alire. *He Forgot to Say Goodbye* (8–11). 2008, Simon & Schuster $16.99 (978-1-4169-6228-1). Ramiro, from the poor sec-tion of El Paso, becomes friends with privileged Jake, the two fatherless young men forming a bond that is stronger than class or circumstance. (Rev: BL 4/15/08)

1655 Saldana, Rene. *The Whole Sky Full of Stars* (8–12). 2007, Random $15.99 (978-0-385-73053-2). Barry agrees to a risky boxing match to help pay off a friend's gambling debt — and to help his own family after his father's death. (Rev: BCCB 5/07; BL 3/15/07; SLJ 5/07)

1656 Salinger, J. D. *The Catcher in the Rye* (7–12). 1951, Little, Brown $25.95 (978-0-316-76953-2). For mature readers, the saga of Holden Caulfield and his three days in New York City. (Rev: BL 10/1/88)

1657 Say, Allen. *The Sign Painter* (5–9). Illus. 2000, Houghton $17.00 (978-0-395-97974-7). An Asian American youth who wants to be a serious artist gets a job painting signboards scattered through the desert. (Rev: BL 10/1/00; HB 9–10/00; HBG 3/01; SLJ 9/00)

1658 Schmidt, Gary D. *Trouble* (7–10). 2008, Clari-on paper $16.00 (978-0-618-92766-1). A multilay-ered novel in which Henry's brother dies after being hit by a truck driven by a classmate, a Cambodian immigrant named Chay; Henry later finds himself accepting a ride from Chay and the two learn more about each other. (Rev: BL 3/1/08; SLJ 4/08)

1659 Schmidt, Gary D. *The Wednesday Wars* (6–9). 2007, Clarion $16.00 (978-0-618-72483-3). In sub-urban Long Island during the late 1960s, Presbyterian 7th-grader Holling Hoodhood must spend Wednesday afternoons alone with his teacher while his Jewish and Catholic classmates attend religious instruction, and she teaches him about Shakespeare, life, and stretching beyond his limits. Newbery Honor Book, 2008. (Rev: BL 6/1–15/07; HB 7–8/07)

1660 Schreck, Karen Halvorsen. *Dream Journal* (7–10). 2006, . Sixteen-year-old Livy's dream journal records the happy times before her mother became terminally ill, and before Livy tried to renew her friendship with Ruth with "fun" that turns into tragedy. (Rev: SLJ 11/06)

1661 Schumacher, Julie. *The Book of One Hundred Truths* (5–8). 2006, Delacorte $15.95 (978-0-385-73290-1). While spending the summer with her grandparents at the Jersey shore, 12-year-old Thea finds herself baby-sitting her younger cousin Jocelyn and struggling to keep private the truths she is listing in her diary. (Rev: BL 11/1/06)

1662 Scott, Elizabeth. *Stealing Heaven* (7–10). 2008, HarperTeen $16.99 (978-0-06-112280-4). Dani, weary from the life of crime she and her mother have long lived, yearns for normalcy when they move to the town of Heaven. (Rev: BL 4/15/08; SLJ 8/08)

1663 Scott, Kieran. *I Was a Non-Blonde Cheerleader* (7–10). 2005, Penguin $16.99 (978-0-399-24279-3). As a brunette, Annisa has a hard time fitting in at her new high school where almost everybody else is blond. (Rev: BL 1/1–15/05; SLJ 1/05; VOYA 4/05)

1664 Scott, Kieran. *A Non-Blonde Cheerleader in Love* (8–12). 2007, Putnam $16.99 (978-0-399-24494-0). Annisa's cheerleading squad goes coed in this sequel to *I Was a Non-Blonde Cheerleader* (2005) and *Brunettes Strike Back* (2006). (Rev: BL 8/07; SLJ 6/07)

1665 Sebestyen, Ouida. *Out of Nowhere* (6–9). 1994, Orchard LB $17.99 (978-0-531-08689-6). The story of the bonding into a sort of family of a quirky group of characters, among them Harley, 13, who's left home; his dog Ishmael; Bill, a junk collector; and May, the "queen of clean." (Rev: BL 4/1/94; SLJ 3/94; VOYA 4/94)

1666 Sefton, Catherine. *Island of the Strangers* (7–9). 1985, Harcourt $12.95 (978-0-15-239100-3). City kids from Belfast clash with town toughs in this novel set on an island off Northern Ireland. (Rev: BL 1/1/86; SLJ 1/86)

1667 Selvadurai, Shyam. *Swimming in the Monsoon Sea* (8–11). 2005, Tundra $18.95 (978-0-88776-735-7). In Sri Lanka in 1980, Amrith's expected quiet summer is enlivened by the arrival from Canada of his cousin Niresh, a boy with whom he soon falls in love but who does not share his feelings. (Rev: BL 9/15/05*; SLJ 11/05)

1668 Seymour, Tres. *The Revelation of Saint Bruce* (7–12). 1998, Orchard paper $16.95 (978-0-531-30109-8). Because of his honesty, Bruce is responsible for the expulsion of several friends from school. (Rev: BL 10/15/98; HBG 3/99; SLJ 9/98; VOYA 2/99)

1669 Shanahan, Lisa. *The Sweet, Terrible, Glorious Year I Truly, Completely Lost It* (7–10). 2007, Delacorte $15.99 (978-0-385-75316-2). In this coming-of-age novel set in small-town Australia, 14-year-old Gemma deals with her emotional family, her sister's wedding, the school play, and shifting romantic attractions. (Rev: BL 8/07; SLJ 8/07)

1670 Shaw, Susan. *Safe* (7–10). 2007, Dutton $16.99 (978-0-525-47829-4). Thirteen-year-old Tracy, whose mother died when she was 3, is overwhelmed by fears after she is raped by the older brother of a classmate. (Rev: BL 9/15/07; SLJ 12/07)

1671 Shaw, Tucker. *Confessions of a Backup Dancer* (8–12). 2004, Simon & Schuster paper $8.99 (978-0-689-87075-0). Seventeen-year-old Kelly Kimball, a talented dancer, suddenly finds herself thrust into a close relationship with pop diva Darcy Barnes; in this journal-like novel, Kelly dishes the dirt on Darcy and the diva's entourage. (Rev: BL 9/15/04; SLJ 8/04)

1672 Sheldon, Dyan. *Planet Janet* (6–10). 2003, Candlewick $14.99 (978-0-7636-2048-6). Janet pours out to her diary the frustrations she and her friend Disha face in their dealings with family and friends in this entertaining novel set in London. (Rev: BCCB 3/03; BL 3/15/03; HBG 4/04; SLJ 5/03)

1673 Shoup, Barbara. *Stranded in Harmony* (7–10). 1997, Hyperion LB $18.49 (978-0-7868-2284-3). Lucas, an 18-year-old popular senior in high school, is discontented until he meets and becomes friendly with an older woman. (Rev: BL 7/97; HBG 3/98; SLJ 6/97*)

1674 Shreve, Susan. *Kiss Me Tomorrow* (5–8). 2006, Scholastic $16.99 (978-0-439-68047-9). Alyssa (aka Blister) is not having a good 7th grade; she feels abandoned by best friend Jonah although she's quick to help him when he's in trouble; she is unhappy about her mother's new boyfriend; and she worries about everything else from clothes to sex. (Rev: BL 9/15/06; SLJ 10/06)

1675 Shura, Mary Francis. *The Sunday Doll* (5–7). 1988, Avon paper $2.95 (978-0-380-70618-1). Thirteen-year-old Emmy is miffed when the family won't tell her what has happened to upset her older sister Jayne, until she learns that Jayne's boyfriend has committed suicide. (Rev: BCCB 7–8/88; BL 7/88; SLJ 8/88)

1676 Shyer, Marlene Fanta. *The Rainbow Kite* (6–8). 2002, Marshall Cavendish $15.95 (978-0-

7614-5122-8). Matthew tells of his gay brother Bennett's "coming out," a process that began painfully but ended happily when Bennett was accepted by his family and friends. (Rev: BCCB 12/02; BL 12/15/02; HBG 3/03; SLJ 11/02; VOYA 6/03)

1677 Siebold, Jan. *My Nights at the Improv* (4–8). 2005, Whitman $14.95 (978-0-8075-5630-6). Lizzie, a shy 8th-grader whose father died two years before, learns how to speak out by eavesdropping on an improvisational theater class, in the process also learning about bullying Vanessa. (Rev: BCCB 7–8/05; SLJ 11/05)

1678 Silverman. *Mirror Mirror: Twisted Tales* (5–8). 2002, Scholastic paper $15.95 (978-0-439-29593-2). Disturbing stories serve as metaphors for the problems of drug use, divorce, homelessness, and other ills. (Rev: BL 9/1/02; HBG 10/02; SLJ 8/02; VOYA 6/02)

1679 Silvey, Anita, ed. *Help Wanted: Short Stories About Young People Working* (6–12). 1997, Little, Brown $16.95 (978-0-316-79148-9). A collection of 12 short stories by such writers as Michael Dorris, Norma Fox Mazer, and Gary Soto that deal with teenagers at work. (Rev: BL 11/1/97; HBG 3/98; SLJ 11/97; VOYA 12/97)

1680 Singer, Marilyn, ed. *Stay True: Short Stories for Strong Girls* (7–12). 1998, Scholastic paper $16.95 (978-0-590-36031-9). There are 11 new short stories in this collection that explores the problems girls face growing up and how they discover inner strength. (Rev: BL 4/1/98; HB 3–4/98; SLJ 5/98; VOYA 4/98)

1681 Slepian, Jan. *The Broccoli Tapes* (5–8). 1989, Scholastic paper $3.50 (978-0-590-43473-7). Sara uses tapes during her stay in Hawaii to keep up with her class oral history project. (Rev: BCCB 4/89; BL 4/15/89; SLJ 4/89; VOYA 6/89)

1682 Smith, Kirsten. *The Geography of Girlhood* (8–11). 2006, Little, Brown $16.99 (978-0-316-16021-6). High schooler Penny documents in verse her unhappy family, school, and friendship experiences, all overshadowed by her mother's abandonment when she was young. (Rev: BCCB 5/06; BL 2/1/06; SLJ 5/06)

1683 Sonenklar, Carol. *My Own Worst Enemy* (5–8). 1999, Holiday $15.95 (978-0-8234-1456-7). In this first-person narrative, Eve Belkin finds there is a price to pay when she outdoes herself to be popular in her new school. (Rev: BL 5/15/99; HBG 9/99; SLJ 8/99; VOYA 10/99)

1684 Sones, Sonya. *What My Mother Doesn't Know* (6–10). 2001, Simon & Schuster $17.00 (978-0-689-84114-9). Sophie, 14, expresses her feelings about falling in and out of love in a poetic narrative that is humorous and romantic. (Rev: BCCB 12/01; BL 11/1/01; HBG 10/02; SLJ 10/01; VOYA 10/01)

1685 Soto, Gary. *Accidental Love* (7–10). 2006, Harcourt $16.00 (978-0-15-205497-7). Something clicks when 14-year-old Marisa meets wimpy Rene and she is inspired to transfer to his school, where, despite complications, she finds herself blossoming socially and academically -- and enjoying her first love. (Rev: BL 1/1–15/06; SLJ 1/06; VOYA 2/06)

1686 Soto, Gary. *Buried Onions* (8–12). 1997, Harcourt $17.00 (978-0-15-201333-2). A junior college dropout, 19-year-old Eddie is trying to support himself in this story set in the barrio of Fresno, California. (Rev: BL 11/15/97; HBG 3/98; SLJ 1/98; VOYA 10/97)

1687 Soto, Gary. *Mercy on These Teenage Chimps* (5–8). 2007, Harcourt $16.00 (978-0-15-206022-0). Friends Ronnie Gonzalez and Joey Rios have just turned 13 and are wrestling with physical and emotional changes. (Rev: BL 12/1/06; SLJ 2/07)

1688 Soto, Gary. *The Pool Party* (4–7). Illus. by Robert Casilla. 1992, Delacorte $13.95 (978-0-385-30890-8). Rudy, part of a Mexican American family, has growing-up problems. (Rev: SLJ 6/93)

1689 Spencer, Katherine. *More Than Friends* (7–10). 2008, Harcourt paper $6.95 (978-0-15-205746-6). The death of her brother Matt hit Grace hard, and she is now trying to clean up her life and enjoying her growing affection for Matt's friend Jackson. But is Jackson stealing? Can the mysterious (guardian angel?) Philomena help? (Rev: BL 8/08)

1690 Spinelli, Jerry. *Eggs* (4–7). 2007, Little, Brown $15.99 (978-0-316-16646-1). Two troubled children — 9-year-old David and 13-year-old Primrose — forge an unlikely friendship. (Rev: BL 4/1/07; SLJ 7/07)

1691 Spinelli, Jerry. *Jason and Marceline* (7–10). 2000, Little, Brown paper $6.99 (978-0-316-80662-6). Jason, now in the 9th grade, sorts out his feelings toward girls in general and Marceline in particular. Preceded by *Space Station Seventh Grade*. (Rev: BL 1/1/87; SLJ 2/87)

1692 Spinelli, Jerry. *Love, Stargirl* (7–10). 2007, Knopf $16.99 (978-0-375-81375-7). In this sequel to the 2000 novel, 15-year-old Stargirl has moved to Pennsylvania and writes letters to her former boyfriend Leo, describing her new life and the very varied friends she has made in her new home. (Rev: BL 8/07; HB 9–10/07; SLJ 9/07) 🌑

1693 Spinelli, Jerry. *Space Station Seventh Grade* (6–8). 2000, Little, Brown paper $6.99 (978-0-316-80605-3). Jason has many adventures, mostly hilarious, during his 7th-grade year.

1694 Spinelli, Jerry. *Stargirl* (6–9). 2000, Knopf $15.95 (978-0-679-88637-2). When the unusual Stargirl appears at Mica High School, things change and social relationships are questioned. (Rev: BL 6/1–15/00; HB 7–8/00; HBG 3/01; SLJ 8/00)

1695 Spinelli, Jerry. *Wringer* (4–7). 1997, Harper-Collins LB $17.89 (978-0-06-024914-4). A sensitive boy must participate in the massacre of thousands of pigeons released at an annual fair. (Rev: BL 9/1/97*; HB 9–10/97; HBG 3/98; SLJ 9/97*)

1696 Stanley, Diane. *A Time Apart* (6–9). 1999, Morrow $15.95 (978-0-688-16997-8). A 13-year-old girl discovers she has inner strengths when she spends a summer with her father on an archaeological project to replicate an Iron Age village in England. (Rev: BCCB 10/99; BL 6/1–15/99; HBG 4/00; SLJ 9/99)

1697 Stevenson, Robin. *Impossible Things* (5–7). 2008, Orca paper $8.95 (978-1-55143-736-1). Cassidy befriends a new girl in town who claims to have magical powers in the hopes that she can become magical too and overpower mean girls and bullies. (Rev: BL 4/15/08; SLJ 8/08)

1698 Stevenson, Robin. *Out of Order* (8–11). 2007, Orca paper $8.95 (978-1-55143-693-7). Sophie, newly slim, is starting high school in a new town and is attracted to classmate Zelia's wild ways until Zelia attempts suicide in this novel about self-perception, sexual identity, and self-respect. (Rev: BL 1/1–15/08)

1699 Stewart, Jennifer J. *The Bean King's Daughter* (5–7). 2002, Holiday $15.95 (978-0-8234-1644-8). Phoebe, a 12-year-old heiress, reluctantly learns about herself and her young stepmother while at an Arizona ranch. (Rev: BL 9/1/02; HBG 10/02; SLJ 7/02)

1700 Strasser, Todd. *Boot Camp* (8–12). 2007, Simon & Schuster $15.99 (978-1-4169-0848-7). After several warnings about his behavior (dating a teacher), Garrett's parents decide to send the 15-year-old to a disciplinary boot camp; Garrett's descriptions of the mental and physical abuse he undergoes at this camp are realistic. (Rev: BL 8/07; LMC 11–12/07; SLJ 4/07)

1701 Strasser, Todd. *Can't Get There from Here* (7–12). 2004, Simon & Schuster $15.95 (978-0-689-84169-9). A teenage girl who has been thrown out by an abusive mother tries to survive on the streets of New York City. (Rev: BL 3/15/04; SLJ 3/04; VOYA 6/04)

1702 Strasser, Todd. *CON-fidence* (5–8). 2002, Holiday $16.95 (978-0-8234-1394-2). Shy Lauren falls under the spell of the dazzling Celeste, failing to perceive Celeste's underlying motives. (Rev: BCCB 2/03; BL 4/15/03; HBG 10/03; SLJ 1/03; VOYA 4/03)

1703 Strauss, Peggy Guthart. *Getting the Boot* (8–12). Series: Students Across the Seven Seas. 2005, Penguin paper $6.99 (978-0-14-240414-0). A light story about popular high school junior Kelly Brandt's summer as an exchange student in Italy. (Rev: BL 5/15/05; SLJ 8/05)

1704 Summer, Jane. *Not the Only One: Lesbian and Gay Fiction for Teens* (7–12). 2004, Alyson paper $13.95 (978-1-55583-834-8). This revised edition includes 10 new stories featuring gay and lesbian teens. (Rev: BL 12/15/04; VOYA 2/05)

1705 Supplee, Suzanne. *Artichoke's Heart* (7–10). 2008, Dutton $16.99 (978-0-525-47902-4). Overweight Rosemary is trying to deal with kids at school teasing her when her mother is diagnosed with cancer. (Rev: BL 5/1/08; SLJ 8/08)

1706 Swallow, Pamela Curtis. *It Only Looks Easy* (4–7). 2003, Millbrook $15.95 (978-0-7613-1790-6). Kat's problems start when her dog is hit by a car and she "borrows" a bicycle to get to the vet only to have it stolen from her. (Rev: BL 4/15/03; HBG 10/03; SLJ 4/03)

1707 Sweeney, Joyce. *Waiting for June* (8–11). 2003, Marshall Cavendish $15.95 (978-0-7614-5138-9). High school senior Sophie is pregnant, reluctant to disclose the identity of the father, and in danger in this complex, suspenseful novel. (Rev: BL 9/1/03; HBG 4/04; SLJ 10/03; VOYA 4/04)

1708 Tamar, Erika. *The Things I Did Last Summer* (7–9). 1994, Harcourt $10.95 (978-0-15-282490-7). A teenager spending the summer on Long Island with his pregnant stepmother loses his virginity when he meets a deceptive older woman. (Rev: BL 3/15/94; SLJ 4/94; VOYA 6/94)

1709 Thesman, Jean. *Cattail Moon* (6–9). 1994, Avon paper $4.50 (978-0-380-72504-5). Julia, 14, is at odds with her mother, who wants to transform her from a classical musician into a cheerleader. (Rev: BL 4/1/94; SLJ 5/94; VOYA 8/94)

1710 Thesman, Jean. *Couldn't I Start Over?* (7–10). 1989, Avon paper $2.95 (978-0-380-75717-6). Growing up in a caring family situation, teenager Shiloh still faces many problems in her coming of age. (Rev: BL 11/15/89; VOYA 2/90)

1711 Thomas, Joyce C. *When the Nightingale Sings* (6–8). 1992, HarperCollins paper $3.95 (978-0-06-440524-9). Marigold's only joy in her stepfamily is singing, which leads her to audition for a Baptist church choir, where she discovers self-worth, her family, and happiness. (Rev: BL 1/1/93; SLJ 2/93)

1712 Thompson, Julian. *Facing It* (7–9). 1989, Avon paper $2.95 (978-0-380-84491-3). An accident ruins the baseball chances of the star at Camp Raycroft. A reissue.

1713 Thompson, Julian. *Philo Fortune's Awesome Journey to His Comfort Zone* (8–12). 1995, Hyperion $16.95 (978-0-7868-0067-4). A story of a youth who discovers the possibilities of the man he might become. (Rev: BL 5/1/95; SLJ 5/95; VOYA 2/96)

1714 Tolan, Stephanie S. *Listen!* (4–7). 2006, HarperCollins $15.99 (978-0-06-057925-8). Lonely after the death of her mother and the departure of her best friend for the summer, 12-year-old Charley finds solace in a stray dog. (Rev: BL 4/1/06)

1715 Torres, Laura. *November Ever After* (8–12). 1999, Holiday $16.95 (978-0-8234-1464-2). Still recovering from her mother's death, 16-yer-old Amy discovers that her best friend, Sara, is a lesbian and in love with a girl in her class. (Rev: BL 12/1/99; HBG 4/00; SLJ 1/00)

1716 Toten, Teresa. *The Onlyhouse* (5–8). 1996, Red Deer paper $7.95 (978-0-88995-137-2). Eleven-year-old Lucija, whose family was originally from Croatia, relocates to a new house in suburban Toronto after several years in a dense downtown neighborhood with a large immigrant population, and must adjust to a new school, peer pressures, and bullies. (Rev: SLJ 7/96)

1717 Townley, Roderick. *Sky: A Novel in 3 Sets and an Encore* (7–10). 2004, Simon & Schuster $16.95 (978-0-689-85712-6). Angered by his father's opposition to his interest in jazz, 15-year-old Sky runs away from home and moves in with the blind jazz pianist whose life he saved. (Rev: BL 8/04; SLJ 7/04)

1718 Trembath, Don. *The Tuesday Cafe* (6–9). 1996, Orca paper $6.95 (978-1-55143-074-4). Harper Winslow, a disaffected, wealthy teenager, learns about life and grows up when he is forced to join a local writing group called "The Tuesday Cafe." (Rev: BL 8/97; SLJ 9/96; VOYA 2/97)

1719 Trueman, Terry. *7 Days at the Hot Corner* (8–11). 2007, HarperTempest $16.99 (978-0-06-057494-9). The "hot corner" of the title is third base, Scott's position on the varsity baseball team, which is threatened when Scott fears he may have contracted AIDS while tending to an injured teammate and friend who is gay. (Rev: BCCB 4/07; BL 2/1/07; SLJ 4/07)

1720 Tullson, Diane. *Edge* (7–10). 2003, Fitzhenry & Whiteside paper $6.95 (978-0-7737-6230-5). Tired of being bullied, Marlie Peters, 14, joins a group of other outcast students only to realize that they are involved in a dangerous plot. (Rev: BL 3/1/03; SLJ 10/03; VOYA 6/03)

1721 Vail, Rachel. *Ever After* (5–9). 1994, Orchard LB $16.99 (978-0-531-08688-9). Fourteen-year-old Molly is trying to act maturely but always seems to mess things up. (Rev: BCCB 4/94; BL 3/1/94; HB 5–6/94, 7–8/94; SLJ 5/94*; VOYA 6/94)

1722 Vail, Rachel. *If We Kiss* (7–10). 2005, HarperCollins LB $16.89 (978-0-06-056915-0). Fourteen-year-old Charlie struggles with feelings of guilt after she kisses Kevin, who just happens to be her best friend's steady. (Rev: BCCB 5/05; BL 3/15/05; HB 7–8/05; SLJ 5/05)

1723 Vail, Rachel. *Lucky* (7–10). 2008, HarperTeen $16.99 (978-0-06-089043-8). Fourteen-year-old

Phoebe's family has never had to worry about money, so when her mother loses her job, Phoebe's new reality changes how she looks at the world and how her friends look at her. (Rev: BL 3/1/08; SLJ 4/08)

1724 Vail, Rachel. *You, Maybe: The Profound Asymmetry of Love in High School* (8–11). 2006, HarperCollins $15.99 (978-0-06-056917-4). Smart, secure teen Josie's confidence is shattered when a boy she casually "hooks up" with gains her trust and then breaks her heart. (Rev: BL 5/1/06; HB 5–6/06; SLJ 7/06)

1725 Vande Velde, Vivian. *Curses, Inc.: And Other Stories* (6–10). 1997, Harcourt $16.00 (978-0-15-201452-0). In the title story in this collection of tales with surprise endings, Bill Essler thinks he has found the perfect way to get even with his girlfriend, who humiliated him, by utilizing a web site, Curses, Inc. (Rev: SLJ 6/97*; VOYA 6/97)

1726 van Diepen, Allison. *Snitch* (7–10). 2007, Simon & Schuster paper $6.99 (978-1-4169-5030-1). Julia is reluctantly caught up in the world of gang violence when she falls in love with a Crip in this cautionary tale. (Rev: BL 1/1–15/08)

1727 Velasquez, Gloria. *Tommy Stands Alone* (7–10). 1995, Arte Publico paper $9.95 (978-1-55885-147-4). An engaging story about a Latino gay teen who is humiliated and rejected but finds understanding from a Chicano therapist. (Rev: BL 10/15/95; SLJ 11/95; VOYA 12/95)

1728 Walker, Paul R. *The Method* (8–12). 1990, Harcourt $14.95 (978-0-15-200528-3). A candid novel about a 15-year-old boy, his acting aspirations, and his sexual problems. (Rev: BL 8/90; SLJ 6/90)

1729 Wallace, Bill. *Aloha Summer* (7–9). 1997, Holiday $15.95 (978-0-8234-1306-5). Fourteen-year-old John Priddle moves with his family to Hawaii in 1925 and finds less than the island paradise he expected. However, his friendship with a Hawaiian classmate brings new meaning to his life. (Rev: BL 10/1/97; HBG 3/98; SLJ 10/97; VOYA 12/97)

1730 Wallace, Rich. *Losing Is Not an Option* (6–10). 2003, Knopf $15.95 (978-0-375-81351-1). Nine stories follow Ron, a high school athlete, through coming-of-age experiences including family problems, budding sexual attractions, and competition with his peers. (Rev: BL 8/03; HB 9–10/03; HBG 4/04; SLJ 9/03; VOYA 10/03)

1731 Walpole, Peter. *The Healer of Harrow Point* (4–7). 2000, Hampton Roads paper $11.95 (978-1-57174-167-7). A novel of love and compassion about a boy who is promised a hunting trip for his twelfth birthday but wonders if he can kill a deer, particularly after seeing one killed by poachers and after meeting Emma, who can heal animals with her touch. (Rev: SLJ 10/00)

1732 Walters, Eric. *Sketches* (7–10). 2008, Viking $15.99 (978-0-670-06294-2). Runaway Dana, 14, finds solace at Sketches, an art center for homeless teens in Toronto. (Rev: BL 1/1–15/08; SLJ 4/08)

1733 Waltman, Kevin. *Nowhere Fast* (8–12). 2002, Scholastic paper $7.99 (978-0-439-41424-1). After stealing a car for joyriding, teenagers Gary and Wilson become entrapped in the activities of a former teacher with a dangerous agenda. (Rev: BL 2/1/03; SLJ 4/03; VOYA 4/03)

1734 Wartski, Maureen C. *My Name Is Nobody* (7–10). 1988, Walker $15.95 (978-0-8027-6770-7). A victim of child abuse survives a suicide attempt and is given a second chance by a tough ex-cop. (Rev: BL 2/1/88; SLJ 3/88; VOYA 4/88)

1735 Wasserman, Robin. *Lust* (8–11). Series: Seven Deadly Sins. 2005, Simon & Schuster paper $7.99 (978-0-689-87782-7). In an entertaining opening volume of a soap-opera-like series, several sex-obsessed high school seniors in a small California town ruthlessly scheme to win the girl or guy of their dreams. (Rev: BL 12/1/05; SLJ 1/06)

1736 Weaver, Beth Nixon. *Rooster* (7–12). 2001, Winslow $16.95 (978-1-58837-001-3). In the 1960s, 15-year-old Kady is growing up in a confusing mix of poverty at home on a struggling orange grove, a devoted but disabled neighboring child, and a wealthy boyfriend who introduces her to marijuana. (Rev: BL 7/01; HB 7–8/01; HBG 10/01; SLJ 6/01; VOYA 2/02)

1737 Weaver, Will. *Full Service* (7–10). 2005, Farrar $17.00 (978-0-374-32485-8). Paul, a sheltered Christian 15-year-old, discovers hippies, alcohol, and sex when he takes a job at a gas station in the summer of 1965. (Rev: BL 9/1/05; SLJ 11/05; VOYA 10/05)

1738 Weinheimer, Beckie. *Converting Kate* (7–10). 2007, Viking $16.99 (978-0-670-06152-5). Her parents' divorce and her father's death have led Kate, 16, to question her faith in the religious sect in which she has grown up, and a move to Maine exposes her to a world outside her strict upbringing. (Rev: BCCB 3/07; BL 3/1/07; SLJ 4/07)

1739 Wetter, Bruce. *The Boy with the Lampshade on His Head* (5–8). 2004, Simon & Schuster $16.95 (978-0-689-85032-5). Painfully shy, 11-year-old Stanley Krakow maintains a low profile but a rich inner life until he makes friends with an abused girl and finds the inner strength to be a real hero. (Rev: BL 5/1/04; SLJ 8/04)

1740 Whelan, Gloria. *Listening for Lions* (6–9). 2005, HarperCollins LB $16.89 (978-0-06-058175-6). Rachel, the orphaned daughter of missionary parents, gets pulled into an elaborate scheme to get her money-grubbing neighbors reinstated in the will of an ailing Englishman. (Rev: BCCB 9/05; BL 5/15/05*; HB 9–10/05; SLJ 8/05; VOYA 8/05)

1741 Whittenberg, Allison. *Life Is Fine* (8–12). 2008, Delacorte $15.99 (978-0-385-73480-6). Samara, a sad, neglected 15-year-old, develops a crush on a substitute teacher who introduces her to poetry. (Rev: BL 1/1–15/08; SLJ 2/08)

1742 Wieler, Diana. *RanVan: The Defender* (7–12). 1997, Douglas & McIntyre $16.95 (978-0-88899-270-3). Orphaned Rhan Van, who lives with his grandmother in a city apartment, begins hanging out in bad company and soon finds he is vandalizing school and private property. (Rev: BL 2/1/98; SLJ 3/98)

1743 Wilhelm, Doug. *Falling* (7–10). 2007, Farrar $17.00 (978-0-374-32251-9). Two troubled teens — Matt, whose first year in high school is ruined by his brother's heroin addiction, and Katie — connect through the Internet in this coming-of-age story set in Vermont. (Rev: BL 3/15/07; SLJ 7/07)

1744 Williams, Lori Aurelia. *Shayla's Double Brown Baby Blues* (7–12). 2003, Pulse $17.00 (978-0-689-85670-9). In this sequel to *When Kambia Elaine Flew in from Neptune* (2000), 13-year-old Shayla must cope with problems including the arrival of a new half-sister, her friend Kambia's traumatic and abusive past, and her friend Lemm's alcoholism. (Rev: BL 7/01; HB 9–10/01; SLJ 8/01)

1745 Williams, Lori Aurelia. *When Kambia Elaine Flew in from Neptune* (7–12). 2001, Pulse paper $17.00 (978-0-689-84593-2). In this first-person narrative, 12-year-old Shayla adjusts to the unhappy departure from the family of her older sister and finds escape in her friendship with an imaginative girl named Kambia. (Rev: BL 2/15/00)

1746 Wilson, Budge. *Sharla* (7–10). 1998, Stoddart paper $6.95 (978-0-7736-7467-7). A run-in with a polar bear, adjusting to a new school, trying to make friends, and getting used to severe weather are some of the problems 15-year-old Sharla faces when she moves with her family from Ottawa to Churchill, a small community in northern Manitoba. (Rev: SLJ 8/98)

1747 Wilson, Johnniece M. *Poor Girl* (5–7). 1992, Scholastic $13.95 (978-0-590-44732-4). A first-person story about Miranda, who spends the summer trying to earn money for contact lenses before the fall. (Rev: BCCB 4/92; BL 8/92; SLJ 4/92)

1748 Winton, Tim. *Lockie Leonard, Human Torpedo* (6–8). 1992, Little, Brown $13.95 (978-0-316-94753-4). Set in Australia, the story of a 14-year-old surfer and his confusion as he begins a more intimate relationship with his girlfriend. (Rev: BL 12/15/91; SLJ 12/91)

1749 Withrow, Sarah. *What Gloria Wants* (7–10). 2005, Groundwood paper $6.95 (978-0-88899-692-3). Gloria always seems to be a step behind her best friend Shawna, so Gloria initially exults when she is first to land a boyfriend. (Rev: BCCB 11/05; BL 12/1/05; HB 1–2/06; SLJ 2/06; VOYA 12/05)

1750 Wittlinger, Ellen. *Hard Love* (8–12). 1999, Simon & Schuster paper $8.00 (978-0-689-84154-5). Two outsiders, John, a high school junior and fan of "zines," and Marisol, a self-proclaimed virgin lesbian, form an unusual relationship in this well-crafted novel that explores many teenage problems. (Rev: BL 10/1/99*; HB 7–8/99; HBG 9/99; SLJ 7/99; VOYA 8/99)

1751 Wittlinger, Ellen. *Sandpiper* (8–12). 2005, Simon & Schuster $16.95 (978-0-689-86802-3). Her promiscuous past has severely tarnished 16-year-old Sandpiper's reputation, but when she develops a friendship with Walker, both troubled teens begin to make some important discoveries about the ways in which the past is shaping their future. (Rev: BL 6/1–15/05; SLJ 7/05; VOYA 8/05)

1752 Wittlinger, Ellen. *Zigzag* (8–12). 2003, Simon & Schuster $16.95 (978-0-689-84996-1). A summer cross-country car trip with her recently widowed aunt and two cousins poses many challenges for 17-year-old Robin. (Rev: BL 9/1/03; HB 7–8/03; HBG 4/04; SLJ 8/03; VOYA 10/03)

1753 Wojciechowska, Maia. *Shadow of a Bull* (5–8). Illus. by Alvin Smith. 1964, Macmillan $16.95 (978-0-689-30042-4). Manolo, surviving son of a great bullfighter, has his own "moment of truth" when he faces his first bull. Newbery Medal winner, 1965.

1754 Wolfson, Jill. *Home, and Other Big, Fat Lies* (5–7). 2006, Holt $16.95 (978-0-8050-7670-7). Shuttled through the foster care system for much of her life, 11-year-old Whitney isn't expecting much out of her latest stop with a family in remote northern California, but her interest in nature — and some new friendships — open her eyes to the importance of fighting for what you believe in. (Rev: SLJ 12/06)

1755 Wolfson, Jill. *What I Call Life* (5–8). 2005, Holt $16.95 (978-0-8050-7669-1). Five young girls — all refugees from troubled families — find friendship and strength during their stay in a group home run by a wise Knitting Lady. (Rev: BCCB 9/05; BL 11/1/05; HBG 4/06; LMC 4–5/06; SLJ 9/05; VOYA 12/05)

1756 Wong, Joyce Lee. *Seeing Emily* (6–9). 2005, Abrams $16.95 (978-0-8109-5757-2). This appealing free-verse novel chronicles the coming of age of 16-year-old Emily Wu, a promising artist and the daughter of Chinese immigrants. (Rev: BCCB 11/05; SLJ 12/05)

1757 Woodson, Jacqueline. *The House You Pass on the Way* (6–9). Illus. 1997, Puffin paper $5.99 (978-0-14-250191-7). A young girl from an interracial marriage feels left out and becomes a loner until she

falls in love with a girl cousin who comes to visit. (Rev: BL 8/97; SLJ 10/97; VOYA 10/97)

1758 Wright, Betty R. *The Summer of Mrs. MacGregor* (5–8). 1986, Holiday $15.95 (978-0-8234-0628-9). Meeting an exotic teenager who calls herself Mrs. Lillina MacGregor helps Linda solve her problem of jealousy toward her older sister. (Rev: BCCB 12/86; BL 11/1/86; SLJ 11/86; VOYA 4/87)

1759 Wyss, Thelma Hatch. *Ten Miles from Winnemucca* (6–8). 2002, HarperCollins $15.95 (978-0-06-029783-1). When his mother and new husband leave on their honeymoon, 16-year-old Martin decides to take a break from his new stepbrother and starts a new life for himself in Idaho. (Rev: BCCB 7–8/02; BL 2/1/02; HB 7–8/02; HBG 10/02; SLJ 6/02; VOYA 2/02)

1760 Yang, Margaret. *Locked Out* (6–9). 1996, Tudor $17.95 (978-0-936389-40-0). Gina is outraged and goaded into activism when she learns that the principal of her school, in an effort to curb smoking, has closed all the bathrooms except those close to his office. (Rev: SLJ 5/96)

1761 Young, Ronder T. *Moving Mama to Town* (5–8). 1997, Orchard LB $18.99 (978-0-531-33025-8). Although his father is a gambler and a failure, Fred never loses faith in him in this story of a boy who must help support his family although he's only 13. (Rev: BL 6/1–15/97; HB 7–8/97; SLJ 6/97)

1762 Zalben, Jane Breskin. *Water from the Moon* (8–10). 1987, Random paper $4.99 (978-0-440-22855-4). Nicky Berstein, a high school sophomore, tries too hard to make friends and is hurt in the process. (Rev: BL 5/15/87; SLJ 5/87; VOYA 8/87)

1763 Zeises, Lara M. *Contents Under Pressure* (6–9). 2004, Delacorte $15.95 (978-0-385-73047-1). In this appealing coming-of-age novel, 14-year-old Lucy experiences dramatic changes in her life when she starts to date Tobin. (Rev: BCCB 5/04; BL 3/15/04; HB 3–4/04; SLJ 4/04; VOYA 6/04)

1764 Zindel, Bonnie, and Paul Zindel. *A Star for the Latecomer* (7–10). 1980, HarperCollins $12.95 (978-0-06-026847-3). When her mother dies, Brooke is freed of the need to pursue a dancing career.

1765 Zindel, Lizabeth. *The Secret Rites of Social Butterflies* (7–10). 2008, Viking $16.99 (978-0-670-06217-1). At her new girls' school in New York City, Maggie breaks into the popular clique and soon finds that betrayal is her new friends' pastime. (Rev: BL 5/15/08)

1766 Zinnen, Linda. *The Truth About Rats, Rules, and Seventh Grade* (5–7). 2001, HarperCollins LB $15.89 (978-0-06-028800-6). Larch, who faces multiple problems at home and at school, tries to live her life by a set of unemotional rules, but a friendly stray dog and the discovery of the truth about her father's death make these rules hard to keep. (Rev: BCCB 6/01; BL 4/1/01*; HBG 10/01; SLJ 2/01)

1767 Zolotow, Charlotte, ed. *Early Sorrow: Ten Stories of Youth* (8–12). 1986, HarperCollins $12.95 (978-0-06-026936-4). This excellent collection of 12 adult stories about growing up is a companion piece to *An Overpraised Season* (o.p.), another anthology about adolescence. (Rev: BL 10/1/86; SLJ 1/87; VOYA 2/87)

World Affairs and Contemporary Problems

1768 Abelove, Joan. *Go and Come Back* (8–10). 1998, Puffin paper $5.99 (978-0-14-130694-0). The story of two female anthropologists studying a primitive Peruvian Indian village, written from the perspective of Alicia, one of the village teenagers. (Rev: BL 3/1/98; SLJ 3/98*; VOYA 10/98)

1769 Adoff, Jaime. *Names Will Never Hurt Me* (7–10). 2004, Dutton $16.99 (978-0-525-47175-2). As their high school marks the first anniversary of the shooting death of a fellow student, four very different teenagers express their feelings about school, their classmates, and themselves. (Rev: BCCB 4/04; BL 4/1/04; HB 7–8/04; SLJ 4/04; VOYA 4/04)

1770 Bledsoe, Lucy Jane. *Cougar Canyon* (5–8). 2001, Holiday $16.95 (978-0-8234-1599-1). A family story and environmental tale about a 13-year-old girl named Izzy who fights to save a cougar in the local park. (Rev: BCCB 2/02; BL 2/1/02; HBG 3/02; SLJ 2/02; VOYA 4/02)

1771 Budhos, Marina. *Ask Me No Questions* (7–10). 2006, Simon & Schuster $16.95 (978-1-4169-0351-2). Fourteen-year-old Nadira describes the legal and emotional upheavals her family faces as Bangladeshis living illegally in the United States. (Rev: BCCB 3/06; BL 12/15/05*; HB 3–4/06; SLJ 4/06; VOYA 2/06)

1772 Carmi, Daniella. *Samir and Yonatan* (4–8). Trans. from Hebrew by Yael Lotan. 2000, Scholastic paper $15.95 (978-0-439-13504-7). Samir, a young Palestinian, is sent to a Jewish hospital for surgery and there he meets some Jewish contemporaries. (Rev: BCCB 4/00; BL 2/1/00; HBG 10/00; SLJ 3/00; VOYA 6/00)

1773 Castaneda, Omar S. *Among the Volcanoes* (7–10). 1996, Bantam paper $4.50 (978-0-440-91118-0). Set in a remote Guatemalan village, this story is about a Mayan woodcutter's daughter, Isabel, who is caught between her respect for the old ways and her yearning for something more. (Rev: BL 5/15/91; SLJ 3/91)

1774 Clinton, Cathryn. *A Stone in My Hand* (6–12). 2002, Candlewick $15.99 (978-0-7636-1388-4). Eleven-year-old Maalak's father is killed in the violence of 1988 Gaza, and she must worry about her

brother's future. (Rev: BL 9/15/02; HBG 3/03; SLJ 11/02*; VOYA 2/03)

1775 Collins, Pat Lowery. *The Fattening Hut* (8–12). 2003, Houghton $15.00 (978-0-618-30955-9). Fourteen-year-old Helen sets off on a dangerous journey, running away from the tropical tribe that requires her to undergo female circumcision before her impending marriage. (Rev: BL 11/1/03; HBG 4/04; SLJ 11/03; VOYA 2/04)

1776 Cooney, Caroline B. *Diamonds in the Shadow* (8–12). 2007, Delacorte $15.99 (978-0-385-73261-1). Jared and Mopsy have different experiences when their family hosts a refugee family from Sierra Leone. (Rev: BL 9/1/07; SLJ 9/07)

1777 Covington, Dennis. *Lasso the Moon* (7–10). 1996, Bantam $20.95 (978-0-385-30991-2). After April and her divorced doctor father move to Saint Simons Island, April takes a liking to Fernando, an illegal alien from El Salvador being treated by her father. (Rev: BL 1/15/95; SLJ 3/95; VOYA 4/95)

1778 Craig, Colleen. *Afrika* (7–12). 2008, Tundra paper $9.95 (978-0-88776-807-1). Kim, a 13-year-old who has grown up in Canada, travels to South Africa with her journalist mother, a white South African, to cover the Truth and Reconciliation Commission hearings; while there she learns about her father's African roots and finds out why her mother left him. (Rev: BL 6/1–15/08; SLJ 7/08)

1779 D'Adamo, Francesco. *Iqbal: A Novel* (4–7). 2003, Simon & Schuster $15.95 (978-0-689-85445-3). The sad story of the death of Iqbal, the young child labor activist, is brought to life through the fictional narrative of a young Pakistani girl who worked with him in the carpet factories. (Rev: BL 11/1/03; HB 11–12/03; HBG 4/04; SLJ 11/03)

1780 Davis, Jenny. *Checking on the Moon* (6–9). 1991, Orchard LB $17.99 (978-0-531-08560-8). A 13-year-old, forced to spend the summer in a run-down Pittsburgh neighborhood with a grandmother she has never met, discovers community activism and her own abilities. (Rev: BL 9/15/91; SLJ 10/91*)

1781 Doherty, Berlie. *The Girl Who Saw Lions* (6–12). 2008, Roaring Brook $16.95 (978-1-59643-377-9). Abela, 9, and Rosa, 13, tell their contrasting stories in alternating chapters. Abela is an AIDS orphan in Tanzania, whose uncle plans to sell her for adoption in England; in London, Rosa is unhappy when she learns that her single-parent mother plans to adopt a child. (Rev: BL 2/15/08; SLJ 7/08)

1782 Ellis, Deborah. *Mud City* (4–7). Series: Breadwinner Trilogy. 2003, Douglas & McIntyre $15.95 (978-0-88899-518-6). Feisty Afghan refugee Shauzia sets off on her own, dreaming of a life of freedom in France and prepared to dress as a boy and beg, but circumstances force her back to the camp on the Pakistan border in this final novel in the trilogy. (Rev: BL 11/15/03; HBG 4/04; SLJ 11/03)

1783 Ellis, Deborah, and Eric Walters. *Bifocal* (7–10). 2007, Fitzhenry & Whiteside $18.95 (978-1-55455-036-4). When a Muslim student is arrested, suspected of being a terrorist, his school is abuzz, and various groups take sides. (Rev: BL 1/1–15/08; SLJ 3/08)

1784 Flegg, Aubrey. *The Cinnamon Tree* (7–10). 2002, O'Brien paper $7.95 (978-0-86278-657-1). The horror of the injuries inflicted by landmines is brought to life in this story of a girl who loses a leg and goes on to teach others about the dangers of these weapons. (Rev: BL 8/02; SLJ 8/02)

1785 Fox, Paula. *Lily and the Lost Boy* (6–9). 1987, Watts LB $17.99 (978-0-531-08320-8). Using the tiny island of Thasos in Greece as a setting the author tells a story of the maturation of a 12-year-old American girl and her older brother. (Rev: BL 7/87; VOYA 2/88)

1786 Golio, Janet, and Mike Golio. *A Present from the Past* (6–8). 1995, Portunus paper $8.95 (978-0-9641330-5-1). In this blend of fact and fiction, Sarah and her friend become concerned about their environment after they discover some petroglyphs. (Rev: BL 1/1–15/96)

1787 Griffin, Paul. *Ten Mile River* (8–12). 2008, Dial $16.99 (978-0-8037-3284-1). Ray, 14, and José, 15, live together in an abandoned building in west Harlem and survive on odd jobs and what they can steal; when they meet the lovely Trini, complications of romance and opportunity test their friendship. (Rev: BL 6/1–15/08; SLJ 9/08)

1788 Hentoff, Nat. *The Day They Came to Arrest the Book* (7–10). 1983, Dell paper $5.50 (978-0-440-91814-1). Some students at George Mason High think *Huckleberry Finn* is a racist book.

1789 Hesse, Karen. *Phoenix Rising* (6–8). 1994, Holt $16.95 (978-0-8050-3108-9). A 13-year-old and her grandmother on a Vermont farm hope to avoid radiation contamination from a nuclear plant. They are visited by Boston evacuees, one of them a boy with whom the girl falls in love. (Rev: BL 5/15/94; SLJ 6/94*; VOYA 8/94)

1790 Hiaasen, Carl. *Hoot* (5–8). 2002, Knopf $15.95 (978-0-375-82181-3). Roy Eberhart, the new kid in Coconut Cove, finds himself embroiled in a battle to save some owls. Newbery Honor Book, 2003. (Rev: BCCB 11/02; BL 10/15/02; HB 11–12/02; HBG 3/03; SLJ 8/02)

1791 Ho, Minfong. *Rice Without Rain* (7–12). 1990, Lothrop $17.99 (978-0-688-06355-9). Jinda, a 17-year-old girl, experiences personal tragedy and the awakening of love in this novel set during revolutionary times in Thailand during the 1970s. (Rev: BL 7/90; SLJ 9/90)

1792 Hobbs, Will. *Crossing the Wire* (5–8). 2006, HarperCollins $15.99 (978-0-06-074138-9). Victor, a teenage Mexican boy who is the sole support for his family, decides to risk the dangerous crossing into the United States in search of work. (Rev: BL 5/1/06; SLJ 5/06; VOYA 4/06) ⬿

1793 Hopkins, Ellen. *Crank* (8–12). 2004, Simon & Schuster paper $6.99 (978-0-689-86519-0). In this debut novel written in verse, Hopkins introduces readers to Kristina Snow and how the high school junior became addicted to crystal meth. (Rev: BL 11/15/04; SLJ 11/04; VOYA 2/05)

1794 James, Brian. *Tomorrow, Maybe* (7–12). 2003, Scholastic paper $6.99 (978-0-439-49035-1). Living a hard life on the streets of New York, 15-year-old Gretchen, a.k.a. Chan, finds a purpose when she takes charge of an 11-year-old in the same predicament. (Rev: LMC 10/03; SLJ 6/03; VOYA 8/03)

1795 Jennings, Richard W. *Stink City* (5–8). 2006, Houghton $16.00 (978-0-618-55248-1). Cade Carlsen, heir to his family's successful — but smelly — catfish bait business, becomes an anti-fishing activist. (Rev: BL 10/15/06)

1796 Kilbourne, Christina. *Dear Jo: The Story of Losing Leah . . . and Searching for Hope* (6–8). 2007, Lobster paper $9.95 (978-1-897073-51-3). A cautionary tale that maintains its readability, this novel focuses on two 12-year-old girl with online boyfriends; one friend disappears, and the other copes by keeping a diary and helping to catch the predator. (Rev: SLJ 7/07)

1797 Laird, Elizabeth, and Sonia Nimr. *A Little Piece of Ground* (6–9). 2006, Haymarket paper $9.95 (978-1-931859-38-7). Karim, 12, and his friends hope to create a soccer field in Ramallah so they have a place to escape from the war surrounding them. (Rev: BL 10/15/06)

1798 Levine, Anna. *Running on Eggs* (5–9). 1999, Front St. $15.95 (978-0-8126-2875-3). The story of two girls — one Jewish and the other Palestinian — and a friendship that withstands cultural and political differences. (Rev: BCCB 11/99; BL 1/1–15/00; HBG 3/00; SLJ 12/99; VOYA 2/00)

1799 Levitin, Sonia. *The Return* (6–10). 1987, Fawcett paper $5.99 (978-0-449-70280-2). Seen from the viewpoint of a teenage girl, this is the story of a group of African Jews who journey from Ethiopia to the Sudan to escape persecution. (Rev: BL 4/15/87; SLJ 5/87; VOYA 6/87)

1800 Lynch, Janet Nichols. *Peace Is a Four-Letter Word* (7–10). 2005, Heyday paper $9.95 (978-1-59714-014-0). The carefully ordered life of high school cheerleader Emily Rankin is shattered when a history teacher inspires her to get involved in the peace movement on the eve of the Gulf War. (Rev: BL 10/1/05; SLJ 10/05)

1801 McDaniel, Lurlene. *Baby Alicia Is Dying* (8–10). 1993, Bantam paper $4.99 (978-0-553-29605-1). In an attempt to feel needed, Desi volunteers to care for HIV-positive babies and discovers a deep commitment in herself. (Rev: BL 10/1/93; SLJ 7/93; VOYA 8/93)

1802 Mankell, Henning. *Secrets in the Fire* (4–8). 2003, Annick $14.95 (978-1-55037-801-6); paper $7.95 (978-1-55037-800-9). This is the true story of Sofia, a courageous Mozambican girl who lost both legs — and her sister — when a landmine exploded. (Rev: BL 12/15/03*; SLJ 5/04)

1803 Martin, Nora. *Perfect Snow* (8–12). 2002, Bloomsbury $16.95 (978-1-58234-788-2). Ben feels strong and confident when he participates in the violent intolerance of the local white supremacists until he meets Eden, a new — and Jewish — girl at school, in this novel set in a small Montana community. (Rev: BL 8/02; SLJ 9/02)

1804 Mosher, Richard. *Zazoo* (6–9). 2001, Clarion $16.00 (978-0-618-13534-9). Zazoo, a French girl adopted from Vietnam, comes to understand the complexities of her adoptive Grand-Pierre's past in this absorbing, multilayered novel. (Rev: BL 12/15/01; HBG 3/02; SLJ 11/01*; VOYA 10/01)

1805 Nelson, Blake. *They Came from Below* (7–12). 2007, Tor $17.95 (978-0-7653-1423-9). Steve and Dave initially seem to be two cute boys, but Emily and Reese come to realize that they are actually creatures from another world intent on persuading humans to save the oceans from pollution. (Rev: BCCB 9/07; SLJ 8/07)

1806 Neville, Emily C. *The China Year* (5–8). 1991, HarperCollins $15.95 (978-0-06-024383-8). Henri, 14, has left his New York City home, school, and friends to go to Peking University for a year with his father. (Rev: BL 5/1/91; SLJ 5/91)

1807 Nye, Naomi Shihab. *Going Going* (7–10). 2005, Greenwillow LB $16.89 (978-0-06-029366-6). Angered by the exodus of small businesses from her hometown, 16-year-old Florrie launches a grassroots campaign against the giant chain stores that she believes are responsible. (Rev: BCCB 7–8/05; BL 4/1/05; HB 7–8/05; SLJ 5/05; VOYA 10/05)

1808 Paulsen, Gary. *Sentries* (8–12). 1986, Penguin paper $3.95 (978-0-317-62279-9). The stories of four different young people are left unresolved when they are all wiped out by a superbomb. (Rev: BL 5/1/86; SLJ 8/86; VOYA 8/86)

1809 Prose, Francine. *After* (8–10). 2003, HarperCollins LB $17.89 (978-0-06-008082-2). A school district hires an over-the-top crisis counselor to impose order in the name of safety after a massacre at a nearby high school. (Rev: HB 5–6/03; HBG 10/03; SLJ 5/03; VOYA 6/03)

1810 Rochman, Hazel, ed. *Somehow Tenderness Survives: Stories of Southern Africa* (8–12). 1988, HarperCollins $12.95 (978-0-06-025022-5); paper $5.99 (978-0-06-447063-6). Ten stories by such writers as Nadine Gordimer about growing up in South Africa. (Rev: BL 8/88; SLJ 12/88; VOYA 12/88)

1811 Rosen, Roger, and Patra McSharry, eds. *Border Crossings: Emigration and Exile* (8–12). Series: Icarus World Issues. 1992, Rosen LB $21.95 (978-0-8239-1364-0); paper $8.95 (978-0-8239-1365-7). Twelve fiction and nonfiction selections that illustrate the lives of those affected by geopolitical change. (Rev: BL 11/1/92)

1812 Ruby, Lois. *Skin Deep* (8–12). 1994, Scholastic paper $14.95 (978-0-590-47699-7). Dan, the frustrated new kid in town, falls in love with popular senior Laurel, but he destroys their relationship when he joins a neo-Nazi skinhead group. (Rev: BL 11/15/94*; SLJ 3/95; VOYA 12/94)

1813 Sitomer, Alan Lawrence. *Homeboyz* (7–10). 2007, Hyperion $16.99 (978-1-4231-0030-0). When his little sister Tina is gunned down by gang members, 17-year-old Teddy quickly seeks revenge and ends up arrested for attempted homicide in this novel that looks at the causes of inner-city violence; the third volume in the trilogy that started with *The Hoopster* (2005) and *Hip-Hop High School* (2006). (Rev: BL 7/07; LMC 10/07; SLJ 8/07)

1814 Sleator, William. *Test* (7–10). 2008, Abrams $16.95 (978-0-8109-9356-3). In a near-future United States, Ann discovers that a test that high school students must pass is part of a larger, corrupt government plan. (Rev: BL 5/1/08; SLJ 7/08)

1815 Temple, Frances. *Grab Hands and Run* (6–12). 1993, Orchard LB $16.99 (978-0-531-08630-8). Jacinto opposes the oppressive government of El Salvador. When he disappears, his wife, Paloma, and their son, 12-year-old Felipe, try to escape to freedom in Canada. (Rev: BL 5/1/93*; SLJ 4/93*)

1816 Temple, Frances. *Tonight, by Sea* (6–10). 1995, Orchard LB $16.99 (978-0-531-08749-7). A docunovel about Haitian boat people who struggle for social justice and attempt harrowing escapes to freedom. (Rev: BL 3/15/95; SLJ 4/95)

1817 Williams, Dar. *Lights, Camera, Amalee* (5–7). 2006, Scholastic $16.99 (978-0-439-80352-6). A modest inheritance from a grandmother she barely knew gives 12-year-old Amalee the funds she needs to make a documentary about endangered species. (Rev: SLJ 9/06)

1818 Woods, Brenda. *Emako Blue* (7–10). 2004, Penguin $15.99 (978-0-399-24006-5). After Emako, a talented singer, is mistakenly killed in a drive-by shooting in Los Angeles, her surviving friends — Eddie, Jamal, and Monterey — share their thoughts about what she meant to them. (Rev: BL 7/04; SLJ 7/04)

1819 Zenatti, Valérie. *A Bottle in the Gaza Sea* (7–12). Trans. by Adriana Hunter. 2008, Blooms-bury $16.95 (978-1-59990-200-5). A Jewish girl in Israel puts a message in a bottle that is thrown into the sea and makes its way to Naïm, a Palestinian in Gaza; Tal and Naïm correspond and develop a rela-tionship despite the wide gulf between their peoples. (Rev: BL 4/1/08; SLJ 5/08)

Fantasy

1820 Abbott, Tony. *Kringle* (5–8). 2005, Scholastic $14.99 (978-0-439-74942-8). In early Britain a 12-year-old orphan named Kringle battles dark forces and discovers his true destiny. (Rev: BCCB 12/05; BL 10/15/05; HBG 4/06; SLJ 10/05; VOYA 2/06)

1821 Abouzeid, Chris. *Anatopsis* (6–8). 2006, Dut-ton $16.99 (978-0-525-47583-5). Princess Anatop-sis, an immortal with magical powers, questions her mother's plans for her future and considers the plight of the mere mortals in her land. (Rev: BCCB 4/06; SLJ 3/06; VOYA 4/06)

1822 Adams, Richard. *Tales from Watership Down* (7–12). 1996, Avon paper $7.99 (978-0-380-72934-0). Nineteen tales keep readers abreast of develop-ments on Watership Down and provide information on the exploits of El-ahrairah, the rabbit folk hero. (Rev: BL 9/1/96; SLJ 1/97)

1823 Adams, Richard. *Watership Down* (7–12). 1996, Scribner $30.00 (978-0-684-83605-8); Simon & Schuster Adult Publishing Group paper $16 (978-0-7432-7770-9). In this fantasy first published in 1974, a small group of male rabbits sets out to find a new home.

1824 Adler, C. S. *Good-bye Pink Pig* (5–7). 1986, Avon paper $2.75 (978-0-380-70175-9). Shy Aman-da takes comfort in the make-believe world of her miniature pink pig — away from the elegant world of her mother and easygoing life of her brother — until trouble enters her real and imaginary worlds and she learns to assert herself. (Rev: BCCB 2/86; BL 12/15/85)

1825 Adler, C. S. *Help, Pink Pig!* (5–7). 1991, Avon paper $2.95 (978-0-380-71156-7). Unsure of herself with her mother, Amanda retreats into the world of her miniature pink pig. (Rev: BL 5/1/90; SLJ 5/90)

1826 Adlington, L. J. *Cherry Heaven* (8–11). 2008, Greenwillow $16.99 (978-0-06-143180-7). In a strange world where cities and towns war against each other and hide disturbing secrets, three girls tell about their lives — one as a slave, two sisters as new citizens of the town of Meander. A companion

to *The Diary of Pelly D.* (Rev: BCCB 6/08; BL 12/15/07; HB 3–4/08; LMC 10/08; SLJ 3/08)

1827 Alcock, Vivien. *The Haunting of Cassie Palmer* (5–8). 1997, Houghton paper $6.95 (978-0-395-81653-0). Cassie finds she is blessed with sec-ond sight.

1828 Alexander, Alma. *Gift of the Unmage* (7–10). Series: Worldweavers Trilogy. 2007, HarperTeen $16.99 (978-0-06-083955-0). Thea, the seventh child of two seventh children, unexpectedly shows no magical ability until Grandma Spider uncovers her power as a dream weaver and Thea enters Wandless Academy for remedial magic. (Rev: BCCB 6/07; BL 3/1/07; SLJ 8/07)

1829 Alexander, Alma. *Spellspam* (7–10). Series: Worldweavers. 2008, Eos $17.99 (978-0-06-083958-1). E-mails that cast spells on unsuspecting people are endangering computer users around the world; can Thea use her magic to stop them? (Rev: BL 2/8/08; SLJ 7/08)

1830 Alexander, Lloyd. *The Iron Ring* (6–9). 1997, Puffin paper $7.99 (978-0-14-130348-2). When he loses in a dice game, Tamar must fulfill a promise to journey to the kingdom of King Jaya in this fanta-sy based on Indian mythology. (Rev: BL 5/15/97; SLJ 5/97*; VOYA 10/97)

1831 Alexander, Lloyd. *The Rope Trick* (4–7). 2002, Dutton $16.99 (978-0-525-47020-5). A young magician sets out on a challenging journey to master the difficult rope trick. (Rev: BCCB 1/03; BL 10/15/02; HB 11–12/02; HBG 3/03; SLJ 9/02; VOYA 12/02)

1832 Allen, Will. *Swords for Hire: Two of the Most Unlikely Heroes You'll Ever Meet* (5–8). Illus. by David Michael Beck. 2003, CenterPunch paper $6.95 (978-0-9724882-0-4). A spoof of a fantasy in which inexperienced warrior 16-year-old Sam Hatcher and his eccentric mentor Rigby Skeet set off to rescue King Olive, who has been unseated by his evil brother. (Rev: BCCB 6/03; SLJ 8/03)

1833 Almond, David. *Clay* (6–9). 2006, Delacorte $15.95 (978-0-385-73171-3). Themes of religion, art and the nature of evil are predominant in this tale of two English boys who create a modern-day Frankenstein-like monster. (Rev: BCCB 9/06; BL 6/1–15/06; HB 7–8/06; LMC 8-9/06; SLJ 8/06)

1834 Almond, David. *Skellig* (5–8). 1999, Delacorte $16.95 (978-0-385-32653-7). Michael discovers a ragged man in his garage existing on dead flies in this novel that is part fantasy, part mystery, and part family story. (Rev: BL 2/1/99*; HB 5–6/99; HBG 10/99; SLJ 2/99)

1835 Alter, Stephen. *Ghost Letters* (5–8). 2008, Bloomsbury $16.95 (978-1-58234-739-4). Gil toss-es a message in a bottle into the sea off the Massa-chusetts coast and receives a reply from a boy living

100 years in the past; fantasy and the supernatural combine for a chilling and thrilling story. (Rev: BL 1/1–15/08; SLJ 5/08)

1836 Alton, Steve. *The Firehills* (6–9). 2005, Carolrhoda $15.95 (978-1-57505-798-9). Sam, Charley, and Amergin — three teens with magical powers — do battle against a group of evil fairies known as the Sidhe. (Rev: BL 10/1/05; SLJ 1/06; VOYA 10/05)

1837 Alton, Steve. *The Malifex* (5–8). 2002, Carolrhoda LB $14.95 (978-0-8225-0959-2). Sam's vacation in contemporary England is complicated by a Wiccan's daughter, the release of the ghost of Merlin's apprentice, and a battle between good and evil. (Rev: BL 9/1/02; HBG 10/03; SLJ 11/02)

1838 Amoss, Berthe. *Lost Magic* (5–7). 1993, Hyperion $14.95 (978-1-56282-573-7). Fantasy and history mingle in this story set in the Middle Ages about a young girl who knows how to use both healing herbs and magic. (Rev: BL 11/1/93)

1839 Andersen, Jodi. *May Bird and the Ever After* (4–7). Illus. by Leonid Gore. 2005, Simon & Schuster $15.95 (978-0-689-86923-5). After falling into a lake near her home, 10-year-old May Bird finds herself in Ever After, a fantasy underworld inhabited by the souls of the dead. (Rev: BCCB 12/05; BL 10/15/05; HBG 4/06; SLJ 12/05; VOYA 12/05)

1840 Anderson, Jodi Lynn. *May Bird, Warrior Princess* (4–7). Series: May Bird. 2007, Atheneum $16.99 (978-0-689-86925-9). Three years after returning from the land of the dead, May Bird and Somber Kitty return to Ever After after falling from a rooftop in the final installment in this inventive fantasy series. (Rev: BL 11/1/07; SLJ 10/07)

1841 Anderson, John David. *Standard Hero Behavior* (6–9). 2007, Clarion $16.00 (978-0-618-75920-0). There's a shortage of heroes in Highsmith, and someone needs to fight the giants and ogres, so Mason sets out to find a hero to save the day. (Rev: BL 10/15/07; SLJ 1/08)

1842 Arkin, Alan. *The Lemming Condition* (4–7). Illus. by Joan Sandin. 1989, HarperCollins paper $9.95 (978-0-06-250048-9). Bubber opposes the mass suicide of his companions in this interesting fable.

1843 Armstrong, Alan. *Whittington* (5–8). Illus. by S. D. Schindler. 2005, Random LB $16.99 (978-0-375-92864-2). Happy to have found a place to live, Whittington the cat regales the other barnyard animals with tales of his famous forebears. (Rev: BL 5/15/05; SLJ 8/05*)

1844 Atwater-Rhodes, Amelia. *Hawksong* (7–10). 2003, Delacorte $9.95 (978-0-385-73071-6). A gripping fantasy about two young leaders who seek to end the long war between their peoples — avian shapeshifters and serpent shapeshifters — and are

prepared to consider marriage for the sake of peace. (Rev: HBG 4/04; SLJ 8/03*; VOYA 6/03)

1845 Atwater-Rhodes, Amelia. *Midnight Predator* (7–9). 2002, Delacorte $9.95 (978-0-385-32794-7). In a world where humans are slaves to vampires, teen vampire hunter Turquoise and her colleague pose as slaves in order to defeat an evil tyrant. (Rev: BL 8/02; HBG 10/02; SLJ 5/02; VOYA 6/02)

1846 Augarde, Steve. *Celandine* (7–10). 2006, Random $16.95 (978-0-385-75048-6). Celandine escapes the cruel boarding school she attends during World War I and returns to the village of the little people, the Various, that live near her family's farm where she discovers her special powers. (Rev: BL 8/06; SLJ 11/06)

1847 Augarde, Steve. *The Various* (4–8). 2004, Random LB $17.99 (978-0-385-75037-0). Midge, a 12-year-old girl on vacation in the countryside, discovers a tribe of little people known as the Various, who are not as helpless as they seem. (Rev: BL 12/15/03; SLJ 3/04)

1848 Avi. *Bright Shadow* (5–8). 1994, Simon & Schuster paper $4.99 (978-0-689-71783-3). At the death of the great wizard, Morenna finds she possesses the last five wishes in the world. (Rev: SLJ 12/85)

1849 Avi. *The Man Who Was Poe* (7–10). 1991, Avon paper $6.99 (978-0-380-71192-5). When Edmund goes out to search for his missing mother and sister, he encounters Edgar Allan Poe in disguise as detective Auguste Dupin. (Rev: BL 10/1/89; SLJ 9/89; VOYA 2/90)

1850 Avi. *Strange Happenings: Five Tales of Transformation* (4–7). 2006, Harcourt $15.00 (978-0-15-205790-9). Shape-shifting and invisibility are among the transformations in this collection of five fantasy tales. (Rev: BL 3/15/06; SLJ 5/06)

1851 Babbitt, Natalie. *The Search for Delicious* (4–7). Illus. by author. 1969, Farrar $17.00 (978-0-374-36534-9). The innocent task of polling the kingdom's subjects for personal food preferences provokes civil war in a zestful spoof of taste and society.

1852 Baker, E. D. *Dragon's Breath* (5–7). 2003, Bloomsbury $15.95 (978-1-58234-858-2). Esmeralda and Eadric help Aunt Grassina find ingredients needed to break the spell that turned Grassina's true love, Haywood, into an otter in this humorous sequel to *The Frog Princess* (2002). (Rev: BL 4/15/04; SLJ 12/03; VOYA 4/04)

1853 Baker, E. D. *The Frog Princess* (5–8). 2002, Bloomsbury $15.95 (978-1-58234-799-8). When Princess Esmeralda kisses the frog, she turns into one herself in this humorous twist on the traditional saga. (Rev: BCCB 2/03; BL 11/15/02; SLJ 1/03; VOYA 12/02)

1854 Baker, E. D. *The Salamander Spell* (4–7). 2007, Bloomsbury $16.95 (978-1-59990-018-6). In this prequel to *The Frog Princess* (2002), 13-year-old Grassina is tired of being overshadowed by her older sister Chartreuse and, accompanied by her snake friend Pippa, runs away to the swamp where she discovers her powers, meets a young magician, and saves the kingdom from werewolves. (Rev: BL 9/15/07; SLJ 12/07)

1855 Baker, E. D. *Wings: A Fairy Tale* (5–8). 2008, Bloomsbury $16.95 (978-1-59990-193-0). Could Tamisin really be a goblin? When she grows wings, she realizes she must be from another world. (Rev: BL 5/15/08)

1856 Banks, Lynne Reid. *Angela and Diabola* (5–8). 1997, Avon $15.95 (978-0-380-97562-4). A wicked romp that chronicles the lives of twins, the angelic Angela and the truly horrible and destructive Diabola. (Rev: SLJ 7/97)

1857 Banks, Lynne Reid. *The Key to the Indian* (4–8). Illus. Series: Indian in the Cupboard. 1998, Avon $16.00 (978-0-380-97717-8). In the fifth book of the Indian in the Cupboard series, Omri and Dad return to the time of Little Bear to help the Iroquois deal with European meddlers. (Rev: BL 11/15/98; HBG 3/99; SLJ 12/98)

1858 Banks, Lynne Reid. *The Mystery of the Cupboard* (4–8). Illus. Series: Indian in the Cupboard. 1993, HarperCollins paper $5.99 (978-0-380-72013-2). In this, the fourth book in the series, the young hero Omri uncovers a diary that reveals secrets about his magical cupboard. (Rev: BCCB 6/93; BL 4/1/93; HB 7–8/93; SLJ 6/93; VOYA 10/93)

1859 Banks, Lynne Reid. *The Return of the Indian* (5–7). Illus. by William Celdart. Series: Indian in the Cupboard. 1986, Doubleday $16.95 (978-0-385-23497-9); Avon paper $5.99 (978-0-380-70284-8). Omri brings his plastic Indian figures to life and discovers that his friend Little Bear has been wounded and needs his help. (Rev: BL 9/15/86; HB 11–12/86; SLJ 11/86)

1860 Banner, Catherine. *The Eyes of a King* (7–11). Series: The Last Descendants. 2008, Random $16.99 (978-0-375-83875-0). An intricate and many-layered fantasy in which teenaged Leo discovers that the true ruler of Malonia has been exiled to England. (Rev: BL 5/15/08; SLJ 8/08)

1861 Barker, Clive. *Days of Magic, Nights of War* (7–12). Series: Abarat. 2004, HarperCollins $24.99 (978-0-06-029170-9). In the second installment in the series, Candy Quackenbush makes discoveries about herself and the islands of Abarat as she tries to stay one step ahead of the Lord of Midnight. (Rev: BL 9/1/04; SLJ 11/04)

1862 Barnes, Jennifer Lynn. *Tattoo* (8–11). 2007, Delacorte LB $11.99 (978-0-385-90363-9); paper $7.99 (978-0-385-73347-2). Four 15-year-old girls buy temporary tattoos and discover each of them now has a superpower that will help the quartet battle an ancient force that plans to create mayhem at their school dance. (Rev: BCCB 3/07; BL 1/1–15/07; SLJ 1/07)

1863 Barrett, Tracy. *On Etruscan Time* (5–8). 2005, Holt $16.95 (978-0-8050-7569-4). Hector, 11, finds himself struggling to rescue an Etruscan boy from execution, in this time-travel fantasy set on an archaeological dig in Italy. (Rev: BL 6/1–15/05; SLJ 7/05)

1864 Barron, T. A. *The Ancient One* (6–9). 1992, Putnam $20.99 (978-0-399-21899-6). A fight to save a stand of Oregon redwoods occupies Kate, 13, in this time-travel fantasy. (Rev: BL 9/1/92; SLJ 11/92)

1865 Barron, T. A. *The Eternal Flame* (7–10). Series: Great Tree of Avalon. 2006, Philomel $19.99 (978-0-399-24213-7). This final book in the trilogy follows Tamwyn, Elli, and Scree as they make their final, dramatic efforts to fend off the evil Rhita Gawr. (Rev: BL 9/1/06; SLJ 11/06)

1866 Barron, T. A. *The Fires of Merlin* (7–10). Illus. Series: Lost Years of Merlin. 1998, Putnam $20.99 (978-0-399-23020-2). A complex sequel to *The Seven Songs of Merlin,* in which young Merlin once again faces the threat of the dragon Valdearg, who is preparing to conquer the land of Fincayra. (Rev: BL 9/1/98; HBG 3/99; SLJ 3/99; VOYA 2/99)

1867 Barron, T. A. *The Great Tree of Avalon* (6–12). Series: Great Tree of Avalon. 2004, Penguin $19.99 (978-0-399-23763-8). The fate of Avalon, which the Lady of the Lake has prophesied will be destroyed by the Dark Child, rests in the hands of two 17-year-old boys: Tamwyn and Scree. (Rev: BL 9/1/04*; SLJ 10/04)

1868 Barron, T. A. *The Lost Years of Merlin* (7–10). Series: Lost Years of Merlin. 1996, Putnam $19.99 (978-0-399-23018-9). The author has created a magical land populated by remarkable creatures in this first book of a trilogy about the early years of the magician Merlin. (Rev: BL 9/1/96; SLJ 9/96; VOYA 10/96)

1869 Barron, T. A. *The Merlin Effect* (6–9). 1994, Putnam $19.99 (978-0-399-22689-2). Kate, 13, accompanies her father, a King Arthur expert, to a remote lagoon where they search a sunken ship for the magical horn of Merlin. A sequel to *Heartlight* (1990) and *The Ancient One* (1992). (Rev: BL 11/1/94; SLJ 11/94; VOYA 12/94)

1870 Barron, T. A. *The Mirror of Merlin* (7–10). Series: Lost Years of Merlin. 1999, Putnam $20.99 (978-0-399-23455-2). Young Merlin faces a deadly disease and confronts his future self as he continues his dangerous search for his sword. (Rev: BL 10/1/99; HBG 4/00; SLJ 10/99; VOYA 2/00)

1871 Barron, T. A. *The Seven Songs of Merlin* (7–10). Series: Lost Years of Merlin. 1997, Putnam $19.99 (978-0-399-23019-6). In this sequel to *The Lost Years of Merlin,* Emrys, who will become Merlin, must travel to the Otherworld to save his mother who has been poisoned. (Rev: BL 9/1/97; HBG 3/98; SLJ 9/97)

1872 Barron, T. A. *Shadows on the Stars* (7–10). Series: Great Tree of Avalon. 2005, Philomel $19.99 (978-0-399-23764-5). In the year 1002 Tamwyn, Elli, and Scree set off on separate quests to conquer the evil Rhita Gawr and save Avalon in this sequel to *Child of the Dark Prophecy* (2004). (Rev: BL 9/15/05; SLJ 12/05)

1873 Barron, T. A. *Tree Girl* (4–8). 2001, Putnam $14.99 (978-0-399-23457-6). Rowanna, 9, discovers she is descended from tree spirits after she is lured into the woods by a shape-shifting bear cub in this book for middle-graders. (Rev: BCCB 10/01; BL 11/1/01; HBG 3/02; SLJ 10/01; VOYA 10/01)

1874 Barron, T. A. *The Wings of Merlin* (7–10). Series: Lost Years of Merlin. 2000, Philomel $21.99 (978-0-399-23456-9). In this, the concluding volume of the saga, Merlin faces his most difficult decision. (Rev: BL 10/1/00; HBG 3/01; SLJ 11/00; VOYA 12/00)

1875 Barry, Dave, and Ridley Pearson. *Peter and the Secret of Rundoon* (4–7). Illus. by Greg Call. Series: Starcatchers. 2007, Hyperion $18.99 (978-0-7868-3788-5). In this action-packed conclusion to the Starcatchers trilogy, Peter (Pan, that is) saves the world long before ever meeting Wendy and her siblings. (Rev: BL 11/15/07; SLJ 10/07)

1876 Barry, Dave, and Ridley Pearson. *Peter and the Shadow Thieves* (5–8). Illus. by Greg Call. 2006, Hyperion $18.99 (978-0-7868-3787-8). In this sequel to *Peter and the Starcatchers* (2005), the forever-young Peter and Tinker Bell race to foil the evil plans of Lord Ombra. (Rev: BL 6/1–15/06; SLJ 8/06; VOYA 8/06)

1877 Bateman, Colin. *Running with the Reservoir Pups* (4–7). 2005, Delacorte LB $17.99 (978-0-440-42048-4). Eddie becomes involved with a gang of tough Belfast kids and ends up rescuing kidnapped babies from a horrible fate in this action-packed fantasy, the first installment in a trilogy. (Rev: BL 3/1/05; SLJ 1/05)

1878 Batson, Wayne Thomas. *The Rise of the Wyrm Lord* (6–8). Series: The Door Within. 2006, Tommy Nelson $16.99 (978-1-4003-0737-1). This is the second volume in a trilogy that weaves Christian undertones into the adventures of friends Aidan and Antoinette, who are called to unite a world called The Realm after the death of King Eliam, to rescue Aidan's friend Robby before he is pulled into the dark side, and to defeat the plans of the evil Paragor

the Betrayer and his secret weapon, the Wyrm Lord. (Rev: SLJ 8/06)

1879 Bauer, Marion Dane. *Touch the Moon* (5–7). Illus. by Alix Berenzy. 1987, Houghton $15.00 (978-0-89919-526-1). Angry when she doesn't get a real horse, Jennifer throws away her toy horse gift and learns a lesson in responsibility. (Rev: BCCB 9/87; BL 9/15/87; HB 9–10/87)

1880 Baum, L. Frank. *The Wonderful Wizard of Oz* (4–8). Illus. by W. W. Denslow. 2000, Harper-Collins $24.99 (978-0-06-029323-9). A handsome facsimile of the 1900 publication on high-quality paper and featuring 24 original color plates and 130 two-color drawings. (Rev: BL 12/1/00)

1881 Baum, L. Frank. *The Wonderful Wizard of Oz: A Commemorative Pop-Up* (4–8). Illus. by Robert Sabuda. 2001, Simon & Schuster $24.95 (978-0-689-81751-9). An extraordinary pop-up version of the classic fantasy told in a condensed text. (Rev: BL 12/1/00; HB 9–10/00; HBG 3/01; SLJ 11/00)

1882 Beck, Ian. *The Secret History of Tom Trueheart* (4–7). Illus. 2007, HarperCollins $16.99 (978-0-06-115210-8). Twelve-year-old Tom Trueheart must try to track down his six older brothers when they mysteriously disappear, suspected victims of the enemy of storytelling. (Rev: SLJ 2/07) ⊚

1883 Becker, Tom. *Darkside* (7–10). 2008, Scholastic $16.99 (978-0-545-03739-6). Darkside is a dangerous and magical underground London that Jonathan discovers is connected to his family (specifically, his mentally troubled father) in mysterious ways. (Rev: BL 2/1/08; SLJ 5/08)

1884 Bedard, Michael. *A Darker Magic* (6–8). 1987, Avon paper $2.95 (978-0-380-70611-2). An intricate fantasy about the strange effects of a magic show run by Professor Mephisto. (Rev: BL 9/1/87; SLJ 9/87)

1885 Beddor, Frank. *The Looking Glass Wars* (6–9). 2006, Dial $17.99 (978-0-8037-3153-0). When she is forced to flee from Wonderland by her evil aunt Redd, young Alyss Heart finds a home in Victorian Oxford, where she persuades Charles Dodgson to write her story and dreams of reclaiming her throne. The sequel is *Seeing Redd* (2007). (Rev: BL 9/1/06; LMC 4/07; SLJ 10/06) ⊚

1886 Belden, Wilanne Schneider. *Mind-Hold* (6–9). 1987, Harcourt $14.95 (978-0-15-254280-1). After a violent earthquake, Carson and his sister, who has the gift of ESP, move into the desert hoping to find new friends. (Rev: BL 2/15/87; SLJ 3/87)

1887 Bell, Clare. *Ratha and Thistle-Chaser* (7–12). 2007, Penguin paper $8.99 (978-0-14-240944-2). Further adventures of the clan of intelligent cats and their search for new land in this continuation (first published in 1990) of *Ratha's Creature* (1983) and

Clan Ground (1984). (Rev: BL 2/1/90; SLJ 6/90; VOYA 6/90)

1888   Bell, Hilari. *Forging the Sword* (7–10). Series: Farsala Trilogy. 2006, Simon & Schuster $17.99 (978-0-689-85416-3). The final book in the Farsala trilogy finds Jiaan, Kavi, and Soraya fighting the Hrum with magic and a newly forged sword. (Rev: BL 12/15/06; SLJ 3/07)

1889   Bell, Hilari. *The Last Knight: A Knight and Rogue Novel* (8–10). 2007, HarperCollins $16.99 (978-0-06-082503-4). Eighteen-year-old Sir Michael Sevenson, a throwback knight errant, and 17-year-old Fisk, his squire, have many adventures as they tangle with the less-noble-than-they-initially-thought Lady Ceciel; the narration alternates between the honest knight and the slippery squire in this blend of fantasy, adventure, and mystery, with humor and "magica" thrown in. (Rev: BL 10/1/07; HB 9–10/07; LMC 2/08; SLJ 9/07)

1890   Bell, Hilari. *The Prophecy* (6–9). 2006, Eos $15.99 (978-0-06-059943-0). Prince Perryn must find his true self while saving his father's kingdom from a dragon and a vicious traitor. (Rev: BL 6/1–15/06; SLJ 10/06)

1891   Bell, Hilari. *Shield of Stars* (5–8). Series: The Shield, the Sword and the Crown. 2007, Simon & Schuster $16.99 (978-1-4169-0594-3). Weasel, 14 and a reformed pickpocket, sets out to rescue Justice Holis, who has given him a home and a job, from the wicked ruler of Deorthas. (Rev: BL 5/15/07; SLJ 5/07)

1892   Bell, Hilari. *The Wizard Test* (5–8). 2005, HarperCollins LB $16.89 (978-0-06-059941-6). Fourteen-year-old Dayven is not thrilled when he learns he has magical abilities until he undergoes wizard training. (Rev: BL 2/1/05; SLJ 3/05)

1893   Bell, Ted. *Nick of Time* (5–8). 2008, St. Martin's $17.95 (978-0-312-38068-7). Villains from the past and present (that is, 1939) show up when plucky young Nick opens a sea chest washed up near his family's lighthouse. (Rev: BL 4/1/08; SLJ 5/08)

1894   Bellairs, John. *The Ghost in the Mirror* (5–8). 1994, Puffin paper $5.99 (978-0-14-034934-4). Fourteen-year-old Rose and white witch Mrs. Zimmerman are transported in time to 1828 on a secret mission. (Rev: SLJ 3/93)

1895   Bennett, Cherie. *Love Never Dies* (7–10). Series: Teen Angels. 1996, Avon paper $3.99 (978-0-380-78248-2). In this fantasy, a teen angel is sent back to earth to help a rock star bent on self-destruction. (Rev: VOYA 6/96)

1896   Bennett, Holly. *The Bonemender* (6–9). 2005, Orca paper $7.95 (978-1-55143-336-3). When Gabrielle, a princess and healer, falls in love with Feolan, an elf, she sees little future for the romance because of the sharp differences between their basic natures. (Rev: BL 11/1/05; SLJ 12/05; VOYA 12/05)

1897   Bennett, Holly. *The Bonemender's Choice* (7–10). Series: Bonemender. 2007, Orca paper $8.95 (978-1-55143-718-7). Gabrielle and her elfen husband race to rescue young Matthieu and Madeline from pirates and from a spreading affliction called the Gray Veil in this third book in the series. (Rev: BL 11/1/07; SLJ 12/07)

1898   Bennett, Holly. *The Bonemender's Oath* (7–12). 2006, Orca paper $8.95 (978-1-55143-443-8). Gabrielle faces a new threat as she heads home from the war in this satisfying sequel to *The Bonemender* (2005). (Rev: SLJ 2/07)

1899   Bennett, Holly. *The Warrior's Daughter* (7–10). 2007, Orca paper $8.95 (978-1-55143-607-4). With its roots in Irish mythology, this tale about the courageous daughter of a famous warrior will satisfy readers in search of adventure; a pronunciation guide helps with the many Gaelic names. (Rev: LMC 8–9/07; SLJ 6/07)

1900   Berkeley, Jon. *The Palace of Laughter: The Wednesday Tales No. 1* (4–7). Illus. by Brandon Dorman. Series: Julie Andrews Collection. 2006, HarperCollins $16.99 (978-0-06-075507-2). Miles Wednesday, an 11-year-old orphan, joins forces with a talking tiger and a diminutive angel named Little to rescue Little's mentor from the Palace of Laughter. (Rev: SLJ 8/06)

1901   Berman, Steve, ed. *Magic in the Mirrorstone* (8–11). 2008, Mirrorstone $14.95 (978-0-7869-4732-4). Fifteen authors — among them Holly Black and Nina Kiriki Hoffman — contribute fantasy stories on topics that interest teens (bullies, friendship, cheating boyfriends, and so forth). (Rev: BL 2/15/08; SLJ 3/08)

1902   Berry, Liz. *The China Garden* (8–12). 1996, HarperCollins paper $7.99 (978-0-380-73228-9). Mysterious occurrences involving villagers who appear to know Clare and a handsome young man on a motorcycle happen when she accompanies her mother to an estate named Ravensmere. (Rev: BL 3/15/96; SLJ 5/96; VOYA 6/96)

1903   Berryhill, Shane. *Chance Fortune and the Outlaws* (5–8). Series: Adventures of Chance Fortune. 2006, Tom Doherty Assoc. $17.95 (978-0-7653-1468-0). Despite his lack of superpowers, 14-year-old Josh Blevins manages to bluff his way into Burlington Academy for the Superhuman, and there discovers that evil is afoot. (Rev: SLJ 1/07)

1904   Bertagna, Julie. *Exodus* (6–10). 2008, Walker $16.95 (978-0-8027-9745-2). In 2100, when the rising waters of global warming threaten her island world, 15-year-old Mara persuades her people to journey to the new sky cities and seek refuge there;

but when they arrive they find only rejection. (Rev: BL 2/15/08; SLJ 3/08)

1905 Bildner, Phil, and Loren Long. *The Barnstormers: Tales of Travelin' Nine Game 1* (4–7). Illus. by Loren Long. 2007, Simon & Schuster $9.99 (978-1-4169-1863-9). On the road with their late father's traveling baseball team, siblings Griffith, Ruby, and Graham discover a ragged baseball with magical powers. (Rev: BL 4/1/07; SLJ 4/07)

1906 Billingsley, Franny. *The Folk Keeper* (5–8). 1999, Simon & Schuster $16.00 (978-0-689-82876-8); Aladdin paper $4.99 (978-0-689-84461-4). Orphaned Corinna disguises herself as a boy to become a Folk Keeper, one who guards the fierce Folk who live underground. (Rev: BCCB 10/99; BL 9/1/99; HB 11–12/99; HBG 3/00; SLJ 10/99; VOYA 12/99)

1907 Birney, Betty G. *The Princess and the Peabodys* (5–8). 2007, HarperCollins $15.99 (978-0-06-084720-3). Casey Peabody, a no-nonsense sports-loving 8th grader, is an unlikely constant companion for Princess Eglantine, who is accidentally released from 700 years of imprisonment, but the two do become good friends while efforts are made to return Egg to her medieval home. (Rev: BCCB 11/07; SLJ 1/08)

1908 Black, Holly. *Tithe: A Modern Faerie Tale* (8–12). 2002, Simon & Schuster $16.95 (978-0-689-84924-4). Sixteen-year-old Kaye's adventures include rescuing a knight, Roiben, and being caught up in the battles between faerie kingdoms. (Rev: BL 2/15/03; HBG 3/03; SLJ 10/02)

1909 Black, Holly. *Valiant: A Modern Tale of Faerie* (8–11). 2005, Simon & Schuster $16.95 (978-0-689-86822-1). In this dark fantasy featuring drugs and homeless teens in New York City, 17-year-old Val becomes involved with trolls and faeries. (Rev: BL 7/05; SLJ 6/05)

1910 Blackman, Malorie. *Naughts and Crosses* (8–11). 2005, Simon & Schuster $15.95 (978-1-4169-0016-0). Callum, a 15-year-old, pale-skinned Naught in a world dominated by the dark-skinned Crosses, falls in love with Sephy, daughter of the Cross politician for whom Callum's mother works. (Rev: BL 6/1–15/05*; SLJ 6/05; VOYA 8/05)

1911 Blackwood, Gary. *The Year of the Hangman* (6–9). 2002, Dutton $16.99 (978-0-525-46921-6). After the British have defeated the colonists and captured General Washington, a 15-year-old English boy faces questions of loyalty in this exciting alternate history. (Rev: BCCB 12/02; BL 8/02; HBG 3/03; SLJ 9/02*)

1912 Blair, Margaret Whitman. *Brothers at War* (4–7). 1997, White Mane paper $7.95 (978-1-57249-049-9). Two brothers and their friend Sarah find themselves transported back in time to the Battle of Antietam in 1862. (Rev: BL 8/97)

1913 Block, Francesca L. *I Was a Teenage Fairy* (8–12). 1998, HarperCollins LB $14.89 (978-0-06-027748-2). Barbie Marks, at 16 a successful model, sorts herself out with the help of a fairy named Mab, after her father leaves and she is molested by a photographer. (Rev: BL 10/15/98; HB 11–12/98; HBG 3/99; SLJ 12/98*; VOYA 10/98)

1914 Bode, N. E. *The Slippery Map* (5–8). 2007, HarperCollins $16.99 (978-0-06-079108-7). Orphan Oyster R. Motel, 10, enters the imaginary world of Boneland and discovers that his parents are in danger and that the slippery map has fallen into the hands of evil Dark Mouth. (Rev: BL 11/1/07; SLJ 12/07)

1915 Bode, N. E. *The Somebodies* (5–8). Illus. by Peter Ferguson. 2006, HarperCollins $16.99 (978-0-06-079111-7). Fern and her best friend Howard are determined to foil the Blue Queen's plan to destroy the home of the Anybodies who live in a city beneath Manhattan; the final book in a fast-paced trilogy. (Rev: SLJ 9/06)

1916 Bondoux, Anne-Laure. *Vasco: Leader of the Tribe* (4–7). 2007, Delacorte $15.99 (978-0-385-73363-2). Vasco, a rat with hopes for the future, escapes extermination by humans and boards an ocean liner, where he encounters more obstacles before tackling a dangerous rainforest. (Rev: BL 12/1/07; LMC 1/08; SLJ 3/08)

1917 Bradbury, Ray. *The Illustrated Man* (7–12). 1990, Bantam paper $7.50 (978-0-553-27449-3). A tattooed man tells a story for each of his tattoos.

1918 Bray, Libba. *A Great and Terrible Beauty* (8–12). 2003, Delacorte LB $17.99 (978-0-385-90161-1). Gemma, a troubled student in London, learns to control her visions and enter the Realms, a place of magic, in this multilayered novel that combines fantasy, mystery, and romance with a look at 19th-century manners. (Rev: BCCB 5/04; BL 11/15/03; SLJ 2/04; VOYA 4/04) ⑨

1919 Bray, Libba. *The Sweet Far Thing* (8–10). Series: Gemma Doyle . 2007, Delacorte $17.99 (978-0-385-73030-3). This final installment in the series finds Gemma wondering whom she can trust with the magic of the Realms even as the Realms themselves are transforming. (Rev: BL 11/15/07; SLJ 1/08) ⑨

1920 Breathed, Berkeley. *The Last Basselope: One Ferocious Story* (4–7). Illus. 2001, Little, Brown paper $5.95 (978-0-316-12664-9). In this imaginative picture book for older readers, Opus and his reluctant adventurers are after the nearly extinct basselope. (Rev: BCCB 1/93; BL 12/15/92; SLJ 1/93)

1921 Brennan, Herbie. *Faerie Lord* (6–8). Series: Faerie War Chronicles. 2007, Bloomsbury $18.95 (978-1-59990-120-6). Henry travels to the far reaches of the realm to stop a plague that threatens all its denizens. (Rev: BL 1/1–15/08; SLJ 1/08) ⊚

1922 Brennan, Herbie. *Faerie Wars* (6–8). 2003, Bloomsbury $17.95 (978-1-58234-810-0). Henry Atherton becomes involved with an escaped fairy crown prince in this complex tale of parallel worlds. (Rev: BL 4/15/03; HBG 10/03; SLJ 7/03; VOYA 6/03)

1923 Brennan, Herbie. *The Purple Emperor: Faerie Wars II* (6–8). 2004, Bloomsbury $17.95 (978-1-58234-880-3). In a sequel to *Faerie Wars* (2003) full of humor and adventure, Henry Atherton returns to the Faerie Realm to help royal siblings Pyrgus Malvae and Holly Blue. (Rev: BL 9/15/04; SLJ 12/04; VOYA 2/05)

1924 Brennan, Herbie. *Ruler of the Realm* (7–10). Series: The Faerie Wars Chronicles. 2006, Bloomsbury $18.95 (978-1-58234-881-0). This action-packed third installment of the series that blends fantasy and science fiction has Queen Blue investigating an office of peace from the Faeries of the Night and Henry (a human) being abducted by aliens. (Rev: SLJ 2/07)

1925 Brown, Joseph F. *Dark Things* (6–9). 1995, Royal Fireworks paper $9.99 (978-0-88092-110-7). A fantasy that spans 130 years, from the Civil War to the present, about a boy who never grows old and who possesses magical powers. (Rev: VOYA 4/96)

1926 Browne, N. M. *Silverboy* (6–9). 2007, Bloomsbury $16.95 (978-1-58234-780-6). Akenna and Tommo—a 15-year-old spellgrinder's apprentice—are fleeing the powers of the spellstones and the Protector, pursued by a flock of human-looking birds. (Rev: BL 2/1/07; LMC 8-9/07; SLJ 5/07)

1927 Browne, N. M. *Warriors of Alavna* (7–10). 2002, Bloomsbury $16.95 (978-1-58234-775-2). This historical fantasy pits 15-year-olds Dan and Ursula against invaders in Roman Britain. A sequel is *Warriors of Camlann* (2003). (Rev: BCCB 10/02; SLJ 1/03; VOYA 2/03)

1928 Bruchac, Josephine. *Wabi: A Hero's Tale* (7–10). 2006, Dial $16.99 (978-0-8037-3098-4). A white great horned owl named Wabi has the power to transform himself into a human being and falls in love with an Abenaki girl named Dojihla. (Rev: BL 2/15/06; SLJ 4/06*; VOYA 4/06)

1929 Buckingham, Jane. *The Hound of Rowan* (6–9). Illus. by author. 2007, Random $17.99 (978-0-375-83894-1). Max McDaniels attends Rowan Academy in New England, where apprentices learn magical skills, train to fight an unnamed enemy, and are paired with unusual animals. (Rev: BL 9/1/07; SLJ 3/08)

1930 Buckley-Archer, Linda. *The Time Thief* (6–9). Series: Gideon Trilogy. 2007, Simon & Schuster $17.99 (978-1-4169-1527-0). Peter's father and

Kate travel through time to save Peter but end up meeting him at age 41 instead of 12, the age he was at the end of *Gideon the Cutpurse* (2006). (Rev: BL 3/1/08; SLJ 2/08)

1931 Buffie, Margaret. *Angels Turn Their Backs* (7–9). 1998, Kids Can $16.95 (978-1-55074-415-6). When 15-year-old Addy moves with her mother to Winnipeg, she suffers panic attacks at the thought of going to a new school and trying to make new friends, but she gets help from a ghost who speaks through a parrot. (Rev: BCCB 11/98; HBG 3/99; SLJ 11/98; VOYA 4/99)

1932 Buffie, Margaret. *The Finder* (6–10). Series: The Watcher's Quest. 2004, Kids Can $16.95 (978-1-55337-671-2). In the final volume of the trilogy, shape-changing heroine Emma Sweeny defies her training master and passes through a magical portal where she must get to four hidden power wands before they're found by the evil Eefa. (Rev: BL 10/15/04; SLJ 1/05; VOYA 2/05)

1933 Buffie, Margaret. *The Seeker* (5–8). 2002, Kids Can $16.95 (978-1-55337-358-2). Emma is involved in a quest to reunite her family and becomes embroiled in interplanetary intrigue and gaming in this sequel to *The Watcher* (2000). (Rev: BL 10/1/02; HBG 10/03; SLJ 11/02; VOYA 4/03)

1934 Buffie, Margaret. *The Watcher* (5–8). 2000, Kids Can $16.95 (978-1-55074-829-1). Sixteen-year-old Emma discovers that she is really a changeling, a Watcher, whose mission is to protect her younger sister from warring factions. (Rev: BL 11/1/00; HBG 3/01; SLJ 10/00; VOYA 2/01)

1935 Bunce, Elizabeth C. *A Curse as Dark as Gold* (7–10). 2008, Scholastic $17.99 (978-0-439-89576-7). Charlotte and her sister Rosie make a bargain with a man named Spinner to save themselves from a curse in this take on the Rumplestiltskin story. (Rev: BL 5/1/08; SLJ 5/08)

1936 Bunting, Eve. *The Lambkins* (7–10). Illus. by Jonathan Keegan. 2005, HarperCollins LB $16.89 (978-0-06-059907-2). Kyle's offer to help a woman with a flat tire goes awry when she kidnaps him and shrinks him to the size of a Coke bottle. (Rev: BL 8/05; SLJ 8/05)

1937 Burden, Meg. *Northlander: Tales of the Borderlands* (5–8). Series: Tales of the Borderlands. 2007, Brown Barn paper $8.95 (978-0-9768126-8-5). Ellin, a Southling with healing powers and other mystical abilities, is torn between her homeland and her friends in the Northlands. (Rev: BL 1/1–15/08; SLJ 2/08)

1938 Buzbee, Lewis. *Steinbeck's Ghost* (5–8). 2008, Feiwel and Friends $17.95 (978-0-312-37328-3). Thirteen-year-old Travis is unhappy when his family moves to a new subdivision and he drifts back to his old neighborhood in Salinas, California, John Steinbeck's hometown; there he works to save the

Steinbeck Library from closure and finds that characters from Steinbeck novels are coming to life. (Rev: BL 8/08; SLJ 9/08) 🌐

1939 Cabot, Meg. *Jinx* (6–10). 2007, HarperTeen $16.99 (978-0-06-083764-8). Unlucky Jinx is sent to live with her relatives in New York City, where she discovers her supernatural powers and that her cousin Tory has sinister intentions. (Rev: BL 9/1/07; SLJ 9/07) 🌐

1940 Calhoun, Dia. *Aria of the Sea* (6–9). 2003, Farrar paper $7.95 (978-0-374-40454-3). In the kingdom of Windward, 13-year-old Cerinthe joins the Royal Dancing School and finds herself having to choose between her talents: dancing and healing. (Rev: SLJ 9/00)

1941 Calhoun, Dia. *Avielle of Rhia* (8–11). 2006, Marshall Cavendish $16.99 (978-0-7614-5320-8). Princess Avielle of Rhia has the physical characteristics of Dredonians (fearful doers of magic) but when all of her royal family is murdered she must use her magic to save the people of Rhia, despite their hatred toward her. (Rev: BL 10/1/06; LMC 2/07; SLJ 11/06)

1942 Calhoun, Dia. *Firegold* (7–12). 1999, Winslow $15.95 (978-1-890817-10-7). A fantasy in which a 13-year-old boy is persecuted in his village because of his different looks and behavior and is forced to travel to the Red Mountains, home of fierce barbarians. (Rev: BL 5/15/99; SLJ 6/99; VOYA 8/99)

1943 Carey, Janet Lee. *The Beast of Noor* (6–9). 2006, Simon & Schuster $16.95 (978-0-689-87644-8). Miles and his sister Hanna are impelled to break their family curse and defeat the Shriker, a vicious dog that feeds on human prey that was supposedly brought to the area by their ancestors. (Rev: BL 8/06; SLJ 11/06)

1944 Carey, Janet Lee. *Dragon's Keep* (7–10). 2007, Harcourt $17.00 (978-0-15-205926-2). Rosland discovers that she is part dragon and that she is destined to care for a brood of dragon children in this action-filled fantasy. (Rev: BCCB 5/07; BL 2/1/07; SLJ 4/07*) 🌐

1945 Carman, Patrick. *Rivers of Fire* (5–8). Series: Atherton. 2008, Little, Brown $16.99 (978-0-316-16672-0). The planet of Atherton is still in trouble, and Edgar, Samuel, and Isabel fight to save it in this continuation of the story that began in *The House of Power*. (Rev: BL 5/15/08; SLJ 8/08)

1946 Carmody, Isobelle. *Winter Door* (7–12). Series: Gateway Trilogy. 2006, Random $16.95 (978-0-375-83018-1). In this second installment in the trilogy, Rage attempts to combat an unusually severe winter while also dealing with a bully; readers will want to read the first volume before tackling this one. (Rev: SLJ 7/06)

1947 Carroll, Thomas. *The Colony* (4–7). 2000, Sunstone $18.95 (978-0-86534-295-8). Fifth-grader Tony and his bullying arch-enemy Lawrence are shrunk to the size of ants by a Navajo charm and in their new environment join opposing forces. (Rev: HBG 3/01; SLJ 7/00)

1948 Catanese, P. W. *The Mirror's Tale: A Further Tales Adventure* (4–7). 2006, Simon & Schuster paper $4.99 (978-1-4169-1251-4). When their father decides to separate his mischievous 13-year-old twin sons for the summer, they switch places and one is sent to the castle of his aunt and uncle where he discovers and falls under the spell of a bewitching mirror. (Rev: SLJ 8/06)

1949 Caveney, Philip. *Prince of Fools* (7–12). Series: Sebastian Darke. 2008, Delacorte $15.99 (978-0-385-73467-7). Would-be (but not very funny) jester Sebastian, 17 and half-elf, travels with his (quite funny) buffalope and the tiny Captain Cornelius, to the court of King Septimus in hopes of gaining employment; along the way they rescue a princess and find themselves embroiled in intrigue. (Rev: BL 3/15/08; SLJ 9/08)

1950 Chan, Gillian. *The Carved Box* (5–8). 2001, Kids Can $16.95 (978-1-55074-895-6). The acquisition of a dog and a carved box ease the transition for orphaned Callum, 15, who has moved from Scotland to Canada to live with his uncle, in this novel which has an element of fantasy that comes to the fore in the dramatic ending. (Rev: BL 10/01; HBG 3/02; SLJ 10/01; VOYA 4/02)

1951 Charnas, Suzy McKee. *The Kingdom of Kevin Malone* (7–10). 1993, Harcourt $16.95 (978-0-15-200756-0). This novel melds the world of the teenage problem novel with that of fantasy in a story that pokes gentle fun at the conventions of fantasy fiction. (Rev: BL 6/1–15/93; SLJ 1/94; VOYA 8/93)

1952 Chima, Cinda Williams. *The Wizard Heir* (8–11). 2007, Hyperion $17.99 (978-1-4231-0487-2). When Seph's magical mishaps (he has had no wizard training) lead to a death, he's sent to a boys' school named the Havens, where he's offered training but at a cost Seph must reject; a companion to *The Warrior Heir* (2006). (Rev: BL 5/15/07; SLJ 12/07)

1953 Cle, Troy. *The Marvelous Effect* (6–9). Series: Marvelous World. 2007, Simon & Schuster $14.99 (978-1-4169-3958-0). Louis goes to an amusement park one day and receives special powers to fight the Galonious Imperial Evil in a video-game like battle. (Rev: BL 7/07; LMC 10/07; SLJ 11/07)

1954 Clement-Davies, David. *Fell* (7–12). 2007, Abrams $19.95 (978-0-8109-1185-7). Alina travels through Transylvania with Fell, a wolf, to defeat Lord Vladeran and his dark powers in order to save the natural world; a sequel to *The Sight*. (Rev: BL 10/15/07; SLJ 1/08) ⑨

1955 Clement-Davies, David. *The Telling Pool* (6–9). 2005, Abrams $19.95 (978-0-8109-5758-9). In this historical fantasy set in 12th-century England, young Rhodri Falcon must defeat the evil sorceress who has cast a spell on his father. (Rev: BCCB 1/06; BL 10/1/05; SLJ 11/05; VOYA 12/05)

1956 Coleman, Alice Scovell. *Engraved in Stone* (4–7). Illus. by Anjal Ren e Armand. 2003, Tiara Bks. $14.95 (978-0-9729846-0-7). A prince and princess who will do anything to avoid their planned marriage set off on a quest to get their fate changed in this humorous fantasy. (Rev: SLJ 12/03)

1957 Colfer, Eoin. *The Arctic Incident* (6–9). Series: Artemis Fowl. 2002, Hyperion $16.99 (978-0-7868-0855-7). Another madcap adventure in which Artemis and Captain Holly combine their talents to combat forces as diverse as the Russian mafia and a band of dangerous smugglers. (Rev: BCCB 7–8/01; BL 5/1/02; HBG 10/02; SLJ 7/02; VOYA 8/02)

1958 Colfer, Eoin. *Artemis Fowl* (6–9). Series: Artemis Fowl. 2001, Hyperion $16.95 (978-0-7868-0801-4). Twelve-year-old genius and adventurous criminal entrepreneur Artemis Fowl captures a fairy investigator, with lively and hilarious results. (Rev: BL 4/15/01; HB 7–8/01; HBG 10/01; SLJ 5/01; VOYA 8/01)

1959 Colfer, Eoin. *The Eternity Code* (6–9). Series: Artemis Fowl. 2003, Hyperion $16.95 (978-0-7868-1914-0). An action-packed adventure in which Artemis creates an unauthorized groundbreaking supercomputer with fairy technology, which becomes a threat when it is stolen. (Rev: BL 6/1–15/03; HBG 10/03; SLJ 7/03)

1960 Colfer, Eoin. *The Lost Colony* (6–9). Series: Artemis Fowl. 2006, Hyperion $16.95 (978-0-7868-4956-7). Artemis, 14, faces new challenges when he must stop demons that are seeking their revenge on humans and threatening to expose the whole fairy world. (Rev: BL 11/1/06)

1961 Colfer, Eoin. *The Opal Deception* (6–9). Series: Artemis Fowl. 2005, Hyperion $16.95 (978-0-7868-5289-5). In the fourth volume of the series, Artemis, his mind wiped clean of memories about the fairy world, reverts to a life of crime and provides an easy target for his nemesis, Opal Koboi. (Rev: BL 5/15/05; SLJ 7/05)

1962 Collins, Suzanne. *Gregor and the Code of Claw* (5–9). Series: The Underland Chronicles. 2007, Scholastic $17.99 (978-0-439-79143-4). A mysterious prophecy makes Gregor question himself in this adventure-filled fifth title in the series. (Rev: SLJ 7/07)

1963 Collins, Suzanne. *Gregor and the Marks of Secret* (5–8). Series: The Underland Chronicles.

2006, Scholastic $16.99 (978-0-439-79145-8). Gregor, accompanied by his little sister Boots, joins forces with Queen Luxa to defend Underland from attacks by the rat army. (Rev: SLJ 9/06; VOYA 8/06)

1964 Collins, Suzanne. *Gregor the Overlander* (4–7). 2003, Scholastic $17.99 (978-0-439-43536-9). When his baby sister disappears into an air vent, 11-year-old Gregor doesn't hesitate to follow and finds himself in a whole new world, an Underland where an unexpected role awaits him. (Rev: BCCB 1/04; BL 11/15/03*; HB 9–10/03; HBG 9–10/03; LMC 11–12/03; SLJ 11/03; VOYA 10/03)

1965 Collodi, Carlo. *The Adventures of Pinocchio*. Rev. ed. (4–10). Trans. from Italian by M. A. Murray. Illus. by Roberta Innocenti. 2005, Creative Editions $19.95 (978-1-56846-190-8). Nineteenth-century European landscapes provide the backdrop for this appealing retelling of the classic story about the puppet that longed to become a little boy; a revision of the 1988 edition. (Rev: SLJ 12/05)

1966 Conly, Jane L. *Racso and the Rats of NIMH* (5–7). Illus. by Leonard Lubin. 1986, HarperCollins LB $17.89 (978-0-06-021362-6). This sequel to the Newbery Medal winner involves once again the smart rodents who wish to live in peace in Thorn Valley. (Rev: BCCB 6/86; BL 6/1/86; SLJ 4/86)

1967 Constable, Kate. *The Singer of All Songs* (7–10). Series: Chanters of Tremaris. 2004, Scholastic $16.95 (978-0-439-55478-7). In this impressive fantasy, Calwyn, a novice priestess, is able to control all things cold and uses this power to fight an evil sorcerer. (Rev: BL 2/1/04*; SLJ 4/04; VOYA 4/04)

1968 Constable, Kate. *The Tenth Power* (7–10). Series: Chanters of Tremaris. 2006, Scholastic $16.99 (978-0-439-55482-4). Mourning the loss of her nine powers of chantment, 18-year-old Calwyn returns to Antaris to discover she must go in search of the key to the mysterious tenth, healing, power. (Rev: BL 3/15/06; SLJ 3/06)

1969 Constable, Kate. *The Waterless Sea* (8–11). Series: Chanters of Tremaris. 2005, Scholastic $16.95 (978-0-439-55480-0). In the second volume of the trilogy, Calwyn and her friends travel to the desolate Merithuran Empire on a mission to rescue some children with magical powers. (Rev: BL 5/15/05; SLJ 8/05; VOYA 8/05)

1970 Cooney, Caroline B. *Prisoner of Time* (6–10). Series: Time Travel. 1998, Laurel Leaf paper $5.50 (978-0-440-22019-0). In this conclusion to the trilogy, there is again a contrast between the lifestyles of today and those of 100 years ago as a girl is rescued from an unsuitable marriage. (Rev: BL 6/1–15/98; HBG 3/02; SLJ 5/98; VOYA 6/98)

1971 Cooper, Susan. *Green Boy* (4–8). 2002, Simon & Schuster $16.00 (978-0-689-84751-6). Two young boys discover a futuristic world in which natural resources are depleted and a war to save the environment is being waged. (Rev: BCCB 5/02; BL 3/1/02; HB 5–6/02; HBG 10/02; SLJ 2/02)

1972 Cooper, Susan. *King of Shadows* (5–8). Illus. by John Clapp. 1999, Simon & Schuster $16.00 (978-0-689-82817-1). Nat Field time-travels to 1599 London and assumes the child-actor role of Puck in *A Midsummer Night's Dream.* (Rev: BL 10/15/99*; HB 11–12/99; HBG 3/00; SLJ 11/99)

1973 Cooper, Susan. *Over Sea, Under Stone* (6–9). Illus. Series: The Dark Is Rising. 1966, Harcourt $18.00 (978-0-15-259034-5). Three contemporary children enter the world of King Arthur in this first volume of a series. Followed by *The Dark Is Rising* (1973), *Greenwitch* (1985), *The Grey King* (1975), and *Silver on the Tree* (1977).

1974 Cooper, Susan. *Silver on the Tree* (5–7). 1980, Macmillan $18.00 (978-0-689-50088-6). In this fifth and last volume of a series, Will Stanton and his friends wage a final battle against the Dark, the powers of evil. The first four volumes are *Over Sea, Under Stone* (1966), *The Dark Is Rising* (1973), *The Grey King* (1975), and *Greenwitch* (1985). *The Grey King* won the 1976 Newbery Medal.

1975 Cooper, Susan. *Victory* (4–7). 2006, Simon & Schuster $16.95 (978-1-4169-1477-8). Homesick Molly finds her fate is intertwined with that of Sam, a child sailor of the 19th century who fought in the Battle of Trafalgar; chapters alternate between the present and the past. (Rev: BL 5/1/06; LMC 11/12/06; SLJ 7/06)

1976 Corder, Zizou. *Lionboy: The Truth* (5–8). 2005, Dial $16.99 (978-0-8037-2985-8). In the final installment in the trilogy, Charlie Ashanti, reunited with his parents in Morocco, is kidnapped by the Corporacy and put on a boat bound for the Caribbean, but the boy wonder calls on his animal friends for help. (Rev: BL 10/1/05; SLJ 9/05; VOYA 12/05)

1977 Cornish, D. M. *Foundling* (7–10). Illus. Series: Monster Blood Tattoo. 2006, Penguin $18.99 (978-0-399-24638-8). Rossamund Bookchild, a foundling boy with a girl's name, sets off from the orphanage to his new job as a lamplighter and finds himself in a perilous world (called Half-Continent) full of monsters. (Rev: BL 4/1/06*; SLJ 7/06*)

1978 Cornish, D. M. *Lamplighter* (7–10). Series: Monster Blood Tattoo. 2008, Putnam $19.99 (978-0-399-24639-5). In the second book of the trilogy that began with *Foundling*, Rossamund Bookchild is joined in his lamplighting by Threnody and the two face even more danger. (Rev: BL 4/15/08; SLJ 7/08)

1979 Coville, Bruce, ed. *A Glory of Unicorns* (5–8). Illus. 1998, Scholastic paper $16.95 (978-0-590-95943-8). A collection of stories by fantasy authors, including the editor and his wife, that deal with unicorns. (Rev: BL 6/1–15/98; HBG 10/98; SLJ 5/98; VOYA 8/98)

1980 Coville, Bruce. *Goblins in the Castle* (5–7). Illus. 1992, Pocket paper $4.99 (978-0-671-72711-6). William, now 11, has grown up in Toad-in-a-Cage Castle and knows many of its secret passages. (Rev: BL 2/1/93)

1981 Coville, Bruce. *Juliet Dove, Queen of Love: A Magic Shop Book* (4–8). 2003, Harcourt $17.00 (978-0-15-204561-6). Life changes for shy Juliet, 12, when she is given an amulet and the boys suddenly come flocking to her side. (Rev: BL 1/1–15/04; HBG 4/04; SLJ 12/03)

1982 Cowell, Cressida. *How to Train Your Dragon: By Hiccup Horrendous Haddock III: Translated from an Old Norse Legend by Cressida Cowell* (4–8). Illus. 2004, Little, Brown paper $10.95 (978-0-316-73737-1). The hilarious account of the fumbling efforts of nerdy Hiccup to capture and train a dragon and to take his rightful place as the next Warrior Chief. Also use *How to Be a Pirate: By Hiccup Horrendous Haddock III* (2005). (Rev: BL 4/15/04; SLJ 7/04)

1983 Cox, Judy. *The Mystery of the Burmese Bandicoot: The Tails of Frederick and Ishbu* (4–7). Illus. by Omar Rayyan. Series: The Tails of Frederick and Ishbu. 2007, Marshall Cavendish $16.99 (978-0-7614-5376-5). Rats Frederick and Ishbu escape their schoolroom cage and embark on an adventure that involves a shipwreck and a statue with the power to end the world. (Rev: BL 10/1/07; SLJ 12/07)

1984 Crew, Gary. *The Viewer* (5–9). Illus. by Shaun Tan. 2003, Lothian $16.95 (978-0-85091-828-1). A well-illustrated dark fantasy linked to world catastrophes caused by mankind, from religious persecution to atomic war. (Rev: SLJ 3/04)

1985 Croggon, Alison. *The Crow: The Third Book of Pellinor* (7–10). Series: Pellinor. 2007, Candlewick $18.99 (978-0-7636-3409-4). Hem becomes a warrior in the fight against the Nameless One and goes in search of kidnapped Zelika in this third installment in the series. (Rev: BL 2/1/08; SLJ 2/08)

1986 Croggon, Alison. *The Naming* (7–10). 2005, Candlewick $17.99 (978-0-7636-2639-6). The life of 16-year-old Maerad, a slave, changes dramatically after she meets Cadvan, who tells her of her epic destiny. (Rev: BCCB 9/05; BL 5/1/05; SLJ 10/05*; VOYA 8/05)

1987 Croggon, Alison. *The Riddle: The Second Book of Pellinor* (7–10). Series: Pellinor. 2006, Candlewick $17.99 (978-0-7636-3015-7). In this second installment in the series, Maerad continues on her quest to find the Treesong, battling the Nameless One along the way, and discovering more about herself and her powers. (Rev: BL 11/1/06; LMC 4/07; SLJ 1/07)

1988 Cross, Gillian. *The Nightmare Game* (6–9). Series: Dark Ground. 2007, Dutton $18.99 (978-0-525-47923-9). The final volume in the trilogy is a multilayered blend of fantasy and mystery in which Robert and friends discover a frightening connection between their own world and the parallel underground world. (Rev: BL 1/1–15/08; LMC 1-2/08; SLJ 12/07)

1989 Cross, Gillian. *Pictures in the Dark* (5–8). 1996, Holiday $16.95 (978-0-8234-1267-9). A boy whose life is miserable uses supernatural means to escape the pressures. (Rev: BCCB 1/97; BL 1/1–15/97)

1990 Crossley-Holland, Kevin. *King of the Middle March* (6–9). 2004, Scholastic $17.95 (978-0-439-26600-0). In the final volume of the trilogy that started with *The Seeing Stone* (2001), 16-year-old Arthur de Caldicot watches the disintegration of King Arthur's court in his seeing stone as he waits in Venice for the start of the Fourth Crusade. (Rev: BL 9/1/04*; SLJ 11/04)

1991 Curley, Marianne. *The Named* (7–11). 2002, Bloomsbury $16.95 (978-1-58234-779-0). Ethan and Isabel time-travel through history on a difficult quest in this first volume of a multilayered trilogy recounting the battle against the Order of Chaos. (Rev: BL 11/15/02; SLJ 1/03)

1992 Curry, Jane Louise. *The Black Canary* (5–8). 2005, Simon & Schuster $16.95 (978-0-689-86478-0). Twelve-year-old James, from a biracial family of musicians, resists pressure to develop his own musical abilities until he travels back in time to Elizabethan London and discovers he is also talented. (Rev: BL 2/15/05*; SLJ 3/05)

1993 Dadey, Debbie, and Marcia T. Jones. *Leprechauns Don't Play Basketball* (5–8). Illus. by John S. Gurney. 1992, Scholastic paper $3.99 (978-0-590-44822-2). The Bailey Elementary 3rd grade thinks the gym teacher is a leprechaun. (Rev: BL 9/15/92)

1994 Datlow, Ellen, and Terri Windling, eds. *Swan Sister: Fairy Tales Retold* (5–10). 2003, Simon & Schuster $16.95 (978-0-689-84613-7). Retellings by well-known authors of traditional stories are inventive and entertaining. (Rev: BCCB 11/03; BL 9/15/03; HBG 4/04; SLJ 12/03)

1995 Dekker, Ted. *Chosen* (7–10). Series: The Lost Books. 2008, Thomas Nelson $12.99 (978-1-59554-359-2). A football game is used to choose four new forest guards who must find the seven lost Books of History. (Rev: BL 3/15/08)

1996 Del Vecchio, Gene. *The Pearl of Anton* (7–10). 2004, Pelican $16.95 (978-1-58980-172-1). In this complex, gripping fantasy, Jason inherits the Wizard's Stone when he turns 15, but the stone's powers cannot be realized until it is joined with the Pearl of Anton, which is hidden in a mountain cave and guarded by two fearsome beasts. (Rev: BL 6/1–15/04*; VOYA 10/04)

1997 de Lint, Charles. *Dingo* (7–10). 2008, Penguin $11.99 (978-0-14-240816-2). Miguel falls in love with a girl who happens to be an Aboriginal shape-shifter and who, along with her twin, is in danger and needs Miguel's help. (Rev: BL 5/15/08; SLJ 8/08)

1998 de Lint, Charles. *Little (Grrl) Lost* (7–10). 2007, Viking $17.99 (978-0-670-06144-0). T.J., 14, misses her old friends and her horse after her family moves to the suburbs, but then she meets and befriends Elizabeth, a 16-year-old "Little" who is only 6 inches high but has an oversized personality. (Rev: BL 8/07; SLJ 11/07)

1999 De Mari, Silvana. *The Last Dragon* (5–8). Trans. by Shaun Whiteside. 2006, Hyperion $16.95 (978-0-7868-3636-9). To fulfill a prophecy in which he will play a key role, a young elf named Yorsh, the last of his kind in a world hostile to elves, sets off in search of the last dragon. (Rev: BL 11/1/06; SLJ 1/07)

2000 Deming, Sarah. *Iris, Messenger* (5–8). 2007, Harcourt $16.00 (978-0-15-205823-4). Iris is a miserable outcast whose life takes a turn for the better when the mythology book she gets for her birthday leads her to an amazing discovery. (Rev: SLJ 7/07)

2001 DeVita, James. *The Silenced* (8–12). 2007, HarperCollins $17.99 (978-0-06-078462-1). Under the new Zero Tolerance government, Marina attends a Youth Training Facility where she is educated under strict regulations but follows her heart and starts a resistance movement named the White Rose. (Rev: BL 6/1–15/07; SLJ 9/07)

2002 Dickinson, Peter. *Angel Isle* (7–10). 2007, Random $17.99 (978-0-385-74690-8). Maja and her companions make an arduous journey to find the Ropemaker so he can use his magic to defy the Watchers; a sequel to *The Ropemaker* (2001). (Rev: BL 10/15/07; HB 11–12/07; LMC 1/08; SLJ 11/07)

2003 DiTocco, Robyn, and Tony DiTocco. *Atlas' Revenge: Another Mad Myth Mystery* (7–12). 2005, Brainstorm $19.95 (978-0-9723429-2-6); paper $11.95 (978-0-9723429-3-3). PJ Allen, a carefree college senior, is called upon to travel to the world of mythology to complete the legendary Twelve Labors of Hercules and solve a cryptic riddle in this fast-paced novel full of legendary characters and literary references. (Rev: SLJ 6/05)

2004 Divakaruni, Chitra Banerjee. *The Mirror of Fire and Dreaming* (5–8). 2005, Roaring Brook $16.95 (978-1-59643-067-9). In this sequel to *The Conch Bearer* (2003), 12-year-old Anand continues his magic studies and travels back to Moghul times, where he encounters powerful sorcerers and evil jinns. (Rev: BL 9/1/05; SLJ 12/05)

2005 D'Lacey, Chris. *Fire Star* (7–12). Series: The Dragon Trilogy. 2007, Scholastic $15.99 (978-0-439-84582-3). David Rain faces a major dragon challenge in this conclusion to the trilogy; readers familiar with the earlier books will enjoy this most. (Rev: SLJ 4/07)

2006 D'Lacey, Chris. *The Fire Within* (5–8). 2005, Scholastic $12.95 (978-0-439-67343-3). A multilayered fantasy in which British college student David Rain comes to board at the home of Liz Pennykettle and her daughter, Lucy, and discovers that the clay dragons crafted by Liz have magical properties. (Rev: SLJ 10/05)

2007 D'Lacey, Chris. *Icefire* (7–12). Series: The Dragon Trilogy . 2006, Scholastic $14.99 (978-0-439-67245-0). In this action-packed sequel to *The Fire Within* (2005), David researches dragons for an essay that might win him a trip to the Arctic. (Rev: SLJ 11/06)

2008 Downer, Ann. *The Dragon of Never-Was* (4–7). Illus. by Omar Ryyan. 2006, Simon & Schuster $16.95 (978-0-689-85571-9). In this lively sequel to *Hatching Magic* (2003), 12-year-old Theodora Oglethorpe accompanies her father to Scotland to investigate the origin of a mysterious scale and there learns more about her own magical powers. (Rev: BL 6/1–15/06; SLJ 12/06)

2009 Downer, Ann. *Hatching Magic* (4–7). Illus. by Omar Rayyan. 2003, Simon & Schuster $16.95 (978-0-689-83400-4). A procession of a pet dragon, a wizard, and his archenemy travel through time from the 13th century to the 21st century, where an 11-year-old Bostonian becomes involved in their disputes. (Rev: BL 4/15/03; HB 7–8/03; HBG 10/03; SLJ 8/03)

2010 Doyle, Marissa. *Bewitching Season* (7–10). 2008, Holt $16.95 (978-0-8050-8251-7). Set during the reign of Queen Victoria, this novel about twins Persephone and Penelope as they ready for their London debut combines historical romance with mystery and a touch of fantasy. (Rev: BL 1/1–15/08; LMC 11–12/08; SLJ 3/08)

2011 *Dr. Ernest Drake's Dragonology: The Complete Book of Dragons* (5–12). Illus. 2003, Candlewick $18.99 (978-0-7636-2329-6). Presented as the recently discovered research of a 19th-century scientist, this richly illustrated volume presents a very realistic encyclopedia of dragon facts and figures. (Rev: BL 4/15/04; SLJ 4/04)

2012 Drexler, Sam, and Fay Shelby. *Lost in Spillville* (5–9). Series: Erika and Oz Adventures in American History. 2000, Aunt Strawberry paper $6.99 (978-0-9669988-1-8). Two teenagers accidentally are transported to the 1930s and must locate an important clock maker to be returned to the 1990s. (Rev: SLJ 11/00; VOYA 12/00)

2013 Duane, Diane. *Deep Wizardry* (5–8). Series: Young Wizards. 2001, Magic Carpet Books LB $15.25 (978-0-613-36059-3); Harcourt paper $6.95 (978-0-15-216257-3). Nita and Kit, the two young wizards of *So You Want to Be a Wizard,* again use their powers to prevent a great catastrophe. (Rev: HB 5–6/85)

2014 Duane, Diane. *So You Want to Be a Wizard* (5–8). Series: Young Wizards. 2003, Harcourt $16.95 (978-0-15-204738-2); paper $6.95 (978-0-15-216250-4). Nita and friends embark on a journey to retrieve the Book of Night with Moon.

2015 Duane, Diane. *A Wizard Alone* (6–10). Series: Young Wizards. 2002, Harcourt $17.00 (978-0-15-204562-3). The sixth book in the series of Nita and Kit's adventures in magic finds wizard Kit working on his own while Nita mourns the death of her mother. (Rev: BL 11/15/02; HBG 3/03; SLJ 2/03; VOYA 4/03)

2016 Duane, Diane. *Wizard's Holiday* (6–9). Series: Young Wizards. 2003, Harcourt $17.00 (978-0-15-204771-9). Plotlines alternate between teen wizards Nita and Kit's exploits on a distant planet and Nita's little sister and her father, who are hosting alien exchange students, as disaster approaches. (Rev: BL 1/1–15/04; SLJ 12/03)

2017 Duel, John. *Wide Awake in Dreamland* (5–8). Illus. 1992, Stargaze $15.95 (978-0-9630923-0-4). An evil warlock threatens to steal a 9-year-old's imagination unless the young boy can find a friendly wizard first. (Rev: BL 3/1/92; SLJ 5/92)

2018 Duey, Kathleen. *Skin Hunger* (7–10). Illus. by Sheila Rayyan. Series: A Resurrection of Magic. 2007, Atheneum $17.99 (978-0-689-84093-7). The story of Sadima, a teenage girl who can communicate with animals, as she lives with magician outlaws; interwoven with the story of Hahp, generations later, as he deals with attending a harsh wizardry school. (Rev: BL 6/1–15/07; HB 7–8/07; SLJ 11/07) 🗐

2019 Dunkle, Clare B. *Close Kin* (6–9). Series: Hollow Kingdom. 2004, Holt $16.95 (978-0-8050-7497-0). In this sequel to *The Hollow Kingdom* (2003), Kate's younger sister Emily realizes the depth of her feelings for Seylin, who has gone in search of his elfin roots, and she sets off to find him. (Rev: BL 10/1/04; SLJ 10/04; VOYA 12/04)

2020 Dunkle, Clare B. *The Hollow Kingdom* (5–8). 2003, Holt $16.95 (978-0-8050-7390-4). A beauty-and-the-beast story with a twist, in which Kate is persuaded to marry a goblin king and move to his underground world. (Rev: BL 11/15/03; HBG 4/04; SLJ 12/03)

2021 Dunkle, Clare B. *In the Coils of the Snake* (7–10). Series: Hollow Kingdom. 2005, Holt $16.95 (978-0-8050-7747-6). When human girl Miranda learns she will not after all marry the new goblin king, she flees from the kingdom; this final volume in the trilogy is set 30 years after *Close Kin* (2004). (Rev: BL 1/1–15/06*; SLJ 10/05; VOYA 10/05)

2022 Dunlop, Eileen. *Websters' Leap* (4–7). 1995, Holiday $15.95 (978-0-8234-1193-1). In this time-slip fantasy, Jill gets involved with people who owned a Scottish castle 400 years before. (Rev: BL 10/1/95; SLJ 10/95)

2023 Dunmore, Helen. *Ingo* (5–8). 2006, Harper-Collins $16.99 (978-0-06-081852-4). As they search for their missing father, 11-year-old Sapphire and her brother Conor find themselves torn between their home on England's Cornish coast and the Mer people and magical sea world of Ingo. (Rev: BCCB 10/06; BL 9/1/06; HBG 4/07; SLJ 8/06; VOYA 4/06)

2024 Dunmore, Helen. *The Tide Knot* (5–8). 2008, HarperCollins $16.99 (978-0-06-081855-5). Part-mermaid siblings Sapphire and Conor, introduced in *Ingo* (2006), must save humans from a huge tidal wave. (Rev: BL 1/1–15/08; HB 1–2/08; SLJ 2/08)

2025 DuPrau, Jeanne. *The City of Ember* (5–7). Series: Books of Ember. 2003, Random LB $17.99 (978-0-375-92274-9). Lina and Doon work to find a way out of their isolated and decaying city, where the population is beginning to panic. (Rev: BL 4/15/03; HB 5–6/03; HBG 10/03; SLJ 5/03; VOYA 6/03)

2026 DuPrau, Jeanne. *The People of Sparks* (5–7). Series: Books of Ember. 2004, Random $15.95 (978-0-375-82824-9). In this sequel to *The City of Ember,* Doon and Lina, plus the 400 people they have led from Ember to the surface of the Earth, seek aid from the people of Sparks. (Rev: BL 4/15/04; HB 7–8/04; SLJ 5/04)

2027 DuPrau, Jeanne. *The Prophet of Yonwood* (4–7). Series: Books of Ember. 2006, Random $15.95 (978-0-375-87526-7). About 50 years before the time of the Embers series, 11-year-old Nickie hides out at her great-grandfather's estate in Yonwood, North Carolina, and thinks about good and evil as she watches her neighbors react to predictions of doom. (Rev: BL 5/15/06; SLJ 6/06; VOYA 4/06) ⊘

2028 Durst, Sarah Beth. *Into the Wild* (6–9). 2007, Penguin $15.99 (978-1-59514-156-9). Rapunzel and her 12-year-old daughter Julie have escaped the enchanted forest known as the Wild and are trying to lead normal lives; but now the Wild is loose and Julie must rescue others before they become trapped in fairy tales. (Rev: BL 6/1–15/07; LMC 11/07; SLJ 9/07)

2029 Eaton, Jason Carter. *The Facttracker* (4–7). Illus. by Pascale Constantin. 2008, HarperCollins $15.99 (978-0-06-056434-6). The library turns into the "liebrary" when the town of Traäkerfaxx decides to deal in lies rather than facts in this imagi-native and clever story. (Rev: BL 1/1–15/08; SLJ 3/08)

2030 Ende, Michael. *The Neverending Story* (7–12). Trans. by Ralph Manheim. 1984, Penguin paper $15.00 (978-0-14-007431-4). An overweight boy with many problems enters the magic world of Fantastica in this charming fantasy.

2031 Etchemendy, Nancy. *The Power of Un* (4–7). 2000, Front St. $14.95 (978-0-8126-2850-0). Gib, a young boy, meets a strange old man who gives him an "unner," which can send him back in time in this thought-provoking fantasy. (Rev: BCCB 7–8/00; BL 5/1/00; HBG 10/00; SLJ 6/00; VOYA 6/00)

2032 Ewing, Lynne. *Barbarian* (8–12). Series: Sons of the Dark. 2004, Hyperion $9.99 (978-0-7868-1811-2). Four gorgeous and immortal teens with magical powers escape slavery in the parallel universe of Nefandus and must deal with life in modern Los Angeles before fulfilling their destinies. (Rev: SLJ 10/04; VOYA 2/05)

2033 Ewing, Lynne. *Into the Cold Fire* (7–12). Series: Daughters of the Moon. 2000, Hyperion LB $9.99 (978-0-7868-0654-6). In this latest light-hearted tale about four Los Angeles girls with extraordinary powers, Serena is faced with a difficult choice: to succumb to the dark and seductive power of the Atrox or to remain loyal to her sister goddesses. (Rev: HBG 3/01; VOYA 6/01)

2034 Farjeon, Eleanor. *The Glass Slipper* (6–9). 1986, HarperCollins LB $11.89 (978-0-397-32181-0). A romantic retelling in prose of the Cinderella story. (Rev: BL 10/15/86)

2035 Farland, David. *Of Mice and Magic* (5–8). Illus. by Howard Lyon. Series: Ravenspell. 2005, Covenant Communications $16.95 (978-1-57734-918-1). Ben's magical mouse Amber turns Ben into a mouse and together the two set out to rescue the animals from the pet store. (Rev: SLJ 1/06)

2036 Farley, Terri. *Seven Tears into the Sea* (7–10). 2005, Simon & Schuster paper $6.99 (978-0-689-86442-1). Working at her clairvoyant grandmother's seaside inn for the summer, 17-year-old Gwen becomes attracted to Jesse, a strange boy with secrets. (Rev: BCCB 4/05; BL 4/1/05; SLJ 6/05; VOYA 6/05)

2037 Farmer, Nancy. *The Land of the Silver Apples* (6–9). 2007, Atheneum $18.99 (978-1-4169-0735-0). In this sequel to *The Sea of Trolls* (2004), young poet Jack is faced with new revelations about his sister Lucy as he travels underground to the Land of the Silver Apples. (Rev: BL 8/07; HB 7–8/07; LMC 11/07; SLJ 8/07)

2038 Farmer, Nancy. *The Sea of Trolls* (6–9). 2004, Atheneum $17.95 (978-0-689-86744-6). In this thrill-packed Viking fantasy, 11-year-old Jack must embark on a dangerous quest into troll country to save his little sister's life. (Rev: BL 11/1/04; SLJ 10/04)

2039 Favole, Robert J. *Through the Wormhole* (5–8). 2001, Flywheel $17.95 (978-1-930826-00-7). Detailed endnotes add historical weight to this story of Michael and Kate, who travel through time to 1778 to aid the Marquis de Lafayette and rescue one of Michael's ancestors. (Rev: BL 3/1/01; SLJ 4/01; VOYA 4/01)

2040 Federici, Debbie, and Susan Vaught. *L.O.S.T* (8–12). 2004, Llewellyn paper $9.95 (978-0-7387-0561-3). Fantasy and romance are intertwined in this fast-paced story about 17-year-old Bren, who is kidnapped by Jazz, 16-year-old Queen of the Witches, because she believes he is the long-prophesied Shadowalker. (Rev: SLJ 1/05)

2041 Fienberg, Anna. *The Witch in the Lake* (5–8). 2002, Annick LB $18.95 (978-1-55037-723-1); paper $7.95 (978-1-55037-722-4). This story of magic and suspense in 16th-century Italy interweaves fantasy with facts about the time. (Rev: HBG 3/03; SLJ 8/02; VOYA 8/02)

2042 Findon, Joanne. *When Night Eats the Moon* (4–7). 2000, Red Deer paper $7.95 (978-0-88995-212-6). Her flute music and some magic take Holly, a Canadian girl visiting England, back to prehistoric times at Stonehenge when the locals are being threatened with a Celtic invasion. (Rev: BL 8/00; VOYA 6/00)

2043 Fisher, Catherine. *Day of the Scarab* (6–9). Series: Oracle Prophecies. 2006, Greenwillow $16.99 (978-0-06-057163-4). The final volume of the complex trilogy set in an imaginary classical world. (Rev: BL 5/15/06; HB 5–6/06; SLJ 7/06)

2044 Fisher, Catherine. *The Oracle Betrayed* (5–8). 2004, Greenwillow $16.99 (978-0-06-057157-3). This suspenseful story set in an imaginary country that combines aspects of ancient Greece and ancient Egypt involves a young heroine, Mirany, on a dangerous quest. (Rev: BL 2/15/04; HB 3–4/04; SLJ 3/04; VOYA 4/04)

2045 Fisher, Catherine. *Snow-Walker* (6–9). 2004, HarperCollins $17.99 (978-0-06-072474-0). Gudrun, an evil witch and the title character of this fantasy novel that draws on Norse and Celtic legends, faces a stiff challenge from the people of Jarshold as they fight to oust her and restore the rightful rulers to the throne. (Rev: BL 9/1/04; SLJ 11/04)

2046 Fisher, Catherine. *The Sphere of Secrets* (5–8). Series: Oracle Prophecies Trilogy. 2005, Greenwillow LB $18.89 (978-0-06-057162-7). Alexos, introduced in *The Oracle Betrayed* (2004), embarks on a journey to the Well of Songs while his friend Mirany serves the Oracle. (Rev: BL 3/15/05; SLJ 3/05)

2047 Flanagan, John. *The Battle for Skandia* (4–7). Series: Ranger's Apprentice. 2008, Philomel $16.99 (978-0-399-24457-5). In book four of the series, Will is saved from death by Halt and Horace, Evanlyn is captured, and the Temujai army closes in. (Rev: BL 4/1/08)

2048 Flanagan, John. *The Burning Bridge* (5–8). Series: Ranger's Apprentice. 2006, Philomel $16.99 (978-0-399-24455-1). Will and his friend Horace again face war and find the safety of the kingdom depends on them. (Rev: BL 5/15/06; SLJ 8/06)

2049 Flanagan, John. *The Icebound Land* (4–7). Series: Ranger's Apprentice. 2007, Philomel $16.99 (978-0-399-24456-8). Will, the ranger's apprentice, and Princess Evanlyn are captives on a ship that takes them to Skandia to work as slaves; while the ranger Halt and knight-in-training Horace journey to rescue them but face many obstacles. (Rev: BL 6/1–15/07; SLJ 8/07)

2050 Flanagan, John. *The Ruins of Gorlan* (5–8). 2005, Philomel $15.99 (978-0-399-24454-4). Will becomes an apprentice ranger and plays a key role in protecting his kingdom in this memorable first installment in a new fantasy series. (Rev: BL 6/1–15/05*; SLJ 6/05)

2051 Fletcher, Charlie. *Ironhand* (5–8). Series: The Stoneheart Trilogy. 2008, Hyperion $16.99 (978-1-4231-0177-2). In this sequel to *Stoneheart*, George races against three gruesome veins that have appeared on his body as he takes the Hard Way and searches for the Stoneheart. (Rev: BL 4/15/08; SLJ 6/08)

2052 Fletcher, Charlie. *Stoneheart* (5–8). 2007, Hyperion $16.99 (978-1-4231-0175-8). At the Natural History Museum in London 12-year-old George stumbles upon a parallel world where good statues (or spits) and evil taints are at war. (Rev: BL 5/15/07; SLJ 8/07)

2053 Flinn, Alex. *Beastly* (7–10). 2007, HarperTeen $16.99 (978-0-06-087416-2). Popular, snooty Kyle is transformed into a beast when he insults a classmate in this modern adaptation of "Beauty and the Beast." (Rev: BL 2/1/08; SLJ 11/07)

2054 Foon, Dennis. *The Dirt Eaters* (5–10). Series: Longlight Legacy Trilogy. 2003, Annick $19.95 (978-1-55037-807-8); paper $9.95 (978-1-55037-806-1). In this well-written first installment of a trilogy, 15-year-old Roan finds himself torn between the peaceful ways of his upbringing and a desire to avenge a murderous attack on his village. (Rev: SLJ 1/04; VOYA 2/04)

2055 Forester, Victoria. *The Girl Who Could Fly* (4–7). 2008, Feiwel and Friends $16.95 (978-0-312-37462-4). Piper McCloud can fly — an ability that unsettles her community — and she is taken to a school for children with unusual abilities, which she soon senses is not quite what it seems. (Rev: BL 6/1–15/08; SLJ 9/08)

2056 Fox, Helen. *Eager's Nephew* (5–8). 2006, Random LB $17.99 (978-0-385-90904-4). In this sequel to *Eager* (2004), Eager the robot and his nephew Jonquil pay a forbidden visit to Eager's human friends, the Bells; mystery and adventure ensue. (Rev: BL 10/15/06; SLJ 1/07)

2057 Friesner, Esther. *Nobody's Princess* (6–10). 2007, Random $16.99 (978-0-375-87528-1). The romantic, exciting, and dangerous childhood of Helen of Troy, whose face launched all those ships when she grew up. The sequel *Nobody's Prize* (2008) continues the story. (Rev: BCCB 7–8/07; BL 3/15/07; LMC 4–5/07; SLJ 7/07)

2058 Friesner, Esther. *Nobody's Prize* (8–12). 2008, Random $16.99 (978-0-375-87531-1). Princess Helen of Sparta (the future Helen of Troy), longing for adventure, disguises herself as a boy and stows away on the *Argo* in this exciting sequel to *Nobody's Princess*. (Rev: BL 2/1/08; SLJ 6/08)

2059 Friesner, Esther. *Temping Fate* (7–10). 2006, Dutton $16.99 (978-0-525-47730-3). Unsuspecting teenager Ilana finds that her summer employer, Divine Relief Temp Agency, has genuine Greek gods and goddesses among its clientele. (Rev: BL 5/15/06; SLJ 8/06)

2060 Fromental, Jean-Luc. *Broadway Chicken* (5–8). Trans. by Suzi Baker. Illus. 1995, Hyperion LB $15.49 (978-0-7868-2048-1). A tale of success and failure with, yes, a dancing chicken as the protagonist. (Rev: BL 12/15/95; SLJ 2/96)

2061 Funke, Cornelia. *Inkheart* (6–12). 2003, Scholastic $24.99 (978-0-439-53164-1). Twelve-year-old Meggie, the key character in this complex novel, is the daughter of a bookbinder who can release fictional characters from their books. (Rev: BL 9/1/03; HBG 4/04; SLJ 10/03; VOYA 12/03)

2062 Funke, Cornelia. *Inkspell* (6–9). 2005, Scholastic $24.99 (978-0-439-55400-8). In this gripping sequel to *Inkheart*, the magical process is reversed and earlier characters find themselves in a fictional world of violence. (Rev: BL 10/1/05*; SLJ 10/05; VOYA 10/05)

2063 Furey, Maggie. *Heart of Myrial* (7–12). Series: Shadowleague. 2000, Bantam paper $6.99 (978-0-553-57938-3). As catastrophic events threaten Myrial, a firedrake, a telepathic dragon, and a woman warrior seek to avert destruction. (Rev: VOYA 6/00)

2064 Gaiman, Neil. *Coraline* (5–8). Illus. by Dave McKean. 2002, HarperCollins LB $17.89 (978-0-06-623744-2). An Alice-in-Wonderland type of tale for older readers in which a girl finds an alternate world in the empty apartment next door. (Rev: BCCB 11/02; BL 8/02; HB 11–12/02; HBG 3/03; SLJ 8/02*)

2065 Gaiman, Neil. *M Is for Magic* (7–10). Illus. by Teddy Kristiansen. 2007, HarperCollins $16.99 (978-0-06-118642-4). This collection of previously published stories (many from *Fragile Things*) includes twisted fairy tales, stories based on myth and legend (from aliens to the Holy Grail), and quirky illustrations. (Rev: BCCB 9/07; BL 4/15/07; SLJ 8/07)

2066 Galloway, Priscilla. *Truly Grim Tales* (7–12). 1998, Random paper $NIS (978-0-440-22728-1). Familiar folk tales get new twists in this collection. (Rev: BL 9/15/95; SLJ 9/95)

2067 García, Laura Gallego. *The Legend of the Wandering King* (6–9). Trans. by Dan Bellm. 2005, Scholastic $16.95 (978-0-439-58556-9). Jealous of the carpet weaver who has bested him in the annual poetry competition for three consecutive years, an Arabian prince orders his rival to weave a carpet that chronicles the complete history of humankind. (Rev: BL 10/15/05; SLJ 10/05)

2068 García, Laura Gallego. *The Valley of the Wolves* (5–8). Trans. by Margaret Sayers Peden. 2006, Scholastic $16.99 (978-0-439-58553-8). Dana, 10, learns to use her magical powers at an academy of sorcery and wonders about the origins of her best friend and constant companion Kai, visible only to Dana. (Rev: BL 5/15/06; SLJ 6/06; VOYA 6/06)

2069 Gardner, Lyn. *Into the Woods* (4–7). Illus. by Mini Grey. 2007, Random $16.99 (978-0-385-75115-5). After their mother's death, Storm and her sisters flee the evil Dr. DeWilde and his pack of wolves and find themselves facing many dangers that will be familiar to readers of fairy tales. (Rev: BL 5/1/07; HB 7–8/07; LMC 10/07; SLJ 6/07)

2070 Gardner, Sally. *I, Coriander* (7–10). 2005, Dial $16.99 (978-0-8037-3099-1). In a fantasy full of the atmosphere of 17th-century England, Coriander is the daughter of a human father and a fairy princess. (Rev: BL 8/05; SLJ 9/05; VOYA 10/05)

2071 Garfield, Henry. *Tartabull's Throw* (7–10). 2001, Simon & Schuster $15.00 (978-0-689-83840-8). A 19-year-old baseball player and a mysterious young woman called Cassandra are the principal characters in this multifaceted story set in 1967 that entwines baseball, werewolves, romance, and suspense. (Rev: BL 5/15/01; HBG 10/01; SLJ 6/01; VOYA 8/01)

2072 George, Jessica Day. *Dragon Flight* (6–9). 2008, Bloomsbury $16.95 (978-1-59990-110-7). In a world populated by people and dragons, orphan Creel is drawn into a war and a romance. (Rev: BL 5/15/08)

2073 George, Jessica Day. *Dragon Slippers* (6–9). 2007, Bloomsbury $16.95 (978-1-59990-057-5). After befriending a dragon, orphan Creel unwittingly acquires an intriguing pair of slippers with the power to determine the future of her kingdom. (Rev: BL 5/15/07; SLJ 10/07)

2074 George, Jessica Day. *Sun and Moon, Ice and Snow* (7–10). 2008, Bloomsbury $16.95 (978-1-59990-109-1). Based on Norse myth, this is a story of a girl who lives in an ice palace with a white bear after being rejected by her mother. (Rev: BL 2/1/08; SLJ 3/08)

2075 Gilmore, Rachna. *The Sower of Tales* (6–9). 2005, Fitzhenry & Whiteside $15.95 (978-1-55041-945-0). In a land where the Plainsfolk are nourished by stories, Calantha, who dreams of following in the footsteps of the Gatherer who harvests the story pods, must act to save them all. (Rev: BL 12/15/05; SLJ 1/06; VOYA 12/05)

2076 Going, K. L. *The Garden of Eve* (5–8). 2007, Harcourt $17.00 (978-0-15-205986-6). When Evie and her father move to a house with an enchanted apple orchard after Evie's mother dies, a ghost and a magical seed help to ease Evie's grief. (Rev: BL 10/1/07; HB 11–12/07; LMC 1/08; SLJ 12/07) ❷

2077 Golding, Julia. *The Gorgon's Gaze* (4–7). Series: Companions Quartet. 2007, Marshall Cavendish $16.99 (978-0-7614-5377-2). This sequel to *Secret of the Sirens* finds both Connie and the Society for the Protection of Mythical Creatures in danger. (Rev: BL 1/1–15/08)

2078 Gopnik, Adam. *The King in the Window* (5–8). 2005, Hyperion $19.95 (978-0-7868-1862-4). Mistaken by window wraiths as their king, 11-year-old Oliver Parker struggles to resist their efforts to pull him into their world. (Rev: BL 10/1/05; SLJ 11/05; VOYA 2/06)

2079 Gordon, Lawrence. *User Friendly* (7–10). Series: Ghost Chronicles. 1999, Karmichael paper $11.95 (978-0-9653966-0-8). Frank, a teenage ghost in limbo, contacts Eddie through the computer to get help to free himself and his friend, a runaway slave, from the purgatory in which they are living. (Rev: BL 1/1–15/99; SLJ 1/99)

2080 Gordon, Roderick, and Brian Williams. *Tunnels: Book 1* (6–9). Series: Tunnels. 2008, Scholastic $17.99 (978-0-439-87177-8). Will, 14, and his friend Chester discover secret worlds beneath London when they investigate the disappearance of Will's archaeologist father; the first volume in a series. (Rev: BL 2/15/08; SLJ 3/08)

2081 Gormley, Beatrice. *Best Friend Insurance* (5–7). Illus. by Emily Arnold McCully. 1988, Avon paper $2.50 (978-0-380-69854-7). Maureen finds that her mother has been transformed into a new friend named Kitty. (Rev: SLJ 8/04)

2082 Goto, Hiromi. *The Water of Possibility* (5–7). Illus. by Aries Cheung. Series: In the Same Boat. 2002, Coteau paper $8.95 (978-1-55050-183-4). Sayuri, 12, and her younger brother discover a magical world full of danger in this fantasy that includes many elements of Japanese folklore. (Rev: SLJ 8/02)

2083 Grant, Vicki. *The Puppet Wrangler* (6–8). 2004, Orca paper $6.95 (978-1-55143-304-2). A humorous, offbeat modern fantasy in which 12-year-old Telly, unfairly banished from home because of her older sister's misdeeds, finds herself befriending a live puppet from her aunt's television show. (Rev: BCCB 7–8/04; SLJ 8/04)

2084 Gray, Anne. *Rites of the Healer* (6–10). 2007, Sumach paper $11.95 (978-1-894549-59-2). This imaginative book tells the story of Dovella, a villager who is sent on a dangerous quest to find the source of a water supply shortage. (Rev: SLJ 3/08)

2085 Gray, Claudia. *Evernight* (8–11). 2008, Harper-Teen $16.99 (978-0-06-128439-7). Bianca's new boarding school is populated with beautiful vampires, and she and her boyfriend Lucas face danger as they uncover the school's secrets. (Rev: BL 5/15/08; SLJ 6/08)

2086 Gray, Luli. *Falcon and the Carousel of Time* (4–7). 2005, Houghton $15.00 (978-0-618-44895-1). Falcon, 13, and her Aunt Emily travel back to 1903 New York City in this novel that blends elements of *Timespinners* (2003) and the two previous Falcon novels. (Rev: BL 6/1–15/05; SLJ 7/05)

2087 Gray, Luli. *Falcon and the Charles Street Witch* (4–7). 2002, Houghton $16.00 (978-0-618-16410-3). In this fantasy follow-up to 1995's *Falcon's Egg*, a 12-year-old girl becomes reacquainted with a dragon she released over New York City and befriends a witch who lives in Greenwich Village. (Rev: BL 3/15/02*; HBG 10/02; SLJ 4/02; VOYA 4/02)

2088 Greer, Gery, and Bob Ruddick. *Max and Me and the Time Machine* (5–8). 1983, HarperCollins paper $4.99 (978-0-06-440222-4). Steve and Max travel back in time to England during the Middle Ages.

2089 Griffin, Peni R. *Switching Well* (5–9). 1993, Penguin paper $5.99 (978-0-14-036910-6). Two girls from different centuries trade places but soon regret their decisions. (Rev: BCCB 7–8/93; BL 6/1–15/93*; SLJ 6/93*; VOYA 8/93)

2090 Gutman, Dan. *Abner and Me* (5–8). Series: Baseball Card Adventure. 2005, HarperCollins LB $17.89 (978-0-06-053444-8). Stosh and his mother travel back to visit the Battle of Gettysburg in an effort to learn more about baseball's origins. (Rev: BL 1/1–15/05)

2091 Gutman, Dan. *Babe and Me* (4–7). Illus. 2000, Avon $16.99 (978-0-380-97739-0). Joe and his dad time-travel to the 1932 World Series to witness a historic moment with hitter Babe Ruth. (Rev: BL 2/1/00; HBG 10/00; SLJ 2/00; VOYA 4/00)

2092 Gutman, Dan. *Honus and Me: A Baseball Card Adventure* (4–7). 1997, Avon paper $5.99 (978-0-380-78878-1). Young Joe Stoshack finds a magical baseball card that allows him to travel through time and participate in the 1909 World Series. (Rev: BL 4/15/97; SLJ 6/97)

2093 Gutman, Dan. *Jackie and Me: A Baseball Card Adventure* (4–7). Illus. 1999, Avon $16.99 (978-0-380-97685-0). While time-traveling to research a paper on Jackie Robinson, Joe Stoshack becomes an African American and experiences prejudice first hand. (Rev: BL 2/1/99; HBG 10/99; SLJ 3/99)

2094 Gutman, Dan. *Satch and Me* (4–7). Series: Baseball Card Adventure. 2005, HarperCollins LB $16.89 (978-0-06-059492-3). Stosh travels back to 1942 to establish whether Satchel Paige was the fastest pitcher in history and learns about racial discrimination in the process. (Rev: SLJ 2/06; VOYA 4/06)

2095 Haddix, Margaret P. *Escape from Memory* (6–9). 2003, Simon & Schuster $16.95 (978-0-689-85421-7). Under hypnosis, Kira reveals memories of another place in another time, one that threatens both herself and her mother. (Rev: BL 9/1/03; SLJ 3/04; VOYA 10/03)

2096 Haddix, Margaret P. *Running Out of Time* (4–7). 1995, Simon & Schuster $16.95 (978-0-689-80084-9). Living in a historical site where the time is the 1840s, Jessie escapes into the present in this fantasy. (Rev: BCCB 11/95; BL 10/1/95; SLJ 10/95*)

2097 Hague, Michael, ed. *The Book of Dragons* (4–7). Illus. by Michael Hague. 1995, Morrow $21.99 (978-0-688-10879-3). Seventeen classic tales about dragons by such authors as Tolkien and Kenneth Grahame are included in this interesting anthology. (Rev: BL 10/1/95; SLJ 10/95)

2098 Hale, Shannon. *Book of a Thousand Days* (7–10). Illus. by James Noel Smith. 2007, Bloomsbury $17.95 (978-1-59990-051-3). As punishment for refusing to marry, Lady Saren and her servant Dashti are sentenced to seven years in a sealed tower, where Dashti writes in her diary about their imprisonment, her secret love for a lord, and their escape; based on a fairy tale from the Brothers Grimm. (Rev: BL 9/15/07; SLJ 10/07) ⊚

2099 Hale, Shannon. *Enna Burning* (8–11). Series: Books of Bayern. 2004, Bloomsbury $17.95 (978-1-58234-889-6). In this companion to *The Goose Girl*, Enna returns to her home in the forest and learns to wield the power of fire, but she must struggle to use that power wisely without risking her life or those of her people. (Rev: BL 9/15/04; SLJ 9/04; VOYA 12/04)

2100 Hale, Shannon. *The Goose Girl* (6–10). Series: Books of Bayern. 2003, Bloomsbury $17.95 (978-1-58234-843-8). Crown Princess Ani, who can talk to the animals, is betrayed by her guards and disguises herself as a goose girl until she can reclaim her crown. (Rev: BL 8/03; HBG 4/04; SLJ 8/03*; VOYA 10/03)

2101 Hale, Shannon. *Princess Academy* (6–9). 2005, Bloomsbury $16.95 (978-1-58234-993-0). Fantasy, feminism, adventure, and romance are combined in the story of 14-year-old Miri, prize student in the Princess Academy and advocate for the miners of the stone called *under*. Newbery Honor Book, 2006. (Rev: BL 6/1–15/05; SLJ 8/05; VOYA 8/05)

2102 Hale, Shannon. *River Secrets* (7–10). Series: Books of Bayern. 2006, Bloomsbury $17.95 (978-1-58234-901-5). Razo, a teenage soldier from Bazo, is surprised to learn he's being sent on a mission to Tira after the war, to help keep peace. But someone is trying to sabotage the peace and Razo must figure out who. A sequel to *The Goose Girl* (2003) and *Enna Burning* (2004). (Rev: BL 9/15/06; SLJ 10/06*)

2103 Hamilton, Virginia. *Justice and Her Brothers* (7–10). Series: The Justice Cycle. 1978, Scholastic paper $4.99 (978-0-590-36214-6). Four children with supernatural powers move in time in this complex novel. Sequels are *Dustland* (1980) and *The Gathering* (1981).

2104 Hanley, Victoria. *The Healer's Keep* (7–12). 2002, Holiday $17.95 (978-0-8234-1760-5). A princess, a former slave girl, and their companions battle evil in a land full of magic. (Rev: BCCB 1/03; HBG 3/03; SLJ 12/02; VOYA 2/03)

2105 Hanley, Victoria. *The Seer and the Sword* (6–10). 2000, Holiday $17.95 (978-0-8234-1532-8). Romance, court politics, battles, and suspense all are essential parts of this fantasy featuring Princess Torina and Prince Landen. (Rev: BCCB 2/01; BL 12/15/00; HBG 10/01; SLJ 3/01; VOYA 4/01)

2106 Haptie, Charlotte. *Otto and the Flying Twins* (4–7). 2004, Holiday $17.95 (978-0-8234-1826-8). In the City of Trees, Otto is shocked to discover his father is king of the magical Karmidee. The sequel is *Otto and the Bird Charmers* (2005). (Rev: BL 4/15/04; SLJ 6/04)

2107 Hardinge, Frances. *Fly by Night* (6–9). 2006, HarperCollins $16.99 (978-0-06-087627-2). Set in an oppressive medieval kingdom, this multilayered novel features Mosca Mye, 12, an orphan with courage and an usual ability — the gift of reading. (Rev: BL 8/06; SLJ SLJ 7/06) ⊚

2108 Hardinge, Frances. *Well Witched* (5–8). 2008, HarperCollins LB $17.89 (978-0-06-088039-2); paper $16.99 (978-0-06-088038-5). Ryan, Josh, and Chelle steal from a wishing well and discover that the act has given them undesirable wish-granting powers in this intriguing story. (Rev: BL 5/15/08; SLJ 8/08)

2109 Harrison, Mette Ivie. *The Princess and the Hound* (6–9). 2007, Eos $17.99 (978-0-06-113187-5). In a kingdom where magical communication with animals is forbidden, Prince George manages to hide his talent until he meets the Princess Beatrice and her beloved dog, Marit. (Rev: BCCB 6/07; BL 7/07; SLJ 9/07)

2110 Hartinger, Brent. *Dreamquest: Tales of Slumberia* (4–8). 2007, Tom Doherty Assoc. $16.95 (978-0-7653-1397-3). Julie, 11, is suffering — her parents fight all day and she has nightmares every night — until she wakes up in Slumberia, where her dreams are created, and must escape while there's still a chance. (Rev: LMC 1/08*; SLJ 2/08)

2111 Haydon, Elizabeth. *The Floating Island* (6–9). Illus. by Brett Helquist. 2006, Tor $17.95 (978-0-7653-0867-2). The adventures of Ven Polypheme, a Nain (a dwarf-like creature) with a seafaring heritage; here he ends up fighting Fire Pirates, is rescued by a mermaid, and visits an inn populated by ghosts and other strange characters. (Rev: BL 9/1/06; SLJ 12/06)

2112 Haydon, Elizabeth. *The Thief Queen's Daughter* (6–9). Illus. by Jason Chan. Series: Lost Journals of Ven Polypheme. 2007, Tor $17.95 (978-0-7653-0868-9). King Vandemere sends Ven and four of his friends on a mission to the Gated City to solve the riddle of a mysterious light stone. (Rev: BL 5/15/07; SLJ 7/07)

2113 Hearn, Julie. *Sign of the Raven* (7–10). 2005, Simon & Schuster $16.95 (978-0-689-85734-8). Living with his grandmother in London while his mother recovers from cancer, 12-year-old Tom finds a portal into an 18th-century world far different from his own. (Rev: BCCB 12/05; HB 1–2/06; SLJ 11/05; VOYA 10/05)

2114 Helgerson, Joseph. *Horns and Wrinkles* (4–7). 2006, Houghton $16.00 (978-0-618-61679-4). Mysterious events are taking place in Blue Wing, Minnesota — the nose of a bully named Duke turns into a rhino horn, and his parents turn to stone — and 12-year-old Claire is drawn into an adventure involving fairies and trolls. (Rev: BL 9/1/06; SLJ 9/06)

2115 Hennesy, Carolyn. *Pandora Gets Jealous* (4–7). Series: Mythic Misadventures. 2008, Bloomsbury $12.95 (978-1-59990-196-1). A lighthearted take on the myth of Pandora in which Pandy takes a special box to school for show-and-tell. (Rev: BL 11/15/07; LMC 4-5/08; SLJ 3/08)

2116 Hess, Nina. *A Practical Guide to Monsters* (4–7). Illus. 2007, Mirrorstone $12.95 (978-0-7869-4809-3). A tongue-in-cheek field guide to common monsters, this companion to the series Knights of the Silver Dragon is geared toward young wizards and features detailed illustrations. (Rev: BL 1/1–15/08)

2117 Hightman, Jason. *The Saint of Dragons* (6–8). 2004, Morrow $16.99 (978-0-06-054011-1). Enrolled at an elite boarding school, 13-year-old Simon St. George is approached by a man claiming to be his father who asks for the boy's help in vanquishing the last surviving dragons; a sequel is *Samurai* (2006). (Rev: BL 8/04; SLJ 9/04)

2118 Highwater, Jamake. *Rama: A Legend* (5–9). 1997, Replica LB $24.95 (978-0-7351-0001-5). When he's wrongfully banished from his father's kingdom and his wife, Sita, is kidnapped, valiant Prince Rama charges back to avenge the evil that's befallen his world. (Rev: BL 11/15/94; SLJ 12/94; VOYA 2/95)

2119 Hill, Laban Carrick. *Casa Azul: An Encounter with Frida Kahlo* (7–10). 2005, Watson-Guptill $15.95 (978-0-8230-0411-9). In this appealing novel, two country children roaming the streets of Mexico City in search of their mother are befriended by artist Frida Kahlo and introduced to the magical world in which she dwells. (Rev: BL 10/1/05; SLJ 9/05)

2120 Hill, Pamela Smith. *The Last Grail Keeper* (7–10). 2001, Holiday $17.95 (978-0-8234-1574-8). While visiting England with her mother, 16-year-old Felicity discovers she is an Arthurian "grail keeper" with magical powers. (Rev: BCCB 2/02; BL 11/15/01; HBG 3/02; SLJ 12/01; VOYA 6/02)

2121 Hill, Stuart. *Blade of Fire* (7–10). Series: The Icemark Chronicles. 2007, Scholastic $18.99 (978-0-439-84122-1). Charlemagne, the youngest child of Queen Thirrin and Oskan Witchfather, is now an adult and finds himself at war with his own sister, who has joined the evil forces of Scipio Bellorum. (Rev: BL 3/15/07; LMC 8–9/07; SLJ 6/07)

2122 Hill, Stuart. *The Cry of the Icemark* (8–11). Series: The Icemark Chronicles. 2005, Scholastic $18.95 (978-0-439-68626-6). In this sprawling military fantasy, 13-year-old Thirrin succeeds her fallen father as ruler of Icemark and sets off to forge alliances with werewolves, vampires, and talking snow leopards to help her defend her tiny country. (Rev: BCCB 4/05; BL 2/15/05; SLJ 5/05; VOYA 6/05)

2123 Hite, Sid. *The Distance of Hope* (6–8). 1998, Holt $16.95 (978-0-8050-5054-7). Young prince Yeshe embarks on a perilous journey to find the White Bean Lama who will help him save his diminishing eyesight. (Rev: BL 3/15/98; HBG 9/98; SLJ 5/98; VOYA 6/98)

2124 Hite, Sid. *Dither Farm* (6–10). 1992, Holt $15.95 (978-0-8050-1871-4). An 11-year-old orphan is taken in by a farm family and discovers joys and miracles. (Rev: BL 5/15/92*; SLJ 5/92)

2125 Hoban, Russell. *The Mouse and His Child* (4–8). Illus. by David Small. 2001, Scholastic paper $16.99 (978-0-439-09826-7). A toy mouse and his child embark on a quest to become "self-winding" and have sometimes scary, sometimes humorous adventures in this enchanting fantasy first published in 1967 and now updated with new illustrations. (Rev: BL 12/1/01; HBG 3/02)

2126 Hodges, Margaret. *Gulliver in Lilliput: From Gulliver's Travels by Jonathan Swift* (4–7). Illus. by Kimberly B. Root. 1995, Holiday $17.95 (978-0-8234-1147-4). The story of Gulliver in the land of the little people is retold with bright, detailed illustrations. (Rev: BCCB 6/95; BL 4/15/95; HB 7–8/95; SLJ 6/95*)

2127 Hoeye, Michael. *No Time Like Show Time* (5–8). Series: A Hermux Tantamoq Adventure. 2004, Putnam $14.99 (978-0-399-23880-2). Hermux the mouse investigates who is responsible for sending threatening letters to famous director Fluster Varmint. (Rev: SLJ 11/04)

2128 Hoeye, Michael. *The Sands of Time* (5–8). Series: A Hermux Tantamoq Adventure. 2002, Putnam $14.99 (978-0-399-23879-6). In this sequel to *Time Stops for No Mouse* (2002), the mouse watchmaker and a chipmunk friend believe that mice were once the slaves of cats. (Rev: HBG 3/03; SLJ 10/02; VOYA 12/02)

2129 Hoeye, Michael. *Time Stops for No Mouse* (5–9). Series: A Hermux Tantamoq Adventure. 2002, Putnam $14.99 (978-0-399-23878-9). Hermux Tantamoq, a mouse, leads a quiet life as a watchmaker until Linka Perflinger turns up and Hermux becomes entangled in mystery and suspense. (Rev: BL 3/15/02*; HB 7–8/02; HBG 10/02; SLJ 5/02; VOYA 6/02)

2130 Hoeye, Michael. *Time to Smell the Roses: A Hermux Tantamoq Adventure* (7–10). Series: Hermux Tantamoq Adventures. 2007, Putnam $15.99 (978-0-399-24490-2). Our mouse detective must solve a mystery at Thorny End while planning his wedding to Linka Perflinger and dodging mutant bees. (Rev: BL 10/1/07)

2131 Hoffman, Alice. *Aquamarine* (4–7). 2001, Scholastic paper $16.95 (978-0-439-09863-2). Twelve-year-old friends Hailey and Claire find a lonely mermaid named Aquamarine, and they try to give her love and adventure. (Rev: BCCB 2/01; BL 3/1/01; HBG 10/01; SLJ 3/01; VOYA 4/01)

2132 Hoffman, Mary. *Stravaganza: City of Flowers* (7–10). Series: Stravaganza. 2005, Bloomsbury $17.95 (978-1-58234-887-2). In the final volume of the trilogy, Sky Meadows, a 17-year-old biracial

Londoner, travels back in time to 16th-century Talia, where many of the characters become involved in multilayered intrigue. (Rev: BL 3/1/05; SLJ 5/05)

2133 Hoobler, Dorothy, and Thomas Hoobler. *The Ghost in the Tokaido Inn* (6–12). 1999, Putnam $17.99 (978-0-399-23330-2). Set in 18th-century Japan, this is the story of 14-year-old Seikei, his dreams of becoming a samurai, and what happened after he saw a legendary ghost stealing a valuable jewel. (Rev: BL 6/1–15/99; HBG 4/00; SLJ 6/99; VOYA 10/99)

2134 Horowitz, Anthony. *Evil Star* (5–8). Series: The Gatekeepers. 2006, Scholastic $17.99 (978-0-439-67996-1). In the second installment of this action-packed fantasy series, 14-year-old Matt Freeman travels to Peru to learn more about the possible opening of another gate to the underworld. (Rev: BL 6/1–15/06; SLJ 7/06)

2135 Horowitz, Anthony. *Nightrise* (6–9). Series: The Gatekeepers. 2007, Scholastic $17.99 (978-0-439-68001-1). An organization called Nightrise is after telepathic twins Jamie and Scott, 14, in this third exciting volume in the struggle to keep the world safe from the Old Ones. (Rev: SLJ 1/08) ⑨

2136 Hoving, Isabel. *The Dream Merchant* (8–12). Trans. from Dutch by Hester Velmans. 2005, Candlewick $17.99 (978-0-7636-2880-2). An action-packed, intricately plotted adventure involving three young people in time travel and a world of collective dreams called *umaya*. (Rev: SLJ 1/06; VOYA 12/05)

2137 Huff, Tanya. *The Second Summoning: The Keeper's Chronicles #2* (7–12). 2001, DAW paper $7.99 (978-0-88677-975-7). Claire, a Keeper entrusted with protecting Canada, allows an angel and a demon to enter with humorous results. (Rev: VOYA 12/01)

2138 Hughes, Carol. *Dirty Magic* (5–8). 2006, Random $17.95 (978-0-375-83187-4). In a desperate attempt to save his little sister's life, 10-year-old Joe Brooks enters a shadowy world where ill children are held captive. (Rev: BL 10/1/06; SLJ 2/07)

2139 Hughes, Monica, sel. *What If? Amazing Stories* (5–10). 1998, Tundra paper $6.95 (978-0-88776-458-5). Fourteen fantasy and science fiction short stories by noted Canadian writers are included in this anthology, plus a few related poems. (Rev: BL 2/15/99; SLJ 6/99; VOYA 6/99)

2140 Hulme, John, and Michael Wexler. *The Glitch in Sleep* (5–8). Series: Seems. 2007, Bloomsbury $16.95 (978-1-59990-129-9). When 12-year-old Becker gets a job at the Institute for Fixing and Repair, he discovers that the world as we know it is under the control of the Seems; a humorous and thought-provoking story with plenty of illustrations and lots of entertaining gadgets. (Rev: BL 11/15/07; LMC 1/08; SLJ 11/07)

2141 Humphreys, Chris. *Vendetta* (8–11). Series: Runestone Saga. 2007, Knopf $15.99 (978-0-375-83293-2). Fifteen-year-old Sky March heads to Corsica to find a way to free his cousin Kristin from his evil Norwegian grandfather's spell. (Rev: BL 8/07; SLJ 1/08)

2142 Hunter, Erin. *A Dangerous Path* (6–9). Series: Warriors. 2004, HarperCollins LB $17.89 (978-0-06-052564-4). In the fifth installment in the series, Fireheart, deputy leader of ThunderClan, worries about the future of all the cats in the forest now that Tigerstar has taken over the leadership of ShadowClan. (Rev: BL 8/04)

2143 Hunter, Erin. *Dawn* (6–9). Series: Warriors: The New Prophecy. 2006, HarperCollins LB $17.89 (978-0-06-074456-4). In the third volume of the series, humans are encroaching further into the habitat of the four cat clans and there is pressure to unite and seek a new home. (Rev: BL 12/1/05)

2144 Hunter, Erin. *Fire and Ice* (6–9). Series: Warriors. 2003, HarperCollins $16.99 (978-0-06-000003-5). Ex-kittypet Firepaw (now known as Fireheart) is eager to prove himself on his first mission — to bring WindClan back to their territory — but faces many obstacles. (Rev: BL 9/1/03; HBG 10/03; SLJ 9/03)

2145 Hunter, Erin. *Firestar's Quest* (6–9). Series: Warriors. 2007, HarperCollins $17.99 (978-0-06-113164-6). Leader of the ThunderClan and proud of the current era of peace, Firestar sets out on a dangerous journey to discover what happened to the SkyClan cats. (Rev: BL 9/15/07)

2146 Hunter, Erin. *Forest of Secrets* (6–9). Series: Warriors. 2003, HarperCollins $16.99 (978-0-06-000004-2). Firepaw suspects Tigerclaw of treachery and works to expose him in this exciting installment featuring a flood, a tragic death, and clan rivalries. (Rev: BL 9/15/03; SLJ 10/03)

2147 Hunter, Erin. *Into the Wild* (6–9). Series: Warriors. 2003, HarperCollins $16.99 (978-0-06-000002-8). A young cat named Firepaw, formerly a pet, becomes an apprentice in the ThunderClan of wild warrior cats, which is in the midst of a struggle to retain its territory. (Rev: BL 2/15/03; HBG 10/03; SLJ 5/03)

2148 Hunter, Erin. *Moonrise* (6–9). Series: Warriors: The New Prophecy. 2005, HarperCollins LB $17.89 (978-0-06-074453-3). The cats of the StarClan take advice from a badger named Midnight and on the ensuing journey through the mountains meet a new and unusual tribe of cats. (Rev: BL 9/1/05)

2149 Hunter, Erin. *Rising Storm* (6–9). Series: Warriors. 2004, HarperCollins LB $17.89 (978-0-06-052562-0). In this fourth volume of the series, Fireheart the cat faces a number of daunting challenges in his new position as deputy leader of the ThunderClan. (Rev: BL 1/1–15/04; VOYA 4/04)

2150 Hunter, Erin. *The Sight* (5–7). Series: Warriors: The Power of Three. 2007, HarperCollins $16.99 (978-0-06-089201-2). Three kits — Hollypaw, Jaypaw, and Lionpaw — whose parents were members of the Thunderclan are endowed with special abilities in this series opener that follows the New Prophecy cycle. (Rev: BL 8/07; LMC 11-12/08)

2151 Hunter, Erin. *Sunset* (6–9). Series: Warriors: The New Prophecy. 2007, HarperCollins paper $6.99 (978-0-06-082771-7). The dead Tigerstar plots against Firestar; will Tigerstar's son Brambleclaw, Firestar's good friend, remain true to Firestar? (Rev: BL 2/1/08)

2152 Hunter, Mollie. *The Mermaid Summer* (5–8). 1988, HarperCollins $15.89 (978-0-06-022628-2). Eric Anderson refuses to recognize the power of the mermaid and leaves his Scottish fishing village after his boat is dashed to pieces on the rocks. (Rev: BCCB 5/88; BL 6/1/88; SLJ 6–7/88)

2153 Hunter, Mollie. *A Stranger Came Ashore* (7–9). 1977, HarperCollins paper $6.99 (978-0-06-440082-4). In this fantasy set in the Shetland Islands, a bull seal takes human form and comes ashore.

2154 Hussey, Charmain. *The Valley of Secrets* (4–7). Illus. by Christopher Crump. 2005, Simon & Schuster $16.95 (978-0-689-87862-6). A detailed, multifaceted novel about an orphan who inherits his great-uncle's estate and, through his uncle's journal, learns about the plight of the Amazon Indians. (Rev: BL 3/1/05; SLJ 2/05)

2155 Irving, Washington. *Rip Van Winkle and the Legend of Sleepy Hollow* (5–7). Illus. by Felix O. Darley. 1980, Sleepy Hollow $19.95 (978-0-912882-42-0). A handsome edition of these two classics.

2156 Iserles, Inbali. *The Tygrine Cat* (5–8). 2008, Candlewick $15.99 (978-0-7636-3798-9). Mati, the son of the slain queen of the Tygrine Cats, is being pursued by a killer sent by Suzerain in this feline fantasy. (Rev: BL 5/15/08)

2157 Jablonski, Carla. *Silent Echoes* (7–10). 2007, Penguin $16.99 (978-1-59514-082-1). Lucy, a 19th-century spiritualist, is astonished when she finds herself communicating with Lindsay, a modern-day teenager, in this time travel novel that will have readers learning about life in the 1880s. (Rev: BCCB 4/07; BL 3/1/07; SLJ 3/07)

2158 Jacques, Brian. *The Angel's Command: A Tale from the Castaways of the Flying Dutchman* (5–9). 2003, Putnam $23.99 (978-0-399-23999-1). This action-packed fantasy, set in the 17th century, is the sequel to *Castaways of the Flying Dutchman*. (Rev:

BL 2/1/03; HB 3–4/03; HBG 10/03; SLJ 3/03; VOYA 4/03)

2159 Jacques, Brian. *The Bellmaker* (5–7). Illus. Series: Redwall. 1995, Putnam $24.99 (978-0-399-22805-6). This seventh tale in the series of animal fantasies features Mariel, a courageous, outspoken mouse. (Rev: BCCB 4/95; BL 4/1/95; HB 5–6/95; SLJ 8/95)

2160 Jacques, Brian. *Castaways of the Flying Dutchman* (5–9). 2001, Putnam $23.99 (978-0-399-23601-3). A mute boy stows away on the *Flying Dutchman*, a ship that is condemned to sail the seas forever, and there he meets the ghostly crew and the crazed captain in this story in which the boy has many adventures and eventually gains the power of speech and the gift of staying young forever. (Rev: BCCB 3/01; BL 3/1/01; HB 3–4/01; HBG 10/01; SLJ 3/01; VOYA 4/01)

2161 Jacques, Brian. *Eulalia!* (5–8). Series: Redwall. 2007, Philomel $23.99 (978-0-399-24209-0). Lord Asheye, Badger Lord of Salamandastron, wishes to find his successor in this satisfying installment in the long-running series. (Rev: BL 8/07; SLJ 5/08) ✪

2162 Jacques, Brian. *High Rhulain* (5–8). Illus. by David Elliot. Series: Redwall. 2005, Philomel $23.99 (978-0-399-24208-3). In this eighteenth installment, ottermaid Tiria bravely journeys to the Green Isle to rescue otter kinsmen from evil wildcats. (Rev: BL 9/1/05; SLJ 9/05)

2163 Jacques, Brian. *The Legend of Luke: A Tale from Redwall* (5–8). Illus. Series: Redwall. 2000, Putnam $23.99 (978-0-399-23490-3). This book focuses on the building of the abbey, Martin's search for his father Luke, and Luke's heroic career. (Rev: BL 12/15/99; HBG 10/00; SLJ 2/00; VOYA 4/00)

2164 Jacques, Brian. *Loamhedge* (5–8). Series: Redwall. 2003, Putnam $23.99 (978-0-399-23724-9). As Redwall stalwarts including Bragoon and Sarobando seek a cure for a haremaid's ills at Loamhedge Abbey, Redwall itself comes under attack. (Rev: BL 9/15/03; HB 11–12/03; HBG 4/04; SLJ 10/03)

2165 Jacques, Brian. *The Long Patrol* (5–8). Illus. Series: Redwall. 1998, Putnam $23.99 (978-0-399-23165-0). In this tenth adventure, the villainous Rapscallions decide to attack the peaceful Abbey of Redwall. (Rev: BCCB 4/98; BL 12/15/97; HB 3–4/98; HBG 10/98; SLJ 1/98)

2166 Jacques, Brian. *Lord Brocktree* (5–8). Series: Redwall. 2000, Putnam $23.99 (978-0-399-23590-0). The villainous Ungatt Trunn and his Blue Hordes invade and capture the mountain fortress Salamandastron. (Rev: BCCB 9/00; BL 9/1/00; HB 9–10/00; HBG 3/01; SLJ 9/00)

2167 Jacques, Brian. *Mariel of Redwall* (5–7). Illus. by Gary Chalk. Series: Redwall. 1992, Putnam $24.99 (978-0-399-22144-6). Fourth in the saga of the animals of Redwall Abbey, this story tells how the great Joseph Bell is brought to the abbey. (Rev: BCCB 3/92; BL 1/15/92*; HB 9–10/92; SLJ 3/92)

2168 Jacques, Brian. *Marlfox* (5–8). Illus. Series: Redwall. 1999, Putnam $22.99 (978-0-399-23307-4). The famous tapestry depicting Martin and Warrior has been stolen from Redwall Abbey, and four young would-be heroes set out to recover it. (Rev: BL 12/15/98; HB 1–2/99; HBG 10/99; SLJ 4/99; VOYA 2/99)

2169 Jacques, Brian. *Martin the Warrior* (5–7). Illus. by Gary Chalk. Series: Redwall. 1994, Putnam $23.99 (978-0-399-22670-0). This volume tells how the mouse Martin the Warrior became the bold, courageous fighter that he is. (Rev: BCCB 1/94; BL 3/1/94; HB 9–10/94; SLJ 1/94)

2170 Jacques, Brian. *Mattimeo* (5–8). Series: Redwall. 1990, Putnam $23.99 (978-0-399-21741-8). The evil fox kidnaps the animal children of Redwall Abbey in this continuation of *Mossflower* (1988) and *Redwall* (1987). (Rev: BL 4/15/90; SLJ 9/90; VOYA 8/90)

2171 Jacques, Brian. *Mossflower* (5–7). Illus. by Gary Chalk. Series: Redwall. 1988, Putnam $24.99 (978-0-399-21549-0); Avon paper $5.99 (978-0-380-70828-4). How a brave and resourceful mouse took power from the evil wildcat. (Rev: BCCB 12/88; BL 11/1/88; SLJ 11/88)

2172 Jacques, Brian. *Outcast of Redwall* (5–8). Illus. Series: Redwall. 1996, Philomel $24.99 (978-0-399-22914-5). This episode in the Redwall saga involves the badger Sunflash, his buddy Skarlath the kestrel, and their enemy the ferret Swartt Sixclaw. (Rev: BCCB 3/96; BL 3/1/96; SLJ 5/96; VOYA 10/96)

2173 Jacques, Brian. *The Pearls of Lutra* (5–8). Series: Redwall. 1997, Putnam $23.99 (978-0-399-22946-6). The evil marten Mad Eyes threatens the peaceful Redwall Abbey in this ninth book in the series. (Rev: BCCB 4/97; BL 2/15/97; SLJ 3/97*; VOYA 6/97)

2174 Jacques, Brian. *Rakkety Tam* (5–8). Illus. by David Elliot. Series: Redwall. 2004, Putnam $23.99 (978-0-399-23725-6). When Redwall is threatened by a murderous wolverine called Gulo the Savage, two warrior squirrels — Rakkety Tam McBurl and Wild Doogy Plumm — take action. (Rev: BL 9/15/04; SLJ 9/04)

2175 Jacques, Brian. *Salamandastron* (5–7). Illus. by Gary Chalk. Series: Redwall. 1993, Putnam $23.99 (978-0-399-21992-4). These tales are centered on the badgers and hares of the castle of Salamandastron near the sea. (Rev: BCCB 7–8/93; BL 3/15/93; HB 5–6/93; SLJ 3/93)

2176 Jacques, Brian. *Taggerung* (5–8). Illus. Series: Redwall. 2001, Putnam $23.99 (978-0-399-23720-1). The 14th book in the series features an otter named Taggerung who was kidnapped from the abbey as a baby and raised by an outlaw ferret. (Rev: BL 8/01; HB 11–12/01; HBG 3/02; SLJ 10/01; VOYA 10/01)

2177 Jacques, Brian. *Triss* (5–8). 2002, Putnam $23.99 (978-0-399-23723-2). An action-packed installment in the Redwall series in which squirrel Triss, an escaped slave, meets up with the badger Sagax and his friend Scarum. (Rev: BL 9/1/02; HB 1–2/03; HBG 3/03; SLJ 10/02; VOYA 12/02)

2178 James, Mary. *Frankenlouse* (5–8). 1994, Scholastic paper $13.95 (978-0-590-46528-1). Nick, 14, is enrolled at Blister Military Academy, which is run by his father. He escapes into his own comic book creations featuring an insect named Frankenlouse. (Rev: BCCB 11/94; BL 10/15/94; SLJ 11/94; VOYA 12/94)

2179 James, Mary. *The Shuteyes* (4–7). 1994, Scholastic paper $3.25 (978-0-590-45070-6). Chester has some unusual experiences when he journeys to Alert, a land where no one sleeps. (Rev: SLJ 4/93)

2180 Jarvis, Robin. *The Whitby Witches* (4–7). Illus. by Jess Petersen. 2006, Chronicle $17.95 (978-0-8118-5413-9). Sent to live with their elderly Aunt Alice in the English seaside village of Whitby, 8-year-old Ben — who can see the invisible — and 12-year-old Jennet find themselves swept up in a struggle between good and evil. (Rev: BL 10/1/06; SLJ 10/06)

2181 Jenkins, A. M. *Night Road* (8–12). 2008, HarperTeen $16.99 (978-0-06-054604-5). Cole and Sandor, both hemovores (as these vampires prefer to be called), are assigned the project of helping young Gordon adjust to the difficult life of a vampire. (Rev: BL 5/15/08; SLJ 8/08)

2182 Jenkins, Jerry B., and Chris Fabry. *The Book of the King* (5–8). Series: The Wormling. 2007, Tyndale paper $5.99 (978-1-4143-0155-6). Owen discovers that there is another world beneath his family's bookstore and that he must battle with dragons to overcome evil forces. (Rev: BL 10/15/07)

2183 Jenkins, Martin. *Jonathan Swift's Gulliver* (5–8). Illus. by Chris Riddell. 2005, Candlewick $19.99 (978-0-7636-2409-5). A retelling of the classic tale using contemporary language and striking artwork. (Rev: BL 3/15/05; SLJ 3/05)

2184 Johansen, K. V. *Nightwalker* (5–8). 2007, Orca paper $8.95 (978-1-55143-481-0). Thrown into the dungeon when it's discovered that he possesses a powerful magical ring, young Maurey escapes with the help of a baroness and travels to Talverdin in an effort to find out if he is a nightwalker. (Rev: BL 4/1/07; SLJ 9/07)

2185 Johnson, Jane. *The Shadow World: The Eidolon Chronicles* (4–7). Illus. by Adam Stower. Series: Eidolon Chronicles. 2007, Simon & Schuster $15.99 (978-1-4169-1783-0). The second book in the series finds Ben entering Eidolon to bring back his sister Ellie, who is being held by the evil Dodman. (Rev: BL 12/1/07; SLJ 11/07)

2186 Johnson, Kathleen Jeffrie. *A Fast and Brutal Wing* (8–11). 2004, Roaring Brook $16.95 (978-1-59643-013-6). In a series of e-mails, journal entries, and newspaper stories, three teens recount the mysterious and fantastic events that led to a Halloween disappearance. (Rev: BL 12/15/04; SLJ 12/04; VOYA 12/04)

2187 Jones, David. *Baboon* (6–9). 2007, Annick $21.95 (978-1-55451-054-2); paper $11.95 (978-1-55451-053-5). After a plane crash in Africa, Gerry, 14, finds himself in a baboon body, part of a baboon troop, and progressively becoming more baboon and less human; the baboon behavior is very realistic. (Rev: BL 5/1/07; SLJ 6/07)

2188 Jones, Diana Wynne. *Cart and Cwidder* (8–10). 1995, Greenwillow $15.00 (978-0-688-13360-3); paper $4.95 (978-0-688-13399-3). When his father dies, 11-year-old Moril becomes heir to the family's cwidder, a musical instrument that has magical powers.

2189 Jones, Diana Wynne. *The Crown of Dalemark* (6–9). Series: Dalemark Quartet. 1995, Greenwillow $17.00 (978-0-688-13363-4). Readers familiar with the first three books in this quartet will enjoy its conclusion about Noreth, a teen who believes she is destined to become queen, and Maewen, who is sent to impersonate her. New readers should start with book one. (Rev: BL 12/15/95; SLJ 8/96)

2190 Jones, Diana Wynne. *House of Many Ways* (6–9). Series: Howl's Moving Castle. 2008, Greenwillow $17.99 (978-0-06-147795-9). Characters from *Howl's Moving Castle* and *Castle in the Air* populate this story about Charmain, who is sent to live in her great-uncle William's magical house and ends up helping to save High Norland. (Rev: BL 5/15/08; SLJ 6/08)

2191 Jones, Diana Wynne. *Howl's Moving Castle* (7–12). 1986, Greenwillow $16.95 (978-0-688-06233-0). A fearful young girl is changed into an old woman and in that disguise moves into the castle of Wizard Howl. (Rev: BL 6/1/86; SLJ 8/86; VOYA 8/86)

2192 Jones, Diana Wynne. *The Merlin Conspiracy* (6–10). 2003, HarperCollins LB $17.89 (978-0-06-052319-0). Three teenagers blessed with magical powers collaborate to save the islands of Blest, an alternate England, from attack by wizards in this complex novel full of humor. (Rev: BL 4/15/03; HB 5–6/03; HBG 10/03; SLJ 5/03; VOYA 8/03)

2193 Jones, Diana Wynne. *The Pinhoe Egg* (5–8). Series: Chrestomanci. 2006, Greenwillow $18.89 (978-0-06-113125-7). In this compelling addition to the Chrestomanci series, Marianne Pinhoe and Cat Chant find a strange egg with magical properties. (Rev: BL 9/15/06; SLJ 10/06) 🍂

2194 Jones, Diana Wynne. *The Time of the Ghost* (6–9). 1996, Greenwillow $15.00 (978-0-668-14598-5). Sally, the ghost of one of four sisters whose parents run a school for boys, tries to undo a bargain she made with an evil goddess when she was young. (Rev: BL 8/96; SLJ 11/96; VOYA 4/97)

2195 Jones, Diana Wynne. *Unexpected Magic: Collected Stories* (5–10). 2004, Greenwillow $16.99 (978-0-06-055533-7). An exciting anthology of 16 tales of mystery and magic by a master of fantasy. (Rev: BL 4/15/04; SLJ 9/04)

2196 Jones, Diana Wynne. *Year of the Griffin* (7–10). 2000, Greenwillow LB $15.89 (978-0-06-029158-7). Pirates, assassins, and plain old magic are among the challenges faced by students at Wizard's University — including Elda, griffin daughter of the wizard Derk — in this sequel to the humorous *Dark Lord of Derkholm* (1998). (Rev: BL 11/1/00; HB 11–12/00; HBG 3/01; SLJ 10/00; VOYA 12/00)

2197 Jones, Frewin. *The Faerie Path* (6–9). 2007, HarperCollins $16.99 (978-0-06-087102-4). After a car accident on the eve of her 16th birthday, Anita wakes up to find that she is in Faerie and has been transformed into Princess Tania, who has been missing for 500 years; what's more, her boyfriend Evan (who was in the car with her) is now Edric, servant to a faerie lord. (Rev: BCCB 3/07; BL 1/1–15/07; SLJ 3/07)

2198 Jones, Frewin. *The Lost Queen* (6–9). Series: The Faerie Path. 2007, Eos $16.99 (978-0-06-087105-5). Tania, who lives a double life in the faerie world and the mortal world, goes in search of the long-lost Queen Titania in this sequel to *The Faerie Path*. (Rev: BL 11/1/07; SLJ 11/07)

2199 Jones, Frewin. *The Sorcerer King* (6–9). Series: Faerie Path. 2008, Eos $16.99 (978-0-06-087108-6). With their king kidnapped and the faerie people enslaved, Princess Tania, Queen Titania, and Edric go to war to save their culture and their world; the final volume in the trilogy. (Rev: BL 2/1/08; SLJ 2/08)

2200 Jordan, Robert. *A Crown of Swords* (8–12). Series: Wheel of Time. 1996, Tor $29.95 (978-0-312-85767-7). In this seventh book of this series, Rand and his army of Aiel warriors prepare to do battle with the Dark One. (Rev: VOYA 2/97)

2201 Jordan, Sherryl. *The Hunting of the Last Dragon* (6–10). 2002, HarperCollins LB $15.89 (978-0-06-028903-4). In 14th-century England a monk records young peasant Jude's story of his quest, accompanied by a young Chinese woman, to kill a dragon. (Rev: BCCB 9/02; BL 4/15/02; HBG 10/02; SLJ 7/02)

2202 Jordan, Sherryl. *Secret Sacrament* (8–12). 2001, HarperCollins LB $17.89 (978-0-06-028905-8). In an ancient time, Gabriel trains at the Citadel to become a healer, hoping to intervene in the violence that surrounds him. (Rev: BCCB 3/01; BL 2/15/01; HBG 10/01; SLJ 2/01; VOYA 6/01)

2203 Jordan, Sherryl. *Time of the Eagle* (7–10). 2007, Eos $16.99 (978-0-06-059554-8). As the daughter of Gabriel Eshban Vala (hero of the 2001 *Secret Sacrament*, Avala is a healer and the Chosen One, who must bring about the uprising of the persecuted Shinali people. (Rev: BL 5/15/07; LMC 11/07; SLJ 9/07)

2204 Kaaberbol, Lene. *The Serpent Gift* (6–9). Series: Shamer Chronicles. 2006, Holt $17.95 (978-0-8050-7770-4). In this third book in the series, Dina and her family escape their Blackmaster father only to find themselves enslaved by the Foundation. (Rev: BL 5/15/06; HB 5–6/06; SLJ 1/07)

2205 Kaaberbol, Lene. *The Shamer's Daughter* (6–8). 2004, Holt $16.95 (978-0-8050-7541-0). Dina has inherited her mother's powers as a Shamer, able to ferret out the shameful truths that others try to hide; the 10-year-old sees her gift as a burden until she's called upon to use her powers to save her mother's life. The sequel is *The Shamer's Signet* (2005). (Rev: BL 4/15/04; HB 5–6/04; SLJ 6/04; VOYA 6/04)

2206 Kaaberbol, Lene. *The Shamer's War* (6–10). Series: The Shamer's Chronicles. 2006, Holt $17.95 (978-0-8050-7771-1). The final volume in this action-packed series featuring a battle between Prince Nicodemus and his acquisitive relative Drakan. (Rev: HB 11–12/06; SLJ 1/07)

2207 Kalman, Maira. *Swami on Rye: Max in India* (4–8). Illus. 1995, Viking $14.99 (978-0-670-84646-7). A sophisticated comic novel about a dog who goes to India to find the meaning of life. (Rev: BL 10/15/95; SLJ 11/95)

2208 Kassem, Lou. *A Summer for Secrets* (5–7). 1989, Avon paper $2.95 (978-0-380-75759-6). Laura's ability to communicate with animals causes complications. (Rev: BL 10/1/89)

2209 Kay, Elizabeth. *The Divide* (5–9). 2003, Scholastic $15.95 (978-0-439-45696-8). Felix, a 13-year-old with a heart problem, passes out while on a trip to Costa Rica and wakes up in a world full of mythical creatures. The sequel is *Back to the Divide* (2004). (Rev: BL 6/1–15/03; HBG 4/04; SLJ 9/03; VOYA 8/03)

2210 Keehn, Sally M. *Magpie Gabbard and the Quest for the Buried Moon* (5–8). 2007, Philomel $16.99 (978-0-399-24340-0). Thirteen-year-old Magpie Gabbard must fulfill a prophecy and put aside her cussedness in order to save the moon in this exuberant and complex tall tale. (Rev: BL 4/15/07; SLJ 2/07)

2211 Kelleher, Victor. *Brother Night* (7–9). 1991, Walker $16.95 (978-0-8027-8100-0). Rabon, 15, was raised by a foster father in a small town and ends up on a quest to the city with his dark, ugly twin, both learning about their heritage along the way. (Rev: BL 6/15/91; SLJ 5/91)

2212 Kempton, Kate. *The World Beyond the Waves: An Environmental Adventure* (5–7). Illus. 1995, Portunus $14.95 (978-0-9641330-6-8); paper $8.95 (978-0-9641330-1-3). After being washed overboard during a violent storm, Sam visits a land where she meets ocean animals that have been misused by humans. (Rev: BL 4/15/95; SLJ 3/95)

2213 Kendall, Carol. *The Gammage Cup* (4–7). Illus. by Erik Blegvad. 1990, Harcourt paper $6.00 (978-0-15-230575-8). A fantasy of the Minnipins, a small people of the "land between the mountains."

2214 Kennedy, James. *The Order of Odd-Fish* (7–12). 2008, Delacorte $15.99 (978-0-385-73543-8). A 13-year-old girl is transported to a strange world where she will play a key role in this involved tale full of absurdities and eccentricities. (Rev: BCCB 7–8/08; BL 8/08; LMC 8/08; SLJ 9/08)

2215 Kerr, P. B. *The Blue Djinn of Babylon* (5–8). Series: Children of the Lamp. 2006, Scholastic $16.99 (978-0-439-67021-0). Philippa Gaunt, 12, is wrongly convicted of cheating and her twin John must rescue her in this action-packed sequel to *The Akhenatan Adventure* (2005). (Rev: BL 3/15/06; SLJ 3/06; VOYA 2/06)

2216 Kessler, Liz. *Emily Windsnap and the Monster from the Deep* (4–7). Series: Emily Windsnap. 2006, Candlewick $15.99 (978-0-7636-2504-7). Half-human and half-mermaid, Emily Windsnap enjoys an idyllic life on Allpoints Island until she inadvertently awakens an evil monster named Kraken; a sequel to *The Tail of Emily Windsnap* (2004). (Rev: BL 6/1–15/06; SLJ 7/06)

2217 Kessler, Liz. *The Tail of Emily Windsnap* (4–7). Illus. by Sarah Gibb. Series: Emily Windsnap. 2004, Candlewick $15.99 (978-0-7636-2483-5). Twelve-year-old Emily Windsnap, who turns into a mermaid when she gets into the water, learns the truth about her parents. (Rev: BL 5/1/04; SLJ 6/04; VOYA 6/04)

2218 Kimmel, Elizabeth C. *The Ghost of the Stone Circle* (5–8). 1998, Scholastic paper $15.95 (978-0-590-21308-0). Fourteen-year-old Cristyn, who is spending the summer in Wales with her historian father, discovers a ghost in the house her father has rented. (Rev: BCCB 3/98; BL 4/15/98; HBG 10/98; SLJ 4/98; VOYA 8/98)

2219 Kindl, Patrice. *Goose Chase* (6–9). 2001, Houghton $16.00 (978-0-618-03377-5). A lively romp in true fairy-tale style that involves an enchanted Goose Girl who must escape a difficult choice between two unappealing suitors. (Rev: BCCB 4/01; BL 4/15/01; HB 7–8/01; HBG 10/01; SLJ 4/01; VOYA 6/01)

2220 King-Smith, Dick. *The Roundhill* (5–7). Illus. 2000, Random paper $4.99 (978-0-440-41844-3). In the English countryside in 1936, 14-year-old Evan meets a mysterious girl who seems to be the Alice of *Alice in Wonderland*. (Rev: BL 1/1–15/01; HBG 3/01; SLJ 12/00)

2221 Kirwan-Vogel, Anna. *The Jewel of Life* (6–8). Illus. 1991, Harcourt $15.95 (978-0-15-200750-8). Young orphan Duffy travels to other worlds, brings back a precious cockatrice feather, and creates the Philosopher's Stone. (Rev: BL 6/15/91; SLJ 6/91)

2222 Kluger, Jeffrey. *Nacky Patcher and the Curse of the Dry-Land Boats* (4–7). 2007, Philomel $18.99 (978-0-399-24604-3). When thief Nacky Patcher and orphan Teedie find a sailing ship floating in the lake, they try to persuade the hapless inhabitants of Yole to rally together to rebuild the vessel and escape their oppression by the cruel Baloo family. (Rev: BL 6/1–15/07; SLJ 7/07)

2223 Kluver, Cayla. *Legacy* (6–9). 2008, Forsooth $17.95 (978-0-9802089-7-9). In this romantic fantasy by a teen author, Princess Alera of Hytanica battles the requirement that she marry, while a boy named Narian, ostensibly from the enemy land of Cokyr, fights his destiny that he destroy Alera's kingdom. (Rev: BLO 6/17/08)

2224 Knox, Elizabeth. *Dreamquake: Book Two of the Dreamhunter Duet* (8–11). Series: Dreamhunter Duet. 2007, Farrar $19.00 (978-0-374-31854-3). Laura and her family are troubled by the government's dream-harvesting program in this follow-up to *Dreamhunter*. (Rev: BL 1/1–15/07; HB 3–4/07; SLJ 6/07)

2225 Koller, Jackie F. *If I Had One Wish . . .* (5–8). 1991, Little, Brown $14.95 (978-0-316-50150-7). When 8th-grader Alec is granted his wish that his little brother had never been born, he learns a lesson about charity, kindness, and old-fashioned family values. (Rev: BCCB 12/91; BL 11/1/91; SLJ 11/91)

2226 Konwicki, Tadeusz. *The Anthropos-Specter-Beast* (7–9). Trans. by George and Audrey Korwin-Rodziszewski. 1977, S. G. Phillips $26.95 (978-0-87599-218-1). Peter is transported to a remote place by the talking dog Sebastian.

2227 Kortum, Jeanie. *Ghost Vision* (5–8). Illus. by Dugald Stermer. 1983, Scholastic paper $3.50 (978-0-614-19197-4). A Greenland Inuit realizes that his son has special mystical powers.

2228 Kostick, Conor. *Epic* (7–10). 2007, Viking $17.99 (978-0-670-06179-2). Readers who enjoy role-playing games will love this book, a fantasy that takes place on New Earth, where violence occurs only in the computer game Epic. (Rev: BL 3/1/07; SLJ 5/07)

2229 Kostick, Conor. *Saga* (7–10). 2008, Viking $18.99 (978-0-670-06280-5). The world of Saga is a virtual reality, role-playing game that has its players captive, and it is up to 15-year-old Ghost and Eric to stop the Dark Queen, who is using Saga to control New Earth. A sequel to *Epic*. (Rev: BL 5/15/08; SLJ 7/08)

2230 Lally, Soinbhe. *A Hive for the Honeybee* (8–12). Illus. 1999, Scholastic paper $16.95 (978-0-590-51038-7). An allegory about life and work that takes place in a beehive with such characters as Alfred, the bee poet, and Mo, a radical drone. (Rev: BL 2/1/99; HB 3–4/99; HBG 10/99; SLJ 5/99*; VOYA 4/99)

2231 Landy, Derek. *Playing with Fire* (5–8). Series: Skulduggery Pleasant. 2008, HarperCollins $16.99 (978-0-06-124088-1). Skulduggery and 13-year-old Valkyrie (formerly known as Stephanie) must curb the evil Baron Vengeous, who plans to bring back to life a terrifying monster called the Grotesquery. (Rev: BL 6/1–15/08; SLJ 7/08)

2232 Landy, Derek. *Skulduggery Pleasant* (5–8). Illus. Series: Skulduggery Pleasant. 2007, Harper-Collins $17.99 (978-0-06-123115-5). When she inherits her Uncle Gordon's property, plucky 12-year-old Stephanie finds herself swept into an adventure combining magic, mystery, and violence in which her companion is a skeleton named Skulduggery Pleasant. (Rev: BL 5/1/07; HB 7–8/07; SLJ 6/07)

2233 Langrish, Katherine. *Troll Mill* (5–8). 2006, HarperCollins LB $17.89 (978-0-06-058308-8). In this sequel to *Troll Fell* (2004), 15-year-old Peer Ulfsson, who still worries about his cruel uncles and is increasingly involved with Hilde, must help protect a half-selkie baby from trolls and other threats. (Rev: BCCB 3/06; BL 2/1/06*; HBG 10/06; LMC 2/07; SLJ 3/06; VOYA 2/06)

2234 Langton, Jane. *The Fledgling* (5–7). 1980, HarperCollins LB $17.89 (978-0-06-023679-3); paper $6.99 (978-0-06-440121-0). A young girl learns to fly with her Goose Prince. A sequel is *The Fragile Flag* (1984). Also use *The Diamond in the Window* (1962).

2235 Larbalestier, Justine. *Magic or Madness* (8–11). 2005, Penguin $16.99 (978-1-59514-022-7). Australian 15-year-old Reason resists the idea of magic until she is transported from her grandmother's home to New York City and finds herself tackling new realities. (Rev: BCCB 3/05; BL 3/15/05*; SLJ 3/05; VOYA 2/05)

2236 Larbalestier, Justine. *Magic's Child* (8–11). Series: Magic or Madness. 2007, Penguin $16.99 (978-1-59514-064-7). Reason, now 15, pregnant, and on her own, struggles with her magical abilities in this final installment in the trilogy. (Rev: BCCB 6/07; BL 4/15/07; SLJ 5/07)

2237 Lasky, Kathryn. *Blood Secret* (6–10). 2004, HarperCollins LB $16.89 (978-0-06-000065-3). Silent since the sudden disappearance of her mother eight years earlier, 14-year-old Jerry Luna goes to live with a great-aunt where a trunk draws her into the time of the Spanish Inquisition and long-hidden secrets about her ancestors. (Rev: BL 10/1/04; SLJ 8/04; VOYA 10/04)

2238 Lasky, Kathryn. *The Capture* (5–8). 2003, Scholastic paper $5.99 (978-0-439-40557-7). Soren, a happy, well-adjusted young barn owl, falls from his nest and is stolen away by a group of owlet thieves bent on reeducation. (Rev: BL 9/15/03; SLJ 10/03)

2239 Law, Ingrid. *Savvy* (5–7). 2008, Dial $16.99 (978-0-8037-3306-0). On her 13th birthday, Mississippi ("Mibs" for short) is to find out what her "savvy," or ability, will be, and she ends up in a series of adventures on the road to this discovery. Newbery Honor Book, 2009. (Rev: BL 5/15/08; HB 1–2/08; LMC 8/08; SLJ 5/08)

2240 Lawrence, Michael. *A Crack in the Line* (8–12). Series: Withern Rise. 2004, HarperCollins $15.99 (978-0-06-072477-1). Still mourning his mother's death, 16-year-old Alaric discovers how to travel to an alternate reality where his mother is still alive. (Rev: BL 6/1–15/04*; SLJ 8/04)

2241 Lawrence, Michael. *The Underwood See* (8–11). Series: Withern Rise. 2007, Greenwillow $16.99 (978-0-06-072483-2). Readers of the previous books in the series (*The Crack in the Line* and *Small Eternities*, 2004 and 2005 respectively) will enjoy this final volume in which Naia, now pregnant, returns to the Underwood See to have her child there. (Rev: BL 5/15/07; SLJ 10/07)

2242 Lawson, Robert. *Rabbit Hill* (4–7). Illus. by author. 1944, Puffin paper $5.99 (978-0-14-031010-8). A warm and humorous story about the small creatures of a Connecticut countryside — each with a distinct personality. Newbery Medal winner, 1945.

2243 Laybourne, Emma. *Missing Magic* (4–7). 2007, Dial $16.99 (978-0-8037-3219-3). Ned, 11, is one of the few students at Leodwych who has no magic, but his practical abilities prove useful when he and two of his classmates are kidnapped. (Rev: BL 7/07; SLJ 9/07)

2244 Layefsky, Virginia. *Impossible Things* (5–8). 1998, Marshall Cavendish $14.95 (978-0-7614-5038-2). Twelve-year-old Brady has several personal and family problems to solve along with taking care of the dragonlike creature that he is hiding. (Rev: HBG 3/99; SLJ 11/98)

2245 Leavitt, Martine. *Keturah and Lord Death* (8–11). 2006, Front St. $16.95 (978-1-932425-29-1). After Keturah becomes lost in the woods and encounters Lord Death she must use her storytelling skills to convince him to let her go and in the process he falls in love with her. (Rev: BL 9/15/06)

2246 Le Guin, Ursula K. *Gifts* (6–10). 2004, Harcourt $17.00 (978-0-15-205123-5). In this engaging fantasy, Gry and Orrec, two Uplanders with supernatural abilities, are hesitant to use their awesome powers for fear that they will cause more harm than good. (Rev: BL 8/04*; SLJ 9/04; VOYA 12/04)

2247 Le Guin, Ursula K. *Powers* (8–12). Series: Annals of the Western Shore. 2007, Harcourt $17.00 (978-0-15-205770-1). The third book in the series continues the theme of a society based on slavery, with slave Gavir —who was kidnapped from his tribe as a child — running from his masters after his sister is raped. (Rev: BL 10/1/07; HB 9–10/07; SLJ 9/07) 🐾

2248 Le Guin, Ursula K. *Voices* (7–10). 2006, Harcourt $17.00 (978-0-15-205678-0). Seventeen-year-old Memer resents the conquerors who oppress her land and ban books and writing and goes on a quest to get revenge; a thought-provoking companion to *Gifts*. (Rev: BL 8/06; HB 9–10/06; LMC 3/07; SLJ 8/06*; VOYA) 🐾

2249 Le Guin, Ursula K. *A Wizard of Earthsea* (8–12). Illus. Series: Earthsea. 1968, Bantam paper $7.50 (978-0-553-26250-6). An apprentice wizard accidentally unleashes an evil power onto the land of Earthsea. Followed by *The Tombs of Atuan* and *The Farthest Shore.*

2250 L'Engle, Madeleine. *An Acceptable Time* (8–12). 1989, Farrar $18.00 (978-0-374-30027-2). Polly O'Keefe time-travels (as her parents did years before in the Time trilogy) but this time to visit a civilization of Druids that lived 3,000 years ago. (Rev: BL 1/1/90; SLJ 1/90; VOYA 4/90)

2251 Leonard, Elmore. *A Coyote's in the House* (5–8). 2004, HarperEntertainment $22.00 (978-0-06-072882-3). A coyote named Antwan strikes up a friendship with a couple of pampered dogs from Hollywood. (Rev: BL 5/15/04*)

2252 Levine, Gail Carson. *Ever* (6–10). 2008, HarperCollins $16.99 (978-0-06-122962-6). Olus, a god, is in love with Kezi, a human girl who is fated to be sacrificed to Admat, the god of oaths. (Rev: BL 4/1/08; SLJ 6/08)

2253 Levine, Gail Carson. *Fairest* (7–10). 2006, HarperCollins paper $17.00 (978-0-06-073408-4). An unattractive 15-year-old girl gains confidence as she comes to recognize her own strengths in this imaginative fairy tale. (Rev: BL 7/06; SLJ 9/06) 🐾

2254 Levine, Gail Carson. *The Two Princesses of Bamarre* (4–7). 2001, HarperCollins LB $17.89 (978-0-06-029316-1). Princess Addie sets out on a quest to find a cure for the Grey Death, a sickness that is destroying her older sister. (Rev: BCCB 10/01; BL 4/15/01; HB 5–6/01; HBG 10/01; SLJ 5/01)

2255 Lewis, C. S. *The Lion, the Witch and the Wardrobe* (5–8). Illus. Series: Narnia. 1988, Macmillan LB $22.95 (978-0-02-758200-0). Four children enter the kingdom of Narnia through the back of an old wardrobe. A special edition illustrated by Michael Hague. The other six volumes in this series are *Prince Caspian*, *The Voyage of the Dawn Treader*, *The Silver Chair*, *The Horse and His Boy*, *The Magician's Nephew*, and *The Last Battle*.

2256 Lewis, C. S. *The Lion, the Witch and the Wardrobe: A Story for Children* (4–7). Illus. by Pauline Baynes. 1988, Macmillan paper $7.95 (978-0-02-044490-9). A beautifully written adventure featuring four children who go into the magical land of Narnia.

2257 Lewis, Richard. *The Demon Queen* (8–11). 2008, Simon & Schuster $15.99 (978-1-4169-6226-7). Jesse, who appears to all to be a regular high-schooler, has a mysterious past that is made clear when it is revealed that he must fight a demon queen to save the world. (Rev: BL 5/15/08)

2258 Lindbergh, Anne. *The Hunky-Dory Dairy* (5–7). Illus. by Julie Brinckloe. 1986, Harcourt $14.95 (978-0-15-237449-5); Dell paper $2.75 (978-0-380-70320-3). Zannah visits a community magically removed from the 20th century and enjoys introducing the people to bubble gum, tacos, and other "modern" things. (Rev: BCCB 9/86; BL 4/1/86; SLJ 8/86)

2259 Lindbergh, Anne. *The Prisoner of Pineapple Place* (5–7). 1988, Harcourt $13.95 (978-0-15-263559-6); Avon paper $2.95 (978-0-380-70765-2). Pineapple Place is invisible to everyone except the inhabitants, and somehow finds itself landing in Connecticut. (Rev: BL 7/88; SLJ 8/88)

2260 Lindgren, Astrid. *Ronia, the Robber's Daughter* (4–7). 1985, Puffin paper $5.99 (978-0-14-031720-6). Ronia becomes friendly with the son of her father's rival in this fantasy.

2261 Lisle, Holly. *The Ruby Key* (6–10). Series: Moon & Sun. 2008, Scholastic $16.99 (978-0-545-00012-3). Genna and Danrith discover that the local nightlings have hatched an evil plan to do away with the nocturnal humans in their village in this first installment in the series. (Rev: BL 5/15/08; SLJ 6/08)

2262 Littlefield, Bill. *The Circus in the Woods* (6–10). 2001, Houghton $15.00 (978-0-618-06642-1). Mystery and fantasy are combined in this quiet, reflective story about a 13-year-old girl who finds a strange circus in the Vermont woods where she spends her summers. (Rev: BCCB 12/01; HBG 10/02; SLJ 11/01; VOYA 12/01)

2263 London, Dena. *Shapeshifter's Quest* (7–10). 2005, Dutton $16.99 (978-0-525-47310-7). Syanthe, a shape-shifting teenager, ventures outside the forest that has always been her home on a mission to unravel the secret of the king's black magic. (Rev: BL 10/1/05; SLJ 10/05; VOYA 8/05)

2264 Lott, Tim. *Fearless* (6–9). 2007, Candlewick $15.99 (978-0-7636-3637-1). In a dystopian future, orphan Little Fearless plans an escape from the workhouse in which she and a thousand other girls are imprisoned under the Controller. (Rev: BL 11/15/07; LMC 1/08; SLJ 3/08)

2265 Lowry, Lois. *Gathering Blue* (5–9). 2000, Houghton $16.00 (978-0-618-05581-4). In an inhospitable future world, young Kira must use her courage and her artistic talents. (Rev: BL 6/1–15/00*; HB 9–10/00; HBG 3/01; SLJ 8/00*)

2266 Lowry, Lois. *The Giver* (6–9). 1993, Houghton $16.00 (978-0-395-64566-6). A dystopian fantasy in which Jonas receives his life assignment as Receiver of Memory and learns that a land with no war, poverty, fear, or hardship is also one where "misfits" are killed. (Rev: BL 4/15/93*; SLJ 5/93*; VOYA 8/93)

2267 Lowry, Lois. *Gossamer* (5–8). 2006, Houghton $16.00 (978-0-618-68550-9). A spirit called Littlest One learns to mix memories that will heal people while they sleep. (Rev: BL 2/15/06; SLJ 5/06*; VOYA 8/06)

2268 Lowry, Lois. *Messenger* (6–10). 2004, Houghton $16.00 (978-0-618-40441-4). In the Village where teenage Matty is a caregiver, the residents decide to build a wall to keep out undesirables in this fantasy filled with truth and symbolism. (Rev: BL 2/15/04*; HB 5–6/04; SLJ 4/04; VOYA 6/04)

2269 Lyon, George E. *Here and Then* (6–8). 1994, Orchard paper $15.95 (978-0-531-06866-3). Abby, 13, becomes connected across time to Eliza, a nurse she portrays in a Civil War reenactment, and goes back in time to help her. (Rev: BL 10/1/94; SLJ 10/94; VOYA 10/94)

2270 Lyon, Steve. *The Gift Moves* (6–9). 2004, Houghton $15.00 (978-0-618-39128-8). In this quiet, futuristic novel set in an America devoid of wealth and materialism, Path Down the Mountain, a weaver's apprentice, and Bird Speaks, son of the local baker, strike up a friendship. (Rev: BL 6/1–15/04; SLJ 6/04; VOYA 6/04)

2271 Lyons, Mary. *Knockabeg: A Famine Tale* (4–7). 2001, Houghton $15.00 (978-0-618-09283-3). In order to protect the people of Knockabeg, faeries battle with the creatures who are causing the

blight during the great Irish potato famine. (Rev: BL 11/15/01; HBG 3/02; SLJ 9/01; VOYA 10/01)

2272 Lytle, Robert A. *Three Rivers Crossing* (5–8). 2000, River Road $15.95 (978-0-938682-55-4). After he suffers an accident while fishing, 7th-grader Walker wakes to find he is in the 1820s village of his ancestors. (Rev: BL 5/15/00; SLJ 6/00)

2273 McAllister, M. I. *Urchin of the Riding Stars* (5–8). Series: Mismantle Chronicles. 2005, Hyperion $17.95 (978-0-7868-5486-8). When his mentor, Captain Crispin, is unjustly accused of slaying the infant prince of Mismantle, Urchin the squirrel is determined to find out who is responsible for the crime. (Rev: BL 10/1/05; SLJ 11/05; VOYA 2/06)

2274 Macaulay, David. *Baaa* (6–10). Illus. 1985, Houghton paper $6.95 (978-0-395-39588-2). An allegory about the world after humans have left and intelligent sheep take control. (Rev: BL 9/1/85; SLJ 10/85)

2275 McCaffrey, Laura Williams. *Alia Waking* (5–7). 2003, Clarion $16.00 (978-0-618-19461-2). Alia, 12, and her best friend Kay long to become "keenten," or warrior women. (Rev: BL 3/1/03; HBG 10/03; SLJ 6/03; VOYA 10/03)

2276 McCaffrey, Laura Williams. *Water Shaper* (6–9). 2006, Clarion $16.00 (978-0-618-61489-9). Princess Margot leaves her father's strict kingdom in an adventure-laden search for her true home. (Rev: BL 5/15/06; SLJ 7/06)

2277 McCaughrean, Geraldine. *A Pack of Lies* (5–7). 1990, Macmillan $16.95 (978-0-7451-1154-4). Stories told by mysterious M.C.C. Berkshire, who wanders into an antique store run by adolescent Ailsa and her mother. (Rev: BCCB 5/89)

2278 McCaughrean, Geraldine. *Peter Pan in Scarlet* (6–9). Illus. by Scott M. Fischer. 2006, Simon & Schuster $17.99 (978-1-4169-1808-0). In this authorized sequel to J. M. Barrie's *Peter Pan,* the adventure continues — at breakneck speed — for Peter, Wendy, John, and the Lost Boys as they return to Neverland. (Rev: BL 11/15/06; HB 1–2/07; LMC 4-5/07; SLJ 12/06*) **⊘**

2279 McGann, Oisín. *The Gods and Their Machines* (8–11). 2004, Tor $19.95 (978-0-7653-1159-7). Fantasy and allegory are blended in this story about Chamus, a teenage Altiman fighter pilot trainee, whose denigration of the people of nearby Bartokhrin as ignorant religious fanatics is revised when a Bartokhrin girl helps him after his plane is forced to land near her home. (Rev: BL 12/15/04)

2280 MacHale, D. J. *The Lost City of Faar* (5–8). Series: Pendragon. 2003, Simon & Schuster paper $5.99 (978-0-7434-3732-5). After saving Denduron from Saint Dane in *The Merchant of Death* (2002), 14-year-old Bobby must confront the shape-changer again in Cloral, a world covered by water. (Rev: SLJ 5/03)

2281 MacHale, D. J. *The Rivers of Zadaa* (5–8). Series: Pendragon. 2005, Simon & Schuster $14.95 (978-1-4169-0710-7). Bobby Pendragon teams up with Loor to foil the villainous Saint Dane's plan to cut off the water supply to Loor's people in Zadaa. (Rev: SLJ 7/05)

2282 McKinley, Robin. *The Blue Sword* (7–10). 1982, Greenwillow $16.99 (978-0-688-00938-0). The king of Damar kidnaps a girl to help in his war against the Northerners. A prequel to *The Hero and the Crown*. Newbery Medal 1985. (Rev: BL 12/15/89)

2283 McKinley, Robin. *The Door in the Hedge* (6–9). 2003, Firebird paper $6.99 (978-0-698-11960-4). Four tales, two of which originated in the folklore of the Grimm Brothers.

2284 McKinley, Robin. *Dragonhaven* (8–11). 2007, Putnam $17.99 (978-0-399-24675-3). Jake, who lives on the dragon preserve at Smokehill National Park, rescues and cares for an orphaned dragon in this realistic novel with an environmental message. (Rev: BL 10/1/07; HB 9–10/07; LMC 3/08; SLJ 9/07)

2285 McKinley, Robin. *Rose Daughter* (6–12). Illus. 1997, Greenwillow $16.95 (978-0-688-15439-4). As in her award-winning *Beauty,* (1955) the author returns to the Beauty and the Beast fairy tale in this outstanding reworking of the traditional story. (Rev: BL 8/97; HBG 3/98; SLJ 9/97; VOYA 2/98) [398.2]

2286 McMann, Lisa. *Wake* (8–10). Series: Wake. 2008, Simon & Schuster $15.99 (978-1-4169-5969-4). Janie, 17, feels both cursed and blessed by her ability to enter and experience other people's dreams; then she begins to learn how to use her skill to help herself and others, including a boy named Cabel whose dreams include her. (Rev: BL 4/15/08; LMC 8//08; SLJ 3/08)

2287 McNamee, Eoin. *City of Time* (5–8). Series: The Navigator Trilogy. 2008, Random $16.99 (978-0-375-83912-2). The moon is inching toward Owen's home planet, causing panic and environmental changes, and Owen travels to the City of Time to try to set things right. (Rev: BL 5/15/08; SLJ 8/08)

2288 McNaughton, Janet. *An Earthly Knight* (7–10). 2004, HarperCollins $15.99 (978-0-06-008992-4). In this romantic fantasy, 16-year-old Jennie in Scotland falls in love with an enchanted lord and their love is so strong that it shatters a powerful curse. (Rev: BL 2/15/04; SLJ 3/04)

2289 McNish, Cliff. *Angel* (7–10). 2008, Carolrhoda $16.95 (978-0-8225-8900-6). Freya's belief in angels has led her into trouble in the past; now, at the age of 14, she realizes that the angels are real. (Rev: BL 6/1–15/08; SLJ 6/08)

2290 McNish, Cliff. *Breathe: A Ghost Story* (4–8). 2006, Carolrhoda LB $15.95 (978-0-8225-6443-0). After the death of his father, young Jack moves with his mother to an old farmhouse in the English countryside, a home that they share with the spirits of four children and the Ghost Mother who enslaved them. (Rev: SLJ 11/06)

2291 McNish, Cliff. *The Silver Child* (6–9). 2005, Carolrhoda $15.95 (978-1-57505-825-2). Mysteriously drawn to a huge garbage dump known as Coldharbour, six children undergo fantastic transformations. (Rev: BCCB 4/05; BL 4/15/05; SLJ 6/05; VOYA 6/05)

2292 McNish, Cliff. *Silver City* (5–8). Series: Silver Sequence. 2006, Carolrhoda $15.95 (978-1-57505-926-6). As the fearsome Roar draws closer to the Earth, Milo, Thomas, Helen, and their friends use their magical powers to keep the threat at bay; a sequel to *The Silver Child* (2005). (Rev: BL 6/1–15/06; SLJ 9/06)

2293 McNish, Cliff. *Silver World* (5–8). Series: The Silver Sequence. 2007, Carolrhoda LB $15.95 (978-1-57505-897-9). In this third volume in the series, Milo and the other children of Coldharbour use their extraordinary powers to protect the Earth from being destroyed by the terrifying monster called "The Roar." (Rev: SLJ 6/07)

2294 Maguire, Gregory. *What the Dickens* (6–9). 2007, Candlewick $15.99 (978-0-7636-2961-8). While seeking shelter from a storm, Gage tells his younger cousins an imaginative story about tooth fairies What-the-Dickens and Pepper. (Rev: BL 10/1/07; HB 9–10/07; LMC 1/08; SLJ 11/07)

2295 Mahy, Margaret. *Maddigan's Fantasia* (5–8). 2007, Simon & Schuster $17.99 (978-1-4169-1812-7). When 12-year-old Garland's father is killed, messengers from the future arrive to urge her to travel to a far-off town in search of a solar converter that will prevent future catastrophe. (Rev: BL 12/15/07; HB 11–12/07; LMC 2/08; SLJ 11/07)

2296 Malley, Gemma. *The Declaration* (6–10). 2007, Bloomsbury $16.95 (978-1-59990-119-0). In a world where people exchange childlessness for immortality, Surplus Anna should never have been born and lives a life of servitude. (Rev: BL 11/15/07; SLJ 2/08) 🏵

2297 Marillier, Juliet. *Wildwood Dancing* (8–11). 2007, Knopf $16.99 (978-0-375-83364-9). Five Transylvanian sisters live lives filled with magic, danger, and romance when they enter a portal into the Other Kingdom. (Rev: BCCB 3/07; BL 2/1/07; HB 3–4/07; LMC 4–5/07; SLJ 2/07*)

2298 Marr, Melissa. *Wicked Lovely* (7–12). 2007, HarperTeen $16.99 (978-0-06-121465-3). Aislinn, who can see fairies, is faced with a very difficult choice that involves all of humanity and faerie when the Summer King asks her to be his queen. (Rev: SLJ 7/07)

2299 Marriott, Zoë. *The Swan Kingdom* (6–9). 2008, Candlewick $16.99 (978-0-7636-3481-0). A fairy-tale-like fantasy in which 15-year-old Alexandra's mother is killed by a shapeshifter and her brothers changed into swans. Can Alexandra save them with her magic? (Rev: BL 1/1–15/08; SLJ 8/08)

2300 Marrone, Amanda. *Uninvited* (7–10). 2007, Simon & Schuster paper $8.99 (978-1-4169-3978-8). Jordan decides to clean up her act (really, her acting out with drugs and sex) when her vampire ex-boyfriend returns to haunt her. (Rev: BL 1/1–15/08; SLJ 11/07)

2301 Marsden, John. *Burning for Revenge* (8–12). Series: Tomorrow. 2000, Houghton $17.00 (978-0-395-96054-7). Ellie and her four Australian friends attack an airfield held by the enemy in this continuing saga. (Rev: BL 10/1/00; HBG 3/01; SLJ 10/00)

2302 Marsden, John. *The Night Is for Hunting* (8–12). Series: Tomorrow. 2001, Houghton $16.00 (978-0-618-07026-8). This sixth book in the Tomorrow series continues the action-packed story of a group of teenagers fighting to defend Australia against a band of invaders. (Rev: BCCB 2/02; BL 11/1/01; HBG 10/02; SLJ 10/01; VOYA 12/01)

2303 Marsh, Katherine. *The Night Tourist* (6–9). 2007, Hyperion $17.99 (978-1-4231-0689-0). Literate and erudite Jack finds he can see the dead after he is hit by a car and is led to another world via the New York subway and a girl called Euri; references to classic literature and mythology add depth to this story. (Rev: BL 11/1/07; SLJ 11/07)

2304 Martin, Rafe. *Birdwing* (5–8). 2005, Scholastic $16.99 (978-0-459-21167-7). This appealing fantasy picks up where "The Six Swans" by the Brothers Grimm ends, chronicling the story of Ardwin, the prince who was turned into a swan and then restored to human form apart from his left arm, which remains a swan's wing. (Rev: BCCB 12/05; BL 11/15/05; HB 1–2/06; SLJ 12/05; VOYA 12/05)

2305 Martini, Clem. *The Mob* (5–8). Series: Feather and Bone: The Crow Chronicles. 2004, Kids Can $16.95 (978-1-55337-574-6). As hundreds of crows of the Kinaar clan come together for their annual socialization at the Gathering Tree, internal conflicts threaten to tear the avian family apart in this first volume in a trilogy. (Rev: BL 10/1/04; SLJ 12/04)

2306 Masson, Sophie. *Serafin* (5–8). 2000, Saint Mary's paper $5.50 (978-0-88489-567-1). After he saves Calou from being lynched as a witch, Frederick is forced to flee his 17th-century French village with Calou and soon afterward realizes that the girl

is a matagot, a half-angel half-human creature. (Rev: SLJ 8/00)

2307 Masson, Sophie. *Snow, Fire, Sword* (6–9). 2006, HarperCollins $15.99 (978-0-06-079091-2). Teens Adi and Dewi must discern right from wrong in their quest to defeat a villainous sorcerer seeking to destroy the forces of good on their island nation of Jayanga. (Rev: BL 5/15/06; SLJ 10/06)

2308 Matas, Carol, and Perry Nodelman. *Out of Their Minds* (5–8). Illus. Series: Minds. 1998, Simon & Schuster $16.00 (978-0-689-81946-9). In this fantasy (the third in the series), Princess Lenora and Prince Coren journey to Andilla to marry but find that some force is upsetting The Balance. (Rev: HBG 3/99; SLJ 9/98; VOYA 2/99)

2309 Matthews, L. S. *A Dog for Life* (5–7). 2006, Delacorte $14.95 (978-0-385-73366-3). Tom is sick and Mouse the dog is banished on grounds of possible infection, so John and Mouse, who can communicate psychically, set out to find Mouse a new home. (Rev: BL 12/1/06*; SLJ 10/06) ⊚

2310 Mebus, Scott. *Gods of Manhattan* (5–8). Series: Gods of Manhattan. 2008, Dutton $17.99 (978-0-525-47955-0). Rory discovers that he has the ability to see figures from New York history (such as Peter Stuyvesant and Babe Ruth) and that he must use this power to save Manhattan. (Rev: BL 5/15/08; SLJ 4/08)

2311 Melling, O. R. *The Light-Bearer's Daughter* (7–11). Series: Chronicles of Faerie. 2007, Abrams $16.95 (978-0-8109-0781-2). In a forest in the fairy realm, 12-year-old Dana embarks on a dangerous mission to deliver a message to the fairy High King; and in contemporary Ireland activists work to save the forest from developers. (Rev: BL 5/15/07)

2312 Melling, O. R. *The Summer King* (8–11). 2005, Abrams $16.95 (978-0-8109-5969-9). Laurel visits her grandparents in Ireland a year after her twin sister's death and discovers a hidden world of fairies, who enlist her help to save their kingdom. (Rev: BL 4/15/06; SLJ 8/06)

2313 Melling, Orla. *The Druid's Tune* (6–10). 1993, O'Brien paper $9.95 (978-0-86278-285-6). Peter, a Druid lost in the 20th century, involves two teenagers in a time-travel spell that sends them back to Ireland's Iron Age. (Rev: BL 2/15/93)

2314 Meyer, Kai. *Pirate Curse* (6–9). Trans. by Elizabeth D. Crawford. Series: Wave Walkers. 2006, Simon & Schuster $15.95 (978-1-4169-2421-0). This first book in the series features the adventures of Jolly, a 14-year-old girl who has the ability to walk on water. (Rev: BL 6/1–15/06; LMC 2/07; SLJ 6/06)

2315 Meyer, Kai. *Pirate Emperor* (6–9). Trans. from German by Elizabeth D. Crawford. Series: Wave Walkers. 2007, Simon & Schuster $16.99

(978-1-4169-2474-6). Readers of *Pirate Curse* will enjoy this sequel in which the magical pirate characters encounter thrilling battles and adventures. (Rev: SLJ 6/07)

2316 Meyer, Kai. *The Stone Light* (5–7). Trans. from German by Elizabeth D. Crawford. Series: The Dark Reflections Trilogy. 2006, Simon & Schuster $16.95 (978-0-689-87789-6). Desperately searching for help in their fight to free Venice from the evil Egyptian pharaoh, Merle travels on Vermithrax, the flying lion, to Hell in hopes of convincing Lucifer to ally himself with their cause; the sequel to *The Water Mirror* (2005). (Rev: BL 3/15/07; SLJ 1/07)

2317 Meyer, Kai. *The Water Mirror* (4–7). Trans. by Elizabeth D. Crawford. Series: Dark Reflections. 2005, Simon & Schuster $15.95 (978-0-689-87787-2). In an alternate Venice in danger of destruction, 14-year-old Merle, a plucky orphan, finds herself playing a central role; the first volume in a series noted for its setting; sequels are *The Stone Light* (2007) and *The Glass Word* (2008). (Rev: BL 1/1–15/06; SLJ 11/05*; VOYA 12/05) ⊚

2318 Michael, Livi. *City of Dogs* (5–8). 2007, Putnam $16.99 (978-0-399-24356-1). Sam has always wanted a dog and is happy when Jenny comes to live with him, but Jenny's mission becomes overarching and she must take on friends and foes in this fantasy full of mythological references. (Rev: BCCB 11/07; LMC 11-12/07; SLJ 11/07)

2319 Miéville, China. *Un Lun Dun* (5–9). 2007, Del Rey $17.95 (978-0-345-49516-7). In contemporary London, Zanna and her friend Deeba find themselves on the edge of a strange Unlondon that is awaiting a chosen one. (Rev: SLJ 4/07*)

2320 Mitchell, Todd. *The Traitor King* (7–10). 2007, Scholastic $16.99 (978-0-439-82788-1). Darren and Jackie discover their uncle in Maine is missing; their search for him leads them to family secrets, magical powers, and an alternate world. (Rev: BL 6/1–15/07; LMC 10/07; SLJ 5/07)

2321 Moesta, Rebecca, and Kevin J. Anderson. *Crystal Doors* (6–9). 2006, Little, Brown $15.99 (978-0-316-01055-9). Fourteen-year-old cousins Gwen and Vic are transported to the island world of Elantya, where they find magic and conflict. (Rev: BL 7/06; LMC 2/07; SLJ 9/06)

2322 Molloy, Michael. *The House on Falling Star Hill* (4–8). 2004, Scholastic $16.95 (978-0-439-57740-3). While spending a vacation with his grandparents in a peaceful English village, Tim discovers an alternate world called Tallis and becomes involved in the turmoil taking place there. (Rev: BL 4/15/04; SLJ 4/04)

2323 Molloy, Michael. *The Time Witches* (5–8). 2002, Scholastic paper $4.99 (978-0-439-42090-7). The characters from *The Witch Trade* (2002) return in this sequel in which Abby, a Light Witch, and her friends must travel into the past to foil a plot hatched by the nefarious Wolfbane. (Rev: BL 1/1–15/03; SLJ 8/03)

2324 Moore, Perry. *Hero* (8–11). 2007, Hyperion $16.99 (978-1-4231-0195-6). Thom, who hides his developing superpowers and his homosexual feelings from his once superhero father, joins the League as an apprentice. (Rev: BL 8/07; HB 9–10/07; LMC 11/07; SLJ 9/07)

2325 Morden, Simon. *The Lost Art* (7–10). 2008, Random $16.99 (978-0-385-75147-6). The world has entered a new dark age, with books and knowledge locked away, and it is up to Va and Benzamir Michael Mahmood to rescue them in this fantasy with action, suspense and romance. (Rev: BL 5/15/08; LMC 4–5/08; SLJ 11/08)

2326 Moredun, P. R. *The Dragon Conspiracy* (5–8). Series: World of Eldaterra. 2005, HarperCollins LB $17.89 (978-0-06-076664-1). A complex first installment in which a British schoolboy in 1910 must battle female dragons to save both our world and the magical parallel world of Eldaterra. (Rev: BL 6/1–15/05; SLJ 10/05)

2327 Morpurgo, Michael. *Little Foxes* (6–9). 1987, David & Charles $15.95 (978-0-7182-3972-5). Two orphans — a boy and a fox — are helped by a swan in this magical story. (Rev: SLJ 9/87)

2328 Morris, Gerald. *Parsifal's Page* (5–8). 2001, Houghton $16.00 (978-0-618-05509-8). Piers becomes a page to Parsifal and accompanies the innocent young man on his quest to become a knight. (Rev: BCCB 4/01; BL 4/15/01; HB 5–6/01; HBG 10/01; SLJ 4/01; VOYA 6/01)

2329 Morris, Gerald. *The Princess, the Crone, and the Dung-Cart Knight* (6–9). 2004, Houghton $17.00 (978-0-618-37823-4). In this absorbing Arthurian fantasy, 13-year-old Sarah enlists help from others in her quest to identify those who instigated the murderous riot that took the lives of her mother and their Jewish friend. (Rev: BCCB 3/04; BL 4/15/04; HB 5–6/04; SLJ 5/04; VOYA 6/04)

2330 Morris, Gerald. *The Savage Damsel and the Dwarf* (5–8). 2000, Houghton $16.00 (978-0-395-97126-0). Sixteen-year-old Lady Lynet travels to Camelot, in the company of a dwarf, to ask King Arthur's aid in defeating her sister's suitor. (Rev: BL 3/1/00; HB 5–6/00; HBG 10/00; SLJ 5/00; VOYA 6/00)

2331 Mullin, Caryl Cude. *A Riddle of Roses* (4–7). 2000, Second Story paper $6.95 (978-1-896764-28-3). Meryl, who has been expelled from school for a year, goes on a quest to Avalon to find her own wisdom. (Rev: BL 2/15/01; VOYA 4/01)

2332 Murdock, Catherine Gilbert. *Princess Ben* (8–11). 2008, Houghton $16.00 (978-0-618-95971-6). The princess of the title (whose full name is

Benevolence) must take on new responsibilities when her parents and her uncle are killed and she learns magic secrets. (Rev: BL 5/15/08; SLJ 6/08)

2333 Myers, Edward. *Storyteller* (6–9). 2008, Clarion $16.00 (978-0-618-69541-6). A 17-year-old storyteller sets off to seek his fortune, gathering stories from characters he meets and finding work, romance, and trouble — and in the process teaching the reader about the value of stories. (Rev: BL 8/08; SLJ 9/08)

2334 Myers, Walter Dean. *The Legend of Tarik* (6–9). 1991, Scholastic paper $3.50 (978-0-590-44426-2). Tarik, a black teenager in Africa of years ago, acquires a magic sword.

2335 Neumeier, Rachel. *The City in the Lake* (8–11). 2008, Knopf $15.99 (978-0-375-84704-2). When Prince Cassiel disappears from the City in the Lake, so does the city's life and magic. Neill and Timou set off in search of him and learn about their heritage as they battle the forces that threaten the kingdom. (Rev: BL 5/15/08; SLJ 9/08)

2336 Nicholson, William. *Noman* (7–10). Series: Noble Warriors. 2008, Harcourt paper $14.00 (978-0-15-206005-3). In the third book of this unusually contemplative trilogy, Seeker, Morning Star and the Wildman search for a new leader. (Rev: BL 5/15/08; SLJ 8/08)

2337 Nicholson, William. *Seeker* (6–9). 2006, Harcourt $17.00 (978-0-15-205768-8). This fantasy with a religious theme tells the story of Seeker, a 16-year old who tries to protect his religion from those who wish to destroy it; the sequel is *Jango* (2007). (Rev: BL 6/1–15/06; LMC 1/07; SLJ 8/06)

2338 Nigg, Joseph. *How to Raise and Keep a Dragon* (5–10). Illus. by Dan Malone. 2006, Barron's $18.99 (978-0-7641-5920-6). This whimsical guide to the care and feeding of dragons offers tips for selecting just the right type of dragon, finding the correct equipment and supplies, establishing good modes of communication, and training for competitions. (Rev: SLJ 11/06)

2339 Nimmo, Jenny. *Charlie Bone and the Time Twister* (5–7). 2003, Scholastic $10.99 (978-0-439-49687-2). In 1916 Henry Yewbeam finds a strange marble and is transported to the present-day Bloor's Academy, where Charlie Bone tests his magical abilities in an effort to send him home. A sequel to *Midnight for Charlie Bone* (2003). (Rev: BL 9/15/03; HBG 4/04; SLJ 10/03)

2340 Nimmo, Jenny. *Griffin's Castle* (5–8). 1997, Orchard LB $17.99 (978-0-531-33006-7). When Dinah and her young mother, Rosalie, move into the rundown mansion owned by Rosalie's boyfriend, Dinah brings to life several carved animals for protection. (Rev: SLJ 6/97; VOYA 8/97)

2341 Nix, Garth. *Above the Veil* (5–7). Series: The Seventh Tower. 2001, Scholastic paper $5.99 (978-0-439-17685-9). In episode four in this series, Tal and Milla continue their otherworldly adventures full of action, secrets, and surprising twists and turns. (Rev: SLJ 9/01)

2342 Nix, Garth. *Grim Tuesday* (5–8). Series: Keys to the Kingdom. 2004, Scholastic paper $7.99 (978-0-439-43655-7). Arthur Penhaligon returns in this second installment in the series to the house that holds an alternate universe and there must challenge the evil Grim Tuesday, who threatens to destroy everything; the next volume is *Drowned Wednesday* (2005). (Rev: SLJ 8/04)

2343 Nix, Garth. *Lady Friday* (6–9). Series: The Keys to the Kingdom. 2007, Scholastic $17.99 (978-0-439-70088-7). A funny, well-written tale in the popular but complex series that finds Arthur challenged by Lady Friday for control of the Middle House. (Rev: SLJ 6/07)

2344 Nix, Garth. *Mister Monday* (5–8). Series: The Keys to the Kingdom. 2003, Scholastic paper $6.99 (978-0-439-55123-6). When 7th-grader Arthur Penhaligon receives a healing key from a mysterious stranger, the gift turns out to be a mixed blessing that brings illness and strange creatures seeking to reclaim the key. (Rev: BCCB 1/04; SLJ 12/03)

2345 Nix, Garth. *One Beastly Beast: Two Aliens, Three Inventors, Four Fantastic Tales* (5–7). Illus. by Brian Biggs. 2007, Eos $15.99 (978-0-06-084319-9). Four short stories accompanied by cartoonish illustrations for readers who enjoy fantasy that's not too far out or too scary. (Rev: BCCB 10/07; BL 7/07; SLJ 9/07)

2346 Nyoka, Gail. *Mella and the N'anga: An African Tale* (5–8). 2006, Sumach paper $9.95 (978-1-894549-49-3). Mella, the daughter of a king in ancient Zimbabwe, with the help of the magical powers she learns from the spiritual adviser called N'anga, strives to save her father's life and realm. (Rev: BL 3/1/06; SLJ 7/06)

2347 O'Brien, Robert C. *Mrs. Frisby and the Rats of NIMH* (5–7). Illus. by Zena Bernstein. 1971, Macmillan $18.00 (978-0-689-20651-1); paper $5.50 (978-0-689-71068-1). Saga of a group of rats made literate and given human intelligence by a series of experiments, who escape from their laboratory to found their own community. Newbery Medal winner, 1972.

2348 Okorafor-Mbachu, Nnedi. *The Shadow Speaker* (5–8). 2007, Hyperion $16.99 (978-1-4231-0033-1). West Africa is a very different place in 2070 in this futuristic tale in which Muslim Ejii, 15, shadow-speaks with the queen who had her father killed years earlier. (Rev: BL 3/1/08; SLJ 2/08)

2349 Okorafor-Mbachu, Nnedi. *Zahrah the Windseeker* (5–8). 2005, Houghton $16.00 (978-0-618-

34090-3). In this appealing debut novel, 13-year-old Zahrah, a "dada girl" readily identifiable by her telltale vine-entwined dreadlocks, struggles to come to terms with her magical powers. (Rev: BL 11/15/05; SLJ 12/05)

2350 Orgel, Doris. *The Princess and the God* (7–10). 1996, Orchard LB $16.99 (978-0-531-08866-1). A handsome retelling of the Cupid and Psyche myth in novel format, in which the power of pure love is shown conquering overwhelming obstacles. (Rev: BL 2/1/96; SLJ 4/96)

2351 Osborne, Mary Pope. *Haunted Waters* (6–8). 2006, Candlewick $14.99 (978-0-7636-2995-3). The story, based on an old fairy tale and beautifully written, of the troubled marriage of a mermaid and a human; by the author of the Magic Treehouse books. (Rev: SLJ 9/06)

2352 Osterweil, Adam. *The Amulet of Komondor* (5–7). 2003, Front St. $15.95 (978-1-886910-81-2). Finding themselves in a parallel world of "Japanimations," Joe and Katie face a mighty challenge, worry about how to get home, and continue their real-world romance in this lighthearted fantasy with *anime*-style illustrations. (Rev: BL 11/15/03; HBG 4/04; SLJ 12/03)

2353 Owen, James A. *Here, There Be Dragons* (8–11). Illus. Series: Chronicles of Imaginarium Geographica. 2006, Simon & Schuster $9.99 (978-1-4169-1227-9). John, Jack, and Charles — English intellectuals who will one day be known as J. R. R. Tolkien, C. S. Lewis, and Charles Williams — sail to the Archipelago of Dreams to defeat the Winter King. (Rev: BL 12/15/06; LMC 2/07; SLJ 11/06)

2354 Owen, James A. *The Search for the Red Dragon* (8–11). Illus. by author. Series: Chronicles of the Imaginarium Geographica. 2008, Simon & Schuster $17.99 (978-1-4169-4850-6). In this sequel to *Here, There Be Dragons*, the caretakers of the Imaginarium must solve the mystery behind the disappearance of the Archipelago's children. (Rev: BL 4/15/08; SLJ 2/08)

2355 Page, Jan. *Rewind* (7–10). 2005, Walker $16.95 (978-0-8027-8995-2). When he is injured in an accident while playing drums onstage, Liam finds himself back in time watching his parents as teenagers, when they had a band whose drummer was killed. (Rev: BL 9/1/05; SLJ 11/05; VOYA 10/05)

2356 Paolini, Christopher. *Eldest* (8–11). Series: Inheritance. 2005, Knopf LB $24.99 (978-0-375-92670-9). Eragon continues his training as a Dragon Rider while his cousin Roran is under threat in this second installment in the trilogy. (Rev: BL 8/05; SLJ 10/05; VOYA 12/05)

2357 Paolini, Christopher. *Eragon* (7–12). Series: Inheritance. 2003, Knopf LB $20.99 (978-0-375-92668-6). A 15-year-old boy called Eragon finds a

stone that hatches a magnificent blue dragon, drawing him into a series of dangerous adventures as the two hunt killers and in turn are hunted. (Rev: BL 8/03*; HBG 4/04; SLJ 9/03; VOYA 8/03)

2358 Papademetriou, Lisa. *The Wizard, the Witch, and Two Girls from Jersey* (6–9). 2006, Penguin paper $8.99 (978-1-59514-074-6). Veronica and Heather find themselves transported into the fantasy world of a novel they're reading for a high school English class. (Rev: BL 5/15/06; LMC 2/07; SLJ 10/06)

2359 Park, Linda Sue. *Archer's Quest* (4–7). 2006, Clarion $16.00 (978-0-618-59631-7). An ancient Korean ruler suddenly appears in the New York State bedroom of 12-year-old Kevin and the two must work out how to get him back home before the Year of the Tiger ends. (Rev: BL 3/15/06; SLJ 5/06)

2360 Patterson, James. *Maximum Ride: School's Out — Forever* (7–10). 2006, Little, Brown $16.99 (978-0-316-15559-5). In this sequel to *The Angel Experiment* (2004), Max and her fellow bird-humans try to integrate into mainstream society but must overcome unexpected danger and betrayal. (Rev: BL 5/15/06; SLJ 8/06)

2361 Patterson, James. *Maximum Ride: The Angel Experiment* (7–9). 2005, Little, Brown $16.99 (978-0-316-15556-4). An engaging tale about a group of children, part human and part bird, who escape from the lab where they were bred and now must track down one of their number who's been kidnapped. (Rev: BCCB 4/05; BL 2/1/05; SLJ 5/05; VOYA 4/06)

2362 Pattou, Edith. *East* (6–10). 2003, Harcourt $18.00 (978-0-15-204563-0). A great white bear carries Rose away from home to her destiny in this romantic novelization of the East o' the Sun and West o' the Moon fairy tale. (Rev: BL 9/1/03*; HBG 4/04; SLJ 12/03; VOYA 12/03)

2363 Paul, Donita K. *Dragonspell* (4–8). 2004, WaterBrook paper $12.99 (978-1-57856-823-9). Fourteen-year-old Kale is the protagonist of this classic quest tale, set in the world of Amara, with Christian overtones reminiscent of C. S. Lewis. (Rev: SLJ 11/04)

2364 Paver, Michelle. *Soul Eater* (6–9). Illus. by Geoff Taylor. Series: Chronicles of Ancient Darkness. 2007, HarperCollins $16.99 (978-0-06-072831-1). The third book in the series finds Torak and Renn traveling north to rescue Wolf, who has been taken into the icy wilderness by Soul Eaters. (Rev: BL 3/15/07; SLJ 5/07)

2365 Paver, Michelle. *Spirit Walker* (6–9). Series: Chronicles of Ancient Darkness. 2006, HarperCollins LB $17.89 (978-0-06-072829-8). Young Stone Age survivor Torak seeks a remedy for the epidemic affecting the clans and is reunited with his beloved Wolf in this sequel to *Wolf Brother* (2005). (Rev: BL 2/15/06; SLJ 6/06; VOYA 2/06)

2366 Pearce, Philippa. *Tom's Midnight Garden* (4–7). Illus. by Susan Einzig. 1959, Dell paper $6.99 (978-0-06-440445-7). When the clock strikes 13, Tom visits his garden and meets Hatty, a strange mid-Victorian girl.

2367 Peck, Dale. *The Drift House: The First Voyage* (8–11). 2005, Bloomsbury $16.95 (978-1-58234-969-5). The Oakenfield siblings are sent to live with their Uncle Farley in Canada, and when their uncle's ship-like home is swept away in a flood, they enjoy a magical journey on the Sea of Time. (Rev: BL 10/1/05; SLJ 11/05; VOYA 10/05)

2368 Peck, Dale. *The Lost Cities: A Drift House Voyage* (8–11). 2007, Bloomsbury $16.95 (978-1-58234-859-9). Siblings Susan and Charles, who first traveled the Sea of Time in *The Drift House: The First Voyage* (2005), are afloat again in this action-packed sequel, this time battling Vikings and a time jetty. (Rev: BL 4/1/07; SLJ 4/07)

2369 Pemberton, Bonnie. *The Cat Master* (5–8). 2007, Marshall Cavendish $16.99 (978-0-7614-5340-6). A dying Cat Master's telepathic message to his successor — indoor cat but formerly feral Buddy — is intercepted by the evil cat Jett, and Buddy and his friends must fight for justice to be fulfilled. (Rev: BL 6/1–15/07; SLJ 6/07)

2370 Perrin, Randy, et al. *Time Like a River* (5–7). 1997, RDR $14.95 (978-1-57143-061-8). Margie travels back in time to find a cure for her mother's mysterious illness. (Rev: HBG 3/98; SLJ 3/98)

2371 Pierce, Tamora. *Briar's Book* (5–9). Series: Circle of Magic. 1999, Scholastic paper $15.95 (978-0-590-55359-9). In this fantasy, Briar, a former street urchin and petty thief, and his teacher, Rosethorn, search for the cause of a deadly plague that is sweeping through their land. (Rev: BL 2/15/99; HBG 10/99; SLJ 3/99; VOYA 6/99)

2372 Pierce, Tamora. *Cold Fire* (6–10). Series: The Circle Opens. 2002, Scholastic $16.95 (978-0-590-39655-4). Daja is studying in the chilly northern city of Kugisko, where her ability to handle fire comes in handy but also draws her into a relationship with an arsonist. (Rev: BL 9/1/02; HB 7–8/02; HBG 10/02; SLJ 8/02; VOYA 6/02)

2373 Pierce, Tamora. *Daja's Book* (5–9). Series: Circle of Magic. 1998, Scholastic paper $15.95 (978-0-590-55358-2). Daja, a mage-in-training, uses her magical powers to create a living vine out of metal, and soon members of the nomadic Traders want to possess it. (Rev: BCCB 12/98; BL 12/1/98; HBG 3/99; SLJ 12/98; VOYA 2/99)

2374 Pierce, Tamora. *Lady Knight* (6–9). Series: Protector of the Small. 2002, Random $16.95 (978-0-375-81465-5). Now a knight, Kel is disappointed when her first assignment is to command a refugee camp. (Rev: BL 10/1/02; HBG 3/03; SLJ 12/02; VOYA 2/03)

2375 Pierce, Tamora. *Magic Steps* (5–9). Series: The Circle Opens. 2000, Scholastic paper $16.95 (978-0-590-39588-5). Fourteen-year-old Sandry and her friend Pasco use their magic to stop the murders of local merchants. (Rev: BCCB 3/00; BL 3/1/00; HB 5–6/00; HBG 10/00; SLJ 4/00)

2376 Pierce, Tamora. *Shatterglass* (6–9). Series: The Circle Opens. 2003, Scholastic $16.95 (978-0-590-39683-7). Tris, 14, joins forces with another mage, Kethlun, whose glass-blowing skills help them solve a series of murders. (Rev: BL 3/1/03; HB 5–6/03; HBG 10/03; SLJ 7/03; VOYA 6/03)

2377 Pierce, Tamora. *Terrier* (7–10). 2006, Random $18.95 (978-0-375-81468-6). Sixteen-year-old orphan Beka Cooper becomes a trainee (or Puppy) with the city guards (Dogs) and uses her magical abilities to good effect, relating her exploits in her journal. (Rev: BL 11/15/06; HB 1–2/07; SLJ 2/07*)

2378 Pierce, Tamora. *Trickster's Queen* (7–12). 2004, Random LB $19.99 (978-0-375-81467-9). In this thrilling sequel to *Trickster's Choice*, Aly must call upon her magical powers to protect the Balitang children and ensure that one of them — Dove — ascends to the throne of the Copper Isles. (Rev: BCCB 10/04; BL 10/1/04; SLJ 9/04; VOYA 2/05)

2379 Pierce, Tamora. *Tris's Book* (5–9). Series: Circle of Magic. 1998, Scholastic paper $15.95 (978-0-590-55357-5). Tris and her three fellow mages combine forces to fight the pirates who are threatening to destroy their home in this sequel to *Sandry's Book*. (Rev: BCCB 4/98; BL 8/98; HBG 10/98; SLJ 4/98; VOYA 8/98)

2380 Pierce, Tamora. *The Will of the Empress* (8–11). 2005, Scholastic $17.99 (978-0-439-44171-1). Bowing to the will of the Empress of Namorn, Sandry, accompanied by her mage friends from the Winding Circle, embarks on a perilous journey to visit her cousin, the empress; this stand-alone novel comes after the Circle of Magic and The Circle Opens quartets. (Rev: BCCB 1/06; BL 11/15/05*; HB 11–12/05; SLJ 11/05; VOYA 10/05)

2381 Popescu, Petru. *Birth of the Pack* (8–11). Series: Weregirls. 2007, Tor $12.95 (978-0-7653-1641-7). The members of the Weregirls soccer team find that they have magical powers to fight evil — and the mean girls at school. (Rev: BL 10/1/07; LMC 1/08; SLJ 12/07)

2382 Porte, Barbara Ann. *Hearsay: Tales from the Middle Kingdom* (5–8). Illus. 1998, Greenwillow $15.00 (978-0-688-15381-6). Each of these 15 entertaining fantasies contains elements of Chinese folklore and culture. (Rev: BCCB 5/98; HBG 10/98; SLJ 6/98)

2383 Pratchett, Terry. *A Hat Full of Sky* (6–10). 2004, HarperCollins $16.99 (978-0-06-058660-7). Witch-in-training Tiffany Aching battles a monster with help from the wee men and head witch Granny Weatherwax in the sequel to *The Wee Free Men*. (Rev: BCCB 5/04; BL 4/15/04; HB 7–8/04; SLJ 7/04; VOYA 6/04)

2384 Pratchett, Terry. *Wintersmith* (7–10). 2006, HarperTempest $16.99 (978-0-06-089031-5). Tiffany Aching, a 13-year-old witch, must find a way to bring back spring, with the help of her friends the Wee Free Men, after the god of winter falls in love with her and will do anything to keep her in his frozen world. (Rev: BL 9/1/06; SLJ 11/06)

2385 Prevost, Guillaume. *The Book of Time* (5–8). Trans. by William Rodarmor. Series: The Book of Time. 2007, Scholastic $16.99 (978-0-439-88375-7). Sam travels through time — to medieval Scotland, World War I France, and ancient Egypt — to find his missing father and finally discovers he's being held captive in Dracula's castle in this first installment in the series. (Rev: BCCB 9/07; BL 7/07; HB 9–10/07; SLJ 11/07) 🏅

2386 Prue, Sally. *Cold Tom* (4–8). 2003, Scholastic $15.95 (978-0-439-48268-4). Tom has disabilities that make him an outcast, and he flees from his elfin tribe to the city inhabited by demons (humans), where he is confronted with his human side. (Rev: BL 9/15/03; HB 7–8/03*; HBG 10/03; SLJ 9/03*; VOYA 10/03)

2387 Pullman, Philip. *The Amber Spyglass* (7–12). Series: His Dark Materials. 2000, Knopf $19.95 (978-0-679-87926-8). Lyra and Will are key figures in the battle between good and evil in this final volume in the prize-winning trilogy. (Rev: BL 10/1/00; HB 11–12/00; HBG 3/01; SLJ 10/00)

2388 Pullman, Philip. *The Golden Compass* (7–12). Series: His Dark Materials. 1996, Knopf $20.00 (978-0-679-87924-4). In this first book of a fantasy trilogy, young Lyra and her alter ego, a protective animal named Pantalaimon, escape from the child-stealing Gobblers and join a group heading north to rescue a band of missing children. (Rev: BL 3/1/96*; SLJ 4/96)

2389 Pullman, Philip. *Lyra's Oxford* (5–8). Illus. by John Lawrence. 2003, Knopf $10.95 (978-0-375-82819-5). This slim volume takes readers back to the world of Pullman's His Dark Materials trilogy, with maps, postcards, and other ephemera. (Rev: BL 2/1/04; SLJ 1/04; VOYA 6/04)

2390 Pullman, Philip. *Once Upon a Time in the North* (7–10). Illus. by John Lawrence. Series: His Dark Materials. 2008, Knopf $12.99 (978-0-375-84510-9). The story of how Lee Scoresby and bear Iorke Byrnison — of the His Dark Materials trilogy — met for the first time in an arctic frontier town; a board game is included with the book. (Rev: BL 5/15/08; LMC 10/08; SLJ 8/08; VOYA 4/08) 🏅

2391 Pullman, Philip. *The Subtle Knife* (7–12). Series: His Dark Materials. 1997, Random $20.00 (978-0-679-87925-1). In this second volume of a trilogy, Will and Lyra travel from world to world searching for the mysterious Dust and Will's long-lost father. (Rev: BL 7/97; HBG 3/98; SLJ 10/97)

2392 Purtill, Richard. *Enchantment at Delphi* (6–9). 1986, Harcourt $14.95 (978-0-15-200447-7). On a trip to Delphi, Alice finds herself transported back in time to the days of Apollo and other Greek gods. (Rev: SLJ 11/86)

2393 Randall, David. *Chandlefort: In the Shadow of the Bear* (7–12). 2006, Simon & Schuster $16.95 (978-0-689-87870-1). In this sequel to *Clovermead* (2004), the title character discovers she is really the royal Demoiselle Cerelune Cindertallow and the 13-year-old must learn a whole new way of living; a complex and multilayered fantasy. (Rev: SLJ 7/07)

2394 Reeve, Philip. *A Darkling Plain* (7–10). Series: The Hungry City Chronicles. 2007, Eos $18.99 (978-0-06-089055-1). Cities are still gobbling one another up in this final installment in the Hungry City Chronicles, and the reappearance of the Stalker Fang threatens all human beings on Earth. (Rev: BL 7/07; HB 9–10/07; SLJ 6/07)

2395 Reiss, Kathryn. *Pale Phoenix* (7–10). 1994, Harcourt paper $3.95 (978-0-15-200031-8). Miranda Browne's parents take in an orphan girl who can disappear at will and who was the victim of a tragedy in a past life in Puritan Massachusetts. (Rev: BL 3/15/94; SLJ 5/94; VOYA 6/94)

2396 Resnick, Mike. *Lady with an Alien: An Encounter with Leonardo da Vinci* (6–9). Series: Art Encounters. 2005, Watson-Guptill $15.95 (978-0-8230-0323-5). Elements of fantasy, time travel, history, art, and philosophy are all present in this novel about da Vinci and his supposed substitution of an alien for an ermine. (Rev: BL 11/1/05; SLJ 10/05)

2397 Richardson, Bill. *After Hamelin* (4–8). 2000, Annick $19.95 (978-1-55037-629-6). In this entertaining fantasy that is a follow-up to the Pied Piper of Hamelin story, Penelope gets the gift of Deep Dreaming and is able to enter the Piper's secret world in the hope of rescuing the children. (Rev: BL 2/15/01; SLJ 4/01; VOYA 4/01)

2398 Riordan, Rick. *The Lightning Thief* (6–9). Series: Percy Jackson and the Olympians. 2005, Hyperion $17.95 (978-0-7868-5629-9). Perseus (aka Percy) Jackson, a New York 12-year-old with problems, has action-packed adventures after he is sent to Camp Half Blood — a summer camp for demigods — and discovers his father is Poseidon. (Rev: BL 9/15/05; SLJ 8/05*)

2399 Riordan, Rick. *The Sea of Monsters* (6–9). Series: Percy Jackson and the Olympians. 2006, Hyperion $17.95 (978-0-7868-5686-2). The 13-year-old son of Poseidon tries to save his friends and summer camp from danger in this second volume in the series. Also use *The Titan's Curse* (2007). (Rev: BL 7/06; HB 5–6/06; SLJ 5/06) 🌀

2400 Roberts, Katherine. *Crystal Mask* (5–8). Series: The Echorium Sequence. 2002, Scholastic paper $15.95 (978-0-439-33864-6). The Singers, a group of people who maintain peace in the world through their unusual powers, are confronted by evildoers known as the Frazhin. Also use *Dark Quetzal* (2003). (Rev: BL 4/15/02; HBG 10/02; SLJ 3/02)

2401 Rodda, Emily. *The Key to Rondo* (4–7). 2008, Scholastic $16.99 (978-0-545-03535-4). A magic music box takes Leo and his cousin Mimi to the land of Rondo, home to fairy-tale characters and an evil queen. (Rev: BL 12/15/07; SLJ 4/08)

2402 Rowling, J. K. *Harry Potter and the Chamber of Secrets* (4–8). 1999, Scholastic $22.99 (978-0-439-06486-6). During his second year at Hogwarts School of Witchcraft and Wizardry, Harry is baffled when he hears noises no one else can. (Rev: BCCB 9/99; BL 5/15/99*; HB 7–8/99; HBG 10/99; SLJ 7/99; VOYA 10/99)

2403 Rowling, J. K. *Harry Potter and the Deathly Hallows* (6–12). Illus. by Mary GrandPré. 2007, Scholastic $34.99 (978-0-545-01022-1). The seventh and final book in the series ties up all the plot threads and ends with an epilogue updating readers on the main characters 19 years later. (Rev: BCCB 10/07; BL 8/07*; HB 9–10/07; SLJ 9/07) 🌀

2404 Rowling, J. K. *Harry Potter and the Goblet of Fire* (4–9). 2000, Scholastic $29.99 (978-0-439-13959-5). This, the fourth installment of Harry Potter's adventures, begins when Voldemort tries to regain the power he lost in his failed attempt to kill Harry. (Rev: BL 8/00*; HB 11–12/00; HBG 3/01; SLJ 8/00)

2405 Rowling, J. K. *Harry Potter and the Half-Blood Prince* (5–12). Illus. by Mary GrandPré. 2005, Scholastic LB $34.99 (978-0-439-78677-5). In this sixth and penultimate volume, Harry, now 16, begins mapping a strategy to defeat the evil Lord Voldemort. (Rev: BL 8/05*; SLJ 9/05; VOYA 10/05)

2406 Rowling, J. K. *Harry Potter and the Order of the Phoenix* (4–12). 2003, Scholastic LB $34.99 (978-0-439-56761-9). Adolescence, adult hypocrisy, and the deadly threat of Voldemort and his evil supporters combine to make Harry's fifth year at Hogwarts as eventful as ever. (Rev: BL 7/03; HB 9–10/03; HBG 10/03; SLJ 8/03; VOYA 8/03)

2407 Rowling, J. K. *Harry Potter and the Prisoner of Azkaban* (4–8). Illus. by Mary GrandPré. 1999,

Scholastic $22.99 (978-0-439-13635-8). In this third thrilling adventure, a murderer has escaped from prison and is after our young hero. (Rev: BCCB 10/99; BL 9/1/99*; HB 11–12/99; HBG 3/00; SLJ 10/99)

2408 Rowling, J. K. *Harry Potter and the Sorcerer's Stone* (4–8). Illus. 1998, Scholastic $22.99 (978-0-590-35340-3). In this humorous and suspenseful story, 11-year-old Harry Potter attends the Hogwarts School for Witchcraft and Wizardry, where he discovers that he is a wizard just as his parents had been and that someone at the school is trying to steal a valuable stone with the power to make people immortal. (Rev: BCCB 11/98; BL 9/15/98; HB 1–2/99; HBG 3/99; SLJ 10/98; VOYA 12/98)

2409 Rubenstein, Gillian. *Foxspell* (7–9). Illus. 1996, Simon & Schuster $16.00 (978-0-689-80602-5). In this fantasy, a troubled boy is tempted by a fox spirit to receive peace and immortality if he will assume a fox shape forever. (Rev: BL 10/15/96; SLJ 9/96; VOYA 12/96)

2410 Ruby, Laura. *The Chaos King* (5–8). 2007, HarperCollins $16.99 (978-0-06-075258-3). In this sequel to *The Wall and the Wing* (2006), Gurl — called Georgie now that she has been reunited with her parents — and her friend Bug must put aside their temporary differences and cope with myriad challenges. (Rev: BCCB 9/07; SLJ 11/07) 🌀

2411 Russell, Barbara T. *The Taker's Stone* (7–12). 1999, DK $16.95 (978-1-78942-568-0). When 14-year-old Fischer steals some glowing red gemstones from a man at a campsite, he unleashes the terrible evil of Belial, some catastrophic weather, and the beginning of the end of the world. (Rev: VOYA 10/99)

2412 Rylant, Cynthia. *The Heavenly Village* (4–7). 1999, Scholastic paper $15.95 (978-0-439-04096-9). A special book about the Heavenly Village — a place where some people stay who are not sure about going to heaven — and about some of the people who live in this in-between world. (Rev: BL 12/1/99*; HBG 3/00; SLJ 3/00; VOYA 2/00)

2413 Sage, Angie. *Flyte* (5–8). Illus. by Mark Zug. Series: Septimus Heap. 2006, HarperCollins $17.99 (978-0-06-057734-6). In this fast-paced sequel to *Magyk* (2005), wizard Septimus must protect Princess Jenna from numerous dangers; a CD includes games. (Rev: BL 5/15/06; SLJ 6/06; VOYA 2/06)

2414 Sage, Angie. *Physik* (5–8). Series: Septimus Heap. 2007, HarperCollins $17.99 (978-0-06-057737-7). When Septimus Heap, apprenticed to a wizard, inadvertently releases the spirit of an evil queen who lived centuries earlier, the ill-tempered monarch unleashes chaos in the kingdom; the third book in the series. (Rev: BL 4/1/07; SLJ 6/07) 🌀

2415 Sage, Angie. *Queste* (5–8). Series: Septimus Heap. 2008, HarperCollins $17.99 (978-0-06-088207-5). In the fourth book of the series, Septimus is sent on a dangerous Queste and tries to rescue his brother Nicko. (Rev: BL 5/15/08; SLJ 6/08)

2416 St. John, Lauren. *The White Giraffe* (5–8). Illus. by David Dean. 2007, Dial $16.99 (978-0-8037-3211-7). After the tragic death of her parents, 11-year-old Martine is sent to live with her grandmother on a large game preserve in South Africa, where she discovers her mystical gifts and exposes poachers who are hunting a rare white giraffe. (Rev: BL 6/1–15/07; LMC 11/07; SLJ 6/07)

2417 Sampson, Fay. *Pangur Ban: The White Cat* (5–8). Series: Pangur Ban. 2003, Lion paper $7.95 (978-0-7459-4763-1). A Welsh cat and an Irish monk encounter princesses and mermaids in this fantasy set in the Middle Ages. (Rev: BL 5/15/03; SLJ 11/03)

2418 Sampson, Fay. *Shape-Shifter: The Naming of Pangur Ban* (5–8). Series: Pangur Ban. 2003, Lion paper $7.95 (978-0-7459-4762-4). A Welsh cat pursued by witches befriends an Irish monk in this first book in the series. (Rev: BL 5/15/03)

2419 Sanderson, Brandon. *Alcatraz Versus the Evil Librarians* (5–8). 2007, Scholastic $16.99 (978-0-439-92550-1). Alcatraz is a 13-year-old boy with unusual powers and a tendency to insert his own thoughts into the narrative, and the librarians are insidious censors of information; fast-paced antics ensure. (Rev: BCCB 2/08; HB 1-2/08; SLJ 11/07)

2420 Sargent, Pamela. *Farseed* (7–10). Series: Seed Trilogy. 2007, Tor $17.95 (978-0-7653-1427-7). The offspring of the genetically engineered humans sent to the planet Home to create a new society have split into two factions in this second book in the trilogy. (Rev: BL 3/15/07; LMC 11–12/07; SLJ 10/07)

2421 Schade, Susan. *Travels of Thelonious* (4–7). Illus. by Jon Buller. 2006, Simon & Schuster $14.95 (978-0-689-87684-4). This is the engaging, imaginative story of Thelonious, a squirrel who discovers the ruins of a city and searches for clues to the mystery of why humans disappeared. (Rev: BL 4/15/06; SLJ 7/06)

2422 Schaeffer, Susan F. *The Dragons of North Chittendon* (5–7). Illus. by Darcy May. 1986, Simon & Schuster paper $2.95 (978-0-685-14462-6). The story of Arthur, an unruly dragon, and his ESP relationship with the boy Patrick in a story of humans and dragons in and above North Chittendon, Vermont. (Rev: BL 8/86; SLJ 9/86)

2423 Schmidt, Gary D. *Straw into Gold* (5–8). 2001, Clarion $15.00 (978-0-618-05601-9). Two boys set off to find the answer to the king's riddle and thereby save the lives of rebels, only to discover much

more than they had expected. (Rev: BCCB 9/01; HBG 10/01; SLJ 8/01; VOYA 2/02)

2424 Scott, Deborah. *The Kid Who Got Zapped Through Time* (4–7). 1997, Avon $14.00 (978-0-380-97356-9). In this humorous time-travel fantasy, Flattop Kincaid is transported to England during the Middle Ages, where he becomes a serf. (Rev: BL 11/1/97; SLJ 9/97)

2425 Scott, Michael. *The Alchemyst: The Secrets of the Immortal Nicholas Flamel* (7–12). 2007, Delacorte $16.99 (978-0-385-73357-1). Fifteen-year-old twins Sophie and Josh find themselves caught up in a deadly, ancient struggle over a Codex, the Book of Abraham the Mage, that holds the promise of eternal youth. (Rev: BL 5/1/07; LMC 10/07; SLJ 5/07) ❧

2426 Seabrooke, Brenda. *Stonewolf* (5–8). 2005, Holiday $16.95 (978-0-8234-1848-0). Young orphan Nicholas is taken captive by a group called the Synod but manages to escape, taking with him a sought-after secret formula. (Rev: BL 3/15/05; SLJ 3/05)

2427 Selfors, Suzanne. *Saving Juliet* (7–10). 2008, Walker $16.95 (978-0-8027-9740-7). Mimi, a reluctant actress in her family's theater, is transported to medieval Verona, where she meets the real Juliet (and her Romeo). (Rev: BL 1/1–15/08; LMC 2/08; SLJ 3/08)

2428 Shan, Darren. *Lord of the Shadows* (5–10). Series: Cirque du Freak. 2006, Little, Brown $15.99 (978-0-316-15628-8). In the 11th book in the series, part-vampire Darren faces off against Steve Leopard, leader of the Vampaneze, in a battle to determine who will be the next Lord of the Shadows. (Rev: SLJ 9/06)

2429 Sherman, Delia. *Changeling* (5–8). 2006, Viking $16.99 (978-0-670-05967-6). Neef, kidnapped as a baby by fairies, faces exile from her home in New York Between — an alternate Manhattan inhabited by elves, pixies, fairies, and other spirits — when she breaks the rules. (Rev: SLJ 10/06)

2430 Sherman, Josepha. *Windleaf* (7–12). 1993, Walker $14.95 (978-0-8027-8259-5). Count Thierry falls in love with half-faerie Glinfinial, only to have her father, the Faerie Lord, steal her away. (Rev: BL 11/1/93*; SLJ 12/93; VOYA 2/94)

2431 Shetterly, Will. *Elsewhere* (8–12). 1991, Harcourt $16.95 (978-0-15-200731-7). Set in Bordertown, between the real world and Faerie world, home to runaway elves and humans, this is a fantasy of integration, survival, and coming of age. (Rev: BL 10/15/91; SLJ 11/91)

2432 Shetterly, Will. *Nevernever* (8–12). 1993, Tor paper $4.99 (978-0-8125-5151-8). This sequel to *Elsewhere* (1991) shows Wolfboy trying to protect

Florida, the heir of Faerie, from gangs of Elves out to get her, while one of his friends is framed for murder. (Rev: BL 9/15/93; SLJ 10/93; VOYA 12/93)

2433 Shinn, Sharon. *The Dream-Maker's Magic* (7–10). 2006, Viking $16.99 (978-0-670-06070-2). In this novel set in the same world as *The Safe-Keeper's Secret* (2004) and *The Truth-Teller's Tale* (2005), Kellen, who was brought up as a boy, matures and offers comfort to her deformed and abused friend Gryffin who turns out to be the new Dream-Maker. (Rev: BL 5/15/06; SLJ 7/06)

2434 Shinn, Sharon. *The Safe-Keeper's Secret* (7–12). 2004, Viking $16.99 (978-0-670-05910-2). Truth and justice are themes in this fantasy about Fiona, a girl whose family has many secrets, and Reed, a boy without an identity, who was left as a baby with Fiona's mother. (Rev: BL 4/15/04; SLJ 6/04; VOYA 6/04)

2435 Shinn, Sharon. *The Truth-Teller's Tale* (7–10). 2005, Viking $16.99 (978-0-670-06000-9). Twin sisters Eleda and Adele are mirror images — Eleda can neither tell nor hear a lie, while Adele can be trusted to keep secret anything she is told. (Rev: BCCB 9/05; BL 4/15/05*; SLJ 7/05; VOYA 8/05)

2436 Shusterman, Neal. *Dread Locks* (6–9). Series: Dark Fusion. 2005, Dutton $15.99 (978-0-525-47554-5). When Tara, with her thick golden hair and dark sunglasses, moves in next door to the family of 14-year-old Parker Baer, bad things start to happen in this novel based on the story of Medusa. (Rev: BL 6/1–15/05; SLJ 6/05; VOYA 6/05)

2437 Shusterman, Neal. *Duckling Ugly* (7–10). Series: Dark Fusion. 2006, Dutton $15.99 (978-0-525-47585-9). Apart from her ability to spell, Cara DeFido has no known attributes until she finds herself in a magic kingdom; her successes there prompt her to return home, however. (Rev: BL 2/1/06; SLJ 7/06)

2438 Shusterman, Neal. *Red Rider's Hood* (6–9). 2005, Dutton $15.99 (978-0-525-47562-0). A dark variation on the Red Riding Hood story in which Red Rider, a 16-year-old boy, vows to seek revenge after a group of werewolves attack his grandmother and steal his beloved Mustang; this will appeal to reluctant readers. (Rev: BL 10/15/05; SLJ 12/05; VOYA 10/05)

2439 Shusterman, Neal. *Unwind* (6–9). 2007, Simon & Schuster $16.99 (978-1-4169-1204-0). Unwinds are teenagers whose organs are to be harvested in this disturbing story set after the Second Civil War. (Rev: BL 10/15/07; HB 3–4/08; LMC 1/08; SLJ 1/08)

2440 Silberberg, Alan. *Pond Scum* (4–7). 2005, Hyperion $15.99 (978-0-7868-5634-3). Ten-year-old Oliver gains a whole new appreciation for his animal neighbors after he finds a magical gem that

allows him to assume the shape of various creatures. (Rev: BL 12/1/05; SLJ 11/05)

2441 Singleton, Linda Joy. *Last Dance* (6–8). Series: The Seer. 2005, Llewellyn paper $6.99 (978-0-7387-0638-2). Sabine goes in search of a possible cure for her desperately ill grandmother but is sidetracked by the ghost of a young girl who reportedly committed suicide. (Rev: SLJ 7/05)

2442 Skelton, Matthew. *Endymion Spring* (6–9). 2006, Delacorte $17.95 (978-0-385-73380-9). While visiting Oxford, England, an American teen discovers part of a rare, centuries-old book that holds many secrets and is sought by sinister forces. (Rev: BL 6/1–15/06; LMC 4-5/07; SLJ 9/06) ✏

2443 Slepian, Jan. *Back to Before* (5–7). 1994, Scholastic paper $3.25 (978-0-590-48459-6). Cousins Linny and Hilary travel back to a time before Linny's mother's death and Hilary's parents' separation. (Rev: BCCB 9/93; BL 9/1/93*; SLJ 10/93)

2444 Smith, Gordon. *The Forest in the Hallway* (6–9). 2006, Clarion $16.00 (978-0-618-68847-0). On the 19th floor of her uncle's apartment building, Beatriz finds a path that leads her to a magical world on a quest to find her missing parents. (Rev: BL 11/15/06; SLJ 12/06)

2445 Smith, Sherwood. *Wren's Quest* (5–8). 1993, Harcourt $16.95 (978-0-15-200976-2). Wren takes time out from magician school to search for clues to her parentage. Sequel to *Wren to the Rescue* (1990). (Rev: BL 4/1/93*; SLJ 6/93)

2446 Smith, Sherwood. *Wren's War* (5–8). 1995, Harcourt $17.00 (978-0-15-200977-9). In this sequel to *Wren to the Rescue* and *Wren's Quest*, Princess Teressa struggles to control herself and her destiny when she finds her parents murdered. (Rev: BL 3/1/95*; SLJ 5/95)

2447 Somary, Wolfgang. *Night and the Candlemaker* (4–8). Illus. 2000, Barefoot Bks. $16.99 (978-1-84148-137-1). In this allegory, a candle maker continues with his trade in spite of threats he receives from Night. (Rev: BL 9/15/00; HBG 10/01; SLJ 1/01)

2448 Spicer, Dorothy. *The Humming Top* (6–8). 1968, Phillips $26.95 (978-0-87599-147-4). An orphan finds she is able to predict future events.

2449 Spiegler, Louise. *The Amethyst Road* (8–11). 2005, Clarion $16.00 (978-0-618-48572-7). In this cautionary futuristic novel, siblings Serena and Willow, half-Gorgio and half-Yulang, struggle to survive the violence of their urban neighborhood and the ostracism caused by their mixed blood. (Rev: BL 12/1/05; SLJ 11/05; VOYA 2/06)

2450 Springer, Nancy. *Dussie* (5–8). 2007, Walker $16.95 (978-0-8027-9649-3). When she hits puberty, Dussie, a New York City 13-year-old named for her aunt Medusa, discovers she is a gorgon — and that the talkative snakes that have sprouted from her head may be an inconvenience, as is her ability to turn people to stone. (Rev: BL 11/15/07; SLJ 12/07)

2451 Stanley, Diane. *Bella at Midnight* (5–8). Illus. by Bagram Ibatoulline. 2006, HarperCollins LB $17.89 (978-0-06-077574-2). A fine retelling of the Cinderella story featuring a plucky Bella and a storytelling format. (Rev: BCCB 4/06; BL 2/1/06*; HB 3–4/06; HBG 10/06; LMC 2/07; SLJ 3/06*; VOYA 2/06)

2452 Stead, Rebecca. *First Light* (5–8). 2007, Random $15.99 (978-0-375-84017-3). On a scientific expedition to Greenland with his parents, 12-year-old Peter meets 14-year-old Thea, a member of a secret society that lives beneath the ice. (Rev: BL 4/15/07; SLJ 8/07)

2453 Steele, Mary Q. *Journey Outside* (5–8). Illus. by Rocco Negri. 1984, Peter Smith $21.75 (978-0-8446-6169-8); Puffin paper $5.99 (978-0-14-030588-3). Young Dilar, believing that his Raft People have been circling endlessly in their quest for a "Better Place," sets out to discover the origin and fate of his kind.

2454 Steer, Dugald A. *The Dragon's Eye* (5–8). Series: Dragonology Chronicles. 2006, Candlewick $15.99 (978-0-7636-2810-9). In the late 19th century, Daniel Cook, 12, and his sister Beatrice attend a dragon school run by Dr. Ernest Drake and accompany him on search for the important Dragon's Eye. (Rev: BL 1/1–15/07; SLJ 1/07)

2455 Stewart, Sharon. *Raven Quest* (5–8). 2005, Carolrhoda LB $15.95 (978-1-57505-894-8). Tok the raven seeks to restore his good name after being falsely accused of murder and sets off to find the legendary Grey Lords. (Rev: SLJ 1/06; VOYA 12/05)

2456 Stone, David Lee. *The Shadewell Shenanigans* (6–9). Series: Illmoor Chronicles. 2006, Hyperion $16.99 (978-0-7868-3795-3). How to get rid of Groan Teethgrit and his barbarian sidekicks? The lords of Illmoor do their best in this funny, edgy final book of the series. (Rev: BL 5/15/06; LMC 2/05; SLJ 8/06)

2457 Stone, David Lee. *The Yowler Foul-up* (5–8). 2006, Hyperion $16.99 (978-0-7868-5597-1). A motley group of would-be heroes tries to stop a plot to turn the people of Dullitch into rocks in this sequel to *The Ratastrophe Catastrophe* (2004). (Rev: BL 4/15/06)

2458 Strickland, Brad. *The Curse of the Midions* (5–8). Series: Grimoire. 2006, Dial $12.99 (978-0-8037-3060-1). A trip to London with his parents goes terribly awry when Jarvey Midion finds himself transported to an alternate universe where he must confront the villainous wizard Tantalus Mideon. (Rev: BL 6/1–15/06; SLJ 11/06)

2459 Strickland, Brad. *Tracked by Terror* (5–8). Series: Grimoire. 2007, Dial $15.99 (978-0-8037-3061-8). This sequel to *Curse of the Midions* (2006) finds 12-year-old Jarvey and his friend Betsy navigating a haunted theater and being hunted by animals. (Rev: BL 11/15/07; LMC 11/07; SLJ 2/08)

2460 Stroud, Jonathan. *The Amulet of Samarkand* (6–12). Series: The Bartimaeus Trilogy. 2003, Hyperion $17.95 (978-0-7868-1859-4). Nathaniel, an apprentice magician, plots to steal an amulet and sets powerful forces in motion in this fantasy set in London. (Rev: BL 9/1/03*; HB 11–12/03; HBG 4/04; SLJ 1/04; VOYA 12/03)

2461 Stroud, Jonathan. *The Golem's Eye* (7–12). Series: The Bartimaeus Trilogy. 2004, Miramax $17.95 (978-0-7868-1860-0). In this sequel to *The Amulet of Samarkand*, 14-year-old Nathaniel, a magician's apprentice, joins forces with the mischievous djinni Bartimaeus to foil the evil plot of a golem. (Rev: BL 8/04; SLJ 10/04)

2462 Sutherland, Tui T. *Shadow Falling: Avatars Book Two* (7–9). Series: Avatars. 2007, Eos $16.99 (978-0-06-085146-0). Beings from different eras of history and prehistory threaten teens Gus, Tigre, Kali, and Diana in the second book in the series. (Rev: BL 12/1/07)

2463 Swados, Elizabeth. *Dreamtective: The Dreamy and Daring Adventures of Cobra Kite* (6–9). 1999, Genesis paper $5.95 (978-1-885478-54-2). A humorous and unusual adventure in which 12-year-old Cobra discovers she can visit other people's dreams. (Rev: SLJ 10/99)

2464 Sweeney, Joyce. *Shadow* (7–10). 1995, Bantam $20.95 (978-0-385-30988-2). Sarah's cat, Shadow, has mysteriously returned from the dead. Sarah and Cissy, the psychic housemaid, try to figure out why. (Rev: BL 7/94; SLJ 9/94; VOYA 10/94)

2465 Taylor, G. P. *The Shadowmancer Returns: The Curse of Salamander Street* (6–10). 2007, Putnam $17.99 (978-0-399-24346-2). This sequel to *Shadowmancer* follows Kate and Thomas as they avoid the evil Obadiah only to be caught in a trap, and Beadle and Raphah as they try to distinguish good from evil as they journey to London. (Rev: BL 5/15/07; SLJ 9/07)

2466 Taylor, Laini. *Faeries of Dreamdark: Blackbringer* (5–8). 2007, Putnam $17.99 (978-0-399-24630-2). With the help of her band of crows, a faerie named Magpie must hunt down devils that the humans have released and keep the dark from consuming the world. (Rev: BL 5/15/07; SLJ 8/07)

2467 Thesman, Jean. *The Other Ones* (7–9). 1999, Puffin paper $5.99 (978-0-14-131246-0). Bridget must decide if she should try to be a normal human or, because she possesses supernatural powers, remain part of the Other Ones. (Rev: BL 5/99; SLJ 6/99; VOYA 8/99)

2468 Thompson, Kate. *The Last of the High Kings* (7–10). 2008, Greenwillow $16.99 (978-0-06-117595-4). J.J. Liddy, introduced in *The New Policeman*, is now married and a father of four, one of whom is a fairy, having been traded for one of J.J.'s children at birth. (Rev: BL 5/15/08; SLJ 7/08)

2469 Thompson, Kate. *The New Policeman* (7–10). 2007, Greenwillow $16.99 (978-0-06-117427-8). J.J., hoping to grant his mother's wish for "more time," goes out into his Irish town to find out just where all the time has gone and discovers the land of eternal youth in this music-filled story. (Rev: BCCB 4/07; BL 2/1/07; HB 3–4/07; LMC 8–9/07; SLJ 3/07*) 🎵

2470 Thompson, Kate. *Only Human* (6–9). Series: Missing Link. 2006, Bloomsbury $16.95 (978-1-58234-651-9). Part human and part animal, characters in this second volume of the trilogy attempt to learn more about human evolution by hunting for the yeti. (Rev: BL 5/15/06; HB 5–6/06)

2471 Thompson, Kate. *Origins* (6–9). Series: Missing Link. 2007, Bloomsbury $16.95 (978-1-58234-652-6). In this final volume in the trilogy, the story alternates between Christie's life at the Fourth World laboratory in 2009 and a post-nuclear-disaster future in which Dogs and Cats have been at war. (Rev: BL 3/3/08; SLJ 12/07)

2472 Thornton, Duncan. *Kalifax* (5–9). Illus. by Yves Noblet. 2000, Coteau paper $8.95 (978-1-55050-152-0). In this fantasy novel, young Tom, with the help of Grandfather Frost, saves the crew of his ship after it becomes trapped in ice. (Rev: SLJ 1/01)

2473 Thornton, Duncan. *The Star-Glass* (5–8). Illus. by Yves Noblet. 2004, Coteau paper $10.95 (978-1-55050-269-5). Tom and Jenny face new challenges in this sequel to the fantasies *Kalifax* and *Captain Jenny and the Sea of Wonders*. (Rev: SLJ 4/04; VOYA 6/04)

2474 Tiernan, Cate. *A Chalice of Wind* (8–11). Series: Balefire. 2005, Penguin paper $6.99 (978-1-59514-045-6). Thais discovers that she has a twin — and that she is a witch — when her father dies and she is sent to live in New Orleans. (Rev: BL 9/1/05; SLJ 8/05)

2475 Tiernan, Cate. *Night's Child* (7–12). Series: Sweep. 2003, Penguin paper $7.99 (978-0-14-250119-1). In this 15th installment — a double-length, stand-alone novel — Moira, 15-year-old daughter of the powerful blood witch Morgan, learns about her heritage and faces danger and treachery as well as romance. (Rev: SLJ 2/04)

2476 Tolkien, J. R. R. *The Hobbit: Or, There and Back Again* (7–12). Illus. 1938, Houghton $16.00 (978-0-395-07122-9); Ballantine paper $7.99 (978-0-345-33968-3). In this prelude to *The Lord of the Rings*, the reader meets Bilbo Baggins, a hobbit, in a land filled with dwarfs, elves, goblins, and dragons.

2477 Tolkien, J. R. R. *Roverandom* (4–9). 1998, Houghton $17.00 (978-0-395-89871-0); paper $12.95 (978-0-395-95799-8). This fantasy deals with a dog named Roverandom who has the misfortune of insulting a wizard and having to pay the consequences. (Rev: BL 7/98; SLJ 6/98; VOYA 10/98)

2478 Tolkien, J. R. R. *Unfinished Tales of Numenor and Middle-Earth* (8–12). Ed. by Christopher Tolkien. 2001, Houghton $26.00 (978-0-618-15404-3); paper $14.95 (978-0-618-15405-0). A collection of previously unpublished fantasy writings by this English master.

2479 Tomlinson, Heather. *The Swan Maiden* (6–10). 2007, Holt $16.95 (978-0-8050-8275-3). Swan maiden Doucette, who only discovers her natural magic in her teens, is in love with the shepherd Jaume, who must complete a series of trials to win her hand in this story based on French fairy tales. (Rev: BL 10/1/07; SLJ 12/07)

2480 Townley, Roderick. *Into the Labyrinth* (5–7). 2002, Simon & Schuster $16.95 (978-0-689-84615-1). In this sequel to *The Great Good Thing* (2001), Princess Sylvie and the other characters in their novel become exhausted as their popularity grows and they must rush from chapter to chapter; when the book goes digital, things spiral out of control and Sylvie must defeat an evil "bot" that threatens to destroy them. (Rev: BL 11/1/02; HBG 10/03; SLJ 10/02)

2481 Townsend, John Rowe. *The Fortunate Isles* (7–12). 1989, HarperCollins LB $13.89 (978-0-397-32366-1). Eleni and her friend Andreas seek the living god in this novel set in a mythical land. (Rev: BL 10/15/89; SLJ 10/89)

2482 Townsend, Tom. *The Trouble with an Elf* (5–8). Series: Fairie Ring. 1999, Royal Fireworks paper $9.99 (978-0-88092-525-9). The adopted daughter of the king of the elves, Elazandra, journeys through a ring of mushrooms to the world of humans to stop the evil that will destroy both worlds. (Rev: SLJ 4/00)

2483 Tunnell, Michael O. *Moon without Magic* (6–9). 2007, Dutton $17.99 (978-0-525-47729-7). Aminah and her jinni travel through the Middle East searching for the lamp that once belonged to Aladdin in this sequel to *Wishing Moon* (2004). (Rev: LMC 1/08; SLJ 12/07)

2484 Tunnell, Michael O. *The Wishing Moon* (6–9). 2004, Penguin $17.99 (978-0-525-47193-6). Struggling to survive after the death of her parents, 14-year-old Aminah is begging for alms outside the sultan's palace when the sultan's daughter throws an old oil lamp at her, not realizing the lamp's magical properties. (Rev: BL 8/04; SLJ 7/04; VOYA 6/04)

2485 Turner, Ann. *Rosemary's Witch* (5–8). 1991, HarperCollins paper $3.95 (978-0-06-440494-5). Rosemary discovers that her new home is haunted by the spirit of a girl named Mathilda, who's become a witch because of her pain and anger. (Rev: BL 4/1/91; SLJ 5/91*)

2486 Turner, Megan W. *The Queen of Attolia* (5–8). 2000, Greenwillow $15.95 (978-0-688-17423-1). In this sequel to *The Thief*, Gen, a slippery rogue, once more gets involved in the rivalry between two city states. (Rev: BL 4/15/00; HB 7–8/00; HBG 10/00; SLJ 5/00)

2487 Turner, Megan W. *The Thief* (5–8). 1996, Greenwillow $17.99 (978-0-688-14627-6). To escape life imprisonment, Gen must steal a legendary stone in this first-person fantasy set in olden days. (Rev: BCCB 11/96; BL 1/1–15/97; HB 11–12/96; SLJ 10/96; VOYA 6/97)

2488 Uehashi, Nahoko. *Moribito: Guardian of the Spirit* (6–9). Trans. by Cathy Hirano. 2008, Scholastic $17.99 (978-0-545-00542-5). Balsa, a 30-year-old woman, is hired to protect the son of the Mikado in this fantasy involving lots of magic and martial arts. Batchelder Award, 2009. (Rev: BL 8/08; SLJ 9/08)

2489 Ursu, Anne. *The Shadow Thieves* (5–8). 2006, Simon & Schuster $16.95 (978-1-4169-0587-5). A plot to reanimate the dead using the essence of living children is foiled by cousins Charlotte and Zee in this story of heroism and mythology that ranges from the Midwest to England to Hades. (Rev: BL 3/1/06; SLJ 4/06)

2490 Ursu, Anne. *The Siren Song* (5–8). Series: Cronus Chronicles. 2007, Atheneum $16.99 (978-1-4169-0589-9). Charlotte, just back from the Underworld (in 2007's *The Shadow Thieves*), goes on a cruise with her cousin Zee and finds herself battling Poseidon and the sea monster Ketos; the second installment in the series that uses elements of Greek mythology. (Rev: BL 11/1/07; HB 7–8/07; SLJ 8/07)

2491 Van Belkom, Edo. *Lone Wolf* (5–8). 2005, Tundra paper $8.95 (978-0-88776-741-8). The four teen werewolves adopted by Ranger Brock in *Wolf Pack* (2004) defend their beloved woods against a corrupt developer. (Rev: SLJ 1/06; VOYA 4/06)

2492 Vande Velde, Vivian. *Now You See It . . .* (5–8). 2005, Harcourt $17.00 (978-0-15-205311-6). Wendy, 15, puts on a pair of sunglasses and a whole new fantasy world is revealed. (Rev: BL 1/1–15/05; SLJ 1/05)

2493 Vande Velde, Vivian. *Witch Dreams* (5–8). 2005, Marshall Cavendish $15.95 (978-0-7614-5235-5). Nyssa, a 16-year-old witch, seeks justice

for her parents, who were murdered six years earlier. (Rev: BL 12/15/05; SLJ 11/05; VOYA 12/05)

2494 Vansickle, Lisa. *The Secret Little City* (5–8). 2000, Palmae $15.95 (978-1-930167-11-7). When 11-year-old Mackenzie moves with her family to a small town in Oregon, she discovers a whole civilization of inch-high people living beneath the floorboards of her new room. (Rev: SLJ 8/00)

2495 Vaupel, Robin. *The Rules of the Universe by Austin W. Hale* (5–8). 2007, Holiday $16.95 (978-0-8234-1811-4). When Austin, 13, discovers that he can alter the molecular structures of people and animals, he conducts careful experiments to determine the limits of this power — and to see if he can save his dying grandfather. (Rev: BL 11/1/07)

2496 Verrillo, Erica. *Elissa's Odyssey* (5–8). Series: Phoenix Rising. 2008, Random $16.99 (978-0-375-83948-1). The second book in the trilogy, following *Elissa's Quest*, finds Elissa in Alhamazar, her mysterious power to speak to animals expanding. (Rev: BL 5/15/08)

2497 Verrillo, Erica. *Elissa's Quest* (5–8). Series: Phoenix Rising. 2007, Random $16.99 (978-0-375-83946-7). Thirteen-year-old Elissa struggles to control her destiny when she finds out that she is the princess of Castlemar and that her father the king plans to trade her to a desert warlord. (Rev: BL 6/1–15/07; LMC 10/07; SLJ 8/07)

2498 Vick, Helen H. *Tag Against Time* (6–9). 1996, Harbinger $15.95 (978-1-57140-006-2); paper $9.95 (978-1-57140-007-9). In this third volume about Tag, our hero thinks it is time to leave the 1200s and the Hopi culture he has grown to love and return to the present. (Rev: SLJ 10/96; VOYA 2/97)

2499 Vick, Helen H. *Walker's Journey Home* (7–10). 1995, Harbinger $14.95 (978-1-57140-000-0); paper $9.95 (978-1-57140-001-7). Walker leads the Sinagua Indians through treacherous challenges from both old enemies and new, and learns that greed and jealousy have been destructive forces throughout history. Sequel to *Walker of Time* (1993). (Rev: BL 8/95)

2500 Voake, Steve. *The Dreamwalker's Child* (5–8). 2006, Bloomsbury $16.95 (978-1-58234-661-8). After being hit by a car, Sam Palmer finds himself in the alternate world of Aurobon, where he learns of a deadly plot to wipe out human life on Earth using a virus transmitted by mosquitoes. (Rev: SLJ 8/06; VOYA 6/06)

2501 Voelkel, Jon, and Pamela Voelkel. *Middleworld* (5–8). Illus. Series: Jaguar Stones Trilogy. 2007, Smith & Kraus $17.95 (978-1-57525-561-3). Fourteen-year-old Max's parents disappear while working in Central America, and he searches for them with the help of local girl Lola and her knowledge of the mystical elements of Mayan culture. (Rev: BL 11/15/07; SLJ 10/07)

2502 Voigt, Cynthia. *The Wings of a Falcon* (7–12). 1993, Scholastic $15.95 (978-0-590-46712-4). Two boys escape from a remote island and face danger and adventure in this multilayered tale that includes themes of friendship, romance, and heroism. (Rev: SLJ 10/93*; VOYA 12/93)

2503 Walsh, Jill Paton. *A Chance Child* (7–9). 1978, Avon paper $1.95 (978-0-380-48561-1). In this English novel, a young boy who has been a prisoner all his life suddenly travels back in time. (Rev: BL 5/1/89)

2504 Wangerin, Walter, Jr. *The Book of the Dun Cow* (7–10). 1978, HarperCollins $12.95 (978-0-06-026346-1). A farmyard fable with talking animals that retells the story of Chanticleer the Rooster.

2505 Ward, David. *Escape the Mask* (5–8). Series: The Grassland Trilogy. 2008, Abrams $15.95 (978-0-8109-9477-5). Coriko and Pippa escape the Spears, who have been keeping them as slaves, when the Spears are attacked by a mysterious group of warriors; but their adventures do not end there. (Rev: BL 4/15/08)

2506 Waugh, Sylvia. *The Mennyms* (4–8). 1994, Greenwillow $16.00 (978-0-688-13070-1). When their owner dies, a family of rag dolls comes to life and takes over her house in this beginning volume of an extensive series. (Rev: BCCB 5/94; HB 7–8/94; SLJ 4/94)

2507 Weatherill, Cat. *Barkbelly* (4–7). Illus. by Peter Brown. 2006, Knopf $15.95 (978-0-375-83327-4). A wooden boy being raised by normal parents flees after he accidentally causes a tragedy and searches for his own family. (Rev: BL 5/15/06; SLJ 7/06)

2508 Weatherill, Cat. *Snowbone* (4–7). Illus. by Peter Brown. 2007, Knopf $15.99 (978-0-375-83328-1). Snowbone rallies her fellow Ashenpeakers (a race of wooden beings that are used as slaves) to escape their bondage and end slavery; a companion to *Barkbelly* (2006). (Rev: BL 6/1–15/07; SLJ 12/07)

2509 Weaver, Will. *Defect* (6–9). 2007, Farrar $16.00 (978-0-374-31725-6). David's defects include strange-looking, supersensitive ears and an even stranger set of wings that he tries to hide; when they are eventually discovered, he must deal with the repercussions of being different. (Rev: BCCB 9/07; BL 7/07; HB 9–10/07; SLJ 3/08)

2510 Weinberg, Karen. *Window of Time* (5–7). Illus. by Annelle W. Ratcliffe. 1991, White Mane paper $9.95 (978-0-942597-18-9). Ben climbs through a window and finds himself 125 years back in time. (Rev: SLJ 7/91)

2511 Weiss, M. Jerry, and Helen S. Weiss, eds. *Dreams and Visions: Fourteen Flights of Fancy* (7–10). 2006, Tor $19.95 (978-0-7653-1249-5). A collection of 14 appealing fantasy short stories by writers including Joan Bauer and Tamora Pierce; includes short biographies of the authors. (Rev: BL 4/15/06; SLJ 4/06)

2512 Wersba, Barbara. *Walter: The Story of a Rat* (4–7). Illus. by Donna Diamond. 2005, Front St. $16.95 (978-1-932425-41-3). Miss Pomeroy, a children's author, develops a friendship with a literary rat named Walter who shares her house in this thoughtful and sophisticated book. (Rev: BCCB 2/06; BL 11/15/05; SLJ 12/05)

2513 Weyn, Suzanne. *Reincarnation* (7–10). 2008, Scholastic $17.99 (978-0-545-01323-9). A fantasy in which a boy and girl are repeatedly reincarnated throughout history and manage to find each other over and over again although impediments to their love sadly also arise. (Rev: BL 6/1–15/08)

2514 White, T. H. *The Sword in the Stone* (7–12). 1993, Putnam $24.99 (978-0-399-22502-4). In this, the first part of *The Once and Future King,* the career of Wart is traced until he becomes King Arthur.

2515 Whitlock, Dean. *Raven* (6–9). 2007, Clarion $16.00 (978-0-618-70224-4). Raven, a 15-year-old bird mage, tries to rescue her mother, Roxaine, and reunite her with her new baby after the overlord Barron Cutter dies, leaving Roxaine vulnerable to the evil estate manager; a companion to *Sky Carver* (2005). (Rev: BL 5/15/07; SLJ 8/07)

2516 Whittemore, JoAnne. *Escape from Arylon* (5–8). Series: The Silverskin Legacy. 2006, Llewellyn paper $8.95 (978-0-7387-0869-0). Ainsley and Megan, neighbors with an uneasy friendship, find themselves transported through a portal to Arylon, where they meet many magical characters and must save the Staff of Lexiam from thieves. (Rev: SLJ 6/06; VOYA 6/06)

2517 Wilce, Ysabeau S. *Flora Segunda: Being the Magical Mishaps of a Girl of Spirit, Her Glass-Gazing Sidekick, Two Ominous Butlers (One Blue), a House with Eleven Thousand Rooms, and a Red Dog* (6–9). Series: Tygers of Wrath. 2007, Harcourt $17.00 (978-0-15-205433-5). Flora, a plucky 13-year-old who lives in the gigantic, magical Crackpot Hall, enters a library she didn't know about and finds herself on a wild adventure. (Rev: BL 11/15/06; SLJ 2/07)

2518 Williams, Maiya. *The Golden Hour* (4–8). 2004, Abrams $16.95 (978-0-8109-4823-5). Thirteen-year-old Rowan and his 11-year-old sister Nina are sent to live with two great-aunts after the death of their mother and find themselves — with their new friends Xanthe and Xavier — transported through a time portal to 1789 Paris. (Rev: BL 3/15/04; SLJ 4/04; VOYA 6/04)

2519 Williams, Maiya. *The Hour of the Cobra* (4–7). 2006, Abrams $16.95 (978-0-8109-5970-5).

Xanthe, Xavier, Rowan, and Nina time-travel to ancient Egypt and narrowly avoid altering history in this sequel to *The Golden Hour* (2004). (Rev: BL 5/15/06; SLJ 7/06; VOYA 6/06)

2520 Williams, Maiya. *The Hour of the Outlaw* (4–7). 2007, Abrams $16.95 (978-0-8109-9355-6). Xavier and Xanthe, Rowan and Nina travel back in time again — this time to the Old West during the California Gold Rush. (Rev: BL 1/1–15/08; SLJ 1/08)

2521 Williams, Mark London. *Trail of Bones* (5–8). Series: Danger Boy. 2005, Candlewick $9.99 (978-0-7636-2154-4). Eli, Thea, and Clyne — three characters of very different backgrounds — travel back in time from 2019 to early 19th-century America and become involved with Lewis and Clark and the plight of escaping slaves. (Rev: SLJ 7/05)

2522 Wilson, N. D. *100 Cupboards* (4–7). Series: 100 Cupboards. 2007, Random $16.99 (978-0-375-83881-1). Henry, a timid 12-year-old, and his braver cousin Henrietta discover a wall of cupboards that lead to alternate worlds. (Rev: BL 12/1/07; HB 1–2/08; LMC 4-5/08; SLJ 4/08)

2523 Winterson, Jeanette. *Tanglewreck* (4–7). 2006, Bloomsbury $16.95 (978-1-58234-919-0). After "time tornadoes" upset the delicate balance of time and space in and around London, 11-year-old Silver embarks on a fantastic odyssey in search of the Timekeeper that, hopefully, can set things right again. (Rev: BL 10/1/06; SLJ 10/06; VOYA 8/06)

2524 Winthrop, Elizabeth. *The Battle for the Castle* (4–7). 1993, Holiday $16.95 (978-0-8234-1010-1). William and friend Jason time-travel to the Middle Ages, where they become involved in a struggle to prevent the return of evil as a ruling power. A sequel to *The Castle in the Attic* (1985). (Rev: BL 9/1/93; HB 7–8/93; SLJ 5/93)

2525 Winthrop, Elizabeth. *The Castle in the Attic* (5–7). 1985, Holiday $16.95 (978-0-8234-0579-4). In an effort to keep his sitter from returning to England, William miniaturizes her and then must find a way to undo the deed. (Rev: BCCB 10/85; BL 1/15/86; SLJ 2/86)

2526 Wood, Beverley, and Chris Wood. *Dog Star* (5–8). 1998, Orca paper $6.95 (978-0-89609-537-3). On a cruise to Alaska with his family, 13-year-old Jeff Beacon encounters a magical pet bull terrier who transports him back in time to the Juneau of 1932. (Rev: VOYA 8/98)

2527 Wood, Beverley, and Chris Wood. *Jack's Knife* (5–9). Series: A Sirius Mystery. 2006, Raincoast paper $7.95 (978-1-55192-709-1). This sequel to *Dog Star* (1998) finds Jack time-traveling with bull terrier Patsy Ann to 1930s Alaska to help solve a mystery at sea. (Rev: SLJ 5/06)

2528 Wooding, Chris. *Poison* (6–9). 2005, Scholastic $16.99 (978-0-439-75570-2). Poison sets out to rescue her little sister from the phaeries and faces many challenges in this rich gothic fantasy. (Rev: BL 8/05; SLJ 9/05; VOYA 12/05)

2529 Woodruff, Elvira. *Orphan of Ellis Island* (4–7). 1997, Scholastic paper $15.95 (978-0-590-48245-5). Left alone on Ellis Island, Dominic finds himself transported in time to the village in Italy his family came from. (Rev: BCCB 3/97; BL 6/1–15/97; SLJ 5/97)

2530 Wrede, Patricia C. *Searching for Dragons* (6–10). Series: Enchanted Forest Chronicles. 1991, Harcourt $16.95 (978-0-15-200898-7). Cimorene goes on a quest with Mendanbar, king of the forest, to find the dragon king Kazul by borrowing a faulty magic carpet from a giant. (Rev: BL 10/1/91; SLJ 12/91)

2531 Wrede, Patricia C. *Talking to Dragons* (6–10). Series: Enchanted Forest Chronicles. 1993, Harcourt $16.95 (978-0-15-284247-5). The fourth book in the series opens 16 years after *Calling on Dragons* with King Menenbar still imprisoned in his castle by a wizard's spells. (Rev: BL 8/93; VOYA 12/93)

2532 Wrede, Patricia C., and Caroline Stevermer. *The Grand Tour or the Purloined Coronation Regalia: Being a Revelation of Matters of High Confidentiality and Greatest Importance, Including Extracts from the Intimate Diary of a Noblewoman and the Sworn Testimony of a Lady of Quality* (6–9). 2004, Harcourt $17.00 (978-0-15-204616-3). In this sequel to *Sorcery and Cecelia* (2003) set in 1817 and blending adventure, humor, fantasy, mystery, and romance, two English cousins, honeymooning in Europe with their husbands, uncover a plot by evil wizards to create a new empire. (Rev: BL 9/1/04; SLJ 11/04)

2533 Wrede, Patricia C., and Caroline Stevermer. *The Mislaid Magician or Ten Years After* (7–10). 2006, Harcourt $17.00 (978-0-15-205548-6). Two cousins investigate a wizard's disappearance in this novel set in 1828 in a magical version of England; this sequel to *Sorcery and Cecelia* (2003) and *The Grand Tour* (2004) is told in the form of letters. (Rev: BL 1/1–15/07; SLJ 1/07)

2534 Wright, Nina. *Homefree* (6–12). 2006, Flux paper $8.95 (978-0-7387-0927-7). Easter is having "astral experiences" in which she travels to her own past; could this have something to do with Homefree, an organization for teenagers with unusual talents? (Rev: SLJ 10/06)

2535 Wright, Randall. *The Silver Penny* (4–7). 2005, Holt $16.95 (978-0-8050-7391-1). In this compelling fantasy set in the 19th century, Jacob — after breaking his leg and facing disability — receives from his great-grandfather a lucky silver penny that gives him access to a supernatural world. (Rev: BCCB 7–8/05; SLJ 8/05; VOYA 10/05)

2536 Wynne-Jones, Tim. *Some of the Kinder Planets* (5–8). 1995, Orchard LB $16.99 (978-0-531-08751-0). Nine imaginative stories about ordinary boys and girls in offbeat situations. (Rev: BCCB 5/95; BL 3/1/95*; HB 1–2/95, 5–6/95, 9–10/95; SLJ 4/95*)

2537 Yancey, Rick. *Alfred Kropp: The Seal of Solomon* (8–11). 2007, Bloomsbury $16.95 (978-1-59990-045-2). Alfred, awkward high school sophomore and descendant of Sir Lancelot, has many adventures as he struggles to battle the forces of evil in this sequel to *The Extraordinary Adventures of Alfred Kropp* (2005). (Rev: BL 5/15/07; SLJ 6/07)

2538 Yarbro, Chelsea Q. *Beyond the Waterlilies* (6–10). Illus. 1997, Simon & Schuster $17.00 (978-0-689-80732-9). Geena Howe has a unique talent — blending into paintings — and has an amazing adventure when she enters a huge Monet painting of water lilies in a castle moat. (Rev: BL 6/1–15/97; SLJ 6/97; VOYA 8/97)

2539 Yep, Laurence. *Dragon of the Lost Sea* (5–8). 1982, HarperCollins paper $6.99 (978-0-06-440227-9). Shimmer, a dragon, in the company of a boy, Thorn, sets out to destroy the villain Civet. (Rev: BL 4/15/04)

2540 Yep, Laurence. *Dragon Steel* (6–10). 1985, HarperCollins $12.95 (978-0-06-026748-3). The dragon princess Shimmer tries to save her people who are forced to work in an undersea volcano in this sequel to *Dragon of the Lost Sea*. (Rev: BL 5/15/85; SLJ 9/85; VOYA 8/85)

2541 Yolen, Jane, et al., eds. *Dragons and Dreams* (6–10). 1986, HarperCollins $12.95 (978-0-06-026792-6). A collection of 10 fantasy and some science fiction stories that can be a fine introduction to these genres. (Rev: SLJ 5/86; VOYA 6/86)

2542 Yolen, Jane. *Merlin* (5–8). Series: Young Merlin Trilogy. 1997, Harcourt $16.00 (978-0-15-200814-7). In this concluding volume of a trilogy, Hawk-Hobby (Merlin) escapes from his enemies with a young friend who will later become King Arthur. (Rev: BL 4/15/97; SLJ 5/97)

2543 Yolen, Jane. *The One-Armed Queen* (8–10). 1998, Tor $23.95 (978-0-312-85243-6). Scillia, the adopted daughter of Queen Jenna, is being groomed to rule when her younger brother decides that he should become king. (Rev: BL 10/1/98; VOYA 4/99)

2544 Yolen, Jane. *Passager* (4–7). Series: Young Merlin Trilogy. 1996, Harcourt $16.00 (978-0-15-200391-3). In medieval England, an abandoned 8-year-old boy named Merlin is taken in by a friendly man who becomes his master. Book two of the trilo-

gy is *Hobby* (1996). (Rev: BL 5/1/96; HB 7–8/96; SLJ 5/96*)

2545 Yolen, Jane, and Adam Stemple. *Pay the Piper* (6–9). 2005, Tor $16.95 (978-0-7653-1158-0). Fourteen-year-old Callie discovers the secret of a member of the Brass Rat when the town's children disappear on Halloween night in this lighthearted version of the Pied Piper tale. (Rev: BL 6/1–15/05; SLJ 8/05; VOYA 8/05)

2546 Yolen, Jane, and Adam Stemple. *Trollbridge: A Rock n' Roll Fairy Tale* (6–9). 2006, Tor $16.95 (978-0-7653-1426-0). Moira, a princess and harpist, and three brothers from a popular band called the Griffsons, are transported to the strange wilderness world of Trollholm where they must rescue the other princesses from Aenmarr, a colossal troll. (Rev: BL 9/1/06; SLJ 8/06)

2547 Yoshi. *The Butterfly Hunt* (5–8). Illus. 1991, Picture Book paper $14.95 (978-0-88708-137-8). In this fantasy, a young boy releases a butterfly and forevermore it becomes his own. (Rev: SLJ 6/91)

2548 Young, Steve. *15 Minutes* (5–8). 2006, HarperCollins $15.99 (978-0-06-072508-2). Casey, a 7th-grader who's always late for almost everything, discovers that his grandfather's watch gives him the power to go back 15 minutes. (Rev: SLJ 9/06)

2549 Zahn, Timothy. *Dragon and Herdsman: The Fourth Dragonback Adventure* (5–8). 2006, Tom Doherty Assoc. $17.95 (978-0-7653-1417-8). With the help of a shape-changing dragon and his friend Alison, 14-year-old Jack Morgan escapes from the Malison Ring. (Rev: SLJ 9/06; VOYA 6/06)

2550 Zappa, Ahmet. *The Monstrous Memoirs of a Mighty McFearless* (4–7). Illus. by author. 2006, Random $12.95 (978-0-375-83287-1). Written and illustrated by the son of Frank Zappa, this rollicking fantasy follows Mini and Max McFearless, monster-minators who must rescue their father from kidnappers. (Rev: BL 5/15/06; SLJ 7/06) ⓦ

2551 Zevin, Gabrielle. *Elsewhere* (7–10). 2005, Farrar $16.00 (978-0-374-32091-1). After dying of a head injury, 15-year-old Liz Hall does not adapt easily to afterlife in Elsewhere and at first spends a lot of time watching what's going on on Earth. (Rev: BL 8/05*; SLJ 10/05*)

2552 Zuckerman, Linda. *A Taste for Rabbit* (6–10). 2007, Scholastic $16.99 (978-0-439-86977-5). This fable of civilized animals can be disturbing in its violence as a group of rabbits begins selling its young to hungry foxes. (Rev: BL 11/15/07; HB 11–12/07; LMC 1/08; SLJ 11/07)

Graphic Novels

2553 Abadzis, Nick. *Laika* (8–12). Illus. by author. 2007, Roaring Brook paper $17.95 (978-1-59643-101-0). A fictionalized account of the little dog named Laika, the first living creature launched into space by the Russians, and her trainer, Yelena Dubrovsky. (Rev: BL 9/1/07; SLJ 11/07)

2554 Abe, Yoshitoshi. *New Feathers* (6–9). Illus. Series: Haibane Renmei. 2006, Dark Horse $14.95 (978-1-59307-520-0). Rakka awakes as a member of the Haibane, angel-like people who live among humans in a walled city, with no recollection of her past. (Rev: BL 11/1/06)

2555 Akimoto, Nami. *Ultra Cute, Vol. 1* (5–8). Trans. from Japanese by Emi Onishi. Illus. by author. 2006, TokyoPop paper $9.99 (978-1-59532-956-1). Ami and Noa, more rivals than friends, compete with each other over two guys who are not as nice as they seem. (Rev: SLJ 7/06)

2556 Alexovich, Aaron. *Kimmie66* (8–12). Illus. by author. 2007, DC Comics paper $9.99 (978-1-4012-0373-3). In the technologically advanced 23rd century, Telly receives a suicide note from a friend — or is it from her friend's digital duplicate? (Rev: BL 1/1–15/08; SLJ 3/08)

2557 *All Star Comics: Archives, Vol. 11* (7–12). Illus. by Arthur Peddy and Bernard Sachs. Series: Archive Editions. 2005, DC Comics $49.95 (978-1-4012-0403-7). The final volume of the Archive Editions series continues the adventures of the Justice Society of America, a band of comic book superheroes that includes the Green Lantern, Flash, Wonder Woman, Atom, and Hawkman. (Rev: BL 7/05; SLJ 9/05)

2558 Altman, Steven-Elliot, et al. *The Irregulars: . . . In the Service of Sherlock Holmes* (7–12). Illus. 2005, Dark Horse paper $12.95 (978-1-59307-303-9). In this suspenseful graphic novel, Holmes assigns the Baker Street Irregulars to find out who's responsible for a murder for which Dr. Watson has been charged. (Rev: BL 5/1/05)

2559 Ando, Natsumi, and Miyuki Kobayashi. *Kitchen Princess* (6–9). Illus. by Natsumi Ando. 2007, Ballantine paper $10.95 (978-0-345-49659-1). A student at a prestigious cooking academy is on the trail of a mysterious stranger from her past in this girls' manga. (Rev: BL 4/1/07; SLJ 9/07)

2560 Appignanesi, Richard, adapt. *A Midsummer Night's Dream* (8–12). Illus. by Kate Brown. Series: Manga Shakespeare. 2008, Abrams paper $9.95 (978-0-8109-9475-1). A manga retelling of the comedy featuring fairies and lovers; illustrated by Kate Brown. (Rev: BL 3/15/08; SLJ 5/08)

2561 Asamiya, Kia. *Dark Angel: The Path to Destiny* (8–12). Illus. Series: Dark Angel. 2000, CPM Comics paper $15.95 (978-1-56219-827-5). In this first volume of a series of graphic novels, a young swordsman named Dark travels through time and different worlds to complete his moral journey. (Rev: BL 12/1/00)

2562 Avi. *City of Light, City of Dark: A Comic-Book Novel* (6–9). Illus. 1995, Orchard paper $8.99 (978-0-531-07058-1). In black-and-white comic book format, Sarah and her friend Carlos must save her father from the evil Underton and pay tribute to the Kurbs before Manhattan freezes. (Rev: BL 9/15/93; VOYA 2/94)

2563 Beechen, Adam. *Robin: Teenage Wasteland* (8–11). Illus. by Freddie Williams. 2007, DC Comics paper $17.99 (978-1-4012-1480-7). A collection of nine issues of well-written comic book stories featuring the boy wonder. (Rev: BL 1/15/08)

2564 Bilgrey, Marc, and Rob Vollmar. *Ghouls Gone Wild!* (6–8). Illus. by Exes. Series: Tales from the Crypt. 2007, Papercutz $12.95 (978-1-59707-083-6); paper $7.95 (978-1-59707-082-9). Four stories from the classic Tales from the Crypt series of the 1950s, with new illustrations. (Rev: BL 1/1–15/08; SLJ 3/08)

2565 Bishop, Debbie. *Black Tide: Awakening of the Key* (6–10). Illus. by Mike S. Miller. 2004, Angel Gate paper $19.99 (978-1-932431-00-1). In this gripping graphic novel, which collects the first eight issues of an ongoing comic book series, past and present collide when Justin Braddock embarks on a mission to solve a series of international murders. (Rev: BL 4/15/04)

2566 Blackman, Haden, et al. *Clone Wars Adventures* (4–7). Series: Star Wars Clone Wars Adventures. 2006, Dark Horse paper $6.95 (978-1-59307-483-8). This fifth volume of the fantasy series, based on the TV cartoon show, includes four fast-paced stories of graphic novel action and adventure. (Rev: BL 6/1–15/06)

2567 Bradbury, Ray. *The Best of Ray Bradbury: The Graphic Novel* (6–12). Illus. 2003, iBooks paper $18.95 (978-0-7434-7476-4). Some of the best artists working in the graphic novels field have adapted Bradbury's works. (Rev: BL 2/1/04)

2568 Brennan, Michael. *Electric Girl, Vol. 2* (5–8). Illus. 2002, Mighty Gremlin paper $13.95 (978-0-9703555-1-5). In this graphic novel, Virginia, who can release bursts of electricity at will, locks horns with evil gremlin Oogleeoog. (Rev: BL 5/1/02; SLJ 5/02)

2569 Brooks, Terry. *Dark Wraith of Shannara* (6–9). Illus. by David Edwin. Series: Shannara. 2008, Del Rey paper $13.95 (978-0-345-49462-7). This graphic novel, which first recaps relevant Shannara history, takes place after the events of *The*

Wishsong of Shannara (1988) as Jair uses the power of wishsong to continue to battle the Ildatch. (Rev: BL 3/15/08; SLJ 7/08)

2570 Brown, Jeffrey. *Incredible Change-Bots* (8–12). Illus. 2007, Top Shelf paper $15.00 (978-1-891830-91-4). Change-Bots, who can morph from robots into vehicles, trash their own planet and then arrive on Earth with a continuing appetite for a fight in this funny, action-filled fantasy. (Rev: BL 11/15/07)

2571 Cabot, Meg. *The Merlin Prophecy* (6–8). Illus. by Jinky Coronado. 2007, TokyoPop paper $7.99 (978-0-06-117707-1). A graphic novel version of Meg Cabot's *Avalon High* (2006) about Ellie and her boyfriend Will, who is unaware that he's the reincarnation of King Arthur. (Rev: BL 9/1/07; SLJ 9/07)

2572 Cammuso, Frank. *Max Hamm, Fairy Tale Detective, Vol. 1* (8–12). Illus. Series: Fairy Tale Detectives. 2005, Nite Owl paper $14.95 (978-0-9720061-4-9). Max Hamm, a pig, is also a private eye in a cycle of pulp-novel-style stories involving fairy tale characters and much clever wordplay. (Rev: BL 8/05; SLJ 11/05)

2573 Carey, Mike. *Re-Gifters* (7–9). Illus. by Sonny Liew. 2007, DC Comics paper $9.99 (978-1-4012-0371-9). Jen Dik Seong, known as Dixie, and her friend Avril want to enter a hapkido (a martial art) tournament but when Dixie foolishly spends her entry fee on a gift for Adam she risks losing her chance to compete. (Rev: BL 6/1–15/07; LMC 11/07; SLJ 1/08)

2574 Carey, Mike, and Louise Carey. *Confessions of a Blabbermouth* (7–12). Illus. by Aaron Alexovich. 2007, Minx paper $9.99 (978-1-4012-1148-6). Blabbermouth is the name of Tasha's blog, and it's an appropriate name for an effective tool that lets important people in her life know how she's feeling; a humorous, well-illustrated graphic novel. (Rev: LMC 1/08; SLJ 11/07)

2575 Chantler, Scott. *The Annotated Northwest Passage* (8–12). Illus. by author. 2007, Oni $19.95 (978-1-932664-61-4). This action-packed graphic novel, set in northern Canada in 1755, tells of the fierce competition between the French, British, and other private interests to control the fur trade. (Rev: BL 8/07; SLJ 11/07)

2576 Clugston, Chynna. *Queen Bee* (5–8). Illus. 2005, Scholastic paper $8.99 (978-0-439-70987-3). In this humorous graphic novel about school cliques, Haley and Alexa, two middle school students with psychokinetic powers, battle each other to become the school's most popular girl. (Rev: BL 9/15/05; SLJ 1/06; VOYA 12/05)

2577 Colfer, Eoin, and Andrew Donkin. *Artemis Fowl: The Graphic Novel* (5–7). Illus. by Giovanni Rigano. 2007, Hyperion $18.99 (978-0-7868-4881-

2); paper $9.99 (978-0-7868-4882-9). A well-illustrated graphic novel rendering of the 2001 novel about the 12-year-old genius and adventurous criminal entrepreneur Artemis Fowl. (Rev: BL 11/15/07; LMC 2/08; SLJ 1/08)

2578 Cover, Arthur Byron. *Macbeth* (6–9). Illus. by Tony Leonard Tamai. 2005, Penguin paper $9.99 (978-0-14-240409-6). This imaginative graphic novel adaptation transports Shakespeare's *Macbeth* to a futuristic setting in outer space. (Rev: BL 10/15/05; SLJ 3/06)

2579 Crilley, Mark. *Autumn* (7–9). Illus. by author. Series: Miki Falls. 2007, HarperTeen paper $7.99 (978-0-06-084618-3). In this manga sequel to *Spring* and *Summer* (both 2007), Miki and Hiro continue to break the rules of Hiro's Deliverer organization (a secret group whose members may not fall in love with humans) and decide to run away. (Rev: BL 2/8/08; SLJ 5/08)

2580 Crilley, Mark. *Miki Falls: Summer* (7–12). Illus. by author. 2007, HarperTeen paper $7.99 (978-0-06-084617-X). This well-illustrated volume in the manga style follows Miki, a Japanese teen who falls in love with a superhuman entity. (Rev: SLJ 7/07)

2581 Crilley, Mark. *Spring* (4–7). Illus. Series: Miki Falls. 2007, HarperTempest paper $7.99 (978-0-06-084616-9). In this manga-style romance novel, high school senior Miki is determined to break through the defenses of the gorgeous but secretive new boy called Hiro. (Rev: BL 3/15/07; SLJ 7/07)

2582 David, Peter. *Final Exam* (6–9). Illus. Series: SpyBoy. 2005, Dark Horse paper $12.95 (978-1-59307-017-5). SpyBoy Alex Fleming faces off against a villainous substitute teacher who threatens to derail Alex's plans to attend his senior prom and graduate from high school. (Rev: BL 3/15/05)

2583 d'Errico, Camilla, and Joshua Dysart. *Avril Lavigne's Make 5 Wishes, v.2* (6–9). Illus. 2007, Del Rey paper $12.95 (978-0-345-50079-3). Hana gets through her family and school problems with the help of her imaginary friend (a version of pop star Avril Lavigne); but then genie/demon Romeo comes along and grants Hana five wishes that have disastrous results. (Rev: BL 8/07)

2584 Dezago, Todd. *Spider-Man: The Terrible Threat of the Living Brain!* (5–8). Illus. by Jonboy Meyers, et al. Series: Spider-Man. 2006, ABDO LB $21.35 (978-1-59961-008-5). Spider-Man, with a little help from Flash, foils the theft of the Living Brain, a powerful robot-like computer. (Rev: SLJ 11/06)

2585 Dezago, Todd. *Spider-Man and Captain America: Stars, Stripes, and Spiders!* (5–8). Series: Spider-Man Team Up. 2006, ABDO LB $21.35 (978-1-59961-001-6). In this action-packed comic-book fantasy, superheroes Spider-Man and Captain

America team up to battle the Grey Gargoyle. (Rev: SLJ 11/06)

2586 Dixon, Chuck. *Nightwing: On the Razor's Edge* (8–12). Illus. by Greg Land and Drew Geraci. 2005, DC Comics paper $14.99 (978-1-4012-0437-2). Robin, Batman's former sidekick, now takes on the superhero identity of Nightwing and must defend himself against his foes. (Rev: SLJ 11/05)

2587 Dixon, Chuck. *Way of the Rat: The Walls of Zhumar* (7–12). Illus. 2003, CrossGeneration paper $15.95 (978-1-931484-51-0). Boon has stolen a scholar's magic ring and the Book of Hell and is now being chased by villains in this fantasy set in Asia and enhanced by dynamic illustrations. (Rev: BL 2/1/03)

2588 Eisner, Will. *Moby Dick* (6–12). Illus. 2001, NBM $15.95 (978-1-56163-293-0). A faithful retelling of Melville's famous novel in full-color graphic novel format. (Rev: BL 11/15/01; HBG 3/02; SLJ 1/02)

2589 Eisner, Will. *The Princess and the Frog: By the Grimm Brothers* (4–7). Illus. 1999, NBM $15.95 (978-1-56163-244-2). A retelling of the familiar fairy tale in graphic novel style. (Rev: BL 12/15/99; HBG 3/00) [398.2]

2590 Eisner, Will. *Will Eisner's The Spirit Archives, Vol. 12* (8–12). Illus. 2003, DC Comics $49.95 (978-1-4012-0006-0). This collection of comic strips covers the full 12-year career of the Spirit, a masked crime fighter. (Rev: BL 2/1/04)

2591 Espinosa, Rod. *Neotopia Color Manga* (6–12). Series: Neotopia. 2004, Antarctic paper $9.99 (978-1-932453-57-7). In the opening volume of the graphic novel series, Nalyn, a servant girl, takes over her spoiled mistress's responsibilities as grand duchess of Mathenia, but the going gets tough when Mathenia comes under attack from the evil empire of Krossos. (Rev: BL 12/1/04)

2592 *Fairy Tales of Oscar Wilde* (5–8). Illus. by P. Craig Russell. 1992, Nantier $15.95 (978-1-56163-056-1). Graphic novel treatment enlivens this retelling of two of Wilde's short stories. (Rev: BL 1/15/93)

2593 Fisher, Jane Smith. *WJHC: Hold Tight* (4–7). Illus. 2005, Wilson Place paper $11.95 (978-0-9744235-1-7). This graphic-novel sequel to *WJHC: On the Air* (2003) continues the adventures of six diverse teenage friends who launched a high school radio station, following them through a reality TV show, a celebrity fashion show, and a trip to a rock concert. (Rev: BL 11/1/05; SLJ 1/06)

2594 Fisher, Jane Smith. *WJHC: On the Air!* (4–8). Illus. 2003, Wilson Place paper $11.95 (978-0-9744235-0-0). Six episodes catalog the entertaining misadventures of a diverse band of teens who

launch a high school radio station. (Rev: BL 2/1/04; VOYA 12/03)

2595 Frampton, Otis. *Oddly Normal, Vol. 1* (4–7). Illus. 2006, Viper paper $11.95 (978-0-9777883-0-9). Half-human and half-witch, unhappy 10-year-old Oddly Normal struggles to find a place where she fits in; a collection of four issues of a mini-series published by Viper Comics. Also use *Family Reunion* (2007). (Rev: BL 11/1/06)

2596 Friedman, Aimee. *Breaking Up* (8–11). Illus. by Christine Norrie. 2007, Scholastic paper $8.99 (978-0-439-74867-4). Romance, sex, and fashion at the Georgia O'Keeffe School for the Arts. (Rev: BL 3/15/07; SLJ 3/07)

2597 Friesen, Ray. *A Cheese Related Mishap and Other Stories* (5–8). Illus. 2005, Don't Eat Any Bugs paper $8.95 (978-0-9728177-6-9). This collection of zany tales full of entertaining characters and situations was created by a teenage author/illustrator. (Rev: BL 11/15/05; SLJ 3/06)

2598 Fujino, Moyamu. *The First King Adventure, Vol. 1* (4–8). Trans. from Japanese by Kay Bertrand. Illus. by author. 2004, ADV paper $9.99 (978-1-4139-0194-8). Prince Tiltu cannot succeed his father as king until he's made contracts with all of the spirit masters that inhabit the kingdom. (Rev: SLJ 7/05)

2599 Gaiman, Neil. *Coraline* (4–7). Illus. by P. Craig Russell. 2008, HarperCollins LB $19.89 (978-0-06-082544-7); paper $18.99 (978-0-06-082543-0). This adaptation of the 2002 novel by the same name graphically captures Coraline's horror as her nightmares become real behind a strange door. (Rev: BL 3/15/08; SLJ 7/08)

2600 Gallardo, Adam. *Gear School* (4–7). Illus. by Nuria Peris. 2007, Dark Horse paper $7.95 (978-1-59307-854-6). Teresa, 13, is being trained to operate huge robotic attack machines called Gear when aliens attack and she and her classmates must defend themselves. (Rev: BL 11/15/07)

2601 Geary, Rick. *The Case of Madeleine Smith* (7–12). Illus. by author. Series: Treasury of Victorian Murder. 2006, NBM $15.95 (978-1-56163-467-5). Based on actual events in Victorian Glasgow, this story of an affair between an upper-class young woman and a merchant's son ends in murder. (Rev: BL 6/1–15/06; SLJ 9/06)

2602 Geary, Rick. *Great Expectations*. Rev. ed. (4–7). Illus. by author. Series: Classics Illustrated. 2008, Papercutz $9.95 (978-1-59707-097-3). The Dickens classic is retold in graphic novel format with illustrations that highlight the key parts of the story. (Rev: BL 3/15/08)

2603 Gownley, Jimmy. *Superheroes* (4–7). Illus. by author. Series: Amelia Rules! 2007, Renaissance paper $14.95 (978-0-9712169-6-9). Amelia's life is a blend of comedy and angst as she faces life after her parents' divorce, a new neighborhood, and new friends. (Rev: BL 9/1/07)

2604 Grant, Alan. *Kidnapped: The Graphic Novel* (5–8). Illus. by Cam Kennedy. 2007, Tundra paper $11.95 (978-0-88776-843-9). A graphic novel adaptation of the story by Robert Louis Stevenson that captures the spirit of the original. (Rev: BL 10/1/07; SLJ 1/08)

2605 Grayson, Devin. *X-Men: Evolution: Hearing Things* (5–8). Illus. by UDON, et al. Series: X-Men Evolution. 2006, ABDO LB $21.35 (978-1-59961-053-5). In this comic-book adventure from the early years of the X-Men series, Jean Grey comes to grips with her telepathic and telekinetic powers. (Rev: SLJ 11/06)

2606 *Green Lantern* (4–10). Series: Showcase Presents. 2005, DC Comics paper $9.99 (978-1-4012-0759-5). A collection of black-and-white reprints of the early comics about the handsome crime fighter. (Rev: SLJ 5/06)

2607 Hague, Michael. *In the Small* (7–10). Illus. by author. 2008, Little, Brown $12.99 (978-0-316-01323-9). In a flash of blue light, the people of the earth are shrunk to a height of six inches or less, changing their lives and leaving them vulnerable to animals — even the household cat; a teen brother and sister seem to offer the only path to salvation. (Rev: BL 3/15/08; SLJ 5/08)

2608 Harper, Charise Mericle. *Fashion Kitty Versus the Fashion Queen* (4–7). Illus. by author. 2007, Hyperion paper $8.99 (978-0-7868-3726-7). Superhero Fashion Kitty (Kiki Kittie's alter ego) continues to rescue victims of fashion emergencies in this funny sequel to *Fashion Kitty* (2005). (Rev: BCCB 7-8/07; SLJ 11/07)

2609 Hinds, Gareth. *Beowulf* (6–9). Illus. 2007, Candlewick $21.99 (978-0-7636-3022-5). This atmospheric graphic novel treatment is abridged but faithful to the original themes. (Rev: BL 5/1/07; HB 7–8/07; LMC 10/07; SLJ 5/07)

2610 Hinds, Gareth. *King Lear* (7–10). Illus. by author. 2007, Thecomic.com $30.00 (978-1-893131-07-1); paper $15.95 (978-1-893131-06-4). This graphic adaptation of the Shakespeare play brings visual drama to the abridged story, adding interest to pull in reluctant readers. (Rev: BL 2/1/08)

2611 Hinds, Gareth. *The Merchant of Venice* (8–12). Illus. by author. 2008, Candlewick $21.99 (978-0-7636-3024-9); paper $11.99 (978-0-7636-3025-6). Gray, moody illustrations of characters in modern dress combine with a pared-down story to make this a very engaging version of the play. (Rev: BL 3/15/08; SLJ 5/08)

2612 Horowitz, Anthony, and Antony Johnston. *Point Blank: The Graphic Novel* (6–9). Illus. by

Kanako Damerum. Series: Alex Rider. 2008, Philomel paper $14.99 (978-0-399-25026-2). A graphic novel presentation of the adventure in which the young British spy infiltrates an exclusive Swiss boarding school. (Rev: BL 3/15/08)

2613 Horowitz, Anthony, and Antony Johnston. *Stormbreaker* (6–9). Illus. by Kanako Damerum. Series: Alex Rider. 2006, Philomel paper $14.99 (978-0-399-24633-3). In this manga-style graphic novel, the infamous young spy named Alex Rider is recruited to work for Britain's elite spy agency after the death of his uncle and must investigate the Stormbreaker computers; this is based on the movie rather than the novel by the same name. (Rev: BL 11/15/06; LMC 11/07)

2614 Hosler, Jay. *Clan Apis* (5–7). Illus. 2001, Active Synapse paper $15.00 (978-0-9677255-0-5). Nyuki, a honeybee, describes his hive's history and migration to a new location in a text presented in graphic novel style that includes information about bees and their environment. (Rev: BL 7/01)

2615 Hugo, Victor. *The Hunchback of Notre Dame* (5–12). Retold by Michael Ford. Illus. by Penko Gelev. Series: Graphic Classics. 2007, Barron's $15.99 (978-0-7641-5979-4). The classic story about the misshapen bell ringer is presented in graphic novel format. (Rev: SLJ 5/07)

2616 Hurd, Damon, and Tatiana Gill. *A Strange Day* (8–12). Illus. 2005, Alternative Comics paper $3.95 (978-1-891867-74-3). This appealing graphic novella tells a story of instant attraction between two teens who share the same tastes in music. (Rev: BL 5/1/05)

2617 Ikezawa, Satomi. *Guru Guru Pon-Chan, Vol. 1* (5–12). Trans. from Japanese by Douglas Varenas. Illus. by author. 2005, Del Rey paper $10.95 (978-0-345-48095-8). In this whimsical shape-changing story, Ponta, a Labrador retriever puppy, nibbles on a newly invented "chit-chat" bone and turns into a human girl who comically retains doggy behavior. (Rev: SLJ 11/05)

2618 Ikumi, Mia. *Tokyo Mew Mew a la Mode, Vol. 1* (5–8). Trans. from Japanese by Yoohae Yang. Illus. by author. 2005, TokyoPop paper $9.99 (978-1-59532-789-5). In the opening volume of the Tokyo Mew Mew a la Mode series, 12-year-old Berry Shirayuki is shanghaied into a team of girl superheroes and soon finds herself doing battle with dragons and the evil Saint Rose Crusaders. (Rev: SLJ 11/05)

2619 Irwin, Jane, and Jeff Berndt. *Vogelein: Clockwork Faerie* (5–12). Illus. 2003, Fiery Studios paper $12.95 (978-0-9743110-0-5). A beautiful 17th-century mechanical fairy who is immortal but depends on others to wind her up stars in this graphic novel. (Rev: BL 11/1/03)

2620 Jacobs, Philip. *Mouse Guard: Fall 1152* (7–12). Illus. by Philip Jacobs,. 2007, Archaia Studios $24.95 (978-1-932386-57-8). The excellent art will draw readers into this story of about three mice — Saxon, Kenzie and Lieam — who, as part of the Mouse Guard, patrol the Mouse Territories borders, and battle to keep the inhabitants safe. (Rev: BL 9/1/07; LMC 1/08)

2621 Jacques, Brian. *Redwall: The Graphic Novel* (4–7). Illus. by Bret Blevins. Series: Redwall. 2007, Philomel paper $12.99 (978-0-399-24481-0). Redwall makes an effective transition to the graphic novel format with this spirited adaptation. (Rev: BL 9/1/07; SLJ 9/07)

2622 Johns, Geoff. *Infinite Crisis* (7–12). Illus. 2006, DC Comics $24.99 (978-1-4012-0959-9). Adapted from the DC Comics miniseries, this is a novel of a nasty era for Superman, Batman, Wonderwoman, and other superheros known as the Justice League: already at odds with each other, being hunted down by cyborgs, and having to deal with parallel realities; fans familiar with DC back stories will appreciate this novel. (Rev: BL 11/15/06; SLJ 3/07)

2623 Johns, Geoff. *JSA: Black Reign* (7–12). Illus. by Rags Morales, et al. 2005, DC Comics paper $12.99 (978-1-4012-0480-8). In a setting reminiscent of present-day Iraq, superhero Black Adam fights for an unpopular cause and faces strong opposition from the people he's trying to help. (Rev: SLJ 11/05)

2624 Johns, Geoff, et al. *Teen Titans: The Future Is Now* (5–8). Illus. Series: Teen Titans. 2005, DC Comics paper $9.99 (978-1-4012-0475-4). In volume four of the series, the title characters return from a mission into the future to learn that Robin's father died while they were away. (Rev: BL 3/15/06)

2625 Johnson, Dan Curtis, and J. H. Williams. *Snow: Batman* (6–12). Illus. 2007, DC Comics paper $14.99 (978-1-4012-1265-0). Early in his crime-fighting career, Batman confronts a super-powered villain named Mr. Freeze. (Rev: BL 5/15/07)

2626 Joong-Ki, Park. *Shaman Warrior, Vol. 1* (7–12). Illus. by author. 2007, Dark Horse paper $12.95 (978-1-59307-638-2). A battle-filled Korean manhwa tale featuring Shaman Warrior Master Yarong and his devoted servant Batu. (Rev: BL 8/07)

2627 Kelly, Joe. *Justice League Elite, Vol. 1* (8–12). Illus. by Doug Mahnke and John Byrne,. 2005, DC Comics paper $19.99 (978-1-4012-0481-5). Superman and other members of the Justice League clash with the rival Justice League Elite over strategies for dealing with evildoers. (Rev: BL 10/1/05; SLJ 11/05)

2628 Kesel, Barbara. *Meridian: Flying Solo* (7–12). Illus. Series: Meridian. 2003, CrossGeneration paper $9.95 (978-1-931484-54-1). Sephie inherits her father's position as first minister of Meridian, a floating city, and must use her magical powers to battle an evil uncle. (Rev: BL 4/1/03)

2629 Kibuishi, Kazu. *The Stonekeeper* (4–7). Illus. by author. Series: Amulet. 2008, Scholastic $21.99 (978-0-439-84680-6); paper $9.99 (978-0-439-84681-3). Emily's father is killed in a car crash and her mother swallowed by a monster after opening a doorway to another world in this first volume in the series. (Rev: BL 12/1/07; LMC 2/08; SLJ 1/08)

2630 Kindt, Matt. *2 Sisters* (8–12). Illus. 2004, Top Shelf paper $19.95 (978-1-891830-58-7). In this graphic novel thriller, set in Europe during World War II, Elle, a volunteer ambulance driver, is recruited as a spy and dispatched on perilous missions behind enemy lines. (Rev: BL 11/1/04)

2631 Knaak, Richard A. *Dragon Hunt* (7–10). Illus. by Jae-Hwan Kim. Series: Warcraft Sunwell. 2005, TokyoPop paper $9.99 (978-1-59532-712-3). In the first volume of a graphic novel trilogy, Kalec, a shape-changing dragon, and Anveena race to reach the all-powerful Sunwell before the villainous Dar'khan can get to it. (Rev: BL 6/1–15/05; SLJ 7/05)

2632 Kobayashi, Jin. *School Rumble, Vol. 1* (7–12). Adapted by William Flanagan. 2006, Del Rey paper $10.95 (978-0-345-49147-3). This romantic manga-style comedy features high school student Tsukamoto Tenma, who has a crush on the oblivious Karasuma Oji and is meanwhile the object of Harima Kenji's desires. (Rev: SLJ 7/06)

2633 Kobayashi, Makoto. *Planet of the Cats* (5–8). Series: What's Michael? 2006, Dark Horse paper $9.95 (978-1-59307-525-5). In this 11th, concluding volume of the graphic novel series first published in Japan, Hanako, a human exobiologist, and her spaceship crew find themselves stranded on a planet ruled by house cats. (Rev: BL 9/1/06)

2634 Kobayashi, Makoto. *Sleepless Nights* (5–8). Illus. Series: What's Michael? 2005, Dark Horse paper $8.95 (978-1-59307-337-4). Volume ten of the continuing adventures of the house cat who has been described as "Japan's version of Garfield, Heathcliff, and Krazy Kat all rolled into one." (Rev: BL 9/1/05)

2635 Krueger, Jim. *Justice 1* (7–12). Illus. 2006, DC Comics $19.99 (978-1-4012-0969-8). Lex Luthor, the Riddler, and other villains join forces to eradicate the Justice League superheroes in this volume illustrated by the award-winning Alex Ross. (Rev: BL 11/15/06)

2636 Kubert, Joe. *Yossel: April 19, 1943: A Story of the Warsaw Ghetto Uprising* (8–12). Illus. 2003, iBooks $24.95 (978-0-7434-7516-7). In this graphic novel, Yossel and his friends fight to the death against their Nazi oppressors. (Rev: BL 2/1/04; SLJ 7/04)

2637 Kurata, Hideyuki. *Train + Train, Vol. 1* (8–11). Illus. by Tomomasa Takuma. 2007, Go! Comi paper $10.99 (978-1-933617-18-3). On the way to school on the distant planet of Deloca, Rei-ichi Sakakusa meets a wild teen named Arena, who changes his life. (Rev: BL 8/07)

2638 Kusakawa, Nari. *The Recipe for Gertrude* (6–9). 2006, DC Comics paper $9.99 (978-1-4012-1110-3). Gertrude, who looks like a teenage boy but is really a man-made demon built from parts of other demons, is searching for the recipe that made him with the help of a high school girl named Sahara. (Rev: BL 10/1/06; LMC 3/07; SLJ 11/06)

2639 Kye, Seung-Hui. *Recast* (8–11). Illus. 2006, TokyoPop $9.99 (978-1-59816-664-4). JDs grandfather, a master magician, is in danger of assassination in this action- and humor-filled manga. (Rev: BL 2/1/07)

2640 Kyoko, Ariyoshi. *The Swan* (6–9). Illus. 2004, DC Comics paper $9.95 (978-1-4012-0535-5). In this appealing shoujo — manga designed to appeal especially to girls — a young Japanese girl from a rural area seeks to realize her dreams of becoming a prima ballerina. (Rev: BL 2/15/05)

2641 Larson, Hope. *Chiggers* (6–8). Illus. by author. 2008, Atheneum $17.99 (978-1-4169-3584-1); paper $9.99 (978-1-4169-3587-2). Summer is different this year for Abby, as last year's camp friendships shift and change. (Rev: BL 4/15/08; SLJ 7/08)

2642 Lat. *Kampung Boy* (8–11). Illus. 2006, Roaring Brook paper $16.95 (978-1-59643-121-8). This funny and eloquent autobiographical graphic novel follows the childhood of a Muslim boy named Mat as he grows up in a small Malaysian town in the 1950s, giving details on the traditions of his kampung (village), and ending with his departure to attend a boarding school. (Rev: BL 9/15/06; SLJ 11/06*)

2643 London, Jack. *The Call of the Wild: The Graphic Novel* (6–9). Ed. by Neil Kleid. Illus. by Alex Niño. Series: Puffin Graphics. 2006, Penguin paper $10.99 (978-0-14-240571-0). Jack London's classic tale in graphic format. (Rev: BL 4/1/06; SLJ 3/06)

2644 Love, Courtney, and D. J. Milky. *Princess Ai: Lumination, Vol. 2* (7–12). Trans. from Japanese by Kimiko Fujikawa and Yuki N. Johnson. Illus. by Misaho Kujiradou. 2005, TokyoPop paper $9.99 (978-1-59182-670-5). In volume two of the Princess Ai series, the title character, an aspiring rock star, turns ever more angelic as her music career begins to take off. (Rev: SLJ 11/05)

2645 Lutes, Jason, and Nick Bertozzi. *Houdini: The Handcuff King* (6–9). Illus. 2007, Hyperion $16.99 (978-0-7868-3902-5). This graphic novel centers on Houdini's jump into the Boston River in 1908 and provides information on his character and achievements. (Rev: BCCB 6/07; BL 3/15/07; LMC 8-9/07; SLJ 7/07)

2646 Ma, Wing Shing. *Storm Riders: Invading Sun, Vol. 1* (8–12). Illus. 2003, ComicsOne paper $9.95 (978-1-58899-359-5). Martial arts and an alternate China are featured in this graphic novel about two expert fighters who set out to find their former master named Conquer. (Rev: BL 2/1/04)

2647 McCaffrey, Anne. *Dragonflight* (6–12). Adapted by Brynne Stephens. Illus. Series: Dragonriders of Pern. 1991, Eclipse Books $4.95 (978-1-56060-074-9). Book one of a three-part graphic novel based on *Dragonflight* from the Dragonriders of Pern series. (Rev: BL 9/1/91)

2648 McCloud, Scott. *The New Adventures of Abraham Lincoln* (7–10). 1998, Homage Comics paper $19.00 (978-1-887279-87-1). Time travel, an encounter with Abraham Lincoln, and an alien attempt to rule America are some of the adventures faced by a middle-school student when he is sent to detention. (Rev: BL 2/1/03)

2649 MacDonald, Fiona. *Dracula* (6–9). Illus. by Penko Gelev. Series: Graphic Classics. 2007, Barron's LB $15.99 (978-0-7641-6054-7). A graphic retelling of the classic story, with illustrations that will draw in reluctant readers plus a biography of Stoker, a history of vampires, and highlighting of SAT vocabulary words. (Rev: BL 2/8/08; SLJ 1/08)

2650 Marunas, Nathaniel. *Manga Claus: The Blade of Kringle* (5–8). Illus. by Erik Craddock. 2006, Penguin $12.99 (978-1-59514-134-7). In this graphic novel Christmas tale, a disgruntled elf triggers a series of events that wrecks Santa's North Pole workshop and threatens to ruin Christmas for millions of children around the world. (Rev: BL 10/15/06; SLJ 10/06)

2651 Mashima, Hiro. *Fairy Tail, Vol. 1* (7–12). Trans. and adapted from Japanese by William Flanagan. Illus. by author. 2008, Del Rey paper $10.95 (978-0-345-50133-2). Lucy wants to join a wizards club called the Fairy Tail in this boisterous fantasy full of oddball characters; the first in a series. (Rev: SLJ 5/08)

2652 Melville, Herman. *Moby Dick* (5–12). Retold by Sophie Furse. Illus. by Penko Gelev. Series: Graphic Classics. 2007, Barron's $15.99 (978-0-7641-5977-0). The classic story about the giant white whale is presented in graphic novel format. (Rev: SLJ 5/07)

2653 Misako Rocks!. *Biker Girl* (5–8). Illus. 2006, Hyperion paper $7.99 (978-0-7868-3676-5). Aki, a shy, bookish girl, is transformed into a superhero after finding a discarded bicycle in her grandfather's garage. (Rev: BL 3/15/06; SLJ 9/06)

2654 Mizuno, Ryo. *Record of Lodoss War: The Grey Witch — Birth of a New Knight* (7–12). Illus. by Yoshihiko Ochi. Series: Grey Witch Trilogy. 2000, CPM Comics $15.95 (978-1-56219-928-9). This graphic novel is the second volume of the Grey Witch Trilogy and tells how Pam struggles to learn the identity of his father in a universe where gods, goddesses, and goblins exist. (Rev: BL 12/1/00)

2655 Monroe, Kevin. *El Zombo Fantasma* (7–10). Illus. 2005, Dark Horse paper $9.95 (978-1-59307-284-1). In this eye-popping superhero graphic novel, Mexican wrestler El Zombo Fantasma, murdered for throwing a match, seeks to avoid eternal damnation by becoming guardian angel to a feisty 10-year-old and tracking down his own killer. (Rev: BL 3/15/05; VOYA 8/05)

2656 Morrison, Grant. *Vimanarama* (8–12). Illus. by Philip Bond. 2006, Vertigo paper $12.99 (978-1-4012-0496-9). In Bradford, England, Ali — 19-year-old son of Pakistani immigrants — and his arranged bride-to-be Sofia become embroiled in a battle against evil when an ancient spirit is released. (Rev: BL 2/1/06; SLJ 5/06)

2657 Murakami, Maki. *Kanpai! Vol. 1* (8–12). Trans. from Japanese by Christine Schilling. Illus. by author. 2005, TokyoPop paper $9.99 (978-1-59532-317-0). Yamada finds himself torn between his rigid training to be a monster guardian and his infatuation with attractive Taino Municipal Middle School classmate Nao. (Rev: SLJ 1/06)

2658 Muth, Jon. *Swamp Thing: Roots* (8–12). 1998, DC Comics paper $7.95 (978-1-56389-377-3). Visual images enhance this story of the supernatural elements that influence life in a small community. (Rev: BL 2/1/03)

2659 Neri, Filippo. *Steam Park* (6–9). Illus. by Piero Ruggeri. 2007, Simply Read $16.95 (978-1-894965-63-7). A carnival turns sinister in this wordless, darkly humorous story in which children are saved from a menacing carnival worker by the attractions themselves. (Rev: BL 3/15/07)

2660 Nicieza, Fabian, et al. *A Stake to the Heart* (8–12). Illus. 2004, Dark Horse paper $12.95 (978-1-59307-012-0). Angel's efforts to help Buffy and Dawn cope with their parents' problems backfire in this graphic novel that precedes the events of the TV show. (Rev: BL 6/1–15/04)

2661 Niles, Steve, and Scott Hampton. *Gotham County Line: Batman* (7–12). Illus. 2006, DC Comics paper $17.99 (978-1-4012-0905-6). Batman takes on a mysterious case of suburban murders, finds that logic (his usual method) is not leading to the solution this time, and must deal with the supernatural in this well-illustrated story. (Rev: BL 12/1/06)

2662 Nishiyama, Yuriko. *Harlem Beat* (8–12). 1999, TokyoPop paper $9.95 (978-1-892213-04-4). Created and produced in Japan, this graphic novel follows the adventures of an urban, teenage boy who loves basketball. (Rev: BL 2/1/03)

2663 No, Yee-Jung. *Visitor, Vol. 1* (7–10). Trans. from Japanese by Jennifer Hahm. Illus. by author. 2005, TokyoPop paper $9.99 (978-1-59532-342-2). On her first day at a new school, Hyo-Bin attracts a number of admirers, but she rebuffs them all, fearful that they could be harmed by the magical powers she's not yet learned to control. (Rev: SLJ 9/05)

2664 Okamoto, Kazuhiro. *Translucent, Vol. 1* (6–10). Trans. by Heidi Plechl. Illus. by author. Series: Translucent. 2007, Dark Horse paper $9.95 (978-1-59307-647-4). Quiet 8th-grader Shizuka is slowly becoming invisible as a result of a strange disease called the Translucent Syndrome but Mamoru — a possible romantic interest? — and Keiko both help her cope and give her hope for the future. (Rev: BL 2/13/08)

2665 Ono, Fuyumi. *Ghost Hunt, Vol. 3* (8–12). Trans. from Japanese by Akira Tsubasa. Illus. by Shiho Inada. 2006, Del Rey paper $10.95 (978-0-345-48626-4). Seventeen-year-old Naru and his paranormal detective agency investigate strange goings-on at the local high school. (Rev: SLJ 5/06)

2666 Park, Sang-Sun. *Ark Angels, Vol. 1* (6–12). Trans. from Japanese by Monica Seya. Illus. by author. 2005, TokyoPop paper $9.99 (978-1-59816-262-2). Three superhero sisters try to juggle being normal teenagers and saving the world from destruction. (Rev: SLJ 5/06)

2667 Pérez, George. *Wonder Woman: Destiny Calling, Vol. 4* (8–12). Illus. by author et al., et al. 2006, DC Comics paper $19.99 (978-1-4012-0943-8). Collects the last five issues of Wonder Woman, in which she investigates the death of her publicist, reveals much about her early home on Themyscira, and must rescue Earth from the god Hermes. (Rev: SLJ 11/06)

2668 Petrucha, Stefan. *Nancy Drew: The Demon of River Heights* (4–9). Series: Nancy Drew, Girl Detective. 2005, Papercutz $12.95 (978-1-59707-004-1). The familiar heroine returns in graphic-novel format with this story in which Nancy, Bess, George discover the secret behind a legendary monster. (Rev: SLJ 8/05)

2669 Plessix, Michel. *The Wind in the Willows*. Rev. ed. (4–7). Illus. by author. Series: Classics Illustrated Deluxe. 2008, Papercutz $17.95 (978-1-59707-095-9); paper $13.95 (978-1-59707-096-6). The classic animal story, presented in a graphic format with beautiful illustrations. (Rev: BL 3/18/08)

2670 Pomplun, Tom, ed. *Arthur Conan Doyle* (8–11). Ed. by Tom Pomplun. 2d ed. Illus. Series: Graphic Classics. 2005, Eureka paper $11.95 (978-

0-9746648-5-9). This revised edition adds several non-Holmes stories to the collection. (Rev: BL 9/15/05; SLJ 11/05; VOYA 4/06)

2671 Pomplun, Tom, ed. *Gothic Classics, vol. 14* (8–12). Illus. by Anne Timmons, et al. Series: Graphic Classics. 2007, Eureka paper $11.95 (978-0-9787919-0-2). Poe, Austen, and Radcliffe are only three of the authors whose works are adapted here with effective illustrations. (Rev: BL 9/1/07; SLJ 9/07)

2672 Pomplun, Tom, ed. *Graphic Classics: Edgar Allan Poe* (8–12). 2006, Eureka paper $11.95 (978-0-9746648-7-3). This is a graphic novel collection of classic Poe stories. (Rev: BL 6/1–15/06; LMC 1/07)

2673 Raicht, Mike. *Spider-Man: Kraven the Hunter* (5–8). Illus. by Jamal Igle, et al. Series: Spider-Man. 2006, ABDO LB $21.35 (978-1-59961-009-2). Spider-Man once again does battle with Kraven the Hunter, one of his oldest enemies. (Rev: SLJ 11/06)

2674 Raymond, Alex, and Don Moore. *Alex Raymond's Flash Gordon, Vol. 2* (8–12). Illus. 2004, Checker paper $19.95 (978-0-9741664-6-9). The second volume of the Flash Gordon series collects comic strips that first appeared in 1935 and 1936. (Rev: BL 10/1/04)

2675 Reed, Gary. *Mary Shelley's Frankenstein: The Graphic Novel* (7–10). Illus. by Frazer Irving. Series: Puffin Graphics. 2005, Penguin paper $10.99 (978-0-14-240407-2). This graphic novel adaptation accurately conveys the dominant themes of the classic. (Rev: BL 3/15/05; SLJ 9/05; VOYA 8/05)

2676 Renier, Aaron. *Spiral Bound: Top Secret Summer* (4–7). Illus. 2005, Top Shelf paper $14.95 (978-1-891830-50-1). This delightful graphic novel chronicles the summer adventures of the animal residents of the Town, a community with a monster in its pond. (Rev: BL 11/1/05)

2677 Rodi, Rob. *Crossovers* (5–12). Illus. 2003, CrossGeneration paper $15.95 (978-1-931484-85-5). This graphic novel is an entertaining look at a suburban family whose members possess a unique power. (Rev: BL 2/1/04)

2678 Roman, Dave. *Agnes Quill: An Anthology of Mystery* (8–10). Illus. by John Ho. 2006, SLG paper $10.95 (978-1-59362-052-3). Agnes — a girl with the ability to speak to the dead — investigates the supernatural and the gory in this anthology, illustrated by four different artists. (Rev: BL 2/1/07)

2679 Rucka, Greg. *The Omac Project* (7–12). Illus. by Jesus Saiz and Cliff Richards. 2005, DC Comics paper $14.99 (978-1-4012-0837-0). Blue Beetle discovers that Max Lord, the millionaire who took over the surveillance camera Brother I, knows the identity of every superhero. (Rev: SLJ 5/06)

2680 Rucka, Greg, and Michael Lark. *The Quick and the Dead: Gotham Central* (7–12). Illus. 2006, Vertigo paper $14.99 (978-1-4012-0912-4). The police force of Gotham is the central focus here — rather than the masked and caped hero who typically comes to their aid in crime-fighting — partially the Bat-Signal has been removed from police HQ following a dispute with Batman. (Rev: BL 12/15/06)

2681 Russell, P. Craig. *The Birthday of the Infanta: Fairy Tales of Oscar Wilde, Vol. 3* (5–8). Illus. 1998, NBM $15.95 (978-1-56163-213-8). A graphic novel version of Wilde's fairy tale about the misshapen dwarf who dies of a broken heart. (Rev: BL 4/1/99)

2682 Russell, P. Craig. *The Fairy Tales of Oscar Wilde: The Devoted Friend, The Nightingale and the Rose* (5–8). Illus. by author. 2004, NBM $15.95 (978-1-56163-391-3). Two of Oscar Wilde's fairy tales — "The Devoted Friend" and "The Nightingale and the Rose" — are presented in a rich, picture-book-size graphic novel format. (Rev: BL 8/04; SLJ 11/04)

2683 Saenagi, Ryo. *Psychic Power Nanaki, Vol. 1* (7–12). Trans. from Japanese by Elina Ishikawa. Illus. by author. 2007, TokyoPop paper $9.99 (978-1-4278-0304-7). In this well-illustrated manga book, a Japanese teen acquires psychic powers and uses them to investigate ghosts and supernatural phenomena. (Rev: SLJ 3/08)

2684 Sahara, Mizu. *The Voices of a Distant Star* (7–10). Illus. 2006, TokyoPop paper $9.99 (978-1-59816-529-6). When Mikako, 15, leaves Earth to travel through space and fight Tarsians (an alien race), she stays in contact with her boyfriend, Noboru, through text messages; but years pass and he must decide if he can wait for her any longer. (Rev: BL 11/1/06)

2685 Sakai, Stan. *Usagi Yojimbo: Glimpses of Death, Vol. 20* (8–11). Series: Usagi Yojimbo. 2006, Dark Horse $15.95 (978-1-59307-549-1). This newest installment in the series finds the samurai rabbit granting a dying man's last request and embarking on a danger-filled quest to deliver a mysterious package to the man's daughter. (Rev: BL 11/1/06)

2686 Sakai, Stan. *Usagi Yojimbo: Travels with Jotaro, Vol. 18* (8–12). 2004, Dark Horse paper $15.95 (978-1-59307-220-9). In the 18th volume of the series, the title character, a rabbit samurai in feudal Japan, encounters a series of adventures while traveling with Jotaro, who is Usagi's son but doesn't know it. (Rev: BL 9/15/04; SLJ 10/04)

2687 Sakura, Tsukuba. *Land of the Blindfolded* (8–11). Illus. 2004, DC Comics paper $9.95 (978-1-4012-0524-9). This manga designed primarily for girls tells of two Japanese high school friends (boy and girl) who become close as they decide how to use their conflicting super powers. (Rev: BL 2/15/05)

2688 Schrag, Ariel, ed. *Stuck in the Middle: Seventeen Comics from an Unpleasant Age* (7–10). 2007, Viking $18.99 (978-0-670-06221-8). Is middle school really that bad? Yes, say these artists, who present their versions of this "unpleasant age" in various artistic styles. (Rev: BCCB 9/07; BL 3/15/07; LMC 11–12/07; SLJ 7/07)

2689 Schreiber, Ellen. *Blood Relatives* (6–9). Illus. by Rem. 2007, TokyoPop paper $7.99 (978-0-06-134081-9). Raven's perfect relationship with her vampire boyfriend is threatened when Claude and his Goth friends come to town. (Rev: BL 1/15/08; SLJ 1/08)

2690 Sfar, Joann. *The Rabbi's Cat* (8–12). Illus. 2005, Pantheon $21.95 (978-0-375-42281-2). The entertaining and sophisticated adventures of a talking cat who lives with a rabbi and his daughter in 1930s Algeria. (Rev: BL 7/05; SLJ 3/06)

2691 Shanower, Eric. *Adventures in Oz* (4–7). Illus. by author. 2007, IDW $75.00 (978-1-60010-071-0); paper $39.99 (978-1-933239-61-3). Dorothy and her friends from Oz return in this beautifully drawn collection of five graphic novel adventures. (Rev: BL 3/15/07; SLJ 3/07; VOYA 4/07)

2692 Shimizu, Aki. *Qwan, Vol. 1* (7–12). Trans. from Japanese by Mike Kief. Illus. by author. 2005, TokyoPop paper $9.99 (978-1-59532-534-1). This compelling graphic novel follows Qwan and his friend as they embark on a magical journey to uncover Qwan's destiny. (Rev: SLJ 7/05)

2693 Shone, Rob. *Greek Myths* (5–9). Illus. by author. Series: Graphic Mythology. 2006, Rosen LB $29.25 (978-1-4042-0801-8). "Jason and the Golden Fleece," "Icarus," and "The Labors of Hercules" are the three tales presented here in graphic novel format. (Rev: SLJ 9/06) [292.1]

2694 *Showcase Presents the House of Mystery, Vol. 1* (5–9). 2006, DC Comics paper $16.99 (978-1-4012-0786-1). A collection of relatively tame horror comics that first appeared in the 1960s, in black and white. (Rev: SLJ 7/06)

2695 Singer, Bryan, and Justin Gray. *Superman Returns: The Prequels* (7–12). Illus. 2006, DC Comics paper $12.99 (978-1-4012-1146-2). *Superman Returns,* the film, is enhanced by these stories that occur in the five years before his return to Earth and involve his adoptive mother Martha, his nemesis Lex Luthor, and his heartbroken love interest Lois Lane; they also bridge some scenes from the 1978 *Superman* film for a better continuity. (Rev: BL 12/1/06)

2696 Siu-Chong, Ken. *Round One: Fight!* (6–9). Illus. Series: Street Fighter. 2004, DDP paper $9.99 (978-1-932796-08-7). The opening volume in the

series brings to life the characters and action of the popular video game of the same name and will appeal to reluctant readers. (Rev: SLJ 7/05)

2697 Smith, Jeff. *Eyes of the Storm, Vol. 3* (4–8). Illus. by author. Series: Bone. 2006, Scholastic $19.99 (978-0-439-70625-4); paper $9.99 (978-0-439-70638-4). The final book in the first Bone trilogy, this comic-book fantasy has funny moments, suspense and dream sequences that fans will love. (Rev: SLJ 7/06)

2698 Smith, Jeff. *Old Man's Cave* (5–12). Illus. by author. Series: Bone. 2007, Scholastic $18.99 (978-0-439-70628-5); paper $9.99 (978-0-439-70635-3). Episode six of this series that combines goofy-looking characters with dramatic fantasy plots finds Phoney Bone and Thorn in grave danger. (Rev: BL 11/1/07)

2699 Smith, Jeff. *Shazam! The Monster Society of Evil* (7–12). Illus. 2007, DC Comics $29.99 (978-1-4012-1466-1). Young Billy Batson, an orphan living in unpleasant circumstances, only has to say Shazam to be transformed into Captain Marvel; but Billy is hampered by his own behavior and his younger sister and now faces an alien invasion and the Monster Society of Evil. (Rev: BL 10/15/07; SLJ 3/08)

2700 Soo, Kean. *Jellaby* (4–7). Illus. by author. 2008, Hyperion $18.99 (978-1-4231-0337-0); paper $9.99 (978-1-4231-0303-5). A gentle purple monster changes the lives of 10-year-old Portia and her friend Jason. (Rev: BL 3/15/08; SLJ 1/08)

2701 Spiegelman, Art. *Little Lit: Folklore and Fairy Tale Funnies* (4–9). Illus. 2000, HarperCollins $19.95 (978-0-06-028624-8). In this presentation in graphic novel format, 15 different artists create brilliant variations on standard fairy and folk tales. (Rev: BL 1/1–15/01*; HB 9–10/00; HBG 3/01; SLJ 12/00) [398.2]

2702 Spradlin, Michael P. *Chase for the Chalice* (6–8). Illus. by Rainbow Buddy. Series: Spy Goddess. 2008, TokyoPop paper $9.99 (978-0-06-136299-6). In this installment, the first in manga form and full of details about Japan, Rachel and her friends are on a mission to thwart Simon Blankenship. (Rev: BL 6/1–15/08; SLJ 9/08)

2703 Stanley, John, and Irving Tripp. *Color Special: Little Lulu* (7–12). Illus. 2006, Dark Horse paper $13.95 (978-1-59307-613-9). Little Lulu is back in vibrant color reproductions of selected stories from issues 4 through 86. (Rev: BL 10/1/06)

2704 Stevenson, Robert Louis. *Treasure Island* (5–9). Adapted and illus. by Tim Hamilton. Series: Puffin Graphics. 2005, Puffin paper $10.99 (978-0-14-240470-6). Robert Louis Stevenson's adventure classic springs to life in this striking graphic novel adaptation that remains faithful to the original text. (Rev: SLJ 11/05)

2705 Stoker, Bram. *Dracula* (7–12). Adapted by Gary Reed. Illus. by Becky Cloonan. Series: Puffin Graphics. 2006, Puffin paper $10.99 (978-0-14-240572-7). A compelling graphic novel version of the famous vampire story. (Rev: SLJ 3/06)

2706 Storrie, Paul D. *Yu the Great: Conquering the Flood* (4–7). Illus. by Sandy Carruthers. Series: Graphic Myths and Legends. 2007, Lerner LB $26.60 (978-0-8225-3088-6). In this graphic novel adaptation of an ancient Chinese folk tale, the emperor Shun asks Yu to save China and its people from the floods that are ravaging the land. (Rev: BL 3/15/07; SLJ 5/07) [398.2]

2707 Sturm, James. *Satchel Paige: Striking Out Jim Crow* (6–12). Illus. by Rich Tommaso. 2007, Hyperion $16.99 (978-0-7868-3900-1); paper $9.99 (978-0-7868-3901-8). This graphic novel serves up a slice of segregated Southern history in which a fictional Negro League player named Emmet Wilson goes up against Paige — a high point in Wilson's life before he returns to farming. (Rev: BL 11/1/07; SLJ 1/08)

2708 Sugisaki, Yukiro. *Rizelmine* (8–12). Trans. from Japanese by Alethea Nibley and Athena Nibley. Illus. by author. 2005, TokyoPop paper $9.99 (978-1-59532-901-1). Fifteen-year-old Iwaki Tomonori rejects the advances of robot-like Rizel, who's become his bride by government decree. (Rev: SLJ 11/05)

2709 Tan, Shaun. *The Arrival* (6–12). Illus. by author. 2007, Scholastic $19.99 (978-0-439-89529-3). Leaving his family behind, an immigrant travels to a strange new world where he struggles but finds friendship and builds a new life for his family; this wordless graphic novel features powerful sepia illustrations. (Rev: BL 9/1/07; SLJ 9/07)

2710 Taniguchi, Tomoko. *Call Me Princess* (5–8). Trans. from Japanese by Mutsumi Masuda and C. B. Cebulski. Illus. by author. 2003, CPM Manga paper $9.99 (978-1-58664-898-5). This graphic novel, set in Japan, centers on the young heroine's romantic attachments but gets a "G" rating. (Rev: SLJ 3/04)

2711 *Teen Titans: Jam Packed Action!* (4–8). 2005, DC Comics paper $7.99 (978-1-4012-0902-5). Two exciting technology-oriented stories are drawn from the Cartoon Network show. (Rev: SLJ 5/06)

2712 Tetzner, Lisa. *The Black Brothers* (6–9). Trans. by Peter F. Neumeyer. Illus. by Hannes Binder. 2004, Front St. $16.95 (978-1-932425-04-8). This striking graphic novel adaptation of Lisa Tetzner's 1941 novel recounts the trials and tribulations of 13-year-old Giorgio, a young chimney sweep in 19th-century Europe whose friendship with the leader of a secret society called the Black Brothers ultimately leads him to happiness. (Rev: BL 9/1/04; SLJ 11/04; VOYA 2/05)

2713 Tinsley, Kevin, and Phil Singer. *Milk Cartons and Dog Biscuits* (7–12). Illus. 2004, Stickman Graphics paper $19.95 (978-0-9675423-4-8). People and elf-like creatures mingle in this adventure mystery about a state ranger who is searching for a runaway daughter. (Rev: BL 2/1/04)

2714 Tolkien, J. R. R. *The Hobbit; or, There and Back Again* (5–10). Adapted by Charles Dixon. Illus. 1990, Eclipse Books paper $12.95 (978-0-345-36858-4). The classic story of Bilbo Baggins and his companions is introduced to reluctant readers in this full-color graphic novel. (Rev: BL 9/1/91)

2715 Toume, Kei. *Kurogane, Vol. 1* (7–12). Trans. from Japanese by Akira Tsubasa. Adapted by Alex Kent. Illus. by author. 2006, Del Rey paper $10.95 (978-0-345-49203-6). Jintetsu, with a steel body and a talking sword, sets out to avenge his father's death in this story set in feudal Japan. (Rev: SLJ 9/06)

2716 Toyoda, Minoru. *Love Roma, Vol. 1* (8–11). Illus. 2005, Del Rey paper $10.95 (978-0-345-48262-4). This delightful manga chronicles the budding romance of teenagers Hoshino and Negishi. (Rev: BL 10/15/05; SLJ 1/06)

2717 Tran, Thien, and Keith Giffen. *Road Trip* (6–9). Illus. by Cully Hamner. Series: Blue Beetle. 2007, DC Comics paper $12.99 (978-1-4012-1361-9). An alien scarab has attached itself to a young Latino named Jaime Reyes, giving him an armor-like shell and superhero abilities; in this second volume in the series, Jaime tries to find out more about what's happening to him. (Rev: BL 9/1/07)

2718 Trondheim, Lewis. *Mister O* (4–8). Illus. by author. 2004, NBM $13.95 (978-1-56163-382-1). Mister O, portrayed in wordless rectangular cartoons, is a round caricature who — à la Wile E. Coyote — can't seem conquer a chasm, no matter how many successful crossings he views. (Rev: SLJ 9/04)

2719 Trondheim, Lewis. *Tiny Tyrant* (4–7). Illus. by Fabrice Parme. 2007, Roaring Brook paper $12.95 (978-1-59643-094-5). Ethelbert, the diminutive and willful 6-year-old child-king of Portocristo, is used to getting his own way in this series of funny episodes. (Rev: BL 3/15/07; SLJ 9/07)

2720 Tsukiji, Toshihiko. *Maburaho, Vol. 1* (8–12). Trans. from Japanese by Kay Bertrand. Illus. by Miki Miyashita. 2005, ADV paper $9.99 (978-1-4139-0293-8). Kazuki, a hapless magician-in-training, is pursued by three female students who know that he is destined to father a child who'll become a powerful wizard. (Rev: SLJ 7/05)

2721 Uderzo, Albert. *Asterix and the Actress* (4–7). Trans. by Anthea Bell and Derek Hockridge. Illus. 2001, Sterling $12.95 (978-0-7528-4657-6). These pun-filled, graphic novel exploits of Asterix the Gaul include a boisterous shared birthday with the rotund Obelix and a daring rescue of prisoners in a Roman jail. (Rev: BL 8/01)

2722 Urushibara, Yuki. *Mushishi, Vol. 1* (8–12). Adapted by William Flanagan. Illus. by author. 2007, Del Rey paper $10.95 (978-0-345-49621-8). Mushi are parasitic, supernatural beings that invade human victims, and Ginko's job is to control them in this compelling manga. (Rev: SLJ 7/07)

2723 Varon, Sara. *Robot Dreams* (6–12). Illus. by author. 2007, Roaring Brook paper $16.95 (978-1-59643-108-9). Poor lonely Dog is very happy when Robot arrives, but Dog doesn't realize Robot can't go swimming in this appealing almost-wordless graphic novel that provides both humor and poignancy. (Rev: BL 8/07; LMC 11/07; SLJ 9/07)

2724 Vollmar, Rob. *The Castaways* (6–9). Illus. by Pablo G. Callejo. 2007, ComicsLit $17.95 (978-1-56163-492-7). Tucker's life is changed when he meets a hobo on a freight train during the Great Depression; this new edition adds a color wash to the black-and-white illustrations as well as an epilogue. (Rev: BL 3/15/07; LMC 11-12/07; SLJ 5/07)

2725 Von Sholly, Pete. *Dead But Not Out! Pete Von Sholly's Morbid 2* (7–12). Illus. 2005, Dark Horse paper $14.95 (978-1-59307-289-6). Cheap horror movies are the target of this entertaining parody. (Rev: BL 3/15/05)

2726 Waid, Mark. *Legion of Super-Heroes: Teenage Revolution* (8–11). Illus. by Barry Kitson. 2005, DC Comics paper $14.99 (978-1-4012-0482-2). In this comic book vision of the future, teenage superheroes rebel against their parents' utopian government. (Rev: BL 1/1–15/06; SLJ 3/06)

2727 Waid, Mark. *Ruse: Inferno of Blue* (7–12). Illus. by Butch Guice. 2002, CrossGeneration paper $15.95 (978-1-931484-19-0). Mystery, action, and magical powers abound in this graphic novel set in an alternate universe and starring detective Simon Archard and sidekick Emma Bishop. (Rev: BL 8/02)

2728 Wein, Len. *Secret of the Swamp Thing* (7–12). Illus. by Berni Wrightson. 2005, DC Comics paper $9.99 (978-1-4012-0798-4). A collection of the first ten issues of the original comics about the legendary hero called Swamp Thing. (Rev: SLJ 5/06)

2729 Wells, H. G. *The Invisible Man* (7–12). Retold by Terry Davis. Illus. by Dennis Calero. Series: Graphic Revolve. 2008, Stone Arch LB $23.93 (978-1-59889-831-6); paper $6.95 (978-1-59889-887-3). This somewhat altered retelling of Wells's story is concise and easy to understand. (Rev: SLJ 3/08)

2730 Wells, H. G. *The Time Machine* (7–12). Retold by Terry Davis. Illus. by Josée Alfonso and Ocampo Ruiz. Series: Graphic Revolve. 2008, Stone Arch LB $23.93 (978-1-59889-833-0); paper $6.95 (978-

1-59889-889-7). Simpler in its retelling, this version of Wells's classic will attract a wide audience. (Rev: SLJ 3/08)

2731 West, David. *Mesoamerican Myths* (5–9). Illus. by Mike Taylor. Series: Graphic Mythology. 2006, Rosen LB $29.25 (978-1-4042-0802-5). Presented in graphic novel format are three tales from the mythology of Mexico and Central America — two creation stories and a hero tale. (Rev: SLJ 9/06) [398.2]

2732 Williams, Rob. *Star Wars Rebellion: My Brother, My Enemy, Vol. 1* (8–12). Illus. by Brandon Badeaux. 2007, Dark Horse paper $14.95 (978-1-59307-711-2). This first volume in a new graphic novel series follows Luke Skywalker after he joins the rebellion and must decide whether to trust his old friend Tank, who is now an Imperial Officer. (Rev: BL 8/07)

2733 Willingham, Bill. *Robin: To Kill a Bird* (8–11). Illus. by Damion Scott. 2006, DC Comics paper $14.99 (978-1-4012-0909-4). In this Batman and Robin adventure, Robin learns to fight for himself as he's attacked by the Penguin's hit men. (Rev: BL 7/06)

2734 Winick, Judd. *Pedro and Me: Friendship, Loss, and What I Learned* (8–12). Illus. 2000, Holt paper $16.00 (978-0-8050-6403-2). A graphic novel tribute to Pedro Zamora, an AIDS educator and actor who died of HIV complications at the age of 22. (Rev: BL 9/15/00; HB 11–12/00; HBG 3/01; SLJ 10/00)

2735 Wolfman, Marv. *The New Teen Titans Archives, Vol. 3* (7–12). Illus. 2006, DC Comics $49.99 (978-1-4012-1144-8). This collection includes the most popular stories from the 1980s comics that updated the 1960s tales about teen sidekicks of superheroes — Robin, Wonder Girl, Starfire, Cyborg, Raven, the Changeling, and Kid Flash. (Rev: BL 12/1/06)

2736 Yagami, Yu. *Hikkatsu, Vol. 1* (6–10). Illus. by author. 2007, Go! Comi paper $10.99 (978-1-933617-29-9). A wacky manga story of a martial artist gone wild, karate-chopping small electrical appliances. (Rev: BL 1/1–15/08)

2737 Yamada, Norie. *Someday's Dreamers, Vol. 1* (8–12). Trans. from Japanese by Jeremiah Bourque. Illus. by Kumichi Yoshizuki. 2006, TokyoPop paper $9.99 (978-1-59816-178-6). Yume is a "magic user" who is paid by the government to use her skills for the good of others. (Rev: SLJ 9/06)

2738 Yoshizaki, Mine. *Sgt. Frog, Vol. 1* (8–11). Illus. 2004, TokyoPop paper $9.99 (978-1-59182-703-0). In this *manga* work, a young brother and sister are dealing with an uninvited guest, an invader from another planet. (Rev: BL 3/15/04)

2739 Young-You, Lee. *Moon Boy* (6–9). 2006, Ice Kunion paper $10.95 (978-8-9527460-4-7). Myung-

Ee meets and likes Yu-da, also realizes he too is a moon rabbit (a being hiding in human form); later she must rescue him from their predators, the moon foxes. (Rev: BL 9/15/06; SLJ 1/07)

2740 Yune, Tommy. *From the Stars* (7–12). Illus. 2003, DC Comics paper $9.95 (978-1-4012-0144-9). When an alien ship crashes on earth, Roy Fokker signs up to be a test pilot and then learns a great deal about alien technology. (Rev: BL 2/1/04)

2741 Zirkel, Huddleston. *A Bit Haywire* (4–7). Illus. 2006, Viper paper $11.95 (978-0-977788-35-4). Owen has many extraordinary powers, but he's having trouble figuring out how to control them. (Rev: BL 3/15/07)

2742 Zornow, Jeff. *The Legend of Sleepy Hollow* (5–7). Illus. by author. Series: Graphic Planet: Graphic Horror. 2008, ABDO LB $18.95 (978-1-60270-060-4). A graphic adaptation of the classic story with satisfyingly creepy illustrations. (Rev: BL 3/15/08; SLJ 5/08)

Historical Fiction and Foreign Lands

Prehistory

2743 Brennan, J. H. *Shiva Accused: An Adventure of the Ice Age* (6–9). 1991, HarperCollins LB $16.89 (978-0-06-020742-7). In this sequel to *Shiva* (o.p.), a prehistoric orphan girl is accused of murder by a rival tribe. (Rev: BL 8/91; SLJ 11/91)

2744 Brennan, J. H. *Shiva's Challenge: An Adventure of the Ice Age* (6–9). 1992, HarperCollins LB $16.89 (978-0-06-020826-4). In the third entry in the series, Cro-Magnon Shiva is spirited away by the shamanistic Crones to test her powers and see if she can survive the ordeals that will make her a Crone, too. (Rev: BL 12/15/92)

2745 Denzel, Justin. *Boy of the Painted Cave* (5–7). 1988, Putnam $17.99 (978-0-399-21559-9). The story of a boy who longs to be a cave artist, set in Cro Magnon times. (Rev: BL 11/1/88; SLJ 11/88)

2746 Dickinson, Peter. *A Bone from a Dry Sea* (7–10). 1993, Dell paper $4.99 (978-0-440-21928-6). The protagonists are Li, a girl in a tribe of "sea apes" living four million years ago, and Vinny, the teenage daughter of a modern-day paleontologist. (Rev: BL 2/1/93; SLJ 4/93*)

2747 Levin, Betty. *Thorn* (7–10). 2005, Front St. $16.95 (978-1-932425-46-8). Thorn, a young boy with an atrophied leg, is befriended by Willow but still feels uncomfortable and plans his escape. (Rev: BL 12/15/05; SLJ 1/06)

2748 Paver, Michelle. *Wolf Brother* (6–9). Illus. by Geoff Taylor. Series: Chronicles of Ancient Darkness. 2005, HarperCollins LB $17.89 (978-0-06-

072826-7). In the distant prehistoric past, 12-year-old Torak and his wolf cub companion set off on a perilous journey to destroy a demon-possessed bear. (Rev: BCCB 2/05; BL 3/1/05; SLJ 2/05)

2749 Williams, Susan. *Wind Rider* (6–9). 2006, HarperCollins $16.99 (978-0-06-087236-6). In Central Asia about 6,000 years ago, a teenage girl named Fern befriends and tames a horse, showing her tribe how useful the animals can be and challenging the standards set for women at that time. (Rev: BL 10/15/06; SLJ 11/06)

Ancient and Medieval History

GENERAL AND MISCELLANEOUS

2750 Cadnum, Michael. *Raven of the Waves* (7–10). 2001, Scholastic $17.95 (978-0-531-30334-4). In this gory tale set in the 8th century, 17-year-old Viking Lidsmod takes part in a bloodthirsty raid on an English community but later helps a boy who is taken captive. (Rev: BL 4/1/01; HB 9–10/01; HBG 3/02; SLJ 7/01; VOYA 8/01)

2751 Carter, Dorothy Sharp. *His Majesty, Queen Hatshepsut* (6–9). 1987, HarperCollins LB $16.89 (978-0-397-32179-7). A fictionalized biography of Queen Hatshepsut, daughter of Thutmose I and the only female pharaoh of Egypt. (Rev: SLJ 10/87; VOYA 12/87)

2752 Chen, Da. *Sword* (6–9). Series: Forbidden Tales. 2008, HarperCollins $16.99 (978-0-06-144758-7). Fifteen-year-old Miu Miu must avenge her father's murder at the hand of the emperor in this novel set in ancient China and featuring lots of martial arts. (Rev: BL 8/08)

2753 Gregory, Kristiana. *Cleopatra VII: Daughter of the Nile* (5–8). Series: Royal Diaries. 1999, Scholastic paper $10.95 (978-0-590-81975-6). This mock-diary recounts various events in the life of 12-year-old Cleopatra who, even at that age, was involved in palace intrigue. (Rev: BL 1/1–15/00; HBG 3/00; SLJ 10/99)

2754 Harvey, Gill. *Orphan of the Sun* (6–9). 2006, Bloomsbury $16.95 (978-1-58234-685-4). Thirteen-year-old Meryt-Re, an orphaned girl living in ancient Egypt, is kicked out of her uncle's home and embarks on a road to self-discovery. (Rev: BL 7/06; LMC 10/06; SLJ 1/07)

2755 Lasky, Kathryn. *The Last Girls of Pompeii* (7–10). 2007, Viking $15.99 (978-0-670-06196-9). Julia and her slave (and best friend) Sura do not have bright futures in Pompeii but together they manage to escape the smothering ash of erupting Vesuvius. (Rev: BL 4/15/07; LMC 11–12/07; SLJ 8/07)

2756 McCaughrean, Geraldine. *Casting the Gods Adrift: A Tale of Ancient Egypt* (5–8). Illus. by

Patricia D. Ludlow. 2003, Cricket $15.95 (978-0-8126-2684-1). History and fiction are intertwined in this well-illustrated, suspenseful novel about two boys who are content to be taken in by the Pharoah Akhenaten, and a father enraged by the Pharaoh's refusal to worship the traditional Egyptian gods. (Rev: BCCB 10/03; BL 10/15/03; HBG 4/04; SLJ 8/03)

2757 McCaughrean, Geraldine. *Not the End of the World* (7–10). 2005, HarperCollins LB $17.89 (978-0-06-076031-1). A harrowing but thought-provoking story of what it was really like aboard Noah's ark, with terrified animals and humans unhinged by their circumstances. (Rev: BL 8/05; SLJ 8/05*; VOYA 8/05)

2758 Miklowitz, Gloria D. *Masada: The Last Fortress* (7–10). 1998, Eerdmans $16.00 (978-0-8028-5165-9). The siege of Masada comes alive through the eyes of a young Jewish man and a Roman commander. (Rev: BCCB 10/98; BL 10/1/98; HBG 3/99; SLJ 12/98; VOYA 2/99)

2759 Pinsker, Marlee. *In the Days of Sand and Stars* (6–9). Illus. by Francois Thisdale. 2006, Tundra $22.95 (978-0-88776-724-1). Ten imagined stories about the lives of legendary women of the Bible such as Eve, Sarah, and Rachel. (Rev: BL 10/1/06; SLJ 1/07)

2760 Roberts, Judson. *Dragons from the Sea* (8–11). Series: Strongbow Saga. 2007, HarperCollins $16.99 (978-0-06-081300-0). In A.D. 845, a young Viking named Halfden, who is skilled at the longbow, joins the crew of the *Gull* and struggles to uphold his honor as he's involved in the violent invasion of France. (Rev: BL 5/15/07; SLJ 9/07)

2761 Roberts, Katherine. *I Am the Great Horse* (8–11). 2006, Scholastic $16.99 (978-0-439-82163-6). The life of Alexander the Great is related from the viewpoint of his famous horse, Bucephalus. (Rev: BL 10/15/06; SLJ 12/06)

2762 Speare, Elizabeth G. *The Bronze Bow* (7–10). 1961, Houghton paper $6.95 (978-0-395-13719-2). A Jewish boy seeks revenge against the Romans who killed his parents, but finally his hatred abates when he hears the messages and teachings of Jesus. Newbery Medal winner, 1962. (Rev: BL 9/1/95)

GREECE AND ROME

2763 Lawrence, Caroline. *The Charioteer of Delphi* (5–8). Series: Roman Mysteries. 2007, Roaring Brook $16.95 (978-1-59643-085-3). Flavia, Jonathan, Nubia, and Lupus find themselves involved in chariot racing in Rome. (Rev: BL 8/07)

2764 Lawrence, Caroline. *Gladiators from Capua* (5–8). Series: Roman Mysteries. 2005, Roaring Brook $16.95 (978-1-59643-074-7). In their search for Jonathan, who may be alive after all, Flavia,

Lupus, and Nubia venture into the coliseum and witness gladiator fights. (Rev: BL 12/1/05; SLJ 2/06)

2765 McLaren, Clemence. *Aphrodite's Blessings: Love Stories from the Greek Myths* (7–12). 2002, Simon & Schuster $16.00 (978-0-689-84377-8). The lot of women in ancient Greece comes to life in three stories, based on mythology, about Atalanta, Andromeda, and Psyche. (Rev: BL 3/1/02; HBG 10/02; SLJ 1/02; VOYA 4/02)

2766 Mitchell, Jack. *The Roman Conspiracy* (5–9). 2005, Tundra paper $8.95 (978-0-88776-713-5). In this compelling historical thriller set in the Roman Empire, young Aulus Spurinna travels to Rome in a desperate attempt to protect his homeland of Etruria from military pillagers. (Rev: SLJ 11/05)

2767 Napoli, Donna Jo. *The Great God Pan* (7–10). 2003, Random $15.95 (978-0-385-32777-0). A beautifully written novel about the life and aspirations of Pan, who was half man and half goat. (Rev: BL 4/15/03; SLJ 6/03)

2768 Napoli, Donna Jo. *Sirena* (7–12). 1998, Scholastic $15.95 (978-0-590-38388-2). This romantic expansion of the Greek myth of the Sirens describes the dilemma of an immortal mermaid who loves a mortal. (Rev: BL 1/1–15/03; HBG 3/99; SLJ 10/98; VOYA 12/98)

2769 Rao, Sirish, and Gita Wolf. *Sophocles' Oedipus the King* (7–10). Illus. by Indrapramit Roy. 2004, Getty $18.95 (978-0-89236-764-1). This retelling of Sophocles' tragic tale of Oedipus is highlighted by the striking illustrations of Indrapromit Roy. (Rev: BL 1/1–15/05)

2770 Rubalcaba, Jill. *The Wadjet Eye* (5–8). 2000, Clarion $15.00 (978-0-395-68942-4). After mummifying his dead mother, Damon sets off to find his father and is later hired by Cleopatra as a spy in this action-filled novel set in the Roman Empire of 45 B.C. (Rev: BL 5/15/00; HBG 10/00; SLJ 6/00; VOYA 6/00)

2771 Sutcliff, Rosemary. *The Eagle of the Ninth* (7–12). 1993, Farrar paper $5.95 (978-0-374-41930-1). A reissue of the historical novel about the Roman legion that went to battle and disappeared.

MIDDLE AGES

2772 Alder, Elizabeth. *The King's Shadow* (7–12). 1995, Bantam paper $5.50 (978-0-440-22011-4). In medieval Britain, mute Evyn is sold into slavery, but as Earl Harold of Wessex's squire and eventual foster son, he chronicles the king's life and becomes a storyteller. (Rev: BL 7/95; SLJ 7/95)

2773 Avi. *Crispin: At the Edge of the World* (5–8). 2006, Hyperion $16.99 (978-0-7868-5152-2). In this compelling sequel to *Crispin: The Cross of Lead*, Bear, who Crispin now regards as a father, is seriously wounded and they make friends with a disfigured girl named Troth; Crispin now finds himself making decisions for the three. (Rev: BCCB 1/07; BL 9/15/06; HB 9–10/06; HBG 4/07; LMC 2/07; SLJ 10/06*; VOYA 10/06) ⊘

2774 Cadnum, Michael. *Forbidden Forest* (7–10). 2002, Scholastic $17.95 (978-0-439-31774-0). The story of Little John's entry into Robin Hood's band of merry men is told from John's point of view and combines realistic descriptions of medieval life with adventure and romance. (Rev: BL 4/15/02; HB 7–8/02; HBG 10/02; SLJ 6/02; VOYA 4/02)

2775 Cadnum, Michael. *In a Dark Wood* (7–10). 1998, Orchard LB $18.99 (978-0-531-33071-5). The story of Robin Hood as seen through the eyes of the sheriff of Nottingham and his young squire, Hugh. (Rev: BL 3/1/98; HB 3–4/98; HBG 9/98; SLJ 4/98; VOYA 8/98)

2776 Cadnum, Michael. *The King's Arrow* (7–10). 2008, Viking $16.99 (978-0-670-06331-4). This story of young Simon, a nobleman who is present during the shooting of King William II with an arrow, will bring the harsh and intriguing Middle Ages to life for its readers. (Rev: BL 12/15/07; HB 3–4/08; LMC 10/08; SLJ 3/08)

2777 Cushman, Karen. *Catherine, Called Birdy* (6–9). 1994, Clarion $16.00 (978-0-395-68186-2). Life in the last decade of the 12th century as seen through the eyes of a teenage girl. (Rev: BL 4/15/94; SLJ 6/94*; VOYA 6/94)

2778 Cushman, Karen. *Matilda Bone* (4–8). 2000, Clarion $15.00 (978-0-395-88156-9). Set in the 14th century, this novel describes the development of Matilda, 13, who serves as an assistant to the local bone setter in exchange for food and shelter. (Rev: BCCB 12/00; BL 8/00; HB 11–12/00; HBG 3/01; SLJ 9/00*; VOYA 12/00)

2779 Cushman, Karen. *The Midwife's Apprentice* (7–12). 1995, Clarion $13.00 (978-0-395-69229-5). A homeless young woman in medieval England becomes strong as she picks herself up and learns from a midwife to be brave. (Rev: BL 3/15/95*; SLJ 5/95)

2780 Dana, Barbara. *Young Joan* (6–10). 1991, HarperCollins $17.95 (978-0-06-021422-7). A fictional account of Joan of Arc that questions how a simple French farm girl hears, assimilates, and acts upon a message from God. (Rev: BL 5/15/91*; SLJ 5/91)

2781 Decker, Timothy. *Run Far, Run Fast* (8–12). Illus. by author. 2007, Front St. $17.95 (978-1-59078-469-3). In 14th-century Europe a young girl's mother tells her to "run far, run fast" to escape the plague; the stark illustrations and simple text add to the setting and the tension. (Rev: BL 9/15/07; SLJ 1/08)

2782 Goodman, Joan Elizabeth. *Peregrine* (7–10). 2000, Houghton $16.00 (978-0-395-97729-3). Fifteen-year-old Lady Edith, who has lost her husband and baby, escapes her problems by going on a pilgrimage from England to the Holy Land. (Rev: BL 4/1/00; HBG 9/00; SLJ 5/00; VOYA 6/00)

2783 Grant, K. M. *Blaze of Silver* (6–9). Series: The de Granville Trilogy. 2007, Walker $16.95 (978-0-8027-9625-7). Will is betrayed by Kamil and must save the king from an assassination plot in this sweeping story that horse-lovers will adore; the final book in the trilogy set in the time of the Crusades, following *Blood Red Horse* (2005) and *Green Jasper* (2006). (Rev: BL 2/1/07; SLJ 5/07)

2784 Grant, K. M. *Blood Red Horse* (6–9). 2005, Walker $16.95 (978-0-8027-8960-0). This epic historical novel chronicles the adventures of English brothers Gavin and William de Granville as they leave home to join the Third Crusade under the leadership of King Richard I. (Rev: BCCB 5/05; BL 4/1/05*; SLJ 5/05; VOYA 6/05)

2785 Grant, K. M. *Green Jasper* (5–9). Series: The de Granville Trilogy. 2006, Walker $16.95 (978-0-8027-8073-7). Will and Gavin, introduced in *Blood Red Horse* (2005), come home from the crusade to find England in chaos and Gavin's beloved Ellie abducted by Constable de Scabious; a multilayered medieval adventure story. (Rev: SLJ 6/06; VOYA 8/06)

2786 Gray, Elizabeth Janet. *Adam of the Road* (5–8). Illus. by Robert Lawson. 1942, Puffin paper $7.99 (978-0-14-032464-8). Adventures of a 13th-century minstrel boy. Newbery Medal winner, 1943.

2787 Grey, Christopher. *Leonardo's Shadow: or, My Astonishing Life as Leonardo da Vinci's Servant* (7–10). 2006, Simon & Schuster $16.95 (978-1-4169-0543-1). Fifteen-year-old Giacomo, a servant to the great Leonardo da Vinci, wards off the artist's creditors while also trying to uncover the truth about his own origins. (Rev: BL 8/06; SLJ 10/06)

2788 Grove, Vicki. *Rhiannon* (6–9). 2007, Putnam $18.99 (978-0-399-23633-4). Rhiannon, her mother, and her grandmother care for the sick and outcast in their medieval Welsh village, even defending one against a murder charge, in this novel that beautifully captures the feel of the times. (Rev: BL 11/15/07; SLJ 12/07)

2789 Jinks, Catherine. *Pagan's Vows* (8–10). 2005, Candlewick $16.99 (978-0-7636-2021-9). Seventeen-year-old Pagan Kidrouk, squire to Lord Roland, joins his master at the Abbey of St. Martin where they are to begin training as monks, but Pagan soon finds that he has trouble adjusting to all the rules of his new life. (Rev: BL 10/1/04; SLJ 9/04; VOYA 10/04)

2790 Karr, Kathleen. *Fortune's Fool* (7–12). 2008, Knopf $15.99 (978-0-375-84816-2). Set in 14th-century Germany, this story of a court jester in search of a new master is full of medieval flavor and humor. (Rev: BL 3/1/08; SLJ 7/08)

2791 Leeds, Constance. *The Silver Cup* (6–9). 2007, Viking $16.99 (978-0-670-06157-0). Anna's family takes in an orphaned Jewish girl in this novel that captures the danger and difficulties of everyday life in 1095 Germany. (Rev: BL 2/15/07; SLJ 7/07)

2792 Morressy, John. *The Juggler* (7–10). 1996, Holt $16.95 (978-0-8050-4217-7). In this adventure story set in the Middle Ages, a young man regrets the bargain he has made with the devil to become the world's greatest juggler in exchange for his soul. (Rev: SLJ 6/96; VOYA 8/96)

2793 Morris, Gerald. *The Ballad of Sir Dinadan* (5–9). 2003, Houghton $16.00 (978-0-618-19099-7). An amusing retelling from Arthurian legend that features the younger brother of Sir Tristram as a music lover and reluctant knight. (Rev: BL 5/1/03; HB 5–6/03; HBG 10/03; SLJ 4/03*; VOYA 6/03)

2794 Morris, Gerald. *The Squire, His Knight, and His Lady* (5–9). 1999, Houghton $16.00 (978-0-395-91211-9). This is a retelling, from the perspective of a knight's squire, of the classic story of Sir Gawain and the Green Knight. (Rev: BL 5/1/99; HBG 10/99; SLJ 5/99; VOYA 8/99)

2795 Morris, Gerald. *The Squire's Tale* (5–9). 1998, Houghton $16.00 (978-0-395-86959-8). The peaceful existence of 14-year-old Terence is shattered when he becomes the squire of Sir Gawain and becomes involved in a series of quests. (Rev: BL 4/15/98; HB 7–8/98; SLJ 7/98; VOYA 8/98)

2796 Napoli, Donna Jo. *Hush: An Irish Princess' Tale* (8–11). 2007, Atheneum $16.99 (978-0-689-86176-5). Melkorka, an Irish princess, is captured by Russian slave traders and refuses to speak in this present-tense story set in the 10th century. (Rev: BL 11/1/07; SLJ 12/07)

2797 Pernoud, Regine. *A Day with a Miller* (4–7). Trans. by Dominique Clift. Illus. by Giorgio Bacchin. 1997, Runestone LB $22.60 (978-0-8225-1914-0). A description of the life of a miller and his family in the 12th century and how hydraulic energy was being introduced at that time. (Rev: HBG 3/98; SLJ 3/98)

2798 Pyle, Howard. *Otto of the Silver Hand* (6–8). Illus. by author. 1967, Dover paper $8.95 (978-0-486-21784-0). Life in feudal Germany, the turbulence and cruelty of robber barons, and the peaceful, scholarly pursuits of the monks are presented in the story of the kidnapped son of a robber baron.

2799 Reeve, Philip. *Here Lies Arthur* (7–10). 2008, Scholastic $16.99 (978-0-545-09334-7). A compelling and inventive retelling of the Arthurian legend from the point of view of a young girl named Gwyna. (Rev: BL 8/08)

2800 Rosen, Sidney, and Dorothy S. Rosen. *The Magician's Apprentice* (5–8). 1994, Carolrhoda LB $19.95 (978-0-87614-809-9). An orphan in a French abbey in the Middle Ages is accused of having a heretical document in his possession and is sent to spy on Roger Bacon, the English scientist. (Rev: BL 5/1/94; SLJ 6/94)

2801 Russell, Christopher. *Hunted* (5–8). 2007, HarperCollins $15.99 (978-0-06-084119-5). Set in the Middle Ages, this is the exciting tale of two teens who run away after being falsely accused of bringing the Black Death to the manor in which they work. (Rev: SLJ 6/07)

2802 Sauerwein, Leigh. *Song for Eloise* (8–10). 2003, Front St. $15.95 (978-1-886910-90-4). In the Middle Ages, an unhappy wife falls for a passing troubadour in a rich text full of historical detail. (Rev: BL 12/1/03; HBG 4/04; SLJ 12/03; VOYA 4/04)

2803 Shulevitz, Uri. *The Travels of Benjamin of Tudela: Through Three Continents in the Twelfth Century* (4–7). Illus. 2005, Farrar $17.00 (978-0-374-37754-0). Based on Benjamin's diaries, this picture book, which is incredibly detailed in both illustrations and text, tells of his perilous journey through parts of Europe, the Mediterranean, and the Middle East. (Rev: BL 3/15/05*; SLJ 4/05)

2804 Temple, Frances. *The Beduins' Gazelle* (7–10). 1996, Orchard LB $16.99 (978-0-531-08869-2). In this 14th-century adventure, a companion piece to *The Ramsey Scallop*, young scholar Etienne becomes involved in the lives of two lovers when he goes to Fez to study at the university. (Rev: BL 2/15/96; SLJ 4/96*; VOYA 12/96)

2805 Temple, Frances. *The Ramsay Scallop* (7–10). 1994, Orchard LB $19.99 (978-0-531-08686-5). In 1299, 14-year-old Elenor and her betrothed nobleman are sent on a chaste pilgrimage to Spain and hear the stories of their fellow travelers. (Rev: BL 3/15/94*; SLJ 5/94; VOYA 4/94)

2806 Thal, Lilli. *Mimus* (8–11). Trans. by John Brownjohn. 2005, Annick $19.95 (978-1-55037-925-9); paper $9.95 (978-1-55037-924-2). Prince Florin is taken captive and made a jester when the kingdom of Vinland overpowers Moltovia in this novel of the Middle Ages. (Rev: BL 9/1/05*; SLJ 12/05*; VOYA 2/06)

2807 Thomson, Sarah L. *The Dragon's Son* (7–12). 2001, Scholastic $17.95 (978-0-531-30333-7). This historical novel, based on Welsh legends about King Arthur, tells the stories of family members and others who were involved in Arthur's life. (Rev: BCCB 7–8/01; BL 5/1/01; HBG 10/01; SLJ 7/01; VOYA 6/01)

2808 Tingle, Rebecca. *Far Traveler* (7–10). 2005, Penguin $18.99 (978-0-399-23890-1). In this historical novel set in 10th-century England, 16-year-old

Aelfwyn flees when her uncle, West Saxon King Edward, tells her she must marry one of his allies or enter a convent. (Rev: BCCB 3/05; BL 2/1/05; SLJ 2/05; VOYA 8/05)

2809 Tomlinson, Theresa. *The Forestwife* (8–12). 1995, Orchard LB $17.99 (978-0-531-08750-3). A Robin Hood legend with Marian as the benevolent Green Lady of the forest. (Rev: BL 3/1/95*; SLJ 3/95; VOYA 5/95)

2810 Wein, Elizabeth E. *A Coalition of Lions* (7–12). Series: The Winter Prince. 2003, Viking $16.99 (978-0-370-03618-2). In the 6th century, a princess named Goewin travels from Britain to Africa on her way to an arranged marriage, in this absorbing sequel to *The Winter Prince* (1993). (Rev: BCCB 4/03; BL 2/15/03; SLJ 4/03)

2811 Williams, Marcia. *Chaucer's Canterbury Tales* (4–8). Illus. 2007, Candlewick $16.99 (978-0-7636-3197-0). The exploits of Chaucer's pilgrims are recounted in age-appropriate double-page spreads that are alive with action and humor; the illustrations help to define the more difficult words. (Rev: BL 2/15/07; HB 3-4/07; LMC 8-9/07; SLJ 3/07*)

2812 Wright, Randall. *Hunchback* (6–9). 2004, Holt $16.95 (978-0-8050-7232-7). Fourteen-year-old Hodge, a hunchbacked orphan in medieval times, dreams that one day he will be a servant to royalty, and when his dream comes true Hodge finds himself drawn into a series of intrigues and adventures. (Rev: BCCB 6/04; BL 5/1/04; SLJ 4/04; VOYA 6/04)

Africa

2813 Burns, Khephra. *Mansa Musa: The Lion of Mali* (4–7). Illus. by Diane Dillon and Leo Dillon. 2001, Harcourt $18.00 (978-0-15-200375-3). Lavish illustrations complement this handsome, challenging book about Mansa Musa's journey from a rural village boyhood to becoming the king of Mali. (Rev: BL 12/1/01; HB 11–12/01; HBG 3/02; SLJ 10/01)

2814 Ellis, Deborah. *The Heaven Shop* (5–8). 2004, Fitzhenry & Whiteside $16.95 (978-1-55041-908-5). The AIDS epidemic has a devastating impact on the family of Binti, a 13-year-old Malawi girl. (Rev: BL 9/1/04; SLJ 10/04)

2815 Farmer, Nancy. *A Girl Named Disaster* (6–10). 1996, Orchard paper $19.95 (978-0-531-09539-3). Set in modern-day Africa, this is the story, with fantasy undertones, of Nhamo, who flees from her home in Mozambique to escape a planned marriage and settles with her father's family in Zimbabwe. (Rev: BL 9/1/96; SLJ 10/96*; VOYA 12/96)

2816 Glass, Linzi Alex. *The Year the Gypsies Came* (8–11). 2006, Holt $16.95 (978-0-8050-7999-9). An elderly Zulu watchman turns out to be young

Emily's strongest anchor in this moving story about a 12-year-old in 1960s Johannesburg, whose life is changed when a family of Australian vagabonds arrives, bringing additional tensions. (Rev: BL 3/1/06; SLJ 5/06)

2817 Kurtz, Jane. *The Storyteller's Beads* (5–8). Illus. 1998, Harcourt $15.00 (978-0-15-201074-4). Two Ethiopian refugees, one a girl from a traditional Ethiopian culture and the other a blind Jewish girl, overcome generations of prejudice against Jews when they face common danger as they flee war and famine during the 1980s. (Rev: BCCB 9/98; BL 5/1/98; HBG 10/98; SLJ 7/98; VOYA 10/98)

2818 Levitin, Sonia. *Dream Freedom* (5–9). 2000, Harcourt $17.00 (978-0-15-202404-8). A novel that graphically portrays the plight of Sudanese slaves, juxtaposed with the story of an American 5th-grade class that joins the fight to free them. (Rev: BL 11/1/00; HBG 3/01; SLJ 10/00; VOYA 12/00)

2819 McDaniel, Lurlene. *Angel of Hope* (7–10). 2000, Bantam paper $8.95 (978-0-553-57148-6). In this sequel to *Angel of Mercy,* Heather returns from missionary work in Uganda and, in her place, her younger, spoiled sister, Amber, continues the work in Africa. (Rev: BL 5/1/00; HBG 9/00)

2820 McKissack, Patricia C. *Nzingha: Warrior Queen of Matamba* (5–8). Illus. Series: Royal Diaries. 2000, Scholastic paper $10.95 (978-0-439-11210-9). Based on fact, this is the story of 17th-century African queen Nzingha who, in present-day Angola, resisted the Portuguese colonizers and slave traders. (Rev: BL 11/1/00; HBG 3/01; SLJ 12/00)

2821 Marston, Elsa. *The Ugly Goddess* (5–8). 2002, Cricket $16.95 (978-0-8126-2667-4). In 523 B.C. Egypt, a 14-year-old Egyptian princess, a young Greek soldier who is in love with her, and an Egyptian boy become embroiled in a mystery adventure that blends fact, fiction, and fantasy. (Rev: BL 1/1–15/03; HBG 3/03; SLJ 12/02)

2822 Mwangi, Meja. *The Mzungu Boy* (5–8). 2005, Groundwood $15.95 (978-0-88899-653-4). In 1950s Kenya, a 12-year-old Kenyan boy becomes friendly with the white landowner's son despite both families' disapproval. (Rev: BL 8/05; SLJ 11/05)

2823 Naidoo, Beverley. *No Turning Back* (5–9). 1997, HarperCollins $15.89 (978-0-06-027506-8). Jaabu, a homeless African boy, looks for shelter in contemporary Johannesburg. (Rev: BCCB 2/97; BL 12/15/96*; HB 3–4/97; SLJ 2/97; VOYA 10/97)

2824 Nanji, Shenaaz. *Child of Dandelions* (7–12). 2008, Front St. $17.95 (978-1-932425-93-2). In 1972, the privileged life of 15-year-old Sabine, member of a wealthy Indian family, is turned upside down when President Idi Amin gives all Indians 90 days to leave the country. (Rev: BL 6/1–15/08; SLJ 5/08)

2825 Stolz, Joelle. *The Shadows of Ghadames* (6–10). 2004, Random LB $17.99 (978-0-385-73104-1). In late-19th-century Libya, Malika dreads the restricted life her 12th birthday will bring, but her father's two wives defy convention and nurse a wounded man back to health within the women's community, opening new horizons for Malika. (Rev: BL 12/1/04*; SLJ 11/04)

2826 Stratton, Allan. *Chanda's Wars* (8–12). 2008, HarperTeen $17.99 (978-0-06-087262-5). Chanda, the African AIDS orphan introduced in *Chanda's Secret,* tracks down her younger brother and sister after they are kidnapped and forced to become vicious child soldiers. (Rev: BL 12/1/07; HB 3–4/08; SLJ 3/08)

2827 Wein, Elizabeth E. *The Lion Hunter* (7–10). Series: The Mark of Solomon. 2007, Viking $16.99 (978-0-670-06163-1). To escape threats made against his aristocratic family, Telemakos (half-Ethiopian grandson of Britain's King Artos) and his young sister Athena are sent to a new community where new friendships are not what they seem in this first volume in a series set in 6th-century Africa and drawing on the author's preceding Arthurian-Aksumite cycle, which ended with *The Sunbird* (2004). (Rev: BL 6/1–15/07; HB 7–8/07; SLJ 9/07)

2828 Wein, Elizabeth E. *The Sunbird* (7–12). Series: The Winter Prince. 2004, Viking $16.99 (978-0-670-03691-2). Telemakos, grandson of noblemen, undertakes a perilous journey to the African kingdom of Aksum to find those responsible for allowing the plague to enter the kingdom in this third volume in the saga. (Rev: BL 6/1–15/04; HB 3–4/04; SLJ 5/04; VOYA 4/04)

2829 Zemser, Amy B. *Beyond the Mango Tree* (6–12). 1998, Greenwillow $14.95 (978-0-688-16005-0). Trapped in her home by a domineering mother, Sarina, a 12-year-old white American girl living in Liberia, befriends a gentle African boy named Boima. (Rev: BL 11/1/98; HB 11–12/98; HBG 3/99; SLJ 10/98; VOYA 4/99)

Asia and the Pacific

2830 Antieau, Kim. *Broken Moon* (6–9). 2007, Simon & Schuster $15.99 (978-1-4169-1767-0). Set in Pakistan, this story of Nadira and her younger brother, who is carried off to become a camel jockey, is disturbing yet not graphic in its descriptions of violence. (Rev: BL 12/15/06; HB 5–6/07; SLJ 5/07)

2831 Bosse, Malcolm. *The Examination* (8–12). 2008, Paw Prints $17.95 (978-1-4352-4634-8). During the Ming Dynasty, two very different Chinese brothers try to understand one another as they travel to Beijing, where one brother hopes to pass a government examination. (Rev: BL 11/1/94*; SLJ 12/94)

2832 Bosse, Malcolm. *Tusk and Stone* (6–10). 1995, Front St. $15.95 (978-1-886910-01-0). Set in 7th-century India, this story tells about a young Brahman who is separated from his sister and sold to the military as a slave, goes on to gain recognition and fame for his skills and bravery as a warrior, and ultimately discovers his true talents and nature as a sculptor and stonecarver. (Rev: BL 12/1/95; VOYA 2/96)

2833 Choi, Sook N. *Year of Impossible Goodbyes* (6–10). 1991, Houghton $16.00 (978-0-395-57419-5). An autobiographical novel of two children in North Korea following World War II who become separated from their mother while attempting to cross the border into South Korea. (Rev: BL 9/15/91; SLJ 10/91*)

2834 Clarke, Judith. *Kalpana's Dream* (6–9). 2005, Front St. $16.95 (978-1-932425-22-2). A visit from her Indian great-grandmother and a school essay assignment help Australian teen Neema to make some important discoveries about who she is. (Rev: BCCB 4/05; BL 5/1/05*; HB 1–2/06; SLJ 8/05; VOYA 8/05)

2835 Compestine, Ying Chang. *Revolution Is Not a Dinner Party* (6–9). 2007, Holt $16.95 (978-0-8050-8207-4). Nine-year-old Ling, a privileged child growing up in China during the Cultural Revolution, learns her family's vulnerability to the political regime; based on Compestine's own youth. (Rev: BL 8/07; SLJ 8/07) 🔊

2836 Conlogue, Ray. *Shen and the Treasure Fleet* (5–8). 2007, Annick $21.95 (978-1-55451-104-4); paper $11.95 (978-1-55451-103-7). Shen and his sister Chang try to free their mother and learn their father's fate while at sea with Zheng He's "treasure fleet" in early 15th-century China. (Rev: BL 11/15/07)

2837 Crew, Gary. *Mama's Babies* (6–9). 2002, Annick $18.95 (978-1-55037-725-5); paper $6.95 (978-1-55037-724-8). Set in Australia in 1897, this absorbing story of cruelty toward foster children — told from the point of view of 9-year-old Sarah — is based on true stories of "baby farmer" mothers who killed their young charges. (Rev: BCCB 9/02; BL 8/02; HBG 10/02; SLJ 6/02; VOYA 8/02)

2838 Crew, Gary. *Troy Thompson's Excellent Poetry Book* (4–7). Illus. by Craig Smith. 2003, Kane/Miller $14.95 (978-1-929132-52-2). Troy Thompson, an 11-year-old Australian boy, uses different forms of poetry to express his feelings about various elements of his life, participating in a yearlong literature assignment and, we learn at the end, winning the grand prize. (Rev: SLJ 1/04)

2839 Ellis, Deborah. *The Breadwinner* (5–7). 2001, Groundwood $15.95 (978-0-88899-419-6). In Kabul under the strict rule of the Taliban, Parvana dresses as a boy so she can work to feed the remaining women in her family. (Rev: BL 3/1/01; HBG 10/01; SLJ 7/01; VOYA 6/01)

2840 Garland, Sherry. *Song of the Buffalo Boy* (7–10). 1992, Harcourt paper $6.00 (978-0-15-200098-1). Loi, the spurned daughter of an American G.I. and a disgraced Vietnamese woman, escapes to Ho Chi Minh City to avoid an arranged marriage. (Rev: BL 4/15/06)

2841 Gratz, Alan. *Samurai Shortstop* (8–11). 2006, Dial $15.99 (978-0-8037-3075-5). Even though the samurai traditions have been outlawed, 16-year-old Toyo is educated in the ancient ways and applies his discipline to the game of baseball in this novel set in 1890 Tokyo). (Rev: BL 4/15/06*; LMC 11–12/06; SLJ 7/06) ⊚

2842 Haugaard, Erik C. *The Revenge of the Forty-Seven Samurai* (7–12). 1995, Houghton $16.00 (978-0-395-70809-5). In a true story set in feudal Japan, a young servant is a witness to destiny when his master meets an unjust death. (Rev: BL 5/15/95; SLJ 4/95)

2843 Herrick, Steven. *The Simple Gift* (8–10). 2004, Simon Pulse paper $14.95 (978-0-689-86867-2). In this compelling free-verse novel told in three voices, Australian 16-year-old Billy escapes an unhappy family life and takes up residence in an abandoned freight car where he finds both friendship and love. (Rev: BL 8/04; SLJ 9/04; VOYA 2/05)

2844 Ho, Minfong. *The Clay Marble* (5–9). 1991, Houghton $12.00 (978-0-395-77155-6). After fleeing from her Cambodian home in the early 1980s, 12-year-old Dara is separated from her family during an attack on a refugee camp on the Thailand border. (Rev: BL 11/15/91; SLJ 10/91)

2845 Ho, Minfong. *Gathering the Dew* (6–9). 2003, Scholastic $16.95 (978-0-439-38197-0). Twelve-year-old Nakri loses her beloved sister to the brutal Khmer Rouge regime in Cambodia and starts a new life in America, determined to uphold her sister's dedication to dance. (Rev: BL 3/1/03; HB 5–6/03; SLJ 3/03)

2846 Hollyer, Belinda. *River Song* (5–8). 2008, Holiday $16.95 (978-0-8234-2149-7). Set in New Zealand, this story of a half-Maori girl torn between two cultures is infused with magical elements from Maori legend. (Rev: BL 5/1/08; SLJ 6/08)

2847 Hoobler, Dorothy, and Thomas Hoobler. *In Darkness, Death* (7–10). 2004, Putnam $16.99 (978-0-399-23767-6). Set in 18th-century Japan like the authors' previous *The Ghost in the Tokaido Inn* (1999), this novel tells how 14-year-old Seikei and his adopted father set out to discover who murdered a powerful warlord. (Rev: BL 5/1/04; SLJ 3/04; VOYA 4/04)

2848 Hoobler, Dorothy, and Thomas Hoobler. *A Samurai Never Fears Death* (6–9). Series: The Samurai Mysteries. 2007, Philomel $12.99 (978-0-399-24609-8). Seikei, who is now a samurai, must clear the name of a puppeteer implicated in a crime in this sequel to *The Ghost in the Tokaido Inn* (1999). (Rev: BL 3/15/07; SLJ 4/07)

2849 Hoobler, Dorothy, and Thomas Hoobler. *The Sword That Cut the Burning Grass* (5–8). Series: The Samurai Mysteries. 2005, Philomel $10.99 (978-0-399-24272-4). In this fourth book about the aspiring young samurai, Seikei tackles a challenging task involving the teenage emperor. (Rev: BL 5/1/05; SLJ 10/05)

2850 Huynh, Quang Nhuong. *The Land I Lost: Adventures of a Boy in Vietnam* (5–8). Illus. by Mai Vo-Dinh. 1990, HarperCollins $15.89 (978-0-397-32448-4); paper $5.99 (978-0-06-440183-8). The story of a boy's growing up in rural Vietnam before the war.

2851 Lasky, Kathryn. *Jahanara: Princess of Princesses* (4–8). Series: Royal Diaries. 2002, Scholastic paper $10.95 (978-0-439-22350-8). Princess Jaharana, the daughter of Shah Jahan (who built the Taj Mahal) writes detailed diary accounts of her 17th-century life, with rich descriptions of her surroundings, palace intrigues, and dealing with her family. (Rev: BL 1/1–15/03; HBG 3/03; SLJ 1/03)

2852 Lewis, Richard. *The Killing Sea: A Story of the Tsunami That Stunned the World* (6–9). 2006, Simon & Schuster $15.95 (978-1-4169-1165-4). This novel based on the devastating 2004 tsunami spares none of the horrifying details of the disaster as it follows survivors Ruslan and Sarah as they search for family and for help. (Rev: BL 12/15/06; SLJ 2/07)

2853 Marchetta, Melina. *Looking for Alibrandi* (8–10). 1999, Orchard LB $17.99 (978-0-531-33142-2). In this novel set in Sydney, Australia, teenage Josie Alibrandi is torn between her family's cultural ties to Italy and her Australian environment. (Rev: BL 2/15/99; HB 5–6/99; HBG 9/99; SLJ 7/99; VOYA 6/99)

2854 Newton, Robert. *Runner* (7–10). 2007, Knopf $15.99 (978-0-375-83744-9). Set in Australia in 1919, this novel is about 15-year-old Charlie and his dangerous efforts to lift himself and his mother from poverty. (Rev: BCCB 7–8/07; BL 4/15/07; SLJ 4/07)

2855 Park, Linda Sue. *Seesaw Girl* (4–7). Illus. 1999, Clarion $14.00 (978-0-395-91514-1). In 17th-century Korea, 12-year-old Jade Blossom wanders away from her aristocratic palace and discovers the reality and poverty of the world outside. (Rev: BCCB 12/99; BL 9/1/99; HBG 3/00; SLJ 9/99)

2856 Park, Linda Sue. *A Single Shard* (4–8). 2001, Clarion $15.00 (978-0-395-97827-6). This Newbery Medal winner describes a Korean boy's journey through unknown territory to deliver two valuable pots. (Rev: BCCB 3/01; BL 4/1/01*; HBG 10/01; SLJ 5/01*)

2857 Park, Linda Sue. *When My Name Was Keoko* (5–9). 2002, Clarion $16.00 (978-0-618-13335-2). A young brother and sister tell, in first-person accounts, what life was like during the Japanese occupation of Korea. (Rev: BCCB 5/02; BL 3/1/02; HB 5–6/02; HBG 10/02; SLJ 4/02)

2858 Paterson, Katherine. *The Master Puppeteer* (4–7). Illus. by Haru Wells. 1989, HarperCollins paper $5.99 (978-0-06-440281-1). Feudal Japan is the setting for this story about a young apprentice puppeteer and his search for a mysterious bandit.

2859 Paterson, Katherine. *Of Nightingales That Weep* (4–7). Illus. by Haru Wells. 1974, Harper-Collins paper $6.99 (978-0-06-440282-8). A story set in feudal Japan tells of Takiko, a samurai's daughter, who is sent to the royal court when her mother remarries.

2860 Paterson, Katherine. *Rebels of the Heavenly Kingdom* (7–9). 1983, Avon paper $2.95 (978-0-380-68304-8). In 19th-century China a 15-year-old boy and a young girl engage in activities to overthrow the Manchu government.

2861 Paterson, Katherine. *The Sign of the Chrysanthemum* (5–7). Illus. by Peter Landa. 1973, Harper-Collins LB $14.89 (978-0-690-04913-8); paper $5.99 (978-0-06-440232-3). At the death of his mother, a young boy sets out to find his samurai father in 12th-century Japan.

2862 Place, Francois. *The Old Man Mad About Drawing* (5–8). Trans. by William Rodarmor. Illus. 2003, Godine $19.95 (978-1-56792-260-8). In 19th-century Edo (now Tokyo), Tojiro, a 9-year-old orphan who sells rice cakes, becomes the assistant to a famous old artist. (Rev: BL 3/15/04*; HB 3–4/04; SLJ 5/04)

2863 Qamar, Amjed. *Beneath My Mother's Feet* (7–10). 2008, Atheneum $16.99 (978-1-4169-4728-8). Fourteen-year-old Nazia's life changes dramatically when her family's economic well-being spirals downward and she finds herself cleaning houses in this novel set in Karachi, Pakistan. (Rev: BL 8/08; SLJ 7/08)

2864 Russell, Ching Yeung. *Child Bride* (4–7). Illus. 1999, Boyds Mills $15.95 (978-1-56397-748-0). Set in China in the early 1940s, this is the story of 11-year-old Ying, her arranged marriage, and an understanding bridegroom who allows her to go home to her ailing grandmother. (Rev: BL 3/1/99; HBG 10/99; SLJ 4/99)

2865 Russell, Ching Yeung. *Lichee Tree* (4–7). 1997, Boyds Mills $15.95 (978-1-56397-629-2). Growing up in China during the 1940s, Ying

dreams of selling lichee nuts and visiting Canton. (Rev: BCCB 4/97; BL 3/15/97; SLJ 6/97)

2866 Sayres, Meghan Nuttall. *Anahita's Woven Riddle* (8–12). 2006, Abrams $16.95 (978-0-8109-5481-6). In early-20th-century Iran, Anahita, a teenage nomad, resists an arranged marriage and seeks a mate who can solve the riddles woven into her wedding carpet. (Rev: SLJ 1/07)

2867 Sheth, Kashmira. *Keeping Corner* (7–12). 2007, Hyperion $15.99 (978-0-7868-3859-2). A 12-year-old widow, Leela is forced to mourn in her family's home for a year but dreams of reforms that would allow her to get an education and a career in this story set in 1918 India. (Rev: BL 10/15/07; LMC 1/08; SLJ 12/07)

2868 Sheth, Kashmira. *Koyal Dark, Mango Sweet* (8–11). 2006, Hyperion $15.99 (978-0-7868-3857-8). At the age of 16, Jeeta, who lives in Mumbai (formerly Bombay), finds many of the traditions that preoccupy her mother to be old-fashioned and inappropriate. (Rev: BL 4/1/06; SLJ 4/06)

2869 Snow, Maya. *Sisters of the Sword* (6–9). Series: Sisters of the Sword. 2008, HarperCollins $16.99 (978-0-06-124387-5). In 13th-century Japan two sisters — Kimi and Hana — disguise themselves as boys to attend samurai school and avenge their father, who was killed by their uncle; an action-packed first volume that offers good historical detail. (Rev: BL 6/1–15/08; SLJ 9/08)

2870 Sparrow, Rebecca. *The Year Nick McGowan Came to Stay* (8–11). 2008, Knopf $15.99 (978-0-375-84570-3). When Nick comes to live with her family after being kicked out of boarding school, Rachel finds out that under his cool, unapproachable exterior is a boy with serious problems; set in Australia in the late 1980s. (Rev: BL 4/15/08; SLJ 5/08)

2871 Sreenivasan, Jyotsna. *Aruna's Journeys* (4–7). Illus. 1997, Smooth Stone paper $6.95 (978-0-9619401-7-1). Aruna denies her Indian heritage until she spends a summer in Bangalore, India. (Rev: BL 7/97)

2872 Staples, Suzanne Fisher. *The House of Djinn* (7–12). 2008, Farrar $16.95 (978-0-374-39936-8). Set in Pakistan, this family drama (and follow-up to 1989's *Shabanu* and 1993's *Haveli*) about Mumtaz and Jameel, young cousins who are ordered to marry, shows the conflicts between generations in traditional Pakistani families. (Rev: BL 2/15/08; SLJ 4/08)

2873 Stone, Jeff. *Tiger* (6–9). Series: The Ancestors. 2005, Random LB $17.99 (978-0-375-93071-3). Five young warrior monk trainees survive a deadly attack on their monastery and use their martial arts skills to avenge their beloved grandmaster, who was killed in the attack. (Rev: BCCB 2/05; BL 2/15/05; SLJ 2/05)

2874 Vejjajiva, Jane. *The Happiness of Kati* (4–7). Trans. by Prudence Borthwick. 2006, Simon & Schuster $15.95 (978-1-4169-1788-5). Nine-year-old Kati's mother is dying and the identity of her father is a mystery in this story set in Thailand. (Rev: BL 5/15/06; SLJ 6/06)

2875 Venkatraman, Padma. *Climbing the Stairs* (6–9). 2008, Putnam $16.99 (978-0-399-24746-0). Vidya's life changes when her father is injured while protesting against the British occupation of India during World War II. (Rev: BL 4/15/08; SLJ 5/08)

2876 Whelan, Gloria. *Chu Ju's House* (6–9). 2004, HarperCollins $16.99 (978-0-06-050724-4). To save her baby sister, destined to be put up for adoption to comply with China's limits on a family's number of children, 14-year-old Chu Ju leaves home and is forced to fend for herself. (Rev: BCCB 5/04; BL 3/15/04; HB 5–6/04; SLJ 5/04; VOYA 10/04)

2877 Whelan, Gloria. *Goodbye, Vietnam* (5–8). 1992, Turtleback paper $11.65 (978-0-606-05848-3). Young Mai and her family escape from Vietnam to Hong Kong, suffering through a difficult boat journey; originally published in 1992. (Rev: BL 4/15/06; HB 1/93; SLJ 9/92)

2878 Whitesel, Cheryl Aylward. *Blue Fingers: A Ninja's Tale* (5–8). 2004, Clarion $15.00 (978-0-618-38139-5). In 16th-century Japan, 12-year-old Koji is trained to become a ninja warrior. (Rev: BL 3/15/04; SLJ 3/04)

2879 Whitesel, Cheryl Aylward. *Rebel: A Tibetan Odyssey* (5–8). 2000, HarperCollins $16.99 (978-0-688-16735-6). In Tibet about a century ago, a young boy named Thunder is sent to live with his uncle, an important lama in a Buddhist monastery. (Rev: BCCB 5/00; BL 4/15/00; HBG 3/01; SLJ 7/00)

2880 Wu, Priscilla. *The Abacus Contest: Stories from Taiwan and China* (5–8). Illus. 1996, Fulcrum $15.95 (978-1-55591-243-7). Six simple short stories explore life in a Taiwanese city. (Rev: BL 7/96; SLJ 6/96)

2881 Wulffson, Don. *The Golden Rat* (6–9). 2007, Bloomsbury $16.95 (978-1-59990-000-1). In 12th-century China, 16-year-old Baoliu is wrongly accused of murdering his stepmother; his father, although rejecting Baoliu, arranges for a stand-in to be executed in Baoliu's place and Baoliu must then make his own way in the world, eager to prove his innocence. (Rev: BL 9/1/07; SLJ 1/08)

2882 Yep, Laurence. *Lady of Ch'iao Kuo: Warrior of the South* (5–8). Illus. Series: Royal Diaries. 2001, Scholastic $10.95 (978-0-439-16483-2). In this volume of the Royal Diaries series, the teenage Princess Redbird of the Hsien tribe must use her diplomatic skills to save the lives of both her own people and Chinese colonists in the 6th century A.D.

Historical notes add background information. (Rev: BL 11/1/01)

2883 Yep, Laurence. *Mountain Light* (8–12). 1997, HarperCollins paper $8.99 (978-0-06-440667-3). Yep continues to explore life in 19th-century China through the experience of a girl, Cassia, her father and friends, and their struggle against the Manchus in this sequel to *The Serpent's Children* (1984). (Rev: BL 9/15/85; SLJ 1/87; VOYA 12/85)

Europe and the Middle East

2884 Armstrong, Alan. *Raleigh's Page* (5–7). Illus. by Tim Jessell. 2007, Random $16.99 (978-0-375-83319-9). As page to Walter Raleigh, 11-year-old Andrew learns about court life, becomes embroiled in intrigues, and has adventures that include visiting the New World. (Rev: BL 8/07; HB 11–12/07; LMC 11/07; SLJ 11/07)

2885 Avi. *The Traitors' Gate* (6–9). 2007, Simon & Schuster $17.99 (978-0-689-85335-7). Victorian England comes to life in this story about 14-year-old John's efforts to save his father from debtors' prison and to find out why he's being spied on. (Rev: BCCB 7-8/07; BL 4/15/07; HB 9–10/07; SLJ 5/07) 🐝

2886 Bajoria, Paul. *The God of Mischief* (7–10). Illus. by Bret Bertholf. 2007, Little, Brown $16.99 (978-0-316-01091-7). Orphans Mog and Nick, the twin discovered in *The Printer's Devil* (2005), are sent to live with their uncle, Sir Septimus Cloy, at Kniveacres Hall and there have further spooky adventures and investigate their past; this series is set in early-19th-century England. (Rev: BL 1/1–15/07; HB 1–2/07; SLJ 3/07)

2887 Banks, Lynne Reid. *The Dungeon* (6–9). 2002, HarperCollins $16.99 (978-0-06-623782-4). Retribution is at the heart of this dark story about a bereaved 14th-century laird whose anger spurs him to abuse a Chinese child. (Rev: BL 10/1/02; HB 9/02; HBG 3/03; SLJ 12/02)

2888 Banks, Lynne Reid. *Tiger, Tiger* (5–8). 2005, Delacorte LB $17.99 (978-0-385-90264-9). Two tiger cubs arrive in Rome destined for different fates; Brute is trained to be a killer of men in the Colosseum while Boots becomes a pet for the caesar's daughter, a decision with dangerous consequences. (Rev: BL 5/15/05; SLJ 6/05)

2889 Bawden, Nina. *The Real Plato Jones* (5–8). 1993, Clarion $15.00 (978-0-395-66972-3). British teen Plato Jones and his mother return to Greece for his grandfather's funeral, where Plato discovers that his grandfather may have been a coward and traitor while serving in the Greek Resistance. (Rev: BCCB 11/93; BL 10/15/93; SLJ 11/93*)

2890 Beaufrand, Mary Jane. *Primavera* (8–10). 2008, Little, Brown $16.99 (978-0-316-01644-5).

While Sandro Botticelli uses Flora's sister Domenica as inspiration for his painting "Primavera," Flora plots an escape from her powerful family and a future in a convent. (Rev: BL 1/1–15/08; LMC 1/08; SLJ 2/08)

2891 Blackwood, Gary. *Shakespeare's Spy* (5–8). 2003, Dutton $16.99 (978-0-525-47145-5). Romance and intrigue are at hand as Widge continues his career at the Globe Theatre in this sequel to *The Shakespeare Stealer* (1998) and *Shakespeare's Scribe* (2000). (Rev: BL 9/1/03; HB 11–12/03; HBG 4/04; SLJ 10/03)

2892 Blackwood, Gary L. *Shakespeare Stealer* (5–8). 1998, NAL $16.99 (978-0-525-45863-0). A 14-year-old apprentice at the Globe Theater is sent by a rival theater company to steal Shakespeare's plays. (Rev: BL 6/1–15/98; HB 7–8/98; HBG 10/98; SLJ 6/98; VOYA 8/98)

2893 Bradley, Kimberly Brubaker. *The Lacemaker and the Princess* (4–8). 2007, Simon & Schuster $16.99 (978-1-4169-1920-9). As the French Revolution gathers strength, a young lace maker becomes the companion of Princess Marie-Thérèse, daughter of Marie Antoinette and King Louis XVI, and witness the growing social unrest. (Rev: BL 4/15/07; SLJ 7/07)

2894 Cadnum, Michael. *Ship of Fire* (6–8). 2003, Viking $16.99 (978-0-670-89907-4). Apprentice surgeon Thomas, 17, has to learn medicine and seafaring fast when he sails with Sir Francis Drake's fleet. (Rev: BL 9/15/03; SLJ 10/03)

2895 Cassidy, Cathy. *Scarlett* (5–8). 2006, Viking $16.99 (978-0-670-06068-9). Much to her surprise (and with some help from a mysterious boy), 12-year-old Scarlett actually enjoys living in Ireland with her father and his new family. (Rev: BL 12/1/06)

2896 Conlon-McKenna, Marita. *Fields of Home* (6–10). Illus. 1997, Holiday paper $15.95 (978-0-8234-1295-2). In this sequel to *Under the Hawthorn Tree* (1990) and *Wildflower Girl* (1992), the Irish O'Driscoll family saga continues as Michael and Eily try to make progress in spite of the hard times in Ireland. (Rev: BCCB 7–8/97; BL 4/15/97; SLJ 6/97)

2897 Cooney, Caroline B. *Enter Three Witches* (8–11). 2007, Scholastic $16.99 (978-0-439-71156-2). A novel based on Shakespeare's play *Macbeth* in which the action centers on 14-year-old Lady Mary, ward of Lord and Lady Macbeth. (Rev: BCCB 5/07; BL 3/1/07; HB 5–6/07; LMC 10/07; SLJ 5/07)

2898 Cottrell Boyce, Frank. *Framed* (4–7). 2006, HarperCollins $16.99 (978-0-06-073402-2). Life changes dramatically for 9-year-old Dylan Hughes and his quiet Welsh village when priceless art from London's National Gallery is temporarily stored in a nearby quarry. (Rev: BL 9/1/06; SLJ 8/06*) ⏚

2899 Creech, Sharon. *The Castle Corona* (4–7). Illus. by David Diaz. 2007, HarperCollins $18.99 (978-0-06-084621-3). This lively and entertaining fairy tale set in medieval Italy follows a pair of orphaned peasant children named Pia and Enzio who become tasters for the royal family of Castle Corona. (Rev: BL 9/1/07; SLJ 10/07) ⏚

2900 Cullen, Lynn. *I Am Rembrandt's Daughter* (8–12). 2007, Bloomsbury $16.95 (978-1-59990-046-9). The daughter of the famous artist feels adrift when her mother dies, leaving only her poor, unconventional father to raise her; Rembrandt's art and times are revealed in this compelling story. (Rev: BCCB 9/07; BL 4/15/07; LMC 1/08; SLJ 8/07)

2901 Curtis, Chara M. *No One Walks on My Father's Moon* (4–8). Illus. 1996, Voyage LB $16.95 (978-0-9649454-1-8). A Turkish boy is accused of blasphemy when he states that a man has walked on the moon. (Rev: BL 11/15/96)

2902 De Angeli, Marguerite. *The Door in the Wall* (5–7). Illus. by author. 1990, Dell paper $5.50 (978-0-440-40283-1). Crippled Robin proves his courage in plague-ridden 19th-century London. Newbery Medal winner, 1950.

2903 DeJong, Meindert. *Wheel on the School* (4–7). Illus. by Maurice Sendak. 1954, HarperCollins LB $18.89 (978-0-06-021586-6); paper $6.95 (978-0-06-440021-3). The storks are brought back to their island by the schoolchildren in a Dutch village. Newbery Medal winner, 1955.

2904 Dhami, Narinder. *Bhangra Babes* (5–8). Series: Babes. 2006, Delacorte $14.95 (978-0-385-73318-2). Their troublesome auntie's marriage plans go awry in this funny, engaging final volume of the trilogy about the Bindi sisters who are adapting their Indian heritage to life in England. (Rev: BL 4/15/06; SLJ 6/06)

2905 Dickinson, Peter. *Shadow of a Hero* (7–12). 1995, Doubleday $20.95 (978-0-385-30976-9). Letta's grandfather fights for the freedom of Varina, her family's Eastern European homeland. Living in England, she becomes interested in Varina's struggle. (Rev: BL 9/15/94*; SLJ 11/94; VOYA 10/94)

2906 Doherty, Berlie. *Street Child* (5–7). 1994, Orchard LB $18.99 (978-0-531-08714-5). The story of a street urchin in Victorian London who is forced to work on a river barge until he escapes. (Rev: BCCB 11/94; BL 9/1/94; SLJ 10/94)

2907 Dowd, Siobhan. *Bog Child* (8–11). 2008, Random $16.99 (978-0-385-75169-8). Set in 1981 in politically troubled Northern Ireland, this richly told story weaves together two historical eras through 18-year-old Fergus, who finds the body of a girl in the peat bogs — apparently murdered perhaps 2000 years before — and begins to dream of her past. (Rev: BL 8/08; SLJ 8/08)

2908 Dowswell, Paul. *Powder Monkey: Adventures of a Young Sailor* (5–9). 2005, Bloomsbury $16.95 (978-1-58234-675-5). In this stirring historical novel set in the opening years of the 19th century, 13-year-old Sam Witchall begins his career at sea as a "powder monkey," assisting the gun crews on a warship. (Rev: SLJ 11/05; VOYA 10/05)

2909 Dowswell, Paul. *Prison Ship: Adventures of a Young Sailor* (5–9). 2006, Bloomsbury $16.95 (978-1-58234-676-2). In this action-packed sequel to *Powder Monkey* set at the beginning of the 19th century, 13-year-old English sailor Sam Witchall is falsely convicted of theft and sent off to prison in Australia, where he escapes into the Outback. (Rev: SLJ 12/06)

2910 Dunlop, Eileen. *Tales of St. Patrick* (6–9). 1996, Holiday $15.95 (978-0-8234-1218-1). Using original sources when possible, the author has fashioned a fictionalized biography of Saint Patrick that focuses on his return to Ireland as a bishop and his efforts to convert the Irish. (Rev: BL 4/15/96; VOYA 8/96)

2911 Eisner, Will. *The Last Knight: An Introduction to Don Quixote by Miguel de Cervantes* (4–8). Illus. 2000, NBM $15.95 (978-1-56163-251-0). Using an engaging text and a comic book format, this is a fine retelling of Cervantes' classic. (Rev: BL 6/1–15/00; HBG 10/00; SLJ 7/00)

2912 Ellis, Deborah. *A Company of Fools* (5–8). 2002, Fitzhenry & Whiteside $15.95 (978-1-55041-719-7). Quiet Henri and free-spirited Micah try to cheer the people of a France devastated by the Black Death of 1348 by singing. (Rev: BCCB 1/03; BL 1/1–15/03; HB 1–2/03; HBG 3/03; VOYA 2/03)

2913 Flegg, Aubrey. *Katie's War* (5–8). 2000, O'Brien paper $7.95 (978-0-86278-525-3). Set during Ireland's fight for independence from England, this story shows a girl torn between two sides when her father wants peace and her brother is preparing to use force. (Rev: BL 12/1/00)

2914 Fletcher, Susan. *Alphabet of Dreams* (6–9). 2006, Simon & Schuster $16.95 (978-0-689-85042-4). Mitra and her brother Babak, who can see the future in his dreams, go from being Persian royalty to beggars on the street after their father's death; they join Melchior and two other magi when Babak dreams of a bright star. (Rev: BL 9/1/06; SLJ 11/06) ⊚

2915 Forsyth, Kate. *The Gypsy Crown* (6–9). 2008, Hyperion $16.99 (978-1-4231-0494-0). Set in England in the 17th century, this story of Emilia and Luka tells of the Puritan persecution of Gypsies during that time. (Rev: BL 4/15/08)

2916 French, Jackie. *Rover* (5–8). 2007, HarperCollins $17.99 (978-0-06-085078-4). When Vikings raid Hekja's Scottish village, she and her puppy are taken to Greenland, where she's enslaved to Frey-dis, Leif Erikson's sister; Hekja's dog can spot icebergs, and the two accompany Freydis on her voyage to North America in this compelling, historically accurate story. (Rev: BL 1/1–15/07; SLJ 6/07)

2917 Frost, Helen. *The Braid* (7–10). 2006, Farrar $16.00 (978-0-374-30962-6). Set in 1850, this moving tale of two Scottish sisters who become separated — Jeannie moving to Canada with her parents and younger siblings and Sarah staying behind with their grandmother — is told in narrative poems in alternating voices. (Rev: BL 6/1–15/06; HB 11–12/06; LMC 3/07; SLJ 10/06*)

2918 Gilman, Laura Anne. *Grail Quest: The Camelot Spell* (5–8). Series: Grail Quest. 2006, HarperCollins LB $14.89 (978-0-06-077280-2). On the eve of King Arthur's quest for the Holy Grail, three young teens of different backgrounds — Gerard, Newt, and Ailias — must reverse a spell crippling all adults. (Rev: BL 2/1/06; SLJ 6/06)

2919 Gilson, Jamie. *Stink Alley* (4–7). 2002, HarperCollins LB $15.89 (978-0-06-029217-1). Twelve-year-old orphan Lizzy Tinker, a Separatist who fled England with her family for Holland in 1608, is befriended by the boy who would one day be known as Rembrandt. (Rev: BCCB 9/02; BL 4/15/02; HB 9–10/02; HBG 3/03; SLJ 7/02)

2920 Grant, K. M. *How the Hangman Lost His Heart* (7–12). 2007, Walker $16.95 (978-0-8027-9672-1). Alice is on a mission — to bury the head of her Uncle Frank, who was executed and beheaded for treason — and danger and romance won't stop her in this funny, action-packed tale set in England in 1746 and inspired by the fate of one of the author's ancestors. (Rev: BL 11/15/07; SLJ 12/07)

2921 Gregory, Kristiana. *Catherine: The Great Journey* (4–7). Series: Royal Diaries. 2005, Scholastic $10.99 (978-0-439-25385-7). The imagined diary of Catherine the Great's teenage years and her engagement to the Grand Duke of Russia; plenty of historical background gives readers a sense of Catherine's times. (Rev: SLJ 5/06)

2922 Harris, Robert, and Jane Yolen. *Prince Across the Water* (6–10). 2004, Penguin $18.99 (978-0-399-23897-0). Thirteen-year-old Duncan shares his countrymen's pride at Bonnie Prince Charlie's struggle to reclaim the crown of England and Scotland from German-born George II, but when the boy runs away from home to join the battle, he discovers the true horrors of war. (Rev: BL 11/15/04; SLJ 12/04; VOYA 10/04)

2923 Harrison, Cora. *The Famine Secret* (5–7). Illus. by Orla Roche. Series: Drumshee Timeline. 1998, Irish American paper $6.95 (978-0-86327-649-1). In 1847 the four McMahon children are orphaned and sent to an Irish workhouse, but their determination prevails and they are soon plotting to regain their home. (Rev: SLJ 12/98)

2924 Harrison, Cora. *The Secret of Drumshee Castle* (5–7). Illus. by Orla Roche. Series: Drumshee Timeline. 1998, Irish American paper $6.95 (978-0-86327-632-3). Grace Barry, the orphaned heiress to a castle in Ireland during Elizabethan times, flees to England to escape threats by her acquisitive guardians. (Rev: SLJ 12/98)

2925 Harrison, Cora. *The Secret of the Seven Crosses* (4–7). Illus. 1998, Wolfhound paper $6.95 (978-0-86327-616-3). In medieval Ireland, three youngsters hope to find hidden treasure by examining sources in their monastery library. Preceded by *Nauala and Her Secret Wolf* and followed by *The Secret of Drumshee Castle*. (Rev: BL 12/15/98)

2926 Hassinger, Peter W. *Shakespeare's Daughter* (7–12). 2004, HarperCollins $15.99 (978-0-06-028467-1). An assortment of historical figures make appearances, including papa, in this story about the 14-year-old daughter of William Shakespeare. (Rev: BL 3/1/04; SLJ 4/04)

2927 Havill, Juanita. *Eyes Like Willy's* (6–9). Illus. by David Johnson. 2004, HarperCollins LB $16.89 (978-0-688-13673-4). Guy, who lives in Paris, and Willy, an Austrian, have been friends since they met in the summer of 1906; now they may face each other across the trenches of World War I. (Rev: BCCB 9/04; BL 3/1/04*; SLJ 7/04)

2928 Hawes, Louise. *The Vanishing Point* (8–10). 2004, Houghton $17.00 (978-0-618-43423-7). In this appealing historical novel that imagines the adolescence of Italian Renaissance artist Lavinia Fontana, young Vini resorts to subterfuge to get her father to let her paint in his studio. (Rev: BL 11/1/04; SLJ 12/04; VOYA 12/04)

2929 Hearn, Julie. *Ivy* (8–10). 2008, Atheneum $17.99 (978-1-4169-2506-4). In 19th-century London, Ivy struggles with addiction to laudanum as she earns a living as a model for a pre-Raphaelite painter. (Rev: BL 6/1–15/08; SLJ 7/08)

2930 Hendry, Frances Mary. *Quest for a Maid* (8–10). 1992, Farrar, Straus and Giroux paper $6.95 (978-0-374-46155-3). The story of an 8-year-old princess and her maid who travel to Britain during the 13th century. (Rev: BL 7/90)

2931 Heneghan, James. *Safe House* (5–8). 2006, Orca paper $7.95 (978-1-55143-640-1). Twelve-year-old Liam Fogarty is forced to go on the run after he sees the face of one of the gunmen who killed his mother and father in their Belfast home. (Rev: BL 11/1/06; SLJ 1/07)

2932 Hoffman, Mary. *The Falconer's Knot* (8–11). 2007, Bloomsbury $16.95 (978-1-59990-056-8). Silvano, 16, is suspected of murder when Angelica's husband is stabbed in this multilayered mystery set in Renaissance Italy. (Rev: BCCB 6/07; BL 3/15/07; LMC 8–9/07; SLJ 4/07)

2933 Holmes, Victoria. *The Horse from the Sea* (5–8). 2005, HarperCollins LB $16.89 (978-0-06-052029-8). In 1588, Nora, an Irish girl, defies the English and helps a young Spanish sailor and a beautiful stallion, survivors of a shipwreck. (Rev: BL 5/15/05; SLJ 8/05)

2934 Holub, Josef. *An Innocent Soldier* (8–11). Trans. by Michael Gofmann. 2005, Scholastic $16.99 (978-0-439-62771-9). Pressed into Napoleon's army for the ill-fated Russian campaign, Adam, a teenage farmhand, is selected as a personal servant by Konrad, an officer from a wealthy family, and the two develop a strong friendship. Batchelder Award, 2006. (Rev: BL 11/15/05; SLJ 12/05; VOYA 2/06)

2935 Holub, Josef. *The Robber and Me* (5–8). Trans. from German by Elizabeth D. Crawford. 1997, Holt $16.95 (978-0-8050-5591-7). On his way to live with his uncle, an orphan is helped by a mysterious stranger and he must later make a decision about whether to stand up to his uncle and the town authorities to clear the name of this man in this novel set in 19th-century Germany. (Rev: SLJ 12/97*)

2936 Hooper, Mary. *At the Sign of the Sugared Plum* (5–8). 2003, Bloomsbury $16.95 (978-1-58234-849-0). The horrors of the bubonic plague and the squalor of 17th-century London are brought to life in this story of Hannah and her sister Sarah, owner of a sweetmeats shop. (Rev: BL 9/15/03; HBG 4/04; SLJ 8/03; VOYA 10/03)

2937 Hopkins, Cathy. *The Princess of Pop* (6–8). Series: Truth or Dare. 2004, Simon & Schuster paper $5.99 (978-0-689-87002-6). On a dare, Becca competes in the British version of "American Idol." (Rev: SLJ 7/04)

2938 Hunter, Mollie. *The King's Swift Rider* (7–12). 1998, HarperCollins $16.95 (978-0-06-027186-2). A fast-paced historical novel about a young Scot, Martin Crawford, who became Robert the Bruce's page, confidante, and spy. (Rev: BL 9/15/98; HB 1–2/99; HBG 3/99; SLJ 12/98)

2939 Hunter, Mollie. *You Never Knew Her as I Did!* (7–10). Illus. 1981, HarperCollins $13.95 (978-0-06-022678-7). A historical novel about a plan to help the imprisoned Mary, Queen of Scots, to escape from prison.

2940 Ibbotson, Eva. *The Star of Kazan* (4–8). Illus. by Kevin Hawkes. 2004, Dutton $16.99 (978-0-525-47347-3). Set in the Austro-Hungarian empire, this richly detailed and very readable novel tells the story of 12-year-old Annika, who gets a rude awakening when her aristocratic mother whisks her away from her adoptive family. (Rev: BL 10/15/04*; SLJ 10/04*)

2941 Jennings, Patrick. *The Wolving Time* (6–8). 2003, Scholastic $15.95 (978-0-439-39555-7). Fantasy and historical fiction are interwoven in this tale, set in 16th-century France, of two werewolves and their son. (Rev: BL 9/15/03; SLJ 1/04)

2942 Jones, Terry. *The Lady and the Squire* (5–7). Illus. 2001, Pavilion $22.95 (978-1-86205-417-2). A beautiful aristocrat joins Tom and Ann as they make their way through a war-torn countryside to the papal court at Avignon. (Rev: BL 2/15/01; SLJ 3/01)

2943 Juster, Norton. *Alberic the Wise* (4–8). Illus. by Leonard Baskin. 1992, Picture Book $16.95 (978-0-88708-243-6). In this picture book set in the Renaissance, Alberic becomes an apprentice to a stained-glass maker. (Rev: BCCB 2/93; BL 1/15/93; SLJ 3/93)

2944 Kanefield, Teri. *Rivka's Way* (4–8). 2001, Front St. $15.95 (978-0-8126-2870-8). Daily life inside and outside the Prague ghetto in 1778 is explored in this novel about an unconventional Jewish girl, 15-year-old Rivka Liebermann. (Rev: BCCB 3/02; BL 4/1/01; HBG 10/01; SLJ 3/01; VOYA 10/01)

2945 Karr, Kathleen. *The 7th Knot* (6–9). 2003, Marshall Cavendish $15.95 (978-0-7614-5135-8). Brothers Wick, 15, and Miles, 12, romp through a series of adventures involving art and politics when they set off across Europe in pursuit of their uncle's kidnapped valet in the late 19th century. (Rev: BL 7/03; HBG 10/03; SLJ 8/03)

2946 Kelly, Eric P. *The Trumpeter of Krakow* (5–9). Illus. by Janina Domanska. 1966, Macmillan $17.95 (978-0-02-750140-7); paper $4.99 (978-0-689-71571-6). Mystery surrounds a precious jewel and the youthful patriot who stands watch over it in a church tower in this novel of 15th-century Poland. Newbery Medal winner, 1929.

2947 Kirwan, Anna. *Victoria: May Blossom of Britannia* (5–8). Series: Royal Diaries. 2001, Scholastic paper $10.95 (978-0-439-21598-5). Young Victoria's fictional diary describes her over-regimented life at the ages of 10 and 11; background material adds some historical context to this account of the girl who grew up to rule England. (Rev: BL 12/1/01; HBG 10/02; SLJ 1/02; VOYA 2/02)

2948 Konigsburg, E. L. *A Proud Taste for Scarlet and Miniver* (7–9). Illus. 1973, Macmillan $18.95 (978-0-689-30111-7). Eleanor of Aquitaine tells her story in heaven while awaiting her second husband, Henry II.

2949 Kujer, Guus. *The Book of Everything* (8–11). 2006, Scholastic $16.99 (978-0-439-74918-3). Thomas, a 9-year-old living in Amsterdam in 1951, strives to be happy in spite of his difficult, deeply religious father in this compelling and often humorous novel. (Rev: BCCB 5/06; BL 6/1–15/06; HB 7–8/06; LMC 10/06; SLJ 7/06)

2950 Lasky, Kathryn. *Broken Song* (5–8). 2005, Viking $15.99 (978-0-670-05931-7). Reuven Bloom, a 15-year-old Jew and promising violinist, escapes from late 19th-century Russia with his baby sister, the only surviving member of his family. (Rev: BL 1/1–15/05; SLJ 3/05)

2951 Lasky, Kathryn. *Dancing Through Fire* (4–7). Series: Portraits. 2005, Scholastic paper $9.99 (978-0-439-71009-1). The Franco-Prussian War interrupts the dreams of 13-year-old Sylvie, a student at the Paris Opera Ballet in the 1870s. (Rev: BCCB 1/06; BL 12/1/05; SLJ 11/05)

2952 Lasky, Kathryn. *Elizabeth I: Red Rose of the House of Tudor* (4–7). Series: Royal Diaries. 1999, Scholastic paper $10.95 (978-0-590-68484-2). Told in diary form, this is a fictionalized account of Elizabeth I's childhood after her mother was killed and she lived with her father, Henry VIII, and Catherine Parr. (Rev: BCCB 12/99; BL 9/15/99; HBG 3/00; SLJ 10/99)

2953 Lasky, Kathryn. *Marie Antoinette: Princess of Versailles* (5–8). Series: Royal Diaries. 2000, Scholastic paper $10.95 (978-0-439-07666-1). This fictional diary covers two years in the life of Marie Antoinette, beginning in 1769 when the 13-year-old was preparing for her fateful marriage. (Rev: BL 4/15/00; HBG 10/00; SLJ 5/00; VOYA 6/00)

2954 Lasky, Kathryn. *Mary, Queen of Scots: Queen Without a Country* (5–8). Illus. Series: Royal Diaries. 2002, Scholastic paper $10.95 (978-0-439-19404-4). Part of the Royal Diary series, this is a fictional diary of the year 1553, when Mary was betrothed to the son of King Henry II of France. (Rev: BL 5/15/02; HBG 10/02; SLJ 6/02)

2955 Lawlor, Laurie. *The Two Loves of Will Shakespeare* (8–11). 2006, Holiday $16.95 (978-0-8234-1901-2). This well-written story imagines the wild love life of young William Shakespeare, based on historical records. (Rev: BL 4/15/06; SLJ 6/06)

2956 Lawrence, Iain. *The Smugglers* (5–8). 1999, Delacorte $15.95 (978-0-385-32663-6). In this continuation of *The Wreckers*, 16-year-old John Spencer faces more adventures aboard the *Dragon*, where he faces powerful enemies and must bring the ship safely to port. (Rev: BCCB 7–8/99; BL 4/1/99*; HB 5–6/99; HBG 10/99; SLJ 6/99)

2957 Lawrence, Iain. *The Wreckers* (5–8). 1998, Bantam paper $5.50 (978-0-440-41545-9). In this historical novel, young John Spencer narrowly escapes with his life after the ship on which he is traveling is wrecked off the Cornish coast, lured to its destruction by a gang seeking to plunder its cargo. (Rev: BCCB 6/98; BL 6/1–15/98; HB 7–8/98*; HBG 10/98; SLJ 6/98; VOYA 2/99)

2958 Lisson, Deborah. *Red Hugh* (6–12). 2001, O'Brien paper $7.95 (978-0-86278-604-5). A exciting tale of 16th-century Ireland's Hugh Roe O'Donnell, a teen whose life is endangered when he is caught up in clan violence. (Rev: BL 12/1/01; SLJ 12/01)

2959 McCaughrean, Geraldine. *Cyrano* (7–10). 2006, Harcourt $16.00 (978-0-15-205805-0). McCaughrean retells the classic tale of Cyrano de Bergerac, a famous swordsman and romantic poet with a very large nose, who lets a fellow French soldier use his poems and letters to win the love of Roxanne, the woman he secretly loves. (Rev: BL 9/15/06; SLJ 10/06)

2960 MacKall, Dandi Daley. *Eva Underground* (8–11). 2006, Harcourt $17.00 (978-0-15-205462-5). In 1978, Eva Lott's father moves her from her high school life in Chicago to Communist Poland, where she initially rebels but later meets a young political activist named Tomek and develops a strong affection for him and an understanding of the oppression he is fighting. (Rev: BL 3/1/06; SLJ 6/06)

2961 McKenzie, Nancy. *Guinevere's Gift* (5–8). 2008, Knopf $15.99 (978-0-375-84345-7). As a young orphan, the plucky Guinevere lives with her aunt, Queen Alyse, and involves herself in castle intrigue, coming to realize that her destiny may be closer to prophecy than she thought. (Rev: BL 6/1–15/08; SLJ 4/08)

2962 Magorian, Michelle. *Back Home* (7–9). 1992, HarperCollins paper $6.95 (978-0-06-440411-2). A young English girl who returns to Britain after World War II wants to go back to her second home in the United States.

2963 Marston, Elsa. *Figs and Fate: Stories About Growing Up in the Arab World Today* (6–9). 2005, George Braziller $22.50 (978-0-8076-1551-5); paper $15.95 (978-0-8076-1554-6). A revealing collection of stories portraying contemporary Arab teens living in Egypt, Iraq, Lebanon, Palestine, and Syria. (Rev: BL 2/15/05; HB 5–6/05; SLJ 3/05; VOYA 10/05)

2964 Meyer, Carolyn. *Anastasia: The Last Grand Duchess, Russia, 1914* (4–8). Series: Royal Diaries. 2000, Scholastic paper $10.95 (978-0-439-12908-4). Anastasia's fictional diary begins when she is 12 in 1914 and ends with her captivity in 1918. (Rev: HBG 10/01; SLJ 10/00; VOYA 4/01)

2965 Meyer, Carolyn. *In Mozart's Shadow* (7–12). 2008, Harcourt $17.00 (978-0-15-205594-3). The fictionalized story of Wolfgang's older sister, Nannerl, who was also a talented musician but remains virtually unknown. (Rev: BL 4/15/08; SLJ 6/08; VOYA 4/08)

2966 Meyer, Carolyn. *Loving Will Shakespeare* (8–11). 2006, Harcourt $17.00 (978-0-15-205451-9). Follows Anne Hathaway's difficult life until her marriage to William Shakespeare. (Rev: BL 9/15/06; LMC 3/07; SLJ 10/06; VOYA)

2967 Meyer, Carolyn. *Marie, Dancing* (6–9). 2005, Harcourt $17.00 (978-0-15-205116-7). Marie van Goethem, the girl who posed for Degas' famous *Little Dancer, Aged Fourteen* sculpture, is at the center of this moving novel about the lives of three sisters struggling to make their way in the artistic world of 19th-century Paris. (Rev: BCCB 1/06; BL 11/1/05; SLJ 11/05)

2968 Meyer, Carolyn. *Patience, Princess Catherine* (6–9). 2004, Harcourt $17.00 (978-0-15-216544-4). This appealing historical novel recounts the confusion surrounding the future of 15-year-old Catherine of Aragon, alone in England when she is widowed only six months after her marriage to Prince Arthur, heir to the British throne. (Rev: BL 3/15/04; SLJ 7/04)

2969 Meyer, L. A. *Bloody Jack: Being an Account of the Curious Adventures of Mary "Jacky" Faber, Ship's Boy* (6–9). 2002, Harcourt $17.00 (978-0-15-216731-8). Orphaned by the plague, Mary Faber disguises herself as a boy and signs up to work on the *HMS Dolphin* to escape life on the streets of 18th-century London. (Rev: BL 3/1/03; HB 1–2/03; HBG 3/03; SLJ 9/02; VOYA 12/02)

2970 Molloy, Michael. *Peter Raven Under Fire* (6–9). 2005, Scholastic $17.95 (978-0-439-72454-8). A fast-paced multilayered story featuring midshipman Peter Raven, 13, who becomes embroiled in international politics during the Napoleonic Wars. (Rev: BL 8/05; SLJ 10/05; VOYA 10/05)

2971 Morgan, Nicola. *The Highwayman's Footsteps* (7–9). 2007, Candlewick $16.99 (978-0-7636-3472-8). Based on the poem by Alfred Noyes, this thrilling novel set in 18th-century England centers on Bess, the highwayman's daughter, and Will, a runaway who becomes Bess's friend and confidant. (Rev: BL 11/15/07; HB 1–2/08; LMC 2/08; SLJ 12/07)

2972 Morris, Gerald. *The Lioness and Her Knight* (6–9). 2005, Houghton $16.00 (978-0-618-50772-6). Lady Luneta, 16 and headstrong, travels to Camelot with her cousin Ywain and a fool named Rhience and finds adventure and romance. (Rev: BL 9/15/05; SLJ 9/05; VOYA 12/05)

2973 Morris, Gerald. *The Quest of the Fair Unknown* (5–8). 2006, Houghton $16.00 (978-0-618-63152-0). To fulfill the deathbed plea of his mother, Beaufils sets off to find his long-absent father, a knight in the court of King Arthur. (Rev: BL 10/15/06; SLJ 11/06)

2974 Napoli, Donna Jo. *Breath* (8–12). 2003, Simon & Schuster $16.95 (978-0-689-86174-1). Salz, a sickly youth, seems to be immune to the sufferings of the people of Hameln in this reinterpretation of the Pied Piper story that conveys much of the atmosphere of 13th-century Europe. (Rev: BL 9/15/03; HBG 4/04; SLJ 11/03; VOYA 12/03)

2975 Newbery, Linda. *At the Firefly Gate* (5–8). 2007, Random $15.99 (978-0-385-75113-1). Henry befriends a neighbor who was once engaged to another Henry, a Royal Air Force pilot who failed to return from a mission in World War II. When Henry begins to see a mysterious figure at his gate and reenacts the pilot's final flight on a simulator, the war seems not so long ago. (Rev: BCCB 4/07; BL 2/15/07; HB 3-4/07; SLJ 3/07)

2976 Orgad, Dorit. *The Boy from Seville* (6–8). 2007, Kar-Ben $16.95 (978-1-58013-253-4). Readers will learn what life was like for Jews in Spain during the Inquisition through the story of Manuel and his family, who risk being burned at the stake if they are found out. (Rev: BL 10/1/07; LMC 1/08; SLJ 11/07)

2977 Orlev, Uri. *The Lady with the Hat* (7–10). Trans. by Hillel Halkin. 1995, Houghton $16.00 (978-0-395-69957-7). Yulek, a concentration camp survivor, encounters anti-Semitism on her return to Poland, while another Jewish girl, hidden from the Nazis, wants to be a nun. (Rev: BL 3/15/95; SLJ 5/95)

2978 Ortiz, Michael J. *Swan Town: The Secret Journal of Susanna Shakespeare* (7–10). 2006, HarperCollins LB $16.89 (978-0-06-058127-5). Shakespeare's teenage daughter Susanna writes in her diary about her current circumstances and her literary and acting ambitions, revealing much about Elizabethan life. (Rev: BL 2/15/06; SLJ 3/06; VOYA 2/06)

2979 Pennington, Kate. *Brief Candle* (6–9). 2005, Hodder paper $12.50 (978-0-340-87370-0). Fourteen-year-old Emily Brontë helps two hapless lovers in this novel set in Yorkshire and featuring the whole Brontë family. (Rev: BL 12/1/05; SLJ 11/05)

2980 Priestley, Chris. *Redwulf's Curse* (6–9). Series: Tom Marlowe Adventure. 2005, Doubleday $16.99 (978-0-385-60695-0). When the elderly Dr. Harker and 18-year-old Tom Marlowe travel from London to the English countryside in the early 18th century, they become swept up in intrigues surrounding the looting of the grave of Redwulf, a 7th-century East Anglian king. (Rev: BL 11/1/05; SLJ 12/05)

2981 Priestley, Chris. *The White Rider* (5–8). 2005, Corgi paper $8.99 (978-0-440-86608-4). In this riveting sequel to *Death and the Arrow*, 16-year-old Tom Marlowe is swept up in a series of intrigues in early 18th-century London. (Rev: BL 10/15/05)

2982 Rees, Elizabeth M. *The Wedding: An Encounter with Jan van Eyck* (8–11). Series: Art Encounters. 2005, Watson-Guptill $15.95 (978-0-8230-0407-2). In this novel set in 15th-century Bruges and channeling Jan van Eyck's *The Arnolfini Portrait*, 14-year-old Giovanna falls in love with a troubador called Angelo even as her father plans her marriage to a wealthy man. (Rev: BL 9/15/05; SLJ 9/05)

2983 Richter, Jutta. *The Summer of the Pike* (4–7). Trans. by Anna Brailovsky. Illus. by Quint Buchholz. 2006, Milkweed $16.95 (978-1-57131-671-4); paper $6.95 (978-1-57131-672-1). Anna, Daniel, and Lucas, who live on the grounds of a German manor, spend a difficult summer as Anna wishes for a closer relationship with her mother and the boys' mother is slowly dying of cancer; translated from German. (Rev: BL 1/1–15/07; SLJ 12/06)

2984 Rinaldi, Ann. *Nine Days a Queen: The Short Life and Reign of Lady Jane Grey* (6–8). 2005, HarperCollins $16.89 (978-0-06-054924-4). This fictionalized first-person account of the tragically brief life of Lady Jane Grey relates the complex palace intrigues that brought the 16-year-old Jane to the throne of England for nine days. (Rev: BL 12/1/04; SLJ 3/05; VOYA 2/05)

2985 Rinaldi, Ann. *The Redheaded Princess* (6–9). 2008, HarperCollins $15.99 (978-0-06-073374-2). An enjoyable novel about the dangerous and intrigue-filled life of Elizabeth I from her childhood until she became queen. (Rev: BL 10/15/07; SLJ 3/08)

2986 Roy, Jennifer. *Yellow Star* (5–8). 2006, Marshall Cavendish $16.95 (978-0-7614-5277-5). The fictionalized story, told in first-person free-verse chapters introduced by historical notes, of the author's aunt Syvia, a Holocaust survivor who spent much of her childhood in the grim Lodz ghetto. (Rev: BL 4/15/06; SLJ 7/06*; VOYA 6/06) 🏵

2987 Rushton, Rosie. *The Dashwood Sisters' Secrets of Love* (6–9). 2005, Hyperion $15.99 (978-0-7868-5136-2). In the wake of their father's remarriage and sudden death, the three Dashwood sisters experience a humbling reversal of fortunes. (Rev: BCCB 3/05; BL 3/1/05; SLJ 4/05; VOYA 6/05)

2988 Schmidt, Gary D. *Anson's Way* (5–9). 1999, Houghton $16.00 (978-0-395-91529-5). During the reign of George II, Anson begins his proud career in the British army as part of the forces occupying Ireland, then becomes disillusioned as he develops a growing respect and concern for the Irish. (Rev: BL 4/1/99*; HBG 10/99; SLJ 4/99; VOYA 8/99)

2989 Scott, Elaine. *Secrets of the Cirque Medrano* (5–8). 2008, Charlesbridge $15.95 (978-1-57091-712-7). In Montmartre, Paris, in 1904, 14-year-old Brigitte works in her aunt's cafe and meets the young artist Pablo Picasso and the circus performers who posed for his painting *Family of Saltambiques*. (Rev: BL 1/1–15/08; LMC 10/08; SLJ 3/08)

2990 *Sir Gawain and the Green Knight* (4–7). Retold by Michael Morpurgo. Illus. by Michael Foreman. 2005, Candlewick $18.99 (978-0-7636-2519-1). Morpurgo retells in contemporary prose the story of the Green Knight's challenge to the court of King Arthur. (Rev: BL 11/1/04*; SLJ 10/04)

2991 Sturtevant, Katherine. *A True and Faithful Narrative* (6–9). 2006, Farrar $17.00 (978-0-374-37809-7). In 17th-century London, 16-year-old Meg has abandoned some of her early dreams but still hopes to be a writer and not just a wife in this sequel to *At the Sign of the Star* (2000). (Rev: BL 3/1/06*; SLJ 5/06*)

2992 Sutcliff, Rosemary. *The Shining Company* (7–12). 1990, Farrar paper $6.95 (978-0-374-46616-9). A novel set in early Britain about a young man who with his friends confronts the enemy Saxons. (Rev: BL 6/15/90; SLJ 7/90)

2993 Szablya, Helen M., and Peggy K. Anderson. *The Fall of the Red Star* (7–9). 1996, Boyds Mills paper $9.95 (978-1-56397-977-4). A novel, partially based on fact, about a 14-year-old Hungarian boy who becomes a freedom fighter during the rebellion against the Soviets in 1956. (Rev: BL 2/1/96; SLJ 2/96; VOYA 6/96)

2994 Thomas, Jane Resh. *The Counterfeit Princess* (5–8). 2005, Clarion $15.00 (978-0-395-93870-6). Iris, a young English girl with an uncanny resemblance to Princess Elizabeth (soon to be Elizabeth I), finds herself embroiled in intrigue in this novel set in the 16th century. (Rev: BL 11/15/05; SLJ 10/05)

2995 Thomson, Sarah L. *The Secret of the Rose* (6–9). 2006, Greenwillow $16.99 (978-0-06-087250-2). In Elizabethan England, 14-year-old Rosalind must protect herself by hiding the fact that she's a Catholic and a female; however, she stumbles on more danger when she becomes servant to playwright Christopher Marlowe, who has his own secrets to hide. (Rev: BL 5/1/06; HB 7–8/06; SLJ 9/06)

2996 Town, Florida Ann. *With a Silent Companion* (7–12). 2000, Red Deer paper $7.95 (978-0-88995-211-9). Beginning in 1806, this novel based on fact tells how a young Irish girl hides her identity and becomes a "man" to pursue a medical career. (Rev: BL 4/15/00; VOYA 6/00)

2997 Updale, Eleanor. *Montmorency* (6–9). 2004, Scholastic $16.95 (978-0-439-58035-9). After surviving a near-fatal accident, a petty thief in Victorian London creates a double life and in the process becomes a criminal mastermind. (Rev: BCCB 4/04; BL 5/1/04; HB 3–4/04; SLJ 4/04; VOYA 6/05)

2998 Vande Velde, Vivian. *The Book of Mordred* (8–11). 2005, Houghton $18.00 (978-0-618-50754-2). A multilayered account of Mordred's acts, seen through the eyes of three women who know him well. (Rev: BL 9/15/05; SLJ 10/05; VOYA 10/05)

2999 Vogiel, Eva. *Friend or Foe?* (5–8). 2001, Judaica $19.95 (978-1-880582-66-4). In this novel set in London during 1948, the girls of the Migdal Binoh School for Orthodox Jewish girls notice

strange happenings when the Campbell family moves next door. (Rev: BL 4/1/01)

3000 Wallace, Karen. *The Unrivalled Spangles* (7–10). 2006, Simon & Schuster $16.95 (978-1-4169-1503-4). Ellen and Lucy Spangle, teenaged circus performers in 19th-century England, long to live new lives outside of the three rings. (Rev: BL 12/1/06; SLJ 12/06)

3001 Weatherly, Lee. *Breakfast at Sadie's* (6–9). 2006, Random $15.95 (978-0-385-75094-3). When her mother becomes very ill and her aunt skips town, Sadie is left to run her family's bed-and-breakfast all on her own in this upbeat story set in Wales. (Rev: SLJ 9/06)

3002 Wheeler, Thomas Gerald. *All Men Tall* (7–9). 1969, Phillips $26.95 (978-0-87599-157-3). An adventure tale set in early England about a 15-year-old boy's search for security.

3003 Wheeler, Thomas Gerald. *A Fanfare for the Stalwart* (7–9). 1967, Phillips $26.95 (978-0-87599-139-9). An injured Frenchman is left behind when Napoleon retreats from Russia.

3004 Whelan, Gerard. *The Guns of Easter* (6–10). 2000, O'Brien paper $7.95 (978-0-86278-449-2). Twelve-year-old Jimmy Conway grapples with the reasons for, and impact of, the violence erupting in Ireland in the early 20th century. (Rev: BL 3/1/01)

3005 Whelan, Gerard. *A Winter of Spies* (6–10). 2002, O'Brien paper $6.95 (978-0-86278-566-6). The story of the Conway family, begun in *The Guns of Easter* (2000), continues in this novel as 11-year-old Sarah sees spies and counterspies all around her in 1920 Dublin. (Rev: BL 6/1–15/02)

3006 Whelan, Gloria. *Parade of Shadows* (7–10). 2007, HarperCollins $15.99 (978-0-06-089028-5). Julia learns about the harsh realities of 1907 Turkish-occupied Syria while traveling across the country with her British father. (Rev: BL 11/15/07; SLJ 10/07)

3007 Whitehouse, Howard. *The Strictest School in the World: Being the Tale of a Clever Girl, a Rubber Boy and a Collection of Flying Machines, Mostly Broken* (5–8). Illus. by Bill Slavin. 2006, Kids Can $16.95 (978-1-55337-882-2); paper $6.95 (978-1-55337-883-9). Raised in India where her father is a British colonial official, Emmaline Cayley is upset when her parents send her to a strict school in England, so she hatches a plan to escape; an appealing blend of humor, fantasy, and Gothic atmosphere. (Rev: SLJ 11/06)

3008 Williams, Laura E. *The Spider's Web* (5–7). Illus. 1999, Milkweed paper $6.95 (978-1-57131-622-6). Lexi, a modern German girl, joins a racist skinhead organization and discovers the consequences of irrational hatred — from her own actions and from speaking with an older woman who was once a member of Hitler's Youth. (Rev: BL 6/1–15/99; HBG 10/99)

3009 Woodruff, Elvira. *Fearless* (5–8). 2008, Scholastic $16.99 (978-0-439-67703-5). Young brothers Digory and Cubby are befriended by Henry Winstanley, the builder of a unusual lighthouse on the Cornish coast, in this intriguing and action-packed story, set in 1703, about bravery and sacrifice. (Rev: BL 5/1/08; LMC 4-5/08; SLJ 4/08)

3010 Woodruff, Elvira. *The Ravenmaster's Secret* (4–7). 2003, Scholastic $15.95 (978-0-439-28133-1). Eleven-year-old Forrest becomes embroiled in dangerous intrigue in this story set inside the Tower of London in the early 18th century, with a glossary and historical notes appended. (Rev: BL 1/1–15/04; SLJ 1/04; VOYA 4/04)

3011 Wulf, Linda Press. *The Night of the Burning: Devorah's Story* (7–10). 2006, Farrar $16.00 (978-0-374-36419-9). Devorah and her younger sister Nechama are the only survivors left in their Polish town after a pogrom but are rescued and taken to a safe community in South Africa. They begin to build a new life and find happiness when they are adopted by families there. (Rev: BL 8/06; SLJ 1/07)

Latin America and Canada

3012 Belpre, Pura. *Firefly Summer* (5–8). 1996, Piñata paper $9.95 (978-1-55885-180-1). This gentle novel depicts family and community life in rural Puerto Rico at the turn of the 20th century as experienced by young Teresa Rodrigo, who has just completed 7th grade. (Rev: SLJ 2/97; VOYA 4/97)

3013 Brandis, Marianne. *The Quarter-Pie Window* (6–8). 2003, Tundra paper $9.95 (978-0-88776-624-4). Fourteen-year-old Emma and her younger brother, recently orphaned, go to live with their aunt and soon discover that the aunt is exploiting them in this novel set in 1830 Canada. (Rev: BL 7/03; VOYA 8/03)

3014 Cardenas, Teresa. *Old Dog* (7–12). Trans. by David Unger. 2007, Groundwood $16.95 (978-0-88899-757-9); paper $8.95 (978-0-88899-836-1). Seventy-year-old Cuban slave Perro Viejo helps to shelter 10-year-old runaway slave Aisa on the sugar plantation where Perro has lived a difficult life since childhood. (Rev: BL 12/15/07)

3015 Caswell, Maryanne. *Pioneer Girl* (5–8). Illus. by Lindsay Grater. 2001, Tundra $16.95 (978-0-88776-550-6). In letters to her grandmother, a 14-year-old girl describes the hardships and interesting experiences of her journey from Ontario to the prairies in the late 1880s. (Rev: HBG 10/01; SLJ 10/01)

3016 Clare, John D. *Aztec Life* (5–8). Illus. 2006, Saddleback paper $8.95 (978-1-59905-050-8). Covers the lifestyle, culture, and traditions of the Aztecs, with quotations from poems and sayings. (Rev: SLJ 9/06) [972]

3017 Clark, Ann Nolan. *Secret of the Andes* (6–8). 1970, Penguin paper $5.99 (978-0-14-030926-3). In this Newbery Medal winner (1953), a young Inca boy searches for his birthright and his identity.

3018 Collison, Linda. *Star-Crossed* (7–10). 2006, Knopf $16.95 (978-0-375-83363-2). After her father's death in 1760, Patricia stows away on a ship bound for Barbados to claim his estate; there she finds romance and learns a valuable trade. (Rev: BL 9/15/06; SLJ 12/06)

3019 Crook, Connie Brummel. *The Hungry Year* (5–8). 2001, Stoddart paper $7.95 (978-0-7737-6206-0). Twelve-year-old Kate must care for her brothers and handle the household chores during a severe Canadian winter in the late 1700s. (Rev: BL 1/1–15/02; SLJ 11/01)

3020 Crook, Connie Brummel. *The Perilous Year* (5–7). 2003, Fitzhenry & Whiteside paper $8.95 (978-1-55041-818-7). In this fast-paced sequel to *The Hungry Year* (2001), 11-year-old twins Alex and Ryan face constant challenges and adventures — including more encounters with pirates — in 18th-century Canada. (Rev: SLJ 3/04)

3021 Curtis, Christopher Paul. *Elijah of Buxton* (6–8). 2007, Scholastic $16.99 (978-0-439-02344-3). Eleven-year-old Elijah, the first child born in the Buxton Settlement for former slaves in Ontario, describes his life and those of the residents and newcomers to the settlement. Coretta Scott King Author Award, 2008; Newbery Honor Book, 2008. (Rev: BL 9/1/07; SLJ 10/07)

3022 Danticat, Edwidge. *Anacaona, Golden Flower: Haiti, 1490* (5–8). Series: Royal Diaries. 2005, Scholastic $10.95 (978-0-439-49906-4). In 15th-century Haiti, Anacaona, a girl of royal heritage, records her people's struggles against the Spanish explorers. (Rev: BL 5/15/05)

3023 Downie, Mary Alice, and John Downie. *Danger in Disguise* (5–8). Series: On Time's Wing. 2001, Roussan paper $6.95 (978-1-896184-72-2). Young Jamie, a Scot raised in Normandy in secrecy, is scooped up to serve in the British navy and sent to Quebec to fight the French in this complex tale of adventure and intrigue set in the mid-18th century. (Rev: SLJ 5/01)

3024 Eboch, Chris. *The Well of Sacrifice* (5–8). Illus. 1999, Houghton $16.00 (978-0-395-90374-2). In this novel set during Mayan times, Eveningstar Macaw sets out to avenge the death of her older brother, Smoke Shell. (Rev: BL 4/1/99; HBG 10/99; SLJ 5/99; VOYA 2/00)

3025 Ellis, Deborah. *I Am a Taxi* (6–9). 2006, Groundwood $16.95 (978-0-88899-735-7). Twelve-year-old Diego lives in a Bolivian prison with his parents, who were wrongfully accused of drug smuggling, and runs errands for prisoners but his life is forever changed when he's lured into working for an illegal cocaine operation deep in the jungle. (Rev: BL 11/15/06; HB 1–2/07; LMC 4–5/07; SLJ 12/06)

3026 Ellis, Deborah. *Sacred Leaf: The Cocalero Novels* (5–8). Series: The Cocalera Novels. 2007, Groundwood $16.95 (978-0-88899-751-7). Twelve-year-old Diego is living with a family of poor Bolivian coca farmers when their crop is destroyed by soldiers and they join a national protest. (Rev: BL 1/1–15/08; SLJ 12/07)

3027 Gantos, Jack. *Jack's New Power: Stories from a Caribbean Year* (5–8). 1995, Farrar $16.00 (978-0-374-33657-8); paper $5.95 (978-0-374-43715-2). Eight stories about the interesting people Jack meets when his family moves to the Caribbean. A sequel to *Heads or Tails* (1994). (Rev: BCCB 12/95; BL 12/1/95; SLJ 11/95*)

3028 Harrison, Troon. *A Bushel of Light* (5–8). 2001, Stoddart paper $7.95 (978-0-7737-6140-7). Fourteen-year-old orphan Maggie juggles her need to search for her twin sister and her responsibilities for 4-year-old Lizzy, in this novel set in Canada in the early 1900s. (Rev: SLJ 10/01)

3029 Haworth-Attard, Barbara. *Home Child* (5–8). 1996, Roussan paper $6.95 (978-1-896184-18-0). Set in Canada during the early 1900s, this is the story of 13-year-old Arthur Fellowes, a London orphan who is treated like an outcast when he joins the Wilson family as a home child (that is, a cheap farm laborer). (Rev: VOYA 8/97)

3030 Holeman, Linda. *Promise Song* (5–8). 1997, Tundra paper $6.95 (978-0-88776-387-8). In 1900, Rosetta, an English orphan who has been sent to Canada, becomes an indentured servant. (Rev: BL 6/1–15/97; SLJ 10/97)

3031 Ibbotson, Eva. *Journey to the River Sea* (5–8). 2002, Dutton $17.99 (978-0-525-46739-7). Orphaned Maia journeys from 1910 London to live with relatives in Brazil in this complex story that involves an unwelcoming family, a beloved governess, a child actor, a runaway, and the wonders of Brazil, all presented with a mix of drama and humor. (Rev: BCCB 4/02; BL 12/15/01; HB 1–2/02; HBG 10/02; SLJ 1/02*; VOYA 12/01)

3032 Jocelyn, Marthe. *Mable Riley: A Reliable Record of Humdrum, Peril, and Romance* (5–10). Illus. 2004, Candlewick $15.99 (978-0-7636-2120-9). This is a charming, humorous diary set in 1901 by a 14-year-old girl who accompanies her sister when she becomes a teacher in Stratford, Ontario. (Rev: BL 3/1/04; HB 5–6/04; SLJ 3/04; VOYA 6/04)

3033 Kositsky, Lynne. *Claire by Moonlight* (7–10). 2005, Tundra paper $9.95 (978-0-88776-659-6).

History and romance are interwoven in this story of 15-year-old Claire's struggle to return to Acadia with her brother and sister after their deportation in the 1750s. (Rev: BL 7/05; SLJ 10/05)

3034 Lawson, Julie. *Goldstone* (5–8). 1998, Stoddart paper $7.95 (978-0-7737-5891-9). Karin, a 13-year-old Swedish Canadian girl, lives with her family in a mountainous town in British Columbia in 1910 when heavy winter snows bring avalanches that cause death and destruction. (Rev: BL 7/97; SLJ 5/98)

3035 Limón, Graciela. *Song of the Hummingbird* (6–10). 1996, Arte Publico paper $12.95 (978-1-55885-091-0). The conquest of the Aztec Empire by Cortes is told through the experiences of Huizitzilin (Hummingbird), a descendent of Mexican kings. (Rev: VOYA 8/97)

3036 Lowery, Linda. *Truth and Salsa* (4–7). 2006, Peachtree $14.95 (978-1-59145-366-6). Staying with her grandmother in Mexico after her parents separate, Haley makes a new friend and learns about people living on the edge of poverty. (Rev: SLJ 7/06)

3037 Major, Kevin. *Ann and Seamus* (5–9). Illus. by David Blackwood. 2003, Groundwood $16.95 (978-0-88899-561-2). Based on an early 19th-century shipwreck off the coast of Newfoundland, this historical novel in verse chronicles the romance that develops between 17-year-old Ann Harvey and the Irish teenager she rescues from the ship. (Rev: BL 3/1/04; HB 3–4/04; SLJ 2/04; VOYA 4/04)

3038 Mikaelsen, Ben. *Tree Girl* (7–12). 2004, HarperTempest $16.99 (978-0-06-009004-3). Through the first-person narrative of Mayan teenager Gabriela Flores, the reader experiences the civil war in Guatemala. (Rev: BL 2/15/04; SLJ 4/04; VOYA 6/04)

3039 Noël, Michel. *Good for Nothing* (8–11). 2004, Douglas & McIntyre $18.95 (978-0-88899-478-3). In this powerful coming-of-age novel set in northern Quebec in the late 1950s and early 1960s, 15-year-old Nipishish, part Algonquin and part white, struggles to find his own identity. (Rev: BL 1/1–15/05; SLJ 1/05; VOYA 2/05)

3040 O'Dell, Scott. *The Captive* (7–9). 1979, Houghton $17.00 (978-0-395-27811-6). During a voyage in the 1500s, a young Jesuit seminarian discovers that the crew of his ship plans to enslave a colony of Mayans. A sequel is *The Feathered Serpent* (1981).

3041 O'Dell, Scott. *The King's Fifth* (7–10). 1966, Houghton $17.00 (978-0-395-06963-9). In a story told in flashbacks, Esteban explains why he is in jail in the Mexico of the Conquistadors. Also use *The Hawk That Dare Not Hunt by Day* (1975).

3042 Porter, Pamela. *The Crazy Man* (6–8). 2005, Douglas & McIntyre $15.95 (978-0-88899-694-7). In appealing free verse, this novel set in 1960s Saskatchewan tells the story of young Emaline, who has been crippled in a farm accident and who befriends Angus, a mental patient who's been hired to help out around the farm. (Rev: BL 11/1/05; SLJ 12/05; VOYA 2/06)

3043 Schwartz, Virginia Frances. *Messenger* (5–9). 2002, Holiday $17.95 (978-0-8234-1716-2). This story of the hardships and joys of a Croatian family living in Ontario's mining towns in the 1920s and 1930s is based on the lives of the author's mother and grandmother. (Rev: HBG 3/03; SLJ 11/02; VOYA 12/02)

3044 Slaughter, Charles H. *The Dirty War* (6–9). 1994, Walker $15.95 (978-0-8027-8312-7). Arte, 14, lives in Buenos Aires, Argentina. When his father is taken prisoner by the government, his grandmother stages public protests. (Rev: BL 11/1/94; SLJ 12/94; VOYA 2/95)

3045 Stenhouse, Ted. *Across the Steel River* (6–8). 2001, Kids Can $16.95 (978-1-55074-891-8). In 1952, a Canadian boy and his Indian friend find the badly beaten body of an Indian man and, in the process of investigating his death, reassess their own relationship. (Rev: BCCB 1/02; BL 1/1–15/02; HBG 3/02; SLJ 10/01; VOYA 2/02)

3046 Stenhouse, Ted. *A Dirty Deed* (6–8). 2003, Kids Can $16.95 (978-1-55337-360-5). In this sequel to *Across the Steel River* (2001), friends Will Samson and Arthur, a Blackfoot Indian, have exciting adventures as they struggle to return a deed to its rightful owners. (Rev: BL 3/15/03; HBG 10/03; SLJ 5/03; VOYA 10/03)

3047 Taylor, Joanne. *There You Are: A Novel* (4–7). 2004, Tundra paper $8.95 (978-0-88776-658-9). On post-World War II Cape Breton Island, 12-year-old Jeannie lives in a remote community and longs for a friend. (Rev: SLJ 11/04)

3048 Temple, Frances. *Taste of Salt: A Story of Modern Haiti* (7–12). 1992, Orchard LB $17.99 (978-0-531-08609-4). A first novel simply told in the voices of two Haitian teenagers who find political commitment and love. (Rev: BL 8/92; SLJ 9/92*)

3049 Trottier, Maxine. *A Circle of Silver* (5–8). 2000, Stoddart paper $7.95 (978-0-7737-6055-4). Set in the 1760s, this is the story of 13-year-old John MacNeil who is sent to Canada by his father to toughen him up. (Rev: SLJ 9/00)

3050 Trottier, Maxine. *Sister to the Wolf* (6–9). 2004, Kids Can $16.95 (978-1-55337-519-7). In this engaging historical novel, which begins in Quebec in the early 18th century, Cecile, the teenage daughter of a fur trader, buys an Indian slave to save him from further abuse. (Rev: BL 1/1–15/05; SLJ 12/04)

3051 Weir, Joan. *The Brideship* (7–9). 1999, Stoddart paper $5.95 (978-0-7736-7474-5). Three plucky British teens journey to British Columbia as mail-order brides in the 1860s. (Rev: SLJ 10/99)

3052 Whelan, Gloria. *The Disappeared* (8–12). 2008, Dial $16.99 (978-0-8037-3275-9). Silvia tries to save her brother Eduardo when he is imprisoned for protesting against the government in Argentina in the 1970s. (Rev: BL 4/15/08; LMC 10/08*; SLJ 7/08)

United States

NATIVE AMERICANS

3053 Armstrong, Nancy M. *Navajo Long Walk* (4–7). Illus. 1994, Roberts Rinehart $8.95 (978-1-879373-56-3). The story of the Long Walk of the Navajo in 1864 and their confinement in an internment camp are vividly told. (Rev: BL 10/1/94; SLJ 1/95)

3054 Bruchac, Joseph. *A Boy Called Slow: The True Story of Sitting Bull* (5–8). Illus. by Rocco Baviera. 1995, Putnam $17.99 (978-0-399-22692-2). The story of the boyhood of Sitting Bull, who, because of his sluggishness, had been called Slow. (Rev: BCCB 4/95; BL 3/15/95; HB 9–10/95; SLJ 10/95)

3055 Bruchac, Joseph. *Geronimo* (7–10). 2006, Scholastic $16.99 (978-0-439-35360-1). Geronimo's fictional adopted grandson narrates the tragic story of Geronimo's final surrender and the subsequent treatment of his people in this well-researched novel. (Rev: BL 3/15/06; SLJ 4/06)

3056 Bruchac, Joseph. *The Journal of Jesse Smoke: The Trail of Tears, 1838* (5–8). Illus. Series: My Name Is America. 2001, Scholastic paper $10.95 (978-0-439-12197-2). Jesse, a 16-year-old Cherokee, chronicles in his diary the tribe's forced journey to Oklahoma and tries to understand the reasons behind this cruel action. (Rev: BL 7/01; HBG 10/01; SLJ 7/01; VOYA 8/01)

3057 Burks, Brian. *Runs with Horses* (5–9). 1995, Harcourt paper $6.00 (978-0-15-200994-6). An adventure story set in 1886 in which 16-year-old Runs with Horses completes his Apache warrior training by performing feats of endurance, survival, and daring, and partly as a result of information he gathers during raids, his tribe realizes that they can no longer continue to resist the white man. (Rev: BL 11/1/95; SLJ 11/95; VOYA 2/96)

3058 Carvell, Marlene. *Sweetgrass Basket* (7–10). 2005, Dutton $16.99 (978-0-525-47547-7). Mohawk sisters Mattie and Sarah describe the abuse they endure at the Carlisle Indian Industrial School at the turn of the 20th century. (Rev: BL 8/05*; SLJ 12/05)

3059 Creel, Ann Howard. *Under a Stand Still Moon* (6–10). 2005, Brown Barn paper $8.95 (978-0-9746481-8-7). In this captivating story set among the ancient Anasazi of the American Southwest, a young girl uses her magical powers to preserve her people's way of life. (Rev: SLJ 11/05)

3060 Doughty, Wayne Dyre. *Crimson Moccasins* (7–9). 1980, HarperCollins paper $2.95 (978-0-06-440015-2). During the Revolutionary War a white boy is raised as the son of an Indian chief.

3061 Driving Hawk Sneve, Virginia. *Lana's Lakota Moons* (5–8). 2008, Univ. of Nebraska paper $12.95 (978-0-8032-6028-3). Lori and Lana, Lakotas whose lives are a combination of Native American tradition and modern American culture, have disturbing premonitions about the future that sadly come true in this thoughtful, moving story. (Rev: BL 5/1/08)

3062 Erdrich, Louise. *The Game of Silence* (5–8). 2005, HarperCollins LB $16.89 (978-0-06-029790-9). As 9-year-old Omakayas is coming of age, the intrusion of the European settlers increasingly impacts the Ojibwe lifestyle in this sequel to *The Birchbark House* (1999). (Rev: BL 5/15/05*; SLJ 7/05)

3063 Erdrich, Louise. *The Porcupine Year* (4–7). Illus. by author. 2008, HarperCollins $15.99 (978-0-06-029787-9). In this sequel to *The Birchbark House* (1999) and *The Game of Silence* (2005), Omakayas is now 12 and the family is traveling north, looking for a new home far from the intruding white settlers. (Rev: BL 6/1–15/08; SLJ 9/08)

3064 Gall, Grant. *Apache: The Long Ride Home* (7–10). 1988, Sunstone paper $9.95 (978-0-86534-105-0). Pedro was only nine when Apache raiders kidnapped him and renamed him Cuchillo. (Rev: BL 9/15/87)

3065 Gregory, Kristiana. *The Legend of Jimmy Spoon* (6–8). 1990, Harcourt $15.95 (978-0-15-200506-1). The story of a 12-year-old white boy who is adopted by the Shoshoni in 1855. (Rev: BL 7/90)

3066 Grutman, Jewel H., and Gay Matthaei. *The Ledgerbook of Thomas Blue Eagle* (4–8). Illus. by Adam Cvijanovic. 1994, Thomasson-Grant $17.95 (978-1-56566-063-2). A young Native American boy attends a white man's school but tries to retain his own identity and culture in this story that takes place in the West 100 years ago. (Rev: SLJ 12/94)

3067 Hausman, Gerald. *The Coyote Bead* (7–12). 1999, Hampton Roads paper $11.95 (978-1-57174-145-5). With the help of his grandfather and Indian magic, a young Navajo boy evades the American soldiers who killed his parents. (Rev: SLJ 1/00; VOYA 4/00)

3068 Highwater, Jamake. *Legend Days* (7–10). Series: Ghost Horse. 1984, HarperCollins $12.95 (978-0-06-022303-8). This story about a young Indian girl begins a moving trilogy about three generations of Native Americans and their fate in a white man's world. Followed by *The Ceremony of Innocence* and *I Wear the Morning Star*.

3069 Homstad, Daniel W. *Horse Dreamer* (7–12). 2001, PublishAmerica paper $27.95 (978-1-58851-042-6). A historical adventure in which 16-year-old Zakarias, son of a white father and a Dakota mother, serves as a scout for the army in the early 1860s until he is captured by renegade Dakotas and decides to join their cause. (Rev: VOYA 4/02)

3070 Hudson, Jan. *Sweetgrass* (5–8). 1989, Scholastic paper $3.99 (978-0-590-43486-7). A description of the culture of the Dakota Indians in the 1830s. (Rev: BCCB 4/89; BL 4/1/89; SLJ 4/89)

3071 Matthaei, Gay, and Jewel Grutman. *The Sketchbook of Thomas Blue Eagle* (4–7). Illus. 2001, Chronicle $16.95 (978-0-88182-908-2). Through drawings and narration, the Lakota artist Thomas Blue Eagle tells how he joined Buffalo Bill's show, traveled to Europe, and made enough money to marry. (Rev: BCCB 5/01; BL 4/1/01)

3072 O'Dell, Scott. *Sing Down the Moon* (6–9). 1970, Houghton $18.00 (978-0-395-10919-9); Dell paper $5.99 (978-0-440-97975-3). A young Navajo girl sees her culture destroyed by Spanish slavers and white soldiers. (Rev: BL 11/1/87)

3073 O'Dell, Scott, and Elizabeth Hall. *Thunder Rolling in the Mountains* (5–9). 1992, Dell paper $5.50 (978-0-440-40879-6). From the viewpoint of Chief Joseph's daughter, this historical novel concerns the forced removal of the Nez Perce from their homeland in 1877. (Rev: BL 6/15/92*; SLJ 8/92)

3074 Patent, Dorothy Hinshaw. *The Buffalo and the Indians: A Shared Destiny* (4–8). Illus. by William Muñoz. 2006, Clarion $18.00 (978-0-618-48570-3). This beautifully illustrated title explores the unique bonds — both spiritual and economic — between Native Americans and the American bison. (Rev: BL 6/1/06*; HBG 4/07; LMC 2/07; SLJ 8/06*) [978.004]

3075 Rees, Celia. *Sorceress* (7–11). 2002, Candlewick $15.99 (978-0-7636-1847-6). Agnes, a Native American who is beginning college, researches Mary Newbury, first seen in *Witch Child* (2001), and discovers a connection that results in a vision quest. (Rev: BL 1/1–15/03; HB 1–2/03; HBG 3/03; SLJ 12/02; VOYA 4/03)

3076 Sandoz, Mari. *The Horsecatcher* (7–9). 1957, Univ. of Nebraska paper $13.95 (978-0-8032-9160-7). A Cheyenne youth gains stature with his tribe and earns the name of Horsecatcher. (Rev: BL 11/1/87)

3077 Schwartz, Virginia Frances. *Initiation* (5–8). Illus. 2003, Fitzhenry & Whiteside $15.95 (978-1-55005-053-0). Kwakiuti Indian twins Nana and Nanolatch prepare to face the responsibilities of adulthood in this story set on the West Coast of North America in the 15th century. (Rev: SLJ 3/04) [813]

3078 Shefelman, Janice. *Comanche Song* (6–9). 2000, Eakin $17.95 (978-1-57168-397-7). Tsena, 16, is imprisoned with other Comanches after peace talks falter and 12 Indian chiefs are killed in this story based on a real event in 1840. (Rev: BL 2/15/01; HBG 10/01; SLJ 10/00)

3079 Smith, Patricia Clark. *Weetamoo: Heart of the Pocassets, Massachusetts — Rhode Island, 1653* (5–8). Illus. Series: Royal Diaries. 2003, Scholastic $10.95 (978-0-439-12910-7). Weetamoo prepares to succeed her father as leader of the tribe and describes relationships with the European settlers and how daily life changes with the seasons. (Rev: BL 12/15/03; HBG 4/04; SLJ 1/04)

3080 Spooner, Michael. *Last Child* (8–11). 2005, Holt $16.95 (978-0-8050-7739-1). Rosalie, who is part Mandan and part Scottish American, is caught up in the conflicts between the Native Americans and the whites in 1837 North Dakota. (Rev: BL 9/1/05; SLJ 11/05; VOYA 8/05)

3081 Vick, Helen H. *Shadow* (5–7). Series: Courage of the Stone. 1998, Roberts Rinehart $15.95 (978-1-57098-218-7); paper $9.95 (978-1-57098-195-1). Shadow, an independent Pueblo Indian girl in pre-Columbian Arizona, leaves her home to rescue her father. (Rev: SLJ 10/98)

3082 Wyss, Thelma Hatch. *Bear Dancer: The Story of a Ute Girl* (4–7). 2005, Simon & Schuster $15.95 (978-1-4169-0285-0). In this fact-based historical novel, life is turned upside down for Elk Girl, a member of the Tabaguache Ute, when she is kidnapped by a rival tribe. (Rev: BL 10/15/05; SLJ 10/05)

DISCOVERY AND EXPLORATION

3083 Carbone, Elisa. *Blood on the River: James Town, 1607* (5–8). 2006, Viking $16.99 (978-0-670-06060-3). As a page for Captain John Smith in the Jamestown Colony, 11-year-old Samuel Collier experiences firsthand the hardships and adventures that confront the settlers; a powerful, historically detailed novel. (Rev: BL 4/15/06; LMC 1/07; SLJ 7/06*)

3084 Duble, Kathleen Benner. *Quest* (5–8). 2008, Simon & Schuster $16.99 (978-1-4169-3386-1). Through the thoughts of four characters, two of them on Henry Hudson's ship *Discovery*, readers will learn of the significance of the voyage to find the Northwest Passage and why it failed. (Rev: BL 4/15/08; SLJ 8/08)

3085 Kudlinski, Kathleen V. *My Lady Pocahontas* (7–10). 2006, Marshall Cavendish $16.95 (978-0-7614-5293-5). This fictional account of the life of Pocahontas from the time of the Jamestown settlement until her death focuses on her strength and inner conflicts. (Rev: BL 5/1/06; LMC 11–12/06; SLJ 12/06)

COLONIAL PERIOD AND FRENCH AND INDIAN WARS

3086 Avi. *Night Journeys* (6–9). 1994, Morrow paper $4.95 (978-0-688-13628-4). In the Pennsylvania of 1767, a 12-year-old orphan boy joins a hunt for escaped bondsmen. Another novel set at the same time by this author is *Encounter at Easton* (1994).

3087 Bruchac, Joseph. *Pocahontas* (6–12). 2003, Harcourt $17.00 (978-0-15-216737-0). Pocahontas and John Smith take turns describing the relationship between the Jamestown colonists and the Powhatan Indians. (Rev: BL 9/15/03; HBG 4/04; SLJ 5/04; VOYA 4/04)

3088 Bruchac, Joseph. *The Winter People* (6–10). 2002, Dial $18.99 (978-0-8037-2694-9). A 14-year-old Abenaki boy searches for his mother and sisters after they are kidnapped by English soldiers in the French and Indian War. (Rev: BL 10/1/02*; HBG 3/03; SLJ 11/02*)

3089 Butler, Amy. *Virginia Bound* (4–7). 2003, Clarion $15.00 (978-0-618-24752-3). Thirteen-year-old Rob is kidnapped in London and shipped to Virginia as an indentured servant to work on a tobacco farm in 1627. (Rev: BL 3/1/03; HBG 10/03; SLJ 6/03)

3090 Collier, James Lincoln. *The Corn Raid: A Story of the Jamestown Settlement* (5–9). 2000, Jamestown paper $5.95 (978-0-8092-0619-3). History and fiction mix in this adventure tale set in the Jamestown settlement and featuring a 12-year-old indentured servant and his cruel master. (Rev: SLJ 4/00)

3091 Coombs, Karen M. *Sarah on Her Own* (6–10). 1996, Avon paper $3.99 (978-0-380-78275-8). Through the eyes of a sensitive English teenager who voyaged to America in 1620, the reader relives the harsh realities and joys of life in an early Virginia settlement. (Rev: SLJ 9/96)

3092 Duble, Kathleen Benner. *The Sacrifice* (6–9). 2005, Simon & Schuster $15.95 (978-0-689-87650-9). Strong-minded Abigail, 10, and her older sister are accused of witchcraft in 1692 Massachusetts in this compelling novel full of social history. (Rev: BL 9/15/05*; SLJ 12/05)

3093 Durrant, Lynda. *The Beaded Moccasins: The Story of Mary Campbell* (5–9). 1998, Clarion $15.00 (978-0-395-85398-6). Told in the first person, this is a fictionalized account of the true story of 12-year-old Mary Campbell who was captured by the Delaware Indians in 1759. (Rev: BCCB 5/98; BL 3/15/98; HBG 10/98; SLJ 6/98; VOYA 12/98)

3094 Edmonds, Walter. *The Matchlock Gun* (5–7). Illus. by Paul Lantz. 1941, Putnam $16.99 (978-0-399-21911-5). Exciting, true story of a courageous boy who protected his mother and sister from the Indians of the Hudson Valley. Newbery Medal winner, 1942.

3095 Field, Rachel. *Calico Bush* (5–7). Illus. by Allen Louis. 1987, Macmillan $17.95 (978-0-02-734610-7). This 1932 Newbery Honor Book is an adventure story of a French girl "loaned" to a family of American pioneers in Maine in the 1740s.

3096 Greene, Jacqueline D. *Out of Many Waters* (6–8). 1988, Walker $16.95 (978-0-8027-6811-7). A historical novel that begins in Brazil and ends with a group of Jewish settlers who, after landing in New Amsterdam, began the first synagogue in America. (Rev: BL 1/15/89; SLJ 10/88; VOYA 12/88)

3097 Grote, JoAnn A. *Queen Anne's War* (5–8). Series: The American Adventure. 1998, Chelsea LB $15.95 (978-0-7910-5045-3). During Queen Anne's War in 1710, Will Smith's family becomes involved in the attempt to drive the French out of New England, but 11-year-old Will is preoccupied with a jealous classmate. (Rev: HBG 3/99; SLJ 1/99)

3098 Hermes, Patricia. *Salem Witch* (5–8). Series: My Side of the Story. 2006, Kingfisher paper $7.95 (978-0-7534-5991-1). Two teenage friends develop different views during the witch trials in 17th-century Salem, and readers can flip the book to read each person's opinion. (Rev: SLJ 2/07)

3099 Hurst, Carol Otis, and Rebecca Otis. *A Killing in Plymouth Colony* (5–7). 2003, Houghton $15.00 (978-0-618-27597-7). John Bradford, the son of the governor of Plymouth Colony, has always struggled to gain his father's approval and feels an affinity toward an outcast who is accused of murder. (Rev: BL 12/1/03; HBG 4/04; SLJ 10/03)

3100 Karr, Kathleen. *Worlds Apart* (4–7). 2005, Marshall Cavendish $15.95 (978-0-7614-5195-2). In 1670 South Carolina, Christopher — a teenage settler — and Sewee Indian Asha-po become friends. (Rev: BCCB 5/05; SLJ 5/05)

3101 Karwoski, Gail Langer. *Surviving Jamestown: The Adventures of Young Sam Collier* (5–7). Illus. by Paul Casale. 2001, Peachtree $14.95 (978-1-56145-239-2); paper $8.95 (978-1-56145-245-3). Full of facts, this novel tells the story of a 12-year-old English boy who sails in 1606 for the colony of Virginia, with details of the struggles the colonists faced. (Rev: HBG 10/01; SLJ 8/01; VOYA 8/01)

3102 Keehn, Sally M. *Moon of Two Dark Horses* (6–9). 1995, Puffin paper $6.99 (978-0-698-11949-9). A sensitively drawn friendship between a Native American boy and a white settler. (Rev: BL 11/15/95*; SLJ 11/95; VOYA 12/95)

3103 Ketchum, Liza. *Where the Great Hawk Flies* (4–7). 2005, Clarion $16.00 (978-0-618-40085-0). The Coombs family and the Tuckers have trouble getting along — even the young boys — because Mrs. Tucker is a Pequot Indian and the Coombs suffered mightily during an Indian raid seven years before. (Rev: BCCB 12/05; BL 9/15/05*; HB 1–2/06; LMC 1/06; SLJ 1/06; VOYA 4/06)

3104 Laird, Marnie. *Water Rat* (7–9). Illus. 1998, Winslow $15.95 (978-1-890817-08-4). An action-filled adventure story set in colonial times about Matt, a 14-year-old orphan, and his struggle to survive and prove his worth. (Rev: SLJ 1/99; VOYA 2/99)

3105 Lasky, Kathryn. *Beyond the Burning Time* (7–12). 1994, Scholastic paper $14.95 (978-0-590-47331-6). In this docunovel that captures the ignorance, violence, and hysteria of the Salem witch trials, Mary, 12, tries to save her mother, accused of witchcraft. (Rev: BL 10/15/94; SLJ 1/95; VOYA 12/94)

3106 Lasky, Kathryn. *A Journey to the New World: The Diary of Remember Patience Whipple* (4–7). Series: Dear America. 1996, Scholastic paper $10.95 (978-0-590-50214-6). Using diary entries as a format, this is the story of 12-year-old Mem Whipple, her journey on the *Mayflower*, and her first year in the New World. (Rev: BCCB 10/96; HB 9–10/96; SLJ 8/96; VOYA 10/96)

3107 Moore, Robin. *The Man with the Silver Oar* (6–12). 2002, HarperCollins LB $15.89 (978-0-06-000048-6). Daniel, a Quaker 15-year-old, stows away on a ship hunting pirates in this fine adventure story set in 1718. (Rev: BL 6/1–15/02; HBG 10/02; SLJ 7/02; VOYA 8/02)

3108 Ovecka, Janice. *Cave of Falling Water* (4–8). Illus. by David K. Fadden. 1992, New England Pr. paper $10.95 (978-0-933050-98-3). A cave in the hills of Vermont plays a part in the lives of three girls, one an Indian and one white, both from colonial times, and the last, a contemporary adolescent. (Rev: BL 5/1/93)

3109 Rinaldi, Ann. *The Journal of Jasper Jonathan Pierce: A Pilgrim Boy, Plymouth, 1620* (4–8). 2000, Scholastic paper $10.95 (978-0-590-51078-3). This fictionalized account of the Pilgrims in journal format follows the adventures of a 14-year-old indentured servant aboard the *Mayflower* and during his first year in the New World. (Rev: BL 2/15/00; HBG 10/00; SLJ 7/00)

3110 Rinaldi, Ann. *Or Give Me Death: A Novel of Patrick Henry's Family* (7–9). 2003, Harcourt

$17.00 (978-0-15-216687-8). The treatment of the mentally ill in the colonial era is shown in this novel narrated by the daughters of an insane mother. (Rev: BL 5/15/03; SLJ 7/03; VOYA 8/03)

3111 Rinaldi, Ann. *A Stitch in Time* (7–10). Series: Quilt Trilogy. 1994, Scholastic paper $13.95 (978-0-590-46055-2). This historical novel set in 18th-century Salem, Massachusetts, concerns the tribulations of a 16-year-old girl and her family. (Rev: BL 3/1/94; SLJ 5/94; VOYA 4/94)

3112 Schwabach, Karen. *A Pickpocket's Tale* (5–8). 2006, Random LB $17.99 (978-0-375-93379-0). After being caught picking pockets on the streets of London in 1730, 10-year-old orphan Molly is exiled to America where she learns many new things from the Jewish family to which she is indentured. (Rev: BL 11/15/06; SLJ 11/06)

3113 Speare, Elizabeth George. *The Sign of the Beaver* (6–9). 1983, Houghton $16.00 (978-0-395-33890-2); Dell paper $5.99 (978-0-440-47900-0). In Maine in 1768, Matt, though only 12, is struggling to survive on his own until the Indians help him. (Rev: BL 3/1/88)

3114 Speare, Elizabeth George. *The Witch of Blackbird Pond* (6–9). 1958, Houghton $16.00 (978-0-395-07114-4); Dell paper $5.99 (978-0-440-99577-7). Historical romance set in Puritan Connecticut with the theme of witchcraft. Newbery Medal winner, 1959. (Rev: BL 7/88)

3115 Stainer, M. L. *The Lyon's Cub* (5–9). Illus. 1998, Chicken Soup Pr. LB $9.95 (978-0-9646904-5-5); paper $6.95 (978-0-9646904-6-2). This novel, a continuation of *The Lyon's Roar* (1997), tells what happened to the settlers of the lost colony of Roanoke and their life with peaceful Indian tribes. Continued in *The Lyon's Pride* (1998). (Rev: SLJ 8/98)

3116 Strickland, Brad. *The Guns of Tortuga* (5–8). 2003, Simon & Schuster paper $4.99 (978-0-689-85297-8). Young Davy helps the crew of the *Aurora* defeat a band of pirates in this sequel to *Mutiny!* (Rev: BL 2/1/03; SLJ 3/03)

3117 Wisler, G. Clifton. *This New Land* (5–9). 1987, Walker LB $14.85 (978-0-8027-6727-1). Twelve-year-old Richard and his family begin a new life in Plymouth, Massachusetts, in 1620. (Rev: BL 3/15/88; SLJ 11/87)

REVOLUTIONARY PERIOD AND THE YOUNG NATION (1775–1809)

3118 Alsheimer, Jeanette E., and Patricia J. Friedle. *The Trouble with Tea* (5–8). 2002, Pentland $15.95 (978-1-57197-299-6). When Patience visits her friend Anne in Boston in 1773, she witnesses many of the events that led to the American Revolution. (Rev: BL 6/1–15/02)

3119 Anderson, Joan. *1787* (7–10). 1987, Harcourt $14.95 (978-0-15-200582-5). The story of a teenager who became James Madison's aide during the 1787 Constitutional Convention in Philadelphia. (Rev: BL 5/87; VOYA 12/87)

3120 Anderson, Laurie Halse. *Fever 1793* (6–10). 2000, Simon & Schuster $16.00 (978-0-689-83858-3). Matilda must find the strength to go on when her family is killed by yellow fever in a 1793 outbreak in Philadelphia. (Rev: BCCB 10/00; BL 10/1/00; HB 9–10/00; HBG 3/01; SLJ 8/00*)

3121 Armstrong, Jennifer. *Thomas Jefferson: Letters from a Philadelphia Bookworm* (5–8). Illus. Series: Dear Mr. President. 2001, Winslow $8.95 (978-1-890817-30-5). Twelve-year-old Amelia and President Jefferson discuss the events of the times in a continuing exchange of letters. (Rev: BL 5/15/01; HBG 10/01; SLJ 6/01; VOYA 8/01)

3122 Avi. *The Fighting Ground* (5–9). Illus. by Ellen Thompson. 1984, HarperCollins LB $16.89 (978-0-397-32074-5); paper $5.99 (978-0-06-440185-2). Thirteen-year-old Jonathan marches off to fight the British. (Rev: BL 4/87)

3123 Bruchac, Joseph. *The Arrow over the Door* (4–7). Illus. 1998, Dial $15.99 (978-0-8037-2078-7). Two boys, one a Quaker and the other a Native American, share the narration of this story that takes place immediately before the Battle of Saratoga in 1777. (Rev: BCCB 4/98; BL 2/15/98; HBG 10/98; SLJ 4/98)

3124 Collier, James Lincoln, and Christopher Collier. *My Brother Sam Is Dead* (6–9). 1984, Simon & Schuster $17.95 (978-0-02-722980-6); Scholastic paper $5.99 (978-0-590-42792-0). The story, based partially on fact, of a Connecticut family divided in loyalties during the Revolutionary War.

3125 Demas, Corinne. *If Ever I Return Again* (5–8). 2000, HarperCollins LB $15.89 (978-0-06-028718-4). Twelve-year-old Celia describes life aboard a whaling ship in letters home to her cousin. (Rev: BCCB 6/00; BL 4/1/00; HBG 10/00; SLJ 8/00)

3126 Durrant, Lynda. *Betsy Zane, the Rose of Fort Henry* (5–8). 2000, Clarion $15.00 (978-0-395-97899-3). Toward the end of the Revolutionary War, Betsy sets out alone from Philadelphia to rejoin her five brothers in western Virginia. (Rev: BCCB 10/00; BL 9/15/00; HBG 3/01; SLJ 4/01)

3127 Elliott, L. M. *Give Me Liberty* (5–8). 2006, HarperCollins $16.99 (978-0-06-074421-2). Nathaniel Dunn, a 13-year-old indentured servant in colonial Virginia, is taken under the wing of an elderly schoolmaster and watches as the revolutionary movement grows and affects his own behavior. (Rev: BL 10/1/06; SLJ 9/06)

3128 Fleischman, Paul. *Path of the Pale Horse* (7–9). 1992, HarperCollins paper $3.95 (978-0-06-

440442-6). Dr. Peale and his apprentice help fight a yellow fever epidemic in 1793 Philadelphia.

3129 Forbes, Esther. *Johnny Tremain: A Novel for Old and Young* (6–9). Illus. by Lynd Ward. 1943, Houghton $17.00 (978-0-395-06766-6); Dell paper $6.50 (978-0-440-94250-4). The story of a young silversmith's apprentice who plays an important part in the American Revolution. Newbery Medal winner, 1944. (Rev: BL 1/1/90)

3130 Goodman, Joan E. *Hope's Crossing* (5–8). 1998, Houghton $16.00 (978-0-395-86195-0). Kidnapped by British loyalists during the Revolution, Hope must try to escape and find her way home. (Rev: BCCB 7–8/98; BL 6/1–15/98; HBG 10/98; SLJ 5/98; VOYA 8/98)

3131 Guzman, Lila, and Rick Guzman. *Lorenzo's Revolutionary Quest* (6–9). 2003, Piñata paper $9.95 (978-1-55885-392-8). In this sequel to *Lorenzo's Secret Mission* (2001), Lorenzo has exciting adventures when he is charged with buying 500 head of cattle for the Revolutionary Army. (Rev: SLJ 5/03)

3132 Guzman, Lila, and Rick Guzman. *Lorenzo's Secret Mission* (6–9). 2001, Piñata paper $9.95 (978-1-55885-341-6). In 1776, 15-year-old Lorenzo Bannister leaves Texas in search of his Virginia grandfather he has never known, and finds himself working on behalf of the American rebels. (Rev: SLJ 12/01)

3133 Meyer, L. A. *Curse of the Blue Tattoo: Being an Account of the Misadventures of Jacky Faber, Midshipman and Fine Lady* (6–9). 2004, Harcourt $17.00 (978-0-15-205115-0). Forced to leave her ship after being exposed as a girl, Jacky Faber enrolls in an elite Boston girls' school but frustrates all attempts to make a lady out of her in this sequel to *Bloody Jack* (2002). (Rev: BL 5/15/04*; HB 7–8/04; SLJ 7/04; VOYA 8/04)

3134 Moore, Ruth Nulton. *Distant Thunder* (5–8). Illus. by Allan Eitzen. 1991, Herald paper $6.99 (978-0-8361-3557-2). During the Revolution, when wounded Americans are sent to Pennsylvania to recover, young Kate experiences the horrors of war. (Rev: BCCB 1/92; SLJ 1/92)

3135 Nordan, Robert. *The Secret Road* (5–9). 2001, Holiday $16.95 (978-0-8234-1543-4). Young Laura helps an escaped slave on a long and suspenseful journey to freedom by posing as her sister. (Rev: BL 9/15/01; HBG 3/02; SLJ 10/01; VOYA 12/01)

3136 O'Dell, Scott. *Sarah Bishop* (6–9). 1980, Scholastic paper $5.99 (978-0-590-44651-8). A first-person narrative of a girl who lives through the American Revolution and its toll of suffering and misery. (Rev: BL 3/1/88)

3137 Reit, Seymour. *Guns for General Washington: A Story of the American Revolution* (6–8). 1992, Harcourt paper $6.00 (978-0-15-232695-1). The true account of Colonel Henry Knox's attempt to bring cannons and artillery to the Continental Army during the blockade of 1775-1776. (Rev: BL 1/1/91; SLJ 1/91)

3138 Rinaldi, Ann. *Taking Liberty: The Story of Oney Judge, George Washington's Runaway Slave* (7–12). 2002, Simon & Schuster $16.95 (978-0-689-85187-2). An elderly Oney looks back on her life as Martha's personal slave, her initial acceptance of her lot, and her final decision to trade comfort for freedom. (Rev: HBG 3/03; SLJ 1/03; VOYA 2/03)

3139 Rinaldi, Ann. *Wolf by the Ears* (8–12). 1991, Scholastic $13.95 (978-0-590-43413-3). Harriet Hemings — the alleged daughter of Thomas Jefferson and his slave mistress — faces moral dilemmas in regard to freedom, equal rights, and her future. (Rev: BL 2/1/91; SLJ 4/91)

3140 Roop, Peter, and Connie Roop. *An Eye for an Eye: A Story of the Revolutionary War* (5–9). 2000, Jamestown paper $5.95 (978-0-8092-0628-5). During the Revolutionary War, Samantha, disguised as boy, sets out to save her brother who is being held prisoner on a British ship. (Rev: BCCB 7–8/00; SLJ 4/00)

3141 Rosenburg, John. *First in War: George Washington in the American Revolution* (7–10). Illus. 1998, Millbrook LB $25.90 (978-0-7613-0311-4). This second part of the fictionalized biography of George Washington covers his career from 1775, when he was elected commander-in-chief, to the end of 1783, when he resigned from his military duties. (Rev: HBG 9/98; SLJ 7/98; VOYA 4/99)

3142 Schwartz, Virginia Frances. *Send One Angel Down* (5–8). 2000, Holiday $16.95 (978-0-8234-1484-0). This is the story of a young slave girl, Eliza, the skills she learns on the plantation, and how this knowledge helps her when she gains freedom. (Rev: BL 6/1–15/00; HB 7–8/00; HBG 10/00; SLJ 8/00)

3143 Thomas, Velma M. *Lest We Forget: The Passage from Africa to Slavery and Emancipation* (5–8). Illus. 1997, Crown $29.95 (978-0-609-60030-6). An interactive book about slavery based on material from the Black Holocaust Museum. (Rev: BL 12/15/97) [973.6]

3144 Wait, Lea. *Seaward Born* (4–7). 2003, Simon & Schuster $16.95 (978-0-689-84719-6). Michael, a young slave, makes a dangerous journey to Canada and freedom in this dramatic historical novel. (Rev: BL 2/15/03; HBG 10/03; SLJ 1/03)

NINETEENTH CENTURY TO THE CIVIL WAR (1809–1861)

3145 Armstrong, Jennifer. *Steal Away* (6–9). 1993, Scholastic paper $4.50 (978-0-590-46921-0). Two unhappy 13-year-old girls — one a slave, the other a white orphan — disguise themselves as boys and run away. (Rev: BL 2/1/92; SLJ 2/92)

3146 Avi. *Beyond the Western Sea: Book Two: Lord Kirkle's Money* (6–9). 1996, Orchard LB $19.99 (978-0-531-08870-8). In this sequel to *Beyond the Western Sea: The Escape from Home* (1996), Patrick and Maura O'Connell and their two friends arrive in America, end up in the mill town of Lowell, Massachusetts, and encounter the villains that pursued them in the first book. (Rev: SLJ 10/96; VOYA 12/96)

3147 Avi. *The True Confessions of Charlotte Doyle* (6–9). 1990, Watts LB $17.99 (978-0-531-08493-9). An adventure story set in the 1850s about a 13-year-old girl and her voyage to America on a ship with a murderous crew. (Rev: BL 9/1/90; SLJ 9/90)

3148 Barker, M. P. *A Difficult Boy* (5–9). 2008, Holiday $16.95 (978-0-8234-2086-5). Indentured to a shopkeeper against his will, Ethan befriends young Daniel, a young Irishman, and the two find friendship and a joint love of horses in this story set in 1839 Massachusetts. (Rev: BL 4/15/08; SLJ 5/08)

3149 Blos, Joan W. *A Gathering of Days: A New England Girl's Journal, 1830–32* (6–8). 1979, Macmillan $16.00 (978-0-684-16340-6); paper $4.99 (978-0-689-71419-1). A fictional diary kept by 13-year-old Catherine Cabot, who is growing up in the town of Meredith, New Hampshire. Newbery Medal winner, 1980.

3150 Blos, Joan W. *Letters from the Corrugated Castle: A Novel of Gold Rush California, 1850–1852* (4–8). 2007, Simon & Schuster $17.99 (978-0-689-87077-4). Reunited with a mother long believed to be dead, 13-year-old Eldora must learn to adjust to living a life of comfort in San Francisco; newspaper articles and her correspondence with Luke, who hopes to find a fortune, reveal much about life during the Gold Rush. (Rev: BL 4/15/07; SLJ 6/07)

3151 Bryant, Louella. *The Black Bonnet* (6–9). 1996, New England Pr. paper $12.95 (978-1-881535-22-5). An exciting story of two young escaped slaves, Charity and her older sister Bea, and their last stop on the Underground Railroad in Burlington, Vermont, which they find is crawling with slave hunters. (Rev: BL 2/1/97; SLJ 2/97)

3152 Bryant, Louella. *Father by Blood* (6–9). 1999, New England Pr. paper $12.95 (978-1-881535-33-1). The story of John Brown and his raid on Harper's Ferry as seen through the eyes of his daughter Annie. (Rev: SLJ 9/99)

3153 Charbonneau, Eileen. *Honor to the Hills* (8–10). 1996, Tor $18.95 (978-0-312-86094-3). Returning to her home in the Catskill Mountains in 1851, 15-year-old Lily Woods finds that her family is involved in the Underground Railroad. (Rev: VOYA 6/96)

3154 Coleman, Wim, and Pat Perrin. *The Amazing Erie Canal and How a Big Ditch Opened Up the West* (4–7). Illus. Series: Wild History of the American West. 2006, Enslow LB $33.27 (978-1-59845-017-0). Why was the Erie Canal built? What was its impact on American commerce and history? This richly illustrated profile answers those questions and offers a general overview of canals; 30 Internet links are provided for further research. (Rev: BL 10/15/06) [386]

3155 Dahlberg, Maurine F. *The Story of Jonas* (4–7). 2007, Farrar $16.00 (978-0-374-37264-4). In the mid-1800s, Jonas, a 13-year-old slave, is sent on an expedition to find gold in the Kansas Territory and realizes that freedom is not beyond his grasp. (Rev: BL 4/07; SLJ 4/07)

3156 Donaldson, Joan. *A Pebble and a Pen* (5–8). 2000, Holiday $15.95 (978-0-8234-1500-7). In 1853, to avoid an arranged marriage, 14-year-old Matty runs away to study penmanship at Mr. Spencer's famous Ohio school. (Rev: BCCB 12/00; BL 1/1–15/01; HBG 10/01; SLJ 12/00; VOYA 2/01)

3157 Duble, Kathleen Benner. *Hearts of Iron* (5–8). 2006, Simon & Schuster $15.95 (978-1-4169-0850-0). In a Connecticut iron-working community in the early 19th century, two young lovers rebel against their families' plans for their future. (Rev: BL 9/15/06; SLJ 11/06)

3158 Duey, Kathleen, and Karen A. Bale. *Hurricane: Open Seas, 1844* (5–7). Series: Survival! 1999, Simon & Schuster paper $4.50 (978-0-689-82544-6). This exciting sea story, set in 1844, tells of two youngsters who are on a whaler when a killer hurricane strikes. (Rev: SLJ 8/99)

3159 Ferris, Jean. *Underground* (6–9). 2007, Farrar $16.00 (978-0-374-37243-9). Charlotte, a 16-year-old slave, is sold to the owner of a hotel near Kentucky's Mammoth Cave and soon discovers that the cave is part of the Underground Railroad. (Rev: BL 11/15/07; SLJ 12/07)

3160 Garland, Sherry. *In the Shadow of the Alamo* (5–8). Series: Great Episodes. 2001, Harcourt $17.00 (978-0-15-201744-6). Fifteen-year-old Lorenzo Bonifacio, a conscript in the Mexican army of Santa Ana, describes the harsh life of the soldiers and the family members who follow them on the trek to Texas and the battle of the Alamo. (Rev: BCCB 1/02; BL 10/15/01; HB 11–12/01; HBG 3/02; SLJ 12/01; VOYA 10/01)

3161 Guccione, Leslie D. *Come Morning* (4–7). 1995, Carolrhoda LB $19.15 (978-0-87614-892-1). A young boy takes over his father's duties as a conductor on the Underground Railroad. (Rev: BCCB 1/96; HB 11–12/95; SLJ 11/95)

3162 Hill, Donna. *Shipwreck Season* (5–8). 1998, Clarion $16.00 (978-0-395-86614-6). In the 1800s, 16-year-old Daniel joins a crew of seamen who patrol America's eastern coastline, rescuing people and cargo from shipwrecks. (Rev: BCCB 7–8/98; BL 6/1–15/98; HBG 3/99; SLJ 6/98)

3163 Hilts, Len. *Timmy O'Dowd and the Big Ditch: A Story of the Glory Days on the Old Erie Canal* (5–7). 1988, Harcourt $13.95 (978-0-15-200606-8). Timmy and his cousin Dennis don't get along, but when the canals threaten to flood, they realize each other's strengths and stamina. (Rev: BCCB 12/88; BL 10/1/88; SLJ 12/88)

3164 Houston, Gloria. *Bright Freedom's Song: A Story of the Underground Railroad* (4–7). 1998, Harcourt $17.00 (978-0-15-201812-2). A tense, dramatic story about a girl who helps her parents operate a North Carolina station on the Underground Railroad. (Rev: BCCB 1/99; BL 11/1/98; HBG 3/99; SLJ 12/98; VOYA 2/99)

3165 Hurst, Carol Otis. *Through the Lock* (5–8). 2001, Houghton $15.00 (978-0-618-03036-1). In this novel set in Connecticut in the first half of the 19th century, a young orphan named Etta shares many adventures with a boy who lives in an abandoned cabin by a canal. (Rev: BCCB 3/01; BL 4/1/01; HB 3–4/01; HBG 10/01; SLJ 3/01; VOYA 4/01)

3166 Ketchum, Liza. *Orphan Journey Home* (5–7). Illus. 2000, Avon $15.99 (978-0-380-97811-3). When their parents die in southern Illinois in 1828, Jesse and her three siblings must find their way to their grandmother in eastern Kentucky. (Rev: BCCB 6/00; BL 6/1–15/00; HBG 10/00; SLJ 8/00)

3167 Krisher, Trudy. *Uncommon Faith* (7–10). 2003, Holiday $17.95 (978-0-8234-1791-9). The year 1837–1838 is a time of change in Millbrook, Massachusetts, and 10 of the residents narrate their experiences in a collage that connects the reader to the townspeople and to the history. (Rev: BL 10/15/03; HBG 4/04; SLJ 10/03*; VOYA 10/03)

3168 Lester, Julius. *Day of Tears: A Novel in Dialogue* (6–9). 2005, Hyperion $15.99 (978-0-7868-0490-0). In this heart-rending novel based on a real event and told mostly in present-tense dialogue, a slave named Emma is torn from the life she knows when her master puts her up for sale at the biggest slave auction in American history. Coretta Scott King Author Award, 2006. (Rev: BCCB 7–8/05; BL 2/1/05*; HB 7–8/05; SLJ 3/05; VOYA 6/05)

3169 Lester, Julius. *The Old African* (4–7). Illus. by Jerry Pinkney. 2005, Dial $19.99 (978-0-8037-2564-5). An elderly slave who never speaks uses his acute mental powers to relieve the pain of his people on a Georgia plantation. (Rev: BL 7/05*; SLJ 9/05; VOYA 12/05)

3170 Lyons, Mary. *Letters from a Slave Boy: The Story of Joseph Jacobs* (6–9). 2007, Simon & Schuster $15.99 (978-0-689-87867-1). Joseph's story, told through letters as he learns to read and write, describes events in the life of the actual slave who was the son of Harriet Jacobs, the subject of *Letters from a Slave Girl: The Story of Harriet Jacobs* (1992). (Rev: BCCB 5/07; BL 1/1–15/07; HB 3-4/07; LMC 4-5/07; SLJ 2/07)

3171 McGill, Alice. *Miles' Song* (6–9). 2000, Houghton $15.00 (978-0-395-97938-9). The story of a slave, Miles, who secretly learns to read and write and later plans a daring escape. (Rev: BL 4/1/00; HBG 9/00; SLJ 4/00; VOYA 6/00)

3172 McKissack, Patricia C., and Fredrick McKissack. *Let My People Go* (5–8). Illus. 1998, Simon & Schuster $20.00 (978-0-689-80856-2). This novel set in the early 19th century combines Bible stories and the hardships endured by slaves as told by Price Jefferson, a former slave who is now an abolitionist living in South Carolina. (Rev: BCCB 12/98; BL 10/1/98; HBG 3/99; SLJ 11/98)

3173 Moses, Shelia P. *I, Dred Scott* (8–11). Illus. by Bonnie Christensen. 2005, Simon & Schuster $16.95 (978-0-689-85975-5). In this fictionalized account, Dred Scott, born a slave, chronicles the ultimately unsuccessful 11-year legal battle to win his freedom. (Rev: BCCB 4/05; BL 3/15/05; SLJ 2/05; VOYA 4/05)

3174 Murphy, Jim. *Desperate Journey* (6–9). 2006, Scholastic $16.99 (978-0-439-07806-1). On the Erie Canal in 1848, 12-year-old Maggie Haggerty faces huge challenges when her father and uncle are arrested, her mother falls ill, and Maggie must save the family's barge by delivering a shipment to Buffalo on time. (Rev: BL 10/15/06; LMC 3/07; SLJ 11/06)

3175 Paterson, Katherine. *Jip: His Story* (5–9). 1998, Puffin paper $6.99 (978-0-14-038674-5). Jip, a foundling boy in Vermont of the 1850s, wonders about his origins, particularly after he finds he is being watched by a mysterious stranger. (Rev: BCCB 12/96; BL 9/1/96*; HB 11–12/96; SLJ 10/96*; VOYA 4/97)

3176 Paulsen, Gary. *Nightjohn* (6–12). 1993, Delacorte $15.95 (978-0-385-30838-0). Told in the voice of Sarny, 12, Paulsen exposes the myths that African American slaves were content, well cared for, ignorant, and childlike, and that brave, resourceful slaves easily escaped. (Rev: BL 12/15/92)

3177 Prince, Bryan. *I Came as a Stranger: The Underground Railroad* (7–12). 2004, Tundra paper $15.95 (978-0-88776-667-1). This account tells what happened after the runaway slaves reached Canada and contains material both about famous leaders and about ordinary people involved in the Underground Railroad. (Rev: BL 5/1/04; SLJ 6/04) [971.1]

3178 Rinaldi, Ann. *The Blue Door* (5–8). Series: Quilt. 1996, Scholastic paper $15.95 (978-0-590-46051-4). In this final volume of the Quilt trilogy — following *A Stitch in Time* (1994) and *Broken Days* — Amanda is forced to take a mill job in Lowell, Massachusetts, after an adventurous trip north from her South Carolina home. (Rev: BL 11/1/96; VOYA 2/97)

3179 Rinaldi, Ann. *Broken Days* (6–10). Series: Quilt. 1995, Scholastic $14.95 (978-0-590-46053-8). When her cousin steals the piece of quilt that will establish her identity, Walking Breeze, who has come to live with her white family in Massachusetts at the age of 14 after being raised by Shawnees, is demoted to servant status in this story that takes place during the War of 1812. The second part of the Quilt trilogy. (Rev: VOYA 4/96)

3180 Rinaldi, Ann. *The Ever-After Bird* (5–8). 2007, Harcourt $17.00 (978-0-15-202620-2). CeCe travels with her uncle, an abolitionist and ornithologist, to Georgia to search for a rare bird and help slaves get to the Underground Railroad. (Rev: BL 11/1/07; LMC 1/08; SLJ 12/07)

3181 Rinaldi, Ann. *Mine Eyes Have Seen* (8–12). 1998, Scholastic paper $16.95 (978-0-590-54318-7). The story of the raid at Harper's Ferry is retold through the eyes of John Brown's daughter Annie. (Rev: BL 2/15/98; HBG 9/98; SLJ 2/98; VOYA 4/98)

3182 Schneider, Mical. *Annie Quinn in America* (5–9). 2001, Carolrhoda LB $15.95 (978-1-57505-510-7). In 1847, young Annie and her brother travel from Ireland, a land ravaged by the potato famine, to America, a land fraught with dangers of its own. (Rev: BL 11/15/01; HBG 3/02; SLJ 9/01)

3183 Schwartz, Virginia Frances. *If I Just Had Two Wings* (6–10). 2001, Stoddart $15.95 (978-0-7737-3302-2). Accompanied by a friend and her two children, a young slave named Phoebe makes a daring escape to Canada and freedom via the Underground Railroad. (Rev: BL 12/1/01; SLJ 12/01; VOYA 12/01)

3184 Siegelson, Kim L. *Honey Bea* (7–10). 2006, Hyperion $15.99 (978-0-7868-0853-3). Beatrice, a young slave in Louisiana, relies on the magic of bees as her work in the master's house leads to discoveries about her past. (Rev: BL 4/15/06)

3185 Stowe, Cynthia M. *The Second Escape of Arthur Cooper* (5–7). 2000, Marshall Cavendish LB $14.95 (978-0-7614-5069-6). Based on a true story, this novel tells of Arthur Cooper, an escaped slave, and the Quakers on Nantucket Island who saved him from slave catchers in 1822. (Rev: BL 8/00; HBG 3/01; SLJ 10/00)

3186 Torrey, Michele. *Voyage of Midnight* (8–11). 2006, Knopf $15.95 (978-0-375-82382-4). In the early 19th century, orphan Philip joins his uncle's crew and is shocked to find that his uncle is a slave trader; when the crew and slaves are blinded by a disease, Philip takes matters into his own hands and steers the ship back to Africa. (Rev: BL 12/15/06; SLJ 1/07)

3187 Trottier, Maxine. *Under a Shooting Star* (5–8). Series: The Circle of Silver Chronicles. 2002, Stoddart paper $7.95 (978-0-7737-6228-2). During the War of 1812, a 15-year-old boy who is half English and half Oneida Indian struggles with conflicting loyalties as he tries to protect the two American girls he is escorting. (Rev: SLJ 5/02)

3188 Turner, Glennette Tilley. *Running for Our Lives* (5–7). Illus. 1994, Holiday $16.95 (978-0-8234-1121-4). A thoroughly researched novel about a boy and his family who escape slavery in the 1850s and traveled on the Underground Railroad to Canada. (Rev: BCCB 6/94; BL 6/1–15/94; SLJ 4/94)

3189 Wait, Lea. *Finest Kind* (4–7). 2006, Simon & Schuster $16.95 (978-1-4169-0952-1). When his family falls on hard times and is forced to move from Boston to Maine in the 1830s, 12-year-old Jake Webber finds himself shouldering new responsibilities, including looking after his disabled younger brother. (Rev: BL 10/15/06; SLJ 11/06)

3190 Wall, Bill. *The Cove of Cork* (5–9). 1999, Irish American paper $7.95 (978-0-85635-225-6). In this novel, the third in a trilogy revolving around the War of 1812, an Irish lad, the first mate of the American schooner *Shenandoah*, sees action in a battle against a British vessel and eventually wins the hand of the granddaughter of a shipbuilding magnate. (Rev: SLJ 7/99)

3191 Wanttaja, Ronald. *The Key to Honor* (5–9). 1996, Royal Fireworks paper $9.99 (978-0-88092-270-8). During the War of 1812, midshipman Nate Lawton has doubts about his courage in battle and worries about his father, who has been taken prisoner by the British. (Rev: VOYA 8/96)

3192 Whelan, Gloria. *Farewell to the Island* (5–8). 1998, HarperCollins $16.95 (978-0-06-027751-2). In this sequel to *Once on This Island,* Mary leaves her Michigan home after the War of 1812 and travels to England where she falls in love with Lord Lindsay. (Rev: BL 12/1/98; HBG 3/99; SLJ 1/99)

3193 Whelan, Gloria. *Once on This Island* (4–7). 1995, HarperCollins LB $14.89 (978-0-06-026249-5). In 1812, Mary and her older brother and sister must tend the family farm on Mackinac Island when their father goes off to war. (Rev: BCCB 11/95; BL 10/1/95; SLJ 11/95; VOYA 2/96)

3194 Wiley, Melissa. *On Tide Mill Lane* (4–8). Illus. 2001, HarperCollins $16.95 (978-0-06-027013-1). Charlotte experiences a number of household crises in Roxbury, Massachusetts, where she lives with her blacksmith father at the time of the War of 1812. (Rev: BL 2/15/01; HBG 10/01)

3195 Wilson, Diane Lee. *Black Storm Comin'* (7–10). 2005, Simon & Schuster $16.95 (978-0-689-87137-5). Son of a white father and a freed-slave mother, 12-year-old Colton Westcott joins the Pony Express in an effort to make sure his mother and siblings finally make it to the West Coast. (Rev: BL 8/05*; SLJ 7/05; VOYA 10/05)

3196 Woods, Brenda. *My Name Is Sally Little Song* (4–7). 2006, Putnam $15.99 (978-0-399-24312-7). Eleven-year-old Sally, a slave on a Georgia plantation at the beginning of the 19th century, escapes with her family and heads south to seek refuge with the Seminole Indians. (Rev: BCCB 11/06; BL 8/06; HBG 4/07; SLJ 9/06)

THE CIVIL WAR (1861–1865)

3197 Avi. *Iron Thunder* (5–8). 2007, Hyperion $14.99 (978-1-4231-0446-9). Tom, a 13-year-old naval yard worker and later crew member, describes the construction of the *Monitor,* the perilous voyage to the Union blockade, and the ensuing battle with the *Merrimac*; period photographs and newspaper headlines add historic context. (Rev: BL 8/07; LMC 11/07; SLJ 9/07)

3198 Beatty, Patricia. *Jayhawker* (6–9). 1995, Morrow paper $6.99 (978-0-688-14422-7). The story of 12-year-old Elijah, son of a Kansas abolitionist, who becomes a spy and infiltrates Charles Quantrill's infamous Bushwhacker network. (Rev: BL 9/1/91*; SLJ 9/91*)

3199 Brill, Marlene T. *Diary of a Drummer Boy* (4–7). 1998, Millbrook LB $23.90 (978-0-7613-0118-9). Using a diary format, this novel tells of a 12-year-old's experiences as a drummer in the Union Army during the Civil War. (Rev: BL 3/1/98; HBG 10/98; SLJ 5/98)

3200 Bruchac, Joseph. *March Toward the Thunder* (7–10). 2008, Dial $16.99 (978-0-8037-3188-2). In this story of a Canadian Indian who enters the Civil War with the Irish Brigade, readers are introduced to many important figures, issues, and lessons of the war. (Rev: BL 4/15/08; SLJ 7/08)

3201 Collier, James Lincoln, and Christopher Collier. *With Every Drop of Blood: A Novel of the Civil War* (6–10). 1994, Dell paper $5.99 (978-0-440-21983-5). A Civil War docunovel about Johnny, a young Confederate soldier, and Cush, a black Union soldier who captures him. Together, the two experience the horrors of war and bigotry. (Rev: BL 7/94; SLJ 8/94; VOYA 12/94)

3202 Crist-Evans, Craig. *Moon over Tennessee: A Boy's Civil War Journal* (4–7). 1999, Houghton $15.00 (978-0-395-91208-9). In free-verse diary entries, 13-year-old Crist-Evans reports on the Civil War from his vantage point in a camp behind the front lines. (Rev: BCCB 6/99; BL 5/15/99; HBG 10/99; SLJ 8/99; VOYA 10/99)

3203 Donahue, John. *An Island Far from Home* (4–7). 1994, Carolrhoda LB $15.95 (978-0-87614-859-4). Joshua, a Union supporter, forms an unusual friendship through corresponding with a young Southern soldier who is a prisoner of war. (Rev: BCCB 2/95; BL 2/15/95; SLJ 2/95)

3204 Durrant, Lynda. *My Last Skirt* (5–8). 2006, Clarion $16.00 (978-0-618-57490-2). After migrating from Ireland to America, Jennie Hodgers, who prefers wearing pants to skirts, adopts the persona of Albert Cashier and joins the Union army in this novel based on a true story. (Rev: BL 2/15/06; SLJ 4/06*)

3205 Elliott, Laura Malone. *Annie, Between the States* (7–11). 2004, HarperCollins LB $16.99 (978-0-06-001211-3). As the Civil War rages around her northern Virginia home, 15-year-old Annie finds her feelings about the North-South conflict evolving. (Rev: BL 12/1/04; SLJ 11/04)

3206 Ernst, Kathleen. *The Bravest Girl in Sharpsburg* (6–9). 1998, White Mane paper $8.95 (978-1-57249-083-3). Told from the viewpoint of three girls in Maryland during the Civil War, this is the story of friendships that are tested when the the girls support different sides and what happens when the Confederate Army marches through their town, thrusting the community into the middle of the war. (Rev: SLJ 9/98)

3207 Ernst, Kathleen. *Ghosts of Vicksburg* (6–10). 2003, White Mane paper $8.95 (978-1-57249-322-3). Jamie and Elisha, 15-year-old Union Army soldiers from Wisconsin, experience the horrors of war as their forces march to Mississippi. (Rev: SLJ 12/03)

3208 Ernst, Kathleen. *Hearts of Stone* (5–8). 2006, Dutton $16.99 (978-0-525-47686-3). Fifteen-year-old Hannah and her three younger siblings struggle to survive after they're orphaned in Civil War Tennessee. (Rev: BL 11/1/06; SLJ 12/06)

3209 Ernst, Kathleen. *The Night Riders of Harper's Ferry* (6–8). Illus. 1996, White Mane paper $7.95 (978-1-57249-013-0). Told from the standpoint of 17-year-old Solomon, this is a story of romance, divided families, and dangerous secrets, set on the border between North and South during the Civil War. (Rev: BL 1/1–15/97; SLJ 5/97)

3210 Ernst, Kathleen. *Retreat from Gettysburg* (5–8). Illus. 2000, White Mane LB $17.95 (978-1-57249-187-8). When a doctor orders 14-year-old Chig and his mother to care for a wounded Confederate soldier, the boy finds it hard to be kind to a man who belongs to the side that killed his father and brothers. (Rev: BL 9/15/00; HBG 10/01; SLJ 12/00)

3211 Fleischner, Jennifer. *Nobody's Boy* (5–8). Illus. 2006, Missouri Historical Society $12.95 (978-1-883982-58-4). George's mother buys freedom for herself and her son; she goes on to work for Mrs. Lincoln in the White House while George chooses the more dangerous avenue of helping slaves find freedom. (Rev: BL 2/1/07)

3212 Garrity, Jennifer Johnson. *The Bushwhacker: A Civil War Adventure* (5–8). Illus. by Paul Bachem. 1999, Peachtree paper $8.95 (978-1-56145-201-9). The clash of divided loyalties is the main conflict in this story of a boy torn between his Unionist feelings and the friendship he feels towards his protector, a Confederate sympathizer. (Rev: SLJ 4/00)

3213 Greenberg, Martin H., and Charles G. Waugh, eds. *Civil War Women II: Stories by Women About Women* (7–10). 1997, August House paper $9.95 (978-0-87483-487-1). A collection of short stories by such female writers as Louisa May Alcott and Edith Wharton that deal with women's lives during the Civil War. (Rev: SLJ 8/97)

3214 Hahn, Mary Downing. *Hear the Wind Blow: A Novel of the Civil War* (6–9). 2003, Clarion $16.00 (978-0-618-18190-2). A moving novel of the Civil War in which 13-year-old Haswell searches for his wounded older brother after his mother is killed and his farm destroyed. (Rev: BCCB 7–8/03; BL 5/15/03; HB 5–6/03; HBG 5–6/03; SLJ 5/03; VOYA 10/03)

3215 Hart, Alison. *Fires of Jubilee* (5–7). 2003, Simon & Schuster paper $4.99 (978-0-689-85528-3). Abby, 13, is suddenly a free person when the Civil War ends and finally able to search for her mother, who left long before. (Rev: BL 11/1/03; SLJ 3/04)

3216 Hart, Alison. *Gabriel's Horses* (6–9). 2007, Peachtree $14.95 (978-1-56145-398-6). Twelve-year-old Gabriel, a slave during the Civil War, cares for the racehorses on his master's plantation and dreams of becoming a jockey in this exciting story based on fact. (Rev: BL 5/15/07; LMC 10/07; SLJ 6/07)

3217 Hart, Alison. *Gabriel's Triumph* (6–9). Series: Racing to Freedom. 2007, Peachtree $14.95 (978-1-56145-410-5). Young freed slave Gabriel (first seen in *Gabriel's Horses* (2007) gets a chance to race a horse at Saratoga and is surprised by the racial climate he meets in the North. (Rev: BL 12/1/07; SLJ 1/08)

3218 Hill, Pamela S. *A Voice from the Border* (6–8). 1998, Holiday $16.95 (978-0-8234-1356-0). Set in Missouri, a border state during the Civil War, this novel introduces 15-year-old Reeves, whose family owns slaves and whose house is commandeered by Union forces after Reeves' father dies in battle. (Rev: BCCB 9/98; HBG 3/99; SLJ 9/98)

3219 Hughes, Pat. *Guerrilla Season* (7–12). 2003, Farrar $18.00 (978-0-374-32811-5). This multilayered novel clearly conveys the confusion that Matt, 15, feels in the face of the approaching violence of the Civil War. (Rev: BL 8/03; HBG 4/04; SLJ 11/03; VOYA 12/03)

3220 Hurst, Carol Otis. *Torchlight* (4–7). 2006, Houghton $16.00 (978-0-618-27601-1). As tension mounts between the Yankee and Irish immigrant settlers in a Massachusetts town in 1864, Charlotte and Maggie struggle to maintain their friendship. (Rev: BL 12/1/06; SLJ 1/07)

3221 Johnson, Nancy. *My Brother's Keeper: A Civil War Story* (6–10). 1997, Down East $14.95 (978-0-89272-414-7). Two orphaned brothers from upstate New York, ages 15 and 13, join the Union Army, one as a soldier, the other as a drummer boy, and soon find themselves surrounded by the blood and tragedy of battle in this story based on the experiences of the author's great-great-uncles. (Rev: HBG 9/98; SLJ 1/98)

3222 Joslyn, Mauriel Phillips. *Shenandoah Autumn: Courage Under Fire* (6–10). 1999, White Mane paper $8.95 (978-1-57249-137-3). During the Civil War, young Mattie and her mother, though afraid of the Union troops around their Virginia home, save a wounded Confederate soldier and return him to his companions. (Rev: BL 5/1/99)

3223 Keehn, Sally M. *Anna Sunday* (4–8). 2002, Putnam $18.99 (978-0-399-23875-8). In 1863, 12-year-old Anna travels with her younger brother from Pennsylvania to Virginia to find her wounded father. (Rev: BCCB 9/02; BL 6/1–15/02; HBG 10/02; SLJ 6/02; VOYA 8/02)

3224 Keith, Harold. *Rifles for Watie* (6–9). 1957, HarperCollins paper $6.99 (978-0-06-447030-8). Jeff, a Union soldier, learns about the realities of war when he becomes a spy. Newbery Medal winner, 1958.

3225 Love, D. Anne. *Three Against the Tide* (5–8). 1998, Holiday $15.95 (978-0-8234-1400-0). In this Civil War novel, 12-year-old Confederate Susanna Simons must care for her two younger brothers when Yankee troops invade South Carolina. (Rev: BL 12/1/98; HBG 10/99; SLJ 1/99)

3226 Lyons, Mary E., and Muriel M. Branch. *Dear Ellen Bee: A Civil War Scrapbook of Two Union Spies* (5–8). Illus. 2000, Atheneum $17.00 (978-0-689-82379-4). Set in Richmond, Virginia, before and during the Civil War, this novel, based on fact, tells how a strong-willed lady and her emancipated slave get involved in a spying adventure. (Rev: BCCB 10/00; BL 11/1/00; HBG 3/01; SLJ 10/00; VOYA 2/01)

3227 McGowen, Tom. *Jesse Bowman: A Union Boy's War Story* (5–8). Series: Historical Fiction Adventure. 2008, Enslow LB $20.95 (978-0-7660-2929-3). The story of a young soldier who is horrified by the brutality of the Civil War. (Rev: BL 4/15/08; SLJ 7/08)

3228 McMullan, Margaret. *How I Found the Strong: A Civil War Story* (5–9). 2004, Houghton $15.00 (978-0-618-35008-7). The Civil War changes the way a boy looks at life when it takes away his father and brother and comes close to his Mississippi home. (Rev: BL 2/15/04; SLJ 4/04; VOYA 6/04)

3229 Myers, Anna. *Assassin* (7–12). 2005, Walker $16.95 (978-0-8027-8989-1). The events surrounding the assassination of Abraham Lincoln are explored in this fictionalized account, narrated in alternating chapters by a teenage White House seamstress and assassin John Wilkes Booth. (Rev: BL 10/1/05; SLJ 12/05; VOYA 10/05)

3230 Nixon, Joan Lowery. *A Dangerous Promise* (6–8). Series: Orphan Train Adventures. 1996, Bantam paper $4.99 (978-0-440-21965-1). Mike Kelly, 12, and his friend Todd Blakely run away to help the Union forces in the Civil War and experience the terrors of war. (Rev: BL 9/1/94; SLJ 11/94; VOYA 10/94)

3231 Paulsen, Gary. *Soldier's Heart* (5–8). 1998, Delacorte $15.95 (978-0-385-32498-4). A powerful novel about the agony of the Civil War, based on the real-life experiences of a Union soldier who was only 15 when he went to war. (Rev: BCCB 9/98; BL 6/1–15/98*; HB 11–12/98; HBG 3/99; SLJ 9/98; VOYA 10/98)

3232 Peck, Richard. *The River Between Us* (7–12). 2003, Dial $16.99 (978-0-8037-2735-9). In 1861 Illinois, Tilly's family makes room for two young women of different complexions from the South. (Rev: BL 9/15/03*; HB 9–10/03; HBG 4/04; SLJ 9/03; VOYA 10/03)

3233 Pinkney, Andrea Davis. *Abraham Lincoln: Letters from a Slave Girl* (4–7). Illus. Series: Dear Mr. President. 2001, Winslow $8.95 (978-1-890817-60-2). Twelve-year-old Lettie Tucker, a slave, exchanges thought-provoking letters with President Abraham Lincoln in this story set in the 1860s packed with interesting illustrations. (Rev: BCCB 2/02; BL 9/1/01; HBG 3/02; SLJ 9/01)

3234 Reeder, Carolyn. *Before the Creeks Ran Red* (6–9). 2003, HarperCollins $16.99 (978-0-06-623615-5). Three stories examine the impact of the Civil War on three young men, who all come to reassess their perspectives on war, valor, and duty. (Rev: BCCB 3/03; BL 2/15/03; HBG 10/03; SLJ 2/03)

3235 Reeder, Carolyn. *Captain Kate* (6–8). 1999, Avon $15.00 (978-0-380-97628-7). This is an unusual Civil War story about 12-year-old Kate, her

stepbrother Seth, and their dangerous trip down the C&O Canal on the family's coal boat. (Rev: BL 1/1–15/99; HBG 10/99; SLJ 1/99)

3236 Richardson, George C. *Drummer* (6–9). 2001, Writer's Showcase paper $9.95 (978-0-595-15359-6). A young slave survives a dangerous journey north and joins a Colored Infantry unit in Philadelphia, becoming a drummer boy. (Rev: SLJ 12/01)

3237 Rinaldi, Ann. *Come Juneteenth* (8–11). 2007, Harcourt $17.00 (978-0-15-205947-7). The news of emancipation was slow to arrive to parts of Texas, and when it did, not everyone believed it, as readers will learn from this story of young slaves Luli and Sis Goose. (Rev: BCCB 9/07; BL 2/15/07; LMC 8–9/07; SLJ 5/07)

3238 Rinaldi, Ann. *In My Father's House* (7–10). 1993, Scholastic paper $14.95 (978-0-590-44730-0). A coming-of-age novel set during the Civil War about 7-year-old Oscie. (Rev: BL 2/15/93)

3239 Rinaldi, Ann. *Juliet's Moon* (5–8). Series: Great Episodes. 2008, Harcourt paper $17.00 (978-0-15-206170-8). Juliet's home and family are destroyed by the Civil War, and she and her brother, Seth, must fight and even kill to survive in this novel, which is loosely based on actual events. (Rev: BL 4/15/08)

3240 Rinaldi, Ann. *Sarah's Ground* (6–9). 2004, Simon & Schuster $15.95 (978-0-689-85924-3). In this appealing Civil War novel based on a true story, 18-year-old Sarah leaves her New York home in 1861 to take a job as a caretaker at Mount Vernon, but as the war intensifies, Sarah and the rest of the staff face mounting challenges to ensure the plantation's security and neutrality. (Rev: BL 2/1/04; SLJ 5/04; VOYA 4/04)

3241 Sappey, Maureen Stack. *Letters from Vinnie* (7–10). 1999, Front St. $16.95 (978-1-886910-31-7). A novel that mixes fact and fiction to tell the story of the tiny woman who sculpted the large statue of Abraham Lincoln found in the Capitol Building in Washington. (Rev: BL 9/15/99; HBG 4/00; SLJ 11/99; VOYA 2/00)

3242 Severance, John B. *Braving the Fire* (7–12). 2002, Clarion $15.00 (978-0-618-22999-4). Jem finds war is far from the "glory" described by others in this coming-of-age story set in the realistic horrors of the Civil War. (Rev: BL 10/1/02; HBG 10/03; SLJ 11/02)

3243 Spain, Susan Rosson. *The Deep Cut* (5–8). 2006, Marshall Cavendish $16.99 (978-0-7614-5316-1). Thirteen-year-old Lonzo, often considered "slow," finally gains the respect of his father for his actions during the hostilities. (Rev: BL 12/1/06*; SLJ 12/06)

3244 Thomas, Carroll. *Blue Creek Farm* (4–8). 2001, Smith & Kraus paper $9.95 (978-1-57525-

243-8). In Kansas of the 1860s, Matty Trescott and her father manage a farm and feel the effects of the Civil War. (Rev: BL 4/1/01; VOYA 6/01)

3245 Wells, Rosemary. *Red Moon at Sharpsburg* (6–9). 2007, Viking $16.99 (978-0-670-03638-7). Young India Moody hopes to attend college one day even though this is virtually unheard-of, but her goal must be put on hold when the Civil War breaks out and its bloody and frightening realities alter her world. (Rev: BCCB 7-8/07; BL 4/15/07; HB 5-6/07; SLJ 3/07*)

3246 Williams, Jeanne. *The Confederate Fiddle* (6–9). 1997, Hendrick-Long $16.95 (978-1-885777-04-1). On his wagon train taking cotton to Mexico in 1862, 17-year-old Vin Clayburn is torn between fulfilling his duty to his family and joining his brother fighting for the South in the Civil War. (Rev: BL 3/15/98; HBG 9/98)

3247 Wisler, G. Clifton. *Red Cap* (6–8). 1991, Penguin paper $5.99 (978-0-14-036936-6). An adolescent boy lies about his age to join the Union Army and ends up as a prisoner of war in the infamous Andersonville camp. (Rev: BL 8/91; SLJ 8/91)

WESTWARD EXPANSION AND PIONEER LIFE

3248 Altsheler, Joseph A. *Kentucky Frontiersman: The Adventures of Henry Ware, Hunter and Border Fighter* (6–10). Illus. 1988, Voyageur $16.95 (978-0-929146-01-0). A reissue of a fine frontier adventure story featuring young Henry Ware who is captured by an Indian hunting party. (Rev: SLJ 3/89)

3249 Applegate, Stan. *The Devil's Highway* (5–8). Illus. by James Watling. 1998, Peachtree paper $8.95 (978-1-56145-184-5). In this adventure novel set in the early 1800s, 14-year-old Zeb and his horse, Christmas, set out on the bandit-infested Natchez Trail to search for the boy's grandfather. (Rev: SLJ 2/99)

3250 Bauer, Marion Dane. *Land of the Buffalo Bones: The Diary of Mary Elizabeth Rodgers, an English Girl in Minnesota* (4–8). Series: Dear America. 2003, Scholastic $12.95 (978-0-439-22027-9). Based on real-life events, Polly Rodgers's diary reveals the hardships endured by a group of English settlers who arrived in Minnesota in 1873. (Rev: BL 5/15/03; HBG 10/03; SLJ 9/01)

3251 Benchley, Nathaniel. *Gone and Back* (7–9). 1971, HarperCollins paper $1.95 (978-0-06-440016-9). Obed's family moves west to take advantage of the Homestead Act, and he soon finds he must assume new family responsibilities.

3252 Benner, J. A. *Uncle Comanche* (5–8). 1996, Texas Christian Univ. paper $12.95 (978-0-87565-152-1). Based on fact, this is the story of the adventures of 12-year-old Sul Ross, who runs away from home in pre-Civil War Texas and is pursued by a family friend nicknamed Uncle Comanche. (Rev: VOYA 10/96)

3253 Blakeslee, Ann R. *A Different Kind of Hero* (5–7). 1997, Marshall Cavendish $14.95 (978-0-7614-5000-9). In 1881 Colorado, Renny is criticized for befriending and helping a Chinese boy new to town. (Rev: BL 9/1/97; HBG 3/98; SLJ 1/98)

3254 Bowers, Terrell L. *Ride Against the Wind* (7–10). 1996, Walker $21.95 (978-0-8027-4156-1). Set in Eden, Kansas, in the late 1800s, this sequel to *The Secret of Snake Canyon* (1993) involves Jerrod Danmyer and his attachment to Marion Gates, daughter of his family's sworn enemies. (Rev: BL 12/15/96; VOYA 8/97)

3255 Bruchac, Joseph. *Sacajawea: The Story of Bird Woman and the Lewis and Clark Expedition* (7–10). 2000, Harcourt $17.00 (978-0-15-202234-1). Told in alternating chapters by Sacajawea and William Clark, this novel re-creates the famous cross-country journey of Lewis and Clark. (Rev: BL 4/1/00; HBG 9/00; SLJ 5/00)

3256 Burks, Brian. *Soldier Boy* (6–9). 1997, Harcourt paper $6.00 (978-0-15-201219-9). To escape a crooked boxing ring in 1870s Chicago, Johnny joins the army to fight Indians and eventually finds himself at Little Big Horn with Custer. (Rev: BL 5/15/97; SLJ 5/97; VOYA 8/97)

3257 Collier, James Lincoln. *Me and Billy* (6–9). 2004, Marshall Cavendish $15.95 (978-0-7614-5174-7). In the Old West, Billy and Possum, best friends who grew up together in the same orphanage, escape and head for a legendary lake full of gold. (Rev: BL 9/15/04; SLJ 1/05)

3258 Collier, James Lincoln. *Wild Boy* (5–8). 2002, Marshall Cavendish $15.95 (978-0-7614-5126-6). After knocking his father out during an argument, 12-year-old Jesse runs away from his frontier home to live in the mountains, where he has many adventures, learns many skills, and reflects on his own characteristics before finally deciding to return home in this story that appears to be set in the 19th century. (Rev: BL 11/1/02; HBG 10/03; SLJ 11/02)

3259 Couloumbis, Audrey. *The Misadventures of Maude March, or, Trouble Rides a Fast Horse* (5–8). 2005, Random LB $17.99 (978-0-375-93245-8). When their aunt and sole guardian is killed, Maude and Sallie March rebel against their new foster family and set off on their own in this rollicking tale of the Old West. (Rev: SLJ 9/05)

3260 Cullen, Lynn. *Nelly in the Wilderness* (5–8). 2002, HarperCollins LB $15.89 (978-0-06-029134-1). Set in the Indiana frontier of 1821, 12-year-old Nelly and her brother, Cornelius, must adjust to a new stepmother after their beloved Ma dies. (Rev:

BCCB 5/02; BL 4/1/02; HB 7–8/02; HBG 10/02; SLJ 2/02)

3261 Cushman, Karen. *The Ballad of Lucy Whipple* (5–8). 1996, Clarion $16.00 (978-0-395-72806-2). Lucy hates being stuck in the California wilderness with an overbearing mother who runs a boarding house. (Rev: BCCB 9/96; BL 8/96*; HB 9–10/96; SLJ 8/96*; VOYA 12/96)

3262 Donahue, Marilyn Cram. *The Valley in Between* (6–9). 1987, Walker LB $15.85 (978-0-8027-6733-2). In a story that spans a four-year period, a young girl comes of age in California of the 1850s. (Rev: BL 11/1/87; SLJ 11/87; VOYA 12/87)

3263 Durrant, Lynda. *The Sun, the Rain, and the Apple Seed: A Novel of Johnny Appleseed's Life* (5–8). 2003, Clarion $15.00 (978-0-618-23487-5). This fictionalized biography of John Chapman's life focuses on his eccentricities. (Rev: BL 5/15/03; HBG 10/03; SLJ 5/03)

3264 Ferris, Jean. *Much Ado About Grubstake* (5–8). 2006, Harcourt $17.00 (978-0-15-205706-0). Sixteen-year-old Arley, owner of her family's mine and boarding house in 1888 Grubstake, Colorado, becomes suspicious when a stranger takes an unusual interest in the rundown mining town; adventure, romance, and humor are combined in this mystery. (Rev: BL 8/06; SLJ 11/06)

3265 Finley, Mary Peace. *Meadow Lark* (5–8). Series: Santa Fe Trail trilogy. 2003, Filter $15.95 (978-0-86541-070-1). In this sequel to *Soaring Eagle* (1993) and *White Grizzly* (2000) set in 1845, Teresita Montoya, 13, has various adventures on the Santa Fe Trail as she searches for her older brother and for a new life for herself. (Rev: BL 12/1/03; HBG 4/04; SLJ 2/04)

3266 Finley, Mary Peace. *White Grizzly* (5–9). 2000, Filter $15.95 (978-0-86541-053-4); paper $8.95 (978-0-86541-058-9). Fifteen-year-old Julio sets out on an arduous journey along the Santa Fe Trail to discover his true identity. (Rev: BL 12/1/00; HBG 10/01; SLJ 1/01; VOYA 2/01)

3267 Fleischman, Paul. *The Borning Room* (5–8). 1991, HarperCollins paper $4.99 (978-0-06-447099-5). Georgina remembers important turning points in her life and the role played by the room set aside for giving birth and dying in her grandfather's house in 19th-century rural Ohio. (Rev: BCCB 9/91; BL 10/1/91*; HB 11–12/91*; SLJ 9/91*)

3268 Garland, Sherry. *Valley of the Moon: The Diary of Rosalia de Milagros* (5–8). Illus. 2001, Scholastic paper $10.95 (978-0-439-08820-6). Rosalia, a 13-year-old orphan, keeps a diary about working on a California ranch in 1846. (Rev: BL 4/1/01; HBG 3/02; SLJ 4/01; VOYA 8/01)

3269 Gray, Dianne E. *Tomorrow, the River* (6–9). 2006, Houghton $16.00 (978-0-618-56329-6). Life

on a Mississippi steamboat in 1896 is rough and dirty, but young Megan finds romance and other rewards among the hard work. (Rev: BL 12/1/06; HB 1–2/07; SLJ 12/06)

3270 Gregory, Kristiana. *Across the Wide and Lonesome Prairie: The Oregon Trail Diary of Hattie Campbell* (4–7). Illus. Series: Dear America. 1997, Scholastic paper $10.95 (978-0-590-22651-6). In a diary format, this novel chronicles the hardships that pioneers endured during a trip west on the Oregon Trail. (Rev: SLJ 3/97)

3271 Gregory, Kristiana. *Jimmy Spoon and the Pony Express* (6–8). 1997, Scholastic paper $4.50 (978-0-590-46578-6). Jimmy answers an ad for Pony Express riders, but he's haunted by his previous life with the Shoshoni (see *The Legend of Jimmy Spoon*, Harcourt, 1991), especially the beautiful Nahanee. (Rev: BL 11/15/94; SLJ 11/94; VOYA 4/95)

3272 Gregory, Kristiana. *Seeds of Hope: The Gold Rush Diary of Susanna Fairchild* (4–8). 2001, Scholastic paper $10.95 (978-0-590-51157-5). After Susanna's mother dies in 1849, the 14-year-old takes over her journal and describes the hardships she and her sisters face when their father decides to move the family to California in search of gold. (Rev: BL 9/1/01; HBG 10/01; SLJ 7/01; VOYA 10/01)

3273 Hahn, Mary D. *The Gentleman Outlaw and Me — Eli: A Story of the Old West* (5–8). 1996, Clarion $16.00 (978-0-395-73083-6). In frontier days, Eliza, masquerading as a boy, travels west in search of her father. (Rev: BCCB 4/96; BL 4/1/96; HB 9–10/96; SLJ 5/96; VOYA 6/96)

3274 Heisel, Sharon E. *Precious Gold, Precious Jade* (5–8). 2000, Holiday $16.95 (978-0-8234-1432-1). At the end of the Gold Rush in southern Oregon, two sisters create hostilities when they befriend a Chinese family that has moved to town. (Rev: BCCB 4/00; HBG 10/00; SLJ 4/00)

3275 Hill, Pamela S. *Ghost Horses* (6–9). 1996, Holiday $15.95 (978-0-8234-1229-7). In this novel set in the late 19th century, Tabitha rebels at her preacher father's old-fashioned ideas and, disguised as a boy, joins an expedition digging for dinosaur bones in the American West. (Rev: BL 4/15/96; SLJ 3/96)

3276 Holland, Isabelle. *The Promised Land* (5–8). 1996, Scholastic paper $15.95 (978-0-590-47176-3). Orphaned Maggie and Annie, who have been happily living with the Russell family on the Kansas frontier for three years, are visited by an uncle who wants them to come home with him to Catholicism and their Irish heritage in New York City. A sequel to *The Journey Home*. (Rev: BL 4/15/96; SLJ 8/96; VOYA 6/96)

3277 Holling, Holling C. *Tree in the Trail* (4–7). Illus. by author. 1942, Houghton $20.00 (978-0-

395-18228-4); paper $11.95 (978-0-395-54534-8). The history of the Santa Fe Trail, described through the life of a cottonwood tree, a 200-year-old landmark to travelers and a symbol of peace to the Indians.

3278 Holm, Jennifer L. *Boston Jane: An Adventure* (5–8). 2001, HarperCollins LB $17.89 (978-0-06-028739-9). A well-bred young woman faces hardships as she searches the 19th-century Washington Territory for her lost fiancé. (Rev: BL 9/1/01; HB 9–10/01; HBG 3/02; SLJ 8/01)

3279 Holm, Jennifer L. *Boston Jane: The Claim* (5–8). 2004, HarperCollins $15.99 (978-0-06-029045-0). In the third installment in Jane's story, an old rival named Sally and a former suitor cause difficulties for Jane. (Rev: BL 3/1/04; SLJ 5/04; VOYA 4/04)

3280 Holm, Jennifer L. *Boston Jane: Wilderness Days* (5–8). 2002, HarperCollins LB $18.89 (978-0-06-029044-3). Jane's continued adventures in 1854 Washington Territory include helping to stop a murderer and adjusting to the hardships of pioneer life. (Rev: BL 9/1/02; HB 9–10/02; HBG 3/03; SLJ 10/02)

3281 Holmas, Stig. *Apache Pass* (6–8). Trans. from Norwegian by Anne Born. Illus. Series: Chiricahua Apache. 1996, Harbinger $15.95 (978-1-57140-010-9); paper $9.95 (978-1-57140-011-6). The kidnapping of a white boy by Indians leads to confrontations and killings in this novel set in what is now New Mexico. (Rev: SLJ 1/97; VOYA 4/97)

3282 Karr, Kathleen. *Exiled: Memoirs of a Camel* (4–8). 2004, Marshall Cavendish $15.95 (978-0-7614-5164-8). This fascinating story of the U.S. Camel Corps is told from the viewpoint of Ali, an Egyptian camel drafted for service in this shortlived branch of the United States Army. (Rev: BL 5/1/04; SLJ 5/04)

3283 Karr, Kathleen. *Oregon Sweet Oregon* (5–8). Series: Petticoat Party. 1997, HarperCollins LB $14.89 (978-0-06-027234-0). This novel, set in Oregon City, Oregon, from 1846 through 1848, recounts the adventures of 13-year-old Phoebe Brown and her family when they stake a land claim along the Willamette River. (Rev: BL 7/97; SLJ 7/98)

3284 Karwoski, Gail L. *Seaman: The Dog Who Explored the West with Lewis and Clark* (4–8). 1999, Peachtree paper $8.95 (978-1-56145-190-6). This historical novel dramatizes the story of Seaman, the Newfoundland dog that accompanied Lewis and Clark on their expedition. (Rev: BL 8/99; HBG 10/03; SLJ 10/99)

3285 Kerr, Rita. *Texas Footprints* (4–7). Illus. 1988, Eakin $13.95 (978-0-89015-676-6). A tale of the author's great-great-grandparents who went to Texas in 1823. (Rev: BL 3/1/89)

3286 Kirkpatrick, Katherine. *The Voyage of the Continental* (6–9). 2002, Holiday $16.95 (978-0-8234-1580-9). A 17-year-old girl relates in her diary the events of her journey by ship from New England to Seattle in 1866, which involve her in adventure, mystery, and romance. (Rev: BL 12/15/02; HBG 3/03; SLJ 11/02; VOYA 12/02)

3287 Laxalt, Robert. *Dust Devils* (6–10). 1997, Univ. of Nevada paper $16.00 (978-0-87417-300-0). A Native American teenager named Ira sets out to retrieve his prize-winning horse that has been stolen by a rustler named Hawkeye. (Rev: BL 10/15/97; VOYA 12/98)

3288 Levine, Ellen. *The Journal of Jedediah Barstow: An Emigrant on the Oregon Trail* (4–7). Series: My Name Is America. 2002, Scholastic $10.95 (978-0-439-06310-4). Jedediah continues his mother's journal about their experiences on the Oregon Trail after she and the rest of his family are drowned while crossing a river. (Rev: BL 2/15/03; HBG 10/03; SLJ 11/02)

3289 Levitin, Sonia. *Clem's Chances* (4–7). 2001, Scholastic paper $17.95 (978-0-439-29314-3). Fourteen-year-old Clem becomes acquainted with the hardships and rewards of frontier life when he travels to California to find his father in 1860. (Rev: BL 9/15/01; HB 11–12/01; HBG 3/02; SLJ 10/01)

3290 Luger, Harriett M. *The Last Stronghold: A Story of the Modoc Indian War, 1872–1873* (5–8). 1995, Linnet paper $17.50 (978-0-208-02403-9). The Modoc Indian War of 1872–1873 is re-created in this story involving three young people: Charka, a Modoc youth; Ned, a frontier boy; and Yankel, a Russian Jew who has been tricked into joining the army. (Rev: VOYA 6/96)

3291 MacBride, Roger L. *New Dawn on Rocky Ridge* (4–7). Illus. Series: Rocky Ridge. 1997, HarperCollins paper $7.99 (978-0-06-440581-2). This part of the Wilder family story covers 1900–1903 and focuses on Rose's difficult early teen years. (Rev: BL 11/1/97; HBG 3/98; SLJ 2/98)

3292 McClain, Margaret S. *Bellboy: A Mule Train Journey* (6–10). Illus. 1989, New Mexico $17.95 (978-0-9622468-1-4). Set in California in the 1870s, this is the story of a 12-year-old boy and his first job on a mule train. (Rev: BL 3/1/90; SLJ 3/90)

3293 McDonald, Brix. *Riding on the Wind* (5–10). 1998, Avenue paper $5.95 (978-0-9661306-0-7). In frontier Wyoming during the early 1860s, 15-year-old Carrie Sutton is determined to become a rider in the Pony Express after her family's ranch has been chosen as a relay station. (Rev: SLJ 1/99)

3294 McKissack, Patricia C. *Run Away Home* (4–7). 1997, Scholastic paper $14.95 (978-0-590-46751-3). In 1888 rural Alabama, a young African American girl helps shelter a fugitive Apache boy. (Rev: BL 10/1/97; HB 11–12/97; HBG 3/98; SLJ 11/97)

3295 Meyer, Carolyn. *Where the Broken Heart Still Beats: The Story of Cynthia Ann Parker* (7–12). 1992, Harcourt paper $7.00 (978-0-15-295602-8). A fictional retelling of the abduction of Cynthia Parker, who was stolen by Comanches as a child and lived with them for 24 years, first as a slave, then as a chief's wife. (Rev: BL 12/1/92; SLJ 9/92)

3296 Milligan, Bryce. *With the Wind, Kevin Dolan: A Novel of Ireland and Texas* (5–7). Illus. 1987, Corona paper $7.95 (978-0-931722-45-5). The story of Kevin and Tom, brothers who leave the famine in Ireland in the 1830s and head for America. (Rev: BL 8/87; SLJ 9/87)

3297 Moeri, Louise. *Save Queen of Sheba* (5–7). 1990, Avon paper $3.50 (978-0-380-71154-3). Young David survives a wagon train massacre and must take care of his young sister.

3298 Moore, Robin. *The Bread Sister of Sinking Creek* (7–10). 1990, HarperCollins LB $14.89 (978-0-397-32419-4). An orphaned 14-year-old girl becomes a servant in Pennsylvania during pioneer days. (Rev: BL 7/90; SLJ 4/90; VOYA 8/90)

3299 Nixon, Joan Lowery. *In the Face of Danger* (5–8). 1996, Bantam paper $4.99 (978-0-440-22705-2). Megan fears she will bring bad luck to her adoptive family in this story set in the prairies of Kansas. This is the third part of the Orphan Train Quartet. (Rev: SLJ 12/88; VOYA 12/88)

3300 Oatman, Eric. *Cowboys on the Western Trail: The Cattle Drive Adventures of Josh McNabb and Davy Bartlett* (4–7). Illus. Series: I Am America. 2004, National Geographic paper $6.99 (978-0-7922-6553-5). The excitement of a cattle drive is shown in the journals and letters of two young teen boys in this blend of fact and fiction set in 1887 and presented in an appealing magazine format. (Rev: BL 5/15/04)

3301 O'Dell, Scott. *Streams to the River, River to the Sea: A Novel of Sacagawea* (5–9). 1986, Houghton $16.00 (978-0-395-40430-0). A fictionalized portrait of the real-life Indian woman who traveled west with Lewis and Clark on their famous journey. (Rev: BL 3/15/86; HB 9–10/86; SLJ 5/86; VOYA 6/86)

3302 Patrick, Denise Lewis. *The Longest Ride* (6–9). 1999, Holt $15.95 (978-0-8050-4715-8). This sequel to *The Adventures of Midnight Son* explores slavery and Indian-black relations when escaped Texas slave Midnight Sun becomes lost during a long cattle drive and is rescued by some Arapahos at the time of the Civil War. (Rev: BL 6/1–15/99; HBG 3/00; SLJ 12/99; VOYA 2/00)

3303 Paulsen, Gary. *The Legend of Bass Reeves* (5–8). 2006, Random $15.95 (978-0-385-74661-8). This fictionalized biography profiles the little-known life and career of Bass Reeves, the former slave who became one of the West's most effective

lawmen. (Rev: BCCB 10/06; BL 6/1–15/06; HBG 10/07; SLJ 8/06)

3304 Philbrick, Rodman. *The Journal of Douglas Allen Deeds: The Donner Party Expedition* (5–7). Series: My Name Is America. 2001, Scholastic paper $10.95 (978-0-439-21600-5). A fictional account of the Donner Party's hardships as written in a 15-year-old orphaned boy's journal. (Rev: BL 1/1–15/02; HBG 3/02; SLJ 12/01)

3305 Rinaldi, Ann. *The Second Bend in the River* (5–9). 1997, Scholastic paper $15.95 (978-0-590-74258-0). In Ohio in 1798, 7-year-old Rebecca begins a long-lasting friendship with the Shawnee chief Tecumseh that eventually leads to a marriage proposal. (Rev: BCCB 3/97; BL 2/15/97; HBG 3/98; SLJ 6/97)

3306 Schultz, Jan Neubert. *Battle Cry* (5–9). 2006, Carolrhoda LB $15.95 (978-1-57505-928-0). Native American Chaska and white settler Johnny are drawn into the bloody 1862 Dakota Conflict in this dramatic tale. (Rev: SLJ 7/06)

3307 Schultz, Jan Neubert. *Horse Sense* (5–7). 2001, Carolrhoda LB $15.95 (978-1-57505-998-3); paper $6.95 (978-1-57505-999-0). Fourteen-year-old Will and his father do not get along, but they join a posse tracking dangerous outlaws in this adventure based on a true story. (Rev: BL 8/01; HBG 3/02; VOYA 12/01)

3308 Seeley, Debra. *Grasslands* (5–8). 2002, Holiday $16.95 (978-0-8234-1731-5). The hard life on the prairie disappoints a 13-year-old newcomer from Virginia until he has the chance to ride as a cowboy in this novel set in the late 19th century. (Rev: BL 11/1/02; HBG 3/03; SLJ 1/03*; VOYA 12/02)

3309 Sommerdorf, Norma. *Red River Girl* (4–7). 2006, Holiday $16.95 (978-0-8234-1903-6). In 1846 after her Ojibwa mother dies, 12-year-old Metis girl Josette starts a journal that documents her family's journey by wagon train from Canada to St. Paul, Minnesota, where they settle and she becomes a teacher. (Rev: BL 11/15/06; SLJ 12/06)

3310 Taylor, Theodore. *Billy the Kid* (6–9). 2005, Harcourt $17.00 (978-0-15-204930-0). In this fictionalized account, author Theodore Taylor provides a different twist on the story of Old West outlaw Billy the Kid. (Rev: BCCB 9/05; BL 5/15/05; SLJ 7/05; VOYA 4/06)

3311 Vick, Helen H. *Charlotte* (6–8). Series: Courage of the Stone. 1999, Roberts Rinehart $15.95 (978-1-57098-278-1); paper $9.95 (978-1-57098-282-8). After her parents are killed by Apache warriors in frontier Arizona Territory, 13-year-old Charlotte learns the ways of survival from an elderly Native American woman. (Rev: HBG 9/99; SLJ 7/99)

3312 Wallace, Bill. *Buffalo Gal* (6–8). 1992, Holiday $16.95 (978-0-8234-0943-3). Amanda's plans for an elegant 16th birthday party evaporate when her mother drags her to the wilds of Texas to search for buffalo with cowboys. (Rev: BL 6/15/92; SLJ 5/92)

3313 Whelan, Gloria. *Miranda's Last Stand* (4–7). 1999, HarperCollins LB $14.89 (978-0-06-028252-3). After her husband was killed at Little Big Horn, Miranda's mother can't bear to be around Indians, including Sitting Bull, who works with her at Buffalo Bill's Wild West Show. (Rev: BL 11/1/99; HBG 3/00; SLJ 11/99)

3314 Whelan, Gloria. *Return to the Island* (4–7). 2000, HarperCollins LB $15.89 (978-0-06-028254-7). In the early 19th century on Mackinac Island, Mary must decide between two men who love her: White Hawk, an orphan raised by a white family, and James, an English painter. (Rev: BL 1/1–15/01; HBG 3/01; SLJ 12/00)

3315 Wilder, Laura Ingalls. *The Long Winter* (5–8). Illus. 1953, HarperCollins LB $17.89 (978-0-06-026461-1). Number six in the Little House books. In this one, the Ingalls face a terrible winter with only seed grain for food.

3316 Wisler, G. Clifton. *All for Texas: A Story of Texas Liberation* (4–8). 2000, Jamestown paper $5.95 (978-0-8092-0629-2). A thirteen-year-old boy tells about moving west with his family in 1838 to Texas, where his father has been promised land if he will fight against Mexico. (Rev: BCCB 7–8/00; SLJ 8/00)

3317 Wolf, Allan. *New Found Land: Lewis and Clark's Voyage of Discovery* (7–12). 2004, Candlewick $18.99 (978-0-7636-2113-1). Seaman the dog, here called Oolum, is the primary narrator of this verse account of the famous expedition that draws heavily on such primary source documents as letters and journals. (Rev: BL 9/04; SLJ 9/04)

3318 Yep, Laurence. *Dragon's Gate* (6–9). 1993, HarperCollins $17.99 (978-0-06-022971-9). The adventures of a privileged Chinese teenager who travels to California in 1865 to join his father and uncle working on the transcontinental railroad. (Rev: BL 1/1/94; SLJ 1/94; VOYA 12/93)

3319 Yep, Laurence. *The Journal of Wong Ming-Chung* (4–7). Illus. 2000, Scholastic paper $10.95 (978-0-590-38607-4). Told in diary format beginning in October 1851, this is the story of a Chinese boy nicknamed Runt who travels from his native country to join an uncle in the gold mining fields of America. (Rev: BL 4/1/00; HBG 10/00; SLJ 4/00; VOYA 6/00)

RECONSTRUCTION TO WORLD WAR I (1865–1914)

3320 Alter, Judith. *Luke and the Van Zandt County War* (5–9). Illus. 1984, Texas Christian Univ. $14.95 (978-0-912646-88-6). Life in Reconstruction Texas as seen through the eyes of two 14-year-olds. (Rev: SLJ 3/85)

3321 Arato, Rona. *Ice Cream Town* (5–8). Illus. 2007, Fitzhenry & Whiteside paper $11.95 (978-1-55041-591-9). Ten-year-old Sammy Levin, a recent Jewish immigrant from Poland, finds it tough to adjust to his new life on the streets of New York City's Lower East Side in the early 1900s. (Rev: BL 4/1/07; SLJ 6/07)

3322 Bass, Ruth. *Sarah's Daughter* (8–10). 2007, Gadd $14.95 (978-0-9774053-4-3). When 14-year-old Rose's mother dies, she must look after her family and the farm while her father goes out carousing in this novel set in the 1800s. (Rev: BL 7/07)

3323 Boling, Katharine. *January 1905* (4–7). 2004, Harcourt $16.00 (978-0-15-205119-8). In alternating voices, 11-year-old mill worker Pauline and her deformed, stay-at-home twin sister Arlene describe the harsh circumstances of their early 20th-century life. (Rev: BL 5/15/04; HB 7–8/04; SLJ 7/04)

3324 Brown, Don. *The Notorious Izzy Fink* (6–9). 2006, Roaring Brook $16.95 (978-1-59643-139-3). On the Lower East Side of New York in the 1890s, 13-year-old Sam, half Irish and half Jewish, struggles to make ends meet and to avoid the racism and violence that are rampant. (Rev: BL 11/15/06; LMC 2/07; SLJ 9/06)

3325 Burleigh, Robert. *Into the Air: The Story of the Wright Brothers' First Flight* (5–8). Illus. by Bill Wylie. Series: American Heroes. 2002, Harcourt paper $6.00 (978-0-15-216803-2). A high-interest, comic-book presentation of the first flight with fictionalized dialogue. (Rev: HBG 3/03; SLJ 9/02)

3326 Byars, Betsy. *Keeper of the Doves* (5–8). 2002, Viking $14.99 (978-0-670-03576-2). Young Amie McBee is a thoughtful child who loves to write and — unlike her older twin sisters — has the sensitivity to see the softer side of the mysterious Polish immigrant who lives on their estate and keeps doves in this story set at the turn of the 20th century and presented in 26 short, alphabetical chapters. (Rev: BCCB 1/03; BL 10/1/02*; HB 9–10/02*; HBG 3/03; SLJ 10/02)

3327 Carter, Alden R. *Crescent Moon* (5–8). 1999, Holiday $16.95 (978-0-8234-1521-2). In the early part of the 20th century, Jeremy joins Great-Uncle Mac on a log drive where they become friends with a Native American and his daughter and, through them, experience the shame of racial prejudice. (Rev: BCCB 1/00; BL 2/15/00; HB 3–4/00; HBG 10/00; SLJ 3/00; VOYA 6/00)

3328 Cindrich, Lisa. *In the Shadow of the Pali: A Story of the Hawaiian Leper Colony* (6–9). 2002, Putnam $18.99 (978-0-399-23855-0). Liliha is only 12 when she is sent in the mid-19th century to the leper colony on the island of Molokai and must deal with the lawless thugs who live there. (Rev: BCCB 10/02; HBG 10/02; SLJ 6/02; VOYA 8/02)

3329 Clark, Clara Gillow. *Hattie on Her Way* (4–7). Series: Hattie. 2005, Candlewick $15.99 (978-0-7636-2286-2). The sequel to *Hill Hawk Hattie* (2003) finds Hattie living with her grandmother after her mother's death and seeking to solve a family mystery. (Rev: BL 3/1/05; SLJ 3/05)

3330 Cross, Gillian. *The Great American Elephant Chase* (5–8). 1993, Holiday $17.95 (978-0-8234-1016-3). In 1881, Tad, 15, and young friend Cissie attempt to get to Nebraska with her showman father's elephant, pursued by two unsavory characters who claim they have bought the animal. (Rev: BCCB 6/93; BL 3/15/93*; SLJ 5/93*; VOYA 10/93)

3331 Cushman, Karen. *Rodzina* (5–9). 2003, Clarion $16.00 (978-0-618-13351-2). On an orphan train going from Chicago to California in 1881, plucky Rodzina worries about her fate and aims to find a better life than some of the other children on the train. (Rev: BCCB 3/03; BL 3/1/03*; HB 5–6/03; HBG 10/03; SLJ 4/03*)

3332 Easton, Richard. *A Real American* (4–7). 2002, Clarion $15.00 (978-0-618-03339-3). Against his father's wishes, 11-year-old Nathan befriends Arturo, the son of Italian immigrants newly arrived in a Pennsylvania coal-mining town. (Rev: BCCB 9/02; BL 5/15/02; SLJ 3/02)

3333 Giff, Patricia Reilly. *Water Street* (5–8). 2006, Random $15.95 (978-0-385-73068-6). In this poignant sequel to *Nory Ryan's Song* (2000) and *Maggie's Door* (2003), set in late 19th-century Brooklyn and told from alternating points of view, 13-year-old Bird Ryan and her new upstairs neighbor Thomas develop a close friendship. (Rev: BCCB 1/07; BL 8/06; HB 9–10/06; HBG 4/07; LMC 2/07; SLJ 9/06) 🎗

3334 Gray, Dianne E. *Together Apart* (5–9). 2002, Houghton $16.00 (978-0-618-18721-8). After surviving the blizzard of 1888, Isaac and Hannah discover their love for each other while working for feminist publisher Eliza Moore. (Rev: BCCB 11/02; BL 9/15/02; HB 11–12/02; HBG 3/03; SLJ 12/02; VOYA 2/03)

3335 Greenwood, Barbara. *Factory Girl* (5–8). Illus. 2007, Kids Can $18.95 (978-1-55337-648-4); paper $12.95 (978-1-55337-649-1). A story about 12-year-old Emily, who in the early 20th century must take a job in a sweatshop and suffer intolerable conditions, is accompanied by historic photographs of children at work and details of key events on the

road to reform. (Rev: BL 2/15/07; LMC 8-9/07; SLJ 5/07)

3336 Gregory, Kristiana. *Earthquake at Dawn* (5–9). Series: Great Episodes. 2003, Harcourt paper $6.99 (978-0-15-204681-1). Based on actual letters and photographs, this historical novel depicts the devastating 1906 San Francisco earthquake. (Rev: BL 4/15/92; SLJ 8/92)

3337 Gregory, Kristiana. *Orphan Runaways* (5–7). 1998, Scholastic paper $15.95 (978-0-590-60366-9). Two brothers run away from a San Francisco orphanage in 1879 to look for an uncle in the gold fields. (Rev: BCCB 3/98; BL 2/15/98; HBG 10/98; SLJ 3/98)

3338 Gundisch, Karin. *How I Became an American* (4–8). Trans. by James Skofield. 2001, Cricket $15.95 (978-0-8126-4875-1). This is the story of Johann, a young German immigrant, who arrives in an Ohio steel town in the early 20th century. (Rev: BL 11/15/01; HBG 3/02; SLJ 12/01; VOYA 4/02)

3339 Gutman, Dan. *Race for the Sky: The Kitty Hawk Diaries of Johnny Moore* (4–7). 2003, Simon & Schuster $15.95 (978-0-689-84554-3). Fact and fiction are interwoven in this diary by 14-year-old John Moore, recording his firsthand observations of the Wright brothers' progress. (Rev: BL 1/1–15/04; SLJ 1/04)

3340 Haas, Jessie. *Chase* (5–9). 2007, HarperCollins $16.99 (978-0-06-112850-9). In mid-19th-century Pennsylvania, Phin Chase witnesses a murder and flees, pursued by a stranger and a horse that seems to have tracking abilities. (Rev: BL 2/1/07; SLJ 4/07)

3341 Haas, Jessie. *Westminster West* (6–9). 1997, Greenwillow $15.00 (978-0-688-14883-6). This novel, set in 1884 Vermont, features two very different sisters and their struggle for position and control within their farming family. (Rev: BL 4/15/97; SLJ 5/97)

3342 Haddix, Margaret P. *Uprising* (5–8). 2007, Simon & Schuster $16.99 (978-1-4169-1171-5). Three very different young girls — 15-year-old Italian immigrant Bella, Russian Jewish immigrant Yetta, and privileged Jane — give their perspective of the strike that occurred 13 months before the Triangle Shirtwaist Fire in 1911, protesting working conditions in the garment industry. (Rev: BL 9/15/07; SLJ 9/07)

3343 Hale, Marian. *Dark Water Rising* (6–8). 2006, Holt $16.95 (978-0-8050-7585-4). Seth, 17, lives in Galveston, TX, in the year 1900 and dreams of being a carpenter although his parents want him to be a doctor; when the deadly hurricane hits, Seth struggles to help where he can. (Rev: BL 10/15/06; SLJ 10/06) 🎗

3344 Hansen, Joyce. *The Heart Calls Home* (6–9). 1999, Walker $16.95 (978-0-8027-8636-4). In this, the third story about Obi and Easter, the two black lovers have survived the Civil War and are trying to build a new life in Reconstruction America. (Rev: BL 12/1/99; HBG 4/00)

3345 Hansen, Joyce. *I Thought My Soul Would Rise and Fly: The Diary of Patsy, a Freed Girl* (4–8). Series: Dear America. 1997, Scholastic paper $10.95 (978-0-590-84913-5). In this novel in the form of a diary, a freed slave girl wonders what to do with her life after leaving the plantation. (Rev: BL 12/15/97; HBG 3/98; SLJ 11/97)

3346 Harris, Carol Flynn. *A Place for Joey* (4–8). 2001, Boyds Mills $15.95 (978-1-56397-108-2). Twelve-year-old Joey, an Italian immigrant living in Boston in the early 20th century, learns an important lesson through a heroic act. (Rev: BL 9/1/01; HBG 3/02; SLJ 9/01; VOYA 10/01)

3347 Hesse, Karen. *Brooklyn Bridge* (7–12). 2008, Feiwel and Friends $17.95 (978-0-312-37886-8). Set in 1903 Brooklyn, this story alternates chapters about 14-year-old Joe, whose immigrant family manufactures America's first teddy bears, and abandoned children fending for themselves in the shadow of the Brooklyn Bridge; includes interesting final notes about the history of teddy bears. (Rev: BL 8/08; SLJ 9/08) 🌑

3348 Hill, Kirkpatrick. *Dancing at the Odinochka* (4–7). 2005, Simon & Schuster $15.95 (978-0-689-87388-1). An atmospheric life of Erinia — daughter of a Russian father and Athabascan mother — growing up in the 1860s in what is now Alaska. (Rev: BL 8/05; SLJ 8/05)

3349 Hurwitz, Johanna. *Faraway Summer* (5–7). Illus. by Mary Azarian. 1998, Morrow $14.95 (978-0-688-15334-2). In 1910, a Jewish orphan who lives in a tenement in New York City is thrilled at the thought of spending two weeks on a farm in Vermont, thanks to the Fresh Air Fund. (Rev: BL 3/1/98; HB 7–8/98; HBG 10/98; SLJ 5/98)

3350 Hurwitz, Johanna. *The Unsigned Valentine: And Other Events in the Life of Emma Meade* (6–9). Illus. by Mary Azarian. 2006, HarperCollins LB $16.89 (978-0-06-056054-6). Emma, 15, has left school to work on her family's Vermont farm in 1911 and is dismayed when her father won't allow handsome Cole Berry to court her. (Rev: BL 3/1/06; SLJ 1/06)

3351 Jocelyn, Marthe. *Earthly Astonishments* (4–8). 2000, Tundra paper $7.95 (978-0-88776-628-2). The setting is New York City in the 1880s and the novel involves a girl who is only 22 inches tall and her career in a glorified freak show. (Rev: BCCB 2/00; HBG 10/00; SLJ 4/00)

3352 Klass, Sheila S. *A Shooting Star: A Novel About Annie Oakley* (4–8). 1996, Holiday $15.95 (978-0-8234-1279-2). A fictionalized biography of the woman who rose from poverty to become a famous show-business sharpshooter. (Rev: BL 12/15/96; SLJ 5/97)

3353 Lasky, Kathryn. *Dreams in the Golden Country: The Diary of Zipporah Feldman, a Jewish Immigrant Girl* (4–8). 1998, Scholastic paper $10.95 (978-0-590-02973-5). Twelve-year-old Zipporah Feldman, a Jewish immigrant from Russia, keeps a diary about her life with her family on New York's Lower East Side around 1910. (Rev: BL 4/1/98; HBG 9/98; SLJ 5/98)

3354 Lerangis, Peter. *Smiler's Bones* (7–10). 2005, Scholastic $16.95 (978-0-439-34485-2). Lerangis brings alive the sad story, based on truth, of an Inuit boy named Minik, who, with his father and four others, was brought to New York City in the late 19th century by explorer Robert Peary. (Rev: BCCB 6/05; BL 4/1/05; SLJ 6/05; VOYA 8/05)

3355 Lowry, Lois. *The Silent Boy* (6–10). 2003, Houghton $15.00 (978-0-618-28231-9). Young Katy, who has a comfortable existence as a doctor's daughter in early-20th-century New England, makes friends with a mentally backward boy and learns that there are tragedies in life. (Rev: BL 4/15/03; HB 5–6/03; HBG 10/03; SLJ 4/03)

3356 McMullan, Margaret. *When I Crossed No-Bob* (5–8). 2007, Houghton $16.00 (978-0-618-71715-6). Addy O'Donnell, 12, manages to separate herself from her violent and racist family in this novel about post-Civil War Mississippi and the beginnings of the Ku Klux Klan. (Rev: BL 10/1/07; HB 1–2/08; SLJ 11/07)

3357 Marshall, Catherine. *Christy* (8–12). 1976, Avon paper $7.99 (978-0-380-00141-5). This story set in Appalachia in 1912 tells about a spunky young girl who goes there to teach. (Rev: BL 5/1/89)

3358 Massie, Elizabeth. *1870: Not with Our Blood* (6–9). Series: Young Founders. 2000, Tor paper $4.99 (978-0-312-59092-5). After his father dies in the Civil War, Patrick and his family seek mill work, which is so discouraging that Patrick considers turning to burglary. (Rev: BL 4/1/00; SLJ 6/00)

3359 Mattern, Joanne. *Coming to America: The Story of Immigration* (4–8). Illus. by Margaret Sanfilippo. 2000, Perfection Learning $17.95 (978-0-7807-9715-4); paper $8.95 (978-0-7891-2851-5). A fictional presentation centering on the Martini family and their journey from Italy at the turn of the 20th century to find a new home in America. (Rev: HBG 3/01; SLJ 2/01)

3360 Myers, Anna. *Hoggee* (5–7). 2004, Walker $16.95 (978-0-8027-8926-6). Despite all his own problems, 14-year-old mule driver Howard decides to do what he can to help a deaf mute girl in this novel set in 19th-century New York State. (Rev: SLJ 11/04)

3361 Napoli, Donna Jo. *The King of Mulberry Street* (6–9). 2005, Random LB $17.99 (978-0-385-90890-0). In the 1890s, 9-year-old Italian Jew Beniamino travels alone by ship from Naples to New York, where he assumes the name of Dom and tries to make his way while longing for his home. (Rev: BL 8/05; SLJ 10/05; VOYA 12/05)

3362 Nixon, Joan Lowery. *Land of Hope* (6–9). Series: Ellis Island. 1993, Dell paper $4.99 (978-0-440-21597-4). Rebekah, 15, and her family escape persecution in Russia in the early 1900s and flee to New York City, where life is harsh but hopeful. (Rev: BL 12/15/92; SLJ 10/92)

3363 Paterson, Katherine. *Bread and Roses, Too* (5–8). 2006, Clarion $16.00 (978-0-618-65479-6). Jake and Rosa, children from different backgrounds, suffer from the effects of the textile workers' strike in early 20th-century Massachusetts. (Rev: BCCB 3/07; BL 8/06; HB 9–10/06; HBG 4/07; LMC 2/07; SLJ 9/06; VOYA 12/06) ⊙

3364 Paterson, Katherine. *Preacher's Boy* (5–8). 1999, Clarion $15.00 (978-0-395-83897-6). In small-town Vermont in 1899, a time of new ideas and technological change, Robbie, the restless, imaginative, questioning son of a preacher, causes unforeseen trouble when he plans his own kidnapping for profit. (Rev: BCCB 10/99; BL 8/99; HB 9–10/99; HBG 3/00; SLJ 8/99)

3365 Peck, Richard. *Here Lies the Librarian* (5–8). 2006, Dial $16.99 (978-0-8037-3080-9). Four young female librarians arrive in a small town in Indiana in 1914 and inspire 14-year-old Peewee McGrath to consider her future in different ways. (Rev: BL 3/1/06; SLJ 4/06*; VOYA 2/06)

3366 Porter, Tracey. *Billy Creekmore* (5–7). 2007, HarperCollins $16.99 (978-0-06-077570-4). From a grim orphanage to the mines of West Virginia and on to a life in the circus, 10-year-old Billy describes in picaresque style the difficult life of the young and poor in the early 20th century. (Rev: BL 4/15/07; SLJ 7/07)

3367 Raphael, Marie. *A Boy from Ireland* (6–9). 2007, Persea $19.95 (978-0-89255-331-0). Liam, son of an Englishman, has grown up in Ireland and learned to face prejudice over his heritage; moving to New York City in 1901, he finds himself in a similar situation. (Rev: BL 1/15/08; SLJ 2/08)

3368 Raphael, Marie. *Streets of Gold* (7–9). 1998, TreeHouse paper $7.95 (978-1-883088-05-7). After fleeing Poland and conscription in the Russian czar's army, Stefan and his sister Marisia begin a new life in America on the Lower East Side of New York City at the turn of the 20th century. (Rev: SLJ 12/98)

3369 Reich, Susanna. *Penelope Bailey Takes the Stage* (4–7). 2006, Marshall Cavendish $16.95 (978-0-7614-5287-4). A frustrated Penny takes a role in the school play against the wishes of her aunt in this novel set in Victorian San Francisco. (Rev: BL 5/15/06; SLJ 5/06)

3370 Robinet, Harriette G. *Forty Acres and Maybe a Mule* (4–7). 1998, Simon & Schuster $16.00 (978-0-689-82078-6). After the Civil War, Gideon and other freed slaves begin working the 40 acres of land each has been promised in spite of the opposition of white settlers. (Rev: BL 1/1–15/99; HBG 3/99; SLJ 11/98)

3371 Rogers, Lisa Waller. *Get Along, Little Dogies: The Chisholm Trail Diary of Hallie Lou Wells: South Texas, 1878* (4–7). 2001, Texas Tech Univ. $14.50 (978-0-89672-446-4); paper $8.95 (978-0-89672-448-8). Feisty 14-year-old Hallie Lou records in her diary the details and dangers of a cattle drive from Texas to Kansas. (Rev: HBG 10/01; SLJ 7/01)

3372 Schlitz, Laura Amy. *A Drowned Maiden's Hair* (6–9). 2006, Candlewick $15.99 (978-0-7636-2930-4). Orphan Maud is happy to be adopted by the spinster Hawthorne sisters, until she discovers they plan to use her to trick trusting people out of their money in this novel set in Victorian times. (Rev: BL 12/15/06; HB 11–12/06; LMC 2/07; SLJ 10/06)

3373 Schmidt, Gary D. *Lizzie Bright and the Buckminster Boy* (7–12). 2004, Clarion $15.00 (978-0-618-43929-4). When Turner, son of a rigid minister, moves with his family to a small town in Maine during 1912, he doesn't fit in. (Rev: BL 5/15/04*; SLJ 5/04)

3374 Sherman, Eileen B. *Independence Avenue* (5–9). 1990, Jewish Publication Soc. $14.95 (978-0-8276-0367-7). This story of Russian Jews who immigrate to Texas in 1907 has a resourceful, engaging hero, an unusual setting, and plenty of action. (Rev: BL 2/15/91; SLJ 1/91)

3375 Tal, Eve. *Double Crossing: A Jewish Immigration Story* (7–10). 2005, Cinco Puntos $16.95 (978-0-938317-94-4). At the beginning of the 20th century, young Raizel and her Orthodox Jewish grandfather travel from Europe to New York only to find they are rejected by immigration officials. (Rev: BL 8/05*; SLJ 10/05; VOYA 4/06)

3376 Taylor, Kim. *Bowery Girl* (8–11). 2006, Viking $16.99 (978-0-670-05966-9). A realistic story about orphaned teen girls who resort to picking pockets and prostitution to survive in late-19th-century New York City. (Rev: BL 3/1/06; SLJ 3/06; VOYA 4/06)

3377 Taylor, Mildred D. *The Land* (7–12). 2001, Penguin $17.99 (978-0-8037-1950-7). In this prequel to *Roll of Thunder, Hear My Cry* (1976), Taylor weaves her own family history into a moving story of a young man of mixed parentage facing prejudice, cruelty, and betrayal during the time of Reconstruction. (Rev: BCCB 10/01; BL 8/01; HB 9–10/01; HBG 3/02; SLJ 8/01; VOYA 10/01)

3378 Tucker, Terry Ward. *Moonlight and Mill Whistles* (5–7). 1998, Summerhouse $15.00 (978-1-887714-32-7). Thirteen-year-old Tommy is unaware how his life will change after he meets a gypsy girl named Rhona in this novel set in an early 1900s South Carolina cotton mill town. (Rev: BL 3/1/99; SLJ 5/99)

3379 Twomey, Cathleen. *Charlotte's Choice* (6–8). 2001, Boyds Mills $15.95 (978-1-56397-938-5). In 1905 Missouri, 13-year-old Charlotte must decide whether to betray her friend Jesse's trust and reveal why Jesse has committed murder. (Rev: BL 1/1–15/02; HBG 3/02; SLJ 12/01; VOYA 2/02)

3380 Warner, Sally. *Finding Hattie* (5–8). 2001, HarperCollins $15.95 (978-0-06-028464-0). Hattie Knowlton's 1882 journal describes Miss Bulkey's school in Tarrytown, New York, and the people she meets there, including her sophisticated, shallow but popular cousin Sophie. (Rev: BCCB 6/01; BL 2/1/01; HB 5–6/01; HBG 10/01; SLJ 2/01; VOYA 8/01)

3381 Welsh, T. K. *The Unresolved* (7–12). 2006, Dutton $15.99 (978-0-525-47731-0). The story of the *General Slocum* steamship disaster of 1904, told from the point of view of Mallory, the ghost of one of the victims. (Rev: SLJ 9/06)

3382 Wemmlinger, Raymond. *Booth's Daughter* (8–11). 2007, Boyds Mills $17.95 (978-1-932425-86-4). The niece of John Wilkes Booth, who assassinated Lincoln, and the daughter of famous actor Edwin Booth, Edwina must find an identity apart from her famous family in this novel set in the Gilded Age. (Rev: BCCB 6/07; BL 2/15/07; LMC 10/07; SLJ 9/07)

3383 Wilson, Diane Lee. *Firehorse* (7–10). 2006, Simon & Schuster $16.95 (978-1-4169-1551-5). Rachel, 15, living in 1872 Boston, loves horses and dreams of becoming a veterinarian, despite what her family and society thinks; when she saves a fire-station horse that has been severely burned, opportunities appear to open. (Rev: BL 10/15/06; LMC 4–5/07; SLJ 1/07)

3384 Winthrop, Elizabeth. *Counting on Grace* (6–9). 2006, Random LB $18.99 (978-0-385-90878-8). In the early 20th century, 12-year-old Grace chafes against her long hours working in the textile mill and longs to go back to school in this story based on a 1910 photograph by Lewis Hines. (Rev: BL 2/15/06; SLJ 3/06*; VOYA 4/06)

BETWEEN THE WARS AND THE GREAT DEPRESSION (1919–1941)

3385 Beard, Darleen Bailey. *The Babbs Switch Story* (5–8). 2002, Farrar $16.00 (978-0-374-30475-1). A young girl saves her sister from a fire on Christmas Eve in 1924 in this fictional account of a real event. (Rev: BL 3/15/02; HBG 10/02; SLJ 3/02; VOYA 4/02)

3386 Blackwood, Gary L. *Moonshine* (5–8). 1999, Marshall Cavendish $14.95 (978-0-7614-5056-6). Thirteen-year-old Thad, growing up with his mother in rural Mississippi during the Depression, makes a little extra money by running an illegal still that produces moonshine for the locals. (Rev: BCCB 11/99; BL 9/1/99; HBG 3/00; SLJ 10/99)

3387 Blakeslee, Ann R. *Summer Battles* (5–8). 2000, Marshall Cavendish $14.95 (978-0-7614-5064-1). The story of Kath, age 11, growing up in a small town in Indiana in 1926 and of her father, a preacher, who is attacked for opposing the Ku Klux Klan. (Rev: BCCB 3/00; BL 4/1/00; HBG 10/00; SLJ 4/00)

3388 Bornstein, Ruth Lercher. *Butterflies and Lizards, Beryl and Me* (5–7). 2002, Marshall Cavendish LB $14.95 (978-0-7614-5118-1). Eleven-year-old Charley befriends an odd woman named Beryl while her mother works hard to make it through the Great Depression. (Rev: BL 5/15/02; HBG 10/02; SLJ 5/02)

3389 Brown, Don. *The Train Jumper* (6–9). 2007, Roaring Brook $16.95 (978-1-59643-218-5). During the Depression, 14-year-old Collie sets out to find his troubled older brother and encounters both danger and friendship on his journey. (Rev: BL 8/07; LMC 11/07)

3390 Bryant, Jen. *Ringside, 1925: Views from the Scopes Trial* (8–12). 2008, Knopf $15.99 (978-0-375-84047-0). In first-person free-verse poems, real and fictional figures at the 1925 trial provide a unique perspective. (Rev: HB 5–6/08; LMC 4–5/08; SLJ 3/08)

3391 Burandt, Harriet, and Shelley Dale. *Tales from the Homeplace: Adventures of a Texas Farm Girl* (4–8). 1997, Holt $15.95 (978-0-8050-5075-2). A family story that takes place on a Texas cotton farm during the Depression and features spunky 12-year-old heroine Irene and her six brothers and sisters. (Rev: BCCB 7–8/97; HB 5–6/97; SLJ 4/97*; VOYA 12/97)

3392 Cummings, Priscilla. *Saving Grace* (4–7). 2003, Dutton $17.99 (978-0-525-47123-3). Eleven-year-old Grace faces a tough dilemma when a wealthy family offers to adopt her while her own family is suffering grinding poverty and illness during the Depression. (Rev: BCCB 9/03; BL 5/15/03; HBG 10/03; SLJ 6/03; VOYA 10/03)

3393 Currier, Katrina Saltonstall. *Kai's Journey to Gold Mountain* (4–7). Illus. by Gabhor Utomo. 2005, Angel Island $16.95 (978-0-9667352-7-7); paper $10.95 (978-0-9667352-4-6). Based on the experiences of a Chinese immigrant to the United States in the 1930s, this troubling tale describes the internment of 12-year-old Kai on Angel Island in San Francisco Bay. (Rev: BL 2/15/05*)

3394 Dotty, Kathryn Adams. *Wild Orphan* (5–8). 2006, Edinborough $14.95 (978-1-889020-20-4). In the Midwest in the 1920s, Lizbeth's friendship with an independent-minded orphan named Georgiana gives her courage. (Rev: BL 6/1–15/06)

3395 Dudley, David L. *The Bicycle Man* (5–8). 2005, Clarion $16.00 (978-0-618-54233-8). In this poignant portrait of African American life in the rural South during the late 1920s, 12-year-old Carissa develops a mutually beneficial relationship with Bailey, an elderly jack-of-all-trades to whom she and her mother offer a home. (Rev: BL 11/15/05; SLJ 11/05)

3396 Easton, Kelly. *Walking on Air* (6–8). 2004, Simon & Schuster $16.95 (978-0-689-84875-9). Traveling the 1930s revival circuit and performing as an aerialist to draw people into her father's tent shows, unhappy 12-year-old June makes some important discoveries about her birth and faith. (Rev: BCCB 7–8/04; BL 4/1/04; SLJ 7/04; VOYA 6/04)

3397 Erickson, John R. *Moonshiner's Gold* (5–9). 2001, Viking $15.99 (978-0-670-03502-1). Fourteen-year-old Riley becomes embroiled in exciting intrigue involving moonshiners and corruption in this novel set in Texas in the 1920s. (Rev: HBG 3/02; SLJ 8/01; VOYA 10/01)

3398 Fisher, Leonard E. *The Jetty Chronicles* (5–9). Illus. 1997, Marshall Cavendish $15.95 (978-0-7614-5017-7). A series of vignettes based on fact about the unusual people the author met while growing up in Sea Gate, New York, at a time when the United States was drifting into World War II. (Rev: BL 10/15/97; HBG 3/98; SLJ 12/97; VOYA 2/98)

3399 Franklin, Kristine L. *Grape Thief* (5–9). 2003, Candlewick $16.99 (978-0-7636-1325-9). In 1925 Washington State, a boy of Croatian heritage tries to find a way to stay in school even though his family is in financial difficulty. (Rev: BL 10/1/03; SLJ 9/03)

3400 Fuqua, Jonathon. *Darby* (4–7). 2002, Candlewick $15.99 (978-0-7636-1417-1). A 9-year-old white girl, Darby, and her family become the target of KKK violence after she protests the killing of a black sharecropper's son in 1926 South Carolina. (Rev: BCCB 7–8/02; BL 3/15/02; HB 3–4/02; HBG 10/02; SLJ 3/02; VOYA 4/02)

3401 Hesse, Karen. *Letters from Rifka* (4–8). 1992, Holt $16.95 (978-0-8050-1964-3). In letters back to Russia, Rifka, 12, recounts her long journey to the United States in 1919, starting with the dangerous escape over the border. (Rev: BCCB 10/92; BL 7/92; HB 9–10/92*; SLJ 8/92*)

3402 Hesse, Karen. *Out of the Dust* (6–12). 1997, Scholastic $16.95 (978-0-590-36080-7). In free verse, 15-year-old Billie Jo describes the tragedies that befall her family during the Dust Bowl years in Oklahoma. Newbery Medal, 1998. (Rev: HBG 3/98)

3403 Hesse, Karen. *A Time of Angels* (5–8). 1995, Hyperion LB $16.49 (978-0-7868-2072-6). As influenza sweeps her city in 1918, killing thousands, Hannah tries to escape its ravages by moving to Vermont, where an old farmer helps her. (Rev: BCCB 1/96; BL 12/1/95; SLJ 12/95)

3404 Hesse, Karen. *Witness* (7–12). 2001, Scholastic paper $16.95 (978-0-439-27199-8). Hesse uses fictional first-person accounts in free verse to describe Ku Klux Klan activity in a 1924 Vermont town. (Rev: BCCB 11/01; BL 9/1/01; HB 11–12/01; HBG 3/02; SLJ 9/01*; VOYA 10/01)

3405 Hunt, Irene. *No Promises in the Wind* (6–8). 1987, Berkley paper $4.99 (978-0-425-09969-8). During the Great Depression, Josh must assume responsibilities far beyond his years. A reissue.

3406 Ingold, Jeanette. *Hitch* (8–11). 2005, Harcourt $17.00 (978-0-13-204747-0). When he loses his job during the Great Depression, 17-year-old Moss Trawley leaves home in search of his father and ends up in an interesting job with the Civilian Conservation Corps. (Rev: BCCB 9/05; BL 5/15/05; SLJ 8/05)

3407 Jackson, Alison. *Rainmaker* (5–8). 2005, Boyds Mills $16.95 (978-1-59078-309-2). The farmers in Pidge Martin's town hire a rainmaker in the hopes that she will save their crops in this story set in 1939 Florida. (Rev: BL 3/15/05; SLJ 4/05)

3408 Jocelyn, Marthe. *How It Happened in Peach Hill* (5–9). 2007, Random $15.99 (978-0-375-83701-2). Fifteen-year-old Annie, who does research for her "clairvoyant" mother mainly by pretending she is stupid, longs for a normal life in this compelling novel set in the 1920s. (Rev: BL 1/1–15/07; SLJ 4/07*)

3409 Kidd, Ronald. *Monkey Town: The Summer of the Scopes Trial* (6–9). 2006, Simon & Schuster $15.95 (978-1-4169-0572-1). This fictionalized account of the 1925 Scopes Monkey Trial in Dayton, Tennessee, is narrated by the perceptive 15-year-old Frances Robinson, daughter of the man primarily responsible for taking the evolution test case to the courts. (Rev: BL 12/15/05; SLJ 2/06*; VOYA 2/06)

3410 Koller, Jackie F. *Nothing to Fear* (5–7). 1991, Harcourt $14.95 (978-0-15-200544-3); paper $8.00 (978-0-15-257582-3). Danny Garvey is a first-generation Catholic Irish American growing up in New York City in the 1930s. (Rev: BCCB 3/91; BL 3/1/91; SLJ 5/91)

3411 Kudlinski, Kathleen. *The Spirit Catchers: An Encounter with Georgia O'Keeffe* (6–9). Series: Art Encounters. 2004, Watson-Guptill $16.95 (978-0-8230-0408-9); paper $6.99 (978-0-8230-0412-6). Fact and fiction are mixed in this story of 15-year-old Parker, a Dust Bowl refugee who finds himself on Georgia O'Keeffe's New Mexico ranch and becomes her assistant. (Rev: SLJ 10/04)

3412 Laskas, Gretchen Moran. *The Miner's Daughter* (6–9). 2007, Simon & Schuster $15.99 (978-1-4169-1262-0). Willa, 16, must disguise herself as a boy to get work when her father loses his mining job during the Depression. (Rev: BCCB 5/07; BL 2/15/07; LMC 8-9/07; SLJ 2/07)

3413 Laxalt, Robert. *Time of the Rabies* (7–12). 2000, Univ. of Nevada $16.00 (978-0-87417-350-5). Set in 1920s Nevada, this novella recalls a harrowing fight against a rabies epidemic. (Rev: VOYA 4/01)

3414 Meltzer, Milton. *Tough Times* (5–8). 2007, Clarion $16.00 (978-0-618-87445-3). With detailed historical background, this novel describes the struggles and despair experienced by high school senior Joey Singer and his family as the Depression deepens. (Rev: BL 9/1/07; SLJ 12/07)

3415 Mills, Claudia. *What About Annie?* (6–8). 1985, Walker $9.95 (978-0-8027-6573-4). A harrowing story of a family in Baltimore living through the Depression as seen through the eyes of a young teenage girl. (Rev: BL 9/1/85)

3416 Myers, Anna. *Tulsa Burning* (8–10). 2002, Walker $16.95 (978-0-8027-8829-0). In 1921 Oklahoma, a 15-year-old boy helps an African American man who is injured during race riots. (Rev: BCCB 12/02; BL 10/1/02*; HBG 3/03; SLJ 9/02; VOYA 12/02)

3417 Myers, Walter Dean. *Harlem Summer* (7–10). 2007, Scholastic $16.99 (978-0-439-36843-8). The atmosphere of 1925 Harlem is strongly evoked in this story of 16-year-old Mark Purvis, an aspiring jazz saxophonist, who takes a job at the NAACP magazine *The Crisis* but soon becomes involved with mobsters. (Rev: BCCB 4/07; BL 2/1/07; HB 5–6/07; LMC 8–9/07; SLJ 3/07)

3418 Naylor, Phyllis Reynolds. *Blizzard's Wake* (7–12). 2002, Simon & Schuster $16.95 (978-0-689-85220-6). In a blizzard in 1941, 15-year-old Kate comes face to face with the man who caused her mother's death. (Rev: BCCB 1/03; BL 10/15/02; HBG 3/03; SLJ 12/02)

3419 O'Sullivan, Mark. *Wash-Basin Street Blues* (7–10). 1996, Wolfhound paper $6.95 (978-0-86327-467-1). In 1920s New York City, 16-year-old Nora is reunited with her two younger brothers but the reunion causes unforeseen problems. A sequel to *Melody for Nora* (1994). (Rev: BL 6/1–15/96)

3420 Peck, Robert Newton. *Arly* (5–8). 1989, Walker $16.95 (978-0-8027-6856-8). A teacher changes the life of a young boy in a migrant camp in Florida in 1927. (Rev: BL 7/89; VOYA 8/89)

3421 Porter, Tracey. *Treasures in the Dust* (5–7). 1997, HarperCollins LB $14.89 (978-0-06-027564-8). With alternating points of view, two girls from poor families in Oklahoma's Dust Bowl tell their stories. (Rev: BL 8/97; HB 9–10/97; HBG 3/98; SLJ 12/97*; VOYA 10/98)

3422 Rabe, Berniece. *Hiding Mr. McMulty* (5–8). 1997, Harcourt $18.00 (978-0-15-201330-1). This novel, set in southeast Missouri in 1937, tells a story of race and class conflicts as experienced by 11-year-old Rass. (Rev: BL 10/15/97; HBG 3/98; SLJ 12/97; VOYA 2/98)

3423 Ray, Delia. *Ghost Girl: A Blue Ridge Mountain Story* (5–8). 2003, Clarion $16.00 (978-0-618-33377-6). In rural Virginia during the Depression, young April longs to go to the new school built by President Hoover and learn to read, but her family circumstances do not make this easy. (Rev: BCCB 11/03; BL 11/15/03; HB 1–2/04*; HBG 4/04; SLJ 11/03*)

3424 Rostkowski, Margaret I. *After the Dancing Days* (6–9). 1986, HarperCollins paper $5.99 (978-0-06-440248-4). Annie encounters the realities of war when she helps care for wounded soldiers after World War I. (Rev: BL 10/15/86; SLJ 12/86; VOYA 4/87)

3425 Ryan, Pam M. *Esperanza Rising* (5–8). 2000, Scholastic paper $17.99 (978-0-439-12041-8). During the Great Depression, poverty forces Esperanza and her mother to leave Mexico and seek work in an agricultural labor camp in California. (Rev: BCCB 12/00; BL 12/1/00; HB 1–2/01; HBG 3/01; SLJ 10/00; VOYA 12/00)

3426 Sternberg, Libby. *The Case Against My Brother* (6–9). 2007, Bancroft $19.95 (978-1-890862-51-0). Carl Matuski, 15 and from a Polish Catholic family, sets out to solve a mystery and encounters prejudice and ethnic hatred in this story set in Oregon in 1922. (Rev: BL 11/15/07)

3427 Stolz, Mary. *Ivy Larkin* (7–9). 1986, Harcourt $13.95 (978-0-15-239366-3). During the Depression in New York City, 15-year-old Ivy's father loses his job and the family moves to the Lower East Side. (Rev: BL 11/1/86; SLJ 12/86)

3428 Tate, Eleanora. *Celeste's Harlem Renaissance* (4–7). 2007, Little, Brown $15.99 (978-0-316-

52394-3). In the early 1920s Celeste arrives in New York from North Carolina and discovers that her aunt is not the famous singer and dancer she was told but that the lively spirit of the Harlem Renaissance brings her rewards. (Rev: BL 2/1/07; SLJ 5/07)

3429 Taylor, Kim. *Cissy Funk* (6–9). 2001, HarperCollins LB $15.89 (978-0-06-029042-9). Cissy is neglected and abused until her Aunt Vera arrives in this novel of complex family relationships that evokes the privations of the Depression years in Colorado. (Rev: BCCB 5/01; BL 8/01; HBG 10/01; SLJ 5/01; VOYA 8/01)

3430 Winthrop, Elizabeth. *Franklin Delano Roosevelt: Letters from a Mill Town Girl* (5–7). Illus. Series: Dear Mr. President. 2001, Winslow $9.95 (978-1-890817-61-9). Fictional letters between Franklin Delano Roosevelt and a 12-year-old girl illustrate living conditions and government policy during the Depression. (Rev: BL 2/1/02; HBG 3/02; SLJ 12/01)

3431 Wolfert, Adrienne. *Making Tracks* (5–7). Illus. Series: Adventures in America. 2000, Silver Moon LB $14.95 (978-1-893110-16-8). In this novel set in the Depression, young Henry leaves his foster home to ride the rails to Chicago to find his father. (Rev: BL 7/00; HBG 3/01; SLJ 11/00)

3432 Wyatt, Leslie J. *Poor Is Just a Starting Place* (5–8). 2005, Holiday $16.95 (978-0-8234-1884-8). In rural Kentucky during the Great Depression, 12-year-old Artie longs for a different life. (Rev: BL 6/1–15/05; SLJ 7/05)

POST WORLD WAR II UNITED STATES (1945–)

3433 Armistead, John. *The Return of Gabriel* (6–9). 2002, Milkweed $17.95 (978-1-57131-637-0); paper $6.95 (978-1-57131-638-7). Friendships and family loyalties are tested when the civil rights movement comes to Mississippi and parents take sides in this story set in 1964. (Rev: BL 12/15/02; HBG 3/03; SLJ 12/02)

3434 Baker, Julie. *Up Molasses Mountain* (6–9). 2002, Random LB $17.99 (978-0-385-90048-5). Clarence and Elizabeth find themselves on opposite sides of a labor dispute involving their coal-mining fathers in this multilayered novel set in 1953 West Virginia. (Rev: BL 5/15/02; HBG 10/02; SLJ 7/02; VOYA 8/02)

3435 Banks, Steven. *King of the Creeps* (6–9). 2006, Knopf $15.95 (978-0-375-83291-8). Set in 1963, this is the story of 17-year-old Tom, a geeky teen who discovers he can attract girls — and attention — by playing guitar and playing up his resemblance to folk star Bob Dylan. (Rev: BL 5/1/06; LMC 10/06; SLJ 6/06)

3436 Bauer, Marion Dane. *Killing Miss Kitty and Other Sins* (8–11). 2007, Clarion $16.00 (978-0-618-69000-8). Five interconnected stories about Claire, a girl growing up in the 1950s and exploring life and sexuality. (Rev: BCCB 9/07; BL 2/15/07; LMC 8–9/07; SLJ 5/07)

3437 Burg, Shana. *A Thousand Never Evers* (7–12). 2008, Delacorte $15.99 (978-0-385-73470-7). African American Addie finds all aspects of life in her Mississippi town are affected by the civil rights movement of the 1960s. (Rev: BL 4/15/08; LMC 4–5/08*; SLJ 7/08) ⚓

3438 Cheng, Andrea. *Eclipse* (5–8). 2006, Front St. $16.95 (978-1-932425-21-5). In 1952 Cincinnati, 8-year-old immigrant Peti is disappointed when his relatives arrive to live with them; his cousin is a bully and his mother still worries about her father, who cannot get out of Hungary. (Rev: BL 11/1/06)

3439 Coleman, Evelyn. *Freedom Train* (5–8). 2008, Simon & Schuster $15.99 (978-1-4169-5211-4). Clyde, who comes from a poor white family, stands up for himself by refusing to join his father in harassing a black family in this story set in 1947 Atlanta. (Rev: BL 2/1/08)

3440 Crowe, Chris. *Mississippi Trial, 1955* (7–12). 2002, Penguin $17.99 (978-0-8037-2745-8). The story of the racist murder in 1955 of a 14-year-old black boy called Emmett Till is told through the eyes of Hiram, a white teenager. (Rev: BCCB 4/02; BL 2/15/02; HBG 10/02; SLJ 5/02; VOYA 4/02)

3441 Crum, Shutta. *Spitting Image* (5–8). 2003, Clarion $15.00 (978-0-618-23477-6). Jessie has a busy summer in 1967 in her Kentucky hometown, tackling family problems and dealing with well-meaning volunteers and reporters who view them as "rural poor." (Rev: BL 3/1/03; HBG 10/03; SLJ 4/03*)

3442 Cushman, Karen. *The Loud Silence of Francine Green* (6–9). 2006, Clarion $16.00 (978-0-618-50455-8). Francine, an 8th-grader in a Catholic girls school in Los Angeles, befriends a headstrong, opinionated girl whose father is suspected of being a Communist in this McCarthy-era novel. (Rev: BL 7/06; HB 9–10/06; LMC 11-12/06; SLJ 8/06*) ⚓

3443 Harrar, George. *The Wonder Kid* (4–7). Illus. by Anthony Winiarski. 2006, Houghton $16.00 (978-0-618-56317-3). As a kid growing up in the 1950s, Jesse contracts polio and with the encouragement of a friend passes the time creating a comic strip hero called the Wonder Kid. (Rev: SLJ 3/07)

3444 Hemphill, Helen. *Long Gone Daddy* (8–11). 2006, Front St. $16.95 (978-1-932425-38-3). Set in the late 1960s, this is the story of Harlan, a 14-year-old funeral home worker who reconciles with his hard-line-preacher father when the two take a road trip to Las Vegas to transport Harlan's grandfather's body and collect their inheritance. (Rev: BL 5/1/06; HB 11–12/06; SLJ 7/06)

3445 Hemphill, Helen. *Runaround* (5–8). 2007, Front St. $16.95 (978-1-932425-83-3). In 1960s Kentucky, motherless 11-year-old Sassy needs more information about love but has trouble finding a source as her Dad is busy with other things, her housekeeper wants her just to act like a young lady, and her sister may be involved with the same handsome neighbor. (Rev: BL 3/1/07*; SLJ 4/07)

3446 Holm, Jennifer L. *Penny from Heaven* (5–8). 2006, Random $15.95 (978-0-375-83687-9). Set in 1953, this is the story of how 12-year-old Penny gets to know her late father's lively Italian American family and comes to understand the circumstances surrounding her father's death. Newbery Honor Book, 2007. (Rev: BL 4/15/06; HB 3–4/07; SLJ 7/06)

3447 Houston, Julian. *New Boy* (8–11). 2005, Houghton $16.00 (978-0-618-43253-0). In the late 1950s, Rob Garrett, an African American teen from Virginia, is the first black student at a tony Connecticut prep school, where he learns about different forms of prejudice and watches civil rights developments in the South. (Rev: BL 11/15/05*; SLJ 3/06; VOYA 2/06)

3448 Kadohata, Cynthia. *Kira-Kira* (6–12). 2004, Simon & Schuster $15.95 (978-0-689-85639-6). Poverty, exploitation, and racial prejudice form a backdrop to this moving story of two Japanese American sisters growing up in a small Georgia town in the late 1950s and facing the older sister's death from lymphoma. Newbery Medal, 2005. (Rev: BCCB 1/04; BL 1/1–15/04; HB 3–4/04; SLJ 3/04; VOYA 8/04)

3449 Klages, Ellen. *White Sands, Red Menace* (5–8). 2008, Viking $16.99 (978-0-670-06235-5). In this riveting sequel to *The Green Glass Sea* (2006), Dewey's father has died and she is living near Los Alamos with her friend Suze, whose father is working on a new rocket for the space race. (Rev: BL 8/08)

3450 Krisher, Trudy. *Fallout* (7–10). 2006, Holiday $17.95 (978-0-8234-2035-3). Growing up during the Cold War in a very conservative coastal town in North Carolina, Genevieve is struck by the ideas introduced by the outspoken Brenda Womper, a new student who has arrived from California. (Rev: BL 11/15/06; SLJ 11/06)

3451 Lawrence, Iain. *Gemini Summer* (4–7). 2006, Delacorte $15.95 (978-0-385-73089-1). In the mid-1960s, soon after Danny's brother Beau dies in an accident, a stray dog appears and adopts Danny; Danny becomes devoted to the dog and, because he sees much of Beau in Rocket, he and Rocket set off for Cape Canaveral to realize Beau's dream of see-

ing the Gemini mission. (Rev: BL 12/15/06; SLJ 11/06)

3452 Lemna, Don. *When the Sergeant Came Marching Home* (4–7). Illus. by Matt Colins. 2008, Holiday $16.95 (978-0-8234-2083-4). Set in the 1940s, this novel of a family that moves to a farm in Montana paints a realistic picture of the hardships and joys of rural life at that time. (Rev: BL 4/15/08; SLJ 7/08)

3453 Levine, Ellen. *Catch a Tiger by the Toe* (5–8). 2005, Viking $15.99 (978-0-670-88461-2). Jamie's world is turned upside down when her father is put in jail for refusing to reveal the names of other Communists to the House Un-American Activities Committee. (Rev: BL 3/15/05*; SLJ 6/05)

3454 Lurie, April. *Brothers, Boyfriends and Other Criminal Minds* (7–10). 2007, Delacorte $15.99 (978-0-385-73124-9). April is growing up in Brooklyn in the 1970s, and makes accommodations with the local Mafia partly to support her older brother. (Rev: BL 7/07; SLJ 10/07)

3455 Madden, Kerry. *Gentle's Holler* (5–8). Series: Maggie Valley. 2005, Viking $16.99 (978-0-670-05998-0). Livy Two, part of a large, poor family living in the North Carolina mountains, learns a lesson when her father is injured. (Rev: BL 3/1/05; SLJ 6/05)

3456 Madden, Kerry. *Jessie's Mountain* (5–8). Series: Maggie Valley. 2008, Viking $16.99 (978-0-670-06154-9). Livy Two and her family are still struggling to make it in this final installment in the series, but they start to turn things around using their love of music. (Rev: BL 2/8/08; SLJ 3/08)

3457 Madden, Kerry. *Louisiana's Song* (5–8). Series: Maggie Valley. 2007, Viking $16.99 (978-0-670-06153-2). Their father is home from the hospital but cannot work, so Livy Two and her nine siblings do everything they can to support their family in this sequel to *Gentle's Holler* (2005) set in North Carolina in 1963. (Rev: BL 6/1–15/07; SLJ 8/07)

3458 Matthews, Kezi. *Scorpio's Child* (7–10). 2001, Cricket $15.95 (978-0-8126-2890-6). In South Carolina in 1947, 14-year-old Afton has difficulty welcoming a taciturn, previously unknown uncle into her home despite her mother's pleas for compassion. (Rev: BCCB 10/01; BL 9/15/01; HB 1–2/02; HBG 3/02; SLJ 10/01; VOYA 4/02)

3459 Moranville, Sharelle Byars. *A Higher Geometry* (8–11). 2006, Holt $16.95 (978-0-8050-7470-3). Fifteen-year-old Anna's love for mathematics sets her apart from her peers in this thoughtful novel about romance and identity in the rural Midwest of 1959. (Rev: BL 4/15/06; SLJ 6/06)

3460 Moses, Shelia P. *The Baptism* (6–9). 2007, Simon & Schuster $15.99 (978-1-4169-0671-1).

Leon and Luke must cope with the hardships that are part of being black in South Carolina in the 1940s in this companion to the author's two Buddy Bush novels. (Rev: BCCB 5/07; BL 2/1/07; LMC 10/07; SLJ 3/07)

3461 Moses, Shelia P. *The Legend of Buddy Bush* (6–9). 2004, Simon & Schuster $15.95 (978-0-689-85839-0). In this poignant, fact-based novel, 12-year-old Pattie Mae Sheals faces many challenges when her beloved Uncle Buddy is accused of the attempted rape of a white woman in 1940s North Carolina. (Rev: BCCB 4/04; BL 3/1/04; SLJ 2/04; VOYA 2/04)

3462 Nemeth, Sally. *The Heights, the Depths, and Everything in Between* (5–8). 2006, Knopf LB $17.99 (978-0-375-93458-2). Jake Little, a dwarf, and Lucy Small, who despite her name is unusually tall, become friends and navigate the rough waters of middle school and dealing with parents in this story set in the 1970s. (Rev: BL 7/06)

3463 Nolan, Han. *A Summer of Kings* (6–9). 2006, Harcourt $17.00 (978-0-15-205108-2). When her family takes in an African American man fleeing the South in the summer of 1963, 14-year-old Esther questions her own feelings and beliefs. (Rev: BL 4/15/06; SLJ 4/06*)

3464 Noonan, Brandon. *Plenty Porter* (7–10). 2006, Abrams $16.95 (978-0-8109-5996-5). Set in 1950s Illinois, this is the story of 12-year-old Plenty, the 11th child of a sharecropper, who struggles to find a sense of belonging within her family and the secretive rural community in which they live. (Rev: BL 4/15/06; LMC 11–12/06; SLJ 8/06)

3465 Pérez, L. King. *Remember as You Pass Me By* (5–8). 2007, Milkweed $16.95 (978-1-57131-677-6); paper $6.95 (978-1-57131-678-3). In 1950s Texas racial tensions come between 12-year-old Silvy Lane and her black friend Mabelee. (Rev: LMC 2/08; SLJ 11/07)

3466 Ray, Delia. *Singing Hands* (4–7). 2006, Clarion $16.00 (978-0-618-65762-9). Gussie's parents are deaf, which means she can be even more mischievous than the average child in this book set in the 1940s American South. (Rev: BL 5/1/06; SLJ 7/06)

3467 Rodman, Mary Ann. *Yankee Girl* (4–8). 2004, Farrar $17.00 (978-0-374-38661-0). In 1964, Alice's family moves from Chicago to Mississippi and 6th-grader Alice must cope not only with the stress of a new school but also with her ambivalence about the only black girl in her class; newspaper headlines introducing each chapter keep the racial violence of the time in the reader's mind. (Rev: BL 3/1/04; SLJ 4/04)

3468 Rogers, Kenny, and Donald Davenport. *Christmas in Canaan* (5–8). 2002, HarperCollins $15.99 (978-0-06-000746-1). In 1960s Texas, after a black

boy and a white boy fight on the school bus, the adults decree that the two boys must spend time together, and a difficult start ends in the boys becoming fast friends when they help a wounded dog. (Rev: BL 11/1/02; HBG 3/03; SLJ 10/02; VOYA 4/03)

3469 Sharenow, Robert. *My Mother the Cheerleader* (7–10). 2007, HarperCollins $16.99 (978-0-06-114896-5). Louise's mother pulls her out of school when young African American Ruby Bridges enrolls in their New Orleans school district in 1960. (Rev: BCCB 9/07; BL 7/07; LMC 10/07; SLJ 7/07)

3470 Smith, D. James. *The Boys of San Joaquin* (5–8). 2005, Simon & Schuster $15.95 (978-0-689-87606-6). An episodic tale set in the 1950s, in which 12-year-old Paolo describes events of his life and a mystery involving a half-eaten $20 bill. (Rev: BL 3/1/05; SLJ 1/05)

3471 Smith, D. James. *Probably the World's Best Story About a Dog and the Girl Who Loved Me* (5–8). 2006, Simon & Schuster $15.95 (978-1-4169-0542-4). In 1951 California, 12-year-old Paolo's beloved dog Rufus is dognapped and he enlists the help of his younger brother and a deaf cousin to unravel the mystery while also coping with a new paper route and a budding romance; this sequel to *The Boys of San Joaquin* (2004) introduces a sign language word with each chapter. (Rev: BL 9/1/06; SLJ 8/06)

3472 Sullivan, Jacqueline Levering. *Annie's War* (4–7). 2007, Eerdmans $15.00 (978-0-8028-5325-7). In 1946, 10-year-old Annie is having a hard time coping with her father's MIA status and her 19-year-old uncle's emotional problems, and she finds some comfort in imagined conversations with President Truman. (Rev: BL 8/07; SLJ 9/07)

3473 Watkins, Steve. *Down Sand Mountain* (7–12). 2008, Candlewick $16.99 (978-0-7636-3839-9). A loss-of-innocence story set in 1966, simply yet beautifully told, in which a 12-year-old boy discovers the cruelty of racism in his small Florida hometown. (Rev: BL 8/08)

3474 White, Ruth. *Way Down Deep* (4–7). 2007, Farrar $16.00 (978-0-374-38251-3). In 1944 West Virginia, the arrival of a new family in a town called Way Down Deep suddenly raises questions about the origins of Ruby June, a foundling who has lived there for 10 years. (Rev: BL 3/1/07; SLJ 4/07)

3475 Woods, Brenda. *The Red Rose Box* (5–8). 2002, Putnam $16.99 (978-0-399-23702-7). In 1953, Leah, a southern black girl, and her family travel to Los Angeles where they find a different culture and more progressive attitudes. (Rev: BCCB 7–8/02; BL 6/1–15/02; HBG 10/02; SLJ 6/02; VOYA 6/02)

Twentieth-Century Wars

WORLD WAR I

3476 Hamley, Dennis. *Without Warning: Ellen's Story, 1914–1918* (7–12). 2007, Candlewick $17.99 (978-0-7636-3338-7). World War I hits close to home for Ellen, whose brother is wounded and boyfriend is killed in the fighting; she later works as a nurse on the front, ministering to English soldiers and even a German prisoner of war. Although long, this first-person narrative is very readable. (Rev: BL 10/1/07; SLJ 2/08)

3477 Hartnett, Sonya. *The Silver Donkey* (5–8). Illus. by Don Powers. 2006, Candlewick $15.99 (978-0-7636-2937-3). Two young French children find and help a wounded World War I soldier in the woods near their home, and as he heals he tells them stories about the tiny silver donkey he carries with him. (Rev: BL 11/15/06; SLJ 12/06)

3478 Jorgensen, Norman. *In Flanders Fields* (4–7). Illus. by Brian Harrison-Lever. 2002, Fremantle Arts Centre $22.95 (978-1-86368-369-2). During a Christmas Day ceasefire in the World War I trenches, a soldier rescues a trapped robin. (Rev: SLJ 2/03)

3479 McKay, Sharon E. *Charlie Wilcox* (5–8). 2000, Stoddart paper $7.95 (978-0-7737-6093-6). This is the story of a 14-year-old Canadian boy who becomes involved in the trench warfare in France during World War I. (Rev: SLJ 11/00)

3480 Magorian, Michelle. *Good Night, Mr. Tom* (7–9). 1981, HarperCollins paper $7.99 (978-0-06-440174-6). A quiet recluse takes in an abused 8-year-old who has been evacuated from World War II London.

3481 Morpurgo, Michael. *Private Peaceful* (7–12). 2004, Scholastic $16.95 (978-0-439-63648-3). Fifteen-year-old Thomas, who lied about his age to follow his beloved older brother into combat in World War I, reflects on the life he left behind in England and the horrors of life on the front lines. (Rev: BL 10/1/04*; SLJ 11/04; VOYA 12/04)

3482 Morpurgo, Michael. *War Horse* (5–8). 2007, Scholastic $16.99 (978-0-439-79663-7). This gripping tale of World War I and all its horrors is told from the point of view of Joey, an English farm horse that's been drafted for service on the battlefront. (Rev: BL 4/1/07)

3483 Sedgwick, Marcus. *The Foreshadowing* (8–11). 2006, Random LB $18.99 (978-0-385-90881-8). Plagued by premonitions about her brother, 17-year-old Sasha signs up as a nurse so that she can look for him on the grim battlefields of World War I France. (Rev: BL 4/1/06*; SLJ 7/06)

3484 Slade, Arthur. *Megiddo's Shadow* (8–11). 2006, Random $15.95 (978-0-385-74701-1). Edward, a 16-year-old Canadian, enlists in the army to avenge his brother's death and ends up fighting in a bloody battle against the Turks in this World War I novel. (Rev: BL 12/15/06; HB 11–12/06; SLJ 12/06*)

3485 Spillebeen, Geert. *Kipling's Choice* (7–10). Trans. by Terese Edelstein. 2005, Houghton $16.00 (978-0-618-43124-3). In this fictionalized biography of John Kipling, the son of the world-famous British author uses his father's influence to get into the army despite his poor eyesight, giving the teen a chance to do battle with the "barbaric Huns" in World War I. (Rev: BCCB 6/05; BL 5/15/05; SLJ 6/05; VOYA 12/05)

3486 Wilson, John. *And in the Morning* (8–12). 2003, Kids Can $16.95 (978-1-55337-400-8). This absorbing story of fighting in the trenches of World War I, told in diary form by a teenage boy, is enhanced by newspaper headlines and clippings. (Rev: BL 3/15/03; HBG 10/03; SLJ 6/03)

WORLD WAR II AND THE HOLOCAUST

3487 Adler, David A. *Don't Talk to Me About the War* (4–7). 2008, Viking $15.99 (978-0-670-06307-9). Tommy tries hard to ignore the problems overseas and at home in this novel set in the Bronx in 1940. (Rev: BL 4/15/08; SLJ 3/08)

3488 Atlema, Martha. *A Time to Choose* (8–12). 1995, Orca paper $7.95 (978-1-55143-045-4). While growing up in Holland under the Nazi occupation, 16-year-old Johannes tries to separate himself from his father, who is considered a collaborator. (Rev: VOYA 10/97)

3489 Avi. *Who Was That Masked Man, Anyway?* (5–7). 1992, Orchard LB $17.99 (978-0-531-08607-0). In a story told through dialogue, 6th-grader Frankie lives through World War II by immersing himself in his beloved radio serials. (Rev: BCCB 10/92*; BL 8/92*; HB 3–4/93; SLJ 10/92*)

3490 Bartoletti, Susan Campbell. *The Boy Who Dared* (6–12). 2008, Scholastic $16.99 (978-0-439-68013-4). This compelling story of a German teenager who was executed for resisting the Nazis is based on a true story. (Rev: BL 2/15/08; SLJ 5/08)

3491 Bawden, Nina. *Carrie's War* (6–9). Illus. 1973, HarperCollins LB $14.89 (978-0-397-31450-8). Carrie relives her days during World War II when she and her brothers were evacuated to Wales. (Rev: BL 3/1/88)

3492 Benchley, Nathaniel. *Bright Candles: A Novel of the Danish Resistance* (6–9). 1974, HarperCollins $13.95 (978-0-06-020461-7). The Danish underground during World War II. (Rev: BL 7/88)

3493 Bloor, Edward. *London Calling* (6–9). 2006, Knopf $16.95 (978-0-375-83635-0). Seventh-grader Martin Conway travels back to World War II-era

London and uncovers hidden truths about the past while at the same time dealing in the present with problems plaguing his father; this is a multilayered novel combining magical realism and history. (Rev: BL 7/06; LMC 1/07; SLJ 9/06)

3494 Boyne, John. *The Boy in the Striped Pajamas: A Fable* (7–10). 2006, Random $15.95 (978-0-385-75106-3). The 9-year old son of a Nazi commandant befriends a Jewish boy he meets through the fence of a concentration camp. (Rev: BL 7/06; HB 9–10/06; LMC 1/07; SLJ 9/06)

3495 Bruchac, Joseph. *Code Talker* (6–9). 2005, Dial $16.99 (978-0-8037-2921-6). This inspiring novel chronicles the experiences of one of the Navajo code talkers who played a crucial role in the American victory in World War II. (Rev: BCCB 2/05; BL 2/15/05*; SLJ 5/05; VOYA 4/05)

3496 Buckvar, Felice. *Dangerous Dream* (6–9). 1998, Royal Fireworks paper $9.99 (978-0-88092-277-7). In postwar Germany, 13-year-old Hella, a concentration camp survivor, mistakenly believes that a new arrival in the infirmary is her father. (Rev: SLJ 4/99; VOYA 8/99)

3497 Bunting, Eve. *Spying on Miss Miller* (6–8). 1995, Clarion $15.00 (978-0-395-69172-4). During World War II in Belfast, Jessie, 13, believes her half-German teacher is a spy. (Rev: BL 3/15/95*; SLJ 5/95)

3498 Chan, Gillian. *A Foreign Field* (7–10). 2002, Kids Can $16.95 (978-1-55337-349-0). Friendship develops into love for 14-year-old Ellen and a young British pilot who is training at an air base near her home in Canada. (Rev: BCCB 12/02; BL 9/15/02; HBG 3/03; SLJ 11/02; VOYA 2/03)

3499 Cheng, Andrea. *Marika* (7–12). 2002, Front St. $16.95 (978-1-886910-78-2). Marika's earlier preoccupations disappear when the arrival of Nazis in 1944 Budapest changes her life. (Rev: BL 11/15/02; HB 11–12/02; HBG 3/03; SLJ 12/02; VOYA 2/03)

3500 Coerr, Eleanor. *Mieko and the Fifth Treasure* (4–7). 2003, Puffin paper $5.99 (978-0-698-11990-1). A Japanese girl believes that she will never draw again after she is injured during the atomic bomb attack on Nagasaki. (Rev: BCCB 4/93; BL 4/1/93*; SLJ 7/93)

3501 Copeland, Cynthia. *Elin's Island* (5–7). 2003, Millbrook LB $22.90 (978-0-7613-2522-2). Raised since infancy by lighthouse keepers, 13-year-old Elin is left on her own to tend the house and light on an eventful night in 1941. (Rev: BL 3/15/03; HBG 10/03; SLJ 7/03)

3502 Davies, Jacqueline. *Where the Ground Meets the Sky* (6–9). 2002, Marshall Cavendish $14.95 (978-0-7614-5105-1). During World War II, 12-year-old Hazel lives a lonely life in a compound in the New Mexico desert while her father works on a

top secret project, until she makes a friend and uncovers a secret. (Rev: BL 9/1/02; HBG 10/02; SLJ 4/02)

3503 DeJong, Meindert. *The House of Sixty Fathers* (6–9). Illus. by Maurice Sendak. 1956, HarperCollins LB $17.89 (978-0-06-021481-4); paper $5.95 (978-0-06-440200-2). In war-torn China, a young boy searches for his family as the Japanese invade his country.

3504 Drucker, Malka, and Michael Halperin. *Jacob's Rescue: A Holocaust Story* (6–10). 1993, Dell paper $4.99 (978-0-440-40965-6). The fictionalized true story of two Jewish children saved from the Holocaust in Poland by "righteous Gentiles." (Rev: BL 2/15/93; SLJ 5/93)

3505 Durbin, William. *The Winter War* (6–9). 2008, Random $15.99 (978-0-385-74652-6). When Russia invades Finland during World War II, Marko — who is an excellent skier despite his crippled leg — enlists in the Junior Civil Guard and endures unspeakable horrors in the winter of 1939–1940. (Rev: BL 11/15/07; LMC 4-5/08; SLJ 3/08)

3506 Elmer, Robert. *Into the Flames* (5–7). Series: Young Underground. 1995, Bethany paper $5.99 (978-1-55661-376-0). Danish twins are captured by the Gestapo while trying to rescue their uncle during World War II. (Rev: BL 5/15/95; SLJ 8/95)

3507 Fox, Robert Barlow. *To Be a Warrior* (6–9). 1997, Sunstone paper $12.95 (978-0-86534-253-8). A Navajo boy joins the marines after the bombing of Pearl Harbor and becomes one of the celebrated "code talkers." (Rev: BL 9/1/97)

3508 Friedman, D. Dina. *Escaping into the Night* (7–10). 2006, Simon & Schuster $14.95 (978-1-4169-0258-4). Based on true events, this is the story of Halina Rudowski's escape into the forest during a Nazi roundup of Jews, and her subsequent efforts to survive. (Rev: BL 1/1–15/06; SLJ 3/06; VOYA 4/06)

3509 Giff, Patricia Reilly. *Lily's Crossing* (5–8). 1997, Delacorte $15.95 (978-0-385-32142-6). During World War II, motherless Lily loses her father when he is sent to fight in France but becomes friendly with Albert, an orphaned Hungarian refugee. (Rev: BCCB 4/97; BL 2/1/97; HB 3–4/97; SLJ 2/97)

3510 Glatshteyn, Yankev. *Emil and Karl* (5–8). Ed. by Jeffrey Shandler. 2006, Roaring Brook $16.95 (978-1-59643-119-5). Two 9-year-old friends — one Jewish, one Aryan — try to elude the Nazis on the streets of Vienna shortly after Germany's invasion; a fast-paced, moving story initially published in 1940. (Rev: BL 4/15/06; SLJ 6/06*; VOYA 4/06)

3511 Graber, Janet. *Resistance* (7–10). 2005, Marshall Cavendish $15.95 (978-0-7614-5214-0). In this suspenseful World War II novel, 15-year-old

Marianne reluctantly joins her mother and brother in fighting for the French Resistance despite her fears that they will be found out by the German soldier billeted in their home. (Rev: BCCB 6/05; BL 5/15/05; SLJ 8/05)

3512 Graff, Nancy Price. *Taking Wing* (5–8). 2005, Clarion $15.00 (978-0-618-53591-0). A multilayered story set in 1942 Vermont and featuring 13-year-old Gus, who, over the course of the book, learns about prejudice, and about killing and death. (Rev: BL 5/15/05*; SLJ 5/05)

3513 Griffis, Molly Levite. *The Feester Filibuster* (4–8). 2002, Eakin $17.95 (978-1-57168-541-4); paper $8.95 (978-1-57168-694-7). John Allen Feester is determined to show he's not a spy in this sequel to *The Rachel Resistance* (2001). (Rev: BL 11/1/02; HBG 10/01)

3514 Gwaltney, Doris. *Homefront* (5–8). 2006, Simon & Schuster $15.95 (978-0-689-86842-9). A young girl must cope with the diverse effects of World War II on her Virginia farming family. (Rev: BCCB 10/06; BL 7/06; SLJ 7/06*)

3515 Hahn, Mary D. *Stepping on the Cracks* (5–8). 1991, Houghton $16.00 (978-0-395-58507-8); Avon paper $5.99 (978-0-380-71900-6). The compelling story of a 6th-grade girl during World War II and her difficult decision whether to help a pacifist deserter. (Rev: BCCB 12/91*; BL 10/15/91*; HB 11–12/91; SLJ 12/91*)

3516 Harlow, Joan Hiatt. *Shadows on the Sea* (7–10). 2003, Simon & Schuster $16.95 (978-0-689-84926-8). Fourteen-year-old Jill, staying with her grandmother in Maine in 1942, finds a pigeon carrying a message in German and suspects U-boats may be close. (Rev: BL 9/15/03; HBG 4/04; SLJ 9/03)

3517 Hertenstein, Jane. *Beyond Paradise* (6–10). 1999, Morrow $16.00 (978-0-688-16381-5). This historical novel recounts the horrors of life in Japanese internment camps in the Pacific during World War II as seen through the eyes of a missionary's daughter. (Rev: BCCB 9/99; BL 8/99; HBG 4/00; SLJ 9/99)

3518 Hinton, Nigel. *Time Bomb* (5–8). 2006, Tricycle $15.95 (978-1-58246-186-1). Coming of age in post-World War II London, four 12-year-old friends who have lost their trust in adults discover an unexploded German bomb and set in motion a chain of events. (Rev: SLJ 12/06)

3519 Hostetter, Joyce Moyer. *Blue* (4–7). 2006, Boyds Mills $16.95 (978-1-59078-389-4). When her father leaves for World War II, Ann Fay, the oldest of four children, struggles to keep up with the chores in their North Carolina home until polio strikes the community. (Rev: BL 2/15/06; SLJ 6/06)

3520 Hughes, Dean. *Soldier Boys* (7–9). 2001, Simon & Schuster $16.00 (978-0-689-81748-9). Parallel stories follow two teenage boys — one American, one German — through the horrors of World War II and the Battle of the Bulge. (Rev: BCCB 3/02; HB 1–2/02; HBG 3/02; SLJ 11/01; VOYA 2/02)

3521 Hull, Nancy L. *On Rough Seas* (6–9). 2008, Clarion $16.00 (978-0-618-89743-8). Alec becomes a galley boy on the *Britannia* to prove himself to his father and ends up helping in the evacuation at Dunkirk early in World War II. (Rev: BL 4/15/08; SLJ 5/08)

3522 Hunter, Bernice Thurman. *The Girls They Left Behind* (7–10). 2005, Fitzhenry & Whiteside paper $9.95 (978-1-55041-927-6). This coming-of-age novel, set in Toronto against the backdrop of World War II, paints a vivid portrait of what life was like for the teenage girls left behind on the home front. (Rev: BCCB 7–8/05; BL 5/15/05; SLJ 8/05; VOYA 8/05)

3523 Kacer, Kathy. *The Night Spies* (4–7). 2003, Second Story paper $5.95 (978-1-896764-70-2). Hiding from the Nazis, Gabi and her family can leave their cramped quarters only at night, but Gabi and her cousin Max manage to help the partisans. (Rev: BL 1/1–15/04; SLJ 3/04)

3524 Kadohata, Cynthia. *Weedflower* (5–8). 2006, Simon & Schuster $16.95 (978-0-689-86574-9). Sumiko and her Japanese American family are moved from their California flower farm to an internment camp in Arizona after the attack on Pearl Harbor; there she grows a garden and befriends a local Mojave boy. (Rev: BL 4/15/06*; HB 7–8/06; SLJ 7/06*) ⬤

3525 Klages, Ellen. *The Green Glass Sea* (4–7). 2006, Viking $16.99 (978-0-670-06134-1). In 1943, talented 10-year-old Dewey goes to live with her father at the Los Alamos compound, a tense place where she initially has trouble making friends. (Rev: BL 11/15/06; SLJ 11/06) ⬤

3526 Kositsky, Lynne. *The Thought of High Windows* (8–12). 2004, Kids Can $16.95 (978-1-55337-621-7). A Jewish refugee named Esther describes her experiences in France during World War II — lice and other discomforts, loneliness, longing for her family, her differences from the other refugees — and her involvement in the Resistance in this affecting novel based on true events. (Rev: HB 5–6/04; SLJ 5/04)

3527 Levitin, Sonia. *Journey to America* (5–8). Illus. by Charles Robinson. 1970, Macmillan paper $4.99 (978-0-689-71130-5). A Jewish mother and her three daughters flee Nazi Germany in 1938 and undertake a long and difficult journey to join their father in America. (Rev: BL 9/1/93)

3528 Lowry, Lois. *Number the Stars* (5–7). 1989, Houghton $16.00 (978-0-395-51060-5); Dell paper $5.99 (978-0-440-40327-2). The story of war-torn Denmark and best friends Annemarie Johansen and Ellen Rosen. Newbery Medal winner, 1990. (Rev: BCCB 3/89; BL 3/1/89; SLJ 3/89)

3529 McSwigan, Marie. *Snow Treasure* (4–7). Illus. by Andre Le Blanc. 1986, Scholastic paper $4.99 (978-0-590-42537-7). Children smuggle gold out of occupied Norway on their sleds.

3530 Manley, Joan B. *She Flew No Flags* (7–10). 1995, Houghton $16.00 (978-0-395-71130-9). A strongly autobiographical World War II novel about a 10-year-old's voyage from India to her new home in the United States and the people she meets on the ship. (Rev: BL 3/15/95; SLJ 4/95; VOYA 5/95)

3531 Matas, Carol. *Daniel's Story* (6–9). 1994, Scholastic paper $6.99 (978-0-590-46588-5). In this companion to an exhibit at the U.S. Holocaust Memorial Museum, Daniel symbolizes the millions of young people who suffered or died under Hitler's regime. (Rev: BL 5/15/93)

3532 Matas, Carol. *The Whirlwind* (6–9). 2007, Orca paper $8.95 (978-1-55143-703-3). Ben, a young German Jew, survives World War II and arrives in Seattle only to be faced with discrimination and hardship there. (Rev: BCCB 7-8/07; BL 3/1/07; SLJ 5/07)

3533 Mazer, Harry. *A Boy at War: A Novel of Pearl Harbor* (7–9). 2001, Simon & Schuster $15.00 (978-0-689-84161-3). Young Adam Pelko, new to Honolulu, is pressed into action on the morning of the attack on Pearl Harbor while trying to find his father, in this absorbing novel that also looks at relations with Japanese Americans. (Rev: BL 4/1/01; HB 5–6/01; HBG 10/01; SLJ 5/01; VOYA 6/01)

3534 Mazer, Harry. *A Boy No More* (7–9). 2004, Simon & Schuster $15.95 (978-0-689-85533-7). In this poignant sequel to *A Boy at War*, Adam Pelko, who lost his father in the Japanese bombing of Pearl Harbor, moves with his mother and sister from Hawaii to California where a Japanese American friend's request presents Adam with a moral dilemma. (Rev: BL 9/1/04; SLJ 9/04)

3535 Mazer, Harry. *Heroes Don't Run: A Novel of the Pacific War* (7–10). 2005, Simon & Schuster $15.95 (978-0-689-85534-4). In this gripping sequel to *A Boy at War* (2001) and *A Boy No More* (2004), 17-year-old Adam Pelko lies about his age to join the U.S. Marines and fights in a climactic battle with the Japanese on Okinawa. (Rev: BL 5/15/05; SLJ 8/05; VOYA 8/05)

3536 Mazer, Harry. *The Last Mission* (7–10). 1981, Dell paper $5.50 (978-0-440-94797-4). An underage Jewish American boy joins the Air Corps and is taken prisoner by the Germans. (Rev: BL 5/1/88)

3537 Melnikoff, Pamela. *Prisoner in Time: A Child of the Holocaust* (6–10). 2001, Jewish Publication Soc. paper $9.95 (978-0-8276-0735-4). Melnikoff combines history, fantasy, and Jewish legend in this story of 12-year-old Jan, in hiding from the Nazis in 1942 Czechoslovakia. (Rev: BL 10/1/01; SLJ 12/01)

3538 Morpurgo, Michael. *The Amazing Story of Adolphus Tips* (4–7). 2006, Scholastic $16.99 (978-0-439-79661-3). This is the story of Lily, a 12-year-old British girl who struggles with anger as her father is sent to war in 1943 and her family is relocated to make room for Allied rehearsals of the Normandy invasion. (Rev: BL 4/15/06; SLJ 8/06)

3539 Morpurgo, Michael. *The Mozart Question* (6–9). Illus. by Michael Foreman. 2008, Candlewick $15.99 (978-0-7636-3552-7). A famous violinist reveals the horrifying reason why he never plays Mozart, dating back to the Holocaust and his father's experiences in the death camps. (Rev: BL 3/15/08; SLJ 5/08)

3540 Myers, Walter Dean. *The Journal of Scott Pendleton Collins: A World War II Soldier* (5–9). Illus. Series: My Name Is America. 1999, Scholastic paper $10.95 (978-0-439-05013-5). Through a series of letters, readers get to know 17-year-old Collins, an American soldier who participates in the D-Day invasion of Europe. (Rev: BL 6/1–15/99; HBG 10/99; SLJ 7/99)

3541 Napoli, Donna Jo. *Fire in the Hills* (5–8). 2006, Dutton $16.99 (978-0-525-47751-8). In this fact-based sequel to *Stones in Water* (1997), 14-year-old Roberto returns to Italy after escaping from a Nazi prison camp and joins the resistance movement. (Rev: BL 9/1/06; SLJ 9/06)

3542 Orgel, Doris. *Daniel, Half Human: And the Good Nazi* (7–12). 2004, Simon & Schuster $17.95 (978-0-689-85747-8). Daniel and Armin, best friends in Germany in the early 1930s, both admire Hitler, but their friendship is tested when Daniel learns that he is half-Jewish. (Rev: BL 9/15/04; SLJ 12/04)

3543 Orlev, Uri. *The Island on Bird Street* (7–9). 1984, Houghton $16.00 (978-0-395-33887-2); paper $6.95 (978-0-395-61623-9). A young Jewish boy struggles to survive inside the Warsaw ghetto during World War II. (Rev: BL 11/1/88)

3544 Orlev, Uri. *The Man from the Other Side* (6–10). Trans. by Hillel Halkin. 1991, Houghton $16.00 (978-0-395-53808-1). The story of a teenager in Nazi-occupied Warsaw who helps desperate Jews despite his dislike of them. (Rev: BL 6/15/91*; SLJ 9/91*)

3545 Orlev, Uri. *Run, Boy, Run* (7–12). 2003, Houghton $15.00 (978-0-618-16465-3). A Polish boy survives the Holocaust by pretending to be a Catholic in this harrowing book full of historical detail. (Rev: BCCB 12/03; BL 10/15/03*; HB 11–12/03; HBG 4/04; SLJ 11/03; VOYA 12/03)

3546 Parker, Marjorie Hodgson. *David and the Mighty Eighth* (4–7). Illus. by Mark Postlethwaite. 2007, Bright Sky $17.95 (978-1-931721-93-6). David is sent to stay on his grandparents' farm in rural England and there befriends an American soldier stationed with the U.S. Eighth Air Force in this novel set in 1944. (Rev: BL 12/15/07)

3547 Parkinson, Curtis. *Domenic's War: A Story of the Battle of Monte Cassino* (6–9). 2006, Tundra paper $9.95 (978-0-88776-751-7). Domenic and his family are caught up in one of the most heartbreaking battles of World War II as Allied Forces and Germans fight at Monte Cassino in Italy, destroying the Benedictine monastery that was supposed to be a safe haven for Italian civilians. (Rev: SLJ 8/06)

3548 Patneaude, David. *Thin Wood Walls* (6–10). 2004, Houghton $16.00 (978-0-618-34290-7). In this poignant tale set against the backdrop of an America reeling from the Japanese attack on Pearl Harbor, Joe Hanada and his Japanese American family feel the rising tide of prejudice and are eventually sent to an internment camp in California. (Rev: BL 9/15/04; SLJ 10/04; VOYA 12/04)

3549 Pausewang, Gudrun. *Dark Hours* (5–8). Trans. from German by John Brownjohn. 2006, Annick $21.95 (978-1-55451-042-9). In Germany during the closing days of World War II, Gisela and her younger siblings become trapped in an air raid shelter after being separated from their mother and grandmother. (Rev: BL 11/1/06; SLJ 2/07)

3550 Pausewang, Gudrun. *Traitor* (7–10). 2006, Carolrhoda $16.95 (978-0-8225-6195-8). Young Anna, a German girl whose family is involved in the Nazi movement, shelters a Russian soldier at great risk to herself in this novel set in 1944. (Rev: BL 12/1/06; SLJ 11/06)

3551 Peet, Mal. *Tamar* (8–12). 2007, . With parallel narratives set in Nazi-occupied Holland and 1995 England, this award-winning novel is about resistance fighters in World War II and the curiosity of a granddaughter on inheriting a box of memorabilia. (Rev: BL 2/1/07*; SLJ 4/07*)

3552 Pressler, Mirjam. *Malka* (6–10). Trans. by Brian Murdoch. 2003, Putnam $18.99 (978-0-399-23984-7). Escaping from the Nazis in Poland, a mother is forced to leave one daughter behind in this story based on truth that alternates between the difficult experiences of the anguished mother and the abandoned child. (Rev: BL 4/1/03; HB 5–6/03*; HBG 10/03; SLJ 5/03; VOYA 10/03)

3553 Ray, Karen. *To Cross a Line* (7–10). 1994, Orchard LB $16.99 (978-0-531-08681-0). The story of a 17-year-old Jewish boy who is pursued by the Gestapo and encounters barriers in his desperate attempts to escape Nazi Germany. (Rev: BL 2/15/94; SLJ 6/94; VOYA 6/94)

3554 Richter, Hans Peter. *Friedrich* (7–9). Trans. by Edite Kroll. 1987, Penguin $5.99 (978-0-14-032205-7). The story of a Jewish boy and his family caught in the horror of the rise of the Nazi party and the Holocaust. (Rev: BL 4/1/90)

3555 Rodman, Mary Ann. *Jimmy's Stars* (5–8). 2008, Farrar $16.95 (978-0-374-33703-2). Ellie's beloved brother Jimmy's deferments run out and he is sent off to fight in World War II; when news arrives that he has been killed, Ellie finds it almost impossible to believe. (Rev: BL 4/1/08; SLJ 6/08)

3556 Ruby, Lois. *Shanghai Shadows* (7–10). 2006, Holiday $16.95 (978-0-8234-1960-9). Ilse and her Jewish family flee Vienna during the Nazi regime and settle in Japanese-occupied Shanghai, where they face many hardships and fears. (Rev: BL 11/1/06; SLJ 9/07)

3557 Salisbury, Graham. *House of the Red Fish* (5–8). 2006, Random $16.95 (978-0-385-73121-8). After his father is sent to an internment camp, Japanese American teen Tomi rallies the community to help raise his father's sunken fishing boat in this inspiring sequel to *Under the Blood-Red Sun* (2005). (Rev: BL 4/15/06; LMC 10/06; SLJ 8/06)

3558 Saroyan, William. *The Human Comedy* (7–12). 1973, Dell paper $6.50 (978-0-440-33933-5). Homer Macauley is growing up during World War II in America, part of the everyday life that is the human comedy.

3559 Say, Allen. *Music for Alice* (4–7). Illus. 2004, Houghton $17.00 (978-0-618-31118-7). Based on a real story, this is the moving portrait of a Japanese American couple who make the best of the challenges forced upon them during World War II. (Rev: BL 2/1/04; HB 5–6/04; SLJ 4/04)

3560 Serraillier, Ian. *The Silver Sword* (6–8). Illus. by C. Walter Hodges. 1959, Phillips $32.95 (978-0-87599-104-7). A World War II story of Polish children who are separated from their parents and finally reunited.

3561 Smith, Roland. *Elephant Run* (5–8). 2007, Hyperion $15.99 (978-1-4231-0402-5). During World War II, 14-year-old Nick is sent to his father's plantation in Burma to escape the London Blitz but ends up running from cruel Japanese occupiers in this suspenseful historical novel. (Rev: BL 2/15/08; SLJ 1/08)

3562 Spinelli, Jerry. *Milkweed* (6–10). 2003, Knopf LB $17.99 (978-0-375-91374-7). A boy who is uncertain of his ethnic background and adopts the name of Misha struggles to survive in the Warsaw ghetto and is befriended by a generous family. (Rev: BCCB 11/03; BL 10/15/03*; HB 11–12/03; HBG 4/04; SLJ 11/03)

3563 Tamar, Erika. *Good-bye, Glamour Girl* (7–10). 1984, HarperCollins LB $12.89 (978-0-397-32088-2). Liesl and her family flee from Hitler's Europe and Liesl must now become Americanized. (Rev: BL 1/1/85)

3564 Taylor, Marilyn. *Faraway Home* (5–8). 2000, O'Brien paper $7.95 (978-0-86278-643-4). Taken from his Austrian homeland by the Kindertransport, 13-year-old Karl is sent to County Down in Ireland where he endures the hardship of country life and the hostility of the locals. (Rev: BL 3/1/01)

3565 Thesman, Jean. *Molly Donnelly* (6–9). 1993, Houghton $16.00 (978-0-395-64348-8); Avon paper $4.50 (978-0-380-72252-5). The saga of a young girl growing up in Seattle during World War II and coping not only with the changes wrought by war but also with typical adolescent concerns. (Rev: BL 4/1/93; SLJ 5/93; VOYA 8/93)

3566 Toksvig, Sandi. *Hitler's Canary* (5–8). 2007, Roaring Brook $16.95 (978-1-59643-247-5). A Danish family decides to risk everything in order to help Jews escape the Nazis. (Rev: BL 1/1–15/07; SLJ 4/07)

3567 Tunnell, Michael O. *Brothers in Valor: A Story of Resistance* (6–10). 2001, Holiday $16.95 (978-0-8234-1541-0). Tunnell interweaves history and fiction in this account of three young Germans, members of the Mormon Church, who protest Hitler's actions and put their own lives at risk. (Rev: BL 5/1/01; HBG 3/02; SLJ 6/01; VOYA 8/01)

3568 Twomey, Cathleen. *Beachmont Letters* (8–12). 2003, Boyds Mills $16.95 (978-1-59078-050-3). During World War II, 17-year-old Eleanor reaches out to a soldier through the letters that she writes him although she holds back those that deal with her own pain and suffering. (Rev: BL 3/1/03; HBG 10/03; SLJ 3/03)

3569 Van Dijk, Lutz. *Damned Strong Love: The True Story of Willi G. and Stefan K.* (8–12). Trans. by Elizabeth D. Crawford. 1995, Holt $15.95 (978-0-8050-3770-8). Nazi persecution of homosexuals, based on the life of Stefan K., a Polish teenager. (Rev: BL 5/15/95; SLJ 8/95)

3570 Vander Els, Betty. *The Bombers' Moon* (5–7). 1992, Farrar paper $4.50 (978-0-374-30877-3). Missionary children Ruth and Simeon are evacuated to escape the Japanese invasion of China; they will not see their parents for four years. A sequel is *Leaving Point* (1987). (Rev: BCCB 9/85; BL 11/1/85; HB 9–10/85)

3571 Van Steenwyk, Elizabeth. *A Traitor Among Us* (6–9). 1998, Eerdmans $15.00 (978-0-8028-5150-5). Set in Nazi-occupied Holland in 1944, this thriller describes the resistance activities of 13-year-old Pieter including his hiding of a wounded American soldier. (Rev: BL 8/98; HBG 9/98; SLJ 8/98)

3572 Waters, Zack C. *Blood Moon Rider* (5–8). 2006, Pineapple $13.95 (978-1-56164-350-9). Abandoned by his stepmother after his father is killed in World War II, 14-year-old Harley Wallace survives an eventful journey to the home of a grandfather he's never met and there finds more excitement waiting. (Rev: SLJ 8/06)

3573 Watts, Irene. *Good-bye Marianne: A Story of Growing Up in Nazi Germany* (5–8). 1998, Tundra paper $7.95 (978-0-88776-445-5). In this autobiographical novel, 11-year-old Marianne Kohn is Jewish and experiencing Nazi persecution in 1938 Berlin when her parents decide to sent her to Britain as part of the Kindertransport rescue operation. (Rev: BCCB 7–8/98; BL 8/98; SLJ 8/98)

3574 Watts, Irene N. *Finding Sophie: A Search for Belonging in Postwar Britain* (5–8). 2002, Tundra paper $6.95 (978-0-88776-613-8). In this sequel to *Remember Me* (2000), World War II has ended and 13-year-old Sophie waits anxiously to hear news of her Jewish family in Germany, at the same time hoping she will not have to leave her happy life in London. (Rev: BL 1/1–15/03; SLJ 3/03; VOYA 8/03)

3575 Watts, Irene N. *Remember Me: A Search for Refuge in Wartime Britain* (5–8). 2000, Tundra paper $7.95 (978-0-88776-519-3). A heart-tugging story of an 11-year-old Jewish girl who, at the beginning of World War II, is transported from her home in Berlin to live in a Welsh mining town where she knows no one and speaks no English. (Rev: BL 12/1/00; SLJ 1/01; VOYA 2/01)

3576 Weston, Elise. *The Coastwatcher* (5–8). 2005, Peachtree $14.95 (978-1-56145-350-4). Vacationing on the South Carolina coast with his family in 1943, 11-year-old Hugh sees some signs that Germans are nearby and is determined to convince the doubting adults that he is right. (Rev: BL 11/1/05; SLJ 3/06)

3577 Whelan, Gloria. *Summer of the War* (6–9). 2006, HarperCollins $15.99 (978-0-06-008072-3). In the summer of 1942 a relaxing vacation in Michigan becomes stressful for 14-year-old Belle and her family when her snobby cousin comes to visit. (Rev: BL 4/15/06; SLJ 8/06)

3578 Williams, Laura E. *Behind the Bedroom Wall* (5–8). Illus. 1996, Milkweed paper $6.95 (978-1-57131-606-6). Korinna, a young Nazi, discovers that her parents are hiding a Jewish couple in wartime Germany. (Rev: BL 8/96; SLJ 9/96)

3579 Wilson, John. *Flames of the Tiger* (5–8). 2003, Kids Can $16.95 (978-1-55337-618-7). The horrors of World War II are seen through the eyes of 17-year-old Dieter, who with his younger sister is fleeing his native Germany as the war nears an end. (Rev: SLJ 1/04; VOYA 6/04) [813]

3580 Wilson, John. *Four Steps to Death* (7–9). 2005, Kids Can $16.95 (978-1-55337-704-7); paper

$6.95 (978-1-55337-705-4). The horrors of war are plain in this story of the Battle of Stalingrad in 1942, featuring 17-year-old Vasily, a Russian defending his soil; 18-year-old Conrad, a committed German tank officer; and 8-year-old Sergei, who is simply trying to survive. (Rev: SLJ 2/06; VOYA 2/06)

3581 Wiseman, Eva. *Kanada* (7–10). 2006, Tundra paper $9.95 (978-0-88776-729-6). Jutka, a young Hungarian Jew, loses her family at Auschwitz and barely survives herself; after she is released, she must decide whether to settle in Israel with a young man with whom she has fallen in love or to join relatives in Canada. (Rev: BL 2/15/07)

3582 Wiseman, Eva. *My Canary Yellow Star* (8–12). Illus. 2002, Tundra paper $7.95 (978-0-88776-533-9). Marta Weisz's privileged life as the daughter of a wealthy Jewish surgeon comes to an abrupt end when Hitler invades Hungary, but her life is spared through the efforts of Raoul Wallenberg. (Rev: BL 1/1–15/02; SLJ 6/02)

3583 Wolf, Joan M. *Someone Named Eva* (6–9). 2007, Clarion $16.00 (978-0-618-53579-8). At the age of 11, Milada, a blonde and blue-eyed Czechoslovakian girl, is seized by the Nazis and renamed Eva. (Rev: BL 9/15/07; SLJ 9/07)

3584 Wulffson, Don. *Soldier X* (8–12). 2001, Viking $16.99 (978-0-670-88863-4). After a battle in World War II, a 16-year-old German boy switches uniforms with a dead Russian in a desperate effort to survive. (Rev: BCCB 3/01; BL 5/1/01; HB 7–8/01; HBG 10/01; SLJ 3/01; VOYA 4/01)

3585 Yep, Laurence. *Hiroshima* (4–7). 1995, Scholastic paper $9.95 (978-0-590-20832-1). A powerful work of fiction that explores the bombing of Hiroshima in 1945 and its aftermath. (Rev: BCCB 6/95; BL 3/15/95*; HB 9–10/95; SLJ 5/95)

3586 Yolen, Jane. *The Devil's Arithmetic* (7–12). 1988, Puffin paper $6.99 (978-0-14-034535-3). This time-warp story transports a young Jewish girl back to Poland in the 1940s, conveying the horrors of the Holocaust. (Rev: BL 9/1/88; SLJ 11/88)

3587 Zeinert, Karen. *To Touch the Stars: A Story of World War II* (5–8). Series: Jamestown's American Portraits. 2000, Jamestown paper $5.95 (978-0-8092-0630-8). Eighteen-year-old Liz Erickson, who loves to fly airplanes, longs for independence while she investigates possible sabotage in the Women's Airforce Service pilots program. (Rev: SLJ 9/00)

3588 Zucker, Jonny. *The Bombed House* (5–8). Illus. by Paul Savage. Series: Keystone Books. 2006, Stone Arch LB $21.26 (978-1-59889-092-1). This fast-paced story, which will attract reluctant readers, features brothers Ned and Harry Jennings, who find a German soldier hiding in London during World War II. (Rev: SLJ 1/07)

KOREAN, VIETNAM, AND OTHER WARS

3589 Brown, Don. *Our Time on the River* (7–10). 2003, Houghton $15.00 (978-0-618-31116-3). Two brothers learn more about each other on a canoe trip that precedes the older brother's departure to fight in Vietnam. (Rev: BL 4/1/03; HBG 10/03; SLJ 4/03)

3590 Crist-Evans, Craig. *Amaryllis* (7–12). 2003, Candlewick paper $7.99 (978-0-7636-2990-8). Jimmy—who is facing problems at home including his alcoholic father's behavior—learns that his older brother Frank, off fighting in Vietnam, has become depressed and drug-addicted as a result of the war. (Rev: BCCB 1/04; BL 4/15/06; LMC 1/04; SLJ 4/05)

3591 Dorros, Arthur. *Under the Sun* (6–9). 2004, Abrams $16.95 (978-0-8109-4933-1). Thirteen-year-old Ehmet and his mother flee war-torn Sarajevo in search of refuge in Croatia; after soldiers kill his mother, the boy struggles on alone until he reaches a multiethnic orphan community. (Rev: BL 9/15/04; SLJ 12/04; VOYA 12/04)

3592 Dowell, Frances O'Roark. *Shooting the Moon* (4–8). 2008, Atheneum $16.99 (978-1-4169-2690-0). Jamie is surprised when her military father is not pleased about her big brother volunteering to go to Vietnam, until TJ sends home increasingly disturbing photographs of the war. (Rev: BL 3/15/08; SLJ 5/08)

3593 Hughes, Dean. *Search and Destroy* (7–10). 2006, Simon & Schuster $16.95 (978-0-689-87023-1). Rick Ward, who joined the army during the Vietnam War to escape his home life, returns from a tour of duty unable to adjust to normal life. (Rev: BL 2/1/06; SLJ 1/06; VOYA 2/06)

3594 Kadohata, Cynthia. *Cracker!* (6–9). 2007, Simon & Schuster $16.99 (978-1-4169-0637-7). Cracker is trained to be part of a military canine unit and becomes 17-year-old handler Rick's lifeline on the front lines of the Vietnam War. (Rev: BL 2/15/07; HB 3–4/07; LMC 4-5/07; SLJ 2/07) ⚫

3595 Myers, Walter Dean. *Patrol: An American Soldier in Vietnam* (4–8). Illus. by Ann Grifalconi. 2002, HarperCollins LB $17.89 (978-0-06-028364-3). A penetrating picture book for older readers told in narrative verse from the perspective of a teenage soldier in Vietnam. (Rev: BL 3/15/02; HB 7–8/02; HBG 10/02; SLJ 5/02)

3596 Nelson, Theresa. *And One for All* (7–12). 1989, Scholastic paper $16.95 (978-0-531-05804-6). Wing faces the disapproval of his best friend, a pacifist, when he decides to sign up to fight in Vietnam. (Rev: BL 4/15/06; SLJ 9/97)

3597 Rostkowski, Margaret I. *The Best of Friends* (7–12). 1989, HarperCollins $12.95 (978-0-06-025104-8). Three Utah teenagers have a growing interest in the Vietnam War and how it affects each of them. (Rev: BL 9/1/89; SLJ 9/89; VOYA 12/89)

3598 Sherlock, Patti. *Letters from Wolfie* (6–9). 2004, Penguin $16.99 (978-0-670-03694-3). In a moment of patriotic fervor, 13-year-old Mark lends his beloved dog Wolfie to the U.S. Army for use in its scout program in Vietnam; Mark's struggles to get his dog back play out against the backdrop of family disagreements about the war. (Rev: BL 7/04; SLJ 6/04; VOYA 8/04)

3599 White, Ellen Emerson. *The Journal of Patrick Seamus Flaherty: United States Marine Corps* (6–9). Illus. Series: Dear America. 2002, Scholastic $10.95 (978-0-439-14890-0). White uses Patrick's journal to portray the life of a soldier in Vietnam, describing the horrors of war and the questions surrounding American involvement in the conflict. (Rev: BL 7/02; HBG 10/02; SLJ 10/02)

3600 White, Ellen Emerson. *The Road Home* (8–12). 1995, Scholastic paper $15.95 (978-0-590-46737-7). This story re-creates a Vietnam War medical base in claustrophobic and horrific detail, and features army nurse Rebecca Phillips, from the Echo Company book series. (Rev: BL 1/15/95; SLJ 4/95; VOYA 4/95)

3601 White, Ellen Emerson. *Where Have All the Flowers Gone? The Diary of Molly Mackenzie Flaherty* (7–10). 2002, Scholastic paper $10.95 (978-0-439-14889-4). Molly, whose brother Patrick is off fighting in the Vietnam War, sees firsthand the casualties of the conflict while working in a Boston hospital. This book is a companion to the story of her brother, *The Journal of Patrick Seamus Flaherty, United States Marine Corps, Khe Sanh, Vietnam, 1968* (2002). (Rev: BL 4/15/06)

3602 Woodworth, Chris. *Georgie's Moon* (5–8). 2006, Farrar $16.00 (978-0-374-33306-5). Seventh-grader Georgie Collins lives her life waiting for her father to return from Vietnam, and is unable to accept his death at first. (Rev: BL 3/1/06; SLJ 4/06)

TWENTY-FIRST CENTURY CONFLICTS

3603 Myers, Walter Dean. *Sunrise over Fallujah* (8–11). 2008, Scholastic $17.99 (978-0-439-91624-0). Robin — nephew of Richie, the young black Vietnam War soldier in 1988's *Fallen Angels* — is serving in Operation Iraqi Freedom and now understands his uncle's reluctance to talk about his experiences. (Rev: BL 2/15/08; SLJ 4/08) 🔊

Horror Stories and the Supernatural

3604 Alphin, Elaine M. *Ghost Soldier* (5–7). 2001, Holt $16.95 (978-0-8050-6158-1). Alex, who has special powers, meets a Civil War ghost and helps

him discover what happened to his family. (Rev: BCCB 7–8/01; BL 8/01; HBG 10/02; SLJ 8/01; VOYA 8/01)

3605 Alter, Stephen. *The Phantom Isles* (4–7). Illus. 2007, Bloomsbury $16.95 (978-1-58234-738-7). Sixth-graders Courtney, Orion, and Ming join with the librarian of their Massachusetts town in an effort to free ghosts that have become trapped in books. (Rev: BL 2/1/07; SLJ 3/07)

3606 Anderson, Jodi Lynn. *May Bird Among the Stars* (4–7). 2006, Simon & Schuster $16.95 (978-0-689-86924-2). In this sequel to *May Bird and the Ever After*, 10-year-old May Bird and her cat Somber Kitty remain trapped in the Afterlife torn between finding a way home and helping to save Ever After from the villainous Bo Cleevil. (Rev: BL 12/1/06; SLJ 11/06)

3607 Anderson, M. T. *The Game of Sunken Places* (5–8). 2004, Scholastic $16.95 (978-0-439-41660-3). Brian and Gregory, both 13, find themselves embroiled in a dangerous and suspenseful game during a stay at the spooky mansion of Gregory's eccentric Uncle Max. (Rev: BL 4/15/04*; SLJ 9/04; VOYA 6/04)

3608 Asimov, Isaac, et al., eds. *Young Witches and Warlocks* (6–9). 1987, HarperCollins $12.95 (978-0-06-020183-8). A collection of 10 stories, most of them scary, about witches. (Rev: BL 7/87; SLJ 1/88)

3609 Avi. *Devil's Race* (7–9). 1984, Avon paper $3.50 (978-0-380-70406-4). John Proud is in constant battle with a demon who has the same name and was hanged in 1854.

3610 Avi. *The Seer of Shadows* (4–7). 2008, HarperCollins $16.99 (978-0-06-000015-8). Horace, a photographer's apprentice in 1872, is told by his boss to fake photographs of ghosts, but discovers that he has the ability to conjure actual ghosts with his camera. (Rev: BL 2/15/08; SLJ 2/08) 🔊

3611 Avi. *Something Upstairs: A Tale of Ghosts* (5–7). 1988, Orchard LB $16.99 (978-0-531-08382-6); Avon paper $5.99 (978-0-380-70853-6). Kenny moves into a house in Rhode Island that is haunted by the ghost of a slave who was murdered in 1800. (Rev: BCCB 9/88; BL 11/1/88; SLJ 10/88)

3612 Barrett, Tracy. *Cold in Summer* (4–7). 2003, Holt $16.95 (978-0-8050-7052-1). An enjoyable story about a lonely girl who slowly comes to realize that her new friend is a ghost. (Rev: BL 4/1/03; HB 5–6/03; HBG 10/03; SLJ 7/03; VOYA 6/03)

3613 Bawden, Nina. *Devil by the Sea* (6–8). 1976, HarperCollins $12.95 (978-0-397-31683-0). Is the strange old man Hilary sees at the beach really the devil?

3614 Belkom, Edo Van, ed. *Be Afraid! Tales of Horror* (8–12). 2000, Tundra $6.95 (978-0-88776-

496-7). Fifteen horror stories for and about teens feature sinister twists, hauntings, and violence. (Rev: BL 2/1/01; SLJ 3/01; VOYA 2/01)

3615 Bial, Raymond. *The Fresh Grave: And Other Ghostly Stories* (5–7). 1997, Midwest Traditions paper $13.95 (978-1-883953-22-5). A series of ten short, humorous ghost stories featuring two teenage heroes and their escapades in a small midwestern town. (Rev: SLJ 12/97)

3616 Bial, Raymond. *The Ghost of Honeymoon Creek* (5–8). Illus. 1999, Midwest Traditions paper $13.95 (978-1-883953-27-0). While investigating a strange light in a neighboring farm, 15-year-old Hank encounters a ghost. (Rev: BL 9/1/00; HBG 3/01; SLJ 1/01)

3617 Bradbury, Ray. *The Halloween Tree* (7–12). 1972, Knopf $19.95 (978-0-394-82409-3). Nine boys discover the true meaning — and horror — of Halloween.

3618 Bradman, Tony. *Voodoo Child* (4–7). Illus. by Martin Chatterton. Series: Tales of Terror. 2005, Egmont paper $7.50 (978-1-4052-1126-0). Megan hopes a voodoo doll will get rid of her father's girlfriend. Other scary titles in this series are *Deadly Game* and *Final Cut* (both 2005). (Rev: SLJ 6/05)

3619 Brown, Roberta Simpson. *The Queen of the Cold-Blooded Tales* (6–9). 1993, August House $19.95 (978-0-87483-332-4). A collection of 23 contemporary horror stories. (Rev: BL 9/1/93; VOYA 4/94)

3620 Bruchac, Joseph. *Whisper in the Dark* (5–8). 2005, HarperCollins $16.99 (978-0-06-058087-2). A frightening Native American legend seems to be coming true for 13-year-old Maddie, descended from a Narragansett chief. (Rev: BL 9/1/05; SLJ 8/05)

3621 Buckingham, Royce. *Demonkeeper* (4–7). 2007, Putnam $15.99 (978-0-399-24649-4). Nat lives in Seattle and looks after mostly harmless demons in his creaky old house — until the day when the scary Beast gets loose and Nat must try to retrieve this orphan-eating demon; this fast-paced romp will please reluctant readers. (Rev: SLJ 9/07)

3622 Buffie, Margaret. *The Dark Garden* (6–10). 1997, Kids Can $16.95 (978-1-55074-288-6). Thea, who suffers from amnesia after an accident, begins hearing voices, one of which belongs to a young woman who died tragically years before. (Rev: BL 10/15/97; HBG 3/98; SLJ 10/97)

3623 Bunting, Eve. *The Presence: A Ghost Story* (6–10). 2003, Clarion $16.00 (978-0-618-26919-8). Catherine, 17, who is still grieving over the death of a friend, finds solace in a handsome young man but at the same time senses that something isn't quite right. (Rev: BL 10/15/03; HBG 4/04; SLJ 10/03; VOYA 2/04)

3624 Byng, Georgia. *Molly Moon Stops the World* (5–8). 2004, HarperCollins LB $18.89 (978-0-06-051413-6). Molly Moon, a girl of unusual hypnotic powers, is dispatched to California to foil a power-mad hypnotist called Primo Cell. (Rev: BL 5/1/04; SLJ 5/04)

3625 Cabot, Meg. *Twilight* (7–10). Series: The Mediator. 2005, HarperCollins LB $16.89 (978-0-06-072468-9). Suze, deeply in love with a ghost named Jesse, faces a real dilemma when she discovers a way to give Jesse back his life that would mean losing him as a boyfriend; the sixth installment in the series. (Rev: SLJ 2/05)

3626 Cameron, Eleanor. *The Court of the Stone Children* (5–7). 1990, Puffin paper $6.99 (978-0-14-034289-5). Nina's move with her family to San Francisco is a disaster until she encounters a young ghost in a small museum.

3627 Cargill, Linda. *The Surfer* (6–9). 1995, Scholastic paper $3.99 (978-0-590-22215-0). After Nick meets Marina, a strange but beautiful surfer, he realizes that she is an immortal who has plotted against male members of his family for generations. (Rev: SLJ 1/96)

3628 Carter, Dean Vincent. *The Hand of the Devil* (8–11). 2006, Delacorte LB $9.99 (978-0-385-90386-8); paper $7.95 (978-0-385-73371-7). Young journalist Ashley Reeves travels to an island in Britain's Lake District to investigate an unusual mosquito and finds himself in dire straits. (Rev: BL 10/1/06; LMC 2/07; SLJ 1/07)

3629 Carus, Marianne, ed. *That's Ghosts for You: 13 Scary Stories* (4–7). Illus. by YongSheng Xuan. 2000, Front St. $15.95 (978-0-8126-2675-9). A fine collection of 13 chilling stories set in locations around the world, each with a supernatural twist. (Rev: BL 12/1/00; HBG 3/01; SLJ 12/00)

3630 Citra, Becky. *Never to Be Told* (6–12). 2006, Orca paper $7.95 (978-1-55143-567-1). A ghost story set in a small town called Cold Creek and featuring a 12-year-old girl named Asia who faces upheavals in her life. (Rev: SLJ 12/06)

3631 Clarke, Judith. *Starry Nights* (5–9). 2003, Front St. $15.95 (978-1-886910-82-9). When Jess's family moves to a new house, a ghost seems to be involved in the family's emotional upheavals. (Rev: BL 6/1–15/03; HB 9–10/03; HBG 4/04)

3632 Colfer, Eoin. *The Wish List* (6–9). 2003, Hyperion $16.95 (978-0-7868-1863-1). Meg's mix of good and bad deeds leaves her poised between Heaven and Hell, and she is sent on a mission that will tip the balance one way or the other. (Rev: BL 10/1/03; SLJ 12/03*)

3633 Cooney, Caroline B. *Night School* (7–10). 1995, Scholastic paper $3.50 (978-0-590-47878-6). Four California teens enroll in a mysterious night school course and encounter an evil instructor and their own worst character defects. (Rev: BL 5/1/95)

3634 Coville, Bruce. *Oddly Enough* (6–9). 1994, Harcourt $15.95 (978-0-15-200093-6). Nine short horror stories involving blood drinking, elves, unicorns, ghosts, werewolves, and executioners. (Rev: BL 10/1/94; SLJ 12/94; VOYA 2/95)

3635 Cray, Jordan. *Gemini 7* (6–10). 1997, Simon & Schuster paper $4.50 (978-0-689-81432-7). In this horror story, Jonah Lanier begins to realize that his new friend, Nicole, might be responsible for the mysterious disasters that are befalling his family and other friends. (Rev: SLJ 1/98)

3636 Creedon, Catherine. *Blue Wolf* (4–8). 2003, HarperCollins LB $16.89 (978-0-06-050869-2). Fantasy lurks around each corner of this story of Jamie, a 14-year-old for whom running is a retreat from life and who sometimes feels that wolves are right at his heels. (Rev: BCCB 1/04; BL 11/15/03; SLJ 10/03)

3637 Crowley, Bridget. *Step into the Dark* (5–7). 2003, Hodder & Stoughton paper $8.95 (978-0-340-84416-8). This ghost story is set in a theater and conveys the attraction of the stage. (Rev: BL 12/1/03)

3638 Cusick, Richie Tankersley. *The House Next Door* (6–12). 2002, Simon & Schuster paper $4.99 (978-0-7434-1838-6). Emma dares to spend a night in a haunted house and becomes caught up in a struggle to free a spirit from the past in this tale of supernatural suspense. (Rev: BL 1/1–15/02; SLJ 2/02; VOYA 6/02)

3639 Del Negro, Janice M. *Passion and Poison: Tales of Shape-Shifters, Ghosts, and Spirited Women* (5–8). Illus. by Vince Natale. 2007, Marshall Cavendish $16.99 (978-0-7614-5361-1). A collection of seven creepy supernatural tales, each featuring females who face peril and challenges. (Rev: BL 9/1/07; SLJ 12/07)

3640 Delaney, Joseph. *Curse of the Bane* (6–9). Illus. by Patrick Arrasmith. Series: The Last Apprentice. 2006, Greenwillow $16.99 (978-0-06-076621-4). On their second adventure Tom and the Spook encounter the Bane and also fall afoul of the Quisitor; when the Spook gets arrested, it's up to Tom and his friend Alice, to save him. (Rev: BL 8/06; SLJ 11/06)

3641 Delaney, Joseph. *Night of the Soul Stealer* (6–9). Series: Last Apprentice. 2007, Greenwillow $16.99 (978-0-06-076624-5). Tom Ward, the 13-year-old apprentice to Mr. Gregory (a Spook who rids the country of ghosts, witches, and boggarts) must decide what to do when the former apprentice, Morgan, tortures his deceased father from beyond the grave. (Rev: BL 8/07; SLJ 2/08) 🐱

3642 Delaney, Joseph. *Revenge of the Witch* (5–8). Illus. by Patrick Arrasmith. Series: The Last Apprentice. 2005, Greenwillow LB $17.89 (978-0-06-076619-1). A scary story in which young Tom, seventh son of a seventh son, becomes an apprentice spook and must protect the people from ghouls, boggarts, and beasties. (Rev: BCCB 10/05; BL 8/05*; HB 11–12/05; HBG 4/06; LMC 3/06; SLJ 11/05; VOYA 8/06)

3643 de Lint, Charles. *The Blue Girl* (8–11). 2004, Penguin $17.99 (978-0-670-05924-9). Imogene, determined to turn over a new leaf at her new high school, strikes up an alliance with loner Maxine and meets the ghost of a former pupil, foreshadowing a struggle between an evil underworld and an inhospitable reality. (Rev: BL 11/15/04; SLJ 11/04; VOYA 12/04)

3644 Duncan, Lois. *Gallows Hill* (6–9). 1997, Bantam paper $4.99 (978-0-440-22725-0). Sarah is alarmed when her harmless "future telling" turns out to be true and she begins dreaming of the Salem witch trials. (Rev: BL 4/15/97; HBG 3/98; SLJ 5/97; VOYA 4/97)

3645 Duncan, Lois. *Locked in Time* (7–10). 1985, Dell paper $4.99 (978-0-440-94942-8). Nore's father marries into a family that somehow never seems to age. (Rev: BL 7/85; SLJ 11/85)

3646 Duncan, Lois. *Stranger with My Face* (7–10). 1984, Dell paper $5.50 (978-0-440-98356-9). A girl encounters her evil twin, who wishes to take her place.

3647 Duncan, Lois. *Summer of Fear* (7–10). 1976, Dell paper $5.50 (978-0-440-98324-8). An orphaned cousin who comes to live with Rachel's family is really a witch.

3648 Dunkle, Clare B. *By These Ten Bones* (6–9). 2005, Holt $16.95 (978-0-8050-7496-3). Maddie, the weaver's daughter in a medieval Scottish village, finds herself drawn to a mysterious young wood carver who has newly arrived in her town only to discover that he is in fact a werewolf. (Rev: BCCB 5/05; BL 5/1/05; SLJ 6/05; VOYA 6/05)

3649 Enthoven, Sam. *The Black Tattoo* (5–8). 2006, Penguin $19.99 (978-1-59514-114-9). In this action-packed fantasy epic set in London and Hell, three teenage friends — Esme, Charlie, and Jack — work together to defeat a demonic entity that has taken possession of Charlie. (Rev: BL 9/1/06; SLJ 1/07) 🐱

3650 Fahy, Thomas. *The Unspoken* (8–12). 2008, Simon & Schuster $15.99 (978-1-4169-4007-4). Allison escaped from a deadly cult years ago, but today she and other teenage survivors are facing mysterious and gory deaths. (Rev: BL 1/1–15/08; LMC 4–5/08; SLJ 4/08)

3651 Falcone, L. M. *Walking with the Dead* (5–8). 2005, Kids Can $16.95 (978-1-55337-708-5). Alex finds himself entangled in the world of Greek mythology when a mummy in his father's museum awakens to take care of some unfinished business in the underworld. (Rev: BL 3/15/05; SLJ 6/05)

3652 Fleischman, Sid. *The Entertainer and the Dybbuk* (6–9). 2007, Greenwillow $16.99 (978-0-06-134445-9). In postwar Europe, Freddie, an ex-GI who's a struggling ventriloquist, meets the ghost of a Jewish child killed in the Holocaust and agrees to help him find the SS officer who murdered him in exchange for help with his act. (Rev: BL 9/1/07; SLJ 8/07)

3653 Gabhart, Ann. *Wish Come True* (7–10). 1988, Avon paper $2.50 (978-0-380-75653-7). Lyssie receives as a gift a mirror that grants her wishes. (Rev: VOYA 6/89)

3654 Garretson, Jerri. *The Secret of Whispering Springs* (7–12). 2002, Ravenstone paper $6.99 (978-0-9659712-4-9). A ghost and a mysterious stranger alert Cassie to potential danger, and a potential fortune, in this suspenseful adventure. (Rev: BL 8/02; SLJ 8/02)

3655 Gifaldi, David. *Yours Till Forever* (7–10). 1989, HarperCollins LB $13.89 (978-0-397-32356-2). In this easily read novel, a high school senior sees disturbing similarities between his friends and his dead parents. (Rev: BL 10/1/89; SLJ 11/89; VOYA 2/90)

3656 Gonick, Larry. *Attack of the Smart Pies* (4–7). Illus. by author. 2005, Cricket $15.95 (978-0-8126-2740-4). This complex novel with graphic elements blends fantasy, horror, mystery, and humor in the story of Emma, a 12-year-old orphan who flees from her threatening foster father and finds herself in Kokonino County, land of the New Muses. (Rev: SLJ 6/05)

3657 Gorog, Judith. *Please Do Not Touch* (6–12). 1995, Scholastic paper $3.50 (978-0-590-46683-7). The reader enters a different fantasy for each of the 11 horror stories. (Rev: BL 9/1/93; VOYA 12/93)

3658 Gorog, Judith. *When Nobody's Home* (6–12). 1996, Scholastic paper $15.95 (978-0-590-46862-6). A collection of 15 terrifying (supposedly true) tales on the theme of baby-sitting. (Rev: BL 5/1/96; SLJ 4/96; VOYA 12/96)

3659 Grabenstein, Chris. *The Crossroads* (5–8). Illus. 2008, Random $16.99 (978-0-375-84697-7). Zack sees creepy faces in trees in this ghost story full of action, suspense, and likable characters. (Rev: BL 5/1/08)

3660 Griffin, Adele. *Vampire Island* (4–7). 2007, Putnam $14.99 (978-0-399-23785-0). Three Manhattan youngsters — vegetarian vampire siblings Lexington, Madison, and Hudson — try to behave like normal people but their respective vampire traits keep getting in the way in this lighthearted, action-packed story. (Rev: BL 8/07; LMC 11-12/08; SLJ 8/07)

3661 Hahn, Mary D. *Look for Me by Moonlight* (7–10). 1995, Clarion $16.00 (978-0-395-69843-3). A 16-year-old girl seeking friendship meets a boy whose attention has dangerous strings attached. (Rev: BL 3/15/95; SLJ 5/95)

3662 Hahn, Mary D. *Wait Till Helen Comes: A Ghost Story* (5–7). 1986, Houghton $15.00 (978-0-89919-453-0); Avon paper $5.99 (978-0-380-70442-2). Things go from bad to worse for Molly and Michael and their stepsister Heather when Heather becomes involved in a frightening relationship with the ghost of a dead child. (Rev: BCCB 10/86; BL 9/1/86; SLJ 10/86)

3663 Hahn, Mary Downing. *All the Lovely Bad Ones* (4–7). 2008, Clarion $16.00 (978-0-618-85467-7). Travis and Corey encounter ghosts at their grandmother's bed-and-breakfast, which was a poor house long ago. (Rev: BL 5/1/08; SLJ 5/08)

3664 Hahn, Mary Downing. *Deep and Dark and Dangerous* (5–8). 2007, Clarion $16.00 (978-0-618-66545-7). While spending the summer at her aunt's cottage in Maine, 13-year-old Ali meets a mysterious girl named Sissie who seems to know a great deal about a tragic accident that occurred three decades earlier. (Rev: BL 3/15/07; SLJ 5/07)

3665 Hahn, Mary Downing. *Witch Catcher* (4–7). 2006, Clarion $16.00 (978-0-618-50457-2). When Jen and her widowed father move into a rambling old mansion, the 12-year-old girl disregards warnings and investigates an old stone tower behind the house. (Rev: BL 6/1–15/06; SLJ 8/06)

3666 Hamilton, Virginia. *Sweet Whispers, Brother Rush* (7–10). 1982, Putnam $21.99 (978-0-399-20894-2). A 14-year-old girl who cares for her older retarded brother meets a charming ghost who reveals secrets of her past.

3667 Harper, Suzanne. *The Secret Life of Sparrow Delaney* (7–10). 2007, Greenwillow $16.99 (978-0-06-113158-5). Sparrow is a reluctant psychic who must face up to her abilities when she begins seeing a ghost named Luke, the dead brother of a friend at school, who needs help. (Rev: BCCB 9/07; BL 7/07; SLJ 11/07)

3668 Hawes, Louise. *Rosey in the Present Tense* (8–12). 1999, Walker $15.95 (978-0-8027-8685-2). After the death of his girlfriend, Rosey, 17-year-old Franklin can't stop living in the past until the ghost of Rosey and his family and friends help him accept his loss and begin to think of the present. (Rev: BL 4/1/99; HBG 9/99; SLJ 5/99; VOYA 10/99)

3669 Hightman, J. P. *Spirit* (6–10). 2008, Harper-Teen $16.99 (978-0-06-085063-0). In 1892 Massachusetts a 17-year-old married couple, ghost-hunters Tess and Tobias Goodraven, very nearly meet their match in a murderous witch. (Rev: BL 8/08; SLJ 9/08)

3670 Hodges, Margaret, ed. *Hauntings: Ghosts and Ghouls from Around the World* (5–8). Illus. by David Wenzel. 1991, Little, Brown $16.95 (978-0-316-36796-7). A diverse collection of 16 familiar and lesser-known tales about the supernatural. (Rev: BL 11/15/91; HB 11–12/91; SLJ 11/91) [398.2]

3671 Hoffman, Nina Kiriki. *Spirits That Walk in Shadow* (8–11). 2006, Viking $17.99 (978-0-670-06071-9). In alternating narratives, roommates Kim and Jaimie describe their story; Jaimie, blessed with unusual powers, is determined to rid Kim of a tiresome "viri." (Rev: BL 11/1/06; SLJ 1/07)

3672 Horowitz, Anthony. *Horowitz Horror: Stories You'll Wish You'd Never Read* (6–9). 2006, Philomel $9.99 (978-0-399-24489-6). A collection of nine creepy tales — about a camera that kills its subjects, a haunted bathtub that drips blood, and more; also use *More Horowitz Horror* (2007). (Rev: BL 9/1/06; SLJ 10/06)

3673 Horowitz, Anthony. *Raven's Gate* (5–8). Series: The Gatekeepers. 2005, Scholastic $17.95 (978-0-439-67995-4). Faced with a choice between jail and life in a remote Yorkshire village, 14-year-old Matt chooses the latter, unaware that he's about to enter a world of frightening evil. (Rev: BL 7/05*; SLJ 7/05; VOYA 10/05)

3674 Jacobs, Deborah Lynn. *Powers* (7–10). 2006, Roaring Brook $16.95 (978-1-59643-112-6). When Gwen meets Adrian they feel a powerful connection between themselves, and their powers — hers to see future tragedies and his to read others' minds — are increased; but can they learn to trust each other and work together? (Rev: BL 8/06; LMC 2/07; SLJ 10/06; VOYA)

3675 Jacques, Brian. *Seven Strange and Ghostly Tales* (4–7). 1991, Avon paper $3.99 (978-0-380-71906-8). Seven genuinely scary stories with touches of humor. (Rev: BCCB 12/91; BL 1/1/91*; HB 5–6/92; SLJ 12/91)

3676 Jarvis, Robin. *Thomas: Book Three of the Deptford Histories* (5–8). 2006, Chronicle $17.95 (978-0-8118-5412-2). This prequel to the Deptford Mice trilogy, written as the memoirs of an old sea mouse, contains plenty of battles, storms and heroic deeds and can be read as a stand-alone novel. (Rev: BL 1/1–15/07)

3677 Jennings, Patrick. *Wish Riders* (5–8). 2006, Hyperion $15.99 (978-1-4231-0010-2). Combining historical fiction and fantasy, this tale of transformation focuses on Edith, 15, who slaves with four other foster children, cooking and cleaning in a Depression-era logging camp until a mysterious seed pod grows into five horses that spirit the children away to forest adventures. (Rev: BL 1/1–15/07)

3678 Johnson, Charles. *Pieces of Eight* (5–7). Illus. by Jennie Anne Nelson. 1989, Discovery $9.95 (978-0-944770-00-9). David and Mitchell rouse a sea captain's ghost and get to meet Blackbeard the pirate. (Rev: BL 3/15/89)

3679 Johnson, Maureen. *Devilish* (8–11). 2006, Penguin $16.99 (978-1-59514-060-9). Jane, a high school senior, finds out that her best friend Ally has sold her soul to a demon in exchange for popularity; Jane's efforts to help lead her into real danger. (Rev: BL 10/15/06; HB 11–12/06; SLJ 10/06)

3680 Jones, Claudia. *Riding Out the Storm* (6–8). 2006, Llewellyn paper $8.95 (978-0-7387-0867-6). Thirteen-year-old Emily attends therapy after a near-drowning incident gives her constant nightmares; here she uncovers that she is the reincarnation of a man who died in a boating accident and goes on a search for more information on her past life. (Rev: SLJ 5/06)

3681 Jones, Diana Wynne. *The Game* (5–8). 2007, Penguin $11.99 (978-0-14-240718-9). Hayley, an orphan who has been raised by her difficult grandparents, now finds herself amid a large, happy family in Ireland with cousins who love to play in the mythosphere, a land of stories where secrets about her past reside. (Rev: BL 12/1/06; SLJ 3/07)

3682 Keehn, Sally M. *Gnat Stokes and the Foggy Bottom Swamp Queen* (5–8). 2005, Putnam $16.99 (978-0-399-24287-8). This fantasy, set in the Appalachian mountains, features a 12-year-old girl named Gnat who faces swamp creatures and spells in her quest to rescue Goodlow Pryce. (Rev: BL 3/1/05; SLJ 4/05)

3683 Kehret, Peg. *Ghost's Grave* (5–8). 2005, Dutton $16.99 (978-0-525-46162-3). Josh expects to be bored when he stays in his aunt's old house, but the ghost of a coal miner who died in 1903 livens things up. (Rev: BL 5/15/05; SLJ 10/05)

3684 Kelleher, Victor. *Del-Del* (7–12). Illus. 1992, Walker $17.95 (978-0-8027-8154-3). A family believes its son is possessed by an evil alien. (Rev: BL 3/1/92; SLJ 6/92)

3685 Klause, Annette Curtis. *The Silver Kiss* (8–12). 1992, Bantam paper $5.50 (978-0-440-21346-8). A teenage girl, beset with personal problems, meets a silver-haired boy who is a vampire in this suspenseful, sometimes gory, novel. (Rev: BL 10/15/90; SLJ 9/90)

3686 Koontz, Dean. *Life Expectancy* (8–12). 2004, Bantam $27.00 (978-0-553-80414-0). Jimmy is stalked by a mad clown from the moment of his birth in this novel that spoofs cinematic and literary conventions. (Rev: BL 11/1/04)

3687 Langrish, Katherine. *Troll Fell* (5–7). 2004, HarperCollins $16.99 (978-0-06-058304-0). Sent to live with his evil twin uncles after his father's death, 12-year-old Peer Ulfsson seeks a way to foil their plan to sell children to the trolls. (Rev: BL 4/15/04*; SLJ 7/04; VOYA 6/04)

3688 Langston, Laura. *Exit Point* (8–12). 2006, Orca $14.95 (978-1-55143-525-1); paper $7.95 (978-1-55143-505-3). When Logan wakes up dead, he watches over his family in spirit form, and commits himself to saving his younger sister from abuse before he moves on forever; for reluctant readers. (Rev: SLJ 8/06)

3689 Lubar, David. *The Curse of the Campfire Weenies: And Other Warped and Creepy Tales* (5–7). 2007, Tor $15.95 (978-0-7653-1807-7). Thirty-five creepy stories combine scariness and dark humor in a way that will attract reluctant readers. (Rev: SLJ 12/07)

3690 Lubar, David. *True Talents* (5–8). 2007, Tor $17.95 (978-0-7653-0977-8). In this sequel to *Hidden Talents* (1999), the paranormally gifted student friends from Edgeview Alternative School flex their extraordinary powers in a series of interconnected adventures; memos, e-mails, and illustrations add to the action-packed narrative. (Rev: BL 3/15/07; SLJ 4/07)

3691 MacDonald, Caroline. *Hostilities: Nine Bizarre Stories* (7–10). 1994, Scholastic paper $13.95 (978-0-590-46063-7). A collection of nine tales with strange, unsettling themes and Australian locales. (Rev: BL 1/15/94; SLJ 3/94; VOYA 10/94)

3692 McKissack, Patricia C. *The Dark-Thirty: Southern Tales of the Supernatural* (5–8). Illus. 1992, Knopf $17.99 (978-0-679-91863-9). Ten original stories, rooted in African American history and the oral-storytelling tradition, deal with such subjects as slavery, belief in "the sight," and the Montgomery bus boycott. (Rev: BCCB 12/92; BL 12/15/92; HB 3–4/93; SLJ 12/92*)

3693 Mahy, Margaret, and Susan Cooper. *Don't Read This! And Other Tales of the Unnatural* (7–10). 1998, Front St. $15.95 (978-1-886910-22-5). Great stories of ghosts and the supernatural are included in this international collection that represents some of the top writers of scary fiction at work today. (Rev: BL 4/1/99; HBG 9/99; SLJ 7/99; VOYA 6/99)

3694 Matthews, L. S. *The Outcasts* (7–10). 2007, Delacorte $15.99 (978-0-385-73367-0). Five misfit students wonder why they have been chosen for a field trip to a mysterious estate — until they discover that they must endure surreal trials to make it back alive. (Rev: BL 11/15/07; SLJ 1/08)

3695 Medearis, Angela Shelf. *Haunts: Five Hair-Raising Tales* (4–7). Illus. by Trina S. Hyman. 1996, Holiday $15.95 (978-0-8234-1280-8). Five stories that contain elements of horror and the supernatural. (Rev: BL 2/1/97; SLJ 4/97)

3696 Meyer, Stephenie. *Eclipse* (8–11). Series: Twilight. 2007, Little, Brown $18.99 (978-0-316-16020-9). Human teen Bella and vampire Edward continue their relationship in the face of opposition from werewolf Jacob (who's in love with Bella too) while Bella also faces decisions about college and her future. (Rev: BL 9/15/07; SLJ 10/07) 🐾

3697 Meyer, Stephenie. *New Moon* (8–11). Series: Twilight. 2006, Little, Brown $17.99 (978-0-316-16019-3). In this sequel to *Twilight* (2005), Bella laments boyfriend Edward's departure and engages in dangerous behavior. (Rev: BL 7/06; SLJ 8/06) 🐾

3698 Moloney, James. *Trapped* (4–8). Illus. by Shaun Tan. 2008, Stone Arch LB $16.95 (978-1-59889-863-7). David, a skateboarder, can't resist exploring a huge drainpipe even though he knows that two boys once died there in this illustrated book that will appeal to reluctant readers. (Rev: BL 12/15/07; SLJ 2/08)

3699 Montes, Marisa. *A Circle of Time* (6–8). 2002, Harcourt $17.00 (978-0-15-202626-4). In a coma after an accident, 14-year-old Allison Blair travels back in time to 1906 California to help two young people in trouble there. (Rev: BL 5/1/02; HBG 10/02; SLJ 8/02; VOYA 6/02)

3700 Morpurgo, Michael, ed. *Ghostly Haunts* (6–9). 1997, Trafalgar paper $16.95 (978-1-85793-833-3). Some of Britain's best writers for young people, including Dick King-Smith and Joan Aiken, have contributed to this collection of supernatural stories. (Rev: BL 3/15/97)

3701 Myracle, Lauren. *Rhymes with Witches* (8–11). 2005, Abrams $16.95 (978-0-8109-5859-3). Invited to join a super-popular clique at her high school, Jane is at first flattered but soon discovers that she's involved in something sinister. (Rev: BCCB 5/05; BL 3/15/05; SLJ 4/05)

3702 Nance, Andrew. *Daemon Hall* (7–10). Illus. by Coleman Polhemus. 2007, Holt $16.95 (978-0-8050-8171-8). Three teenaged writers win a night at a haunted mansion with a horror writer, and each contestant must tell a spooky story by candlelight. Will all the contestants survive? (Rev: BCCB 6/07; BL 7/07; SLJ 12/07)

3703 Naylor, Phyllis Reynolds. *Jade Green: A Ghost Story* (5–8). 2000, Simon & Schuster $16.00 (978-0-689-82005-2). Set in South Carolina about 100 years ago, this ghost story involves Judith Sparrow, age 15, and the mystery surrounding the gruesome death of a girl named Jade Green. (Rev: BL 12/15/99; HBG 10/00; SLJ 2/00; VOYA 6/00)

3704 Newbery, Linda. *Lost Boy* (5–8). 2008, Random $15.99 (978-0-375-84574-1). New to the town of Hay-on-Wye in Wales, Matt feels the presence of a boy who died there several years before. (Rev: BCCB 3/08; BL 4/1/08; LMC 4-5/08; SLJ 3/08)

3705 Nixon, Joan Lowery. *Whispers from the Dead* (7–12). 1991, Bantam paper $4.99 (978-0-440-20809-9). After being saved from drowning, Sarah is able to communicate with dead spirits. (Rev: BL 9/15/89; SLJ 9/89; VOYA 12/89)

3706 Norton, Andre, and Phyllis Miller. *House of Shadows* (7–9). 1984, Tor paper $2.95 (978-0-8125-4743-6). While staying with a great-aunt, three children learn about the family curse.

3707 Noyes, Deborah. *Gothic! Ten Original Dark Tales* (7–10). 2005, Candlewick $15.99 (978-0-7636-2243-5). Ten Gothic tales by contemporary authors embody the dark fantasy and the fairy tale aspects of the genre as well as offering supernatural horror plus humor. (Rev: BL 10/15/04; SLJ 1/05)

3708 Noyes, Deborah, ed. *The Restless Dead: Ten Original Stories of the Supernatural* (8–12). 2007, Candlewick $16.99 (978-0-7636-2906-9). Vampires, corpses, ghosts, and more appear in these scary stories by well-known YA authors. (Rev: BL 5/15/07; HB 9–10/07; LMC 11/07; SLJ 9/07)

3709 Olson, Arielle North, and Howard Schwartz, eds. *Ask the Bones: Scary Stories from Around the World* (5–9). 1999, Viking $16.99 (978-0-670-87581-8). A collection of 22 scary stories about subjects ranging from ghosts to witches and voodoo spells, accompanied by spooky illustrations. (Rev: BCCB 4/99; BL 5/1/99; HB 5–6/99; HBG 10/99; SLJ 4/99)

3710 Peck, Richard. *The Ghost Belonged to Me* (5–8). 1997, Viking paper $5.99 (978-0-14-038671-4). Richard unwillingly receives the aid of his nemesis, Blossom Culp, in trying to solve the mystery behind the ghost of a young girl. Two sequels are *Ghosts I Have Been* (1977); *The Dreadful Future of Blossom Culp* (1983).

3711 Pendleton, Thomas. *Mason* (8–10). 2008, HarperCollins paper $8.99 (978-0-06-117736-1). Cruel and violent Gene terrorizes his brother Mason, as well as Mason's friends, until Mason begins to use his mind to retaliate. (Rev: BL 5/15/08)

3712 Pines, T., ed. *Thirteen: 13 Tales of Horror by 13 Masters of Horror* (8–12). 1991, Scholastic paper $6.99 (978-0-590-45256-4). Popular horror writers' stories of revenge, lust, and betrayal. (Rev: BL 3/1/92)

3713 Pipe, Jim. *The Werewolf* (4–7). Illus. Series: In the Footsteps Of. 1996, Millbrook LB $24.90 (978-0-7613-0450-0). A horror story in which Bernard, a werewolf, commits terrible acts under the influence of a full moon. (Rev: SLJ 7/96)

3714 Poe, Edgar Allan. *The Cask of Amontillado* (8–12). Illus. by Gary Kelley. Series: Creative Short Stories. 2008, Creative Education LB $19.95 (978-1-58341-580-1). This chilling short story of revenge is accompanied by illustrations and brief biographical information about the author. (Rev: BL 4/30/08; SLJ 8/08)

3715 Potter, Ellen. *Olivia Kidney and the Exit Academy* (4–7). Illus. by Peter H. Reynolds. Series: Olivia Kidney. 2005, Putnam $15.99 (978-0-399-24162-8). After her brother's death, Olivia and her father move into a creepy apartment building where, she discovers, people go to rehearse their deaths. (Rev: BL 3/15/05; SLJ 5/05)

3716 Potter, Ellen. *Olivia Kidney and the Secret Beneath the City* (5–7). Series: Olivia Kidney. 2007, Philomel $16.99 (978-0-399-24701-9). Twelve-year-old Olivia is starting 7th grade at a new arts school and also dealing with other problems real and surreal in this third book in the series. (Rev: BL 5/1/07; SLJ 6/07)

3717 Pratchett, Terry. *Johnny and the Dead* (5–8). Series: Johnny Maxwell. 2006, HarperCollins LB $16.89 (978-0-06-054189-7). In the funny second volume of this trilogy, ghosts of the "post-senior citizens" buried in a local cemetery ask the title character to help block plans to bulldoze their final resting place. (Rev: BL 12/15/05; HB 1–2/06; SLJ 12/05; VOYA 2/06)

3718 Preussler, Otfried. *The Satanic Mill* (7–10). 1987, Peter Smith $31.50 (978-0-8446-6196-4). A young apprentice outwits a strange magician in this fantasy first published in 1972. (Rev: BL 6/1–15/98)

3719 Primavera, Elise. *The Secret Order of the Gumm Street Girls* (4–7). Illus. 2006, HarperCollins $16.99 (978-0-06-056946-4). Four girls who live on Gumm Street have little in common until a series of incidents appear to threaten their picturesque town of Sherbet and Franny, Pru, Cat, and Ivy find themselves on a very Oz-like adventure. (Rev: BL 12/15/06; SLJ 12/06)

3720 Rees, Celia. *The Soul Taker* (5–8). 2004, Hodder paper $7.95 (978-0-340-87817-0). Lewis, overweight and lacking confidence, finds himself in thrall to a sinister toy maker. (Rev: BL 1/1–15/04)

3721 Rees, Douglas. *Vampire High* (6–9). 2003, Delacorte $15.95 (978-0-385-73117-1). A flunking Cody is sent to Vlad Dracul Magnet School where he finds his classmates very strange, but he soon adapts to their vampire nature. (Rev: BCCB 11/03; BL 8/03; HB 9–10/03; SLJ 11/03)

3722 Reiss, Kathryn. *Sweet Miss Honeywell's Revenge* (4–7). 2004, Harcourt $17.00 (978-0-15-216574-1). A haunted dollhouse, a parallel story about the original owner of the antique, and the problems of blended family life are intertwined in this story about 12-year-old Zibby Thorne. (Rev: BL 5/1/04; SLJ 8/04)

3723 Richardson, E. E. *Devil's Footsteps* (8–11). 2005, Delacorte LB $17.99 (978-0-385-90279-3). Still troubled by his brother's disappearance at the hands of the Dark Man five years earlier, 15-year-old Bryan meets two other teens struggling with the effects of similar attacks. (Rev: BCCB 10/05; BL 5/1/05; SLJ 1/06)

3724 Richardson, E. E. *The Intruders* (6–9). 2006, Delacorte $15.95 (978-0-385-73264-2). Joel and his new stepfamily move into a spooky old mansion filled with mysterious spirits in this suspenseful tale. (Rev: BL 6/1–15/06; SLJ 9/06)

3725 Roach, Marilynne K. *Encounters with the Invisible World* (5–9). Illus. by author. 1977, Amereon $18.95 (978-0-89190-874-6). Spooky stories about witches, demons, spells, and ghosts in New England.

3726 Rupp, Rebecca. *Journey to the Blue Moon: In Which Time Is Lost and Then Found Again* (5–8). 2006, Candlewick $15.99 (978-0-7636-2544-3). A multilayered story in which Alex loses his grandfather's pocket watch and takes a trip to the blue moon, where all things lost go; there he finds other searchers and a group that threatens his chances of returning home. (Rev: BL 12/1/06; SLJ 10/06)

3727 Sage, Angie. *Book One: Magyk* (5–8). Illus. by Mark Zug. 2005, HarperCollins LB $18.89 (978-0-06-057732-2). A fantasy of magic, spells, and evil forces, focusing on young Jenna, who was raised by Septimus Heap's family and who now must flee the evil Supreme Custodian. (Rev: BL 3/15/05; SLJ 4/05)

3728 San Souci, Robert D. *Dare to Be Scared: Thirteen Stories to Chill and Thrill* (4–8). Illus. by David Ouimet. 2003, Cricket $15.95 (978-0-8126-2688-9). A baker's dozen of spooky stories suitable for this age group that feature diverse characters. (Rev: BL 10/1/03; HBG 10/03; SLJ 9/03)

3729 San Souci, Robert D. *Triple-Dare to Be Scared: Thirteen Further Freaky Tales* (6–9). Illus. by David Ouimet. 2007, Cricket $16.95 (978-0-8126-2749-7). Well-written and illustrated, this third book of stories by San Souci in which the protagonists don't always escape will give readers the creeps. (Rev: SLJ 6/07)

3730 *Scary Stories* (6–9). Illus. by Barry Moser. 2006, Chronicle $16.95 (978-0-8118-5414-6). A collection of twenty classic creepy stories — many by well-known authors — accompanied by stark black-and-white illustrations. (Rev: BL 12/1/06; SLJ 1/07)

3731 Schreiber, Ellen. *Vampireville* (7–10). 2006, HarperCollins $15.99 (978-0-06-077625-1). Raven and her vampire boyfriend Alexander must get rid of the bad vampire twins Luna and Jagger before they sink their fangs into soccer star Trevor and try

and take over the town of Dullsville. (Rev: BL 8/06; SLJ 11/06)

3732 Schwartz, Alvin. *Scary Stories 3: More Tales to Chill Your Bones* (4–7). Illus. by Stephen Gammell. 1991, HarperCollins LB $17.89 (978-0-06-021795-2); paper $5.99 (978-0-06-440418-1). A modernized version of spooky tales handed down through the years. (Rev: BL 8/91; HB 11–12/91; SLJ 11/91)

3733 Seabrooke, Brenda. *The Vampire in My Bathtub* (4–7). 1999, Holiday $16.95 (978-0-8234-1505-2). After 13-year-old Jeff moves to a new home with his mother, he finds a friendly vampire hidden inside an old trunk. (Rev: BL 1/1–15/00; HBG 3/00; SLJ 12/99)

3734 Shan, Darren. *Blood Beast, Book 5* (7–10). Series: Demonata. 2007, Little, Brown $16.99 (978-0-316-00377-3). Grubbs worries that he too will become a werewolf in this gripping fifth installment in the series. (Rev: SLJ 2/08)

3735 Shan, Darren. *Demon Thief* (7–12). Series: Demonata. 2006, Little, Brown $15.99 (978-0-316-01237-9). An inventive horror story in which a boy who is able to construct windows from light discovers that demons live behind them. (Rev: SLJ 9/06)

3736 Shan, Darren. *A Living Nightmare* (5–8). Series: Cirque du Freak. 2001, Little, Brown $15.95 (978-0-316-60340-9). A supernatural story about a young boy who visits the Cirque Du Freak and is turned into a vampire. (Rev: BL 4/15/01; HBG 10/01; SLJ 5/01; VOYA 4/01)

3737 Shan, Darren. *Tunnels of Blood* (5–8). Series: Cirque du Freak. 2002, Little, Brown $15.95 (978-0-316-60763-6). Darren Shan, teenage half-vampire, sets out to investigate a spate of recent killings for which he believes his vampire master might be responsible. (Rev: BL 8/02; HBG 10/02; SLJ 5/02; VOYA 6/02)

3738 Shan, Darren. *Vampire Mountain* (5–8). Series: Cirque du Freak. 2002, Little, Brown $15.95 (978-0-316-60806-0). Darren Shan, teenage half-vampire, and his mentor travel to Vampire Mountain. The fifth, sixth, and seventh installments in the series are *Trials of Death*, *The Vampire Prince* (both 2003), and *Hunters of the Dusk* (2004). (Rev: BL 8/02; HBG 3/03; SLJ 9/02; VOYA 12/02)

3739 Shan, Darren. *The Vampire's Assistant* (5–8). Series: Cirque du Freak. 2001, Little, Brown $15.95 (978-0-316-60610-3). The creepy, suspenseful second installment about a boy who is "half vampire" and his efforts to adjust to the world of a traveling freak show. (Rev: BL 10/15/01; HBG 3/02; SLJ 8/01; VOYA 10/01)

3740 Shreve, Susan. *Ghost Cats* (4–7). 1999, Scholastic paper $14.95 (978-0-590-37131-5). A boy, who is trying to adjust to a new family home and the loss of his five cats, is helped when the cats return as ghosts. (Rev: BCCB 12/99; BL 9/1/99; HBG 3/00; SLJ 11/99; VOYA 6/00)

3741 Shusterman, Neal. *Darkness Creeping: Twenty Twisted Tales* (5–8). 2007, Penguin paper $6.99 (978-0-14-240721-9). Four of these creepy stories were written for this collection; others have been published before but are not easily found. (Rev: BL 5/15/07; SLJ 7/07)

3742 Shusterman, Neal. *Everlost* (7–10). 2006, Simon & Schuster $16.95 (978-0-689-87237-2). Nick and Allie are killed in an automobile accident and end up in Everlost, a world for lost souls, where they must learn to survive. Nick accepts the situation but Allie will do anything to escape. (Rev: BL 9/15/06; SLJ 10/06*)

3743 Shusterman, Neal. *Full Tilt* (6–10). 2003, Simon & Schuster $16.95 (978-0-689-80374-1). A suspenseful drama in which 16-year-old Blake must tackle frightening rides at a mysterious carnival and face his own worst fears in order to save his daredevil older brother Quinn. (Rev: BCCB 9/03; BL 5/15/03; HB 7–8/03; HBG 10/03; SLJ 6/03; VOYA 10/03)

3744 Sierra, Judy. *The Gruesome Guide to World Monsters* (5–8). Illus. by Henrik Drescher. 2005, Candlewick $17.99 (978-0-7636-1727-1). A wonderfully ghoulish field guide to more than 60 monsters from world folklore, complete with Gruesomeness Ratings and Survival Tips if appropriate. (Rev: BCCB 9/05; BL 9/15/05*; HBG 4/06; LMC 2/06; SLJ 9/05)

3745 Singer, Nicky. *The Innocent's Story* (7–10). 2007, Holiday $16.95 (978-0-8234-2082-7). After dying in a suicide bomb attack, 13-year-old Cassina becomes a vapor and enters into the mind and hearts of living characters including her parents and the terrorists responsible for her death. (Rev: BL 5/15/07; SLJ 9/07)

3746 Sinykin, Sheri. *Giving Up the Ghost* (5–8). 2007, Peachtree $15.95 (978-1-56145-423-5). Davia is only 13, has asthma, is worried about her mother's cancer, and afraid of various things; now her dying Aunt Mari wants Davi to help Emilie, a young Creole ghost, to find peace. (Rev: LMC 2/08; SLJ 2/08)

3747 Sleator, William. *Hell Phone* (5–8). 2006, Abrams $16.95 (978-0-8109-5479-3). In this dark, suspenseful novel, 17-year-old Nick discovers that the cell phone he bought at a bargain price constantly rings with frightening requests. (Rev: BL 10/1/06; SLJ 11/06)

3748 Snyder, Zilpha Keatley. *The Headless Cupid* (4–7). 1971, Dell paper $4.99 (978-0-440-43507-5). Amanda, a student of the occult, upsets her new family. A sequel is *The Famous Stanley Kidnapping Case* (1985).

3749 Somper, Justin. *Demons of the Ocean* (6–9). Series: Vampirates. 2006, Little, Brown $15.99 (978-0-316-01373-4). Young twins Connor and Grace, attracted to the sea by stories they heard as children, decide to make it their life when their father dies; early on they are separated in a storm and find themselves on very different ships. (Rev: SLJ 11/06)

3750 Somper, Justin. *Tide of Terror* (6–9). Series: Vampirates. 2007, Little, Brown $15.99 (978-0-316-01374-1). Grace and Connor Tempest, 14-year-old orphan twins, leave their dangerous life aboard the pirate ship *Diablo* and spend time at the elite Pirate Academy; but Grace yearns to go back to the vampirate way of life. (Rev: BL 5/1/07; SLJ 8/07)

3751 Soto, Gary. *The Afterlife* (7–10). 2003, Harcourt $16.00 (978-0-15-204774-0). After he is stabbed to death, 17-year-old Chuy lingers long enough to watch the reactions of family and friends while getting to know some other ghosts. (Rev: BL 8/03*; HB 11–12/03; HBG 4/04; SLJ 11/03; VOYA 2/04)

3752 Springer, Nancy. *Sky Rider* (5–8). 2000, HarperCollins paper $4.95 (978-0-380-79565-9). In this contemporary supernatural mystery, Dusty's beloved horse Tazz is cured by a visitor who turns out to be the angry ghost of a teenage boy recently killed on her father's property. (Rev: BCCB 10/99; HBG 3/00; SLJ 8/99)

3753 Stahler, David. *A Gathering of Shades* (7–10). 2005, HarperCollins LB $16.89 (978-0-06-052295-7). Sixteen-year-old Aidan, who moves to rural Vermont with his mother after his father's death, discovers that his grandmother is secretly feeding ghosts with a mixture of her own blood and spring water. (Rev: BCCB 5/05; BL 5/1/05; SLJ 8/05)

3754 Starkey, Dinah, ed. *Ghosts and Bogles* (5–10). Illus. 1987, David & Charles $17.95 (978-0-434-96440-6). A collection of 16 British ghost stories, each nicely presented with illustrations. (Rev: SLJ 9/87)

3755 Staub, Wendy Corsi. *Lily Dale: Awakening* (7–10). 2007, Walker $15.95 (978-0-8027-9654-7). At the age of 17, following her mother's accidental death and on a visit to the spiritualist community of Lily Dale, Calla discovers her psychic abilities. (Rev: BL 11/1/07; LMC 1/08; SLJ 11/07)

3756 Stewart, Trenton Lee. *The Mysterious Benedict Society* (4–7). Illus. by Carson Ellis. 2007, Little, Brown $16.99 (978-0-316-05777-6). Orphan Reynie Muldoon is one of a number of gifted children selected to take part in an effort to infiltrate the Learning Institute for the Very Enlightened; a complex story of mystery and adventure. (Rev: BL 1/1–15/07; SLJ 3/07*)

3757 Stine, R. L. *The Haunting Hour: Chill in the Dead of Night* (5–8). Illus. 2001, HarperCollins

$14.89 (978-0-06-623605-6). Ten chilling short stories, each with an introduction by the author. (Rev: BCCB 11/01; BL 1/1–15/02; HBG 3/02)

3758 Stine, R. L. *Nightmare Hour* (4–7). Illus. 1999, HarperCollins $16.99 (978-0-06-028688-0). Ten scary stories by a master of mystery, with characters that include aliens, sorcerers, werewolves, witches, and ghosts. (Rev: BL 10/15/99; HBG 3/00; SLJ 12/99)

3759 Stolarz, Laurie Faria. *Project 17* (7–10). 2007, Hyperion $15.99 (978-0-7868-3856-1). Five teenagers spend a spooky night at the ghost-filled Danvers State Insane Asylum. (Rev: BL 11/15/07; LMC 1/08; SLJ 12/07)

3760 Strasser, Todd. *Hey Dad, Get a Life!* (5–8). 1996, Holiday $15.95 (978-0-8234-1278-5). Twelve-year-old Kelly and her younger sister use the ghost of their dead father to accomplish their everyday chores and finally let their mother know about their secret helper. (Rev: BCCB 3/97; BL 2/15/97; SLJ 3/97)

3761 Strickland, Brad. *The Whistle, the Grave, and the Ghost* (5–8). Series: Lewis Barnevalt. 2003, Dial $16.99 (978-0-8037-2622-2). A silver whistle frees a woman vampire, drawing Lewis Barnevalt and his friends into suspenseful adventures battling an ancient threat. (Rev: BL 8/03; HBG 4/04; SLJ 8/03)

3762 Teitelbaum, Michael. *The Scary States of America* (5–8). 2007, Delacorte LB $12.99 (978-0-385-90348-6); paper $7.99 (978-0-385-73331-1). A collection of short stories about paranormal events that take place in each of the 50 states. (Rev: BL 6/1–15/07; SLJ 8/07)

3763 Tolan, Stephanie S. *The Face in the Mirror* (6–9). 1998, Morrow $15.00 (978-0-688-15394-6). When Jared goes to live with his father, a theater director, he isn't prepared for the malicious pranks of his stepbrother or the encounters with George Marsden, a sympathetic ghost. (Rev: BCCB 9/98; BL 9/1/98; HBG 3/99; SLJ 11/98; VOYA 4/99)

3764 Tolan, Stephanie S. *Who's There?* (5–8). 1994, Morrow $15.00 (978-0-688-04611-8); paper $4.95 (978-0-688-15289-5). Fourteen-year-old Drew is convinced that there is a ghost in her crusty grandfather's house, where she and her brother Evan, who has been mute since their parents' deaths, are currently living. (Rev: BCCB 12/94; BL 9/1/94; SLJ 10/94)

3765 Tunnell, Michael O. *School Spirits* (5–8). 1997, Holiday $15.95 (978-0-8234-1310-2). Three students at creepy Craven Hill School, including the son of the new principal, discover a ghost and solve a decades-old murder mystery involving an 8-year-old boy. (Rev: BCCB 3/98; BL 2/15/98; HBG 3/98; SLJ 3/98; VOYA 8/98)

3766 Vande Velde, Vivian. *All Hallows' Eve: 13 Stories* (7–10). 2006, Harcourt $17.00 (978-0-15-205576-9). Thirteen chilling horror stories that take place on Halloween night feature teens and their encounters with vampires, killers, ghosts, and more. (Rev: BL 10/1/06; HB 9–10/06; LMC 4–5/07; SLJ 11/06)

3767 Wade, Rebecca. *The Theft and the Miracle* (5–8). 2007, HarperCollins $16.99 (978-0-06-077493-6). Mystery and supernatural are combined in this story of Hannah, a plain, overweight 12-year-old with artistic abilities, who — with her friend Sam — finds herself on a hunt for a missing religious statue. (Rev: BL 11/15/06; SLJ 1/07)

3768 Watts, Leander. *Beautiful City of the Dead* (8–11). 2006, Houghton $16.00 (978-0-618-59443-6). Zee and her fellow heavy metal bandmates discover they have unsuspected powers and must battle the evil forces around them that want to take these powers away. (Rev: BL 9/15/06)

3769 Welch, R. C. *Scary Stories for Stormy Nights* (5–7). Illus. 1995, Lowell House paper $5.95 (978-1-56565-262-0). Ten contemporary horror stories that involve such characters as a werewolf and some pirates. (Rev: BL 5/1/95)

3770 Welvaert, Scott R. *The Curse of the Wendigo: An Agate and Buck Adventure* (5–9). Illus. by Brann Garvey. 2006, Stone Arch LB $23.93 (978-1-59889-066-2). Searching for their parents in the vast Canadian wilderness in the late 19th century, 16-year-old Buck and his younger sister Agate find themselves being pursued by the mythical Wendigo; suitable for reluctant readers. (Rev: SLJ 1/07)

3771 Westall, Robert. *Ghost Abbey* (5–9). 1990, Scholastic paper $3.25 (978-0-590-41693-1). Maggi realizes that the abbey her father is restoring seems to have a life of its own. (Rev: BCCB 2/89; BL 2/1/89; SLJ 3/89; VOYA 6/89)

3772 Westall, Robert. *Shades of Darkness: More of the Ghostly Best Stories of Robert Westall* (7–12). 1994, Macmillan paper $11.95 (978-0-330-35318-2). Eleven eerie tales, not the guts-and-gore variety of supernatural fiction but haunting and insightful stories. (Rev: BL 4/15/94; SLJ 5/94; VOYA 8/94)

3773 Westerfeld, Scott. *Blue Noon* (6–12). Series: Midnighters. 2006, HarperCollins $15.99 (978-0-06-051957-5). In this action-packed third volume in the series, the darklings have found a way to expand their time, threatening all human beings. (Rev: SLJ 7/06)

3774 Westerfeld, Scott. *The Secret Hour* (6–10). Series: Midnighters. 2004, HarperCollins LB $17.89 (978-0-06-051952-0). In this exciting first volume, 15-year-old Jessica Day discovers that — like several others — she has special abilities to battle supernatural creatures. (Rev: SLJ 6/04; VOYA 4/04)

3775 Westerfeld, Scott. *Touching Darkness* (6–10). Illus. Series: Midnighters. 2005, HarperCollins LB $16.89 (978-0-06-051955-1). In volume two of the Midnighters series, five teens born at the stroke of midnight learn about the hidden past of their Oklahoma hometown and a frightening conspiracy that threatens them all. (Rev: SLJ 3/05)

3776 Westwood, Chris. *Calling All Monsters* (7–12). 1993, HarperCollins LB $14.89 (978-0-06-022462-2). Joanne is a huge fan of a horror writer, so when she starts seeing nightmare creatures from his books, she recognizes them. (Rev: BL 6/1–15/93; SLJ 7/93; VOYA 12/93)

3777 Westwood, Chris. *He Came from the Shadows* (5–8). 1991, HarperCollins LB $14.89 (978-0-06-021659-7). In a cautionary tale about the dangers of wishing for too much, odd things start to happen after a stranger comes to town. (Rev: BL 4/1/91; SLJ 6/91)

3778 Whelan, Gerard. *Dream Invader* (5–7). 2002, O'Brien paper $7.95 (978-0-86278-516-1). Only Simon's grandmother can break the spell behind the bad dreams he's been having in this supernatural tale set in Ireland. (Rev: BL 9/1/02)

3779 Wild, Margaret. *Woolvs in the Sitee* (6–9). Illus. by Anne Spudvilas. 2007, Front St. $17.95 (978-1-59078-500-3). A strange and disturbing picture book, in which a boy living in a post-apocalyptic world writes in scrawled, desperate-looking handwriting about terrifying "woolvs" that the reader never sees. (Rev: BL 11/15/07; HB 11–12/07; SLJ 9/07)

3780 Wright, Betty R. *Crandalls' Castle* (4–7). 2003, Holiday $16.95 (978-0-8234-1726-1). This gripping suspense story combines supernatural elements with a look at teen girls' yearning to belong. (Rev: BL 4/1/03; HBG 10/03; SLJ 5/03)

3781 Wright, Betty R. *A Ghost in the House* (5–7). 1991, Scholastic paper $13.95 (978-0-590-43606-9). Bizarre happenings take place when Sarah's elderly aunt moves in. (Rev: BCCB 11/91; BL 1/1/91; SLJ 11/91)

3782 Wright, Nina. *Sensitive* (8–10). 2007, Flux paper $9.95 (978-0-7387-1170-6). Cal and Easter, who have supernatural abilities, make contact with the dead and, more romantically, with each other in this novel set in ghost-filled St. Augustine, Florida; the sequel to *Homefree* (2006). (Rev: BL 11/1/07; SLJ 3/08)

3783 Yashinsky, Dan, ed. *Ghostwise: A Book of Midnight Stories* (7–12). 1997, August House $11.95 (978-0-87483-499-4). A collection of 35 short but chilling stories of the supernatural and ghosts. (Rev: BCCB 3/98; VOYA 2/98)

3784 Yee, Paul. *The Bone Collector's Son* (6–9). 2005, Marshall Cavendish $15.95 (978-0-7614-5242-3). In early 20th-century Vancouver, Bing is ashamed of his father's occupation as shipper of bones back to China for burial in this novel that interweaves the real and supernatural worlds. (Rev: BCCB 11/05; BL 12/1/05; HB 11–12/05; VOYA 12/05)

3785 Yolen, Jane, and Martin H. Greenberg, eds. *Werewolves: A Collection of Original Stories* (6–9). 1988, HarperCollins $13.95 (978-0-06-026798-8). Fifteen mostly scary stories about all kinds of werewolves. (Rev: BL 7/88; SLJ 9/88; VOYA 8/88)

3786 Young, Richard, and Judy Dockery Young. *Ozark Ghost Stories* (6–12). 1995, August House paper $12.95 (978-0-87483-410-9). Spooky Ozark stories are the focus of this horror anthology, including old favorites and less-well-known jokes and tales. (Rev: BL 6/1–15/95)

3787 Young, Richard, and Judy Dockery Young. *The Scary Story Reader* (6–9). 1993, August House $19.00 (978-0-87483-271-6). Forty-one scary urban legends are presented, including traditional tales of horror as well as less-well-known stories from Alaska and Hawaii. (Rev: BL 11/15/93; SLJ 5/94)

3788 Zindel, Paul. *Loch* (7–10). 1994, HarperCollins LB $15.89 (978-0-06-024543-6). Lovable, though human-eating, creatures trapped in a Vermont lake become prey for a ruthless man. (Rev: BL 11/15/94; SLJ 1/95; VOYA 4/95)

Humor

3789 Acampora, Paul. *Defining Dulcie* (7–10). 2006, Dial $16.99 (978-0-8037-3046-5). Dulcie may only be 16 but she knows her own mind, and when her mother moves her to California following her janitor father's death, Dulcie drives home to Connecticut and lives with her janitor grandfather. (Rev: BL 4/1/06*; SLJ 4/06*; VOYA 4/06)

3790 Ardagh, Philip. *Dreadful Acts* (4–7). Illus. by David Roberts. Series: Eddie Dickens. 2003, Holt $14.95 (978-0-8050-7155-9). This zany sequel to *A House Called Awful End* (2002) throws more wild adventures at 12-year-old Eddie Dickens. (Rev: BL 4/15/03; HBG 10/03; SLJ 5/03)

3791 Ardagh, Philip. *Terrible Times* (4–7). Illus. by David Roberts. 2003, Holt $12.95 (978-0-8050-7156-6). Young Eddie Dickens sails for America and encounters all sorts of zany situations in this last installment in the trilogy set in Victorian England. (Rev: BL 2/1/04; SLJ 12/03)

3792 Avi. *Punch with Judy* (6–8). Illus. 1993, Bradbury LB $14.95 (978-0-02-707755-1). The orphan boy Punch encounters tragedy and comedy in his attempt to keep a medicine show alive with the help of the owner's daughter. (Rev: BL 3/15/93; SLJ 6/93; VOYA 8/93)

3793 Avi. *Romeo and Juliet: Together (and Alive) at Last!* (6–8). 1987, Watts LB $16.99 (978-0-531-08321-5); Avon paper $5.99 (978-0-380-70525-2). Ed Sitrow decides to help true love along by casting his friends as Romeo and Juliet in a school play. Sitrow is also the "genius" behind the soccer escapades in *S.O.R. Losers*. (Rev: BL 8/87; SLJ 10/87)

3794 Bath, K. P. *Escape from Castle Cant* (6–9). Illus. by Leah Palmer Preiss. 2006, Little, Brown $16.99 (978-0-316-10857-7). A civil war over chewing gum has Pauline and her half-sister Lucy on the run in this sequel to *The Secret of Castle Cant* (2006). (Rev: SLJ 10/06)

3795 Binder, Mark. *The Brothers Schlemiel* (6–9). Illus. by Zevi Blum. 2008, Jewish Publication Soc. $19.95 (978-0-8276-0865-8). Identical twin brothers Abraham and Adam grow up in the town of Chelm, Poland, where their pranks and pratfalls keep everyone laughing; full-color illustrations add to the fun. (Rev: BL 3/1/08)

3796 Blume, Judy. *Starring Sally J. Freedman as Herself* (4–7). 1977, Dell paper $5.99 (978-0-440-48253-6). A story of a 5th-grader's adventures in New Jersey and Florida in the late 1940s.

3797 Bradley, Alex. *24 Girls in 7 Days* (8–11). 2005, Dutton $15.99 (978-0-525-47369-5). Dateless only two weeks before the senior prom, Jack is desperate, so desperate that two of his friends run a personal ad in the school paper in an effort to get Jack a date. (Rev: BL 1/1–15/05; SLJ 3/05; VOYA 2/05)

3798 Brockmeier, Kevin. *Grooves: A Kind of Mystery* (4–7). 2006, HarperCollins LB $17.89 (978-0-06-073692-7). In this funny mystery with science fiction overtones, unprepossessing 7th-grader Dwayne Ruggles finds out that the sounds coming from his blue jeans are really cries for help from imprisoned factory workers. (Rev: BL 2/1/06; SLJ 3/06)

3799 Brooke, William J. *A Is for AARRGH!* (5–8). 1999, HarperCollins LB $14.89 (978-0-06-023394-5). A humorous story about a prehistoric boy, Mog, and his amazing discoveries about language and communication. (Rev: BCCB 11/99; BL 10/15/99; HB 9–10/99; HBG 3/00; SLJ 9/99)

3800 Burnham, Niki. *Royally Jacked* (8–10). 2004, Simon & Schuster paper $5.99 (978-0-689-86668-5). Valerie, a 15-year-old product of divorce accompanies her father to live in a castle in Europe in this lively, humorous story. (Rev: BL 3/1/04; SLJ 2/04)

3801 Burnham, Niki. *Spin Control* (8–10). 2005, Simon & Schuster paper $5.99 (978-0-689-86669-2). Valerie is desperately unhappy when she's forced to leave Schwerinborg and her prince

boyfriend and return to Virginia, but a reunion with an old boyfriend soon eases her pain in this sequel to *Royally Jacked* (2004). (Rev: SLJ 2/05)

3802 Byars, Betsy. *Bingo Brown's Guide to Romance* (5–8). 2000, Puffin paper $5.99 (978-0-14-036080-6). Romance, confusion, and comedy occur when Bingo Brown meets his true love in the produce section of the grocery store. (Rev: BL 4/1/92; SLJ 4/92)

3803 Byars, Betsy. *The Burning Questions of Bingo Brown* (6–8). 1990, Puffin paper $6.99 (978-0-14-032479-2). During Bingo's 6th-grade year, he falls in love three times for starters. (Rev: BCCB 4/88; BL 4/15/88; SLJ 5/88)

3804 Cabot, Meg. *Airhead* (7–10). 2008, Scholastic $16.99 (978-0-545-04052-5). Feminist loner Em's brain is transplanted into the body of a famous model, allowing her to experience life as one of the beautiful people. (Rev: BL 4/15/08; SLJ 8/08)

3805 Cabot, Meg. *The Princess Diaries* (7–10). Series: Princess Diaries. 2000, HarperCollins LB $17.89 (978-0-06-029210-2). Fourteen-year-old Mia's diary reveals a fairly interesting life even before she learns that she is actually a royal princess, heir to the throne of Genovia. (Rev: BCCB 12/00; BL 9/15/00; HBG 3/01; SLJ 10/00; VOYA 4/01)

3806 Cabot, Meg. *Princess in Love: The Princess Diaries, Vol. 3* (6–9). Series: The Princess Diaries. 2002, HarperCollins $16.99 (978-0-06-029467-0). This action-packed installment follows Mia's life from Thanksgiving through her December departure for Genovia, with details of typical teen life and of her efforts to learn about her new country. (Rev: BCCB 5/02; BL 7/02; HBG 10/02; SLJ 10/02; VOYA 6/02)

3807 Cabot, Meg. *Princess in Pink* (7–10). Series: Princess Diaries. 2004, HarperCollins $15.99 (978-0-06-009610-6). In this, the fifth volume of the Princess Diaries series, Mia celebrates her 15th birthday and her pregnant mom is about to give birth. (Rev: BL 4/15/04; SLJ 8/04)

3808 Cabot, Meg. *Princess in Training* (7–10). Series: Princess Diaries. 2005, HarperCollins $16.99 (978-0-06-009613-7). Princess Mia's current worries range from English and geometry, running for student council president, and her college boyfriend's expectations, to her new baby brother and the ecology of the Bay of Genovia. (Rev: BL 8/05; SLJ 6/05; VOYA 8/05)

3809 Cabot, Meg. *Princess in Waiting* (5–7). Series: Princess Diaries. 2003, HarperCollins $16.99 (978-0-06-009607-6). Princess Mia gets in a royal mess when her duties interfere with her love life. (Rev: BL 5/15/03; HBG 10/03; SLJ 5/03; VOYA 6/03)

3810 Cabot, Meg. *Princess on the Brink* (8–11). Series: Princess Diaries. 2007, HarperCollins $16.99 (978-0-06-072456-6). Princess Mia contemplates the pros and cons of having sex with her boyfriend in this continuation of the series. (Rev: BL 12/15/06) ⊚

3811 Cheshire, Simon. *The Prince and the Snowgirl* (6–9). 2007, Delacorte LB $12.99 (978-0-385-90359-2); paper $8.99 (978-0-385-73342-7). Tom has been earning money impersonating Prince George (heir to the British throne) and hoping at the same time to impress the lovely Louise, but fate intervenes at a skiing championship and Tom must make a quick decision. (Rev: BCCB 3/07; SLJ 5/07)

3812 Collins, Ross. *Medusa Jones* (4–7). Illus. by author. 2008, Scholastic $16.99 (978-0-439-90100-0). Yes, Medusa does have snakes for hair, and her friend Mino is half bull; they are part of the outcast group at school, where Theseus and his friends push them around. A trip to Mount Olympus changes all that, since the students must pull together. (Rev: BL 12/1/07; LMC 3/08; SLJ 1/08)

3813 Conford, Ellen. *The Alfred G. Graebner Memorial High School Handbook of Rules and Regulations* (6–9). 1976, Little, Brown $14.95 (978-0-316-15293-8). The trials and tribulations of student life in a typical high school. (Rev: BL 7/88)

3814 Conford, Ellen. *Dear Lovey Hart, I Am Desperate* (6–7). 1975, Little, Brown $14.95 (978-0-316-15306-5). Freshman reporter Carrie Wasserman gets into trouble with her advice column in the school newspaper. (Rev: BL 10/15/87)

3815 Conford, Ellen. *Seven Days to Be a Brand-New Me* (6–9). 1990, Scholastic paper $3.50 (978-0-590-43824-7). Maddy knows she will become a teenage vamp after following Dr. Dudley's program.

3816 Conford, Ellen. *Why Me?* (6–9). 1985, Little, Brown $14.95 (978-0-316-15326-3). G.G. Graffman has a crush on Hobie, who only has eyes for Darlene, who is ga-ga over Warren. (Rev: BL 10/15/85; SLJ 11/85; VOYA 2/86)

3817 Dent, Grace. *LBD: Friends Forever!* (7–10). Series: LBD. 2006, Putnam $16.99 (978-0-399-24189-5). Claude enters a modeling contest while the girls are working and vacationing at Destiny Bay in the latest installment of the LBD (Les Bambinos Dangereuses) series. (Rev: SLJ 10/06)

3818 Feiffer, Jules. *The Man in the Ceiling* (5–7). Illus. 1993, HarperCollins paper $9.99 (978-0-06-205907-9). Jimmy turns to cartooning in an effort to gain some recognition in a family that is intent on ignoring him. (Rev: BCCB 12/93; BL 11/15/93; SLJ 2/94*)

3819 Fleischman, Sid. *Chancy and the Grand Rascal* (5–7). Illus. by Eric Von Schmidt. 1966, Little, Brown $14.95 (978-0-316-28575-9); paper $4.95 (978-0-316-26012-1). The boy and his uncle, the grand rascal, combine hard work and quick wits to outsmart a scoundrel, hoodwink a miser, and capture a band of outlaws.

3820 Foley, June. *Susanna Siegelbaum Gives Up Guys* (5–8). 1992, Scholastic paper $3.25 (978-0-590-43700-4). Susanna, a flirt, makes a bet that she can give up guys for three months. (Rev: SLJ 8/91)

3821 Gonzalez, Julie. *Imaginary Enemy* (6–10). 2008, Delacorte $15.99 (978-0-385-73552-0). Jane, 16, is shocked when her imaginary enemy, Bubba (whom she has blamed for any misbehavior since second grade), responds to one of her letters; a rich and funny novel. (Rev: BL 3/15/08)

3822 Gorman, Carol. *Lizard Flanagan, Supermodel??* (4–7). 1998, HarperCollins $14.95 (978-0-06-024868-0). Sixth-grader Lizard Flanagan will do anything to make enough money to go by bus from her home in Iowa to a game in Wrigley Field, but is entering a local fashion show for teens going too far? (Rev: BL 11/15/98; HBG 3/99; SLJ 10/98)

3823 Griggs, Terry. *Cat's Eye Corner* (6–8). 2003, Raincoast paper $7.95 (978-1-55192-350-5). Wordplay stars in this entertaining novel full of eccentric characters whom Olivier finds on a scavenger hunt through his grandfather's old mansion; a sequel is *Invisible Ink* (2006). (Rev: BL 6/1–15/03; SLJ 8/03)

3824 Harmel, Kristin. *When You Wish* (7–10). 2008, Delacorte $15.99 (978-0-385-73475-2). Beck is tired of being a pop star and rebels against her manager mother by disguising herself and hopping on a bus to Florida. (Rev: BL 4/1/08; SLJ 5/08)

3825 Hautman, Pete. *Godless* (7–10). 2004, Simon & Schuster $15.95 (978-0-689-86278-6). Rebelling against his devoutly Catholic father, 16-year-old Jason Block and his best friend Shin create a religion of their own with the town's water tower as the deity. (Rev: BL 6/1–15/04*; HB 7–8/04; SLJ 8/04; VOYA 10/04)

3826 Hayes, Daniel. *Eye of the Beholder* (5–8). 1992, Fawcett paper $6.99 (978-0-449-00235-3). Tyler and Lymie are in trouble again when they fake some works of a famous sculptor. (Rev: BL 2/1/93; SLJ 12/92)

3827 Henry, Chad. *DogBreath Victorious* (6–10). 1999, Holiday $16.95 (978-0-8234-1458-1). Tim's rock band, DogBreath, ends up competing against his mom's group, the Angry Housewives, in this entertaining story. (Rev: HBG 9/00; SLJ 2/00; VOYA 6/00)

3828 Hite, Sid. *Those Darn Dithers* (5–8). 1996, Holt $15.95 (978-0-8050-3838-5). A humorous novel about the dithering Dithers with adventures involving Porcellina the dancing pig and an eccentric who drifts out to sea on a rubber raft. (Rev: BL 12/15/96; SLJ 12/96; VOYA 10/97)

3829 Horvath, Polly. *When the Circus Came to Town* (5–8). 1996, FSG paper $5.95 (978-0-374-48367-8). Opinion is sharply divided in Ivy's town when a circus troupe decides to relocate there. (Rev: BCCB 12/96; BL 11/15/96; SLJ 12/96*)

3830 Howe, James. *Bunnicula Meets Edgar Allan Crow* (4–7). Illus. by Eric Fortune. 2006, Simon & Schuster $15.95 (978-1-4169-1458-7). When world-famous author M. T. Graves and his pet, Edgar Allan Crow, come to stay with the Monroe family, Bunnicula the vampire bunny suspects that the household guests are up to no good. (Rev: BL 1/1–15/07; SLJ 2/07)

3831 Howe, James. *The New Nick Kramer or My Life as a Baby-Sitter* (5–9). 1995, Hyperion LB $14.49 (978-0-7868-2053-5). Nick and rival Mitch make an unusual bet on who will win the affections of newcomer Jennifer. (Rev: BL 12/15/95; SLJ 1/96)

3832 Ives, David. *Monsieur Eek* (4–7). 2001, Harper-Collins LB $15.89 (978-0-06-029530-1). Thirteen-year-old Emmaline defends a monkey against criminal charges in the not-quite-right town of MacOongafoondsen, population 21. (Rev: BL 6/1–15/01; HBG 3/02; SLJ 6/01)

3833 Ives, David. *Scrib* (6–9). 2005, HarperCollins LB $17.89 (978-0-06-059842-6). His spelling and grammar may leave a lot to be desired, but 16-year-old Billy Christmas enjoys an adventure-filled life as he travels the Old West writing and delivering letters. (Rev: BCCB 4/05; BL 3/1/05; SLJ 2/05; VOYA 6/05)

3834 Jennings, Richard W. *Ferret Island* (5–7). 2007, Houghton $16.00 (978-0-618-80632-4). Will and a huge, friendly ferret named Jim are on the run from a ferret gang that has been trained to attack McDonald's restaurants. (Rev: BCCB 5/07; BL 7/07; HB 5–6/07; SLJ 5/07)

3835 Jennings, Richard W. *My Life of Crime* (4–8). 2002, Houghton $15.00 (978-0-618-21433-4). Nothing goes right when 6th-grader Fowler decides to "rescue" a caged parrot. (Rev: BL 1/1–15/03; HBG 3/03; VOYA 2/03)

3836 Juby, Susan. *Miss Smithers* (7–12). 2004, HarperCollins LB $16.89 (978-0-06-051547-8). Told through journal articles and a zine, this is the story of Alice of *Alice, I Think* (2003) and how she enters a beauty contest in spite of her mother's opposition. (Rev: BL 5/1/04; HB 7–8/04; SLJ 10/04)

3837 Kidd, Ronald. *Sammy Carducci's Guide to Women* (5–7). 1995, Dramatic Publg. $6.25 (978-0-87129-522-4). A somewhat sexist 6th grader discovers that, where women are concerned, perhaps

he is not as irresistible as he thinks he is. (Rev: BCCB 1/92; BL 1/1/92; SLJ 1/92)

3838 Kiesel, Stanley. *The War Between the Pitiful Teachers and the Splendid Kids* (7–9). 1980, Avon paper $3.50 (978-0-380-57802-3). A humorous fantasy about schoolchildren who decide to wage war on their teachers.

3839 Kinney, Jeff. *Rodrick Rules* (5–8). Illus. by author. 2008, Abrams $12.95 (978-0-8109-9473-7). Twelve-year-old Greg Heffley of *Diary of a Wimpy Kid* (2007) will make readers laugh again with this diary that recounts his struggles at home and at school, particularly those involving his annoying older brother Rodrick. (Rev: BL 2/1/08; SLJ 3/08)

3840 Kline, Suzy. *Orp Goes to the Hoop* (5–7). 1993, Avon paper $3.50 (978-0-380-71829-0). Seventh-grader Orp gets a chance to play a big part in the basketball team's big game. (Rev: BCCB 7–8/91; BL 7/91; SLJ 7/91)

3841 Korman, Gordon. *Don't Care High* (7–10). 1986, Scholastic paper $2.50 (978-0-590-40251-4). A new student in a high school where apathy is so rife it's nicknamed Don't Care High decides to infuse some school spirit into the student body. (Rev: BL 10/15/85)

3842 Korman, Gordon. *Losing Joe's Place* (7–10). 1991, Scholastic paper $5.99 (978-0-590-42769-2). Three teenage boys take over an apartment for the summer with hilarious results. (Rev: BL 3/1/90; SLJ 5/90; VOYA 6/90)

3843 Lawson, Robert. *Ben and Me* (5–8). Illus. by author. 1939, Little, Brown $16.95 (978-0-316-51732-4); paper $5.99 (978-0-316-51730-0). The events of Benjamin Franklin's life, as told by his good mouse Amos, who lived in his old fur cap.

3844 Lawson, Robert. *Mr. Revere and I* (5–8). Illus. by author. 1953, Little, Brown paper $6.99 (978-0-316-51729-4). A delightful account of certain episodes in Revere's life, as revealed by his horse Scheherazade. (Rev: SLJ 1/05)

3845 Limb, Sue. *Girl, Barely 15: Flirting for England* (7–10). Series: Jess Jordan. 2008, Delacorte $15.99 (978-0-385-73538-4). Jess's class welcomes a group of French exchange students, and romance and hijinks ensue on a combined camping trip in this funny British import. (Rev: BL 1/1–15/08; SLJ 4/08)

3846 Limb, Sue. *Girl, Going on 17: Pants on Fire* (7–10). Series: Jess Jordan. 2006, Delacorte $15.95 (978-0-385-73218-5). Jess copes with love and school difficulties with her usual humor and fortitude. (Rev: BL 7/06; SLJ 9/06)

3847 Lockhart, E. *Fly on the Wall: How One Girl Saw Everything* (7–10). 2006, Delacorte LB $17.99 (978-0-385-90299-1). Gretchen Yee's wish to be a fly on the wall of the boys' locker room comes true and in the process she gains confidence and learns a lot about boys and friendship. (Rev: BCCB 4/06; BL 7/06; HB 3–4/06; SLJ 3/06)

3848 Lowry, Brigid. *Follow the Blue* (8–12). 2004, Holiday $16.95 (978-0-8234-1827-5). A delightful novel from Australia about 15-year-old Bec, who, with her two younger siblings, is left in the care of a dowdy housekeeper while her parents are away. (Rev: BL 5/1/04*; HB 7–8/04; SLJ 5/04)

3849 Lowry, Lois. *Anastasia at This Address* (5–9). 1991, Houghton $16.00 (978-0-395-56263-5); Dell paper $4.50 (978-0-440-40652-5). The irrepressible Anastasia answers a personal ad, using her mother's picture instead of her own, with typically hilarious results. (Rev: BCCB 3/91; BL 4/1/91; SLJ 8/91)

3850 Lowry, Lois. *Anastasia on Her Own* (5–7). Illus. 1985, Houghton $16.00 (978-0-395-38133-5); Dell paper $4.50 (978-0-440-40291-6). Seventh-grader Anastasia Krupnik must face both domestic crisis and romance. Another chapter in Anastasia's busy life is recounted in *Anastasia Has the Answers* (1986). (Rev: BL 5/15/85; HB 9–10/85; SLJ 8/85)

3851 Lowry, Lois. *Anastasia's Chosen Career* (5–7). 1987, Houghton $16.00 (978-0-395-42506-0); Bantam paper $4.50 (978-0-440-40100-1). Thirteen-year-old Anastasia gets some surprises when she begs to go to charm school to change her freaky looks. Anastasia's baby brother is featured in *All About Sam* (1988). (Rev: BCCB 9/87; BL 9/1/87; SLJ 9/87)

3852 Lowry, Lois. *Switcharound* (5–7). 1985, Houghton $16.00 (978-0-395-39536-3). Caroline and her nemesis brother J.P. must spend the summer with their divorced father's new family in Des Moines. A sequel to *The One Hundredth Thing About Caroline* (1983). (Rev: BCCB 1/86; BL 10/1/85; HB 1–2/86)

3853 Lowry, Lois. *Your Move, J.P.!* (6–8). 1990, Houghton $16.00 (978-0-395-53639-1). J. P. Tate, a 7th grader, is hopelessly in love with Angela. (Rev: BL 3/1/90; SLJ 5/90; VOYA 4/90)

3854 Lubar, David. *Punished!* (4–7). 2006, Darby Creek $15.95 (978-1-58196-042-6). Thanks to a curse, Logan becomes a non-stop punster and must uncover oxymorons, anagrams, and palindromes to break the spell. (Rev: BL 5/1/06; SLJ 5/06*)

3855 MacDonald, Amy. *No More Nice* (4–7). Illus. 1996, Orchard LB $15.99 (978-0-531-08892-0). A humorous story about a spring vacation spent by a boy with his eccentric great-aunt and -uncle. (Rev: BCCB 10/96; BL 9/1/96; SLJ 9/96)

3856 McFann, Jane. *Deathtrap and Dinosaur* (7–12). 1989, Avon paper $2.75 (978-0-380-75624-7). An unlikely pair works to force the departure of a disliked history teacher. (Rev: SLJ 10/89; VOYA 10/89)

3857 Mackay, Claire, sel. *Laughs* (5–8). 1997, Tundra paper $6.95 (978-0-88776-393-9). An anthology of humorous stories (and some poems) by several well-known Canadian writers. (Rev: SLJ 9/97)

3858 McKenna, Colleen O'Shaughnessy. *Mother Murphy* (5–7). 1993, Scholastic paper $2.95 (978-0-590-44856-7). With her mother confined to bed, 12-year-old Collette volunteers as mother-for-a-day with disasterous and funny results. (Rev: BCCB 2/92; BL 2/1/92; SLJ 2/92)

3859 MacLeod, Doug. *I'm Being Stalked by a Moon Shadow* (7–10). 2007, Front St. $16.95 (978-1-59078-501-0). Seth, the son of hippies, falls in love with tough-girl Miranda, the daughter of an uptight neighbor in this funny Australian novel. (Rev: BL 10/1/07; SLJ 1/08)

3860 McManus, Patrick F. *Never Cry "Arp!" and Other Great Adventures* (6–9). 1996, Holt $16.95 (978-0-8050-4662-5). Based on fact, the 12 stories in this collection deal humorously with the problems of growing up in the mountains of Idaho. (Rev: BL 8/96; SLJ 7/96)

3861 Maguire, Gregory. *One Final Firecracker* (4–7). Illus. by Elaine Clayton. Series: The Hamlet Chronicles. 2005, Clarion $17.00 (978-0-618-27480-2). In the final pun-filled installment in the series, the rival Tattletales and Copycats must cooperate to defend the class and the soon-to-be-wed Miss Earth from myriad threats. (Rev: SLJ 5/05)

3862 Manes, Stephen. *Comedy High* (7–10). 1992, Scholastic paper $13.95 (978-0-590-44436-1). A comic story of a new high school designed to graduate jocks, performers, gambling experts, and hotel workers. (Rev: BL 12/1/92; SLJ 11/92)

3863 Many, Paul. *These Are the Rules* (7–10). 1997, Walker $15.95 (978-0-8027-8619-7). In this hilarious first-person narrative, Colm tries to figure out the rules of dating, driving, girls, and getting some direction in his life. (Rev: BL 5/1/97; HBG 3/98; SLJ 5/97)

3864 Maxwell, Katie. *They Wear What Under Their Kilts?* (8–11). 2004, Dorchester paper $5.99 (978-0-8439-5258-2). Emily Williams, the 16-year-old American introduced in the riotous *The Year My Life Went Down the Loo*, is off to a Scottish sheep farm on a month-long work-study program. (Rev: BL 1/1–15/04)

3865 Meacham, Margaret. *A Fairy's Guide to Understanding Humans* (5–8). 2007, Holiday $16.95 (978-0-8234-2078-0). Morgan's unreliable fairy godmother tries to improve 14-year-old Morgan's life after her move to a new house and new school in this sequel to *A Mid-Semester Night's Dream* (2004). (Rev: BL 2/1/08; SLJ 2/08)

3866 Meehl, Brian. *Suck It Up* (8–11). 2008, Delacorte $15.99 (978-0-385-73300-7). Sixteen-year-old

Morning is an unlikely vampire — he drinks only blood substitute and is something of a nerd — but he is chosen to be the first of his kind to reveal his true nature to humans; romance and humor add to the appeal. (Rev: BL 3/1/08)

3867 Merrill, Jean. *The Pushcart War* (6–9). Illus. by Ronni Solbert. 1987, Dell paper $5.50 (978-0-440-47147-9). Mack, driving a Mighty Mammoth, runs down a pushcart belonging to Morris the Florist and starts a most unusual war that is humorous and also reveals many human foibles. (Rev: BL 4/87)

3868 Mills, Claudia. *Alex Ryan, Stop That!* (4–7). Series: West Creek Middle School. 2003, Farrar $16.00 (978-0-374-34655-3). All Alex's efforts to attract classmate Marcia go awry in this humorous account of 7th-grade and son-father relations. (Rev: BL 4/1/03; HBG 10/03; SLJ 4/03)

3869 Mlynowski, Sarah. *Frogs and French Kisses* (7–10). 2006, Delacorte $15.95 (978-0-385-73182-9). This funny, cleverly written sequel to *Bras and Broomsticks* (2005) features Rachel's efforts to control her family members' overuse of magic while she copes with the consequences. (Rev: BL 7/06; SLJ 9/06)

3870 Mlynowski, Sarah. *Spells and Sleeping Bags* (6–9). 2007, Delacorte $16.99 (978-0-385-73387-8). In this third book about witch sisters Rachel and Miri, the girls go to a summer camp in the Adirondacks and Rachel tries to keep her powers under cover. (Rev: SLJ 8/07)

3871 Montgomery, Claire, and Monte Montgomery. *Hubert Invents the Wheel* (4–7). Illus. by Jeff Shelly. 2005, Walker $16.95 (978-0-8027-8990-7). Hubert, a struggling 15-year-old inventor in ancient Sumeria, finally finds success when he invents the wheel, but things quickly spin out of control. (Rev: SLJ 11/05)

3872 Mulford, Philippa Greene. *Making Room for Katherine* (5–9). 1994, Macmillan $14.95 (978-0-02-767652-5). A 16-year-old is recovering from her father's death when a 13-year-old cousin arrives from Paris to visit for the summer. (Rev: BL 4/15/94; SLJ 5/94; VOYA 8/94)

3873 Naylor, Phyllis Reynolds. *Alice Alone* (6–10). 2001, Simon & Schuster $15.00 (978-0-689-82634-4). Alice's story continues as she starts high school and deals with the misery of breaking up with her boyfriend. (Rev: BCCB 5/01; BL 5/15/01; HB 7–8/01; HBG 10/01; SLJ 6/01; VOYA 8/01)

3874 Naylor, Phyllis Reynolds. *Alice in April* (5–8). 1993, Dell paper $4.50 (978-0-440-91032-9). Alice is back, this time caught between her desire to be a perfect housekeeper and her fascination with her developing body. (Rev: BL 3/1/93; SLJ 6/93)

3875 Naylor, Phyllis Reynolds. *Alice in Lace* (6–8). 1996, Simon & Schuster $17.00 (978-0-689-80358-1). Alice, in her usual bumbling, endearing way, confronts society's greatest problems when her health class does a unit on "Critical Choices." (Rev: BL 3/1/96; SLJ 4/96; VOYA 8/96)

3876 Naylor, Phyllis Reynolds. *Alice the Brave* (5–7). 1995, Simon & Schuster paper $4.99 (978-0-689-80598-1). Alice conquers her fear of deep water and also feels the pangs of growing up in this amusing continuation of a popular series. (Rev: BCCB 4/95; BL 5/1/95; HB 7–8/95; SLJ 5/95)

3877 Naylor, Phyllis Reynolds. *All But Alice* (5–8). 1992, Macmillan $15.95 (978-0-689-31773-6). Alice, now a 7th grader and still motherless, deals with the challenges of friendship and popularity. (Rev: BCCB 5/92; BL 3/1/92; HB 7–8/92; SLJ 5/92*)

3878 Naylor, Phyllis Reynolds. *The Grooming of Alice* (6–9). 2000, Simon & Schuster $16.00 (978-0-689-82633-7). In this, the twelfth Alice story, our heroine discovers what is meant by "normal" for girls and also helps a friend who is having trouble at home. (Rev: BL 6/1–15/00; HB 7–8/00; HBG 9/00; SLJ 5/00)

3879 Naylor, Phyllis Reynolds. *Including Alice* (6–9). 2004, Simon & Schuster $15.95 (978-0-689-82637-5). Alice has trouble adjusting to life with her new stepmother as well as the usual problems of a sophomore. (Rev: HB 7–8/04; SLJ 5/04; VOYA 8/04)

3880 Naylor, Phyllis Reynolds. *Outrageously Alice* (6–8). 1997, Simon & Schuster $15.95 (978-0-689-80354-3); paper $4.99 (978-0-689-80596-7). Thirteen-year-old Alice, now in the 8th grade, decides that she is too ordinary and wants to do something about it. (Rev: BCCB 7–8/97; BL 5/15/97; HB 7–8/98; SLJ 6/97; VOYA 10/97)

3881 Naylor, Phyllis Reynolds. *Patiently Alice* (6–9). 2003, Simon & Schuster $15.95 (978-0-689-82636-8). Alice spends summer as a camp counselor and despite a lack of romance has lots of fun (including talk of sex) and learns about her disadvantaged charges. (Rev: BL 8/03; HB 7–8/03; HBG 10/03; SLJ 5/03; VOYA 8/03)

3882 Naylor, Phyllis Reynolds. *Reluctantly Alice* (5–8). 1991, Macmillan $16.00 (978-0-689-31681-4). Alice's life in the 7th grade seems full of embarrassment. (Rev: BCCB 4/91*; BL 2/1/91; HB 7–8/91; SLJ 3/91*)

3883 Naylor, Phyllis Reynolds. *Simply Alice* (6–9). 2002, Simon & Schuster $16.00 (978-0-689-82635-1). Now 14, Alice is in 9th grade and living a full life while learning to deal with family, friendships, and embarrassing situations. (Rev: BCCB 6/02; BL 6/1–15/02; HB 7–8/02; HBG 10/02; SLJ 5/02; VOYA 6/02)

3884 Naylor, Phyllis Reynolds. *Who Won the War?* (4–7). 2006, Delacorte LB $17.99 (978-0-385-90172-7). In the last weeks before they return to Ohio (and the last volume in the series), the Malloy sisters mount a last-ditch campaign to prove their superiority over the Hatford boys. (Rev: BL 11/1/06; SLJ 9/06)

3885 Park, Barbara. *Buddies* (5–8). 1986, Avon paper $2.95 (978-0-380-69992-6). Dinah's dreams of being popular at camp are dashed in this humorous novel because she is forever being accompanied by Fern, the camp nerd. (Rev: BCCB 5/85; BL 4/15/85; SLJ 5/85)

3886 Paulsen, Gary. *Harris and Me: A Summer Remembered* (6–10). 1993, Harcourt $16.00 (978-0-15-292877-3). A humorous story in which the 11-year-old narrator often gets the blame for mischief caused by troublemaker Harris. (Rev: BL 12/1/93*; SLJ 2/00; VOYA 2/94)

3887 Paulsen, Gary. *Lawn Boy* (5–8). 2007, Random $12.99 (978-0-385-74686-1). Given his late grandfather's somewhat battered riding mower as a gift, a 12-year-old entrepreneur launches a phenomenally successful lawn care business in this zany, tongue-in-cheek story. (Rev: BL 4/15/07; HB 7–8/07; SLJ 6/07)

3888 Peck, Richard. *A Long Way from Chicago* (6–10). 1998, Dial $16.99 (978-0-8037-2290-3). Seven stories are included in this book, each representing a different summer from 1929 to 1935 that Joey spent visiting in Illinois with his lying, cheating, conniving, and thoroughly charming grandmother. (Rev: BCCB 10/98; BL 9/1/98; HB 11–12/98; HBG 3/99; SLJ 10/98*; VOYA 12/98)

3889 Peck, Richard. *A Year Down Yonder* (6–10). 2000, Dial $16.99 (978-0-8037-2518-8). In this 2001 Newbery Medal winner, 15-year-old Mary Alice visits her feisty, independent, but lovable Grandma Dowdel in rural Illinois during the Great Depression. A sequel to *A Long Way from Chicago* (1998). (Rev: BCCB 1/01; BL 10/15/00*; HB 11–12/00; HBG 3/01; SLJ 9/00; VOYA 12/00)

3890 Peck, Robert Newton. *Higbee's Halloween* (5–7). 1990, Walker LB $14.85 (978-0-8027-6969-5). Higbee decides something must be done about the unruly Striker children. (Rev: SLJ 10/90)

3891 Petty, J. T. *The Squampkin Patch: A Nasselrogt Adventure* (4–7). Illus. by David Michael Friend. 2006, Simon & Schuster $15.95 (978-1-4169-0274-4). A funny, far-fetched fantasy about two children who escape hard labor at the zipper factory/orphanage (their parents are tied up in tanning beds) and find themselves pursued by squampkins — pumpkin-like creatures — that are out for blood. (Rev: SLJ 7/06)

3892 Pinder, Margaret. *But I Don't Want to Be a Movie Star* (6–9). 2006, Dutton $15.99 (978-0-525-

47634-4). This is the wildly funny story of Kat, a 15-year-old English girl who visits her Oscar-winning grandmother in California and, after the grandmother breaks an ankle, decides to impersonate her. (Rev: BL 4/15/06; SLJ 4/06)

3893 Pinkwater, Daniel. *The Neddiad: How Neddie Took the Train, Went to Hollywood, and Saved Civilization* (6–9). 2007, Houghton $16.00 (978-0-618-59444-3). A sacred stone turtle, ghosts, movie stars, and woolly mammoths are some of the characters that enter into this story of Neddie Wentworthstein and his travels with his family across 1940s America on the way to have dinner in Los Angeles. (Rev: BL 2/1/07; HB 5-6/07; SLJ 4/07) ⑨

3894 Pratchett, Terry. *Going Postal* (8–12). Series: Discworld. 2004, HarperCollins $24.95 (978-0-06-001313-4). In this humorous and inventive 29th Discworld novel, career criminal Moist von Lipwig escapes hanging by accepting the job of postmaster for Ankh-Morpork, a job he intends to leave far behind as soon as he can. (Rev: BL 9/1/04; SLJ 2/05)

3895 Rennison, Louise. *Angus, Thongs and Full-Frontal Snogging: Confessions of Georgia Nicolson* (6–9). 2000, HarperCollins $16.99 (978-0-06-028814-3). In her diary, 14-year-old Georgia Nicolson writes with humor and charm of her latest crush, learning to kiss, hunting for her cat, and other teen concerns. (Rev: BL 7/00; HB 5–6/00; HBG 9/00; SLJ 7/00; VOYA 6/00)

3896 Rennison, Louise. *Startled by His Furry Shorts: Confessions of Georgia Nicolson* (7–10). 2006, HarperTempest $16.99 (978-0-06-085384-6). Georgia, a British teenager, gives her hilarious views about dealing with boys, her family, having fun with friends, and getting stuck with a part in her school's play. (Rev: BL 10/15/06; SLJ 7/06) ⑨

3897 Rennison, Louise. *Then He Ate My Boy Entrancers: More Mad, Marvy Confessions of Georgia Nicolson* (7–10). 2005, HarperCollins $15.99 (978-0-06-058937-0). In her sixth volume of diaries, Georgia travels to and critiques the United States as well as cataloging her usual problems at home with friends, boyfriends, siblings, and cats. (Rev: BL 8/05; SLJ 8/05; VOYA 10/05)

3898 Riggs, Bob. *My Best Defense* (6–10). 1996, Ward Hill paper $5.95 (978-1-886747-01-2). Sarcasm is the best defense of the narrator in this humorous story of a family and the unusual characters they attract. (Rev: SLJ 8/96; VOYA 10/96)

3899 Robertson, Keith. *Henry Reed, Inc.* (5–7). Illus. by Robert McCloskey. 1989, Puffin paper $6.99 (978-0-14-034144-7). Told deadpan in diary form, this story of Henry's enterprising summer in New Jersey presents one of the most amusing boys since Tom and Huck. Others in the series *Henry*

Reed's Journey (1963); *Henry Reed's Baby-Sitting Service* (1966); *Henry Reed's Big Show* (1970).

3900 Rodgers, Mary. *Freaky Friday* (4–7). 1972, HarperCollins LB $16.89 (978-0-06-025049-2); paper $5.99 (978-0-06-440046-6). Thirteen-year-old Annabel learns some valuable lessons during the day she becomes her mother. Two sequels are *A Billion for Boris* (1974) and *Summer Switch* (1982). (Rev: BL 4/15/89)

3901 Ryan, Mary C. *Who Says I Can't?* (7–10). 1988, Little, Brown $12.95 (978-0-316-76374-5). Tessa decides to get revenge on a boy who shows too much ardor in his romancing. (Rev: SLJ 11/88)

3902 Sachar, Louis. *Sideways Arithmetic from Wayside School* (4–8). Series: Wayside School. 1992, Scholastic paper $4.99 (978-0-590-45726-2). Sue learns a new kind of math and encounters some humorous brainteasers when she transfers to Wayside School. (Rev: BL 12/15/89)

3903 Scrimger, Richard. *Noses Are Red* (4–7). 2002, Tundra paper $7.95 (978-0-88776-590-2). Norbert, the alien who likes to live in Alan's nose, works to Alan's benefit once again when Alan and a friend meet a variety of perils on a camping trip. (Rev: BL 1/1–15/03; HBG 3/03; SLJ 12/02; VOYA 2/03)

3904 Selzer, Adam. *Pirates of the Retail Wasteland* (6–9). 2008, Delacorte $15.99 (978-0-385-73482-0). Leon, an inventive 14-year-old, and a group of friends in his gifted class decide to stage a protest against the big-business coffee shop that is threatening their downtown favorite. (Rev: BL 3/15/08; SLJ 7/08)

3905 Sheldon, Dyan. *Confessions of a Hollywood Star* (7–10). 2006, Candlewick $208.00 (978-0-7636-3075-1). In this funny follow-up to *Confessions of a Teenage Drama Queen* (1999), Lola schemes to get a part in a Hollywood movie being filmed in her suburban New Jersey hometown. (Rev: BL 6/1–15/06; HB 7–8/06; LMC 11–12/06; SLJ 10/06)

3906 Shields, Gillian. *The Actual Real Reality of Jennifer James* (7–10). 2006, HarperCollins $16.99 (978-0-06-082240-8). Unpopular British high school student Jennifer James becomes a contestant on a TV reality show in this funny story told through diary entries (with helpful definitions of British slang). (Rev: BL 5/15/06; SLJ 6/06)

3907 Shipton, Paul. *The Pig Scrolls* (6–9). 2005, Candlewick $15.99 (978-0-7636-2702-7). Shipton turns ancient Greek history and mythology on its ear to create this rollicking tale of Gryllus, who is transformed into a talking pig by Circe and goes on to save the world. (Rev: BL 10/15/05; SLJ 12/05)

3908 Shipton, Paul. *The Pig Who Saved the World: By Gryllus the Pig* (5–8). 2007, Candlewick $15.99 (978-0-7636-3446-9). In this sequel to *The Pig Scrolls* (2005), Gryllus the pig and his mythological friends — including the young poet Homer — are searching for Circe, the sorceress who can make Gryllus human again. (Rev: BL 10/1/07; SLJ 11/07)

3909 Shusterman, Neal. *The Schwa Was Here* (6–9). 2004, Penguin $16.99 (978-0-525-47182-0). The virtual invisibility of 8th-grader Calvin Schwa proves profitable for newfound friend Anthony Bonano, who takes wagers on how much his new pal can get away with. (Rev: BL 12/1/04; SLJ 10/04; VOYA 10/04)

3910 Sleator, William. *Oddballs* (8–12). 1995, Penguin paper $5.99 (978-0-14-037438-4). A collection of stories based on experiences from the author's youth and peopled with an unusual assortment of family and friends.

3911 Smith, Edwin R. *Blue Star Highway: A Tale of Redemption from North Florida, Vol. 1* (7–12). 1997, Mile Marker Twelve Publg. paper $9.95 (978-0-9659054-0-4). In this humorous novel, 14-year-old Marty Crane tells of the events in his life leading up to being sentenced to a detention home in 1962. (Rev: BL 2/15/99)

3912 Snicket, Lemony. *The Bad Beginning* (4–7). Illus. Series: A Series of Unfortunate Events. 1999, HarperCollins $12.99 (978-0-06-440766-3). A humorous story about the ill-fated Beaudelaire orphans and the creepy, wicked villains they never seem to avoid. (Rev: BL 12/1/99; HBG 3/00; SLJ 11/99)

3913 Snicket, Lemony. *The Carnivorous Carnival* (4–8). Illus. by Brett Helquist. Series: A Series of Unfortunate Events. 2002, HarperCollins LB $15.89 (978-0-06-029640-7). The Baudelaire orphans pose as carnival freaks in the ninth volume of this unhappily-ever-after series. (Rev: BL 12/15/02; HBG 3/03; SLJ 1/03)

3914 Snicket, Lemony. *The End* (5–8). Illus. by Brett Helquist. Series: A Series of Unfortunate Events. 2006, HarperCollins $12.99 (978-0-06-441016-8). The Baudelaire orphans find themselves stranded on an island with none other than the villainous Count Olaf; will this be the last installment in the series? (Rev: BL 10/15/06)

3915 Snicket, Lemony. *The Wide Window* (4–7). Illus. Series: A Series of Unfortunate Events. 2000, HarperCollins LB $15.89 (978-0-06-028314-8). The three Baudelaire children have a new guardian, timid cousin Josephine, but they are pursued by former keeper Count Olaf. (Rev: BL 2/1/00; HBG 10/00; SLJ 1/00)

3916 Soto, Gary. *Summer on Wheels* (5–8). 1995, Scholastic paper $13.95 (978-0-590-48365-0). In this sequel to *Crazy Weekend* (1994), Hector and Mando take a bike ride from their barrio home in Los Angeles to Santa Monica. (Rev: BL 1/15/95; SLJ 4/95; VOYA 4/95)

3917 Spinelli, Jerry. *The Library Card* (4–8). 1997, Scholastic paper $15.95 (978-0-590-46731-5). Four humorous, poignant stories about how books changed the lives of several youngsters. (Rev: BCCB 3/97; BL 2/1/97; HB 3–4/97; SLJ 3/97; VOYA 10/97)

3918 Standford, Natalie. *Blonde at Heart* (5–8). Series: Elle Woods. 2006, Hyperion $4.99 (978-0-7868-3843-1). How Elle Woods, the central character of the 2001 movie *Legally Blonde*, became a blond bombshell in her effort to attract the attention of her crush. (Rev: BL 7/06; SLJ 5/06)

3919 Stanley, George E. *Hershell Cobwell and the Miraculous Tattoo* (4–8). 1991, Avon paper $2.95 (978-0-380-75897-5). A junior high boy decides to gain popularity by getting a tattoo. (Rev: BL 3/15/91)

3920 Taha, Karen T. *Marshmallow Muscles, Banana Brainstorms* (6–8). 1988, Harcourt $13.95 (978-0-15-200525-2). A puny youngster tries a regime of body development through the help of his dream girl. (Rev: BL 1/1/89)

3921 Trahey, Jane. *The Clovis Caper* (5–8). 1990, Avon paper $2.95 (978-0-380-75914-9). Martin is so upset at leaving his dog, Clovis, when going to England that Aunt Hortense plots to smuggle the dog out of the country. (Rev: BL 7/90)

3922 Trembath, Don. *A Fly Named Alfred* (7–10). 1997, Orca paper $6.95 (978-1-55143-083-6). In this sequel to *The Tuesday Cafe*, Harper Winslow gets into more trouble when he write an anonymous column in the school newspaper that enrages the school bully. (Rev: BL 8/97; SLJ 9/96)

3923 Tulloch, Richard. *Weird Stuff* (5–8). Illus. by Shane Nagle. 2006, Walker $16.95 (978-0-8027-8058-4). A borrowed pen gives school soccer star Brian Hobble amazing new writing abilities, but they're limited to a single genre — romantic fiction. (Rev: SLJ 8/06)

3924 Uderzo, Albert. *Asterix and Son* (4–8). Trans. by Anthea Bell and Derek Hockridge. Illus. 2002, Orion paper $9.95 (978-0-7528-4775-7). In comic-book format, this is the entertaining story of French heroes Asterix and Obelix and how they became guardians of a kidnapped baby. Also use *Asterix and the Black Gold* (2002) and *Asterix and the Great Divide* (2002). (Rev: BL 4/15/02)

3925 Ware, Cheryl. *Venola in Love* (4–7). Illus. by Kristin Sorra. 2000, Orchard LB $16.99 (978-0-531-33306-8). Told through diary entries, e-mail messages, and class notes, this humorous novel tells how 7th-grader Venola discovers the problems of falling in love. (Rev: BCCB 10/00; HBG 10/01; SLJ 10/00)

3926 Wersba, Barbara. *You'll Never Guess the End* (7–12). 1992, HarperCollins $14.00 (978-0-06-020448-8). A send-up of the New York City literary scene, rich dilettantes, and scientology. (Rev: BL 11/15/92; SLJ 9/92)

3927 Weyn, Suzanne. *The Makeover Club* (7–9). 1986, Avon paper $2.50 (978-0-380-75007-8). Three girls decide they are going to be glamorous by forming the Makeover Club. (Rev: SLJ 1/87; VOYA 12/86)

3928 Whytock, Cherry. *My Scrumptious Scottish Dumplings: The Life of Angelica Cookson Potts* (6–9). 2004, Simon & Schuster $14.95 (978-0-689-86549-7). In this rollicking sequel to *My Cup Runneth Over* (2003), poor privileged — and unsylphlike — Angel finds herself barred from the Harrods' food halls after her Scottish-born father stages a protest against the quality of the big store's haggis. (Rev: BL 1/1–15/05; SLJ 1/05)

3929 Wibberley, Leonard. *The Mouse That Roared* (7–12). 1992, Buccaneer LB $27.95 (978-0-89966-887-1). To get foreign aid, the tiny Duchy of Grand Fenwick declares war on the United States.

3930 Wood, Maryrose. *Sex Kittens and Horn Dawgs Fall in Love* (7–10). 2006, Delacorte LB $17.99 (978-0-385-90296-0). To get closer to Matthew, the object of her affection, 14-year-old Felicia suggests that the two of them work together on a science fair project investigating the workings of love's "X-factor." (Rev: BL 11/15/05; SLJ 2/06)

3931 Yee, Lisa. *So Totally Emily Ebers* (5–8). 2007, Scholastic $16.99 (978-0-439-83847-4). In this companion to *Millicent Min, Girl Genius* (2003) and *Stanford Wong Flunks Big-Time* (2005), Emily writes a series of letters to her absent father, telling him about her friends Millicent and Stanford and their tutoring arrangement. (Rev: BL 3/15/07; SLJ 4/07)

3932 Yee, Lisa. *Stanford Wong Flunks Big-Time* (4–7). 2005, Scholastic $16.99 (978-0-439-62247-9). In this rollicking sequel to *Millicent Minn, Girl Genius*, Stanford Wong is upset when his parents hire Millicent, his arch-nemesis, to tutor him in English. (Rev: BL 11/15/05; SLJ 12/05)

3933 Ziegler, Jennifer. *Alpha Dog* (8–11). 2006, Delacorte paper $7.99 (978-0-385-73285-7). When Katie learns to be alpha dog and control her adopted mutt, she also learns to assert herself with her mother and friends in this funny novel. (Rev: BL 7/06; LMC 10/06)

3934 Ziegler, Jennifer. *How Not to Be Popular* (7–10). 2008, Delacorte $15.99 (978-0-385-73465-3). When her family moves yet again, Sugar Magnolia (Maggie) ditches her usual effort to make friends and instead decides to become an outsider at school. (Rev: BL 4/1/08; SLJ 3/08)

Mysteries, Thrillers, and Spy Stories

3935 Abbott, Tony. *The Postcard* (6–9). 2008, Little, Brown $15.99 (978-0-316-01172-3). When Jason discovers an old postcard that belonged to his recently deceased grandmother, he is drawn into a mystery that mirrors a story in an old magazine. (Rev: BL 5/1/08; SLJ 4/08)

3936 Abrahams, Peter. *Down the Rabbit Hole* (7–10). Series: Echo Falls. 2005, HarperCollins LB $17.89 (978-0-06-073702-3). Thirteen-year-old Ingrid Levin-Hill takes a page from her idol Sherlock Holmes and sets out to track down the murderer of an eccentric townswoman. (Rev: BCCB 4/05; BL 5/1/05*; SLJ 5/05; VOYA 6/05)

3937 Abrahams, Peter. *Into the Dark* (5–12). Series: Echo Falls. 2008, HarperCollins $15.99 (978-0-06-073708-5). Ingrid's grandfather, a World War II veteran, is a suspect in a murder committed using a World War II-era rifle. Can Ingrid solve the mystery and clear her grandfather's name? (Rev: BL 5/1/08; SLJ 3/08)

3938 Aiken, Joan. *The Teeth of the Gale* (7–9). 1988, HarperCollins $14.95 (978-0-06-020044-2). Eighteen-year-old Felix tries to rescue three children who have been kidnapped. A sequel to *Go Saddle the Sea* and *Bridle the Wind*. (Rev: BL 9/15/88; SLJ 11/88; VOYA 12/88)

3939 Allison, Jennifer. *Gilda Joyce: Psychic Investigator* (5–7). 2005, Dutton $13.99 (978-0-525-47375-6). Thirteen-year-old Gilda Joyce and a new friend, Juliet, look into the suicide of Juliet's aunt in this richly layered mystery. (Rev: BL 5/1/05*; SLJ 7/05*)

3940 Allison, Jennifer. *Gilda Joyce: The Ghost Sonata* (5–8). 2007, Dutton $15.99 (978-0-525-47808-9). Gilda's psychic abilities come in handy as she accompanies her friend Wendy to a piano competition in England and discovers that Wendy is being haunted. (Rev: SLJ 8/07) 🌢

3941 Alphin, Elaine Marie. *The Perfect Shot* (8–12). 2005, Carolrhoda LB $16.95 (978-1-57505-862-7). Brian, a high school basketball star, learns important lessons about justice, racial prejudice, and civic responsibility when his girlfriend's father is charged with the murder of his wife and two daughters and an African American teammate is arrested on trumped-up charges. (Rev: SLJ 10/05*; VOYA 12/05)

3942 Anastasio, Dina. *The Case of the Glacier Park Swallow* (4–7). Illus. 1994, Roberts Rinehart paper $6.95 (978-1-879373-85-3). Juliet, who wants to be a veterinarian, stumbles upon a drug-smuggling ring in this tightly knit mystery. (Rev: BL 12/1/94; SLJ 10/94)

3943 Anastasio, Dina. *The Case of the Grand Canyon Eagle* (5–8). Series: Juliet Stone Environmental Mystery. 1994, Roberts Rinehart paper $6.95 (978-1-879373-84-6). In this ecological mystery, 17-year-old Juliet Stone investigates the disappearance of eagle eggs. (Rev: SLJ 10/94)

3944 Anderson, M. T. *The Clue of the Linoleum Lederhosen: M. T. Anderson's Thrilling Tales* (4–7). Illus. by Kurt Cyrus. 2006, Harcourt $15.00 (978-0-15-205352-9). Jasper Dash, Boy Technonaut, Katie, and Lily are caught up in an exciting mystery at Moose Tongue Lodge in this zany sequel to *Whales on Stilts* (2005). (Rev: BCCB 7–8/06; BL 5/1/06*; HB 5–6/06; HBG 10/06; SLJ 6/06; VOYA 6/06) 🌢

3945 Apone, Claudio. *My Grandfather, Jack the Ripper* (6–12). 2000, Herodias $19.00 (978-1-928746-16-4). Thirteen-year-old Andy Dobson, a clairvoyant Londoner, travels back in time — with the help of hallucinogenic drugs — to discover the true identity of the legendary murderer. (Rev: HBG 10/01; SLJ 6/01; VOYA 6/01)

3946 Arnold, Tedd. *Rat Life: A Mystery* (7–10). 2007, Dial $16.99 (978-0-8037-3020-5). Todd, 14, loves to write funny, crude stories to entertain his classmates until he befriends a Vietnam veteran named Rat; his writing takes on a new perspective while he also begins to uncover clues to an unsolved murder. (Rev: BL 5/1/07; SLJ 5/07)

3947 Balliett, Blue. *Chasing Vermeer* (5–8). Illus. by Brett Helquist. 2004, Scholastic $16.95 (978-0-439-37294-7). Petra and Calder, brainy 12-year-old classmates at the University of Chicago Lab School, join forces to find out what happened to a missing Vermeer painting. (Rev: BL 4/1/04*; HB 7–8/04; SLJ 7/04)

3948 Bauer, Joan. *Peeled* (6–9). 2008, Putnam $16.99 (978-0-399-23475-0). Hildy and her friends start up an underground newspaper when the principal shuts down the school paper following inflammatory articles about mysterious happenings around town. (Rev: BL 4/15/08; SLJ 4/08)

3949 Bell, Hilari. *Rogue's Home* (7–10). Series: Knight and Rogue. 2008, Eos $17.99 (978-0-06-082506-5). The second adventure in the series, this buddy story has the "knight" Mike and his sidekick squire Fisk returning to Fisk's hometown to investigate blackmail and arson. (Rev: BL 8/08; SLJ 9/08)

3950 Bennett, Jay. *Coverup* (8–10). 1992, Fawcett paper $5.99 (978-0-449-70409-7). Realizing his friend has killed a pedestrian on a deserted road after a party, Brad returns to the accident scene and meets a girl searching for her homeless father. (Rev: BL 11/1/91)

3951 Bloor, Edward. *Taken* (5–8). 2007, Knopf $16.99 (978-0-375-83636-7). In Florida in the year 2035, where kidnapping has become a common crime with recognized procedures, 13-year-old Charity must find a way to escape and survive when her wealthy family's payoff to the kidnappers goes wrong. (Rev: BL 9/1/07; SLJ 12/07)

3952 Bosch, Pseudonymous. *The Name of This Book Is Secret* (4–7). Illus. 2007, Little, Brown $16.99 (978-0-316-11366-3). What's inside this book is secret, too, and only after much cautioning does the narrator begin to tell the story of a group trying to discover the key to immortality. (Rev: BL 7/07; SLJ 1/08) 📖

3953 Bossley, Michele Martin. *Swiped* (6–8). Series: Orca Currents. 2006, Orca paper $8.95 (978-1-55143-646-3). Even though their efforts meet with suspicion and disapproval, middle-schoolers Trevor, Nick, and Robyn investigate mysteries — missing sandwiches, stolen books — with gusto; for reluctant and challenged readers. (Rev: SLJ 3/07)

3954 Bowler, Tim. *Frozen Fire* (7–10). 2008, Philomel $17.99 (978-0-399-25053-8). Set in a wintry England, this is a disquieting and complex story of a ghostlike boy whom Dusty suspects knows the whereabouts of her missing brother. (Rev: BL 5/15/08; SLJ 7/08)

3955 Bowler, Tim. *Storm Catchers* (6–10). 2003, Simon & Schuster $16.95 (978-0-689-84573-4). A multilayered, suspenseful story of the kidnapping of a 13-year-old girl on the Cornwall coast, her brother's agonized guilt, and the discovery of a dark family secret. (Rev: BL 9/1/03; HBG 4/04; SLJ 5/03; VOYA 8/03)

3956 Bradbury, Jennifer. *Shift* (7–12). 2008, Atheneum $16.99 (978-1-4169-6219-9). Friends Chris and Win take a cross-country bike trip the summer after high school; but Win disappears in Montana and Chris becomes the focus of an FBI investigation. (Rev: BL 3/1/08)

3957 Broach, Elise. *Shakespeare's Secret* (6–9). 2005, Holt $16.95 (978-0-8050-7387-4). Hero, a 6th-grade misfit named for a character in a Shakespeare play, embarks on a search for a diamond with links to the Elizabethan era. (Rev: BCCB 6/05; BL 5/1/05; SLJ 6/05; VOYA 8/05)

3958 Bunting, Eve. *The Haunting of Safe Keep* (7–10). 1985, HarperCollins LB $12.89 (978-0-397-32113-1). In this romantic mystery, two college friends work out their family problems while investigating strange occurrences where they work. (Rev: BL 4/15/85; SLJ 5/85; VOYA 8/85)

3959 Burgess, Melvin. *Sara's Face* (8–12). 2007, Simon & Schuster $16.99 (978-1-4169-3295-6). Wealthy rock star Jonathan Heat, whose obsession with plastic surgery has left him without a face, offers to pay for surgery for pretty teen Sara; could his motives be less than generous? (Rev: BL 5/15/07; SLJ 6/07)

3960 Butcher, A. J. *Spy High: Mission One* (7–10). 2004, Little, Brown paper $6.99 (978-0-316-73760-9). This thriller is set in the year 2060 and deals with a group of students at a school known as Spy High who are training to become secret agents. (Rev: BL 5/1/04; SLJ 7/04)

3961 Butler, Dori Hillestad. *Do You Know the Monkey Man?* (5–7). 2005, Peachtree $14.95 (978-1-56145-340-5). After a psychic says that her twin sister — believed drowned 10 years before — is not dead at all, 13-year-old Samantha sets off with a friend to investigate. (Rev: BL 5/1/05; SLJ 6/05)

3962 Cargill, Linda. *Pool Party* (7–10). 1996, Scholastic paper $3.99 (978-0-590-58111-0). Sharon's beach party at a resort with a reputation for being haunted ends in murder. (Rev: SLJ 1/97)

3963 Carter, Ally. *Cross My Heart and Hope to Spy* (6–9). 2007, . Espionage and intrigue are interwoven with romance in this second (after 2006's *I'd Tell You I Love You, But Then I'd Have to Kill You*) story about Cammie Morgan and the other students at the Gallagher spy camp. (Rev: SLJ 10/07)

3964 Chandler, Elizabeth. *Dark Secrets: Legacy of Lies* (6–12). Series: Dark Secrets. 2000, Pocket paper $4.99 (978-0-7434-0028-2). Megan, 16, has finally met her grandmother, but she still feels like an outsider and her frightening dreams become more and more intense. (Rev: BCCB 2/01; BL 2/1/01; SLJ 1/01; VOYA 12/00)

3965 Clark, Mary Higgins, ed. *The International Association of Crime Writers Presents Bad Behavior* (8–12). 1995, Harcourt $20.00 (978-0-15-200179-7). Features many stories with young characters and less overt violence than adult fare. Includes works by Sara Paretsky, P. D. James, Lawrence Block, and Liza Cody. (Rev: BL 7/95)

3966 Coburn, Ann. *Glint* (6–9). 2007, HarperCollins LB $17.89 (978-0-06-084724-1). Ellie's younger brother is kidnapped and Ellie sets out to find him, inspired by a story the two siblings had read years before. (Rev: BL 1/1–15/07; SLJ 6/07)

3967 Collier, James Lincoln. *The Dreadful Revenge of Ernest Gallen* (5–8). 2008, Bloomsbury $16.95 (978-1-59990-220-3). Gene, the main character in this Depression-era mystery, is haunted by a ghost looking for revenge and searches for the role his family and neighbors played in a horrible crime. (Rev: BL 8/08; SLJ 9/08)

3968 Comino, Sandra. *The Little Blue House* (4–7). 2003, Douglas & McIntyre $15.95 (978-0-88899-504-9). Young Cintia and her friend Bruno investigate why an abandoned house in their small town in Argentina turns blue for one day each year in this suspenseful novel that contains some violence. (Rev: BL 2/15/04)

3969 Conly, Jane Leslie. *In the Night, on Lanvale Street* (6–8). 2005, Holt $16.95 (978-0-8050-7464-2). When their next-door neighbor is murdered, 13-year-old Charlie and her younger brother are swept up in a mystery that envelops the whole community. (Rev: SLJ 6/05)

3970 Copeland, Mark. *The Bundle at Blackthorpe Heath* (4–7). 2006, Houghton $15.00 (978-0-618-56302-9). With the help of a spyglass he receives as a birthday present, 12-year-old Arthur Piper uncovers a conspiracy to undermine his grandfather's traveling insect circus. (Rev: BL 6/1–15/06; SLJ 7/06)

3971 Cray, Jordan. *Dead Man's Hand* (5–9). Series: danger.com. 1998, Simon & Schuster paper $3.99 (978-0-689-82383-1). In this light read, Nick Annunciato and his stepsister, Annie Hanley, use their brains and a computer to solve a murder and escape a biological-weapons smuggling ring. (Rev: SLJ 2/99)

3972 Cray, Jordan. *Shiver* (5–8). Series: danger.com. 1998, Simon & Schuster paper $3.99 (978-0-689-82384-8). Six drama students are spending a weekend in the Green Mountains of Vermont, when one of the group is murdered. (Rev: SLJ 2/99)

3973 Cross, Gillian. *Phoning a Dead Man* (6–10). 2002, Holiday $16.95 (978-0-8234-1685-1). This suspenseful novel set in Russia alternates between the story of John, an amnesiac who is fleeing danger, and that of his sister and wheelchair-bound fiancee who are searching for him. (Rev: BCCB 5/02; BL 5/1/02; HB 7–8/02; HBG 10/02; SLJ 5/02; VOYA 6/02)

3974 Crossman, David A. *The Mystery of the Black Moriah* (5–8). Series: A Bean and Ab Mystery. 2002, Down East $16.95 (978-0-89272-536-6). The ever-curious Bean and Ab become caught up in a mystery adventure involving pirates, kidnappers, and a legendary ghost. (Rev: HBG 3/03; SLJ 12/02)

3975 Crossman, David A. *The Secret of the Missing Grave* (5–8). Series: A Bean and Ab Mystery. 1999, Down East $16.95 (978-0-89272-456-7). Two girls investigate a haunted house and become involved in a mystery concerning a missing treasure and stolen paintings in this fast-paced novel set in Maine. (Rev: HBG 3/00; SLJ 1/00)

3976 Davidson, Nicole. *Dying to Dance* (8–12). 1996, Avon paper $3.99 (978-0-380-78152-2). Carrie, a competitor on the ballroom-dance circuit, is suspected of murdering her archrival. (Rev: SLJ 7/96)

3977 Dean, Claire. *Girlwood* (6–9). 2008, Houghton $16.00 (978-0-618-88390-5). Mystery, New Age mysticism, environmentalism, and magic are intertwined in this story of 12-year-old Polly and her older sister, Bree, who has run away and may be living in a forest threatened by developers. (Rev: BL 2/15/08; SLJ 6/08)

3978 DeFelice, Cynthia. *The Missing Manatee* (5–8). 2005, Farrar $16.00 (978-0-374-31257-2). Skeet Waters sets out to solve the mystery of a murdered manatee he finds near his Florida home. (Rev: BL 3/1/05; SLJ 6/05)

3979 Delaney, Mark. *Of Heroes and Villains* (7–10). 1999, Peachtree paper $5.95 (978-1-56145-178-4). Using the world of comic books as a backdrop, this mystery features four teen sleuths known as the Misfits and the puzzle of a stolen film starring comic book hero Hyperman. (Rev: BL 7/99)

3980 Delaney, Mark. *The Protester's Song* (5–9). Series: Misfits, Inc. 2001, Peachtree paper $5.95 (978-1-56145-244-6). Four teens keep themselves busy investigating an incident that occurred during riots in Ohio in 1970 and, in a subplot, try to stop the new principal from removing books from the library. (Rev: SLJ 8/01)

3981 Delaney, Mark. *The Vanishing Chip* (5–8). Series: Misfits, Inc. 1998, Peachtree paper $5.95 (978-1-56145-176-0). Four teens who don't fit in at school investigate the disappearance of the world's most powerful computer chip. (Rev: BL 12/15/98; SLJ 2/99)

3982 Doctorow, Cory. *Little Brother* (8–12). 2008, Tor $17.95 (978-0-7653-1985-2). A terrorist attack on the San Francisco of the not-too-distant future results in Marcus being detained by the Department of Homeland Security and organizing a group of hackers to fight the powers that be. (Rev: BL 4/1/08; SLJ 5/08)

3983 Dowd, Siobhan. *The London Eye Mystery* (5–8). 2008, Random $15.99 (978-0-375-84976-3). Ted and Kat's cousin Salim disappears after entering a ride called the London Eye, and Ted relies on his unusual intellectual abilities to try to find him. (Rev: BL 1/1–15/08; HB 5–6/08; LMC 3/08; SLJ 2/08)

3984 Draanen, Wendelin Van. *Sammy Keyes and the Skeleton Man* (5–8). 1998, Knopf paper $4.99 (978-0-375-80054-2). Sammy, the youthful sleuth, is challenged when she tries to solve the mystery of a man dressed in a skeleton costume. (Rev: BL 9/1/98; HBG 3/99; SLJ 9/98)

3985 Duncan, Lois. *Daughters of Eve* (7–10). 1979, Dell paper $4.99 (978-0-440-91864-6). A group of girls comes under the evil influence of the faculty sponsor of their club.

3986 Duncan, Lois. *Down a Dark Hall* (7–10). 1974, Little, Brown paper $5.50 (978-0-440-91805-9). From the moment of arrival, Kit feels uneasy at her new boarding school.

3987 Duncan, Lois. *Killing Mr. Griffin* (7–10). 1978, Dell paper $5.50 (978-0-440-94515-4). A kidnapping plot involving a disliked English teacher leads to murder. (Rev: BL 10/15/88)

3988 Duncan, Lois. *The Third Eye* (7–10). 1984, Little, Brown $15.95 (978-0-316-19553-9); Dell paper $5.50 (978-0-440-98720-8). Karen learns that she has mental powers that enable her to locate missing children. (Rev: BL 7/87)

3989 Duncan, Lois. *The Twisted Window* (7–10). 1987, Dell paper $5.50 (978-0-440-20184-7). Tracy grows to regret the fact that she has helped a young man kidnap his 2-year-old half-sister. (Rev: BL 9/1/87; SLJ 9/87; VOYA 11/87)

3990 Eden, Alexandra. *Holy Smoke: A Bones and Duchess Mystery* (5–7). 2004, Alien A. Knoll $16.00 (978-1-888310-46-7). Ex-cop Bones Fatzinger and Verity Buscador, a 12-year-old girl with Asperger's syndrome, work together to track down the person responsible for setting fire to a local church. (Rev: BL 5/1/04)

3991 Ehrenhaft, Daniel. *Drawing a Blank: or, How I Tried to Solve a Mystery, End a Feud, and Land the Girl of My Dreams* (8–11). Illus. by Trevor Ristow. 2006, HarperCollins $15.99 (978-0-06-075252-1). In this clever novel, with the narrative switching from first person to comic book panels, boarding school student Carlton travels to Scotland to solve a mystery and find his kidnapped father; footnotes are both informative and amusing. (Rev: BL 5/1/06; SLJ 6/06*)

3992 Elmer, Robert. *Far from the Storm* (4–7). Series: Young Underground. 1995, Bethany paper $5.99 (978-0-556-61377-0). At the end of World War II, Danish twins Peter and Elise set out to find the culprit who set their uncle's boat on fire. (Rev: BL 2/15/96)

3993 Emerson, Kathy L. *The Mystery of the Missing Bagpipes* (5–7). 1991, Avon paper $2.95 (978-0-380-76138-8). Kim tries to find the real culprit when a young boy is wrongfully accused of stealing a set of ancient bagpipes and some precious daggers. (Rev: BL 9/15/91)

3994 Emerson, Scott. *The Case of the Cat with the Missing Ear: From the Notebooks of Edward R. Smithfield, D.V.M.* (5–7). 2003, Simon & Schuster LB $15.95 (978-0-689-85861-1). This canine takeoff of the Sherlock Holmes format features Yorkshire terrier Samuel Blackthorne and his sidekick and chronicler Dr. Edward Smithfield, who investigate mysteries with humor and deductive prowess. (Rev: BCCB 10/02; BL 12/1/03; HBG 4/04; SLJ 3/04)

3995 Erickson, John R. *Discovery at Flint Springs* (5–8). 2004, Viking $16.99 (978-0-670-05946-1). In 1927, 14-year-old Riley and his younger brother Coy join in an exciting search for archaeological sites on their Texas ranch. (Rev: BL 2/1/05; SLJ 12/04)

3996 Evarts, Hal G. *Jay-Jay and the Peking Monster* (7–9). 1984, Peter Smith $15.75 (978-0-8446-6166-7). Two teenagers discover the bones of a prehistoric man, and then the criminals move in.

3997 Falcone, L. M. *The Mysterious Mummer* (5–7). 2003, Kids Can $16.95 (978-1-55337-376-6). When Joey, 13, arrives in Newfoundland to spend Christmas with his aunt, he finds some very mysterious goings-on. (Rev: HBG 4/04; SLJ 10/03)

3998 Feder, Harriet K. *Death on Sacred Ground* (6–10). Series: Vivi Hartman. 2001, Lerner $14.95 (978-0-8225-0741-3). Teen sleuth Vivi Hartman encounters a mystery at the funeral of an Orthodox Jewish girl who died on sacred Indian ground. (Rev: BCCB 3/01; BL 11/15/01; HBG 10/01; SLJ 3/01)

3999 Feder, Harriet K. *Mystery of the Kaifeng Scroll* (6–9). 1995, Lerner LB $14.95 (978-0-8225-0739-0). In this sequel to *Mystery in Miami Beach*, Vivi Hartman, 15, must use her wits and knowledge of the Torah to save her mother from Palestinian terrorists. (Rev: BL 6/1–15/95)

4000 Feinstein, John. *Cover-Up: Mystery at the Super Bowl* (6–9). 2007, Knopf $16.99 (978-0-375-84247-4). After being fired from Kid Sports, teen reporter Steve meets up with his former co-host Susan Carol at the Super Bowl, where they uncover another sports scandal. (Rev: BL 9/1/07; SLJ 12/07) ✍

4001 Feinstein, John. *Vanishing Act* (6–9). 2006, Knopf LB $18.99 (978-0-375-83592-6). Susan Carol Anderson and Stevie Thomas, 13-year-old sports reporters, are covering the U.S. Open tennis championships when one of the star players is kidnapped. (Rev: BL 9/1/06; SLJ 10/06)

4002 Ferguson, Alane. *The Christopher Killer* (7–10). Series: Forensic Mystery. 2006, Viking $15.99 (978-0-670-06008-5). In this CSI-like story, a serial killer is on the loose and 17-year-old Cameryn, an aspiring forensic pathologist, helps her coroner father investigate. (Rev: BL 7/06; LMC 10/06; SLJ 8/06)

4003 Ferguson, Alane. *Overkill* (7–10). 1992, Avon paper $3.99 (978-0-380-72167-2). Lacey is seeing a therapist about nightmares in which she stabs her friend Celeste; when Celeste is found dead, Lacey is falsely arrested for the crime. (Rev: BL 1/1/93; SLJ 1/93)

4004 Ferguson, Alane. *Show Me the Evidence* (7–12). 1989, Avon paper $3.99 (978-0-380-70962-5). In this mystery story, a 17-year-old girl is fearful that her best friend might be involved in the mysterious deaths of several children. (Rev: BL 4/1/89; SLJ 3/89; VOYA 6/89)

4005 Fields, Terri. *Holdup* (6–10). 2007, Roaring Brook $16.95 (978-1-59643-219-2). Nine teen characters give their first-person accounts of the evening of a holdup of a fast-food restaurant. (Rev: BL 5/1/07; LMC 8–9/07; SLJ 4/07)

4006 Finney, Patricia. *Feud* (4–7). Series: Lady Grace Mysteries. 2006, Delacorte $7.95 (978-0-385-73323-6); paper $9.99 (978-0-385-90342-4). Lady Grace, maid of honor to Queen Elizabeth I, attempts to unravel the mystery surrounding the poisoning of another maid of honor. (Rev: BL 10/15/06)

4007 Foyt, Victoria. *The Virtual Life of Lexie Diamond* (6–8). 2007, HarperCollins $16.99 (978-0-06-082563-8). Lexie's recently deceased mother appears on Lexie's computer screen and reveals that she was murdered, and Lexie sets out to find out who killed her. (Rev: BCCB 6/07; BL 4/1/07; SLJ 5/07)

4008 Fusilli, Jim. *Marley Z. and the Bloodstained Violin* (5–8). 2008, Dutton $16.99 (978-0-525-47907-9). Marley's musician friend Marisol is accused of stealing a valuable violin, and Marley is determined to prove her innocence in this mystery set in New York City. (Rev: BL 5/1/08; SLJ 9/08)

4009 Gerber, Linda. *Death by Bikini* (7–10). 2008, Penguin paper $7.99 (978-0-14-241117-9). A murder mystery complicates the romance between Aphra and Adam, a guest at the resort that Aphra's father runs. (Rev: BL 5/1/08; SLJ 8/08)

4010 Gerson, Corrine. *My Grandfather the Spy* (5–7). 1990, Walker $14.95 (978-0-8027-6955-8). When a man arrives on the family farm in Vermont with a briefcase full of money, Danny suspects his grandfather is a spy. (Rev: BL 6/15/90; SLJ 8/90)

4011 Giles, Gail. *Dead Girls Don't Write Letters* (6–9). 2003, Millbrook $15.95 (978-0-7613-1727-2). Sunny, a 9th grader, is dealing with the aftermath of her 18-year-old sister Jazz's death in an apartment fire — until one day, a mysterious new Jazz appears. (Rev: BCCB 3/03; BL 3/15/03; HBG 10/03; SLJ 5/03; VOYA 6/03)

4012 Giles, Gail. *What Happened to Cass McBride?* (8–11). 2006, Little, Brown $16.99 (978-0-316-16638-6). When a cruel note from Cass pushes classmate David over the edge to suicide, David's older brother Kyle takes Cass captive in this suspenseful novel. (Rev: BCCB 12/06; BL 1/1–15/07; LMC 4–5/07; SLJ 2/07)

4013 Godwin, Jane. *Falling from Grace* (6–9). 2007, Holiday $16.95 (978-0-8234-2105-3). Thirteen-year-old Grace disappears into the surf off an Australian beach at the same moment a boy is rescued from drowning in this suspenseful thriller. (Rev: BL 10/1/07; LMC 1/08; SLJ 11/07)

4014 Golden, Christopher, and Rick Hautala. *Throat Culture* (8–11). Series: Body of Evidence. 2005, Simon & Schuster paper $5.99 (978-0-689-86527-5). College sophomore Jenna Blake investigates the mysterious illness that has stricken her father's new bride. (Rev: BL 5/1/05; SLJ 7/05)

4015 Golding, Julia. *The Diamond of Drury Lane* (7–10). Series: Cat Royal Adventures. 2008, Roaring Brook $12.50 (978-1-59643-351-9). Catherine Royal, called Cat, lives with danger and intrigue in the Drury Lane theater in London in 1790. Her life is further complicated when she learns that a diamond is hidden somewhere in the theater. (Rev: BL 4/15/08; SLJ 6/08)

4016 Gordon, Lawrence. *Haunted High* (6–9). Series: Ghost Chronicles. 2000, Karmichael paper $11.95 (978-0-9653966-1-5). Eddie discovers he is receiving messages on his computer from long-dead high school students. (Rev: SLJ 7/00; VOYA 4/00)

4017 Grant, Vicki. *Quid Pro Quo* (7–10). 2005, Orca $16.95 (978-1-55143-394-3); paper $7.95 (978-1-55143-370-7). When his mother — newly graduated from law school — suddenly disappears, 13-year-old Cyril Floyd MacIntyre tries to unravel the mystery surrounding her disappearance. (Rev: SLJ 6/05)

4018 Green, Timothy. *Twilight Boy* (7–10). 1998, Northland LB $12.95 (978-0-87358-670-2); paper $6.95 (978-0-87358-640-5). Navajo folkways form the background of this gripping mystery about a boy who is haunted by the memory of his dead brother and an evil that is preying on his Navajo community. (Rev: BL 4/15/98; HBG 9/98; VOYA 8/98)

4019 Greene, Michele Dominguez. *Chasing the Jaguar* (7–10). 2006, HarperCollins $15.99 (978-0-06-076353-4). Strange dreams lead Martika, a Mexican American teenager living in Los Angeles, to discover she is descended from Mayan healers and has psychic powers that may help her solve a kidnapping. (Rev: BL 5/1/06; LMC 2/07; SLJ 7/06)

4020 Gutman, Dan. *Shoeless Joe and Me* (4–7). Series: Baseball Card Adventure. 2002, HarperCollins LB $17.89 (978-0-06-029254-6). Thirteen-year-old Joe travels back in time to remedy the 1919 Black Sox scandal and save Shoeless Joe's reputation. (Rev: BL 1/1–15/02; HBG 10/02; SLJ 3/02)

4021 Hahn, Mary D. *The Dead Man in Indian Creek* (6–8). 1990, Clarion $15.00 (978-0-395-52397-1). On a harmless camping trip, Matt and friend Parker find a body floating in Indian Creek. (Rev: BL 2/15/90; SLJ 4/90)

4022 Hall, Lynn. *A Killing Freeze* (6–10). 1990, Avon paper $2.95 (978-0-380-75491-5). A loner endangers her own life to find a murderer. (Rev: BL 8/88; SLJ 9/88; VOYA 12/88)

4023 Hall, Lynn. *Ride a Dark Horse* (7–10). 1987, Avon paper $2.95 (978-0-380-75370-3). A teenage girl is fired from her job on a horse-breeding farm because she is getting too close to solving a mystery. (Rev: BL 9/15/87; SLJ 12/87; VOYA 10/87)

4024 Hamilton, Virginia. *The House of Dies Drear* (6–9). Illus. 1968, Macmillan paper $5.99 (978-0-02-043520-4). First-rate suspense as history professor Small and his young son Thomas investigate their rented house, formerly a station on the Underground Railroad, unlocking the secrets and dangers from attitudes dating back to the Civil War. (Rev: BL 10/15/87)

4025 Hautman, Pete, and Mary Logue. *Doppelganger* (6–9). Series: Bloodwater Mysteries. 2008, Putnam $16.99 (978-0-399-24379-0). Could Roni's private-eye partner, Brian, have been kidnapped as a child? Roni sets out to find the truth about Brian's past as an orphan adopted from Korea in this fast-paced adventure. (Rev: BL 5/1/08; SLJ 7/08)

4026 Hautman, Pete, and Mary Logue. *Skullduggery* (6–9). Series: Bloodwater Mysteries. 2007, Putnam $16.99 (978-0-399-24378-3). Young sleuths Roni and Brian — first seen in *Snatched* (2006) — investigate a local land development scheme after they find an archaeologist lying injured in a cave. (Rev: BL 5/1/07; SLJ 6/07)

4027 Hautman, Pete, and Mary Logue. *Snatched* (7–10). Series: Bloodwater Mysteries. 2006, Philomel $15.99 (978-0-399-24377-6). High school students Roni and Brian investigate the mystery of the missing Alicia in this suspenseful novel that holds readers' interest. (Rev: BL 5/1/06; HB 7–8/06; SLJ 6/06)

4028 Hayes, Daniel. *The Trouble with Lemons* (5–8). 1991, Random paper $5.99 (978-0-449-70416-5). Tyler, 14, has all kinds of problems — allergies, asthma, and nightmares — and then he finds a dead body. (Rev: BL 5/1/91; SLJ 6/91)

4029 Heyes, Eileen. *O'Dwyer and Grady Starring in Tough Act to Follow* (4–7). Illus. by Eric Bowman. Series: O'Dwyer and Grady. 2003, Simon & Schuster paper $4.99 (978-0-689-84920-6). Young actors Billy and Virginia stumble into a mystery while searching for props for a show in this action-packed story set in the 1930s. (Rev: BL 5/15/03; SLJ 7/03)

4030 Hill, William. *The Vampire Hunters* (7–12). 1998, Otter Creek $19.95 (978-1-890611-05-7); paper $12.95 (978-1-890611-02-6). Members of a gang called the Graveyard Armadillos are convinced that Marcus Chandler is a vampire, and 15-year-old Scooter Keyshaw is determined to find the truth. (Rev: BL 10/15/98; SLJ 2/99)

4031 Holm, Jennifer L. *The Creek* (6–8). 2003, HarperCollins $15.99 (978-0-06-000133-9). When local bad boy Caleb Devlin returns to town, he quickly gains 12-year-old Penny's fascinated attention, but his return coincides with a series of increasingly alarming events. (Rev: BCCB 7–8/03; BL 8/03; HBG 10/03; SLJ 7/03; VOYA 10/03)

4032 Hopper, Nancy J. *Ape Ears and Beaky* (4–7). 1987, Avon paper $2.50 (978-0-380-70270-1). Scott and Beaky solve the mystery of the robberies in a condominium.

4033 Horowitz, Anthony. *Alex Rider: The Gadgets* (5–8). Illus. by John Lawson. 2006, Philomel $15.99 (978-0-399-24486-5). A look at all the gadgets used in the first five Alex Rider mysteries — including such wonders as a radio mouth brace, exploding ear stud, and pizza delivery assassin kit — with diagrams and details of how they were used. (Rev: BL 4/1/06; SLJ 4/06)

4034 Horowitz, Anthony. *Ark Angel* (6–9). Series: Alex Rider. 2006, Philomel $17.99 (978-0-399-24152-9). Alex Rider battles "eco warriors" and becomes involved in the projected first hotel in space in this action- and gadget-packed sixth installment in the series. (Rev: BL 4/15/06; SLJ 4/06)

4035 Horowitz, Anthony. *Eagle Strike* (7–12). Series: Alex Rider Adventure. 2004, Putnam $17.99 (978-0-399-23979-3). Alex Rider, the hero of many adventures, recognizes a famous Russian assassin while Alex is vacationing in France, and a new thriller begins. (Rev: BL 5/1/04; SLJ 3/04; VOYA 4/04)

4036 Horowitz, Anthony. *Point Blank* (6–10). Series: Alex Rider Adventure. 2002, Putnam $17.99 (978-0-399-23621-1). Alex, the young British spy, infiltrates an exclusive Swiss boarding school in this action-filled adventure. (Rev: BL 4/1/02; HBG 10/02; SLJ 3/02; VOYA 2/02)

4037 Horowitz, Anthony. *Scorpia* (8–11). Series: Alex Rider Adventure. 2005, Penguin $17.99 (978-0-399-24151-2). Teenage spy Alex Rider infiltrates a terrorist organization called Scorpia. (Rev: BL 2/1/05; SLJ 3/05; VOYA 4/05)

4038 Horowitz, Anthony. *Skeleton Key* (6–9). Series: Alex Rider. 2003, Philomel $17.99 (978-0-399-23777-5). Alex confronts and confounds a former Russian commander who intends to resurrect the Soviet Union in this action-packed novel a la James Bond. (Rev: BL 5/15/03; HBG 10/03; SLJ 5/03; VOYA 6/03)

4039 Horowitz, Anthony. *South by Southeast* (4–7). Series: Diamond Brothers. 2005, Philomel $16.99 (978-0-399-24155-0); paper $5.99 (978-0-14-240374-7). Hapless private eye Tim Diamond and his brother Nick find themselves drawn into a labyrinthine mystery after a visit from a stranger. (Rev: BL 12/1/05; SLJ 12/05)

4040 Horowitz, Anthony. *Stormbreaker* (5–9). Series: Alex Rider. 2001, Philomel $17.99 (978-0-399-23620-4). Fourteen-year-old Alex becomes embroiled in dangerous undercover exploits when his MI6 uncle is murdered. (Rev: BCCB 9/01; BL 9/1/01; HBG 10/01; SLJ 6/01; VOYA 8/01)

4041 Horowitz, Anthony. *Three of Diamonds* (5–8). Series: Diamond Brothers. 2005, Philomel $16.99

(978-0-399-24157-4). Tim and Nick succeed in solving crimes despite Tim's blunderings in these three fast-paced and entertaining mystery stories full of wordplay. (Rev: BL 5/15/05; SLJ 5/05)

4042 Hrdlitschka, Shelley. *Tangled Web* (6–12). 2000, Orca paper $6.95 (978-1-55143-178-9). Telepathic twins Alex and Tanner again tangle with their former kidnapper in this fast-paced sequel to *Disconnected* (1999). (Rev: BL 10/15/00; SLJ 10/00; VOYA 12/00)

4043 Jennings, Richard W. *Mystery in Mt. Mole* (6–9). 2003, Houghton $15.00 (978-0-618-28478-8). The assistant principal has disappeared but nobody seems to care much except 13-year-old Andy. (Rev: BL 9/15/03*; SLJ 12/03)

4044 Johns, Linda. *Hannah West on Millionaire's Row* (5–8). Series: Hannah West. 2007, Puffin paper $5.99 (978-0-14-240824-7). Girl sleuth Hannah West, who was adopted from China, solves a mystery involving feng shui, antiques, and old mansions in this fourth installment in the series. (Rev: BL 10/1/07)

4045 Johnson, Henry, and Paul Hoppe. *Travis and Freddy's Adventures in Vegas* (5–8). 2006, Dutton $15.99 (978-0-525-47646-7). A lighthearted, fast-paced adventure in which preteens Travis and Freddy head to Las Vegas to win enough money to save Travis's home; there they win big but soon find they have the mob at their heels. (Rev: BL 2/15/06; SLJ 4/06; VOYA 4/06)

4046 Johnson, Rodney. *The Secret of Dead Man's Mine* (5–7). Illus. by Jill Thompson. Series: Rinnah Two Feathers Mystery. 2001, Uglytown paper $12.00 (978-0-9663473-3-3). Rinnah Two Feathers and two friends set out to solve the mystery of a suspicious stranger and find themselves in danger. (Rev: SLJ 9/01)

4047 Jorgensen, Christine T. *Death of a Dustbunny: A Stella the Stargazer Mystery* (8–12). 1998, Walker $22.95 (978-0-8027-3315-3). An uncomplicated mystery in which sleuth Stella the Stargazer, who writes a combination astrology and advice-to-the-lovelorn column for a local newspaper, investigates the disappearance of her friend Elena Ruiz, an employee of the Dustbunnies housekeeping and nanny agency. (Rev: BL 4/15/98; VOYA 8/98)

4048 Jubert, Hervé. *Devil's Tango* (8–11). 2006, HarperCollins $16.99 (978-0-06-077720-3). Crime is virtually impossible in the futuristic city of Basle, Switzerland, thanks to tracers that monitor all parts of the city, but when a serial killer called the Baron of the Mists goes on a killing spree and can't be detected it's up to detective Roberta Morgenstern and her partner Clement to track him; this is a complex novel of suspense with elements of fantasy, science fiction, and romance. (Rev: BL 10/1/06; SLJ 2/07)

4049 Karas, Phyllis. *The Hate Crime* (7–10). 1995, Avon paper $3.99 (978-0-380-78214-7). A docu-novel/whodunit about a teen who scrawls the names of seven concentration camps on a Jewish temple. (Rev: BL 12/1/95; VOYA 2/96)

4050 Karbo, Karen. *Minerva Clark Gets a Clue* (6–9). 2005, Bloomsbury $16.95 (978-1-58234-677-9). An electric shock changes 7th-grader Minerva from a self-concious but humorous worrier into a self-confident solver of mysteries. (Rev: BL 9/15/05; SLJ 10/05)

4051 Karbo, Karen. *Minerva Clark Gives Up the Ghost* (6–8). Series: Minerva Clark Mysteries. 2007, Bloomsbury $16.95 (978-1-58234-679-3). This time, Minerva is tackling a mystery in a haunted grocery store — and dealing with the return of her long-lost, newly remarried mother. (Rev: BL 11/15/07; SLJ 6/08)

4052 Keene, Carolyn. *Where's Nancy?* (4–7). Series: Nancy Drew Super Mystery. 2005, Simon & Schuster paper $4.99 (978-0-416-90034-7). Nancy herself is missing in this first installment of a new series. (Rev: BL 5/1/05)

4053 Kerr, M. E. *Fell* (8–12). 1987, HarperCollins paper $4.95 (978-0-06-447031-5). In a bizarre identity switch, a teenager from a middle-class background enters a posh prep school. Followed by *Fell Back* and *Fell Down*. (Rev: BL 6/1/87; SLJ 8/87; VOYA 10/87)

4054 Kerr, M. E. *Fell Down* (7–12). 1991, Harper-Collins $15.00 (978-0-06-021763-1). Fell has dropped out of prep school but is haunted by the death of his best friend there, so he returns, to find kidnapping, murder, and obsession. (Rev: BL 9/15/91*; SLJ 10/91)

4055 Klise, Kate. *Trial by Jury Journal* (5–8). Illus. by M. Sarah Klise. 2001, HarperCollins LB $16.89 (978-0-06-029541-7). When she is given the opportunity to serve as her state's first juvenile juror, 12-year-old Lily's sleuthing skills solve a murder mystery and save the day. (Rev: BCCB 4/01; BL 9/1/01; HB 5–6/01; HBG 10/01; SLJ 6/01)

4056 Konigsburg, E. L. *Silent to the Bone* (5–9). 2000, Simon & Schuster $16.00 (978-0-689-83601-5). A mystery story filled with suspense about a baby who's been dropped and a 13-year-old suspect who has lost his ability to speak. (Rev: BL 8/00*; HB 11–12/00; HBG 3/01; SLJ 9/00; VOYA 12/00)

4057 Kotzwinkle, William. *Trouble in Bugland: A Collection of Inspector Mantis Mysteries* (6–8). Illus. by Joe Servello. 1996, Godine paper $14.95 (978-1-56792-070-3). An all-insect cast in a takeoff on Sherlock Holmes mysteries.

4058 Lachtman, Ofelia Dumas. *Looking for La Única* (6–9). 2004, Arte Publico paper $9.95 (978-1-55885-412-3). In the summer before her senior year at high school, Monica gets swept into a series of adventures after a treasured guitar disappears from a shop owned by family friends in this sequel to *The Summer of El Pintor* (2001). (Rev: BL 1/1–15/05)

4059 Lachtman, Ofelia Dumas. *The Summer of El Pintor* (7–10). 2001, Arte Publico paper $9.95 (978-1-55885-327-0). Sixteen-year-old Monica's father loses his job and the two move from their wealthy neighborhood to the barrio house in which her dead mother grew up, where Monica searches for a missing neighbor and discovers the truth of her past. (Rev: BL 8/01; SLJ 7/01; VOYA 12/01)

4060 Lachtman, Ofelia Dumas. *The Truth About Las Mariposas* (7–10). 2007, Arte Publico paper $9.95 (978-1-55885-494-9). While Caroline (called Caro) is spending the summer with Tía Matilde, helping her run her bed-and-breakfast in the tiny town of Two Sands, she stumbles on a mystery that could affect her aunt's livelihood. (Rev: BL 12/15/07)

4061 Lafevers, R. L. *Theodosia and the Serpents of Chaos* (5–8). Illus. by Yoko Tanaka. 2007, Houghton $16.00 (978-0-618-75638-4). In the early 20th century, precocious 11-year-old Theodosia finds herself embroiled in a supernatural mystery involving Egyptian artifacts. (Rev: BL 5/1/07*; SLJ 4/07)

4062 Lalicki, Tom. *Shots at Sea: A Houdini and Nate Mystery* (4–7). Series: Houdini and Nate. 2007, Farrar $15.95 (978-0-374-31679-2). In the second book in the series, Nate, 13, is aboard the *Lusitania* and finds among his fellow-passengers both Harry Houdini and Teddy Roosevelt; Nate and the former rescue the latter from an assassination attempt. (Rev: BL 1/1–15/08; SLJ 11/07)

4063 Lawrence, Iain. *The Séance* (5–7). 2008, Delacorte $15.99 (978-0-385-73375-5). Scooter, whose spiritualist mother performs fake séances, is caught up in a murder mystery involving his idol, Houdini, in this novel that captures the tone of 1920s New York City. (Rev: BL 5/1/08; SLJ 8/08)

4064 L'Engle, Madeleine. *Troubling a Star* (7–10). 1994, Farrar $19.00 (978-0-374-37783-0). Vicki Austin, 16, travels to Antarctica and meets a Baltic prince looking for romance, and the two try to solve a mystery involving nuclear waste. (Rev: BL 8/94; SLJ 10/94; VOYA 12/94)

4065 Lisle, Janet Taylor. *Black Duck* (7–10). 2006, Philomel $15.99 (978-0-399-23963-2). In hopes of getting his story published, a teen boy interviews his elderly neighbor about the days of Prohibition and learns of lawlessness and mysterious events occurring in their Rhode Island town. (Rev: BL 5/1/06; HB 7–8/06; LMC 1/07; SLJ 5/06*) ⚓

4066 Littke, Lael. *Lake of Secrets* (7–10). 2002, Holt $16.95 (978-0-8050-6730-9). Carlene experiences strong and puzzling feelings of deja vu when she and her mother go to the town where Carlene's

brother died 18 years earlier, before Carlene's birth. (Rev: BCCB 4/02; BL 3/1/02; HB 5–6/02; HBG 10/02; SLJ 3/02; VOYA 6/02)

4067 Lucashenko, Melissa. *Killing Darcy* (8–10). 1998, Univ. of Queensland paper $13.95 (978-0-7022-3041-7). In this complex supernatural murder mystery set in New South Wales, 16-year-old Filomena uncovers a family murder, discovers a camera that can take pictures of the past, and is helped by a gay Aboriginal boy to solve the mystery. (Rev: SLJ 2/99)

4068 McClintock, Norah. *Dooley Takes the Fall* (8–12). 2008, Red Deer $12.95 (978-0-88995-403-8). Ryan Dooley, a 17-year-old with a record, is a suspect in two deaths and, to complicate matters, is attracted to the sister of one of the victims; eventually it seems that only he can clear himself. (Rev: BLO 6/17/08)

4069 Machado, Ana Maria. *From Another World* (4–7). Illus. by Lucia Brandao. 2005, Douglas & McIntyre $15.95 (978-0-88899-597-1). Spending a night in an outbuilding of an old farmhouse, Mariano and his three friends meet the ghost of a 19th-century slave girl and promise to help in this story set in Brazil. (Rev: BL 5/1/05; SLJ 6/05)

4070 McNab, Andy, and Robert Rigby. *Avenger* (7–12). 2007, Putnam $16.99 (978-0-399-24685-2). In this sequel to *Traitor* (2005) and *Payback* (2006), Danny, his grandfather Fergus, and his friend Elena pit their skills under Black Star, an evil computer expert. (Rev: SLJ 12/07; VOYA date)

4071 Madison, Bennett. *Lulu Dark and the Summer of the Fox* (6–9). 2006, Razorbill $10.99 (978-1-59514-086-9). Spunky, likable heroine Lulu investigates after her boyfriend is kidnapped and her mother disappears. (Rev: BL 5/1/06; LMC 8-9/06)

4072 Marks, Graham. *Omega Place* (8–11). 2007, Bloomsbury $16.95 (978-1-59990-127-5). Paul, 17, runs away from home and joins a resistance group in London—Omega Place—that is bent on destroying the ubiquitous closed-circuit cameras that keep tabs on the nation's citizens. (Rev: BL 10/15/07; LMC 1/08; SLJ 4/08)

4073 Marks, Graham. *Zoo* (8–11). 2005, Bloomsbury paper $8.95 (978-1-58234-991-6). A complex and suspenseful adventure story in which 17-year-old Cam escapes from kidnappers only to find that he has a mysterious chip in his arm and his parents may have been involved in his capture. (Rev: BL 9/15/05; SLJ 10/05; VOYA 8/05)

4074 Martin, Terri. *A Family Trait* (5–7). 1999, Holiday $15.95 (978-0-8234-1467-3). In this fast-paced story, Iris, 11 years old and incurably curious, has a number of mysteries to solve while trying to finish a book report. (Rev: BL 10/1/99; HBG 3/00; SLJ 10/99)

4075 Michaels, Rune. *Genesis Alpha* (7–10). 2007, Atheneum $15.99 (978-1-4169-1886-8). Josh was a designer baby whose stem cells saved his older brother Max from cancer; now Max is accused of murder — is Josh in some way guilty too? (Rev: BCCB 9/07; BL 5/1/07; LMC 8–9/07; SLJ 7/07)

4076 Miller, Kirsten. *Kiki Strike: The Empress's Tomb* (5–8). 2007, Bloomsbury $16.95 (978-1-59990-047-6). Kiki and the Irregulars tackle assorted bad guys in this sequel to *Kiki Strike: Inside the Shadow City,* again set in the world under New York City. (Rev: SLJ 12/07)

4077 Mitchard, Jacquelyn. *Now You See Her* (8–11). 2007, HarperTempest $15.99 (978-0-06-111683-4). Is 15-year-old Hope telling the truth about her affair with the leading man in the school play? Was she truly abducted? Readers will have a hard time separating Hope's truth from the lies in this suspenseful psychological thriller. (Rev: BCCB 4/07; BL 2/15/07; SLJ 3/07)

4078 Mitchell, Marianne. *Finding Zola* (5–8). 2003, Boyds Mills $16.95 (978-1-59078-070-1). A 13-year-old girl in a wheelchair investigates the disappearance of an elderly woman who has been staying with her. (Rev: BL 5/15/03; HBG 10/03; SLJ 2/03; VOYA 10/03)

4079 Mitchell, Marianne. *Firebug* (5–8). 2004, Boyds Mills $16.95 (978-1-59078-170-8). Twelve-year-old Haley investigates a suspicious fire at her Uncle Jake's Arizona ranch. (Rev: BL 3/15/04; SLJ 2/04)

4080 Moloney, James. *Black Taxi* (8–11). 2005, HarperCollins LB $16.89 (978-0-06-055938-0). When her grandfather is sent to jail for six months, 16-year-old Rosie Sinclair is appointed caretaker of his eye-catching black Mercedes; she enlists the help of her friends — one an attractive young man — when she starts getting threatening phone calls. (Rev: BCCB 5/05; BL 3/1/05; SLJ 3/05; VOYA 8/05)

4081 Mundis, Hester. *My Chimp Friday* (4–7). 2002, Simon & Schuster $16.00 (978-0-689-83837-8). Rachel and her family grow to love their new pet, a chimp named Friday, but when kidnappers try to steal Friday, Rachel realizes he is not an ordinary chimp. (Rev: BL 6/1–15/02; HBG 10/02; SLJ 6/02)

4082 Murphy, T. M. *The Secrets of Code Z* (4–8). Series: A Belltown Mystery. 2001, J. N. Townsend paper $9.95 (978-1-880158-33-3). Orville Jacques becomes embroiled in a fast-paced mystery involving CIA cover-ups, a death powder, and an evil Russian. (Rev: BL 5/15/01; SLJ 7/01)

4083 Murray, Susan, and Robert Davies. *Panic in Puerto Vallarta* (7–9). Series: K. C. Flanagan, Girl Detective. 1998, Robert Davies Multimedia paper $8.99 (978-1-55207-015-4). After witnessing a mur-

der in Puerto Vallarta, young K. C. Flanagan finds that the killers are out to get her. (Rev: SLJ 12/98)

4084 Naylor, Phyllis Reynolds. *Bernie Magruder and the Bats in the Belfry* (4–7). 2003, Simon & Schuster $16.95 (978-0-689-85066-0). Bernie is investigating a bat with a fatal bite; could it be connected to the fact that the bells in the belfry are annoyingly stuck on the same tune? (Rev: BL 1/1–15/03; HBG 10/03; SLJ 4/03)

4085 Nickerson, Sara. *How to Disappear Completely and Never Be Found* (4–8). Illus. by Sally Wern Comport. 2002, HarperCollins LB $17.89 (978-0-06-029772-5). Two youngsters with problems, 12-year-old Margaret and her friend Boyd, explore a deserted mansion and solve the mystery of the supernatural terrors it supposedly contains. (Rev: BCCB 5/02; BL 4/1/02; HB 7–8/02; HBG 10/02; SLJ 4/02)

4086 Nixon, Joan Lowery. *A Candidate for Murder* (6–12). 1991, Dell paper $4.99 (978-0-440-21212-6). While Cary's father enters the political limelight, his daughter becomes embroiled in a series of strange events. (Rev: BL 3/1/91)

4087 Nixon, Joan Lowery. *The Dark and Deadly Pool* (7–12). 1989, Bantam paper $4.99 (978-0-440-20348-3). Mary Elizabeth becomes aware of strange happenings at the health club where she works. (Rev: BL 11/1/87; SLJ 2/88; VOYA 12/87)

4088 Nixon, Joan Lowery. *The Ghosts of Now* (7–10). 1984, Dell paper $4.99 (978-0-440-93115-7). Angie investigates a hit-and-run accident that has left her brother in a coma.

4089 Nixon, Joan Lowery. *Murdered, My Sweet* (6–9). 1997, Delacorte $15.95 (978-0-385-32245-4). The son of a millionaire is murdered and young Jenny and her mystery-writer mother try to solve the case. (Rev: BL 9/1/97; HBG 3/98; SLJ 9/97; VOYA 2/98)

4090 Nixon, Joan Lowery. *The Name of the Game Was Murder* (6–8). 1994, Dell paper $4.99 (978-0-440-21916-3). Teenager Samantha must work with her uncle's houseguests to find a damning manuscript and uncover the murderer of its author. (Rev: BL 3/1/93)

4091 Nixon, Joan Lowery. *Nightmare* (6–10). 2003, Delacorte LB $17.99 (978-0-385-90151-2). This suspenseful mystery features 10th-grader Emily, who has suffered a recurring nightmare since childhood and now finds herself facing a killer at her summer camp. (Rev: BL 10/15/03; HBG 4/04; SLJ 10/03; VOYA 10/03)

4092 Nixon, Joan Lowery. *The Other Side of Dark* (7–10). 1986, Dell paper $4.99 (978-0-440-96638-8). After waking from a four-year coma, Stacy is now the target of the man who wounded her and killed her mother. (Rev: BL 9/15/86; SLJ 9/86; VOYA 12/86)

4093 Nixon, Joan Lowery. *Shadowmaker* (7–9). 1995, Dell paper $4.99 (978-0-440-21942-2). When Katie's mother, an investigative journalist, probes evidence of toxic-waste dumping, Katie discovers that events at her school are related. (Rev: BL 3/1/94; SLJ 5/94; VOYA 8/94)

4094 Nixon, Joan Lowery. *The Weekend Was Murder!* (6–10). 1992, Dell paper $4.99 (978-0-440-21901-9). A teen sleuth and her boyfriend attend a murder mystery enactment weekend and discover a real murder. (Rev: BL 2/15/92; SLJ 3/92)

4095 Oliver, Andrew. *If Photos Could Talk* (4–7). Series: A Sam and Stephanie Mystery. 2005, Adams-Pomeroy paper $12.95 (978-0-9661009-6-9). Twelve-year-olds Sam and Stephanie investigate the disappearance of an elderly man in their small Wisconsin town in this well-plotted novel. (Rev: SLJ 1/06)

4096 Orenstein, Denise Gosliner. *The Secret Twin* (7–10). 2007, HarperCollins $16.99 (978-0-06-078564-2). Skinny, sickly Noah, whose twin died at birth, is thrown for a loop when hearty Grace comes to take care of him after his grandmother's facelift in this suspenseful and complex novel. (Rev: BL 12/15/06; SLJ 3/07)

4097 Parkinson, Curtis. *Death in Kingsport* (6–8). 2007, Tundra paper $11.95 (978-0-88776-827-9). This fast-paced mystery set in Canada in 1941 starts with 15-year-old Neil hearing thumping sounds from his uncle's coffin. (Rev: SLJ 12/07)

4098 Pascal, Francine. *Fearless FBI: Kill Game* (8–11). Series: Fearless FBI. 2005, Simon & Schuster paper $7.99 (978-0-689-87821-3). Despite her unreliability, the FBI invites intrepid Gaia — of the earlier Fearless series — to try their boot camp training program. (Rev: BL 8/05; SLJ 6/05)

4099 Peacock, Shane. *Eye of the Crow* (7–10). Series: The Boy Sherlock Holmes. 2007, Tundra $19.95 (978-0-88776-850-7). Named one of the *Booklist* Top Ten in Young Mysteries, this first book in the series begins in 1867, when Sherlock is 13 and accused of murder, launching his career of detective work. (Rev: BL 11/1/07; SLJ 11/07)

4100 Pearson, Ridley. *The Challenge* (5–8). 2008, Disney $16.99 (978-1-4231-0640-1). Steve is caught up in a terrorist kidnapping plot when he looks inside an abandoned briefcase in this fast-paced adventure. (Rev: BL 1/1–15/08; LMC 4-5/08)

4101 Penn, Audrey. *Mystery at Blackbeard's Cove* (5–8). Illus. by Joshua Miller. 2004, Tanglewood $14.95 (978-0-9749303-1-2). The death of Mrs. McNemmish, a descendant of Blackbeard the pirate, sets in motion a series of adventures for four young residents of Okracoke Island. (Rev: BL 1/1–15/05)

4102 Pike, Christopher. *Gimme a Kiss* (7–12). 1991, Pocket paper $4.50 (978-0-671-63682-1). A girl fakes her own death in a wild plot to get revenge. (Rev: BL 10/15/88; VOYA 4/89)

4103 Pike, Christopher. *Slumber Party* (7–10). 1985, Scholastic paper $5.99 (978-0-590-43014-2). Six teenage girls stranded in a winter vacation home experience mysterious occurrences that bring terror into their lives. (Rev: SLJ 12/86)

4104 Plum-Ucci, Carol. *The Body of Christopher Creed* (8–12). 2000, Harcourt $17.00 (978-0-15-202388-1). Torey and his friends are implicated in the disappearance of his classmate Chris, causing Torey to examine his life while trying to find Chris. (Rev: HBG 9/00; SLJ 7/00)

4105 Plum-Ucci, Carol. *The She* (8–12). 2003, Harcourt $17.00 (978-0-15-216819-3). Evan, his brother, and a friend set out to find the truth behind the disappearance of Evan's parents years before. (Rev: BL 9/15/03*; SLJ 10/03; VOYA 12/03)

4106 Plum-Ucci, Carol. *Streams of Babel* (8–11). 2008, Harcourt $17.00 (978-0-15-216556-7). A Palestinian teenager working for the U.S. government uncovers a terrorist plot to poison drinking water that has already sickened and killed two people in New York. (Rev: BL 4/15/08; SLJ 7/08)

4107 Plummer, Louise. *Finding Daddy* (6–9). 2007, Delacorte $15.99 (978-0-385-73092-1). Nearly 16, Mira decides to track down her long-absent father, but soon after she finds him on the Internet things begin to happen; someone seems to be watching — and threatening — her and her family. (Rev: BL 12/1/07; SLJ 12/07)

4108 Pow, Tom. *Captives* (6–9). 2007, Roaring Brook $17.95 (978-1-59643-201-7). The story of a deadly kidnapping of American tourists by Caribbean guerrillas is told by one of the fathers and amplified by 16-year-old Martin, whose perspective is quite different. (Rev: BCCB 9/07; BL 5/15/07; SLJ 5/07)

4109 Raskin, Ellen. *The Westing Game* (6–9). 1978, Avon paper $3.50 (978-0-380-67991-1). Sixteen possible heirs try to decipher an enigmatic will. Newbery Medal, 1979.

4110 Reaver, Chap. *A Little Bit Dead* (8–12). 1992, Delacorte $15.00 (978-0-385-30801-4). When Reece saves an Indian boy from lynching by U.S. marshals, lawmen claim that Reece murdered one of the marshals and he must clear himself. (Rev: BL 9/1/92; SLJ 9/92)

4111 Richards, Justin. *The Death Collector* (6–9). 2006, Bloomsbury $16.95 (978-1-58234-721-9). In this creepy, page-turner mystery set in Victorian Britain, three teenagers try to prevent a monster-creating villain from taking over the world. (Rev: BL 5/15/06; LMC 10/06; SLJ 7/06)

4112 Richardson, Nigel. *The Wrong Hands* (8–11). 2006, Knopf $15.95 (978-0-375-83459-2). Fourteen-year-old Graham has large, strange hands and an even bigger secret — with these hands, he can fly; when he rescues a baby and is considered a hero, this ability becomes harder for the British boy to conceal. (Rev: BL 8/06; SLJ 10/06) ⟲

4113 Ripslinger, Jon. *Last Kiss* (8–12). 2007, Flux paper $9.95 (978-0-7387-1072-3). Billy, a simple farm boy, is the prime suspect when his girlfriend — from a wealthy and prominent family — is found murdered. (Rev: BL 11/1/07; SLJ 2/08)

4114 Roberts, Willo Davis. *Baby-Sitting Is a Dangerous Job* (5–7). 1987, Fawcett paper $6.50 (978-0-449-70177-5). Darcy tries to cope with three bratty children, but a kidnapping puts her and her charges in the hands of three dangerous men. (Rev: BCCB 3/85; BL 5/1/85; SLJ 5/85)

4115 Roberts, Willo Davis. *The One Left Behind* (4–7). 2006, Simon & Schuster $16.95 (978-0-689-85075-2). Mandy, an 11-year-old mourning her dead twin sister, is accidentally left home alone for the weekend and pluckily investigates when there's a break-in downstairs. (Rev: BL 4/1/06; SLJ 5/06)

4116 Roberts, Willo Davis. *Undercurrents* (7–10). 2002, Simon & Schuster $16.00 (978-0-689-81671-0). Fourteen-year-old Nikki is troubled when her father remarries only months after her mother's death and his new wife seems to be hiding facts about her unhappy past. (Rev: BCCB 4/02; BL 2/15/02; HBG 10/02; SLJ 2/02; VOYA 2/02)

4117 Roberts, Willo Davis. *The View from the Cherry Tree* (7–9). 1994, Simon & Schuster paper $4.99 (978-0-689-71784-0). A boy who witnesses a murder becomes targeted as the next victim.

4118 Rose, Malcolm. *Blood Brother* (4–7). Series: Traces. 2008, Kingfisher paper $5.95 (978-0-7534-6170-9). Luke and his robot sidekick are investigating 26 mysterious deaths at York Hospital; could Luke's doctor father, the principal investigator on a clinical trial at the hospital, somehow be responsible? (Rev: BL 11/15/07)

4119 Rose, Malcolm. *Final Lap* (8–12). 2007, Kingfisher paper $5.95 (978-0-7534-6005-4). Luke and his robot use their forensic skills in investigating sabotage at the Youth International Games. (Rev: SLJ 3/07)

4120 Rose, Malcolm. *Lost Bullet* (6–9). Series: Traces. 2005, Kingfisher paper $5.95 (978-0-7534-5830-3). In a futuristic London, forensic investigator Luke Harding and his robotic sidekick try to find out who's responsible for the murder of a doctor and find themselves facing a cult. (Rev: BL 6/1–15/05; SLJ 7/05)

4121 Runholt, Susan. *The Mystery of the Third Lucretia* (7–10). 2008, Viking $16.99 (978-0-670-

06252-2). Two young artists are caught up in an international mystery when they pursue a painter who has forged a Rembrandt work; set in Minneapolis, London, and Amsterdam, this mystery combines art history with intrigue. (Rev: BL 5/1/08; SLJ 3/08)

4122 Schmidt, Gary. *First Boy* (7–10). 2005, Holt $16.95 (978-0-8050-7859-6). With the help of kind neighbors, 14-year-old Cooper hopes to be able to live alone on his grandparents' farm, but questions about his missing parents seem linked to politics and the presidential elections. (Rev: BCCB 2/06; BL 9/15/05; HB 9–10/05; SLJ 10/05; VOYA 4/06)

4123 Scrimger, Richard. *From Charlie's Point of View* (7–10). 2005, Dutton $10.99 (978-0-525-47374-9). Fourteen-year-old Charlie is blind, but best friend Bernadette acts as his eyes, and together they set out to prove that Charlie's dad had nothing to do with a series of neighborhood ATM thefts. (Rev: BCCB 9/05; BL 5/1/05; SLJ 8/05)

4124 Shaw, Diana. *Lessons in Fear* (6–9). 1987, Little, Brown $12.95 (978-0-316-78341-5). An unpopular teacher has a series of mysterious accidents and one of her students, Carter Colborn, decides she must investigate them. (Rev: BL 4/15/88; SLJ 10/87)

4125 Shearer, Alex. *Canned* (6–9). 2008, Scholastic $16.99 (978-0-439-90309-7). Fergal finds a finger in an old can, and Charlotte finds a ring in another — a grisly opening to a mystery story full of black humor. (Rev: BL 2/15/08; SLJ 2/08)

4126 Simmons, Michael. *Finding Lubchenko* (7–10). 2005, Penguin paper $16.99 (978-1-59514-021-0). Evan Macalister, a 16-year-old slacker, steals high-value computer equipment from his father's business and sells it for spending cash, but he faces a moral dilemma when he discovers evidence that could clear his father of murder charges on a laptop he's stolen; a funny, offbeat novel. (Rev: BCCB 7–8/05; SLJ 6/05; VOYA 12/04)

4127 Simmons, Michael. *The Rise of Lubchenko* (8–11). 2006, Penguin $16.99 (978-1-59514-061-6). in this sequel to *Finding Lubchenko* (2005), wealthy Evan Macalister is informed that his father's business partner is planning to smuggle a live smallpox virus into Europe. (Rev: BL 9/1/06; SLJ 9/06)

4128 Skurzynski, Gloria, and Alane Ferguson. *Buried Alive* (4–7). Series: Mysteries in Our National Parks. 2003, National Geographic $15.95 (978-0-7922-6966-3). A hit man and an avalanche are only two of the challenges Jack and Ashley face while on vacation with their parents in Denali National Park. (Rev: HBG 10/03; SLJ 12/03)

4129 Skurzynski, Gloria, and Alane Ferguson. *Deadly Waters* (4–7). Illus. Series: Mysteries in Our National Parks. 1999, National Geographic $15.95 (978-0-7922-7037-9). The Landon kids — Jack,

Ashley, and foster brother, Bridger — travel to the Florida Everglades where their parents are investigating the mysterious deaths of some manatees. (Rev: BL 10/15/99; HBG 3/00; SLJ 10/99)

4130 Skurzynski, Gloria, and Alane Ferguson. *The Hunted* (5–8). Illus. Series: Mysteries in Our National Parks. 2000, National Geographic $15.95 (978-0-7922-7053-9). The Landon family sets out to discover why young grizzly bears are disappearing from Glacier National Park. (Rev: BL 6/1–15/00; HBG 10/00; SLJ 8/00)

4131 Skurzynski, Gloria, and Alane Ferguson. *Wolf Stalker* (5–8). Series: Mysteries in Our National Parks. 1997, National Geographic $15.00 (978-0-7922-7034-8). Three youngsters solve the mystery of who is killing the wolves of Yellowstone Park. (Rev: HBG 3/98; SLJ 1/98)

4132 Smith, Roland. *Jack's Run* (5–8). 2005, Hyperion $15.99 (978-0-7868-5592-6). Last seen adapting to being in the witness protection program in *Zach's Lie* (2001), Jack and Joanne are now in danger after Joanne has blown their cover in this fast-paced, suspenseful story. (Rev: BL 8/05; SLJ 12/05; VOYA 10/05)

4133 Sniegoski, Tom. *Sleeper Code* (8–12). Series: Sleeper Conspiracy. 2006, Penguin paper $6.99 (978-1-59514-052-4). In this suspenseful adventure, Tom discovers that his narcolepsy is the result of government intervention and realizes he cannot trust anyone. (Rev: SLJ 8/06)

4134 Sorrells, Walter. *Club Dread* (8–11). 2006, Dutton paper $10.99 (978-0-525-47618-4). In this thrilling, action-packed sequel to *Fake I.D.* (2004), 16-year-old Chass has formed a band in San Francisco but witnesses a murder and becomes drawn into the investigation. (Rev: BL 1/1–15/06; SLJ 3/06)

4135 Sorrells, Walter. *Fake I.D.* (8–11). 2005, Dutton $12.99 (978-0-525-47514-9). On the run with her mother since she was a baby, 16-year-old Chastity Pureheart has only six days to find out what happened to her mother or face placement in foster care. (Rev: BL 5/1/05*; SLJ 6/05)

4136 Sorrells, Walter. *First Shot* (7–12). 2007, Dutton $16.99 (978-0-525-47801-0). In this taut teen thriller set at a New England boarding school, a young man named David Crandall is beset with problems: his own feelings of inadequacy; his mother's murder, his father's emotional and physical abuse, and above all the suspicion that his father is the murderer. (Rev: BL 9/15/07; SLJ 3/08)

4137 Sorrells, Walter. *The Silent Room* (8–11). 2006, Dutton $16.99 (978-0-525-47697-9). Oz is wrongly sent to an institution for wayward boys in a remote Florida swamp and hatches a desperate plot to escape after learning that he and his roommates are in danger. (Rev: BL 5/1/06; SLJ 7/06)

4138 Spirn, Michele. *The Bridges in London: Going to London* (5–7). Series: Going To. 2000, Four Corners paper $7.95 (978-1-893577-00-8). When two sisters fly to London with their parents, they become involved in a mystery when they find a suitcase full of knives. (Rev: SLJ 3/00)

4139 Spizman, Robyn Freedman, and Mark Johnston. *The Secret Agents Strike Back* (5–8). 2007, Simon & Schuster $16.99 (978-1-4169-0086-3). Information about a possible cure for cancer is stolen and Kyle and his friends chase clues all over New York City in this entertaining mystery. (Rev: SLJ 6/07)

4140 Spradlin, Michael P. *To Hawaii, with Love* (7–10). Series: Spy Goddess. 2006, HarperCollins $15.99 (978-0-06-059410-7). This latest action-filled thriller has 15-year-old Rachel racing to recover an ancient Hawaiian artifact before it is seized by an evil foe. (Rev: BL 5/1/06)

4141 Springer, Nancy. *The Case of the Bizarre Bouquets* (6–9). Series: Enola Holmes. 2008, Philomel $14.99 (978-0-399-24518-3). Enola Holmes uses her knowledge of the Victorian language of flowers to solve the case of the missing Dr. Watson. (Rev: BL 2/1/08; SLJ 1/08)

4142 Springer, Nancy. *The Case of the Left-Handed Lady* (6–9). Series: Enola Holmes. 2007, Philomel $12.99 (978-0-399-24517-6). Enola Holmes, Sherlock's younger sister, disguises herself to find a missing person in this story set in 19th-century London. (Rev: BL 3/15/07; SLJ 3/07)

4143 Springer, Nancy. *The Case of the Missing Marquess: An Enola Holmes Mystery* (5–8). Series: Enola Holmes. 2006, Philomel paper $10.99 (978-0-399-24304-2). Enola Holmes, the much younger sister of Sherlock and Mycroft, embarks on a search for her mother, who disappears on Enola's 14th birthday. (Rev: BCCB 2/06; BL 12/1/05*; HBG 10/06; SLJ 2/06*)

4144 Stanley, Diane. *The Mysterious Case of the Allbright Academy* (4–7). 2008, HarperCollins $15.99 (978-0-06-085817-9). What's going on at Allbright Academy? Frannie suspects that her "perfect" classmates are being brainwashed and placed into positions of authority in the U.S. government, and she sets out to foil the plot. (Rev: BL 11/15/07; SLJ 3/08)

4145 Steiner, Barbara. *Dreamstalker* (8–12). 1992, Avon paper $3.50 (978-0-380-76611-6). A girl wonders if she's psychic when her terrifying nightmares start coming true. (Rev: BL 3/15/92)

4146 Steiner, Barbara. *Spring Break* (7–10). 1996, Scholastic paper $3.99 (978-0-590-54419-1). Five high schoolers rent a haunted house where they contend with odd appearances and disappearances, arson, and a skeleton. (Rev: SLJ 12/96)

4147 Stengel, Joyce A. *Mystery of the Island Jewels* (5–8). 2002, Simon & Schuster paper $4.99 (978-0-689-85049-3). On a cruise to Martinique with her father and new stepfamily, 14-year-old Cassie and new friend Charles uncover a mystery. (Rev: SLJ 6/02)

4148 Sternberg, Libby. *The Case Against My Brother* (6–9). 2007, Bancroft $19.95 (978-1-890962-51-7). In Oregon in 1922, Carl Matuski, a 15-year-old Polish Catholic boy, is determined to clear his older brother Adam of stealing in this mystery that exposes prejudice and racism. (Rev: BL 11/15/07; SLJ 1/08)

4149 Sternberg, Libby. *Finding the Forger* (6–9). 2004, Bancroft $19.95 (978-1-890862-32-9); paper $14.95 (978-1-890862-37-4). Bianca Balducci, 15-year-old wannabe detective, gets caught up in the investigation of an art forgery at the local museum while at the same time worrying in humorous first-person narrative about friends, boyfriends, and family. (Rev: BL 2/1/05; SLJ 4/05; VOYA 8/05)

4150 Sternberg, Libby. *Uncovering Sadie's Secrets: A Bianca Balducci Mystery* (6–9). Series: Bianca Balducci Mystery. 2003, Bancroft $16.95 (978-1-890862-23-7). Bianca Balducci is a sophomore in high school with all of the everyday teen anxieties as well as an interest in the mysterious circumstances surrounding her new friend, Sadie. (Rev: BL 1/1–15/03; SLJ 3/03; VOYA 4/03)

4151 Stine, R. L. *The Wrong Number* (5–9). 1990, Pocket paper $4.99 (978-0-671-69411-1). While making a crank telephone call, a teenager hears a murder being committed. (Rev: SLJ 6/90)

4152 Sukach, Jim. *Clever Quicksolve Whodunit Puzzles* (4–7). Illus. by Lucy Corvino. Series: Mini-Mysteries for You to Solve. 1999, Sterling $14.95 (978-0-8069-6569-7). Thirty-five mini-mysteries are presented with answers appended. (Rev: SLJ 1/00)

4153 Taylor, Cora. *Murder in Mexico* (4–7). Series: The Spy Who Wasn't There. 2007, Coteau paper $7.95 (978-1-55050-353-1). In this second, fast-paced installment in the mystery series, twins Jennifer and Maggie are visiting ruins in the Yucatan when Jennifer must use her ability to become invisible to solve a crime. (Rev: SLJ 4/07)

4154 Taylor, G. P. *Mariah Mundi: The Midas Box* (6–9). Series: Mariah Mundi. 2008, Putnam $17.99 (978-0-399-24347-9). In Victorian England, Mariah finds himself working at a creepy hotel where something very odd is going on. (Rev: BL 5/1/08; SLJ 8/08)

4155 Thesman, Jean. *Rachel Chance* (6–9). 1990, Houghton $16.00 (978-0-395-50934-0). Rachel's young brother has been kidnapped, but no one seems to be taking any action. (Rev: BL 5/1/90; SLJ 4/90)

4156 Thurlo, David, and Aimée Thurlo. *The Spirit Line* (6–10). 2004, Viking $16.99 (978-0-670-03645-5). Fifteen-year-old Crystal Manyfeathers solves a theft and in so doing begins to question her Navajo beliefs. (Rev: BL 5/1/04; SLJ 6/04; VOYA 6/04)

4157 Trembath, Don. *Emville Confidential* (5–8). 2007, Orca paper $8.95 (978-1-55143-671-5). A tongue-in-cheek hard-boiled detective novel featuring 7th-graders Baron, Myles, and Rebecca. (Rev: BL 11/1/07; SLJ 2/08)

4158 Trout, Richard E. *Czar of Alaska: The Cross of Charlemagne* (5–8). Series: MacGregor Family Adventure. 2005, Pelican $15.95 (978-1-58980-328-2). In volume four of the series, the five MacGregors travel to Alaska to assess the environmental impact of drilling for oil and become entangled with ecoterrorists and priests seeking an ancient cross. (Rev: SLJ 12/05)

4159 Twain, Mark. *The Stolen White Elephant* (4–8). Illus. 1882, Ayer $19.95 (978-0-8369-3486-1). The tale of the elephant's guardian who naively is impressed by a corrupt police detective. (Rev: BL 5/1/88; SLJ 2/88)

4160 Updale, Eleanor. *Montmorency and the Assassins* (7–10). 2006, Scholastic $16.99 (978-0-439-68343-2). Montmorency and Lord George Fox-Selwyn, plus some teen helpers, investigate bomb-planting anarchists in this Victorian mystery that ranges from London to Florence to New Jersey. (Rev: BL 3/15/06; SLJ 5/06; VOYA 2/06)

4161 Updale, Eleanor. *Montmorency on the Rocks: Doctor, Aristocrat, Murderer?* (6–9). 2005, Scholastic $16.95 (978-0-439-60676-9). Montmorency, recovering from opium addiction, and sidekicks Lord George Fox-Selwyn and Dr. Fawcett must unravel a London bomb plot and mysterious deaths in Scotland. (Rev: BL 5/15/05; SLJ 4/05)

4162 Updale, Eleanor. *Montmorency's Revenge* (7–10). Series: Montmorency. 2007, Scholastic $16.99 (978-0-439-81373-0). Lord George Fox-Selwyn has been murdered, and this leads to the pursuit of revenge by his powerful group of friends in this fourth installment in the action-packed series. (Rev: BCCB 5/07; BL 7/07; HB 7–8/07; SLJ 8/07)

4163 Van Draanen, Wendelin. *Sammy Keyes and the Art of Deception* (5–8). Series: Sammy Keyes. 2003, Knopf $15.95 (978-0-375-81176-0). Sammy (with some help from Grams) solves a mystery involving an art thief. (Rev: BL 2/1/03; HBG 10/03; SLJ 3/03; VOYA 8/03)

4164 Van Draanen, Wendelin. *Sammy Keyes and the Dead Giveaway* (5–8). 2005, Knopf LB $17.99 (978-0-375-92350-0). Seventh-grade sleuth Sammy tackles personal problems — should she make a confession that would exonerate her archenemy? —

and community ones as she investigates abuse of eminent domain. (Rev: BL 9/1/05; SLJ 11/05)

4165 Van Draanen, Wendelin. *Sammy Keyes and the Wild Things* (6–9). Series: Sammy Keyes. 2007, Knopf $18.99 (978-0-375-93525-1). While on a Girl Scout camping trip, Sammy does some detective work to help save an endangered condor. (Rev: BL 5/1/07; SLJ 6/07)

4166 Varrato, Tony. *Fakie* (7–10). 2008, Lobster paper $7.95 (978-1-897073-79-7). Danny and his mother, in the Witness Protection Program since Danny's father's murder, stay one step ahead of the bad guys in this suspenseful story. (Rev: BL 4/1/08)

4167 Voigt, Cynthia. *The Vandemark Mummy* (6–9). 1991, Atheneum $18.95 (978-0-689-31476-6). This story involves a break-in at a museum of Egyptian antiquities and two teenage siblings who attempt to solve the mystery. (Rev: BL 9/1/91; SLJ 9/91)

4168 Vrettos, Adrienne Maria. *Sight* (8–10). 2007, Simon & Schuster $16.99 (978-1-4169-0657-5). Dylan, 16, is able to picture the details of the murders that took place in her town years before; when the killing begins again she must try to use her talent to bring the murderer to justice before the town splits apart. (Rev: BL 1/1–15/08; SLJ 3/08)

4169 Wahl, Mats. *The Invisible* (8–11). Trans. by Katarina E. Tucker. 2007, Farrar $17.00 (978-0-374-33609-7). A teenage Swedish boy named Hilmer is thought to be missing but has merely become invisible. Could neo-Nazis be responsible? (Rev: BCCB 4/07; BL 3/15/07; SLJ 4/07)

4170 Walden, Mark. *H.I.V.E: The Higher Institute of Villainous Education* (5–8). Series: H.I.V.E. 2007, Simon & Schuster $15.99 (978-1-4169-3571-1). Kidnapped along with three of his friends and enrolled in an academy that grooms students in the villainous arts, 13-year-old brilliant orphan Otto maps a plan to escape, a feat never before accomplished. (Rev: BL 4/1/07; SLJ 6/07)

4171 Walden, Mark. *H.I.V.E: The Overlord Protocol* (5–8). Series: H.I.V.E. 2008, Simon & Schuster $15.99 (978-1-4169-6016-4). Wing and Otto, students at the Higher Institute of Villainous Education (H.I.V.E.), travel to Japan for Wing's father's funeral and realize they have fallen into an evil trap. (Rev: BL 3/1/08)

4172 Weir, Joan. *The Mysterious Visitor* (5–7). Series: Lion and Bobbi. 2002, Raincoast paper $6.99 (978-1-55192-404-5). Two Canadian youngsters, Lion and sister Bobbi, try to solve the mystery of strange events occurring on a friend's land. (Rev: BL 5/1/02)

4173 Weltman, June. *Mystery of the Missing Candlestick* (5–8). 2004, Mayhaven $23.95 (978-1-878044-98-3). Miranda, 17, and her friends Leila and Rebecca join forces to solve the mystery of a valuable antique candlestick that has been stolen from Rebecca's grandfather. (Rev: BL 5/1/04)

4174 Werlin, Nancy. *Black Mirror* (7–12). 2001, Dial $16.99 (978-0-8037-2605-5). Lonely Frances, 16, struggles with her Jewish-Japanese heritage and with her guilt and puzzlement over her brother's suicide in this intriguing and suspenseful novel set in a private boarding school. (Rev: BCCB 10/01; BL 9/15/01; HB 9–10/01; HBG 3/02; SLJ 9/01*; VOYA 10/01)

4175 Westerfeld, Scott. *So Yesterday* (7–12). 2004, Penguin $16.99 (978-1-59514-000-5). Two teenagers who help big companies identify coming trends in the consumer marketplace find themselves caught up in a mystery when their boss disappears. (Rev: BL 9/15/04; SLJ 10/04; VOYA 10/04)

4176 White, Ruth. *The Search for Belle Prater* (4–7). 2005, Farrar $16.00 (978-0-374-30853-7). In this sequel to *Belle Prater's Boy*, 13-year-old Woodrow and his cousin Gypsy continue to search for Woodrow's missing mother against the backdrop of mid-1950s segregation. (Rev: BL 2/15/05*; SLJ 4/05)

4177 Whitehouse, Howard. *The Faceless Fiend: Being the Tale of a Criminal Mastermind, His Masked Minions and a Princess with a Butter Knife, Involving Explosives and a Certain Amount of Pushing and Shoving* (4–7). Illus. by Bill Slavin. 2007, Kids Can $16.95 (978-1-55453-130-1); paper $7.95 (978-1-55453-180-6). In this sequel to *The Strictest School in the World* (2006), Emmaline and her friend Princess Purnah escape from St. Grimelda's School for Young Ladies and — with a motley crew of supporters and many comical mishaps along the way — manage to foil a kidnapping. (Rev: LMC 1/08; SLJ 11/07)

4178 Whyman, Matt. *Icecore: A Carl Hobbes Thriller* (8–12). 2007, Simon & Schuster $16.99 (978-1-4169-4907-7). British Carl Hobbes, 17, hacks into the security system at Fort Knox — just to prove he can do it — and soon finds himself a prisoner at a maximum-security American site above the Arctic Circle — and that's just the beginning of the plot-driven adventure. (Rev: BCCB 2/08; SLJ 1/08)

4179 Wilson, Eric. *Code Red at the Supermall* (6–8). Illus. by Richard Row. Series: A Tom and Liz Austen Mystery. 2000, Orca paper $4.99 (978-1-55143-172-7). The intrepid Tom and Liz Austen investigate criminal activities at the Edmonton supermall. Also recommended in this series is *Disneyland Hostage* (2000). (Rev: SLJ 6/00)

4180 Wilson, Eric. *Murder on the Canadian: A Tom Austen Mystery* (4–8). Illus. by Richard Row. 2000, Orca paper $4.99 (978-1-55143-151-2). A fast-moving mystery starring an intrepid hero who is also featured in *Vancouver Nightmare: A Tom Austen Mystery* (2000). (Rev: SLJ 1/01)

4181 Wilson, F. Paul. *Jack: Secret Histories* (6–9). 2008, Tor $15.95 (978-0-7653-1854-1). When members of a mysterious cult in Jack's town are found dead, he and his friends find a strange box that may hold the answer. (Rev: BL 5/1/08)

4182 Wright, Betty R. *The Dollhouse Murders* (4–7). 1983, Holiday $16.95 (978-0-8234-0497-1). Dolls in a dollhouse come to life in this mystery about long-ago murders.

4183 Yep, Laurence. *The Case of the Firecrackers* (4–7). 1999, HarperCollins LB $15.89 (978-0-06-024452-1). In this Chinatown mystery, Tiger Lil and her great-niece Lily are on the trail of the murderer who killed the star of the television show in which they were extras. (Rev: BL 9/15/99; HBG 3/00; SLJ 9/99)

4184 Young, E. L. *The Infinity Code* (5–8). 2008, Dial $16.99 (978-0-8037-3265-0). Young computer whizzes Andrew, Will, Gaia, and Caspian make up the group STORM ("Science and Technology to Over-Rule Misery") and find themselves in a tech-driven battle against a group that has kidnapped Caspian's father. (Rev: BL 3/1/08; SLJ 5/08)

4185 Zambreno, Mary F. *Journeyman Wizard* (4–7). 1994, Harcourt $16.95 (978-0-15-200022-6). Student wizard Jeremy is studying the casting of spells with Lady Allons when an unfortunate death occurs and he is accused of murder. (Rev: BL 5/1/94; SLJ 6/94)

Romances

4186 Applegate, Katherine, et al. *See You in September* (7–9). 1995, Avon paper $3.99 (978-0-380-78088-4). Four chaste and charming short stories by four popular YA romance authors. (Rev: BL 1/1–15/96; SLJ 3/96)

4187 Bat-Ami, Miriam. *Two Suns in the Sky* (8–12). 1999, Front St. $15.95 (978-0-8126-2900-2). A docunovel set in upstate New York during 1944 about the love between a Catholic teenage girl and a Jewish Holocaust survivor from Yugoslavia who is living in a refugee camp. (Rev: BL 4/15/99; HB 7–8/99; HBG 9/99; SLJ 7/99; VOYA 10/99)

4188 Bernardo, Anilú. *Loves Me, Loves Me Not* (7–10). 1998, Arte Publico $16.95 (978-1-55885-258-7). A teen romance that involves Cuban American Maggie, a basketball player named Zach, newcomer Justin, and Maggie's friend, Susie. (Rev: BL 1/1–15/99)

4189 Bertrand, Diane Gonzales. *Lessons of the Game* (7–10). 1998, Arte Publico paper $9.95 (978-

1-55885-245-7). Student teacher Kaylene Morales is attracted to the freshman football coach but wonders if romance and her school assignments will mix. (Rev: BL 1/1–15/99; VOYA 10/99)

4190 Brooks, Martha. *Two Moons in August* (7–12). 1992, Little, Brown $15.95 (978-0-316-10979-6). A midsummer romance in the 1950s between a newcomer to a small Canadian community and a 16-year-old girl who is mourning her mother's death. (Rev: BL 11/15/91*; SLJ 3/92*)

4191 Burnham, Niki, et al. *Fireworks: Four Summer Stories* (7–12). 2007, Scholastic paper $8.99 (978-0-439-90300-4). Well-written with believable characters, these stories of summer romances occur in varied locales and are sure to please a wide spectrum of readers. (Rev: SLJ 7/07)

4192 Cann, Kate. *Grecian Holiday: Or, How I Turned Down the Best Possible Thing Only to Have the Time of My Life* (7–12). 2002, Avon paper $5.99 (978-0-06-447302-6). In addition to the beach, the food, and the drink, Kelly's vacation in Greece is a time of learning about herself, friendship, romance, and sex; for mature teens. (Rev: VOYA 2/03)

4193 Cann, Kate. *Ready? Love Trilogy #1* (8–12). 2001, HarperCollins paper $6.95 (978-0-06-440869-1). In the first book of a British romantic trilogy, 16-year-old Collette falls for Art, who is both rich and handsome, but she is troubled by his unrelenting pressure for physical intimacy. The sequels are *Sex* (2001) and *Go!* (2001). (Rev: HBG 10/02; SLJ 8/01; VOYA 10/01)

4194 Cleary, Beverly. *Fifteen* (7–9). 1956, Avon paper $6.99 (978-0-380-72804-6). A young adolescent discovers that having a boyfriend isn't the answer to all her social problems.

4195 Cleary, Beverly. *The Luckiest Girl* (7–9). 1958, Avon paper $6.99 (978-0-380-72806-0). New social opportunities arise when a young girl spends her senior year at a school in California.

4196 Coffey, Jan. *Tropical Kiss* (8–11). 2005, HarperCollins paper $5.99 (978-0-06-076003-8). Morgan's summer on Aruba with her father turns out to be more fun than she expected, but the discovery that her dad may be in trouble casts a cloud over her enjoyment of a new friend and boyfriend. (Rev: SLJ 8/05)

4197 Cooney, Caroline B. *Both Sides of Time* (6–10). 1997, Delacorte paper $4.99 (978-0-440-21932-3). Annie Lockwood, who has been yearning for love, suddenly finds herself in the 1890s, in a much more appealing era; however, traveling through time can lack romance. (Rev: BL 9/15/95; HB 11/95; HBG 3/02; SLJ 7/95)

4198 Daly, Maureen. *Seventeenth Summer* (6–8). 1981, Harmony LB $19.95 (978-0-89967-029-4); Archway paper $5.99 (978-0-671-61931-2). Angie experiences an idyllic summer after she meets Jack in this classic 1942 novel.

4199 Davis, Leila. *Lover Boy* (7–12). 1989, Avon paper $2.95 (978-0-380-75722-0). Ryan finds that his racy reputation is keeping him from the girl he really loves. (Rev: SLJ 10/89; VOYA 8/89)

4200 Dessen, Sarah. *This Lullaby* (8–12). 2002, Viking $16.99 (978-0-670-03530-4). Eighteen-year-old Remy's complex family life leads her to avoid deep romantic attachments until she meets Dexter. (Rev: BCCB 5/02; BL 4/1/02; HB 7–8/02; HBG 10/02; SLJ 4/02; VOYA 6/02)

4201 DuJardin, Rosamond. *Boy Trouble* (7–9). 1988, HarperCollins LB $12.89 (978-0-397-32263-3). A harmless romance first published in the 1960s and now back in print. (Rev: SLJ 2/88)

4202 Echols, Jennifer. *Major Crush* (8–12). 2006, Simon & Schuster paper $5.99 (978-1-4169-1830-1). Virginia wants to become the drum major in her high school band but finds she has competition in the form of the exasperating but very cute Drew. (Rev: SLJ 9/06)

4203 Fiedler, Lisa. *Romeo's Ex: Rosaline's Story* (8–11). 2006, Holt $16.95 (978-0-8050-7500-7). A retelling of *Romeo and Juliet* from the point of view of Rosaline, Juliet's cousin and Romeo's first love. (Rev: BL 9/15/06; SLJ 11/06)

4204 Filichia, Peter. *Not Just Another Pretty Face* (7–10). 1988, Avon paper $2.50 (978-0-380-75244-7). A high school story in which the course of true love does not run smoothly for Bill Richards. (Rev: BL 3/1/88; SLJ 5/88)

4205 Frank, Lucy. *Will You Be My Brussels Sprout?* (7–10). 1996, Holiday $15.95 (978-0-8234-1220-4). In this continuation of *I Am an Artichoke*, Emily, now 16, studies the cello at a New York music conservatory and falls in love for the first time. (Rev: BL 4/15/96; SLJ 4/96; VOYA 10/96)

4206 Fredericks, Mariah. *In the Cards: Love* (5–8). Illus. 2007, Simon & Schuster $15.99 (978-0-689-87654-7). Three eighth-grade girls in Manhattan use tarot cards to discover whether Anna will succeed in turning her crush on Declan into a romance; likable, believable characters populate this funny novel. (Rev: BL 1/1–15/07; SLJ 4/07)

4207 Friedman, Aimee. *A Novel Idea* (7–11). 2006, Simon & Schuster paper $5.99 (978-1-4169-0785-5). A light romantic comedy in which Norah's focus switches from her college resumé to the attractive James. (Rev: SLJ 2/06)

4208 Geras, Adele. *Pictures of the Night* (7–12). 1993, Harcourt $16.95 (978-0-15-261588-8). A modern version of *Snow White*, with the heroine an 18-year-old singer in London and Paris. (Rev: BL 3/1/93; SLJ 6/93)

4209 Geras, Adele. *The Tower Room* (7–12). 1992, Harcourt $15.95 (978-0-15-289627-0). The fairy tale *Rapunzel* is updated and set in an English girls' boarding school in the 1960s. (Rev: BL 2/15/92; SLJ 5/92)

4210 Gunn, Robin Jones. *I Promise* (6–12). Series: Christy and Todd, The College Years. 2001, Bethany $10.99 (978-0-7642-2274-0). Christy and Todd are finally engaged, but the complicated wedding plans and accompanying turmoil threaten to derail their happiness. (Rev: BL 1/1–15/02; VOYA 12/01)

4211 Hahn, Mary D. *The Wind Blows Backward* (8–12). 1993, Clarion $16.00 (978-0-395-62975-8). Spencer's downward emotional spiral and Lauren's deep commitment evoke a fantasy love gone awry. (Rev: BL 5/1/93; SLJ 5/93)

4212 Hart, Bruce, and Carole Hart. *Sooner or Later* (8–12). 1978, Avon paper $2.95 (978-0-380-42978-3). In order to fool her 17-year-old boyfriend into thinking she is older than 13, Jessie begins an intricate pattern of lies.

4213 Hart, Bruce, and Carole Hart. *Waiting Games* (7–10). 1981, Avon paper $3.50 (978-0-380-79012-8). Jessie and Michael are in love and must make difficult decisions about sex.

4214 Hobbs, Valerie. *Anything but Ordinary* (8–12). 2007, Farrar $16.00 (978-0-374-30374-7). High school sweethearts Bernie and Winifred are separated when Winifred goes off to college and Bernie stays behind; the distance between them increases when Winifred is "madeover" at school. (Rev: BCCB 5/07; BL 4/15/07; SLJ 3/07)

4215 Jacobs, Holly. *Pickup Lines* (8–12). 2005, Avalon $21.95 (978-0-8034-9704-7). A comic romance in which teacher Mary Rosenthal and businessman Ethan Westbrook vie to win a pickup truck. (Rev: BL 4/1/05)

4216 Johnson, Kathleen Jeffrie. *Dumb Love* (8–11). 2005, Roaring Brook $16.95 (978-1-59643-062-4). A funny romance in which high school student Carlotta aspires both to win the heart of Pete and to write a novel. (Rev: BL 9/15/05; SLJ 11/05)

4217 Kantor, Melissa. *Confessions of a Not It Girl* (7–12). 2004, Hyperion $15.99 (978-0-7868-1837-2). Jan Miller has high hopes that love will come her way during her senior year in high school, but it's soon obvious that it won't be easy in this entertaining, true-to-life romantic comedy. (Rev: BL 6/1–15/04; HB 7–8/04; SLJ 4/04; VOYA 6/04)

4218 Kaplow, Robert. *Alessandra in Love* (8–10). 1989, HarperCollins LB $12.89 (978-0-397-32282-4). Alessandra's boyfriend turns out to be a self-centered disappointment. (Rev: BL 4/15/89; SLJ 4/89; VOYA 8/89)

4219 Kerr, M. E. *Someone Like Summer* (7–12). 2007, HarperTempest $15.99 (978-0-06-114100-3). Annabel, 17, falls in love with Esteban, an illegal alien working for her father, in this novel set in the Hamptons. (Rev: BCCB 9/07; BL 4/1/07; SLJ 11/07)

4220 Klass, David. *Screen Test* (7–9). 1997, Scholastic paper $16.95 (978-0-590-48592-0). Sixteen-year-old Liz Weaton is whisked off to Hollywood, where she almost falls in love with her costar. (Rev: BL 12/1/97; HBG 3/98; SLJ 10/97)

4221 Knudson, R. R. *Just Another Love Story* (7–10). 1983, Avon paper $2.50 (978-0-380-65532-8). Dusty takes up body building to help forget the girlfriend who has spurned him.

4222 Lachtman, Ofelia Dumas. *The Girl from Playa Bianca* (7–12). 1995, Arte Publico paper $9.95 (978-1-55885-149-8). A gothic romance in which a Mexican teenager and her young brother travel to Los Angeles in search of their father. (Rev: BL 11/15/95; SLJ 10/95; VOYA 12/95)

4223 Lenhard, Elizabeth. *Knit Two Together* (6–9). Series: Chicks with Sticks. 2006, Dutton $16.99 (978-0-525-47764-8). The knitting foursome is back, and this time boys and romance take up as many pages as knitting and chatting. (Rev: BL 12/15/06; SLJ 2/07)

4224 McClymer, Kelly. *Getting to Third Date* (8–11). 2006, Simon & Schuster paper $5.99 (978-1-4169-1479-2). College advice columnist Katelyn is forced to take a dose of her own medicine and give her ex-boyfriends another chance. (Rev: BL 4/15/06)

4225 McDaniel, Lurlene. *Don't Die, My Love* (7–12). 1995, Bantam paper $4.99 (978-0-553-56715-1). A young couple, Julie and Luke, "engaged" since 6th grade, discover that Luke has Hodgkin's lymphoma. (Rev: BL 9/15/95; SLJ 10/95; VOYA 12/95)

4226 McFann, Jane. *Maybe by Then I'll Understand* (7–9). 1987, Avon paper $2.50 (978-0-380-75221-8). Cath and Tony become a pair but Tony demands more attention and loyalty than she can give. (Rev: BL 11/15/87; SLJ 1/88; VOYA 12/87)

4227 Malcolm, Jahnna N. *Mixed Messages* (6–9). Series: Love Letters. 2005, Simon & Schuster paper $5.99 (978-0-689-87222-8). Jade, a high school senior, has had a crush on Zephyr Strauss for years, but when she finally writes him a love letter, it ends up in the wrong hands. (Rev: SLJ 1/05)

4228 Malcolm, Jahnna N. *Perfect Strangers* (6–9). Series: Love Letters. 2005, Simon & Schuster paper $5.99 (978-0-689-87221-1). There's no love lost between high school juniors Madison and Jeremy, who are running against each other for class president, until they're secretly paired up in their school's Heart-2-Heart e-mail-pal program. (Rev: SLJ 1/05)

4229 Martin, Ann M. *Just a Summer Romance* (6–8). 1987, Holiday $13.95 (978-0-8234-0649-4). While spending a summer on Fire Island, 14-year-old Melanie becomes attracted to Justin. (Rev: BL 4/1/87; SLJ 6/87; VOYA 10/87)

4230 Matthews, Phoebe. *The Boy on the Cover* (6–8). 1988, Avon paper $2.75 (978-0-380-75407-6). Cyndi falls in love with a boy whose picture is on the cover of a book she owns. (Rev: VOYA 2/89)

4231 Mauser, Pat Rhoads. *Love Is for the Dogs* (7–10). 1989, Avon paper $2.50 (978-0-380-75723-7). Janna realizes that Brian, the boy next door, can be very desirable. (Rev: BL 4/15/89; SLJ 4/89)

4232 Mines, Jeanette. *Risking It* (7–9). 1988, Avon paper $2.75 (978-0-380-75401-4). Jeannie is attracted to Trent Justin, who has joined her senior class. (Rev: BL 9/1/88; SLJ 1/89; VOYA 6/88)

4233 *Mistletoe: Four Holiday Stories* (7–10). 2006, Scholastic paper $8.99 (978-0-439-86368-1). A collection of four different winter holiday stories about love by YA authors. (Rev: BL 11/1/06; SLJ 10/06)

4234 O'Connell, Tyne. *True Love, the Sphinx and Other Unsolvable Riddles* (7–10). 2007, Bloomsbury $16.95 (978-1-59990-050-6). A ritzy school trip to Egypt brings together students from an American boys' school and an English girls' school in this romance that offers humor and informative travelogue. (Rev: BL 11/1/07; SLJ 3/08)

4235 Osterlund, Anne. *Aurelia* (7–12). 2008, Penguin paper $8.99 (978-0-14-240579-6). Princess Aurelia's life is in danger and she faces a marriage arranged by her father; can her childhood friend Robert save her? (Rev: BL 5/1/08)

4236 Plummer, Louise. *The Unlikely Romance of Kate Bjorkman* (7–10). 1997, Bantam paper $4.50 (978-0-440-22704-5). A brainy teen foils a beautiful, evil temptress and gets the man of her dreams. (Rev: SLJ 10/95; VOYA 12/95)

4237 Rallison, Janette. *It's a Mall World After All* (8–11). 2006, Walker $16.95 (978-0-8027-8853-5). Charlotte is so busy trying to catch Bryant cheating on her friend that she doesn't notice what a nice guy Bryant's best friend Colton is. (Rev: BL 1/1–15/07; SLJ 12/06)

4238 Reinhardt, Dana. *How to Build a House* (8–12). 2008, Random $15.99 (978-0-375-84453-9). Harper sends a summer helping to build houses in Tennessee and learns that happiness is always possible. (Rev: BL 4/15/08; HB 7–8/08; SLJ 6/08) ✎

4239 Ryan, Mary C. *Frankie's Run* (6–8). 1987, Little, Brown $12.95 (978-0-316-76370-7). In this teen novel, Mary Frances falls for the new boy in town but also organizes a run to aid her local library. (Rev: BL 8/87; SLJ 5/87)

4240 Schreiber, Ellen. *Teenage Mermaid* (6–8). 2003, HarperCollins LB $16.89 (978-0-06-008205-5). Romance and entertainment abound in this story of a teen mermaid who rescues a young surfer. (Rev: BL 7/03; HBG 10/03; SLJ 8/03; VOYA 8/03)

4241 Shinn, Sharon. *General Winston's Daughter* (7–10). 2007, Viking $16.99 (978-0-670-06248-5). Averie, whose father is a general in the Aebrian military, goes to visit a colonized land named Chiarrin and as she learns more about its culture, finds her views of many things in life — love, politics, even her father — are changing. (Rev: BL 8/07; SLJ 1/08)

4242 Sierra, Patricia. *One-Way Romance* (7–10). 1986, Avon paper $2.50 (978-0-380-75107-5). A talented girl who does well with carpentry and track seems to be losing out with her boyfriend. (Rev: BL 8/86; SLJ 11/86; VOYA 12/86)

4243 Sones, Sonya. *What My Girlfriend Doesn't Know* (7–10). 2007, Simon & Schuster paper $7.99 (978-0-689-87603-5). Popular Sophie falls for geeky Robin despite disapproval and disbelief from their friends in this stand-alone follow-up to *What My Mother Doesn't Know* (2001), narrated by Robin in first-person free verse. (Rev: BL 4/1/07*; SLJ 6/07)

4244 Stacey, Cherylyn. *Gone to Maui* (7–9). 1996, Roussan paper $8.95 (978-1-896184-14-2). In this novel, teenage Becky accompanies her mother on a trip to Maui, and there finds romance. (Rev: VOYA 4/97)

4245 Stanek, Lou W. *Katy Did* (8–12). 1992, Avon paper $2.99 (978-0-380-76170-8). A shy country girl and popular city boy fall in love, with tragic consequences. (Rev: BL 3/15/92)

4246 Sunshine, Tina. *An X-Rated Romance* (7–9). 1982, Avon paper $2.50 (978-0-380-79905-3). Two 13-year-old girls have a crush on their English teacher. A reissue.

4247 Thesman, Jean. *Who Said Life Is Fair?* (7–9). 1987, Avon paper $3.50 (978-0-380-75088-7). Teddy is trying to cope with work on the school newspaper while keeping her love life in order. (Rev: BL 5/87; VOYA 8/87)

4248 Trembath, Don. *A Beautiful Place on Yonge Street* (8–10). 1999, Orca paper $6.95 (978-1-55143-121-5). Budding writer Harper Winslow falls in love with Sunny Taylor when he attends a summer writing camp, and experiences all the angst that goes with it. (Rev: BL 3/1/99; SLJ 7/99; VOYA 6/99)

4249 Weyn, Suzanne. *The Makeover Summer* (6–8). 1988, Avon paper $2.95 (978-0-380-75521-9). An exchange student who needs help joins the three girls of the Makeover Club. (Rev: BL 2/15/89)

4250 Wittlinger, Ellen. *Lombardo's Law* (7–10). 1993, Morrow paper $4.95 (978-0-688-05294-2). The conventions of romance are thrown aside when sophomore Justine and 8th-grader Mike find themselves attracted to each other, despite obstacles. (Rev: BL 9/15/93; VOYA 12/93)

4251 Woodson, Jacqueline. *If You Come Softly* (7–10). 1998, Putnam $17.99 (978-0-399-23112-4). The story of the love between a black boy and a white girl, their families, and the prejudice they encounter. (Rev: BL 10/1/98; HBG 9/99; SLJ 12/98; VOYA 12/98)

Science Fiction

4252 Allen, Roger MacBride. *David Brin's Out of Time: The Game of Worlds* (7–12). Series: David Brin's Out of Time. 1999, Avon paper $4.99 (978-0-380-79969-5). Adam O'Connor, a mischievous high school student in the late 20th century, finds himself facing a whole new set of problems when he's yanked 350 years into the future. (Rev: VOYA 4/00)

4253 Anderson, Kevin J., ed. *War of the Worlds: Global Dispatches* (7–12). 1996, Bantam $22.95 (978-0-553-10352-6). This tribute to H. G. Wells's *War of the Worlds* features stories of Martian invasions that are either take-offs on the writing styles of such famous authors as Conrad, London, Verne, and Kipling, or the experiences of famous individuals, such as Teddy Roosevelt and Pablo Picasso, during a Martian invasion. (Rev: VOYA 10/96)

4254 Applegate, K. A. *Animorphs #1: The Invasion* (5–8). 1996, Scholastic paper $4.99 (978-0-590-62977-5). Jake, an average suburban kid, is confronted one night by a creature from space who teaches him how to morph into the forms of other creatures. (Rev: VOYA 12/96)

4255 Armstrong, Jennifer, and Nancy Butcher. *The Kindling* (7–10). Series: Fire-Us. 2002, Harper-Collins LB $16.89 (978-0-06-029411-3). In 2007, after a virus has killed the adults, a small band of children join together in a Florida town and try to carry on with life. (Rev: BCCB 6/02; BL 4/15/02; HBG 10/02; SLJ 10/02)

4256 Asimov, Isaac. *Caves of Steel* (7–12). 1955, Spectra paper $6.99 (978-0-553-29034-9). A human and a robot combine forces in this science fiction classic to work together to help mankind. Part of Asimov's well-written Robot series. (Rev: BL BL 5/1/00)

4257 Asimov, Isaac. *Fantastic Voyage: A Novel* (8–12). 1966, Houghton paper $6.99 (978-0-553-

27572-8). Five people are miniaturized to enter the body of a sick man and save his life.

4258 Asimov, Isaac, et al., eds. *Young Extraterrestrials* (7–9). 1984, HarperCollins paper $7.95 (978-0-06-020167-8). Eleven stories by well-known authors about youngsters who are aliens from space.

4259 Asimov, Janet. *Norby and the Terrified Taxi* (4–8). 1997, Walker $15.95 (978-0-8027-8642-5). Norby, the bungling robot, is kidnapped, and while trying to find him, Jeff and his friends stumble on a plot by Garc the Great to take over the Federation. This is one of a large series of Norby books suitable for middle school readers. (Rev: BL 1/1–15/98; SLJ 12/97)

4260 Asimov, Janet. *The Package in Hyperspace* (5–7). Illus. 1988, Walker LB $14.85 (978-0-8027-6823-0). Two space-wrecked children must fend for themselves as they try to reach Merkina. (Rev: BL 1/1/89; SLJ 11/88)

4261 Asimov, Janet, and Isaac Asimov. *Norby and the Invaders* (5–8). 1985, Walker LB $10.85 (978-0-8027-6607-6). Jeff and his unusual robot Norby travel to a planet to help one of Norby's ancestors. Part of a series that includes *Norby's Other Secret*. (Rev: BL 3/1/86; SLJ 2/86)

4262 Asimov, Janet, and Isaac Asimov. *Norby and Yobo's Great Adventure* (5–8). 1989, Walker LB $13.85 (978-0-8027-6894-0). Norby the robot time-travels to help Admiral Yobo of Mars to trace his family roots. Part of a series that also includes *Norby Down to Earth*. (Rev: BL 10/15/89)

4263 Asimov, Janet, and Isaac Asimov. *Norby Finds a Villain* (4–8). 1987, Walker LB $13.85 (978-0-8027-6711-0). Norby the robot and his human friends set out to free Pera, who has been robot-napped by the traitor Ing, in this sixth book of the Norby series. Also use *Norby and the Queen's Necklace* (1986). (Rev: BL 1/1/88; SLJ 11/87)

4264 Ball, Justin, and Evan Croker. *Space Dogs* (4–7). 2006, Knopf $15.95 (978-0-375-83256-7). When a powerful force threatens to destroy Gersbach, the planet's inhabitants dispatch dog-shaped vehicles to Earth in a desperate attempt to head off disaster; they end up battling in the front yard of Amy and Lucy Buckley in this humorous, action-packed story. (Rev: BL 6/1–15/06; SLJ 8/06)

4265 Ball, Margaret. *Lost in Translation* (8–12). 1995, Baen $5.99 (978-0-671-87638-8). American teenager Allie flies to France to attend a university but lands in a fantasy world filled with spells of every kind, where people communicate through voice-bubbles and a group of terrifying monsters controls an important subterranean substance called landvirtue. (Rev: VOYA 4/96)

4266 Bawden, Nina. *Off the Road* (5–9). 1998, Clarion $16.00 (978-0-395-91321-5). In this science fic-

tion novel set in a time when the elderly are exterminated, 11-year-old Tom follows his grandfather to the "savage jungle" Outside the Wall, where the old man hopes to escape his fate, and discovers a different kind of society. (Rev: BCCB 10/98; BL 9/15/98; HBG 10/99; SLJ 11/98)

4267 Bechard, Margaret. *Spacer and Rat* (6–9). 2005, Roaring Brook $16.95 (978-1-59643-058-7). Space resident Jack revises his views about Earth "rats" when he meets Kit and her highly intelligent bot Waldo in this novel full of references to classic works and entertaining jargon. (Rev: BL 9/1/05; SLJ 11/05; VOYA 10/05)

4268 Belden, Wilanne Schneider. *Mind-Find* (6–9). 1988, Harcourt $14.95 (978-0-15-254270-2). A 13-year-old girl adjusts with difficulty to her amazing powers of ESP. (Rev: BL 2/15/88; SLJ 8/88)

4269 Boulle, Pierre. *Planet of the Apes* (7–12). 2001, Random paper $6.99 (978-0-345-44798-2). Stranded on the planet Soror, Ulysse Merou discovers a civilization ruled by apes.

4270 Bradbury, Ray. *Fahrenheit 451* (7–12). 1953, Ballantine paper $6.99 (978-0-345-34296-6). In this futuristic novel, book reading has become a crime.

4271 Bradbury, Ray. *The October Country* (7–12). 1999, Avon $15.95 (978-0-380-97387-3). Ordinary people are caught up in unreal situations in these 19 strange stories.

4272 Buckley-Archer, Linda. *Gideon the Cutpurse* (6–9). 2006, Simon & Schuster $17.95 (978-1-4169-1525-6). Two 12-year-olds named Kate and Peter find themselves transported back to 1763 London where the only person to offer them help is a cutpurse named Gideon. (Rev: BL 8/06; SLJ 7/06*)

4273 Bunting, Eve. *The Cloverdale Switch* (7–9). 1979, HarperCollins LB $12.89 (978-0-397-31867-4). John and Cindy encounter unusual changes in their world and find a mysterious black box.

4274 Butts, Nancy. *The Door in the Lake* (5–8). 1997, Front St. $17.95 (978-1-886910-27-0). Twenty-seven months after being abducted by aliens, Joey returns home to find that everything has changed while he has remained the same. (Rev: BCCB 7–8/98; BL 5/15/98; HBG 10/98; SLJ 6/98; VOYA 10/98)

4275 Card, Orson Scott. *First Meetings: In the Enderverse* (6–12). 2003, Tor $17.95 (978-0-7653-0873-3). Contains the novella "Ender's Game," first published in 1977, and three other stories, one previously unpublished. (Rev: SLJ 1/04)

4276 Carman, Patrick. *Atherton: The House of Power* (5–8). 2007, Little, Brown $16.99 (978-0-316-16670-6). Atherton is a socially divided world under threat and 12-year-old Edgar has a book that contains key secrets. (Rev: BL 5/15/07; LMC 11/07; SLJ 6/07)

4277 Carmichael, Claire. *Leaving Simplicity* (6–9). 2007, Annick $21.95 (978-1-55451-090-0); paper $10.95 (978-1-55451-089-4). In a future where advertising and marketing are king, teenagers Taylor and Barrett find themselves in danger when they decide to resist. (Rev: BL 12/15/07)

4278 Cart, Michael, ed. *Tomorrowland: 10 Stories About the Future* (7–10). 1999, Scholastic paper $15.95 (978-0-590-37678-5). Ten writers, including Ron Koertge, Lois Lowry, and Katherine Paterson, have contributed original stories to this anthology that reflect their concepts of the future. (Rev: BCCB 12/99; BL 8/99; HBG 4/00; SLJ 9/99; VOYA 12/99)

4279 Castro, Adam-Troy. *Spider-Man: Secret of the Sinister Six* (7–12). Illus. by Mike Zeck. 2002, BP $24.95 (978-0-7434-4464-4). Six supervillians attack New York City and Spider-Man comes to the rescue in this humorous and action-packed final installment in a trilogy. (Rev: SLJ 7/02)

4280 Clancy, Tom, and Steve Pieczenik. *Virtual Vandals* (7–12). Series: Net Force. 1999, Berkley paper $4.99 (978-0-425-16173-9). In 2025, after Matt Hunter and his computer friends attend an all-star virtual reality baseball game where terrorists shoot wildly at the stands, our hero and his pals set out to catch the culprits. Followed by *The Deadliest Game*. (Rev: BL 3/15/99)

4281 Clarke, Arthur C. *Childhood's End* (7–12). 1963, Ballantine paper $6.99 (978-0-345-34795-4). The overlords' arrival on Earth marks the beginning of the end for humankind.

4282 Clements, Andrew. *Things Not Seen* (7–10). 2002, Putnam $16.99 (978-0-399-23626-6). Bobby, 15, suddenly becomes invisible and must deal with all the problems his "disappearance" causes. (Rev: BCCB 6/02; BL 4/15/02; HB 3–4/02; HBG 10/02; SLJ 3/02; VOYA 2/02)

4283 Colfer, Eoin. *The Supernaturalist* (6–9). 2004, Hyperion $16.95 (978-0-7868-5148-5). In this action-packed futuristic novel, 14-year-old Cosmo Hill escapes from an orphanage and is befriended by an unlikely trio known as the Supernaturalists, who draft the teen to join them in their campaign against the invisible but deadly Parasites. (Rev: BCCB 9/04; BL 8/04; SLJ 7/04; VOYA 8/04)

4284 Collins, Paul. *The Skyborn* (8–11). 2005, Tor $17.95 (978-0-7653-1273-0). Accepted by the Earthborn after his ship *Colony* crashed on post-holocaust Earth, 14-year-old Welkin, born a Skyborn, learns the Earthborn are in danger from the Skyborn; a sequel to *The Earthborn* (2003). (Rev: BL 2/15/06)

4285 Cooper, Clare. *Ashar of Qarius* (5–8). 1990, Harcourt $14.95 (978-0-15-200409-5). A teenage girl, two children, and their pets are left alone in a space dome and must find a way to survive. (Rev: BL 5/15/90; SLJ 7/90)

4286 Cowley, Joy. *Starbright and the Dream Eater* (5–8). 2000, HarperCollins LB $14.89 (978-0-06-028420-6). A child born to a mentally disabled teenage mother and named Starbright is destined to save the earth from the Dream Eater. (Rev: BCCB 7–8/00; BL 4/15/00; HBG 10/00; SLJ 6/00)

4287 Craig, Joe. *Jimmy Coates: Assassin?* (4–7). 2005, HarperCollins LB $16.89 (978-0-06-077264-2). Thirty-five percent human and 65 percent technologically engineered assassin, 11-year-old Jimmy Coates faces external dangers and internal struggles, all with action, suspense, and humor. (Rev: BL 5/1/05; SLJ 6/05)

4288 Craig, Joe. *Jimmy Coates: Target* (5–8). 2007, HarperCollins $16.99 (978-0-06-077266-6). Jimmy Coates, mostly robot but part human, chooses his human side and ends up on the run from the government that wants him assassinated. (Rev: BL 6/1–15/07)

4289 Czerneda, Julie E. *In the Company of Others* (7–12). 2001, DAW paper $7.99 (978-0-88677-999-3). Biologist Gail Smith embarks on the space ship Seeker to track down Aaron Pardell, whose help she needs in her mission to find and destroy a deadly life form called the Quill. (Rev: VOYA 2/02)

4290 Daley, Michael J. *Shanghaied to the Moon* (5–8). 2007, Putnam $16.99 (978-0-399-24619-7). In the year 2165, 13-year-old Stewart Hale wants above all to become a space pilot like his mother was before she died in a crash; when his father refuses to help him, he runs away and finds himself on a secret mission to the moon. (Rev: BL 5/1/07; SLJ 5/07)

4291 Dickinson, Peter. *Eva* (8–12). 1990, Dell paper $5.50 (978-0-440-20766-5). When Eva wakes up after an accident she finds that she has retained her memory but been given the body of a chimpanzee. (Rev: HB 7/89; SLJ 4/89)

4292 Dicks, Terrance. *Doctor Who and the Genesis of the Daleks* (7–9). 1979, Amereon $18.95 (978-0-8488-0151-9). Based on the TV series, this is the story of an unusual Time Lord and his adventures in space.

4293 Doyle, Debra, and James D. MacDonald. *Groogleman* (5–8). 1996, Harcourt $15.00 (978-0-15-200235-0). In this novel set in the future, 13-year-old Dan is immune to the plague that is devastating the countryside and sets out with friend Leesie to help tend the sick. (Rev: BCCB 12/96; SLJ 12/96; VOYA 6/97)

4294 Dunkle, Clare B. *The Sky Inside* (4–8). 2008, Atheneum $16.99 (978-1-4169-2422-7). Martin discovers the terrible truth about his flawless, enclosed suburb when he gathers the courage to venture outside it. (Rev: BL 5/15/08; SLJ 5/08)

4295 Enthoven, Sam. *Tim, Defender of the Earth* (5–8). 2008, Penguin $19.99 (978-1-59514-184-2). Tim, a huge, T. rex-type fighting monster, breaks out of his underground lab to save London and the world from a crazy scientist — with the help of 14-year-old Anna and her friend Chris. (Rev: BL 1/1–15/08; SLJ 3/08)

4296 Farmer, Nancy. *The Ear, the Eye and the Arm* (7–10). 1994, Orchard LB $19.99 (978-0-531-08679-7). In Zimbabwe in 2194, the military ruler's son, 13, and his younger siblings leave their technologically overcontrolled home and embark on a series of perilous adventures. (Rev: BL 4/1/94; SLJ 6/94; VOYA 6/94)

4297 Farmer, Nancy. *House of the Scorpion* (7–10). 2002, Simon & Schuster $17.95 (978-0-689-85222-0). Young Matt, who has spent his childhood in cruel circumstances, discovers he is in fact a clone of the 142-year-old ruler of Opium, a land south of the U.S. border. (Rev: BL 9/15/02; HB 11–12/02; HBG 3/03; SLJ 9/02)

4298 Fisher, Catherine. *Corbenic* (8–11). 2006, Greenwillow $16.99 (978-0-06-072470-2). Cal leaves his alcoholic mother to live with his uncle but on the train ride there is transported to a mythical place called Corbenic, where the fate of the Fisher King lies in his hands. (Rev: BL 8/06; HB 9–10/06; SLJ 11/06)

4299 Follett, Ken. *The Power Twins* (4–8). 1991, Scholastic paper $2.75 (978-0-590-42507-0). Three youngsters travel to a planet where large, gentle worms live. (Rev: SLJ 1/91)

4300 Foster, Alan Dean. *The Hand of Dinotopia* (6–10). Series: Dinotopia. 1999, HarperCollins $22.99 (978-0-06-028005-5). In this adventure involving dinosaurs, our heroes journey through the Great Desert and Outer Island to find the key to a sea route that will link Dinotopia to the rest of the world. (Rev: BL 5/1/99; HBG 10/99; SLJ 4/99)

4301 Foster, Alan Dean. *Splinter of the Mind's Eye* (8–12). 1978, Ballantine paper $6.99 (978-0-345-32023-0). A novel about Luke Skywalker and Princess Leia of *Star Wars* fame and their battle against the Empire.

4302 Fukui, Isamu. *Truancy* (8–12). 2008, Tor $17.95 (978-0-7653-1767-4). Fifteen-year-old Tack joins a children's resistance movement called the Truancy that is bent on violently overthrowing the establishment. (Rev: BL 4/15/08; LMC 4–5/08; SLJ 6/08)

4303 Gaiman, Neil, and Michael Reaves. *InterWorld* (5–8). 2007, Eos $16.99 (978-0-06-123896-3). Joey, 16, discovers that he can walk into alternate dimensions where he finds other versions of himself and is recruited into an army of Joeys that battles Lord Dogknife and Lady Indigo, two evil magicians. (Rev: BL 9/1/07; SLJ 11/07) ⑨

4304 Gerrold, David. *Blood and Fire* (8–12). 2004, BenBella paper $14.95 (978-1-932100-11-2). In this story that is a metaphor for the AIDS problem, a starship happens on another one, adrift in space, that contains blood worms, a deadly parasite. (Rev: BL 1/1–15/04)

4305 Gerrold, David. *Chess with a Dragon* (8–12). 1988, Avon paper $3.50 (978-0-380-70662-4). The entire human race becomes slaves of giant slugs and Yake must save them. (Rev: BL 6/15/87; SLJ 9/87)

4306 Gideon, Melanie. *Pucker* (8–11). 2006, Penguin $16.99 (978-1-59514-055-5). Nicknamed "Pucker" by his classmates for the horrible burn scars on his face, 17-year-old Thomas Quicksilver has even larger issues to confront as he returns to his home world of Isaura on a mission to save his mother's life. (Rev: BL 4/15/06; SLJ 5/06)

4307 Gilden, Mel. *Outer Space and All That Junk* (5–7). Illus. 1989, HarperCollins LB $12.89 (978-0-397-32307-4). Myron's uncle is collecting junk, which he believes will help aliens return to their home in outer space. (Rev: BL 12/1/89; SLJ 12/89)

4308 Gilmore, Kate. *The Exchange Student* (6–9). 1999, Houghton $15.00 (978-0-395-57511-6). Set in the year 2094, this novel describes the problems faced by a group of exchange students from the planet Chela who are studying on Earth. (Rev: BL 9/15/99; HB 9–10/99; HBG 4/00; SLJ 10/99)

4309 Grant, Michael. *Gone* (6–9). 2008, HarperTeen $17.99 (978-0-06-144876-8). When everyone older than 13 simply vanishes one day, the children are left to fend for themselves and realize that strange things are happening to the humans and animals left behind. (Rev: BL 5/15/08*; SLJ 8/08)

4310 Guibert, Emmanuel, and Joann Sfar. *Sardine in Outer Space 3* (5–8). Trans. by Elisabeth Brizzi. Illus. 2007, Roaring Brook paper $12.95 (978-1-59643-128-7). Sardine and her space-pirate friends tackle Supermuscleman among others in this series of zany adventures. (Rev: BL 3/15/07; SLJ 7/07)

4311 Gutman, Dan. *Cyberkid* (4–8). 1998, Hyperion LB $14.49 (978-0-7868-2344-4). Yip, a computer-savvy 12-year-old, and his sister, Paige, create a "virtual actor," or "vactor," who breaks out of cyberspace and reveals a serious flaw: his database does not include a conscience. (Rev: BL 6/1–15/98; SLJ 8/98)

4312 Haarsma, P. J. *Betrayal on Orbis 2* (5–8). Series: The Softwire. 2008, Candlewick $16.99 (978-0-7636-2710-2). This sequel to *Virus on Orbis 1* finds JT and his friends enslaved to aquatic aliens called Samirans on a wormhole ring. (Rev: BL 5/15/08; SLJ 7/08)

4313 Haarsma, P. J. *Virus on Orbis 1* (6–9). 2006, Candlewick $15.99 (978-0-7636-2709-6). Johnny, 12, and his sister have spent their lives traveling with other children on a spaceship to Orbis, where Johnny learns that he has the ability to communicate telepathically with computers, an ability that puts him in danger. (Rev: BL 11/15/06; LMC 2/07; SLJ 12/06)

4314 Haddix, Margaret P. *Among the Barons* (5–8). 2003, Simon & Schuster $16.95 (978-0-689-83906-1). Luke, a third child who has been living underground in this two-child society, comes close to exposure in this exciting installment in the series that began with *Among the Hidden* (1998). (Rev: BL 5/15/03; HBG 10/03; SLJ 6/03; VOYA 8/03)

4315 Haddix, Margaret P. *Among the Betrayed* (5–9). 2002, Simon & Schuster $16.95 (978-0-689-83905-4). In this third novel in the series that started with *Among the Hidden* (1998), illegal third child Nina faces danger and difficult decisions. (Rev: BCCB 10/02; HBG 10/02; SLJ 6/02; VOYA 6/02)

4316 Haddix, Margaret P. *Among the Brave* (4–7). Series: Shadow Children. 2004, Simon & Schuster $15.95 (978-0-689-85794-2). This sequel to *Among the Barons* (2003) features Trey's efforts to rescue Luke and other third-born children. (Rev: BL 5/15/04; SLJ 6/04)

4317 Haddix, Margaret P. *Among the Enemy* (5–8). Series: Shadow Children. 2005, Simon & Schuster $15.95 (978-0-689-85796-6). Matthias, one of the third children illegal in his society, is mistakenly welcomed into the Population Police; there he is confused by divided loyalties. (Rev: BL 6/1–15/05; SLJ 6/05)

4318 Haddix, Margaret P. *Among the Free* (5–8). Series: Shadow Children. 2006, Simon & Schuster $16.95 (978-0-689-85798-0). Illegal third child Luke inadvertently sets off an uprising that leads to the overthrow of his country's oppressive government. (Rev: BL 6/1–15/06; SLJ 8/06)

4319 Haddix, Margaret P. *Among the Hidden* (5–8). 1998, Simon & Schuster $16.95 (978-0-689-81700-7). In a society where only two children are allowed per family, Luke, the third, endures a secret life hidden from authorities. (Rev: HBG 3/99; SLJ 9/98; VOYA 10/98)

4320 Haddix, Margaret P. *Among the Impostors* (5–7). 2001, Simon & Schuster $16.00 (978-0-689-83904-7). As a third child in a society that allows only two per family, Luke has assumed a new identity and at age 12 enrolls in a nightmarish boarding school. (Rev: BCCB 9/01; BL 4/15/01; HBG 10/01; SLJ 7/01; VOYA 8/01)

4321 Haddix, Margaret P. *Double Identity* (5–8). 2005, Simon & Schuster $15.95 (978-0-689-87374-4). In this science fiction page-turner, 12-year-old Bethany Cole, left with her aunt after her mother

suffers a nervous breakdown, uncovers some shocking family secrets. (Rev: BL 10/1/05; SLJ 11/05; VOYA 10/05)

4322 Haddix, Margaret P. *Found* (6–12). Series: The Missing. 2008, Simon & Schuster $15.99 (978-1-4169-6227-4). Thirteen-year-old Jonah, who was adopted, receives strange notes referring to his past and discovers that, as babies, he and 35 other children traveled through time and arrived on an unpiloted airplane. (Rev: BL 5/1/08; LMC 4–5/08; SLJ 5/08) ◐

4323 Hayden, Patrick Nielsen, ed. *New Skies: An Anthology of Today's Science Fiction* (7–12). 2003, Tor $19.95 (978-0-7653-0010-2). Short stories that were originally published in science fiction magazines include pieces by Orson Scott Card, Philip K. Dick, and Connie Willis. (Rev: BL 1/1–15/04)

4324 Heinlein, Robert A. *The Star Beast* (7–10). 1977, Macmillan $15.00 (978-0-684-15329-2). A pet smuggled to Earth never seems to stop growing.

4325 Heintze, Ty. *Valley of the Eels* (5–8). 1993, Eakin $15.95 (978-0-89015-904-0). A dolphin leads two boys to an underwater station where friendly aliens are cultivating trees to replant on their own planet. (Rev: BL 3/1/94)

4326 Henderson, J. A. *Bunker 10* (6–9). 2007, Harcourt $17.00 (978-0-15-206240-8). To survive the coming destruction of their military installation, a group of techno-genius teens must use all their skills — in both reality and virtual reality. (Rev: BL 10/1/07; LMC 1/08; SLJ 1/08)

4327 Hill, William. *The Magic Bicycle* (5–8). 1998, Otter Creek paper $13.95 (978-1-890611-00-2). For helping an alien escape, Danny receives a magical bicycle that is capable of transporting him through time and space. (Rev: BL 1/1–15/98; SLJ 3/98)

4328 Hobbs, Will. *Go Big or Go Home* (5–8). 2008, HarperCollins $15.99 (978-0-06-074141-9). A meteorite crashes into Brady's bedroom in South Dakota, and Brady soon finds that something in the space debris has changed him. (Rev: BL 4/1/08; HB 5-6/08; SLJ 4/08)

4329 Hughes, Monica. *Invitation to the Game* (7–10). 1991, Simon & Schuster paper $4.99 (978-0-671-86692-1). In 2154, a high school graduate and her friends face life on welfare in a highly robotic society and are invited to participate in a sinister government "game." (Rev: BL 9/15/91)

4330 Hughes, Monica. *The Keeper of the Isis Light* (7–9). 2008, Atheneum paper $11.99 (978-1-4169-8963-9). A 16-year-old girl's lonely existence on planet Isis comes to an end when settlers arrive; first published in 1981.

4331 Jeapes, Ben. *The Xenocide Mission* (7–10). 2002, Viking $15.95 (978-0-385-75007-3). A complex and exciting adventure set in the distant future in which humans and their quadruped companions must fight against ferocious aliens known as the Kin. (Rev: BCCB 6/02; BL 4/15/02; HBG 3/03; SLJ 6/02; VOYA 8/02)

4332 Jeter, K. W. *The Mandalorian Armor* (7–9). Series: The Bounty Hunter Wars. 1998, Bantam paper $6.99 (978-0-553-57885-0). This first installment in a trilogy involves Boba Fett, the bounty hunter who captured Han Solo in *The Empire Strikes Back.* (Rev: VOYA 2/99)

4333 Johansen, K. V. *The Cassandra Virus* (5–8). 2006, Orca paper $7.95 (978-1-55143-497-1). Computer geek Jordan designs a powerful computer program that takes on a life of its own, spreading via the Internet to other computers and taking control of their operations. (Rev: SLJ 11/06; VOYA 8/06)

4334 Jones, Diana Wynne. *Hexwood* (8–12). 1994, Greenwillow $16.00 (978-0-688-12488-5). A complex science fiction story about virtual realism, time manipulation, and a young girl who investigates the disappearance of guests at Hexwood Farm. (Rev: BL 6/1–15/94; SLJ 3/94; VOYA 10/94)

4335 Keaney, Brian. *The Hollow People* (6–9). Illus. by Nicoletta Ceccoli. Series: The Promises of Dr. Sigmundus. 2007, Knopf $16.99 (978-0-375-84332-7). Dante and Beatrice, both 13, attempt to escape from Tarnegar island, where dreams and subversive thoughts are controlled by medication under the supervision of Dr. Sigmundus. (Rev: BL 11/1/07; SLJ 1/08)

4336 Key, Alexander. *The Forgotten Door* (5–7). 1986, Scholastic paper $4.99 (978-0-590-43130-9). When little Jon falls to earth from another planet, he encounters suspicion and hostility as well as sympathy. A reissue.

4337 Kiesel, Stanley. *Skinny Malinky Leads the War for Kidness* (6–8). 1984, Avon paper $2.50 (978-0-380-69875-2). Skinny is about to be captured by a powerful mutant red ant.

4338 Kilworth, Garry. *The Electric Kid* (6–9). 1995, Orchard LB $15.99 (978-0-531-08786-2). Two homeless young people struggle for survival in a large city's oppressive underworld in this bleak novel set in the horrifying world of 2061. (Rev: BL 1/1–15/96; SLJ 10/95; VOYA 12/95)

4339 Klass, David. *Firestorm* (8–11). 2006, Farrar $17.00 (978-0-374-32307-3). A thrilling adventure about Jack who learns that he has special powers and was sent back from the future to save the dying planet. (Rev: BL 9/15/06; SLJ 9/06)

4340 Lassiter, Rhiannon. *Shadows* (7–10). 2002, Simon & Schuster paper $4.99 (978-0-7434-2212-3). Raven, the superhacker introduced in *Hex*, faces new dangers as the government seeks to destroy her and her fellow mutants. The last volume in the trilogy is *Ghosts* (2002). (Rev: BL 4/15/02; SLJ 4/02)

4341 Lawrence, Louise. *Andra* (6–10). 1991, Harper-Collins $14.95 (978-0-06-023685-4). This novel is set 2,000 years in the future, when humanity, having destroyed Earth's environment, lives in rigidly governed, sealed underground cities. (Rev: BL 5/1/91; SLJ 5/91)

4342 Layne, Steven L. *This Side of Paradise* (7–10). 2001, North Star $15.99 (978-0-9712336-9-0). Jack, a junior in high school, soon questions his father's motives for moving the family into a town called Paradise, where things are definitely not what they seem. (Rev: BL 2/1/02; SLJ 1/02; VOYA 2/02)

4343 Lee, Tanith. *Indigara* (4–7). 2007, Penguin $11.99 (978-0-14-240922-0). Jet and her dog Otis encounter mindless celebrities in the underworld of Planet Obelisk in this humorous meeting of science fiction and pop culture. (Rev: BL 12/15/07; SLJ 12/07)

4344 Le Guin, Ursula K. *The Left Hand of Darkness* (7–12). 1969, Ace paper $7.99 (978-0-441-47812-5). An envoy is sent to the ice-covered planet Gethen where people can be either male or female at will.

4345 L'Engle, Madeleine. *Many Waters* (7–10). 1986, Farrar $18.00 (978-0-374-34796-3). The Murry twins, from the author's Wrinkle in Time trilogy, time-travel to the Holy Land prior to the Great Flood. (Rev: BL 8/86; SLJ 11/86; VOYA 12/86)

4346 L'Engle, Madeleine. *A Wrinkle in Time* (6–9). 1962, Farrar $17.00 (978-0-374-38613-9). Meg and Charles Wallace Murry, with the help of Calvin O'Keefe, set out in space to find their scientist father. Newbery Medal 1963. Followed by *A Wind in the Door* (1973), *A Swiftly Tilting Planet* (1978), and *A Ring of Endless Light* (1981).

4347 Lennon, Joan. *Questors* (5–8). 2007, Simon & Schuster $16.99 (978-1-4169-3658-9). When an energy leak threatens the existence of three separate worlds, three youthful half siblings — Bryn, Madlen, and Cam — find they bear a heavy responsibility. (Rev: BL 8/07; HB 1–2/08; LMC 1/08; SLJ 12/07)

4348 Lowenstein, Sallie. *Evan's Voice* (5–8). Illus. 1998, Lion Stone paper $15.00 (978-0-9658486-1-9). Teenager Jake cares for his catatonic younger brother while seeking civilization's last chance for survival in an area known as the Dead Zone. (Rev: BL 3/1/99; VOYA 6/99)

4349 Lowenstein, Sallie. *Focus* (5–9). Illus. 2001, Lion Stone paper $15.00 (978-0-9658486-3-3). The Haldrans leave their planet and relocate to Miners World, where humans live, in order to save their son from discrimination because of his creative intelligence. (Rev: BL 4/15/01; SLJ 8/01; VOYA 8/01)

4350 McCaffrey, Anne, and Todd McCaffrey. *Dragon's Fire* (7–12). Series: Dragonriders of Pern. 2006, Del Rey $24.95 (978-0-345-48028-6). The series continues as the MacCaffreys return to Pern and as the colonists prepare for a phenomenon known as the Thread that follows the Red Star every 50 years and falls onto the planet killing all organic material that it touches; this preparation proves dangerous for the miners of explosive firestone and for the dragons who must chew it to burn the Thread from the sky. (Rev: BL 6/1–15/06; SLJ 8/06)

4351 Mackel, Kathy. *Alien in a Bottle* (4–8). 2004, HarperCollins LB $16.89 (978-0-06-029282-9). An entertaining and action-packed novel in which 8th-grader Sean Winger, an aspiring glassblower, mistakes an alien space ship for an ornate glass bottle and becomes swept up in intergalactic intrigue. (Rev: BL 5/1/04; SLJ 4/04)

4352 McKinty, Adrian. *The Lighthouse Land* (5–8). 2006, Abrams $16.95 (978-0-8109-5480-9). In this first installment in an action-packed science fiction series, Jamie (a 13-year-old who is mute after losing his left arm to bone cancer) and his mother move to an Irish island, where he and a new friend discover an artifact that transports them to a far-off planet in time to help a girl named Wishaway. (Rev: BL 11/15/06; SLJ 1/07)

4353 McNamee, Eoin. *The Navigator: Chosen to Save the World* (5–8). 2007, Random $15.99 (978-0-375-83910-8). Owen finds himself suddenly in a different world where he and a girl named Cati must battle the Harsh, evil beings who freeze all that they touch and have set time running backward. (Rev: BL 12/1/06; SLJ 3/07)

4354 Marley, Louise. *The Glass Harmonica* (7–12). 2000, Ace paper $16.00 (978-0-441-00729-5). In an appealing blend of science fiction, mystery, romance, and historical fiction, two related stories — one from the 18th century and the other from the not-so-distant future — feature young girls and a glass harmonica. (Rev: VOYA 2/01)

4355 Nelson, O. T. *The Girl Who Owned a City* (7–9). 1977, Dell paper $4.99 (978-0-440-92893-5). A mysterious virus kills off Earth's population except for children under the age of 13.

4356 Nix, Garth. *Shade's Children* (7–12). 1997, HarperCollins LB $15.89 (978-0-06-027325-5). In this science fiction novel, when a person reaches age 16, he or she is sent to the Meat Factory, where body parts are turned into hideous creatures. (Rev: BL 10/1/97; SLJ 8/97; VOYA 6/98)

4357 Norton, Andre. *Key Out of Time* (7–12). 1978, Ultramarine $25.00 (978-0-89366-186-1). Two Time Agents re-create the conflict that destroyed life on the planet Hawaika.

4358 Norton, Andre. *Time Traders II* (8–12). Series: Time Traders. 2001, Baen $24.00 (978-0-671-

31968-7). This single volume contains two of Norton's Time Traders novellas: *Key Out of Time* and *The Defiant Agents*. (Rev: BL 2/1/01)

4359 Oldham, June. *Found* (7–12). 1996, Orchard LB $17.99 (978-0-531-08893-7). In this novel set in the 21st century, Ren becomes lost in a bleak countryside, gets involved with three other misfits, and finds an abandoned baby. (Rev: BL 9/15/96; SLJ 10/96; VOYA 2/97)

4360 Oppel, Kenneth. *Skybreaker* (6–9). 2005, HarperCollins LB $17.89 (978-0-06-053228-4). In this action-packed sequel to *Airborn* (2003), Matt Cruse, now an officer trainee at Airship Academy, races to locate the long-lost *Hyperion* before pirates can loot the ghost ship. (Rev: BCCB 2/06; BL 11/15/05; HB 1–2/06; SLJ 12/05; VOYA 12/05)

4361 Patterson, James. *Maximum Ride: Saving the World and Other Extreme Sports* (6–9). Series: Maximum Ride. 2007, Little, Brown $16.99 (978-0-316-15560-1). This third installment in the series follows Max and her winged mutant flock as they run from the scientists who created and now want to exterminate them, while they also try to stop the Itex Corporation's evil plot. (Rev: BL 8/07; SLJ 7/07)

4362 Pearson, Mary E. *The Adoration of Jenna Fox* (8–12). 2008, Holt $16.95 (978-0-8050-7668-4). Jenna, 17, awakens from a coma to find her brain has been altered in this first-person narrative set in a not-too-distant future in which bioengineering has made great strides. (Rev: BL 3/1/08; SLJ 5/08) ❧

4363 Peel, John. *The Zanti Misfits* (6–10). 1997, Tor paper $3.99 (978-0-8125-9063-0). This quick read, a product of *The Outer Limits* television show, tells how the planet Zanti sent to Earth a shipload of its worst criminals and how three teenagers wander into the landing area. Also use *The Choice* and *The Time Shifter* (both 1997). (Rev: VOYA 4/98)

4364 Pfeffer, Susan Beth. *Life as We Knew It* (7–10). 2006, Harcourt $17.00 (978-0-15-205826-5). Miranda, 16, describes the drastic changes in her life after a meteor hits the moon and causes major weather and other catastrophes on Earth. (Rev: BL 9/1/06; SLJ 10/06)

4365 Pierce, Tamora. *Street Magic* (5–9). Series: The Circle Opens. 2001, Scholastic paper $16.95 (978-0-590-39628-8). Briar, a 14-year-old former gang member, finds he is again caught between warring gangs when he helps a female street urchin in this futuristic novel. (Rev: BL 4/15/01; HB 3–4/01; HBG 10/01; SLJ 7/01; VOYA 4/01)

4366 Pow, Tom. *The Pack* (6–9). 2006, Roaring Brook $16.95 (978-1-59643-159-1). After the collapse of civilization as we know it, three children — Bradley, Victor, and Floris —and three dogs struggle to survive in the dangerous and chaotic world of the near-future, watched over by an Old Woman whose stories may bring salvation. (Rev: BL 5/15/06; SLJ 9/06)

4367 Powell, J. *Big Brother at School* (5–8). Illus. by Paul Savage. Series: Keystone Books. 2006, Stone Arch LB $21.26 (978-1-59889-091-4). At a school where cameras watch students' every move, Lee becomes convinced that the principal and a visiting doctor are aliens and takes step to save his fellow students from abduction. (Rev: SLJ 1/07)

4368 Pratchett, Terry. *Only You Can Save Mankind* (5–8). 2005, HarperCollins LB $17.89 (978-0-06-054186-6). It's up to Johnny to save the aliens in a new computer game, and the situation forces him to do some thinking about the very nature of war. (Rev: BL 4/15/05*; SLJ 10/05)

4369 Price, Susan. *The Sterkarm Handshake* (7–10). 2000, HarperCollins LB $18.89 (978-0-06-029392-5). Violent confrontations result when a 21st-century corporation makes inroads into the 16th-century Scottish Borders. (Rev: BL 10/1/00; HBG 3/01; SLJ 12/00)

4370 Read Magazine, ed. *Read into the Millennium: Tales of the Future* (6–8). 1999, Millbrook LB $24.90 (978-0-7613-0962-8). This collection of 10 science fiction stories includes works by Robert Lipsyte, Kurt Vonnegut, and Lois Lowry, plus adaptations of Wells's *The Time Machine* and Shelley's *Frankenstein*. (Rev: BL 5/15/99; HBG 9/99; SLJ 6/99)

4371 Reeve, Philip. *Infernal Devices* (7–10). Series: Hungry City Chronicles. 2006, HarperCollins $16.99 (978-0-06-082635-2). In this gripping third book of the post-apocalyptic series that started with *Mortal Engines*, adventure-seeking 15-year-old Wren is kidnapped and her parents must come to her rescue. (Rev: BL 5/15/06; HB 7–8/06; SLJ 6/06)

4372 Reeve, Philip. *Larklight, or, The Revenge of the White Spiders!, or, To Saturn's Rings and Back!* (5–8). Illus. by David Wyatt. 2006, Bloomsbury $16.95 (978-1-59990-020-9). Art and Myrtle Mumby, who live with their father in a Victorian mansion orbiting the earth, become embroiled in a plot to destroy the solar system; a science fiction romp with a touch of romance and a dollop of Victorian manners. (Rev: BCCB 2/07; BL 10/1/06; HB 11–12/06; HBG 4/07; LMC 2/07; SLJ 11/06*; VOYA 12/06)

4373 Reeve, Philip. *Starcross* (5–8). Illus. by David Wyatt. 2007, Bloomsbury $16.95 (978-1-59990-121-3). Starcross is the name of the asteroid belt hotel where Art, Myrtle, and their mother go for a holiday that turns into a strange journey through time; the sequel to *Larklight* (2006). (Rev: BL 11/1/07; HB 1–2/08; SLJ 12/07)

4374 Regan, Dian C. *Princess Nevermore* (5–7). 1995, Scholastic $14.95 (978-0-590-47582-2). A princess from another world gets her wish to visit Earth, where she is befriended by two teenagers, Sarah and Adam. (Rev: BCCB 11/95; SLJ 9/95)

4375 Reisman, Michael. *Simon Bloom, the Gravity Keeper* (4–7). 2008, Dutton $15.99 (978-0-525-47922-2). When a book teaches 11-year-old Simon how to control gravity, velocity, friction, and other physical properties; magic, adventure, and suspense ensue. (Rev: BL 3/1/08; SLJ 4/08)

4376 Rex, Adam. *The True Meaning of Smekday* (5–8). 2007, Hyperion $16.99 (978-0-7868-4900-0). Gratuity (called Tip) resents having to write an essay about the day aliens took over America in this funny and visually engaging story. (Rev: BL 10/1/07; HB 11–12/07; LMC 1/08; SLJ 11/07)

4377 Rubenstein, Gillian. *Galax-Arena* (7–10). 1995, Simon & Schuster paper $15.00 (978-0-689-80136-5). A 13-year-old girl and 20 other children from Earth are removed to another planet and trained to perform dangerous acrobatic tricks. (Rev: BL 10/15/95*; SLJ 10/95)

4378 Sargent, Pamela. *Alien Child* (8–12). 1988, HarperCollins $13.95 (978-0-06-025202-1). A teenage girl raised in an alien world discovers there is another human living in her complex. (Rev: BL 2/1/88; SLJ 4/88; VOYA 8/88)

4379 Schmid, Susan Maupin. *Lost Time* (5–8). 2008, Philomel $16.99 (978-0-399-24460-5). On the sparsely populated planet Lindos, Violynne searches for her lost parents while living with her aunt Madelyn. (Rev: BL 5/15/08; SLJ 9/08)

4380 Scrimger, Richard. *The Nose from Jupiter* (5–8). 1998, Tundra paper $5.95 (978-0-88776-428-8). Alan doesn't mind that Norbert, an alien from Jupiter, is living in his nose, but Norbert's outspoken remarks often get Alan into trouble. Also use *The Boy from Earth* (2004). (Rev: BL 7/98)

4381 Simons, Jamie, and E. W. Scollon. *Goners: The Hunt Is On* (4–7). Illus. 1998, Avon paper $3.99 (978-0-380-79730-1). Four alien teens from the planet Roma time-travel to Monticello to fetch Thomas Jefferson. (Rev: BL 5/15/98)

4382 Skurzynski, Gloria. *The Choice* (5–8). Series: The Virtual War Chronologs. 2006, Simon & Schuster $16.95 (978-0-689-84267-2). In the fast-paced concluding installment in the series, 16-year-old Corgan has a final confrontation with the murderous Brigand. (Rev: SLJ 10/06)

4383 Skurzynski, Gloria. *The Clones* (6–9). Series: The Virtual War Chronologs. 2002, Simon & Schuster $16.00 (978-0-689-84463-8). In this sequel to *Virtual War* (1997), in which Corgan successfully defended the Western Hemisphere Federation, Corgan's peaceful life is disturbed by the arrival of a pair of surprisingly different clones. (Rev: BL 4/15/02; VOYA 8/02)

4384 Skurzynski, Gloria. *The Revolt* (8–12). Series: The Virtual War Chronologs. 2005, Simon & Schuster $16.95 (978-0-689-84265-8). In this action-packed third volume in the series, Corgan flees to Florida to put an end to his battle with Brigand but is soon followed there by his violent enemy. (Rev: SLJ 7/05)

4385 Sleator, William. *The Boy Who Reversed Himself* (8–12). 1998, Puffin paper $5.99 (978-0-14-038965-4). Laura travels into the fourth dimension with her gifted neighbor and literally everything in her life becomes upside-down. (Rev: BL 10/15/86; SLJ 11/86; VOYA 6/87)

4386 Sleator, William. *House of Stairs* (7–10). 1991, Puffin paper $5.99 (978-0-14-034580-3). Five teenage orphans are kidnapped to become part of an experiment on aggression.

4387 Sleator, William. *Interstellar Pig* (7–10). 1996, Peter Smith $22.25 (978-0-8446-6898-7); Puffin paper $6.99 (978-0-14-037595-4). Barney plays an odd board game with strangers who are actually aliens from space.

4388 Sleator, William. *The Last Universe* (6–9). 2005, Abrams $16.95 (978-0-8109-5858-6). Quantum mechanics plays a key role in the tension in this story of 14-year-old Susan who must care for her 16-year-old, wheelchair-bound brother Gary; they spend a lot of time in a maze that seems to allow travel to other dimensions. (Rev: BCCB 4/05; BL 4/15/05; SLJ 7/05; VOYA 4/05)

4389 Sleator, William. *Parasite Pig* (7–10). 2002, Dutton $15.99 (978-0-525-46918-6). Barney and Katie continue playing the board game they began in *Interstellar Pig* and wind up on a planet called J'koot, threatened by crablike aliens with cannibal tendencies. (Rev: BCCB 2/03; BL 11/15/02; HB 11–12/02*; HBG 3/03; SLJ 10/02; VOYA 12/02)

4390 Sleator, William. *Singularity* (7–12). 1995, Puffin paper $6.99 (978-0-14-037598-5). Twin boys discover a playhouse on the property they have inherited that contains a mystery involving monsters from space and a new dimension in time. (Rev: BL 4/1/85; SLJ 8/85)

4391 Slote, Alfred. *My Robot Buddy* (5–8). Illus. 1986, HarperCollins $12.95 (978-0-397-31641-0). An easily read novel about Danny and the robot that is created for him. (Rev: BL 11/1/87)

4392 Stackpole, Michael A. *I, Jedi* (8–12). 1998, Random paper $6.99 (978-0-553-57873-7). In order to find his wife, Corran must take a quick course at the Jedi Academy founded by Luke Skywalker and learn to use his hidden powers. (Rev: VOYA 12/98)

4393 Stahler, David. *Truesight* (5–7). Series: The Truesight Trilogy. 2004, HarperCollins LB $16.89 (978-0-06-052286-5). A race of blind people living in a colony on a distant planet includes one teenager who discovers he can see, and he sees all sorts of flaws in the people of his community. (Rev: SLJ 3/04; VOYA 4/04)

4394 Stahler, David, Jr. *The Seer* (5–7). Series: The Truesight Trilogy. 2007, HarperCollins $16.99 (978-0-06-052288-9). Jacob, 13, leaves the colony of Harmony, where he is the only person who can see, and seeks both a new life and his childhood friend Delaney, who is a talented musician. (Rev: BCCB 5/07; SLJ 8/07)

4395 Sutherland, Tui T. *So This Is How It Ends* (8–11). Series: Avatars. 2006, HarperCollins $16.99 (978-0-06-075024-4). Five teenagers are the only young people left in a future world, and their special powers will help them survive among crystal monsters and old, confused humans. (Rev: BCCB 2/07; BL 1/1–15/07; SLJ 11/06)

4396 Thompson, Kate. *Fourth World* (5–8). Series: Missing Link. 2005, Bloomsbury $16.95 (978-1-58234-650-2). Christie and his older stepbrother Danny go from Ireland to Scotland, where they discover strange developments at Fourth World, the compound where Danny's scientist mother lives and works, in this first volume of a trilogy. (Rev: BL 5/15/05; SLJ 10/05)

4397 Tolan, Stephanie S. *Welcome to the Ark* (7–10). 1996, Morrow $15.00 (978-0-688-13724-3). Science fiction and adventure combine in the story of four young people who are able to act for good or evil through telecommunications. (Rev: BL 10/15/96; SLJ 10/96; VOYA 4/97)

4398 Townsend, John Rowe. *The Creatures* (7–10). 1980, HarperCollins $12.95 (978-0-397-31864-3). Earth is dominated by creatures from another planet who believe in mind over emotion.

4399 Ure, Jean. *Plague* (7–12). 1991, Harcourt $16.95 (978-0-15-262429-3). Three teenagers must band together to survive in a hostile, nearly deserted London after a catastrophe has killed almost everyone. (Rev: BL 11/15/91*; SLJ 10/91)

4400 Vande Velde, Vivian. *Heir Apparent* (6–9). 2002, Harcourt $17.00 (978-0-15-204560-9). When Giannine, 14, enters a virtual reality game set in medieval times, she doesn't expect the game to be damaged or her playing skill to become a matter of life and death. (Rev: BCCB 12/02; BL 2/1/03; HB 11–12/02; HBG 3/03; SLJ 10/02; VOYA 12/02)

4401 Verne, Jules. *Around the Moon* (8–12). 1968, Airmont paper $1.50 (978-0-8049-0182-6). An early science fiction relic about a trip to the moon. Also use *From the Earth to the Moon* (1984).

4402 Voake, Steve. *The Web of Fire* (5–8). Illus. by Mark Watkinson. 2007, Bloomsbury $17.95 (978-1-58234-737-0). Sam and Skipper are back with new adventures and gadgetry in this fast-paced sequel to *The Dreamwalker's Child* (2006). (Rev: SLJ 6/07)

4403 Walsh, Jill Paton. *The Green Book* (4–7). Illus. by Lloyd Bloom. 1982, Farrar paper $4.95 (978-0-374-42802-0). The exodus of a group of Britons from dying Earth to another planet.

4404 Wells, H. G. *First Men in the Moon* (7–12). 1993, Tuttle paper $7.95 (978-0-460-87304-8). The first men on the moon discover strange creatures living there.

4405 Wells, H. G. *The Invisible Man* (8–12). 1987, Buccaneer LB $21.95 (978-0-89966-377-7); Bantam paper $4.95 (978-0-553-21353-9). Two editions of many available of the story of a scientist who finds a way to make himself invisible.

4406 Wells, H. G. *Time Machine* (7–12). 1984, Bantam paper $4.95 (978-0-553-21351-5). This is one of the earliest novels to use traveling through time as its subject.

4407 Wells, H. G. *The War of the Worlds* (7–12). 1988, Bantam paper $4.95 (978-0-553-21338-6). In this early science fiction novel, first published in 1898, strange creatures from Mars invade England.

4408 Westerfeld, Scott. *Extras* (7–10). Series: The Uglies. 2007, Simon & Schuster $16.99 (978-1-4169-5117-9). In the future world in which human worth is now based on celebrity, Aya, an Ugly and now an Extra, discovers the underside to her city while she chases popularity. (Rev: BL 1/1–15/08; HB 11–12/07; SLJ 1/08)

4409 Westerfeld, Scott. *Pretties* (8–11). Series: The Uglies. 2005, Simon & Schuster paper $6.99 (978-0-689-86539-8). In the sequel to *Uglies* (2005), Tally enjoys her transformation into a Pretty and the accompanying hedonistic lifestyle until she is reminded of her underlying purpose and faces real danger. (Rev: BL 9/15/05; SLJ 12/05; VOYA 10/05)

4410 Westerfeld, Scott. *Specials* (7–10). Series: The Uglies. 2006, Simon & Schuster $15.95 (978-1-4169-2165-3). Sixteen-year-old Tally (of *Uglies* and *Pretties,* 2004 and 2005 respectively) transforms yet again, this time becoming a Special, part of her government's high-powered commando unit that enforces adherence to the norms. (Rev: BL 5/15/06; HB 9–10/06) ♦

4411 Westerfeld, Scott. *Uglies* (7–10). Series: The Uglies. 2005, Simon & Schuster paper $6.99 (978-0-689-86538-1). In a futuristic dystopia, 15-year-old Tally is counting the days until she turns 16 and is transformed from ugly to pretty but events threaten this happening on schedule; a thought-provoking novel about the importance of image and ethics. (Rev: BCCB 2/05; BL 3/15/05*; SLJ 3/05; VOYA 6/05)

4412 White, Andrea. *No Child's Game: Reality TV 2083* (7–10). 2005, HarperCollins LB $16.89 (978-0-06-055455-2). In this chilling look at a future in which television is used to distract the populace from grim reality, five teens will live or die while reenacting a historic Antarctic expedition for the entertainment of the viewing audience. (Rev: BL 4/15/05; SLJ 7/05)

4413 Wismer, Donald. *Starluck* (6–8). 1982, Ultramarine $20.00 (978-0-89366-255-4). A boy with unusual powers tries to overthrow a wicked emperor.

4414 Wooding, Chris. *Storm Thief* (6–9). 2006, Scholastic $16.99 (978-0-439-86513-5). Rail and Moa are two thieves trying to live in the city of Orokos, which is plagued with probability storms; they will need the help of a golem named Vago to survive and unlock the secrets of the city and its tempests. (Rev: BL 9/1/06; SLJ 10/06)

4415 Yolen, Jane, et al., eds. *Spaceships and Spells* (5–9). 1987, HarperCollins $12.95 (978-0-06-026796-4). A collection of 13 original tales, mostly science fiction but also some fantasy. (Rev: BL 1/15/88; SLJ 11/87)

4416 Zakour, John. *Baxter Moon: Galactic Scout* (4–7). 2008, Brown Barn paper $8.95 (978-0-9768126-9-2). Baxter and his crew travel through space to rescue an Aquarian ship from robotic aliens in this entertaining romp. (Rev: BL 5/15/08; SLJ 6/08)

Sports

4417 Altman, Millys N. *Racing in Her Blood* (7–12). 1980, HarperCollins LB $12.89 (978-0-397-31895-7). A junior novel about a young girl who wants to succeed in the world of automobile racing.

4418 Barwin, Steven. *Icebreaker* (4–8). Series: Sports Stories. 2007, Lorimer paper $7.95 (978-1-55028-950-3). Hockey fans will love this book featuring Greg, a junior high school hockey player whose year gets complicated when his stepsister tries out for the team. (Rev: SLJ 7/07)

4419 Barwin, Steven, and Gabriel David Tick. *Slam Dunk* (5–7). Series: Sports Stories. 1999, Orca paper $5.50 (978-1-55028-598-7). An easy read about a junior high basketball team in Canada that goes coed and the problems that result. (Rev: SLJ 1/00)

4420 Baskin, Nora Raleigh. *Basketball (or Something Like It)* (6–9). 2005, HarperCollins LB $16.89 (978-0-06-059611-8). In alternating chapters, three 6th-grade basketball players — and the basketball-loving sister of one team member — tell stories of parental interference or indifference and how these have taken away some of the fun of the game. (Rev: BCCB 3/05; BL 2/1/05; SLJ 2/05; VOYA 6/05)

4421 Bledsoe, Lucy Jane. *Hoop Girlz* (5–7). 2002, Holiday $16.95 (978-0-8234-1691-2). When 11-year-old River is denied a place on the girls' basketball team, she forms her own team, with her brother as the coach. (Rev: BL 9/1/02; HBG 10/03; SLJ 12/02)

4422 Bo, Ben. *The Edge* (5–8). 1999, Lerner LB $14.95 (978-0-8225-3307-8). Conflicted Declan is sent to a rehabilitation program in Canada's Glacier National Park, where he learns to snowboard and is drawn into a duel with the local champion. (Rev: BCCB 1/00; BL 10/15/99; HBG 3/00; SLJ 1/00; VOYA 4/00)

4423 Bo, Ben. *Skullcrack* (7–12). 2000, Lerner LB $14.95 (978-0-8225-3308-5). Jonah, an avid surfer, travels with his father to Florida to be united with his twin sister who was put up for adoption at birth. (Rev: BL 6/1–15/00; HBG 9/00; SLJ 6/00)

4424 Bowen, Fred. *The Final Cut* (4–7). Illus. by Ann Barrow. Series: AllStar Sport Story. 1999, Peachtree paper $4.95 (978-1-56145-192-0). A fast-paced novel about four friends and their efforts to make the junior high school basketball team. (Rev: SLJ 7/99)

4425 Bowen, Fred. *On the Line* (4–7). Illus. by Ann Barrow. 1999, Peachtree paper $4.95 (978-1-56145-199-9). A young boy learns about self-image and open-mindedness while trying to improve his foul shots in this novel about an 8th grader and his basketball skills. (Rev: SLJ 4/00)

4426 Brooks, Bruce. *Dooby* (5–8). Series: Wolfbay Wings. 1998, HarperCollins LB $14.89 (978-0-06-027898-4); paper $4.50 (978-0-06-440708-3). Dooby sulks when he is not made captain of his Peewee hockey team, but is completely humiliated to learn he has lost out to a girl. Also recommended in this series is *Reed* (1998). (Rev: HBG 3/99; SLJ 2/99)

4427 Brooks, Bruce. *The Moves Make the Man* (7–9). 1984, HarperCollins paper $6.99 (978-0-06-447022-3). Jerome, the only African American student in his high school and a star basketball player, forms an unusual friendship with Bix. (Rev: BL 3/87)

4428 Brooks, Bruce. *Prince* (5–8). Series: Wolfbay Wings. 1998, HarperCollins paper $4.50 (978-0-06-440600-0). Prince, the only African American boy on the Wolfbay Wings hockey team, is pressured by his middle school coach to switch to basketball. (Rev: HBG 10/98; SLJ 6/98)

4429 Brooks, Bruce. *Reed* (5–8). Series: Wolfbay Wings. 1998, HarperCollins LB $14.89 (978-0-06-028055-0). Reed, a member of the Wolfbay Wings hockey team, is considered a "puck-hog" and must learn to be more of a team player. (Rev: HBG 3/99; SLJ 2/99)

4430 Brooks, Bruce. *Shark* (5–8). Series: Wolfbay Wings. 1998, HarperCollins LB $14.89 (978-0-06-027570-9); paper $4.50 (978-0-06-440681-9). In spite of being fat, slow, and confused, Shark becomes a valuable player on the Wolfbay Wings hockey team. (Rev: HBG 10/98; SLJ 6/98)

4431 Bruchac, Joseph. *The Warriors* (5–8). 2003, Darby Creek $15.95 (978-1-58196-002-0). Jake Forrest, a Native American teenager and lacrosse whiz, leaves the reservation to attend a private school and encounters many new situations, including a different attitude toward sports. (Rev: BL 12/1/03; HBG 10/01; SLJ 10/03)

4432 Butcher, Kristin. *Cairo Kelly and the Man* (4–8). 2002, Orca paper $6.95 (978-1-55143-211-3). When Midge discovers that his baseball team's umpire, Hal Mann, is illiterate, Midge and his friend Kelly set out to solve the problem. (Rev: BL 9/1/02; VOYA 4/03)

4433 Butler, Dori Hillestad. *Sliding into Home* (5–8). 2003, Peachtree $14.95 (978-1-56145-222-4). Joelle, 13, refuses to accept a ban on girls playing baseball when she moves to a small town in Iowa. (Rev: BL 5/1/03; HBG 10/03; SLJ 1/04)

4434 Carter, Alden R. *Bull Catcher* (7–10). 1997, Scholastic paper $15.95 (978-0-590-50958-9). High school friends Bull and Jeff seem to live for baseball and plan their futures around the sport, but one of them begins to move in a different direction. (Rev: BL 4/15/97; SLJ 5/97; VOYA 10/97)

4435 Carter, Alden R. *Love, Football, and Other Contact Sports* (8–11). 2006, Holiday House $16.95 (978-0-8234-1975-3). The football team at Argyle West High School is at the center of these entertaining short stories. (Rev: BL 3/15/06*; SLJ 6/06)

4436 Christopher, Matt. *Mountain Bike Mania* (5–7). 1998, Little, Brown paper $4.50 (978-0-316-14292-2). Will is at loose ends with no after-school activities until he becomes involved in a mountain bike club. (Rev: BL 2/1/99; HBG 10/99; SLJ 3/99)

4437 Christopher, Matt. *Prime-Time Pitcher* (4–7). 1998, Little, Brown paper $4.50 (978-0-316-14213-7). Koby Caplin becomes arrogant about his winning streak on the baseball team and soon loses games because of his lack of teamwork. (Rev: HBG 3/99; SLJ 12/98)

4438 Christopher, Matt. *Return of the Home Run Kid* (4–7). Illus. by Paul Casale. 1994, Little, Brown paper $4.50 (978-0-316-14273-1). In this sequel to *The Kid Who Only Hit Homers* (1972), Sylvester learns to be more aggressive on the field but gets criticism from his friends. (Rev: BL 4/15/92; SLJ 5/92)

4439 Christopher, Matt. *Snowboard Maverick* (4–7). 1997, Little, Brown paper $4.50 (978-0-316-14203-

8). Dennis overcomes his fears and begins snow-boarding. (Rev: BL 4/1/98; HBG 3/98; SLJ 3/98)

4440 Clare, Cassandra. *Toby Wheeler: Eighth-Grade Bench Warmer* (5–8). 2007, Delacorte $14.99 (978-0-385-73390-8). Toby, an 8th-grader, joins the basketball team to be closer to his best friend but find himself stuck on the bench, the 12th man. (Rev: BL 9/1/07; SLJ 9/07)

4441 Clippinger, Carol. *Open Court* (5–8). 2007, Knopf $15.99 (978-0-375-84049-4). Thirteen-year-old Holloway ("Hall") is only 13 but must deal with the pressures of competitive tennis as well as every-day stresses of being a teenager. (Rev: SLJ 7/07)

4442 Corbett, Sue. *Free Baseball* (4–7). 2006, Dutton $15.99 (978-0-525-47120-2). An endearing 11-year-old called Felix, who loves baseball and is annoyed that his mother won't tell him more about his Cuban outfielder father, is thrilled when he gets the chance to be batboy for a minor league Florida team. (Rev: BCCB 2/06; SLJ 2/06; VOYA 4/06)

4443 Coy, John. *Crackback* (8–11). 2005, Scholastic $16.99 (978-0-439-69733-0). High school football player Miles Manning faces many challenges including difficult relationships with his father and his coach, girl problems, and whether to join his teammates in using steroids. (Rev: BL 9/1/05*; SLJ 12/05; VOYA 12/05)

4444 Crutcher, Chris. *The Crazy Horse Electric Game* (7–12). 1987, Greenwillow $16.99 (978-0-688-06683-3). A motorboat accident ends the comfortable life and budding baseball career of a teenage boy. (Rev: BL 4/15/87; SLJ 5/87; VOYA 6/87)

4445 Crutcher, Chris. *Ironman* (8–12). 1995, Greenwillow $17.99 (978-0-688-13503-4). A psychological sports novel in which a 17-year-old carries an attitude that fuels the plot. (Rev: BL 3/1/95*; SLJ 3/95; VOYA 5/95)

4446 Crutcher, Chris. *Running Loose* (7–10). 1983, Greenwillow $18.99 (978-0-688-02002-6). A senior in high school faces problems when he opposes the decisions of a football coach. (Rev: BL 3/87)

4447 Crutcher, Chris. *Stotan!* (8–12). 2008, Harper-Tempest paper $7.99 (978-0-06-009492-8). A group of boys from different backgrounds but all close friends sign up for a brutally taxing physical program run by their school coach; first published in 1986. (Rev: BL 3/15/86; SLJ 5/86; VOYA 4/86)

4448 Crutcher, Chris. *Whale Talk* (8–12). 2001, HarperTeen $15.95 (978-0-688-18019-5). Well-adjusted and academically able, T. J. is not into sports, which goes against the grain at his high school; he eventually is persuaded to form a swimming team and deliberately picks members from who buck the sports formula. (Rev: BL 4/1/01; HB 5–6/01; SLJ 4/01) 🐝

4449 Day, Karen. *No Cream Puffs* (6–9). 2008, Random $15.99 (978-0-375-83775-3). Talented player Madison becomes the first girl to play on a boys' Little League baseball team in this story set in Michigan in 1980. (Rev: BL 5/15/08; SLJ 7/08)

4450 Deuker, Carl. *Gym Candy* (8–11). 2007, Houghton $16.00 (978-0-618-77713-6). To improve his high school football performance, Mick begins using steroids ("gym candy") and suffers physical and emotional consequences. (Rev: BL 9/1/07; SLJ 10/07)

4451 Deuker, Carl. *Night Hoops* (7–11). 2000, Houghton $15.00 (978-0-395-97936-5). When older brother Scott gives up basketball for music, Nick develops his own presence on the court. (Rev: BL 5/1/00; HB 5–6/00; HBG 9/00; SLJ 5/00)

4452 Deuker, Carl. *On the Devil's Court* (8–12). 1991, Avon paper $5.99 (978-0-380-70879-6). In this variation on the Faust legend, a senior high basketball star believes he has sold his soul to have a perfect season. (Rev: BL 12/15/88; SLJ 1/89; VOYA 4/89)

4453 Drumtra, Stacy. *Face-Off* (4–8). 1992, Avon paper $3.50 (978-0-380-76863-9). T.J. and his twin Brad become rivals for friends and for status on the hockey team. (Rev: BL 4/1/93; SLJ 1/05; VOYA 8/93)

4454 Durant, Alan, sel. *Sports Stories* (5–9). Illus. by David Kearney. Series: Story Library. 2000, Kingfisher $14.95 (978-0-7534-5322-3). A collection of 21 previously published short stories by well-known authors dealing with a variety of sports. (Rev: HBG 10/01; SLJ 11/00)

4455 Dygard, Thomas J. *Second Stringer* (6–12). 1998, Morrow $15.99 (978-0-688-15981-8). A star quarterback's knee injury gives second-stringer Kevin Taylor the opportunity of a lifetime during his senior year in high school. (Rev: BL 9/1/98; HBG 3/99; SLJ 12/98; VOYA 2/99)

4456 Esckilsen, Erik E. *Offsides* (6–10). 2004, Houghton $15.00 (978-0-618-46284-1). Tom Gray, a top-notch soccer player, is proud of his Mohawk heritage and when he moves to a new town where the school's mascot is an Indian, he refuses to play. (Rev: BL 9/1/04; SLJ 1/05; VOYA 12/04)

4457 Esckilsen, Erik E. *The Outside Groove* (7–10). 2006, Houghton $16.00 (978-0-618-66854-0). Casey's family only cares about her brother and his stock-car racing career, ignoring all of her accomplishments, so she decides to start racing, finding out a lot of family secrets in the process. (Rev: BL 9/15/06)

4458 Fehler, Gene. *Beanball* (7–9). 2008, Clarion $16.00 (978-0-618-84348-0). In free verse, witnesses to a baseball accident describe what happened (a popular, talented player is blinded in one eye) and how it affected them. (Rev: BL 2/15/08; SLJ 5/08)

4459 Fitzgerald, Dawn. *Getting in the Game* (4–7). 2005, Roaring Brook $15.95 (978-1-59643-044-0). In first-person narrative, Joanna Giordano describes her difficult experiences as the only girl on a 7th-grade ice hockey team that doesn't want her, plus her problems with peers, parents, and ailing grandfather. (Rev: BCCB 9/05; BL 3/1/05; SLJ 7/05; VOYA 6/05)

4460 Fitzgerald, Dawn. *Soccer Chick Rules* (5–8). 2006, Roaring Brook $16.95 (978-1-59643-137-9). When her school's sports program is threatened, Tess Munro, a talented 13-year-old soccer player, joins the campaign to win approval for the school levy. (Rev: BL 9/1/06; SLJ 10/06)

4461 Flynn, Pat. *Alex Jackson: SWA* (6–10). 2002, Univ. of Queensland paper $13.50 (978-0-7022-3307-4). Alex flirts with physical danger and trouble with the police when he joins up with Skate-boarders with Attitude. (Rev: SLJ 1/03)

4462 Godfrey, Martyn. *Ice Hawk* (7–12). Illus. 1986, EMC paper $13.50 (978-0-8219-0235-6). An easy-to-read story about a young minor league hockey player who balks at unnecessary use of violence. (Rev: BL 2/1/87)

4463 Green, Tim. *Football Genius* (5–8). 2007, HarperCollins $16.99 (978-0-06-112270-5). Troy's football skills are ignored until a linebacker for the Atlanta Falcons sees his ability to predict upcoming plays and uses him as the team's secret weapon. (Rev: BL 5/1/07; SLJ 7/07)

4464 Guest, Jacqueline. *Racing Fear* (7–10). Series: SideStreets. 2004, Lorimer paper $4.99 (978-1-55028-838-4). Trent and Adam are best friends and car racing buddies until an accident puts a strain on their friendship; suitable for reluctant readers. (Rev: SLJ 1/05)

4465 Hale, Daniel J., and Matthew LaBrot. *Red Card* (4–7). Series: Zeke Armstrong Mystery. 2002, Top paper $8.95 (978-1-929976-15-7). Someone is trying to kill the soccer coach, and young Zeke sets out to discover who and why. (Rev: SLJ 12/02; VOYA 12/02)

4466 Hampshire, Anthony. *Fast Track* (6–12). Series: Redline Racing. 2006, Fitzhenry & Whiteside paper $6.95 (978-1-55041-570-4). For reluctant readers, this is an action-packed story with good car racing scenes. Also use *Full Throttle* and *On the Limit* (both 2006). (Rev: SLJ 2/07; VOYA)

4467 Harkrader, L. D. *Airball: My Life in Briefs* (4–7). 2005, Roaring Brook $15.95 (978-1-59643-060-0). Kirby's middle school basketball team begins to improve when their coach — whom Kirby secretly believes is his father — insists the boys

practice in their underwear. (Rev: BL 9/1/05; SLJ 11/05; VOYA 10/05)

4468 Haven, Paul. *Two Hot Dogs with Everything* (4–7). Illus. by Tim Jessell. 2006, Random LB $17.99 (978-0-375-93350-9). Danny, 11, follows many superstitious rituals each time the Sluggers play, but his efforts seem to have no effect until he chews some 108-year-old gum that belonged to the team's founder. (Rev: BL 4/1/06)

4469 Hirschfeld, Robert. *Goalkeeper in Charge* (5–7). Series: Christopher Sports. 2002, Little, Brown paper $4.50 (978-0-316-07548-0). Seventh-grader Tina works to overcome her shyness on and off the soccer field. (Rev: BL 9/1/02; HBG 3/03)

4470 Holohan, Maureen. *Catch Shorty by Rosie* (4–8). Series: The Broadway Ballplayers. 1999, Broadway Ballplayers paper $6.95 (978-0-9659091-6-7). Sixth-grader Rosie Jones devotes her time to organizing an all-girls football league while coping with a series of minor personal problems at home and school. (Rev: SLJ 3/00)

4471 Johnson, Scott. *Safe at Second* (5–8). 2001, Penguin paper $7.99 (978-0-698-11877-5). The story of the friendship between Paulie and Todd, their love of baseball, and what happens after Todd is hit during a game and loses an eye. (Rev: BL 6/1–15/99; SLJ 7/99; VOYA 8/99)

4472 King, Donna. *Double Twist* (5–8). 2007, King-fisher paper $5.95 (978-0-7534-6023-8). When her ice-dancing partner injures his knee, 12-year-old Laura Lee scrambles to replace him just one month before the Junior Grand Prix. (Rev: BL 1/1–15/07)

4473 Klass, David. *Danger Zone* (7–12). 1996, Scholastic paper $16.95 (978-0-590-48590-6). Jimmy Doyle, a young basketball star, tries to prove to himself as well as to his mostly African American teammates that he deserves a place on the American High School Dream Team. (Rev: BL 4/1/96; SLJ 3/96; VOYA 4/96)

4474 Knudson, R. R. *Fox Running* (7–9). Illus. 1977, Avon paper $2.50 (978-0-380-00930-5). Kathy and an Apache Indian girl find friendship and inspiration in their mutual love of running.

4475 Korman, Gordon. *The Zucchini Warriors* (6–8). 1991, Scholastic paper $4.50 (978-0-590-44174-2). Hank, a former football player, promises to build Bruno and Boots's school a recreation hall if their team has a winning season. (Rev: VOYA 10/88)

4476 Levy, Elizabeth. *Tackling Dad* (5–8). 2005, HarperCollins LB $16.89 (978-0-06-000050-9). Cassie, 13, has won a place on the football team but her father won't sign the consent form. (Rev: BL 9/1/05; SLJ 8/05)

4477 Levy, Marilyn. *Run for Your Life* (7–9). 1997, Penguin paper $6.99 (978-0-698-11608-5). Thirteen-year-old Kisha tries to escape the Oakland projects and her parents' crumbling marriage by joining a track team that has been started by a new community center director. (Rev: BL 4/1/96; BR 9–10/96; SLJ 3/96; VOYA 6/96)

4478 Lipsyte, Robert. *Yellow Flag* (8–11). 2007, HarperTeen $16.99 (978-0-06-055707-2). When his brother, a NASCAR driver, is injured, Kyle takes his place and does so well that he must decide whether to continue racing or instead pursue his love of music. (Rev: BL 9/1/07; SLJ 9/07)

4479 Lupica, Mike. *The Big Field* (5–8). 2008, Philomel $17.99 (978-0-399-24625-8). Fourteen-year-old Hutch and his team are going to the Florida State finals, but Hutch's happiness is marred by troubled relationships with his father and a new, difficult teammate. (Rev: BL 12/1/07; SLJ 2/08)

4480 Lupica, Mike. *Heat* (6–9). 2006, Philomel $16.99 (978-0-399-24301-1). Cuban American Michael Arroyo, who has been hiding his father's death to avoid the attention of the social services, finds his Little League pitching career in jeopardy when he can't produce a birth certificate. (Rev: BL 4/1/06*; SLJ 4/06; VOYA 4/06)

4481 Lupica, Mike. *Summer Ball* (5–8). 2007, Philomel $17.99 (978-0-399-24487-2). Even though his coach offers little encouragement, Danny Walker's determination helps him lead his summer basketball team to victory. (Rev: BL 4/15/07; SLJ 6/07)

4482 Lupica, Mike. *Travel Team* (6–8). 2004, Penguin $16.99 (978-0-399-24150-5). Twelve-year-old Danny Walker, cut from the 7th-grade basketball travel team, fights back with a team of his own. (Rev: BL 9/1/04; SLJ 11/04; VOYA 12/04)

4483 McGinley, Jerry. *Joaquin Strikes Back* (6–9). 1998, Tudor $18.95 (978-0-936389-58-5). Joaquin forms a soccer team in his new school that eventually plays the team from his former school. (Rev: BL 3/15/98; SLJ 3/99)

4484 Maddox, Jake. *Full Court Dreams* (4–7). Illus. by Tuesday Mourning. Series: Impact. 2008, Stone Arch LB $16.95 (978-1-4342-0469-1). Megan is determined to make the basketball team this year and gives the tryouts her all; for reluctant readers. (Rev: BL 4/1/08)

4485 Mercado, Nancy E., ed. *Baseball Crazy: Ten Short Stories That Cover All the Bases* (6–9). 2008, Dial $16.99 (978-0-8037-3162-2). An eclectic mix of baseball-related stories (plus a play) by writers including Ron Koertge and Joseph Bruchac, some of which range far from the sport itself. (Rev: BL 1/1–15/08; LMC 11–12/08; SLJ 5/08)

4486 Myers, Walter Dean. *Game* (8–12). 2008, HarperTeen $16.99 (978-0-06-058294-4). Harlem born and bred, Drew hopes to become an NBA star, but the appearance of a talented white player on his team threatens his future. (Rev: BL 2/1/08; SLJ 2/08) ⊚

4487 Myers, Walter Dean. *Hoops* (7–10). 1981, Dell paper $5.50 (978-0-440-93884-2). Lonnie plays basketball in spite of his coach, a has-been named Cal. Followed by *The Outside Shot* (1987).

4488 Myers, Walter Dean. *Me, Mop, and the Moondance Kid* (5–7). Illus. 1988, Dell paper $4.99 (978-0-440-40396-8). The efforts of T.J. and Moondance to get their friend Mop adopted. (Rev: BCCB 12/88; BL 2/1/89; SLJ 1/88)

4489 Nicholson, Lorna Schultz. *Roughing* (5–8). 2005, Lorimer paper $5.50 (978-1-55028-858-2). This story set in a hockey camp in Calgary, Alberta, features Josh, a boy with type 1 diabetes; Peter, a native Canadian; and Peter, a bully who plans to teach Peter a lesson. (Rev: BL 5/15/05; SLJ 9/05)

4490 Nicholson, Lorna Schultz. *Too Many Men* (4–8). Series: Sports Stories. 2007, Lorimer paper $7.95 (978-1-55028-948-0). Hockey player Sam juggles his busy home life with hockey practice as starting goalie. (Rev: SLJ 7/07)

4491 Nitz, Kristin Wolden. *Defending Irene* (5–7). 2004, Peachtree $14.95 (978-1-56145-309-2). When her family moves to Italy for a year, 13-year-old Irene is determined to continue playing soccer, even if it's on the boys' team. (Rev: SLJ 9/04)

4492 Norman, Rick. *Cross Body Block* (8–10). 1996, Colonial Pr. paper $9.95 (978-1-56883-060-5). An anguished story about a middle-aged football coach and his personal family tragedies, including the brutal death of a son. (Rev: VOYA 8/96)

4493 Park, Linda Sue. *Keeping Score* (4–7). 2008, Clarion $16.00 (978-0-618-92799-9). In 1951 fireman Jim teaches Brooklyn Dodgers fan Maggie, 9, how to score a game and the two remain friends even when Jim is sent to Korea; when Jim is horribly injured, Maggie is determined to help. (Rev: BL 2/1/08; SLJ 3/08)

4494 Parker, Robert B. *Edenville Owls* (6–9). 2007, Philomel $17.99 (978-0-399-24656-2). Eighth-grader Bobby tries to help an abused teacher and solve the mystery of her past while also starting a basketball team with his friends and dreaming of winning a local tournament. (Rev: BL 5/1/07; HB 7–8/07; SLJ 7/07)

4495 Patneaude, David. *Haunting at Home Plate* (4–7). 2000, Albert Whitman LB $15.99 (978-0-8075-3181-5). Twelve-year-old Nelson is amazed when mysterious instructions are left on the playing field in this baseball novel about a losing team that suddenly seems to be getting help from a ghost. (Rev: BCCB 11/00; BL 9/1/00; HBG 3/01; SLJ 9/00)

4496 Peers, Judi. *Shark Attack* (5–7). Series: Sports Stories. 1999, Orca paper $6.50 (978-1-55028-620-

5). An easily read story set in Canada, in which a young baseball player wants to impress his father but doesn't think he can ever reach his older brother's record. (Rev: SLJ 1/00)

4497 Platt, Kin. *Brogg's Brain* (6–9). 1981, Harper-Collins LB $11.89 (978-0-397-31946-6). Monty is a runner who is pushed by his father and his coach to win.

4498 Powell, Randy. *Dean Duffy* (8–12). 1995, Farrar paper $5.95 (978-0-374-41698-0). A Little League baseball great has problems with his pitching arm and sees his career collapse. (Rev: BL 4/15/95; SLJ 5/95)

4499 Powell, Randy. *The Whistling Toilets* (7–10). 1996, Farrar paper $5.95 (978-0-374-48369-2). When Stan tries to help his friend Ginny with her tennis game, he finds that something strange is troubling the rising young tennis star. (Rev: BL 9/15/96; SLJ 10/96; VOYA 12/96)

4500 Preller, James. *Six Innings* (5–8). 2008, Feiwel and Friends $16.95 (978-0-312-36763-3). Six innings of a Little League game reveal much about the game's young players and about the young announcer, a player side-lined by cancer. (Rev: BL 4/1/08; SLJ 4/08)

4501 Ritter, John H. *The Boy Who Saved Baseball* (5–7). 2003, Putnam $17.99 (978-0-399-23622-8). A small town depends on its baseball team to rescue it from big developers. (Rev: BL 5/1/03*; HBG 4/04; SLJ 6/03; VOYA 8/03)

4502 Ritter, John H. *Choosing Up Sides* (5–9). 1998, Putnam $18.99 (978-0-399-23185-8). Jake is a great southpaw in baseball, but his preacher father forbids the boy to use his left hand for pitching as it is the instrument of Satan. (Rev: BCCB 6/98; BL 5/1/98; HBG 10/98; SLJ 6/98; VOYA 12/98)

4503 Roberts, Kristi. *My Thirteenth Season* (5–8). 2005, Holt $15.95 (978-0-8050-7495-6). When Fran, whose mother has recently died, tries to play baseball for the boys' team in her new town, she is in for a world of trouble. (Rev: BL 3/15/05*; SLJ 3/05)

4504 Romain, Joseph. *The Mystery of the Wagner Whacker* (7–12). 1997, Warwick paper $8.95 (978-1-895629-94-1). Matt, a baseball enthusiast, is upset at moving to a small Canadian town where the sport is all but unknown, but an accidental travel in time to 1928 changes the situation. (Rev: BL 7/98; SLJ 7/98)

4505 Rottman, S. L. *Slalom* (6–8). 2004, Penguin $16.99 (978-0-670-05913-3). Seventeen-year-old Sandro, raised in the shadow of a posh ski resort by his single mother, is shaken when the handsome Italian skier who is his father turns up and reunites with his mother. (Rev: BL 9/1/04; SLJ 11/04; VOYA 10/04)

4506 Rud, Jeff. *In the Paint* (5–8). 2005, Orca paper $7.95 (978-1-55143-337-0). Matt is glad to make the basketball team but soon finds there are pressures he would prefer to avoid. (Rev: BL 7/05)

4507 Strasser, Todd. *Cut Back* (7–12). Series: Impact Zone. 2004, Simon & Schuster paper $5.99 (978-0-689-87030-9). In this action-packed series installment, 15-year-old Kai faces off against his nemesis, Lucas Frank, in a surfing competition; a sequel is *Take Off* (2004). (Rev: BL 7/04; SLJ 8/04)

4508 Swan, Bill. *The Enforcer* (5–8). Series: Canadian Sports Stories. 2008, James Lorimer $8.95 (978-1-55028-981-7); paper $8.95 (978-1-55028-979-4). Hockey is the focus in this book about Jake, a boy with three grandfathers who all intrude into his life in different ways. (Rev: BL 6/1–15/08)

4509 Sweeney, Joyce. *Players* (6–12). 2000, Winslow $16.95 (978-1-890817-54-1). Corey, leader of the basketball team, is determined to find out who is sabotaging its chances of success. (Rev: BL 10/1/00; HBG 10/01; SLJ 9/00; VOYA 12/00)

4510 Tharp, Tim. *Knights of the Hill Country* (8–11). 2006, Knopf $16.95 (978-0-375-83653-4). In his senior year, Hampton, the star linebacker in a school and town that live for football, begins to deal with his uncertainties and realize that he is more than just an athlete. (Rev: BL 10/1/06; LMC 1/07; SLJ 9/06)

4511 Tocher, Timothy. *Chief Sunrise, John McGraw, and Me* (6–9). 2004, Cricket $15.95 (978-0-8126-2711-4). In this appealing baseball tale set in 1919, 15-year-old Hank Cobb escapes from an abusive father, joins forces with a 19-year-old baseball hopeful who claims to be a Seminole, and travels to New York in search of a career playing ball. (Rev: BCCB 7–8/04; BL 5/15/04; SLJ 9/04)

4512 Trembath, Don. *Frog Face and the Three Boys* (4–7). Series: Black Belt. 2001, Orca paper $6.95 (978-1-55143-165-9). Three very different 7th-graders are enrolled in a karate class to teach them discipline. (Rev: BL 3/1/01; SLJ 9/01; VOYA 8/02)

4513 Tunis, John R. *The Kid from Tomkinsville* (6–9). 1990, Harcourt $14.95 (978-0-15-242568-5). This novel, first published in 1940, introduces Roy Tucker and his remarkable pitching arm. It is continued in *The Kid Comes Back* (1946). Also use *Rookie of the Year* (1944). (Rev: BL 8/87)

4514 Wallace, Bill. *Never Say Quit* (5–7). 1993, Holiday $16.95 (978-0-8234-1013-2). A group of misfits who don't make the soccer team decide to form one of their own. (Rev: BL 4/15/93)

4515 Walters, Eric. *Juice* (6–9). 2005, Orca paper $7.95 (978-1-55143-351-6). Moose gets caught up in his high school football team's doping scandal in this novel for reluctant readers. (Rev: BL 9/1/05; VOYA 8/05)

4516 Weaver, Will. *Hard Ball* (7–12). 1998, Harper-Collins LB $15.89 (978-0-06-027122-0). Billy Baggs discovers that his rival for the star position on the freshman baseball team is also his rival for the attention of the girl he is attracted to. (Rev: BL 1/1–15/98; HBG 9/98; SLJ 4/98; VOYA 6/98)

4517 Weaver, Will. *Saturday Night Dirt* (8–11). Series: Motor. 2008, Farrar $14.95 (978-0-374-35060-4). A racetrack in rural Minnesota is the setting for this story about a group of people who share a love of racing. (Rev: BL 3/1/08; SLJ 4/08)

4518 Weaver, Will. *Striking Out* (8–12). 1993, HarperCollins paper $7.99 (978-0-06-447113-8). When Minnesota farmboy Billy Baggs picks up a stray baseball and fires it back to the pitcher, his baseball career begins, but his family isn't enthusiastic. (Rev: BL 11/1/93; SLJ 10/93; VOYA 12/93)

4519 Webster-Doyle, Terrence. *Breaking the Chains of the Ancient Warrior: Tests of Wisdom for Young Martial Artists* (5–8). Illus. 1995, Martial Arts for Peace paper $14.95 (978-0-942941-32-6). A collection of inspirational stories, karate parables, and tests that promote ethical behavior, with accompanying follow-up questions and a message for adult readers. (Rev: SLJ 1/96)

4520 Withers, Pam. *Skater Stuntboys* (6–9). Series: Take It to the Xtreme. 2005, Walrus paper $6.95 (978-1-55285-647-5). An action-filled novel about 15-year-olds Jake and Peter, who take jobs as skate-boarding stunt doubles on the set of an extreme-sports film and find they're in the middle of a mystery. (Rev: SLJ 11/05)

4521 Wolff, Virginia E. *Bat 6* (5–9). 1998, Scholastic paper $16.95 (978-0-590-89799-0). In this novel narrated by the members of the opposing teams, a Japanese American girl just out of an internment camp meets a bitter girl whose father was killed at Pearl Harbor, and the two become rivals in baseball. (Rev: BCCB 6/98; BL 5/1/98*; HBG 10/98; SLJ 5/98; VOYA 6/98)

4522 Wooldridge, Frosty. *Strike Three! Take Your Base* (5–9). Illus. by Pietri Freeman. 2001, Brookfield Reader $16.95 (978-1-930093-01-0); paper $6.95 (978-1-930093-07-2). Baseball provides the setting as two brothers deal individually with the sudden death of their umpire father. (Rev: SLJ 3/02)

4523 Wunderli, Stephen. *The Heartbeat of Halftime* (6–9). 1996, Holt $14.95 (978-0-8050-4713-4). Wing tries to forget his father's declining health by becoming totally absorbed in football. (Rev: BL 10/1/96; SLJ 11/96; VOYA 10/96)

4524 Zirpoli, Jane. *Roots in the Outfield* (5–7). 1988, Houghton $16.00 (978-0-395-45184-7). Josh spends a summer with his newly married father in Wisconsin and discovers some baseball memorabilia that help him overcome his own fears and ineptness in right field. (Rev: BL 4/1/88; SLJ 5/88)

4525 Zusak, Markus. *Fighting Ruben Wolfe* (8–12). 2001, Scholastic $15.95 (978-0-439-24188-5). Two brothers, Ruben and Cameron, try to assist their struggling family by boxing under the direction of an unethical promoter. (Rev: BL 2/15/01; HB 3–4/01; HBG 10/01; SLJ 3/01; VOYA 4/01)

Short Stories and General Anthologies

4526 Abrahams, Peter, et al. *Up All Night: A Short Story Collection* (7–12). 2008, HarperCollins $16.99 (978-0-06-137076-2). "What keeps you up all night?" Popular YA authors — including Libba Bray, David Levithan, and Patricia McCormick — contribute quite different answers to the question. (Rev: BL 4/1/08; SLJ 4/08)

4527 Asher, Sandy, and David L. Harrison, eds. *Dude! Stories and Stuff for Boys* (4–7). 2006, Dutton $17.99 (978-0-525-47684-9). Selections for boys — poems, short stories, and other works — offer diverse experiences; authors include Sneed B. Collard III, Clyde Robert Bulla, Jane Yolen, and Ron Koertge. (Rev: BL 7/06; HBG 4/07; LMC 1/07; SLJ 8/06; VOYA 12/06)

4528 Avi, sel. *Best Shorts: Favorite Short Stories for Sharing* (5–9). Ed. by Carolyn Shute. Illus. by Chris Raschka. 2006, Houghton $16.95 (978-0-618-47603-9). The 24 short stories in this anthology provide a sampling of some of the best writing in a wide variety of genres. (Rev: SLJ 10/06)

4529 Bauer, Marion Dane, ed. *Am I Blue?* (8–12). 1995, HarperCollins paper $7.99 (978-0-06-440587-4). Sixteen short stories from well-known YA writers who have something meaningful to share about gay awareness and want to present positive, credible gay role models. (Rev: BL 5/1/94*; SLJ 6/94; VOYA 8/94)

4530 *The Big Book of Horror: 21 Tales to Make You Tremble* (5–7). Illus. by Pedro Rodriguez. 2007, Sterling $12.95 (978-1-4027-3860-9). This collection of 21 horror tales includes stories by Edgar Allan Poe, Charles Dickens, Robert Louis Stevenson, and H. P. Lovecraft. (Rev: BL 3/15/07; SLJ 7/07)

4531 Bradman, Tony, ed. *My Dad's a Punk: 12 Stories about Boys and Their Fathers* (7–10). 2006, Kingfisher paper $7.95 (978-0-7534-5870-9). The complexities of father/son relationships are explored in this collection of 12 short stories by writers including Ron Koertge and Tim Wynne-Jones. (Rev: BL 5/1/06; HB 7–8/06; SLJ 8/06)

4532 Brooks, Bruce. *All That Remains* (7–12). 2001, Simon & Schuster $16.00 (978-0-689-83351-9). Three darkly entertaining novellas tackle the topic of death and how young people cope with it. (Rev: BCCB 6/01; BL 5/1/01; HB 7–8/01; HBG 10/01; SLJ 5/01; VOYA 6/01)

4533 Busby, Cylin, ed. *First Kiss (Then Tell): A Collection of True Lip-Locked Moments* (7–10). 2008, Bloomsbury $15.95 (978-1-59990-199-2); Bloomsbury Children's paper $8.95 (978-1-59990-241-8). Popular YA authors including Jon Scieszka, David Levithan, Deb Caletti, and Justine Larbalestier describe their first kisses — some romantic, some sloppy, some embarrassing, some clumsy. (Rev: BL 2/1/08; SLJ 2/08)

4534 Canfield, Jack, et al., eds. *Chicken Soup for the Kid's Soul: 101 Stories of Courage, Hope and Laughter* (4–7). 1998, Health Communications paper $14.95 (978-1-55874-609-1). A collection of inspiring true stories, some by well-known people, but mostly by children who sent them to the editors. (Rev: BL 9/1/98; HBG 3/99) [158.1]

4535 Canfield, Jack, et al., eds. *Chicken Soup for the Preteen Soul: 101 Stories of Changes, Choices and Growing Up for Kids Ages 9–13* (5–7). Illus. 2000, Health Communications $24.00 (978-1-55874-801-9); paper $14.95 (978-1-55874-800-2). The usual mix of verse and prose written by and for preteens, with the aim of offering inspiration, comfort, and practical advice. (Rev: HBG 10/01; SLJ 4/01) [158.1]

4536 Carter, Anne Laurel. *No Missing Parts and Other Stories About Real Princesses* (7–12). 2003, Red Deer paper $9.95 (978-0-88995-253-9). Ten thoughtful stories from Canada portray young women who rely on their own resources in difficult situations. (Rev: BL 5/1/03; SLJ 5/03; VOYA 10/03)

4537 Carver, Peter, ed. *Close-Ups: Best Stories for Teens* (6–8). 2000, Red Deer paper $9.95 (978-0-88995-200-3). Self-image, sexuality, and a variety of other teen topics are presented in this collection of stories by Canadian authors. (Rev: BL 2/15/01; VOYA 4/01)

4538 *Cowboy Stories* (7–12). Illus. by Barry Moser. 2007, Chronicle $16.95 (978-0-8118-5418-4). A collection of traditional western stories featuring cowboys, gunslingers, and lawmen by famous authors including Louis L'Amour and Elmer Kelton. (Rev: BL 9/15/07; SLJ 9/07)

4539 Crebbin, June, ed. *Horse Tales* (4–7). Illus. by Inga Moore. 2005, Candlewick $18.99 (978-0-7636-2657-0). Diverse short stories about horses, with color illustrations. (Rev: BL 9/1/05; SLJ 8/05)

4540 Dahl, Roald. *Skin and Other Stories* (7–12). 2000, Viking $15.99 (978-0-670-89184-9). Selected from the author's short stories for adults, these 13 bizarre tales will also delight younger readers. (Rev: BL 10/1/00; HBG 3/01; VOYA 12/00)

4541 Datlow, Ellen, and Terri Windling, eds. *The Green Man: Tales from the Mythic Forest* (7–12). 2002, Viking $18.99 (978-0-670-03526-7). Mythical beings with special relevance to the natural world are portrayed in a collection of stories and poems. (Rev: BL 4/15/02; HBG 10/02; SLJ 7/02; VOYA 6/02)

4542 Davis, Donald. *Mama Learns to Drive and Other Stories: Stories of Love, Humor, and Wisdom* (4–7). 2005, August House $17.95 (978-0-87483-745-2). Brief, slow-paced short stories based on his mother, who grew up in the Smoky Mountains in the 1930s, are mixed with tales about the author's own youth in the 1950s. (Rev: BL 8/05; SLJ 10/05)

4543 Editors of McSweeney's. *Noisy Outlaws, Unfriendly Blobs, and Some Other Things* (4–7). Illus. 2005, McSweeney's $22.00 (978-1-932416-35-0). Kid-friendly stories by well-known authors including Nick Hornby, Neil Gaiman, and Jon Scieszka. (Rev: BL 9/1/05)

4544 Estevis, Anne. *Down Garrapata Road* (6–12). 2003, Arte Publico paper $12.95 (978-1-55885-397-3). In this collection of closely linked short stories, Estevis paints an appealing portrait of life in a small Mexican American community in South Texas during the 1930s and 1940s. (Rev: BL 1/1–15/04)

4545 Fleischman, Paul. *Graven Images: Three Stories* (7–9). Illus. 1982, HarperCollins paper $4.95 (978-0-06-440186-9). Three stories that explore various aspects of human nature.

4546 Fox, Carol, et al. *In Times of War: An Anthology of War and Peace in Children's Literature* (6–12). Illus. 2001, Pavilion $24.95 (978-1-86205-446-2). Educators in the United Kingdom, Belgium, and Portugal worked together on this anthology of fiction, memoirs, and poetry — most of which deals with World Wars I and II in Europe — that is presented in thematic groupings. (Rev: BL 4/15/01; SLJ 6/01)

4547 Gac-Artigas, Alejandro. *Off to Catch the Sun* (5–8). 2001, Ediciones Nuevo Espacio paper $11.95 (978-1-930879-28-7). Thirteen-year-old author Gac-Artigas explores serious issues through poetry, essays, and short stories. (Rev: BL 1/1–15/02)

4548 Gallo, Donald R., ed. *What Are You Afraid Of? Stories About Phobias* (7–10). 2006, Candlewick $15.99 (978-0-7636-2654-9). This is a collection of short stories (by well-known authors) about a variety of phobias, how their victims' day-to-day lives are affected, and how they cope with their fears. (Rev: BL 9/1/06; SLJ 9/06)

4549 Hearne, Betsy. *Hauntings and Other Tales of Danger, Love, and Sometimes Loss* (5–8). 2007, Greenwillow $15.99 (978-0-06-123910-6). A collection of 15 eerie stories set in the past (mostly in Ireland), in the present (mostly America), and in the hereafter (mostly Heaven and Hell). (Rev: BL 8/07; LMC 9-10/07; SLJ 11/07)

4550 Hollander, John, ed. *O. Henry* (5–8). Illus. by Miles Hyman. 2006, Sterling $14.95 (978-1-4027-0988-3). A collection of seven O. Henry short stories, including "The Gift of the Magi," with helpful introductions before each story. (Rev: BL 4/15/06; SLJ 5/06)

4551 Holt, Kimberly Willis. *Part of Me: Stories of a Louisiana Family* (5–8). 2006, Holt $16.95 (978-0-8050-6360-8). Reading is the thread that links this collection of short stories that spans four generations of a Louisiana family, from 1939 to the early 21st century. (Rev: BL 9/1/06; SLJ 9/06)

4552 Howe, James, ed. *13: Thirteen Stories That Capture the Agony and Ecstasy of Being Thirteen* (6–9). 2003, Simon & Schuster $16.95 (978-0-689-82863-8). This collection of short stories by such popular authors as Ann Martin, Alex Sanchez, and Ellen Wittlinger beautifully captures what it means to be 13 years old. (Rev: BCCB 1/04; BL 1/1–15/04; SLJ 10/03; VOYA 12/03)

4553 Hudson, Wade, and Cheryl W. Hudson, eds. *In Praise of Our Fathers and Our Mothers* (6–12). Illus. 1997, Just Us Bks. $29.95 (978-0-940975-59-0); paper $17.95 (978-0-940975-60-6). Nearly 50 well-known African American writers, among them Walter Dean Myers, Virginia Hamilton, and Brian Pinkney, recall their family life in this anthology of poetry, essays, paintings, and interviews. (Rev: BL 4/1/97; HB 3–4/97; SLJ 6/97) [920]

4554 Jocelyn, Marthe, sel. *Secrets* (5–8). 2005, Tundra paper $8.95 (978-0-88776-723-4). A collection of 12 short stories that reveal the importance of secrets. (Rev: SLJ 2/06)

4555 Kulpa, Kathryn, ed. *Something Like a Hero* (6–10). 1995, Merlyn's Pen paper $9.95 (978-1-886427-03-7). A collection of 11 short stories from different genres, reprinted from the national magazine of student writing *Merlyn's Pen*. (Rev: VOYA 2/96)

4556 Lanagan, Margo. *White Time* (8–11). 2006, HarperCollins $15.99 (978-0-06-074393-2). From the author of Black Juice comes a thought-provoking collection of 10 short stories with topics on death, love, and more set in alternate realities. (Rev: BL 8/06; SLJ 11/06)

4557 Levithan, David, ed. *Where We Are, What We See: Poems, Stories, Essays, and Art from the Best Young Writers and Artists in America* (8–11). 2005, Scholastic paper $7.99 (978-0-439-73646-6). Winning entries in the Scholastic Art and Writing Awards program. (Rev: BL 9/15/05; SLJ 1/06) [810]

4558 London, Jack. *The Portable Jack London* (8–12). Ed. by Earle Labor. 1994, Penguin paper $18.00 (978-0-14-017969-9). As well as several short stories and the full text of *The Call of the Wild,* this anthology contains some letters and general nonfiction. [818]

4559 Lord, Christine, ed. *Eighth Grade: Stories of Friendship, Passage and Discovery by Eighth Grade Writers* (6–12). Series: American Teen Writer. 1996, Merlyn's Pen paper $9.95 (978-1-886427-08-2). This is a group of short stories collected by *Merlyn's Pen* magazine that were written by 8th-graders. Also in this series are *Freshman: Fiction, Fantasy, and Humor by Ninth Grade Writers* and *Sophomores: Tales of Reality, Conflict, and the Road,* plus eight other volumes (all 1996). Each is accompanied by an audiotape. (Rev: VOYA 6/98)

4560 Lubar, David. *Invasion of the Road Weenies and Other Warped and Creepy Tales* (4–7). 2005, Tor $16.95 (978-0-7653-1447-5). Entertaining stories about how things don't always work out how you hope or expect; suitable for reluctant readers. (Rev: BL 8/05; SLJ 9/05; VOYA 10/05)

4561 McKinley, Robin, and Peter Dickinson. *Water: Tales of Elemental Spirits* (7–12). 2002, Putnam $18.99 (978-0-399-23796-6). Six captivating and imaginative stories feature magical sea-beings and the humans who love or fight them. (Rev: BL 4/15/02; HB 7–8/02; HBG 10/02; SLJ 6/02*; VOYA 6/02)

4562 Macy, Sue, ed. *Girls Got Game: Sports Stories and Poems* (6–9). 2001, Holt $15.95 (978-0-8050-6568-8). A collection of original stories and poems about girls playing sports that range from team games to individual pursuits. (Rev: BL 6/1–15/01; HB 7–8/01; HBG 10/01; SLJ 7/01; VOYA 8/01)

4563 Mazer, Anne, ed. *America Street: A Multicultural Anthology of Stories* (5–8). 1993, Persea paper $7.95 (978-0-89255-191-0). Fourteen short stories about growing up in America's diverse society by Robert Cormier, Langston Hughes, Grace Paley, Gary Soto, and others. (Rev: BCCB 11/93; BL 9/1/93; SLJ 11/93; VOYA 12/93)

4564 Miller-Lachmann, Lyn, ed. *Once Upon a Cuento* (6–9). 2003, Curbstone paper $15.95 (978-1-880684-99-3). A diverse collection of short stories by Hispanic American authors, each preceded by editor's comments that add context. (Rev: SLJ 1/04; VOYA 12/04)

4565 Mooney, Ben, ed. *You Never Did Learn to Knock: 14 Stories about Girls and Their Mothers* (7–10). 2006, Kingfisher paper $7.95 (978-0-7534-5877-8). Fourteen enjoyable stories about all types of mothers and the relationships — be they strained, loving, or complicated — they have with their daughters. (Rev: BL 4/15/06; LMC 8–9/06; SLJ 6/06)

4566 Morpurgo, Michael, comp. *The Kingfisher Book of Great Boy Stories: A Treasury of Classics* *from Children's Literature* (4–8). Illus. 2000, Kingfisher $19.95 (978-0-7534-5320-9). An attractively illustrated collection of stories from authors including Carlo Collodi, Roald Dahl, Ted Hughes, C. S. Lewis, A. A. Milne, Donald Sobol, and Mark Twain. (Rev: HBG 10/01; SLJ 4/01)

4567 Myers, Walter Dean. *What They Found: Love on 145th Street* (7–11). 2007, Random $15.99 (978-0-385-32138-9). A collection of 15 interrelated stories about love of family among African Americans, many dealing with poverty, drug addiction, incarceration, and other hardships. (Rev: BCCB 11/07; BL 7/07; SLJ 8/07)

4568 Naidoo, Beverley. *Out of Bounds: Seven Stories of Conflict and Hope* (6–10). 2003, HarperCollins LB $17.89 (978-0-06-050800-5). The seven stories in this book, with a foreword by Archbishop Desmond Tutu, look at the racism, apartheid, discrimination, and progress in South Africa from the 1950s to the present. (Rev: BL 2/15/03; HB 3–4/03*; HBG 10/03; SLJ 1/03; VOYA 6/03)

4569 Nix, Garth. *Across the Wall: A Tale of the Abhorsen and Other Stories* (7–10). 2005, HarperCollins LB $17.89 (978-0-06-074714-5). In this collection of short stories, Garth offers an eclectic mix of genres and settings — only the first is related to Abhorsen — suitable for a range of readers. (Rev: BL 6/1–15/05; SLJ 11/05; VOYA 10/05)

4570 November, Sharyn, ed. *Firebirds* (7–12). 2003, Putnam $19.99 (978-0-14-250142-9). An excellent collection of stories by authors who publish with the Firebird imprint, including Michael Cadnum, Garth Nix, and Meredith Ann Pierce. (Rev: BL 10/15/03; HBG 4/04; VOYA 12/03)

4571 November, Sharyn, ed. *Firebirds Rising: An Anthology of Original Science Fiction and Fantasy* (7–10). 2006, Penguin $19.99 (978-0-14-240549-9). Contributors to this anthology of 16 original stories include Tamora Pierce, Charles de Lint, Patricia A. McKillip, Kara Dalkey, and Tanith Lee. (Rev: BL 4/1/06; SLJ 4/06; VOYA 4/06)

4572 Oldfield, Jenny, comp. *The Kingfisher Book of Horse and Pony Stories* (4–7). Illus. 2005, Kingfisher $16.95 (978-0-7534-5850-1). The special relationship between horses and humans is celebrated in this collection of 12 contemporary, fantasy, and historical short stories. (Rev: SLJ 12/05)

4573 Paulsen, Gary, ed. *Shelf Life: Stories by the Book* (4–7). 2003, Simon & Schuster $16.95 (978-0-689-84180-4). Books are the stars of these 10 stories by well-known authors that show that reading can change lives. (Rev: BL 8/03; HBG 4/04; SLJ 8/03; VOYA 8/03)

4574 Peck, Richard. *Past Perfect, Present Tense* (5–12). 2004, Dial $16.99 (978-0-8037-2998-8). This anthology includes 11 previously published stories and two new ones, with comments on each story's inspiration and tips on writing fiction. (Rev: BL 4/1/04; HB 3–4/04; SLJ 4/04; VOYA 6/04)

4575 Pullman, Philip, sel. *Whodunit? Detective Stories* (6–12). 2007, Kingfisher paper $6.95 (978-0-7534-6142-6). Pullman introduces this collection of stories — by the likes of Arthur Conan Doyle, Agatha Christie, Isaac Asimov, and Damon Runyon — with a history of the genre. (Rev: SLJ 11/07)

4576 Rosen, Roger, and Patra M. Sevastiades, eds. *On Heroes and the Heroic: In Search of Good Deeds* (7–12). Series: Icarus World Issues. 1993, Rosen LB $21.95 (978-0-8239-1384-8); paper $11.95 (978-0-8239-1385-5). Nine fiction and nonfiction pieces explore the concepts of heroes and antiheroes. (Rev: BL 9/15/93; SLJ 1/94; VOYA 12/93)

4577 Salisbury, Graham. *Blue Skin of the Sea* (8–12). 1992, Delacorte $15.95 (978-0-385-30596-9). These 11 stories contain a strong sense of time and place, fully realized characters, stylish prose, and universal themes. (Rev: BL 6/15/92*; SLJ 6/92*)

4578 Sherman, Josepha, ed. *Orphans of the Night* (6–10). 1995, Walker $16.95 (978-0-8027-8368-4). Brings together 11 short stories and two poems about creatures from folklore, most with teen protagonists. (Rev: BL 6/1–15/95; SLJ 6/95; VOYA 12/95)

4579 *Shining On: 11 Star Authors' Illuminating Stories* (7–10). 2007, Delacorte LB $11.99 (978-0-385-90470-4); paper $8.99 (978-0-385-73472-1). A collection of 11 short stories by well-known British and American authors — Lois Lowry, Celia Rees, and Meg Cabot, among them — with the theme of growing up and dealing with problems. (Rev: BL 6/1–15/07; LMC 10/07; SLJ 4/07)

4580 Singer, Isaac Bashevis. *Stories for Children* (7–9). 1984, Farrar paper $14.00 (978-0-374-46489-9). This collection includes 36 stories, most of which are fantasies about Jewish life in old Europe.

4581 Singer, Marilyn, comp. *I Believe in Water: Twelve Brushes with Religion* (7–10). 2000, HarperCollins LB $15.89 (978-0-06-028398-8). Short stories by writers including Virginia Euwer Wolff and M. E. Kerr look at religion from varied viewpoints. (Rev: BL 10/1/00; HBG 3/01; SLJ 11/00; VOYA 4/01)

4582 Singer, Marilyn. *Make Me Over: 11 Original Stories About Transforming Ourselves* (7–10). 2005, Dutton $17.99 (978-0-525-47480-7). Teenage transformations and the importance of relationships are themes of these stories by writers including Joseph Bruchac, Margaret Peterson Haddix, and Joyce Sweeney. (Rev: BL 9/15/05; SLJ 2/06)

4583 Soto, Gary. *Help Wanted* (7–10). 2005, Harcourt $17.00 (978-0-15-205201-0). In this collection of ten short stories, Soto explores the dreams and struggles of Mexican American teens living in central California. (Rev: BCCB 5/05; BL 5/1/05; HB 5–6/05; SLJ 5/05)

4584 Spiegelman, Art, and Francoise Mouly, eds. *Little Lit: Strange Stories for Strange Kids* (4–9). Illus. 2001, HarperCollins paper $19.95 (978-0-06-028626-2). This collection of offbeat, imaginative, graphic stories includes something for everyone, from humor to fantasy to horror, from Maurice Sendak to David Sedaris. (Rev: BL 12/15/01; HB 1–2/02; HBG 3/02; SLJ 3/02)

4585 *Sports Shorts* (4–7). 2005, Darby Creek $15.99 (978-1-58196-040-2). Eight writers contribute "semi-autobiographical" tales about their sporting achievements at school, many humorously revealing failings rather than triumphs. (Rev: BL 9/1/05; SLJ 11/05)

4586 *Twice Told: Original Stories Inspired by Original Artwork* (7–10). Illus. by Scott Hunt. 2006, Dutton $19.99 (978-0-525-46818-9). Nine charcoal drawings by Scott Hunt were provided as inspiration to pairs of popular YA writers; the resulting short stories cover a wide range of styles and themes. (Rev: BL 2/15/06*; SLJ 4/06)

4587 Weiss, M. Jerry, and Helen S. Weiss, eds. *Big City Cool: Short Stories About Urban Youth* (7–12). 2002, Persea paper $8.95 (978-0-89255-278-8). A variety of urban settings and cultural and racial experiences are portrayed in these 14 stories, half of which have previously appeared in print. (Rev: BL 10/15/02; SLJ 11/02; VOYA 12/02)

4588 White, Trudy. *Table of Everything* (7–12). Illus. 2001, Allen & Unwin paper $16.95 (978-1-86508-135-9). Australian writer White captivates readers with this collection of offbeat short stories. (Rev: VOYA 8/02)

4589 Yee, Paul. *Dead Man's Gold and Other Stories* (6–12). Illus. by Harvey Chan. 2002, Groundwood $16.95 (978-0-88899-475-2). A collection of disturbing ghost stories featuring Chinese immigrants to America and Canada. (Rev: BL 11/1/02; HB 1–2/03*; HBG 3/03; SLJ 1/03)

4590 Yee, Paul. *What Happened This Summer* (7–10). 2006, Tradewind $10.95 (978-1-896580-88-3). A collection of nine short stories about Chinese Canadian teens and the particular tensions they face. (Rev: BL 11/1/06; LMC 4–5/07; SLJ 2/07)

Plays

General and Miscellaneous Collections

4591 Bansavage, Lisa, and L. E. McCullough, eds. *111 Shakespeare Monologues for Teens: The Ultimate Audition Book for Teens, Vol. V* (7–12). Series: Young Actors. 2003, Smith & Kraus paper $11.95 (978-1-57525-356-5). Monologues ranging from 15 seconds to 2 minutes and chosen for the youthful speakers or topics of interest to young people are arranged in three sections: for female actors, for male actors, and for male or female; an introduction explains Shakespeare's language and rhythms. (Rev: SLJ 7/04) [808.82]

4592 Bert, Norman A., and Deb Bert. *Play It Again! More One-Act Plays for Acting Students* (8–12). 1993, Meriwether paper $14.95 (978-0-916260-97-2). This is a collection of 21 one-act plays and monologs for young actors. [812.008]

4593 Dabrowski, Kristen. *Teens Speak, Boys Ages 16 to 18: Sixty Original Character Monologues* (7–12). Series: Kids Speak. 2005, Smith & Kraus paper $11.95 (978-1-57525-415-9). A collection of brief, varied monologues for teenage boys from 16 to 18. Also in the series are *Teens Speak, Boys Ages 13 to 15: Sixty Original Character Monologues*, *Teens Speak, Girls Ages 16 to 18: Sixty Original Character Monologues*, and *Teens Speak, Girls Ages 13 to 15: Sixty Original Character Monologues* (all 2005). (Rev: SLJ 7/05) [808.82]

4594 Ellis, Roger, ed. *Audition Monologs for Student Actors II: Selections from Contemporary Plays* (8–12). 2001, Meriwether paper $15.95 (978-1-56608-073-6). Fifty monologues for both sexes from ages 10 to mid-20s are accompanied by scene-setting notes and acting tips. (Rev: SLJ 4/02)

4595 Ellis, Roger, ed. *International Plays for Young Audiences: Contemporary Works from Leading Playwrights* (7–12). 2000, Meriwether paper $16.95 (978-1-56608-065-1). The 12 short plays in this collection come from varied cultures and deal with situations of interest to young people. (Rev: SLJ 2/01)

4596 Fairbanks, Stephanie S. *Spotlight: Solo Scenes for Student Actors* (7–12). 1996, Meriwether paper $14.95 (978-1-56608-020-0). This book contains 55 excellent one- to three-page monologues, some specifically for girls, others for boys, and others nonspecific. (Rev: BL 12/1/96; SLJ 5/97) [812]

4597 Fredericks, Anthony D. *Tadpole Tales and Other Totally Terrific Treats for Readers Theatre* (4–8). 1997, Libraries Unlimited paper $23.00 (978-1-56308-547-5). A delightful collection of scripts for young performers that are spin-offs from folktales, fables, and nursery rhymes. (Rev: BL 3/1/98) [372.67]

4598 Gallo, Donald R., ed. *Center Stage: One-Act Plays for Teenage Readers and Actors* (7–12). 1990, HarperCollins $17.00 (978-0-06-022170-6); paper $8.99 (978-0-06-447078-0). A collection of 10 one-act plays especially written for this collection by such authors as Walter Dean Myers and Ouida Sebestyen. (Rev: BL 12/1/90; SLJ 9/90) [812]

4599 *Great Scenes for Young Actors* (7–12). Series: Young Actors. 1997, Smith & Kraus paper $14.95 (978-1-57525-107-3). A variety of scenes representing different forms of drama are reprinted from such playwrights as Arthur Miller, George S. Kaufman, Horton Foote, and Paul Zindel. (Rev: BL 3/1/99; SLJ 6/99) [808.82]

4600 Hamlett, Christina. *Humorous Plays for Teen-Agers* (7–10). 1987, Plays paper $12.95 (978-0-8238-0276-0). Easily read one-act plays for beginners in acting. (Rev: BL 5/1/87; SLJ 11/87) [812]

4601 Henderson, Heather H. *The Flip Side II: 60 More Point-of-View Monologs for Teens* (6–9). 2001, Meriwether paper $15.95 (978-1-56608-074-3). A second collection of paired monologues that present two sides of a variety of situations. (Rev: SLJ 7/02) [812]

4602 Jennings, Coleman A., and Aurand Harris, eds. *A Treasury of Contemporary and Classic Plays for Children: Plays Children Love, Vol. II* (5–8). Illus. by Susan Swan. 1988, St. Martin's $19.95 (978-0-312-01490-2). A group of 20 plays requiring royalties based on such stories as Charlotte's Web, The Wizard of Oz, and The Wind in the Willows. [812.00809282]

4603 Kamerman, Sylvia, ed. *The Big Book of Large-Cast Plays: 27 One-Act Plays for Young Actors* (5–10). 1994, Plays $12.95 (978-0-8238-0302-6). Thirty short plays on varied subjects, arranged according to audience appeal. (Rev: BL 3/15/95) [812]

4604 Lamedman, Debbie. *The Ultimate Audition Book for Teens: 111 One-Minute Monologues, Vol. 4* (7–12). Series: Young Actors. 2003, Smith & Kraus paper $11.95 (978-1-57525-353-4). Monologues for both girls and boys give young actors ample opportunity to display their talent in a range of selections. (Rev: SLJ 4/03) [812]

4605 Latrobe, Kathy Howard, and Mildred Knight Laughlin. *Readers Theatre for Young Adults: Scripts and Script Development* (7–12). 1989, Libraries Unlimited paper $22.00 (978-0-87287-743-6). A collection of short scripts based on literary classics, plus tips on how to do one's own adaptations. (Rev: BL 1/1/90) [808.5]

4606 Nolan, Paul T. *Folk Tale Plays Round the World: A Collection of Royalty-Free, One-Act Plays About Lands Far and Near* (4–7). 1982, Plays paper $15.00 (978-0-8238-0253-1). Johnny Appleseed and Robin Hood are heroes featured in two of the 17 plays in this collection.

4607 Ratliff, Gerald L., ed. *Millennium Monologs: 95 Contemporary Characterizations for Young Actors* (8–12). 2002, Meriwether paper $15.95 (978-1-56608-082-8). High school thespians will appreciate this collection of monologues, which are arranged by theme, as well as the advice on auditions. (Rev: BL 3/15/03; SLJ 5/03) [792]

4608 Ratliff, Gerald L., and Theodore O. Zapel, eds. *Playing Contemporary Scenes: 31 Famous Scenes and How to Play Them* (8–12). 1996, Meriwether paper $16.95 (978-1-56608-025-5). A selection of scenes by contemporary playwrights, arranged according to age and gender. (Rev: VOYA 6/97) [812]

4609 Slaight, Craig, and Jack Sharrar, eds. *Great Scenes and Monologues for Children* (5–8). Series: Young Actors. 1993, Smith & Kraus paper $12.95

(978-1-880399-15-6). Includes selections from children's novels and fairy tales, as well as adult drama and short stories. (Rev: BL 10/1/93; SLJ 11/93) [808.82]

4610 Slaight, Craig, and Jack Sharrar, eds. *Short Plays for Young Actors* (8–12). 1996, Smith & Kraus paper $16.95 (978-1-880399-74-3). An impressive collection of short plays in a variety of genres, plus material on how to approach acting as a serious pursuit. (Rev: BL 9/15/96) [812]

4611 Stevens, Chambers. *Magnificent Monologues for Kids* (4–8). Ed. by Renee Rolle-Whatley. 1999, Sandcastle paper $13.95 (978-1-883995-08-9). A collection of 51 monologues — some best for girls, others for boys — representing different situations and emotions. (Rev: BL 4/1/99; SLJ 8/99) [808.82]

4612 Surface, Mary Hall. *Short Scenes and Monologues for Middle School Actors* (6–9). 2000, Smith & Kraus paper $11.95 (978-1-57525-179-0). This is an excellent collection of monologues and scenes for two actors on a variety of subjects and settings that are suitable for 12- to14-year-old actors. (Rev: BL 2/15/00; SLJ 7/00; VOYA 6/00) [812.5408.]

4613 Vigil, Angel. *¡Teatro! Hispanic Plays for Young People* (4–8). Illus. 1996, Teacher Ideas paper $25.00 (978-1-56308-371-6). This collection contains 14 English-language scripts that integrate elements of the Hispanic traditions of the Southwest. (Rev: BL 3/1/97; VOYA 6/97) [812]

Geographical Regions

Europe

GREAT BRITAIN AND IRELAND

4614 Birch, Beverley. *Shakespeare's Stories: Histories* (5–8). Illus. 1988, Bedrick paper $6.95 (978-0-87226-226-3). Retelling the classic stories of Shakespeare. (Rev: BL 2/15/89; SLJ 2/89) [813.54]

4615 Birch, Beverley. *Shakespeare's Stories: Tragedies* (5–8). Illus. 1988, Bedrick paper $6.95 (978-0-87226-227-0). Retelling the great tragedies. (Rev: BL 2/15/89; SLJ 2/89) [813.54]

4616 Birch, Beverley. *Shakespeare's Tales* (5–8). Illus. by Stephen Lambert. 2002, Hodder $22.95 (978-0-340-79725-9). This appealing and accessible large-format book introduces modern teens to the plots and language of four Shakespeare plays — *Hamlet, Othello, Antony and Cleopatra*, and *The Tempest*. (Rev: BL 1/1–15/03; SLJ 4/03) [823.914]

4617 Coville, Bruce. *William Shakespeare's Hamlet* (4–8). Illus. by Leonid Gore. 2004, Dial $18.99 (978-0-8037-2708-3). This masterful prose retelling makes the famous play accessible to young people. (Rev: BL 5/15/04; SLJ 2/04) [822.3]

4618 Coville, Bruce. *William Shakespeare's Macbeth* (4–8). Illus. 1997, Dial $18.99 (978-0-8037-1899-9). Using a picture-book format, the story of Macbeth is retold with emphasis on the supernatural aspects. (Rev: BL 11/1/97; HBG 3/98; SLJ 12/97) [822.3]

4619 Coville, Bruce. *William Shakespeare's The Winter's Tale* (4–7). Illus. by LeUyen Pham. 2007, Dial $16.99 (978-0-8037-2709-0). An illustrated prose retelling of the classic tale of jealousy and renewal. (Rev: BL 11/1/07; SLJ 12/07) [822.3]

4620 Kahle, Peter V. T. *Shakespeare's The Tempest: A Prose Narrative* (5–8). Illus. by Barbara Nickerson. 1999, Seventy Fourth Street $22.95 (978-0-9655702-2-0). An illustrated retelling of Shakespeare's play that uses much of its dialogue. (Rev: SLJ 1/00) [822.3]

4621 Kindermann, Barbara. *William Shakespeare's Romeo and Juliet* (4–7). Trans. by J. Alison James. Illus. by Christa Unzner. 2006, North-South $17.95 (978-0-7358-2090-6). This well-phrased prose retelling of the ill-fated romance is enhanced by the Renaissance-style illustrations. (Rev: BL 8/06; SLJ 12/06)

4622 Lamb, Charles, and Mary Lamb. *Tales from Shakespeare* (7–9). Illus. 1993, Buccaneer LB $24.95 (978-1-56849-117-2). The famous retelling of 20 of Shakespeare's plays in a version first published in 1807. [822.3]

4623 McKeown, Adam. *Julius Caesar* (5–8). Illus. by Janet Hamlin. Series: Young Reader's Shakespeare. 2008, Sterling $14.95 (978-1-4027-3579-0). An accessible retelling to assist students of the play, with engaging illustrations and a tone that is respectful to the original. (Rev: BL 5/15/08; SLJ 6/08) [813.6]

4624 McKeown, Adam, retel. *Macbeth* (5–10). Illus. by Lynne Cannoy. Series: The Young Reader's Shakespeare. 2005, Sterling $14.95 (978-1-4027-1116-9). This conversational prose retelling includes an introduction to the play and incorporates many of the important poetic passages. (Rev: BL 3/1/05; SLJ 5/05) [822.3]

4625 McKeown, Adam. *Romeo and Juliet: Young Reader's Shakespeare* (5–10). Illus. by Peter Fiore. 2004, Sterling $14.95 (978-1-4027-0004-0). Faithful to the original, this retelling uses finely crafted prose and interweaves many of the best-known poetic stanzas. (Rev: BL 8/04; SLJ 10/04) [822.3]

4626 Miles, Bernard. *Favorite Tales from Shakespeare* (7–10). Illus. 1993, Checkerboard $14.95 (978-1-56288-257-0). Shakespeare's most famous plays in a modern retelling. [822.3]

4627 Rosen, Michael. *Shakespeare's Romeo and Juliet* (7–10). Illus. by lane Ray. 2004, Candlewick $17.99 (978-0-7636-2258-9). Vivid, evocative illustrations and a conversational narrative accompany passages of Shakespeare in an appealing retelling of the popular story that includes references and glossaries. (Rev: BL 12/1/03; SLJ 2/04) [823]

4628 Schlitz, Laura Amy. *Good Masters! Sweet Ladies!* (5–8). Illus. by Robert Byrd. 2007, Candlewick $19.99 (978-0-7636-1578-9). Providing a glimpse into medieval life, a series of interconnected monologues and dialogues feature 23 young people in medieval England and convey information about society at the time. Newbery Medal, 2008. (Rev: BL 8/07*; HB 11–12/07; LMC 11/07; SLJ 8/07) [812.6] 🏆

4629 Shakespeare, William. *William Shakespeare* (5–7). Ed. by David Scott Kastan and Marina Kastan. Illus. Series: Poetry for Young People. 2000, Sterling $14.95 (978-0-8069-4344-2). In a large format illustrated by paintings, this volume contains three sonnets and 23 short excerpts from the plays of William Shakespeare. (Rev: BL 1/1–15/01; HBG 3/01; SLJ 1/01) [821]

OTHER COUNTRIES

4630 Goodrich, Frances. *The Diary of Anne Frank* (7–12). Illus. 1958, Dramatists Play Service paper $6.50 (978-0-8222-0307-0). This is the prize-winning play based on the diary. [812]

4631 Perry, Mark. *A Dress for Mona* (7–12). 2002, Fifth Epoch $10.00 (978-1-931492-02-7). Iranian persecution of people of the Baha'i faith is illustrated in this moving play that features Mona, a 16-year-old who will die for her beliefs; staging advice and a pronunciation guide are among the aids provided. (Rev: VOYA 6/03)

4632 Wasserman, Dale. *Man of La Mancha* (7–12). Illus. 1966, Random paper $9.95 (978-0-394-40619-0). Based loosely on Cervantes's novel, this is a musical play of the adventures of Don Quixote and his servant Sancho Panza. [812]

United States

4633 Chanda, Justin, ed. *Acting Out* (4–8). 2008, Atheneum $16.99 (978-1-4169-6213-7). Young people challenge authority in these one-act plays written by six Newbery Medal winners. (Rev: BL 6/1–15/08) [812]

4634 Kamerman, Sylvia, ed. *The Big Book of Holiday Plays* (6–9). 1990, Plays $16.95 (978-0-8238-0291-3). An assortment of one-act plays and adaptations, both dramas and comedies, related to 14 holidays. (Rev: BL 2/1/91; SLJ 1/91) [812]

4635 Kamerman, Sylvia, ed. *Great American Events on Stage: 15 Plays to Celebrate America's Past* (5–8). 1996, Plays paper $15.95 (978-0-8238-0305-7). A collection of short plays, each of which revolves around a single incident or individual important in U.S. history. (Rev: SLJ 5/97) [812]

4636 Kamerman, Sylvia, ed. *Plays of Black Americans: The Black Experience in America, Dramatized for Young People* (7–12). 1994, Plays paper $13.95 (978-0-8238-0301-9). Eleven dramas focus on the history of African Americans. (Rev: BL 5/15/95; SLJ 2/95) [812]

4637 McCullough, L. E. *Plays of America from American Folklore for Young Actors* (7–12). Series: Young Actors. 1996, Smith & Kraus paper $14.95 (978-1-57525-040-3). Ten original short plays based on folk traditions are included, along with suggestions for staging and costumes. (Rev: BL 8/96; SLJ 8/96) [812]

4638 Mason, Timothy. *The Children's Theatre Company of Minneapolis: 10 Plays for Young Audiences* (6–9). Series: Young Actors. 1997, Smith & Kraus paper $19.95 (978-1-57525-120-2). This is a collection of 10 plays, each about an hour long, adapted from such classics as *Pinocchio, Aladdin*, and *Huckleberry Finn*. (Rev: SLJ 8/98) [812]

4639 Smith, Marisa, ed. *Seattle Children's Theatre: Six Plays for Young Audiences* (7–12). 1996, Smith & Kraus $21.95 (978-1-57525-008-3). A collection of six plays commissioned and performed by the Seattle Children's Theatre that explore adolescence, its problems and concerns. (Rev: BL 6/1–15/97; SLJ 6/97) [812]

4640 Smith, Ronn. *Nothing but the Truth* (7–10). 1997, Avon paper $4.99 (978-0-380-78715-9). This is a play version of Avi's novel about a 9th-grader whose suspension from school becomes a national issue. (Rev: VOYA 8/97) [812]

4641 Soto, Gary. *Nerdlandia: A Play* (8–12). 1999, Penguin paper $5.99 (978-0-698-11784-6). Young love causes transformations in nerdy Martin and cool Ceci in this hip play full of Spanish dialogue. (Rev: BL 10/1/99) [812.4]

4642 Thoms, Annie, ed. *With Their Eyes: September 11th: The View from a High School at Ground Zero* (7–12). Photos by Ethan Moses. 2002, HarperCollins paper $7.99 (978-0-06-051718-2). A collection of moving and dramatic monologues created after students at a high school near Ground Zero interviewed fellow students, faculty, and others about their experiences that day. (Rev: BL 9/1/02; SLJ 1/03) [812]

Poetry

General and Miscellaneous Collections

4643 Alexander, Kwame. *Crush: Love Poems* (8–12). 2007, Word of Mouth paper $10.00 (978-1-888018-40-0). An anthology of varied poems about love. (Rev: SLJ 10/07) [811]

4644 Anaya, Rudolfo A. *Elegy on the Death of Cesar Chavez* (4–7). Illus. 2000, Cinco Puntos $16.95 (978-0-938317-51-7). This is an elegiac poem that celebrates the life, work, and struggle of the respected labor leader. (Rev: BL 12/15/00; HBG 3/01; SLJ 1/01) [811]

4645 Appelt, Kathi. *Poems from Homeroom: A Writer's Place to Start* (7–12). 2002, Holt $16.95 (978-0-8050-6978-5). Poems that speak to the adolescent experience are accompanied by encouraging writing tips from the poet. (Rev: BL 11/15/02; SLJ 9/02) [811]

4646 Argueta, Jorge. *A Movie in My Pillow / Una Pelicula en Mi Almohada* (4–8). Illus. by Elizabeth Gomez. 2001, Children's $15.95 (978-0-89239-165-3). The author remembers in poetry his family's immigration to the United States from El Salvador, with each poem accompanied by the translation and rich illustrations. (Rev: BL 10/1/01; HBG 10/01; SLJ 5/01*) [861]

4647 Berry, James, ed. *Classic Poems to Read Aloud* (4–8). Illus. 1995, Kingfisher $18.95 (978-1-85697-987-0). Jamaican writer Berry has collected old favorites, mostly British, along with new voices usually excluded from the literary canon. (Rev: BL 5/1/95; SLJ 5/95) [811]

4648 Bloom, Harold, ed. *Poets of World War I: Wilfred Owen and Isaac Rosenberg* (7–12). Series: Bloom's Major Poets. 2002, Chelsea LB $31.95 (978-0-7910-5932-6). This introduction to the work of these two poets includes four poems by each, with analysis. (Rev: SLJ 7/02) [821]

4649 Brewton, Sara, et al., eds. *My Tang's Tungled and Other Ridiculous Situations* (6–9). 1973, HarperCollins $12.95 (978-0-690-57223-0). A wonderful collection of humorous verse. [811]

4650 Brewton, Sara, et al., eds. *Of Quarks, Quasars and Other Quirks: Quizzical Poems for the Supersonic Age* (5–8). Illus. by Quentin Blake. 1977, HarperCollins LB $13.89 (978-0-690-04885-8). Contemporary poems that poke fun at such modern innovations as transplants and water beds.

4651 Donegan, Patricia. *Haiku: Asian Arts and Crafts for Creative Kids* (4–8). Illus. 2004, Tuttle $14.95 (978-0-8048-3501-5). Haiku advice and exercises follow an introduction to the verse form. (Rev: BL 3/15/04; SLJ 8/04) [372.6]

4652 Dunning, Stephen, et al., eds. *Reflections on a Gift of Watermelon Pickle and Other Modern Verse* (6–8). Illus. 1967, Lothrop $19.99 (978-0-688-41231-9). An attractive volume of 114 expressive poems by recognized modern poets, illustrated with striking photographs.

4653 Fleischman, Paul. *Big Talk: Poems for Four Voices* (4–7). Illus. 2000, Candlewick $17.99 (978-0-7636-0636-7). This collection of spirited, evocative poems for four voices to read aloud covers a variety of topics. (Rev: BCCB 4/00; BL 6/1–15/00; HB 5–6/00; HBG 10/00; SLJ 6/00) [811]

4654 Fletcher, Ralph. *Have You Been to the Beach Lately? Poems* (4–7). Photos by Andrea Sperling. 2001, Scholastic paper $15.95 (978-0-531-30330-6). More than 30 chatty poems, illustrated with black-and-white photographs, are written from the perspective of a smart and funny 11-year-old. (Rev: HBG 10/01; SLJ 8/01) [811]

4655 Fletcher, Ralph. *Relatively Speaking: Poems About Family* (5–7). Illus. 1999, Orchard LB $15.99 (978-0-531-33141-5). From an 11-year-old boy's point of view, these original poems explore relationships as family members go through periods of change. (Rev: BCCB 5/99; BL 7/99; HBG 10/99; SLJ 4/99) [811]

4656 Frost, Helen. *Spinning Through the Universe: A Novel in Poems from Room 214* (5–7). 2004, Farrar $16.00 (978-0-374-37159-3). A variety of poetic forms — including haiku, tercelle, sonnet, pantoun, and tanka — are used in these diverse and compelling poems about the lives of a fifth-grade teacher and her students. (Rev: BL 4/1/04; SLJ 4/04) [811]

4657 George, Kristine O'Connell. *Swimming Upstream: Middle School Poems* (5–8). Illus. by Debbie Tilley. 2002, Clarion $14.00 (978-0-618-15250-6). Brief poems describe how one girl navigates the rapids of middle school, discussing everything from school lunches and lockers to making friends and relationships with boys. (Rev: BL 1/1–15/03; HB 1–2/03; HBG 3/03; SLJ 9/02) [811]

4658 Gillooly, Eileen, ed. *Rudyard Kipling* (4–8). Illus. by Jim Sharpe. 2000, Sterling $14.95 (978-0-8069-4484-5). This book contains complete poems or excerpts from 28 poems by this well-liked writer including "If" and "The Ballad of East and West." (Rev: HBG 3/01; SLJ 5/00) [821]

4659 Gordon, Ruth, ed. *Peeling the Onion* (8–12). 1993, HarperCollins $15.89 (978-0-06-021728-0). A collection of 66 poems with multilayered meanings by world-famous contemporary poets. (Rev: BL 6/1–15/93*; SLJ 7/93; VOYA 8/93) [808.81]

4660 Gordon, Ruth, sel. *Under All Silences: Shades of Love* (8–12). 1987, HarperCollins $13.00 (978-0-06-022154-6). Sixty-six love poems, dating from ancient Egypt to modern days. (Rev: BL 9/15/87; SLJ 10/87; VOYA 4/88) [808.1]

4661 Grandits, John. *Blue Lipstick: Concrete Poems* (5–9). Illus. by author. 2007, Clarion $15.00 (978-0-618-56860-4); paper $5.95 (978-0-618-85132-4). A visually entertaining collection of poems about Jessie, a 9th-grader whose main concerns are clothes, friends, and conflicts with her parents. (Rev: SLJ 7/07) [811]

4662 Greenberg, Jan, ed. *Heart to Heart: New Poems Inspired by Twentieth-Century American Art* (5–10). Illus. 2001, Abrams $19.95 (978-0-8109-4386-5). This book contains specially commissioned poems from well-known writers to accompany some of the finest artworks of the 20th century. (Rev: BL 3/15/01*; HBG 10/01; SLJ 4/01*; VOYA 8/01) [811]

4663 Greenberg, Jan, ed. *Side by Side: New Poems Inspired by Art from around the World* (8–12). 2008, Abrams $19.95 (978-0-8109-9471-3). Poems in many languages (with English translations) and inspired by art of all kinds are featured in this book that includes maps pinpointing each poet's country. (Rev: BL 5/1/08; SLJ 7/08) [811]

4664 Grimes, Nikki. *At Jerusalem's Gate: Poems of Easter* (5–8). Illus. by David Frampton. 2005, Eerdmans $20.00 (978-0-8028-5183-3). More than 20 poems are introduced by thoughtful paragraphs and enhanced by handsome illustrations. (Rev: BL 2/15/05; SLJ 3/05) [232.96]

4665 Grimes, Nikki. *Tai Chi Morning: Snapshots of China* (4–8). Illus. by Ed Young. 2004, Cricket $15.95 (978-0-8126-2707-7). Grimes's journal in verse describes her impressions on a tour of China. (Rev: BL 3/1/04; SLJ 5/04) [811]

4666 Grimes, Nikki. *What Is Goodbye?* (4–8). Illus. by Raul Colon. 2004, Hyperion $15.99 (978-0-7868-0778-9). A brother and sister mourn the death of their older brother in poems in alternating voices. (Rev: BL 5/1/04; SLJ 6/04) [811]

4667 Hall, Donald. *The Man Who Lived Alone* (4–7). Illus. 1998, Godine paper $11.95 (978-1-56792-050-5). A narrative poem concerning a man who ran away from abuse to see the world and returns in later life.

4668 Harrison, Michael, and Christopher Stuart-Clark, comps. *The Oxford Treasury of Time Poems* (4–9). 1999, Oxford LB $25.00 (978-1—7). From John Milton and William Blake to W. H. Auden and Sylvia Plath, this anthology contains poetry and thoughts about time. (Rev: SLJ 7/99) [811]

4669 Hollander, John, ed. *Animal Poems* (5–7). Illus. by Simona Mulazzani. Series: Poetry for Young People. 2005, Sterling $14.95 (978-1-4027-0926-5). A collection of classic poems (by such poets as Blake, Frost, Melville, and Yeats) accompanied by artwork and explanatory notes. (Rev: BL 4/1/05; SLJ 3/05) [808.81]

4670 Hollyer, Belinda, sel. *She's All That! Poems About Girls* (4–7). Illus. by Susan Hellard. 2006, Kingfisher $14.95 (978-0-7534-5852-5). Poems celebrate today's diverse girls and their interests and concerns, with breezy, hip illustrations. (Rev: SLJ 7/06) [811]

4671 Hopkins, Lee Bennett, ed. *America at War: Poems Selected by Lee Bennett Hopkins* (5–8). Illus. by Stephen Alcorn. 2008, Simon & Schuster $21.99 (978-1-4169-1832-5). A collection of 50-plus poems about American wars from the Revolutionary War to the conflict in Iraq, many centered on the pain felt by soldiers and their families. (Rev: BL 3/1/08; SLJ 3/08) [811]

4672 Hopkins, Lee Bennett, ed. *Days to Celebrate: A Full Year of Poetry, People, Holidays, History, Fascinating Facts, and More* (4–7). Illus. by Stephen Alcorn. 2005, Greenwillow LB $19.89

(978-0-06-000766-9). A wide-ranging collection organized by month, each introduced by a calendar page that highlights important dates. (Rev: BL 1/1–15/05; SLJ 1/05) [811]

4673 Hopkins, Lee Bennett, ed. *Got Geography!* (4–7). Illus. by Philip Stanton. 2006, Greenwillow LB $17.89 (978-0-06-055602-0). Poems celebrate the joys of travel and the maps that guide the way. (Rev: BL 2/1/06; SLJ 5/06) [811]

4674 Janeczko, Paul B. *The Place My Words Are Looking For: What Poets Say About and Through Their Work* (4–9). Illus. 1990, Macmillan $17.95 (978-0-02-747671-2). A collection of works by some of the best contemporary poets. (Rev: BCCB 7–8/90; BL 5/1/90; HB 5–6/90*; SLJ 5/90; VOYA 6/90) [811]

4675 Janeczko, Paul B., ed. *Stone Bench in an Empty Park* (5–12). Illus. 2000, Orchard LB $16.99 (978-0-531-33259-7). An inspired collection of haiku from a variety of poets, illustrated with stunning black-and-white photographs. (Rev: BCCB 6/00; BL 3/15/00*; HB 3–4/00; HBG 10/00; SLJ 3/00) [811]

4676 Janeczko, Paul B., ed. *Wherever Home Begins: 100 Contemporary Poems* (8–12). 1995, Orchard LB $17.99 (978-0-531-08781-7). One hundred poems that express various approaches to a sense of place. (Rev: BL 10/1/95; SLJ 11/95; VOYA 12/95) [811]

4677 Kennedy, Caroline, ed. *A Family of Poems: My Favorite Poetry for Children* (4–7). Illus. by Jon J Muth. 2005, Hyperion $19.95 (978-0-7868-5111-9). This collection of poems for children includes a number of Kennedy family favorites. (Rev: BL 10/15/05; SLJ 12/05*) [811]

4678 Lawson, JonArno. *Black Stars in a White Night Sky* (4–7). Illus. by Sherwin Tjia. 2008, Boyds Mills $16.95 (978-1-59078-521-8). An eclectic collection of poems — some silly, some serious, and all full of unusual turns of phrase and wordplay. (Rev: BL 2/15/08; SLJ 4/08) [811]

4679 Lewis, J. Patrick. *Heroes and She-roes: Poems of Amazing and Everyday Heroes* (4–7). Illus. by Jim Cooke. 2005, Dial $16.99 (978-0-8037-2925-4). Helen Keller, Rosa Parks, and Gandhi are among the courageous individuals featured in this collection of poems. (Rev: BL 1/1–15/05; SLJ 3/05) [811]

4680 Lewis, J. Patrick. *Vherses: A Celebration of Outstanding Women* (4–7). Illus. by Mark Summers. 2005, Creative $18.95 (978-1-56846-185-4). The accomplishments of 14 notable and diverse women — including Emily Dickinson, Georgia O'Keeffe, and Venus and Serena Williams — are celebrated in an appealing blend of poetry and art. (Rev: BL 12/15/05) [811]

4681 Lewis, J. Patrick, and Rebecca Kai Dotlich. *Castles: Old Stone Poems* (4–7). Illus. by Dan Burr. 2006, Boyds Mills $18.95 (978-1-59078-380-1). The poems in this attractive collection celebrate castles of past and present. (Rev: BL 10/1/06; SLJ 10/06) [811]

4682 Little, Jean. *I Gave My Mom a Castle* (4–7). Illus. by Kady MacDonald Denton. 2004, Orca paper $7.95 (978-1-55143-253-3). Gifts — expected and unexpected, rewarding and trying — are the theme of this diverse collection of prose poems. (Rev: BL 3/1/04; SLJ 4/04) [811]

4683 McCord, David. *All Day Long: Fifty Rhymes of the Never Was and Always Is* (4–7). Illus. by Henry B. Kane. 1975, Little, Brown paper $6.95 (978-0-316-55532-6). A collection of poems on a variety of subjects, chiefly times that are important in childhood.

4684 McCullough, Frances, ed. *Love Is Like a Lion's Tooth: An Anthology of Love Poems* (7–12). 1984, HarperCollins $12.95 (978-0-06-024138-4). A collection of love poems that span time from ancient days to the 20th century. [808.81]

4685 McGough, Roger, sel. *The Kingfisher Book of Funny Poems* (4–7). Illus. by Caroline Holden. 2002, Kingfisher $19.00 (978-0-7534-5480-0). An anthology of poems arranged by theme that includes many by familiar names such as Ogden Nash, Lewis Carroll, and Shel Silverstein. (Rev: SLJ 6/02) [811]

4686 McGough, Roger, ed. *Wicked Poems* (4–8). Illus. by Neal Layton. 2005, Bloomsbury paper $15.00 (978-0-7475-6195-8). Misbehavior of varying degrees is displayed in this varied collection of poems accompanied by cartoons. (Rev: SLJ 1/05) [811]

4687 Mark, Jan, ed. *A Jetblack Sunrise: Poems About War and Conflict* (7–10). Illus. by John Yates. 2005, Hodder paper $8.99 (978-0-340-89379-1). This anthology of poems explores not only the barbarity and savagery of war but also the courage, selflessness, and valor that sometimes shine through. (Rev: BL 9/1/05) [808.9]

4688 Miller, Kate. *Poems in Black and White* (4–7). Illus. 2007, Boyds Mills $17.95 (978-1-59078-412-9). The poems and striking artwork in this slim volume explore images in black and white. (Rev: BL 4/1/07; SLJ 5/07) [811]

4689 Morgenstern, Constance. *Waking Day* (4–7). Illus. 2006, North Word $17.95 (978-1-55971-919-3). In a picture book for older readers, Morgenstern melds Impressionist works with lines from her own poetry. (Rev: BL 2/15/06) [811]

4690 Morrison, Lillian. *Way to Go! Sports Poems* (4–8). Illus. by Susan Spellman. 2001, Boyds Mills $16.95 (978-1-56397-961-3). Sport lovers will appreciate this collection of poems full of rhythm and life, with vibrant illustrations. (Rev: HBG 3/02; SLJ 10/01) [811]

4691 Myers, Walter Dean. *Blues Journey* (5–8). Illus. by Christopher Myers. 2003, Holiday $18.95 (978-0-8234-1613-4). Poems reflecting the soulfulness of blues music, accompanied by illustrations. (Rev: BL 2/15/03; HB 5–6/03; HBG 10/03; SLJ 4/03*; VOYA 4/03) [811]

4692 Nye, Naomi Shihab. *Honeybee: Poems and Short Prose* (7–12). 2008, Greenwillow $16.99 (978-0-06-085390-5). A collection of poems and short pieces of prose that use honeybee imagery as a metaphor for human experiences and resilience. (Rev: BL 8/08; SLJ 3/08) [811]

4693 *Once Upon a Poem: Favorite Poems That Tell Stories* (4–7). Illus. 2004, Scholastic $18.95 (978-0-439-65108-0). This appealing collection of 15 narrative poems includes offerings from Lewis Carroll, Longfellow, C. S. Lewis, Roald Dahl, Edward Lear, and Robert Service. (Rev: BL 1/1–15/05; SLJ 1/05) [811]

4694 Philip, Neil, ed. *War and the Pity of War* (6–12). 1998, Clarion $20.00 (978-0-395-84982-8). An outstanding collection of poetry from different times and cultures that explores the cruelty, bravery, and tragedy of war. (Rev: BL 9/15/98; HBG 10/99; SLJ 9/98; VOYA 2/99) [808.81]

4695 Prelutsky, Jack. *Nightmares: Poems to Trouble Your Sleep* (5–8). Illus. by Arnold Lobel. 1976, Greenwillow LB $17.89 (978-0-688-84053-2). Shuddery, macabre poems that will frighten but amuse a young audience. A sequel is *The Headless Horseman Rides Tonight: More Poems to Trouble Your Sleep* (1980).

4696 Prelutsky, Jack, ed. *The Random House Book of Poetry for Children* (6–9). Illus. 1983, Random LB $21.99 (978-0-394-95010-5). A selection of verse suitable for children that concentrates on light verse written recently. [821.08]

4697 Rogasky, Barbara, ed. *Leaf by Leaf: Autumn Poems* (5–8). Illus. by Marc Tauss. 2001, Scholastic paper $16.95 (978-0-590-25347-5). Verses by poets including Shelley, Yeats, and Whitman accompany stunning autumnal photographs. (Rev: BL 7/01; HBG 3/02; SLJ 9/01*) [811.008]

4698 Rosen, Michael, ed. *Classic Poetry: An Illustrated Collection* (6–8). 1998, Candlewick $21.99 (978-1-56402-890-7). A fine selection of poems by major writers, supplying a brief biography of each, plus one or two poems or excerpts from poems, and an illustration that evokes the poet's times or the mood of the poems. (Rev: BL 1/1–15/99; HBG 3/99; SLJ 5/99) [821.008]

4699 Rosenberg, Liz, ed. *Light-Gathering Poems* (6–12). 2000, Holt $15.95 (978-0-8050-6223-6). An excellent anthology of high-quality poems, mainly

from classic writers such as Byron and Frost but also from some newer voices. (Rev: BL 3/15/00; HB 5–6/00; HBG 9/00; SLJ 6/00; VOYA 6/00) [808.81]

4700 Rowden, Justine. *Paint Me a Poem: Poems Inspired by Masterpieces of Art* (4–7). Illus. 2005, Boyds Mills $16.95 (978-1-59078-289-7). Each of the 14 poems in this collection is inspired by a famous painting from the National Gallery of Art. (Rev: BL 11/1/05; SLJ 10/05) [811.54]

4701 Sidman, Joyce. *This Is Just to Say: Poems of Apology and Forgiveness* (4–7). Illus. by Pamela Zagarenski. 2007, Houghton $16.00 (978-0-618-61680-0). Poems of all kinds written by a fictional 6th-grade class to say "sorry" are paired with responses from the recipients. (Rev: BL 5/15/07; SLJ 5/07) [811]

4702 Simon, Seymour, ed. *Star Walk* (4–8). Illus. 1995, Morrow LB $14.93 (978-0-688-11887-7). Simple poems and outstanding photographs create an impressive introduction to stars and outer space. (Rev: BL 3/1/95; SLJ 4/95) [811]

4703 Smith, Charles R. *Hoop Kings* (4–7). Illus. 2004, Candlewick $14.99 (978-0-7636-1423-2). This celebration of basketball, presented in a blend of rap-style poetry with eye-catching photographs, focuses on 12 of the biggest stars. (Rev: BL 2/15/04; SLJ 3/04) [811]

4704 Smith, Hope Anita. *Keeping the Night Watch* (5–8). Illus. by E. B. Lewis. 2008, Holt $18.95 (978-0-8050-7202-0). In this equally poetic and well-illustrated sequel to *The Way a Door Closes* (2003), 13-year-old C.J.'s father is back home but the family's foundation remains shaky at first. Coretta Scott King Author Honor Book, 2009. (Rev: BL 3/15/08; SLJ 6/08) [811]

4705 Strand, Mark, ed. *100 Great Poems of the Twentieth Century* (8–12). 2005, Norton $24.95 (978-0-393-05894-9). Pulitzer Prize-winning poet Strand offers his selection of the 100 best poems of the 20th century. (Rev: BL 5/15/05) [821]

4706 Swenson, May. *The Complete Poems to Solve* (5–8). Illus. by Christy Hale. 1993, Macmillan $13.95 (978-0-02-788725-9). From simple riddles to more complex questions, each of these poems contains a puzzle. (Rev: HB 3–4/93; SLJ 5/93) [811]

4707 Thomas, Joyce Carol. *A Mother's Heart, A Daughter's Love* (6–12). 2001, HarperCollins LB $14.89 (978-0-06-029650-6). Two poetic voices — a mother's and a daughter's — describe their life together from the birth of the daughter through the death of the mother. (Rev: BL 3/15/01; HBG 10/01; SLJ 9/01) [811]

4708 Vecchione, Patrice, ed. *Faith and Doubt: An Anthology of Poems* (8–12). 2007, Holt $16.95

(978-0-8050-8213-5). Poems by authors of many faiths both challenge and embrace traditional religion; prayers, reflections, and supplications will appeal to readers with all sorts of spiritual lives. (Rev: BL 4/1/07; LMC 10/07; SLJ 6/07) [808.81]

4709 Vecchione, Patrice, ed. *Revenge and Forgiveness: An Anthology of Poems* (8–12). 2004, Holt $16.95 (978-0-8050-7376-8). This anthology on war, violence, and the search for peace contains poems from many lands and times. (Rev: BL 3/15/04; HB 3–4/04; SLJ 7/04; VOYA 6/04) [808.81]

4710 Viorst, Judith. *If I Were in Charge of the World and Other Worries: Poems for Children and Their Parents* (5–8). Illus. 1984, Macmillan paper $5.99 (978-0-689-70770-4). Easily read poems focus on topics familiar to young people. [811]

4711 Wallace, Daisy, ed. *Ghost Poems* (4–7). Illus. by Tomie dePaola. 1979, Holiday paper $4.95 (978-0-8234-0849-8). New and old poems to delight and frighten young readers.

4712 Waters, Fiona, comp. *Dark as a Midnight Dream: Poetry Collection 2* (5–8). Illus. by Zara Slattery. 1999, Evans Brothers $24.95 (978-0-237-51845-5). An extensive anthology of poetry arranged by subjects such as "Mythical Creatures" and "City Life" that features such writers as Robert Browning, William Shakespeare, William Butler Yeats, William Wordsworth, Langston Hughes, and Carl Sandburg. (Rev: SLJ 11/99) [811]

4713 Watson, Esther Pearl, and Mark Todd, sels. *The Pain Tree: And Other Teenage Angst-Ridden Poetry* (7–12). Illus. by Esther Pearl Watson and Mark Todd. 2000, Houghton paper $6.95 (978-0-618-04758-1). Poems collected from teen Web sites and magazines and illustrated with paintings express a wide range of emotions. (Rev: HBG 9/00; SLJ 9/00; VOYA 6/00) [811]

4714 Willard, Nancy, ed. *Step Lightly: Poems for the Journey* (7–12). 1998, Harcourt paper $12.00 (978-0-15-202052-1). These works from the pens of about 40 poets represent the poems that the editor particularly loves. (Rev: BL 10/1/98; HBG 3/99; SLJ 11/98; VOYA 4/99) [811:008]

4715 Worth, Valerie. *Animal Poems* (4–7). Illus. 2007, Farrar $17.00 (978-0-374-38057-1). A diverse, sometimes challenging collection of poems highlighting animals' individual characteristics. (Rev: BL 4/1/07; SLJ 4/07*) [811]

4716 Worthen, Tom, ed. *Broken Hearts . . . Healing: Young Poets Speak Out on Divorce* (5–9). Illus. by Kyle Hernandez. Series: Young Poets Speak Out. 2001, Poet Tree $26.95 (978-1-58876-150-7); paper $14.95 (978-1-58876-151-4). This large selection of poems written by their peers about divorce, family breakups, and blended families will resonate with young readers. (Rev: SLJ 9/01; VOYA 10/01) [811]

4717 Yolen, Jane. *Sacred Places* (5–9). Illus. 1996, Harcourt $16.00 (978-0-15-269953-6). An international collection of informational poems about the places sacred to various faiths. (Rev: BCCB 12/00; BL 10/1/96; SLJ 3/96) [811]

Geographical Regions

Europe

GREAT BRITAIN AND IRELAND

4718 Chaucer, Geoffrey. *The Canterbury Tales* (5–9). Adapted by Geraldine McCaughrean. Illus. 1985, Checkerboard $14.95 (978-1-56288-259-4). An adaptation for young readers of 13 tales that still keep the flavor and spirit of the originals. (Rev: SLJ 2/86) [826]

4719 Coleridge, Samuel Taylor. *Samuel Taylor Coleridge* (6–10). Ed. by James Engell. Illus. by Harvey Chan. Series: Poetry for Young People. 2003, Sterling $14.95 (978-0-8069-6951-0). Biographical information introduces a sampling of Coleridge's most famous poems, which are accompanied by editorial notes and full-color illustrations. Also use *William Wordsworth* and *William Butler Yeats* (both 2003). (Rev: BL 4/1/03; HBG 4/04; SLJ 9/03) [821]

4720 Corrin, Sara, and Stephen Corrin. *The Pied Piper of Hamelin* (6–9). Illus. 1989, Harcourt $14.95 (978-0-15-261596-3). A fine edition of the Browning poem with stunning illustrations by Errol Le Cain. (Rev: BL 4/1/89) [398.2]

4721 Dahl, Roald. *Vile Verses* (5–8). Illus. 2005, Viking $25.00 (978-0-670-06042-9). New illustrations adorn the poems in this aptly titled collection. (Rev: BL 11/1/05; SLJ 11/05*) [811]

4722 Gillooly, Eileen, ed. *Robert Browning* (7–12). Illus. by Joel Spector. Series: Poetry for Young People. 2001, Sterling $14.95 (978-0-8069-5543-8). A fine, well-illustrated introduction to the works of the English poet that gives historical context, references, and explanations of terms. (Rev: HBG 10/01; SLJ 10/01) [811]

4723 Hughes, Ted. *Collected Poems for Children* (4–8). Illus. by Raymond Briggs. 2007, Farrar $18.00 (978-0-374-31429-3). A nicely illustrated collection of 250 British-flavored children's poems by the late Hughes, some funny, some serious, some even scary. (Rev: BL 2/15/07; HB 7–8/07; LMC 11–12/07; SLJ 3/07) [811]

4724 Lear, Edward. *The Owl and the Pussycat* (5–10). Illus. by Stephane Jorisch. Series: Visions in Poetry. 2007, Kids Can $16.95 (978-1-55337-828-

0); paper $9.95 (978-1-55453-232-2). A charmingly illustrated version of Lear's classic poem using watercolor and ink. (Rev: SLJ 1/08)

4725 Livingston, Myra Cohn, comp. *Poems of Lewis Carroll* (7–9). Illus. 1986, HarperCollins LB $11.89 (978-0-690-04540-6). A complete collection of rhymes, poems, and riddles from the creator of Alice. (Rev: SLJ 8/86) [821]

4726 Maynard, John, ed. *Alfred, Lord Tennyson* (5–8). Illus. by Allen Garns. Series: Poetry for Young People. 2004, Sterling $14.95 (978-0-8069-6612-0). This large-format introduction to Tennyson's works includes an informative profile of the poet, selections accompanied by notes, and rich illustrations. (Rev: BL 2/15/04) [821]

4727 Noyes, Alfred. *The Highwayman* (7–10). Illus. by Murray Kimber. Series: Visions in Poetry. 2005, Kids Can $16.95 (978-1-55337-425-1). In this beautifully illustrated Art Deco version of Noyes's immortal poem, the title character is transformed into a motorcycle-riding thief who roams the streets of New York City, while his beloved Bess is now a voluptuous glamour girl. (Rev: BL 5/1/05; SLJ 8/05; VOYA 10/05) [821]

4728 Opie, Iona, and Peter Opie. *I Saw Esau: The Schoolchild's Pocket Book* (7–12). Illus. 1992, Candlewick $19.99 (978-1-56402-046-8). Traces schoolyard folk rhymes to their roots. (Rev: BL 4/15/92*; SLJ 6/92) [821]

4729 Tennyson, Alfred Lord. *The Lady of Shalott* (5–7). Illus. by Genevieve Cote. 2005, Kids Can $16.95 (978-1-55337-874-7). The setting of Tennyson's "The Lady of Shalott" is moved from the England of King Arthur to the streets of an early 20th-century city in this beautifully illustrated adaptation. (Rev: BL 10/1/05; SLJ 12/05) [821]

4730 Thomas, Dylan. *A Child's Christmas in Wales* (5–8). Illus. by Trina S. Hyman. 1985, Holiday $16.95 (978-0-8234-0565-7). A prose poem about the poet's childhood in a small Welsh village. [821.912]

United States

4731 Alexander, Elizabeth, and Marilyn Nelson. *Miss Crandall's School for Young Ladies and Little Misses of Color* (6–10). Illus. by Floyd Cooper. 2007, Boyds Mills $17.95 (978-1-59078-456-3). Told in poetry, this is the true story of a Connecticut teacher who founded a school for black girls in 1833 and faced cruel opposition. (Rev: BCCB 11/07; BL 10/1/07; HB 9–10/07; LMC 11–12/07; SLJ 9/07) [811]

4732 Carlson, Lori, ed. *Red Hot Salsa: Bilingual Poems on Being Young and Latino in the United States* (8–11). 2005, Holt $14.95 (978-0-8050-7616-5). Poems in Spanish and English voice issues

important to teens and the joys and sorrows of straddling two cultures. (Rev: BL 8/05; SLJ 8/05*) [811]

4733 Clinton, Catherine, ed. *I, Too, Sing America: Three Centuries of African American Poetry* (6–10). Illus. 1998, Houghton $22.00 (978-0-395-89599-3). This heavily illustrated volume of 36 poems by 25 authors traces the history of African American poetry, from Phillis Wheatley to Rita Dove. (Rev: BL 11/15/98; HBG 3/99; SLJ 11/98; VOYA 8/99) [712.2]

4734 Clinton, Catherine, ed. *A Poem of Her Own: Voices of American Women Yesterday and Today* (6–9). Illus. by Stephen Alcorn. 2003, Abrams $17.95 (978-0-8109-4240-0). Biographical profiles enhance this collection of poems by 25 women in U.S. history. (Rev: BL 4/1/03*; HBG 10/03; SLJ 5/03; VOYA 8/03) [811.008]

4735 DeDonato, Collete. *City of One: Young Writers Speak to the World* (7–12). 2004, Aunt Lute paper $10.95 (978-1-879960-69-5). In this moving collection of poetry from San Francisco-based WritersCorps, scores of young people give voice to their feelings about peace and violence. (Rev: BL 8/04; SLJ 8/04; VOYA 10/04) [810.8]

4736 Dickinson, Emily. *I'm Nobody! Who Are You?* (6–9). Illus. 1978, Stemmer $21.95 (978-0-916144-21-0); paper $19.75 (978-0-916144-22-7). A well-illustrated edition of poems that young people can appreciate. [811]

4737 Dunbar, Paul Laurence. *The Complete Poems of Paul Laurence Dunbar* (7–12). 1980, Dodd paper $10.95 (978-0-396-07895-1). The definitive collection, first published in 1913, of this African American poet's work. [811]

4738 Fleischman, Paul. *I Am Phoenix: Poems for Two Voices* (4–9). Illus. 1985, HarperCollins paper $5.99 (978-0-06-446092-7). A group of love poems about birds that are designed to be read by two voices or groups of voices. (Rev: BL 12/1/85) [811]

4739 Fletcher, Ralph. *Buried Alive: The Elements of Love* (5–8). 1996, Simon & Schuster $14.00 (978-0-689-80593-6). A series of free-verse poems that explore various aspects of love — puppy and otherwise. (Rev: BCCB 6/96; BL 5/1/96; SLJ 5/96; VOYA 10/96) [811]

4740 Frost, Robert. *A Swinger of Birches* (6–9). Illus. 1982, Stemmer $21.95 (978-0-916144-92-0); paper $19.75 (978-0-916144-93-7). A collection of Frost's poems suitable for young readers in a well-illustrated edition. [811]

4741 Gardner, Joann, ed. *Runaway with Words: Poems from Florida's Youth Shelters* (6–12). 1996, Anhinga Pr. paper $14.95 (978-0-938078-47-0). Joy, anger, confusion, and fear are some of the emotions expressed in this collection of poems culled from writing workshops for teens in Florida's shelters. (Rev: BL 6/1–15/97) [811]

4742 Glenn, Mel. *Jump Ball: A Basketball Season in Poems* (6–12). 1997, Dutton $15.99 (978-0-525-67554-9). In a series of poems, people involved in an inner-city high school are introduced, including basketball players, parents, teachers, and friends. (Rev: BL 10/15/97; SLJ 11/97*; VOYA 12/97) [811]

4743 Grimes, Nikki. *A Dime a Dozen* (5–8). Illus. 1998, Dial $17.99 (978-0-8037-2227-9). Through a series of original poems, the writer explores her childhood: its happy moments, its painful memories — including divorce, foster homes, and parents with drinking and gambling problems — and her search for herself as a teenager. (Rev: BL 12/1/98; HBG 3/99; SLJ 11/98; VOYA 4/99) [811]

4744 Grimes, Nikki. *Stepping Out with Grandma Mac* (4–7). Illus. 2001, Orchard paper $16.95 (978-0-531-30320-7). A loving 10-year-old girl describes a very independent grandmother. (Rev: BL 5/15/01*; HBG 10/01; SLJ 7/01) [811.54]

4745 Hayford, James. *Knee-Deep in Blazing Snow: Growing Up in Vermont* (4–7). Illus. by Michael McCurdy. 2005, Boyds Mills $17.95 (978-1-59078-338-2). Hayford's simple, quiet poems evoke a simpler country life. (Rev: BL 1/1–15/06; SLJ 11/05) [811]

4746 Herrera, Juan F. *Laughing Out Loud, I Fly (A Caracajadas Yo Vuelo): Poems in English and Spanish* (6–10). Illus. 1998, HarperCollins $16.99 (978-0-06-027604-1). In this series of poems in both languages, the poet celebrates incidents in his childhood. (Rev: SLJ 5/98; VOYA 6/99) [811]

4747 Holbrook, Sara. *Walking on the Boundaries of Change: Poems of Transition* (8–12). 1998, Boyds Mills paper $9.95 (978-1-56397-737-4). In this collection of 53 poems, the author explores the problems of being a teen with amazing insight into concerns and decisions. (Rev: VOYA 2/99) [811]

4748 Hollander, John, ed. *American Poetry* (4–10). Illus. by Sally Wern Comport. Series: Poetry for Young People. 2004, Sterling $14.95 (978-1-4027-0517-5). A colorful celebration of American life, containing 26 poems by well-known poets including Robert Frost, Walt Whitman, Maya Angelou, and Langston Hughes. (Rev: SLJ 8/04) [811]

4749 Hopkins, Lee Bennett, ed. *Hand in Hand* (5–8). 1994, Simon & Schuster $21.95 (978-0-671-73315-5). An overview of the history of American poetry, with an interesting selection of poems arranged chronologically. (Rev: BCCB 1/95; BL 1/1/95; SLJ 12/94; VOYA 4/95) [811]

4750 Hudson, Wade, ed. *Poetry from the Masters: The Pioneers* (6–12). Illus. by Stephan J. Hudson. 2003, Just Us Bks. paper $9.95 (978-0-940975-96-

5). Two-page biographical profiles introduce 11 African Americans and their works; among them are Phillis Wheatley, Paul Laurence Dunbar, Countee Cullen, Langston Hughes, and Gwendolyn Brooks. (Rev: SLJ 2/04) [811]

4751 Hughes, Langston. *The Dream Keeper and Other Poems* (6–12). Illus. 1994, Knopf LB $14.99 (978-0-679-94421-8). A classic collection by the renowned African American poet, originally published in 1932, is presented in an updated, illustrated edition. (Rev: BL 3/15/94; VOYA 6/94) [811]

4752 Johnson, Angela. *The Other Side: Shorter Poems* (6–12). 1998, Orchard LB $16.99 (978-0-531-33114-9). This African American poet gives us glimpses of her childhood in Alabama, her family life, and her views on such issues as the Vietnam War, racism, and the Black Panthers. (Rev: BL 11/15/98; HB 11–12/98; HBG 3/99; SLJ 9/98; VOYA 2/99) [811]

4753 Johnson, Dave, ed. *Movin': Teen Poets Take Voice* (5–10). Illus. by Chris Raschka. 2000, Orchard $15.95 (978-0-531-30258-3); paper $6.95 (978-0-531-07171-7). An anthology of poems by teens who participated in New York Public Library workshops or submitted their work via the Web. (Rev: BL 3/15/00; HBG 10/00; SLJ 5/00; VOYA 6/00) [811]

4754 Knudson, R. R., and May Swenson, eds. *American Sports Poems* (7–12). 1988, Watts LB $19.99 (978-0-531-08353-6). An excellent collection that concentrates on such popular sports as baseball, football, and swimming. (Rev: BL 8/88; SLJ 11/88; VOYA 10/88) [811]

4755 Levin, Jonathan, ed. *Walt Whitman: Poetry for Young People* (5–9). Illus. 1997, Sterling $14.95 (978-0-8069-9530-4). After a brief biographical sketch, this volume contains 26 poems and excerpts from longer poems, each introduced with an analysis. (Rev: HBG 3/98; SLJ 11/97) [811]

4756 Lewis, J. Patrick. *The Brothers' War: Civil War Voices in Verse* (6–9). Illus. 2007, National Geographic $17.95 (978-1-4263-0036-3). Eleven powerful poems about the pain and tragedy of the Civil War; reproductions of photographs from the war add to the poignancy. (Rev: BL 12/15/07; HB 1–2/08; LMC 2/08; SLJ 1/08) [811]

4757 Lewis, J. Patrick. *Freedom Like Sunlight: Praisesongs for Black Americans* (5–12). Illus. 2000, Creative $17.95 (978-1-56846-163-2). This collection of original poems pays tribute to such important African Americans as Sojourner Truth, Arthur Ashe, Rosa Parks, Marian Anderson, Malcolm X, and Langston Hughes. (Rev: BL 9/15/00*; HBG 3/01; SLJ 12/00) [811]

4758 Loewen, Nancy, ed. *Walt Whitman* (7–12). 1994, Creative Editions LB $23.95 (978-0-88682-608-6). A dozen selections from *Leaves of Grass* are juxtaposed with biographical vignettes and sepia photographs. (Rev: SLJ 7/94*) [811]

4759 Longfellow, Henry Wadsworth. *The Children's Own Longfellow* (5–8). Illus. 1908, Houghton $20.00 (978-0-395-06889-2). Eight selections from the best-known and best-loved of Longfellow's poems. (Rev: BL 2/15/04*; SLJ 3/04)

4760 Longfellow, Henry Wadsworth. *Hiawatha and Megissogwon* (4–7). Illus. by Jeffrey Thompson. 2001, National Geographic $16.95 (978-0-7922-6676-1). Artwork with an authentic Native American feel illustrates Hiawatha's exciting adventures in the "Pearl-Feather" section of Longfellow's epic poem. (Rev: BCCB 3/02; BL 11/15/01; HBG 3/02; SLJ 9/01) [811]

4761 Meltzer, Milton, ed. *Hour of Freedom: American History in Poetry* (6–12). Illus. by Marc Nadel. 2003, Boyds Mills $16.95 (978-1-59078-021-3). Brief histories introduce many classic and some less-familiar poems — plus lyrics and speeches — that are grouped in chronological chapters, ranging from the colonial period to the 20th century. (Rev: BL 9/1/03; HBG 4/04; SLJ 7/03; VOYA 2/04) [811.54]

4762 Millay, Edna St. Vincent. *Edna St. Vincent Millay's Poems Selected for Young People* (7–10). Illus. 1979, HarperCollins $14.00 (978-0-06-024218-3). A fine selection of the poet's work, illustrated with woodcuts. [811]

4763 Mora, Pat. *My Own True Name: New and Selected Poems for Young Adults, 1984–1999* (6–12). Illus. 2000, Arte Publico paper $11.95 (978-1-55885-292-1). The Mexican American poet looks at her bilingual heritage, the beauty of the desert country in which she was raised, her love of language, and racial discrimination. (Rev: SLJ 7/00; VOYA 12/00) [811]

4764 Mullins, Tom, ed. *Running Lightly . . . : Poems for Young People* (4–9). 1998, Mercier paper $12.95 (978-1-85342-193-8). A charming collection of old songs and ballads, nonsense rhymes, and lyrics. (Rev: BL 5/15/98; SLJ 7/98) [811]

4765 Myers, Walter Dean. *Angel to Angel: A Mother's Gift of Love* (4–8). Illus. 1998, HarperCollins LB $15.89 (978-0-06-027722-2). A photo/poetry montage with 10 distinctly styled poems and photographs focusing on African American mothers and children, and reflecting the relationship between words and pictures. (Rev: BL 2/15/98; HBG 10/98; SLJ 6/98) [811]

4766 Myers, Walter Dean. *Voices from Harlem: Poems in Many Voices* (7–10). 2004, Holiday House $16.95 (978-0-8234-1853-4). In this appealing collection of 54 poems, modeled on Edgar Lee Masters's *Spoon River Anthology*, Myers speaks in the diverse voices of imagined Harlem residents from many walks of life. (Rev: BCCB 12/04; BL 11/1/04*; HB 1–2/05; SLJ 12/04; VOYA 2/05) [811]

4767 Nelson, Marilyn. *Fortune's Bones: The Manumission Requiem* (7–12). 2005, Front St. $16.95 (978-1-932425-12-3). Six poems celebrate the life of Fortune, a slave who died in 1798 but continued to serve his master, who rendered his bones and used Fortune's skeleton to teach anatomy. (Rev: BCCB 2/05; BL 11/15/04; HB 1–2/05; SLJ 12/04) [811]

4768 Poe, Edgar Allan. *Complete Poems* (8–12). Ed. by Thomas Ollive Mabbott. 2000, Univ. of Illinois paper $25.00 (978-0-252-06921-5). This is an exhaustive collection of Poe's poems, totaling 101 works. [811]

4769 Poe, Edgar Allan. *The Raven* (6–9). Illus. by Ryan Price. 2006, Kids Can $16.95 (978-1-55337-473-2). Edgar Allen Poe's famous poem is accompanied by the dry point printmaking art of Ryan Price in this new edition. (Rev: BL 9/1/06; SLJ 12/06) [811]

4770 Roessel, David, and Arnold Rampersad, eds. *Poetry for Young People: Langston Hughes* (7–10). Illus. by Benny Andrews. 2006, Sterling $14.95 (978-1-4027-1845-8). An illustrated picture-book-format collection of 26 poems with a useful introduction, a biography, and notes. Coretta Scott King Illustrator Honor Award, 2007. (Rev: BL 2/1/06*; SLJ 5/06) [811]

4771 Rosenberg, Liz, ed. *The Invisible Ladder: An Anthology of Contemporary American Poems for Young Readers* (6–10). 1996, Holt $19.95 (978-0-8050-3836-1). As well as an excellent anthology of modern American poetry, this volume provides commentary by the poets, photographs of them, and suggestions for using each of the poems. (Rev: BL 9/15/96; SLJ 2/97; VOYA 2/97) [811]

4772 Rylant, Cynthia. *Boris* (7–10). 2005, Harcourt $16.00 (978-0-15-205412-0). This collection of free-verse poems celebrates the life and times of Boris, a big, gray cat adopted from a humane shelter. (Rev: BCCB 4/05; BL 2/15/05; HB 5–6/05; SLJ 4/05; VOYA 4/05) [811]

4773 Rylant, Cynthia. *Soda Jerk* (7–12). Illus. 1990, Watts LB $16.99 (978-0-531-08464-9). A group of poems about the inhabitants of a small town, written from the viewpoint of a teenage soda jerk. (Rev: BL 2/15/90; SLJ 4/90; VOYA 6/90) [811]

4774 Rylant, Cynthia. *Something Permanent* (7–12). Illus. 1994, Harcourt $18.00 (978-0-15-277090-7). Combines Rylant's poetry with Walker Evans's photographs to evoke strong emotions of southern life during the Depression. (Rev: BL 7/94*; SLJ 8/94; VOYA 12/94) [811]

4775 Schmidt, Gary D., ed. *Robert Frost* (5–7). Illus. by Henri Sorensen. Series: Poetry for Young

People. 1994, Sterling $14.95 (978-0-8069-0633-1). An anthology of 25 poems suitable for young people, with watercolor illustrations that picture the New England landscape that Frost loved. (Rev: BL 12/1/94; SLJ 2/95) [811]

4776 Schoonmaker, Frances, ed. *Henry Wadsworth Longfellow* (4–8). Illus. Series: Poetry for Young People. 1999, Sterling $14.95 (978-0-8069-9417-8). A generous, carefully selected presentation of Longfellow's poetry illustrated by full-color paintings and accompanied by biographical notes. (Rev: BL 3/15/99; HBG 9/99; SLJ 3/99) [811]

4777 Shields, Carol Diggory. *BrainJuice: American History Fresh Squeezed!* (4–8). Illus. by Richard Thompson. 2002, Handprint $14.95 (978-1-929766-62-8). A timeline runs across the tops of these pages of poems about events in American history. (Rev: HBG 3/03; SLJ 1/03) [811]

4778 Siebert, Diane. *Tour America: A Journey Through Poems and Art* (4–7). 2006, Chronicle $17.95 (978-0-8118-5056-8). Natural and manmade sights across America are celebrated in this appealing collection of poetry and art. (Rev: BL 6/1–15/06; SLJ 6/06*) [811]

4779 Silverstein, Shel. *A Light in the Attic* (6–9). Illus. 1981, HarperCollins LB $19.89 (978-0-06-025674-6). More than 100 humorous poems that deal with children's interests and need for fun. Also use the author's earlier *Where the Sidewalk Ends* (1974). [811]

4780 Smith, Hope Anita. *The Way a Door Closes* (5–8). Illus. by Shane W. Evans. 2003, Holt $18.95 (978-0-8050-6477-3). A series of poems convey the feelings of a 13-year-old African American boy whose warm, loving home is destroyed when his father loses his job. (Rev: BL 5/1/03; HBG 10/03; SLJ 5/03*) [811]

4781 Soto, Gary. *A Fire in My Hands*. Rev. ed. (6–9). 2006, Harcourt $16.00 (978-0-15-205564-6). The joys and agonies of everyday life are captured in these poems, half of them new to this edition. (Rev: BL 4/1/06; SLJ 5/06) [811]

4782 Stavans, Ilan, ed. *Wachale! Poetry and Prose About Growing Up Latino in America* (5–8). 2001, Cricket $16.95 (978-0-8126-4750-1). A bilingual anthology about Latino experiences, both in the past and in the present. (Rev: BCCB 2/02; BL 2/1/02; HBG 10/02; SLJ 2/02; VOYA 6/02) [810.8]

4783 Steig, Jeanne. *Alpha Beta Chowder* (5–8). Illus. 1992, HarperCollins LB $14.89 (978-0-06-205007-6). A collection of nonsense verses celebrating the joy of words — their sound and meaning — with each verse playing with a letter of the alphabet. (Rev: BL 11/15/92; SLJ 12/92) [811]

4784 Stepanek, Mattie J. T. *Hope Through Heartsongs* (6–12). Illus. 2002, Hyperion $14.95 (978-0-7868-6944-2). Hope and courage are central to this third collection of poems by Mattie Stepanek, who died of muscular dystrophy in June 2004, less than a month before his 14th birthday. (Rev: SLJ 8/02; VOYA 8/02) [811]

4785 Strickland, Michael R., ed. *My Own Song: And Other Poems to Groove To* (6–12). Illus. 1997, Boyds Mills $14.95 (978-1-56397-686-5). A collection of poems about music and its relationship to such subjects as love, cities, and birds. (Rev: BL 10/15/97; HBG 3/98; SLJ 12/97) [811]

4786 Thayer, Ernest L. *Casey at the Bat* (5–10). Illus. by Joe Morse. Series: Visions in Poetry. 2006, Kids Can $16.95 (978-1-55337-827-3). The famous poem is reimagined in a contemporary setting, with a multicultural crowd and modern technology grounding the poem in the here-and-now. (Rev: SLJ 6/06) [811]

4787 Thayer, Ernest L. *Casey at the Bat: A Ballad of the Republic Sung in the Year 1888* (4–8). Illus. by C. F. Payne. 2003, Simon & Schuster $16.95 (978-0-689-85494-1). An impossibly muscular Casey is the star of this version of the classic baseball poem. (Rev: BCCB 1/01*; BL 2/1/03; HBG 10/03; SLJ 3/03*) [811]

4788 Turner, Ann. *Grass Songs: Poems* (7–12). Illus. 1993, Harcourt $16.95 (978-0-15-136788-7). Dramatic monologues in poetic form that express courage and despair, passion and loneliness, and the struggle to find a home in the wilderness. (Rev: BL 6/1–15/93; VOYA 8/93) [811]

4789 Turner, Ann W. *A Lion's Hunger: Poems of First Love* (8–12). Illus. 1999, Marshall Cavendish $15.95 (978-0-7614-5035-1). Written from a young woman's point of view, this is a collection of poems by the author chronicling the joys and sorrows of first love. (Rev: BL 3/1/99; HBG 3/99; SLJ 1/99; VOYA 2/99) [811]

4790 Weatherford, Carole Boston. *Remember the Bridge: Poems of a People* (7–12). Illus. 2002, Putnam $17.99 (978-0-399-23726-3). This collection of poems celebrates African Americans from the era of slavery through today, with accompanying archival images. (Rev: BL 2/15/02; HBG 10/02; SLJ 1/02; VOYA 8/02) [811]

4791 Whitman, Walt. *Voyages: Poems by Walt Whitman* (7–12). Illus. 1988, Harcourt $15.95 (978-0-15-294495-7). An introductory biographical sketch is followed by 53 representative poems selected by Lee Bennett Hopkins. (Rev: BL 11/15/88; SLJ 12/88; VOYA 1/89) [811.3]

4792 Wong, Janet S. *Behind the Wheel* (7–12). 1999, Simon & Schuster $15.00 (978-0-689-82531-6). In a series of free-verse poems, the author explores individuals and their relationships within families. (Rev: BL 1/1–15/00*; HB 11–12/99; HBG 4/00; VOYA 2/00) [811]

4793 Yolen, Jane, sel. *Once Upon Ice: And Other Frozen Poems* (4–8). 1997, Boyds Mills $19.95 (978-1-56397-408-3). A collection of 17 poems inspired by photographs of ice formations, which are also included. (Rev: BL 2/1/97; SLJ 3/97) [811]

Other Regions

4794 Agard, John. *Half-Caste and Other Poems* (4–7). 2005, Hodder $16.99 (978-0-340-89382-1). Guyana-born Agard offers a collection of his saucy, Caribbean-flavored poetry dealing with topics such as tolerance and diversity that young people will recognize. (Rev: BL 10/15/05; HB 1–2/06; HBG 4/06; SLJ 1/06; VOYA 2/06) [811]

4795 Brand, Dionne. *Earth Magic* (4–7). Illus. by Eugenie Fernandes. 2006, Kids Can $14.95 (978-1-55337-706-1). In her first collection of poetry for young people, Brand writes about life in Trinidad, the island of her birth. (Rev: BL 4/1/06; SLJ 7/06) [811]

4796 Engle, Margarita. *The Surrender Tree: Poems of Cuba's Struggle for Freedom* (6–12). 2008, Holt $17.95 (978-0-8050-8674-4). Poems about Cuba in the late 19th century center on Rosa, a former slave, and the violence of the nation's efforts to achieve independence. (Rev: BL 3/15/08; SLJ 6/08) [811]

4797 Johnston, Tony. *The Ancestors Are Singing* (4–8). Illus. by Karen Barbour. 2003, Farrar $16.00 (978-0-374-30347-1). Mexico's geography, history, and culture are portrayed in poems full of vivid images. (Rev: BL 4/1/03; HBG 10/03; SLJ 4/03; VOYA 10/03) [811]

4798 Liu, Siyu, and Orel Protopopescu. *A Thousand Peaks: Poems from China* (6–10). Illus. by Siyu Liu. 2002, Pacific View $19.95 (978-1-881896-24-1). Thirty-five translations of Chinese poems are accompanied by information giving historical and cultural context, the original in Chinese characters and pinyin transliteration, a literal translation, and black-and-white drawings. (Rev: BL 3/15/02; SLJ 2/02*) [895.1]

4799 Nye, Naomi S., ed. *The Space Between Our Footsteps: Poems and Paintings from the Middle East* (8–12). Illus. 1998, Simon & Schuster $21.95 (978-0-689-81233-0). More than 100 poets and artists from 19 countries in the Middle East are featured in this handsome volume of verse about families, friends, and everyday events. (Rev: BCCB 5/98; BL 3/1/98; HB 3–4/98; SLJ 5/98; VOYA 10/98) [808.81]

4800 Tadjo, Veronique, ed. *Talking Drums: A Selection of Poems from Africa South of the Sahara* (4–8). Illus. by Veronique Tadjo. 2004, Bloomsbury $15.95 (978-1-58234-813-1). Arranged by theme, these 75 poems — traditional and contemporary — cover a broad range of topics. (Rev: BL 3/1/04; SLJ 4/04; VOYA 4/04) [811]

Folklore and Fairy Tales

General and Miscellaneous

4801 Caduto, Michael J. *Earth Tales from Around the World* (5–8). Illus. 1997, Fulcrum paper $17.95 (978-1-55591-968-9). This collection of 48 folktales from around the world emphasizes respect for the natural world. (Rev: BL 4/1/98; SLJ 5/98; VOYA 4/98) [398.27]

4802 Cole, Joanna, ed. *Best-Loved Folktales of the World* (7–12). Illus. 1982, Doubleday paper $17.00 (978-0-385-18949-1). A collection of 200 tales from around the globe, arranged geographically. [398.2]

4803 Coombs, Kate. *The Runaway Princess* (4–7). 2006, Farrar $17.00 (978-0-374-35546-3). In this entertaining takeoff on traditional fairy tales, 15-year-old Princess Meg, angry over being sequestered while princes from far and wide compete for her hand in marriage, escapes and takes matters into her own hands. (Rev: BL 9/1/06; SLJ 9/06) [398.2]

4804 Dokey, Cameron. *Before Midnight: A Retelling of "Cinderella"* (6–10). Series: Once upon a Time. 2007, Simon & Schuster paper $5.99 (978-1-4169-3471-4). Dokey adds details to the Cinderella tale, explaining that the girl's father left her in his grief over his wife's death in childbirth. (Rev: SLJ 4/07)

4805 Dokey, Cameron. *Golden* (6–10). 2006, Simon & Schuster paper $5.99 (978-1-4169-0580-6). Obviously based on the Rapunzel fairy tale, but with several interesting twists on the original, this story tells of a bald Rapunzel whom her mother gave up to sorceress Melisande, who raised her as her own, having lost her own daughter Rue to a wizard who cursed her and imprisoned her in a magic tower. Rapunzel — in the midst of feelings of jealousy — leads the effort to save Rue before it is too late. (Rev: SLJ 8/06*)

4806 Dokey, Cameron. *Sunlight and Shadow* (6–10). Series: Once upon a Time. 2004, Simon & Schuster paper $5.99 (978-0-689-86999-0). Mina — daughter of Pamina, the Queen of the Night, and of Sarastro, the Mage of the Day — falls in love with a prince called Tern and together the two face obstacles in this reworking of "The Magic Flute." (Rev: SLJ 11/04; VOYA 12/04)

4807 Ferris, Jean. *Once Upon a Marigold* (5–8). 2002, Harcourt $17.00 (978-0-15-216791-2). Christian falls in love with Princess Marigold and wins her heart through his bravery in this fairy tale full of fun. (Rev: BCCB 2/03; BL 9/15/02; HB 9–10/02; HBG 3/03; SLJ 11/02; VOYA 12/02)

4808 Ferris, Jean. *Twice Upon a Marigold: Part Comedy, Part Tragedy, Part Two* (5–8). 2008, Harcourt $17.00 (978-0-15-206382-5). Queen Marigold and King Christian, introduced in *Once upon a Marigold*, are now married and Queen Olympia, who fell into a river at the end of the first book, is now dried off and back to her wicked ways. (Rev: BL 4/15/08; SLJ 6/08)

4809 Forest, Heather. *Wisdom Tales from Around the World* (4–7). 1996, August House $27.95 (978-0-87483-478-9); paper $19.95 (978-0-87483-479-6). Fifty fables, folktales, and myths from around the world. (Rev: BCCB 2/97; BL 3/1/97; SLJ 4/97) [398.2]

4810 Hamilton, Martha, and Mitch Weiss. *How and Why Stories: World Tales Kids Can Read and Tell* (5–10). Illus. 1999, August House $21.95 (978-0-87483-562-5); paper $12.95 (978-0-87483-561-8). This excellent collection of 25 pourquoi (how and why) stories from around the world also contains a useful introduction on folklore, plus tips on delivering each of the tales. (Rev: BL 5/15/00; HBG 3/00; SLJ 1/00) [398.2]

4811 Jaffe, Nina, and Steve Zeitlin. *The Cow of No Color: Riddle Stories and Justice Tales from Around the World* (5–8). Illus. 1998, Holt $17.00 (978-0-8050-3736-4). A collection of folktales from around the world that deal with the theme of justice. (Rev: BCCB 12/98; BL 11/1/98; HBG 3/99; SLJ 12/98) [398.2]

4812 Lupton, Hugh, ed. *The Songs of Birds: Stories and Poems from Many Cultures* (4–7). Illus. 2000, Barefoot Bks. $19.95 (978-1-84148-045-9). A beautifully illustrated collection of stories (mostly creation myths) and poems about birds culled from a wide range of cultures. (Rev: BL 3/15/00; SLJ 9/00) [808.819]

4813 MacDonald, Margaret Read. *Peace Tales: World Folktales to Talk About* (5–7). Illus. 1992, Shoe String LB $25.00 (978-0-208-02328-5); paper $17.50 (978-0-208-02329-2). Stories and proverbs directed toward achieving world peace. (Rev: BL 6/15/92; SLJ 10/92) [398.2]

4814 MacDonald, Margaret Read. *Three Minute Tales: Stories from Around the World to Tell or Read When Time Is Short* (8–12). 2004, August House $24.95 (978-0-87483-728-5); paper $17.95 (978-0-87483-729-2). Brief tales that are easy to learn come with notes about sources and tips about effective telling. (Rev: BL 9/15/04; SLJ 10/04) [398.2]

4815 Matthews, John. *The Barefoot Book of Knights* (4–7). Illus. by Giovanni Manna. 2002, Barefoot Bks. $19.99 (978-1-84148-064-0). This book contains retellings of seven tales of knights and chivalry from countries around the world. (Rev: BCCB 9/02; BL 4/15/02; HBG 10/02; SLJ 6/02) [398.2]

4816 Mutén, Burleigh. *Grandfather Mountain: Stories of Gods and Heroes from Many Cultures* (4–7). Retold by Burleigh Muten. Illus. by Siân Bailey. 2004, Barefoot Bks. $19.99 (978-1-84148-789-2). Strong male protagonists are featured in folktales from England, Greece, Ireland, Japan, Mexico, New Zealand, Nigeria, and the Seneca Indians. (Rev: BL 11/15/04; SLJ 1/05) [398.2]

4817 Oberman, Sheldon. *Solomon and the Ant* (5–8). 2006, Boyds Mills $19.95 (978-1-59078-307-8). Nearly 50 traditional Jewish stories are arranged chronologically and accompanied by notes and commentary. (Rev: BL 2/1/06; SLJ 3/06) [398.2]

4818 Opie, Iona, and Peter Opie, eds. *The Classic Fairy Tales* (6–12). Illus. 1987, Oxford paper $19.99 (978-0-19-520219-9). The definitive retelling of 24 of the most popular fairy tales of all time. [398.2]

4819 Pearson, Maggie. *The Headless Horseman and Other Ghoulish Tales* (4–7). Illus. 2001, Interlink $18.95 (978-1-56656-377-2). From Bluebeard to Baba Yaga and Ichabod Crane, this is a collection of 14 tales about eerie beings. (Rev: BL 3/1/01; HBG 10/01; SLJ 1/01) [398.2]

4820 Rosen, Michael J. *How the Animals Got Their Colors* (5–8). Illus. by John Clemenston. 1992, Harcourt $14.95 (978-0-15-236783-1). Tales from around the world that explain such things as a leopard's spots and the green on a frog's back. (Rev: BCCB 7–8/92; BL 6/15/92; SLJ 9/91) [398.2]

4821 Rossel, Seymour. *Sefer Ha-Aggadah: The Book of Legends for Young Readers* (4–7). Illus. by Judy Dick. 1996, UAHC paper $14.00 (978-0-8074-0603-8). A collection of legends based on stories about the Jewish people from the Old Testament. (Rev: SLJ 3/97) [398.2]

4822 Sherman, Josepha. *Merlin's Kin: World Tales of the Heroic Magician* (5–8). 1998, August House paper $11.95 (978-0-87483-519-9). A splendid international collection of folktales that feature magicians, sorcerers, shamans, healers, and wizards. (Rev: BL 4/15/99; SLJ 3/99; VOYA 12/98) [398.21]

4823 Thompson, Stith, ed. *One Hundred Favorite Folktales* (5–8). Illus. by Franz Altschuler. 1968, Indiana Univ. $39.95 (978-0-253-15940-3); paper $19.95 (978-0-253-20172-0). A selection from an international store of folktales. [398.2]

4824 Yolen, Jane, ed. *Mightier than the Sword: World Folktales for Strong Boys* (4–8). Illus. by Raul Colon. 2003, Harcourt $20.00 (978-0-15-216391-4). Yolen has collected stories from countries including Afghanistan, Angola, and China that portray intelligence as an invaluable asset. (Rev: BL 4/1/03; HB 5–6/03; HBG 10/03; SLJ 5/03) [398.2]

4825 Yolen, Jane, and Shulamith Oppenheim. *The Fish Prince and Other Stories* (7–12). Illus. by Paul Hoffman. 2001, Interlink $29.95 (978-1-56656-389-5); paper $15.00 (978-1-56656-390-1). An absorbing and informative collection of stories of mermaids and mermen from around the world, accompanied by black-and-white illustrations. (Rev: BL 11/15/01) [398.21]

4826 Young, Richard A., and Judy Dockery Young, eds. *Stories from the Days of Christopher Columbus: A Multicultural Collection for Young Readers* (5–9). 1992, August House paper $8.95 (978-0-87483-198-6). An anthology of stories translated from a variety of languages, including Italian, Spanish, Portuguese, and Aztec. (Rev: BL 9/15/92; SLJ 7/92) [398.2]

Geographical Regions

Africa

4827 Abrahams, Roger D., ed. *African Folktales: Traditional Stories of the Black World* (7–12). Illus. 1983, Pantheon paper $18.00 (978-0-394-72117-0).

A collection of about 100 tales from south of the Sahara. [398.2]

4828 Arkhurst, Joyce Cooper. *The Adventures of Spider: West African Folktales* (4–7). Illus. by Jerry Pinkney. 1992, Little, Brown paper $8.99 (978-0-316-05107-1). Six humorous stories featuring the crafty spider. [398.2]

4829 Ashabranner, Brent, and Russell Davis. *The Lion's Whiskers and Other Ethiopian Tales* (4–7). Illus. 1997, Linnet LB $19.95 (978-0-208-02429-9). A classic collection of 16 Ethiopian folktales originally published in 1995. (Rev: BL 10/1/97; SLJ 5/97*) [398.2]

4830 Eisner, Will. *Sundiata: A Legend of Africa* (5–8). Illus. 2003, NBM $15.95 (978-1-56163-332-6). A retelling, in comic book style, of an African folktale about a lame prince who conquers an evil king. (Rev: BL 2/1/03; HBG 10/03; SLJ 2/03) [398.2]

4831 Giles, Bridget. *Myths of West Africa* (6–10). Series: Mythic World. 2002, Gale LB $27.12 (978-0-7398-4976-7). A general introduction to this area of Africa through text and pictures is followed by retellings of important myths and relevant background information. (Rev: BL 7/02; HBG 10/02; SLJ 5/02) [398.2]

4832 Greaves, Nick. *When Hippo Was Hairy: And Other Tales from Africa* (4–8). Illus. 1988, Barron's paper $11.95 (978-0-8120-4548-2). Thirty-one traditional African tales, a combination of folklore and fact. (Rev: BL 2/15/89; SLJ 2/89) [398.2]

4833 Green, Roger L. *Tales of Ancient Egypt* (5–9). 1972, Penguin paper $4.99 (978-0-14-036716-4). A collection of folktales from ancient Egypt including one about the source of the Nile. [398]

4834 Kituku, Vincent Muli Wa, retel. *East African Folktales: From the Voice of Mukamba* (6–9). Illus. 1997, August House $9.95 (978-0-87483-489-5). This bilingual book contains 18 folktales in English and Kikamba, the language of the Kamba community in Kenya. (Rev: SLJ 8/97) [398.2]

4835 McCall Smith, Alexander. *The Girl Who Married a Lion and Other Tales from Africa* (8–12). 2004, Pantheon $20.00 (978-0-375-42312-3). Traditional tales feature characterful animals and humans. (Rev: BL 11/1/04) [398.2]

4836 McIntosh, Gavin. *Hausaland Tales from the Nigerian Marketplace* (4–9). Illus. 2002, Linnet $22.50 (978-0-208-02523-4). This collection of 12 Nigerian folktales skillfully interweaves details of contemporary Hausa society. (Rev: HBG 3/03; SLJ 11/02) [398.2]

4837 Mama, Raouf, retel. *Why Goats Smell Bad and Other Stories from Benin* (4–8). Illus. 1998, Linnet LB $21.50 (978-0-208-02469-5). A delightful collection of 20 folktales from the Fon culture of Benin, handsomely illustrated with woodcuts. (Rev: BCCB 5/98; BL 2/15/98; HBG 9/98; SLJ 4/98) [398.2]

4838 *Nelson Mandela's Favorite African Folktales* (6–12). Illus. 2002, Norton $24.95 (978-0-393-05212-1). Thirty-two folktales from the African continent are complemented by artwork as diverse as the stories. (Rev: BL 12/1/02; HBG 10/03; SLJ 2/03) [398.2]

4839 Tchana, Katrin. *The Serpent Slayer and Other Stories of Strong Women* (4–7). Illus. 2000, Little, Brown $21.95 (978-0-316-38701-9). A collection of 18 folktales from around the world featuring brave, creative, and strong women and girls. (Rev: BCCB 11/00*; BL 12/15/00; HB 11–12/00; HBG 3/01; SLJ 11/00) [398.2]

Asia and the Middle East

4840 Bedard, Michael, ed. *The Painted Wall and Other Strange Tales* (4–7). 2003, Tundra $16.95 (978-0-88776-652-7). Chinese folktales collected centuries ago are full of action and the supernatural. (Rev: BL 1/1–15/04; SLJ 1/04) [398.2]

4841 Carpenter, F. R. *Tales of a Chinese Grandmother* (5–7). Illus. by Malthe Hasselriis. 1973, Amereon LB $24.95 (978-0-89190-481-6); Tuttle paper $8.95 (978-0-8048-1042-5). A boy and a girl listen to 30 classic Chinese tales. [398.2]

4842 Chin, Yin-lien C., ed. *Traditional Chinese Folktales* (5–8). Illus. by Lu Wang. 1989, East Gate $44.95 (978-0-87332-507-3). This is a collection of 12 Chinese folktales that express a variety of themes and genres from faithful lovers to trickster tales. (Rev: SLJ 8/89) [398.2]

4843 Conover, Sarah, ed. *Kindness: A Treasury of Buddhist Wisdom for Children and Parents* (4–7). Illus. 2001, Eastern Washington Univ. paper $19.95 (978-0-910055-67-3). Thirty-one stories related to Buddhism, including Jataka tales about the Buddha's incarnations, have been effectively translated and adapted for this anthology. (Rev: BL 2/15/01; SLJ 3/01) [294.3]

4844 Fu, Shelley. *Ho Yi the Archer and Other Classic Chinese Tales* (6–9). Illus. 2001, Linnet LB $22.50 (978-0-208-02487-9). This collection of folktales and myths, some of which may be familiar, is introduced by a look at Chinese folklore and the influence of Taoism and Buddhism and includes a pronunciation guide, and list of characters. (Rev: BL 7/01; HB 9–10/01; HBG 3/02; SLJ 7/01) [398.2]

4845 Jaffrey, Madhur. *Seasons of Splendor: Tales, Myths, and Legends from India* (5–8). Illus. by Michael Foreman. 1985, Puffin paper $7.95 (978-0-317-62172-3). Folktales and family stories as well as accounts of Rama and Krishna. (Rev: BCCB 1/86; BL 1/15/86) [398.2]

4846 Kendall, Carol, retel. *Haunting Tales from Japan* (6–9). Illus. 1985, Spencer Museum Publns. paper $6.00 (978-0-913689-22-6). A retelling of six Japanese folktales, some of which deal with murder and suicide. (Rev: SLJ 2/86) [398]

4847 Krishnaswami, Uma, retel. *Shower of Gold: Girls and Women in the Stories of India* (6–10). 1999, Linnet LB $21.50 (978-0-208-02484-8). All of the enchanting tales in this fine collection of Indian folklore feature wise and powerful women. (Rev: BCCB 5/99; BL 3/15/99; HBG 3/00; SLJ 8/99) [891]

4848 Lang, Andrew. *The Arabian Nights Entertainments* (5–9). Illus. 1969, Dover paper $12.95 (978-0-486-22289-9). Aladdin and Sinbad are only two of the characters in these 26 tales of Arabia and the East. (Rev: BL 9/1/89) [398.2]

4849 Lee, Jeanne M. *The Song of Mu Lan* (5–8). Illus. 1995, Front St. $17.95 (978-1-886910-00-3). Mu Lan disguises herself as a boy and joins the emperor's army in this traditional Chinese tale. (Rev: BL 11/15/95; SLJ 12/95) [398.2]

4850 Lee, Jeanne M., retel. *Toad Is the Uncle of Heaven: A Vietnamese Folk Tale* (4–7). Illus. by Jeanne M. Lee. 1985, Holt paper $6.95 (978-0-8050-1147-0). This book tells the story of Toad who collects companions on his way to see the King of Heaven, who makes rain. (Rev: BL 11/1/85; HB 3–4/86) [398.2]

4851 McCaughrean, Geraldine. *Gilgamesh the Hero* (6–9). Illus. by David Parkins. 2003, Eerdmans $20.00 (978-0-8028-5262-5). McCaughrean retells the ancient epic story of Gilgamesh, a Sumerian king around 3000 B.C.E., in this volume illustrated with evocative paintings. (Rev: BL 9/1/03*; HB 9–10/03; SLJ 12/03*) [398.]

4852 Meeker, Clare Hodgson. *A Tale of Two Rice Birds: A Folktale from Thailand* (4–8). Illus. by Christine Lamb. 1994, Sasquatch $14.95 (978-1-57061-008-0). Two rice birds are reincarnated as a princess and a farmer's son in this Thai folktale. (Rev: BL 1/15/95; SLJ 11/94) [398.2]

4853 Merrill, Jean. *The Girl Who Loved Caterpillars: A Twelfth-Century Tale from Japan* (5–8). Illus. by Floyd Cooper. 1992, Putnam $16.99 (978-0-399-21871-2). The story of a young Izumi who has no interest in lute playing or writing poetry but is fascinated with "creepy crawlies" instead. (Rev: BCCB 11/92; BL 9/1/92*; SLJ 9/92) [398.2]

4854 Napoli, Donna Jo. *Bound* (7–12). 2004, Simon & Schuster $16.95 (978-0-689-86175-8). In this multilayered and thought-provoking Cinderella tale that draws on traditional Chinese elements, Xing Xing is mistreated by her stepmother and stepsister after the death of the girl's beloved father, but she escapes the cruel foot binding inflicted on her stepsister. (Rev: BL 12/1/04*; SLJ 11/04; VOYA 2/05)

4855 Riordan, James. *Tales from the Arabian Nights* (7–9). Illus. 1985, Checkerboard $14.95 (978-1-56288-258-7). Among the 10 stories retold are those of Sinbad, Ali Baba, and Aladdin. (Rev: SLJ 3/86) [398.2]

4856 Vuong, Lynette Dyer. *The Brocaded Slipper and Other Vietnamese Tales* (5–7). Illus. by Vo-Dinh Mai. 1982, HarperCollins paper $4.95 (978-0-06-440440-2). Five Vietnamese fairy tales, some of which are similar to our own. [398.2]

4857 Yep, Laurence. *The Rainbow People* (7–10). Illus. 1989, HarperCollins $16.00 (978-0-06-026760-5); paper $6.99 (978-0-06-440441-9). The retelling of 20 Chinese folktales with illustrations by David Wiesner. (Rev: BL 4/1/89; SLJ 5/89) [398.2]

Australia and the Pacific Islands

4858 Flood, Bo, and Beret E. Strong. *Pacific Island Legends: Tales from Micronesia, Melanesia, Polynesia, and Australia* (6–12). Illus. by Connie J. Adams. 1999, Bess $22.95 (978-1-57306-084-4); paper $14.95 (978-1-57306-078-3). The ocean's impact on island life is a theme that runs through many of these tales, which are organized in geographical groupings with introductions on each area's culture and history. (Rev: HBG 4/00; SLJ 10/99) [398.2]

4859 Oodgeroo. *Dreamtime: Aboriginal Stories* (6–10). Illus. 1994, Lothrop $16.00 (978-0-688-13296-5). Traditional and autobiographical stories of aboriginal culture and its roots. Also examines current aboriginal life alongside white civilization. (Rev: BCCB 1/99; BL 10/1/94; SLJ 10/94) [398.2]

4860 Te Kanawa, Kiri. *Land of the Long White Cloud: Maori Myths, Tales and Legends* (7–12). Illus. 1997, Pavilion paper $17.95 (978-1-86205-075-4). A group of magical Maori folktales about sea gods, fairies, monsters, and fantastic voyages, retold by the famous opera singer from New Zealand. (Rev: BL 9/1/97) [398.2]

Europe

4861 Afanasév, Aleksandr. *Russian Fairy Tales* (7–12). 1976, Pantheon paper $18.00 (978-0-394-73090-5). This is a standard collection of traditional Russian tales. [398]

4862 Collodi, Carlo. *The Adventures of Pinocchio* (5–7). Illus. by Iassen Ghiuselev. 2002, Simply Read $29.95 (978-0-9688768-0-0). The full text of the original is used here with effective black-and-white illustrations and several full-page watercolors. (Rev: BL 4/1/02)

4863 Delamare, David. *Cinderella* (7–12). 1993, Simon & Schuster paper $15.00 (978-0-671-76944-

4). The familiar story is set in a locale much like Venice and enhanced by Delamare's paintings, both realistic and surreal. (Rev: BCCB 11/00; BL 9/15/93; SLJ 12/93) [398.2]

4864 Green, Roger L. *Adventures of Robin Hood* (5–9). 1994, Knopf $15.00 (978-0-679-43636-2); Puffin paper $4.99 (978-0-14-036700-3). The exploits of this folk hero are retold in this reissue of a classic version. [398]

4865 Grimm Brothers. *Household Stories of the Brothers Grimm* (4–7). Illus. by Walter Crane. 1963, Dover paper $9.95 (978-0-486-21080-3). First published in the United States in 1883. [398.2]

4866 Grimm Brothers. *The Three Feathers* (5–8). Illus. by Eleonore Schmid. 1984, Creative Editions LB $13.95 (978-0-87191-941-0). A version for older readers that is faithful to the original. [398.2]

4867 Kilgannon, Eily. *Folktales of the Yeats Country* (5–8). Illus. 1990, Mercier paper $10.95 (978-0-85342-861-9). Seventeen folktales that originate in County Sligo in Ireland. (Rev: BL 8/90; SLJ 2/91) [398.2]

4868 Krull, Kathleen, ed. *A Pot o' Gold: A Treasury of Irish Stories, Poetry, Folklore and (of Course) Blarney* (4–8). Illus. by David McPhail. 2004, Hyperion $16.99 (978-0-7868-0625-6). This is a comprehensive collection — including riddles, blessing, and battle cries — with attractive and appropriate illustrations. (Rev: BL 2/15/04; SLJ 3/04) [820.8]

4869 Leavy, Una. *Irish Fairy Tales and Legends* (4–8). Illus. 1997, Roberts Rinehart $18.95 (978-1-57098-177-7). An attractive book that contains 10 Irish legends, some going back 2,000 years. (Rev: BL 2/1/98; HBG 10/98; SLJ 2/98) [398.2]

4870 Levine, Gail C. *Ella Enchanted* (5–8). 1997, HarperCollins LB $17.89 (978-0-06-027511-2). A spirited, cleverly plotted retelling of the Cinderella story in which Ella is finally paired with the Prince Charmant. (Rev: BCCB 5/97; BL 4/15/97*; HB 5–6/97; SLJ 4/97*; VOYA 8/97)

4871 Miles, Bernard. *Robin Hood: His Life and Legend* (7–9). Illus. 1979, Checkerboard $12.95 (978-1-56288-412-3). A collection of tales about this English folk hero and his merry men. [398.2]

4872 Molnar, Irma. *One-Time Dog Market at Buda and Other Hungarian Folktales* (5–8). Illus. by Georgeta-Elena Enesel. 2001, Linnet $25.00 (978-0-208-02505-0). A collection of 23 clever, thought-provoking Hungarian folktales for older readers. (Rev: BL 1/1–15/02; HBG 3/02; SLJ 2/02) [398.2]

4873 Morpurgo, Michael. *Beowulf* (7–10). Illus. by Michael Foreman. 2006, Candlewick $17.99 (978-0-7636-3206-9). A retelling of the ancient story that does not leave out any gory details and that captures the atmosphere of the original through both prose

and illustrations. (Rev: BL 3/1/07; LMC 4–5/07; SLJ 12/06) [398.2]

4874 Nye, Robert. *Beowulf: A New Telling* (7–9). 1982, Dell paper $4.99 (978-0-440-90560-8). A retelling in modern English of the monster Grendel and the hero Beowulf. [398.2]

4875 Prokofiev, Sergei. *Peter and the Wolf* (4–8). Adapted by Miguelanxo Prado. Illus. by author. 1998, NBM $15.95 (978-1-56163-200-8). A somber version of the Russian folktale filled with menacing situations and scary settings. (Rev: HBG 10/98; SLJ 6/98) [398.2]

4876 Pyle, Howard. *The Merry Adventures of Robin Hood of Great Renown in Nottinghamshire* (7–9). Illus. n.d., Peter Smith $29.25 (978-0-8446-2765-6); Dover paper $10.95 (978-0-486-22043-7). The classic (first published in 1883) retelling of 22 of the most famous stories. [398.2]

4877 Pyle, Howard. *The Story of King Arthur and His Knights* (8–12). Illus. 1973, Peter Smith $25.75 (978-0-8446-2766-3); Dover paper $12.95 (978-0-486-21445-0). A retelling that has been in print since its first publication in 1903. [398.2]

4878 Pyle, Howard. *The Story of Sir Launcelot and His Companions* (7–12). Illus. 1991, Dover paper $13.95 (978-0-486-26701-2). This book of episodes in the Arthurian legend is noteworthy because of the illustrations of Howard Pyle. [398.2]

4879 Pyle, Howard. *The Story of the Grail and the Passing of Arthur* (5–8). Illus. by author. 1985, Macmillan paper $12.95 (978-0-486-27361-7). The last title of a four-volume King Arthur series, first published in 1910. (Rev: BL 12/15/85) [398.2]

4880 Radunsky, Vladimir. *The Mighty Asparagus* (4–7). Illus. 2004, Harcourt $16.00 (978-0-15-216743-1). In this entertaining version of the Russian folktale "The Enormous Turnip" with eye-catching illustrations full of artistic allusions, a gigantic stalk of asparagus sprouts in the courtyard of an Italian king. (Rev: BL 5/15/04; SLJ 7/04) [398.2]

4881 Raven, Nicky. *Beowulf: A Tale of Blood, Heat, and Ashes* (6–12). Illus. by John Howe. 2007, Candlewick $18.99 (978-0-7636-3647-0). This is a beautifully illustrated retelling of the epic story. (Rev: BL 11/15/07; SLJ 2/08) [398.2]

4882 Rumford, James. *Beowulf: A Hero's Tale Retold* (5–8). Illus. by reteller. 2007, Houghton $17.00 (978-0-618-75637-7). Beautifully illustrated, this is a simplified retelling of the ancient tale about the warrior who defeats the monster Grendel. (Rev: BCCB 11/07; BL 8/07; HB 7-8/07; SLJ 8/07) [398.2]

4883 Sauvant, Henriette. *Rapunzel and Other Magic Fairy Tales* (4–7). Trans. by Anthea Bell. Illus. by author. 2008, Egmont $15.95 (978-1-4052-2702-5). Retellings of fourteen fairy tales, many of them by the Grimm brothers, and some of them grim or even grisly, accompanied by lush illustrations. (Rev: BL 5/1/08; SLJ 7/08) [398.2]

4884 Spariosu, Mihai I., and Dezso Benedek. *Ghosts, Vampires, and Werewolves: Eerie Tales from Transylvania* (6–10). 1994, Orchard LB $19.99 (978-0-531-08710-7). An anthology of horror tales by two authors who heard the stories as children living in the Transylvanian Alps. (Rev: BL 10/15/94; SLJ 10/94) [398.2]

4885 Sutcliff, Rosemary, retel. *Beowulf* (5–8). Illus. by Charles Keeping. 1984, Smith $24.50 (978-0-8446-6165-0). This is a reissue of the Anglo-Saxon tale published originally in 1962. Also use the King Arthur story, *The Sword and the Circle* (1981, Dutton). [398.2]

4886 Talbott, Hudson. *Lancelot* (5–7). Illus. 1999, Morrow LB $15.89 (978-0-688-14833-1). A retelling of the life of Lancelot, from his rescue as a child by the Lady of the Lake to his love for Guinevere, marriage to Elaine, and fathering of Galahad. (Rev: BL 9/1/99; HBG 3/00; SLJ 10/99) [398.2]

4887 Vivian, E. Charles. *The Adventures of Robin Hood* (6–9). n.d., Airmont paper $1.75 (978-0-8049-0067-6). The principal stories about Robin Hood and his men are retold in this inexpensive edition. [398]

4888 Walker, Barbara K., ed. *A Treasury of Turkish Folktales for Children* (4–7). 1988, Shoe String LB $25.00 (978-0-208-02206-6). A witty collection interspersed with riddles. (Rev: BL 10/15/88; SLJ 10/88) [398.2]

4889 Whipple, Laura. *If the Shoe Fits* (5–8). Illus. by Laura Beingessner. 2002, Simon & Schuster $17.95 (978-0-689-84070-8). A handsome retelling of the Cinderella story using blank verse. (Rev: BCCB 3/02; BL 5/1/02; HBG 10/02; SLJ 8/02) [398.2]

4890 Wolfson, Evelyn. *King Arthur and His Knights in Mythology* (6–9). Series: Mythology. 2002, Enslow LB $26.60 (978-0-7660-1914-0). The myths and legends surrounding King Arthur are retold with valuable historical background material. (Rev: BL 12/15/02; HBG 3/03) [398]

4891 Wyly, Michael. *King Arthur* (7–10). Series: Mystery Library. 2001, Lucent LB $27.45 (978-1-56006-771-9). An engrossing account that explores the fact and fiction surrounding this legendary king and his knights. (Rev: BL 9/15/01) [942]

North America

GENERAL AND MISCELLANEOUS

4892 Gerson, Mary-Joan. *Fiesta Feminina: Celebrating Women in Mexican Folktales* (4–8). Illus. 2001, Barefoot Bks. $19.99 (978-1-84148-365-8).

This volume includes eight tales from Mexican folklore about strong and magical women, presented with bold illustrations, a pronunciation guide, and a glossary. (Rev: BL 9/15/01; HBG 3/02; SLJ 10/01) [398.2]

4893 Kirwan, Anna. *Lady of Palenque: Flower of Bacal, Mesoamerica, C.E. 749* (6–9). Illus. 2004, Scholastic $10.95 (978-0-439-40971-1). In this gripping adventure, ShahnaK'in Yaxchel Pacal, a 13-year-old Maya princess, embarks on a dangerous journey to meet her future husband. (Rev: BL 5/15/04; SLJ 7/04)

4894 McManus, Kay. *Land of the Five Suns* (6–8). Series: Looking at Myths and Legends. 1997, NTC $12.95 (978-0-8442-4762-5). Classic Aztec myths, including creation stories and tales of Aztec gods, are retold in novelized format. (Rev: SLJ 4/98) [398.2]

4895 Madrigal, Antonio H. *The Eagle and the Rainbow: Timeless Tales from México* (4–7). Illus. by Tomie dePaola. 1997, Fulcrum $15.95 (978-1-55591-317-5). A collection of wise, wonderful, but little-known folktales from Mexico. (Rev: BL 7/97; HBG 4/04) [398.2]

4896 Montejo, Victor, retel. *Popol Vuh: A Sacred Book of the Maya* (5–8). Trans. by David Under. Illus. by Luis Garay. 1999, Groundwood $19.95 (978-0-88899-334-2). A creation story from the Mayans in a beautifully designed book that features gods, giants, mortals, and animals. (Rev: HBG 3/00; SLJ 12/99) [398.2]

4897 Philip, Neil, ed. *Horse Hooves and Chicken Feet: Mexican Folktales* (4–8). Illus. by Jacqueline Main. 2003, Clarion $19.00 (978-0-618-19463-6). Bright folk-art illustrations accompany 14 stories that feature humor and the importance of the Catholic church. (Rev: BL 10/15/03; HBG 4/04; SLJ 9/03) [398.2]

4898 Turenne Des Pres, Francois. *Children of Yayoute: Folktales of Haiti* (6–9). 1994, Universe $19.95 (978-0-87663-791-3). Traditional folktales that depict Haitian history and customs. Includes paintings that illustrate island life. (Rev: BL 10/1/94; SLJ 1/95) [398.2]

NATIVE AMERICANS

4899 Bierhorst, John. *The Way of the Earth: Native America and the Environment* (7–12). 1994, Morrow $15.00 (978-0-688-11560-9). Explores the mythologic and folkloric patterns of Native American belief systems. (Rev: BL 5/15/94; SLJ 5/94; VOYA 10/94) [179]

4900 Bruchac, Joseph. *Native American Animal Stories* (5–8). Illus. 1992, Fulcrum paper $12.95 (978-1-55591-127-0). Animal stories from various Native

American tribes, for reading aloud and storytelling. (Rev: BL 9/1/92; SLJ 11/92) [398.2]

4901 Bruchac, Joseph. *Native Plant Stories* (4–8). Illus. 1995, Fulcrum paper $12.95 (978-1-55591-212-3). A collection of stories about plants that come from various Native American cultures in North and Central America. (Rev: BL 9/1/95) [398.24]

4902 Connolly, James E. *Why the Possum's Tail Is Bare: And Other North American Indian Nature Tales* (4–7). Illus. 1992, Stemmer $15.95 (978-0-88045-069-0); paper $7.95 (978-0-88045-107-9). Nature and folklore are combined in 13 Native American animal tales. (Rev: BL 9/1/85; SLJ 10/85) [398.2]

4903 Goble, Paul. *The Legend of the White Buffalo Woman* (4–8). Illus. 1998, National Geographic $16.95 (978-0-7922-7074-4). In this picture book for older readers recounting a Lakata Indian tale, an earth woman and an eagle mate after a great flood to produce a new people. (Rev: BL 3/15/98; HBG 10/98; SLJ 5/98) [398.2]

4904 Highwater, Jamake. *Anpao: An American Indian Odyssey* (5–8). Illus. by Fritz Scholder. 1993, HarperCollins paper $8.99 (978-0-06-440437-2). A young hero encounters great danger on his way to meet his father, the Sun, in this dramatic American Indian folktale. [398.2]

4905 Hillerman, Tony, ed. *The Boy Who Made Dragonfly: A Zuni Myth* (5–7). Illus. by Laszlo Kubinyi. 1986, Univ. of New Mexico paper $11.95 (978-0-8263-0910-5). A Zuni boy and his little sister are left behind by their tribe and survive hunger and deprivation through the intervention of the Cornstalk Being. [398.2]

4906 Martin, Rafe. *The World Before This One* (5–8). Illus. by Calvin Nichols. 2002, Scholastic paper $16.95 (978-0-590-37976-2). Crow, a Seneca Indian, comes upon a storytelling stone that tells him about the origins of the earth in this series of stories. (Rev: BL 2/15/03; HBG 3/03; SLJ 12/02; VOYA 2/03) [398.2]

4907 Mayo, Gretchen Will. *Star Tales: North American Indian Stories About the Stars* (4–7). Illus. by author. 1987, Walker LB $13.85 (978-0-8027-6673-1). Fourteen tales, each introduced by a one-page commentary on a constellation. (Rev: BL 6/15/87; SLJ 5/87) [398.2]

4908 Philip, Neil, ed. *The Great Mystery: Myths of Native America* (8–12). Illus. 2001, Clarion $25.00 (978-0-395-98405-5). A collection of creation and other stories from many Native American tribes, organized by region. (Rev: BL 11/15/01; HBG 10/02; SLJ 11/01) [398.2]

4909 Pijoan, Teresa. *White Wolf Woman: Native American Transformation Myths* (7–12). 1992,

August House paper $11.95 (978-0-87483-200-6). Drawn from a wide range of Indian tribes, a collection of 37 stories about animal and human transformations and connections. (Rev: BL 10/1/92) [398.2]

4910 Shenandoah, Joanne, and Douglas M. George-Kanentiio. *Skywoman: Legends of the Iroquois* (4–8). Illus. 1998, Clear Light $14.95 (978-0-940666-99-3). Good writing and effective artwork are combined in this retelling of nine traditional Iroquois tales, including a series of creation stories. (Rev: HBG 10/99; SLJ 2/99) [398.2]

4911 Tingle, Tim. *Spirits Dark and Light: Supernatural Tales from the Five Civilized Tribes* (6–9). 2006, August House $15.95 (978-0-87483-778-0). A collection of 25 Native American folk tales from the southeastern United States that involve supernatural creatures and themes. (Rev: BL 11/1/06; LMC 2/07; SLJ 1/07) [398.2]

4912 Tingle, Tim. *Walking the Choctaw Road* (6–12). 2003, Cinco Puntos $16.95 (978-0-938317-74-6). A collection of stories that convey Choctaw traditions and culture, including experiences on the Trail of Tears. (Rev: BL 6/1–15/03; HBG 4/04; VOYA 2/04) [398.2]

4913 Van Etten, Teresa. *Ways of Indian Magic* (7–12). Illus. 1985, Sunstone paper $8.95 (978-0-86534-061-9). A fine retelling of six legends of the Pueblo Indians. [398.2]

4914 Van Etten, Teresa. *Ways of Indian Wisdom* (7–10). 1987, Sunstone paper $10.95 (978-0-86534-090-9). A collection of 20 Pueblo tales that reflect the Southeastern Indians' culture and customs. [398.2]

4915 Webster, M. L., retel. *On the Trail Made of Dawn: Native American Creation Stories* (4–9). 2001, Linnet LB $19.50 (978-0-208-02497-8). The author retells 13 creation stories and places them in cultural context. (Rev: HBG 3/02; SLJ 12/01) [398.2]

4916 Wolfson, Evelyn. *Inuit Mythology* (5–9). Illus. by William Sauts Bock. Series: Mythology. 2001, Enslow LB $26.60 (978-0-7660-1559-3). Seven tales from Inuit folklore are accompanied by information on the history and culture of the Inuit peoples. (Rev: BL 4/15/02; HBG 3/02; SLJ 3/02) [398.2]

UNITED STATES

4917 Anaya, Rudolfo A. *My Land Sings: Stories from the Rio Grande* (5–9). 1999, Morrow $17.00 (978-0-688-15078-5). A magical collection of 10 stories, set mostly in New Mexico, that deal with Mexican and Native American folklore. (Rev: BL 8/99; HBG 10/00; SLJ 9/99) [398.2]

4918 Avila, Alfred. *Mexican Ghost Tales of the Southwest* (7–9). Ed. by Kat Avila. 1994, Arte Publico paper $9.95 (978-1-55885-107-8). A collection of Mexican tales of ghosts and the spirit world from the Southwest. (Rev: BL 10/1/94; SLJ 9/94; VOYA 4/95) [398.25]

4919 Brown, Marcia. *Backbone of the King: The Story of Paka'a and His Son Ku* (5–7). Illus. by author. 1984, Univ. of Hawaii $19.00 (978-0-8248-0963-8). A reissue of the book based on a Hawaiian legend of a boy who wants to help his exiled father. [398.2]

4920 Cohen, Daniel. *Southern Fried Rat and Other Gruesome Tales* (6–10). Illus. 1989, Avon paper $3.50 (978-0-380-70655-6). A collection of stories — some funny, some grisly — about people living in urban areas today. [398.2]

4921 Hamilton, Virginia. *Her Stories: African American Folktales, Fairy Tales, and True Tales* (5–8). Illus. 1995, Scholastic paper $22.95 (978-0-590-47370-5). Nineteen tales about African American females are retold in the wonderful style of Virginia Hamilton. (Rev: BL 11/1/95*; SLJ 11/95*) [398.2]

4922 Hamilton, Virginia. *The People Could Fly: American Black Folk Tales* (4–9). Illus. by Leo Dillon and Diane Dillon. 1985, Knopf LB $18.99 (978-0-394-96925-1); paper $13.00 (978-0-679-84336-8). A retelling of 24 folktales — some little known, others familiar, such as Tar Baby. (Rev: BCCB 7/85; BL 7/85; SLJ 11/85) [398.2]

4923 Jacobs, Jimmy. *Moonlight Through the Pines: Tales from Georgia Evenings* (5–7). Illus. 2000, Franklin-Sarrett paper $11.95 (978-0-9637477-3-0). A collection of humorous reminiscences, family stories, tall tales, and other examples of folklore, all from the South. (Rev: BL 8/00) [398.2]

4924 Reneaux, J. J. *Cajun Folktales* (6–8). 1992, August House $19.95 (978-0-87483-283-9); paper $11.95 (978-0-87483-282-2). An assortment of Cajun folktales divided into broad groups: animal tales, fairy tales, funny folk tales, and ghost stories. (Rev: BL 9/15/92) [398.2]

4925 Reneaux, J. J. *Haunted Bayou: And Other Cajun Ghost Stories* (4–8). 1994, August House paper $9.95 (978-0-87483-385-0). Thirteen scary, entertaining folktales from Cajun country are retold effectively. (Rev: SLJ 12/94) [398.2]

4926 Rhyne, Nancy. *More Tales of the South Carolina Low Country* (7–9). 1984, Blair paper $9.95 (978-0-89587-042-1). A collection of eerie and unusual folktales. [398.2]

4927 Rounds, Glen. *Ol' Paul, the Mighty Logger* (6–8). Illus. 1976, Holiday paper $5.95 (978-0-8234-0713-2). The colorful saga of the great tall-tale hero of American folklore. [398.2]

4928 Schwartz, Alvin. *More Scary Stories to Tell in the Dark* (4–7). Illus. by Stephen Gammell. 1984, HarperCollins LB $16.89 (978-0-397-32082-0); paper $5.99 (978-0-06-440177-7). Brief tales from folk stories and hearsay with a scary bent. [398.2]

4929 Schwartz, Alvin. *Scary Stories to Tell in the Dark* (6–9). Illus. 1981, HarperCollins LB $16.89 (978-0-397-31927-5). Stories about ghosts and witches that are mostly scary but often also humorous. Continued in *More Scary Stories to Tell in the Dark* (1984). [398.2]

4930 Shepherd, Esther. *Paul Bunyan* (7–10). Illus. 1941, Harcourt paper $6.95 (978-0-15-259755-9). The tall-tale lumberjack is brought to life by the text and the stunning illustrations by Rockwell Kent. [398.2]

South and Central America

4931 Aldana, Patricia, ed. *Jade and Iron: Latin American Tales from Two Cultures* (5–8). Trans. by Hugh Hazelton. Illus. 1996, Douglas & McIntyre $18.95 (978-0-88899-256-7). Fourteen folktales on a variety of subjects and from many regions in Latin America are retold in this large-format picture book. (Rev: BCCB 1/97; BL 12/1/96) [398.2]

4932 Delacre, Lulu, retel. *Golden Tales: Myths, Legends, and Folktales from Latin America* (4–8). Illus. 1996, Scholastic paper $18.95 (978-0-590-48186-1). Twelve important Latin American folktales from before and after the time of Columbus are featured. (Rev: BL 12/15/96; SLJ 9/96) [398.2]

4933 Dorson, Mercedes, and Jeanne Wilmot. *Tales from the Rain Forest: Myths and Legends from the Amazonian Indians of Brazil* (5–8). Illus. 1997, Ecco $18.00 (978-0-88001-567-7). Ten entertaining folktales from the Amazonian Indians of Brazil. (Rev: BL 2/15/98; HB 3–4/98; HBG 10/98) [398.2]

4934 Ehlert, Lois. *Moon Rope: A Peruvian Folktale* (4–8). Illus. 1992, Harcourt $17.00 (978-0-15-255343-2). In both English and Spanish, this is the story of Fox, who wants to go to the moon and persuades his friend Mole to go along. (Rev: BCCB 12/92; BL 10/15/92*; HB 11–12/92; SLJ 10/92*) [398.2]

4935 Kimmel, Eric A. *The Witch's Face: A Mexican Tale* (7–12). Illus. 1993, Holiday $15.95 (978-0-8234-1038-5). Kimmel uses a picture book format for this Mexican tale of a man who rescues his love from becoming a witch, only to lose her to his own doubt. (Rev: BL 11/15/93; SLJ 2/94) [398.22]

4936 Munduruku, Daniel. *Tales of the Amazon: How the Munduruku Indians Live* (5–8). Trans. by Jane Springer. Illus. by Laurabeatriz. 2000, Groundwood $18.95 (978-0-88899-392-2). This is an interesting view of the life of the human inhabitants of the Amazon rain forest with material on lifestyles, houses, languages, myths, and marriage. (Rev: BL 9/1/03; HBG 3/01; SLJ 9/00) [981]

4937 Schuman, Michael A. *Mayan and Aztec Mythology* (6–9). Series: Mythology. 2002, Enslow LB $26.60 (978-0-7660-1409-1). As well as retelling famous myths from the Aztec and Mayan cultures, this account gives good historical background information. (Rev: BL 4/15/02; HBG 10/02) [398.2]

Mythology

General and Miscellaneous

4938 Berk, Ari. *The Runes of Elfland* (7–12). Illus. by Brian Froud. 2003, Abrams $25.00 (978-0-8109-4612-5). Brief stories and wonderful art highlighting the rune's significance and associations accompany each of 24 runes. (Rev: SLJ 5/04; VOYA 2/04) [398.2]

4939 Bingham, Ann. *South and Meso-American Mythology A to Z* (6–12). Series: Mythology A to Z. 2004, Facts on File $40.00 (978-0-8160-4889-2). A handsome and thorough guide to the legends and folklore of early civilizations in Central and South America. (Rev: BL 10/1/04; SLJ 2/05) [398.2]

4940 Bini, Renata. *A World Treasury of Myths, Legends, and Folktales: Stories from Six Continents* (6–9). Illus. 2000, Abrams $24.95 (978-0-8109-4554-8). Stories from around the world are organized geographically in this handsome, large-format volume full of rich illustrations. (Rev: BL 1/1–15/01; HBG 3/01; SLJ 12/00) [291.1]

4941 Boughn, Michael. *Into the World of the Dead: Astonishing Adventures in the Underworld* (5–8). Illus. 2006, Annick LB $24.95 (978-1-55037-959-4); paper $12.95 (978-1-55037-958-7). This illustrated collection of myths and legends from diverse cultures includes a variety of gods, monsters, and heroes who survived travels to the Underworld. (Rev: SLJ 1/07) [398.2]

4942 Dalal, Anita. *Myths of Oceania* (5–8). Series: Mythic World. 2002, Raintree LB $27.12 (978-0-7398-4978-1). Information about Oceania and its people is included as well as 10 myths about the sea, fishing, and other unique aspects of island living. (Rev: BL 7/02; HBG 10/02) [398.3]

4943 Dalal, Anita. *Myths of Russia and the Slavs* (5–8). Series: Mythic World. 2002, Raintree LB $27.12 (978-0-7398-4979-8). This lavishly illustrated, oversize volume contains 10 myths from Eastern Europe as well as material on the society that created them. (Rev: BL 7/02; HBG 10/02; SLJ 5/02) [398.2]

4944 Echlin, Kim. *Inanna: From the Myths of Ancient Sumer* (7–12). Illus. by Linda Wolfsgruber. 2003, Groundwood $19.95 (978-0-88899-496-7). The stories of the powerful goddess Inanna and her adventures in love and war, based on 4,000-year-old sources. (Rev: BL 3/1/04; HBG 4/04; SLJ 3/04; VOYA 12/03) [398.2]

4945 Evslin, Bernard. *Pig's Ploughman* (7–12). Illus. 1990, Chelsea LB $19.95 (978-1-55546-256-7). In Celtic mythology, Pig's Ploughman is the huge hog who fights Finn McCool. (Rev: BL 8/90; SLJ 3/91) [398.2]

4946 Fisher, Leonard Everett. *Gods and Goddesses of the Ancient Maya* (4–7). Illus. 1999, Holiday $16.95 (978-0-8234-1427-7). This book provides a fascinating introduction to Mayan mythology by describing 10 gods and two goddesses. (Rev: BL 2/1/00; HBG 3/00; SLJ 12/99) [299]

4947 Green, Jen. *Myths of China and Japan* (5–8). Series: Mythic World. 2002, Raintree LB $27.12 (978-0-7398-4977-4). This handsome, oversize book explores the ancient mythology of China and Japan and, in addition to the retelling of 10 myths, contains information on the societies that created them. (Rev: BL 7/02; HBG 10/02) [398.2]

4948 Hamilton, Dorothy. *Mythology* (8–12). Illus. 1942, Little, Brown $27.95 (978-0-316-34114-1). An introduction to the mythology of Greece and Scandinavia, plus a retelling of the principal myths. [292]

4949 Harpur, James. *Celtic Myth: A Treasury of Legends, Art, and History* (8–12). Illus. Series: World Mythology. 2007, M.E. Sharpe LB $35.95

(978-0-7656-8102-7). A collection of artifacts of ancient Celtic culture, including myths (some violent), weapons, and artwork. (Rev: BL 12/15/07; LMC 2/08; SLJ 4/08) [299]

4950 Harris, Geraldine. *Gods and Pharaohs from Egyptian Mythology* (5–8). Illus. by David O'Connor and John Sibbick. 1992, Bedrick LB $24.95 (978-0-87226-907-1). A collection of myths and legends from ancient Egypt. [398.2]

4951 January, Brendan. *The New York Public Library Amazing Mythology: A Book of Answers for Kids* (5–8). Illus. 2000, Wiley paper $14.95 (978-0-471-33205-3). This compendium of information covers Middle Eastern, African, Mediterranean, Asian, Pacific, Northern European, and North and Central American mythology. (Rev: BL 11/1/00; SLJ 9/00) [291.1]

4952 Lynch, Patricia Ann. *Native American Mythology A to Z* (6–12). Series: Mythology A to Z. 2004, Facts on File $40.00 (978-0-8160-4891-5). A handsome and thorough guide to Native American legends and folklore. (Rev: BL 10/1/04; SLJ 2/05) [398.2]

4953 Mutén, Burleigh, retel. *The Lady of Ten Thousand Names: Goddess Stories from Many Cultures* (4–7). Illus. by Helen Cann. 2001, Barefoot Bks. $19.99 (978-1-84148-048-0). Eight myths that feature goddesses from cultures around the world are retold in this appealing volume. (Rev: HBG 3/02; SLJ 11/01) [291.2]

4954 Nardo, Don. *Egyptian Mythology* (6–12). Illus. Series: Mythology. 2001, Enslow $26.60 (978-0-7660-1407-7). Eight Egyptian myths are related here, with background historical and cultural information, question-and-answer sections, and commentary from scholars. (Rev: BL 5/15/01; SLJ 5/01) [299]

4955 Philip, Neil. *The Illustrated Book of Myths: Tales and Legends of the World* (5–8). Illus. by Nilesh Mistry. 1995, DK paper $19.99 (978-0-7894-0202-8). Ancient myths from both the Old World and the New World have been collected under such headings as creation, destruction, and fertility. (Rev: BL 12/1/95; SLJ 12/95; VOYA 4/96) [291.1]

4956 Philip, Neil. *Mythology of the World* (8–12). 2004, Houghton $24.95 (978-0-7534-5779-5). An excellent and thorough overview of world mythology, introducing readers to the plots and characters of myth and legend and examining the historical, cultural, and spiritual aspects of mythology. (Rev: BL 12/1/04; SLJ 10/04) [398.2]

4957 Roberts, Jeremy. *Japanese Mythology A to Z* (6–12). Illus. Series: Mythology A to Z. 2003, Facts on File $40.00 (978-0-8160-4871-7). An easy-to-use alphabetically arranged volume introducing important places, practices and rituals, people, crea-

tures, and so forth, with guidance on pronunciation. (Rev: SLJ 4/04) [299]

4958 Ross, Anne. *Druids, Gods and Heroes of Celtic Mythology* (6–10). Illus. 1994, Bedrick LB $24.95 (978-0-87226-918-7); paper $14.95 (978-0-87226-919-4). An oversized book that gives detailed information on Irish and Welsh Celtic mythology as well as material on King Arthur. (Rev: SLJ 2/87) [291.1]

4959 Schomp, Virginia. *The Ancient Egyptians* (5–7). Series: Myths of the World. 2007, Marshall Cavendish LB $22.95 (978-0-7614-2549-6). Schomp provides background information on the myths of ancient Egypt and retells several of the best-known ones; full-color illustrations add to the appeal. (Rev: LMC 3/08; SLJ 1/08)

4960 Schomp, Virginia. *The Native Americans* (5–7). Series: Myths of the World. 2007, Marshall Cavendish LB $22.95 (978-0-7614-2550-2). Schomp provides background information on the myths of the Native Americans and retells several of the best-known ones; full-color illustrations add to the appeal. (Rev: LMC 3/08; SLJ 1/08)

4961 Tchana, Katrin Hyman. *Changing Woman and Her Sisters* (5–8). Illus. by Trina Schart Hyman. 2006, Holiday $18.95 (978-0-8234-1999-9). An illustrated collection of traditional stories about ten goddesses from a variety of lesser-known cultures, including Celtic, ancient Mayan, Shinto, Buddhist, and Navajo. (Rev: BCCB 9/06; BL 6/1–15/06; HB 7–8/06; HBG 10/06; LMC 1/07; SLJ 8/06) [398.2]

4962 Tomlinson, Theresa. *The Moon Riders* (6–9). 2006, HarperCollins $16.99 (978-0-06-084736-4). Myrina, 13, a member of the Moon Riders (a group of warrior women better known as the Amazons), tells about the Trojan War and the role the Moon Riders play as allies to the Trojans. (Rev: BL 11/1/06; SLJ 12/06)

Classical

4963 Aesop. *Aesop's Fables* (7–12). 1988, Scholastic paper $4.50 (978-0-590-43880-3). This is one of many editions of the short moral tales from ancient Greece. (Rev: BCCB 12/00) [398.2]

4964 Cadnum, Michael. *Nightsong: The Legend of Orpheus and Eurydice* (7–10). 2006, Scholastic $16.99 (978-0-439-54535-8). The story of Orpheus traveling to the underworld to bring back his bride, Eurydice, only to lose her is retold as a novel. (Rev: BL 12/15/06; LMC 3/07; SLJ 4/07)

4965 Catran, Ken. *Voyage with Jason* (5–8). 2003, Lothian paper $10.95 (978-0-7344-0151-9). A new twist on the story of Jason and the Argonauts, narrated by a youth who is part of the eventful three-year quest for the Golden Fleece and concentrating on character as well as adventure. (Rev: SLJ 4/04) [398.2]

4966 Curlee, Lynn. *Mythological Creatures: A Classical Bestiary* (4–8). Illus. by author. 2008, Atheneum $17.99 (978-1-4169-1453-2). A beautiful book with dreamy color illustrations of creatures that roam through classical mythology, such as gryphons, the Minotaur, Cerberus, and centaurs; each illustration is accompanied by comments about the creature's part in mythology. (Rev: BL 4/1/08; SLJ 5/08) [292.2]

4967 Daly, Kathleen N. *Greek and Roman Mythology A to Z*. Rev. ed. (6–12). Illus. Series: Mythology A to Z. 2003, Facts on File $40.00 (978-0-8160-5155-7). A newly updated, easy-to-use volume containing more than 500 entries of differing lengths covering places, practices and rituals, people, creatures, and so forth. (Rev: BL 3/1/04; SLJ 4/04; VOYA 6/04) [292]

4968 Evslin, Bernard. *The Adventures of Ulysses: The Odyssey of Homer* (8–12). 1989, Scholastic paper $5.99 (978-0-590-42599-5). A modern retelling of the adventures of Ulysses during the 10 years he wandered after the Trojan War. [292]

4969 Evslin, Bernard. *Anteus* (6–9). Illus. 1988, Chelsea LB $19.95 (978-1-55546-241-3). A retelling of the story of Hercules and his battle against the horrible giant Anteus. Also use by the same author *Hecate* (1988). (Rev: BL 9/1/88) [292]

4970 Evslin, Bernard. *Cerberus* (6–12). Illus. 1987, Chelsea LB $19.95 (978-1-55546-243-7). The story of the three-headed dog in Greek mythology that guards the gates of Hell. Also in this series are *The Dragons of Boeotia* and *Geryon* (both 1987). (Rev: BL 11/15/87; SLJ 1/88) [398.2]

4971 Evslin, Bernard. *The Chimaera* (6–10). Illus. 1987, Chelsea LB $19.95 (978-1-55546-244-4). This ugly, dangerous creature is composed of equal parts lion, goat, and reptile. Another in the series is *The Sirens* (1987). (Rev: BL 3/1/88) [398.2]

4972 Evslin, Bernard. *The Cyclopes* (6–12). Illus. 1987, Chelsea LB $19.95 (978-1-55546-236-9). The story of the ferocious one-eyed monster and how he was blinded by Ulysses. Others in this series about mythical monsters are *Medusa, The Minotaur,* and *Procrustes* (all 1987). (Rev: BL 6/15/87; SLJ 8/87) [398.2]

4973 Evslin, Bernard. *The Furies* (7–12). Illus. 1989, Chelsea LB $19.95 (978-1-55546-249-9). In Greek mythology the Furies were three witches. This retelling also includes the story of Circe, the famous sorceress. (Rev: BL 12/15/89; SLJ 4/90) [398.21]

4974 Evslin, Bernard. *Heroes, Gods and Monsters of Greek Myths* (8–12). Illus. 1984, Bantam paper $5.99 (978-0-553-25920-9). The most popular Greek myths are retold in modern language. (Rev: SLJ 2/06) [292]

4975 Evslin, Bernard. *Ladon* (7–12). Illus. 1990, Chelsea LB $19.95 (978-1-55546-254-3). A splendid retelling of the Greek myth about the sea serpent called up by Hera to fight Hercules. (Rev: BL 8/90) [398.24]

4976 Evslin, Bernard. *The Trojan War: The Iliad of Homer* (8–12). 1988, Scholastic paper $2.95 (978-0-590-41626-9). The story of the 10-year war between the Greeks and the Trojans is retold for the modern reader. [292]

4977 Graves, Robert. *Greek Gods and Heroes* (6–8). 1973, Dell paper $5.50 (978-0-440-93221-5). Tales of 12 of the most important figures in Greek mythology in 27 short chapters. (Rev: SLJ 2/06) [292]

4978 Green, Jen. *Myths of Ancient Greece* (5–8). Illus. Series: Mythic World. 2001, Raintree LB $27.12 (978-0-7398-3191-5). This volume for older readers separates myth from reality about ancient Greece. (Rev: BL 3/1/02; HBG 3/02; SLJ 12/01) [398.2]

4979 Harris, John. *Strong Stuff: Herakles and His Labors* (4–7). Illus. by Gary Baseman. 2005, Getty $16.95 (978-0-89236-784-9). A lively, tongue-in-cheek account of the 12 labors of ancient Greece's mythical strongman, Herakles (known to the ancient Romans as Hercules). (Rev: BL 11/15/05; SLJ 11/05) [398.2]

4980 Hawthorne, Nathaniel. *Wonder Book and Tanglewood Tales* (5–7). 1972, Ohio State Univ. $72.95 (978-0-8142-0158-9). This is a highly original retelling of the Greek myths, originally published in 1853. (Rev: BL 2/15/04; SLJ 4/04) [398.2]

4981 Kindl, Patrice. *Lost in the Labyrinth* (6–10). 2002, Houghton $16.00 (978-0-618-16684-8). Told by Xenodice, a 14-year-old princess and the younger sister of Ariadne, this is an expanded version of the legend of Theseus and the Minotaur. (Rev: BCCB 11/02; BL 1/1–15/03; HB 11–12/02; HBG 3/03; SLJ 11/02; VOYA 2/03)

4982 McCarty, Nick, retel. *The Iliad* (4–8). Illus. by Victor G. Ambrus. 2000, Kingfisher paper $15.95 (978-0-7534-5321-6). This account of the Trojan War uses an exciting text and action-packed illustrations. (Rev: SLJ 1/01) [398.2]

4983 *Odysseus* (4–8). Retold by Geraldine McCaughrean. 2004, Cricket $15.95 (978-0-8126-2721-3). Homer's dramatic story is retold in rhythmic prose. (Rev: BL 12/15/04; SLJ 12/04)

4984 Pickels, Dwayne E. *Roman Myths, Heroes, and Legends* (5–8). Series: Costume, Tradition, and Culture: Reflecting on the Past. 1998, Chelsea $28.00 (978-0-7910-5164-1). Using double-page spreads and old collectors' cards as illustrations, this work retells the major Roman myths and introduces their important characters. (Rev: BL 3/15/99; HBG 10/99) [398.2]

4985 Schomp, Virginia. *The Ancient Greeks* (5–7). Series: Myths of the World. 2007, Marshall Cavendish LB $22.95 (978-0-7614-2547-2). Schomp provides background information on the myths of ancient Greece and retells several of the best-known ones; full-color illustrations add to the appeal. (Rev: LMC 3/08; SLJ 1/08)

4986 Spies, Karen Bornemann. *Heroes in Greek Mythology* (6–9). Series: Mythology. 2002, Enslow LB $26.60 (978-0-7660-1560-9). Through an introduction to the heroes in Greek mythology, many of the most famous myths are retold. (Rev: BL 4/15/02; HBG 10/02) [292]

4987 Spies, Karen Bornemann. *The Iliad and the Odyssey in Greek Mythology* (6–9). Series: Mythology. 2002, Enslow LB $26.60 (978-0-7660-1561-6). The two great epics of Homer are retold with many original illustrations and with useful historical background material. (Rev: BL 12/15/02; HBG 3/03; VOYA 8/03) [292]

4988 Spinner, Stephanie. *Quicksilver* (8–11). 2005, Knopf LB $17.99 (978-0-375-92638-9). Hermes, son of Zeus and quite a character in this incarnation, describes his participation in various well-known myths. (Rev: BCCB 4/05; BL 4/15/05; HB 3–4/05; SLJ 9/05; VOYA 4/05)

4989 Spinner, Stephanie. *Quiver* (7–12). 2002, Knopf LB $17.99 (978-0-375-91489-8). A deft retelling of the Greek myth of Atalanta, who will marry only a man who can outrun her. (Rev: BCCB 2/03; BL 1/1–15/03*; HB 1–2/03; HBG 3/03; SLJ 10/02; VOYA 12/02)

4990 Usher, Kerry. *Heroes, Gods and Emperors from Roman Mythology* (8–12). Illus. 1992, NTC LB $24.95 (978-0-87226-909-5). The origins of Roman mythology are given, accompanying retellings of famous myths. [292]

4991 Woff, Richard. *A Pocket Dictionary of Greek and Roman Gods and Goddesses* (4–8). 2003, Getty $9.95 (978-0-89236-706-1). Varied reproductions from the British Museum add visual appeal to this brief who's who. (Rev: SLJ 2/04) [292.2]

4992 Wolfson, Evelyn. *Roman Mythology* (6–9). Series: Mythology. 2002, Enslow LB $26.60 (978-0-7660-1558-6). This is a general introduction to Roman mythology with a retelling of the major stories and an introduction to important characters. (Rev: BL 12/15/02; HBG 3/03) [398]

Scandinavian

4993 Coville, Bruce. *Thor's Wedding Day* (4–7). 2005, Harcourt $15.00 (978-0-15-201455-1). A hilarious retelling of an ancient Norse poem, in which Thor's goat boy describes how he helped Thor to retrieve his stolen magic hammer. (Rev: BL 8/05) [398.2]

4994 Daly, Kathleen N. *Norse Mythology A to Z*. Rev. ed. (6–12). Illus. Series: Mythology A to Z. 2003, Facts on File $40.00 (978-0-8160-5156-4). A newly updated, easy-to-use volume containing approximately 400 entries covering places, practices and rituals, people, creatures, and so forth. (Rev: BL 3/1/04; SLJ 4/04; VOYA 6/04) [292.1]

4995 Schomp, Virginia. *The Norsemen* (5–7). Series: Myths of the World. 2007, Marshall Cavendish LB $22.95 (978-0-7614-2548-9). Schomp provides background information on the myths of Scandinavia and retells several of the best-known ones; full-color illustrations add to the appeal. (Rev: LMC 3/08; SLJ 1/08)

Humor and Satire

4996 Mash, Robert. *How to Keep Dinosaurs*. Rev. ed. (7–12). Illus. 2003, Weidenfeld & Nicolson $14.99 (978-0-297-84347-4). A tongue-in-cheek cleverly illustrated guide to the selection and care of your own pet prehistoric animal. (Rev: SLJ 4/04; VOYA 8/04)

4997 Schulz, Charles M. *The Complete Peanuts: 1961 to 1962* (7–12). Illus. 2006, Fantagraphics $28.95 (978-1-56097-672-1). This collection of comic strips from the early 1960s includes well-known episodes: Linus and the Great Pumpkin, Lucy pulling the football away from Charlie Brown, Schroeder's celebration of Beethoven's birthday, and the baseball team's defeats; just one of a series of *Peanuts* volumes. (Rev: BL 11/1/06)

Speeches, Essays, and General Literary Works

4998 Davis, Jill, ed. *Open Your Eyes: Extraordinary Experiences in Faraway Places* (8–12). 2003, Viking $16.99 (978-0-670-03616-5). Ten writers, among them Lois Lowry and Harry Mazer, tell stories about how travel changed their lives. (Rev: BL 1/1–15/04; HBG 4/04; SLJ 1/04; VOYA 4/04) [910.4]

4999 Halliburton, Warren J., ed. *Historic Speeches of African Americans* (7–12). Series: African American Experience. 1993, Watts LB $24.00 (978-0-531-11034-8). Chronologically organized speeches by such leaders as Sojourner Truth, Frederick Douglass, Marcus Garvey, James Baldwin, Angela Davis, and Jesse Jackson. (Rev: BL 4/15/93; SLJ 7/93) [815]

5000 *Lines in the Sand: New Writing on War and Peace* (6–10). 2003, Disinformation paper $7.95 (978-0-9729529-1-0). More than 150 children from around the world have written essays, stories, and memoirs or drawn pictures calling for peace. (Rev: BL 2/1/04) [808.803]

5001 McIntire, Suzanne, ed. *The American Heritage Book of Great American Speeches for Young People* (7–12). 2001, Wiley paper $14.95 (978-0-471-38942-2). More than 100 key speeches by individuals ranging from politicians to athletes are provided in this single volume. (Rev: SLJ 12/01) [815.008]

5002 *Merlyn's Pen: Fiction, Essays, and Poems by American Teens* (6–12). Illus. 2001, Merlyn's Pen paper $15.95 (978-1-886427-50-1). This annual anthology of teen writings offers selected poetry, fiction, and essays written by students in middle school and high school. (Rev: VOYA 8/01)

5003 Meyer, Stephanie H., and John Meyer, eds. *Teen Ink: Friends and Family* (6–12). 2001, Health Communications paper $12.95 (978-1-55874-931-3). This collection of fiction, poetry, and essays written by young people that appeared in *Teen Ink* magazine is organized by themes such as "Snapshots: Friends and Family" and "Out of Focus: Facing Challenges." (Rev: BL 1/1–15/02; SLJ 12/01) [810.8]

5004 Meyer, Stephanie H., and John Meyer, eds. *Teen Ink: Love and Relationships* (6–12). 2002, Health Communications paper $12.95 (978-1-55874-969-6). In this collection of poems, essays, and photographs, teens give voice to their thoughts about love in all its many forms. (Rev: SLJ 8/02; VOYA 8/02) [810.8]

5005 Meyer, Stephanie H., and John Meyer, eds. *Teen Ink 2: More Voices, More Visions* (6–12). 2001, Health Communications paper $12.95 (978-1-55874-913-9). This collection of teen creativity includes poems, essays, short stories, and photographs that reflect their views on such themes as Family, Love, Friends, Challenges, Imagination, Fitting In, Memories, and School Days. (Rev: SLJ 8/01; VOYA 12/01)

5006 Rosen, Roger, and Patra McSharry, eds. *East-West: The Landscape Within* (7–12). Series: World Issues. 1992, Rosen LB $21.95 (978-0-8239-1375-6); paper $11.95 (978-0-8239-1376-3). Short stories and nonfiction selections by diverse authors of varied nationalities on their cultures' beliefs and values, among them the Dalai Lama, Joseph Campbell, Lydia Minatoya, and Aung Aung Taik. (Rev: BL 12/15/92; SLJ 2/93) [909]

5007 Sedaris, David. *Dress Your Family in Corduroy and Denim* (8–12). 2004, Little, Brown $24.95 (978-0-316-14346-2). In this collection of 27 essays, David Sedaris mines humor from a series of incidents in his personal life, some of which were not at all funny when they happened. (Rev: SLJ 1/05) [813]

5008 Stone, Miriam. *At the End of Words: A Daughter's Memoir* (6–12). 2003, Candlewick $14.00 (978-0-7636-1854-4). Moving poetry and narrative describe the author's grief and emotional upheaval over her mother's death from cancer. (Rev: BL 4/15/03; HBG 10/03; SLJ 5/03; VOYA 12/03) [362.1]

5009 WritersCorps Youth. *Smart Mouth: Poetry and Prose by WritersCorps Youth* (7–12). 2000, San Francisco WritersCorps paper $12.95 (978-1-888048-05-6). This anthology offers multiple selections of both prose and poetry written by students who participated in the WritersCorps program. (Rev: VOYA 6/01)

Literary History and Criticism

Fiction

General and Miscellaneous

5010 Barlowe, Wayne Douglas, and Neil Duskis. *Barlowe's Guide to Fantasy* (7–12). Illus. 1996, HarperCollins paper $19.95 (978-0-06-100817-7). Using double-page spreads, this handsome book covers the history of fantasy literature from ancient times to the present by highlighting 50 examples, among them *Beowulf, Wind in the Willows,* and *Mists of Avalon.* (Rev: VOYA 10/97)

5011 Miller, Ron. *The History of Science Fiction* (6–10). Illus. 2001, Watts LB $30.00 (978-0-531-11866-5). An enticing overview of the genre, its development, recurring themes, primary authors, TV and movie presentations, and most important awards. (Rev: BL 7/01; SLJ 7/01; VOYA 6/02) [809.3]

5012 Rainey, Richard. *The Monster Factory* (6–12). 1993, Macmillan LB $19.00 (978-0-02-775663-0). A discussion of seven famous monster-story writers and their most-loved works. (Rev: BL 8/93; VOYA 10/93) [809.3]

5013 Reid, Suzanne Elizabeth. *Presenting Young Adult Science Fiction* (7–12). Series: Twayne's United States Authors. 1998, Twayne $35.00 (978-0-8057-1653-5). This comprehensive introduction to science fiction describes the history of the genre, profiles such classical masters as Asimov, Bradbury, Heinlein, and Le Guin, and presents members of the new generation, among them Orson Scott Card, Pamela Service, Piers Anthony, and Douglas Adams. (Rev: SLJ 6/99) [808.3]

5014 Rovin, Jeff. *Aliens, Robots, and Spaceships* (7–12). Illus. 1995, Facts on File $38.50 (978-0-8160-3107-8). Alphabetically arranged entries on characters, creatures, and places in the world of sci-ence fiction, with more than 100 black-and-white illustrations. (Rev: SLJ 12/95; VOYA 4/96) [813]

5015 Smith, Lucinda I. *Women Who Write, Vol. 2* (8–12). 1994, Messner $15.00 (978-0-671-87253-3). Interviews and short biographies of contemporary women writers, including Margaret Atwood and Sue Grafton. Addresses the desire to write and provides tips for aspiring authors. (Rev: BL 10/15/94; SLJ 11/94; VOYA 12/94) [809.8]

Europe

Great Britain and Ireland

5016 Beahm, George. *Muggles and Magic: J. K. Rowling and the Harry Potter Phenomenon* (7–12). Illus. 2004, Hampton Roads paper $16.95 (978-1-57174-412-8). An impressive collection of information about the boy-wizard, his world, and his creator, J. K. Rowling. (Rev: SLJ 2/05)

5017 Bloom, Harold, ed. *Charlotte Brontë's Jane Eyre* (8–12). Series: Bloom's Notes. 1996, Chelsea LB $21.95 (978-0-7910-4063-8). In addition to a collection of critical essays on *Jane Eyre,* there is a biography of the author, a plot summary, and character sketches. (Rev: BL 1/1–15/97; SLJ 4/97) [823]

5018 Brontë, Charlotte. *Jane Eyre* (8–12). Series: Case Studies in Contemporary Criticism. 1964, Airmont paper $4.95 (978-0-8049-0017-1). An author biography is accompanied by brief critical comments, plot and theme analysis, and a list of characters.

5019 Brown, Alan. *The Story Behind George Orwell's Animal Farm* (6–9). Series: History in Literature. 2006, Heinemann LB $32.86 (978-1-4034-8203-7). Brown introduces readers to Orwell's life, times, and influences. (Rev: SLJ 2/07)

5020 Swisher, Clarice. *Understanding The Canterbury Tales* (8–12). Series: Understanding Great Literature. 2003, Gale LB $29.95 (978-1-56006-782-5). Background on Chaucer and medieval life precedes discussion of the themes, characters, and literary devices found in the tales. (Rev: SLJ 1/04) [821]

United States

5021 Bernard, Catherine. *Understanding To Kill a Mockingbird* (7–10). Series: Understanding Great Literature. 2003, Gale LB $29.95 (978-1-56006-860-0). Provides a biography of Harper Lee, historical background, and discussion of the plot and characters in addition to study questions and quotations from reviews and articles. (Rev: SLJ 3/04) [813]

5022 Bloom, Harold, ed. *Maya Angelou's I Know Why the Caged Bird Sings* (8–12). Series: Bloom's Notes. 1996, Chelsea LB $30.00 (978-0-7910-3666-2). A collection of critical essays on this work by Maya Angelou, plus a detailed analysis of the book and its characters, accompanied by material on the author's life. (Rev: BL 1/1–15/97; SLJ 3/97) [818]

5023 Cart, Michael. *Presenting Robert Lipsyte* (8–12). 1995, Twayne $29.00 (978-0-8057-4151-3). A probing look at Lipsyte's life and work. (Rev: BL 6/1–15/95; VOYA 6/96) [813]

5024 Crowe, Chris. *Presenting Mildred D. Taylor* (6–12). Illus. Series: United States Authors. 1999, Twayne $39.00 (978-0-8057-1687-0). As well as some biographical material, this book gives an analysis of Taylor's works, their historical context, and a history of racism and the civil rights movement in Mississippi. (Rev: BL 2/15/00; VOYA 6/00) [813]

5025 Curry, Barbara K., and James Michael Brodie. *Sweet Words So Brave: The Story of African American Literature* (5–8). Illus. 1996, Zino $24.95 (978-1-55933-179-1). An outline of African American literature, from slave narratives to the great writers of today, such as Nikki Giovanni and Toni Morrison. (Rev: BL 2/15/97*; SLJ 4/97) [810.9]

5026 Diorio, Mary Ann L. *A Student's Guide to Nathaniel Hawthorne* (7–10). Series: Understanding Literature. 2004, Enslow LB $27.93 (978-0-7660-

2283-6). The plot, characters, themes, and literary devices found in Hawthorne's works are discussed, and there are details of his life and major influences. (Rev: SLJ 6/04) [813]

5027 Johnson-Feelings, Dianne. *Presenting Laurence Yep* (8–12). 1995, Twayne $35.00 (978-0-8057-8201-1). A biocritical study that uses material from the Chinese American's autobiography, *The Lost Garden*. (Rev: BL 12/15/95) [813]

5028 MacRae, Cathi Dunn. *Presenting Young Adult Fantasy Fiction* (7–12). 1998, Twayne $35.00 (978-0-8057-8220-2). An excellent survey of current writers of fantasy plus in-depth interviews with Terry Brooks, Barbara Hambly, Jane Yolen, and Meredith Ann Pierce. (Rev: BL 1/1–15/99; VOYA 8/98) [813]

5029 Newman, Gerald, and Eleanor Newman Layfield. *A Student's Guide to John Steinbeck* (8–12). Series: Understanding Literature. 2004, Enslow LB $27.93 (978-0-7660-2259-1). This guide examines the writer's life as well as the characters, themes, and symbolism found in his novels. (Rev: SLJ 3/05) [813]

5030 Pingelton, Timothy J. *A Student's Guide to Ernest Hemingway* (7–12). Series: Understanding Literature. 2005, Enslow LB $27.93 (978-0-7660-2431-1). Introduces Hemingway's life and works, with analysis of some of his best-known writings. (Rev: SLJ 10/05) [813]

5031 *A Student's Guide to Jack London* (7–12). Illus. Series: Understanding Literature. 2007, Enslow LB $20.95 (978-0-7660-2707-7). Provides summaries and critical analysis of London's most famous books as well as information on his life and beliefs. (Rev: BL 9/1/07) [813]

5032 Vickers, Rebecca. *The Story Behind Mark Twain's The Adventures of Huckleberry Finn* (6–9). Series: History in Literature. 2006, Heinemann LB $32.86 (978-1-4034-8206-8). Vickers introduces readers to Twain's life, times, and influences. (Rev: SLJ 2/07)

5033 Williams, Brian. *The Story Behind John Steinbeck's Of Mice and Men* (6–9). Series: History in Literature. 2006, Heinemann LB $32.86 (978-1-4034-8207-5). Williams introduces readers to Steinbeck's life, times, and influences. (Rev: SLJ 2/07)

Plays and Poetry

General and Miscellaneous

5034 Adoff, Jaime. *The Song Shoots out of My Mouth: A Celebration of Music* (6–9). Illus. by Martin French. 2002, Dutton $17.99 (978-0-525-46949-0). Colorful illustrations accompany free-verse poems celebrating music from classical and jazz to reggae and hip hop. (Rev: BL 1/1–15/03; HBG 3/03; SLJ 10/02; VOYA 4/03) [811.6]

5035 Deutsch, Babette. *Poetry Handbook: A Dictionary of Terms*. 4th ed. (7–12). 1981, Barnes & Noble paper $14.00 (978-0-06-463548-6). The standard introduction to the technical aspects of poetry through definitions of terms with examples. [808.1]

5036 Lithgow, John, ed. *The Poet's Corner: The One-and-Only Poetry Book for the Whole Family* (7–12). 2007, Grand Central $24.99 (978-0-446-58002-1). Well-known poems by English and American poets are accompanied by conversational commentary, quotations, and other items of interest. (Rev: BL 10/15/07) [821.008] 🔊

5037 Vecchione, Patrice, ed. *The Body Eclectic: An Anthology of Poems* (8–12). 2002, Holt $16.95 (978-0-8050-6935-8). A collection of poems, both contemporary and classic, that look at parts of the body from serious, comic, tragic, reflective, and romantic points of view. (Rev: BL 7/02; HB 7–8/02; HBG 10/02; SLJ 8/02; VOYA 8/02) [808.81]

Europe

Shakespeare

5038 Allison, Amy. *Shakespeare's Globe* (7–10). Series: Building History. 1999, Lucent LB $27.45 (978-1-56006-526-5). The story of the theater built on the south bank of the Thames in London by Shakespeare and his partners and how this building became a landmark in theatrical history. (Rev: BL 10/15/99; HBG 9/00; SLJ 2/00) [822.3]

5039 Birch, Beverley, retel. *Shakespeare's Stories: Comedies* (5–9). Illus. 1990, Bedrick paper $6.95 (978-0-87226-225-6). This is the first of three volumes that retell in attractive, straightforward prose the most popular of his plays. The others are *Shakespeare's Stories: Histories* and *Shakespeare's Stories: Tragedies* (both 1988). (Rev: BL 2/15/89; SLJ 2/89) [813]

5040 Greenhill, Wendy, and Paul Wignall. *Macbeth*. Rev. ed. (6–9). Series: Shakespeare Library. 2006, Heinemann LB $29.29 (978-1-4034-8606-6). Information on *Macbeth* is abundant in this slim book, covering the plot, characters, historical background, actors' viewpoints, themes, and past productions; it also includes illustrations and photographs of recent plays. Also use *Romeo and Juliet* and *A Midsummer Night's Dream* (both 2006). (Rev: SLJ 8/06)

5041 Olster, Fredi, and Rick Hamilton. *A Midsummer Night's Dream: A Workbook for Students* (8–12). Series: Discovering Shakespeare. 1996, Smith & Kraus paper $19.95 (978-1-57525-042-7). The text of the play is presented in a double-page, four-column format that provides stage directions, scene description, and the original text, plus a version in the vernacular. Supplemental background material is also appended. (Rev: BL 1/1–15/97; SLJ 12/96; VOYA 2/97) [822.3]

5042 Olster, Fredi, and Rick Hamilton. *Romeo and Juliet: A Workbook for Students* (8–12). Series: Discovering Shakespeare. 1996, Smith & Kraus paper $19.95 (978-1-57525-044-1). This Shakespearean tragedy is presented in a four-column format that gives the original text, stage directions, scene descriptions, and a reworking into modern English. (Rev: BL 1/1–15/97; VOYA 2/97) [822.3]

5043 Olster, Fredi, and Rick Hamilton. *The Taming of the Shrew* (7–12). Series: Discovering Shakespeare. 1997, Smith & Kraus paper $19.95 (978-1-57525-046-5). This guide to Shakespeare's comedy uses a paraphrased text opposite the original script with details on stage directions. (Rev: BL 2/15/97; SLJ 6/97; VOYA 2/97) [822.3]

5044 Page, Philip, and Marilyn Pettit, eds. *Romeo and Juliet* (8–11). Illus. Series: Picture This! Shakespeare. 2005, Barron's paper $7.99 (978-0-7641-3144-8). This attractive title uses both straight text and cartoon characters to present not only the full text of Shakespeare's tragic romance but also notes on devices and related information. (Rev: BL 3/15/05; SLJ 9/05) [745.1]

5045 Thrasher, Thomas. *Romeo and Juliet* (7–12). Series: Understanding Great Literature. 2001, Lucent $27.45 (978-1-56006-787-0). After introducing the life and times of Shakespeare, this work discusses, in depth, the background, plot, characters, and themes of this classic play. (Rev: BL 8/01; SLJ 6/01) [822.3]

United States

5046 Borus, Audrey. *A Student's Guide to Emily Dickinson* (7–12). Series: Understanding Literature. 2005, Enslow LB $27.93 (978-0-7660-2285-0). Introduces Dickinson's life and poetry, with discussion of key themes, how to analyze the poems, and a glossary of terms. (Rev: SLJ 10/05) [813]

5047 Bush, Valerie Chow, ed. *Believe Me, I Know: Poetry and Photographs by WritersCorps Youth* (6–12). Illus. 2002, WritersCorps paper $14.95 (978-1-888048-08-7). These poems and photographs dealing with a wide range of subjects were created during a WritersCorps workshop attended by a multicultural group of students. (Rev: BL 8/02; SLJ 11/02*; VOYA 12/02) [811]

5048 Dunkleberger, Amy. *A Student's Guide to Arthur Miller* (7–12). Series: Understanding Literature. 2005, Enslow LB $27.93 (978-0-7660-2432-8). Combines biographical information and discussion of Miller's key works. (Rev: SLJ 10/05) [813]

5049 MacGowan, Christopher, ed. *Poetry for Young People: William Carlos Williams* (6–12). Illus. by Robert Crockett. 2004, Sterling $14.95 (978-1-4027-0006-4). Thirty-one poems by Williams plus biographical and critical material are included in this excellent collection. (Rev: BL 3/1/04) [811]

Language and Communication

Signs and Symbols

5050 Ferry, Joseph. *The American Flag* (5–7). Series: American Symbols and Their Meanings. 2002, Mason Crest LB $18.95 (978-1-59084-026-9). Designs that preceded the familiar flag accompany material on Betsy Ross and Francis Scott Key, illustrations of important flag raisings, and discussion of proper use and treatment of the flag, all in a package that will appeal to reluctant readers. (Rev: SLJ 4/02) [929.9]

5051 Radlauer, Ruth. *Honor the Flag: A Guide to Its Care and Display* (4–7). Illus. by J. J. Smith-Moore. 1992, Forest LB $14.95 (978-1-878363-61-9). Lots of information about the American flag and its care. (Rev: BL 10/15/92) [929.92]

5052 Warner, Penny. *Signing Fun: American Sign Language Vocabulary, Phrases, Games and Activities* (4–8). Illus. by Paula Gray. 2006, Gallaudet Univ. paper $19.95 (978-1-56368-292-6). This fun-filled introduction to American Sign Language introduces the basic vocabulary of ASL and offers a wide selection of related games and puzzles. (Rev: SLJ 12/06) [419]

5053 Williams, Earl P. *What You Should Know About the American Flag* (4–8). Illus. 1989, Thomas paper $5.95 (978-0-939631-10-0). A comprehensive guide to facts and legends, history and traditions concerning the U.S. flag. (Rev: BL 11/15/87) [929.9]

5054 Woods, Mary B., and Michael Woods. *Ancient Communication: From Grunts to Graffiti* (5–8). Series: Ancient Technologies. 2000, Runestone LB $25.26 (978-0-8225-2996-5). Beginning with cave paintings and hieroglyphics and ending with modern alphabets and universal languages, this account of the history of communication emphasizes ancient cultures. (Rev: BL 9/15/00; HBG 3/01; SLJ 1/01) [652]

Words and Languages

5055 *The Art of Reading: Forty Illustrators Celebrate RIF's 40th Anniversary* (7–10). Illus. 2005, Dutton $19.99 (978-0-525-47484-5). To mark Reading Is Fundamental's 40th birthday, 40 illustrators choose a favorite children's book, talk about its importance, and create an image that captures the spirit of the book; a large, attractive volume. (Rev: BL 7/05; SLJ 8/05*) [745.6]

5056 Bailey, LaWanda. *Miss Myrtle Frag, the Grammar Nag* (5–9). Illus. by Brian Strassburg. 2000, Absey paper $13.95 (978-1-888842-19-7). A clever book that explains key grammar rules through a series of witty letters from Miss Myrtle Frag. (Rev: SLJ 2/01) [415]

5057 Baker, Rosalie. *In a Word: 750 Words and Their Fascinating Stories and Origins* (4–8). Illus. by Tom Lopes. 2003, Cobblestone $17.95 (978-0-8126-2710-7). Useful for reference, this guide to the origins and meanings of words and phrases is drawn from a monthly column in *Cobblestone*. (Rev: BL 2/15/04; SLJ 4/04) [422]

5058 Casagrande, June. *Grammar Snobs Are Great Big Meanies: A Guide to Language for Fun and Spite* (8–12). 2006, Penguin paper $14.00 (978-0-14-303683-8). A lighthearted review of the rules of grammar, from prepositions and split infinitives to new conventions for e-mail and text messaging. (Rev: BL 4/1/06) [428]

5059 Cooper, Kay. *Why Do You Speak as You Do? A Guide to World Languages* (5–8). Illus. by Brandon Kruse. 1992, Children's LB $14.85 (978-0-8027-8165-9). A simple yet lively presentation of linguistics. (Rev: BCCB 2/93; BL 1/15/93) [400]

5060 Cox, Brenda S. *Who Talks Funny? A Book About Languages for Kids* (7–12). 1995, Linnet LB $25.00 (978-0-208-02378-0). Explores the importance of learning other languages, describes the development of languages and common elements, and provides interesting information, such as how to say the days of the week in 27 languages. (Rev: BL 7/95; SLJ 4/95) [400]

5061 Edwards, Wallace. *Monkey Business* (4–8). Illus. 2004, Kids Can $16.95 (978-1-55337-462-6). Whimsical artwork introduces such common idioms as "opening a can of worms" and "a bull in a china shop"; readers will also enjoy looking for hidden monkeys. (Rev: BL 11/1/04; SLJ 9/04*) [423]

5062 Espinasse, Kristin. *Words in a French Life: Lessons in Love and Language from the South of France* (7–12). 2006, Simon & Schuster $18.00 (978-0-7432-8728-9). Beef up French vocabulary with this collection of amusing stories by an American living in France combined with useful lists of words and phrases. (Rev: BL 4/15/06) [305.81]

5063 *In Few Words / En Pocas Palabras: A Compendium of Latino Folk Wit and Wisdom* (6–12). Trans. by Jose A. Burciaga. 1996, Mercury House paper $14.95 (978-1-56279-093-6). This bilingual collection features popular sayings, proverbs, maxims, and adages that permeate Hispanic culture. (Rev: VOYA 6/97) [468.1]

5064 Johnson, Stephen T. *Alphabet City* (4–7). Illus. 1995, Viking $16.99 (978-0-670-85631-2). A sophisticated alphabet book that consists of a series of paintings, each of which represents a letter. (Rev: BCCB 11/95; BL 1/1–15/96; HB 11–12/95; SLJ 1/96*) [421]

5065 Lederer, Richard. *The Circus of Words: Acrobatic Anagrams, Parading Palindromes, Wonderful Words on a Wire, and More Lively Letter Play* (5–8). Illus. by Dave Morice. 2001, Chicago Review paper $12.95 (978-1-55652-380-9). Lovers of words will find lots of entertainment in this selection of challenging exercises. (Rev: SLJ 8/01) [428.1]

5066 Schwartz, Alvin. *Chin Music: Tall Talk and Other Talk* (7–9). Illus. 1979, HarperCollins LB $12.89 (978-0-397-31870-4). A collection of folk words and their meanings. [410]

5067 Shields, Carol Diggory. *English, Fresh Squeezed! 40 Thirst-for-Knowledge-Quenching Poems* (4–7). Illus. by Tony Ross. Series: Brain-Juice. 2005, Handprint $14.95 (978-1-59354-053-1). A humorous, rhyming look at annoying grammatical and other rules of language, with appealing illustrations and useful mnemonic devices. (Rev: BL 2/15/04; HB 5–6/04; SLJ 5/05)

5068 Terban, Marvin. *Building Your Vocabulary* (4–8). Illus. Series: Scholastic Guides. 2002, Scholastic paper $12.95 (978-0-439-28561-2). In addition to techniques for increasing vocabulary, Terban discusses etymology and how to use a dictionary and thesaurus, giving clear, often entertaining examples throughout. (Rev: SLJ 8/02) [428.1]

5069 Terban, Marvin. *The Dove Dove: Funny Homograph Riddles* (4–7). Illus. by Tom Huffman. 1988, Houghton paper $7.95 (978-0-89919-810-1).

Making homographs less puzzling. Also use *Mad As a Wet Hen! and Other Funny Idioms* (1987). (Rev: BL 1/1/89) [818.5402]

5070 Vinton, Ken. *Alphabetic Antics: Hundreds of Activities to Challenge and Enrich Letter Learners of All Ages* (5–8). Illus. 1996, Free Spirit paper $19.95 (978-1-57542-008-0). For each letter of the alphabet, there is a history, how it appears in different alphabets, important words that begin with the letter, a quotation from someone whose name starts with it, and a number of interesting related projects. (Rev: SLJ 1/97) [411]

5071 Wilbur, Richard. *Opposites* (5–7). Illus. by author. 1991, Harcourt $11.95 (978-0-15-258720-8). Through verses and cartoonlike illustrations, antonyms are given for a series of words. [811.52]

5072 Young, Ed. *Voices of the Heart* (4–8). Illus. 1997, Scholastic paper $17.95 (978-0-590-50199-6). In this sumptuous picture book, the author lists and explains 26 Chinese characters, each of which expresses a different emotion. (Rev: BCCB 4/97; BL 4/15/97; HB 5–6/97; SLJ 6/97) [179]

Writing and the Media

General and Miscellaneous

5073 Bauer, Marion Dane. *Our Stories: A Fiction Workshop for Young Authors* (6–10). 1996, Clarion paper $6.95 (978-0-395-81599-1). Using critiques of 30 selections by students, the author explores such writing techniques as character development, dialogue, and point of view. (Rev: BL 10/15/96; SLJ 12/96; VOYA 12/96) [808.3]

5074 Bush, Valerie Chow, ed. *Jump: Poetry and Prose by WritersCorps Youth* (6–12). 2001, WritersCorps Bks. $12.95 (978-1-888048-06-3). This collection of prose and poetry showcases the creativity of teenage members of the San Francisco-based WritersCorps youth writing program. (Rev: VOYA 6/02)

5075 Currie, Stephen, ed. *Terrorism* (7–10). Illus. Series: Writing the Critical Essay. 2005, Gale LB $29.95 (978-0-7377-3206-1). Opposing viewpoints on terrorism are combined with tips for writing a succinct essay on the subject. (Rev: BL 3/1/06) [363.32]

5076 Donoughue, Carol. *The Story of Writing* (4–7). Illus. 2007, Firefly $19.95 (978-1-55407-306-1). From early alphabets through tablets and scrolls, illuminated manuscripts, and the printing press, this is an appealing introduction to the development of writing. (Rev: BL 1/1–15/08) [411.09]

5077 Farrell, Tish. *Write Your Own Fantasy Story* (4–8). Series: Write Your Own. 2006, Compass Point LB $33.26 (978-0-7565-1639-0). Covering characters, viewpoint, plot, and speech, this is a helpful guide to writing fantasy literature. Also use *Write Your Own Mystery Story* and *Write Your Own Science Fiction Story* (both 2006). (Rev: SLJ 8/06) [808.3]

5078 Francis, Barbara. *Other People's Words: What Plagiarism Is and How to Avoid It* (6–12). Series: Issues in Focus Today. 2005, Enslow LB $31.93 (978-0-7660-2525-7). Practical suggestions about avoiding plagiarism are accompanied by examples of plagiarism through history and current instances of "borrowing" ideas and words. (Rev: SLJ 12/05)

5079 Harper, Timothy, and Elizabeth Harper. *Your Name in Print: A Teen's Guide to Publishing for Fun, Profit and Academic Success* (8–12). 2005, St. Martin's paper $13.95 (978-0-312-33759-9). The Harpers (father and daughter) offer alternating how-to advice on writing and getting published in a variety of formats. (Rev: BL 9/1/05; SLJ 11/05; VOYA 8/05) [808]

5080 Jean, Georges. *Writing: The Story of Alphabets and Scripts* (7–12). Series: Discoveries. 1992, Abrams paper $12.95 (978-0-8109-2893-0). Traces the beginnings of writing from the development of alphabets to printing and bookmaking, emphasizing the technological rather than intellectual aspects of the process. (Rev: BL 7/92) [652.1]

5081 Levine, Gail Carson. *Writing Magic: Creating Stories That Fly* (5–10). 2006, HarperCollins $16.99 (978-0-06-051961-2); paper $5.99 (978-0-06-051960-5). Well-known author Levine provides upbeat, practical tips on such topics as finding story ideas, character and plot development, and investigating the possibility of publication. (Rev: BL 12/15/06; SLJ 2/07*) [808.3]

5082 Otfinoski, Steven. *Extraordinary Short Story Writing* (5–8). Illus. by Kevin Pope. Series: F. W. Prep. 2005, Watts LB $31.00 (978-0-531-16760-1). Tips and activities reinforce the information on writing different types of stories, choosing ideas, and using available resources effectively; a sample short story offers step-by-step guidance. (Rev: SLJ 2/06) [808]

5083 Rivera, Shelia. *The Media War* (5–8). Illus. Series: World in Conflict. 2004, ABDO LB $25.65 (978-1-59197-418-5). A brief overview of American journalism's impact on war from the Civil War to the U.S. invasion of Afghanistan. (Rev: BL 4/1/04) [070.1]

5084 Roy, Jennifer Rozines. *You Can Write a Story or Narrative* (4–8). Illus. Series: You Can Write! 2003, Enslow LB $22.60 (978-0-7660-2085-6). Sound advice for plotting and writing a wide array of different narratives, including adventure, history, fantasy, and folklore. (Rev: SLJ 1/04; VOYA 4/04) [808]

5085 Senn, Joyce. *The Young People's Book of Quotations* (5–10). 1999, Millbrook LB $39.90 (978-0-7613-0267-4). Beginning with "accomplishment" and ending with "zoos," this is a collection of 2,000 quotations of special interest to young people, arranged by topic. (Rev: BL 3/1/99*; SLJ 4/99) [082]

5086 Trueit, Trudi Strain. *Keeping a Journal* (4–8). Illus. 2004, Watts LB $20.50 (978-0-531-12262-4). Trueit encourages readers to keep journals, offering tips on getting started, writing prompts and exercises, a calendar of ideas, and alternatives for those who don't enjoy writing, such as scrapbooks and drawing. (Rev: BL 10/15/03; SLJ 3/05) [808]

5087 Van Allsburg, Chris. *The Mysteries of Harris Burdick* (7–9). Illus. 1984, Houghton LB $18.95 (978-0-395-35393-6). Fourteen drawings and captions invite the reader to write stories that explain them. (Rev: BL 9/86) [808]

5088 Wolf, Allan. *Immersed in Verse: An Informative, Slightly Irreverent and Totally Tremendous Guide to Living the Poet's Life* (6–12). Illus. by Tuesday Mourning. 2006, Sterling LB $14.95 (978-1-57990-628-3). A humorous and inspirational guide for young people interested in writing poetry, this is full of helpful tips and ends with useful appendixes. (Rev: SLJ 6/06*)

Books and Publishing

5089 *Dear Author: Students Write About the Books That Changed Their Lives* (5–9). 1995, Conari paper $9.95 (978-1-57324-003-1). A collection of young adults' letters to authors, both dead and alive, expressing, with wit and honesty, how the authors' books have affected them. (Rev: BL 1/1–15/96; SLJ 11/95) [028.5]

5090 Garcia, John. *The Success of Hispanic Magazine* (7–10). Illus. Series: Success. 1996, Walker LB $16.85 (978-0-8027-8310-3). A behind-the-scenes look at the magazine business, from starting out to marketing research, staffing, sales, circulation, and

distribution. Traces an article from initial conception to final version and publication. (Rev: BL 5/15/96; SLJ 4/96) [051]

5091 Swain, Gwenyth. *Bookworks: Making Books by Hand* (4–7). Illus. 1995, Carolrhoda LB $22.60 (978-0-87614-858-7). After a brief history of books and printing, this account gives directions for making paper and various kinds of books. (Rev: BL 7/95; SLJ 8/95*) [745.5]

Print and Other Media

5092 Bausum, Ann. *Muckrakers: How Ida Tarbell, Upton Sinclair, and Lincoln Steffens Helped Expose Scandal, Inspire Reform, and Invent Investigative Journalism* (6–9). Illus. 2007, National Geographic $21.95 (978-1-4263-0137-7). An inspiring introduction to the work of writers who exposed scandals including conditions in the meatpacking industry and immoral practices by Standard Oil. (Rev: BL 11/1/07; LMC 4-5/08; SLJ 11/07) [070.4]

5093 Botzakis, Stergios. *Pretty in Print: Questioning Magazines* (4–7). Illus. Series: Fact Finders. Media Literacy. 2006, Capstone LB $22.60 (978-0-7368-6764-1). This book explores how magazines capture readers' attention, why they need to do so, and the influences they may have on society; it includes colorful graphics and interesting sidebars. (Rev: SLJ 6/07) [050]

5094 Cohen, Daniel. *Yellow Journalism: Scandal, Sensationalism, and Gossip in the Media* (6–12). Illus. 2000, Twenty-First Century LB $22.90 (978-0-7613-1502-5). The history of tabloid journalism and sensation-driven media is the focus of this fascinating book that uses many modern cases as examples. (Rev: BL 5/15/00; SLJ 8/00) [302.23]

5095 Day, Nancy. *Sensational TV: Trash or Journalism?* (7–10). Illus. Series: Issues in Focus. 1996, Enslow LB $26.60 (978-0-89490-733-3). A history of tabloid journalism both in print and on TV, plus a discussion of present-day controversies surrounding it. (Rev: BL 4/1/96; SLJ 4/96; VOYA 6/96) [791.45]

5096 DeFalco, Tom. *Hulk: The Incredible Guide* (6–12). Illus. 2003, DK $24.99 (978-0-7894-9771-0). Full-color illustrations spanning 40 years of comics portray the Hulk's life and escapades in this oversize volume. Also use *X-Men: The Ultimate Guide* (2003). (Rev: BL 5/1/03) [741.5]

5097 Fleming, Thomas. *Behind the Headlines: The Story of American Newspapers* (6–10). 1989, Walker LB $15.85 (978-0-8027-6891-9). A lively history of American newspapers from the Revolution on and an indication of their continued importance today. (Rev: BL 1/1/90; SLJ 1/90; VOYA 12/90) [071.3]

5098 Gourley, Catherine. *War, Women, and the News: How Female Journalists Won the Battle to Cover World War II* (6–9). 2007, Simon & Schuster $19.99 (978-0-689-87752-0). Readers will be fascinated by the obstacles that women journalists had to overcome to become war correspondents; photographs add interest. (Rev: BCCB 5/07; BL 1/1–15/07; LMC 8-9/07; SLJ 2/07) [070]

5099 Ketcham, Hank. *Hank Ketcham's Complete Dennis the Menace: 1955–1956* (7–12). Illus. 2006, Fantagraphics $24.95 (978-1-56097-770-4). A collection of the funny cartoons about Dennis and his antics. (Rev: BL 1/1–15/07) [741.5]

5100 Krensky, Stephen. *Comic Book Century: The History of American Comic Books* (5–8). Illus. Series: People's History. 2007, Lerner LB $30.60 (978-0-8225-6654-0). The history of comics is presented as a part of America's history in this illustration- and photo-filled volume. (Rev: BL 10/1/07; LMC 1/08; SLJ 11/07) [741.5]

5101 Rollins, Prentis. *The Making of a Graphic Novel* (7–12). Illus. by author. 2006, Watson-Guptill paper $19.95 (978-0-8230-3053-8). One side of this "double-sided flip book" contains the text of a graphic novel called *The Resonator*; the other side holds a detailed account of the construction of this novel and the inspirations for the designs. (Rev: SLJ 3/06) [741.5]

5102 Schulz, Charles M. *The Complete Peanuts: 1950 to 1952* (7–12). Ed. by Gary Groth. Illus. 2004, Fantagraphics paper $28.95 (978-1-56097-589-2). The first volume of a series that will eventually include the entire 50 years of this classic comic strip. (Rev: BL 4/1/04)

5103 Segar, E. C. *"I Yam What I Yam!": E.C. Segar's Popeye, , Vol. 1* (7–12). Illus. 2006, Fantagraphics $29.95 (978-1-56097-779-7). An oversize volume collecting the first two years of the Popeye comic strip. (Rev: BL 1/1–15/07) [741.5]

5104 Somervill, Barbara A. *Backstage at a Newscast* (5–8). Illus. Series: Backstage Pass. 2003, Children's LB $24.50 (978-0-516-24326-9); paper $6.95 (978-0-516-24388-7). Somerville provides information on how a newscast is created, along with guidance on careers in journalism. (Rev: BL 5/1/03) [070.1]

5105 Stay, Byron L., ed. *Mass Media* (8–12). 1999, Greenhaven LB $32.45 (978-0-7377-0055-8); paper $21.20 (978-0-7377-0054-1). How does television affect society? Is advertising harmful? How do the media influence politics? Should pornography on the Internet be regulated? Do TV content labels benefit children? These are some of the questions explored in this collection of writings about the mass media. (Rev: BL 4/15/99) [303.6]

5106 Streissguth, Thomas. *Media Bias* (8–12). Series: Open for Debate. 2006, Benchmark LB $27.95 (978-0-7614-2296-9). After a discussion of media bias in America (from the first newspaper in 1690), Streissguth illustrates how public opinion can be swayed. (Rev: SLJ 4/07) [302.23]

5107 Sullivan, George. *Journalists at Risk: Reporting America's Wars* (6–9). Series: People's History. 2005, Twenty-First Century LB $29.27 (978-0-7613-2745-5). A look at the historical role of journalists in reporting on U.S. wars in far-flung corners of the globe, including information on the embedded journalists covering the war in Iraq. (Rev: BL 10/15/05; SLJ 12/05; VOYA 2/06)

5108 Wakin, Edward. *How TV Changed America's Mind* (7–12). 1996, Lothrop $15.00 (978-0-688-13482-2). This book chronicles the impact of television journalism on U.S. history over the past 50 years by analyzing how the major news stories of the time were reported. (Rev: SLJ 7/96) [070.1]

5109 Wan, Guofang. *Virtually True: Questioning Online Media* (4–7). Illus. Series: Fact Finders. Media Literacy. 2006, Capstone LB $22.60 (978-0-7368-6767-2). Designed to awaken skepticism about online media, this book discusses the motivations of those who produce online content and the influence this media has on society. (Rev: SLJ 6/07)

Biography, Memoirs, Etc.

General and Miscellaneous

5110 Berson, Robin Kadison. *Young Heroes in World History* (7–12). 1999, Greenwood $57.95 (978-0-313-30257-2). Real people — of both sexes and many nationalities — who achieved amazing things before the age of 25 are profiled, with quotations and black-and-white illustrations. (Rev: SLJ 1/00; VOYA 4/00) [920.02]

5111 Gifford, Clive, et al. *1000 Years of Famous People* (6–10). Illus. 2002, Kingfisher $24.95 (978-0-7534-5540-1). Brief descriptions of famous men and women in sports, medicine, politics, the arts, and other fields are included in this large-format book that is organized by subject and provides historical overviews of each discipline. (Rev: BL 12/1/02; HBG 3/03; SLJ 2/03; VOYA 6/03) [920.02]

5112 Hatch, Robert, and William Hatch. *The Hero Project: How We Met Our Greatest Heroes and What We Learned from Them* (8–12). Illus. 2005, McGraw-Hill paper $16.95 (978-0-07-144904-5). Fascinating interviews with such luminaries as Jackie Chan, Lance Armstrong, Orson Scott Card, Yo-Yo Ma, and Jimmy Carter result from the Hatch brothers' "hero project," which started when William was only 11 years old. (Rev: BL 9/15/05; SLJ 1/06) [920]

5113 Hazell, Rebecca. *Heroes: Great Men Through the Ages* (5–8). Illus. 1997, Abbeville $19.95 (978-0-7892-0289-5). A collection of 12 biographies, from Socrates to Martin Luther King, Jr., and including Shakespeare, Mohandas Gandhi, Leonardo da Vinci, and Jorge Louis Borges. (Rev: SLJ 6/97) [920]

Adventurers and Explorers

Collective

5114 Bledsoe, Karen E. *Daredevils of the Air: Thrilling Tales of Pioneer Aviators* (7–12). Series: Avisson Young Adult. 2003, Avisson paper $19.95 (978-1-888105-58-2). The Wright brothers, Eddie Rickenbacker, Bessie Coleman, and Beryl Markham are among the early flyers profiled in stories of exciting aerial exploits. (Rev: SLJ 1/04) [920]

5115 Colman, Penny. *Adventurous Women: Eight True Stories About Women Who Made a Difference* (6–9). Illus. 2006, Holt $17.95 (978-0-8050-7744-5). Letters and other primary sources add to these accessible profiles of women adventurers, many of whom are not well-known. (Rev: BL 2/15/06; SLJ 3/06) [920.72]

5116 Doherty, Kieran. *Ranchers, Homesteaders, and Traders: Frontiersmen of the South-Central States* (6–10). Illus. 2001, Oliver LB $22.95 (978-1-881508-53-3). Seven important settlers — including Sam Houston, Daniel Boone, and Eli Thayer — are introduced with plenty of historical and geographical background material. (Rev: BL 5/1/02; HBG 10/02; SLJ 1/02) [976]

5117 Holden, Henry M. *American Women of Flight: Pilots and Pioneers* (7–12). Series: Collective Biographies. 2003, Enslow LB $26.60 (978-0-7660-2005-4). This collection of profiles includes sketches on Harriet Quimby, Bessie Coleman, Amelia Earhart, Anne Morrow Lindbergh, and Jacqueline Cochran. (Rev: BL 6/1–15/03; HBG 10/03) [920]

5118 Jones, Charlotte Foltz. *Westward Ho! Explorers of the American West* (5–8). Illus. 2005, Holiday $22.95 (978-0-8234-1586-1). Intriguing narrative describes the lives and adventures of 11 explorers, including Zebulon Pike and John Wesley Powell. (Rev: BL 5/1/05; SLJ 8/05) [920]

5119 Kimmel, Elizabeth Cody. *The Look-It-Up-Book of Explorers* (5–9). Illus. 2004, Random LB $17.99 (978-0-375-92478-1); paper $10.99 (978-0-375-82478-4). Chronologically arranged spreads introduce explorers from Leif Eriksson to Robert Ballard, with maps, illustrations, and historical context. (Rev: SLJ 1/05) [920]

5120 McLean, Jacqueline. *Women of Adventure* (5–9). Series: Profiles. 2003, Oliver LB $19.95 (978-1-881508-73-1). Seven 19th- and 20th-century women with diverse interests who broke social barriers by exploring far from home are profiled here, with biographical information, photographs, and maps. (Rev: BCCB 5/03; HBG 10/03; SLJ 7/03; VOYA 8/03) [910]

5121 Murphy, Claire R., and Jane G. Haigh. *Gold Rush Women* (7–12). Illus. 1997, Alaska Northwest paper $16.95 (978-0-88240-484-4). A collective biography of several women in the late 19th century who went to the Yukon and Alaska, where they panned for gold, ran boarding houses, and worked as dance hall girls and prostitutes. (Rev: BL 8/97; SLJ 11/97*) [920]

5122 Richie, Jason. *Spectacular Space Travelers* (6–10). Series: Profiles. 2001, Oliver LB $19.95 (978-1-881508-71-7). Three Soviet cosmonauts and four American astronauts are profiled in this volume that provides a brief history of the space race. (Rev: HBG 10/02; SLJ 4/02) [629.45]

5123 Rooney, Frances. *Extraordinary Women Explorers* (5–8). Illus. Series: Women's Hall of Fame. 2005, Second Story paper $7.95 (978-1-896764-98-6). Women endowed with curiosity and courage are celebrated in this text-dense volume. (Rev: BL 3/1/06; SLJ 12/05) [910]

5124 Schraff, Anne. *American Heroes of Exploration and Flight* (5–9). Illus. Series: Collective Biographies. 1996, Enslow LB $26.60 (978-0-89490-619-0). From the Wright Brothers, Lindbergh, and Earhart to Neil Armstrong and Sally Ride, this is a history of 12 Americans who dared the unknown. (Rev: BL 4/15/96; SLJ 5/96; VOYA 6/96) [920]

5125 Sharp, Anne Wallace. *Daring Pirate Women* (5–8). Series: Biography. 2002, Lerner LB $27.93 (978-0-8225-0031-5). Profiles are given of notorious and ruthless female pirates such as Anne Bonny, Mary Read, and Grace O'Malley. (Rev: BL 6/1–15/02; HBG 10/02; SLJ 8/02) [920]

5126 Stefoff, Rebecca. *Vasco da Gama and the Portuguese Explorers* (6–9). Series: World Explorers. 1993, Chelsea LB $14.95 (978-0-7910-1303-8). An account of how different Portuguese explorers beginning with Vasco da Gama were able to visit unknown territories, particularly in the New World. (Rev: BL 3/15/93) [920]

5127 Twist, Clint. *Magellan and da Gama: To the Far East and Beyond* (4–7). Illus. Series: Beyond the Horizons. 1994, Raintree LB $24.26 (978-0-8114-7254-8). Describes the period in which these two explorers lived, as well as their voyages and accomplishments. (Rev: BL 8/94) [920]

5128 Weatherly, Myra. *Women Pirates: Eight Stories of Adventure* (4–7). Illus. 1998, Morgan Reynolds LB $21.95 (978-1-883846-24-4). These stories of eight women pirates from the 17th and 18th centuries — including Grace O'Malley, Maria Cobham, and Rachel Wall — are enlivened by period prints and portraits and good maps. (Rev: BCCB 4/98; BL 4/15/98; HBG 3/99; SLJ 7/98; VOYA 10/98) [920]

5129 Wren, Laura Lee. *Pirates and Privateers of the High Seas* (6–10). Series: Collective Biographies. 2003, Enslow LB $26.60 (978-0-7660-1542-5). The piratical exploits of seafarers including Sir Francis Drake, Jean Laffite, Anne Bonny, and Mary Read are related in a lively narrative. (Rev: BL 6/1–15/03; HBG 10/03; SLJ 9/03) [910.4]

5130 Yolen, Jane. *Sea Queens: Women Pirates around the World* (4–7). Illus. by Christine Joy Pratt. 2008, Charlesbridge $18.95 (978-1-58089-131-8). Yolen introduces 12 women pirates — from Artemisia in the 5th century B.C. to Madame Ching in the 19th century and including the well-known Anne Bonny. (Rev: BL 6/1–15/08; SLJ 7/08) [920]

5131 Yount, Lisa. *Women Aviators* (6–9). 1995, Facts on File $25.00 (978-0-8160-3062-0). Profiles of 11 prominent female aviators. (Rev: BL 4/1/95) [920]

Individual

ANZA, JUAN BAUTISTA DE

5132 Bankston, John. *Juan Bautista de Anza* (5–7). Series: Latinos in American History. 2003, Mitchell Lane LB $29.95 (978-1-58415-196-8). The biography of the Spanish explorer of the American Southwest who was a governor of New Mexico in the late 18th century. (Rev: BL 1/1–15/04) [921]

ARMSTRONG, NEIL

5133 Byers, Ann. *Neil Armstrong: The First Man on the Moon* (4–7). Illus. Series: The Library of Astronaut Biographies. 2004, Rosen LB $29.25 (978-0-8239-4461-3). A lively overview focusing mainly on Armstrong's education and training. (Rev: SLJ 1/05) [921]

5134 Kramer, Barbara. *Neil Armstrong: The First Man on the Moon* (5–7). Illus. Series: People to Know. 1997, Enslow LB $26.60 (978-0-89490-828-6). This biography covers Armstrong's public and private life, with details on his specialized training and many space missions. (Rev: HBG 3/98; SLJ 12/97) [921]

BALBOA, VASCO NUNEZ DE

5135 Otfinoski, Steven. *Vasco Nunez de Balboa: Explorer of the Pacific* (5–8). Series: Great Explorations. 2004, Benchmark LB $29.93 (978-0-7614-1609-8). After material on Balboa's early life, Otfinoski looks at the Spanish explorer's trip to the Pacific. (Rev: SLJ 3/05) [921]

BLUFORD, GUION

5136 Haskins, Jim, and Kathleen Benson. *Space Challenger: The Story of Guion Bluford* (4–7). Illus. 1984, Carolrhoda LB $27.93 (978-0-87614-259-2). The story of the first African American man in space. [629.4540924]

BURTON, RICHARD FRANCIS

5137 Young, Serinity. *Richard Francis Burton: Explorer, Scholar, Spy* (5–9). Series: Great Explorations. 2006, Benchmark LB $32.79 (978-0-7614-2222-8). This biography chronicles the English adventurer's explorations in Africa, the Middle East, South Asia, and South America and looks at his interest in the cultures of the people he encountered there. (Rev: SLJ 1/07) [921]

BYRD, ADMIRAL RICHARD EVELYN

5138 Burleigh, Robert. *Black Whiteness: Admiral Byrd Alone in the Antarctic* (4–8). Illus. by Walter

L. Krudop. 1998, Simon & Schuster $16.95 (978-0-689-81299-6). An outstanding picture biography, with generous quotations from Byrd's diary that describe his great endurance and his lonely vigil in a small underground structure in the Antarctic. (Rev: BL 1/1–15/98*; HB 3–4/98; HBG 10/98; SLJ 3/98) [921]

CABEZA DE VACA, ALVAR NUNEZ

5139 Menard, Valerie. *Alvar Nunez Cabeza de Vaca* (5–7). Series: Latinos in American History. 2002, Mitchell Lane LB $29.95 (978-1-58415-153-1). A biography of the 16th-century Spanish nobleman who lived with Native Americans for eight years and who claimed Florida, Louisiana, and Texas for Spain. (Rev: BL 2/15/03; HBG 10/03) [921]

5140 Waldman, Stuart. *We Asked for Nothing: The Remarkable Journey of Cabeza de Vaca* (5–8). Illus. by Tom McNeely. Series: A Great Explorers Book. 2003, Mikaya $19.95 (978-1-931414-07-4). Drawing on the writings of Cabeza de Vaca, Waldman tells the riveting story of the Spaniard's eight years in 16th-century Texas and Mexico. (Rev: SLJ 2/04) [921]

CABOT, JOHN

5141 Shields, Charles J. *John Cabot and the Rediscovery of North America* (4–8). Series: Explorers of New Worlds. 2001, Chelsea $25.00 (978-0-7910-6438-2); paper $25.00 (978-0-7910-6439-9). An absorbing biography that focuses on Cabot's expeditions at the end of the 15th century in search of a passage to Asia. (Rev: SLJ 3/02) [921]

CHAMPLAIN, SAMUEL DE

5142 Faber, Harold. *Samuel de Champlain: Explorer of Canada* (5–8). Series: Great Explorations. 2004, Benchmark LB $29.93 (978-0-7614-1608-1). Drawing on Champlain's own accounts, this well-illustrated volume examines his voyages to Canada and achievements as governor of New France. (Rev: SLJ 3/05) [921]

5143 Sherman, Josepha. *Samuel de Champlain: Explorer of the Great Lakes Region and Founder of Quebec* (4–7). Series: The Library of Explorers and Exploration. 2003, Rosen LB $33.25 (978-0-8239-3629-8). In addition to covering Champlain's life, this volume places his explorations in historical context and gives interesting information on the fur trade and relations with Native Americans. (Rev: SLJ 9/03) [971.01]

CID, EL

5144 Koslow, Philip. *El Cid* (5–8). Illus. Series: Hispanics of Achievement. 1993, Chelsea LB $21.95 (978-0-7910-1239-0). The story of Spain's national hero, who gained fame fighting the Moors. (Rev: BL 9/15/93) [921]

COCHRAN, JACQUELINE

5145 Smith, Elizabeth Simpson. *Coming Out Right: The Story of Jacqueline Cochran, the First Woman Aviator to Break the Sound Barrier* (5–8). Illus. 1991, Walker LB $15.85 (978-0-8027-6989-3). From her impoverished childhood to her triumphs in the air and later, this is the story of a female aviation pioneer. (Rev: BL 4/15/91; SLJ 5/91) [921]

COLEMAN, BESSIE

5146 Fisher, Lillian M. *Brave Bessie: Flying Free* (4–7). Illus. 1995, Hendrick-Long $16.95 (978-0-937460-94-8). This biography tells of the struggles of Bessie Coleman, who became the first African American aviatrix in the United States. (Rev: BL 2/15/96; SLJ 2/96) [921]

5147 Hart, Philip S. *Up In the Air: The Story of Bessie Coleman* (5–8). 1996, Carolrhoda LB $16.95 (978-0-87614-949-2). Forced by restrictions in the United States to get her training in France in the 1920s, Coleman became the first African American female airplane pilot. (Rev: BL 8/96; SLJ 8/96) [921]

5148 Plantz, Connie. *Bessie Coleman: First Black Woman Pilot* (4–8). 2001, Enslow LB $26.60 (978-0-7660-1545-6). This is a readable biography that breathes life into Coleman's childhood, training as a pilot, and tragic death. (Rev: HBG 3/02; SLJ 1/02) [921]

COLUMBUS, CHRISTOPHER

5149 Clare, John D., ed. *The Voyages of Christopher Columbus* (5–8). Illus. Series: Living History. 1992, Harcourt $16.95 (978-0-15-200507-8). Using actors and backdrops of the period, this account reconstructs each of Columbus's New World voyages. (Rev: SLJ 11/92) [921]

5150 Pelta, Kathy. *Discovering Christopher Columbus: How History Is Invented* (5–7). Illus. 1991, Lerner LB $23.93 (978-0-8225-4899-7). After telling what we know about Columbus, the author examines how myths and legends about him have grown over the years. (Rev: BL 10/1/91) [921]

5151 Sundel, Al. *Christopher Columbus and the Age of Exploration in World History* (8–12). Illus. Series: In World History. 2001, Enslow LB $26.60 (978-0-7660-1820-4). A detailed biography of Columbus that looks at the political climate of the time and discusses the atrocities inflicted on native peoples. (Rev: BL 3/1/02; HBG 10/02) [970.01]

COOK, CAPTAIN JAMES

5152 Gaines, Ann Graham. *Captain Cook Explores the Pacific* (8–12). Series: In World History. 2002, Enslow LB $26.60 (978-0-7660-1823-5). A mature account of the life and exploits of the famous British explorer known principally for his voyages in the Pacific Ocean. (Rev: BL 4/1/02; HBG 10/02; SLJ 8/02) [921]

5153 Lawlor, Laurie. *Magnificent Voyage: An American Adventurer on Captain James Cook's Final Expedition* (7–12). Illus. 2002, Holiday $22.95 (978-0-8234-1575-5). This absorbing account of Captain Cook's ill-fated efforts to locate the Northwest Passage gives details of the various difficulties encountered and of Cook's violent death. (Rev: BL 1/1–15/03; HBG 10/03; SLJ 2/03; VOYA 4/03) [910]

5154 Meltzer, Milton. *Captain James Cook: Three Times Around the World* (5–8). Series: Great Explorations. 2001, Marshall Cavendish LB $28.50 (978-0-7614-1240-3). Using both text and illustrations, this is a fine biography of the English mariner and explorer who, among other feats, explored the west coast of North America. (Rev: BL 4/1/02; HBG 3/02) [921]

DA GAMA, VASCO

5155 Calvert, Patricia. *Vasco da Gama: So Strong a Spirit* (5–8). Series: Great Explorations. 2004, Benchmark LB $29.93 (978-0-7614-1611-1). After material on da Gama's early life, Calvert looks at the 15th-century Portuguese explorer's voyages. (Rev: SLJ 3/05) [921]

5156 Draper, Allison Stark. *Vasco da Gama: The Portuguese Quest for a Sea Route from Europe to India* (5–8). Illus. Series: Library of Explorers and Exploration. 2003, Rosen LB $33.25 (978-0-8239-3632-8). Da Gama's achievements and brutal behavior are given equal exposure in this well-illustrated volume. (Rev: BL 6/1–15/03) [910]

5157 Kratoville, Betty Lou. *Vasco da Gama* (4–7). Series: Trade Route Explorers. 2000, High Noon paper $17.00 (978-1-57128-168-5). The story of the famous explorer who rounded the Cape of Good Hope and visited India, told in a simple, interesting account. (Rev: SLJ 3/01) [921]

DE SOTO, HERNANDO

5158 Gaines, Ann Graham. *Hernando de Soto and the Search for Gold* (8–12). Series: In World History. 2002, Enslow LB $26.60 (978-0-7660-1821-1). The story of the famous Spanish conquistador who explored the southeastern United States in his search for gold. (Rev: BL 4/1/02; HBG 10/02; SLJ 8/02) [921]

5159 Whiting, Jim. *Hernando de Soto* (5–7). Series: Latinos in American History. 2002, Mitchell Lane LB $29.95 (978-1-58415-147-0). A simple biography of the Spanish explorer who discovered the Mississippi River in the 16th century while traveling through what is now the southern United States. (Rev: BL 2/15/03; HBG 10/03; SLJ 6/03) [921]

DRAKE, SIR FRANCIS

5160 Duncan, Alice Smith. *Sir Francis Drake and the Struggle for an Ocean Empire* (6–9). Series: World Explorers. 1993, Chelsea LB $32.00 (978-0-7910-1302-1). The story of the intrepid Elizabethan explorer and adventurer who helped establish England's claims in the New World. (Rev: BL 3/15/93) [921]

5161 Gallagher, Jim. *Sir Francis Drake and the Foundation of a World Empire* (4–8). Series: Explorers of New Worlds. 2000, Chelsea $31.00 (978-0-7910-5950-0); paper $25.00 (978-0-7910-6160-2). This appealing and readable biography of Sir Francis Drake presents his life from childhood and details his major accomplishments, with photographs, sidebar features, documents, and maps. (Rev: HBG 10/01; SLJ 4/01) [921]

5162 Rice, Earle, Jr. *Sir Francis Drake: Navigator and Pirate* (5–8). Series: Great Explorations. 2002, Benchmark LB $29.93 (978-0-7614-1483-4). A profile of the 16th-century British explorer who circumnavigated the globe and fought the Spanish Armada, with maps, timeline, and reproductions. (Rev: HBG 10/03; SLJ 6/03) [942.05]

5163 Whitfield, Peter. *Sir Francis Drake* (8–12). Illus. Series: British Library Historic Lives. 2004, New York Univ. $25.00 (978-0-8147-9403-6). Drake's great naval accomplishments are balanced against less admirable activities. (Rev: BL 10/15/04) [942.05]

EARHART, AMELIA

5164 Lauber, Patricia. *Lost Star: The Story of Amelia Earhart* (5–7). Illus. 1988, Scholastic paper $4.50 (978-0-590-41159-2). A candid biography of the famed lost aviator. (Rev: BL 10/1/88; SLJ 12/88) [921]

5165 Leder, Jane. *Amelia Earhart* (6–9). Illus. 1990, Greenhaven LB $16.95 (978-0-89908-070-3). A thorough biography and good coverage of theories about Earhart's disappearance. (Rev: BL 3/1/90; SLJ 5/90) [921]

5166 Micklos, John, Jr. *Unsolved: What Really Happened to Amelia Earhart?* (4–8). 2006, Enslow LB $31.93 (978-0-7660-2365-9). The mystery of Earhart's last flight makes this a compelling read, even for researchers, and it provides what they need in terms of information about her childhood and motivations, photographs, maps, and so forth. (Rev: SLJ 7/07) [921]

5167 Sloate, Susan. *Amelia Earhart: Challenging the Skies* (5–8). Illus. 1990, Fawcett paper $6.99 (978-0-449-90396-4). The aviator's life story is told along with an examination of all the theories concerning her disappearance. (Rev: SLJ 6/90) [921]

EXQUEMELIN

5168 Exquemelin, A. O. *Exquemelin and the Pirates of the Caribbean* (5–8). Ed. by Jane Shuter. Illus. Series: History Eyewitness. 1995, Raintree LB $24.26 (978-0-8114-8282-0). An edited version of the exciting journal of the 17th-century Frenchman who joined a pirate gang as a barber-surgeon. (Rev: BL 4/15/95) [921]

FREMONT, JOHN C.

5169 Faber, Harold. *John Charles Fremont: Pathfinder to the West* (5–8). Series: Great Explorations. 2002, Benchmark LB $29.93 (978-0-7614-1481-0). A profile of the 19th-century explorer who helped open the American West to settlers, with maps, timeline, and reproductions. (Rev: HBG 10/03; SLJ 6/03) [979]

GRAHAM, ROBIN LEE

5170 Graham, Robin Lee, and Derek Gill. *Dove* (7–12). Illus. 1991, HarperCollins paper $13.00 (978-0-06-092047-0). A five-year solo voyage around the world and a tender romance with a girl the author met in Fiji. [921]

HENRY THE NAVIGATOR

5171 Gallagher, Aileen. *Prince Henry the Navigator: Pioneer of Modern Exploration* (5–8). Illus. Series: Library of Explorers and Exploration. 2003, Rosen LB $33.25 (978-0-8239-3621-2). During the 15th century, Prince Henry of Portugal spurred others to seek a route to India, claim new territory, and spread Christianity. (Rev: BL 6/1–15/03) [946.9]

HENSON, MATTHEW

5172 Gilman, Michael. *Matthew Henson* (6–10). Illus. 1988, Chelsea LB $21.95 (978-1-55546-590-2). The life story of the African American explorer who accompanied Peary on expeditions in search of the North Pole. (Rev: BL 6/15/88; SLJ 4/88) [921]

5173 Hoena, B. A. *Matthew Henson: Arctic Adventurer* (4–7). Illus. by Phil Miller. Series: Graphic Biographies. 2005, Capstone LB $26.60 (978-0-7368-4634-9). The life of the African American explorer is presented in speedy, user-friendly, classic comic book format. (Rev: BL 11/1/05) [910]

5174 Johnson, Dolores. *Onward: A Photobiography of African-American Polar Explorer Matthew Henson* (5–8). Illus. Series: National Geographic Photobiography. 2005, National Geographic LB $27.90 (978-0-7922-7915-0). The extraordinary life and achievements of African American explorer Matthew Henson are beautifully documented in this volume that also discusses the racism that Henson faced. (Rev: BCCB 5/06; BL 12/15/05*; HB 5–6/06; HBG 10/06; LMC 8–9/06; SLJ 3/06*; VOYA 6/06) [910]

HUDSON, HENRY

5175 Saffer, Barbara. *Henry Hudson: Ill-Fated Explorer of North America's Coast* (4–8). Series: Explorers of New Worlds. 2001, Chelsea $25.00 (978-0-7910-6436-8); paper $25.00 (978-0-7910-6437-5). This absorbing biography focuses on Hudson's early 17th-century expeditions from England in search of a sea route to the Far East. (Rev: HBG 10/02; SLJ 3/02) [921]

JOHNSON, OSA

5176 Arruda, Suzanne Middendorf. *From Kansas to Cannibals: The Story of Osa Johnson* (6–8). Series: Avisson Young Adult. 2001, Avisson paper $19.95 (978-1-888105-50-6). This is the biography of an intrepid woman who, with her husband, traveled to remote areas of Africa and the South Pacific from the 1920s to the 1940s, coming across wild beasts and cannibal headhunters. (Rev: SLJ 11/01) [910]

LA SALLE, CAVELIER DE

5177 Faber, Harold. *La Salle: Down the Mississippi* (5–8). Series: Great Explorations. 2001, Marshall Cavendish LB $29.93 (978-0-7614-1239-7). The exciting story of the French explorer who traveled down the Mississippi River to the Gulf of Mexico and named the region Louisiana. (Rev: BL 4/1/02; HBG 3/02; SLJ 3/02) [921]

LEWIS AND CLARK

5178 Edwards, Judith. *Lewis and Clark's Journey of Discovery* (6–10). Series: In American History. 1998, Enslow LB $26.60 (978-0-7660-1127-4). This story of the overland expedition to find the Pacific Ocean begins with Lewis and Clark getting their commission from Jefferson and ends with their return home two years later. (Rev: BL 2/15/99; HBG 9/99) [921]

5179 Streissguth, Thomas. *Lewis and Clark: Explorers of the Northwest* (4–9). Series: Historical American Biographies. 1998, Enslow LB $26.60 (978-0-7660-1016-1). The story of the two intrepid explorers who made their way overland to the Pacific Ocean. (Rev: BL 8/98) [921]

LINDBERGH, CHARLES

5180 Denenberg, Barry. *An American Hero: The True Story of Charles A. Lindbergh* (8–12). Illus. 1996, Scholastic paper $16.95 (978-0-590-46923-4). Beginning with Lindbergh's transatlantic flight, this fascinating biography then recounts the story of his early years followed by details about his multifaceted life. (Rev: BL 3/15/96*; SLJ 7/96; VOYA 6/96) [921]

5181 Giblin, James Cross. *Charles A. Lindbergh: A Human Hero* (6–12). Illus. 1997, Clarion $22.00 (978-0-395-63389-2). A book about the public and private life of one of America's heroes that deals with his pro-Nazi sympathies and anti-Semitism, the adoration he received for his transatlantic flight, and pity the public felt for the kidnapping and murder of his child. (Rev: BL 9/15/97; HBG 3/98; SLJ 11/97*; VOYA 6/98) [921]

5182 Kent, Zachary. *Charles Lindbergh and the Spirit of St. Louis* (6–10). Series: In American History. 2001, Enslow LB $26.60 (978-0-7660-1683-5). Lindbergh's life and accomplishments are re-created, including the first solo trip by airplane across the Atlantic Ocean, made when he was only 25 years old. (Rev: BL 8/01; HBG 10/01) [921]

5183 Meachum, Virginia. *Charles Lindbergh: American Hero of Flight* (6–10). Series: People to Know. 2002, Enslow LB $26.60 (978-0-7660-1535-7). A well-illustrated, appealing biography of the American hero of aviation with insights into his personal life. (Rev: BL 9/15/02; HBG 10/02; SLJ 9/02) [921]

LIVINGSTONE, DAVID

5184 Otfinoski, Steven. *David Livingstone: Deep in the Heart of Africa* (5–9). Series: Great Explorations. 2006, Benchmark LB $32.79 (978-0-7614-2226-6). This biography focuses on the three decades during which the Scottish-born adventurer explored central Africa. (Rev: SLJ 1/07) [921]

MCNAIR, RONALD

5185 Naden, Corinne J. *Ronald McNair* (5–8). Illus. Series: Black Americans of Achievement. 1991, Chelsea LB $21.95 (978-0-7910-1133-1). An inspirational biography of the second African American astronaut, a victim of the *Challenger* disaster. (Rev: BL 4/1/91; SLJ 3/91) [921]

MAGELLAN, FERDINAND

5186 Burnett, Betty. *Ferdinand Magellan: The First Voyage Around the World* (4–7). Series: The Library of Explorers and Exploration. 2003, Rosen LB $33.25 (978-0-8239-3617-5). In addition to covering Magellan's life, this volume places his 16th-century voyage in historical context and gives interesting information on the funding of such expeditions and life at sea. (Rev: SLJ 9/03) [910]

5187 Levinson, Nancy Smiler. *Magellan and the First Voyage Around the World* (5–8). Illus. 2001, Clarion $19.00 (978-0-395-98773-5). A straightforward biography of Magellan, with information on his times and insightful analysis of his character. (Rev: BCCB 2/02; BL 2/1/02; HB 1–2/02; HBG 3/02; SLJ 1/02) [910.92]

5188 Meltzer, Milton. *Ferdinand Magellan: First to Sail Around the World* (5–8). Illus. Series: Great Explorations. 2001, Benchmark LB $29.93 (978-0-7614-1238-0). An encompassing look at Magellan's achievements is complemented by excellent illustrations, a timeline, and Web site information. (Rev: BL 1/1–15/02; HBG 3/02; SLJ 3/02) [910]

5189 Stefoff, Rebecca. *Ferdinand Magellan and the Discovery of the World Ocean* (7–12). Illus. 1990, Chelsea LB $32.00 (978-0-7910-1291-8). Using many quotations from original sources, this is an engrossing account of the explorer and his voyage. (Rev: BL 6/15/90) [921]

5190 Waldman, Stuart. *Magellan's World* (4–7). Illus. by Gregory Manchess. Series: Great Explorers. 2007, Mikaya $22.95 (978-1-931414-19-7). "Magellan was driven to ever-greater extremes of brilliance, courage, brutality and madness as he sailed around the world," states this book, which offers an unvarnished portrait of the explorer as well as beautiful illustrations and maps. (Rev: BL 11/1/07) [921]

MALLORY, GEORGE

5191 Salkeld, Audrey. *Mystery on Everest: A Photobiography of George Mallory* (5–8). Illus. Series: Photobiography. 2000, National Geographic $17.95 (978-0-7922-7222-9). The life of the famous English mountain climber George Mallory, who died in 1924 in a climbing accident on Mount Everest, written by a member of the team that discovered his body in 1999. (Rev: BCCB 9/00; BL 11/1/00; HBG 3/01; SLJ 11/00) [921]

MARKHAM, BERYL

5192 Gourley, Catherine. *Beryl Markham: Never Turn Back* (6–10). Series: Bernard Biography. 1997, Conari paper $11.95 (978-1-57324-073-4). An exciting biography of the unconventional Englishwoman who was the first person to fly the Atlantic from east to west. (Rev: BL 3/15/97; SLJ 5/97; VOYA 12/97) [921]

MARTIN, JESSE

5193 Martin, Jesse. *Lionheart: A Journey of the Human Spirit* (8–12). 2002, Allen & Unwin paper $14.95 (978-1-86508-347-6). Martin details the exciting events and extreme isolation of his inspiring round-the-world solo voyage at the age of 17. (Rev: SLJ 5/02; VOYA 6/02) [910.4]

OCHOA, ELLEN

5194 Iverson, Teresa. *Ellen Ochoa* (4–8). Series: Hispanic-American Biographies. 2005, Raintree LB $32.86 (978-1-4109-1299-2). The personal and professional life of the first Hispanic American woman astronaut. (Rev: SLJ 1/06) [921]

5195 Paige, Joy. *Ellen Ochoa: The First Hispanic Woman in Space* (4–7). Illus. Series: The Library of Astronaut Biographies. 2004, Rosen LB $29.25 (978-0-8239-4457-6). A lively overview focusing mainly on Ochoa's education and training. (Rev: SLJ 1/05) [921]

PEARY, ROBERT E.

5196 Calvert, Patricia. *Robert E. Peary: To the Top of the World* (5–8). Series: Great Explorations. 2001, Marshall Cavendish LB $29.93 (978-0-7614-1242-7). The exciting story of the Arctic explorer who, after several attempts, reached the North Pole in 1909. (Rev: BL 4/1/02; HBG 3/02; SLJ 3/02) [921]

5197 Dwyer, Christopher. *Robert Peary and the Quest for the North Pole* (6–9). Series: World Explorers. 1992, Chelsea LB $14.95 (978-0-7910-1316-8). Courage and endurance are highlighted in this account of Peary's expeditions to reach the South Pole. (Rev: BL 2/1/93) [921]

PIKE, ZEBULON

5198 Calvert, Patricia. *Zebulon Pike: Lost in the Rockies* (5–8). Series: Great Explorations. 2004, Benchmark LB $29.93 (978-0-7614-1612-8). Presents the life and career of the army officer who explored the West and Southwest. (Rev: SLJ 3/05) [921]

POLO, MARCO

5199 Freedman, Russell. *The Adventures of Marco Polo* (7–10). Illus. by Bagram Ibatoulline. 2006, Scholastic $17.99 (978-0-439-52394-3). Vivid illustrations accompany the descriptions of Marco Polo's exciting journey to Kublai Khan's court. (Rev: BL 10/15/06; HB 11–12/06; SLJ 11/06*) [910.4]

5200 Otfinoski, Steven. *Marco Polo: To China and Back* (4–8). Series: Great Explorations. 2002, Benchmark LB $29.93 (978-0-7614-1480-3). Readable text accompanied by many illustrations and sidebar features traces Polo's life and adventures. (Rev: HBG 10/03; SLJ 5/03) [915.04]

PONCE DE LEON, JUAN

5201 Dolan, Sean. *Juan Ponce de León* (5–9). Series: Hispanics of Achievement. 1995, Chelsea LB $14.95 (978-0-7910-2023-4). The story of the Spanish explorer who after accompanying Columbus on his second voyage set out on his own and eventually became the discoverer of Florida. (Rev: BL 10/15/95) [921]

5202 Otfinoski, Steven. *Juan Ponce de Leon: Discoverer of Florida* (5–8). Series: Great Explorations. 2004, Benchmark LB $29.93 (978-0-7614-1610-4). A well-illustrated account of the explorer's life and discoveries, dismissing the idea that he was really searching for the fountain of youth. (Rev: SLJ 3/05) [921]

5203 Whiting, Jim. *Juan Ponce de Leon* (5–7). Series: Latinos in American History. 2002, Mitchell Lane LB $29.95 (978-1-58415-149-4). This is the story of the man who is credited with discovering Florida in 1513 while searching for the fountain of youth. (Rev: BL 2/15/03; HBG 10/03; SLJ 6/03) [921]

5204 Worth, Richard. *Ponce de Leon and the Age of Spanish Exploration in World History* (5–9). Series: In World History. 2003, Enslow LB $26.60 (978-0-7660-1940-9). As well as a biography of this great adventurer from Spain, this book describes the work of other Spanish explorers in the Americas. (Rev: BL 11/15/03; HBG 4/04) [921]

POWELL, JOHN WESLEY

5205 Bruns, Roger A. *John Wesley Powell: Explorer of the Grand Canyon* (5–8). Illus. Series: Historical American Biographies. 1997, Enslow LB $26.60 (978-0-89490-783-8). This biography tells about Powell's youth, education, and Civil War days, as well as his many expeditions and research activities. (Rev: SLJ 10/97) [921]

RALEIGH, SIR WALTER

5206 Aronson, Marc. *Sir Walter Ralegh and the Quest for El Dorado* (7–10). 2000, Clarion $20.00 (978-0-395-84827-2). The fascinating life and times of the colorful Elizabethan explorer, with illustrations, maps, and quotations from Sir Walter himself. (Rev: BL 8/00; HB 9–10/00; HBG 9/00; SLJ 7/00*) [942.05]

RAMON, ILAN

5207 Sofer, Barbara. *Ilan Ramon: Israel's Space Hero* (4–8). 2004, Lerner LB $16.95 (978-1-58013-115-5); paper $6.95 (978-1-58013-116-2). The story of the first Israeli astronaut, from his early life and schooling to his selection for the crew of the ill-fated Columbia space shuttle that broke apart on re-entry in 2003. (Rev: SLJ 6/04) [921]

RIDE, SALLY

5208 Camp, Carole Ann. *Sally Ride: First American Woman in Space* (6–10). Illus. Series: People to Know. 1997, Enslow LB $20.95 (978-0-89490-829-3). A lively account of Sally Ride's work as an astronaut and astrophysicist, with material on her training, shuttle flight, and life in microgravity. (Rev: BL 1/1–15/98; HBG 3/98; SLJ 12/97) [921]

5209 Hurwitz, Jane, and Sue Hurwitz. *Sally Ride: Shooting for the Stars* (5–8). 1989, Ballantine paper $6.99 (978-0-449-90394-0). An interestingly written account in paperback format of the female space pioneer. (Rev: BL 12/15/89; SLJ 2/90; VOYA 2/90) [921]

5210 Kramer, Barbara. *Sally Ride: A Space Biography* (4–8). Illus. Series: Countdown to Space. 1998, Enslow LB $23.93 (978-0-89490-975-7). A brief, well-written biography of Sally Ride that describes her training, experience, and space flights. (Rev: BL 4/1/98; HBG 9/98; SLJ 5/98) [921]

SACAGAWEA

5211 White, Alana J. *Sacagawea: Westward with Lewis and Clark* (4–8). Series: Native American Biographies. 1997, Enslow LB $26.60 (978-0-89490-867-5). A well-written account of this gallant woman's life, accompanied by a reading list, chapter notes, and a chronology. (Rev: BL 4/15/97; SLJ 8/97; VOYA 8/97) [921]

SELKIRK, ALEXANDER

5212 Kraske, Robert. *Marooned: The Strange but True Adventures of Alexander Selkirk, the Real Robinson Crusoe* (5–8). Illus. by Robert Andrew Parker. 2005, Clarion $15.00 (978-0-618-56843-7). The adventurous life of Alexander Selkirk, the Scottish navigator who served as the model for Daniel Defoe's *Robinson Crusoe*. (Rev: BL 11/15/05; SLJ 12/05) [996.1]

SERRA, JUNÍPERO

5213 Dolan, Sean. *Junípero Serra* (5–9). Series: Hispanics of Achievement. 1991, Chelsea LB $21.95 (978-0-7910-1255-0). The story of the devoted Spanish Franciscan missionary who was responsible for founding the famous missions on the coast of California. (Rev: BL 11/1/91; SLJ 2/92) [921]

5214 Genet, Donna. *Father Junípero Serra* (6–9). Illus. Series: Hispanic Biographies. 1996, Enslow LB $26.60 (978-0-89490-762-3). This book divides its contents equally between a biography of Father Junípero Serra and the story of the founding, history, and significance of the California missions. (Rev: BL 10/15/96; SLJ 9/96) [979.4]

5215 Whiting, Jim. *Junípero José Serra* (5–7). Series: Latinos in American History. 2003, Mitchell Lane LB $29.95 (978-1-58415-187-6). Profiles the monk who was responsible for founding nine California missions and converting thousands of Native Americans to Christianity. (Rev: BL 1/1–15/04; SLJ 3/00) [921]

SHACKLETON, SIR ERNEST

5216 Calvert, Patricia. *Sir Ernest Shackleton: By Endurance We Conquer* (4–8). Series: Great Explorations. 2002, Benchmark LB $29.93 (978-0-7614-1485-8). Readable text accompanied by many illustrations and sidebar features traces Shackleton's life and adventures. (Rev: HBG 10/03; SLJ 5/03) [919.8904]

5217 Johnson, Rebecca. *Ernest Shackleton: Gripped by the Antarctic* (6–10). Illus. Series: Trailblazer Biographies. 2003, Carolrhoda LB $30.60 (978-0-87614-920-1). Photographs, anecdotes, and quotations are sprinkled throughout this exciting account of Shackleton's youth and famous expeditions. (Rev: BL 6/1–15/03; HBG 10/03; SLJ 8/03; VOYA 8/03) [919.8]

5218 Kostyal, K. M. *Trial by Ice: A Photobiography of Sir Ernest Shackleton* (4–8). Illus. 1999, National Geographic $17.95 (978-0-7922-7393-6). A biography that details the life of Sir Ernest Shackleton, his 1915 Antarctic expedition, and the survival of the explorers aboard the *Endurance*. (Rev: BCCB 12/99; BL 12/1/99; HBG 3/00; SLJ 3/00) [921]

5219 Riffenburgh, Beau. *Shackleton's Forgotten Expedition: The Voyage of the Nimrod* (8–12). 2004, Bloomsbury $25.95 (978-1-58234-488-1). This story of Shackleton's first expedition to the Antarctic aboard the *Nimrod* underlines its significant scientific and exploratory achievements. (Rev: BL 10/15/04) [919.8]

SHEPARD, ALAN

5220 Orr, Tamra. *Alan Shepard: The First American in Space* (4–7). Illus. Series: The Library of Astronaut Biographies. 2004, Rosen LB $29.25 (978-0-8239-4455-2). A lively overview focusing mainly on Shepard's education and training. (Rev: SLJ 1/05) [921]

SMITH, JOHN

5221 Doherty, Kieran. *To Conquer Is to Live: The Life of Captain John Smith of Jamestown* (6–8). 2001, Twenty-First Century LB $23.90 (978-0-7613-1820-0). A compelling biography that includes details of Smith's adventures before coming to the New World. (Rev: HBG 3/02; SLJ 12/01) [973.2]

WHITMAN, NARCISSA

5222 Harness, Cheryl. *The Tragic Tale of Narcissa Whitman and a Faithful History of the Oregon Trail* (4–7). Illus. 2006, National Geographic $16.95 (978-0-7922-5920-6). A biography of Narcissa Whitman, the first woman to cross the Rockies on the perilous Oregon Trail in order to bring her Christian beliefs to the Indians of that area. (Rev: BL 12/1/06) [917.804]

Artists, Authors, Composers, and Entertainers

Collective

5223 Aronson, Virginia. *Literature* (6–9). Series: Female Firsts in Their Fields. 1999, Chelsea $18.65 (978-0-7910-5146-7). Biographies of pioneering women authors Phillis Wheatley, Edith Wharton, Pearl Buck, Toni Morrison, Alice Walker, and Judy Blume. (Rev: BL 5/15/99; HBG 9/99) [920]

5224 Ball, Heather. *Magnificent Women in Music* (4–7). Series: The Women's Hall of Fame. 2006, Second Story paper $7.95 (978-1-897187-02-9). Ten women from different times and with different musical gifts are profiled here, including Clara Schumann, Marian Anderson, and k.d. lang. (Rev: SLJ 7/06)

5225 Barnes, Rachel. *Abstract Expressionists* (6–8). Series: Artists in Profile. 2003, Heinemann LB $28.50 (978-1-58810-644-5). An introduction to the art and artists of this period, with profiles of major artists and examples of their works. Also use *Harlem Renaissance Artists* (2003). (Rev: HBG 10/03; LMC 10/03; SLJ 7/03) [759.13]

5226 Benedict, Kitty, and Karen Covington. *The Literary Crowd: Writers, Critics, Scholars, Wits* (5–9). Series: Remarkable Women. 2000, Raintree LB $32.82 (978-0-8172-5732-3). Profiles of 150 women writers and others associated with the literary world, including Virginia Woolf, Jane Austen, and Maya Angelou. (Rev: SLJ 8/00) [920]

5227 Bostrom, Kathleen Long. *Winning Authors: Profiles of the Newbery Medalists* (5–10). Series: Popular Authors. 2003, Libraries Unlimited $52.00 (978-1-56308-877-3). Report writers will find useful information on the authors who won this prestigious award, including quotations and material on experiences that relate to the winning books. (Rev: SLJ 6/04; VOYA 6/04) [920]

5228 Bredeson, Carmen. *American Writers of the 20th Century* (5–8). Illus. 1996, Enslow LB $20.95 (978-0-89490-704-3). Ten writers for adults, including Toni Morrison and F. Scott Fitzgerald, are introduced in brief profiles. (Rev: BL 6/1–15/96; SLJ 9/96) [920]

5229 Chiu, Christina. *Lives of Notable Asian Americans: Literature and Education* (6–10). Illus. Series: Asian American Experience. 1995, Chelsea LB $19.95 (978-0-7910-2182-8). Brief biographies of important Asian American writers and educators. (Rev: BL 1/1–15/96) [920]

5230 Covington, Karen. *Creators: Artists, Designers, Craftswomen* (5–9). Series: Remarkable Women. 2000, Raintree LB $32.85 (978-0-8172-5725-5). Mary Cassatt, Georgia O'Keefe, Frido Kahlo, and Beatrix Potter are four of the 150 female artists celebrated in this collective biography. (Rev: BL 6/1–15/00; SLJ 8/00) [920]

5231 Datnow, Claire. *American Science Fiction and Fantasy Writers* (5–8). Illus. Series: Collective Biographies. 1999, Enslow LB $26.60 (978-0-7660-1090-1). Science fiction and fantasy writers profiled in this book include Asimov, Heinlein, Bradbury, Anderson, Norton, L'Engle, and Le Guin. (Rev: BL 4/15/99; VOYA 6/99) [920]

5232 Davidson, Sue. *Getting the Real Story: Nellie Bly and Ida B. Wells* (6–10). 1992, Seal paper $8.95 (978-1-878067-16-6). A dual biography of two women who broke down barriers in journalism and how their different races shaped their individual stories. (Rev: BL 3/1/92; SLJ 7/92) [920]

5233 De Angelis, Gina. *Motion Pictures: Making Cinema Magic* (6–10). Series: Innovators. 2004, Oliver LB $21.95 (978-1-881508-78-6). Profiles eight inventors of motion picture technology, including Auguste and Louis Lumière, Lee de Forest, and Mike Todd. (Rev: BCCB 5/04; SLJ 9/04) [920]

5234 Earls, Irene. *Young Musicians in World History* (7–12). 2002, Greenwood $51.95 (978-0-313-31442-1). Thirteen musicians whose skills were recognized before the age of 25 are profiled, ranging from Bach and Beethoven to Louis Armstrong, Bob Dylan, and John Lennon. (Rev: LMC 2/03; SLJ 1/03) [780]

5235 Ford, Carin T. *Legends of American Dance and Choreography* (5–7). Series: Collective Biographies. 2000, Enslow LB $26.60 (978-0-7660-1378-0). This collective work presents 10 short biographies of such dance luminaries as George Balanchine and Martha Graham. (Rev: BL 6/1–15/00; HBG 10/00; SLJ 7/00) [920]

5236 Gaines, Ann. *Entertainment and Performing Arts* (6–9). Series: Female Firsts in Their Fields. 1999, Chelsea $18.95 (978-0-7910-5145-0). Emphasizing their importance as role models, this book discusses the lives of six pioneering women in the fields of the performing arts and entertainment. (Rev: BL 5/15/99; HBG 9/99) [920]

5237 Gaines, Ann Graham. *American Photographers: Capturing the Image* (4–7). Series: Collective Biographies. 2002, Enslow LB $26.60 (978-0-7660-1833-4). The lives and contributions of 10 well-known photographers are presented with photographs and a brief history of photography. (Rev: HBG 10/02; SLJ 10/02) [921]

5238 Gourse, Leslie. *Sophisticated Ladies: The Great Women of Jazz* (5–8). Illus. by Martin French. 2007, Dutton $19.99 (978-0-525-47198-1). Profiles 14 female jazz singers, with full-color portraits, biographical details, and comments on vocal style and importance. (Rev: BL 12/15/06; SLJ 5/07) [920]

5239 Govenar, Alan. *Extraordinary Ordinary People: Five American Masters of Traditional Arts* (5–8). 2006, Candlewick $19.99 (978-0-7636-2047-9). Five American artists, recipients of National Endowment for the Arts fellowships, who practice unique — but traditional — art forms are profiled here. (Rev: BL 9/1/06; SLJ 8/06*) [920]

5240 Halliwell, Sarah, ed. *The 18th Century: Artists, Writers, and Composers* (6–9). Series: Who and When? 1997, Raintree LB $29.97 (978-0-8172-4727-0). A discussion of the lives and works of artists including Watteau, Hogarth, and David; composers including Vivaldi, Bach, and Haydn; and writers including Defoe, Swift, and Voltaire. (Rev: BL 12/15/97; SLJ 2/98) [700]

5241 Halliwell, Sarah, ed. *The 17th Century: Artists, Writers, and Composers* (6–9). Series: Who and When? 1997, Raintree LB $29.97 (978-0-8172-4726-3). This work profiles artists including Caravaggio, Rubens, Velazquez, and Rembrandt and

discusses works by such writers as Shakespeare, Donne, and Milton and the composer Monteverdi. (Rev: BL 12/15/97; SLJ 2/98) [700]

5242 Hasday, Judy L. *Extraordinary People in the Movies* (5–9). Series: Extraordinary People. 2003, Children's LB $40.00 (978-0-516-22348-3); paper $16.95 (978-0-516-27857-5). Brief biographies of individuals associated with the movie business are arranged chronologically by date of birth and interspersed with short essays on related topics. (Rev: SLJ 7/03) [791.43]

5243 Hill, Anne E. *Broadcasting and Journalism* (6–9). Series: Female Firsts in Their Fields. 1999, Chelsea $28.00 (978-0-7910-5139-9). The biographies of six pioneering women in the mass media and how their work became an inspiration for other women. (Rev: BL 5/15/99; HBG 9/99) [920]

5244 Hill, Anne E. *Ten American Movie Directors: The Men Behind the Camera* (7–12). Series: Collective Biographies. 2003, Enslow LB $26.60 (978-0-7660-1836-5). This collective biography features profiles of 10 famous movie directors, including Alfred Hitchcock, Frank Capra, Woody Allen, Martin Scorsese, George Lucas, Spike Lee, and Steven Spielberg. (Rev: BL 6/1–15/03; HBG 10/03) [920]

5245 Hill, Christine M. *Ten Hispanic American Authors* (6–12). Illus. Series: Collective Biographies. 2002, Enslow LB $26.60 (978-0-7660-1541-8). Ten Hispanic Americans — including Sandra Cisneros, Gary Soto, and Piri Thomas — are introduced here, with information on how they became successful writers. (Rev: BL 5/1/02; HBG 10/02; SLJ 6/02) [810.9]

5246 Hill, Christine M. *Ten Terrific Authors for Teens* (5–7). Series: Collective Biographies. 2000, Enslow LB $26.60 (978-0-7660-1380-3). Among the authors profiled are Judy Blume, Virginia Hamilton, Julius Lester, Lois Lowry, Katherine Paterson, Gary Soto, and Lawrence Yep. (Rev: BL 9/15/00; HBG 10/01; SLJ 12/00; VOYA 8/01) [920]

5247 Hirschfelder, Arlene. *Artists and Craftspeople* (8–12). Illus. Series: American Indian Lives. 1994, Facts on File $25.00 (978-0-8160-2960-0). Profiles 18 historical and contemporary Native Americans including Nampeyo, Maria Martinez, and Oscar Howe, who are famous for their contributions to craftwork and art. (Rev: BL 11/15/94; SLJ 11/94; VOYA 4/95) [920]

5248 Holme, Merilyn, and Bridget McKenzie. *Expressionists* (5–9). Series: Artists in Profile. 2002, Heinemann LB $28.50 (978-1-58810-647-6). Introduces the movement and gives biographical information on the major artists and their key works, with reproductions and photographs. Also use *Impressionists* and *Pop Artists* (both 2002). (Rev: HBG 3/03; SLJ 3/03) [759.06]

5249 Ishizuka, Kathy. *Asian American Authors* (5–9). Series: Collective Biographies. 2000, Enslow LB $26.60 (978-0-7660-1376-6). Writers for children (including Laurence Yep) and for adults (such as Amy Tan) are included in this collective biography of 10 Asian American writers. (Rev: HBG 10/01; SLJ 3/01) [920]

5250 Kallen, Stuart A. *Great Composers* (6–9). Series: History Makers. 2000, Lucent LB $27.45 (978-1-56006-669-9). Music is covered from the Renaissance through jazz and rock through brief profiles of such composers as Bach, Mozart, and Andrew Lloyd Webber. (Rev: BL 6/1–15/00; HBG 3/01) [920]

5251 Knapp, Ron. *American Legends of Rock* (6–9). Illus. 1996, Enslow LB $26.60 (978-0-89490-709-8). Brief biographies of such personalities as Chuck Berry, Elvis Presley, Buddy Holly, and Jimi Hendrix. (Rev: BL 11/15/96; SLJ 12/96; VOYA 2/97) [920]

5252 Koopmans, Andy. *Filmmakers* (7–10). Illus. Series: History Makers. 2005, Gale LB $29.95 (978-1-59018-598-8). Profiles five of the world's most influential filmmakers — Alfred Hitchcock, Stanley Kubrick, Francis Ford Coppola, Spike Lee, and Peter Jackson. (Rev: BL 6/1–15/05) [920]

5253 Krull, Kathleen. *Lives of the Musicians: Good Times, Bad Times (And What the Neighbors Thought)* (5–8). Illus. 1993, Harcourt $20.00 (978-0-15-248010-3). Biographies of 16 musical giants, from Vivaldi, Mozart, and Beethoven to Gershwin, Joplin, and Woody Guthrie. (Rev: BL 4/1/93*; SLJ 5/93*) [920]

5254 Madison, Bob. *American Horror Writers* (7–12). Series: Collective Biographies. 2001, Enslow LB $26.60 (978-0-7660-1379-7). Edgar Allan Poe, H. P. Lovecraft, Dean Koontz, R. L. Stine, Anne Rice, and Stephen King are among the 10 writers profiled here. (Rev: HBG 10/01; SLJ 4/01) [813]

5255 Marcus, Leonard. *Pass It Down: Five Picture-Book Families Make Their Mark* (5–8). 2007, Walker $19.95 (978-0-8027-9600-4). Multigenerational families of picture book authors/illustrators are featured here: Donald Crews, Ann Jonas, and Nina Crews; Clement, Edith, and Thacher Hurd; Walter Dean and Christopher Myers; Jerry and Brian Pinkney; and Harlow, Anne, and Lizzy Rockwell. (Rev: BL 12/15/06; SLJ 1/07) [920]

5256 Marcus, Leonard S., ed. *The Wand in the Word: Conversations with Writers of Fantasy* (6–9). 2006, Candlewick $19.99 (978-0-7636-2625-9). This is a collection of interviews with 13 top authors of fantasy fiction (including Susan Cooper, Tamora Pierce, Philip Pullman, and Madeleine l'Engle), with profiles of the writers, discussion of their inspiration, and advice for young writers. (Rev: BL

5/15/06; HB 7–8/06; LMC 2/07; SLJ 5/06*) [813.009]

5257 Marquez, Heron. *Latin Sensations* (5–9). 2001, Lerner LB $27.93 (978-0-8225-4993-2); paper $7.95 (978-0-8225-9695-0). A collective biography that features profiles of Selena, Ricky Martin, Jennifer Lopez, Marc Anthony, and Enrique Iglesias. (Rev: HBG 10/01; SLJ 3/01) [920]

5258 Mass, Wendy. *Great Authors of Children's Literature* (6–10). Series: History Makers. 2000, Lucent LB $28.70 (978-1-56006-589-0). From early children's books to the present, this is a collection of brief biographies of trailblazers in the field of children's literature including Milne, Dahl, Dr. Seuss, Sendak, and Judy Blume. (Rev: BL 3/15/00; HBG 9/00; SLJ 6/00) [920]

5259 Mazer, Anne, ed. *Going Where I'm Coming From: Memoirs of American Youth* (8–12). 1995, Persea paper $7.95 (978-0-89255-206-1). Writers from different cultures talk about growing up and the incidents in their lives that helped to establish their identities. (Rev: BL 1/15/95; VOYA 5/95) [818]

5260 Meehan, Elizabeth. *Twentieth-Century American Writers* (6–9). Series: History Makers. 2000, Lucent LB $27.45 (978-1-56006-671-2). This brief volume contains profiles of a few of the major American writers of the past century. (Rev: BL 9/15/00; HBG 3/01; SLJ 11/00) [920]

5261 Mour, Stanley L. *American Jazz Musicians* (6–9). Series: Collective Biographies. 1998, Enslow LB $26.60 (978-0-7660-1027-7). Ten greats of jazz are profiled chronologically, including Scott Joplin, Louis Armstrong, Duke Ellington, Charlie Parker, Miles Davis, and John Coltrane. (Rev: HBG 3/99; SLJ 1/99) [920]

5262 Nathan, Amy. *Meet the Dancers: From Ballet, Broadway, and Beyond* (6–12). 2008, Holt $19.95 (978-0-8050-8071-1). Sixteen very different dancers describe their training and their careers, which run the gamut from Broadway to MTV. (Rev: BL 5/1/08; SLJ 4/08) [792.802]

5263 Otfinoski, Steven. *African Americans in the Performing Arts* (8–12). Illus. Series: A to Z of African Americans. 2003, Facts on File $45.00 (978-0-8160-4807-6). Profiles of African American actors, dancers, choreographers, composers, musicians, and singers, mostly from the 20th century, give personal and career information. (Rev: BL 8/03; SLJ 6/03) [791]

5264 Price-Groff, Claire. *Extraordinary Women Journalists* (7–10). Series: Extraordinary People. 1997, Children's Pr. LB $40.00 (978-0-516-20474-1). More than 50 well-known and lesser-known female reporters, publishers, humorists, columnists, photographers, and television journalists from colonial times to the present are profiled, including Nellie Bly, Hedda Hopper, Ann Landers, Abigail Van Buren, and Barbara Walters. (Rev: SLJ 3/98; VOYA 4/98) [920]

5265 Rennert, Richard, ed. *Female Writers* (6–9). Series: Profiles of Great Black Americans. 1994, Chelsea paper $5.95 (978-0-7910-2064-7). Biographical overviews of such writers as Alice Walker, Maya Angelou, and Toni Morrison. (Rev: BL 2/15/94; SLJ 3/94) [920]

5266 Rennert, Richard, ed. *Jazz Stars* (6–9). Series: Profiles of Great Black Americans. 1993, Chelsea LB $18.65 (978-0-7910-2059-3). Profiles of eight jazz greats: Louis Armstrong, Count Basie, Charlie Parker, Ella Fitzgerald, Billie Holiday, Duke Ellington, Dizzy Gillespie, and John Coltrane. (Rev: BL 1/1/94; SLJ 12/93) [781.65]

5267 Rennert, Richard, ed. *Male Writers* (6–9). Series: Profiles of Great Black Americans. 1994, Chelsea LB $14.95 (978-0-7910-2061-6); paper $7.65 (978-0-7910-2062-3). Biographical overviews of such writers as James Baldwin, Alex Haley, and Richard Wright. (Rev: BL 2/15/94) [920]

5268 Rennert, Richard, ed. *Performing Artists* (6–9). Illus. Series: Profiles of Great Black Americans. 1994, Chelsea paper $7.65 (978-0-7910-2070-8). Alvin Ailey, Marian Anderson, Josephine Baker, Bill Cosby, Katerine Dunham, Lena Horne, Sidney Poitier, and Paul Robeson are the performing artists included in this collective biography. (Rev: BL 6/1–15/94) [920]

5269 Satter, James. *Journalists Who Made History* (7–12). Illus. Series: Profiles. 1998, Oliver LB $19.95 (978-1-881508-39-7). Ten journalists famous for their fearless reporting are profiled, including Horace Greeley, Ida Tarbell, Carl Bernstein and Bob Woodward, William Randolph Hearst, and Edward R. Murrow. (Rev: BL 10/15/98; SLJ 11/98) [920]

5270 Scieszka, Jon, ed. *Guys Write for Guys Read: Favorite Authors Write About Being Boys* (6–9). 2005, Viking $16.99 (978-0-670-06007-8). Well-known male authors and illustrators share boyhood memories in this delightful collection of stories, anecdotes, poems, drawings, and comics. (Rev: BL 4/15/05; SLJ 4/05) [810.8]

5271 Sills, Leslie. *In Real Life: Six Women Photographers* (6–12). Illus. 2000, Holiday $19.95 (978-0-8234-1498-7). This broad-ranging collective biography not only looks at the lives and works of artists including Dorothea Lange and Carrie Mae Weems but also gives the reader guidance on appreciating the women's technique and artistry. (Rev: BL 12/1/00; HB 1–2/01; HBG 3/01; SLJ 2/01; VOYA 2/01) [770]

5272 Steffens, Bradley, and Robyn M. Weaver. *Cartoonists* (6–9). Series: History Makers. 2000, Lucent LB $27.45 (978-1-56006-668-2). Charles Schulz

and Garry Trudeau are among the cartoonists featured in this volume that also traces the history of cartooning and the genre's importance in our society. (Rev: BL 6/1–15/00; HBG 9/00; SLJ 8/00) [920]

5273 Strickland, Michael R. *African-American Poets* (5–10). Illus. Series: Collective Biographies. 1996, Enslow LB $26.60 (978-0-89490-774-6). The lives and works of 10 prominent African American poets from Phillis Wheatley to Rita Dove are covered, with quotations from their works and a single full-length poem from each. (Rev: BL 2/15/97; SLJ 1/97) [920]

5274 Stux, Erica. *Eight Who Made a Difference: Pioneer Women in the Arts* (7–10). 1999, Avisson LB $19.95 (978-1-888105-37-7). Profiles eight famous women in the arts: Marian Anderson, Mary Cassatt, Nadia Boulanger, Margaret Bourke-White, Julia Morgan, Louise Nevelson, Beverly Sills, and Maria Tallchief. (Rev: BL 2/15/99; SLJ 5/99; VOYA 10/99) [920]

5275 Tate, Eleanora E. *African American Musicians* (4–7). Series: Black Stars. 2000, Wiley $24.95 (978-0-471-25356-3). This collective biography highlights both past and present contributions to different kinds of music by several African Americans. (Rev: BL 7/00; HBG 3/01; SLJ 7/00) [920]

5276 Terkel, Studs, and Milly Hawk Daniel. *Giants of Jazz*. 2nd ed. (7–10). 1992, HarperCollins LB $16.89 (978-0-690-04917-6). Thirteen subjects are highlighted, including Benny Goodman, Louis Armstrong, Bessie Smith, and Dizzy Gillespie. [920]

5277 Tessitore, John. *Extraordinary American Writers* (6–12). 2004, Children's Pr. LB $40.00 (978-0-516-22656-9). Writers profiled here "examined and analyzed American society in their works" and range from Benjamin Franklin to Philip Roth; biographical essays include information on important works and a brief excerpt. (Rev: SLJ 9/04) [920]

5278 Wilds, Mary. *Raggin' the Blues: Legendary Country Blues and Ragtime Musicians* (6–9). Illus. 2001, Avisson paper $19.95 (978-1-888105-47-6). Although many readers will not be familiar with these musicians — including Lightnin' Hopkins, Skip James, Libba Cotton, and Blind Willie Johnson — they will appreciate their contributions to the foundations of modern blues, jazz, and improvisational music. (Rev: BL 2/15/03) [781]

5279 Wilkinson, Brenda. *African American Women Writers* (4–7). Illus. Series: Black Stars. 1999, Wiley $22.95 (978-0-471-17580-3). Arranged chronologically, this collective biography contains short profiles of more than 20 important female African American writers. (Rev: BL 2/15/00; HBG 10/00; SLJ 2/00) [910]

5280 Woog, Adam. *Magicians and Illusionists* (6–10). Series: History Makers. 1999, Lucent LB

$28.70 (978-1-56006-573-9). Eight illusionists — including Houdini and David Copperfield — are profiled, with discussion of their performances and many quotations from original sources. (Rev: BL 10/15/99; HBG 9/00; SLJ 3/00) [793.8]

5281 Woog, Adam. *Rock and Roll Legends* (6–9). Series: History Makers. 2001, Lucent $24.95 (978-1-56606-741-6). Included in this book of short profiles are Elvis Presley, John Lennon, Janis Joplin, Jimi Hendrix, Bruce Springsteen, and Kurt Cobain. (Rev: BL 8/1/01) [920]

Artists and Architects

ABBOTT, BERENICE

5282 Sullivan, George. *Berenice Abbott, Photographer: An Independent Vision* (6–9). 2006, Clarion $20.00 (978-0-618-44026-9). A comprehensive look at the life and work of Abbott, an accomplished 20th-century photographer, with excellent reproductions. (Rev: BL 6/1–15/06; SLJ 8/06) [921]

ADAMS, ANSEL

5283 Gherman, Beverly. *Ansel Adams: America's Photographer* (6–10). Illus. 2002, Little, Brown $19.95 (978-0-316-82445-3). This splendid introduction to Adams's photography includes high-quality reproductions of his work and a lively account of his life and love of the natural world. (Rev: BL 6/1–15/03*; HBG 10/03) [770.92]

5284 Strangis, Joel. *Ansel Adams: American Artist with a Camera* (6–8). Series: People to Know. 2003, Enslow LB $26.60 (978-0-7660-1847-1). The life of the famous American photographer of landscapes who died in 1984. (Rev: BL 6/1–15/03; HBG 10/03) [921]

AUDUBON, JOHN JAMES

5285 Roop, Peter, and Connie Roop, eds. *Capturing Nature* (5–7). Illus. by Rick Farley. 1993, Walker LB $17.85 (978-0-8027-8205-2). Audubon's prints and original paintings and excerpts from his journals are combined to produce a stunning biography. (Rev: BCCB 12/93; BL 12/15/93; SLJ 1/94) [921]

BAMA, JAMES

5286 Kane, Brian M. *James Bama: American Realist* (8–12). Illus. 2006, Flesk $34.95 (978-0-9723758-8-7). This is a tribute to James Bama, a triumphantly successful illustrator who did hundreds of paperback covers during the 1960s and 1970s as well as artwork for magazines, advertising, military, and sports publications. (Rev: BL 11/1/06) [759.13]

BEARDEN, ROMARE

5287 Brown, Kevin. *Romare Bearden* (7–10). Series: Black Americans of Achievement. 1995, Chelsea LB $19.95 (978-0-7910-1119-5). The story of the Harlem-raised African American painter who tries to portray the everyday experiences of African Americans. (Rev: BL 3/15/95; SLJ 3/95) [921]

BOTTICELLI, SANDRO

5288 Connolly, Sean. *Botticelli* (4–8). Illus. Series: Lives of the Artists. 2005, World Almanac LB $31.00 (978-0-8368-5648-4). A tall, slender volume full of facts about Botticelli's life and times, with many color reproductions. (Rev: BL 6/1–15/04; SLJ 3/05) [921]

BOURGEOIS, LOUISE

5289 Greenberg, Jan, and Sandra Jordan. *Runaway Girl: The Artist Louise Bourgeois* (8–12). Illus. 2003, Abrams $19.95 (978-0-8109-4237-0). The life of the famous sculptor, with details of her youth and her difficult relations with her parents, is accompanied by many black-and-white and color photographs. (Rev: BL 4/15/03*; HB 7–8/03; HBG 10/03; SLJ 5/03*; VOYA 8/03) [730]

BOURKE-WHITE, MARGARET

5290 Daffron, Carolyn. *Margaret Bourke-White* (7–12). Illus. 1988, Chelsea LB $19.95 (978-1-55546-644-2). The life story of this famous photographer in an account well illustrated with the artist's work. (Rev: BL 5/1/88; SLJ 8/88) [921]

5291 Rubin, Susan G. *Margaret Bourke-White: Her Pictures Were Her Life* (6–12). Illus. 1999, Abrams $19.95 (978-0-8109-4381-0). An excellent biography of a courageous, highly disciplined photographer whose work remains a hallmark of quality in the field. (Rev: BL 11/1/99* ; HBG 4/00) [770]

5292 Welch, Catherine A. *Margaret Bourke-White: Racing with a Dream* (4–8). Illus. 1998, Carolrhoda LB $30.35 (978-1-57505-049-2). A fine biography of the important photographer whose subjects included skyscrapers, the Depression, Buchenwald, and South African miners. (Rev: BL 10/1/98; HBG 3/99; SLJ 7/98) [921]

5293 Wooten, Sara McIntosh. *Margaret Bourke-White: Daring Photographer* (6–10). Series: People to Know. 2002, Enslow LB $26.60 (978-0-7660-1534-0). An accessible biography of the adventurous photographer with many examples of her work. (Rev: BL 9/15/02; HBG 3/03; SLJ 11/02; VOYA 6/03) [921]

BRADY, MATHEW

5294 Pflueger, Lynda. *Mathew Brady* (5–8). Series: Historical American Biographies. 2001, Enslow LB $26.60 (978-0-7660-1444-2). A biography of the photographer known primarily for his coverage of the Civil War, illustrated with many of his works. (Rev: BL 1/1–15/02; HBG 10/01; SLJ 9/01; VOYA 2/02) [921]

CALDECOTT, RANDOLPH

5295 Hegel, Claudette. *Randolph Caldecott: An Illustrated Life* (5–9). Series: Avisson Young Adult. 2004, Avisson $27.50 (978-1-888105-60-5). Many of Caldecott's drawings are included in this account of the artist's life and work, with coverage of the children's award named in his honor. (Rev: BL 10/1/04; SLJ 11/04) [741.6]

CALDER, ALEXANDER

5296 Lipman, Jean, and Margaret Aspinwall. *Alexander Calder and His Magical Mobiles* (6–9). Illus. 1981, Hudson Hills $19.95 (978-0-933920-17-0). A biography of the noted sculptor with many interesting incidents from his childhood. [921]

CANALETTO

5297 Rice, Earle, Jr. *Canaletto* (7–12). Series: Art Profiles for Kids. 2007, Mitchell Lane LB $29.95 (978-1-58415-561-4). Report writers will appreciate this thorough introduction to the artist's life and work, with interesting "FYI" sections and small color reproductions. (Rev: SLJ 1/08)

CARLE, ERIC

5298 Carle, Eric. *Flora and Tiger: 19 Very Short Stories from My Life* (4–8). Illus. 1997, Putnam $17.99 (978-0-399-23203-9). An autobiography of the famous picture-book artist who was born in Germany but who has lived in the United States since 1952. (Rev: BL 12/15/97; HBG 3/98; SLJ 2/98) [921]

CARR, EMILY

5299 Bogart, Jo Ellen. *Emily Carr: At the Edge of the World* (4–8). Illus. by Maxwell Newhouse. 2003, Tundra $18.95 (978-0-88776-640-4). This picture book for older readers presents the life and work of the Canadian artist and writer who became famous for her depictions of the native peoples of the Pacific Coast. (Rev: BL 11/1/03; HBG 4/04; SLJ 12/03) [759.11]

5300 Debon, Nicolas. *Four Pictures by Emily Carr* (5–9). Illus. 2003, Douglas & McIntyre $15.95 (978-0-88899-532-2). This small comic-book biography uses four of Carr's paintings to introduce chapters that trace the Canadian artist's life and interest in Native Americans. (Rev: BL 12/1/03; HB 1–2/04; HBG 3/02; SLJ 11/03) [759.11]

CASSATT, MARY

5301 Ferrara, Cos. *Mary Cassatt: The Life and Art of a Genteel Rebel* (5–8). Illus. Series: Girls Explore, Reach for the Stars. 2005, Girls Explore $20.00 (978-0-9749456-3-7). Cassatt's art, shown in small full-color reproductions, is introduced in this biography that also discusses her independence and feminist views. (Rev: BL 2/15/05) [921]

5302 Streissguth, Thomas. *Mary Cassatt* (4–8). Series: Trailblazers. 1999, Lerner LB $27.93 (978-1-57505-291-5). Full-color illustrations enhance this biography of the American painter who was associated with the Impressionists and spent most of her adult life in France. (Rev: BL 5/1/99; HBG 10/99; SLJ 9/99) [921]

CATLIN, GEORGE

5303 Reich, Susanna. *Painting the Wild Frontier: The Art and Adventures of George Catlin* (7–12). Illus. 2008, Clarion $21.00 (978-0-618-71470-4). This excellent introduction to the artwork and life of George Catlin, a 19th-century painter of Native Americans, includes prints and photographs of his work and extensive back matter. (Rev: BL 6/1–15/08; SLJ 8/08) [921]

CÉZANNE, PAUL

5304 Burleigh, Robert. *Paul Cézanne: A Painter's Journey* (4–7). Illus. 2006, Abrams $17.95 (978-0-8109-5784-8). A lavishly illustrated and thoughtfully written profile of Cézanne's life and art. (Rev: BL 2/15/06; SLJ 3/06) [759.4]

5305 Sellier, Marie. *Cézanne from A to Z* (4–8). Trans. from French by Claudia Zoe Bedrick. Illus. Series: Artists from A to Z. 1996, Bedrick LB $14.95 (978-0-87226-476-2). An imaginative, well-executed account of the life and works of Cézanne, enhanced by reproductions of many of his paintings. (Rev: SLJ 5/96) [921]

5306 Tracy, Kathleen. *Paul Cézanne* (4–7). Series: Art Profiles for Kids. 2007, Mitchell Lane LB $29.95 (978-1-58415-565-2). Suitable for both research and browsing, this examination of the artist's life and times includes many reproductions and interesting sidebars. (Rev: LMC 2/08; SLJ 12/07) [921]

CHAGALL, MARC

5307 Hopler, Brigitta. *Marc Chagall: Life Is a Dream* (4–7). Trans. by Catherine McCreadie. Illus. Series: Adventures in Art. 1999, Prestel $14.95

(978-3-7913-1986-5). This biography of the surrealist painter not only relates the artist's life story but also encourages the reader to discover the meanings behind the images. (Rev: BL 2/1/99; SLJ 2/99) [921]

5308 Lemke, Elisabeth, and Thomas David. *Marc Chagall: What Colour Is Paradise?* (4–8). Illus. Series: Adventures in Art. 2001, Prestel $14.95 (978-3-7913-2393-0). Using Chagall's biographical paintings as a focus, this innovative biography tells of his life, career, and work. (Rev: BL 1/1–15/01; SLJ 4/01) [921]

5309 Mason, Antony. *Marc Chagall* (4–8). Illus. Series: Lives of the Artists. 2005, World Almanac LB $31.00 (978-0-8368-5649-1). A tall, slender volume full of facts about Chagall's life and times, with many color reproductions. (Rev: BL 6/1–15/04; SLJ 3/05) [921]

CHANG, WAH MING

5310 Riley, Gail B. *Wah Ming Chang: Artist and Master of Special Effects* (4–8). Illus. Series: Multicultural Junior Biographies. 1995, Enslow LB $26.60 (978-0-89490-639-8). A thorough, well-documented biography of this Chinese American who has gained prominence in the field of special effects. (Rev: BL 2/15/96; SLJ 2/96) [921]

CHONG, GORDON H.

5311 *The Success of Gordon H. Chong and Associates: An Architecture Success Story* (7–10). Illus. Series: Success. 1996, Walker $15.95 (978-0-8027-8307-3). The amazing rise of the contemporary American architect, with examples of his work. (Rev: BL 5/15/96; SLJ 9/96) [921]

COROT, JEAN CAMILLE

5312 Larroche, Caroline. *Corot from A to Z* (5–8). Trans. from French by Claudia Zoe Bedrick. Series: Artists from A to Z. 1996, Bedrick LB $14.95 (978-0-87226-477-9). Although the text is somewhat confusing, the strength of this account of Corot's life and work is the full-color reproductions of his work. (Rev: SLJ 1/97) [921]

CURTIS, EDWARD S.

5313 Lawlor, Laurie. *Shadow Catcher: The Life and Work of Edward S. Curtis* (6–12). 1994, Walker LB $20.85 (978-0-8027-8289-2). The personal and professional highlights of the life of this little-known, largely unappreciated photojournalist who was determined to preserve the lore of Native Americans. (Rev: BL 12/1/94; SLJ 2/95; VOYA 12/94) [921]

DA VINCI, LEONARDO

5314 Herbert, Janis. *Leonardo da Vinci for Kids: His Life and Ideas* (4–8). Illus. 1998, Chicago Review paper $16.95 (978-1-55652-298-7). This biography of Leonardo da Vinci contains background information on history, art techniques, science, and philosophy. (Rev: BL 3/1/99; SLJ 4/99) [921]

5315 Kallen, Stuart A., and P. M. Boekhoff. *Leonardo da Vinci* (7–12). Series: The Importance Of. 2000, Lucent LB $27.45 (978-1-56006-604-0). The life, accomplishments, and significance of this multi-talented genius are covered in this fine biography. (Rev: BL 8/00; HBG 9/00) [921]

5316 Krull, Kathleen. *Leonardo da Vinci* (5–8). Illus. by Boris Kulikov. Series: Giants of Science. 2005, Viking $15.99 (978-0-670-05920-1). The less attractive features of da Vinci's times are covered here, along with the artist's childhood and adolescence and his development into both an artist and a scientist, drawing connections between the two disciplines and incorporating much from da Vinci's notebooks. (Rev: BL 9/1/05; SLJ 10/05*) [921]

5317 Kuhne, Heinz. *Leonardo da Vinci: Dreams, Schemes, and Flying Machines* (4–8). Illus. Series: Adventures in Art. 2000, Prestel $14.95 (978-3-7913-2166-0). This well-illustrated biography covers da Vinci's accomplishments as a scientist, engineer, inventor, and artist. (Rev: BL 7/00) [921]

5318 Mason, Antony. *Leonardo da Vinci* (4–8). Illus. 1994, Barron's paper $8.99 (978-0-8120-1997-1). A brief biography that chronicles the achievements of this multifaceted genius and supplies pictures of some of his great triumphs. (Rev: BL 12/1/94) [921]

5319 O'Connor, Barbara. *Leonardo da Vinci: Renaissance Genius* (5–8). Series: Trailblazer Biographies. 2002, Carolrhoda LB $27.93 (978-0-87614-467-1). An excellent biography that details Leonardo's life from childhood, discusses some of his famous paintings, and looks at his inventions and experiments. (Rev: BL 3/15/03; HBG 3/03; SLJ 11/02; VOYA 8/03) [921]

5320 Reed, Jennifer. *Leonardo da Vinci: Genius of Art and Science* (4–7). Illus. Series: Great Minds of Science. 2005, Enslow LB $26.60 (978-0-7660-2500-4). Reed describes da Vinci's wide-ranging achievements — showing, for example, his urban planning ideas, his design for a flying machine, and his anatomical drawings — and emphasizes his originality and creativity. (Rev: SLJ 6/05) [921]

DALI, SALVADOR

5321 Anderson, Robert. *Salvador Dali* (5–8). Illus. Series: Artists in Their Time. 2002, Watts LB $24.00 (978-0-531-12231-0). This volume presents

Dali's life and influence with many illustrations, news clippings, and useful information. (Rev: BL 10/15/02) [709]

DESJARLAIT, PATRICK

5322 Williams, Neva. *Patrick DesJarlait: Conversations with a Native American Artist* (5–7). Illus. 1994, Lerner LB $22.60 (978-0-8225-3151-7). A beautifully illustrated biography of the Native American artist who worked at the Red Lake Indian Reservation in Minnesota. (Rev: BL 1/1/95; SLJ 1/95) [921]

DISNEY, WALT

5323 Cole, Michael D. *Walt Disney: Creator of Mickey Mouse* (4–7). Illus. Series: People to Know. 1996, Enslow LB $26.60 (978-0-89490-694-7). A thoughtful biography of the great animator, perfectionist, and founder of an entertainment empire. (Rev: BL 6/1–15/96; SLJ 8/96) [921]

5324 Ford, Barbara. *Walt Disney* (4–8). Illus. 1989, Walker LB $17.00 (978-0-8027-6865-0). The story of Disney's youth and his struggle to fulfill his dreams. (Rev: BL 5/15/89) [791.430924]

ELLABBAD, MOHIEDDIN

5325 Ellabbad, Mohieddin. *The Illustrator's Notebook* (5–10). Trans. from French by Sarah Quinn. Illus. by author. 2006, Groundwood $16.95 (978-0-88899-700-5). In this fascinating journal printed from right to left, Egyptian-born illustrator Ellabbad reflects on the influences that led him to a life in art and offers valuable insights into Arabic cultural sensibilities. (Rev: SLJ 8/06) [921]

EVANS, WALKER

5326 Nau, Thomas. *Walker Evans: Photographer of America* (6–9). Illus. 2007, Roaring Brook $19.95 (978-1-59643-225-3). A profile of Evans is accompanied by reproductions of many of his photographs, arranged to show how his work changed and progressed during his career. (Rev: BL 3/1/07; HB 5-6/07; LMC 8-9/07; SLJ 3/07) [921]

GAUGUIN, PAUL

5327 Anderson, Robert. *Paul Gauguin* (4–8). Series: Artists in Their Time. 2003, Watts LB $24.00 (978-0-531-12239-6); paper $6.95 (978-0-531-16647-5). An interesting life of Gauguin, with reproductions of his works and of those of fellow painters, with a timeline that adds historical context. (Rev: SLJ 6/03) [759.4]

GEHRY, FRANK

5328 Lazo, Caroline Evensen. *Frank Gehry* (7–10). Series: A&E Biography. 2005, Twenty-First Century LB $29.27 (978-0-8225-2649-0); paper $7.95 (978-0-8225-3388-7). Introduces the architect and his most famous structures, with full-color photos and reproductions. (Rev: SLJ 2/06) [921]

GIACOMETTI, ALBERTO

5329 Gaff, Jackie. *Alberto Giacometti* (5–8). Series: Artists in Their Time. 2002, Watts LB $24.00 (978-0-531-12224-2); paper $6.95 (978-0-531-16617-8). The life of this Italian artist noted for his elongated sculptures is re-created with comments on his social period and reproductions of his work. (Rev: BL 10/15/02) [921]

GORMAN, R. C.

5330 Hermann, Spring. *R. C. Gorman: Navajo Artist* (4–8). Illus. Series: Multicultural Junior Biographies. 1995, Enslow LB $20.95 (978-0-89490-638-1). The story of this contemporary Native American artist, who reflects his heritage in his work. (Rev: BL 2/15/96; SLJ 3/96) [921]

HOPPER, EDWARD

5331 Foa, Emma. *Edward Hopper* (4–8). Series: Artists in Their Time. 2003, Watts LB $24.00 (978-0-531-12240-2); paper $6.95 (978-0-531-16641-3). An interesting life of Hopper, with reproductions of his works and of those of fellow painters, and a timeline that adds historical context. (Rev: SLJ 6/03) [759.13]

5332 Lyons, Deborah. *Edward Hopper: Summer at the Seaside* (4–8). Series: Adventures in Art. 2003, Prestel $14.95 (978-3-7913-2737-2). The story of the American painter who died in 1967, with a good analysis of many of his important works. (Rev: BL 11/15/03; SLJ 9/03) [921]

5333 Rubin, Susan G. *Edward Hopper: Painter of Light and Shadow* (5–8). Illus. 2007, Abrams $18.95 (978-0-8109-9347-1). Along with a life of the painter, Rubin provides good reproductions of his work plus discussion of his themes, images, and technique. (Rev: BL 9/1/07; SLJ 10/07) [921]

HUNTER, CLEMENTINE

5334 Lyons, Mary E. *Talking with Tebe: Clementine Hunter, Memory Artist* (7–12). 1998, Houghton $17.00 (978-0-395-72031-8). This richly illustrated book, which quotes extensively from taped interviews and is as much about social history as about painting, tells the story of the first illiterate, self-taught African American folk artist to receive national attention for her work. (Rev: BCCB 1/99; BL 8/98; HB 9–10/98; HBG 3/99; SLJ 9/98) [921]

JACKSON, WILLIAM HENRY

5335 Lawlor, Laurie. *Window on the West: The Frontier Photography of William Henry Jackson* (5–8). 1999, Holiday $18.95 (978-0-8234-1380-5). In addition to tracing the life of this famous photographer who captured the life and spirit of frontier America, this account covers the history and development of the West and pioneer life. (Rev: BL 2/15/00; HB 3–4/00; HBG 10/00; SLJ 3/00; VOYA 12/00) [921]

KAHLO, FRIDA

5336 Bernier-Grand, Carmen T. *Frida: Viva la vida! Long Live Life!* (7–12). Illus. by Frida Kahlo. 2007, Marshall Cavendish $18.99 (978-0-7614-5336-9). Free-verse poems about the art and life of Frida Kahlo accompany reproductions of her artwork and photographs of the artist and her family; some poems deal with adult subjects such as a troubled marriage and a pregnancy loss. (Rev: BL 11/1/07; SLJ 12/07) [921]

5337 Cruz, Barbara C. *Frida Kahlo: Portrait of a Mexican Painter* (6–9). Illus. Series: Hispanic Biographies. 1996, Enslow LB $26.60 (978-0-89490-765-4). A biography of one of Mexico's greatest artists that includes material on her relationship with artist Diego Rivera. (Rev: BL 11/1/96; SLJ 10/96) [921]

5338 Frazier, Nancy. *Frida Kahlo: Mysterious Painter* (5–7). Illus. Series: Library of Famous Women. 1993, Rosen $24.95 (978-1-56711-012-8). A biography of this enigmatic artist with examples of her work. (Rev: BL 2/15/93) [921]

5339 Garza, Hedda. *Frida Kahlo* (5–9). Series: Hispanics of Achievement. 1994, Chelsea LB $21.95 (978-0-7910-1698-5); paper $9.95 (978-0-7910-1699-2). Known once only as the wife of Diego Rivera, this painter, who lived most of her life in Mexico, is now considered a great artist. (Rev: BL 3/1/94) [921]

5340 Holzhey, Magdalena. *Frida Kahlo: The Artist in the Blue House* (4–8). Series: Adventures in Art. 2003, Prestel $14.95 (978-3-7913-2863-8). A colorful introduction to this Mexican painter with an interesting analysis of individual paintings. (Rev: BL 11/15/03; SLJ 9/03) [921]

5341 Laidlaw, Jill A. *Frida Kahlo* (5–8). Series: Artists in Their Time. 2003, Watts LB $24.00 (978-0-531-12236-5); paper $6.95 (978-0-531-16642-0). An interesting life of Kahlo, with reproductions of her works and a timeline and informative sidebars that add historical context. (Rev: SLJ 6/03) [759]

KIRBY, JACK

5342 Hamilton, Sue. *Jack Kirby* (4–8). Illus. Series: Comic Book Creators. 2007, ABDO LB $16.95 (978-1-59928-298-5). A biography of comic book legend Kirby, with information on his childhood, early career, and work on comics such as the *Incredible Hulk* and *Captain America*. (Rev: BL 5/1/07) [921]

KLEE, PAUL

5343 Laidlaw, Jill A. *Paul Klee* (5–8). Series: Artists in Their Time. 2002, Watts LB $24.00 (978-0-531-12230-3). Photographs, reproductions, maps, and a timeline that links world events with events in the artist's life make this suitable both for browsing and report writing. (Rev: BL 10/15/02; SLJ 1/03) [921]

LANGE, DOROTHEA

5344 Partridge, Elizabeth. *Restless Spirit: The Life and Work of Dorothea Lange* (6–12). 1998, Viking $22.99 (978-0-670-87888-8). Using over 60 photographs, this photoessay tells of the personal and professional life of photographer Lange, her many problems, and her artistic accomplishments, particularly during the Depression and World War II. (Rev: BCCB 12/98; BL 10/15/98; HB 3–4/99; HBG 3/99; SLJ 10/98; VOYA 8/99) [921]

LAWRENCE, JACOB

5345 Duggleby, John. *Story Painter: The Life of Jacob Lawrence* (5–8). Illus. 1998, Chronicle $16.95 (978-0-8118-2082-0). Using 50 color reproductions, this biography of the great African American illustrator and painter tells how he moved to Harlem in the 1930s and developed his own techniques and style. (Rev: BCCB 1/99; BL 10/15/98; HB 3–4/99; HBG 3/99; SLJ 12/98) [921]

5346 Leach, Deba Foxley. *I See You I See Myself: The Young Life of Jacob Lawrence* (5–9). Illus. by Jacob Lawrence. 2002, Phillips Collection $20.00 (978-0-943044-26-2). A look at the early life and work of the African American artist, with information on his paintings as a teen. (Rev: SLJ 12/02) [759.13]

LEE, STAN

5347 Miller, Raymond H. *Stan Lee: Creator of Spider-Man* (4–8). Series: Inventors and Creators. 2006, Gale LB $26.20 (978-0-7377-3447-8). Superhero fans will enjoy this biography of the man behind Spider-Man and other comic-book characters. (Rev: SLJ 6/06) [921]

LEWIN, TED

5348 Lewin, Ted. *Touch and Go: Travels of a Children's Book Illustrator* (6–9). Illus. 1999, Lothrop $15.00 (978-0-688-14109-7). The noted picture book illustrator tells about his unusual experiences around the world in search of subjects for his books. (Rev: BL 4/15/99; SLJ 7/99) [921]

LIN, MAYA

5349 Lashnits, Tom. *Maya Lin* (6–10). Series: Asian Americans of Achievement. 2007, Chelsea House LB $30.00 (978-0-7910-9268-2). This is an attractive biography of the designer of the Vietnam Veterans Memorial in Washington, D.C. (Rev: SLJ 8/07) [921]

5350 Ling, Bettina. *Maya Lin* (5–7). Illus. Series: Contemporary Asian Americans. 1997, Raintree LB $17.98 (978-0-8172-3992-3). A profile of the Asian American architect and an introduction to many of her projects, including the Vietnam War Memorial in Washington, D.C. (Rev: BL 5/1/97) [921]

MARTINEZ, MARIA

5351 Morris, Juddi. *Tending the Fire: The Story of Maria Martinez* (5–8). 1997, Northland paper $6.95 (978-0-87358-654-2). The life story of New Mexico's most famous potter, who was born in an Indian pueblo in 1887. (Rev: BL 12/1/97; HBG 3/98; SLJ 12/97) [921]

MATISSE, HENRI

5352 Hollein, Max, and Nina Hollein. *Matisse: Cut-Out Fun with Matisse* (4–8). Series: Adventures in Art. 2003, Prestel $14.95 (978-3-7913-2858-4). This large-formatted book that originated in Germany, successfully introduces the life and work of the great French master. (Rev: BL 11/15/03; HBG 3/02; SLJ 8/01) [921]

5353 Welton, Jude. *Henri Matisse* (5–8). Series: Artists in Their Time. 2002, Watts LB $24.00 (978-0-531-12228-0); paper $6.95 (978-0-531-16621-5). The artistic and social periods during which Matisse worked are re-created along with a biography and several color examples of his work. (Rev: BL 10/15/02; SLJ 1/03) [921]

MICHELANGELO

5354 *Michelangelo* (5–8). Series: The Lives of the Artists. 2004, World Almanac LB $31.00 (978-0-8368-5600-2). A tall, slender volume full of facts about Michelangelo's life and times, with many color reproductions. (Rev: SLJ 8/04) [921]

5355 Somervill, Barbara A. *Michelangelo: Sculptor and Painter* (6–9). Illus. Series: Signature Lives. 2005, Compass Point LB $34.60 (978-0-7565-0814-

2). Michelangelo comes to life in this readable biography that includes color images. (Rev: BL 8/05) [709]

5356 Whiting, Jim. *Michelangelo* (4–7). Series: Art Profiles for Kids. 2007, Mitchell Lane LB $29.95 (978-1-58415-562-1). Suitable for both research and browsing, this examination of the artist's life and times includes many reproductions and interesting sidebars. (Rev: LMC 2/08; SLJ 12/07) [921]

MONET, CLAUDE

5357 Connolly, Sean. *Claude Monet* (4–8). Illus. Series: Lives of the Artists. 2005, World Almanac LB $31.00 (978-0-8368-5650-7). A tall, slender volume full of facts about Monet's life and times, with many color reproductions. (Rev: BL 6/1–15/04; SLJ 3/05) [921]

5358 Hodge, Susie. *Claude Monet* (5–8). Illus. Series: Artists in Their Time. 2002, Watts LB $24.00 (978-0-531-12226-6). Photographs, reproductions, maps, and a timeline that links world events with events in the artist's life make this suitable both for browsing and report writing. (Rev: SLJ 1/03) [921]

5359 Waldron, Ann. *Claude Monet* (7–12). Series: First Impressions. 1991, Abrams $19.95 (978-0-8109-3620-1). This illustrated biographical study of the pioneering Impressionist painter explores his fascination with nature and his experimentation with the effects of light. (Rev: BL 11/15/91; SLJ 1/92) [921]

5360 Whiting, Jim. *Claude Monet* (4–7). Series: Art Profiles for Kids. 2007, Mitchell Lane LB $29.95 (978-1-58415-563-8). Suitable for both research and browsing, this examination of the artist's life and times includes many reproductions and interesting sidebars. (Rev: LMC 2/08; SLJ 12/07) [921]

MORGAN, JULIA

5361 James, Cary. *Julia Morgan: Architect* (7–10). Illus. 1990, Chelsea LB $30.00 (978-1-55546-669-5). The story of the outstanding female architect who now has more than 700 projects to her credit. (Rev: SLJ 8/90) [921]

MOSES, GRANDMA

5362 Biracree, Tom. *Grandma Moses* (7–10). Illus. 1989, Chelsea LB $19.95 (978-1-55546-670-1). This primitive artist's life and works are discussed, and insets are provided of some of her paintings. (Rev: BL 12/1/89; SLJ 1/90; VOYA 2/90) [921]

MOUNT, WILLIAM SIDNEY

5363 Howard, Nancy S. *William Sidney Mount: Painter of Rural America* (4–7). Illus. 1994, Sterling

$14.95 (978-1-871922-75-2). An interactive book that explores the work and paintings of the 19th-century American painter William Sidney Mount. (Rev: BL 1/15/95) [921]

NAST, THOMAS

5364 Pflueger, Lynda. *Thomas Nast: Political Cartoonist* (5–8). Series: Historical American Biographies. 2000, Enslow LB $26.60 (978-0-7660-1251-6). An informative, entertaining, and well-written biography of this influential political cartoonist and critic. (Rev: BL 9/15/00; HBG 10/01; SLJ 11/00) [921]

NOGUCHI, ISAMU

5365 Tiger, Caroline. *Isamu Noguchi* (6–12). Series: Asian Americans of Achievement. 2007, Chelsea House LB $30.00 (978-0-7910-9276-7). This is the fascinating story of Noguchi's search for an identity and a place to call home as well as his development into an internationally renowned sculptor. (Rev: SLJ 10/07) [921]

O'KEEFFE, GEORGIA

5366 Berry, Michael. *Georgia O'Keeffe: Painter* (7–12). Illus. 1988, Chelsea LB $30.00 (978-1-55546-673-2). Illustrated chiefly in black and white, this is the story of the artist who reached maturity painting subjects in the southwestern states. (Rev: BL 9/15/88; SLJ 9/88; VOYA 2/89) [921]

5367 Shull, Jodie A. *Georgia O'Keeffe: Legendary American Painter* (6–8). Illus. Series: People to Know. 2004, Enslow LB $26.60 (978-0-7660-2104-4). Events that tilted O'Keeffe in the direction of her artistic style are revealed in this appealing biography. (Rev: BL 11/1/04) [921]

OROZCO, JOSE

5368 Cruz, Barbara C. *Jose Clemente Orozco: Mexican Artist* (7–12). Series: Hispanic Biographies. 1998, Enslow LB $26.60 (978-0-7660-1041-3). The story of the great artist Orozco, as well as an introduction to the mural painters of Mexico and how they used designs from Aztec and Mayan art. (Rev: BL 1/1–15/99; HBG 3/99; SLJ 3/99) [921]

PICASSO, PABLO

5369 Hodge, Susie, and Pablo Picasso. *Pablo Picasso* (4–8). Series: Lives of the Artists. 2004, Gareth Stevens LB $11.95 (978-0-8368-5606-4). Works by the young Picasso are a feature of this well illustrated profile. (Rev: BL 6/1–15/04) [921]

5370 MacDonald, Patricia A. *Pablo Picasso: Greatest Artist of the 20th Century* (7–10). Illus. Series: Giants of Art and Culture. 2001, Blackbirch LB

$29.94 (978-1-56711-504-8). Picasso's life and career are placed in historical context, with photographs, a timeline, a glossary, and lists of resources. (Rev: BL 8/01; HBG 3/02) [709]

5371 Meadows, Matthew. *Pablo Picasso* (5–7). Illus. Series: Art for Young People. 1996, Sterling $14.95 (978-0-8069-6160-6). In double-page spreads, presents the life and work of this multitalented Spanish artist. (Rev: BL 2/1/97; HB 5–6/96; SLJ 3/97) [921]

5372 Pfleger, Susanne. *A Day with Picasso* (4–7). Series: Adventures in Art. 2000, Prestel $14.95 (978-3-7913-2165-3). An introduction to the life and work of Picasso, including many full-color reproductions. (Rev: BL 2/15/00; SLJ 2/00) [921]

5373 *Picasso: Soul on Fire* (4–7). Trans. by Rick Jacobson. Illus. by Rick Jacobson and Laura Fernandez. 2004, Tundra $15.95 (978-0-88776-599-5). Oil paintings of the Spanish-born artist, along with reproductions of some of his best-known pieces, introduce his work and brief facts about his life. (Rev: BL 11/1/04) [921]

5374 Scarborough, Kate. *Pablo Picasso* (5–8). Series: Artists in Their Time. 2002, Watts LB $24.00 (978-0-531-12229-7); paper $6.95 (978-0-531-16622-2). This biography of the 20th century's most famous artist is accompanied by material on the social conditions of his time. (Rev: BL 10/15/02; SLJ 1/03) [921]

5375 Selfridge, John W. *Pablo Picasso* (5–9). Series: Hispanics of Achievement. 1993, Chelsea LB $32.00 (978-0-7910-1777-7). A colorful biography of this great Spanish painter, who lived most of his life as a political exile in France, with some examples of his enormous output. (Rev: BL 3/1/94) [9212]

5376 Wallis, Jeremy. *Pablo Picasso* (5–8). Series: Creative Lives. 2001, Heinemann LB $27.07 (978-1-58810-206-5). Picasso's eccentricities are highlighted in this volume that covers his life, his family, and his work. (Rev: HBG 10/02; SLJ 3/02) [921]

POLITI, LEO

5377 Stalcup, Ann. *Leo Politi: Artist of the Angels* (4–9). Illus. by Leo Politi. 2004, Silver Moon $24.95 (978-1-893110-38-0). The life of the American-born man who spent his formative years in Italy and returned as an adult to make his home in Los Angeles and protray the ethnic communities there in his books for children. (Rev: SLJ 4/05) [921]

POLLOCK, JACKSON

5378 Oliver, Clare. *Jackson Pollock* (5–8). Series: Artists in Their Time. 2003, Watts LB $24.00 (978-0-531-12237-2). An interesting life of Pollock, with reproductions of his works and of those of fellow painters, and a timeline that adds historical context. (Rev: SLJ 5/03) [759]

REMBERT, WINFRED

5379 Rembert, Winfred. *Don't Hold Me Back: My Life and Art* (4–7). Illus. 2003, Cricket $19.95 (978-0-8126-2703-9). Rembert reflects on his life in the South as a sharecropper's son — picking cotton, dealing with racism, the civil rights movement — and displays his evocative works of art with comments on their creation. (Rev: BL 11/1/03*; HBG 4/04; SLJ 12/03*) [759.1]

REMBRANDT VAN RIJN

5380 Mason, Antony. *Rembrandt* (4–8). Illus. Series: Lives of the Artists. 2005, World Almanac LB $31.00 (978-0-8368-5651-4). A tall, slender volume full of facts about Rembrandt's life and times, with many color reproductions. (Rev: BL 6/1–15/04; SLJ 3/05) [921]

5381 Schwartz, Gary. *Rembrandt* (7–12). Series: First Impressions. 1992, Abrams $19.95 (978-0-8109-3760-4). This jargon-free, accessible biography presents Rembrandt with all his flaws and quirks. (Rev: BL 5/1/92; SLJ 6/92*) [921]

REMINGTON, FREDERIC

5382 Plain, Nancy. *Frederic Remington* (6–8). Illus. Series: Historical American Biographies. 2003, Enslow LB $26.60 (978-0-7660-1975-1). This look at Remington's life and accomplishments includes black-and-white reproductions of his works and period photographs that convey the flavor of the 1880s. (Rev: BL 6/1–15/03; SLJ 6/03) [709]

RENOIR, PIERRE-AUGUSTE

5383 Parsons, Tom. *Pierre Auguste Renoir* (5–7). Illus. Series: Art for Young People. 1996, Sterling $14.95 (978-0-8069-6162-0). The life and work of this prolific French artist are examined in a series of double-page spreads. (Rev: BL 2/1/97; SLJ 3/97) [921]

5384 Somervill, Barbara. *Pierre-Auguste Renoir* (5–8). Illus. Series: Art Profiles for Kids. 2007, Mitchell Lane LB $29.95 (978-1-58415-566-9). A brief introduction to the artist's life and work and the times in which he lived, with reproductions of his art. (Rev: BL 1/1–15/08; LMC 2/08; SLJ 12/07) [921]

RIVERA, DIEGO

5385 Bankston, John. *Diego Rivera* (5–7). Series: Latinos in American History. 2003, Mitchell Lane LB $29.95 (978-1-58415-208-8). A biography of the famous 20th-century Mexican artist who is best known for his murals with political overtones. (Rev: BL 1/1–15/04; HBG 4/04; SLJ 2/04) [921]

5386 Cockcroft, James D. *Diego Rivera* (5–9). Series: Hispanics of Achievement. 1991, Chelsea LB $21.95 (978-0-7910-1252-9). The life of this Mexican artist and activist, with several illustrations. (Rev: BL 11/1/91; SLJ 1/92) [921]

5387 Goldstein, Ernest. *The Journey of Diego Rivera* (7–10). Illus. 1996, Lerner LB $23.93 (978-0-8225-2066-5). Though short on biographical material, this profusely illustrated volume is a fine introduction to Rivera's art and its connections to the history of Mexico. (Rev: BL 4/15/96; SLJ 1/96; VOYA 10/96) [921]

5388 Gonzales, Doreen. *Diego Rivera: His Art, His Life* (6–9). Illus. Series: Hispanic Americans. 1996, Enslow LB $26.60 (978-0-89490-764-7). The story of the great Mexican painter and muralist and his relationship with Frida Kahlo. (Rev: BL 11/1/96; SLJ 10/96) [921]

5389 Litwin, Laura Baskes. *Diego Rivera: Legendary Mexican Painter* (7–10). Illus. Series: Latino Biography. 2005, Enslow LB $31.93 (978-0-7660-2486-1). The life, art, and controversial politics of Mexican artist Diego Rivera are explored in this attractive and readable title. (Rev: BL 11/1/05; SLJ 4/06) [759.972]

ROCKWELL, NORMAN

5390 Gherman, Beverly. *Norman Rockwell: Storyteller with a Brush* (4–7). Illus. 2000, Simon & Schuster $19.95 (978-0-689-82001-4). An appealing biography of this New England artist who reflected mid-20th-century American life and values in his many paintings. (Rev: BCCB 7–8/00; BL 2/15/00; HB 3–4/00; HBG 10/00; SLJ 2/00) [921]

ROUSSEAU, HENRI

5391 Pfleger, Susanne. *Henri Rousseau: A Jungle Expedition* (4–7). Trans. by Catherine McCreadie. Illus. Series: Adventures in Art. 1999, Prestel $14.95 (978-3-7913-1987-2). The story of Henri Rousseau and the art that evolved from his visits to a botanical garden. (Rev: BL 2/1/99; SLJ 2/99) [921]

SCHULKE, FLIP

5392 Schulke, Flip. *Witness to Our Times: My Life as a Photojournalist* (6–12). Illus. 2003, Cricket $19.95 (978-0-8126-2682-7). In this volume full of examples of his work, Schulke describes his early life and his career covering events of the 20th century including the space program and the civil rights movement. (Rev: BL 4/15/03; HBG 10/03; SLJ 6/03; VOYA 2/04) [070.4]

SCHULZ, CHARLES

5393 Marvis, Barbara. *Charles Schulz: The Story of the Peanuts Gang* (4–8). Illus. Series: Robbie Reader. 2004, Mitchell Lane LB $25.70 (978-1-58415-289-7). This photo-filled biography traces Schulz's life and his love of cartoons; it is especially suitable for reluctant readers. (Rev: BL 9/1/05)

5394 Schuman, Michael A. *Charles M. Schulz: Cartoonist and Creator of Peanuts* (6–10). Series: People to Know. 2002, Enslow LB $26.60 (978-0-7660-1846-4). A fine biography of the creator of Peanuts, complete with many illustrations and cartoons. (Rev: BL 9/15/02; HBG 10/02) [921]

SIMMONS, PHILIP

5395 Lyons, Mary E. *Catching the Fire: Philip Simmons, Blacksmith* (4–8). 1997, Houghton $17.00 (978-0-395-72033-2). A biography of the contemporary African American craftsman and artist from Charleston, South Carolina, with extensive quotations from personal interviews. (Rev: BL 9/1/97; HBG 3/98; SLJ 9/97) [921]

THIEBAUD, WAYNE

5396 Rubin, Susan G. *Delicious: The Life and Art of Wayne Thiebaud* (5–8). Illus. 2007, Chronicle $15.95 (978-0-8118-5168-8). Paintings (by Thiebaud, of course) of gum balls and cupcakes on the cover of this nicely designed volume draw readers in to the story of a man who paints "happy pictures." (Rev: BL 2/15/08; SLJ 3/08) [921]

UNGERER, TOMI

5397 Ungerer, Tomi. *Tomi: A Childhood Under the Nazis* (6–10). 1998, Roberts Rinehart $29.95 (978-1-57098-163-0). Using many memorabilia of the time, this is the illustrator's story of his life during World War II after the Germans entered his Alsace town in 1940 when he was 8 years old. (Rev: BL 12/15/98; SLJ 3/99) [921]

VAN GOGH, VINCENT

5398 Bonafoux, Pascal. *Van Gogh: The Passionate Eye* (7–12). Series: Discoveries. 1992, Abrams paper $12.95 (978-0-8109-2828-2). An overview of the life and work of this disturbed Dutch painter. (Rev: BL 7/92) [021]

5399 Green, Jen. *Vincent van Gogh* (5–8). Series: Artists in Their Time. 2002, Watts LB $24.00 (978-0-531-12238-9). The life and times of this 20th-century artistic genius are covered, with a number of reproductions of his paintings. (Rev: BL 10/15/02) [921]

5400 Tyson, Peter. *Vincent van Gogh: Artist* (8–12). Illus. Series: Great Achievers: Lives of the Physically Challenged. 1996, Chelsea LB $21.95 (978-0-7910-2422-5). This mature biography discusses van Gogh's life and work and his contributions to Impressionism, achieved despite the deterioration of his mental health. (Rev: BL 5/1/96; SLJ 8/96) [921]

5401 Whiting, Jim. *Vincent Van Gogh* (7–12). Series: Art Profiles for Kids. 2007, Mitchell Lane LB $29.95 (978-1-58415-564-5). Report writers will appreciate this thorough introduction to the artist's life and work, with interesting "FYI" sections and small color reproductions. (Rev: SLJ 1/08)

WALDMAN, NEIL

5402 Waldman, Neil. *Out of the Shadows: An Artist's Journey* (5–8). Illus. 2006, Boyds Mills $21.95 (978-1-59078-411-2). In this candid memoir, Waldman describes how his challenging childhood experiences influenced him as an artist. (Rev: BL 4/15/06; SLJ 5/06) [741.6]

WANG YANI

5403 Zhensun, Zheng, and Alice Low. *A Young Painter: The Life and Paintings of Wang Yani — China's Extraordinary Young Artist* (5–8). 1991, Scholastic paper $17.95 (978-0-590-44906-9). The story of a self-taught prodigy whose paintings are highly regarded in China. Includes many examples of her unique work, based on the traditional Chinese style. (Rev: BCCB 9/91; BL 10/1/91*; SLJ 8/91) [921]

WARHOL, ANDY

5404 Bolton, Linda. *Andy Warhol* (5–8). Series: Artists in Their Time. 2002, Watts LB $24.00 (978-0-531-12225-9); paper $6.95 (978-0-531-16618-5). This biography includes material on the social period in which Warhol worked. (Rev: BL 10/15/02) [921]

5405 Greenberg, Jan, and Sandra Jordan. *Andy Warhol, Prince of Pop* (8–12). 2004, Random LB $18.99 (978-0-385-73056-3). Warhol had a successful career in commercial art before rising to fame as a pop icon; this volume covers his youth, early career, love of celebrity, and early death as well as his art and its lasting influence. (Rev: BCCB 12/04; BL 6/1–15/04*; HB 1–2/05; SLJ 11/04; VOYA 10/04) [709]

5406 Rubin, Susan G. *Andy Warhol: Pop Art Painter* (4–7). Illus. 2006, Abrams $18.95 (978-0-8109-5477-9). This picture-book biography chronicles Warhol's life and career, focusing in particular on his art and his childhood in Pittsburgh; there are many reproductions plus a timeline and a glossary. (Rev: BL 11/1/06; SLJ 11/06) [700]

WOOD, GRANT

5407 Duggleby, John. *Artist in Overalls: The Life of Grant Wood* (4–8). 1996, Chronicle $15.95 (978-0-8118-1242-9). The life of this American artist tells of his difficult struggle with poverty and his great attachment to the Midwest. (Rev: BCCB 6/96; BL 4/15/96; HB 7–8/96; SLJ 5/96) [921]

WOOD, MICHELE

5408 Igus, Toyomi. *Going Back Home: An Artist Returns to the South* (4–8). Illus. 1996, Children's $16.95 (978-0-89239-137-0). The author re-creates the family history and life of the African American illustrator Michele Wood. (Rev: BCCB 12/96; BL 9/15/96; SLJ 7/97) [921]

WRIGHT, FRANK LLOYD

5409 Adkins, Jan. *Frank Lloyd Wright* (7–12). Illus. Series: Up Close. 2007, Viking $16.99 (978-0-670-06138-9). The biographer does not gloss over the architect's infamously prickly nature but also emphasizes Wright's talent and his influence on building design. (Rev: BL 11/1/07; SLJ 11/07) [921]

5410 Davis, Frances A. *Frank Lloyd Wright: Maverick Architect* (5–9). Illus. 1996, Lerner LB $30.35 (978-0-8225-4953-6). A well-documented life of this influential 20th-century architect, with many black-and-white photographs of his most important buildings. (Rev: BL 1/1–15/97; SLJ 1/97) [921]

5411 Fandel, Jennifer. *Frank Lloyd Wright* (7–12). Series: Xtraordinary Artists. 2005, Creative Education LB $21.95 (978-1-58341-378-4). This well-illustrated life of the visionary architect draws on comments from his students, contemporaries, and admirers. (Rev: SLJ 12/05) [921]

5412 Mayo, Gretchen Will. *Frank Lloyd Wright* (5–8). Series: Trailblazers of the Modern World. 2004, World Almanac LB $31.00 (978-0-8368-5101-4). Report writers will find useful information on Wright's life, achievements, and lasting contributions. (Rev: SLJ 7/04) [921]

5413 Middleton, Haydn. *Frank Lloyd Wright* (5–8). Series: Creative Lives. 2001, Heinemann LB $27.07 (978-1-58810-203-4). An attractive look at the architect's life and career with illustrations and a useful timeline. (Rev: HBG 10/02; SLJ 3/02) [921]

ZHANG, ANGE

5414 Zhang, Ange. *Red Land, Yellow River: A Story from the Cultural Revolution* (5–8). 2004, Groundwood $16.95 (978-0-88899-489-9). In this compelling autobiography, artist Ange Zhang tells how he came of age during one of the most turbulent periods in modern Chinese history — the Cultural Revolution of the late 1960s. (Rev: BL 12/1/04*; SLJ 12/04) [921]

Authors

ALCOTT, LOUISA MAY

5415 Ruth, Amy. *Louisa May Alcott* (4–7). Series: A&E Biography. 1999, Lerner LB $27.93 (978-0-8225-4938-3). A clear, readable life of the author who wrote from personal experience about family life at the time of the Civil War and later. (Rev: BL 3/15/00; HBG 3/99; SLJ 1/99) [921]

5416 Silverthorne, Elizabeth. *Louisa May Alcott* (4–7). Illus. Series: Who Wrote That? 2002, Chelsea $30.00 (978-0-7910-6721-5). A look at the life and works of author Louisa May Alcott, with particular emphasis on how her family influenced her work. (Rev: BL 10/15/02; HBG 3/03; SLJ 10/02) [813]

5417 Warrick, Karen Clemens. *Louisa May Alcott: Author of Little Women* (5–8). Series: Historical American Biographies. 2000, Enslow LB $26.60 (978-0-7660-1254-7). Using many direct quotations from Alcott, along with fact boxes, maps, a chronology, and chapter notes, this is an interesting biography of the prolific writer from Pennsylvania. (Rev: BL 3/15/00; HBG 10/00) [921]

ALLENDE, ISABEL

5418 Main, Mary. *Isabel Allende: Award-Winning Latin American Author* (6–9). Series: Latino Biography Library. 2005, Enslow LB $31.93 (978-0-7660-2488-5). An engaging life of the writer that gives readers a perspective on life in Chile and on the world affairs that have impacted Allende. (Rev: SLJ 1/06) [921]

ALVAREZ, JULIA

5419 Aykroyd, Clarissa. *Julia Alvarez: Novelist and Poet* (7–10). Illus. Series: 20th Century's Most Influential Hispanics. 2007, Gale LB $32.45 (978-1-4205-0022-6). The poet's life and work, with many quotations from Alvarez and excerpts from her poems. (Rev: BL 2/15/08) [921]

ANDERSEN, HANS CHRISTIAN

5420 Varmer, Hjordis. *Hans Christian Andersen: His Fairy Tale Life* (4–7). Trans. by Tina Nunnally. Illus. by Lilian Bregger. 2005, Groundwood $19.95 (978-0-88899-670-1). This large-format, lively biography presents the Danish storyteller's single-minded struggle to rise above adversity. (Rev: BL 11/1/05; SLJ 6/06) [839.81]

ANGELOU, MAYA

5421 Cuffie, Terrasita A. *Maya Angelou* (4–8). Series: The Importance Of. 1999, Lucent LB $27.45 (978-1-56006-532-6). A biography that traces Maya Angelou's life from her childhood exposure to poverty and bigotry in the rural South to her eventual fame as a writer. (Rev: BL 9/15/99; SLJ 11/99) [921]

5422 Kirkpatrick, Patricia. *Maya Angelou* (5–9). Illus. by John Thompson. Series: Voices in Poetry. 2003, Creative LB $19.95 (978-1-58341-281-7). This picture-book biography introduces readers to Angelou's poetry and life from childhood. (Rev: BL 12/1/03; SLJ 12/03) [811]

5423 Kite, L. Patricia. *Maya Angelou* (6–9). Series: A&E Biography. 1999, Lerner LB $27.93 (978-0-8225-4944-4). Beginning in 1993, when Maya Angelou read her poetry at President Clinton's inauguration, this biography flashes back to her birth in 1928 and continues through 1996, covering personal aspects of her life and honors she has received, and including brief descriptions of her poetry and other writing. (Rev: BL 3/15/00; SLJ 7/99) [921]

5424 Lisandrelli, Elaine S. *Maya Angelou: More than a Poet* (7–12). Illus. Series: African-American Biographies. 1996, Enslow LB $20.95 (978-0-89490-684-8). A biography of the famous African American writer that includes her work as a dancer, singer, actress, and spokesperson for African American causes. (Rev: BL 9/1/96; SLJ 6/96; VOYA 10/96) [921]

5425 Raatma, Lucia. *Maya Angelou: Author and Documentary Filmmaker* (4–8). Series: Ferguson Career Biographies. 2001, Ferguson LB $25.00 (978-0-89434-336-0). As well as a life of Maya Angelou, this book includes information on how to become a writer, filmmaker, and director. (Rev: SLJ 2/01) [921]

5426 Shapiro, Miles. *Maya Angelou* (7–10). Illus. Series: Black Americans of Achievement. 1994, Chelsea LB $21.95 (978-0-7910-1862-0). A chronological narrative of the life of this amazing African American writer that describes her hardships and triumphs. (Rev: BL 6/1–15/94; SLJ 6/94) [921]

ASIMOV, ISAAC

5427 Boerst, William J. *Isaac Asimov: Writer of the Future* (5–9). Illus. 1998, Morgan Reynolds LB $23.95 (978-1-883846-32-9). An engaging biography of the amazingly prolific author and scientist who was considered a misfit in his youth. (Rev: BL 12/1/98; SLJ 1/99) [921]

5428 Judson, Karen. *Isaac Asimov: Master of Science Fiction* (5–9). Illus. 1998, Enslow LB $26.60 (978-0-7660-1031-4). A biography of Asimov that includes two chapters particularly helpful to researchers: on his importance as a writer of science fiction and on his work in other genres. (Rev: BL 12/1/98; HBG 3/99; SLJ 2/99) [921]

AUSTEN, JANE

5429 Locke, Juliane. *England's Jane: The Story of Jane Austen* (8–11). Illus. 2006, Morgan Reynolds LB $26.95 (978-1-931798-82-2). The parallels between Austen's life and novels are evident in this appealing biography. (Rev: BL 2/15/06; SLJ 2/06) [823]

5430 Ruth, Amy. *Jane Austen* (5–8). Series: A&E Biography. 2001, Lerner LB $27.93 (978-0-8225-4992-5). This is the intriguing story of Jane Austen, who lived a quiet, obscure life yet produced some of the world's greatest novels. (Rev: BL 6/1–15/01; HBG 10/01; SLJ 11/01) [921]

5431 Wagner, Heather Lehr. *Jane Austen* (7–10). Series: Who Wrote That? 2003, Chelsea House LB $30.00 (978-0-7910-7623-1). Details of Austen's family life and education and of the mores of the time give insight into her humorous attitude toward society and romance. (Rev: SLJ 6/04) [921]

AVI

5432 Markham, Lois. *Avi* (5–8). 1996, Learning Works paper $7.99 (978-0-88160-280-7). This profile of the gifted writer recounts his triumph over dysgraphia, a learning disability that makes writing difficult, and explores his creative process and the major themes of his work. (Rev: BL 4/1/96; SLJ 8/96) [921]

5433 Mercier, Cathryn M., and Susan P. Bloom. *Presenting Avi* (6–10). Series: Twayne's United States Authors. 1997, Macmillan $35.00 (978-0-8057-4569-6). This biography of the noted writer of books for children and young adults is divided into chapters based on roles he has assumed as a writer, including storyteller, stylist, magician, and historian, and explores his many beliefs about the significance of literature. (Rev: SLJ 6/98) [921]

5434 Sommers, Michael A. *Avi* (5–8). Series: The Library of Author Biographies. 2004, Rosen LB $27.95 (978-0-8239-4522-1). Covers Avi's life and career as a YA author, with analysis of his work, an interview, and lists of works and awards. (Rev: SLJ 1/05) [921]

BARRIE, J. M.

5435 Aller, Susan Bivin. *J. M. Barrie: The Magic Behind Peter Pan* (6–8). 1994, Lerner LB $25.26 (978-0-8225-4918-5). This biography of the author reveals Barrie's similarities to his character Peter Pan and also gives details of his failed marriages. (Rev: BL 11/1/94; SLJ 12/94) [921]

BORGES, JORGE LUÍS

5436 Lennon, Adrian. *Jorge Luís Borges* (5–9). Series: Hispanics of Achievement. 1991, Chelsea LB $19.95 (978-0-7910-1236-9). A simple account that describes the life and work of one of South America's great contemporary writers. (Rev: BL 3/15/92; SLJ 7/92) [921]

BRADBURY, RAY

5437 Mass, Wendy. *Ray Bradbury: Master of Science Fiction and Fantasy* (6–9). Illus. Series: Authors Teens Love. 2004, Enslow LB $26.60 (978-0-7660-2240-9). Report writers will find ample details about Bradbury's life and career, with plot summaries of his most famous books. (Rev: BL 11/1/04; SLJ 12/04) [921]

BRONTË FAMILY

5438 Kenyon, Karen Smith. *The Brontë Family: Passionate Literary Geniuses* (5–9). Series: Lerner Biographies. 2002, Lerner LB $30.35 (978-0-8225-0071-1). An absorbing introduction to the individual members of this literary family, with many illustrations and quotations from letters. (Rev: HBG 3/03; SLJ 1/03; VOYA 2/03) [921]

BROOKS, GWENDOLYN

5439 Hill, Christine M. *Gwendolyn Brooks: "Poetry Is Life Distilled"* (7–10). Illus. Series: African-American Biography Library. 2005, Enslow LB $31.93 (978-0-7660-2292-8). Poet Gwendolyn Brooks, the first African American to win the Pulitzer Prize, is profiled in accessible text with lots of photos and background information. (Rev: BL 11/1/05; SLJ 11/05) [811]

5440 Rhynes, Martha E. *Gwendolyn Brooks: Poet from Chicago* (6–10). Illus. Series: World Writers. 2003, Morgan Reynolds LB $23.95 (978-1-931798-05-1). The chronological presentation in this biography provides readers with an understanding of Brooks's changing views and themes. (Rev: BL 2/15/03; HBG 10/03; SLJ 4/03; VOYA 6/03) [811]

BUCK, PEARL S.

5441 La Farge, Ann. *Pearl Buck* (7–10). Illus. 1988, Chelsea LB $19.95 (978-1-55546-645-9). The life of the writer who introduced pre-Revolutionary China to millions of American readers. (Rev: BL 8/88) [921]

BURNETT, FRANCES HODGSON

5442 Carpenter, Angelica S., and Jean Shirley. *Frances Hodgson Burnett: Beyond the Secret Gar-*den (4–8). Illus. 1990, Lerner LB $27.93 (978-0-8225-4905-5). A glimpse into the private life of the woman who wrote *The Secret Garden*. (Rev: BCCB 12/90; BL 1/1/91; SLJ 3/91*) [921]

BURROUGHS, EDGAR RICE

5443 Boerst, William J. *Edgar Rice Burroughs: Creator of Tarzan* (5–8). Illus. Series: World Writers. 2000, Morgan Reynolds LB $23.95 (978-1-883846-56-5). A concise biography of the prolific author who created Tarzan and was a pioneer of the science fiction genre. (Rev: BL 7/00; HBG 3/01; SLJ 1/01) [921]

BYARS, BETSY

5444 Byars, Betsy. *The Moon and I* (4–7). Illus. 1996, Morrow paper $5.99 (978-0-688-13704-5). A memoir from this well-known children's author, which gives her the opportunity to tell how she likes both writing and snakes. (Rev: BCCB 3/92*; BL 5/15/92; SLJ 4/92) [921]

5445 Cammarano, Rita. *Betsy Byars* (4–7). Series: Who Wrote That? 2002, Chelsea $30.00 (978-0-7910-6720-8). A profile in text and pictures of one of America's best-loved authors and winner of the Newbery and other prizes. (Rev: BL 10/15/02; HBG 3/03) [921]

CARD, ORSON SCOTT

5446 Willett, Edward. *Orson Scott Card: Architect of Alternate Worlds* (7–9). Series: Authors Teens Love. 2006, Enslow LB $31.93 (978-0-7660-2354-3). A thorough profile of the creator of the "Enderverse." (Rev: SLJ 1/07) [921]

CARROLL, LEWIS

5447 Carpenter, Angelica Shirley. *Lewis Carroll: Through the Looking Glass* (6–9). Series: Lerner Biographies. 2002, Lerner LB $27.93 (978-0-8225-0073-5). The mathematician and author who created Alice is introduced through a look at his youth, education, university career, and Oxford friendships. (Rev: BCCB 1/03; HBG 3/03; SLJ 3/03; VOYA 8/03) [828]

CATHER, WILLA

5448 Keene, Ann T. *Willa Cather* (7–12). 1994, Messner LB $15.00 (978-0-671-86760-7). A biography examining the writer's childhood, college years, jobs as editor and teacher, travels, and friends, as well as her reputed lesbianism. (Rev: BL 10/1/94; SLJ 11/94; VOYA 4/95) [813]

5449 Ling, Bettina. *Willa Cather: Author and Critic* (6–9). Series: Great Life Stories. 2003, Watts LB $30.50 (978-0-531-12316-4). Sidebar features provide background information on society and politics in the late 19th and early 20th centuries, adding depth to this life of the author of *My Antonia* and other classics. (Rev: SLJ 1/04) [305.235]

5450 Meltzer, Milton. *Willa Cather* (7–12). Illus. Series: Literary Greats. 2008, Lerner LB $33.26 (978-0-8225-7604-4). An easy-to-understand profile that describes Cather's upbringing on the plains and provides historical context. (Rev: BL 4/15/08; SLJ 6/08) [921]

5451 O'Brien, Sharon. *Willa Cather* (7–12). Series: Lives of Notable Gay Men and Lesbians. 1994, Chelsea LB $19.95 (978-0-7910-2302-0); paper $9.95 (978-0-7910-2877-3). Focuses on the author's reputed lesbianism and shows how Cather created a nurturing network of women friends and lovers. (Rev: BL 11/1/94; SLJ 11/94; VOYA 2/95) [921]

5452 Streissguth, Thomas. *Writer of the Plains: A Story About Willa Cather* (4–7). Illus. 1997, Carolrhoda LB $22.60 (978-1-57505-015-7). A simple introduction to the works of Willa Cather and the places where she lived and wrote. (Rev: BL 6/1–15/97; SLJ 10/97) [921]

CERVANTES, MIGUEL DE

5453 Goldberg, Jake. *Miguel de Cervantes* (5–9). Series: Hispanics of Achievement. 1993, Chelsea LB $21.95 (978-0-7910-1238-3). The absorbing story of the Spanish writer whose life rivaled that of his adventurous hero, Don Quixote. (Rev: BL 9/15/93) [921]

CHAUCER, GEOFFREY

5454 Hubbard-Brown, Janet. *Chaucer: Celebrated Poet and Author* (6–9). Series: Makers of the Middle Ages and Renaissance. 2005, Chelsea House LB $30 (978-0-7910-8635-3). A biography of the famous medieval writer, with information on his childhood, background, influences, career, and works. (Rev: SLJ 5/06) [921]

CHESNUTT, CHARLES

5455 Thompson, Cliff. *Charles Chesnutt* (7–10). Series: Black Americans of Achievement. 1992, Chelsea LB $19.95 (978-1-55546-578-0). The life of this pioneering African American writer who explored themes relating to slavery and the Reconstruction period in his fiction. (Rev: BL 12/1/92) [921]

CHRISTIE, AGATHA

5456 Dommermuth-Costa, Carol. *Agatha Christie: Writer of Mystery* (5–9). Series: Biographies. 1997, Lerner LB $30.35 (978-0-8225-4954-3). A biography of the "First Lady of Crime," with material on

her personal life, including her two marriages. (Rev: SLJ 8/97; VOYA 4/98)

CISNEROS, SANDRA

5457 Brackett, Virginia. *A Home in the Heart: The Story of Sandra Cisneros* (7–12). Series: World Writers. 2004, Morgan Reynolds LB $23.95 (978-1-931798-42-6). The life and literary career of Mexican American author Sandra Cisneros. (Rev: BL 12/1/04; SLJ 3/05) [921]

5458 Mirriam-Goldberg, Caryn. *Sandra Cisneros: Latina Writer and Activist* (5–8). Illus. Series: Hispanic Biographies. 1998, Enslow LB $19.95 (978-0-7760-1045-8). A biography, enlivened with many quotations, of the woman who received Cs and Ds in school and later became a first-rate author and leading Hispanic American activist. (Rev: BL 1/1–15/99; VOYA 10/99) [921]

CONRAD, JOSEPH

5459 Fletcher, Chris. *Joseph Conrad* (7–9). Illus. 1999, Oxford LB $32.95 (978-0-19-521441-3). Using many quotations from Conrad's letters and works plus excellent illustrations, this biography traces the life of the adventurous author whose second language was English. (Rev: BL 1/1–15/00; HBG 4/00; SLJ 1/00) [921]

COURLANDER, HAROLD

5460 Jaffe, Nina. *A Voice for the People: The Life and Work of Harold Courlander* (7–10). Illus. 1997, Holt $16.95 (978-0-8050-3444-8). A biography of the famous collector of folk tales from minority groups who was also a noted writer and storyteller. (Rev: BL 11/1/97; HBG 3/98; SLJ 12/97) [921]

COVILLE, BRUCE

5461 Marcovitz, Hal. *Bruce Coville* (6–9). Series: Who Wrote That? 2005, Chelsea House LB $30 (978-0-7910-8656-8). A biography of author Bruce Coville, covering his childhood, life experiences, career, how books and reading affected his life, and his inspirations. (Rev: SLJ 5/06) [921]

CRANE, STEPHEN

5462 Kepnes, Caroline. *Stephen Crane* (5–8). Series: Classic Storytellers. 2004, Mitchell Lane LB $29.95 (978-1-58415-272-9). An introduction to Crane's life, work, and legacy, with background information on relevant historical, cultural, and economic factors. (Rev: BL 1/05; SLJ 1/05) [921]

CRUTCHER, CHRIS

5463 Davis, Terry. *Presenting Chris Crutcher* (6–10). 1997, Macmillan $29.00 (978-0-8057-8223-3). A warm biography of this important young adult author who combines sports stories with important themes such as tolerance and the meaning of friendship. (Rev: SLJ 6/98; VOYA 6/98) [921]

5464 Summers, Michael A. *Chris Crutcher* (5–8). Series: The Library of Author Biographies. 2005, Rosen LB $27.95 (978-1-4042-0325-9). An interview with Crutcher is an interesting addition to this description of the author's life — including his experiences as a novelist, educator, therapist, and child protection advocate — and his works for children. (Rev: SLJ 9/05) [921]

CUMMINGS, E. E.

5465 Reef, Catherine. *E. E. Cummings: A Poet's Life* (8–11). 2006, Clarion $21.00 (978-0-618-56849-9). In addition to Cummings's poetry, Reef looks at his difficult teen years and romantic relationships and at the culture of the time. (Rev: BL 11/15/06; HB 11–12/06; SLJ 3/07*) [921]

DAHL, ROALD

5466 Cooling, Wendy. *D Is for Dahl: A Gloriumptious A–Z Guide to the World of Roald Dahl* (5–8). Illus. by Quentin Blake. 2005, Viking $15.99 (978-0-670-06023-8). For Dahl fans, this is an alphabetically arranged collection of trivia about his life and writings. (Rev: BL 8/05; SLJ 10/05) [823]

5467 Dahl, Roald. *Boy: Tales of Childhood* (7–12). Illus. 1984, Farrar $17.00 (978-0-374-37374-0). The famous author's autobiography — sometimes humorous, sometimes touching — of growing up in Wales and spending summers in Norway. (Rev: BL 6/87) [921]

5468 Gelletly, LeeAnne. *Gift of Imagination: The Story of Roald Dahl* (7–10). 2006, Morgan Reynolds $26.95 (978-1-59935-026-4). Dahl's early life and career are detailed in this profile that includes many photographs, a timeline, and a bibliography of the author's works. (Rev: BL 11/1/06; SLJ 12/06) [823]

5469 Houle, Michelle M. *Roald Dahl: Author of Charlie and the Chocolate Factory* (6–9). Series: Authors Teens Love. 2006, Enslow LB $23.95 (978-0-7660-2353-6). Covers Dahl's life and work, with glossary, chapter notes, and bibliography. (Rev: BL 7/06; SLJ 7/06) [921]

5470 Shields, Charles J. *Roald Dahl* (4–7). Series: Who Wrote That? 2002, Chelsea $30.00 (978-0-7910-6722-2). A brief biography of the master of whimsical stories that involve such strange elements as secretive chocolate factories and giant peaches. (Rev: BL 10/15/02; HBG 3/03) [921]

D'ANGELO, PASCAL

5471 Murphy, Jim. *Pick and Shovel Poet: The Journeys of Pascal D'Angelo* (6–12). Illus. 2000, Clarion $20.00 (978-0-395-77610-0). The story of the short, hard life of the Italian American poet who wrote an important autobiography about coming to the New World. (Rev: BCCB 12/00; BL 3/1/01; HB 1–2/01; HBG 3/01; SLJ 1/01; VOYA 2/02) [973.04]

DANTE ALIGHIERI

5472 Davenport, John C. *Dante: Poet, Author, and Proud Florentine* (6–9). Series: Makers of the Middle Ages and Renaissance. 2005, Chelsea House LB $30 (978-0-7910-8634-6). Describes the childhood, background, influences, career, and works of the Italian author. (Rev: SLJ 5/06) [921]

DANZIGER, PAULA

5473 Krull, Kathleen. *Presenting Paula Danziger* (6–12). Series: United States Authors. 1995, Twayne $35.00 (978-0-8057-4153-7). Examines writer Danziger's personal problems, humorous teaching experiences, and group discussions of her books in six thematic chapters. (Rev: BL 9/1/95; VOYA 2/96) [921]

5474 Reed, Jennifer. *Paula Danziger: Voice of Teen Troubles* (5–8). Series: Authors Teens Love. 2006, Enslow LB $31.93 (978-0-7660-2444-1). This profile of the popular author includes interviews in which she discusses her dysfunctional family and her struggles with depression and bulimia. (Rev: BL 9/15/06) [921]

DEPAOLA, TOMIE

5475 dePaola, Tomie. *Christmas Remembered* (5–8). 2006, Putnam $19.99 (978-0-399-24622-7). Folk artist dePaola recalls some of the most memorable Christmases from his past. (Rev: BL 10/1/06; SLJ 10/06) [813]

DICKENS, CHARLES

5476 Caravantes, Peggy. *Best of Times: The Story of Charles Dickens* (7–10). Illus. Series: Writers of Imagination. 2005, Morgan Reynolds LB $26.95 (978-1-931798-68-6). Examines the events in the author's life that led to his literary preoccupation with social injustices. (Rev: BL 8/05; SLJ 12/05) [823]

5477 Collins, David R. *Tales for Hard Times: A Story About Charles Dickens* (4–8). Illus. by David Mataya. Series: Creative Minds. 1991, Carolrhoda LB $22.60 (978-0-87614-433-6). The life of Charles Dickens, including his poverty-ridden childhood. (Rev: SLJ 3/91) [921]

5478 Rosen, Michael. *Dickens: His Work and His World* (4–7). Illus. by Robert Ingpen. 2005, Candlewick $19.99 (978-0-7636-2752-2). Before reviewing Dickens's major works, Rosen discusses the author's difficult childhood and the social conditions of his times. (Rev: BCCB 3/06; BL 9/15/05*; HBG 4/06; LMC 3/06; SLJ 11/05*) [921]

DICKINSON, EMILY

5479 Dommermuth-Costa, Carol. *Emily Dickinson: Singular Poet* (6–9). 1998, Lerner LB $27.93 (978-0-8225-4958-1). Extensive quotations from poems and letters add interesting details to this biography of Emily Dickinson. (Rev: BL 12/15/98; HBG 3/99; SLJ 11/98) [921]

5480 Herstek, Amy Paulson. *Emily Dickinson: Solitary and Celebrated Poet* (7–10). Series: Historical American Biographies. 2003, Enslow LB $26.60 (978-0-7660-1977-5). A life of Dickinson, describing her childhood, the development of her beliefs, her love of nature, family, and friends, and her work. (Rev: SLJ 5/04; VOYA 4/04) [921]

5481 Meltzer, Milton. *Emily Dickinson* (8–11). Illus. Series: American Literary Greats. 2006, Lerner LB $31.93 (978-0-7613-2949-7). Dickinson's life story is interwoven with quotes from her poetry and excerpts from primary sources including letters. (Rev: BL 2/15/06; SLJ 6/06; VOYA 4/06) [811]

5482 Olsen, Victoria. *Emily Dickinson* (7–12). Illus. 1990, Chelsea LB $30.00 (978-1-55546-649-7). An illustrated biography that describes the life of Emily Dickinson as well as her work. (Rev: BL 7/90) [921]

DINESEN, ISAK

5483 Leslie, Roger. *Isak Dinesen: Gothic Storyteller* (8–12). Illus. 2004, Morgan Reynolds LB $23.95 (978-1-931798-17-4). Danish-born author Isak Dinesen, best known for *Out of Africa*, a memoir of her years spent in Kenya, is profiled in this engaging volume that emphasizes her battle with syphilis. (Rev: BL 4/1/04; SLJ 5/04) [921]

DORRIS, MICHAEL

5484 Weil, Ann. *Michael Dorris* (4–7). Illus. Series: Contemporary Native Americans. 1997, Raintree LB $17.98 (978-0-8172-3994-7). The life story of the late Native American writer and teacher and his crusade to fight alcohol abuse. (Rev: BL 6/1–15/97) [921]

DOYLE, SIR ARTHUR CONAN

5485 Adams, Cynthia. *The Mysterious Case of Sir Arthur Conan Doyle* (5–8). Illus. Series: World Writers. 1999, Morgan Reynolds LB $21.95 (978-1-883846-34-3). This book traces the life of Sir Arthur Conan Doyle from his Scottish boyhood and failed medical practice to success as a writer and creator of Sherlock Holmes. (Rev: BL 3/1/99; SLJ 9/99; VOYA 10/99) [921]

5486 Pascal, Janet B. *Arthur Conan Doyle: Beyond Baker Street* (7–12). Illus. 2000, Oxford $32.95 (978-0-19-512262-6). This biography of the creator of Sherlock Holmes tells how he was also a defender of those unjustly accused of crimes, a spiritualist, and a prolific author in various genres. (Rev: BL 2/15/00; HBG 9/00; SLJ 6/00) [921]

DUNBAR, PAUL LAURENCE

5487 Gentry, Tony. *Paul Laurence Dunbar* (7–12). Illus. 1988, Chelsea LB $32.00 (978-1-55546-583-4). A richly illustrated biography of one of the chief poets of the Harlem Renaissance of the 1920s. (Rev: BL 2/15/89; SLJ 3/89; VOYA 2/89) [921]

5488 Reef, Catherine. *Paul Laurence Dunbar: Portrait of a Poet* (6–9). Series: African-American Biographies. 2000, Enslow $26.60 (978-0-7660-1350-6). Dunbar's experiences with injustice are described in this biography of the poet who dedicated his work to portraying the lives of African Americans. (Rev: HBG 9/00; SLJ 9/00) [811]

FITZGERALD, F. SCOTT

5489 Bankston, John. *F. Scott Fitzgerald* (5–8). Series: Classic Storytellers. 2004, Mitchell Lane LB $29.95 (978-1-58415-249-1). An introduction to Fitzgerald's life, work, and legacy, with background information on relevant historical, cultural, and economic factors. (Rev: BL 1/05; SLJ 1/05) [921]

5490 Boon, Kevin Alexander. *F. Scott Fitzgerald* (7–10). Series: Writers and Their Works. 2005, Benchmark LB $25.95 (978-0-7614-1947-1). *The Great Gatsby* is discussed in some detail in this overview of Fitzgerald's life and works. (Rev: SLJ 3/06) [921]

5491 Lazo, Caroline Evensen. *F. Scott Fitzgerald: Voice of the Jazz Age* (6–9). Series: Lerner Biographies. 2002, Lerner LB $27.93 (978-0-8225-0074-2). Fitzgerald's life from childhood, marriage, and work are covered in this interesting account that includes many black-and-white photographs. (Rev: HBG 3/03; SLJ 12/02; VOYA 2/03) [813]

5492 Stewart, Gail B. *F. Scott Fitzgerald* (4–8). Series: The Importance Of. 1999, Lucent LB $27.45 (978-1-56006-541-8). The story of the famous Jazz Age author whose enduring works reflect American life in his era. (Rev: BL 9/15/99) [921]

FLEISCHMAN, SID

5493 Fleischman, Sid. *The Abracadabra Kid: A Writer's Life* (6–12). Illus. 1996, Greenwillow $16.99 (978-0-688-14859-1). The exciting autobiography of the famous author who was also a magician, gold miner, and World War II sailor. (Rev: BL 9/1/96*; SLJ 8/96*; VOYA 4/97) [921]

5494 Freedman, Jeri. *Sid Fleischman* (5–9). Series: The Library of Author Biographies. 2004, Rosen LB $27.95 (978-0-8239-4019-6). Traces the popular, Newbery-winning author's life and looks at his works, writing process, and inspirations, concluding with an interview and reference material. (Rev: SLJ 9/04) [921]

FOX, PAULA

5495 Daniel, Susanna. *Paula Fox* (5–8). Series: The Library of Author Biographies. 2004, Rosen LB $27.95 (978-0-8239-4525-2). Covers Fox's life and career, with analysis of her work and its themes, an interview, and lists of works and awards. (Rev: SLJ 1/05) [921]

FRITZ, JEAN

5496 Fritz, Jean. *China Homecoming* (8–12). Illus. 1985, Putnam $19.99 (978-0-399-21182-9). This autobiographical account describes the author's return to China, where she spent her childhood. (Rev: SLJ 8/85) [921]

5497 Fritz, Jean. *Homesick: My Own Story* (7–12). Illus. by Margot Tomes. 1982, Putnam $17.99 (978-0-399-20933-8). Growing up in the troubled China of the 1920s. (Rev: BL 2/1/89) [921]

FROST, ROBERT

5498 Caravantes, Peggy. *Deep Woods: The Story of Robert Frost* (7–10). Illus. 2006, Morgan Reynolds LB $26.95 (978-1-931798-92-1). An introduction to the poet's life and successful career. (Rev: BL 9/15/06; SLJ 6/06) [921]

5499 Wooten, Sara McIntosh. *Robert Frost: The Life of America's Poet* (5–8). Series: People to Know Today. 2006, Enslow LB $31.93 (978-0-7660-2627-8). A fine introduction to the New England poet whose poetry is loved by young people and adults, with information on his difficult childhood and continuing struggles with depression and financial woes. (Rev: SLJ 1/07) [921]

GANTOS, JACK

5500 Gantos, Jack. *Hole in My Life* (8–12). 2002, Farrar $16.00 (978-0-374-39988-7). The gritty story of the author's experiences in prison after being convicted for drug smuggling — and his successful efforts to live a better life. (Rev: BCCB 5/02; BL

4/1/02; HB 5–6/02*; HBG 10/02; SLJ 5/02*; VOYA 6/02) [813.54]

GEISEL, THEODOR

5501 Cohen, Charles D. *The Seuss, the Whole Seuss, and Nothing but the Seuss* (8–12). Illus. 2004, Random $35.00 (978-0-375-82248-3). This oversize, abundantly illustrated book gives a profile of the great author/illustrator and an analysis of his ideas and work. (Rev: BL 3/15/04; SLJ 6/04) [921]

5502 Dean, Tanya. *Theodor Geisel (Dr. Seuss)* (4–7). Illus. Series: Who Wrote That? 2002, Chelsea $30.00 (978-0-7910-6724-6). A look at the life and works of the author and illustrator known as Dr. Seuss. (Rev: BL 10/15/02; HBG 3/03) [813]

GIFF, PATRICIA REILLY

5503 Giff, Patricia Reilly. *Don't Tell the Girls: A Family Memoir* (4–7). Illus. 2005, Holiday $16.95 (978-0-8234-1813-8). The author tells of the search for her family's roots that led her to Ireland. (Rev: BL 3/1/05; SLJ 7/05) [813]

GIOVANNI, NIKKI

5504 Josephson, Judith Pinkerton. *Nikki Giovanni: Poet of the People* (7–12). Series: African-American Biographies. 2000, Enslow LB $26.60 (978-0-7660-1238-7). The life and work of one of the most popular living poets, who has written both for adults and children, is covered in prose and pictures. (Rev: BL 9/15/00; HBG 3/01; SLJ 1/01) [921]

GRIMM BROTHERS

5505 Hettinga, Donald R. *The Brothers Grimm: Two Lives, One Legacy* (5–8). Illus. 2001, Clarion $22.00 (978-0-618-05599-9). An interesting biography that places the brothers' lives in the context of their time and discusses their skills as lexicographers and scholars. (Rev: BL 7/01; HB 1–2/02; HBG 3/02; SLJ 10/01) [430]

HALEY, ALEX

5506 Shirley, David. *Alex Haley* (7–10). Series: Black Americans of Achievement. 1993, Chelsea LB $30.00 (978-0-7910-1979-5); paper $8.95 (978-0-7910-1980-1). The story of the African American writer who gave us the family saga *Roots*. (Rev: BL 2/15/94) [921]

HANSBERRY, LORRAINE

5507 McKissack, Patricia C., and Fredrick McKissack. *Young, Black, and Determined: A Biography of Lorraine Hansberry* (8–12). Illus. 1997, Holiday $18.95 (978-0-8234-1300-3). The story of the late

African American playwright who skyrocketed to fame in 1959 when she was only 28 for the play *A Raisin in the Sun*, which opened on Broadway and won the Drama Critics Award. (Rev: BCCB 5/98; BL 2/15/98; SLJ 4/98; VOYA 8/98) [921]

5508 Scheader, Catherine. *Lorraine Hansberry: Playright and Voice of Justice* (7–10). Illus. Series: African-American Biographies. 1998, Enslow LB $26.60 (978-0-89490-945-0). Raised on Chicago's South Side, Lorraine Hansberry, writer and civil rights activist, used this setting for her prize-winning play *A Raisin in the Sun*. (Rev: BL 9/1/98; HBG 3/99; SLJ 11/98) [921]

5509 Sinnott, Susan. *Lorraine Hansberry: Award-Winning Playwright and Civil Rights Activist* (7–12). 1998, Conari paper $11.95 (978-1-57324-093-2). This story of the great African American playwright who grew up with a passion for theater and politics conveys a sense of the politics from the 1930s to the 1960s and the pressures of fame on an artist. (Rev: BL 2/15/99) [921]

HAWTHORNE, NATHANIEL

5510 Meltzer, Milton. *Nathaniel Hawthorne: A Biography* (6–12). 2006, Twenty-First Century LB $31.93 (978-0-7613-3459-0). Hawthorne had an event-filled life according to thisbiography that covers both triumphs and blemishes and puts the whole in historical context. (Rev: SLJ 11/06)

HEMINGWAY, ERNEST

5511 McDaniel, Melissa. *Ernest Hemingway: The Writer Who Suffered from Depression* (8–12). Series: Great Achievers: Lives of the Physically Challenged. 1996, Chelsea LB $14.95 (978-0-7910-2420-1). This personal and literary biography emphasizes the way Hemingway contributed to and changed American literature, using many excerpts from his works as well as quotations from reviewers and critics, while also discussing his alcoholism and the emotional problems that eventually led to his suicide. (Rev: SLJ 3/97) [921]

5512 Whiting, Jim. *Ernest Hemingway* (6–8). Series: Classic Storytellers. 2005, Mitchell Lane LB $29.95 (978-1-58415-376-4). A concise and readable introduction to the author's life and works. (Rev: SLJ 12/05) [921]

5513 Yannuzzi, Della A. *Ernest Hemingway: Writer and Adventurer* (6–10). Series: People to Know. 1998, Enslow LB $26.60 (978-0-89490-979-5). An engrossing biography of the tempestuous writer whose life and loves were as exciting as his novels. (Rev: BL 11/15/98; HBG 3/99; SLJ 4/99) [921]

HENRY, MARGUERITE

5514 Collins, David R. *Write a Book for Me: The Story of Marguerite Henry* (7–10). Illus. Series: World Writers. 1999, Morgan Reynolds LB $23.95 (978-1-883846-39-8). A short, simple biography of the writer of such memorable books for young people as *King of the Wind*. (Rev: BL 3/15/99; SLJ 9/99; VOYA 10/99) [921]

HINTON, S. E.

5515 Kjelle, Marylou Morano. *S. E. Hinton: Author of The Outsiders* (5–8). Series: Authors Teens Love. 2007, Enslow LB $31.93 (978-0-7660-2720-6). A life of the author of the well-known novel, with an "In Her Own Words" section that researchers will find useful. (Rev: SLJ 11/07) [921]

HOMER

5516 Tracy, Kathleen. *The Life and Times of Homer* (5–8). Series: Biography from Ancient Civilizations: Legends, Folklore, and Stories of Ancient Worlds. 2004, Mitchell Lane LB $29.95 (978-1-58415-260-6). Drawing on ancient legends, this is a profile of ancient Greek poet and storyteller Homer. (Rev: BL 10/15/04; SLJ 12/04)

HOPKINS, LEE BENNETT

5517 Strong, Amy. *Lee Bennett Hopkins: A Children's Poet* (5–8). Series: Great Life Stories. 2003, Watts LB $30.50 (978-0-531-12315-7). An inspiring biography that chronicles Hopkins's early struggles and his love for his work. (Rev: SLJ 2/04) [921]

HOROWITZ, ANTHONY

5518 Abrams, Dennis. *Anthony Horowitz* (6–9). Series: Who Wrote That? 2006, Chelsea House LB $30.00 (978-0-7910-8968-2). This biography of British horror and spy fiction author Horowitz explores how his unhappy childhood experiences influenced his books. (Rev: BL 6/1–15/06) [921]

HUGHES, LANGSTON

5519 Hill, Christine M. *Langston Hughes: Poet of the Harlem Renaissance* (6–10). Series: African-American Biographies. 1997, Enslow LB $26.60 (978-0-89490-815-6). An easy-to-read, accurate look at the poet's life and times, with good-quality black-and-white photographs. (Rev: SLJ 1/98) [921]

5520 Meltzer, Milton. *Langston Hughes: An Illustrated Edition* (6–12). Illus. 1997, Millbrook paper $20.95 (978-0-7613-0327-5). A new, large, well-illustrated edition of the highly respected 1968 biography of Langston Hughes. (Rev: BL 8/97; SLJ 11/97; VOYA 2/98) [920]

5521 Osofsky, Audrey. *Free to Dream: The Making of a Poet, Langston Hughes* (6–10). Illus. 1996, Lothrop $16.00 (978-0-688-10605-8). An attractive biography that covers the writer's life and works as well as providing general information on the Harlem Renaissance. (Rev: BL 4/1/96; SLJ 7/96) [921]

5522 Rummel, Jack. *Langston Hughes: Poet.* Rev. ed. (7–12). Series: Black Americans of Achievement. 2005, Chelsea House LB $30.00 (978-0-7910-8250-8). A revised edition of the highly readable and well illustrated biography of the African American poet and fiction writer, containing excerpts from his writings. (Rev: SLJ 11/05) [921]

5523 Wallace, Maurice. *Langston Hughes: The Harlem Renaissance* (8–12). Illus. Series: Writers and Their Works. 2007, Marshall Cavendish LB $27.95 (978-0-7614-2591-5). Accessible analysis of Hughes's works is combined with information about his life and the environment in which he worked. (Rev: BL 2/1/08; SLJ 2/08) [921]

HURSTON, ZORA NEALE

5524 Calvert, Roz. *Zora Neale Hurston* (5–8). Illus. Series: Black Americans of Achievement. 1993, Chelsea LB $15.95 (978-0-7910-1766-1). A lively account of the life of the famous writer and folklorist. (Rev: BL 5/1/93; SLJ 6/93) [921]

5525 Litwin, Laura Baskes. *Zora Neale Hurston: "I Have Been in Sorrow's Kitchen"* (7–10). Illus. 2007, Enslow LB $23.95 (978-0-7660-2536-3). Presents the life of legendary author and folklorist Zora Neale Hurston, including her childhood, her influences, and her remarkable career. (Rev: BL 6/1–15/07; SLJ 7/07) [921]

5526 Porter, A. P. *Jump at de Sun: The Story of Zora Neale Hurston* (7–12). 1992, Carolrhoda paper $27.93 (978-0-87614-546-3). A brief, easy-to-read biography that places Hurston within the context of the racism of her era. (Rev: BL 12/15/92; SLJ 1/93*) [921]

5527 Sapet, Kerrily. *Rhythm and Folklore: The Story of Zora Neale Hurston* (7–12). Illus. 2008, Morgan Reynolds LB $27.95 (978-1-59935-067-7). This vibrant biography of the author of *Their Eyes Were Watching God* contains plenty of personal quotes, full-page photographs, and complete back matter. (Rev: BL 6/1–15/08; SLJ 8/08) [921]

5528 Yannuzzi, Della A. *Zora Neale Hurston: Southern Storyteller* (7–12). Illus. Series: African-American Biographies. 1996, Enslow LB $26.60 (978-0-89490-685-5). The story of the Harlem Renaissance author who died penniless but left a priceless legacy in her writings. (Rev: BL 9/1/96; SLJ 6/96) [921]

IRVING, WASHINGTON

5529 Collins, David R. *Washington Irving: Storyteller for a New Nation* (4–8). Illus. Series: World Writers. 2000, Morgan Reynolds LB $23.95 (978-1-883846-50-3). This biography introduces the globe-trotting American writer and gives details of his work and personality. (Rev: BL 4/1/00; HBG 3/00; SLJ 5/00; VOYA 6/01) [921]

KEHRET, PEG

5530 Kehret, Peg. *Five Pages a Day: A Writer's Journey* (4–7). 2002, Albert Whitman LB $15.99 (978-0-8075-8650-1). Aspiring young writers will particularly enjoy Kehret's account of her writing life, from starting a newspaper about the neighborhood dogs to entering writing contests to her career as an author of children's books. (Rev: BL 12/15/02; HBG 3/03; SLJ 9/02) [813]

KERR, M. E.

5531 Nilsen, Alleen P. *Presenting M. E. Kerr.* Rev. ed. (8–12). Series: Twayne's United States Authors. 1997, Twayne $35.00 (978-0-8057-9248-5). A biography of this popular young adult writer that also discusses her works, with a detailed analysis of her five most popular books. (Rev: SLJ 4/98; VOYA 4/98) [810]

KING, STEPHEN

5532 Keyishian, Amy, and Marjorie Keyishian. *Stephen King* (7–12). Series: Pop Culture Legends. 1995, Chelsea LB $21.95 (978-0-7910-2340-2). Gives insight into the life of one of the world's most successful writers, covering King's childhood poverty and abandonment by his father, support by his mother, and influences on his work by such giants as C. S. Lewis, H. G. Wells, and Bram Stoker. (Rev: BL 12/15/95; SLJ 1/96) [921]

5533 Whitelaw, Nancy. *Dark Dreams: The Story of Stephen King* (7–10). Illus. Series: World Writers. 2005, Morgan Reynolds $26.95 (978-1-931798-77-8). An inviting introduction to King and to his writing, with lots of interesting anecdotes and snippets of his work. (Rev: BL 11/15/05; VOYA 2/06) [813]

5534 Wukovits, John F. *Stephen King* (6–10). Illus. Series: People in the News. 1999, Lucent LB $27.45 (978-1-56006-562-3). A biography of the rags-to-riches prize-winning author whose mysteries and supernatural stories have thrilled millions. (Rev: BL 12/15/99; HBG 4/00; SLJ 11/99) [921]

LEE, HARPER

5535 Shields, Charles. *I Am Scout: The Biography of Harper Lee* (7–12). 2008, Holt $18.95 (978-0-8050-8334-7). The story of Lee's life, written by the author of *Mockingbird* (2006), a biography of Lee for adults. (Rev: BL 3/1/08; SLJ 4/08) [921]

L'ENGLE, MADELEINE

5536 McClellan, Marilyn. *Madeleine L'Engle: Banned, Challenged, and Censored* (8–12). Illus. Series: Authors of Banned Books. 2008, Enslow LB $25.95 (978-0-7660-2708-4). Why do some groups question if the author's *A Wrinkle in Time* is appropriate for young readers? This book examines the objections and the author's defense of her award-winning book. (Rev: BL 4/1/08) [921]

LEWIS, C. S.

5537 Parker, Vic. *C. S. Lewis* (4–7). Series: Writers Uncovered. 2006, Heinemann LB $23.00 (978-1-4034-7336-3). In addition to providing biographical information on Lewis, Parker looks at his books, especially the Narnia series, giving plot outlines and discussing the stories and themes. (Rev: BL 8/06) [921]

LONDON, JACK

5538 Bankston, John. *Jack London* (4–7). Illus. Series: Classic Storytellers. 2005, Mitchell Lane LB $29.95 (978-1-58415-263-7). An introduction to London's life, work, and legacy, with background information on relevant historical, cultural, and economic factors. (Rev: BL 1/05) [921]

5539 Dyer, Daniel. *Jack London: A Biography* (7–10). Illus. 1997, Scholastic paper $17.95 (978-0-590-22216-7). The hard life and early death of author Jack London, an adventurous, passionate lover of life. (Rev: BL 9/15/97; SLJ 9/97; VOYA 10/98) [921]

5540 Stefoff, Rebecca. *Jack London: An American Original* (7–10). Series: Oxford Portraits. 2002, Oxford LB $32.95 (978-0-19-512223-7). A profile of this American original, his life, his work, and his lasting importance. (Rev: BL 7/02; HBG 10/02; SLJ 8/02) [921]

5541 Streissguth, Thomas. *Jack London* (4–7). Series: A&E Biography. 2000, Lucent LB $27.93 (978-0-8225-4987-1). The story of an adventurer and author who battled personal hardships and wrote eloquently about nature and survival. (Rev: BL 12/15/00; HBG 3/01; SLJ 3/01) [921]

LOVECRAFT, H. P.

5542 Schoell, William. *H. P. Lovecraft: Master of Weird Fiction* (5–8). Illus. 2003, Morgan Reynolds LB $23.95 (978-1-931798-15-0). Lovecraft, known for his stories of horror and the supernatural, was born into privilege that ended with his parents' early deaths; his works only received real acclaim after

his death. (Rev: BL 9/15/03; HBG 4/04; SLJ 12/03) [813]

LOWRY, LOIS

5543 Lowry, Lois. *Looking Back: A Book of Memories* (4–8). Illus. 1998, Houghton $17.00 (978-0-395-89543-6). This autobiographical work centers around a series of photographs and the author's comments on each. (Rev: BL 11/1/98; HB 1–2/99; HBG 3/99; SLJ 9/98; VOYA 4/99) [921]

5544 Markham, Lois. *Lois Lowry* (5–8). Series: Meet the Author. 1995, Learning Works paper $7.99 (978-0-88160-278-4). This biography of the Newbery Medal–winning author tells how she became a writer and looks at the personal experiences that are reflected in her books. (Rev: SLJ 1/96) [921]

MCCAFFREY, ANNE

5545 Trachtenberg, Martha P. *Anne McCaffrey: Science Fiction Storyteller* (6–10). Illus. Series: People to Know. 2001, Enslow LB $26.60 (978-0-7660-1151-9). Trachtenberg introduces readers to McCaffrey's life and writing career, detailing the setbacks the author faced before winning the Hugo Award in 1968. (Rev: BL 7/01; HBG 3/02; SLJ 9/01) [813]

MAGEE, JOHN

5546 Granfield, Linda. *High Flight: A Story of World War II* (5–7). Illus. 1999, Tundra $15.95 (978-0-88776-469-1). The moving story of John Magee, a young Canadian Air Force pilot who was killed in World War II and who is best known for writing the poem "High Flight." (Rev: BCCB 12/99; BL 1/1–15/00; HBG 3/00; SLJ 2/00) [921]

MANZANO, JUAN FRANCISCO

5547 Engle, Margarita. *The Poet Slave of Cuba: A Biography of Juan Francisco Manzano* (7–10). Illus. by Sean Quails. 2006, Holt $16.95 (978-0-8050-7706-3). This lyrical free-verse biography tells the story of the poet born into slavery in Cuba in 1797, describing his early talent with languages and how it helped him survived amazing brutality. (Rev: BL 2/15/06*; SLJ 4/06*) [811]

MARTI, JOSE

5548 Goodnough, David. *Jose Marti: Cuban Patriot and Poet* (6–10). Illus. Series: Hispanic Biographies. 1996, Enslow LB $26.60 (978-0-89490-761-6). This biography of the Cuban revolutionary who fought against Spanish rule also contains samples of his poetry in both Spanish and English. (Rev: BL 9/1/96; SLJ 6/96) [921]

MARTÍ, JOSÉ J.

5549 West, Alan. *José Martí: Man of Poetry, Soldier of Freedom* (5–8). Illus. Series: Hispanic Heritage. 1994, Millbrook LB $23.90 (978-1-56294-408-7). The life story of the famous 19th-century Cuban poet, with excerpts from his work in both Spanish and English. (Rev: SLJ 1/95) [921]

MELTZER, MILTON

5550 Meltzer, Milton. *Milton Meltzer: Writing Matters* (8–11). Illus. 2004, Watts LB $29.00 (978-0-531-12257-0). Meltzer combines recollections of his childhood, adolescence, and working days with details of his progression as a writer. (Rev: BL 1/1–15/05; SLJ 4/05) [973.07]

MELVILLE, HERMAN

5551 Meltzer, Milton. *Herman Melville: A Biography* (8–12). Series: American Literary Greats. 2005, Twenty-First Century LB $31.93 (978-0-7613-2749-3). Traces the writer's difficult life and links his struggles to passages from his works, in particular *Moby Dick*. (Rev: SLJ 1/06) [921]

MILLAY, EDNA ST. VINCENT

5552 Daffron, Carolyn. *Edna St. Vincent Millay* (7–12). Illus. 1989, Chelsea LB $19.95 (978-1-55546-668-8). The life and career of this noted poet with examples of her work. (Rev: BL 12/1/89; SLJ 3/90) [921]

MILLER, ARTHUR

5553 Andersen, Richard. *Arthur Miller* (7–10). Series: Writers and Their Works. 2005, Benchmark LB $25.95 (978-0-7614-1946-4). *The Crucible* and *Death of a Salesman* are discussed in some detail in this overview of Miller's life and works. (Rev: SLJ 3/06) [921]

MOEYAERT, BART

5554 Moeyaert, Bart. *Brothers: The Oldest, the Quietest, the Realest, the Farthest, the Nicest, the Fastest, and I* (7–9). Trans. from Flemish by Wanda J. Boeke. Illus. by Cercla Dendooven. 2005, Front St. $16.95 (978-1-932425-18-5). The Belgian author offers candid and often wistful vignettes of growing up the youngest of seven brothers and the incidents that seemed of utmost importance to him. (Rev: SLJ 1/06; VOYA 4/06) [921]

MONTGOMERY, L. M.

5555 Kjelle, Marylou Morano. *L. M. Montgomery* (6–9). Illus. Series: Who Wrote That? 2005, Chelsea House LB $30.00 (978-0-7910-8234-8). This inter-

esting profile shows the parallels between Montgomery and her most famous character, Anne of Green Gables. (Rev: BL 11/1/05) [813]

MORRISON, TONI

5556 Andersen, Richard. *Toni Morrison* (7–10). Series: Writers and Their Works. 2005, Benchmark LB $25.95 (978-0-7614-1945-7). *Sula* and *The Bluest Eye* are discussed in some detail in this overview of Morrison's life and works. (Rev: SLJ 3/06) [921]

5557 Century, Douglas. *Toni Morrison* (8–12). Series: Black Americans of Achievement. 1994, Chelsea LB $30.00 (978-0-7910-1877-4). A biography of the Nobel Prize–winning African American author, examining her life and the major themes of her novels. (Rev: BL 9/1/94; SLJ 7/94; VOYA 8/94) [921]

5558 Haskins, Jim. *Toni Morrison: Telling a Tale Untold* (7–12). Illus. 2002, Millbrook LB $26.90 (978-0-7613-1852-1). Haskins adds discussion of each of Morrison's books to this account of her life and literary career. (Rev: BL 10/1/02; HBG 3/03; VOYA 12/02) [813]

5559 Kramer, Barbara. *Toni Morrison: Nobel Prize–Winning Author* (7–12). Series: African-American Biographies. 1996, Enslow LB $26.60 (978-0-89490-688-6). Using many quotations and first-person comments, this biography re-creates the life and important works of this African American Nobel Prize winner. (Rev: BL 9/15/96; SLJ 11/96; VOYA 6/97) [921]

MYERS, WALTER DEAN

5560 Burshtein, Karen. *Walter Dean Myers* (7–10). Series: The Library of Author Biographies. 2004, Rosen LB $27.95 (978-0-8239-4020-2). A look at the life and work of the well-known author, with many quotations. (Rev: SLJ 9/04) [921]

5561 Jordan, Denise M. *Walter Dean Myers: Writer for Real Teens* (7–10). Series: African-American Biographies. 1999, Enslow LB $26.60 (978-0-7660-1206-6). Jordan tells the story of the prolific African American writer who continues a storytelling tradition. (Rev: BL 11/15/99; HBG 4/00; SLJ 1/00) [921]

NAYLOR, PHYLLIS REYNOLDS

5562 Naylor, Phyllis Reynolds. *How I Came to Be a Writer*. Rev. ed. (4–9). 2001, Simon & Schuster paper $4.99 (978-0-689-83887-3). Naylor describes the joys and difficulties of life as a writer and includes excerpts of her work in this autobiographical account. (Rev: SLJ 5/01) [921]

NERUDA, PABLO

5563 Goodnough, David. *Pablo Neruda: Nobel Prize–Winning Poet* (6–12). Illus. Series: Hispanic Biographies. 1998, Enslow LB $26.60 (978-0-7660-1042-0). A brief, interesting biography of the great Chilean poet that includes good background material on the rise and fall of the dictator Allende. (Rev: BL 8/98; HBG 3/99; SLJ 9/98; VOYA 10/98) [921]

NIXON, JOAN LOWERY

5564 Wade, Mary Dodson. *Joan Lowery Nixon: Masterful Mystery Writer* (5–8). Series: Authors Teens Love. 2004, Enslow LB $26.60 (978-0-7660-2194-5). Examines Nixon's life, writings, and her focus on girls of character and strength. (Rev: SLJ 11/04) [921]

ORWELL, GEORGE

5565 Agathocleous, Tanya. *George Orwell: Battling Big Brother* (8–12). Illus. Series: Oxford Portraits. 2000, Oxford $32.95 (978-0-19-512185-8). A concise, well-written life of this fascinating English writer and his contributions to world literature. (Rev: BL 10/1/00; HBG 10/01) [921]

5566 Boerst, William J. *Generous Anger: The Story of George Orwell* (6–9). 2001, Morgan Reynolds $23.95 (978-1-883846-74-9). Report writers will find this a useful source of information on Orwell's life and career, with quotations from primary sources and full chapter notes. (Rev: BL 6/1–15/01; HBG 10/02; SLJ 10/01) [828]

PAREDES, AMERICO

5567 Murcia, Rebecca Thatcher. *Americo Paredes* (5–7). Series: Latinos in American History. 2003, Mitchell Lane LB $29.95 (978-1-58415-207-1). The story of the Mexican American author, folklorist, and professor at the University of Texas in Austin who is also famous for establishing a center for intercultural studies. (Rev: BL 1/1–15/04) [921]

PATERSON, KATHERINE

5568 Cary, Alice. *Katherine Paterson* (5–8). Illus. Series: Meet the Author. 1997, Learning Works paper $7.99 (978-0-88160-281-4). A biography of the two-time Newbery winner, with many quotations from interviews and autobiographical essays. (Rev: BL 5/1/97; SLJ 7/97) [921]

5569 Kjelle, Marylou Morano. *Katherine Paterson* (4–7). Illus. Series: Classic Storytellers. 2004, Mitchell Lane LB $29.95 (978-1-58415-268-2). Examines the life and times of the award-winning children's author, including her work as a missionary in Japan and how religious faith informs her writing. (Rev: BL 1/1–15/05; SLJ 3/05) [921]

5570 McGinty, Alice B. *Katherine Paterson* (5–8). Series: The Library of Author Biographies. 2005, Rosen LB $27.95 (978-1-4042-0328-0). An interview with Paterson is an interesting addition to this description of the author's life and works for children. (Rev: SLJ 9/05) [921]

PAULSEN, GARY

5571 Fine, Edith Hope. *Gary Paulsen: Author and Wilderness Adventurer* (5–8). Series: People to Know. 2000, Enslow LB $26.60 (978-0-7660-1146-5). The story of an outdoorsman who turned many of his exciting adventures into stories for children and young adults. (Rev: BL 9/15/00; HBG 10/00; SLJ 9/00) [921]

5572 Paterra, Elizabeth. *Gary Paulsen* (4–7). Series: Who Wrote That? 2002, Chelsea $30.00 (978-0-7910-6723-9). A profile of the prolific author (of almost 200 books) who is best known for his young adult outdoor survival stories. (Rev: BL 10/15/02; HBG 3/03) [921]

5573 Paulsen, Gary. *Caught by the Sea* (5–8). 2001, Delacorte $15.95 (978-0-385-32645-2). The author describes his ongoing love of the sea and the adventures he's had, some funny, some scary. (Rev: BL 9/15/01; HBG 3/02; SLJ 10/01; VOYA 12/01) [818]

5574 Peters, Stephanie True. *Gary Paulsen* (4–8). Illus. 1999, Learning Works paper $7.99 (978-0-88160-324-8). A straightforward biography of the outdoorsman and author that tells about his books, his interests, his alcoholism, and his continuing health problems. (Rev: BL 6/1–15/99; SLJ 6/99) [921]

POE, EDGAR ALLAN

5575 Frisch, Aaron. *Edgar Allan Poe* (5–9). Photos by Tina Mucci. Illus. by Gary Kelley. Series: Voices in Poetry. 2005, Creative Education LB $31.35 (978-1-58341-344-9). A brief biography that adds atmospheric paintings and photographs to a chronological narrative and excerpts from Poe's works. (Rev: SLJ 3/06) [921]

5576 Kent, Zachary. *Edgar Allan Poe* (5–8). Series: Historical American Biographies. 2001, Enslow LB $26.60 (978-0-7660-1600-2). An informative, well-presented biography of this writer whose unique stories changed the history of American literature. (Rev: BL 1/1–15/02; HBG 3/02; SLJ 9/01) [921]

5577 Meltzer, Milton. *Edgar Allan Poe* (6–12). Illus. 2003, Millbrook LB $31.90 (978-0-7613-2910-7). Poe's difficult life and literary accomplishments are described within the larger context of early 19th-century society in this well-illustrated and well-documented biography. (Rev: BL 11/15/03; HBG 4/04; VOYA 2/04) [818]

5578 Peltak, Jennifer. *Edgar Allan Poe* (6–8). Series: Who Wrote That? 2003, Chelsea House LB $30.00 (978-0-7910-7622-4). The dark details of Poe's personal life provide insight into the themes of his stories and poems; a well-written and attractive volume. (Rev: SLJ 6/04; VOYA 6/04) [921]

5579 Schoell, William. *Mystery and Terror: The Story of Edgar Allan Poe* (7–12). Illus. Series: Writers of Imagination. 2004, Morgan Reynolds LB $23.95 (978-1-931798-39-6). Poe's unhappy childhood, marriage, and alcoholism are among the personal aspects covered in this biography that also talks about his work and his continuing need to earn enough money. (Rev: BL 10/1/04; SLJ 12/04) [921]

5580 Streissguth, Thomas. *Edgar Allan Poe* (5–8). Series: A&E Biography. 2001, Lerner LB $27.93 (978-0-8225-4991-8). The tortured life of this early master of the short story is brought to life in an interesting text and many black-and-white illustrations. (Rev: BL 6/1–15/01; HBG 10/01; SLJ 8/01) [921]

PULLMAN, PHILIP

5581 Yuan, Margaret Speaker. *Philip Pullman* (7–10). Illus. Series: Who Wrote That? 2005, Chelsea House LB $30.00 (978-0-7910-8658-2). In addition to profiling this author of award-winning books, this biography describes his writing methods. (Rev: BL 3/15/06; SLJ 5/06) [823]

PYLE, ERNIE

5582 O'Connor, Barbara. *The Soldiers' Voice: The Story of Ernie Pyle* (4–7). Illus. 1996, Carolrhoda LB $30.35 (978-0-87614-942-3). The story of the renowned World War II correspondent who died in the South Pacific while covering the war. (Rev: BCCB 10/96; BL 9/1/96; SLJ 8/96) [921]

RIIS, JACOB

5583 Pascal, Janet B. *Jacob Riis: Reporter and Reformer* (8–11). Series: Oxford Portraits. 2006, Oxford LB $28.00 (978-0-19-514527-4). Riis's groundbreaking photography and journalism exposing 19th-century living and working conditions is explored in this well-balanced biography of the Danish American. (Rev: BL 6/1–15/06; SLJ 7/06) [921]

RODRIGUEZ, LUIS

5584 Schwartz, Michael. *Luis Rodriguez* (4–8). Illus. Series: Contemporary Hispanic Americans. 1997, Raintree LB $17.98 (978-0-8172-3990-9). The life of this contemporary Hispanic American who went from gang leader and drug addict to writer, journalist, publisher, speaker, and youth activist. (Rev: BL 4/15/97; SLJ 6/97) [921]

ROWLING, J. K.

5585 Chippendale, Lisa A. *Triumph of the Imagination: The Story of Writer J. K. Rowling* (7–10). Illus. Series: Overcoming Adversity. 2001, Chelsea LB $30.00 (978-0-7910-6312-5). Rowling's period on public assistance and the legal challenges to the Harry Potter books are among the topics touched on in this biography. (Rev: BL 3/15/02; HBG 10/02; SLJ 5/02) [823]

5586 Harmin, Karen Leigh. *J. K. Rowling: Author of Harry Potter* (4–7). Series: People to Know Today. 2006, Enslow LB $31.93 (978-0-7660-1850-1). An attractive and accessible biography of the creator of the wildly popular series, with details of her youth, career, and the impact success has had on her life; plus information on aspects of British life that will interest young readers. (Rev: BL 11/1/06) [921]

SACHAR, LOUIS

5587 Greene, Meg. *Louis Sachar* (5–9). Series: The Library of Author Biographies. 2004, Rosen LB $26.50 (978-0-8239-4017-2). Traces the popular, Newbery-winning author's life and looks at his works, writing process, and inspirations, concluding with an interview and reference material. (Rev: SLJ 9/04) [921]

SANDBURG, CARL

5588 Meltzer, Milton. *Carl Sandburg: A Biography* (5–10). Illus. 1999, Millbrook LB $31.90 (978-0-7613-1364-9). The story of a literary giant who, in addition to his poetry, is noted for nonfiction works including a biography of Abraham Lincoln. (Rev: BL 12/15/99; HBG 10/00; VOYA 6/00) [921]

SEBESTYEN, OUIDA

5589 Monseau, Virginia R. *Presenting Ouida Sebestyen* (6–12). Series: United States Authors. 1995, Twayne $28.00 (978-0-8057-8224-0). Sebestyen's unorthodox writing habits enliven this text, with biographical information and detailed analysis of six novels. (Rev: BL 9/1/95) [921]

SENDAK, MAURICE

5590 Marcovitz, Hal. *Maurice Sendak* (6–9). 2006, Chelsea House LB $30.00 (978-0-7910-8796-1). A look at the life of Maurice Sendak, with information on his childhood, his art and stories, and his concern with the Holocaust. (Rev: BL 9/1/06) [921]

SHAKESPEARE, WILLIAM

5591 Aliki. *William Shakespeare and the Globe* (4–7). Illus. 1999, HarperCollins LB $18.89 (978-0-06-027821-2). Shakespeare and Elizabethan England come to life in this detailed picture book that uses many quotations from his plays and also tells of the recent rebuilding of the Globe theater. (Rev: BCCB 4/99; BL 6/1–15/99*; HB 5–6/99; HBG 10/99; SLJ 5/99) [921]

5592 Bryson, Bill. *Shakespeare: The World as Stage* (8–12). 2007, HarperCollins $19.95 (978-0-06-074022-1). Bryson has created an unusual and enjoyable survey of Shakespeare's life and times, explaining his research as he goes and disproving earlier claims. (Rev: BL 10/15/07) [921] ⑨

5593 Dommermuth-Costa, Carol. *William Shakespeare* (5–8). Series: Biography. 2001, Lerner LB $27.93 (978-0-8225-4996-3). A readable, well-illustrated biography of the Bard of Avon with material on many of his plays. (Rev: BL 4/1/02; HBG 10/02; SLJ 3/02) [921]

5594 Fandel, Jennifer. *William Shakespeare* (5–9). Photos by Marcel Imsand. Series: Voices in Poetry. 2003, Creative Editions LB $19.95 (978-1-58341-283-1). A brief and appealing introduction to Shakespeare's life and work, with examples of his poems, excerpts from his plays, and illustrations. (Rev: SLJ 12/03) [822.3]

5595 Hilliam, David. *William Shakespeare: England's Greatest Playwright and Poet* (5–8). Illus. Series: Rulers, Scholars, and Artists of the Renaissance. 2005, Rosen LB $33.25 (978-1-4042-0318-1). Information on Shakespeare's life and on the theater scene in 16th-century London is interwoven with quotes from the plays and poems. (Rev: BL 8/05) [822.3]

5596 Nettleton, Pamela Hill. *William Shakespeare: Playwright and Poet* (5–9). Series: Signature Lives. 2005, Compass Point $34.60 (978-0-7565-0816-6). Nettleton places facts about Shakespeare's life within the context of everyday life of the time, with details about the theater and publishing. (Rev: SLJ 6/05) [921]

5597 Thrasher, Thomas. *The Importance of William Shakespeare* (4–8). Series: The Importance Of. 1998, Lucent LB $27.45 (978-1-56006-374-2). This work discusses Shakespeare and his contribution to world culture. (Rev: BL 12/15/98; VOYA 6/99) [921]

SHELLEY, MARY WOLLSTONECRAFT

5598 Darrow, Sharon. *Through the Tempests Dark and Wild: A Story of Mary Shelley, Creator of Frankenstein* (4–7). Illus. by Angela Barren. 2003, Candlewick $16.99 (978-0-7636-0835-4). The dramatic story of Mary Shelley's troubled youth is told in this beautifully illustrated, fictionalized picture-book biography. (Rev: BL 6/1–15/03; HBG 10/03; SLJ 6/03) [823]

5599 Miller, Calvin C. *Spirit Like a Storm: The Story of Mary Shelley* (7–10). Illus. 1996, Morgan Reynolds LB $21.95 (978-1-883846-13-8). The life story of the fascinating, talented creator of *Frankenstein,* who was also the wife of poet Percy Bysshe Shelley. (Rev: BL 2/15/96; SLJ 3/96; VOYA 6/96) [921]

SINGER, ISAAC BASHEVIS

5600 Singer, Isaac Bashevis. *A Day of Pleasure: Stories of a Boy Growing Up in Warsaw* (6–8). Illus. by Roman Vishniac. 1969, Farrar paper $8.95 (978-0-374-41696-6). A Hasidic Jew's fond remembrances of the world in which he grew up. [921]

SÍS, PETER

5601 Sís, Peter. *The Wall: Growing Up Behind the Iron Curtain* (7–10). Illus. by author. 2007, Farrar $18.00 (978-0-374-34701-7). This autobiographical picture book portrays Sis's childhood in Czechoslovakia and the impact of Soviet rule on life in the nation. Sibert Medal, 2008. (Rev: BL 9/1/07; SLJ 8/07) [943.7]

SPINELLI, JERRY

5602 Seidman, David. *Jerry Spinelli* (5–9). Series: The Library of Author Biographies. 2004, Rosen LB $27.95 (978-0-8239-4016-5). Traces the popular, Newbery-winning author's life and looks at his works, writing process, and inspirations, concluding with an interview and reference material. (Rev: SLJ 9/04) [921]

5603 Spinelli, Jerry. *Knots in My Yo-Yo String: The Autobiography of a Kid* (5–8). 1998, Knopf paper $10.95 (978-0-679-88791-1). A frank, delightful memoir of growing up in Norristown, Pennsylvania, during the 1950s by the renowned Newbery Medal–winning writer of fiction for young people. (Rev: BCCB 7–8/98; BL 5/1/98; HBG 10/98; SLJ 6/98; VOYA 12/98) [921]

STEINBECK, JOHN

5604 Florence, Donne. *John Steinbeck: America's Author* (6–8). Illus. Series: People to Know. 2000, Enslow LB $26.60 (978-0-7660-1150-2). A biography of the American Nobel Prize winner for literature with material on each of his great works. (Rev: BL 4/15/00; HBG 9/00) [921]

5605 Meltzer, Milton. *John Steinbeck* (6–9). Illus. Series: Up Close. 2008, Viking $16.99 (978-0-670-06139-6). Meltzer provides good background information on the time and society in which Steinbeck lived. (Rev: BL 3/15/08; SLJ 1/08) [921]

5606 Reef, Catherine. *John Steinbeck* (7–12). Illus. 1996, Clarion $17.95 (978-0-395-71278-8). A handsome photobiography that not only covers salient aspects of Steinbeck's life but also explores the themes and locales of his work. (Rev: BL 5/1/96; SLJ 3/96; VOYA 8/96) [921]

5607 Tracy, Kathleen. *John Steinbeck* (5–8). Series: Classic Storytellers. 2004, Mitchell Lane LB $29.95 (978-1-58415-271-2). An introduction to Steinbeck's life, work, and legacy, with background information on relevant historical, cultural, and economic factors. (Rev: BL 1/05; SLJ 1/05) [921]

STEVENSON, ROBERT LOUIS

5608 Carpenter, Angelica S., and Jean Shirley. *Robert Louis Stevenson: Finding Treasure Island* (5–8). Illus. 1997, Lerner LB $27.93 (978-0-8225-4955-0). A lively biography of this great writer, who was a disappointment to his family because he did not become a minister. (Rev: BL 11/15/97; HBG 3/98; SLJ 12/97) [921]

STINE, R. L.

5609 Cohen, Joel H. *R. L. Stine* (5–8). Series: People in the News. 2000, Lucent LB $28.70 (978-1-56006-608-8). This well-documented biography, illustrated with several black-and-white photographs, tells the story of an author who enjoys scaring his readers. (Rev: BL 6/1–15/00; HBG 10/00; SLJ 8/00) [921]

5610 Parker-Rock, Michelle. *R. L. Stine: Creator of Creepy and Spooky Stories* (5–8). Series: Authors Teens Love. 2005, Enslow LB $26.60 (978-0-7660-2445-8). Stine's writing career is the main focus of this biography that includes an interview. (Rev: SLJ 1/06) [921]

STOWE, HARRIET BEECHER

5611 Fritz, Jean. *Harriet Beecher Stowe and the Beecher Preachers* (5–9). 1994, Putnam $15.99 (978-0-399-22666-3). In addition to covering *Uncle Tom's Cabin*, this biography gives a full account of Harriet Beecher's private life, marriage, and extended family. (Rev: BCCB 10/94; BL 8/94; HB 9–10/94; SLJ 9/94*; VOYA 8/94) [921]

5612 Griskey, Michèle. *Harriet Beecher Stowe* (5–7). Series: Classic Storytellers. 2005, Mitchell Lane LB $29.95 (978-1-58415-375-7). Good historical and social context makes clear the importance of Stowe's achievements. (Rev: SLJ 11/05) [921]

5613 Jakoubek, Robert E. *Harriet Beecher Stowe: Author and Abolitionist* (6–9). Illus. 1989, Chelsea LB $30.00 (978-1-55546-680-0). This account is valuable not only as a biography of this famous writer but also as an insight into the horrors of slavery. (Rev: SLJ 6/89) [921]

TAN, AMY

5614 Kramer, Barbara. *Amy Tan: Author of the Joy Luck Club* (6–12). Illus. 1996, Enslow LB $20.95 (978-0-89490-699-2). The story of the Chinese American writer who at first denied her immigrant background and later grew to accept and celebrate it in her fiction. (Rev: BL 6/1–15/96; SLJ 10/96; VOYA 10/96) [921]

5615 Shields, Charles J. *Amy Tan* (7–10). Illus. Series: Women of Achievement. 2001, Chelsea LB $30.00 (978-0-7910-5889-3); paper $30.00 (978-0-7910-5890-9). An appealing biography of Amy Tan that explores Tan's relationship with her mother and interest in her Chinese heritage. (Rev: BL 3/1/02; HBG 10/02; SLJ 6/02) [813]

TARBELL, IDA

5616 Somervill, Barbara A. *Ida Tarbell: Pioneer Investigative Reporter* (6–9). Illus. Series: World Writers. 2002, Morgan Reynolds LB $23.95 (978-1-883846-87-9). In addition to giving details of Tarbell's life and career as an influential journalist, Somervill's interesting text introduces the reader to labor conditions in the early 20th century. (Rev: BL 3/1/02; HBG 10/02; SLJ 6/02) [070.92]

TAYLOR, MILDRED

5617 Houghton, Gillian. *Mildred Taylor* (5–8). Series: The Library of Author Biographies. 2005, Rosen LB $27.95 (978-1-4042-0330-3). An interview with Taylor is an interesting addition to this description of the African American author's life and writings. (Rev: SLJ 9/05) [921]

THOREAU, HENRY DAVID

5618 Hausman, Gerald, and Loretta Hausman. *A Mind with Wings: The Story of Henry David Thoreau* (6–9). Illus. 2006, Shambhala $15.95 (978-1-59030-228-6). Told in a series of anecdotes, this is a lively portrayal of Thoreau's life that uses dialogue based on his own statements. (Rev: BL 3/1/06; SLJ 9/06) [921]

5619 McCarthy, Pat. *Henry David Thoreau* (6–8). Illus. Series: Historical American Biographies. 2003, Enslow LB $26.60 (978-0-7660-1978-2). A detailed introduction to Thoreau's life, work, and legacy, with brief excerpts from his writings. (Rev: BL 6/1–15/03; HBG 10/03) [921]

5620 Meltzer, Milton. *Henry David Thoreau* (8–11). Illus. Series: American Literary Greats. 2007, Lerner LB $31.93 (978-0-8225-5893-4). A clear examination of Thoreau's life and work, exploring his philosophy and wit and their continuing relevance today. (Rev: BL 6/1–15/07; SLJ 5/07) [818]

5621 Thoreau, Henry David. *Thoreau at Walden* (8–12). Illus. by John Porcellino. Series: Center for Cartoon Studies. 2008, Hyperion $16.99 (978-1-4231-0038-6); paper $9.99 (978-1-4231-0039-3). Using Thoreau's words and spare, clean illustrations, this is a graphic novel-style introduction to the philosopher's beliefs about leading a simple life. (Rev: BL 3/15/08; SLJ 3/08) [921]

TOLKIEN, J. R. R.

5622 Lynch, Doris. *J. R. R. Tolkien* (5–8). Illus. 2003, Watts LB $30.50 (978-0-531-12253-2). An attractive biography that reveals how much the author of *The Lord of the Rings* was influenced by his surroundings and experiences. (Rev: BL 12/15/03; SLJ 7/04) [828]

5623 Willett, Edward. *J. R. R. Tolkien: Master of Imaginary Worlds* (6–9). Illus. Series: Authors Teens Love. 2004, Enslow LB $26.60 (978-0-7660-2246-1). Tolkien's interesting life will grab readers' attention, as will the quotations in the "In His Own Words" section. (Rev: BCCB 9/04; BL 11/1/04; SLJ 12/04) [921]

TWAIN, MARK

5624 Aller, Susan Bivin. *Mark Twain* (5–8). Series: A&E Biography. 2001, Lerner LB $27.93 (978-0-8225-4994-9). The colorful life of one of America's favorite authors is re-created in accessible text, black-and-white photographs, and such additions as interesting sidebars and extensive reading lists. (Rev: BL 6/1–15/01; HBG 10/01) [921]

5625 Cox, Clinton. *Mark Twain: America's Humorist, Dreamer, Prophet* (5–9). 1995, Scholastic paper $14.95 (978-0-590-45642-5). A biography that includes a discussion of Twain's views on race and how they changed. (Rev: BL 9/15/95; SLJ 9/95; VOYA 12/95) [921]

5626 Fleischman, Sid. *The Trouble Begins at 8: A Life of Mark Twain in the Wild, Wild West* (5–8). Illus. 2008, Greenwillow $18.99 (978-0-06-134431-2). This is a spirited account of Twain's adventurous early years and how they formed the foundation for his writing. (Rev: BL 6/1–15/08; SLJ 7/08) [921]

5627 Howard, Todd, ed. *Mark Twain* (7–12). Series: People Who Made History. 2002, Gale paper $36.20 (978-0-7377-0897-4). Detailed essays that explore various aspects of Twain's life and writing are preceded by a general introductory that gives an overview of his life and times. (Rev: BL 4/1/02) [921]

5628 Lasky, Kathryn. *A Brilliant Streak: The Making of Mark Twain* (4–7). Illus. by Barry Moser. 1998, Harcourt $18.00 (978-0-15-252110-3). Using many quotations and anecdotes from the author's

work, this nicely illustrated biography of Mark Twain concentrates on his first 30 years when he was a steamboat pilot, prospector, reporter, and budding writer. (Rev: BCCB 7–8/98; BL 4/1/98; HB 5–6/98; HBG 10/98; SLJ 4/98) [921]

5629 Pflueger, Lynda. *Mark Twain* (5–8). Series: Historical American Biographies. 1999, Enslow LB $26.60 (978-0-7660-1093-2). A balanced, well-documented biography that includes chapter notes, a bibliography, glossary, and some period black-and-white illustrations. (Rev: BL 1/1–15/00; HBG 3/00; SLJ 1/00) [921]

5630 Rasmussen, R. Kent. *Mark Twain for Kids: His Life and Times, 21 Activities* (4–7). Illus. Series: For Kids. 2004, Chicago Review paper $14.95 (978-1-55652-527-8). An engaging biography that reveals interesting details of Twain's life and shows how many of the episodes in his books were based on his own experiences. (Rev: BL 9/15/04; SLJ 9/04) [921]

5631 Ward, Geoffrey C., et al. *Mark Twain* (8–12). Illus. 2001, Knopf $40.00 (978-0-375-40561-7). As well as a good text, this biography contains a treasure trove of photographs and other illustrations that depict the life and times of Mark Twain. (Rev: BL 10/15/01; SLJ 6/02) [921]

VERNE, JULES

5632 Schoell, William. *Remarkable Journeys: The Story of Jules Verne* (4–8). Series: World Writers. 2002, Morgan Reynolds LB $23.95 (978-1-883846-92-3). Writing was not Verne's first love, as Schoell explains in this accessible biography. (Rev: BL 6/1–15/02; HBG 10/02; SLJ 9/02) [843.8]

5633 Teeters, Peggy. *Jules Verne: The Man Who Invented Tomorrow* (5–7). Illus. 1993, Walker LB $14.85 (978-0-8027-8191-8). The life of the famous writer of science fiction, including his childhood in France. (Rev: BL 3/15/93; SLJ 5/93) [921]

WALKER, ALICE

5634 Lazo, Caroline Evensen. *Alice Walker: Freedom Writer* (6–12). Illus. Series: Lerner Biographies. 2000, Lerner LB $25.26 (978-0-8225-4960-4). The personal life and literary career of the woman who won the Pulitzer Prize for *The Color Purple* is enhanced by the frequent use of quotations. (Rev: BL 8/00; HBG 9/00; SLJ 8/00; VOYA 2/01) [921]

WELLS, H. G.

5635 Boerst, William J. *Time Machine: The Story of H. G. Wells* (5–8). Illus. Series: World Writers. 1999, Morgan Reynolds LB $23.95 (978-1-883846-40-4). The story of the intriguing English author, including material on his childhood, romances, political views, and literary works. (Rev: BL 1/1–15/00; HBG 3/00) [921]

WHEATLEY, PHILLIS

5636 Kent, Deborah. *Phillis Wheatley: First Published African-American Poet* (4–7). Series: Our People. 2003, The Child's World LB $27.07 (978-1-59296-009-5). The life of the 18th-century poet is outlined in this well-illustrated work that features large type and includes historical background. (Rev: SLJ 4/04) [921]

5637 McLendon, Jacquelyn. *Phillis Wheatley: A Revolutionary Poet* (4–7). Series: Library of American Lives and Times. 2003, Rosen LB $34.60 (978-0-8239-5750-7). Kidnapped into slavery from Senegal, Phillis Wheatley became a major voice in the American literary scene. (Rev: BL 6/1–15/03; SLJ 5/03) [921]

5638 Richmond, Merle. *Phillis Wheatley* (7–10). Illus. 1988, Chelsea LB $30.00 (978-1-55546-683-1). A heavily illustrated account of this poet who triumphed over slavery. (Rev: BL 2/15/88; SLJ 4/88) [921]

5639 Salisbury, Cynthia. *Phillis Wheatley: Legendary African-American Poet* (5–8). Series: Historical American Biographies. 2001, Enslow LB $26.60 (978-0-7660-1394-0). The life story of the first important African American poet, who was brought to America as a slave and bought by a Quaker family who allowed her to develop her talents. (Rev: BL 3/1/01; HBG 10/01; SLJ 7/01) [921]

WHITE, E. B.

5640 Bernard, Catherine. *E. B. White: Spinner of Webs and Tales* (5–8). Series: Authors Teens Love. 2005, Enslow LB $26.60 (978-0-7660-2350-5). An introductory chapter that gives a good overview of White's life is followed by chapters that delve into more detail plus a timeline and an excerpt from a 1969 interview that adds a more personal dimension. (Rev: BCCB 12/05; SLJ 10/05) [921]

5641 Murcia, Rebecca Thatcher. *E. B. White* (5–8). Series: Classic Storytellers. 2004, Mitchell Lane LB $29.95 (978-1-58415-273-6). An introduction to White's life, work, and legacy, with background information on relevant historical, cultural, and economic factors. (Rev: BL 1/05; SLJ 1/05) [921]

5642 Tingum, Janice. *E. B. White: The Elements of a Writer* (7–10). 1995, Lerner LB $30.35 (978-0-8225-4922-2). This quiet biography of the author of the much-beloved *Charlotte's Web* and other books discusses the underside of White's success: his shyness and depression. (Rev: BL 11/1/95) [921]

WHITMAN, WALT

5643 Kerley, Barbara. *Walt Whitman: Words for America* (4–8). Illus. by Brian Selznick. 2004, Scholastic $16.95 (978-0-439-35791-3). Whitman's experiences during the Civil War, including his service as a nurse to injured and dying soldiers, are highlighted in this picture-book biography. (Rev: BL 11/15/04; SLJ 11/04) [811]

5644 Meltzer, Milton. *Walt Whitman: A Biography* (6–12). Illus. 2002, Millbrook LB $31.90 (978-0-7613-2272-6). This life story of the American poet emphasizes his place in the country's history. (Rev: BL 4/1/02; HB 9–10/02; HBG 3/03; SLJ 3/02; VOYA 6/03) [921]

5645 Reef, Catherine. *Walt Whitman* (7–12). 1995, Clarion $16.95 (978-0-395-68705-5). A biography of the 19th-century poet who sang of America and the self. (Rev: BL 5/1/95; SLJ 5/95) [921]

WILDER, LAURA INGALLS

5646 Berne, Emma Carlson. *Laura Ingalls Wilder* (5–8). Illus. Series: Essential Lives. 2007, ABDO LB $22.95 (978-1-59928-843-7). The life of the author of the beloved Little House books, with an emphasis on the hard realities that she faced both as a pioneer child and as an adult during the Great Depression. (Rev: BL 2/1/08; SLJ 3/08) [813]

5647 Wadsworth, Ginger. *Laura Ingalls Wilder: Storyteller of the Prairie* (5–8). Series: Biography. 1997, Lerner LB $27.93 (978-0-8225-4950-5). A solid, readable biography of this author that clarifies the chronology in the Little House books. (Rev: BL 3/1/97; SLJ 4/97) [921]

5648 Wilder, Laura Ingalls. *A Little House Traveler: Writings from Laura Ingalls Wilder's Journeys Across America* (5–8). 2006, HarperCollins $16.99 (978-0-06-072491-7). Three of Wilder's diaries — one never before published — chronicle the Little House author's travels with her husband Almanzo and daughter Rose. (Rev: BL 12/15/05; VOYA 4/06) [813]

WILLIAMS, WILLIAM CARLOS

5649 Berry, S. L. *William Carlos Williams* (5–9). Illus. by Yan Nascimbene. Series: Voices in Poetry. 2003, Creative LB $19.95 (978-1-58341-284-8). This picture-book biography introduces readers to Williams's poetry and life from childhood. (Rev: BL 12/1/03; HBG 4/04) [808]

WOODSON, CARTER G.

5650 Durden, Robert F. *Carter G. Woodson: Father of African-American History* (6–10). Series: African-American Biographies. 1998, Enslow LB $26.60 (978-0-89490-946-7). This balanced, documented account focuses on the successes and failures of this historian, pioneering writer, and publisher, who devoted his life to the study of African American history and culture. (Rev: SLJ 1/99) [921]

WOODSON, JACQUELINE

5651 Hinton, KaaVonia. *Jacqueline Woodson* (5–8). Illus. Series: Classic Storytellers. 2008, Mitchell Lane LB $20.95 (978-1-58415-533-1). The story of Woodson's life, from her childhood in the 1960s to her adulthood — including her lesbian relationship — with photographs and discussions of her work. (Rev: BL 3/3/08; SLJ 8/08) [921]

WOOLF, VIRGINIA

5652 Brackett, Virginia. *Restless Genius: The Story of Virginia Woolf* (7–12). Series: Writers of Imagination. 2004, Morgan Reynolds LB $23.95 (978-1-931798-37-2). Woolf's personal life — her relationship with Vita Sackville-West is touched on — and mental stability are the main focus of this brief, interesting biography that also discusses her writing and its influence. (Rev: BCCB 11/04; BL 10/1/04; SLJ 11/04) [921]

WRIGHT, RICHARD

5653 Hart, Joyce. *Native Son: The Story of Richard Wright* (6–10). Illus. Series: World Writers. 2002, Morgan Reynolds LB $23.95 (978-1-931798-06-8). This biography describes best-selling African American author Richard Wright's controversial works and his development as a writer. (Rev: BL 2/15/03; HBG 3/03; SLJ 4/03) [921]

5654 Levy, Debbie. *Richard Wright* (7–12). Illus. Series: Literary Greats. 2007, Lerner LB $33.26 (978-0-8225-6793-6). The life and times of the author of *Native Son* and *Black Boy,* with photographs and a timeline. (Rev: BL 12/1/07; SLJ 12/07) [921]

5655 Urban, Joan. *Richard Wright* (7–10). Illus. 1989, Chelsea LB $19.95 (978-1-55546-618-3). A well-illustrated biography that also tells a little about the author's work. (Rev: BL 6/15/89; SLJ 8/89) [921]

5656 Westen, Robin. *Richard Wright: Author of Native Son and Black Boy* (7–10). Series: African-American Biographies. 2002, Enslow LB $26.60 (978-0-7660-1769-6). The life and achievements of the African American novelist known for opposition to racial discrimination. (Rev: HBG 3/03; SLJ 1/03) [921]

5657 Wright, Richard. *Black Boy: A Record of Childhood and Youth* (8–12). 1998, HarperCollins paper $13.95 (978-0-06-092978-7). The tortured boyhood of the great black writer growing up in the South. This autobiography is continued in *American Hunger* (1977). [921]

YEATS, WILLIAM BUTLER

5658 Allison, Jonathan, ed. *William Butler Yeats* (6–12). Illus. by Glenn Harrington. Series: Poetry for Young People. 2003, Sterling $14.95 (978-0-8069-6615-1). A handsomely illustrated collection of Yeats's poems, each introduced with commentary and followed by explanations of any challenging vocabulary. (Rev: BL 4/1/03; HBG 10/03; SLJ 2/03) [921]

ZINDEL, PAUL

5659 Daniel, Susanna. *Paul Zindel* (5–8). Series: The Library of Author Biographies. 2004, Rosen LB $27.95 (978-0-8239-4524-5). Covers Zindel's career as a YA author, with analysis of his work, an interview, and lists of works and awards. (Rev: SLJ 1/05) [921]

Composers

BACH, JOHANN SEBASTIAN

5660 Getzinger, Donna, and Daniel Felsenfeld. *Johann Sebastian Bach and the Art of Baroque Music* (6–12). Illus. Series: Classical Composers. 2004, Morgan Reynolds LB $26.95 (978-1-931798-22-8). This biography reviews Bach's life and times, emphasizing in particular his musical education and commitment and his love for this family. (Rev: BL 6/1–15/04; SLJ 8/04) [780]

BEETHOVEN, LUDWIG VAN

5661 Balcavage, Dynise. *Ludwig Van Beethoven: Composer* (4–8). Series: Great Achievers: Lives of the Physically Challenged. 1997, Chelsea LB $21.95 (978-0-7910-2082-1). This is an information-rich account of the composer's public and private life, with good coverage of his compositions. (Rev: SLJ 7/97) [921]

5662 Viegas, Jennifer. *Beethoven's World* (5–8). Series: Music Throughout History. 2007, Rosen LB $29.25 (978-1-4042-0724-0). Six biographical chapters cover the composer's early life, family, personal life, musical training, compositions, and influences, with photographs of key people and places. (Rev: SLJ 1/08)

BERLIN, IRVING

5663 Furstinger, Nancy. *Say It with Music: The Story of Irving Berlin* (5–9). Illus. Series: Masters of Music. 2003, Morgan Reynolds LB $23.95 (978-1-

931798-12-9). Well-researched and very readable, this account traces Berlin's life from Russia to the United States and his popular and lasting success as a songwriter. (Rev: BL 6/1–15/03; HBG 4/04; SLJ 10/03) [780.92]

BERLIOZ, HECTOR

5664 Whiting, Jim. *The Life and Times of Hector Berlioz* (5–7). Series: Masters of Music: The World's Greatest Composers. 2004, Mitchell Lane LB $20.95 (978-1-58415-259-0). A brief biography of the talented and troubled creator of the *Symphonie fantastique*. (Rev: SLJ 2/05) [921]

BERNSTEIN, LEONARD

5665 Blashfield, Jean F. *Leonard Bernstein: Composer and Conductor* (4–7). Series: Ferguson Career Biographies. 2001, Ferguson LB $25.00 (978-0-89434-337-7). Numerous black-and-white photographs accompany the easily read text in this interesting account of Bernstein's life and career. (Rev: SLJ 7/01) [780]

5666 Hurwitz, Johanna. *Leonard Bernstein: A Passion for Music* (4–8). Illus. by Sonia O. Lisker. 1993, Jewish Publication Soc. $14.95 (978-0-8276-0501-5). The career of this amazing conductor and composer who was also a gifted pianist and teacher. (Rev: BL 2/15/94; SLJ 12/93) [921]

5667 Lazo, Caroline Evensen. *Leonard Bernstein: In Love with Music* (7–12). Illus. 2002, Lerner LB $27.93 (978-0-8225-0072-8). This detailed portrait of Bernstein's life and musical accomplishments includes many black-and-white photographs. (Rev: BL 10/15/02; HBG 3/03; VOYA 12/02) [780]

CHOPIN, FREDERIC

5668 Malaspina, Ann. *Chopin's World* (5–8). Series: Music Throughout History. 2007, Rosen LB $29.25 (978-1-4042-0723-3). Six biographical chapters cover the composer's early life, family, personal life, musical training, compositions, and influences, with photographs of key people and places. (Rev: SLJ 1/08)

DVORAK, ANTONIN

5669 Horowitz, Joseph. *Dvorak in America* (6–12). Illus. 2003, Cricket $17.95 (978-0-8126-2481-6). Dvorak's life in the United States (he arrived from Prague in the 1890s) is the focus of this narrative, which also covers the composition of the New World symphony. (Rev: BL 6/1–15/03) [780]

GERSHWIN, GEORGE

5670 Reef, Catherine. *George Gershwin: American Composer* (5–8). Illus. Series: Masters of Music.

2000, Morgan Reynolds LB $23.95 (978-1-883846-58-9). This biography traces the life one of America's great composers, giving insight into his personality, family, and times. (Rev: BL 2/15/00; HBG 10/00; SLJ 3/00) [921]

GUTHRIE, WOODY

5671 Partridge, Elizabeth. *This Land Was Made for You and Me: The Life and Songs of Woodie Guthrie* (6–12). Illus. 2002, Viking $21.99 (978-0-670-03535-9). The life, work, and times of the folk singer, from his childhood in the Dust Bowl to his death from Huntington's Disease. (Rev: BL 4/1/02; HB 3–4/02*; HBG 10/02; SLJ 4/02; VOYA 8/02) [782.42162]

5672 Yates, Janelle. *Woody Guthrie: American Balladeer* (6–10). 1995, Ward Hill LB $14.95 (978-0-9623380-0-7); paper $10.95 (978-0-9623380-5-2). Describes Guthrie's creative life and provides important historical information, including the many tragedies suffered by his family and his friendly relationship with labor, members of the Communist Party, and other musicians. (Rev: BL 2/1/95; SLJ 3/95) [921]

HANDEL, GEORGE FRIDERIC

5673 Getzinger, Donna, and Daniel Felsenfeld. *George Frideric Handel and Music for Voices* (6–10). Series: Classical Composers. 2004, Morgan Reynolds LB $26.95 (978-1-931798-23-5). Handel's life and career are placed in historical context. (Rev: SLJ 11/04) [921]

5674 Lee, Lavina. *Handel's World* (5–8). Series: Music Throughout History. 2007, Rosen LB $29.25 (978-1-4042-0726-4). Six biographical chapters cover the composer's early life, family, personal life, musical training, compositions, and influences, with photographs of key people and places. (Rev: LMC 1/08; SLJ 1/08)

HAYDN, FRANZ JOSEPH

5675 Norton, James R. *Haydn's World* (5–8). Series: Music Throughout History. 2007, Rosen LB $29.25 (978-1-4042-0727-1). Six biographical chapters cover the composer's early life, family, personal life, musical training, compositions, and influences, with photographs of key people and places. (Rev: SLJ 1/08)

JONES, QUINCY

5676 Kavanaugh, Lee H. *Quincy Jones: Musician, Composer, Producer* (5–8). 1998, Enslow LB $20.95 (978-0-89490-814-9). This biography describes Quincy Jones's 50-year career in music and how he overcame poverty, racism, and health problems to become a musical director, composer, producer, arranger, and driving force behind many award-winning recordings. (Rev: VOYA 8/98) [921]

JOPLIN, SCOTT

5677 Bankston, John. *The Life and Times of Scott Joplin* (5–7). Series: Masters of Music: The World's Greatest Composers. 2004, Mitchell Lane LB $20.95 (978-1-58415-270-5). Joplin's career as a ragtime piano player and composer is documented, with coverage of his African American heritage. (Rev: SLJ 2/05) [921]

5678 Preston, Katherine. *Scott Joplin: Composer* (7–10). Illus. 1988, Chelsea LB $21.95 (978-1-55546-598-8). The story of the talented musician, composer, and performer and the legacy of ragtime music he has left us. (Rev: BL 2/1/88; SLJ 5/88) [921]

MENDELSSOHN, FANNY

5679 Shichtman, Sandra, and Dorothy Indenbaum. *Gifted Sister: The Story of Fanny Mendelssohn* (8–11). Illus. 2007, Morgan Reynolds LB $27.95 (978-1-59935-038-7). Fanny, the sister of the noted musician, was very talented herself and composed throughout her life; this biography shows how her life evolved under the social constraints of the early 1800s. (Rev: BL 9/15/07; SLJ 9/07) [921]

MESSIAEN, OLIVIER

5680 Bryant, Jen. *Music for the End of Time* (4–7). Illus. by Beth Peck. 2005, Eerdmans $17.00 (978-0-8028-5229-8). This fictionalized picture-book biography tells how French soldier Olivier Messiaen composed and performed music while in a German prison camp during World War II. (Rev: BL 9/1/05; SLJ 12/05) [921]

MOZART, WOLFGANG AMADEUS

5681 Weeks, Marcus. *Mozart: The Boy Who Changed the World with His Music* (5–8). Series: World History Biographies. 2007, National Geographic $17.95 (978-1-4263-0002-8). An attractive, well-organized life of the young composer, with details of his music lessons and instruments, his first job, and his later financial worries. (Rev: SLJ 6/07) [921]

STILL, WILLIAM GRANT

5682 Reef, Catherine. *William Grant Still: African American Composer* (6–9). Illus. 2003, Morgan Reynolds LB $23.95 (978-1-931798-11-2). Still, who was born in 1895, shunned his mother's advice and devoted himself to music, learning to play, compose, and arrange. (Rev: BL 7/03; HBG 10/03; SLJ 9/03) [780.9]

VIVALDI, ANTONIO

5683 Getzinger, Donna, and Daniel Felsenfeld. *Antonio Vivaldi and the Baroque Tradition* (6–10). Series: Classical Composers. 2004, Morgan Reynolds LB $26.95 (978-1-931798-20-4). The story of the rise and fall of this prolific composer as well as of his music world and the importance of Venice in this sphere. (Rev: BL 4/15/04; SLJ 6/04) [921]

WAGNER, RICHARD

5684 Getzinger, Donna, and Daniel Felsenfeld. *Richard Wagner and German Opera* (6–10). Series: Classical Composers. 2004, Morgan Reynolds LB $26.95 (978-1-931798-24-2). A well-written, balanced biography that discusses Wagner's flaws as well as his great achievements. (Rev: SLJ 11/04) [921]

Performers (Actors, Musicians, etc.)

ABDUL, PAULA

5685 Zannos, Susan. *Paula Abdul* (4–8). Series: Real-Life Reader Biographies. 1999, Mitchell Lane LB $15.95 (978-1-883845-74-2). A brief biography of this choreographer and recording artist that recounts her many problems, including a struggle with bulimia and a series of failed marriages. (Rev: BL 6/1–15/99) [921]

AILEY, ALVIN

5686 Cruz, Barbara C. *Alvin Ailey: Celebrating African-American Culture in Dance* (5–9). Series: African-American Biographies. 2004, Enslow LB $26.60 (978-0-7660-2293-5). Ailey's life and contributions to dance are detailed, including a chapter on the classic "Revelations" and information on his contemporaries. (Rev: SLJ 1/05) [921]

ALLEN, TIM

5687 Wukovits, John. *Tim Allen* (6–9). Illus. Series: Overcoming Adversity. 1998, Chelsea paper $9.95 (978-0-7910-4697-5). A sympathetic portrait of the show business star who once went to jail for selling cocaine and rebounded to gain success on TV's *Home Improvement*. (Rev: HBG 3/99; SLJ 11/98) [921]

ALONSO, ALICIA

5688 Arnold, Sandra M. *Alicia Alonso: First Lady of the Ballet* (6–10). 1993, Walker LB $15.85 (978-0-8027-8243-4). Overcoming the lack of dance schools in her native Cuba and going blind in her 20s, Alicia Alonso became a prima ballerina and went on to teach, study, and perform in Cuba. (Rev: BL 12/15/93; SLJ 11/93; VOYA 2/94) [921]

ANDERSON, MARIAN

5689 Broadwater, Andrea. *Marian Anderson: Singer and Humanitarian* (7–12). Series: African-American Biographies. 2000, Enslow LB $26.60 (978-0-7660-1211-0). The story of the great African American singer who broke many color barriers in the world of music. (Rev: BL 4/15/00; HBG 9/00) [921]

5690 Freedman, Russell. *The Voice That Challenged a Nation: Marian Anderson and the Struggle for Equal Rights* (4–8). 2004, Houghton $18.00 (978-0-618-15976-5). Beautifully illustrated with period photographs, this picture-book biography of the African American vocalist describes her life and the events leading up to her historic concert at the Lincoln Memorial. (Rev: BL 6/1–15/04; HB 5–6/04; SLJ 7/04) [921]

5691 Jones, Victoria Garrett. *Marian Anderson: A Voice Uplifted* (6–9). Illus. Series: Sterling Biographies. 2008, Sterling $12.95 (978-1-4027-5802-7); paper $5.95 (978-1-4027-4239-2). The inspiring story of the African American singer is presented in historical context. (Rev: BL 2/1/08; SLJ 8/08) [921]

5692 Tedards, Anne. *Marian Anderson* (6–10). Illus. 1987, Chelsea LB $19.95 (978-1-55546-638-1). The life story of the great singer-artist who helped tear down many color barriers. (Rev: BL 2/1/88; SLJ 4/88) [921]

ARMSTRONG, LOUIS

5693 Old, Wendie C. *Louis Armstrong: King of Jazz* (5–9). Series: African-American Biographies. 1998, Enslow LB $26.60 (978-0-89490-997-9). The life and accomplishments of the legendary jazz trumpeter know as Satchmo who lived from 1900 to 1971. (Rev: BL 11/15/98; SLJ 11/98) [921]

5694 Tanenhaus, Sam. *Louis Armstrong* (7–10). Illus. 1989, Chelsea LB $30.00 (978-1-55546-571-1). The story of the African American musician who rose from poverty in New Orleans to the heights of the jazz world. (Rev: BL 3/15/89) [921]

BALANCHINE, GEORGE

5695 Gottlieb, Robert. *George Balanchine: The Ballet Maker* (8–12). 2004, HarperCollins $19.95 (978-0-06-075070-1). Balanchine's ballet talent was recognized at a young age; this biography follows his progress from St. Petersburg to New York and worldwide fame. (Rev: BL 11/1/04) [792.8]

5696 Kristy, Davida. *George Balanchine: American Ballet Master* (5–9). Illus. Series: Biographies. 1996, Lerner LB $27.93 (978-0-8225-4951-2). The

story of the Russian émigré choreographer and how he changed the world of American ballet. (Rev: BL 9/1/96; SLJ 8/96) [921]

5697 Seibert, Brian. *George Balanchine* (6–9). Illus. Series: Library of American Choreographers. 2005, Rosen LB $23.95 (978-0-404-20447-1). The life and career of the Russian-born ballet choreographer; there are no source notes. (Rev: BL 11/1/05) [792.8]

BANKS, TYRA

5698 Levin, Pam. *Tyra Banks* (5–8). Illus. Series: Black Americans of Achievement. 1999, Chelsea $30.00 (978-0-7910-5195-5); paper $30.00 (978-0-7910-4964-8). This is the story of an "ugly duckling" who was awkward and uncoordinated as a child but who later became a supermodel. (Rev: BL 2/15/00; HBG 3/00) [921]

BARR, ROSEANNE

5699 Gaines, Ann. *Roseanne: Entertainer* (5–8). Series: Overcoming Adversity. 1999, Chelsea LB $21.95 (978-0-7910-4706-4); paper $8.95 (978-0-7910-4707-1). The story of how this overweight housewife made difficult decisions and many sacrifices to achieve her goal of becoming successful not just in show business, but also in the difficult field of comedy, and later as a TV personality. (Rev: VOYA 8/98) [921]

BASIE, COUNT

5700 Kliment, Bud. *Count Basie* (7–10). Series: Black Americans of Achievement. 1992, Chelsea LB $30.00 (978-0-7910-1118-8). The story of this trailblazing band leader and his contributions to jazz and popular music. (Rev: BL 9/15/92) [921]

BEATLES (MUSICAL GROUP)

5701 Roberts, Jeremy. *The Beatles* (5–8). Series: Biography. 2001, Lerner LB $27.93 (978-0-8225-4998-7). This is the story of the Beatles, from Liverpool to international stardom and eventual separation. (Rev: BL 4/1/02; HBG 10/02) [921]

5702 Sawyers, June S., ed. *Read the Beatles: Classic and New Writings on the Beatles, Their Legacy, and Why They Still Matter* (8–12). 2006, Penguin paper $16.00 (978-0-14-303732-3). A compilation of articles and essays about the Beatles, by writers including Gloria Steinem, Allen Ginsberg, and Philip Glass. (Rev: BL 11/1/06) [920]

5703 Spitz, Bob. *Yeah! Yeah! Yeah!* (7–10). Illus. 2007, Little, Brown $18.99 (978-0-316-11555-1). A fluent history of the Beatles, with information on the group's beginnings, influences, growth, and worldwide legacy, enhanced by black-and-white photographs; from the author of the adult book *The*

Beatles (2005). (Rev: BL 11/1/07; SLJ 12/07) [782.421]

5704 Woog, Adam. *The Beatles* (4–8). Series: Importance Of. 1997, Lucent LB $28.70 (978-1-56006-088-8). Outlines the lives and careers of these four Liverpool natives and their many achievements. (Rev: BL 10/15/97; SLJ 12/97) [921]

BLADES, RUBEN

5705 Cruz, Barbara C. *Ruben Blades: Salsa Singer and Social Activist* (4–9). Series: Hispanic Biographies. 1997, Enslow LB $26.60 (978-0-89490-893-4). The inspiring story of the Panama-born musician and his involvement in social activism and politics. (Rev: HBG 3/98; SLJ 1/98; VOYA 2/98) [921]

5706 Marton, Betty A. *Rubén Blades* (5–9). Series: Hispanics of Achievement. 1992, Chelsea LB $32.00 (978-0-7910-1235-2). The story of the Panamanian salsa singer who is also a poet and activist. (Rev: BL 10/1/92; SLJ 11/92) [921]

BOONE, JOHN WILLIAM

5707 Harrah, Madge. *Blind Boone* (5–8). Illus. 2003, Carolrhoda LB $30.60 (978-1-57505-057-7). The son of a runaway slave, Boone became blind as an infant but soon revealed a musical talent and went on to become a composer and concert pianist. (Rev: BL 12/1/03; HBG 3/02; SLJ 10/01) [781.64]

BRANDY (SINGER)

5708 Newman, Michael. *Brandy* (5–8). Series: Galaxy of Superstars. 2000, Chelsea $25.00 (978-0-7910-5781-0). A biography of the famous singer and star of *Moesha*. (Rev: BL 12/15/00; HBG 10/01) [921]

BROOKS, GARTH

5709 Powell, Phelan. *Garth Brooks: Award-Winning Country Music Star* (4–7). Series: Real-Life Reader Biographies. 1999, Mitchell Lane LB $15.95 (978-1-58415-004-6). A biography of the award-winning country music star and how he got there. (Rev: SLJ 1/00)

5710 Wren, Laura Lee. *Garth Brooks: Country Music Superstar* (6–10). Series: People to Know. 2002, Enslow LB $26.60 (978-0-7660-1672-9). The story of the country music star and his incredible rise to fame is told in text and pictures. (Rev: BL 9/15/02; HBG 3/03; SLJ 1/03) [921]

BULLOCK, SANDRA

5711 Hill, Anne E. *Sandra Bullock* (5–8). Series: People in the News. 2000, Lucent LB $27.45 (978-1-56006-711-5). Quotations from Bullock and oth-

ers expand this biography and explain how and why she has gained prominence as a Hollywood actress. (Rev: BL 9/15/00) [921]

BURKE, CHRIS

5712 Geraghty, Helen M. *Chris Burke* (5–9). Series: Great Achievers: Lives of the Physically Challenged. 1994, Chelsea LB $19.95 (978-0-7910-2081-4). This biography of the star of TV's *Life Goes On* looks at Burke's family life and career success despite Down's syndrome. (Rev: BL 10/15/94) [921]

CARREY, JIM

5713 Wukovits, John. *Jim Carrey* (5–9). Series: People in the News. 1999, Lucent LB $28.70 (978-1-56006-561-6). From his boyhood in Canada to stardom in such movies as *The Truman Show*, this biography reveals Carrey's efforts to become a multidimensional actor. (Rev: BL 8/99; HBG 3/00) [921]

CASALS, PABLO

5714 Garza, Hedda. *Pablo Casals* (5–9). Series: Hispanics of Achievement. 1993, Chelsea LB $21.95 (978-0-7910-1237-6). The story of the legendary Spanish cellist and his exile from his homeland during Franco's regime. (Rev: BL 4/1/93; SLJ 7/93; VOYA 8/93) [921]

CASH, JOHNNY

5715 Neimark, Anne E. *Johnny Cash* (6–9). Series: Up Close. 2007, Viking $15.99 (978-0-670-06215-7). This account of the complicated and difficult life of the famous musician discusses Cash's admirable traits (such as musical talent and compassion for the downtrodden) as well as his less-admirable (such as drug use and a quick temper). (Rev: BL 2/1/07; HB 3-4/07; SLJ 4/07) [921]

CHAPLIN, CHARLIE

5716 Turk, Ruth. *Charlie Chaplin: Genius of the Silent Screen* (5–9). 2000, Lerner LB $30.35 (978-0-8225-4957-4). A competent overview of this great movie maker's life from his childhood in England to his exile in Switzerland. (Rev: BL 2/15/00; HBG 10/00; SLJ 4/00) [921]

CHARLES, RAY

5717 Duggleby, John. *Uh Huh! The Story of Ray Charles* (6–12). 2005, Morgan Reynolds LB $26.95 (978-1-931798-65-5). In addition to an account of Ray Charles's life and music, this volume reveals much about the social context of his times. (Rev: BL 6/1–15/05; SLJ 10/05) [921]

5718 Ritz, David. *Ray Charles: Voice of Soul* (6–10). 1994, Chelsea LB $32.00 (978-0-7910-2080-7); paper $8.95 (978-0-7910-2093-7). The story of Ray Charles Robinson, who overcame the hardships of poverty, racism, drug addiction, and blindness to become one of America's influential musicians. (Rev: BL 11/15/94) [921]

5719 Turk, Ruth. *Ray Charles: Soul Man* (5–8). Illus. Series: Newsmakers. 1996, Lerner LB $30.35 (978-0-8225-4928-4). A candid biography of the great blind entertainer that includes compelling details about his childhood. (Rev: SLJ 8/96) [921]

5720 Woog, Adam. *Ray Charles and the Birth of Soul* (7–12). 2006, Gale LB $28.70 (978-1-59018-844-6). Covering Charles's life from a child of poverty in Florida to the legendary soul musician, Woog touches on his mother's influence and chronicles the development of his talents and innovations despite his blindness. (Rev: SLJ 6/06)

CHO, MARGARET

5721 Tiger, Caroline. *Margaret Cho* (7–12). Illus. Series: Asian Americans of Achievement . 2007, Chelsea House LB $30.00 (978-0-7910-9275-0). This biography of the edgy Asian American comedian will appeal to all teenagers who feel marginalized or who simply appreciate Cho's brand of angry but hilarious humor. (Rev: BL 4/15/07) [921]

COBAIN, KURT

5722 Burlingame, Jeff. *Kurt Cobain: "Oh Well, Whatever, Nevermind"* (8–11). Series: American Rebels. 2006, Enslow $20.95 (978-0-7660-2426-7). The author has the inside scoop on the rocker's adolescence, and he delves into what influenced Cobain's troubled youth and sad death. (Rev: BL 1/1–15/07) [921]

CODY, BUFFALO BILL

5723 Spies, Karen B. *Buffalo Bill Cody: Western Legend* (5–8). Series: Historical American Biographies. 1998, Enslow LB $26.60 (978-0-7660-1015-4). An in-depth look at this legendary frontiersman and the Wild West show he founded. (Rev: BL 3/15/98; SLJ 5/98) [921]

COLTRANE, JOHN

5724 Barron, Rachel Stiffler. *John Coltrane: Jazz Revolutionary* (6–10). 2001, Morgan Reynolds LB $23.95 (978-1-883846-57-2). Coltrane's love of music and jazz innovations are the main focus of this biography. (Rev: HBG 3/02; SLJ 1/02; VOYA 10/03) [921]

COSBY, BILL

5725 Haskins, Jim. *Bill Cosby: America's Most Famous Father* (5–7). Illus. 1988, Walker LB $17.00 (978-0-8027-6786-8). The childhood and career of this famous entertainer. (Rev: BL 6/1/88) [921]

5726 Schuman, Michael A. *Bill Cosby: Actor and Comedian* (6–12). Series: People to Know. 1995, Enslow LB $26.60 (978-0-89490-548-3). Describes the life and career of one of the most successful comedians in modern times. (Rev: BL 9/15/95; SLJ 2/96; VOYA 2/96) [921]

CRUISE, TOM

5727 Powell, Phelan. *Tom Cruise* (6–9). Series: Overcoming Adversity. 1999, Chelsea LB $30.00 (978-0-7910-4940-2); paper $30.00 (978-0-7910-4941-9). The story of this famous actor, his struggle with dyslexia and his parents' divorce, and his eventual fame in film. (Rev: BL 5/15/99; HBG 9/99) [921]

DAMON, MATT

5728 Greene, Meg. *Matt Damon* (5–8). Series: Galaxy of Superstars. 2000, Chelsea $25.00 (978-0-7910-5779-7). An entertaining biography of the actor who gained star status as the cowriter and lead actor in *Good Will Hunting*. (Rev: BL 12/15/00; HBG 10/01) [921]

DAVIS, MILES

5729 Dell, Pamela. *Miles Davis: Jazz Master* (5–8). Series: Journey to Freedom. 2005, Child's World LB $28.50 (978-1-59296-232-7). An easy-to-read biography that deals frankly with the trumpeter's addiction to heroin and his difficult personality. (Rev: SLJ 8/05) [921]

5730 Frankl, Ron. *Miles Davis* (7–10). Series: Black Americans of Achievement. 1995, Chelsea LB $30.00 (978-0-7910-2156-9). The story of the famous African American trumpeter and his contributions to jazz. (Rev: BL 11/15/95) [921]

DEAN, JAMES

5731 Oleksy, Walter. *The Importance of James Dean* (7–12). Series: The Importance Of. 2000, Lucent LB $27.45 (978-1-56006-698-9). Using a number of firsthand quotations, this book traces the life of James Dean, his tragic death, and his impact on motion pictures. (Rev: BL 3/1/01) [921]

DICAPRIO, LEONARDO

5732 Stauffer, Stacey. *Leonardo DiCaprio* (5–8). Illus. Series: Galaxy of Superstars. 1999, Chelsea

$25.00 (978-0-7910-5151-1); paper $25.00 (978-0-7910-5326-3). The story of this young actor's life, with special attention to his role in *Titanic*. (Rev: BL 4/15/99; HBG 10/99; SLJ 5/99) [921]

DION, CELINE

5733 Lutz, Norma Jean. *Celine Dion* (5–8). Series: Galaxy of Superstars. 2000, Chelsea $25.00 (978-0-7910-5777-3). The story of the amazing career of this French Canadian singer and how she gained worldwide popularity. (Rev: BL 10/15/00; HBG 10/01) [921]

DOMINGO, PLÁCIDO

5734 Stefoff, Rebecca. *Plácido Domingo* (5–9). Series: Hispanics of Achievement. 1992, Chelsea LB $14.95 (978-0-7910-1563-6). The story of the amazing Spanish-born tenor and his sensational international career, with some information on his private life. (Rev: BL 12/1/92; SLJ 1/93) [921]

DOWD, OLYMPIA

5735 Dowd, Olympia. *A Young Dancer's Apprenticeship: On Tour with the Moscow City Ballet* (6–9). 2003, Twenty-First Century LB $24.90 (978-0-7613-2917-6). Dowd tells the story of how, at the age of only 14, she was offered the opportunity to dance with the Moscow City Ballet. (Rev: HBG 10/03; SLJ 5/03; VOYA 10/03) [792.8]

DUNCAN, ISADORA

5736 O'Connor, Barbara. *Barefoot Dancer: The Story of Isadora Duncan* (5–7). Illus. 1994, Carolrhoda LB $27.93 (978-0-87614-807-5). The story of this eccentric individualist who influenced and liberated a generation of dancers. (Rev: BCCB 10/94; BL 7/94) [921]

DUNHAM, KATHERINE

5737 O'Connor, Barbara. *Katherine Dunham: Pioneer of Black Dance* (5–8). Illus. 2000, Carolrhoda LB $30.35 (978-1-57505-353-0). A fine biography of the African American choreographer who used her study of anthropology to create works for her own dance company and for stage and screen productions. (Rev: BL 5/15/00; HBG 10/00; SLJ 7/00; VOYA 2/01) [921]

DYLAN, BOB

5738 Richardson, Susan. *Bob Dylan* (7–12). Series: Pop Culture Legends. 1995, Chelsea paper $8.95 (978-0-7910-2360-0). The life of this creative icon who influenced both country and pop music. (Rev: BL 8/95) [921]

5739 Roberts, Jeremy. *Bob Dylan: Voice of a Generation* (8–11). Illus. Series: Lerner Biographies. 2005, Lerner LB $27.93 (978-0-8225-1368-1). This evenhanded biography chronicles the folk singer's transformation from Bobby Zimmerman in small-town Minnesota to cultural icon. (Rev: BL 6/1–15/05) [921]

ELLINGTON, DUKE

5740 Frankl, Ron. *Duke Ellington: Bandleader and Composer* (6–10). Illus. 1988, Chelsea LB $21.95 (978-1-55546-584-1). The story of the evolution of a great composer and of his life in music. (Rev: SLJ 8/88) [921]

5741 Old, Wendie C. *Duke Ellington: Giant of Jazz* (7–12). Series: African-American Biographies. 1996, Enslow LB $26.60 (978-0-89490-691-6). An attractive biography of this giant of jazz who was a brilliant composer and arranger as well as an outstanding performer. (Rev: BL 9/15/96) [921]

ESTEFAN, GLORIA

5742 Gonzales, Doreen. *Gloria Estefan: Singer and Entertainer* (5–9). Series: Hispanic Biographies. 1998, Enslow LB $26.60 (978-0-89490-890-3). This story of the singer who started with the Miami Sound Machine and then branched out as a soloist also reveals her devotion to her family and many social causes. (Rev: HBG 3/99; SLJ 10/98; VOYA 10/98) [921]

5743 Rodriguez, Janel. *Gloria Estefan* (4–8). Illus. Series: Contemporary Hispanic Americans. 1995, Raintree LB $24.26 (978-0-8172-3982-4). A fine biography of this Cuban American entertainer who, at the height of her career, overcame severe medical problems and remained a star singer. (Rev: BL 3/15/96; SLJ 1/96) [921]

5744 Shirley, David. *Gloria Estefan* (4–7). Illus. Series: Hispanics of Achievement. 1994, Chelsea LB $15.95 (978-0-7910-2114-9); paper $7.65 (978-0-7910-2117-0). A nicely illustrated biography of the Cuban-born rock star. (Rev: BL 11/15/94; SLJ 10/94) [921]

5745 Stefoff, Rebecca. *Gloria Estefan* (5–9). Series: Hispanics of Achievement. 1991, Chelsea LB $21.95 (978-0-7910-1244-4). The story of the singer who broke her back in a 1990 accident but bounced back to success. (Rev: BL 8/91; SLJ 12/91) [782.42164]

FITZGERALD, ELLA

5746 Stone, Tanya Lee. *Ella Fitzgerald* (7–10). Illus. Series: Up Close. 2008, Viking $16.99 (978-0-670-06149-5). The singer's hard work and exceptional voice are the main focus of this biography. (Rev: BL 2/1/08; SLJ 2/08) [782.421]

FREEMAN, MORGAN

5747 De Angelis, Gina. *Morgan Freeman* (7–12). Series: Black Americans of Achievement. 1999, Chelsea LB $30.00 (978-0-7910-4963-1). The life and career of the African American actor who has starred on Broadway, on television, and in movies. (Rev: HBG 4/00; SLJ 1/00) [791.43]

GILLESPIE, DIZZY

5748 Gourse, Leslie. *Dizzy Gillespie and the Birth of Bebop* (6–10). 1994, Atheneum $14.95 (978-0-689-31869-6). Bebop became a national music trend due in part to the influence of this trumpet-playing jazz legend. (Rev: BL 1/1/95; SLJ 3/95) [921]

GOH, CHAN HON

5749 Goh, Chan Hon, and Cary Fagan. *Beyond the Dance: A Ballerina's Life* (6–12). 2002, Tundra LB $15.95 (978-0-88776-596-4). A readable account of Goh's childhood in Vancouver and rapid rise as a ballet dancer to become a prima ballerina with the National Ballet of Canada. (Rev: HBG 10/03; SLJ 4/03; VOYA 4/03) [921]

GOLDBERG, WHOOPI

5750 Blue, Rose, and Corinne J. Naden. *Whoopi Goldberg* (7–10). Series: Black Americans of Achievement. 1995, Chelsea LB $30.00 (978-0-7910-2152-1); paper $8.95 (978-0-7910-2153-8). A biography that tells how, in spite of great odds, this unusual comedian and actress rose to the top. (Rev: BL 3/15/95) [921]

5751 Caper, William. *Whoopi Goldberg: Comedian and Movie Star* (6–9). Illus. 1999, Enslow LB $26.60 (978-0-7660-1205-9). Goldberg's journey from the New York housing projects to Hollywood is detailed here with black-and-white photographs and a chronology and filmography. (Rev: BL 10/1/99) [791.43]

5752 Gaines, Ann. *Whoopi Goldberg* (6–9). Series: Overcoming Adversity. 1999, Chelsea LB $21.95 (978-0-7910-4938-9); paper $6.65 (978-0-7910-4939-6). The story of Whoopi Goldberg, her struggle with dyslexia, and how she dropped out of school at the age of 13 and turned to a life of drugs and sex before finding acting and a new life. (Rev: BL 5/15/99; HBG 9/99) [921]

5753 Katz, Sandor. *Whoopi Goldberg: Performer with a Heart* (5–8). Series: Junior Black Americans of Achievement. 1996, Chelsea $18.65 (978-0-7910-2396-9). A look at Whoopi Goldberg's life and career, focusing on how she feels about her profession and the causes she believes in. (Rev: BL 10/15/96; SLJ 1/97) [921]

GRAHAM, MARTHA

5754 Freedman, Russell. *Martha Graham: A Dancer's Life* (4–8). 1998, Clarion $19.00 (978-0-395-74655-4). Martha Graham's amazing talents, driving force, and complex personality are well depicted in this handsomely illustrated biography. (Rev: BCCB 6/98; BL 4/1/98; SLJ 5/98; VOYA 8/98) [921]

GRATEFUL DEAD (MUSICAL GROUP)

5755 *The Grateful Dead* (7–9). Illus. Series: Pop Culture Legends. 1997, Chelsea $21.95 (978-0-7910-3250-3); paper $8.95 (978-0-7910-4454-4). A colorful portrait of this band that has become a rock and roll legend and of its many dedicated fans, who are known as Deadheads. (Rev: BL 7/97; SLJ 7/97) [782.42]

HANKS, TOM

5756 Kramer, Barbara. *Tom Hanks: Superstar* (6–8). Series: People to Know. 2000, Enslow LB $26.60 (978-0-7660-1436-7). A portrait of this amazing multi-talented superstar is presented in a heavily-illustrated account. (Rev: BL 3/1/01; HBG 10/01) [921]

HANSON (MUSICAL GROUP)

5757 Powell, Phelan. *Hanson* (5–8). Series: Galaxy of Superstars. 1999, Chelsea $25.00 (978-0-7910-5148-1); paper $25.00 (978-0-7910-5325-6). An attractive volume with information on the three-brother singing group that hails from Tulsa, Oklahoma. (Rev: BL 4/15/98; HBG 10/99) [921]

HENDRIX, JIMI

5758 Markel, Rita J. *Jimi Hendrix* (7–10). Illus. Series: A&E Biography. 2001, Lerner LB $27.93 (978-0-8225-4990-1); paper $7.95 (978-0-8225-9697-4). The unhappy life and drug-related death of rock guitarist Jimi Hendrix are related with evocative descriptions of his music, a bibliography, Web sites, and discography. (Rev: BL 2/15/01; HBG 10/01; SLJ 3/01) [921]

5759 Piccoli, Sean. *Jimi Hendrix* (6–9). 1996, Chelsea LB $30.00 (978-0-7910-2042-5). An objective account of Hendrix's phenomenal music career and the unfortunate circumstances surrounding his death. (Rev: SLJ 11/96) [921]

5760 Stockdale, Tom. *Jimi Hendrix* (7–9). Illus. Series: They Died Too Young. 1999, Chelsea LB $18.65 (978-0-7910-4632-6). Early musical influences, career-related events, and the effects of drugs and alcohol are covered in this biography of the entertainer and singer whose career highlights included a tour in 1968 and a performance at Woodstock. (Rev: SLJ 7/98) [921]

5761 Willett, Edward. *Jimi Hendrix: "Kiss the Sky"* (7–10). Illus. Series: American Rebels. 2006, Enslow LB $20.95 (978-0-7660-2449-6). From the musician's childhood to his death at the age of 27, this biography does not shy away from describing Hendrix's destructive behavior, including the use of alcohol and drugs. (Rev: BL 2/1/07) [921]

HILL, FAITH

5762 Hinman, Bonnie. *Faith Hill* (5–9). 2001, Chelsea $25.00 (978-0-7910-6471-9). A look at the life and career of the country music star, with information on Nashville's Grand Ole Opry. (Rev: HBG 10/02; SLJ 4/02) [921]

HILL, LAURYN

5763 Greene, Meg. *Lauryn Hill* (5–8). Series: Galaxy of Superstars. 1999, Chelsea $25.00 (978-0-7910-5495-6). A biography of the music superstar who won five Grammy Awards for her breakout solo album. (Rev: BL 3/15/00; HBG 10/00) [921]

HINES, GREGORY

5764 DeAngelis, Gina. *Gregory Hines* (4–7). Illus. Series: Black Americans of Achievement. 1999, Chelsea $30.00 (978-0-7910-5197-9); paper $9.95 (978-0-7910-5198-6). Though he is known primarily as a dancer, this biography of Gregory Hines points out his many other talents, including acting. (Rev: BL 2/15/00; HBG 3/00) [921]

HITCHCOCK, ALFRED

5765 Adair, Gene. *Alfred Hitchcock: Filming Our Fears* (7–10). Series: Oxford Portraits. 2002, Oxford LB $32.95 (978-0-19-511967-1). Hitchcock's youth in England is covered in addition to chronological details of his career from the silent movies through his classic creations. (Rev: HBG 3/03; SLJ 11/02) [921]

HOLIDAY, BILLIE

5766 Kliment, Bud. *Billie Holiday* (8–12). Illus. 1990, Chelsea LB $30.00 (978-1-55546-592-6). A stirring biography of one of the great ladies of song whose life ended tragically. (Rev: BL 2/15/90; SLJ 5/90; VOYA 5/90) [921]

HOUSTON, WHITNEY

5767 Cox, Ted. *Whitney Houston: Singer Actress* (5–8). Illus. Series: Black Americans of Achievement. 1997, Chelsea LB $30.00 (978-0-7910-4455-1); paper $8.95 (978-0-7910-4456-8). A readable

biography that shows Whitney Houston growing up in New Jersey, the major influences in her life, her rise to fame, marriage, and philanthropic endeavors. (Rev: BL 8/98; HBG 10/98) [921]

HOWARD, RON

5768 Kramer, Barbara. *Ron Howard: Child Star and Hollywood Director* (7–10). Series: People to Know. 1998, Enslow LB $26.60 (978-0-89490-981-8). Using many photographs of Howard at work, this book traces his career from sitcoms such as *Happy Days* to becoming the director of fine films including *Apollo 13*. (Rev: BL 2/15/99; HBG 3/99; SLJ 3/99) [921]

JACKSON, JANET

5769 Dyson, Cindy. *Janet Jackson* (4–7). Series: Black Americans of Achievement. 2000, Chelsea $32.00 (978-0-7910-5283-9). The life story of the popular singer and the ups and downs of her career. (Rev: BL 6/1–15/00; HBG 10/00) [921]

JACKSON, MAHALIA

5770 Kramer, Barbara. *Mahalia Jackson: The Voice of Gospel and Civil Rights* (6–10). Illus. Series: African-American Biographies. 2004, Enslow LB $26.60 (978-0-7660-2115-0). This biography traces the life of the singer and civil rights activist from her childhood in New Orleans to her great successes as a gospel singer. (Rev: BL 2/15/04; HBG 4/04) [921]

JACKSON, MICHAEL

5771 Graves, Karen Marie. *Michael Jackson* (5–8). Series: People in the News. 2001, Lucent LB $35.15 (978-1-56006-707-8). The unusual life of this show business legend is outlined in text and photographs. (Rev: BL 4/1/02) [921]

5772 Nicholson, Lois. *Michael Jackson* (4–8). Illus. Series: Black Americans of Achievement. 1994, Chelsea paper $8.95 (978-0-7910-1930-6). A biography of the pop star that examines his loneliness and his family ties, and touches on the allegations against him of sexual abuse. (Rev: BL 10/15/94; SLJ 10/94) [921]

JACKSON, SAMUEL L.

5773 Dils, Tracey E. *Samuel L. Jackson* (4–7). Series: Black Americans of Achievement. 2000, Chelsea $30.00 (978-0-7910-5281-5). The life story of the African American actor who has portrayed diverse characters in films including *Pulp Fiction* and *A Time to Kill*. (Rev: BL 6/1–15/00; HBG 10/00) [921]

JOHNSON, ROBERT

5774 Lewis, J. Patrick. *Black Cat Bone* (7–12). Illus. by Gary Kelley. 2006, Creative LB $19.95 (978-1-56846-194-6). A picture book for big kids, this story in poetry of blues musician Robert Johnson alludes to the legend that he sold his soul to the devil in exchange for some wicked skills on the guitar. (Rev: BL 1/1–15/07; LMC 8–9/07; SLJ 12/06*) [921]

JONES, JAMES EARL

5775 Hasday, Judy. *James Earl Jones: Actor* (7–10). Illus. Series: Overcoming Adversity. 1999, Chelsea LB $32.00 (978-0-7910-4702-6). A story of the great African American actor, noted for his deep, resonant voice, who conquered stuttering and muteness as a child. (Rev: HBG 9/98; SLJ 8/98; VOYA 8/98) [921]

JULIA, RAUL

5776 Perez, Frank, and Ann Well. *Raul Julia* (4–8). Illus. Series: Contemporary Hispanic Americans. 1995, Raintree LB $28.80 (978-0-8172-3984-8). The story of the brilliant stage and film actor who gained fame in *The Addams Family* and on *Sesame Street*. This biography was written before his untimely death. (Rev: BL 3/15/96; SLJ 1/96) [921]

KELLY, EMMETT, SR.

5777 Wilkerson, J. L. *Sad-Face Clown: Emmett Kelly* (5–8). Illus. Series: The Great Heartlanders. 2004, Acorn paper $9.95 (978-0-9664470-9-5). The story of Emmett Kelly, Sr., who — as Weary Willie — became possibly the world's most famous circus clown. (Rev: SLJ 4/04) [791.3]

LANG, LANG

5778 Lang, Lang, and Michael French. *Lang Lang: Playing with Flying Keys* (7–10). Illus. 2008, Delacorte $16.99 (978-0-385-73578-0). The internationally respected pianist recalls the stresses of his childhood, his unending training schedule, and his triumphs. (Rev: BL 6/1–15/08; SLJ 9/08) [921]

LATIFAH, QUEEN

5779 Bloom, Sara R. *Queen Latifah* (4–7). Series: Black Americans of Achievement. 2001, Chelsea $30.00 (978-0-7910-6287-6). Numerous photographs add interest to this biography of the amazing singer-actress and her rise to fame. (Rev: BL 4/1/02; HBG 10/02; SLJ 6/02) [921]

5780 Ruth, Amy. *Queen Latifah* (5–8). Series: A&E Biography. 2000, Lerner LB $27.93 (978-0-8225-4988-8). The story of the female rap singer who used her positive attitudes, hard work, and determi-

nation to get ahead. (Rev: BL 3/1/01; HBG 10/01) [921]

LED ZEPPELIN (MUSICAL GROUP)

5781 Hoskyns, Barney. *Led Zeppelin IV* (8–12). Illus. 2006, Rodale $16.95 (978-1-59486-370-7). This profile of the rock band looks behind the scenes, especially at the making of its classic fourth album. (Rev: BL 11/15/06) [921]

LEE, BRUCE

5782 Little, John, ed. *Bruce Lee: The Celebrated Life of the Golden Dragon* (6–12). 2000, Charles E. Tuttle $24.95 (978-0-8048-3230-4). Stunning photographs and excerpts from Lee's own writings paint an absorbing portrait of the late martial arts film star. (Rev: VOYA 8/01) [921]

5783 Tagliaferro, Linda. *Bruce Lee* (5–10). Series: A&E Biography. 2000, Lerner LB $27.93 (978-0-8225-4948-2); paper $7.95 (978-0-8225-9688-2). This colorful biography of the famous action star is filled with information about him, his films, and his family. (Rev: HBG 10/00; SLJ 5/00) [921]

LEE, SPIKE

5784 Hardy, James Earl. *Spike Lee* (7–10). Series: Black Americans of Achievement. 1995, Chelsea LB $30.00 (978-0-7910-1875-0); paper $30.00 (978-0-7910-1904-7). The story of the African American film producer and director who has fought for the right to express his ideas in a tough motion picture world. (Rev: BL 11/15/95; SLJ 12/95) [921]

5785 Haskins, Jim. *Spike Lee: By Any Means Necessary* (6–10). Illus. 1997, Walker LB $16.85 (978-0-8027-8496-4). Compiling previously published biographical material, the author has produced an interesting profile of this important African American filmmaker, including a behind-the-cameras view of each of Lee's 10 films. (Rev: BL 5/1/97; SLJ 6/97; VOYA 10/97) [921]

5786 Shields, Charles J. *Spike Lee* (5–7). Illus. 2002, Chelsea $30.00 (978-0-7910-6715-4). This look at Spike Lee's career, working methods, and importance includes both strengths and weaknesses and includes many photographs and quotations. (Rev: BL 11/1/02; HBG 3/03) [791.43]

LENNON, JOHN

5787 Conord, Bruce W. *John Lennon* (7–12). Series: Pop Culture Legends. 1993, Chelsea LB $21.95 (978-0-7910-1739-5); paper $8.95 (978-0-7910-1740-1). Looks at Lennon's childhood in Liverpool, his career with the Beatles, and his life after their breakup. (Rev: BL 12/15/93; SLJ 11/93) [921]

5788 Wright, David K. *John Lennon: The Beatles and Beyond* (6–10). Series: People to Know. 1996, Enslow LB $26.60 (978-0-89490-702-9). This biography of the legendary founder of one of the most popular music groups of all time explores Lennon's background and his development as a songwriter and as a political activist, as well as recounting the history of the Beatles. (Rev: BL 10/15/96; SLJ 12/96; VOYA 2/97) [921]

LETTERMAN, DAVID

5789 Lefkowitz, Frances. *David Letterman* (7–9). Series: Pop Culture Legends. 1996, Chelsea LB $21.95 (978-0-7910-3252-7); paper $8.95 (978-0-7910-3253-4). This show-business biography traces Letterman's career and the evolution of his style, with an emphasis on entertainers who influenced him. (Rev: SLJ 12/96) [921]

LOPEZ, JENNIFER

5790 Hill, Anne E. *Jennifer Lopez* (5–8). Series: Galaxy of Superstars. 2000, Chelsea $25.00 (978-0-7910-5775-9). This book chronicles the career of the young Latina star who is a fine singer and actress. (Rev: BL 10/15/00; HBG 10/01) [921]

LUCAS, GEORGE

5791 Rau, Dana Meachen, and Christopher Rau. *George Lucas: Creator of Star Wars* (5–8). Series: Book Report Biographies. 1999, Watts LB $22.00 (978-0-531-11457-5). An entertaining look at the popular filmmaker's life and accomplishments, illustrated with black-and-white photographs. (Rev: HBG 10/99; SLJ 7/99) [921]

5792 Shields, Charles J. *George Lucas* (5–7). Illus. Series: Behind the Camera. 2002, Chelsea $30.00 (978-0-7910-6712-3). A profile of the famous filmmaker, with information on his strengths and weaknesses, his working methods, and his importance to the American film industry, backed up by many photographs and quotations. (Rev: BL 11/1/02; HBG 3/03) [791.43]

5793 White, Dana. *George Lucas* (5–8). Series: A&E Biography. 1999, Lerner LB $27.93 (978-0-8225-4975-8); paper $7.95 (978-0-8225-9684-4). This book covers the childhood and early career of this filmmaker but concentrates on his masterpiece, the creation of the *Star Wars* saga. (Rev: HBG 3/00; SLJ 3/00) [921]

MA, YO-YO

5794 Chippendale, Lisa A. *Yo-Yo Ma: A Cello Superstar Brings Music to the World* (6–8). Illus. Series: People to Know. 2004, Enslow LB $26.60 (978-0-7660-2286-7). Traces the life of cellist Yo-Yo Ma, from child prodigy to internationally recognized musical virtuoso. (Rev: BL 11/1/04; SLJ 2/05) [921]

5795 Worth, Richard. *Yo-Yo Ma* (6–10). Series: Asian Americans of Achievement. 2007, Chelsea House LB $30.00 (978-0-7910-9270-5). This attractive profile recounts the highlights of Ma's personal life and covers his career as a cellist and his work with young people. (Rev: SLJ 8/07) [921]

MCGREGOR, EWAN

5796 Jones, Veda Boyd. *Ewan McGregor* (5–8). Series: Galaxy of Superstars. 1999, Chelsea $25.00 (978-0-7910-5501-4). A well-illustrated biography of the Scottish-born actor in the *Star Wars* prequels. (Rev: BL 3/15/00; HBG 10/00) [921]

MADONNA

5797 Claro, Nicole. *Madonna* (7–10). Series: Pop Culture Legends. 1994, Chelsea LB $21.95 (978-0-7910-2330-3); paper $8.95 (978-0-7910-2355-6). Examines the pop diva's childhood, the early death of her mother, her rise to stardom, her love affairs, and her controversial personality. (Rev: BL 10/15/94; SLJ 11/94; VOYA 12/94) [021]

5798 Gnojewski, Carol. *Madonna: "Express Yourself"* (8–11). Illus. 2007, Enslow LB $25.95 (978-0-7660-2442-7). Covers the life and career of musical icon Madonna from childhood. (Rev: BL 8/07) [921]

MARLEY, BOB

5799 Dolan, Sean. *Bob Marley* (6–9). Series: Black Americans of Achievement. 1996, Chelsea LB $30.00 (978-0-7910-2041-8); paper $8.95 (978-0-7910-3255-8). The life story of the Jamaican entertainer, with historical background about his island home. (Rev: SLJ 11/96) [921]

5800 Miller, Calvin Craig. *Reggae Poet: The Story of Bob Marley* (7–10). Illus. 2007, Morgan Reynolds LB $27.95 (978-1-59935-071-4). A look at the good and the bad about the late reggae musician, including his influential style, his drug use, and his difficult childhood; with photographs. (Rev: BL 11/15/07; SLJ 2/08) [921]

MARTIN, RICKY

5801 Zymet, Cathy Alter. *Ricky Martin* (7–10). Series: Latinos in the Limelight. 2001, Chelsea House LB $27.50 (978-0-7910-6100-8). From his debut in the Menudo group to the year 2000, this is the story of the famous Puerto Rican singer. (Rev: HBG 10/01) [921]

MARX, GROUCHO

5802 Tyson, Peter. *Groucho Marx* (7–12). Illus. Series: Pop Culture Legends. 1995, Chelsea $19.95 (978-0-7910-2341-9). The story of Groucho Marx, from his childhood on the Lower East Side of Manhattan to stardom with his brothers and, lastly, to fame as a quiz show host. (Rev: BL 7/95) [921]

MILLER, NORMA

5803 Govenar, Alan, ed. *Stompin' at the Savoy: The Story of Norma Miller* (5–8). Illus. by Martin French. 2006, Candlewick $16.99 (978-0-7636-2244-2). The energy of Norma Miller, who was still going strong in her early 80s, infuses the pages of this brief biography, made up largely of excerpts from interviews with the legendary African American swing dancer. (Rev: BL 2/1/06; SLJ 3/06) [792.8]

MONROE, MARILYN

5804 Krohn, Katherine E. *Marilyn Monroe: Norma Jeane's Dream* (6–9). Series: Newsmakers Biographies. 1997, Lerner LB $30.35 (978-0-8225-4930-7). A well-illustrated biography that gives a good overview of the actress's life without probing into the mystery surrounding her death. (Rev: SLJ 7/97) [921]

5805 Lefkowitz, Frances. *Marilyn Monroe* (7–12). Series: Pop Culture Legends. 1995, Chelsea LB $21.95 (978-0-7910-2342-6); paper $8.95 (978-0-7910-2367-9). The story of the Hollywood star who, despite immense popularity, had a tragic life. (Rev: BL 8/95) [921]

5806 Woog, Adam. *Marilyn Monroe* (6–10). Series: Mysterious Deaths. 1996, Lucent LB $27.45 (978-1-56006-265-3). After a brief overview of the star's life and career, this account describes her last night alive and the many theories surrounding her death. (Rev: SLJ 3/97; VOYA 8/97) [921]

MORENO, RITA

5807 Suntree, Susan. *Rita Moreno* (5–9). Series: Hispanics of Achievement. 1992, Chelsea LB $21.95 (978-0-7910-1247-5). A biography of the Puerto Rican entertainer and her successes on stage and screen. (Rev: BL 2/1/93) [921]

MORRISON, JIM

5808 Lewis, Jon E. *Jim Morrison* (7–9). Illus. Series: They Died Too Young. 1997, Chelsea LB $21.95 (978-0-7910-4631-9). The great talent of this rock legend is highlighted in this biography that does not minimize the effects of drugs and alcohol on his life. (Rev: SLJ 7/98) [921]

MURPHY, EDDIE

5809 Wilburn, Deborah A. *Eddie Murphy* (7–10). Series: Black Americans of Achievement. 1993, Chelsea LB $30.00 (978-0-7910-1879-8); paper $9.95 (978-0-7910-1908-5). A nicely illustrated introduction to the life of this talented actor/comedian. (Rev: BL 1/1/94; SLJ 1/94) [921]

NEW KIDS ON THE BLOCK (MUSICAL GROUP)

5810 McGibbon, Robin. *New Kids on the Block: The Whole Story* (5–8). Illus. 1990, Avon paper $6.95 (978-0-380-76344-3). Stories about members of this band have been collected from a variety of sources, including the members themselves. (Rev: BL 10/1/90) [921]

NUREYEV, RUDOLF

5811 Maybarduk, Linda. *The Dancer Who Flew: A Memoir of Rudolf Nureyev* (5–9). Illus. 1999, Tundra $18.95 (978-0-88776-415-8). The author, a friend and colleague of Nureyev, not only gives a straightforward biography of the dancer but also tells many backstage stories and introduces his most important roles. (Rev: BL 1/1–15/00; HBG 3/00; SLJ 2/00; VOYA 4/00) [921]

OAKLEY, ANNIE

5812 Flynn, Jean. *Annie Oakley: Legendary Sharpshooter* (4–9). Series: Historical American Biographies. 1998, Enslow LB $26.60 (978-0-7660-1012-3). Using a concise text, fact boxes, and a chronology, this is the story of the star attraction of Buffalo Bill's Wild West Show. (Rev: BL 8/98; SLJ 8/98) [921]

5813 Macy, Sue. *Bull's-Eye: A Photobiography of Annie Oakley* (5–8). Illus. 2001, National Geographic $17.95 (978-0-7922-7008-9). This book separates fact from fiction in the life of Phoebe Ann Moses Butler, who came to be known as Annie Oakley. (Rev: BL 11/15/01; HBG 3/02; SLJ 10/01; VOYA 4/02) [799.3]

5814 Wukovits, John. *Annie Oakley* (4–8). Series: Legends of the West. 1997, Chelsea LB $18.65 (978-0-7910-3906-9). A profile of the famous sharpshooter and her career with Buffalo Bill's Wide West Show. (Rev: SLJ 10/97) [921]

O'DONNELL, ROSIE

5815 Kallen, Stuart A. *Rosie O'Donnell* (4–8). Series: People in the News. 1999, Lucent LB $27.45 (978-1-56006-546-3). An interesting, well-researched biography of this popular actress, comedienne, and talk-show host, covering her personal and professional life. (Rev: BL 8/99; HBG 3/00) [921]

5816 Krohn, Katherine E. *Rosie O'Donnell* (4–8). Series: A&E Biography. 1998, Lerner LB $27.93 (978-0-8225-4939-0). A breezy look at O'Donnell's rise from stand-up comic to TV fame with glimpses into her personal life, her mother's death when she was a child, and her fulfilling adoption of two children. (Rev: HBG 3/99; SLJ 2/99) [921]

5817 Stone, Tanya L. *Rosie O'Donnell: America's Favorite Grown-Up Kid* (4–7). Illus. 2000, Millbrook LB $23.90 (978-0-7613-1724-1). A well-designed, chatty biography of the popular talk-show host and comedienne. (Rev: BL 12/15/00; HBG 3/01) [792.7]

OLMOS, EDWARD JAMES

5818 Carrillo, Louis. *Edward James Olmos* (4–8). Illus. Series: Contemporary Hispanic Americans. 1997, Raintree LB $17.98 (978-0-8172-3989-3). Along with a timeline and glossary, this account traces the life of this contemporary human rights activist and actor. (Rev: BL 4/15/97) [921]

OZAWA, SEIJI

5819 Tan, Sheri. *Seiji Ozawa* (5–7). Illus. Series: Contemporary Asian Americans. 1997, Raintree LB $17.98 (978-0-8172-3993-0). A profile of the Asian American musician who has been the chief conductor of the Boston Symphony for more than 20 years. (Rev: BL 5/1/97; SLJ 9/97) [921]

PARKER, CHARLIE

5820 Frankl, Ron. *Charlie Parker* (7–10). Series: Black Americans of Achievement. 1992, Chelsea LB $30.00 (978-0-7910-1134-8). The story of the "Bird," his alto sax, and his contributions to jazz, particularly bebop. (Rev: BL 2/1/93) [921]

PITT, BRAD

5821 Dempsey, Amy. *Brad Pitt* (6–8). Illus. Series: Superstars of Film. 1999, Chelsea LB $18.65 (978-0-7910-4649-4). An easy-to-read biography about the teen idol and the hard work and seized opportunities that made him a star. (Rev: SLJ 10/98) [921]

PRESLEY, ELVIS

5822 Brown, Adele Q. *Elvis Presley* (6–9). Series: Trailblazers of the Modern World. 2003, World Almanac paper $11.95 (978-0-8368-5245-5). A biography of the international pop music star who reigned as king for many years. (Rev: BL 6/1–15/03) [921]

5823 Gentry, Tony. *Elvis Presley* (7–12). Series: Pop Culture Legends. 1994, Chelsea LB $14.95 (978-0-7910-2329-7); paper $8.95 (978-0-7910-2354-9). The life of the "King" is re-created in this nicely illustrated biography. (Rev: BL 9/15/94) [921]

5824 Hampton, Wilborn. *Elvis Presley* (6–9). Illus. Series: Up Close. 2007, Viking $15.99 (978-0-670-06166-2). Hampton covers Elvis's rise to fame, his personal life and drug-related downfall, and his influence on music and culture. (Rev: BL 5/1/07; HB 7–8/07; SLJ 6/07) [921]

5825 Krohn, Katherine E. *Elvis Presley: The King* (5–7). Illus. 1994, Lerner LB $18.60 (978-0-8225-2877-7). A somewhat sanitized biography of Elvis Presley that highlights important events in his career. (Rev: BL 7/94; SLJ 7/94) [921]

PUENTE, TITO

5826 Olmstead, Mary. *Tito Puente* (4–7). Illus. Series: Hispanic-American Biographies. 2004, Raintree LB $32.86 (978-1-4109-0713-4). A concise account of the life and career of Tito Puente, the popular American bandleader and percussionist who in the 1950s was nicknamed the Mambo King. (Rev: BL 2/1/05; SLJ 8/05) [784.4]

QUINN, ANTHONY

5827 Amdur, Melissa. *Anthony Quinn* (5–9). Series: Hispanics of Achievement. 1993, Chelsea LB $19.95 (978-0-7910-1251-2). The life of this Mexican American actor is told with many interesting asides concerning his career and black-and-white stills from his movies. (Rev: BL 9/15/93) [921]

REESE, DELLA

5828 Dean, Tanya. *Della Reese* (4–7). Series: Black Americans of Achievement. 2001, Chelsea $30.00 (978-0-7910-6291-3). The life and career of this show business giant are outlined with special coverage on her recent successes in television. (Rev: BL 4/1/02) [921]

REEVE, CHRISTOPHER

5829 Finn, Margaret L. *Christopher Reeve: Actor and Activist* (6–10). 1997, Chelsea LB $32.00 (978-0-7910-4446-9); paper $8.95 (978-0-7910-4447-6). The story of the gallant film actor, his tragic accident, and the causes he champions. (Rev: HBG 3/98; VOYA 2/98) [921]

5830 Howard, Megan. *Christopher Reeve* (6–9). 1999, Lerner LB $27.93 (978-0-8225-4945-1). This is an inspiring portrait of the film star, his career, and the emotional and physical hardships he faced following his crippling horse-riding accident. Despite limitations and initial depression, Reeve has learned to focus on what he can do, rather than on what he can't. (Rev: BL 8/99) [921]

RIMES, LEANN

5831 Zymet, Cathy Alter. *LeAnn Rimes* (5–8). Series: Galaxy of Superstars. 1999, Chelsea $25.00 (978-0-7910-5152-8); paper $25.00 (978-0-7910-5327-0). This book covers the rise to stardom and the career of this country-western singer who hails from Jackson, Mississippi. (Rev: BL 4/15/98; HBG 10/99) [921]

ROBESON, PAUL

5832 Wright, David K. *Paul Robeson: Actor, Singer, Political Activist* (5–9). Illus. Series: African-American Biographies. 1998, Enslow LB $26.60 (978-0-89490-944-3). This book details Robeson's personal and professional life and the hardships he faced because of his race and beliefs. (Rev: BL 11/15/98; SLJ 11/98) [921]

ROCK, CHRIS

5833 Blue, Rose, and Corinne J. Naden. *Chris Rock* (4–7). Series: Black Americans of Achievement. 2000, Chelsea $30.00 (978-0-7910-5277-8). The story of the comedian and actor who began his career on *Saturday Night Live* and is noted for his acerbic wit. (Rev: BL 6/1–15/00; HBG 10/00) [921]

RODRIGUEZ, ROBERT

5834 Marvis, Barbara. *Robert Rodriguez* (5–10). Series: A Real-Life Reader Biography. 1997, Mitchell Lane LB $15.95 (978-1-883845-48-3). This simple, attractive biography of the successful movie maker focuses on his problems growing up in a large family and clinging to his career dreams. (Rev: BL 6/1–15/98; HBG 3/98; SLJ 2/98) [921]

ROGERS, WILL

5835 Donovan, Sandy. *Will Rogers: Cowboy, Comedian, and Commentator* (4–8). Series: Signature Lives. 2007, Compass Point LB $31.93 (978-0-7565-2542-9). This detailed biography of Will Rogers will be useful for report writers. (Rev: SLJ 6/07) [921]

5836 Malone, Mary. *Will Rogers: Cowboy Philosopher* (4–7). Illus. Series: People to Know. 1996, Enslow LB $20.95 (978-0-89490-695-4). A lively look at the life and accomplishments of this cowboy and show business idol. (Rev: BL 5/15/96; SLJ 6/96) [921]

RONSTADT, LINDA

5837 Amdur, Melissa. *Linda Ronstadt* (5–9). Series: Hispanics of Achievement. 1993, Chelsea LB $14.95 (978-0-7910-1781-4). This biography of the popular Mexican American singer describes her roots and pride in her Hispanic heritage. (Rev: BL 9/15/93; SLJ 10/93) [921]

SANDLER, ADAM

5838 Seldman, David. *Adam Sandler* (5–8). Series: Galaxy of Superstars. 2000, Chelsea $25.00 (978-0-7910-5773-5). An entertaining biography of the actor and comedian who gained notoriety from his roles in *The Waterboy* and *Big Daddy*. (Rev: BL 12/15/00; HBG 10/01) [921]

SCHUMANN, CLARA

5839 Allman, Barbara. *Her Piano Sang: A Story About Clara Schumann* (4–7). Illus. 1996, Carolrhoda LB $25.55 (978-1-57505-012-6). The story of this groundbreaking composer and pianist who also championed her husband's music. (Rev: BL 1/1–15/97; SLJ 1/97) [921]

5840 Reich, Susanna. *Clara Schumann: Piano Virtuoso* (5–8). 1999, Houghton $18.00 (978-0-395-89119-3). A thorough, well-researched biography of this amazing pianist and composer that describes her life as a child prodigy, her marriage to Robert Schumann, and her life promoting his music after his death. (Rev: BL 8/99; HB 3–4/99; HBG 10/99; SLJ 4/99*; VOYA 4/00) [921]

SELENA

5841 Jones, Veda Boyd. *Selena* (6–9). Series: Latinos in the Limelight. 2001, Chelsea LB $31.00 (978-0-7910-6112-1). The life and work of the award-winning Texas singer who was shot by the president of her fan club. (Rev: HBG 10/01; SLJ 8/01) [782.42164]

5842 Marvis, Barbara. *Selena* (5–10). Series: A Real-Life Reader Biography. 1997, Mitchell Lane LB $15.95 (978-1-883845-47-6). A simple, attractive biography of the singer, her supportive family, and her tragic death. (Rev: BL 6/1–15/98; HBG 3/98; SLJ 2/98) [921]

SIEGEL, SIENA CHERSON

5843 Siegel, Siena Cherson. *To Dance: A Ballerina's Graphic Novel* (5–8). Illus. by Mark Siegel. 2006, Simon & Schuster $17.95 (978-0-689-86747-7). In graphic novel format, Siegel tells the story of her dance career, from her introduction to ballet at the age of 6 to her stage debut with the New York City Ballet. Sibert Honor Book, 2007. (Rev: BCCB 1/07; BL 9/1/06; LMC 1/07; SLJ 11/06*; VOYA 4/07) [921]

SMITH, WILL

5844 Anderson, Marilyn D. *Will Smith* (6–10). Series: People in the News. 2003, Gale LB $27.45 (978-1-59018-140-9). The story of Will Smith's youth, life as a rapper, and stardom in movies including *Men in Black* will appeal to his many fans. (Rev: SLJ 3/03) [921]

5845 Stauffer, Stacey. *Will Smith* (6–10). Series: Black Americans of Achievement. 1998, Chelsea $30.00 (978-0-7910-4914-3); paper $30.00 (978-0-7910-4915-0). A serious biography of this popular star, beginning with *Independence Day* then moving back to Smith's childhood. (Rev: HBG 3/99; VOYA 8/99) [921]

SPEARS, BRITNEY

5846 Lutz, Norma Jean. *Britney Spears* (5–8). Series: Galaxy of Superstars. 1999, Chelsea $25.00 (978-0-7910-5499-4). A profile of the popular entertainer, telling how her childhood influenced her career path. (Rev: BL 3/15/00; HBG 10/00) [921]

SPICE GIRLS (MUSICAL GROUP)

5847 Shore, Nancy. *Spice Girls* (5–8). Series: Galaxy of Superstars. 1999, Chelsea $25.00 (978-0-7910-5149-8); paper $25.00 (978-0-7910-5328-7). Biographies of members of the popular singing group that took first Britain and then the world by storm. (Rev: BL 4/15/98; HBG 10/99; SLJ 5/99) [921]

SPIELBERG, STEVEN

5848 Edge, Laura B. *Steven Spielberg: Director of Blockbuster Films* (5–8). Illus. Series: People to Know Today. 2008, Enslow LB $23.95 (978-0-7660-2888-3). With many photographs and lists of print and Web resources, this profile provides up-to-date information on the filmmaker's career, personal life, work ethic, and storytelling skills. (Rev: BL 6/1–15/08) [921]

5849 Ferber, Elizabeth. *Steven Spielberg* (7–12). Illus. Series: Pop Culture Legends. 1996, Chelsea LB $21.95 (978-0-7910-3256-5); paper $9.95 (978-0-7910-3257-2). An account of America's popular filmmaker that includes material on *Jaws*, *E.T.*, and *Jurassic Park*, and ends with *Schindler's List*. (Rev: BL 11/15/96; SLJ 1/97) [921]

5850 Schoell, William. *Magic Man: The Life and Films of Steven Spielberg* (4–7). Illus. 1998, Tudor $18.95 (978-0-936389-57-8). This biography of Spielberg concentrates on how he produces the astonishing special effects for his movies. (Rev: BL 5/15/98; SLJ 2/99) [921]

SPRINGSTEEN, BRUCE

5851 Frankl, Ron. *Bruce Springsteen* (7–10). Illus. Series: Pop Culture Legends. 1994, Chelsea paper $9.95 (978-0-7910-2352-5). The compelling story of the famous rocker who has never forgotten his working-class roots. (Rev: BL 6/1–15/94) [921]

SUMMER, DONNA

5852 Haskins, Jim, and J. M. Stifle. *Donna Summer: An Unauthorized Biography* (7–12). Illus. 1983, Little, Brown $14.95 (978-0-316-35003-7). Covers Summer's life and rise from a bit part in *Hair* to full stardom. [921]

SUPREMES (MUSICAL GROUP)

5853 Rivera, Ursula. *The Supremes* (4–8). Illus. Series: Rock and Roll Hall of Famers. 2002, Rosen LB $29.25 (978-0-8239-3527-7). The Supremes' rise to stardom — and eventual fall from fame without leader Diana Ross — is chronicled here with photographs, glossary, discography, and bibliography. (Rev: BL 10/1/02; SLJ 5/02) [782.421644]

TEMPTATIONS (MUSICAL GROUP)

5854 Cox, Ted. *The Temptations* (6–10). Series: African-American Achievers. 1997, Chelsea LB $21.95 (978-0-7910-2587-1); paper $30.00 (978-0-7910-2588-8). A chronicle of the rise and fall of this musical group, with profiles of each of the members and insights into the influence of Motown records on the careers of many African American musicians in the 1960s. (Rev: HBG 3/98; SLJ 1/98) [921]

THREE STOOGES

5855 Scordato, Mark, and Ellen Scordato. *The Three Stooges* (7–12). Series: Pop Culture Legends. 1995, Chelsea LB $14.95 (978-0-7910-2344-0); paper $9.95 (978-0-7910-2369-3). A look at the six men who composed the Three Stooges at various times. Includes black-and-white photographs, a filmography, and a chronology. (Rev: BL 6/1–15/95) [921]

TWAIN, SHANIA

5856 Gallagher, Jim. *Shania Twain: Grammy Award-Winning Singer* (4–7). Series: Real-Life Reader Biographies. 1999, Mitchell Lane LB $15.95 (978-1-58415-000-8). The story of the entertainer who was adopted into the Ojibwa tribe, began singing in bars at age eight, and went on to marry producer Mutt Lange. (Rev: SLJ 1/00) [921]

VALENS, RITCHIE

5857 Mendheim, Beverly. *Ritchie Valens: The First Latino Rocker* (8–12). Illus. 1987, Bilingual paper

$15.00 (978-0-916950-79-8). The story of the popular Latino rocker who died in a plane crash in 1959. (Rev: BL 12/15/87) [921]

WALTERS, BARBARA

5858 Remstein, Henna. *Barbara Walters* (5–8). 1998, Chelsea $21.95 (978-0-7910-4716-3); paper $9.95 (978-0-7910-4717-0). The life story of Barbara Walters, who broke many barriers for women in the communications field and has become an icon in the field of journalism. (Rev: HBG 3/99; VOYA 4/99) [921]

WASHINGTON, DENZEL

5859 Hill, Anne E. *Denzel Washington* (7–10). Series: Black Americans of Achievement. 1998, Chelsea $32.00 (978-0-7910-4692-0); paper $9.95 (978-0-7910-4693-7). A complimentary biography of this versatile, attractive actor who quickly rose to the top of the acting profession. (Rev: HBG 3/99; SLJ 3/99) [921]

WILLIAMS, VANESSA

5860 Boulais, Sue. *Vanessa Williams* (4–8). Series: Real-Life Reader Biographies. 1999, Mitchell Lane LB $15.95 (978-1-883845-75-9). The life story of the African American who lost her title of Miss America in 1983 but rebounded with a brilliant career in show business. (Rev: BL 6/1–15/99) [921]

WINFREY, OPRAH

5861 Cooper, Ilene. *Up Close: Oprah Winfrey* (7–12). Series: Up Close. 2007, Viking $15.99 (978-0-670-06162-4). Cooper focuses on Winfrey's unhappy childhood and her philanthropic work when she became successful. (Rev: SLJ 5/07) [921]

5862 Krohn, Katherine. *Oprah Winfrey* (6–9). Illus. Series: Just the Facts Biographies. 2005, Lerner LB $27.93 (978-0-8225-2472-4). Simple text and clear definitions make this biography suitable for reluctant and ESL readers. (Rev: BL 4/1/05) [794.4502]

5863 Krohn, Katherine. *Oprah Winfrey* (5–8). Series: Biography. 2001, Lerner LB $27.93 (978-0-8225-4999-4). The media genius and talk-show hostess is profiled in an interesting text with many photographs. (Rev: BL 4/1/02; HBG 10/02) [921]

5864 Nicholson, Lois. *Oprah Winfrey: Talking with America* (5–8). Series: Junior Black Americans of Achievement. 1997, Chelsea LB $28.00 (978-0-7910-2390-7); paper $4.95 (978-0-7910-4460-5). A biography that skims the life of this personality, with material on her difficult childhood, sexual abuse, college experiences, early career, weight problems, and success on television. (Rev: SLJ 8/97) [921]

5865 Stone, Tanya Lee. *Oprah Winfrey: Success with an Open Heart* (4–7). Illus. Series: Gateway Biographies. 2001, Millbrook LB $23.90 (978-0-7613-1814-9). Oprah's story, with concise text and excellent photographs, will attract and inspire young readers. (Rev: BL 6/1–15/01; HBG 10/01) [791.45]

5866 Westen, Robin. *Oprah Winfrey: "I Don't Believe in Failure"* (5–8). Series: African-American Biography Library. 2005, Enslow LB $31.93 (978-0-7660-2462-5). Winfrey's phenomenal rise to success in the worlds of business and entertainment is placed in social context. (Rev: SLJ 11/05; VOYA 6/06) [921]

5867 Wooten, Sara McIntosh. *Oprah Winfrey: Talk Show Legend* (6–10). Illus. Series: African-American Biographies. 1999, Enslow LB $26.60 (978-0-7660-1207-3). The story of the amazing television personality who rose from a background of poverty, loneliness, and sexual abuse to become world-famous. (Rev: BL 9/15/99; HBG 4/00; VOYA 12/99) [921]

WONDER, STEVIE

5868 Williams, Tenley. *Stevie Wonder* (7–10). Illus. Series: Overcoming Adversity. 2001, Chelsea LB $30.00 (978-0-7910-5903-6). This look at the musician's life and career puts an emphasis on the difficulties he has had to overcome. (Rev: BL 3/15/02; HBG 10/02) [782.421644]

Miscellaneous Artists

BARNUM, P. T.

5869 Barnum, P. T. *Barnum's Own Story* (7–12). Illus. 1962, Peter Smith $20.50 (978-0-8446-4001-3). The autobiography of the showman who could fool people like no one else. [921]

5870 Fleming, Alice. *P. T. Barnum: The World's Greatest Showman* (5–8). 1993, Walker LB $15.85 (978-0-8027-8235-9). A look at the circus owner's childhood and various successful entrepreneurial ventures. (Rev: BL 1/15/94; SLJ 12/93; VOYA 2/94) [921]

5871 Warrick, Karen Clemens. *P. T. Barnum: Genius of the Three-Ring Circus* (5–8). Series: Historical American Biographies. 2001, Enslow LB $26.60 (978-0-7660-1447-3). The story of the showman and creator of "The Greatest Show on Earth" who presented such attractions as General Tom Thumb and Jenny Lind. (Rev: BL 4/15/01; HBG 10/01; SLJ 7/01) [921]

GALAN, NELY

5872 Rodriguez, Janel. *Nely Galan* (4–8). Illus. Series: Contemporary Hispanic Americans. 1997, Raintree LB $17.98 (978-0-8172-3991-6). The life of this contemporary Hispanic American who, as a Hollywood producer, is responsible for developing TV and video projects for other Hispanic Americans. (Rev: BL 4/15/97) [921]

Contemporary and Historical Americans

Collective

5873 Alegre, Cèsar. *Extraordinary Hispanic Americans* (6–9). Series: Extraordinary People. 2006, Children's Pr. LB $40.00 (978-0-516-25343-5). More than 200 Hispanic Americans are introduced in brief profiles with black-and-white photographs. (Rev: BL 3/1/07; SLJ 5/07) [920]

5874 Ashby, Ruth. *Extraordinary People* (5–8). Series: Civil War Chronicles. 2002, Smart Apple LB $28.50 (978-1-58340-182-8). Key military and civilian figures from both North and South are profiled. (Rev: HBG 3/03; SLJ 2/03; VOYA 4/03) [973.7]

5875 Bailey Hutchinson, Kay. *Leading Ladies: American Trailblazers* (7–12). Illus. 2007, Harper-Collins $25.95 (978-0-06-113824-9). Pioneering American women in all walks of lives are celebrated in this collective biography that includes wives of presidents, activists, scientists, doctors, and journalists. (Rev: BL 12/1/07) [920]

5876 Barber, James, and Amy Pastan. *Presidents and First Ladies* (4–8). Illus. 2002, DK paper $12.99 (978-0-7894-8453-6). For each president and his First Lady, there are biographies, a list of key events, and a box highlighting an important event during that administration, plus plenty of color illustrations. (Rev: BL 4/1/02; HBG 10/02; SLJ 5/02) [920]

5877 Bausum, Ann. *Our Country's First Ladies* (4–8). 2007, National Geographic $19.95 (978-1-4263-0006-6). These profiles of America's first ladies provide material for report writers and enough interest for browsers. (Rev: SLJ 1/07) [920]

5878 Blassingame, Wyatt. *The Look-It-Up Book of Presidents* (6–9). Illus. 1990, Random paper $9.95 (978-0-679-80358-4). The author devotes two to six pages to each president and covers all the salient facts about each. (Rev: HBG 10/01; SLJ 5/90) [920]

5879 Brooks, Philip. *Extraordinary Jewish Americans* (5–9). Series: Extraordinary People. 1998, Children's LB $40.00 (978-0-516-20609-7). In chronological order, this book presents brief biographical sketches of 60 prominent Jews from a wide variety of fields including science, business, sports, the arts, entertainment, and politics. (Rev: HBG 3/99; SLJ 10/98; VOYA 6/99) [920]

5880 Bruning, John Robert. *Elusive Glory: African-American Heroes of World War II* (5–8). Illus. Series: Avisson Young Adult. 2001, Avisson paper $19.95 (978-1-888105-48-3). The true stories of African American servicemen, including six Tuskegee Airmen, who served the United States during World War II. (Rev: BL 1/1–15/02; SLJ 4/02) [940.54]

5881 Buller, Jon, et al. *Smart About the Presidents* (4–7). Illus. by authors. Series: Smart About History. 2004, Penguin paper $5.99 (978-0-448-43372-1). Pertinent facts about each president are conveyed in an informative, accessible style. (Rev: BL 9/1/04; SLJ 4/05) [920]

5882 Caravantes, Peggy. *Petticoat Spies: Six Women Spies of the Civil War* (5–8). Illus. 2002, Morgan Reynolds LB $23.95 (978-1-883846-88-6). An exciting volume about six women who spied for the Union and Confederacy during the Civil War, with photographs, source notes, a glossary, and a bibliography. (Rev: BL 3/15/02; HBG 10/02; SLJ 8/02) [973.7]

5883 Delano, Marfé Ferguson. *American Heroes* (5–8). Illus. 2005, National Geographic LB $45.90 (978-0-7922-7215-1). Fifty men and women whose heroism has helped to shape America are profiled in this attractive large-format volume. (Rev: BL 12/1/05; SLJ 2/06) [920.073]

5884 Doherty, Kieran. *Explorers, Missionaries, and Trappers: Trailblazers of the West* (5–8). Series: Shaping America. 2000, Oliver LB $22.95 (978-1-881508-52-6). Nine important pioneers of the American West are profiled including a Spanish conquistador, two Spanish priests, John Sutter, Marcus and Narcissa Whitman, and Brigham Young. (Rev: HBG 10/00; SLJ 5/00) [920]

5885 Doherty, Kieran. *Voyageurs, Lumberjacks, and Farmers: Pioneers of the Midwest* (5–8). Series: Shaping America. 2004, Oliver LB $22.95 (978-1-881508-54-0). The lives and accomplishments of eight individuals — including Antoine Cadillac, Jean du Sable, and Josiah and Abigail Snelling — who played key roles in the settlement of the Midwest are placed in historical context, with discussion of the plight of Native Americans in the region. (Rev: SLJ 9/04) [920]

5886 Emert, Phyllis R. *Top Lawyers and Their Famous Cases* (6–10). Series: Profiles. 1996, Oliver LB $19.95 (978-1-881508-31-1). Profiles of eight notable lawyers and their outstanding legal cases, from colonial days to the present, including Alexander Hamilton, Morris Dees, Abraham Lincoln, Robert H. Jackson, Joseph Welsh, and Belva Lockwood. (Rev: SLJ 11/96; VOYA 6/97) [920]

5887 Fradin, Dennis Brindell. *The Founders: The 39 Stories Behind the U.S. Constitution* (4–7). Illus. by Michael McCurdy. 2005, Walker $22.95 (978-0-8027-8972-3). The 39 men who signed the Constitution are profiled in brief chapters that include information on their home states. (Rev: BL 10/15/05; SLJ 9/05) [973.3]

5888 Franklin, John Hope, and August Meier, eds. *Black Leaders of the Twentieth Century* (7–12). Illus. 1982, Univ. of Illinois $34.95 (978-0-252-00870-2); paper $18.95 (978-0-252-00939-6). A total of 15 African Americans, including W. E. B. Du Bois, Marcus Garvey, and Whitney Young, Jr., are highlighted. A companion volume is *Black Leaders of the Nineteenth Century*. [920]

5889 Freedman, Russell. *Indian Chiefs* (6–9). Illus. 1987, Holiday $22.95 (978-0-8234-0625-8). Brief biographies of six Indian chiefs including Red Cloud, Sitting Bull, and Joseph of the Nez Perce. (Rev: BL 5/1/87; SLJ 5/87; VOYA 8/87) [920]

5890 Furbee, Mary R. *Women of the American Revolution* (7–9). Series: History Makers. 1999, Lucent LB $27.45 (978-1-56006-489-3). Profiles of six women — Abigail Smith Adams, Peggy Shippen Arnold, Esther DeBerdt Reed, Deborah Sampson, Mercy Otis Warren, and Phillis Wheatley — who played very different roles during the American Revolution, with material on the general role of women during the Revolution and an overview of events leading up to it. (Rev: HBG 4/00; SLJ 9/99) [920]

5891 Gilbreth, Frank B., and Ernestine Gilbreth Carey. *Cheaper by the Dozen*. Rev. ed. (8–12). 1963, Crowell paper $11.95 (978-0-06-008460-8). A biographical account of the Gilbreth family, whose 12 children were reared by a father who believed in time and efficiency applications even in the home. [920]

5892 Gourley, Catherine. *Society's Sisters: Stories of Women Who Fought for Social Justice in America* (6–9). Illus. 2003, Millbrook LB $25.90 (978-0-7613-2865-0). An oversize collective biography concentrating on 19th-century women reformers who may not be familiar to readers. (Rev: BL 11/15/03) [303.48]

5893 Green, Carl R., and William R. Sanford. *Confederate Generals of the Civil War* (5–8). Illus. Series: Collective Biographies. 1998, Enslow LB $26.60 (978-0-7660-1029-1). After a brief introduction to the Civil War, this book highlights the careers of 10 Southern generals and their contributions to the Confederate cause. (Rev: BL 8/98) [920]

5894 Green, Carl R., and William R. Sanford. *Union Generals of the Civil War* (5–8). Illus. 1998, Enslow LB $26.60 (978-0-7660-1028-4). Using period photographs and prints plus a concise text, this book outlines the careers of 10 Union generals and supplies background material on the Civil War, including charts and maps. (Rev: BL 8/98) [920]

5895 Hacker, Carlotta. *Great African Americans in History* (5–8). Series: Outstanding African Americans. 1997, Crabtree LB $22.60 (978-0-86505-805-7); paper $8.95 (978-0-86505-819-4). There are profiles of 13 great African Americans in American history, including Frederick Douglass, Harriet Tubman, W. E. B. Du Bois, Mary McLeod Bethune, and George Washington Carver. (Rev: BL 9/15/97; SLJ 1/98) [920]

5896 Hancock, Sibyl. *Famous Firsts of Black Americans* (7–12). Illus. 1983, Pelican $14.95 (978-0-88289-240-5). Biographies of 20 famous African Americans who have contributed in a unique way to our culture. [920]

5897 Hansen, Joyce. *Women of Hope: African Americans Who Made a Difference* (6–12). 1998, Scholastic paper $16.95 (978-0-590-93973-7). A large-size volume that celebrates the lives and accomplishments of 13 female African American leaders from various walks of life, including civil rights activists such as Fannie Lou Hamer and writers such as Maya Angelou. (Rev: BL 12/1/98; HBG 3/99; SLJ 10/98; VOYA 4/99) [920]

5898 Harmon, Rod. *American Civil Rights Leaders* (5–7). Series: Collective Biographies. 2000, Enslow LB $26.60 (978-0-7660-1381-0). This collective biography profiles 10 individuals who are currently or once were active in the civil rights movement in the United States. (Rev: BL 12/15/00; HBG 10/01) [920]

5899 Harness, Cheryl. *Remember the Ladies* (4–7). Illus. 2001, HarperCollins $16.99 (978-0-688-17017-2). Brief profiles of 100 important American women are each accompanied by a portrait. (Rev: BL 4/15/01; HBG 10/01; SLJ 2/01) [920]

5900 Haskins, Jim. *African American Military Heroes* (7–12). Series: Black Stars. 1998, Wiley $24.95 (978-0-471-14577-6). Profiles of 33 African American servicemen and servicewomen and their contributions, from the 1760s to the 1990s, are given in this book that stresses the struggle for equality. (Rev: BL 9/1/98; HBG 3/99; SLJ 11/98) [920]

5901 Haskins, Jim. *One More River to Cross: The Stories of Twelve Black Americans* (4–8). Illus. 1992, Scholastic $13.95 (978-0-590-42896-5). Eight men and four women who defied the odds to achieve prominence in their fields are introduced, including Ralph Bunche, Shirley Chisholm, and Ron McNair. (Rev: BCCB 4/92; BL 2/1/92; SLJ 4/92) [920]

5902 Haskins, Jim, and Kathleen Benson. *African-American Religious Leaders* (7–10). Illus. Series: Black Stars. 2008, Wiley LB $24.95 (978-0-471-73632-5). Leaders of the black church in America since the days of slavery are profiled in this book.that is organized in five chronological sections. (Rev: BL 2/1/08; SLJ 7/08) [277.3]

5903 Hoose, Phillip. *We Were There, Too! Young People in U.S. History* (5–8). Illus. 2001, Farrar $28.00 (978-0-374-38252-0). Hoose tells the stories of dozens of young people who contributed to the making of America — some famous but many who will be new to readers. (Rev: BCCB 10/01; BL 8/01; HB 9–10/01*; HBG 3/02; SLJ 8/01*) [973]

5904 Hudson, Wade, and Valerie Wesley Wilson. *Afro-Bets Book of Black Heroes from A to Z: An Introduction to Important Black Achievers* (4–7). Illus. 1988, Just Us Bks. paper $7.95 (978-0-940975-02-6). Forty-nine African American men and women of outstanding accomplishment. (Rev: BL 1/1/89; SLJ 12/88) [920]

5905 Hughes, Chris. *The Constitutional Convention* (5–9). Series: People at the Center Of. 2005, Gale LB $24.95 (978-1-56711-918-3). After an overview of the convention, this volume provides biographical information on key figures including George Washington, Benjamin Franklin, James Madison, and Alexander Hamilton. (Rev: SLJ 6/05) [920]

5906 Jones, Veda Boyd. *Government and Politics* (6–9). Series: Female Firsts in Their Fields. 1999, Chelsea $12.95 (978-0-7910-5140-5). Using black-and-white illustrations and clear, concise prose, this book profiles six women who were pioneers in

American politics and government. (Rev: BL 5/15/99; HBG 9/99; VOYA 8/99) [920]

5907 Kallen, Stuart A. *Native American Chiefs and Warriors* (6–10). Illus. Series: History Makers. 1999, Lucent LB $28.70 (978-1-56006-364-3). This collective biography gives basic information on some historically important Native American leaders. (Rev: BL 1/1–15/00; HBG 4/00; SLJ 1/00) [920]

5908 Kallen, Stuart A. *Women of the Civil Rights Movement* (7–12). Series: Women in History. 2005, Gale LB $32.45 (978-1-59018-569-8). Women who made important contributions to the U.S. civil rights movement are celebrated in chapters devoted to organizations, protests, education, voting rights, radicals, and so forth. (Rev: SLJ 11/05) [920]

5909 Katz, William L. *Black People Who Made the Old West* (6–9). Illus. 1992, Africa World $35.00 (978-0-86543-363-2); paper $14.95 (978-0-86543-364-9). Sketches of 35 black explorers, pioneers, etc., who helped open up the West. [920]

5910 Keenan, Sheila. *Scholastic Encyclopedia of Women in United States History* (4–9). 1996, Scholastic paper $17.95 (978-0-590-22792-6). More than 200 brief biographies of American women representing a variety of professions and accomplishments, organized into six chronologically arranged chapters. (Rev: SLJ 2/97) [920]

5911 Kennedy, John F. *Profiles in Courage*. Memorial Ed. (7–12). 1964, Perennial paper $7.00 (978-0-06-080698-9). Sketches of several famous Americans who took unpopular stands during their lives. (Rev: BL 4/87) [920]

5912 Kimmel, Elizabeth Cody. *Ladies First: 40 Daring American Women Who Were Second to None* (4–7). 2006, National Geographic $18.95 (978-0-7922-5393-8). From well-known women such as Sacagawea and Helen Keller to racing driver Shirley Muldowney and rabbi Sally Priesand, this is a well-written and informative resource. (Rev: SLJ 10/06; VOYA 8/06) [920]

5913 Knapp, Ron. *American Generals of World War II* (5–8). Series: Collective Biographies. 1998, Enslow LB $26.60 (978-0-7660-1024-6). The 10 U.S. generals profiled here are Henry Arnold, Omar Bradley, Dwight Eisenhower, Curtis LeMay, Douglas MacArthur, George Marshall, George Patton, Matthew Ridgway, Holland Smith, and Joseph Stilwell. (Rev: SLJ 9/98) [920]

5914 Kramer, Barbara. *Trailblazing American Women* (5–7). Series: Collective Biographies. 2000, Enslow LB $26.60 (978-0-7660-1377-3). This collection of biographies profiles women who dared to branch out into new fields and break new ground. (Rev: BL 9/15/00; HBG 10/01; SLJ 12/00) [920]

5915 Krull, Kathleen. *Lives of the Presidents: Fame, Shame (and What the Neighbors Thought)* (4–8). Illus. by Kathryn Hewitt. 1998, Harcourt $20.00 (978-0-15-200808-6). An entertaining collective biography that stresses the human side of U.S. presidents, with interesting, insightful tidbits and details that bring the presidents to life. (Rev: BL 8/98; HB 11–12/98; HBG 3/99; SLJ 9/98) [920]

5916 Langley, Wanda. *Women of the Wind: Early Women Aviators* (6–9). Illus. 2006, Morgan Reynolds LB $26.95 (978-1-931798-81-5). From childhood through achievements in the air, this attractive collective biography covers nine American women flyers. (Rev: BL 2/15/06; SLJ 2/06) [629.13]

5917 Lindop, Edmund. *Dwight D. Eisenhower, John F. Kennedy, Lyndon B. Johnson* (4–7). Illus. Series: Presidents Who Dared. 1996, Twenty-First Century LB $23.90 (978-0-8050-3404-2). The highlights of these three administrations are presented, preceded by an introduction to the American presidency. (Rev: BL 4/15/96; SLJ 6/96) [920]

5918 Lindop, Edmund. *George Washington, Thomas Jefferson, Andrew Jackson* (4–7). Illus. Series: Presidents Who Dared. 1995, Twenty-First Century LB $23.90 (978-0-8050-3401-1). After a general introduction on the duties of the president, brief biographies of three are given, with emphasis on their accomplishments in office. (Rev: BL 1/1–15/96; SLJ 11/95) [920]

5919 Lindop, Edmund. *James K. Polk, Abraham Lincoln, Theodore Roosevelt* (4–7). Illus. Series: Presidents Who Dared. 1995, Twenty-First Century LB $23.90 (978-0-8050-3402-8). Highlights and evaluations of the presidencies of Polk, Lincoln, and Theodore Roosevelt. (Rev: BL 1/1–15/96; SLJ 11/95) [920]

5920 Lindop, Edmund. *Richard M. Nixon, Jimmy Carter, Ronald Reagan* (4–8). Series: Presidents Who Dared. 1996, Twenty-First Century LB $23.90 (978-0-8050-3405-9). This account traces salient events in each of these presidents' terms, for example: Nixon and Watergate and relations with China; Carter and ending the war between Egypt and Israel; and Reagan and his arms agreement with the Soviet Union. (Rev: BL 4/15/96; SLJ 6/96) [920]

5921 Lindop, Edmund. *Woodrow Wilson, Franklin D. Roosevelt, Harry S. Truman* (5–8). Illus. Series: Presidents Who Dared. 1995, Twenty-First Century LB $23.90 (978-0-8050-3403-5). After an overview of the presidency and brief profiles of these men, this account looks at daring decisions they made as presidents. (Rev: BL 1/1–15/96; SLJ 11/95; VOYA 6/96) [920]

5922 Lindop, Laurie. *Champions of Equality* (7–10). Illus. Series: Dynamic Modern Women. 1997, Twenty-First Century LB $24.90 (978-0-8050-4165-1). A look at 10 women activists for human and equal rights, among them Margarethe Cammermeyer, Marian Wright Edelman, Wilma Mankiller, and Eleanor Holmes Norton. (Rev: BL 9/1/97; SLJ 9/97) [303.48]

5923 Lindop, Laurie. *Political Leaders* (6–12). Illus. Series: Dynamic Modern Women. 1996, Twenty-First Century LB $24.90 (978-0-8050-4164-4). Elizabeth Dole, Dianne Feinstein, Geraldine Ferraro, Ruth Bader Ginsburg, and Barbara Jordan are five of the 10 prominent women in politics profiled in this book, with details on the childhood, influences, education, and political career of each. (Rev: BL 1/1–15/97; SLJ 1/97; VOYA 2/97) [320]

5924 Lynne, Douglas. *Contemporary United States: 1968 to the Present* (5–8). Illus. Series: Presidents of the United States. 2007, Weigl LB $20.35 (978-1-59036-753-7). The lives and times of recent U.S. presidents — from Nixon to George W. Bush — are covered in this eighth volume in the series. (Rev: BL 10/15/07) [973.92092]

5925 McCullough, Noah. *The Essential Book of Presidential Trivia* (7–12). Illus. 2006, Random paper $9.95 (978-1-4000-6482-3). Written by a 10-year-old presidential hopeful and historian, this book gives a short presidential biography per chapter, a "Did You Know?" section of trivia, and a black-and-white drawing for each. (Rev: SLJ 6/06)

5926 McLean, Jacqueline. *Women with Wings* (4–7). Illus. Series: Profiles. 2001, Oliver $19.95 (978-1-881508-70-0). An absorbing account of the achievements of women pilots, including Bessie Coleman, Amelia Earhart, and Anne Morrow Lindbergh. (Rev: BL 5/15/01; HBG 10/01; SLJ 10/01) [629.13]

5927 Marvis, Barbara. *Famous People of Asian Ancestry, Vol. 4* (4–7). Illus. Series: Contemporary American Success Stories. 1994, Mitchell Lane paper $10.95 (978-1-883845-09-4). A collective biography of Asian Americans, including actor Dustin Nguyen, novelist Amy Tan, and businessman Rocky Aoki. Also use volumes 1 through 3 (2nd ed., 1997). (Rev: BL 10/1/94; SLJ 11/94) [920]

5928 Marvis, Barbara. *Famous People of Hispanic Heritage, Vol. 1* (4–7). Illus. Series: Contemporary American Success Stories. 1995, Mitchell Lane LB $21.95 (978-1-883845-21-6); paper $18.95 (978-1-883845-20-9). This is the first of three volumes that give brief biographies of Hispanic Americans from all walks of life who have made significant contributions to our country. (Rev: BL 11/15/95; SLJ 1/96) [920]

5929 Marvis, Barbara. *Famous People of Hispanic Heritage, Vol. 4* (5–9). Illus. 1996, Mitchell Lane paper $12.95 (978-1-883845-29-2). The lives of two Hispanic men and two women who have succeeded in their careers are presented in an easy-to-read style. Other volumes in this series by the same author are available. (Rev: BL 12/15/96; SLJ 1/97; VOYA 2/97) [920]

5930 Masters, Nancy Robinson. *Extraordinary Patriots of the United States of America: Colonial Times to Pre-Civil War* (5–8). Series: Extraordinary People. 2005, Children's Pr. LB $40.00 (978-0-516-24404-4). Interesting 3- to 5-page profiles are arranged chronologically by year of birth. (Rev: SLJ 2/06) [920]

5931 Meisner, James, and Amy Ruth. *American Revolutionaries and Founders of the Nation* (5–7). Series: Collective Biographies. 1999, Enslow LB $26.60 (978-0-7660-1115-1). Ten brief biographies of prominent leaders of the American Revolution, each with a black-and-white portrait. (Rev: BL 9/15/99) [920]

5932 Morey, Janet Nomura, and Wendy Dunn. *Famous Hispanic Americans* (7–10). Illus. 1996, Dutton $16.99 (978-0-525-65190-1). Fourteen men and women of Hispanic heritage from science, sports, the arts, and other professions are featured in this collective biography. (Rev: BL 2/15/96; SLJ 2/96; VOYA 8/96) [920]

5933 Morin, Isobel V. *Women Chosen for Public Office* (5–7). Illus. 1995, Oliver LB $19.95 (978-1-881508-20-5). Nine biographies of women who are involved in the federal government from the superintendent of army nurses to Supreme Court Justice Ruth Bader Ginsburg. (Rev: BL 5/1/95; SLJ 6/95) [920]

5934 Morin, Isobel V. *Women of the U.S. Congress* (6–10). 1994, Oliver LB $19.95 (978-1-881508-12-0). Lists all the women who have served in Congress as of 1994 and provides political biographies of seven of them, citing their accomplishments and their different backgrounds and views. (Rev: BL 7/94; SLJ 5/94; VOYA 6/94) [920]

5935 Morin, Isobel V. *Women Who Reformed Politics* (7–12). 1994, Oliver LB $19.95 (978-1-881508-16-8). Describes the political activism of eight American women, including Abby Foster's abolition fight, Carrie Catt's suffrage battle, and Gloria Steinem's feminist crusade. (Rev: BL 10/15/94; SLJ 11/94; VOYA 2/95) [920]

5936 Morris, Juddi. *At Home with the Presidents* (4–8). 1999, Wiley paper $13.95 (978-0-471-25300-6). In three to five pages each, this account profiles the presidents of the United States from Washington through Clinton. (Rev: SLJ 3/00) [920]

5937 Munson, Sammye. *Today's Tejano Heroes* (5–8). Illus. 2000, Eakin $13.95 (978-1-57168-328-1). In alphabetical order, this volume introduces 16 important 20th-century Mexican Americans who have contributed to the history and culture of Texas, including Vikki Carr, Attorney General Dan Morales, and federal judge Hilda Tagle. (Rev: BL 2/1/01) [920]

5938 Netzley, Patricia D. *Presidential Assassins* (6–9). Series: History Makers. 2000, Lucent LB $27.45 (978-1-56006-623-1). Profiles of people who have assassinated or attempted to assassinate American presidents are profiled with material on the consequences of their action on the nation. (Rev: BL 6/1–15/00; HBG 9/00; SLJ 8/00) [920]

5939 O'Connor, Jane. *If the Walls Could Talk: Family Life at the White House* (4–7). Illus. by Gary Hovland. 2004, Simon & Schuster $16.95 (978-0-689-86863-4). This inside view of family life within the White House — with caricatures and interesting trivia — is similar to Judith St. George's *So You Want to Be President* (Putnam, 2000). (Rev: BL 8/04; SLJ 9/04)

5940 Pinkney, Andrea D. *Let It Shine: Stories of Black Women Freedom Fighters* (5–8). Illus. 2000, Harcourt $20.00 (978-0-15-201005-8). This work contains chatty profiles of 10 important African American women, including Sojourner Truth, Rosa Parks, and Shirley Chisholm. (Rev: BCCB 11/00; BL 11/15/00; HB 11–12/00; HBG 3/01; SLJ 10/00; VOYA 12/00) [921]

5941 Rappaport, Doreen. *In the Promised Land: Lives of Jewish Americans* (4–7). Illus. by Cornelius Van Wright. 2005, HarperCollins LB $16.89 (978-0-06-059395-7). A look at the lives and diverse accomplishments of 13 notable Jewish Americans, including Asser Levy, Harry Houdini, Jonas Salk, and Steven Spielberg. (Rev: BL 1/1–15/05; SLJ 5/05) [920]

5942 Rennert, Richard, ed. *Book of Firsts: Leaders of America* (6–9). Illus. Series: Profiles of Great Black Americans. 1994, Chelsea paper $7.65 (978-0-7910-2066-1). This collective biography profiles the lives and works of nine African American leaders, including Ralph Bunche, Shirley Chisholm, William H. Hastie, Colin Powell, and L. Douglas Wilder. (Rev: BL 6/1–15/94) [920]

5943 Roberts, Russell. *Presidents and Scandals* (6–9). Series: History Makers. 2001, Lucent $28.70 (978-1-56006-642-2). This work discusses five American presidents whose term of office was tainted by scandal, including Grant, Harding, Nixon, Reagan, and Clinton. (Rev: BL 8/1/01; SLJ 6/01) [920]

5944 Rodriguez, Robert, and Tamra Orr. *Great Hispanic-Americans* (6–12). 2005, Publications Int'l LB $15.98 (978-1-4127-1148-7). More than 50 Hispanic Americans from different walks of life are profiled in accessible text. (Rev: SLJ 1/06) [920]

5945 Straub, Deborah G., ed. *Hispanic American Voices* (6–12). 1997, Gale $52.00 (978-0-8103-9827-6). Profiles of 16 Hispanic Americans, most of whom are civil and human rights leaders, politicians, attorneys, or civil rights activists. (Rev: SLJ 11/97) [920]

5946 Streissguth, Thomas. *Legendary Labor Leaders* (7–12). Illus. Series: Profiles. 1998, Oliver LB $19.95 (978-1-881508-44-1). The eight labor leaders profiled in this collective biography are Samuel Gompers, Cesar Chavez, A. Philip Randolph, Jimmy Hoffa, Eugene Debs, William Haywood, Mother Jones, and John L. Lewis. (Rev: BL 10/15/98; SLJ 1/99) [920]

5947 Sullivan, Otha Richard. *African American Millionaires* (5–10). Series: Black Stars. 2004, Wiley $24.95 (978-0-471-46928-5). Tyra Banks and Oprah Winfrey are included here, but so are many names that may be unfamiliar to readers, such as William Alexander Leidesdorff and Annie Turnbo Malone. (Rev: SLJ 5/05) [920]

5948 Taylor, Kimberly H. *Black Abolitionists and Freedom Fighters* (6–10). 1996, Oliver LB $19.95 (978-1-881508-30-4). Profiles are given for eight African Americans who fought to end slavery, some well-known (including Nat Turner and Harriet Tubman) and others less familiar, such as Richard Allen and Mary Terrell. (Rev: SLJ 10/96) [920]

5949 Taylor, Kimberly H. *Black Civil Rights Champions* (6–12). Illus. 1995, Oliver LB $19.95 (978-1-881508-22-9). In separate chapters, seven civil rights leaders, including W. E. B. Du Bois, James Farmer, Ella Baker, and Malcolm X, are profiled, with a final chapter that gives thumbnail sketches of many more. (Rev: BL 1/1–15/96; SLJ 3/96; VOYA 6/96) [920]

5950 Thimmesh, Catherine. *Madam President: The Extraordinary, True (and Evolving) Story of Women in Politics*. Rev. ed. (4–7). Illus. by Douglas B. Jones. 2008, Houghton $17.00 (978-0-618-39666-5); paper $8.95 (978-0-618-97143-5). This update includes profiles of more than 20 women who have been influential in the political arena, including Margaret Chase Smith, Sirimavo Bandaranaike, Margaret Thatcher, Nancy Pelosi, Hillary Clinton, and Condoleezza Rice. (Rev: BL 10/1/04; SLJ 5/08) [920]

5951 Thrasher, Thomas. *Gunfighters* (6–9). Series: History Makers. 2000, Lucent LB $28.70 (978-1-56006-570-8). A fascinating collective biography that introduces the West of olden days and gives profiles of Wild Bill Hickok, Ben Thompson, Wyatt Earp, John Wesley Hardin, Billy the Kid, and Tom Horn. (Rev: BL 3/15/00; HBG 10/00; SLJ 9/00) [920]

5952 Thro, Ellen. *Twentieth-Century Women Politicians* (7–12). Series: American Profiles. 1998, Facts on File $25.00 (978-0-8160-3758-2). Beginning in the mid-20th century, this work features 10 women who were elected to important public offices, including Margaret Chase Smith, Geraldine Ferraro, Dianne Feinstein, Christine Todd Whitman, and Ann Richards. (Rev: BL 12/15/98) [920]

5953 Ungar, Harlow G. *Teachers and Educators* (7–10). Illus. Series: American Profiles. 1994, Facts on File $25.00 (978-0-8160-2990-7). This book profiles eight great American educators of the past, including John Dewey, Horace Mann, Emma Willard, Booker T. Washington, and Henry Barnard. (Rev: BL 7/95; VOYA 5/95) [920]

5954 Weatherford, Carole Boston. *Great African-American Lawyers: Raising the Bar of Freedom* (7–12). Illus. Series: Collective Biographies. 2003, Enslow $26.60 (978-0-7660-1837-2). From Macon Allen, the first black lawyer in America, through more familiar names such as Thurgood Marshall and Marian Wright Edelman, this is an overview of the accomplishments of African American lawyers. (Rev: BL 2/15/03; HBG 10/03) [340.09]

5955 Wheeler, Jill C. *America's Leaders* (4–7). Series: War on Terrorism. 2002, ABDO LB $25.65 (978-1-57765-661-6). This book contains brief profiles of important American figures in the war against terrorism such as President Bush, Colin Powell, John Ashcroft, and Rudy Giuliani. (Rev: BL 5/15/02; HBG 10/02) [920]

5956 Woog, Adam. *Gangsters* (6–9). Series: History Makers. 2000, Lucent LB $27.45 (978-1-56006-638-5). A collective biography featuring gangsters including Al Capone. (Rev: BL 9/15/00; HBG 3/01) [920]

5957 Zimmerman, Dwight Jon. *First Command: Paths to Leadership* (7–12). 2005, Vandamere $22.95 (978-0-918339-62-1). A collective biography of 23 American soldiers and marines who went on to become generals, focusing on their early commands and the leadership qualities that helped them advance. (Rev: SLJ 5/06)

Civil and Human Rights Leaders

ADDAMS, JANE

5958 Caravantes, Peggy. *Waging Peace: The Story of Jane Addams* (5–8). 2004, Morgan Reynolds LB $23.95 (978-1-931798-40-2). Covers Addams's life and achievements, with good material on her youth and the lessons she learned from her Quaker father. (Rev: SLJ 2/05) [921]

5959 Fradin, Judith Bloom, and Dennis Brindell Fradin. *Jane Addams: Champion of Democracy* (6–9). 2006, Clarion $21.00 (978-0-618-50436-7). This account of the fascinating life of Jane Addams, social activist and Nobel Peace Prize winner, provides lots of historical context and clearly shows her legacy today. (Rev: BL 10/15/06; HB 11–12/06; LMC 3/07; SLJ 11/06*) [361.2]

5960 Harvey, Bonnie Carman. *Jane Addams: Nobel Prize Winner and Founder of Hull House* (5–8).

Illus. Series: Historic American Biographies. 1999, Enslow LB $26.60 (978-0-7660-1094-9). This biography of the Nobel Peace Prize winner and founder of Hull House traces her life and her outstanding achievements as a social worker. (Rev: BL 11/1/99; HBG 3/00; SLJ 11/99) [921]

5961 Kittredge, Mary. *Jane Addams* (6–10). Illus. 1988, Chelsea LB $19.95 (978-1-55546-636-7). Jane Addams helped immigrants by founding the first settlement house, Hull House, in Chicago; this is a comprehensive profile that will be useful for report writers. (Rev: BL 6/15/88; SLJ 1/89) [921]

5962 McPherson, Stephanie S. *Peace and Bread: The Story of Jane Addams* (5–8). 1993, Carolrhoda LB $27.93 (978-0-87614-792-4). An introduction to Jane Addams's work among the poor of Chicago and her leadership in international organizations on behalf of world peace. (Rev: BL 1/15/94; SLJ 2/94) [921]

ANTHONY, SUSAN B.

5963 Kendall, Martha E. *Susan B. Anthony: Voice for Women's Voting Rights* (6–8). Series: Historical American Biographies. 1997, Enslow LB $26.60 (978-0-89490-780-7). A biography of this amazing woman who campaigned for women's right to vote, hold political office, divorce, and own property, and for an end to slavery. (Rev: SLJ 8/97) [921]

5964 Orr, Tamra. *The Life and Times of Susan B. Anthony* (5–8). Illus. Series: Profiles in American History. 2007, Mitchell Lane LB $19.95 (978-1-58415-445-7). This biography of Anthony traces her life and work in the women's rights movement and contains supplemental facts that will interest readers. (Rev: SLJ 7/07) [921]

5965 Weisberg, Barbara. *Susan B. Anthony* (6–10). Illus. 1988, Chelsea LB $30.00 (978-1-55546-639-8). A life of the woman who led the early suffragette movement. (Rev: BL 12/1/88) [921]

BAKER, ELLA

5966 Bohannon, Lisa Frederiksen. *Freedom Cannot Rest: Ella Baker and the Civil Rights Movement* (7–12). Illus. Series: Civil Rights Leaders. 2005, Morgan Reynolds LB $26.95 (978-1-931798-71-6). A well-illustrated and evenhanded introduction to the life and accomplishments of Ella Baker, a major — but often overlooked — player in the U.S. civil rights movement. (Rev: SLJ 12/05) [921]

BATES, DAISY

5967 Fradin, Judith Bloom, and Dennis Brindell Fradin. *The Power of One: Daisy Bates and the Little Rock Nine* (8–11). Illus. 2004, Clarion $19.00 (978-0-618-31556-7). A detailed profile of Daisy Bates, who as president of the Arkansas chapter of

the NAACP played a pivotal role in the 1957 integration of Central High School in Little Rock. (Rev: BL 2/1/05; SLJ 4/05) [323]

5968 Polakow, Amy. *Daisy Bates: Civil Rights Crusader* (6–12). Illus. 2003, Linnet $25.00 (978-0-208-02513-5). In 1957, Bates supported the Little Rock Nine students who were the first African Americans to take advantage of school integration. (Rev: BL 6/1–15/03; HBG 10/03; SLJ 8/03; VOYA 6/04) [921]

BETHUNE, MARY MCLEOD

5969 Halasa, Malu. *Mary McLeod Bethune* (6–10). Illus. 1988, Chelsea LB $30.00 (978-1-55546-574-2). A stirring biography of the African American woman who fought for the right to a quality education for her people. (Rev: BL 3/15/89) [921]

5970 Meltzer, Milton. *Mary McLeod Bethune: Voice of Black Hope* (4–7). Illus. 1988, Puffin paper $4.99 (978-0-14-032219-4). An effective profile of the African American educator. (Rev: BCCB 5/87; BL 3/15/87; SLJ 3/87) [370.0924]

5971 Somervill, Barbara A. *Mary McLeod Bethune: African-American Educator* (4–7). Series: Our People. 2003, The Child's World LB $27.07 (978-1-59296-008-8). A profile of the African American educator and leader, with sidebars that add historical context. (Rev: SLJ 4/04) [921]

BOND, JULIAN

5972 Jordan, Denise M. *Julian Bond: Civil Rights Activist and Chairman of the NAACP* (6–8). 2001, Enslow LB $26.60 (978-0-7660-1549-4). A concise overview of the life and political career of the African American who protested against the Vietnam War and against racial discrimination. (Rev: HBG 3/02; SLJ 3/02) [323.1]

BROWN, JOHN

5973 Cox, Clinton. *Fiery Vision: The Life and Death of John Brown* (7–10). Illus. 1997, Scholastic paper $15.95 (978-0-590-47574-7). A well-researched, detailed account of the life of the abolitionist who was hanged for the raid at Harper's Ferry. (Rev: BL 2/15/97; HBG 3/98; SLJ 6/97; VOYA 10/98) [921]

5974 Reynolds, David S. *John Brown, Abolitionist: The Man Who Killed Slavery, Sparked the Civil War, and Seeded Civil Rights* (8–12). 2005, Knopf $30.00 (978-0-375-41188-5). This insightful biography adds fuel to the continuing debate over what motivated the fiery abolitionist. (Rev: BL 2/1/05) [973.7]

CATT, CARRIE CHAPMAN

5975 Somervill, Barbara A. *Votes for Women! The Story of Carrie Chapman Catt* (5–8). Illus. 2002, Morgan Reynolds LB $23.95 (978-1-883846-96-1). This is the story of Carrie Chapman Catt, who devoted her early life to the quest for women's right to vote and later turned her energies to helping Jewish refugees. (Rev: BL 11/15/02; HBG 3/03; SLJ 1/03; VOYA 2/03) [324.6]

CHAVEZ, CESAR

5976 Brown, Jonatha A. *Cesar Chavez* (5–8). Series: Trailblazers of the Modern World. 2004, World Almanac LB $31.00 (978-0-8368-5097-0). Report writers will find lots of suitable information in this work that covers Chavez's life and accomplishments. (Rev: SLJ 7/04) [921]

5977 Gonzales, Doreen. *Cesar Chavez: Leader for Migrant Farm Workers* (6–10). Illus. Series: Hispanic Biographies. 1996, Enslow LB $26.60 (978-0-89490-760-9). This biography concentrates on Chavez's struggle to organize California farmworkers, his belief in nonviolence, and his inspirational leadership. (Rev: BL 10/1/96; SLJ 6/96) [921]

5978 Houle, Michelle E., ed. *Cesar Chavez* (7–12). Series: People Who Made History. 2003, Gale paper $24.95 (978-0-7377-1299-5). A compilation of essays about the champion of migrant workers that show his achievements from various points of view. (Rev: SLJ 10/03) [921]

5979 Tracy, Kathleen. *Cesar Chavez* (5–7). Series: Latinos in American History. 2003, Mitchell Lane LB $29.95 (978-1-58415-224-8). This biography covers the life and accomplishments of the Mexican American labor leader who founded the United Farm Workers. (Rev: BL 1/1–15/04) [921]

5980 Young, Jeff C. *Cesar Chavez* (7–10). Illus. Series: American Workers. 2007, Morgan Reynolds $27.95 (978-1-59935-036-3). The activist's early life and inspirations as well as his influence on labor practices are well presented in this easy-to-read biography. (Rev: BL 3/15/07; SLJ 4/07) [331.88]

CHILD, LYDIA MARIA

5981 Kenschaft, Lori. *Lydia Maria Child: The Quest for Racial Justice* (6–10). Illus. Series: Oxford Portraits. 2002, Oxford LB $32.95 (978-0-19-513257-1). Lydia Maria Child, an activist for civil rights in the early and middle 1800s, is also known for her literary career. (Rev: BL 3/1/03; HBG 3/03; SLJ 1/03) [303.48]

DAY, DOROTHY

5982 Kent, Deborah. *Dorothy Day: Friend to the Forgotten* (7–12). Illus. 1996, Eerdmans $15.00 (978-0-8028-5117-8). A profile of the great friend of the poor and helpless whose own life's drama involved an abortion, a short-lived marriage, imprisonment, political involvement, and questioning of her deep religious beliefs. (Rev: BL 6/1–15/96; SLJ 8/96) [921]

DIX, DOROTHEA

5983 Herstek, Amy Paulson. *Dorothea Dix* (5–8). Series: Historical American Biographies. 2001, Enslow LB $26.60 (978-0-7660-1258-5). The life of this militant reformer who fought for more humane treatment of the insane. (Rev: BL 1/1–15/02; HBG 3/02; SLJ 1/02) [921]

DOUGLASS, FREDERICK

5984 Meltzer, Milton, ed. *Frederick Douglass: In His Own Words* (8–12). Illus. 1995, Harcourt $22.00 (978-0-15-229492-2). An introduction to the articles and speeches of the great 19th-century abolitionist leader, arranged chronologically. (Rev: BL 12/15/94; SLJ 2/95) [305.8]

DU BOIS, W. E. B.

5985 Moss, Nathaniel. *W. E. B. Du Bois: Civil Rights Leader* (5–8). Series: Junior World Biography. 1996, Chelsea LB $15.95 (978-0-7910-2382-2). A brief, somewhat superficial overview of this great pioneer in the civil rights movement and his accomplishments. (Rev: SLJ 7/96) [921]

5986 Rowh, Mark. *W. E. B. Du Bois: Champion of Civil Rights* (7–12). Series: African-American Biographies. 1999, Enslow LB $26.60 (978-0-7660-1209-7). The inspiring biography of the African American educator and writer who helped found the NAACP. (Rev: BL 11/15/99; HBG 4/00) [921]

FARRAKHAN, LOUIS

5987 Haskins, Jim. *Louis Farrakhan and the Nation of Islam* (7–12). Illus. 1996, Walker LB $16.85 (978-0-8027-8423-0). Beginning with a history of African American nationalism and the Nation of Islam, this biography places the life of Farrakhan within the movement for black solidarity. (Rev: BL 10/1/96; SLJ 1/97) [921]

FREEMAN, ELIZABETH

5988 Wilds, Mary. *MumBet: The Life and Times of Elizabeth Freeman: The True Story of a Slave Who Won Her Freedom* (7–12). Illus. 1999, Avisson LB $19.95 (978-1-888105-40-7). The story of MumBet (Elizabeth Freeman), a slave who sued for her freedom in Massachusetts in 1781 after hearing a reading of the Declaration of Independence and won, helping to set the legal precedents that ended slavery in New England. (Rev: BL 6/1–15/99; SLJ 6/99; VOYA 2/00) [921]

GARVEY, MARCUS

5989 Caravantes, Peggy. *Marcus Garvey: Black Nationalist* (6–10). Series: Twentieth Century Leaders. 2004, Morgan Reynolds LB $23.95 (978-1-931798-14-3). A biography of this black nationalist, Pan-Africanist, and exponent of black civil rights. (Rev: BL 2/15/04; HBG 4/04; SLJ 11/03; VOYA 6/04) [921]

5990 Kallen, Stuart A. *Marcus Garvey and the Back to Africa Movement* (7–12). 2006, Gale LB $28.70 (978-1-59018-838-5). An excellent account of Garvey's contributions to the black pride and power movements, touching on his charisma but also on his deficiencies. (Rev: SLJ 8/06)

5991 Lawler, Mary. *Marcus Garvey* (7–10). Illus. Series: Black Americans of Achievement. 1987, Chelsea LB $30.00 (978-1-55546-587-2). The story of the black leader who preached black separation and founded the Universal Negro Improvement Association. (Rev: BL 12/1/87; VOYA 10/88) [921]

5992 Schraff, Anne. *Marcus Garvey: Controversial Champion of Black Pride* (6–10). Illus. Series: African-American Biographies. 2004, Enslow LB $26.60 (978-0-7660-2168-6). This is a fine biography of the controversial leader of the early 20th-century Pan-African movement with discussion of his opinions, including his separatist views on race. (Rev: BL 2/15/04) [921]

GONZALEZ, HENRY B.

5993 Haugen, Brenda. *Henry B. Gonzalez: Congressman of the People* (6–9). 2005, Compass Point LB $30.60 (978-0-7565-0996-5). In his 37 years as a representative in the U.S. Congress, Henry Gonzalez (a Democrat from Texas) fought for racial equality, civil rights, and efforts to end poverty. (Rev: SLJ 8/06) [921]

GRIMKE, SARAH AND ANGELINA

5994 McPherson, Stephanie S. *Sisters Against Slavery: A Story About Sarah and Angelina Grimke* (4–7). Illus. by Karen Ritz. Series: Creative Minds Biographies. 1999, Carolrhoda LB $21.27 (978-1-57505-361-5). The story of the remarkable Grimke sisters from South Carolina who fought against slavery and later became suffragettes. (Rev: BCCB 1/00; HBG 3/00; SLJ 12/99) [921]

HAMER, FANNIE LOU

5995 Fiorelli, June Estep. *Fannie Lou Hamer: A Voice for Freedom* (5–10). Series: Avisson Young Adult. 2005, Avisson paper $19.95 (978-1-888105-

62-9). Hamer's life, including her youth, are described and placed in the context of events in the United States at the time. (Rev: SLJ 2/06) [921]

HARRIS, LA DONNA

5996 Schwartz, Michael. *La Donna Harris* (4–7). Illus. Series: Contemporary Native Americans. 1997, Raintree LB $17.98 (978-0-8172-3995-4). The life story and accomplishments of this Native American, who has openly championed her people's rights before the Senate. (Rev: BL 6/1–15/97) [921]

HAYDEN, LEWIS

5997 Strangis, Joel. *Lewis Hayden and the War Against Slavery* (7–12). 1998, Shoe String LB $25.00 (978-0-208-02430-5). The dramatic story of the former slave who became an active abolitionist and a stationmaster on the Underground Railroad. (Rev: BL 2/15/99; HBG 9/99; SLJ 5/99; VOYA 10/99) [921]

HESCHEL, ABRAHAM JOSHUA

5998 Rose, Or. *Abraham Joshua Heschel* (4–8). Illus. 2003, Jewish Publication Soc. paper $9.95 (978-0-8276-0758-3). A portrait of the rabbi and teacher who was born in Poland, emigrated to the United States, and became a leader in the civil rights movement. (Rev: BL 6/1–15/03; HBG 10/01) [921]

HUERTA, DOLORES

5999 Murcia, Rebecca Thatcher. *Dolores Huerta* (5–7). Series: Latinos in American History. 2002, Mitchell Lane LB $29.95 (978-1-58415-155-5). The story of the gallant woman who worked along with Cesar Chavez to protect the rights of farm workers. (Rev: BL 2/15/03; HBG 10/03) [921]

6000 Perez, Frank. *Dolores Huerta* (4–8). Illus. Series: Contemporary Hispanic Americans. 1995, Raintree LB $28.80 (978-0-8172-3981-7). The accomplishments of Dolores Huerta, a Hispanic American who cofounded the United Farm Workers, are described in this informative biography. (Rev: BL 3/15/96) [921]

IDAR, JOVITA

6001 Gibson, Karen Bush. *Jovita Idar* (5–7). Series: Latinos in American History. 2002, Mitchell Lane LB $29.95 (978-1-58415-151-7). The inspiring story of the Latin American woman who started San Antonio's first free kindergarten and who founded the League of Mexican American women in 1911 to educate poor children. (Rev: BL 2/15/03; HBG 10/03) [921]

JACKSON, JESSE

6002 Haskins, James. *Jesse Jackson: Civil Rights Activist* (6–10). Series: African-American Biographies. 2000, Enslow LB $26.60 (978-0-7660-1390-2). A biography of the man who has been a defender of the poor, minorities, and underprivileged. (Rev: BL 9/15/00; HBG 3/01; SLJ 11/00) [921]

6003 Steffens, Bradley, and Dan Wood. *Jesse Jackson* (5–8). Series: People in the News. 2000, Lucent LB $32.45 (978-1-56006-631-6). This well-documented look at the life of the religious and civil rights leader gives interesting information on the events and people who influenced him. (Rev: BL 6/1–15/00; HBG 10/00) [921]

JACOBS, HARRIET A.

6004 Fleischner, Jennifer. *I Was Born a Slave: The Story of Harriet Jacobs* (4–8). Illus. 1997, Millbrook LB $26.90 (978-0-7613-0111-0). The turbulent life of Harriet Jacobs, who was born into slavery and lived for many years as a fugitive before winning her freedom and becoming an abolitionist. (Rev: BL 9/15/97; HBG 3/98; SLJ 1/98) [921]

JONES, MOTHER

6005 Josephson, Judith P. *Mother Jones: Fierce Fighter for Workers' Rights* (6–10). Illus. 1997, Lerner LB $27.93 (978-0-8225-4924-6). The story of this early labor leader in coal country is also a history of the struggle against long work hours, unsafe working conditions, poor wages, and child labor. (Rev: BL 2/1/97; SLJ 4/97*) [921]

KING, CORETTA SCOTT

6006 Bankston, John. *Coretta Scott King and the Story Behind the Coretta Scott King Award* (4–8). Series: Great Achievement Awards. 2003, Mitchell Lane $29.95 (978-1-58415-202-6). The story of the widow of Martin Luther King, Jr., her continuing fight for civil rights, and the children's book prize named after her are covered in this biography. (Rev: BL 10/15/03; SLJ 10/03) [921]

6007 Rhodes, Lisa R. *Coretta Scott King* (5–8). Illus. Series: Black Americans of Achievement. 1999, Chelsea LB $30.00 (978-0-7910-4690-6); paper $6.65 (978-0-7910-4691-3). This biography of Coretta Scott King describes her childhood, education, marriage, participation in the civil rights movement, and her work since her husband's assassination. (Rev: BL 8/98; HBG 10/98; SLJ 8/98) [323.092]

6008 Rhodes, Lisa Renee. *Coretta Scott King: Civil Rights Activist* (7–12). Illus. Series: Black Americans of Achievement. 2005, Chelsea House LB $30.00 (978-0-7910-8251-5). This revised edition of King's life adds new photographs and information

boxes to the description of her childhood, education, marriage, participation in the civil rights movement, and work after her husband's assassination. (Rev: SLJ 11/05) [921]

6009 Schraff, Anne. *Coretta Scott King: Striving for Civil Rights* (7–12). Series: African-American Biographies. 1997, Enslow LB $26.60 (978-0-89490-811-8). The life story of the gallant woman who has, with her family, continued the struggle for civil rights begun by her husband. (Rev: BL 6/1–15/97) [921]

KING, MARTIN LUTHER, JR.

6010 Bolden, Tonya. *M. L. K: Journey of a King* (7–10). Illus. 2007, Abrams $19.95 (978-0-8109-5476-2). An inspiring biography of the civil rights leader that emphasizes his influences and legacy. (Rev: BCCB 3/07; BL 2/1/07; LMC 8–9/07; SLJ 2/07*) [921]

6011 Darby, Jean. *Martin Luther King, Jr.* (4–8). Illus. Series: Lerner Biographies. 1990, Lerner LB $27.93 (978-0-8225-4902-4). An in-depth look at King's life and the civil rights movement. (Rev: BL 7/90; SLJ 11/90) [921]

6012 Haskins, Jim. *I Have a Dream: The Life and Words of Martin Luther King, Jr.* (6–12). 1993, Millbrook LB $29.90 (978-1-56294-087-4). Describes King's early life, family, and education, and the impact of the civil rights movement and beliefs that he espoused. (Rev: BL 2/15/93; SLJ 6/93*) [921]

6013 Jakoubek, Robert E. *Martin Luther King, Jr.* (6–9). Illus. 1989, Chelsea LB $30.00 (978-1-55546-597-1). A stirring biography that also gives a good history of the nonviolent civil rights movement. (Rev: BL 12/15/89; SLJ 3/90; VOYA 2/90) [921]

6014 January, Brendan. *Martin Luther King Jr.: Minister and Civil Rights Activist* (4–8). Series: Ferguson Career Biographies. 2001, Ferguson LB $25.00 (978-0-89434-342-1). This concise account focuses on King's career as a minister as well as his work as an advocate of civil rights and includes a section on training for the ministry. (Rev: SLJ 4/01) [921]

6015 Lambert, Kathy K. *Martin Luther King, Jr.* (4–7). Illus. Series: Junior World Biography. 1992, Chelsea LB $12.00 (978-0-7910-1759-3). A well-designed biography using many photographs to recreate the life of the great civil rights leader. (Rev: BL 11/1/92) [921]

6016 Pastan, Amy. *Martin Luther King, Jr.* (5–10). Illus. Series: DK Biography. 2004, DK LB $14.99 (978-0-7566-0491-2); paper $4.99 (978-0-7566-0342-7). A heavily illustrated, attractive biography of King that offers broad historical background. (Rev: BL 6/1–15/04) [921]

6017 Schuman, Michael A. *Martin Luther King, Jr.: Leader for Civil Rights* (5–8). Series: African-American Biographies. 1996, Enslow LB $26.60 (978-0-89490-687-9). A straightforward biography that covers the important events in King's life. (Rev: SLJ 12/96) [921]

LADUKE, WINONA

6018 Silverstone, Michael. *Winona LaDuke: Restoring Land and Culture in Native America* (5–8). Series: Women Changing the World. 2001, Feminist $19.95 (978-1-55861-260-0). A candidate for the vice presidency under Ralph Nader in 2000, this author and environmental and Native American rights activist lives on a reservation in Minnesota, where she is dedicated to restoring the land and the culture. (Rev: BL 12/15/01; HBG 10/02) [921]

LYON, MARITCHA REYMOND

6019 Bolden, Tonya. *Maritcha: A Nineteenth-Century American Girl* (4–7). Illus. 2005, Abrams $17.95 (978-0-8109-5045-0). Drawing on primary sources, Bolden tells the story of Maritcha Remond Lyon, a free black girl who succeeded in her fight to attend an all-white high school in Rhode Island in the mid-19th century. Coretta Scott King Illustrator Award and Author Honor Book, 2006. (Rev: BL 2/1/05*; SLJ 2/05) [921]

LYON, MARY

6020 Rosen, Dorothy S. *A Fire in Her Bones: The Story of Mary Lyon* (5–7). Illus. 1995, Carolrhoda LB $30.35 (978-0-87614-840-2). A biography of the woman who defied social barriers and founded Mount Holyoke Female Seminary, now known as Mount Holyoke College. (Rev: BL 6/1–15/95; SLJ 4/95) [921]

MALCOLM X

6021 Benson, Michael. *Malcolm X* (5–8). Series: Biography. 2001, Lerner LB $27.93 (978-0-8225-5025-9). An accessible text and many photographs are used to enliven this biography of the African American civil rights leader who was assassinated in 1965. (Rev: BL 4/1/02; HBG 3/02; SLJ 3/02) [921]

6022 Diamond, Arthur. *Malcolm X: A Voice for Black America* (6–12). Illus. Series: People to Know. 1994, Enslow $18.95 (978-0-89490-453-0). A sympathetic but unbiased account of the man, once a convict, who became an important African American leader. (Rev: BL 6/1–15/94) [921]

6023 Malcolm X, and Alex Haley. *The Autobiography of Malcolm X* (7–12). 1999, Ballantine $20.00 (978-0-345-91536-8); paper $12.00 (978-0-345-91503-0). The story of the man who turned from Harlem drug pusher into a charismatic leader of his people. [921]

6024 Rummel, Jack. *Malcolm X* (6–9). Illus. 1989, Chelsea LB $30.00 (978-1-55546-600-8). A heavily illustrated portrait of the African American leader and the movement for civil rights for his people. (Rev: BL 5/15/89; SLJ 6/89; VOYA 8/89) [921]

PARKS, ROSA

6025 Davis, Kenneth C. *Don't Know Much About Rosa Parks* (4–7). Illus. by Sergio Martinez. Series: Don't Know Much About. 2005, HarperCollins paper $4.99 (978-0-06-442126-3). A question-and-answer format, interesting sidebars, and news photographs enliven this profile of Parks, which emphasizes her long-term commitment to civil rights. (Rev: BL 2/1/05) [323]

6026 Hull, Mary. *Rosa Parks* (7–10). Illus. Series: Black Americans of Achievement. 1994, Chelsea LB $21.95 (978-0-7910-1881-1). The story of the seemingly ordinary African American woman who had the courage to fight bus segregation in Montgomery, Alabama. (Rev: BL 6/1–15/94; SLJ 8/94; VOYA 8/94) [921]

6027 Parks, Rosa, and Jim Haskins. *Rosa Parks: My Story* (6–10). 1992, Dial $17.99 (978-0-8037-0673-6). This autobiography of the civil rights hero becomes an oral history of the movement, including her recollections of Martin Luther King, Jr., Roy Wilkins, and others. (Rev: BL 12/15/91; SLJ 2/92) [921]

6028 Schraff, Anne. *Rosa Parks: "Tired of Giving In"* (4–8). Series: African-American Biography Library. 2005, Enslow LB $31.93 (978-0-7660-2463-2). An accessible profile of Parks and her importance. (Rev: SLJ 10/05) [921]

6029 Siegel, Beatrice. *The Year They Walked: Rosa Parks and the Montgomery Bus Boycott* (6–8). 1992, Four Winds $16.00 (978-0-02-782631-9). The story behind the historic bus boycott and the committed work of African Americans and whites who made it a success. (Rev: BL 2/15/92; SLJ 8/92) [921]

RANDOLPH, A. PHILIP

6030 Hanley, Sally. *A. Philip Randolph* (5–9). 1988, Chelsea LB $19.95 (978-1-55546-607-7); paper $8.95 (978-0-7910-0222-3). A life of the African American labor leader who founded the Brotherhood of Sleeping Car Porters. (Rev: BL 10/1/88; VOYA 2/89) [921]

6031 Miller, Calvin Craig. *A. Philip Randolph and the African-American Labor Movement* (7–10). Illus. Series: Civil Rights Leaders. 2005, Morgan Reynolds $26.95 (978-1-931798-50-1). The life and achievements of the founding president of the

Brotherhood of Sleeping Car Porters. (Rev: BL 2/15/05; SLJ 5/05) [323]

RUSTIN, BAYARD

6032 Brimner, Larry Dane. *We Are One: The Story of Bayard Rustin* (5–8). Illus. 2007, Boyds Mills $17.95 (978-1-59078-498-3). With lively text, photographs, quotations, and song lyrics, Brimner explains Bayard Rustin's importance in the struggle for civil rights. (Rev: BL 9/1/07; SLJ 11/07) [921]

6033 Miller, Calvin Craig. *No Easy Answers: Bayard Rustin and the Civil Rights Movement* (7–10). Illus. Series: Civil Rights Leaders. 2005, Morgan Reynolds LB $26.95 (978-1-931798-43-3). Rustin's significant achievements in the field of civil rights are discussed along with his homosexuality, which was a large factor in his relative obscurity. (Rev: BL 2/1/05; SLJ 6/05; VOYA 8/05) [323]

SHABAZZ, BETTY

6034 Jeffrey, Laura S. *Betty Shabazz: Sharing the Vision of Malcolm X* (6–10). Series: African-American Biographies. 2000, Enslow LB $26.60 (978-0-7660-1210-3). The wife of Malcolm X was only 31 years old when her husband was assassinated and she was left to raise six children and continue his fight for civil rights. (Rev: BL 9/15/00; HBG 3/01; SLJ 1/01) [921]

STANTON, ELIZABETH CADY

6035 Bohannon, Lisa Frederiksen. *Women's Rights and Nothing Less: The Story of Elizabeth Cady Stanton* (6–12). Illus. 2000, Morgan Reynolds LB $23.95 (978-1-883846-66-4). An engrossing biography of this great fighter for human rights and her relations with such people as Susan B. Anthony and Frederick Douglass. (Rev: BL 12/15/00; HBG 3/01; SLJ 12/00) [921]

6036 Fritz, Jean. *You Want Women to Vote, Lizzie Stanton?* (4–7). Illus. 1995, Putnam $18.99 (978-0-399-22786-8). An exciting, witty re-creation of the life of Elizabeth Cady Stanton, fighter for women's rights, including suffrage. (Rev: BCCB 10/95; BL 8/95*; SLJ 9/95*) [921]

6037 Loos, Pamela. *Elizabeth Cady Stanton* (5–8). Illus. Series: Women of Achievement. 2000, Chelsea $30.00 (978-0-7910-5293-8). Drawing largely on Stanton's autobiography, this is the life story of the well-known suffragist of the 19th century. (Rev: BL 2/15/01; HBG 10/01) [921]

6038 Salisbury, Cynthia. *Elizabeth Cady Stanton: Leader of the Fight for Women's Rights* (5–8). Series: Historical American Biographies. 2002, Enslow LB $26.60 (978-0-7660-1616-3). The life of the fighter for women's suffrage and the organizer

of the first women's rights convention. (Rev: BL 4/1/02; HBG 10/02; SLJ 5/02) [921]

6039 Sigerman, Harriet. *Elizabeth Cady Stanton: The Right Is Ours* (6–10). Illus. Series: Oxford Portraits. 2001, Oxford $32.95 (978-0-19-511969-5). The life of the pioneering suffragist, accompanied by photographs and historic documents such as newspaper articles and cartoons. (Rev: BL 12/15/01; HBG 3/02; SLJ 11/01; VOYA 2/02) [921]

STEINEM, GLORIA

6040 Daffron, Carolyn. *Gloria Steinem* (7–12). Illus. 1988, Chelsea LB $19.95 (978-1-55546-679-4). The story of the influential feminist leader who founded *Ms.* magazine. (Rev: BL 11/1/87; VOYA 2/89) [921]

6041 Hoff, Mark. *Gloria Steinem: The Women's Movement* (6–12). Series: New Directions. 1991, Millbrook LB $21.90 (978-1-878841-19-3). A biography of the famous feminist. (Rev: BL 2/1/91) [921]

6042 Lazo, Caroline. *Gloria Steinem: Feminist Extraordinaire* (5–7). Illus. Series: Lerner Biographies. 1998, Lerner LB $27.93 (978-0-8225-4934-5). The story of Steinem, who overcame a troubled childhood to become a great humanitarian, writer, and leader of the feminist movement. (Rev: BL 7/98; SLJ 7/98) [921]

6043 Wheaton, Elizabeth. *Ms: The Story of Gloria Steinem* (6–9). Illus. Series: Feminist Voices. 2002, Morgan Reynolds LB $23.95 (978-1-883846-82-4). A very readable account of Steinem's life that gives a clear portrait of her character as well as her many accomplishments. (Rev: BL 3/1/02; HBG 10/02; SLJ 6/02; VOYA 2/03) [305.42]

TERRELL, MARY CHURCH

6044 Fradin, Dennis Brindell, and Judith Bloom Fradin. *Fight On! Mary Church Terrell's Battle for Integration* (5–9). Illus. 2003, Clarion $18.00 (978-0-618-13349-9). Terrell's efforts to end discrimination are detailed in a readable, large-format biography that includes primary sources and lots of illustrations. (Rev: BL 6/1–15/03; HB 7–8/03; HBG 10/03; SLJ 5/03*; VOYA 6/03) [323]

6045 Lommel, Cookie. *Mary Church Terrell: Speaking Out for Civil Rights* (4–7). Series: African-American Biographies. 2003, Enslow LB $26.60 (978-0-7660-2116-7). This interesting account of Terrell's life and her passion for education and activism contains many black-and-white photographs. (Rev: HBG 4/04; SLJ 10/03) [323]

TRUTH, SOJOURNER

6046 Bernard, Catherine. *Sojourner Truth: Abolitionist and Women's Rights Activist* (5–8). Series: Historical American Biographies. 2001, Enslow LB $26.60 (978-0-7660-1257-8). The life story of the freed slave who traveled throughout the North preaching emancipation and women's rights before the Civil War. (Rev: BL 4/15/01; HBG 10/01) [921]

6047 Brezina, Corona. *Sojourner Truth's "Ain't I a Woman?" Speech: A Primary Source Investigation* (6–9). Illus. Series: Great Historic Debates and Speeches. 2005, Rosen LB $29.25 (978-1-4042-0154-5). A fascinating account of Truth's historic 1851 speech to the Women's Convention in Akron, Ohio; the primary sources offer insight into the words of a woman who could neither read nor write. (Rev: BL 2/15/05; SLJ 5/05) [306.3]

6048 Butler, Mary G. *Sojourner Truth: From Slave to Activist for Freedom* (4–8). Series: Library of American Lives and Times. 2003, Rosen LB $34.60 (978-0-8239-5736-1). A forerunner of the modern civil rights movement, Sojourner Truth rose from slavery to become a crusader for good race relations and women's rights. (Rev: BL 6/1–15/03; SLJ 5/03; VOYA 6/03) [921]

6049 Krass, Peter. *Sojourner Truth* (7–12). Illus. 1988, Chelsea LB $30.00 (978-1-55546-611-4). The life of a woman who began as a slave and ended as a respected abolitionist and feminist. (Rev: BL 10/1/88) [921]

6050 Rockwell, Anne. *Only Passing Through* (4–8). Illus. 2000, Knopf $16.95 (978-0-679-89186-4). A moving picture-book biography of Sojourner Truth, who was a pioneer in the struggle for racial equality and devoted her life to the abolitionist movement. (Rev: BCCB 1/01; BL 11/15/00; HB 11–12/00; HBG 3/01; SLJ 12/00) [921]

TUBMAN, HARRIET

6051 Bradford, Sarah. *Harriet Tubman, the Moses of Her People* (7–12). Illus. 1961, Peter Smith $18.75 (978-0-8446-1717-6). A biography first published in 1869 of this former slave who brought hundreds of slaves north to freedom. [921]

6052 Burns, Bree. *Harriet Tubman* (4–7). Illus. Series: Junior World Biography. 1992, Chelsea LB $12.00 (978-0-7910-1751-7). This is a straightforward account of the escaped slave who helped free more than 300 slaves via the Underground Railroad. (Rev: BL 10/1/92; SLJ 12/92) [921]

6053 Schraff, Anne. *Harriet Tubman: Moses of the Underground Railroad* (4–8). Series: African-American Biographies. 2001, Enslow LB $26.60 (978-0-7660-1548-7). This is an absorbing account of the life of the Underground Railroad leader that

covers her work as a nurse, a scout, and a spy. (Rev: HBG 3/02; SLJ 10/01) [921]

6054 Taylor, M. W. *Harriet Tubman* (5–8). Illus. Series: Black Americans of Achievement. 1990, Chelsea LB $30.00 (978-1-55546-612-1). The story of the famous conductor on the Underground Railroad. (Rev: SLJ 1/91) [921]

TURNER, NAT

6055 Bisson, Terry. *Nat Turner: Slave Revolt Leader* (6–9). Illus. Series: Black Americans of Achievement. 2004, Chelsea House LB $30.00 (978-0-7910-8167-9). New illustrations, essays on related figures, and a list of Web sites enhance this new edition of a profile of Nat Turner, who led a bloody Virginia slave uprising in 1831. (Rev: BL 2/1/05) [975.5]

6056 Edwards, Judith. *Nat Turner's Slave Rebellion* (7–12). Illus. Series: In American History. 2000, Enslow LB $26.60 (978-0-7660-1302-5). After some general material on slavery and other slave rebellions, this account stresses the life of Nat Turner and the consequences of his belief that he was sent by God to free the slaves. (Rev: BL 2/15/00; HBG 9/00; SLJ 7/00) [921]

6057 Hendrickson, Ann-Marie. *Nat Turner: Rebel Slave* (4–7). Illus. Series: Junior World Biography. 1995, Chelsea LB $18.65 (978-0-7910-2386-0). An attractive biography of this slave who led a revolution and became a symbol of heroism for his people. (Rev: BL 10/15/95) [921]

VESEY, DENMARK

6058 Edwards, Lillie J. *Denmark Vesey: Slave Revolt Leader* (6–9). Illus. 1990, Chelsea LB $19.95 (978-1-55546-614-5). The story of the slave who bought his freedom and was later hanged for plotting a slave rebellion. (Rev: BL 7/90; SLJ 7/90) [921]

WASHINGTON, BOOKER T.

6059 Washington, Booker T. *Up from Slavery: An Autobiography by Booker T. Washington* (7–12). Illus. 1963, Airmont paper $3.95 (978-0-8049-0157-4). The story of the slave who later organized the Tuskegee Institute. [921]

WELLS, IDA B.

6060 Fradin, Dennis Brindell, and Judith B. Fradin. *Ida B. Wells: Mother of the Civil Rights Movement* (5–10). 2000, Clarion $19.00 (978-0-395-89898-7). An inspiring biography of the African American who was born a slave and went on to become a school teacher, journalist, and an activist who fought for black women's right to vote and helped found the NAACP. (Rev: BL 2/15/00; HB 5–6/00; HBG 10/00; SLJ 4/00*) [921]

6061 Schraff, Anne. *Ida B. Wells-Barnett: "Strike a Blow against a Glaring Evil"* (6–9). Illus. Series: African-American Biography Library. 2008, Enslow LB $23.95 (978-0-7660-2704-6). This book about the journalist and activist will give readers a glimpse into the days before civil rights were granted to all and what it took to achieve those rights. (Rev: BL 2/1/08) [921]

6062 Welch, Catherine A. *Ida B. Wells-Barnett: Powerhouse with a Pen* (5–8). Illus. Series: Trailblazer Biographies. 2000, Carolrhoda LB $30.35 (978-1-57505-352-3). This book introduces Wells-Barnett, who was born a slave and became a powerful journalist and activist as well as a spokesperson for all African Americans. (Rev: BL 6/1–15/00; HBG 10/00; SLJ 7/00; VOYA 2/01) [921]

WOODHULL, VICTORIA

6063 Brody, Miriam. *Victoria Woodhull: Free Spirit for Women's Rights* (7–12). Series: Oxford Portraits. 2004, Oxford LB $32.95 (978-0-19-514367-6). Presenting historical and social context, this biography covers the American reformer's difficult childhood and complex adult life. (Rev: SLJ 2/05) [921]

6064 Havelin, Kate. *Victoria Woodhull: Fearless Feminist* (7–10). Series: Trailblazer Biographies. 2006, Twenty-First Century LB $30.60 (978-0-8225-5986-3). A concise, well-researched biography of the ardent suffragist who ran for U.S. president in 1872. (Rev: SLJ 11/06) [921]

6065 McLean, Jacqueline. *Victoria Woodhull: First Woman Presidential Candidate* (7–12). 1999, Morgan Reynolds LB $23.95 (978-1-883846-47-3). The fascinating story of Victoria Woodhull, an ardent suffragist and feminist who was nominated by the Equal Rights Party in 1872 as its presidential candidate. (Rev: BL 8/99; HBG 4/00; SLJ 10/99; VOYA 12/99) [921]

Presidents and Their Families

ADAMS, ABIGAIL

6066 Ching, Jacqueline. *Abigail Adams: A Revolutionary Woman* (4–7). Series: Library of American Lives and Times. 2001, Rosen $34.60 (978-0-8239-5723-1). This biography of Abigail Adams stresses the fact that her husband, John Adams, relied heavily on her advice and that her vision of equality and justice inspired the early consideration of women's rights. (Rev: BCCB 4/01; BL 10/15/01) [921]

6067 Davis, Kate. *Abigail Adams* (6–8). Series: Triangle Histories of the Revolutionary War: Leaders. 2003, Gale LB $28.70 (978-1-56711-610-6). The life and times of the influential wife of President John Adams and mother of President John Quincy Adams. (Rev: LMC 8–9/03; SLJ 5/03) [973.4]

6068 McCarthy, Pat. *Abigail Adams: First Lady and Patriot* (5–8). Series: Historical American Biographies. 2002, Enslow LB $26.60 (978-0-7660-1618-7). The life story of the prolific letter-writer who was wife of the second president of the United States, John Adams. (Rev: BCCB 4/01; BL 4/1/02; HBG 10/02; SLJ 7/02) [921]

6069 Osborne, Angela. *Abigail Adams* (6–10). Illus. 1988, Chelsea LB $19.95 (978-1-55546-635-0). The life of the early feminist who was a strong influence on her husband John and a fine recorder of American history. (Rev: BL 12/1/88; SLJ 1/89) [921]

ADAMS, JOHN

6070 Behrman, Carol H. *John Adams* (5–8). Illus. Series: Presidential Leaders. 2003, Lerner LB $29.27 (978-0-8225-0820-5). This biography provides lots of details and illustrations, covering Adams's life and career. (Rev: BL 1/1–15/04) [973.4]

6071 Feinberg, Barbara S. *John Adams* (5–8). Illus. Series: Encyclopedia of Presidents. 2003, Children's Pr. LB $34.00 (978-0-516-22680-4). An informative and appealing account of Adams's life and achievements, with glossary, timeline, and lists of books and Web sites. (Rev: BL 1/1–15/04) [973.4]

6072 Feinstein, Stephen. *John Adams* (5–9). 2002, Enslow LB $25.26 (978-0-7660-5001-3). A well-written and accessible overview of Adams's life and contributions that is extended by a number of recommended Web sites. (Rev: SLJ 6/02) [921]

6073 Lukes, Bonnie L. *John Adams: Public Servant* (8–12). Illus. Series: Notable Americans. 2000, Morgan Reynolds LB $23.95 (978-1-883846-80-0). An excellent biography of the second president of the United States that reveals both his virtues and his flaws. (Rev: BL 12/1/00; HBG 3/01; SLJ 2/01) [921]

6074 Yoder, Carolyn P., ed. *John Adams The Writer: A Treasury of Letters, Diaries, and Public Documents* (7–10). Illus. 2007, Boyds Mills $16.95 (978-1-59078-247-7). Selected writings of the second president of the United States are drawn from speeches, diaries, letters, and other sources, providing a full picture of this important figure from his own words. (Rev: BL 12/1/07; LMC 1/08; SLJ 4/08) [793.4]

ADAMS, JOHN AND ABIGAIL

6075 Ashby, Ruth. *John and Abigail Adams* (5–8). Illus. Series: Presidents and First Ladies. 2005, Gareth Stevens LB $31.00 (978-0-8368-5755-9). An accessible, balanced, and attractive discussion of the Adamses and the contributions each made to their joint lives. (Rev: BL 3/1/05) [921]

6076 St. George, Judith. *John and Abigail Adams: An American Love Story* (6–9). Illus. 2001, Holiday $22.95 (978-0-8234-1571-7). This story of the Adamses' partnership, drawing extensively on their letters to each other, will be useful for report writers. (Rev: BL 11/1/01; HB 1–2/02; HBG 3/02; SLJ 12/01; VOYA 2/02) [973.4]

ADAMS, JOHN QUINCY

6077 Feinstein, Stephen. *John Quincy Adams* (5–9). 2002, Enslow LB $25.26 (978-0-7660-5002-0). Adams's early and later life are covered in this concise biography that includes several pages of annotated Web site recommendations. (Rev: HBG 10/02; SLJ 10/02) [921]

ARTHUR, CHESTER A.

6078 Young, Jeff C. *Chester A. Arthur* (4–7). Series: Presidents. 2002, Enslow LB $25.26 (978-0-7660-5077-8). As well as an overview of the life and accomplishments of Chester A. Arthur, this book gives a pre-evaluated listing of Web sites where more material can be found. (Rev: BL 12/15/02) [921]

BUCHANAN, JAMES

6079 Young, Jeff C. *James Buchanan* (4–7). Series: Presidents. 2003, Enslow LB $25.26 (978-0-7660-5101-0). The story of the fifteenth president who had an extensive political career before becoming president. (Rev: BL 6/1–15/03; HBG 10/03) [921]

BUSH, GEORGE H. W.

6080 Anderson, Ken. *George Bush: A Lifetime of Service* (6–12). Illus. 2003, Eakin $16.95 (978-1-57168-663-3); paper $12.95 (978-1-57168-600-8). George Herbert Walker Bush, the 41st president, is profiled in this biography that gives insights into his relationship with his son, George W. Bush. (Rev: BL 1/1–15/03; HBG 10/03; SLJ 2/03) [921]

6081 Pemberton, William E. *George Bush* (6–12). Series: World Leaders. 1993, Rourke LB $25.27 (978-0-86625-478-6). A biography of the former president and an assessment of his accomplishments in office. (Rev: BL 12/1/93) [921]

6082 Schuman, Michael A. *George H. W. Bush* (6–12). Illus. Series: United States Presidents. 2002, Enslow LB $26.60 (978-0-7660-1702-3). Bush's youth, family, education, career, and presidency are all covered here, as is his role raising children with strong political agendas. (Rev: BL 3/1/03; HBG 10/03) [921]

BUSH, GEORGE W.

6083 Jones, Veda Boyd. *George W. Bush* (5–8). Illus. Series: Modern World Leaders. 2006, Chelsea House $30.00 (978-0-7910-9217-0). This biography traces Bush's life and political career from his 1946 birth in New Haven, Connecticut, through the first five years of his presidency. (Rev: BL 10/15/06) [973.9]

6084 Kachurek, Sandra J. *George W. Bush* (4–7). Series: United States Presidents. 2004, Enslow LB $26.60 (978-0-7660-2040-5). A balanced and well-documented profile with plenty of photographs plus lists of Web sites and places to visit. (Rev: BL 9/15/04) [921]

6085 McNeese, Tim. *George W. Bush: First President of the New Century* (6–10). Series: Notable Americans. 2001, Morgan Reynolds LB $21.95 (978-1-883846-85-5). This biography of the former Texas governor covers his life from childhood and gives details of the controversial 2000 presidential election. (Rev: HBG 3/02; SLJ 4/02) [921]

6086 Marquez, Heron. *George W. Bush* (5–8). Illus. Series: Presidential Leaders. 2006, Lerner LB $29.27 (978-0-8225-1507-4). A balanced profile that examines Bush's childhood and adolescence as well as his accomplishments and the controversies surrounding some of his decisions. (Rev: BL 10/15/06) [921]

6087 Thompson, Bill, and Dorcas Thompson. *George W. Bush* (4–8). Illus. Series: Childhoods of the Presidents. 2003, Mason Crest $17.95 (978-1-59084-281-2). Bush's privileged childhood and education, his role as eldest son, and the death of his sister from leukemia are covered in an interesting narrative that highlights his character. (Rev: BL 6/1–15/03; SLJ 2/03) [973.931]

6088 Wheeler, Jill C. *George W. Bush* (4–7). Series: War on Terrorism. 2002, ABDO LB $25.65 (978-1-57765-662-3). A brief profile of President Bush with particular emphasis on his war on terrorism. (Rev: BL 5/15/02; HBG 10/02) [921]

6089 Wukovits, John F. *George W. Bush* (5–8). Series: People in the News. 2000, Lucent LB $32.45 (978-1-56006-693-4). Published before the 2000 election, this biography uses extensive quotations from Mr. Bush, his friends, and critics. (Rev: BL 9/15/00; HBG 3/01; SLJ 10/00) [921]

BUSH, LAURA WELCH

6090 Gormley, Beatrice. *Laura Bush: America's First Lady* (5–8). Illus. 2003, Simon & Schuster paper $4.99 (978-0-689-85366-1). A chronological account of Laura Bush's life, with information on her childhood as well as her later public life. (Rev: BL 3/1/03; HBG 10/03; SLJ 5/03) [973.931]

CARTER, JIMMY

6091 Kent, Deborah. *Jimmy Carter* (4–7). Illus. Series: Encyclopedia of Presidents — Second Series. 2005, Children's Pr. LB $34.00 (978-0-516-22975-1). Updated from the 1989 volume, this new, redesigned edition covers the former president's life and career and adds information about his recent work. (Rev: BL 6/1–15/05) [973.926]

6092 O'Shei, Tim. *Jimmy Carter* (5–9). 2002, Enslow LB $25.26 (978-0-7660-5051-8). This introduction to Carter's life, including his childhood, and his contributions contains a long list of recommended Web sites that extend the printed material. (Rev: HBG 10/02; SLJ 6/02) [921]

6093 Richman, Daniel A. *James E. Carter* (5–8). Series: Presidents of the United States. 1989, GEC LB $21.27 (978-0-944483-24-4). The story of this former U.S. president, his political career, family, and present charitable activities. (Rev: SLJ 9/89) [921]

6094 Santella, Andrew. *James Earl Carter Jr.* (4–7). Series: Profiles of the Presidents. 2002, Compass Point LB $26.60 (978-0-7565-0283-6). A straightforward profile that touches on Carter's southern roots, his successes and failures as president, and his subsequent work in the fields of human rights and democracy. (Rev: SLJ 1/03) [921]

6095 Slavin, Ed. *Jimmy Carter* (4–8). Illus. 1989, Chelsea LB $19.95 (978-1-55546-828-6). Introducing the 39th president of the United States. (Rev: BL 7/89) [921]

6096 Smith, Betsy. *Jimmy Carter, President* (5–7). Illus. 1986, Walker LB $13.85 (978-0-8027-6652-6). A profile of Jimmy Carter and his one-term presidency. (Rev: BL 2/15/87; SLJ 12/86) [921]

6097 Whitelaw, Nancy. *Jimmy Carter: President and Peacemaker* (7–10). Illus. 2003, Morgan Reynolds LB $23.95 (978-1-931798-18-1). From childhood in rural Georgia to his current work for charities and international peace, this is the story of the 39th president. (Rev: BL 12/15/03; HBG 4/04; VOYA 12/03) [921]

CLEVELAND, GROVER

6098 Collins, David R. *Grover Cleveland: 22nd and 24th President of the United States* (7–9). Illus. 1988, Garrett LB $21.27 (978-0-944483-01-5). A fine introduction to this president and his career, with interesting sidebar features. (Rev: SLJ 9/88) [921]

CLINTON, BILL

6099 Cole, Michael D. *Bill Clinton: United States President* (6–9). 1994, Enslow LB $20.95 (978-0-89490-437-0). Surveys Clinton's life and accomplishments prior to his presidential election, emphasizing his tenure as governor of Arkansas. (Rev: BL 7/94; SLJ 7/94) [921]

6100 Cwiklik, Robert. *Bill Clinton: President of the 90's*. Rev. ed. (4–8). Series: Gateway Biographies. 1997, Millbrook $22.90 (978-0-7613-0129-5); paper $8.95 (978-0-7613-0146-2). A readable biography that concentrates on Clinton's career as governor of Arkansas and his early years as president. (Rev: BL 9/15/97; SLJ 7/97) [921]

6101 Heinrichs, Ann. *William Jefferson Clinton* (4–8). Series: Profiles of the Presidents. 2002, Compass Point LB $26.60 (978-0-7565-0207-2). This absorbing account of Clinton's life and career covers both the good and bad sides of his presidency and includes a discussion of Hillary's role. (Rev: SLJ 6/02) [921]

6102 Kelly, Michael. *Bill Clinton* (6–10). Series: Overcoming Adversity. 1998, Chelsea LB $30.00 (978-0-7910-4700-2). This book describes Bill Clinton's difficult childhood but focuses on his political career, emphasizing the important role Hillary Rodham Clinton has played in his success, with a good balance between coverage of Clinton's achievements and problems. (Rev: HBG 3/99; SLJ 2/99) [921]

6103 Marcovitz, Hal. *Bill Clinton* (4–8). Illus. Series: Childhoods of the Presidents. 2003, Mason Crest LB $17.95 (978-1-59084-273-7). This brief, well-illustrated overview of Clinton's childhood and adolescence looks in particular at his relationships with family members, his support for civil rights, and his popularity. (Rev: BL 6/1–15/03; SLJ 2/03) [973.929]

COOLIDGE, CALVIN

6104 Allen, Michael Geoffrey. *Calvin Coolidge* (6–12). Illus. Series: United States Presidents. 2002, Enslow LB $26.60 (978-0-7660-1703-0). Coolidge's youth, family, education, career, and presidency are all covered here, as are his character and his legacy. (Rev: BL 3/1/03; HBG 3/03; SLJ 2/03) [921]

EISENHOWER, DWIGHT D.

6105 Darby, Jean. *Dwight D. Eisenhower: A Man Called Ike* (6–9). Illus. Series: Lerner Biographies. 1989, Lerner LB $30.35 (978-0-8225-4900-0). An easily read account of the highlights in the life of this general and president. (Rev: BL 11/15/89; SLJ 9/89) [921]

6106 Deitch, Kenneth, and Joanne B. Weisman. *Dwight D. Eisenhower: Man of Many Hats* (5–7).

Illus. by Jay Connolly. 1990, Discovery LB $14.95 (978-1-878668-02-8). Each stage of Eisenhower's multifaceted career is represented. (Rev: SLJ 2/91) [921]

6107 Raatma, Lucia. *Dwight D. Eisenhower* (4–7). Series: Profiles of the Presidents. 2002, Compass Point LB $26.60 (978-0-7565-0279-9). A straightforward account that focuses on Eisenhower's military career and successes in World War II. (Rev: SLJ 1/03) [921]

6108 Sandberg, Peter Lars. *Dwight D. Eisenhower* (7–12). Illus. 1986, Chelsea LB $19.95 (978-0-87754-521-7). A brief biography of the president and war leader that emphasizes his human side. (Rev: SLJ 11/86) [921]

6109 Van Steenwyk, Elizabeth. *Dwight David Eisenhower, President* (5–8). Illus. 1987, Walker LB $13.85 (978-0-8027-6671-7). The focus is on the career of this war-hero president. (Rev: BL 5/15/87) [921]

6110 Young, Jeff C. *Dwight D. Eisenhower: Soldier and President* (6–12). Illus. 2001, Morgan Reynolds LB $23.95 (978-1-883846-76-3). This well-written and interesting biography of the 34th president covers his life from boyhood, his career, and his personality. (Rev: BL 11/15/01; HBG 3/02; SLJ 2/02) [921]

FILLMORE, MILLARD

6111 Gottfried, Ted. *Millard Fillmore* (4–7). Series: Presidents and Their Times. 2007, Marshall Cavendish LB $22.95 (978-0-7614-2431-4). A clear and thorough life of the president, describing his early years, presidential career, and later life, with discussion of important events that took place during his life. (Rev: SLJ 1/08)

GARFIELD, JAMES A.

6112 Kingsbury, Robert. *The Assassination of James A. Garfield* (6–9). Series: The Library of Political Assassinations. 2002, Rosen LB $27.95 (978-0-8239-3540-6). The life and death of this lesser-known President are examined with material on the strange life of the assassin, Charles Guiteau. (Rev: BL 8/02) [921]

6113 Young, Jeff C. *James A. Garfield* (4–7). Series: Presidents. 2003, Enslow LB $25.26 (978-0-7660-5100-3). The story of the twentieth president of the U.S. who served as a major general during the Civil War and was assassinated while he was still in office. (Rev: BL 6/1–15/03) [921]

GORE, TIPPER

6114 Kramer, Barbara. *Tipper Gore* (4–7). Illus. Series: People to Know. 1999, Enslow LB $26.60

(978-0-7660-1142-7). The story of the life of the former vice president's wife and her activities as a mother, professional photographer, and social issues advocate. (Rev: BL 8/99) [921]

GRANT, ULYSSES S.

6115 Alter, Judy. *Ulysses S. Grant* (5–9). 2002, Enslow LB $25.26 (978-0-7660-5014-3). Grant's early and later life are covered in this concise and balanced biography that includes several pages of annotated Web site recommendations. (Rev: SLJ 10/02) [921]

6116 Rice, Earle, Jr. *Ulysses S. Grant: Defender of the Union* (8–11). Illus. Series: Civil War Leaders. 2005, Morgan Reynolds LB $26.95 (978-1-931798-48-8). A vivid portrait of Grant, who rose from humble beginnings in his native Ohio to achieve acclaim as a military leader and ascend to the highest office in the land. (Rev: BL 3/15/05; SLJ 11/05) [973.8]

6117 Sapp, Richard. *Ulysses S. Grant and the Road to Appomattox* (5–8). Series: In the Footsteps of American Heroes. 2006, World Almanac LB $34.00 (978-0-8368-6431-1). This life of Grant includes information on historical sites in sidebar features. (Rev: SLJ 9/06) [921]

HOOVER, HERBERT

6118 Hilton, Suzanne. *The World of Young Herbert Hoover* (4–8). Illus. 1987, Walker LB $13.85 (978-0-8027-6709-7). This brief biography takes Hoover through his college years and gives some indication of events to follow. (Rev: SLJ 1/88) [921]

6119 Holford, David M. *Herbert Hoover* (5–8). Series: United States Presidents. 1999, Enslow LB $26.60 (978-0-7660-1035-2). An insightful look at the president who was orphaned as a child and gained a reputation for being rigid and insensitive. (Rev: SLJ 1/00) [921]

6120 Ruth, Amy. *Herbert Hoover* (5–8). Series: Presidential Leaders. 2004, Lerner LB $29.27 (978-0-8225-0821-2). Quotations, photographs, and informative sidebars add to the engaging text about Hoover's life and times. (Rev: SLJ 1/05) [921]

HOOVER, LOU

6121 Colbert, Nancy A. *Lou Hoover: The Duty to Serve* (5–8). Illus. 1997, Morgan Reynolds LB $21.95 (978-1-883846-22-0). President Hoover's wife was a most interesting person, who, among other accomplishments, was the first woman to get a degree in geology in this country, was the translator — with her husband — of a 16th-century Latin mining text, was an advocate of physical education for women, and was fluent in seven languages, including Chinese. (Rev: BL 2/15/98; HBG 3/98; SLJ 3/98) [973.91]

JACKSON, ANDREW

6122 Behrman, Carol H. *Andrew Jackson* (5–8). Series: Presidential Leaders. 2002, Lerner LB $29.27 (978-0-8225-0093-3). Jackson's life and character are brought to life in this narrative that points out his failings as well as his achievements. (Rev: HBG 3/03; SLJ 1/03) [921]

6123 Feinstein, Stephen. *Andrew Jackson* (5–9). 2002, Enslow LB $25.26 (978-0-7660-5003-7). A well-written and accessible overview of Jackson's life and contributions that is extended by a number of recommended Web sites. (Rev: SLJ 6/02; VOYA 8/02) [921]

6124 Marrin, Albert. *Old Hickory: Andrew Jackson and the American People* (6–12). 2004, Penguin $35.00 (978-0-525-47293-3). The life and times of a colorful president are presented in a suitably vivid biography. (Rev: BL 12/1/04; SLJ 12/04; VOYA 6/05) [921]

6125 Whitelaw, Nancy. *Andrew Jackson: Frontier President* (7–10). Illus. Series: Notable Americans. 2000, Morgan Reynolds LB $23.95 (978-1-883846-67-1). A fine biography of an interesting, multifaceted man who overcame many obstacles to achieve prominence. (Rev: BL 11/1/00; HBG 3/01; SLJ 2/01) [921]

JEFFERSON, THOMAS

6126 Davis, Kenneth C. *Don't Know Much About Thomas Jefferson* (4–7). Illus. by Rob Shepperson. Series: Don't Know Much About. 2005, HarperTrophy paper $4.99 (978-0-06-442128-7). Jefferson's many accomplishments and contributions are presented in a question-and-answer format amplified by sidebar features, maps, and quotations that add context. (Rev: BL 2/1/05; SLJ 5/05) [921]

6127 Ferris, Jeri. *Thomas Jefferson: Father of Liberty* (5–8). 1998, Lerner LB $30.35 (978-1-57505-009-6). This readable biography covers both the public and the private sides of Jefferson's life, with details on his personality and his family. (Rev: BL 3/1/99; HBG 3/99; SLJ 12/98) [921]

6128 Harness, Cheryl. *Thomas Jefferson* (4–7). Illus. 2004, National Geographic $17.95 (978-0-7922-6496-5). Harness paints a personal portrait of Jefferson and his various roles in this picture book, enhanced by maps and eye-catching illustrations. (Rev: BL 2/1/04; SLJ 2/04) [973.4]

6129 Mullin, Rita Thievon. *Thomas Jefferson: Architect of Freedom* (7–10). Illus. Series: Sterling Biographies. 2007, Sterling paper $5.95 (978-1-4027-3397-0). Report writers will find a wealth of information on the president's prolific and remark-

able life, as well as drawings and photographs to enhance the text. (Rev: BL 4/1/07; SLJ 5/07) [973.4]

6130 Old, Wendie C. *Thomas Jefferson* (5–8). Series: United States Presidents. 1997, Enslow LB $26.60 (978-0-89490-837-8). An account of the life and career of the multifaceted Jefferson. (Rev: BL 2/1/98; HBG 3/98; SLJ 3/98) [921]

6131 Reiter, Chris. *Thomas Jefferson* (4–7). Illus. Series: MyReportLinks.com. 2002, Enslow LB $25.26 (978-0-7660-5071-6). A concise biography suitable for students doing reports that provides extensive Web links for further research and uses Web site images among the many illustrations. (Rev: BL 9/1/02; HBG 3/03) [973.4]

6132 Severance, John B. *Thomas Jefferson: Architect of Democracy* (7–12). 1998, Clarion $18.00 (978-0-395-84513-4). A thoughtful, well-rounded biography that focuses on Jefferson's accomplishments and his beliefs, with many quotations from his writings. (Rev: BL 9/1/98; HBG 3/99; SLJ 12/98; VOYA 4/99) [921]

6133 Whitelaw, Nancy. *Thomas Jefferson: Philosopher and President* (7–10). 2001, Morgan Reynolds LB $23.95 (978-1-883846-81-7). This concise and thorough biography, which covers Jefferson's strengths and weaknesses, will be useful for report writers. (Rev: HBG 3/02; SLJ 3/02) [921]

JOHNSON, ANDREW

6134 Alter, Judy. *Andrew Johnson* (5–8). 2002, Enslow LB $25.26 (978-0-7660-5007-5). This overview of Johnson's life and career contains a listing of about 30 Web sites that will extend the information contained in the book. (Rev: SLJ 6/02) [921]

6135 Stevens, Rita. *Andrew Johnson: 17th President of the United States* (5–7). Illus. 1989, Garrett LB $21.27 (978-0-944483-16-9). Story of the man who became president on Lincoln's assassination. (Rev: BL 5/1/89) [973.810924]

JOHNSON, LYNDON B.

6136 Colbert, Nancy A. *Great Society: The Story of Lyndon Baines Johnson* (4–8). Illus. 2002, Morgan Reynolds LB $23.95 (978-1-883846-84-8). A solid, readable life of the hardworking president that presents fairly both his virtues and defects. (Rev: BL 4/15/02; HBG 3/03; SLJ 8/02) [921]

6137 Falkof, Lucille. *Lyndon B. Johnson: 36th President of the United States* (5–8). Illus. 1989, Garrett LB $21.27 (978-0-944483-20-6). An informative biography that covers both the public and private life of this president. (Rev: BL 5/1/89; SLJ 8/89) [921]

6138 Kaye, Tony. *Lyndon B. Johnson* (6–10). Illus. 1987, Chelsea LB $19.95 (978-0-87754-536-1). A biography of the president associated with Great Society legislation and the Vietnam War. (Rev: BL 1/15/88; SLJ 4/88) [921]

6139 Levy, Debbie. *Lyndon B. Johnson* (5–9). Series: Presidential Leaders. 2003, Lerner LB $29.27 (978-0-8225-0097-1). A look at the fascinating personal and political life of the president known for his support for civil rights and for increasing the U.S. involvement in Vietnam. (Rev: HBG 10/03; SLJ 2/03) [921]

6140 Schuman, Michael A. *Lyndon B. Johnson* (6–10). Series: United States Presidents. 1998, Enslow LB $26.60 (978-0-89490-938-2). Johnson's public career, presidential administration, and legacy are the focus of this biography. (Rev: HBG 3/99; SLJ 3/99) [921]

KENNEDY FAMILY

6141 Uschan, Michael V. *The Kennedys* (7–12). 2001, Gale LB $28.70 (978-1-56006-875-4). The Kennedys presented here — with their achievements and their failings — are Joseph P.; his sons John, Robert, and Ted; and John's wife Jacqueline and son John Jr. (Rev: SLJ 1/02) [920]

KENNEDY, JOHN F.

6142 Anderson, Catherine Corley. *John F. Kennedy* (5–8). Series: Presidential Leaders. 2004, Lerner LB $29.27 (978-0-8225-0812-0). Quotations, photographs, and informative sidebars add to the engaging text about Kennedy's life and times. (Rev: SLJ 1/05) [921]

6143 Cole, Michael D. *John F. Kennedy: President of the New Frontier* (4–7). Illus. Series: People to Know. 1996, Enslow LB $20.95 (978-0-89490-693-0). A profile of the life and accomplishments of this charismatic president. (Rev: BL 5/15/96; SLJ 6/96) [921]

6144 Cooper, Ilene. *Jack: The Early Years of John F. Kennedy* (7–12). 2003, Dutton $22.99 (978-0-525-46923-0). Jack's youth and school years — in particular his rivalry with his older brother — are described in a narrative peppered with anecdotes and quotations from family and friends. (Rev: BCCB 2/03; BL 1/1–15/03; HB 3–4/03; HBG 10/03; SLJ 2/03; VOYA 4/03) [921]

6145 Falkof, Lucille. *John F. Kennedy: 35th President of the United States* (6–9). Illus. 1988, Garrett LB $21.27 (978-0-944483-03-9). As well as the life and career of this president, the author gives good background material on the issues and general events of the times. (Rev: SLJ 10/88) [921]

6146 Hodge, Marie. *John F. Kennedy: Voice of Hope* (5–8). Series: Sterling Biographies. 2007, Sterling $12.95 (978-1-4027-4749-6); paper $5.95 (978-1-4027-3232-4). This generally admiring, well-illustrated profile covers Kennedy's life from childhood. (Rev: SLJ 5/07) [921]

6147 Kaplan, Howard S. *John F. Kennedy* (5–10). Illus. Series: DK Biography. 2004, DK paper $4.99 (978-0-7566-0340-3). A heavily illustrated, attractive biography of Kennedy that offers broad historical background. (Rev: BL 6/1–15/04) [921]

6148 Randall, Marta. *John F. Kennedy* (6–10). Illus. 1987, Chelsea LB $19.95 (978-0-87754-586-6). A biography of this beloved president that includes coverage of domestic and international crises. (Rev: BL 1/15/88; VOYA 10/88) [921]

6149 Schultz, Randy. *John F. Kennedy* (4–7). Illus. Series: MyReportLinks.com. 2002, Enslow LB $25.26 (978-0-7660-5012-9). A basic, illustrated account of Kennedy's life and accomplishments that provides extensive Web links for students to do further research. (Rev: BL 9/1/02) [973.922]

6150 Spencer, Lauren. *The Assassination of John F. Kennedy* (6–10). Series: Library of Political Assassinations. 2001, Rosen LB $27.95 (978-0-8239-3541-3). This is a highly readable account of the assassination, its political buildup, and the social fallout. (Rev: BL 3/15/02; SLJ 6/02) [921]

6151 Swisher, Clarice, ed. *John F. Kennedy* (8–12). Illus. Series: People Who Made History. 1999, Greenhaven LB $32.45 (978-0-7377-0225-5); paper $21.20 (978-0-7377-0224-8). This collection of essays covers such topics as major influences on JFK, the presidential debates, the new frontier, foreign policy, and assessments of his presidency. (Rev: BL 2/1/00) [921]

6152 Uschan, Michael V. *John F. Kennedy* (6–10). Illus. 1998, Lucent LB $27.45 (978-1-56006-482-4). An objective account that uses quotations from many original sources, chronicling fairly and honestly Kennedy's rise to power, his triumphs, and his faults. (Rev: SLJ 4/99; VOYA 8/99) [921]

KENNEDY, JOHN F., JR.

6153 Landau, Elaine. *John F. Kennedy Jr.* (6–9). Illus. Series: Great Americans. 2000, Twenty-First Century LB $26.90 (978-0-7613-1857-6). Beginning with the tragic plane crash that ended his life, and moving back in time, this biography of JFK Jr. captures his personality and the aura that surrounded him. (Rev: BL 12/15/00; HBG 3/01; SLJ 3/01) [921]

LINCOLN, ABRAHAM

6154 Barter, James. *Abraham Lincoln* (7–12). Series: The Importance Of. 2003, Gale LB $32.45 (978-1-56006-965-2). This biography of Lincoln uses ample quotations from important sources and tries to evaluate Lincoln's importance by present-day standards. (Rev: BL 3/15/03) [921]

6155 Bracken, Thomas. *Abraham Lincoln: U.S. President* (7–9). Illus. Series: Overcoming Adversity. 1999, Chelsea paper $30.00 (978-0-7910-4705-7). A biography of Lincoln that stresses the many obstacles he overcame, including lack of formal education, financial difficulties, and bouts of depression. (Rev: HBG 3/99; SLJ 10/98) [921]

6156 Davis, Kenneth C. *Don't Know Much About Abraham Lincoln* (4–8). Illus. by Rob Shepperson. Series: Don't Know Much About. 2004, Harper-Collins LB $15.89 (978-0-06-028820-4). A question-and-answer format gives easy access to key details about Lincoln's life. (Rev: BL 2/1/05; SLJ 2/04) [921]

6157 Freedman, Russell. *Lincoln: A Photobiography* (4–8). Illus. 1987, Houghton $20.00 (978-0-89919-380-9); paper $9.95 (978-0-395-51848-9). A no-nonsense, unromanticized look at this beloved president. Newbery Medal winner, 1988. (Rev: BL 12/15/87; SLJ 12/87) [921]

6158 Herbert, Janis. *Abraham Lincoln for Kids: His Life and Times with 21 Activities* (4–8). Illus. 2007, Chicago Review paper $14.95 (978-1-55652-656-5). With many quotations, illustrations, and sidebars, this volume covers Lincoln's life, beliefs, and contributions and includes activities (such as drawing a cartoon and learning Morse code). (Rev: SLJ 10/07) [921]

6159 Holzer, Harold. *Abraham Lincoln: The Writer* (6–10). Illus. 2000, Boyds Mills $16.95 (978-1-56397-772-5). Following a brief biography, this resource contains letters, excerpts from speeches, notes, debates, and inaugural addresses, each with explanatory introductions that connect the snippet to his life. (Rev: BL 5/1/00; HBG 9/00; SLJ 6/00) [921]

6160 Holzer, Harold. *The President Is Shot! The Assassination of Abraham Lincoln* (5–8). Illus. 2004, Boyds Mills $17.95 (978-1-56397-985-9). A riveting account of Lincoln's assassination, with archival illustrations and historical context. (Rev: BL 3/1/04*; SLJ 2/04) [973.7]

6161 Roberts, Jeremy. *Abraham Lincoln* (5–7). Series: Presidential Leaders. 2003, Lerner LB $29.27 (978-0-8225-0817-5). From childhood through assassination, this is a thorough, well-illustrated, and well-organized account of Lincoln's life. (Rev: SLJ 2/04) [921]

6162 Sandburg, Carl. *Abe Lincoln Grows Up* (6–9). 1975, Harcourt paper $6.99 (978-0-15-602615-4). From the pen of one of America's great poets, this is an account of the boyhood of his great hero. [921]

6163 Sloate, Susan. *Abraham Lincoln: The Freedom President* (5–8). 1989, Ballantine paper $15.00 (978-0-449-90375-9). An accessible account of the president who led his country through division back to unity. (Rev: BL 12/15/89) [921]

6164 Stone, Tanya Lee. *Abraham Lincoln* (5–10). Illus. Series: DK Biography. 2005, DK $14.99 (978-0-7566-0833-0); paper $4.99 (978-0-7566-0834-7). A heavily illustrated, attractive biography of Lincoln that offers broad historical background. (Rev: BL 6/1–15/04) [921]

6165 Sullivan, George. *Picturing Lincoln: Famous Photographs That Popularized the President* (5–8). Illus. 2000, Clarion $16.00 (978-0-395-91682-7). Using five images of Lincoln taken between 1846 and 1864, this book gives historical and biographical information on each and tells how they have been used for posters, button, ribbons, postage stamps, and currency. (Rev: BL 2/1/01; HB 3–4/01; HBG 10/01; SLJ 3/01) [921]

LINCOLN, MARY TODD

6166 Hull, Mary E. *Mary Todd Lincoln* (5–8). Series: Historical American Biographies. 2000, Enslow LB $26.60 (978-0-7660-1252-3). This biography faithfully records the tragic life of Lincoln's widow, whose emotional health declined after the deaths of her son and her husband. (Rev: BL 1/1–15/00; HBG 10/00; SLJ 5/00) [921]

MCKINLEY, WILLIAM

6167 Wilson, Antoine. *The Assassination of William McKinley* (6–9). Series: The Library of Political Assassinations. 2002, Rosen LB $27.95 (978-0-8239-3546-8). The life of this President is re-created with emphasis on details leading up to the crime and the characters involved. (Rev: BL 8/02) [921]

MADISON, DOLLEY

6168 Pflueger, Lynda. *Dolley Madison: Courageous First Lady* (5–8). Series: Historical American Biographies. 1999, Enslow LB $26.60 (978-0-7660-1092-5). An interesting biography of the woman who defined the role of First Lady and who was known for her political acumen and diplomatic and social skills as well as her patriotism and her ability to inspire others. (Rev: SLJ 1/99) [921]

6169 Weatherly, Myra. *Dolley Madison: America's First Lady* (5–8). Illus. Series: Founders of the Republic. 2002, Morgan Reynolds LB $23.95 (978-1-883846-95-4). This portrait of Dolley Madison conveys her popularity and courage, with reproductions of period paintings, prints, and maps. (Rev: BL 11/1/02; HBG 3/03; SLJ 3/03) [973.5]

MADISON, JAMES

6170 Elish, Dan. *James Madison* (4–7). Series: Presidents and Their Times. 2007, Marshall Cavendish LB $22.95 (978-0-7614-2432-1). A clear and thorough profile of the president, describing his early years, presidential career, and later life, with discussion of important events that took place during his life. (Rev: LMC 4-5/08; SLJ 1/08)

6171 Kent, Zachary. *James Madison: Creating a Nation* (5–8). Series: America's Founding Fathers. 2004, Enslow LB $26.60 (978-0-7660-2180-8). This profile of Madison focuses largely on his public life from the period leading up to the American Revolution through his presidency. (Rev: BL 6/1–15/04) [921]

6172 Malone, Mary. *James Madison* (7–9). Series: United States Presidents. 1997, Enslow LB $26.60 (978-0-89490-834-7). This objective biography emphasizes Madison's intellectual and public-service contributions, with details on his role in drafting the Constitution and his two terms as president. (Rev: BL 9/15/97; HBG 3/98; SLJ 9/97) [921]

MADISON, JAMES AND DOLLEY

6173 Ashby, Ruth. *James and Dolley Madison* (5–8). Illus. Series: Presidents and First Ladies. 2005, Gareth Stevens LB $31.00 (978-0-8368-5757-3). An accessible, balanced, and attractive discussion of the Madisons and the contributions each made to their joint lives. (Rev: BL 3/1/05; SLJ 8/05) [921]

MONROE, JAMES

6174 Wetzel, Charles. *James Monroe* (6–10). Illus. 1989, Chelsea LB $19.95 (978-1-55546-817-0). The life of the Revolutionary War hero and details of his presidency and the foreign policy named after him. (Rev: BL 7/89) [921]

NIXON, RICHARD M.

6175 Aronson, Billy. *Richard M. Nixon* (5–8). Illus. Series: Presidents and Their Times. 2007, Marshall Cavendish LB $22.95 (978-0-7614-2428-4). This biography of the 37th president covers his childhood, his candidacy, and his accomplishments in office, as well as his downfall and impeachment. (Rev: BL 10/15/07; SLJ 1/08) [921]

6176 Marquez, Heron. *Richard M. Nixon* (5–7). Series: Presidential Leaders. 2003, Lerner LB $29.27 (978-0-8225-0098-8). The Vietnam War, relations with China, and Watergate all feature prominently in this look at Nixon's private and public life. (Rev: BL 4/15/03; HBG 10/03; SLJ 2/03) [921]

6177 Randolph, Sallie. *Richard M. Nixon, President* (6–9). Illus. 1989, Walker LB $14.85 (978-0-8027-6849-0). A straightforward account using many original sources that doesn't skirt the controversial issues. (Rev: BL 1/15/90; SLJ 12/90; VOYA 2/90) [921]

6178 Ripley, C. Peter. *Richard Nixon* (6–10). Illus. 1987, Chelsea LB $19.95 (978-0-87754-585-9). Beginning with his 1974 resignation, Nixon's life is retraced and an assessment of his career is given. (Rev: BL 12/1/87; SLJ 12/87) [921]

OBAMA, BARACK

6179 Brill, Marlene Targ. *Barack Obama: Working to Make a Difference* (5–8). Illus. Series: Gateway Biography. 2006, Lerner LB $23.93 (978-0-8225-3417-4). Obama, the U.S. senator from Illinois, is profiled with details of his family life, education, and entrance to politics. (Rev: BL 3/15/06; SLJ 8/06) [328.73]

6180 Davis, William Michael. *Barack Obama: The Politics of Hope* (6–9). Illus. Series: Shapers of America. 2007, OTTN $25.95 (978-1-59556-024-7); paper $16.99 (978-1-59556-032-2). Published before Obama was elected to the office of president in 2008, this biography looks at the former senator's early life, service, and writings, as well as his motivations and inspirations. (Rev: BL 2/1/08; SLJ 6/08) [921]

6181 Schuman, Michael A. *Barack Obama: "We Are One People"* (5–8). Illus. Series: African-American Biography Library. 2008, Enslow LB $23.95 (978-0-7660-2891-3). Opening with Obama's speech at the 2004 Democratic Convention, this biography goes on to cover his life chronologically from childhood through running for president. (Rev: BL 6/1–15/08) [328.730]

PIERCE, FRANKLIN

6182 Brown, Fern G. *Franklin Pierce* (5–8). Series: Presidents of the United States. 1989, GEC LB $21.27 (978-0-944483-25-1). The story of Pierce, his political life and presidency, plus material on his personal life. (Rev: SLJ 9/89) [921]

REAGAN, RONALD

6183 Hinkle, Donald Henry. *Ronald Reagan* (4–7). Series: Presidents. 2003, Enslow LB $25.26 (978-0-7660-5112-6). The life story of the fortieth president with material on the successes and failures of his two terms. (Rev: BL 6/1–15/03; HBG 10/03) [921]

6184 Sullivan, George. *Ronald Reagan* (5–8). Illus. 1991, Simon & Schuster $14.98 (978-0-671-74537-0). This revised edition adds new material on Reagan's second term. (Rev: BL 1/15/92) [921]

6185 Sutherland, James. *Ronald Reagan* (6–9). Series: Up Close. 2008, Viking $16.99 (978-0-670-06345-1). A thought-provoking character portrait as well an account of the president's life and career. (Rev: BL 6/1–15/08) [921]

6186 Young, Jeff C. *Great Communicator: The Story of Ronald Reagan* (6–10). Illus. Series: Twentieth-Century Leaders. 2003, Morgan Reynolds LB $23.95 (978-1-931798-10-5). Reagan's career is the main focus of this biography that includes many quotations and black-and-white photographs and deals objectively with the former president's strengths and weaknesses. (Rev: BL 6/1–15/03; HBG 10/03; SLJ 10/03; VOYA 12/03) [921]

ROOSEVELT, ELEANOR

6187 Fleming, Candace. *Our Eleanor: A Scrapbook Look at Eleanor Roosevelt's Remarkable Life* (6–9). Illus. 2005, Simon & Schuster $19.95 (978-0-689-86544-2). Archival photos, first-person accounts, direct quotes, and informative sidebars document Roosevelt's life and cover her character and questions about her sexuality. (Rev: BL 9/1/05; SLJ 11/05*; VOYA 10/05) [973.917]

6188 Freedman, Russell. *Eleanor Roosevelt: A Life of Discovery* (5–9). 1993, Clarion $17.95 (978-0-89919-862-0). This admiring photobiography captures Roosevelt's public role and personal sadness. (Rev: BL 7/93*; SLJ 8/93*; VOYA 2/94) [921]

6189 Jones, Victoria Garrett. *Eleanor Roosevelt: A Courageous Spirit* (5–8). Series: Sterling Biographies. 2007, Sterling $12.95 (978-1-4027-4746-5); paper $5.95 (978-1-4027-3371-0). This well-illustrated profile covers Eleanor Roosevelt's life from childhood and discusses her contributions as First Lady, a position she transformed. (Rev: SLJ 5/07) [921]

6190 Koestler-Grack, Rachel A. *The Story of Eleanor Roosevelt* (4–7). Illus. Series: Breakthrough Biographies. 2004, Chelsea House LB $23.00 (978-0-7910-7313-1). This brief biography covers Roosevelt's early years as well as her later contributions to her country and to the world. (Rev: BL 3/1/04) [973917]

6191 Lassieur, Allison. *Eleanor Roosevelt: Activist for Social Change* (5–8). Series: Great Life Stories. 2006, Watts LB $30.50 (978-0-531-13871-7). This biography of Eleanor Roosevelt focuses on the first lady's personal life and on her social activism while in the White House and later as an envoy to the United Nations. (Rev: SLJ 2/07) [921]

6192 Somervill, Barbara A. *Eleanor Roosevelt: First Lady of the World* (5–8). Illus. Series: Signature Lives: Modern America. 2005, Compass Point $34.60 (978-0-7565-0992-7). An appealing biography that traces the First Lady's life and focuses on her tireless efforts to make life better for America's disadvantaged minorities. (Rev: BL 10/15/05) [973.917]

6193 Toor, Rachel. *Eleanor Roosevelt* (6–10). Illus. 1989, Chelsea LB $19.95 (978-1-55546-674-9). An affectionate portrait of a first lady who was also a great humanitarian and internationalist. (Rev: BL 4/1/89; SLJ 5/89; VOYA 8/89) [921]

6194 Westervelt, Virginia Veeder. *Here Comes Eleanor: A New Biography of Eleanor Roosevelt for Young People* (5–8). Series: Avisson Young Adult. 1999, Avisson paper $16.00 (978-1-888105-33-9). A clear account of the life of Eleanor Roosevelt that gives a fine assessment of her many contributions to humankind. (Rev: BL 2/15/99; SLJ 7/99; VOYA 10/99) [921]

6195 Winget, Mary. *Eleanor Roosevelt* (5–8). Series: A&E Biography. 2000, Lerner LB $27.93 (978-0-8225-4985-7). Growing up in a troubled but loving family, Eleanor Roosevelt showed that an ordinary woman can achieve greatness. (Rev: BL 3/1/01; HBG 10/01) [921]

ROOSEVELT, FRANKLIN D.

6196 Allport, Alan. *Franklin Delano Roosevelt* (5–7). Series: Great American Presidents. 2003, Chelsea House LB $30.00 (978-0-7910-7598-2). A concise life of the longest-serving president in U.S. history, from his childhood through his years in the White House, with a foreword by Walter Cronkite. (Rev: SLJ 4/04) [921]

6197 Bardhan-Quallen, Sudipta. *Franklin Delano Roosevelt: A National Hero* (5–8). Series: Sterling Biographies. 2007, Sterling $12.95 (978-1-4027-4747-2); paper $5.95 (978-1-4027-3545-5). The author emphasizes the contrast between Roosevelt's privileged background and his concern about social injustice. (Rev: SLJ 5/07) [921]

6198 Burgan, Michael. *Franklin D. Roosevelt* (4–8). Series: Profiles of the Presidents. 2002, Compass Point LB $26.60 (978-0-7565-0203-4). An absorbing introduction to Roosevelt's life and career, with details of his youth and education and the role that his illness played in shaping his character. (Rev: SLJ 6/02) [973.917092]

6199 Devaney, John. *Franklin Delano Roosevelt, President* (6–10). Illus. 1987, Walker $12.95 (978-0-8027-6713-4). A detailed account of Roosevelt's personality and career. (Rev: SLJ 1/88; VOYA 12/87) [921]

6200 Freedman, Russell. *Franklin Delano Roosevelt* (5–8). Illus. 1990, Houghton $20.00 (978-0-89919-379-3). A carefully researched and well-illustrated account of the man and the times. (Rev: HB 3–4/90; SLJ 12/90*) [921]

6201 Greenblatt, Miriam. *Franklin D. Roosevelt: 32nd President of the United States* (5–8). Illus.

1989, Garrett LB $21.27 (978-0-944483-06-0). A clearly written, objective biography of the man who guided the country through World War II, with information on his family life. (Rev: BL 5/1/89; SLJ 8/89) [921]

6202 Haugen, Brenda. *Franklin Delano Roosevelt: The New Deal President* (4–8). Series: Signature Lives. 2006, Compass Point LB $34.60 (978-0-7565-1586-7). Slim but fact-filled, this is a useful biography for report writers, with excerpts from speeches and writings and full discussion of key events in Roosevelt's life. (Rev: SLJ 9/06) [921]

6203 Knapp, Ron. *Franklin D. Roosevelt* (5–9). 2002, Enslow LB $25.26 (978-0-7660-5009-9). A listing of recommended Web sites extends the contents of this introduction to Roosevelt's life and presidency. (Rev: HBG 10/02; SLJ 6/02) [921]

6204 Morris, Jeffrey. *The FDR Way* (5–8). Illus. Series: Great Presidential Decisions. 1996, Lerner LB $23.93 (978-0-8225-2929-3). A straightforward, incisive analysis of far-reaching, often painful decisions that FDR made, and an assessment of their consequences. (Rev: BL 3/15/96) [921]

6205 Nardo, Don. *Franklin D. Roosevelt: U.S. President* (7–10). Series: Great Achievers: Lives of the Physically Challenged. 1995, Chelsea LB $14.95 (978-0-7910-2406-5). This biography stresses the physical challenges Roosevelt faced and the strong personality that allowed him to achieve great success. (Rev: SLJ 1/96) [921]

6206 Panchyk, Richard. *Franklin Delano Roosevelt for Kids: His Life and Times with 21 Activities* (6–9). Illus. 2007, Chicago Review paper $14.95 (978-1-55652-657-2). In addition to an informative biography that places FDR's life in historical context, this volume includes such activities as giving a "fireside chat," collecting stamps, and researching genealogy. (Rev: BL 11/15/07; SLJ 10/07) [921]

6207 Schuman, Michael A. *Franklin D. Roosevelt: The Four-Term President* (4–7). Illus. Series: People to Know. 1996, Enslow LB $26.60 (978-0-89490-696-1). A thoughtful, serious look at this great president, his important decisions, and his significance in history. (Rev: BL 6/1–15/96; SLJ 8/96) [921]

ROOSEVELT, FRANKLIN D. AND ELEANOR

6208 Ashby, Ruth. *Franklin and Eleanor Roosevelt* (5–8). Illus. Series: Presidents and First Ladies. 2005, Gareth Stevens LB $31.00 (978-0-8368-5758-0). An accessible, balanced, and attractive discussion of the Roosevelts and the contributions each made to their joint lives. (Rev: BL 3/1/05) [921]

ROOSEVELT, THEODORE

6209 Donnelly, Matt. *Theodore Roosevelt: Larger Than Life* (6–9). Illus. 2003, Linnet $27.50 (978-0-208-02510-4). Information about the presidency of Theodore Roosevelt is presented along with coverage of his childhood and early experiences in the West and as a public servant. (Rev: BL 1/1–15/03; HB 3–4/03; HBG 10/03; SLJ 3/03; VOYA 10/03) [973.91]

6210 Elish, Dan. *Theodore Roosevelt* (4–7). Series: Presidents and Their Times. 2007, Marshall Cavendish LB $22.95 (978-0-7614-2429-1). A clear and thorough profile of the president, describing his early years, presidential career, and later life, with discussion of important events that took place during his life. (Rev: SLJ 1/08)

6211 Kelley, Alison Turnbull. *Theodore Roosevelt* (5–7). Series: Great American Presidents. 2003, Chelsea House LB $30.00 (978-0-7910-7606-4). An illustrated profile of the 26th president, from his childhood through his public life and legacy. (Rev: SLJ 4/04) [921]

6212 Kraft, Betsy Harvey. *Theodore Roosevelt: Champion of the American Spirit* (5–9). Illus. 2003, Clarion $19.00 (978-0-618-14264-4). The determination that carried Roosevelt through a difficult childhood and drove his successful career is emphasized in this engrossing biography of his life and survey of his diverse accomplishments. (Rev: BL 10/15/03; HB 11–12/03; HBG 4/04; SLJ 12/03*; VOYA 10/03) [973.9]

6213 Marrin, Albert. *The Great Adventure: Theodore Roosevelt and the Rise of Modern America* (8–11). Illus. 2007, Dutton $30.00 (978-0-525-47659-7). Marrin provides excellent, balanced information on Roosevelt's life and political career, giving good background on the social and political mores of the time and covering the president's achievements and peculiarities. (Rev: BL 9/1/07; SLJ 12/07) [973.91]

6214 Schuman, Michael A. *Theodore Roosevelt* (5–8). Series: United States Presidents. 1997, Enslow LB $26.60 (978-0-89490-836-1). An objective biography of the life of this active president whose life spanned both the Civil War and World War I, with good background information. (Rev: BL 2/1/98; HBG 3/98; SLJ 2/98) [921]

6215 Whitelaw, Nancy. *Theodore Roosevelt Takes Charge* (6–9). 1992, Albert Whitman LB $16.99 (978-0-8075-7849-0). A clear, credible biography of a larger-than-life American hero who was full of contradictions. (Rev: BL 6/1/92*; SLJ 7/92*) [921]

TAYLOR, ZACHARY

6216 Collins, David R. *Zachary Taylor: 12th President of the United States* (5–7). Illus. 1989, Garrett LB $21.27 (978-0-944483-17-6). Tells the life story of a military man elected president in 1848. (Rev: BL 5/1/89) [921]

TRUMAN, HARRY S

6217 Fleming, Thomas. *Harry S Truman, President* (6–12). 1993, Walker LB $15.85 (978-0-8027-8269-4). The author of this uncritical biography of the former president had access to family photographs and documents. (Rev: BL 1/1/94; SLJ 12/93; VOYA 2/94) [921]

6218 Lazo, Caroline Evensen. *Harry S Truman* (5–7). Illus. Series: Presidential Leaders. 2003, Lerner LB $29.27 (978-0-8225-0096-4). Truman's youth, education, family life, and career are all covered in this concise biography full of photographs. (Rev: BL 4/15/03; HBG 10/03) [973.918]

VAN BUREN, MARTIN

6219 Doak, Robin. *Martin Van Buren* (4–7). 2003, Compass Point LB $26.60 (978-0-7565-0256-0). Van Buren's strengths and weakness receive equal weight in this balanced and readable biography that covers his life from a young age. (Rev: SLJ 11/03) [973.5]

6220 Ellis, Rafaela. *Martin Van Buren: 8th President of the United States* (5–7). Illus. 1989, Garrett LB $21.27 (978-0-944483-12-1). The story of a New York governor who became president. (Rev: BL 5/1/89) [921]

WASHINGTON, GEORGE

6221 Adler, David A. *George Washington: An Illustrated Biography* (5–7). 2004, Holiday House $24.95 (978-0-8234-1838-1). Adler presents a balanced and well-researched biography of Washington, giving details of his character as well as information on key events of his time. (Rev: BL 9/15/04; SLJ 12/04) [973.4]

6222 Bruns, Roger. *George Washington* (6–10). Illus. 1986, Chelsea LB $19.95 (978-0-87754-584-2). A solid, readable biography of the first president. (Rev: BL 3/1/87; SLJ 5/87) [921]

6223 Falkof, Lucille. *George Washington: 1st President of the United States* (5–8). Illus. 1989, Garrett LB $21.27 (978-0-944483-19-0). An objective, readable portrait of the life and times of our first president. (Rev: BL 5/1/89; SLJ 8/89) [921]

6224 Hilton, Suzanne. *The World of Young George Washington* (5–8). 1987, Walker $12.95 (978-0-8027-6657-1). Washington as a youth plus detailed information on life in pre-Revolutionary America. (Rev: SLJ 4/87) [921]

6225 Hort, Lenny. *George Washington* (5–10). Illus. Series: DK Biography. 2005, DK $14.99 (978-0-7566-0832-3); paper $4.99 (978-0-7566-0835-4). A

heavily illustrated, attractive biography of the man born in Virginia. (Rev: BL 6/1–15/04) [921]

6226 McClung, Robert M. *Young George Washington and the French and Indian War: 1753–1758* (6–9). Illus. 2002, Linnet $22.50 (978-0-208-02509-8). A portrait of Washington as a military leader who matures from youthful impetuosity to a more thoughtful outlook on life. (Rev: BL 8/02; HBG 3/03; SLJ 10/02) [973.2]

6227 McNeese, Tim. *George Washington: America's Leader in War and Peace* (4–8). Series: Leaders of the American Revolution. 2005, Chelsea House LB $30.00 (978-0-7910-8619-3). An even-handed introduction to Washington's life and contributions, presented chronologically with occasional factboxes; suitable for report writers. (Rev: SLJ 1/06) [921]

6228 Marrin, Albert. *George Washington and the Founding of a Nation* (7–12). Illus. 2001, Dutton $30.00 (978-0-525-46481-5). A detailed account of this complex leader that examines the facts and the myths. (Rev: BCCB 2/01; BL 1/1–15/01; HB 5–6/01; HBG 10/01; SLJ 1/01) [921]

6229 Old, Wendie C. *George Washington* (5–8). Illus. Series: United States Presidents. 1997, Enslow LB $26.60 (978-0-89490-832-3). Washington's personal life and political career are dealt with equally in this thoughtful biography. (Rev: BL 9/15/97; SLJ 12/97) [921]

6230 Roberts, Jeremy. *George Washington* (5–7). Series: Presidential Leaders. 2003, Lerner LB $29.27 (978-0-8225-0818-2). This engaging biography chronicles the life and achievements of America's first president and dispels some widely believed myths. (Rev: SLJ 2/04) [921]

6231 Rosenburg, John. *First in Peace: George Washington, the Constitution, and the Presidency* (7–10). 1998, Millbrook LB $25.90 (978-0-7613-0422-7). The last of a trilogy about Washington, this installment describes the emergence of the new nation and the role played by the first president. (Rev: HBG 3/99; SLJ 1/99) [921]

6232 Yoder, Carolyn P., ed. *George Washington: The Writer: A Treasury of Letters, Diaries, and Public Documents* (7–10). Illus. 2003, Boyds Mills $16.95 (978-1-56397-199-0). Washington's speeches, letters, will, and other documents — many excerpted — reveal much about his life and career. (Rev: BL 3/15/03; HBG 10/03; SLJ 2/03; VOYA 12/03) [921]

WASHINGTON, MARTHA

6233 McPherson, Stephanie S. *Martha Washington: First Lady* (7–9). Series: Historical American Biographies. 1998, Enslow LB $26.60 (978-0-7660-1017-8). An affectionate portrait of the first First

Lady, who was not well educated but put the skills she learned to good use running a household and living in polite society. (Rev: BL 1/1–15/99; SLJ 1/99) [921]

WILSON, WOODROW

6234 Collins, David R. *Woodrow Wilson: 28th President of the United States* (5–8). Illus. 1989, Garrett LB $21.27 (978-0-944483-18-3). A compact biography of a Nobel Peace Prize–winning president. (Rev: BL 5/1/89; SLJ 8/89) [921]

6235 Lukes, Bonnie L. *Woodrow Wilson and the Progressive Era* (6–10). Series: World Leaders. 2005, Morgan Reynolds LB $26.95 (978-1-931798-79-2). A chronological survey of Wilson's life from birth in 1856 through his death in 1924, with discussion of his achievements in light of the global events of the time. (Rev: SLJ 2/06) [921]

6236 Randolph, Sallie. *Woodrow Wilson, President* (5–9). Series: Presidential Biography. 1992, Walker LB $15.85 (978-0-8027-8144-4). Offers a concise overview of Wilson's tragic personal and political struggles, his achievements, and his place in history. (Rev: BL 12/15/91; SLJ 3/92) [921]

6237 Schraff, Anne. *Woodrow Wilson* (5–8). Series: United States Presidents. 1998, Enslow LB $26.60 (978-0-89490-936-8). The story of the brilliant 28th president, his initial opposition to entering World War I, the defeat of his proposals concerning the League of Nations, and the stroke he suffered. (Rev: SLJ 9/98) [921]

WILSON, WOODROW AND EDITH

6238 Ashby, Ruth. *Woodrow and Edith Wilson* (5–8). Illus. Series: Presidents and First Ladies. 2005, Gareth Stevens LB $31.00 (978-0-8368-5759-7). An accessible, balanced, and attractive discussion of the Wilsons and the contributions each made to their joint lives. (Rev: BL 3/1/05; SLJ 8/05) [921]

Other Government and Public Figures

ADAMS, SAMUEL

6239 Burgan, Michael. *Samuel Adams: Patriot and Statesman* (4–7). Illus. Series: Signature Lives (Revolutionary War Era). 2005, Compass Point LB $34.60 (978-0-7565-0823-4). Profiles the man who played a key role in the tax rebellion and Boston Tea Party. (Rev: BL 4/1/05) [921]

6240 Fradin, Dennis Brindell. *Samuel Adams: The Father of American Independence* (5–9). Illus. 1998, Houghton $20.00 (978-0-395-82510-5). An

attractive biography of the amazing Sam Adams, whom Jefferson called "the Man of the Revolution." (Rev: BCCB 7–8/98; BL 7/98; SLJ 7/98; VOYA 2/99) [921]

ALBRIGHT, MADELEINE

6241 Burgan, Michael. *Madeleine Albright* (8–10). 1998, Millbrook LB $24.90 (978-0-7613-0367-1). This life of the first woman U.S. secretary of state describes her European childhood, her arrival as a refugee in this country, and her experiences as a student, journalist, activist, teacher, mother, ambassador, and, finally, cabinet member. (Rev: SLJ 6/99) [921]

6242 Byman, Jeremy. *Madam Secretary: The Story of Madeleine Albright* (5–9). Series: Notable Americans. 1997, Morgan Reynolds LB $21.95 (978-1-883846-23-7). The emphasis in this biography is on Albright's public life, first as adviser to various political figures, then as ambassador to the United Nations, and finally as secretary of state. (Rev: BL 12/15/97; SLJ 4/98; VOYA 6/98) [921]

6243 Hasday, Judy. *Madeleine Albright* (8–12). Series: Women of Achievement. 1998, Chelsea $30.00 (978-0-7910-4708-8); paper $30.00 (978-0-7910-4709-5). A well-rounded biography of Madeleine Albright, covering her career in American public service and her childhood in Eastern Europe. (Rev: HBG 3/99; SLJ 3/99) [921]

6244 Kramer, Barbara. *Madeleine Albright: First Woman Secretary of State* (6–9). Illus. Series: Poeple to Know. 2000, Enslow LB $26.60 (978-0-7660-1143-4). This account traces the life and career of Albright through early 1999 and the Kosovo bombings. (Rev: BL 1/1–15/00; HBG 9/00) [327.73.]

ALLEN, ETHAN

6245 Haugen, Brenda. *Ethan Allen: Green Mountain Rebel* (4–7). Illus. Series: Signature Lives (Revolutionary War Era). 2005, Compass Point LB $34.60 (978-0-7565-0824-1). Traces the life of the man who, along with Benedict Arnold, led the Green Mountain Boys in capturing Fort Ticonderoga from the British. (Rev: BL 4/1/05; SLJ 8/05) [921]

6246 Raabe, Emily. *Ethan Allen: The Green Mountain Boys and Vermont's Path to Statehood* (4–7). Series: Library of American Lives and Times. 2001, Rosen LB $34.60 (978-0-8239-5722-4). Extraordinary illustrations and fine text tell the story of the controversial founder of Vermont who led the Green Mountain Boys in the capture of Fort Ticonderoga and Crown Point. (Rev: BL 10/15/01) [921]

ARNOLD, BENEDICT

6247 Dell, Pamela. *Benedict Arnold: From Patriot to Traitor* (4–7). Illus. Series: Signature Lives (Revolutionary War Era). 2005, Compass Point LB $34.60 (978-0-7565-0825-8). A well-designed and informative profile of the man who betrayed his country. (Rev: BL 4/1/05) [921]

6248 Fritz, Jean. *Traitor: The Case of Benedict Arnold* (7–9). Illus. 1981, Putnam $16.99 (978-0-399-20834-8). A biography that tries to probe the many reasons for Arnold's actions. [921]

6249 Gaines, Ann Graham. *Benedict Arnold: Patriot or Traitor?* (5–8). Series: Historical American Biographies. 2001, Enslow LB $26.60 (978-0-7660-1393-3). Many facets of the character of this controversial American are examined in this well-illustrated volume. (Rev: BL 4/15/01; HBG 10/01; SLJ 6/01) [921]

6250 King, David C. *Benedict Arnold and the American Revolution* (5–9). Series: Notorious Americans and Their Times. 1998, Blackbirch LB $28.70 (978-1-56711-221-4). Benedict Arnold's life and military accomplishments are placed in the context of the period in which he lived and the conflicts he faced. (Rev: BL 12/15/98; HBG 3/99; SLJ 12/98) [921]

6251 Murphy, Jim. *The Real Benedict Arnold* (7–10). Illus. 2007, Clarion $20.00 (978-0-395-77609-4). An examination of Arnold's character reveals what may have led him to become a traitor. (Rev: BL 10/1/07; HB 1–2/08; LMC 2/08; SLJ 12/07) [921]

6252 Powell, Walter L. *Benedict Arnold: Revolutionary War Hero and Traitor* (5–8). Series: Library of American Lives and Times. 2004, Rosen LB $34.60 (978-0-8239-6627-1). The life of Benedict Arnold, the American patriot who switched his allegiance to the British cause. (Rev: SLJ 7/04) [921]

6253 Sonneborn, Liz. *Benedict Arnold: Hero and Traitor* (4–8). Series: Leaders of the American Revolution. 2005, Chelsea House LB $30.00 (978-0-7910-8617-9). An even-handed introduction to Arnold's life, presented chronologically with occasional factboxes; suitable for report writers. (Rev: SLJ 1/06) [921]

AUSTIN, STEPHEN F.

6254 Haley, James L. *Stephen F. Austin and the Founding of Texas* (5–8). Series: The Library of American Lives and Times. 2003, Rosen LB $34.60 (978-0-8239-5738-5). A concise biography of the pioneer who became one of the founders of Texas. (Rev: SLJ 5/03) [976.4]

BOOTH, EDWIN AND JOHN WILKES

6255 Giblin, James Cross. *Good Brother, Bad Brother: The Story of Edwin Booth and John Wilkes Booth* (5–8). Illus. 2005, Clarion $22.00 (978-0-618-09642-8). In a compelling and highly readable narrative, Giblin reveals the alcoholism and depression that plagued the theatrical Booth family, the disagreement between the two brothers over the Civil War, and the effects of the assassination on Edwin's later life. (Rev: BL 5/1/05*; SLJ 5/05) [921]

BRADFORD, WILLIAM

6256 Doherty, Kieran. *William Bradford: Rock of Plymouth* (5–9). 1999, Twenty-First Century LB $24.90 (978-0-7613-1304-5). Using Bradford's own writings and other contemporary accounts as sources, this is an objective biography of the man who was the governor of the Plymouth Plantation. (Rev: BL 12/1/99; HBG 3/00; SLJ 1/00) [921]

BRADLEY, BILL

6257 Buckley, James, Jr. *Bill Bradley* (5–8). Illus. Series: Basketball Hall of Famers. 2002, Rosen LB $29.25 (978-0-8239-3479-9). An easy-to-read, detailed biography of the former athlete, with plenty of photographs. (Rev: BL 9/1/02) [921]

6258 Jaspersohn, William. *Senator: A Profile of Bill Bradley in the U.S. Senate* (6–10). 1992, Harcourt $19.95 (978-0-15-272880-9). An in-depth photoessay about Congress in general and Senator Bradley of New Jersey in particular, showing how his sports career led to the Senate. (Rev: BL 7/92; SLJ 10/92) [921]

BRANDEIS, LOUIS

6259 Freedman, Suzanne. *Louis Brandeis* (4–9). Illus. Series: Justices of the Supreme Court. 1996, Enslow LB $26.60 (978-0-89490-678-7). A biography of the great justice who advocated many public causes and was known as the "people's attorney." (Rev: BL 8/96; SLJ 11/96) [921]

BUNCHE, RALPH

6260 Schraff, Anne. *Ralph Bunche: Winner of the Nobel Peace Prize* (7–12). Series: African-American Biographies. 1999, Enslow LB $26.60 (978-0-7660-1203-5). The story of the great American diplomat who helped mediate several international disputes and won the Nobel peace prize in 1950. (Rev: BL 11/15/99; SLJ 8/99) [921]

BURR, AARON

6261 Ingram, W. Scott. *Aaron Burr and the Young Nation* (5–8). Series: Major World Leaders. 2002,

Chelsea $28.70 (978-1-56711-250-4). The story of the controversial political leader who killed Alexander Hamilton in a duel and later was tried and found guilty of treason. (Rev: BL 1/1–15/03; SLJ 10/02) [921]

6262 Melton, Buckner F. *Aaron Burr: The Rise and Fall of an American Politician* (5–8). Series: Library of American Lives and Times. 2004, Rosen LB $34.60 (978-0-8239-6626-4). This engaging biography chronicles the rise and fall of the Revolutionary War hero who was later branded a traitor. (Rev: SLJ 7/04) [921]

CAMPBELL, BEN NIGHTHORSE

6263 Henry, Christopher. *Ben Nighthorse Campbell: Cheyenne Chief and U.S. Senator* (5–8). Illus. Series: North American Indians of Achievement. 1994, Chelsea $19.95 (978-0-7919-2046-6). The story of the Cheyenne leader who gained prominence not only among his own people but also in the U.S. Congress. (Rev: BL 6/1–15/93) [921]

CLINTON, HILLARY RODHAM

6264 Burgan, Michael. *Hillary Rodham Clinton: First Lady and Senator* (6–9). Illus. Series: Modern America: Signature Lives. 2008, Compass Point LB $25.95 (978-0-7565-1588-1). Clinton's childhood, early political activity, and time as First Lady are covered (including a mention of the Lewinsky scandal); the book ends with her attempt to become a presidential candidate in 2008. An appealing design makes this a friendly choice for researchers. (Rev: BL 4/15/08) [921]

6265 Guernsey, JoAnn Bren. *Hillary Rodham Clinton* (5–8). Illus. 2005, Lerner LB $29.27 (978-0-8225-2372-7); paper $7.95 (978-0-8225-9613-4). Traces Clinton's life from childhood, and covers the trials of her husband's second term in office in some detail. (Rev: BL 6/1–15/05; SLJ 7/05) [921]

6266 Wells, Catherine. *Hillary Clinton* (5–8). Illus. Series: Political Profiles. 2007, Morgan Reynolds LB $27.95 (978-1-59935-047-9). Readers will learn of the former First Lady and presidential hopeful's life and achievements from this positive portrait. (Rev: BL 11/15/07) [921]

CRAZY HORSE (SIOUX CHIEF)

6267 Brennan, Kristine. *Crazy Horse* (4–7). Series: Famous Figures of the American Frontier. 2001, Chelsea $25.00 (978-0-7910-6493-1); paper $25.00 (978-0-7910-6494-8). Report writers will find this a useful source of information on this Native American leader's adult life and achievements in battle. (Rev: HBG 10/02; SLJ 4/02) [921]

6268 Freedman, Russell. *The Life and Death of Crazy Horse* (6–12). Illus. 1996, Holiday $24.95

(978-0-8234-1219-8). This biography of Crazy Horse tells an uncompromising story of bloody wars, terrible grief, tragedy, and the Sioux's losing battle to preserve their independence and their land. (Rev: BL 6/1–15/96*; SLJ 6/96*; VOYA 10/96) [921]

6269 Haugen, Brenda. *Crazy Horse: Sioux Warrior* (5–8). Series: Signature Lives. 2005, Compass Point LB $34.60 (978-0-7565-0999-6). Crazy Horse's life and efforts to save his native lands and way of life are documented here. (Rev: SLJ 2/06) [921]

CROW, JOSEPH MEDICINE

6270 Medicine Crow, Joseph. *Counting Coup: Becoming a Crow Chief on the Reservation and Beyond* (5–8). Illus. 2006, National Geographic LB $23.90 (978-0-7922-8328-7); paper $6.95 (978-0-7922-7297-7). The memoirs of a Crow chief who was educated in mission and boarding schools and went on to fight in World War II. (Rev: BCCB 5/06; BL 4/15/06; LMC 11-12/06; SLJ 7/06) [967.62]

CUSTER, GEORGE ARMSTRONG

6271 Anderson, Paul Christopher. *George Armstrong Custer: The Indian Wars and the Battle of the Little Big Horn* (4–8). Series: The Library of American Lives and Times. 2004, Rosen LB $34.60 (978-0-8239-6631-8). The importance of understanding history is emphasized in this balanced and well-illustrated look at Custer's life and stance at Little Big Horn. (Rev: SLJ 7/04) [920]

6272 Kent, Zachary. *George Armstrong Custer* (5–8). Series: Historical American Biographies. 2000, Enslow LB $26.60 (978-0-7660-1255-4). Using extensive chapter notes, a glossary, bibliography, and index, this is a well-documented and objective assessment of Custer's life and deeds. (Rev: BL 1/1–15/00; HBG 10/00) [921]

DAVIS, JEFFERSON

6273 Burch, Joann J. *Jefferson Davis: President of the Confederacy* (5–8). Series: Historical American Biographies. 1998, Enslow LB $26.60 (978-0-7660-1064-2). Using personal documents and well-chosen illustrations, this lively biography describes Jefferson Davis's life as well as the causes and major events of the Civil War. (Rev: BL 10/15/98; SLJ 1/99) [921]

6274 King, Perry Scott. *Jefferson Davis* (7–10). Illus. 1990, Chelsea LB $21.95 (978-1-55546-806-4). With many illustrations, King re-creates the life and times of the president of the Confederacy. (Rev: BL 8/90; SLJ 8/90) [921]

DE ZAVALA, LORENZO

6275 Tracy, Kathleen. *Lorenzo de Zavala* (5–7). Series: Latinos in American History. 2002, Mitchell Lane LB $29.95 (978-1-58415-154-8). The biography of the 19th-century Mexican who became vice president of the Republic of Texas and was one of the signers of its constitution. (Rev: BL 2/15/03; HBG 10/03) [921]

FRANKLIN, BENJAMIN

6276 Adler, David A. *B. Franklin, Printer* (4–8). Illus. 2001, Holiday $19.95 (978-0-8234-1675-2). Quotations, anecdotes, and wonderful illustrations round out this excellent volume about the life and accomplishments of Benjamin Franklin. (Rev: BCCB 2/02; BL 1/1–15/02; HBG 10/02; SLJ 2/02*; VOYA 4/02) [973.3]

6277 Cousins, Margaret. *Ben Franklin of Old Philadelphia* (6–8). 1963, Random paper $5.99 (978-0-394-84928-7). A well-rounded portrait of this major figure in American history. [921]

6278 Dash, Joan. *A Dangerous Engine: Benjamin Franklin, from Scientist to Diplomat* (6–10). Illus. by Dusan Petricic. 2006, Farrar $17.00 (978-0-374-30669-4). Franklin's keen interest in science and the development of new technology is emphasized in this lively biography illustrated with pen-and-ink drawings. (Rev: BCCB 1/06; BL 3/1/06; HB 3–4/06; SLJ 2/06) [921]

6279 Fleming, Candace. *Ben Franklin's Almanac: Being a True Account of the Gentleman's Life* (6–9). Illus. 2003, Simon & Schuster $19.95 (978-0-689-83549-0). Compiled in scrapbook style, this is an appealing biography full of anecdotes and graphic elements and covering Franklin's family life and scientific, literary, and political achievements. (Rev: BL 8/03; HB 9–10/03; SLJ 9/03*) [973.3]

6280 Foster, Leila M. *Benjamin Franklin: Founding Father and Inventor* (5–8). Series: Historical American Biographies. 1997, Enslow LB $26.60 (978-0-89490-784-5). An admiring biography that describes Franklin's many talents — as a printer, businessman, scientist, inventor, and statesman. (Rev: SLJ 11/97) [921]

6281 Gaustad, Edwin S. *Benjamin Franklin: Inventing America* (7–10). Series: Oxford Portraits. 2004, Oxford LB $32.95 (978-0-19-515732-1). The life and achievements of Benjamin Franklin are described using many quotations from Franklin's autobiography. (Rev: SLJ 2/05) [921]

6282 Lee, Tanja, ed. *Benjamin Franklin* (7–12). Series: People Who Made History. 2002, Gale LB $24.95 (978-0-7377-0898-1); paper $36.20 (978-0-7377-0899-8). After a general introduction to Franklin, his life, and his times, essays explore his talents, contributions, accomplishments, and his place in world history. (Rev: BL 4/1/02) [921]

6283 Looby, Chris. *Benjamin Franklin* (6–10). Illus. 1990, Chelsea LB $21.95 (978-1-55546-808-8). A well-illustrated account of the life of this complex man that also introduces many of his contemporaries. (Rev: BL 8/90; SLJ 7/90; VOYA 8/90) [921]

6284 Streissguth, Thomas. *Benjamin Franklin* (5–8). Series: Biography. 2001, Lerner LB $27.93 (978-0-8225-4997-0). A readable biography of the many-faceted genius of the newly formed United States. (Rev: BL 4/1/02; HBG 10/02) [921]

6285 Van Vleet, Carmella. *Amazing Ben Franklin Inventions You Can Build Yourself* (4–8). Illus. 2007, Nomad paper $14.95 (978-0-9771294-7-8). Activities — making invisible ink, wave bottles, kites, and so forth — and the accompanying narrative bring Franklin's inquisitive nature to light. (Rev: LMC 2/08; SLJ 11/07) [921]

GERONIMO

6286 Haugen, Brenda. *Geronimo: Apache Warrior* (5–8). Series: Signature Lives. 2005, Compass Point LB $34.60 (978-0-7565-1002-2). Geronimo's unsuccessful efforts to secure freedom for his people are documented in this attractive book. (Rev: SLJ 2/06) [921]

6287 Hermann, Spring. *Geronimo: Apache Freedom Fighter* (6–9). Series: Native American Biographies. 1997, Enslow LB $26.60 (978-0-89490-864-4). This is a fine, well-rounded portrait of the man who became an Apache leader, fought at Little Bighorn, and died a prosperous man at age 85. (Rev: BL 4/15/97; SLJ 6/97) [921]

6288 Thompson, Bill, and Dorcas Thompson. *Geronimo* (4–7). Series: Famous Figures of the American Frontier. 2001, Chelsea $25.00 (978-0-7910-6491-7); paper $8.95 (978-0-7910-6492-4). A balanced biography of the Apache leader that report writers will find a useful resource. (Rev: HBG 10/02; SLJ 4/02) [921]

GIULIANI, RUDOLPH W.

6289 Sharp, Anna Layton. *Rudy Giuliani* (6–9). Illus. Series: Political Profiles. 2007, Morgan Reynolds LB $27.95 (978-1-59935-048-6). An evenhanded look at the former mayor of New York City, with details about his shortcomings as well as his successes. (Rev: BL 1/1–15/08; SLJ 1/08) [921]

GLENN, JOHN

6290 Cole, Michael D. *John Glenn: Astronaut and Senator* (5–8). Series: People to Know. 2000, Enslow LB $26.60 (978-0-7660-1532-6). A biography of the astronaut and politician with coverage of his two trips into space. (Rev: BL 9/15/00; HBG 3/01) [921]

6291 Streissguth, Thomas. *John Glenn* (5–8). Series: A&E Biography. 1999, Lerner LB $25.26 (978-0-8225-4947-5); paper $7.95 (978-0-8225-9685-1). This account of John Glenn's life includes childhood influences, his career with NASA, and his political life as a senator. (Rev: HBG 3/00; SLJ 3/00) [921]

6292 Vogt, Gregory L. *John Glenn's Return to Space* (4–7). Illus. 2000, Twenty-First Century LB $24.90 (978-0-7613-1614-5). As well as describing John Glenn's two space flights on the *Mercury* capsule and later the *Discovery,* this biography gives information on astronauts' training and equipment. (Rev: BL 9/15/00; HBG 10/01; SLJ 1/01) [921]

GREENE, NATHANAEL

6293 Mierka, Gregg A. *Nathanael Greene: The General Who Saved the Revolution* (5–8). Illus. Series: Forgotten Heroes of the American Revolution. 2006, OTTN LB $23.95 (978-1-59556-012-4). Employing primary and previously unpublished sources, Mierka's lively text examines Greene's pivotal role as quartermaster general and southern commander in Washington's Revolutionary army. (Rev: BL 1/1–15/07) [973.3]

HAMILTON, ALEXANDER

6294 DeCarolis, Lisa. *Alexander Hamilton: Federalist and Founding Father* (4–7). Series: Library of American Lives and Times. 2003, Rosen LB $31.95 (978-0-8239-5735-4). The story of the military hero of the American Revolution who was the first secretary of the treasury and helped write the Federalist Papers. (Rev: BL 6/1–15/03; SLJ 4/03) [921]

6295 Haugen, Brenda. *Alexander Hamilton: Founding Father and Statesman* (4–7). Illus. Series: Signature Lives (Revolutionary War Era). 2005, Compass Point LB $34.60 (978-0-7565-0827-2). Traces the life of the man who became the first secretary of the treasury. (Rev: BL 4/1/05; SLJ 8/05) [921]

HANCOCK, JOHN

6296 Kjelle, Marylou Morano. *The Life and Times of John Hancock* (5–8). Illus. Series: Profiles in American History. 2007, Mitchell Lane LB $19.95 (978-1-58415-443-3). Little-known facts about John Hancock's life make this well-organized biography an interesting read. (Rev: SLJ 7/07) [921]

HENRY, PATRICK

6297 Kukla, Amy, and Jon Kukla. *Patrick Henry: Voice of the Revolution* (4–7). Illus. Series: Library

of American Lives and Times. 2001, Rosen $31.95 (978-0-8239-5725-5). Detailed text, a variety of illustrations, and a timeline give readers a good understanding of Henry's importance. (Rev: BL 10/15/01) [973.3]

HOLLIDAY, DOC

6298 Green, Carl R., and William R. Sanford. *Doc Holliday* (5–8). Series: Outlaws and Lawmen of the Wild West. 1995, Enslow LB $21.26 (978-0-89490-589-6). The life and exploits of this colorful western hero are reproduced with the help of photographs and maps. (Rev: BL 6/1–15/95) [921]

HOOVER, J. EDGAR

6299 Cunningham, Kevin. *J. Edgar Hoover: Controversial FBI Director* (5–8). Series: Signature Lives. 2005, Compass Point LB $34.60 (978-0-7565-0997-2). This introduction to Hoover's career provides limited personal details, concentrating instead on his political ambitions and tendency to ignore ethical standards. (Rev: SLJ 1/06) [921]

6300 Streissguth, Thomas. *J. Edgar Hoover: Powerful FBI Director* (5–8). Series: Historical American Biographies. 2002, Enslow LB $26.60 (978-0-7660-1623-1). Streissguth looks at Hoover's life from youth, his personality, and his work as head of the FBI, and explores the areas in which his influence was felt, including civil rights and politics. (Rev: HBG 10/02; SLJ 8/02) [363.25092]

HOUSTON, SAM

6301 Caravantes, Peggy. *An American in Texas: The Story of Sam Houston* (5–8). Series: Founders of the Republic. 2003, Morgan Reynolds LB $23.95 (978-1-931798-19-8). A portrait of the colorful general who became the first president of the Republic of Texas. (Rev: SLJ 5/04) [921]

6302 Woodward, Walter M. *Sam Houston: For Texas and the Union* (5–8). Series: The Library of American Lives and Times. 2003, Rosen LB $34.60 (978-0-8239-5739-2). A concise biography of the man credited with gaining Texas's independence. (Rev: SLJ 5/03) [976.4]

INOUYE, DANIEL K.

6303 Slavicek, Louise Chipley. *Daniel Inouye* (6–10). Series: Asian Americans of Achievement. 2007, Chelsea House LB $30.00 (978-0-7910-9271-2). A useful profile of the first Japanese American elected to the U.S. Congress, with information on his family's arrival in Hawaii and Inouye's experiences in World War II. (Rev: SLJ 8/07) [921]

JACKSON, STONEWALL

6304 Brager, Bruce L. *There He Stands: The Story of Stonewall Jackson* (8–10). Illus. Series: Civil War Leaders. 2005, Morgan Reynolds LB $26.95 (978-1-931798-44-0). The life and military career of Stonewall Jackson, one of the Civil War's most skilled tacticians; photographs, reproductions, and maps complement the well-written text. (Rev: SLJ 11/05) [921]

6305 Pflueger, Lynda. *Stonewall Jackson: Confederate General* (5–8). Illus. Series: Historical American Biographies. 1997, Enslow LB $26.60 (978-0-89490-781-4). This sympathetic biography of Jackson, who favored neither slavery nor secession but became a Confederate general in the Civil War, provides good material on his personal life and beliefs, quoting generously from firsthand sources. (Rev: BL 10/1/97) [921]

JONES, JOHN PAUL

6306 Bradford, James C. *John Paul Jones and the American Navy* (4–7). Series: Library of American Lives and Times. 2001, Rosen $34.60 (978-0-8239-5726-2). This attractively designed volume combines the life story of the naval hero of the American Revolution with a history of the birth and growth of the American navy. (Rev: BL 10/15/01) [921]

6307 Brager, Bruce L. *John Paul Jones: America's Sailor* (7–10). 2006, Morgan Reynolds LB $26.95 (978-1-931798-84-6). The naval commander's life (flaws and attributes) and times are covered in well-organized text plus maps, timeline, sources, and a bibliography. (Rev: BL 7/06; SLJ 5/06) [921]

6308 Cooper, Michael L. *Hero of the High Seas: John Paul Jones* (4–7). 2006, National Geographic $21.95 (978-0-7922-5547-5). This biography focuses on the Scottish immigrant's naval heroics during the American Revolution and includes a detailed timeline and a useful listing of "Words and Expressions from the Days of Sailing Ships." (Rev: BL 6/1–15/06; SLJ 9/06) [973.3]

6309 Tibbitts, Alison Davis. *John Paul Jones: Father of the American Navy* (5–8). Series: Historical American Biographies. 2002, Enslow LB $26.60 (978-0-7660-1448-0). The life of the American naval officer noted for his role in the Revolution and for the statement, "I have not yet begun to fight." (Rev: BL 4/1/02; HBG 10/02; SLJ 5/02) [921]

JORDAN, BARBARA

6310 Blue, Rose, and Corinne J. Naden. *Barbara Jordan* (7–10). Series: Black Americans of Achievement. 1992, Chelsea LB $30.00 (978-0-7910-1131-7). The colorful life of this former congresswoman

and educator is re-created in this illustrated biography. (Rev: BL 9/15/92; SLJ 11/92) [921]

6311 Jeffrey, Laura S. *Barbara Jordan: Congresswoman, Lawyer, Educator* (7–12). Illus. Series: African-American Biographies. 1997, Enslow LB $20.95 (978-0-89490-692-3). This biography covers both the personal and professional life of this amazing woman who overcame great obstacles to fulfill a multi-faceted career. (Rev: BL 5/15/97; SLJ 3/97) [921]

JOSEPH (NEZ PERCE CHIEF)

6312 Yates, Diana. *Chief Joseph: Thunder Rolling from the Mountains* (7–12). 1992, Ward Hill LB $14.95 (978-0-9623380-9-0); paper $10.95 (978-0-9623380-8-3). A sensitive distillation of the life and times of Chief Joseph of the Nez Perce. (Rev: BL 12/15/92; SLJ 12/92) [921]

KENNEDY, ROBERT F.

6313 Aronson, Marc. *Robert F. Kennedy* (8–11). Illus. Series: Up Close. 2007, Viking $15.99 (978-0-670-06066-5). True to the series' title, this book looks at Robert F. Kennedy up close, examining his personal life more than his public achievements. (Rev: BCCB 6/07; BL 3/1/07; HB 3–4/07; SLJ 5/07) [921]

6314 Koestler-Grack, Rachel A. *The Assassination of Robert F. Kennedy* (5–8). Series: American Moments. 2005, ABDO LB $25.65 (978-1-59197-931-9). Kennedy's assassination is placed in historical context, with a brief biography and discussion of the aftermath of this tragedy. (Rev: SLJ 11/05) [921]

6315 Mills, Judie. *Robert Kennedy* (8–12). Illus. 1998, Millbrook LB $36.90 (978-1-56294-250-2). A useful, informative biography that tells of Robert Kennedy's life and career and places them in the context of other historical events. (Rev: BL 8/98; SLJ 9/98) [921]

KERRY, JOHN

6316 Brager, Bruce L. *John Kerry: Senator from Massachusetts* (6–10). 2005, Morgan Reynolds LB $23.95 (978-1-931798-64-8). Kerry's life and military service are presented along with his career in politics and unsuccessful bid for the presidency in 2004. (Rev: SLJ 8/05) [921]

LEE, ROBERT E.

6317 Anderson, Paul Christopher. *Robert E. Lee: Legendary Commander of the Confederacy* (4–7). Series: Library of American Lives and Times. 2003, Rosen LB $34.60 (978-0-8239-5748-4). Extensive original sources are used to re-create the life of this

Confederate general and the times in which he lived. (Rev: BL 6/1–15/03) [921]

6318 Brown, Warren. *Robert E. Lee* (6–10). Series: World Leaders — Past and Present. 1991, Chelsea LB $19.95 (978-1-55546-814-9). Using many illustrations and maps, this volume re-creates the life of the Confederate Civil War general. (Rev: BL 11/15/91) [921]

6319 Kerby, Mona. *Robert E. Lee: Southern Hero of the Civil War* (5–8). Illus. Series: Historical American Biographies. 1997, Enslow LB $26.60 (978-0-89490-782-1). This thorough, sympathetic biography of Lee points out that he did not approve of slavery or the South's secession from the Union. (Rev: BL 10/1/97; SLJ 9/97) [921]

6320 Rice, Earle, Jr. *Robert E. Lee: First Soldier of the Confederacy* (8–10). Illus. Series: Civil War Leaders. 2005, Morgan Reynolds LB $26.95 (978-1-931798-47-1). Lee's childhood, adult life, and military career are covered; photographs, reproductions, and maps complement the well-written text. (Rev: SLJ 11/05) [921]

6321 Robertson, James I. *Robert E. Lee: Virginian Soldier, American Citizen* (7–10). Illus. 2005, Simon & Schuster $21.95 (978-0-689-85731-7). A rich and even-handed portrait of Robert E. Lee, including a number of excerpts from such primary sources as letters and diaries. (Rev: BL 11/15/05; SLJ 1/06; VOYA 10/05) [973.7]

LITTLE CROW

6322 Swain, Gwenyth. *Little Crow: Leader of the Dakota* (6–12). 2004, Minnesota Historical Soc. $22.95 (978-0-87351-502-3). Little Crow, who died in 1863, did all in his power to keep his people from war but joined them on the front lines when they chose to disregard his counsel. (Rev: BL 7/04; SLJ 7/04) [978.004]

LONG, HUEY

6323 La Vert, Suzanne. *Huey Long: The Kingfish of Louisiana* (8–12). Series: Makers of America. 1995, Facts on File $25.00 (978-0-8160-2880-1). Looks at the motivations and political life of Huey Long, including his assassination. (Rev: BL 6/1–15/95) [921]

MACARTHUR, DOUGLAS

6324 Darby, Jean. *Douglas MacArthur* (6–9). Illus. Series: Lerner Biographies. 1989, Lerner LB $30.35 (978-0-8225-4901-7). The career of the controversial general who led the war in the Pacific is outlined in this volume. (Rev: BL 11/15/89; SLJ 9/89) [921]

6325 Fox, Mary V. *Douglas MacArthur* (4–8). Series: The Importance Of. 1999, Lucent LB $27.45 (978-1-56006-545-6). The story of one of the nation's most prominent generals, whose unorthodox actions made him a controversial figure. (Rev: BL 9/15/99) [921]

6326 Gaines, Ann Graham. *Douglas MacArthur: Brilliant General, Controversial Leader* (5–8). Series: Historical American Biographies. 2001, Enslow LB $26.60 (978-0-7660-1445-9). Using many black-and-white photographs as illustrations, this account gives a well-rounded, unbiased picture of this controversial general. (Rev: BL 4/15/01; HBG 10/01; SLJ 6/01) [921]

6327 Haugen, Brenda. *Douglas MacArthur: America's General* (5–8). Series: Signature Lives. 2005, Compass Point LB $34.60 (978-0-7565-0994-1). This introduction to MacArthur's career provides limited personal details but concentrates instead on his leadership abilities and military achievements. (Rev: SLJ 1/06) [921]

MCCAIN, JOHN

6328 Feinberg, Barbara S. *John McCain: Serving His Country* (4–7). Illus. Series: Gateway. 2000, Millbrook LB $23.90 (978-0-7613-1974-0). A biography of the senator that tells about his youth and later political career but concentrates on his stint in the navy and his imprisonment during the Vietnam War. (Rev: BL 3/1/01; HBG 10/01) [921]

6329 Kozar, Richard. *John McCain* (8–12). Series: Overcoming Adversity. 2002, Chelsea LB $30.00 (978-0-7910-6299-9). The story of the prominent U.S. politician and how he survived the ordeal of a POW camp in Vietnam. (Rev: BL 4/15/02; HBG 10/02) [921]

6330 Wells, Catherine. *John McCain* (5–8). Illus. Series: Political Profiles. 2008, Morgan Reynolds LB $27.95 (978-1-59935-046-2). Beginning with his early years and ending just before his nomination as a presidential candidate, this book examines McCain's life as well as his public and military service. (Rev: BL 5/15/08; SLJ 1/08) [921]

MCCARTHY, JOSEPH

6331 Cohen, Daniel. *Joseph McCarthy: The Misuse of Political Power* (7–12). Illus. 1996, Millbrook LB $23.90 (978-1-56294-917-4). The dramatic story of the U.S. senator who used the threat of communism to gain power and ruin innocent lives. (Rev: BL 10/1/96; SLJ 10/96) [921]

MANKILLER, WILMA

6332 Glassman, Bruce. *Wilma Mankiller: Chief of the Cherokee Nation* (5–7). Illus. Series: Library of Famous Women. 1992, Blackbirch $24.94 (978-1-

56711-032-6). This is an inspiring biography of the amazing woman who led her Cherokee Indians through difficult crises. (Rev: BL 6/1/92; SLJ 4/92) [921]

MARSHALL, THURGOOD

6333 Crowe, Chris. *Thurgood Marshall* (6–12). Series: Up Close. 2008, Viking $16.99 (978-0-670-06228-7). Using many quotations, Crowe covers Marshall's life, work as an NAACP lawyer, civil rights activism, and career on the Supreme Court. (Rev: BL 6/1–15/08) [921]

6334 Herda, D. J. *Thurgood Marshall: Civil Rights Champion* (6–10). Illus. Series: Justices of the Supreme Court. 1995, Enslow LB $26.60 (978-0-89490-557-5). The story of the first African American Supreme Court justice and his lifelong fight to champion the rights of the oppressed. (Rev: BL 3/15/96) [921]

6335 Prentzas, G. S. *Thurgood Marshall: Champion of Justice* (4–8). Illus. Series: Junior World Biography. 1993, Chelsea LB $15.95 (978-0-7910-1769-2); paper $4.95 (978-0-7910-1969-6). An interesting biography of Thurgood Marshall that touches on his civil rights work but focuses on his years as a Supreme Court justice. (Rev: SLJ 11/93) [921]

6336 Rowh, Mark. *Thurgood Marshall: Civil Rights Attorney and Supreme Court Justice* (6–8). Series: African-American Biographies. 2002, Enslow LB $26.60 (978-0-7660-1547-0). Marshall's youth, education, early career, family life, and experiences as a Supreme Court judge are all covered in this readable biography. (Rev: HBG 10/02; SLJ 10/02) [347.73]

MORRIS, GOUVERNOR

6337 Crompton, Samuel Willard. *Gouverneur Morris: Creating a Nation* (5–8). Series: America's Founding Fathers. 2004, Enslow LB $26.60 (978-0-7660-2213-3). An introduction to the life and legacy of Gouvernor Morris, who helped to edit the final draft of the Declaration of Independence. (Rev: SLJ 7/04) [973.4]

NADER, RALPH

6338 Bowen, Nancy. *Ralph Nader: Man with a Mission* (6–10). Illus. 2002, Millbrook LB $24.90 (978-0-7613-2365-5). An absorbing biography of the consumer advocate, environmentalist, and politician, with photographs. (Rev: BL 4/1/02; HBG 10/02; SLJ 4/02) [921]

6339 Celsi, Teresa. *Ralph Nader: The Consumer Revolution* (6–12). Series: New Directions. 1991, Millbrook LB $21.90 (978-1-56294-044-7). The story of the consumer advocate who has taken on some of the largest corporations in America and won. (Rev: BL 10/1/91; SLJ 10/91) [921]

6340 Graham, Kevin. *Ralph Nader: Battling for Democracy* (6–12). 2000, Windom paper $9.95 (978-0-9700323-0-0). A readable biography of the man who has devoted his life to fighting for liberty and justice for all. (Rev: BL 12/1/00; SLJ 11/00) [921]

NAVA, JULIAN

6341 Nava, Julian. *Julian Nava: My Mexican-American Journey* (7–12). 2002, Arte Publico $16.95 (978-1-55885-364-5); paper $9.95 (978-1-55885-351-5). Nava tells the story of his life and his journey from the barrio to become the first Mexican American ambassador to Mexico. (Rev: BL 10/15/02) [921]

NORTON, ELEANOR HOLMES

6342 Marcovitz, Hal. *Eleanor Holmes Norton* (7–12). Series: African-American Leaders. 2003, Chelsea House LB $30.00 (978-0-7910-7682-8). Profiles the woman representing Washington, D.C. in the House of Representatives, and discusses her work on sexual harassment in the workplace. (Rev: SLJ 4/04) [921]

O'CONNOR, SANDRA DAY

6343 Herda, D. J. *Sandra Day O'Connor: Independent Thinker* (6–10). Illus. Series: Justices of the Supreme Court. 1995, Enslow LB $17.95 (978-0-89480-558-5). The story of the first female Supreme Court justice, including her personal life and some key decisions since becoming a Supreme Court member in 1981. (Rev: BL 2/15/96) [921]

6344 Macht, Norman L. *Sandra Day O'Connor: Supreme Court Justice* (4–7). Illus. Series: Junior World Biography. 1992, Chelsea paper $8.95 (978-0-7910-0448-7). In clear text with many photographs, this is a simple account of the first female Supreme Court Justice. (Rev: BL 8/92; SLJ 8/92) [921]

PAINE, THOMAS

6345 Burgan, Michael. *Thomas Paine: Great Writer of the Revolution* (4–7). Illus. Series: Signature Lives (Revolutionary War Era). 2005, Compass Point LB $34.60 (978-0-7565-0830-2). A well-designed profile of the revolutionary thinker. (Rev: BL 4/1/05) [921]

6346 Kaye, Harvey J. *Thomas Paine: Firebrand of the Revolution* (6–10). Illus. 2000, Oxford LB $32.95 (978-0-19-511627-4). A readable, well-illustrated biography on the career, accomplishments, and lasting importance of this Revolutionary War personality, with material on the social and political conditions of the period. (Rev: BL 3/1/00; HBG 9/00; SLJ 4/00) [921]

6347 McCarthy, Pat. *Thomas Paine: Revolutionary Patriot and Writer* (5–8). Series: Historical American Biographies. 2001, Enslow LB $26.60 (978-0-7660-1446-6). A balanced, well-researched biography of the American political theorist and writer who created controversy throughout his lifetime. (Rev: BL 4/15/01; HBG 10/01) [921]

6348 McCartin, Brian. *Thomas Paine: Common Sense and Revolutionary Pamphleteering* (4–7). Series: Library of American Lives and Times. 2001, Rosen $34.60 (978-0-8239-5729-3). The story of the British-born colonialist who heard the cries for liberty around him and whose writings set the stage for the Declaration of Independence. (Rev: BL 10/15/01) [921]

6349 Vail, John. *Thomas Paine* (6–10). Illus. 1990, Chelsea LB $19.95 (978-1-55546-819-4). The story of the outspoken radical whose writings influenced the development of the American Revolution. (Rev: BL 8/90; SLJ 6/90; VOYA 8/90) [921]

PELOSI, NANCY

6350 Shichtman, Sandra H. *Nancy Pelosi* (5–8). Series: Political Profiles. 2007, Morgan Reynolds LB $27.95 (978-1-59935-049-3). An admiring portrait of this important political figure, with photographs. (Rev: BL 11/15/07; SLJ 1/08) [328.7]

PENN, WILLIAM

6351 Somervill, Barbara A. *William Penn: Founder of Pennsylvania* (7–9). 2006, Compass Point LB $30.60 (978-0-7565-1598-0). A straightforward profile of the colonial figure, covering his childhood, his reasons for leaving England, and his commitment to religious freedom. (Rev: SLJ 7/06) [921]

PERKINS, FRANCES

6352 Keller, Emily. *Frances Perkins: First Woman Cabinet Member* (8–12). 2006, Morgan Reynolds LB $27.95 (978-1-931798-91-4). Perkins, a social reformer, served as Secretary of Labor under Franklin D. Roosevelt; this thorough biography documents her achievements and covers her personal life. (Rev: SLJ 5/07) [921]

PHILIP (SACHEM OF THE WAMPANOAGS)

6353 Averill, Esther. *King Philip: The Indian Chief* (5–8). Illus. by Vera Belsky. 1993, Shoe String LB $20.00 (978-0-208-02357-5). The story of the Wampanoag chief who befriended the Pilgrims and later waged war against the settlers. (Rev: BL 7/93) [921]

POWELL, COLIN

6354 Blue, Rose, and Corinne J. Naden. *Colin Powell: Straight to the Top.* Rev. ed. (4–8). Series: Gateway Biographies. 1997, Millbrook LB $23.90 (978-0-7613-0256-8); paper $9.95 (978-0-7613-0242-1). A balanced biography of Colin Powell that focuses on his adult life and his stint as chairman of the Joint Chiefs of Staff. (Rev: BL 9/15/97; SLJ 1/98) [921]

6355 Brown, Warren. *Colin Powell* (7–10). Series: Black Americans of Achievement. 1992, Chelsea LB $30.00 (978-0-7910-1647-3). A nicely illustrated account of the African American general who distinguished himself during the Persian Gulf War. (Rev: BL 8/92) [921]

6356 Finlayson, Reggie. *Colin Powell* (5–8). Series: A&E Biography. 2003, Lerner LB $27.93 (978-0-8225-4966-6); paper $7.95 (978-0-8225-9698-1). Documents Powell's rise through the military and transition into the political and diplomatic world. (Rev: BL 1/1–15/04; HBG 4/04) [921]

6357 Finlayson, Reggie. *Colin Powell: People's Hero* (5–8). Series: Achievers Biographies. 1997, Lerner LB $25.55 (978-0-8225-2891-3). From his birth in Harlem to his distinguished military career, this is a fine biography of Colin Powell. (Rev: SLJ 4/97; VOYA 6/97) [921]

6358 Schraff, Anne. *Colin Powell: Soldier and Patriot* (7–12). Illus. Series: African-American Biographies. 1997, Enslow LB $26.60 (978-0-89490-810-1). A profile of the career soldier who led U.S. forces in war and peace. (Rev: BL 5/15/97; SLJ 3/97; VOYA 6/97) [921]

6359 Senna, Carl. *Colin Powell: A Man of War and Peace* (4–8). Illus. 1992, Walker LB $16.85 (978-0-8027-8181-9). The life of the general who became the first African American chairman of the Joint Chiefs of Staff. (Rev: BL 3/15/93) [921]

6360 Shichtman, Sandra H. *Colin Powell: "Have a Vision. Be Demanding."* (5–8). Series: African-American Biography Library. 2005, Enslow LB $31.93 (978-0-7660-2464-9). Sandra H. Shichtman profiles former Secretary of State Colin Powell in this title from the African-American Biography Library series. (Rev: SLJ 11/05) [921]

RANKIN, JEANNETTE

6361 Woelfle, Gretchen. *Jeannette Rankin: Political Pioneer* (6–9). Illus. 2007, Boyds Mills $18.95 (978-1-59078-437-2). Jeannette Rankin became Montana's representative in Congress in 1916 and went on to advocate for women's rights; this is an informative and interesting profile. (Rev: BL 2/15/07) [921]

RICE, CONDOLEEZZA

6362 Ditchfield, Christin. *Condoleezza Rice: America's Leading Stateswoman*. Rev. ed. (5–8). Series: Great Life Stories. 2006, Watts LB $30.50 (978-0-531-13874-8). An updated version of the 2003 biography, adding information on Rice's role as secretary of state and the continuing events in Iraq. (Rev: SLJ 2/07) [921]

6363 Ryan, Bernard. *Condoleezza Rice: National Security Advisor and Musician* (5–8). 2003, Ferguson LB $25.00 (978-0-8160-5480-0). Rice's life and career are detailed, up to the invasion of Iraq. (Rev: SLJ 5/04) [921]

6364 Wade, Mary Dodson. *Condoleezza Rice: Being the Best* (4–7). Illus. 2003, Millbrook LB $23.90 (978-0-7613-2619-9). An interesting profile with a focus on Rice's talented youth and southern upbringing. (Rev: BL 3/1/03; HBG 10/03; SLJ 4/03) [355]

RICHARDS, ANN

6365 Siegel, Dorothy S. *Ann Richards: Politician, Feminist, Survivor* (4–7). Illus. Series: People to Know. 1996, Enslow LB $20.95 (978-0-89490-497-4). In a conversational style, this biography covers the important events in the life of this Texas politician. (Rev: BL 5/15/96; SLJ 10/96) [921]

SCHWARZENEGGER, ARNOLD

6366 Sexton, Colleen A. *Arnold Schwarzenegger* (5–8). Series: A&E Biography. 2004, Lerner LB $29.27 (978-0-8225-1634-7). This evenhanded profile, with many photographs and quotations, covers Schwarzenegger's life from his childhood in Austria to his election as governor of California and appends a list of his films. (Rev: BL 11/1/04) [921]

SCHWARZKOPF, NORMAN

6367 McNeese, Tim. *H. Norman Schwarzkopf* (6–9). Series: Great Military Leaders of the 20th Century. 2003, Chelsea House LB $30.00 (978-0-7910-7406-0). Schwarzkopf's personal life and military career are explored in this admiring biography of the Persian Gulf War general. (Rev: SLJ 2/04) [921]

SEWARD, WILLIAM

6368 Kent, Zachary. *William Seward: The Mastermind of the Alaska Purchase* (6–10). Series: Historical American Biographies. 2001, Enslow LB $26.60 (978-0-7660-1391-9). The story of the man who was appointed secretary of state by Lincoln and who engineered the purchase of Alaska is the focus of this biography full of period illustrations, maps, and cartoons. (Rev: BL 3/1/01; HBG 10/01; SLJ 5/01) [921]

SHARPTON, AL

6369 Mallin, Jay. *Al Sharpton: Community Activist* (6–12). Series: Great Life Stories. 2006, Watts LB $30.50 (978-0-531-13872-4). Mallin looks at Sharpton's personal and professional life from childhood to his bid for the presidency. (Rev: SLJ 3/07) [921]

SITTING BULL

6370 Schleichert, Elizabeth. *Sitting Bull: Sioux Leader* (6–9). Series: Native American Biographies. 1997, Enslow LB $26.60 (978-0-89490-868-2). A well-documented account of this important Sioux leader, including his reasons for participating in Buffalo Bill's Wild West Show. (Rev: BL 4/15/97; SLJ 6/97) [921]

STUART, JEB

6371 Pflueger, Lynda. *Jeb Stuart: Confederate Cavalry General* (5–8). Series: Historical American Biographies. 1998, Enslow LB $20.95 (978-0-7660-1013-0). The life of the brilliant general who had successes at the battles of Bull Run, Antietam, and Fredericksburg, but who committed a tactical error at Gettysburg. (Rev: BL 8/98; SLJ 8/98) [921]

SUTTER, JOHN

6372 Engstrand, Iris, and Ken Owens. *John Sutter: Sutter's Fort and the California Gold Rush* (4–8). Series: The Library of American Lives and Times. 2004, Rosen LB $34.60 (978-0-8239-6630-1). The importance of understanding history is emphasized in this balanced and well-illustrated look at Sutter's life. (Rev: SLJ 7/04) [921]

THOMAS, CLARENCE

6373 Macht, Norman L. *Clarence Thomas* (6–9). 1995, Chelsea LB $30.00 (978-0-7910-1883-5); paper $30.00 (978-0-7910-1912-2). Details Thomas's life, culminating in his controversial appointment to the Supreme Court, with frank coverage of the congressional hearings. (Rev: BL 8/95; SLJ 9/95) [347.73]

VALLEJO, MARIANO GUADALUPE

6374 Tracy, Kathleen. *Mariano Guadalupe Vallejo* (5–7). Series: Latinos in American History. 2002, Mitchell Lane LB $29.95 (978-1-58415-152-4). The story of the 19th-century military man who supported the U.S. annexation of California and later served in the state's first Senate. (Rev: BL 2/15/03; HBG 10/03) [921]

401

WARD, NANCY

6375 Furbee, Mary R. *Wild Rose: Nancy Ward and the Cherokee Nation* (6–9). Illus. Series: Women of the Frontier. 2001, Morgan Reynolds LB $23.95 (978-1-883846-71-8). This is the absorbing story of the Cherokee woman who became a much-respected leader and advocate for peaceful coexistence with the white settlers. (Rev: HBG 3/02; SLJ 9/01; VOYA 6/02) [975]

WARREN, EARL

6376 Compston, Christine L. *Earl Warren: Justice for All* (7–10). Illus. Series: Oxford Portraits. 2002, Oxford $32.95 (978-0-19-513001-0). In addition to Warren's family life and career, this portrait presents his belief in the rule of law and his dealings with successive presidents. (Rev: BL 4/15/02; HBG 10/02; SLJ 6/02) [921]

6377 Herda, D. J. *Earl Warren: Chief Justice for Social Change* (6–10). Illus. Series: Justices of the Supreme Court. 1995, Enslow LB $20.95 (978-0-89490-556-8). The story of the chief justice who led the Supreme Court during a period of great change and who headed the commission that investigated President Kennedy's death. (Rev: BL 3/15/96; SLJ 3/96) [921]

WATTS, J. C.

6378 Lutz, Norma Jean. *J. C. Watts* (4–7). Series: Black Americans of Achievement. 2000, Chelsea $30.00 (978-0-7910-5338-6). The story of a former Oklahoma University football player who entered politics and was first elected to the House of Representatives in 1994. (Rev: BL 6/1–15/00; HBG 10/00) [921]

WEBSTER, DANIEL

6379 Harvey, Bonnie Carman. *Daniel Webster* (5–8). Series: Historical American Biographies. 2001, Enslow LB $26.60 (978-0-7660-1392-6). An engrossing biography of the American statesman, lawyer, and orator who fought to save the Union. (Rev: BL 1/1–15/02; HBG 3/02; SLJ 12/01) [921]

WILLIAMS, ROGER

6380 Burgan, Michael. *Roger Williams: Founder of Rhode Island* (7–9). 2006, Compass Point LB $30.60 (978-0-7565-1596-6). A straightforward profile of the colonial figure, covering his childhood, his reasons for leaving England, and his belief in separation of church and state. (Rev: SLJ 7/06) [921]

WINTHROP, JOHN

6381 Burgan, Michael. *John Winthrop: Colonial Governor of Massachusetts* (7–9). 2006, Compass Point LB $30.60 (978-0-7565-1591-1). A straightforward profile of the governor, covering his childhood, his reasons for leaving England, and his Puritan beliefs. (Rev: SLJ 7/06) [921]

Miscellaneous Persons

ALLEN, RICHARD

6382 Klots, Steve. *Richard Allen* (5–8). Illus. Series: Black Americans of Achievement. 1990, Chelsea LB $19.95 (978-1-55546-570-4). Born a slave in 1780, this convert to Christianity founded the first African American Methodist Church. (Rev: SLJ 2/91) [921]

BAILEY, ANNE

6383 Furbee, Mary R. *Anne Bailey: Frontier Scout* (6–12). Illus. 2001, Morgan Reynolds $21.95 (978-1-883846-70-1). This is the absorbing story of a courageous woman who became a scout in the Revolutionary War. (Rev: BL 12/1/01; HBG 3/02; SLJ 3/02) [921]

BALL, CHARLES

6384 Shuter, Jane, ed. *Charles Ball and American Slavery* (5–8). Illus. Series: History Eyewitness. 1995, Raintree LB $24.26 (978-0-8114-8281-3). This autobiographical account in simple language brings the horrors of slavery to life, with period prints and maps. (Rev: BL 4/15/95; SLJ 5/95) [975]

BARTON, CLARA

6385 Hamilton, Leni. *Clara Barton* (5–10). Illus. 1987, Chelsea LB $19.95 (978-1-55546-641-1). The story of the Civil War nurse and how she prepared for the founding of the American Red Cross. (Rev: BL 11/1/87) [921]

6386 Koestler-Grack, Rachel A. *The Story of Clara Barton* (4–7). Illus. Series: Breakthrough Biographies. 2004, Chelsea House LB $23.00 (978-0-7910-7312-4). From her childhood and early career to her founding of the American Red Cross, this profile gives personal details and historical context. (Rev: BL 3/1/04; SLJ 9/04) [361.763]

6387 Somervill, Barbara A. *Clara Barton: Founder of the American Red Cross* (5–8). Illus. Series: Signature Lives: Civil War Era. 2007, Compass Point LB $23.95 (978-0-7565-1888-2). Chronicles the life of Clara Barton and provides information on the time in which she worked. (Rev: BL 6/1–15/07) [921]

6388 Whitelaw, Nancy. *Clara Barton: Civil War Nurse* (5–9). Series: Historical American Biographies. 1997, Enslow LB $26.60 (978-0-89490-778-4). Using material from her diaries and published books, this biography relates Barton's life story and amazing accomplishments. (Rev: BL 3/15/98; SLJ 2/98) [921]

BECKWOURTH, JAMES

6389 Gregson, Susan R. *James Beckwourth: Mountaineer, Scout, and Pioneer* (5–8). Series: Signature Lives. 2005, Compass Point LB $34.60 (978-0-7565-1000-8). Beckwourth was one of the first African Americans to play a role in the exploration of the West. (Rev: SLJ 2/06) [921]

BILLY THE KID

6390 Bruns, Roger A. *Billy the Kid* (5–8). Series: Historical American Biographies. 2000, Enslow LB $26.60 (978-0-7660-1091-8). A well-researched and thoroughly documented biography of America's famous outlaw. (Rev: BL 1/1–15/00; HBG 10/00; SLJ 5/00) [921]

6391 Cline, Don. *Alias Billy the Kid, the Man Behind the Legend* (8–12). Illus. 1986, Sunstone paper $12.95 (978-0-86534-080-0). The real story of Billy the Kid, clearing up many misconceptions. [921]

6392 Green, Carl R., and William R. Sanford. *Billy the Kid* (4–8). Illus. Series: Outlaws and Lawmen of the Wild West. 1992, Enslow LB $21.26 (978-0-89490-364-9). The life story of the outlaw William H. Bonney, who lived from 1859 to 1881. (Rev: BL 7/92; SLJ 8/92) [921]

BLY, NELLIE

6393 Fredeen, Charles. *Nellie Bly: Daredevil Reporter* (5–9). Series: Lerner Biographies. 2000, Lerner LB $25.26 (978-0-8225-4956-7). The story of the daring reporter who traveled around the world in 72 days and was a champion of the women's suffrage movement. (Rev: HBG 10/00; SLJ 3/00) [921]

6394 Peck, Ira, and Nellie Bly. *Nellie Bly's Book: Around the World in 72 Days* (6–8). 1998, Twenty-First Century LB $27.90 (978-0-7613-0971-0). An abridged version of the account written by the famous muckraking journalist about her trip around the world in which she beat Phileas Fogg's record by six days. (Rev: BL 2/15/99; HBG 10/99; SLJ 4/99) [921]

BOONE, DANIEL

6395 Calvert, Patricia. *Daniel Boone: Beyond the Mountains* (5–8). Series: Great Explorations. 2001, Marshall Cavendish LB $29.93 (978-0-7614-1243-4). An attractive biography of the American pioneer who explored the Cumberland Gap region and helped settlers in the Kentucky region. (Rev: BCCB 3/02; BL 4/1/02; HBG 3/02; SLJ 3/02) [921]

6396 Faragher, John Mack. *Daniel Boone: The Life and Legend of an American Pioneer* (7–12). 1992, Holt paper $18.00 (978-0-8050-3007-5). A biography of the complex frontier pioneer/politician/maverick. (Rev: BL 11/1/92*; SLJ 5/93*) [921]

6397 Green, Carl R. *Blazing the Wilderness Road with Daniel Boone* (6–10). Series: In American History. 2000, Enslow LB $26.60 (978-0-7660-1346-9). The story of Daniel Boone, his contributions to opening up the West, and his role in the American Revolution. (Rev: BL 12/15/00; HBG 3/01) [921]

6398 McCarthy, Pat. *Daniel Boone* (5–8). Series: Historical American Biographies. 2000, Enslow LB $26.60 (978-0-7660-1256-1). A well-organized and thoroughly documented biography of the legendary pioneer and hero of the American Revolution who died in 1820. (Rev: BL 1/1–15/00; HBG 10/00; SLJ 5/00) [921]

BOWIE, JIM

6399 Edmondson, J. R. *Jim Bowie: Frontier Legend, Alamo Hero* (4–7). Series: Library of American Lives and Times. 2003, Rosen LB $34.60 (978-0-8239-5734-7). As well as being a rogue, slave trader, and murderer, Jim Bowie was also a hero of the famous battle of the Alamo. (Rev: BL 6/1–15/03; SLJ 7/03) [921]

6400 Gaines, Ann Graham. *Jim Bowie* (5–8). Series: Historical American Biographies. 2000, Enslow LB $26.60 (978-0-7660-1253-0). A well-documented biography of Jim Bowie, a hero of the revolution in Texas who was best known for fighting in the battle of the Alamo. (Rev: BL 1/1–15/00; HBG 10/00; SLJ 5/00) [921]

BRIDGMAN, LAURA

6401 Alexander, Sally Hobart, and Robert Alexander. *She Touched the World: Laura Bridgman, Deaf-Blind Pioneer* (5–8). Illus. 2008, Clarion $18.00 (978-0-618-85299-4). A little-known pioneer in the education of the deaf-blind, Bridgman (two generations older than Helen Keller) is an important figure, and this book ably introduces her to young readers. (Rev: BL 3/1/08; SLJ 3/08) [921]

BROADWICK, GEORGIA "TINY"

6402 Roberson, Elizabeth Whitley. *Tiny Broadwick: The First Lady of Parachuting* (4–8). Illus. 2001, Pelican paper $9.95 (978-1-56554-780-3). Less than 5 feet tall, "Tiny" Broadwick joined a hot-air balloon act as a teenager and became the first woman to jump with a parachute. (Rev: BL 7/01) [797.5]

CAPONE, AL

6403 King, David C. *Al Capone and the Roaring Twenties* (5–9). Illus. Series: Notorious Americans and Their Times. 1998, Blackbirch LB $28.70 (978-1-56711-218-4). In this biography of the gangster, the reader also gets information on the Jazz Age, the Ku Klux Klan, and other personalities of the time, such as Earhart and Lindbergh. (Rev: BL 12/15/98; HBG 3/99; SLJ 12/98) [921]

CASSIDY, BUTCH

6404 Green, Carl R., and William R. Sanford. *Butch Cassidy* (4–8). Series: Outlaws and Lawmen of the Wild West. 1995, Enslow LB $21.26 (978-0-89490-587-2). The Wild West is re-created in this brief account of the life of this colorful outlaw, whose death remains a mystery. (Rev: BL 6/1–15/95; SLJ 7/95) [921]

6405 Wukovits, John F. *Butch Cassidy* (4–7). Series: Legends of the West. 1997, Chelsea $18.65 (978-0-7910-3857-4). This biography of Robert Leroy Parker, who is better known as Butch Cassidy, emphasizes the fact that he was a ruthless criminal and not the idealized character of the movies. (Rev: HBG 3/98; SLJ 4/98) [921]

CHAPMAN, JOHN

6406 Warrick, Karen Clemens. *John Chapman: The Legendary Johnny Appleseed* (5–8). Series: Historical American Biographies. 2001, Enslow LB $26.60 (978-0-7660-1443-5). An engrossing, nicely illustrated portrait of the man who wandered the Midwest promoting apple cultivation. (Rev: BL 4/15/01; HBG 10/01; SLJ 4/01) [921]

CHIPETA

6407 Krudwig, Vickie Leigh. *Searching for Chipeta: The Story of a Ute and Her People* (4–7). 2004, Fulcrum paper $12.95 (978-1-55591-466-0). In the second half of the 19th century, Chipeta and her Ute husband worked tirelessly — but ultimately unsuccessfully — to forge an agreement with the U.S. government that would allow the tribe to remain in its traditional homeland. (Rev: BL 9/1/04) [921]

CRANDALL, PRUDENCE

6408 Jurmain, Suzanne. *The Forbidden Schoolhouse: The True and Dramatic Story of Prudence Crandall and Her Students* (5–8). Illus. 2005, Houghton $19.00 (978-0-618-47302-1). The inspiring story of Prudence Crandall, who in the 1830s risked ostracism — and worse — from the townspeople of Canterbury, Connecticut, when she opens her academy to young African American women. (Rev: BCCB 11/05; BL 10/1/05*; HB 11–12/05; HBG 4/06; LMC 8–9/05; SLJ 11/05) [370]

EARP, WYATT

6409 Green, Carl R., and William R. Sanford. *Wyatt Earp* (4–8). Illus. Series: Outlaws and Lawmen of the Wild West. 1992, Enslow LB $21.26 (978-0-89490-367-0). With maps and authentic illustrations, this biography tells the story of the deputy marshal who tried to clean up Tombstone, Arizona. (Rev: BL 10/1/92; SLJ 11/92) [921]

EDMONDS, EMMA

6410 Reit, Seymour. *Behind Rebel Lines: The Incredible Story of Emma Edmonds, Civil War Spy* (5–8). 1988, Harcourt $12.95 (978-0-15-200416-3); paper $6.00 (978-0-15-200424-8). The remarkable Canadian-born spy who helped to defend the Union in the Civil War. (Rev: BL 3/1/88; SLJ 3/88) [973.785]

EDWARDS, JONATHAN

6411 Lutz, Norma Jean. *Jonathan Edwards: Colonial Religious Leader* (5–7). Series: Colonial Leaders. 2001, Chelsea $27.50 (978-0-7910-5961-6). The life of Edwards, a leader in the Great Awakening spiritual movement and preacher among Native American tribes, is presented here with discussion of his contributions and his failings. (Rev: SLJ 5/01) [921]

ESCALANTE, JAIME

6412 Byers, Ann. *Jaime Escalante: Sensational Teacher* (6–10). Illus. Series: Hispanic Biographies. 1996, Enslow LB $26.60 (978-0-89490-763-0). A profile of the unique, inspiring teacher whose career became the basis of the film *Stand and Deliver*. (Rev: BL 10/1/96; SLJ 9/96; VOYA 12/96) [921]

FORTUNE, AMOS

6413 Yates, Elizabeth. *Amos Fortune, Free Man* (6–9). Illus. by Nora S. Unwin. 1950, Dutton $16.99 (978-0-525-25570-3); Puffin paper $6.99 (978-0-14-034158-4). The simplicity and dignity of the human spirit and its triumph over degradation are movingly portrayed in this portrait of a slave who bought his freedom. Newbery Medal winner, 1951. [974.4]

FRAUNCES, PHOEBE

6414 Griffin, Judith Berry. *Phoebe the Spy* (7–9). 1989, Scholastic paper $3.99 (978-0-590-42432-5). The story of the 13-year-old black girl who saved George Washington's life from an assassination attempt. [921]

FRY, VARIAN

6415 McClafferty, Carla Killough. *In Defiance of Hitler: The Secret Mission of Varian Fry* (7–12). Illus. 2008, Farrar $19.95 (978-0-374-38204-9). This is the amazing story of a New York journalist who helped to save more than 2,000 — Jews and non-Jews — from Nazi-occupied France. (Rev: BL 6/1–15/08; SLJ 9/08) [921]

GATES, HENRY LOUIS, JR.

6416 Kjelle, Marylou Morano. *Henry Louis Gates, Jr.* (6–12). Series: African-American Leaders. 2003, Chelsea House LB $30.00 (978-0-7910-7687-3). A life of the influential historian and author who teaches at Harvard. (Rev: SLJ 4/04) [921]

GRAHAM, BILLY

6417 Wooten, Sara McIntosh. *Billy Graham: World-Famous Evangelist* (6–10). Illus. Series: People to Know. 2001, Enslow LB $26.60 (978-0-7660-1533-3). A well-rounded and interesting account of Graham's life, education, and career, with coverage of his boisterous youth. (Rev: BL 10/1/01; HBG 3/02) [921]

HALE, NATHAN

6418 Krizner, L. J., and Lisa Sita. *Nathan Hale: Patriot and Martyr of the American Revolution* (4–7). Series: Library of American Lives and Times. 2001, Rosen $31.95 (978-0-8239-5724-8). Nathan Hale, executed by the British in 1776, represented the life-and-death issues fought for in the Revolution and became a symbol of courage and patriotism. (Rev: BL 10/15/01) [921]

6419 Tracy, Kathleen. *The Life and Times of Nathan Hale* (5–8). Illus. Series: Profiles in American History. 2007, Mitchell Lane LB $19.95 (978-1-58415-447-1). This is an appealing life of Nathan Hale, from his childhood through his execution by the British. (Rev: SLJ 7/07) [921]

HALE, SARAH JOSEPHA BUELL

6420 Dubois, Muriel L. *To My Countrywomen: The Life of Sarah Josepha Hale* (6–9). 2006, Apprentice

Shop Books $15.00 (978-0-9723410-1-1). This is the story of Sarah Hale, who successfully used her skills as a writer after her husband died in 1822, leaving her to raise their small children on her own. (Rev: BL 9/15/06) [921]

HAYSLIP, LE LY

6421 Englar, Mary. *Le Ly Hayslip* (5–8). Series: Asian-American Biographies. 2005, Raintree LB $23.00 (978-1-4109-1055-4). An interesting profile of the Vietnamese-born woman who started the East Meets West Foundation. (Rev: SLJ 3/06) [921]

HEARST, WILLIAM RANDOLPH

6422 Whitelaw, Nancy. *William Randolph Hearst and the American Century* (6–12). Illus. 1999, Morgan Reynolds $21.95 (978-1-883846-46-6). Hearst's eccentricities and lively, thrusting approach to life are well portrayed in this vivid biography. (Rev: BL 10/1/99; HBG 4/00; VOYA 6/00) [921]

HICKOK, WILD BILL

6423 Green, Carl R., and William R. Sanford. *Wild Bill Hickok* (4–8). Illus. Series: Outlaws and Lawmen of the Wild West. 1992, Enslow LB $21.26 (978-0-89490-366-3). The life story of the famous frontier marshal in Kansas is retold in text and pictures. (Rev: BL 7/92; SLJ 8/92) [921]

6424 Rosa, Joseph G. *Wild Bill Hickok: Sharpshooter and U.S. Marshal of the Wild West* (4–8). Series: The Library of American Lives and Times. 2004, Rosen LB $34.60 (978-0-8239-6632-5). The importance of understanding history is emphasized in this balanced and well-illustrated look at Hickok's life. (Rev: SLJ 7/04) [921]

HOUDINI, HARRY

6425 Cox, Clinton. *Houdini: Master of Illusion* (5–9). Illus. 2001, Scholastic paper $16.95 (978-0-590-94960-6). A fast-paced account of the life of the world-famous magician from childhood on, with eight pages of photographs and reproductions. (Rev: BL 11/15/01; HB 1–2/02; HBG 3/02; SLJ 12/01; VOYA 2/02) [793.8]

6426 Fleischman, Sid. *Escape! The Story of the Great Houdini* (4–8). 2006, HarperCollins $18.99 (978-0-06-085694-6). A lively and entertaining biography by a great writer and professional magician, who reveals just enough of the magic behind the tricks; includes many photographs. (Rev: SLJ 8/06*; VOYA 6/06) [921]

6427 Lalicki, Tom. *Spellbinder: The Life of Harry Houdini* (5–8). Illus. 2000, Holiday $18.95 (978-0-8234-1499-4). A biography of Elrich Weiss, aka Harry Houdini, and his career as a magician and escape artist. (Rev: BCCB 3/01; BL 9/1/00; HBG 3/01; SLJ 9/00; VOYA 12/00) [921]

HUTCHINSON, ANNE

6428 Ilgenfritz, Elizabeth. *Anne Hutchinson* (5–8). Illus. Series: American Women of Achievement. 1990, Chelsea LB $19.95 (978-1-55546-660-2). The story of the woman in pre-Revolutionary days who stood trial to defend religious liberty. (Rev: SLJ 4/91) [921]

INGLES, MARY DRAPER

6429 Furbee, Mary R. *Shawnee Captive: The Story of Mary Draper Ingles* (5–8). Illus. 2001, Morgan Reynolds LB $23.95 (978-1-883846-69-5). The tragic and exciting story of a pioneer woman captured by Shawnee Indians, her daring escape, and her long and difficult journey home. (Rev: BL 5/15/01; HBG 10/01; SLJ 6/01) [975.5]

JAMES, JESSE

6430 Bruns, Roger. *Jesse James: Legendary Outlaw* (5–8). Series: Historical American Biographies. 1998, Enslow LB $26.60 (978-0-7660-1055-0). Using fact boxes, maps, a chronology, and chapter notes as well as an interesting text and black-and-white photographs, this book gives a fine biography of Jesse James and his exploits. (Rev: BL 10/15/98; SLJ 8/98) [921]

6431 Green, Carl R., and William R. Sanford. *Jesse James* (4–8). Illus. Series: Outlaws and Lawmen of the Wild West. 1992, Enslow LB $21.26 (978-0-89490-365-6). This easy-to-read text portrays the legendary gunman as both outlaw and hero. (Rev: BL 3/1/92; SLJ 5/92) [921]

6432 Wukovits, John F. *Jesse James* (5–8). Illus. Series: Legends of the West. 1996, Chelsea $18.65 (978-0-7910-3876-5). An action-packed biography that tries to probe the complex nature of the famous Western outlaw. (Rev: SLJ 4/97) [921]

JOHN HENRY (LEGENDARY CHARACTER)

6433 Nelson, Scott Reynolds, and Marc Aronson. *Ain't Nothing But a Man: My Quest to Find the Real John Henry* (6–9). Illus. 2008, National Geographic $18.95 (978-1-4263-0000-4). This first-person narrative combines biographical information about the real John Henry with details of the research Nelson conducted and how setbacks and disappointments sometimes led to breakthroughs. (Rev: BL 2/1/08; SLJ 12/07) [921]

KANDER, LIZZIE

6434 Kann, Bob. *A Recipe for Success: Lizzie Kander and Her Cookbook* (5–8). Illus. Series: Badger

Biographies. 2006, Wisconsin Historical Soc. paper $12.95 (978-0-87020-373-2). Lizzie Kander was a social reformer in the mid-19th century, responsible among other things for a successful cookbook that benefited the Milwaukee Settlement House; in addition to a profile of Kander, this volume offers interesting information on the time she lived in. (Rev: BL 2/15/07) [921]

KELLER, HELEN

6435 Ford, Carin T. *Helen Keller: Lighting the Way for the Blind and Deaf* (6–9). Series: People to Know. 2001, Enslow LB $20.95 (978-0-7660-1530-2). Ford traces Keller's life from birth through her college education, activism, and fund-raising work in a narrative that is both interesting and detailed enough for report writers. (Rev: HBG 10/01; SLJ 5/01) [362.4]

6436 Garrett, Leslie. *Helen Keller: Biography* (5–10). Series: DK Biography. 2004, DK paper $5.99 (978-0-7566-0339-7). Keller's struggles to conquer her physical disabilities and her worldwide recognition as a political activist and public speaker are covered in the usual rich DK format. (Rev: BL 6/1–15/04) [921]

6437 Keller, Helen. *The Story of My Life: The Restored Classic, Complete and Unabridged, Centennial Edition* (8–12). 2003, Norton $21.95 (978-0-393-05744-7). The autobiography of the blind and deaf women who overcame her handicaps through the help of a devoted teacher, Anne Sullivan. Originally published in 1903. [921]

6438 Lawlor, Laurie. *Helen Keller: Rebellious Spirit* (4–8). Illus. 2001, Holiday $22.95 (978-0-8234-1588-5). This account puts Keller's life in the context of her time and looks at the opinions and beliefs that made her a "rebellious spirit," with photographs, quotations, a bibliography, and the manual alphabet. (Rev: BL 9/1/01; HB 9–10/01; HBG 3/02; SLJ 9/01*; VOYA 2/02) [362.4]

6439 Nicholson, Lois. *Helen Keller: Humanitarian* (7–10). Series: Great Achievers: Lives of the Physically Challenged. 1995, Chelsea LB $21.95 (978-0-7910-2086-9). The strong personality traits that allowed Keller to rise above her physical handicaps are stressed in this biography of a remarkable woman. (Rev: SLJ 1/96) [921]

6440 Wepman, Dennis. *Helen Keller* (6–10). Illus. 1987, Chelsea LB $30.00 (978-1-55546-662-6). The inspiring story of this handicapped woman and her struggle to help people like herself. (Rev: BL 8/87; SLJ 9/87) [921]

KLECKLEY, ELIZABETH

6441 Rutberg, Becky. *Mary Lincoln's Dressmaker: Elizabeth Kleckley's Remarkable Rise from Slave to*

White House Confidante (6–10). 1995, Walker $15.95 (978-0-8027-8224-3). The story of a slave, a fine seamstress, who was freed and became Mary Todd Lincoln's dressmaker. (Rev: BL 10/15/95; SLJ 12/95; VOYA 12/95) [921]

KOVIC, RON

6442 Moss, Nathaniel. *Ron Kovic: Antiwar Activist* (7–12). Series: Great Achievers: Lives of the Physically Challenged. 1994, Chelsea LB $19.95 (978-0-7910-2076-0). A biography of the disabled Vietnam veteran, antiwar activist, and author. (Rev: BL 1/15/94) [921]

LANDERS, ANN AND ABIGAIL VAN BUREN

6443 Aronson, Virginia. *Ann Landers and Abigail Van Buren* (6–9). Series: Women of Achievement. 2003, Chelsea $32.00 (978-0-7910-5297-6). A look at the lives from childhood of the twin sisters who have offered advice to millions, with excerpts from their columns and many photographs. (Rev: HBG 9/00; SLJ 7/00) [070]

LINDBERGH, ANNE MORROW

6444 Gherman, Beverly. *Anne Morrow Lindbergh: Between the Sea and the Stars* (6–9). Illus. 2007, Lerner LB $27.93 (978-0-8225-5970-2). Gherman looks at Lindbergh's character and emotions as well as her youth, marriage, the murder of her son, and her accomplishments as a pilot and writer. (Rev: BL 9/1/07) [921]

MARION, FRANCIS

6445 Towles, Louis P. *Francis Marion: The Swamp Fox of the American Revolution* (4–7). Series: Library of American Lives and Times. 2001, Rosen LB $34.60 (978-0-8239-5728-6). The life of the Revolutionary War hero known as the Swamp Fox because of his stealthy retreats into the swamp lands. (Rev: BL 1/1–15/02) [921]

NATION, CARRY A.

6446 Harvey, Bonnie Carman. *Carry A. Nation: Saloon Smasher and Prohibitionist* (5–8). Series: Historical American Biographies. 2002, Enslow LB $26.60 (978-0-7660-1907-2). A lively and balanced biography of the prohibitionist who fought alcohol with violence. (Rev: HBG 3/03; SLJ 1/03) [921]

NEWTON, JOHN

6447 Granfield, Linda. *Amazing Grace: The Story of the Hymn* (4–8). Illus. 1997, Tundra $15.95 (978-0-88776-389-2). The life story of John Newton, a sea captain in the slave trade who later rejected slavery,

became a minister, and wrote several hymns, including "Amazing Grace." (Rev: SLJ 8/97) [921]

PINKERTON, ALLAN

6448 Green, Carl R., and William R. Sanford. *Allan Pinkerton* (4–8). Illus. Series: Outlaws and Lawmen of the Wild West. 1995, Enslow LB $16.95 (978-0-89490-590-2). A profile of the Scottish immigrant who organized Pinkerton's National Detective Agency, whose specialty was antiunion actions. (Rev: BL 11/15/95) [921]

6449 Josephson, Judith P. *Allan Pinkerton: The Original Private Eye* (5–8). Illus. 1996, Lerner $17.21 (978-0-8225-4923-9). The story of the famed criminal-catcher who founded the world-famous detective agency. (Rev: BL 10/15/96; SLJ 10/96) [921]

POCAHONTAS

6450 Holler, Anne. *Pocahontas: Powhatan Peacemaker* (7–10). Series: North American Indians of Achievement. 1992, Chelsea $21.95 (978-0-7910-1705-0). A colorful re-creation of the life of this legendary Native American woman, how she saved Captain John Smith's life, and her death in England before she could return home. (Rev: BL 2/1/93) [921]

6451 Iannone, Catherine. *Pocahontas* (4–7). Illus. Series: Junior World Biography. 1995, Chelsea LB $18.65 (978-0-7910-2496-6); paper $18.65 (978-0-7910-2497-3). The fascinating story of the Native American who married a white man and was received by English royalty. (Rev: BL 10/15/95; SLJ 10/95) [921]

PRINTZ, MICHAEL

6452 Bankston, John. *Michael L. Printz and the Story of the Michael L. Printz Award* (4–8). Illus. Series: Great Achievement Awards. 2003, Mitchell Lane LB $19.95 (978-1-58415-182-1). Printz's career as a high school librarian is highlighted in this account of his establishment of the well-known award for YA literature, which includes a list of prize winners. (Rev: BL 10/15/03; SLJ 10/03) [020]

QUINTANILLA, GUADALUPE

6453 Wade, Mary D. *Guadalupe Quintanilla: Leader of the Hispanic Community* (4–8). Illus. Series: Multicultural Junior Biographies. 1995, Enslow LB $26.60 (978-0-89490-637-4). An inspiring story of a woman who once was considered mentally disabled and now is a leader in her Spanish American community. (Rev: BL 3/1/96; SLJ 2/96) [921]

REVERE, PAUL

6454 Giblin, James Cross. *The Many Rides of Paul Revere* (4–7). Illus. 2007, Scholastic $17.99 (978-0-439-57290-3). This well-illustrated, large-format book provides lots of often overlooked information on Paul Revere, covering his childhood, training, career, and role in the American Revolution. (Rev: BL 9/1/07; SLJ 11/07) [973.3]

6455 Randolph, Ryan P. *Paul Revere and the Minutemen of the American Revolution* (4–7). Series: Library of American Lives and Times. 2001, Rosen $34.60 (978-0-8239-5727-9). Fairly large type and many illustrations bring to life Paul Revere, a businessman and family man but also a soldier and spy, and the group of patriots known as the Minutemen. (Rev: BL 10/15/01) [921]

ROGERS, ROBERT

6456 Quasha, Jennifer. *Robert Rogers: Rogers' Rangers and the French and Indian War* (4–7). Series: Library of American Lives and Times. 2001, Rosen $34.60 (978-0-8239-5731-6). A beautifully illustrated biography of Major Robert Rogers, who recruited companies of soldiers known as Rogers' Rangers to fight for the British in the French and Indian War. (Rev: BL 10/15/01) [921]

ROSS, BETSY

6457 Harkins, Susan Sales, and William H. Harkins. *The Life and Times of Betsy Ross* (5–8). Illus. 2007, Mitchell Lane LB $19.95 (978-1-58415-446-4). This profile provides a balanced account of what is known about the life of Betsy Ross and her role, if any, in creating the American flag. (Rev: SLJ 7/07) [921]

6458 Randolph, Ryan P. *Betsy Ross: The American Flag and Life in a Young America* (4–7). Series: Library of American Lives and Times. 2001, Rosen $34.60 (978-0-8239-5730-9). This contemporary of George Washington was supposedly the seamstress of the American flag. (Rev: BL 1/1–15/02) [921]

SEQUOYAH

6459 Basel, Roberta. *Sequoyah: Inventor of Written Cherokee* (5–8). Series: Signature Lives. 2007, Compass Point LB $31.93 (978-0-7565-1887-5). A life of the Cherokee leader whose efforts to transcribe spoken Cherokee into a written language were not greatly appreciated; this volume will be useful for report writers. (Rev: SLJ 7/07) [921]

6460 Klausner, Janet. *Sequoyah's Gift: A Portrait of the Cherokee Leader* (4–7). Illus. 1993, HarperCollins LB $16.89 (978-0-06-021236-0). The life of this Cherokee leader is retold, with material on his

invention of a written alphabet and his behavior during the Trail of Tears journey. (Rev: BL 9/1/93; HB 9–10/93; SLJ 11/93) [921]

SHERBURNE, ANDREW

6461 Sherburne, Andrew. *The Memoirs of Andrew Sherburne: Patriot and Privateer of the American Revolution* (5–8). Ed. by Karen Zeinert. Illus. 1993, Linnet LB $17.50 (978-0-208-02354-4). This excerpt from Sherburne's autobiography of the war years describes his early life at sea and his capture and imprisonment by the British. (Rev: BL 5/15/93; SLJ 7/93) [921]

SHREVE, HENRY MILLER

6462 McCall, Edith. *Mississippi Steamboatman: The Story of Henry Miller Shreve* (5–8). Illus. 1986, Walker $11.95 (978-0-8027-6597-0). The story of Henry Shreve, whose freight and passenger boats helped open up the Midwest. (Rev: SLJ 3/86; VOYA 4/86) [921]

STANDISH, MYLES

6463 Harness, Cheryl. *The Adventurous Life of Myles Standish and the Amazing-but-True Survival Story of Plymouth Colony* (6–9). Illus. Series: Cheryl Harness Histories. 2006, National Geographic $16.95 (978-0-7922-5918-3). A reader-friendly, well-illustrated account of how the Pilgrims (just barely) survived in the New World with Standish's guidance. (Rev: BL 12/15/06; SLJ 1/07) [921]

STEWART, BRIDGETT

6464 Stewart, Bridgett, and Franklin White. *No Matter What* (7–12). 2002, Blue/Black $12.99 (978-0-9652827-1-0). In diary form, Stewart relates the hardships of growing up poor in a shack in Georgia and the uphill battle she faced in her effort to get a full education. (Rev: BL 7/02) [921]

STILL, PETER

6465 Fradin, Dennis Brindell. *My Family Shall Be Free! The Life of Peter Still* (6–12). Illus. 2001, HarperCollins LB $17.89 (978-0-06-029328-4). Along with his brother, Peter Still was taken and sold into slavery; this compelling story of his struggle to win freedom and reunite with his family incorporates historical documents, interviews, and maps. (Rev: BCCB 5/01; BL 2/15/01; HBG 10/01; SLJ 4/01; VOYA 8/01) [921]

STINSON, KATHERINE

6466 Winegarten, Debra L. *Katherine Stinson: The Flying Schoolgirl* (4–7). 2001, Eakin $26.95 (978-1-57168-459-2). An absorbing introduction to Stinson's accomplishments, which include a whole series of "firsts," that interweaves fiction and fact. (Rev: HBG 10/01; SLJ 6/01) [629.13092]

STUYVESANT, PETER

6467 Krizner, L. J., and Lisa Sita. *Peter Stuyvesant: New Amsterdam, and the Origins of New York* (4–7). Series: Library of American Lives and Times. 2001, Rosen LB $34.60 (978-0-8239-5732-3). The story of New Amsterdam's best-known leader and how the Dutch presence in America influenced our culture for years to come. (Rev: BL 10/15/01; SLJ 7/01*) [921]

SULLIVAN, ANNIE

6468 Delano, Marfé Ferguson. *Helen's Eyes: A Photobiography of Annie Sullivan, Helen Keller's Teacher* (4–7). Illus. 2008, National Geographic $17.95 (978-1-4263-0209-1). Full of photographs, this attractive, oversize book tells the story of Sullivan's often-sad life. (Rev: BL 6/1–15/08; SLJ 9/08) [921]

TILLAGE, LEON

6469 Tillage, Leon W. *Leon's Story* (4–9). Illus. 1997, Farrar $15.00 (978-0-374-34379-8). An autobiographical account of growing up African American and poor in the segregated South and of participating in the civil rights movement. (Rev: BL 10/1/97*; HB 11–12/97; HBG 3/98; SLJ 12/97) [975.6]

TWEED, WILLIAM "BOSS"

6470 Johnson, Suzan. *Boss Tweed and Tammany Hall* (5–8). Series: Major World Leaders. 2002, Chelsea LB $27.44 (978-1-56711-224-5). The amazing life of the corrupt New York politician who defrauded the city of more than $30 million and whose life ended in prison. (Rev: BL 1/1–15/03) [921]

WEBER, EDNAH NEW RIDER

6471 Weber, EdNah New Rider. *Rattlesnake Mesa: Stories from a Native American Childhood* (4–8). 2004, Lee & Low $18.95 (978-1-58430-231-5). In this poignant memoir, Weber tells of her life as a student at a government-run boarding school for Native Americans during the 1920s. (Rev: BL 12/15/04; SLJ 12/04) [921]

WEST, CORNEL

6472 Morrison, John. *Cornel West* (7–12). Series: African-American Leaders. 2003, Chelsea House LB $30.00 (978-0-7910-7686-6). West's commitment to populism and improved race relations is the focus of this biography of the African American Ivy League professor. (Rev: SLJ 4/04) [921]

WILSON, BILL

6473 White, Tom. *Bill W., a Different Kind of Hero* (4–7). Illus. 2003, Boyds Mills $16.95 (978-1-59078-067-1). The founder of Alcoholics Anonymous is the subject of this biography that describes his long battle with addiction. (Rev: BL 4/15/03; HBG 10/03; SLJ 2/03) [362.292]

Science, Medicine, Industry, and Business Figures

Collective

6474 Aaseng, Nathan. *Black Inventors* (6–12). Illus. Series: American Profiles. 1997, Facts on File $25.00 (978-0-8160-3407-9). This work profiles 10 African American inventors, including Lewis Temple, Elijah McCoy, and Sarah Breedlove Walker, and tells how they overcame social and economic obstacles to achieve success but were denied recognition for their achievements. (Rev: BL 2/15/98) [920]

6475 Aaseng, Nathan. *Business Builders in Broadcasting* (7–10). Series: Business Builders. 2005, Oliver LB $24.95 (978-1-881508-83-0). From Morse and Marconi to Sarnoff and Rupert Murdoch, this is a useful overview of key figures in broadcasting. (Rev: SLJ 3/06) [920]

6476 Aaseng, Nathan. *Business Builders in Computers* (5–8). Series: Business Builders. 2000, Oliver LB $22.95 (978-1-881508-57-1). Bill Gates, Steve Jobs of Apple, and Steve Case of AOL are among the individuals profiled in this interesting volume on the growth of the computer industry. (Rev: BL 2/1/01; HBG 10/01; SLJ 5/01) [338.4]

6477 Aaseng, Nathan. *Business Builders in Fast Food* (5–8). Series: Business Builders. 2001, Oliver $22.95 (978-1-881508-58-8). An interesting look at the creators of fast food empires such as McDonald's and Wendy's. (Rev: BL 9/15/01; HBG 10/01; SLJ 9/01) [381]

6478 Aaseng, Nathan. *Business Builders in Oil* (5–8). Series: Business Builders. 2000, Oliver LB $22.95 (978-1-881508-56-4). This lively introduction to the oil industry provides profiles of key individuals such as John D. Rockefeller, Andrew Mellon, and J. Paul Getty. (Rev: BL 2/1/01; HBG 10/01; SLJ 5/01) [338.2]

6479 Aaseng, Nathan. *Construction: Building the Impossible* (5–9). Illus. 2000, Oliver LB $21.95 (978-1-881508-59-5). This book profiles eight famous builders — from Imhotep, who built the first stone pyramids in Egypt, to Frank Crowe, the visionary behind the Hoover Dam. (Rev: BL 5/1/00; HBG 10/00; SLJ 10/00) [920]

6480 Anderson, Margaret J., and Karen F. Stephenson. *Scientists of the Ancient World* (6–9). Series: Collective Biographies. 1999, Enslow LB $26.60 (978-0-7660-1111-3). Ten early scientists are profiled, including Pythagoras, Hippocrates, Aristotle, Archimedes, Pliny, Galen, and Al-Khwarizmi. (Rev: BL 12/1/98) [920]

6481 Armstrong, Mabel. *Women Astronomers: Reaching for the Stars* (7–10). Illus. Series: Discovering Women in Science. 2008, Stone Pine paper $16.95 (978-0-9728929-5-7). Readers may be surprised to learn that women have been studying the skies since 2350 b.c. and that many of them made important discoveries; this volume has a browser-friendly format. (Rev: BL 4/1/08; SLJ 1/08) [508.2]

6482 Balchin, Jon. *Science: 100 Scientists Who Changed the World* (6–12). 2003, Enchanted Lion $18.95 (978-1-59270-017-2). Two-page chapters introduce 100 scientists and their accomplishments, grouped by century. (Rev: SLJ 1/04) [920]

6483 Bankston, John. *Francis Crick and James Watson: Pioneers in DNA Research* (5–7). Series: Unlocking the Secrets of Science. 2002, Mitchell Lane LB $17.95 (978-1-58415-122-7). An accessible account of the discovery of the structure of DNA and the lives of the two scientists involved. (Rev: HBG 10/03; SLJ 1/03) [576.5]

6484 Bradley, Michael J. *The Birth of Mathematics: Ancient Times to 1300* (6–9). Illus. Series: Pioneers in Mathematics. 2006, Ferguson $29.95 (978-0-8160-5423-7). Covers the contributions and discoveries of 10 important early mathematicians (such as Archimedes, Euclid, Hypatia of Alexandria, and Fibonacci). (Rev: BL 10/15/06; SLJ 5/07) [510.9]

6485 Buchanan, Doug. *Air and Space* (6–9). Series: Female Firsts in Their Fields. 1999, Chelsea $18.65 (978-0-7910-5141-2). The biographies of six women who were pioneers in air and space technology. (Rev: BL 5/15/99; HBG 9/99) [920]

6486 Bussing-Burks, Marie. *Influential Economists* (7–12). Illus. 2003, Oliver $19.95 (978-1-881508-72-4). The historical perspective of this book provides insights into economic theories and introduces some of the key people — including John Maynard Keynes and Milton Friedman — who have shaped the world's economy. (Rev: BL 3/1/03; HBG 10/03; SLJ 12/03) [920]

6487 Byrnes, Patricia. *Environmental Pioneers* (6–10). 1998, Oliver LB $19.95 (978-1-881508-45-8). This collective biography of early environmentalists includes profiles of John Muir, David Brower, Rachel Carson, Jay Darling, Rosalie Edge, Aldo Leopold, and Gaylord Nelson. (Rev: BL 9/15/98; SLJ 11/98) [920]

6488 Camp, Carole Ann. *American Astronomers: Searchers and Wonderers* (5–8). Series: Collective Biographies. 1996, Enslow LB $26.60 (978-0-89490-631-2). This volume presents brief profiles of important astronomers including Maria Mitchell, Edwin Hubble, and Carl Sagan. (Rev: BL 4/15/96; SLJ 5/96) [920]

6489 Camp, Carole Ann. *American Women Inventors* (5–10). Illus. Series: Collective Biographies. 2004, Enslow LB $26.60 (978-0-7660-1913-3). A collective biography of 10 important American female inventors, their lives, and their discoveries. (Rev: BL 3/1/04) [920]

6490 Cooney, Miriam P. *Celebrating Women in Mathematics and Science* (6–10). 1996, National Council of Teachers of Math paper $26.95 (978-0-87353-425-3). Covering ancient times to the present, this collective biography highlights the struggles and triumphs of women in the fields of mathematics and sciences. (Rev: SLJ 10/96) [920]

6491 Cox, Clinton. *African American Healers* (4–7). Illus. Series: Black Stars. 1999, Wiley $24.95 (978-0-471-24650-3). Using entries of two to three pages each, this work profiles more than 20 African Americans who have achieved prominence in medicine and related areas. (Rev: BL 2/15/00; HBG 10/00; SLJ 2/00) [910]

6492 Cullen, Katherine. *Science, Technology, and Society: The People Behind the Science* (8–11). Illus. Series: Pioneers in Science. 2006, Chelsea House $29.95 (978-0-8160-5468-8). Pioneers whose biographies appear in this volume include Marie Curie, Louis Pasteur, Guglielmo Marconi, Rachel Carson, and J. Robert Oppenheimer. Also use *Earth

Science: The People Behind the Science and *Marine Science: The People Behind the Science* (both 2006). (Rev: BL 4/1/06) [509]

6493 Currie, Stephen. *Women Inventors* (6–9). Series: History Makers. 2001, Lucent $27.45 (978-1-56006-865-5). This collective biography highlights the lives and accomplishments of five American female inventors including Grace Hopper and Madam C. J. Walker. (Rev: BL 8/1/01; SLJ 12/01) [920]

6494 Dash, Joan. *The Triumph of Discovery: Four Nobel Women* (7–12). 1991, Messner paper $8.95 (978-0-671-69333-6). Highlights the work of four women who won the Nobel Prize in science, including Rita Levi-Montalcini and Barbara McClintock. (Rev: BL 3/15/91) [920]

6495 DeAngelis, Gina. *Science and Medicine* (5–9). Series: Female Firsts in Their Fields. 1999, Chelsea $28.00 (978-0-7910-5143-6). The six women profiled here are Elizabeth Blackwell, Clara Barton, Marie Curie, Margaret Mead, Rachel Carson, and Antonia Novello. (Rev: BL 5/15/99; HBG 10/99; SLJ 9/99; VOYA 8/99) [920]

6496 De Angelis, Gina, and David J. Bianco. *Computers: Processing the Data* (7–10). Illus. Series: Innovators. 2005, Oliver LB $24.95 (978-1-881508-87-8). Profiles of computer pioneers including Charles Babbage, Steve Wozniak, and Tim Berners-Lee are accompanied by explanations of the technology involved. (Rev: BL 12/1/05; SLJ 1/06) [004]

6497 Di Domenico, Kelly. *Super Women in Science* (6–8). Illus. 2002, Second Story paper $10.95 (978-1-896764-66-5). Ten women are featured for their contributions to the scientific community, among them environmentalist Rachel Carson, physicist Chien-Shiung Wu, researcher Rosalind Franklin, and astronaut Mae Jemison. (Rev: BL 3/1/03) [509]

6498 Evans, Harold. *They Made America: From the Steam Engine to the Search Engine: Two Centuries of Innovators* (8–12). Illus. 2004, Little, Brown $40.00 (978-0-316-27766-2). For both browsing and research, this is an interesting and information-packed celebration of American inventiveness, focusing as much on the entrepreneurs as on the products. (Rev: BL 10/1/04) [609.2]

6499 Evernden, Margery. *The Experimenters: Twelve Great Chemists* (6–8). Illus. 2001, Avisson paper $19.95 (978-1-888105-49-0). The lives and research of 12 chemists are introduced in this accessible volume that is suitable for report writers. (Rev: BL 1/1–15/01) [540]

6500 Fortey, Jacqueline. *Great Scientists* (5–8). Illus. Series: Eyewitness. 2007, DK $15.99 (978-0-7566-2974-8). From Aristotle to Stephen Hawking, this volume offers brief introductions to 30 great scientists, discussing their accomplishments and providing personal information, a timeline, and a few photographs with captions adding historical details. (Rev: BL 9/1/07) [500]

6501 French, Laura. *Internet Pioneers: The Cyber Elite* (5–9). Series: Collective Biographies. 2001, Enslow LB $26.60 (978-0-7660-1540-1). French tells the stories of 10 Internet innovators — including Andrew Grove, Bill Gates, Larry Ellison, and Jeff Bezos — detailing their successes and revealing their very different backgrounds. (Rev: HBG 3/02; SLJ 9/01) [920]

6502 Green, Carl R., and William R. Sanford. *American Tycoons* (6–9). Series: Collective Biographies. 1999, Enslow LB $26.60 (978-0-7660-1112-0). The stories of 10 businessmen — including Henry Ford and Bill Gates — who built fortunes in America. (Rev: HBG 4/00; SLJ 3/00) [970]

6503 Hansen, Ole Steen. *The Wright Brothers and Other Pioneers of Flight* (4–7). Series: The Story of Flight. 2003, Crabtree $25.27 (978-0-7787-1200-8). In text and pictures, this book introduces the pioneers of flight, with a concentration on the Wright brothers. (Rev: BL 10/15/03) [921]

6504 Harris, Laurie L., ed. *Biography Today: Profiles of People of Interest to Young Readers* (4–7). Illus. Series: Scientists and Inventors. 1996, Omnigraphics LB $39.00 (978-0-7808-0068-7). Profiles of 14 important contemporaries including Carl Sagan and Jane Goodall are accompanied by those of some lesser-known figures, such as geneticist and AIDS fighter Mathilde Krim. (Rev: SLJ 2/97) [920]

6505 Haskins, Jim. *African American Entrepreneurs* (6–12). Illus. Series: Black Stars. 1998, Wiley $24.95 (978-0-471-14576-9). A collective biography of more than 30 African Americans who have made their mark on the business community. (Rev: BL 2/15/98; SLJ 7/98) [920]

6506 Haskins, Jim. *Outward Dreams: Black Inventors and Their Inventions* (7–12). 1991, Walker LB $14.85 (978-0-8027-6994-7). Examines the lives and inventions of African American men and women did not receive recognition for their contributions until after the Civil War. (Rev: BL 5/15/91) [920]

6507 Hatt, Christine. *Scientists and Their Discoveries* (6–9). Illus. Series: Documenting History. 2001, Watts LB $24.50 (978-0-531-14614-9). An overview of the work of a number of famous scientists in various disciplines, drawing from sources including advertisements, interviews, and personal diaries. (Rev: BL 12/15/01) [509.2]

6508 Henderson, Harry. *Modern Mathematicians* (7–12). Illus. 1995, Facts on File LB $25.00 (978-0-8160-3235-8). Profiles of the lives and accomplishments of nine men and four women, among them George Boole, Alan Turing, and Sophia Kovalevsky, who have contributed to the development of modern mathematics. (Rev: BL 1/1–15/96; SLJ 2/96; VOYA 2/96) [920]

6509 Hudson, Wade. *Book of Black Heroes: Scientists, Healers and Inventors* (5–8). Illus. 2002, Just Us Bks. $9.95 (978-0-940975-97-2). One historic or present-day African American figure is presented on each page of this collective biography of doctors, engineers, and inventors. (Rev: BL 2/15/03) [925]

6510 Jeffrey, Laura S. *American Inventors of the 20th Century* (6–9). Illus. Series: Collective Biographies. 1996, Enslow LB $26.60 (978-0-89490-632-9). Ten short biographies of famous modern inventors such as Philo Farnsworth (television) and William Lear (Learjet) are presented in this easily read book. (Rev: BL 7/96; SLJ 5/96) [920]

6511 Jeffrey, Laura S. *Great American Businesswomen* (4–7). Illus. 1996, Enslow LB $26.60 (978-0-89490-706-7). Profiles of 10 successful American businesswomen, including Maggie L. Walker and Katharine Graham. (Rev: BL 9/1/96; SLJ 9/96) [920]

6512 Kent, Jacqueline C. *Business Builders in Cosmetics* (6–9). Series: Business Builders. 2004, Oliver LB $22.95 (978-1-881508-82-3). Entrepreneurs including Elizabeth Arden, Max Factor, and Anita Roddick are profiled here, with a history of cosmetics dating back to Queen Nefertiti and sidebars on companies such as Clinique and Gillette. (Rev: SLJ 9/04) [920]

6513 Kent, Jacqueline C. *Business Builders in Fashion* (6–9). Illus. Series: Business Builders. 2003, Oliver LB $22.95 (978-1-881508-80-9). Chanel, Dior, Worth, Mary Quant, and Ralph Lauren are among the designers introduced. (Rev: BL 5/1/03; HBG 10/03; SLJ 6/03) [746.9]

6514 Kimmel, Elizabeth Cody. *Dinosaur Bone War: Cope and Marsh's Fossil Feud* (4–7). Illus. 2006, Random $11.99 (978-0-375-91349-5); paper $5.99 (978-0-375-81349-8). The story of American fossil hunters Edward Cope and Othniel Charles Marsh and the bitter rivalry that led to many dinosaur fossil discoveries and spurred the development of paleontology as a science. (Rev: BL 12/1/06) [560.92]

6515 Kirsh, Shannon, and Florence Kirsh. *Fabulous Female Physicians* (4–8). 2002, Second Story paper $7.95 (978-1-896764-43-6). Using short chapters and black-and-white photographs, this account profiles 10 mostly unknown female doctors and their accomplishments. (Rev: BL 6/1–15/02; VOYA 8/02) [921]

6516 Lindop, Laurie. *Scientists and Doctors* (6–10). Series: Dynamic Women. 1997, Twenty-First Century LB $24.90 (978-0-8050-4166-8). Biographies of women who have excelled in such areas as archaeology, physics, astronautics, and genetics feature Mae Jemison, Susan Love, and Rosalyn Yalow, among others. (Rev: SLJ 9/97) [920]

6517 Lomask, Milton. *Great Lives: Invention and Technology* (5–8). Series: Invention and Technology. 1991, Scribner $23.00 (978-0-684-19106-5). Profiles of great names in invention and technology around the world. (Rev: BL 11/1/91; SLJ 1/92) [920]

6518 Lutz, Norma Jean. *Business and Industry* (6–9). Series: Female Firsts in Their Fields. 1999, Chelsea $12.95 (978-0-7910-5142-9). Six trail-blazing females in the business world are profiled: Madam C. J. Walker, Katharine Graham, Mary Kay Ash, Martha Stewart, Oprah Winfrey, and Sherry Lansing. (Rev: BL 5/15/99; HBG 10/99; SLJ 9/99; VOYA 8/99) [920]

6519 McClure, Judy. *Healers and Researchers: Physicians, Biologists, Social Scientists* (5–9). Series: Remarkable Women. 2000, Raintree LB $32.85 (978-0-8172-5734-7). This book profiles 150 women from the scientific community including Barbara McClintock, Anna Freud, Jocelyn Elders, and Sushila Nyir. (Rev: SLJ 8/00) [920]

6520 Marshall, David, and Bruce Harper. *Wild About Flying: Dreamers, Doers, and Daredevils* (8–12). 2003, Firefly $35.00 (978-1-55297-849-8). Brief biographies of key figures in the history of aviation are grouped in three categories: Dreamers, Doers, and Daredevils. (Rev: SLJ 3/04; VOYA 6/04) [920]

6521 Mayberry, Jodine. *Business Leaders Who Built Financial Empires* (5–8). Illus. Series: 20 Events. 1995, Raintree LB $27.12 (978-0-8114-4934-2). The biographies of 19 financial wizards and entrepreneurs, beginning with Levi Strauss and Andrew Carnegie and ending with Steven Jobs and Anita Roddick. (Rev: SLJ 7/95) [920]

6522 Mulcahy, Robert. *Medical Technology: Inventing the Instruments* (5–8). Illus. Series: Innovators. 1997, Oliver LB $21.95 (978-1-881508-34-2). Seven short biographies of scientists who were responsible for such inventions as the X-ray, stethoscope, thermometer, and electrocardiograph. (Rev: BCCB 7–8/97; SLJ 7/97) [920]

6523 Northrup, Mary. *American Computer Pioneers* (6–12). Illus. Series: Collective Biographies. 1998, Enslow LB $26.60 (978-0-7660-1053-6). Profiles individuals who revolutionized modern technology and gives a concise history of the evolution of computers and their capabilities. (Rev: BL 10/15/98; HBG 3/99; SLJ 8/98) [920]

6524 Oleksy, Walter. *Hispanic-American Scientists* (7–10). Illus. Series: American Profiles. 1998, Facts on File $25.00 (978-0-8160-3704-9). Ten Hispanic American scientists are profiled, including Pedro Sanchez, Henry Diaz, Adriana Ocampo, and Francisco Dallmeier. (Rev: BL 3/1/99; SLJ 2/99) [920]

6525 Pile, Robert B. *Top Entrepreneurs and Their Business* (6–12). 1993, Oliver LB $19.95 (978-1-

881508-04-5). The rags-to-riches stories of nine entrepreneurs, among them L. L. Bean, Walt Disney, and Sam Walton. With photographs. (Rev: BL 11/15/93; SLJ 1/94) [920]

6526 Pile, Robert B. *Women Business Leaders* (6–12). Illus. Series: Profiles. 1995, Oliver LB $19.95 (978-1-881508-24-3). Profiles of eight women, most of them not well known (except for Mary Kay Ash of the cosmetics firm), who have the "creativity, strength, and determination to run thriving businesses." (Rev: BL 1/1–15/96; SLJ 5/96; VOYA 4/96) [920]

6527 Polking, Kirk. *Oceanographers and Explorers of the Sea* (5–9). Series: Collective Biographies. 1999, Enslow LB $20.95 (978-0-7660-1113-7). Profiles 10 scientists and adventurers who have devoted their lives to the oceans, marine life, and ocean-related pursuits, including Maurice Ewing, who mapped the ocean floor, and Robert Ballard, discoverer of the *Titanic*. (Rev: BL 8/99; SLJ 9/99) [920]

6528 Rennert, Richard, ed. *Pioneers of Discovery* (6–9). Illus. Series: Profiles of Great Black Americans. 1994, Chelsea paper $7.65 (978-0-7910-2068-5). Eight African American leaders in science and technology profiled here, among them Benjamin Banneker, James Beckwourth, George Washington Carver, Charles Drew, and Matthew Henson. (Rev: BL 6/1–15/94) [920]

6529 Richie, Jason. *Space Flight: Crossing the Last Frontier* (5–9). Illus. Series: Innovators. 2002, Oliver LB $21.95 (978-1-881508-77-9). Biographies of seven men who were instrumental in the development of space flight — including Robert Goddard, Wernher von Braun, and Sergei Korolev — are arranged in chronological order. (Rev: HBG 3/03; LMC 4–5/03; SLJ 4/03) [629.4]

6530 Shell, Barry. *Sensational Scientists: The Journeys and Discoveries of 24 Men and Women of Science* (8–11). Illus. 2006, Raincoast paper $15.95 (978-1-55192-727-5). Profiles of 24 scientists associated with Canada cover a wide range of interests. (Rev: BL 2/15/06) [509]

6531 Sherman, Josepha. *Jerry Yang and David Filo: Chief Yahoos of Yahoo* (5–8). Series: Techies. 2001, Millbrook LB $23.90 (978-0-7613-1961-0). This is the story of the creators of Yahoo!, the world's most heavily trafficked Web site. (Rev: BL 4/1/02; HBG 3/02; SLJ 12/01) [921]

6532 Stanley, Phyllis M. *American Environmental Heroes* (4–7). Illus. 1996, Enslow LB $26.60 (978-0-89490-630-5). John Muir, Barry Commoner, Sylvia Earle, and seven other environmentalists are profiled. (Rev: BL 9/1/96; SLJ 7/96) [920]

6533 Sullivan, Otha R. *African American Inventors* (5–8). Ed. by Jim Haskins. Illus. Series: Black Stars. 1998, Wiley $24.95 (978-0-471-14804-3). Among the African American inventors profiled in two- and three-page spreads are Benjamin Banneker, Madam C. J. Walker, and Dr. Charles Drew, whose research laid the basis for blood donation. (Rev: BL 7/98; SLJ 6/98) [920]

6534 Sullivan, Otha Richard. *African American Women Scientists and Inventors* (7–10). Series: Black Stars. 2001, Wiley $24.95 (978-0-471-38707-7). Twenty-six African American women born between 1849 and 1967 are profiled in this accessible book, with details of their lives and accomplishments. (Rev: SLJ 4/02) [920]

6535 Thimmesh, Catherine. *The Sky's the Limit: Stories of Discovery by Women and Girls* (5–7). Illus. by Melissa Sweet. 2002, Houghton $16.00 (978-0-618-07698-7). Details discoveries in the sciences, all made by women and girls. A sequel to *Girls Think of Everything* (2000). (Rev: BL 3/1/02; HB 5–6/02; HBG 10/02; SLJ 5/02; VOYA 6/02) [500]

6536 VanCleave, Janice. *Janice VanCleave's Scientists Through the Ages* (4–7). Illus. 2003, Wiley paper $12.95 (978-0-471-25222-1). A collective biography profiling 25 scientists, with explanations of each one's important work and a relevant experiment for the reader to perform. (Rev: BL 12/1/03) [509]

6537 White, Casey. *Sergey Brin and Larry Page: The Founders of Google* (5–9). Illus. Series: Internet Career Biographies. 2006, Rosen LB $31.95 (978-1-4042-0716-5). The interesting story of the two Stanford graduates who created a company that added a new word to our vocabulary. (Rev: LMC 8-9/07; SLJ 5/07) [920]

6538 Yount, Lisa. *Asian-American Scientists* (6–10). Series: American Profiles. 1998, Facts on File $25.00 (978-0-8160-3756-8). This work features 12 Asian American scientists who have contributed to major scientific advances in the past century, among them Flossie Wong-Staal, Subrahmanyan Chandrasekhar, Tsutomo Shimomura, and David Da-i Ho. (Rev: BL 12/15/98; SLJ 7/99) [920]

6539 Yount, Lisa. *Disease Detectives* (6–9). Series: History Makers. 2000, Lucent LB $28.70 (978-1-56006-738-2). This is a collection of profiles of medical pioneers who worked in the discovery, prevention, and treatment of diseases. (Rev: BL 1/1–15/01) [920]

6540 Yount, Lisa. *Twentieth-Century Women Scientists* (7–12). Illus. 1995, Facts on File $25.00 (978-0-8160-3173-3). Provides details of the obstacles these 11 women faced, as well as information on their contributions and diverse backgrounds. (Rev: BL 4/15/96; SLJ 2/96; VOYA 4/96) [920]

6541 Zach, Kim K. *Hidden from History: The Lives of Eight American Women Scientists* (6–12). Illus. 2002, Avisson paper $19.95 (978-1-888105-54-4). The important achievements of eight women who made often unacknowledged contributions to the sciences are accompanied by some personal details. (Rev: BL 12/1/02; SLJ 4/03; VOYA 12/03) [920]

Individual

AL-HAYTHAM, IBN

6542 Steffens, Bradley. *Ibn Al-Haytham: First Scientist* (8–11). Illus. Series: Profiles in Science. 2007, Morgan Reynolds $27.95 (978-1-59935-024-0). A Muslim who was born in A.D. 965 in the Middle East, Ibn al-Haytham made important contributions to science. (Rev: BL 12/1/06; SLJ 7/07) [921]

ALVAREZ, LUIS

6543 Allison, Amy. *Luis Alvarez and the Development of the Bubble Chamber* (5–8). Series: Unlocking the Secrets of Science. 2002, Mitchell Lane LB $25.70 (978-1-58415-140-1). Alvarez was a scientist of wide-ranging interests who won a Nobel Prize for developing a bubble chamber to track atomic particles. (Rev: HBG 3/03; SLJ 2/03; VOYA 6/03) [921]

ANDREESSEN, MARC

6544 Ehrenhaft, Daniel. *Marc Andreessen: Web Warrior* (5–8). Illus. Series: The Techies. 2001, Twenty-First Century LB $23.90 (978-0-7613-1964-1). This biography introduces Marc Andreessen, who coauthored the Web-browsing software Mosaic, cofounded the firm Netscape, and was a multimillionaire at age 24. (Rev: BL 3/15/01; HBG 10/01; SLJ 7/01; VOYA 8/01) [921]

ANDREWS, ROY CHAPMAN

6545 Bausum, Ann. *Dragon Bones and Dinosaur Eggs: A Photobiography of Explorer Roy Chapman Andrews* (5–8). Illus. 2000, National Geographic $17.95 (978-0-7922-7123-9). A biography of the famous paleontologist who made several important dinosaur discoveries in central Asia and later became director of the American Museum of Natural History in New York City. (Rev: BCCB 5/00*; BL 3/15/00; HBG 10/00; SLJ 3/00) [921]

ANNING, MARY

6546 Goodhue, Thomas. *Curious Bones: Mary Anning and the Birth of Paleontology* (5–8). Illus. 2002, Morgan Reynolds LB $23.95 (978-1-883846-93-0). A readable biography of the groundbreaking female paleontologist (1799–1847) that places her achievements in historical context, with a glossary, bibliography, and timeline. (Rev: BL 7/02; HBG 3/03; SLJ 9/02) [560.92]

ARCHIMEDES

6547 Gow, Mary. *Archimedes: Mathematical Genius of the Ancient World* (5–8). Illus. Series: Great Minds of Science. 2005, Enslow LB $26.60 (978-0-7660-2502-8). Archimedes' mathematical discoveries are explained and placed in social, scientific, and cultural context. (Rev: SLJ 12/05) [921]

6548 Hasan, Heather. *Archimedes: The Father of Mathematics* (6–10). Series: The Library of Greek Philosophers. 2006, Rosen LB $33.25 (978-1-4042-0774-5). The importance of this ancient thinker is explained, and readers learn of his times and his influence. (Rev: SLJ 9/06)

AVERY, OSWALD

6549 Severs, Vesta-Nadine, and Jim Whiting. *Oswald Avery and the Story of DNA* (4–7). Series: Unlocking the Secrets of Science. 2002, Mitchell Lane LB $25.70 (978-1-58415-110-4). The importance of Avery's early research is reinforced by a description of DNA evidence being used to free wrongly accused prisoners. (Rev: HBG 10/02; SLJ 6/02) [579.3092]

BANNEKER, BENJAMIN

6550 Conley, Kevin. *Benjamin Banneker* (5–9). Illus. 1989, Chelsea LB $30.00 (978-1-55546-573-5). Banneker was a remarkable 18th-century African American who excelled in mathematics and science. (Rev: BL 1/1/90; SLJ 5/90; VOYA 4/90) [921]

6551 Litwin, Laura Baskes. *Benjamin Banneker: Astronomer and Mathematician* (6–10). Illus. Series: African-American Biographies. 1999, Enslow LB $26.60 (978-0-7660-1208-0). The story of the self-taught African American scientist who lived during the days of slavery and was responsible for some brilliant scientific inventions. (Rev: BL 9/15/99; HBG 4/00) [921]

BELL, ALEXANDER GRAHAM

6552 Bankston, John. *Alexander Graham Bell and the Story of the Telephone* (5–8). Illus. Series: Uncharted, Unexplored, and Unexplained. 2004, Mitchell Lane LB $29.95 (978-1-58415-243-9). As a teacher of the deaf and son of a deaf mother, Bell had a special interest in finding new and better ways to communicate. (Rev: BL 10/15/04) [921]

6553 Carson, Mary Kay. *Alexander Graham Bell: Giving Voice to the World* (5–8). Series: Sterling Biographies. 2007, Sterling LB $12.95 (978-1-4027-4951-3); paper $5.95 (978-1-4027-3230-0).

Covers Bell's childhood and his lifelong commitment to improving communication. (Rev: SLJ 10/07) [921]

6554 Pasachoff, Naomi. *Alexander Graham Bell: Making Connections* (6–9). Series: Oxford Portraits in Science. 1996, Oxford $32.95 (978-0-19-509908-9). A fine biography that focuses on Bell's work as a teacher of the deaf and his career as an inventor. (Rev: SLJ 2/97*) [921]

6555 Pollard, Michael. *Alexander Graham Bell: Father of Modern Communication* (5–7). Series: Giants of Science. 2000, Blackbirch LB $27.44 (978-1-56711-334-1). Known primarily for the invention of the telephone, Bell also invented the first hydrofoil, an air-conditioning system, and an early fax machine. (Rev: BL 1/1–15/01; HBG 3/01) [921]

6556 Shulman, Seth. *The Telephone Gambit: Chasing Alexander Graham Bell's Secret* (8–12). 2008, Norton $24.95 (978-0-393-06206-9). Did Bell really invent the telephone? History and science students will find this well-written investigation riveting. (Rev: BL 12/1/07) [921]

BENZ, KARL

6557 Bankston, John. *Karl Benz and the Single Cylinder Engine* (5–8). Illus. Series: Uncharted, Unexplored, and Unexplained. 2004, Mitchell Lane LB $29.95 (978-1-58415-244-6). The first person to build a three-wheeled automobile, Benz went on to design many more-sophisticated cars. (Rev: BL 10/15/04) [921]

BERNERS-LEE, TIM

6558 Gaines, Ann. *Tim Berners-Lee and the Development of the World Wide Web* (4–7). Series: Unlocking the Secrets of Science. 2001, Mitchell Lane LB $25.70 (978-1-58415-096-1). A profile of the man who created the user-friendly way of accessing much of the information on the Internet. (Rev: HBG 10/02; SLJ 2/02) [921]

6559 Stewart, Melissa. *Tim Berners-Lee: Inventor of the World Wide Web* (4–7). Series: Ferguson Career Biographies. 2001, Ferguson LB $25.00 (978-0-89434-367-4). Young readers will be fascinated by the details of Berners-Lee's life and career and the accompanying information on the skills needed to become a computer programmer. (Rev: SLJ 10/01) [921]

BEZOS, JEFF

6560 Garty, Judy. *Jeff Bezos* (5–8). Illus. Series: Internet Biographies. 2003, Enslow LB $23.93 (978-0-7660-1972-0). A reader-friendly biography of the creator of Amazon.com, with plenty of information on his youth. (Rev: BL 3/15/03; HBG 10/03) [380.1]

6561 Sherman, Josepha. *Jeff Bezos: King of Amazon* (5–8). Illus. 2001, Twenty-First Century LB $23.90 (978-0-7613-1963-4). Jeff Bezos, the genius behind Amazon.com, is introduced along with information on his struggle to found a book company on the Web. (Rev: BL 3/15/01; HBG 10/01; SLJ 7/01; VOYA 8/01) [921]

BLACKWELL, ELIZABETH

6562 Brown, Jordan. *Elizabeth Blackwell* (7–10). Illus. 1989, Chelsea LB $19.95 (978-1-55546-642-8). The life story of the first woman doctor; she also organized a nursing service during the Civil War and helped provide educational opportunities for other young women. (Rev: BL 5/15/89) [921]

6563 Kline, Nancy. *Elizabeth Blackwell: A Doctor's Triumph* (5–9). Series: Barnard Biography. 1997, Conari paper $11.95 (978-1-57324-057-4). The story of the first woman doctor in America, with generous excerpts from her journal and letters. (Rev: BL 2/15/97; SLJ 6/97; VOYA 12/97) [921]

BOHR, NIELS

6564 Pasachoff, Naomi. *Niels Bohr: Physicist and Humanitarian* (7–10). Illus. Series: Great Minds of Science. 2003, Enslow $26.60 (978-0-7660-1997-3). An appealing biography that explains Bohr's scientific achievements in clear, understandable terms and covers his protests against the Nazis and against the use of nuclear weapons. (Rev: BL 6/1–15/03; HBG 10/03; VOYA 6/04) [530]

BOYLE, ROBERT

6565 Baxter, Roberta. *Skeptical Chemist: The Story of Robert Boyle* (8–11). Illus. 2006, Morgan Reynolds $26.95 (978-1-59935-025-7). Boyle's natural curiosity led to his developing an important methodology for scientific experimentation, and his biography will inspire students interested in both science and history. (Rev: BL 12/1/06; SLJ 1/07) [921]

6566 Gow, Mary. *Robert Boyle: Pioneer of Experimental Chemistry* (6–9). Illus. Series: Great Minds of Science. 2005, Enslow LB $26.60 (978-0-7660-2501-1). Pioneering 17th-century chemist Robert Boyle is profiled in this volume that will be useful for report writers. (Rev: BL 3/15/05; SLJ 6/05) [530]

BRAHE, TYCHO

6567 Boerst, William J. *Tycho Brahe: Mapping the Heavens* (6–9). Illus. 2003, Morgan Reynolds LB $26.95 (978-1-883846-97-8). A concise biography with many illustrations of the man whose research on astronomy in the 1500s provided the foundation for future scientific inquiry. (Rev: BL 3/15/03; HBG 10/03; SLJ 8/03) [520]

6568 Nardo, Don. *Tycho Brahe: Pioneer of Astronomy* (5–8). Illus. Series: Signature Lives: Scientific Revolution. 2007, Compass Point LB $23.95 (978-0-7565-3309-0). In addition to this Danish scientist's career and discoveries, this well-designed volume explores the basics of scientific investigation and the nature of his breakthroughs. (Rev: BL 12/1/07; SLJ 1/08) [921]

BREAZEAL, CYNTHIA

6569 Brown, Jordan D. *Robo World: The Story of Robot Designer Cynthia Breazeal* (6–10). Series: Women's Adventures in Science. 2005, Watts LB $31.50 (978-0-531-16782-3). An interesting biography that blends personal information with scientific facts. (Rev: SLJ 2/06) [921]

BROWN, HELEN GURLEY

6570 Falkof, Lucille. *Helen Gurley Brown: The Queen of Cosmopolitan* (5–8). Series: Wizards of Business. 1992, Garrett LB $17.26 (978-1-56074-013-1). An interesting, accessible, and inspiring biography of the magazine magnate. (Rev: BL 6/15/92; SLJ 7/92) [921]

BURROUGHS, JOHN

6571 Wadsworth, Ginger. *John Burroughs: The Sage of Slabsides* (5–8). Illus. 1997, Clarion $16.95 (978-0-395-77830-2). A biography of the American naturalist and essayist who lived in a cabin in the Catskill Mountains and wrote about his observations. (Rev: BCCB 5/97; BL 3/15/97; HB 7–8/97; SLJ 5/97) [508.73]

CARNEGIE, ANDREW

6572 Edge, Laura B. *Andrew Carnegie: Industrial Philanthropist* (7–10). Series: Lerner Biography. 2004, Lerner LB $27.93 (978-0-8225-4965-9). The fascinating story of Carnegie's progress from poor Scottish immigrant to wealthy industrialist and generous philanthropist. (Rev: BL 6/1–15/04; SLJ 2/04) [936.2]

CARSON, RACHEL

6573 Jezer, Marty. *Rachel Carson* (6–9). 1988, Chelsea LB $30.00 (978-1-55546-646-6). The biography of the scientist who was one of the first to warn us of our environmental problems. (Rev: BL 9/1/88; VOYA 2/89) [921]

6574 Levine, Ellen. *Rachel Carson* (7–10). Illus. Series: Up Close. 2007, Viking $15.99 (978-0-670-

06220-1). A well-documented biography of the groundbreaking environmentalist that provides details of her personal life as well as her career and of the obstacles she faced. (Rev: BL 2/15/07; HB 3–4/07; SLJ 4/07*) [921]

6575 Wadsworth, Ginger. *Rachel Carson: Voice for the Earth* (5–7). Illus. Series: Lerner Biographies. 1992, Lerner LB $27.93 (978-0-8225-4907-9). The life and work of the conservationist and author, best known for *Silent Spring*. (Rev: BL 6/1/92; HB 7–8/92; SLJ 7/92) [921]

CARVER, GEORGE WASHINGTON

6576 MacLeod, Elizabeth. *George Washington Carver: An Innovative Life* (4–7). Illus. 2007, Kids Can $14.95 (978-1-55337-906-5); paper $6.95 (978-1-55337-907-2). Well-organized with attractive graphics, this biography of Carver provides interesting details about his life as well as his major accomplishments. (Rev: SLJ 6/07) [921]

CASE, STEVE

6577 Ashby, Ruth. *Steve Case: America Online Pioneer* (5–8). Series: Techies. 2002, Millbrook LB $23.90 (978-0-7613-2655-7). The story of the Honolulu native who was a leader of AOL and the driving force behind its merger with Time-Warner. (Rev: BL 4/1/02; HBG 10/02) [921]

CHANEL, COCO

6578 Gaines, Ann. *Coco Chanel* (6–12). Series: Women in the Arts. 2003, Chelsea House LB $30.00 (978-0-7910-7455-8). Introduces the life of the famous designer, attempting to distinguish between fact and Chanel's own fictions about herself. (Rev: SLJ 2/04) [921]

CHIEN-SHIUNG WU

6579 Cooperman, Stephanie H. *Chien-Shiung Wu: Pioneering Physicist and Atomic Researcher* (5–8). Illus. Series: Women Hall of Famers in Mathematics and Science. 2004, Rosen LB $29.25 (978-0-8239-3875-9). This biography describes Wu's life and achievements, explaining how she found a flaw in a widely held assumption about atoms. (Rev: BL 3/1/04; SLJ 9/04) [921]

CLARK, EUGENIE

6580 Butts, Ellen R., and Joyce R. Schwartz. *Eugenie Clark: Adventures of a Shark Scientist* (5–8). Illus. 2000, Linnet $19.50 (978-0-208-02440-4). An interesting biography of a contemporary American scientist — an ichthyologist who has produced some startling research on sharks. (Rev: BCCB 2/00; BL 2/15/00; HBG 10/00; SLJ 7/00) [921]

COPERNICUS

6581 Andronik, Catherine M. *Copernicus: Founder of Modern Astronomy* (4–8). Illus. Series: Great Minds of Science. 2002, Enslow LB $26.60 (978-0-7660-1755-9). This absorbing biography that covers Copernicus's youth and succeeds in explaining necessary scientific concepts also includes activities that reinforce this understanding. (Rev: HBG 10/02; SLJ 6/02) [520.92]

6582 Goble, Todd. *Nicholas Copernicus and the Founding of Modern Astronomy* (6–8). 2003, Morgan Reynolds LB $26.95 (978-1-883846-99-2). The 16th-century Polish astronomer's life and work are placed in historical context, revealing the upsurge in scientific inquiry that took place during the Renaissance. (Rev: SLJ 10/03) [520]

6583 Ingram, Scott. *Nicolaus Copernicus: Father of Modern Astronomy* (5–9). Series: Giants of Science. 2004, Gale LB $26.20 (978-1-56711-489-8). Copernicus's life, the influences of the church, and his important contributions to science are presented in clear prose and historical context. (Rev: SLJ 6/05) [921]

CURIE, MARIE

6584 Birch, Beverley. *Marie Curie: Courageous Pioneer in the Study of Radioactivity* (5–7). Illus. Series: Giants of Science. 2000, Blackbirch LB $24.95 (978-1-56711-333-4). This biography of Marie Curie covers her youth, her struggles to get an education, her marriage, and her scientific career and accomplishments. (Rev: BL 1/1–15/01; HBG 3/01) [921]

6585 Birch, Beverley. *Marie Curie, Spanish and English* (5–8). Series: Giants of Science Bilingual. 2005, Gale LB $28.70 (978-1-4103-0505-3). English and Spanish versions of this life of Curie are presented side by side, and the timeline, glossary, and index are also bilingual. (Rev: SLJ 2/06) [921]

6586 Goldsmith, Barbara. *Obsessive Genius: The Inner World of Marie Curie* (8–12). Illus. 2004, Norton $23.95 (978-0-393-05137-7). Curie's personal triumphs are also covered in this account of her scientific achievements. (Rev: BL 12/1/04) [540]

6587 Healy, Nick. *Marie Curie* (6–9). Illus. Series: Genius. 2005, Creative Education LB $21.95 (978-1-58341-332-6). This attractive picture-book biography will interest readers but report writers will want more documentation. (Rev: BL 2/15/06) [540]

6588 Krull, Kathleen. *Marie Curie* (5–8). Illus. by Boris Kulikov. Series: Giants of Science. 2007, Viking $15.99 (978-0-670-05894-5). This biography of the Nobel Prize-winning scientist supplies plenty of information about her family life and personality as well as her discoveries and her legacy.

(Rev: BL 12/15/07; HB 11–12/07; SLJ 12/07) [540.92]

6589 Lassieur, Allison. *Marie Curie: A Scientific Pioneer* (6–9). Series: Great Life Stories. 2003, Watts LB $30.50 (978-0-531-12270-9). Curie's ability to succeed in a man's world is underlined in this well-written biography. (Rev: SLJ 1/04) [921]

6590 McClafferty, Carla Killough. *Something Out of Nothing: Marie Curie and Radium* (7–10). Illus. 2006, Farrar $18.00 (978-0-374-38036-6). This readable biography examines Curie's personal life and her valuable contributions to scientific knowledge. (Rev: BL 3/1/06; SLJ 5/06*) [540]

6591 Poynter, Margaret. *Marie Curie: Discoverer of Radium* (4–7). Illus. Series: Great Minds of Science. 1994, Enslow LB $26.60 (978-0-89490-477-6). The life and significance of this discoverer of radium are covered, with a chapter of suggested activities. (Rev: BL 1/1/95; SLJ 10/94) [921]

6592 Yannuzzi, Della. *New Elements: The Story of Marie Curie* (5–10). Illus. Series: Profiles in Science. 2006, Morgan Reynolds $26.95 (978-1-59935-023-3). More about the scientist's life than about the significance of her research, this introduction will be helpful to report writers. (Rev: BL 12/1/06; SLJ 1/07) [921]

DAMADIAN, RAYMOND

6593 Kjelle, Marylou Morano. *Raymond Damadian and the Development of MRI* (5–7). Series: Unlocking the Secrets of Science. 2002, Mitchell Lane LB $25.70 (978-1-58415-141-8). This account focuses on Damadian's scientific accomplishments. (Rev: HBG 10/03; SLJ 1/03) [921]

DARWIN, CHARLES

6594 Anderson, Margaret J. *Charles Darwin: Naturalist* (4–7). Illus. Series: Great Minds of Science. 1994, Enslow LB $26.60 (978-0-89490-476-9). In addition to a biography of this controversial naturalist, there is a chapter on activities for the reader. (Rev: BL 1/1/95; SLJ 10/94) [921]

6595 Evans, J. Edward. *Charles Darwin: Revolutionary Biologist* (6–9). Series: Lerner Biographies. 1993, Lerner LB $23.93 (978-0-8225-4914-7). An account of Darwin's life that includes interesting anecdotes, such as the fact that he dropped out of medical school and that his father thought he would never amount to anything. (Rev: BL 12/1/93; SLJ 11/93) [921]

6596 Greenberger, Robert. *Darwin and the Theory of Evolution* (5–8). Series: Primary Sources of Revolutionary Scientific Discoveries and Theories. 2005, Rosen LB $29.25 (978-1-4042-0306-8). Profiles English naturalist Charles Darwin and the events that led up to his groundbreaking theory of

evolution; useful for brief reports. (Rev: SLJ 11/05) [921]

6597 Lawson, Kristan. *Darwin and Evolution for Kids: His Life and Ideas with 21 Activities* (5–9). Illus. 2003, Chicago Review paper $16.95 (978-1-55652-502-5). The naturalist's life and work are examined in clear, interesting text, with thorough coverage of his five-year research voyage on *H.M.S. Beagle* and the continuing controversy over his theories. (Rev: SLJ 4/04) [921]

6598 Patent, Dorothy Hinshaw. *Charles Darwin: The Life of a Revolutionary Thinker* (7–12). Illus. 2001, Holiday $22.95 (978-0-8234-1494-9). An absorbing portrait of the man who came late to the career that made him famous, with information on his youth, education, family life, and interests in science and literature. (Rev: BL 8/01; HB 9–10/01; HBG 3/02; SLJ 8/01) [921]

6599 Senker, Cath. *Charles Darwin* (4–8). Illus. Series: Scientists Who Made History. 2002, Raintree LB $27.12 (978-0-7398-4843-2). Darwin's life and contributions are presented in clear text and ample illustrations, with historical detail that places the information in context. (Rev: HBG 10/02; SLJ 9/02) [576.8092]

6600 Sís, Peter. *The Tree of Life: Charles Darwin* (4–7). Illus. 2003, Farrar $18.00 (978-0-374-45628-3). Highly illustrated, this imaginative and visual biography traces Darwin's life and development as a naturalist, with a focus on his voyages on the *Beagle*. (Rev: BL 10/15/03; HB 11–12/03*; HBG 4/04; SLJ 10/03*) [576.8]

6601 Sproule, Anna. *Charles Darwin: Visionary Behind the Theory of Evolution* (4–7). Illus. Series: Giants of Science. 2003, Gale $26.20 (978-1-56711-655-7). Darwin's life and accomplishments are presented in concise text. (Rev: SLJ 1/03) [921]

DE LA RENTA, OSCAR

6602 Carrillo, Louis. *Oscar de la Renta* (4–8). Illus. Series: Contemporary Hispanic Americans. 1995, Raintree LB $28.80 (978-0-8172-3980-0). This account focuses on the professional life of the renowned Hispanic American fashion designer who was born in the Dominican Republic. (Rev: BL 3/15/96; SLJ 1/96) [921]

DE PASSE, SUZANNE

6603 Mussari, Mark. *Suzanne De Passe: Motown's Boss Lady* (5–8). Illus. Series: Wizards of Business. 1992, Garrett LB $17.26 (978-1-56074-026-1). The story of the woman who helped make Motown the great name in the music industry. (Rev: BL 6/15/92) [921]

DREW, CHARLES

6604 Mahone-Lonesome, Robyn. *Charles Drew* (6–10). Illus. 1990, Chelsea LB $30.00 (978-1-55546-581-0). The biography of the African American scientist who did pioneer work in blood preservation and the establishment of blood banks. (Rev: BL 2/15/90) [921]

DYSON, ESTHER

6605 Jablonski, Carla. *Esther Dyson: Web Guru* (5–8). Series: Techies. 2002, Millbrook LB $23.90 (978-0-7613-2657-1). A leading light in the computer world, Dyson is the owner of EDventure Holdings, and is an active developer of emerging technologies and companies. (Rev: BL 4/1/02; HBG 10/02) [921]

6606 Morales, Leslie. *Esther Dyson: Internet Visionary* (5–8). Series: Internet Biographies. 2003, Enslow LB $23.93 (978-0-7660-1973-7). Dyson, a skillful businesswoman, has played an influential role in the development of the Internet as a tool suitable for everyday use. (Rev: HBG 10/03; SLJ 10/03) [338.4]

EARLE, SYLVIA

6607 Baker, Beth. *Sylvia Earle: Guardian of the Sea* (4–7). Illus. Series: Lerner Biographies. 2000, Lerner LB $27.93 (978-0-8225-4961-1). This is a thrilling biography of the famous underwater explorer and marine scientist who was one of the first humans to swim with whales. (Rev: BL 10/15/00; HBG 3/01; SLJ 11/00) [921]

EASTMAN, GEORGE

6608 Pflueger, Lynda. *George Eastman: Bringing Photography to the People* (7–10). Series: Historical American Biographies. 2002, Enslow LB $26.60 (978-0-7660-1617-0). Eastman's success in bringing photography to the masses is described, as are his philanthropy and personal life. (Rev: HBG 3/03; SLJ 11/02) [921]

EDISON, THOMAS ALVA

6609 Carlson, Laurie. *Thomas Edison for Kids: His Life and Ideas: 21 Activities* (4–7). Illus. 2006, Chicago Review paper $14.95 (978-1-55652-584-1). Activities allow readers to try some of the inventor's experiments; the biography section covers Edison's personal life as well as his achievements and introduces some of his contemporaries. (Rev: BL 2/15/06; SLJ 6/06) [621.3]

6610 Dolan, Ellen M. *Thomas Alva Edison: Inventor* (5–8). Series: Historical American Biographies. 1998, Enslow LB $26.60 (978-0-7660-1014-7). Direct quotations, fact boxes, a chronology, and

chapter notes make this an attractive life of the great inventor. (Rev: BL 8/98) [921]

6611 Graham, Amy. *Thomas Edison: Wizard of Light and Sound* (5–8). Illus. Series: Inventors Who Changed the World. 2007, Enslow LB $24.95 (978-1-59845-052-1). The text of this profile of Edison and his achievements is augmented by links to carefully evaluated Web sites. (Rev: SLJ 11/07) [921]

6612 Sproule, Anna. *Thomas Edison: The World's Greatest Inventor* (5–7). Series: Giants of Science. 2000, Blackbirch paper $24.95 (978-1-56711-331-0). A prolific inventor, Edison not only worked on the electric light bulb but also the phonograph, the movie projector, and an early answering machine. (Rev: BL 1/1–15/01; HBG 3/01; SLJ 1/01) [921]

6613 Tagliaferro, Linda. *Thomas Edison: Inventor of the Age of Electricity* (6–9). 2003, Lerner LB $27.93 (978-0-8225-4689-4). Clear, lively language is used to give details of Edison's youth and trace his interest in science and invention throughout his life. (Rev: HBG 10/03; SLJ 7/03) [621.3]

6614 Woodside, Martin. *Thomas A. Edison: The Man Who Lit Up the World* (5–8). Series: Sterling Biographies. 2007, Sterling LB $12.95 (978-1-4027-4955-1); paper $5.95 (978-1-4027-3229-4). A concise account of Edison's life from childhood and his many achievements in varied fields. (Rev: SLJ 10/07) [921]

EINSTEIN, ALBERT

6615 Bankston, John. *Albert Einstein and the Theory of Relativity* (5–8). Series: Unlocking the Secrets of Science. 2002, Mitchell Lane LB $25.70 (978-1-58415-137-1). Einstein's accomplishments and the many challenges he faced are explored in concise text with many black-and-white photographs. (Rev: SLJ 2/03) [921]

6616 Delano, Marfé Ferguson. *Genius: A Photobiography of Albert Einstein* (5–8). Illus. 2005, National Geographic $17.95 (978-0-7922-9544-0). Photographs of the scientist's life, as well as brief explanations of his work, help to make the man and his theories more accessible to young readers; an oversized and engaging volume. (Rev: BL 4/1/05*; SLJ 5/05) [921]

6617 Hasday, Judy L. *Albert Einstein: The Giant of 20th Century Science* (7–12). Series: Nobel Prize–Winning Scientists. 2004, Enslow LB $26.60 (978-0-7660-2185-3). Report writers will find this a useful source of material on Einstein's breakthrough achievements in physics. (Rev: SLJ 4/04) [921]

6618 Lassieur, Allison. *Albert Einstein: Genius of the Twentieth Century* (5–8). Series: Great Life Stories. 2005, Watts LB $30.50 (978-0-531-12401-7). In addition to placing Einstein's life (including his childhood) and contributions in historical and social context, Lassieur explains his theories and their application. (Rev: SLJ 9/05) [921]

6619 MacDonald, Fiona. *Albert Einstein: The Genius Behind the Theory of Relativity* (5–7). Illus. Series: Giants of Science. 2000, Blackbirch LB $27.44 (978-1-56711-330-3). As well as his childhood, education, theories, personal life, and international awards, this biography of Albert Einstein assesses his lasting contributions to physics and mathematics. (Rev: BL 1/1–15/01; HBG 3/01; SLJ 1/01) [921]

6620 MacLeod, Elizabeth. *Albert Einstein: A Life of Genius* (5–7). Illus. 2003, Kids Can $14.95 (978-1-55337-396-4); paper $6.95 (978-1-55337-397-1). Small photographs and illustrations accompany this attractive chronological introduction to the life of Einstein that focuses on the man rather than his theories. (Rev: BL 3/1/03; HBG 10/03; SLJ 5/03) [530]

6621 McPherson, Stephanie S. *Ordinary Genius: The Story of Albert Einstein* (4–7). Illus. 1995, Carolrhoda LB $27.93 (978-0-87614-788-7). Good historical background information is given on the life of Einstein plus a clear explanation of his discoveries. (Rev: BL 6/1–15/95; SLJ 9/95) [921]

6622 Pirotta, Saviour. *Albert Einstein* (6–8). Illus. Series: Scientists Who Made History. 2002, Raintree LB $27.12 (978-0-7398-4844-9). A thorough account of Einstein's life and well-known contributions, with clear scientific explanations and discussion of his legacy. (Rev: HBG 10/02; SLJ 7/02) [530]

6623 Severance, John B. *Einstein: Visionary Scientist* (7–12). Illus. 1999, Clarion $18.00 (978-0-395-93100-4). This book covers Einstein's academic theories as well as his private life and his celebrity. (Rev: BCCB 9/99; BL 9/1/99; HB 9–10/99; HBG 4/00; SLJ 9/99) [921]

6624 Speregen, Devra Newberger. *Albert Einstein: The Jewish Man behind the Theory* (6–9). 2006, Jewish Publication Soc. $12.95 (978-0-8276-0824-5). This book explores the development of Einstein's sense of identity as a Jew as he became aware of Nazi anti-Semitism. (Rev: BL 6/1–15/06) [921]

6625 Yeatts, Tabatha. *Albert Einstein: The Miracle Mind* (7–12). Illus. Series: Sterling Biography. 2007, Sterling LB $12.95 (978-1-4027-4950-6); paper $5.95 (978-1-4027-3228-7). Covers the life and scientific accomplishments of Albert Einstein, as well as his stand against racism and nuclear war. (Rev: BL 9/1/07) [921]

ELION, GERTRUDE

6626 MacBain, Jennifer. *Gertrude Elion: Nobel Prize Winner in Physiology and Medicine* (5–8). Illus. Series: Women Hall of Famers in Mathemat-

ics and Science. 2004, Rosen LB $29.25 (978-0-8239-3876-6). Elion, a biochemist and pharmacologist who never earned a doctorate, won a Nobel Prize for her advances in the field of chemotherapy. (Rev: BL 3/1/04; SLJ 9/04) [615]

ELLISON, LARRY

6627 Ehrenhaft, Daniel. *Larry Ellison: Sheer Nerve* (5–8). Series: Techies. 2001, Millbrook LB $23.90 (978-0-7613-1962-7). The life story of one of the world's richest men and co-founder of Oracle, the world's leading supplier of software for information management. (Rev: BL 4/1/02; HBG 3/02; SLJ 12/01) [921]

6628 Peters, Craig. *Larry Ellison: Database Genius of Oracle* (5–8). Series: Internet Biographies. 2003, Enslow LB $23.93 (978-0-7660-1974-4). A look at the life and accomplishments of the cofounder of Oracle Corporation. (Rev: HBG 10/03; SLJ 10/03) [338.7]

EUCLID

6629 Hayhurst, Chris. *Euclid: The Great Geometer* (6–10). 2006, Rosen LB $33.25 (978-1-4042-0497-3). The importance of this ancient thinker (who is called the father of geometry) is explained, and readers learn of his times and his influence. (Rev: SLJ 9/06) [921]

FANNING, SHAWN

6630 Mitten, Christopher. *Shawn Fanning: Napster and the Music Revolution* (5–8). Series: Techies. 2002, Millbrook LB $23.90 (978-0-7613-2656-4). Using many photographs and an interesting text, this is the biography of the creator of Napster, a software package for downloading music from computers. (Rev: BL 4/1/02; HBG 10/02; SLJ 6/02) [921]

FARADAY, MICHAEL

6631 Russell, Colin A. *Michael Faraday: Physics and Faith* (8–12). Illus. Series: Oxford Portraits in Science. 2001, Oxford Univ. LB $32.95 (978-0-19-511763-9). The story of the inventor of the electric transformer and the dynamo is placed in interesting historical context. (Rev: HBG 10/01; SLJ 3/01) [921]

FARNSWORTH, PHILO

6632 McPherson, Stephanie S. *TV's Forgotten Hero: The Story of Philo Farnsworth* (4–7). Illus. 1996, Carolrhoda LB $27.93 (978-1-57505-017-1). The biography of the genius who invented electronic television when he was only 14. (Rev: BL 2/1/97; SLJ 2/97) [921]

FERMI, ENRICO

6633 Cooper, Dan. *Enrico Fermi: And the Revolutions of Modern Physics* (8–12). Series: Oxford Portraits in Science. 1999, Oxford $32.95 (978-0-19-511762-2). A readable biography of the Italian scientist who immigrated to the United States in 1939 and worked on the first atomic bomb. Some of the coverage of quantum and nuclear physics is challenging. (Rev: SLJ 6/99) [921]

6634 Stux, Erica. *Enrico Fermi: Trailblazer in Nuclear Physics* (7–12). Illus. Series: Nobel Prize–Winning Scientists. 2004, Enslow LB $26.60 (978-0-7660-2177-8). This review of Fermi's achievements in nuclear physics offers good material for report writers. (Rev: BL 6/1–15/04; SLJ 4/04) [921]

FLEMING, ALEXANDER

6635 Bankston, John. *Alexander Fleming and the Story of Penicillin* (5–8). Series: Unlocking the Secrets of Science. 2001, Mitchell Lane LB $25.70 (978-1-58415-106-7). This absorbing biography of the Scottish Nobel Prize winner covers his personal life as well as his scientific career. (Rev: HBG 3/02; SLJ 1/02) [616.014092]

6636 Birch, Beverley. *Alexander Fleming: Pioneer with Antibiotics* (4–7). Illus. Series: Giants of Science. 2003, Gale $26.20 (978-1-56711-656-4). Fleming's life, education, research, and discovery of penicillin are presented in concise text. (Rev: SLJ 1/03) [921]

6637 Tocci, Salvatore. *Alexander Fleming: The Man Who Discovered Penicillin* (5–8). Series: Great Minds of Science. 2002, Enslow LB $26.60 (978-0-7660-1998-0). An absorbing account of Fleming's childhood and later life, with solid information on his contributions to medical science and his legacy. (Rev: HBG 10/02; SLJ 9/02) [921]

FORD, HENRY

6638 McCarthy, Pat. *Henry Ford: Building Cars for Everyone* (5–8). Series: Historical American Biographies. 2002, Enslow LB $26.60 (978-0-7660-1620-0). Ford is shown as an eccentric but successful father, engineer, and businessman, who made the automobile widely available but expected his workers to suffer difficult conditions. (Rev: HBG 3/03; SLJ 1/03) [338.76292092]

FOSSEY, DIAN

6639 Gogerly, Liz. *Dian Fossey* (5–8). Illus. Series: Scientists Who Made History. 2003, Raintree LB $27.12 (978-0-7368-5225-8). A riveting profile of the woman who became an expert on gorillas and the militant stance that may have led to her murder. (Rev: BL 3/1/03) [599.884]

6640 Nicholson, Lois P. *Dian Fossey: Primatologist* (7–12). Series: Women in Science. 2003, Chelsea LB $30.00 (978-0-7910-6907-3). An absorbing portrait of the woman who overcame obstacles to study and protect mountain gorillas in central Africa. (Rev: LMC 11–12/03; SLJ 7/03) [599.884]

FRANCE, DIANE

6641 Hopping, Lorraine Jean. *Bone Detective: The Story of Forensic Anthropologist Diane France* (7–10). Illus. Series: Women's Adventures in Science. 2005, Watts LB $31.50 (978-0-531-16776-2). Part of the Women's Adventures in Science series, this compelling biography of Diane France traces the forensic anthropologist's life from her childhood in Colorado to her role in identifying victims of the 9/11 terrorist attacks. (Rev: BL 10/15/05; SLJ 2/06) [363.25]

FRANKLIN, ROSALIND

6642 Polcovar, Jane. *Rosalind Franklin and the Structure of Life* (8–11). Illus. Series: Profiles in Science. 2006, Morgan Reynolds LB $26.95 (978-1-59935-022-6). Franklin had a small part in the discovery of DNA — she took the image that set Watson and Crick on the path to found the field of genetics; this profile looks at her advancement in a profession generally closed to women and at the competitive nature of the search for the double helix. (Rev: BL 12/1/06; SLJ 3/07) [921]

6643 Senker, Cath. *Rosalind Franklin* (5–8). Illus. Series: Scientists Who Made History. 2003, Raintree $27.12 (978-0-7398-5226-2). An interesting biography of the woman who never gained credit for her contributions to the discovery of the structure of DNA. (Rev: BL 3/1/03; HBG 10/03; SLJ 4/03) [572.8]

FREUD, SIGMUND

6644 Krull, Kathleen. *Sigmund Freud* (6–9). Illus. by Boris Kulikov. Series: Giants of Science. 2006, Viking $15.99 (978-0-670-05892-1). This book examines the complex life of the father of psychoanalysis — his flaws as well as his virtues — and the enormous influence his theories have had on modern life. (Rev: BL 12/1/06; HB 9–10/06; SLJ 12/06) [921]

6645 Reef, Catherine. *Sigmund Freud: Pioneer of the Mind* (7–12). Illus. 2001, Clarion $19.00 (978-0-618-01762-1). Reef looks at Freud's life and career, showing the ways in which his ideas evolved over time and the initial rejection of many of his revolutionary thoughts. (Rev: BL 7/01; HB 7–8/01*; HBG 10/01; SLJ 8/01; VOYA 10/01) [921]

FULTON, ROBERT

6646 Flammang, James M. *Robert Fulton: Inventor and Steamboat Builder* (5–8). Illus. Series: Historical American Biographies. 1999, Enslow LB $26.60 (978-0-7660-1141-0). Beginning with Fulton's 1807 demonstration of his steamboat, this biography moves back and forth in time to trace the complete career of this man who changed America's transportation history. (Rev: BL 11/1/99; HBG 3/00) [921]

6647 Pierce, Morris A. *Robert Fulton and the Development of the Steamboat* (4–8). Series: Library of American Lives and Times. 2003, Rosen LB $34.60 (978-0-8239-5737-8). The inventor of the steamboat was a man of determination and wide interests who also worked on naval weapons. (Rev: BL 6/1–15/03; SLJ 4/03) [921]

FUNG, INEZ

6648 Skelton, Renee. *Forecast Earth: The Story of Climate Scientist Inez Fung* (6–10). Illus. Series: Women's Adventures in Science. 2005, Watts LB $31.50 (978-0-531-16777-9). An interesting biography that blends personal information with scientific facts. (Rev: SLJ 2/06) [921]

GALILEO

6649 Boerst, William J. *Galileo Galilei and the Science of Motion* (6–10). Illus. Series: Great Scientists. 2003, Morgan Reynolds LB $26.95 (978-1-931798-00-6). Galileo's early insistence on adherence to scientific verification is emphasized in this detailed yet accessible biography that includes color period reproductions and a timeline. (Rev: BL 11/1/03; HBG 4/04; SLJ 12/03) [921]

6650 Hightower, Paul. *Galileo: Astronomer and Physicist* (4–7). Illus. Series: Great Minds of Science. 1997, Enslow LB $26.60 (978-0-89490-787-6). This biography not only includes material on the life and accomplishments of this courageous scientist but also contains several activities that give an understanding of his work. (Rev: BL 6/1–15/97) [921]

6651 Hilliam, Rachel. *Galileo Galilei: Father of Modern Science* (5–8). Series: Rulers, Scholars, and Artists of the Renaissance. 2005, Rosen LB $33.25 (978-1-4042-0314-3). Ford places Galileo's life and accomplishments in the context of culture and politics of the time. (Rev: SLJ 10/05) [921]

6652 Mason, Paul. *Galileo* (6–8). Illus. Series: Groundbreakers. 2001, Heinemann LB $25.64 (978-1-58810-052-8). Galileo's life, times, and achievements are covered here, with discussion of his failings as well as his attributes. (Rev: HBG 10/01; SLJ 7/01) [520]

6653 Panchyk, Richard. *Galileo for Kids: His Life and Ideas* (5–9). Illus. 2005, Chicago Review paper $16.95 (978-1-55652-566-7). A clearly written and well-illustrated overview of Galileo's life and scientific achievements, with excerpts from Galileo's writings and suggested activities. (Rev: SLJ 9/05) [921]

GATES, BILL

6654 Boyd, Aaron. *Smart Money: The Story of Bill Gates* (6–10). 1995, Morgan Reynolds LB $21.95 (978-1-883846-09-1). A biography of Microsoft's billionaire mogul. (Rev: BL 4/1/95; SLJ 4/95; VOYA 2/96) [921]

6655 Dickinson, Joan D. *Bill Gates: Billionaire Computer Genius* (5–8). Series: People to Know. 1997, Enslow LB $26.60 (978-0-89490-824-8). This biography of the computer genius traces his life from his birth in 1955, showing how his personal drive made him into the richest man in America. (Rev: BL 10/15/97; HBG 3/98; SLJ 12/97; VOYA 2/98) [921]

6656 Lockwood, Brad. *Bill Gates: Profile of a Digital Entrepreneur* (5–8). 2007, Rosen LB $31.95 (978-1-4042-1906-9). Well-written and updated, this volume on Gates focuses on his career. (Rev: LMC 1/08; SLJ 3/08)

6657 Peters, Craig. *Bill Gates* (5–8). Illus. Series: Internet Biographies. 2003, Enslow LB $23.93 (978-0-7660-1969-0). A reader-friendly biography of the creator of Microsoft, with information on his youth as well as his successful later life. (Rev: BL 3/15/03; HBG 10/03) [338.7]

6658 Schuman, Michael A. *Bill Gates: Computer Mogul and Philanthropist* (5–8). 2007, Enslow LB $31.93 (978-0-7660-2693-3). Gates and his wife Melinda and their far-reaching philanthropic efforts are covered in this clearly written volume. (Rev: SLJ 3/08) [921]

6659 Woog, Adam. *Bill Gates* (4–7). Illus. Series: Famous People. 2003, Gale $26.20 (978-0-7377-1400-5). Woog covers Gates's childhood, education, interest in computers, and career, with photographs. (Rev: BL 6/1–15/03) [338.7]

GETTY, JOHN PAUL

6660 Glassman, Bruce S. *John Paul Getty: Billionaire Oilman* (7–10). Illus. Series: Giants of American Industry. 2001, Blackbirch LB $27.45 (978-1-56711-513-0). Glassman covers Getty's life from childhood, describing how he became a millionaire in his 20s and later was known for his philanthropy and art collection. (Rev: BL 10/15/01; HBG 3/02) [921]

GODDARD, ROBERT

6661 Bankston, John. *Robert Goddard and the Liquid Rocket Engine* (4–7). Series: Unlocking the Secrets of Science. 2001, Mitchell Lane LB $17.95 (978-1-58415-107-4). Bankston combines an introduction to Goddard's commitment to rocketry and his difficulty finding funding with an understandable explanation of the scientific challenges. (Rev: HBG 3/02; SLJ 2/02) [621.43]

6662 Streissguth, Thomas. *Rocket Man: The Story of Robert Goddard* (5–7). Illus. Series: Trailblazers. 1995, Carolrhoda LB $27.93 (978-0-87614-863-1). A history of rocketry, with emphasis on the life and accomplishments of Goddard. (Rev: BL 10/15/95; SLJ 9/95) [921]

GOODALL, JANE

6663 Bardhan-Quallen, Sudipta. *Jane Goodall: Primatologist* (6–9). Illus. Series: Up Close. 2008, Viking $16.99 (978-0-670-06263-8). This sometimes very detailed profile that covers Goodall's life from childhood will be useful for report writers. (Rev: BL 6/1–15/08; SLJ 9/08) [921]

6664 January, Brendan. *Jane Goodall: Animal Behaviorist and Writer* (4–7). Series: Ferguson Career Biographies. 2001, Ferguson LB $25.00 (978-0-89434-370-4). This easily read biography will appeal in particular to reluctant readers and students seeking quick information for a report. (Rev: SLJ 9/01) [921]

6665 Kozleski, Lisa. *Jane Goodall: Primatologist/Naturalist* (7–12). Series: Women in Science. 2003, Chelsea LB $30.00 (978-0-7910-6905-9). An absorbing biography that discusses the primatologist's personal life as well as her dedicated work with chimpanzees in Tanzania. (Rev: LMC 11–12/03; SLJ 7/03) [921]

6666 Meachum, Virginia. *Jane Goodall: Protector of Chimpanzees* (6–10). Illus. Series: People to Know. 1997, Enslow LB $26.60 (978-0-89490-827-9). The story of the great naturalist who fulfilled her childhood dream and made groundbreaking observations of chimpanzee behavior. (Rev: BL 1/1–15/98; HBG 3/98) [921]

6667 Pratt, Paula B. *Jane Goodall* (4–8). Illus. Series: The Importance Of. 1997, Lucent LB $27.45 (978-1-56006-082-6). The story of the great naturalist who studied and protected the primates of Africa. (Rev: BL 1/1–15/97; SLJ 2/97) [921]

GRAHAM, KATHARINE

6668 Asirvatham, Sandy. *Katharine Graham* (7–10). Illus. Series: Women of Achievement. 2001, Chelsea LB $30.00 (978-0-7910-6310-1); paper $9.95 (978-0-7910-6311-8). A concise and readable account of Graham's life and her success in taking over the *Washington Post* after her husband's suicide. (Rev: BL 3/1/02; HBG 10/02; SLJ 6/02) [921]

6669 Whitelaw, Nancy. *Let's Go! Let's Publish! Katharine Graham and the Washington Post* (7–10). 1998, Morgan Reynolds LB $21.95 (978-1-883846-37-4). The life story of the famous woman editor of the *Washington Post,* who led it through such turbulent times as the Pentagon Papers and Watergate. (Rev: BL 1/1–15/99; HBG 3/99; SLJ 5/99; VOYA 6/00) [921]

GROVE, ANDREW

6670 Byman, Jeremy. *Andrew Grove and the Intel Corporation* (6–12). 1999, Morgan Reynolds LB $23.95 (978-1-883846-38-1). From hiding with his mother in Nazi-occupied Budapest to the founding of Intel, the company that changed computer history, this is the story of Andrew Grove. (Rev: BL 3/15/99; SLJ 5/99) [921]

GUTENBERG, JOHANN

6671 Pollard, Michael. *Johann Gutenberg: Master of Modern Printing* (5–7). Series: Giants of Science. 2001, Blackbirch LB $27.44 (978-1-56711-335-8). Good use of illustrations and an interesting text are highlights of this life of the German printer who first used movable type. (Rev: BL 8/1/01; HBG 3/02) [921]

HALLEY, EDMOND

6672 Fox, Mary Virginia. *Scheduling the Heavens: The Story of Edmond Halley* (6–9). Illus. 2007, Morgan Reynolds LB $27.95 (978-1-59935-021-9). Details the life, career, and achievements of the scientist best known for calculating the orbit and accurately predicting the return of the eponymous comet. (Rev: BL 6/1–15/07; SLJ 4/07) [921]

HAMMEL, HEIDI

6673 Bortz, Fred. *Beyond Jupiter: The Story of Planetary Astronomer Heidi Hammel* (6–10). Illus. Series: Women's Adventures in Science. 2005, Watts LB $31.50 (978-0-531-16775-5). An interesting biography that blends personal information with scientific facts. (Rev: SLJ 2/06) [921]

HARVEY, WILLIAM

6674 Yount, Lisa. *William Harvey: Discoverer of How Blood Circulates* (4–8). Illus. Series: Great Minds of Science. 1994, Enslow LB $26.60 (978-0-89490-481-3). A biography of the 17th-century scientist that describes early theories about the blood system and the importance of Harvey's discoveries. (Rev: SLJ 2/95) [921]

HAWKING, STEPHEN

6675 Bankston, John. *Stephen Hawking: Breaking the Boundaries of Time and Space* (6–9). Series: Great Minds of Science. 2005, Enslow LB $26.60 (978-0-7660-2281-2). The life and scientific career of British physicist Stephen Hawking are presented in clear and simple text. (Rev: SLJ 6/05) [921]

HEWLETT, WILLIAM

6676 Tracy, Kathleen. *William Hewlett: Pioneer of the Computer Age* (5–7). Series: Unlocking the Secrets of Science. 2002, Mitchell Lane LB $25.70 (978-1-58415-142-5). This accessible account focuses on Hewlett's scientific accomplishments and career in business. (Rev: SLJ 1/03) [921]

HOOKE, ROBERT

6677 Gow, Mary. *Robert Hooke: Creative Genius, Scientist, Inventor* (5–9). Series: Great Minds of Science. 2006, Enslow LB $31.93 (978-0-7660-2547-9). A biography of the 17th-century man of science and arts who made discoveries in many fields and also helped to redesign London after the fire of 1666. (Rev: SLJ 6/07) [921]

HUBBLE, EDWIN

6678 Datnow, Claire. *Edwin Hubble: Discoverer of Galaxies* (4–8). Illus. Series: Great Minds of Science. 1997, Enslow LB $26.60 (978-0-89490-934-4). A portrait of the great astronomer, noted for his amazing scientific abilities and quirky pretentions. (Rev: BL 12/1/97; HBG 3/98; SLJ 3/98; VOYA 12/97) [921]

6679 Kupperberg, Paul. *Hubble and the Big Bang* (6–9). Illus. Series: Primary Sources of Revolutionary Scientific Discoveries and Theories. 2005, Rosen LB $29.25 (978-1-4042-0307-5). A profile of American astronomer Edwin Hubble with an easy-to-understand explanation of his theory of the expanding universe and reproductions of newspaper and journal articles. (Rev: BL 9/1/05; SLJ 11/05; VOYA 12/05) [921]

6680 MacDonald, Fiona. *Edwin Hubble* (6–8). Illus. Series: Groundbreakers. 2001, Heinemann LB $25.64 (978-1-58810-054-2). MacDonald takes a frank look at Hubble's life, times, and achievements, discussing his difficult character as well as his important contributions. (Rev: SLJ 7/01) [520]

IVE, JONATHAN

6681 Hirschmann, Kris. *Jonathan Ive: Designer of the iPod* (5–8). Illus. Series: Innovators. 2007, Gale LB $27.45 (978-0-7377-3533-8). Introduces the man behind this popular gadget; the inside info on

Apple is also fascinating. (Rev: BL 12/15/07) [745.2092]

JACKSON, SHIRLEY ANN

6682 O'Connell, Diane. *Strong Force: The Story of Physicist Shirley Ann Jackson* (5–8). Series: Women's Adventures in Science. 2005, Watts LB $31.50 (978-0-531-16784-7). The life and scientific career of Jackson, physicist and former chairman of the U.S. Nuclear Regulatory Commission. (Rev: SLJ 12/05) [921]

JEMISON, MAE

6683 Jemison, Mae. *Find Where the Wind Goes* (7–12). 2001, Scholastic $16.95 (978-0-439-13195-7). The fascinating autobiography of the first African American woman in space. (Rev: BL 11/1/01; HBG 10/01; SLJ 4/01; VOYA 8/01) [629.45]

JOBS, STEVE

6684 Brashares, Ann. *Steve Jobs: Thinks Different* (5–8). Series: Techies. 2001, Twenty-First Century LB $23.90 (978-0-7613-1959-7). The life story of the amazing creator of Apple computers and his phenomenal success as a businessman and entrepreneur. (Rev: BL 3/15/01; HBG 10/01) [921]

6685 Corrigan, Jim. *Steve Jobs* (6–9). Illus. Series: Business Builders. 2008, Morgan Reynolds $27.95 (978-1-59935-076-9). A somewhat critical look at the founder of Apple, focusing on his career and management approach. (Rev: BL 6/1–15/08; SLJ 8/08) [338.7]

6686 Wilson, Suzan. *Steve Jobs: Wizard of Apple Computer* (5–8). Series: People to Know. 2001, Enslow LB $26.60 (978-0-7660-1536-4). An engrossing biography that will attract computer-lovers, in which Jobs's early passion for electronics is shown as paving the way for his success — and failures — at Apple and other companies. (Rev: HBG 3/02; SLJ 3/02) [921]

JONES, CAROLINE

6687 Fleming, Robert. *The Success of Caroline Jones Advertising, Inc.* (7–10). Illus. Series: Success. 1996, Walker LB $16.85 (978-0-8027-8354-7). The story of Jones's rapid rise in the world of advertising. (Rev: BL 1/1–15/96; SLJ 4/96) [921]

KARAN, DONNA

6688 Tippins, Sherill. *Donna Karan: Designing an American Dream* (5–8). Illus. Series: Wizards of Business. 1992, Garrett LB $17.26 (978-1-56074-019-3). Along with the life story of one of America's top fashion designers is advice for those who wish to enter the field. (Rev: BL 6/15/92) [921]

KEPLER, JOHANNES

6689 Boerst, William J. *Johannes Kepler: Discovering the Laws of Celestial Motion* (6–9). Illus. Series: Renaissance Scientists. 2003, Morgan Reynolds LB $26.95 (978-1-883846-98-5). Astronomer and mathematician Kepler's life and achievements are placed in historical context, with details of the religious tensions of the time and the uncertainty of a scientific career. (Rev: BL 6/1–15/03; HBG 10/03; SLJ 8/03) [520]

KOEHL, MIMI

6690 Parks, Deborah. *Nature's Machines: The Story of Biomechanist Mimi Koehl* (6–10). Illus. Series: Women's Adventures in Science. 2005, Watts LB $31.50 (978-0-531-16780-9). An interesting biography that blends personal information with scientific facts. (Rev: SLJ 2/06) [921]

KOLFF, WILLEM

6691 Tracy, Kathleen. *Willem Kolff and the Invention of the Dialysis Machine* (5–8). Illus. Series: Unlocking the Secrets of Science. 2002, Mitchell Lane LB $25.70 (978-1-58415-135-7). Kolff invented the dialysis machine in 1942 in the Nazi-occupied Netherlands. (Rev: HBG 3/03; SLJ 12/02) [617.461059092]

LATIMER, LEWIS

6692 Norman, Winifred Latimer, and Lily Patterson. *Lewis Latimer* (7–10). Series: Black Americans of Achievement. 1993, Chelsea LB $21.95 (978-0-7910-1977-1). Follows Latimer's career from Civil War veteran to executive at the Edison Company, where he helped Thomas Edison improve the light bulb and supervised the installation of electrical systems in several cities. (Rev: BL 11/15/93) [921]

LAVOISIER, ANTOINE

6693 Yount, Lisa. *Antoine Lavoisier: Founder of Modern Chemistry* (4–7). Illus. Series: Great Minds of Science. 1997, Enslow LB $26.60 (978-0-89490-785-2). In addition to providing an assessment of the life and works of Lavoisier, called the Father of Chemistry, this book includes several hands-on activities that depend on an understanding of his work. (Rev: BL 6/1–15/97) [921]

LEAKEY, LOUIS AND MARY

6694 Poynter, Margaret. *The Leakeys: Uncovering the Origins of Humankind* (5–8). Illus. Series: Great Minds of Science. 1997, Enslow LB $26.60 (978-0-89490-788-3). The story of the famous husband-and-wife team of scientists, Louis and Mary Leakey, and how they expanded our knowledge of evolution. (Rev: BL 12/1/97; HBG 3/98; SLJ 12/97) [921]

LEEUWENHOEK, ANTONI VAN

6695 Yount, Lisa. *Antoni van Leeuwenhoek: First to See Microscopic Life* (4–8). Series: Great Minds of Science. 1996, Enslow LB $26.60 (978-0-89490-680-0). A brief biography of the Dutch maker of microscopes, who was also the first to examine closely bacteria and blood cells. (Rev: BL 10/15/96; SLJ 12/96) [921]

LEOPOLD, ALDO

6696 Lorbiecki, Marybeth. *Of Things Natural, Wild, and Free: A Story About Aldo Leopold* (4–7). Illus. 1993, Carolrhoda LB $15.95 (978-0-87614-797-9). The story of a man who was a great hunter until he realized the importance of the balance in nature, and then turned a tract of farmland into a nature refuge. (Rev: BL 11/1/93; SLJ 11/93) [921]

LINNAEUS, CARL

6697 Anderson, Margaret J. *Carl Linnaeus: Father of Classification* (4–8). Series: Great Minds of Science. 1997, Enslow LB $26.60 (978-0-89490-786-9). This biography discusses the personal life of Linnaeus, including his explorations in Lapland, but the focus is on the development of his important biological classification system. (Rev: BL 12/1/97; HBG 3/98; SLJ 9/97) [921]

MCCLINTOCK, BARBARA

6698 Cullen, J. Heather. *Barbara McClintock: Geneticist* (6–12). Illus. Series: Women in Science. 2003, Chelsea LB $30.00 (978-0-7910-7248-6). Cullen explores the life and achievements of McClintock, who won a Nobel Prize in 1983 for research in genetics that she conducted decades earlier. (Rev: HBG 10/03; SLJ 10/03) [921]

6699 Fine, Edith Hope. *Barbara McClintock: Nobel Prize Geneticist* (6–8). Series: People to Know. 1998, Enslow LB $26.60 (978-0-89490-983-2). This biography of the famous female geneticist whose work on maize earned her a Nobel Prize gives interesting details on her youth and the many honors she received later in life. (Rev: BL 1/1–15/99; HBG 3/99; SLJ 3/99) [921]

6700 Spangenburg, Ray, and Diane Kit Moser. *Barbara McClintock: Pioneering Geneticist* (8–11). Illus. Series: Makers of Modern Science. 2008, Chelsea House LB $29.95 (978-0-8160-6172-3). A biography of the 1983 winner of a Nobel Prize for her work on the genetics of maize. (Rev: BL 4/15/08) [576.5092]

6701 Tracy, Kathleen. *Barbara McClintock: Pioneering Geneticist* (4–7). Series: Unlocking the Secrets of Science. 2001, Mitchell Lane LB $25.70 (978-1-58415-111-1). An absorbing look at the life and research of this Nobel Prize winner. (Rev: HBG 3/02; SLJ 2/02) [921]

MALONE, ANNIE TURNBO

6702 Wilkerson, J. L. *Story of Pride, Power and Uplift: Annie T. Malone* (4–8). Illus. 2003, Acorn $9.95 (978-0-9664470-8-8). Malone, a child of slaves, created beauty products for African American women at the turn of the 20th century and became a wealthy woman and philanthropist. (Rev: BL 3/1/03; SLJ 7/03) [646.7]

MAYER, MARIA GOEPPERT

6703 Ferry, Joseph P. *Maria Goeppert Mayer: Physicist* (6–12). Series: Women in Science. 2003, Chelsea LB $30.00 (978-0-7910-7247-9). Ferry explores the life and achievements of Mayer, who won a Nobel Prize in 1963 for research into the atomic nucleus. (Rev: HBG 10/03; SLJ 10/03) [921]

MEAD, MARGARET

6704 Horn, Geoffrey M. *Margaret Mead* (5–8). Series: Trailblazers of the Modern World. 2004, World Almanac LB $31.00 (978-0-8368-5099-4). Report writers will find useful information on Mead's life, achievements, and lasting contributions. (Rev: SLJ 7/04) [921]

6705 Mark, Joan. *Margaret Mead: Coming of Age in America* (6–10). Ed. by Owen Gingerich. Illus. Series: Oxford Portraits in Science. 1999, Oxford $32.95 (978-0-19-511679-3). An introduction to the life and work of the pioneering anthropologist and her research with the peoples of the South Seas, particularly in Samoa. (Rev: BL 4/1/99; SLJ 3/99) [921]

6706 Ziesk, Edra. *Margaret Mead* (5–8). Illus. Series: American Women of Achievement. 1990, Chelsea LB $19.95 (978-1-55546-667-1). A useful volume covering the career and personal life of this unconventional anthropologist. (Rev: BL 2/15/90; SLJ 9/90; VOYA 8/90) [921]

MEITNER, LISE

6707 Barron, Rachel Stiffler. *Lise Meitner: Discoverer of Nuclear Fission* (7–12). Series: Great Scientists. 2000, Morgan Reynolds LB $23.95 (978-1-883846-52-7). The story of the Jewish scientist who fled Nazi Germany to the U.S., where her findings concerning nuclear fission led to the first atomic bomb. (Rev: BL 3/15/00; HBG 4/00; SLJ 6/00) [921]

6708 Hamilton, Janet. *Lise Meitner: Pioneer of Nuclear Fission* (6–10). Illus. Series: Great Minds of Science. 2002, Enslow LB $26.60 (978-0-7660-1756-6). This readable biography of the nuclear physicist who fled Nazi Germany before the outbreak of World War II, and who subsequently refused to work on developing nuclear weapons, is notable for placing her life and work in historical context. (Rev: HBG 10/02; SLJ 10/02) [921]

MENDEL, GREGOR

6709 Bankston, John. *Gregor Mendel and the Discovery of the Gene* (5–8). Illus. Series: Uncharted, Unexplored, and Unexplained. 2004, Mitchell Lane LB $29.95 (978-1-58415-266-8). Profiles the 19th-century Austrian monk who discovered the laws of genetics. (Rev: BL 10/15/04; SLJ 12/04) [921]

6710 Edelson, Edward. *Gregor Mendel: And the Roots of Genetics* (7–10). Series: Oxford Portraits in Science. 1999, Oxford $34.99 (978-0-19-512226-8). Describes Mendel's life and his work on plant heredity and the study of genetics in the context of the social, scientific, and political events of his time. (Rev: SLJ 7/99) [921]

6711 Klare, Roger. *Gregor Mendel: Father of Genetics* (5–7). Illus. Series: Great Minds of Science. 1997, Enslow LB $26.60 (978-0-89490-789-0). The science of genetics is introduced through the life of Mendel and his experimentation with peas. (Rev: BL 12/1/97; HBG 3/98; SLJ 12/97; VOYA 12/97) [921]

MENDELEYEV, DMITRI

6712 Zannos, Susan. *Dmitri Mendeleyev and the Periodic Table* (5–8). Series: Uncharted, Unexplored, and Unexplained. 2004, Mitchell Lane LB $29.95 (978-1-58415-267-5). This brief biography looks at the life of the inventor of the periodic table, focusing initially on his childhood and offering political context. (Rev: BL 10/15/04) [540]

MERCATOR, GERARDUS

6713 Heinrichs, Ann. *Gerardus Mercator: Father of Modern Mapmaking* (5–12). Series: Signature Lives. 2007, Compass Point LB $31.93 (978-0-7565-3312-0). Scientific concepts are presented clearly in this profile that covers Mercator's life, with excerpts from his writing and a timeline that adds historical context. (Rev: SLJ 1/08)

MEXIA, YNES

6714 Anema, Durlynn. *Ynes Mexia: Botanist and Adventurer* (6–9). 2005, Morgan Reynolds $26.95

(978-1-931798-67-9). Mexia is known for her adventurous spirit and her important collections of plants from North and South America, which she started in her mid-50s. (Rev: SLJ 1/06) [921]

MITCHELL, MARIA

6715 Gormley, Beatrice. *Maria Mitchell: The Soul of an Astronomer* (6–9). 1995, Eerdmans paper $8.00 (978-0-8028-5099-7). An authentic, interesting biography of the 19th-century female astronomer, with details on her accomplishments and an accompanying 16-page centerfold of photographs. (Rev: BL 9/1/95; SLJ 1/96) [921]

MORGAN, J. P.

6716 Byman, Jeremy. *J. P. Morgan: Banker to a Growing Nation* (6–10). Series: American Business Leaders. 2001, Morgan Reynolds LB $23.95 (978-1-883846-60-2). An easily read introduction to Morgan's importance that places his contributions in political and social context. (Rev: HBG 10/01; SLJ 7/01) [021]

MUIR, JOHN

6717 Wadsworth, Ginger. *John Muir: Wilderness Protector* (6–12). 1992, Lerner LB $18.95 (978-0-8225-4912-3). Original photographs and Muir's letters, journals, and writings provide an overview of the conservationist's personal life, achievements, and contributions to the environmental movement. (Rev: BL 8/92) [921]

MURRAY, JOSEPH E.

6718 Mattern, Joanne. *Joseph E. Murray and the Story of the First Human Kidney Transplant* (5–8). Illus. Series: Unlocking the Secrets of Science. 2002, Mitchell Lane LB $25.70 (978-1-58415-136-4). A look at the work of the surgeon who performed the first successful kidney transplant. (Rev: SLJ 12/02; VOYA 6/03) [617.95092]

NEWTON, ISAAC

6719 Allan, Tony. *Isaac Newton* (6–8). Illus. Series: Groundbreakers. 2001, Heinemann LB $25.64 (978-1-58810-053-5). MacDonald takes a frank look at Newton's life, times, and achievements, discussing his unpopularity as a teacher and his interest in alchemy. (Rev: SLJ 7/01) [530]

6720 Anderson, Margaret J. *Isaac Newton: The Greatest Scientist of All Time* (4–7). Illus. Series: Great Minds of Science. 1996, Enslow LB $26.60 (978-0-89490-681-7). The life of the great English mathematician and physicist who formulated the laws of motion and gravity. (Rev: BL 10/15/96; SLJ 12/96) [921]

6721 Boerst, William J. *Isaac Newton: Organizing the Universe* (6–10). Illus. Series: Renaissance Scientists. 2004, Morgan Reynolds LB $26.95 (978-1-931798-01-3). A fine biography of Newton that includes good explanations of the laws of motion and excellent color reproductions of period paintings. (Rev: BL 2/1/04; SLJ 4/04) [921]

6722 Christianson, Gale E. *Isaac Newton and the Scientific Revolution* (8–12). Illus. Series: Oxford Portraits in Science. 1996, Oxford $32.95 (978-0-19-509224-0). A challenging biography that gives the scientist's life history plus detailed explanations of theories of gravity, relativity, and calculus. (Rev: BL 12/1/96; SLJ 1/97; VOYA 2/97) [921]

6723 Krull, Kathleen. *Isaac Newton* (5–8). Illus. by Boris Kulikov. Series: Giants of Science. 2006, Viking $15.99 (978-0-670-05921-8). Newton's childhood and adult personality are highlighted in this readable biography that gives good explanations of his scientific theories. (Rev: BL 4/1/06; SLJ 3/06*; VOYA 6/06) [530]

6724 Mason, Paul. *Isaac Newton* (4–8). Illus. Series: Scientists Who Made History. 2002, Raintree LB $27.12 (978-0-7398-4845-6). Newton's life and contributions are presented in clear text and ample illustrations, with historical detail that places the information in context. (Rev: HBG 10/02; SLJ 9/02) [530.092]

6725 Steele, Philip. *Isaac Newton: The Scientist Who Changed Everything* (4–7). Illus. Series: National Geographic World History Biographies. 2007, National Geographic $17.95 (978-1-4263-0114-8). A colorful, well-designed survey of Newton's life and legacy. (Rev: BL 12/1/07; SLJ 6/07) [921]

OMIDYAR, PIERRE

6726 Viegas, Jennifer. *Pierre Omidyar: The Founder of eBay* (5–8). Illus. Series: Internet Career Biographies. 2006, Rosen LB $31.95 (978-1-4042-0715-8). A look at the successful founder of eBay and his hopes for the future. (Rev: BL 10/15/06; SLJ 5/07) [921]

OPPENHEIMER, J. ROBERT

6727 Allman, Toney. *J. Robert Oppenheimer: Father of the Atomic Bomb* (5–9). Series: Giants of Science. 2005, Gale $26.20 (978-1-56711-889-6). Controversial physicist Oppenheimer, who played a key role in the development of the atomic bomb, is profiled in readable text with lots of details for report writers. (Rev: SLJ 7/05) [921]

6728 Scherer, Glenn, and Marty Fletcher. *J. Robert Oppenheimer: The Brain Behind the Bomb* (6–10). Illus. Series: Inventors Who Changed the World. 2007, Enslow LB $33.27 (978-1-59845-050-7). The story of the physicist who shepherded the Manhattan Project, with discussion of the science involved and the key political and social factors. (Rev: BL 7/07; SLJ 11/07) [921]

PASTEUR, LOUIS

6729 Ackerman, Jane. *Louis Pasteur and the Founding of Microbiology* (7–12). Illus. Series: Great Scientists. 2004, Morgan Reynolds $26.95 (978-1-931798-13-6). Using his microscope, Pasteur developed the fields of immunology and microbiology and invented the pasteurization of milk. (Rev: BL 2/1/04; SLJ 4/04) [921]

6730 Birch, Beverley. *Louis Pasteur: Father of Modern Medicine* (5–7). Series: Giants of Science. 2001, Blackbirch LB $27.44 (978-1-56711-336-5). A readable, well-organized biography of the French chemist whose varied accomplishments include discovery of the process known now as pasteurization. (Rev: BL 8/1/01; HBG 3/02) [921]

6731 Gogerly, Liz. *Louis Pasteur* (6–8). Illus. Series: Scientists Who Made History. 2002, Raintree LB $27.12 (978-0-7398-4846-3). Information on Pasteur's youth and his early fascination with science is included in this readable account of his life and accomplishments. (Rev: HBG 10/02; SLJ 7/02) [579]

6732 Robbins, Louise E. *Louis Pasteur and the Hidden World of Microbes* (8–12). Series: Oxford Portraits in Science. 2001, Oxford $34.99 (978-0-19-512227-5). A look at the life of the famous scientist, with glimpses of his personality as well as his research and discoveries. (Rev: BL 12/1/01; HBG 3/02; SLJ 12/01) [921]

6733 Smith, Linda W. *Louis Pasteur: Disease Fighter* (4–8). Illus. Series: Great Minds of Science. 1997, Enslow LB $26.60 (978-0-89490-790-6). The story of the "father of microbiology," who discovered pasteurization while working on a wine problem for Napoleon. (Rev: BL 12/1/97; HBG 3/98; SLJ 12/97) [921]

PAULING, LINUS

6734 Pasachoff, Naomi. *Linus Pauling: Advancing Science, Advocating Peace* (7–12). Illus. Series: Nobel Prize–Winning Scientists. 2004, Enslow LB $26.60 (978-0-7660-2130-3). Pauling's scientific errors are not dismissed in this biography that relates the Nobel prize winner's achievements in science and his campaign against nuclear weapons. (Rev: BL 6/1–15/04) [921]

PAVLOV, IVAN

6735 Saunders, Barbara R. *Ivan Pavlov: Exploring the Mysteries of Behavior* (5–9). Series: Great Minds of Science. 2006, Enslow LB $31.93 (978-0-

7660-2506-6). This well-written profile chronicles Pavlov's famous experiments and discoveries and shows how his work influenced other branches of science. (Rev: SLJ 6/07) [921]

PLOTKIN, MARK

6736 Pascoe, Elaine, adapt. *Mysteries of the Rain Forest: 20th Century Medicine Man* (4–8). Series: The New Explorers. 1997, Blackbirch LB $18.95 (978-1-56711-229-0). An exploration of the life and discoveries of Mark Plotkin, an ethnobotanist fascinated by the plants and people of the Amazon. (Rev: HBG 3/98; SLJ 2/98) [921]

PRIESTLEY, JOSEPH

6737 Conley, Kate A. *Joseph Priestley and the Discovery of Oxygen* (6–8). Series: Uncharted, Unexplored, and Unexplained: Scientific Advancements of the 19th Century. 2005, Mitchell Lane LB $19.95 (978-1-58415-367-2). An introduction to the scientist Joseph Priestley, including his childhood in England, setting his life and discoveries in historical context. (Rev: SLJ 5/06) [921]

PULITZER, JOSEPH

6738 Whitelaw, Nancy. *Joseph Pulitzer and the New York World* (7–10). Illus. Series: Makers of the Media. 1999, Morgan Reynolds LB $21.95 (978-1-883846-44-2). The life story of the founder of "tabloid journalism," who revolutionized the newspaper industry by combining sensational news, visuals, and reports on political corruption to both attract readers and encourage social change, and for whom the Pulitzer Prize is named. (Rev: BL 6/1–15/99; SLJ 9/99) [921]

6739 Zannos, Susan. *Joseph Pulitzer and the Story Behind the Pulitzer Prize* (4–8). Illus. Series: Great Achievement Awards. 2003, Mitchell Lane LB $29.95 (978-1-58415-179-1). Pulitzer's difficulty personality and passion for journalism are highlighted in this account of his establishment of the well-known awards. (Rev: BL 10/15/03; SLJ 9/03) [070.9]

ROBERTS, EDWARD

6740 Zannos, Susan. *Edward Roberts and the Story of the Personal Computer* (5–7). Series: Unlocking the Secrets of Science. 2002, Mitchell Lane LB $25.70 (978-1-58415-118-0). This accessible account focuses on Roberts's accomplishments as an electronic engineer. (Rev: HBG 10/03; SLJ 1/03) [921]

ROCKEFELLER, JOHN D.

6741 Laughlin, Rosemary. *John D. Rockefeller: Oil Baron and Philanthropist* (5–8). Illus. Series: American Business Leaders. 2001, Morgan Reynolds LB $21.95 (978-1-883846-59-6). A biography of the determined and skilled businessman who made Standard Oil the dominant company in the oil industry and who was later noted for his philanthropy. (Rev: BL 3/1/01; HBG 10/01; SLJ 7/01) [921]

RUTHERFORD, ERNEST

6742 Pasachoff, Naomi. *Ernest Rutherford: Father of Nuclear Science* (6–12). Series: Great Minds of Science. 2005, Enslow LB $26.60 (978-0-7660-2441-0). The life and scientific career of the New Zealand-born physicist who helped to pave the way for the development of nuclear physics. (Rev: SLJ 8/05) [921]

SAGAN, CARL

6743 Butts, Ellen R., and Joyce R. Schwarts. *Carl Sagan* (5–8). Series: A&E Biography. 2000, Lerner LB $27.93 (978-0-8225-4986-4). The story of the great astronomer who interested millions in the study of the stars and the question of whether there is life elsewhere in our universe. (Rev: BL 10/15/00; HBG 3/01; SLJ 10/00) [921]

6744 Byman, Jeremy. *Carl Sagan: In Contact with the Cosmos* (5–8). Illus. Series: Great Scientists. 2000, Morgan Reynolds LB $21.95 (978-1-883846-55-8). An informative biography of the scientist who popularized astronomy while maintaining a highly productive scholarly life. (Rev: BL 11/1/00; HBG 10/00; SLJ 8/00) [921]

SALK, JONAS

6745 McPherson, Stephanie Sammartino. *Jonas Salk: Conquering Polio* (5–8). Series: Lerner Biographies. 2001, Lerner LB $27.93 (978-0-8225-4964-2). An absorbing account of Salk's life and contributions to medicine that discusses his confrontation with Sabin and the early failures of Salk's vaccine. (Rev: HBG 3/02; SLJ 4/02) [921]

6746 Tocci, Salvatore. *Jonas Salk: Creator of the Polio Vaccine* (4–7). Illus. Series: Great Minds of Science. 2003, Enslow LB $26.60 (978-0-7660-2097-9). This book covers the life of the scientist and the importance and impact of the vaccine he developed. (Rev: BL 5/15/03; HBG 10/03) [610]

STEWART, MARTHA

6747 Meachum, Virginia. *Martha Stewart: Successful Businesswoman* (6–10). Series: People to Know. 1998, Enslow LB $26.60 (978-0-89490-984-9). A well-documented biography of Martha Kostyra Stewart, the human dynamo who has achieved fame as a model, master chef, expert homemaker, entertainer, author, and TV celebrity. (Rev: HBG 3/99; SLJ 1/99) [921]

STRAUSS, LEVI

6748 Van Steenwyk, Elizabeth. *Levi Strauss: The Blue Jeans Man* (5–9). 1988, Walker LB $14.85 (978-0-8027-6796-7). A biography of the Bavarian immigrant, Levi Strauss, who became the blue jeans king of the western world. (Rev: BL 6/15/88; SLJ 10/88; VOYA 8/88) [921]

TELLER, EDWARD

6749 Bankston, John. *Edward Teller and the Development of the Hydrogen Bomb* (5–8). Series: Unlocking the Secrets of Science. 2001, Mitchell Lane LB $25.70 (978-1-58415-108-1). The life of the scientist born in Hungary who played a key role in the development of the H-bomb. (Rev: HBG 3/02; SLJ 1/02) [539.7092]

TESLA, NIKOLA

6750 Aldrich, Lisa J. *Nikola Tesla and the Taming of Electricity* (8–11). Illus. Series: Modern Scientists. 2005, Morgan Reynolds LB $26.95 (978-1-931798-46-4). The life and many inventions — including radio — of the Croatian-born electrical engineer. (Rev: BL 5/1/05; SLJ 10/05; VOYA 10/05) [621.3]

6751 Dommermuth-Costa, Carol. *Nikola Tesla: A Spark of Genius* (5–9). 1994, Lerner LB $27.93 (978-0-8225-4920-8). Traces the life and career of this pioneer in the field of electricity. (Rev: BL 12/15/94; SLJ 2/95) [921]

TIENDA, MARTA

6752 O'Connell, Diane. *People Person: The Story of Sociologist Marta Tienda* (5–8). Series: Women's Adventures in Science. 2005, Watts LB $31.50 (978-0-531-16781-6). An informative and accessible profile of sociologist Marta Tienda and her work to create opportunities for people around the world. (Rev: SLJ 12/05) [921]

TORVALDS, LINUS

6753 Brashares, Ann. *Linus Torvalds: Software Rebel* (5–8). Series: Techies. 2001, Millbrook LB $23.90 (978-0-7613-1960-3). The story of the computer genius who created the Linux operating system. (Rev: BL 4/1/02; HBG 3/02; SLJ 12/01) [921]

TURING, ALAN

6754 Corrigan, Jim. *Alan Turing* (7–10). 2008, Morgan Reynolds LB $27.95 (978-1-59935-064-6). This biography of "the father of computer science" goes beyond his work in mathematics into his private life, discussing how his homosexuality affected his career. (Rev: BL 6/1–15/08) [921]

TURNER, TED

6755 Byman, Jeremy. *Ted Turner: Cable Television Tycoon* (7–10). Illus. 1998, Morgan Reynolds LB $23.95 (978-1-883846-25-1). Known as the "mouth of the south," media mogul Ted Turner, a born rebel, introduced CNN in 1980. (Rev: BL 4/1/98; HBG 9/98; SLJ 8/98) [921]

VEDDER, AMY

6756 Ebersole, Rene. *Gorilla Mountain: The Story of Wildlife Biologist Amy Vedder* (5–8). Series: Women's Adventures in Science. 2005, Watts LB $31.50 (978-0-531-16779-3). An informative and accessible account of Vedder's efforts to protect the endangered mountain gorillas of Rwanda. (Rev: SLJ 12/05)

WAKSMAN, SELMAN

6757 Gordon, Karen. *Selman Waksman and the Discovery of Streptomycin* (5–7). Series: Unlocking the Secrets of Science. 2002, Mitchell Lane LB $25.70 (978-1-58415-138-8). An accessible account of Waksman's life and scientific research. (Rev: HBG 10/03; SLJ 1/03) [921]

WALKER, MADAM C. J.

6758 Bundles, A'Lelia Perry. *Madam C. J. Walker* (5–10). Series: Black Americans of Achievement. 1993, Chelsea LB $32.00 (978-1-55546-615-2); paper $30.00 (978-0-7910-0251-3). Written by Walker's great-great-granddaughter, this volume describes the developer of a line of hair-care products whose entrepreneurial ability made her into the "foremost colored businesswoman in America." (Rev: BL 3/1/94) [921]

6759 Yannuzzi, Della A. *Madam C. J. Walker: Self-Made Businesswoman* (6–9). Illus. 2000, Enslow LB $26.60 (978-0-7660-1204-2). Born into poverty, the daughter of freed slaves, Walker made a fortune as an entrepreneur in hair-care products for African American women. (Rev: BL 2/15/00; HBG 9/00; SLJ 7/00) [921]

WALKER, MAGGIE

6760 Branch, Muriel M., and Dorothy M. Rice. *Pennies to Dollars: The Story of Maggie Lena Walker* (4–8). 1997, Linnet LB $19.50 (978-0-208-02453-

4); paper $13.95 (978-0-208-02455-8). Maggie Walker, the daughter of a former slave, helped African Americans through her financial schemes, including the founding of the Penny Savings Bank. (Rev: BL 11/1/97; SLJ 10/97) [921]

WALKER, MARY

6761 Joinson, Carla. *Civil War Doctor: The Story of Mary Walker* (8–11). Illus. 2007, Morgan Reynolds LB $27.95 (978-1-59935-028-8). Walker studied medicine at a time when this was very unusual for a woman; she later served as a surgeon in the Union Army and in 1865 was the first woman to be awarded the Congressional Medal of Honor. (Rev: BL 1/1–15/07) [921]

WANG, VERA

6762 Todd, Anne M. *Vera Wang* (6–10). Series: Asian Americans of Achievement. 2007, Chelsea House LB $30.00 (978-0-7910-9272-9). This attractive profile recounts the highlights of Wang's personal life and covers her work for *Vogue* and Ralph Lauren before starting her own business. (Rev: SLJ 8/07) [921]

WEINBERG, ROBERT A.

6763 Gaines, Ann, and Jim Whiting. *Robert A. Weinberg and the Search for the Cause of Cancer* (4–7). Series: Unlocking the Secrets of Science. 2002, Mitchell Lane LB $25.70 (978-1-58415-095-4). The life and achievements of the scientist who specializes in the genetic causes of disease. (Rev: HBG 10/02; SLJ 6/02) [616.9940092]

WEXLER, NANCY

6764 Glimm, Adele. *Gene Hunter: The Story of Neuropsychologist Nancy Wexler* (6–10). Illus. Series: Women's Adventures in Science. 2005, Watts LB $31.50 (978-0-531-16778-6). An interesting biography that blends personal information with scientific facts. (Rev: SLJ 2/06) [921]

WHITNEY, ELI

6765 Gibson, Karen Bush. *The Life and Times of Eli Whitney* (5–8). Illus. Series: Profiles in American History. 2006, Mitchell Lane LB $20.95 (978-1-58415-434-1). An interesting profile of the cotton gin inventor, with period reproductions and relevant sidebar features. (Rev: BL 10/15/06) [609.2]

WILLIAMS, DANIEL HALE

6766 Kaye, Judith. *The Life of Daniel Hale Williams* (5–8). Illus. Series: Pioneers in Health and Medicine. 1993, Twenty-First Century LB $16.90 (978-0-8050-2302-2). The life story of the famous doctor who pioneered heart surgery and also helped open up the medical profession to African Americans. (Rev: SLJ 1/94) [921]

WOZNIAK, STEPHEN

6767 Kendall, Martha E. *Steve Wozniak: Inventor of the Apple Computer* (6–9). 1995, Walker $15.85 (978-0-8027-8342-4). A biography of the eccentric genius who revolutionized personal computing. (Rev: BL 3/1/95; SLJ 3/95) [921]

6768 Riddle, John, and Jim Whiting. *Stephen Wozniak and the Story of Apple Computer* (4–7). Series: Unlocking the Secrets of Science. 2001, Mitchell Lane LB $17.95 (978-1-58415-109-8). A profile of the life and achievements of the co-founder of Apple, who is known for his philanthropy and teaching in elementary schools. (Rev: HBG 10/02; SLJ 2/02) [921]

WRIGHT, WILBUR AND ORVILLE

6769 Collins, Mary. *Airborne: A Photobiography of Wilbur and Orville Wright* (4–8). Illus. 2003, National Geographic $18.95 (978-0-7922-6957-1). Sixty photographs are only the beginning of this intriguing book packed with information about the brothers and their famous flight. (Rev: BL 2/1/03*; HB 3–4/03; HBG 10/03; SLJ 3/03) [629.13]

6770 Crompton, Samuel Willard. *The Wright Brothers: First in Flight* (6–12). Series: Milestones in American History. 2007, Chelsea House LB $35.00 (978-0-7910-9356-6). An accessible account of the lives of the two brothers and their contributions to aviation. (Rev: LMC 1/08; SLJ 10/07) [921]

6771 Dixon-Engel, Tara, and Mike Jackson. *The Wright Brothers: First in Flight* (5–8). Series: Sterling Biographies. 2007, Sterling LB $12.95 (978-1-4027-4954-4); paper $5.95 (978-1-4027-3231-7). The brothers' early life, inspiration, and eventual success are all covered here. (Rev: SLJ 10/07) [921]

6772 Freedman, Russell. *The Wright Brothers: How They Invented the Airplane* (6–10). 1991, Holiday $22.95 (978-0-8234-0875-7). Chronicles the achievements of two brothers who built the first flying machine in an Ohio bicycle shop and ultimately saw their dream come true. (Rev: BL 6/15/91*; SLJ 6/91*) [921]

6773 McPherson, Stephanie Sammartino, and Joseph Sammartino Gardner. *Wilbur and Orville Wright: Taking Flight* (4–7). Illus. Series: Trailblazer Biographies. 2003, Carolrhoda LB $30.60 (978-1-57505-443-8). A well-written, detailed account of the Wright brothers' landmark experiments, enlivened with period photographs and other illustrations. (Rev: SLJ 4/04) [921]

6774 Martin, Michael J. *The Wright Brothers* (7–12). Series: The Importance Of. 2003, Gale LB $32.45 (978-1-56006-847-1). With lengthy quotations from primary and secondary sources, this is a lively biography of Wilbur and Orville Wright and how they changed history at Kitty Hawk. (Rev: BL 6/1–15/03) [921]

6775 Old, Wendie C. *The Wright Brothers* (5–8). Series: Historical American Biographies. 2000, Enslow LB $26.60 (978-0-7660-1095-6). An accurate and objective biography of the heroes of Kitty Hawk, containing chapter notes, a bibliography, and a glossary. (Rev: BL 1/1–15/00; HBG 10/00; SLJ 7/00) [921]

6776 Reynolds, Quentin. *The Wright Brothers* (5–8). 1963, Random paper $5.99 (978-0-394-84700-9). An easily read account of the two young men and their dream of flight. [921]

6777 Sproule, Anna. *The Wright Brothers: The Birth of Modern Aviation* (5–8). Series: Giants of Science. 1999, Blackbirch LB $24.95 (978-1-56711-328-0). This slim biography with an inviting format stresses the lasting contributions of the Wright brothers to world transportation. (Rev: HBG 10/00; SLJ 2/00) [921]

Sports Figures

Collective

6778 Aaseng, Nathan. *African-American Athletes* (8–12). Series: A to Z of African Americans. 2003, Facts on File $45.00 (978-0-8160-4805-2). Profiles of more than 150 African American athletes, past and present and representing all kinds of sports, give personal and career information. (Rev: SLJ 6/03) [920]

6779 Aaseng, Nathan. *Athletes* (7–12). Series: American Indian Lives. 1995, Facts on File $25.00 (978-0-8160-3019-4). A collective biography that highlights the lives of 11 Native American athletes, including Jim Thorpe, Kitty O'Neil, Sonny Sixkiller, Billy Mills, and Henry Boucha. (Rev: BL 4/1/95) [920]

6780 Aaseng, Nathan. *Top 10 Basketball Scoring Small Forwards* (4–7). Series: Sports Top 10. 1999, Enslow LB $23.93 (978-0-7660-1152-6). Each of these 10 basketball forwards is covered by a two-page biography, a full-page picture, and a page of sports statistics. (Rev: BL 11/15/99; HBG 10/00) [920]

6781 Aaseng, Nathan. *True Champions* (5–9). 1993, Walker LB $15.85 (978-0-8027-8247-2). Tales of legendary athletes who have demonstrated heroism and self-sacrifice off the field. (Rev: BL 8/93; SLJ 6/93) [921]

6782 Breton, Marcos. *Home Is Everything: The Latino Baseball Story* (7–12). Trans. by Daniel Santacruz. Photos by Jos Luis Villegas. 2003, Cinco Puntos paper $25.95 (978-0-938317-70-8). The story of Miguel Tejada is spotlighted in this photoessay that also profiles other Latino baseball players including Jose Santana, Orlando Cepeda, and Roberto Clemente. (Rev: SLJ 12/03; VOYA 12/03) [920]

6783 Bryant, Jill. *Amazing Women Athletes* (4–8). Illus. Series: Women's Hall of Fame. 2002, Second Story paper $7.95 (978-1-896764-44-3). This book contains profiles of 10 distinguished women athletes including mountain climber Annie Smith Peck and tennis stars Venus and Serena Williams. (Rev: BL 6/1–15/02; SLJ 8/02) [920]

6784 Christopher, Andre. *Top 10 Men's Tennis Players* (4–7). Series: Sports Top 10. 1998, Enslow LB $17.95 (978-0-7600-1009-9). Brief biographies of past and present tennis greats, with fact boxes, career statistics, and chapter notes. (Rev: BL 3/15/98) [920]

6785 Deane, Bill. *Top 10 Baseball Home Run Hitters* (4–7). Illus. Series: Sports Top 10. 1997, Enslow LB $23.93 (978-0-89490-804-0). Ten brief biographies of baseball hitters, e.g., Hank Aaron, Mickey Mantle, Jimmie Foxx, and Frank Thomas. (Rev: BL 9/15/97; HBG 3/98) [920]

6786 Deane, Bill. *Top 10 Men's Baseball Hitters* (4–7). Series: Sports Top 10. 1998, Enslow LB $17.95 (978-0-7600-1007-5). Brief biographies of great past and present baseball hitters, with fact boxes, career statistics, and chapter notes. (Rev: BL 3/15/98) [920]

6787 Ditchfield, Christin. *Top 10 American Women's Olympic Gold Medalists* (4–7). Illus. Series: Sports Top 10. 2000, Enslow LB $23.93 (978-0-7660-1277-6). Along with the profiles of 10 female athletes, this book contains fact boxes, career statistics, and chapter notes. (Rev: BL 9/15/00; HBG 10/01) [920]

6788 Gaines, Ann. *Sports and Activities* (6–9). Series: Female Firsts in Their Fields. 1999, Chelsea $12.95 (978-0-7910-5144-3). A collection of six biographies of outstanding female trail blazers in athletics, focusing on how each achieved firsts for their sex. (Rev: BL 5/15/99; HBG 9/99) [920]

6789 Green, Septima. *Top 10 Women Gymnasts* (4–7). Series: Sports Top 10. 1999, Enslow LB $23.93 (978-0-89490-809-5). Each of these star gymnasts from the past and present gets a two-page biography, a page of important statistics, and a black-and-white photograph. (Rev: BL 11/15/99; HBG 10/00) [920]

6790 Gutman, Bill. *Teammates: Michael Jordan and Scottie Pippen* (7–10). 1998, Millbrook LB $23.90 (978-0-7613-0420-3). A look at the life stories of these two NBA stars with emphasis on their personal and professional development and their dedication to basketball and team spirit. (Rev: HBG 3/99; SLJ 1/99; VOYA 4/99) [920]

6791 Halberstam, David. *The Teammates* (8–12). 2003, Hyperion $22.95 (978-1-4013-0057-9). The story of the lives and friendships of four Boston Red Sox players: Ted Williams, Dominic DiMaggio, Johnny Pesky, and Bobby Doerr. [920]

6792 Hasday, Judy L. *Extraordinary Women Athletes* (6–12). Illus. Series: Extraordinary People. 2000, Children's LB $16.95 (978-0-516-27039-5). A collective biography of 45 women who have gained recognition in a wide variety of sports. (Rev: BL 10/1/00; VOYA 2/01) [920]

6793 Hotchkiss, Ron. *The Matchless Six: The Story of Canada's First Women's Olympic Team* (5–8). Illus. 2006, Tundra $16.95 (978-0-88776-738-8). Profiles the individual athletes and achievements of Canada's groundbreaking women's Olympic team of 1928. (Rev: BL 3/15/06; SLJ 6/06) [796.48]

6794 Kaminsky, Marty. *Uncommon Champions: Fifteen Athletes Who Battled Back* (5–8). Illus. 2000, Boyds Mills $14.95 (978-1-56397-787-9). Profiles of 15 athletes in several different sports who have conquered such mental and physical problems as blindness and drug addiction to achieve their goals. (Rev: BCCB 1/01; BL 11/1/00; HBG 3/01; SLJ 10/00; VOYA 12/00) [921]

6795 Knapp, Ron. *Top 10 American Men Sprinters* (4–7). Series: Sports Top 10. 1999, Enslow LB $23.93 (978-0-7660-1074-1). Profiles and photographs are given of 10 important American male sprinters past and present. (Rev: BL 3/15/99; HBG 10/99) [920]

6796 Knapp, Ron. *Top 10 American Men's Olympic Gold Medalists* (4–7). Illus. Series: Sports Top 10. 2000, Enslow LB $23.93 (978-0-7660-1274-5). This book of 10 American male Olympic stars covers a number of sports, including track and field and diving. (Rev: BL 9/15/00; HBG 10/00) [920]

6797 Knapp, Ron. *Top 10 NFL Super Bowl Most Valuable Players* (4–7). Series: Sports Top 10. 2000, Enslow LB $23.93 (978-0-7660-1273-8). This book profiles 10 of the past and present most valuable players in the National Football League's Super Bowl. (Rev: BL 12/15/00; HBG 10/01) [920]

6798 Krull, Kathleen. *Lives of the Athletes* (4–7). Illus. by Kathryn Hewitt. 1997, Harcourt $20.00 (978-0-15-200806-2). A collective biography that describes the public and private lives of 20 famous athletes, including Johnny Weissmuller, Red Grange, Babe Didrikson Zaharias, Sonja Henie, and Bruce Lee. (Rev: BCCB 6/97; BL 3/15/97; HB 5–6/97; SLJ 5/97) [920]

6799 Kuhn, Betsy. *Top 10 Jockeys* (4–7). Series: Sports Top 10. 1999, Enslow LB $23.93 (978-0-7660-1130-4). Important jockeys, both past and present, are featured with a short biography, a portrait, and a page of pertinent statistics. (Rev: BL 11/15/99; HBG 10/00) [920]

6800 Lipsyte, Robert. *Heroes of Baseball: The Men Who Made It America's Favorite Game* (4–7). Illus. 2006, Simon & Schuster $19.95 (978-0-689-86741-5). As well as introducing key players of the game, this volume presents a concise history of the sport itself. (Rev: BL 2/15/06; SLJ 4/06) [796.357]

6801 Molzahn, Arlene Bourgeois. *Top 10 American Women Sprinters* (4–8). Series: Sports Top 10. 1998, Enslow LB $23.93 (978-0-7660-1011-6). An easily read survey of the lives and accomplishments of 10 important women runners in track and field. (Rev: BL 8/98; HBG 10/99; SLJ 1/99) [920]

6802 Pietrusza, David. *Top 10 Baseball Managers* (4–7). Series: Sports Top 10. 1999, Enslow LB $23.93 (978-0-7660-1076-5). This work gives brief profiles of 10 famous past and present managers of American baseball teams. (Rev: BL 1/1–15/99; HBG 10/99) [920]

6803 Poynter, Margaret. *Top 10 American Women's Figure Skaters* (4–7). Series: Sports Top 10. 1998, Enslow LB $23.93 (978-0-7660-1075-8). This work offers brief profiles and photographs of 10 female figure skaters. (Rev: BL 11/15/98; HBG 10/99) [920]

6804 Rappoport, Ken. *Guts and Glory: Making It in the NBA* (4–8). 1997, Walker LB $16.85 (978-0-8027-8431-5). The 10 basketball players profiled in this book had to overcome obstacles to get to the top. (Rev: BL 8/97; SLJ 7/97) [920]

6805 Rappoport, Ken. *Ladies First: Women Athletes Who Made a Difference* (5–8). Illus. 2005, Peachtree $14.95 (978-1-56145-338-2). Gymnast Nadia Comaneci and dogsled racer Susan Butcher are only two of the many women in diverse sports featured in this collective biography that also gives a brief history of women's participation in sports. (Rev: BL 5/1/05; SLJ 6/05) [920]

6806 Rappoport, Ken. *Profiles in Sports Courage* (4–7). 2006, Peachtree $15.95 (978-1-56145-368-9). Twelve stories of bravery on and off the playing field (or court, ring, or track) by men and women from all types of sport and from all around the world. (Rev: BL 7/06; SLJ 6/06) [796.092]

6807 Rennert, Richard S., ed. *Book of Firsts: Sports Heroes* (5–8). Illus. Series: Profiles of Great Black Americans. 1993, Chelsea LB $15.95 (978-0-7910-2055-5); paper $7.65 (978-0-7910-2056-2). Contains profiles of these great African American athletes: Arthur Ashe, Chuck Cooper, Althea Gibson, Jesse Owens, Jackie Robinson, Jack Johnson, Frank Robinson, and Bill Russell. (Rev: SLJ 12/93) [920]

6808 Rutledge, Rachel. *The Best of the Best in Figure Skating* (4–7). Series: Women of Sports. 1998, Millbrook LB $24.90 (978-0-7613-1302-1). After a brief history of figure skating and mention of its women pioneers, this book devotes separate chapters to the sport's present-day female leaders. (Rev: BL 2/15/99; HBG 10/99) [920]

6809 Rutledge, Rachel. *The Best of the Best in Gymnastics* (5–8). Series: Women of Sports. 1999, Millbrook LB $24.90 (978-0-7613-1321-2); paper $7.95 (978-0-7613-0784-6). After an overview of the sport and its history, the author profiles eight important contemporary female gymnasts, five of whom are American. (Rev: HBG 10/99; SLJ 7/99; VOYA 2/00) [920]

6810 Rutledge, Rachel. *The Best of the Best in Soccer* (4–7). Series: Women of Sports. 1998, Millbrook LB $24.90 (978-0-7613-1315-1). A revised edition of the 1998 title, containing a brief history of women's soccer and profiles of the top women players of yesterday, today, and tomorrow. (Rev: BL 2/15/99; HBG 10/99) [920]

6811 Rutledge, Rachel. *The Best of the Best in Track and Field* (5–8). Series: Women of Sports. 1999, Millbrook LB $24.90 (978-0-7613-1300-7); paper $7.95 (978-0-7613-0446-3). A brief history of track and field is followed by profiles of eight female athletes from the United States and abroad, with material on their careers and off-the-field lives. (Rev: HBG 10/99; SLJ 7/99; VOYA 2/00) [920]

6812 Savage, Jeff. *Top 10 Basketball Point Guards* (4–7). Series: Sports Top 10. 1997, Enslow LB $23.93 (978-0-89490-807-1). Each of the athletes is presented in four pages containing a biography, statistics, and two photographs. Also use *Top 10 Basketball Power Forwards* (1997). (Rev: BL 9/15/97; VOYA 10/97) [920]

6813 Savage, Jeff. *Top 10 Football Sackers* (4–7). Series: Sports Top 10. 1997, Enslow LB $23.93 (978-0-89490-805-7). Each of the 10 football stars highlighted is covered in four pages that include a short biography, two photographs, and a statistics table. (Rev: BL 9/15/97) [920]

6814 Savage, Jeff. *Top 10 Heisman Trophy Winners* (4–7). Series: Sports Top 10. 1999, Enslow LB $23.93 (978-0-7660-1072-7). This work profiles 10 winners of the trophy given each year to the most

outstanding college football player in America. (Rev: BL 1/1–15/99; HBG 10/99) [920]

6815 Savage, Jeff. *Top 10 Physically Challenged Athletes* (4–7). Series: Sports Top 10. 2000, Enslow LB $23.93 (978-0-7660-1272-1). Each of the 10 short biographies in this book on physically handicapped athletes has an accompanying photo (usually in color) and a page of statistics. (Rev: BL 2/15/00; HBG 10/00; SLJ 10/00) [920]

6816 Savage, Jeff. *Top 10 Professional Football Coaches* (6–9). Series: Sports Top 10. 1998, Enslow LB $23.93 (978-0-7660-1006-2). Profiles of 10 top football coaches are accompanied by statistics and photographs. (Rev: HBG 10/98; SLJ 9/98; VOYA 12/98) [920]

6817 Schnakenberg, Robert E. *Teammates: Karl Malone and John Stockton* (5–7). Illus. 1998, Millbrook LB $23.90 (978-0-7613-0300-8). Despite very different backgrounds, these two leading players on the Utah Jazz basketball team have become close personal friends. (Rev: BL 8/98; HBG 10/98; SLJ 5/98) [920]

6818 Spiros, Dean. *Top 10 Hockey Goalies* (6–9). Series: Sports Top 10. 1998, Enslow LB $23.93 (978-0-7660-1010-9). This book profiles 10 top hockey goalies, with brief biographical sketches and career statistics. (Rev: BL 8/98; HBG 9/99; VOYA 12/98) [920]

6819 Staples, Bill, and Rich Herschlag. *Before the Glory: 20 Baseball Heroes Talk about Growing Up and Turning Hard Times into Home Runs* (8–12). 2007, Health Communications paper $14.95 (978-0-7573-0626-6). Twenty major-league players talk about their childhoods and relate anecdotes that influenced their future careers. (Rev: BLO 5/22/07) [796.357]

6820 Torres, John A. *Top 10 Basketball Three-Point Shooters* (4–7). Series: Sports Top 10. 1999, Enslow LB $23.93 (978-0-7660-1071-0). A profile and a photograph of 10 star basketball players make up this slender volume. (Rev: BL 1/1–15/99; HBG 10/99) [920]

6821 Torres, John A. *Top 10 NBA Finals Most Valuable Players* (4–7). Illus. Series: Sports Top 10. 2000, Enslow LB $23.93 (978-0-7660-1276-9). Short profiles of these NBA players also include photographs and some sports statistics. (Rev: BL 9/15/00; HBG 10/00) [920]

6822 Young, Jeff C. *Top 10 Basketball Shot-Blockers* (4–7). Series: Sports Top 10. 2000, Enslow LB $23.93 (978-0-7660-1275-2). For each of the basketball stars profiled, there is a full-page picture, a two-page biography, and a page of statistics. (Rev: BL 2/15/00; HBG 10/00) [920]

Automobile Racing

ANDRETTI, MARIO

6823 Prentzas, G. S. *Mario Andretti* (6–9). Series: Car Racing Legends. 1996, Chelsea LB $25.00 (978-0-7910-3176-6). This biography of the racing hero reveals Andretti's drive and endurance in his rise to the top. (Rev: SLJ 8/96) [921]

EARNHARDT, DALE, JR.

6824 Stewart, Mark. *Dale Earnhardt Jr.: Driven by Destiny* (5–8). Series: Auto Racing's New Wave. 2003, Millbrook LB $22.90 (978-0-7613-2908-4). An exciting biography of the NASCAR driver who was voted the most popular driver of 2003. (Rev: BL 6/1–15/03; HBG 10/03; SLJ 10/03) [796.72]

GORDON, JEFF

6825 Gitlin, Marty. *Jeff Gordon: Racing's Brightest Star* (5–8). Illus. Series: Heroes of Racing. 2008, Enslow LB $23.95 (978-0-7660-2997-2). For NASCAR fans, a biography that concentrates on Gordon's victories and charisma. (Rev: BL 4/1/08) [796.72]

LABONTE, TERRY AND BOBBY

6826 Hubbard-Brown, Janet. *The Labonte Brothers* (4–8). Series: Race Car Legends: Collector's Edition. 2005, Chelsea House LB $25.00 (978-0-7910-8767-1). The famous brothers Terry and Bobby Labonte and their racing rivalry and successes are the focus of this readable, photo-filled volume. (Rev: SLJ 5/06) [921]

PATRICK, DANICA

6827 Mello, Tara Baukus. *Danica Patrick* (5–8). Illus. Series: Race Car Legends Collector's Edition. 2008, Chelsea House LB $25.00 (978-0-7910-9126-5). An attractive portrait of this history-making race car driver. (Rev: BL 4/15/08) [921]

PETTY FAMILY

6828 Stewart, Mark. *The Pettys: Triumphs and Tragedies of Auto Racing's First Family* (4–8). Illus. 2001, Millbrook LB $24.90 (978-0-7613-2273-3). Photographs, quotations, anecdotes, and informative text introduce readers to the famous Petty family and their sometimes tragic involvement in automobile racing. (Rev: BL 9/1/01; HBG 3/02) [796.72]

STEWART, TONY

6829 Leebrick, Kristal. *Tony Stewart* (4–7). Illus. Series: NASCAR Racing. 2004, Capstone LB $23.93 (978-0-7368-2425-5). This profile of auto racing star Tony Stewart chronicles his meteoric rise from go-karts and midget racers to the top ranks of NASCAR. (Rev: BL 4/1/04) [790.72]

UNSER FAMILY

6830 Bentley, Karen. *The Unsers* (4–8). Series: Race Car Legends: Collector's Edition. 2005, Chelsea House LB $25.00 (978-0-7910-8764-0). The famous Unser automobile racing family is the focus of this book that describes their rivalries with the Andretti family and their victories at important races including the Indianapolis 500. (Rev: SLJ 5/06) [921]

Baseball

AARON, HANK

6831 Rennert, Richard. *Henry Aaron* (7–10). Series: Black Americans of Achievement. 1993, Chelsea LB $30.00 (978-0-7910-1859-0). The story of the African American baseball great who broke Babe Ruth's batting record in 1974. (Rev: BL 5/1/93) [921]

6832 Spencer, Lauren. *Hank Aaron* (4–7). Series: Baseball Hall of Famers. 2003, Rosen LB $29.25 (978-0-8239-3600-7). In 1974, Hank Aaron, an African American, was crowned home run king, taking the title away from Babe Ruth. This is his story. (Rev: BL 6/1–15/03; SLJ 6/03) [921]

ABBOTT, JIM

6833 Savage, Jeff. *Jim Abbott* (5–8). Series: Sports Greats. 1993, Enslow LB $22.60 (978-0-89490-395-3). The amazing career of the one-handed pitcher who came up with the California Angels and threw a no-hitter for the New York Yankees. (Rev: BL 3/1/93) [921]

ALOMAR, ROBERTO

6834 Macht, Norman L. *Roberto Alomar* (6–10). Series: Latinos in Baseball. 1999, Mitchell Lane LB $18.95 (978-1-883845-84-1). Using extensive interviews with Alomar, his family, friends, and colleagues, this profile of the famous Puerto Rican baseball player shows his strong self-discipline, work ethic, and close family ties. (Rev: BL 4/15/99; HBG 10/99; SLJ 5/99) [921]

ALOU, MOISES

6835 Muskat, Carrie. *Moises Alou* (6–10). Illus. Series: Latinos in Baseball. 1999, Mitchell Lane LB $18.95 (978-1-883845-86-5). This is the story of the baseball giant who came from a sports-minded family, and who faced a number of personal tragedies on his way to the top. (Rev: BL 4/15/99; HBG 9/99) [921]

BELL, COOL PAPA

6836 McCormack, Shaun. *Cool Papa Bell* (4–7). Series: Baseball Hall of Famers of the Negro Leagues. 2002, Rosen LB $29.25 (978-0-8239-3474-4). A biography of James Thomas "Cool Papa" Bell of Negro League baseball, who is said to have stolen 175 bases in one season. (Rev: BL 7/02) [921]

BONDS, BARRY

6837 Savage, Jeff. *Barry Bonds: Mr. Excitement* (4–8). Series: Sports Achievers. 1996, Lerner paper $5.95 (978-0-8225-9748-3). The story of this fantastic baseball player who has won the Most Valuable Player Award three times and who grew up in the shadow of a famous father. (Rev: BL 4/15/97; SLJ 2/97) [921]

BONILLA, BOBBY

6838 Knapp, Ron. *Bobby Bonilla* (5–8). Illus. Series: Sports Greats. 1993, Enslow LB $22.60 (978-0-89490-417-2). Using easy-to-read prose and a number of action photographs, this is a lively introduction to baseball star Bobby Bonilla. (Rev: BL 9/15/93) [921]

6839 Rappoport, Ken. *Bobby Bonilla* (5–9). 1993, Walker LB $15.85 (978-0-8027-8256-4). A biography of the baseball player who rose from poverty in the South Bronx to superstardom and multimillionaire status. (Rev: BL 5/15/93; SLJ 5/93; VOYA 8/93) [921]

CANSECO, JOSÉ

6840 Aaseng, Nathan. *Jose Canseco: Baseball's Forty-Forty Man* (4–7). Illus. 1989, Lerner paper $4.95 (978-0-8225-9586-1). The ups and downs of this sometimes controversial baseball star of the Oakland A's. (Rev: BCCB 9/89; BL 7/89; SLJ 8/89) [921]

CLEMENTE, ROBERTO

6841 Gilbert, Tom. *Roberto Clemente* (5–8). Illus. 1991, Chelsea LB $32.00 (978-0-7910-1240-6). The life of the first Hispanic in the Baseball Hall of Fame. (Rev: BL 8/91) [921]

6842 Kingsbury, Robert. *Roberto Clemente* (4–7). Series: Baseball Hall of Famers. 2003, Rosen LB $29.25 (978-0-8239-3602-1). The story of the National League battling champion who faced racism and discrimination because of his Hispanic background. (Rev: BL 6/1–15/03; SLJ 6/03) [921]

6843 Marquez, Heron. *Roberto Clemente: Baseball's Humanitarian Hero* (4–7). Illus. 2005, Carolrhoda LB $30.60 (978-1-57505-767-5). The story of the ballplayer, from his birth in Puerto Rico to his death in a plane crash, with photographs. (Rev: BL 3/15/05; SLJ 5/05) [796.357]

6844 Walker, Paul R. *Pride of Puerto Rico: The Life of Roberto Clemente* (4–7). 1988, Harcourt paper $6.00 (978-0-15-263420-9). The life of a baseball star and hero who died trying to help others. (Rev: BL 10/1/88; HB 9–10/88; SLJ 1/89) [921]

GEHRIG, LOU

6845 Viola, Kevin. *Lou Gehrig* (4–7). Series: Sports Heroes and Legends. 2004, Lerner LB $8.95 (978-0-8225-5311-3). Starting with Gehrig's sad retirement and his "Luckiest Man" speech, this well-written and informative biography goes back to look at his life and successful career. (Rev: BL 9/1/04) [921]

GIBSON, JOSH

6846 Holway, John B. *Josh Gibson* (7–10). Series: Black Americans of Achievement. 1995, Chelsea LB $19.95 (978-0-7910-1872-9). The inspiring story of this African American baseball hero. (Rev: BL 8/95) [921]

6847 Twemlow, Nick. *Josh Gibson* (4–7). Series: Baseball Hall of Famers of the Negro Leagues. 2002, Rosen LB $29.25 (978-0-8239-3475-1). In addition to racial prejudice in the world of baseball, Josh Gibson suffered many personal misfortunes as this life story recounts. (Rev: BL 7/02) [921]

HERSHISER, OREL

6848 Knapp, Ron. *Orel Hershiser* (5–8). Series: Sports Greats. 1993, Enslow LB $17.95 (978-0-89490-389-2). An easily read sports biography that re-creates the great moments in this baseball star's career up to 1993. (Rev: BL 4/1/93) [921]

IRVIN, MONTE

6849 Haegele, Katie. *Monte Irvin* (4–7). Series: Baseball Hall of Famers of the Negro Leagues. 2002, Rosen LB $29.25 (978-0-8239-3477-5). Though recruited into the Negro leagues when he was 17, Irvin, a very talented player, was past his prime when he finally became a major leaguer. (Rev: BL 7/02) [921]

JETER, DEREK

6850 Robinson, Tom. *Derek Jeter: Captain On and Off the Field* (5–8). Series: Sports Stars with Heart. 2006, Enslow LB $31.93 (978-0-7660-2819-7). This biography focuses primarily on Jeter's career in baseball and his work with the philanthropic Turn 2 Foundation. (Rev: BL 9/1/06) [921]

JOHNSON, JUDY

6851 Billus, Kathleen. *Judy Johnson* (4–7). Illus. Series: Baseball Hall of Famers of the Negro Leagues. 2002, Rosen LB $29.25 (978-0-8239-3476-8). A biography of Johnson covering his years as player, coach, manager, and scout, with black-and-white photographs, glossary, timeline, and lists of additional resources. (Rev: BL 7/02) [796.357]

JOHNSON, MAMIE "PEANUT"

6852 Green, Michelle Y. *A Strong Right Arm: The Story of Mamie "Peanut" Johnson* (4–7). 2002, Dial $15.99 (978-0-8037-2661-1). The life story of the woman who was one of three to play professional baseball and of her career as pitcher with the Negro Leagues' Indianapolis Clowns. (Rev: BL 6/1–15/02*; HBG 3/03; SLJ 8/02; VOYA 8/02) [921]

JOHNSON, WALTER

6853 Kavanagh, Jack. *Walter Johnson* (4–8). Illus. Series: Baseball Legends. 1991, Chelsea LB $18.65 (978-0-7910-1179-9). A biography of a baseball giant, including coverage of important games and many black-and-white photographs. (Rev: BL 1/15/92) [921]

LEONARD, BUCK

6854 Payment, Simone. *Buck Leonard* (4–7). Series: Baseball Hall of Famers of the Negro Leagues. 2002, Rosen LB $29.25 (978-0-8239-3473-7). The story of one of the greatest baseball players of all time, who missed worldwide fame because of his color. (Rev: BL 7/02) [921]

MCGWIRE, MARK

6855 Thornley, Stew. *Mark McGwire: Star Home Run Hitter* (4–8). Series: Sports Reports. 1999, Enslow LB $20.95 (978-0-7660-1329-2). A look at the life and accomplishments of this exciting baseball player. (Rev: BL 3/15/99; HBG 9/99; SLJ 7/99; VOYA 8/99) [921]

MADDUX, GREG

6856 Thornley, Stew. *Greg Maddux* (5–8). Illus. Series: Sports Greats. 1997, Enslow LB $22.60

(978-0-89490-873-6). The life of this baseball great, supplemented by career statistics and many action photographs. (Rev: BL 2/15/97; VOYA 6/97) [921]

MANTLE, MICKEY

6857 Marlin, John. *Mickey Mantle* (4–7). Series: Sports Heroes and Legends. 2004, Lerner LB $27.93 (978-0-8225-1796-2). A concise, well-written biography that focuses on Mantle's illustrious career. (Rev: BL 9/1/04; SLJ 11/04) [921]

MARTINEZ, PEDRO

6858 Gallagher, Jim. *Pedro Martinez* (6–10). Series: Latinos in Baseball. 1999, Mitchell Lane LB $18.95 (978-1-883845-85-8). The life history and career highlights of Pedro Martinez, one of the many Hispanic Americans to become baseball stars. (Rev: BL 4/15/99; HBG 9/99) [921]

6859 Lashnits, Tom. *Pedro Martinez* (6–10). Series: Great Hispanic Heritage. 2006, Chelsea House LB $30 (978-0-7910-8840-1). Baseball fans will enjoy this account of the Red Sox player's life and career. (Rev: SLJ 9/06) [921]

MATSUI, HIDEKI

6860 Beach, Jerry. *Godzilla Takes the Bronx: The Inside Story of Hideki Matsui* (8–12). 2004, Taylor $24.95 (978-1-58979-113-8). A biography of the Japanese baseball player who recently joined the Yankees. (Rev: BL 3/15/04) [921]

PAIGE, SATCHEL

6861 Schmidt, Julie. *Satchel Paige* (4–7). Illus. Series: Baseball Hall of Famers of the Negro Leagues. 2002, Rosen LB $29.25 (978-0-8239-3478-2). A biography of the famous pitcher who became the oldest rookie ever, with black-and-white photographs, glossary, timeline, and lists of additional resources. (Rev: BL 7/02; VOYA 6/02) [796.357]

6862 Shirley, David. *Satchel Paige* (7–10). Series: Black Americans of Achievement. 1993, Chelsea LB $19.95 (978-0-7910-1880-4). The story of the baseball Hall of Famer who was the first African American to pitch in the American League. (Rev: BL 5/1/93) [921]

PUJOLS, ALBERT

6863 Buckingham, Mark. *Albert Pujols: MVP On and Off the Field* (4–7). Illus. 2007, Enslow LB $23.95 (978-0-7660-2866-1). Presents facts on the life of the baseball legend, including his childhood in the Dominican Republic, his move to the United States, his career and accomplishments with the St.

Louis Cardinals, and his family. (Rev: BL 9/1/07) [921]

RIPKEN, CAL, JR.

6864 Macnow, Glen. *Cal Ripken, Jr.* (5–8). Series: Sports Greats. 1993, Enslow LB $17.95 (978-0-89490-387-8). The story of the baseball giant who gained fame as the star shortstop for the Baltimore Orioles. (Rev: BL 4/1/93) [921]

ROBINSON, JACKIE

6865 Coombs, Karen Mueller. *Jackie Robinson: Baseball's Civil Rights Legend* (5–7). Illus. Series: African-American Biographies. 1997, Enslow LB $26.60 (978-0-89490-690-9). The story of the baseball great who stood up to racism in athletics. (Rev: BL 6/1–15/97) [921]

6866 DeAngelis, Gina. *Jackie Robinson: Overcoming Adversity* (5–8). Illus. Series: Overcoming Adversity. 2000, Chelsea $30.00 (978-0-7910-5897-8). Using a highly readable text and black-and-white photographs, this book gives a real picture of Robinson that touches on the reasons he felt extreme anger and his great determination to make a difference. (Rev: BL 2/15/01; HBG 10/01) [921]

6867 Scott, Richard. *Jackie Robinson* (5–10). Illus. 1987, Chelsea LB $30.00 (978-1-55546-609-1). A well-researched biography giving good material on Robinson's life outside baseball. (Rev: BL 9/1/87; SLJ 9/87) [921]

6868 Weidhorn, Manfred. *Jackie Robinson* (6–12). 1993, Atheneum LB $15.95 (978-0-689-31644-9). This biography of the African American legend who integrated baseball in 1947 focuses on the personal qualities of the boy, the man, and the athlete. (Rev: BL 3/15/94; SLJ 2/94; VOYA 4/94) [921]

6869 Wukovits, John F. *Jackie Robinson and the Integration of Baseball* (5–8). Series: The Lucent Library of Black History. 2006, Gale LB $28.70 (978-1-59018-913-9). The social background to Robinson's achievements is well laid out in this biography suitable for report writers. (Rev: SLJ 3/07) [921]

RODRIGUEZ, ALEX

6870 Macnow, Glen. *Alex Rodriguez* (5–8). Series: Sports Greats. 2002, Enslow LB $22.60 (978-0-7660-1845-7). An easy-to-read yet fairly detailed biography of the baseball player, with plenty of statistics and quotations. (Rev: BL 9/1/02; HBG 10/02) [796.357]

RUTH, BABE

6871 Nicholson, Lois. *Babe Ruth: Sultan of Swat* (5–8). Illus. 1995, Goodwood $17.95 (978-0-

9625427-1-8). This well-written account of the famous slugger explains his lasting influence on baseball. (Rev: SLJ 7/95) [921]

RYAN, NOLAN

6872 Lace, William W. *Nolan Ryan* (5–8). Series: Sports Greats. 1993, Enslow LB $22.60 (978-0-89490-394-6). The amazing story of this baseball phenomenon who became the baseball strike-out king. (Rev: BL 6/1–15/93) [921]

SOSA, SAMMY

6873 Muskat, Carrie. *Sammy Sosa* (6–10). Illus. Series: Latinos in Baseball. 1999, Mitchell Lane LB $18.95 (978-1-883845-92-6). This account of Sosa's life tells of his beginning as a poor shoeshine boy in the Dominican Republic and his rise in baseball to his record-setting home run at age 29. (Rev: BL 4/15/99; HBG 10/99; SLJ 5/99) [921]

SUZUKI, ICHIRO

6874 Levin, Judith. *Ichiro Suzuki* (5–8). Illus. Series: Baseball Superstars. 2007, Chelsea House LB $30.00 (978-0-7910-9440-2). A biography of the record-setting, award-winning Seattle Mariners player from Japan. (Rev: BL 3/18/08) [921]

6875 Stewart, Mark. *Ichiro Suzuki: Best in the West* (4–7). Illus. Series: Sports New Wave. 2002, Millbrook LB $22.90 (978-0-7613-2616-8). A well-constructed biography of the famous Japanese Seattle Mariners player that offers information on the game itself as well as statistics, color photographs, and quotations that illustrate his achievements. (Rev: BL 9/1/02; HBG 3/03) [796.357]

Basketball

ABDUL-JABBAR, KAREEM

6876 Kneib, Martha. *Kareem Abdul-Jabbar* (5–8). Series: Basketball Hall of Famers. 2002, Rosen LB $29.25 (978-0-8239-3483-6). An in-depth look at this basketball great's life, with highlights from his childhood through his NBA career. (Rev: BL 9/1/02) [921]

BARKLEY, CHARLES

6877 Dolan, Sean. *Charles Barkley* (5–7). Illus. Series: Basketball Legends. 1996, Chelsea LB $18.65 (978-0-7910-2433-1). The life of this basketball superstar, with details on his record on the court. (Rev: BL 7/96) [921]

6878 Macnow, Glen. *Charles Barkley* (5–8). Series: Sports Greats. 1992, Enslow LB $17.95 (978-0-

89490-386-1). A short biography of this basketball star, with career statistics and action photographs. (Rev: BL 10/15/92) [921]

BIRD, LARRY

6879 Kavanagh, Jack. *Larry Bird* (4–8). Illus. Series: Sports Greats. 1992, Enslow LB $22.60 (978-0-89490-368-7). The extraordinary story of the basketball player who drove his team, the Boston Celtics, to five NBA finals. (Rev: BL 7/92; SLJ 10/92) [921]

BRYANT, KOBE

6880 Kennedy, Nick. *Kobe Bryant: Star Guard* (4–8). Series: Sports Reports. 2002, Enslow LB $26.60 (978-0-7660-1828-0). An accessible biography of the basketball player, with detailed descriptions of career highlights. (Rev: BL 9/1/02; HBG 3/03) [796.323]

6881 Savage, Jeff. *Kobe Bryant: Basketball Big Shot* (4–7). Illus. Series: Sports Biography. 2000, Lerner LB $22.60 (978-0-8225-3680-2). A very readable, attractive biography of the new NBA sensation that ends with the 1999–2000 season. (Rev: BL 1/1–15/01; HBG 10/01) [921]

6882 Stewart, Mark. *Kobe Bryant: Hard to the Hoop* (4–8). Series: Basketball's New Wave. 2000, Millbrook LB $20.90 (978-0-7613-1800-2). The life story of this basketball star who was the son of an NBA player and who became the youngest player in league history to star in the All-Star Game. (Rev: HBG 10/00; SLJ 8/00) [921]

CARTER, VINCE

6883 Savage, Jeff. *Vince Carter* (5–8). Series: Sports Greats. 2002, Enslow LB $22.60 (978-0-7660-1767-2). An accessible biography of the Toronto Raptors basketball player that will be useful for students writing reports. (Rev: BL 9/1/02; HBG 10/02) [796.323]

COOPER, CYNTHIA

6884 Schnakenberg, Robert E. *Cynthia Cooper* (5–9). Series: Women Who Win. 2000, Chelsea $25.00 (978-0-7910-5796-4). A biography of this basketball star that focuses on her career and game-related information. (Rev: HBG 3/01; SLJ 2/01; VOYA 4/01) [921]

DUNCAN, TIM

6885 Adams, Sean. *Tim Duncan* (4–7). Illus. Series: Sports Heroes and Legends. 2004, Lerner LB $27.93 (978-0-8225-1793-1). A balanced, well-crafted life of the basketball star. (Rev: BL 9/1/04) [921]

6886 Byman, Jeremy. *Tim Duncan* (4–8). Illus. Series: Great Athletes. 2000, Morgan Reynolds LB $18.95 (978-1-883846-43-5). This biography about a basketball hero who has been playing professionally for only a short time focuses on his college years, his outstanding talent, and his determination. (Rev: BL 6/1–15/00; HBG 3/01) [921]

6887 Rappoport, Ken. *Tim Duncan: Star Forward* (5–8). Series: Sports Reports. 2000, Enslow LB $20.95 (978-0-7660-1334-6). A look at one of basketball's star forwards, accompanied by statistics and action photographs. (Rev: BL 10/15/00; HBG 3/01) [921]

6888 Stewart, Mark. *Tim Duncan: Tower of Power* (4–8). Series: Basketball's New Wave. 1999, Millbrook LB $22.90 (978-0-7613-1513-1). Although this biography of basketball's rising star is brief, the information is ample and important topics are all covered. (Rev: HBG 10/00; SLJ 7/00) [921]

6889 Torres, John Albert. *Tim Duncan* (5–8). Series: Sports Greats. 2002, Enslow LB $22.60 (978-0-7660-1766-5). The life of this basketball star is re-created using an easy-reading text and many photographs. (Rev: BL 9/1/02; HBG 10/02) [921]

EWING, PATRICK

6890 Kavanagh, Jack. *Patrick Ewing* (5–8). Illus. Series: Sports Greats. 1992, Enslow LB $22.60 (978-0-89490-369-4). An easily read, candid look at the basketball great from Jamaica. (Rev: BL 9/1/92) [921]

GARNETT, KEVIN

6891 Bernstein, Ross. *Kevin Garnett: Star Forward* (4–8). Series: Sports Reports. 2002, Enslow LB $26.60 (978-0-7660-1829-7). An in-depth look at the life of this basketball star in a simple account suitable for reluctant readers. (Rev: BL 9/1/02; HBG 3/03) [921]

6892 Stewart, Mark. *Kevin Garnett: Shake Up the Game* (4–7). Series: Sports New Wave. 2002, Millbrook LB $22.90 (978-0-7613-2615-1). A short biography that chronicles the career of the new star of the Minnesota Timberwolves. (Rev: BL 9/1/02; HBG 10/02) [921]

HARDAWAY, ANFERNEE

6893 Rekela, George R. *Anfernee Hardaway* (5–8). Illus. Series: Sports Greats. 1996, Enslow LB $17.95 (978-0-89490-758-6). Career statistics and many black-and-white photographs enliven the biography of this famous basketball star. (Rev: BL 3/15/96) [921]

439

HILL, GRANT

6894 Rappoport, Ken. *Grant Hill* (6–9). Illus. 1996, Walker LB $16.85 (978-0-8027-8456-8). The story of the basketball star, from the AAU National Basketball Championship at age 13 through high school, where he played on the varsity team as a freshman, and his college years playing at Duke, to the Detroit Pistons, where he was the NBA Rookie of the Year. (Rev: BL 1/1–15/97; SLJ 1/97; VOYA 8/97) [796.323]

HOWARD, JUWAN

6895 Savage, Jeff. *Juwan Howard* (5–8). Series: Sports Greats. 1998, Enslow LB $22.60 (978-0-7660-1065-9). The Washington Wizards basketball star is profiled in this lively account, supplemented by many black-and-white photographs. (Rev: BL 2/15/99; HBG 10/99; VOYA 6/99) [921]

6896 Sirak, Ron. *Juwan Howard* (5–8). 1998, Chelsea LB $18.65 (978-0-7910-4575-6). A biography of one of the great basketball players of the 1990s, with good material on his early years and the influence of his grandmother. (Rev: HBG 3/99; VOYA 6/99) [921]

JAMES, LEBRON

6897 Morgan, David Lee. *LeBron James* (7–12). Illus. 2003, Gray & Company paper $14.95 (978-1-886228-74-0). The biography of the African American basketball superstar who came from a culture of poverty and drugs to reach the peak of the sports world. (Rev: BL 2/15/04; SLJ 6/04) [921]

JOHNSON, MAGIC

6898 Dolan, Sean. *Magic Johnson* (7–10). 1993, Chelsea LB $21.95 (978-0-7910-1975-7). The story to 1992 of the Los Angeles Lakers star and his battle after testing HIV-positive. (Rev: BL 9/15/93) [921]

6899 Greenberg, Keith E. *Magic Johnson: Champion with a Cause* (4–7). Illus. Series: Achievers. 1992, Lerner LB $27.15 (978-0-8225-0546-4). The story of the gifted athlete for the L.A. Lakers, whose career was cut short when he discovered he was HIV-positive. (Rev: BL 8/92; SLJ 7/92) [921]

6900 Haskins, Jim. *Magic Johnson*. Rev. ed. (5–8). Series: Sports Greats. 1992, Enslow LB $22.60 (978-0-89490-348-9). This revised and updated edition includes a discussion of the basketball star's HIV status, his 1991 retirement from the Lakers, and his role in the fight against AIDS. (Rev: BL 10/15/92) [921]

JORDAN, MICHAEL

6901 Aaseng, Nathan. *Michael Jordan* (5–8). Illus. Series: Sports Greats. 1992, Enslow LB $17.95 (978-0-89490-370-0). Michael Jordan's life, his successes as guard of the Chicago Bulls, and his commercials for TV are discussed in this easily read book. (Rev: BL 10/15/92) [921]

6902 Berger, Phil, and John Rolfe. *Michael Jordan* (4–7). Illus. 1990, Little, Brown paper $4.95 (978-0-316-09229-6). This account covers Jordan's childhood and his career development. (Rev: BL 12/15/90; SLJ 4/91) [921]

6903 Dolan, Sean. *Michael Jordan* (7–10). Series: Black Americans of Achievement. 1993, Chelsea paper $9.95 (978-0-7910-2151-4). The life of this basketball legend to 1992 and how his determination and family support helped him rise to the top. (Rev: BL 3/1/94; VOYA 6/94) [921]

6904 Lovitt, Chip. *Michael Jordan* (6–10). 1998, Scholastic paper $4.50 (978-0-590-59644-2). This quick read, an update of the 1993 edition, traces Jordan's remarkable career from a young age to the end of the Chicago Bulls' 1998 season. (Rev: VOYA 4/99) [921]

KIDD, JASON

6905 Gray, Valerie A. *Jason Kidd: Star Guard* (5–8). Series: Sports Reports. 2000, Enslow LB $20.95 (978-0-7660-1333-9). The story of the basketball superstar with behind-the-scenes reporting on his life and career. (Rev: BL 10/15/00; HBG 10/00) [921]

6906 Torres, John A. *Jason Kidd* (5–8). Series: Sports Greats. 1998, Enslow LB $22.60 (978-0-7660-1001-7). An action-filled biography of this basketball star, complete with career statistics and black-and-white photographs of Kidd on the court. (Rev: BL 7/98; HBG 10/98) [921]

LESLIE, LISA

6907 Kelley, Brent. *Lisa Leslie* (5–9). Series: Women Who Win. 2000, Chelsea $25.00 (978-0-7910-5794-0). This profile of a pioneer in the Women's National Basketball Association contains much game-related information. (Rev: HBG 3/01; SLJ 2/01) [921]

LIEBERMAN-CLINE, NANCY

6908 Greenberg, Doreen, and Michael Greenberg. *A Drive to Win: The Story of Nancy Lieberman-Cline* (4–8). Illus. by Phil Velikan. Series: Anything You Can Do — New Sports Heroes for Girls. 2000, Wish paper $9.95 (978-1-930546-40-0). Based on personal interviews, this is an informative biography of the basketball star Lieberman-Cline. (Rev: SLJ 3/01; VOYA 2/01) [921]

MILLER, REGGIE

6909 Thornley, Stew. *Reggie Miller* (5–8). Series: Sports Greats. 1996, Enslow LB $22.60 (978-0-89490-874-3). The life of this basketball star is traced, with special emphasis on key games. (Rev: BL 9/15/96) [921]

MING, YAO

6910 Krawiec, Richard. *Yao Ming: Gentle Giant of Basketball* (6–8). Illus. 2004, Avisson paper $19.95 (978-1-888105-63-6). This story of the Chinese basketball player's path to stardom brings up interesting questions about the business and patriotic aspects of professional sports. (Rev: BL 2/15/04; SLJ 3/04) [790.323]

6911 Ming, Yao, and Ric Bucher. *Yao: A Life in Two Worlds* (8–12). Illus. 2004, Miramax $22.95 (978-1-4013-5214-1). Yao Ming writes of his success in the NBA and also of the sharp contrast between the culture of his native China and that of the United States. (Rev: BL 9/1/04) [796.323]

MOURNING, ALONZO

6912 Fortunato, Frank. *Alonzo Mourning* (5–8). Illus. Series: Sports Greats. 1997, Enslow LB $22.60 (978-0-89490-875-0). An easily read biography of this amazing basketball star. (Rev: BL 2/15/97; VOYA 6/97) [921]

MULLIN, CHRIS

6913 Morgan, Terri, and Shmuel Thaler. *Chris Mullin: Sure Shot* (4–8). Illus. Series: Sports Achievers. 1994, Lerner LB $10.13 (978-0-8225-2887-6). The story of this amazing basketball star who overcame many obstacles, including alcoholism. (Rev: BL 1/1/95; SLJ 1/95) [921]

NUNEZ, TOMMY

6914 Marvis, Barbara. *Tommy Nunez, NBA Referee: Taking My Best Shot* (6–10). Illus. 1996, Mitchell Lane paper $12.95 (978-1-883845-28-5). The story of the youngster who grew up in the poverty of Phoenix's barrio to become the first Mexican American referee in the NBA. (Rev: BL 5/15/96; SLJ 3/96; VOYA 6/96) [921]

OLAJUWON, HAKEEM

6915 McMane, Fred. *Hakeem Olajuwon* (5–7). Series: Basketball Legends. 1997, Chelsea LB $18.65 (978-0-7910-4385-1). The story of this basketball star of the Houston Rockets, his boyhood in

Nigeria, and his role as part of the U.S. Olympic "Dream Team." (Rev: BL 9/15/97) [921]

O'NEAL, SHAQUILLE

6916 Sullivan, Michael J. *Shaquille O'Neal* (5–8). Series: Sports Greats. 1998, Enslow LB $22.60 (978-0-7660-1003-1). The life and career of this well-known basketball star are covered in this easily read biography containing career statistics and many illustrations. (Rev: BL 2/15/99; HBG 10/99) [921]

6917 Ungs, Tim. *Shaquille O'Neal* (5–7). Illus. Series: Basketball Legends. 1996, Chelsea LB $18.65 (978-0-7910-2437-9). An interesting portrait of the unstoppable Lakers basketball superstar. (Rev: BL 7/96) [921]

PIPPEN, SCOTTIE

6918 Bjarkman, Peter C. *Scottie Pippen* (5–8). Series: Sports Greats. 1996, Enslow LB $22.60 (978-0-89490-755-5). Action photographs, career statistics, and an account of important games are highlights of this basketball biography. (Rev: BL 9/15/96) [921]

6919 McMane, Fred. *Scottie Pippen* (5–7). Illus. Series: Basketball Legends. 1996, Chelsea LB $12.95 (978-0-7910-2498-0). The life of this basketball star, highlighting his special abilities and his court record. (Rev: BL 7/96) [921]

6920 Pippen, Scottie, and Greg Brown. *Reach Higher* (4–7). 1997, Taylor $14.95 (978-0-87833-981-5). The story of the famous Chicago Bulls basketball star, who came from a family of 12 and whose original sports were baseball and football. (Rev: BL 10/1/97) [921]

RICHMOND, MITCH

6921 Grody, Carl W. *Mitch Richmond* (5–8). Series: Sports Greats. 1998, Enslow LB $17.95 (978-0-7660-1070-3). Using many black-and-white photographs and a lively text, this book re-creates the life of the basketball great. (Rev: BL 2/15/99; HBG 10/99) [921]

ROBINSON, DAVID

6922 Aaseng, Nathan. *David Robinson* (5–8). Illus. Series: Sports Greats. 1992, Enslow LB $17.95 (978-0-89490-373-1). This easily read biography highlights David Robinson of the San Antonio Spurs, the 1990 Rookie of the Year. (Rev: BL 10/15/92) [921]

6923 Bock, Hal. *David Robinson* (5–7). Series: Basketball Legends. 1997, Chelsea LB $18.65 (978-0-7910-4387-5). The story of this star of the San Antonio Spurs, who was a brilliant student and an officer in the U.S. Navy before turning to professional sports. (Rev: BL 9/15/97) [921]

RODMAN, DENNIS

6924 Frank, Steven. *Dennis Rodman* (4–8). Series: Basketball Legends. 1997, Chelsea LB $18.65 (978-0-7910-4388-2). A candid look at the bad boy of basketball, his troubled youth, and rebellious attitudes. (Rev: HBG 3/98; SLJ 4/98) [921]

6925 Thornley, Stew. *Dennis Rodman* (5–8). Illus. Series: Sports Greats. 1996, Enslow LB $22.60 (978-0-89490-759-3). The life of this controversial basketball star is told in a brisk text with many black-and-white photographs. (Rev: BL 3/15/96) [921]

STILES, JACKIE

6926 Stewart, Mark. *Jackie Stiles: Gym Dandy* (4–7). Illus. Series: Sports New Wave. 2002, Millbrook LB $22.90 (978-0-7613-2614-4). A biography of the WNBA star, with information on her childhood and family, statistics, color photographs, and general material on the game itself. (Rev: BL 9/1/02; HBG 3/03) [796.323]

STOCKTON, JOHN

6927 Aaseng, Nathan. *John Stockton* (5–8). Illus. Series: Sports Greats. 1995, Enslow LB $17.95 (978-0-89490-598-8). A short biography of the basketball great John Stockton, with sports action and lively photographs. (Rev: BL 9/15/95) [921]

SWOOPES, SHERYL

6928 Rappoport, Ken. *Sheryl Swoopes* (4–8). Illus. Series: Sports Reports. 2002, Enslow LB $26.60 (978-0-7660-1827-3). An accessible biography of the basketball player, with detailed descriptions of career highlights. (Rev: BL 9/1/02; HBG 3/03) [976.323]

THOMAS, ISIAH

6929 Knapp, Ron. *Isiah Thomas* (5–8). Illus. Series: Sports Greats. 1992, Enslow LB $22.60 (978-0-89490-374-8). Using a standard chronological approach and many photographs, this is an accurate, appealing biography of this great African American basketball player. (Rev: BL 9/1/92) [921]

WEST, JERRY

6930 Ramen, Fred. *Jerry West* (5–8). Series: Basketball Hall of Famers. 2002, Rosen LB $29.25 (978-0-8239-3482-9). Facts, stories, and full-color photographs are used to bring alive the story of this

basketball great, with material on his NBA career and beyond. (Rev: BL 9/1/02) [921]

WILKINS, DOMINIQUE

6931 Bjarkman, Peter C. *Dominique Wilkins* (5–8). Series: Sports Greats. 1996, Enslow LB $22.60 (978-0-89490-754-8). The story of this basketball star, with profiles of his most exciting games and career statistics. (Rev: BL 9/15/96) [921]

Boxing

ALI, MUHAMMAD

6932 Random House, eds. *Muhammad Ali* (6–10). 1997, Random $20.00 (978-0-517-20080-3). Using plenty of sidebars, quotations from his poetry, and photographs, this excellent biography, based on A&E cable TV's *Biography* show, traces the boxer's life from his days as a scrawny kid named Cassius Clay, Jr. to his becoming "the greatest," ending with the 1996 lighting of the Olympic torch in Atlanta. (Rev: VOYA 8/98) [921]

6933 Rummel, Jack. *Muhammad Ali* (6–10). Illus. 1988, Chelsea LB $30.00 (978-1-55546-569-8). A biography that emphasizes the boxer's professional career rather than his personal life. (Rev: BL 6/15/88) [921]

6934 Smith, Charles R. *Twelve Rounds to Glory: The Story of Muhammad Ali* (5–8). Illus. by Bryan Collier. 2007, Candlewick $19.99 (978-0-7636-1692-2). Twelve poems and dynamic mixed-media pictures illustrate the drama of Ali's victories and his life's struggles. Coretta Scott King Author Honor Book, 2008. (Rev: BL 2/1/08; SLJ 12/07) [921]

CHAVEZ, JULIO CESAR

6935 Dolan, Terrance. *Julio Cesar Chavez* (5–8). Illus. Series: Hispanics of Achievement. 1994, Chelsea LB $21.95 (978-0-7910-2021-0). A biography of the fighting boxer and his struggle to get to the top. (Rev: BL 9/15/94) [921]

DE LA HOYA, OSCAR

6936 Torres, John A. *Oscar De La Hoya* (5–8). Series: Sports Greats. 1998, Enslow LB $22.60 (978-0-7660-1066-6). A brief biography of the boxing sensation, with action photographs and career statistics. (Rev: BL 2/15/98; HBG 10/99) [921]

HAWKINS, DWIGHT

6937 Hawkins, Dwight, and Morrie Greenberg. *Survival in the Square* (7–10). Illus. 1989, Brooke-

Richards paper $5.95 (978-0-9622652-0-4). The story of an African American who overcame a physical handicap and became a boxing champion. (Rev: BL 11/15/89; VOYA 12/89) [921]

LOUIS, JOE

6938 Jakoubek, Robert E. *Joe Louis* (6–9). Illus. 1990, Chelsea LB $19.95 (978-1-55546-599-5). Both the professional career of Joe Louis and his often unfortunate personal life are handled in this account. (Rev: BL 5/1/90) [921]

Football

AIKMAN, TROY

6939 Macnow, Glen. *Troy Aikman* (5–8). Illus. Series: Sports Greats. 1995, Enslow LB $17.95 (978-0-89490-593-3). The life story of the football great Troy Aikman, with good action photographs and sports statistics. (Rev: BL 9/15/95) [921]

BETTIS, JEROME

6940 Majewski, Stephen. *Jerome Bettis* (5–8). Illus. Series: Sports Greats. 1997, Enslow LB $17.95 (978-0-89490-872-9). The great football hero Jerome Bettis and his amazing career are highlighted in this easily read biography. (Rev: BL 2/15/97; VOYA 6/97) [921]

BRADY, TOM

6941 Stewart, Mark. *Tom Brady: Heart of the Huddle* (4–7). Series: Sports New Wave. 2003, Millbrook LB $22.90 (978-0-7613-2907-7). The story of the popular young football player who is quarterback for the New England Patriots. (Rev: BL 6/1–15/03; HBG 10/03) [921]

BRUNELL, MARK

6942 Steenkamer, Paul. *Mark Brunell: Star Quarterback* (4–8). Series: Sports Reports. 2002, Enslow LB $26.60 (978-0-7660-1830-3). The life story of the Jacksonville Jaguars quarterback, told with detailed summaries of his greatest moments. (Rev: BL 9/1/02; HBG 3/03) [921]

BRYANT, PAUL W.

6943 Smith, E. S. *Bear Bryant: Football's Winning Coach* (6–8). Illus. 1984, Walker $11.95 (978-0-8027-6526-0). The story of one of the most famous coaches in football history. [921]

CULPEPPER, DAUNTE

6944 Stewart, Mark. *Daunte Culpepper: Command and Control* (4–7). Series: Sports New Wave. 2002, Millbrook LB $22.90 (978-0-7613-2613-7). This brief biography celebrates the career of the young African American footballer and his achievements as quarterback of the Minnesota Vikings. (Rev: BL 9/1/02; HBG 10/02) [921]

DAVIS, TERRELL

6945 Stewart, Mark. *Terrell Davis: Toughing It Out* (4–8). Series: Football's New Wave. 1999, Millbrook LB $22.90 (978-0-7613-1514-8). A brief biography of this football hero that uses color photographs and many fact boxes. (Rev: HBG 10/00; SLJ 7/00) [921]

FAVRE, BRETT

6946 Mooney, Martin. *Brett Favre* (5–7). Illus. Series: Football Legends. 1997, Chelsea LB $18.65 (978-0-7910-4396-7). The story of the famous quarterback who took the Green Bay Packers to victory in the 1997 Super Bowl. (Rev: BL 1/1–15/98; HBG 3/98) [921]

6947 Rekela, George R. *Brett Favre: Star Quarterback* (5–8). Series: Sports Reports. 2000, Enslow LB $26.60 (978-0-7660-1332-2). A brief biography of one of football's star quarterbacks that provides good career statistics and behind-the-scenes reporting. (Rev: BL 10/15/00; HBG 10/00) [921]

6948 Savage, Jeff. *Brett Favre* (5–8). Series: Sports Greats. 1998, Enslow LB $17.95 (978-0-7660-1000-0). An exciting biography of the star quarterback of the Green Bay Packers. (Rev: BL 3/15/98; HBG 10/98) [921]

JACKSON, BO

6949 Devaney, John. *Bo Jackson: A Star for All Seasons* (5–7). Illus. 1992, Walker LB $15.85 (978-0-8027-8179-6). Biography of the Kansas City Royals baseball star, who also played pro football for the Los Angeles Raiders. (Rev: BL 2/15/89; SLJ 1/89) [921]

6950 Knapp, Ron. *Bo Jackson* (5–8). Illus. Series: Sports Greats. 1990, Enslow LB $22.60 (978-0-89490-281-9). A standard biography that includes unexpected aspects of Jackson's personality. (Rev: BL 10/15/90; SLJ 3/91) [921]

KELLY, JIM

6951 Harrington, Denis J. *Jim Kelly* (5–8). Illus. Series: Sports Greats. 1996, Enslow LB $17.95 (978-0-89490-670-1). A short, action-filled biography of this former star quarterback, complete with career statistics. (Rev: BL 3/15/96) [921]

LOMBARDI, VINCE

6952 Roensch, Greg. *Vince Lombardi* (4–7). Series: Football Hall of Famers. 2003, Rosen LB $29.25 (978-0-8239-3610-6). A lively, detailed, and inspiring biography of the legendary coach for whom the Super Bowl trophy is named. (Rev: SLJ 4/03) [796.332]

MANNING, PEYTON

6953 Savage, Jeff. *Peyton Manning: Precision Passer* (4–7). Series: Sports Achievers. 2001, Lerner LB $22.60 (978-0-8225-3683-3); paper $5.95 (978-0-8225-9865-7). Sports statistics, action photographs, and an accessible text highlight this biography of the Indianapolis Colts quarterback. (Rev: BL 4/1/02; HBG 10/02) [921]

6954 Stewart, Mark. *Peyton Manning: Rising Son* (4–8). Series: Football's New Wave. 2000, Millbrook LB $22.90 (978-0-7613-1517-9). An easily read account of the professional football player's life and family, including a father who also played in the NFL. (Rev: HBG 10/00; SLJ 1/01) [921]

MONTANA, JOE

6955 Kavanagh, Jack. *Joe Montana* (4–8). Illus. Series: Sports Greats. 1992, Enslow LB $22.60 (978-0-89490-371-7). In simple text, this is the story of the quarterback who led his San Francisco 49ers to four Super Bowl championships. (Rev: BL 7/92; SLJ 10/92) [921]

MOSS, RANDY

6956 Bernstein, Ross. *Randy Moss: Star Wide Receiver* (4–8). Series: Sports Reports. 2002, Enslow LB $26.60 (978-0-7660-1503-6). A well-illustrated account of the life of this Minnesota Vikings star, told with plenty of sports action. (Rev: BL 9/1/02; HBG 10/02) [921]

6957 Stewart, Mark. *Randy Moss: First in Flight* (4–8). Illus. Series: Football's New Wave. 2000, Millbrook LB $22.90 (978-0-7613-1518-6). The story of the footballer who came from a poor, segregated West Virginia town, was arrested as a young man, but went on to attend college and play professional football. (Rev: HBG 10/00; SLJ 1/01) [921]

RICE, JERRY

6958 Dickey, Glenn. *Jerry Rice* (5–8). Illus. Series: Sports Greats. 1993, Enslow LB $17.95 (978-0-89490-419-6). A brief biography of the star football player who gained fame with the San Francisco 49ers. (Rev: BL 9/15/93) [921]

SANDERS, BARRY

6959 Aaseng, Nathan. *Barry Sanders: Star Running Back* (4–7). Illus. Series: Sports Reports. 1994, Enslow LB $20.95 (978-0-89490-484-4). This biography of the football star of the Detroit Lions contains many quotations about him from his associates. (Rev: SLJ 8/94) [921]

6960 Knapp, Ron. *Barry Sanders* (5–8). Illus. Series: Sports Greats. 1993, Enslow LB $17.95 (978-0-89490-418-9). This brief biography of the star football player contains many action photographs and a separate section on his career statistics. (Rev: BL 9/15/93) [921]

SMITH, EMMITT

6961 Grabowski, John. *Emmitt Smith* (5–8). Series: Sports Greats. 1998, Enslow LB $17.95 (978-0-7660-1002-4). A high-interest biography of this football great that contains career statistics, action photographs, and exciting game action. (Rev: BL 7/98; HBG 10/98) [921]

6962 Thornley, Stew. *Emmitt Smith: Relentless Rusher* (4–8). Series: Sports Achievers. 1996, Lerner LB $27.15 (978-0-8225-2897-5). The professional life of one of the Dallas Cowboys is highlighted, supplemented by career statistics and action photographs. (Rev: BL 4/15/97; SLJ 8/97) [921]

TARKENTON, FRAN

6963 Hulm, David. *Fran Tarkenton* (4–7). Series: Football Hall of Famers. 2003, Rosen LB $29.25 (978-0-8239-3608-3). A lively, detailed, and inspiring biography of the star of the Minnesota Vikings and the New York Giants who went on to become a successful businessman. (Rev: SLJ 4/03; VOYA 4/03) [796.332]

THOMAS, THURMAN

6964 Savage, Jeff. *Thurman Thomas: Star Running Back* (4–7). Illus. Series: Sports Reports. 1994, Enslow LB $26.60 (978-0-89490-445-5). This life story of the football hero also contains action photographs, fact boxes, and statistics. (Rev: SLJ 8/94) [921]

WALKER, HERSCHEL

6965 Benagh, Jim. *Herschel Walker* (5–8). Illus. Series: Sports Greats. 1990, Enslow LB $22.60 (978-0-89490-207-9). This account tells how Walker grew up in Georgia and went on to a career in professional football. (Rev: BL 10/15/90; SLJ 3/91) [921]

YOUNG, STEVE

6966 Morgan, Terri, and Shmuel Thaler. *Steve Young: Complete Quarterback* (4–8). Illus. Series: Sports Achievers. 1995, Lerner paper $9.55 (978-0-8225-9716-2). A profile of the San Francisco 49ers quarterback, with material on his professional career, his character, and outside interests. (Rev: BL 11/15/95) [921]

Gymnastics

MOCEANU, DOMINIQUE

6967 Durrett, Deanne. *Dominique Moceanu* (5–8). Series: People in the News. 1999, Lucent LB $32.45 (978-1-56006-099-4). Drawing heavily on Moceanu's autobiography, this is the life story of the phenomenal gymnast, with behind-the scenes glimpses of competitions, training, scoring, and routines. (Rev: HBG 3/00; SLJ 8/99) [921]

6968 Quiner, Krista. *Dominique Moceanu: A Gymnastics Sensation* (4–7). Illus. 1997, Bradford paper $12.95 (978-0-9643460-3-1). The story of the United States' youngest gold medal winner in gymnastics, with a special 24-page insert of photographs. (Rev: SLJ 3/97) [921]

Ice Skating and Hockey

BOITANO, BRIAN

6969 Boitano, Brian, and Suzanne Harper. *Boitano's Edge: Inside the Real World of Figure Skating* (4–8). Illus. 1997, Simon & Schuster $25.00 (978-0-689-81915-5). In this autobiography, Boitano tells about his life, the 1988 Olympics, his training programs, touring, and preparing for competitions. (Rev: BCCB 3/98; BL 2/15/98; SLJ 4/98; VOYA 4/98) [921]

FORREST, ALBERT

6970 McFarlane, Brian. *The Youngest Goalie* (6–9). 1997, Warwick paper $8.95 (978-1-895629-95-8). This is an exciting, fictionalized biography of Albert Forrest, who was born in 1887 and became the youngest goalie to play in a Stanley Cup final. (Rev: VOYA 2/99) [921]

GORDEEVA, EKATERINA

6971 Hill, Anne E. *Ekaterina Gordeeva* (6–9). Series: Overcoming Adversity. 1999, Chelsea LB $30.00 (978-0-7910-4948-8); paper $9.95 (978-0-7910-4949-5). The story of the amazing Russian ice skater, her Olympic triumphs, and her adjustment to the sudden death of her husband and partner, who was also a gold-medal winner. (Rev: BL 5/15/99) [921]

6972 Shea, Pegi Deitz. *Ekatarina Gordeeva* (4–8). Series: Female Figure Skating Legends. 1999, Chelsea LB $12.95 (978-0-7910-5027-9). Sports lovers will enjoy this look at the life of the famous skater before and after the death of her partner and husband, Sergei Grinkov. (Rev: SLJ 4/99) [921]

GRETZKY, WAYNE

6973 Rappoport, Ken. *Wayne Gretzky* (5–8). Illus. Series: Sports Greats. 1996, Enslow LB $17.95 (978-0-89490-757-9). A brief biography of this hockey phenomenon, illustrated with black-and-white action photographs. (Rev: BL 3/15/96) [921]

HAMILTON, SCOTT

6974 Brennan, Kristine. *Scott Hamilton* (6–9). Series: Overcoming Adversity. 1999, Chelsea LB $30.00 (978-0-7910-4944-0); paper $9.95 (978-0-7910-4945-7). A biography of the 4-time winner of the men's world figure skating championship between 1981 and 1984, and his gallant battle against cancer. (Rev: BL 5/15/99) [921]

KWAN, MICHELLE

6975 James, Laura. *Michelle Kwan: Heart of a Champion* (4–8). Illus. 1997, Scholastic paper $14.95 (978-0-590-76340-0). A highly personal account of this figure-skating champion, who describes how she succeeded in placing second at the World Championships in 1997 only one month after two falls cost her the position of U.S. women's champion, and who reveals a maturity beyond her years. (Rev: BL 11/15/97; HBG 3/98; SLJ 11/97) [921]

6976 Koestler-Grack, Rachel A. *Michelle Kwan* (7–10). Illus. 2007, Chelsea House LB $30.00 (978-0-7910-9273-6). Details the accomplishments of figure skater Kwan and provides information about her training, competition, and her life off the ice. (Rev: BL 9/1/07) [920]

LEMIEUX, MARIO

6977 O'Shei, Tim. *Mario Lemieux* (8–12). Series: Overcoming Adversity. 2002, Chelsea LB $30.00 (978-0-7910-6305-7). This biography of the renowned hockey legend tells how he made an amazing comeback from Hodgkin's Disease. (Rev: BL 4/15/02; HBG 10/02) [921]

6978 Rossiter, Sean. *Mario Lemieux* (4–8). Illus. Series: Hockey Heroes. 2001, Sterling $12.95 (978-1-55054-870-9). A detailed look at the career of

Pittsburgh Penguin Mario Lemieux. (Rev: BL 2/15/02) [796.962]

6979 Stewart, Mark. *Mario Lemieux: Own the Ice* (5–8). Illus. 2002, Millbrook LB $24.90 (978-0-7613-2555-0); paper $8.95 (978-0-7613-1687-9). A readable biography of the ice hockey star, with photographs, statistics, and information about the athlete's personal life and work ethic. (Rev: BL 9/15/02; HBG 3/03) [796.962]

LINDROS, ERIC

6980 Rappoport, Ken. *Eric Lindros* (5–8). Series: Sports Greats. 1997, Enslow LB $22.60 (978-0-89490-871-2). A biography of the famous hockey star that includes career statistics and action photographs. (Rev: BL 10/15/97) [921]

WICKENHEISER, HAYLEY

6981 Etue, Elizabeth. *Hayley Wickenheiser: Born to Play* (4–7). Illus. 2005, Kids Can paper $6.95 (978-1-55337-791-7). The story of Canadian-born Wickenheiser, a member of Canada's gold medal-winning women's ice hockey team at the Salt Lake City Olympics, who went on to become the first woman to play professional hockey. (Rev: BL 9/1/05) [921]

WITT, KATARINA

6982 Coffey, Wayne. *Katarina Witt* (4–7). Illus. 1992, Blackbirch $16.45 (978-1-56711-001-2). This biography highlights the 1988 Olympic Games, where this figure skater became a star. (Rev: SLJ 11/92) [921]

6983 Kelly, Evelyn B. *Katarina Witt* (6–9). Series: Female Figure Skating Legends. 1999, Chelsea LB $18.65 (978-0-7910-5026-2). This is the story of figure skating champion Katerina Witt, from her childhood in East Germany under Communist rule to her many Olympic competitions. (Rev: BL 3/1/99; VOYA 6/99) [921]

Tennis

AGASSI, ANDRE

6984 Knapp, Ron. *Andre Agassi: Star Tennis Player* (5–8). Series: Sports Reports. 1997, Enslow LB $26.60 (978-0-89490-798-2). An in-depth look at the life and career of this tennis star, with details of his childhood and his father's influence. (Rev: BL 8/97; SLJ 8/97) [921]

6985 Savage, Jeff. *Andre Agassi: Reaching the Top — Again* (4–8). Series: Sports Achievers. 1997, Lerner paper $9.55 (978-0-8225-9750-6). A short,

easily read biography of this volatile tennis star. (Rev: BL 1/1–15/98; HBG 3/98) [921]

ASHE, ARTHUR

6986 Cunningham, Kevin. *Arthur Ashe: Athlete and Activist* (5–8). Illus. Series: Journey to Freedom: The African American Library. 2005, Child's World LB $28.50 (978-1-59296-228-0). Chronicles the Virginia-born athlete's rise to tennis stardom and his involvement in the fight against apartheid. (Rev: BL 2/1/05) [921]

6987 Lazo, Caroline. *Arthur Ashe* (4–7). Series: A&E Biography. 1999, Lerner $25.26 (978-0-8225-1932-4). The inspiring story of this great African American tennis star and humanitarian is told in a clear, well-organized text with several black-and-white photographs. (Rev: BL 3/15/00) [921]

6988 Wright, David K. *Arthur Ashe: Breaking the Color Barrier in Tennis* (7–12). Illus. Series: African-American Biographies. 1996, Enslow LB $20.95 (978-0-89490-689-3). A look at the life of this revered tennis star, his professional career, and his valiant struggle against AIDS. (Rev: BL 12/15/96; SLJ 10/96) [921]

CHANG, MICHAEL

6989 Ditchfield, Christin. *Michael Chang* (5–8). Series: Sports Greats. 1999, Enslow LB $22.60 (978-0-7660-1223-3). A biography of this tennis phenomenon, with career statistics and plenty of action photographs. (Rev: BL 3/15/99; HBG 10/99) [921]

GIBSON, ALTHEA

6990 Biracree, Tom. *Althea Gibson* (7–12). Illus. 1989, Chelsea LB $19.95 (978-1-55546-654-1). The rags-to-riches story of the African American athlete who was once the best woman tennis player in the world. (Rev: BL 2/15/90; SLJ 2/90; VOYA 2/90) [921]

SELES, MONICA

6991 Blue, Rose, and Corinne J. Naden. *Monica Seles* (8–12). Series: Overcoming Adversity. 2002, Chelsea LB $30.00 (978-0-7910-5899-2). The biography of the courageous tennis star who returned to competition after being stabbed during a match. (Rev: BL 4/15/02; HBG 10/02) [921]

6992 Murdico, Suzanne J. *Monica Seles* (5–8). Illus. Series: Overcoming the Odds. 1998, Raintree $28.80 (978-0-8172-4128-5). The story of the great tennis player and the courtside stabbing that resulted in a trauma difficult to overcome. (Rev: HBG 9/98; VOYA 8/98) [921]

WILLIAMS, VENUS AND SERENA

6993 Aronson, Virginia. *Venus Williams* (5–8). Illus. Series: Galaxy of Superstars. 1999, Chelsea $25.00 (978-0-7910-5153-5); paper $25.00 (978-0-7910-5329-4). The story of this superstar of tennis, how her father trained her, and how he made her education more important than her tennis. (Rev: BL 4/15/99; HBG 10/99; SLJ 5/99; VOYA 4/00) [921]

6994 Fillon, Mike. *Young Superstars of Tennis: The Venus and Serena Williams Story* (4–8). Series: Avisson Young Adult. 1999, Avisson LB $19.95 (978-1-888105-43-8). This biography of the Williams sisters tells about their childhood, the influence of their father, and their determination to get to the top in tennis. (Rev: BL 12/15/99; SLJ 3/00; VOYA 4/00) [921]

6995 Morgan, Terri. *Venus and Serena Williams: Grand Slam Sisters* (4–7). Series: Sports Achievers. 2001, Lerner LB $22.60 (978-0-8225-3684-0); paper $5.95 (978-0-8225-9866-4). An action-packed biography of the amazing tennis duo that covers their careers and their family. (Rev: BL 4/1/02; HBG 10/02) [921]

6996 Stewart, Mark. *Venus and Serena Williams: Sisters in Arms* (4–7). Series: Tennis's New Wave. 2000, Millbrook LB $22.90 (978-0-7613-1803-3). A simple biography of the amazing tennis-playing sisters with good coverage of their early lives. (Rev: HBG 3/01; SLJ 3/01) [921]

Track and Field

DEVERS, GAIL

6997 Worth, Richard. *Gail Devers* (8–12). Series: Overcoming Adversity. 2002, Chelsea LB $30.00 (978-0-7910-6307-1). While battling Bright's Disease, a serious thyroid disorder, Gail Devers won a gold medal in the 100-meter sprint at the 1992 Olympics. (Rev: BL 4/15/02; HBG 10/02) [921]

JONES, MARION

6998 Rutledge, Rachel. *Marion Jones: Fast and Fearless* (4–7). 2000, Millbrook LB $22.90 (978-0-7613-1870-5). A biography of the track-and-field star of the 2000 Sydney Olympics that stresses her drive and tenacity. (Rev: HBG 3/01; SLJ 3/01) [921]

JOYNER-KERSEE, JACKIE

6999 Harrington, Geri. *Jackie Joyner-Kersee: Champion Athlete* (6–10). 1995, Chelsea LB $21.95 (978-0-7910-2085-2). Describes Joyner-Kersee's

four Olympic championships, despite asthma attacks. (Rev: BL 10/1/95) [921]

LEWIS, CARL

7000 Aaseng, Nathan. *Carl Lewis: Legend Chaser* (4–8). Illus. 1985, Lerner LB $18.60 (978-0-8225-0496-2). Childhood, college, and Olympic performances are covered in this biography, including both praise and criticism about Lewis's attempt at the long-jump record. (Rev: BCCB 11/85; BL 7/85; SLJ 8/85) [796.420924]

LEWIS, RAY

7001 Cooper, John. *Rapid Ray: The Story of Ray Lewis* (5–9). 2002, Tundra paper $8.95 (978-0-88776-612-1). An absorbing profile of the Canadian-born black athlete (and train porter) who won a bronze medal in the 1932 Olympics and the racial hurdles he had to overcome. (Rev: SLJ 6/03) [796.42]

LONGBOAT, TOM

7002 Batten, Jack. *The Man Who Ran Faster Than Everyone: The Story of Tom Longboat* (7–12). Illus. 2002, Tundra paper $12.95 (978-0-88776-507-0). A straightforward biography of the Onondaga Indian distance runner who won fame in the early 20th century. (Rev: BL 4/1/02; SLJ 6/02) [796.42]

O'BRIEN, DAN

7003 Gutman, Bill. *Dan O'Brien* (5–8). Series: Overcoming the Odds. 1998, Raintree $28.80 (978-0-8172-4129-2). A biography of this great decathlete that describes his struggles to overcome attention-deficit hyperactivity disorder as well as various injuries. (Rev: HBG 9/98; VOYA 8/98) [921]

OWENS, JESSE

7004 Gentry, Tony. *Jesse Owens: Champion Athlete* (6–9). Illus. 1990, Chelsea LB $30.00 (978-1-55546-603-9). The story of the African American track star who upset Hitler's master race theory at the Olympics. (Rev: SLJ 7/90; VOYA 8/90) [921]

7005 Josephson, Judith P. *Jesse Owens: Track and Field Legend* (6–10). Series: African-American Biographies. 1997, Enslow LB $20.95 (978-0-89490-812-5). The life of this track star is retold with details about the prejudice he faced throughout his personal and professional life and his performance at the 1936 Berlin Olympics, where he won four gold medals, defying Adolf Hitler's view of Aryans as the "Master Race." (Rev: SLJ 1/98) [921]

7006 Rennert, Richard S. *Jesse Owens* (4–7). Illus. Series: Junior World Biography. 1991, Chelsea LB

$16.95 (978-0-7910-1570-4). An attractive, well-illustrated account of this famous track-and-field star who embarrassed Hitler by winning four gold medals at the 1936 Olympic Games. (Rev: BL 9/1/91; SLJ 9/91) [921]

RUDOLPH, WILMA

7007 Biracree, Tom. *Wilma Rudolph* (7–12). Illus. 1987, Chelsea LB $19.95 (978-1-55546-675-6). The inspiring story of the African American athlete who conquered polio and won three Olympic gold medals in track in a single year. (Rev: BL 8/88) [921]

7008 Schraff, Anne. *Wilma Rudolph: The Greatest Woman Sprinter in History* (6–9). Series: African-American Biographies. 2004, Enslow LB $26.60 (978-0-7660-2291-1). Rudolph's childhood battle with polio, pregnancy at the age of 17, and struggles to deal with racism and supporting her family make a poignant background to her athletic achievements. (Rev: SLJ 8/04) [921]

THORPE, JIM

7009 Bruchac, Joseph. *Jim Thorpe: Original All-American* (5–8). 2006, Dial $16.99 (978-0-8037-3118-9). Using the first person, this biography chronicles the Native American's youth, his amazing sporting abilities, and his quiet determination to overcome barriers. (Rev: BL 6/1–15/06; SLJ 8/06) [921]

7010 Crawford, Bill. *All American: The Rise and Fall of Jim Thorpe* (8–12). Illus. 2004, Wiley $32.50 (978-0-471-55732-6). An in-depth look at the tumultuous life of the Native American athlete who triumphed on the world's playing fields but ultimately died in relative obscurity. (Rev: BL 11/15/04) [796]

7011 Long, Barbara. *Jim Thorpe: Legendary Athlete* (5–7). Illus. Series: Native American Biographies. 1997, Enslow LB $20.95 (978-0-89490-865-1). The story of the amazing Native American athlete whose career had tremendous highs and lows. (Rev: BL 6/1–15/97) [921]

Miscellaneous Sports

ARMSTRONG, LANCE

7012 Benson, Michael. *Lance Armstrong: Cyclist* (5–8). Series: Ferguson Career Biographies. 2003, Ferguson LB $25.00 (978-0-8160-5479-4). Traces the inspiring life of the great bicycle-racer through his fifth Tour de France win, with an emphasis on his perseverance and optimism. (Rev: SLJ 5/04) [796.6]

7013 Coyle, Daniel. *Lance Armstrong's War: One Man's Battle Against Fate, Fame, Love, Death, Scandal, and a Few Other Rivals on the Road to the Tour de France* (8–12). Illus. 2005, HarperCollins $25.95 (978-0-06-073794-8). Traces Armstrong's winning 2004 season and reviews the daunting challenges the cyclist has had to overcome in his life. (Rev: BL 6/1–15/05) [796.6]

7014 Stewart, Mark. *Sweet Victory: Lance Armstrong's Incredible Journey* (6–10). Illus. Series: Inspiring People. 2000, Millbrook LB $24.90 (978-0-7613-1861-3). The inspiring story of Lance Armstrong who became an American hero when he fought and won a battle with cancer and triumphed at the Tour de France in 1999. (Rev: BL 8/00; HBG 10/00; SLJ 8/00) [921]

7015 Thompson, John. *Lance Armstrong* (6–12). Series: Overcoming Adversity. 2001, Chelsea House LB $30.00 (978-0-7910-5879-4). An inspiring account of Armstrong's triumph over multiple challenges — including testicular cancer — to climb to the top ranks of cycling. (Rev: HBG 3/02; SLJ 12/01; VOYA 4/02) [921]

BASS, TOM

7016 Wilkerson, J. L. *From Slave to World-Class Horseman: Tom Bass* (4–8). 2000, Acorn paper $9.95 (978-0-9664470-3-3). A fast-paced narrative about the man who was born a slave and later became such a renowned horseman that he performed for Queen Victoria. (Rev: SLJ 4/00) [921]

BUTCHER, SUSAN

7017 Wadsworth, Ginger. *Susan Butcher: Sled Dog Racer* (4–7). Illus. Series: Sports Achievers. 1994, Lerner LB $18.60 (978-0-8225-2878-4). This exciting biography brings to life the four-time Iditarod winner and the rigors and courage each race involved. (Rev: SLJ 6/94) [921]

HAMILTON, BETHANY

7018 Hamilton, Bethany. *Soul Surfer: A True Story of Faith, Family, and Fighting to Get Back on the Board* (6–9). Illus. 2004, Pocket $18.00 (978-0-7434-9922-4). Bethany Hamilton, the teenage surfer who lost an arm in a shark attack off Kauai in 2003, tells how her family and faith helped to sustain her and give her the courage to return to surfing. (Rev: BL 1/1–15/05) [797.1]

HAWK, TONY

7019 Hawk, Tony, and Sean Mortimer. *Hawk: Occupation, Skateboarder* (8–12). 2000, Regan paper $15.00 (978-0-06-095831-2). The biography of a man who, during a rebellious youth, discovered skateboarding and was determined to excel at it. [921]

7020 Peterson, Todd. *Tony Hawk: Skateboarder and Businessman* (8–11). Illus. Series: Ferguson Career Biographies. 2005, Ferguson LB $25.00 (978-0-8160-5893-8). Skateboarder Tony Hawk's childhood, skating career, and business achievements are all covered in this readable volume. (Rev: BL 9/1/05) [796.22]

HILLARY, SIR EDMUND

7021 Brennan, Kristine. *Sir Edmund Hillary: Modern-Day Explorer* (4–8). Series: Explorers of New Worlds. 2000, Chelsea $25.00 (978-0-7910-5953-1); paper $25.00 (978-0-7910-6163-3). An appealing overview of the life and accomplishments of the mountaineer and explorer, with photographs and maps. (Rev: SLJ 4/01) [796.52]

7022 Coburn, Broughton. *Triumph on Everest: A Photobiography of Sir Edmund Hillary* (5–8). 2000, National Geographic $17.95 (978-0-7922-7114-7). Using many quotations and excellent photographs, this work records the lifetime accomplishments of one of the first men to reach the top of Mount Everest. (Rev: BCCB 9/00; HBG 3/01; SLJ 10/00) [921]

7023 Elish, Dan. *Edmund Hillary: First to the Top* (5–9). Series: Great Explorations. 2006, Benchmark LB $32.79 (978-0-7614-2224-2). This biography focuses on the New Zealand mountain climber's 1953 conquest of Mount Everest and includes coverage of Sherpa Tenzing Norgay. (Rev: SLJ 1/07) [921]

7024 Stewart, Whitney. *Sir Edmund Hillary: To Everest and Beyond* (5–8). Photos by Anne B. Keiser. Illus. Series: Newsmakers. 1996, Lerner LB $30.35 (978-0-8225-4927-7). The life of this famous mountain climber is presented with interesting details about his other interests, including bee keeping, conservation, and helping the Sherpa people. (Rev: SLJ 9/96) [921]

KAHANAMOKU, DUKE

7025 Crowe, Ellie. *Surfer of the Century: The Life of Duke Kahanamoku* (4–7). Illus. by Richard Waldrep. 2007, Lee & Low $18.95 (978-1-58430-276-6). A wonderfully illustrated picture-book biography of Duke Kahanamoku, an Olympic Gold Medal swimmer and well-known surfer from Hawaii who was born in 1890. (Rev: BL 9/1/07; SLJ 10/07) [921]

LEMOND, GREG

7026 Porter, A. P. *Greg LeMond: Premier Cyclist* (4–7). Illus. Series: Sports Achievers. 1990, Lerner LB $18.60 (978-0-8225-0476-4). Although he suffered severe injuries in a hunting accident, LeMond

won the Tour de France bicycle race. (Rev: BL 6/15/90; SLJ 9/90) [921]

MONPLAISIR, SHARON

7027 Greenberg, Doreen, and Michael Greenberg. *Sword of a Champion: The Story of Sharon Monplaisir* (4–8). Illus. by Phil Velikan. Series: Anything You Can Do — New Sports Heroes for Girls. 2000, Wish paper $9.95 (978-1-930546-39-4). The life story of the timid, shy high schooler who found her place in fencing via a coach who encouraged her to develop her natural talents. (Rev: SLJ 3/01; VOYA 2/01) [796.8]

NASH, KEVIN

7028 Mudge, Jacqueline. *Kevin Nash* (4–7). Series: Pro Wrestling Legends. 2000, Chelsea paper $25.00 (978-0-7910-5828-2). This is the biography of the wrestler known as "Diesel." (Rev: BL 10/15/00; HBG 3/01) [921]

PAK, SE RI

7029 Stewart, Mark. *Se Ri Pak: Driven to Win* (4–8). Series: Golf's New Wave. 2000, Millbrook LB $22.90 (978-0-7613-1519-3). The story of the South Korean who won the Ladies Professional Golf Association Championship in 1998. (Rev: HBG 10/00; SLJ 8/00) [921]

PELE (SOCCER PLAYER)

7030 Buckley, James. *Pele* (6–9). Illus. Series: DK Biographies. 2007, DK $14.99 (978-0-7566-2996-0); paper $4.99 (978-0-7566-2987-8). Profiles the childhood, life, and extraordinary career of the Brazilian soccer legend. (Rev: BL 9/1/07) [921]

REECE, GABRIELLE

7031 Morgan, Terri. *Gabrielle Reece: Volleyball's Model Athlete* (4–7). Illus. Series: Sports Achievers. 1999, Lerner LB $22.60 (978-0-8225-3667-3). An accessible biography of the woman who is not only a volleyball champ but also a fashion model and TV personality. (Rev: BL 10/15/99; HBG 3/00) [921]

ROSENFELD, FANNY BOBBIE

7032 Dublin, Anne. *Bobbie Rosenfeld: The Olympian Who Could Do Everything* (5–8). 2004, Second Story paper $11.95 (978-1-896764-82-5). Fanny Bobbie Rosenfeld migrated from the Ukraine to Canada in 1905, became an outstanding athlete excelling in many sports, and led the Canadian women's relay team to an Olympic gold in 1928. (Rev: BL 9/1/04) [921]

TAYLOR, MARSHALL

7033 Brill, Marlene Targ. *Marshall "Major" Taylor: World Champion Bicyclist, 1899–1901* (5–8). Illus. Series: Trailblazer Biographies. 2007, Lerner LB $31.93 (978-0-8225-6610-6). An inspiring profile of the first African American world cycling champion and his struggles with racism. (Rev: BL 9/1/07) [921]

TREVINO, LEE

7034 Gilbert, Thomas. *Lee Trevino* (5–9). Series: Hispanics of Achievement. 1991, Chelsea LB $19.95 (978-0-7910-1256-7). The story of one of golf's all-time greats to 1990. (Rev: BL 3/15/92) [796.352]

VENTURA, JESSE

7035 Cohen, Daniel. *Jesse Ventura: The Body, the Mouth, the Mind* (6–10). Illus. 2001, Millbrook LB $25.90 (978-0-7613-1905-4). A comprehensive profile of Ventura's private life and his stints as Navy Seal, talk-show host, actor, wrestler, and politician. (Rev: BL 10/1/01; HBG 3/02; SLJ 12/01; VOYA 12/01) [977.6]

7036 Greenberg, Keith E. *Jesse Ventura* (5–8). Illus. Series: A&E Biography. 1999, Lerner LB $27.93 (978-0-8225-4977-2); paper $7.95 (978-0-8225-9680-6). A look at this larger-than-life pop culture hero who has been an actor, a professional wrestler, a Navy SEAL, and the governor of Minnesota. (Rev: BL 3/1/00; HBG 3/00; SLJ 2/00) [921]

7037 Uschan, Michael V. *Jesse Ventura* (5–8). Series: People in the News. 2001, Lucent LB $35.15 (978-1-56006-777-1). From a career in wrestling to a state governorship, this is the story of the amazing Jesse Ventura. (Rev: BL 4/1/02) [921]

WOODS, TIGER

7038 Boyd, Aaron. *Tiger Woods* (5–10). 1997, Morgan Reynolds LB $18.95 (978-1-883846-19-0). A brief, straightforward biography of this amazing golfer who was a young prodigy. (Rev: BL 5/1/97; HBG 3/98; SLJ 8/97; VOYA 10/97) [921]

7039 Collins, David R. *Tiger Woods, Golfing Champion* (5–8). Illus. by Larry Nolte. 1999, Pelican $14.95 (978-1-56554-322-5). A chronologically arranged book ending in 1999 that reveals Tiger Woods's determination and love of the game. (Rev: SLJ 1/00) [921]

7040 Roberts, Jeremy. *Tiger Woods* (5–8). Series: Biography. 2002, Lerner LB $27.93 (978-0-8225-0030-8). The story of the likable wonder boy of golf is told in text and pictures. (Rev: BL 4/1/02; HBG 10/02) [921]

7041 Teague, Allison L. *Prince of the Fairway: The Tiger Woods Story* (8–12). 1997, Avisson LB $18.50 (978-1-888105-22-3). Written for young adults, this biography probes into Woods's childhood and the cultural values of his family as well as describing his golf training and career. (Rev: SLJ 10/97; VOYA 10/97) [921]

ZAHARIAS, BABE DIDRIKSON

7042 Cayleff, Susan E. *Babe Didrikson: The Greatest All-Sport Athlete of All Time* (7–12). Illus. 2000, Conari paper $8.95 (978-1-57324-194-6). A candid, honest look at the life of this difficult, brash, competitive golf legend. (Rev: BL 10/1/00; VOYA 8/01) [921]

7043 Freedman, Russell. *Babe Didrikson Zaharias: The Making of a Champion* (6–12). 1999, Clarion $19.00 (978-0-395-63367-0). Although she was known to most for her golf career, this entertaining biography points out that Babe Didrikson Zaharias was also an Olympic athlete, a track star, leader of a women's amateur basketball team, and an entrepreneur. (Rev: BCCB 10/99; BL 7/99; HB 9–10/99; HBG 3/00; SLJ 7/99; VOYA 12/00) [921]

7044 Lynn, Elizabeth A. *Babe Didrikson Zaharias* (6–10). Illus. 1988, Chelsea LB $19.95 (978-1-55546-684-8). The story of the all-around athlete best known for her accomplishments in golf. (Rev: BL 12/1/88) [921]

7045 Wakeman, Nancy. *Babe Didrikson Zaharias: Driven to Win* (4–7). Illus. Series: Biography. 2000, Lerner LB $27.93 (978-0-8225-4917-8). The account focuses on this sportswoman's professional career and her strong personality plus her accomplishments in track and field, basketball, and baseball. (Rev: BL 6/1–15/00; HBG 10/00; SLJ 7/00; VOYA 12/00) [921]

World Figures

Collective

7046 Aaseng, Nathan. *The Peace Seekers: The Nobel Peace Prize* (5–8). Illus. 1987, Lerner paper $7.95 (978-0-8225-9604-2). Martin Luther King, Jr., and Lech Walesa are among those whose lives and works are introduced. (Rev: BL 2/1/88) [327.1720922]

7047 Avakian, Monique. *Reformers: Activists, Educators, Religious Leaders* (5–9). Series: Remarkable Women. 2000, Raintree LB $32.85 (978-0-8172-5733-0). This book contains 150 profiles of woman who, throughout history and from many cultures, have fought for human rights, including Harriet Tubman, Mother Teresa, and Dolores Huerta. (Rev: SLJ 8/00) [920]

7048 Axelrod-Contrada, Joan. *Women Who Led Nations* (7–10). Series: Profiles. 1999, Oliver LB $19.95 (978-1-881508-48-9). Corazon Aquino, Benazir Bhutto, and Golda Meir are among the seven women profiled in detail in this collective biography. (Rev: HBG 4/00; SLJ 10/99) [920]

7049 Baker, Rosalie, and Charles Baker. *Ancient Egyptians: People of the Pyramids* (6–12). Illus. Series: Oxford Profiles. 2001, Oxford $55.00 (978-0-19-512221-3). Detailed biographies of key figures such as Nefertiti, Hatshepsut, Tutankhamen, and Ramses give plenty of background social and cultural information and are accompanied by sidebar features and black-and-white photographs. (Rev: BL 9/15/01; HBG 10/02; SLJ 11/01) [920.032]

7050 Bardhan-Quallen, Sudipta. *The Mexican-American War* (5–9). Series: People at the Center Of. 2005, Gale LB $24.95 (978-1-56711-927-5). After an overview of the war, this volume provides biographical information on key figures including James K. Polk, Abraham Lincoln, Santa Anna, and Zachary Taylor. (Rev: SLJ 6/05) [920]

7051 Benson, Sonia G. *Korean War: Biographies* (6–10). 2001, Gale LB $70.00 (978-0-7876-5692-8). A collection of 25 biographies of individuals — Koreans, Americans, and other nationalities — who participated in or affected the course of the Korean War. (Rev: BL 3/15/02; SLJ 5/02) [920]

7052 Billinghurst, Jane. *Growing Up Royal: Life in the Shadow of the British Throne* (4–7). Illus. 2001, Annick $22.95 (978-1-55037-623-4); paper $12.95 (978-1-55037-622-7). A look at what it's like to be young and royal, with a focus on the lives of today's British royalty, with color photographs and interesting anecdotes. (Rev: BL 9/1/01; HBG 3/02; SLJ 11/01; VOYA 4/02) [971.082]

7053 Blue, Rose, and Corinne J. Naden. *People of Peace* (4–7). Illus. 1994, Millbrook LB $26.90 (978-1-56294-409-4). Brief biographies of 10 people in modern history who have made great sacrifices for world peace, including Mohandas Gandhi and Desmond Tutu. (Rev: BL 12/15/94; SLJ 2/95) [920]

7054 Butts, Ed. *She Dared: True Stories of Heroines, Scoundrels, and Renegades* (6–9). Illus. by Heather Collins. 2005, Tundra paper $8.95 (978-0-88776-718-0). Engaging profiles of 15 diverse women who defied social norms. (Rev: BL 12/1/05; SLJ 12/05) [920.72]

7055 Chin-Lee, Cynthia. *Amelia to Zora: Twenty-Six Women Who Changed the World* (4–7). Illus. 2005, Charlesbridge $15.95 (978-1-57091-522-2). Brief information on 26 remarkable and varied women (scientists, artists, athletes, inventors) along with beautiful artwork and quotations from the subjects. (Rev: BL 4/1/05*; SLJ 4/05) [920.72]

7056 Cotter, Charis. *Kids Who Rule: The Remarkable Lives of Five Child Monarchs* (5–8). Illus. 2007, Annick $24.95 (978-1-55451-062-7); paper $14.95 (978-1-55451-061-0). King Tutankhamen,

Mary Queen of Scots, Queen Christina of Sweden, Emperor Puyi of China, and the fourteenth Dalai Lama are the young rulers included in this interesting book that provides historical context. (Rev: BL 12/15/07) [920.0068]

7057 Green, Robert. *Dictators* (6–9). Series: History Makers. 2000, Lucent LB $28.70 (978-1-56006-594-4). Several 20th-century dictators such as Stalin, Hitler, Mao Zedong, Franco, and Saddam Hussein are profiled. (Rev: BL 6/1–15/00; HBG 9/00) [920]

7058 Haskins, Jim. *African Heroes* (5–8). Series: Black Stars. 2005, Wiley $24.95 (978-0-471-46672-7). Profiles 27 important Africans, both contemporary and from the past, in entries of varying length. (Rev: SLJ 7/05) [920]

7059 Hazell, Rebecca. *The Barefoot Book of Heroic Children* (4–7). Illus. 2000, Barefoot Bks. $19.95 (978-1-902283-23-4). This book presents the lives of 12 heroic children from different times and places, among them Anne Frank, Fanny Mendelssohn, Annie Sullivan, and Iqbal Masih. (Rev: BL 4/15/00) [920]

7060 Hazell, Rebecca. *Heroines: Great Women Through the Ages* (5–8). Illus. 1996, Abbeville $19.95 (978-0-7892-0210-9). This is a collective biography of 12 great women spanning the period from ancient Greece to modern times, including Sacagawea, Madame Sun Yat-Sen, Frido Kahlo, Joan of Arc, Harriet Tubman, and Marie Curie. (Rev: SLJ 12/96) [920]

7061 Humphrey, Sandra McLeod. *Dare to Dream! 25 Extraordinary Lives* (4–7). 2005, Prometheus paper $15.98 (978-1-59102-280-0). Twenty-five individuals — including artists, athletes, politicians, and scientists — who overcame obstacles to achieve greatness are profiled, with information on childhood and adult life. (Rev: BL 3/1/05; SLJ 6/05) [920]

7062 Hunter, Ryan Ann. *In Disguise: Stories of Real Women Spies* (5–8). Illus. 2004, Beyond Words paper $9.95 (978-1-58270-095-3). Profiles 26 women who risked their lives to spy for causes in which they believed, from 1640 to the Cold War. (Rev: SLJ 8/04) [920]

7063 James, Lesley. *Women in Government: Politicians, Lawmakers, Law Enforcers* (6–10). Illus. Series: Remarkable Women. 2000, Raintree LB $32.85 (978-0-8172-5730-9). A collection of illustrated, alphabetically arranged biographies of famous queens, presidents, activists, and empresses. (Rev: BL 6/1–15/00) [920]

7064 Krull, Kathleen. *Lives of Extraordinary Women: Rulers, Rebels (and What the Neighbors Thought)* (5–8). Illus. Series: Extraordinary Lives. 2000, Harcourt $20.00 (978-0-15-200807-9). Short biographies of women who affected the course of

history, from Cleopatra to contemporary Burma's Aung San Suu Kyi. (Rev: BCCB 9/00; BL 9/1/00; HB 11–12/00; HBG 3/01; SLJ 9/00; VOYA 6/01) [920]

7065 Lace, William W. *Leaders and Generals* (5–10). Series: American War. 2000, Lucent LB $28.70 (978-1-56006-664-4). The following World War II leaders are profiled: Erwin Rommel, Georgi Zhukov, Erich von Manstein, Yamamoto Isoroku, Douglas MacArthur, Chester Nimitz, Dwight Eisenhower, and Bernard Law Montgomery. (Rev: BL 4/15/00; HBG 10/00; SLJ 6/00) [920]

7066 Leon, Vicki. *Outrageous Women of Ancient Times* (4–7). Illus. 1997, Wiley paper $12.95 (978-0-471-17006-8). Fifteen unusual women from ancient civilizations in Asia, Europe, and Africa are profiled, among them warriors, philosophers, empresses, artists, and professional poisoners, and including Cleopatra and Sappho. (Rev: BL 11/1/97; SLJ 12/97) [920]

7067 Leon, Vicki. *Outrageous Women of the Middle Ages* (4–7). Illus. 1998, Wiley paper $12.95 (978-0-471-17004-4). Using a witty writing style and modern comparisons, this fascinating book profiles a diverse group of amazing women who lived from the 6th through the 14th centuries in Europe, Asia, and Africa. (Rev: BL 4/15/98; SLJ 8/98) [920]

7068 Meltzer, Milton. *Ten Kings and the Worlds They Ruled* (5–8). Illus. by Bethanne Andersen. 2002, Scholastic paper $21.95 (978-0-439-31293-6). Ten kings from around the world and across the ages are discussed in this attractive book that includes impressive portraits and other illustrations. Also use *Ten Queens* (1998). (Rev: BCCB 9/02; BL 7/02; HBG 10/02; SLJ 10/02*) [920.02]

7069 Nardo, Don. *Women Leaders of Nations* (6–10). Illus. Series: History Makers. 1999, Lucent LB $27.45 (978-1-56006-397-1). An overview of women in government, followed by chapters on several female leaders of nations, among them Cleopatra and Margaret Thatcher, and a chapter on other women leaders, including Amazon warriors and Queen Boudicca. (Rev: BL 6/1–15/99) [920]

7070 Phibbs, Cheryl Fisher, ed. *Pioneers of Human Rights* (8–11). Illus. Series: Profiles in History. 2005, Gale LB $36.20 (978-0-7377-2146-1). Among the figures profiled in this volume are Mohandas Gandhi, Frederick Douglass, Nelson Mandela, and Eleanor Roosevelt. (Rev: BL 7/05) [323]

7071 Price-Groff, Claire. *Great Conquerors* (6–10). Series: History Makers. 2000, Lucent LB $18.96 (978-1-56006-612-5). This work profiles seven world conquerors, including Alexander the Great and Napoleon, each representing a different time period and a different culture. (Rev: BL 3/15/00; SLJ 8/00) [920]

7072 Price-Groff, Claire. *Twentieth-Century Women Political Leaders* (7–10). Series: Global Profiles. 1998, Facts on File LB $25.00 (978-0-8160-3672-1). A look at 12 women political leaders in the second half of the 20th century: Golda Meir, Indira Gandhi, Eva Peron, Margaret Thatcher, Corazon Aquino, Winnie Mandela, Barbara Jordan, Violeta Chamorro, Wilma Mankiller, Gro Harlem Brundtland, Aung San Suu Kyi, and Benazir Bhutto. (Rev: SLJ 1/99) [920]

7073 Sanderson, Ruth. *More Saints: Lives and Illuminations* (4–7). Illus. 2007, Eerdmans $20.00 (978-0-8028-5272-4). A sequel to *Saints: Lives and Illuminations* (2003), this volume adds profiles of 36 saints, this time of the second millennium. (Rev: BL 2/1/07) [270]

7074 Scandiffio, Laura. *Evil Masters: The Frightening World of Tyrants* (7–10). 2005, Annick $24.95 (978-1-55037-895-5); paper $12.95 (978-1-55037-894-8). Nero, Ivan the Terrible, Hitler, Stalin, and Saddam Hussein are five of the seven rulers profiled; an introduction discusses personality traits and the reasons why such men are able to assume power. (Rev: SLJ 1/06) [920]

7075 Shaw, Maura D. *Ten Amazing People: And How They Changed the World* (4–7). Illus. 2002, SkyLight Paths $17.95 (978-1-893361-47-8). Shaw presents 10 well-illustrated biographies of 20th-century religious figures, each with timelines, a quotation, a glossary, and an emphasis on the individual's beliefs. (Rev: BL 10/1/02; HBG 3/03; SLJ 12/02) [200]

7076 Traub, Carol G. *Philanthropists and Their Legacies* (7–12). Illus. Series: Profiles. 1997, Oliver LB $19.95 (978-1-881508-42-7). Profiles — warts and all — of nine of the world's greatest benefactors, including Alfred Nobel, Andrew Carnegie, Cecil Rhodes, George Eastman, and Will Kellogg. (Rev: BL 2/15/98; SLJ 2/98) [920]

7077 Wakin, Edward. *Contemporary Political Leaders of the Middle East* (6–12). Illus. Series: Global Profiles. 1996, Facts on File $25.00 (978-0-8160-3154-2). Profiles of eight Israeli and Arab leaders who have shaped events in the Middle East, including Saddam Hussein, Mubarak, Qadafi, Rabin, and Peres. (Rev: BL 4/15/96; SLJ 3/96; VOYA 4/96) [920]

7078 Weatherly, Myra. *Women of the Sea: Ten Pirate Stories* (6–9). Illus. 2006, Morgan Reynolds LB $26.95 (978-1-931798-80-8). This revised edition of a 1998 publication (*Women Pirates: Eight Stories of Adventure*) adds information on two women pirates plus source notes and additional resources. (Rev: BL 12/15/05; SLJ 4/06) [910.4]

7079 Zalben, Jane Breskin. *Paths to Peace: People Who Changed the World* (4–7). Illus. 2006, Dutton $18.99 (978-0-525-47734-1). Zalben profiles 16

individuals who have devoted much of their lives to the goal of making peace a reality. (Rev: BL 1/1–15/06; SLJ 2/06) [920]

Africa

AMIN, IDI

7080 Allen, John. *Idi Amin* (6–9). Series: History's Villains. 2004, Gale LB $28.70 (978-1-56711-759-2). An interesting profile of the Ugandan leader that describes the atrocities committed under his regime. (Rev: SLJ 5/04) [921]

CLEOPATRA

7081 Hoobler, Dorothy, and Thomas Hoobler. *Cleopatra* (6–10). Illus. 1986, Chelsea LB $21.95 (978-0-87754-589-7). Through recounting the story of this amazing queen, the author tells about life in ancient Egypt. (Rev: BL 2/1/87; SLJ 2/87) [921]

7082 Nardo, Don, ed. *Cleopatra* (7–12). Series: People Who Made History. 2000, Greenhaven paper $14.96 (978-0-7377-0321-4). This collection of essays focuses on the life of Cleopatra, her contributions, and her place in history. (Rev: BL 3/1/01; SLJ 3/01) [921]

7083 Nardo, Don. *Cleopatra: Egypt's Last Pharaoh* (6–10). Series: The Lucent Library of Historical Eras. 2005, Gale LB $32.45 (978-1-59018-660-2). Presenting many quotations from ancient writings about Cleopatra, Nardo discusses their biases plus the importance of the Egyptian leader's relationships with Julius Caesar and Marc Antony. (Rev: SLJ 11/05) [921]

7084 Sapet, Kerrily. *Cleopatra: Ruler of Egypt* (8–12). Illus. 2007, Morgan Reynolds LB $27.95 (978-1-59935-035-6). Presents the fascinating details of the life of the Egyptian queen, with descriptions of the cultural wealth of the ancient world, the role of women, and life along the Nile. (Rev: BL 6/1–15/07; SLJ 7/07) [921]

7085 Streissguth, Thomas. *Queen Cleopatra* (4–7). Series: A&E Biography. 2000, Lerner LB $27.93 (978-0-8225-4946-8). The story of Cleopatra and her impact on world history. (Rev: BL 3/15/00; HBG 10/00; SLJ 5/00) [921]

HATSHEPSUT

7086 Greenblatt, Miriam. *Hatshepsut and Ancient Egypt* (6–8). Series: Rulers and Their Times. 1999, Benchmark LB $29.93 (978-0-7614-0911-3). To give the reader a feel for ancient Egypt, this biography of Hatshepsut also compares Hatshepsut's life with the life of a typical Egyptian. (Rev: HBG 9/00; SLJ 2/00) [932]

MANDELA, NELSON

7087 Connolly, Sean. *Nelson Mandela: An Unauthorized Biography* (5–7). 2000, Heinemann LB $24.22 (978-1-57572-225-2). An appealing biography that contains good background material on South Africa, past and present. (Rev: SLJ 1/01) [921]

7088 Finlayson, Reggie. *Nelson Mandela* (4–8). Illus. Series: A&E Biography. 1999, Lerner LB $27.93 (978-0-8225-4936-9). An overview that concentrates on Mandela's childhood, his training as a lawyer, and his rise through the ranks of the African National Congress, with only brief coverage of his imprisonment, release, and presidency. (Rev: BL 2/15/00; HBG 3/99; SLJ 2/99) [921]

7089 Keller, Bill. *Tree Shaker: The Story of Nelson Mandela* (6–12). Illus. 2008, Kingfisher $16.95 (978-0-7534-5992-8). The accomplishments of the South African leader are related by a former *New York Times* Johannesburg bureau chief. An explanation of the history of apartheid helps readers to understand what Mandela was fighting for. (Rev: BL 11/1/07; SLJ 8/08) [921]

7090 Kramer, Ann. *Nelson Mandela* (6–10). Illus. Series: Twentieth Century History. 2003, Raintree LB $32.85 (978-0-7398-5258-3). An attractive and absorbing account of Mandela's life and efforts to bring equality to his country. (Rev: BL 6/1–15/03; SLJ 7/03) [968.06]

MUGABE, ROBERT

7091 Worth, Richard. *Robert Mugabe of Zimbabwe* (5–8). Illus. Series: In Focus Biographies. 1990, Silver Burdett LB $13.95 (978-0-671-68987-2); paper $7.95 (978-0-671-70684-5). Tells the story of Zimbabwe's first prime minister, along with a history of this emerging country. (Rev: SLJ 2/91) [921]

TUTANKHAMEN, KING

7092 Hawass, Zahi. *Tutankhamun: The Mystery of the Boy King* (4–7). Illus. 2005, National Geographic $17.95 (978-0-7922-8354-6). The director of excavations at key Egyptian archaeological sites offers a fascinating account of the life, death, and burial of King Tut and of new revelations about his fate. (Rev: BL 11/1/05; SLJ 10/05*) [932]

Asia and the Middle East

AHMADINEJAD, MAHMOUD

7093 Broyles, Matthew. *Mahmoud Ahmadinejad: President of Iran* (8–12). Illus. Series: Newsmakers. 2007, Rosen LB $31.95 (978-1-4042-1900-7).

Readers are introduced to the president of Iran, whose provocative and challenging statements have enraged many and impressed others; Iran's current political climate and its history are covered as well. (Rev: BL 10/15/07) [955.05]

ARAFAT, YASIR

7094 Ferber, Elizabeth. *Yasir Arafat: The Battle for Peace in Palestine* (7–12). 1995, Millbrook $23.90 (978-1-56294-585-5). A balanced presentation of Arafat's political career. (Rev: BL 10/1/95; SLJ 12/95) [921]

7095 Headlam, George. *Yasser Arafat* (5–8). Series: A&E Biography. 2003, Lerner LB $29.27 (978-0-8225-5004-4); paper $7.95 (978-0-8225-9902-9). The story of the Palestinian leader, his rise to power, and his current status. (Rev: BL 1/1–15/04; HBG 4/04; SLJ 2/04)

7096 Williams, Colleen Madonna Flood. *Yasir Arafat* (5–8). Illus. 2002, Chelsea $30.00 (978-0-7910-6941-7); paper $30.00 (978-0-7910-7186-1). The controversial PLO leader is shown as a man of conviction who struggles to balance the desires of his people and of the rest of the world. (Rev: BL 1/1–15/03; HBG 3/03; SLJ 2/03) [956.9405]

BEGIN, MENACHEM

7097 Brackett, Virginia. *Menachem Begin* (5–8). Series: Major World Leaders. 2002, Chelsea $30.00 (978-0-7910-6946-2). The life of the important Israeli prime minister who was in office when peace was declared between Israel and Egypt. (Rev: BL 1/1–15/03; SLJ 2/03) [921]

BHATT, ELA

7098 Sreenivasan, Jyotsna. *Ela Bhatt: Uniting Women in India* (5–8). Illus. Series: Women Changing the World. 2000, Feminist $19.95 (978-1-55861-229-7). Inspired by Gandhi, this Indian lawyer founded an organization to help and protect the lives of her country's poorest women and organized a labor union for them. (Rev: BL 9/15/00; HBG 3/01; SLJ 12/00) [921]

BIN LADEN, OSAMA

7099 Landau, Elaine. *Osama bin Laden: A War Against the West* (6–10). Illus. 2002, Millbrook LB $23.90 (978-0-7613-1709-8). Landau combines what is known of Bin Laden's youth, fundamentalist beliefs, and terrorist organization with a look at his assumed involvement in the September 11, 2001, and other attacks. (Rev: BL 1/1–15/02; HBG 10/02; SLJ 3/02) [921]

7100 Louis, Nancy. *Osama bin Laden* (4–7). Series: War on Terrorism. 2002, ABDO LB $25.65 (978-1-

57765-663-0). A brief biography of the terrorist leader told through a matter-of-fact text and many color photographs. (Rev: BL 5/15/02; HBG 10/02) [921]

7101 Woolf, Alex. *Osama Bin Laden* (5–8). Series: A&E Biography. 2003, Lerner LB $29.27 (978-0-8225-5003-7); paper $7.95 (978-0-8225-9900-5). The story of the leader of the Al Qaeda terrorist movement and his family background in Saudi Arabia. (Rev: BL 1/1–15/04; HBG 4/04; SLJ 2/04) [921]

BUDDHA

7102 Gedney, Mona. *The Life and Times of Buddha* (5–7). Series: Biography from Ancient Civilizations: Legends, Folklore, and Stories of Ancient Worlds. 2005, Mitchell Lane LB $29.95 (978-1-58415-342-9). Gedney recounts what is known of the life of Siddartha Gautama, whose search for a better way of living led to the founding of Buddhism. (Rev: SLJ 9/05) [921]

CONFUCIUS

7103 Freedman, Russell. *Confucius: The Golden Rule* (4–8). Illus. by Frederic Clement. 2002, Scholastic paper $17.99 (978-0-439-13957-1). This absorbing account of the life and philosophy of Confucius gives new insight into the character of the man who had so much influence on China. (Rev: BL 10/1/02*; HB 1–2/03; HBG 3/03; SLJ 9/02*) [181]

DALAI LAMA

7104 Perez, Louis G. *The Dalai Lama* (6–12). Series: World Leaders. 1993, Rourke LB $25.27 (978-0-86625-480-9). Tells of the Dalai Lama's lonely childhood, nonviolent struggle for his people, years in exile, his impact and life through 1992. (Rev: BL 12/1/93) [921]

7105 Stewart, Whitney. *The 14th Dalai Lama: Spiritual Leader of Tibet* (5–8). Series: Newsmakers. 1996, Lerner LB $30.35 (978-0-8225-4926-0). As well as describing the life and spiritual beliefs of the 14th Dalai Lama, this account describes the political situation in Tibet at the time. (Rev: SLJ 6/96; VOYA 10/96) [921]

GANDHI, INDIRA

7106 Dommermuth-Costa, Carol. *Indira Gandhi: Daughter of India* (7–12). Series: Lerner Biographies. 2001, Lerner LB $6.95 (978-0-8225-4963-5). A thorough profile that places Gandhi's life in historical context and provides a good history of modern India. (Rev: HBG 3/02; SLJ 3/02) [921]

GANDHI, MAHATMA

7107 Martin, Christopher. *Mohandas Gandhi* (4–7). Series: A&E Biography. 2000, Lucent LB $27.93 (978-0-8225-4984-0). The story of the man who sought to unite and free his people not through violence but by prayer, civil disobedience, and communication. (Rev: BL 12/15/00; HBG 3/01; SLJ 1/01) [921]

7108 Severance, John B. *Gandhi, Great Soul* (6–9). Illus. 1997, Clarion $19.00 (978-0-395-77179-2). The life and times of Gandhi are covered in this attractive, informative book, which explains Gandhi's philosophy of peaceful resistance and describes the evolution of his beliefs. (Rev: BL 2/15/97; SLJ 4/97*) [921]

7109 Shields, Charles J. *Mohandas K. Gandhi* (8–12). Illus. Series: Overcoming Adversity. 2001, Chelsea LB $30.00 (978-0-7910-6301-9). This thorough account of Gandhi's beliefs and work also discusses his influence on other leaders and opposition to his ideas. (Rev: BL 2/15/02; HBG 10/02) [921]

7110 Wilkinson, Philip. *Gandhi: The Young Protestor Who Founded a Nation* (4–7). Illus. Series: World History Biographies. 2005, National Geographic LB $27.90 (978-0-7922-3648-1). Gandhi's character shines through the straightforward text and interesting anecdotes in this biography that gives historical context plus maps and photographs. (Rev: BL 6/1–15/05) [954.03]

GENGHIS KHAN

7111 Goldberg, Enid A., and Norman Itzkowitz. *Genghis Khan: 13th-Century Mongolian Tyrant* (5–7). Illus. Series: Wicked History. 2007, Scholastic LB $30.00 (978-0-531-12596-0). The bloody deeds of the tyrant are emphasized (this is the Wicked History series, after all), but readers will also learn about ancient Mongolia and its people as well as the few positive results of Genghis Khan's rule. (Rev: BL 12/15/07; LMC 2/08; SLJ 1/08) [921]

7112 Humphrey, Judy. *Genghis Khan* (6–10). Illus. 1987, Chelsea LB $21.95 (978-0-87754-527-9). The story of the fierce warrior who shaped the Mongolian empire in the 12th century. (Rev: BL 11/15/87; SLJ 12/87) [921]

7113 Rice, Earle, Jr. *Empire in the East: The Story of Genghis Khan* (7–11). Illus. Series: World Leaders. 2005, Morgan Reynolds LB $26.95 (978-1-931798-62-4). A life of Genghis Khan, who rose from obscurity to become leader of the Great Mongol Nation and ruler of vast territories that stretched from the Adriatic to the Pacific. (Rev: BL 8/05; SLJ 8/05) [950]

HERZL, THEODOR

7114 Finkelstein, Norman H. *Theodor Herzl: Architect of a Nation* (7–12). 1991, Lerner LB $6.95 (978-0-8225-4913-0). The story of the respected playwright/journalist who dedicated himself to helping the Jewish people obtain their own country. (Rev: BL 4/15/92; SLJ 7/92) [921]

HUSSEIN, SADDAM

7115 Anderson, Dale. *Saddam Hussein* (5–8). Series: A&E Biography. 2003, Lerner LB $29.27 (978-0-8225-5005-1); paper $7.95 (978-0-8225-9901-2). This biography of the Iraqi despot tells his story up to the decision that led to the American invasion. (Rev: BL 1/1–15/04; HBG 4/04; SLJ 2/04) [921]

7116 Claypool, Jane. *Saddam Hussein* (6–12). Series: World Leaders. 1993, Rourke LB $25.27 (978-0-86625-477-9). Describes Hussein's violent childhood, his rise to power, his impact, and his life to 1992. (Rev: BL 12/1/93; SLJ 1/94) [921]

7117 Shields, Charles J. *Saddam Hussein* (5–8). Illus. Series: Major World Leaders. 2002, Chelsea $30.00 (978-0-7910-6943-1). An account of the Iraqi leader's regime, with information on the Iran-Iraq and Persian Gulf wars and on United Nations sanctions and weapons inspections. (Rev: BL 2/1/03; HBG 3/03; SLJ 4/03) [956.7044]

7118 Stewart, Gail B. *Saddam Hussein* (8–12). Series: Heroes and Villains. 2004, Gale LB $29.95 (978-1-59018-350-2). Ending before Saddam Hussein's capture by U.S. forces, this is a portrait of a ruthless dictator and his ascent to and maintenance of power. (Rev: SLJ 4/04) [921]

KARZAI, HAMID

7119 Abrams, Dennis. *Hamid Karzai* (8–12). Series: Modern World Leaders. 2007, Chelsea House LB $30.00 (978-0-7910-9267-5). Karzai was sworn in as the first democratically elected president of Afghanistan in 2004, and since then has faced many challenges in the struggle to rebuild the war-torn country. (Rev: SLJ 10/07) [921]

KHAMENEI, ALI

7120 Murphy, John. *Ali Khamenei* (8–12). Illus. Series: Modern World Leaders. 2007, Chelsea House LB $30.00 (978-0-7910-9517-1). A look at the rise to power of Ali Khamenei, who became the Grand Ayatollah of Iran upon Khomeini's death. (Rev: BL 4/10/08) [955.05]

KIM IL SUNG

7121 Ingram, Scott. *Kim Il Sung* (6–12). Illus. Series: History's Villains. 2004, Gale LB $28.70 (978-1-4103-0259-5). Profiles North Korean dictator Kim Il Sung, who ruled his country with a brutal hand for more than 40 years. (Rev: BL 7/04; SLJ 5/04) [951.930]

KIM JONG IL

7122 Behnke, Alison. *Kim Jong Il's North Korea* (7–12). Illus. 2007, Lerner LB $38.60 (978-0-8225-7282-4). Extensive background about North Korea gives the reader a foundation for understanding Kim Jong Il's dictatorship. (Rev: BL 10/15/07; SLJ 11/07) [921]

KOLLEK, TEDDY

7123 Rabinovich, Abraham. *Teddy Kollek: Builder of Jerusalem* (5–8). Illus. 1996, Jewish Publication Soc. $14.95 (978-0-8276-0559-6); paper $9.95 (978-0-8276-0561-9). The story of the former mayor of Jerusalem, who supervised the city's unification after the Six Days War in 1967. (Rev: BL 5/15/96) [921]

LAO TZU

7124 Demi. *The Legend of Lao Tzu and the Tao Te Ching* (4–7). Illus. by author. 2007, Simon & Schuster $21.99 (978-1-4169-1206-4). A well-designed introduction to the legendary Chinese religious figure Lao Tzu, with 20 verses from the book of wisdom associated with him. (Rev: BL 5/15/07; HB 7–8/07; LMC 11/07; SLJ 5/07) [921]

MUBARAK, HOSNI

7125 Darraj, Susan Muaddi. *Hosni Mubarak* (8–12). Series: Modern World Leaders. 2007, Chelsea House LB $30.00 (978-0-7910-9280-4). Events in Egypt during Mubarak's presidency are the main focus of this profile. (Rev: SLJ 10/07) [921]

MUHAMMAD

7126 Demi. *Muhammad* (4–7). Illus. 2003, Simon & Schuster $19.95 (978-0-689-85264-0). This readable account of the life of the founding prophet of Islam is accompanied by quotations from the Koran and intricate illustrations. (Rev: BL 6/1–15/03*; HB 7–8/03; HBG 4/04; SLJ 8/03) [297.6]

NOOR, QUEEN

7127 Raatma, Lucia. *Queen Noor: American-Born Queen of Jordan* (6–9). Illus. Series: Signature Lives. 2006, Compass Point LB $34.60 (978-0-7565-1595-9). The life of the American-born woman who became the queen of Jordan. (Rev: BL 4/1/06; SLJ 6/06) [956.9504]

PAHLAVI, MOHAMMED REZA

7128 Barth, Linda. *Mohammed Reza Pahlavi* (5–8). Series: Major World Leaders. 2002, Chelsea $30.00 (978-0-7910-6948-6). An engrossing biography of the last Shah of Iran, who ruled during a tumultuous time in the region. (Rev: BL 1/1–15/03) [921]

RIZAL, JOSE

7129 Arruda, Suzanne Middendorf. *Freedom's Martyr: The Story of José Rizal, National Hero of the Philippines* (6–12). Series: Avisson Young Adult. 2003, Avisson paper $19.95 (978-1-888105-55-1). A patriot and activist on behalf of the native peoples of the Philippines, Rizal was executed by the Spanish for treason in 1896 and remains the country's national hero. (Rev: SLJ 5/04) [921]

SADAT, ANWAR

7130 Kras, Sara Louise. *Anwar Sadat* (5–8). Series: Major World Leaders. 2002, Chelsea $30.00 (978-0-7910-6949-3). An absorbing account of the life of the famous Egyptian leader who shared the 1978 Nobel Peace Prize with Israeli Prime Minister Menachem Begin. (Rev: BL 1/1–15/03; HBG 3/03) [921]

SUU KYI, AUNG SAN

7131 Stewart, Whitney. *Aung San Suu Kyi: Fearless Voice of Burma* (6–9). 1997, Lerner LB $30.35 (978-0-8225-4931-4). A thorough, well-documented biography of the Nobel Peace Prize winner and fearless Burmese leader in the struggle for democracy. (Rev: BL 4/1/97; SLJ 5/97; VOYA 12/97) [921]

TAMERLANE

7132 Wepman, Dennis. *Tamerlane* (6–10). Illus. 1987, Chelsea LB $19.95 (978-0-87754-442-5). The story of the barbaric Mongol chieftain who lived in the 14th century and was responsible for the deaths of millions. (Rev: BL 7/87; SLJ 8/87) [921]

TERESA, MOTHER

7133 Dils, Tracey E. *Mother Teresa* (4–8). Series: Women of Achievement. 2001, Chelsea $30.00 (978-0-7910-5887-9). An absorbing account of the humanitarian's life from her childhood in Albania through her early years in India and her international work with the Missionaries of Charity. (Rev: HBG 3/02; SLJ 11/01) [921]

7134 Johnson, Linda C. *Mother Teresa: Protector of the Sick* (5–8). Illus. Series: Library of Famous Women. 1991, Blackbirch $24.95 (978-1-56711-034-0). Tracing Mother Teresa's life from her childhood in Yugoslavia to her renowned efforts to aid the sick around the world. (Rev: BL 3/15/93) [921]

7135 Morgan, Nina. *Mother Teresa: Saint of the Poor* (4–7). Illus. 1998, Raintree paper $7.95 (978-0-8172-7848-9). A biography of the nun whose work with the poor of India made her an international celebrity and earned her a Nobel Peace Prize. (Rev: BL 7/98; HBG 10/98; SLJ 7/98) [921]

7136 Pond, Mildred. *Mother Teresa: A Life of Charity* (4–7). Illus. Series: Junior World Biography. 1992, Chelsea LB $15.95 (978-0-7910-1755-5). The inspiring life story of the nun who gave her life to serve and help the poor, particularly in India. (Rev: BL 8/92; SLJ 7/92) [921]

7137 Rice, Tanya. *Mother Teresa* (5–8). Illus. Series: The Life and Times Of. 1999, Chelsea LB $12.95 (978-0-7910-4637-1). A straightforward account of the life of Mother Teresa, from her birth in Albania to devout Catholic parents and her religious calling as a child, to her work in India and her commitment to helping the poor, to the winning of the Nobel Peace Prize, and her death. (Rev: SLJ 8/98) [921]

7138 Slavicek, Louise Chipley. *Mother Teresa: Caring for the World's Poor* (8–12). Series: Modern Peacemakers. 2007, Chelsea House LB $30.00 (978-0-7910-9433-4). An evenhanded profile of the Nobel Peace Prize winner, including the text of her acceptance speech. (Rev: SLJ 8/07) [921]

7139 Tilton, Rafael. *Mother Teresa* (4–8). Series: The Importance Of. 2000, Lucent LB $27.45 (978-1-56006-565-4). This thoroughly researched account describes the life of Mother Teresa and gives an honest appraisal of her importance. (Rev: BL 1/1–15/00; HBG 9/00) [921]

XIAOPING, DENG

7140 Stewart, Whitney. *Deng Xiaoping: Leader in a Changing China* (4–7). Series: Lerner Biographies. 2001, Lerner LB $30.35 (978-0-8225-4962-8). An accessible biography of the most powerful man in China from the 1970s until his death, with details of how his reputation was tarnished by the Tiananmen Square massacre. (Rev: BL 9/15/01; HBG 10/01; SLJ 7/01) [921]

ZEDONG, MAO

7141 Slavicek, Louise Chipley. *Mao Zedong* (6–9). Series: Great Military Leaders of the 20th Century. 2003, Chelsea House LB $30.00 (978-0-7910-7407-7). Mao's beliefs, personal life, and political career are clearly described, with maps, photographs, and reproductions. (Rev: SLJ 3/04) [921]

7142 Stefoff, Rebecca. *Mao Zedong: Founder of the People's Republic of China* (7–12). Illus. 1996, Millbrook LB $22.40 (978-1-56294-531-2). A well-documented biography of this important Chinese politician that covers childhood influences, contributions to the development of his nation, and his lasting impact on world history. (Rev: BL 5/1/96; SLJ 6/96) [921]

Australia and the Pacific Islands

KA'IULANI, PRINCESS

7143 Linnea, Sharon. *Princess Ka'iulani: Hope of a Nation, Heart of a People* (5–8). 1999, Eerdmans $18.00 (978-0-8028-5145-1). The story of the Hawaiian princess who tried to prevent the annexation of her country by the United States and of her untimely death at age 22. (Rev: BL 7/99; SLJ 6/99; VOYA 10/99) [921]

Europe

ALEXANDER THE GREAT

7144 Adams, Simon. *Alexander: The Boy Soldier Who Conquered the World* (5–7). Series: National Geographic World History Biographies. 2005, National Geographic LB $27.90 (978-0-7922-3661-0). An attractive, well-illustrated account of Alexander's life and accomplishments, with references to his less-appealing characteristics. (Rev: HBG 4/06; SLJ 9/05) [921]

7145 Behnke, Alison. *The Conquests of Alexander the Great* (6–12). Series: Pivotal Moments in History. 2007, Twenty-First Century LB $38.60 (978-0-8225-5920-7). A thorough biography of Alexander's life and achievements, with background information on the time as well as details of battles, maps, a timeline, and key figures. (Rev: SLJ 9/07) [921]

7146 Greenblatt, Miriam. *Alexander the Great and Ancient Greece* (5–8). Illus. Series: Rulers and Their Times. 1999, Marshall Cavendish LB $29.93 (978-0-7614-0913-7). The first part of this biography introduces Alexander the Great and his accomplishments and the second tells about daily life in ancient Greece. (Rev: BL 1/1–15/00; HBG 10/00; SLJ 2/00) [921]

7147 McGowen, Tom. *Alexander the Great: Conqueror of the Ancient World* (5–8). Series: Rulers of the Ancient World. 2006, Enslow LB $27.93 (978-0-7660-2560-8). Excellent for report writers, this biography covers Alexander the Great's life and distinguishes between fact and legend. (Rev: BL 6/1–15/06; SLJ 6/06) [921]

7148 Saunders, Nicholas. *The Life of Alexander the Great* (5–8). Illus. Series: Stories from History. 2006, School Specialty $9.95 (978-0-7696-4713-5); paper $6.95 (978-0-7696-4694-7). Full-color illus-

trations and graphic-novel format make this engaging biography — which covers the bond between Alexander and his horse as well as his relationship with Hephaestion — attractive to reluctant readers. (Rev: SLJ 1/07) [921]

7149 Shecter, Vicky Alvear. *Alexander the Great Rocks the World* (5–8). Illus. by Terry Naughton. 2006, Darby Creek $18.95 (978-1-58196-045-7). Shecter employs an irreverent, kid-appealing tone to accurately present Alexander's amazing travels; cartoons, historical depictions, detailed notes, and resources round out the volume. (Rev: BL 1/1–15/07; SLJ 12/06) [921]

ANIELEWICZ, MORDECHAI

7150 Callahan, Kerry P. *Mordechai Anielewicz: Hero of the Warsaw Uprising* (5–8). Series: Holocaust Biographies. 2001, Rosen LB $31.95 (978-0-8239-3377-8). The story of Anielewicz and other members of the Jewish resistance in the Warsaw ghetto is told in gripping text accompanied by black-and-white photographs. (Rev: BL 10/15/01) [921]

ARISTOTLE

7151 Anderson, Margaret J., and Karen F. Stephenson. *Aristotle: Philosopher and Scientist* (5–8). Series: Great Minds of Science. 2004, Enslow LB $26.60 (978-0-7660-2096-2). Aristotle's life, times, and contributions to philosophy and science are examined in concise text. (Rev: SLJ 7/04) [921]

ARTHUR, KING

7152 Nardo, Don. *King Arthur* (6–9). Illus. Series: Heroes and Villains. 2003, Gale LB $27.45 (978-1-56006-948-5). This biography recounts Arthur's story and examines the combination of legend and fact. (Rev: BL 1/1–15/03; SLJ 3/03) [942.01]

ATATURK, KEMAL

7153 Tachau, Frank. *Kemal Ataturk* (6–10). Illus. 1987, Chelsea LB $19.95 (978-0-87754-507-1). A biography of the man who transformed Turkey and brought it into the 20th century. (Rev: BL 1/1/88; SLJ 3/88) [921]

BLAIR, TONY

7154 Hinman, Bonnie. *Tony Blair*. Rev. ed. (7–10). Series: Major World Leaders. 2006, Chelsea House $30.00 (978-0-7910-9216-3). An updated profile (to 2006, before his resignation) of the leader of the British Labour Party who in 1997 became the youngest prime minister in nearly 200 years. (Rev: BL 1/1–15/07) [921]

BRAILLE, LOUIS

7155 Bryant, Jennifer. *Louis Braille: Inventor* (5–7). Illus. 1994, Chelsea LB $21.95 (978-0-7910-2077-7). This well-researched biography of Braille tells about the horror of his own blindness as well as the development of the alphabet that allows blind people to read. (Rev: BL 7/94; SLJ 8/94) [921]

7156 Freedman, Russell. *Out of Darkness: The Story of Louis Braille* (4–8). Illus. 1997, Clarion $16.00 (978-0-395-77516-5). The story of the blind Frenchman who, more than 170 years ago, invented a system of reading using raised dots. (Rev: BCCB 5/97; BL 3/1/97; HB 5–6/97; SLJ 3/97*) [686.2]

CAESAR, AUGUSTUS

7157 Forsyth, Fiona. *Augustus: The First Emperor* (6–9). Series: Leaders of Ancient Rome. 2003, Rosen LB $33.25 (978-0-8239-3588-8). A balanced biography of the emperor's achievements and failings. (Rev: LMC 8–9/03; SLJ 6/03) [937]

7158 Greenblatt, Miriam. *Augustus and Imperial Rome* (6–8). Series: Rulers and Their Times. 1999, Benchmark LB $29.93 (978-0-7614-0912-0). To give the reader a feel for ancient Rome, this biography of Caesar Augustus also compares his life with the life of a typical Roman. (Rev: HBG 9/00; SLJ 2/00) [937]

CAESAR, JULIUS

7159 Barter, James. *Julius Caesar and Ancient Rome in World History* (8–12). Illus. Series: In World History. 2001, Enslow LB $26.60 (978-0-7660-1461-9). A detailed look at Caesar's life and accomplishments, along with information about the empire he ruled and the political and social climate of the time; with quotations from primary sources. (Rev: BL 3/1/02; HBG 3/02; SLJ 1/02) [921]

7160 Bruns, Roger. *Julius Caesar* (6–10). Illus. 1987, Chelsea LB $21.95 (978-0-87754-514-9). Using many sources, the author creates an accurate picture of the rise and fall of this Roman leader. (Rev: BL 11/15/87; SLJ 12/87; VOYA 10/88) [921]

7161 Galford, Ellen. *Julius Caesar: The Boy Who Conquered an Empire* (5–8). Series: World History Biographies. 2007, National Geographic $17.95 (978-1-4263-0064-6). A brief but well-organized biography of Caesar, covering his childhood, adolescence, marriage, military career, rise to power, and murder, and offering pertinent historical context. (Rev: SLJ 6/07) [921]

7162 Kent, Zachary. *Julius Caesar: Ruler of the Roman World* (6–9). 2006, Enslow LB $20.95 (978-0-7660-2563-9). Using both modern and ancient sources, Kent introduces one of the most powerful leaders in the history of Western civilization. (Rev: SLJ 8/06) [921]

7163 Saunders, Nicholas. *The Life of Julius Caesar* (5–8). Illus. Series: Stories from History. 2006, School Specialty $9.95 (978-0-7696-4717-3); paper $6.95 (978-0-7696-4697-8). Full-color illustrations and graphic-novel format make this engaging biography attractive to reluctant readers. (Rev: SLJ 1/07) [921]

CALVIN, JOHN

7164 Stepanek, Sally. *John Calvin* (6–10). Illus. 1986, Chelsea LB $21.95 (978-0-87754-515-6). A well-researched biography of the 16th-century leader of the Protestant Reformation. (Rev: BL 3/1/87; SLJ 3/87) [921]

CATHERINE THE GREAT

7165 Whitelaw, Nancy. *Catherine the Great and the Enlightenment in Russia* (8–12). Illus. Series: European Queens. 2004, Morgan Reynolds LB $26.95 (978-1-931798-27-3). The colorful life of the Russian empress from childhood in her native Germany to her pivotal role in leading her adopted country into full participation in the cultural and political life of Europe. (Rev: BL 12/15/04; SLJ 12/04) [921]

CAVELL, EDITH

7166 Batten, Jack. *Silent in an Evil Time: The Brave War of Edith Cavell* (6–9). Illus. 2007, Tundra paper $16.95 (978-0-88776-737-1). Cavell, a British nurse who was executed by the Germans in World War I for her resistance activities, is remembered in this biography that explains the tenor of the times in which she lived and worked. (Rev: BL 11/1/07; SLJ 11/07) [921]

CHARLEMAGNE

7167 Greenblatt, Miriam. *Charlemagne and the Early Middle Ages* (8–12). Series: Rulers and Their Times. 2002, Marshall Cavendish LB $29.93 (978-0-7614-1487-2). The story of the King of the Franks and the founder of the Holy Roman Empire, who ruled at the beginning of the Middle Ages. (Rev: BL 1/1–15/03; HBG 3/03; SLJ 3/03) [921]

7168 Westwood, Jennifer. *Stories of Charlemagne* (7–9). 1976, Phillips $26.95 (978-0-87599-213-6). A biography of the famous emperor of the Holy Roman Empire, who was one of the most influential men of the Middle Ages. [921]

CHURCHILL, SIR WINSTON

7169 Ashworth, Leon. *Winston Churchill* (5–8). Illus. Series: British History Makers. 2002, Cherrytree $17.95 (978-1-84234-072-1). A balanced look at the life and career of the British statesman, with a useful timeline and excellent illustrations. (Rev: SLJ 8/02) [941.082092]

7170 Binns, Tristan Boyer. *Winston Churchill* (5–8). Series: Great Life Stories. 2004, Watts LB $30.50 (978-0-531-12361-4). The complex life of Churchill is well portrayed in this biography that covers his youth and career, triumphs and losses, and many and varied interests. (Rev: SLJ 3/05) [921]

7171 Haugen, Brenda. *Winston Churchill: British Soldier, Writer, Statesman* (4–8). 2006, Compass Point LB $34.60 (978-0-7565-1582-9). Slim but fact-filled, this is a useful biography for report writers, with excerpts from speeches and writings and full discussion of key events in Churchill's life. (Rev: SLJ 9/06) [921]

7172 Severance, John B. *Winston Churchill: Soldier, Statesman, Artist* (5–8). Illus. 1996, Clarion $19.00 (978-0-395-69853-2). A well-organized, clearly written account of the life and works of Britain's great statesman. (Rev: BL 4/15/96; HB 7–8/96; SLJ 4/96*; VOYA 6/96) [941.084]

CLEISTHENES

7173 Parton, Sarah. *Cleisthenes: Founder of Athenian Democracy* (7–10). Series: Leaders of Ancient Greece. 2004, Rosen LB $33.25 (978-0-8239-3826-1). Information about Cleisthenes and his times is carefully couched in discussion of the sources used and the ways in which this material has been gathered and analyzed. (Rev: SLJ 9/04) [921]

CLEMENCEAU, GEORGES

7174 Gottfried, Ted. *Georges Clemenceau* (6–10). Illus. 1987, Chelsea LB $21.95 (978-0-87754-518-7). A biography of the French political leader who served his country with distinction during World War I. (Rev: BL 11/15/87; SLJ 3/88) [921]

CONSTANTINE I, EMPEROR

7175 Morgan, Julian. *Constantine: Ruler of Christian Rome* (6–9). Series: Leaders of Ancient Rome. 2003, Rosen LB $33.25 (978-0-8239-3592-5). The story of the 4th-century emperor who was the first Roman ruler to convert to Christianity. (Rev: SLJ 6/03) [937]

DIANA, PRINCESS OF WALES

7176 Brennan, Kristine. *Diana, Princess of Wales* (5–8). Series: Women of Achievement. 1998, Chelsea $32.00 (978-0-7910-4714-9); paper $30.00 (978-0-7910-4715-6). This book covers the facts about Diana's life, disappointing marriage, struggle for happiness, and untimely death. (Rev: HBG 3/99; VOYA 4/99) [921]

7177 Oleksy, Walter. *Princess Diana* (5–8). Series: People in the News. 2001, Lucent LB $27.45 (978-1-56006-579-1). A well-documented life of this tragic, troubled princess, with many quotations and black-and-white photographs. (Rev: BCCB 10/98; BL 4/1/02; HBG 3/01) [921]

7178 Wood, Richard. *Diana: The People's Princess* (4–7). Illus. 1998, Raintree paper $7.95 (978-0-8172-7849-6). A biography that reveals some personal information about this multifaceted woman and details the many causes she supported. (Rev: BL 7/98; HBG 10/98; SLJ 8/98) [921]

ELEANOR OF AQUITAINE

7179 Hilliam, David. *Eleanor of Aquitaine: The Richest Queen in Medieval Europe* (6–9). Illus. Series: Leaders of the Middle Ages. 2005, Rosen LB $33.25 (978-1-4042-0162-0). A readable life of the wealthy monarch, underlining her unusual accomplishments. (Rev: BL 4/1/05; SLJ 6/05) [942.03]

7180 Sapet, Kerrily. *Eleanor of Aquitaine: Medieval Queen* (8–11). 2006, Morgan Reynolds $26.95 (978-1-931798-90-7). A look at the rise and fall of Eleanor of Aquitaine, who was Queen of France and then Queen of England during the Middle Ages. (Rev: BL 8/06; SLJ 8/06) [921]

ELIZABETH I

7181 Havelin, Kate. *Elizabeth I* (5–8). Series: Biography. 2002, Lerner LB $27.93 (978-0-8225-0029-2). The story of one of the most powerful queens in history and how she learned, at an early age, the politics of survival. (Rev: BCCB 12/99; BL 6/1–15/02; HBG 10/02; SLJ 7/02) [921]

7182 Price-Groff, Claire. *The Importance of Queen Elizabeth I* (7–12). Series: The Importance Of. 2000, Lucent LB $28.70 (978-1-56006-700-9). As well as tracing the life of this famous monarch, this account comments on her lasting importance in world history. (Rev: BL 3/1/01; SLJ 2/01) [921]

7183 Thomas, Jane Resh. *Behind the Mask: The Life of Queen Elizabeth I* (5–8). Illus. 1998, Clarion $20.00 (978-0-395-69120-5). A behind-the-scenes look at the long-lived queen, discussing her childhood, how she overcame opposition to become queen, and her subsequent manipulation of people, the court, and foreigners to attain greatness. (Rev: BL 12/15/98; HB 1–2/99; HBG 3/99; SLJ 12/98*; VOYA 4/99) [921]

7184 Weatherly, Myra. *Elizabeth I: Queen of Tudor England* (6–8). Series: Signature Lives. 2005, Compass Point LB $34.60 (978-0-7565-0988-0). A clearly written and well illustrated life of the fascinating queen. (Rev: SLJ 1/06) [921]

ELIZABETH II

7185 Auerbach, Susan. *Queen Elizabeth II* (6–12). Series: World Leaders. 1993, Rourke LB $25.27 (978-0-86625-481-6). Queen Elizabeth's childhood during World War II, how she came to the throne, and the major events in her reign up to 1993. (Rev: BL 12/1/93) [921]

FRANCIS OF ASSISI, SAINT

7186 dePaola, Tomie. *Francis: The Poor Man of Assisi* (4–7). Illus. by author. 1982, Holiday $18.95 (978-0-8234-0435-3); paper $9.95 (978-0-8234-0812-2). A simple retelling of the life of St. Francis with fine pictures by dePaola. [921]

THE FRANK FAMILY

7187 Denenberg, Barry. *Shadow Life: A Portrait of Anne Frank and Her Family* (6–10). 2005, Scholastic $16.95 (978-0-439-41678-8). In this engaging title from the Shadow Life series, author Barry Denenberg tells the complete story of Anne Frank and her family from their earlier life in Frankfurt to their eventual transport to Nazi concentration camps. (Rev: BL 2/1/05*; SLJ 4/05; VOYA 4/05) [940.53]

FRANK, ANNE

7188 Alagna, Magdalena. *Anne Frank: Young Voice of the Holocaust* (5–8). Series: Holocaust Biographies. 2001, Rosen LB $26.50 (978-0-8239-3373-0). This book describes Anne's childhood, her time spent in hiding, her diary, and her life in the concentration camps. (Rev: BL 10/15/01) [921]

7189 Frank, Anne. *Anne Frank: The Diary of a Young Girl* (5–8). 1967, Pocket paper $3.95 (978-0-685-05466-6). The moving diary of a young Jewish girl hiding from the Nazis in World War II Amsterdam. [921]

7190 Frank, Anne. *The Diary of a Young Girl: The Definitive Edition* (7–12). Trans. by Susan Massotty. 1995, Doubleday $27.50 (978-0-385-47378-1). This edition contains all of the writings of Anne Frank, including some short passages in the diary that had been formerly suppressed. (Rev: BL 4/15/95) [921]

7191 Gold, Alison L. *Memories of Anne Frank: Reflections of a Childhood Friend* (4–8). Illus. 1997, Scholastic paper $16.95 (978-0-590-90722-4). Anne Frank's story as told through recollections of her best friend in Amsterdam, Hannah Goslar, a survivor of the Holocaust. (Rev: BL 9/1/97; HBG 3/98; SLJ 11/97) [921]

7192 Hermann, Spring. *Anne Frank: Hope in the Shadows of the Holocaust* (5–7). Series: Holocaust Heroes and Nazi Criminals. 2005, Enslow LB $27.93 (978-0-7660-2531-8). The story of Anne Frank before, during, and after the two years she and her family hid from the Nazis. (Rev: SLJ 11/05) [921]

7193 Hurwitz, Johanna. *Anne Frank: Life in Hiding* (4–7). Illus. by Vera Rosenberry. 1989, Jewish Publication Soc. $13.95 (978-0-8276-0311-0). This biography describes Anne's life in hiding. (Rev: BL 4/15/89) [921]

7194 Lee, Carol Ann. *Anne Frank and the Children of the Holocaust* (7–10). 2006, Viking $16.99 (978-0-670-06107-5). Lee describes Anne Frank's life before she went into hiding, providing historical context and stories of other children who suffered. (Rev: BL 10/1/06; HB 3–4/05; LMC 4–5/07; SLJ 12/06) [940.53]

7195 Lindwer, Willy. *The Last Seven Months of Anne Frank* (8–12). 1992, Doubleday paper $12.95 (978-0-385-42360-1). Moving testimony from six women interned in a concentration camp with Anne Frank tells of the tragic conclusion of the young diarist's life. (Rev: BL 3/15/91) [921]

GARIBALDI, GIUSEPPI

7196 Viola, Herman J., and Susan P. Viola. *Giuseppi Garibaldi* (6–10). Illus. 1987, Chelsea LB $21.95 (978-0-87754-526-2). Garibaldi was a hero, patriot, and the man who led the movement to unify his country, Italy. (Rev: BL 11/15/87; SLJ 3/88) [921]

HAMMARSKJOLD, DAG

7197 Sheldon, Richard N. *Dag Hammarskjold* (6–10). Illus. 1987, Chelsea LB $19.95 (978-0-87754-529-3). The life story of the Swedish man who served as the secretary general of the United Nations for eight years. (Rev: BL 9/1/87; SLJ 10/87) [921]

HANNIBAL

7198 Warrick, Karen Clemens. *Hannibal: Great General of the Ancient World* (5–8). Series: Rulers of the Ancient World. 2006, Enslow LB $27.93 (978-0-7660-2564-6). The story of Hannibal's life and successes against the Romans are placed in historical context, with details of important battles as well as insight into his character. (Rev: SLJ 6/06) [921]

HAVEL, VACLAV

7199 Duberstein, John. *A Velvet Revolution: Vaclav Havel and the Fall of Communism* (8–11). 2006, Morgan Reynolds $26.95 (978-1-931798-85-3). This profile of the magnetic Czech leader cleverly interweaves history with biographical information (includes photos and resource lists). (Rev: BL 7/06; SLJ 9/06) [921]

HENRY VIII, KING OF ENGLAND

7200 Dwyer, Frank. *Henry VIII* (7–12). Illus. 1988, Chelsea LB $21.95 (978-0-87754-530-9). A fact-filled biography with a great deal of English history given for background. (Rev: BL 1/15/88; SLJ 3/88) [921]

HIMMLER, HEINRICH

7201 Worth, Richard. *Heinrich Himmler: Murderous Architect of the Holocaust* (8–11). Illus. Series: Holocaust Heroes and Nazi Criminals. 2005, Enslow LB $27.93 (978-0-7660-2532-5). A profile of the career of the architect of Nazi Germany's lethally effective campaign against the Jews and other victims of the Holocaust. (Rev: BL 10/15/05; SLJ 1/06) [940.53]

HINDENBURG, PAUL VON

7202 Berman, Russell A. *Paul von Hindenburg* (6–10). Illus. 1987, Chelsea LB $19.95 (978-0-87754-532-3). The story of the German military and political leader who became famous during World War I. (Rev: BL 8/87; SLJ 11/87) [921]

HITLER, ADOLF

7203 Ayer, Eleanor. *Adolf Hitler* (4–8). Illus. Series: The Importance Of. 1996, Lucent LB $27.45 (978-1-56006-072-7). This study of Hitler's rise and impact on Germany and the world includes analyses of the dictator's mental state, leadership qualities, and personality traits. (Rev: BL 3/15/96; SLJ 1/96) [921]

7204 Giblin, James Cross. *The Life and Death of Adolf Hitler* (7–9). 2002, Clarion $21.00 (978-0-395-90371-1). This absorbing biography examines the forces that shaped Hitler's personality and philosophy and rise to power, covers Hitler's behavior during the war, and looks at today's neo-Nazis. (Rev: BL 4/1/02; HB 5–6/02; HBG 10/02; SLJ 5/02*; VOYA 6/02) [943.086]

7205 Harris, Nathaniel. *Hitler* (8–12). Illus. 1989, David & Charles $19.95 (978-0-7134-5961-6). This biography surveys the life and times of Hitler and his impact on history. (Rev: SLJ 12/89) [921]

7206 Rice, Earle, Jr. *Adolf Hitler and Nazi Germany* (6–9). Series: World Leaders. 2005, Morgan Reynolds LB $26.95 (978-1-931798-78-5). This accessible biography traces Hitler's progress from a modest childhood and uncertain adolescence through his army career, rise to power, and crafting of the German war machine. (Rev: BL 1/1–15/06; SLJ 1/06) [921]

7207 Stalcup, Brenda, ed. *Adolf Hitler* (7–12). Series: People Who Made History. 2000, Greenhaven LB $32.45 (978-0-7377-0223-1); paper $21.20 (978-0-7377-0222-4). The dictator's life is depicted through a collection of documents that give special emphasis to his role in World War II and the Holocaust and the impact on the German people. (Rev: BL 4/15/00; SLJ 11/00) [921]

JAMES I, KING OF ENGLAND

7208 Dwyer, Frank. *James I* (6–10). Illus. 1988, Chelsea LB $19.95 (978-1-55546-811-8). The story of the first Stuart king of both England and Scotland. (Rev: BL 6/15/88) [921]

JOAN OF ARC

7209 Lee, William W. *Joan of Arc and the Hundred Years' War in World History* (5–9). Series: In World History. 2003, Enslow LB $26.60 (978-0-7660-1938-6). This combination of biography and history tells the story of Joan of Arc and gives details on the long conflict between France and England. (Rev: BL 6/1–15/03; HBG 10/03; SLJ 9/03) [921]

7210 Stanley, Diane. *Joan of Arc* (4–8). Illus. 1998, Morrow $16.89 (978-0-688-14330-5). Using glorious illustrations, this picture book for older readers gives a detailed history of the life and times of Joan of Arc. (Rev: BCCB 9/98; BL 8/98; HB 9–10/98*; HBG 3/99; SLJ 9/98) [921]

JOHN PAUL II, POPE

7211 Behnke, Alison. *Pope John Paul II* (7–10). Illus. Series: A&E Biography. 2005, Lerner paper $7.95 (978-0-8225-3387-0). This very human portrait of Pope John Paul II traces his life and presents the views of his critics as well as his supporters. (Rev: BL 10/1/05; SLJ 9/05) [282]

7212 Mainardi, Alessandro. *The Life of Pope John Paul II . . . in Comics!* (7–10). Illus. by Werner Maresta. 2006, Papercutz $16.95 (978-1-59707-039-3); paper $9.95 (978-1-59707-057-7). A biography of the life of Pope John Paul II, told in graphic novel format, covering his childhood, journey into priesthood, his accomplishments, and leadership as the Pope. (Rev: BL 10/1/06; LMC 4–5/07; SLJ 1/07) [921]

7213 Sullivan, George. *Pope John Paul II: The People's Pope* (7–9). Illus. 1984, Walker $11.95 (978-0-8027-6523-9). A very readable biography of this beloved pope and his activities for world peace. [921]

KOLBE, SAINT MAXIMILIAN

7214 Mohan, Claire J. *Saint Maximilian Kolbe: The Story of the Two Crowns* (4–8). Illus. 1999, Young Sparrow paper $8.95 (978-0-9621500-3-6). The story of a Polish Catholic monk who took the place of a fellow prisoner who was condemned to die at Auschwitz. (Rev: BL 2/1/00) [921]

LAFAYETTE, MARQUIS DE

7215 Fritz, Jean. *Why Not, Lafayette?* (5–8). Illus. 1999, Putnam $17.99 (978-0-399-23411-8). Using plenty of quotations, interesting anecdotes, and dry humor, this is a fine biography of General Lafayette, the French-born hero of the American Revolution. (Rev: BCCB 12/99; BL 9/15/99; HB 11–12/99; HBG 3/00; SLJ 12/99) [921]

7216 Payan, Gregory. *Marquis de Lafayette: French Hero of the American Revolution* (4–7). Illus. Series: Library of American Lives and Times. 2001, Rosen $34.60 (978-0-8239-5733-0). Payan introduces the French general who assisted the American cause, with illustrations, maps, and other aids to understanding his times. (Rev: BL 10/15/01) [944.04]

LENIN, VLADIMIR ILICH

7217 Haney, John. *Vladimir Ilich Lenin* (6–10). Illus. 1988, Chelsea LB $19.95 (978-0-87754-570-5). A biography of the man who led the Russian Revolution and established the U.S.S.R. (Rev: BL 4/1/88) [921]

7218 Naden, Corinne J., and Rose Blue. *Lenin* (6–10). Series: Importance Of. 2005, Gale $32.45 (978-1-59018-233-8). The life and political career of Vladimir Lenin, founder of the Russian Communist Party. (Rev: BL 6/1–15/04) [921]

7219 Rawcliffe, Michael. *Lenin* (7–10). Illus. 1989, David & Charles $19.95 (978-0-7134-5611-0). Besides supplying a biography of this Russian leader, this book evaluates Lenin's significance in history. (Rev: SLJ 5/89) [921]

LLOYD GEORGE, DAVID

7220 Shearman, Deidre. *David Lloyd George* (7–12). Illus. 1987, Chelsea LB $21.95 (978-0-87754-581-1). The life of the Welsh statesman who was British prime minister during World War I. (Rev: BL 1/15/88) [921]

MACHIAVELLI, NICCOLÒ

7221 Ford, Nick. *Niccolò Machiavelli: Florentine Statesman, Playwright, and Poet* (5–8). Series: Rulers, Scholars, and Artists of the Renaissance. 2005, Rosen LB $33.25 (978-1-4042-0316-7). Ford places Machiavelli's life and accomplishments in

the context of culture and politics of the time. (Rev: SLJ 10/05) [921]

MARIE ANTOINETTE

7222 Lotz, Nancy, and Carlene Phillips. *Marie Antoinette and the Decline of the French Monarchy* (8–12). Illus. Series: European Queens. 2004, Morgan Reynolds LB $26.95 (978-1-931798-28-0). The turbulent life of Marie Antoinette from her birth in Vienna to her death on the guillotine in October 1793. (Rev: BL 12/15/04; SLJ 12/04) [921]

MARSHAL, WILLIAM

7223 Weatherly, Myra. *William Marshal: Medieval England's Greatest Knight* (5–8). Illus. 2001, Morgan Reynolds LB $23.95 (978-1-883846-48-0). The story of the brave medieval English knight whose accomplishments numbered fighting in tournaments, traveling to the Holy Land, helping to draw up the Magna Carta, and serving as regent when Henry III was a child. (Rev: BCCB 3/01; BL 1/1–15/01; HBG 10/01; SLJ 3/01) [921]

MARY, QUEEN OF SCOTS

7224 Lotz, Nancy, and Carlene Phillips. *Mary Queen of Scots* (7–10). Illus. Series: European Queens. 2007, Morgan Reynolds LB $27.95 (978-1-59935-040-0). Chronicling the life of Mary Queen of Scots and her involvement in politics, conspiracies, and religious conflict, this volume will be helpful for report writers. (Rev: BL 6/1–15/07; SLJ 9/07) [921]

7225 Stepanek, Sally. *Mary, Queen of Scots* (6–10). Illus. 1987, Chelsea LB $21.95 (978-0-87754-540-8). The tragic story of this ill-fated queen, in prose and many pictures. (Rev: BL 6/1/87; SLJ 12/87) [921]

MEDICI, LORENZO DE

7226 Greenblatt, Miriam. *Lorenzo de' Medici* (8–12). Series: Rulers and Their Times. 2002, Marshall Cavendish LB $29.93 (978-0-7614-1490-2). This towering figure of the Renaissance was known as the Magnificent because he was a great politician, patron, poet, and scholar. (Rev: BL 1/1–15/03; HBG 3/03) [921]

7227 Hancock, Lee. *Lorenzo De' Medici: Florence's Great Leader and Patron of the Arts* (5–8). Series: Rulers, Scholars, and Artists of the Renaissance. 2005, Rosen LB $33.25 (978-1-4042-0315-0). Ford places de Medici's life and accomplishments in the context of culture and politics of the time. (Rev: SLJ 10/05) [921]

MENGELE, JOSEF

7228 Cefrey, Holly. *Dr. Josef Mengele: The Angel of Death* (6–9). Series: Holocaust Biographies. 2001, Rosen LB $26.50 (978-0-8239-3374-7). Mengele's interest in genetics and natural selection and his activities at Auschwitz are the focus of this frank biography. (Rev: SLJ 1/02) [921]

7229 Grabowski, John F. *Josef Mengele* (8–12). Series: Heroes and Villains. 2004, Gale LB $29.95 (978-1-59018-425-7). A life of the Nazi who committed atrocities during World War II but escaped to South America. (Rev: SLJ 4/04) [921]

MUSSOLINI, BENITO

7230 Hartenian, Larry. *Benito Mussolini* (6–10). Illus. 1988, Chelsea LB $19.95 (978-0-87754-572-9). A fascinating biography of the Italian Fascist leader who brought his country to defeat in World War II. (Rev: BL 6/1/88) [921]

NAPOLEON I

7231 Burleigh, Robert. *Napoleon: The Story of the Little Corporal* (5–8). Illus. 2007, Abrams $18.95 (978-0-8109-1378-3). This informative and attractive biography of Napoleon from his childhood through his final defeat and exile uses an accessible, conversational style. (Rev: BL 6/1–15/07; SLJ 7/07) [921]

7232 Landau, Elaine. *Napoleon Bonaparte* (7–10). 2006, Twenty-First Century LB $27.93 (978-0-8225-3420-4). This biography of Bonaparte chronicles his most important milestones with the help of a timeline, map, quotations, and black-and-white photographs. (Rev: SLJ 6/06) [921]

7233 Obstfeld, Raymond, and Loretta Obstfeld, eds. *Napoleon Bonaparte* (7–12). Series: People Who Made History. 2001, Greenhaven paper $14.96 (978-0-7377-0422-8). After an introductory overview chapter covering Napoleon's career, there are a number of specialized essays that focus on his contributions and place in history. (Rev: BL 4/15/01) [921]

NOBEL, ALFRED

7234 Bankston, John. *Alfred Nobel and the Story of the Nobel Prize* (4–8). Series: Great Achievement Awards. 2003, Mitchell Lane LB $29.95 (978-1-58415-168-5). An intriguing biography of the inventor of dynamite and the founder of the famous prizes. (Rev: BL 10/15/03; SLJ 9/03) [921]

PETER THE GREAT

7235 Greenblatt, Miriam. *Peter the Great and Tsarist Russia* (5–8). Illus. Series: Rulers and Their Times. 1999, Marshall Cavendish LB $29.93 (978-0-7614-0914-4). A biography of the czar who westernized Russia is followed by a section on daily life during his reign. (Rev: BL 1/1–15/00; HBG 10/00; SLJ 2/00) [921]

PULASKI, CASIMIR

7236 Collins, David R. *Casimir Pulaski: Soldier on Horsback* (4–8). Illus. 1995, Pelican $14.95 (978-1-56554-082-8). A smoothly written biography of the Polish patriot who, though he could scarcely speak English, became an important figure helping the colonists during the Revolutionary War. (Rev: BL 2/15/96) [921]

PUTIN, VLADIMIR

7237 Shields, Charles J. *Vladimir Putin* (5–8). Illus. Series: Major World Leaders. 2002, Chelsea $30.00 (978-0-7910-6945-5). Putin's family life, ambitions to be a spy, and accession to power are all covered in this fine biography. (Rev: BL 2/1/03; HBG 3/03; SLJ 3/03) [947.086]

7238 Streissguth, Thomas. *Vladimir Putin* (7–10). Illus. Series: A&E Biography. 2005, Lerner LB $29.27 (978-0-8225-2374-1); paper $7.95 (978-0-8225-9630-1). Putin's professional and political life take center stage in this biography that will be useful for report writers. (Rev: BL 9/1/05) [947.086]

RASPUTIN, GRIGORY

7239 Goldberg, Enid A., and Norman Itzkowitz. *Grigory Rasputin: Holy Man or Mad Monk?* (6–8). 2007, Watts LB $30.00 (978-0-531-12594-6). This biography of Rasputin provides a full account of his background and rise to power, and leads readers to ponder his true nature. (Rev: SLJ 3/08) [921]

RINGELBLUM, EMMANUEL

7240 Beyer, Mark. *Emmanuel Ringelblum: Historian of the Warsaw Ghetto* (5–8). Illus. Series: Holocaust Biographies. 2001, Rosen LB $31.95 (978-0-8239-3375-4). This true story of a man who recorded events in the Warsaw Ghetto during the Holocaust includes black-and-white photographs. (Rev: BL 10/15/01) [940.53]

ROBINSON, MARY

7241 Friedman, Lita. *Mary Robinson: Fighter for Human Rights* (6–9). Series: Avisson Young Adult. 2004, Avisson paper $19.95 (978-1-888105-65-0). In 1990 Robinson became the first female president of Ireland; subsequently she served as the United Nations High Commissioner for Human Rights. (Rev: SLJ 10/04) [921]

SCHINDLER, OSKAR

7242 Thompson, Bruce, ed. *Oskar Schindler* (7–12). Series: People Who Made History. 2002, Gale LB $24.95 (978-0-7377-0894-3); paper $36.20 (978-0-7377-0895-0). The life and times of a hero of the Jewish Holocaust are explored in a series of essays that deal with different aspects of his career and contributions. (Rev: BL 4/1/02; SLJ 7/02) [921]

SCHOLL, HANS AND SOPHIE

7243 Axelrod, Toby. *Hans and Sophie Scholl: German Resisters of the White Rose* (7–12). Series: Holocaust Biographies. 2001, Rosen LB $31.95 (978-0-8239-3316-7). The Scholls, brother and sister, were arrested and executed for their role in organizing the group known as the White Rose, which worked to expose the Nazis' atrocities. (Rev: SLJ 6/01) [921]

SOCRATES

7244 Dell, Pamela. *Socrates: Ancient Greek in Search of Truth* (5–8). Illus. Series: Signature Lives. 2006, Compass Point LB $34.60 (978-0-7565-1874-5). A solid profile of the Greek philosopher that underlines his importance and provides insight into life in ancient Athens. (Rev: BL 10/15/06) [183]

SOLON

7245 Randall, Bernard. *Solon: The Lawmaker of Athens* (7–10). Series: Leaders of Ancient Greece. 2004, Rosen LB $33.25 (978-0-8239-3829-2). Information about Solon and his times is carefully introduced with discussion of the sources used and the ways in which this material has been gathered and analyzed. (Rev: SLJ 9/04) [921]

SULEIMAN THE MAGNIFICENT

7246 Greenblatt, Miriam. *Süleyman the Magnificent and the Ottoman Empire* (8–12). Series: Rulers and Their Times. 2002, Marshall Cavendish LB $29.93 (978-0-7614-1489-6). The story of the great sultan who ruled during the 16th century and brought the Ottoman Empire to its height of power. (Rev: BL 1/1–15/03; HBG 3/03) [921]

THEMISTOCLES

7247 Morris, Ian Macgregor. *Themistocles: Defender of Greece* (7–10). Series: Leaders of Ancient Greece. 2004, Rosen LB $33.25 (978-0-8239-3830-8). Information about Themistocles and his times is carefully couched in discussion of the sources used and the ways in which this material has been gathered and analyzed. (Rev: SLJ 9/04) [921]

TITO, JOSIP BROZ

7248 Schiffman, Ruth. *Josip Broz Tito* (6–10). Illus. 1987, Chelsea LB $19.95 (978-0-87754-443-2). The story of this unusual Yugoslavian leader and of the unique Communist regime he founded. (Rev: BL 6/15/87; SLJ 8/87) [921]

VAN BEEK, CATO BONTJES

7249 Friedman, Ina R. *Flying Against the Wind: The Story of a Young Woman Who Defied the Nazis* (6–10). 1995, Lodgepole Pr. paper $11.95 (978-1-886721-00-5). The story of Cato Bontjes van Beek, who grew up in a progressive German household and was executed by the Nazis with her boyfriend for joining an underground movement. (Rev: BL 7/95; VOYA 4/96) [921]

VICTORIA, QUEEN

7250 Price-Groff, Claire. *Queen Victoria and Nineteenth-Century England* (8–12). Series: Rulers and Their Times. 2002, Marshall Cavendish LB $29.93 (978-0-7614-1488-9). The story of the great British monarch who gave her name to the age she dominated. (Rev: BL 1/1–15/03; HBG 3/03) [921]

WALLENBERG, RAOUL

7251 Linnea, Sharon. *Raoul Wallenberg: The Man Who Stopped Death* (5–7). Illus. 1993, Jewish Publication Soc. paper $9.95 (978-0-8276-0448-3). This Swedish architect saved thousands of Jews in Hungary from the Nazi Holocaust. (Rev: BL 6/1–15/93) [940]

7252 McArthur, Debra. *Raoul Wallenberg: Rescuing Thousands from the Nazis' Grasp* (5–7). Series: Holocaust Heroes and Nazi Criminals. 2005, Enslow LB $27.93 (978-0-7660-2530-1). A well-documented profile of the courageous Swedish diplomat who saved thousands of Hungarian Jews and disappeared after the end of the war. (Rev: SLJ 11/05) [921]

7253 Streissguth, Thomas. *Raoul Wallenberg: Swedish Diplomat and Humanitarian* (7–12). Series: Holocaust Biographies. 2001, Rosen LB $31.95 (978-0-8239-3318-1). Wallenberg's efforts to save Hungarian Jews during World War II and his subsequent disappearance are described here. (Rev: SLJ 6/01) [921]

WIESENTHAL, SIMON

7254 Jeffrey, Laura S. *Simon Wiesenthal: Tracking Down Nazi Criminals* (6–9). Series: People to Know. 1997, Enslow LB $26.60 (978-0-89490-830-9). The story of the great investigator of Holocaust crimes who was responsible for bringing to justice such infamous war criminals as Adolph Eichmann. (Rev: HBG 3/98; SLJ 3/98) [921]

WILLIAM, PRINCE

7255 Dougherty, Terry. *Prince William* (5–8). Series: People in the News. 2001, Lucent LB $32.45 (978-1-56006-982-9). Using many quotes, good photographs, and an interesting text, this is a biography of the royal Prince Charming. (Rev: BL 4/1/02) [921]

7256 Wyborny, Sheila. *Prince William* (4–7). Illus. Series: Famous People. 2003, Gale $26.20 (978-0-7377-1401-2). An interesting biography of the young prince that covers his mother's death and the difficulties of living in the limelight, with lots of color photographs. (Rev: BL 6/1–15/03) [941.085]

WOLLSTONECRAFT, MARY

7257 Miller, Calvin C. *Mary Wollstonecraft and the Rights of Women* (7–12). Illus. 1999, Morgan Reynolds LB $23.95 (978-1-883846-41-1). This is a biography of the passionate English fighter for women's rights who was motivated by the grinding poverty, discrimination, and lack of opportunity suffered by women in the late 18th and early 19th centuries. (Rev: BL 5/1/99; SLJ 5/99; VOYA 12/99) [921]

YELTSIN, BORIS

7258 Miller, Calvin C. *Boris Yeltsin: First President of Russia* (6–9). 1994, Morgan Reynolds LB $20.95 (978-1-883846-08-4). The biography of the controversial Russian leader up to 1993. (Rev: BL 12/1/94; SLJ 4/95; VOYA 2/95) [921]

South and Central America, Canada, and Mexico

BOLIVAR, SIMON

7259 Goodnough, David. *Simon Bolivar: South American Liberator* (7–12). Series: Hispanic Biographies. 1998, Enslow LB $26.60 (978-0-7660-1044-4). The inspiring story of the young military leader who led the fight to free several South American countries from the oppression of the Spaniards. (Rev: BL 1/1–15/99; HBG 3/99; VOYA 10/99) [921]

CASTRO, FIDEL

7260 Bentley, Judith. *Fidel Castro of Cuba* (7–12). Series: In Focus Biographies. 1991, Messner LB $13.95 (978-0-671-70198-7); paper $7.95 (978-0-671-70199-4). Relates the Cuban leader's personal story to a detailed history of his country, its problems and achievements, and the changing international scene up to 1991. (Rev: BL 11/1/91) [921]

7261 Platt, Richard. *Fidel Castro: From Guerrilla to World Statesman* (5–7). Series: Twentieth-Century History Makers. 2003, Raintree LB $32.85 (978-0-7398-6141-7). Platt traces Castro's life from childhood through today, presenting opposing opinions of his achievements in a chapter called "Hero or Monster?" (Rev: HBG 4/04; SLJ 9/03) [973.9106]

7262 Press, Petra. *Fidel Castro: An Unauthorized Biography* (5–7). Series: Heinemann Profiles. 2000, Heinemann LB $24.22 (978-1-57572-497-3). An interesting introduction to the life of Cuba's dictator, with photographs that show urban and rural Cuba. (Rev: SLJ 6/01) [972.91064092]

7263 Woog, Adam. *Fidel Castro* (6–8). Series: The Importance Of. 2003, Gale LB $32.45 (978-1-59018-231-4). A thorough and readable biography that looks objectively at Castro and his country and wonders what the future will bring. (Rev: BL 6/1–15/03; SLJ 9/03) [973.9106]

CHAVEZ, HUGO

7264 Young, Jeff C. *Hugo Chavez: Leader of Venezuela* (6–12). Illus. 2007, Morgan Reynolds LB $27.95 (978-1-59935-068-4). Covers the life of Venezuela's leader from his childhood to the present, as well as his military career, brief imprisonment, presidency, and attitude toward the United States. (Rev: BL 8/07) [921]

DE PORTOLA, GASPAR

7265 Whiting, Jim. *Gaspar de Portola* (5–7). Series: Latinos in American History. 2002, Mitchell Lane LB $29.95 (978-1-58415-148-7). The story of the Latino governor of "Las Californias" from 1768 to 1770 who was responsible for expelling Jesuits from the area. (Rev: BL 2/15/03; HBG 10/03) [921]

DUVALIER, FRANÇOIS AND JEAN-CLAUDE

7266 Condit, Erin. *The Duvaliers* (6–9). Illus. 1989, Chelsea $21.95 (978-1-55546-832-3). A history of modern Haiti is given as well as the life stories of these two dictators. (Rev: BL 8/89; VOYA 12/89) [921]

FOX, VICENTE

7267 Paprocki, Sherry Beck. *Vicente Fox* (5–8). Series: Major World Leaders. 2002, Chelsea $30.00 (978-0-7910-6944-8). The story of the man who became president of Mexico in July 2000, the first opposition candidate to gain presidential office in more than 70 years. (Rev: BL 1/1–15/03) [921]

GUEVARA, CHE

7268 Havelin, Kate. *Che Guevara* (7–12). Series: Biography. 2006, Twenty-First Century LB $27.93 (978-0-8225-5951-1). This is a brief but thorough profile of the revolutionary who had so much impact in his short life. (Rev: SLJ 3/07) [921]

7269 Miller, Calvin Craig. *Che Guevara: In Search of the Revolution* (7–10). 2006, Morgan Reynolds LB $26.95 (978-1-931798-93-8). A captivating biography of Che Guevara, with details on his personal life, his role as a revolutionary leader in Cuba, and the time he spent working with Castro. (Rev: BL 8/06; SLJ 3/07) [921]

7270 Neimark, Anne E. *Ch'e! Latin America's Legendary Guerrilla Leader* (7–10). Illus. 1989, HarperCollins LB $13.89 (978-0-397-32309-8). A portrait of the Latin American revolutionary who tried to help the oppressed and poor of the nations in Spanish America. (Rev: BL 5/15/89; SLJ 5/89) [921]

7271 Uschan, Michael V. *Che Guevara, Revolutionary* (8–11). Illus. Series: The 20th Century's Most Influential Hispanics. 2006, Gale LB $31.20 (978-1-59018-970-2). A balanced profile of the socialist rebel who has become a popular icon. (Rev: BL 4/1/07) [921]

MARIN, LUIS MUNOZ

7272 Bernier-Grand, Carmen T. *Poet and Politician of Puerto Rico: Don Luis Muñoz Marín* (5–8). 1995, Orchard LB $16.99 (978-0-531-08737-4). This story of the life of the man who helped make Puerto Rico a commonwealth also includes a history of the island. (Rev: BL 5/15/95; SLJ 4/95) [921]

MENCHU, RIGOBERTA

7273 Kallen, Stuart A. *Rigoberta Menchú: Indian Rights Activist* (6–12). Series: The 20th Century's Most Influential Hispanics. 2006, Gale LB $32.45 (978-1-59018-975-7). A life of the Nobel laureate and advocate for human rights. (Rev: SLJ 9/07) [921]

7274 Menchú, Rigoberta, and Dante Liano. *The Girl from Chimel* (4–7). Trans. by David Unger. Illus. by Domi. 2005, Groundwood $16.95 (978-0-88899-666-4). Rigoberta Menchu, winner of the 1992 Nobel Peace Prize and Maya activist, tells about growing up in the Guatemalan Indian village of Chimel. (Rev: BL 11/1/05; SLJ 2/06) [868]

7275 Schulze, Julie. *Rigoberta Menchú Túm: Champion of Human Rights* (8–12). Illus. Series: Contemporary Profile and Policy. 1998, John Gordon Burke $20.00 (978-0-934272-42-1); paper $12.95 (978-0-934272-43-8). This biography combines the life story of Nobel Peace Prize-winner Rigoberta Menchu Tum with the story of the struggle of the Mayan people for equality in Guatemala and throughout Central America. (Rev: BL 4/1/98) [921]

7276 Wagner, Heather Lehr. *Rigoberta Menchú Tum: Activist for Indigenous Rights in Guatemala* (8–12). Illus. 2007, Chelsea House LB $30.00 (978-0-7910-8998-9). An introduction to the life of the 1992 Nobel Peace Prize winner, from her impoverished childhood in a Mayan-K'iche community, through the murder of her activist parents and siblings, to her fight for the rights of indigenous people. (Rev: BL 6/1–15/07) [921]

NEZAHUALCOYOTL

7277 Serrano, Francisco. *The Poet King of Tezcoco: A Great Leader of Ancient Mexico* (5–8). Trans. by Trudy Balch. Illus. by Pablo Serrano. 2007, Groundwood $18.95 (978-0-88899-787-6). This picture book for older readers introduces the life of Nezahualcoyotl, a 15th-century Toltec royal and poet who brought much advancement to his kingdom. (Rev: BL 6/1–15/07; SLJ 12/07) [972]

SANTA ANNA, ANTONIO LOPEZ DE

7278 Bankston, John. *Antonio López de Santa Anna* (5–7). Series: Latinos in American History. 2003, Mitchell Lane LB $29.95 (978-1-58415-209-5). A biography of the Mexican general, president, and statesman who is best known for his part in the Battle of the Alamo. (Rev: BL 1/1–15/04; HBG 4/04; SLJ 2/04) [921]

SILVA, MARINA

7279 Hildebrant, Ziporah. *Marina Silva: Defending Rainforest Communities in Brazil* (5–8). Series: Women Changing the World. 2001, Feminist $19.95 (978-1-55861-292-1). Though battling a serious illness, this gallant women, once a leader of the native Amazonians, has become a leading figure in protecting the forests of Brazil. (Rev: BL 12/15/01) [921]

VILLA, PANCHO

7280 O'Brien, Steven. *Pancho Villa* (5–9). Series: Hispanics of Achievement. 1994, Chelsea LB $21.95 (978-0-7910-1257-4). The life and accomplishments of this Mexican freedom fighter. (Rev: BL 9/15/94; VOYA 8/94) [921]

Miscellaneous Interesting Lives

Collective

7281 Cox, Clinton. *African American Teachers* (4–7). Series: Black Stars. 2000, Wiley $22.95 (978-0-471-24649-7). A collection of short profiles of important African American teachers who have inspired their students and championed the cause of education. (Rev: BL 7/00; HBG 3/01; SLJ 7/00) [920]

7282 Fleischman, John. *Black and White Airmen: Their True History* (5–8). Illus. 2007, Houghton $20.00 (978-0-618-56297-8). At a reunion decades later, white bomber pilot Herb Heilbrun and Tuskegee Airman John Leahr discover how much of World War II they shared although separated by segregation. (Rev: BL 2/1/07) [920]

7283 Gonzales, Doreen. *AIDS: Ten Stories of Courage* (6–10). Illus. Series: Collective Biographies. 1996, Enslow LB $26.60 (978-0-89490-766-1). A collection of 10 biographies of individuals, including Ryan White and Magic Johnson, who have helped people understand AIDS and its effects. (Rev: BL 4/15/96; SLJ 5/96; VOYA 6/96) [920]

7284 Warren, Andrea. *We Rode the Orphan Trains* (4–8). Illus. 2001, Houghton $18.00 (978-0-618-11712-3). Eight moving biographical accounts of men and women, now in their 80s and 90s, who traveled to the Midwest to find new homes and families. (Rev: BCCB 11/01; BL 11/1/01; HBG 3/02; SLJ 11/01; VOYA 12/01) [362.73]

Individual

APPELT, KATHI

7285 Appelt, Kathi. *My Father's Summers: A Daughter's Memoir* (6–12). 2004, Holt $15.95 (978-0-8050-7362-1). In a series of prose poems, Appelt paints a poignant portrait of her life growing up in Houston and the pain caused by the extended absences of her father. (Rev: BCCB 7–8/04; BL 6/1–15/04; SLJ 6/04; VOYA 6/04) [813]

BARAKAT, IBTISAM

7286 Barakat, Ibtisam. *Tasting the Sky: A Palestinian Childhood* (7–10). 2007, Farrar $16.00 (978-0-374-35733-7). A memoir of the author's war-torn youth, which included running from bomb attacks, living at detention centers, and uneven schooling. (Rev: BL 3/15/07; LMC 10/07; SLJ 5/07*) [921]

BLOOMER, ELIZABETH

7287 Reed, Jennifer. *Elizabeth Bloomer: Child Labor Activist* (4–8). Series: Young Heroes. 2006, Gale LB $23.70 (978-0-7377-3615-1). Bloomer became an activist against child labor when she was in middle school and learned about Iqbal Masih, a Pakistani boy sold into slavery. (Rev: SLJ 5/07) [921]

BONETTA, SARAH FORBES

7288 Myers, Walter Dean. *At Her Majesty's Request: An African Princess in Victorian England* (5–8). Illus. 1999, Scholastic paper $17.95 (978-0-590-48669-9). The intriguing story of the African princess who at age 7 was saved from becoming a sacrifice and sent her to England, where she became the ward of Queen Victoria. (Rev: BCCB 2/99; BL 4/1/99; HBG 10/99; SLJ 1/99; VOYA 4/99) [921]

DEMALLIE, HOWARD R.

7289 DeMallie, Howard R. *Behind Enemy Lines: A Young Pilot's Story* (7–9). 2007, Sterling paper $6.95 (978-1-4027-4137-1). DeMallie tells the true story of his capture and imprisonment by the Nazis in occupied Holland after his B-17 ran into trouble in 1944. (Rev: BL 6/1–15/07; SLJ 8/07) [921]

GAC-ARTIGAS, ALEJANDRO

7290 Gac-Artigas, Alejandro. *Yo, Alejandro* (5–7). 2000, Ediciones Nuevo Espacio paper $11.95 (978-1-930879-21-8). This is a collection of personal essays written by the author before his 12th birthday about his life in Puerto Rico, the state of Georgia, and later New York City. (Rev: BL 3/1/01) [921]

GARNER, ELEANOR

7291 Garner, Eleanor Ramrath. *Eleanor's Story: An American Girl in Hitler's Germany* (7–12). 1999, Peachtree $15.95 (978-1-56145-193-7). The author recounts her family's struggle to survive in Germany during World War II. (Rev: BL 10/1/99*; HBG 4/00; SLJ 3/00) [940.54]

GRIMBERG, TINA

7292 Grimberg, Tina. *Out of Line: Growing Up Soviet* (8–12). 2007, Tundra $22.95 (978-0-88776-803-3). Grimberg, now a rabbi in Canada, recalls her life as a girl in a Jewish family in the Soviet Union in the 1960s and 1970s. (Rev: BL 12/1/07; SLJ 1/08) [305.2]

HALILBEGOVICH, NADJA

7293 Halilbegovich, Nadja. *My Childhood Under Fire: A Sarajevo Diary* (4–7). 2006, Kids Can $14.95 (978-1-55337-797-9). As a 12-year-old, Halilbegovich kept a diary that reveals the frightening details of her life during the Balkans war. (Rev: BL 5/15/06; SLJ 6/06) [949.703]

HAUTZIG, ESTHER

7294 Hautzig, Esther. *The Endless Steppe: Growing Up in Siberia* (7–12). 1968, HarperCollins paper $5.99 (978-0-06-447027-8). The autobiography of a Polish girl who, with her family, was exiled to Siberia during World War II. [921]

JACOBSEN, RUTH

7295 Jacobsen, Ruth. *Rescued Images: Memories of a Childhood in Hiding* (6–12). 2001, Mikaya $19.95 (978-1-931414-00-5). The author, who was 8 years old when her family fled the Nazis and went into hiding in the Netherlands, relates memories evoked by family photographs, which are also included. (Rev: BCCB 2/02; BL 1/1–15/02; HBG 3/02; SLJ 1/02; VOYA 2/02) [921]

JIANG, JI-LI

7296 Jiang, Ji-li. *Red Scarf Girl: A Memoir of the Cultural Revolution* (6–10). 1997, HarperCollins $17.99 (978-0-06-027585-3). An engrossing memoir of a Chinese girl, her family, and how their lives became a nightmare during Chairman Mao's Cultural Revolution of the late 1960s. (Rev: BL 10/1/97; SLJ 12/97; VOYA 6/98) [921]

KHERDIAN, JERON

7297 Kherdian, Jeron. *The Road from Home: The Story of an Armenian Girl* (6–8). 1979, Morrow paper $6.99 (978-0-688-14425-8). A portrait of the youth of the author's mother, an Armenian girl who suffered many hardships and finally arrived in America as a mail-order bride. [921]

KOSSMAN, NINA

7298 Kossman, Nina. *Behind the Border* (5–7). 1994, Lothrop $14.00 (978-0-688-13494-5). This book contains 12 episodes about the author's childhood in Communist Russia before emigrating to the United States. (Rev: BCCB 10/94; BL 8/94; SLJ 10/94) [921]

LAMBKE, BRYAN

7299 Lambke, Bryan, and Tom Lambke. *I Just Am: A Story of Down Syndrome Awareness and Tolerance* (4–10). 2006, Five Star $14.99 (978-1-58985-020-0). In this compelling photoessay, a young adult with Down syndrome — with some help from his father — explains what it's like to live with this disability. (Rev: SLJ 10/06) [921]

LEKUTON, JOSEPH LEMASOLAI

7300 Lekuton, Joseph Lemasolai. *Facing the Lion: Growing Up Maasai on the African Savanna* (5–12). 2003, National Geographic $15.95 (978-0-7922-5125-5). Lekuton, a member of a nomadic Masai tribe and now a teacher in Virginia, remembers his youth in Kenya. (Rev: BCCB 5/06; BL 9/15/03; HBG 4/04; LMC 11–12/06; SLJ 10/03*) [967.62]

LI, MOYING

7301 Li, Moying. *Snow Falling in Spring: Coming of Age in China during the Cultural Revolution* (7–12). Illus. 2008, Farrar $16.00 (978-0-374-39922-1). Moying Li tells the story of her childhood during the Great Leap Forward, followed by the shock of the Cultural Revolution, during which her mother was sent to the countryside and her father to a labor camp; Li's remarkable grandmother and Li's own love of literature nurtured her through this difficult time. (Rev: BL 2/15/08; SLJ 4/08) [951.05]

MACDONALD, WARREN

7302 Macdonald, Warren. *A Test of Will: One Man's Extraordinary Story of Survival* (8–12). 2004, Douglas & McIntyre paper $14.95 (978-1-55365-064-5). The riveting story of Macdonald's survival after his legs were pinned under a massive rock on an island off Australia. (Rev: BL 9/15/04) [790.5]

MANJIRO

7303 Blumberg, Rhoda. *Shipwrecked! The True Adventures of a Japanese Boy* (5–9). Illus. 2001, HarperCollins $16.95 (978-0-688-17484-2). The story of a shipwrecked Japanese boy who was adopted by an American sea captain, brought to Massachusetts for an education, and became the first Japanese person to live in the United States. (Rev: BCCB 3/01; BL 2/1/01*; HB 3–4/01; HBG 10/01; SLJ 2/01) [921]

MILLMAN, ISAAC

7304 Millman, Isaac. *Hidden Child* (4–7). Illus. 2005, Farrar $18.00 (978-0-374-33071-2). The author relates his experiences as a child in World War II, when he was hidden in various homes in France to save him from the Nazis. (Rev: BL 6/1–15/05*; SLJ 9/05) [921]

MOHAPATRA, JYOTIRMAYEE

7305 Woog, Adam. *Jyotirmayee Mohapatra: Advocate for India's Young Women* (4–8). Illus. Series: Young Heroes. 2006, Gale LB $27.45 (978-0-7377-3611-3). From a village in rural India, Mohapatra became worried at a young age about the challenges facing girls and young women; she went on to found the network of Meena Clubs for which she received the prestigious Youth Action Network award. (Rev: BL 1/1–15/07; SLJ 4/07) [921]

MONTESSORI, MARIA

7306 Shephard, Marie T. *Maria Montessori: Teacher of Teachers* (5–7). Illus. 1996, Lerner LB $30.35 (978-0-8225-4952-9). A biography of the Italian educator and her unusual teaching methods for the young. (Rev: BL 8/96; SLJ 9/96) [921]

PAYNE, LUCILLE M. W.

7307 Rice, Dorothy M., and Lucille Payne. *The Seventeenth Child* (7–12). 1998, Linnet LB $18.50 (978-0-208-02414-5). The story of an African American woman growing up in rural Virginia during the 1930s and 1940s, as recorded and edited by her daughter. (Rev: HBG 3/99; SLJ 1/99; VOYA 6/99) [921]

PEARY, MARIE AHNIGHITO

7308 Kirkpatrick, Katherine. *The Snow Baby: The Arctic Childhood of Robert E. Peary's Daring Daughter* (5–8). Illus. 2007, Holiday $16.95 (978-0-8234-1973-9). This engaging account of a child growing up partly among the Inuit and partly in her mother's nice home in the United States is based on the autobiography, published in 1934, of Marie Ahnighito Peary, daughter of explorer Robert E. Peary, who was born north of the Arctic Circle in 1893. (Rev: BL 4/15/07; SLJ 3/07) [921]

QUADRINO, JAMES

7309 Pearce, Q. L. *James Quadrino: Wildlife Protector* (4–7). Series: Young Heroes. 2006, Gale LB $23.70 (978-0-7377-3612-0). At age 13, James Quadrino took it upon himself to save a fire-ravaged bird sanctuary by building nesting boxes. (Rev: SLJ 6/07) [921]

REISS, JOHANNA

7310 Reiss, Johanna. *The Upstairs Room* (7–10). 1972, HarperCollins $19.99 (978-0-690-85127-4); paper $6.99 (978-0-06-447043-8). The author's story of her years spent hiding from the Nazis in occupied Holland. Followed by *The Journey Back* (1976). (Rev: BL 3/1/88) [921]

RHODES-COURTER, ASHLEY

7311 Rhodes-Courter, Ashley. *Three Little Words* (8–12). 2008, Atheneum $17.99 (978-1-4169-4806-3). A product of the U.S. foster care system describes her childhood with foster parents, some who were kind, others who were abusive; a disturbing story, explicitly told. (Rev: BL 1/1–15/08; LMC 2/08; SLJ 1/08) [362.73]

RUNYAN, BRENT

7312 Runyon, Brent. *The Burn Journals* (8–12). 2004, Random LB $19.99 (978-0-375-82621-4). In this powerful memoir, Runyon recounts his journey to recovery from life-threatening burns suffered in a teenage suicide attempt. (Rev: BL 6/1–15/04; SLJ 11/04) [362.28]

SIEGAL, ARANKA

7313 Siegal, Aranka. *Memories of Babi* (4–7). 2008, Farrar $16.00 (978-0-374-39978-8). The author recalls her pleasant, simple life as a child in Hungary and her closeness to her Jewish grandmother in the years preceding those covered in *Upon the Head of a Goat* (1981). (Rev: BL 12/15/07; HB 9–10/08) [947.7]

SIMMONS, RUSSELL

7314 Lommel, Cookie. *Russell Simmons* (7–10). Illus. Series: Hip-Hop Stars. 2007, Chelsea House LB $30.00 (978-0-7910-9467-9). Lommel includes lots of hip-hop history in this profile of the founder of Def Jam records. (Rev: BL 3/1/08) [921]

STEINER, MATTHEW

7315 Warren, Andrea. *Escape from Saigon: How a Vietnam War Orphan Became an American Boy* (5–12). Illus. 2004, Farrar $17.00 (978-0-374-32224-3). An inspiring account of a young Amerasian war orphan's long journey from Vietnam to a new and successful life in the United States; Long was part of the 1975 Operation Babylift and took the name of Matt Steiner when he was adopted by an American family. (Rev: BL 6/1–15/04*; SLJ 10/04) [959.704]

SUGIHARA, CHIUNE

7316 Gold, Alison L. *A Special Fate: Chiune Sugihara: Hero of the Holocaust* (5–10). 2000, Scholastic paper $15.95 (978-0-590-39525-0). The life story of the Japanese diplomat who saved thousands of Jewish lives during the Holocaust while he was stationed in Lithuania. (Rev: BCCB 5/00; BL 4/1/00; HB 5–6/00; HBG 10/00; SLJ 5/00; VOYA 6/00) [921]

SUZUKI, SHINICHI

7317 Collins, David R. *Dr. Shinichi Suzuki: Teaching Music from the Heart* (4–8). 2001, Morgan Reynolds LB $23.95 (978-1-883846-49-7). This account covers Suzuki's childhood, his interest in music, and his development of a successful method of teaching music, especially the violin, to young children. (Rev: BL 12/15/01; HBG 3/02; SLJ 4/02; VOYA 10/03) [780]

SWADOS, ELIZABETH

7318 Swados, Elizabeth. *My Depression: A Picture Book* (8–12). Illus. 2005, Hyperion $16.95 (978-1-4013-0789-9). In a candid yet entertaining cartoon picture-book format, Swados reveals her struggles with severe depression. (Rev: BL 3/15/05) [818]

TAMANG, JHALAK MAN

7319 Miller, Raymond H. *Jhalak Man Tamang: Slave Labor Whistleblower* (4–7). Series: Young Heroes. 2006, Gale LB $23.70 (978-0-7377-3616-8). This biography chronicles the life of Tamang, who was able to escape a life as a child weaving carpets in Nepal and bring to light the abuses of the industry. (Rev: SLJ 6/07) [921]

VINCENT, ERIN

7320 Vincent, Erin. *Grief Girl* (8–11). 2007, Delacorte $15.99 (978-0-385-73353-3). An account of how the author, then 14, and her siblings coped with the deaths of their parents in a car crash in 1983. (Rev: BCCB 4/07; BL 2/1/07; LMC 8–9/07; SLJ 2/07) [155.9]

WEINSTEIN, LAUREN

7321 Weinstein, Lauren. *Girl Stories* (7–10). Illus. 2006, Holt paper $16.95 (978-0-8050-7863-3). Episodic graphic novel-format vignettes paint a vivid portrait of the author's 8th- and 9th-grade years. (Rev: BL 3/15/06; SLJ 7/06; VOYA 4/06) [741.5]

WONG, LI KENG

7322 Wong, Li Keng. *Good Fortune: My Journey to Gold Mountain* (4–7). 2006, Peachtree $14.95 (978-1-56145-367-2). Wong, who migrated to the United States from China with her mother and sister in 1933, writes about the challenges of adjusting to a new culture. (Rev: BL 3/1/06; SLJ 7/06) [979.4]

YEBOAH, EMMANUEL OFOSU

7323 Currie-Mcghee, Leanne K. *Emmanuel Ofosu Yeboah: Champion for Ghana's Disabled* (4–7). Series: Young Heroes. 2006, Gale LB $23.70 (978-0-7377-3614-4). The inspiring story of a disabled Ghanaian who fought for equal rights in a culture that discriminated against the physically challenged. (Rev: SLJ 6/07)

YU, CHUN

7324 Yu, Chun. *Little Green: Growing Up During the Chinese Cultural Revolution* (7–10). 2005, Simon & Schuster $15.95 (978-0-689-86943-3). Chun Yu, who was born the year that China's Cultural Revolution began, recounts in poetry what life was like during one of the most tumultuous periods in Chinese history. (Rev: BL 1/1–15/05; SLJ 3/05; VOYA 10/05) [951.05]

ZENATTI, VALÉRIE

7325 Zenatti, Valérie. *When I Was a Soldier* (8–11). Trans. by Adriana Hunter. 2005, Bloomsbury $16.95 (978-1-58234-978-7). In this compelling memoir, Valérie Zenatti, an immigrant to Israel from France, chronicles her two years of compulsory service in the Israeli army. (Rev: BCCB 7–8/05; BL 5/1/05*; SLJ 5/05) [921]

The Arts and Entertainment

General and Miscellaneous

7326 Marcovitz, Hal. *Anime* (6–9). Illus. Series: Eye on Art. 2007, Gale LB $32.45 (978-1-59018-995-5). Fans of Japanese comics will enjoy this history of the genre. (Rev: BL 2/15/08) [791.43]

7327 O'Kane, Bernard. *Treasures of Islam: Artistic Glories of the Muslim World* (8–12). Illus. 2007, Sterling $35.00 (978-1-84483-483-9). With about 170 color photographs, this handsome volume traces Islamic art and architecture from the 7th to 19th centuries and discusses political and religious aspects throughout. (Rev: BL 10/1/07) [709]

Architecture and Building

General and Miscellaneous

7328 Arbogast, Joan Marie. *Buildings in Disguise: Architecture That Looks Like Animals, Food, and Other Things* (4–7). 2004, Boyds Mills $16.95 (978-1-59078-099-2). Buildings in the shapes of milk bottles, elephants, wigwams, and baskets are among the wonders shown in many period and contemporary photographs. (Rev: BL 11/1/04; SLJ 1/05) [720]

7329 Glenn, Patricia Brown. *Under Every Roof: A Kid's Style and Field Guide to the Architecture of American Houses* (5–8). 1993, Preservation $16.95 (978-0-89133-214-5). An introduction to the history and styles of architecture of American homes, with a look at more than 70 houses. (Rev: BL 7/94; SLJ 6/94) [728]

7330 Pascoe, Elaine, ed. *The Pentagon* (4–7). Series: Super Structures of the World. 2003, Gale LB $24.95 (978-1-56711-867-4). An architectural tour of the Pentagon, headquarters of the U.S. Department of Defense. (Rev: SLJ 4/04) [355.6]

7331 Rubin, Susan G. *There Goes the Neighborhood: Ten Buildings People Loved to Hate* (4–7). 2001, Holiday $18.95 (978-0-8234-1435-2). Many buildings create an uproar from their earliest design but later become nostalgic favorites, among them the Eiffel Tower and Guggenheim Museum, which are profiled here in an absorbing, colorful account that discusses materials and methods of construction. (Rev: BCCB 9/01; BL 8/01; HBG 3/02; SLJ 9/01; VOYA 10/01) [720]

History of Architecture

7332 Curlee, Lynn. *Parthenon* (5–8). Illus. by author. 2004, Simon & Schuster $17.95 (978-0-689-84490-4). A beautifully composed overview of the construction and history of the temple built by the ancient Greeks to honor the goddess Athena. (Rev: BL 9/15/04*; HB 7–8/04; SLJ 6/04) [726]

7333 De Medeiros, James. *Parthenon* (6–9). Illus. Series: Structural Wonders. 2007, Weigl LB $26.00 (978-1-59036-727-8); paper $7.95 (978-1-59036-728-5). This interesting account of the construction of the Parthenon also discusses its current status and includes excellent full-color photographs. (Rev: SLJ 12/07) [726]

7334 DuTemple, Lesley A. *The Pantheon* (6–9). Illus. Series: Great Building Feats. 2003, Lerner LB $27.93 (978-0-8225-0376-7). An interesting look at the Pantheon, with background information on Rome at the time of its construction and Thomas Jefferson's admiration of the design. (Rev: HBG 10/03; LMC 4–5/03; SLJ 4/03*) [726]

7335 Lace, William W. *The Medieval Cathedral* (7–10). Series: Building History. 2000, Lucent LB $32.45 (978-1-56006-720-7). The whys and hows of cathedral building in the Middle Ages are explained with many color illustrations, diagrams, and examples of existing structures. (Rev: BL 4/15/01) [726]

7336 Macaulay, David. *Building the Book Cathedral* (5–9). 1999, Houghton $29.95 (978-0-395-92147-0). The author retells the fascinating story behind the creation of the original *Cathedral* book 25 years ago and adds numerous changes as he leads a tour of the cathedral, such as alterations in scale and page placement. (Rev: BCCB 12/99; BL 11/15/99; HB 9–10/99; SLJ 9/99) [726]

7337 Macaulay, David. *Castle* (5–8). Illus. by author. 1977, Houghton $20.00 (978-0-395-25784-5); paper $9.95 (978-0-395-32920-7). Another of the author's brilliant, detailed works, this one on the planning and building of a Welsh castle. [940.1]

7338 Macaulay, David. *Cathedral: The Story of Its Construction* (6–8). Illus. by author. 1973, Houghton $18.00 (978-0-395-17513-2). Gothic architecture as seen through a detailed examination of the construction of an imaginary cathedral. [726]

7339 Macaulay, David. *Mill* (5–8). Illus. by author. 1983, Houghton $19.00 (978-0-395-34830-7); paper $9.95 (978-0-395-52019-2). Rhode Island textile mills of the 19th century are described in text and excellent drawings. [690]

7340 Macaulay, David. *Mosque* (6–12). Illus. 2003, Houghton $18.00 (978-0-618-24034-0). Macaulay follows a 16th-century mosque through initial design and planning, construction, and the uses of the finished structure and all its associated support buildings. (Rev: BL 10/1/03*; HB 11–12/03; SLJ 11/03*) [726]

7341 Macaulay, David. *Pyramid* (7–12). Illus. 1975, Houghton $20.00 (978-0-395-21407-7); paper $9.95 (978-0-395-32121-8). In beautiful line drawings, the author describes how an ancient Egyptian pyramid was constructed. [726]

7342 Mann, Elizabeth. *The Parthenon: The Height of Greek Civilization* (4–7). Illus. by Yuan Lee. 2006, Mikaya $22.95 (978-1-931414-15-9). The engineering feats involved in the construction of the Parthenon are placed in historical and cultural context; includes a foldout spread, a useful map, and many illustrations. (Rev: BL 12/1/06; SLJ 3/07) [938.5]

7343 Nardo, Don. *Artistry in Stone: Great Structures of Ancient Egypt* (6–10). Illus. Series: The Lucent Library of Historical Eras. 2005, Gale LB $32.45 (978-1-59018-661-9). Photographs, reproductions, and film and documentary stills illustrate this well-documented examination of massive ancient Egyptian structures such as the pyramids and the Sphinx. (Rev: SLJ 11/05) [932]

7344 Nardo, Don. *Greek Temples* (5–7). Illus. Series: Famous Structures. 2002, Watts LB $25.50

(978-0-531-12035-4). Nardo looks at the construction, elements, use, and importance of ancient Greek temples, with illustrations. (Rev: BL 9/1/02; SLJ 8/02) [726]

7345 Nardo, Don. *The Medieval Castle* (6–10). Illus. Series: Building History. 1997, Lucent LB $28.70 (978-1-56006-430-5). This study presents a history of the medieval European castle, including its structure, design, usage, and construction. (Rev: SLJ 5/98) [940.1]

7346 Shuter, Jane. *The Acropolis* (5–7). Series: Visiting the Past. 1999, Heinemann LB $24.22 (978-1-57572-855-1). As well as describing the main buildings found in ancient Greece, this account uses double-page spreads to introduce the daily life and culture of the Athenians. (Rev: SLJ 3/00) [938]

7347 Weaver, Janice. *Building America* (5–8). Illus. by Bonnie Shemie. 2002, Tundra $17.95 (978-0-88776-606-0). This brief history of architecture in America, from the 17th century to today, features detailed renderings, an illustrated timeline, and a useful glossary. (Rev: HBG 3/03; SLJ 5/03) [721]

7348 Webster, Christine. *Great Wall of China* (6–9). Illus. Series: Structural Wonders. 2007, Weigl LB $26.00 (978-1-59036-723-0); paper $7.95 (978-1-59036-724-7). This interesting account of the construction of the Great Wall also discusses its current status and includes excellent full-color photographs. (Rev: SLJ 12/07) [623]

Various Types of Buildings

7349 Forward, Toby. *Shakespeare's Globe: An Interactive Pop-up Theatre* (5–8). Illus. by Juan Wijngaard. 2005, Candlewick $19.99 (978-0-7636-2694-5). A large-format pop-up model of the Globe Theatre, with narrative by a Shakespeare colleague and scenes from Shakespeare's plays. (Rev: BL 5/1/05; SLJ 11/05) [792]

7350 George, Charles. *Pyramids* (5–9). Series: Mysterious and Unknown. 2007, Reference Point LB $24.95 (978-1-60152-027-2). Pyramids around the world are addressed in this well-written text with color photographs; useful for reports. (Rev: SLJ 2/08)

Painting, Sculpture, and Photography

General and Miscellaneous

7351 Aldana, Patricia, ed. *Under the Spell of the Moon: Art for Children from the World's Great Illustrators* (6–12). Trans. by Stan Dragland. 2004, Groundwood $25.00 (978-0-88899-559-9). Artwork by children's book illustrators from around the world celebrates children's literature and the work of the International Board on Books for Young People. (Rev: BL 12/15/04; SLJ 1/05) [741.6]

7352 Ancona, George. *Murals: Walls That Sing* (5–8). Illus. 2003, Marshall Cavendish $17.95 (978-0-7614-5131-0). A photoessay showing murals stretching back from today's urban frescos to the cave paintings of Lascaux. (Rev: BL 4/15/03; HBG 4/04; SLJ 5/03) [751.7]

7353 *Artist to Artist: 23 Major Illustrators Talk to Children about Their Art* (5–8). Illus. 2007, Philomel $30.00 (978-0-399-24600-5). More than 20 children's book illustrators (including Quentin Blake, Leo Lionni, and Tomie dePaola) contribute creative self-portraits and insightful thoughts to this beautiful gatefolded book. (Rev: BL 11/1/07; SLJ 10/07) [741.6]

7354 Billout, Guy. *Something's Not Quite Right* (6–12). Illus. 2002, Godine $20.95 (978-1-56792-230-1). The detailed illustrations in this book, reminiscent of Dali and Escher, offer intriguing perspectives on the world and will encourage creative writing. (Rev: BL 2/15/03; HB 1–2/03; HBG 3/03; SLJ 1/03) [741.6]

7355 Capek, Michael. *Artistic Trickery: The Tradition of Trompe l'Oeil Art* (5–8). Illus. 1995, Lerner LB $22.60 (978-0-8225-2064-1). The art of creating images so perfect that the viewer thinks they are real is introduced, with many historical and contemporary examples. (Rev: BCCB 7–8/95; BL 6/1–15/95; SLJ 7/95) [758]

7356 Coyne, Jennifer Tarr. *Come Look with Me: Discovering Women Artists for Children* (4–7). Illus. Series: Come Look with Me. 2005, Lickle $15.95 (978-1-890674-08-3). Beautifully reproduced examples of works by women artists are paired with brief biographical information and questions that direct the reader's attention to different aspects of art. (Rev: BL 5/1/05; SLJ 6/05) [709]

7357 Delafosse, Claude. *Landscapes* (4–7). Illus. Series: First Discovery Art. 1996, Scholastic $11.95 (978-0-590-50216-0). The art and techniques of landscape painting are introduced, with many examples from the masters in various historical periods. (Rev: BL 6/1–15/96; SLJ 7/96) [750]

7358 Delafosse, Claude. *Paintings* (4–7). Illus. Series: First Discovery Art. 1996, Scholastic $11.95 (978-0-590-55201-1). A general introduction to painting, with many reproductions and lessons in art appreciation. (Rev: BL 6/1–15/96; SLJ 7/96) [750]

7359 de Rynck, Patrick, ed. *How to Read a Painting: Lessons from the Old Masters* (8–12). Illus. 2004, Abrams $35.00 (978-0-8109-5576-9). Introduces readers to the symbols, themes, and motifs that aid understanding of the great masters' art; two-page spreads display 150 paintings and frescoes. (Rev: BL 12/15/04) [753]

7360 Fritz, Jean. *Leonardo's Horse* (4–7). Illus. by Hudson Talbott. 2001, Putnam $18.99 (978-0-399-23576-4). The story of a Leonardo da Vinci sculpture that was begun in 1493 and finally completed — thanks to the efforts of Charles Dent — in 1999, along with biographical information about da Vinci and examples of his work. (Rev: BCCB 10/01; BL 10/15/01; HB 9–10/01; HBG 3/02; SLJ 9/01) [730]

7361 Ganz, Nicholas. *Graffiti World: Street Art from Five Continents* (8–12). Ed. by Tristan Manco.

Illus. 2004, Abrams $35.00 (978-0-8109-4979-9). Graffiti from around the world is organized by continent and then by artist, with more than 2,000 color photos showing the common themes and wonderful inventiveness of these artists. (Rev: BL 1/1–15/05; SLJ 5/05) [751.7]

7362 Greenway, Shirley. *Art: An A–Z Guide* (6–12). 2000, Watts LB $34.00 (978-0-531-11729-3). An alphabetical introduction to art history and techniques, with full-color photographs. (Rev: SLJ 4/01)

7363 Hand, John Oliver. *National Gallery of Art: Master Paintings from the Collection* (8–12). Illus. 2004, Abrams $60.00 (978-0-8109-5619-3). Four hundred paintings from the National Gallery serve as the base for a satisfying review of European and American art. (Rev: BL 11/15/04) [750]

7364 Kallen, Stuart A. *Photography* (7–12). Illus. Series: Eye on Art. 2007, Gale LB $32.45 (978-1-59018-986-3). Tracing the history of the camera and of photography as an art form, this volume includes plenty of photographs that illustrate concepts and styles. (Rev: BL 11/1/07; LMC 2/08; SLJ 12/07) [770]

7365 *Life: The Platinum Anniversary Collection* (7–12). Illus. 2006, Time-Life $29.95 (978-1-933405-17-9). This is a showcase of the best of 70 years of *Life* photography. (Rev: BL 11/15/06) [070.4]

7366 Nilsen, Anna. *Art Auction Mystery* (5–8). Illus. 2005, Kingfisher $16.95 (978-0-7534-5842-6). Wannabe art sleuths are challenged to find forgeries hidden in a selection of world-famous paintings. (Rev: BL 11/1/05; SLJ 1/06; VOYA 12/05) [759]

7367 Nilsen, Anna. *The Great Art Scandal: Solve the Crime, Save the Show!* (4–9). Illus. 2003, Kingfisher $16.95 (978-0-7534-5587-6). Readers must solve a mystery involving an art exhibition in this comic-book-format work that introduces many famous paintings and artists. (Rev: SLJ 3/04) [759.06]

7368 Raczka, Bob. *Unlikely Pairs: Fun with Famous Works of Art* (4–10). 2005, Millbrook LB $23.93 (978-0-7613-2936-7); paper $9.95 (978-0-7613-2378-5). Raczka pairs famous works from different eras and styles (Rodin's "The Thinker" appears to be considering a move on Klee's chessboard, for example); a closing catalog offers factual information. (Rev: SLJ 12/05) [750]

7369 Raczka, Bob. *Where in the World? Around the Globe in 13 Works of Art* (5–8). Illus. Series: Art Adventures. 2007, Lerner LB $23.93 (978-0-8225-6371-6). Full-page reproductions and lively text introduce 13 famous works of art, with information on the artist. (Rev: BL 6/1–15/07; SLJ 8/07) [709]

7370 Roalf, Peggy. *Dogs* (5–8). Illus. Series: Looking at Paintings. 1993, Hyperion paper $6.95 (978-

1-56282-530-0). Various ways that dogs have been represented in paintings are reproduced, with explanations, in this attractive book on art appreciation. (Rev: BL 2/15/94; SLJ 2/94) [758.3]

7371 Ross, Stewart. *Art and Architecture* (5–8). Series: Medieval Realms. 2004, Gale LB $29.95 (978-1-59018-534-6). Romanesque, Gothic, Moorish, and Islamic art and architecture are covered in this well-organized and well-illustrated volume that includes discussions of houses of the poor as well as castles, manors, monasteries, and cathedrals. (Rev: SLJ 3/05) [720]

7372 Sousa, Jean. *Faces, Places, and Inner Spaces* (5–8). Illus. 2006, Abrams $18.95 (978-0-8109-5966-8). The director of interpretive exhibitions and family programs at the Art Institute of Chicago introduces a variety of works — portraits, landscapes, and abstract pieces — and asks questions that stimulate analysis. (Rev: BL 5/15/06; SLJ 7/06) [701]

7373 White, Matt. *Cameras on the Battlefield: Photos of War* (5–7). Series: High Five Reading. 2002, Capstone LB $23.93 (978-0-7368-4004-0). For reluctant readers, this is an appealing look at photographs of war, both those that celebrate war and those that document its horrors. (Rev: SLJ 8/02) [779.9355]

History of Art

7374 Barter, James. *A Renaissance Painter's Studio* (5–9). Series: The Working Life. 2003, Gale LB $29.95 (978-1-59018-178-2). An exploration of daily life for a painter at a time when art was growing in social importance. (Rev: HBG 10/03; SLJ 5/03) [759.5]

7375 Baskett, John. *The Horse in Art* (8–12). Illus. 2006, Yale $45.00 (978-0-300-11740-0). Representations of horses in both two- and three-dimensional art are presented here, from ancient Greek and Roman battle scenes to medieval, Renaissance, Baroque, 19th-century, and modern-day works, including pieces by Stubbs, Rubens, and Remington. (Rev: BL 11/1/06) [704.94]

7376 Belloli, Andrea. *Exploring World Art* (7–12). Illus. 1999, J. Paul Getty Museum $27.50 (978-0-89236-510-4). Using examples from world art and artifacts, this work introduces a variety of media and images under such chapter headings as "Daily Life" and "History and Myth." (Rev: BL 1/1–15/00; HBG 4/00; SLJ 4/00) [709]

7377 Bingham, Jane. *Science and Technology* (4–7). Series: Through Artists' Eyes. 2006, Raintree LB $32.86 (978-1-4109-2241-0). A brief but interesting exploration of the ways in which artists have documented the progress of science and technology over the years. Also use *Landscape and the Environment* and *Society and Class* (both 2006). (Rev: SLJ 1/07)

7378 Capek, Michael. *Murals: Cave, Cathedral, to Street* (5–8). Illus. 1996, Lerner LB $28.80 (978-0-8225-2065-8). A history of mural painting, from cave painting to such modern masters as Diego Rivera. (Rev: BL 6/1–15/96; SLJ 10/96; VOYA 10/96) [751.7]

7379 Chrisp, Peter. *Ancient Rome* (4–8). Series: History in Art. 2004, Raintree LB $29.93 (978-1-4109-0520-8). A look at what art can reveal about the culture and technology of a society. (Rev: SLJ 4/05) [709]

7380 Demilly, Christian. *Pop Art* (6–9). Illus. Series: Adventures in Art. 2007, Prestel $14.95 (978-3-7913-3894-1). Beautiful reproductions of many of the most important and most memorable works of Pop Art will draw readers in to this book, which traces the early-20th-century movement from its origins to its influence. (Rev: BL 11/1/07; SLJ 4/08) [709]

7381 D'Harcourt, Claire. *Masterpieces Up Close: Western Painting from the 14th to 20th Centuries* (4–8). Trans. from French by Shoshanna Kirk. Series: Up Close. 2006, Chronicle $22.95 (978-0-8118-5403-0). An oversize volume that challenges readers to analyze major works of Western art. (Rev: SLJ 7/06) [759]

7382 Halliwell, Sarah, ed. *Impressionism and Postimpressionism: Artists, Writers, and Composers* (6–9). Illus. Series: Who and When? 1998, Raintree LB $19.98 (978-0-8172-4730-0). Clear reproductions and a concise text introduce such artists as Pissarro, Monet, Renoir, Gauguin, and van Gogh as well as writers including Zola and the composer Debussy. (Rev: BL 12/15/97) [700]

7383 Harris, Nathaniel. *Renaissance Art* (6–10). Series: Art and Artists. 1994, Thomson Learning LB $24.26 (978-1-56847-217-1). A general overview of this rich period in art history, with illustrations of paintings, sculpture, and architecture. (Rev: BL 11/15/94; SLJ 10/94) [709]

7384 Heslewood, Juliet. *The History of Western Painting: A Young Person's Guide* (5–9). Illus. 1995, Raintree LB $25.68 (978-0-8172-4000-4). Beginning with cave paintings, this large-format book gives a cursory overview of Western painting, with several pages devoted to contemporary artists and movements. (Rev: BL 1/1–15/96; SLJ 12/95) [759]

7385 Heslewood, Juliet. *The History of Western Sculpture* (5–9). Illus. 1995, Raintree LB $25.68 (978-0-8172-4001-1). This oversize, heavily illustrated book traces the history of Western sculpture from the ancient Greeks to contemporary masters. (Rev: BL 1/1–15/96; SLJ 12/95) [730]

7386 Khalili, Nasser D. *Islamic Art and Culture: A Visual History* (8–12). Illus. 2006, Overlook $60.00 (978-1-58567-839-6). This is a large and varied collection of examples of Islamic art, ranging from carpets and textiles, paintings, jewelry, and lacquer to calligraphy, metal work, scientific instruments, and weapons; a good introduction to the culture of Islam. (Rev: BL 11/1/06) [709]

7387 Knapp, Ruthie, and Janice Lehmberg. *Greek and Roman Art* (5–9). Series: Off the Wall Museum Guides for Kids. 2001, Davis paper $9.95 (978-0-87192-549-7). Using many photographs, this account highlights a number of art objects, explains relevant terms associated with them, describes their uses, and gives details on Greek and Roman culture. (Rev: BL 8/1/01) [936]

7388 Knapp, Ruthie, and Janice Lehmberg. *Impressionist Art* (5–9). Illus. Series: Off the Wall Museum Guides for Kids. 1999, Davis paper $9.95 (978-0-87192-385-1). This pocket-size guide supplies an overview of Impressionism and brief introductions to major artists, including Sisley and Monet. (Rev: BL 1/1–15/99) [709.03]

7389 Knapp, Ruthie, and Janice Lehmberg. *Modern Art* (5–9). Series: Off the Wall Museum Guides for Kids. 2001, Davis paper $9.95 (978-0-87192-458-2). A lively and colorful survey of 20th-century art including examples from expressionists, cubists, surrealists, and pop artists. (Rev: BL 8/1/01) [709]

7390 Langley, Andrew. *Ancient Greece* (4–8). Series: History in Art. 2004, Raintree LB $29.93 (978-1-4109-0517-8). A look at what art can reveal about the culture and technology of a society. (Rev: SLJ 4/05) [709]

7391 Mason, Antony. *A History of Western Art: From Prehistory to the 20th Century* (7–10). Illus. 2007, Abrams $22.50 (978-0-8109-9421-8). A sweeping overview of important sculpture, architecture, painting, and other works from Western culture from the ancient to the postmodern, presented in a pleasing, uncrowded design. (Rev: BL 2/1/08; SLJ 4/08) [709]

7392 Mason, Antony. *In the Time of Michelangelo: The Renaissance Period* (7–10). Series: Art Around the World. 2001, Millbrook LB $23.90 (978-0-7613-2455-3). Full of full-color reproductions, this volume not only looks at the work of major artists of the Renaissance but also profiles artists in other parts of the world during the 15th and 16th centuries. Also use *In the Time of Renoir: The Impressionist Era* (2001). (Rev: HBG 10/02; SLJ 3/02) [709]

7393 Opie, Mary-Jane. *Sculpture* (7–12). Series: Eyewitness Art. 1994, DK $16.95 (978-1-56458-613-1). A handsome book filled with color illustrations introducing the world of sculpture, its history, and its various forms and materials. (Rev: BL 12/1/94; SLJ 6/95; VOYA 5/95) [730]

7394 Powell, Jillian. *Ancient Art* (6–10). Series: Art and Artists. 1994, Thomson Learning LB $24.26 (978-1-56847-216-4). This book covers the ancient civilizations and their contributions to the history of art. (Rev: BL 11/15/94; SLJ 10/94) [709]

7395 Rebman, Renee C. *The Sistine Chapel* (7–10). Series: Building History. 2000, Lucent LB $28.70 (978-1-56006-640-8). This account includes material on Michelangelo's original creation, his conflicts with the Pope, and the recent restorations of the ceiling. (Rev: BL 9/15/00; HBG 3/01) [945]

7396 Robinson, Shannon. *Cubism* (6–12). Series: Movements in Art. 2005, Creative Education LB $31.35 (978-1-58341-347-0). A review of cubism from the works of Picasso and Braque through the movement's influence on sculpture and architecture, with large, clear reproductions. (Rev: SLJ 2/06)

7397 Sabbeth, Carol. *Monet and the Impressionists for Kids* (6–9). Illus. 2002, Chicago Review paper $17.95 (978-1-55652-397-7). Sabbeth introduces the life and work of seven impressionist artists — Monet, Renoir, Degas, Cassatt, Cezanne, Gauguin, and Seurat — and provides 21 related activities. (Rev: BL 7/02; SLJ 6/02) [759.05]

7398 Salvi, Francesco. *The Impressionists*. Rev. ed. (5–8). Illus. by L. R. Galante. Series: Art Masters. 2008, Oliver LB $24.95 (978-1-934545-03-4). A look at the work of the main artists contributing to this movement: Manet, Monet, Renoir, Degas, Cezanne, Pissaro, Sisley, Morisot, Cassatt, Guillaumin, and Caillebotte; the appealing design will please report writers. (Rev: BL 4/15/08) [759.054]

7399 Sandler, Martin W. *Photography: An Illustrated History* (6–12). Illus. 2002, Oxford $39.99 (978-0-19-512608-2). An overview of photography's major figures and developments, from its invention to new technologies, featuring many photographs. (Rev: BL 4/15/02; HBG 3/03; SLJ 6/02; VOYA 4/02) [770.9]

7400 Steffens, Bradley. *Photography: Preserving the Past* (6–10). Series: Encyclopedia of Discovery and Invention. 1991, Lucent LB $52.44 (978-1-56006-212-7). A history of photography that describes its impact on the modern world and profiles men and women involved in it. (Rev: BL 4/15/92) [770]

7401 *30,000 Years of Art: The Story of Human Creativity across Time and Space* (7–12). 2007, Phaidon $49.95 (978-0-7148-4789-4). Arranged chronologically, 1,000 beautifully reproduced pieces of art illustrate the evolution of creativity around the world. (Rev: BL 11/1/07) [700]

7402 Wakin, Edward, and Daniel Wakin. *Photos That Made U.S. History, Vol. 1: From the Civil War Era to the Atomic Age* (6–9). 1993, Walker LB $13.85 (978-0-8027-8231-1). Photographs that altered the perceptions of people and governments during times of military and social crisis. Also use *Photos That Made U.S. History, Vol. 2: From the Cold War to the Space Age* (1993). (Rev: BL 5/1/94; SLJ 2/94) [973.9]

7403 Zuffi, Stefano. *The Cat in Art* (8–12). Trans. by Simon Jones. 2007, Abrams $35.00 (978-0-8109-9328-0). A survey of art featuring cats serves to introduce a wide variety of artists — from Raphael and Rembrandt to Picasso and Warhol — and art forms. (Rev: BL 5/1/07) [704.9]

Regions

Africa

7404 Finley, Carol. *The Art of African Masks: Exploring Cultural Traditions* (5–9). Series: Art Around the World. 1999, Lerner LB $23.93 (978-0-8225-2078-8). This account on African mask making past and present focuses on the western Sudan, the Guinea Coast, and Central Africa. (Rev: HBG 10/99; SLJ 11/99) [745.5]

7405 Knapp, Ruthie, and Janice Lehmberg. *Egyptian Art* (5–9). Illus. Series: Off the Wall Museum Guides for Kids. 1999, Davis paper $9.95 (978-0-87192-384-4). This pocket-size art appreciation book discusses mummies, sculpture, hieroglyphs, and other artifacts from Egyptian art. (Rev: BL 1/1–15/99) [709.32]

Asia and the Middle East

7406 Barber, Nicola. *Islamic Art and Culture* (5–8). Illus. Series: World Art and Culture. 2005, Raintree LB $32.86 (978-1-4109-1105-6). High-quality color photographs document the architecture, sculpture, painting, pottery, music, dance, and other art forms found in the Islamic world from early times to the present. (Rev: BL 4/1/04)

7407 Bingham, Jane. *Indian Art and Culture* (5–8). Illus. Series: World Art and Culture. 2004, Raintree LB $29.99 (978-0-7398-6607-8). High-quality color photographs document the architecture, sculpture, painting, pottery, music, dance, and other art forms found in India from early times to the present. Also use *Aboriginal Art and Culture* (2004). (Rev: BL 4/1/04; SLJ 2/04) [709]

7408 Finley, Carol. *Aboriginal Art of Australia: Exploring Cultural Traditions* (5–9). Series: Art Around the World. 1999, Lerner LB $23.93 (978-0-8225-2076-4). The author covers aboriginal art, aboriginal beliefs, and the contemporary works that reflect the Australian natives' struggle for equality. (Rev: HBG 3/00; SLJ 11/99) [701]

7409 Finley, Carol. *Art of Japan: Wood Block Color Prints* (6–9). Series: Art Around the World. 1998, Lerner LB $28.75 (978-0-8225-2077-1). This richly illustrated book describes the 18th- and 19th-century wood block prints made in Japan, with background material on Japanese history and culture. (Rev: BL 4/1/99; HBG 3/99) [769.952]

7410 Hibbert, Clare. *Chinese Art and Culture* (5–8). Illus. Series: World Art and Culture. 2005, Raintree LB $29.99 (978-1-4109-1107-0). High-quality color photographs document the architecture, sculpture, painting, pottery, music, dance, and other art forms found in China from early times to the present. (Rev: BL 4/1/04)

7411 Khanduri, Kamini. *Japanese Art and Culture* (5–8). Illus. Series: World Art and Culture. 2004, Raintree LB $29.99 (978-0-7398-6609-2). High-quality color photographs document the architecture, sculpture, painting, pottery, music, dance, and other art forms found in Japan from early times to the present. (Rev: BL 4/1/04)

Europe

7412 Blanquet, Claire-Helene. *Miró: Earth and Sky* (5–7). Trans. from French by John Goodman. Illus. Series: Art for Children. 1994, Chelsea LB $15.95 (978-0-7910-2813-1). Using a conversational style and some fictitious characters, the life and works of the famous 20th-century French painter Miró are introduced. (Rev: SLJ 12/94) [709]

7413 Impelluso, Lucia. *Nature and Its Symbols* (8–12). Trans. by Stephen Sartarelli. Illus. 2004, J. Paul Getty Museum paper $24.95 (978-0-89236-772-6). A helpful guide to the symbols found in European painters' depictions of the natural world from the 14th through the 17th centuries. (Rev: BL 12/15/04) [704.9]

7414 Jockel, Nils. *Bruegel's Tower of Babel: The Builder with the Red Hat* (4–7). Illus. Series: Adventures in Art. 1998, Prestel $14.95 (978-3-7913-1941-4). A detailed analysis of Pieter Bruegel's surreal masterpiece, using one of the characters in the painting to supply a point of view and an examination of the meaning of its contents. (Rev: BL 8/98; SLJ 8/98) [759.9493]

7415 Loumaye, Jacqueline. *Chagall: My Sad and Joyous Village* (4–8). Trans. from French by John Goodman. Illus. by Veronique Boiry. Series: Art for Children. 1994, Chelsea LB $25.00 (978-0-7910-2807-0). A youngster learns about Chagall and his paintings from a violinist who grew up in the artist's home town in Russia. (Rev: SLJ 8/94) [709]

7416 Loumaye, Jacqueline. *Degas: The Painted Gesture* (4–8). Trans. from French by John Good-

man. Illus. by Nadine Massart. Series: Art for Children. 1994, Chelsea LB $25.00 (978-0-7910-2809-4). Using a series of workshops for children at the Orsay Museum (Paris) as a focus, the life and works of Degas are introduced. (Rev: SLJ 8/94) [709]

7417 Loumaye, Jacqueline. *Van Gogh: The Touch of Yellow* (4–8). Trans. from French by John Goodman. Illus. by Claudine Roucha. Series: Art for Children. 1994, Chelsea LB $31.00 (978-0-7910-2817-9). Two youngsters visit the museums in Amsterdam to learn about van Gogh, his tragic life, and his paintings. (Rev: SLJ 8/94) [709]

7418 Wenzel, Angela. *Rene Magritte: Now You See It — Now You Don't* (4–7). Illus. Series: Adventures in Art. 1998, Prestel $14.95 (978-3-7913-1873-8). An examination of some of the works of Belgian surrealist Rene Magritte. (Rev: BL 8/98; SLJ 8/98) [759.949]

North America

UNITED STATES

7419 Amaki, Amalia K., ed. *A Century of African American Art: The Paul R. Jones Collection* (8–12). Illus. 2004, Rutgers paper $29.95 (978-0-8135-3457-2). The work of 66 African American artists is showcased in this attractive volume that includes profiles and commentary. (Rev: BL 2/1/05) [704.03]

7420 Butler, Jerry. *A Drawing in the Sand: A Story of African American Art* (4–7). Illus. 1999, Zino $24.95 (978-1-55933-216-3). This oversize book contains two narratives; the first is a history of African American art and artists, the second, an autobiography of Jerry Butler, the African American artist. (Rev: BL 2/15/99*) [704.03]

7421 Clee, Paul. *Photography and the Making of the American West* (6–9). 2003, Linnet LB $27.50 (978-0-208-02512-8). Clee explores the photographs that documented the exploration of the West and the impact they had on Americans' perceptions. (Rev: SLJ 1/04; VOYA 4/04) [770]

7422 Cockcroft, James D., and Jane Canning. *Latino Visions: Contemporary Chicano, Puerto Rican, and Cuban American Artists* (7–12). 2000, Watts LB $26.00 (978-0-531-11312-7). The central themes of modern Latino art and the interests of individual artists are explored in this comprehensive survey that includes sections of full-color plates and many black-and-white illustrations and photographs. (Rev: SLJ 2/01; VOYA 6/01) [704.03]

7423 Cummings, Pat. *Talking with Artists, Vol. 3* (4–8). Series: Talking with Artists. 1999, Clarion $22.00 (978-0-395-89132-2). This is the third volume of interviews with children's artists and includes Peter Sis, Betsy Lewin, and Paul O. Zelinsky, with examples of their works. (Rev: BCCB

4/99; BL 3/15/99; HB 5–6/99; HBG 10/99; SLJ 4/99) [741.6]

7424 Curlee, Lynn. *Skyscraper* (4–7). Illus. 2007, Simon & Schuster $17.99 (978-0-689-84489-8). Accompanied by striking acrylic paintings, Curlee's detailed narrative explores the architectural history and engineering of skyscrapers. (Rev: BL 1/1–15/07; SLJ 3/07) [720]

7425 Curtis, Edward S., and Christopher Cardozo. *Edward S. Curtis: The Women* (8–12). Illus. 2005, Bulfinch $35.00 (978-0-8212-2895-1). This stunning volume showcases 100 of photographer Edward S. Curtis's portraits of Native American women. (Rev: BL 4/1/05) [779]

7426 Horwitz, Elinor Lander. *Contemporary American Folk Artists* (7–9). Illus. 1975, HarperCollins paper $3.95 (978-0-397-31627-4). An explanation of what folk art is plus samples of the products of many artists. [709]

7427 Howard, Nancy S. *Jacob Lawrence: American Scenes, American Struggles* (4–7). Illus. 1996, Davis $14.95 (978-0-87192-302-8). The narrative paintings of this contemporary African American artist are featured, with several suggested follow-up activities. (Rev: BL 11/1/96) [759.13]

7428 January, Brendan. *Native American Art and Culture* (5–8). Series: World Art and Culture. 2005, Raintree LB $32.86 (978-1-4109-1108-7). Pottery, textiles, carving, painting, textiles, and architecture are all discussed, along with body art, ceremonies, songs, and dances; many color photographs are included and a list of museums is appended. (Rev: BL 4/1/04; SLJ 6/05)

7429 Knapp, Ruthie, and Janice Lehmberg. *American Art* (5–9). Series: Off the Wall Museum Guides for Kids. 1999, Davis paper $9.95 (978-0-87192-386-8). An informal pocket-size art appreciation book that features portraits from several centuries of American art, plus various artifacts and furniture. (Rev: BL 1/1–15/99) [709.73]

7430 Panchyk, Richard. *American Folk Art for Kids: With 21 Activities* (6–12). 2004, Chicago Review paper $16.95 (978-1-55652-499-8). This historical survey of American folk art is supplemented by detailed instructions for projects that readers can make for themselves. (Rev: BL 11/1/04; SLJ 11/04) [745]

7431 Sandler, Martin W. *America Through the Lens: Photographers Who Changed the Nation* (6–9). Illus. 2005, Holt $18.95 (978-0-8050-7367-6). Profiles 11 American photographers whose inspiring works may have influenced how America perceives itself and its actions. (Rev: BL 9/1/05; SLJ 11/05; VOYA 8/05) [770]

7432 Slowik, Theresa J. *America's Art: Smithsonian American Art Museum* (8–12). Illus. 2006, Abrams $65.00 (978-0-8109-5532-5). An oversize volume showcasing some of the best-known works in the collection of the Smithsonian American Art Museum. (Rev: BL 3/15/06) [709]

South and Central America

7433 Chaplik, Dorothy. *Latin American Arts and Cultures* (5–8). Illus. 2001, Davis $26.95 (978-0-87192-547-3). An encompassing look at Latin American art, architecture, and culture, from pre-Columbian to present-day, complete with pronunciation guide and captioned reproductions or photographs on each page. (Rev: BL 11/1/01) [700.9]

7434 Lane, Kimberly. *Come Look with Me: Latin American Art* (4–8). Illus. Series: Come Look with Me. 2007, Charlesbridge $15.95 (978-1-890674-20-5). An oversize introduction to Latin American art over the last two centuries, with color reproductions and information on the artists' lives and techniques. (Rev: BL 8/07; LMC 1/08; SLJ 8/07) [709.8]

7435 Presilla, Maricel E. *Mola: Cuna Life Stories and Art* (5–7). Illus. 1996, Holt $17.95 (978-0-8050-3801-9). An examination of the life and art of the Cuna Indians, who live on islands off the coast of Panama. (Rev: BCCB 1/97; BL 10/1/96; SLJ 10/96) [305.48]

Decorative Arts

7436 Emert, Phyllis Raybin. *Art in Glass* (7–12). Series: Eye on Art. 2007, Gale LB $32.45 (978-1-59018-983-2). This book reviews the history of glassmaking from ancient times through Venetian glass to art nouveau and art deco to contemporary styles and techniques. (Rev: LMC 2/08; SLJ 12/07) [748]

Music

General and Miscellaneous

7437 Cefrey, Holly. *Backstage at a Music Video* (5–8). Illus. Series: Backstage Pass. 2003, Children's paper $6.95 (978-0-516-24386-3). The history of music videos is coupled with information on how they are financed and produced, along with guidance on careers in the music business. (Rev: BL 5/1/03) [791.45]

7438 Ench, Rick, and Jay Cravath. *North American Indian Music* (5–7). Illus. Series: Watts Library: Indians of the Americas. 2002, Watts LB $25.50 (978-0-531-11772-9); paper $8.95 (978-0-531-16230-9). This title looks at the importance of music in the rituals of North American Indian tribes and describes the forms of beat, rhythm, and melody, with illustrations, a glossary, bibliography, and timeline. (Rev: BL 7/02) [782.62]

7439 Evans, Roger. *How to Read Music: For Singing, Guitar, Piano, Organ, and Most Instruments* (8–12). 1979, Crown paper $10.00 (978-0-517-88438-6). An easily understood introduction to music notation and score reading for the beginner. [781.4]

7440 Garty, Judy. *Marching Band Competition* (6–9). Series: Let's Go Team. 2003, Mason Crest LB $19.95 (978-1-59084-539-4). Students considering joining a marching band will learn about the kinds of competitions that take place and the planning and rehearsing necessary. Also use *Techniques of Marching Bands* (2003). (Rev: SLJ 11/03) [784.8]

7441 Garty, Judy. *Techniques of Marching Bands* (5–8). Series: Let's Go Team. 2003, Mason Crest LB $19.95 (978-1-59084-538-7). The slim volume supplies a look at the functions of a marching band, how they operate, and the joys of playing in one. (Rev: BL 10/15/03; SLJ 11/03) [785.06]

7442 Igus, Toyomi. *I See the Rhythm* (5–8). Illus. 1998, Children's $15.95 (978-0-89239-151-6). Using a timeline to set the social context, this title traces African American contributions to such musical forms as the blues, big band, jazz, bebop, gospel, and rock. (Rev: BCCB 7–8/98; BL 2/15/98; SLJ 6/98) [780]

7443 Rowe, Julian. *Music* (4–7). Illus. Series: Science Encounters. 1997, Rigby paper $25.55 (978-1-57572-091-3). This book shows how scientific principles are used in music, musical instruments, hearing, and recording devices. (Rev: SLJ 10/97) [780]

7444 Schaefer, A. R. *Forming a Band* (5–8). Illus. Series: Rock Music Library. 2003, Capstone LB $23.93 (978-0-7368-2146-9). A hip and practical guide suitable for reluctant readers. Also use *Booking a First Gig* (2003). (Rev: BL 12/1/03) [784.100]

History of Music

7445 Kallen, Stuart A. *The History of Classical Music* (6–10). Illus. Series: Music Library. 2002, Gale LB $32.45 (978-1-59018-123-2). This overview covers classical music and composers starting with the Middle Ages, providing interesting excerpts from primary documents. Also use *The History of Jazz* (2002). (Rev: BL 11/1/02) [781.6]

Jazz and Popular Music (Country, Rap, Rock, etc.)

7446 Aquila, Richard. *That Old Time Rock and Roll: A Chronicle of an Era, 1954–1963* (8–12). 1989, Schirmer $25.00 (978-0-02-870082-3). A history complete with important biographies from the first decade of rock. (Rev: BL 9/15/89) [784.5]

7447 Asirvatham, Sandy. *The History of the Blues* (6–10). Series: American Mosaic. 2003, Chelsea LB $30.00 (978-0-7910-7266-0). The origin, style, and technique of blues, along with its evolution and key figures, are presented with drawings and photographs. Also use *The History of Jazz* (2003). (Rev: BL 10/15/03; HBG 10/03; SLJ 8/03) [781.643]

7448 Ayazi-Hashjin, Sherry. *Rap and Hip Hop: The Voice of a Generation* (4–7). Illus. Series: Library of African American Arts and Culture. 1999, Rosen LB $26.50 (978-0-8239-1855-3). This account traces the history of rap and hip hop music from their origins in spirituals, jazz, blues, and storytelling traditions; it also gives some information on musicians. (Rev: BL 2/15/00; SLJ 1/00) [782.4]

7449 Bertholf, Bret. *The Long Gone Lonesome History of Country Music* (5–8). Illus. 2007, Little, Brown $18.99 (978-0-316-52393-6). A chatty survey of country music, discussing its roots and early instruments, tracing the evolution to today's sounds, and introducing some of its greatest performers. (Rev: BL 4/1/07; SLJ 4/07*) [781.642]

7450 Bolden, Tonya. *Take-Off: American All-Girl Bands during WWII* (6–9). Illus. 2007, Knopf $18.99 (978-0-375-82797-6). Women on the homefront during World War II stepped in and formed their own bands when male swing musicians went off to fight. This book and music CD celebrates their sound; photographs, newspaper accounts, and other elements add interest. (Rev: BL 2/15/07; SLJ 6/07) [784.4]

7451 Delancey, Morgan. *Dave Matthews Band: Step Into the Light.* Rev. 2nd ed. (7–12). 2001, ECW paper $16.95 (978-1-55022-443-6). In addition to a detailed history of the band, this revised edition includes interviews with band members. (Rev: VOYA 8/02) [782.42]

7452 Elmer, Howard. *Blues: Its Birth and Growth* (6–9). Illus. Series: Library of African American Arts and Culture. 1999, Rosen LB $26.50 (978-0-8239-1853-9). This book traces the blues back to the song traditions of Africa, shows how it was influenced by the African American experience, and highlights the careers of such pioneers as Robert Johnson, Bessie Smith, and Muddy Waters. (Rev: SLJ 8/99; VOYA 8/99) [781.66]

7453 George-Warren, Holly. *Shake, Rattle and Roll: The Founders of Rock and Roll* (4–7). 2001, Houghton $16.00 (978-0-618-05540-1). After an informative introduction on the history of rock and roll, there is a series of one-page biographies of famous personalities. (Rev: BL 3/1/01; HBG 10/01; SLJ 5/01*) [781.66]

7454 Handyside, Christopher. *Country* (5–9). Series: A History of American Music. 2006, Heinemann LB $31.43 (978-1-4034-8151-1). This history of country music traces the genre from its hillbilly roots to the present and introduces some of its most influential figures, including the Carter family, Johnny Cash, Loretta Lynn, and John Denver. (Rev: SLJ 9/06) [781.642]

7455 Kallen, Stuart A. *The History of Rock and Roll* (6–10). Series: Music Library. 2002, Gale LB $32.45 (978-1-59018-126-3). Beginning in the early 1950s, this account traces the history of rock and roll, profiles many musicians involved, and describes the unique characteristics of this form of music. (Rev: BL 3/15/03) [781.66]

7456 Keeley, Jennifer. *Rap Music* (6–12). Series: Overview. 2001, Lucent LB $29.95 (978-1-56006-504-3). This richly illustrated book gives an in-depth overview of rap music and profiles of many celebrities connected with it. (Rev: BL 9/15/01; SLJ 10/01) [782.42]

7457 Lee, Jeanne. *Jam! The Story of Jazz Music* (4–7). Illus. Series: Library of African American Arts and Culture. 1999, Rosen LB $26.50 (978-0-8239-1852-2). This book tells about the African American musicians who were responsible for the early development of jazz and blues. (Rev: BL 2/15/00; SLJ 1/00) [781.65]

7458 Lommel, Cookie. *The History of Rap Music* (8–12). Series: African-American Achievers. 2001, Chelsea House $30.00 (978-0-7910-5820-6). The history of rap music from its origins in the hip hop of the 1970s through its growing popularity through the 1990s to 2000. (Rev: HBG 10/01) [782.42]

7459 Marsalis, Wynton. *Jazz A B Z: An A to Z Collection of Jazz Portraits* (7–12). Illus. by Paul Rogers. 2005, Candlewick $24.99 (978-0-7636-2135-3). Arranged in alphabet-book format, this strikingly illustrated volume celebrates jazz and its best-known practitioners. (Rev: BL 1/1–15/06; SLJ 1/06*) [811]

7460 Reisfeld, Randi. *This Is the Sound: The Best of Alternative Rock* (7–9). Illus. 1996, Simon & Schuster paper $7.99 (978-0-689-80670-4). Although it is now somewhat dated, this is a rundown on the hottest alternative rock bands as of 1996. (Rev: BL 6/1–15/96; SLJ 7/96; VOYA 12/96) [791.66]

Opera and Musicals

7461 Englander, Roger. *Opera: What's All the Screaming About?* (7–12). Illus. 1983, Walker $12.95 (978-0-8027-6491-1). After a general introduction to the history and conventions of opera, 50 popular operas are introduced. (Rev: BL 9/1/87) [782.1]

7462 Gatti, Anne, retel. *The Magic Flute* (4–8). Illus. by Peter Malone. 1997, Chronicle $17.95 (978-0-8118-1003-6). An elegant retelling of the Mozart opera, with each scene given a full-color painting and a page of text. The accompanying CD has 16 selections coded to each page. (Rev: SLJ 1/98*) [782.1]

Orchestra and Musical Instruments

7463 Dearling, Robert, ed. *The Illustrated Encyclopedia of Musical Instruments* (8–12). 1996, Schirmer $90.00 (978-0-02-864667-1). In addition to material on the history, development, and characteristics of each musical instrument, this oversize, well-illustrated book gives a history of music-making, plus coverage of composers and performers. (Rev: BL 1/1–15/97; SLJ 5/97) [784.19]

7464 Evans, Roger. *How to Play Guitar: A New Book for Everyone Interested in Guitar* (8–12). Illus. 1980, St. Martin's paper $9.95 (978-0-312-36609-4). An easily followed basic guidebook on how to play the guitar with information on such topics as buying equipment and reading music. [787.6]

7465 Helsby, Genevieve. *Those Amazing Musical Instruments!* (4–9). Illus. 2007, Sourcebooks $19.95 (978-1-4022-0825-6). A CD-ROM is included with this engaging and comprehensive guide to orchestral instruments. (Rev: SLJ 3/08) [784.3]

7466 Levine, Robert. *The Story of the Orchestra* (5–7). Illus. by Meredith Hamilton. 2001, Black Dog & Leventhal $19.98 (978-1-57912-148-8). Orchestra Bob introduces young readers to orchestra history, famous conductors and their eras, and instruments, in a guided tour that includes amusing cartoons, illustrations, and links to selections on the accompanying CD. (Rev: BL 12/15/01; SLJ 9/01) [784.2]

7467 Sabbeth, Alex. *Rubber-Band Banjos and a Java Jive Bass: Projects and Activities on the Science of Music and Sound* (4–7). Illus. 1997, Wiley paper $12.95 (978-0-471-15675-8). Describes the basic elements of music while giving directions for making a variety of homemade instruments. (Rev: BL 3/15/97; SLJ 6/97) [781]

7468 Thyacott, Louise. *Musical Instruments* (5–7). Illus. Series: Traditions Around the World. 1995, Thomson Learning LB $24.26 (978-1-56847-228-7). A continent-by-continent survey of the many kinds of musical instruments found in various cultures. (Rev: BCCB 11/94; BL 9/15/95) [784.3]

Songs and Folk Songs

7469 Berger, Melvin. *The Story of Folk Music* (6–9). Illus. 1976, Phillips LB $29.95 (978-0-87599-215-0). The story of the origins and characteristics of American folk music, with biographical information on singers from Woody Guthrie to John Denver. [781.7]

7470 Blood-Patterson, Peter, ed. *Rise Up Singing* (8–12). Illus. 1988, Sing Out paper $17.95 (978-0-9626704-9-7). Words, chords, and some background material on 1,200 songs, some folk, others pop. (Rev: BL 12/15/88) [784.5]

7471 Cooper, Michael L. *Slave Spirituals and the Jubilee Singers* (6–9). Illus. 2001, Clarion $16.00 (978-0-395-97829-0). All about the songs of American slavery and the Fisk University Jubilee Singers, who kept the songs alive after slavery ended. With photographs and sheet music. (Rev: BL 12/1/01; HB 1–2/02; HBG 3/02; SLJ 12/01; VOYA 2/02) [782.42162]

7472 Handyside, Christopher. *Folk* (5–9). 2006, Heinemann LB $31.43 (978-1-4034-8150-4). This attractive volume traces the evolution of American folk music from its post-Civil War roots to its influence on the contemporary music scene and introduces some of its most influential figures, including Leadbelly, Woody Guthrie, Joan Baez, and Bob Dylan. (Rev: SLJ 9/06) [781.62]

7473 McGill, Alice. *In the Hollow of Your Hand: Slave Lullabies* (5–7). Illus. 2000, Houghton $18.00 (978-0-395-85755-7). Family life in the days of slavery is revealed in this moving collection of 13 folk lullabies; a CD of the songs is also included. (Rev: BCCB 1/01; BL 11/15/00; HBG 3/01; SLJ 12/00) [811.008]

7474 McNeil, Keith, and Rusty McNeil, eds. *California Songbook with Historical Commentary* (6–10). Illus. 2001, WEM Records $15.95 (978-1-878360-27-4). Music, chords, lyrics, and background information are given for a large selection of songs that originated in California. (Rev: BL 8/01) [782.42]

7475 McNeil, Keith, and Rusty McNeil. *Colonial and Revolution Songbook: With Historical Commentary* (4–7). 1996, WEM Records paper $11.95 (978-1-878360-08-3). This songbook contains 39 traditional songs from the 17th century through the

War of 1812, with brief historical comments for each. (Rev: SLJ 12/96) [973]

7476 McNeil, Keith, and Rusty McNeil. *Moving West Songbook: With Historical Commentary* (7–10). Illus. 2003, WEM Records $15.95 (978-1-878360-30-4). Historical information, anecdotes, illustrations, and guitar chords accompany this large-format selection of about 50 songs of the early to mid-19th century. (Rev: BL 7/03; SLJ 11/03) [782.42]

7477 Sandburg, Carl. *The American Songbag* (7–12). Illus. 1970, Harcourt paper $35.00 (978-0-15-605650-2). A fine collection of all kinds of American folk songs with music and background notes from Mr. Sandburg. [784.7]

7478 Sieling, Peter. *Folk Music* (6–9). Illus. Series: North American Folklore. 2003, Mason Crest LB $22.95 (978-1-59084-342-0). Sieling defines the essence of folk music, looks at the instruments used, and explores its roots in the Old World, and the ways in which it has evolved in the New World. Also use *Folk Songs* (2003), which has a chapter on children's songs. (Rev: SLJ 6/03) [781.62]

7479 Silverman, Jerry. *Songs and Stories of the Civil War* (6–9). Illus. 2002, Twenty-First Century LB $29.90 (978-0-7613-2305-1). Lyrics, music, and recommended recordings are given for a dozen Civil War songs, each introduced by information on its history and on its relevance to the soldiers and civilians of the time. (Rev: BL 2/1/02; HBG 10/02; SLJ 7/02) [782.42]

7480 Yolen, Jane. *Apple for the Teacher: Thirty Songs for Singing While You Work* (4–7). Illus. 2005, Abrams $24.95 (978-0-8109-4825-9). This collection of work songs, compiled by Yolen and featuring music arrangements by her son Adam Stemple, celebrates 30 diverse occupations from astronaut to weaver. (Rev: BL 10/1/05; SLJ 10/05) [782.42]

Theater, Dance, and Other Performing Arts

General and Miscellaneous

7481 Amendola, Dana. *A Day at the New Amsterdam Theatre* (4–9). Photos by Gino Domenico. 2004, Disney $24.95 (978-0-7868-5438-7). A behind-the-scenes look at a production of a musical in the renovated theater in New York City, introducing the wide variety of individuals involved. (Rev: SLJ 1/05) [792]

Dance (Ballet, Modern, etc.)

7482 Anderson, Janet. *Modern Dance* (7–12). Series: World of Dance. 2003, Chelsea House LB $30.00 (978-0-7910-7644-6). Traces the history of modern dance, describing key personalities and innovations and looking at a modern dance class. (Rev: SLJ 3/04; VOYA 8/04) [792.8]

7483 Augustyn, Frank, and Shelley Tanaka. *Footnotes: Dancing the World's Best-Loved Ballets* (5–8). Illus. 2001, Millbrook LB $24.90 (978-0-7613-2323-5). A readable account that introduces ballet from a backstage perspective, with material on how it feels to be a dancer in a large ballet company. (Rev: BL 4/15/01; HBG 10/01; SLJ 6/01*; VOYA 8/01) [792.8]

7484 Balanchine, George, and Francis Mason. *101 Stories of the Great Ballets* (7–12). 1975, Doubleday paper $16.00 (978-0-385-03398-5). Both the classics and newer ballets are introduced plus general background material such as a brief history of ballet. [792.8]

7485 Berger, Melvin. *The World of Dance* (6–8). Illus. 1978, Phillips $29.95 (978-0-87599-221-1). An overview of the subject that begins in prehistoric times and ends with today's social dancing and ballet. [792]

7486 Dillman, Lisa. *Ballet* (4–7). Illus. Series: Get Going! Hobbies. 2005, Heinemann LB $27.79 (978-1-4034-6115-5). A photo-filled introduction to ballet, with historical information plus basic positions and steps and exercises to help would-be dancers get in shape; also use *Tap Dancing* (2005). (Rev: BL 11/1/05; SLJ 3/06) [792.8]

7487 Haskins, Jim. *Black Dance in America: A History Through Its People* (7–12). 1990, HarperCollins LB $14.89 (978-0-690-04659-5). Beginning with the dances brought from Africa by the slaves, this history moves to the present with the contributions of such people as Gregory Hines and Alvin Ailey. (Rev: BL 8/90; SLJ 6/90; VOYA 6/90) [792.8]

7488 Johnson, Anne E. *Jazz Tap: From African Drums to American Feet* (4–7). Series: The Library of African American Arts and Culture. 1999, Rosen LB $27.95 (978-0-8239-1856-0). This book traces the history of jazz tap from a variety of African dances to its emergence in the 1920s and its later development in night clubs, on Broadway, and in movies. (Rev: SLJ 1/00) [793.3]

7489 Kuklin, Susan. *Reaching for Dreams: A Ballet from Rehearsal to Opening Night* (7–12). Illus. 2001, iUniverse paper $13.95 (978-0-595-17081-4). Using the introduction of a new ballet into the Alvin Ailey dance company's repetoire as a springboard, this is the account of the pangs of creation in the ballet world; first published in 1987. (Rev: BL 3/1/87; BR 11–12/87; SLJ 5/87; VOYA 12/87) [792.8]

7490 Rinaldi, Robin. *Ballet* (7–12). Series: World of Dance. 2003, Chelsea House LB $30.00 (978-0-7910-7640-8). Traces the history of ballet, describing key personalities and innovations and looking at a modern ballet class. (Rev: SLJ 3/04; VOYA 8/04) [792.8]

7491 Schorer, Suki, and School of American Ballet. *Put Your Best Foot Forward: A Young Dancer's Guide to Life* (4–8). Photos by Chris Carroll. Illus. by Donna Ingemanson. 2005, Workman $9.95 (978-0-7611-3795-5). Practical tips are combined with artistic advice in this helpful guide for young ballet dancers, written by a former principal dancer. (Rev: SLJ 3/06) [792.8]

7492 Tythacott, Louise. *Dance* (5–7). Illus. Series: Traditions Around the World. 1995, Thomson Learning LB $24.26 (978-1-56847-275-1). The ways people dance around the world and the reasons they do are presented with many color photographs. (Rev: BL 6/1–15/95; SLJ 9/95) [793.3]

7493 Yolen, Jane, and Heidi Stemple. *The Barefoot Book of Ballet Stories* (5–7). Illus. by Rebecca Guay. 2004, Barefoot Bks. $19.99 (978-1-84148-229-3). The stories behind seven of the world's classic ballets — including "Cinderella," "The Nutcracker," "Coppelia," and "Sleeping Beauty" — are introduced by a general discussion of ballet as an art form and accompanied by production notes on each work. (Rev: BL 11/1/04; SLJ 12/04) [792.8]

Motion Pictures

7494 Brackett, Leigh, and Lawrence Kasdan. *The Empire Strikes Back: The Illustrated Screenplay* (8–12). 1998, Ballantine paper $12.00 (978-0-345-42070-1). The shooting script for the second of the original *Star Wars* trilogy, with action direction and drawings of action scenes, preceded by an introduction that includes background and thoughts about the movie trilogy from the perspectives of people who were involved with the first release of the films. (Rev: SLJ 12/98) [791.43]

7495 Burtt, Ben. *Star Wars Galactic Phrase Book and Travel Guide: Beeps, Bleats, and Other Common Intergalactic Verbiage* (7–12). Illus. 2001, Ballantine $8.00 (978-0-345-44074-7). A small-format, travel guide/phrase book that will fascinate devotees of Star Wars. (Rev: SLJ 12/01; VOYA 6/02) [791.43]

7496 Clee, Paul. *Before Hollywood: From Shadow Play to the Silver Screen* (7–12). Illus. 2005, Clarion $22.00 (978-0-618-44533-2). Early technologies and the reactions of early audiences are the focus of this fascinating account. (Rev: BCCB 7–8/05; HB 9–10/05; SLJ 7/05) [791.43]

7497 Fingeroth, Danny. *Backstage at an Animated Series* (4–8). Series: Backstage Pass. 2003, Children's paper $6.95 (978-0-516-24385-6). Fingeroth explores the world of animated films, discussing

their history, recent technological advances, and the mechanics of production, and suggesting ways to become involved. Also use *Backstage at a Movie Set* (2003). (Rev: SLJ 10/03) [791.43]

7498 Jones, Sarah. *Film* (7–10). Illus. Series: Media-Wise. 2003, Smart Apple LB $28.50 (978-1-58340-256-6). The world of film making is clearly explained, with information on everything from initial concept to financing to the mechanics of production. (Rev: BL 10/15/03; SLJ 11/03) [791.43]

7499 McCaig, Iain, et al. *Star Wars Visionaries* (7–10). Illus. 2005, Dark Horse paper $17.95 (978-1-59307-311-4). Artists who worked on *The Revenge of the Sith* showcase their individual artistic styles in this gallery of Star Wars scenarios. (Rev: BL 5/15/05; SLJ 11/05) [741.5]

7500 Mast, Gerald. *A Short History of the Movies*. 6th ed. (8–12). Illus. 1992, Macmillan $35.00 (978-0-02-580510-1). A lavishly illustrated history that deals with both the creative and technical aspects of movie history. (Rev: BL 1/15/87) [791.43]

7501 Miller, Ron. *Special Effects: An Introduction to Movie Magic* (7–10). Illus. 2006, Lerner LB $26.60 (978-0-7613-2918-3). Covers both the history of special effects and the techniques used today; boxed features discuss key figures and offer career advice. (Rev: BL 3/15/06; SLJ 6/06) [778.5]

7502 Osborne, Robert A. *75 Years of the Oscar: The Official History of the Academy Awards* (8–12). 2003, Abbeville $75.00 (978-0-7892-0787-6). A history of the Oscars through 2003, with asides about the ceremonies, winners, nominees, and the Academy of Motion Picture Arts and Sciences. [791.43]

7503 Reynolds, David West. *Star Wars: Incredible Cross-Sections* (4–8). 1998, DK $19.95 (978-1-78943-480-4). This large-format book includes cross-sections of the TIE fighter, the X-wing fighter, the AT-AT, the Millennium Falcon, Jabba's sail barge, and the Death Star. (Rev: BL 12/15/98) [791.43]

7504 Reynolds, David West. *Star Wars: The Visual Dictionary* (4–8). 1998, DK $19.99 (978-0-7894-3481-4). Using a large-format dictionary approach, the people, creatures, and droids of the *Star Wars* saga are presented, with large photographs of the characters and many stills from the movies. (Rev: BL 12/15/98; HBG 3/99; SLJ 2/99) [791.43]

7505 Reynolds, David West. *Star Wars Episode I: Incredible Cross-Sections: The Definitive Guide to the Craft of Star Wars Episode I* (4–8). Illus. by Hans Jenssen and Richard Chasemore. 1999, DK $19.95 (978-0-7894-3962-8). An excellent guidebook that features cross-sections of vehicles and spacecraft featured in *Star Wars: Episode I*. (Rev: HBG 3/00; SLJ 12/99) [791]

7506 Reynolds, David West. *Star Wars Episode I: The Visual Dictionary* (4–8). Illus. 1999, DK $19.95 (978-0-7894-4701-2). In this large-format book, a follow-up to *Star Wars: The Visual Dictionary,* the author, an archaeologist, reports on creatures and events in *Episode 1,* using movie stills and posed photographs to explain the galaxy's history, technology, anthropology, and politics. (Rev: BL 8/99) [791.43]

7507 Richards, Andrea. *Girl Director: A How-to Guide for the First-Time Flat-Broke Film Maker (and Video Maker)* (7–12). Illus. by Elizabeth McCallie. 2001, Alloy $17.95 (978-1-931497-00-8). Technical tips, inspiration, and instruction for would-be directors, with plenty of illustrations and other graphic elements. (Rev: BL 11/1/01; VOYA 6/01) [791.43]

7508 Salisbury, Mark. *Planet of the Apes: Re-Imagined by Tim Burton* (6–12). Illus. 2001, Newmarket $32.95 (978-1-55704-487-7); paper $22.95 (978-1-55704-486-0). A richly illustrated look behind the scenes at film director Tim Burton's recent remake of *The Planet of the Apes.* (Rev: VOYA 2/02)

7509 Vaz, Mark Cotta, et al. *The Art of The Incredibles* (8–12). Illus. 2004, Chronicle $40.00 (978-0-8118-4433-8). Many illustrations enhance this look at the making of the popular animated motion picture. (Rev: BL 10/15/04) [791.43]

7510 Wallace, Daniel. *Star Wars: The Essential Guide to Planets and Moons* (6–12). Illus. 1998, Del Rey paper $19.95 (978-0-345-42068-8). This volume provides fascinating information on 110 different planets and moons in the *Star Wars* universe, arranged alphabetically from Abregado-rae, a popular stop for smugglers, to Zhar, a gas-filled giant, covering each world's inhabitants, climate, language, points of interest, and history. (Rev: VOYA 6/99) [791.45]

Radio, Television, and Video

7511 Killick, Jane. *Babylon 5: The Coming of Shadows* (7–12). 1998, Ballantine paper $11.00 (978-0-345-42448-8). This is the second of a five-volume guide to this popular television series. (Rev: VOYA 12/98) [791.45]

7512 Kraus, Lawrence M. *The Physics of Star Trek* (7–12). Illus. 1996, HarperPerennial paper $13.00 (978-0-06-097710-8). Warp, transporter beams, antimatter, and other scientific concepts popularized in the TV series are examined, with speculations on their possible application in the future. (Rev: VOYA 8/97) [791.45]

7513 Lommel, Cookie. *African Americans in Film and Television* (7–12). Series: American Mosaic. 2003, Chelsea LB $30.00 (978-0-7910-7268-4). The history of the struggle of African Americans to be accepted in films and television and their position in these media today. (Rev: BL 10/15/03; HBG 10/03) [791.45]

7514 Riess, Jana. *What Would Buffy Do? The Vampire Slayer as Spiritual Guide* (7–12). 2004, Jossey-Bass paper $14.95 (978-0-7879-6922-6). For fans of the TV series, this is a guide to the first seven seasons with material on the show's values and characters. (Rev: BL 5/1/04) [791.45]

7515 Schieffer, Bob. *Face the Nation: My Favorite Stories from the First 50 Years of the Award-Winning News Broadcast* (8–12). Illus. 2004, Simon & Schuster $26.95 (978-0-7432-6585-0). Highlights from the first 50 years of CBS's popular *Face the Nation.* (Rev: BL 9/1/04) [791.45]

7516 Wallner, Rosemary. *Fresh Prince of Bel-Air: The History of the Future* (7–10). 1992, ABDO LB $18.48 (978-1-56239-140-9). The story behind the TV series, now in reruns, that made a star of Will Smith. (Rev: BL 3/1/93; SLJ 11/93) [791.45]

7517 Wan, Guofang. *TV Takeover: Questioning Television* (4–7). Illus. Series: Fact Finders. Media Literacy. 2006, Capstone LB $22.60 (978-0-7368-6763-4). In alerting readers to the motivations behind those who produce television shows, this book fosters critical thinking about the mass media. (Rev: SLJ 6/07) [384.55]

Theater and Other Dramatic Forms

7518 Bany-Winters, Lisa. *On Stage: Theater Games and Activities for Kids* (4–7). Illus. 1997, Chicago Review paper $14.95 (978-1-55652-324-3). This book provides a number of theater games involving improvisation, creating characters, using and becoming objects, and ideas for pantomime and puppetry. (Rev: BL 2/1/98; SLJ 3/98) [327.12]

7519 Caruso, Sandra, and Susan Kosoff. *The Young Actor's Book of Improvisation: Dramatic Situations from Shakespeare to Spielberg: Ages 12–16* (6–12). 1998, Heinemann paper $22.95 (978-0-325-00049-7). This work supplies hundreds of situations suitable for improvisation culled from all forms of literature, plays, and movie scripts, arranged by themes such as confrontation and relationships. (Rev: BL 9/15/98; SLJ 1/99) [793]

7520 Currie, Stephen. *An Actor on the Elizabethan Stage* (7–10). Illus. 2003, Gale LB $29.95 (978-1-59018-174-4). An entertaining look at the Elizabethan theater and the skills that the all-male actors required. (Rev: SLJ 11/03) [792]

7521 Cushman, Kathleen, and Montana Miller. *Circus Dreams* (6–12). Illus. 1990, Little, Brown

$15.95 (978-0-316-16561-7). A look at the professional college for circus artists in France, following the experiences of one of its students. (Rev: BL 1/15/91; SLJ 1/91) [791.3]

7522 Dunleavy, Deborah. *The Jumbo Book of Drama* (4–8). Illus. by Jane Kurisu. 2004, Kids Can paper $14.95 (978-1-55337-008-6). Divided into Acts, this volume covers all aspects of drama and stagecraft, from body movement to lighting and props. (Rev: BL 5/1/04; SLJ 6/04) [372.66]

7523 Friedman, Lise. *Break a Leg! The Kid's Guide to Acting and Stagecraft* (4–7). Illus. by Mary Dowdle. 2002, Workman paper $14.95 (978-0-7611-2208-1). Some of the topics covered for young would-be actors include analyzing a script, memorizing lines, stage fright, body language, and monologues. (Rev: BL 5/1/02; HBG 10/02) [292]

7524 Haskins, Jim, and Kathleen Benson. *Conjure Times: Black Magicians in America* (6–12). Illus. 2001, Walker LB $17.85 (978-0-8027-8763-7). The authors explore the substantial contributions of black performers to the early theater in America. (Rev: BL 7/01; HBG 3/02; SLJ 11/01; VOYA 4/02) [793.8]

7525 Kipnis, Claude. *The Mime Book* (7–12). Illus. 1988, Meriwether paper $16.95 (978-0-916260-55-2). One of the world's greatest mimes explains what it is and how it is done. [792.3]

7526 Lee, Robert L. *Everything About Theatre! The Guidebook of Theatre Fundamentals* (7–12). Illus.

1996, Meriwether paper $19.95 (978-1-56608-019-4). This excellent introduction to the backstage world includes material ranging from theater history to stagecraft, acting, and play production. (Rev: BL 12/1/96; SLJ 2/97) [792]

7527 Miller, Kimberly M. *Backstage at a Play* (4–8). Series: Backstage Pass. 2003, Children's LB $24.50 (978-0-516-24327-6). Miller explores the world of theater, discussing how they are produced and the degree of commitment necessary, and suggesting ways to become involved. (Rev: SLJ 10/03) [792]

7528 Stevens, Chambers. *Sensational Scenes for Teens: The Scene Studyguide for Teen Actors!* (7–10). Illus. Series: Hollywood 101. 2001, Sandcastle paper $14.95 (978-1-883995-10-2). Acting coach Stevens includes more than 30 scenes — both comedy and drama — suitable for two teen actors, with choices for boy-girl, boy-boy, and girl-girl combinations. (Rev: BL 5/15/01; SLJ 4/01) [812.6]

7529 Stolzenberg, Mark. *Be a Clown!* (7–12). Illus. 1989, Sterling paper $10.95 (978-0-8069-5804-0). A how-to manual that describes how to create a clown character and supplies a number of routines. (Rev: BL 1/1/90) [791.3]

7530 Straub, Cindie, and Matthew Straub. *Mime: Basics for Beginners* (7–12). Illus. 1984, Plays paper $13.95 (978-0-8238-0263-0). The fundamentals of traditional mime are explained in text, line drawings, and photographs. (Rev: BL 2/1/85) [792.3]

History and Geography

General History and Geography

Miscellaneous Works

7531 Aaseng, Nathan. *You Are the Explorer* (4–8). Illus. Series: Great Decisions. 2000, Oliver LB $19.95 (978-1-881508-55-7). In this interactive book about famous explorers, the reader is asked to make decisions similar to those made by real explorers such as Columbus, Cortes, Champlain, and Robert Scott. (Rev: BL 5/1/00; HBG 10/00; SLJ 9/00) [910]

7532 Arnold, Caroline. *The Geography Book: Activities for Exploring, Mapping, and Enjoying Your World* (4–7). Illus. by Tina Cash-Walsh. 2001, Wiley paper $14.95 (978-0-471-41236-6). An organized introduction to several geography concepts along with step-by-step instructions for projects and experiments. (Rev: BL 2/15/02; SLJ 3/02) [910]

7533 Burger, Leslie, and Debra L. Rahm. *Sister Cities in a World of Difference* (4–8). Illus. 1996, Lerner LB $22.60 (978-0-8225-2697-1). The pairing of cities internationally is covered with material on the results, mostly positive. (Rev: BL 9/1/96; SLJ 9/96; VOYA 4/97) [303.48]

7534 Pascoe, Elaine, and Deborah Kops. *Scholastic Kid's Almanac for the 21st Century* (4–7). Illus. by Bob Italiano and David C. Bell. 1999, Scholastic paper $12.95 (978-0-590-30724-6). An almanac that covers subjects including aerospace, animals, chemistry, computers, energy, geography, plants, religion, and sports. (Rev: SLJ 2/00) [900]

Atlases, Maps, and Mapmaking

7535 Bramwell, Martyn. *How Maps Are Made* (5–8). Illus. Series: Maps and Mapmakers. 1998, Lerner LB $22.60 (978-0-8225-2920-0). The difficulties in representing the globe on a flat surface are explored, plus details on how maps are made — both by hand and by computer — and on the use of aerial photography in mapmaking. (Rev: BL 3/15/99; HBG 3/99; SLJ 2/99) [526]

7536 Bramwell, Martyn. *Mapping Our World* (4–8). Illus. Series: Maps and Mapmakers. 1998, Lerner LB $22.60 (978-0-8225-2924-8). This work shows how different kinds of maps can be used to illustrate topography, geology, climate, vegetation, population, geography, minerals, trade, pollution, and habitat. (Rev: BL 3/15/99; SLJ 2/99) [912]

7537 Bramwell, Martyn. *Mapping the Seas and Airways* (5–8). Series: Maps and Mapmakers. 1998, Lerner LB $22.60 (978-0-8225-2921-7). This volume deals with special kinds of maps prepared and used by oceanographers and by airline cartographers. (Rev: BL 3/15/99; HBG 3/99) [912]

7538 Bramwell, Martyn. *Maps in Everyday Life* (5–8). Illus. Series: Maps and Mapmakers. 1998, Lerner LB $22.60 (978-0-8225-2923-1). This book explains how different maps are used for different purposes, e.g., tourist maps and climate maps. (Rev: BL 3/15/99; HBG 3/99; SLJ 10/96) [912]

7539 Jouris, David. *All over the Map: An Extraordinary Atlas of the United States* (8–10). 1994, Ten Speed paper $11.95 (978-0-89815-649-2). A U.S.

atlas that explores the history of the names of towns and cities, including such places as Peculiar, Ding Dong, Vendor, and Joy. (Rev: BL 7/94) [910]

7540 Oleksy, Walter. *Mapping the World* (5–7). Series: Watts Library: Geography. 2002, Watts LB $25.50 (978-0-531-12029-3); paper $8.95 (978-0-531-16636-9). A history of how maps have been made, from the explorers, merchants, and mapmakers of old to the accurate modern products that use new technology. Also use *Mapping the Seas* and *Maps in History* (both 2002). (Rev: BL 10/15/02) [912]

7541 Pratt, Paula B. *Maps: Plotting Places on the Globe* (6–10). Series: Encyclopedia of Discovery and Invention. 1995, Lucent LB $29.95 (978-1-56006-255-4). Traces the evolution of mapmaking/cartography from ancient times to the present. (Rev: BL 4/15/95; SLJ 3/95) [912]

7542 Ritchie, Robert. *Historical Atlas of the Renaissance* (8–12). Illus. Series: Historical Atlas. 2004, Facts on File $35.00 (978-0-8160-5731-3). Art, culture, politics, literature, science, and key figures are all covered in this chronologically organized atlas. (Rev: SLJ 2/05)

7543 Ross, Val. *The Road to There: Mapmakers and Their Stories* (7–10). Illus. 2003, Tundra $19.95 (978-0-88776-621-3). Mapmakers of different eras and nationalities, well-known figures such as Henry the Navigator and less familiar individuals, and the charts they created are featured in this interesting volume with period illustrations and many maps. (Rev: BCCB 1/04; BL 12/15/03; HBG 4/04; SLJ 12/03*) [912]

7544 Smith, A. G. *Where Am I? The Story of Maps and Navigation* (4–8). Illus. 1997, Stoddart paper $13.95 (978-0-7737-5836-0). Important discoveries and innovations in the history of mapmaking are explained. (Rev: BL 9/1/97) [910]

7545 Wilkinson, Philip. *The Kingfisher Student Atlas* (5–8). 2003, Kingfisher $24.95 (978-0-7534-5589-0). An atlas of the earth, with detail on each area's physical characteristics and political boundaries and material on such problems as pollution and deforestation. An accompanying CD offers printable maps. (Rev: SLJ 4/04)

Paleontology

7546 Aaseng, Nathan. *American Dinosaur Hunters* (6–9). Illus. 1996, Enslow LB $26.60 (978-0-89490-710-4). A history of paleontology, the story of major discoveries, and brief biographies of such scientists as Edward Hitchcock and Roy Chapman Andrews. (Rev: BL 11/15/96; SLJ 12/96) [560]

7547 Agenbroad, Larry D., and Lisa Nelson. *Mammoths: Ice-Age Giants* (5–8). Illus. Series: Discovery! 2002, Lerner LB $31.95 (978-0-8225-2862-3). A detailed look at mammoths, theories on mammoth extinction, and mammoth discoveries, with sidebar features on topics such as human hunters in the Ice Age, and geologic timelines. (Rev: BL 6/1–15/02; HBG 10/02; SLJ 7/02) [569]

7548 Barrett, Paul. *National Geographic Dinosaurs* (6–10). Illus. 2001, National Geographic $29.95 (978-0-7922-8224-2). This comprehensive and attractive guide provides a wealth of information about dinosaurs, their timeframe and evolution, individual species, and eventual extinction, with maps, fact boxes, and graphics. (Rev: BL 7/01; SLJ 10/01) [567.9]

7549 Berger, Melvin. *Mighty Dinosaurs* (4–8). Illus. 1990, Avon paper $2.95 (978-0-380-76052-7). Covers various kinds of dinosaurs and includes the latest research on their extinction. (Rev: BL 12/15/90) [567.9]

7550 Bradley, Timothy J. *Paleo Bugs: Survival of the Creepiest* (5–8). Illus. by author. 2008, Chronicle $15.99 (978-0-8118-6022-2). The author provides information about prehistoric bugs alongside his own illustrations imagining what they might have looked like in those long-ago days. A companion to *Paleo Sharks*. (Rev: BL 5/15/08; SLJ 7/08) [565]

7551 Bradley, Timothy J. *Paleo Sharks: Survival of the Strangest* (4–7). Illus. 2007, Chronicle $15.95 (978-0-8118-4878-7). Well-arranged double-page spreads introduce sharks of prehistoric times and examine how they compare to their modern descendants. (Rev: BL 4/1/07; SLJ 6/07) [567]

7552 Brett-Surman, Michael, and Thomas R. Holtz, Jr. *James Gurney: The World of Dinosaurs* (5–8). Illus. by James Gurney. 1998, GWP paper $19.95 (978-0-86713-046-1). This story of the 15 dinosaur stamps designed for the U.S. Postal Service includes a description of each of the beasts. (Rev: SLJ 9/98) [567.9]

7553 Christian, Spencer, and Antonia Felix. *Is There a Dinosaur in Your Backyard? The World's Most Fascinating Fossils, Rocks, and Minerals* (5–8). Series: Spencer Christian's World of Wonders. 1998, Wiley paper $12.95 (978-0-471-19616-7). In addition to discussing dinosaurs, this fascinating book introduces earth science, with interesting details about rocks, minerals, and fossils. (Rev: BL 9/1/98; SLJ 10/98) [552]

7554 Cooley, Brian, and Mary Ann Wilson. *Make-a-Saurus: My Life with Raptors and Other Dinosaurs* (4–8). Photos by Gary Campbell. 2000, Annick paper $14.95 (978-1-55037-644-9). A two-part book giving a step-by step description of how museum-quality models of dinosaurs are made using the latest discoveries in paleontology, followed by an exploration of how these techniques can be adapted so the reader can make models at home. (Rev: HBG 3/01; SLJ 9/00) [567.9]

7555 Currie, Philip, and Kevin Padian, eds. *Encyclopedia of Dinosaurs* (8–12). Illus. 1997, Academic Pr. $148.00 (978-0-12-226810-6). An adult reference book, written by scientists, with interesting, alphabetically arranged articles on dinosaurs, digs, and sites. (Rev: BL 11/1/97; SLJ 5/98) [567.9]

7556 Currie, Philip J., and Colleayn O. Mastin. *The Newest and Coolest Dinosaurs* (4–8). Illus. 1998, Grasshopper $18.95 (978-1-895910-41-4). Using double-page spreads, this useful volume introduces 15 of the most recent finds in the world of dinosaurs. (Rev: SLJ 1/99) [560]

7557 Cutchins, Judy, and Ginny Johnston. *Giant Predators of the Ancient Seas* (4–7). Illus. Series: Southern Fossil Discoveries. 2001, Pineapple $14.95 (978-1-56164-237-3). A look at the reptiles, fish, whales, sharks, and sea snakes that were found in the seas that once covered much of North America, as well as a discussion of the methods scientists used to reconstruct them. (Rev: HBG 3/02; SLJ 12/01) [566]

7558 Dal Sasso, Cristiano. *Animals: Origins and Evolution* (4–8). Illus. Series: Beginnings — Origins and Evolution. 1995, Raintree LB $24.26 (978-0-8114-3333-4). This well-illustrated account traces the development of animals from bacteria to the invertebrates and then fish, amphibians, reptiles, birds, and mammals. (Rev: BL 5/1/95; SLJ 6/95) [591]

7559 Dingus, Lowell. *Dinosaur Eggs Discovered!* (6–9). Illus. 2007, Lerner LB $30.60 (978-0-8225-6791-2). Describes the discovery of Titanosaur fossils and what the evidence has revealed about the huge prehistoric creatures. (Rev: BL 9/1/07; SLJ 10/07) [567.909]

7560 Dixon, Dougal. *Amazing Dinosaurs: More Feathers, More Claws, Big Horns, Wide Jaws!* 2nd ed. (5–7). 2007, Boyds Mills $19.95 (978-1-59078-537-9). This carefully updated edition provides new illustrations and text reflecting recent discoveries about dinosaurs. (Rev: SLJ 3/08) [567.9]

7561 Dixon, Dougal. *The Search for Dinosaurs* (4–7). Illus. Series: Digging Up the Past. 1995, Thomson Learning LB $24.26 (978-1-56847-396-3). A history of the various discoveries that paleontologists have made about dinosaurs and other prehistoric beasts. (Rev: SLJ 2/96) [567.9]

7562 Dixon, Dougal, and John Malam. *Dinosaur* (7–12). Illus. Series: DK/Google e.guides. 2004, DK $17.99 (978-0-7566-0761-6). An attractive, highly illustrated yet informative overview of dinosaurs and dinosaur discoveries, with a link to a Web site that offers additional material. (Rev: BL 12/1/04) [567.9]

7563 Farlow, James O. *Bringing Dinosaur Bones to Life: How Do We Know What Dinosaurs Were Like?* (4–7). Illus. 2001, Watts LB $26.00 (978-0-531-11403-2). An interesting look at the life of dinosaurs and at the methods paleontologists use to learn about the beasts, pointing out that although scientists can reconstruct animals from skeletons and fossil evidence, they must always differentiate between fact and educated guesses. (Rev: BL 12/15/01; SLJ 12/01) [567.9]

7564 Gallant, Jonathan R. *The Tales Fossils Tell* (5–9). Series: The Story of Science. 2000, Benchmark LB $29.93 (978-0-7614-1153-6). A fascinating introduction to paleontology that explains how the importance of fossils was only clearly understood after the ideas of evolution and extinction were accepted. (Rev: BL 12/15/00; HBG 10/01; SLJ 2/01) [560]

7565 Gee, Henry. *A Field Guide to Dinosaurs: The Essential Handbook for Travelers in the Mesozoic* (6–12). Illus. by Luis V. Rey. 2003, Barron's $24.95 (978-0-7641-5511-6). Fact and speculation are interwoven in this guide to dinosaur species that follows the format of a field guide to birds. (Rev: BL 8/03; HBG 10/03; SLJ 9/03) [567.9]

7566 Holmes, Thom, and Laurie Holmes. *Armored, Plated, and Bone-Headed Dinosaurs: The Ankylosaurs, Stegosaurs, and Pachycephalosaurs* (6–10). Illus. by Michael William Skrepnick. Series: Dinosaur Library. 2002, Enslow LB $26.60 (978-0-7660-1453-4). A well-organized introduction to these dinosaurs and their adaptation of anatomical defenses, with illustrations, graphic elements, a timeline of scientific discoveries, and a glossary. (Rev: BL 8/02; HBG 10/02; SLJ 10/02) [567.915]

7567 Holmes, Thom, and Laurie Holmes. *Feathered Dinosaurs: The Origin of Birds* (6–10). Illus. by Michael William Skrepnick. Series: Dinosaur Library. 2002, Enslow LB $26.60 (978-0-7660-1454-1). A well-organized introduction to these dinosaurs and their relationship to today's birds, with illustrations, graphic elements, a timeline of scientific discoveries, and a glossary. (Rev: BL 8/02; HBG 10/02; SLJ 10/02) [567.9]

7568 Holmes, Thom, and Laurie Holmes. *Horned Dinosaurs: The Ceratopsians* (6–10). Illus. by Michael William Skrepnick. Series: Dinosaur Library. 2001, Enslow LB $26.60 (978-0-7660-1451-0). A detailed survey of psittacosaurs, protoceratopsids, and ceratopsids. Other recommended titles in this series are *Meat-Eating Dinosaurs: The Theropods* and *Peaceful Plant-Eating Dinosaurs: The Iguanodonts, Duckbills, and Other Ornithopods* (2001). (Rev: HBG 3/02; SLJ 11/01) [567.915]

7569 Holtz, Thomas R., Jr. *Dinosaurs: The Most Complete, Up-to-Date Encyclopedia for Dinosaur Lovers of All Ages* (5–12). Illus. by Luis V. Rey. 2007, Random $34.99 (978-0-375-82419-7). Paleontologist Holtz offers a well-organized overview of dinosaurs and everything dinosaur-related in a well-illustrated volume that will be appreciated by users of many ages (those not interested in cladistics, for example, may find just the information they need on dinosaur eggs). (Rev: HB 1–2/08; SLJ 12/07) [567.9]

7570 Krueger, Richard. *The Dinosaurs* (5–8). Illus. Series: Prehistoric North America. 1996, Millbrook LB $22.90 (978-1-56294-548-0). With plenty of color illustrations, this chatty overview tells about

North American dinosaurs. (Rev: BL 5/15/96; SLJ 4/96) [567.9]

7571 Lambert, David. *A Field Guide to Dinosaurs* (7–12). Illus. 1983, Avon paper $9.95 (978-0-380-83519-5). A well-illustrated guide to more than 340 different dinosaurs arranged by family groups. [567.9]

7572 Larson, Peter, and Kristin Donnan. *Bones Rock! Everything You Need to Know to Be a Paleontologist* (5–9). Illus. 2004, Invisible Cities paper $19.95 (978-1-931229-35-7). A comprehensive, accessible guide to paleontology, describing how to dig for fossils, clean them, keep records, and develop and test theories, with interesting accounts of the authors' experiences. (Rev: SLJ 11/04) [560]

7573 Lessem, Don. *Dinosaur Worlds: New Dinosaurs, New Discoveries* (5–8). Illus. 1996, Boyds Mills $19.95 (978-1-56397-597-4). The reader visits various dinosaur digs worldwide in a review of what we know about these amazing creatures. (Rev: BL 11/15/96; SLJ 12/96*) [567.9]

7574 Llamas, Andreu. *The Era of the Dinosaurs* (4–8). Illus. Series: Development of the Earth. 1996, Chelsea LB $17.55 (978-0-7910-3452-1). Various kinds of dinosaurs are introduced, with an emphasis on their evolution and on how geology and climate affected their development. (Rev: SLJ 7/96) [567.9]

7575 Llamas, Andreu. *The First Amphibians* (4–8). Illus. Series: Development of the Earth. 1996, Chelsea LB $17.55 (978-0-7910-3453-8). Using many color illustrations, this book begins with the earliest land vertebrates and gives clear explanations of their adaptations over time. (Rev: SLJ 7/96) [567.9]

7576 Malam, John. *Dinosaur* (5–8). Illus. 2006, DK $15.99 (978-0-7566-1412-6). Tyrannosaurus rex is the star of this attractive book that covers the dinosaur's anatomy, life cycle, and hunting techniques plus archaeological findings and the science that has allowed us to reconstruct the animal from what we know today. (Rev: SLJ 4/07) [567.9]

7577 Manning, Phillip Lars. *Dinomummy: The Life, Death, and Discovery of Dakota, a Dinosaur from Hell Creek* (5–8). Illus. 2007, Kingfisher $18.95 (978-0-7534-6047-4). The 2006 discovery of a hadrosaur fossil — so complete its skin was still intact — is the subject of this dramatically designed book that takes readers into the world of paleontology. (Rev: BL 3/3/08) [567.914]

7578 Nardo, Don. *Dinosaurs: Unearthing the Secrets of Ancient Beasts* (6–10). Series: Encyclopedia of Discovery and Invention. 1995, Lucent LB $29.95 (978-1-56006-253-0). Describes dinosaurs and their habitats and highlights the dedicated men and women who have made significant discoveries about them. (Rev: BL 4/15/95) [567.9]

7579 Patent, Dorothy Hinshaw. *In Search of Maiasaurs* (4–7). Series: Frozen in Time. 1998, Benchmark LB $28.50 (978-0-7614-0787-4). This book on dinosaurs describes the recent find of a huge bed of bones and Jack Horner's work to retrieve the fossils and learn from them. (Rev: HBG 10/99; SLJ 3/99) [567.9]

7580 Sloan, Christopher. *Supercroc and the Origin of Crocodiles* (5–8). Illus. 2002, National Geographic $18.95 (978-0-7922-6691-4). A fascinating account of the discovery in Africa of the fossil *Sarcosuchus*, or Supercroc, with additional information on paleontology and crocodile evolution. (Rev: BCCB 5/02; BL 9/15/02; HBG 10/02; SLJ 7/02*) [567.9]

7581 Stein, Wendy. *Dinosaurs* (6–10). Series: Great Mysteries. 1994, Greenhaven $18.96 (978-1-56510-096-1). An introduction to dinosaurs and an examination of the various theories about their extinction. (Rev: BL 4/15/94) [567.9]

7582 Thompson, Ida. *The Audubon Society Field Guide to North American Fossils* (7–12). Illus. 1982, Knopf $19.95 (978-0-394-52412-2). An illustrated guide to the identification of North American fossils plus some background information on their formation. [560]

7583 Thompson, Sharon E. *Death Trap: The Story of the La Brea Tar Pits* (4–8). Illus. 1995, Lerner LB $28.75 (978-0-8225-2851-7). A history of the 40,000-year-old tar pits in Los Angeles and of the many species of prehistoric animals that were trapped in them, with color photographs. (Rev: BL 6/1–15/95; SLJ 5/95) [560]

7584 VanCleave, Janice. *Dinosaurs for Every Kid: Easy Activities That Make Learning Science Fun* (4–7). Illus. Series: Science for Every Kid. 1994, Wiley paper $12.95 (978-0-471-30812-6). With accompanying activities, this book explores the world of dinosaurs and how paleontology has discovered, through fossils, how they lived. (Rev: BL 4/1/94; SLJ 7/94) [567.9]

7585 Williams, Judith. *The Discovery and Mystery of a Dinosaur Named Jane* (5–7). Illus. 2007, Enslow LB $23.93 (978-0-7660-2730-5); paper $13.26 (978-0-7660-2709-1). A straightforward account of the discovery, excavation and installation of this important fossil find. (Rev: SLJ 7/07)

Anthropology and Evolution

7586 Batten, Mary. *Anthropologist: Scientist of the People* (4–7). Illus. Series: Scientists in the Field. 2001, Houghton $16.00 (978-0-618-08368-8). Striking photographs of a Paraguayan tribe of hunter-gatherers serve as a powerful backdrop to this explanation of the work of anthropologists. (Rev: BL 8/01; HB 1–2/02*; HBG 3/02; SLJ 9/01) [627]

7587 Corbishley, Mike. *What Do We Know About Prehistoric People?* (4–7). Illus. Series: What Do We Know About. 1996, Bedrick LB $18.95 (978-0-87226-383-3). Using double-page spreads, this book explores the known facts about human prehistoric life around the world. (Rev: BL 6/1–15/96) [930.1]

7588 Crump, Donald J., ed. *Giants from the Past: The Age of Mammals* (7–10). Illus. 1983, National Geographic LB $12.50 (978-0-87044-429-6). A description of early animals, such as the mastodon, and how they evolved during the Ice Age. [569]

7589 Facchini, Fiorenzo. *Humans: Origins and Evolution* (4–8). Illus. Series: Beginnings — Origins and Evolution. 1995, Raintree LB $24.26 (978-0-8114-3336-5). Theories and facts explaining human evolution are presented in a straightforward way, with extensive artwork and diagrams. (Rev: BL 4/15/95; SLJ 6/95) [573.2]

7590 Gallant, Roy A. *Early Humans* (5–8). Series: The Story of Science. 1999, Benchmark LB $29.93 (978-0-7614-0960-1). Neanderthals, Homo erectus, and early hominids are covered in this work on human evolution and important anthropological finds. (Rev: BL 2/15/00; HBG 3/00; SLJ 3/00) [573.2]

7591 Gallant, Roy A. *The Origins of Life* (6–10). Series: Story of Science. 2000, Marshall Cavendish LB $29.93 (978-0-7614-1151-2). This prize-winning author presents a clear, attractive introduction to the beginning of life on this earth. (Rev: BL 12/15/00; HBG 10/01) [575]

7592 Garassino, Alessandro. *Life, Origins and Evolution* (5–8). Series: Beginnings — Origins and Evolution. 1995, Raintree LB $24.26 (978-0-8114-3335-8). Using informative visuals, the author presents theories concerning the beginnings of life in the world. (Rev: BL 5/1/95) [575]

7593 Goldenberg, Linda. *Little People and a Lost World: An Anthropological Mystery* (5–8). Illus. 2006, Twenty-First Century LB $29.27 (978-0-8225-5983-2). In 2003, a team of archaeologists and anthropologists discovered the skeleton of what's believed to be a small human being who lived more than 12,000 years ago on Flores Island in Indonesia; this book looks at the controversy over the discovery and the insights it has given into early human life. (Rev: BL 12/1/06; SLJ 4/07) [569.909598]

7594 Lauber, Patricia. *Who Came First? New Clues to Prehistoric Americans* (5–10). Illus. 2003, National Geographic $18.95 (978-0-7922-8228-0). An attractive, oversized volume that encompasses anthropology, archaeology, genetics, and linguistics in its discussion of the provenance of the peoples of the Americas. (Rev: BL 7/03*; HB 7–8/03; HBG 10/03; SLJ 8/03*) [970.01]

7595 McCutcheon, Marc. *The Beast in You! Activities and Questions to Explore Evolution* (4–8). Illus. by Michael Kline. Series: A Kaleidoscope Kids Book. 1999, Williamson paper $10.95 (978-1-885593-36-8). In a humorous, creative presentation, the author shows the similarities between humans and other animals and introduces the topic of evolution, our early ancestors, and their development. (Rev: SLJ 3/00) [575]

7596 McGowen, Tom. *Giant Stones and Earth Mounds* (4–8). Illus. 2000, Millbrook LB $25.90 (978-0-7613-1372-4). A history of the New Stone Age of about 9,000 years ago and the constructions that still exist in the United States today from that period. (Rev: BL 10/1/00; HBG 10/01; SLJ 10/00) [930.1]

7597 Naff, Clay Farris, ed. *Evolution* (7–12). Series: Exploring Science and Medical Discoveries. 2005, Gale LB $34.95 (978-0-7377-2823-1). This collection of writings documents the history of theories about human origins from ancient Greece to the 20th century. (Rev: SLJ 12/05)

7598 Patent, Dorothy Hinshaw. *Mystery of the Lascaux Cave* (4–7). Series: Frozen in Time. 1998, Benchmark LB $28.50 (978-0-7614-0784-3). As well as displaying these remarkable cave paintings, this book covers what is known or surmised about the prehistoric people who produced these artistic wonders. (Rev: HBG 10/99; SLJ 3/99) [930.12]

7599 Patent, Dorothy Hinshaw. *Secrets of the Ice Man* (4–7). Series: Frozen in Time. 1998, Benchmark LB $28.50 (978-0-7614-0782-9). The author discusses life during the Ice Age with material from recent discoveries. (Rev: HBG 10/99; SLJ 3/99) [937]

7600 Pickering, Robert. *The People* (5–8). Illus. Series: Prehistoric North America. 1996, Millbrook LB $22.90 (978-1-56294-550-3). An account of the development of the prehistoric North American tribes that may have crossed the land bridge from Asia to the Americas. (Rev: SLJ 4/96) [973.01]

7601 Pye, Claire. *The Wild World of the Future* (4–8). Illus. 2003, Firefly $24.95 (978-1-55297-727-9); paper $14.95 (978-1-55297-725-5). This lively, attractive volume speculates on the animals of the future, basing the projections on previous evolutionary development. (Rev: BL 7/03; SLJ 6/03) [576.8]

7602 Robertshaw, Peter, and Jill Rubalcaba. *The Early Human World* (8–12). Series: The World in Ancient Times. 2005, Oxford LB $32.95 (978-0-19-516157-1). Using primary sources and good illustrations, this volume looks at the world's earliest hominids and the evidence that they evolved from more primitive primates. (Rev: SLJ 6/05; VOYA 8/04) [599]

7603 Sloan, Christopher. *Bury the Dead: Tombs, Corpses, Mummies, Skeletons, and Rituals* (5–9). Illus. 2002, National Geographic $18.95 (978-0-7922-7192-5). Young readers will be fascinated by this serious account of burial practices throughout the ages, with timelines, color photographs, diagrams, and clear descriptions of rites around the world. (Rev: BL 12/1/02; HBG 3/03; SLJ 10/02*) [393]

7604 Thorndike, Jonathan L. *Epperson v. Arkansas: The Evolution–Creationism Debate* (6–10). Series: Landmark Supreme Court Cases. 1999, Enslow LB $20.95 (978-0-7660-1084-0). This book examines the issues involved in this case of evolution versus creationism, traces the case from lower courts to the Supreme Court, and discusses the present-day impact of the court's decision. (Rev: BL 3/15/99) [116]

7605 Westrup, Hugh. *The Mammals* (5–8). Illus. Series: Prehistoric North America. 1996, Millbrook LB $22.90 (978-1-56294-546-6). The woolly mammoth and saber-toothed tiger are two of the prehistoric mammals described in words and pictures. (Rev: BL 5/15/96; SLJ 4/96) [569]

7606 Wilkinson, Philip, and Jacqueline Dineen. *The Early Inventions* (5–8). Illus. 1995, Chelsea LB $21.95 (978-0-7910-2766-0). A look at the invention of early tools and processes, mostly for human survival purposes — eating and staying warm. (Rev: SLJ 11/95; VOYA 2/96) [930]

Archaeology

7607 Arnold, Caroline. *Stone Age Farmers Beside the Sea: Scotland's Prehistoric Village of Skara Brae* (5–8). 1997, Clarion $16.00 (978-0-395-77601-8). A stunning volume that tells the story of the Stone Age village of Skara Brae, dating to about 3000 B.C., that was unearthed in the Orkney Islands in 1850. (Rev: BCCB 4/97; BL 4/15/97; SLJ 7/97) [930]

7608 Avi-Yonah, Michael. *Dig This! How Archaeologists Uncover Our Past* (5–8). Series: Buried Worlds. 1993, Lerner LB $28.75 (978-0-8225-3200-2). A history of the discipline of archaeology, an examination of excavating methods, and a look at several ancient civilizations. (Rev: BL 1/15/94; SLJ 2/94) [930.1]

7609 Buell, Janet. *Ancient Horsemen of Siberia* (6–9). Series: Time Travelers. 1998, Millbrook LB $25.90 (978-0-7613-3005-9). This account describes the excavation of a 2,500-year-old burial site in the Altai Mountains in southern Siberia and recounts how the Russian archeologists were able to re-create the life of these primitive peoples through an examination of their artifacts. (Rev: SLJ 10/98) [930]

7610 Buell, Janet. *Greenland Mummies* (5–8). Series: Time Travelers. 1998, Twenty-First Century LB $25.90 (978-0-7613-3004-2). By examining mummified human corpses found in Greenland, archaeologists have been able to reconstruct the life and culture of Inuits who lived 500 years ago. (Rev: SLJ 10/98) [930]

7611 Buell, Janet. *Ice Maiden of the Andes* (5–8). Illus. Series: Time Travelers. 1997, Twenty-First Century paper $25.90 (978-0-8050-5185-8). The story of the discovery of the frozen body of a young Inca girl who died 500 years ago and of how forensic methods such as DNA testing have revealed insights into Inca society, its religion, and gender roles. (Rev: BL 2/1/98; SLJ 3/98) [985]

7612 *Dazzling! Jewelry of the Ancient World* (5–8). Illus. Series: Buried Worlds. 1995, Lerner LB $28.75 (978-0-8225-3203-3). An exploration of the jewels that archaeologists have retrieved from various ancient sites. (Rev: BL 7/95; SLJ 4/95) [739.27]

7613 Dean, Arlan. *Terra-Cotta Soldiers: Army of Stone* (4–7). Illus. Series: High Interest Books: Digging Up the Past. 2005, Children's Pr. LB $24.50 (978-0-516-25124-0); paper $6.95 (978-0-516-25093-9). For reluctant readers, this is a useful introduction to one of the world's most extraordinary archaeological finds: the 8,000 terracotta warriors of China. (Rev: BL 10/15/05; SLJ 2/06) [931]

7614 Echo-Hawk, Roger C., and Walter R. Echo-Hawk. *Battlefields and Burial Grounds: The Indian Struggle to Protect Ancestral Graves in the United States* (7–10). 1994, Lerner LB $22.60 (978-0-8225-2663-6); paper $8.95 (978-0-8225-9722-3). A solid discussion of the conflict over Indian graves that have been plundered in the name of scientific research. (Rev: BL 5/15/94; SLJ 7/94*) [393]

7615 Funston, Sylvia. *Mummies* (5–7). Illus. by Joe Weissmann. Series: Strange Science. 2000, Owl $19.95 (978-1-894379-03-8); paper $9.95 (978-1-894379-04-5). All kinds of mummified human remains are discussed, from those in ancient Egypt to the 1999 discovery of George Mallory's body on Mount Everest. (Rev: HBG 3/01; SLJ 11/00) [909]

7616 Greene, Meg. *Buttons, Bones, and the Organ-Grinder's Monkey: Tales of Historical Archaeology* (5–8). Illus. 2001, Linnet LB $25.00 (978-0-208-02498-5). This introduction to historical archaeology looks at finds at five different sites in the United States. (Rev: BL 10/1/01; HBG 10/02; SLJ 1/02; VOYA 4/02) [973]

7617 Guiberson, Brenda Z. *Mummy Mysteries: Tales from North America* (4–7). Illus. by author. Series: A Redfeather Chapter Book. 1998, Holt

$15.95 (978-0-8050-5369-2). Reading like a mystery story, this book focuses on mummies found in North America, how and where they were found, and the information they reveal. (Rev: BCCB 2/99; HBG 3/99; SLJ 12/98) [937]

7618 Harris, Nathaniel. *Ancient Maya: Archaeology Unlocks the Secrets of the Maya's Past* (5–8). Illus. Series: National Geographic Investigates. 2008, National Geographic $17.95 (978-1-4263-0227-5). With photographs, illustrations, and maps, this book shows how archaeology has uncovered information about the Maya and their culture. (Rev: BL 3/3/08) [972.8]

7619 Hoobler, Dorothy. *Lost Civilizations* (5–7). Illus. by Thomas Hoobler. 1992, Walker LB $15.85 (978-0-8027-8153-6). Interesting discussion of Stonehenge, the Mound Builders, and other lost ancient civilizations. (Rev: BL 5/1/92; SLJ 9/92) [930]

7620 Jameson, W. C. *Buried Treasures of the Atlantic Coast: Legends of Sunken Pirate Treasures, Mysterious Caches, and Jinxed Ships — From Maine to Florida* (4–8). Series: Buried Treasure. 1997, August House $11.95 (978-0-87483-484-0). An account of how buried treasures were acquired and lost and the modern efforts to locate and retrieve them. Also use *Buried Treasures of New England* (1997). (Rev: SLJ 10/97) [910.4]

7621 Kallen, Stuart A. *Mummies* (4–7). Illus. Series: Wonders of the World. 2003, Gale LB $18.96 (978-0-7377-1031-1). Coverage of various types of mummies, the mummification process, and mummies of note will be especially useful for report writers. (Rev: BL 5/1/03; SLJ 4/03) [393]

7622 Kops, Deborah. *Palenque* (5–8). Illus. Series: Unearthing Ancient Worlds. 2008, Twenty-First Century LB $30.60 (978-0-8225-7504-7). With many large photographs and interesting text, this volume traces the discovery of the ruins at Palenque in the mid-19th century and the work that has been done since then on this Mayan site. (Rev: LMC 11-12/08; SLJ 2/08)

7623 Lourie, Peter. *The Mystery of the Maya: Uncovering the Lost City of Palenque* (5–8). Illus. 2001, Boyds Mills $19.95 (978-1-56397-839-5). The author relates his interesting and often exciting experiences at a dig in Mexico and describes the work of the archaeologists and the history of the site. (Rev: BL 9/15/01; HBG 3/02; SLJ 11/01) [972.75]

7624 Malam, John. *Mummies* (5–8). Illus. Series: Kingfisher Knowledge. 2003, Kingfisher $11.95 (978-0-7534-5623-1). A highly illustrated, readable exploration of preserved bodies of all eras and areas of the world. (Rev: HBG 4/04; SLJ 12/03) [393]

7625 Panchyk, Richard. *Archaeology for Kids: Uncovering the Mysteries of Our Past with 25 Activities* (5–8). Illus. 2001, Chicago Review paper $14.95 (978-1-55652-395-3). An introduction for older readers to the history and scientific method of archaeology, full of illustrations and with interesting activities. (Rev: BL 1/1–15/02; SLJ 12/01) [930.1]

7626 Place, Robin. *Bodies from the Past* (4–7). Illus. Series: Digging Up the Past. 1995, Thomson Learning LB $24.26 (978-1-56847-397-0). Explores the preserved remains of people around the world from burial sites in China and mummies in peat bogs to the Ice Man recently discovered in the Alps. (Rev: SLJ 2/96) [567.9]

7627 Reid, Struan. *The Children's Atlas of Lost Treasures* (4–7). Illus. Series: Children's Atlases. 1997, Millbrook paper $14.95 (978-0-7613-0240-7). Using a double-page spread for each site, this book supplies a survey of the world-famous discoveries of treasures that began as religious offerings, pirate booty, and items lost in war or by natural disasters. (Rev: HBG 3/98; SLJ 3/98) [930.1]

7628 Scarre, Chris, and Rebecca Stefoff. *Palace of Minos at Knossos* (7–10). Series: Digging for the Past. 2002, Oxford $23.95 (978-0-19-514272-3). After a map and timeline, this account describes various archaeological digs at Knossos, tells how the palace was built, and gives material on the original structure. (Rev: BL 10/15/02; HBG 4/04; SLJ 2/04) [930]

7629 Scheller, William. *Amazing Archaeologists and Their Finds* (6–10). 1994, Oliver LB $19.95 (978-1-881508-17-5). This work presents eight archaeologists' discoveries, including the walls of Troy, the tomb of King Tut, Jericho, and Incan ruins. (Rev: BL 11/1/94; SLJ 2/95; VOYA 2/95) [930.1]

7630 Smith, K. C. *Exploring for Shipwrecks* (5–7). Series: Shipwrecks. 2000, Watts LB $25.50 (978-0-531-20377-4). This book explains and explores the world of underwater archaeology, the techniques and training involved, and gives many examples from specific shipwreck studies. (Rev: BL 10/15/00) [930.1]

7631 Smith, K. C. *Shipwrecks of the Explorers* (5–7). Illus. Series: Watts Library: Shipwrecks. 2000, Watts LB $25.50 (978-0-531-20378-1). A look at underwater archaeology tells how scientists locate shipwrecks and what the ships reveal about the explorers who sailed in them. There are also descriptions of famous voyages including those of Columbus and Amundsen. (Rev: BL 10/15/00) [910.4]

7632 Sonneborn, Liz. *Pompeii* (5–8). Illus. Series: Unearthing Ancient Worlds. 2008, Lerner LB $30.60 (978-0-8225-7505-4). Concentrating on the original excavation of Pompeii in the 18th century, this book explains how early archaeological digs were conducted. (Rev: BL 4/1/08; SLJ 2/08) [937]

7633 Tanaka, Shelley. *Mummies: The Newest, Coolest and Creepiest from Around the World* (4–7). Illus. 2005, Abrams $16.95 (978-0-8109-5797-8). Mummies from across history and around the world are on display in the colorful — and often graphic — pages of this fascinating book. (Rev: BL 12/1/05*; HBG 4/06; LMC 4–5/06; SLJ 12/05*) [393]

7634 Vivian, R. Gwinn, and Margaret Anderson. *Chaco Canyon* (7–10). Illus. Series: Digging for the Past. 2002, Oxford $23.95 (978-0-19-514280-8). An interesting overview of Chaco Canyon's history and the work of archaeologists there over the years. (Rev: BL 10/15/02; HBG 10/02; SLJ 10/02) [973]

7635 Wheatley, Abigail, and Struan Reid. *The Usborne Introduction to Archaeology: Internet-Linked* (6–9). Illus. Series: Archaeology. 2005, EDC $19.95 (978-0-7945-0806-7). This excellent, large-format introduction to archaeology explores the discipline itself, the various techniques used to date and preserve artifacts, and significant discoveries around the world. (Rev: BL 4/1/05) [930.1]

7636 Wilcox, Charlotte. *Mummies and Their Mysteries* (5–7). Illus. 1993, Carolrhoda LB $23.93 (978-0-87614-767-2). An account of how throughout history many civilizations and religions have attempted to preserve bodies. (Rev: BCCB 7–8/93*; BL 6/1–15/93*) [393.3]

7637 Wilcox, Charlotte. *Mummies, Bones, and Body Parts* (4–7). Illus. 2000, Lerner paper $7.95 (978-1-57505-486-5). The study of human remains is covered, including material on how death is treated in various cultures, embalming practices, and the work of archaeologists and anthropologists. (Rev: BCCB 9/00; BL 9/1/00; HBG 10/01; SLJ 10/00) [393]

World History and Geography

7638 Aaseng, Nathan. *You Are the General II: 1800–1899* (6–9). Series: Great Decisions. 1995, Oliver LB $19.95 (978-1-881508-25-0). In this account of famous battles such as Waterloo, Gettysburg, and Little Bighorn, the reader is asked to become a field marshal and interact with history. (Rev: SLJ 2/96) [900]

7639 Andryszewski, Tricia. *Walking the Earth: The History of Human Migration* (5–9). 2006, Twenty-First Century LB $27.93 (978-0-7613-3458-3). A thorough introduction to the movements of human population across more than 150,000 years, with many illustrations, maps, and charts. (Rev: HBG 4/07; LMC 3/07; SLJ 1/07; VOYA 12/06) [304.8]

7640 Beller, Susan Provost. *The History Puzzle: How We Know What We Know about the Past* (8–11). Illus. 2006, Lerner LB $26.60 (978-0-7613-2877-3). This concise overview of how archaeology and other methods allow historians to piece together the past includes sepia photographs, illustrations, and paintings. (Rev: BL 4/15/06; LMC 11–12/06; SLJ 5/06) [901]

7641 Beyer, Rick. *The Greatest Stories Never Told: 100 Tales from History to Astonish, Bewilder, and Stupefy* (6–12). Illus. 2003, HarperCollins $18.95 (978-0-06-001401-8). Browsers will enjoy this well-illustrated and well-researched chronological overview of historical tidbits. (Rev: VOYA 10/03)

7642 Blackwood, Gary L. *Enigmatic Events* (5–8). Illus. Series: Unsolved History. 2005, Marshall Cavendish LB $20.95 (978-0-7614-1889-4). Explores some of history's most enduring mysteries — the disappearance of the dinosaurs and of the *Mary Celeste*, to name only two. (Rev: BL 3/1/06; SLJ 3/06) [904]

7643 Blackwood, Gary L. *Highwaymen* (5–8). Illus. Series: Bad Guys. 2001, Marshall Cavendish LB $29.93 (978-0-7614-1017-1). Period artwork, photographs, and intriguing tales bring real highway robbers, and the times they lived in, to life. (Rev: BL 1/1–15/02; HBG 3/02; SLJ 1/02) [364.15]

7644 Blackwood, Gary L. *Swindlers* (5–8). Illus. Series: Bad Guys. 2001, Marshall Cavendish LB $29.93 (978-0-7614-1031-7). The author presents famous swindlers and cheats throughout history, providing illustrations, source notes, and recommended Web sites and further reading. (Rev: BL 1/1–15/02; HBG 3/02) [364.16]

7645 Burgan, Michael. *The Spanish Conquest of America: Prehistory to 1775* (5–8). Series: Latino-American History. 2006, Chelsea House LB $35.00 (978-0-8160-6440-3). A thorough and clear account of Spain's influence on the Americas, with discussion of individual explorers as well as the impact on native peoples and the conflicts with other colonial powers. (Rev: BL 3/15/07) [979]

7646 Butts, Ed. *SOS: Stories of Survival* (6–9). Illus. 2007, Tundra paper $12.95 (978-0-88776-786-9). Thirteen historic and modern-day disasters, both acts of God (such as the 2004 tsunami) and acts of man (such as the Triangle Shirtwaist factory fire), are included in this book that emphasizes brave acts and survivors. (Rev: BL 7/07; SLJ 8/07) [363.34]

7647 Cawthorne, Nigel. *Military Commanders: The 100 Greatest Throughout History* (6–12). 2004, Enchanted Lion $18.95 (978-1-59270-029-5). This chronology identifies the greatest military battles in world history and the men who led their forces to victory in those battles. (Rev: BL 6/1–15/04; SLJ 4/04) [355]

7648 Chisholm, Jane. *The Usborne Book of World History Dates: The Key Events in History* (4–8). 1998, EDC paper $22.95 (978-0-7460-2318-1).

Timelines and double-page spreads with brief topical essays present a panorama of world history. (Rev: SLJ 5/99) [910]

7649 Christie, Peter. *The Curse of Akkad: Climate Upheavals That Rocked Human History* (5–8). Illus. 2008, Annick $19.95 (978-1-55451-119-8); paper $11.95 (978-1-55451-118-1). The effects of climate change through history are described in segments of one to three pages, making this a good choice for reluctant readers. (Rev: BL 8/08) [551.609]

7650 Claybourne, Anna, and Caroline Young. *The Usborne Book of Treasure Hunting* (4–7). Illus. 1999, Usborne paper $14.95 (978-0-7460-3445-3). In a series of short chapters, this book covers famous treasures that were buried underground, lost at sea, or existed in ancient times — with coverage of such subjects as the clay soldiers in Huang Di's tomb and the restoration of the Tudor ship *Mary Rose*. (Rev: BL 4/1/99) [622.19]

7651 Connolly, Sean. *Gender Equality* (5–8). Series: Campaigns for Change. 2005, Smart Apple Media LB $29.95 (978-1-58340-515-4). An exploration of women's status and struggles to improve it throughout history; also use *The Right to Vote* (2005). (Rev: SLJ 5/06) [305.42]

7652 Cox, Caroline, and Ken Albala. *Opening Up North America, 1497–1800* (6–12). Series: Discovery and Exploration. 2005, Facts on File $40.00 (978-0-8160-5261-5). Chronicles the arrival of Europeans in North America and their progression across the continent, with maps, illustrations, and excerpts from primary sources. (Rev: SLJ 8/05) [973]

7653 Currie, Stephen. *Pirates* (6–10). Series: World History. 2001, Lucent LB $27.45 (978-1-56006-807-5). Although pirates of all eras are mentioned, the "Golden Age of Piracy" in the 17th and 18th centuries is the focus of this detailed overview. (Rev: SLJ 7/01) [910.4]

7654 Deary, Terry. *The Wicked History of the World: History with the Nasty Bits Left In!* (4–7). Illus. by Martin Brown. 2006, Scholastic $10.99 (978-0-439-87786-2). This pun-filled survey of world history, with its emphasis on the shadier side, will attract reluctant readers with sections on "Beastly Barbarians," "Rotten Rules," and "Vicious Villains." (Rev: SLJ 12/06) [909]

7655 Defries, Cheryl L. *Seven Natural Wonders of the United States and Canada* (4–7). Illus. Series: Seven Wonders of the World. 2005, Enslow LB $25.26 (978-0-7660-5291-8). This tour of seven of North America's natural wonders, including the Grand Canyon, Everglades, and Niagara Falls, is extended by constantly updated links to Web sites. (Rev: SLJ 11/05) [557]

7656 De Porti, Andrea. *Explorers: The Most Exciting Voyages of Discovery — from the African Expeditions to the Lunar Landing* (8–12). Illus. 2005, Firefly $49.95 (978-1-55407-101-2). Rare archival photos document the history of exploration over the past 150 years, telling 53 stories of discovery — some well-known and others more obscure. (Rev: BL 12/1/05) [910.92]

7657 Gelber, Carol. *Masks Tell Stories* (5–7). Illus. Series: Beyond Museum Walls. 1993, Millbrook LB $24.90 (978-1-56294-224-3). Explores the nature, meaning, and uses of masks in different cultures at various times. (Rev: BL 8/93) [391]

7658 Gilpin, Daniel. *Food and Clothing* (6–9). Illus. Series: History of Invention. 2004, Facts on File $35.00 (978-0-8160-5441-1). A slim introductory overview of advances in food and clothing from prehistoric times to today, with maps, illustrations, and profiles of key figures. (Rev: SLJ 12/04) [973]

7659 Gold, Susan Dudley. *Governments of the Western Hemisphere* (5–8). Illus. Series: Comparing Continents. 1997, Twenty-First Century LB $24.90 (978-0-8050-5602-0). This book examines the struggles for independence in the United States, Canada, Mexico, Central America, and South America and the different directions taken by each once independence was achieved, highlighting the diversity across the nations. (Rev: BL 2/1/98; SLJ 3/98) [320.3]

7660 Graham, Amy. *Seven Wonders of the Natural World* (4–7). Illus. Series: Seven Wonders of the World. 2005, Enslow LB $25.26 (978-0-7660-5290-1). A tour of seven of the world's natural wonders, including Mount Everest, the Great Barrier Reef, and the Grand Canyon; the text is extended by constantly updated links to Web sites. (Rev: SLJ 11/05)

7661 Grant, Kevin Patrick. *Exploration in the Age of Empire, 1750–1953* (6–10). Series: Discovery and Exploration. 2004, Facts on File $40.00 (978-0-8160-5260-8). A look at the exploration that took place during these two centuries and the underlying political and religious motivations, in clear, informative text plus photographs, illustrations, and excerpts from primary sources. (Rev: SLJ 12/04) [973]

7662 Hannigan, Des. *One People: Many Journeys* (8–12). Illus. 2005, Lonely Planet $40.00 (978-1-74104-600-7). Striking photographs from around the world capture the universality of the human experience and demonstrate the wide diversity of resources. (Rev: BL 1/1–15/06) [910]

7663 Hart, Avery, and Paul Mantell. *Who Really Discovered America? Unraveling the Mystery and Solving the Puzzle* (5–7). Illus. by Michael Kline. Series: A Kaleidoscope Kids Book. 2001, Williamson paper $12.95 (978-1-885593-46-7). Several theories are presented about the discovery of America, and students are urged to examine them with open minds, using activities that help them to question and explore. (Rev: SLJ 10/01) [970.01]

7664 Hinds, Kathryn. *The Celts of Northern Europe* (7–10). Series: Cultures of the Past. 1996, Benchmark LB $29.93 (978-0-7614-0092-9). This book gives a history of the Celts, their religion, social structure, art, folklore, and how they helped keep Christianity alive in Ireland. (Rev: SLJ 3/97) [940.1]

7665 Huff, Toby. *An Age of Science and Revolutions: 1600–1800* (7–10). Illus. Series: Medieval and Early Modern World. 2005, Oxford $32.95 (978-0-19-517724-4). A sweeping overview of history in both the East and West from the beginning of the 17th century through the end of the 18th century, with color photographs, maps, profiles of key figures, and so forth. (Rev: BL 10/15/05; SLJ 7/06) [909]

7666 Kachur, Matthew. *The Slave Trade* (6–9). Series: Slavery in the Americas. 2006, Chelsea House $35.00 (978-0-8160-6134-1). Provides a broad overview of the transatlantic slave trade and how it affected both Africa and the Americas, with discussion of the Middle Passage, sugar production, and other related issues. (Rev: BL 7/06) [306.3]

7667 Kallen, Stuart A. *Life Among the Pirates* (6–10). Series: The Way People Live. 1998, Lucent LB $28.70 (978-1-56006-393-3). A fascinating history of world piracy with an emphasis on the "Golden Age" from 1519 until the 1720s. (Rev: BL 11/15/98; SLJ 3/99) [910.45]

7668 Kyi, Tanya L. *Fires!* (6–9). Series: True Stories from the Edge. 2004, Annick $18.95 (978-1-55037-877-1); paper $8.95 (978-1-55037-876-4). The stories behind ten of history's most horrific fires — including the Great Fire of London in 1666 and the Chernobyl nuclear plant explosion in 1986 — are recounted in this compelling title. (Rev: BL 1/1–15/05; VOYA 6/05) [363.37]

7669 Lassieur, Allison. *The Celts* (6–9). Series: Lost Civilizations. 2001, Lucent LB $24.95 (978-1-56006-746-7). This well-researched account covers the history, culture and artistic contributions of the ancient Celts during the period from 600 B.C. through 600 A.D. (Rev: BL 8/1/01) [940.1]

7670 Levy, Elizabeth. *Awesome Ancient Ancestors! Mound Builders, Maya, and More* (5–8). Illus. by Daniel McFeely. Series: America's Horrible Histories. 2001, Scholastic $12.95 (978-0-439-30349-1); paper $4.99 (978-0-590-10795-2). A humorous and chatty cockroach introduces the early inhabitants of North America and Mesoamerica. (Rev: HBG 10/02; SLJ 5/02) [970.01]

7671 Llewellyn, Claire. *Great Discoveries and Amazing Adventures: The Stories of Hidden Marvels and Lost Treasures* (4–7). Illus. 2004, Kingfisher $18.95 (978-0-7534-5783-2). Important discover-

ies — and hoaxes — are described in inviting text, plus many illustrations, factoids, and a foreword by Robert Ballard. (Rev: SLJ 1/05) [509]

7672 Markle, Sandra. *Rescues!* (4–7). Illus. 2006, Lerner LB $25.26 (978-0-8225-3413-6). Markle covers rescue efforts in 11 recent disasters (2004 to 2005), giving details of technology used and providing accounts by victims, rescuers, and eyewitnesses. (Rev: BL 4/1/06*; HBG 10/06; LMC 11–12/06; SLJ 8/06; VOYA 6/06) [363.34]

7673 Mason, Antony. *People Around the World* (5–7). Illus. 2002, Kingfisher $24.95 (978-0-7534-5497-8). An oversize guide to people of different cultures around the world, organized by continent, featuring hundreds of full-color photographs and illustrations, and detailing such topics as diet, language, employment, and leisure of urban and rural dwellers. (Rev: BL 5/1/03; HBG 10/03; SLJ 4/03; VOYA 6/03) [305.8]

7674 Maynard, Christopher. *The History News: Revolution* (4–7). Illus. 1999, Candlewick $16.99 (978-0-7636-0491-2). Using a tabloid-newspaper format, this book covers four revolutions: the American, French, Russian, and Chinese. (Rev: BL 12/15/99; HBG 3/00; SLJ 10/99) [909]

7675 Millard, Anne. *A Street Through Time* (4–8). Illus. 1998, DK $17.99 (978-0-7894-3426-5). Western European history is traced in this oversize book that contains 14 views of the same riverside location at various times in history, including the Stone Age, Viking times, the Roman period, the Middle Ages, and modern times. (Rev: BL 1/1–15/99; HB 1–2/99; HBG 3/99; SLJ 12/98) [936]

7676 O'Brien, Patrick. *Mutiny on the Bounty* (4–7). Illus. 2007, Walker $17.95 (978-0-8027-9587-8). Clear, balanced narrative and vivid illustrations tell both sides of the story of the famous mutiny and its aftermath. (Rev: BL 1/1–15/07; SLJ 3/07) [910.4]

7677 Phillips, Dee, et al. *People of the World* (4–7). Illus. Series: Just the Facts. 2006, School Specialty paper $9.95 (978-0-7696-4257-4). Statistics and fast facts on the countries and peoples of the world are presented on double-page spreads. (Rev: BL 4/1/06) [305.8]

7678 Ross, Stewart. *Conquerors and Explorers* (5–7). Illus. Series: Fact or Fiction? 1996, Millbrook LB $26.90 (978-0-7613-0532-3). The subtitle of this work is "The Greed, Cunning, and Bravery of the Travelers and Plunderers Who Opened Up the World." (Rev: BL 10/15/96; SLJ 4/97) [910]

7679 Ruggiero, Adriane. *The Ottoman Empire* (5–8). Series: Cultures of the Past. 2002, Marshall Cavendish $29.93 (978-0-7614-1494-0). A handsome account that traces the rise and fall of the great Ottoman Empire from its beginning in the 15th century to its collapse and the formation of modern

Turkey after World War I. (Rev: BL 1/1–15/03; HBG 3/03; SLJ 2/03) [956]

7680 Rutsala, David. *The Sea Route to Asia* (4–7). Series: Exploration and Discovery. 2002, Mason Crest LB $19.95 (978-1-59084-046-7). Rutsala presents Portuguese explorers' efforts to find a route around Africa to Asia, with information on Prince Henry the Navigator, Bartholomeu Dias, and Vasco da Gama. (Rev: SLJ 12/02) [910]

7681 St. Antoine, Sara, ed. *Stories from Where We Live: The Great North American Prairie* (4–8). 2001, Milkweed $19.95 (978-1-57131-630-1). A collection of historical and contemporary stories, poems, essays, and journal entries about life on the prairie, with informative appendixes. (Rev: BL 5/15/01) [978]

7682 Scandiffio, Laura. *Escapes!* (5–9). Illus. by Stephen MacEachern. Series: True Stories from the Edge. 2004, Annick $18.95 (978-1-55037-823-8); paper $7.95 (978-1-55037-822-1). Ten stories of great escapes and escape attempts, from the first century B.C. to the late 1970s, with a concentration on resourcefulness and bravery. (Rev: SLJ 6/04) [904]

7683 Shapiro, Stephen. *Battle Stations! Fortifications Through the Ages* (5–8). Illus. 2005, Annick LB $19.95 (978-1-55037-889-4); paper $7.95 (978-1-55037-888-7). A tall, slim, and very visual overview of fortifications around the world and throughout history. (Rev: BL 9/15/05) [355.7]

7684 Smith, Bonnie G. *Imperialism: A History in Documents* (6–12). Series: Pages from History. 2000, Oxford $39.95 (978-0-19-510801-9). This detailed account of how powerful nations spread their influence around the globe draws on many primary sources and includes eye-catching photographs and a useful timeline. (Rev: BL 11/15/00; HBG 10/01; SLJ 4/01) [325]

7685 Stefoff, Rebecca. *Exploration* (6–9). Series: World Historical Atlases. 2004, Marshall Cavendish $27.07 (978-0-7614-1640-1). A brief overview of world exploration, with many clear maps, chronicling voyages of discovery from ancient times through the polar explorations of Amundsen and Shackleton. (Rev: BL 1/05) [910]

7686 Stewart, Robert, et al. *Mysteries of History* (7–12). Illus. 2003, National Geographic $29.95 (978-0-7922-6232-9). Such controversial topics as Stonehenge, Napoleon's death, and Custer's Last Stand are presented with 16 others in this well-illustrated book. (Rev: BL 2/1/04; HBG 4/04) [902]

7687 Swanson, Diane. *Tunnels!* (5–8). Series: True Stories from the Edge. 2003, Annick $18.95 (978-1-55037-781-1); paper $6.95 (978-1-55037-780-4). Ten thrilling stories of tunnel escapes and escapades are accompanied by maps. (Rev: BL 4/15/03; SLJ 5/03) [624.1]

7688 Wells, Don. *The Spice Trade* (5–8). Illus. Series: Great Journeys. 2004, Weigl $26.00 (978-1-59036-208-2); paper $7.95 (978-1-59036-261-7). Colorful illustrations and an attractive format will appeal to browsers seeking information about the spice trade; a useful timeline and links to Web sites are included. (Rev: BL 11/1/04)

7689 Wiesner-Hanks, Merry E. *An Age of Voyages, 1350–1600* (7–12). 2006, Oxford Univ. LB $32.95 (978-0-19-517672-8). Exploration from Europe to Asia, Africa, the Middle East, and the Americas is examined with many illustrations and extracts from primary sources, including letters and diaries, and text that discusses the accompanying discoveries, inventions, and social changes. (Rev: LMC 11–12/06; SLJ 7/06)

7690 Williams, Brian. *The Modern World: From the French Revolution to the Computer Age* (5–8). Illus. by James Field. Series: Timelink. 1994, Bedrick LB $18.95 (978-0-87226-312-3). An overview of the 200 years of world history that outlines major events, with useful timelines and maps. (Rev: SLJ 1/95) [909]

7691 Williams, Brian, and Brenda Williams. *The Age of Discovery: From the Renaissance to American Independence* (5–8). Illus. by James Field. Series: Timelink. 1994, Bedrick LB $18.95 (978-0-87226-311-6). An overview of world history from the Renaissance through the American Revolution presented in 50-year segments. (Rev: SLJ 1/95) [909]

7692 Wojtanik, Andrew. *Afghanistan to Zimbabwe: Country Facts That Helped Me Win the National Geographic Bee* (5–12). 2005, National Geographic paper $12.95 (978-0-7922-7981-5). Facts and figures about the world's 192 independent countries are organized into three categories: Physical, Political, and Environmental/Economic. (Rev: SLJ 10/05; VOYA 8/05) [910]

7693 Worth, Richard. *The Great Empire of China and Marco Polo in World History* (5–8). Illus. Series: In World History. 2003, Enslow LB $26.60 (978-0-7660-1939-3). Quotations from primary documents and excerpts from Polo's own writings add context to this account of his 13th-century journeys to the Far East. (Rev: SLJ 3/04) [915.04]

7694 Worth, Richard. *New France 1534–1763: Featuring the Region That Now Includes All or Parts of Michigan, Minnesota, Wisconsin, Illinois, Indiana, Ohio, Pennsylvania, Vermont, Maine, and Canada from Manitoba to Newfoundland* (6–9). Illus. Series: Voices from Colonial America. 2007, National Geographic $21.95 (978-1-4263-0147-6). As the title indicates, a huge part of North America was once the colony of New France; this book uses quotations from colony residents as well as other primary and secondary sources to introduce the territory. (Rev: BL 2/15/08) [971.01]

Ancient History

General and Miscellaneous

7695 Avi-Yonah, Michael. *Piece by Piece! Mosaics of the Ancient World* (5–8). Illus. Series: Buried Worlds. 1993, Lerner LB $28.75 (978-0-8225-3204-0). This book shows how and where mosaics were made in the ancient world and how, through the wonders of archaeology, they are still being uncovered today. (Rev: BL 1/15/94; SLJ 3/94) [738.5]

7696 Ball, Jacqueline, and Richard H. Levey. *Ancient China: Archaeology Unlocks the Secrets of China's Past* (5–8). Illus. Series: National Geographic Investigates. 2006, National Geographic $17.95 (978-0-7922-7783-5). After an introduction to China and its history, this volume looks at individual archaeological finds and at the lives revealed; vivid illustrations and good descriptions of archaeological techniques add to the value. (Rev: BL 10/15/06) [931]

7697 Barter, James. *The Ancient Persians* (5–8). Series: Lost Civilizations. 2005, Gale LB $29.95 (978-1-59018-621-3). The lost civilization of the ancient Persians, with information about the society's people, customs, monetary system, and military, with maps and illustrations. (Rev: SLJ 6/06) [935]

7698 Bingham, Jane. *The Ancient World* (5–8). Illus. Series: A History of Fashion and Costume. 2005, Facts on File $35.00 (978-0-8160-5944-7). A broad overview of the clothing and personal adornment worn during ancient times, with many visual aids. (Rev: SLJ 5/06) [391]

7699 Bowman, John S., and Maurice Isserman, eds. *Exploration in the World of the Ancients* (6–10). Series: Discovery and Exploration. 2004, Facts on File $40.00 (978-0-8160-5257-8). A look at the voyages and routes of explorers from prehistoric times to the beginning of the Middle Ages. (Rev: SLJ 12/04) [973]

7700 Brewer, Paul. *Warfare in the Ancient World* (7–10). Series: History of Warfare. 1999, Raintree LB $29.97 (978-0-8172-5442-1). This account describes important wars and battles in the ancient world, from Egypt through the Roman Empire. (Rev: HBG 3/99; SLJ 3/99) [930]

7701 Calvert, Patricia. *The Ancient Celts* (5–8). Series: People of the Ancient World. 2005, Watts LB $30.50 (978-0-531-12359-1); paper $9.95 (978-0-531-16845-5). Introduces readers to the arts, religious beliefs, and society of the ancient Celts, with discussion of individual occupations and of the discoveries by archaeologists and anthropologists. (Rev: SLJ 9/05) [973]

7702 Caselli, Giovanni. *The First Civilizations* (6–8). Illus. 1985, Bedrick $18.95 (978-0-911745-

59-7). This account traces the early history of man, from the first toolmakers to the civilizations of Egypt and Greece, through the objects that were made and used. (Rev: BL 11/15/85; SLJ 1/87) [930]

7703 Corbishley, Mike. *How Do We Know Where People Came From?* (5–8). Series: How Do We Know. 1995, Raintree LB $24.26 (978-0-8114-3880-3). Using double-page spreads, this book covers early cultures and touches on such subjects as early writing, Stonehenge, the Great Wall of China, the Easter Island statues, and the pyramids. (Rev: SLJ 1/96) [930]

7704 DeAngelis, Therese. *Wonders of the Ancient World* (5–8). Illus. Series: Costume, Tradition, and Culture: Reflecting on the Past. 1998, Chelsea $19.75 (978-0-7910-5170-2). This work features, in double-page spreads, such wonders as the Great Pyramids, Easter Island, and Stonehenge. (Rev: BL 3/15/99; HBG 10/99) [930]

7705 Fagan, Brian M., ed. *The Seventy Great Inventions of the Ancient World* (7–12). Illus. 2004, Thames & Hudson $40.00 (978-0-500-05130-6). This photo-filled volume explores inventions in categories ranging from hunting and farming to artwork and communications. (Rev: BL 12/1/04) [609]

7706 Gaines, Ann. *Herodotus and the Explorers of the Classical Age* (6–9). Illus. Series: World Explorers. 1993, Chelsea LB $32.00 (978-0-7910-1293-2). A description of the exploration of the Mediterranean Sea region by adventurers of the ancient world, including the "father of history," Herodotus. (Rev: BL 12/15/93; SLJ 11/93) [909]

7707 Gonen, Rivka. *Fired Up! Making Pottery in Ancient Times* (5–8). Illus. Series: Buried Worlds. 1993, Lerner LB $28.75 (978-0-8225-3202-6). This book explains how pottery was made in ancient times, showing examples from different cultures, and tells how archaeologists are uncovering more and more examples. (Rev: BL 1/15/94; SLJ 4/94) [738.3]

7708 Greene, Jacqueline D. *Slavery in Ancient Greece and Rome* (4–7). Series: Watts Library: History of Slavery. 2000, Watts LB $25.50 (978-0-531-11693-7). Topics covered include the treatment of slaves in Greece and Rome, how they thrived in Greece's democracy, the slave fire brigades, battles of slave gladiators, and the attitudes toward slavery in the early Christian church. (Rev: BL 3/1/01; SLJ 3/01) [930]

7709 Hall, Eleanor J. *Ancient Chinese Dynasties* (7–10). Series: World History. 2000, Lucent LB $27.45 (978-1-56006-624-8). This well-illustrated account describes the dynasties that laid the foundations of Chinese culture and highlights their unsurpassed works of art, architecture, and philosophy. (Rev: BL 6/1–15/00; HBG 9/00; SLJ 6/00) [951]

7710 Haywood, John. *The Encyclopedia of Ancient Civilizations of the Near East and the Mediterranean* (8–12). Illus. 1997, M.E. Sharpe $95.00 (978-1-56324-799-6). Divided into three parts — ancient Near East and Egypt, the Greek world, and the Roman world — this adult narrative presents basic history and, through the use of sidebars, provides material on important places, cultural advances, scientific progress, religious practices, and military advances. (Rev: SLJ 8/98) [909]

7711 Hunter, Erica C. D., and Mike Corbishley. *First Civilizations*. Rev. ed. (5–8). Illus. Series: Cultural Atlas for Young People. 2003, Facts on File $35.00 (978-0-8160-5149-6). Colorful topical spreads introduce readers to the culture, geography, history, and politics of Mesopotamia, Persia, and Assyria. (Rev: SLJ 1/04) [939]

7712 Lourie, Peter. *Hidden World of the Aztec* (5–8). Illus. 2006, Boyds Mills $17.95 (978-1-59078-069-5). This lavishly illustrated title uses modern archaeological projects to introduce the history and culture of the ancient Aztec civilization. (Rev: BL 10/15/06; SLJ 10/06) [972]

7713 Mellor, Ronald, and Amanda H. Podany. *The World in Ancient Times: Primary Sources and Reference Volume* (6–12). Series: The World in Ancient Times. 2006, Oxford Univ. LB $32.95 (978-0-19-522220-3). More than 75 selections from poems, letters, inscriptions, and other accounts introduce civilizations and everyday life in ancient times. (Rev: SLJ 5/06) [930]

7714 Perl, Lila. *The Ancient Maya* (5–8). Series: People of the Ancient World. 2005, Watts LB $30.50 (978-0-531-12381-2); paper $9.95 (978-0-531-16848-6). Introduces readers to the arts, religious beliefs, and society of the Maya, with discussion of individual occupations and of the discoveries by archaeologists and anthropologists. (Rev: SLJ 9/05) [973]

7715 Richardson, Hazel. *Life in Ancient Africa* (4–7). Illus. Series: Peoples of the Ancient World. 2005, Crabtree LB $26.60 (978-0-7787-2043-0); paper $8.95 (978-0-7787-2073-7). Introduces the early civilizations of Africa, examining their arts, spiritual beliefs, government, language, and technology; color photographs, sidebars, and timelines add information and appeal. (Rev: SLJ 11/05) [973]

7716 Richardson, Hazel. *Life in Ancient Japan* (4–7). Illus. Series: Peoples of the Ancient World. 2005, Crabtree LB $26.60 (978-0-7787-2041-6); paper $8.95 (978-0-7787-2071-3). Introduces ancient Japan's arts, spiritual beliefs, government, language, and technology; color photographs, sidebars, and timelines add information and appeal. (Rev: SLJ 11/05) [952]

7717 Richardson, Hazel. *Life in the Ancient Indus River Valley* (4–7). Illus. Series: Peoples of the

Ancient World. 2005, Crabtree LB $26.60 (978-0-7787-2040-9); paper $8.95 (978-0-7787-2070-6). Introduces life in the earliest urban civilization on the Indian subcontinent, examining the arts, spiritual beliefs, government, language, and technology; color photographs, sidebars, and timelines add information and appeal. (Rev: SLJ 11/05) [973]

7718 Richardson, Hazel. *Life of the Ancient Celts* (4–7). Illus. Series: Peoples of the Ancient World. 2005, Crabtree LB $26.60 (978-0-7787-2045-4); paper $8.95 (978-0-7787-2075-1). Introduces the early Celtic civilization, examining arts, spiritual beliefs, government, language, and technology; color photographs, sidebars, and timelines add information and appeal. (Rev: SLJ 11/05) [973]

7719 Schomp, Virginia. *Ancient India* (6–8). Series: People of the Ancient World. 2005, Watts LB $30.50 (978-0-531-12379-9). Readable text and attractive illustrations introduce readers to ancient India and its art, culture, religion, government, agriculture, and societal levels. (Rev: SLJ 6/05) [954]

7720 Schomp, Virginia. *The Vikings* (6–8). Series: People of the Ancient World. 2005, Watts LB $30.50 (978-0-531-12382-9). The culture, literature, arts, religious beliefs, and government of the Vikings are explored in readable text and attractive illustrations. (Rev: SLJ 6/05) [948]

7721 Service, Pamela F. *300 B.C.* (5–8). Series: Around the World In. 2002, Benchmark $29.93 (978-0-7614-1080-5). The author explores what was going on in Europe, Africa, Asia, and the Americas in the year 300 B.C. Also use *1200* (2002). (Rev: HBG 3/03; SLJ 2/03) [930]

7722 Smith, K. C. *Ancient Shipwrecks* (5–7). Series: Shipwrecks. 2000, Watts LB $25.50 (978-0-531-20381-1). From the Bronze Age through the Roman Empire, this volume explores the fascinating stories behind ancient wrecks found in the Mediterranean and explored by archaeologists. (Rev: BL 10/15/00) [930]

7723 Sonneborn, Liz. *The Ancient Aztecs* (6–8). Series: People of the Ancient World. 2005, Watts LB $30.50 (978-0-531-12362-1). The culture, arts, literature, religious beliefs, and government of the Aztecs are explored in readable text accompanied by attractive illustrations. (Rev: SLJ 6/05) [972]

7724 Sonneborn, Liz. *The Ancient Kushites* (5–8). Series: People of the Ancient World. 2005, Watts LB $30.50 (978-0-531-12380-5). Explores the arts, religious beliefs, and culture of Africa's ancient Kushites, who were also known as Nubians. (Rev: SLJ 9/05) [973]

7725 Stefoff, Rebecca. *The Ancient Mediterranean* (5–8). Series: World Historical Atlases. 2004, Benchmark LB $27.07 (978-0-7614-1641-8). Maps, text, and illustrations give a broad overview of the cultures found in the ancient Mediterranean. Also use *The Ancient Near East* and *The Asian Empires* (both 2004). (Rev: SLJ 2/05) [930]

7726 Wells, Donald. *The Silk Road* (5–8). Series: Great Journeys. 2004, Weigl LB $26.00 (978-1-59036-207-5). Colorful illustrations and an attractive format will appeal to browsers seeking information on this ancient trade route; a useful timeline and links to Web sites are included. (Rev: BL 11/1/04) [950]

7727 Wilkinson, Philip, and Jacqueline Dineen. *The Mediterranean* (4–7). Illus. by Robert Ingpen. Series: Mysterious Places. 1994, Chelsea LB $21.95 (978-0-7910-2751-6). Ten sites around the Mediterranean are investigated, including Knossos, Rhodes, Delphi, Mistra, the Topkapi Palace, and Hagia Sophia. (Rev: BL 1/15/94; SLJ 5/94) [930.3]

7728 Woods, Michael, and Mary Woods. *Ancient Agriculture: From Foraging to Farming* (5–8). Series: Ancient Technologies. 2000, Runestone LB $25.26 (978-0-8225-2995-8). Beginning with prehistoric food-gathering peoples, this book traces the history of plant cultivation and agriculture through each of the great ancient civilizations. (Rev: BL 8/00; HBG 10/00; SLJ 6/00) [630]

7729 Woods, Michael, and Mary Woods. *Ancient Machines from Wedges to Waterwheels* (5–8). Series: Ancient Technologies. 1999, Lerner LB $25.26 (978-0-8225-2994-1). This heavily illustrated account describes the important machines that came into being from ancient history to the fall of the Western Roman Empire. (Rev: BL 1/1–15/00; HBG 10/00; SLJ 6/00; VOYA 6/00) [936]

7730 Woods, Michael, and Mary B. Woods. *Ancient Medicine: From Sorcery to Surgery* (5–8). Illus. Series: Ancient Technologies. 2000, Lerner LB $25.26 (978-0-8225-2992-7). Medical practices in ancient times and cultures — the Stone Age, ancient Egypt, and early Hindu cultures, for example — are discussed in this volume. (Rev: BL 1/1–15/00; HBG 10/00; SLJ 5/00; VOYA 6/00) [610]

7731 Woods, Michael, and Mary B. Woods. *Ancient Transportation: From Camels to Canals* (5–8). Illus. Series: Ancient Technologies. 2000, Lerner LB $25.26 (978-0-8225-2993-4). This book covers such topics related to early transportation as the first bridges and roads, early skis and sleds, primitive wagons, and the beginnings of maps. (Rev: BL 1/1–15/00; HBG 10/00; SLJ 6/00; VOYA 6/00) [629.04]

Egypt and Mesopotamia

7732 Alcraft, Rob. *Valley of the Kings* (5–7). Series: Visiting the Past. 1999, Heinemann LB $24.22 (978-1-57572-860-5). This account uses double-page spreads to cover topics including the history,

landscape, beliefs, and daily life of the ancient Egyptians. (Rev: SLJ 3/00) [932]

7733 Berger, Melvin, and Gilda Berger. *Mummies of the Pharaohs: Exploring the Valley of the Kings* (4–7). Illus. 2001, National Geographic $17.95 (978-0-7922-7223-6). Beginning with King Tut's tomb and continuing through other sites, this book uses stunning photographs and a clear text to describe workings of archaeological digs that are studying Egypt's past. (Rev: BL 2/1/01) [932]

7734 Broida, Marian. *Ancient Egyptians and Their Neighbors: An Activity Guide* (4–8). Illus. 1999, Chicago Review paper $16.95 (978-1-55652-360-1). The lives and times of the ancient Egyptians, Nubians, Hittites, and Mesopotamians are examined using text and a series of 40 fascinating projects. (Rev: BL 3/15/00; SLJ 2/00) [939]

7735 Chapman, Gillian. *The Egyptians* (4–8). Series: Crafts from the Past. 1997, Heinemann LB $25.64 (978-1-57572-556-7). A variety of craft projects related to the ancient Egyptians are introduced and placed within their cultural context. (Rev: SLJ 4/98) [932]

7736 Chrisp, Peter. *Mesopotamia: Iraq in Ancient Times* (4–7). Illus. Series: Picturing the Past. 2004, Enchanted Lion $15.95 (978-1-59270-024-0). History and archaeology are the highlights of this nicely illustrated overview of Mesopotamian civilization. (Rev: BL 10/15/04; SLJ 11/04) [935]

7737 Chrisp, Peter. *Pyramid* (4–8). Illus. Series: DK Experience. 2006, DK $15.99 (978-0-7566-1410-2). Full-color illustrations, 3-D diagrams, and CT scans make this survey of the construction and importance of the Great Pyramid of Giza informative and attractive. (Rev: SLJ 11/06) [932]

7738 Cline, Eric H., and Jill Rubalcaba. *The Ancient Egyptian World* (5–10). Series: The World in Ancient Times. 2005, Oxford LB $32.95 (978-0-19-517391-8). An overview of ancient Egyptian history and culture, with chronologically arranged chapters covering religion, medicine, clothing, arts, and so forth and introducing key figures such as Hatshepsut, Tutankhamen, and Cleopatra. (Rev: SLJ 1/06) [932]

7739 Crosher, Judith. *Technology in the Time of Ancient Egypt* (4–8). Series: Technology in the Time Of. 1998, Raintree LB $27.12 (978-0-8172-4875-8). Each double-page spread presents an aspect of technology in ancient Egypt in such areas as food production, transportation, and building. (Rev: HBG 10/98; SLJ 3/99) [932]

7740 Day, Nancy. *Your Travel Guide to Ancient Egypt* (4–8). Series: Passport to History. 2000, Runestone LB $26.50 (978-0-8225-3075-6). Written in the style of a modern-day travel guide, this book on ancient Egypt covers such subjects as sites to see, food, clothing, religious beliefs, politics, and daily life. (Rev: BL 11/15/00; HBG 3/01; SLJ 5/01; VOYA 8/01) [932]

7741 Giblin, James Cross. *Secrets of the Sphinx* (7–12). Illus. by Bagram Ibatoulline. 2004, Scholastic LB $17.95 (978-0-590-09847-2). Full of interesting facts and details of archaeological discoveries, this is a handsome, well-illustrated picture-book-format account of the mysteries that still surround the Sphinx and the facts that are known. (Rev: BL 9/15/04; HB 11–12/04; SLJ 11/04) [932]

7742 Greene, Jacqueline D. *Slavery in Ancient Egypt and Mesopotamia* (4–7). Series: Watts Library: History of Slavery. 2000, Watts LB $25.50 (978-0-531-11692-0). This unusual book covers the earliest forms of slavery, how the pharaohs used slaves to construct the pyramids, and the place of slavery in Hebrew society. (Rev: BL 3/1/01; SLJ 3/01) [930]

7743 Harris, Geraldine. *Ancient Egypt.* Rev. ed. (5–8). Illus. Series: Cultural Atlas for Young People. 2003, Facts on File $35.00 (978-0-8160-5148-9). Colorful topical spreads introduce readers to the culture, history, and politics of ancient Egypt. (Rev: SLJ 1/04; VOYA 2/04) [932]

7744 Hawass, Zahi. *Tutankhamun and the Golden Age of the Pharaohs* (8–12). Illus. 2005, National Geographic $35.00 (978-0-7922-3873-7). Companion to a traveling exhibit, this volume highlights the importance of items retrieved from Tutankhamen's tomb. (Rev: BL 6/1–15/05) [932]

7745 Hinds, Kathryn. *The City* (6–9). Series: Life in Ancient Egypt. 2006, Benchmark LB $22.95 (978-0-7614-2184-9). This handsome, well-illustrated volume describes city life in Egypt's New Kingdom (from 1550 B.C. to 1070 B.C.) from numerous perspectives and includes interesting in-depth sidebar features; also recommended in this series are *The Countryside, The Pharaoh's Court,* and *Religion* (all 2006). (Rev: SLJ 5/07) [932]

7746 Hynson, Colin. *The Building of the Great Pyramid* (5–8). Illus. Series: Stories from History. 2006, School Specialty $9.95 (978-0-7696-4708-1); paper $6.95 (978-0-7696-4692-3). Full-color illustrations and graphic novel format make this survey of the ancient engineering feat attractive to reluctant readers. (Rev: SLJ 1/07)

7747 Jovinelly, Joann, and Jason Netelkos. *The Crafts and Culture of the Ancient Egyptians* (5–8). Series: Crafts of the Ancient World. 2002, Rosen LB $29.25 (978-0-8239-3509-3). As well as learning about the mysteries of ancient Egypt, readers can engage in such craft projects as designing a pharaoh's headdress and necklace and re-creating an ancient marbles game. (Rev: BL 5/15/02; SLJ 6/02) [932]

7748 Kallen, Stuart A. *Pyramids* (7–10). Series: Mystery Library. 2002, Gale LB $29.95 (978-1-56006-773-3). This work explores the mysterious and intriguing aspects of the purposes behind and construction of the Egyptian pyramids. (Rev: BL 7/02; SLJ 7/02) [932]

7749 Kaplan, Sarah Pitt. *The Great Pyramid at Giza: Tomb of Wonders* (5–8). Series: Digging Up the Past. 2005, Children's Pr. LB $24.50 (978-0-516-25131-8); paper $6.95 (978-0-516-25095-3). A richly illustrated survey of the important pyramid and the reasons for its creation; suitable for reluctant readers. (Rev: SLJ 2/06) [932]

7750 Kennett, David. *Pharaoh: Life and Afterlife of a God* (4–7). Illus. by author. 2008, Walker $18.95 (978-0-8027-9567-0). This attractive book introduces readers to the elaborate burial of Seti I and in doing so also explains many aspects of life in ancient Egypt, for royalty as well as common people. (Rev: BL 5/1/08; SLJ 2/08) [932]

7751 Lace, William W. *The Curse of King Tut* (5–8). Illus. Series: Mysterious & Unknown. 2007, Reference Point LB $24.95 (978-1-60152-024-1). Readers will learn factual information about the discovery of King Tutankhamen's tomb while searching for the truth about his "curse." (Rev: BL 10/15/07; LMC 2/08; SLJ 2/08) [932]

7752 McNeese, Tim. *The Pyramids of Giza* (6–8). Series: Building History. 1997, Lucent LB $27.45 (978-1-56006-426-8). Although crammed with too much detail, this volume gives interesting information on what is known, and theorized, about how these massive monuments to the dead were built. (Rev: HBG 3/98; SLJ 8/97) [932]

7753 McNeill, Sarah. *Ancient Egyptian People* (4–8). Illus. Series: People and Places. 1997, Millbrook LB $21.90 (978-0-7613-0056-4). This basic introduction to the people of ancient Egypt and how they lived consists of several attractive double-page spreads and a brief text. (Rev: BL 2/15/97; SLJ 3/97) [932]

7754 McNeill, Sarah. *Ancient Egyptian Places* (4–8). Illus. Series: People and Places. 1997, Millbrook LB $21.90 (978-0-7613-0057-1). Some of the great constructions of ancient Egypt are pictured in a series of elegant double-page spreads with a simple text. (Rev: BL 2/15/97; SLJ 3/97) [932]

7755 Malam, John. *Ancient Egypt* (5–8). Series: Remains to Be Seen. 1998, Evans Brothers $19.95 (978-0-237-51839-4). This introduction to ancient Egypt's culture and history is organized in double-page spreads and is noteworthy for its many sidebars, charts, and illustrations. (Rev: SLJ 9/98) [932]

7756 Malam, John. *Ancient Egyptian Jobs* (5–7). Illus. 2002, Heinemann LB $27.07 (978-1-4034-0311-7). The daily activities of workers such as scribes, bakers, dancers, jewelers, pyramid builders, and embalmers are described in this slim volume that also offers a general introduction to ancient Egypt. (Rev: HBG 10/03; SLJ 4/03) [331.7]

7757 Malam, John. *Mesopotamia and the Fertile Crescent: 10,000 to 539 B.C.* (5–8). Series: Looking Back. 1999, Raintree $19.98 (978-0-8172-5434-6). The story of the ancient civilizations that grew up in the rich area around the Tigris and Euphrates rivers. (Rev: BL 5/15/99; SLJ 7/99) [930]

7758 Mann, Elizabeth. *The Great Pyramid* (4–7). Illus. Series: Wonders of the World. 1996, Mikaya $19.95 (978-0-9650493-1-3). The building of this architectural marvel is told graphically, with details on the society of ancient Egypt. (Rev: BL 2/1/97; SLJ 6/97*) [932]

7759 Manning, Ruth. *Ancient Egyptian Women* (5–8). Illus. Series: People in the Past. 2002, Heinemann LB $27.07 (978-1-4034-0313-1). A look at the life of, and options open to, women in ancient Egypt. (Rev: BL 3/1/03; SLJ 4/03) [305.42]

7760 Marston, Elsa. *The Ancient Egyptians* (5–8). Series: Cultures of the Past. 1995, Benchmark LB $29.93 (978-0-7614-0073-8). With photographs of artifacts, monuments, and historical scenes, this book tells of ancient Egyptian history and culture, the rise and fall of the dynasties, and the people's religious beliefs and practices. (Rev: SLJ 6/96) [932]

7761 Matthews, Sheelagh. *Pyramids of Giza* (6–9). Illus. Series: Structural Wonders. 2007, Weigl LB $26.00 (978-1-59036-725-4); paper $7.95 (978-1-59036-726-1). This interesting account of the construction of the pyramids at Giza also discusses their current status and includes excellent full-color photographs. (Rev: SLJ 12/07) [932]

7762 Morgan, Julian. *Cleopatra: Ruling in the Shadow of Rome* (6–8). Series: Leaders of Ancient Egypt. 2003, Rosen LB $33.25 (978-0-8239-3591-8). Cleopatra's relations with Julius Caesar and Mark Anthony are central to this account that homes in on their individual characteristics and provides ample historical context. (Rev: SLJ 9/03) [921]

7763 Nardo, Don. *Ancient Alexandria* (6–10). Illus. Series: A Travel Guide To. 2003, Gale LB $29.95 (978-1-59018-142-3). Readers are treated to a guidebook-style survey of ancient Alexandria's attractions, with a focus on weather, transport, hotels, shopping, festivals and sporting events, institutions, and people. (Rev: SLJ 6/03) [962]

7764 Nardo, Don. *Ancient Egypt* (7–12). Illus. Series: History of Weapons and Warfare. 2003, Gale LB $27.45 (978-1-59018-066-2). The Battle of Kadesh is a central part of this account that discusses the ancient Egyptians' military weapons and techniques. (Rev: SLJ 2/03) [355]

7765 Nardo, Don. *Arts, Leisure, and Sport in Ancient Egypt* (6–10). Illus. Series: The Lucent Library of Historical Eras. 2005, Gale LB $32.45 (978-1-59018-706-7). Photographs, reproductions, and film and documentary stills illustrate this well-documented examination of the art and leisure activities of ancient Egyptians, from music and dance to hunting and fishing. Also use *Mummies, Myth, and Magic: Religion in Ancient Egypt* (2005). (Rev: SLJ 11/05) [932]

7766 Nardo, Don. *Empires of Mesopotamia* (6–9). Series: Lost Civilizations. 2001, Lucent LB $28.70 (978-1-56006-820-4). A well-researched account that traces the history and accomplishments of the various peoples who controlled the fertile crescent in ancient times. (Rev: BL 8/1/01; SLJ 6/01) [930]

7767 Payne, Elizabeth. *The Pharaohs of Ancient Egypt* (6–8). Illus. 1981, Random paper $5.99 (978-0-394-84699-6). A fascinating study of this important period in Egyptian history. [932]

7768 Perl, Lila. *The Ancient Egyptians* (4–7). Series: People of the Ancient World. 2004, Watts LB $30.50 (978-0-531-12345-4). Pharaohs, mummy makers, farmers, and brewers are among the people presented in this overview of life in ancient Egypt. (Rev: SLJ 2/05) [930]

7769 Podany, Amanda H., and Marni McGee. *The Ancient Near Eastern World* (8–12). Series: The World in Ancient Times. 2005, Oxford LB $32.95 (978-0-19-516159-5). Using primary sources and useful illustrations, this volume explores the ancient civilizations that flourished in the Fertile Crescent until the region was conquered by Alexander the Great in the 4th century B.C. (Rev: SLJ 6/05; VOYA 10/04) [935]

7770 Putnam, James. *The Ancient Egypt Pop-Up Book* (5–8). Illus. 2003, Universe $29.95 (978-0-7893-0985-3). Seven imaginatively designed pop-up spreads introduce ancient Egypt, including its pyramids, pharaohs, and mummies. (Rev: SLJ 3/04)

7771 Roberts, Russell. *Rulers of Ancient Egypt* (7–10). Series: History Makers. 1999, Lucent LB $28.70 (978-1-56006-438-1). The author uses both primary and secondary sources to describe the contributions and personalities of Hatshepsut, Akhenaten, Tutankhamon, Ramses II, and Cleopatra and to provide further insight into this period's culture and power structure. (Rev: SLJ 8/99) [932]

7772 Schomp, Virginia. *Ancient Mesopotamia: The Sumerians, Babylonians, and Assyrians* (5–8). Series: People of the Ancient World. 2004, Watts LB $30.50 (978-0-531-11818-4). This fascinating volume covers the history and culture of the Sumerians, Babylonians, and Assyrians, looking at writing, warfare, and the daily life of people ranging from farmers and traders to warriors and nobles. (Rev: SLJ 3/05) [935]

7773 Service, Pamela F. *Ancient Mesopotamia* (6–9). Series: Cultures of the Past. 1998, Marshall

Cavendish LB $29.93 (978-0-7614-0301-2). This book explores the cultures of ancient Mesopotamia, their sacred tales and legends, their histories, and their legacy. (Rev: BL 12/15/98; HBG 9/99; SLJ 4/99) [935]

7774 Shuter, Jane. *Egypt* (5–10). Series: Ancient World. 1998, Raintree LB $27.12 (978-0-8172-5058-4). Ancient Egypt's mysterious hieroglyphics, treasure-filled tombs, puzzling pyramid construction, and embalming techniques, as well as its history, politics, ideas, religion, art, architecture, science, and everyday life are covered in this introductory volume. (Rev: BL 1/1–15/99; HBG 3/99; SLJ 3/99) [932]

7775 Streissguth, Thomas. *Life in Ancient Egypt* (6–10). Series: The Way People Live. 2000, Lucent LB $29.95 (978-1-56006-643-9). Everyday life within the different social classes that existed in ancient Egypt is covered in this account that contains many black-and-white illustrations. (Rev: BL 3/1/01) [932]

7776 Tiano, Oliver. *Ramses II and Egypt* (6–10). Series: W5. 1996, Holt $19.95 (978-0-8050-4659-5). Using all sorts of gimmicky illustrations and diagrams, this work presents basic facts about ancient Egypt, its culture, and its people. (Rev: SLJ 12/96) [932]

7777 Tyldesley, Joyce. *Egypt* (5–8). Illus. Series: Insiders. 2007, Simon & Schuster $16.99 (978-1-4169-3858-3). An introduction to ancient Egypt — the pyramids, mummies, Abu Simbel, transportation, arts and crafts, and so forth — with eye-catching illustrations. (Rev: LMC 10/07; SLJ 12/07) [932]

7778 Woods, Geraldine. *Science in Ancient Egypt* (4–8). Series: Science of the Past. 1998, Watts paper $8.95 (978-0-531-15915-6). The many contributions to science by the ancient Egyptians, including architecture, astronomy, and mathematics, are outlined in this richly illustrated volume. (Rev: BL 6/1–15/98; HBG 10/98; SLJ 6/98) [932]

Greece

7779 Chapman, Gillian. *The Greeks* (4–7). Series: Crafts from the Past. 1998, Heinemann LB $25.64 (978-1-57572-733-2). Double-page spreads each outline a project inspired by an art object, i.e. a Greek vase yields pâpier-maché pottery. (Rev: SLJ 2/99) [938]

7780 Day, Nancy. *Your Travel Guide to Ancient Greece* (4–8). Illus. Series: Passport to History. 2000, Runestone LB $26.50 (978-0-8225-3076-3). An outstanding introduction to ancient Greece arranged in the format of a guided tour and covering topics including geography, history, customs, and

places to visit in an exciting, interesting way. (Rev: BL 10/15/00*; HBG 3/01; SLJ 2/01) [938]

7781 Hart, Avery, and Paul Mantell. *Ancient Greece! 40 Hands-On Activities to Experience This Wondrous Age* (4–7). Illus. 1999, Williamson paper $14.25 (978-1-885593-25-2). A concise text and several craft projects introduce us to the world of ancient Greece, its geography, history, people, culture, and lasting contributions. (Rev: BL 9/15/99; SLJ 8/99) [938]

7782 Hodge, Susie. *Ancient Greek Art* (4–8). Series: Art in History. 1998, Heinemann LB $24.22 (978-1-57572-551-2). A solid introduction to ancient Greek art, covering painting, mosaics, pottery, architecture, and sculpture. (Rev: HBG 3/98; SLJ 5/98) [938]

7783 Hull, Robert. *Greece* (5–10). Series: Ancient World. 1998, Raintree LB $27.12 (978-0-8172-5055-3). This brief introduction to ancient Greece touches on its religion and mythology, its great philosophers, important historical events, and its contributions to world culture. (Rev: BL 1/1–15/99; HBG 3/99) [938]

7784 Jovinelly, Joann, and Jason Netelkos. *The Crafts and Culture of the Ancient Greeks* (5–8). Series: Crafts of the Ancient World. 2002, Rosen LB $29.25 (978-0-8239-3510-9). As well as basic information on ancient Greece, this book outlines many craft projects. (Rev: BL 5/15/02) [938]

7785 Malam, John. *Ancient Greece* (4–7). Series: Picturing the Past. 2004, Enchanted Lion $15.95 (978-1-59270-022-6). This photo-filled volume uses images of ancient Greek artifacts and structures to introduce the civilization's governmental organization, religion, mythology, recreation, and theater. (Rev: BL 10/15/04; SLJ 11/04) [938]

7786 Malam, John. *Exploring Ancient Greece* (5–8). Series: Remains to Be Seen. 1999, Evans Brothers $19.95 (978-0-237-51994-0). Particularly noteworthy in this basic account of the history of ancient Greece are the stunning photographs of temples, theaters, artifacts, and landscapes. (Rev: SLJ 1/00) [938]

7787 Martell, Hazel M. *The Myths and Civilization of the Ancient Greeks* (4–8). Illus. Series: Myths and Civilization. 1999, Bedrick $16.95 (978-0-87226-283-6). A handsome volume that combines Greek myths and legends with information about ancient Greek artifacts, culture, and history. (Rev: HBG 10/99; SLJ 3/99) [938]

7788 Nardo, Don. *Ancient Athens* (5–8). Illus. Series: A Travel Guide To. 2002, Gale $28.70 (978-1-59018-016-7). This fact-filled "guidebook" introduces aspiring travelers to everyday life in ancient Athens, in addition to information on climate, geography, important sights, and so forth. (Rev: BL 1/1–15/03; SLJ 2/03) [914.75]

7789 Nardo, Don. *Ancient Greece* (7–10). Series: History of Weapons and Warfare. 2003, Gale LB $27.45 (978-1-59018-004-4). A look at weapons, techniques, and strategies of the ancient Greeks — both on land and at sea — with quotations from a variety of sources and maps, diagrams, and other illustrations. (Rev: SLJ 1/03) [355]

7790 Nardo, Don. *A History of the Ancient Greeks* (8–12). Illus. Series: The Lucent Library of Historical Eras. 2004, Gale LB $32.45 (978-1-59018-525-4). An excellent overview of ancient Greek history. (Rev: SLJ 1/05) [938]

7791 Nardo, Don. *Life in Ancient Athens* (6–10). Series: The Way People Live. 1999, Lucent LB $27.45 (978-1-56006-494-7). This account describes how people lived in ancient Athens with material on how they dressed, worked, ate, socialized, played, and went to school. (Rev: BL 10/15/99; HBG 9/00) [938]

7792 Nardo, Don. *The Parthenon of Ancient Greece* (6–10). 1998, Lucent LB $27.45 (978-1-56006-431-2). The how and why of the construction of the Parthenon, its legacy as a symbol of classical Greek society and artistry, and its influence on Roman, American, and European architecture. (Rev: BL 12/15/98; SLJ 3/99) [726]

7793 Nardo, Don. *Philip II and Alexander the Great Unify Greece in World History* (6–10). Illus. Series: In World History. 2000, Enslow LB $26.60 (978-0-7660-1399-5). Primary and secondary sources are used in this survey of relations between the city-states of Greece in the 4th century B.C. (Rev: HBG 9/00; SLJ 6/00) [938]

7794 Nardo, Don. *Scientists of Ancient Greece* (7–12). Illus. 1998, Lucent LB $27.45 (978-1-56006-362-9). An introduction to the development of scientific thought in ancient Greece precedes chapters on the scientific theories and work of Democritus, Plato, Aristotle, Theophrastus, Archimedes, Ptolemy, and Galen. (Rev: SLJ 4/99) [938]

7795 Nardo, Don. *Women of Ancient Greece* (7–10). Series: World History. 2000, Lucent LB $32.45 (978-1-56006-646-0). The story of the place of women in ancient Greek society, how they lacked political rights and lived sheltered lives yet performed many important duties. (Rev: BL 6/1–15/00; HBG 3/01) [938]

7796 Powell, Anton. *Ancient Greece*. Rev. ed. (5–8). Illus. Series: Cultural Atlas for Young People. 2003, Facts on File $35.00 (978-0-8160-5146-5). Colorful topical spreads introduce readers to the culture, history, and politics of ancient Greece, with information on the Olympics, daily life, and women's role. (Rev: SLJ 1/04) [938]

7797 Roberts, Jennifer T., and Tracy Barrett. *The Ancient Greek World* (7–10). Series: The World in Ancient Times. 2004, Oxford LB $32.95 (978-0-19-

515696-6). The authors take a lively and humorous approach to their carefully researched account of political and cultural life in ancient Greece. (Rev: SLJ 8/04) [938]

7798 Robinson, C. E. *Everyday Life in Ancient Greece* (7–12). Illus. 1933, AMS $45.00 (978-0-404-14592-7). The classic account, first published in 1933, of how people lived during various periods in ancient Greek history. [938]

7799 Schomp, Virginia. *The Ancient Greeks* (5–8). Series: Cultures of the Past. 1995, Benchmark LB $29.93 (978-0-7614-0070-7). Using quotations from period literature and many photographs and drawings, this volume examines the history of ancient Greece, its culture, and the importance of the numerous Greek gods and goddesses. (Rev: SLJ 6/96) [938]

7800 Woodford, Susan. *The Parthenon* (6–10). Illus. 1983, Cambridge Univ. paper $19.00 (978-0-521-22629-5). A history of the famous temple in Athens and of the religion of ancient Greece. [938]

7801 Wright, Anne. *Art and Architecture* (7–10). Illus. Series: Inside Ancient Greece. 2007, M.E. Sharpe LB $31.45 (978-0-7656-8130-0). Focusing on practical and decorative art and architecture in ancient Greece, this volume describes in detail how art was produced during this time. (Rev: BL 10/15/07; LMC 2/08; SLJ 12/07) [709.38]

Middle East

7802 Broida, Marian. *Ancient Israelites and Their Neighbors: An Activity Guide* (4–7). Illus. 2003, Chicago Review paper $16.95 (978-1-55652-457-8). Readers will find out what life was like for the ancient Israelis, Phoenicians, and Philistines through the information and activities in this attractive book. (Rev: BL 5/15/03; SLJ 8/03) [933]

7803 Jenkins, Earnestine. *A Glorious Past: Ancient Egypt, Ethiopia and Nubia* (7–10). Series: Milestones in Black History. 1995, Chelsea LB $21.95 (978-0-7910-2258-0); paper $8.95 (978-0-7910-2684-7). A social and political survey of ancient Egypt, Nubia, the civilization to the south, and Ethiopia. (Rev: BL 4/15/95; SLJ 4/95) [932]

7804 Jovinelly, Joann, and Jason Netelkos. *The Crafts and Culture of the Ancient Hebrews* (5–8). Illus. Series: Crafts of the Ancient World. 2002, Rosen LB $29.25 (978-0-8239-3511-6). The crafts of the ancient Hebrews and projects related to them are used to give basic information on their history and how they lived. (Rev: BL 4/1/02) [932]

7805 Mann, Kenny. *The Ancient Hebrews* (6–9). Series: Cultures of the Past. 1998, Marshall Cavendish LB $29.93 (978-0-7614-0302-9). A fine introduction to the history of the ancient Jews, their culture, religion, and legacy. (Rev: BL 12/15/98; HBG 9/99; SLJ 4/99) [909]

7806 Trumble, Kelly. *The Library of Alexandria* (5–7). Illus. by Robina MacIntyre Marshall. 2003, Clarion $17.00 (978-0-395-75832-8). An introduction to the famous library, its collection, its scholars, and its destruction by fire. (Rev: BCCB 1/04; BL 11/15/03; HBG 4/04; SLJ 1/04) [027.032]

7807 Zeinert, Karen. *The Persian Empire* (7–10). Series: Cultures of the Past. 1996, Benchmark LB $29.93 (978-0-7614-0089-9). A brief history of the Persian Empire, with material on the kings Cyrus, Darius, and Xerxes, is followed by chapters on daily life, culture, religion, and lasting contributions the empire made to human achievement. (Rev: SLJ 3/97) [935]

Rome

7808 Beller, Susan Provost. *Roman Legions on the March: Soldiering in the Ancient Roman Army* (5–8). 2007, Twenty-First Century LB $33.26 (978-0-8225-6781-3). After background information on the Roman army, this volume examines the life of the soldiers and provides interesting sidebar features and photographs. (Rev: SLJ 1/08)

7809 Blacklock, Dyan. *The Roman Army* (5–8). Illus. by David Kennett. 2004, Walker $17.95 (978-0-8027-8896-2). The soldiers, weaponry, fighting techniques, and ingenuity of the Romans are detailed here in clear text and effective cartoon-style illustrations. (Rev: BL 3/1/04*; SLJ 4/04) [355]

7810 Chapman, Gillian. *The Romans* (4–7). Series: Crafts from the Past. 1998, Heinemann LB $25.64 (978-1-57572-734-9). Using double-page spreads, this work describes Roman culture while outlining several craft projects inspired by art objects, places, or people. (Rev: HBG 10/99; SLJ 2/99) [937]

7811 Corbishley, Mike. *Ancient Rome*. Rev. ed. (5–8). Illus. Series: Cultural Atlas for Young People. 2003, Facts on File $35.00 (978-0-8160-5147-2). Colorful topical spreads introduce readers to the culture, history, and politics of ancient Rome, with information on architecture and major cities of the provinces. (Rev: SLJ 1/04) [937]

7812 Deem, James M. *Bodies from the Ash: Life and Death in Ancient Pompeii* (5–8). Illus. 2005, Houghton $17.00 (978-0-618-47308-3). This photoessay full of vivid illustrations outlines what archaeologists have uncovered about the destruction of Pompeii when Mount Vesuvius erupted nearly 2,000 years ago. (Rev: BL 11/1/05; SLJ 12/05*) [937]

7813 DuTemple, Lesley A. *The Colosseum* (4–7). Series: Great Building Feats. 2003, Lerner LB $27.93 (978-0-8225-4693-1). Using many colorful diagrams and illustrations, this is the story of the construction of the famous colosseum in Rome. (Rev: BL 11/15/03; HBG 4/04) [937]

7814 Hanel, Rachael. *Gladiators* (5–8). Series: Fearsome Fighters. 2007, Creative Education LB $31.35 (978-1-58341-535-1). Weapons, armor, fighting techniques, and motivation are all discussed in this description of gladiators in ancient Rome and the kinds of people who were tempted to this career. (Rev: SLJ 1/08)

7815 Hinds, Kathryn. *The Ancient Romans* (7–10). Series: Cultures of the Past. 1996, Benchmark LB $29.93 (978-0-7614-0090-5). A well-illustrated volume that tells about the Roman Empire, the architectural feats of the Romans, their religion and entertainment, and their lasting contributions to world civilization. (Rev: SLJ 3/97) [937]

7816 Hodge, Susie. *Ancient Roman Art* (4–8). Series: Art in History. 1997, Heinemann LB $24.22 (978-1-57572-552-9). This slim, well-illustrated volume outlines Roman contributions to architecture, sculpture, pottery, and mosaics. (Rev: SLJ 5/98) [937.6]

7817 Jovinelly, Joann, and Jason Netelkos. *The Crafts and Culture of the Romans* (5–8). Series: Crafts of the Ancient World. 2002, Rosen LB $29.25 (978-0-8239-3513-0). The daily life and contributions of the ancient Romans are covered, as well as such craft projects as designing a toga. (Rev: BL 5/15/02; SLJ 6/02) [937]

7818 Lassieur, Allison. *The Ancient Romans* (6–8). Illus. Series: People of the Ancient World. 2004, Watts LB $30.50 (978-0-531-12338-6); paper $9.95 (978-0-531-16742-7). Government, the arts, social life — from aristocrats to slaves — and women's rights are among the topics discussed in this lively and accessible text. (Rev: BL 10/15/04; SLJ 1/05) [937]

7819 Macaulay, David. *City: A Story of Roman Planning and Construction* (6–10). Illus. 1974, Houghton $18.00 (978-0-395-19492-8); paper $9.95 (978-0-395-34922-9). In text and detailed drawing, the artist explores an imaginary Roman city over approximately 125 years. [711]

7820 Mann, Elizabeth. *The Roman Colosseum* (4–7). Illus. Series: Wonders of the World. 1998, Mikaya $19.95 (978-0-9650493-3-7). An oversize book that is crammed with factual material on the Colosseum in Rome. (Rev: BL 12/15/98; SLJ 2/99) [937]

7821 Mellor, Ronald, and Marni McGee. *The Ancient Roman World* (7–10). Illus. Series: The World in Ancient Times. 2004, Oxford LB $32.95 (978-0-19-515380-4). This attractive and accessible volume introduces readers to the history, people, and culture of ancient Rome, using many quotations and illustrations. (Rev: BL 4/1/04; SLJ 7/04) [937]

7822 Nardo, Don. *The Battle of Zama* (6–10). Illus. 1996, Lucent LB $34.95 (978-1-56006-420-6). An exciting account of the 202 B.C. battle in North Africa in which Hannibal's forces were defeated by the Romans during the second Punic War. (Rev: BL 4/15/96; SLJ 4/96) [937]

7823 Nardo, Don. *The Fall of the Roman Empire* (7–12). Illus. Series: Opposing Viewpoints Digests. 1997, Greenhaven LB $27.45 (978-1-56510-739-7). Theories about why Rome fell are presented in a pro and con format. (Rev: BL 3/1/98) [937]

7824 Nardo, Don. *Games of Ancient Rome* (6–10). Series: The Way People Live. 2000, Lucent LB $28.70 (978-1-56006-655-2). Nardo gives an interesting overview of popular sports in ancient Rome (gladiators, wild animal shows, and chariot races, for example), their importance in daily life, and the reasons for their decline. (Rev: BL 1/1–15/00; HBG 9/00; SLJ 5/00) [937]

7825 Nardo, Don. *Roman Amphitheaters* (5–7). Illus. Series: Famous Structures. 2002, Watts LB $25.50 (978-0-531-12036-1); paper $8.95 (978-0-531-16224-8). A clear overview of the construction, elements, use, and importance of ancient Roman amphitheaters, with illustrations. (Rev: BL 9/1/02; SLJ 8/02) [725]

7826 Nardo, Don. *The Roman Army: Instrument of Power* (8–12). Illus. Series: The Lucent Library of Historical Eras. 2003, Gale LB $32.45 (978-1-59018-316-8). An interesting survey of Roman military power and tactics, with comparisons to other systems of the time and helpful diagrams of famous battles. Also in this series are *Arts, Leisure, and Entertainment: Life of the Ancient Romans* and *From Founding to Fall: A History of Rome* (both 2003). (Rev: SLJ 5/04)

7827 Nardo, Don. *A Roman Gladiator* (6–10). Series: The Working Life. 2004, Gale LB $29.95 (978-1-59018-480-6). Gladiators' recruitment, training, living conditions, and status are all covered here. (Rev: SLJ 1/05) [937]

7828 Nardo, Don. *A Roman Senator* (6–9). Illus. Series: Working Life. 2004, Gale LB $29.95 (978-1-59018-481-3). Black-and-white illustrations add to this account of the evolution of the Roman senate over almost 12 centuries. (Rev: BL 2/1/05) [328]

7829 Nardo, Don. *Women of Ancient Rome* (6–10). Illus. Series: Women in History. 2002, Gale LB $27.45 (978-1-59018-169-0). The daily lives of Roman women, from slaves to aristocrats, are portrayed here, with details of social status, work, attire, religion, and even sexuality. (Rev: BL 10/15/02; SLJ 1/03) [305.4]

7830 Patent, Dorothy Hinshaw. *Lost City of Pompeii* (4–7). Series: Frozen in Time. 1999, Benchmark LB $27.07 (978-0-7614-0785-0). The story of the ancient city of Pompeii, its destruction, and how its excavation has given us a wealth of information about ancient Rome. (Rev: BL 2/1/00; HBG 10/00; SLJ 3/00) [937]

7831 Ridd, Stephen, ed. *Julius Caesar in Gaul and Britain* (5–8). Illus. Series: History Eyewitness. 1995, Raintree LB $24.26 (978-0-8114-8283-7). An edited version of Caesar's fascinating accounts of the Gallic Wars, with pictures and maps. (Rev: BL 4/15/95; SLJ 5/95) [937.05]

7832 Sheehan, Sean, and Pat Levy. *Rome* (5–10). Series: Ancient World. 1998, Raintree LB $27.12 (978-0-8172-5057-7). A brief history of Rome and the Roman Empire, including its culture, buildings, amusements, and emperors. (Rev: BL 1/1–15/99; HBG 3/99; SLJ 3/99) [937]

7833 Snedden, Robert. *Technology in the Time of Ancient Rome* (4–8). Series: Technology in the Time Of. 1998, Raintree LB $27.12 (978-0-8172-4876-5). Weaving, food production, construction, transportation, and metalwork are covered in this discussion of Roman technology. (Rev: HBG 10/98; SLJ 3/99) [937]

7834 Solway, Andrew. *Rome: In Spectacular Cross-Section* (4–7). Illus. by Stephen Biesty. 2003, Scholastic paper $18.95 (978-0-439-45546-6). An inside look at life in ancient Rome, with views of a private home, the Colosseum, the docks, and a bustling festival. (Rev: BL 2/15/03; HBG 10/03; SLJ 7/03) [937]

7835 Stroud, Jonathan. *Ancient Rome: A Guide to the Glory of Imperial Rome* (4–7). Series: Sightseers. 2000, Kingfisher $8.95 (978-0-7534-5235-6). This book on ancient Rome is presented like a handbook for tourists, with material on such topics as accommodations, shopping, key sites, etc. (Rev: HBG 3/01; SLJ 9/00) [937]

7836 Williams, Brian. *Ancient Roman Women* (5–8). Illus. Series: People in the Past. 2002, Heinemann LB $27.07 (978-1-58810-632-2). A look at the life of, and options open to, women in ancient Rome. (Rev: BL 3/1/03; HBG 10/03; SLJ 4/03) [305.8]

Middle Ages Through the Renaissance (500–1700)

7837 Aronson, Marc. *John Winthrop, Oliver Cromwell, and the Land of Promise* (7–10). 2004, Houghton $20.00 (978-0-618-18177-3). In this fascinating historical study, Aronson explores the interrelationship between John Winthrop, 17th-century governor of the Massachusetts Bay Colony, and Oliver Cromwell, who led the successful Puritan revolt against Britain's King Charles I. (Rev: BL 6/1–15/04; HB 7–8/04; SLJ 9/04) [974.4]

7838 Barter, James. *Artists of the Renaissance* (6–10). Illus. Series: History Makers. 1999, Lucent LB $28.70 (978-1-56006-439-8). Following an overview of the Renaissance, including explanations of humanism and classicism, this book focuses on several great artists, among them Giotto, Leonardo da Vinci, and Michelangelo. (Rev: BL 6/1–15/99; SLJ 7/99) [709]

7839 Barter, James. *A Medieval Knight* (6–9). Illus. Series: Working Life. 2005, Gale LB $29.95 (978-1-59018-580-3). A medieval knight's life involves training, tournaments, fighting, and administration and legal duties as laid out in this thorough overview that includes relevant images and excerpts from primary sources. (Rev: SLJ 11/05) [940]

7840 Blackwood, Gary L. *Life in a Medieval Castle* (6–10). Series: The Way People Live. 1999, Lucent LB $28.70 (978-1-56006-582-1). The daily life and personal problems involved in living in a castle during the Middle Ages are two of the topics discussed in this book that uses quotations from original sources. (Rev: BL 11/15/99) [940.1]

7841 Brewer, Paul. *Warfare in the Renaissance World* (7–10). Series: History of Warfare. 1999, Raintree LB $29.97 (978-0-8172-5444-5). Using diagrams and other illustrations, this is an account of the wars and battles fought during the Renaissance. (Rev: HBG 3/99; SLJ 3/99) [940.2]

7842 Claybourne, Anna. *The Renaissance* (5–9). Series: Time Travel Guides. 2007, Raintree LB $34.29 (978-1-4109-2910-5); paper $9.99 (978-1-4109-2916-7). With chapter headings like "Facts," "Everyday Life," and "Things to See and Do," this volume takes an effective travel-guide approach to the Renaissance, incorporating many visual elements. (Rev: SLJ 1/08)

7843 Corbishley, Mike. *The Medieval World* (5–7). Illus. Series: Timelink. 1993, Bedrick LB $18.95 (978-0-87226-362-8). Using a chronological approach, this book covers the years 450 through 1500 in Europe, Asia, Africa, and the Americas. (Rev: SLJ 8/93) [940.1]

7844 Crompton, Samuel Willard. *The Third Crusade: Richard the Lionhearted vs. Saladin* (7–12). Series: Great Battles Through the Ages. 2003, Chelsea House LB $30.00 (978-0-7910-7437-4). A useful survey of the First and Second Crusades is followed by details of the third campaign and portrayals of Richard and Saladin. (Rev: SLJ 5/04) [909.07]

7845 Currie, Stephen. *Miracles, Saints, and Superstition: The Medieval Mind* (5–9). 2006, Gale LB $32.45 (978-1-59018-861-3). Describes the Middle Ages and the role of Christianity at that time. (Rev: SLJ 3/07*) [940.1]

7846 Davenport, John. *The Age of Feudalism* (8–11). Illus. Series: World History. 2007, Gale LB $32.45 (978-1-59018-649-7). A look at the feudal social and economic system in Europe, which lasted from the 5th century until the rise of nation-states. (Rev: BL 2/1/08) [940.1]

7847 Day, Nancy. *Your Travel Guide to Renaissance Europe* (4–8). Series: Passport to History. 2000, Lerner LB $26.50 (978-0-8225-3080-0). This book uses a travel guide format to introduce the reader to the life and people of Europe from 1350 to 1550 with coverage of culture, style, inventions, religious beliefs, and scientific discoveries. (Rev: BL 3/1/01; HBG 10/01) [940.2]

7848 De Hahn, Tracee. *The Black Death* (6–8). Series: Great Disasters. 2001, Chelsea LB $30.00 (978-0-7910-6326-2). The story of the terrible plague that swept through Europe and parts of Asia in the 14th century and of the changes it produced in society. (Rev: BL 6/1–15/02; HBG 10/02) [614.5]

7849 Doherty, Katherine M., and Craig A. Doherty. *King Richard the Lionhearted and the Crusades* (8–12). Series: In World History. 2002, Enslow LB $26.60 (978-0-7660-1459-6). Combining both biography and history, this account re-creates the life of Richard the Lionhearted and his contributions to freeing the Holy Land during the Crusades. (Rev: BL 4/1/02; HBG 10/02; SLJ 6/02) [921]

7850 Dunn, John M. *Life During the Black Death* (5–9). Series: The Way People Live. 2000, Lucent LB $28.70 (978-1-56006-542-5). This account traces the spread of the Black Death from Mongolia in 1320 to Western Europe and its lasting effects on history, society, and culture. (Rev: HBG 10/00; SLJ 6/00) [940]

7851 Ford, Nick. *Jerusalem Under Muslim Rule in the Eleventh Century: Christian Pilgrims Under Islamic Government* (5–9). Series: The Library of the Middle Ages. 2004, Rosen LB $29.25 (978-0-8239-4216-9). Useful for report writers, this volume looks at life in Jerusalem for people of all religions, providing details from primary sources. (Rev: SLJ 8/04) [956.94]

7852 George, Linda S. *800* (5–8). Illus. Series: Around the World. 2003, Marshall Cavendish LB $29.93 (978-0-7614-1085-0). This absorbing look at civilizations around the world in the year 800 includes color reproductions, photographs, a timeline, a glossary, and lists of resources. (Rev: BL 6/1–15/03; HBG 3/03) [909.07]

7853 Halliwell, Sarah, ed. *The Renaissance: Artists and Writers* (6–9). Illus. Series: Who and When? 1998, Raintree LB $19.98 (978-0-8172-4725-6). This account covers the artistic life of the Renaissance and includes profiles of 13 artists and writers, including Giotto, Botticelli, Bosch, Dante, Chaucer, and Cervantes. (Rev: BL 12/15/97; SLJ 1/98) [700]

7854 Hanawalt, Barbara. *The Middle Ages: An Illustrated History* (8–12). Illus. 1999, Oxford $37.99

(978-0-19-510359-5). A carefully researched account of the Roman Empire and its gradual fall, the rise of the church, its use of power, and feudal society, including such topics as castles, the Crusades, the Black Death, the rise of guilds and universities, and the growth of the middle class. (Rev: BL 3/1/99; HBG 3/99; SLJ 4/99) [909.07]

7855 Hancock, Lee. *Saladin and the Kingdom of Jerusalem: The Muslims Recapture the Holy Land in AD 1187* (5–9). Series: The Library of the Middle Ages. 2004, Rosen LB $29.25 (978-0-8239-4217-6). Useful for report writers, this volume looks at life in Jerusalem under the Crusaders, providing details from primary sources. (Rev: SLJ 8/04) [956]

7856 Hanel, Rachael. *Knights* (5–8). Series: Fearsome Fighters. 2007, Creative Education LB $31.35 (978-1-58341-536-8). Weapons, armor, fighting techniques, and motivation are all discussed in this description of the knights of the Middle Ages and the kinds of people who were tempted to this career. (Rev: SLJ 1/08)

7857 Hay, Jeff, ed. *The Early Middle Ages* (7–12). Series: Turning Points in World History. 2001, Greenhaven paper $21.20 (978-0-7377-0481-5). After a general introduction to this period in western history, several detailed essays present various aspects of the culture and social conditions of the time. (Rev: BL 6/1–15/01) [940.1]

7858 Haywood, John. *Medieval Europe* (5–9). Series: Time Travel Guides. 2007, Raintree LB $34.29 (978-1-4109-2909-9); paper $9.99 (978-1-4109-2915-0). With chapter headings like "Facts," "Everyday Life," and "Things to See and Do," this volume takes an effective travel-guide approach to the Middle Ages, incorporating many visual elements. (Rev: SLJ 1/08)

7859 Hilliam, Paul. *Islamic Weapons, Warfare, and Armies: Muslim Military Operations Against the Crusaders* (5–9). Series: The Library of the Middle Ages. 2004, Rosen LB $29.25 (978-0-8239-4215-2). Useful for report writers, this volume looks at the spread of Islam and the conflicts with the Crusaders. (Rev: SLJ 8/04) [355]

7860 Hinds, Kathryn. *The Castle* (5–8). Series: Life in the Middle Ages. 2000, Marshall Cavendish LB $29.93 (978-0-7614-1007-2). A book that explores the construction and parts of the medieval castle as well as the lifestyles of those who lived in them, from kings and knights to humble servants. (Rev: BL 3/1/01; HBG 3/01; SLJ 3/01) [940]

7861 Hinds, Kathryn. *The Church* (6–9). Series: Life in the Renaissance. 2003, Benchmark LB $29.93 (978-0-7614-1679-1). Hinds describes life for men and women involved in the church, both Catholic and Protestant, during the upheavals of the Renaissance; a recipe for hot-cross buns is included. (Rev: SLJ 4/04)

7862 Hinds, Kathryn. *The Church* (5–8). Series: Life in the Middle Ages. 2000, Marshall Cavendish LB $29.93 (978-0-7614-1008-9). Explains the role of the church and the clergy in medieval life as well as giving examples of church construction. (Rev: BL 3/1/01; HBG 3/01; SLJ 3/01) [940]

7863 Hinds, Kathryn. *The City* (6–8). Series: Life in Elizabethan England. 2007, Marshall Cavendish LB $22.95 (978-0-7614-2544-1). Details of city life in Elizabethan England, including living conditions, food and sanitation, are discussed in this well-illustrated volume. (Rev: LMC 4/08; SLJ 3/08)

7864 Hinds, Kathryn. *The City* (5–8). Illus. Series: Life in the Middle Ages. 2000, Marshall Cavendish LB $29.93 (978-0-7614-1005-8). A beautifully designed book that describes daily life in medieval cities and explores their roles as centers of learning, commerce, worship, construction, and recreation as well as disease and disaster. (Rev: BL 2/15/01; HBG 3/01; SLJ 3/01) [940.1]

7865 Hinds, Kathryn. *The Countryside* (6–8). Series: Life in Elizabethan England. 2007, Marshall Cavendish LB $22.95 (978-0-7614-2543-4). A handsome representation of country life in Elizabethan England. (Rev: LMC 4/08; SLJ 3/08)

7866 Hinds, Kathryn. *The Countryside* (6–9). Series: Life in the Renaissance. 2003, Benchmark LB $29.93 (978-0-7614-1677-7). A handsome and detailed portrayal of life in rural Europe during the Renaissance, covering both landowners and peasants. (Rev: SLJ 4/04)

7867 Hinds, Kathryn. *The Countryside* (5–8). Illus. Series: Life in the Middle Ages. 2000, Marshall Cavendish LB $29.93 (978-0-7614-1006-5). The author explains manorialism — a primary social structure in rural areas during the Middle Ages — and describes a medieval village, its residents, and their work and pastimes. (Rev: BL 2/15/01; HBG 3/01; SLJ 3/01) [940.1]

7868 Hinds, Kathryn. *Elizabeth and Her Court* (6–8). Series: Life in Elizabethan England. 2007, Marshall Cavendish LB $22.95 (978-0-7614-2542-7). A look at the queen and royal court in Elizabethan times. (Rev: SLJ 3/08)

7869 Jones, Madeline. *Knights and Castles* (6–9). Series: How It Was. 1991, Batsford $19.95 (978-0-7134-6352-1). A re-creation of castles and knights and the time in which they existed. (Rev: BL 1/15/92; SLJ 3/92) [941]

7870 Kallen, Stuart A. *A Medieval Merchant* (6–9). Illus. Series: The Working Life. 2005, Gale LB $29.95 (978-1-59018-581-0). Trade routes, guilds, training, fairs, and the banking system are all covered in this thorough overview that includes relevant images and excerpts from primary sources. (Rev: SLJ 11/05) [909]

7871 Knight, Judson. *Middle Ages: Almanac* (6–10). Series: UXL Middle Ages Reference Library. 2000, Gale LB $70.00 (978-0-7876-4856-5). A comprehensive review of events around the world during the Middle Ages, with material on Africa and Asia as well as on Europe and the Middle East. Also use *Middle Ages: Biographies* and *Middle Ages: Primary Sources* (both 2000). (Rev: BL 4/1/01; SLJ 5/01) [940.1]

7872 Knight, Judson. *Middle Ages: Primary Sources* (8–12). 2000, U.X.L $70.00 (978-0-7876-4860-2). This book includes 19 entire or excerpted documents from the Middle Ages by such authors as Dante and Marco Polo. (Rev: BL 4/1/01; SLJ 5/01) [909.07]

7873 Lace, William W. *Elizabethan England* (8–12). 2005, Gale LB $31.20 (978-1-59018-655-8). The major issues and figures important in Queen Elizabeth I's reign — as well as the social, scientific, and geographic developments of the 1500s — are described in this book, with lots of color reproductions, a timeline, sidebars, and a further reading section. (Rev: SLJ 6/06)

7874 MacDonald, Fiona. *Knights, Castles, and Warfare in the Middle Ages* (5–8). Series: World Almanac Library of the Middle Ages. 2005, World Almanac LB $31.00 (978-0-8368-5895-2). Describes the role of knights, the equipment they used, and their lives and homes. Also use *The Plague and Medicine in the Middle Ages* (2005). (Rev: SLJ 1/06) [940.1]

7875 Marshall, Chris. *Warfare in the Medieval World* (7–10). Series: History of Warfare. 1999, Raintree LB $29.97 (978-0-8172-5443-8). The Hundred Years' War is one of the wars highlighted in this book that focuses on individual battles and is illustrated with many full-color maps and reproductions. (Rev: HBG 3/99; SLJ 3/99; VOYA 2/00) [940.1]

7876 Marston, Elsa. *The Byzantine Empire* (5–8). Series: Cultures of the Past. 2002, Marshall Cavendish $29.93 (978-0-7614-1495-7). Well-written text and colorful graphics present the history and culture of the surviving eastern part of the Roman Empire. (Rev: BL 1/1–15/03; HBG 3/03; SLJ 2/03) [949.5]

7877 Martin, Alex. *Knights and Castles: Exploring History Through Art* (5–8). Illus. Series: Picture That! 2004, Two-Can $19.95 (978-1-58728-441-0). Paintings serve as the vehicle to draw students into the discussion of life in Europe during the late medieval period. (Rev: BL 11/1/04; SLJ 2/05) [940.1]

7878 Morgan, Gwyneth. *Life in a Medieval Village* (5–7). Illus. by author. 1991, HarperCollins paper $14.95 (978-0-06-092046-3). A story of activities in a medieval village and of the church's importance in life in the Middle Ages. [306.094265]

7879 Nardo, Don. *Lords, Ladies, Peasants, and Knights: Class in the Middle Ages* (7–10). Series: The Lucent Library of Historical Eras — Middle Ages. 2006, Gale LB $28.70 (978-1-59018-928-3). Nardo describes the social classes of medieval Europe — from kings and popes down through knights and clergy to the peasants and serfs. (Rev: SLJ 4/07)

7880 Padrino, Mercedes. *Cities and Towns in the Middle Ages* (5–8). Series: World Almanac Library of the Middle Ages. 2005, World Almanac LB $31.00 (978-0-8368-5893-8). A look at medieval urban living — social structure, government structure, employment, education, religion, food and clothing, and so forth. Also use *Feudalism and Village Life in the Middle Ages* (2005). (Rev: SLJ 1/06) [940.1]

7881 Pernoud, Regine. *A Day with a Noblewoman* (5–8). Trans. by Dominique Clift. Illus. Series: A Day With. 1997, Runestone LB $27.15 (978-0-8225-1916-4). After a brief introduction to the Middle Ages, this book describes a busy day in the life of Blanche, the countess of Champagne, a French widow in the 13th century. (Rev: BL 1/1–15/98; HBG 3/98; SLJ 2/98) [940.1]

7882 Prum, Deborah Mazzotta. *Rats, Bulls, and Flying Machines: A History of Renaissance and Reformation* (4–8). Illus. Series: Core Chronicles. 1999, Core Knowledge $21.95 (978-1-890517-19-9); paper $11.95 (978-1-890517-18-2). A handsome volume that gives a basic history of the Renaissance and Reformation and highlights the accomplishments of people such as the Medici family, Machiavelli, Michelangelo, Cervantes, Shakespeare, and Gutenberg. (Rev: BL 12/15/99) [909.08]

7883 Ross, Stewart. *Monarchs* (5–8). Illus. Series: Medieval Realms. 2004, Gale $29.95 (978-1-59018-535-3). This colorfully illustrated, oversize volume explores the structure of European governments during the Middle Ages and such topics as the birth of new nations, wars, and the Crusades. (Rev: BL 10/15/04) [940.1]

7884 Schomp, Virginia. *1500* (5–8). Illus. Series: Around the World. 2003, Marshall Cavendish LB $29.93 (978-0-7614-1082-9). This absorbing look at civilizations around the world in the year 1500 includes color reproductions, photographs, a timeline, a glossary, and lists of resources. (Rev: BL 6/1–15/03; HBG 3/03) [909]

7885 Schomp, Virginia. *The Italian Renaissance* (5–8). Series: Cultures of the Past. 2002, Marshall Cavendish $29.93 (978-0-7614-1492-6). A handsome volume that gives a balanced, well-organized account of the Italian Renaissance, its history, personalities, art, and artifacts. (Rev: BL 1/1–15/03; HBG 3/03) [940.2]

7886 Senker, Cath. *The Black Death 1347–1350: The Plague Spreads Across Europe* (4–7). Series: When Disaster Struck. 2006, Raintree LB $32.86 (978-1-4109-2278-6). Documents the widespread devastation caused by the plague that spread across Europe in the mid-14th century causing an estimated 20 million deaths and discusses current medical understanding and practices. (Rev: SLJ 1/07) [614.5732]

7887 Steele, Philip. *Castles* (5–7). Illus. 1995, Kingfisher $16.95 (978-1-85697-547-6). In this oversized, well-designed book, castles, jousting, armor, and feast days are described. (Rev: BL 8/95; SLJ 4/95) [940.1]

7888 Steele, Philip. *The Medieval World* (5–8). Illus. Series: A History of Fashion and Costume. 2005, Facts on File $35.00 (978-0-8160-5945-4). A broad overview of the clothing and personal adornment worn during this time period, with many visual aids. (Rev: SLJ 5/06) [391]

7889 Sypeck, Jeff. *The Holy Roman Empire and Charlemagne in World History* (8–12). Series: In World History. 2002, Enslow LB $26.60 (978-0-7660-1901-0). This combination of biography and history tells the story of the life and reign of Charlemagne and the foundation of the Holy Roman Empire, which lasted for more than 700 years. (Rev: BL 3/15/03; HBG 3/03) [940.1]

7890 Thomson, Melissa, and Ruth Dean. *Women of the Renaissance* (7–12). Series: Women in History. 2004, Gale LB $32.45 (978-1-59018-473-8). A look at women's lives during the Renaissance, covering such topics as work, religion, and art. (Rev: SLJ 3/05)

7891 Waldman, Nomi J. *The Italian Renaissance* (5–7). Series: Daily Life. 2004, Gale LB $26.20 (978-0-7377-1398-5). In simple language, this slim volume describes Italy's rebirth, the blossoming of commerce and culture, and daily life for people of different backgrounds. (Rev: SLJ 2/05) [945]

7892 White, Pamela. *Exploration in the World of the Middle Ages, 500–1500* (6–12). Illus. Series: Discovery and Exploration. 2005, Facts on File $40.00 (978-0-8160-5264-6). The expeditions of Marco Polo, the Vikings, and other explorers of the Middle Ages are chronicled in clear, informative text plus maps, illustrations, and excerpts from primary sources. (Rev: SLJ 8/05) [973]

7893 Wood, Tim. *The Renaissance* (5–8). Series: See Through History. 1993, Viking $19.99 (978-0-670-85149-2). A series of double-page spreads explore the day-to-day lives of people during the Renaissance, including Far East trade, Italian city-states, women at court, art, and technology. (Rev: BL 12/15/93; SLJ 2/94) [940.2]

7894 Woolf, Alex. *Education* (5–8). Series: Medieval Realms. 2004, Gale LB $29.95 (978-1-59018-532-

2). Discusses the forms of education available during the Middle Ages — including apprenticeships, song schools, monastic schools, universities — and who was able to enjoy them and what they learned, ending with material on the rise of humanism. (Rev: SLJ 3/05) [370]

Eighteenth Through Nineteenth Centuries (1700–1900)

7895 Dunn, John M. *The Enlightenment* (6–9). Series: World History. 1998, Lucent LB $28.70 (978-1-56006-242-4). A look at Western Europe's emergence from the Dark Ages and the rediscovery of ancient scholarship. (Rev: BL 12/15/98) [940.2]

7896 Haskins, Jim, and Kathleen Benson. *Bound for America: The Forced Migration of Africans to the New World* (4–9). Illus. by Floyd Cooper. Series: From African Beginnings. 1999, Lothrop LB $17.89 (978-0-688-10259-3). This stirring account traces the fate of African slaves from capture, imprisonment, and branding to the brutal conditions on slave ships and finally to the survivors' arrival in the New World. (Rev: BCCB 3/99; BL 12/15/98; HBG 10/99; SLJ 1/99*) [382]

7897 Killingray, David. *The Transatlantic Slave Trade* (7–12). Illus. 1987, Batsford $19.95 (978-0-7134-5469-7). This book gives detailed coverage of the causes, history, and end of the international slave trade and how it has affected demographics today. (Rev: SLJ 1/88) [380.1]

7898 Monaghan, Tom. *The Slave Trade* (6–10). Series: Events and Outcomes. 2002, Raintree LB $31.42 (978-0-7398-5802-8). An interesting overview of the supply of slaves to the New World from its early days through its abolition, with information on key abolitionists and discussion of the economic reasons for this trade. (Rev: HBG 3/03; SLJ 4/03) [306.3]

7899 Sharp, S. Pearl, and Virginia Schomp. *The Slave Trade and the Middle Passage* (5–8). Series: Drama of African-American History. 2006, Benchmark LB $23.95 (978-0-7614-2176-4). A brief overview of the triangular trade between Africa, the American colonies, and Europe, looking at conditions aboard the slave ships. (Rev: SLJ 5/07) [306.3]

7900 Sommerville, Donald. *Revolutionary and Napoleonic Wars* (8–10). Series: History of Warfare. 1998, Raintree LB $29.97 (978-0-8172-5446-9). This well-illustrated book looks at the wars fought from the late-18th through mid-19th centuries, focusing primarily on the Americans and the French and their wars of independence and subsequent battles with other enemies. (Rev: HBG 3/99; SLJ 1/99) [909]

7901 Westwell, Ian. *Warfare in the 18th Century* (8–10). Series: History of Warfare. 1998, Raintree LB $29.97 (978-0-8172-5445-2). A look at wars fought from the Great Northern War in 1700 to the death of Catherine the Great in 1796, including wars fought with Native Americans and over the fate of India. (Rev: HBG 3/99; SLJ 1/99) [909]

7902 Wilkinson, Philip, and Jacqueline Dineen. *The Industrial Revolution* (6–9). Illus. 1995, Chelsea LB $21.95 (978-0-7910-2767-7). This simple account shows how harnessing energy and the development of industry during the 19th century and afterward changed the way people lived and created a new social structure. (Rev: VOYA 2/96) [909.8]

Twentieth Century

General and Miscellaneous

7903 Crew, David F. *Hitler and the Nazis: A History in Documents* (8–12). 2006, Oxford Univ. $36.95 (978-0-19-515285-2). Government documents, propaganda, letters, articles, personal memoirs, and trial testimony reveal much about the growth, success, and eventual defeat of the Nazis. (Rev: SLJ 6/06)

7904 Jedicke, Peter. *Great Inventions of the 20th Century* (5–8). Series: Scientific American. 2007, Chelsea House LB $30.00 (978-0-7910-9048-0). With plenty of photographs and clear text, this volume — produced in association with *Scientific American* — presents inventions of the 20th century including cellophane and the microwave in chapters such as "On the Road," "At Home," and "In the Air." (Rev: SLJ 2/08)

7905 McGowen, Tom. *Assault from the Sea: Amphibious Invasions in the Twentieth Century* (5–8). Series: Military Might. 2002, Twenty-First Century LB $26.90 (978-0-7613-1811-8). Invasions launched from the sea during World Wars I and II and the Korean War are the subject of this introduction that includes black-and-white photographs and maps. Also use *Assault from the Sky: Airborne Infantry of World War II* (2002). (Rev: HBG 10/02; SLJ 6/02) [355.460904]

7906 Wilson, Janet. *Imagine That!* (4–8). Illus. by author. 2000, Stoddart $14.95 (978-0-7737-3221-6). In the form of a reminiscence by 100-year-old Auntie Violet, this is a brief history of the past century, with major events highlighted. (Rev: SLJ 11/00) [909]

World War I

7907 Clare, John D., ed. *First World War* (5–8). Illus. Series: Living History. 1995, Gulliver $16.95

(978-0-15-200087-5). Excellent visuals and a vivid text are used in this history of World War I. (Rev: SLJ 6/95) [940.53]

7908 Coetzee, Frans, and Marilyn Shevin-Coetzee. *World War I: A History in Documents* (7–12). Series: Pages from History. 2002, Oxford LB $39.95 (978-0-19-513746-0). Letters, poems, posters, quotations, and other documents are accompanied by advice on evaluating their content. (Rev: SLJ 8/02) [940.3]

7909 Gay, Kathlyn, and Martin Gay. *World War I* (5–8). Illus. Series: Voices from the Past. 1995, Twenty-First Century LB $25.90 (978-0-8050-2848-5). The causes, major battles, and effects of World War I are covered, with many excerpts from personal accounts. (Rev: BL 12/15/95; SLJ 2/96) [940.3]

7910 George, Linda S. *World War I* (5–8). Series: Letters from the Homefront. 2001, Benchmark LB $29.93 (978-0-7614-1096-6). Life at the front and at home during the First World War is depicted through letters and other firsthand accounts. (Rev: BL 10/15/01; HBG 3/02) [973.9]

7911 Granfield, Linda. *Where Poppies Grow: A World War I Companion* (4–7). 2002, Stoddart $16.95 (978-0-7737-3319-0). The horrors of war in the trenches are portrayed in this scrapbook full of photographs, propaganda, and ephemera that includes accounts of two Canadian soldiers. (Rev: BL 6/1–15/02; HBG 10/02; SLJ 7/02) [940.3]

7912 Grant, Reg. *World War I: Armistice 1918* (5–8). Series: The World Wars. 2001, Raintree LB $27.12 (978-0-7398-2753-6). The negotiations that ended World War I are detailed here, with discussion of the failure of the League of Nations and the lead-up to World War II. (Rev: SLJ 6/01) [940.3]

7913 Hamilton, John. *Aircraft of World War I* (5–8). Illus. Series: World War I. 2003, ABDO LB $24.21 (978-1-57765-912-9). How aircraft became a valuable military tool for the first time in World War I, and how some of the pilots became internationally famous. (Rev: SLJ 6/04) [940.4]

7914 Hamilton, John. *Battles of World War I* (5–8). Illus. Series: World War I. 2003, ABDO LB $24.21 (978-1-57765-913-6). A review of key battles that took place during the three years before the United States entered the conflict in 1917, with information on key figures. (Rev: SLJ 6/04) [940.4]

7915 Hamilton, John. *Events Leading to World War I* (5–8). Illus. Series: World War I. 2003, ABDO LB $24.21 (978-1-57765-914-3). An evenhanded description of events and circumstances during the years leading up to World War I in each of the countries that became involved in the conflict. (Rev: SLJ 6/04) [940.3]

7916 Hansen, Ole Steen. *Military Aircraft of WWI* (4–7). Series: The Story of Flight. 2003, Crabtree $25.27 (978-0-7787-1201-5). This book introduces in text and pictures the aircraft used by the allies and enemies during World War I. (Rev: BL 10/15/03) [940.3]

7917 Hansen, Ole Steen. *World War I: War in the Trenches* (5–8). Series: The World Wars. 2001, Raintree LB $27.12 (978-0-7398-2752-9). The causes of World War I are introduced, followed by information on the major battles and descriptions of the misery of life in the trenches, with plenty of photographs, reproductions, maps, sidebars, and excerpts from primary sources. (Rev: SLJ 6/01) [940.3]

7918 Hatt, Christine. *World War I: 1914–18* (6–9). Illus. Series: Documenting History. 2001, Watts LB $24.50 (978-0-531-14611-8). This overview of the war draws on sources including advertisements, interviews, and personal diaries, and offers maps, charts, and photographs. (Rev: BL 12/15/01; SLJ 12/01) [940.3]

7919 Murphy, Donald J., ed. *World War I* (7–12). Series: Turning Points in World History. 2002, Gale LB $31.20 (978-0-7377-0932-2); paper $37.45 (978-0-7377-0933-9). The causes, campaigns, battles, effects, and personal aspects of World War I are explored in this anthology of important essays for the serious student. (Rev: BL 6/1–15/02) [940.3]

7920 Myers, Walter Dean, and Bill Miles. *The Harlem Hellfighters: When Pride Met Courage* (5–8). Illus. 2006, HarperCollins LB $18.89 (978-0-06-001137-6). A tribute to the World War I heroism of the 369th Infantry Regiment, which was made up entirely of African Americans. (Rev: BL 2/1/06; SLJ 4/06) [940.4]

7921 Preston, Diana. *Remember the Lusitania!* (5–8). Illus. 2003, Walker LB $21.85 (978-0-8027-8847-4). This gripping account of the sinking of the *Lusitania* includes many personal stories that will hold young readers' attention. (Rev: BL 4/15/03; HB 7–8/03; HBG 10/03; SLJ 7/03) [940.4]

7922 Rice, Earle, Jr. *The Battle of Belleau Wood* (6–10). Illus. Series: Great Battles in History. 1996, Lucent LB $34.95 (978-1-56006-424-4). The story of the victory over the Germans in June 1918 by chiefly American troops is told with generous use of illustrations, maps, and a timeline. (Rev: BL 4/15/96) [940.4]

7923 Ross, Stewart. *Assassination in Sarajevo: The Trigger for World War I* (4–9). Illus. by Stefan Chabluk. Series: Point of Impact. 2001, Heinemann LB $24.22 (978-1-58810-074-0). The assassination of the Archduke of Austria, a precipitating factor in World War I, is put into context and the alliances among the world's nations at the time are clearly explained. (Rev: HBG 10/01; SLJ 7/01) [940.3]

7924 Ross, Stewart. *The Battle of the Somme* (5–8). Series: The World Wars. 2003, Raintree LB $28.56 (978-0-7398-5479-2). An examination of the first Battle of the Somme in 1916, an all-out assault on entrenched German forces in northern France by British and French troops, and of the enormous carnage involved. (Rev: SLJ 5/04) [940.4]

7925 Ross, Stewart. *Causes and Consequences of World War I* (7–10). Series: Causes and Consequences. 1998, Raintree LB $29.97 (978-0-8172-4057-8). This volume analyzes the factors that led to World War I and the conflict's short-term and long-term effects, with illustrations. (Rev: BL 8/98; SLJ 6/98) [940.311]

7926 Ross, Stewart. *Leaders of World War I* (4–8). Illus. Series: World Wars. 2003, Raintree LB $28.56 (978-0-7398-5481-5). Stewart presents concise details on the large cast of world and military leaders involved in this conflict. (Rev: BL 12/1/03; HBG 10/03) [023]

7927 Ross, Stewart. *The Technology of World War I* (4–8). Illus. Series: World Wars. 2003, Raintree LB $28.56 (978-0-7398-5482-2). New technologies used during World War I included torpedoes, mines, submarines, tanks, planes with machine guns, and mustard gas; all are shown here with maps, diagrams, period reproductions, and posters. (Rev: BL 12/1/03; HBG 10/03; SLJ 7/03) [023]

7928 Schomp, Virginia. *World War I* (6–8). Illus. Series: Letters from the Battlefront. 2004, Marshall Cavendish LB $29.93 (978-0-7614-1661-6). History and firsthand accounts are combined into a memorable overview of World War I. (Rev: BL 4/1/04; SLJ 2/04) [940.3]

World War II and the Holocaust

7929 Aaseng, Nathan. *Navajo Code Talkers* (6–9). 1992, Walker LB $16.85 (978-0-8027-8183-3). Describes how Navajos were recruited during World War II to create an unbreakable code that allowed the marines to transmit information quickly, accurately, and safely. (Rev: BL 12/1/92; SLJ 12/92) [940.54]

7930 Aaseng, Nathan. *Paris* (6–12). Series: Cities at War. 1992, Macmillan LB $18.00 (978-0-02-700010-8). Remembrances from people who experienced World War II in Paris. (Rev: BL 10/15/92) [944]

7931 Adams, Simon. *World War II* (4–8). Illus. 2000, DK $15.95 (978-0-7894-3298-8). Each double-page spread presents a different aspect of World War II, such as the Battle of Britain, military equipment, women at work, and conditions inside the Soviet Union. (Rev: BL 11/1/00) [940.53]

7932 Adler, David A. *We Remember the Holocaust* (4–7). 1995, Holt paper $14.95 (978-0-8050-3715-

9). Through interview excerpts, the terrible days of the Holocaust are remembered. (Rev: SLJ 12/89) [940.54]

7933 Allen, Thomas B. *Remember Pearl Harbor: American and Japanese Survivors Tell Their Stories* (5–9). Illus. 2001, National Geographic $17.95 (978-0-7922-6690-7). First-person accounts by Japanese and American men and women give readers a close-up view of the 1941 Japanese attack on Pearl Harbor, with maps and photographs. (Rev: BL 9/1/01; HBG 3/02; SLJ 9/01*; VOYA 10/01) [940.54]

7934 Altman, Linda J. *Crimes and Criminals of the Holocaust* (5–10). Illus. Series: Holocaust in History. 2004, Enslow LB $26.60 (978-0-7660-1995-9). This book focuses on the end of World War II and the war crimes trials in Nuremberg as well as other cases such as that of Adolf Eichmann. (Rev: BL 5/1/04) [940.53]

7935 Altman, Linda J. *The Forgotten Victims of the Holocaust* (5–10). Illus. Series: Holocaust in History. 2003, Enslow LB $26.60 (978-0-7660-1993-5). Altman looks at populations victimized by the Nazis that are often overlooked: Poles, Russians, gypsies, homosexuals, and the disabled. Also use *The Jewish Victims of the Holocaust* (2003), which describes Hitler's genocide of the Jews. (Rev: BL 7/03; HBG 4/04; SLJ 10/03) [940.53]

7936 Altman, Linda J. *The Holocaust Ghettos* (8–12). Series: Holocaust Remembered. 1998, Enslow LB $26.60 (978-0-89490-994-8). This volume explains the role that ghettos played in the Nazis' scheme to isolate and control the Jews in preparation for relocation to death camps. (Rev: SLJ 7/98; VOYA 8/98) [940.54]

7937 Altman, Linda J. *The Holocaust, Hitler, and Nazi Germany* (6–12). Illus. Series: Holocaust Remembered. 1999, Enslow LB $26.60 (978-0-7660-1230-1). This book explores the many causes and forces that produced the Holocaust. (Rev: BL 4/1/00; HBG 4/00; SLJ 5/00) [943.08]

7938 Altman, Linda J. *Impact of the Holocaust* (5–10). Illus. Series: Holocaust in History. 2004, Enslow LB $26.60 (978-0-7660-1996-6). Dscusses the Holocaust's influence in the creation of a homeland for the Jews and a Universal Declaration of Human Rights. (Rev: BL 5/1/04) [940.53]

7939 Altshuler, David A. *Hitler's War Against the Jews: A Young Reader's Version of The War Against the Jews, 1933–1945, by Lucy S. Dawidowicz* (7–10). Illus. 1995, Behrman paper $14.95 (978-0-87441-298-7). The tragic story of Hitler's Final Solution and its aftermath. [940.54]

7940 Ambrose, Stephen E. *The Good Fight: How World War II Was Won* (7–12). Illus. 2001, Simon & Schuster $19.95 (978-0-689-84361-7). Historian Ambrose presents an appealing and well-written

overview of World War II, from its origins through the Marshall Plan, with many photographs, fact boxes, and maps. (Rev: BL 7/01; HBG 10/01; SLJ 5/01; VOYA 6/01) [940.53]

7941 Anflick, Charles. *Resistance: Teen Partisan and Resisters Who Fought Nazi Tyranny* (5–9). Series: Teen Witnesses to the Holocaust. 1999, Rosen LB $26.50 (978-0-8239-2847-7). This volume celebrates the teenagers who fought against the Nazis in ghettos, concentration camps, inside Germany, and in the lands that the Nazis conquered. (Rev: BL 4/15/98; VOYA 8/99) [940.54]

7942 Anthony, Nathan, and Robert Gardner. *The Bombing of Pearl Harbor in American History* (6–10). Series: In American History. 2001, Enslow LB $26.60 (978-0-7660-1126-7). This is a well-researched account that covers the bombing of Pearl Harbor by the Japanese in 1941 and the consequences. (Rev: BL 3/1/01; HBG 10/01) [940.54]

7943 Auerbacher, Inge. *I Am a Star: Child of the Holocaust* (5–7). Illus. 1993, Puffin paper $5.99 (978-0-14-036401-9). The memoirs of a former child survivor of the Terezin concentration camp in Czechoslovakia. (Rev: BCCB 7–8/87; BL 6/1/87; SLJ 4/87) [940.5]

7944 Axelrod, Toby. *In the Camps: Teens Who Survived the Nazi Concentration Camps* (5–9). Series: Teen Witnesses to the Holocaust. 1999, Rosen LB $26.50 (978-0-8239-2844-6). These are the stories of teenagers who survived the death camps, their despair and sadness, and the hope they maintained despite the horror around them. (Rev: BL 7/99) [940.54]

7945 Axelrod, Toby. *Rescuers Defying the Nazis: Non-Jewish Teens Who Rescued Jews* (5–8). Series: Teen Witnesses to the Holocaust. 1999, Rosen LB $26.50 (978-0-8239-2848-4). Inspiring stories of teenage gentiles in Poland, Denmark, and Germany who risked their lives to rescue Jews from the Holocaust. (Rev: BL 7/99; SLJ 8/99) [940.54]

7946 Ayer, Eleanor. *Berlin* (6–12). Series: Cities at War. 1992, Macmillan LB $18.00 (978-0-02-707800-8). A photoessay on the lives of ordinary people in Berlin during World War II, with eyewitness quotations. (Rev: BL 6/15/92; SLJ 9/92) [940.53]

7947 Ayer, Eleanor. *In the Ghettos: Teens Who Survived the Ghettos of the Holocaust* (5–8). Series: Teens Witnesses to the Holocaust. 1999, Rosen LB $27.95 (978-0-8239-2845-3). The harrowing stories of courageous teenagers who survived life in the ghettos of Lodz, Theresienstadt, and Warsaw. (Rev: BL 7/99; SLJ 8/99) [940.54]

7948 Bachrach, Susan D. *Tell Them We Remember: The Story of the Holocaust* (5–9). 1994, Little, Brown $21.95 (978-0-316-69264-9). A photohistory focusing on the young who struggled through the brutality of the Holocaust following the destruction of their world of family and friends. (Rev: BL 7/94*; SLJ 11/94; VOYA 12/94) [940.54]

7949 Bard, Mitchell G., ed. *The Holocaust* (6–12). Illus. Series: Complete History Of. 2001, Greenhaven LB $123.75 (978-0-7377-0373-3). A well-organized and balanced look at the Holocaust comprising more than 90 entries. (Rev: BL 11/1/01; SLJ 8/01) [940.53]

7950 Bard, Mitchell G., ed. *The Holocaust* (7–12). Series: Turning Points in World History. 2001, Greenhaven LB $37.45 (978-0-7377-0576-8); paper $24.95 (978-0-7377-0575-1). The Jewish genocide in Nazi Germany is explored in an anthology of essays, each of which examines a different aspect of this terrible period in history. (Rev: BL 6/1–15/01) [940.54]

7951 Barr, Gary E. *Pearl Harbor* (6–8). Series: Witness to History. 2004, Heinemann LB $27.07 (978-1-4034-4569-8). Eyewitness accounts add to this overview of the attack on Pearl Harbor; readers are asked to consider the lessons that have been learned from this event. Also in this series: *World War II Home Front* (2004). (Rev: SLJ 10/04) [940.54]

7952 Beller, Susan Provost. *Battling in the Pacific: Soldiering in World War II* (5–8). 2007, Twenty-First Century LB $33.26 (978-0-8225-6381-5). After background information on the war, this volume examines the life of soldiers in the Pacific and provides interesting sidebar features and photographs. (Rev: SLJ 1/08)

7953 Bodden, Valerie. *The Bombing of Hiroshima and Nagasaki* (5–9). Illus. Series: Days of Change. 2007, Creative Education LB $21.95 (978-1-58341-545-0). Survivors of the bombings in both cities recall the horrors of the attacks; a brief background on World War II will help readers to place the bombings in context. (Rev: BL 12/15/07; SLJ 3/08) [940.54]

7954 Boraks-Nemetz, Lillian, and Irene N. Watts, eds. *Tapestry of Hope: Holocaust Writing for Young People* (6–12). 2003, Tundra $24.99 (978-0-88776-638-1). Two Holocaust survivors have collected fiction, poetry, drama, and nonfiction excerpts that detail the experiences of those who went into hiding, were sent to the camps, joined the resistance movement, and made their way to other countries. (Rev: BL 6/1–15/03; HBG 10/03; SLJ 8/03; VOYA 10/03) [810.8]

7955 Brager, Bruce L. *The Trial of Adolf Eichmann: The Holocaust on Trial* (8–12). Series: Famous Trials. 1999, Lucent LB $27.45 (978-1-56006-469-5). The story of the search for the infamous war criminal and of his trial in Israel in 1961, during which the horror of the Holocaust was relived. (Rev: BL 5/1/99; SLJ 8/99) [364.15]

7956 Byers, Ann. *The Holocaust Camps* (8–12). Series: Holocaust Remembered. 1998, Enslow LB $18.95 (978-0-89490-955-9). This work traces the evolution of political prison camps to labor camps and eventually to death camps during the Nazi regime. (Rev: SLJ 12/98; VOYA 8/98) [940.54]

7957 Clive, A. Lawton. *Hiroshima* (6–12). 2004, Candlewick $18.99 (978-0-7636-2271-8). This powerful photoessay presents the history of the development and dropping of the first atom bomb, documenting with many quotations the misgivings of some of the key figures. (Rev: BL 7/04; SLJ 11/04) [940.54]

7958 Cox, Jeromy. *Holocaust: The Events and Their Impact on Real People* (6–12). Illus. 2007, DK $29.99 (978-0-7566-2535-1). Using DK's usual layout and accompanying DVD with narratives by Holocaust survivors and eyewitnesses, this volume provides a well-rounded overview of anti-Semitism in world history and of the events of the Holocaust itself. (Rev: BL 9/1/07; SLJ 8/07) [940.53]

7959 Cretzmeyer, Stacy. *Your Name Is Renée: Ruth Kapp Hartz's Story as a Hidden Child in Nazi-Occupied France* (5–8). 2003, Bt. Bound $22.20 (978-0-613-56879-1). The story of a German Jewish family living in France during the Holocaust, how they survived, and how young Ruth hid in an orphanage run by Catholic nuns. (Rev: BCCB 7–8/99; SLJ 8/99) [940.54]

7960 Cross, Robin. *Children and War* (4–7). Illus. Series: World War II. 1994, Thomson Learning LB $24.26 (978-1-56847-180-8). True case histories of children in various circumstances during World War II, including in a gulag, the resistance movement, and a death camp. (Rev: BL 12/15/94; SLJ 2/95) [940.53]

7961 De Angelis, Therese. *Pearl Harbor: Deadly Surprise Attack* (6–9). Illus. Series: American Disasters. 2002, Enslow LB $23.93 (978-0-7660-1783-2). A concise account of the attack that brought the United States into World War II. (Rev: BL 1/1–15/03; HBG 3/03; SLJ 10/02) [940.54]

7962 DeSaix, Deborah Durland, and Karen Gray Ruelle. *Hidden on the Mountain: Stories of Children Sheltered from the Nazis in Le Chambon* (6–9). Illus. 2007, Holiday $24.95 (978-0-8234-1928-9). First-person accounts by the former children and profiles of their rescuers give a compelling portrait of the courage of the residents of this small French town and the resilience of the children. (Rev: BCCB 9/07; BL 3/15/07; SLJ 5/07) [940.53]

7963 Devaney, John. *America Fights the Tide: 1942* (6–10). 1991, Walker $17.95 (978-0-8027-6997-8). Using a diary format and anecdotal accounts, this volume focuses on the United States' entry into World War II in both the European and the Pacific theaters. (Rev: BL 10/15/91; SLJ 10/91) [940.54]

7964 Devaney, John. *America Goes to War: 1941* (5–8). 1991, Walker LB $17.85 (978-0-8027-6980-0). An illustrated, datelined, day-by-day account that covers personal and public events of America's first year of World War II. (Rev: BL 10/1/91; SLJ 8/91) [940.53]

7965 Devaney, John. *America on the Attack: 1943* (6–10). Series: Walker's World War II. 1992, Walker LB $18.85 (978-0-8027-8195-6). This well-illustrated account describes America's active participation in World War II once the war effort got under way. (Rev: BL 12/1/92) [940.53]

7966 Devaney, John. *America Storms the Beaches: 1944* (6–10). Series: World War II. 1993, Walker LB $18.85 (978-0-8027-8245-8). The story of D Day and the other invasions that spelled the beginning of the end of Nazi Germany. (Rev: BL 12/15/93; SLJ 12/93; VOYA 2/94) [940.54]

7967 Downing, David. *The Origins of the Holocaust* (7–10). Illus. Series: World Almanac Library of the Holocaust. 2005, World Almanac LB $31.00 (978-0-8368-5943-0). Downing looks at the roots of anti-Semitism and the continuing persecution of the Jews over the centuries, connecting this history with the rise of the Nazi Party. (Rev: BL 10/15/05; SLJ 3/06) [940.53]

7968 Drez, Ronald J. *Remember D-Day: The Plan, the Invasion, Survivor Stories* (4–8). 2004, National Geographic $17.95 (978-0-7922-6666-2). Filled with period photographs and personal stories, this large-format survey of the Allied invasion of Normandy focuses on the military operation and on the strategic planning that preceded it. (Rev: BL 7/04; SLJ 7/04) [940.54]

7969 Drucker, Olga L. *Kindertransport* (5–8). 1995, Holt paper $8.95 (978-0-8050-4251-1). A true account of a Jewish girl sent from Germany to live in England until she could join her parents in New York City in 1945. (Rev: BCCB 1/93; SLJ 11/92) [940.54]

7970 Dvorson, Alexa. *The Hitler Youth: Marching Toward Madness* (5–9). Illus. Series: Teen Witnesses to the Holocaust. 1999, Rosen LB $27.95 (978-0-8239-2783-8). This volume describes how thousands of German boys and girls joined the Hitler Youth, why they were seduced into obeying the Nazis, and how their dreams were eventually shattered. (Rev: BL 4/15/99) [943.086]

7971 Fisch, Robert O. *Light from the Yellow Star: A Lesson of Love from the Holocaust* (7–12). Illus. 1996, Univ. of Minnesota $14.95 (978-1-885116-00-0); paper $9.95 (978-0-9644896-0-8). A biographical account that uses the author's abstract paintings to tell about his childhood in Budapest and his death camp experiences. (Rev: BL 4/15/96) [940.53]

7972 Fox, Anne L., and Eva Abraham-Podietz. *Ten Thousand Children: True Stories Told by Children Who Escaped the Holocaust on the Kindertransport* (5–8). Illus. 1998, Behrman paper $12.95 (978-0-87441-648-0). The moving stories of 21 survivors who were part of the rescue operation known as the Kindertransport that took 10,000 Jewish children from Nazi-occupied Europe to freedom during late 1938 and 1939. (Rev: BL 1/1–15/99) [940.53]

7973 Freeman, Charles. *The Rise of the Nazis* (7–12). Series: New Perspectives. 1998, Raintree $28.54 (978-0-8172-5015-7). Presents differing views on Hitler and the Nazi Party as expressed by German politicians, leaders, and ordinary citizens. (Rev: BL 3/15/98; HBG 9/98; SLJ 7/98) [940.54]

7974 Fremon, David K. *The Holocaust Heroes* (6–10). Series: Holocaust Remembered. 1998, Enslow LB $26.60 (978-0-7660-1046-8). This account of the Holocaust focuses on Resistance fighters, such as the people of the Warsaw Ghetto, and on individuals including Raoul Wallenberg and the Danish nation who took risks to help Jews escape. (Rev: BL 9/15/98; HBG 3/99; SLJ 12/98) [940.5318]

7975 Friedman, Ina R. *The Other Victims: First-Person Stories of Non-Jews Persecuted by the Nazis* (7–12). 1995, Houghton paper $7.99 (978-0-395-74515-1). This account deals with the other victims of the Holocaust — including Gypsies, homosexuals, dissenters, and some religious minorities. (Rev: BL 6/15/90; SLJ 4/90; VOYA 6/90) [940.53]

7976 Fuller, William, and Jack James. *Reckless Courage: The True Story of a Norwegian Boy Under Nazi Rule* (8–11). 2005, Taber Hall paper $13.95 (978-0-9769252-0-0). The true story of a Norwegian boy's participation in the resistance against his country's Nazi occupiers. (Rev: BL 9/15/05) [940.53]

7977 Galloway, Priscilla, ed. *Too Young to Fight: Memories from Our Youth During World War II* (6–12). 2000, Stoddart $22.95 (978-0-7737-3190-5). Eleven Canadian authors of books for young people describe what it was like growing up on the home front during World War II. (Rev: BL 5/1/00; SLJ 7/00) [940.53]

7978 Giddens, Sandra. *Escape: Teens Who Escaped the Holocaust to Freedom* (5–9). Series: Teen Witnesses to the Holocaust. 1999, Rosen LB $27.95 (978-0-8239-2843-9). This volume focuses on the ordeals of four Jewish teens who were able to elude the Nazis during the Holocaust. (Rev: BL 4/15/98; VOYA 8/99) [940.54]

7979 Gies, Miep, and Alison L. Gold. *Anne Frank Remembered: The Story of Miep Gies, Who Helped to Hide the Frank Family* (8–12). Illus. 1987, Simon & Schuster paper $14.00 (978-0-671-66234-9). The story of the woman who helped the Frank family during World War II and of the Resistance movement in the Netherlands. (Rev: BL 4/1/87; SLJ 11/87; VOYA 12/87) [940.53]

7980 Gonzales, Doreen. *The Manhattan Project and the Atomic Bomb in American History* (6–12). Illus. Series: American History. 2000, Enslow LB $26.60 (978-0-89490-879-8). This work traces the events that produced the atomic bomb, introduces the people involved, and gives details on the impact of its use during World War II. (Rev: BL 1/1–15/00; HBG 9/00; SLJ 9/00) [355.8]

7981 Gottfried, Ted. *Children of the Slaughter: Young People of the Holocaust* (7–12). Illus. Series: Holocaust. 2001, Twenty-First Century LB $28.90 (978-0-7613-1716-6). Gottfried provides a clear and thought-provoking account of the suffering of children at the hands of the Nazis, looking not only at the genocide of Jewish children but also at the experiences of German youngsters forced into Hitler Youth, spying on their families, and dying in battle. Also use *Heroes of the Holocaust* (2001), which tells the stories of heroic rescuers. (Rev: BL 5/15/01; HBG 10/01; SLJ 6/01) [940.53]

7982 Gottfried, Ted. *Displaced Persons: The Liberation and Abuse of Holocaust Survivors* (6–12). Illus. 2001, Twenty-First Century LB $29.90 (978-0-7613-1924-5). Survivors of the Holocaust went on to suffer many indignities and rejections, as Gottfried shows in this account of continued racism, displaced persons camps, and denial of shelter by countries including the United States. (Rev: BL 9/1/01; HBG 3/02) [940]

7983 Gottfried, Ted. *Martyrs to Madness: The Victims of the Holocaust* (8–12). Illus. Series: Holocaust. 2000, Twenty-First Century LB $21.68 (978-0-7613-1715-9). After a brief overview of the Holocaust, the author devotes separate chapters to each group of victims including Jews, Slavs, gypsies, homosexuals, and POWs. (Rev: BL 7/00; HBG 10/01; SLJ 12/00; VOYA 6/01) [940.53]

7984 Gottfried, Ted. *Nazi Germany: The Face of Tyranny* (8–12). Illus. Series: Holocaust. 2000, Twenty-First Century LB $21.68 (978-0-7613-1714-2). Gottfried describes the Nazis' rise to power, their expansion through Europe, and the systematic attacks against Jews and other groups. (Rev: BL 7/00; HBG 10/01; SLJ 12/00; VOYA 6/01) [940.53]

7985 Grant, R. G. *Hiroshima and Nagasaki* (7–12). Illus. Series: New Perspectives. 1998, Raintree $28.54 (978-0-8172-5013-3). This account of the dropping of atomic bombs on Japan examines the different viewpoints of the scientists, politicians, and air crews involved, and the people who survived it. (Rev: BL 3/15/98; HBG 9/98) [940.54]

7986 Grant, R. G. *The Holocaust* (7–12). Series: New Perspectives. 1998, Raintree $19.98 (978-0-

8172-5016-4). The story of the Holocaust, one of history's darkest moments, as shaped by the German perpetrators, witnessed by onlookers, and recalled by survivors. (Rev: BL 3/15/98; HBG 9/98; SLJ 7/98) [940.54]

7987 Hama, Larry, and Anthony Williams. *The Battle of Iwo Jima: Guerrilla Warfare in the Pacific* (5–8). Illus. Series: Graphic Battles of World War II. 2007, Rosen LB $29.25 (978-1-4042-0781-3). After background text to provide context, this graphic novel account of the battle of Iwo Jima takes readers behind the lines on both sides of the bloody conflict. (Rev: BL 4/1/07; SLJ 7/07) [940.54]

7988 Hanmer, Trudy J. *Leningrad* (6–12). Series: Cities at War. 1992, Macmillan $18.00 (978-0-02-742615-1). The story of the city of Leningrad during World War II and the terrible siege that destroyed a large percentage of the city and its inhabitants. (Rev: BL 10/15/92) [947]

7989 Heyes, Eileen. *Children of the Swastika: The Hitler Youth* (7–12). 1993, Millbrook LB $22.40 (978-1-56294-237-3). A study of the Hitler Youth's structure, purpose, impact on the war effort, and effects on the youth. (Rev: BL 2/15/93) [324.243]

7990 Hill, Jeff, ed. *The Holocaust* (7–12). 2006, Omnigraphics LB $65 (978-0-7808-0935-2). Provides primary sources that will help students researching the various stages of the Holocaust from its roots through the camps for displaced persons and the aftermath of the war. (Rev: SLJ 1/07)

7991 Hillman, Laura. *I Will Plant You a Lilac Tree: A Memoir of a Schindler's List Survivor* (8–11). 2005, Simon & Schuster $16.95 (978-0-689-86980-8). In this inspiring true story of Holocaust survival, Hannelore escapes the Nazi gas chambers when her name is added to Schindler's list. (Rev: BCCB 7–8/05; BL 5/1/05*; HB 7–8/05; SLJ 9/05; VOYA 8/05) [940.5]

7992 Hills, C. A. R. *The Second World War* (7–12). Illus. 1986, David & Charles $19.95 (978-0-7134-4531-2). A brief but comprehensive history of World War II as seen through the eyes of its leaders. (Rev: SLJ 11/86) [940.53]

7993 Hipperson, Carol Edgemon. *The Belly Gunner* (6–9). Illus. 2001, Twenty-First Century LB $27.90 (978-0-7613-1873-6). This is the absorbing story, told in the first person and enhanced by informative side notes, of one man's experiences in World War II as a B-17 gunner and in a German prison camp. (Rev: HBG 3/02; SLJ 8/01) [940.54]

7994 Hook, Jason. *Hiroshima: August 6, 1945* (6–8). Series: Days That Shook the World. 2003, Raintree LB $27.12 (978-0-7398-5234-7). With many color and black-and-white photographs, this slim volume looks at the development of the atom bomb, the circumstances that led to its use, the destruction it caused in Hiroshima, and the aftermath. (Rev: HBG 10/03; SLJ 10/03) [940.54]

7995 Isserman, Maurice. *World War II* (7–12). Series: America at War. 1991, Facts on File $25.00 (978-0-8160-2374-5). The major battles and personalities of World War II, events leading to war, and discussion of changes following the conflict. (Rev: BL 10/15/91; SLJ 8/92) [940.53]

7996 Jones, Catherine. *Navajo Code Talkers: Native American Heroes* (6–10). 1998, Tudor $12.95 (978-0-936389-51-6); paper $7.95 (978-0-936389-52-3). This is the story of the Navajo Code Talkers of the Marine Corps who, during World War II in the Pacific, communicated in a code that neither the Japanese nor the Americans could decipher. (Rev: SLJ 4/98) [940.54]

7997 Jones, Steven L. *The Red Tails: World War II's Tuskegee Airmen* (4–8). Illus. Series: Cover-to-Cover. 2002, Perfection Learning $17.95 (978-0-7569-0251-3); paper $8.95 (978-0-7891-5487-3). The story of the heroic African American squadron of World War II fighter pilots, their successful missions, and the prejudices they faced. (Rev: BL 5/1/02) [940.5404]

7998 Kacer, Kathy. *Hiding Edith: A Holocaust Remembrance Book for Young Readers* (4–7). Illus. 2006, Second Story $10.95 (978-1-897187-06-7). Focusing on a young Jewish girl named Edith Schwalb, this is the story of a French couple who hid 100 Jewish refugee children during World War II with the help of their town. (Rev: BL 12/1/06; SLJ 12/06) [940.53]

7999 Kacer, Kathy. *The Underground Reporters: A True Story* (5–8). Illus. 2005, Second Story $11.95 (978-1-896764-85-6). Based on real events, this inspiring story tells how a newspaper, published by a group of Jewish teenagers in Budejovice, Czechoslovakia, helped to lift the spirits of the Jewish community during the years of Nazi occupation. (Rev: BL 2/15/05; SLJ 8/05) [940.53]

8000 Keeley, Jennifer. *Life in the Hitler Youth* (7–12). Illus. Series: The Way People Live. 1999, Lucent LB $27.45 (978-1-56006-613-2). A compelling narrative, using many eyewitness accounts, of the training and indoctrination of Hitler's Youth and the part its members played in World War II. (Rev: BL 1/1–15/00; HBG 9/00; SLJ 3/00) [943.086]

8001 Kodama, Tatsuharu. *Shin's Tricycle* (5–8). Trans. by Kazuko Hokumen-Jones. Illus. by Noriyuki Ando. 1995, Walker LB $16.85 (978-0-8027-8376-9). A father recalls the life of his young son, who was killed in the bombing of Hiroshima. (Rev: BCCB 12/95; BL 9/1/95*; SLJ 12/95) [940.54]

8002 Krinitz, Esther Nisenthal, and Bernice Steinhardt. *Memories of Survival* (6–9). Illus. 2005, Hyperion $15.99 (978-0-7868-5126-3). Steinhardt adds commentary to her mother's affecting hand-

embroidered panels depicting her experiences during the Holocaust. (Rev: BL 10/15/05*; SLJ 11/05*) [910]

8003 Kronenwetter, Michael. *London* (6–12). Series: Cities at War. 1992, Macmillan $18.00 (978-0-02-751050-8). A photoessay on the lives of ordinary people in London during World War II, with eyewitness quotations. (Rev: BL 6/15/92; SLJ 9/92) [942.1084]

8004 Kuhn, Betsy. *Angels of Mercy* (5–8). Illus. 1999, Simon & Schuster $18.00 (978-0-689-82044-1). A series of narratives on courage and bravery gives us a fascinating look at the contributions of nurses in World War II. (Rev: BCCB 12/99; BL 10/15/99; HBG 3/00; SLJ 11/99; VOYA 4/00) [940.54]

8005 Kustanowitz, Esther. *The Hidden Children of the Holocaust: Teens Who Hid from the Nazis* (5–9). Series: Teen Witnesses to the Holocaust. 1999, Rosen LB $26.50 (978-0-8239-2562-9). Many first-person narratives are used in this account of teenage Jews who hid in homes, barns, and forests or disguised themselves as non-Jews to escape the Nazis. (Rev: BL 7/99; SLJ 8/99) [940.54]

8006 Lace, William W. *Hitler and the Nazis* (6–12). Series: American War Library. 2000, Lucent LB $27.45 (978-1-56006-372-8). The story of the rise of Adolf Hitler and the emergence of the Nazi Party. (Rev: BL 4/15/00; HBG 9/00) [940.54]

8007 Landau, Elaine. *The Warsaw Ghetto Uprising* (7–10). 1992, Macmillan LB $19.00 (978-0-02-751392-9). Recounts the horrors of the month-long battles between Nazis and Jews in 1943 Poland. (Rev: BL 2/15/93) [940.53]

8008 Langley, Wanda. *Flying Higher: The Women Airforce Service Pilots of World War II* (5–8). Illus. 2002, Linnet $25.00 (978-0-208-02506-7). The women who flew in World War II gained little glory for performing many vital tasks; this arresting volume focuses on the director of the service, Jacqueline Cochran, and one of the pilots. (Rev: BL 11/1/02; HBG 3/03; SLJ 8/02; VOYA 12/02) [940.54]

8009 Lawson, Don. *The French Resistance* (5–9). 1984, Messner LB $8.79 (978-0-671-50832-6). The story of the many gallant French men and women who defied death to oppose the German forces that occupied their country. [940.53]

8010 Levine, Ellen. *Darkness over Denmark: The Danish Resistance and the Rescue of the Jews* (6–12). Illus. 2000, Holiday $22.95 (978-0-8234-1447-5). This is a straightforward history that uses many first-person accounts to relate the Danish people's remarkable efforts to save their Jewish citizens during World War II. (Rev: BL 7/00*; HB 9–10/00; HBG 10/00; SLJ 8/00; VOYA 2/01) [940.531809489]

8011 Levine, Karen. *Hana's Suitcase* (5–8). Illus. 2003, Albert Whitman $15.95 (978-0-8075-3148-8). A Japanese curator of a Holocaust exhibit traces the owner of a suitcase and learns the story of young Hana, who died in Auschwitz. (Rev: BL 3/15/03; HB 5–6/03; HBG 10/03) [940.53]

8012 Levy, Pat. *Causes* (5–9). Series: The Holocaust. 2001, Raintree LB $28.54 (978-0-7398-3257-8). Levy discusses the causes of the Holocaust, looking at historical, religious, political, social, and economic factors. Also use *The Death Camps* (2002). (Rev: HBG 10/02; SLJ 2/02; VOYA 4/02) [940.5318]

8013 Levy, Pat. *The Home Front in World War II* (5–8). Series: The World Wars. 2003, Raintree LB $28.56 (978-0-7398-6065-6). A description of life on the home front in World War II, both in the Allied countries and the Axis countries, including the bombing, refugees, and various shortages. (Rev: SLJ 5/04) [940.53]

8014 McGowen, Tom. *Carrier War: Aircraft Carriers in World War II* (5–7). Series: Military Might. 2001, Twenty-First Century LB $26.90 (978-0-7613-1808-8). An introduction to the importance of aircraft carriers in World War II, with coverage of Pearl Harbor and major battles in the Pacific. (Rev: HBG 10/01; SLJ 6/01) [940.54]

8015 McGowen, Tom. *Germany's Lightning War: Panzer Divisions of World War II* (5–8). Series: Military Might. 1999, Twenty-First Century LB $26.90 (978-0-7613-1511-7). After a general history of tank warfare, this account focuses on the Germans' Panzer tank divisions and the part they played in World War II. (Rev: HBG 3/00; SLJ 9/99) [940.54]

8016 McGowen, Tom. *Sink the Bismarck: Germany's Super-Battleship of World War II* (5–8). Series: Military Might. 1999, Twenty-First Century LB $26.90 (978-0-7613-1510-0). A history of German sea power during World War II and the many (eventually successful) British efforts to sink the *Bismarck*. (Rev: HBG 3/00; SLJ 9/99) [940.54]

8017 McKain, Mark, ed. *Making and Using the Atomic Bomb* (8–12). Series: History Firsthand. 2003, Gale LB $32.45 (978-0-7377-1412-8). A collection of documents relating to the discovery of fission, the Manhattan Project, the decision to use the bomb and the choice of targets, and stories of survivors of Hiroshima and Nagasaki. (Rev: SLJ 7/03) [355.8]

8018 McKissack, Patricia C., and Fredrick McKissack. *Red-Tail Angels: The Story of the Tuskegee Airmen of World War II* (6–8). Illus. 1995, Walker LB $20.85 (978-0-8027-8293-9). A carefully researched account of the formation and training of the 332nd Fighter Group of African American aviators and their exploits during World War II in the

North African and European theaters of war. (Rev: BL 2/15/96*; SLJ 2/96; VOYA 4/96) [940.54]

8019 McNeese, Tim. *The Attack on Pearl Harbor* (5–8). Illus. Series: First Battles. 2001, Morgan Reynolds LB $23.95 (978-1-883846-78-7). This book details the 1941 attack on Pearl Harbor and explains the conditions in Japan that led to the assault. (Rev: BL 10/1/01; HBG 3/02; SLJ 1/02; VOYA 12/01) [940.54]

8020 Maruki, Toshi. *Hiroshima No Pika* (7–10). Illus. 1982, Lothrop $17.99 (978-0-688-01297-7). One family's experiences during the day the bomb dropped on Hiroshima, told in text and moving illustrations by the author. (Rev: BL 3/87) [940.54]

8021 Marx, Trish. *Echoes of World War II* (5–8). Illus. 1994, Lerner LB $14.95 (978-0-8225-4898-0). The true stories of six children around the world whose lives were changed dramatically by World War II. (Rev: BCCB 5/94; BL 9/15/94; SLJ 5/94) [940.53]

8022 Meltzer, Milton. *Rescue: The Story of How Gentiles Saved Jews in the Holocaust* (6–9). 1988, HarperCollins paper $9.99 (978-0-06-446117-7). The uplifting story of those courageous few who helped save Jews from Nazi death camps. (Rev: BL 10/1/88; SLJ 8/88; VOYA 8/88) [940.53]

8023 Miller, Donald L. *D-Days in the Pacific* (8–12). Illus. 2005, Simon & Schuster paper $16.00 (978-0-7432-6929-2). The Allied military offensives that finally brought an end to World War II in the Pacific are described in readable text with excellent illustrations. (Rev: BL 3/15/05) [940.54]

8024 Milman, Barbara. *Light in the Shadows* (5–9). Illus. 1997, Jonathan David paper $14.95 (978-0-8246-0401-1). Illustrated with powerful woodcut prints, this book tells the story of five Holocaust survivors. (Rev: BL 11/15/97) [940.53]

8025 Nardo, Don. *World War II in the Pacific* (7–10). Series: World History. 2002, Gale LB $28.70 (978-1-59018-015-0). From Pearl Harbor to Japan's surrender, this is a history of the battles, decisions, and important people involved in the war in the Pacific. (Rev: BL 8/02) [940.54]

8026 Nathan, Amy. *Yankee Doodle Gals: Women Pilots of World War II* (6–9). Illus. 2001, National Geographic $21.00 (978-0-7922-8216-7). The fascinating story of the Women's Airforce Service Pilots (WASPs) of World War II, with photographs and biographical information on individuals. (Rev: BL 12/15/01; VOYA 8/02) [940.54]

8027 Newton, David E. *Tokyo* (6–12). Series: Cities at War. 1992, Macmillan LB $18.00 (978-0-02-768235-9). Remembrances from people who experienced World War II in Tokyo. (Rev: BL 10/15/92; SLJ 1/93) [952]

8028 Nicholson, Dorinda Makanaonalani. *Remember World War II: Kids Who Survived Tell Their Stories* (5–8). Illus. Series: Remember. 2005, National Geographic LB $27.90 (978-0-7922-7191-8). First-person accounts of World War II are given historical context plus illustrations, maps, and so forth; Madeleine Albright contributes an effective introduction. (Rev: BL 7/05; SLJ 8/05) [940.53]

8029 Panchyk, Richard. *World War II for Kids: A History with 21 Activities* (5–7). Illus. 2002, Chicago Review paper $14.95 (978-1-55652-455-4). Features on such topics as living on rations for a day, growing a victory garden, and tracking a ship's movements depict conditions in America and Europe during the war. (Rev: SLJ 12/02) [940.53]

8030 Payment, Simone. *American Women Spies of World War II* (6–9). Series: American Women at War. 2004, Rosen LB $31.95 (978-0-8239-4449-1). A well-written account of the exploits of women spies — including a fashion model and entertainer Josephine Baker — during World War II. (Rev: BL 10/15/04; SLJ 12/04) [940.54]

8031 Perl, Lila, and Marion B. Lazan. *Four Perfect Pebbles: A Holocaust Story* (5–9). Illus. 1996, Greenwillow $16.99 (978-0-688-14294-0). A memoir of the horror and incredible tribulations suffered by the author's family in the detention camps and later death camps during the Holocaust. (Rev: BL 4/1/96; SLJ 5/96) [940.53]

8032 Pfeifer, Kathryn B. *The 761st Tank Battalion* (5–8). Series: African American Soldiers. 1994, Twenty-First Century LB $24.90 (978-0-8050-3057-0). The history of an outfit of African American soldiers who served with distinction during World War II but were marginalized by racism. (Rev: BL 9/1/94; SLJ 11/94) [940.54]

8033 Rice, Earle, Jr. *The Battle of Britain* (6–10). Illus. Series: Great Battles in History. 1996, Lucent LB $19.95 (978-1-56006-414-5). This account of the air battle in the skies over Britain during 1940 quotes many primary sources and uses extensive illustrations. (Rev: BL 4/15/96) [940.54]

8034 Rice, Earle, Jr. *Blitzkrieg! Hitler's Lightning War* (5–8). Illus. Series: Monumental Milestones: Great Events of Modern Times. 2008, Mitchell Lane LB $20.95 (978-1-58415-542-3). The joint air-and-ground attacks that brought Hitler great success at the outset of World War II are the focus of this book that will interest reluctant readers. (Rev: BL 2/15/08) [940.54]

8035 Rice, Earle, Jr. *Strategic Battles in the Pacific* (6–12). Series: American War Library. 2000, Lucent LB $28.70 (978-1-56006-537-1). Beginning with the rise of Japanese power in the Pacific, this account traces the war in this area from Pearl Harbor through such crucial battles as Midway. (Rev: BL 4/15/00; HBG 9/00) [940.54]

8036 Rochman, Hazel, and Darlene Z. McCampbell, eds. *Bearing Witness: Stories of the Holocaust* (7–12). 1995, Orchard LB $16.99 (978-0-531-08788-6). This anthology of 24 works revolving around the Holocaust includes memoirs, poetry, short stories, a film script, a letter, and a comic strip. (Rev: BL 6/1–15/95; SLJ 9/95; VOYA 12/95) [808]

8037 Rogasky, Barbara. *Smoke and Ashes: The Story of the Holocaust*. Rev. ed. (6–12). 2002, Holiday $27.50 (978-0-8234-1612-7); paper $14.95 (978-0-8234-1677-6). In this new edition, Rogasky updates information where new facts have come to light and expands the details of resistance efforts. (Rev: BL 10/15/02; HBG 3/03; SLJ 10/02) [940.53]

8038 Rogers, James T. *The Secret War* (8–12). Series: World Espionage. 1991, Facts on File LB $16.95 (978-0-8160-2395-0). A well-supported thesis stating that the British and Americans were more successful at espionage, counterespionage, and detection than either the Germans or the Japanese. (Rev: BL 3/1/92; SLJ 5/92) [940.54]

8039 Rogow, Sally M. *Faces of Courage: Young Heroes of World War II* (5–9). 2003, Granville Island $12.95 (978-1-894694-20-9). Based on true stories, this volume presents 12 fictionalized accounts of heroic actions by teenagers under Nazi rule in Europe. (Rev: BL 10/15/03) [940.53]

8040 Ross, Stewart. *World War II* (7–12). Series: Causes and Consequences. 1995, Raintree LB $29.97 (978-0-8172-4050-9). This book identifies the factors that led to the outbreak of World War II and discusses its outcome, using eyewitness accounts. (Rev: BL 12/15/95) [940.53]

8041 Rubin, Susan G. *Fireflies in the Dark: The Story of Friedl Dicker-Brandeis and the Children of Terezin* (5–10). Illus. 2000, Holiday $18.95 (978-0-8234-1461-1). A heartbreaking picture book that reproduces some of the artwork and writings of the children imprisoned at the Terezin concentration camp, where only 100 of 15,000 children survived. (Rev: BCCB 11/00; BL 7/00*; HB 9–10/00; HBG 10/00; SLJ 8/00) [940.53]

8042 Rubin, Susan G. *Searching for Anne Frank: Letters from Amsterdam to Iowa* (5–12). 2003, Abrams $19.95 (978-0-8109-4514-2). A brief pen-pal exchange between two sisters in Iowa and Anne Frank and her sister serves as the basis for a comparison between life in America and life for Jews in Europe. (Rev: BL 11/1/03; HB 11–12/03; HBG 4/04; SLJ 11/03; VOYA 10/03) [940.5]

8043 Schomp, Virginia. *World War II* (6–8). Illus. Series: Letters from the Battlefront. 2003, Marshall Cavendish LB $29.93 (978-0-7614-1662-3). History and letters by men and women who served in the U.S. armed forces are combined into a memorable overview of World War II. (Rev: BL 4/1/04; SLJ 2/04) [940.54]

8044 Schroeder, Peter W., and Dagmar Schroeder-Hildebrand. *Six Million Paper Clips: The Making of a Children's Holocaust Memorial* (5–8). Illus. 2004, Kar-Ben $17.95 (978-1-58013-169-8); paper $7.95 (978-1-58013-176-6). This is the story of a Tennessee school project in which students collected 11 million paper clips to help them grasp the magnitude of the Holocaust's human toll. (Rev: BL 1/1–15/05; SLJ 7/05) [940.53]

8045 Shapiro, Stephen, and Tina Forrester. *Hoodwinked: Deception and Resistance* (7–10). Illus. by David Craig. Series: Outwitting the Enemy: Stories from World War II. 2004, Annick paper $14.95 (978-1-55037-832-0). This compelling title explores some of the inventive deceptive strategies that Allied forces employed against the Axis powers. (Rev: BL 1/1–15/05; SLJ 1/05) [940.54]

8046 Shapiro, Stephen, and Tina Forrester. *Ultra Hush-Hush: Espionage and Special Missions* (5–8). Illus. by David Craig. Series: Outwitting the Enemy. 2003, Annick LB $29.95 (978-1-55037-779-8); paper $14.95 (978-1-55037-778-1). Undercover activities during World War II are the focus of this volume that covers such groups and missions as the Navajo Code Talkers and Britain's double agents. (Rev: BL 8/03; SLJ 5/04) [940.54]

8047 Sheehan, Sean. *D-Day: June 6, 1944* (6–8). Series: Days That Shook the World. 2003, Raintree LB $27.12 (978-0-7398-5232-3). With many color and black-and-white photographs and quotations from combatants on both sides, this slim volume looks at the Allied landings in Normandy. (Rev: HBG 10/03; SLJ 10/03) [940.54]

8048 Sheehan, Sean. *The Technology of World War II* (5–8). 2003, Raintree LB $28.56 (978-0-7398-6064-9). New technologies introduced during World War II include radar, microwave transmissions, V-1 and V-2 rockets, the jet, codes, chemical and biological weapons, and the atom bomb. (Rev: HBG 10/03; SLJ 7/03) [940.54]

8049 Sherrow, Victoria. *Amsterdam* (6–12). Series: Cities at War. 1992, Macmillan LB $18.00 (978-0-02-782465-0). A photoessay on the lives of ordinary people in Amsterdam during World War II, with quotations by eyewitnesses. (Rev: BL 6/15/92; SLJ 9/92) [940.53]

8050 Shuter, Jane. *The Camp System* (7–12). Illus. Series: Holocaust. 2003, Heinemann LB $28.50 (978-1-4034-0809-9). This book explores the horrors of life in the concentration camps of the Holocaust. (Rev: BL 3/1/03; SLJ 4/03) [940.53]

8051 Shuter, Jane, ed. *Christabel Bielenberg and Nazi Germany* (5–8). Illus. Series: History Eyewitness. 1996, Raintree LB $24.26 (978-0-8114-8285-1). Using a first-person narrative as a framework, this account traces the growth, flowering, and defeat

of Nazism in Germany. (Rev: BL 5/15/96; SLJ 6/96) [943.086]

8052 Shuter, Jane. *Resistance to the Nazis* (7–12). Illus. Series: Holocaust. 2003, Heinemann LB $28.50 (978-1-4034-0814-3). An account of the acts of heroism by the many people who risked and lost their lives resisting the Nazis and their Holocaust agenda. (Rev: BL 3/1/03; SLJ 4/03) [943.086]

8053 Soumerai, Eve Nussbaum, and Carol D. Schulz. *A Voice from the Holocaust* (6–9). Series: Voices of Twentieth-Century Conflict. 2003, Greenwood $41.95 (978-0-313-32358-4). Photographs and diary entries help to tell the story of Soumerai's childhood as a privileged Jewish girl in Nazi Berlin, her years as a refugee, and her later experiences, all introduced with background information and a timeline of Nazi history. (Rev: SLJ 4/04) [940.53]

8054 Stalcup, Ann. *On the Home Front: Growing up in Wartime England* (6–10). Illus. 1998, Shoe String LB $19.50 (978-0-208-02482-4). A vivid first-person account about growing up in a small town in Shropshire during World War II. (Rev: BCCB 9/98; BL 10/15/98; HBG 9/98; SLJ 7/98) [940.54]

8055 Stein, R. Conrad. *World War II in Europe: "America Goes to War"* (5–7). Illus. Series: American War. 1994, Enslow LB $26.60 (978-0-89490-525-4). An unbiased account of the European theater of war during World War II, with emphasis on American participation. (Rev: BL 10/15/94; SLJ 1/95) [940.54]

8056 Stein, R. Conrad. *World War II in the Pacific: Remember Pearl Harbor* (5–7). Illus. Series: American War. 1994, Enslow LB $26.60 (978-0-89490-524-7). A well-organized, concise account of the Pacific war from the attack on Pearl Harbor to V-J Day that describes key battles and important personnel. (Rev: BL 7/94; SLJ 7/94) [940.54]

8057 Steins, Richard. *The Allies Against the Axis: World War II (1940–1950)* (5–8). Series: First Person America. 1994, Twenty-First Century LB $20.90 (978-0-8050-2586-6). An introduction to World War II and early postwar conditions, with generous use of primary sources. (Rev: BL 5/15/94; SLJ 12/94) [940.53]

8058 Strahinich, Helen. *The Holocaust: Understanding and Remembering* (6–10). Illus. Series: Issues in Focus. 1996, Enslow LB $26.60 (978-0-89490-725-8). A fully documented account that covers such topics as the roots of anti-Semitism, the rise of Nazism, ghetto life, the roundups, death camps, liberation, and the Nuremberg trials. (Rev: BL 9/15/96; SLJ 10/96; VOYA 10/96) [940.53]

8059 Sullivan, George. *Strange but True Stories of World War II* (7–12). Illus. 1983, Walker $14.95 (978-0-8027-6489-8). Eleven true stories of bizarre incidents during World War II. [940.53]

8060 Talbott, Hudson. *Forging Freedom* (4–7). Illus. 2000, Putnam $15.99 (978-0-399-23434-7). This is the story of Jaap Penraat, a young architectural student in Amsterdam during the Nazi occupation who saved hundreds of Jews from deportation by forging papers and smuggling them out of the city. (Rev: BCCB 11/00; BL 7/00; HB 1–2/01; HBG 3/01; SLJ 11/00) [940.53]

8061 Tames, Richard. *Fascism* (6–8). Series: Ideas of the Modern World. 2001, Raintree LB $25.69 (978-0-7398-3159-5). The story of the regimes in Germany, Italy, and Japan that promoted one-person rule and aggressive military policies. (Rev: BL 4/15/02; VOYA 4/02) [940.54]

8062 Tanaka, Shelley. *Attack on Pearl Harbor: The True Story of the Day America Entered World War II* (5–8). Illus. Series: I Was There. 2001, Hyperion $19.99 (978-0-7868-0736-9). An absorbing account of Pearl Harbor that presents the real-life, and very different, experiences of four young men who were there. (Rev: BL 8/01; HBG 10/01; SLJ 11/01; VOYA 12/01) [940.54]

8063 Taylor, Theodore. *Air Raid — Pearl Harbor: The Story of December 7, 1941* (5–8). 1991, Harcourt paper $6.00 (978-0-15-201655-5). A fine account of why the attack occurred and the effects that were felt around the world. A revised edition. (Rev: SLJ 12/91) [940.54]

8064 Taylor, Theodore. *Battle in the English Channel* (7–10). Illus. 1983, Avon paper $3.50 (978-0-380-85225-3). A retelling of the exciting World War II incident when Hitler tried to free three of his battleships from French waters. [940.54]

8065 Taylor, Theodore. *The Battle of Midway Island* (7–10). Illus. 1981, Avon paper $3.95 (978-0-380-78790-6). The story of the brilliant victory of U.S. forces at Midway is excitingly retold. [940.54]

8066 Taylor, Theodore. *H.M.S. Hood vs. Bismarck: The Battleship Battle* (7–10). Illus. 1982, Avon paper $3.95 (978-0-380-81174-8). The subject of this book is the sinking of the battleship *Bismarck* by the Royal Navy. [940.54]

8067 Tito, E. Tina. *Liberation: Teens in the Concentration Camps and the Teen Soldiers Who Liberated Them* (5–9). Illus. Series: Teen Witnesses to the Holocaust. 1999, Rosen LB $26.50 (978-0-8239-2846-0). A harrowing account in which two teenage Nazi camp survivors and two American soldiers who were also teenagers during World War II tell their respective stories. (Rev: BL 4/15/99; VOYA 8/99) [940.53]

8068 Tregaskis, Richard. *Guadalcanal Diary* (6–9). Illus. 1993, Buccaneer LB $25.95 (978-1-56849-231-5). This is a simplified version of the adult book that tells of the Marine landing at Guadalcanal in 1942. [940.54]

8069 van Maarsen, Jacqueline, and Carol Ann Lee. *A Friend Called Anne: One Girl's Story of War, Peace, and a Unique Friendship with Anne Frank* (5–8). 2005, Viking $15.99 (978-0-670-05958-4). Anne Frank's ordinary life before the war, and how things changed once the Nazis arrived, told by Anne's childhood friend. (Rev: BL 4/1/05; SLJ 4/05) [940.53]

8070 Warren, Andrea. *Surviving Hitler: A Boy in the Nazi Death Camps* (5–10). Illus. 2001, HarperCollins LB $17.89 (978-0-06-029218-8). The true story of Jack Mandelbaum, who as a teenager survived three years in Nazi death camps through a combination of luck, courage, and friendship. (Rev: BCCB 3/01; BL 1/1–15/01; HB 3–4/01; HBG 10/01; SLJ 3/01) [940.53]

8071 Wassiljewa, Tatjana. *Hostage to War: A True Story* (6–10). 1997, Scholastic paper $15.95 (978-0-590-13446-0). The World War II diary of a young Russian girl who endured hunger, cold, disease, and brutality during the German occupation of Leningrad and then spent years in forced labor camps and factories in Germany. (Rev: BL 4/15/97; SLJ 6/97; VOYA 12/98) [940.54]

8072 White, Steve. *The Battle of Midway: The Destruction of the Japanese Fleet* (5–9). Illus. by Richard Elson. 2007, Rosen LB $29.25 (978-1-4042-0783-7). This history of the Battle of Midway in comic book form will draw readers in with dramatic and detailed illustrations. (Rev: SLJ 7/07) [940.54265933]

8073 Whiteman, Dorit Bader. *Lonek's Journey: The True Story of a Boy's Escape to Freedom* (5–8). Illus. 2005, Star Bright $15.95 (978-1-59572-021-4). In this gripping true story that starts in 1939, a young Jew named Lonek survives the Nazis' arrival in Poland, a slave labor camp in Siberia, and the long, perilous journey to Palestine. (Rev: BL 11/15/05*; HBG 4/06; LMC 4–5/06; SLJ 1/06) [940.53]

8074 Whiting, Jim. *The Story of the Holocaust* (5–7). Series: Monumental Milestones: Great Events of Modern Times. 2006, Mitchell Lane LB $29.95 (978-1-58415-400-6). Although slim, this volume conveys a lot of information about the roots and atrocities of the Holocaust. (Rev: SLJ 5/06) [940.53]

8075 Whitman, Sylvia. *Uncle Sam Wants You!* (5–7). Illus. 1993, Lerner LB $30.35 (978-0-8225-1728-3). This work describes the experiences of the many men and women who served in the various armed forces during World War II. (Rev: BL 5/1/93) [940.54]

8076 Williams, Barbara. *World War II: Pacific* (6–8). Series: Chronicle of America's Wars. 2004, Lerner LB $27.93 (978-0-8225-0138-1). The major events of the war in the Pacific theater are covered in this well-documented brief overview. (Rev: SLJ 2/05) [940.54]

8077 Wukovits, John F. *Life of an American Soldier in Europe* (6–10). Series: American War Library. 2000, Lucent LB $27.45 (978-1-56006-666-8). As well as giving a history of World War II and the major battles involving Americans in Europe, this account describes the soldiers' training, daily life, and living conditions. (Rev: BL 4/15/00; HBG 10/00; SLJ 6/00) [940.54]

8078 Yancey, Diane. *The Internment of the Japanese* (7–10). Series: World History. 2002, Gale LB $32.45 (978-1-59018-013-6). An accessible account of the causes of the internment of many Japanese Americans during World War II, the conditions they endured, and the aftermath. (Rev: BL 8/02; SLJ 8/02) [940.54]

Modern World History (1945–)

8079 Benson, Sonia G. *Korean War: Almanac and Primary Sources* (6–10). 2001, Gale LB $70.00 (978-0-7876-5691-1). After an almanac section that traces the progress of the war, a selection of primary materials — speeches, memoirs, government documents, and so forth — are presented with introductions that place them in historical context. (Rev: SLJ 5/02) [951.904]

8080 Bjornlund, Britta. *The Cold War* (7–10). Series: World History. 2002, Gale LB $27.45 (978-1-59018-003-7). With ample quotations from original sources and a timeline, Bjornlund looks at the origins and development of the Cold War, and details the crises and periods of reduced tension that marked the length of the conflict. (Rev: BL 8/02; SLJ 10/02) [909.83]

8081 Brubaker, Paul. *The Cuban Missile Crisis in American History* (6–10). Series: In American History. 2001, Enslow LB $26.60 (978-0-7660-1414-5). This is a gripping account of how diplomacy and quick-thinking averted a war when the Soviets brought missiles to Cuba in 1962. (Rev: BL 8/01; HBG 10/01; SLJ 7/01) [973.992]

8082 Burgan, Michael. *The Berlin Airlift* (4–7). Series: We the People. 2006, Compass Point LB $26.60 (978-0-7565-2024-3). The story of the Berlin Airlift is told in straightforward text, with photographs and useful "Did You Know?" features. (Rev: SLJ 1/07) [943]

8083 Carlisle, Rodney P. *Iraq War* (6–12). Illus. Series: America at War. 2007, Facts on File LB $35.00 (978-0-8160-7129-6). An update of a 2004 title, this straightforward volume covers developments in the war from 2003 to 2006. (Rev: BL 11/1/07) [946.002]

8084 Denenberg, Barry. *Voices from Vietnam* (7–12). 1995, Scholastic paper $16.95 (978-0-590-

44267-1). Personal narratives of the Vietnam War from the late 1940s to 1975. (Rev: BL 2/15/95*; SLJ 3/95) [959.704]

8085 Dolan, Edward. *America in the Korean War* (7–12). 1998, Millbrook LB $30.90 (978-0-7613-0361-9). This study of the Korean War focuses on the battles, strategies, technological limitations, and personalities involved. (Rev: BL 1/1–15/99; HBG 3/99; SLJ 3/99) [951.904]

8086 Fisher, Trevor. *The 1960s* (8–12). Illus. 1989, David & Charles $19.95 (978-0-7134-5603-5). Under a broad subject arrangement, the major news stories and trends of the 1960s are chronicled. (Rev: SLJ 5/89) [973.92]

8087 Gallagher, Jim. *Causes of the Iraq War* (5–8). Illus. Series: Road to War. 2005, OTTN LB $22.95 (978-1-59556-009-4). Explores the case put forward for the recent Iraq War, along with the views of those who oppose the conflict with good illustrations and appended material. (Rev: BL 10/15/05) [956.7044]

8088 Gay, Kathlyn, and Martin Gay. *Korean War* (6–8). Illus. Series: Voices from the Past. 1996, Twenty-First Century LB $25.90 (978-0-8050-4100-2). A discussion of the often forgotten Korean War — its causes, its battles, and the people involved. (Rev: BL 11/15/96; SLJ 12/96; VOYA 4/97) [951.904]

8089 Gay, Kathlyn, and Martin Gay. *Persian Gulf War* (6–8). Illus. Series: Voices from the Past. 1996, Twenty-First Century LB $25.90 (978-0-8050-4102-6). A clearly written, objective overview of the Gulf War that gives material on the recent history of Iraq and Saddam Hussein's rise to power and contains many quotations from reporters, soldiers, military leaders, and ordinary people on every aspect of the war. (Rev: BL 11/15/96; SLJ 2/97; VOYA 6/97) [956.7044]

8090 Gay, Kathlyn, and Martin Gay. *Vietnam War* (6–8). Illus. Series: Voices from the Past. 1996, Twenty-First Century LB $25.90 (978-0-8050-4101-9). An objective overview of the Vietnam War, illustrated with black-and-white photographs. (Rev: BL 11/15/96; SLJ 12/96; VOYA 2/97) [959.704]

8091 Gerdes, Louise I., ed. *The Cold War* (6–12). Series: Great Speeches in History. 2003, Gale LB $36.20 (978-0-7377-0869-1); paper $24.95 (978-0-7377-0868-4). Winston Churchill and Che Guevara are among the world leaders whose words are given in this collection that examines the confrontation between East and West. (Rev: BL 5/1/03; SLJ 9/03) [909.82]

8092 Gunderson, Cory. *The Need for Oil* (5–8). Illus. Series: World in Conflict. 2004, ABDO LB $25.65 (978-1-59197-417-8). This history of conflicts over oil includes useful statistics and will be helpful to students seeking information for reports or background context before the recent Iraq war. (Rev: BL 4/1/04; SLJ 3/04) [338.2]

8093 Hillstrom, Kevin, and Laurie Collier Hillstrom. *Vietnam War: Almanac* (7–12). Series: UXL Vietnam War Reference Library. 2000, Gale LB $70.00 (978-0-7876-4883-1). An absorbing and comprehensive overview of the causes, conduct, and aftermath of the war that includes interesting sidebars and black-and-white photographs. Also use *Vietnam War: Biographies* and *Vietnam War: Primary Sources* (both 2000). (Rev: BL 3/15/01; SLJ 5/01) [959.704]

8094 Holden, Henry M. *The Persian Gulf War* (4–8). Series: U.S. Wars. 2003, Enslow LB $25.26 (978-0-7660-5109-6). This concise, interesting account of the conflict in the early 1990s is enhanced by Internet access to a set of monitored Web links. (Rev: HBG 10/03; SLJ 8/03) [956.7]

8095 Isserman, Maurice. *The Korean War* (7–12). Series: America at War. 1992, Facts on File $25.00 (978-0-8160-2688-3). A thorough re-creation of the Korean War, the first armed conflict of the Cold War. (Rev: BL 11/1/92) [951.904]

8096 Isserman, Maurice. *The Vietnam War: America at War* (7–12). Series: America at War. 1992, Facts on File $25.00 (978-0-8160-2375-2). A riveting account of the Vietnam War from its roots after World War II to U.S. withdrawal in 1975, and a review of the lessons learned. (Rev: BL 3/1/92) [959.7]

8097 Kent, Zachary. *The Persian Gulf War: "The Mother of All Battles"* (5–7). Illus. 1994, Enslow LB $26.60 (978-0-89490-528-5). The story of the 1991 Gulf War, its causes and effects, told with striking action photographs. (Rev: BL 4/15/95; SLJ 2/95) [956.7]

8098 Langley, Andrew. *The Collapse of the Soviet Union: The End of an Empire* (7–12). Series: Snapshots in History. 2006, Compass Point LB $31.93 (978-0-7565-2009-0). This is an informative survey of the events that led to the disintegration of the Soviet empire. (Rev: SLJ 2/07)

8099 Levy, Pat, and Sean Sheehan. *From Punk Rock to Perestroika: The Mid 1970s to the Mid 1980s* (6–9). Series: Modern Eras Uncovered. 2005, Raintree LB $32.86 (978-1-4109-1789-8). Focuses on the mid-1970s through mid-1980s, presenting the major social, political, economic, and technological changes as well as fashion and pop culture. Also use *From Compact Discs to the Gulf War: The Mid 1980s to the Early 1990s* and *From the World Wide Web to September 11: The Early 1990s to 2001* (2005). (Rev: SLJ 5/06)

8100 McArthur, Debra. *Desert Storm: The First Persian Gulf War in American History* (6–8). Series: In American History. 2004, Enslow LB $26.60 (978-0-7660-2149-5). Surveys the regional history that laid the groundwork for this conflict, the war itself, and its uncertain conclusion. (Rev: SLJ 1/05) [956.7]

8101 Mead, Alice. *Dawn and Dusk* (6–9). 2007, Farrar $16.00 (978-0-374-31708-9). Azad's Iranian Kurdish family is torn apart during the Iran-Iraq war when his father becomes an informer for Iran's secret police, and Saddam Hussein's gas attack prompts the 13-year-old to flee to Turkey. (Rev: BCCB 5/07; BL 2/15/07; LMC 10/07; SLJ 4/07)

8102 Murdico, Suzanne J. *The Gulf War* (5–9). Illus. Series: War and Conflict in the Middle East. 2004, Rosen LB $27.95 (978-0-8239-4551-1). Examines the 1991 war between Iraq and a coalition of nations. (Rev: BL 11/1/04) [956.7]

8103 Nakaya, Andrea C., ed. *Iraq* (8–12). Series: Current Controversies. 2004, Gale LB $36.20 (978-0-7377-2210-9); paper $24.95 (978-0-7377-2211-6). Statements by key U.S. figures including President Bush and Colin Powell are included in this survey of opinions about the Iraq war. (Rev: SLJ 12/04; VOYA 6/05) [956]

8104 Nardo, Don. *The War Against Iraq* (6–12). Series: American War Library: The Persian Gulf War. 2000, Lucent LB $29.95 (978-1-56006-715-3). This vividly written and nonjudgmental account of the Gulf War of 1991 includes a good final chapter on the results of the war. (Rev: BL 3/1/01; SLJ 3/01) [956.7]

8105 Rice, Earle, Jr. *Point of No Return: Tonkin Gulf and the Vietnam War* (7–12). Illus. 2003, Morgan Reynolds LB $23.95 (978-1-931798-16-7). Rice presents the events that led up to the passage in 1964 of the Tonkin Gulf Resolution, which gave Lyndon Johnson authority to take action against North Vietnam. (Rev: BL 9/1/03; HBG 4/04; SLJ 11/03) [959.704]

8106 Roberts, Russell. *Leaders and Generals* (6–12). Series: American War Library: The Vietnam War. 2001, Lucent LB $19.96 (978-1-56006-717-7). Ho Chi Minh, Lyndon Johnson, Richard Nixon, and Henry Kissinger are among the leaders whose roles in the Vietnam War are examined here. (Rev: BL 3/15/01; SLJ 6/01) [957.704]

8107 Ross, Stewart. *The Collapse of Communism* (6–8). Series: Witness to History. 2004, Heinemann LB $27.07 (978-1-4034-4865-1); paper $8.95 (978-1-4034-5525-3). Examines the forces that led to the decline of communism in the Soviet Union and Eastern Europe during the late 1980s and early 1990s, drawing on primary sources. (Rev: SLJ 1/05) [947]

8108 Schaffer, David. *The Iran-Iraq War* (5–8). Illus. Series: World History. 2002, Gale LB $32.45 (978-1-59018-184-3). Schaffer traces the causes and progress of this long war, incorporating useful primary and secondary source material plus interesting sidebar features. (Rev: BL 5/1/03) [955.05]

8109 Sherman, Josepha. *The Cold War* (6–12). Illus. Series: Chronicle of America's Wars. 2003, Lerner LB $27.93 (978-0-8225-0150-3). The half-century standoff between the United States and the Soviet Union is briefly chronicled, with coverage of the Korean and Vietnam wars, the Cuban Missile Crisis, and the Soviet invasion of Afghanistan. (Rev: BL 4/1/04) [909.82]

8110 Sirimarco, Elizabeth. *The Cold War* (6–9). Illus. Series: American Voices From. 2004, Benchmark LB $34.21 (978-0-7614-1694-4). Primary source documents and excellent illustrations are accompanied by good introductory text and "Think about This" questions. (Rev: SLJ 2/05) [973]

8111 Stanley, George E. *America and the Cold War (1949–1969)* (5–8). Illus. Series: A Primary Source History of the United States. 2005, World Almanac LB $31.00 (978-0-8368-5830-3). A simple narrative links well-chosen primary sources documenting the key events of the Cold War. Also use *America in Today's World (1969–2004)* (2005). (Rev: BL 4/1/05)

8112 Stein, R. Conrad. *The Korean War: "The Forgotten War"* (5–7). Illus. 1994, Enslow LB $26.60 (978-0-89490-526-1). This well-organized account of the Korean War presents a balanced picture of the war and includes personal observations. (Rev: BL 4/15/95; SLJ 2/95) [951]

8113 Taylor, David. *The Cold War* (5–9). Illus. Series: 20th Century Perspectives. 2001, Heinemann LB $25.64 (978-1-57572-434-8). An easily understood account of the causes of tension between the Soviet Union and the West and the major crises of the "war." (Rev: HBG 3/02; SLJ 11/01) [909.825]

8114 Willoughby, Douglas. *The Vietnam War* (5–9). Series: 20th Century Perspectives. 2001, Heinemann LB $25.64 (978-1-57572-439-3). An easily understood and attractive account of Vietnam's relations with China, and of French and U.S. involvement in the country's affairs. (Rev: SLJ 11/01) [959]

8115 Wukovits, John F. *Leaders and Generals* (6–12). Series: American War Library: The Persian Gulf War. 2001, Lucent LB $27.45 (978-1-56006-714-6). Key personnel who led the army during the Persian Gulf War of 1991 are profiled in this work that comments on the contributions of each. (Rev: BL 3/15/01) [956.7044]

8116 Yeatts, Tabatha. *The Holocaust Survivors* (6–10). Series: Holocaust Remembered. 1998, Enslow LB $26.60 (978-0-89490-993-1). This work concentrates on the liberation of the Nazi death camps, the capture of war criminals, the Nuremberg trials, the founding of Israel, and the lives of individual survivors. (Rev: BL 9/15/98; HBG 3/99; SLJ 12/98) [940.5318]

8117 Young, Marilyn B., and John J. Fitzgerald. *The Vietnam War: A History in Documents* (6–12). Series: Pages from History. 2002, Oxford $39.95 (978-0-19-512278-7). Primary sources cover the conflict in Vietnam from French involvement through the U.S. withdrawal and include everything from official documents, speeches, and transcripts of White House tapes to North Vietnamese political cartoons and U.S. anti-war posters. (Rev: BCCB 9/02; BL 6/1–15/02; HBG 10/02; SLJ 9/02) [959.704]

Geographical Regions

Africa

General and Miscellaneous

8118 Baroin, Catherine. *Tubu: The Teda and the Daza* (7–12). Illus. Series: Heritage Library of African Peoples. 1997, Rosen LB $29.25 (978-0-8239-2000-6). The history and contemporary life of these peoples of Chad, Libya, Niger, and the Sudan are presented in easy-reading text. (Rev: BL 4/15/97) [967.43]

8119 Beckwith, Carol, and Angela Fisher. *Faces of Africa: Thirty Years of Photography* (8–12). Illus. 2004, National Geographic $35.00 (978-0-7922-6830-7). Eye-catching photographs document the traditional life of diverse African peoples. (Rev: BL 9/1/04) [305.896]

8120 Bingham, Jane. *African Art and Culture* (5–8). Illus. Series: World Art and Culture. 2004, Raintree LB $29.99 (978-0-7398-6606-1). The indigenous art and culture of Africa from prehistoric times to the present are beautifully captured in this handsome and comprehensive overview. (Rev: BL 4/1/04; SLJ 2/04) [709]

8121 Bowden, Rob. *Africa* (5–8). Series: Continents of the World. 2006, World Almanac LB $34.00 (978-0-8368-5910-2). Factboxes and "In Focus" articles add to this overview of the history, geography, people, culture, and so forth of the continent of Africa. (Rev: SLJ 2/06)

8122 Bowden, Rob. *The Nile* (5–7). Series: A River Journey. 2003, Raintree LB $28.56 (978-0-7398-6072-4). A trip down the length of East Africa's Nile, from its source to the sea, and a look at its importance to the people who live along it and the challenge of pollution, with photographs, maps, and charts. (Rev: SLJ 3/04) [916.2]

8123 Croze, Harvey. *Africa for Kids: Exploring a Vibrant Continent* (4–7). Illus. 2006, Chicago Review paper $17.95 (978-1-55652-598-8). Africa's diversity is highlighted in this accessible volume that covers history, nature, key individuals, and contemporary problems such as poverty, war, AIDS, and the environment; there are 19 activities. (Rev: BL 8/06) [916.22]

8124 Downing, David. *Africa: Postcolonial Conflict* (6–8). Series: Troubled World. 2003, Raintree LB $28.56 (978-1-4109-0183-5). Covers conflicts since the end of colonial rule in countries lying south of the Sahara apart from South Africa; factboxes, maps, and color insets defining terms and concepts add to the presentation. (Rev: SLJ 3/04) [960]

8125 Habeeb, Mark W. *Africa: Facts and Figures* (7–10). Illus. Series: Continent in the Balance: Africa. 2005, Mason Crest LB $21.95 (978-1-59084-817-3). An excellent overview of the continent, including its natural features, climate, cultural diversity, history, and economy. (Rev: BL 4/1/05*) [960]

8126 Hall, Linley Erin. *Starvation in Africa* (6–9). Series: In the News. 2007, Rosen LB $27.95 (978-1-4042-0976-3). For reluctant readers, this is a good introduction to the continent of Africa and the reasons why starvation is so prevalent there; wars and internal unrest are underlined as aggravating factors. (Rev: SLJ 8/07) [363.8096]

8127 Harrison, Peter, ed. *African Nations and Leaders* (7–12). Illus. Series: History of Africa. 2003, Facts on File $30.00 (978-0-8160-5066-6). Double-page spreads provide a wealth of information on the nations of Africa, their leaders, and important historical events. (Rev: BL 9/15/03) [900]

8128 Holmes, Martha, et al. *Nile* (7–12). Illus. 2004, BBC $35.00 (978-0-563-48713-5). From the BBC, this is a richly illustrated guide to the history and geology of the world's longest river. (Rev: BL 11/1/04) [902]

8129 Reader, John. *Africa* (8–12). Illus. by Michael Lewis. 2001, National Geographic $50.00 (978-0-7922-7681-4). A lavishly illustrated overview of Africa with sections on each of the many ecological divisions, such as savanna, desert, mountains, and coast. (Rev: BL 8/01) [960]

8130 Rich, Susan, et al. *Africa South of the Sahara: Understanding Geography and History Through Art* (5–9). Series: Artisans Around the World. 1999, Raintree LB $27.12 (978-0-7398-0118-5). After a brief overview of the history and geography of southern Africa, this book presents a colorful introduction to such crafts as beadwork from Kenya, a carved wooden mask from Congo, and a wire toy from South Africa. Most will require adult help or supervision. (Rev: HBG 3/00; SLJ 1/00) [960]

8131 Sheehan, Sean. *Great African Kingdoms* (5–10). Series: Ancient World. 1998, Raintree LB $27.12 (978-0-8172-5124-6). Coverage of the great African kingdoms includes the spectacular palace of Great Zimbabwe, the majestic sculptures of Benin, and the Zulu empire's struggle for survival. (Rev: BL 1/1–15/99; HBG 3/99) [960]

8132 Shillington, Kevin. *Causes and Consequences of Independence in Africa* (6–9). Series: Causes and Consequences. 1998, Raintree LB $29.97 (978-0-8172-4060-8). A concise overview of African history before, during, and after colonialism. (Rev: BL 7/98; SLJ 6/98) [960.32]

8133 Weintraub, Aileen. *Discovering Africa's Land, People, and Wildlife* (5–8). Series: Continents of the World. 2004, Enslow LB $25.26 (978-0-7660-5204-8). An introduction to the geography, history, economy, plants and animals, culture, and peoples of the continent, with discussion of the continuing need for foreign aid in many countries. (Rev: SLJ 11/04) [916]

8134 Wekesser, Carol, and Christina Pierce. *Africa* (7–12). Series: Opposing Viewpoints. 1992, Greenhaven paper $16.20 (978-0-89908-161-8). The history and present conditions of Africa, from politics to social issues, are discussed in essays offering varying perspectives. (Rev: BL 5/15/92; SLJ 7/92) [960]

8135 Wolfe, Art, and Michelle A. Gliders. *Africa* (8–12). Illus. 2001, Wildlands $75.00 (978-0-9675918-1-0). Magnificent photographs are the highlight of this expensive book that introduces Africa by five separate ecosystems: savanna, woodland, rain forest, wetland, and desert. (Rev: BL 9/15/01) [960]

8136 Worth, Richard. *Stanley and Livingstone and the Exploration of Africa in World History* (6–9). Series: In World History. 2000, Enslow LB $26.60 (978-0-7660-1400-8). Worth chronicles the explor-

ers' expeditions into Africa and their historical context and consequences. (Rev: HBG 9/00; SLJ 7/00) [916.704]

Central and Eastern Africa

8137 Allen, Christina. *Hippos in the Night: Autobiographical Adventures in Africa* (4–8). Illus. by Rob Shepperson. 2003, HarperCollins LB $17.89 (978-0-688-17827-7). An appealing account of a camping trip through Kenya and Tanzania, with details of the exciting animals and fascinating people encountered on the way. (Rev: BL 4/15/03; HBG 10/03; SLJ 4/03) [591.96]

8138 Ayodo, Awuor. *Luo* (4–7). Illus. Series: Heritage Library of African Peoples. 1995, Rosen LB $29.25 (978-0-8239-1758-7). A portrait of the culture, history, and society of the Luo people, who lived on the shores of Lake Victoria in Kenya. (Rev: BL 3/1/96) [967.8]

8139 Bangura, Abdul Karim. *Kipsigis* (5–8). Illus. Series: Heritage Library of African Peoples. 1994, Rosen LB $29.25 (978-0-8239-1765-5). An attractive title that deals with the history and present status of the Kipsigis people of Kenya. (Rev: SLJ 5/95) [967.62]

8140 Beard, Peter. *Zara's Tales: Perilous Escapades in Equatorial Africa* (8–12). Illus. 2004, Knopf $26.95 (978-0-679-42659-2). In this compelling memoir, Beard talks about his many encounters — some life-threatening — with the animals of East Africa. (Rev: BL 10/15/04) [967.70]

8141 Bessire, Aimee, and Mark Bessire. *Sukuma* (5–8). Series: Heritage Library of African Peoples. 1997, Rosen LB $29.25 (978-0-8239-1992-5). Describes the history, culture, leaders, customs, and present situation of the Sukuma people of Tanzania. (Rev: BL 9/15/97; VOYA 12/97) [967.6]

8142 Bodnarchuk, Kari. *Rwanda: Country Torn Apart* (7–10). Illus. Series: World in Conflict. 1999, Lerner LB $25.26 (978-0-8225-3557-7). This history of Rwanda concentrates on the Tutsi/Hutu civil war in 1994 that left over a million people dead. (Rev: BL 1/1–15/00; HBG 4/00) [967.571]

8143 Bowden, Rob. *Kenya* (6–10). Illus. Series: Countries of the World. 2003, Facts on File $30.00 (978-0-8160-5384-1). This profile of an impoverished nation gives material on physical geography, resources, population, tourism, commerce, and geography. (Rev: BL 2/1/04) [967.62]

8144 Broberg, Catherine. *Kenya in Pictures* (6–10). Series: Visual Geography. 2002, Lerner LB $27.93 (978-0-8225-1957-7). Information on all aspects of life in this African country, including extensive coverage of its history, is accompanied by plenty of photographs and a Web site that offers up-to-date links. (Rev: BL 10/15/02; HBG 3/03; SLJ 12/02) [967]

8145 Burnham, Philip. *Gbaya* (7–12). Illus. Series: Heritage Library of African Peoples. 1997, Rosen LB $29.25 (978-0-8239-1995-6). These African people who live in Cameroon, Central African Republic, Congo, and Zaire, are introduced through illustrations and simple text. (Rev: BL 4/15/97) [967]

8146 Corona, Laurel. *Ethiopia* (5–8). Series: Modern Nations of the World. 2000, Lucent LB $29.95 (978-1-56006-823-5). An attractive, well-organized introduction to Ethiopia that gives its history, geography, and culture plus national statistics, a chronology, and bibliographies. (Rev: BL 3/1/01) [963]

8147 Corona, Laurel. *Kenya* (5–8). Illus. Series: Modern Nations of the World. 1999, Lucent LB $27.45 (978-1-56006-590-6). A profile of this poor African country that is a study in contrasts and cultures, with material on such subjects as geography, economics, people, and current problems. (Rev: BL 2/15/00; HBG 10/00) [967.62]

8148 Creed, Alexander. *Uganda* (6–12). Series: Major World Nations. 1998, Chelsea LB $21.95 (978-0-7910-4770-5). This book presents background material on the history and geography of Uganda and good current information on the country's economic, cultural, and social conditions. (Rev: BL 9/15/98) [967.61]

8149 Diouf, Sylviane. *Kings and Queens of Central Africa* (4–7). Series: Watts Library: Africa — Kings and Queens. 2000, Watts LB $25.50 (978-0-531-20372-9). This look at the political and social evolution of central Africa describes some of its important royalty including the 15th-century Afonso and Bolongongo, the legendary Bakuba king, with a final chapter on the region today. (Rev: BL 3/1/01) [960]

8150 Diouf, Sylviane. *Kings and Queens of East Africa* (4–7). Illus. Series: Watts Library: Africa — Kings and Queens. 2000, Watts LB $25.50 (978-0-531-20373-6). This book gives biographical information about royalty in East Africa and through these sketches re-creates the history of this part of Africa. (Rev: BL 2/15/01) [967.6]

8151 *Ethiopia in Pictures* (5–8). Illus. Series: Visual Geography. 1994, Lerner LB $21.27 (978-0-8225-1836-5). Land, history and government, culture, education, religion, and health are covered. (Rev: BL 2/1/89) [963]

8152 Freeman, Charles. *Crisis in Rwanda* (7–12). Series: New Perspectives. 1998, Raintree LB $28.54 (978-0-8172-5020-1). This book tells of the genocide of the Tutsi, the movements of Hutu refugees, and the actions of the international community from the viewpoints of survivors, aid workers, politicians,

historians, and journalists. (Rev: BL 12/15/98; HBG 3/99; SLJ 2/99) [967.57]

8153 Gaertner, Ursula. *Elmolo* (7–10). Series: Heritage Library of African Peoples. 1995, Rosen LB $29.25 (978-0-8239-1764-8). Looks at the customs, daily life, and values of the Elmolo tribe in Kenya. (Rev: BL 7/95; SLJ 5/95) [967.62]

8154 Giles, Bridget. *Kenya* (4–8). Series: Nations of the World. 2001, Raintree LB $34.26 (978-0-7398-1290-7). From snow-capped mountains to scorching deserts, this geographically and culturally diverse African nation is attractively introduced in this volume. (Rev: BL 12/15/01; HBG 3/02; SLJ 12/01) [967.62]

8155 Gish, Steven. *Ethiopia* (4–7). Illus. Series: Cultures of the World. 1996, Marshall Cavendish LB $37.07 (978-0-7614-0276-3). After general background information on Ethiopia, such topics as lifestyles, religion, and language are discussed. (Rev: BL 8/96; SLJ 8/96) [963]

8156 Hall, Martin, and Rebecca Stefoff. *Great Zimbabwe: Digging for the Past* (7–10). Series: Digging for the Past. 2006, Oxford $21.95 (978-0-19-515773-4). Traces our knowledge of the ancient city-state that lies in present-day Mozambique, with an emphasis on the archaeological discoveries and discussion of racial preconceptions that blurred understanding. (Rev: BL 6/1–15/06; SLJ 11/06) [968.91]

8157 *History of Central Africa* (7–12). Illus. Series: History of Africa. 2003, Facts on File $30.00 (978-0-8160-5064-2). A historical overview of the region that includes information on the Atlantic slave trade and on European colonial rule. Also use *History of East Africa* (2003). (Rev: SLJ 1/04) [967]

8158 Holtzman, Jon. *Samburu* (7–10). Series: Heritage Library of African Peoples. 1995, Rosen LB $29.25 (978-0-8239-1759-4). Discusses in detailed but simple text the culture and lifestyle of the Samburu people of Kenya. (Rev: BL 7/95; SLJ 5/95) [967]

8159 Hussein, Ikram. *Teenage Refugees from Somalia Speak Out* (7–12). Series: Teenage Refugees Speak Out. 1997, Rosen LB $27.95 (978-0-8239-2444-8). Teenage refugees from Somalia recount the violent anarchy and acute famine in their country and their journey from Africa to the United States. (Rev: BL 12/15/97; SLJ 12/97) [967]

8160 Ifemesia, Chieka. *Turkana* (7–10). Illus. Series: Heritage Library of African Peoples. 1996, Rosen LB $29.25 (978-0-8239-1761-7). Using a simple text and color photographs, this account describes the past and present of the Turkana people, who now live in Ethiopia, Kenya, Sudan, and Uganda. (Rev: BL 2/15/95) [960]

8161 Jansen, Hanna. *Over a Thousand Hills I Walk with You* (7–10). Trans. by Elizabeth D. Crawford. 2006, Carolrhoda $16.95 (978-1-57505-927-3). The heartbreaking story of 8-year-old Jeanne, the only member of her family to survive the Rwandan genocide of 1994, is told by the girl's adoptive mother. (Rev: BL 4/1/06*; SLJ 6/06*) [833]

8162 Jones, Schuyler. *Pygmies of Central Africa* (5–8). Illus. 1989, Rourke LB $16.67 (978-0-86625-268-3). A vivid look into the lives of these fascinating people. (Rev: BL 5/15/89) [967.00496]

8163 Kabira, Wanjiku M. *Agikuyu* (7–10). Series: Heritage Library of African Peoples. 1995, Rosen LB $29.25 (978-0-8239-1762-4). Presents social and cultural aspects of the Agikuyu community of Kenya in ways that make them accessible to Western readers. (Rev: BL 7/95; SLJ 6/95) [967]

8164 Koopmans, Andy. *Rwanda* (7–10). Illus. Series: Africa. 2005, Mason Crest LB $21.95 (978-1-59084-812-8). Covers the geography, history, politics, government, economy, people, and culture of Rwanda, providing a map, flag, recipes, glossary, timeline, and colorful photographs. (Rev: SLJ 3/05) [967.571]

8165 MacDonald, Joan Vos. *Tanzania* (7–10). Illus. Series: Africa. 2005, Mason Crest LB $21.95 (978-1-59084-813-5). Covers the geography, history, politics, government, economy, people, and culture of Tanzania, providing a map, flag, recipes, glossary, timeline, and colorful photographs. (Rev: SLJ 3/05; VOYA 8/04) [967.8]

8166 McQuail, Lisa. *The Masai of Africa* (4–7). Illus. Series: First Peoples. 2001, Lerner LB $23.93 (978-0-8225-4855-3). McQuail provides information about the Masai people, covering their history, customs, and contemporary daily life, with photographs. (Rev: BL 10/15/01; HBG 3/02; SLJ 3/02) [967.6]

8167 *Malawi in Pictures* (5–8). Illus. Series: Visual Geography. 1989, Lerner LB $25.55 (978-0-8225-1842-6). An overview of climate, history, geography, culture, education, and other aspects of life. (Rev: BL 2/1/89) [968.97]

8168 Nnoromele, Salome. *Somalia* (5–8). Series: Modern Nations of the World. 2000, Lucent LB $27.45 (978-1-56006-396-4). An introduction to this East African country with material on its history and geography and a large section on daily life. (Rev: BL 5/15/00; HBG 10/00) [967.73]

8169 Nwaezeigwe, Nwankwo T. *Ngoni* (7–12). Illus. Series: Heritage Library of African Peoples. 1997, Rosen LB $29.25 (978-0-8239-2006-8). The history, traditions, and struggle for freedom of this African group in Malawi are laid out in accessible text. (Rev: BL 4/15/97) [968.97]

8170 Oghojafor, Kingsley. *Uganda* (5–8). Series: Countries of the World. 2004, Gareth Stevens LB $31.00 (978-0-8368-3112-2). Introduces readers to the African country's geography, history, people, culture, and government and also takes a look at its relations with other countries and contemporary challenges. (Rev: SLJ 8/04) [967.61]

8171 Ojo, Onukaba A. *Mbuti* (7–10). Illus. Series: Heritage Library of African Peoples. 1996, Rosen LB $29.25 (978-0-8239-1998-7). The Mbuti people of Zaire are introduced with details on their environment, history, customs, and present situation. (Rev: BL 2/15/96; SLJ 7/96) [305.896]

8172 Okeke, Chika. *Kongo* (7–12). Illus. Series: Heritage Library of African Peoples. 1997, Rosen LB $29.25 (978-0-8239-2001-3). The Kongo people of Angola, Congo, and Zaire in Central Africa are featured in easy-reading text with material on their land, kingdoms, political life, and culture. (Rev: BL 4/15/97) [967]

8173 Parris, Ronald. *Rendille* (5–8). Illus. Series: Heritage Library of African Peoples. 1994, Rosen LB $29.25 (978-0-8239-1763-1). With extensive use of black-and-white and color photographs, introduces the history and customs of the Rendille people of Kenya. (Rev: SLJ 5/95) [967.62]

8174 Pateman, Robert. *Kenya* (4–7). Illus. Series: Cultures of the World. 1993, Marshall Cavendish LB $35.64 (978-1-85435-572-0). The background story of Kenya is revealed through color photographs and a text that also covers present concerns. (Rev: BL 8/93) [967.62]

8175 *Peoples of East Africa* (6–12). Series: Peoples of Africa. 1997, Facts on File $28.00 (978-0-8160-3484-0). This book gives a concise overview of 15 ethnic groups of eastern Africa, with details on history, language, way of life, society, religion, and culture. Included are Falasha, Ganda, Hutus and Tutsis, Masai, Nyoro, Somalis, and Swahili. (Rev: SLJ 10/97) [967]

8176 Roberts, Mary N., and Allen F. Roberts. *Luba* (6–10). Series: Heritage Library of African Peoples. 1997, Rosen LB $29.25 (978-0-8239-2002-0). The Luba people of Zaire are introduced with material on their history, present conditions, and cultural resources. (Rev: BL 9/15/97) [967]

8177 Schnapper, LaDena. *Teenage Refugees from Ethiopia Speak Out* (5–10). Series: Teenage Refugees Speak Out. 1997, Rosen LB $27.95 (978-0-8239-2438-7). Ethiopian teens now living in America tell of the violence, famine, and civil war that drove them from their country and of their reception in America. (Rev: SLJ 2/98) [963]

8178 *Sudan in Pictures* (5–8). Illus. Series: Visual Geography. 1990, Lerner LB $25.55 (978-0-8225-1839-6). An overview of history, culture, geography, economy, education, and health. (Rev: BL 2/1/89) [962.4]

8179 Swinimer, Ciarunji C. *Pokot* (5–8). Illus. Series: Heritage Library of African Peoples. 1994, Rosen LB $29.25 (978-0-8239-1756-3). Using a good balance of text and visuals, this account describes the history, culture, and present status of the Pokot people of Kenya. (Rev: SLJ 5/95) [967.62]

8180 Tanguay, Bridget. *Kenya* (4–7). Illus. Series: Countries of the World. 2006, National Geographic $19.95 (978-0-7922-7628-9). An overview of Kenya with information on the country's history, land, people, government, economy and present issues; excellent color photographs and maps are included. (Rev: SLJ 3/07) [967.6]

8181 *Tanzania in Pictures* (5–8). Illus. Series: Visual Geography. 1989, Lerner LB $25.55 (978-0-8225-1838-9). Part of the Visual Geography series, contains information on history, geography, economy, religion, and culture. (Rev: BL 2/1/89) [967.8104]

8182 Twagilimana, Aimable. *Hutu and Tutsi* (5–9). Series: The Heritage Library of African Peoples. 1997, Rosen LB $29.25 (978-0-8239-1999-4). A large section of this book is devoted to the current struggle between the Hutu and Tutsi people of central Africa, along with chapters on art and religion. (Rev: SLJ 3/98) [967]

8183 Twagilimana, Aimable. *Teenage Refugees from Rwanda Speak Out* (5–10). Series: Teenage Refugees Speak Out. 1997, Rosen LB $27.95 (978-0-8239-2443-1). Teenage refugees from Rwanda describe the warfare between Tutsi and Hutu peoples, the terrible living conditions that forced them to leave their country, and the challenges and difficulties they have experienced in the United States. (Rev: SLJ 2/98) [967]

8184 Wangari, Esther. *Ameru* (7–10). Illus. Series: Heritage Library of African Peoples. 1995, Rosen LB $29.25 (978-0-8239-1766-2). An introduction to the history, traditions, and culture of the Ameru people of Kenya in easy-reading text. (Rev: BL 9/15/95; SLJ 11/95) [967.6]

8185 Zeleza, Tiyambe. *Akamba* (7–10). Illus. Series: Heritage Library of African Peoples. 1995, Rosen LB $29.25 (978-0-8239-1768-6). The history, traditions, and fight for freedom of the Akamba people of Kenya are covered in this book with many color illustrations. (Rev: BL 7/95; SLJ 6/95) [960]

8186 Zeleza, Tiyambe. *Maasai* (5–8). Illus. Series: Heritage Library of African Peoples. 1994, Rosen LB $29.25 (978-0-8239-1757-0). An introduction to these people of Kenya and Tanzania, their culture, customs, and history. (Rev: SLJ 5/95) [967.62]

8187 Zeleza, Tiyambe. *Mijikenda* (7–10). Series: Heritage Library of African Peoples. 1995, Rosen

LB $29.25 (978-0-8239-1767-9). Combines history and anthropology to provide an easy-to-read portrait of the Mijikenda people. (Rev: BL 9/15/95; SLJ 11/95) [967]

North Africa

8188 Azuonye, Chukwuma. *Dogon* (7–10). Illus. Series: Heritage Library of African Peoples. 1995, Rosen LB $29.25 (978-0-8239-1976-5). Provides information on the history, culture, and lifestyles of the Dogon people of Mali. (Rev: BL 2/15/96) [966.23]

8189 Blauer, Ettagale, and Jason Lauré. *Morocco* (4–7). Series: Enchantment of the World. 1999, Children's LB $37.00 (978-0-516-20961-6). In this fine introduction to Morocco topics include history, government, economics, people, religion, culture, and the arts. (Rev: BL 9/15/99) [964]

8190 Kagda, Falaq. *Algeria* (4–7). Illus. Series: Cultures of the World. 1997, Marshall Cavendish LB $37.07 (978-0-7614-0680-8). This book on Algeria emphasizes the people and how they live. (Rev: BL 8/97) [965]

8191 Malcolm, Peter. *Libya* (4–7). Illus. 1993, Marshall Cavendish LB $35.64 (978-1-85435-573-7). Well-chosen photographs and readable text give good background information as well as material on present problems. (Rev: BL 8/93) [961.2]

8192 Raskin, Lawrie, and Debora Pearson. *52 Days by Camel: My Sahara Adventure* (4–8). Illus. 1998, Annick $24.95 (978-1-55037-519-0); paper $14.95 (978-1-55037-518-3). An engaging account of a trip from Fez to Timbuktu by bus, jeep, train, truck, and camel, with details on desert life and culture. (Rev: BL 6/1–15/98; SLJ 7/98) [964]

Southern Africa

8193 Barnes-Svarney, Patricia. *Zimbabwe* (5–9). Illus. Series: Major World Nations. 1999, Chelsea LB $29.95 (978-0-7910-4753-8). A good introduction to Zimbabwe's history, geography, government, people, pastimes, economy, and culture. (Rev: SLJ 8/98) [968]

8194 Beecroft, Simon. *The Release of Nelson Mandela* (6–12). Illus. Series: Days that Changed the World. 2004, World Almanac LB $31.00 (978-0-8368-5571-5). The significance of Mandela's release after 27 years of imprisonment is made clear through the explanation of the struggle against apartheid, with discussion of the progress South Africa has made since then. (Rev: BL 4/1/04; SLJ 7/04) [618.1]

8195 Biesele, Megan, and Kxao Royal. *San* (7–10). Series: Heritage Library of African Peoples. 1997, Rosen LB $29.25 (978-0-8239-1997-0). The San people of Botswana, Namibia, and South Africa are featured in this accessible account that describes their rich tradition and struggle for freedom. (Rev: BL 9/15/97) [960]

8196 Blauer, Ettagale, and Jason Lauré. *Madagascar* (4–7). Series: Enchantment of the World. 2000, Children's LB $37.00 (978-0-516-21634-8). Madagascar, the island nation off the coast of Africa, is introduced. Topics addressed include its land and people, wildlife, history, traditions, daily life, and economy. (Rev: BL 12/15/00) [969]

8197 Blauer, Ettagale, and Jason Lauré. *South Africa*. Rev. ed. (6–9). 2006, Children's Pr. LB $25.20 (978-0-516-24853-0). A clear view of modern South Africa — including geography, history, economy, religion, and current challenges — is presented along with maps, photographs, and a timeline. (Rev: BL 7/06; SLJ 8/06) [968]

8198 Bolaane, Maitseo, and Part T. Mgadla. *Batswana* (6–10). Series: Heritage Library of African Peoples. 1997, Rosen LB $29.25 (978-0-8239-2008-2). This work discusses the history, culture, and present status of the Batswana people of southern Africa. (Rev: BL 1/1–15/98) [968]

8199 Brandenburg, Jim. *Sand and Fog: Adventures in Southern Africa* (5–8). Illus. 1994, Walker LB $17.85 (978-0-8027-8233-5). A stunning photoessay about the wildlife found in Namibia. (Rev: BCCB 5/94; BL 3/1/94*; HB 5–6/94; SLJ 5/94) [968.1]

8200 Canesso, Claudia. *South Africa* (6–10). Series: Major World Nations. 1998, Chelsea LB $21.95 (978-0-7910-4766-8). An accurate, informative, and unbiased account of the social, political, and economic conditions in South Africa today, supplemented by illustrations and maps. (Rev: BL 9/15/98; HBG 3/99; SLJ 6/99) [968.06]

8201 Diouf, Sylviane. *Kings and Queens of Southern Africa* (4–7). Illus. Series: Watts Library: Africa — Kings and Queens. 2000, Watts LB $25.50 (978-0-531-20374-3). Through the lives of Shaka the Zulu king, Moshoeshoe of the Sotho kingdom, and others, the reader gets a good history of this region before and during the colonial period. (Rev: BL 2/15/01) [968]

8202 Downing, David. *Apartheid in South Africa* (7–10). Illus. Series: Witness to History. 2004, Heinemann $27.07 (978-1-4034-4870-5). This brief historical survey draws on primary sources — including newspaper articles and full-color photographs — to trace apartheid's rise and fall and its impact on both the country's black and white communities. (Rev: BL 1/05) [323.168]

8203 Fish, Bruce, and Becky Durost Fish. *South Africa: 1880 to the Present: Imperialism, Nationalism, and Apartheid* (6–12). 2000, Chelsea LB $35.00 (978-0-7910-5676-9). This survey of South

African history is careful to highlight changes and achievements that did not involve European influence; it includes many Royal Geographic Society black-and-white photographs. (Rev: HBG 3/01; SLJ 2/01) [968]

8204 Flint, David. *South Africa* (5–8). Illus. Series: Modern Industrial World. 1996, Raintree $24.26 (978-0-8172-4554-2). The present economic status of South Africa is studied through personal narratives and case studies. (Rev: BL 2/15/97; SLJ 8/97) [968]

8205 Green, Jen. *South Africa* (4–8). Series: Nations of the World. 2001, Raintree LB $34.26 (978-0-7398-1282-2). A profile of the strongest industrial nation in Africa, with material on its geography, resources, environment, government, economy, and future. (Rev: BL 6/1–15/01; HBG 10/01) [968]

8206 Green, Rebecca L. *Merina* (7–12). Illus. Series: Heritage Library of African Peoples. 1997, Rosen LB $29.25 (978-0-8239-1991-8). The history and culture of the Merina people of Madagascar are covered in simple text and many illustrations. (Rev: BL 4/15/97; VOYA 6/97) [969.1]

8207 Harrison, Peter, ed. *History of Southern Africa* (7–12). Illus. Series: History of Africa. 2003, Facts on File $30.00 (978-0-8160-5065-9). From prehistory to today, this volume covers in detail the history of southern Africa, detailing in particular European settlement, independence, and apartheid. (Rev: BL 9/15/03; SLJ 5/04) [968]

8208 Inserra, Rose, and Susan Powell. *The Kalahari* (5–8). Series: Ends of the Earth. 1997, Heinemann LB $25.45 (978-0-431-06932-6). An introduction to the history, animal and vegetable life, and future of this desert region of southern Botswana, eastern Namibia, and western South Africa. (Rev: SLJ 11/97) [968]

8209 Kaschula, Russel. *Xhosa* (7–12). Series: Heritage Library of African Peoples. 1997, Rosen LB $23.95 (978-0-8239-2013-6). The Xhosa people of South Africa are introduced with stunning photographs and simple text describing their past and present culture and lifestyles. (Rev: BL 1/1–15/98) [968]

8210 Langley, Andrew. *Cape Town* (4–7). Illus. Series: Great Cities of the World. 2005, World Almanac LB $31.00 (978-0-8368-5045-1). An informative and appealing overview of this major city, with material on its history, its economy, and what it's like to live there. (Rev: BL 4/15/04)

8211 *Madagascar in Pictures* (5–8). Illus. Series: Visual Geography. 1988, Lerner LB $25.55 (978-0-8225-1841-9). Covers geography, history, culture, economics, religion, and health. (Rev: BL 2/1/89) [969.1]

8212 Mitchell, Peter, ed. *Southern Africa* (8–11). Illus. Series: Peoples and Cultures of Africa. 2006, Chelsea House LB $39.00 (978-0-8160-6265-2). A detailed look at the nations of southern Africa (including Madagascar), discussing their culture, history, ethnic groups, religions, languages, and arts and architecture. (Rev: BL 10/15/06) [900]

8213 Nagle, Garrett. *South Africa* (6–12). Series: Country Studies. 1999, Heinemann LB $27.07 (978-1-57572-896-4). An excellent overview of South Africa, with particularly good coverage of current conditions and problems. (Rev: BL 8/99) [968]

8214 Ngwane, Zolani. *Zulu* (7–12). Series: Heritage Library of African Peoples. 1997, Rosen LB $23.95 (978-0-8239-2014-3). This readable work introduces the history and culture of the Zulus of South Africa. (Rev: BL 9/15/97; VOYA 12/97) [968]

8215 Njoku, Onwuka N. *Mbundu* (7–12). Illus. Series: Heritage Library of African Peoples. 1997, Rosen LB $29.25 (978-0-8239-2004-4). An easy-to-read introduction to the history and contemporary culture of this people of Angola. (Rev: BL 4/15/97) [967.3]

8216 Oluikpe, Benson O. *Swazi* (7–12). Illus. Series: Heritage Library of African Peoples. 1997, Rosen LB $29.25 (978-0-8239-2012-9). This accessible book describes the history, traditions, and struggles for freedom of the Swazi people of Swaziland and South Africa. (Rev: BL 4/15/97; SLJ 12/97) [968]

8217 *Peoples of Southern Africa* (6–12). Series: Peoples of Africa. 1997, Facts on File $28.00 (978-0-8160-3487-1). The history, geography, culture, religion, and social life of 17 different South African peoples are highlighted, including Afrikaners, Cape Coloreds, Cape Malays, Indian South Africans, Ndebele, Swazi, Tswana, Venda, and Zulu. (Rev: SLJ 10/97) [968]

8218 Rogers, Barbara Radcliffe, and Stillman D. Rogers. *Zimbabwe* (4–7). Series: Enchantment of the World. 2002, Children's LB $37.00 (978-0-516-21113-8). This troubled African land is introduced with material on topics including history, geography, people, government, and resources. (Rev: BL 5/15/02; SLJ 7/02) [968.9]

8219 Rosemarin, Ike. *South Africa* (4–7). Illus. Series: Cultures of the World. 1993, Marshall Cavendish LB $35.64 (978-1-85435-575-1). Historical and modern concerns are covered in this look at South Africa. (Rev: BL 8/93) [968]

8220 Schneider, Elizabeth Ann. *Ndebele* (7–12). Illus. Series: Heritage Library of African Peoples. 1997, Rosen LB $29.25 (978-0-8239-2009-9). Topics covered about the Ndebele people of South Africa include environment, history, religion, social organization, politics, and customs. (Rev: BL 4/15/97) [968]

8221 Smith, Chris. *Conflict in Southern Africa* (6–12). Series: Conflicts. 1993, Macmillan LB $22.00 (978-0-02-785956-0). An overview of the politics of southern Africa: Angola, Mozambique, Zambia, Namibia, and South Africa. (Rev: BL 7/93; SLJ 12/93) [968]

8222 *South Africa in Pictures* (5–8). Illus. Series: Visual Geography. 1996, Lerner LB $25.55 (978-0-8225-1835-8). Focusing on climate, geography, wildlife, and the history of this troubled country. (Rev: BL 8/88) [968.06]

8223 Udechukwu, Ada. *Herero* (7–10). Series: Heritage Library of African Peoples. 1996, Rosen LB $29.25 (978-0-8239-2003-7). In simple text, this book introduces the three Herero subgroups that share a similar language and culture in today's Botswana, Angola, and Namibia, with an emphasis on their political history. (Rev: BL 3/15/96; SLJ 6/96) [968]

8224 Van Wyk, Gary N. *Basotho* (5–7). Illus. Series: Heritage Library of African Peoples. 1996, Rosen LB $29.25 (978-0-8239-2005-1). Describes the Basotho people, who live in Lesotho and South Africa, with simple text on their history, religion, social organization, and customs. (Rev: BL 11/15/96; SLJ 3/97) [968]

8225 Van Wyk, Gary N., and Robert Johnson. *Shona* (5–7). Series: Heritage Library of African Peoples. 1997, Rosen LB $29.25 (978-0-8239-2011-2). The Shona people of Zimbabwe are presented in outstanding photographs, with a text that covers their past, their culture, and their present living conditions and problems. (Rev: BL 1/1–15/98) [968]

8226 *Zimbabwe in Pictures* (5–8). Illus. Series: Visual Geography. 1997, Lerner LB $25.55 (978-0-8225-1825-9). Many photographs highlight this overview of Zimbabwe's history, climate, wildlife, and culture. (Rev: BL 4/15/88) [968]

West Africa

8227 Adeeb, Hassan, and Bonnetta Adeeb. *Nigeria: One Nation, Many Cultures* (4–8). Illus. Series: Exploring Cultures of the World. 1995, Benchmark LB $27.07 (978-0-7614-0190-2). Opening with an account of a legendary figure, this book continues with an introduction to Nigeria that emphasizes its culture and how the people live. (Rev: SLJ 6/96) [966.9]

8228 Adeleke, Tunde. *Songhay* (5–7). Illus. Series: Heritage Library of African Peoples. 1996, Rosen LB $29.25 (978-0-8239-1986-4). Both historical information and material on contemporary life are given in this account of the African people who live chiefly in Mali, Niger, and Benin. (Rev: BL 11/15/96) [960]

8229 Anda, Michael O. *Yoruba* (7–10). Series: Heritage Library of African Peoples. 1996, Rosen LB $23.95 (978-0-8239-1988-8). This work describes one of the largest sub-Saharan ethnic groups, whose influence, because of the slave trade, spread to the New World, especially Brazil. (Rev: BL 3/15/96; SLJ 6/96) [966.9]

8230 Azuonye, Chukwuma. *Edo: The Bini People of the Benin Kingdom* (7–10). Illus. Series: Heritage Library of African Peoples. 1996, Rosen LB $29.25 (978-0-8239-1985-7). A review of the history, culture, society, and the struggle for freedom of the Bini people, whose empire was part of present-day Nigeria. (Rev: BL 3/15/96) [966.9]

8231 Barnett, Jeanie M. *Ghana* (5–9). Illus. Series: Major World Nations. 1999, Chelsea LB $21.95 (978-0-7910-4739-2). Basic facts about Ghana's history, geography, politics, government, economy, natural resources, education, and people. (Rev: HBG 9/98; SLJ 8/98) [966.7]

8232 Blauer, Ettagale, and Jason Lauré. *Ghana* (4–7). Series: Enchantment of the World. 1999, Children's LB $36.00 (978-0-516-20962-3). A geographical and cultural exploration of the African nation of Ghana, once a center of the slave trade. (Rev: BL 12/15/99) [966.7]

8233 Boateng, Faustine Ama. *Asante* (5–7). Illus. Series: Heritage Library of African Peoples. 1996, Rosen LB $29.25 (978-0-8239-1975-8). This African people living in present-day Ghana is described, with information on history, traditions, and lifestyle. (Rev: BL 11/15/96; SLJ 3/97) [966.7]

8234 Bowden, Rob, and Roy Maconachie. *Nigeria* (5–7). Series: The Changing Face Of. 2003, Raintree LB $28.56 (978-0-7398-6829-4). An examination of modern-day Nigeria, with a look at the nation's past difficulties and how it may benefit from its wealth of natural resources. (Rev: SLJ 4/04) [966.9]

8235 Brace, Steve. *Ghana* (4–8). Illus. Series: Economically Developing Countries. 1995, Thomson Learning LB $24.26 (978-1-56847-242-3). Rich and poor rural and urban families are introduced in this attractive book on Ghana, its past, and its present. (Rev: SLJ 7/95) [966.7]

8236 Brook, Larry. *Daily Life in Ancient and Modern Timbuktu* (5–7). Illus. 1999, Lerner LB $25.26 (978-0-8225-3215-6). A fascinating look at this ancient West African city that was once a center of commerce and learning. (Rev: BL 9/1/99; HBG 10/99; SLJ 7/99) [966.23]

8237 Chambers, Catherine. *West African States: 15th Century to the Colonial Era* (5–8). Series: Looking Back. 1999, Raintree $19.98 (978-0-8172-5427-8). A brief overview of the history and culture of the great empires of West Africa and how they

disappeared with the arrival of the Europeans. (Rev: BL 5/15/99; VOYA 2/00) [966.2]

8238 *Cote d'Ivoire (Ivory Coast) in Pictures* (5–8). Illus. Series: Visual Geography. 1988, Lerner LB $25.55 (978-0-8225-1828-0). Covering all aspects of life in this overview, with pictorial emphasis and coverage of possible future developments. (Rev: BL 4/15/88; SLJ 11/88) [966.68]

8239 Diouf, Sylviane. *Kings and Queens of West Africa* (4–7). Series: Watts Library: Africa — Kings and Queens. 2000, Watts LB $25.50 (978-0-531-20375-0). Some of the royal figures covered in this historical survey of West Africa are Emperor Mansa Musa of Mali and Nsate Yalla Mbodj, queen of the Walo of Senegal. (Rev: BL 3/1/01) [960]

8240 Harmon, Daniel E. *Nigeria: 1880 to the Present: The Struggle, the Tragedy, the Promise* (6–12). 2000, Chelsea LB $35.00 (978-0-7910-5452-9). This survey of Nigerian history is careful to highlight changes and achievements that did not involve European influence; it includes many Royal Geographic Society black-and-white photographs. (Rev: HBG 3/01; SLJ 2/01) [966.9]

8241 Hathaway, Jim. *Cameroon in Pictures* (5–8). Illus. Series: Visual Geography. 1992, Lerner LB $25.55 (978-0-8225-1857-0). With numerous charts, maps, and photographs, the country of Cameroon is introduced. (Rev: BL 9/15/89) [967]

8242 Heale, Jay. *Democratic Republic of the Congo* (5–9). Series: Cultures of the World. 1998, Marshall Cavendish LB $37.07 (978-0-7614-0874-1). A history of this nation that has been stricken with civil wars and political instability, with descriptions of its history, economy, government, people, and culture. (Rev: HBG 9/99; SLJ 6/99) [967]

8243 Heinrichs, Ann. *Niger* (4–7). Series: Enchantment of the World. 2001, Children's LB $37.00 (978-0-516-21633-1). Niger, a predominately Muslim country that is one of the hottest places in the world, is described in this attractive volume with material on topics such as resources, history, and culture. (Rev: BL 1/1–15/02) [967]

8244 Koslow, Philip. *Asante: The Gold Coast* (6–9). Illus. Series: Kingdoms of Africa. 1996, Chelsea LB $17.95 (978-0-7910-3139-1). The history of the mighty West African people who acquired great wealth from their gold mines and who were known worldwide for their artwork. (Rev: BL 6/1–15/96) [966.7018]

8245 Koslow, Philip. *Benin: Lords of the River* (6–9). Illus. Series: Kingdoms of Africa. 1995, Chelsea paper $8.95 (978-0-7910-3134-6). A history of the people who lived around the Benin River, their conflicts with Europeans, and their lasting imperial grandeur. (Rev: BL 6/1–15/96) [966.9]

8246 Koslow, Philip. *Dahomey: The Warrior Kings* (5–8). Illus. Series: The Kingdoms of Africa. 1996, Chelsea LB $20.85 (978-0-7910-3137-7); paper $8.95 (978-0-7910-3138-4). A history of the West African kingdom that flourished in the 17th and 18th centuries, describing how the slave trade affected it. (Rev: SLJ 12/96) [960]

8247 Koslow, Philip. *Lords of the Savanna: The Bambara, Fulani, Igbo, Mossi, and Nupe* (7–10). Series: Kingdoms of Africa. 1997, Chelsea paper $8.95 (978-0-7910-3142-1). A strong narrative style and attractive illustrations are used to present the history and culture of these West African peoples of present-day Nigeria, Cameroon, and Burkina Faso. (Rev: SLJ 1/98) [966]

8248 Koslow, Philip. *Songhay: The Empire Builders* (6–9). Illus. Series: The Kingdoms of Africa. 1995, Chelsea LB $17.95 (978-0-7910-3128-5); paper $8.95 (978-0-7910-2943-5). This account concentrates on the 10th through 15th centuries, and tells about the great Songhay empire in West Africa that flourished under King Sunni Ali and later King Askia Muhammad, and produced such thriving cities as Timbuktu. (Rev: BL 2/15/96) [966.2]

8249 Koslow, Philip. *Yorubaland: The Flowering of Genius* (6–9). Illus. Series: The Kingdoms of Africa. 1995, Chelsea LB $17.95 (978-0-7910-3131-5); paper $9.95 (978-0-7910-3132-2). This account traces the 1,500-year history of the Yorubaland civilization in West Africa that dates back to the 4th century B.C. and produced an early sophisticated system of government. (Rev: BL 2/15/96; SLJ 2/96) [960]

8250 Levy, Patricia. *Nigeria* (4–7). Illus. Series: Cultures of the World. 1993, Marshall Cavendish LB $35.64 (978-1-85435-574-4). Information on history, geography, lifestyles, people, and culture. (Rev: BL 8/93) [966.9]

8251 *Liberia in Pictures* (5–8). Illus. Series: Visual Geography. 1996, Lerner LB $25.55 (978-0-8225-1837-2). Covers climate, geography, wildlife, vegetation, and natural resources. (Rev: BL 8/88) [966.62]

8252 Mack-Williams, Kibibi V. *Mossi* (7–10). Illus. Series: Heritage Library of African Peoples. 1996, Rosen LB $29.25 (978-0-8239-1984-0). The history, social organization, and culture of the Mossi people of West Africa are described. (Rev: BL 3/15/96) [966.25]

8253 Ndukwe, Pat I. *Fulani* (7–10). Illus. Series: Heritage Library of African Peoples. 1995, Rosen LB $29.25 (978-0-8239-1982-6). A description of the history, surroundings, politics, customs, and current conditions of the Fulani people, who live in Cameroon, Mali, and Nigeria. (Rev: BL 2/15/96; SLJ 7/96) [966]

8254 *Nigeria in Pictures* (5–8). Illus. Series: Visual Geography. 1995, Lerner LB $25.55 (978-0-8225-1826-6). A visual focus on this African land. (Rev: BL 8/88) [966.9]

8255 Nnoromele, Salome C. *Life Among the Ibo Women of Nigeria* (8–12). Illus. Series: The Way People Live. 1997, Lucent LB $27.45 (978-1-56006-344-5). Before European contact, Ibo women were equal in power with men in the economy, politics, and the family, but English influences changed this. Today these women are caught between two cultures. (Rev: BL 9/1/98; SLJ 10/98) [966.9]

8256 Nwanunobi, C. O. *Malinke* (5–7). Illus. Series: Heritage Library of African Peoples. 1996, Rosen LB $29.25 (978-0-8239-1979-6). Features the culture, history, and contemporary lifeways of the Malinke people, now living along the western coast of Africa. (Rev: BL 11/15/96) [966.23]

8257 Nwanunobi, C. O. *Soninke* (5–7). Illus. Series: Heritage Library of African Peoples. 1996, Rosen LB $29.25 (978-0-8239-1978-9). A discussion of the African people found in such countries as Ghana, Mali, Nigeria, and Senegal, with material on history, customs, and present living conditions. (Rev: BL 11/15/96) [966]

8258 Ogbaa, Kalu. *Igbo* (7–10). Series: Heritage Library of African Peoples. 1995, Rosen LB $29.25 (978-0-8239-1977-2). An introduction to the Igbo people, one of the three most important ethnic groups in Nigeria. (Rev: BL 9/15/95; SLJ 11/95) [966.9]

8259 Parris, Ronald. *Hausa* (5–7). Illus. Series: Heritage Library of African Peoples. 1996, Rosen LB $29.25 (978-0-8239-1983-3). A look at the Hausa people of Niger and Nigeria, with material on history and contemporary life. (Rev: BL 11/15/96) [966]

8260 *Peoples of West Africa* (6–12). Series: Peoples of Africa. 1997, Facts on File $28.00 (978-0-8160-3485-7). Extensive background material is provided on the history, geography, languages, art, music, religion, and society of 13 West African peoples, including the Asante, Bambara, Dogon, Fon, Hausa, Moors, Mossi, and Yoruba. (Rev: BL 8/97; SLJ 10/97) [966]

8261 Reef, Catherine. *This Our Dark Country: The American Settlers of Liberia* (7–12). 2002, Clarion $17.00 (978-0-618-14785-4). This chronological account of Liberia's history makes good use of excerpts from letters and diaries. (Rev: BL 11/15/02; HBG 3/03; SLJ 12/02; VOYA 6/03) [966.62]

8262 Sallah, Tijan M. *Wolof* (7–12). Series: Heritage Library of African Peoples. 1996, Rosen LB $29.25 (978-0-8239-1987-1). Using maps, many color illustrations, and simple text, this book introduces the Wolof people of Senegal and their history, social and political life, customs, religious beliefs, and relations with other peoples in their region. (Rev: BL 3/15/96; SLJ 7/96) [966.3]

8263 *Senegal in Pictures* (5–8). Illus. Series: Visual Geography. 1989, Lerner LB $25.55 (978-0-8225-1827-3). A look at the geography, history, culture, and economics of Senegal. (Rev: BL 4/15/89; SLJ 11/88) [966.3]

8264 Sheehan, Patricia. *Côte d'Ivoire* (5–8). 1999, Marshall Cavendish LB $37.07 (978-0-7614-0980-9). The Ivory Coast is presented with coverage of its geography, history, government, economy, and social and cultural life. (Rev: HBG 10/00; SLJ 4/00) [966.68]

8265 Tenquist, Alasdair. *Nigeria* (5–8). Illus. Series: Economically Developing Countries. 1996, Raintree LB $24.26 (978-0-8172-4527-6). This introduction to Nigeria emphasizes present-day government and economic conditions. (Rev: BL 3/1/97; SLJ 9/97) [330.9669]

8266 Walker, Ida. *Nigeria* (7–10). Illus. Series: Africa. 2005, Mason Crest LB $21.95 (978-1-59084-811-1). Covers the geography, history, politics, government, economy, people, and culture of Nigeria, providing a map, flag, recipes, glossary, timeline, and colorful photographs. (Rev: SLJ 3/05) [966.9]

Asia

General and Miscellaneous

8267 Bowden, Rob. *Asia* (5–8). Series: Continents of the World. 2006, World Almanac LB $34.00 (978-0-8368-5911-9). Factboxes and "In Focus" articles add to this overview of the history, geography, people, culture, and so forth of the continent of Asia. (Rev: SLJ 2/06) [915]

8268 Bramwell, Martyn. *Southern and Eastern Asia* (4–8). Illus. Series: The World in Maps. 2001, Lerner LB $23.93 (978-0-8225-2916-3). For each country in these geographical areas, readers will find a color map, the flag, a box containing important facts, and brief discussions of geography, industry, and economy. Also use *Northern and Western Asia* (2001). (Rev: HBG 10/01; SLJ 7/01) [915]

8269 Des Forges, Roger V., and John S. Major. *The Asian World, 600–1500* (7–12). 2006, Oxford Univ. LB $32.95 (978-0-19-517843-2). The authors explore the contributions, culture, empires, and conflicts of China, Japan, India, and Korea over nine centuries, with color photographs, artwork, maps, and quotations. (Rev: SLJ 7/06)

8270 Dramer, Kim. *The Mekong River* (4–8). Series: Watts Library. 2001, Watts LB $25.50 (978-0-531-11854-2). A fact-filled introduction to the history of the Mekong and to the landscape and industry found along it. (Rev: SLJ 5/01) [959.7]

8271 Greenblatt, Miriam. *Genghis Khan and the Mongol Empire* (5–8). Series: Rulers and Their Times. 2001, Marshall Cavendish LB $29.93 (978-0-7614-1027-0). This handsomely illustrated book presents, in three parts, a life of Genghis Khan, a section on conditions in Russia during his reign, and a selection of documents of the time. (Rev: BL 1/1–15/02; HBG 3/02; SLJ 2/02) [947]

8272 Hammond, Paula. *China and Japan* (4–8). Illus. Series: Cultures and Costumes: Symbols of Their Period. 2003, Mason Crest LB $19.95 (978-1-59084-436-6). A detailed survey of the history of garments and accessories worn by people of all classes in these two Asian nations prior to the 20th century. (Rev: SLJ 3/04) [391]

8273 Kilgallon, Conor. *India and Sri Lanka* (4–8). Illus. Series: Cultures and Costumes: Symbols of Their Period. 2003, Mason Crest LB $19.95 (978-1-59084-443-4). A look at the history of garments and accessories worn by all classes of people in India and Sri Lanka up to the end of the 19th century. (Rev: SLJ 3/04) [391]

8274 Kort, Michael. *Central Asian Republics* (7–12). Series: Nations in Transition. 2003, Facts on File $40.00 (978-0-8160-5074-1). After a history of the region, each of the independent republics is introduced with discussion of the current challenges it faces; these include border disputes, poor environment, poor health care and quality of life, and government corruption. (Rev: SLJ 4/04)

8275 Major, John S., and Betty J. Belanus. *Caravan to America: Living Arts of the Silk Road* (5–8). Illus. 2002, Cricket $24.95 (978-0-8126-2666-7); paper $15.95 (978-0-8126-2677-3). The traditions and skills emanating from the ancient trade routes are shown as surviving today in the work of a rug restorer in New York, an artist-monk in Los Angeles, a cook from Iran, and other examples in this fascinating approach to an interesting subject. (Rev: BL 11/1/02; HB 1–2/03; HBG 3/03; SLJ 2/03; VOYA 6/03) [745]

8276 Pascoe, Elaine. *The Pacific Rim: East Asia at the Dawn of a New Century* (7–12). 1999, Twenty-First Century LB $25.90 (978-0-7613-3015-8). Brief historical information and current economic figures are given for Japan, China, Taiwan, the Koreas, Indonesia, Singapore, Malaysia, and the Philippines. (Rev: BL 7/99; SLJ 9/99) [950.4]

8277 Sayre, April Pulley. *Asia* (5–8). Illus. Series: Seven Continents. 1999, Twenty-First Century LB $25.90 (978-0-7613-1368-7). Using maps, photographs, and sidebars, this concise work discusses Asia's people, geography and geology, climate and oceans, flora and fauna. (Rev: BL 8/99; HBG 3/00) [915]

8278 Wilkinson, Philip, and Michael Pollard. *The Magical East* (4–7). Illus. by Robert Ingpen. Series: Mysterious Places. 1994, Chelsea LB $21.95 (978-0-7910-2754-7). An oversize volume that highlights several places and cities of importance in the history of the Orient. (Rev: BL 1/15/94; SLJ 4/94) [930.1]

China

8279 Baldwin, Robert F. *Daily Life in Ancient and Modern Beijing* (4–7). Illus. by Ray Webb. Series: Cities Through Time. 1999, Runestone LB $25.26 (978-0-8225-3214-9). Topics introduced in this contrast between Beijing past and present include the arts, religion, school, history, and daily life. (Rev: HBG 10/99; SLJ 7/99) [951]

8280 Barber, Nicola. *Beijing* (4–7). Illus. Series: Great Cities of the World. 2004, World Almanac LB $31.00 (978-0-8368-5028-4). In addition to the usual information on history and people, this attractive volume describes living conditions and leisure time and provides maps and sidebars about contemporary environmental and political issues. (Rev: BL 4/15/04; SLJ 6/04) [951]

8281 Behnke, Alison. *China in Pictures*. Rev. ed. (6–10). Illus. Series: Visual Geography. 2002, Lerner LB $27.93 (978-0-8225-0370-5). An excellent introduction to China that includes material on geography, history, people, economy, and culture with maps, photographs, and illustrations. (Rev: BL 10/15/02; HBG 3/03; SLJ 3/03) [951]

8282 Bingham, Jane. *Tiananmen Square: June 4, 1989* (6–8). Series: Days That Shook the World. 2004, Raintree LB $28.56 (978-0-7398-6649-8). A clear, well-illustrated overview of the events in Beijing's Tiananmen Square and their legacy. (Rev: SLJ 10/04) [951.058]

8283 Bowden, Rob. *The Yangtze* (5–7). Series: A River Journey. 2003, Raintree LB $28.56 (978-0-7398-6074-8). A well-illustrated trip along China's Yangtze River, concentrating on mankind's influence on the river and vice versa, with photographs, maps, and charts. (Rev: SLJ 3/04) [915.1]

8284 DuTemple, Lesley A. *The Great Wall of China* (4–7). Illus. Series: Great Building Feats. 2003, Lerner LB $27.93 (978-0-8225-0377-4). This absorbing account tells the story of the building and importance of the Great Wall of China, with a good selection of illustrations, sidebar features, and maps. (Rev: BL 1/1–15/03; HBG 10/03; SLJ 4/03*) [931]

8285 Ferroa, Peggy. *China* (4–7). Illus. Series: Cultures of the World. 1991, Marshall Cavendish LB $35.64 (978-1-85435-399-3). Unusual facts highlight this look at China, with emphasis on culture. (Rev: BL 2/15/92; SLJ 3/92) [951]

8286 Field, Catherine. *China* (4–8). Illus. Series: Nations of the World. 2000, Raintree LB $34.26 (978-0-8172-5781-1). This is a fine introduction to China's past and present that supplies even more interesting information through the use of sidebars. (Rev: BL 10/15/00; HBG 10/00) [951.21]

8287 Green, Robert. *China* (6–10). Series: Modern Nations of the World. 1999, Lucent LB $28.70 (978-1-56006-440-4). A well-organized overview of China and its emergence as a major political and economic power. (Rev: SLJ 8/99) [051]

8288 Haugen, David M., ed. *China* (8–12). 2006, Gale LB $34.95 (978-0-7377-3389-1); paper $23.70 (978-0-7377-3390-7). China's economic growth, steps toward democracy, military threat, and other important aspects are discussed in this collection of brief articles that present different perspectives. (Rev: SLJ 8/06)

8289 Immell, Myra. *The Han Dynasty* (6–10). Illus. Series: Lost Civilizations. 2003, Gale LB $27.45 (978-1-59018-096-9). An informative and readable overview of the long Han dynasty and the social and agricultural systems of the time. (Rev: SLJ 5/03) [931]

8290 Israel, Fred L., and Arthur M. Schlesinger, Jr., eds. *Peking* (6–10). Illus. Series: The World 100 Years Ago. 1999, Chelsea LB $29.95 (978-0-7910-4666-1). This is an edited version of travel essays by Burton Holmes, a popular traveler-lecturer during the first half of the 20th century, about the sights he saw in Peking. (Rev: SLJ 7/98) [951]

8291 Kagda, Falaq. *Hong Kong* (5–8). Series: Cultures of the World. 1998, Marshall Cavendish LB $37.07 (978-0-7614-0692-1). An attractive book that introduces us to Hong Kong's history and geography, its people, and their culture and lifestyles. (Rev: HBG 3/98; SLJ 6/98) [951]

8292 Langley, Andrew. *The Cultural Revolution: Years of Chaos in China* (6–10). Illus. Series: Snapshots in History. 2008, Compass Point LB $24.95 (978-0-7565-3483-7). A look at the events leading up to the violence in China in the 1960s begins this book, which then delves into what happened during the Cultural Revolution and why. (Rev: BL 3/3/08; SLJ 7/08) [951.05]

8293 Lazo, Caroline. *The Terra Cotta Army of Emperor Qin* (5–8). Illus. 1993, Macmillan LB $14.95 (978-0-02-754631-6). The story of the 7,500 terracotta figures that guard the tomb of China's first emperor. (Rev: BL 7/93; SLJ 8/93) [931]

8294 Malaspina, Ann. *The Chinese Revolution and Mao Zedong in World History* (5–8). Series: World History. 2004, Enslow LB $26.60 (978-0-7660-1935-5). After a brief overview of Chinese history, Malaspina provides a well-researched introduction to Chinese communism under Mao Zedong, from the early days of the party in the 1920s to the post-Mao reforms of recent times. (Rev: SLJ 3/04) [951]

8295 Mann, Elizabeth. *The Great Wall: The Story of Thousands of Miles of Earth and Stone* (4–8). Illus. Series: Wonders of the World. 1997, Mikaya $19.95 (978-0-9650493-2-0). The story behind the building of this massive structure, which began as far back as 200 B.C. and involves historical battles for land and power between the Chinese and the nomadic Mongols. (Rev: BL 1/1–15/98; SLJ 12/97) [951]

8296 Marx, Trish. *Elephants and Golden Thrones: Inside China's Forbidden City* (4–7). Illus. by Ellen B. Senisi. 2008, Abrams $18.95 (978-0-8109-9485-0). Full of photographs, this is an inside look at the sights and history of the huge palace complex. (Rev: BL 6/1–15/08; SLJ 7/08) [951]

8297 Patent, Dorothy Hinshaw. *The Incredible Story of China's Buried Warriors* (4–7). Series: Frozen in Time. 1999, Benchmark LB $27.07 (978-0-7614-0783-6). This book explores the mystery of the creation of China's buried warriors, the thousands of terracotta statues that belonged to the first emperor of China and were uncovered in 1974. (Rev: BL 2/1/00; HBG 10/00; SLJ 3/00) [951]

8298 Pellegrini, Nancy. *Beijing* (4–8). Photos by Adrian Cooper. Series: Global Cities. 2007, Chelsea House LB $30.00 (978-0-7910-8848-7). With plenty of photographs and maps, this volume introduces the history of Beijing as well as its geography, people, environment, transportation, and so forth. (Rev: SLJ 7/07)

8299 Pilon, Pascal, and Elizabeth Thomas. *We Live in China* (4–7). Illus. Series: Kids Around the World. 2006, Abrams $15.95 (978-0-8109-5735-0). Four children from different areas of China introduce their region and everyday life; the lack of an index and photo captions limit the book's usefulness for reports, but it will nevertheless serve as an attractive introduction. (Rev: BL 10/15/06; SLJ 2/07)

8300 Pollard, Michael. *The Yangtze* (5–7). Series: Great Rivers. 1997, Benchmark LB $22.79 (978-0-7614-0505-4). Covers historical and geographical aspects of the Yangtze River and discusses current dam-building projects. (Rev: HBG 3/98; SLJ 4/98) [951]

8301 Qing, Zheng. *China* (4–7). Illus. by Tim Hutchinson. Series: Find Out About. 2007, Barron's $12.99 (978-0-7641-5952-7). This well-organized, attractively illustrated guide looks at China's history and contemporary life, and introduces basic phrases in Mandarin. (Rev: BL 4/1/07; SLJ 2/07) [951]

8302 Schomp, Virginia. *The Ancient Chinese* (4–7). Series: People of the Ancient World. 2004, Watts LB $30.50 (978-0-531-11817-7). Emperors, artisans, inventors, and healers are among the people presented in this overview of life in ancient China. (Rev: SLJ 2/05) [931]

8303 Shuter, Jane. *Ancient China* (5–8). Series: Time Travel Guides. 2007, Raintree LB $34.29 (978-1-4109-2729-3). An attractive trip back in time to ancient China, providing details about daily life there — accommodation, food, shopping, and so forth — and suggesting sights to see. (Rev: SLJ 9/07) [931]

8304 Walker, Kathryn. *Shanghai* (4–7). Illus. Series: Great Cities of the World. 2005, World Almanac LB $31.00 (978-0-8368-5046-8). An informative and appealing overview of this important Chinese city, with material on its history, its economy, and what it's like to live there. (Rev: BL 4/15/04)

8305 Waterlow, Julia. *China* (4–7). Illus. Series: Country Insights. 1997, Raintree LB $27.12 (978-0-8172-4787-4). Compares the social conditions — home life, employment, schooling, and recreation — in a large city and a rural village in China. (Rev: BL 7/97; SLJ 8/97) [951]

8306 Zurlo, Tony. *Life in Hong Kong* (6–10). Series: The Way People Live. 2002, Gale LB $28.70 (978-1-56006-384-1). Contemporary life in Hong Kong at many levels of wealth and position is the topic of this fascinating narrative that includes many illustrations and some historical coverage. (Rev: BL 7/02; SLJ 6/02) [951]

India, Pakistan, and Bangladesh

8307 Arnold, Caroline, and Madeleine Comora. *Taj Mahal* (4–7). Illus. by Rahul Bhushan. 2007, Carolrhoda LB $17.95 (978-0-7613-2609-9). A beautifully designed, oversized picture book, this volume on the Taj Mahal and the story behind its construction includes detailed paintings. (Rev: SLJ 7/07)

8308 Bowden, Rob. *The Ganges* (5–7). Series: A River Journey. 2003, Raintree LB $28.56 (978-0-7398-6070-0). A detailed look at India's most famous river, its importance to the people who live along it, and the challenge of pollution, with photographs, maps, and charts. (Rev: SLJ 3/04) [915.4]

8309 Brace, Steve. *Bangladesh* (4–8). Illus. Series: Economically Developing Countries. 1995, Thomson Learning LB $24.26 (978-1-56847-243-0). An overview of life in Bangladesh told in a simple, large-print text and many color photographs. (Rev: SLJ 7/95) [954.9]

8310 Brace, Steve. *India* (7–10). Series: Country Studies. 1999, Heinemann LB $27.07 (978-1-57572-893-3). An excellent introduction to India that gives current information on such subjects as population, environment, problems, and economy. (Rev: BL 8/99) [954]

8311 Crompton, Samuel Willard. *Pakistan* (7–12). Series: Modern World Nations. 2002, Chelsea LB $30.00 (978-0-7910-7098-7). An overview of the history, geography, people, politics, and religion of

Pakistan, with discussion of current difficulties such as ethnic strife, population problems, and disputes with India. (Rev: SLJ 2/03) [954.91]

8312 Cumming, David. *The Ganges Delta and Its People* (5–8). Illus. Series: People and Places. 1994, Thomson Learning LB $24.26 (978-1-56847-168-6). An introduction to the Ganges delta, the people who live there, the economy it supports, and the tragedy of its frequent flooding. (Rev: BL 10/15/94) [954]

8313 Cumming, David. *India* (4–7). Illus. Series: Our Country. 1998, Raintree LB $27.12 (978-0-8172-4797-3). Several young inhabitants introduce India and describe life, customs, food, and their homes. (Rev: BL 12/1/89; HBG 10/98; SLJ 3/92) [954]

8314 Dalal, Anita. *India* (4–8). Series: Nations of the World. 2001, Raintree LB $34.26 (978-0-7398-1289-1). A fine introduction to this vast, populous country with chapters on the land and cities, past and present, the economy, arts and living, and the future. (Rev: BL 12/15/01; HBG 3/02) [954]

8315 Downing, David. *Conflict: India vs. Pakistan* (6–8). Series: Troubled World. 2003, Raintree LB $28.56 (978-1-4109-0181-1). Covers conflicts between India and Pakistan since the end of colonial rule; factboxes, maps, and color insets defining terms and concepts add to the presentation. (Rev: SLJ 3/04) [954]

8316 DuTemple, Lesley A. *The Taj Mahal* (4–7). Series: Great Building Feats. 2003, Lerner LB $27.93 (978-0-8225-4694-8). Using many illustrations, this account traces the building of the magnificent tomb that was inspired by one man's love for his wife. (Rev: BL 11/15/03) [954]

8317 Goodwin, William. *India* (5–8). Series: Modern Nations of the World. 2000, Lucent LB $27.45 (978-1-56006-598-2). An admirable introduction to India that gives material on the land and its past but concentrates on today's population, living conditions, and problems. (Rev: BL 3/15/00; HBG 10/00) [954]

8318 Goodwin, William. *Pakistan* (6–12). Illus. Series: Modern Nations of the World. 2002, Gale LB $29.95 (978-1-59018-218-5). An overview of Pakistan's geography, history, culture, and society, with biographical information on key individuals. (Rev: BL 11/15/02; SLJ 1/03) [954.91]

8319 Green, Jen. *Mumbai* (4–8). Photos by Chris Fairclough. Series: Global Cities. 2007, Chelsea House LB $30.00 (978-0-7910-8851-7). With plenty of photographs and maps, this overview of the city of Mumbai (formerly Bombay) provides concise information on its history, geography, people, environment, transportation, and so forth. (Rev: SLJ 7/07)

8320 Guile, Melanie. *Culture in India* (4–7). Illus. Series: Culture In. 2005, Raintree LB $25.70 (978-1-4109-1134-6). Customs, holidays, clothing, food, and arts and crafts are well covered in this volume that also provides basic information needed for reports and interesting sidebar features on such topics as ancestor worship and celebrities. (Rev: BL 2/15/04; SLJ 5/05) [954]

8321 Orr, Tamra. *Bangladesh* (5–9). Illus. Series: Enchantment of the World Second Series. 2007, Children's Pr. LB $36.00 (978-0-516-25012-0). Features information on the Asian nation of Bangladesh, including its culture, religion, family life, arts, and sports and looks in particular at the country's struggles with pollution, poor living and working conditions, and political instability. (Rev: BL 8/07) [954.92]

8322 Pollard, Michael. *The Ganges* (5–7). Series: Great Rivers. 1997, Benchmark LB $22.79 (978-0-7614-0504-7). This work describes the course of the Ganges from the Himalayas to its muddy delta, covers its history, and touches on the poverty and pollution that is found around it today. (Rev: HBG 3/98; SLJ 4/98) [954]

8323 Rowe, Percy, and Patience Coster. *Delhi* (4–7). Illus. Series: Great Cities of the World. 2005, World Almanac LB $31.00 (978-0-8368-5037-6). An informative and appealing overview of this major Indian city, with material on its history, its economy, and what it's like to live there. (Rev: BL 4/15/04)

8324 Srinivasan, Radhika, and Leslie Jermyn. *India*. 2nd ed. (4–8). Illus. Series: Cultures of the World. 2001, Benchmark LB $37.07 (978-0-7614-1354-7). An updated edition of the 1990 title, covering the history, geography, politics, people, arts, culture, and environmental concerns of India. (Rev: HBG 3/02; SLJ 3/02) [954]

8325 Swan, Erin Pembrey. *India* (4–7). Series: Enchantment of the World. 2002, Children's LB $37.00 (978-0-516-21121-3). This visually attractive introduction to the past and present of India includes coverage of languages, culture, the people, economy, and government. (Rev: BL 5/15/02) [954]

8326 Valliant, Doris. *Bangladesh* (8–12). Illus. Series: The Growth and Influence of Islam in the Nations of Asia and Central Asia. 2005, Mason Crest LB $25.95 (978-1-59084-879-1). A well-illustrated look at Bangladesh and the importance of Islam in the country's history, politics, economy, and foreign relations. (Rev: SLJ 9/05) [954.9]

8327 Viswanath, R. *Teenage Refugees and Immigrants from India Speak Out* (7–12). Series: Teenage Refugees Speak Out. 1997, Rosen LB $27.95 (978-0-8239-2440-0). A description of the ethnic and religious conflicts and economic conditions that have caused the displacement of tens of thousands of Indians, plus the stories of those who came to the United States, told in first-person teenage accounts. (Rev: BL 12/15/97; SLJ 4/98) [954]

8328 Wagner, Heather Lehr. *India and Pakistan* (6–12). Illus. Series: People at Odds. 2002, Chelsea LB $30.00 (978-0-7910-6709-3). An easy-to-understand, chronological summary of the ongoing conflict between the two nations, with photographs and maps. (Rev: BL 11/1/02; HBG 3/03; SLJ 12/02) [954.03]

8329 Weston, Mark. *The Land and People of Pakistan* (6–9). Series: Land and People Of. 1992, HarperCollins LB $17.89 (978-0-06-022790-6). Pakistan's geography, ethnicity, and history as well as an exploration of political, social, economic, and cultural life. (Rev: BL 8/92; SLJ 12/92*) [954.91]

8330 Whyte, Mariam. *Bangladesh* (5–9). Series: Cultures of the World. 1998, Marshall Cavendish LB $37.07 (978-0-7614-0869-7). A sympathetic look at the history and geography of Bangladesh, with details of the country's rich background and current problems. (Rev: HBG 10/99; SLJ 6/99) [954.9]

Japan

8331 Behnke, Alison. *Japan in Pictures* (6–10). Series: Visual Geography. 2002, Lerner LB $27.93 (978-0-8225-1956-0). This revised edition of an old title contains all new material on Japan's history, government, people, customs, economy, and culture. (Rev: BL 10/15/02; HBG 3/03) [952]

8332 Blumberg, Rhoda. *Commodore Perry in the Land of the Shogun* (5–8). Illus. 1985, Lothrop $21.99 (978-0-688-03723-9). Japan was a mysterious country when Perry arrived in 1853 to open its harbors to American ships. (Rev: BL 11/1/85; SLJ 10/85) [952.025]

8333 Bornoff, Nick. *Japan* (4–7). Illus. Series: Country Insights. 1997, Raintree LB $27.12 (978-0-8172-4786-7). This description of modern life in the city of Okazaki and in the village of Narai compares home life, employment, schooling, and recreation. (Rev: BL 7/97; SLJ 8/97) [952]

8334 Case, Robert. *Japan* (6–10). Series: Countries of the World. 2003, Facts on File $30.00 (978-0-8160-5381-0). An attractive introduction to Japan that includes material on history, geography, economy, people, and culture. (Rev: BL 1/1–15/04) [952]

8335 Donovan, Sandy. *Teens in Japan* (6–9). Series: Global Connections. 2007, Compass Point LB $23.95 (978-0-7565-2444-9). This volume covers many aspects of Japanese culture and traditions practiced by people of all ages, focusing in particular on everyday life for teens and the stresses they suffer. (Rev: BL 4/1/07) [305.2350]

8336 Green, Jen. *Japan* (4–8). Series: Nations of the World. 2001, Raintree LB $34.26 (978-0-8172-5783-5). An attractive, fact-filled introduction to this island nation, its rich culture, advanced technology, and wealthy economy. (Rev: BL 6/1–15/01; HBG 10/01) [952]

8337 Hall, Eleanor J. *Life Among the Samurai* (6–10). Series: The Way People Live. 1998, Lucent LB $28.70 (978-1-56006-390-2). A history of the feudal period in Japanese history that focuses on the warrior class and their exploits. (Rev: BL 11/15/98) [952]

8338 Hanel, Rachael. *Samurai* (5–8). Series: Fearsome Fighters. 2007, Creative Education LB $31.35 (978-1-58341-538-2). Weapons, armor, fighting techniques, and motivation are all discussed in this description of the Japanese feudal warriors and the kinds of people who were tempted to this career. (Rev: SLJ 1/08)

8339 Kallen, Stuart A. *Life in Tokyo* (6–10). Series: The Way People Live. 2001, Lucent LB $29.95 (978-1-56006-797-9). After a brief historical introduction, life in present-day Tokyo is featured with material on such topics as daily life, education, entertainment, jobs, food, and culture. (Rev: BL 6/1–15/01; SLJ 6/01) [952]

8340 Patchett, Kaye. *The Akashi Kaikyo Bridge* (5–8). Illus. Series: Building World Landmarks. 2004, Gale LB $24.95 (978-1-4103-0140-6). A concise account of the amazing construction of the bridge that links Shikoku and Honshu islands. (Rev: BL 4/1/04; SLJ 4/05)

8341 Pilbeam, Mavis. *Japan Under the Shoguns, 1185–1868* (5–8). Series: Looking Back. 1999, Raintree $19.98 (978-0-8172-5431-5). A handsome, detailed overview of the shogun society of Japan from 1185 to 1868, featuring color photographs and reproductions of original art. (Rev: BL 5/15/99) [452]

8342 Roberson, John R. *Japan Meets the World: The Birth of a Super Power* (7–12). 1998, Millbrook LB $24.90 (978-0-7613-0407-4). Beginning with the shoguns of the 16th century, this book traces Japanese history through various stages of progress, its development into an economic superpower, and its current economic crisis and social stresses. (Rev: BL 1/1–15/99; HBG 3/99; SLJ 2/99) [952]

8343 Ross, Stewart. *The Rise of Japan and the Pacific Rim* (7–12). Series: Causes and Consequences. 1995, Raintree LB $29.97 (978-0-8172-4054-7). A thorough, unbiased account of the remarkable history of Japan since World War II, with well-documented details on the political, social, and economic conditions that made it possible, and also including material on the economic rise of other Pacific Rim nations. (Rev: BL 12/15/95; SLJ 2/96) [952]

8344 Say, Allen. *Tea with Milk* (4–8). Illus. 1999, Houghton LB $17.00 (978-0-395-90495-4). A picture book about the author's mother, who was forced by her father to leave her California residence and return to the family's original home in Japan. (Rev: BCCB 6/99; BL 3/15/99*; HB 7–8/99; HBG 10/99; SLJ 5/99) [952]

8345 Schomp, Virginia. *Japan in the Days of the Samurai* (5–8). Illus. Series: Cultures of the Past. 2001, Marshall Cavendish LB $29.93 (978-0-7614-0304-3). A well-illustrated look at the history of Japan, including information on such cultural topics as the tea ceremony and samurai women. (Rev: BL 2/15/02; HBG 3/02; SLJ 3/02) [952]

8346 Shelley, Rex, and Teo Chuu Yong. *Japan.* 2nd ed. (5–8). Illus. Series: Cultures of the World. 2001, Benchmark LB $37.07 (978-0-7614-1356-1). An updated edition of the 1996 title, covering the history, geography, politics, people, arts, culture, and environmental concerns of Japan. (Rev: HBG 3/02; SLJ 3/02) [952]

8347 Stefoff, Rebecca. *Japan* (6–10). Series: Major World Nations. 1998, Chelsea LB $21.95 (978-0-7910-4761-3). With emphasis on social, economic, and cultural conditions, this is a readable, informative introduction to Japan. (Rev: BL 9/15/98) [952.04]

Other Asian Countries

8348 *Afghanistan in Pictures* (5–8). Illus. Series: Visual Geography. 1997, Lerner LB $25.55 (978-0-8225-1849-5). Includes sections on vegetation and wildlife, minerals, cities, history, and government. (Rev: BL 5/1/89) [958.1]

8349 Ali, Sharifah Enayat. *Afghanistan* (4–7). Illus. Series: Cultures of the World. 1995, Marshall Cavendish LB $37.07 (978-0-7614-0177-3). After general background information, this account focuses on the arts, leisure activities, and festivals of the people of Afghanistan. (Rev: BL 1/1–15/96; SLJ 4/96) [958.1]

8350 Ali, Sharifah Enayat. *Afghanistan.* 2nd ed. (5–9). Illus. Series: Cultures of the World. 2006, Benchmark LB $27.95 (978-0-7614-2064-4). A revised and updated edition of the guide to Afghanistan and its history, geography, culture, and government including maps and color photographs. (Rev: SLJ 3/07) [958.1]

8351 Barber, Nicola. *Singapore* (4–7). Illus. Series: Great Cities of the World. 2005, World Almanac LB $31.00 (978-0-8368-5047-5). An informative and appealing overview of one of the world's most famous cities, with material on its history, its economy, and what it's like to live there. (Rev: BL 4/15/04)

8352 Burbank, Jon. *Nepal* (4–7). Illus. Series: Cultures of the World. 1991, Marshall Cavendish LB $35.64 (978-1-85435-401-3). The emphasis is on culture as well as the basics of geography, history, government, and people. (Rev: BL 2/15/92) [954.96]

8353 Clifford, Mary Louise. *The Land and People of Afghanistan* (5–7). Illus. 1989, HarperCollins LB $14.89 (978-0-397-32339-5). An introduction to past life in this central Asian country. A reissue. [958.1]

8354 Cole, Wendy M. *Vietnam* (6–10). Illus. Series: Major World Nations. 1999, Chelsea LB $29.95 (978-0-7910-4751-4). A revised edition of the author's 1989 introduction to Vietnam, with chapters on history, geography, people, culture, cities and villages, government and social services, resources and economy, and transportation and communications. (Rev: SLJ 5/98) [959.7]

8355 Corona, Laurel. *Afghanistan* (6–12). Illus. Series: Modern Nations of the World. 2002, Gale LB $29.95 (978-1-59018-217-8). This book covers cultural, geographical, religious, and other aspects of Afghanistan, with discussion of the Taliban and the role of women. (Rev: BL 11/15/02; SLJ 12/02) [958.1]

8356 Cottrell, Robert C. *Vietnam: 17th Parallel* (7–9). Illus. Series: Arbitrary Borders. 2004, Chelsea House LB $35.00 (978-0-7910-7834-1). This series discusses the importance of borders in the stability (or instability) of a country; this volume looks at Vietnam and the lengthy conflict over the arbitrary division of the nation. (Rev: BL 8/04; SLJ 7/04) [959.70]

8357 Fiscus, James W. *America's War in Afghanistan* (5–9). Illus. Series: War and Conflict in the Middle East. 2004, Rosen LB $27.95 (978-0-8239-4552-8). A well-organized, balanced account of the war between the United States and Afghanistan in the aftermath of the 2001 terrorist attacks on New York and Washington, D.C. (Rev: BL 11/1/04)

8358 Gogol, Sara. *A Mien Family* (4–7). Illus. Series: Journey Between Two Worlds. 1996, Lerner LB $22.60 (978-0-8225-3407-5); paper $8.95 (978-0-8225-9745-2). The story of a refugee family from the mountainous area of Laos and their journey to the United States. (Rev: BL 11/15/96; SLJ 1/97) [306.85]

8359 Goodman, Jim. *Thailand* (5–9). Series: Cultures of the World. 1991, Marshall Cavendish LB $35.64 (978-1-85435-402-0). Thailand's history, land, and culture. (Rev: BL 3/15/92) [959.3]

8360 Gritzner, Jeffrey A. *Afghanistan* (7–12). Series: Modern World Nations. 2002, Chelsea LB $30.00 (978-0-7910-6774-1). An overview of the history, geography, people, politics, and religion of Afghanistan, with discussion of the current antiterrorist and rebuilding efforts. (Rev: SLJ 2/03) [958.1]

8361 Guile, Melanie. *Culture in Malaysia* (4–7). Illus. Series: Culture In. 2005, Raintree LB $25.70 (978-1-4109-1133-9). Customs, holidays, clothing, food, and arts and crafts are well covered in this volume that also provides basic information needed for reports and interesting sidebar features. (Rev: SLJ 5/05)

8362 Hansen, Ole Steen. *Vietnam* (5–8). Illus. Series: Economically Developing Countries. 1996, Raintree LB $24.26 (978-0-8172-4526-9). This introduction to Vietnam includes background information and material on its emerging economy. (Rev: BL 3/1/97) [959.7]

8363 Hanson, Jennifer L. *Mongolia* (7–10). Series: Nations in Transition. 2003, Facts on File $40.00 (978-0-8160-5221-9). A thorough review of Mongolia's history, geography, and culture, detailing the difficulties involved in making a transition to democracy. (Rev: SLJ 5/04; VOYA 6/04) [951]

8364 Jung, Sung-Hoon. *South Korea* (5–8). Series: Economically Developing Countries. 1997, Raintree LB $24.26 (978-0-8172-4530-6). This overview of economic conditions in South Korea describes the country's success with electronic exports and provides case studies of family-run companies. (Rev: BL 5/15/97) [951.95]

8365 Kendra, Judith. *Tibetans* (5–8). Series: Threatened Cultures. 1994, Thomson Learning LB $24.25 (978-1-56847-152-5). Discusses Tibetan culture and religion, with emphasis on the denial by China of Tibetans' rights. Follows the daily lives of two Tibetan children, one living in the country, one in the city. (Rev: BL 7/94) [951]

8366 Kizilos, Peter. *Tibet: Disputed Land* (7–10). Series: World in Conflict. 2000, Lerner LB $25.26 (978-0-8225-3563-8). The history of Tibet and its present political divisions are covered in this well-illustrated account. (Rev: BL 10/15/2000; HBG 3/01) [951.1]

8367 Kummer, Patricia K. *North Korea* (7–12). Illus. Series: Enchantment of the World. 2008, Children's Pr. LB $37.00 (978-0-531-18485-1). Geography, history, economy, religion, sports, and education are all discussed here, along with government oppression, censorship, and the nuclear weapons program; includes numerous maps and photographs. (Rev: BL 8/08) [951.93]

8368 Kummer, Patricia K. *Tibet* (4–8). Series: Enchantment of the World. 2003, Children's Pr. LB $37.00 (978-0-516-22693-4). A visually attractive book that covers such topics as the geography, history, government, culture, and people, with a timeline, fast facts, and a recipe. (Rev: SLJ 1/04) [951]

8369 Layton, Lesley. *Singapore* (5–8). Illus. Series: Cultures of the World. 1990, Marshall Cavendish LB $35.64 (978-1-85435-295-8). As well as history and economy, this introduction to Singapore includes coverage of lifestyles and current problems. (Rev: BL 3/1/91; SLJ 6/91) [959.57]

8370 Levy, Patricia. *Tibet* (4–7). Illus. Series: Cultures of the World. 1996, Marshall Cavendish LB $37.07 (978-0-7614-0277-0). Tibet is introduced with general background information, followed by material on its people and their culture, festivals, and food. (Rev: BL 8/96; SLJ 9/96) [951.1]

8371 Lorbiecki, Marybeth. *Children of Vietnam* (4–7). Photos by Paul P. Rome. Series: The World's Children. 1997, Carolrhoda LB $28.75 (978-1-57505-034-8). Beginning in the north and working south, this photoessay describes the people of Vietnam and the lives of their children. (Rev: HBG 3/98; SLJ 2/98) [959.7]

8372 McNair, Sylvia. *Malaysia* (4–7). Series: Enchantment of the World. 2002, Children's LB $37.00 (978-0-516-21009-4). This Southeast Asian nation is presented in text and many color photographs that introduce its history, geography, people, culture, and present status. (Rev: BL 9/15/02) [959.505]

8373 *Malaysia in Pictures* (5–8). Illus. Series: Visual Geography. 1997, Lerner LB $25.55 (978-0-8225-1854-9). A basic, visual overview of this nation and its people. (Rev: BL 5/1/89) [959.5]

8374 Miller, Raymond H. *The War in Afghanistan* (6–8). Illus. Series: American War Library: The War on Terrorism. 2004, Gale LB $29.95 (978-1-59018-331-1). An account of the U.S.-led campaign to force the Taliban and al-Qaeda out of Afghanistan, the difficulties the military faced, and the resulting political reforms and efforts to rebuild the country and deal with problems such as remaining land mines. (Rev: BL 8/04) [958.10]

8375 Mirpuri, Gouri, and Robert Cooper. *Indonesia.* 2nd ed. (5–8). Illus. Series: Cultures of the World. 2001, Marshall Cavendish LB $37.07 (978-0-7614-1355-4). An encompassing look at the history, culture, society, and geography of Indonesia. (Rev: BL 3/1/02; HBG 3/02; SLJ 4/02) [959.8]

8376 Moiz, Azra. *Taiwan* (4–7). Illus. Series: Cultures of the World. 1995, Marshall Cavendish LB $37.07 (978-0-7614-0180-3). The accomplishments, lifestyle, and religious festivals of the people of Taiwan are covered, along with its history and geography. (Rev: BL 1/1–15/96; SLJ 9/96) [957.24]

8377 Munan, Heidi. *Malaysia* (5–8). Illus. Series: Cultures of the World. 1990, Marshall Cavendish LB $35.64 (978-1-85435-296-5). Cultural diversity and lifestyles of the people are two topics covered in this introduction to Malaysia. (Rev: BL 3/1/91) [959.5]

8378 Otfinoski, Steven. *Afghanistan* (7–12). Series: Nations in Transition. 2003, Facts on File $40.00 (978-0-8160-5056-7). A thorough overview of Afghanistan presenting the current political and security problems — including healthcare needs, opium trade, and reliance on foreign funding — as well as material on the country's history, geography, people, culture, and so forth. (Rev: SLJ 4/04; VOYA 6/04) [958.1]

8379 Pang, Guek-Cheng. *Mongolia* (5–8). Series: Cultures of the World. 1999, Marshall Cavendish LB $37.07 (978-0-7614-0954-0). A clear, well-illustrated introduction to this remote land that includes good background information as well as coverage of modern life. (Rev: HBG 10/99; SLJ 10/99) [957]

8380 Rowell, Jonathan. *Malaysia* (5–8). Illus. Series: Economically Developing Countries. 1997, Raintree LB $24.26 (978-0-8172-4531-3). The growth and development of Malaysia are traced, with material on its high-tech sector. (Rev: BL 5/15/97) [959.505]

8381 Salter, Christopher. *North Korea* (6–12). Illus. 2003, Chelsea LB $30.00 (978-0-7910-7233-2). A thorough and concise overview of North Korea's geography, history, government, politics, economics, language, peoples, and religion, with maps, photographs, and a look at the future. (Rev: BL 9/15/03; HBG 10/03) [951.93]

8382 Sheehan, Sean. *Cambodia* (4–7). Illus. Series: Cultures of the World. 1996, Marshall Cavendish LB $37.07 (978-0-7614-0281-7). The troubled land of Cambodia is introduced, with emphasis on its people, their lifestyles, and culture. (Rev: BL 8/96; SLJ 9/96) [959]

8383 Sheehan, Sean, and Shahrezad Samiuddin. *Pakistan* (5–9). Illus. Series: Cultures of the World. 2004, Benchmark LB $37.07 (978-0-7614-1787-3). Pakistan's geography, history, economy, and people are all examined, with discussion of interesting aspects of Pakistani culture. (Rev: SLJ 2/05) [954.9]

8384 Sís, Peter. *Tibet: Through the Red Box* (7–12). Illus. 1998, Farrar $25.00 (978-0-374-37552-2). Using a journal kept by the author's filmmaker father when he journeyed to Tibet long ago, old tales, and pictures of landscapes and intriguing illustrations inspired by the Tibetan wheel of life, the author writes about the past and present of this land, its culture, and its religion. (Rev: BCCB 12/98; BL 9/15/98; HB 11–12/98; HBG 3/99; SLJ 10/98) [954.96]

8385 *South Korea in Pictures* (5–7). Series: Visual Geography. 1997, Lerner LB $25.55 (978-0-8225-1868-6). An introduction to South Korea that focuses on its politics and economy. (Rev: SLJ 5/90) [951.9]

8386 Stewart, Gail B. *Life Under the Taliban* (6–10). Series: The Way People Live. 2004, Gale

LB $29.95 (978-1-59018-291-8). A look at what life was like in Afghanistan under the repressive Taliban regime. (Rev: SLJ 1/05) [958.1]

8387 Taus-Bolstad, Stacy. *Pakistan in Pictures*. Rev. ed. (5–9). Illus. Series: Visual Geography. 2003, Lerner LB $27.93 (978-0-8225-4682-5). This substantially revised volume covers Pakistan's history, geography, culture, and lifestyle. (Rev: SLJ 7/03) [954.9]

8388 Tull, Mary, et al. *Northern Asia* (4–7). Illus. Series: Artisans Around the World. 1990, Raintree LB $27.12 (978-0-7398-0119-2). This book introduces Mongolia and its neighbors, with descriptions of arts and crafts and many projects. (Rev: BL 10/15/99; HBG 3/00; SLJ 1/00) [745.5]

8389 *Vietnam in Pictures* (5–8). Illus. Series: Visual Geography. 1994, Lerner LB $25.55 (978-0-8225-1909-6). This well-illustrated account of Vietnam covers its history, geography, people, government, and economy. (Rev: BL 11/1/94) [915.97]

8390 Wanasundera, Nanda P. *Sri Lanka* (4–7). Illus. Series: Cultures of the World. 1991, Marshall Cavendish LB $213.86 (978-1-85435-397-9). The history, geography, and culture of Sri Lanka are introduced with an emphasis on contemporary problems. (Rev: BL 2/15/92) [954.93]

8391 Whitehead, Kim. *Afghanistan* (8–12). Illus. Series: The Growth and Influence of Islam in the Nations of Asia and Central Asia. 2005, Mason Crest LB $25.95 (978-1-59084-833-3). A well-illustrated look at Afghanistan and the importance of Islam in the country's history, politics, economy, and foreign relations. (Rev: SLJ 9/05) [958.104]

8392 Willis, Karen. *Vietnam* (5–8). Illus. Series: Modern Nations of the World. 2000, Lucent LB $27.45 (978-1-56006-635-4). A thorough history of Vietnam, this work also focuses on progress after the war and daily life in modern Vietnam. (Rev: BL 9/15/00; HBG 3/01) [959.7]

8393 Willis, Terri. *Vietnam* (4–7). Series: Enchantment of the World. 2002, Children's LB $37.00 (978-0-516-22150-2). This attractive volume presents basic material on Vietnam's history, geography, and culture, with an emphasis on progress after the war. (Rev: BL 9/15/02; SLJ 12/02) [959.7]

8394 Withington, William A. *Southeast Asia* (5–8). Illus. 1988, Gateway $16.95 (978-0-934291-32-3). Sections on lifestyle, land and climate, history and government, festivals, sports, arts, and crafts. (Rev: BL 12/1/88)

8395 Yin, Saw Myat. *Myanmar*. Rev. ed. (4–8). Illus. Series: Cultures of the World. 2001, Benchmark LB $37.07 (978-0-7614-1353-0). An introduction to every aspect of Myanmar with useful information on daily life and phonetic pronunciations of many foreign words. Also use *Indonesia* (2001). (Rev: HBG 3/02; SLJ 4/02) [959.1]

8396 Yu, Ling. *Taiwan in Pictures* (5–8). Illus. Series: Visual Geography. 1997, Lerner LB $25.55 (978-0-8225-1865-5). The history and geography of Taiwan are introduced, with coverage of cities, culture, religion, and economy. (Rev: BL 9/15/89) [915.1]

8397 Zwier, Lawrence J. *Sri Lanka: War Torn Island* (8–12). Illus. Series: World in Conflict. 1998, Lerner LB $25.26 (978-0-8225-3550-8). The author describes the long political struggle in Sri Lanka. (Rev: BL 4/15/98) [305.8]

Australia and the Pacific Islands

8398 Alter, Judy. *Discovering Australia's Land, People, and Wildlife* (5–8). Series: Continents of the World. 2004, Enslow LB $25.26 (978-0-7660-5207-9). An introduction to the geography, history, economy, plants and animals, culture, and people of the continent, showing the contrast between the urban centers on the coasts and the rugged interior. (Rev: SLJ 11/04) [994]

8399 Arnold, Caroline. *Easter Island: Giant Stone Statues Tell of a Rich and Tragic Past* (4–7). Illus. 2000, Clarion LB $15.00 (978-0-395-87609-1). This chronological history of Easter Island tells how the stone statues got there and what they mean. (Rev: BCCB 4/00; BL 3/15/00; HB 5–6/00; HBG 10/00; SLJ 4/00) [996.1]

8400 Arnold, Caroline. *Uluru: Australia's Aboriginal Heart* (4–8). Illus. by Arthur Arnold. 2003, Clarion $16.00 (978-0-618-18181-0). Uluru, formerly known as Ayers Rock, is a giant sandstone monolith that changes color in the setting sun and is a spiritual landmark for the native people of the central Australian desert. (Rev: BCCB 12/03; BL 12/15/03; HB 11–12/03; HBG 11–12/03; SLJ 1/04) [994.01]

8401 Arnold, Caroline. *A Walk on the Great Barrier Reef* (4–7). Illus. 1988, Lerner LB $25.26 (978-0-87614-285-1). Exploring one of the great natural wonders of the world. (Rev: BL 7/88; SLJ 8/88) [574.91943]

8402 Bartlett, Anne. *The Aboriginal Peoples of Australia* (4–7). Illus. Series: First Peoples. 2001, Lerner LB $23.93 (978-0-8225-4854-6). An introduction to the indigenous people of Australia, including their history, customs, and daily life, with photographs. (Rev: BL 10/15/01; HBG 3/02; SLJ 3/02) [994]

8403 Darian-Smith, Kate. *Australia, Antarctica, and the Pacific* (5–8). Series: Continents of the World. 2006, World Almanac LB $34.00 (978-0-8368-

5912-6). Factboxes and "In Focus" articles add to this overview of the history, geography, people, culture, and so forth of the continents of Australia, Antarctica, and island of the Pacific. (Rev: SLJ 2/06)

8404 Darian-Smith, Kate, and David Lowe. *The Australian Outback and Its People* (4–7). Illus. Series: People and Places. 1995, Thomson Learning LB $24.26 (978-1-56847-337-6). A well-organized guide to the Australian outback, its exploration and history, flora and fauna, mining, environmental issues, and people. (Rev: SLJ 7/95) [994]

8405 Darlington, Robert. *Australia* (4–8). Series: Nations of the World. 2001, Raintree LB $34.26 (978-0-7398-1280-8). Australia, the world's largest island, is introduced in this attractive volume that gives material on geography, climate, terrain, history, economy, and lifestyles. (Rev: BL 6/1–15/01; HBG 10/01) [994]

8406 Franklin, Sharon, et al. *Southwest Pacific* (4–7). Series: Artisans Around the World. 1999, Raintree LB $27.12 (978-0-7398-0120-8). The influence of traditions and geography is shown in this survey of folk art from Australia, New Guinea, New Zealand, and Indonesia, with directions for projects such as a Maori woven band and a batik wall hanging. (Rev: BL 10/15/99; HBG 3/00; SLJ 1/00) [994]

8407 Grabowski, John F. *Australia* (5–8). Series: Modern Nations of the World. 2002, Gale LB $27.45 (978-1-56006-566-1). The continent Down Under is introduced with coverage of history, natural resources, landmarks, economy, and people. (Rev: BL 12/15/02) [994]

8408 Lowe, David, and Andrea Shimmen. *Australia* (4–8). Illus. Series: Modern Industrial World. 1996, Raintree LB $24.26 (978-0-8172-4553-5). Australia's economic status, living standards, educational system, and industry are covered. (Rev: BL 2/15/97) [919.4]

8409 Macdonald, Robert. *Islands of the Pacific Rim and Their People* (5–8). Illus. Series: People and Places. 1994, Thomson Learning LB $24.26 (978-1-56847-167-9). An overview of the islands of the Pacific Ocean and their people, different environments, and economies. (Rev: BL 10/15/94; SLJ 10/94) [990]

8410 McGuinn, Taro. *East Timor: Island in Turmoil* (7–10). Series: World in Conflict. 1998, Lerner LB $25.26 (978-0-8225-3555-3). The country of East Timor, an island east of Indonesia, is introduced, with material on its internal ethnic and political conflicts. (Rev: BL 10/15/98; HBG 3/99; SLJ 10/98) [959.86]

8411 Mason, Paul. *Sydney* (4–8). Photos by Rob Bowden. Series: Global Cities. 2007, Chelsea House LB $30.00 (978-0-7910-8849-4). With plenty of photographs and maps, this volume introduces the history of Sydney, Australia, as well as its geography, people, environment, transportation, and so forth. (Rev: SLJ 7/07)

8412 NgCheong-Lum, Roseline. *Tahiti* (4–7). Illus. Series: Cultures of the World. 1997, Marshall Cavendish LB $37.07 (978-0-7614-0682-2). Background material on history and geography is given, with information on how Tahitians live today. (Rev: BL 8/97; HBG 3/98) [919.62]

8413 Nile, Richard. *Australian Aborigines* (4–7). Illus. Series: Threatened Cultures. 1993, Raintree LB $24.26 (978-0-8114-2303-8). The aboriginal culture of Australia is presented. (Rev: BL 8/93; SLJ 8/93) [305]

8414 Oleksy, Walter. *The Philippines* (4–7). Series: Enchantment of the World. 2000, Children's LB $37.00 (978-0-516-21010-0). These South Pacific islands are presented with coverage of history, geography, economy, the people, current problems, culture, and recreation. (Rev: BL 7/00) [959.9]

8415 Pelta, Kathy. *Rediscovering Easter Island* (5–9). Series: How History Is Invented. 2001, Lerner LB $28.75 (978-0-8225-4890-4). An assortment of illustrations, maps, and inserts add to this exploration of the mysteries of Easter Island. (Rev: BCCB 7–8/01; HBG 10/01; SLJ 2/02) [996.18]

8416 Rajendra, Vijeya, and Sundran Rajendra. *Australia* (4–7). Illus. Series: Cultures of the World. 1991, Marshall Cavendish LB $35.64 (978-1-85435-400-6). Beyond the basics, this volume highlights contemporary problems and concerns in the Land Down Under. (Rev: BL 2/15/92; SLJ 3/92) [994]

8417 Shepherd, Donna Walsh. *New Zealand* (4–7). Series: Enchantment of the World. 2002, Children's LB $37.00 (978-0-516-21099-5). Some of the subjects covered in this fine introduction to New Zealand are history, people and languages, economy, government, culture, natural resources, and climate. (Rev: BL 5/15/02; SLJ 10/02) [992]

8418 Tope, Lily R. *Philippines* (4–7). Illus. Series: Cultures of the World. 1991, Marshall Cavendish LB $35.64 (978-1-85435-403-7). With emphasis on contemporary problems and concerns, the land and culture of the Philippines are introduced in text and well-chosen color photographs. (Rev: BL 2/15/92) [959.9]

8419 Turner, Kate. *Australia* (5–8). Series: Countries of the World. 2007, National Geographic LB $27.90 (978-1-4263-0055-4). Excellent photographs and maps make this an appealing introduction to the country's history, geography, government, economy, people, culture, and nature. (Rev: SLJ 10/07) [994]

8420 Vail, Martha, and John S. Bowman, eds. *Exploring the Pacific* (6–12). Illus. Series: Discovery and Exploration. 2005, Facts on File $40.00 (978-0-8160-5258-5). Exploration in the Pacific, from early Polynesians onward and including such figures as Magellan and Cook, is the focus of this volume that contains clear, informative text plus maps, illustrations, and excerpts from primary sources. (Rev: SLJ 8/05) [973]

Europe

General and Miscellaneous

8421 Bowden, Rob. *Istanbul* (4–8). Photos by Edward Parker. Series: Global Cities. 2007, Chelsea House LB $30.00 (978-0-7910-8850-0). With plenty of photographs and maps, this volume introduces the history of Istanbul as well as its geography, people, environment, transportation, and so forth. (Rev: SLJ 7/07)

8422 *Cyprus in Pictures* (5–8). Illus. Series: Visual Geography. 1992, Lerner LB $25.55 (978-0-8225-1910-2). The divided island of Cyprus is introduced, with good background information and material on the standoff between Greece and Turkey up to 1992. (Rev: BL 2/1/93) [956.45]

8423 Feinstein, Steve. *Turkey in Pictures* (5–8). Illus. 1989, Lerner LB $25.55 (978-0-8225-1831-0). An overview of Turkey and its people that includes lots of images. (Rev: BL 8/88) [956.1]

8424 Flint, David. *Europe* (5–8). Series: Continents of the World. 2006, World Almanac LB $34.00 (978-0-8368-5913-3). Factboxes and "In Focus" articles add to this overview of the history, geography, people, culture, and so forth of the continent of Europe. (Rev: SLJ 2/06) [940]

8425 Pollard, Michael. *The Rhine* (5–8). Series: Great Rivers. 1997, Benchmark LB $22.79 (978-0-7614-0500-9). After explaining how the Rhine was formed, this attractive book describes its history, importance, tributaries, tourism, and present-day role. (Rev: HBG 3/98; SLJ 3/98) [943]

8426 Sheehan, Sean. *Malta* (5–9). Series: Cultures of the World. 2000, Marshall Cavendish LB $37.07 (978-0-7614-0993-9). This work covers the culture, geography, and history of Malta with material on such subjects as government, economy, people, lifestyles, and leisure. (Rev: HBG 10/00; SLJ 11/00) [945]

8427 Sheehan, Sean. *Turkey* (4–7). Illus. Series: Cultures of the World. 1993, Marshall Cavendish LB $35.64 (978-1-85435-576-8). This introduction to Turkey covers history, culture, economics, and present-day concerns. (Rev: BL 8/93) [956.1]

8428 Stafford, James. *The European Union: Facts and Figures* (8–11). Illus. Series: European Union. 2006, Mason Crest LB $21.95 (978-1-4222-0045-2). A useful, information-packed guide to the European Union and its origins and goals. (Rev: BL 4/1/06) [641.242]

Eastern Europe and the Balkans

8429 Andryszewski, Tricia. *Kosovo: The Splintering of Yugoslavia* (5–8). Illus. Series: Headliners. 2000, Millbrook LB $25.90 (978-0-7613-1750-0). Introduced by refugees' accounts of the horror in Kosovo, this book traces the origins of ethnic conflicts in Yugoslavia, with a concentration on events of the past 10 years. (Rev: BL 6/1–15/00; HBG 10/00; SLJ 6/00) [949.7]

8430 Bultje, Jan Willem. *Looking at the Czech Republic* (6–9). Series: Looking at Europe. 2006, Oliver LB $22.95 (978-1-881508-29-8). Numerous color photographs enhance the text that covers many aspects — history, geography, culture, economy, and so forth — of this eastern European land. (Rev: BL 10/15/06; SLJ 12/06) [943.71]

8431 Burke, Patrick. *Eastern Europe: Bulgaria, Czech Republic, Hungary, Poland, Romania, Slovakia* (5–8). Series: Country Fact Files. 1997, Raintree LB $27.12 (978-0-8172-4628-0). In chapters two to four pages long, the impact of geography on the landscape, daily life, natural resources, transportation, and other aspects of life is examined for these six countries. (Rev: SLJ 8/97) [947]

8432 Corona, Laurel. *Poland* (5–8). Illus. Series: Modern Nations of the World. 2000, Lucent LB $28.70 (978-1-56006-600-2). A good history of Poland that also covers Polish achievements and daily life. (Rev: BL 9/15/00; HBG 3/01) [943.8]

8433 Fireside, Harvey, and Bryna J. Fireside. *Young People From Bosnia Talk About War* (6–9). Illus. Series: Issues in Focus. 1996, Enslow LB $20.95 (978-0-89490-730-2). Several students from Bosnia who have been brought to this country to study by the Bosnian Student Project tell about the effects of the war on them, their families, and their country. (Rev: BL 10/15/96; SLJ 10/96; VOYA 2/97) [949.702]

8434 Ganeri, Anita. *Focus on Turkey* (6–9). Series: World in Focus. 2007, World Almanac LB $33.27 (978-0-8368-6753-4); paper $11.95 (978-0-8368-6760-2). Turkey's history, geography, economy, culture, and handicrafts are all covered in this survey. (Rev: SLJ 2/08)

8435 Harris, Nathaniel. *The War in Former Yugoslavia* (7–12). Illus. Series: New Perspectives. 1998, Raintree LB $28.54 (978-0-8172-5014-0). Different perspectives on this war are expressed through the viewpoints of political leaders, ordinary citizens,

soldiers, militiamen, foreign diplomats, rescue workers, and news reporters. (Rev: BL 3/15/98; HBG 9/98) [940.54]

8436 *Hungary in Pictures* (5–8). Illus. Series: Visual Geography. 1993, Lerner LB $25.55 (978-0-8225-1883-9). Concise text and extensive photographs introduce the land, history, and people of Hungary. (Rev: BL 12/1/93; SLJ 12/93) [943.9]

8437 King, David C. *Bosnia and Herzegovina* (7–10). Illus. Series: Cultures of the World. 2005, Benchmark LB $37.07 (978-0-7614-1853-5). Explores the geography, history, people, culture, and lifestyles of Bosnia and Herzegovina. (Rev: SLJ 7/05) [949.7]

8438 Nichols, Jeremy, and Emilia Trembicka-Nichols. *Poland* (7–10). Series: Countries of the World. 2005, Facts on File LB $30.00 (978-0-8160-6005-4). History, geography, culture, government, and economy are all covered in this attractive overview of Poland. (Rev: SLJ 1/06) [9.4.3]

8439 Orr, Tamra. *Slovenia* (5–8). Series: Enchantment of the World. 2004, Children's Pr. LB $37.00 (978-0-516-24249-1). Introduces the history, geography, people, and culture of Slovenia, with plenty of clear photographs and an emphasis on contemporary life. (Rev: BL 9/1/04; SLJ 7/04) [949.73]

8440 Otfinoski, Steven. *Bulgaria* (6–10). Series: Nations in Transition. 1998, Facts on File $35.00 (978-0-8160-3705-6). This book reviews the history, politics, people, and culture of Bulgaria, including material on relationships with Gypsies and other minorities. (Rev: BL 3/1/99; SLJ 6/99) [949.903]

8441 Otfinoski, Steven. *The Czech Republic* (7–12). Illus. Series: Nations in Transition. 2004, Facts on File $40.00 (978-0-8160-5083-3). An updated edition that adds more recent events to the 1997 text about the history, people, culture, and government of the Czech Republic. (Rev: BL 12/1/04) [943.7105]

8442 Reger, James P. *The Rebuilding of Bosnia* (6–8). Illus. Series: Overview. 1997, Lucent LB $27.45 (978-1-56006-190-8). After a discussion of the ethnic and religious strife in the Balkans for 1,500 years, this book focuses on the recent war in Bosnia and the uneasy peace following 1995's Dayton Accords. (Rev: BL 9/1/97; SLJ 8/97) [949.703]

8443 Ricchiardi, Sherry. *Bosnia: The Struggle for Peace* (5–8). Illus. 1996, Millbrook LB $25.90 (978-0-7613-0031-1). An account that gives background information but concentrates on the recent (through 1995) history of Bosnia. (Rev: BL 7/96; SLJ 7/96) [949.702]

8444 Rollyson, Carl S. *Teenage Refugees from Eastern Europe Speak Out* (7–12). Series: Teenage Refugees Speak Out. 1997, Rosen LB $27.95 (978-0-8239-2437-0). Young refugees from Slovakia, Bulgaria, Hungary, Romania, Poland, Yugoslavia, and the former East Germany tell about conditions in their homelands and their receptions in the United States. (Rev: BL 12/15/97) [947]

8445 *Romania in Pictures* (5–8). Illus. Series: Visual Geography. 1993, Lerner LB $25.55 (978-0-8225-1894-5). In addition to background material on history and geography, this account gives a good picture of contemporary life in Romania. (Rev: BL 9/1/93) [949.8]

8446 Sioras, Efstathia. *Czech Republic* (7–10). Series: Cultures of the World. 1998, Marshall Cavendish LB $37.07 (978-0-7614-0870-3). An attractive volume that covers the standard topics: geography, history, government, economy, leisure, festivals, and food, and includes full-color photographs, colorful sidebars, maps, charts, and recipes. (Rev: HBG 9/99; SLJ 6/99) [943.7]

8447 Willis, Terri. *Romania* (4–7). Series: Enchantment of the World. 2001, Children's LB $37.00 (978-0-516-21635-5). Packed with photographs, original maps, and browser-friendly sidebars, this is a fine introduction to Romania that explores a number of aspects of the past and present of this country. (Rev: BL 1/1–15/02) [949.8]

France

8448 Barter, James. *The Palace of Versailles* (6–10). Series: Building History. 1998, Lucent LB $27.45 (978-1-56006-433-6). An informative account of the building of the palace for King Louis XIV of France, which took 40 years and represents a pinnacle of opulence and grandeur. (Rev: BL 12/15/98; SLJ 2/99) [944]

8449 Corona, Laurel. *France* (5–8). Series: Modern Nations of the World. 2002, Gale LB $29.95 (978-1-56006-760-3). A comprehensive introduction to the land and people of France with material on history, geography, culture, and lifestyles. (Rev: BL 12/14/02) [944]

8450 Dunford, Mick. *France* (5–8). Illus. Series: Modern Industrial World. 1994, Thomson Learning LB $24.26 (978-1-56847-263-8). An introduction to modern France that gives information about government, people, economic conditions, and recent history. (Rev: BL 1/15/95) [944]

8451 Egendorf, Laura K., ed. *The French Revolution* (7–12). Series: Opposing Viewpoints: World History. 2004, Gale LB $37.45 (978-0-7377-1815-7). Questions about the French Revolution, such as the justification for the many executions, are explored in this collection of different points of view about this turning point in French history. (Rev: BL 2/15/04; SLJ 5/04) [944]

8452 Fisher, Teresa. *France: City and Village Life* (4–7). Illus. Series: Country Insights. 1997, Raintree LB $27.12 (978-0-8172-4788-1). A specific city and village are used to compare and contrast two lifestyles in contemporary France. (Rev: SLJ 8/97) [944]

8453 Gofen, Ethel C. *France* (4–7). Illus. Series: Cultures of the World. 1992, Marshall Cavendish LB $35.64 (978-1-85435-449-5). This account provides information on the history, culture, and people of France and discusses the current problems and concerns. (Rev: BL 10/15/92) [944]

8454 Greene, Meg. *The Eiffel Tower* (7–10). Series: Building History. 2000, Lucent LB $32.45 (978-1-56006-826-6). This account describes the building of this Paris landmark with coverage of the social and technical obstacles that confronted its builders. (Rev: BL 4/15/01; SLJ 6/01) [944]

8455 Hoban, Sarah. *Daily Life in Ancient and Modern Paris* (4–7). Illus. 2000, Runestone LB $25.26 (978-0-8225-3222-4). This well-illustrated history of Paris is divided chronologically into seven sections, beginning with early Paris and working through the Middle Ages to World War II and the Paris of today. (Rev: BL 2/1/01; HBG 3/01; SLJ 2/01) [944]

8456 Ingham, Richard. *France* (4–8). Illus. 2000, Raintree LB $34.26 (978-0-8172-5782-8). A fine introduction to France — its past, its present, and its people — that is particularly noteworthy for its use of graphics. (Rev: BL 10/15/00; HBG 10/00; SLJ 7/00) [944]

8457 Kranz, Nickie. *Teens in France* (7–12). Series: Global Connections. 2006, Compass Point LB $31.93 (978-0-7565-2062-5). Introduces French teens and their schools, family life, hobbies, sports, and so forth, covering both traditional aspects and those that have arrived with new technology and new immigration. (Rev: SLJ 5/07) [305.235]

8458 Plain, Nancy. *Louis XVI, Marie-Antoinette and the French Revolution* (5–8). Series: Rulers and Their Times. 2001, Marshall Cavendish LB $29.93 (978-0-7614-1029-4). In three well-illustrated parts, this book offers a biography of Marie Antoinette, a history of France and its people during the French Revolution, and a generous selection of original documents of the period. (Rev: BL 1/1–15/02; HBG 3/02; SLJ 3/02) [944]

8459 Powell, Jillian. *A History of France Through Art* (5–8). Illus. Series: History Through Art. 1996, Thomson Learning LB $5.00 (978-1-56847-441-0). The basic history of France is covered in 21 double-page spreads, each dealing with an important event or subject and each containing works of art and informative background text. (Rev: BL 3/1/96; SLJ 2/96) [944]

8460 Prosser, Robert. *France* (6–10). Series: Countries of the World. 2003, Facts on File $30.00 (978-0-8160-5380-3). This basic introduction to the land and people of France includes material on economy, culture, and present-day problems. (Rev: BL 1/1–15/04) [944]

8461 Shuter, Jane, ed. *Helen Williams and the French Revolution* (5–8). Illus. Series: History Eyewitness. 1996, Raintree LB $24.26 (978-0-8114-8287-5). An abridged, well-illustrated firsthand account describes the causes and the course of the French Revolution. (Rev: BL 5/15/96; SLJ 6/96) [944.04]

8462 Stacey, Gill. *Paris* (4–7). Illus. 2004, World Almanac LB $31.00 (978-0-8368-5030-7). This attractive introduction to Paris covers the French capital's history and examines some of its modern-day problems. (Rev: BL 4/15/04; SLJ 6/04) [944]

8463 Yuan, Margaret Speaker. *The Arc de Triomphe* (5–8). Series: Building World Landmarks. 2004, Gale LB $24.95 (978-1-4103-0138-3). A concise account of the design and construction of this arch, which met financial, political, and technical difficulties. (Rev: SLJ 4/05)

Germany, Austria, and Switzerland

8464 Barber, Nicola. *Berlin* (4–7). Illus. Series: Great Cities of the World. 2005, World Almanac LB $31.00 (978-0-8368-5043-7). An informative and appealing overview of one of the world's most famous cities, with material on its history, its economy, and what it's like to live there. (Rev: BL 4/15/04)

8465 Bartoletti, Susan Campbell. *Hitler Youth: Growing Up in Hitler's Shadow* (7–10). Illus. 2005, Scholastic $19.95 (978-0-439-35379-3). This chilling look at the Hitler Youth movement, which at its peak boasted a membership of roughly 3.5 million boys and girls, includes excerpts from diaries, letters, oral histories, and the author's interviews with former members and resisters. Newbery Honor Book, 2006. (Rev: BL 4/15/05*; SLJ 6/05; VOYA 8/05) [943.086]

8466 Cartlidge, Cherese, and Charles Clark. *Life of a Nazi Soldier* (6–10). Series: The Way People Live. 2000, Lucent LB $29.95 (978-1-56006-484-8). The living conditions and military requirements of German soldiers during World War II are the primary focus of this volume, which condemns the atrocities that took place while attempting to explain why they were allowed to happen. (Rev: BL 3/1/01; SLJ 7/01) [940.54]

8467 Fuller, Barbara. *Germany* (4–7). Illus. Series: Cultures of the World. 1992, Marshall Cavendish LB $35.64 (978-1-85435-530-0). In addition to the usual information on the history and geography of Germany, this account stresses how the people live and their traditions. (Rev: BL 1/1/93) [943]

8468 *Germany in Pictures* (5–8). Illus. Series: Visual Geography. 1994, Lerner LB $21.27 (978-0-

8225-1873-0). The new united Germany is introduced with a basic text and copious illustrations, including maps, charts, and attractive photographs. (Rev: BL 1/15/95) [943]

8469 Grant, R. G. *The Berlin Wall* (7–12). Series: New Perspectives. 1998, Raintree LB $28.54 (978-0-8172-5017-1). This presentation of various perspectives on the Berlin Wall, its uses, and its destruction in 1989, is also an overview of the Cold War in Europe and the collapse of communism there. (Rev: BL 1/1–15/99; HBG 3/99) [943.1]

8470 Halleck, Elaine, ed. *Living in Nazi Germany* (8–12). Series: Exploring Cultural History. 2004, Gale LB $24.95 (978-0-7377-1732-7). First-person accounts excerpted from other works offer insight into life in Germany under the Nazis, from the point of view of those brutalized and of those who took part in the regime. (Rev: BL 8/04) [943.086]

8471 Levy, Debbie. *The Berlin Wall* (5–8). Series: Building World Landmarks. 2004, Gale LB $24.95 (978-1-4103-0137-6). A concise account of the wall's history and its importance in the struggle between East and West; with a timeline. (Rev: SLJ 4/05)

8472 McGowen, Tom. *Frederick the Great, Bismarck, and the Building of the German Empire in World History* (8–12). Series: In World History. 2002, Enslow LB $26.60 (978-0-7660-1822-8). From Frederick, ruler of Prussia, through the careers of Otto von Bismarck and William I, this is the story of the unification of Germany. (Rev: BL 3/15/03; HBG 3/03; SLJ 12/02) [943]

8473 Nardo, Don, ed. *The Rise of Nazi Germany* (7–12). Series: Turning Points in World History. 1999, Greenhaven LB $32.45 (978-1-56510-965-0); paper $21.20 (978-1-56510-964-3). This anthology of writings examines the emergence of fascism and National Socialism in Germany, the personality of Hitler, his use of propaganda, and his political maneuvering to seize control in 1933. (Rev: BL 6/1–15/99; SLJ 5/99) [943.086]

8474 Netzley, Patricia D. *Switzerland* (5–8). Series: Modern Nations of the World. 2001, Lucent LB $27.45 (978-1-56006-821-1). Interesting sidebars, a chronology, and excellent photographs supplement informative text introducing this small country. (Rev: BL 6/1–15/01) [949.3]

8475 Nickles, Greg, and Niki Walker. *Germany* (4–8). Series: Nations of the World. 2001, Raintree LB $34.26 (978-0-7398-1285-3). A profile of this recently united, highly industrialized, and urbanized country, with material on its past, present, and future. (Rev: BL 6/1–15/01; HBG 10/01) [943]

8476 Rogers, Lura. *Switzerland* (4–7). Series: Enchantment of the World. 2001, Children's LB $37.00 (978-0-516-21080-3). A highly visual introduction to Switzerland that covers such topics as people and languages, history, natural resources, and climate. (Rev: BL 1/1–15/02) [949.4]

8477 Russell, Henry. *Germany* (5–8). Series: Countries of the World. 2007, National Geographic LB $27.90 (978-1-4263-0059-2). Excellent photographs and maps make this an appealing introduction to the country's history, geography, government, economy, people, culture, and nature. (Rev: SLJ 10/07) [943]

8478 Sheehan, Sean. *Austria* (4–7). Illus. Series: Cultures of the World. 1992, Marshall Cavendish LB $35.64 (978-1-85435-454-9). This introduction to Austria covers its history, lifestyles of the people, and contemporary problems. (Rev: BL 10/15/92) [943.6]

8479 Stein, R. Conrad. *Austria* (4–7). Series: Enchantment of the World. 2000, Children's LB $37.00 (978-0-516-21049-0). A thorough introduction to Austria with material on such subjects as history, the land, government, people, culture, cities, and daily life. (Rev: BL 1/1–15/01) [943.6]

8480 *Switzerland in Pictures* (5–8). Series: Visual Geography. 1996, Lerner LB $25.55 (978-0-8225-1895-2). With a generous number of color pictures, this account traces the history and geography of Switzerland, with emphasis on the modern nation and its people. (Rev: BL 9/15/96; SLJ 8/98) [949.4]

Great Britain and Ireland

8481 Allan, Tony. *The Irish Famine: The Birth of Irish America* (4–9). Illus. by Stefan Chabluk. Series: Point of Impact. 2001, Heinemann LB $24.22 (978-1-58810-077-1). Allan traces the causes of the crisis that started in Ireland in 1845, the subsequent wave of emigration to the United States, and the ill feelings created between Britain and Ireland. (Rev: HBG 10/01; SLJ 7/01) [941.5081]

8482 Ashby, Ruth. *Elizabethan England* (5–9). Series: Cultures of the Past. 1998, Benchmark LB $29.93 (978-0-7614-0269-5). Ashby looks at the cultural aspects of Elizabethan England, providing material on the art and literature of the period plus coverage of daily life, religion, and major personalities. (Rev: BL 12/15/98; HBG 10/99; SLJ 2/99) [942]

8483 Ashby, Ruth. *Victorian England* (5–8). Series: Cultures of the Past. 2002, Marshall Cavendish $29.93 (978-0-7614-1493-3). The political, historical, and cultural aspects of life in England during the reign of Victoria are covered in this handsome volume. (Rev: BL 1/1–15/03; HBG 3/03) [942]

8484 Bean, Rachel. *United Kingdom* (4–8). Illus. Series: Countries of the World. 2007, National Geographic LB $27.90 (978-1-4263-0126-1). This attractive volume full of photographs covers the

United Kingdom's geography, history, economy, people, and so forth. (Rev: SLJ 2/08)

8485 Bernard, Catherine. *The British Empire and Queen Victoria in World History* (8–12). Series: In World History. 2002, Enslow LB $26.60 (978-0-7660-1824-2). Combining both biography and history, this account describes Victoria's 63-year reign and how, during it, the British Empire flourished. (Rev: BL 3/15/03; HBG 10/03; SLJ 7/03) [941]

8486 Blashfield, Jean F. *Ireland* (4–7). Series: Enchantment of the World. 2002, Children's LB $37.00 (978-0-516-21127-5). Using many visual aids and a lively text, this is an introduction to Ireland — the land, the people, and the culture. (Rev: BL 5/15/02; SLJ 12/02) [941.5]

8487 Bowden, Rob. *United Kingdom* (6–10). Series: Countries of the World. 2003, Facts on File $30.00 (978-0-8160-5383-4). An attractive volume that presents basic material about Great Britain including history, geography, and present social conditions. (Rev: BL 1/1–15/04) [941]

8488 Buscher, Sarah, and Bettina Ling. *Mairead Corrigan and Betty Williams: Making Peace in Northern Ireland* (5–8). Illus. 1999, Feminist $19.95 (978-1-55861-200-6); paper $9.95 (978-1-55861-201-3). The story of the two women in Northern Ireland who won the Nobel Peace Prize for their efforts to help end the civil strife in their country. (Rev: BL 3/15/00; SLJ 2/00; VOYA 4/00) [941]

8489 Childress, Diana. *Chaucer's England* (7–12). Illus. 2000, Linnet LB $25.00 (978-0-208-02489-3). A fascinating glimpse into the social life, community structure, landscape, and economy of 14th-century England. (Rev: BL 9/15/00; HBG 10/01; SLJ 10/00; VOYA 4/01) [942.03]

8490 Corona, Laurel. *Scotland* (5–8). Series: Modern Nations of the World. 2000, Lucent LB $29.95 (978-1-56006-703-0). The history, geography, and culture of Scotland are discussed along with material on daily life in modern Scotland. (Rev: BL 3/1/01) [941]

8491 Davis, Kenneth C. *Don't Know Much About the Kings and Queens of England* (4–7). Illus. by S. D. Schindler. Series: Don't Know Much About. 2002, HarperCollins LB $15.89 (978-0-06-028612-5). Humorous questions and answers supply information that browsers will enjoy. (Rev: HBG 10/02; SLJ 7/02) [941.0099]

8492 Dolan, Edward F. *The Irish Potato Famine: The Story of Irish-American Immigration* (6–9). Series: Great Journeys. 2002, Marshall Cavendish LB $32.79 (978-0-7614-1323-3). The story of the terrible Irish famine that lasted from 1845 through 1851 and caused a mass exodus, particularly to America. (Rev: BL 3/15/03; HBG 3/03) [941.7]

8493 Elgin, Kathy. *Elizabethan England, Vol. 3* (5–8). Illus. Series: A History of Fashion and Costume. 2005, Facts on File $35.00 (978-0-8160-5946-1). A broad overview of the clothing and personal adornment worn during this time period, with many visual aids. (Rev: SLJ 5/06) [391]

8494 Flint, David. *Great Britain* (5–8). Illus. Series: Modern Industrial World. 1996, Raintree LB $24.26 (978-0-8172-4555-9). Modern Great Britain is the focus of this volume, which concentrates on the economy and industrial development. (Rev: BL 2/15/96; SLJ 8/97) [330.941]

8495 Gallagher, Carole. *The Irish Potato Famine* (6–8). Series: Great Disasters. 2001, Chelsea LB $30.00 (978-0-7910-5788-9). The horrors of the terrible blight that destroyed the potato crops of Ireland from 1845 to 1849 are re-created, with discussion of the monumental changes that followed. (Rev: BL 6/1–15/02; HBG 10/02) [941.7]

8496 Gottfried, Ted. *Northern Ireland: Peace in Our Time?* (5–8). Series: Headliners. 2002, Millbrook LB $25.90 (978-0-7613-2252-8). This attractive book gives current and background information on the struggles within Northern Ireland and the causes and possible solutions. (Rev: BL 4/15/02; HBG 10/02; SLJ 3/02) [941]

8497 Greenblatt, Miriam. *Elizabeth I and Tudor England* (5–8). Series: Rulers and Their Times. 2001, Marshall Cavendish LB $29.93 (978-0-7614-1028-7). After a biography of Elizabeth I, this colorful account traces everyday life in Elizabethan times and supplies a selection of primary documents. (Rev: BL 1/1–15/02; HBG 3/02; SLJ 3/02) [942.1]

8498 Hamilton, Janice. *The Norman Conquest of England* (7–9). Series: Pivotal Moments in History. 2007, Twenty-First Century LB $38.60 (978-0-8225-5902-3). An attractive and interesting account of the Norman invasion of 1066 with maps, photographs, and reproductions of manuscripts. (Rev: SLJ 1/08)

8499 Hestler, Anna. *Wales* (5–9). Illus. Series: Cultures of the World. 2001, Marshall Cavendish LB $37.07 (978-0-7614-1195-6). Geography, history, government, arts and culture, and lifestyle are all covered in this interesting and attractive volume. (Rev: HBG 10/01; SLJ 11/01) [942.9]

8500 Hinds, Kathryn. *The Church* (6–8). Series: Life in Elizabethan England. 2007, Marshall Cavendish LB $22.95 (978-0-7614-2545-8). This visually appealing volume discusses the church during the Elizabethan era. (Rev: SLJ 3/08; VOYA 4/08)

8501 Hynson, Colin. *Elizabeth I and the Spanish Armada* (5–8). Illus. Series: Stories from History. 2006, School Specialty $9.95 (978-0-7696-4703-6); paper $6.95 (978-0-7696-4629-9). A graphic novel presentation of the confrontation between England's

Queen Elizabeth I and the Spanish empire, climaxing in the defeat of the Spanish Armada by the English; full-color depictions of battles, fast facts, and maps aid comprehension. (Rev: BL 10/15/06; SLJ 1/07) [942.05]

8502 Innes, Brian. *United Kingdom* (4–8). Series: Nations of the World. 2001, Raintree LB $34.26 (978-0-7398-1288-4). An in-depth look at the nation's geography, climate. terrain, history, government, and lifestyles. (Rev: BL 12/15/01) [941]

8503 *Ireland in Pictures* (5–8). Illus. Series: Visual Geography. 1997, Lerner LB $25.55 (978-0-8225-1878-5). Contemporary Ireland is highlighted in this illustrated account. (Rev: BL 12/1/90) [941.5]

8504 Jocelyn, Marthe. *A Home for Foundlings* (7–10). Series: Lord Museum. 2005, Tundra paper $15.95 (978-0-88776-709-8). A fascinating history of London's Foundling Hospital, which was opened in the 18th century to provide a home for babies whose mothers were unable to care for them and did not close until 1953. (Rev: BL 3/1/05; SLJ 6/05) [362.7]

8505 Lace, William W. *The British Empire* (6–12). Illus. Series: History's Great Defeats. 2000, Lucent LB $27.45 (978-1-56006-683-5). Subtitled "The End of Colonialism," this account traces the rise and growth of the British Empire, its accomplishments and failures, and its decline and fall. (Rev: BL 11/1/00; HBG 3/01; SLJ 10/00) [909]

8506 Lace, William W. *Elizabeth I and Her Court* (6–10). Series: Lucent Library of Historical Eras: Elizabethan England. 2002, Gale LB $28.70 (978-1-59018-098-3). A well-written account of life at court during Elizabeth I's reign, with black-and-white reproductions and photographs. Also recommended in this series are *Life in Elizabethan London* and *Primary Sources* (both 2002). (Rev: LMC 11–12/03; SLJ 9/03)

8507 Lace, William W. *Oliver Cromwell and the English Civil War in World History* (8–12). Series: In World History. 2002, Enslow LB $26.60 (978-0-7660-1937-9). The story of the English Civil War leader who defeated both Charles I and Charles II and became, for a time, Lord Protector of England. (Rev: BL 3/15/03; HBG 10/03; VOYA 8/03) [941]

8508 Levy, Debbie. *The Signing of the Magna Carta* (7–9). Series: Pivotal Moments in History. 2007, Twenty-First Century LB $38.60 (978-0-8225-5917-7). An attractive and interesting account of the creation and signing of this important document with maps, photographs, and reproductions of manuscripts. (Rev: SLJ 1/08)

8509 Levy, Patricia. *Ireland* (4–7). Illus. Series: Cultures of the World. 1993, Marshall Cavendish LB $25.95 (978-1-85435-580-5). An account that traces the role of women in Irish history to the present day. (Rev: SLJ 2/94) [941]

8510 Lyons, Mary E., ed. *Feed the Children First: Irish Memories of the Great Hunger* (4–8). Illus. 2002, Simon & Schuster $17.00 (978-0-689-84226-9). Text, full-color reproductions, and occasional photographs clearly document the suffering of ordinary people during the Irish potato famine. (Rev: BL 12/15/01; HB 3–4/02; HBG 10/02; SLJ 3/02*) [941.5081]

8511 Mitchell, Graham. *The Napoleonic Wars* (5–9). Illus. 1990, Batsford $19.95 (978-0-7134-5729-2). This British import tells about the war chiefly from the British point of view and uses many quotations from original sources. (Rev: SLJ 3/90) [944.05]

8512 *Northern Ireland in Pictures* (5–8). Series: Visual Geography. 1991, Lerner LB $25.55 (978-0-8225-1898-3). This beautiful but troubled land is introduced in text and pictures. (Rev: BL 2/15/92) [941.6]

8513 Ross, Stewart. *Elizabethan Life* (6–9). Series: How It Was. 1991, Batsford $19.95 (978-0-7134-6356-9). Laws, journals, and other historical sources from the period help re-create a vivid picture of Elizabethan life. (Rev: BL 1/15/92) [941]

8514 Sancha, Sheila. *The Luttrell Village: Country Life in the Middle Ages* (7–10). Illus. 1983, HarperCollins LB $13.89 (978-0-690-04324-2). Life and activities in an English village of 1328 are revealed in words and excellent drawings by the author. [942.03]

8515 Shields, Charles J. *The Great Plague and Fire of London* (6–8). Series: Great Disasters. 2001, Chelsea LB $21.95 (978-0-7910-6324-8). This is the story of the plague that ravished England in 1665 and of the fire the following year that nearly destroyed the entire city of London. (Rev: BL 6/1–15/02; SLJ 6/02) [941]

8516 Stacey, Gill. *London* (4–8). Series: Great Cities of the World. 2003, World Almanac LB $31.00 (978-0-8368-5022-2). In an appealing blend of text, photographs, quotations, and sidebar features, this volume introduces readers to some of London's history and attractions. (Rev: SLJ 1/04) [942.1]

8517 Stein, R. Conrad. *Scotland* (4–7). Series: Enchantment of the World. 2001, Children's LB $37.00 (978-0-516-21112-1). Numerous pictures, charts, maps, and drawings contribute to a fascinating portrait of Scotland's past and present. (Rev: BL 1/1–15/02) [931]

8518 Swisher, Clarice. *Victorian England* (7–10). Series: World History. 2000, Lucent LB $32.45 (978-1-56006-323-0). Quotations and period reproductions enhance this interesting survey of the long and eventful reign of Queen Victoria, a time of technological and social innovation and of growing

power for Great Britain. (Rev: BL 12/15/00; SLJ 3/01) [942]

8519 Toht, Betony, and David Toht. *Daily Life in Ancient and Modern London* (6–9). Series: Cities Through Time. 2001, Lerner LB $25.26 (978-0-8225-3223-1). London's evolution from earliest times to today is presented in double-page spreads, with information on political, social, and religious life. (Rev: BL 4/15/01; HBG 10/01; SLJ 7/01) [942]

8520 *Wales in Pictures* (5–8). Illus. 1994, Lerner LB $25.55 (978-0-8225-1877-8). Wales is introduced and material is given on history and current conditions. (Rev: BL 12/1/90) [942.9]

8521 Yancey, Diane. *Life in Charles Dickens's England* (6–10). Series: The Way People Live. 1998, Lucent LB $27.45 (978-1-56006-098-7). From terrible squalor and grinding poverty to great wealth and comfort, the spectrum of British society, rural and urban, is explored during the days of Charles Dickens. (Rev: BL 10/15/98; SLJ 1/99; VOYA 12/99) [942]

Greece

8522 Dubois, Jill, and Xenia Skoura. *Greece*. 2nd ed. (5–8). Illus. Series: Cultures of the World. 2003, Benchmark LB $37.07 (978-0-7614-1499-5). In addition to coverage of the geography, history, and economics of Greece, this volume looks at the people and the culture of this Mediterranean nation and provides recipes. (Rev: HBG 10/03; SLJ 8/03) [949.5]

8523 *Greece in Pictures* (5–8). Illus. Series: Visual Geography. 1996, Lerner LB $25.55 (978-0-8225-1882-2). Photographs, maps, charts, and concise text introduce the land and people of Greece. (Rev: BL 10/1/92) [949.5]

8524 Heinrichs, Ann. *Greece* (4–7). Series: Enchantment of the World. 2002, Children's LB $37.00 (978-0-516-22271-4). With many color illustrations, this book gives a fascinating portrait of Greece's past and present with coverage of topics including natural resources, culture, climate, and religion. (Rev: BL 9/15/02; SLJ 12/02) [949.5]

8525 Kotapish, Dawn. *Daily Life in Ancient and Modern Athens* (5–8). Illus. by Bob Moulder. Series: Cities Through Time. 2000, Runestone LB $25.26 (978-0-8225-3216-3). Kotapish explores everyday life, government, and culture in Athens through the ages. (Rev: HBG 3/01; SLJ 5/01) [949.5]

8526 Nardo, Don. *Greece* (5–8). Series: Modern Nations of the World. 2000, Lucent LB $27.45 (978-1-56006-587-6). Although there is coverage of ancient Greece, this account stresses modern history, the people today, and current living conditions and problems. (Rev: BL 2/15/00; HBG 10/00; SLJ 6/00) [949.5]

Italy

8527 Barber, Nicola. *Rome* (4–7). Illus. Series: Great Cities of the World. 2005, World Almanac LB $31.00 (978-0-8368-5040-6). An informative and appealing overview of one of the world's most famous cities, with material on its history, its economy, and what it's like to live there. (Rev: BL 4/15/04)

8528 Behnke, Alison. *Italy in Pictures*. Rev. ed. (4–8). Illus. Series: Visual Geography. 2002, Lerner LB $27.93 (978-0-8225-0368-2). An excellent introduction to Italy that includes material on geography, history, people, economy, and culture with maps, photographs, and illustrations. (Rev: HBG 3/03; SLJ 3/03) [914.5]

8529 Cassidy, Picot. *Italy* (4–8). Series: Nations of the World. 2001, Raintree LB $34.26 (978-0-7398-1287-7). A fine overall picture of Italy, its past, its land, its people, its culture, and present-day problems. (Rev: BL 12/15/01; HBG 3/02) [945]

8530 Hinds, Kathryn. *Venice and Its Merchant Empire* (5–8). Illus. Series: Cultures of the Past. 2001, Marshall Cavendish LB $29.93 (978-0-7614-0305-0). A well-illustrated overview of the history of Venice with a focus on the city's glory during the Renaissance. (Rev: BL 2/15/02; HBG 3/02) [945]

8531 Macaulay, David. *Rome Antics* (5–8). Illus. 1997, Houghton $18.00 (978-0-395-82279-1). The reader gets a pigeon-eye view of vistas and buildings as the bird flies over Rome. (Rev: BL 9/15/97; SLJ 11/97*) [945]

8532 Martin, Fred. *Italy* (5–8). Series: Country Studies. 1999, Heinemann LB $27.07 (978-1-57572-894-0). Using double-page spreads filled with charts, graphs, drawings, maps, and photographs, this book provides basic material about Italy with a focus on contemporary issues. (Rev: BL 8/99; SLJ 8/99) [945]

8533 Nardo, Don. *Roman Roads and Aqueducts* (7–10). Series: Building History. 2000, Lucent LB $28.70 (978-1-56006-721-4). This look at the highways, roads, and aqueducts of the ancient Roman Empire combines history and scientific and technological principles. (Rev: BL 4/15/01; SLJ 3/01) [930]

8534 Parker, Vic. *Pompeii AD 79: A City Buried by a Volcanic Eruption* (4–7). Series: When Disaster Struck. 2006, Raintree LB $32.86 (978-1-4109-2276-2). Parker looks at Pompeii both before and after its destruction by the eruption of Mount Vesuvius, discussing the nature (and likelihood) of volcanic eruptions and what archaeologists have

learned from their excavations. (Rev: SLJ 1/07) [937.7]

8535 Winter, Jane K. *Italy* (5–8). Illus. Series: Cultures of the World. 1992, Marshall Cavendish LB $35.64 (978-1-85435-453-2). Gives geographic and historical information about Italy and tells about its people and their concerns. (Rev: BL 10/15/92) [945]

The Netherlands and Belgium

8536 Burgan, Michael. *Belgium* (4–7). Series: Enchantment of the World. 2000, Children's LB $37.00 (978-0-516-21006-3). This new edition of a standard title contains up-to-date material on such topics as geography and climate, plants and animals, people and culture, the arts, and sports. (Rev: BL 7/00) [949.3]

8537 Hintz, Martin. *The Netherlands* (4–7). Series: Enchantment of the World. 1999, Children's LB $36.00 (978-0-516-21053-7). An up-to-date, well-illustrated, and comprehensive introduction to the Netherlands. (Rev: BL 12/15/99) [949.2]

8538 Pateman, Robert. *Belgium* (4–7). Illus. Series: Cultures of the World. 1995, Marshall Cavendish LB $37.07 (978-0-7614-0176-6). After a brief introduction to the history and geography of Belgium, this book focuses on the populace, how they live, and their major contributions to the world. (Rev: BL 1/1–15/96; SLJ 9/96) [949.3]

8539 Sheehan, Patricia. *Luxembourg* (4–7). Illus. Series: Cultures of the World. 1997, Marshall Cavendish LB $37.07 (978-0-7614-0685-3). Includes information on this tiny European country's history, culture, and lifestyles. (Rev: BL 8/97) [914.935]

Russia and Other Former Soviet Republics

8540 Aizpuriete, Amanda. *Latvia* (5–8). Trans. by Katarina Hartgers. Photos by Jan Willem Bultje. Series: Looking at Europe. 2006, Oliver $22.95 (978-1-881508-37-3). This colorful volume with excellent photographs introduces readers to Latvia's geography, history, people, culture, economy, and lifestyle. (Rev: LMC 4/07; SLJ 1/07) [947.96]

8541 *Armenia* (5–8). Series: Then and Now. 1992, Lerner LB $23.93 (978-0-8225-2806-7). The story up to 1991 of the former Soviet republic that faced many internal problems after it gained independence. (Rev: BL 2/1/93; SLJ 3/93) [956.6]

8542 *Azerbaijan* (5–8). Series: Then and Now. 1993, Lerner LB $23.93 (978-0-8225-2810-4). This book introduces the small republic of Azerbaijan, once the Soviet Union's most important oil producing area. (Rev: BL 2/15/93) [947]

8543 Bassis, Volodymyr. *Ukraine* (4–7). Illus. Series: Cultures of the World. 1997, Marshall

Cavendish LB $37.07 (978-0-7614-0684-6). An introduction to this former Soviet state, with emphasis on current history and culture. (Rev: BL 8/97; SLJ 10/97) [947.7]

8544 Batalden, Stephen K., and Sandra L. Batalden. *The Newly Independent States of Eurasia: Handbook of Former Soviet Republics.* 2nd ed. (7–12). 1997, Oryx paper $59.95 (978-0-89774-940-4). Arranged by geographical region, this volume examines each of the newly formed republics created from the former USSR, with details on their past, their culture, and key problems facing each today. (Rev: SLJ 11/97) [947]

8545 *Belarus* (5–8). Series: Then and Now. 1993, Lerner LB $23.93 (978-0-8225-2811-1). An introduction to the history and status as of 1993 of the former Soviet republic of Belarus, which borders on Ukraine. (Rev: BL 5/15/93) [947]

8546 Bultje, Jan Willem. *Lithuania* (5–8). Trans. by Wilma Hoving. Photos by author. Series: Looking at Europe. 2006, Oliver $22.95 (978-1-881508-43-4). This colorful volume with excellent photographs introduces readers to Lithuania's geography, history, people, culture, economy, and lifestyle. (Rev: SLJ 1/07) [947.93]

8547 Carrion, Esther. *The Empire of the Czars* (4–7). Illus. Series: World Heritage. 1994, Children's LB $15.00 (978-0-516-08319-3). An overview of Russian history from early times to the breakup of the Soviet Union, with special material on Russia's famous sights, such as Red Square, the Kremlin, and St. Petersburg. (Rev: SLJ 5/95) [947.07]

8548 Cartlidge, Cherese. *The Central Asian States* (6–12). Illus. Series: Modern Nations of the World: Former Soviet Republics. 2001, Lucent LB $29.95 (978-1-56006-735-1). This well-illustrated introduction to the former Soviet republics of Kazakhstan, Turkmenistan, Uzbekistan, Kyrgyzstan, and Tajikistan presents material on physical features, people, culture, economy, history, and efforts to enter the global market. (Rev: BL 8/01; SLJ 9/01) [958]

8549 Corona, Laurel. *Life in Moscow* (6–10). Series: The Way People Live. 2000, Lucent LB $28.70 (978-1-56006-795-5). After background historical information, this account introduces modern Moscow and the daily lives of its citizens. (Rev: BL 3/1/01; SLJ 3/01) [947]

8550 Corona, Laurel. *The Russian Federation* (6–12). Illus. Series: Former Soviet Republics. 2001, Lucent LB $29.95 (978-1-56006-675-0). Corona introduces readers to the dramatic changes that took place in Russia during the 20th century and looks at the economic and political challenges facing the country today. (Rev: BL 7/01; SLJ 9/01) [958]

8551 Corona, Laurel. *Ukraine* (5–8). Series: Modern Nations of the World. 2001, Lucent LB $29.95

(978-1-56006-737-5). This well-illustrated introduction to the former Soviet republic presents material on the people, culture, economy, history, and physical features. (Rev: BL 6/1–15/01) [947]

8552 Corrigan, Jim. *Kazakhstan* (8–12). Series: The Growth and Influence of Islam in the Nations of Asia and Central Asia. 2005, Mason Crest LB $25.95 (978-1-59084-882-1). A well-illustrated look at Kazakhstan and the importance of Islam in the country's history, politics, economy, and foreign relations. (Rev: SLJ 9/05) [958]

8553 Cumming, David. *Russia* (5–8). Illus. Series: Modern Industrial World. 1994, Thomson Learning LB $24.26 (978-1-56847-240-9). An introduction to Russia that stresses the economic upheaval caused by the breakup of the USSR. (Rev: BL 1/15/95; SLJ 3/95) [947]

8554 Dhilawala, Sakina. *Armenia* (4–7). Illus. Series: Cultures of the World. 1997, Marshall Cavendish LB $37.07 (978-0-7614-0683-9). An introduction to this troubled land that describes how its people live, their lifestyles, and culture. (Rev: BL 8/97; HBG 3/98) [945.56]

8555 *Estonia* (5–8). 1992, Lerner LB $23.93 (978-0-8225-2803-6). Following an introduction about the fall of communism, the book provides an overview of the land and its peoples. (Rev: BL 2/1/93; SLJ 12/92) [914.7]

8556 *Georgia* (5–8). Illus. Series: Then and Now. 1994, Lerner LB $23.93 (978-0-8225-2807-4). This former Soviet republic is introduced, with information on its geography, ethnic makeup, history, economy, and future challenges. (Rev: BL 2/1/94; SLJ 3/94) [947]

8557 Gottfried, Ted. *The Road to Communism* (8–12). Illus. by Melanie Reim. 2002, Millbrook LB $28.90 (978-0-7613-2557-4). This first volume on the rise and fall of the Soviet Union traces in depth the developments that led to the establishment of a communist state. The second volume is titled *Stalinist Empire*. (Rev: BL 10/15/02; HBG 3/03; SLJ 11/02) [957]

8558 Harbor, Bernard. *The Breakup of the Soviet Union* (6–12). Series: Conflicts. 1993, Macmillan LB $22.00 (978-0-02-742625-0). An overview of the conflicts and changes in the region. (Rev: BL 7/93; SLJ 12/93) [947.08]

8559 Harmon, Daniel E. *Kyrgyzstan* (8–12). Illus. Series: The Growth and Influence of Islam in the Nations of Asia and Central Asia. 2005, Mason Crest LB $25.95 (978-1-59084-883-8). A well-illustrated look at Kyrgyzstan and the importance of Islam in the country's history, politics, economy, and foreign relations. (Rev: SLJ 9/05)

8560 Israel, Fred L., and Arthur M. Schlesinger, Jr., eds. *Moscow* (6–10). Illus. Series: The World 100

Years Ago. 1999, Chelsea $29.95 (978-0-7910-4658-6). This book describes what Burton Holmes, a traveler-lecturer during the first half of the 20th century, saw when he visited Moscow around the beginning of the century, including a trip to the Kremlin, a visit to the public baths, and a breakfast with Leo Tolstoy. (Rev: SLJ 7/98) [947]

8561 Kagda, Sakina. *Lithuania* (4–7). Illus. Series: Cultures of the World. 1997, Marshall Cavendish LB $37.07 (978-0-7614-0681-5). An introduction to Lithuania, with material on geography, history, government, culture, daily life, and festivals. (Rev: BL 8/97; SLJ 10/97) [947.93]

8562 *Kazakhstan* (5–8). Series: Then and Now. 1993, Lerner LB $23.93 (978-0-8225-2815-9). An introduction to the second-largest republic in the former USSR, with information on its status as of 1993. (Rev: BL 9/1/93; SLJ 9/93) [958]

8563 Kollár, Daniel. *Slovakia* (4–7). Series: Looking at Europe. 2006, Oliver $22.95 (978-1-881508-49-6). This photo-filled introduction to Slovakia explores its geography, history, people, culture, cuisine, economy, transportation, tourism, and natural resources. (Rev: SLJ 12/06) [943.73]

8564 Kort, Michael G. *The Handbook of the Former Soviet Union* (7–12). Illus. 1997, Millbrook LB $39.90 (978-0-7613-0016-8). An expert in Russian history gives an overview of the former Soviet Union, the problems each state faces today and the important personalities involved. (Rev: BL 2/1/98; SLJ 1/98; VOYA 6/98) [947]

8565 Kort, Michael G. *Russia*. Rev. ed. (7–12). Series: Nations in Transition. 1998, Facts on File $25.00 (978-0-8160-3776-6). This book explains the rapid changes in Russia's economy, politics, social conditions, and daily life in recent years and reviews the country's complex history and importance today. (Rev: BL 3/15/99; SLJ 4/99) [947.085]

8566 Kummer, Patricia K. *Ukraine* (4–7). Series: Enchantment of the World. 2001, Children's LB $37.00 (978-0-516-21101-5). A fine introduction to the past and present of the Ukraine with well-chosen illustrations and material on such topics as resources, daily life, landmarks, languages, and economy. (Rev: BL 1/1–15/02; SLJ 12/01) [947.7]

8567 *Lithuania* (5–8). Series: Then and Now. 1992, Lerner LB $23.93 (978-0-8225-2804-3). This Baltic Sea republic is described, including its history, people, and conditions in the period immediately following its independence in 1990. (Rev: BL 2/1/93) [947]

8568 Lugovskaya, Nina. *I Want to Live: The Diary of a Young Girl in Stalin's Russia* (8–11). Trans. by Andrew Bromfeld. 2007, Houghton $17.00 (978-0-618-60575-0). This diary of a teenage girl living in a Soviet gulag is remarkable for its passages (in bold type) that were censored by police who seized it, and also for the fact that its author survived. (Rev: BL 4/15/07; SLJ 8/07) [946.0842]

8569 Lustig, Michael M. *Ukraine* (7–12). Series: Nations in Transition. 1999, Facts on File $35.00 (978-0-8160-3757-5). A slim volume that traces the history of Ukraine and its people, with emphasis on today — its faltering economy, corruption in government, Crimean independence, and other problems. (Rev: BL 4/15/99; SLJ 6/99) [947.7]

8570 McCray, Thomas. *Russia and the Former Soviet Republics* (7–10). 2006, Chelsea House LB $30.00 (978-0-7910-8144-0). Examines many aspects of Russia including its geography, economy, history, politics, people, and culture with additional information on some of the surrounding countries that also belonged to the former Soviet Union. (Rev: BL 9/1/06; SLJ 9/06) [947]

8571 *Moldova* (5–8). Series: Then and Now. 1992, Lerner LB $23.93 (978-0-8225-2809-8). The history of this small, landlocked republic, parts of which at one time or another have belonged to the Ottoman Turks, Romania, Russia, and the USSR, and which is now independent. (Rev: BL 2/1/93; SLJ 3/93) [947]

8572 Otfinoski, Steven. *The Baltic Republics* (7–10). Series: Nations in Transition. 2004, Facts on File LB $40.00 (978-0-8160-5117-5). Introduces the Baltic republics of Estonia, Latvia, and Lithuania, and the geography, history, people, culture, religious beliefs, and economy of each. (Rev: SLJ 1/05) [947]

8573 Pavlenkov, Victor, and Peter Pappas, eds. *Russia: Yesterday, Today, Tomorrow: Voice of the Young Generation* (8–12). Illus. 1997, FC-Izdat paper $12.95 (978-0-9637035-5-2). This is a collection of essays written by Russian high school students who reflect on the past, present, and future of their country. (Rev: BL 2/15/97) [947.08]

8574 Robbins, Gerald. *Azerbaijan* (8–12). Series: The Growth and Influence of Islam in the Nations of Asia and Central Asia. 2005, Mason Crest LB $25.95 (978-1-59084-878-4). A well-illustrated look at Azerbaijan and the importance of Islam in the country's history, politics, economy, and foreign relations. (Rev: SLJ 9/05) [947]

8575 Rogers, Stillman D. *Russia* (4–7). Series: Enchantment of the World. 2002, Children's LB $37.00 (978-0-516-22494-7). This portrait of Russia in text and illustrations covers such basic subjects as history, resources, geography, people, problems, economy, and culture. (Rev: BL 9/15/02; SLJ 10/02) [947]

8576 *Russia* (5–8). Series: Then and Now. 1992, Lerner LB $23.93 (978-0-8225-2805-0). A brief history of Russia with emphasis on its status in the period immediately following the fall of the USSR in 1991. (Rev: BL 2/1/93; SLJ 12/92) [947]

8577 Sallnow, John, and Tatyana Saiko. *Russia* (5–8). Series: Country Fact Files. 1997, Raintree LB $27.12 (978-0-8172-4625-9). The impact of geography on different aspects of life in Russia, including natural resources, daily life, the landscape, and transportation, is explored. (Rev: SLJ 8/97) [947]

8578 Schemann, Serge. *When the Wall Came Down* (6–9). Illus. 2006, Kingfisher $15.95 (978-0-7534-5994-2). Primary sources, personal insights, and edited *New York Times* columns make this a useful account of the fall of the Berlin Wall and its impact on the whole Eastern Bloc. (Rev: BL 2/15/06; SLJ 7/06) [943]

8579 Sheehan, Patricia. *Moldova* (5–9). Series: Cultures of the World. 2000, Marshall Cavendish LB $37.07 (978-0-7614-0997-7). This book on the former Soviet republic that borders on the Ukraine covers such topics as culture, land, people, history, resources, and government. (Rev: HBG 10/00; SLJ 11/00) [947]

8580 Spilling, Michael. *Estonia* (7–10). Series: Cultures of the World. 1999, Marshall Cavendish LB $37.07 (978-0-7614-0951-9). An overview of this Baltic land that covers basic information and contemporary life and culture. (Rev: HBG 9/99; SLJ 7/99) [947]

8581 Spilling, Michael. *Georgia* (6–10). Series: Cultures of the World. 1997, Marshall Cavendish LB $37.07 (978-0-7614-0691-4). A detailed introduction to the former Soviet republic of Georgia, its geography, history, government, and culture. (Rev: HBG 3/98; SLJ 2/98) [947]

8582 Streissguth, Thomas. *Life in Communist Russia* (6–10). Series: The Way People Live. 2001, Lucent LB $29.95 (978-1-56006-378-0). From the 1917 revolution through the collapse of the regime in the 1980s, the history of Communist Russia is told with emphasis on social and economic conditions and everyday life. (Rev: BL 6/1–15/01; SLJ 7/01) [947]

8583 Streissguth, Thomas, ed. *The Rise of the Soviet Union* (7–12). Series: Turning Points in World History. 2002, Gale LB $24.95 (978-0-7377-0928-5). Following an overview of Russian and Soviet history, each of the essays in this anthology explores a different aspect of the rise of Communism and the creation of the Soviet Union. (Rev: BL 6/1–15/02; SLJ 6/02) [947]

8584 *Tajikistan* (5–8). Illus. Series: Then and Now. 1993, Lerner LB $23.93 (978-0-8225-2816-6). An introduction to the land and people of this remote former Soviet republic located north of Afghanistan. (Rev: BL 10/15/93; SLJ 11/93) [958.6]

8585 Taylor, Peter Lane, and Christos Nicola. *The Secret of Priest's Grotto* (7–10). Illus. 2007, KarBen $18.95 (978-1-58013-260-2); paper $8.95 (978-1-58013-261-9). The true story of how 38 members

of three Ukrainian Jewish families survived nearly a year hiding from the Nazis in a cave; photographs add impact. (Rev: BL 3/1/07; HB 7–8/07; LMC 10/07; SLJ 4/07) [940.53]

8586 *Ukraine* (5–8). Series: Then and Now. 1992, Lerner LB $23.93 (978-0-8225-2808-1). The history of this Black Sea republic and its status in the period immediately following its independence in 1991. (Rev: BCCB 3/93; BL 2/1/93; SLJ 3/93) [947]

8587 *Uzbekistan* (5–8). Series: Then and Now. 1993, Lerner LB $23.93 (978-0-8225-2812-8). A history of this Muslim republic, its economic situation, and prospects for the future as of 1993. (Rev: BL 5/15/93) [958.7]

8588 Vail, John. *"Peace, Land, Bread?": A History of the Russian Revolution* (7–12). Illus. Series: World History Library. 1996, Facts on File $25.00 (978-0-8160-2818-4). This volume, illustrated with photographs and maps, covers the period in Russian history from the revolt against the czar to the rise of Joseph Stalin. (Rev: BL 2/15/96; SLJ 2/96; VOYA 4/96) [947.084]

8589 Veceric, Danica. *Slovenia* (4–7). Series: Looking at Europe. 2006, Oliver $22.95 (978-1-881508-74-8). A tour of Slovenia, examining the country's geography, history, people, culture, cuisine, economy, transportation, tourism, and natural resources. (Rev: SLJ 12/06) [949.73]

8590 Wilson, Neil. *Russia* (4–8). Series: Nations of the World. 2001, Raintree LB $34.26 (978-0-7398-1281-5). Colorful photographs, charts, and maps enrich chapters on Russia's past and present, land and cities, economy, art and culture, and possible future developments. (Rev: BL 6/1–15/01; HBG 10/01) [947]

Scandinavia, Iceland, and Greenland

8591 Berger, Melvin, and Gilda Berger. *The Real Vikings: Craftsmen, Traders, and Fearsome Raiders* (4–8). Illus. 2003, National Geographic $18.95 (978-0-7922-5132-3). A highly illustrated introduction to the Vikings and their world, with information on their political and social ideals — including democracy — as well as their more fearsome and acquisitive traits. (Rev: BL 12/1/03; HBG 4/04; SLJ 1/04) [948]

8592 Blashfield, Jean F. *Norway* (4–7). Series: Enchantment of the World. 2000, Children's LB $37.00 (978-0-516-20651-6). An introduction to Norway that covers such subjects as geography and climate, history and government, mythology and culture, and people and economy. (Rev: BL 7/00) [948.1]

8593 Butler, Robbie. *Sweden* (4–8). Series: Nations of the World. 2001, Raintree LB $34.26 (978-0-8172-5784-2). Colorful maps, charts and graphs, and photographs supplement the text in this fine profile of Sweden. (Rev: BL 6/1–15/01; HBG 10/01) [948.5]

8594 Carlsson, Bo Kage. *Sweden* (5–8). Series: Modern Industrial World. 1995, Thomson Learning LB $24.26 (978-1-56847-436-6). A survey of modern Sweden and its industries, economy, resources, and people. (Rev: BL 12/15/95) [949.4]

8595 Casanova, Mary. *The Klipfish Code* (4–7). 2007, Houghton $16.00 (978-0-618-88393-6). Marit and her brother Lars struggle under the restrictions of Nazi-occupied Norway in this action- and suspense-filled novel. (Rev: BL 10/15/07; SLJ 10/07)

8596 Corona, Laurel. *Norway* (5–8). Series: Modern Nations of the World. 2000, Lucent LB $29.95 (978-1-56006-647-7). Norway is introduced with coverage of history, geography, and culture plus material on everyday modern life. (Rev: BL 3/1/01) [948.1]

8597 *Denmark in Pictures* (5–8). Illus. Series: Visual Geography. 1997, Lerner LB $25.55 (978-0-8225-1880-8). In photographs, maps, charts, and concise text, the land of Denmark and its people are introduced. (Rev: BL 4/1/91; SLJ 7/91) [948]

8598 DuTemple, Lesley A. *Sweden* (5–8). Series: Modern Nations of the World. 2000, Lucent LB $28.70 (978-1-56006-588-3). A general introduction to Sweden that includes its history and geography but stresses today's living conditions and the people's lifestyles. (Rev: BL 3/15/00; HBG 10/00) [948.5]

8599 Franklin, Sharon, et al. *Scandinavia* (4–7). Series: Artisans Around the World. 1999, Raintree LB $27.12 (978-0-7398-0122-2). This book, which contains many hands-on activities, surveys Scandinavian crafts and shows how geography has influenced this area's artisans. (Rev: BL 10/15/99; HBG 3/00; SLJ 1/00) [948]

8600 Gan, Delice. *Sweden* (4–7). Illus. Series: Cultures of the World. 1992, Marshall Cavendish LB $35.64 (978-1-85435-452-5). This introduction to Sweden gives special coverage of the people and their lifestyles. (Rev: BL 10/15/92) [948.5]

8601 Hansen, Ole Steen. *Denmark* (4–7). Series: Country Insights. 1998, Raintree LB $27.12 (978-0-8172-4794-2). This book provides a broad description of the country — its lifestyle, culture, and traditions — and contrasts Denmark's rural and urban environments. (Rev: BL 6/1–15/98; HBG 10/98) [948]

8602 *Iceland in Pictures* (5–8). Illus. Series: Visual Geography. 1996, Lerner LB $25.55 (978-0-8225-1892-1). The history, government, people, and economy of the northern republic of Iceland are covered in words and pictures. (Rev: BL 8/91) [949.12]

8603 Jovinelly, Joann, and Jason Netelkos. *The Crafts and Culture of the Vikings* (5–8). Series: Crafts of the Ancient World. 2002, Rosen LB $29.25 (978-0-8239-3514-7). In addition to giving a tour of ancient Scandinavia, this book outlines such craft projects as designing a battle shield and helmet, minting coins, and playing an ancient board game. (Rev: BL 5/15/02) [948]

8604 Kagda, Sakina. *Norway* (4–7). Illus. Series: Cultures of the World. 1995, Marshall Cavendish LB $37.07 (978-0-7614-0181-0). After general information on Norway's geography and history, this account concentrates on the Norwegian people, how they live, and their artistic accomplishments. (Rev: BL 1/1–15/96; SLJ 9/96) [948.1]

8605 Lassieur, Allison. *The Vikings* (6–9). Series: Lost Civilizations. 2001, Lucent LB $29.95 (978-1-56006-816-7). Using archaeological evidence, this account re-creates the history and culture of the Vikings from their glory days to their ultimate demise. (Rev: BL 8/1/01) [948]

8606 Lee, Tan Chung. *Finland* (4–7). Illus. Series: Cultures of the World. 1996, Marshall Cavendish LB $37.07 (978-0-7614-0280-0). The small country of Finland with its thousands of lakes is introduced, with emphasis on the people and how they live. (Rev: BL 8/96; SLJ 7/96) [984.97]

8607 Schaffer, David. *Viking Conquests* (7–10). Series: World History. 2002, Gale LB $32.45 (978-1-56006-322-3). Though the Vikings were known mainly for their raids and pillaging, this account also gives details of their lasting contributions to the world. (Rev: BL 8/02) [948]

8608 Streissguth, Thomas. *Life Among the Vikings* (7–10). Series: The Way People Live. 1998, Lucent LB $27.45 (978-1-56006-392-6). Using a topical approach, this book covers the Vikings' everyday life, warfare, ships, farming, language, art, and poetry. (Rev: SLJ 6/99) [948]

8609 *Sweden in Pictures* (5–8). Illus. Series: Visual Geography. 1993, Lerner LB $21.27 (978-0-8225-1872-3). Gives the background geography and history of Sweden, along with contemporary material. (Rev: BL 12/1/90) [948.5]

8610 Wilcox, Jonathan. *Iceland* (4–7). Series: Cultures of the World. 1996, Marshall Cavendish LB $37.07 (978-0-7614-0279-4). The history, geography, people, and culture of this remote island republic are introduced, with many color photographs. (Rev: SLJ 7/96) [949.12]

Spain and Portugal

8611 Anderson, Wayne. *The ETA: Spain's Basque Terrorists* (4–8). Series: Inside the World's Most Infamous Terrorist Organizations. 2003, Rosen LB $27.95 (978-0-8239-3818-6). This is the history and present status of the violent organization committed to creating an ethnic homeland separate from Spain. (Rev: BL 10/15/03; SLJ 9/03) [946]

8612 Blauer, Ettagale, and Jason Lauré. *Portugal* (4–7). Series: Enchantment of the World. 2002, Children's LB $37.00 (978-0-516-21109-1). This highly visual introduction to Portugal includes accessible information on topics including history, people and language, customs, and economy. (Rev: BL 9/15/02) [946.9]

8613 Champion, Neil. *Portugal* (5–8). Illus. Series: Modern Industrial World. 1995, Thomson Learning LB $24.26 (978-1-56847-435-9). Modern Portugal is highlighted in text and pictures, with coverage of its economy, industries, and resources. (Rev: BL 12/15/95) [946.904]

8614 Goodman, Joan Elizabeth. *A Long and Uncertain Journey: The 27,000-Mile Voyage of Vasco da Gama* (4–8). Illus. by Tom McNeely. 2001, Mikaya $19.95 (978-0-9650493-7-5). Details of Vasco da Gama's explorations and their historical context are accompanied by biographical information, illustrations, journal entries, a map, and a timeline. (Rev: BL 9/1/01; HBG 10/01; SLJ 6/01*; VOYA 8/01) [910]

8615 Heale, Jay. *Portugal* (5–8). Illus. Series: Cultures of the World. 1995, Marshall Cavendish LB $37.07 (978-0-7614-0169-8). Present-day conditions in Portugal are emphasized in this account, which also covers history, geography, and culture. (Rev: SLJ 11/95) [914.9]

8616 Kohen, Elizabeth. *Spain* (4–7). Illus. Series: Cultures of the World. 1992, Marshall Cavendish LB $35.64 (978-1-85435-451-8). With text, photographs, maps, and fact sheets, the land and people of Spain are introduced. (Rev: BL 10/15/92) [946]

8617 McDowall, David. *The Spanish Armada* (8–12). Illus. 1988, David & Charles $19.95 (978-0-7134-5671-4). A British import that tells about the events surrounding this Spanish fleet and also supplies many short biographies of the people involved. (Rev: SLJ 3/89) [946]

8618 Mann, Kenny. *Isabel, Ferdinand and Fifteenth-Century Spain* (5–8). Series: Rulers and Their Times. 2001, Marshall Cavendish LB $29.93 (978-0-7614-1030-0). Following biographies of these great Spanish rulers, there is a section on the life and culture of their times plus a generous selection of original documents of the period. (Rev: BL 1/1–15/02; HBG 3/02; SLJ 3/02) [946]

8619 Melchiore, Susan McCarthy. *The Spanish Inquisition* (6–8). Series: Great Disasters. 2001, Chelsea LB $32.00 (978-0-7910-6327-9). The story of this institution established by Spanish monarchs in 1478, and its ruthless treatment of Jews and Muslims as well as Christians suspected of heresy. (Rev: BL 6/1–15/02; HBG 10/02; SLJ 6/02) [946]

8620 Millar, Heather. *Spain in the Age of Exploration* (5–8). Series: Cultures of the Past. 1998, Benchmark LB $29.93 (978-0-7614-0303-6). This book covers Spanish history from the time of Columbus to about 1700, with an emphasis on art and literature plus material on daily life and major personalities. (Rev: BL 12/15/98; HBG 10/99; SLJ 2/99) [946]

8621 *Portugal in Pictures* (5–8). Illus. Series: Visual Geography. 1996, Lerner LB $25.55 (978-0-8225-1886-0). Current conditions and problems in Portugal are introduced along with the standard material on history, geography, and social conditions. (Rev: BL 12/15/91) [946.9]

8622 Rogers, Lura. *Spain* (4–7). Series: Enchantment of the World. 2001, Children's LB $37.00 (978-0-516-21123-7). A well-designed book that uses clear text, numerous charts, maps, drawings, and photographs to introduce a number of topics related to Spain and its people. (Rev: BL 1/1–15/02) [946]

8623 Selby, Anna. *Spain* (4–7). Illus. Series: Country Fact Files. 1994, Raintree LB $27.12 (978-0-8114-1848-5). A well-illustrated introduction to Spain, with coverage of such subjects as current social conditions, the economy, food and farming, and the environment. (Rev: SLJ 7/94) [946]

8624 Shubert, Adrian. *The Land and People of Spain* (6–9). Series: Land and People Of. 1992, HarperCollins LB $17.89 (978-0-06-020218-7). A comprehensive, detailed history of Spain. (Rev: BL 8/92) [946]

8625 Skog, Jason. *Teens in Spain* (7–12). Series: Global Connections. 2006, Compass Point LB $31.93 (978-0-7565-2446-3). Introduces Spanish teens and their schools, family life, hobbies, sports, and so forth, covering both traditional aspects and those that have arrived with new technology and new immigration. (Rev: SLJ 5/07) [305.235]

8626 *Spain in Pictures* (5–8). Illus. Series: Visual Geography. 1995, Lerner LB $25.55 (978-0-8225-1887-7). Modern Spain is the focus of this introduction, which includes many photographs, charts, and maps. (Rev: BL 11/15/95) [914.6]

8627 Worth, Richard. *The Spanish Inquisition in World History* (8–12). Series: In World History. 2002, Enslow LB $26.60 (978-0-7660-1825-9). This account describes the formation of the Spanish Inquisition, the work of Torquemada, and how the Catholic Church tried to punish those who went against the teachings of Christianity. (Rev: BL 3/15/03; HBG 10/03; SLJ 4/03) [946]

Middle East

General and Miscellaneous

8628 Broyles, Matthew. *The Six-Day War* (5–9). Illus. Series: War and Conflict in the Middle East. 2004, Rosen LB $27.95 (978-0-8239-4549-8). A well-organized, balanced account of the 1973 war between Israel and its Arab neighbors Egypt, Jordan, and Syria. (Rev: BL 11/1/04; SLJ 1/05)

8629 Dudley, William, ed. *The Middle East* (7–10). Series: Opposing Viewpoints. 1992, Greenhaven paper $16.20 (978-0-89908-160-1). Articles and essays examine the background causes of the Middle East conflicts. (Rev: BL 6/15/92; SLJ 7/92) [320.956]

8630 Einfeld, Jann, ed. *Can Democracy Succeed in the Middle East?* (6–12). Series: At Issue. 2006, Gale LB $28.70 (978-0-7377-3393-8). The title question and many others (can democracy be imposed?) are addressed in this collection of 12 essays. (Rev: SLJ 3/07)

8631 Fiscus, James W. *The Suez Crisis* (5–9). Illus. Series: War and Conflict in the Middle East. 2004, Rosen LB $27.95 (978-0-8239-4550-4). Examines the 1956 conflict over control of the canal, involving Egypt, Israel, Britain, and France. (Rev: BL 11/1/04)

8632 Hampton, Wilborn. *War in the Middle East: A Reporter's Story: Black September and the Yom Kippur War* (6–9). Illus. 2007, Candlewick $19.99 (978-0-7636-2493-4). Reporter Hampton describes the events of the 1970 Jordanian "Black September" civil conflict and of the 1973 Yom Kippur War, giving a personal perspective that will interest students of journalism in particular. (Rev: BL 8/07; LMC 1/08; SLJ 8/07) [956.04]

8633 Harik, Ramsay M., and Elsa Marston. *Women in the Middle East*. Rev. ed. (7–12). Illus. 2003, Watts LB $30.50 (978-0-531-12222-8). A chapter on the women of Afghanistan has been added to this revised and updated edition that looks at topics including health, education, and family and public life. (Rev: BL 4/15/03; SLJ 5/03; VOYA 8/03) [305.42]

8634 Kort, Michael G. *The Handbook of the Middle East* (7–12). Illus. 2002, Twenty-First Century LB $39.90 (978-0-7613-1611-4). History, geography, culture, politics (current and future), and religion are all covered in this overview of the region that includes maps, flags, a timeline, and material on key figures. (Rev: HBG 10/02; SLJ 3/02; VOYA 6/02) [956]

8635 Long, Cathryn J. *The Middle East in Search of Peace*. Rev. ed. (4–7). Illus. Series: Headliners. 1996, Millbrook LB $25.90 (978-0-7613-0105-9). An objective account of the conflict between Arabs and Jews in the Middle East, with good historical information and a description of various peace plans. (Rev: SLJ 1/97) [956]

8636 Steele, Philip. *Middle East* (4–7). Series: Kingfisher Knowledge. 2006, Kingfisher LB $12.95 (978-0-7534-5984-3). Traces the history of the region — extending from Eastern Mediterranean countries into Iraq, Iran, and Afghanistan — as well as its geography, peoples, cultures, religions, economies, and politics. (Rev: SLJ 12/06) [956]

8637 Wagner, Heather Lehr. *Israel and the Arab World* (6–12). Illus. Series: People at Odds. 2002, Chelsea LB $30.00 (978-0-7910-6705-5). An easy-to-understand summary of the conflict between the two groups, with illustrative photographs. (Rev: BL 11/1/02; HBG 3/03) [956.9405]

8638 Worth, Richard. *The Arab-Israeli Conflict* (7–12). Series: Open for Debate. 2006, Benchmark LB $27.95 (978-0-7614-2295-2). Worth gives a balanced overview of this long-running conflict, with historical information, accounts of the key areas of dispute, and explanations of each side's beliefs and goals. (Rev: SLJ 2/07)

Egypt

8639 Barghusen, Joan. *Daily Life in Ancient and Modern Cairo* (6–9). Series: Cities Through Time. 2001, Lerner LB $25.26 (978-0-8225-3221-7). Cairo's evolution from earliest times to today is presented in richly illustrated double-page spreads with information on political, social, and religious life as well as women's issues, with a timeline and quotations. (Rev: BL 4/15/01; HBG 10/01; SLJ 7/01) [962.16]

8640 Bowden, Rob, and Roy Maconachie. *Cairo* (4–7). Illus. Series: Great Cities of the World. 2005, World Almanac LB $31.00 (978-0-8368-5035-2). An informative and appealing overview of one of the world's most famous cities, with material on its history, its economy, and what it's like to live there. (Rev: BL 4/15/04)

8641 Loveridge, Emma. *Egypt* (5–8). Series: Country Fact Files. 1997, Raintree LB $27.12 (978-0-8172-4626-6). This book gives standard basic information about Egypt, including its climate, landscape, trade, industry, and daily life. (Rev: SLJ 9/97) [962]

8642 Orr, Tamra. *Egyptian Islamic Jihad* (4–8). Series: Inside the World's Most Infamous Terrorist Organizations. 2003, Rosen LB $27.95 (978-0-8239-3819-3). Dedicated to the overthrow of the secular Egyptian government, this terrorist organization has links to the Al Qaeda terrorist network. (Rev: BL 10/15/03) [962]

8643 Parks, Peggy J. *The Aswan High Dam* (5–8). Series: Building World Landmarks. 2004, Gale LB

$24.95 (978-1-56711-329-7). This is the fascinating story of the construction of the huge dam on the Nile and the immense technical and social challenges involved. (Rev: SLJ 6/04) [627]

8644 Pateman, Robert. *Egypt* (4–7). Illus. Series: Cultures of the World. 1992, Marshall Cavendish LB $35.64 (978-1-85435-535-5). Egypt past and present is introduced in this account that stresses how the people live. (Rev: BL 1/1/93) [962]

8645 Stewart, Gail. *The Suez Canal* (7–10). Series: Building History. 2001, Lucent $32.45 (978-1-56006-842-6). This is the dramatic story of the construction and utilization of the Suez Canal, one of the great engineering marvels of the 19th century. (Rev: BL 8/01) [962]

8646 Tenquist, Alasdair. *Egypt* (5–7). Illus. Series: Economically Developing Countries. 1995, Thomson Learning LB $24.26 (978-1-56847-385-7). A look at present-day conditions in Egypt and its concerns and problems. (Rev: SLJ 2/96) [962]

8647 Wilson, Neil. *Egypt* (4–8). Series: Nations of the World. 2001, Raintree LB $34.26 (978-0-7398-1283-9). An excellent introduction to the country that housed one of the world's oldest civilizations and is currently a center of Islamic culture and religion. (Rev: BL 6/1–15/01; HBG 10/01) [962]

8648 Zuehlke, Jeffrey. *Egypt in Pictures*. Rev. ed. (4–8). Illus. Series: Visual Geography. 2002, Lerner LB $27.93 (978-0-8225-0367-5). Covers Egypt's geography, history, people, economy, and culture with maps, photographs, and illustrations. (Rev: SLJ 3/03) [962]

Israel and Palestine

8649 Corona, Laurel. *Israel* (6–9). Illus. Series: Modern Nations of the World. 2003, Gale $29.95 (978-1-59018-115-7). A thorough overview of the geography, history, and people of the land of Israel, with informative and interesting sidebars on historical and contemporary topics. (Rev: BL 4/15/03; SLJ 8/03) [956.94]

8650 Dubois, Jill. *Israel* (4–7). Illus. Series: Cultures of the World. 1992, Marshall Cavendish LB $35.64 (978-1-85435-531-7). This introduction to Israel emphasizes its culture and the lifestyles of the people. (Rev: BL 1/1/93) [956.94]

8651 Feinstein, Steve. *Israel in Pictures* (5–8). Illus. 1992, Lerner LB $25.55 (978-0-8225-1833-4). An overview of geography, climate, wildlife, and vegetation with photographs, maps, and charts. (Rev: BL 8/88) [956.9405]

8652 Finkelstein, Norman H. *Friends Indeed: The Special Relationship of Israel and the United States* (7–12). 1998, Millbrook LB $24.90 (978-0-7613-0114-1). This book explores the close, often rocky, relationship between Israel and the U.S. through 10 administrations and several wars. (Rev: BL 8/98; SLJ 6/98) [327.73]

8653 Frank, Mitch. *Understanding the Holy Land: Answering Questions About the Israeli-Palestinian Conflict* (6–9). Illus. 2005, Viking $17.99 (978-0-670-06032-0). In easy-to-read question-and-answer format, author Mitch Frank provides an excellent introduction to the history of the Holy Land and the diverse factors involved in the continuing conflict between Israelis and Palestinians. (Rev: BL 3/1/05*; SLJ 3/05; VOYA 4/05) [956.9405]

8654 Gaughen, Shasta, ed. *The Arab-Israeli Conflict* (7–10). Series: Contemporary Issues Companion. 2004, Gale paper $24.95 (978-0-7377-1616-0). After background on the long-running conflict, this volume provides opposing views about how to resolve the crisis and first-person stories of life amid turmoil. (Rev: SLJ 1/05) [956.04]

8655 Green, Jen. *Israel* (4–8). Series: Nations of the World. 2001, Raintree LB $34.26 (978-0-7398-1286-0). A fine, attractive introduction to the land and people of Israel, the nation that was created as a homeland for the Jewish people after World War II. (Rev: BL 6/1–15/01; HBG 10/01) [956.94]

8656 Greenfeld, Howard. *A Promise Fulfilled: Theodor Herzl, Chaim Weizmann, David Ben-Gurion, and the Creation of the State of Israel* (7–10). Illus. 2005, Greenwillow LB $19.89 (978-0-06-051505-8). This story of the creation of the state of Israel focuses on the contributions of three remarkable and very different men. (Rev: BL 4/15/05; SLJ 7/05) [320.54]

8657 Hayhurst, Chris. *Israel's War of Independence* (5–9). Illus. Series: War and Conflict in the Middle East. 2004, Rosen LB $27.95 (978-0-8239-4548-1). An even-handed overview of Israel's struggle for independence and the ensuing years of violence, with statistics, maps, photographs, and profiles of leaders. (Rev: BL 11/1/04; SLJ 1/05) [956.04]

8658 Katz, Samuel M. *Jerusalem or Death: Palestinian Terrorism* (7–12). Illus. Series: Terrorist Dossiers. 2003, Lerner LB $26.60 (978-0-8225-4033-5). This book focuses on the terrorist groups that have been active in Israel and the West Bank. (Rev: BL 3/15/04; HBG 4/04; SLJ 3/04; VOYA 4/04) [956.9]

8659 Marshood, Nabil. *Palestinian Teenage Refugees and Immigrants Speak Out* (7–12). Series: Teenage Refugees Speak Out. 1997, Rosen LB $27.95 (978-0-8239-2442-4). The exodus of Palestinians, many to the United States, and their reasons for leaving their homes are shown through the stories of several teenage immigrants. (Rev: BL 12/15/97) [956.04]

8660 Ross, Stewart. *The Arab-Israeli Conflict* (7–12). Series: Causes and Consequences. 1995, Raintree LB $29.97 (978-0-8172-4051-6). This conflict is presented in a historical context, using a magazine format, maps, and photographs, laying the basis for understanding the continuing hostility. (Rev: BL 12/15/95; SLJ 2/96) [956.94]

8661 Scharfstein, Sol. *Understanding Israel* (5–7). Illus. 1994, KTAV paper $14.95 (978-0-88125-428-0). A heavily illustrated introduction to Israel that covers history, religion, government, culture, and current concerns. (Rev: SLJ 10/94) [956.94]

8662 Senker, Cath. *The Arab-Israeli Conflict* (5–8). Series: Questioning History. 2004, Smart Apple Media LB $28.50 (978-1-58340-441-6). A clear and balanced discussion of the history and current status of relations between Arabs and Israelis, with a timeline, glossary, and detailed index. (Rev: SLJ 2/05) [956.04]

8663 Sha'Ban, Mervet A., and Galit Fink. *If You Could Be My Friend: Letters of Mervet Akram Sha'Ban and Galit Fink* (6–9). Trans. by Beatrice Khadige. Illus. 1998, Orchard LB $16.99 (978-0-531-33113-2). Two teenage girls — one an Israeli and the other a Palestinian — share their feelings and fears in a series of letters they exchanged from 1988 to 1991. (Rev: BCCB 11/98; BL 10/15/98; HB 9–10/98; HBG 3/99; SLJ 11/98; VOYA 12/98) [956.94054]

8664 Sherman, Josepha. *Your Travel Guide to Ancient Israel* (4–8). Illus. Series: Passport to History. 2003, Lerner LB $26.60 (978-0-8225-3072-5). An illustrated visit to Israel in the time of King Solomon, with description of foods, housing, clothing, customs, and notable people of that era. (Rev: SLJ 4/04) [933]

8665 Silverman, Maida. *Israel: The Founding of a Modern Nation* (4–7). Illus. 1998, Dial LB $15.00 (978-0-8034-2136-3). This account covers 3,000 years of Jewish history, with emphasis on recent centuries, and includes a timeline showing Israel's history from 1948 to 1998. (Rev: BL 5/1/98) [956.94]

8666 Slavik, Diane. *Daily Life in Ancient and Modern Jerusalem* (6–9). Illus. Series: Cities Through Time. 2000, Lerner $25.26 (978-0-8225-3218-7). Slavik traces the history of Jerusalem from the earliest times, exploring what life was like for the inhabitants of each period. (Rev: BL 3/1/01; HBG 10/01; SLJ 9/01) [956.94]

8667 Stefoff, Rebecca. *West Bank / Gaza Strip* (7–12). Series: Major World Nations. 1999, Chelsea LB $21.95 (978-0-7910-4771-2). This work describes the long, confrontational history of this area, with information on its people, economics, geography, and the outlook for the future. (Rev: HBG 3/99; SLJ 6/99) [956.94]

8668 *Three Wishes: Palestinian and Israeli Children Speak* (5–12). 2004, Groundwood $16.95 (978-0-88899-554-4). In an evenhanded presenta-

tion that offers an introductory historical overview, 20 first-person accounts relate the experiences of Christian, Jewish, and Muslim young people during the ongoing conflict between Israelis and Palestinians. (Rev: BL 9/1/04*; SLJ 10/04) [956.04]

8669 Wingate, Katherine. *The Intifadas* (5–9). Illus. Series: War and Conflict in the Middle East. 2004, Rosen LB $27.95 (978-0-8239-4546-7). An evenhanded overview of the events leading up to the Palestinian uprisings, with statistics, maps, photographs, and profiles of leaders. (Rev: BL 11/1/04) [956.95]

Other Middle East Countries

8670 Augustin, Byron. *United Arab Emirates* (4–7). Series: Enchantment of the World. 2002, Children's LB $36.00 (978-0-516-20473-4). This important nation is introduced with material on topics including history, natural resources, climate, and people. (Rev: BL 5/15/02; SLJ 9/02) [953]

8671 Augustin, Byron, and Jake Kubena. *Iraq* (5–8). Illus. Series: Enchantment of the World. 2006, Children's Pr. LB $37.00 (978-0-516-24852-3). An updated version of a 1998 book on the country, with additional information on ethnic groups, the environment, and continuing violence. (Rev: SLJ 7/06) [956.7]

8672 Bodnarchuk, Kari. *Kurdistan: Region Under Siege* (7–10). Series: World in Conflict. 2000, Lerner LB $25.26 (978-0-8225-3556-0). This work gives an unbiased historical picture of this mountainous region of the Middle East and tells of the frequent upheavals that mark its past and present. (Rev: BL 6/1–15/00; HBG 3/01; SLJ 12/00) [955]

8673 Boueri, Marijean, and Jill Boutros. *Lebanon A to Z: A Middle Eastern Mosaic* (4–8). Illus. by Tatiana Sabbagh. 2006, PublishingWorks $25.00 (978-0-9744803-4-3). Eleven-year-old Kareem takes readers on a tour through the country's present and past, with an emphasis on cultural traditions and Lebanon's people. (Rev: SLJ 7/06) [956.92]

8674 Broberg, Catherine. *Saudi Arabia in Pictures* (6–10). Illus. Series: Visual Geography. 2002, Lerner LB $27.93 (978-0-8225-1958-4). Full-color photographs complement information on the country's geography, history, government, economy, people, and culture. (Rev: BL 10/15/02; HBG 3/03) [953.8]

8675 Byers, Ann. *Lebanon's Hezbollah* (4–8). Series: Inside the World's Most Infamous Terrorist Organizations. 2003, Rosen LB $27.95 (978-0-8239-3821-6). This is the story of the Lebanese terrorist organization dedicated to installing a conservative Islamic government in Lebanon and to the destruction of Israel. (Rev: BL 10/15/03; SLJ 9/03) [956.92]

8676 Cartlidge, Cherese. *Iran* (5–8). Series: Modern Nations of the World. 2002, Gale LB $29.95 (978-1-56006-971-3). This colorful account gives a comprehensive overview of Iran, including history, geography, and culture. (Rev: BL 12/15/02; SLJ 1/03) [955]

8677 Clark, Charles. *Iran* (7–12). Series: Nations in Transition. 2002, Gale LB $32.45 (978-0-7377-1096-0). Iran's internal political upheavals and difficult relationship with the rest of the world are the focus of this thorough and concise volume that includes biographical and cultural features. (Rev: SLJ 1/03) [955]

8678 Downing, David. *Iraq: 1968–2003* (6–8). Series: Troubled World. 2003, Raintree LB $28.56 (978-1-4109-0184-2). Covers events in Iraq from the late 1960s until Saddam Hussein's removal from power, discussing factors that will remain of interest including the importance of oil; factboxes, maps, and color insets defining terms and concepts add to the presentation. (Rev: SLJ 3/04) [956.7]

8679 Eboch, Chris. *Turkey* (5–9). Series: Modern Nations of the World. 2003, Gale LB $29.95 (978-1-59018-122-5). This account presents a broad spectrum of material about Turkey including history, geography, and culture. (Rev: BL 11/15/03; SLJ 6/03) [961]

8680 Foster, Leila M. *Oman* (4–7). Series: Enchantment of the World. 1999, Children's LB $37.00 (978-0-516-20964-7). A fine introduction to this oil-producing country, covering topics such as history, geography, government, religion, and the economy. (Rev: BL 9/15/99) [956]

8681 Goodwin, William. *Saudi Arabia* (5–8). Series: Modern Nations of the World. 2001, Lucent LB $29.95 (978-1-56006-763-4). The land ruled by the Saud dynasty is presented with details on history, government, geography, resources, and world importance. (Rev: BL 6/1–15/01) [953.8]

8682 Graham, Amy. *Iran in the News: Past, Present, and Future* (5–8). Illus. Series: Middle East Nations in the News. 2006, Enslow LB $33.27 (978-1-59845-022-4). History, culture, people, and current political issues are all covered in this readable overview of Iran that includes links to Web sites that extend the text. (Rev: BL 4/1/06; SLJ 5/06) [955]

8683 Gray, Leon. *Iran* (4–8). Illus. Series: Countries of the World. 2008, National Geographic LB $27.90 (978-1-4263-0200-8). Useful for researchers, this book provides basic information about the country as well as data and additional facts presented in sidebars and other features. (Rev: BL 4/15/08) [955.22]

8684 Hassig, Susan M. *Iraq* (4–7). Illus. Series: Cultures of the World. 1992, Marshall Cavendish LB $35.64 (978-1-85435-533-1). This introduction

stresses the lifestyles of the people, their religion, and culture. (Rev: BL 1/1/93) [956.7]

8685 Heinrichs, Ann. *Saudi Arabia* (4–7). Series: Enchantment of the World. 2002, Children's LB $37.00 (978-0-516-22287-5). Topics covered in the highly visual introduction to Saudi Arabia include history, religion, language, economy, and government. (Rev: BL 9/15/02) [953.8]

8686 Hestler, Anna. *Yemen* (5–8). Series: Cultures of the World. 1999, Marshall Cavendish LB $37.07 (978-0-7614-0956-4). A fine introduction to this country on the Gulf of Aden with good background information and an overview of modern life. (Rev: HBG 10/99; SLJ 10/99) [956]

8687 *Iran in Pictures* (5–8). Illus. Series: Visual Geography. 1992, Lerner LB $21.27 (978-0-8225-1848-8). Basic coverage on this Middle Eastern land and its people. (Rev: BL 5/1/89) [955]

8688 Isiorho, Solomon A. *Kuwait* (7–12). Series: Modern World Nations. 2002, Chelsea LB $30.00 (978-0-7910-6781-9). An overview of the history, geography, people, politics, and religion of Kuwait, with discussion of the importance of Islam. Also use *Bahrain* (2002). (Rev: SLJ 2/03) [953.67]

8689 Janin, Hunt. *Saudi Arabia* (4–7). Illus. Series: Cultures of the World. 1992, Marshall Cavendish LB $35.64 (978-1-85435-532-4). The history, geography, economy, language, and people are discussed in this book about Saudi Arabia. (Rev: BL 1/1/93) [953.8]

8690 *Jordan in Pictures* (5–8). Illus. 1992, Lerner LB $25.55 (978-0-8225-1834-1). Young readers learn what life is like in this Middle East land. (Rev: BL 2/1/89; SLJ 2/89) [956.9504]

8691 Kheirabadi, Masoud. *Iran* (6–12). Illus. Series: Modern World Nations. 2003, Chelsea LB $30.00 (978-0-7910-7234-9). A thorough and concise overview of Iran's geography, history, government, politics, economics, language, peoples, and religion, with maps, photographs, and a look at the future. (Rev: BL 9/15/03; HBG 10/03) [955]

8692 *Lebanon in Pictures* (5–8). Illus. Series: Visual Geography. 1992, Lerner LB $25.55 (978-0-8225-1832-7). A country torn apart by strife is the focus of this edition. (Rev: BL 2/1/89) [956.9204]

8693 Marcovitz, Hal. *Jordan* (7–12). Series: Creation of the Modern Middle East. 2002, Chelsea LB $35.00 (978-0-7910-6507-5). This volume on the history of Jordan, its importance in the Middle East, and its relations with the United States will be useful for report writers. Also use *Syria*, *Oman*, and *The Kurds* (all 2002). (Rev: LMC 4–5/03; SLJ 2/03) [956.9504]

8694 Marcovitz, Hal. *Kuwait* (5–8). Illus. Series: Modern Middle East Nations. 2003, Mason Crest LB $24.95 (978-1-59084-510-3). A thorough introduction to the geography, history, and people of Kuwait, whose wealth makes it an unusual country. (Rev: BL 6/1–15/03; HBG 4/04; SLJ 10/03) [953.67]

8695 Miller, Debra A. *Iraq* (6–12). Series: The World's Hot Spots. 2004, Gale LB $31.20 (978-0-7377-1813-3); paper $23.70 (978-0-7377-1814-0). Reprinted essays, speeches, and news articles provide a fascinating overview of Iraq's history and the factors that precipitated the American-led invasion in 2003. (Rev: BL 6/1–15/04; SLJ 8/04) [956.704]

8696 Orr, Tamra. *Turkey* (5–8). Illus. Series: Enchantment of the World, Second Series. 2003, Children's LB $37.00 (978-0-516-22679-8). A visually attractive book that covers such topics as the geography, history, government, culture, and people, with a timeline, fast facts, and a recipe. (Rev: SLJ 5/03) [915]

8697 Rajendra, Vijeya, and Gisela Kaplan. *Iran* (4–7). Illus. Series: Cultures of the World. 1992, Marshall Cavendish LB $35.64 (978-1-85435-534-8). As well as standard introductory information about Iran, this book tells about how the people live and what the country's present problems are. (Rev: BL 1/1/93) [955]

8698 Reed, Jennifer Bond. *The Saudi Royal Family* (5–8). Illus. Series: Major World Leaders. 2002, Chelsea $30.00 (978-0-7910-7063-5); paper $30.00 (978-0-7910-7187-8). Saudi Arabia's ruling royal family is profiled, detailing its rise to power, its Islamic policies, and the various individual rulers, with a look at the contrast between the family's extravagant lifestyle and its religious beliefs. (Rev: BL 1/1–15/03; SLJ 4/03) [953.8]

8699 Riverbend. *Baghdad Burning: Girl Blog from Iraq* (8–12). 2005, Feminist paper $14.95 (978-1-55861-489-5). A young Iraqi blogger paints a grim picture of life in her country after the 2003 invasion of U.S. and allied forces. (Rev: BL 4/1/05) [956.7]

8700 Riverbend. *Baghdad Burning II: More Girl Blog from Iraq* (8–12). 2006, Feminist paper $14.95 (978-1-55861-529-8). This second volume of compiled blogs describes the continuing shortages of water, power, and food; religious and political violence at the hands of Iraqi security forces; repression; and the general chaos that has reigned during the U.S. occupation. (Rev: BL 11/1/06) [956.7044]

8701 Sheehan, Sean. *Lebanon* (5–10). Series: Cultures of the World. 1996, Marshall Cavendish LB $37.07 (978-0-7614-0283-1). A lively, well-written introduction to this war-ravaged country with details on history, economy, culture, religion and foods, including a recipe for a typical dish. (Rev: SLJ 6/97) [569.2]

8702 South, Coleman. *Jordan* (5–10). Series: Cultures of the World. 1996, Marshall Cavendish LB $37.07 (978-0-7614-0287-9). Everyday life in Jordan is the focus of this book that also covers history, religion, culture, geography, festivals, and foods; a single recipe is included. (Rev: SLJ 6/97) [569.5]

8703 Spencer, William. *Iraq: Old Land, New Nation in Conflict* (7–12). Illus. 2000, Twenty-First Century LB $23.90 (978-0-7613-1356-4). This account traces the history of Iraq from its Mesopotamian origins to Saddam Hussein's rule prior to the American invasion. (Rev: BL 11/15/00; HBG 3/01; SLJ 12/00) [956.7]

8704 Spencer, William. *The United States and Iran* (7–12). Illus. 2000, Twenty-First Century LB $23.90 (978-0-7613-1554-4). After covering Iranian culture and history, this account explores Iran's rocky relations with the U.S. to the beginning of 2000, with material on the hostage crisis of 1979. (Rev: BL 4/15/00; HBG 9/00; SLJ 7/00; VOYA 6/01) [327.73055]

8705 Wills, Karen. *Jordan* (5–8). Series: Modern Nations of the World. 2001, Lucent LB $29.95 (978-1-56006-822-8). A good profile of Jordan is presented, with basic background material and information on present conditions and the people today. (Rev: BL 6/1–15/01) [956.95]

8706 *Yemen in Pictures* (5–8). Illus. Series: Visual Geography. 1993, Lerner LB $25.55 (978-0-8225-1911-9). In introduction to this Muslim republic on the Gulf of Aden, with material on its economic and social conditions. (Rev: BL 12/1/93; SLJ 12/93) [953.3]

North and South America (excluding the United States)

General and Miscellaneous

8707 Alter, Judy. *Discovering North America's Land, People, and Wildlife* (5–8). Series: Continents of the World. 2004, Enslow LB $25.26 (978-0-7660-5206-2). An introduction to the geography, history, economy, plants and animals, culture, and people of the continent, with brief coverage of the Caribbean and Central America. (Rev: SLJ 11/04) [917]

8708 Aronson, Marc, and John W. Glenn. *The World Made New: Why the Age of Exploration Happened and How It Changed the World* (5–8). 2007, National Geographic $17.95 (978-0-7922-6454-5). This is an enlightening and well-illustrated survey of world exploration — in particular of European expeditions to the Western Hemisphere in the 15th and 16th centuries — looking at key figures and at the lasting consequences for the people, plants, and animals. (Rev: BL 9/15/07; SLJ 8/07) [910.9]

8709 Dalal, Anita. *Myths of Pre-Columbian America* (5–8). Illus. Series: Mythic World. 2002, Raintree LB $27.12 (978-0-7398-3193-9). This volume for older readers separates myth from reality about cultures present in America in pre-Columbian times. (Rev: BL 3/1/02; HBG 3/02; SLJ 12/01) [398.2]

8710 Haas, Robert B. *Through the Eyes of the Condor: An Aerial Vision of Latin America* (8–12). 2007, National Geographic $50.00 (978-1-4262-0132-5). Haas's camera takes a bird's-eye view of Central and South America, showing the diversity of the landscape in vast panoramas. (Rev: BL 9/15/07) [779.36098]

8711 Jones, Charlotte F. *Yukon Gold: The Story of the Klondike Gold Rush* (4–8). 1999, Holiday $18.95 (978-0-8234-1403-1). A solid account of the Alaska/Yukon Gold Rush that is enlivened by black-and-white photographs and intriguing asides and anecdotes. (Rev: BCCB 6/99; HB 7–8/99; HBG 10/99; SLJ 5/99; VOYA 12/99) [979.8]

8712 Long, Cathryn J. *Ancient America* (7–10). Series: World History. 2002, Gale LB $32.45 (978-1-56006-889-1). The story of the hunter-gatherers, agriculturalists, and city dwellers of North and South America from the arrival of the first humans in America to Columbus. (Rev: BL 8/02) [970]

8713 Murphy, Jim. *Gone a-Whaling: The Lure of the Sea and the Hunt for the Great Whale* (7–12). Illus. 1998, Clarion $18.00 (978-0-395-69847-1). Diary entries are used to describe American whale hunting and life aboard whaling vessels from the 19th century to the present. (Rev: BCCB 4/98; BL 3/15/98; HB 5–6/98; SLJ 5/98; VOYA 12/98) [306.3]

8714 O'Neill, Thomas. *Lakes, Peaks, and Prairies: Discovering the United States-Canadian Border* (7–12). Illus. 1984, National Geographic LB $12.95 (978-0-87044-483-8). A trip across the continent that reveals much about the diversity of these regions. [973]

8715 Patent, Dorothy Hinshaw. *Treasures of the Spanish Main* (6–10). Series: Frozen in Time. 1999, Marshall Cavendish LB $28.50 (978-0-7614-0786-7). This lavishly illustrated book describes the sinking of Spanish galleons near the Florida Keys in the 1600s and how their excavation has brought us amazing information about life and culture in the New World at that time. (Rev: BL 2/15/00; HBG 10/00; SLJ 3/00) [930]

8716 Smith, Tom. *Discovery of the Americas, 1492–1800* (6–12). Illus. Series: Discovery and Exploration. 2005, Facts on File $40.00 (978-0-8160-5262-2). European exploration of the New World is the focus of this volume that contains clear, informative text plus maps, illustrations, and excerpts from primary sources. (Rev: SLJ 8/05) [973]

North America

CANADA

8717 Beattie, Owen, and John Geiger. *Buried in Ice: The Mystery of a Lost Arctic Expedition* (4–7). Illus. by Janet Wilson. Series: Time Quest. 1993, Scholastic paper $6.95 (978-0-590-43849-0). The story of Sir John Franklin's unsuccessful 1845 expedition from England to find the Northwest Passage. (Rev: BCCB 3/92; BL 4/1/92; SLJ 4/92*) [919.804]

8718 Braun, Eric. *Canada in Pictures*. Rev. ed. (5–9). Illus. Series: Visual Geography. 2003, Lerner LB $27.93 (978-0-8225-4679-5). An informative and interesting overview of Canada's history, geography, government, economy, and people suitable for both research and browsing. (Rev: HBG 10/03; SLJ 7/03) [971.064]

8719 Campbell, Marjorie Wilkins. *The Nor'westers: The Fight for the Fur Trade* (6–12). Illus. 2003, Fitzhenry & Whiteside paper $12.95 (978-1-894004-97-8). An absorbing account of the Canadian fur trade in the 19th century, with details of company politics and relations between traders and Native Americans. (Rev: BL 4/1/03) [380.1]

8720 Cooper, John. *Season of Rage: Racial Conflict in a Small Town* (6–9). Illus. 2005, Tundra paper $9.95 (978-0-88776-700-5). The arresting story of the fight to win equal treatment for blacks in the small town of Dresden, Ontario, in the 1950s. (Rev: BL 2/1/05; SLJ 7/05; VOYA 4/06) [323.1196]

8721 Cooper, Michael. *Klondike Fever: The Famous Gold Rush of 1898* (5–8). Illus. 1990, Houghton paper $6.95 (978-0-395-54784-7). The events that turned a remote part of the Yukon into a three-ring circus of gold-hungry prospectors. (Rev: BCCB 1/90; BL 11/15/89; HB 1–2/90) [971.9]

8722 Coulter, Tony. *Jacques Cartier, Samuel de Champlain, and the Explorers of Canada* (5–8). Illus. Series: World Explorers. 1993, Chelsea LB $32.00 (978-0-7910-1298-7). This book about the early exploration of Canada includes material on Cartier, Champlain, Cabot, and Hudson, among others. (Rev: BL 1/1/93) [971]

8723 *Destination Vancouver* (6–9). Illus. Series: Port Cities of North America. 1998, Lerner LB $23.93 (978-0-8225-2787-9). A small volume that is full of information about Vancouver, its history, economy, and details about materials and goods that are shipped in and out of this port city. (Rev: HBG 9/98; SLJ 8/98) [971]

8724 Ferry, Steven. *Ontario* (6–9). Illus. Series: Exploring Canada. 2003, Gale LB $29.95 (978-1-59018-050-1). Ontario's geography, history, people, politics, and potential are presented in a well-organized volume that will be useful for report writers. (Rev: BL 7/03; SLJ 6/03) [971.3]

8725 Garrington, Sally. *Canada* (7–10). Series: Countries of the World. 2005, Facts on File LB $30.00 (978-0-8160-6009-2). History, geography, culture, government, and economy are all covered in this attractive overview of Canada. (Rev: SLJ 1/06) [971]

8726 Grabowski, John. *Canada* (5–8). Illus. Series: Overview: Modern Nations of the World. 1997, Lucent LB $27.45 (978-1-56006-520-3). A fine introduction to Canada and its people with coverage of major cities, industry, art and culture, government, and the separatist movement in Quebec. (Rev: BL 6/1–15/98; SLJ 8/98) [971]

8727 Greenwood, Barbara. *Gold Rush Fever: A Story of the Klondike, 1898* (4–7). Illus. by Heather Collins. 2001, Kids Can $18.95 (978-1-55074-852-9); paper $12.95 (978-1-55074-850-5). Thirteen-year-old Tim and his older brother trek to the Yukon to try to win their fortune in this account that interweaves fact and fiction, with many details about the hardships the miners faced. (Rev: BL 12/15/01; HBG 10/02; SLJ 10/01) [971.91]

8728 Hughes, Susan. *Coming to Canada: Building a Life in a New Land* (6–9). Illus. Series: Wow Canada! 2005, Maple Tree $18.95 (978-1-897066-46-1). From the first arrivals thousands of years ago to today's diverse immigrants, this is a fascinating overview of Canadian history that does not whitewash unhappy episodes. (Rev: BL 8/05; SLJ 11/05*) [971.004]

8729 Kizilos, Peter. *Quebec: Province Divided* (7–10). Series: World in Conflict. 2000, Lerner LB $25.26 (978-0-8225-3562-1). The history of the French Canadian province and the separatist movement there. (Rev: BL 10/15/2000; HBG 4/00; VOYA 8/01) [971]

8730 Murphy, Claire R., and Jane G. Haigh. *Children of the Gold Rush* (6–9). 1999, Roberts Rinehart paper $14.95 (978-1-57098-257-6). The story of the Yukon Gold Rush of 1878–1898 from the perspectives of the children involved, using diary excerpts, advertisements of the day, archival photographs, maps, and illustrations. (Rev: HB 7–8/99; HBG 9/99; SLJ 9/99) [971]

8731 Palana, Brett J. *British Columbia* (6–9). Illus. Series: Exploring Canada. 2003, Gale LB $29.95 (978-1-59018-046-4). A concise look at British Columbia's geography, history, people, and politics, with information on the large population of Asian immigrants and on environmental concerns. (Rev: BL 7/03) [971.1]

8732 Pang, Guek-Cheng. *Canada*. 2nd ed. (5–9). Illus. Series: Cultures of the World. 2004, Benchmark LB $37.07 (978-0-7614-1788-0). History, geography, and culture are all covered in this useful volume that attempts to impart a comprehensive understanding of life in all parts of Canada. (Rev: SLJ 2/05) [971]

8733 Renaud, Anne. *Pier 21: Stories from Near and Far* (4–7). Illus. by Aries Cheung. Series: Canadian Immigration. 2008, Lobster $16.95 (978-1-897073-70-4). This book is a collection of documents, memories, photographs, and illustrations relating to the site on Halifax Harbor where thousands of immigrants to Canada (in the years 1928 to 1971) started their new lives. (Rev: BL 4/15/08) [325.71]

8734 Rogers, Barbara Radcliffe, and Stillman D. Rogers. *Canada* (4–7). Series: Enchantment of the World. 2000, Children's LB $37.00 (978-0-516-21076-6). This fine introduction to Canada, its land and its people, also contains coverage of its history, economy, plants and animals, languages, sports, and the arts. (Rev: BL 1/1–15/01) [971]

8735 Thompson, Alexa. *Nova Scotia* (4–8). Series: Hello Canada. 1995, Lerner LB $19.93 (978-0-8225-2759-6). Nova Scotia's history, geography, and the economy are covered, with material on the various peoples and cultures. (Rev: SLJ 3/96) [971.6]

8736 Whitcraft, Melissa. *The Niagara River* (4–8). Series: Watts Library. 2001, Watts LB $25.50 (978-0-531-11903-7). This absorbing and readable account with maps and historical and contemporary photographs looks at the river's history, industry, and impact on the surrounding region. (Rev: SLJ 5/01) [971.3]

8737 Yates, Sarah. *Alberta* (4–8). Series: Hello Canada. 1995, Lerner LB $19.93 (978-0-8225-2763-3). A colorful, slim volume that crams many facts about this western Canadian province's culture, history, geography, and resources into a few attractive pages. (Rev: BL 12/15/95; SLJ 3/96) [971.23]

CENTRAL AMERICA

8738 Day, Nancy. *Your Travel Guide to Ancient Mayan Civilization* (4–8). Series: Passport to History. 2000, Lerner LB $26.50 (978-0-8225-3077-0). Using the format of a modern-day travel guide, this book explores the ancient Mayan cities of Uzmal, Tikal, Copan, and others to discover the lifestyles of the Maya, their food, clothes, religion, discoveries, and behavior. (Rev: BL 3/1/01; HBG 10/01; SLJ 4/01) [972]

8739 Freedman, Russell. *In the Days of the Vaqueros: America's First True Cowboys* (5–9). Illus. 2001, Clarion $18.00 (978-0-395-96788-1). Vivid artwork complements this history of the earliest cowboys, the Central American vaqueros who first rode the range in the late 15th century. (Rev: BL 11/15/01*; HB 1–2/02; HBG 3/02; SLJ 9/01) [636.2]

8740 Gaines, Ann. *The Panama Canal in American History* (4–8). Series: In American History. 1999, Enslow LB $26.60 (978-0-7660-1216-5). This is a carefully researched history of the building of the Panama Canal, including a review of events before U.S. involvement, how the United States established the country of Panama and gained control of the Canal Zone, details of the many difficulties encountered, and a description of how the canal locks operate. (Rev: BL 3/1/99; HBG 10/99; SLJ 8/99) [972.87]

8741 Gold, Susan Dudley. *The Panama Canal Transfer: Controversy at the Crossroads* (7–10). 1999, Raintree $19.98 (978-0-8172-5762-0). The first half of this book describes the building of the canal and the second half traces the process of returning the Canal Zone to Panama, including the 1978 treaty providing for the return and the ill will and controversy that developed. (Rev: SLJ 8/99) [972.8]

8742 Hadden, Gerry. *Teenage Refugees from Guatemala Speak Out* (7–12). Series: Teenage Refugees Speak Out. 1997, Rosen LB $27.95 (978-0-8239-2439-4). Teens from Guatemala who now live in the U.S. describe the violent military campaigns that destroyed villages and lives in their homeland. (Rev: BL 10/15/97; SLJ 1/98) [972.8]

8743 Hassig, Susan M. *Panama* (4–7). Illus. Series: Cultures of the World. 1996, Marshall Cavendish LB $37.07 (978-0-7614-0278-7). The troubled history of Panama is covered, with material on geography and the lifestyle and culture of its people. (Rev: BL 8/96) [972.87]

8744 Haverstock, Nathan A. *Nicaragua in Pictures* (5–8). Illus. 1993, Lerner LB $25.55 (978-0-8225-1817-4). A visit to this controversial country is highlighted by color photographs and clear text. (Rev: BL 10/15/87) [972.85]

8745 *Honduras in Pictures* (4–7). Illus. Series: Visual Geography. 1994, Lerner LB $25.55 (978-0-8225-1804-4). Chapters focus on history, culture, education, people, geography, and lifestyles. (Rev: BL 8/87)

8746 Jermyn, Leslie. *Belize* (5–9). Series: Cultures of the World. 2001, Marshall Cavendish LB $37.07 (978-0-7614-1190-1). Geography, history, government, arts and culture, and lifestyle are all covered in this interesting and attractive volume. (Rev: HBG 10/01; SLJ 11/01) [972.82]

8747 Lindop, Edmund. *Panama and the United States: Divided by the Canal* (5–8). Illus. 1997, Twenty-First Century LB $23.40 (978-0-8050-4768-4). A history of United States-Panama relations, from the building of the canal to the present. (Rev: BL 8/97; SLJ 7/97) [327.7307287]

8748 McGaffey, Leta. *Honduras* (5–9). Series: Cultures of the World. 1999, Marshall Cavendish LB

$37.07 (978-0-7614-0955-7). After background material on the history and geography of Honduras, this book focuses on modern times and such topics as the economy, population, religion, holidays, and recreation. (Rev: HBG 10/99; SLJ 11/99) [972.8]

8749 McNeese, Tim. *The Panama Canal* (5–8). Illus. Series: Building History. 1997, Lucent LB $28.70 (978-1-56006-425-1). A description of the building of the Panama Canal that also supplies valuable insights into the economic and social conditions of the times. (Rev: BL 8/97; HBG 3/98; SLJ 7/97) [386]

8750 Malone, Michael. *A Guatemalan Family* (4–7). Illus. Series: Journey Between Two Worlds. 1996, Lerner paper $8.95 (978-0-8225-9742-1). The story of a refugee family from Guatemala and of its resettlement in the United States. (Rev: BL 11/15/96; SLJ 1/97) [975.9]

8751 Mann, Elizabeth. *Tikal: The Center of the Maya World* (4–8). Illus. by Tom McNeely. Series: Wonders of the World. 2002, Mikaya $19.95 (978-1-931414-05-0). Mann provides an overview for older readers of the Mayan city of Tikal, covering the location, the people, the architecture, the culture, and their sometimes bloodthirsty customs. (Rev: BL 12/15/02; HBG 3/03; SLJ 1/03) [972.81]

8752 Markun, Patricia M. *It's Panama's Canal!* (5–9). Illus. 1999, Linnet LB $22.50 (978-0-208-02499-2). This account gives a good background history of the canal plus current information on Panama's control of the zone and its plans for successful management. (Rev: BL 1/1–15/00; HBG 3/00) [972.87]

8753 Morrison, Marion. *Nicaragua* (4–7). Series: Enchantment of the World. 2002, Children's LB $37.00 (978-0-516-20963-0). Such topics as geography, history, people, language, economy, and government are covered in this introduction to Nicaragua. (Rev: BL 5/15/02) [972.8]

8754 Netzley, Patricia D. *Maya Civilization* (6–9). 2002, Gale LB $32.45 (978-1-56006-806-8). Primary and secondary sources are incorporated into the text of this introduction to the Mayans and their culture that emphasizes the role of historians. (Rev: SLJ 12/02) [972]

8755 *Panama in Pictures* (4–7). Illus. Series: Visual Geography. 1996, Lerner LB $25.55 (978-0-8225-1818-1). The life and culture, history, and geography of the people of Panama. (Rev: BL 8/87) [972.87]

8756 Sheehan, Sean. *Guatemala* (6–10). Series: Cultures of the World. 1998, Marshall Cavendish LB $37.07 (978-0-7614-0812-3). A solid introduction to Guatemala's geography, politics, and culture. (Rev: HBG 9/98; SLJ 2/99) [972.8]

8757 Shields, Charles J. *Belize* (5–7). Illus. Series: Discovering Central America. 2002, Mason Crest LB $19.95 (978-1-59084-092-4). Students needing facts about Belize will find everything here: geography, history, people, and culture, all backed up by maps, photographs, a timeline, and even recipes. (Rev: BL 1/1–15/03) [972.82]

8758 Shields, Charles J. *Central America: Facts and Figures* (5–7). Illus. Series: Discovering Central America. 2002, Mason Crest LB $19.95 (978-1-59084-099-3). This look at Central America as a whole covers history, geography, inhabitants, and cultures. (Rev: BL 1/1–15/03) [972.8]

8759 Silverstone, Michael. *Rigoberta Menchu: Defending Human Rights in Guatemala* (5–8). Illus. 1999, Feminist paper $9.95 (978-1-55861-199-3). In addition to a biography of Nobel Peace Prize winner Rigoberta Menchu, this account presents Guatemala, its civil war, and the efforts to end it. (Rev: BL 3/15/00) [972.81]

MEXICO

8760 Bingham, Jane. *The Aztec Empire* (5–8). Series: Time Travel Guides. 2007, Raintree LB $34.29 (978-1-4109-2730-9). An attractive trip back in time to the Aztec Empire, providing details about daily life there — accommodation, food, shopping, and so forth — as well as the calendar and festivals. (Rev: LMC 11-12/07; SLJ 9/07) [972]

8761 Burr, Claudia, et al. *Broken Shields* (4–8). Illus. 1997, Douglas & McIntyre paper $6.95 (978-0-88899-304-5). From firsthand eyewitness accounts, this is the story of the betrayal of Montezuma at the hands of the Spanish conqueror Cortez. (Rev: BL 12/1/97; HB 11–12/97; HBG 3/98; SLJ 1/98) [972]

8762 Chapman, Gillian. *The Aztecs* (4–8). Series: Crafts from the Past. 1997, Heinemann LB $25.64 (978-1-57572-555-0). A craft book with instructions for a variety of Aztec ornaments and artifacts, including textiles and statues. (Rev: SLJ 4/98) [745]

8763 Flowers, Charles. *Cortés and the Conquest of the Aztec Empire in World History* (6–10). Illus. Series: In World History. 2001, Enslow LB $26.60 (978-0-7660-1395-7). This accessible and interesting account describes Cortes's incursion into the Aztec empire and explains how the Aztecs' beliefs contributed to the ease of this conquest. (Rev: HBG 10/01; SLJ 8/01) [972]

8764 Franklin, Sharon, et al. *Mexico and Central America* (4–7). Illus. Series: Artisans Around the World. 1999, Raintree LB $27.12 (978-0-7398-0121-5). This craft book, with related projects, describes the folk art of each of the countries in Central America and Mexico. (Rev: BL 10/15/99; HBG 3/00; SLJ 1/00) [745.5]

8765 Gruber, Beth. *Mexico* (4–8). Series: Countries of the World. 2006, National Geographic $19.95 (978-0-7922-7629-6). This book covers the geography, people, language, customs, and natural resources of Mexico, with plenty of graphics to add interest to the presentation. (Rev: BL 2/15/07; LMC 4-5/07) [917.2]

8766 Hadden, Gerry. *Teenage Refugees from Mexico Speak Out* (7–12). Series: Teenage Refugees Speak Out. 1997, Rosen LB $27.95 (978-0-8239-2441-7). Teens who have left Mexico and come to the U.S. to escape economic conditions and political instability tell about their experiences. (Rev: BL 10/15/97; SLJ 1/98) [972]

8767 Hamilton, Janice. *Mexico in Pictures*. Rev. ed. (4–8). Illus. Series: Visual Geography. 2002, Lerner LB $27.93 (978-0-8225-1960-7). An excellent introduction to Mexico that includes material on geography, history, people, economy, and culture with maps, photographs, and illustrations. (Rev: HBG 3/03; SLJ 3/03) [972]

8768 Hull, Robert. *The Aztecs* (5–10). Series: Ancient World. 1998, Raintree LB $27.12 (978-0-8172-5056-0). This history of the Aztecs and their culture describes their great pyramids, feathered headdresses, gods, human sacrifices, and the coming of the Spanish. (Rev: BL 1/1–15/99; HBG 3/99) [972]

8769 Jovinelly, Joann, and Jason Netelkos. *The Crafts and Culture of the Aztecs* (5–8). Illus. Series: Crafts of the Ancient World. 2002, Rosen LB $29.25 (978-0-8239-3512-3). The culture of the Aztecs is covered through a discussion of their crafts and a variety of easily accomplished projects related to them. (Rev: BL 4/1/02; VOYA 6/02) [972]

8770 Kent, Deborah. *Mexico: Rich in Spirit and Tradition* (4–8). Series: Exploring Cultures of the World. 1995, Benchmark LB $27.07 (978-0-7614-0187-2). This book begins with a Mexican folktale, then gives an overview of the country's people, culture, history, and problems. (Rev: SLJ 6/96) [972]

8771 Lewington, Anna. *Mexico* (5–8). Illus. Series: Economically Developing Countries. 1996, Raintree LB $24.26 (978-0-8172-4528-3). A fine general profile of Mexico that includes jobs, industries, and other economic indicators. (Rev: BL 3/15/97; SLJ 2/97) [330.972]

8772 Lewis, Elizabeth. *Mexican Art and Culture* (5–8). Illus. Series: World Art and Culture. 2004, Raintree LB $29.99 (978-0-7398-6610-8). The indigenous art and culture of Mexico from prehistoric times to the present are beautifully captured in this handsome and comprehensive overview. (Rev: BL 4/1/04; SLJ 2/04) [709]

8773 Libura, Krystyna, et al. *What the Aztecs Told Me* (4–8). Illus. 1997, Douglas & McIntyre paper

$6.95 (978-0-88899-306-9). Based on an original 12-volume work written in the 16th century, this book describes the Aztec people from observation and eyewitness accounts. (Rev: BL 12/1/97; HB 11–12/97; HBG 3/98; SLJ 12/97) [972]

8774 Marquez, Heron. *Destination Veracruz* (5–8). Series: Port Cities of North America. 1998, Lerner LB $23.93 (978-0-8225-2791-6). A description of this port city on the Gulf of Mexico that reviews its history, everyday life, the effects of development on the environment, and the city's economy, including the impact of NAFTA and a discussion of international trade, economic systems, and free trade. (Rev: HBG 3/99; SLJ 3/99) [972]

8775 Pascoe, Elaine. *Mexico and the United States: Cooperation and Conflict* (7–12). Illus. 1996, Twenty-First Century LB $24.90 (978-0-8050-4180-4). After a history of the stormy relations between Mexico and the U.S., the author discusses current problems, such as drug trafficking, oil, the peso, and immigration. (Rev: BL 12/1/96; SLJ 1/97) [303.48]

8776 Reilly, Mary J. *Mexico* (5–8). Illus. Series: Cultures of the World. 1991, Marshall Cavendish LB $35.64 (978-1-85435-385-6). This account emphasizes the geography, history, economy, and lifestyles of the Mexican people. (Rev: BL 4/1/91) [972]

8777 Rosenblum, Morris. *Heroes of Mexico* (5–8). 1972, Fleet $9.50 (978-0-8303-0082-2). A collected group of profiles of people important in the history of Mexico. (Rev: BL 6/87) [972]

8778 Rummel, Jack. *Mexico* (6–10). Series: Major World Nations. 1998, Chelsea LB $19.95 (978-0-7910-4763-7). A well-illustrated account that emphasizes current economic, political, and cultural conditions, supplemented by good background information. (Rev: BL 9/15/98; HBG 3/99; SLJ 12/98) [917.2]

8779 Sanna, Ellyn. *Mexico: Facts and Figures* (5–8). Series: Mexico: Our Southern Neighbor. 2002, Mason Crest LB $19.95 (978-1-59084-088-7). An introduction to Mexico and its states, with material on history, people and culture today, and issues of importance such as poverty. Also use *The Geography of Mexico*, *The Economy of Mexico*, and *The Government of Mexico*. (Rev: SLJ 12/02) [972]

8780 Stein, R. Conrad. *The Aztec Empire* (5–8). Series: Cultures of the Past. 1995, Benchmark LB $29.93 (978-0-7614-0072-1). The Aztecs' history, beliefs, and lifestyles are examined in this book, with quotations from original sources and many color photographs of artifacts, monuments, and historical sites. (Rev: SLJ 6/96) [972]

8781 Stein, R. Conrad. *The Mexican Revolution* (6–12). 2007, Morgan Reynolds LB $27.95 (978-1-59935-051-6). This comprehensive, well-written book covers the Mexican Revolution in detail and does not gloss over the more violent aspects of the conflict (includes maps, photos, reproductions, bibliography, chronology, index, notes and Web sites). (Rev: SLJ 3/08)

8782 Stein, R. Conrad. *The Mexican War of Independence* (6–12). 2007, Morgan Reynolds LB $27.95 (978-1-59935-054-7). Lively text and illustrations will appeal to readers of this volume, which covers three centuries of Spanish rule of Mexico, from 1521-1855 (includes maps, photos, reproductions, bibliography, chronology, index, notes and Web sites). (Rev: SLJ 3/08)

PUERTO RICO, CUBA, AND OTHER CARIBBEAN ISLANDS

8783 Anthony, Suzanne. *West Indies* (6–12). Series: Major World Nations. 1998, Chelsea LB $19.95 (978-0-7910-4772-9). An introduction to the people, geography, history, and economy of the West Indies, with a focus on current conditions. (Rev: BL 9/15/98) [975.9]

8784 Carey, Charles W., Jr., ed. *Castro's Cuba* (7–12). Series: History Firsthand. 2004, Gale LB $36.20 (978-0-7377-1654-2); paper $24.95 (978-0-7377-1655-9). Historical documents, interviews, and newspaper and magazine articles are used in this account of Castro's takeover in Cuba and developments since then. (Rev: SLJ 11/04) [972]

8785 Fernandez, Ronald M., et al. *Puerto Rico Past and Present: An Encyclopedia* (8–12). 1998, Greenwood $86.95 (978-0-313-29822-6). A browsable book that contains biographies of famous Puerto Ricans as well as political terms and groups, buildings, important court decisions, and other information on the island's cultural and historical developments. (Rev: BL 7/97; VOYA 10/98) [972.95]

8786 Fisanick, Christina. *The Bay of Pigs* (6–12). Series: At Issue in History. 2004, Gale paper $23.70 (978-0-7377-1990-1). The failed Bay of Pigs invasion is described in an introductory overview followed by a collection of essays, speeches, and editorials that provide diverse views about the event. (Rev: BL 9/1/04) [972.910]

8787 Greenberg, Keith E. *A Haitian Family* (4–7). Illus. Series: Journey Between Two Worlds. 1998, Lerner LB $22.60 (978-0-8225-3410-5). The story of the Beaubrun family, the political oppression they suffered in Haiti, and their eventual journey to freedom in the United States. (Rev: BL 3/1/98; HBG 10/98) [305.9]

8788 Harlan, Judith. *Puerto Rico: Deciding Its Future* (7–10). Illus. 1996, Twenty-First Century LB $23.40 (978-0-8050-4372-3). The statehood-commonwealth-independence question is presented with clarity, simplicity, and objectivity. (Rev: BL 1/1–15/97; SLJ 7/97) [972.95]

8789 Haverstock, Nathan A. *Cuba in Pictures* (5–8). Illus. Series: Visual Geography. 1997, Lerner LB $25.55 (978-0-8225-1811-2). A look at America's island neighbor, with color photographs. Also use *Dominican Republic in Pictures* (1997). (Rev: BL 10/15/87) [972.91064]

8790 *Jamaica in Pictures* (5–8). Illus. Series: Visual Geography. 1997, Lerner LB $25.55 (978-0-8225-1814-3). Color photographs highlight this visit to a popular and beautiful island. (Rev: BL 10/15/87) [972.92]

8791 McCarthy, Pat. *The Dominican Republic* (5–8). Illus. Series: Top Ten Countries of Recent Immigrants. 2004, Enslow LB $25.26 (978-0-7660-5179-9). Information on the Dominican Republic — culture, history, climate, and people — accompanies an explanation of the reasons for migration to the United States and discussion of the contributions of this community; supported by Web links. (Rev: SLJ 3/05) [304]

8792 Marquez, Heron. *Destination San Juan* (5–8). Series: Port Cities of North America. 1998, Lerner LB $23.93 (978-0-8225-2792-3). A matter-of-fact introduction to San Juan that describes the city, people, economy, and port activities. (Rev: HBG 3/99; SLJ 3/99) [972.95]

8793 Morrison, Marion. *Cuba* (4–7). Illus. Series: Country Insights. 1998, Raintree LB $27.12 (978-0-8172-4796-6). An introduction to contemporary life in Cuba, showing the contrast between life in a big city (Havana) and in a country village. (Rev: BL 5/1/98; HBG 10/98) [972.91]

8794 *Puerto Rico in Pictures* (4–7). Illus. Series: Visual Geography. 1995, Lerner LB $25.55 (978-0-8225-1821-1). Everyday life, history, culture, and geography are introduced. (Rev: BL 8/87) [972.95]

8795 Sheehan, Sean. *Jamaica* (5–8). Illus. Series: Cultures of the World. 1993, Marshall Cavendish LB $25.95 (978-1-85435-581-2). This informative account describes many facets of Jamaican life, including history, religion, and reggae music. (Rev: SLJ 2/94) [972.92]

8796 Sheehan, Sean, and Leslie Jermyn. *Cuba* (7–10). Illus. Series: Cultures of the World: Second Edition. 2005, Marshall Cavendish LB $25.95 (978-0-7614-1964-8). A frank, balanced, and readable overview of Cuba's history, geography, economy, culture, and people. (Rev: BL 2/15/06) [972.91]

8797 Sherrow, Victoria. *Cuba* (7–12). Illus. 2001, Twenty-First Century LB $24.90 (978-0-7613-1404-2). Fidel Castro is a key figure in this overview of Cuba's internal affairs and relations with the outside world that will be useful for report writers.

(Rev: BL 9/15/01; HBG 3/02; SLJ 12/01; VOYA 12/01) [973.91]

8798 Tuck, Jay, and Norma C. Vergara. *Heroes of Puerto Rico* (5–8). 1969, Fleet $9.50 (978-0-8303-0070-9). A series of profiles of famous Puerto Ricans. (Rev: BL 6/87) [972.9]

8799 Turck, Mary C. *Haiti: Land of Inequality* (8–12). Series: World in Conflict. 1999, Lerner $25.26 (978-0-8225-3554-6). Though now out of date, this well-illustrated book gives good background information on this troubled land and its history. (Rev: BL 10/15/99; HBG 4/00; SLJ 2/00) [975.9]

8800 Will, Emily Wade. *Haiti* (5–8). Series: Modern Nations of the World. 2001, Lucent LB $29.95 (978-1-56006-761-0). The history, geography, and culture of this island country are presented with colorful prose and pictures plus unusual facts contained in sidebars. (Rev: BL 6/1–15/01) [972.94]

8801 Worth, Richard. *Puerto Rico in American History* (7–12). Illus. Series: From Many Cultures, One History. 2008, Enslow LB $23.95 (978-0-7660-2836-4). An interesting overview of an often-overlooked part of the United States, with an attractive layout. (Rev: BL 4/1/08) [972.95]

South America

8802 *Argentina in Pictures* (5–8). Illus. Series: Visual Geography. 1994, Lerner LB $25.55 (978-0-8225-1807-5). An overview of climate, wildlife, cities, vegetation, and mineral resources. (Rev: BL 4/15/88; SLJ 5/88) [982]

8803 Augustin, Byron. *Bolivia* (4–7). Series: Enchantment of the World. 2001, Children's LB $37.00 (978-0-516-21050-6). With each page containing a color illustration, this attractive book introduces the land and people, economy, culture, and natural resources of Bolivia. (Rev: BL 1/1–15/02) [984]

8804 Barter, James. *The Galapagos Islands* (7–10). Series: Endangered Animals and Habitats. 2002, Gale LB $27.45 (978-1-56006-920-1). In text and many color illustrations, this endangered habitat and its history are described with material on the methods employed to save these unique islands from destruction. (Rev: BL 5/15/02) [508.866]

8805 Bender, Evelyn. *Brazil* (6–12). Series: Major World Nations. 1998, Chelsea LB $21.95 (978-0-7910-4758-3). Current economic and social conditions in Brazil are emphasized, supplemented by background material on history and geography. (Rev: BL 9/15/98; HBG 3/99) [981]

8806 Bernhard, Brendan. *Pizarro, Orellana, and the Exploration of the Amazon* (6–9). Series: World Explorers. 1991, Chelsea LB $32.00 (978-0-7910-

1305-2). An account of the hardships, dangers, and rewards faced by the early explorers of the Amazon. (Rev: BL 9/15/91; SLJ 12/91) [981]

8807 Bingham, Jane. *The Inca Empire* (5–8). Series: Time Travel Guides. 2007, Raintree LB $34.29 (978-1-4109-2731-6). An attractive trip back in time to the Inca Empire, providing details about daily life there — accommodation, food, shopping, and so forth. (Rev: SLJ 9/07) [985]

8808 Calvert, Patricia. *The Ancient Inca* (5–8). Series: People of the Ancient World. 2004, Watts LB $30.50 (978-0-531-12358-4). This fascinating volume covers the history and culture of the Inca people, looking at childhood and the daily life of people ranging from farmers to priests, warriors, and emperors. (Rev: SLJ 3/05) [985]

8809 Cameron, Sara. *Out of War: True Stories from the Front Lines of the Children's Movement for Peace in Colombia* (7–12). 2001, Scholastic $15.95 (978-0-439-29721-9). Nine teen members of the Colombian peace movement describe their lives in this war-torn country and express their desire for peace rather than retribution. (Rev: BL 9/1/01; HBG 3/02; SLJ 8/01; VOYA 10/01) [305.23]

8810 Castner, James L. *Native Peoples* (6–12). Illus. Series: Deep in the Amazon. 2001, Marshall Cavendish LB $28.50 (978-0-7614-1128-4). This volume looks at the people of the Amazon, their way of life, and the encroachment of outsiders. Also use *Rainforest Researchers* (2001). (Rev: BL 12/15/01; HBG 3/02) [981]

8811 *Colombia in Pictures* (5–8). Illus. Series: Visual Geography. 1996, Lerner LB $25.55 (978-0-8225-1810-5). Many photographs highlight this visit to a South American nation. (Rev: BL 10/15/87) [986.1]

8812 Corona, Laurel. *Brazil* (5–8). Series: Modern Nations of the World. 1999, Lucent LB $27.45 (978-1-56006-621-7). A lively account of Brazil's history, geography, famous people, and conditions today. (Rev: BL 2/15/00; HBG 10/00) [981]

8813 Corona, Laurel. *Peru* (5–8). Series: Modern Nations of the World. 2001, Lucent LB $28.70 (978-1-56006-862-4). Detailed sidebars, a chronology, and national statistics supplement the general information presented in this colorful introduction to Peru. (Rev: BL 6/1–15/01) [985]

8814 Dalal, Anita. *Argentina* (4–8). Series: Nations of the World. 2001, Raintree LB $34.26 (978-0-7398-1279-2). A colorful, interesting introduction to Argentina that covers its land and cities, history, culture, present economic conditions, and possible future developments. (Rev: BL 6/1–15/01; HBG 10/01) [982]

8815 Dalal, Anita. *Brazil* (4–8). Series: Nations of the World. 2001, Raintree LB $34.26 (978-0-7398-

1284-6). A profile of the home of Carnival, the Amazon, and Pele with material attractively presented on its past and present, its people, and its culture. (Rev: BL 6/1–15/01; HBG 10/01) [981]

8816 Dicks, Brian. *Brazil* (6–10). Illus. Series: Countries of the World. 2003, Facts on File $30.00 (978-0-8160-5382-7). A well-illustrated account that covers all important topics including present-day racial friction and economic inequality. (Rev: BL 2/1/04) [949.12]

8817 Dubois, Jill. *Colombia* (5–8). Illus. Series: Cultures of the World. 1991, Marshall Cavendish LB $35.64 (978-1-85435-384-9). Background information on Colombia is given as well as coverage of contemporary concerns. (Rev: BL 4/1/91) [986.1]

8818 Falconer, Kieran. *Peru* (4–7). Illus. Series: Cultures of the World. 1995, Marshall Cavendish LB $37.07 (978-0-7614-0179-7). The focus of this book is on the people of Peru, their lifestyles, artistic endeavors, religion, and leisure activities. (Rev: BL 1/1–15/96; SLJ 4/96) [985]

8819 Fearns, Les, and Daisy Fearns. *Argentina* (7–10). Series: Countries of the World. 2005, Facts on File LB $30.00 (978-0-8160-6008-5). History, geography, culture, government, and economy are all covered in this attractive overview of Argentina. (Rev: SLJ 1/06) [982]

8820 Foley, Erin. *Ecuador* (5–8). Illus. Series: Cultures of the World. 1995, Marshall Cavendish LB $37.07 (978-0-7614-0173-5). This book supplies good background material on Ecuador but is strongest in describing contemporary conditions. (Rev: SLJ 11/95) [980]

8821 Gofen, Ethel C. *Cultures of the World: Argentina* (5–8). Illus. Series: Cultures of the World. 1991, Marshall Cavendish LB $213.86 (978-1-85435-380-1). This book provides standard information on history and geography and tells about the contemporary lifestyles of the people. (Rev: BL 4/1/91) [962]

8822 Gorrell, Gena K. *In the Land of the Jaguar: South America and Its People* (6–10). Illus. by Andrej Krystoforski. 2007, Tundra $22.95 (978-0-88776-756-2). A beautiful and informative book that covers all the countries of South America, discussing their geography, animals, and natural resources as well as their people and their customs. (Rev: BL 10/1/07; SLJ 11/07) [980]

8823 *Guyana in Pictures* (5–8). Illus. Series: Visual Geography. 1997, Lerner LB $25.55 (978-0-8225-1815-0). History, climate, wildlife, and major cities are covered in this overview. (Rev: BL 4/15/88) [988.1]

8824 Haverstock, Nathan A. *Brazil in Pictures* (4–7). Illus. Series: Visual Geography. 1997, Lerner LB $25.55 (978-0-8225-1802-0). Current data on the political scene, plus chapters on history, people, and culture in this revised text. Also use *Chile in Pictures* (1988). (Rev: BL 8/87)

8825 Haverstock, Nathan A. *Paraguay in Pictures* (5–8). Illus. Series: Visual Geography. 1995, Lerner LB $25.55 (978-0-8225-1819-8). This overview of Paraguay includes its history to 1987 and possible future developments. (Rev: BL 4/15/88) [989.2]

8826 Jermyn, Leslie. *Paraguay* (5–8). 1999, Marshall Cavendish LB $37.07 (978-0-7614-0979-3). This book about Paraguay covers history, geography, government, and economy as well as such social and cultural topics as religion, the arts, food, and recreation. (Rev: HBG 10/00; SLJ 4/00) [989]

8827 Jermyn, Leslie. *Uruguay* (7–10). Series: Cultures of the World. 1998, Marshall Cavendish LB $37.07 (978-0-7614-0873-4). An attractive book that covers all the basic topics relating to Uruguay, plus material on leisure activities, festivals, and food. (Rev: HBG 9/99; SLJ 6/99) [980]

8828 Litteral, Linda L. *Boobies, Iguanas, and Other Critters: Nature's Story in the Galapagos* (6–10). 1994, American Kestrel $23.00 (978-1-883966-01-0). After a historical overview of the Galapagos Islands, this richly illustrated book covers the islands' animals, plants, and geology. (Rev: BL 6/1–15/94; SLJ 9/94) [508.866]

8829 Lourie, Peter. *Lost Treasure of the Inca* (4–7). Illus. 1999, Boyds Mills $18.95 (978-1-56397-743-5). A thrilling narrative of a modern search for the gold supposedly hidden by the Incas in the Ecuadorian mountains. (Rev: BCCB 11/99; BL 10/15/99; HBG 3/00; SLJ 11/99) [986.6]

8830 McNair, Sylvia. *Chile* (4–7). Series: Enchantment of the World. 2000, Children's LB $37.00 (978-0-516-21007-0). This attractive new edition of an old title includes material on Chile's land and people, history and government, economics and landmarks, daily life, and sports. (Rev: BL 7/00) [983]

8831 Martell, Hazel M. *Civilizations of Peru, Before 1535* (5–8). Illus. Series: Looking Back. 1999, Raintree $19.98 (978-0-8172-5428-5). This book covers the history and culture of the Inca empire that stretched far beyond the boundaries of Peru. (Rev: BL 5/15/99; SLJ 7/99) [985]

8832 Morrison, Marion. *Brazil* (4–7). Illus. Series: Country Insights. 1997, Raintree LB $27.12 (978-0-8172-4785-0). Compares the home life, employment, schooling, and recreation in a large city and in a small village in Brazil. (Rev: BL 7/97; SLJ 8/97) [918.1]

8833 Morrison, Marion. *Ecuador* (4–7). Series: Enchantment of the World. 2000, Children's LB $37.00 (978-0-516-21544-0). This book examines the geography and climate of Ecuador, its history,

government, language, economy, and people. (Rev: BL 1/1–15/01) [986]

8834 Morrison, Marion. *Guyana* (5–8). Illus. Series: Enchantment of the World, Second Series. 2003, Children's LB $37.00 (978-0-516-22377-3). A visually attractive book that covers such topics as the geography, history, government, culture, and people with a timeline, fast facts, and a recipe. (Rev: SLJ 5/03) [966.7]

8835 Nishi, Dennis. *The Inca Empire* (7–10). Series: World History. 2000, Lucent LB $27.45 (978-1-56006-538-8). This book discusses the mightiest of the Andean civilizations and how it spread over a great part of South America and created an intricate social structure. (Rev: BL 6/1–15/00; HBG 9/00; SLJ 7/00) [985]

8836 Parker, Edward. *Peru* (5–8). Illus. 1996, Raintree LB $24.26 (978-0-8172-4525-2). After a general introduction to Peru, this account discusses such current economic indicators as the job market, industry, and agriculture. (Rev: BL 3/15/97; SLJ 2/97) [985]

8837 Pateman, Robert. *Bolivia* (4–7). Illus. Series: Cultures of the World. 1995, Marshall Cavendish LB $37.07 (978-0-7614-0178-0). The people of Bolivia, how they live, and their traditions are some of the topics covered in this general introduction. (Rev: BL 1/1–15/96; SLJ 4/96) [984]

8838 Peck, Robert McCracken. *Headhunters and Hummingbirds: An Expedition into Ecuador* (7–10). Illus. 1987, Walker LB $14.85 (978-0-8027-6646-5). An account of an ill-fated scientific expedition into the land of the Jívaro Indians in Ecuador. (Rev: SLJ 6/87; VOYA 8/87) [986]

8839 *Peru in Pictures* (5–8). Illus. Series: Visual Geography. 1997, Lerner LB $25.55 (978-0-8225-1820-4). An introduction to this South American land, highlighted by color photographs. (Rev: BL 10/15/87) [985]

8840 Rawlins, Carol B. *The Orinoco River* (4–7). Illus. Series: World of Water. 1999, Watts LB $25.50 (978-0-531-11740-8). An introduction to this important Venezuelan river, with material on its history and current status and the areas through which it passes. (Rev: BL 1/1–15/00) [987.06]

8841 Rice, Earle, Jr. *A Brief Political and Geographic History of Latin America: Where Are Gran Colombia, La Plata, and Dutch Guiana?* (6–9). Illus. Series: Places in Time. 2007, Mitchell Lane LB $24.95 (978-1-58415-626-0). The history of the region (beginning in the 16th century) as well as information about Latin America's culture, geography, natural resources, and important people, in an attractive format. (Rev: BL 10/15/07; SLJ 8/08) [980]

8842 Richard, Christopher. *Brazil* (5–8). Illus. Series: Cultures of the World. 1991, Marshall Cavendish LB $35.64 (978-1-85435-382-5). Brazil is introduced with information on such topics as history, economics, people, and modern problems. (Rev: BL 4/1/91) [981]

8843 Robinson, Roger. *Brazil* (5–8). Series: Country Studies. 1999, Heinemann LB $27.07 (978-1-57572-892-6). Using colorful charts, graphs, drawings, maps, and photographs in double-page spreads, this book provides basic information about Brazil, with emphasis on regional contrasts and contemporary issues, such as population changes and the growth of agribusiness. (Rev: BL 8/99; SLJ 8/99) [981]

8844 Sayer, Chloe. *The Incas* (5–10). Series: Ancient World. 1998, Raintree LB $27.12 (978-0-8172-5125-3). An in-depth look at Inca life, from their beautiful gold ornaments to their unique form of record keeping and impressive citadels and forts. (Rev: BL 1/1–15/99; HBG 3/99) [985]

8845 Somervill, Barbara A. *Empire of the Inca* (7–10). Illus. Series: Great Empires of the Past. 2004, Facts on File $35.00 (978-0-8160-5560-9). In addition to covering the Inca civilization, Somervill draws connections from that ancient society to contemporary culture. (Rev: BL 2/1/05) [985]

8846 Tagliaferro, Linda. *Galapagos Islands: Nature's Delicate Balance at Risk* (4–8). Illus. 2001, Lerner LB $27.93 (978-0-8225-0648-5). This is a detailed but accessible introduction to the history, geology, wildlife, and ecology of the Galapagos Islands, with maps and photographs. (Rev: BL 9/15/01; HBG 3/02; SLJ 11/01; VOYA 12/01) [561.9866]

8847 *Venezuela in Pictures* (4–7). Illus. Series: Visual Geography. 1993, Lerner LB $21.27 (978-0-8225-1824-2). The land, people, and government of this oil-rich country are explored in maps, text, and photographs. (Rev: BL 1/1/88) [987]

8848 Winter, Jane K. *Chile* (5–8). Illus. Series: Cultures of the World. 1991, Marshall Cavendish LB $35.64 (978-1-85435-383-2). The geography, history, government, and economy of Chile are some of the topics covered in this fine introduction. (Rev: BL 4/1/91) [983]

8849 Winter, Jane K. *Venezuela* (5–8). Illus. Series: Cultures of the World. 1991, Marshall Cavendish LB $35.64 (978-1-85435-386-3). In detailed text and color photographs, the land, people, and contemporary problems and concerns of Venezuela are introduced. (Rev: BL 4/1/91) [987]

8850 Worth, Richard. *Pizarro and the Conquest of the Incan Empire in World History* (6–9). Series: In World History. 2000, Enslow LB $26.60 (978-0-7660-1396-4). The explorer's conquest and its historical context and consequences are described. (Rev: HBG 9/00; SLJ 7/00) [985.019]

Polar Regions

8851 Anderson, Harry S. *Exploring the Polar Regions* (8–11). Illus. Series: Discovery and Exploration. 2004, Facts on File $40.00 (978-0-8160-5259-2). This analytical history of polar exploration looks at the motivations behind the expeditions as well as the specifics of early and modern ventures into new terrain. (Rev: BL 1/05; SLJ 12/04) [910]

8852 Bial, Raymond. *The Inuit* (5–8). Series: Lifeways. 2001, Marshall Cavendish LB $34.21 (978-0-7614-1212-0). Using clear language and many intriguing illustrations, this is a fine introduction to the Inuit that begins with a folk story on the origins of the people and continues with material on a variety of basic topics. (Rev: BL 1/1–15/02; HBG 3/02; SLJ 4/02) [979.8]

8853 Bledsoe, Lucy Jane. *How to Survive in Antarctica* (5–8). 2006, Holiday $16.95 (978-0-8234-1890-9). An account of the author's trips to Antarctica, filled with interesting facts about the frigid land — from wildlife notes to survival tips — plus photographs by the author. (Rev: BCCB 10/06; BL 7/06; HBG 4/07; SLJ 8/06; VOYA 8/06) [919.8]

8854 Bocknek, Jonathan. *Antarctica: The Last Wilderness* (5–8). Series: Understanding Global Issues. 2003, Smart Apple $19.95 (978-1-58340-356-3). This nicely illustrated book introduces Antarctica with material on climate, animals, exploration, and possible future developments. (Rev: BL 11/15/03; HB 9–10/01; HBG 3/02; SLJ 12/03) [998.9]

8855 Bredeson, Carmen. *After the Last Dog Died: The True-Life, Hair-Raising Adventures of Douglas Mawson and his 1911–1914 Antarctic Expedition* (5–8). Illus. 2003, National Geographic $18.95 (978-0-7922-6140-7). This enthralling story of courage in the face of starvation and harsh conditions draws on primary materials including the writings of expedition leader Mawson himself. (Rev: BL 11/1/03; HBG 4/04; SLJ 1/04*) [919.8]

8856 Currie, Stephen. *Antarctica* (7–12). Illus. Series: Exploration and Discovery. 2004, Gale LB $29.95 (978-1-59018-495-0). Currie examines early theories about what lay at the southern end of the Earth and chronicles the early-20th-century expeditions to learn more about the continent. (Rev: BL 10/15/04) [919.8]

8857 Fiennes, Ranulph. *Race to the Pole: Tragedy, Heroism, and Scott's Antarctic Quest* (8–12). 2004, Hyperion $27.95 (978-1-4013-0047-0). Fiennes, a polar explorer himself, offers an in-depth account of Captain Robert Scott's ill-fated 1911–1912 expedition to the South Pole. (Rev: BL 9/15/04) [919.8]

8858 Fine, Jil. *The Shackleton Expedition* (5–8). Series: Survivor. 2002, Children's LB $24.50 (978-

0-516-23904-0); paper $6.95 (978-0-516-23489-2). For reluctant readers, this is an accessible and exciting account of how Shackleton's men survived the perils of shipwreck in the ice. (Rev: SLJ 9/02) [919.8904]

8859 Henderson, Bruce. *True North: Peary, Cook, and the Race to the Pole* (8–12). Illus. 2005, Norton $24.95 (978-0-393-05791-1). Who got to the North Pole first? Henderson offers evidence for the reader to mull over. (Rev: BL 1/1–15/05) [910]

8860 Hooper, Meredith. *Antarctic Journal: The Hidden Worlds of Antarctica's Animals* (5–7). Illus. by Lucia deLeiris. 2001, National Geographic $16.95 (978-0-7922-7188-8). An exciting account of a summer the author spent at Palmer Station in the Antarctic and the wildlife there. (Rev: BL 6/1–15/01; HBG 10/01; SLJ 3/01) [988]

8861 Kimmel, Elizabeth C. *Ice Story: Shackleton's Lost Expedition* (4–7). Illus. 1999, Clarion $19.00 (978-0-395-91524-0). A fine, accurate, and engrossing description of Shackleton's Imperial Transatlantic Expedition to the Antarctic — one of the great survival stories of all time. (Rev: BL 4/1/99; HBG 10/99; SLJ 4/99) [910.9]

8862 Loewen, Nancy, and Ann Bancroft. *Four to the Pole!* (6–9). Illus. 2001, Linnet $25.00 (978-0-208-02518-0). Diary entries, interviews, and expedition newsletters bring to life the physical and mental strength required of the first all-woman team to reach the South Pole. (Rev: BL 9/1/01; HBG 3/02; SLJ 8/01*; VOYA 10/01) [919.8904]

8863 Lynch, Wayne. *The Arctic* (5–9). Series: Our Wild World Ecosystems. 2007, NorthWord $16.95 (978-1-55971-960-5); paper $8.95 (978-1-55971-961-2). Lynch introduces the flora and fauna of the Arctic with interesting anecdotes about his own experiences, color photographs, sidebar features, and eco-fact boxes. (Rev: SLJ 5/07) [577.0911]

8864 Markle, Sandra. *Animals Robert Scott Saw: An Adventure in Antarctica* (4–7). Illus. by Phil. Series: Explorers. 2008, Chronicle LB $16.99 (978-0-8118-4918-0). As the title indicates, this book focuses on the animals that explorer Scott took with him to the South Pole in 1912 and those he observed on the way. (Rev: BL 4/1/08) [919.8]

8865 Oberman, Sheldon. *The Shaman's Nephew: A Life in the Far North* (4–8). Illus. 2000, Stoddart $18.95 (978-0-7737-3200-1). This first-person narrative explores Inuit art and culture as experienced by Tookoome, an Inuit artist, who reflects on the daily life, beliefs, and myths of his people as presented in his work. (Rev: BL 6/1–15/00; SLJ 7/00) [971.9]

8866 Sandler, Martin. *Trapped in Ice! An Amazing True Whaling Adventure* (5–8). Illus. 2006, Scholastic $16.99 (978-0-439-74363-1). A gripping account of 1,219 people forced to abandon ship after their whaling vessels became imprisoned in Arctic ice during the early winter of 1871; includes maps, photographs, and journal accounts. (Rev: BL 4/15/06; SLJ 6/06) [639.2]

8867 Sayre, April P. *Antarctica* (5–8). Series: Seven Continents. 1998, Twenty-First Century LB $25.90 (978-0-7613-3227-5). A well-written and well-illustrated introduction to the Antarctic environment, including its geology, plants, animals, and research facilities. (Rev: BL 2/1/99; HBG 9/99; SLJ 4/99) [919.89]

8868 Scott, Elaine. *Poles Apart: Why Penguins and Polar Bears Will Never Be Neighbors* (4–8). Illus. 2004, Viking $17.99 (978-0-670-05925-6). This fascinating overview of the two polar regions examines their physical characteristics, seasons, wildlife, magnetism, exploration, and the effects of global warming. (Rev: BL 12/1/04; SLJ 12/04) [909]

8869 Senungetuk, Vivian, and Paul Tiulana. *A Place for Winter: Paul Tiulana's Story* (7–12). Illus. 1988, CIRI Foundation $17.95 (978-0-938227-02-1). The story of a King Island Eskimo boy, his childhood, and his people. (Rev: BL 5/15/88) [917.98]

8870 Sommers, Michael A. *Antarctic Melting: The Disappearing Antarctic Ice Cap* (4–8). Series: Extreme Environmental Threats. 2006, Rosen LB $27.95 (978-1-4042-0741-7). An examination of the impact that global warming has had on Antarctica since 1995, with discussion of the research that takes place on the continent and the work of glaciologists. (Rev: LMC 8-9/07; SLJ 8/07) [363.738]

8871 Steger, Will, and Jon Bowermaster. *Over the Top of the World: Explorer Will Steger's Trek Across the Arctic* (4–7). Illus. 1997, Scholastic paper $17.95 (978-0-590-84860-2). Describes the grueling, dangerous adventures involved in a journey across the Arctic Ocean. (Rev: BCCB 2/97; BL 4/15/97; SLJ 4/97*) [919.804]

8872 Tulloch, Coral. *Antarctica: The Heart of the World* (6–9). Illus. by author. 2006, Enchanted Lion $17.95 (978-1-59270-054-7). A continent visited by a tiny percentage of humans is described in this informative, illustrated book that covers historical and contemporary aspects. (Rev: SLJ 8/06) [919.89]

8873 Warrick, Karen Clemens. *The Race for the North Pole in World History* (8–12). Series: In World History. 2002, Enslow LB $26.60 (978-0-7660-1933-1). Various explorers of the Arctic are introduced with emphasis on Robert Peary and Frederick Cook, both of whom claimed to be the first to reach the North Pole. (Rev: BL 3/15/03; HBG 10/03; VOYA 8/03) [979.8]

8874 Winckler, Suzanne. *Our Endangered Planet: Antarctica* (4–7). Illus. Series: Our Endangered Planet. 1992, Lerner LB $27.15 (978-0-8225-2506-6). Introduces the continent of Antarctica, including current environmental concerns. (Rev: BL 5/15/92) [918.8]

8875 Winner, Cherie. *Life in the Tundra* (5–8). Series: Ecosystems in Action. 2003, Lerner LB $26.60 (978-0-8225-4686-3). In text and pictures, the Arctic tundra is presented with material on the organisms that live there and how human life has changed this ecosystem. (Rev: BL 9/15/03; HBG 10/03) [551.4]

8876 Wu, Norbert, and Jim Mastro. *Under Antarctic Ice: The Photographs of Norbert Wu* (8–12). Illus. 2004, Univ. of California $45.00 (978-0-520-23504-5). Life beneath the ice of Antarctica is brilliantly captured in the photographs of Norbert Wu; with a useful introduction. (Rev: BL 10/15/04) [779]

8877 Yue, Charlotte, and David Yue. *The Igloo* (6–8). Illus. 1988, Houghton $16.00 (978-0-395-44613-3). This account describes the geography of the Arctic and the life led by the native Inuit. (Rev: BL 9/1/88; SLJ 12/88) [970.004]

United States

General History and Geography

8878 Andryszewski, Tricia. *Step by Step Along the Appalachian Trail* (4–8). 1998, Twenty-First Century LB $24.90 (978-0-7613-0273-5). A state-by-state tour of the Appalachian Trail, with material on the terrain, elevations, landmarks, and sites along the way. (Rev: BL 3/1/99; HBG 9/99; SLJ 4/99) [973]

8879 Armstrong, Jennifer. *The American Story: 100 True Tales from American History* (4–7). Illus. by Roger Roth. 2006, Knopf $34.95 (978-0-375-81256-9). The 100 stories in this large-format collection bring American history to life and include such diverse events as Paul Revere's midnight ride, the first flight of the Wright brothers, the eruption of Mount St. Helens, and the Supreme Court decision resolving the disputed 2000 presidential election. (Rev: BCCB 10/06; BL 8/06; HBG 4/07; SLJ 8/06*) [973]

8880 Baines, John. *The United States* (4–8). Illus. Series: Country Fact Files. 1994, Raintree LB $27.12 (978-0-8114-1857-7). In a series of double-page spreads, basic information about the United States is given, including geography, economy, population, industry, education, government, and environment. (Rev: SLJ 7/94) [973]

8881 Baker, Patricia. *Fashions of a Decade: The 1940s* (7–12). Illus. Series: Fashions of a Decade. 1992, Facts on File $25.00 (978-0-8160-2467-4). Each book in this series that covers the 1920s through the 1990s connects political and social history with particular modes of dress. (Rev: BL 4/1/92; SLJ 7/07) [391]

8882 Baker, Patricia. *The 1950s* (7–10). Illus. Series: Fashions of a Decade. 2007, Chelsea House $35.00 (978-0-8160-6721-3). Pictures and discussion of the fashions of this decade are accompanied by information about the trends and events of the times and how they affected what Americans wore. (Rev: BL 4/15/07) [391]

8883 Bockenhauer, Mark H., and Stephen F. Cunha. *Our Fifty States* (4–10). Illus. 2004, National Geographic LB $45.90 (978-0-7922-6992-2). Maps of the states are accompanied by basic facts, photographs, and archival reproductions of key historical events; also includes the U.S. territories. (Rev: SLJ 1/05) [973]

8884 Bolden, Tonya, ed. *33 Things Every Girl Should Know About Women's History: From Suffragettes to Skirt Lengths to the E. R. A.* (6–9). Illus. 2002, Random paper $12.95 (978-0-375-81122-7). This well-designed follow-up to *33 Things Every Girl Should Know* (1998) is an appealing compilation of articles, fiction, poetry, diary entries, charts, and a timeline that reveal much about women's roles in America — from the struggle for equal rights to fashion and 1960s singing groups. (Rev: BL 3/1/02; HB 7–8/02; HBG 10/02; SLJ 4/02; VOYA 12/02) [305.4]

8885 Brexel, Bernadette. *The Knights of Labor and the Haymarket Riot: The Fight for an Eight-Hour Workday* (5–8). Illus. Series: America's Industrial Society in the 19th Century. 2004, Rosen LB $22.50 (978-0-8239-4028-8). For reluctant readers, this overview of the struggle to improve working conditions features large print and short chapters. Also use *The Populist Party: A Voice for the Farmers in an Industrial Society* (2004). (Rev: BL 4/1/04)

8886 Brown, Gene. *Conflict in Europe and the Great Depression: World War I (1914–1940)* (5–8). Series: First Person America. 1994, Twenty-First Century LB $20.90 (978-0-8050-2585-9). The period from 1914 to 1940 is re-created through excerpts from original source material and texts describing events and social conditions. (Rev: BL 5/15/94; SLJ 11/94) [973.9]

8887 Buckley, Susan, and Elspeth Leacock. *Journeys for Freedom: A New Look at America's Story* (4–7). Illus. by Rodica Prato. 2006, Houghton $17.00 (978-0-618-22323-7). Twenty stories of personal struggles for freedom — ranging from the early 17th century to the late 20th century — feature quotations from primary sources. (Rev: BL 11/15/06; SLJ 1/07) [973]

8888 Buckley, Susan, and Elspeth Leacock. *Kids Make History: A New Look at America's Story* (4–8). Illus. by Randy Jones. 2006, Houghton $17.00 (978-0-618-22329-9). Twenty stories of young people who experienced milestone events in American history — from Pocahontas in 1607 to a high school senior on 9/11 — are told in text, quotations, fictionalized dialogue, and illustrations. (Rev: SLJ 1/07) [973.09]

8889 Collier, Christopher, and James Lincoln Collier. *The Rise of the Cities: 1820–1920* (5–8). Illus. Series: The Drama of American History. 2001, Marshall Cavendish LB $31.36 (978-0-7614-1051-5). In this highly illustrated volume, the Colliers paint a broad picture of the process of urbanization in the United States, tracing the problems involved and the growing prominence of cities in American life. (Rev: BL 3/15/01; HBG 10/01; SLJ 7/01) [973]

8890 Collier, Christopher, and James Lincoln Collier. *The United States Enters the World Stage: From the Alaska Purchase Through World War I* (5–8). Series: The Drama of American History. 2001, Marshall Cavendish LB $31.36 (978-0-7614-1053-9). Covering the years 1867 through 1918, this well-illustrated account traces America's emergence as a world power. (Rev: BL 3/15/01; HBG 10/01) [973.9]

8891 Colman, Penny. *Girls: A History of Growing Up Female in America* (5–8). Illus. 2000, Scholastic paper $18.95 (978-0-590-37129-2). Using diaries, memoirs, letters, magazine articles, and other sources, the author presents a history of girls in America from the first females to cross the Bering Strait to the present day. (Rev: BCCB 2/00; BL 2/1/00; HBG 10/00; SLJ 3/00) [305.23]

8892 Cooper, Jason. *Árboles / Trees* (4–8). Trans. by Blanca Rey. Illus. Series: La Guía de Rourke Para los Símbolos de los Estados/Rourke's Guide to State Symbols. 2002, Rourke LB $20.95 (978-1-58952-399-9). The 50 state trees are introduced in bilingual text and illustrations. Also use *Aves / Birds*, *Banderas / Flags*, and *Flores / Flowers*. (Rev: SLJ 3/03) [582]

8893 Davenport, John C. *The Mason-Dixon Line* (6–8). Illus. Series: Arbitrary Borders. 2004, Chelsea House LB $35.00 (978-0-7910-7830-3). This series examines the profound effects that artificial boundaries have had on the course of world history; this title looks at the history of the Mason-Dixon Line and the role it played in polarizing sentiments between the North and South in the years leading up to the Civil War. (Rev: BL 8/04; SLJ 9/04) [911]

8894 Dolan, Edward F. *The American Indian Wars* (5–8). Illus. 2003, Millbrook LB $29.90 (978-0-7613-1968-9). Four hundred years of conflict are covered in this volume that looks at the causes, details the key battles and events, and provides portraits of the key participants. (Rev: BL 12/1/03) [973.04]

8895 Dudley, William, ed. *Opposing Viewpoints in American History, Vol. 1: From Colonial Times to Reconstruction* (8–12). Illus. Series: Opposing Viewpoints. 1996, Greenhaven LB $37.44 (978-1-56510-348-1). Alternative primary source opinions are given for such issues in early American history as Native American rights, acceptance of the Bill of Rights, and slavery. (Rev: BL 3/15/96) [973]

8896 Edwards, Judith. *Abolitionists and Slave Resistance: Breaking the Chains of Slavery* (6–12). Series: Slavery in American History. 2004, Enslow LB $26.60 (978-0-7660-2155-6). A well-written survey of the emergence and progress of the anti-slavery movement. (Rev: SLJ 8/04) [326]

8897 Ehlert, Willis J. *America's Heritage: Capitols of the United States* (6–12). 1993, State House paper $10.95 (978-0-9634908-3-4). Provides data on state capitals and capitol buildings, descriptions of architectural details, brief state histories, state symbols, and an extensive bibliography. (Rev: BL 4/15/93) [725]

8898 Feinstein, Stephen. *The 1940s: From World War II to Jackie Robinson* (5–8). Illus. Series: Decades of the 20th Century. 2000, Enslow LB $22.60 (978-0-7660-1428-2). A lively look at events of the 1940s, covering everything from fashion and fads to politics, science, technology, medicine, and sports. Also use *The 1930s: From the Great Depression to the Wizard of Oz* (2001) and *The 1950s: From the Korean War to Elvis* (2000). (Rev: HBG 3/01; SLJ 5/01) [973.9]

8899 Feinstein, Stephen. *The 1990s: Fom the Persian Gulf War to Y2K* (5–8). Series: Decades of the 20th Century. 2001, Enslow LB $22.60 (978-0-7660-1613-2). The events of the 1990s are covered in chapters on lifestyle and fashion; arts and entertainment; sports; politics; and science, technology, and medicine. (Rev: HBG 10/02; SLJ 2/02) [973.9]

8900 Feinstein, Stephen. *The 1970s: From Watergate to Disco* (4–7). Series: Decades of the 20th Century. 2000, Enslow LB $22.60 (978-0-7660-1425-1). This book covers the people and events of the 1970s along with developments in such areas as politics, science, and sports. (Rev: BL 10/15/00; HBG 3/01; SLJ 12/00) [973.9]

8901 Feinstein, Stephen. *The 1960s: From the Vietnam War to Flower Power* (4–7). Illus. Series: Decades of the 20th Century. 2000, Enslow LB $22.60 (978-0-7660-1426-8). An account of America's turbulent 1960s that includes lifestyles, politics, fashion, fads, and entertainment. (Rev: BL 10/15/00; HBG 3/01; SLJ 12/00) [973.92]

8902 Feinstein, Stephen. *The 1910s: From World War I to Ragtime Music* (5–8). Series: Decades of the 20th Century. 2001, Enslow LB $22.60 (978-0-7660-1611-8). The events of the 1910s are covered in chapters on lifestyle and fashion, arts and entertainment, sports, politics, and science, technology, and medicine. Also use *The 1920s: From Prohibition to Charles Lindbergh* (2001). (Rev: HBG 10/02; SLJ 2/02) [973.9]

8903 Fischer, Maureen M. *Nineteenth Century Lumber Camp Cooking* (4–7). Series: Exploring History Through Simple Recipes. 2000, Capstone LB $23.93 (978-0-7368-0604-6). After describing life in a lumber camp more than a hundred years ago, this book supplies some authentic recipes. (Rev: BL 3/1/01; HBG 10/01; SLJ 4/01) [973.8]

8904 Foster, Genevieve, and Joanna Foster. *George Washington's World.* Rev. ed. (5–8). Illus. 1997, Beautiful Feet paper $15.95 (978-0-9643803-4-9). A new edition of this 50-year-old book that re-creates what was happening in the world during Washington's life, now with expanded coverage on minorities. (Rev: SLJ 3/98) [909]

8905 Foster, Mark. *Whale Port: A History of Tuckanucket* (4–7). Illus. by Gerald Foster. 2007, Houghton $18.00 (978-0-618-54722-7). The life and times of a fictitious New England town from 1683 to today reveal how changes in population, technology, commerce, and society all affect a town's growth; detailed illustrations. (Rev: BL 12/1/07; SLJ 11/07) [338.3]

8906 Fyson, Nance Lui. *The 1940s* (6–9). Illus. 1990, Batsford $19.95 (978-0-7134-5628-8). The story of World War II and its aftermath are covered plus developments in such areas as sports, the arts, science, and invention. (Rev: SLJ 7/90) [973.9]

8907 Garrington, Sally. *The United States* (6–10). Series: Countries of the World. 2003, Facts on File $30.00 (978-0-8160-5385-8). This basic work supplies an overview of information on the United States with emphasis on present conditions. (Rev: BL 1/1–15/04) [973]

8908 Gay, Kathlyn, and Martin Gay. *After the Shooting Stops: The Aftermath of War* (7–12). 1998, Millbrook LB $24.90 (978-0-7613-3006-6). A look at the political, economic, and social changes that have followed U.S. involvement in various wars. (Rev: BL 8/98; HBG 3/99; SLJ 9/98) [355.00973]

8909 Gourley, Catherine. *Gibson Girls and Suffragists: Perceptions of Women from 1900 to 1918, Vol. 1* (7–12). Series: Images and Issues of Women in the Twentieth Century. 2007, Twenty-First Century LB $38.60 (978-0-8225-7150-6). With many photographs and reproductions, this volume looks at images and issues relating to women's roles in the early 20th century. Also use *Rosie and Mrs. America: Perceptions of Women in the 1930s and 1940s* (2007). (Rev: SLJ 11/07) [305.4]

8910 Haban, Rita D. *How Proudly They Wave: Flags of the Fifty States* (4–9). Illus. 1989, Lerner LB $23.93 (978-0-8225-1799-3). Pictures of the state flags are accompanied by background information. (Rev: BL 12/15/89; SLJ 3/90) [929.9]

8911 Haskins, James, and Kathleen Benson. *Africa: A Look Back* (5–8). Series: Drama of African-American History. 2006, Benchmark LB $23.95 (978-0-

7614-2148-1). Slave narratives form a substantial portion of this survey of African American culture, tracing its roots back to the western part of Africa. (Rev: SLJ 5/07) [967]

8912 Head, Judith. *America's Daughters: 400 Years of American Women* (6–12). Illus. 1999, Perspectives paper $16.95 (978-0-9622036-8-8). This overview of the part played by women in American history highlights the work of many who have been unjustly ignored. (Rev: BL 1/1–15/00; SLJ 3/00) [305.4]

8913 Heinemann, Sue. *The New York Public Library Amazing Women in History* (6–10). Illus. 1998, Wiley paper $14.95 (978-0-471-19216-9). Using a question-and-answer format, this work supplies hundreds of facts about women in American history, arranged by topics that include activism, sports, recreation, and racial and ethnic groups. (Rev: BL 4/15/98; SLJ 8/98) [973]

8914 Hopkinson, Deborah. *Up before Daybreak: Cotton and People in America* (5–8). Illus. 2006, Scholastic $18.99 (978-0-439-63901-9). A concise, readable history of the American cotton industry with a focus on laborers, especially children; contains archival photographs, reading list, and bibliography. (Rev: BL 4/15/06*; HB 5–6/06; LMC 11-12/06; SLJ 6/06*) [331.7]

8915 Isaacs, Sally Senzell. *America in the Time of Franklin Delano Roosevelt: The Story of Our Nation from Coast to Coast, from 1929 to 1948* (4–8). Series: America in the Time Of. 1999, Heinemann LB $30.35 (978-1-57572-761-5). Using the life of Roosevelt as a framework, this account describes life in America during the Great Depression and World War II. (Rev: SLJ 5/00) [973.9]

8916 Isaacs, Sally Senzell. *America in the Time of Susan B. Anthony: The Story of Our Nation from Coast to Coast, from 1845 to 1928* (4–8). 1999, Heinemann LB $30.35 (978-1-57572-763-9). Using the life of Susan B. Anthony as a framework, this work covers topics including woman's suffrage, poverty, and World War I. (Rev: SLJ 5/00) [973.9]

8917 Johnston, Robert D. *The Making of America* (5–8). Illus. 2002, National Geographic $29.95 (978-0-7922-6944-1). An informative and balanced overview of American history, this appealing volume divides American history into eight periods; in addition to the narrative, each period includes profiles of two major figures and examines important issues of the time. (Rev: BL 1/1–15/03; HBG 3/03; SLJ 12/02*) [973]

8918 Jordan, Anne Devereaux, and Virginia Schomp. *Slavery and Resistance* (5–8). Illus. 2006, Marshall Cavendish LB $23.95 (978-0-7614-2178-8). A well-illustrated, well-organized history of slavery in America from the first colony in Jamestown up until the Civil War. (Rev: BL 2/1/07; SLJ 5/07) [306.3]

8919 Kalman, Bobbie, and Greg Nickles. *Spanish Missions* (4–7). Illus. Series: Historic Communities. 1996, Crabtree LB $25.27 (978-0-86505-436-3); paper $7.95 (978-0-86505-466-0). In double-page spreads, this book covers the building of the mission in the southern United States and of its functions: teaching Christianity, educating children, and supplying housing and food. (Rev: SLJ 4/97) [973]

8920 Katz, William L. *Exploration to the War of 1812, 1492–1814* (7–10). Series: History of Multicultural America. 1993, Raintree LB $27.11 (978-0-8114-6275-4). Discusses America from before European colonization through the formation of the new nation, exploration of new territory, and the War of 1812. Includes the role and treatment of Native Americans, women, slaves, and free blacks. (Rev: BL 6/1–15/93) [973]

8921 King, David C. *World Wars and the Modern Age* (5–8). Illus. Series: American Heritage, American Voices. 2004, Wiley paper $12.95 (978-0-471-44392-6). A concise overview of the profound changes seen in the United States during the decades from 1870 to 1950, with excerpts from primary sources. (Rev: BL 2/1/05; SLJ 5/05) [973]

8922 McCormick, Anita Louise. *The Industrial Revolution in American History* (5–8). Illus. Series: In American History. 1998, Enslow LB $26.60 (978-0-89490-985-6). A description of the causes of the Industrial Revolution and the changes that it brought to the United States up to 1946. (Rev: BL 9/1/98) [338.0973]

8923 McNeese, Tim. *The Rise and Fall of American Slavery: Freedom Denied, Freedom Gained* (6–12). Illus. Series: Slavery in American History. 2004, Enslow LB $26.60 (978-0-7660-2156-3). Traces the growth of the slave trade in the American colonies, as well as the rise of the abolition movement that later pushed for an end to slavery. (Rev: BL 9/1/04; SLJ 8/04) [97]

8924 Masoff, Joy. *We Are All Americans: Understanding Diversity* (4–7). 2006, Five Ponds $26.50 (978-0-9727156-2-1). This celebration of immigration to America — full of photographs, maps, and diagrams — looks at the reasons for migration, the problems involved, and the contributions made by immigrants in all aspects of American life, including music, sports, games, celebrations, literature, food, and art. (Rev: SLJ 1/07) [304.8]

8925 Miller, Marilyn. *Words That Built a Nation: A Young Person's Collection of Historic American Documents* (4–8). Illus. 1999, Scholastic paper $18.95 (978-0-590-29881-0). A collection of 37 documents important in American history — from the Mayflower Compact and the Declaration of Independence to Hillary Rodham Clinton's address to the United Nations Conference on Women and Malcolm X's "The Ballot or the Bullet" speech. (Rev: BL 10/15/99; HBG 3/00; SLJ 2/00) [973]

8926 Miller, Page Putnam. *Landmarks of American Women's History* (5–8). 2004, Oxford Univ. LB $32.95 (978-0-19-514501-4). Landmarks — all on the National Register of Historic Places — highlighted for their importance in women's history include Taos Pueblo, New Mexico, chosen for the strong Native American women who lived there; the Wesleyan Chapel at Seneca Falls, where the first women's rights conference was held; and the Boardinghouse at Boott Cotton Mill in Lowell, Massachusetts, home to many young women who worked in the textile industry. (Rev: SLJ 9/04) [973]

8927 Nash, Gary B. *Landmarks of the American Revolution* (5–8). Series: American Landmarks. 2003, Oxford LB $32.95 (978-0-19-512849-9). Landmark sites such as Independence Hall, Valley Forge National Historic Park, Faneuil Hall, and Yorktown Battlefield are introduced with excerpts from primary documents such as letters and broadsides. (Rev: SLJ 8/03) [973.3]

8928 Nathan, Amy. *Count on Us: American Women in the Military* (6–9). Illus. 2004, National Geographic $21.95 (978-0-7922-6330-2). Nathan celebrates women's diverse contributions to the United States' military causes — from women who disguised themselves as men in the Revolutionary War to World War I nurses to women flying Black Hawk missions today. (Rev: BL 2/15/04; SLJ 3/04) [355]

8929 Pollard, Michael. *The Mississippi* (5–8). Illus. Series: Great Rivers. 1997, Benchmark LB $22.79 (978-0-7614-0502-3). A history of this great river and its influence on American history, with photographs, maps, and diagrams. (Rev: HBG 3/98; SLJ 3/98) [917.7]

8930 Rawlins, Carol B. *The Colorado River* (4–8). Series: Watts Library. 1999, Watts LB $25.50 (978-0-531-11738-5). With full-color photographs and maps that complement the text, this book traces the famous Rocky Mountain waterway from north-central Colorado through the Southwest into the Gulf of California and covers its history and uses. (Rev: BL 1/1–15/00; SLJ 2/00) [973]

8931 Ruth, Maria Mudd. *The Mississippi River* (7–12). Illus. Series: Ecosystems of North America. 2000, Benchmark LB $28.50 (978-0-7614-0934-2). A detailed look at the largest river in North America, its flora and fauna, and the effects of human development on the ecosystem. (Rev: HBG 3/01; SLJ 4/01) [577.6]

8932 Rydell, Robert W., et al. *Fair America: World's Fairs in the United States* (8–12). 2000, Smithsonian $29.95 (978-1-56098-968-4); paper $15.95 (978-1-56098-384-2). This book examines world's fairs held in the United States from 1853 to 1984. [907]

8933 St. George, Judith. *In the Line of Fire* (6–9). Illus. 1999, Holiday $22.95 (978-0-8234-1428-4). This book describes each of the attempts to assassinate U.S. presidents, some successful and some not, and gives information on both the targets and the criminals. (Rev: BCCB 1/00; BL 12/1/99; HBG 4/00) [364.15]

8934 Sandak, Cass R. *The United States* (4–8). Illus. Series: Modern Industrial World. 1996, Raintree LB $24.26 (978-0-8172-4556-6). An examination of the economic and industrial situation in the United States, with additional information on education, living standards, and related subjects. (Rev: BL 2/15/97; SLJ 8/97) [973]

8935 Sheafer, Silvia A. *Women in America's Wars* (6–12). Illus. 1996, Enslow LB $26.60 (978-0-89490-553-7). From the American Revolution to the Persian Gulf War, this account profiles 10 women and the amazingly diversified roles they played in U.S. wars. (Rev: BL 4/15/96; SLJ 5/96; VOYA 6/96) [355]

8936 Sills, Leslie. *From Rags to Riches: A History of Girls' Clothing in America* (4–7). Illus. 2005, Holiday $16.95 (978-0-8234-1708-7). Changes in clothing over the centuries are linked to the social mores of the time in this appealing volume. (Rev: BL 5/1/05; SLJ 8/05) [391]

8937 Stanley, George E. *The New Republic (1763–1815)* (5–8). Illus. Series: A Primary Source History of the United States. 2005, World Almanac LB $31.00 (978-0-8368-5825-9). A simple narrative links well-chosen primary sources documenting the key events of the revolutionary period. (Rev: BL 4/1/05; SLJ 7/05)

8938 Stone, Tanya Lee. *The Great Depression and World War II* (5–8). Series: Making of America. 2001, Raintree LB $28.54 (978-0-8172-5710-1). Concise text and attractive illustrations re-create the history of America from 1929 through World War II. (Rev: BL 9/15/01; HBG 10/01) [973.9]

8939 Stone, Tanya Lee. *The Progressive Era and World War I* (5–8). Series: Making of America. 2001, Raintree LB $28.54 (978-0-8172-5709-5). Roughly the first 20 years of the 20th century in American history are retold in this history that also looks at home life, culture, and entertainment. (Rev: BL 9/15/01; HBG 10/01; SLJ 6/01) [973.9]

8940 Streissguth, Thomas. *Utopian Visionaries* (7–12). Illus. 1999, Oliver LB $19.95 (978-1-881508-47-2). This account presents material on attempts to build utopian communities in the U.S. during the 18th and 19th centuries by such visionaries as Ann Lee, a Shaker, and John Humphrey Noyes, who created the Oneida community. (Rev: BL 12/15/99; HBG 4/00; SLJ 11/99) [321]

8941 Thro, Ellen, and Andrew K. Frank. *Growing and Dividing* (5–8). Series: The Making of America. 2001, Raintree LB $28.54 (978-0-8172-5704-0). The story of the development of the eastern United States from the early days of the Republic through the clashes that led to the Civil War. (Rev: BL 4/15/01; HBG 10/01) [973.5]

8942 *United States in Pictures* (5–8). Illus. Series: Visual Geography. 1995, Lerner LB $25.55 (978-0-8225-1896-9). An attractive basic introduction to the geography, history, and people of the United States. (Rev: BL 8/95) [973]

8943 Uschan, Michael V. *Lynching and Murder in the Deep South* (8–12). Series: Lucent Library of Black History. 2006, Gale LB $28.70 (978-1-59018-845-3). This is a frank discussion of the lynchings and other violence that took place in the South from Reconstruction right up to the 1950s. (Rev: SLJ 4/07) [364.1]

8944 Uschan, Michael V. *The 1910s* (7–10). Illus. 1998, Lucent LB $29.95 (978-1-56006-551-7). This volume presents an overview of the 1910s, highlighting social and technical developments as well as the U.S. role in world affairs and World War I. (Rev: SLJ 4/99) [973.9]

8945 Uschan, Michael V. *The 1940s* (5–10). Series: Cultural History of the United States. 1998, Lucent LB $28.70 (978-1-56510-554-6). Life at home and abroad during World War II dominate this book, which also discusses the Great Depression, the New Deal, events leading up to U.S. participation in the war, the beginnings of the Cold War, the growth of suburban living, and the rise of television, with sidebars on such topics as the Holocaust, the influences of radio, movies, and comics, 1940s slang, and the first computers. (Rev: SLJ 1/99) [973.9]

8946 Van Zandt, Eleanor. *A History of the United States Through Art* (5–8). Illus. Series: History Through Art. 1996, Thomson Learning LB $5.00 (978-1-56847-443-4). American history is covered in 21 double-page spreads that feature text and famous artworks. (Rev: BL 3/1/96; SLJ 2/96) [973]

8947 Wacker, Grant. *Religion in Nineteenth Century America* (5–8). Series: Religion in American Life. 2000, Oxford $32.95 (978-0-19-511021-0). This is the story of how religion in America affected such 19th-century events as the westward movement, the Civil War, and immigration, with additional coverage of the careers of such people as Sojourner Truth and Mary Baker Eddy. (Rev: BL 6/1–15/00; HBG 10/00; SLJ 8/00) [973]

8948 Wilbur, Keith C. *Revolutionary Medicine, 1700–1800* (4–8). Illus. Series: Illustrated Living History. 1996, Chelsea $21.95 (978-0-7910-4532-9). In a large-book format, this account gives a great deal of information — some gruesome, some funny — about medicine in 18th-century America. (Rev: BL 6/1–15/97; SLJ 7/97) [973.3]

8949 Wormser, Richard. *American Childhoods: Three Centuries of Youth at Risk* (7–12). Illus. 1996, Walker LB $17.85 (978-0-8027-8427-8). A graphic, realistic picture of childhood and growing up in America from the repressive Puritans to the present day with chapters on work, crime, disease, education, sex, and related topics. (Rev: BL 9/15/96; SLJ 9/96; VOYA 12/96) [305.23]

8950 Wormser, Richard. *Hoboes: Wandering in America, 1870–1940* (6–12). Illus. 1994, Walker $17.95 (978-0-8027-8279-3). This account covers the history, rules, literature, songs, and customs of those who rode the rails from the end of the Civil War to the outbreak of World War II. (Rev: BL 6/1–15/94; SLJ 7/94) [305.5]

8951 Worth, Richard. *Slave Life on the Plantation: Prisons Beneath the Sun* (6–12). Illus. Series: Slavery in American History. 2004, Enslow LB $26.60 (978-0-7660-2152-5). A vivid portrait of what daily life was like for slaves laboring on the vast plantations of the American South. (Rev: BL 9/1/04; SLJ 12/04) [306.3]

8952 Worth, Richard. *The Slave Trade in America: Cruel Commerce* (6–12). Series: Slavery in American History. 2004, Enslow LB $26.60 (978-0-7660-2151-8). The slave trade is traced back to its origins in the days of early Romans before a more detailed survey of the American slave trade in the 17th and 18th centuries, with attention to the social and economic aspects. (Rev: SLJ 8/04) [382]

8953 Yorinks, Adrienne. *Quilt of States: Piecing Together America* (5–8). Illus. 2005, National Geographic LB $29.90 (978-0-7922-7286-1). With contributions from librarians from all 50 states, this beautifully illustrated volume offers a brief story of each state's accession to the Union, along with other pertinent facts and figures. (Rev: BL 10/1/05; SLJ 12/05) [973]

Historical Periods

NATIVE AMERICANS

8954 Aaseng, Nathan. *Cherokee Nation v. Georgia: The Forced Removal of a People* (6–9). Illus. Series: Famous Trials. 2000, Lucent paper $19.95 (978-1-5600-6628-6). This account chronicles the struggle between settlers and Native Americans that led to the court case and the decision, under President Andrew Jackson, that set the course of Native American relations for the next half century. (Rev: BL 9/15/00; SLJ 7/97) [973]

8955 Anderson, Dale. *The Anasazi Culture at Mesa Verde* (5–8). Series: Landmark Events in American History. 2003, World Almanac LB $31.00 (978-0-8368-5371-1). The story of the native people from the region around the Four Corners and of their many cultural accomplishment including basketry, pottery, and urban architecture. (Rev: BL 10/15/03) [973]

8956 Ayer, Eleanor. *The Anasazi* (6–9). 1993, Walker LB $15.85 (978-0-8027-8185-7). An in-depth look at the Anasazi Indians of the Southwest, who came to this country about 2,000 years ago. (Rev: BL 3/1/93; SLJ 11/93) [979]

8957 Bial, Raymond. *The Apache* (5–8). Series: Lifeways. 2000, Benchmark LB $34.21 (978-0-7614-0939-7). Presents the dramatic, often tragic history of the Apache Indians, with biographies of leaders such as Geronimo and a description of the social and cultural life of these nomadic people. (Rev: BL 11/15/00; HBG 3/01; SLJ 3/01) [973]

8958 Bial, Raymond. *The Cheyenne* (5–8). Series: Lifeways. 2000, Benchmark LB $34.21 (978-0-7614-0938-0). Part of the Great Plains Indian group, the Cheyenne's daily life, religious beliefs, social system, and history are introduced in this book. (Rev: BL 11/15/00; HBG 3/01; SLJ 3/01) [973]

8959 Bial, Raymond. *The Chumash* (6–9). Illus. Series: Lifeways. 2003, Benchmark LB $34.21 (978-0-7614-1681-4). A look at the history, culture, social structure, key figures, and current status of the Chumash tribe of California, with maps, drawings, and photographs. (Rev: SLJ 5/04) [973]

8960 Bial, Raymond. *The Comanche* (4–8). Series: Lifeways. 1999, Benchmark LB $34.21 (978-0-7614-0864-2). This impressive volume gives an accurate picture of the social and political life of the Comanche from their early history to the present day. (Rev: BL 3/15/00; HBG 10/00; SLJ 3/00) [973]

8961 Bial, Raymond. *The Delaware* (5–9). Series: Lifeways. 2005, Benchmark LB $23.95 (978-0-7614-1904-4). The history, culture, traditions, and present-day life of the Native American tribe, with photographs and other visuals. (Rev: SLJ 6/06) [974.004]

8962 Bial, Raymond. *The Haida* (5–8). Series: Lifeways. 2000, Benchmark LB $34.21 (978-0-7614-0937-3). This book describes these Native Americans of the Northwest and introduces their artistic and carving skills, their social system, beliefs, history, and daily life. (Rev: BL 11/15/00; HBG 3/01; SLJ 3/01) [973]

8963 Bial, Raymond. *The Huron* (5–8). Series: Lifeways. 2000, Benchmark LB $34.21 (978-0-7614-0940-3). Color pictures and clear text describe this Indian group's past and present and give details of their daily life, religion, and rituals. (Rev: BL 11/15/00; HBG 3/01; SLJ 3/01) [973]

8964 Bial, Raymond. *The Long Walk: The Story of Navajo Captivity* (6–9). Series: Great Journeys. 2002, Marshall Cavendish LB $32.79 (978-0-7614-1322-6). The story of the Navajo nation and the imprisonment that lasted until 1868 when they were given their own reservation. (Rev: BL 3/15/03; HBG 3/03; SLJ 3/03) [973]

8965 Bial, Raymond. *The Menominee* (5–9). Series: Lifeways. 2005, Benchmark LB $23.95 (978-0-7614-1903-7). The history, culture, traditions and present-day life of the Native American tribe, with photographs and other visuals. (Rev: SLJ 6/06) [977.4004]

8966 Bial, Raymond. *The Nez Perce* (5–8). Series: Lifeways. 2001, Marshall Cavendish LB $34.21 (978-0-7614-1210-6). This attractively illustrated account gives basic material on the historical and social aspects of this Native American tribe, including their food, clothing, and culture. (Rev: BL 1/1–15/02; HBG 3/02; SLJ 4/02) [973]

8967 Bial, Raymond. *The Ojibwe* (5–8). Illus. Series: Lifeways. 1999, Marshall Cavendish LB $34.21 (978-0-7614-0863-5). Topics covered in this introduction to the Ojibwe nation include history, traditions, beliefs, and the nation today. (Rev: BL 3/1/00; HBG 10/00; SLJ 3/00) [977]

8968 Bial, Raymond. *The Powhatan* (5–8). Series: Lifeways. 2001, Marshall Cavendish LB $34.21 (978-0-7614-1209-0). The story of the Powhatan tribe of Virginia, whose members included Pocahontas, with material on their history and various aspects of their culture. (Rev: BL 1/1–15/02; HBG 3/02) [973]

8969 Bial, Raymond. *The Pueblo* (5–8). Illus. Series: Lifeways. 1999, Marshall Cavendish LB $34.21 (978-0-7614-0861-1). Good photographs and a lucid text combine to produce a fine introduction to the Pueblo Indians, their history, culture, traditions, present status, and notable members of the nation. (Rev: BL 3/1/00; HBG 10/00; SLJ 3/00) [978.9]

8970 Bial, Raymond. *The Seminole* (4–8). Series: Lifeways. 1999, Benchmark LB $34.21 (978-0-7614-0862-8). Topics covered in this account of the Seminole Indians include history, daily life, religious beliefs, sacred rituals, and attitudes toward themselves. (Rev: BL 3/15/00; HBG 10/00; SLJ 3/00) [973]

8971 Bial, Raymond. *The Shoshone* (5–8). Series: Lifeways. 2001, Marshall Cavendish LB $34.21 (978-0-7614-1211-3). The story of the Native American tribe of buffalo hunters who lived in the Northwest, with material on their history, culture, language, food, and clothing. (Rev: BL 1/1–15/02; HBG 3/02) [973]

8972 Bial, Raymond. *The Wampanoag* (6–9). Illus. Series: Lifeways. 2003, Benchmark LB $34.21 (978-0-7614-1683-8). A look at the history, culture, social structure, key figures, and current status of the Wampanoag tribe of Massachusetts, with maps, drawings, and photographs. (Rev: SLJ 5/04) [973]

8973 Birchfield, D. L. *The Trail of Tears* (4–7). Series: Landmark Events in American History. 2003, World Almanac LB $31.00 (978-0-8368-5381-0). A brief account of the tragic forced removal of Native American people from their lands by the U.S. government in the mid-19th century. (Rev: SLJ 6/04) [973.04]

8974 Bond, Fred G. *Flatboating on the Yellowstone, 1877* (7–12). 1998, Ward Hill $19.95 (978-1-886747-03-6). A first-person account of the relocation in 1877 of Chief Joseph and other Nez Perce Indians from Oregon to Oklahoma by raft down the Yellowstone and Missouri Rivers, written by their pilot, who documented the trip for the New York Public Library in 1925. (Rev: BL 12/15/98) [973]

8975 Bonvillain, Nancy. *The Inuit* (6–9). Series: Indians of North America. 1995, Chelsea paper $9.95 (978-0-7910-0380-0). A history of the present residents of the tundra and arctic regions of North America, with material on their daily life, beliefs, culture, and origins. (Rev: BL 10/15/95) [971]

8976 Bonvillain, Nancy. *Native American Medicine* (6–9). Series: Indians of North America. 1997, Chelsea LB $21.95 (978-0-7910-4041-6). This volume follows the course of Native American medical practices, healing rituals, and treatments through history and offers an interesting account of America's first doctors. (Rev: BL 11/15/97) [973]

8977 Bonvillain, Nancy. *Native American Religion* (6–10). Series: Indians of North America. 1995, Chelsea LB $21.95 (978-0-7910-2652-6); paper $9.95 (978-0-7910-3479-8). Explains Native American spiritual life, emphasizing the natural world and the earth, and discusses holistic approaches toward illness and well-being. (Rev: BL 3/1/96; SLJ 2/96) [973]

8978 Bonvillain, Nancy. *The Sac and Fox* (6–9). Series: Indians of North America. 1995, Chelsea $19.95 (978-0-7910-1684-8). The tragic story of these Native American peoples whose fight to maintain their lands eventually led to the Black Hawk War and their resettlement in the Midwest. (Rev: BL 7/95) [977.1]

8979 Bonvillain, Nancy. *The Santee Sioux* (6–9). Series: Indians of North America. 1996, Chelsea LB $21.95 (978-0-7910-1685-5). This account of the Native American tribe that lived on the Great Plains covers their way of life, history, and culture, as well as current issues and conflicts. (Rev: BL 12/15/96) [973]

8980 Bonvillain, Nancy. *The Teton Sioux* (6–9). Series: Indians of North America. 1994, Chelsea LB $21.95 (978-0-7910-1688-6). A look at the largest group of the Sioux confederacy, the Teton Dakotas, including the battle at Wounded Knee. (Rev: BL 10/15/94; VOYA 2/95) [977]

8981 Bonvillain, Nancy. *The Zuni* (6–9). Series: Indians of North America. 1995, Chelsea LB $19.95 (978-0-7910-1689-3). The history of the Zuni Indians of western New Mexico, including their crafts such as basket weaving and turquoise jewelry. (Rev: BL 10/15/95) [973]

8982 Bruchac, Joseph. *Navajo Long Walk: The Tragic Story of a Proud People's Forced March from Their Homeland* (4–8). Illus. by Shonto Begay. 2002, National Geographic $18.95 (978-0-7922-7058-4). Using revealing words and pictures, this large picture book for older readers re-creates the shameful story of the deadly marches of the Navajo in the 1860s. (Rev: BL 5/1/02; HBG 10/02; SLJ 7/02) [979.1]

8983 Calvert, Patricia. *Standoff at Standing Rock: The Story of Sitting Bull and James McLaughlin* (6–12). Illus. 2001, Twenty-First Century LB $24.90 (978-0-7613-1360-1). The confrontation between these two determined men serves as the central focus of an examination of the treatment of Native Americans, the Indian Wars, boarding schools, and the efforts to impose new beliefs. (Rev: BL 2/15/01; HBG 10/01; VOYA 12/01) [978.004]

8984 Carew-Miller, Anna. *Native American Cooking* (4–7). Illus. Series: Native American Life. 2002, Mason Crest LB $19.95 (978-1-59084-131-0). The role of the environment in Native American food choices is emphasized in this overview that is organized by region. Also use *Native American Tools and Weapons* and *What the Native Americans Wore* (both 2002). (Rev: SLJ 2/03) [641.5979]

8985 Collins, David R., and Kris Bergren. *Ishi: The Last of His People* (5–8). Illus. 2000, Morgan Reynolds LB $23.95 (978-1-883846-54-1). This is the story of Ishi, the ill-clad and half-starved man who emerged from the wilderness in California in 1911 and who was believed to be a survivor of the lost Yahi tribe. (Rev: BL 12/1/00; HBG 10/00) [979.4004]

8986 Cooper, Michael L. *Indian School: Teaching the White Man's Way* (5–10). Illus. 1999, Clarion $18.00 (978-0-395-92084-8). A moving photoessay about Native American children and how they were removed from their homes and uprooted from their culture to attend Indian boarding schools in an effort to "civilize" them. (Rev: BL 12/1/99; HBG 3/00; SLJ 2/00; VOYA 4/00) [370]

8987 Cornell, George L., and Gordon Henry. *Ojibwa* (8–12). Series: North American Indians Today. 2003, Mason Crest LB $22.95 (978-1-59084-673-5). The contemporary status of Ojibwa Indians is emphasized in this volume that covers religion, government, and the arts. (Rev: SLJ 5/04) [973]

8988 Cory, Steven. *Pueblo Indian* (5–8). Illus. Series: American Pastfinder. 1996, Lerner LB $21.27 (978-0-8225-2976-7). Color illustrations and maps accompany this account of the Pueblo Indians and the incredible cities they built. (Rev: BL 7/96) [973]

8989 Delgado, James P. *Native American Shipwrecks* (5–7). Illus. Series: Watts Library: Shipwrecks. 2000, Watts LB $25.50 (978-0-531-20379-8). This book covers the boats that Native Americans made, their uses and voyages, the culture of these peoples, and how underwater archaeologists have explored their wrecks. (Rev: BL 10/15/00) [623.8]

8990 Denny, Sidney G., and Ernest L. Schusky. *The Ancient Splendor of Prehistoric Cahokia* (4–8). 1997, Ozark paper $3.95 (978-1-56763-272-9). Using the findings at the Cahokia Mounds in southern Illinois as a beginning, the author re-creates the life and culture of these prehistoric American Indians. (Rev: BL 5/1/97) [977.3]

8991 *Do All Indians Live in Tipis? Questions and Answers from the National Museum of the American Indian* (8–12). 2007, Smithsonian paper $14.95 (978-0-06-115301-3). With answers to questions posed by the general public, this book aims to set the facts straight about Native American cultures. (Rev: SLJ 3/08)

8992 Dramer, Kim. *Native Americans and Black Americans* (7–10). Illus. Series: Indians of North America. 1997, Chelsea LB $19.95 (978-0-7910-2653-3). This work gives a historic overview of the relationship between these two groups through slavery, the Civil War, land battles, segregation, and various political movements, as well as a basic history of each group's struggle for civil rights. (Rev: BL 8/97; SLJ 9/97) [303.48]

8993 Durrett, Deanne. *Healers* (8–12). Series: American Indian Lives. 1997, Facts on File $17.95 (978-0-8160-3460-4). This work profiles 12 Native American healers, ranging from the traditional medicine man to modern physicians and nurses. (Rev: VOYA 8/97) [973]

8994 Elish, Dan. *The Trail of Tears: The Story of the Cherokee Removal* (6–9). Illus. Series: Great Journeys. 2001, Marshall Cavendish LB $32.79 (978-0-7614-1228-1). The economic and social reasons for the Cherokees' forced exile to lands in the West are presented in text, quotations from primary sources, and many illustrations and maps. (Rev: BL 1/1–15/02; HBG 10/02; SLJ 3/02) [973]

8995 Ferrell, Nancy W. *The Battle of the Little Bighorn* (5–9). Series: In American History. 1996, Enslow LB $26.60 (978-0-89490-768-5). A detailed account of the Battle of Little Bighorn from various points of view on both sides, along with a review of the conflicts between the U.S. government and Native Americans, the different cultures of various tribes, key figures such as Crazy Horse and Sitting Bull, and the aftermath of the battle. (Rev: SLJ 12/96) [973.8]

8996 Fowler, Verna. *The Menominee* (4–7). Series: Indian Nations. 2000, Raintree LB $25.69 (978-0-8172-5458-2). Opening with a folk tale, this book describes the Menominee Indians, their life and culture, and how they were overrun in the 19th century and pushed onto a reservation in northern Wisconsin. (Rev: BL 3/15/01; HBG 10/01) [973]

8997 Freedman, Russell. *An Indian Winter* (6–9). 1992, Holiday $24.95 (978-0-8234-0930-3); paper $12.95 (978-0-8234-1158-0). A German naturalist/explorer and a Swiss artist recorded in words and pictures their 1832 observations of Mandan and Hidatsa Indian tribes in North Dakota. (Rev: BL 6/1/92*; HB 7–8/92; SLJ 6/92*) [917.804]

8998 Gleason, Katherine. *Native American Literature* (6–9). Series: Junior Library of American Indians. 1996, Chelsea LB $25.00 (978-0-7910-2477-5). This is an excellent introduction to the long history of Native American oral and written literature that begins with chants, myths, and prayers and ends with such famous contemporary writers as Louis Erdrich and Michael Dorris. (Rev: SLJ 3/97) [973]

8999 Gold, Susan Dudley. *Indian Treaties* (5–8). Illus. Series: Pacts and Treaties. 1997, Twenty-First Century LB $24.90 (978-0-8050-4813-1). A history of the successive treaties under which the Native Americans gradually lost their homes and livelihood. (Rev: BL 5/15/97; SLJ 6/97) [323.1]

9000 Gorsline, Marie, and Douglas Gorsline. *North American Indians* (5–8). Illus. by Douglas Gorsline. 1978, Random paper $3.25 (978-0-394-83702-4). Major tribes are identified and briefly described. [973]

9001 Griffin, Lana T. *The Navajo* (4–7). Illus. Series: Indian Nations. 1999, Raintree LB $25.69 (978-0-8172-5463-6). This book describes the history of the Navajo, their everyday life, customs, and tribal government, and includes two Navajo creation stories. (Rev: BL 2/15/00; HBG 10/00; SLJ 4/00) [979.1]

9002 Gunderson, Mary. *American Indian Cooking Before 1500* (4–7). Series: Exploring History Through Simple Recipes. 2000, Capstone LB $23.93 (978-0-7368-0605-3). This book describes the everyday life of Native Americans before Europeans arrived and gives a few simple recipes. (Rev: BL 3/1/01; HBG 10/01; SLJ 7/01) [973]

9003 Holm, Tom. *Code Talkers and Warriors: Native Americans and World War II* (5–9). Illus. Series: Landmark Events in Native American History . 2007, Chelsea House LB $35.00 (978-0-7910-9340-5). How Native Americans have aided their country in wars (many more than WWII are discussed), with an emphasis on Navajo and Comanche code talk. (Rev: BL 12/15/07) [940.54]

9004 Hoyt-Goldsmith, Diane. *Potlatch: A Tsimshian Celebration* (4–8). 1997, Holiday $16.95 (978-0-

8234-1290-7). A 13-year-old boy explains the meaning of potlatch for the Tsimshian tribe in Alaska and describes the many rituals and activities it involves. (Rev: BL 5/1/97; SLJ 6/97) [394.2]

9005 Hubbard-Brown, Janet. *The Shawnee* (6–9). Series: Indians of North America. 1995, Chelsea paper $9.95 (978-0-7910-3475-0). The history of the Native American tribe that resisted white expansion, sided with the British in the American Revolution and again in the War of 1812, and who were led by Tecumseh, the warrior who sought to unite all northwestern Indians to fight for their land. (Rev: BL 7/95) [973]

9006 Jones, Constance. *The European Conquest of North America* (7–12). 1995, Facts on File $25.00 (978-0-8160-3041-5). A detailed account of Native American cultures and the methods used by European conquerors to subdue them. (Rev: BL 5/1/95) [970.01]

9007 Kallen, Stuart A. *Native Americans of the Great Lakes* (7–10). Illus. Series: Indigenous Peoples of North America. 1999, Lucent LB $28.70 (978-1-56006-568-5). This book covers the history, culture, and famous people connected with the Six Nations of the Iroquois in the east around the Great Lakes and the Algonquins in the west. (Rev: BL 3/1/00; HBG 9/00) [977.004]

9008 Kallen, Stuart A. *Native Americans of the Northeast* (7–10). Series: Indigenous Peoples of North America. 2000, Lucent LB $28.70 (978-1-56006-629-3). Kallen looks at the history, culture, religion, and conflicts of these Indians, with material on their daily lives in the past and today. (Rev: BL 3/15/00; HBG 9/00; SLJ 5/00) [973]

9009 Kallen, Stuart A. *The Pawnee* (7–10). Series: Indigenous Peoples of North America. 2002, Gale LB $28.70 (978-1-56006-825-9). The history and contributions of this Native American group who lived in the Midwest and were the enemies of their neighbors, the Cheyenne. (Rev: BL 4/15/02) [970.004]

9010 Katz, Jane B., ed. *We Rode the Wind: Recollections of Native American Life*. Rev. ed. (6–10). 1995, Lerner LB $22.60 (978-0-8225-3154-8). A collection of the autobiographical writings of eight notable Native Americans, among them Charles Eastman and Black Elk, who grew up on the Great Plains. (Rev: BL 2/1/96; SLJ 12/95) [978]

9011 Kavasch, E. Barrie. *The Seminoles* (4–7). Illus. Series: Indian Nations. 1999, Raintree LB $25.69 (978-0-8172-5464-3). This account gives a history of the Seminole Indians, with material on their society, customs, festivals, government, present-day conditions, and one of their creation myths. (Rev: BL 2/15/00; HBG 10/00; SLJ 4/00) [975.9]

9012 Keoke, Emory Dean, and Kay Marie Porterfield. *Trade, Transportation, and Warfare* (7–10).

Illus. Series: American Indian Contributions to the World. 2005, Facts on File $35.00 (978-0-8160-5395-7). Native American accomplishments in both North and South America in the realms of transportation, trade, sports, governance, and military strategy are among the aspects highlighted here. (Rev: BL 4/1/05; SLJ 6/05) [970.004]

9013 King, Sandra. *Shannon: An Ojibway Dancer* (4–7). Illus. by Catherine Whipple. 1993, Lerner $19.95 (978-0-8225-2752-7); paper $21.27 (978-0-8225-9643-1). Thirteen-year-old Shannon Anderson, an Ojibway girl, prepares for the summer powwow and her part in the shawl dance. (Rev: BCCB 1/94; BL 1/15/94; SLJ 2/94) [394]

9014 Kirk, Connie Ann. *The Mohawks of North America* (4–7). Series: First Peoples. 2001, Lerner LB $23.93 (978-0-8225-4853-9). This book focuses on the history and cultural practices of the Mohawk people and their present status in America. (Rev: BL 10/15/01; HBG 3/02) [973]

9015 Klots, Steve. *Native Americans and Christianity* (7–10). Illus. Series: Indians of North America. 1997, Chelsea paper $9.95 (978-0-7910-4463-6). The story of how early explorers and settlers tried to convert Native Americans to Christianity, the forms that this religion took, and the many ways Native Americans practice their religion today. (Rev: BL 8/97; SLJ 9/97) [277]

9016 Krehbiel, Randy. *Little Bighorn* (4–8). Series: Battlefields Across America. 1997, Twenty-First Century LB $26.90 (978-0-8050-5236-7). A review of the historical background and events leading up to the Battle of Little Bighorn, followed by a description of the battle itself and the site as it is today. (Rev: SLJ 1/98) [973.8]

9017 Lacey, Theresa Jensen. *The Blackfeet* (6–9). Series: Indians of North America. 1995, Chelsea LB $14.95 (978-0-7910-1681-7). The story of the nomadic Native Americans of the northern Great Plains and their history of struggles with the European settlers. (Rev: BL 7/95) [970.004]

9018 La Pierre, Yvette. *Native American Rock Art: Messages from the Past* (4–8). Illus. 1994, Thomasson-Grant $16.95 (978-1-56566-064-9). Different types and techniques of Native American rock art are discussed, with additional information on the cultures that produced this phenomenon. (Rev: BL 12/1/94; SLJ 11/94) [709]

9019 Lassieur, Allison. *Before the Storm: American Indians Before the Europeans* (7–12). Series: Library of American Indian History. 1998, Facts on File $25.00 (978-0-8160-3651-6). This unique study reports on the flourishing civilizations of seven "precontact Native American" peoples before contact with the European invaders. (Rev: BL 11/15/98; SLJ 9/98) [970]

9020 Lavender, David. *Mother Earth, Father Sky: Pueblo Indians of the American Southwest* (5–8). Illus. 1998, Holiday $16.95 (978-0-8234-1365-2). After introducing the geographical area of the Southwest known as Four Corners — where Arizona, New Mexico, Colorado, and Utah meet — this book traces the history and culture of the Pueblo Indians who live there. (Rev: BL 9/1/98; HBG 10/99; SLJ 11/98) [978]

9021 Limberland, Dennis, and Mary Em Parrilli. *The Cheyenne* (4–7). Series: Indian Nations. 2000, Raintree LB $25.69 (978-0-8172-5469-8). This history of the Cheyenne Indians begins with a folk tale and goes on to describe their lifestyles before and after being sent to reservations in Oklahoma and Montana. (Rev: BL 3/15/01; HBG 10/01) [973]

9022 Long, Cathryn J. *The Cherokee* (7–10). Series: Indigenous Peoples of North America. 2000, Lucent LB $28.70 (978-1-56006-617-0). The story of the Cherokee from their origins in the southern Appalachian mountains, through the Trail of Tears to Oklahoma, to their present status. (Rev: BL 3/15/00; HBG 9/00; VOYA 6/01) [973]

9023 McCarthy, Cathy. *The Ojibwa* (4–7). Series: Indian Nations. 2000, Raintree LB $25.69 (978-0-8172-5460-5). A history of the Ojibwa Indians that includes material on the daily life and traditions of this group that now lives in Minnesota, Wisconsin, and central Canada. (Rev: BL 3/15/01; HBG 10/01) [973]

9024 McCormick, Anita Louise. *Native Americans and the Reservation in American History* (7–10). Illus. Series: American History. 1996, Enslow LB $26.60 (978-0-89490-769-2). An overview of the relationship between whites and Native Americans that covers hundreds of years of history and discusses the cruelty of forced marches and life on the reservations. (Rev: BL 1/1–15/97; SLJ 2/97) [973]

9025 McIntosh, Kenneth. *Apache* (8–12). Series: North American Indians Today. 2003, Mason Crest LB $22.95 (978-1-59084-664-3). The contemporary status of Apache Indians is emphasized in this volume that covers religion, government, and the arts. (Rev: SLJ 5/04) [973]

9026 McIntosh, Kenneth. *Navajo* (6–9). Illus. Series: North American Indians Today. 2003, Mason Crest LB $22.95 (978-1-59084-672-8). This portrait of the Navajo people offers a brief history of the tribe but focuses primarily on their present-day culture and government. (Rev: BL 4/1/04; SLJ 5/04) [979.1]

9027 McIntosh, Kenneth, and Marsha McIntosh. *Cheyenne* (8–12). Series: North American Indians Today. 2003, Mason Crest LB $22.95 (978-1-59084-666-7). The contemporary status of Cheyenne Indians is emphasized in this volume that covers religion, government, and the arts. Also use *Iroquois* (2003). (Rev: SLJ 5/04) [973]

9028 McLester, L. Gordon, and Elisabeth Towers. *The Oneida* (4–7). Series: Indian Nations. 2000, Raintree LB $25.69 (978-0-8172-5457-5). The Oneida left their New York lands for Wisconsin and Canada. Beginning with a folk tale, this account describes their past and present with some indication of what the future holds. (Rev: BL 3/15/01; HBG 10/01) [973]

9029 Margolin, Malcolm, and Yolanda Montijo, eds. *Native Ways: California Indian Stories and Memories* (5–8). Illus. 1996, Heyday paper $8.95 (978-0-930588-73-1). Reminiscences and stories reflect California Indian culture, both past and present. (Rev: BL 7/96) [979.4]

9030 Mayfield, Thomas Jefferson. *Adopted by Indians: A True Story* (5–8). Ed. by Malcolm Margolin. Illus. 1997, Heyday paper $10.95 (978-0-930588-93-9). This is an adaption of the memoirs of a white man who lived with the Choinumne Indians in California for 10 years, beginning in 1850 when he was 8 years old. (Rev: BL 3/1/98) [979.4]

9031 Meyers, Madeleine, ed. *Cherokee Nation: Life Before the Tears* (4–8). Series: Perspectives on History. 1994, Discovery paper $6.95 (978-1-878668-26-4). A history of the Cherokees that emphasizes the leadership of Sequoyah and the life of the tribe before their forced displacement. (Rev: BL 8/94) [970.3]

9032 Mooney, Martin. *The Comanche Indians* (4–7). Illus. Series: Junior Library of American Indians. 1993, Chelsea LB $25.00 (978-0-7910-1653-4). A historical account of the Comanches from about 1700 to the present. (Rev: SLJ 4/93) [970]

9033 Nies, Judith. *Native American History: A Chronology of a Culture's Vast Achievements and Their Links to World Events* (6–12). 1997, Ballantine paper $15.00 (978-0-345-39350-0). This chronology of Native North American history and culture from 28,000 B.C. through 1996, using a split-page format to juxtapose simultaneous political, social, religious, and military developments occurring in North America and in other parts of the world. (Rev: SLJ 5/97) [970.003]

9034 Philip, Neil, ed. *A Braid of Lives: Native American Childhood* (4–8). Illus. 2000, Clarion $20.00 (978-0-395-64528-4). Twenty vignettes of one or two pages in length give a many-faceted picture of growing up Native American in different parts of the county. (Rev: BL 10/1/00; HBG 10/01; SLJ 6/01; VOYA 4/01) [973]

9035 Philip, Neil. *The Great Circle: A History of the First Nations* (6–9). 2006, Clarion $20.00 (978-0-618-15941-3). An excellent history of Native American tribes — their leaders, beliefs, traditions —

and, in particular, their interactions with white settlers. (Rev: BL 10/1/06; SLJ 11/06*) [973.04]

9036 Philip, Neil, ed. *In a Sacred Manner I Live: Native American Wisdom* (4–8). Illus. 1997, Clarion $20.00 (978-0-395-84981-1). More than 30 Native American leaders — including Geronimo and Cochise — are quoted on topics relating to the conduct of life and their beliefs. (Rev: BL 7/97; HBG 3/98; SLJ 12/97) [973]

9037 Remington, Gwen. *The Cheyenne* (7–10). Series: Indigenous Peoples of North America. 2000, Lucent LB $28.70 (978-1-56006-750-4). The story of the past and present of the nomadic rulers of the High Plains who were considered to be the most civilized of the Great Plains Indians. (Rev: BL 9/15/00) [973]

9038 Roessel, Monty. *Kinaalda: A Navajo Girl Grows Up* (4–7). Illus. 1993, Lerner LB $25.55 (978-0-8225-2655-1); paper $11.15 (978-0-8225-9641-7). Celinda McKelvey, a Navajo girl, returns to the reservation to participate in her Kinaalda, the coming-of-age ceremony. (Rev: BCCB 1/94; BL 1/15/94; SLJ 2/94) [392.1]

9039 Seymour, Tryntje Van Ness. *The Gift of Changing Woman* (5–8). 1993, Holt $16.95 (978-0-8050-2577-4). A description of the Apache initiation rite for young women in picture-book format, illustrated by Apache artists. (Rev: BL 11/15/93; SLJ 3/94) [299]

9040 Sherrow, Victoria. *Cherokee Nation v. Georgia: Native American Rights* (6–10). Series: Landmark Supreme Court Cases. 1997, Enslow LB $26.60 (978-0-89490-856-9). This book re-creates vividly the important case of 1831 when the Supreme Court ruled that the Cherokee tribe was a "domestic, dependent nation" and not liable to regulation by the state of Georgia. (Rev: BL 10/15/97; HBG 3/98) [973]

9041 Shuter, Jane, ed. *Francis Parkman and the Plains Indians* (5–8). Illus. Series: History Eyewitness. 1995, Raintree LB $24.26 (978-0-8114-8280-6). An edited and abridged version of Parkman's autobiographical writing about the social customs, family life, and hunting practices of the Plains Indians. (Rev: BL 4/15/95) [978]

9042 Siegel, Beatrice. *Indians of the Northeast Woodlands* (4–8). Illus. by William Sauts Bock. 1991, Walker LB $14.85 (978-0-8027-8157-4). In question-and-answer format — following the original 1972 edition — this volume contains much information on Native Americans in New England. (Rev: BL 11/15/92) [973]

9043 Sonneborn, Liz. *The New York Public Library Amazing Native American History: A Book of Answers for Kids* (5–8). 1999, Wiley paper $16.95 (978-0-471-33204-6). Organized by regions and using a question-and-answer approach, this is a fine overview of the history of Native Americans, ending with a chapter on contemporary conditions. (Rev: BL 5/1/00; SLJ 7/00) [970.004]

9044 Steele, Philip. *Little Bighorn* (5–8). Illus. by Richard Hook. Series: Great Battles and Sieges. 1992, Macmillan $21.00 (978-0-02-786885-2). How General George Custer was defeated by Cheyenne and Sioux Indians in 1876. (Rev: BL 10/1/92; SLJ 2/93) [973.8]

9045 Stewart, Mark, ed. *The Indian Removal Act: Forced Relocation* (6–8). Illus. 2007, Compass Point LB $23.95 (978-0-7565-2452-4). Presents historical information on the issues and events leading up to the Indian Removal Act of 1830 and the many deaths along the Trail of Tears. (Rev: BL 5/15/07) [973.04]

9046 Stone, Amy M. *Creek* (4–8). Series: Native American Peoples. 2004, Gareth Stevens LB $26.00 (978-0-8368-4217-3). History, tradition, and contemporary life are described with photographs, timeline, fact boxes, and activities. (Rev: SLJ 1/05) [973]

9047 *The Story of the Blackfoot People: Nitsitapi-isinni* (7–12). Illus. 2001, Firefly paper $15.95 (978-1-55297-583-1). Blackfoot leaders reveal details of their people's history, beliefs, social structure, traditions, and culture, with numerous photographs and a glossary of Blackfoot terms. (Rev: BL 2/15/02; SLJ 3/02) [970.004]

9048 Stout, Mary. *Blackfoot* (4–8). Series: Native American Peoples. 2004, Gareth Stevens LB $26.00 (978-0-8368-4216-6). History, tradition, and contemporary life are described with photographs, timeline, fact boxes, and activities. (Rev: SLJ 1/05) [973]

9049 Streissguth, Thomas. *The Comanche* (7–10). Series: Indigenous Peoples of North America. 2000, Lucent LB $28.70 (978-1-56006-633-0). The history of these fierce raiders and expert horsemen who became the "Masters of the South," and one of the most feared of all Native American tribes. (Rev: BL 8/00; HBG 3/01) [973]

9050 Taylor, C. J. *Peace Walker: The Legend of Hiawatha and Tekanawita* (6–9). Illus. 2004, Tundra $15.95 (978-0-88776-547-6). In rhythmic prose and full-page paintings, Taylor retells the story of Hiawatha and places it in cultural context. (Rev: BL 2/15/05; SLJ 4/05) [398.2]

9051 Tehanetorens. *Roots of the Iroquois* (7–10). Illus. 2000, Native Voices paper $9.95 (978-1-57067-097-8). A lively, detailed look at the history of the Iroquois Confederation before and after the arrival of European settlers. (Rev: BL 11/15/00) [974.004]

9052 Thompson, Linda. *The California People* (4–7). Illus. Series: Native People, Native Lands.

2003, Rourke LB $29.93 (978-1-58952-753-9). One of a well-illustrated series on individual groups of native Americans, with attention to the negative impact of the arrival of European settlers. Other titles in the series include *People of the Northwest and Subarctic*, *People of the Great Basin*, *People of the Northeast Woodlands*, and *People of the Plains and Prairies* (all 2003). (Rev: SLJ 4/04) [979.4]

9053 Wolfson, Evelyn. *Growing Up Indian* (5–7). Illus. 1986, Walker LB $11.85 (978-0-8027-6644-1). What it was like to grow up Indian in traditional American culture before the influence of the white race. (Rev: BL 1/15/87; SLJ 3/87) [306.08997073]

9054 Wood, Marion, and Brian Williams. *Ancient America*. Rev. ed. (5–8). Illus. Series: Cultural Atlas for Young People. 2003, Facts on File $35.00 (978-0-8160-5145-8). Colorful topical spreads introduce readers to Native American history from the end of the Ice Age to the arrival of European explorers and conquerers. (Rev: SLJ 1/04) [970.01]

9055 Woods, Geraldine. *The Navajo* (5–7). Illus. Series: Watts Library: Indians of the Americas. 2002, Watts paper $8.95 (978-0-531-16227-9). This account includes information on history and contemporary issues and covers the Navajo code talkers, land disputes, traditions, housing, and clothing. (Rev: BL 7/02) [979.1]

9056 Young, Robert. *A Personal Tour of Mesa Verde* (4–7). Illus. Series: How It Was. 1999, Lerner LB $30.35 (978-0-8225-3577-5). This book gives a special glimpse into the lives of the Native Americans known as the Puebloans, how they lived, and the culture they developed. (Rev: BL 6/1–15/99; HBG 10/99; SLJ 7/99) [978.8]

9057 Yue, Charlotte, and David Yue. *The Wigwam and the Longhouse* (4–9). Illus. by authors. 2000, Houghton $15.00 (978-0-395-84169-3). A well-balanced account that describes the life and history of several tribes of Native Americans from the eastern woodlands. (Rev: HB 7–8/00; HBG 10/00; SLJ 10/00; VOYA 12/00) [973]

DISCOVERY AND EXPLORATION

9058 Arenstam, Peter, et al. *Mayflower 1620: A New Look at a Pilgrim Voyage* (5–9). 2003, National Geographic $17.95 (978-0-7922-6142-1). A large-format photoessay of a voyage of the *Mayflower II* — re-creating the original journey — is the backdrop for detail about the 1620 passengers, supplies, navigation techniques, and the new country they arrived in. (Rev: BL 11/1/03; HBG 4/04; SLJ 11/03) [974.4]

9059 Armentrout, David, and Patricia Armentrout. *The Mayflower Compact* (4–7). 2004, Rourke $20.95 (978-1-59515-229-9). The reasons for the creation of this document — a political statement signed by a group of *Mayflower* passengers — are thoroughly explored in concise text, accompanied by an array of maps and illustrations. (Rev: BL 10/15/04) [974.4]

9060 Aykroyd, Clarissa. *Exploration of the California Coast* (4–7). Series: Exploration and Discovery. 2002, Mason Crest LB $19.95 (978-1-59084-043-6). Explorers such as Cortes and Drake are covered in this look at 16th-century California. (Rev: SLJ 12/02) [917.94041]

9061 Faber, Harold. *The Discoverers of America* (6–12). 1992, Scribner $17.95 (978-0-684-19217-8). Discusses the exploration of North and South America, focusing on the period from Columbus to Lewis and Clark. (Rev: BL 5/15/92; SLJ 6/92) [970.01]

9062 Faber, Harold. *Lewis and Clark: From Ocean to Ocean* (5–8). Illus. Series: Great Explorations. 2001, Benchmark LB $29.93 (978-0-7614-1241-0). This concise, artfully illustrated volume about the journey of Lewis and Clark includes journal entries, a timeline, and Web site information. (Rev: BL 1/1–15/02; HBG 3/02; SLJ 3/02) [917.804]

9063 Foran, Jill. *Search for the Northwest Passage* (5–8). Series: Great Journeys. 2004, Weigl LB $26.00 (978-1-59036-205-1). Colorful illustrations and an attractive format will appeal to browsers seeking information about the search for a sea route to the West; a useful timeline and links to Web sites are included. (Rev: BL 11/1/04) [910]

9064 Freedman, Russell. *Who Was First? Discovering the Americas* (6–9). Illus. 2007, Clarion $19.00 (978-0-618-66391-0). Freedman explores various claims to the discovery of the Americas, providing lots of reader-friendly information plus a good grounding in the purpose of studying history. (Rev: BL 10/1/07; SLJ 11/07) [970.01]

9065 Lepore, Jill. *Encounters in the New World: A History in Documents* (7–12). Series: Pages from History. 1999, Oxford LB $39.95 (978-0-19-510513-1). Documents including letters, journals, and advertisements make relations between Native Americans and European arrivals more real to readers. (Rev: HBG 9/00; SLJ 3/00) [970]

9066 MacGregor, Greg. *Lewis and Clark Revisited: A Photographer's Trail* (8–12). Ed. by Iris Tillman Hill. Illus. 2004, Univ. of Washington $50.00 (978-0-295-98342-4). This book, which contains many eye-catching photographs, traces the route of the Lewis and Clark expedition in 1804-06 and shows the route as it looks today. (Rev: BL 2/15/04) [917.804]

9067 Patent, Dorothy Hinshaw. *Animals on the Trail with Lewis and Clark* (4–8). Illus. by William Muñoz. 2002, Clarion $18.00 (978-0-395-91415-1). A handsome account of the Lewis and Clark expedition with emphasis on the animals that were discovered during the journey. (Rev: BCCB 5/02; BL 4/15/02*; HB 5–6/02; HBG 10/02; SLJ 4/02) [917.804]

9068 Roberts, Russell. *Pedro Menendez de Aviles* (5–7). Illus. Series: Latinos in American History. 2002, Mitchell Lane LB $29.95 (978-1-58415-150-0). This account of explorer Pedro Menendez de Aviles's efforts to procure Florida for Spain uses some fictionalized narrative to illustrate the times. (Rev: BL 10/15/02; HBG 3/03; SLJ 10/02) [975.9]

9069 Roop, Peter, and Connie Roop. *River Roads West* (5–8). Illus. 2007, Boyds Mills $19.95 (978-1-59078-430-3). The Hudson, Ohio, and Mississippi rivers and the Erie Canal are among the American waterways introduced in this large-format book that discusses the Native American peoples who lived along them and the impact of European exploration and settlement. (Rev: BL 9/15/07; SLJ 9/07) [917]

9070 Schouweiler, Thomas. *The Lost Colony of Roanoke* (6–10). Series: Great Mysteries. 1991, Greenhaven LB $22.45 (978-0-89908-093-2). Outlines what is known about the colony that disappeared and poses questions about its unsolved mysteries. (Rev: BL 3/1/92) [975.6]

9071 Stefoff, Rebecca. *Exploring the New World* (4–7). Illus. Series: North American Historical Atlases. 2000, Benchmark LB $27.07 (978-0-7614-1056-0). Using historical maps and reproductions, the important explorers and their accomplishments are covered in this slim, attractive volume. (Rev: HBG 3/01; SLJ 1/01) [970.01]

9072 Stefoff, Rebecca. *Lewis and Clark* (4–7). Illus. 1992, Chelsea LB $28.00 (978-0-7910-1750-0). A simple text and pictures of the Lewis and Clark expedition, which helped open up the West. (Rev: BL 7/92) [978.02]

9073 Steins, Richard. *Exploration and Settlement* (5–8). Illus. Series: Making of America. 2000, Raintree LB $28.54 (978-0-8172-5700-2). This account begins with prehistoric migrations to North America and continues with European explorers, including the Spanish, English, French, and Dutch. (Rev: BL 5/1/00; HBG 10/00; SLJ 9/00) [970.01]

9074 Warrick, Karen Clemens. *The Perilous Search for the Fabled Northwest Passage in American History* (6–9). Series: In American History. 2004, Enslow LB $26.60 (978-0-7660-2148-8). Traces early efforts to find the passage as well as Amundsen's successful 1906 expedition. (Rev: SLJ 10/04) [910]

9075 Whiting, Jim. *Francisco Vasquez de Coronado* (5–7). Illus. Series: Latinos in American History. 2002, Mitchell Lane LB $29.95 (978-1-58415-146-3). This account of Francisco Vasquez de Coronado's search for the lost cities of gold, and his subsequent trial for cruelty to Native Americans, uses some fictionalized narrative. (Rev: BL 10/15/02; HBG 3/03; SLJ 10/02; VOYA 6/03) [979]

9076 Wittmann, Kelly. *The European Rediscovery of America* (4–7). Series: Exploration and Discovery. 2002, Mason Crest LB $19.95 (978-1-59084-052-8). Wittmann looks at the explorers of the 15th and 16th centuries, including Columbus and Cabot. (Rev: SLJ 12/02) [970]

9077 Yero, Judith Lloyd. *The Mayflower Compact* (4–7). Series: American Documents. 2006, National Geographic $15.95 (978-0-7922-5891-9). Yero distinguishes fact from myth in this examination of the *Mayflower*'s voyage, the colony the Separatists create, and the document they drafted as their governing compact. (Rev: BL 9/15/06; SLJ 10/06) [974.4]

COLONIAL PERIOD AND FRENCH AND INDIAN WARS

9078 Allman, Melinda, ed. *Primary Sources* (5–8). Series: Thirteen Colonies. 2002, Gale LB $27.45 (978-1-59018-011-2). A fascinating collection of primary source material for the young researcher. (Rev: BL 9/15/02; SLJ 10/02) [873.2]

9079 Altman, Linda J. *Trade and Commerce* (5–9). Series: Colonial Life. 2007, Sharpe Focus $37.95 (978-0-7656-8111-9). With color illustrations and interesting sidebars, this volume looks at trade and commerce in the colonies. (Rev: SLJ 1/08)

9080 Asirvatham, Sandy. *The Salem Witch Trials* (6–8). Series: Great Disasters. 2001, Chelsea LB $30.00 (978-0-7910-6328-6). A historically accurate account of the hysteria that swept New England and resulted in the execution of 20 suspected witches in 1692. (Rev: BL 6/1–15/02; HBG 10/02) [973.2]

9081 Brown, Gene. *Discovery and Settlement: Europe Meets the New World (1490–1700)* (5–7). Series: First Person America. 1993, Twenty-First Century LB $20.90 (978-0-8050-2574-3). Using excerpts from original documents, this book covers the exploration of the United States, the Puritans, and the role of Native Americans, African Americans, and women in early colonial days. (Rev: SLJ 3/94) [973.2]

9082 Butler, Jon. *Religion in Colonial America* (5–8). Series: Religion in American Life. 2000, Oxford $32.95 (978-0-19-511998-5). This book describes the mix of Catholics, Jews, Africans, Native Americans, Puritans, and various Protestant faiths that coexisted during colonial times. (Rev: BL 6/1–15/00; HBG 10/00) [973.2]

9083 Collier, Christopher, and James Lincoln Collier. *Clash of Cultures: Prehistory–1638* (5–8). Illus. Series: Drama of American History. 1998, Marshall Cavendish LB $31.36 (978-0-7614-0436-1). This well-illustrated examination of the cultures on both sides of the Atlantic — Native American and European — in the years before and during the formation of the colonies. (Rev: BL 4/15/98*; HBG 10/98) [970.00497]

9084 Collier, Christopher, and James Lincoln Collier. *The French and Indian War* (5–8). Illus. Series: Drama of American History. 1998, Marshall Cavendish LB $31.36 (978-0-7614-0439-2). A nicely illustrated book providing a broad perspective on the French and Indian War, and noting the conflict's importance on both sides of the Atlantic. (Rev: BL 4/15/98*; HBG 10/98) [973.2]

9085 Collier, Christopher, and James Lincoln Collier. *The Paradox of Jamestown: 1585–1700* (5–8). Illus. Series: Drama of American History. 1998, Marshall Cavendish LB $31.36 (978-0-7614-0437-8). The paradox of Jamestown's history is that it gave democratic freedom through its elected legislature while introducing the first African slaves into the colonies. (Rev: BL 4/15/98*; HBG 10/98) [975.5]

9086 Collier, Christopher, and James Lincoln Collier. *Pilgrims and Puritans: 1620–1676* (5–8). Illus. Series: Drama of American History. 1997, Marshall Cavendish LB $31.36 (978-0-7614-0438-5). This volume describes the routes the Pilgrims and Puritans took to America, their beliefs and practices, and how present-day American life continues to be influenced by them. (Rev: BL 4/15/98*; HBG 10/98) [974.4]

9087 Cooper, Michael L. *Jamestown 1607* (6–9). Illus. 2007, Holiday $18.95 (978-0-8234-1948-7). The story of the Jamestown colony is told in concise text with excellent illustrations, quotations from primary sources, and background context. (Rev: BCCB 6/07; BL 4/15/07; SLJ 4/07) [973.2]

9088 Daugherty, James. *The Landing of the Pilgrims* (5–7). Illus. by author. 1981, Random paper $5.99 (978-0-394-84697-2). Based on his own writings, this is the story of the Pilgrims from the standpoint of William Bradford. [974.4]

9089 Day, Nancy. *Your Travel Guide to Colonial America* (4–8). Series: Passport to History. 2000, Lerner LB $26.50 (978-0-8225-3079-4). Using a modern-day guidebook format, this account takes the reader back to colonial times with glimpses of the *Mayflower* and visits to such colonies as Jamestown, Virginia, and Plymouth, Massachusetts. (Rev: BL 3/1/01; HBG 10/01; SLJ 4/01) [973.2]

9090 Doherty, Kieran. *Puritans, Pilgrims, and Merchants: Founders of the Northeastern Colonies* (4–8). Illus. 1999, Oliver LB $22.95 (978-1-881508-50-2). A history of each of the northeastern colonies is supplemented with brief biographies of such people as William Bradford, John Winthrop, Peter Stuyvesant, Anne Hutchinson, and William Penn. (Rev: BL 8/99; HBG 3/00; SLJ 1/00) [974]

9091 Doherty, Kieran. *Soldiers, Cavaliers, and Planters: Settlers of the Southeastern Colonies* (4–8). 1999, Oliver LB $22.95 (978-1-881508-51-9). This book focuses on the early southern colonies and their founders and leaders, among them Captain John Smith, Sir Walter Raleigh, and Pedro Menendez de Aviles. (Rev: BL 8/99; HBG 3/00; SLJ 10/99) [975]

9092 Dosier, Susan. *Colonial Cooking* (4–7). Illus. Series: Exploring History Through Simple Recipes. 2000, Capstone LB $23.93 (978-0-7368-0352-6). This work covers the home life of the colonialists in the North, with material on kitchens, celebrations, food, and some recipes. (Rev: BL 8/00; HBG 10/00) [394.1]

9093 Edwards, Judith. *Jamestown: John Smith and Pocahontas in American History* (6–10). Series: In American History. 2002, Enslow LB $26.60 (978-0-7660-1842-6). This is a well-documented account that describes this crucial period in American colonial history and the key people involved. (Rev: BL 5/15/02; HBG 10/02) [973.2]

9094 Egger-Bovet, Howard, and Marlene Smith-Baranzini. *US Kids History: Book of the American Colonies* (5–7). Illus. Series: Brown Paper School. 1996, Little, Brown paper $14.99 (978-0-316-22201-3). In an informal writing style with plenty of drawings and activities, the American colonial period is introduced. (Rev: BL 8/96; SLJ 8/96) [973.2]

9095 Girod, Christina M. *South Carolina* (5–8). Series: Thirteen Colonies. 2002, Gale LB $27.45 (978-1-56006-994-2). A history of the colony of South Carolina and its people from the early settlements to admission into the United States, told in concise prose with numerous black-and-white illustrations. (Rev: BL 9/15/02) [973.2]

9096 Hale, Anna W. *The Mayflower People: Triumphs and Tragedies* (5–8). Illus. 1995, Harbinger $15.95 (978-1-57140-002-4); paper $9.95 (978-1-57140-003-1). A human account of the Pilgrims that begins with their departure from Southampton, England, in 1620 and ends two years later in the New World with the death of Squanto. (Rev: BL 1/1–15/96) [974.4]

9097 Hinds, Kathryn. *Daily Living* (5–9). Series: Colonial Life. 2007, Sharpe Focus $37.95 (978-0-7656-8110-2). With color illustrations and interesting sidebars, this volume looks at social life in the colonies, exploring food, family life, and so forth. (Rev: SLJ 1/08)

9098 Hinman, Bonnie. *Pennsylvania: William Penn and the City of Brotherly Love* (4–7). Series: Building America. 2006, Mitchell Lane LB $19.95 (978-1-58415-463-1). This history of colonial Pennsylvania explores the reasons why William Penn established the colony in the late 17th century. (Rev: SLJ 2/07) [974.8]

9099 Hossell, Karen. *Delaware 1638–1776* (5–8). Series: Voices from Colonial America. 2006, National Geographic $21.95 (978-0-7922-6408-8). This well-illustrated title traces the history of Delaware from the 17th-century massacre of Dutch settlers by Native Americans to the eve of the American Revolution; maps and a timeline make this useful for research. (Rev: SLJ 1/07) [975.1]

9100 Howarth, Sarah. *Colonial Places* (4–8). Illus. Series: People and Places. 1994, Millbrook LB $22.90 (978-1-56294-513-8). Highlights various places of importance in everyday colonial life, such as the meetinghouse and the church. (Rev: BL 5/15/95; SLJ 3/95) [973]

9101 Hubbard-Brown, Janet. *The Secret of Roanoke Island* (4–7). Illus. 1991, Avon paper $3.50 (978-0-380-76223-1). An intriguing look at this bit of history in colonial times. (Rev: BL 12/15/91) [975.63]

9102 Jackson, Shirley. *The Witchcraft of Salem Village* (4–7). Illus. 1963, Random paper $5.99 (978-0-394-89176-7). An account of the witch-hunting hysteria that hit Salem Village. [133.43097445]

9103 Kelly, Martin, and Melissa Kelly. *Government* (5–9). Series: Colonial Life. 2007, Sharpe Focus $37.95 (978-0-7656-8112-6). With color illustrations and interesting sidebars, this volume looks at government in the colonies, exploring the Native American tribal organization as well as the colonial structure. (Rev: SLJ 1/08)

9104 Kent, Deborah. *In Colonial New England* (4–8). Series: How We Lived. 1999, Benchmark LB $28.50 (978-0-7614-0905-2). Topics such as home life, childhood, religion, problems, and amusements are covered for the colonial period in New England. Companion volumes are *In the Middle Colonies* and *In the Southern Colonies* (1999). (Rev: HBG 10/00; SLJ 2/00) [973.2]

9105 Kent, Zachary. *The Mysterious Disappearance of Roanoke Colony in American History* (7–10). Illus. Series: American History. 2004, Enslow LB $26.60 (978-0-7660-2147-1). A detailed account of the settlement on Roanoke Island with recent research material on the fate of the colony. (Rev: BL 3/1/04; SLJ 6/04) [975.6]

9106 Lukes, Bonnie L. *Colonial America* (7–10). Illus. 1999, Lucent LB $27.45 (978-1-56006-321-6). Using extensive quotations from many sources, this book traces the basic history of colonial America, and gives good material on the obstacles settlers faced and their relations with Native Americans. (Rev: BL 2/15/00; HBG 9/00; SLJ 3/00) [940.2]

9107 McKissack, Patricia C., and Fredrick McKissack. *Hard Labor: The First African Americans, 1619* (5–8). Illus. by Joseph Fiedler. Series: Milestone Books. 2004, Simon & Schuster paper $3.99 (978-0-689-86149-9). Drawing on the meager evidence available, the authors reconstruct the story of the first Africans brought to America. (Rev: BL 2/15/04; SLJ 3/04) [306.3]

9108 McNeese, Tim. *Jamestown* (5–8). Illus. Series: Colonial Settlements in America. 2007, Chelsea House $30.00 (978-0-7910-9335-1). This overview of the settlement of the colony will be helpful to report writers and includes maps and other graphics. (Rev: BL 7/07; LMC 11/07; SLJ 7/07) [973]

9109 Marrin, Albert. *Struggle for a Continent: The French and Indian Wars, 1690–1760* (6–9). Illus. 1987, Macmillan LB $15.95 (978-0-689-31313-4). A vivid re-creation of the events and personalities of these wars and how they helped lead to the Revolution. (Rev: BL 1/15/88; SLJ 12/87; VOYA 10/87) [973.2]

9110 Miller, Brandon M. *Good Women of a Well-Blessed Land: Women's Lives in Colonial America* (5–8). Series: People's History. 2003, Lerner LB $29.27 (978-0-8225-0032-2). The lives and roles of women from all layers of early American society are presented in this well-written account that includes many quotations, maps, and period reproductions. (Rev: BL 5/15/03; HBG 10/03; SLJ 7/03) [305.4]

9111 Miller, Brandon M. *Growing Up in a New World* (5–8). Series: Our America. 2002, Lerner LB $26.60 (978-0-8225-0658-4). The thrill of landing in the New World for the first time is re-created through true-life adventures of young people. (Rev: BL 2/15/03; HBG 3/03; SLJ 7/03) [973.2]

9112 Miller, Lee. *Roanoke: The Mystery of the Lost Colony* (4–7). Illus. 2007, Scholastic $18.99 (978-0-439-71266-8). Author Miller presents her theory that the colony at Roanoke was sabotaged. (Rev: BL 6/1–15/07; LMC 10/07) [975.6]

9113 Nardo, Don. *Braving the New World, 1619–1784: From the Arrival of the Enslaved Africans to the End of the American Revolution* (7–10). Series: Milestones in Black History. 1995, Chelsea LB $21.95 (978-0-7910-2259-7); paper $9.95 (978-0-7910-2685-4). How and why the slave trade became established in North America and the legacy of the slave culture. (Rev: BL 4/15/95) [973.2]

9114 O'Neill, Laurie A. *The Boston Tea Party* (4–8). Series: Spotlight on American History. 1996, Millbrook LB $24.90 (978-0-7613-0006-9). The causes and effects of the Boston Tea Party are discussed, along with material on the Battles of Lexington and Concord. (Rev: BL 1/1–15/97; SLJ 3/97) [973.3]

9115 Roop, Connie, and Peter Roop, eds. *Pilgrim Voices: Our First Year in the New World* (4–7). Illus. 1995, Walker LB $17.85 (978-0-8027-8315-8). Using first-person sources, the experiences of the Pilgrims from their sea journey to the first Thanksgiving are re-created. (Rev: BL 2/1/96; SLJ 1/96) [974.4]

9116 Sherrow, Victoria. *Huskings, Quiltings, and Barn Raisings: Work-Play Parties in Early America* (4–7). Illus. by Laura LoTurco. 1992, Walker LB $14.85 (978-0-8027-8188-8). How people in early America helped each other with difficult tasks, such as clearing land and raising barns. (Rev: BL 1/15/93) [973.2]

9117 Smith, Carter, ed. *The Arts and Sciences: A Sourcebook on Colonial America* (5–8). Illus. Series: American Albums. 1991, Millbrook $25.90 (978-1-56294-037-9). Through many well-captioned illustrations and brief text, this sourcebook traces cultural and scientific life during the U.S. colonial period. (Rev: BL 1/1/92) [973.2]

9118 Stefoff, Rebecca. *Cities and Towns* (5–9). Series: Colonial Life. 2007, Sharpe Focus $37.95 (978-0-7656-8109-6). With color illustrations and interesting sidebars, this volume looks at the development of cities and towns from the earlier forts and fishing camps. (Rev: SLJ 1/08)

9119 Stefoff, Rebecca. *The Colonies* (4–7). Series: North American Historical Atlases. 2000, Benchmark LB $27.07 (978-0-7614-1057-7). A slim, clearly written account that gives a history of the American colonies, important places, and outstanding people. (Rev: HBG 3/01; SLJ 1/01) [973.2]

9120 Stefoff, Rebecca. *Exploration and Settlement* (5–9). Series: Colonial Life. 2007, Sharpe Focus $37.95 (978-0-7656-8108-9). With color illustrations and interesting sidebars, this volume looks at the progress of exploration in the 15th and 16th centuries and includes profiles of key explorers. (Rev: SLJ 1/08)

9121 Steins, Richard. *Colonial America* (5–8). Series: Making of America. 2000, Raintree LB $28.54 (978-0-8172-5701-9). A brief history of the colonies from 1607 to 1763 with details of their founding, composition, and history. (Rev: HBG 10/00; SLJ 8/00) [973.2]

9122 Wiener, Roberta, and James R. Arnold. *Connecticut: The History of Connecticut Colony, 1633–1776* (5–8). Series: 13 Colonies. 2004, Raintree LB $31.36 (978-0-7398-6877-5). A fact-filled and balanced discussion of the settlement of this area and the problems — political, social, and religious — that confronted the early European inhabitants. Also use *Delaware* and *Maryland* (both 2004). (Rev: SLJ 4/05) [974.6]

9123 Wilson, Lori L. *The Salem Witch Trials: How History Is Invented* (6–12). Illus. Series: How History Is Invented. 1997, Lerner LB $23.93 (978-0-8225-4889-8). The story of the famous trial of 100 people in Massachusetts during 1692, and the hysteria and falsehoods that led to 20 people being put to death. (Rev: BL 9/1/97; HBG 3/98; SLJ 8/97*) [133.4]

9124 Winters, Kay. *Colonial Voices: Hear Them Speak* (4–7). Illus. by Larry Day. 2008, Dutton $17.99 (978-0-525-47872-0). Fictional residents of colonial Boston offer their opinions on independence and revolution in this illustrated book by the author of *Voices of Egypt*. (Rev: BL 5/15/08; LMC 11-12/08; SLJ 6/08*) [973.3]

9125 Worth, Richard. *Colonial America: Building Toward Independence* (5–8). Series: The American Saga. 2006, Enslow LB $31.93 (978-0-7660-2569-1). Tracing the history of the original 13 colonies from the earliest English settlements through the ratification of the Constitution, this volume will be useful for report writers seeking information on politics, government, economy, and culture. (Rev: SLJ 12/06) [973.2]

REVOLUTIONARY PERIOD AND THE YOUNG NATION (1775–1809)

9126 Allen, Thomas B. *George Washington, Spymaster: How the Americans Outspied the British and Won the Revolutionary War* (6–8). Illus. 2004, National Geographic $16.95 (978-0-7922-5126-2). This interesting volume focuses on the general's strategic use of espionage to win America's freedom from the British, providing details about invisible ink, codes and ciphers, and secret messages. (Rev: BL 4/15/04*; SLJ 5/04) [973.3]

9127 Allen, Thomas B. *Remember Valley Forge: Patriots, Tories, and Redcoats Tell Their Stories* (6–9). Illus. 2007, National Geographic $17.95 (978-1-4263-0149-0). All sorts of facts about what went on at Valley Forge, many drawn from the writings of eyewitnesses; maps, photographs, important documents, and other visuals add interest and information. (Rev: BL 12/15/07; SLJ 2/08) [973.3]

9128 Allison, Robert J., ed. *American Eras: The Revolutionary Era (1754–1783)* (7–12). 1998, Gale $140.00 (978-0-7876-1480-5). A good reference source that opens with an overview of world events during the Revolutionary period, followed by chapters on specific topics such as the arts; business and the economy; law and justice; lifestyles, social trends, and fashions; religion; and sports and recreation. (Rev: BL 3/15/99; SLJ 2/99) [973.3]

9129 Anderson, Dale. *The American Colonies Declare Independence* (5–8). Series: World Almanac Library of the American Revolution. 2005, World Almanac LB $31.00 (978-0-8368-5926-3). Excerpts from primary sources bolster the informative, clearly written text, which is sprinkled with biographical sidebars. Also use *The Causes of the American Revolution, The Patriots Win the American Revolution,* and *Forming a New American Government* (all 2005). (Rev: SLJ 1/06) [973.3]

9130 Beller, Susan Provost. *The Revolutionary War* (5–8). Series: Letters from the Homefront. 2001, Benchmark LB $29.93 (978-0-7614-1094-2). An attractive volume that brings events and living conditions during the Revolution alive through a collec-

tion of letters and other personal documents. (Rev: BL 10/15/01; HBG 3/02) [973.3]

9131 Beller, Susan Provost. *Yankee Doodle and the Redcoats: Soldiering in the Revolutionary War* (5–8). Illus. by Larry Day. 2003, Millbrook LB $26.90 (978-0-7613-2612-0). This attractive book covers the plight of the Revolutionary War soldier, with artwork as well as soldiers' letters and other documents adding to the presentation. (Rev: BL 5/15/03; HBG 10/03; SLJ 9/01) [973.3]

9132 Bliven, Bruce, Jr. *The American Revolution, 1760–1783* (6–9). Illus. 1958, Random paper $5.99 (978-0-394-84696-5). A concise account of the causes, battles, and results of the Revolution. [973.3]

9133 Bobrick, Benson. *Fight for Freedom: The American Revolutionary War* (5–8). 2004, Simon & Schuster $22.95 (978-0-689-86422-3). Full-page illustrations face text and "Quick Facts" about topics ranging from the origins and progress of the war to the Continental Congresses, with profiles of key figures and maps. (Rev: BL 11/15/04; SLJ 11/04) [973.3]

9134 Bohannon, Lisa Frederiksen. *The American Revolution* (5–8). Series: Chronicle of America's Wars. 2003, Lerner LB $27.93 (978-0-8225-4717-4). Illustrations and maps enliven this overview of the American colonies' struggle for independence, covering the two decades from the French and Indian War to the Treaty of Paris. (Rev: SLJ 3/04) [973.3]

9135 Brenner, Barbara. *If You Were There in 1776* (4–8). Illus. 1994, Bradbury $17.95 (978-0-02-712322-7). The year 1776 is explored, with particular emphasis on the everyday life of young people in the colonies. (Rev: BCCB 6/94; BL 5/15/94; SLJ 6/94) [973.3]

9136 Burgan, Michael. *The Louisiana Purchase* (5–8). Series: We the People. 2002, Compass Point LB $26.60 (978-0-7565-0210-2). An accessible, well-illustrated account of the purchase that doubled the size of the United States. (Rev: SLJ 7/02) [973.46]

9137 Chase, John Churchill. *Louisiana Purchase: An American Story.* Rev. ed. (5–8). Illus. 2002, Pelican paper $12.95 (978-1-58980-084-7). The story of the Louisiana Purchase, engagingly told in comic-strip format. (Rev: BL 2/1/03) [973.4]

9138 Collier, Christopher, and James Lincoln Collier. *The American Revolution: 1763–1783* (5–8). Series: Drama of American History. 1998, Marshall Cavendish LB $31.36 (978-0-7614-0440-8). Using period illustrations, this is a basic history of the Revolution, with material on how the colonialists felt, major battles, and major figures. (Rev: BL 4/15/98*; HBG 10/98) [973.3]

9139 Collier, Christopher, and James Lincoln Collier. *Building a New Nation, 1789–1801* (5–8). Illus. Series: Drama of American History. 1998, Marshall Cavendish LB $31.36 (978-0-7614-0777-5). An account of how the Federalists began to use the Constitution as a blueprint for guiding the young nation. (Rev: BL 2/15/99) [973.4]

9140 Collier, Christopher, and James Lincoln Collier. *Slavery and the Coming of the Civil War, 1831–1861* (5–8). Illus. 1999, Marshall Cavendish LB $29.93 (978-0-7614-0817-8). A reliable, interesting account the traces the history of slavery in the United States, with an emphasis on the events leading up to the Civil War. (Rev: BL 2/15/00; HBG 10/00; SLJ 3/00) [973.7]

9141 Deem, James M. *Primary Source Accounts of the Revolutionary War* (5–8). Illus. Series: America's Wars Through Primary Sources. 2006, Enslow LB $33.27 (978-1-59845-004-0). Soldiers' journal entries, letters from home, personal recollections, songs and poetry, and newspaper articles are among the primary sources included in this general history of the war. (Rev: SLJ 4/07) [973.3]

9142 Diouf, Sylviane A. *Growing Up in Slavery* (6–12). 2001, Millbrook LB $25.90 (978-0-7613-1763-0). A compelling account that dispels any myths about happy slave children and describes the hard life on the plantation as well as the atrocious conditions on slave ships. (Rev: BL 3/1/01; HBG 10/01; SLJ 6/01) [380.1]

9143 Doherty, Craig A., and Katherine M. Doherty. *The Erie Canal* (4–7). Illus. Series: Building America. 1996, Blackbirch LB $24.95 (978-1-56711-112-5). Photographs and maps are used effectively in this introduction to the Erie Canal, an engineering marvel. (Rev: BL 2/15/97; SLJ 2/97) [386]

9144 Dolan, Edward F. *The American Revolution: How We Fought the War of Independence* (6–9). 1995, Millbrook LB $30.40 (978-1-56294-521-3). This heavily illustrated, clearly written, battle-by-battle history of the Revolution looks at the causes, places, campaigns, and people, as well as the bloodiest battles. (Rev: BL 12/15/95; SLJ 1/96) [973.3]

9145 Ferrie, Richard. *The World Turned Upside Down: George Washington and the Battle of Yorktown* (5–9). Illus. 1999, Holiday $18.95 (978-0-8234-1402-4). A lavishly illustrated account of the battle that was the turning point in the Revolution, with details on strategies, personalities, and period warfare. (Rev: BL 9/1/99; HBG 3/00; SLJ 10/99) [973.3]

9146 Fleming, Thomas. *Everybody's Revolution* (4–7). Illus. 2006, Scholastic $19.99 (978-0-439-63404-5). A fascinating introduction to the diverse heroes and heroines of many nationalities who contributed to the success of the American Revolution. (Rev: BL 10/15/06; SLJ 11/06) [973.3]

9147 Freedman, Russell. *Give Me Liberty! The Story of the Declaration of Independence* (4–7). Illus. 2000, Holiday $24.95 (978-0-8234-1448-2). Beginning with the Boston Tea Party, this stirring account introduces characters including Patrick Henry and Paul Revere, events such as the battles at Lexington and Concord, and ends with the Continental Congress and the drawing up of the Declaration of Independence. (Rev: BCCB 10/00; BL 10/1/00*; HB 1–2/01; HBG 3/01; SLJ 10/00) [973.3]

9148 Gaines, Ann Graham. *The Louisiana Purchase in American History* (7–10). Series: In American History. 2000, Enslow LB $26.60 (978-0-7660-1301-8). A well-documented and illustrated account of the 1803 purchase of southern land from the French government. (Rev: BL 1/1–15/00; HBG 9/00) [973.5]

9149 Gunderson, Mary. *Southern Plantation Cooking* (4–7). Illus. 2000, Capstone LB $23.93 (978-0-7368-0357-1). This book explores life on Southern plantations during the days of slavery with emphasis on the importance of food and food preparation. A few representative recipes are provided. (Rev: BL 8/00; HBG 10/00) [394.1]

9150 Herbert, Janis. *The American Revolution for Kids* (5–8). Illus. 2002, Chicago Review paper $14.95 (978-1-55652-456-1). A comprehensive look at the American Revolution from its causes through the early 18th century, with biographical information and interesting features. (Rev: BL 10/1/02; SLJ 11/02) [973.3]

9151 Hull, Mary. *The Boston Tea Party in American History* (6–10). Series: In American History. 1999, Enslow LB $26.60 (978-0-7660-1139-7). A look at the events leading up to this act of defiance that sparked the American Revolution. (Rev: BL 2/15/99; HBG 9/99) [973.3115]

9152 Hull, Mary. *Shays' Rebellion and the Constitution in American History* (6–10). Series: In American History. 2000, Enslow LB $26.60 (978-0-7660-1418-3). The story of the economic depression of the 1780s and the resulting violent protests and government reforms. (Rev: BL 2/15/00; HBG 10/00; SLJ 6/00) [973.4]

9153 Karapalides, Harry J. *Dates of the American Revolution: Who, What, and Where in the War for Independence* (7–12). 1998, Burd Street paper $19.95 (978-1-57249-106-9). A chronological record tracing the American Revolution from 1760, when King George II inherited the British throne, to George Washington's death in 1799, with an emphasis on military action and commanders. (Rev: SLJ 2/99) [973.3]

9154 Kent, Deborah. *The American Revolution: "Give Me Liberty, or Give Me Death!"* (5–7). Illus. Series: American War. 1994, Enslow LB $26.60 (978-0-89490-521-6). A succinct history of the Revolution that uses many firsthand quotations and period illustrations and maps. (Rev: BL 7/94; SLJ 7/94) [973.3]

9155 King, David C. *Saratoga* (5–8). Illus. Series: Battlefields Across America. 1998, Twenty-First Century LB $26.90 (978-0-7613-3011-0). The significance of the battle at Saratoga in 1777, in which General Burgoyne's British army was defeated, and where and how the history of this battle is preserved today. (Rev: HBG 9/98; SLJ 8/98) [973.3]

9156 McCullough, David. *1776* (8–12). Illus. 2005, Simon & Schuster $32.00 (978-0-7432-2671-4). McCullough brings to life the key events of the year 1776 for George Washington and the new young nation. (Rev: SLJ 10/05) [973]

9157 McGowen, Tom. *The Revolutionary War and George Washington's Army in American History* (7–10). Illus. Series: American History. 2004, Enslow LB $26.60 (978-0-7660-2143-3). This is a readable account of all the battles in the Revolution plus a great assessment of George Washington's strengths and weaknesses. (Rev: BL 3/1/04; SLJ 3/04) [973.3]

9158 Miller, Brandon M. *Declaring Independence: Life During the American Revolution* (5–8). Series: People's History. 2005, Lerner LB $29.27 (978-0-8225-1275-2). A thorough look at what life was like during the American Revolution, using primary sources. (Rev: SLJ 9/05; VOYA 6/05) [973.3]

9159 Miller, Brandon M. *Growing Up in the Revolution and the New Nation* (4–7). Illus. Series: Our America. 2002, Lerner LB $26.60 (978-0-8225-0078-0). An in-depth examination of the lives of children during and immediately after the American Revolution, including biographical information about real youngsters. (Rev: BL 10/15/02; HBG 3/03; SLJ 12/02) [973.3]

9160 Minks, Louise, and Benton Minks. *The Revolutionary War* (7–12). Series: America at War. 1992, Facts on File $25.00 (978-0-8160-2508-4). A colorful account of the causes, main battles, and outcomes of the Revolutionary War. (Rev: BL 2/1/93) [973.3]

9161 Morton, Joseph C. *The American Revolution* (7–12). Series: Greenwood Guides to Historic Events, 1500–1900. 2003, Greenwood $51.95 (978-0-313-31792-7). A thorough, text-dense overview of the events leading up to the war, the war itself, and its aftermath, with profiles of key individuals. (Rev: SLJ 7/04) [973.3]

9162 Murphy, Jim. *An American Plague: The True and Terrifying Story of the Yellow Fever Epidemic of 1793* (6–12). Illus. 2003, Clarion $18.00 (978-0-395-77608-7). Narrative, newspaper articles, and archival prints and photographs combine to tell the dramatic story of the epidemic that hit Philadelphia in the late 18th century. (Rev: BL 6/1–15/03; HB 7–8/03; HBG 10/03; SLJ 6/03*; VOYA 12/03) [614.5]

9163 Murphy, Jim. *A Young Patriot: The American Revolution as Experienced by One Boy* (5–8). Illus. 1996, Clarion $16.00 (978-0-395-60523-3). The American Revolution as seen through the eyes of a 15-year-old volunteer. (Rev: BCCB 6/96; BL 6/1–15/96*; HB 9–10/96; SLJ 6/96*) [973.3]

9164 Nardo, Don. *The American Revolution* (7–12). Series: Opposing Viewpoints Digests. 1998, Greenhaven paper $17.45 (978-1-56510-754-0). Quoting from dozens of primary and secondary sources, this book explores issues relating to the Revolution, such as prewar disputes, patriotic vs. loyalist views, wartime concerns, and modern attitudes. (Rev: BL 5/15/98; SLJ 6/98) [973.3]

9165 Schanzer, Rosalyn. *George vs. George: The Revolutionary War as Seen by Both Sides* (5–7). Illus. 2004, National Geographic $16.95 (978-0-7922-7349-3). The two sides' differences — and commonalities — are portrayed in an appealing combination of well-written text, colorful art, and speech balloons; sensationalist aspects detract from the overall value. (Rev: BL 11/15/04; SLJ 10/04*) [973.3]

9166 Sheinkin, Steve. *King George: What Was His Problem? Everything Your Schoolbooks Didn't Tell You About the American Revolution* (4–7). Illus. by Tim Robinson. 2008, Roaring Brook $19.95 (978-1-59643-319-9). First published as *The American Revolution* (2005), this is a breezy and often funny collection of stories that history students will remember. (Rev: BL 8/08) [973.3]

9167 Slavicek, Louise Chipley. *The Women of the American Revolution* (6–10). Illus. Series: Women in History. 2002, Gale LB $27.45 (978-1-59018-172-0). An absorbing, well-illustrated account of the roles women played during the Revolutionary War — on the battlefield and on the home front. (Rev: BL 10/15/02) [973.3]

9168 Smith, Carter, ed. *The Revolutionary War: A Sourcebook on Colonial America* (5–8). Series: American Albums. 1991, Millbrook $25.90 (978-1-56294-039-3). This volume illustrates the major events leading up to the Revolution and the battles and personalities involved. (Rev: BL 1/1/92) [973.38]

9169 Stefoff, Rebecca. *Revolutionary War* (4–7). Illus. Series: North American Historical Atlases. 2000, Benchmark LB $27.07 (978-0-7614-1058-4). Using historical maps and reproductions plus a clear text, this is a basic account of the American Revolution. (Rev: HBG 3/01; SLJ 1/01) [973.3]

9170 Stewart, Gail B. *Weapons of War* (6–12). Series: American War Library. 2000, Lucent LB $18.96 (978-1-56006-616-3). This book discusses weapons used during the American Revolution including muskets, swords, rifles, warships, and even intelligence and espionage. (Rev: BL 2/15/00) [973.3]

9171 Weber, Michael. *The American Revolution* (5–8). Series: Making of America. 2000, Raintree LB $28.54 (978-0-8172-5702-6). A fine overview of the American Revolution from the French and Indian War to the creation of the United States. (Rev: BL 7/00; HBG 10/00; SLJ 8/00) [973.3]

9172 Weber, Michael. *Yorktown* (4–7). Illus. Series: Battlefields Across America. 1997, Twenty-First Century LB $26.90 (978-0-8050-5226-8). Background material on the Revolutionary War is given, along with details of the battle and the present-day condition of its site. (Rev: SLJ 1/98) [973.3]

9173 Weber, Michael. *The Young Republic* (5–8). Illus. Series: Making of America. 2000, Raintree LB $28.54 (978-0-8172-5703-3). This well-illustrated account begins in the 1780s with the creation of the federal system, the ratification of the Constitution, and the inauguration of Washington as president in 1789. (Rev: BL 5/1/00; HBG 10/00; SLJ 9/00) [973]

9174 Whitelaw, Nancy. *The Shot Heard Round the World: The Battles of Lexington and Concord* (5–8). Illus. 2001, Morgan Reynolds LB $23.95 (978-1-883846-75-6). Whitelaw details events from the Boston Massacre in 1770 to the first battles of the Revolution in 1775, with profiles of some of the key players. (Rev: BL 5/15/01; HBG 10/01; SLJ 7/01; VOYA 6/01) [973.3]

9175 Wilbur, Keith C. *The Revolutionary Soldier, 1775–1783* (4–8). Series: Illustrated Living History. 1996, Chelsea LB $14.95 (978-0-7910-4533-6). Topics covered in this book about the Continental Army include clothing, weapons, camp life, food, hospitals, and leisure activities. (Rev: BL 6/1–15/97; SLJ 7/97) [973.3]

9176 Zall, P. M. *Becoming American: Young People in the American Revolution* (8–12). 1993, Linnet LB $25.00 (978-0-208-02355-1). Letters, journal entries, and testimony by young people describing their lives, events, and social conditions in the years immediately before, during, and immediately after the Revolution. (Rev: BL 5/1/93; VOYA 8/93) [973.3]

9177 Zeinert, Karen. *Those Remarkable Women of the American Revolution* (5–8). Illus. 1996, Millbrook LB $29.90 (978-1-56294-657-9). A fascinating account of the conditions and status of women in colonial America and their important contributions to the Revolution, from fighting and spying to fund raising. (Rev: BL 12/1/96; SLJ 3/97; VOYA 4/97) [973.3]

NINETEENTH CENTURY TO THE CIVIL WAR (1809–1861)

9178 Baldwin, Robert F. *New England Whaler* (5–8). Illus. Series: American Pastfinder. 1996, Lerner LB $25.55 (978-0-8225-2978-1). Life on a 19th-century whaling ship is detailed, with many maps and color photographs. (Rev: BL 7/96; SLJ 6/96) [638.2]

9179 Bial, Raymond. *The Strength of These Arms: Life in the Slave Quarters* (5–8). 1997, Houghton $16.00 (978-0-395-77394-9). This photoessay recreates daily life in the slave quarters on large plantations, contrasts it with the luxurious lifestyles of the slave holders, and documents how slaves tried to preserve their heritage, dignity, and hope. (Rev: BL 9/15/97; HBG 3/98; SLJ 11/97) [975]

9180 Blight, David W., ed. *Passages to Freedom: The Underground Railroad in History and Memory* (8–12). Illus. 2004, Smithsonian $39.95 (978-1-58834-157-0). Essays, photographs, and illustrations document the reality, rather than the myth, of the Underground Railroad; compiled on behalf of the National Underground Railroad Center in Cincinnati. (Rev: BL 7/04) [973.7]

9181 Bozonelis, Helen Koutras. *Primary Source Accounts of the War of 1812* (5–8). Illus. Series: America's Wars Through Primary Sources. 2006, Enslow LB $33.27 (978-1-59845-006-4). Soldiers' journal entries, letters from the homefront, personal recollections, songs and poetry, and newspaper articles are among the primary sources included in this general history of the war. (Rev: SLJ 4/07) [973.5]

9182 Bredeson, Carmen. *The Battle of the Alamo: The Fight for Texas Territory* (5–8). Series: Spotlight on American History. 1996, Millbrook LB $24.90 (978-0-7613-0019-9). A well-organized account of the causes, events, and campaigns of the war in which much of California, Texas, and the Southwest became part of the United States. (Rev: SLJ 4/97) [973.6]

9183 Carey, Charles W. *The Mexican War: "Mr. Polk's War"* (6–9). Series: American War. 2002, Enslow LB $26.60 (978-0-7660-1853-2). A thorough and very readable account of the Mexican-American War and the key figures of the time. Also in this series is *The War of 1812: "We Have Met the Enemy and They Are Ours"* (2002). (Rev: HBG 3/03; SLJ 1/03) [973.6]

9184 Carson, Mary Kay. *The Underground Railroad for Kids: From Slavery to Freedom* (6–9). Illus. Series: For Kids. 2005, Chicago Review paper $14.95 (978-1-55652-554-4). With an engaging blend of first-person accounts and brief profiles, this is an easy-to-understand history of the Underground Railroad and the men and women who used it to escape from slavery. (Rev: BL 2/1/05; SLJ 3/05) [973.7]

9185 Cloud Tapper, Suzanne. *The Abolition of Slavery: Fighting for a Free America* (7–12). Series: The American Saga. 2006, Enslow LB $31.93 (978-0-7660-2605-6). The history of the abolitionist movement is chronicled in this well-organized book that includes primary source material, photographs, and maps. (Rev: SLJ 7/07) [973.7]

9186 Collier, Christopher, and James Lincoln Collier. *Andrew Jackson's America, 1824–1850* (5–8). Illus. Series: Drama of American History. 1998, Marshall Cavendish LB $29.93 (978-0-7614-0779-9). The Colliers trace American history over an eventful 26 years that encompass great change, from the Industrial Revolution to the Trail of Tears. (Rev: BL 2/15/99; HBG 10/99) [973.56]

9187 Collier, Christopher, and James Lincoln Collier. *Hispanic America, Texas and the Mexican War, 1835–1850* (5–8). Illus. Series: Drama of American History. 1998, Marshall Cavendish LB $31.36 (978-0-7614-0780-5). This account covers the history of Europeans in the Southwest, the Hispanic culture in the region, the doctrine of Manifest Destiny, the Mexican War, and the settling of California. (Rev: BL 2/15/99; HBG 10/99; SLJ 4/99) [979]

9188 Collier, Christopher, and James Lincoln Collier. *The Jeffersonian Republicans, 1800–1823* (5–8). Illus. Series: Drama of American History. 1998, Marshall Cavendish LB $29.93 (978-0-7614-0778-2). This lively account describes 23 eventful years in our history that include the Louisiana Purchase, the Lewis and Clark Expedition, and the War of 1812. (Rev: BL 2/15/99; HBG 10/99; SLJ 4/99) [973.46]

9189 Currie, Stephanie. *Life of a Slave on a Southern Plantation* (6–10). Series: The Way People Live. 1999, Lucent LB $28.70 (978-1-56006-539-5). Using many quotations from original sources, this book about everyday life on a southern slave plantation covers family life, food and housing, work, play, and methods of escape. (Rev: BL 10/15/99; HBG 9/00; SLJ 1/00) [975]

9190 Currie, Stephen. *Escapes from Slavery* (5–9). Series: Great Escapes. 2003, Gale LB $29.95 (978-1-59018-276-5). The stories of six of the approximately 60,000 slaves who escaped from captivity in pre-Civil War America. (Rev: SLJ 4/04) [973.7]

9191 Currie, Stephen. *Thar She Blows: American Whaling in the Nineteenth Century* (6–9). Illus. Series: People's History. 2001, Lerner LB $25.26 (978-0-8225-0646-1). A concise text with many quotations from primary sources such as diaries, letters, and newspaper articles brings to life the grim conditions aboard whaling ships. (Rev: BL 1/1–15/02; HBG 10/02; SLJ 4/02; VOYA 4/02) [639.2]

9192 DeFord, Deborah H. *Life Under Slavery* (6–12). Series: Slavery in the Americas. 2006, Chelsea House $35 (978-0-8160-6135-8). Middle schoolers studying slavery in the United States will be interested to learn how African blacks adapted their culture and traditions in an effort to survive life as captives. (Rev: SLJ 9/06)

9193 Draper, Charla L. *Cooking on Nineteenth-Century Whaling Ships* (4–7). Series: Exploring History Through Simple Recipes. 2000, Capstone LB $23.93 (978-0-7368-0602-2). As well as learning about life on a whaling ship, this book provides a series of simple recipes. (Rev: BL 3/1/01; HBG 10/01; SLJ 4/01) [974.8]

9194 Fleischner, Jennifer. *The Dred Scott Case: Testing the Right to Live Free* (5–8). Series: Spotlight on American History. 1997, Millbrook $24.90 (978-0-7613-0005-2). An account of the life of the slave Dred Scott and the historic court case of 1857 against his owner, John Sanford. (Rev: BL 5/1/97; SLJ 4/97) [342.73]

9195 Fradin, Dennis Brindell. *Bound for the North Star: True Stories of Fugitive Slaves* (8–12). Illus. 2000, Clarion $21.00 (978-0-395-97017-1). Personal experiences form the basis of these moving profiles that spare no details of the horrors suffered by escaping slaves and the courage of their helpers. (Rev: BL 1/1–15/01*; HB 1–2/01; HBG 3/01; SLJ 11/00*; VOYA 10/01) [973.7]

9196 Freedman, Florence B. *Two Tickets to Freedom: The True Story of Ellen and William Craft, Fugitive Slaves* (4–8). Illus. by Ezra Jack Keats. 1971, Bedrick $12.95 (978-0-87226-330-7); paper $5.95 (978-0-87226-221-8). An exciting story of slavery, escape, and pursuit that is based on fact. A reissue. [973.5]

9197 Gay, Kathlyn, and Martin Gay. *War of 1812* (5–8). Series: Voices of the Past. 1995, Twenty-First Century LB $25.90 (978-0-8050-2846-1). Excerpts from letters, memoirs, and official reports highlight this well-illustrated history of the War of 1812 and its consequences. (Rev: BL 12/15/95; SLJ 3/96) [973.5]

9198 Hansen, Joyce, and Gary McGowan. *Freedom Roads: Searching for the Underground Railroad* (5–8). Illus. by James Ransome. 2003, Cricket $18.95 (978-0-8126-2673-5). This look at the history of the Underground Railroad emphasizes how much of our knowledge consists of speculation and anecdotal material rather than hard evidence. (Rev: BL 5/1/03; HB 7–8/03; HBG 10/03; SLJ 9/03*) [973.7]

9199 Heidler, David S., and Jeanne T. Heidler. *The War of 1812* (8–12). Series: Greenwood Guides to Historic Events, 1500–1900. 2002, Greenwood $51.95 (978-0-313-31687-6). This thorough and detailed description of the causes, events, and key figures of the War of 1812 will be useful for report writers. (Rev: BL 10/15/02; SLJ 10/02) [973.5]

9200 Herda, D. J. *The Dred Scott Case: Slavery and Citizenship* (6–10). Illus. Series: Landmark Supreme Court Cases. 1994, Enslow LB $26.60 (978-0-89490-460-8). An examination of the pre-Civil War case in which a slave was denied his freedom, and its consequences. (Rev: BL 6/1–15/94) [342.73]

9201 Kallen, Stuart A. *Life on the Underground Railroad* (6–10). Series: The Way People Live. 2000, Lucent LB $27.45 (978-1-56006-667-5). After a brief history of slavery in America, this account covers the organization of and people involved in the Underground Railroad, the journeys made on it, and its impact on the future. (Rev: BL 2/15/00; HBG 10/00; SLJ 5/00) [973.6]

9202 King, David C. *New Orleans* (5–8). Illus. Series: Battlefields Across America. 1998, Twenty-First Century LB $26.90 (978-0-7613-3010-3). The story of the famous 1815 battle in New Orleans in which the British were decisively defeated, including the background of the War of 1812, the role of Andrew Jackson, and the significance of this defeat to the British. (Rev: HBG 9/98; SLJ 8/98) [973.6]

9203 Landau, Elaine. *Fleeing to Freedom on the Underground Railroad: The Courageous Slaves, Agents, and Conductors* (6–9). Illus. Series: People's History. 2006, Lerner LB $29.27 (978-0-8225-3490-7). Anecdotes about individual contributions and quotations from primary sources add to this account of the Underground Railroad and those who created and used it; excerpts from key legislation round out this useful volume. (Rev: BL 2/1/06; SLJ 5/06) [973.7]

9204 Levy, Janey. *The Alamo: A Primary Source History of the Legendary Texas Mission* (5–8). Illus. Series: Primary Sources in American History. 2003, Rosen LB $29.25 (978-0-8239-3681-6). Primary sources — including maps and paintings — tell the story of the Battle of the Alamo. (Rev: BL 5/15/03; SLJ 5/03) [976.4]

9205 McKissack, Patricia C., and Fredrick McKissack. *Rebels Against Slavery: American Slave Revolts* (5–8). Illus. 1996, Scholastic paper $15.95 (978-0-590-45735-4). A fascinating account of the men and women who led revolts against slavery, including Toussaint L'Ouverture, Cinque, Harriet Tubman, and Nat Turner. (Rev: BCCB 6/96; BL 2/15/96; SLJ 3/96; VOYA 4/96) [970]

9206 McNeese, Tim. *The Abolitionist Movement: Ending Slavery* (8–12). Illus. Series: Reform Movements in American History. 2007, Chelsea House LB $30.00 (978-0-7910-9502-7). An informative survey of the movement and its leaders. (Rev: BL 11/15/07; LMC 4–5/08) [973.7114]

9207 McNeese, Tim. *The Alamo* (6–9). Illus. Series: Sieges That Changed the World. 2003, Chelsea LB $30.00 (978-0-7910-7101-4). The attack on the Alamo that resulted in the death of many Texans at the hands of Santa Ana's troops is placed in historical context. (Rev: HBG 10/03; SLJ 10/03) [976.4]

9208 Mancall, Peter C., ed. *American Eras: Westward Expansion (1800–1860)* (8–12). 1999, Gale $140.00 (978-0-7876-1483-6). The period of growth and change in America from the early 19th century up to the Civil War is examined. (Rev: BL 3/15/99; SLJ 8/99) [973.6]

9209 Marquette, Scott. *War of 1812* (4–7). Illus. Series: America at War. 2002, Rourke LB $20.95 (978-1-58952-389-0). This book for middle-graders studies the war itself and the events that led up to it. (Rev: BL 10/15/02) [973.5]

9210 Morrison, Taylor. *Coast Mappers* (4–8). Illus. 2004, Houghton $16.00 (978-0-618-25408-8). Science and biography are interwoven in this examination of the mid-19th-century mapping of the U.S. Pacific coastline. (Rev: BL 3/15/04; SLJ 5/04) [623.89]

9211 Nardo, Don. *The Mexican-American War* (6–9). Series: World History. 1999, Lucent LB $31.20 (978-1-56006-495-4). The author reviews the events leading up to this war involving Texas, Colorado, and California, the major battles, the large antiwar movement in the United States, and the bitterness that still exists among some Mexicans. (Rev: BL 9/15/99; HBG 4/00; SLJ 9/99) [973.6]

9212 Nofi, Albert A. *The Underground Railroad and the Civil War* (4–8). Series: Untold History of the Civil War. 2000, Chelsea $25.00 (978-0-7910-5434-5). A history of the dangers, devotion, excitement, and daring involved in this collaborative system that was developed to help fugitive Southern slaves reach freedom in the North or in Canada. (Rev: BL 5/15/00; HBG 10/00; SLJ 6/00) [973.7]

9213 Paulson, Timothy J. *Days of Sorrow, Years of Glory, 1831–1850: From the Nat Turner Revolt to the Fugitive Slave Law* (5–9). Series: Milestones in Black American History. 1994, Chelsea paper $14.93 (978-0-7910-2552-9). An examination of the Underground Railroad, slave resistance, the Seminole Wars, and the abolition movement. (Rev: BL 11/1/94; SLJ 4/95; VOYA 12/94) [973]

9214 Richards, Caroline Cowles. *A 19th Century Schoolgirl: The Diary of Caroline Cowles Richards, 1852–1855* (4–8). Ed. by Kerry Graves. Illus. Series: Diaries, Letters, and Memoirs. 2000, Capstone LB $23.93 (978-0-7368-0342-7). This diary of a young girl living in western New York State in the early 1850s describes her daily life, schooling, and her reaction to the women's rights movement. (Rev: BL 10/15/00; HBG 10/00; SLJ 9/00) [974.7]

9215 Sawyer, Kem K. *The Underground Railroad in American History* (7–10). Illus. Series: In American History. 1997, Enslow LB $26.60 (978-0-89490-885-9). A description of the formation of the Underground Railroad, its functions, key people connected with it, and its importance in American history. (Rev: BL 7/97) [973.7]

9216 Schlesinger, Arthur M., Jr., ed. *The Election of 1860 and the Administration of Abraham Lincoln* (8–12). Series: Major Presidential Elections and the Administrations That Followed. 2003, Mason Crest LB $24.95 (978-1-59084-355-0). A good source of speeches, quotations, and excerpts from public documents, with commentary, illustrations, and further reading. (Rev: SLJ 1/04) [973.7]

9217 Sisson, Mary Barr. *The Gathering Storm: From the Framing of the Constitution to Walker's Appeal, 1787–1829* (7–10). Illus. Series: Milestones in Black American History. 1996, Chelsea LB $21.95 (978-0-7910-2252-8); paper $9.95 (978-0-7910-2678-6). The story of slavery in the early days of the Republic with emphasis on civil disobedience, militant action, and important figures of the period. (Rev: BL 10/15/96; SLJ 2/97) [973]

9218 Sorrels, Roy. *The Alamo in American History* (6–8). Illus. Series: In American History. 1996, Enslow LB $26.60 (978-0-89490-770-8). This book gives an account of the events leading up to the battle plus detailed coverage of the siege of the Alamo and its significance in American history. (Rev: BL 3/1/97) [976.4]

9219 Stefoff, Rebecca. *The War of 1812* (4–7). Illus. Series: North American Historical Atlases. 2000, Benchmark LB $27.07 (978-0-7614-1060-7). A clearly written text plus historical maps and reproductions are used to give an easy-to-read account of the War of 1812. (Rev: HBG 3/01; SLJ 1/01) [973.8]

9220 Stein, R. Conrad. *John Brown's Raid on Harpers Ferry* (7–10). Series: In American History. 1999, Enslow LB $26.60 (978-0-7660-1123-6). This account gives an in-depth look at this important moment in American history and its effects on the events to come. (Rev: BL 9/15/99; HBG 4/00) [973.6]

9221 Stewart, Mark. *The Alamo, February 23–March 6, 1836* (5–7). Illus. Series: American Battlefields. 2004, Enchanted Lion $14.95 (978-1-59270-026-4). This overview of the Battle of the Alamo offers a clear account of the conflict and an examination of the developments leading up to it; sidebars, illustrations, a timeline, and other features add to the narrative. (Rev: BL 11/1/04) [976.4]

9222 Swain, Gwenyth. *Dred and Harriet Scott: A Family's Struggle for Freedom* (6–9). 2004, Borealis paper $12.95 (978-0-87351-483-5). The story of the Scotts' desire that their young daughters should not have to live as slaves and the lengthy court battle that they ultimately lost, a battle that brought the Civil War a step closer. (Rev: SLJ 7/04) [973.7]

9223 Turner, Glennette Tilley. *The Underground Railroad in Illinois* (5–8). Illus. 2001, Newman

Educational Publg. paper $16.95 (978-0-938990-05-5). Using a question-and-answer format, this book focuses on the Underground Railroad in Illinois, the historical period, the problems, people who worked on the effort, and the many heroic deeds. (Rev: BL 2/15/01) [973.7]

9224 Walker, Paul Robert. *Remember the Alamo: Texians, Tejanos, and Mexicans Tell Their Stories* (5–8). Illus. 2007, National Geographic $17.95 (978-1-4263-0010-3). A detailed account of the siege of the Alamo, with explanation of the events leading up to the crisis and with many firsthand descriptions. (Rev: BL 5/15/07; SLJ 8/07) [976.4]

9225 Zeinert, Karen. *The Amistad Slave Revolt and American Abolition* (7–10). Illus. 1997, Shoe String LB $21.50 (978-0-208-02438-1); paper $12.95 (978-0-208-02439-8). The dramatic story of Cinque and 52 other slaves onboard the Spanish ship *Amistad* in 1839 and of their historic mutiny and subsequent trial. (Rev: BL 7/97; SLJ 6/97) [326]

9226 Zeinert, Karen. *Tragic Prelude: Bleeding Kansas* (6–10). Illus. 2001, Linnet $25.00 (978-0-208-02446-6). An accessible account of the conflict that erupted in Kansas over the question of slavery, with information on individuals including John Brown and Hannah Ropes, a timeline, extracts from primary documents, photographs, and references. (Rev: BL 6/1–15/01; HBG 10/01; SLJ 6/01; VOYA 2/02) [978.1]

CIVIL WAR (1861–1865)

9227 Allen, Thomas B. *Harriet Tubman, Secret Agent: How Daring Slaves and Free Blacks Spied for the Union During the Civil War* (5–8). Illus. by Carla Bauer. 2006, National Geographic $16.95 (978-0-7922-7889-4). The efforts of Tubman and other slaves to gather important information and pass it to the Union forces is the focus of this volume that includes examples of a code sometimes used. (Rev: BCCB 1/07; BL 12/1/06; HBG 4/07; LMC 4–5/07; SLJ 2/07*) [973.7]

9228 Armentrout, David, and Patricia Armentrout. *The Emancipation Proclamation* (4–7). Series: Documents That Shaped the Nation. 2004, Rourke $20.95 (978-1-59515-233-6). The reasons for the creation of this document and the results of its proclamation are thoroughly explored in concise text, accompanied by an array of maps and illustrations. (Rev: BL 10/15/04) [973.7]

9229 Armstrong, Jennifer. *Photo by Brady: A Picture of the Civil War* (6–9). Illus. 2005, Simon & Schuster $18.95 (978-0-689-85785-0). This photoessay artfully uses the photographs of Mathew Brady to document Civil War history from the inauguration of Abraham Lincoln to his assassination, only days after the end of hostilities. (Rev: BL 3/15/05; SLJ 3/05; VOYA 4/05) [973.7]

9230 Arnold, James R., and Roberta Wiener. *Divided in Two: The Road to Civil War* (4–7). Series: The Civil War. 2002, Lerner LB $25.26 (978-0-8225-2312-3). A well-designed oversize book that describes the events of 1861 that led to the outbreak of the Civil War. (Rev: BL 10/15/02; HBG 10/02; SLJ 7/02) [973.7]

9231 Arnold, James R., and Roberta Wiener. *Life Goes On: The Civil War at Home* (4–7). Series: The Civil War. 2002, Lerner LB $25.26 (978-0-8225-2315-4). Many easy-to-follow maps and illustrations are used with a simple text to describe life on the home front in both South and North during the Civil War. (Rev: BL 10/15/02; HBG 10/02; SLJ 7/02) [973.7]

9232 Arnold, James R., and Roberta Wiener. *Lost Cause: The End of the Civil War* (4–7). Series: The Civil War. 2002, Lerner LB $25.26 (978-0-8225-2317-8). Beginning with the campaign of 1864, this well-illustrated account traces the Civil War to Appomattox and beyond. (Rev: BL 10/15/02; HBG 10/02; SLJ 6/02) [973.7]

9233 Arnold, James R., and Roberta Wiener. *On to Richmond: The Civil War in the East, 1861–1862* (4–7). Illus. Series: Civil War. 2002, Lerner LB $25.26 (978-0-8225-2313-0). Early battles in the Civil War are the subject of this volume for older readers that includes timelines, notes, and lists of Web sites and battlefields to visit. (Rev: BL 10/15/02; HBG 10/02; SLJ 6/02; VOYA 6/03) [973.7]

9234 Arnold, James R., and Roberta Wiener. *River to Victory: The Civil War in the West* (4–7). Series: The Civil War. 2002, Lerner LB $25.26 (978-0-8225-2314-7). The Civil War in the West from 1861 through 1863 is re-created in text and illustrations with many maps and sidebars on personalities and events. (Rev: BL 10/15/02; HBG 10/02; SLJ 6/02; VOYA 6/03) [973.7]

9235 Arnold, James R., and Roberta Wiener. *This Unhappy Country: The Turn of the Civil War* (4–7). Illus. Series: Civil War. 2002, Lerner LB $25.26 (978-0-8225-2316-1). Maps and other period illustrations flesh out the events of 1863, a pivotal year in the Civil War, in this volume for older readers. (Rev: BL 10/15/02; HBG 10/02; SLJ 7/02) [973.7]

9236 Ashby, Ruth. *Gettysburg* (5–8). Series: Civil War Chronicles. 2002, Smart Apple LB $28.50 (978-1-58340-186-6). The three days of battle are covered in some detail, and the text and photographs convey the horrible conditions. (Rev: HBG 3/03; SLJ 2/03; VOYA 4/03) [973]

9237 Bailey, Ronald H. *The Bloodiest Day: The Battle of Antietam* (7–12). Illus. 1984, Silver Burdett LB $25.93 (978-0-8094-4741-1). The story of Lee's defeat in the battle that caused terrible losses on both sides. [973.7]

9238 Barney, William L. *The Civil War and Reconstruction: A Student Companion* (7–12). Series: Oxford Student Companions to American History. 2001, Oxford LB $65.00 (978-0-19-511559-8). An alphabetically arranged series of articles covering all aspects of the Civil War and Reconstruction, illustrated with photographs, maps, and reproductions. (Rev: BL 9/15/01; SLJ 6/01) [973.7]

9239 Beller, Susan P. *Billy Yank and Johnny Reb: Soldiering in the Civil War* (5–8). Illus. 2000, Twenty-First Century LB $26.90 (978-0-7613-1869-9). Solid, interesting information is provided in this illustrated account that describes the everyday life of soldiers on both sides of the Civil War. (Rev: BL 10/15/00; HBG 3/01; SLJ 12/00; VOYA 2/01) [973.7]

9240 Beller, Susan P. *The Confederate Ladies of Richmond* (5–8). Illus. 1999, Twenty-First Century LB $26.90 (978-0-7613-1470-7). The Civil War seen through the eyes and activities of the upper-class women of Richmond, the capital of the Confederacy. (Rev: BCCB 1/00; BL 12/15/99; HBG 3/00; SLJ 1/00) [973.7]

9241 Beller, Susan Provost. *The Civil War* (5–8). Series: American Voices From. 2002, Benchmark LB $34.21 (978-0-7614-1204-5). A collection of primary sources that includes speeches by Lincoln and Lee and represents people from all walks of life commenting on different aspects of the Civil War. (Rev: HBG 10/03; SLJ 4/03) [973.7]

9242 Bolotin, Norman. *Civil War A to Z: A Young Reader's Guide to Over 100 People, Places, and Points of Importance* (4–8). Illus. 2002, Dutton $19.99 (978-0-525-46268-2). An encyclopedia-style text on the Civil War, with brief entries on important battles; politicians, generals, and other key figures; and crucial issues of the time, with photographs, a glossary, a timeline, and information on further resources. (Rev: BL 7/02; SLJ 7/02) [973.7]

9243 Brooks, Victor. *African Americans in the Civil War* (4–8). Illus. Series: Untold History of the Civil War. 2000, Chelsea $25.00 (978-0-7910-5435-2). This book describes African American soldiers' roles in the Civil War, on both the Confederate and Union sides. (Rev: BL 5/15/00; HBG 10/00; SLJ 6/00) [355.7]

9244 Brooks, Victor. *Civil War Forts* (4–8). Illus. Series: Untold History of the Civil War. 2000, Chelsea $25.00 (978-0-7910-5438-3). Describes the important roles played by such forts as Fort Sumter and Fort Wagner in South Carolina, Fort Fischer in North Carolina, Fort Henry and Fort Donelson in Tennessee, and the city of Vicksburg, Mississippi. (Rev: BL 5/15/00; HBG 10/00; SLJ 7/00) [973.7]

9245 Brooks, Victor. *Secret Weapons in the Civil War* (4–8). Series: Untold History of the Civil War. 2000, Chelsea $29.50 (978-0-7910-5433-8). Covers such secret weapons and maneuvers as underwater transportation, advanced artillery, communications devices, and explosive materials. (Rev: BL 5/15/00; HBG 10/00; SLJ 7/00) [973.7]

9246 *Chancellorsville* (7–12). Illus. Series: Voices of the Civil War. 1996, Time-Life Books $24.95 (978-0-7853-4708-8). A handsome description of this key Civil War battle, featuring regimental histories, letters, diaries, and memoirs. (Rev: BL 1/1–15/97) [973.7]

9247 Clinton, Catherine. *Scholastic Encyclopedia of the Civil War* (4–7). Illus. 1999, Scholastic paper $18.95 (978-0-590-37227-5). Using many black-and-white illustrations, this narrative gives a good chronological introduction to the Civil War, with interesting supplementary information. (Rev: BL 1/1–15/00; HBG 3/00; SLJ 5/00) [973.7]

9248 Colbert, Nancy. *The Firing on Fort Sumter: A Splintered Nation Goes to War* (6–12). Illus. 2000, Morgan Reynolds LB $23.95 (978-1-883846-51-0). An intriguing, detailed account, told in lively prose and many photographs, of the incident that began the Civil War. (Rev: BL 10/1/00; HBG 3/01; VOYA 6/01) [973.7]

9249 Collier, Christopher, and James Lincoln Collier. *The Civil War, 1860–1865* (5–8). Series: Drama of American History. 1999, Marshall Cavendish LB $31.36 (978-0-7614-0818-5). A dramatic, accurate account that covers causes, leaders, battles, effects, and the immediate aftermath of the Civil War. (Rev: BL 2/15/00; HBG 10/00; SLJ 3/00) [973.7]

9250 Damon, Duane. *Growing Up In the Civil War: 1861 to 1865* (5–8). Series: Our America. 2002, Lerner LB $26.60 (978-0-8225-0656-0). The lives of children in this period are described with many quotations and excerpts from diaries, letters, and memoirs. (Rev: BL 2/15/03; HBG 3/03; SLJ 2/03) [973.7]

9251 Damon, Duane. *When This Cruel War Is Over* (5–8). Illus. 1996, Lerner LB $30.35 (978-0-8225-1731-3). The human side of the Civil War is stressed as the reader goes behind the scenes at the battlefields and learns about conditions on the home front. (Rev: BL 8/96; SLJ 8/96*) [973.7]

9252 Day, Nancy. *Your Travel Guide to Civil War America* (4–8). Series: Passport to History. 2000, Lerner LB $26.50 (978-0-8225-3078-7). Using the format of a guide book, this account takes the reader back to the Civil War with coverage of topics including food, civil and military clothing, Lincoln's office, Gettysburg, and various battlefields. (Rev: BL 3/1/01; HBG 10/01; SLJ 4/01; VOYA 8/01) [073.7]

9253 DeFord, Deborah H. *African Americans during the Civil War* (6–12). Series: Slavery in the Americas. 2006, Chelsea House $35 (978-0-8160-6138-9). The importance of blacks in America during the

Civil War — as slaves, civilians, and soldiers — is covered, as is the "National Convention of Colored Men" and the effects that the war had on African Americans' rights. (Rev: SLJ 9/06)

9254 Dolan, Edward F. *The American Civil War: A House Divided* (5–8). Illus. 1997, Millbrook LB $29.90 (978-0-7613-0255-1). A chronologically arranged, well-organized account of the Civil War, beginning with the shots fired at Fort Sumter. (Rev: BL 3/1/98; HBG 3/98; SLJ 3/98) [973.7]

9255 Dosier, Susan. *Civil War Cooking: The Confederacy* (4–7). Series: Exploring History Through Simple Recipes. 2000, Capstone LB $23.93 (978-0-7368-0350-2). As well as simple, authentic recipes of Civil War times, this book tells of customs, family roles, and everyday life during this period. Also use *Civil War Cooking: The Union* (2000). (Rev: BL 8/00; HBG 10/00; SLJ 9/00) [973.7]

9256 Egger-Bovet, Howard, and Marlene Smith-Baranzini. *Book of the American Civil War* (5–7). Illus. by D. J. Simison. Series: Brown Paper School. 1998, Little, Brown paper $12.95 (978-0-316-22243-3). Facts, photographs, illustrations, stories and appealing activities are combined in this overview of the Civil War. (Rev: SLJ 12/98) [973.7]

9257 Feinberg, Barbara S. *Abraham Lincoln's Gettysburg Address: Four Score and More . . .* (4–8). Illus. 2000, Twenty-First Century LB $24.40 (978-0-7613-1410-3). Illustrated with period photographs, this well-researched volume reveals surprising facts about the Gettysburg Address and its delivery. (Rev: BL 11/15/00) [973.7]

9258 Fleming, Thomas. *Band of Brothers: West Point in the Civil War* (6–9). Illus. 1988, Walker LB $14.85 (978-0-8027-6741-7). The influence in the Civil War of such men as Grant and Lee, all of whom were graduates of West Point. (Rev: BL 2/1/88) [973.7]

9259 Ford, Carin T. *The American Civil War: An Overview* (5–8). Series: The Civil War Library. 2004, Enslow LB $23.93 (978-0-7660-2255-3). This informative general overview of the war features maps, illustrations, and interesting sidebar features. Also use *Lincoln, Slavery, and the Emancipation Proclamation* (2004). (Rev: SLJ 3/05) [973.7]

9260 Friend, Sandra. *Florida in the Civil War: A State in Turmoil* (5–8). Illus. 2001, Millbrook LB $25.90 (978-0-7613-1973-3). An account of Florida's involvement in the Civil War, with maps and photographs. (Rev: BL 10/15/01; HBG 3/02; SLJ 2/02; VOYA 12/01) [973.7]

9261 Gaines, Ann Graham. *The Battle of Gettysburg in American History* (6–10). Series: In American History. 2001, Enslow LB $26.60 (978-0-7660-1455-8). The causes and events relating to this, the most momentous battle of the Civil War, are retold with a fine interweaving of personal stories. (Rev: BL 8/01; HBG 10/01) [973.7]

9262 Golay, Michael. *The Civil War* (7–12). Series: America at War. 1992, Facts on File $25.00 (978-0-8160-2514-5). A comprehensive chronicle of the war, from the issues that gave rise to it to Lee's surrender at Appomattox. (Rev: BL 10/15/92) [973.7]

9263 Haskins, Jim. *The Day Fort Sumter Was Fired On: A Photo History of the Civil War* (5–8). Illus. 1995, Scholastic paper $6.95 (978-0-590-46397-3). A short, well-illustrated history of the Civil War, with coverage of the roles of women and African Americans. (Rev: BL 7/95) [973.7]

9264 Heinrichs, Ann. *The Emancipation Proclamation* (5–8). Series: We the People. 2002, Compass Point LB $26.60 (978-0-7565-0209-6). An accessible examination of the proclamation's creation that reveals Lincoln's careful attention to detail. (Rev: SLJ 7/02) [973.7]

9265 Herbert, Janis. *The Civil War for Kids: A History with 21 Activities* (4–8). Illus. 1999, Chicago Review paper $14.95 (978-1-55652-355-7). As well as supplying information about leaders, battles, daily life, and the contributions of women and African Americans, this book on the Civil War includes activities such as reenactments of battles, most of which are geared toward groups. (Rev: SLJ 12/99) [973.7]

9266 Holford, David M. *Lincoln and the Emancipation Proclamation in American History* (5–8). Series: In American History. 2002, Enslow LB $26.60 (978-0-7660-1456-5). A well-researched account that gives background material and traces the significance of this document. (Rev: BL 1/1–15/03; HBG 3/03) [973.7]

9267 Hughes, Christopher. *Antietam* (5–8). Series: Battlefields Across America. 1998, Millbrook LB $26.90 (978-0-7613-3009-7). This book describes the battle at Antietam in detail, discusses its impact on the outcome of the war and on the future of the United States, profiles the major people involved, and provides information on where the history of this battle is preserved. (Rev: HBG 9/98; SLJ 8/98) [973.7]

9268 Hull, Mary E. *The Union and the Civil War in American History* (6–10). Series: In American History. 2000, Enslow LB $26.60 (978-0-7660-1416-9). This account explains how the North tried to keep the nation together through the Civil War and highlights how different groups — from nurses and soldiers to people on the home front — helped the war effort. (Rev: BL 7/00; HBG 3/01) [973.7]

9269 January, Brendan. *Gettysburg, July 1–3, 1863* (5–7). Illus. Series: American Battlefields. 2004, Enchanted Lion $14.95 (978-1-59270-025-7). This overview of the Battle of Gettysburg offers a clear account of the bloody conflict and an examination

of the developments leading up to it; sidebars, illustrations, a timeline, and other features add to the narrative. (Rev: BL 11/1/04) [973]

9270 Kantor, MacKinlay. *Gettysburg* (6–9). Illus. 1952, Random paper $5.99 (978-0-394-89181-1). The story of the crucial battle of the Civil War that could have meant a total victory for the Confederacy. [973.7]

9271 Kent, Zachary. *The Civil War: "A House Divided"* (5–7). Illus. Series: American War. 1994, Enslow LB $26.60 (978-0-89490-522-3). Using many original quotations, period illustrations, and maps, this account gives a concise history of the Civil War. (Rev: BL 7/94; SLJ 9/94) [973.7]

9272 Lalicki, Tom. *Grierson's Raid: A Daring Cavalry Strike Through the Heart of the Confederacy* (7–12). 2004, Farrar $18.00 (978-0-374-32787-3). Lalicki recounts Union Colonel Benjamin Grierson's daring 16-day raid through the state of Mississippi in 1863. (Rev: BL 8/04; HB 7–8/04; SLJ 6/04; VOYA 8/04) [973.7]

9273 McComb, Marianne. *The Emancipation Proclamation* (4–7). Illus. Series: American Documents. 2006, National Geographic LB $23.90 (978-0-7922-7936-5). The background, nature, and impact of this important document are explained clearly, with photos and illustrations plus full texts of the Emancipation Proclamation, the Fugitive Slave Law of 1850, and Constitutional Amendments XIII through XV. (Rev: BL 2/1/06; SLJ 2/06; VOYA 8/06) [973.7]

9274 McPherson, James M. *Fields of Fury: The American Civil War* (6–8). Illus. 2002, Simon & Schuster $22.95 (978-0-689-84833-9). Packed with interesting illustrations and sidebars, this large-format book gives an overview of the Civil War that will attract both report writers and casual browsers. (Rev: BL 11/15/02; HBG 3/03; SLJ 10/02*) [973.7]

9275 Marinelli, Deborah A. *The Assassination of Abraham Lincoln* (6–9). Series: The Library of Political Assassinations. 2002, Rosen LB $27.95 (978-0-8239-3539-0). In addition to describing the assassination itself, Marinelli covers the Civil War and Lincoln's legacy. (Rev: BL 8/02; SLJ 8/02) [976]

9276 Murphy, Jim. *The Long Road to Gettysburg* (6–9). 1992, Clarion $18.00 (978-0-395-55965-9). An account of the Civil War from both the Union and Confederate perspectives. (Rev: BL 5/15/92*; SLJ 6/92*) [973.7]

9277 Murray, Aaron R. *Civil War Battles and Leaders* (6–12). Illus. Series: Battles and Leaders. 2004, DK $16.99 (978-0-7894-9890-8); paper $9.99 (978-0-7894-9891-5). A richly illustrated, easily accessed source of reliable information on the battles and key figures of the Civil War. (Rev: BL 4/1/04*) [973.7]

9278 Nofi, Albert A. *Spies in the Civil War* (5–8). Series: Untold History of the Civil War. 2000, Chelsea $25.00 (978-0-7910-5427-7). In this account readers meet famous spies (including Allan Pinkerton and Belle Boyd) and lesser-known spies of the Civil War. (Rev: HBG 10/00; SLJ 7/00) [973.7]

9279 Savage, Douglas J. *Ironclads and Blockades in the Civil War* (4–8). Series: Untold History of the Civil War. 2000, Chelsea $25.00 (978-0-7910-5429-1). A clear text and period illustrations introduce the huge ships used in the Union and Confederate navies and their efforts to block different ports during the Civil War. (Rev: BL 7/00; HBG 10/00; SLJ 9/00) [973.7]

9280 Savage, Douglas J. *Prison Camps in the Civil War* (4–8). Series: Untold History of the Civil War. 2000, Chelsea $25.00 (978-0-7910-5428-4). This account describes the prisoner-of-war camps on both sides during the Civil War, the appalling conditions in them, and the acts of heroism that sometimes occurred. (Rev: BL 7/00; HBG 10/00; SLJ 9/00) [973.7]

9281 Savage, Douglas J. *Women in the Civil War* (4–8). Series: Untold History of the Civil War. 2000, Chelsea $25.00 (978-0-7910-5436-9). This book describes the roles played by women in the Civil War as nurses, suppliers of support services, and crusaders for issues including suffrage and abolition. (Rev: BL 7/00; HBG 10/00; SLJ 9/00) [973.7]

9282 Schomp, Virginia. *The Civil War* (6–8). Illus. Series: Letters from the Battlefront. 2003, Marshall Cavendish LB $29.93 (978-0-7614-1660-9). This collection of first-person accounts offers valuable insights into the Civil War. (Rev: BL 4/1/04; SLJ 4/04) [973.7]

9283 Schomp, Virginia. *The Civil War* (5–8). Illus. Series: Letters from the Homefront. 2001, Marshall Cavendish LB $29.93 (978-0-7614-1095-9). After placing the conflict in historical context, Schomp uses excerpts from letters and other accounts that bring the period to life. (Rev: BL 10/15/01; HBG 3/02; SLJ 3/02) [973.7]

9284 Sheinkin, Steve. *Two Miserable Presidents: Everything Your Schoolbooks Didn't Tell You About the Civil War* (4–8). Illus. by Tim Robinson. 2008, Roaring Brook $19.95 (978-1-59643-320-5). This unusual take on the war and its leaders will attract reluctant history students. It focuses on the personalities but does not leave out the larger issues that led to the war and affected its outcome. (Rev: BL 4/15/08) [973.7]

9285 Smith, Carter, ed. *One Nation Again: A Sourcebook on the Civil War* (5–8). Series: American Albums. 1993, Millbrook LB $25.90 (978-1-56294-266-3). This heavily illustrated sourcebook chroni-

cles the peace at Appomattox and the period immediately following. (Rev: BL 3/1/93) [973.8]

9286 Smith, Carter, ed. *The Road to Appomattox: A Sourcebook on the Civil War* (5–8). Series: American Albums. 1993, Millbrook $25.90 (978-1-56294-264-9). The last battles of the Civil War are covered in this album that uses period illustrations and excerpts from first-person accounts. (Rev: BL 3/1/93) [973.7]

9287 Somerlott, Robert. *The Lincoln Assassination* (5–8). Series: In American History. 1998, Enslow LB $26.60 (978-0-89490-886-6). Using primary sources, the author has created a gripping story of the causes of the assassination, the shooting itself, and its aftermath. (Rev: BL 7/98; SLJ 6/98) [973.7]

9288 Stanchak, John. *Civil War* (5–8). Illus. Series: Eyewitness Books. 2000, DK paper $15.99 (978-0-7894-6302-9). This highly visual treatment presents topics related to the Civil War such as causes, battles, slavery, states' rights, weapons, and uniforms in a series of double-page spreads. (Rev: BL 1/1–15/01; HBG 3/01; SLJ 12/00) [973.7]

9289 Stanley, George E. *The Crisis of the Union (1815–1865)* (5–8). Illus. Series: A Primary Source History of the United States. 2005, World Almanac LB $31.00 (978-0-8368-5826-6). A simple narrative links well-chosen primary sources documenting the key events of the Civil War. (Rev: BL 4/1/05)

9290 Sullivan, George. *The Civil War at Sea* (5–8). Illus. 2001, Twenty-First Century LB $27.90 (978-0-7613-1553-7). This book tells of the struggle between the Union and Confederate forces in American bays, harbors, and rivers with material on famous ships and their commanders, important battles, and the daily life of the sailors. (Rev: BL 2/1/01; HBG 10/01; SLJ 3/01) [973.7]

9291 Tackach, James, ed. *The Battle of Gettysburg* (8–12). Illus. Series: At Issue in History. 2002, Greenhaven paper $18.70 (978-0-7377-0826-4). Excerpts from historical documents and contemporary writings portray events at Gettysburg from both Union and Confederate points of view, with maps, photographs, and other illustrations. (Rev: BL 5/1/02; SLJ 4/02) [973.7]

9292 Weber, Michael. *Civil War and Reconstruction* (5–8). Series: The Making of America. 2001, Raintree LB $19.98 (978-0-8172-5707-1). Using many illustrations, interesting sidebars, and an accessible text, this is a concise history of the Civil War and its immediate aftermath. (Rev: BL 4/15/01) [973.7]

9293 Zeinert, Karen. *The Lincoln Murder Plot* (6–12). 1999, Shoe String LB $22.50 (978-0-208-02451-0). A detailed, well-documented retelling of the first assassination of a U.S. president and its world-shaking results. (Rev: BL 3/1/99; HB 7–8/99; SLJ 5/99; VOYA 4/99) [973.7]

9294 Zeinert, Karen. *Those Courageous Women of the Civil War* (5–8). Illus. 1998, Millbrook LB $29.90 (978-0-7613-0212-4). This account relates the contributions of women during the Civil War, with details on how they served as nurses, spies, writers, and workers on the home front. (Rev: BL 6/1–15/98; HBG 3/99) [973.7]

WESTWARD EXPANSION AND PIONEER LIFE

9295 Altman, Linda J. *The California Gold Rush in American History* (4–8). Illus. Series: In American History. 1997, Enslow LB $26.60 (978-0-89490-878-1). After a brief history of the California Gold Rush, this book covers topics including frontier injustice, racial discrimination, and the place of women. (Rev: HBG 3/98; SLJ 3/98) [979.4]

9296 Anderson, Dale. *Westward Expansion* (5–8). Series: The Making of America. 2001, Raintree LB $28.54 (978-0-8172-5705-7). An attractive, balanced history of the expansion of the United States to the Pacific with many biographies of pioneers given in sidebars. (Rev: BL 4/15/01; HBG 10/01) [978]

9297 Bentley, Judith. *Brides, Midwives, and Widows* (6–9). Series: Settling the West. 1995, Twenty-First Century LB $24.90 (978-0-8050-2994-9). The story of the women who helped settle the West, using diaries and other primary sources. (Rev: BL 8/95; SLJ 9/95) [978]

9298 Bentley, Judith. *Explorers, Trappers, and Guides* (6–9). Series: Settling the West. 1995, Twenty-First Century LB $24.90 (978-0-8050-2995-6). Unusually well-told stories about lesser-known explorers taken from first-person accounts. (Rev: BL 8/95; SLJ 11/95) [979.5]

9299 Blackwood, Gary L. *Life on the Oregon Trail* (5–8). Series: The Way People Live. 1999, Lucent LB $28.70 (978-1-56006-540-1). Using many excerpts from diaries, this is a thorough, appealing account of life on the Oregon Trail, which took pioneers from Missouri to the Pacific Ocean. (Rev: HBG 3/00; SLJ 8/99) [978]

9300 Calabro, Marian. *The Perilous Journey of the Donner Party* (5–8). Illus. 1999, Houghton $20.00 (978-0-395-86610-8). The story of the ill-fated Donner Party, as seen through the eyes of 12-year-old Virginia Reed. (Rev: BL 4/1/99*; HB 5–6/99; SLJ 5/99; VOYA 2/00) [979.4]

9301 Coleman, Wim, and Pat Perrin. *What Made the Wild West Wild* (4–8). Illus. Series: The Wild History of the American West. 2006, Enslow LB $33.27 (978-1-59845-016-3). The myths and legends of the Wild West are debunked in this expansive overview of media portrayals and reality. (Rev: SLJ 1/07) [978]

9302 Collier, Christopher, and James Lincoln Collier. *Indians, Cowboys, and Farmers: And the Battle for the Great Plains* (5–8). Series: The Drama of American History. 2001, Marshall Cavendish LB $31.36 (978-0-7614-1052-2). This excellently written and illustrated account covers the history of the Great Plains from the end of the Civil War to 1910, by which time the Native Americans had been scattered and the ranchers and farmers had reached a truce. (Rev: BL 3/15/01; HBG 10/01; SLJ 7/01) [973.8]

9303 Dary, David. *The Oregon Trail: An American Saga* (8–12). Illus. 2004, Knopf $35.00 (978-0-375-41399-5). A sweeping and very readable history of the Oregon Trail, from its early-19th-century origins through a period of obscurity to its present importance. (Rev: BL 10/15/04) [978]

9304 DeAngelis, Gina. *The Black Cowboys* (4–8). Illus. Series: Legends of the West. 1997, Chelsea LB $30.00 (978-0-7910-2589-5); paper $9.95 (978-0-7910-2590-1). A look at the contributions of African Americans such as Jim Beckwourth and Edward Rose to the exploration and settlement of the American West. (Rev: BL 2/15/98; HBG 3/98) [978]

9305 DeAngelis, Gina. *The Wild West* (5–8). Series: Costume, Tradition, and Culture: Reflecting on the Past. 1998, Chelsea $19.75 (978-0-7910-5169-6). Illustrated with historical collectors' cards, this account relates the legends and stories of the Wild West — its explorers, lawmen, outlaws, and Native Americans. (Rev: BL 3/15/99; HBG 10/99) [978]

9306 Delgado, James P. *Shipwrecks from the Westward Movement* (5–7). Series: Shipwrecks. 2000, Watts LB $25.50 (978-0-531-20380-4). A discussion and exploration of the shipwrecks — from small canoes to steam-powered riverboats — that occurred as European settlers moved across America. (Rev: BL 10/15/00) [978]

9307 Dolan, Edward F. *Beyond the Frontier: The Story of the Trails West* (6–10). Series: Great Journeys. 1999, Benchmark LB $32.79 (978-0-7614-0969-4). As well as describing life on the Santa Fe, Oregon, and California trails, and the sea routes taken west, this account covers such specific topics as the Donner Party and life in western settlements. (Rev: BL 1/1–15/00; HBG 3/00; SLJ 2/00) [978]

9308 Duncan, Dayton. *People of the West* (5–10). Illus. 1996, Little, Brown $19.95 (978-0-316-19627-7). Individual people — both famous and less well known — describe in their own words the opening up of the West. Based on the PBS series. (Rev: BL 8/96; SLJ 10/96) [978]

9309 Freedman, Russell. *Buffalo Hunt* (7–10). 1988, Holiday $21.95 (978-0-8234-0702-6). A history of how the buffalo were hunted from the times of the Indians to the slaughter by whites that brought on the near extinction of this animal. (Rev: BL 10/1/88; SLJ 10/88) [973]

9310 Freedman, Russell. *Children of the Wild West* (5–9). Illus. 1983, Clarion $18.00 (978-0-89919-143-0). A look at the life of the children of pioneers. (Rev: BL 1/1/90) [978]

9311 Freedman, Russell. *Cowboys of the Wild West* (5–8). Illus. 1990, Houghton paper $9.95 (978-0-395-54800-4). Text and excellent historical photographs describe these romantic figures. (Rev: BCCB 12/85; HB 3–4/86) [978.02]

9312 Galford, Ellen. *The Trail West: Exploring History Through Art* (5–8). Illus. Series: Picture That! 2004, Two-Can $19.95 (978-1-58728-442-7). Paintings serve as the vehicle to draw students into the story of westward expansion. (Rev: BL 11/1/04; SLJ 2/05) [978]

9313 Goldsmith, Connie. *Lost in Death Valley: The True Story of Four Families in California's Gold Rush* (5–8). Illus. 2001, Twenty-First Century LB $24.90 (978-0-7613-1915-3). Using original sources, the author has re-created the story of an ill-fated pioneer trek and the shortcut that led them into Death Valley. (Rev: BL 4/1/01; HBG 10/01; SLJ 4/01; VOYA 10/01) [979.4]

9314 Green, Carl R. *The California Trail to Gold in American History* (6–10). Series: In American History. 2000, Enslow LB $26.60 (978-0-7660-1347-6). Searchers for gold in California first used the Oregon Trail to go west, then they made their own separate, more direct trail. This is the history of that trail. (Rev: BL 10/15/2000; HBG 3/01) [978]

9315 Green, Carl R., and William R. Sanford. *The Dalton Gang* (4–8). Illus. Series: Outlaws and Lawmen of the Wild West. 1995, Enslow LB $21.26 (978-0-89490-588-9). The story of the gang of outlaws who roamed the West during pioneer days. (Rev: BL 11/15/95) [978]

9316 Harris, Edward D. *John Charles Fremont and the Great Western Reconnaissance* (6–9). Illus. 1990, Chelsea LB $21.95 (978-0-7910-1312-0). An account of the exploration of the West that concentrates on the five major journeys taken by Fremont. (Rev: BL 9/15/90) [973.6]

9317 Harvey, Brett. *Farmers and Ranchers* (6–9). Illus. Series: Settling the West. 1995, Twenty-First Century LB $24.90 (978-0-8050-2999-4). Westward migration and homesteading are covered in this history that uses first-person accounts and the experiences of people of various backgrounds. (Rev: BL 8/95; SLJ 11/95) [978.02]

9318 Hatt, Christine. *The American West: Native Americans, Pioneers and Settlers* (4–7). Series: History in Writing. 1999, Bedrick $19.95 (978-0-87226-290-4). A broad overview of frontier life in America with material on such topics as the Louisiana

Purchase, Indian relocations, the Gold Rush, and a settler's daily life. (Rev: HBG 3/00; SLJ 5/99) [978]

9319 Hevly, Nancy. *Preachers and Teachers* (6–9). Illus. Series: Settling the West. 1995, Twenty-First Century LB $24.90 (978-0-8050-2996-3). The bringing of religion and education to the western pioneers is the subject of this book that relies heavily of first-person accounts. (Rev: BL 8/95; SLJ 11/95) [278]

9320 Hilton, Suzanne. *Miners, Merchants, and Maids* (6–9). Illus. Series: Settling the West. 1995, Twenty-First Century LB $24.90 (978-0-8050-2998-7). Three kinds of employment that helped open up the West are discussed, with quotations from many primary sources representing people of different backgrounds. (Rev: BL 8/95; SLJ 11/95) [978]

9321 Hirschfelder, Arlene B. *Photo Odyssey: Solomon Cavalho's Remarkable Western Adventure, 1853–54* (6–10). Illus. 2000, Clarion $18.00 (978-0-395-89123-0). The story of the last westward journey of John C. Fremont as seen through the eyes of a painter/photographer who was a member of the expedition. (Rev: BCCB 9/00; BL 7/00; HBG 9/00; SLJ 8/00*; VOYA 12/00) [917.8]

9322 Isserman, Maurice. *Across America: The Lewis and Clark Expedition* (6–10). Series: Discovery and Exploration. 2004, Facts on File $40.00 (978-0-8160-5256-1). A detailed look at the expedition with clear, informative text plus photographs, illustrations, and excerpts from primary sources. (Rev: SLJ 12/04) [973]

9323 Isserman, Maurice. *Exploring North America, 1800–1900* (6–12). Series: Discovery and Exploration. 2005, Facts on File $40.00 (978-0-8160-5263-9). Clear text and primary sources explain the 19th-century explorations of North America by John Fremont, John Wesley Powell, and others, and put them in historical and social context. (Rev: SLJ 8/05) [973]

9324 January, Brendan. *Little Bighorn: June 25, 1876* (5–7). Series: American Battlefields. 2004, Enchanted Lion $14.95 (978-1-59270-028-8). This overview of the Battle of Little Bighorn offers a clear-cut account of the bloody conflict and an examination of the developments leading up to it; sidebars, illustrations, a timeline, and other features add to the narrative. (Rev: BL 11/1/04) [973]

9325 Kallen, Stuart A. *Life on the American Frontier* (6–10). Series: The Way People Live. 1998, Lucent LB $29.95 (978-1-56006-366-7). Thematically arranged chapters offer material on everyday life on the American frontier and on such groups as the trailblazers, the mountain men, the miners, the railroad men, the sodbusters, and the cattlemen. (Rev: BL 10/15/98; SLJ 1/99; VOYA 12/99) [978]

9326 Katz, William L. *Black Pioneers: An Untold Story* (7–12). 1999, Simon & Schuster $17.00 (978-0-689-81410-5). The stories of the many determined African Americans who defied prejudice, slavery, and severe legal restrictions such as the Northwest Territory's "Black Laws" to make a new life for themselves in the frontier of pre-Civil War days. (Rev: BL 7/99; HB 7–8/99; HBG 9/99; SLJ 9/99; VOYA 8/99) [977]

9327 Katz, William L. *Black Women of the Old West* (6–9). 1995, Atheneum $19.95 (978-0-689-31944-0). The role black women played in the settlement of the West — a topic virtually ignored in history books. (Rev: BL 12/15/95; SLJ 12/95; VOYA 4/96) [978]

9328 Katz, William L. *The Civil War to the Last Frontier: 1850–1880s* (7–9). Series: History of Multicultural America. 1993, Raintree LB $27.11 (978-0-8114-6277-8). A history of the United States during this period, from a multicultural perspective. (Rev: BL 9/1/93; VOYA 8/93) [973.5]

9329 Kimball, Violet T. *Stories of Young Pioneers: In Their Own Words* (6–9). Illus. 2000, Mountain Press paper $14.00 (978-0-87842-423-8). Using diaries and memoirs as sources, the editor brings to life the experiences of youngsters who traveled westward in the mid-19th century. (Rev: BL 12/15/00; VOYA 4/01) [978]

9330 Klausmeier, Robert. *Cowboy* (4–7). Illus. Series: American Pastfinder. 1996, Lerner LB $21.27 (978-0-8225-2975-0). This account focuses on the huge cattle drives and the men who led them in the years following the Civil War. (Rev: BL 3/1/96; SLJ 3/96) [636.2]

9331 Landau, Elaine. *The Transcontinental Railroad* (5–8). Illus. Series: Watts Library: American West. 2005, Watts LB $25.50 (978-0-531-12326-3). The story behind the building of the Transcontinental Railroad, with illustrations, maps, a timeline, and sidebar features. (Rev: SLJ 12/05)

9332 Lavender, David. *Snowbound: The Tragic Story of the Donner Party* (6–10). Illus. 1996, Holiday $22.95 (978-0-8234-1231-0). With extensive use of primary documents and excellent illustrations, this account vividly reconstructs the hardships and horror of the Donner Party's attempt to cross the Rockies. (Rev: BL 6/1–15/96; SLJ 7/96; VOYA 8/96) [978]

9333 McCormick, Anita Louise. *The Pony Express in American History* (6–10). Series: In American History. 2001, Enslow LB $26.60 (978-0-7660-1296-7). This account traces the development and the short life of this phenomenon that linked the East to the West and created an American legend. (Rev: BL 8/01; HBG 10/01) [383]

9334 Matthews, Leonard J. *Indians* (6–9). Illus. Series: Wild West in American History. 1988,

Rourke LB $23.93 (978-0-86625-364-2). An overview of how Indians lived during the days of the Wild West. (Rev: SLJ 6/89) [970.004]

9335 Matthews, Leonard J. *Pioneers* (6–9). Illus. Series: Wild West in American History. 1988, Rourke LB $18.00 (978-0-86625-362-8). A tribute to the homesteaders who risked their lives to find a new home in the West. Also use in the same series *Railroaders and Soldiers* (both 1989). (Rev: SLJ 6/89) [973.5]

9336 Miller, Brandon M. *Buffalo Gals: Women of the Old West* (4–7). Illus. 1995, Lerner LB $30.35 (978-0-8225-1730-6). A realistic portrait of the hardships faced by women pioneers during the 19th century on the western frontier. (Rev: BCCB 7–8/95; BL 5/1/95; SLJ 6/95*) [978]

9337 Morris, Juddi. *The Harvey Girls: The Women Who Civilized the West* (6–9). Illus. 1994, Walker $15.95 (978-0-8027-8302-8). The story of the waitresses at Fred Harvey's restaurants along the Santa Fe railroad, and how they left their homes in the East in search of adventure and independence. (Rev: BL 6/1–15/94; SLJ 7/94) [979]

9338 Murphy, Virginia R. *Across the Plains in the Donner Party* (6–10). Ed. by Karen Zeinert. 1996, Linnet LB $21.50 (978-0-208-02404-6). As well as being a condensation of the memoirs of a teenage survivor of the Donner Party, this account gives good background information and excerpts from other original sources. (Rev: BL 6/1–15/96; SLJ 8/96; VOYA 8/96) [979.4]

9339 O'Donnell, Kerri. *The Gold Rush: A Primary Source History of the Search for Gold in California* (4–8). Series: Primary Sources in American History. 2003, Rosen LB $29.25 (978-0-8239-3682-3). Timelines and reproductions of period photographs and relevant items add to the narrative in this introduction to the Gold Rush, the life of the miners, and the lawless character of the West. (Rev: SLJ 5/03) [979.4]

9340 Peavy, Linda, and Ursula Smith. *Frontier Children* (6–12). 1999, Univ. of Oklahoma $24.95 (978-0-8061-3161-0). This richly illustrated volume full of excerpts from primary sources looks at the lives of children on America's frontier during the 19th century. (Rev: BL 10/1/99; VOYA 12/00) [978]

9341 Pelta, Kathy. *Cattle Trails: "Get Along Little Dogies"* (5–8). Series: American Trails. 1997, Raintree LB $19.98 (978-0-8172-4073-8). A discussion of the cattle drives that were part of the history of the American West from 1850 to 1890. (Rev: SLJ 12/97) [978]

9342 Pelta, Kathy. *The Royal Roads: Spanish Trails in North America* (5–8). Series: American Trails. 1997, Raintree LB $19.98 (978-0-8172-4074-5). The story of the Spanish trails in Florida, California,

New Mexico, and Texas, and the people who traveled them looking for spiritual or material gain. (Rev: SLJ 12/97) [970.01]

9343 Rau, Margaret. *The Mail Must Go Through: The Story of the Pony Express* (7–10). Illus. Series: America's Moving Frontier. 2005, Morgan Reynolds LB $26.95 (978-1-931798-63-1). A lively account of the exciting — but brief — history of the Pony Express. (Rev: BL 6/1–15/05; SLJ 10/05) [383]

9344 Reinfeld, Fred. *Pony Express* (7–12). Illus. 1973, Univ. of Nebraska paper $11.95 (978-0-8032-5786-3). A history of the communication system that linked the East and West and the courageous riders who manned it. [383]

9345 Richards, Colin. *Sheriff Pat Garrett's Last Days* (8–12). Illus. 1986, Sunstone paper $8.95 (978-0-86534-079-4). A history of the Wild West drawn into focus by the death of the man who shot Billy the Kid. [978]

9346 Ritchie, David. *Frontier Life* (5–7). Illus. Series: Life in America 100 Years Ago. 1995, Chelsea $21.95 (978-0-7910-2842-1). A concise overview of life on the American frontier that does not gloss over the harsh and often violent aspects. (Rev: SLJ 1/96) [973.5]

9347 Ross, Stewart. *Cowboys* (5–7). Illus. Series: Fact or Fiction? 1995, Millbrook LB $26.90 (978-1-56294-618-0). The life of cowboys during the late 1800s is covered, with information that tries to separate fact from fable. (Rev: BL 7/95; SLJ 5/95) [978.02]

9348 Saffer, Barbara. *The California Gold Rush* (5–7). Series: The American West. 2002, Mason Crest LB $19.95 (978-1-59084-060-3). Reluctant readers will be drawn to this attractive account of the hardships of traveling to California and the life in the mining camps. (Rev: SLJ 4/02) [979.4]

9349 Sanford, William R. *The Chisholm Trail* (6–10). Series: In American History. 2000, Enslow LB $26.60 (978-0-7660-1345-2). A look at this important trail that stretched from Texas to Kansas, and became the main route for driving longhorn cattle to the North. (Rev: BL 7/00; HBG 3/01; SLJ 12/00) [978]

9350 Sanford, William R. *The Natchez Trace Historic Trail* (6–9). Series: In American History. 2001, Enslow LB $26.60 (978-0-7660-1344-5). Sanford looks at the history of this ancient Native American trail that became important from the 1780s to 1830s, the people who used it, and confrontations between newcomers and the indigenous people. (Rev: BL 12/15/01; HBG 3/02; SLJ 3/02) [976]

9351 Sanford, William R. *The Santa Fe Trail in American History* (6–10). Series: In American History. 2000, Enslow LB $26.60 (978-0-7660-1348-3). The story of the trail from Missouri to New Mexico that opened in 1821 and became an important continental trade route. (Rev: BL 10/15/2000; HBG 3/01) [978]

9352 Savage, Candace. *Born to Be a Cowgirl: A Spirited Ride Through the Old West* (6–9). 2001, Tricycle $15.95 (978-1-58246-019-2); paper $10.95 (978-1-58246-020-8). An appealing package of fascinating text, excerpts from letters and journals, and period illustrations that introduces female cowhands and their lifestyle. (Rev: BL 5/15/01; HB 7–8/01; HBG 10/01; SLJ 6/01; VOYA 12/01) [978]

9353 Savage, Jeff. *Cowboys and Cow Towns of the Wild West* (4–7). Illus. Series: Trailblazers of the Wild West. 1995, Enslow LB $21.26 (978-0-89490-603-9). Through the experiences of a single cowboy, the reader learns about his equipment, dangers, leisure time, cattle drives, and roundups. (Rev: SLJ 2/96) [978]

9354 Schaffer, David. *The Louisiana Purchase: The Deal of the Century That Doubled the Nation* (5–8). Illus. Series: The Wild History of the American West. 2006, Enslow LB $33.27 (978-1-59845-018-7). Tells the story behind America's negotiations to buy the vast Louisiana Territory for $15 million, or less than 3 cents an acre; includes a list of carefully selected Web sites that offer additional information. (Rev: SLJ 12/06) [973.4]

9355 Schlaepfer, Gloria G. *The Louisiana Purchase* (5–8). Illus. Series: Watts Library: American West. 2005, Watts LB $25.50 (978-0-531-12300-3). The story behind the Louisiana Purchase and its role in America's westward expansion, with illustrations, maps, a timeline, and sidebar features. (Rev: SLJ 12/05)

9356 Schroeder, Lisa Golden. *California Gold Rush Cooking* (4–7). Series: Exploring History Through Simple Recipes. 2000, Capstone LB $23.93 (978-0-7368-0603-9). This book discusses the California Gold Rush and everyday life of the period with details of the kinds of food eaten and some simple recipes. (Rev: BL 3/1/01; HBG 10/01; SLJ 4/01) [979.4]

9357 Shuter, Jane, ed. *Sarah Royce and the American West* (5–8). Illus. Series: History Eyewitness. 1996, Raintree LB $24.26 (978-0-8114-8286-8). The ordeals and achievements of American pioneers are chronicled in this first-person account, accompanied by many splendid illustrations. (Rev: BL 5/15/96; SLJ 6/96) [978]

9358 Sonneborn, Liz. *The Mormon Trail* (5–8). Illus. Series: Watts Library: American West. 2005, Watts LB $25.50 (978-0-531-12317-1). The story behind the westward trek of thousands of Mormons during the middle of the 19th century, with illustrations, maps, a timeline, and sidebar features. (Rev: SLJ 12/05)

9359 Sonneborn, Liz. *Women of the American West* (4–7). Illus. Series: Watts Library: American West. 2005, Watts LB $25.50 (978-0-531-12318-8). Excerpts from first-person accounts offer a glimpse into what life was like for the women who helped to open the American West. (Rev: BL 10/15/05) [978]

9360 Stefoff, Rebecca. *First Frontier* (4–7). Series: North American Historical Atlases. 2000, Benchmark LB $24.21 (978-0-7614-1059-1). This book presents an illustrated view of the western expansion and its effects on Native Americans, frontiersmen, speculators, and soldiers. (Rev: HBG 3/01; SLJ 1/01) [978]

9361 Stefoff, Rebecca. *The Opening of the West* (5–8). 2002, Benchmark LB $34.21 (978-0-7614-1201-4). A collection of primary sources that includes excerpts from letters, newspaper articles, and journal entries commenting on different aspects of frontier life, exploration, and the plight of Native Americans. (Rev: HBG 10/03; SLJ 4/03) [978]

9362 Stefoff, Rebecca. *The Oregon Trail in American History* (6–10). Illus. Series: In American History. 1997, Enslow LB $26.60 (978-0-89490-771-5). The story of the Oregon Trail and the everyday life of the settlers who traveled it are re-created, with a guide to the trail as it exists today. (Rev: BL 2/1/98; HBG 3/98; SLJ 2/98) [978]

9363 Stefoff, Rebecca. *Women Pioneers* (6–12). Series: American Profiles. 1995, Facts on File $25.00 (978-0-8160-3134-4). Nine profiles of pioneer women noted for their courage, ingenuity, and triumphs are presented in this readable account that gives details of life on the American frontier. (Rev: BL 1/1–15/96; SLJ 2/96; VOYA 4/96) [973.8]

9364 Stein, R. Conrad. *In the Spanish West* (4–8). Series: How We Lived. 1999, Benchmark LB $27.07 (978-0-7614-0906-9). This well-balanced account describes the American West under Spanish control and influence with material on history, social life, agriculture, and home life. (Rev: HBG 10/00; SLJ 3/00) [978]

9365 Stein, R. Conrad. *On the Old Western Frontier* (4–8). Series: How We Lived. 1999, Benchmark LB $28.50 (978-0-7614-0909-0). An interesting book that gives an overview of the history and living conditions on the American frontier with material on everyday life, farming and ranching, social life, religion, Native Americans, and slaves. (Rev: HBG 10/00; SLJ 3/00) [978]

9366 Stovall, TaRessa. *The Buffalo Soldiers* (6–10). Illus. Series: African-American Achievers. 1997, Chelsea LB $30.00 (978-0-7910-2595-6); paper $30.00 (978-0-7910-2596-3). The story of the stirring achievements of the black U.S. Army regiments that distinguished themselves during numerous campaigns and played a vital role in the settlement

of the American West. (Rev: BL 12/1/97; HBG 3/98) [978]

9367 Swanson, Wayne. *Why the West Was Wild* (5–8). 2004, Annick $12.95 (978-1-55037-837-5); paper $12.95 (978-1-55037-836-8). The excitement of the Old West is captured in this lavishly illustrated survey of the region's history during the second half of the 19th century. (Rev: BL 8/04; SLJ 6/04) [978]

9368 Torr, James D., ed. *The American Frontier* (7–12). Series: Turning Points in World History. 2001, Greenhaven LB $24.95 (978-0-7377-0785-4); paper $37.45 (978-0-7377-0786-1). A collection of essays that explores the opening up of the West, the nature of the pioneer spirit, and the changes this development brought to our history. (Rev: BL 3/15/02) [973.7]

9369 Torr, James D., ed. *Westward Expansion* (7–12). Series: Interpreting Primary Documents. 2003, Gale LB $32.45 (978-0-7377-1134-9). A broad selection of primary sources present different perspectives on issues relating to the United States' westward expansion (the Indian Wars, building the transcontinental railroad, the gold rush, and so forth). (Rev: BL 1/1–15/03; SLJ 2/03) [978]

9370 Tunis, Edwin. *Frontier Living* (7–12). 1976, Crowell paper $18.95 (978-1-58574-137-3). Using more than 200 original drawings and a fine text, the author portrays the life, artifacts, and customs of the American frontier. [978]

9371 Uschan, Michael V. *The Transcontinental Railroad* (4–7). Series: Landmark Events in American History. 2003, World Almanac LB $31.00 (978-0-8368-5382-7). In accessible language and with plenty of illustrations, this is the story of the railroad that spanned the nation. (Rev: SLJ 6/04) [385]

9372 Wadsworth, Ginger. *Words West: Voices of Young Pioneers* (5–8). 2003, Clarion $18.00 (978-0-618-23475-2). Excerpts from journals and other documents give a clear picture of the experiences of young people traveling west between 1840 and 1870. (Rev: HBG 4/04; SLJ 12/03) [917.804]

9373 Waldman, Stuart. *The Last River: John Wesley Powell and the Colorado River Exploring Expedition* (4–7). Illus. by Gregory Manchess. 2005, Mikaya $19.95 (978-1-931414-09-8). This is the exciting story of the three-month exploration of the Colorado River led by the one-armed John Wesley Powell in 1869; excerpts from journals and letters reveal details of the dangers faced. (Rev: BL 12/15/05; SLJ 2/06) [550.92]

9374 Werther, Scott P. *The Donner Party* (5–7). Illus. 2002, Children's LB $24.50 (978-0-516-23901-9). The fate of the Donner Party is described against the backdrop of life in America in the 1840s and the dangers of travel to the West and the Pacific. (Rev: SLJ 10/02) [979.4]

9375 Winslow, Mimi. *Loggers and Railroad Workers* (6–9). Illus. Series: Settling the West. 1995, Twenty-First Century LB $24.90 (978-0-8050-2997-0). First-person accounts from workers in logging and on the railroad are woven together to give a portrait of these fledgling industries in the Old West. (Rev: BL 7/95; SLJ 9/95) [338.7]

9376 Worth, Richard. *Westward Expansion and Manifest Destiny in American History* (6–10). Series: In American History. 2001, Enslow LB $26.60 (978-0-7660-1457-2). This account chronicles events after the Revolution when Americans believed that westward expansion was their destiny and acted on this impulse. (Rev: BL 8/01; HBG 10/01; SLJ 7/01) [978]

RECONSTRUCTION TO WORLD WAR I (1865–1914)

9377 Arnold, Caroline. *Children of the Settlement Houses* (4–7). Illus. Series: Picture the American Past. 1998, Carolrhoda LB $27.15 (978-1-57505-242-7). Using historical photographs and a simple text, this book introduces the turn-of-the-20th-century settlement house, where the poor and new immigrants found shelter and a place to learn, explore the arts, and develop a sense of belonging. (Rev: BL 9/15/98; HBG 3/99; SLJ 1/99) [362.5]

9378 Axelrod-Contrada, Joan. *The Lizzie Borden "Axe Murder" Trial: A Headline Court Case* (5–9). Series: Headline Court Cases. 2000, Enslow LB $26.60 (978-0-7660-1422-0). A well-documented account of the famous 1892 trial, the events that led up to it, and its aftermath. (Rev: HBG 3/01; SLJ 1/01) [973.8]

9379 Baker, Julie. *The Bread and Roses Strike of 1912* (6–10). 2007, Morgan Reynolds LB $27.95 (978-1-59935-044-8). Tells the story of the largest textile labor strike in American history, which occurred in Massachusetts in 1912, with profiles of union leaders, photographs of suffering families, and details of the employees' (including children) horrific living and working conditions. (Rev: BL 5/15/07; SLJ 7/07)

9380 Bartoletti, Susan C. *Growing Up in Coal Country* (5–8). Illus. 1996, Houghton $17.00 (978-0-395-77847-0). The life of child laborers in the coal mines of Pennsylvania 100 years ago is covered in this brilliant photoessay. (Rev: BCCB 2/97; BL 12/1/96*; SLJ 2/97*) [331.3]

9381 Bartoletti, Susan C. *Kids on Strike!* (5–8). Illus. 1999, Houghton $20.00 (978-0-395-88892-6). This book chronicles the history of child labor in America during the 19th and early 20th centuries and features such personalities as William Randolph Hearst, Pauline Newman, and Mother Jones. (Rev: BCCB 12/99; BL 12/1/99; HBG 3/00; SLJ 12/99*; VOYA 2/00) [973.8]

9382 Brezina, Corona. *America's Political Scandals in the late 1800s: Boss Tweed and Tammany Hall* (5–8). Illus. Series: America's Industrial Society in the 19th Century. 2004, Rosen LB $22.50 (978-0-8239-4021-9). For reluctant readers, this overview of the political scandals of the late 19th century features large print and short chapters. (Rev: BL 4/1/04)

9383 Cohen, Daniel. *The Alaska Purchase* (4–8). Series: Spotlight on American History. 1996, Millbrook $24.90 (978-1-56294-528-2). The story of the purchase of Alaska from Russia in 1867 and how it changed the course of American history. (Rev: BL 3/15/96; SLJ 5/96) [979.8]

9384 Collier, Christopher, and James Lincoln Collier. *Reconstruction and the Rise of Jim Crow, 1864–1896* (5–8). Series: Drama of American History. 1999, Marshall Cavendish LB $31.36 (978-0-7614-0819-2). A clear, objective account of the problems facing the country after the Civil War and how they were resolved. (Rev: BL 2/15/00; HBG 10/00; SLJ 3/00) [973.8]

9385 Collier, Christopher, and James Lincoln Collier. *The Rise of Industry, 1860–1900* (5–8). Illus. Series: Drama of American History. 1999, Marshall Cavendish LB $31.36 (978-0-7614-0820-8). A readable account of 40 years of industrialism and its effect on the United States. (Rev: BL 2/15/00; HBG 10/00; SLJ 3/00) [338.0973]

9386 Currie, Stephen. *We Have Marched Together: The Working Children's Crusade* (7–12). Series: People's History. 1996, Lerner LB $30.35 (978-0-8225-1733-7). The focus of this book is on child labor in the United States and the protest march from Philadelphia to New York led by Mother Jones in 1903. (Rev: BL 5/1/97; SLJ 7/97) [331.3]

9387 De Angelis, Gina. *The Triangle Shirtwaist Company Fire of 1911* (7–12). Illus. Series: Great Disasters: Reforms and Ramifications. 2000, Chelsea $30.00 (978-0-7910-5267-9). This is a dramatic and detailed account of the fire, the conditions that made such a disaster possible, and the union protests that followed. (Rev: BL 10/15/00; HBG 3/01; SLJ 2/01; VOYA 2/01) [974.7]

9388 Dolan, Edward F. *The Spanish-American War* (5–8). Illus. 2001, Millbrook LB $28.90 (978-0-7613-1453-0). This chronological account of the Spanish-American War includes profiles of military personnel, maps, and historical photographs. (Rev: BL 11/1/01; HBG 3/02; SLJ 11/01) [973.8]

9389 Ferrell, Claudine L. *Reconstruction* (5–10). Series: Greenwood Guides to Historic Events, 1500–1900. 2003, Greenwood $51.95 (978-0-313-32062-0). Covers key individuals involved in Reconstruction and the speeches, proclamations, and other primary documents that cast light on the events of the time. (Rev: SLJ 6/04) [973.8]

9390 Fireside, Bryna J. *The Haymarket Square Riot Trial* (6–10). Series: Headline Court Cases. 2002, Enslow LB $26.60 (978-0-7660-1761-0). This is an account of the trial that resulted from the arrest of several people after a bomb-throwing incident during a labor protest rally in Chicago on May 4, 1886. (Rev: BL 3/15/03; HBG 3/03) [973.8]

9391 Fremon, David K. *The Alaska Purchase in American History* (7–10). Series: In American History. 1999, Enslow LB $26.60 (978-0-7660-1138-0). This account covers both the purchase of Alaska in 1867 and an early history of the Native Americans who lived there. (Rev: BL 11/15/99; HBG 3/00; SLJ 3/00) [979.8]

9392 Gan, Geraldine. *Communication* (6–9). Series: Life in America 100 Years Ago. 1997, Chelsea LB $21.95 (978-0-7910-2845-2). An exploration of the growing importance of mail, books, newspapers, magazines, telegraphs, and telephones at the turn of the 20th century. (Rev: BL 10/15/97; SLJ 9/97) [973.8]

9393 Gourley, Catherine. *Good Girl Work: Factories, Sweatshops, and How Women Changed Their Role in the American Workforce* (7–10). 1999, Millbrook LB $26.90 (978-0-7613-0951-2). This history of the exploitation of female children around the turn of the 20th century includes dramatic, in-depth personal testimonies and first-person accounts from letters, diaries, memoirs, and newspaper interviews. (Rev: BL 5/1/99; SLJ 8/99) [331.3]

9394 Greene, Meg. *Into the Land of Freedom: African Americans in Reconstruction* (5–8). Illus. Series: People's History. 2004, Lerner LB $29.27 (978-0-8225-4690-0). Sepia-toned photographs and historical documents and interviews add to this portrait of the situation of African Americans during Reconstruction. (Rev: BL 2/15/04*; SLJ 5/04) [973]

9395 Greenwood, Janette Thomas. *The Gilded Age: A History in Documents* (6–12). Illus. 2000, Oxford LB $39.95 (978-0-19-510523-0). Documents of all kinds are used to show readers the many changes that took place in American society in the last years of the 19th century. (Rev: BL 10/1/00; HBG 3/01; SLJ 10/00) [973.8]

9396 Hansen, Joyce. *"Bury Me Not in a Land of Slaves": African-Americans in the Time of Reconstruction* (6–10). Illus. 2000, Watts LB $24.00 (978-0-531-11539-8). An excellent overview of the complex era that followed the Civil War and how compromises were reached on giving civil rights to African Americans. (Rev: BL 6/1–15/00; SLJ 6/00) [973]

9397 Haskins, Jim. *Geography of Hope: Black Exodus from the South After Reconstruction* (7–12). Illus. 1999, Twenty-First Century LB $31.90 (978-0-7613-0323-7). After information on slavery and the Reconstruction, the author describes the migra-

tions of African Americans to the North, their leaders, and the politics that made life in the South intolerable. (Rev: BL 10/15/99; HBG 4/00; SLJ 11/99; VOYA 6/00) [973]

9398 Havens, John C. *Government and Politics* (6–9). Illus. Series: Life in America 100 Years Ago. 1997, Chelsea LB $21.95 (978-0-7910-2847-6). This book focuses on the influences on politics at the turn of the 20th century, such as the end of the Civil War, the rise of big business and the growing power of industry, and government scandals. (Rev: BL 6/1–15/97) [973]

9399 *Industry and Business* (6–9). Illus. Series: Life in America 100 Years Ago. 1996, Chelsea LB $21.95 (978-0-7910-2846-9). A look at the Industrial Revolution that transformed the United States from a rural to an urban nation and set it on a course toward becoming a world power. (Rev: BL 6/1–15/97) [338.0973]

9400 Isserman, Maurice. *Journey to Freedom* (7–12). Illus. Series: Library of African American History. 1997, Facts on File $25.00 (978-0-8160-3413-0). An account of the African American men and women who traveled north at the beginning of the 20th century filled with hope and looking for freedom, dignity, and economic opportunity, and of the impact on the nation's politics and culture. (Rev: BL 2/15/98) [975]

9401 Jackson, Robert. *Meet Me in St. Louis: A Trip to the 1904 World's Fair* (4–7). Illus. 2004, HarperCollins $17.99 (978-0-06-009267-2). Jackson beautifully evokes the excitement surrounding the 1904 St. Louis World's Fair, which attracted nearly 20 million people, many of them key figures of the day. (Rev: BL 2/15/04; SLJ 4/04) [907]

9402 Josephson, Judith Pinkerton. *Growing Up in a New Century* (5–8). Illus. Series: Our America. 2002, Lerner LB $26.60 (978-0-8225-0657-7). A look at the lives of American children of different backgrounds and situations at the dawn of the 20th century. (Rev: BL 2/1/03; HBG 3/03; SLJ 7/03) [973.91]

9403 Leuzzi, Linda. *Education* (6–9). Series: Life in America 100 Years Ago. 1998, Chelsea LB $21.95 (978-0-7910-2849-0). With fascinating examples and detailed descriptions, this book discusses practices in turn-of-the-century schools and classrooms. (Rev: BL 3/15/98; HBG 9/98) [973.8]

9404 McNeese, Tim. *Remember the Maine: The Spanish-American War Begins* (6–12). Illus. Series: First Battles. 2001, Morgan Reynolds LB $23.95 (978-1-883846-79-4). The story of the sinking of the battleship *Maine*, an event that led to the Spanish-American War in 1898. (Rev: BL 11/1/01; HBG 3/02; SLJ 4/02) [973.8]

9405 Miller, Marilyn. *The Transcontinental Railroad* (5–8). Illus. 1987, Silver Burdett paper $12.36

(978-0-382-09912-0). The great event that linked East and West by rail is portrayed with numerous illustrations. (Rev: BL 7/87; SLJ 9/87) [385.0979]

9406 Porterfield, Jason. *Problems and Progress in American Politics: The Growth of the Democratic Party in the Late 1800s* (5–8). Illus. Series: America's Industrial Society in the 19th Century. 2004, Rosen LB $22.50 (978-0-8239-4026-4). For reluctant readers, this overview of the growth of the Democratic Party features large print and short chapters. (Rev: BL 4/1/04)

9407 Ruggiero, Adriane. *American Voices from Reconstruction* (8–11). Illus. Series: American Voices. 2006, Marshall Cavendish LB $25.95 (978-0-7614-2168-9). This volume effectively uses primary sources — newspaper accounts, speeches, letters and diary entries, songs, and so forth — to tell the story of Reconstruction, presenting the points of view of key politicians as well as former slaves and slave owners. (Rev: BL 2/1/07) [973.8]

9408 Sandler, Martin W. *Island of Hope: The Story of Ellis Island and the Journey to America* (5–7). Illus. 2004, Scholastic $19.99 (978-0-439-53082-8). Drawing heavily on first-hand accounts, Sandler traces immigrants' progress through the processing at Ellis Island and on into the cities and farms of their new country. (Rev: BL 4/15/04; SLJ 6/04) [304.8]

9409 Schaefer, Adam R. *The Triangle Shirtwaist Factory Fire* (4–7). Series: Landmark Events in American History. 2003, World Almanac LB $31.00 (978-0-8368-5383-4). An accessible account of the tragic 1911 fire in New York City, with material on the horrible working conditions and the resulting reforms in labor law. (Rev: SLJ 6/04) [974.7]

9410 Schwartz, Eric. *Crossing the Seas: Americans Form an Empire 1890–1899* (5–8). Series: How America Became America. 2005, Mason Crest LB $22.95 (978-1-59084-910-1). Schwartz explores America's turn to imperialism in the final decade of the 19th century. Also use *Super Power: Americans Today* (2005). (Rev: SLJ 11/05) [973]

9411 Sherrow, Victoria. *The Triangle Factory Fire* (5–8). Series: Spotlight on American History. 1995, Millbrook LB $24.90 (978-1-56294-572-5). The story of the deadly factory fire that exposed the shameful labor exploitation in this country and led to needed reforms. (Rev: SLJ 3/96) [363.37]

9412 Somerlott, Robert. *The Spanish-American War: "Remember the Maine!"* (6–12). Illus. Series: American War. 2002, Enslow LB $26.60 (978-0-7660-1855-6). This overview of the Spanish-American War's key events and individuals includes information on President William McKinley, Teddy Roosevelt and his Rough Riders, and Clara Barton. (Rev: BL 3/1/03; HBG 3/03; SLJ 6/03) [973.8]

9413 Stanley, George E. *An Emerging World Power (1900–1929)* (5–8). Illus. Series: A Primary Source History of the United States. 2005, World Almanac LB $31.00 (978-0-8368-5828-0). A simple narrative links well-chosen primary sources documenting the key events of the early 20th century. Also use *The Era of Reconstruction and Expansion (1865–1900)* and *The Great Depression and World War II (1929–1949)* (both 2005). (Rev: BL 4/1/05; SLJ 7/05)

9414 Stein, R. Conrad. *The Transcontinental Railroad in American History* (6–10). Illus. Series: In American History. 1997, Enslow LB $26.60 (978-0-89490-882-8). This is a lively account of the building of the transcontinental railroad and the people involved, including the essential role of Chinese Americans. (Rev: BL 2/1/98; HBG 3/98; SLJ 1/98) [385]

9415 Stites, Bill. *The Republican Party in the Late 1800s: A Changing Role for American Government* (5–8). Illus. Series: America's Industrial Society in the 19th Century. 2004, Rosen LB $22.50 (978-0-8239-4030-1). For reluctant readers, this overview of the growth of the Republican Party features large print and short chapters. (Rev: BL 4/1/04)

9416 Stroud, Bettye, and Virginia Schomp. *The Reconstruction Era* (5–8). Series: Drama of African-American History. 2006, Benchmark LB $23.95 (978-0-7614-2181-8). This volume traces the history of Reconstruction and the tensions remaining between the many factions after the Civil War. (Rev: SLJ 5/07) [973.8]

9417 Wells, Donna. *America Comes of Age* (5–8). Series: The Making of America. 2001, Raintree LB $28.54 (978-0-8172-5708-8). A handsomely illustrated account that traces U.S. history from Reconstruction to the beginning of the 20th century. (Rev: BL 4/15/01; HBG 10/01) [973.8]

9418 Wilder, Laura Ingalls. *West from Home: Letters of Laura Ingalls Wilder, San Francisco 1915* (7–9). 1974, HarperCollins paper $5.99 (978-0-06-440081-7). The author describes her trip from Missouri to San Francisco in 1915. [973.9]

9419 Ziff, Marsha. *Reconstruction Following the Civil War in American History* (7–10). Series: In American History. 1999, Enslow LB $26.60 (978-0-7660-1140-3). A look at the events, personalities, and movements associated with the period from 1865 to 1877. (Rev: BL 11/15/99; HBG 4/00; SLJ 3/00) [973.8]

WORLD WAR I

9420 Ruggiero, Adriane. *World War I* (6–9). Series: American Voices From. 2002, Benchmark LB $34.21 (978-0-7614-1203-8). Excerpts from primary documents including letters, newspaper articles, speeches, and journals present a variety of different experiences of those who lived through World War I. (Rev: HBG 10/03; SLJ 3/03) [940.3]

9421 Torr, James D., ed. *Primary Sources* (6–12). Series: American War Library: World War I. 2002, Gale LB $29.95 (978-1-59018-008-2). This is a collection of documents, letters, and memorabilia that describe key events and America's participation in World War I. (Rev: BL 6/1–15/02) [940.1]

9422 Wukovits, John F. *Flying Aces* (6–12). Series: American War Library: World War I. 2002, Gale LB $29.95 (978-1-56006-810-5). With an emphasis on American airmen, this account describes the war in the air and the people involved during World War I. (Rev: BL 6/1–15/02) [940.3]

9423 Wukovits, John F. *Strategic Battles* (6–12). Series: American War Library: World War I. 2002, Gale LB $29.95 (978-1-56006-836-5). The important battles of World War I are described with an emphasis on those involving Americans, with first-hand accounts, maps, and archival photographs. (Rev: BL 6/1–15/02) [940.3]

BETWEEN THE WARS AND THE GREAT DEPRESSION (1918–1941)

9424 Altman, Linda J. *The Decade That Roared: America During Prohibition* (7–10). 1997, Twenty-First Century $23.40 (978-0-8050-4133-0). The excitement and significance of the roaring 20s are conveyed, with vivid depictions of bootleggers, flagpole sitters, mobsters, revivalist preachers, and speakeasy queens, as well as laborers, blues and jazz musicians, participants in the "Scopes monkey trial," and even conservative rural dwellers. (Rev: SLJ 1/98) [973.9]

9425 Appelt, Kathi, and Jeanne Cannella Schmitzer. *Down Cut Shin Creek* (6–9). Illus. 2001, Harper-Collins $16.99 (978-0-06-029135-8). An absorbing account of the dedicated pack-horse librarians who braved difficult conditions to deliver books and other materials to needy families in the hills of Kentucky during the Depression. (Rev: BL 7/01; HB 5–6/01; HBG 10/01; SLJ 5/01*) [716.15]

9426 Blumenthal, Karen. *Six Days in October: The Stock Market Crash of 1929* (7–12). Illus. 2002, Simon & Schuster $17.95 (978-0-689-84276-4). An absorbing look at the factors that led to the infamous crash and the fortunes that were lost, with clear definitions of economic concepts and interesting illustrations. (Rev: BL 11/1/02; HB 1–2/03; HBG 3/03; SLJ 10/02; VOYA 12/02) [332.64]

9427 Bragg, Rick. *Ava's Man* (7–12). 2001, Knopf $25.00 (978-0-375-41062-8). Bragg paints a loving portrait of his maternal grandfather, Charlie Bundrum, a simple backwoods man who, with his wife Ava, struggled to raise seven children to adulthood during the lean years of the Great Depression. (Rev: BL 6/1–15/01*; VOYA 4/02) [975]

9428 Callan, Jim. *America in the 1930s* (7–10). Illus. Series: Decades of American History. 2005, Facts on File $35.00 (978-0-8160-5638-5). Excellent information — especially for report writers — is hampered by poor design. (Rev: BL 1/1–15/06) [973.917]

9429 Candaele, Kerry. *Bound for Glory: From the Great Migration to the Harlem Renaissance, 1910–1930* (7–10). Illus. Series: Milestones in Black American History. 1996, Chelsea LB $21.95 (978-0-7910-2261-0); paper $9.95 (978-0-7910-2687-8). This account covers the mass movement of African Americans from the rural South to the northern cities in the early 20th century and their achievements in the arts, politics, business, and sports, with emphasis on the origins of the Harlem Renaissance. (Rev: BL 10/15/96; SLJ 2/97) [973]

9430 Carter, Ron. *The Youngest Drover* (5–9). 1995, Harbour $19.95 (978-0-9643672-1-0); paper $14.95 (978-0-9643672-0-3). In 1923, when he was 15, the author's father participated in an exciting cattle drive from Alberta to Montana. (Rev: BL 1/1–15/96) [978]

9431 Chambers, Veronica. *The Harlem Renaissance* (7–12). Illus. Series: African-American Achievers. 1997, Chelsea LB $30.00 (978-0-7910-2597-0); paper $9.95 (978-0-7910-2598-7). This history discusses the emergence of Harlem as a cultural center in the 1920s in the context of the social and political forces of the time, weaving in accounts of such greats as Langston Hughes, Countee Cullen, Zora Neale Hurston, and others who were part of this artistic and intellectual movement. (Rev: BL 2/15/98; HBG 3/98; SLJ 4/98) [700]

9432 Collier, Christopher, and James Lincoln Collier. *Progressivism, the Great Depression, and the New Deal* (5–8). Illus. Series: The Drama of American History. 2001, Marshall Cavendish LB $31.36 (978-0-7614-1054-6). A highly readable account that covers such topics as the stock market crash, the reformation of business practices, the Great Depression, and the social policies of the New Deal. (Rev: BL 3/15/01; HBG 10/01) [973.91]

9433 Cooper, Michael L. *Dust to Eat: Drought and Depression in the 1930s* (5–8). Illus. 2004, Clarion $17.00 (978-0-618-15449-4). First-person accounts and period photographs convey the hopelessness of those who were caught in the grip of the Depression and the drought in the Midwest. (Rev: BL 7/04; SLJ 9/04) [973.917]

9434 Costantino, Maria. *Fashions of a Decade: The 1930s* (5–10). 2007, Chelsea House LB $35.00 (978-0-8160-6719-0). With illustrations, photographs, and a helpful chronology of trends and events, this book captures the fashions of the 1930s and relates them to the conditions of the times. (Rev: SLJ 7/07)

9435 Cryan-Hicks, Kathryn, ed. *Pride and Promise: The Harlem Renaisssance* (4–8). Illus. Series: Perspectives on History. 1994, Discovery Enterprises paper $6.95 (978-1-878668-30-1). The story of the great artistic awakening in New York's Harlem and of its many leaders, including Langston Hughes. (Rev: BL 8/94) [305.896]

9436 Damon, Duane. *Headin' for Better Times: The Arts of the Great Depression* (6–8). Illus. Series: People's History. 2002, Lerner LB $25.26 (978-0-8225-1741-2). Damon introduces readers to the wide range of literature, music, art, drama, and entertainment that was produced during this time of hardship in the United States. (Rev: BL 3/15/02; HBG 10/02; SLJ 5/02) [700]

9437 Davis, Barbara J. *The Teapot Dome Scandal: Corruption Rocks 1920s America* (5–8). Series: Snapshots in History. 2007, Compass Point LB $31.93 (978-0-7565-3336-6). Davis traces the corruption in the Harding administration and the scandal that erupted over oil leasing without competitive bidding. (Rev: SLJ 1/08)

9438 DeAngelis, Therese, and Gina DeAngelis. *The Dust Bowl* (6–8). Illus. Series: Great Disasters. 2002, Chelsea LB $30.00 (978-0-7910-6323-1). Photographs and excerpts from letters add realism to this portrait of the hardships of life in the Midwest during the Depression. (Rev: BL 4/15/02; HBG 10/02) [978]

9439 Dudley, William, ed. *The Great Depression: Opposing Viewpoints* (7–12). Illus. Series: Opposing Viewpoints Digests. 1994, Greenhaven LB $17.95 (978-1-56510-084-8). This account uses dozens of quotations from primary and secondary sources to explore various facets of the Great Depression, including its causes, its effects, and the New Deal. (Rev: BL 2/1/94) [973.9]

9440 Edwards, Judith. *The Lindbergh Baby Kidnapping* (7–10). Series: In American History. 2000, Enslow LB $26.60 (978-0-7660-1299-8). The 1932 kidnapping and subsequent trial are covered in detail, followed by a discussion of capital punishment and the pressures involved in this celebrity case. (Rev: BL 1/1–15/00; HBG 9/00; SLJ 4/00) [973.9]

9441 Feinberg, Barbara S. *Black Tuesday: The Stock Market Crash of 1929* (4–7). Illus. Series: Spotlight on American History. 1995, Millbrook LB $24.90 (978-1-56294-574-9). The causes and consequences of the great stock market crash of 1929 are interestingly retold with many photographs and illustrations. (Rev: BL 10/15/95) [338.5]

9442 Freedman, Russell. *Children of the Great Depression* (5–8). Illus. 2005, Clarion $20.00 (978-0-618-44630-8). The works of such notable photographers as Dorothea Lange and Walker Evans, moving quotations, and the accessible text of Freed-

man make this a memorable photoessay. (Rev: BCCB 12/05; BL 12/15/05*; HBG 4/05; LMC 3/06; SLJ 12/05*; VOYA 6/06) [305.23]

9443 Fremon, David K. *The Great Depression* (7–10). Series: In American History. 1997, Enslow LB $26.60 (978-0-89490-881-1). The Great Depression, its causes, its effects, and how it was ended, are covered in a lively text and many black-and-white photographs. (Rev: BL 5/15/97) [338.5]

9444 Harris, Nathaniel. *The Great Depression* (7–12). Illus. 1988, David & Charles $19.95 (978-0-7134-5658-5). This account describes the 1930s in the United States and in Britain and Europe. (Rev: SLJ 1/89) [973.91]

9445 Haskins, Jim. *The Harlem Renaissance* (6–10). Illus. 1996, Millbrook LB $30.90 (978-1-56294-565-7). This book offers a guided tour of the Harlem Renaissance from 1916 through 1940 and an introduction to the artists and writers involved. (Rev: BL 9/1/96; SLJ 9/96; VOYA 12/96) [700]

9446 Herald, Jacqueline. *Fashions of a Decade: The 1920s* (5–10). 2007, Chelsea House LB $35.00 (978-0-8160-6718-3). Photographs, illustrations, and timelines accompany text that relates the fashion of the 1920s to events and the culture of the times. (Rev: SLJ 7/07)

9447 Hill, Laban Carrick. *Harlem Stomp! A Cultural History of the Harlem Renaissance* (7–12). Illus. 2004, Little, Brown $18.95 (978-0-316-81411-9). This illustrated history covers developments during the roaring 1920s and the great creations and creators of the Harlem Renaissance. (Rev: BL 2/15/04*; SLJ 1/04; VOYA 2/04) [810.9]

9448 Hintz, Martin. *Farewell, John Barleycorn: Prohibition in the United States* (6–10). Illus. Series: People's History. 1996, Lerner LB $25.26 (978-0-8225-1734-4). A well-organized, readable account that traces the history of alcohol use in the United States, covers the 18th Amendment and its effects, and ends with repeal of Prohibition. (Rev: BL 8/96; SLJ 10/96) [363.4]

9449 Hoffman, Nancy. *Eleanor Roosevelt and the Arthurdale Experiment* (5–8). Illus. 2001, Linnet LB $22.50 (978-0-208-02504-3). Hoffman includes quotations and black-and-white photographs in her account of the story of Arthurdale, a government-planned community of the 1930s. (Rev: BL 10/15/01; HBG 3/02; SLJ 12/01) [975.4]

9450 Katz, William L. *The New Freedom to the New Deal: 1913–1939* (7–9). Series: History of Multicultural America. 1993, Raintree LB $27.11 (978-0-8114-6279-2). An examination from a multicultural perspective of events inside the U.S. from World War I through the beginning of World War II. (Rev: BL 9/1/93) [973.91]

9451 Lawson, Don. *FDR's New Deal* (7–9). 1979, HarperCollins $12.95 (978-0-690-03953-5). The story of how President Roosevelt's policies helped this country out of the Great Depression. [973.91]

9452 McArthur, Debra. *The Dust Bowl and the Depression* (6–10). Series: In American History. 2002, Enslow LB $26.60 (978-0-7660-1838-9). A well-researched and well-documented account of the Great Depression in the Midwest, the plight of the farmers, and the lasting effects. (Rev: BL 5/15/02; HBG 10/02; SLJ 7/02) [973.91]

9453 Meltzer, Milton. *Driven from the Land: The Story of the Dust Bowl* (4–8). Series: Great Journeys. 1999, Benchmark LB $32.79 (978-0-7614-0968-7). Traces the development of the Dust Bowl, its effects on the land and the people, and how many were forced to leave their farms and seek a new life elsewhere. (Rev: BL 1/1–15/00; HBG 3/00; SLJ 2/00) [973.9]

9454 Nardo, Don, ed. *The Great Depression* (7–12). Series: Turning Points in World History. 2000, Greenhaven LB $32.45 (978-0-7377-0231-6). After a general overview of the Great Depression, this collection of informative essays and eyewitness accounts explores various aspects of this bleak period. (Rev: BL 5/15/00; SLJ 3/00) [338]

9455 Nishi, Dennis, ed. *The Great Depression* (6–12). Illus. Series: History Firsthand. 2001, Greenhaven paper $21.20 (978-0-7377-0410-5). More than 20 first-person accounts introduce readers to life during the Depression — on Wall Street, among the unemployed and the homeless, and the New Deal efforts of President Roosevelt. (Rev: BL 5/15/01) [338.5]

9456 Ross, Stewart. *Causes and Consequences of the Great Depression* (7–10). Series: Causes and Consequences. 1998, Raintree LB $29.97 (978-0-8172-4059-2). A thorough analysis that uses illustrations including cartoons, posters, photographs, and statistical charts as well as quotations from historians and world leaders. (Rev: BL 8/98; SLJ 6/98; VOYA 2/99) [338.542]

9457 Ruggiero, Adriane. *The Great Depression* (6–9). Illus. Series: American Voices From. 2004, Benchmark LB $34.21 (978-0-7614-1696-8). Primary source documents and excellent illustrations are accompanied by good introductory text and "Think about This" questions. (Rev: SLJ 2/05) [973]

9458 Ruth, Amy. *Growing Up in the Great Depression* (5–8). Series: Our America. 2002, Lerner LB $26.60 (978-0-8225-0655-3). With many sidebars and quotations from original sources, this narrative re-creates the despair and courage of children growing up during the Great Depression. (Rev: BL 2/15/03; HBG 3/03) [973.9]

9459 Swisher, Clarice. *Women of the Roaring Twenties* (6–10). Illus. Series: Women in History. 2005, Gale LB $22.96 (978-1-59017-363-3). Using primary sources, this readable volume looks at life for women from diverse backgrounds during the turbulent 1920s. (Rev: BL 2/15/06) [305.4]

9460 Woog, Adam. *Roosevelt and the New Deal* (7–10). Illus. Series: World History. 1997, Lucent LB $32.45 (978-1-56006-324-7). With double-page spreads, sidebars, political cartoons, photographs, reproductions, and first-person accounts, this book discusses Roosevelt's efforts to end the Great Depression through the New Deal and looks at its impact on the nation. (Rev: SLJ 8/98) [973.9]

9461 Wroble, Lisa A. *The New Deal and the Great Depression in American History* (5–8). Series: In American History. 2002, Enslow LB $26.60 (978-0-7660-1421-3). A timeline, maps, chapter notes, and research topics are found in this well-researched account that concentrates on Roosevelt's economic policies during the 1930s. (Rev: BL 1/1–15/03; HBG 3/03) [973.9]

9462 Yancey, Diane. *Life During the Dust Bowl* (7–12). Illus. Series: The Way People Live. 2004, Gale LB $29.95 (978-1-59018-265-9). Black-and-white photographs and excerpts from oral histories add to the narrative overview to paint a vivid portrait of the devastation caused by the Great Plains dust storms of the 1930s. (Rev: BL 8/04; SLJ 8/04) [978]

WORLD WAR II

9463 Alonso, Karen. *Korematsu v. United States: Japanese-American Internment Camps* (7–12). Illus. Series: Landmark Supreme Court Cases. 1998, Enslow LB $26.60 (978-0-89490-966-5). This book discusses the Japanese American internments during World War II and focuses on Fred Korematsu's case challenging the government's right to remove him from his home and imprison him simply because he was a Japanese American. (Rev: BL 5/1/98; SLJ 8/98; VOYA 2/99) [323.1]

9464 Bernstein, Mark, and Alex Lubertozzi. *World War II on the Air: Hear Edward R. Murrow and the Voices That Carried the War Home* (8–12). 2003, Sourcebooks $29.95 (978-1-4022-0026-7). Murrow and other radio greats of the war are featured in this book-and-audio-CD set. (Rev: BL 5/1/03; SLJ 6/03)

9465 Brinkley, Douglas, ed. *The World War II Memorial: A Grateful Nation Remembers* (8–12). Illus. 2004, Smithsonian $39.95 (978-1-58834-210-2). Published in conjunction with the dedication of the World War II Memorial in Washington, D.C., this striking coffee table book is loaded with photos and remembrances of the war and its lasting impact on America. (Rev: BL 9/1/04) [940.54]

9466 Cooper, Michael L. *Fighting for Honor: Japanese Americans and World War II* (6–12). Illus. 2000, Clarion $18.00 (978-0-395-91375-8). The experiences of Japanese Americans who were sent to internment camps or faced anti-Asian attacks in their communities are well-documented here. (Rev: BCCB 2/01; BL 1/1–15/01; HB 3–4/01; HBG 10/01; SLJ 3/01) [940.53]

9467 Cooper, Michael L. *Remembering Manzanar: Life in a Japanese Relocation Camp* (4–8). Illus. 2002, Clarion $15.00 (978-0-618-06778-7). This evocative account of life in a Japanese American World War II internment center tells its tale through personal accounts of survivors, quotations from the camp newspaper, and revealing photographs. (Rev: BL 1/1–15/03; HBG 10/03; SLJ 2/03) [940.54]

9468 Dudley, William, ed. *Japanese American Internment Camps* (7–12). Series: At Issue in History. 2002, Gale LB $27.45 (978-0-7377-0821-9). Primary texts revealing different attitudes toward the internment of Japanese Americans are introduced by statements explaining the historical context. (Rev: SLJ 3/02) [940.53]

9469 Fremon, David K. *Japanese-American Internment in American History* (7–10). Illus. Series: In American History. 1996, Enslow LB $26.60 (978-0-89490-767-8). Drawing on a wide range of personal narratives, the author re-creates the shameful period during World War II when Japanese Americans were forcibly evacuated to internment camps. (Rev: BL 1/1–15/97; SLJ 6/97; VOYA 12/96) [940.53]

9470 Grapes, Bryan J., ed. *Japanese American Internment Camps* (6–12). Series: History Firsthand. 2000, Greenhaven LB $32.45 (978-0-7377-0413-6). Essays, speeches, and firsthand accounts tell the story of the relocation of Japanese Americans during World War II. (Rev: BL 3/1/01; SLJ 4/01) [940.53]

9471 Hasday, Judy L. *The Tuskegee Airmen* (7–12). Series: American Mosaic. 2003, Chelsea LB $30.00 (978-0-7910-7267-7). During World War II, few could match the obstacles and accomplishments of the Tuskegee Airmen, a group of African American pilots. (Rev: BL 10/15/03; HBG 10/03) [940.54]

9472 Josephson, Judith Pinkerton. *Growing Up in World War II* (5–8). Illus. Series: Our America. 2002, Lerner LB $26.60 (978-0-8225-0660-7). A look at the lives of American children of different backgrounds and situations during World War II. (Rev: BL 2/1/03; HBG 3/03) [940.533]

9473 Kallen, Stuart A. *The War at Home* (6–12). Illus. 1999, Lucent LB $27.45 (978-1-56006-531-9). This book describes conditions within the United States during World War II and covers such topics as daily life, the changing workplace and workforce, civil defense, and racial discrimination. (Rev: BL 1/1–15/00; HBG 9/00; SLJ 2/00) [940.53]

9474 Komatsu, Kimberly, and Kaleigh Komatsu. *In America's Shadow* (5–8). Illus. 2003, Thomas George $35.00 (978-0-9709829-0-2). This account of the internment of Japanese Americans during World War II draws on the memories and archives of the authors' family. (Rev: BL 4/1/03) [940.531]

9475 Nicholson, Dorinda M. *Pearl Harbor Child: A Child's View of Pearl Harbor — from Attack to Peace* (5–8). 1998, Woodson House paper $9.95 (978-1-892858-00-9). This photoessay describes a child's experience during the bombing of Pearl Harbor, the temporary evacuation, and everyday life growing up in Hawaii during World War II. (Rev: BL 1/1–15/99) [996.9]

9476 Nobleman, Marc Tyler. *The Sinking of the USS Indianapolis* (4–7). Series: We the People. 2006, Compass Point LB $26.60 (978-0-7565-2031-1). The story of the sinking of the *USS Indianapolis*, two weeks before the end of World War II, is told in straightforward text, with photographs and useful "Did You Know?" features. (Rev: SLJ 1/07)

9477 Perl, Lila. *Behind Barbed Wire: The Story of Japanese-American Internment During World War II* (6–9). Series: Great Journeys. 2002, Marshall Cavendish LB $32.79 (978-0-7614-1321-9). The story of the causes, events, and effects related to the internment of many Japanese Americans during World War II. (Rev: BL 3/15/03; HBG 3/03) [940.5472]

9478 Ruggiero, Adriane. *World War II* (6–9). Series: American Voices From. 2002, Benchmark LB $34.21 (978-0-7614-1206-9). Excerpts from primary documents including letters, newspaper articles, speeches, and journals present a variety of different experiences of those who lived through World War II. (Rev: HBG 10/03; SLJ 3/03) [940.53]

9479 Schomp, Virginia. *World War II* (5–8). Illus. Series: Letters from the Homefront. 2001, Marshall Cavendish LB $29.93 (978-0-7614-1098-0). Schomp uses letters written during World War II, accompanied by relevant illustrations, to give readers a real understanding of the difficulties of life on the homefront. (Rev: BL 10/15/01; HBG 3/02) [940.54]

9480 Stein, R. Conrad. *The World War II D-Day Invasion* (7–10). Series: In American History. 2004, Enslow LB $26.60 (978-0-7660-2136-5). This great landing in Normandy is re-created in pictures and text. (Rev: BL 3/15/04; SLJ 3/04) [940.54]

9481 Streissguth, Thomas, ed. *The Attack on Pearl Harbor* (7–10). Series: At Issue in History. 2002, Gale paper $18.70 (978-0-7377-0751-9). Primary sources present opposing views on the attack and on who was responsible for the lack of preparation for such a possibility. (Rev: SLJ 7/02) [940.54]

9482 Tunnell, Michael O., and George W. Chilcoat. *The Children of Topaz: The Story of a Japanese-American Internment Camp Based on a Classroom*

Diary (6–10). Illus. 1996, Holiday $19.95 (978-0-8234-1239-6). This book consists of 20 excerpts from a classroom diary kept by a 3rd-grade Japanese American schoolteacher during her confinement in a desert relocation camp during 1943. (Rev: BL 7/96; SLJ 8/96*; VOYA 12/96) [769.8]

9483 Whitman, Sylvia. *V Is for Victory: The American Home Front During World War II* (4–7). Illus. 1993, Lerner LB $30.35 (978-0-8225-1727-6). Rosie the Riveter, ration stamps, and the relocation of Japanese Americans are among the topics covered in this look at the United States in another time. (Rev: BL 2/15/93) [973.9]

POST WORLD WAR II UNITED STATES
(1945–)

9484 Alonso, Karen. *The Chicago Seven Political Protest Trial* (6–10). Series: Headline Court Cases. 2002, Enslow LB $26.60 (978-0-7660-1764-1). This is an account of the trial of the Chicago Seven, a group that was arrested during a demonstration at the Democratic National Convention in Chicago. (Rev: BL 3/15/03; HBG 10/03) [973.92]

9485 Anderson, Dale. *America into a New Millennium* (5–8). Series: Making of America. 2001, Raintree LB $28.54 (978-0-8172-5712-5). This last part of a 12-volume series presents American history from the end of the Cold War to the beginning of the 21st century. (Rev: BL 9/15/01; HBG 10/01; SLJ 6/01) [973.9]

9486 Anderson, Dale. *The Cold War Years* (5–8). Series: Making of America. 2001, Raintree LB $28.54 (978-0-8172-5711-8). A concise, easy-to-understand text tells America's story from the end of World War II to the 1990s. (Rev: BL 9/15/01; HBG 10/01; SLJ 6/01) [973.9]

9487 Archer, Jules. *The Incredible Sixties: The Stormy Years That Changed America* (7–12). 1986, Harcourt $17.95 (978-0-15-238298-8). A topically arranged overview of the events, trends, and significance of the 1960s and how they have shaped our future. (Rev: BL 5/15/86; SLJ 9/86; VOYA 4/87) [973.922]

9488 Aretha, David. *Freedom Summer* (7–12). Illus. Series: The Civil Rights Movement. 2007, Morgan Reynolds LB $27.95 (978-1-59935-059-2). The summer of 1964, when white college students traveled to Mississippi to help blacks register to vote, is the focus of this volume in the Civil Rights Movement series. (Rev: BL 2/1/08; SLJ 3/08) [323.1196]

9489 Baker, Patricia. *Fashions of a Decade: The 1950s* (7–12). Series: Fashions of a Decade. 1991, Facts on File $25.00 (978-0-8160-2468-1). An illustrated overview of fashions of the 1950s and the political, economic, and social developments of the time. (Rev: BL 12/15/91; SLJ 2/92) [391]

9490 Brown, Gene. *The Nation in Turmoil: Civil Rights and the Vietnam War (1960–1973)* (5–8). Series: First Person America. 1994, Twenty-First Century LB $20.90 (978-0-8050-2588-0). An overview of the civil rights movement and the Vietnam War, highlighting excerpts from letters, diaries, and speeches. (Rev: BL 5/15/94) [973.92]

9491 Brown, Gene. *The 1992 Election* (5–8). Illus. Series: Headliners. 1993, Millbrook LB $25.90 (978-1-56294-080-5). This book presents the issues and highlights of the campaigns and presidential election. (Rev: BL 4/1/93; SLJ 7/93) [973.9]

9492 Ching, Jacqueline. *The Assassination of Martin Luther King, Jr.* (6–10). Series: The Library of Political Assassinations. 2002, Rosen LB $27.95 (978-0-8239-3543-7). A look at the life and death of Martin Luther King, Jr., and his legacy. (Rev: BL 8/02; SLJ 8/02) [976]

9493 Ching, Juliet. *The Assassination of Robert F. Kennedy* (6–10). Series: The Library of Political Assassinations. 2002, Rosen LB $27.95 (978-0-8239-3545-1). In addition to discussing the assassination and the events preceding it, the author looks at the rumors of a conspiracy and allegations of incompetence on the part of the Los Angeles police force. (Rev: BL 8/02; SLJ 8/02) [976]

9494 Cunningham, Jesse G., ed. *The McCarthy Hearings* (8–12). Series: At Issue in History. 2003, Gale paper $18.70 (978-0-7377-1347-3). An objective look at the activities of the senator from Wisconsin that gives clear historical context. (Rev: SLJ 4/03) [973.921]

9495 Dolan, Sean. *Pursuing the Dream: From the Selma-Montgomery March to the Formation of PUSH (1965–1971)* (7–10). Illus. Series: Milestones in Black American History. 1995, Chelsea LB $19.95 (978-0-7910-2254-2); paper $8.95 (978-0-7910-2680-9). This chronicle of the civil rights movement of the 1960s describes the demonstrations and confrontations and gives background information on participation of African Americans in sports and the arts. (Rev: BL 7/95) [323.1]

9496 Draper, Allison Stark. *The Assassination of Malcolm X* (6–10). Series: The Library of Political Assassinations. 2002, Rosen LB $27.95 (978-0-8239-3542-0). A description of the assassination and its aftermath is followed by information on Malcolm X's life and beliefs. (Rev: BL 2/15/02; SLJ 7/02) [976.2]

9497 Epstein, Dan. *The 80s: The Decade of Plenty* (7–10). Series: 20th Century Pop Culture. 2000, Chelsea LB $22.95 (978-0-7910-6088-9). A mix of popular entertainment and fashion with key news events, all arranged chronologically and accompanied by lots of color photographs. Other books in the series include *The 50s: America Tunes In* and

The 60s: A Decade of Change: The Flintstones to Woodstock. (Rev: SLJ 6/01) [973.9]

9498 Feinstein, Stephen. *The 1980s: From Ronald Reagan to MTV* (4–7). Series: Decades of the 20th Century. 2000, Enslow LB $22.60 (978-0-7660-1424-4). Presents the decade's major events, important people, and developments in such areas as politics, science, the arts, and sports. (Rev: BL 10/15/00; HBG 10/00; SLJ 12/00) [973.9]

9499 Feinstein, Stephen. *The 1950s: From the Korean War to Elvis* (6–9). Illus. Series: Decades of the 20th Century in Color. 2006, Enslow LB $27.93 (978-0-7660-2635-3). Ample illustrations and a useful timeline make this an appealing reference to the events — cultural, scientific, and sporting — of the 1950s. (Rev: BL 4/1/06) [973.92]

9500 Finkelstein, Norman H. *Thirteen Days / Ninety Miles: The Cuban Missile Crisis* (8–12). 1994, Messner LB $18.95 (978-0-671-86622-8). Declassified materials, letters, and memoirs describe the tension-filled Cuban missile crisis, documenting the actions and ideologies of Kennedy and Khrushchev and revealing how narrowly nuclear war was averted. (Rev: BL 7/94*; SLJ 6/94) [973.992]

9501 Fitzgerald, Brian. *McCarthyism: The Red Scare* (7–12). Series: Snapshots in History. 2006, Compass Point LB $31.93 (978-0-7565-2007-6). This is a clear account of the period of anti-Communism in the United States stirred up by Senator Joseph McCarthy, including the impact on the lives of individuals around the country plus quotations from the Army-McCarthy hearings. (Rev: SLJ 2/07)

9502 Fremon, David K. *The Watergate Scandal in American History* (7–10). Series: In American History. 1997, Enslow LB $26.60 (978-0-89490-883-5). A clear, logically arranged, and objective account of the famous political scandal that ended the Nixon presidency. (Rev: BL 4/15/98; SLJ 5/98) [973.9]

9503 Gard, Carolyn. *The Attack on the Pentagon on September 11, 2001* (4–8). Series: Terrorist Attacks. 2003, Rosen LB $27.95 (978-0-8239-3858-2). In addition to describing the attack itself, Gard looks at the organization of Al-Qaeda. (Rev: SLJ 2/04) [975.5]

9504 Hampton, Wilborn. *Kennedy Assassinated! The World Mourns* (5–8). Illus. 1997, Candlewick $17.99 (978-1-56402-811-2). A gripping first-person account of John Kennedy's assassination by a veteran newspaper reporter who was in Dallas that day. (Rev: BL 9/15/97; HBG 3/98; SLJ 10/97) [364.1]

9505 Herda, D. J. *United States v. Nixon: Watergate and the President* (6–10). Illus. Series: Landmark Supreme Court Cases. 1996, Enslow LB $20.95 (978-0-89490-753-1). The Watergate scandal is reviewed with special emphasis on the legal aspects

of this case that brought down the presidency of Richard Nixon. (Rev: BL 8/96; SLJ 7/96) [342.73]

9506 Hull, Mary. *Struggle and Love, 1972–1997* (7–10). Illus. Series: Milestones in Black American History. 1996, Chelsea LB $21.95 (978-0-7910-2262-7); paper $9.95 (978-0-7910-2688-5). This book covers the past quarter of a century in African American history, highlighting the lives and careers of prominent individuals including Jesse Jackson, Colin Powell, and Michael Jordan. (Rev: BL 3/15/97; SLJ 6/97) [973]

9507 Isaacs, Sally Senzell. *America in the Time of Martin Luther King Jr.: The Story of Our Nation from Coast to Coast, from 1948 to 1976* (4–8). Series: America in the Time Of. 1999, Heinemann LB $30.35 (978-1-57572-780-6). As well as describing the accomplishment of Martin Luther King, Jr., this account traces important developments during his time including the 1960s peace movement, the Vietnam War, space travel, and the Watergate scandal. (Rev: SLJ 5/00) [973.9]

9508 Johnson, Darv. *The Reagan Years* (7–10). Series: World History. 2000, Lucent LB $27.45 (978-1-56006-592-0). This account of the two-term president focuses on conservatism, his economic agenda, and relations with the Soviet Union, the Middle East, and Central America. (Rev: BL 6/1–15/00; HBG 9/00; SLJ 9/00) [973.9]

9509 Kallen, Stuart A. *Life in America During the 1960s* (6–10). Series: The Way People Live. 2001, Lucent LB $28.70 (978-1-56006-790-0). Using as a backdrop the presidencies of Kennedy and Johnson, the civil rights movement and the Vietnam War, this work focuses in pictures and text on the daily life of Americans in this difficult period. (Rev: BL 6/1–15/01) [973.9]

9510 Katz, William L. *The Great Society to the Reagan Era: 1964–1990* (7–9). Series: History of Multicultural America. 1993, Raintree LB $27.11 (978-0-8114-6282-2). A history of race relations in the United States that covers the struggles, gains, and setbacks from the mid-1960s to 1990, spanning the Johnson, Nixon, Carter, and Reagan administrations. (Rev: BL 9/1/93) [973.92]

9511 Landsman, Susan. *Who Shot JFK?* (6–8). Series: History Mystery. 1992, Avon paper $3.50 (978-0-380-77063-2). A look at the controversial subject of JFK's assassination, examining the maze of theories, charges, and countercharges. (Rev: BL 4/1/93) [364.1]

9512 Lindop, Edmund. *America in the 1950s* (6–10). Illus. 2002, Millbrook LB $25.90 (978-0-7613-2551-2). Lindop looks at the lighter sides of life in the 1950s — including the influence of TV on popular culture, the move to the suburbs, and sports — as well as the political and social upheavals of the Korean War, the Cold War, McCarthyism, and desegregation. (Rev: BL 9/1/02; HBG 3/03; SLJ 10/02) [973.921]

9513 Maus, Derek C., ed. *Living Through the Red Scare* (8–12). Series: Living Through the Cold War . 2005, Gale LB $32.45 (978-0-7377-2615-2). This fascinating collection of readings revisits the fear of communism that was rampant in the United States at the beginning of the Cold War. (Rev: SLJ 6/06)

9514 Maus, Derek C., ed. *Living Under the Threat of Nuclear War* (7–10). Series: Living Through the Cold War. 2005, Gale LB $33.70 (978-0-7377-2130-0). This title examines how Americans coped with the ever-present threat of nuclear war during the half-century-long Cold War. (Rev: SLJ 10/05) [973]

9515 Morris, Jeffrey. *The Reagan Way* (6–9). Series: Great Presidential Decisions. 1996, Lerner LB $23.93 (978-0-8225-2931-6). By examining Reagan's major presidential decisions, the author presents an even-handed look at Reagan's strengths and weaknesses. (Rev: SLJ 2/96) [973.9]

9516 Ribeiro, Myra. *The Assassination of Medgar Evers* (6–10). Series: The Library of Political Assassinations. 2002, Rosen LB $27.95 (978-0-8239-3544-4). A description of the assassination and its aftermath is followed by information on Evers's life and beliefs. (Rev: BL 2/15/02; SLJ 7/02) [976]

9517 Schlesinger, Arthur M., Jr., ed. *The Election of 1948 and the Administration of Harry S. Truman* (8–12). Series: Major Presidential Elections and the Administrations That Followed. 2003, Mason Crest LB $24.95 (978-1-59084-360-4). A good source of speeches, quotations, and excerpts from public documents, with commentary, illustrations, and further reading. Also use *The Election of 1912 and the Administration of Woodrow Wilson* and *The Election of 1960 and the Administration of John F. Kennedy* (both 2003). (Rev: SLJ 1/04) [973]

9518 Schmidt, Mark Ray, ed. *The 1970s* (6–12). Series: America's Decades. 2000, Greenhaven paper $27.45 (978-0-7377-0307-8). This anthology contains articles on topics including environmental and energy issues, racial integration, the Watergate scandal, and interracial conflicts. (Rev: BL 7/00; SLJ 7/00) [973.9]

9519 Steins, Richard. *The Postwar Years: The Cold War and the Atomic Age (1950–1959)* (5–8). Series: First Person America. 1994, Twenty-First Century LB $20.90 (978-0-8050-2587-3). Coverage of the 1950s includes first-person material on the Cold War and the Korean conflict. (Rev: BL 5/15/94; SLJ 12/94) [973.92]

9520 Tracy, Kathleen. *The Watergate Scandal* (6–9). Series: Monumental Milestones: Great Events of Modern Times. 2006, Mitchell Lane LB $19.95 (978-1-58415-470-9). The complexity of the

Watergate affair will restrict this account to the strongest readers. (Rev: SLJ 11/06)

9521 Walsh, Frank. *The Montgomery Bus Boycott* (5–8). Series: Landmark Events in American History. 2003, World Almanac LB $31.00 (978-0-8368-5375-9). The story of what happened when Rosa Parks refused to give up her seat on a Montgomery, Alabama, bus in 1955. (Rev: BL 10/15/03; SLJ 9/03) [305.8]

9522 Zeinert, Karen. *McCarthy and the Fear of Communism* (7–10). Series: In American History. 1998, Enslow LB $26.60 (978-0-89490-987-0). The story of the reign of terror inflicted on America during the 1950s by the senator from Wisconsin. (Rev: BL 8/98; HBG 9/99; SLJ 12/98) [973.9]

KOREAN, VIETNAM, AND GULF WARS

9523 Al-Windawi, Thura. *Thura's Diary: My Life in Wartime Iraq* (6–12). 2004, Viking $15.99 (978-0-670-05886-0). This diary was kept by a 19-year-old girl in Baghdad from the first bombings to the first days of the occupation by American forces. (Rev: BL 5/15/04; HB 7–8/04; SLJ 7/04) [956]

9524 Canwell, Diane, and Jon Sutherland. *African Americans in the Vietnam War* (5–8). Illus. Series: American Experience in Vietnam. 2005, World Almanac LB $31.00 (978-0-8368-5772-6). Personal stories and full-color photographs add to the information on black Americans' contributions to the conflict and the military's efforts toward integration. Also use *American Women in the Vietnam War* (2005). (Rev: BL 2/1/05) [959.705]

9525 Caputo, Philip. *10,000 Days of Thunder: A History of the Vietnam War* (7–10). Illus. 2005, Simon & Schuster $22.95 (978-0-689-86231-1). In this sweeping overview of the Vietnam War, Caputo traces the fractured country's history from the beginnings of resistance to French colonial rule to the fall of Saigon and also assesses the conflict's enduring impact on Americans. (Rev: BL 10/1/05; SLJ 11/05*; VOYA 10/05) [959.704]

9526 Carter, E. J. *The Cuban Missile Crisis* (4–8). Series: 20th Century Perspectives. 2003, Heinemann LB $27.07 (978-1-4034-3806-5). A review of the 1962 crisis in which Cuba secretly installed missiles capable of carrying nuclear warheads. (Rev: SLJ 5/04) [972.9]

9527 Feldman, Ruth Tenzer. *The Korean War* (6–12). Illus. Series: Chronicle of America's Wars. 2003, Lerner LB $27.93 (978-0-8225-4716-7). Explores events before, during, and after the Korean War and introduces the key individuals involved. (Rev: BL 4/1/04) [951.904]

9528 Freedman, Suzanne. *Clay v. United States: Muhammad Ali Objects to War* (6–10). Series: Landmark Supreme Court Cases. 1997, Enslow LB

$26.60 (978-0-89490-855-2). A thorough examination of Muhammad Ali's court case involving the Vietnam War. (Rev: BL 10/15/97; HBG 3/98; SLJ 12/97) [959.704]

9529 Galt, Margot Fortunato. *Stop This War! American Protest of the Conflict in Vietnam* (8–12). Series: People's History. 2000, Lerner LB $26.60 (978-0-8225-1740-5). The author cites her husband, a conscientious objector, among those who protested the war from the early 1960s until its end, and details key events and student and other groups. (Rev: BL 7/00; HBG 9/00; SLJ 8/00) [959.704]

9530 Granfield, Linda. *I Remember Korea: Veterans Tell Their Stories of the Korean War, 1950–53* (6–12). Illus. 2003, Clarion $16.00 (978-0-618-17740-0). First-person accounts by American combatants that reveal a wide variety of experiences are accompanied by brief introductory notes, photographs, and a short account of the war itself. (Rev: BCCB 2/04; BL 12/15/03; HBG 4/04; SLJ 2/04) [951.904]

9531 Kallen, Stuart A. *The Home Front: Americans Protest the War* (6–12). Series: American War Library: The Vietnam War. 2000, Lucent LB $29.95 (978-1-56006-718-4). Campus protests against the war, peace marches, the burning of draft cards, and Woodstock are among the topics covered in this informative volume. (Rev: BL 3/1/01; SLJ 4/01) [959.704]

9532 Kent, Deborah. *The Vietnam War: "What Are We Fighting For?"* (5–7). Illus. Series: American War. 1994, Enslow LB $26.60 (978-0-89490-527-8). An objective overview of this war, its causes, progression, and results. (Rev: BL 10/15/94; SLJ 11/94) [959.704]

9533 Koestler-Grack, Rachel A. *The Kent State Tragedy* (4–7). Illus. Series: American Moments. 2005, ABDO LB $25.65 (978-1-59197-934-0). A concise overview of the deadly 1970 clash between National Guard troops and war protesters on the campus of Ohio's Kent State University. (Rev: BL 9/1/05; SLJ 11/05) [378.771]

9534 McCloud, Bill. *What Should We Tell Our Children About Vietnam?* (7–12). 1989, Univ. of Oklahoma paper $16.95 (978-0-8061-3240-2). More than 120 individuals, including the first President Bush and Gary Trudeau, tell what they think young people should know about the war. (Rev: BL 9/15/89) [959.704]

9535 McCormick, Anita Louise. *The Vietnam Antiwar Movement* (6–12). Illus. Series: In American History. 2000, Enslow LB $26.60 (978-0-7660-1295-0). Historical photographs and clear prose are used in this account of the many anti-Vietnam War protests in the United States and their effect on the course of history. (Rev: BL 1/1–15/00; HBG 9/00; SLJ 4/00) [959.704]

9536 Mason, Andrew. *The Vietnam War: A Primary Source History* (5–8). Illus. Series: In Their Own Words. 2005, Gareth Stevens LB $27.00 (978-0-8368-5981-2). Primary sources — including letters, articles, speeches, and songs — deliver the views of combatants in Vietnam and people on the home front in this well-illustrated volume. (Rev: BL 10/15/05) [959.704]

9537 Murray, Stuart. *Vietnam War* (6–9). Illus. Series: Eyewitness Books. 2005, DK LB $19.99 (978-0-7566-1165-1). This photo-filled volume introduces the key events, figures, armaments, and political and social issues of the Vietnam War. (Rev: BL 9/1/05) [959.704]

9538 O'Connell, Kim A. *Primary Source Accounts of the Vietnam War* (6–9). Series: America's Wars Through Primary Sources. 2006, Enslow LB $24.95 (978-1-59845-001-9). Learn about the Vietnam War from the perspective of soldiers (American and Vietnamese), nurses, and Vietnamese civilians through diaries, letters, songs, and other documents. (Rev: BL 10/15/06) [959.704]

9539 Pendergast, Tom. *The Vietnam War* (7–10). Series: Defining Moments. 2006, Omnigraphics LB $44.00 (978-0-7808-0954-3). Ten years of the conflict's history are covered in detail and copious background information is provided to help report writers. (Rev: BL 3/15/07) [959.704]

9540 Richie, Jason. *Iraq and the Fall of Saddam Hussein.* Rev. ed. (8–10). Illus. 2004, Oliver LB $24.95 (978-1-881508-63-2). This account traces the story of the invasion of Iraq and ends with the capture of Saddam Hussein in December 2003. (Rev: BL 5/1/04; HBG 4/04; SLJ 1/04) [956.7]

9541 Santella, Andrew. *The Korean War* (4–7). Series: We the People. 2006, Compass Point LB $26.60 (978-0-7565-2027-4). A brief overview of the roots and progress of the conflict between the two parts of a divided nation. (Rev: SLJ 1/07) [951.904]

9542 Schomp, Virginia. *The Vietnam War* (5–8). Series: Letters from the Homefront. 2001, Benchmark LB $29.93 (978-0-7614-1099-7). Conditions on the home front during the Vietnam War are re-created through primary documents such as letters and period photographs. (Rev: BL 10/15/01; HBG 3/02; SLJ 3/02) [973.9]

9543 Zeinert, Karen. *The Valiant Women of the Vietnam War* (5–8). Illus. 2000, Millbrook LB $29.90 (978-0-7613-1268-0). Provides a good overview of the Vietnam War and highlights the contributions of women at home and abroad during this conflict. (Rev: BL 4/1/00; HBG 10/00; SLJ 5/00) [959.704]

Regions

MIDWEST

9544 Anderson, Reuben. *Uniquely Oklahoma* (4–7). Illus. Series: Heinemann State Studies. 2004, Heinemann LB $27.07 (978-1-4034-4658-9). In addition to providing the facts necessary for report writers, this volume emphasizes the features that distinguish Oklahoma from its neighbors. (Rev: BL 10/15/03)

9545 Anderson, Reuben. *Uniquely South Dakota* (4–7). Illus. Series: Heinemann State Studies. 2004, Heinemann LB $31.36 (978-1-4034-4662-6). In addition to providing the facts necessary for report writers, this volume emphasizes the features that distinguish South Dakota from its neighbors. (Rev: BL 10/15/03)

9546 Ash, Stephanie. *Uniquely Minnesota* (4–7). Series: Heinemann State Studies. 2004, Heinemann LB $27.07 (978-1-4034-4494-3). In addition to providing the facts necessary for report writers, this volume emphasizes the features that distinguish Minnesota from its neighbors. (Rev: BL 4/1/04)

9547 Aylesworth, Thomas G., and Virginia L. Aylesworth. *Eastern Great Lakes: Indiana, Michigan, Ohio* (4–7). Illus. Series: State Reports. 1995, Chelsea $19.95 (978-0-7910-3409-5). Information is given for each of the three states covered, including major cities, history, geography, and climate. (Rev: BL 3/15/92) [977]

9548 Balcavage, Dynise. *Iowa* (5–8). Illus. Series: From Sea to Shining Sea, Second Series. 2002, Children's LB $30.50 (978-0-516-22481-7). An attractive overview of Iowa's land, history, culture, economy, and people. (Rev: SLJ 3/03) [977.7]

9549 Baldwin, Guy. *Oklahoma* (4–8). Series: Celebrate the States. 2000, Marshall Cavendish LB $148.29 (978-0-7614-1061-4). The beauties and hidden treasures of Oklahoma are covered in this colorful introduction to the state, its past, its present, and its people. (Rev: BL 12/15/00) [976.6]

9550 Bennett, Michelle. *Missouri* (4–8). Series: Celebrate the States. 2001, Benchmark LB $37.07 (978-0-7614-1063-8). A logically organized, thorough introduction to Missouri with material on such topics as history, people, landmarks, and famous natives. (Rev: BL 9/15/01; HBG 10/01) [977.8]

9551 Bial, Raymond. *Nauvoo: Mormon City on the Mississippi River* (4–7). Illus. 2006, Houghton $17.00 (978-0-618-39685-6). This richly illustrated title profiles the Illinois city of Nauvoo and the important role it played in the history of the Church of Jesus Christ of Latter-day Saints. (Rev: BL 11/1/06; SLJ 12/06) [289.3]

9552 Bjorklund, Ruth. *Kansas* (4–8). Series: Celebrate the States. 2000, Marshall Cavendish LB $37.07 (978-0-7614-0646-4). A broad introduction

to Kansas — its geography and history, its government and people, its songs and folktales, and a few of its recipes. (Rev: BL 6/1–15/00; HBG 10/00) [978.1]

9553 Brill, Marlene T. *Illinois* (4–8). Illus. Series: Celebrate the States. 1996, Marshall Cavendish LB $37.07 (978-0-7614-0113-1). Maps, diagrams, and photographs enliven this introduction to Illinois that gives good coverage of history, geography, and social conditions. (Rev: BL 2/1/97; SLJ 2/97) [913.73]

9554 Brill, Marlene T. *Indiana* (4–8). Illus. Series: Celebrate the States. 1997, Marshall Cavendish LB $37.07 (978-0-7614-0147-6). An introduction to this Midwest state's agriculture, industries, famous natives, history, and geography. (Rev: BL 7/97; SLJ 8/97) [977.2]

9555 Brill, Marlene Targ. *Illinois* (4–7). Illus. Series: Celebrate the States. 2005, Benchmark LB $37.07 (978-0-7614-1735-4). A revised edition of this introduction to the state — including its history, culture, famous sites, and important individuals — with updated illustrations. (Rev: SLJ 5/06) [913.73]

9556 Burgan, Michael. *Illinois* (5–8). Illus. Series: America the Beautiful: Third Series. 2007, Children's Pr. LB $38.00 (978-0-531-18559-9). This new edition of the classic series entry about the state features a new design and layout, definitions of difficult words in the margins, more history and mini biographies, and project ideas in writing, art, and science. (Rev: BL 2/1/08) [8. 977.3]

9557 Carlson, Jeffrey D. *A Historical Album of Minnesota* (5–8). Illus. Series: Historical Albums. 1993, Millbrook LB $24.40 (978-1-56294-006-5). A heavily illustrated volume that traces the history of Minnesota from Native American communities through exploration and settlement to present-day concerns. (Rev: SLJ 10/93) [977.6]

9558 Dornfeld, Margaret. *Wisconsin* (4–7). Series: It's My State! 2003, Marshall Cavendish LB $27.07 (978-0-7614-1524-4). Using many quotations from various sources, this account supplies a basic introduction to Wisconsin, its people, and its past and present. (Rev: BL 9/15/03; HBG 4/04; SLJ 11/03) [977.5]

9559 Edge, Laura B. *A Personal Tour of Hull-House* (4–7). Series: How It Was. 2001, Lerner LB $25.26 (978-0-8225-3583-6). A firsthand account of the settlement house founded in Chicago by Jane Addams. (Rev: BL 8/1/01) [977.3]

9560 Hahn, Laura. *Mount Rushmore* (4–8). Illus. Series: American Symbols and Their Meanings. 2002, Mason Crest LB $18.95 (978-1-59084-027-6). Hahn describes Gutzon Borglum's struggle to build his monument, with a helpful timeline and many illustrations. (Rev: SLJ 9/02) [730]

9561 Jameson, W. C. *Buried Treasures of the Great Plains* (5–8). Series: Buried Treasure. 1997, August House $11.95 (978-0-87483-486-4). Stories of buried treasure are organized by the individual states of the Great Plains region. (Rev: SLJ 7/97) [977]

9562 Martin, Michael A. *Ohio: The Buckeye State* (4–7). Series: World Almanac Library of the States. 2002, World Almanac LB $31.00 (978-0-8368-5124-3). Facts, statistics, a pleasing layout, and color photographs make this a useful choice for report writers. Also use *Iowa: The Hawkeye State* (2002). (Rev: SLJ 9/02) [977.1]

9563 Murphy, Jim. *The Great Fire* (5–9). 1995, Scholastic paper $18.95 (978-0-590-47267-8). A dramatic re-creation of the great Chicago fire that combines documents, personal accounts, illustrations, photographs, and street maps to give an in-depth view of the disaster. (Rev: BCCB 5/95; BL 6/1–15/95; HB 5–6/95, 9–10/95; SLJ 7/95) [977.3]

9564 Opat, Jamie Stockman. *Uniquely Nebraska* (4–7). Illus. Series: Heinemann State Studies. 2004, Heinemann LB $27.07 (978-1-4034-4649-7). In addition to providing the facts necessary for report writers, this volume emphasizes the features that distinguish Nebraska from its neighbors. (Rev: BL 10/15/03)

9565 Presnall, Judith Janda. *Mount Rushmore* (7–10). Series: Building History. 1999, Lucent LB $27.45 (978-1-56006-529-6). Conceived by Doune Robinson and sculpted by Gutzon Borglum, this mountainside monument has become a national landmark. (Rev: BL 10/15/99; HBG 9/00) [978.3]

9566 Redmond, Jim, and D. J. Ross. *Uniquely North Dakota* (4–7). Series: Heinemann State Studies. 2004, Heinemann LB $27.07 (978-1-4034-4657-2). In addition to providing the facts necessary for report writers, this volume emphasizes the features that distinguish North Dakota from its neighbors. (Rev: BL 4/1/04)

9567 Schonberg, Lisa. *People of Ohio* (4–7). Illus. Series: Heinemann State Studies. 2003, Heinemann LB $27.07 (978-1-4034-0668-2). Schonberg looks at groups of Ohioans from the original native peoples to later arrivals and at individuals who have contributed to all fields of endeavor, with many color photographs. (Rev: BL 10/15/03; HBG 4/04; SLJ 10/03) [305.8]

9568 Schwabacher, Martin. *Minnesota* (4–7). Series: Celebrate the States. 1999, Benchmark LB $37.07 (978-0-7614-0658-7). Minnesota is introduced in six chapters that cover history, geography, government and economy, people, achievements, and landmarks. (Rev: HBG 10/99; SLJ 10/99) [977.6]

9569 Steele, Christy Lee. *Uniquely Wisconsin* (4–7). Series: Heinemann State Studies. 2004, Heinemann LB $27.07 (978-1-4034-4499-8). In addition to pro-

viding the facts necessary for report writers, this volume emphasizes the features that distinguish Wisconsin from its neighbors. (Rev: BL 4/1/04)

9570 Wills, Charles A. *A Historical Album of Illinois* (4–8). Illus. Series: Historical Albums. 1994, Millbrook LB $24.40 (978-1-56294-482-7). A brief history of Illinois that touches on the most important events from before the white man to the 1990s. (Rev: SLJ 3/95) [977.3]

9571 Wills, Charles A. *A Historical Album of Michigan* (4–7). Illus. Series: Historical Albums. 1996, Millbrook LB $24.40 (978-0-7613-0036-6). Using many archival prints, drawings, photographs, and ample text, the history of Michigan is told. (Rev: BL 10/15/96) [977]

MOUNTAIN AND PLAINS STATES

9572 Ayer, Eleanor. *Colorado* (4–8). Illus. Series: Celebrate the States. 1997, Marshall Cavendish LB $37.07 (978-0-7614-0148-3). An introduction to the Centennial State, with information on its history, geography, and people. (Rev: BL 7/97; SLJ 8/97) [978.8]

9573 Bograd, Larry. *Uniquely Wyoming* (4–7). Illus. Series: Heinemann State Studies. 2004, Heinemann LB $31.36 (978-1-4034-4666-4). In addition to providing the facts necessary for report writers, this volume emphasizes the features that distinguish Wyoming from its neighbors. (Rev: BL 10/15/03)

9574 Dumas, Bianca, and D. J. Ross. *Uniquely Utah* (4–7). Series: Heinemann State Studies. 2004, Heinemann LB $27.07 (978-1-4034-4663-3). In addition to providing the facts necessary for report writers, this volume emphasizes the features that distinguish Utah from its neighbors. (Rev: BL 4/1/04)

9575 Lynch, Wayne, and Aubrey Lang. *Rocky Mountains* (4–7). Illus. by Wayne Lynch. Series: Our Wild World. 2006, NorthWord $16.95 (978-1-55971-948-3); paper $8.95 (978-1-55971-949-0). An appealing introduction to the geography, animals, and plants of the region, with full-color photographs and first-person anecdotes. (Rev: BL 10/15/06; SLJ 1/07*) [577.5]

9576 McDaniel, Melissa. *Arizona* (4–8). Series: Celebrate the States. 2000, Marshall Cavendish LB $37.07 (978-0-7614-0647-1). This introduction to Arizona discusses its land, history, economy, festivals, cultural diversity, and landmarks. (Rev: BL 6/1–15/00; HBG 10/00; SLJ 9/00) [979.1]

9577 Minor, Wendell. *Grand Canyon: Exploring a Natural Wonder* (4–8). Illus. 1998, Scholastic paper $16.95 (978-0-590-47968-4). In watercolors and lyrical text, the author presents a grand portrait of the Grand Canyon. (Rev: BL 9/15/98; HBG 3/99; SLJ 8/98) [978.8]

9578 O'Connor, Rebecca K., and Dennis Myers. *Uniquely Nevada* (4–7). Illus. Series: Heinemann State Studies. 2004, Heinemann LB $27.07 (978-1-4034-4650-3). In addition to providing the facts necessary for report writers, this volume emphasizes the features that distinguish Nevada from its neighbors. (Rev: BL 10/15/03)

9579 Stefoff, Rebecca. *Idaho* (4–8). Series: Celebrate the States. 2000, Benchmark LB $37.07 (978-0-7614-0663-1). Interesting charts, graphs, and maps are used to illustrate such topics as the people, land, history, and culture of Idaho. (Rev: BL 1/1–15/00; HBG 10/00) [978.8]

9580 Stefoff, Rebecca. *Nevada* (4–8). Series: Celebrate the States. 2001, Benchmark LB $37.07 (978-0-7614-1073-7). This well-organized introduction to Nevada gives general information followed by a timeline and special material on tourist attractions, famous natives of Nevada, and local festivals. (Rev: BL 9/15/01; HBG 10/01) [979.3]

9581 Stefoff, Rebecca. *Utah* (4–8). Series: Celebrate the States. 2000, Marshall Cavendish LB $37.07 (978-0-7614-1064-5). Utah's unique characteristics and places are highlighted in this account that also covers the state's history, geography, and government. (Rev: BL 12/15/00; HBG 3/01; SLJ 2/01) [979.2]

9582 Wills, Charles A. *A Historical Album of Colorado* (4–7). Illus. Series: Historical Albums. 1996, Millbrook $24.40 (978-1-56294-592-3); paper $6.95 (978-1-56294-858-0). Using many old engravings and photographs, the history of Colorado is traced, beginning with its Native American population. (Rev: BL 7/96; SLJ 7/96) [978.8]

NORTHEASTERN AND MID-ATLANTIC STATES

9583 Aaseng, Nathan. *The White House* (7–10). Series: Building History. 2000, Lucent LB $32.45 (978-1-56006-708-5). The history of this Washington landmark is given plus material on the presidents and architects who shaped this building through the years. (Rev: BL 9/15/00) [975.3]

9584 Allen, Thomas B. *The Washington Monument: It Stands for All* (8–12). Illus. 2000, Discovery $29.95 (978-1-56331-921-1). Full of photographs and drawings plus an interesting text that supplies good background material, this is a handsome guide to one of the capital's most famous landmarks. (Rev: BL 6/1–15/00) [975.3]

9585 Arnosky, Jim. *Nearer Nature* (6–12). Illus. 1996, Lothrop $18.00 (978-0-688-12213-3). In 26 short chapters and using his own pencil sketches, the author introduces the animals and the beauty of life on a wooded sheep farm in rural Vermont. (Rev: BL 8/96; SLJ 11/96; VOYA 4/97) [508.743]

9586 Ashabranner, Brent. *Badge of Valor: The National Law Enforcement Officers Memorial* (5–8). Illus. 2000, Twenty-First Century LB $25.90 (978-0-7613-1522-3). This history of the memorial, from the original proposal in the 1970s to its opening in 1991, also discusses what it stands for and reveals the heroic deeds of some important law enforcement officers. (Rev: BL 10/1/00; HBG 3/01; SLJ 1/01) [363.2]

9587 Ashabranner, Brent. *A Date with Destiny: The Women in Military Service for America Memorial* (5–8). Illus. 2000, Twenty-First Century LB $25.90 (978-0-7613-1472-1). This book tells the story of the memorial outside Arlington National Cemetery that honors American women in the military and retells some of the stories of these servicewomen. (Rev: BL 2/1/00; HBG 10/00; SLJ 4/00) [355.1]

9588 Ashabranner, Brent. *No Better Hope: What the Lincoln Memorial Means to America* (4–8). Illus. Series: Great American Memorials. 2001, Twenty-First Century LB $25.90 (978-0-7613-1523-0). As well as telling about Lincoln and his importance to the country, this volume describes the building of the memorial and the important events that have occurred on the site. (Rev: BL 3/1/01; HBG 10/01; SLJ 7/01; VOYA 10/01) [975.3]

9589 Ashabranner, Brent. *On the Mall in Washington, D.C.: A Visit to America's Front Yard* (5–7). Illus. by Jennifer Ashabranner. 2002, Twenty-First Century LB $23.90 (978-0-7613-2351-8). An entertaining and informative tour of the National Mall in Washington, D.C. (Rev: BL 3/15/02; HBG 10/02; SLJ 4/02) [917.5304]

9590 Ashabranner, Brent. *Remembering Korea: The Korean War Veterans Memorial* (4–8). Illus. by Jennifer Ashabranner. Series: Great American Memorials. 2001, Twenty-First Century LB $25.90 (978-0-7613-2156-9). Ashabranner explains who the memorial honors, how much it cost, and what it represents. (Rev: BL 9/15/01; HBG 3/02; SLJ 12/01) [951.904]

9591 Ashabranner, Brent. *The Washington Monument: A Beacon for America* (4–8). Illus. by Jennifer Ashabranner. Series: Great American Memorials. 2002, Millbrook LB $25.90 (978-0-7613-1524-7). Ashabranner presents the story behind the monument, including its planning, design, and construction, with full-color photographs and black-and-white period reproductions. (Rev: BL 9/1/02; HBG 3/03; SLJ 11/02) [975.3]

9592 Attie, Alice. *Harlem on the Verge* (8–12). Illus. 2003, Quantuck Lane $35.00 (978-0-9714548-7-3). After an introductory essay, this book consists of unforgettable color photographs that depict life in Manhattan's Harlem and Spanish Harlem. (Rev: BL 2/15/04*) [974.7]

9593 Avakian, Monique. *A Historical Album of Massachusetts* (4–8). Illus. Series: Historical Albums. 1994, Millbrook LB $24.40 (978-1-56294-481-0). A history of Massachusetts that begins with the Native American culture and ends with the 1900s, including basic material on major events and personalities. (Rev: SLJ 2/95) [974.4]

9594 Avakian, Monique, and Carter Smith, III. *A Historical Album of New York* (5–8). Illus. Series: Historical Albums. 1993, Millbrook $24.40 (978-1-56294-005-8). An overview of New York State history from Native American settlements to the present day, using extensive archival illustrations. (Rev: SLJ 10/93) [974.7]

9595 Barenblat, Rachel. *Massachusetts: The Bay State* (4–7). Series: World Almanac Library of the States. 2002, World Almanac LB $31.00 (978-0-8368-5123-6). History, politics, government, culture, and state symbols are all covered, with charts, maps, photographs, biographical sketches, and a list of important events and attractions. (Rev: SLJ 6/02) [974.4]

9596 Bial, Raymond. *Tenement: Immigrant Life on the Lower East Side* (5–8). Illus. 2002, Houghton $16.00 (978-0-618-13849-4). Historic photographs complement the simple, descriptive text about life in New York City tenement housing in the late 1800s and early 1900s. (Rev: BL 10/15/02; HB 11–12/02; HBG 3/03; SLJ 9/02) [307.76]

9597 Burchard, Sue. *The Statue of Liberty: Birth to Rebirth* (7–9). Illus. 1985, Harcourt $13.95 (978-015279969-4). After a tour of present-day Liberty Island the author describes the history behind the statue. (Rev: BL 12/1/85; SLJ 12/85) [941.7]

9598 Burgan, Michael. *Connecticut* (4–7). Series: It's My State! 2003, Marshall Cavendish LB $27.07 (978-0-7614-1523-7). This New England state is introduced with material on its people, geography, history, cities, products, and resources. (Rev: BL 9/15/03; HBG 4/04) [974.6]

9599 Conway, Lorie. *Forgotten Ellis Island: The Extraordinary Story of America's Immigrant Hospital* (7–12). Photos by Chris Barnes. 2007, Smithsonian $26.95 (978-0-06-124196-3). The story of the construction and use of the Ellis Island hospital facilities is enhanced by archival photographs and many quotations from doctors and immigrants. (Rev: SLJ 10/07) [362.1109747]

9600 Cowan, Mary Morton. *Timberrr: A History of Logging in New England* (5–8). Illus. 2003, Millbrook LB $25.90 (978-0-7613-1866-8). Cowan highlights timber's historical importance in many walks of life — trade, politics, and construction, for example — and looks at changes brought by new technologies and the impact on ecology and the environment. (Rev: BL 11/15/03; HBG 4/04) [634.9]

9601 Cytron, Barry. *Fire! The Library Is Burning* (4–7). Illus. 1988, Lerner LB $15.93 (978-0-8225-0525-9). How workers and volunteers helped to restore the Jewish Theological Seminary in New York City when it was nearly destroyed by fire. (Rev: BL 7/88; SLJ 9/88) [027.63]

9602 Doak, Robin. *New Jersey* (5–8). Illus. Series: Voices from Colonial America. 2005, National Geographic LB $32.90 (978-0-7922-6680-8). A compelling account of life in early New Jersey, from its initial settlement by the Dutch through the adoption of the Constitution. (Rev: BL 6/1–15/05; SLJ 1/06) [974.9]

9603 Doherty, Craig A., and Katherine M. Doherty. *Pennsylvania* (5–9). Illus. Series: The Thirteen Colonies. 2005, Facts on File LB $35.00 (978-0-8160-5413-8). Traces the history of Pennsylvania from the early settlers through 1787, with discussion of the Native American culture, the Quakers, and with excerpts from primary documents, maps, and profiles of key individuals. (Rev: SLJ 8/05) [973]

9604 Doherty, Craig A., and Katherine M. Doherty. *Rhode Island* (5–9). Illus. Series: The Thirteen Colonies. 2005, Facts on File LB $35.00 (978-0-8160-5415-2). Traces the history of Rhode Island from the early settlers through 1787, with discussion of the Native American culture and with excerpts from primary documents, maps, and profiles of key individuals. (Rev: SLJ 8/05) [973]

9605 Dornfeld, Margaret. *Maine* (4–8). Series: Celebrate the States. 2001, Benchmark LB $37.07 (978-0-7614-1071-3). An attractive, fact-filled introduction to the state of Maine with material on history, famous places and people, and current concerns. (Rev: BL 9/15/01; HBG 10/01) [974.1]

9606 Elish, Dan. *New York* (4–7). Illus. Series: My State. 2003, Marshall Cavendish $27.07 (978-0-7614-1419-3). Color photographs accompany information on the state's topography, wildlife, climate, population, government, industries, and resources. (Rev: BL 3/1/03; HBG 10/03) [974.7]

9607 Elish, Dan. *Vermont* (6–9). Series: Celebrate the States. 2006, Marshall Cavendish $25.95 (978-0-7614-2018-7). This revised edition contains more on Vermont's political, economic and social issues as well as its history and traditions. (Rev: BL 6/1–15/06) [974.3]

9608 Elish, Dan. *Washington, D.C.* (5–8). Series: Celebrate the States. 1998, Benchmark LB $37.07 (978-0-7614-0423-1). An attractive introduction to the people and government of the U.S. capital with material on parks, landmarks, history, economics, and racial problems. (Rev: HBG 10/98; SLJ 1/99) [975.3]

9609 Fisher, Leonard E. *Niagara Falls: Nature's Wonder* (7–9). Illus. 1996, Holiday $16.95 (978-0-8234-1240-2). Beginning with the European discovery of the Falls in 1678, the author focuses on this natural wonder as a cultural and historical institution. (Rev: BL 9/1/96; SLJ 10/96) [971.3]

9610 Goldstein, Ernest. *The Statue of Abraham Lincoln: A Masterpiece by Daniel Chester French* (5–8). Series: Art Beyond Borders. 1998, Lerner LB $28.80 (978-0-8225-2067-2). This book provides a detailed description of the Lincoln Memorial and an introduction to the life and accomplishments of its sculptor, Daniel Chester French. (Rev: SLJ 5/98) [975.3]

9611 Graham, Amy. *Maine* (4–7). Illus. Series: States. 2002, Enslow LB $25.26 (978-0-7660-5017-4). This well-illustrated volume offers report writers basic information on the state's land, climate, economy, government, and history, plus recommendations of Web sites that will extend their knowledge. Also use *New York* (2002). (Rev: SLJ 9/02) [974.1]

9612 Hempstead, Anne. *The Statue of Liberty* (4–7). Series: Land of the Free. 2006, Heinemann LB $28.21 (978-1-4034-7004-1). With many illustrations and interesting sidebars, this history of the Statue of Liberty details key events and examines its significance as an American symbol. (Rev: SLJ 10/06) [974.7]

9613 Hempstead, Anne. *The Supreme Court* (4–7). Series: Land of the Free. 2006, Heinemann LB $28.21 (978-1-4034-7001-0). With many illustrations and interesting sidebars, this history of the U.S. Supreme Court details key events and examines its significance as an American symbol. Also use *The U.S. Capitol* and *The White House* (both 2006). (Rev: SLJ 10/06) [347]

9614 Herda, D. J. *Environmental America: The Northeastern States* (4–7). Illus. Series: American Scene. 1991, Millbrook LB $22.40 (978-1-878841-06-3). This volume discusses the condition of the environment and presents information on such topics as water and land pollution in the northeastern states. (Rev: BL 8/91; SLJ 7/91) [639.9]

9615 Herda, D. J. *Ethnic America: The Northeastern States* (5–7). Illus. Series: American Scene. 1991, Millbrook LB $22.40 (978-1-56294-014-0). In this heavily illustrated account, the ethnic groups of the area, including Native Americans, are described and their accomplishments detailed. (Rev: BL 2/1/92; SLJ 2/92) [572.973]

9616 Ingram, Scott. *Pennsylvania: The Keystone State* (4–7). Series: World Almanac Library of the States. 2002, World Almanac LB $31.00 (978-0-8368-5120-5). Facts, statistics, a pleasing layout, and color photographs make this a useful choice for report writers. (Rev: SLJ 9/02) [974.8]

9617 Jameson, W. C. *Buried Treasures of New England: Legends of Hidden Riches, Forgotten War Loots, and Lost Ship Treasures* (4–8). Series: Buried Treasure. 1997, August House $11.95 (978-

0-87483-485-7). This account describes how these treasures were amassed and lost, and furnishes maps to indicate their general location. (Rev: SLJ 10/97) [910.4]

9618 Levert, Suzanne. *Massachusetts* (4–8). Series: Celebrate the States. 2000, Benchmark LB $37.07 (978-0-7614-0666-2). A fine introduction to the people and places of the Bay State that also includes recipes, folktales, and songs. (Rev: BL 1/1–15/00; HBG 10/00; SLJ 5/00) [974.4]

9619 Levy, Janey. *The Erie Canal: A Primary Source History of the Canal That Changed America* (5–8). 2003, Rosen LB $29.25 (978-0-8239-3680-9). The story of the construction of the Erie Canal and its impact on commerce is revealed through primary documents and many period illustrations. (Rev: SLJ 5/03) [974.7]

9620 Locker, Thomas. *In Blue Mountains: An Artist's Return to America's First Wilderness* (6–12). Illus. 2000, Bell Pond $18.00 (978-0-88010-471-5). This picture book is a tribute to nature, chronicling the author-artist's return to Kaaterskill Cove in New York State to find inspiration. (Rev: BL 7/00; SLJ 11/00) [974.7]

9621 Louis, Nancy. *Ground Zero* (4–7). Series: War on Terrorism. 2002, ABDO LB $16.95 (978-1-57765-675-3). This heavily illustrated, factually accurate account describes the search, recovery, and cleanup that took place after September 11, 2001, in New York City. (Rev: BL 5/15/02) [974.7]

9622 Lourie, Peter. *Erie Canal: Canoeing America's Great Waterway* (5–8). Illus. 1997, Boyds Mills $17.95 (978-1-56397-669-8). This colorful book about a journey along the Erie Canal also supplies historical facts about its construction and uses. (Rev: BL 7/97; HBG 3/98; SLJ 9/97) [974.7]

9623 McNeese, Tim. *The New York Subway System* (6–10). Illus. Series: Building History. 1997, Lucent LB $28.70 (978-1-56006-427-5). The story of the building of the 722 miles of tunnels that compose the subway system of New York City, the longest underground system in the world. (Rev: BL 12/1/97; HBG 3/98; SLJ 11/97) [388.4]

9624 Marcovitz, Hal. *The Liberty Bell* (4–8). Illus. Series: American Symbols and Their Meanings. 2002, Mason Crest LB $18.95 (978-1-59084-025-2). The history and condition of the bell are presented through text, illustrations, and a useful timeline. Also use *The White House* (2002). (Rev: SLJ 9/02) [974.8]

9625 Melman, Peter. *Uniquely New Hampshire* (4–7). Series: Heinemann State Studies. 2004, Heinemann LB $27.07 (978-1-4034-4651-0). In addition to providing the facts necessary for report writers, this volume emphasizes the features that distinguish New Hampshire from its neighbors. (Rev: BL 4/1/04)

9626 Moose, Katherine B. *Uniquely Delaware* (4–7). Series: Heinemann State Studies. 2004, Heinemann LB $27.07 (978-1-4034-4644-2). In addition to providing the facts necessary for report writers, this volume emphasizes the features that distinguish Delaware from its neighbors. (Rev: BL 4/1/04)

9627 Moose, Katherine B. *Uniquely Rhode Island* (4–7). Illus. Series: Heinemann State Studies. 2004, Heinemann LB $27.07 (978-1-4034-4660-2). In addition to providing the facts necessary for report writers, this volume emphasizes the features that distinguish Rhode Island from its neighbors. (Rev: BL 10/15/03)

9628 Morgane, Wendy. *New Jersey* (4–8). Series: Celebrate the States. 2000, Benchmark LB $37.07 (978-0-7614-0673-0). This excellent introduction to New Jersey covers its history, land, government, economy, unique characteristics, and famous residents. (Rev: BL 1/1–15/00; HBG 10/00) [974.9]

9629 Myers, Walter Dean. *Harlem* (6–12). Illus. 1997, Scholastic paper $16.95 (978-0-590-54340-8). This book is an impressionistic appreciation of Harlem and its culture as seen through the eyes of author Walter Dean Myers and his artist son, Christopher. (Rev: BL 2/15/97; SLJ 2/97; VOYA 10/97) [811]

9630 *Our White House: Looking In, Looking Out* (5–8). Illus. 2008, Candlewick $29.99 (978-0-7636-2067-7). Essays, historical fiction, and poetry from contemporary children's writers are combined with firsthand accounts from former presidents, their family members, and White House visitors to create this attractive, large-format look at the White House and its place in America's history. (Rev: BL 8/08; SLJ 9/08) [975.3]

9631 Pascoe, Elaine. *History Around You: A Unique Look at the Past, People, and Places of New York* (4–7). Illus. 2004, Gale LB $27.45 (978-1-4103-0490-2). Using a news-style format with maps, charts, and illustrations, Pascoe details the history of New York State and profiles famous individuals. (Rev: SLJ 3/05) [974.7]

9632 Peters, Stephen. *Pennsylvania* (4–7). Series: Celebrate the States. 2000, Marshall Cavendish LB $37.07 (978-0-7614-0644-0). An overview of the history, geography, and culture of Pennsylvania with additional material on state symbols, industry, the people, and the economy. (Rev: BL 6/1–15/00; SLJ 9/00) [974.8]

9633 Raabe, Emily. *Uniquely Vermont* (4–7). Illus. Series: Heinemann State Studies. 2005, Heinemann LB $31.36 (978-1-4034-4664-0). In addition to providing the facts necessary for report writers, this volume emphasizes the features that distinguish Vermont from its neighbors. (Rev: BL 10/15/03)

9634 Rebman, Renee C. *Life on Ellis Island* (5–8). Series: The Way People Live. 1999, Lucent LB $29.95 (978-1-56006-533-3). With extensive use of firsthand accounts, this book relates the purpose of Ellis Island, the processing of immigrants, and the joys and hardships involved. (Rev: BL 10/15/99; HBG 10/00; SLJ 1/00) [325.1]

9635 Rock, Howard B., and Deborah Moore. *Cityscapes: A History of New York in Images* (8–12). Illus. 2001, Columbia $80.50 (978-0-231-10624-5). Using fine prints and photographs, this account traces the evolution of Manhattan from a Dutch settlement to the great modern city of massive towers that it is today. (Rev: BL 12/1/01) [974.7]

9636 Ross, D. J. *Uniquely Maine* (4–7). Series: Heinemann State Studies. 2004, Heinemann LB $27.07 (978-1-4034-4655-8). In addition to providing the facts necessary for report writers, this volume emphasizes the features that distinguish Maine from its neighbors. (Rev: BL 4/1/04)

9637 Schnurnberger, Lynn. *Kids Love New York! The A-to-Z Resource Book* (4–8). Illus. 1990, Congdon & Weed paper $133.65 (978-0-312-92415-7). A group of suggestions for various activities in New York City.

9638 Schomp, Virginia. *New York* (4–7). Illus. Series: Celebrate the States. 2005, Benchmark LB $37.07 (978-0-7614-1738-5). A revised edition of this introduction to the Empire State — including its history, culture, famous sites, and distinguished New Yorkers — with updated illustrations. (Rev: SLJ 5/06) [917.47]

9639 Schuman, Michael. *Delaware* (4–8). Series: Celebrate the States. 2000, Marshall Cavendish LB $37.07 (978-0-7614-0645-7). Beginning with quotations about Delaware and its people, this account covers the basic topics plus information on folklore, food, and festivals. (Rev: BL 6/1–15/00; HBG 10/00) [975.1]

9640 Sullivan, George. *How the White House Really Works* (5–8). Illus. 1990, Scholastic paper $3.95 (978-0-590-43403-4). Home, office, museum, and tourist attraction — how the White House operates. (Rev: BCCB 5/89; BL 5/15/89; HB 7–8/89) [975.3]

9641 Tagliaferro, Linda. *Destination New York* (4–8). Series: Port Cities of North America. 1998, Lerner LB $23.93 (978-0-8225-2793-0). Written with a focus on New York's economic life and its handling of goods moving in and out of the port, this book also gives information on the city's history, geography, and daily life. (Rev: HBG 3/99; SLJ 1/99) [974.7]

9642 Warrick, Karen Clemens. *Independence National Historical Park* (5–8). Illus. Series: Virtual Field Trips. 2005, Enslow LB $25.26 (978-0-7660-5224-6). A visit to Independence Park, using both print and related Web sites, that covers its historical importance, including Independence Hall and the Liberty Bell. (Rev: SLJ 5/05)

9643 Whitcraft, Melissa. *The Hudson River* (4–7). Illus. Series: World of Water. 1999, Watts LB $25.50 (978-0-531-11739-2). A handsome volume that traces the history of New York State's most important river and how it currently affects people's lives. (Rev: BL 1/1–15/00) [974.7]

9644 Wills, Charles A. *A Historical Album of Pennsylvania* (4–8). Series: Historical Albums. 1996, Millbrook LB $24.40 (978-1-56294-595-4). Beginning with its Native American origins and settlement by Europeans and the Quakers, this book traces the history of Pennsylvania from the First Continental Congress and the ratification of the United States Constitution, through the Battle of Gettysburg and President Lincoln's famous Gettysburg Address, and up to today. (Rev: BL 7/96; SLJ 7/96) [974.8]

PACIFIC STATES

9645 Abbink, Emily. *Missions of the Monterey Bay Area* (4–7). Series: California Missions. 1996, Lerner LB $23.93 (978-0-8225-1928-7). Covers the history of the missions at San Carlos Borromeo de Carmelo, San Juan Bautista, and Santa Cruz. (Rev: BL 2/15/97) [979.4]

9646 Altman, Linda J. *California* (5–8). Series: Celebrate the States. 2005, Benchmark LB $37.07 (978-0-7614-1737-8). This revised edition updates facts and adds information on the government and economy plus new, full-color photographs. (Rev: SLJ 3/06) [979.4]

9647 Ansary, Mir Tamim. *People of California* (4–7). Illus. Series: Heinemann State Studies. 2003, Heinemann LB $27.07 (978-1-4034-0342-1). Ansary looks at groups of people who have settled in California and offers brief biographies of individuals who have contributed to all fields of endeavor, with many color photographs. (Rev: BL 10/15/03; HBG 4/04; SLJ 11/03) [305.8]

9648 Barter, James. *Alcatraz* (7–10). Series: Building History. 2000, Lucent LB $28.70 (978-1-56006-596-8). The story of how and why buildings were placed on Alcatraz Island and how it functions today as a popular park. (Rev: BL 1/1–15/00; HBG 9/00) [979.4]

9649 Behler, Deborah. *The Rain Forests of the Pacific Northwest* (7–12). Illus. Series: Ecosystems of North America. 2000, Benchmark LB $27.07 (978-0-7614-0926-7). A detailed look at the flora and fauna of this ecosystem that covers each layer of the forest from top to bottom as well as the impact of human activities. (Rev: HBG 3/01; SLJ 4/01) [577.34]

9650 Behrens, June. *Missions of the Central Coast* (4–7). Series: California Missions. 1996, Lerner LB $23.93 (978-0-8225-1930-0). The missions at Santa Barbara, Santa Ines, and La Purisima Concepción are discussed, with material on their history and importance. (Rev: BL 2/15/97) [979.4]

9651 Boekhoff, P. M., and Stuart A. Kallen. *California* (4–7). Illus. Series: Seeds of a Nation. 2002, Gale LB $23.70 (978-0-7377-0946-9). The history of California before statehood is presented with material on Native Americans, missionaries, settlers, and prospectors. (Rev: BL 4/1/02) [979.4]

9652 Bowermaster, Jon. *Aleutian Adventure* (6–12). Illus. 2001, National Geographic $17.95 (978-0-7922-7999-0). Beautifully illustrated, this book chronicles a harrowing but ultimately successful kayak expedition among the rugged islands of the Aleutian chain. (Rev: VOYA 8/01) [797.1]

9653 Bredeson, Carmen. *Fire in Oakland, California: Billion-Dollar Blaze* (4–8). Series: American Disasters. 1999, Enslow LB $23.93 (978-0-7660-1220-2). A high-interest book that tells of the terrible fire in Oakland and the massive destruction it caused. (Rev: BL 10/15/99; HBG 3/00) [976.8]

9654 Brower, Pauline. *Missions of the Inland Valleys* (4–7). Series: California Missions. 1996, Lerner LB $23.93 (978-0-8225-1929-4). Examines four missions, including San Luis Obispo and San Miguel Arcangel, with material on their early history and their impact on the existing cultures. (Rev: BL 2/15/97) [979.4]

9655 Chippendale, Lisa A. *The San Francisco Earthquake of 1906* (7–12). Series: Great Disasters: Reforms and Ramifications. 2001, Chelsea $30.00 (978-0-7910-5270-9). An interesting account full of photographs, eyewitness accounts, and good background information on earthquakes and California history that focuses on the appropriateness of the responses to the disaster by the various authorities and the lessons learned. (Rev: BL 4/15/01; HBG 10/01; SLJ 6/01) [979.4]

9656 Corral, Kimberly. *A Child's Glacier Bay* (4–8). Illus. 1998, Graphic Arts Center $15.95 (978-0-88240-503-2). A photoessay chronicling a three-week kayak trip in Alaska's Glacier Bay, told from the perspective of a 13-year-old girl. (Rev: BL 7/98; HBG 10/98; SLJ 8/98) [978.652]

9657 Doak, Robin. *California 1542–1850* (5–8). Series: Voices from Colonial America. 2006, National Geographic $21.95 (978-0-7922-6391-3). This well-illustrated title traces the history of California from its 1542 "discovery" by Juan Rodriguez Cabrillo to the frenzied Gold Rush years of the mid-19th century; maps and a timeline make this useful for research. (Rev: SLJ 1/07) [979.4]

9658 Ferrell, Nancy W. *Destination Valdez* (6–9). Illus. Series: Port Cities of North America. 1997,

Lerner LB $23.93 (978-0-8225-2790-9). A fact-filled book that describes the history, economy, and people of the port city of Valdez in Alaska, including an examination of the effect of the billion-dollar oil shipping industry on a tiny, remote town in Alaska. (Rev: HBG 9/98; SLJ 8/98) [979]

9659 Gill, Shelley. *Hawai'i* (5–8). Illus. by Scott Goto. 2006, Charlesbridge paper $6.95 (978-0-88106-297-7). A boy and his father tour the state of Hawaii by kayak; as they pass each island the father tells his son a little about its history, geography, people, culture, and economy. (Rev: SLJ 8/06) [996.9]

9660 Goh, Geok Yian. *Uniquely Hawaii* (4–7). Illus. Series: Heinemann State Studies. 2004, Heinemann LB $27.07 (978-1-4034-4645-9). In addition to providing the facts necessary for report writers, this volume emphasizes the features that make Hawaii unique. (Rev: BL 10/15/03)

9661 Goldberg, Jake. *Hawaii* (5–8). Series: Celebrate the States. 1998, Benchmark LB $37.07 (978-0-7614-0203-9). Using fine illustrations, fact boxes, graphs, and maps, this attractive book gives an excellent introduction to Hawaii, with the added bonus of a recipe and two songs. (Rev: HBG 10/98; SLJ 1/99) [996.9]

9662 Green, Carl R. *The Mission Trails* (6–10). Series: In American History. 2001, Enslow LB $26.60 (978-0-7660-1349-0). A well-researched and well-documented history of the southwestern Spanish missions and the trails that were built to connect them. (Rev: BL 12/15/01; HBG 3/02; SLJ 3/02) [979.4]

9663 Heinrichs, Ann. *The California Missions* (5–8). Series: We the People. 2002, Compass Point LB $26.60 (978-0-7565-0208-9). An accessible, well-illustrated account of the creation of Spanish missions in California and the impact on the native peoples of the region. (Rev: SLJ 7/02) [979.402]

9664 Henry, Judy. *Uniquely Alaska* (4–7). Illus. Series: Heinemann State Studies. 2005, Heinemann LB $31.36 (978-1-4034-4642-8). In addition to providing the facts necessary for report writers, this volume emphasizes the features that make Alaska unique. (Rev: BL 10/15/03)

9665 Herda, D. J. *Environmental America: The Northwestern States* (4–7). Illus. Series: American Scene. 1991, Millbrook LB $22.40 (978-1-878841-10-0). This account presents information on such topics as pollution, waste, logging, and the general condition of the environment in Idaho, Montana, Oregon, Washington, and Wyoming. (Rev: BL 8/91; SLJ 7/91) [639.9]

9666 Knapp, Ron. *Oregon* (4–7). Illus. Series: MyReportLinks.com. 2002, Enslow LB $25.26 (978-0-7660-5021-1). An introduction to the government, geography, and history of the state, with helpful Web sites. (Rev: BL 2/1/03; HBG 3/03; VOYA 4/03) [979.5]

9667 Lemke, Nancy. *Missions of the Southern Coast* (4–7). Illus. Series: California Missions. 1996, Lerner LB $23.93 (978-0-8225-1925-6). The three missions described here are San Diego de Alcala, San Luis Rey de Francia, and San Juan Capistrano. (Rev: BL 9/15/96; SLJ 8/96) [979.4]

9668 Levi, Steven C. *Cowboys of the Sky: The Story of Alaska's Bush Pilots* (5–9). Illus. 1996, Walker LB $18.85 (978-0-8027-8332-5). The exciting life of the people who deliver medical supplies, mail, and passengers to remote areas in Alaska is vividly re-created. (Rev: BL 6/1–15/96; SLJ 7/96; VOYA 8/96) [629.13]

9669 MacMillan, Dianne. *Missions of the Los Angeles Area* (4–7). Illus. Series: California Missions. 1996, Lerner LB $23.93 (978-0-8225-1927-0). This volume gives a description and history of three missions: San Gabriel Arcangel, San Fernando Rey de España, and San Buenaventura. (Rev: BL 9/15/96; SLJ 8/96) [979.4]

9670 Murphy, Claire Rudolf. *Children of Alcatraz: Growing Up on the Rock* (4–7). Illus. 2006, Walker $17.95 (978-0-8027-9577-9). This is the story of the children who have grown up on Alcatraz Island over time — early Native American children, children of lighthouse keepers, children of prison authorities, and so forth — with archival photographs and a timeline. (Rev: BL 12/15/06; SLJ 11/06) [979.4]

9671 Oliver, Marilyn Tower. *Alcatraz Prison* (4–8). Series: In American History. 1998, Enslow LB $26.60 (978-0-89490-990-0). After years as first a settlement and then a fort and a lighthouse, the "Rock" became a military and federal prison. This is its history, including famous prisoners, escape attempts, and its evolution into a top tourist attraction. (Rev: HBG 3/99; SLJ 1/99) [979.4]

9672 Orr, Tamra. *California* (5–8). Illus. Series: America the Beautiful: Third Series. 2007, Children's Pr. LB $38.00 (978-0-531-18557-5). This new edition of the classic series entry about the state features a new design and layout, definitions of difficult words in the margins, more history and mini biographies, and project ideas in writing, art, and science. (Rev: BL 2/1/08) [979.4]

9673 Otfinoski, Steve. *Washington* (4–7). Series: It's My State! 2003, Marshall Cavendish LB $27.07 (978-0-7614-1522-0). The state of Washington, its geography, history, people, and economic development are some of the topics covered in this introduction to this Pacific state. (Rev: BL 9/15/03; HBG 4/04) [979.9]

9674 Pratt, Helen Jay. *The Hawaiians: An Island People* (6–8). Illus. 1991, Tuttle paper $9.95 (978-0-8048-1709-7). An account of early Hawaii and its inhabitants, with emphasis on folk customs.

9675 Rice, Oliver D. *Lone Woman of Ghalas-Hat* (5–7). Illus. by Charles Zafuto. 1993, California Weekly LB $13.00 (978-0-936778-52-5); paper $6.00 (978-0-936778-51-8). The true story of the Indian woman who lived alone on a California island for 18 years. This was the basis of *Island of the Blue Dolphins*. A reissue. [979.7]

9676 Ruth, Maria Mudd. *The Pacific Coast* (7–12). Illus. Series: Ecosystems of North America. 2000, Benchmark LB $28.50 (978-0-7614-0935-9). A detailed look at the tides, plants, animals, and ecosystems found along the Pacific Coast from Alaska south to Mexico. (Rev: HBG 3/01; SLJ 4/01) [577.5]

9677 Seibold, J. Otto, and Vivian Walsh. *Going to the Getty: A Book About the Getty Center in Los Angeles* (4–7). Illus. 1997, Getty Museum $17.50 (978-0-89236-493-0). This introduction to the Getty Museum in Los Angeles is a patchwork of impressions, photographs, drawings, and reproductions of artworks. (Rev: BL 2/15/98; HBG 10/98) [708]

9678 Sherrow, Victoria. *The Exxon Valdez: Tragic Oil Spill* (4–8). Series: American Disasters. 1998, Enslow LB $23.93 (978-0-7660-1058-1). The dramatic story of the *Exxon Valdez* oil spill and the damage it caused to the Alaskan coast and its wildlife. (Rev: BL 1/1–15/99; HBG 3/99; SLJ 3/99; VOYA 4/99) [979.8]

9679 Sherrow, Victoria. *San Francisco Earthquake, 1989: Death and Destruction* (4–8). Illus. Series: American Disasters. 1998, Enslow LB $23.93 (978-0-7660-1060-4). This account of the San Francisco earthquake incorporates many eyewitness reports. (Rev: BL 1/1–15/99; HBG 3/99; SLJ 6/99) [363.34]

9680 Stefoff, Rebecca. *Oregon* (4–8). Illus. Series: Celebrate the States. 1997, Marshall Cavendish LB $37.07 (978-0-7614-0145-2). A look at life in this Pacific state, along with its history, famous sights, cities, and industries. (Rev: BL 7/97; SLJ 7/97) [917.95]

9681 Stepanchuk, Carol. *Exploring Chinatown* (4–8). Illus. by Leland Wong. 2002, Pacific View LB $22.95 (978-1-881896-25-8). This "walk" through San Francisco's Chinatown explores the Chinese culture and customs, and offers historical facts as well as a few hands-on projects. (Rev: BL 8/02; SLJ 9/02) [305.8951073]

9682 Takaki, Ronald. *Raising Cane: The World of Plantation Hawaii* (6–10). Adapted by Rebecca Stefoff. Illus. Series: Asian American Experience. 1994, Chelsea LB $19.95 (978-0-7910-2178-1). A fascinating look at the part that Asian immigrants played in the development of the economy of Hawaii. (Rev: BL 6/1–15/94; SLJ 7/94) [996.9]

9683 Uschan, Michael V. *The California Gold Rush* (5–8). Series: Landmark Events in American History. 2003, World Almanac LB $31.00 (978-0-8368-

5374-2). An attractive account of the California gold rush, famous people involved, and its consequences. (Rev: BL 10/15/03) [979.4]

9684 White, Tekla N. *Missions of the San Francisco Bay Area* (4–7). Illus. Series: California Missions. 1996, Lerner LB $23.93 (978-0-8225-1926-3). The history of five Spanish missions in the San Francisco Bay Area, including Santa Clara de Asis and San Rafael Arcangel. (Rev: BL 9/15/96; SLJ 8/96) [979.4]

9685 Wills, Charles A. *A Historical Album of California* (4–8). Illus. Series: Historical Albums. 1994, Millbrook LB $24.40 (978-1-56294-479-7). A slim volume that covers the basic history of California, with material on major events and important personalities. (Rev: SLJ 3/95) [979.4]

9686 Wills, Charles A. *A Historical Album of Oregon* (4–8). Series: Historical Albums. 1995, Millbrook $24.40 (978-1-56294-594-7). A good, broad overview of Oregon's history and current political and economic situation, places to see, and other information, with many illustrations. (Rev: BL 12/15/95; SLJ 1/96) [979.5]

9687 Young, Robert. *A Personal Tour of La Purisima* (4–7). Series: How It Was. 1999, Lerner LB $30.35 (978-0-8225-3576-8). A you-are-there visit to La Purisima — one of the 21 missions built by the Spanish in California — in which the reader experiences life in the mission as it was in 1820. (Rev: BL 6/1–15/99; HBG 10/99) [979.4]

SOUTH

9688 Altman, Linda J. *Arkansas* (4–8). Series: Celebrate the States. 2000, Benchmark LB $37.07 (978-0-7614-0672-3). An broad introduction to the culture, land, government, history, and unique characteristics of Arkansas, with emphasis on its inhabitants. (Rev: BL 1/1–15/00; HBG 10/00) [976.7]

9689 Barrett, Tracy. *Kentucky* (4–7). Series: Celebrate the States. 1999, Benchmark LB $37.07 (978-0-7614-0657-0). An attractive, concise introduction to Kentucky that covers geography, history, government and economy, people, achievements, and landmarks. (Rev: HBG 10/99; SLJ 10/99) [976.9]

9690 Barrett, Tracy. *Virginia* (4–7). Illus. Series: Celebrate the States. 2005, Benchmark LB $37.07 (978-0-7614-1734-7). A revised edition of this introduction to the state — including its history, culture, famous sites, and important Virginians — with updated illustrations. (Rev: SLJ 5/06) [975.5]

9691 Bredeson, Carmen, and Mary Dodson Wade. *Texas* (5–8). Series: Celebrate the States. 2005, Benchmark LB $37.07 (978-0-7614-1736-1). This revised edition updates facts and adds information on the government and economy plus new, full-color photographs. (Rev: SLJ 3/06) [976.4]

9692 Chang, Perry. *Florida* (5–8). Series: Celebrate the States. 1998, Benchmark LB $37.07 (978-0-7614-0420-0). A fine introduction to the history, geography, people, landmarks, and government of Florida, with material on the cultural diversity of its people. (Rev: HBG 9/98; SLJ 1/99) [975.9]

9693 Cocke, William. *A Historical Album of Virginia* (4–8). Series: Historical Albums. 1995, Millbrook paper $6.95 (978-1-56294-856-6). A broad overview of Virginia's history, using many period prints and paintings, with equal space given to past and current events, and including general information on the state. (Rev: SLJ 1/96) [975.5]

9694 Coleman, Wim, and Pat Perrin. *Colonial Williamsburg* (5–8). Illus. Series: Virtual Field Trips. 2005, Enslow LB $25.26 (978-0-7660-5220-8). A visit to Williamsburg, using both print and related Web sites, that covers its historical importance and its portrayal of colonial life. (Rev: SLJ 5/05)

9695 Cribben, Patrick. *Uniquely West Virginia* (4–7). Illus. Series: Heinemann State Studies. 2005, Heinemann LB $31.36 (978-1-4034-4665-7). In addition to providing the facts necessary for report writers, this volume emphasizes the features that distinguish West Virginia from its neighbors. (Rev: BL 10/15/03)

9696 Doherty, Craig A., and Katherine M. Doherty. *North Carolina* (5–9). Illus. Series: The Thirteen Colonies. 2005, Facts on File LB $35.00 (978-0-8160-5412-1). Traces the history of North Carolina from the early settlers through 1787, with discussion of the Native American culture and with excerpts from primary documents, maps, and profiles of key individuals. (Rev: SLJ 8/05) [973]

9697 Fisher, Leonard Everett. *Monticello* (4–7). Illus. by author. 1988, Holiday $18.95 (978-0-8234-0688-3). Touring the famous home of the third president. (Rev: BCCB 6/88; BL 6/1/88; SLJ 6–7/88) [973.46]

9698 Gaines, Ann Graham. *Kentucky* (4–7). Series: It's My State! 2003, Marshall Cavendish LB $27.07 (978-0-7614-1525-1). Full-color photographs, trivia, and recipes and crafts are included along with the standard information required for reports. (Rev: BL 9/15/03; HBG 4/04; SLJ 9/03) [976.9]

9699 Harkins, Susan Sales, and William H. Harkins. *Georgia: The Debtors Colony* (4–7). Series: Building America. 2006, Mitchell Lane LB $19.95 (978-1-58415-465-5). A look at Georgia's early history — including climate, early industry, and population — with information on James Oglethorpe, a key figure who aimed to provide a haven in America for debtors imprisoned in England. (Rev: SLJ 2/07) [975.8]

9700 Herda, D. J. *Environmental America: The South Central States* (4–7). Illus. Series: American Scene. 1991, Millbrook LB $22.40 (978-1-878841-09-4). This account discusses the general state of the environment and presents information on animal species, pollution, waste, and urban sprawl for 10 states, including Georgia, Kansas, Missouri, and Texas. (Rev: BL 8/91; SLJ 7/91) [639.9]

9701 Hess, Debra. *Florida* (4–7). Series: It's My State! 2003, Marshall Cavendish LB $27.07 (978-0-7614-1527-5). Products, resources, plants and animals, and important background material are some of the topics covered in this general introduction to Florida. (Rev: BL 9/15/03; HBG 4/04; SLJ 9/03) [975.9]

9702 Hoffman, Nancy. *South Carolina* (4–8). Series: Celebrate the States. 2000, Marshall Cavendish LB $37.07 (978-0-7614-1065-2). An interesting introduction to South Carolina, with material on its land and waterways, history, government, economy, landmarks, and success stories. (Rev: BL 12/15/00; HBG 3/01) [975.7]

9703 Leese, Jennifer. *Uniquely Maryland* (4–7). Series: State Studies. 2004, Heinemann LB $27.07 (978-1-4034-4493-6). History, industry, tourism, and culture are among the highlights of this survey of Maryland and its characteristics. (Rev: BL 4/1/04) [975.2]

9704 Levert, Suzanne. *Louisiana* (4–8). Illus. Series: Celebrate the States. 1997, Marshall Cavendish LB $37.07 (978-0-7614-0112-4). An interesting introduction that covers the standard material needed for reports. (Rev: BL 7/97; SLJ 7/97) [976.3]

9705 Lynch, Wayne. *The Everglades* (4–7). Illus. Series: Our Wild World. 2007, NorthWord $16.95 (978-1-55971-970-4); paper $8.95 (978-1-55971-971-1). With eye-catching color photographs and conversational narrative, Lynch introduces the flora and fauna of the Everglades and highlights the threats to this ecosystem. (Rev: BL 9/1/07; SLJ 11/07) [508.759]

9706 McClellan, Adam, and Martin Wilson. *Uniquely North Carolina* (4–7). Series: Heinemann State Studies. 2004, Heinemann LB $27.07 (978-1-4034-4653-4). In addition to providing the facts necessary for report writers, this volume emphasizes the features that distinguish North Carolina from its neighbors. (Rev: BL 4/1/04)

9707 Martin, Michael A. *Alabama: The Heart of Dixie* (4–7). Series: World Almanac Library of the States. 2002, World Almanac LB $31.00 (978-0-8368-5127-4). Full-color photographs and graphic elements this informative introduction to the state. Also use *Virginia* (2002). (Rev: SLJ 2/03) [976.1]

9708 Odinoski, Steve. *Georgia* (4–8). Series: Celebrate the States. 2000, Marshall Cavendish LB $37.07 (978-0-7614-1062-1). An informative, attractive introduction to Georgia with material on its land, history, people, social issues, and hidden treasures. (Rev: BL 12/15/00; HBG 3/01; SLJ 2/01) [975.8]

9709 Owens, Lisa. *Uniquely Missouri* (4–7). Series: Heinemann State Studies. 2004, Heinemann LB $27.07 (978-1-4034-4495-0). In addition to providing the facts necessary for report writers, this volume emphasizes the features that distinguish Missouri from its neighbors. (Rev: BL 4/1/04)

9710 Pobst, Sandy. *Virginia, 1607–1776* (5–8). Illus. Series: Voices from Colonial America. 2005, National Geographic LB $32.90 (978-0-7922-6771-3). A thorough political and social history of early Virginia, with excellent illustrations. (Rev: BL 10/15/05; SLJ 11/05) [975.5]

9711 Rauth, Leslie. *Maryland* (5–9). Series: Celebrate the States. 1999, Benchmark LB $37.07 (978-0-7614-0671-6). This book explores Maryland with material on topics including land and waterways, government, economy, festivals, and people. (Rev: BL 1/1–15/00; HBG 10/00; SLJ 5/00) [975.2]

9712 St. Antoine, Sara, ed. *Stories from Where We Live: The Gulf Coast* (7–12). Illus. 2002, Milkweed $19.95 (978-1-57131-636-3). A variety of literary forms including poetry, essays, and stories describe experiences on the Gulf Coast. (Rev: BL 1/1–15/03; HBG 10/03) [976]

9713 Sherrow, Victoria. *Uniquely South Carolina* (4–7). Illus. Series: Heinemann State Studies. 2005, Heinemann LB $31.36 (978-1-4034-4661-9). In addition to providing the facts necessary for report writers, this volume emphasizes the features that distinguish South Carolina from its neighbors. (Rev: BL 10/15/03)

9714 Shirley, David. *Alabama* (4–8). Series: Celebrate the States. 2000, Marshall Cavendish LB $37.07 (978-0-7614-0648-8). An introduction to Alabama that covers its land and waterways; its history, government, and economy; and its culture and success stories. (Rev: BL 6/1–15/00; HBG 10/00) [976.1]

9715 Shirley, David. *North Carolina* (4–8). Series: Celebrate the States. 2001, Benchmark LB $37.07 (978-0-7614-1072-0). A fine introduction to the land, history, economy, and people of North Carolina. (Rev: BL 9/15/01; HBG 10/01) [975.6]

9716 Stout, Mary. *Atlanta* (4–7). Illus. Series: Great Cities of the World. 2005, World Almanac LB $31.00 (978-0-8368-5042-0). Report writers will find useful information on Atlanta's history, culture, lifestyle, and current problems. (Rev: BL 4/15/04)

9717 Weatherford, Carole Boston. *Sink or Swim: African-American Lifesavers of the Outer Banks* (4–8). Illus. 1999, Coastal Carolina $15.95 (978-1-928556-01-5); paper $12.95 (978-1-928556-03-9). A history of the African Americans who participated in lifesaving efforts on the Outer Banks of North

Carolina, known as "the graveyard of the Atlantic." (Rev: BL 12/15/99) [363.28]

9718 Wills, Charles A. *A Historical Album of Alabama* (4–8). Series: Historical Albums. 1995, Millbrook LB $23.40 (978-1-56294-591-6); paper $6.95 (978-1-56294-854-2). Using many period prints and engravings, the author traces the history of Alabama from prehistoric days to today, including the impact of the shift away from cotton as a main crop, the civil rights movement, and the importance of football in the state. (Rev: BL 12/15/95; SLJ 1/96) [976.1]

9719 Wills, Charles A. *A Historical Album of Florida* (4–8). Illus. Series: Historical Albums. 1994, Millbrook LB $24.40 (978-1-56294-480-3). This compressed history of Florida deals with major events from prehistory through the 1990s. (Rev: SLJ 2/95) [975.9]

9720 Wills, Charles A. *A Historical Album of Georgia* (4–7). Illus. Series: Historical Albums. 1996, Millbrook LB $24.40 (978-0-7613-0035-9). With many period illustrations, some in color, and a simple text, the history and geography of Georgia are presented. (Rev: BL 12/15/96) [975.8]

9721 Wilson, Martin. *Uniquely Alabama* (4–7). Series: Heinemann State Studies. 2004, Heinemann LB $27.07 (978-1-4034-4485-1). In addition to providing the facts necessary for report writers, this volume emphasizes the features that distinguish Alabama from its neighbors. (Rev: BL 4/1/04)

9722 Wilson, Martin. *Uniquely Mississippi* (4–7). Illus. Series: Heinemann State Studies. 2004, Heinemann LB $27.07 (978-1-4034-4656-5). In addition to providing the facts necessary for report writers, this volume emphasizes the features that distinguish Mississippi from its neighbors. (Rev: BL 10/15/03)

9723 Young, Robert. *A Personal Tour of Monticello* (4–7). Illus. Series: How It Was. 1999, Lerner LB $30.35 (978-0-8225-3575-1). Through the eyes of Jefferson, his daughter, and one of his slaves, the reader is introduced to the home of the third president of the United States. (Rev: BL 6/1–15/99; HBG 10/99; SLJ 7/99) [975.5]

SOUTHWEST

9724 Alter, Judy. *New Mexico* (4–7). Illus. Series: MyReportLinks.com. 2002, Enslow LB $25.26 (978-0-7660-5098-3). An introduction to the government, geography, and history of the state, with helpful Web sites. (Rev: BL 2/1/03; SLJ 4/03; VOYA 4/03) [978.9]

9725 Bjorklund, Ruth. *New Mexico* (4–7). Series: It's My State! 2003, Marshall Cavendish LB $27.07 (978-0-7614-1526-8). Actual quotations from both famous and unknown residents of New Mexico are used to introduce this state, its people, history, wildlife, and resources. (Rev: BL 9/15/03; HBG 4/04) [978.9]

9726 Bredeson, Carmen. *The Spindletop Gusher: The Story of the Texas Oil Boom* (4–7). Illus. Series: Spotlight on American History. 1996, Millbrook LB $24.90 (978-1-56294-916-7). A discussion of the Texas oil boom, its effects on the state and its economy, and the present status of the oil industry. (Rev: BL 3/15/96) [338.4]

9727 Coleman, Wim, and Pat Perrin. *The Alamo* (6–9). Illus. Series: Virtual Field Trips. 2005, Enslow LB $25.26 (978-0-7660-5221-5). An attractive overview of the events that make the Alamo an important historical landmark, with Web links for further research. (Rev: BL 8/05; SLJ 5/05) [976.4]

9728 Corrick, James. *Uniquely Arizona* (4–7). Series: Heinemann State Studies. 2004, Heinemann LB $27.07 (978-1-4034-4486-8); paper $8.50 (978-1-4304-4501-2). In addition to providing the facts necessary for report writers, this volume emphasizes the features that distinguish Arizona from its neighbors. (Rev: BL 4/1/04)

9729 Herda, D. J. *Environmental America: The Southwestern States* (4–7). Illus. Series: American Scene. 1991, Millbrook LB $22.40 (978-1-878841-11-7). This account, which discusses the state of the environment and how it can be changed for the better, covers Arizona, California, Colorado, Nevada, New Mexico, and Utah. (Rev: BL 8/91; SLJ 7/91) [639.9]

9730 Lourie, Peter. *The Lost World of the Anasazi: Exploring the Mysteries of Chaco Canyon* (5–8).

Illus. 2003, Boyds Mills $19.95 (978-1-56397-972-9). With many full-color photographs, the author describes his trip to the ruins of Chaco Canyon and discusses the mysterious disappearance of its Anasazi residents. (Rev: BL 9/1/03; HBG 4/04; SLJ 1/04) [978.9]

9731 McCarry, Charles. *The Great Southwest* (7–12). Illus. 1980, National Geographic LB $12.95 (978-0-87044-288-9). In pictures and text, descriptions are given of such states as New Mexico, Colorado, and Arizona. [979.1]

9732 Marcovitz, Hal. *The Alamo* (4–8). Illus. Series: American Symbols and Their Meanings. 2002, Mason Crest LB $18.95 (978-1-59084-037-5). A basic and readable introduction to the history of the Alamo and its importance to Americans, with illuminating illustrations and inset features. (Rev: SLJ 9/02) [976]

9733 Tweit, Susan J. *Meet the Wild Southwest: Land of Hoodoos and Gila Monsters* (4–8). Illus. 1996, Alaska Northwest paper $14.95 (978-0-88240-468-4). An impressive collection of facts and curiosities about the natural history of the Southwest, with many appendixes that supply more-traditional information. (Rev: BL 3/1/96) [508.79]

9734 Wills, Charles A. *A Historical Album of Texas* (4–7). Illus. Series: Historical Albums. 1995, Millbrook LB $24.40 (978-1-56294-504-6). This account of the history of Texas from earliest times to today is also particularly noteworthy for its many illustrations. (Rev: SLJ 6/95) [976.4]

Philosophy and Religion

World Religions and Holidays

General and Miscellaneous

9735 Abrams, Judith Z. *The Secret World of Kabbalah* (5–9). Illus. 2006, Lerner paper $9.95 (978-1-58013-224-4). This interesting introduction to Kabbalah defines this form of Jewish mysticism as "the journey to come as closely in touch with God as you can." (Rev: SLJ 12/06) [296.16]

9736 Andryszewski, Tricia. *Communities of the Faithful: American Religious Movements Outside the Mainstream* (6–10). 1997, Millbrook LB $24.90 (978-0-7613-0067-0). Seven religious orders — Old Order Amish, Shakers, Mormons, Catholic Workers, Nation of Islam, Lubavitcher Hasidim, and Quakers — are introduced, with material on their beliefs and contributions to American culture. (Rev: SLJ 2/98) [200]

9737 Bahree, Patricia. *Hinduism* (6–9). Illus. 1985, Batsford $19.95 (978-0-7134-3654-9). The basic beliefs and gods of Hinduism are discussed under 100 subjects arranged alphabetically. (Rev: BL 5/1/85) [294.5]

9738 Batmanglij, Najmieh. *Happy Nowruz: Cooking with Children to Celebrate the Persian New Year* (4–8). Illus. 2008, Mage $40.00 (978-1-933823-16-4). This attractive spiral-bound book combines the history and customs of the Persian New Year with recipes. (Rev: BL 6/1–15/08) [641.59]

9739 Birdseye, Debbie H., and Tom Birdseye. *What I Believe: Kids Talk About Faith* (4–7). 1996, Holiday $15.95 (978-0-8234-1268-6). Children from six faiths explain what their religion means to them. (Rev: BL 12/15/96; SLJ 2/97) [200]

9740 Braude, Ann. *Women and American Religion* (8–12). Illus. Series: Religion in America. 2000, Oxford LB $32.95 (978-0-19-510676-3). Beginning with Native American and Puritan women and continuing to the present, this account traces the many contributions women have made to religion in America. (Rev: BL 3/15/00; HBG 3/01; SLJ 5/00) [200]

9741 Breuilly, Elizabeth, et al. *Religions of the World: The Illustrated Guide to Origins, Beliefs, Traditions and Festivals* (7–12). Illus. 1997, Facts on File $29.95 (978-0-8160-3723-0). This well-illustrated work defines religion generally, discusses each of the world's major religions, points out similarities, and links each religion to current events and international politics. (Rev: BL 10/1/97; HBG 3/98; SLJ 2/98) [291]

9742 Brown, Alan, and Andrew Langley. *What I Believe: A Young Person's Guide to the Religions of the World* (4–7). Illus. 1999, Millbrook LB $24.90 (978-0-7613-1501-8). Young people of eight major faiths explain their religion's principal tenets, rituals, holy days, and celebrations. (Rev: BL 10/1/99; HBG 3/00; SLJ 2/00) [291]

9743 Brunelli, Roberto. *A Family Treasury of Bible Stories: One for Each Week of the Year* (4–8). Illus. 1997, Abrams $24.95 (978-0-8109-1248-9). A collection of 52 short stories from the Old and New Testaments. (Rev: BL 10/1/97; SLJ 2/98) [220.9]

9744 Chaikin, Miriam. *Angels Sweep the Desert Floor: Bible Legends About Moses in the Wilderness* (4–7). Illus. by Alexander Koshkin. 2002, Clarion $19.00 (978-0-395-97825-2). This collection of stories mixes religious history and rabbinic literature to tell the story of the Israelites' 40 years in the wilderness. (Rev: BL 10/1/02; HB 11–12/02; HBG 3/03; SLJ 9/02) [296.1]

9745 Cotner, June, ed. *Teen Sunshine Reflections: Words for the Heart and Soul* (6–12). 2002, HarperCollins $15.95 (978-0-06-000525-2); paper $9.95 (978-0-06-000527-6). This anthology of poems and quotations that celebrate spiritual beliefs and appreciation of the world about us includes the works of the well-known (such as Saint Francis, Gandhi, and Anne Frank) and the unknown. (Rev: BL 7/02; HBG 10/02; SLJ 8/02; VOYA 8/02) [082]

9746 Dhanjal, Beryl. *Sikhism* (7–10). Illus. 1987, David & Charles $19.95 (978-0-7134-5202-0). The major tenets, doctrines, and personages of this religion are discussed in alphabetical order. (Rev: SLJ 9/87) [294.6]

9747 Dillon, Leo, and Diane Dillon. *To Every Thing There Is a Season: Verses from Ecclesiastes* (4–7). Illus. 1998, Scholastic paper $16.95 (978-0-590-47887-8). Using verses from Ecclesiastes such as "A time to be born and a time to die," the artists have created a stunning picture book on the cycle of life. (Rev: BCCB 11/98; BL 10/1/98*; HB 9–10/98; HBG 3/99; SLJ 9/98) [223]

9748 Ellwood, Robert S., and Gregory D. Alles, eds. *The Encyclopedia of World Religions* (7–12). Illus. 1998, Facts on File $45.00 (978-0-8160-3504-5). Though basically intended as a reference book, this is an absorbing work that offers information on religions past and present and on general topics of interest, such as the sun, moon, music, and science. (Rev: BL 9/1/98; SLJ 11/98) [200]

9749 Gaskins, Pearl Fuyo. *I Believe In . . .: Christian, Jewish, and Muslim Young People Speak About Their Faiths* (7–10). 2004, Cricket $18.95 (978-0-8126-2713-8). Suitable for browsing, this is a collection of interviews with about 100 young adults from diverse religious backgrounds in the Chicago area. (Rev: BCCB 9/04; BL 10/1/04; HB 7–8/04) [200]

9750 Gellman, Marc. *God's Mailbox: More Stories About Stories in the Bible* (4–7). Illus. by Debbie Tilley. 1996, Morrow $15.00 (978-0-688-13169-2). Some stories retold from the Bible, including the Creation, Garden of Eden, Jacob's ladder, the Exodus, and Moses receiving the Ten Commandments. (Rev: BCCB 5/96; SLJ 3/96) [222]

9751 Gellman, Marc, and Thomas Hartman. *How Do You Spell God? Answers to the Big Questions from Around the World* (5–8). Illus. by Joseph A. Smith. 1995, Morrow $17.99 (978-0-688-13041-1). A priest and a rabbi have written this introduction to the world's most important religions: Judaism, Christianity, Islam, Buddhism, and Hinduism. (Rev: BCCB 7–8/95; BL 6/1–15/95; SLJ 5/95) [200]

9752 Gold, Susan Dudley. *Religions of the Western Hemisphere* (5–8). Illus. Series: Comparing Continents. 1997, Twenty-First Century $23.40 (978-0-8050-5603-7). This work explores the history and influence of religions, beliefs, and customs on life in the United States, Canada, and Latin America, with discussion of the roles of religious leaders in government, economy, and everyday life. (Rev: BL 2/1/98; SLJ 3/98) [200]

9753 Hartz, Paula. *Baha'i Faith* (6–10). Series: World Religions. 2002, Facts on File $30.00 (978-0-8160-4729-1). A look at the history and beliefs of the Baha'i Faith and its spread from Persia to the rest of the world. (Rev: HBG 3/03; SLJ 12/02) [297.9]

9754 Hartz, Paula R. *Taoism* (6–9). Illus. Series: World Religions. 1993, Facts on File $30.00 (978-0-8160-2448-3). A clear, objective explanation of the Chinese religion Taoism, with details on its metamorphosis from mysticism to a more secular form. (Rev: BL 7/93) [299]

9755 Hoffman, Nancy. *Sikhism* (6–9). Series: Religions of the World. 2005, Gale LB $29.95 (978-1-59018-453-0). A basic introduction to the beliefs and practices of Sikhism, with a chronology of important events. (Rev: SLJ 2/06) [294.6]

9756 Hoobler, Thomas, and Dorothy Hoobler. *Confucianism* (6–9). Series: World Religions. 1993, Facts on File $30.00 (978-0-8160-2445-2). Describes how the teachings of Confucius evolved from a social order to a religion, permeating all phases of Chinese life for 2,000 years. (Rev: BL 3/1/93) [299]

9757 Ikeda, Daisaku. *The Way of Youth* (6–12). 2000, Middleway paper $14.95 (978-0-9674697-0-6). The great questions of human behavior — such as the nature of love, friendship, and compassion — are discussed from a Buddhist perspective. (Rev: BL 12/1/00) [294.3]

9758 Kallen, Stuart A. *Shinto* (6–9). Series: Religions of the World. 2001, Gale LB $29.95 (978-1-56006-988-1). This book explores the beliefs, customs, and historical roots of Shinto, the indigenous religion of Japan. (Rev: BL 8/02; SLJ 6/02) [299]

9759 Kingsbury, Karen. *A Treasury of Miracles for Teens: True Stories of God's Presence Today* (7–12). 2003, Warner $12.95 (978-0-446-52962-4). Kingsbury recounts stories in which teens seek God's help and are rewarded. (Rev: BL 7/03) [231.7]

9760 Krishnaswami, Uma. *The Broken Tusk: Stories of the Hindu God Ganesha* (4–8). Illus. 1996, Linnet $19.95 (978-0-208-02242-4). A collection of tales about the elephant-headed Hindu god Ganesha, the god of good beginnings. (Rev: SLJ 7/97) [294.5]

9761 Lester, Julius. *When the Beginning Began: Stories About God, the Creatures, and Us* (4–8). Illus. 1999, Harcourt $17.00 (978-0-15-201138-3). Using parts of Genesis and creation stories from Jewish legends, this wondrous retelling adds thought-provoking human interest to the stories that end with Adam and Eve. (Rev: BL 4/15/99*; SLJ 5/99) [296.1]

9762 Lincoln, Frances. *A Family Treasury of Prayers* (4–8). 1996, Simon & Schuster $16.00 (978-0-689-

80956-9). Classic art works illustrate this lovely collection of prayers from famous sources. (Rev: BL 10/1/96; SLJ 10/96; VOYA 6/97) [242]

9763 Lottridge, Celia B. *Stories from Adam and Eve to Ezekiel: Retold from the Bible* (4–7). Illus. by Gary Clement. 2004, Groundwood $24.95 (978-0-88899-490-5). Some of the best-loved stories from the Hebrew Bible are engagingly adapted in this attractively illustrated volume. (Rev: BL 10/1/04; SLJ 4/05) [220]

9764 Lugira, Aloysius. *African Religion* (7–10). Illus. Series: World Religions. 1999, Facts on File $30.00 (978-0-8160-3876-3). The author gives a fine overview of the major religious beliefs of the different ethnic groups in Africa plus material on organized religion, witchcraft, and the influence of Western religions on the area. (Rev: BL 1/1–15/00; HBG 4/00; SLJ 1/00) [299]

9765 MacMillan, Dianne M. *Diwali: Hindu Festival of Lights* (4–8). Series: Best Holiday Books. 1997, Enslow LB $23.93 (978-0-89490-817-0). This book on the Hindu Diwali festival discusses its significance and relationship to the history, culture, and people of India, and includes material on the food, crafts, instruments, and costumes of the festival. (Rev: SLJ 8/97) [294.5]

9766 Mann, Gruinder Singh, et al. *Buddhists, Hindus, and Sikhs in America* (6–12). Illus. Series: Religion in American Life. 2002, Oxford $32.95 (978-0-19-512442-2). Photographs, anecdotes, and excerpts from primary sources add appeal to this survey of how three major religions have affected, and been affected by, life in America. (Rev: BL 1/1–15/02; HBG 10/02; SLJ 1/02; VOYA 4/02) [294]

9767 Martin, Joel W. *Native American Religion* (7–12). 1999, Oxford LB $32.95 (978-0-19-511035-7). An overview of historical and contemporary Native American religious beliefs and practices, their importance in daily life, and the conflicts introduced by the Europeans. (Rev: HBG 4/00; SLJ 9/99; VOYA 10/99) [299]

9768 Mason, Claire. *New Religious Movements: The Impact on Our Lives* (6–10). Series: 21st Century Debates. 2003, Raintree LB $28.56 (978-0-7398-6032-8). Zen Buddhists, Hare Krishnas, Mormons, and Scientologists are all included in this discussion of non-mainstream religious movements and cults around the world. (Rev: SLJ 6/04)

9769 Mayer, Marianna. *Remembering the Prophets of Sacred Scripture* (6–10). Illus. 2003, Penguin $16.99 (978-0-8034-2727-3). Old Testament prophets — from Daniel and Moses to Amos and Obadiah — are introduced in this handsome picture book for older readers. (Rev: BL 7/03; SLJ 8/03) [224]

9770 Metcalf, Franz. *Buddha in Your Backpack: Everyday Buddhism for Teens* (7–12). 2002, Ulysses paper $12.95 (978-1-56975-321-7). This humorous and informative guide will satisfy young adults' interest in the spiritual world of Buddhism. (Rev: BL 1/1–15/03; SLJ 2/03; VOYA 2/04) [294.3]

9771 Morgan, Peggy. *Buddhism* (7–10). Illus. 1987, David & Charles $19.95 (978-0-7134-5203-7). In a dictionary format, the major points concerning this religion and its founder are described. (Rev: SLJ 9/87) [294.3]

9772 Morris, Neil. *The Life of Moses* (6–9). Illus. Series: Art Revelations. 2003, Enchanted Lion $18.95 (9781592700011). The works of artists including Botticelli and Michelangelo, hieroglyphs, and artifacts form a handsome backdrop to the story of Moses in this large-format book that looks at important events in double-page spreads. Also use *The Life of Jesus* (2003). (Rev: BL 8/03) [704.9]

9773 Murphy, Claire Rudolf, et al. *Daughters of the Desert: Stories of Remarkable Women from Christian, Jewish, and Muslim Traditions* (7–10). 2003, SkyLight Paths $19.95 (978-1-893361-72-0). Five authors contributed to these 18 stories, based on the Bible and Koran, of the lives of women including Eve, Esther, Mary Magdalene, Sarah, and Khadiji, the wife of Mohammed. (Rev: BL 10/15/03) [220.9]

9774 Philip, Neil. *In the House of Happiness: A Book of Prayer and Praise* (6–9). Illus. by Isabelle Brent. 2003, Clarion $17.00 (978-0-618-23481-3). Reflective verses are accompanied by images of nature in this book of inspirational messages. (Rev: BL 2/1/03; HBG 10/03; SLJ 7/03) [291.4]

9775 Seeger, Elizabeth. *Eastern Religions* (7–12). Illus. 1973, HarperCollins $14.95 (978-0-690-25342-9). A fine overview of such religions as Hinduism, Buddhism, Confucianism, and Taoism. [291]

9776 Simpson, Nancy. *Face-to-Face with Women of the Bible* (6–8). Illus. 1996, Chariot-Victor $16.99 (978-0-7814-0251-4). Both well-known and obscure women from the Bible are introduced in two or three pages per subject. (Rev: BL 10/15/96) [220.92]

9777 Singh, Nikky-Guninder Kaur. *Sikhism* (6–9). Series: World Religions. 1993, Facts on File $30.00 (978-0-8160-2446-9). Describes the development of Sikhism an outgrowth of Hinduism and discusses its traditions, customs, and beliefs. (Rev: BL 7/93) [294.6]

9778 Sita, Lisa. *Worlds of Belief: Religion and Spirituality* (5–8). Series: Our Human Family. 1995, Blackbirch LB $27.45 (978-1-56711-125-5). Using many illustrations, this book gives a tour of the world's religions, with an emphasis on the similarities rather than the differences. (Rev: SLJ 1/96) [200]

9779 Stein, Stephen J. *Alternative American Religions* (8–12). Series: Religion in American Life. 2000, Oxford LB $32.95 (978-0-19-511196-5). From Puritan dissenters to cults like Heaven's Gate, this is a look at the alternative religions that have attracted followers in the Americas. (Rev: HBG 9/00; SLJ 4/00; VOYA 12/00) [291.9]

9780 Sweeney, Jon M., ed. *God Within: Our Spiritual Future — As Told by Today's New Adults* (8–12). 2001, SkyLight Paths paper $14.95 (978-1-893361-15-7). Writers in their teens and 20s, who reflect a wide variety of beliefs, present very personal essays on their faiths and their paths to spirituality. (Rev: BL 1/1–15/02) [200]

9781 Thompson, Jan. *Islam* (5–8). Series: World Religions. 2005, Walrus paper $12.95 (978-1-55285-654-3). Using a question-and-answer format, this attractive introduction explores the history and beliefs of Islam; a first-person account by a 15-year-old Muslim boy in London starts the book. (Rev: BL 10/15/05) [297]

9782 Wagner, Katherine. *Life in an Amish Community* (6–10). Series: The Way People Live. 2001, Lucent $28.70 (978-1-56006-654-5). Wagner explains the traditions of the Amish, traces their history, and discusses some of the contemporary disagreements within the community and problems with outsiders. (Rev: BL 10/1/01; SLJ 1/02) [973]

9783 Waldman, Neil. *The Promised Land: The Birth of the Jewish People* (4–7). Illus. 2002, Boyds Mills $21.95 (978-1-56397-332-1). Waldman interweaves information on religious tradition and the experiences of the Jewish people over time in this handsome volume. (Rev: BL 10/1/02; HBG 3/03; SLJ 9/02) [909]

9784 Wangu, Madhu Bazaz. *Buddhism* (6–9). Series: World Religions. 1993, Facts on File $30.00 (978-0-8160-2442-1). Describes Buddha's life, the spread of Buddhism, and its existence today. (Rev: BL 3/1/93; SLJ 6/93) [294.3]

9785 Wangu, Madhu Bazaz. *Hinduism* (6–9). Series: World Religions. 1991, Facts on File $26.95 (978-0-8160-2447-6). A detailed, in-depth look at this major religion, with particular emphasis on how it is practiced in India. (Rev: BL 4/15/92; SLJ 3/92) [294.5]

9786 Ward, Elaine. *Old Testament Women* (5–10). Series: Art Revelations. 2004, Enchanted Lion $18.95 (978-1-59270-011-0). Paintings by masters accompany stories about 18 women including Rachel, Ruth, and Bathsheba. (Rev: SLJ 8/04) [224]

9787 Wilkinson, Philip. *Buddhism* (5–8). Illus. 2003, DK $15.99 (978-0-7894-9833-5). An attractive, well-illustrated overview of the teachings and symbols of Buddhism, with information on history, different forms, important sites, and art and artifacts. (Rev: BL 1/1–15/04) [294.3]

9788 Winston, Diana. *Wide Awake: A Buddhist Guide for Teens* (6–10). 2003, Putnam paper $14.95 (978-0-399-52897-2). In a conversational style, the author introduces the tenets of Buddhism, explains her own beliefs and how she arrived at them, and looks at ways teens can apply Buddhist teachings to their own experiences. (Rev: BL 10/1/03) [294]

9789 Zarin, Cynthia. *Saints Among the Animals* (5–8). Illus. by Leonid Gore. 2006, Atheneum $17.95 (978-0-689-85031-8). An attractive collection of ten stories about saints interacting with animals; brief biographies of the saints are appended. (Rev: BL 12/1/06; SLJ 1/07) [270]

Christianity

9790 Aaseng, Rolf E. *Augsburg Story Bible* (4–8). Illus. by Annegert Fuchshuber. 1992, Augsburg LB $19.99 (978-0-8066-2607-9). This copiously illustrated version of the Bible is only slightly abridged. (Rev: SLJ 7/92) [222]

9791 Bolick, Nancy O., and Sallie Randolph. *Shaker Inventions* (6–8). Illus. 1990, Walker LB $13.85 (978-0-8027-6934-3). This book describes the Shaker religion and explores the many contributions of the Shakers to American life, such as the clothespin and washing machine. (Rev: BL 8/90) [289]

9792 Bolick, Nancy O., and Sallie Randolph. *Shaker Villages* (6–8). Illus. 1993, Walker LB $13.85 (978-0-8027-8210-6). This history offers insights into one of the world's longest-lived communal societies, its founder, its faith, its daily life, and its village organization. (Rev: BL 3/15/93; SLJ 6/93) [289]

9793 Capek, Michael. *A Personal Tour of a Shaker Village* (4–7). Series: How It Was. 2001, Lerner LB $30.35 (978-0-8225-3584-3). An account of life in a Shaker village, seen through the eyes of people who lived there. (Rev: BL 8/1/01; HBG 10/01; SLJ 8/01) [289.8]

9794 *Christmas in Colonial and Early America* (4–7). Illus. 1996, World Book $19.00 (978-0-7166-0875-2). The evolution of Christmas celebrations is traced through more than 100 years of American history to the end of the 19th century. (Rev: BL 11/1/96) [394.26]

9795 *Christmas in Greece* (5–10). Illus. Series: Christmas Around the World. 2000, World Book $19.00 (978-0-7166-0859-2). This account focuses on the religious practices of the Greek Orthodox Church at Christmastime, which begins with a long fasting period. (Rev: BL 9/1/00) [398.2]

9796 Connolly, Sean. *New Testament Miracles* (5–10). Series: Art Revelations. 2004, Enchanted Lion $18.95 (978-1-59270-012-7). Presents brief retellings of 12 miracles performed by Jesus Christ, each illustrated by a well-known painting by an eminent artist, such as Rembrandt, El Greco, and Tintoretto. (Rev: SLJ 8/04) [226.7]

9797 Demi. *Mary* (4–7). 2006, Simon & Schuster $19.95 (978-0-689-87692-9). Traces the story of the mother of Jesus from the days preceding her birth through her ascension into heaven. (Rev: BL 10/1/06; SLJ 11/06) [232.91]

9798 Israel, Fred L. *The Amish* (5–8). Illus. Series: Immigrant Experience. 1996, Chelsea LB $14.95 (978-0-7910-3368-5). The story of this conservative division of the Mennonites, why they settled in the United States, and their contributions to the nation. (Rev: BL 7/96; SLJ 10/96) [305.6]

9799 Jeffers, H. Paul. *Legends of Santa Claus* (4–7). Series: A&E Biography. 2000, Lucent LB $27.93 (978-0-8225-4983-3). This book recounts the tales, legends, and myths about Santa Claus and sorts the truth from the fiction. (Rev: BL 12/15/00; HBG 3/01) [394.2]

9800 John Paul II. *Every Child a Light: The Pope's Message to Young People* (4–7). Ed. by Jerome M. Vereb. Illus. 2002, Boyds Mills $16.95 (978-1-56397-090-0). Using photographs and snippets from Pope John Paul II's writings for children and teens, this is an inspirational book of comments and advice for youngsters. (Rev: BL 6/1–15/02; HBG 10/02; SLJ 5/02) [248.8]

9801 Lottridge, Celia B. *Stories from the Life of Jesus* (5–7). Illus. by Linda Wolfsgruber. 2004, Douglas & McIntyre $24.95 (978-0-88899-497-4). Lottridge draws on the first four books of the New Testament for this illustrated collection of stories. (Rev: BL 5/1/04; HB 7–8/04; SLJ 11/04) [232.9]

9802 Lutz, Norma Jean. *The History of the Black Church* (5–8). Illus. Series: African American Achievers. 2001, Chelsea $30.00 (978-0-7910-5822-0). Historical and contemporary photographs illustrate this history of African American religious life and institutions. (Rev: BL 10/1/01; HBG 3/02; SLJ 12/01) [277.3]

9803 Mulvihill, Margaret. *The Treasury of Saints and Martyrs* (5–7). Illus. 1999, Viking $19.99 (978-0-670-88789-7). A handsome, oversize book about the lives of 40 saints from the beginning of Christianity to the present day. (Rev: BL 10/1/99; HBG 10/00; SLJ 3/00) [270.029]

9804 Noll, Mark. *Protestants in America* (7–12). Illus. Series: Religion in America. 2000, Oxford $32.95 (978-0-19-511034-0). From the arrival of the Puritans to today, this is a well-organized overview of Protestantism and how it has evolved, changed, and splintered in America. (Rev: BL 10/1/00; HBG 3/01; SLJ 2/01) [280]

9805 Paul, John. *For the Children: Words of Love and Inspiration from His Holiness John Paul II* (4–7). Illus. 2000, Scholastic paper $16.95 (978-0-439-14902-0). Letters and speeches by Pope John Paul II and photographs of children from around the world are used to illustrate inspirational messages about such subjects as hope, faith, and school. (Rev: BL 3/1/00; HBG 10/00; SLJ 3/00) [248.8]

9806 Penney, Sue. *Christianity* (6–8). Series: World Beliefs and Cultures. 2000, Heinemann LB $25.64 (978-1-57572-355-6). A balanced introduction to the history and practice of this major religion, with material on its sacred texts, worship, pilgrimage sites, key figures, festivals, and subgroups. (Rev: HBG 10/01; SLJ 4/01) [230]

9807 Ross, Lillian H. *Daughters of Eve: Strong Women of the Bible* (5–7). Illus. 2000, Barefoot Bks. $19.99 (978-1-902283-82-1). Fictionalized accounts that expand on the material given in the Bible and Apocrypha about 12 strong women and their deeds. (Rev: BL 10/1/00; HBG 10/01; SLJ 11/00) [220.9]

9808 Schmidt, Gary D., retel. *The Blessing of the Lord: Stories from the Old and New Testaments* (5–8). Illus. 1997, Eerdmans $20.00 (978-0-8028-3789-9). Using 25 Old and New Testament stories as a focus, these insightful accounts describe how biblical personalities react to such events as Daniel's struggle with the lions and Jesus causing nets to be filled with fish. (Rev: BL 11/1/97; HBG 3/98; SLJ 10/97) [222]

9809 Self, David. *Christianity* (5–8). Series: Religions of the World. 2005, World Almanac LB $31.00 (978-0-8368-5866-2). A basic introduction to the beliefs and practices of Christianity, with a chronology of important events. (Rev: SLJ 2/06)

9810 *Stories from the Bible* (5–7). Illus. by Lisbeth Zwerger. 2002, North-South $19.95 (978-0-7358-1413-4). Sophisticated paintings illustrate verbatim excerpts from the King James version of both the Old and New Testaments. (Rev: BCCB 9/02; BL 4/1/02; HB 7–8/02; HBG 10/02; SLJ 5/02) [220.5]

9811 Visconte, Guido. *Clare and Francis* (4–7). Illus. by Bimba Landmann. 2004, Eerdmans $20.00 (978-0-8028-5269-4). Eye-catching artwork highlights the inspiring stories of saints Clare and Francis in this picture book for older readers. (Rev: BL 2/1/04*; SLJ 6/04) [270]

9812 Winthrop, Elizabeth, adapt. *He Is Risen: The Easter Story* (4–7). Illus. by Charles Mikolaycak. 1985, Holiday $17.95 (978-0-8234-0547-3). The Easter story taken from parts of the King James version of the Bible and dramatically illustrated. (Rev: BCCB 4/85; HB 7–8/85; SLJ 4/85)

Islam

9813 Barnes, Trevor. *Islam* (5–8). Illus. Series: World Faiths. 2005, Kingfisher paper $6.95 (978-0-7534-5882-2). Originally published in 1999 as part of *The Kingfisher Book of Religions: Festivals, Ceremonies, and Beliefs from Around the World*, this 40-page expanded volume provides a wide-ranging overview of Islam and its followers. (Rev: BL 10/1/05; SLJ 10/05; VOYA 6/06) [297]

9814 Child, John. *The Rise of Islam* (6–8). 1995, Bedrick $17.95 (978-0-87226-116-7). A historical approach to Islam's impact on world history. Discusses its beginnings and middle development but only briefly discusses Islam today. (Rev: BL 9/1/95; SLJ 8/95) [297]

9815 Clark, Charles. *Islam* (6–9). Illus. Series: Religions of the World. 2002, Gale LB $29.95 (978-1-56006-986-7). Clark explains the history and practice of Islam and discusses the challenges facing this religion today, with interesting sidebars on topics including dietary laws and dress for women. (Rev: BL 8/02; SLJ 7/02) [297]

9816 Conover, Sarah, and Freda Crane. *Beautiful Signs/Ayat Jamilah: A Treasury of Islamic Wisdom for Children and Parents* (5–7). Illus. by Valerie Wahl. Series: Little Light of Mine. 2004, Eastern Washington Univ. paper $19.95 (978-0-910055-94-9). Muslim folktales, fables, stories from the Koran, and historic tales originate from countries around the world. (Rev: BL 10/15/04; SLJ 8/04) [297.1]

9817 Dudley, William. *Islam* (8–12). Series: Opposing Viewpoints. 2004, Gale LB $36.20 (978-0-7377-2238-3); paper $24.95 (978-0-7377-2239-0). Opposing perspectives are offered on wide-ranging topics including the compatibility of Islam with democratic ideals; the status of women; conflicts with Western values; and attitudes toward terrorism and violence. (Rev: BL 10/1/04; SLJ 12/04) [297.2]

9818 Egendorf, Laura K., ed. *Islam in America* (7–12). Series: At Issue. 2005, Gale LB $29.95 (978-0-7377-2727-2). Essays cover topics including discrimination against Muslims, the growing popularity of the religion among Hispanic Americans, and the degree of support of terrorism. (Rev: SLJ 2/06) [297]

9819 Einfeld, Jann, ed. *Is Islam a Religion of War or Peace?* (7–9). Series: At Issue. 2005, Gale LB $28.70 (978-0-7377-3100-2). Opposing perspectives on Islam's attitude toward violence are examined in this thought-provoking collection of essays, many of which quote from the Koran in support of their assertions. (Rev: SLJ 11/05) [297]

9820 Gordon, Matthew S. *Islam*. 3rd ed. (7–10). 2006, Facts on File $30.00 (978-0-8160-6612-4).

An overview of the history of Islam, its branches, the Koran, and Islam's place in the modern world. (Rev: SLJ 3/07) [297]

9821 Hafiz, Dilara, and Imran Hafiz. *The American Muslim Teenager's Handbook* (7–12). 2007, Acacia Pub paper $11.95 (978-0-9792531-2-6). An informative guide to the beliefs and practice of Islam, with tips on prayer, charity, food, entertainment, clothing, and peer pressure plus discussion of Islamic contributions to the world and of misunderstandings on the part of non-Muslims. (Rev: SLJ 10/07) [297.5]

9822 Hurley, Jennifer A., ed. *Islam* (8–12). Illus. Series: Opposing Viewpoints. 2000, Greenhaven LB $32.45 (978-0-7377-0514-0). Essays offer widely contrasting viewpoints on Islam, looking in particular at the religion's basic values, women's role in Muslim society, terrorism, and relations with the West. (Rev: SLJ 2/01) [297]

9823 Jeffrey, Laura S. *Celebrate Ramadan* (5–8). Illus. Series: Celebrate Holidays. 2007, Enslow LB $23.95 (978-0-7660-2774-9). Report writers and others wanting to know about this Muslim holiday will find the facts they need here, as well as more general information about Islam in America. (Rev: BL 10/1/07; SLJ 11/07) [297.3]

9824 Siddiqui, Haroon. *Being Muslim* (8–12). Series: Groundwork Guide. 2006, Groundwood $15.95 (978-0-88899-785-2). This is an objective introduction to the Muslim faith and to related topics of current interest including women's rights and terrorist elements. (Rev: BL 12/15/06; LMC 4–5/07; SLJ 2/07) [297]

9825 Spencer, William. *Islam Fundamentalism in the Modern World* (7–10). 1995, Millbrook LB $24.90 (978-1-56294-435-3). Explains the tenets of Islam and the general nature of religious fundamentalism. (Rev: BL 4/15/95; SLJ 5/95) [320.5]

9826 Tames, Richard. *Islam* (8–10). Illus. 1985, David & Charles $18.95 (978-0-7134-3655-6). A topically arranged overview of Islam that covers such subjects as marriage, mosques, festivals, and beliefs. (Rev: BL 8/85; SLJ 1/86) [297]

9827 Wormser, Richard. *American Islam: Growing Up Muslim in America* (7–12). 1994, Walker $16.85 (978-0-8027-8344-8). A portrait of Muslim American youth and their faith. (Rev: BL 12/15/94; SLJ 3/95; VOYA 2/95) [297]

Judaism

9828 Adler, David A. *The Kids' Catalog of Jewish Holidays* (4–7). Illus. 1996, Jewish Publication Soc. paper $15.95 (978-0-8276-0581-7). Thirteen major and several minor Jewish holidays are introduced, along with activities, songs, and recipes. (Rev: BL 12/15/96; SLJ 3/97) [296.4]

9829 Burstein, Chaya M. *The Jewish Kids Catalog* (7–9). 1983, Jewish Publication Soc. paper $15.95 (978-0-8276-0215-1). All sorts of information is given on Jewish culture and history including holidays, folktales, and even some recipes. [296]

9830 Chaikin, Miriam. *Menorahs, Mezuzas, and Other Jewish Symbols* (5–9). 1990, Clarion $17.00 (978-0-89919-856-9). A Jewish historian explains some of the symbols of the faith. (Rev: BL 1/15/91; HB 5–6/91; SLJ 1/91) [296.4]

9831 Corona, Laurel. *Judaism* (6–9). Series: Religions of the World. 2003, Gale LB $29.95 (978-1-56006-987-4). The history, teachings, and contemporary customs of Judaism are clearly presented, with information on some famous Jews. (Rev: BL 11/15/03; SLJ 11/03) [296]

9832 David, Jo, and Daniel B. Syme. *The Book of the Jewish Life* (5–8). Illus. 1997, UAHC paper $13.95 (978-0-8074-0628-1). This book explores common Jewish traditions in such areas as birth and naming, religious schools, bar/bat mitzvahs, confirmation, marriage, and mourning. (Rev: SLJ 9/98) [296]

9833 Feinstein, Edward. *Tough Questions Jews Ask: A Young Adult's Guide to Building a Jewish Life* (5–7). 2003, Jewish Lights $14.99 (978-1-58023-139-8). Rabbi Feinstein effectively answers hypothetical questions posed by an imagined class of thoughtful young students. (Rev: BL 4/1/03) [296.7]

9834 Fisher, Leonard E. *To Bigotry No Sanction: The Story of the Oldest Synagogue in America* (5–8). Illus. 1998, Holiday $16.95 (978-0-8234-1401-7). Beginning with the expulsion of the Jews from Spain in 1492, the author traces the history of Jews in America, including the 1763 building — with George Washington's blessing — of the Touro Synagogue. (Rev: BCCB 4/99; BL 2/1/99; HBG 10/99; SLJ 3/99) [296.097457]

9835 Isaacs, Ron. *Ask the Rabbi: The Who, What, Where, Why, and How of Being Jewish* (7–12). 2003, Jossey-Bass paper $22.95 (978-0-7879-6784-0). Questions and answers are divided into thematic chapters and provide information on practices in different denominations. (Rev: BL 10/15/03) [296]

9836 Keene, Michael. *Judaism* (5–8). Series: Religions of the World. 2005, World Almanac LB $31.00 (978-0-8368-5869-3). A basic introduction to the beliefs and practices of Judaism around the world, with a chronology of important events. (Rev: SLJ 2/06) [296]

9837 Kimmel, Eric A. *Wonders and Miracles: A Passover Companion* (4–8). Illus. 2004, Scholastic

$18.95 (978-0-439-07175-8). In addition to a description of the holiday and its rituals, Kimmel provides stories, songs, prayers, poems, and recipes. (Rev: BL 2/15/04*; SLJ 2/04) [296.4]

9838 Metter, Bert. *Bar Mitzvah, Bat Mitzvah: The Ceremony, the Party, and How the Day Came to Be* (4–7). Illus. by Joan Reilly. 2007, Clarion $15.00 (978-0-618-76772-4); paper $5.95 (978-0-618-76773-1). This book about the coming-of-age ceremony for Jewish children (and now adults) covers its history but does not leave out the fun part — the party — and even includes details about the parties of some celebrities. (Rev: BL 7/07; SLJ 11/07) [296.4]

9839 Morrison, Martha, and Stephen F. Brown. *Judaism* (6–9). Illus. Series: World Religions. 1991, Facts on File $30.00 (978-0-8160-2444-5). An illustrated study of the impact Judaism has had on civilization and a look at its evolution, branches, holidays, and traditions. (Rev: BL 4/15/92; SLJ 3/92) [296]

9840 Penney, Sue. *Judaism* (6–8). Series: World Beliefs and Cultures. 2000, Heinemann LB $25.64 (978-1-57572-358-7). A balanced introduction to the history and practice of this major religion, with material on its sacred texts, worship, pilgrimage sites, key figures, festivals, and subgroups. (Rev: HBG 10/01; SLJ 4/01) [296]

9841 Scharfstein, Sol. *Understanding Jewish History I* (6–9). Illus. 1996, KTAV paper $15.95 (978-0-88125-545-4). Using many colorful illustrations, this work traces Jewish history from biblical times to the expulsion of the Jews from Spain in the 15th century. (Rev: BL 10/1/96; SLJ 1/97) [909]

9842 Scharfstein, Sol. *Understanding Jewish Holidays and Customs: Historical and Contemporary* (4–7). Illus. 1999, KTAV $27.50 (978-0-88125-634-5); paper $18.95 (978-0-88125-626-0). From ancient Jewish traditions to the present day, this highly visual volume describes the history, customs, and teaching of Judaism. (Rev: BL 10/1/99; HBG 3/00; SLJ 2/00) [296.4]

9843 Wood, Angela. *Being a Jew* (6–10). Illus. 1988, David & Charles $19.95 (978-0-7134-4668-5). This book deals with the history, religion, customs, and traditions of Jewish people around the world. (Rev: SLJ 8/88) [296]

9844 Wood, Angela. *Judaism* (5–8). Illus. Series: World Religions. 1995, Thomson Learning LB $24.26 (978-1-56847-376-5). An informative, clearly written text on Judaism, with a glossary, bibliography, and map of regions in which the religion flourishes. (Rev: BL 9/1/95; SLJ 11/95) [296]

Religious Cults

9845 Barghusen, Joan D. *Cults* (7–12). Illus. Series: Overview. 1997, Lucent LB $29.95 (978-1-56006-199-1). The author recounts the history of cults in America, attempts to demystify them through an examination of their beliefs, recruitment methods, funding, and various practices, and reviews the anti-cult movement, including the practice of de-programming. (Rev: BL 5/1/98; SLJ 8/98) [291.0460973]

9846 Cohen, Daniel. *Cults* (7–10). 1994, Millbrook LB $23.40 (978-1-56294-324-0). This work describes cults throughout American history, including Pilgrims, Quakers, Moonies, and Satanists, and examines their recruiting methods. (Rev: BL 11/1/94; SLJ 2/95; VOYA 2/95) [291.9]

9847 Cole, Michael D. *The Siege at Waco: Deadly Inferno* (5–9). Series: American Disasters. 1999, Enslow LB $23.93 (978-0-7660-1218-9). The story of the disaster that ended the 51-day siege at Waco and resulted in the deaths of cult leader David Koresh and 73 of his followers. (Rev: BL 2/15/99; HBG 10/99) [976.4284063]

9848 De Angelis, Gina. *Jonestown Massacre: Tragic End of a Cult* (6–9). Illus. Series: American Disasters. 2002, Enslow LB $23.93 (978-0-7660-1784-9). The circumstances behind the mass suicide at Jonestown, Guyana, are examined here. (Rev: BL 1/1–15/03; HBG 3/03; SLJ 4/03) [988.1]

9849 Gay, Kathlyn. *Communes and Cults* (7–12). 1997, Twenty-First Century LB $24.40 (978-0-8050-3803-3). After tracing the history of cults that rely on communal living, the author discusses contemporary cults, their similarities and differences, their appeal, and their problems. (Rev: BL 9/1/97; SLJ 7/97; VOYA 10/97) [280]

9850 Goodnough, David. *Cult Awareness: A Hot Issue* (5–8). Series: Hot Issues. 2000, Enslow LB $27.93 (978-0-7660-1196-0). This book explains the nature of cults and how they differ as well as giving information on many groups including Jehovah's Witnesses, Unification Church, Hare Krishna, Shakers, Mormons, and Church of Scientology. (Rev: BL 6/1–15/00; HBG 10/00; SLJ 6/00) [291.9]

9851 Kellaher, Karen Burns. *Cult Leaders* (6–9). Illus. Series: History Makers. 1999, Lucent LB $27.45 (978-1-56006-593-7). This work profiles six cult leaders including Shaker founder Mother Ann Lee, David Koresh of Branch Davidian fame, and Jim Jones who followed his cult members in death. (Rev: BL 3/15/00; HBG 9/00; SLJ 4/00) [200.]

9852 Roleff, Tamara L., ed. *Satanism* (6–12). Series: At Issue. 2002, Gale $29.95 (978-0-7377-0807-3); paper $21.20 (978-0-7377-0806-6). A series of essays examine Satanism and the beliefs and rituals of the Church of Satan. (Rev: BL 5/15/02; SLJ 7/02) [113.4]

9853 Streissguth, Thomas. *Charismatic Cult Leaders* (7–12). 1995, Oliver LB $19.95 (978-1-881508-18-2). A balanced presentation of a potentially sensational topic. Includes biblical references where appropriate in the discussion of various cults and their leaders. (Rev: BL 8/95; SLJ 5/95) [291]

9854 Zeinert, Karen. *Cults* (7–12). Illus. Series: Issues in Focus. 1997, Enslow LB $26.60 (978-0-89490-900-9). Following a history of cults in America from the days of the Salem witches on, this book discusses all forms of present-day cults, from the more establishment (Jehovah's Witnesses and Mormonism) to the extremist (Branch Davidians and the Freemen of Montana). (Rev: BL 6/1–15/97; VOYA 10/97) [291.9]

Society and the Individual

Government and Political Science

General and Miscellaneous

9855 Downing, David. *Democracy* (5–8). Illus. Series: Political and Economic Systems. 2002, Heinemann LB $28.50 (978-1-4034-0317-9). Downing explains the history of democracy and looks at its weaknesses and benefits. Also use *Dictatorship* (2002). (Rev: BL 1/1–15/03; HBG 3/03) [321.8]

9856 Harris, Nathaniel. *Democracy* (6–8). Series: Ideas of the Modern World. 2001, Raintree LB $25.69 (978-0-7398-3160-1). This account traces the history of democracy from ancient Greece through its flowering after the American and French revolutions and ends with the defeat of communism in the Cold War. (Rev: BL 4/15/02) [320.5]

9857 Tames, Richard. *Monarchy* (5–8). Series: Political and Economic Systems. 2002, Heinemann LB $28.50 (978-1-4034-0320-9). A description of the concept of monarchy, followed by a history of its application, its current status, and its various forms. (Rev: BL 1/1–15/03; HBG 3/03) [321.8]

United Nations and Other International Organizations

9858 Burger, Leslie, and Debra L. Rahm. *Red Cross / Red Crescent: When Help Can't Wait* (5–7). Illus. 1996, Lerner $22.60 (978-0-8225-2698-8). The story of the Red Cross and the role it plays in helping people today. (Rev: BL 1/1–15/97; SLJ 1/97; VOYA 4/97) [361.7]

9859 Maddocks, Steven. *UNICEF* (5–8). Series: World Watch. 2004, Raintree LB $271.40 (978-0-7398-6617-7). Introduces UNICEF's history, organ-

ization, and work on behalf of the world's children; sidebars provide key facts and relevant quotations. (Rev: BL 4/1/04; SLJ 6/04) [362.7]

9860 Ostopowich, Melanie. *Greenpeace* (4–8). Series: International Organizations. 2002, Weigl LB $16.95 (978-1-59036-020-0). An introduction to the goals, structure, members, and volunteers who work with this international organization. Also use *Peace Corps* (2003). (Rev: HBG 3/03; SLJ 4/03) [333.72]

9861 Ross, Stewart. *The United Nations* (7–12). Illus. Series: 20th Century Perspectives. 2003, Heinemann LB $27.07 (978-1-4034-0152-6). An overview of the history, importance, abilities, and current activities of the United Nations, including efforts of UN agencies such as the World Health Organization. (Rev: BL 3/1/03; HBG 10/03; SLJ 5/03) [341.23]

9862 Ross, Stewart. *United Nations* (5–8). Illus. Series: World Watch. 2004, Raintree LB $18.99 (978-0-7398-6616-0). Ross explains the role of the United Nations as an international watchdog and provides a brief review of its history and organization. (Rev: BL 4/1/04) [341.23]

International Relations, Peace, and War

9863 Altman, Linda J. *Genocide: The Systematic Killing of a People* (7–12). Series: Issues in Focus. 1995, Enslow LB $20.95 (978-0-89490-664-0). Discusses the history of genocide and explores the Us-Them mentality and racist stereotypes that are still used today to execute genocidal policies. (Rev: BL 10/15/95; SLJ 11/95; VOYA 12/95) [364.15]

9864 Bixler, Mark. *The Lost Boys of Sudan: An American Story of the Refugee Experience* (8–12).

Illus. 2005, Univ. of Georgia $24.95 (978-0-8203-2499-9). Journalist Bixler tracks the progress of four young men — refugees who were part of the so-called Lost Boys of Sudan — as they adjust to their new lives in America. (Rev: BL 2/1/05) [962.404]

9865 Bradman, Tony, ed. *Give Me Shelter: Stories about Children Who Seek Asylum* (5–8). 2007, Frances Lincoln $16.95 (978-1-845\0-752-4). These gripping stories of real children seeking refuge from countries torn apart by war or strife will capture readers' hearts. (Rev: SLJ 3/08)

9866 Chippendale, Neil. *Crimes Against Humanity* (7–10). Series: Crime, Justice, and Punishment. 2001, Chelsea LB $30.00 (978-0-7910-4254-0). A clearly written, informative account that explores such international crimes as genocide. (Rev: BL 6/1–15/01; HBG 3/01; SLJ 2/01) [341]

9867 Dalton, Dave. *Refugees and Asylum Seekers* (7–10). Illus. Series: People on the Move. 2005, Heinemann LB $31.36 (978-1-4034-6961-8). A look at the plight of civilians who have been forced from their native lands by war or ethnic cleansing; a poor layout is offset by the personal stories. (Rev: BL 8/05; SLJ 12/05) [305.9]

9868 Dalton, David. *Living in a Refugee Camp: Carbino's Story* (6–9). Illus. Series: Children in Crisis. 2005, World Almanac LB $31.00 (978-0-8368-5960-7). A Sudanese native tells the story of his 14-year exile from his country; background information and photographs add context. (Rev: SLJ 11/05)

9869 Fridell, Ron. *Spy Technology* (4–7). Series: Cool Science. 2006, Lerner LB $25.26 (978-0-8225-5934-4). A review of the kinds of technology available in the past and today — including gadgets used by the CIA and KGB and spy satellites — is followed by accounts of dangerous missions and discussion of future technologies. (Rev: SLJ 4/07) [623]

9870 Gerdes, Louise, ed. *Rogue Nations* (6–12). Series: Opposing Viewpoints. 2006, Gale LB $34.95 (978-0-7377-3421-8). What is a "rogue" nation? Iran, North Korea, Pakistan, and the United States are among those mentioned in this provocative pro/con discussion. (Rev: SLJ 3/07) [355]

9871 Gold, Susan Dudley. *Arms Control* (6–9). Illus. Series: Pacts and Treaties. 1997, Twenty-First Century LB $24.90 (978-0-8050-4812-4). Beginning with the 1868 Declaration of St. Petersburg calling for a ban on the use of explosive projectiles, the author tells of the many subsequent attempts by world leaders to limit the sale and use of arms. (Rev: BL 9/1/97; SLJ 12/97) [327.1]

9872 Gottfried, Ted. *The Fight for Peace: A History of Antiwar Movements in America* (8–11). Illus. Series: People's History. 2005, Twenty-First Century LB $29.90 (978-0-7613-2932-9). Chronicles the history of American protest movements from the Civil War to the present. (Rev: BL 10/1/05; SLJ 11/05) [303.6]

9873 Grant, R. G. *Genocide* (5–10). Illus. Series: Talking Points. 1999, Raintree LB $27.12 (978-0-8172-5314-1). This book covers the Holocaust in World War II as well as more recent massacres in Cambodia, Rwanda, and Bosnia, and probes such controversies as who is guilty of genocide — the person who pulls the trigger or those who plan and organize it, and what about the bystander? (Rev: BL 9/1/99) [304.6]

9874 Landau, Elaine. *Big Brother Is Watching: Secret Police and Intelligence Services* (7–12). 1992, Walker LB $15.85 (978-0-8027-8161-1). Describes the activities and methods of intelligence and police services in several Western and former Eastern-bloc nations, including the KGB, the Mossad, the CIA, and Honduran death squads. (Rev: BL 6/1/92; SLJ 8/92) [363.2]

9875 *Making It Home: Real Life Stories from Children Forced to Flee* (5–8). Illus. 2006, Dial $17.99 (978-0-8037-3083-0); paper $6.99 (978-0-14-240455-3). The horrific impact of war on children is documented in these first-person accounts, with many photographs, from children who were displaced from their homes in Afghanistan, Bosnia, Burundi, Congo, Iraq, Kosovo, Liberia, and Sudan. (Rev: BL 12/1/05; SLJ 2/06) [305.23]

9876 Ousseimi, Maria. *Caught in the Crossfire: Growing Up in a War Zone* (6–10). 1995, Walker LB $20.85 (978-0-8027-8364-6). Examines the effects of violence on children and how violence changes children's perception of the world. (Rev: BL 9/1/95; SLJ 9/95; VOYA 12/95) [305.23]

9877 Spangenburg, Ray, and Kit Moser. *The Crime of Genocide: Terror Against Humanity* (8–12). Series: Issues in Focus. 2000, Enslow LB $26.60 (978-0-7660-1249-3). Separate chapters address the mass killings of the 20th century — during the Holocaust and in Armenia, Bosnia and Kosovo, Cambodia, and Rwanda. (Rev: HBG 3/01; SLJ 3/01) [364.15]

United States Government and Institutions

General and Miscellaneous

9878 McIntosh, Kenneth, and Marsha McIntosh. *When Religion and Politics Mix: How Matters of Faith Influence Political Policies* (7–10). Illus. Series: Religion and Modern Culture. 2006, Mason Crest LB $22.95 (978-1-59084-971-2). Statistics from the 2004 election provide a basis for this overview of Americans' views on religion and politics. (Rev: BL 4/1/06) [201]

9879 Ventura, Jesse, and Heron Marquez. *Jesse Ventura Tells It Like It Is: America's Most Outspoken Governor Speaks Out About Government* (5–8). Illus. 2002, Lerner LB $15.95 (978-0-8225-0385-9). A look at the U.S. government and politicians from the viewpoint of wrestler-turned-Minnesota-governor Jesse Ventura. (Rev: BL 8/02; HBG 3/03; SLJ 9/02) [977.6]

The Constitution

9880 Banfield, Susan. *The Fifteenth Amendment: African-American Men's Right to Vote* (7–12). Illus. Series: Constitution. 1998, Enslow LB $26.60 (978-0-7660-1033-8). This is the stormy history of the constitutional amendment passed during Reconstruction that barred states from denying voting rights to black males. (Rev: BL 9/1/98) [324.6]

9881 Bjornlund, Lydia. *The Constitution and the Founding of America* (6–9). Series: World History. 2000, Lucent LB $27.45 (978-1-56006-586-9). A clearly written account with many quotations from original sources that traces the development of the U.S. Constitution after the Revolution. (Rev: BL 2/15/00; HBG 9/00) [342.73]

9882 Boaz, John, ed. *Free Speech* (7–12). Series: Current Controversies. 2006, Gale LB $34.95 (978-0-7377-2204-8); paper $23.70 (978-0-7377-2205-5). Previously published articles involving free speech answer four main questions: "Should Free Speech Be Limited? Is Free Speech Threatened? Does the War on Terror Threaten Free Speech?" and "How Should the Right to Free Speech Apply to Corporations?" (Rev: SLJ 6/06)

9883 Collier, Christopher, and James Lincoln Collier. *Creating the Constitution, 1787* (5–8). Illus. Series: Drama of American History. 1998, Marshall Cavendish LB $31.36 (978-0-7614-0776-8). This history of the U.S. Constitution describes the background and importance of the document and the compromises made to win ratification. (Rev: BL 2/15/99) [342.73029]

9884 Eck, Kristin. *Drafting the Constitution: Weighing the Evidence to Draw Sound Conclusions* (5–8). Illus. Series: Critical Thinking in American History. 2005, Rosen LB $26.50 (978-1-4042-0412-6). This slim volume offers a review of the issues debated at the Constitutional Convention, plus study questions, a reading list, and a Web site with links to related online resources. (Rev: BL 10/15/05) [342.7302]

9885 Farish, Leah. *The First Amendment: Freedom of Speech, Religion, and the Press* (6–9). Illus. 1998, Enslow LB $26.60 (978-0-89490-897-2). Using many actual cases as examples, the author explores the complexities of the First Amendment

to the Constitution, which guarantees basic freedoms. (Rev: BL 3/15/98; SLJ 6/98) [342.73]

9886 Feinberg, Barbara S. *The Articles of Confederation: The First Constitution of the United States* (7–10). Illus. 2002, Twenty-First Century LB $24.90 (978-0-7613-2114-9). Feinberg presents the history and text of the constitution that was in force from 1776 to 1787, along with a list of the signers, a timeline, and source notes. (Rev: BL 2/1/02; HBG 10/02; SLJ 3/02) [342.73]

9887 Feinberg, Barbara S. *Constitutional Amendments* (5–8). Series: Inside Government. 1996, Twenty-First Century LB $22.40 (978-0-8050-4619-9). After presenting a brief history of the Constitution, this work examines the Bill of Rights and then covers the remaining amendments in chapters arranged by topic. (Rev: SLJ 12/96) [342.73]

9888 Finkelman, Paul. *The Constitution* (4–8). Series: American Documents. 2006, National Geographic LB $23.90 (978-0-7922-7975-4). An unusually attractive introduction to the Constitution, with reproductions, photographs, and profiles of key individuals. (Rev: SLJ 2/06; VOYA 8/06) [342.73]

9889 Freedman, Russell. *In Defense of Liberty: The Story of America's Bill of Rights* (5–10). 2003, Holiday $24.95 (978-0-8234-1585-4). A succinct explanation of the history of the Bill of Rights, discussing each amendment in turn and its particular relevance to today's controversies, with many references to cases involving young people. (Rev: BCCB 10/03*; BL 10/1/03*; HB 9–10/03*; HBG 4/04; SLJ 10/03*; VOYA 4/04) [342.73]

9890 Friedman, Ian C. *Freedom of Speech and the Press* (7–12). Series: American Rights. 2005, Facts on File $35.00 (978-0-8160-5662-0). Issues relating to the freedoms of speech and the press — in the past, present, and future — are explored in this title. (Rev: SLJ 12/05)

9891 Gerberg, Mort. *The U.S. Constitution for Everyone* (8–12). Illus. 1987, Putnam paper $7.95 (978-0-399-51305-3). The text of the Constitution and amendments is analyzed with many interesting asides and background information. (Rev: BL 5/1/87) [342.73]

9892 Gonzales, Doreen. *A Look at the Second Amendment: To Keep and Bear Arms* (4–7). Illus. Series: MyReportLinks.com. 2007, Enslow LB $24.95 (978-1-59845-061-3). Links to relevant Web sites enhance the text introducing students to the content and intent of the Second Amendment to the United States Constitution. (Rev: BL 10/15/07; LMC 11/07; SLJ 1/08) [344.7305]

9893 Graham, Amy. *A Look at the 18th and 21st Amendments: The Prohibition and Sale of Intoxicating Liquors* (5–8). Illus. Series: The Constitution of the United States. 2007, Enslow LB $33.27 (978-1-59845-063-7). A clear overview of these two amendments with links to Web sites that offer additional information. (Rev: SLJ 1/08)

9894 Haesly, Richard, ed. *The Constitutional Convention* (6–9). Series: History Firsthand. 2001, Gale LB $36.20 (978-0-7377-1072-4). Excerpts from personal accounts bring to life the events and key characters surrounding the writing of the U.S. Constitution. (Rev: SLJ 2/02) [342.73]

9895 Hanson, Freya Ottem. *The Second Amendment: The Right to Own Guns* (6–8). Series: The Constitution. 1998, Enslow LB $26.60 (978-0-89490-925-2). Using historical background material, case studies, legal decisions, and statistics, the author presents a balanced account of the controversy surrounding the owning of arms and the demand for gun control. (Rev: SLJ 12/98) [347]

9896 Haynes, Charles C., and Sam Chaltain. *First Freedoms: A Documentary History of the First Amendment Rights in America* (7–12). 2006, Oxford Univ. $40.00 (978-0-19-515750-5). A look at the key figures in the struggle for First Amendment rights — John Locke, Thomas Jefferson, Elizabeth Cady Stanton, and John Scopes, among them — and at the topics that raised people's ire. (Rev: SLJ 11/06*)

9897 Head, Tom. *Freedom of Religion* (7–10). Illus. Series: American Rights. 2005, Facts on File $35.00 (978-0-8160-5664-4). Examines the significance of freedom of religion as guaranteed by the First Amendment to the Constitution and provides an overview of the role played by religion in America's early history, the Scopes trial, and questions surrounding school prayer. (Rev: BL 10/15/05) [323.44]

9898 Horn, Geoffrey M. *The Bill of Rights and Other Amendments* (5–8). Series: World Almanac Library of American Government. 2004, World Almanac LB $31.00 (978-0-8368-5475-6). A thorough and detailed examination of the process of changing the Constitution and the issues underlying the various amendments. (Rev: SLJ 9/04) [342.73]

9899 Hubbard-Brown, Janet. *How the Constitution Was Created* (5–8). Series: The U.S. Government: How It Works. 2007, Chelsea House LB $30.00 (978-0-7910-9420-4). This is a thorough introduction to the Constitution, with interesting text and accompanying historical and biographical sidebars. (Rev: SLJ 1/08)

9900 Hudson, David L. *The Bill of Rights* (5–8). Illus. Series: The Constitution. 2002, Enslow LB $26.60 (978-0-7660-1903-4). A look at the first 10 amendments to the Constitution and how they have affected the citizens of the United States. (Rev: BL 2/15/03; HBG 3/03) [342.73]

9901 Hudson, David L. *The Fourteenth Amendment: Equal Protection Under the Law* (5–8). Illus. Series: The Constitution. 2002, Enslow LB $26.60 (978-0-7660-1904-1). What the 14th amendment to the

Constitution entails and how it has affected the citizens of the United States. (Rev: BL 2/15/03; HBG 10/03) [342.73]

9902 Johnson, Terry. *Legal Rights* (7–12). Series: American Rights. 2005, Facts on File $35.00 (978-0-8160-5665-1). A look at the controversial issue of legal rights under the U.S. Constitution, with discussion of government initiatives since September 11, 2001. (Rev: SLJ 12/05)

9903 Judson, Karen. *The Constitution of the United States* (7–10). Series: American Government in Action. 1996, Enslow LB $26.60 (978-0-89490-586-5). This book focuses on the historical background of the constitutional convention and the issues that were debated. (Rev: SLJ 5/96) [342.73]

9904 Krull, Kathleen. *A Kids' Guide to America's Bill of Rights: Curfews, Censorship, and the 100-Pound Giant* (5–8). Illus. 1999, Avon $16.99 (978-0-380-97497-9). After a description of the first 10 amendments, this book details famous court cases and what each amendment means to young people. (Rev: BL 12/1/99; HBG 3/00; VOYA 4/00) [342.73]

9905 Lucas, Eileen. *The Eighteenth and Twenty-First Amendments: Alcohol, Prohibition, and Repeal* (7–12). Illus. Series: Constitution. 1998, Enslow LB $26.60 (978-0-89490-926-9). An account of the circumstances that led to the passage of Prohibition, its effects, and later repeal. (Rev: BL 9/1/98) [344.730541]

9906 Richie, Donald A. *Our Constitution* (7–12). 2006, Oxford Univ. $40 (978-0-19-522385-9). From the reasons for having a constitution to the amendments and their relevance to well-known cases, this is a well-presented overview. (Rev: SLJ 12/06)

9907 Schleichert, Elizabeth. *The Thirteenth Amendment: Ending Slavery* (8–10). 1998, Enslow LB $26.60 (978-0-89490-923-8). The stormy history of this constitutional amendment that ended slavery and fundamentally changed American society. (Rev: BL 8/98; HBG 3/99; SLJ 1/99) [342.73]

9908 Weidner, Daniel. *The Constitution: The Preamble and the Articles* (5–8). Series: The Constitution. 2002, Enslow LB $26.60 (978-0-7660-1906-5). The history of the U.S. Constitution and its meanings are explored through personal stories and examples. (Rev: BL 2/15/03; HBG 3/03; SLJ 1/03) [342.73]

9909 Weidner, Daniel. *Creating the Constitution: The People and Events That Formed the Nation* (5–8). Series: The Constitution. 2002, Enslow LB $26.60 (978-0-7660-1905-8). This informative volume describes how the U.S. Constitution was written and the debates that preceded its adoption. (Rev: BL 2/15/03; HBG 3/03; SLJ 1/03) [342.73]

9910 Wetterer, Charles M. *The Fourth Amendment: Search and Seizure* (8–10). 1998, Enslow LB

$26.60 (978-0-89490-924-5). Though enacted early in this country's history, this amendment on privacy has continued to have an important impact throughout the years. (Rev: BL 8/98) [342.73]

The Presidency

9911 Aaseng, Nathan. *You Are the President* (7–10). 1994, Oliver LB $19.95 (978-1-881508-10-6). Devotes one chapter each to a crisis faced by eight presidents in the 20th century, among them Theodore Roosevelt, Eisenhower, and Nixon. (Rev: BL 4/1/94; SLJ 7/94; VOYA 8/94) [973.9]

9912 Aaseng, Nathan. *You Are the President II: 1800–1899* (7–10). Illus. Series: Great Decisions. 1994, Oliver LB $19.95 (978-1-881508-15-1). This work discusses the powers of the presidency during the 19th century and the major decisions made by presidents during that time. (Rev: BL 11/15/94; SLJ 12/94) [973.5]

9913 Bernstein, Richard B., and Jerome Agel. *The Presidency* (8–12). Illus. 1989, Walker LB $13.85 (978-0-8027-6831-5). A basic history of this institution with some biographical information and a final section that explores the advisability of concentrating such power in one office. (Rev: BL 5/1/89; SLJ 1/89; VOYA 4/89) [353.03]

9914 Cohen, Daniel. *The Impeachment of William Jefferson Clinton* (6–12). 2000, Twenty-First Century LB $23.90 (978-0-7613-1711-1). Extensive background information sets the stage for this account of the impeachment proceedings. (Rev: HBG 9/00; SLJ 6/00; VOYA 2/01) [973.929]

9915 Fernandez, Justin. *High Crimes and Misdemeanors: The Impeachment Process* (7–10). Illus. Series: Crime, Justice, and Punishment. 2000, Chelsea LB $30.00 (978-0-7910-5450-5). Attorney Fernandez explains this process, looking at the early history and at the impeachment of Bill Clinton. (Rev: BL 1/1–15/01; HBG 3/01; SLJ 12/00; VOYA 2/01) [342.73]

9916 Hardesty, Von. *Air Force One: The Aircraft That Shaped the Modern Presidency* (6–12). 2003, NorthWord $29.95 (978-1-55971-894-3). From FDR's first presidential flights through today's dependence on air travel, this highly visual book describes the interior redesigns and other evolutions in this symbol of prestige. (Rev: SLJ 11/03*) [387.7]

9917 Judson, Karen. *The Presidency of the United States* (7–10). Series: American Government in Action. 1996, Enslow LB $26.60 (978-0-89490-585-8). This introduction to the American presidency includes material on the roles of the president, the constitutional basis of the office, the operations of the White House, and the organization of the executive branch. (Rev: SLJ 5/96) [353.03]

9918 Morin, Isobel V. *Impeaching the President* (8–12). 1996, Millbrook LB $24.90 (978-1-56294-668-5). This book, written before the Clinton impeachment, explains what impeachment is, its processes, and its role in American history. (Rev: SLJ 6/96; VOYA 10/96) [336.73]

9919 Nardo, Don. *The U.S. Presidency* (6–8). Series: Overview. 1995, Lucent LB $29.95 (978-1-56006-157-1). This book explores the events that shaped the presidency and the changing views of the president's role in legislative affairs, foreign policy, war, and the appointment process. (Rev: BL 7/95) [353.03]

9920 Rubel, David. *Scholastic Encyclopedia of the Presidents and Their Times*. Rev. ed. (4–8). Illus. 1997, Scholastic paper $18.95 (978-0-590-49366-6). This fine reference book introduces each of the presidents and his administration and supplies material on related historical events, movements, and personalities. (Rev: HBG 10/01; SLJ 5/97) [920]

9921 Schlesinger, Arthur M., Jr., ed. *The Election of 2000 and the Administration of George W. Bush* (8–12). Series: Major Presidential Elections and the Administrations That Followed. 2003, Mason Crest LB $24.95 (978-1-59084-365-9). The circumstances of Bush's election and the major events of his administration through 2002 are presented with reference to many primary sources; brief biographical facts about the president and his cabinet are also included. (Rev: HBG 4/04; SLJ 10/03) [324.973]

9922 Smith, Carter, ed. *Presidents in a Time of Change: A Sourcebook on the U.S. Presidency* (5–8). Illus. Series: American Albums. 1993, Millbrook $25.90 (978-1-56294-362-2). A heavily illustrated, attractive review of the presidency from Truman to Clinton. (Rev: BL 12/1/93; SLJ 4/94; VOYA 4/94) [973.92]

9923 Smith, Carter, ed. *Presidents of a Divided Nation: A Sourcebook on the U.S. Presidency* (5–8). Series: American Albums. 1993, Millbrook $25.90 (978-1-56294-360-8). A visual sourcebook about the presidents during the Civil War and immediately after, from the Library of Congress collection on U.S. presidents. Also use *Presidents of a Growing Country*. (Rev: BL 12/1/93) [973.8]

9924 Smith, Carter, ed. *Presidents of a Growing Country: A Sourcebook on the U.S. Presidency* (5–8). Illus. Series: American Albums. 1993, Millbrook $25.90 (978-1-56294-358-5). Through extensive use of pictorials, a thorough timeline, and concise text, this attractive book traces the presidency from Hayes through McKinley. (Rev: BL 12/1/93; SLJ 4/94) [973.8]

9925 Smith, Carter, ed. *Presidents of a Young Republic: A Sourcebook on the U.S. Presidency* (5–8). Illus. Series: American Albums. 1993, Millbrook $25.90 (978-1-56294-359-2). A well-illustrated account that traces U.S. history from the presidency of John Quincy Adams through James Buchanan. (Rev: BL 12/1/93; SLJ 4/94) [973.5]

9926 Waldman, Michael, comp. *My Fellow Americans: The Most Important Speeches of American Presidents from George Washington to George W. Bush* (7–12). 2003, Sourcebooks paper $45.00 (978-1-4022-0027-4). A collection of more than 40 speeches by 17 presidents, some of which are shown with early drafts; two accompanying CDs contain all the speeches, with the actual voices of presidents starting with Teddy Roosevelt. (Rev: BL 10/15/03; SLJ 10/03*) [352.23]

9927 Woronoff, Kristen. *American Inaugurals: The Speeches, the Presidents, and Their Times* (7–10). Illus. 2002, Gale $64.94 (978-1-56711-854-4). An attractive, well-illustrated, large-format presentation of all the inaugural speeches, with background information, fast-fact sidebars, and commentary. (Rev: BL 8/02; SLJ 11/02) [352.23]

Federal Government, Its Agencies, and Public Administration

9928 Aaseng, Nathan. *You Are the Senator* (7–10). Illus. Series: Great Decisions. 1997, Oliver LB $19.95 (978-1-881508-36-6). This book describes the duties and responsibilities of a U.S. senator and the nature of the decisions that senators make. (Rev: BL 4/15/97; SLJ 8/97; VOYA 8/97) [328.73]

9929 Balcavage, Dynise. *The Federal Bureau of Investigation* (7–9). Series: Your Government: How It Works. 2000, Chelsea LB $31.00 (978-0-7910-5530-4). Famous cases introduce this examination of the FBI, its history, and crime detection equipment and strategies. (Rev: HBG 9/00; SLJ 8/00) [363.25]

9930 Bausum, Ann. *Our Country's Presidents* (5–8). Illus. 2005, National Geographic LB $45.90 (978-0-7922-9330-9). Full of interesting facts, quotations, and illustrations, this new edition has been extended with information on vice presidents, the Electoral College, and presidential security. (Rev: BL 5/15/05; SLJ 4/05) [973]

9931 Bernstein, Richard B., and Jerome Agel. *The Congress* (7–12). Illus. 1989, Walker LB $13.85 (978-0-8027-6833-9). An introduction to this branch of the government with material arranged chronologically and including some coverage of scandals and decline in prestige. (Rev: BL 5/1/89; SLJ 1/89; VOYA 4/89) [328.73]

9932 Emert, Phyllis Raybin. *Attorneys General: Enforcing the Law* (6–9). 2005, Oliver LB $24.95 (978-1-881508-66-3). An introduction to the responsibilities of the attorney general and to eight key individuals who have held the position. (Rev: SLJ 6/06)

9933 Esherick, Joan. *The FDA and Psychiatric Drugs: How a Drug Is Approved* (6–10). Illus. Series: Psychiatric Disorders: Drugs and Psychology for the Mind and Body. 2003, Mason Crest LB $24.95 (978-1-59084-578-3). As well as a clear explanation of the drug approval process, this volume contains information on alternative medicines and an interesting look at how treatment of schizophrenia has advanced over time. (Rev: SLJ 5/04)

9934 Harmon, Daniel E. *The Environmental Protection Agency* (6–9). Series: Your Government: How It Works. 2002, Chelsea LB $25.00 (978-0-7910-6792-5). A readable examination of the purpose of the agency and its internal workings, with an emphasis on the kinds of challenges our environment faces. (Rev: HBG 3/03; SLJ 1/03) [354.3]

9935 Harmon, Daniel E. *The FBI* (7–10). Series: Crime, Justice, and Punishment. 2001, Chelsea LB $30.00 (978-0-7910-4289-2). The highest branch of criminal investigation in the United States is discussed with material on powers, methods, and personnel. (Rev: BL 6/1–15/01; HBG 10/01) [363.2]

9936 Horn, Geoffrey M. *The Presidency* (5–8). Series: World Almanac Library of American Government. 2003, World Almanac LB $31.00 (978-0-8368-5458-9). Information on the first lady, the White House, and key presidents add to the coverage here, which includes primary sources as well as many photographs and statistics. (Rev: SLJ 1/04) [973]

9937 Kassinger, Ruth G. *U.S. Census: A Mirror of America* (5–8). Illus. 1999, Raintree $28.54 (978-0-7398-1217-4). Written before the 2000 census began, this book describes the history of the census and the methods used to count Americans. (Rev: BL 12/15/99; HBG 3/00) [304]

9938 Mintzer, Rich. *The National Institutes of Health* (6–9). 2002, Chelsea LB $25.00 (978-0-7910-6793-2). An absorbing overview of the role of this institution and the importance of public health. (Rev: HBG 3/03; SLJ 1/03) [362.1]

9939 Partner, Daniel. *The House of Representatives* (7–12). Series: Your Government — How It Works. 2000, Chelsea House $31.00 (978-0-7910-5535-9). A discussion of the history, structure, functions, and importance of the U.S. House of Representatives. [328.73]

9940 Richie, Jason. *Secretaries of State: Making Foreign Policy* (7–10). Illus. Series: Cabinet. 2002, Oliver LB $22.95 (978-1-881508-65-6). Succinct profiles of eight secretaries of state, ranging chronologically from John Quincy Adams to James Baker, look at their beliefs and how they influenced the nation's foreign policy. Also recommended in this series is *Secretaries of War, Navy, and Defense: Ensuring National Security* (2002). (Rev: BL 10/15/02; HBG 3/03; SLJ 4/03) [327.73]

9941 Sandak, Cass R. *Congressional Committees* (7–9). Series: Inside Government. 1995, Twenty-First Century LB $24.90 (978-0-8050-3425-7). An overview of how congressional committees came into existence and their role, including how they control legislation. (Rev: BL 12/15/95; SLJ 1/96) [336.73]

9942 Sandak, Cass R. *Lobbying* (7–9). Series: Inside Government. 1995, Twenty-First Century LB $24.90 (978-0-8050-3424-0). A look at how legislation is influenced, including a brief history of lobbies and descriptions of domestic and foreign public interest groups. (Rev: BL 12/15/95; SLJ 1/96) [328.73]

9943 Sandak, Cass R. *The National Debt* (5–8). Series: Inside Government. 1996, Twenty-First Century LB $22.40 (978-0-8050-3423-3). The origins and causes of the national debt are covered, with options for the future. (Rev: BL 5/15/96; SLJ 8/96) [336.3]

9944 Teichmann, Iris. *Immigration and the Law* (5–8). Series: Understanding Immigration. 2006, Smart Apple Media LB $31.35 (978-1-58340-970-1). Covers all aspects of immigration including the laws granting admission, visas, and how to gain citizenship. (Rev: SLJ 3/07)

9945 Wagner, Heather Lehr. *The Central Intelligence Agency* (5–8). Illus. Series: The U.S. Government: How It Works. 2007, Chelsea House LB $30.00 (978-0-7910-9282-8). Provides information on the Central Intelligence Agency; its history, how it influences government policies, and the kinds of jobs available there. (Rev: BL 8/07) [327]

State and Municipal Governments and Agencies

9946 Gorrell, Gena K. *Catching Fire: The Story of Firefighting* (7–10). 1999, Tundra paper $16.95 (978-0-88776-430-1). This is a history of firefighting, from the bucket brigades of the past to the sophisticated equipment of today, with related information on how fires burn, important fires in history, equipment, firefighting tactics, forms of arson, wildfires, and more. (Rev: BCCB 5/99; BL 6/1–15/99; SLJ 6/99) [363.3]

9947 Levinson, Isabel Simone. *Gibbons v. Ogden: Controlling Trade Between States* (8–10). Series: Landmark Supreme Court Cases. 1999, Enslow LB $26.60 (978-0-7660-1086-4). States' rights and autonomy were the subject of this important Supreme Court case that focused on trade between the states. (Rev: BL 8/99) [353]

9948 Ryan, Bernard. *Serving with Police, Fire, and EMS* (7–12). Series: Community Service for Teens. 1998, Ferguson LB $19.95 (978-0-89434-232-5). This work explains how teens can play an active and productive role in police, fire, and allied community agencies. (Rev: BL 9/15/98; SLJ 2/99) [361.8]

Libraries and Other Educational Institutions

9949 Lerner, Fred. *Libraries Through the Ages* (7–10). Illus. 1999, Continuum $15.95 (978-0-8264-1201-0). A history of libraries, the books they hold, and their readers, adapted from the adult title *The Story of Libraries*. (Rev: BL 11/15/99) [027]

The Law and the Courts

9950 Aaseng, Nathan. *The O. J. Simpson Trial: What It Shows Us About Our Legal System* (6–9). 1996, Walker LB $16.85 (978-0-8027-8405-6). The author uses the Simpson trial to explain such aspects of the American judicial system as investigative techniques, the grand jury, defense, prosecution, the media's role, and emerging technologies. (Rev: BL 5/1/96; SLJ 4/96) [345.73]

9951 Aaseng, Nathan. *You Are the Juror* (6–10). 1997, Oliver LB $19.95 (978-1-881508-40-3). The author re-creates eight famous criminal trials of the 20th century, including the Lindbergh kidnapping case, the Patty Hearst and O. J. Simpson trials, and the Ford Pinto case, and asks the reader to become a jury member and make a decision. (Rev: SLJ 1/98) [347.73]

9952 Aaseng, Nathan. *You Are the Supreme Court Justice* (7–10). Illus. Series: Great Decisions. 1994, Oliver LB $19.95 (978-1-881508-14-4). A description of how the Supreme Court works and the decisions and responsibilities involved in being a Justice. (Rev: BL 11/15/94; SLJ 12/94) [347.73]

9953 Alonso, Karen. *The Alger Hiss Communist Spy Trial* (6–10). Series: Headline Court Cases. 2001, Enslow LB $26.60 (978-0-7660-1481-7). Alonso provides a clear explanation of the political climate of the time and of the intricacies of this important trial, with a glossary, discussion questions, and excerpts from recently declassified documents. (Rev: BL 12/15/01; HBG 3/02; SLJ 11/01) [345]

9954 Alonso, Karen. *Loving v. Virginia: Interracial Marriage* (7–12). Series: Landmark Supreme Court Cases. 2000, Enslow LB $26.60 (978-0-7660-1338-4). A thorough examination of the case that overturned Virginia's law forbidding interracial marriage. (Rev: HBG 3/01; SLJ 10/00) [346.7301]

9955 Anderson, Kelly C. *Police Brutality* (6–10). Series: Overview. 1995, Lucent LB $27.45 (978-1-56006-164-9). A discussion of the reasons for police behavior, the stress and danger of the job and the possible misuse of power. (Rev: BL 4/15/95; SLJ 3/95) [363.2]

9956 Anderson, Wayne. *Brown v. Board of Education: The Case Against School Segregation* (5–8). Series: Supreme Court Cases Through Primary Sources. 2004, Rosen LB $29.25 (978-0-8239-4009-7). Primary sources — photographs, police records, newspaper clippings, and court documents — provide details of the case and the narrative discusses the historical and social context. Also use *Plessy v. Ferguson: Legalizing Segregation* (2004). (Rev: SLJ 6/04) [345.73]

9957 Anderson, Wayne. *The Chicago Black Sox Trial: A Primary Source Account* (5–8). Illus. Series: Great Trials of the Twentieth Century. 2003, Rosen LB $29.25 (978-0-8239-3969-5). This is a detailed, readable account of the 1919 Chicago Black Sox scandal and the plot to fix the World Series. (Rev: BL 4/1/04; SLJ 6/04; VOYA 4/04) [796.357]

9958 Andryszewski, Tricia. *School Prayer: A History of the Debate* (8–12). Illus. Series: Issues in Focus. 1997, Enslow LB $26.60 (978-0-89490-904-7). A thorough, balanced account that explores all sides of the controversy concerning school prayer, with material on the separation of church and state. (Rev: BL 10/1/97; SLJ 3/98; VOYA 2/98) [344.73]

9959 Aretha, David. *The Trial of the Scottsboro Boys* (7–12). Illus. Series: Civil Rights. 2007, Morgan Reynolds $27.95 (978-1-59935-058-5). A compelling account of what happened to nine young black men in 1930s Alabama. (Rev: BL 11/1/07; SLJ 12/07) [345.761]

9960 Berger, Leslie. *The Grand Jury* (7–12). Illus. Series: Crime, Justice, and Punishment. 2000, Chelsea $30.00 (978-0-7910-4290-8). This work traces the history of the grand jury system, outlines procedures at the local and national level, and cites famous grand jury hearings including the Monica Lewinsky case. (Rev: BL 8/00) [345.73]

9961 Bernstein, Richard B., and Jerome Agel. *The Supreme Court* (8–12). Illus. 1989, Walker LB $13.85 (978-0-8027-6835-3). An account that gives a history of the Supreme Court, details on landmark cases, and an outline of how it operates today. (Rev: BL 5/1/89; SLJ 1/89; VOYA 4/89) [347]

9962 Billitteri, Thomas J. *The Gault Case: Legal Rights for Young People* (7–12). Series: Landmark Supreme Court Cases. 2000, Enslow LB $26.60 (978-0-7660-1340-7). Children's rights and due process were the focus of this 1960s case — involving a 15-year-old — that was eventually decided by the Supreme Court. (Rev: HBG 3/01; SLJ 2/01) [345.73]

9963 Burnett, Betty. *The Trial of Julius and Ethel Rosenberg: A Primary Source Account* (5–8). Illus. Series: Great Trials of the Twentieth Century. 2004, Rosen LB $29.25 (978-0-8239-3976-3). Primary sources — photographs, original transcripts, quota-

tions, and so forth — give depth to this compelling account of the complex trial. (Rev: BL 4/1/04; SLJ 10/04)

9964 Campbell, Andrew. *Rights of the Accused* (7–10). Series: Crime, Justice, and Punishment. 2001, Chelsea LB $30.00 (978-0-7910-4303-5). A cleverly written, informative exploration of how and why the judicial system tries to safeguard the rights of accused criminals. (Rev: BL 6/1–15/01; HBG 3/01; SLJ 2/01; VOYA 12/01) [345]

9965 Carrel, Annette. *It's the Law! A Young Person's Guide to Our Legal System* (8–12). 1994, Volcano paper $12.95 (978-1-884244-01-8). The book's goal is voter responsibility through understanding of the laws, how they developed, and how they can be changed. (Rev: BL 2/15/95; VOYA 12/95) [349.73]

9966 Carroll, Jamuna, ed. *Civil Liberties and War* (7–12). Series: Issues on Trial. 2006, Gale LB $34.95 (978-0-7377-2503-2). Jamuna examines the United States' history of restriction of civil liberties during wartime, looking in depth at four instances in the 20th and 21st centuries. (Rev: SLJ 8/06)

9967 Chadwick, Bruce. *Infamous Trials* (6–9). Illus. Series: Crime, Justice, and Punishment. 1997, Chelsea LB $30.00 (978-0-7910-4293-9). This book highlights eight cases in the history of American justice, from the Salem witchcraft trials to the Chicago Seven, including Benedict Arnold's court-martial, the Scopes "monkey trial," and the Scottsboro boys. (Rev: BL 9/1/97; SLJ 10/97) [345.73]

9968 Ciment, James. *Law and Order* (6–9). Series: Life in America 100 Years Ago. 1995, Chelsea LB $21.95 (978-0-7910-2843-8). An examination of how the rule of law was established in the U.S. and how basic institutions involving the courts, law enforcement officials, and the legal profession evolved. (Rev: BL 2/1/96) [349.73]

9969 Cothran, Helen, ed. *Police Brutality* (7–12). Illus. Series: Opposing Viewpoints. 2001, Greenhaven LB $36.20 (978-0-7377-0516-4); paper $24.95 (978-0-7377-0515-7). Contributors address various aspects of police conduct and overview, with a special interest in the treatment of teen suspects and a focus on New York City and Los Angeles. (Rev: BL 5/15/01) [363.2]

9970 Crewe, Sabrina, and Michael V. Uschan. *The Scottsboro Case* (4–7). Illus. Series: Events That Shaped America. 2005, Gareth Stevens LB $26.00 (978-0-8368-3407-9). A thorough and thought-provoking look at the infamous Scottsboro case in which nine young African Americans were accused of raping two white women. (Rev: BL 1/1–15/05; SLJ 3/05) [345.73]

9971 Day, Nancy. *The Death Penalty for Teens: A Pro/Con Issue* (6–10). Illus. Series: Hot Pro/Con Issues. 2000, Enslow LB $27.93 (978-0-7660-1370-

4). Strong, opposing opinions on juvenile justice and the death penalty are accompanied by a historical overview and comparisons between the United States and other countries. (Rev: BL 2/15/01; HBG 3/01; SLJ 4/01; VOYA 6/01) [364.66]

9972 DeVillers, David. *The John Brown Slavery Revolt Trial: A Headline Court Case* (8–12). 2000, Enslow $26.60 (978-0-7660-1385-8). An account of the trial of the abolitionist who was hanged for treason and murder. (Rev: HBG 3/01; SLJ 9/00) [306.3]

9973 DeVillers, David. *Marbury v. Madison: Powers of the Supreme Court* (6–10). Series: Landmark Supreme Court Cases. 1998, Enslow LB $26.60 (978-0-89490-967-2). A look at the steps, arguments, and personalities in this early court case that helped define the powers of the Supreme Court. (Rev: BL 2/15/98; SLJ 6/98) [343.7]

9974 Donnelly, Karen. *Cruzan v. Missouri: The Right to Die* (5–7). Illus. Series: Supreme Court Cases Through Primary Sources. 2004, Rosen LB $29.25 (978-0-8239-4014-1). The lengthy legal battle for a patient's right to die is chronicled in this account of the Supreme Court's decision in Cruzan v. Missouri. (Rev: BL 6/1–15/04; SLJ 6/04) [344.73]

9975 Dudley, Mark E. *Engel v. Vitale (1962): Religion and the Schools* (5–9). Series: Supreme Court Decisions. 1995, Twenty-First Century LB $25.90 (978-0-8050-3916-0). The story of the Supreme Court case on school prayer that originated with two Jewish youngsters who objected to being forced to pray every morning in a New York City school. (Rev: BL 11/15/95; SLJ 1/96; VOYA 4/96) [347]

9976 Dudley, Mark E. *Gideon v. Wainwright (1963): Right to Counsel* (6–10). Series: Supreme Court Decisions. 1995, Twenty-First Century LB $25.90 (978-0-8050-3914-6). Reviews how the case was built, argued, and decided, and discusses its impact. (Rev: BL 6/1–15/95; SLJ 8/95) [347.3]

9977 Dudley, Mark E. *United States v. Nixon (1974)* (6–10). Illus. Series: Supreme Court Decisions. 1994, Twenty-First Century LB $25.90 (978-0-8050-3658-9). This landmark Supreme Court case concerning the definition of presidential powers is reported on in a step-by-step analysis of the arguments in the Watergate case. (Rev: BL 12/15/94; SLJ 2/95) [342.73]

9978 Egendorf, Laura K., ed. *The Death Penalty* (7–12). Illus. Series: Examining Issues Through Political Cartoons. 2002, Gale paper $21.20 (978-0-7377-1101-1). Egendorf uses cartoons focusing on the death penalty as the basis for a discussion of the controversies surrounding this practice. Also recommended in this series is *Euthanasia* (2002). (Rev: BL 8/02) [364.44]

9979 Fireside, Bryna J. *The Trial of the Police Officers in the Shooting Death of Amadou Diallo: A Headline Court Case* (8–11). Illus. Series: Headline Court Cases. 2004, Enslow LB $26.60 (978-0-7660-2166-2). Covers the trial of four New York City police officers for the 1999 shooting of West African immigrant Amadou Diallo. (Rev: BL 2/1/05) [345.73]

9980 Freedman, Suzanne. *United States v. Amistad: Rebellion on a Slave Ship* (6–9). Series: Landmark Supreme Court Cases. 2000, Enslow LB $26.60 (978-0-7660-1337-7). A look at the slave rebellion from the perspective of the trial that followed, laying out the presentations of the prosecution and defense. (Rev: HBG 3/01; SLJ 2/01)

9981 Fridell, Ron. *Capital Punishment* (8–12). Series: Open for Debate. 2003, Benchmark LB $37.07 (978-0-7614-1587-9). Strong illustrations, graphs, and sidebars add to the narrative on the history of the death penalty, the arguments for and against, and ways to make the system more just and humane. (Rev: SLJ 3/04) [346.66]

9982 Gold, Susan Dudley. *Brown v. Board of Education: Separate But Equal?* (7–12). Series: Supreme Court Milestones. 2004, Benchmark LB $37.07 (978-0-7614-1842-9). An overview of the groundbreaking decision, with information on the key individuals involved and on the legal process itself plus human-interest stories that add depth. (Rev: SLJ 1/05) [344.73]

9983 Gold, Susan Dudley. *Miranda v. Arizona (1966)* (6–10). Series: Supreme Court Decisions. 1995, Twenty-First Century LB $25.90 (978-0-8050-3915-3). This book describes the court case that defined the rights of suspects, with good historical background and a discussion of its impact through 1994. (Rev: BL 6/1–15/95; SLJ 8/95) [345.73]

9984 Gold, Susan Dudley. *The Pentagon Papers: National Security or the Right to Know* (7–12). Series: Supreme Court Milestones. 2004, Benchmark LB $37.07 (978-0-7614-1843-6). An easily understood account of the events surrounding the Pentagon Papers case and the high court's decision that blocked the Nixon administration's efforts to keep the papers secret. (Rev: SLJ 1/05) [342.73]

9985 Gottfried, Ted. *Capital Punishment: The Death Penalty Debate* (6–12). Illus. Series: Issues in Focus. 1997, Enslow LB $20.95 (978-0-89490-899-6). The author presents strong arguments on all sides of the death penalty controversy, including material on its history, moral justification, purpose, legal procedures, and questions of race and geography. (Rev: BL 2/1/97; SLJ 7/97) [345.73]

9986 Gottfried, Ted. *The Death Penalty: Justice or Legalized Murder?* (7–12). Illus. 2002, Twenty-First Century LB $24.90 (978-0-7613-2155-2). Gottfried presents an absorbing and balanced examination of the arguments for and against the death penalty, with historical information and details of specific cases. (Rev: BL 3/15/02; HBG 10/02; SLJ 3/02) [364.66]

9987 Gottfried, Ted. *Police Under Fire* (7–12). Illus. 1999, Twenty-First Century LB $24.90 (978-0-7613-1313-7). A well-balanced account that gives a history of policing, police culture, pressures on police personnel, corruption, and cases of police brutality. (Rev: BL 12/15/99; HBG 4/00; SLJ 1/00) [363.2]

9988 Grabowski, John F. *The Death Penalty* (5–8). Series: Overview. 1999, Lucent LB $29.95 (978-1-56006-371-1). A fair, unbiased review of the history, pro and con arguments, and present status of the death penalty in America. (Rev: BL 8/99) [364.6]

9989 Haas, Carol. *Engel v. Vitale: Separation of Church and State* (6–10). 1994, Enslow LB $26.60 (978-0-89490-461-5). A discussion of the arguments presented by both sides in this landmark Supreme Court case concerning the separation of church and state as it applies to religion in public schools. (Rev: BL 11/15/94; VOYA 12/94) [344.73]

9990 Hanson, Freya Ottem. *The Scopes Monkey Trial: A Headline Court Case* (6–10). Illus. Series: Headline Court Cases. 2000, Enslow LB $26.60 (978-0-7660-1388-9). The story of the famous trial of a Tennessee high school teacher for teaching evolution. (Rev: BL 10/1/00; HBG 3/01; SLJ 9/00) [345.73]

9991 Harmon, Daniel E. *Defense Lawyers* (7–10). Series: Crime, Justice, and Punishment. 2001, Chelsea LB $30.00 (978-0-7910-4284-7). This introduction to the roles of defense attorney and public defender provides brief profiles of figures including Clarence Darrow and Alan Dershowitz. (Rev: HBG 10/02; SLJ 4/02) [345.73]

9992 Henningfeld, Diane Andrews, ed. *The Death Penalty* (7–12). Series: Opposing Viewpoints. 2006, Gale LB $34.95 (978-0-7377-2929-0); paper $23.70 (978-0-7377-2930-6). A thought-provoking collection of essays providing many points of view on the use of the death penalty. (Rev: SLJ 9/06)

9993 Herda, D. J. *Furman v. Georgia: The Death Penalty Case* (6–10). Series: Landmark Supreme Court Cases. 1994, Enslow LB $26.60 (978-0-89490-489-9). Summarizes the historical background of this case, the case itself, and its impact. (Rev: BL 11/15/94; SLJ 11/94) [345.73]

9994 Herda, D. J. *New York Times v. United States: National Security and Censorship* (6–10). Illus. Series: Landmark Supreme Court Cases. 1994, Enslow LB $26.60 (978-0-89490-490-5). This exciting, controversial Supreme Court case involved the Pentagon Papers and helped define freedom of the press when it conflicts with what may be considered national security. (Rev: BL 11/15/94; SLJ 1/95) [342.73]

9995 Herda, D. J. *Roe v. Wade: The Abortion Question* (6–10). Illus. Series: Landmark Supreme Court Cases. 1994, Enslow LB $26.60 (978-0-89490-459-2). This book describes the arguments on both sides of the abortion debate, how the justices of the Supreme Court reacted, their decision, and its consequences. (Rev: BL 6/1–15/94; SLJ 7/94; VOYA 8/94) [344.73]

9996 Himton, Kerry. *The Trial of Sacco and Vanzetti: A Primary Source Account* (5–8). Illus. Series: Great Trials of the Twentieth Century. 2004, Rosen LB $29.25 (978-0-8239-3973-2). Primary sources — photographs, original transcripts, quotations, and so forth — give depth to this compelling account of the complex trial. (Rev: BL 4/1/04; SLJ 6/04)

9997 Horn, Geoffrey M. *The Supreme Court* (5–8). Series: World Almanac Library of American Government. 2003, World Almanac LB $31.00 (978-0-8368-5459-6). An excellent introduction to the U.S. Supreme Court and the important role it plays in interpreting the laws of the land. (Rev: SLJ 1/04)

9998 Hulm, David. *United States v. the Amistad: The Question of Slavery in a Free Country* (6–8). Series: Supreme Court Cases Through Primary Sources. 2004, Rosen LB $29.25 (978-0-8239-4013-4). Using many primary documents, this volume retells the story of the slave revolt aboard the *Amistad* in 1839 and the resulting legal battle that went all the way to the Supreme Court. (Rev: SLJ 6/04) [326]

9999 Jacobs, Thomas A. *Teens on Trial: Young People Who Challenged the Law — and Changed Your Life* (8–12). 2000, Free Spirit paper $14.95 (978-1-57542-081-3). Student rights and responsibilities are explored through this examination of 21 cases in which teens participated in the legal process. (Rev: BL 1/1–15/01; SLJ 1/01; VOYA 4/01) [346.7301]

10000 Jacobs, Thomas A. *They Broke the Law, You Be the Judge: True Cases of Teen Crime* (7–12). 2003, Free Spirit paper $15.95 (978-1-57542-134-6). A former juvenile court judge presents 21 real-life cases involving juveniles, gives the reader the sentencing options, and reveals the actual outcome of each case. (Rev: BL 2/1/04; SLJ 1/04) [345.73]

10001 Jarrow, Gail. *The Printer's Trial: The Case of John Peter Zenger and the Fight for a Free Press* (7–10). Illus. 2006, Boyds Mills $18.95 (978-1-59078-432-7). Covers the events leading up to and the 1735 trial of John Peter Zenger, a printer from New York who was found not guilty of seditious libel against the British government, establishing freedom of the press. (Rev: BL 10/1/06; LMC 2/07; SLJ 11/06) [345.73]

10002 Jones-Brown, Delores D. *Race, Crime, and Punishment* (7–12). Illus. Series: Crime, Justice, and Punishment. 2000, Chelsea $30.00 (978-0-7910-

4273-1). This book explores the double standard often applied to black and white offenders and also discusses police brutality as related to race. (Rev: BL 8/00; HBG 9/00) [364]

10003 Koopmans, Andy. *Leopold and Loeb: Teen Killers* (7–12). Series: Famous Trials. 2004, Gale LB $29.95 (978-1-59018-227-7). The story of the famous trial of two privileged boys for the murder of a third, with details of Clarence Darrow's innovative defense strategy. (Rev: SLJ 6/04) [345.73]

10004 Kowalski, Kathiann M. *Lemon v. Kurtzman and the Separation of Church and State Debate* (8–12). Series: Debating Supreme Court Decisions. 2005, Enslow LB $26.60 (978-0-7660-2391-8). This well-documented title examines the Supreme Court's decision in Lemon *v.* Kurtzman and reviews its impact on the doctrine of separation of church and state. (Rev: SLJ 12/05)

10005 Kronenwetter, Michael. *The Supreme Court of the United States* (7–10). Series: American Government in Action. 1996, Enslow LB $26.60 (978-0-89490-536-0). After presenting an example of the power of the Supreme Court, the author describes the judicial system and a brief history of the court, discusses how it operates and the increasingly political nature of appointments and decisions, and details some of its most significant decisions. (Rev: SLJ 5/96) [347]

10006 McNeese, Tim. *Dred Scott v. Sandford* (7–10). Series: Great Supreme Court Decisions. 2006, Chelsea House LB $30.00 (978-0-7910-9236-1). Illustrations and graphics add interest to this account of the Dred Scott court case and its significance in the nation's division over slavery. (Rev: BL 2/1/07) [342]

10007 Manaugh, Sara. *Judges and Sentencing* (7–10). Series: Crime, Justice, and Punishment. 2001, Chelsea LB $30.00 (978-0-7910-4296-0). An introduction to the role of judges and to the sentencing process, with material on sentencing reform. (Rev: HBG 10/02; SLJ 4/02) [345.73]

10008 Monroe, Judy. *The Sacco and Vanzetti Controversial Murder Trial: A Headline Court Case* (6–10). Illus. Series: Headline Court Cases. 2000, Enslow $26.60 (978-0-7660-1387-2). The story of the murder trials of two Italian immigrants in 1921, the long-questioned conviction, and the abuse and protection of suspects' rights then and today. (Rev: BL 10/1/00; HBG 9/00; SLJ 1/01) [345.73]

10009 Mountjoy, Shane. *Engel v. Vitale: School Prayer and the Establishment Clause* (7–12). Series: Great Supreme Court Decisions. 2006, Chelsea House LB $30.00 (978-0-7910-9241-5). An accessible overview of the ongoing debate about school prayer in the United States. (Rev: SLJ 7/07) [344.73]

10010 Naden, Corinne J., and Rose Blue. *Dred Scott: Person or Property?* (5–8). Illus. Series: Supreme Court Milestones. 2005, Benchmark LB $37.07 (978-0-7614-1841-2). The Supreme Court's 1857 Dred Scott decision, arguably the high court's most misguided ruling ever, is examined in detail. (Rev: BL 2/1/05) [342.7]

10011 Nakaya, Andrea C., ed. *The Environment* (7–12). Series: Issues on Trial. 2006, Gale LB $34.95 (978-0-7377-2797-5). Four benchmark court cases illustrate how environmental laws can become forces for social change. (Rev: SLJ 7/06)

10012 Olson, Steven P. *The Trial of John T. Scopes: A Primary Source Account* (5–8). Series: Great Trials of the Twentieth Century. 2004, Rosen LB $29.25 (978-0-8239-3974-9). Primary sources — photographs, original transcripts, quotations, and so forth — give depth to this compelling account of the complex trial. (Rev: BL 4/1/04; SLJ 8/04) [344.73]

10013 Owens, L. L. *American Justice: Seven Famous Trials of the 20th Century* (6–8). Illus. Series: Cover-to-Cover. 2000, Perfection Learning $17.95 (978-0-7807-7831-3); paper $8.95 (978-0-7891-2869-0). Kidnappings, murder, and a classic civil rights case are among the trials presented here. (Rev: BL 1/1–15/01) [345.73]

10014 Paddock, Lisa. *Facts About the Supreme Court of the United States* (8–12). 1996, H.W. Wilson $105.00 (978-0-8242-0896-7). A one-stop reference source for information about the Supreme Court, from individual justices to the court's history and important cases. (Rev: VOYA 12/96) [347]

10015 Panchyk, Richard. *Our Supreme Court: A History with 14 Activities* (7–10). Illus. 2006, Chicago Review paper $17.95 (978-1-55652-607-7). Focusing on the history and development of the Supreme Court and landmark cases handled, this large-format book with effective illustrations includes interviews with attorneys, politicians, and other related figures as well as a variety of activities, a glossary, and useful facts. (Rev: BL 11/1/06; SLJ 3/07) [347.73]

10016 Payment, Simone. *Roe v. Wade: The Right to Choose* (5–7). Illus. Series: Supreme Court Cases Through Primary Sources. 2004, Rosen LB $29.25 (978-0-8239-4012-7). Illustrations are used to good effect in this overview of the issues raised in the Supreme Court's landmark decision. (Rev: BL 6/1–15/04; SLJ 6/04) [342.73]

10017 Payment, Simone. *The Trial of Leopold and Loeb: A Primary Source Account* (5–8). Illus. Series: Great Trials of the Twentieth Century. 2004, Rosen LB $29.25 (978-0-8239-3970-1). Primary sources — photographs, original transcripts, quotations, and so forth — give depth to this compelling account of the complex trial. (Rev: BL 4/1/04; SLJ 6/04; VOYA 4/04)

10018 Peacock, Nancy. *Great Prosecutions* (8–12). Illus. Series: Crime, Justice, and Punishment. 2001, Chelsea LB $30.00 (978-0-7910-4292-2). Accounts of five famous trials — including those of the Manson "family" and Al Capone — show readers how prosecutors work to prove guilt. (Rev: BL 1/1–15/02) [345]

10019 Pellowski, Michael J. *The O. J. Simpson Murder Trial: A Headline Court Case* (7–12). Series: Headline Court Cases. 2001, Enslow LB $26.60 (978-0-7660-1480-0). An objective summary of the murder investigation, the murder trial and the civil trial, and the personalities involved. (Rev: HBG 3/02; SLJ 12/01) [345.73]

10020 Persico, Deborah A. *Mapp vs. Ohio: Evidence and Search Warrants* (6–10). Illus. Series: Landmark Supreme Court Cases. 1997, Enslow LB $26.60 (978-0-89490-857-6). A step-by-step account of the Supreme Court decision that established a citizen's rights concerning search warrants and the collection of evidence. (Rev: BL 4/15/97; SLJ 6/97) [345.73]

10021 Persico, Deborah A. *New Jersey v. T.L.O.: Drug Searches in Schools* (7–12). Illus. Series: Landmark Supreme Court Cases. 1998, Enslow LB $20.95 (978-0-89490-969-6). This Supreme Court case lasted five years and explored the rights of a student, identified as T.L.O., whose handbag was searched by a school administrator who found marijuana and articles that indicated the student was selling drugs. (Rev: BL 8/98; HBG 9/98; SLJ 8/98; VOYA 2/99) [345.73]

10022 Persico, Deborah A. *Vernonia School District v. Acton: Drug Testing in Schools* (7–12). Series: Landmark Supreme Court Cases. 1999, Enslow LB $26.60 (978-0-7660-1087-1). An examination of an Oregon court case involving random drug testing introduces the reader to important legal concepts. (Rev: HBG 4/00; SLJ 1/00) [344.73]

10023 Ramen, Fred. *The Rights of the Accused* (7–12). Series: Individual Rights and Civic Responsibility. 2001, Rosen LB $26.50 (978-0-8239-3238-2). Real cases illustrate how constitutional provisions play a significant role in protecting the rights of the accused. (Rev: SLJ 8/01; VOYA 12/01) [345.73]

10024 Riley, Gail B. *Miranda v. Arizona: Rights of the Accused* (6–10). Illus. 1994, Enslow LB $18.95 (978-0-89490-404-2). This account analyzes the Supreme Court case that defined the rights of an accused person based on what became known as Miranda rights. (Rev: BL 11/15/94) [345.73]

10025 Roensch, Greg. *The Lindbergh Baby Kidnapping Trial: A Primary Source Account* (5–8). Series: Great Trials of the Twentieth Century. 2004, Rosen LB $29.25 (978-0-8239-3971-8). Primary sources — photographs, original transcripts, handwriting samples, and so forth — give depth to this account

of this controversial trial. (Rev: BL 4/1/04; SLJ 8/04) [345.73]

10026 Scheppler, Bill. *The Mississippi Burning Trial: A Primary Source Account* (5–8). Illus. Series: Great Trials of the Twentieth Century. 2004, Rosen LB $29.25 (978-0-8239-3972-5). Primary sources — photographs, original transcripts, quotations, and so forth — give depth to this compelling account of the complex trial. (Rev: BL 4/1/04; SLJ 10/04)

10027 Schonebaum, Steve, ed. *Does Capital Punishment Deter Crime?* (8–12). Series: At Issue. 1998, Greenhaven LB $26.20 (978-1-56510-791-5); paper $17.45 (978-1-56510-091-6). This anthology presents arguments by those who maintain the death penalty deters crime and by others with statistics, studies, and other evidence that point to the opposite conclusion. (Rev: BL 6/1–15/98) [364.6]

10028 Sonneborn, Liz. *Miranda v. Arizona: The Rights of the Accused* (5–8). Series: Supreme Court Cases Through Primary Sources. 2004, Rosen LB $29.25 (978-0-8239-4010-3). Primary sources — photographs, police records, newspaper clippings, and court documents — provide details of the case and the narrative discusses the historical and social context. (Rev: BL 6/1–15/04; SLJ 6/04) [345.73]

10029 Sorensen, Lita. *The Scottsboro Boys Trial: A Primary Source Account* (5–8). Illus. 2003, Rosen LB $29.25 (978-0-8239-3975-6). Sorensen dissects the sensational Scottsboro Boys rape case in Alabama that attracted media attention from around the globe. (Rev: BL 4/1/04) [345.761]

10030 Steffens, Bradley. *Furman v. Georgia: Fairness and the Death Penalty* (6–9). Series: Famous Trials. 2001, Lucent LB $29.95 (978-1-56006-470-1). The Supreme Court case of 1972 that stuck down the death penalty as cruel and unusual punishment is investigated with good background material and information about this case's significance. (Rev: BL 12/15/01) [345]

10031 Steins, Richard. *The Death Penalty: Is It Justice?* (6–9). Series: Issues of Our Time. 1993, Twenty-First Century LB $22.90 (978-0-8050-2571-2). Jumping off from Gary Gilmore's execution, this book looks at the death penalty through history and presents the current debate. (Rev: BL 11/1/93) [364.6]

10032 Telgen, Diane. *Brown v. Board of Education* (8–12). Series: Defining Moments. 2005, Omnigraphics LB $49.00 (978-0-7808-0775-4). An accessible examination of the landmark Supreme Court decision on school segregation, including many interesting sidebar features and chronicling events before and after the ruling, up to the present day. (Rev: SLJ 12/05*)

10033 Torr, James D. *The Patriot Act* (7–12). Series: The Lucent Terrorism Library. 2005, Gale LB

$29.95 (978-1-59018-774-6). Torr explores the provisions of this controversial piece of legislation and looks at the ongoing criticisms about its threats to privacy and the Fourth Amendment. (Rev: SLJ 3/06) [345.73]

10034 Trespacz, Karen L. *Ferrell v. Dallas I. S. D.* (6–10). Series: Landmark Supreme Court Cases. 1998, Enslow LB $26.60 (978-0-7660-1054-3). The dramatic story of the school district case that was adjudicated by the Supreme Court. (Rev: BL 8/98; HBG 3/99; SLJ 1/99; VOYA 2/99) [347]

10035 Wolf, Robert V. *Capital Punishment* (6–9). Series: Crime, Justice, and Punishment. 1997, Chelsea $30.00 (978-0-7910-4311-0). This book reviews the history of capital punishment, explores the moral, philosophical, and legal issues involved, and presents case studies of several death-row inmates. (Rev: SLJ 2/98) [364.6]

10036 Worth, Richard. *The Insanity Defense* (7–10). Series: Crime, Justice, and Punishment. 2001, Chelsea LB $30.00 (978-0-7910-4294-6). After some historical background material, this account uses specific examples to explore facets of the question of how far mental illness goes in excusing criminal behavior. (Rev: BL 6/1–15/01; HBG 10/01; SLJ 7/01; VOYA 6/02) [345]

Politics

GENERAL AND MISCELLANEOUS

10037 Anderson, Dale. *The Democratic Party: America's Oldest Party* (5–8). Series: Snapshots in History. 2007, Compass Point LB $31.93 (978-0-7565-2450-0). This well-designed book provides a thorough, unbiased history of the Democratic Party and includes sidebars, charts, photographs, maps, and Web sites. (Rev: SLJ 7/07) [324.2736]

10038 Anderson, Dale. *The Republican Party: The Story of the Grand Old Party* (5–8). Series: Snapshots in History. 2007, Compass Point LB $31.93 (978-0-7565-2449-4). This history of the Republican Party presents a balanced view of the how the party formed, its values, and its highs and lows since its formation. (Rev: SLJ 7/07) [324.273]

10039 Archer, Jules. *Special Interests: How Lobbyists Influence Legislation* (7–12). Illus. 1997, Millbrook LB $24.90 (978-0-7613-0060-1). This timely account looks at special interest groups, why lobbyists have so much power, how lobbies were created, and the role they play in influencing policy. (Rev: BL 12/15/97; SLJ 1/98; VOYA 2/98) [324]

10040 Audryszewski, Tricia. *The Reform Party* (5–8). Series: Headliners. 2000, Millbrook LB $25.90 (978-0-7613-1906-1). This book describes the formation of the Reform Party and highlights the work of Ross Perot, Pat Buchanan, and Jesse Ventura. (Rev: BL 8/00; HBG 10/01; SLJ 1/01) [324.273]

10041 Boyers, Sara Jane. *Teen Power Politics: Make Yourself Heard* (7–12). 2000, Twenty-First Century LB $24.90 (978-0-7613-1307-6); paper $9.95 (978-0-7613-1391-5). An in-depth and inspiring look at the ways in which teens too young to vote can nonetheless exert their influence. (Rev: BL 11/15/00; HBG 3/01; SLJ 1/01; VOYA 4/01) [323]

10042 Cox, Vicki. *The History of Third Parties* (7–10). Illus. Series: The U.S. Government: How It Works. 2007, Chelsea House LB $30.00 (978-0-7910-9421-1). Third parties have not seen success in the United States; this volume explores the history of third parties and looks at the reasons why they have had trouble attracting voters. (Rev: BL 2/15/08) [324.273]

10043 Kronenwetter, Michael. *Political Parties of the United States* (6–9). Illus. 1996, Enslow LB $20.95 (978-0-89490-537-7). A history of political parties and how they function plus how they influence every aspect of the country's political life. (Rev: BL 6/1–15/96; SLJ 6/96) [324.273]

10044 Lindop, Edmund. *Political Parties* (5–8). Series: Inside Government. 1996, Twenty-First Century LB $24.90 (978-0-8050-4618-2). This work traces the origins of political parties and the role they play in presidential elections. (Rev: BL 9/15/96; SLJ 12/96) [324.273]

10045 Lutz, Norma Jean. *The History of the Republican Party* (7–9). Series: Your Government: How It Works. 2000, Chelsea LB $25.00 (978-0-7910-5540-3). A look at the history and structure of the Republican Party, with anecdotes and information on key figures. (Rev: HBG 9/00; SLJ 8/00) [324.2734]

10046 Morin, Isobel V. *Politics, American Style: Political Parties in American History* (6–12). Illus. 1999, Twenty-First Century $24.90 (978-0-7613-1267-3). An engaging account of the history of American political parties, accompanied by political cartoons. (Rev: BL 11/15/99; HBG 4/00; SLJ 1/00) [324.273]

10047 Staton, Hilarie. *The Progressive Party: The Success of a Failed Party* (5–8). Series: Snapshots in History. 2007, Compass Point LB $31.93 (978-0-7565-2451-7). This history of the Progressives is well-organized and shows how the party's agenda moved forward even though the party itself didn't survive. (Rev: SLJ 7/07) [324.2732]

10048 Winters, Paul A., ed. *The Media and Politics* (8–12). 1996, Greenhaven LB $11.95 (978-1-56510-383-2); paper $17.45 (978-1-56510-382-5). A collection of articles about the relationship between the media and politics and how messages can be influenced by the agendas of journalists, politicians, and special interest groups. (Rev: BL 3/15/96; SLJ 4/96; VOYA 8/96) [302.23]

10049 Zeinert, Karen. *Women in Politics: In the Running* (6–9). 2002, Twenty-First Century LB $29.90 (978-0-7613-2253-5). From 1774 to the present, the author looks at women who have been elected to office or who have been influential in the political field, and discusses the possibility of a woman president. (Rev: BL 12/1/02; HBG 3/03; SLJ 11/02) [320]

ELECTIONS

10050 Goldman, David J. *Presidential Losers* (6–9). Illus. 2004, Lerner LB $25.26 (978-0-8225-0100-8). From Aaron Burr to Al Gore, this account profiles unsuccessful presidential candidates across two centuries of American history. (Rev: BL 4/1/04) [973]

10051 Gottfried, Ted. *The 2000 Election* (5–8). Illus. 2002, Millbrook LB $25.90 (978-0-7613-2406-5). A well-designed and detailed look at the controversial presidential election of 2000, with background information, sidebars on important people, and an electoral map and other graphics. (Rev: BL 7/02; HBG 10/02; SLJ 4/02) [324.973]

10052 Hewson, Martha S. *The Electoral College* (5–9). 2002, Chelsea $25.00 (978-0-7910-6790-1). Covers the history of the electoral college and details of elections of particular interest, including the 2000 Bush–Gore decision. (Rev: HBG 3/03; SLJ 2/03) [324.6]

10053 Horn, Geoffrey M. *Political Parties, Interest Groups, and the Media* (5–8). Series: World Almanac Library of American Government. 2004, World Almanac LB $31.00 (978-0-8368-5478-7). An engaging introduction to the world of politics, the importance of money and lobbying, and the role of the press. (Rev: SLJ 9/04) [324]

10054 Israel, Fred L. *Student's Atlas of American Presidential Elections 1789 to 1996* (7–12). 1997, Congressional Quarterly $45.00 (978-1-56802-377-9). Each of the 53 presidential elections in U.S. history is described on a page or two, accompanied by maps to illustrate election results. (Rev: BL 11/15/97; SLJ 11/97) [973]

10055 Kowalski, Kathiann M. *Campaign Politics: What's Fair? What's Foul?* (8–12). Series: Pro/Con. 2000, Lerner LB $25.26 (978-0-8225-2630-8). Elections are examined along with the practices, both fair and unfair, that are often used to win them. (Rev: HBG 10/01; SLJ 3/01) [324.7]

10056 Marzilli, Alan. *Election Reform* (7–10). Series: Point/Counterpoint. 2003, Chelsea House LB $32.95 (978-0-7910-7698-9). The thorny topics of voter registration, campaign contributions, and political advertising are discussed after an account of the November 2000 Florida recount. (Rev: SLJ 6/04) [324.6]

10057 Morris-Lipsman, Arlene. *Presidential Races: The Battle for Power in the United States* (5–8). Illus. Series: People's History. 2007, Lerner LB $30.60 (978-0-8225-6783-7). Political cartoons, photographs, and other memorabilia add to the text of this guide to the growth in importance of presidential election campaigns; the author gives pertinent background information on each election and provides a useful chart of election results. (Rev: BL 9/15/07; SLJ 10/07) [324.973]

10058 Wagner, Heather Lehr. *How the President Is Elected* (5–8). Series: The U.S. Government: How It Works. 2007, Chelsea House LB $30.00 (978-0-7910-9418-1). This is a thorough introduction to the presidential election process (using the drama of the 2000 election to draw readers in), with interesting text and accompanying historical and biographical sidebars. (Rev: SLJ 1/08)

The Armed Forces

10059 Aaseng, Nathan. *You Are the General* (7–12). Illus. Series: Great Decisions. 1994, Oliver $19.95 (978-1-881508-11-3). This book deals with decisions that have to be made by members of the military, with many examples. (Rev: BL 6/1–15/94) [355]

10060 Doherty, Kieran. *Congressional Medal of Honor Recipients* (6–9). Illus. 1998, Enslow LB $26.60 (978-0-7660-1026-0). This work profiles 11 winners of this prestigious medal, beginning with Jacob Parrott, who earned the first medal in 1863. (Rev: BL 3/15/98) [355.1]

10061 Goldberg, Jan. *Green Berets: The U.S. Army Special Forces* (5–7). Series: Inside Special Operations. 2003, Rosen LB $26.50 (978-0-8239-3808-7). An overview of the history, mission, training, and equipment of the Special Forces. (Rev: BL 7/03) [356]

10062 McNab, Chris. *Protecting the Nation with the U.S. Army* (6–10). Series: Rescue and Prevention: Defending Our Nation. 2003, Mason Crest LB $22.95 (978-1-59084-414-4). This series about the specific roles the various services play in defending U.S. interests at home and abroad also discusses each service's history, structure, equipment, and recent operations. Also use *Protecting the Nation with the U.S. Air Force* and *Protecting the Nation with the U.S. Navy* (2003). (Rev: HBG 4/04; SLJ 7/03) [355]

10063 Stremlow, Mary V. *Coping with Sexism in the Military* (7–12). 1990, Rosen LB $21.95 (978-0-8239-1025-0). An analysis of the military from the perspective of the female recruit that reflects conditions in the late 1980s. (Rev: BL 2/15/91) [355]

10064 Worth, Richard. *Women in Combat: The Battle for Equality* (7–12). Series: Issues in Focus. 1999, Enslow LB $26.60 (978-0-7660-1103-8). A study of the changing role of women in the armed forces from the First World War to the Gulf War. (Rev: BL 5/1/99) [355]

10065 Zeinert, Karen, and Mary Miller. *The Brave Women of the Gulf Wars: Operation Desert Storm and Operation Iraqi Freedom* (5–8). Illus. Series: Women at War. 2005, Twenty-First Century LB $30.60 (978-0-7613-2705-9). Highlights women's roles in the Persian Gulf military campaigns. (Rev: BL 10/1/05; SLJ 11/05) [956.7]

Citizenship and Civil Rights

General and Miscellaneous

10066 Andryszewski, Tricia. *Same-Sex Marriage: Moral Wrong or Civil Right?* (7–12). 2008, Lerner LB $38.60 (978-0-8225-7176-6). A balanced look at many aspects of this issue in the United States. The author's discussion is enhanced by quotations from people of all opinions on gay marriage. (Rev: BL 5/1/08; SLJ 6/08) [306.84]

10067 Ellis, Richard J. *To the Flag: The Unlikely History of the Pledge of Allegiance* (7–12). Illus. 2005, Univ. Press of Kansas $29.95 (978-0-7006-1372-4). Traces the history of the Pledge of Allegiance and the flap over two words — "under God" — that were inserted into the pledge nearly 60 years after it was written. (Rev: BL 3/1/05) [323.6]

10068 Grodin, Elissa. *D Is for Democracy: A Citizen's Alphabet* (5–8). Illus. by Victor Juhasz. 2004, Sleeping Bear $16.95 (978-1-58536-234-9). From "Amendment" to "Zeitgeist," this is an exploration of key concepts, people, places, and things, with the emphasis on the United States. (Rev: BL 1/1–15/05; SLJ 10/04) [320.973]

10069 Luthringer, Chelsea. *So What Is Citizenship Anyway?* (5–8). Series: A Student's Guide to American Civics. 1999, Rosen LB $23.95 (978-0-8239-3097-5). Describes and defines the roles and responsibilities of citizens in a democracy and encourages young people to become active in political and social affairs and issues. (Rev: HBG 10/00; SLJ 3/00; VOYA 4/00) [323.6]

Civil and Human Rights

10070 Adams, Colleen. *Women's Suffrage: A Primary Source History of the Women's Rights Movement in America* (5–8). Illus. Series: Primary Sources in American History. 2003, Rosen LB $29.25 (978-0-8239-3685-4). Primary sources — including pamphlets and newspaper articles — tell the story of the women's rights movement in America. (Rev: BL 5/15/03) [305.42]

10071 Allen, Zita. *Black Women Leaders of the Civil Rights Movement* (6–9). Illus. 1996, Watts LB $24.00 (978-0-531-11271-7). An overview of the civil rights movement from 1900 to 1964 that focuses on the many and varied contributions that African American women made to the cause. (Rev: BL 2/15/97; SLJ 1/97) [323.3]

10072 Alonso, Karen. *Schenck v. United States: Restrictions on Free Speech* (7–10). Series: Landmark Supreme Court Cases. 1999, Enslow LB $26.60 (978-0-7660-1089-5). A re-creation of this landmark Supreme Court case that explored the limitations of free speech, including a follow-up on its consequences. (Rev: BL 8/99) [323.44]

10073 Altman, Linda J. *Human Rights: Issues for a New Millennium* (7–10). 2002, Enslow LB $26.60 (978-0-7660-1689-7). A general introduction to the topic of human rights, with historical information and a survey of international organizations working in this area today. (Rev: HBG 10/03; SLJ 5/03; VOYA 8/03) [323]

10074 Altman, Linda J. *Slavery and Abolition in American History* (7–10). Series: In American History. 1999, Enslow LB $26.60 (978-0-7660-1124-3). A well-researched and well-documented account of slavery and the abolitionist movement in the

United States. (Rev: BL 11/15/99; HBG 4/00; SLJ 3/00) [973.7]

10075 Andryszewski, Tricia. *Gay Rights* (6–12). Illus. 2000, Twenty-First Century LB $23.90 (978-0-7613-1568-1). The author presents many viewpoints in this book that discusses gay rights in relation to the law, the military, the church, marriage, the family, government, and politics. (Rev: BL 10/15/00; HBG 10/01; SLJ 10/00; VOYA 12/00) [305.9]

10076 Aretha, David. *The Murder of Emmett Till* (7–12). Series: Civil Rights Movement. 2007, Morgan Reynolds LB $27.95 (978-1-59935-057-8). This book explains how the shocking death of Emmett Till sparked outrage around the country and was one factor leading to the civil rights movement. (Rev: BL 12/1/07; SLJ 1/08) [364.1]

10077 Aretha, David. *Selma and the Voting Rights Act* (7–12). Illus. Series: Civil Rights. 2007, Morgan Reynolds LB $27.95 (978-1-59935-056-1). This book explains how events in Alabama in the 1960s led to the 1965 Voting Rights Act. (Rev: BL 12/15/07; SLJ 1/08) [324.6]

10078 Bausum, Ann. *Freedom Riders: John Lewis and Jim Zwerg on the Front Lines of the Civil Rights Movement* (6–9). 2005, National Geographic LB $28.90 (978-0-7922-4174-4). The passion of those involved in the 1961 Freedom Rides is captured in these profiles of two young men — John Lewis and Jim Zwerg — who played key roles in the protests. Sibert Honor Book, 2007. (Rev: BL 2/1/06*; SLJ 5/06*) [323]

10079 Bausum, Ann. *With Courage and Cloth: Winning the Fight for a Woman's Right to Vote* (6–12). 2004, National Geographic $32.90 (978-0-7922-6996-0). A lively, well-illustrated text chronicles the history of the women's suffrage movement in America, focusing in particular on the period between 1913 and 1920 when the more militant National Women's Party, led by Alice Paul, stepped up pressure for women's right to vote. (Rev: BCCB 1/05; BL 10/15/04; SLJ 9/04) [324.6]

10080 Bender, David, and Bruno Leone, eds. *Feminism* (7–12). Series: Opposing Viewpoints. 1995, Greenhaven paper $16.20 (978-1-56510-179-1). Essays supporting different viewpoints are presented. Topics include feminism's effects on women and society and its future and goals. (Rev: BL 7/95; SLJ 2/95) [305.42]

10081 Berg, Barbara J. *The Women's Movement and Young Women Today: A Hot Issue* (6–9). Series: Hot Issues. 2000, Enslow LB $27.93 (978-0-7660-1200-4). A look at the history of the women's movement and at the many inequalities still facing women today. (Rev: HBG 9/00; SLJ 8/00) [305.42]

10082 Boerst, William. *Marching in Birmingham* (7–12). Series: Civil Rights. 2008, Morgan Reynolds LB $27.95 (978-1-59935-055-4). This well-designed volume with firsthand accounts discusses the various efforts to achieve civil rights in Alabama. (Rev: SLJ 3/08)

10083 Bradley, David, and Shelley Fisher Fishkin, eds. *The Encyclopedia of Civil Rights in America* (5–10). 1997, Sharpe Reference $299.00 (978-0-7656-8000-6). This three-volume set contains 683 alphabetically arranged articles that explore the history, meaning, and application of civil rights issues in the United States. (Rev: BL 2/15/98; SLJ 5/98) [323]

10084 Ching, Jacqueline, and Juliet Ching. *Women's Rights* (7–9). Illus. Series: Individual Rights and Civic Responsibility. 2001, Rosen LB $31.95 (978-0-8239-3233-7). A concise account of the struggle for women's rights in America. (Rev: BL 12/1/01) [305.42]

10085 Crowe, Chris. *Getting Away with Murder: The True Story of the Emmett Till Case* (7–12). Illus. 2003, Penguin $18.99 (978-0-8037-2804-2). A gripping and detailed account of the brutal murder of 14-year-old Emmett Till, an African American boy from Chicago who was visiting relatives in Mississippi in 1954, with discussion of the impact of his death and the ensuing trial on the civil rights movement. (Rev: BL 2/15/03; HB 7–8/03; HBG 10/03; SLJ 5/03*) [364.15]

10086 Currie, Stephen. *Slavery* (7–12). Series: Opposing Viewpoints Digests. 1998, Greenhaven LB $31.20 (978-1-56510-881-3). Diverse opinions are presented in this anthology on issues relating to slavery and human rights, morality, justice, abolition, and resistance. (Rev: BL 4/15/99) [177]

10087 Davidson, Tish. *Prejudice* (4–8). Series: Life Balance. 2003, Watts LB $20.50 (978-0-531-12252-5); paper $6.95 (978-0-531-15572-1). This book explore the causes, types, and effects of prejudice, how it can change a person's mental health, and how it has influenced human history. (Rev: BL 10/15/03) [305.8]

10088 Durrett, Deanne. *Teen Privacy Rights: A Hot Issue* (7–9). 2001, Enslow LB $27.93 (978-0-7660-1374-2). Durrett traces the history of efforts to preserve privacy and explores how this issue affects teens today. (Rev: HBG 10/01; SLJ 6/01) [346.7301]

10089 Egendorf, Laura K., ed. *Human Rights* (8–12). Series: Opposing Viewpoints. 2003, Gale LB $36.20 (978-0-7377-1689-4). This collection of essays covers a definition of human rights, the state of these rights today, and ways in which the United States and the world can respond to human rights abuse. (Rev: BL 1/1–15/04) [323.4]

10090 Englebert, Phillis, and Beth Des Chenes, eds. *American Civil Rights: Primary Sources* (7–12). 1999, U.X.L $70.00 (978-0-7876-3170-3). This is a collection of 15 documents relating to the civil rights movement in America, such as speeches, proclamations, and autobiographical texts. (Rev: BL 1/1–15/00; SLJ 5/00; VOYA 4/00) [323.1]

10091 Faherty, Sara. *Victims and Victims' Rights* (7–12). Series: Justice and Punishment. 1998, Chelsea LB $30.00 (978-0-7910-4308-0). A multi-faceted overview of the victims' rights movement in the United States and its development over the past 25 years. (Rev: BL 3/15/99) [362.88]

10092 Farish, Leah. *Tinker vs. Des Moines: Student Protest* (6–10). Illus. Series: Landmark Supreme Court Cases. 1997, Enslow LB $26.60 (978-0-89490-859-0). This book traces step-by-step this case that was argued in the Supreme Court and that determined the rights of students in schools and campuses. (Rev: BL 4/15/97; SLJ 5/97) [341.4]

10093 Finkelstein, Norman H. *Heeding the Call: Jewish Voices in the Civil Rights Struggle* (6–9). 1997, Jewish Publication Soc. $14.95 (978-0-8276-0590-9). Beginning with the 1600s when both Africans and Jews first came to first country, this book traces the bond between these groups as they fought for civil rights. (Rev: BL 2/15/98) [323.1]

10094 Finlayson, Reggie. *We Shall Overcome: The History of the American Civil Rights Movement* (6–10). Illus. Series: People's History. 2003, Lerner $25.26 (978-0-8225-0647-8). In chronological order, this book explores important civil rights events of the 1950s and 1960s — including demonstrations, marches, lynchings, assassinations, and violent protests — and provides historical context and key quotations. (Rev: BL 2/15/03; HBG 3/03; SLJ 1/03; VOYA 12/03) [323.1]

10095 Fireside, Harvey. *The "Mississippi Burning" Civil Rights Murder Conspiracy Trial* (6–10). Series: Headline Court Cases. 2002, Enslow LB $26.60 (978-0-7660-1762-7). This account describes the vicious murder of three young civil rights workers in Mississippi in 1964 and how their killers were brought to justice. (Rev: BL 3/15/03; HBG 3/03; SLJ 3/03) [973.9]

10096 Fireside, Harvey. *New York Times v. Sullivan: Affirming Freedom of the Press* (6–10). Series: Landmark Supreme Court Cases. 1999, Enslow LB $26.60 (978-0-7660-1085-7). The limits to freedom of the press was the subject of this Supreme Court case that had far-reaching results in the world of journalism. (Rev: BL 8/99) [347.3]

10097 Fireside, Harvey. *Plessy vs. Ferguson: Separate but Equal?* (6–10). Illus. Series: Landmark Supreme Court Cases. 1997, Enslow LB $20.95 (978-0-89490-860-6). This book gives a step-by-step account of the hearings in the Supreme Court of this case that challenged the basic underpinnings of segregation laws. (Rev: BL 7/97; HBG 3/98; SLJ 10/97) [342.73]

10098 Fireside, Harvey, and Sarah B. Fuller. *Brown v. Board of Education: Equal Schooling for All* (6–10). Series: Landmark Supreme Court Cases. 1994, Enslow LB $26.60 (978-0-89490-469-1). Presents background information, the case itself, and the far-reaching impact it has had. (Rev: BL 11/15/94) [344.73]

10099 Freedman, Jeri. *America Debates Civil Liberties and Terrorism* (5–8). Series: America Debates. 2007, Rosen LB $29.25 (978-1-4042-1927-4). Presents facts and opinions on both sides of issues including governmental surveillance and homeland security. (Rev: LMC 2/08; SLJ 11/07) [323.4]

10100 Freedman, Jeri. *America Debates Privacy Versus Security* (5–8). Series: America Debates. 2007, Rosen LB $29.25 (978-1-4042-1929-8). Presents facts and opinions on both sides of issues including profiling and the right to privacy. (Rev: LMC 2/08; SLJ 11/07) [323.44]

10101 Freedman, Russell. *Freedom Walkers: The Story of the Montgomery Bus Boycott* (4–7). 2006, Holiday $18.95 (978-0-8234-2031-5). First-person accounts enliven this history of the 381-day Montgomery Bus Boycott of the mid-1950s, which ended segregation on the buses. (Rev: BCCB 12/06; BL 9/15/06; HBG 4/07; LMC 3/07; SLJ 11/06*; VOYA 10/06) [323.1196]

10102 Fremon, David K. *The Jim Crow Laws and Racism* (6–10). Series: In American History. 2000, Enslow LB $26.60 (978-0-7660-1297-4). This is a history of racism in America from the end of the Civil War to the death of Martin Luther King, Jr., in 1968. (Rev: BL 10/15/2000; HBG 3/01; SLJ 12/00) [973]

10103 Fridell, Ron. *Privacy vs. Security: Your Rights in Conflict* (6–9). Series: Issues in Focus. 2004, Enslow LB $26.60 (978-0-7660-2161-7). The importance of protecting privacy is balanced against the interests of national security, with discussion of many topics from hidden cameras to medical records to airport searches. (Rev: SLJ 9/04) [342.7308]

10104 Gay, Kathlyn. *Cultural Diversity: Conflicts and Challenges: The Ultimate Teen Guide* (7–12). Series: It Happened to Me. 2003, Scarecrow paper $25.95 (978-0-8108-4805-4). Prejudice, stereotypes, and intolerance are among the topics discussed in this overview of the challenges faced and the possible solutions; teens' personal stories add immediacy. (Rev: SLJ 5/04; VOYA 4/04) [305.8]

10105 George, Charles. *Life Under the Jim Crow Laws* (6–9). Series: The Way People Live. 1999, Lucent LB $27.45 (978-1-56006-499-2). A look at racial segregation laws and what life was like for African Americans before the civil rights movement. (Rev: BL 10/15/99; HBG 9/00; SLJ 1/00) [305.896075]

10106 George, Charles, ed. *Living through the Civil Rights Movement* (7–12). Series: Living Through the Cold War. 2006, Gale LB $32.45 (978-0-7377-2919-1). Speeches and essays by those who experienced the civil rights movement firsthand lend depth to this overview. (Rev: SLJ 6/07) [323.1196]

10107 Gold, Susan Dudley. *Human Rights* (6–9). Illus. Series: Pacts and Treaties. 1997, Twenty-First Century LB $23.40 (978-0-8050-4811-7). This is a history of the fight for worldwide human rights that begins with the Geneva Convention of 1863 and ends with the present-day efforts by both political and private organizations. (Rev: BL 9/1/97; SLJ 7/97) [341.4]

10108 Gold, Susan Dudley. *In Re Gault (1967): Juvenile Justice* (5–9). Series: Supreme Court Decisions. 1995, Twenty-First Century LB $25.90 (978-0-8050-3917-7). Inequalities in juvenile sentencing were the subject of this Supreme Court case, an appeal of a six-year reform school sentence given to a juvenile for making an obscene phone call. (Rev: BL 11/15/95; SLJ 1/96; VOYA 4/96) [347]

10109 Gottfried, Ted. *Homeland Security Versus Constitutional Rights* (8–12). Illus. 2003, Millbrook LB $24.90 (978-0-7613-2862-9). Gottfried addresses important questions, both historical and contemporary, in the balancing of safety versus civil liberties. (Rev: BL 11/15/03; HBG 4/04; SLJ 12/03; VOYA 2/04) [303.3]

10110 Gottfried, Ted. *Privacy: Individual Rights v. Social Needs* (8–12). 1994, Millbrook LB $25.90 (978-1-56294-403-2). Discusses debates on privacy in relation to law enforcement, surveillance, abortion, AIDS, and the media. (Rev: BL 9/15/94; SLJ 10/94; VOYA 2/95) [342.73]

10111 Greenberg, Keith E. *Adolescent Rights: Are Young People Equal Under the Law?* (5–8). Illus. Series: Issues of Our Time. 1995, Twenty-First Century LB $22.90 (978-0-8050-3877-4). This unbiased account of the controversial subject encourages readers to form their own conclusions. (Rev: SLJ 9/95) [323]

10112 Guernsey, JoAnn B. *Voices of Feminism: Past, Present, and Future* (7–10). Illus. Series: Frontline. 1996, Lerner LB $19.95 (978-0-8225-2626-1). After a 150-year history of feminism, this account covers the complicated issues and concerns surrounding this subject and discusses past and present leaders in the movement. (Rev: BL 9/15/96; SLJ 7/97; VOYA 4/97) [305.42]

10113 Haskins, Jim. *Separate but Not Equal: The Dream and the Struggle* (7–10). Illus. 1998, Scholastic paper $15.95 (978-0-590-45910-5). A history of African Americans' struggle for equality in education beginning from the time of slavery, with coverage of key court cases and incidents and the beliefs of such leaders as W. E. B. Du Bois and Booker T.

Washington. (Rev: BL 2/15/98; HBG 9/98; SLJ 2/98; VOYA 10/98) [379.2]

10114 Heinrichs, Ann. *The Ku Klux Klan: A Hooded Brotherhood* (4–7). Series: Journey to Freedom. 2002, Child's World LB $28.50 (978-1-56766-646-5). This brief introduction to the Klan covers the group's origins and history, and touches on the Internet's role in spreading hate messages. (Rev: SLJ 12/02) [322.420973]

10115 Hu, Evaleen. *A Level Playing Field: Sports and Race* (5–8). Illus. Series: Sports Issues. 1995, Lerner LB $28.75 (978-0-8225-3302-3). A frank, thorough examination of the problems involving race in sports and how different athletes have dealt with them. (Rev: BL 1/1–15/96; SLJ 9/95) [796]

10116 Hudson, David L., Jr. *Gay Rights* (8–12). Series: Point/Counterpoint. 2004, Chelsea House LB $32.95 (978-0-7910-8094-8). Both sides of the heated debate over gay rights are addressed, including the peripheral issues of military service, rights in the workplace, gay marriage, and adoption rights. (Rev: SLJ 4/05) [305.9]

10117 Jacobs, Thomas A. *What Are My Rights? 95 Questions and Answers About Teens and the Law* (7–12). 1997, Free Spirit paper $14.95 (978-1-57542-028-8). Using a question-and-answer format, this topically arranged manual describes in simple terms concerns relating to teens' rights within the family, at school, and on the job. (Rev: BL 4/1/98; SLJ 4/98; VOYA 6/98) [346.7301]

10118 Kafka, Tina. *Gay Rights* (8–11). Illus. 2006, Gale $28.70 (978-1-59018-637-4). A look at the issue of gay rights, with information on historical and contemporary controversies. (Rev: BL 9/15/06; SLJ 1/07) [323.3]

10119 Katz, William L. *World War II to the New Frontier: 1940–1963* (7–9). Series: History of Multicultural America. 1993, Raintree LB $27.11 (978-0-8114-6280-8). From the beginning of World War II through the Kennedy Era, this is a history of race relations and the struggle for civil rights in this country. (Rev: BL 9/1/93) [305.8]

10120 Kendall, Martha E. *Failure Is Impossible: The History of American Women's Rights* (5–8). Illus. Series: People's History. 2001, Lerner LB $30.35 (978-0-8225-1744-3). The status of women in the United States is discussed from the time of the Puritans to the present, including information on life for slaves, Native American women, and mill girls, and on equal pay and equal opportunity. (Rev: BL 5/1/01; HBG 10/01; SLJ 6/01; VOYA 8/01) [305.42]

10121 King, Casey. *Oh, Freedom! Kids Talk About the Civil Rights Movement with the People Who Made It Happen* (5–9). 1997, Random paper $12.95 (978-0-679-89005-8). In 31 interviews, children ask family members, neighbors, and friends about the part they played in the civil rights movement. (Rev: BL 4/1/97; SLJ 6/97*) [973]

10122 King, David C. *Freedom of Assembly* (4–8). Series: Land of the Free. 1997, Millbrook LB $22.90 (978-0-7613-0064-9). This book covers this basic civil right with examples throughout U.S. history and landmark court cases that helped define its limits. (Rev: BL 5/15/97; SLJ 10/97) [342.73]

10123 King, David C. *The Right to Speak Out* (4–8). Series: Land of the Free. 1997, Millbrook LB $22.90 (978-0-7613-0063-2). Background material on the freedom of speech is given, its use and abuse, and landmark courts cases that have defined it. (Rev: BL 5/15/97; SLJ 10/97) [351.81]

10124 King, Martin Luther, Jr. *I Have a Dream* (4–8). Illus. 1997, Scholastic paper $16.95 (978-0-590-20516-0). The full text of Dr. King's speech is reprinted, with illustrations by 15 award-winning African American artists. (Rev: BL 2/15/98; HBG 3/98; SLJ 11/97) [305.896]

10125 King, Martin Luther, Jr. *The Words of Martin Luther King, Jr.* (7–12). Illus. 1983, Newmarket $15.95 (978-0-937858-28-8). A selection from the writings and speeches of Dr. King that covers a great number of topics. [323.4]

10126 Kleinman, Joseph, and Eileen Kurtis-Kleinman. *Life on an African Slave Ship* (6–10). Series: The Way People Live. 2000, Lucent LB $28.70 (978-1-56006-653-8). The author uses quotations from primary sources and many illustrations in this portrayal of the terrible conditions endured by slaves bound for America. (Rev: BL 3/1/01; SLJ 5/01) [973.6]

10127 Kops, Deborah. *Women's Suffrage* (5–8). Illus. Series: People at the Center. 2004, Gale LB $24.95 (978-1-56711-772-1). This brief but fact-filled volume introduces key leaders in the women's suffrage movement in America. (Rev: BL 5/15/04; SLJ 9/04) [324.6]

10128 Kowalski, Kathiann M. *Affirmative Action* (6–9). Series: Open for Debate. 2006, Benchmark LB $27.95 (978-0-7614-2300-3). Kowalski gives a balanced overview of the policy that favors preferential treatment for women and minority groups in employment and education, presenting various opinions for and against that will be useful for research. (Rev: SLJ 2/07)

10129 Kowalski, Kathiann M. *Teen Rights: At Home, at School, Online* (6–12). Illus. Series: Issues in Focus. 2000, Enslow LB $26.60 (978-0-7660-1242-4). The author lays out teens' rights in areas ranging from school drug testing and Internet use to healthcare and freedom of expression. (Rev: BL 8/00; HBG 9/00; SLJ 8/00; VOYA 2/01) [305.235]

10130 Kramer, Ann. *Human Rights: Who Decides?* (5–8). Series: Behind the News. 2006, Heinemann LB $32.86 (978-1-4034-8832-9). With photographs and examples of news stories, this volume offers various viewpoints on the information we receive on human rights and asks readers how they will make up their minds. (Rev: SLJ 4/07) [323]

10131 Landau, Elaine. *Your Legal Rights: From Custody Battles to School Searches, the Headline-Making Cases That Affect Your Life* (6–10). 1995, Walker LB $14.85 (978-0-8027-8360-8). A review of advances in protection of the legal rights of children and teenagers. (Rev: BL 5/15/95; SLJ 8/95) [346.7301]

10132 Levine, Ellen. *Freedom's Children: Young Civil Rights Activists Tell Their Own Stories* (6–12). 1993, Avon paper $4.99 (978-0-380-72114-6). In this collection of oral histories, 30 African Americans who, as children or teenagers, were part of the civil rights struggles in the 1950s–1960s South recall their experiences. (Rev: BL 12/15/92*; SLJ 3/93*) [973]

10133 Levy, Debbie. *Bigotry* (6–12). 2002, Gale LB $29.95 (978-1-56006-500-5). Specific examples of racism, anti-Semitism, and homophobia are accompanied by discussion of the incidence of bigotry in America, its history, and the influence of the media. (Rev: BL 2/1/02) [179]

10134 Levy, Debbie. *Civil Liberties* (7–12). Illus. Series: Overview. 1999, Lucent LB $29.95 (978-1-56006-611-8). This introduction to civil liberties presents the Bill of Rights and covers freedom of speech and assembly, media freedom, religious liberties, and the right to privacy. (Rev: BL 2/1/00; HBG 9/00) [342.73]

10135 Long, Barbara. *United States v. Virginia: Virginia Military Institute Accepts Women* (7–10). Series: Landmark Supreme Court Cases. 2000, Enslow LB $20.95 (978-0-7660-1342-1). Virginia Military Institute's battle to continue excluding women cadets is documented here with quotations and excerpts from primary documents. (Rev: HBG 3/01; SLJ 11/00) [344.73]

10136 Lucas, Eileen. *Civil Rights: The Long Struggle* (6–10). Illus. Series: Issues in Focus. 1996, Enslow LB $20.95 (978-0-89490-729-6). After a discussion of the first 10 amendments to the U.S. Constitution, this account focuses on the civil rights struggles of African Americans. (Rev: BL 9/15/96; SLJ 12/96) [323]

10137 McKissack, Patricia C., and Fredrick McKissack. *Days of Jubilee: The End of Slavery in the United States* (5–8). 2003, Scholastic $19.99 (978-0-590-10764-8). A combination of clear, interesting narrative, relevant quotations from primary sources, thorough historical approach, and well-chosen illustrations make this a worthwhile volume on the gradual end of slavery. (Rev: BCCB 4/03; BL 5/15/03;

HBG 10/03; LMC 8–9/03; SLJ 5/03; VOYA 4/03) [973.7]

10138 McWhorter, Diane. *Dream of Freedom: The Civil Rights Movement from 1954–1968* (6–8). 2004, Scholastic $19.99 (978-0-439-57678-9). A sweeping, chronological survey of the modern civil rights movement, with personal commentary and many photographs. (Rev: BL 11/15/04*; SLJ 12/04; VOYA 4/05) [323.1]

10139 Mayer, Robert H. *The Civil Rights Act of 1964* (6–12). Series: At Issue in History. 2004, Gale LB $33.70 (978-0-7377-2304-5); paper $23.70 (978-0-7377-2305-2). The landmark act is described in an introductory overview followed by a collection of essays, speeches, and editorials that provide diverse views about the legislation and its impact on race relations in the United States. (Rev: BL 9/1/04; SLJ 9/04) [342.73]

10140 Mayer, Robert H. *When the Children Marched: The Birmingham Civil Rights Movement* (6–12). Illus. 2008, Enslow LB $25.95 (978-0-7660-2930-9). A moving account of the role young people played in Birmingham, Alabama, during the violent events of the civil rights movement, with photographs, news reports, quotations, a timeline, and so forth. (Rev: BL 6/1–15/08) [323.1196]

10141 Meltzer, Milton. *They Came in Chains: The Story of the Slave Ships* (6–10). Illus. Series: Great Journeys. 1999, Benchmark LB $32.79 (978-0-7614-0967-0). Slavery is treated in a global context with material on the horrors of the Middle Passage, and the life of slaves before and after the voyage. (Rev: BL 1/1–15/00; HBG 4/00; SLJ 2/00) [382]

10142 Meyers, Madeleine, ed. *Forward into Light: The Struggle for Woman's Suffrage* (4–8). Illus. Series: Perspectives on History. 1994, Discovery paper $6.95 (978-1-878668-25-7). The story of the long struggle for women's right to vote, including the contributions of Elizabeth Cady Stanton, Susan B. Anthony, Sojourner Truth, and other leaders. (Rev: BL 8/94) [324.6]

10143 Milios, Rita. *Working Together Against Racism* (7–12). Series: Library of Social Activism. 1995, Rosen LB $16.95 (978-0-8239-1840-9). A history of civil rights in America and ways to protect citizens from racism. (Rev: BL 4/15/95; SLJ 4/95) [305.8]

10144 Monroe, Judy. *The Nineteenth Amendment: Women's Right to Vote* (6–8). Illus. 1998, Enslow LB $26.60 (978-0-89490-922-1). Beginning with the historic Seneca Falls meeting in 1848, this book highlights the events, movements, and people involved in the passage of the 19th Amendment giving women the right to vote. (Rev: BL 4/15/98; SLJ 6/98; VOYA 4/98) [324-6]

10145 Monroe, Judy. *The Susan B. Anthony Women's Voting Rights Trial* (6–10). Series: Headline Court

Cases. 2002, Enslow LB $26.60 (978-0-7660-1759-7). Monroe explores the fight for women's suffrage and the trial of Susan B. Anthony for voting illegally in the 1872 election. (Rev: BL 3/15/03; HBG 3/03; SLJ 12/02) [324.6]

10146 Morrison, Toni. *Remember: The Journey to School Integration* (5–12). Illus. 2004, Houghton $18.00 (978-0-618-39740-2). With striking archival photographs and a fictionalized narrative based on historical fact, this fascinating book explores the impact of the American struggle for civil rights on the children who were often at its center. (Rev: BL 4/15/04; SLJ 6/04) [379.2]

10147 Nakaya, Andrea C., ed. *Censorship* (7–12). Series: Opposing Viewpoints. 2005, Gale LB $36.20 (978-0-7377-2925-2); paper $24.95 (978-0-7377-2926-9). This new edition adds thoughtful essays on censorship and free speech as they relate to the press, telemarketing, electronic filtering, spam, and other issues. (Rev: SLJ 9/05) [363.3]

10148 Nakaya, Andrea C., ed. *Civil Liberties* (8–12). Series: Introducing Issues with Opposing Viewpoints. 2005, Gale LB $32.45 (978-0-7377-3387-7). A collection of articles and essays by various authors, all debating issues of civil liberties including the Patriot Act. (Rev: SLJ 5/06) [342.7308]

10149 Nakaya, Andrea C., ed. *Civil Liberties and War* (8–11). Illus. Series: Examining Issues Through Political Cartoons. 2005, Gale LB $29.95 (978-0-7377-2517-9). A current hot-button issue — the suspension of civil liberties during wartime — is put into historical perspective in this volume with cartoons dating from the wars as far back as the Civil War. (Rev: BL 2/1/06; SLJ 7/06) [323]

10150 Nash, Carol R. *The Fight for Women's Right to Vote* (7–10). Series: In American History. 1998, Enslow LB $26.60 (978-0-89490-986-3). The struggle for women's right to vote is told concisely and clearly, with thumbnail sketches of the leading personalities involved. (Rev: BL 8/98; HBG 9/99; SLJ 1/99) [324.6]

10151 Ojeda, Auriana, ed. *Slavery Today* (6–12). Series: At Issue. 2004, Gale LB $29.95 (978-0-7377-1613-9). The problem of slavery today, particularly in some African countries, is explored in this collection of writings. (Rev: BL 2/15/04; SLJ 7/04) [326]

10152 Oliver, Marilyn Tower. *Gay and Lesbian Rights: A Struggle* (7–12). 1998, Enslow LB $26.60 (978-0-89490-958-0). After recounting two incidents of gay bashing, the author reviews the history of gay rights from the ancient Greeks to today, with material on discrimination, law, health, and family issues. (Rev: BL 12/1/98; SLJ 2/99; VOYA 10/99) [305.9]

10153 Parks, Rosa, and Gregory J. Reed. *Dear Mrs. Parks: A Dialogue with Today's Youth* (5–8). 1996,

Lee & Low $16.95 (978-1-880000-45-8). This book contains a sampling of the thousands of letters sent to civil rights leader Rosa Parks and her replies. (Rev: BL 12/1/96; SLJ 12/96) [323]

10154 Patterson, Charles. *The Civil Rights Movement* (6–12). Series: Social Reform Movement. 1995, Facts on File $25.00 (978-0-8160-2968-6). Chronicles the civil rights movement in the United States, including a timeline, chapter notes, and a reading list. (Rev: BL 11/15/95; SLJ 11/95; VOYA 12/95) [323.1196]

10155 Peck, Rodney. *Working Together Against Human Rights Violations* (7–12). Series: Library of Social Activism. 1995, Rosen LB $27.95 (978-0-8239-1778-5). Presents the struggles over a wide range of human rights issues. (Rev: BL 4/15/95; SLJ 4/95) [323]

10156 Rappaport, Doreen. *Nobody Gonna Turn Me 'Round* (4–7). Illus. by Shane W. Evans. 2006, Candlewick $19.99 (978-0-7636-1927-5). This concluding volume of a trilogy documenting the black experience in America focuses on the stormy decade between the Montgomery bus boycott and the signing of the Voting Rights Act in August 1965, providing profiles of key figures. (Rev: BL 8/06; SLJ 10/06) [323.1196]

10157 Rasmussen, R. Kent. *Farewell to Jim Crow: The Rise and Fall of Segregation in America* (8–12). Series: Library of African American History. 1997, Facts on File $25.00 (978-0-8160-3248-8). This is a history of segregation in the United States in such areas as housing, education, employment, transportation, and public accommodations, and efforts to end it. (Rev: VOYA 2/98) [973]

10158 Rhym, Darren. *The NAACP* (6–9). Illus. Series: African American Achievers. 2001, Chelsea LB $30.00 (978-0-7910-5812-1). This history of the NAACP and the civil rights movement in America includes black-and-white photographs and a timeline. (Rev: BL 2/15/02; HBG 10/02; SLJ 5/02) [305.896]

10159 Roleff, Tamara L., ed. *Civil Liberties* (8–12). Series: Opposing Viewpoints. 1998, Greenhaven LB $32.45 (978-1-56510-937-7). This collection of essays explores potential restrictions on freedom of expression, the right to privacy, the separation of church and state, and freedom to use the Internet. (Rev: BL 8/98; SLJ 1/99; VOYA 6/99) [342]

10160 Sawvel, Patty Jo, ed. *Student Drug Testing* (7–12). Series: Issues That Concern You. 2006, Gale LB $32.45 (978-0-7377-2424-0). Students, educators, journalists, government officials, and a selection of experts present their opinions on the efficacy and ethics of student drug testing. (Rev: SLJ 2/07)

10161 Seidman, David. *Civil Rights* (7–9). Series: Individual Rights and Civic Responsibility. 2001,

Rosen LB $26.50 (978-0-8239-3231-3). Civil rights are defined, with material on key issues and a discussion of landmark cases including the Civil Rights Act of 1964. (Rev: BL 3/15/02; SLJ 2/02; VOYA 2/02) [323.1]

10162 Sirimarco, Elizabeth. *The Civil Rights Movement* (6–9). Illus. Series: American Voices From. 2004, Benchmark LB $34.21 (978-0-7614-1697-5). Primary source documents and excellent illustrations are accompanied by good introductory text and "Think about This" questions. (Rev: SLJ 2/05) [973]

10163 Somerlott, Robert. *The Little Rock School Desegregation Crisis* (6–10). Series: In American History. 2001, Enslow LB $26.60 (978-0-7660-1298-1). Beginning on September 5, 1957, when nine African American schoolchildren were refused entrance to a Little Rock school, this account looks at the Arkansas school desegregation crisis. (Rev: BL 12/15/01; HBG 3/02; SLJ 9/01) [344.73]

10164 Springer, Jane. *Listen to Us: The World's Working Children* (7–12). Illus. 1997, Douglas & McIntyre $24.95 (978-0-88899-291-8). This impressive photoessay looks at the exploitation of children around the world in industry, agriculture, the home, the military, and on the street. (Rev: BL 1/1–15/98; SLJ 3/98) [331.3]

10165 Stalcup, Brenda, ed. *Women's Suffrage* (8–12). Series: Turning Points in World History. 2000, Greenhaven LB $32.45 (978-0-7377-0326-9); paper $21.20 (978-0-7377-0325-2). This collection of essays traces the history of the women's suffrage movement from the declaration of women's rights signed in New York State in 1848 through the impact of the passage of the 19th Amendment on American history. (Rev: BL 5/15/00; SLJ 8/00) [346]

10166 *Stand Up, Speak Out: A Book About Children's Rights* (6–8). Illus. 2002, Two-Can $14.95 (978-1-58728-540-0); paper $9.95 (978-1-58728-541-7). Children's artwork and writings address children's rights issues around the world, with information on the U.N.'s Convention on the Rights of the Child, UNICEF, and other aid organizations. (Rev: BL 4/15/02; HBG 10/02; SLJ 6/02) [323]

10167 Stearman, Kaye. *Slavery Today* (6–10). Series: Talking Points. 1999, Raintree LB $27.12 (978-0-8172-5320-2). Examples of modern slavery include child labor, trafficking in people, prostitution, migrant workers who are exploited, and other forms of forced labor. (Rev: BL 12/15/99; HBG 9/00; SLJ 5/00) [326]

10168 Stearman, Kaye. *Women's Rights: Changing Attitudes, 1900–2000* (6–9). Series: 20th Century Issues. 2000, Raintree LB $28.54 (978-0-8172-5892-4). Stearman traces the history of the women's rights movement and looks at its achievements, the status of women around the world today, and possible future efforts. (Rev: BL 11/15/00; HBG 9/00; SLJ 4/00) [323.1]

10169 Stokes, John A., and Lois Wolfe. *Students on Strike: Jim Crow, Civil Rights, Brown, and Me* (5–8). Illus. 2008, National Geographic $15.95 (978-1-4263-0153-7). The author recounts his days on strike to protest the conditions at a black high school in Virginia in 1951 and explains how this strike helped lead to school desegregation in the 1960s. (Rev: BL 3/15/08; SLJ 4/08) [371.829]

10170 Sullivan, George. *The Day the Women Got the Vote: A Photo History of the Women's Rights Movement* (5–8). Illus. 1994, Scholastic paper $6.95 (978-0-590-47560-0). The history of the struggle for women's rights is covered in a series of 24 short photoessays. (Rev: BL 6/1–15/94; SLJ 7/94) [323.34]

10171 Turck, Mary C. *The Civil Rights Movement for Kids: A History with 21 Activities* (4–8). 2000, Chicago Review paper $14.95 (978-1-55652-370-0). The story of the civil rights movement with coverage of key events and personalities plus a number of related activities. (Rev: SLJ 10/00) [973.9]

10172 Turner, Chérie. *Everything You Need to Know About the Riot Grrrl Movement: The Feminism of a New Generation* (6–10). Illus. Series: Need to Know Library. 2001, Rosen LB $27.95 (978-0-8239-3400-3). A look at the movement that evolved from a 1970s aggressive punk attitude to a 1990s emphasis on equality and self-esteem. (Rev: SLJ 12/01) [781.66]

10173 Weatherford, Carole Boston. *The African-American Struggle for Legal Equality* (6–10). Series: In American History. 2000, Enslow LB $26.60 (978-0-7660-1415-2). From slavery to the present, the account traces the amazing changes that brought African Americans equality before the law. (Rev: BL 10/15/2000; HBG 3/01) [973]

10174 Weber, Michael. *Causes and Consequences of the African-American Civil Rights Movements* (6–10). Series: Causes and Consequences. 1998, Raintree LB $29.97 (978-0-8172-4058-5). The author traces the legal and social history of African Americans that led up to the historic 1963 March on Washington; recounts events of the 1950s and 1960s such as the integration of schools, the growing urban tensions, and the rise of the black power movement; and discusses the movement's lasting achievements and current problems. (Rev: SLJ 6/98) [973]

10175 Williams, Mary E., ed. *Civil Rights* (7–12). Series: Examining Issues Through Political Cartoons. 2002, Gale LB $29.95 (978-0-7377-1100-4). This limited but unusual approach to exploration of the civil rights movement looks at political cartoons in four thematic chapters. (Rev: SLJ 10/02) [323.1]

10176 Wilson, Reginald. *Our Rights: Civil Liberties and the U.S.* (7–12). Illus. 1988, Walker $14.85 (978-0-8027-6751-6). A book that explains what civil rights are, how we have these freedoms, and how to protect them. (Rev: SLJ 8/88; VOYA 8/88) [323.4]

10177 Wilson, Reginald. *Think About Our Rights: Civil Liberties and the United States* (5–8). Illus. 1991, Walker LB $15.85 (978-0-8027-8127-7); paper $9.95 (978-0-8027-7371-5). The focus is on such civil rights questions as integration, affirmative action, and women's rights. (Rev: SLJ 1/92) [323.4]

10178 Winters, Paul A., ed. *The Civil Rights Movement* (8–12). Series: Turning Points in World History. 2000, Greenhaven LB $37.45 (978-0-7377-0217-0); paper $21.20 (978-0-7377-0216-3). Essays cover the civil rights struggles of the 1950s and 1960s with material on the leaders, important debates, events, and the continuing struggle. (Rev: BL 2/15/00; SLJ 4/00) [323.1]

10179 Worth, Richard. *Cinqué of the Amistad and the Slave Trade* (6–10). Series: In World History. 2001, Enslow LB $26.60 (978-0-7660-1460-2). An accessible overview of slave trading from Roman times through the U.S. Civil War, with black-and-white photographs and reproductions and excerpts from source documents. (Rev: HBG 10/01; SLJ 8/01) [326]

10180 Zeinert, Karen. *Free Speech: From Newspapers to Music Lyrics* (7–10). 1995, Enslow LB $26.60 (978-0-89490-634-3). The censorship battle in the context of various mediums, from a historical perspective. (Rev: BL 4/1/95; SLJ 6/95) [323.44]

Immigration

10181 Ambrosek, Renee. *America Debates United States Policy on Immigration* (6–9). Illus. Series: America Debates. 2007, Rosen LB $21.95 (978-1-4042-1924-3). A thorough and attractive introduction to the issues surrounding immigration into the United States. (Rev: BL 11/15/07; SLJ 11/07) [325.73]

10182 Andryszewski, Tricia. *Immigration: Newcomers and Their Impact on the U.S.* (7–9). 1995, Millbrook $24.90 (978-1-56294-499-5). A detailed study of immigration as it pertains to the United States. (Rev: BL 1/15/95; SLJ 5/95) [304.8]

10183 Archibald, Erika F. *A Sudanese Family* (4–7). Illus. Series: Journey Between Two Worlds. 1997, Lerner paper $8.95 (978-0-8225-9753-7). Introduces Dei Jock Dei and his family, who left Sudan to escape religious persecution and, through the help of a church, settled in Atlanta, Georgia. (Rev: BL 6/1–15/97; SLJ 7/97) [975.8]

10184 Aykroyd, Clarissa. *Refugees* (8–12). Series: The Changing Face of North America: Immigration Since 1965. 2004, Mason Crest LB $24.95 (978-1-59084-692-6). An overview of the origins of refugees to the United States and Canada, the reasons for their flight from their home countries, and the process they must undergo on arrival. (Rev: SLJ 11/04)

10185 Berg, Lois Anne. *An Eritrean Family* (4–7). Illus. Series: Journey Between Two Worlds. 1997, Lerner LB $22.60 (978-0-8225-3405-1); paper $8.95 (978-0-8225-9755-1). The story of the Kiklu family, which fled Eritrea in eastern Africa in 1978, spent 10 years in a refugee camp, and resettled in Minnesota. (Rev: BL 6/1–15/97; SLJ 8/97) [304.895]

10186 Bode, Janet. *The Colors of Freedom: Immigrant Stories* (7–12). 1999, Watts paper $9.95 (978-0-531-15961-3). Using students' writing, artwork, interviews, and poems, the author has collected material on the feelings of young adult immigrants to this country from such areas as Latin America, Europe, and Asia. (Rev: BL 1/1–15/00; SLJ 3/00) [305.8]

10187 Budhos, Marina. *Remix: Conversations with Immigrant Teenagers* (7–12). 1999, Holt $16.95 (978-0-8050-5113-1). This book contains interviews with 20 older teens from around the world who comment on their experiences as immigrants in the United States and the cultural differences they have encountered. (Rev: BL 9/15/99; HBG 4/00; SLJ 11/99; VOYA 12/99) [341.4]

10188 Caroli, Betty Boyd. *Immigrants Who Returned Home* (6–10). Illus. 1990, Chelsea LB $19.95 (978-0-87754-864-5). An account of immigrants who found life in the United States less than expected and returned home to their countries. (Rev: BL 4/15/90; SLJ 8/90) [304.8]

10189 Collier, Christopher, and James Lincoln Collier. *A Century of Immigration, 1820–1924* (5–8). Series: Drama of American History. 1999, Marshall Cavendish LB $31.36 (978-0-7614-0821-5). A compelling account that focuses on 100 years of migration to this country, with material on where the immigrants came from, why they emigrated, where they settled, and the problems of assimilation. (Rev: BL 2/15/00; HBG 10/00; SLJ 3/00) [973]

10190 Cox, Vic. *The Challenge of Immigration* (7–12). Series: Multicultural Issues. 1995, Enslow LB $20.95 (978-0-89490-628-2). An introduction to the controversial issues concerning immigration. (Rev: BL 5/1/95; SLJ 5/95) [325.73]

10191 Daniels, Roger. *American Immigration: A Student Companion* (6–12). Series: Oxford Student Companions to American History. 2001, Oxford LB $65.00 (978-0-19-511316-7). An alphabetically arranged series of articles covering all aspects of immigration to the United States and the various

ethnic groups that have made the journey, illustrated with photographs, maps, and reproductions. (Rev: BL 10/15/01; SLJ 6/01) [304.8]

10192 Dudley, William, ed. *Illegal Immigration* (7–12). Series: Opposing Viewpoints. 2002, Gale LB $31.20 (978-0-7377-0911-7); paper $21.20 (978-0-7377-0910-0). A balanced collection of essays on the topic of illegal arrivals in the United States and the treatment of these immigrants, updated from the 1994 edition. (Rev: BL 4/15/02; SLJ 8/02) [325.73]

10193 Emsden, Katharine, ed. *Coming to America: A New Life in a New Land* (4–8). Series: Perspectives on History. 1993, Discovery paper $6.95 (978-1-878668-23-3). Diaries, journals, and letters of immigrants from many countries are used to provide insights into their lives. (Rev: BL 11/15/93) [325.73]

10194 Goldish, Meish. *Immigration: How Should It Be Controlled?* (6–9). Illus. Series: Issues of Our Time. 1994, Twenty-First Century LB $22.90 (978-0-8050-3182-9). An unbiased, clear look at current positions and solutions to the immigration problem, particularly as they apply to the United States. (Rev: BL 6/1–15/94; SLJ 7/94) [325.73]

10195 Haerens, Margaret, ed. *Illegal Immigration* (7–12). Series: Opposing Viewpoints. 2006, Gale LB $34.95 (978-0-7377-3356-3); paper $23.70 (978-0-7377-3357-0). This collection of essays on illegal immigration captures all sides of the issue, allowing readers to form their own opinions. (Rev: SLJ 10/06)

10196 Hauser, Pierre. *Illegal Aliens* (5–8). Series: Immigrant Experience. 1996, Chelsea LB $14.95 (978-0-7910-3363-0). A history of attitudes toward immigration is followed by a discussion of illegal immigrants, where they come from, why they came, and the government's policy toward them. (Rev: SLJ 2/97) [932]

10197 Hay, Jeff, ed. *Immigration* (7–12). Series: Turning Points in World History. 2001, Greenhaven paper $24.95 (978-0-7377-0638-3). In a series of engaging essays, the phenomenon of immigration is explored and how shifting populations have changing world history. (Rev: BL 3/15/02) [325]

10198 Hopkinson, Deborah. *Shutting Out the Sky* (5–12). Illus. 2003, Scholastic $17.95 (978-0-439-37590-0). Five personal stories of young immigrants, striking photographs, and excerpts from primary documents form the backbone of this history of immigration to New York City in the late 19th century. (Rev: BL 11/1/03*; HBG 4/04; SLJ 12/03*; VOYA 6/04) [307.76]

10199 Knight, Margy B. *Who Belongs Here? An American Story* (4–7). Illus. by Anne S. O'Brien. 1993, Tilbury House $16.95 (978-0-88448-110-2). The story of ten-year-old Nari, who survived the killing fields of Cambodia and found a new life in the United States. (Rev: BL 3/1/94; SLJ 10/93) [305.895]

10200 Kosof, Anna. *Living in Two Worlds: The Immigrant Children's Experience* (7–12). Illus. 1996, Twenty-First Century LB $23.40 (978-0-8050-4083-8). After a brief introduction on the history of immigration, this book describes the problems and the reception of present-day teenage immigrants, using many first-person accounts. (Rev: BL 10/1/96; SLJ 10/96; VOYA 2/97) [305.23]

10201 Levine, Herbert M. *Immigration* (7–12). Illus. Series: American Issues Debated. 1997, Raintree LB $31.40 (978-0-8172-4353-1). Questions involving immigration and the economy, the rights of illegal immigrants, and English-only laws are covered from various points of view. (Rev: BL 11/15/97) [304.873]

10202 Meltzer, Milton. *Bound for America: The Story of the European Immigrants* (6–10). Series: Great Journeys. 2001, Benchmark LB $32.79 (978-0-7614-1227-4). An absorbing examination of the reasons for migration within and from Europe in the 19th and early 20th centuries, and of the hardships these travelers suffered. (Rev: BCCB 3/99; HBG 10/02; SLJ 3/02) [325.73]

10203 Miller, Debra A. *Illegal Immigration* (8–12). Illus. Series: Compact Research: Current Issues. 2007, Reference Point LB $24.95 (978-1-60152-009-8). Will a guest-worker program work? Do illegal aliens strain social services in the United States? All sides of these questions and many more are examined in this overview. (Rev: BL 4/1/07; LMC 10/07; SLJ 5/07) [304.8]

10204 Miller, Debra A., ed. *Illegal Immigration* (6–9). Illus. Series: Current Controversies. 2007, Gale LB $36.20 (978-0-7377-3723-3); paper $24.95 (978-0-7377-3724-0). A collection of writings presenting various points of view about the issues that surround illegal immigration. (Rev: BL 2/1/08) [325.73]

10205 Miller, Karen, ed. *Immigration* (8–12). Series: Social Issues Firsthand. 2006, Gale LB $28.70 (978-0-7377-2893-4). This compilation of 14 previously published essays gives insight into the experiences of varied immigrants to the United States — from Cuba, Vietnam, Bosnia, and Ethiopia, to name just a few nations — and looks at the difficulties they met in their new country. (Rev: SLJ 6/07) [304.8]

10206 Morrow, Robert. *Immigration: Blessing or Burden?* (7–10). Illus. Series: Pro/Con Issues. 1998, Lerner LB $30.35 (978-0-8225-2613-1). This book examines our changing attitudes toward immigration, how we regard immigration laws, and the controversy over multiculturalism vs. assimilation. (Rev: BL 3/15/98; SLJ 4/98) [304.8]

10207 Murphy, Nora. *A Hmong Family* (4–7). Illus. Series: Journey Between Two Worlds. 1997, Lerner LB $27.15 (978-0-8225-3406-8); paper $8.95 (978-0-8225-9756-8). After fleeing Laos in 1975 to escape the Communists, this family spent time in a refugee camp in Thailand before settling in Minneapolis, Minnesota. (Rev: BL 6/1–15/97; SLJ 8/97) [305.895]

10208 O'Connor, Karen. *Dan Thuy's New Life in America* (4–8). Illus. 1992, Lerner LB $19.93 (978-0-8225-2555-4). A photoessay of a 13-year-old Vietnamese girl and her family, newly arrived in San Diego. (Rev: BL 9/15/92; SLJ 9/92) [325]

10209 O'Connor, Karen. *A Kurdish Family* (5–8). Series: Journey Between Two Worlds. 1996, Lerner LB $22.60 (978-0-8225-3402-0); paper $8.95 (978-0-8225-9743-8). This work describes the living conditions endured by a Kurdish family in their homeland and their new life in the United States. (Rev: BCCB 12/96; BL 11/1/96; SLJ 11/96) [305.891]

10210 Outman, James L., and Lawrence W. Baker. *U.S. Immigration and Migration Primary Sources* (7–10). Series: Immigration and Migration Reference Library. 2004, Gale $70.00 (978-0-7876-7669-8). Primary source documents — including articles, letters, and Supreme Court rulings — chronicle the history of immigration to and migration within America. (Rev: SLJ 2/05) [304.8]

10211 Rangaswamy, Padma. *Indian Americans* (8–12). Series: The New Immigrants. 2006, Chelsea House $27.95 (978-0-7910-8786-2). This volume traces the history of immigration from India to the United States — and of Indians who have been living in Africa, Europe, and the Caribbean. (Rev: LMC 8–9/07; SLJ 3/07) [977.3]

10212 Reimers, David M. *A Land of Immigrants* (5–8). Series: Immigrant Experience. 1995, Chelsea LB $21.95 (978-0-7910-3361-6). An overview of immigration to the United States and Canada and how the influx influenced the culture. (Rev: BL 10/15/95; SLJ 12/95) [304.8]

10213 Roleff, Tamara L., ed. *Immigration* (7–12). Series: Opposing Viewpoints: World History. 2004, Gale LB $37.45 (978-0-7377-1701-3). Pros and cons concerning immigration are presented in this collection of opposing viewpoints. (Rev: BL 2/15/04) [325]

10214 Santos, Edward J. *Everything You Need to Know If You and Your Parents Are New Americans* (7–12). Illus. Series: Need to Know Library. 2002, Rosen LB $27.95 (978-0-8239-3547-5). A useful and attractive guide for immigrant teens that gives practical advice on dealing with various facets of American life and emphasizes the possibility of retaining one's heritage while fitting in to a new culture. (Rev: BL 6/1–15/02; SLJ 4/02; VOYA 2/03) [304.8]

10215 Sawyer, Kem K. *Refugees: Seeking a Safe Haven* (7–12). Series: Multicultural Issues. 1995, Enslow LB $20.95 (978-0-89490-663-3). This book describes the lives and problems of refugees admitted into this country, with material on why they left their homelands and their reception here. (Rev: BL 6/1–15/95; SLJ 8/95) [362.87]

10216 Schroeder, Michael J. *Mexican Americans* (6–10). Illus. Series: The New Immigrants. 2007, Chelsea House LB $27.95 (978-0-7910-8785-5). A look at the political and social issues surrounding immigrants to the United States from Mexico, with graphics that will improve readers' understanding. (Rev: BL 7/07) [973]

10217 Sherman, Augustus F. *Augustus F. Sherman: Ellis Island Portraits, 1905–1920* (8–12). Illus. 2005, Aperture $40.00 (978-1-931788-60-1). Moving photographs taken by an Ellis Island immigration clerk spotlight would-be immigrants — many of them young people — who were held for further interrogation. (Rev: BL 5/15/05) [779.9]

10218 Staeger, Rob. *Asylees* (8–12). Series: The Changing Face of North America: Immigration Since 1965. 2004, Mason Crest LB $24.95 (978-1-59084-685-8). An overview of asylum seekers in the United States and Canada and the process they must undergo on arrival. Also use *Deported Aliens* (2004). (Rev: SLJ 11/04)

Ethnic Groups and Prejudice

General and Miscellaneous

10219 Altman, Linda J. *Racism and Ethnic Bias: Everybody's Problem* (6–9). Illus. Series: Teen Issues. 2001, Enslow LB $22.60 (978-0-7660-1578-4). Racism, racial profiling, and ethnic stereotyping are all discussed here, with examples of these behaviors and tips on how people can work against racism. (Rev: BL 1/1–15/02; HBG 3/02) [305.8]

10220 Birdseye, Debbie H., and Tom Birdseye. *Under Our Skin: Kids Talk About Race* (4–8). 1997, Holiday $15.95 (978-0-8234-1325-6). In separate chapters, six 8th-grade students in Oregon from different racial and ethnic backgrounds talk about race and what racism means to them. (Rev: HBG 3/98; SLJ 4/98) [572.973]

10221 Cole, Carolyn Kozo, and Kathy Kobayashi. *Shades of L.A.: Pictures from Ethnic Family Albums* (7–12). 1996, New Pr. paper $20.00 (978-1-56584-313-4). A collection of photographs of African American, Mexican American, Asian American, and Native American family life in Los Angeles'

ethnic and racial neighborhoods prior to 1965. (Rev: BL 8/96; VOYA 2/97) [979.4]

10222 Cruz, Barbara C. *Multiethnic Teens and Cultural Identity: A Hot Issue* (6–10). Series: Hot Issues. 2001, Enslow LB $27.93 (978-0-7660-1201-1). A concise examination of the challenges facing teens of mixed racial heritage that looks at ethnic diversity during American history and profiles individuals such as Tiger Woods and Halle Berry. (Rev: HBG 10/01; SLJ 7/01) [305.23]

10223 Garg, Samidha, and Jan Hardy. *Racism* (6–10). Illus. Series: Global Issues. 1996, Raintree LB $19.98 (978-0-8172-4548-1). This study of racism, supplementing statistics and facts with personal experiences, discusses prejudice, immigration, and citizenship, with separate chapters on Europe, South Africa, the United States, and Australia. (Rev: BL 2/1/97) [305.8]

10224 Gaskins, Pearl Fuyo, ed. *What Are You? Voices of Mixed-Race Young People* (7–12). 1999, Holt $18.95 (978-0-8050-5968-7). In essays, interviews, and poetry, 45 mixed-race young people ages 14 to 26 talk about themselves and growing up. (Rev: BL 5/15/99; HB 7–8/99; SLJ 7/99; VOYA 10/99) [973]

10225 Gillam, Scott. *Discrimination: Prejudice in Action* (7–12). Series: Multicultural Issues. 1995, Enslow LB $20.95 (978-0-89490-643-5). This book shows how racial discrimination is still practiced in this country and discusses how it can be combated. (Rev: BL 6/1–15/95; SLJ 9/95) [303.3]

10226 Grant, R. G. *Racism: Changing Attitudes, 1900–2000* (6–9). Illus. Series: Twentieth Century Issues. 1999, Raintree LB $28.54 (978-0-8172-5567-1). A brief discussion of racism and its various aspects is the focus of this account that includes material on colonialism, civil rights, and black power. (Rev: BL 3/15/00; HBG 9/00; SLJ 4/00) [305.8.]

10227 Haugen, David M., ed. *Interracial Relationships* (7–12). Series: At Issue. 2006, Gale LB $28.70 (978-0-7377-2390-8); paper $19.95 (978-0-7377-2391-5). Pro and con articles present viewpoints on the degree of acceptance of interracial relationships in various sectors of society. (Rev: SLJ 8/07) [306.84]

10228 Hull, Mary. *Ethnic Violence* (5–8). Illus. Series: Overview. 1997, Lucent LB $29.95 (978-1-56006-184-7). Gives a history of racial prejudice that has led to violence and discusses decisions and policies that currently guide our behavior and attitudes toward this problem. (Rev: BL 8/97; SLJ 9/97) [305.8]

10229 Hurley, Jennifer A., ed. *Racism* (7–12). 1998, Greenhaven LB $32.45 (978-1-56510-809-7). How prevalent is racism in U.S. society? How does racism affect minorities? Is affirmative action effective? How can racism be combated? These are some of the questions explored in this collection of essays. (Rev: BL 8/98) [305.8]

10230 Kassam, Nadya, ed. *Telling It Like It Is: Young Asian Women Talk* (7–12). 1998, Livewire paper $11.95 (978-0-7043-4941-4). These 22 short, informal essays reveal various attitudes toward sexism and racism as experienced by Hindu and Moslem girls living in Britain whose families are from the Indian subcontinent. (Rev: BL 9/15/98; SLJ 8/98) [305.8914]

10231 Katz, William L. *The Great Migrations: History of Multicultural America* (7–12). Series: History of Multicultural America. 1993, Raintree LB $22.83 (978-0-8114-6278-5). Shows the impact that women and minorities have had in the formation and development of the United States. (Rev: BL 6/1–15/93; VOYA 10/93) [973]

10232 Newman, Gerald, and Eleanor N. Layfield. *Racism: Divided by Color* (7–12). Series: Multicultural Issues. 1995, Enslow LB $20.95 (978-0-89490-641-1). A well-documented history of color barriers in America and efforts to eradicate them. (Rev: BL 9/15/95; SLJ 12/95; VOYA 2/96) [305.8]

10233 O'Hearn, Claudine Chiawei, ed. *Half and Half: Writers on Growing Up Biracial and Bicultural* (7–12). 1998, Pantheon paper $13.00 (978-0-375-70011-8). This work contains 18 personal essays by people who live and work in the U.S., but who, because they are biracial and bicultural, are not sure where they belong. (Rev: BL 9/1/98) [306.84]

10234 Sharp, Anne Wallace. *The Gypsies* (8–12). Illus. Series: Indigenous Peoples of the World. 2003, Gale $27.45 (978-1-59018-239-0). The history and culture of the Roma are detailed here, with information on the fate of these groups during World War II and on continuing prejudices. (Rev: BL 4/15/03; SLJ 7/03) [909]

10235 Stanford, Eleanor, ed. *Interracial America* (7–12). Series: Opposing Viewpoints. 2006, Gale LB $34.95 (978-0-7377-2943-6); paper $23.70 (978-0-7377-2944-3). A useful compilation of essays and excerpts on racial issues such as equal opportunity, interracial families, immigration, and profiling; each chapter includes a bibliography of related articles. (Rev: SLJ 8/06) [305.8]

10236 Williams, Mary, ed. *Interracial America* (6–12). Illus. Series: Opposing Viewpoints. 2001, Greenhaven LB $32.45 (978-0-7377-0658-1); paper $21.20 (978-0-7377-0657-4). Essays present various viewpoints on such topics as the advisability of emphasizing ethnic differences, affirmative action, interracial marriage, and transracial adoption. (Rev: BL 7/01) [305.8]

10237 Young, Mitchell, ed. *Racial Discrimination* (7–12). Series: Issues on Trial. 2006, Gale LB $34.95 (978-0-7377-2787-6). Young has compiled a useful volume of opinions on cases brought before

the Supreme Court that involved racial discrimination. (Rev: SLJ 1/07)

African Americans

10238 Ashabranner, Brent. *The New African Americans* (5–9). Illus. 1999, Linnet LB $22.50 (978-0-208-02420-6). After a brief history of early African immigration and slavery, this account focuses on present-day immigrants — where they come from and their reception in the United States. (Rev: BCCB 12/99; BL 10/15/99; HB 11–12/99; HBG 3/00; VOYA 12/00) [304.87]

10239 Banks, William H., Jr. *The Black Muslims* (5–10). Series: African-American Achievers. 1996, Chelsea LB $21.95 (978-0-7910-2593-2); paper $30.00 (978-0-7910-2594-9). The story of the founding of the Nation of Islam, its leaders, the Million Man March, and the reign of Louis Farrakhan. (Rev: SLJ 5/97) [323]

10240 Bolden, Tonya. *Tell All the Children Our Story: Memories and Mementos of Being Young and Black in America* (4–8). Illus. 2002, Abrams $24.95 (978-0-8109-4496-1). From the first recorded birth of a black child in the United States to the Million Man March, this book describes the African American experience through both personal and historical accounts, using a scrapbook format. (Rev: BL 2/15/02; HB 3–4/02; HBG 10/02; SLJ 3/02*; VOYA 4/02) [973]

10241 Clinton, Catherine. *The Black Soldier: 1492 to the Present* (5–8). Illus. 2000, Houghton $17.00 (978-0-395-67722-3). This history of African Americans in the army begins with colonial slaves who were given muskets to fight the Indians and continues through each of America's wars to the present with emphasis on the slow progress toward equality in the ranks. (Rev: BCCB 10/00; BL 9/15/00; HBG 3/01; SLJ 10/00; VOYA 2/01) [355]

10242 Cole, Harriette, and John Pinderhuges. *Coming Together: Celebrations for African American Families* (4–12). Illus. 2003, Hyperion $22.99 (978-0-7868-0753-6). Traditions surrounding celebrations including Christmas, Kwanzaa, and naming ceremonies are covered here, with accompanying crafts, menu suggestions, and activities. (Rev: BL 12/15/03; HBG 4/04; VOYA 2/04) [306.8]

10243 Cole, Michael D. *The Los Angeles Riots: Rage in the City of Angels* (5–9). Series: American Disasters. 1999, Enslow LB $23.93 (978-0-7660-1219-6). An account of the police beating of Rodney King in Los Angeles and the subsequent riots, the worst in U.S. history. (Rev: BL 2/1/99; HBG 10/99; SLJ 6/99) [979.494053]

10244 De Angelis, Therese. *Louis Farrakhan* (6–10). Series: Black Americans of Achievement. 1998, Chelsea $32.00 (978-0-7910-4688-3); paper $9.95

(978-0-7910-4689-0). This book provides information about Farrakhan and explains the evolution of his leadership, but it is more a history of the Nation of Islam movement, with information on African American leaders including Malcolm X, Elijah Muhammad, and Roy Wilkins. (Rev: HBG 3/99; SLJ 2/99) [305.8]

10245 Dornfeld, Margaret. *The Turning Tide: From the Desegregation of the Armed Forces to the Montgomery Bus Boycott* (7–10). Series: Milestones in Black American History. 1995, Chelsea LB $21.95 (978-0-7910-2255-9); paper $9.95 (978-0-7910-2681-6). This work surveys the period in African American history from 1948 through 1956 and includes Rosa Parks, Ralph Ellison, Charlie Parker, and Adam Clayton Powell, Jr. (Rev: BL 8/95) [973]

10246 Ebony, eds. *Ebony Pictorial History of Black America* (7–12). Illus. 1971, Johnson $54.95 (978-0-87485-049-9). These three volumes trace African American history from slavery to today's fight for integration and equality. [305.8]

10247 Feelings, Tom. *Tommy Traveler in the World of Black History* (5–8). 1991, Black Butterfly $13.95 (978-0-86316-202-2). A history of African Americans seen through the eyes of a boy who imagines himself participating in the important events. (Rev: BL 9/15/91; SLJ 2/92) [973]

10248 Ferry, Joe. *The History of African-American Civic Organizations* (7–12). Illus. Series: American Mosaic: African-American Contributions. 2003, Chelsea LB $30.00 (978-0-7910-7270-7). Social, business, and other clubs and groups for African American men, women, and children are explored, with information on membership and rituals. (Rev: BL 10/15/03; HBG 4/04) [36]

10249 Fradin, Judith Bloom, and Dennis Brindell Fradin. *5,000 Miles to Freedom: Ellen and William Craft's Flight from Slavery* (6–9). Illus. 2005, National Geographic LB $29.90 (978-0-7922-7886-3). Ellen and William Craft, a married couple, escaped slavery in Georgia only to find they were in danger again in Boston; this appealing volume documents their adventures, including their flight to England. (Rev: BL 3/15/06; SLJ 5/06*) [326.0]

10250 Frank, Andrew. *The Birth of Black America: The Age of Discovery and the Slave Trade* (6–8). Series: Milestones in Black American History. 1996, Chelsea LB $14.95 (978-0-7910-2257-3). This work covers slavery during the colonization of the Americas, the birth of African American culture, and the end of the slave trade. (Rev: SLJ 10/96) [973.2]

10251 Garrison, Mary. *Slaves Who Dared: The Stories of Ten African-American Heroes* (7–12). Illus. 2002, White Mane LB $19.95 (978-1-57249-272-1). Historical prints and quotations from original texts lend authenticity to these moving accounts of

famous and less-well-known men and women who escaped from slavery. (Rev: BL 9/1/02; HBG 3/03; SLJ 7/02) [973]

10252 Greene, Meg. *Slave Young, Slave Long: The American Slave Experience* (5–8). Illus. Series: People's History. 1999, Lerner LB $30.35 (978-0-8225-1739-9). Using quotations from both victims and perpetrators, and illustrated by historical prints and photographs, this book presents the story of slavery in the United States. (Rev: BL 4/1/99; HBG 10/99; SLJ 10/99) [973.0496]

10253 Greenfield, Eloise, and Lessie Jones Little. *Childtimes: A Three-Generation Memoir* (5–8). Illus. by Jerry Pinkney. 1979, HarperCollins LB $16.89 (978-0-690-03875-0); paper $9.99 (978-0-06-446134-4). The childhoods of three generations of African American women.

10254 Haley, James, ed. *Reparations for American Slavery* (6–12). Series: At Issue. 2004, Gale LB $29.95 (978-0-7377-1340-4). The arguments for and against the payments or other compensation for the years of slavery to present-day African Americans are the subject of this collection of writings. (Rev: BL 2/15/04) [326]

10255 Hansen, Joyce, and Gary McGowan. *Breaking Ground, Breaking Silence: The Story of New York's African Burial Ground* (8–12). 1998, Holt $19.95 (978-0-8050-5012-7). The graphic story of the finding, in 1991, of the mid-18th-century African Burial Ground in Manhattan and what it reveals about the lives of slaves in New York. (Rev: BL 5/15/98; HBG 10/98; SLJ 5/98; VOYA 8/98) [974.7]

10256 Haskins, James, and Kathleen Benson. *Out of the Darkness: The Story of Blacks Moving North, 1890–1940* (6–8). Series: Great Journeys. 1999, Benchmark LB $32.79 (978-0-7614-0970-0). The stories of two individuals personalize this discussion of the "Great Migration." (Rev: BL 1/1–15/00; HBG 4/00; SLJ 2/00) [304.8]

10257 Hatt, Christine. *Slavery: From Africa to the Americas* (5–8). 1998, Bedrick $19.95 (978-0-87226-552-3). A broad overview of slavery in America that covers slave ships, plantation life, abolitionism, the Civil War, and Reconstruction, with maps, illustrations, and reproductions of documents. (Rev: HBG 10/98; SLJ 5/98) [973]

10258 Hauser, Pierre. *Great Ambitions: From the "Separate but Equal" Doctrine to the Birth of the NAACP (1896–1909)* (7–10). Series: Milestones in Black American History. 1995, Chelsea $21.95 (978-0-7910-2264-1); paper $9.95 (978-0-7910-2690-8). The history of African Americans at the end of the 19th and beginning of the 20th century, with coverage of such political and cultural pioneers as W. E. B. Du Bois, Charles Chesnutt, Paul Laurence Dunbar, and Scott Joplin. (Rev: BL 2/15/95) [323.1]

10259 Henry, Christopher. *Forever Free: From the Emancipation Proclamation to the Civil Rights Bill of 1875 (1863–1875)* (7–10). Series: Milestones in Black American History. 1995, Chelsea LB $21.95 (978-0-7910-2253-5); paper $8.95 (978-0-7910-2679-3). The history of African Americans during Reconstruction, covering the tearing down of racial barriers and the journey from political impotence to civil power. (Rev: BL 7/95; SLJ 10/95) [323.1]

10260 Hine, Darlene Clark. *The Path to Equality: From the Scottsboro Case to the Breaking of Baseball's Color Barrier* (7–10). Series: Milestones in Black American History. 1995, Chelsea LB $19.95 (978-0-7910-2251-1); paper $9.95 (978-0-7910-2677-9). This section of African American history covers the Great Depression and World War II, and features the accomplishments of individuals including Marian Anderson, Thurgood Marshall, A. Philip Randolph, and Jackie Robinson. (Rev: BL 8/95) [973]

10261 Holliday, Laurel, ed. *Dreaming in Color, Living in Black and White: Our Own Stories of Growing Up Black in America* (8–12). 2000, Pocket paper $4.99 (978-0-671-04127-4). This is a moving collection of first-person accounts by African Americans who tell of the racism they faced while growing up. (Rev: BL 2/15/00; SLJ 4/00; VOYA 4/00) [305.896]

10262 Horton, James Oliver. *Landmarks of African American History* (8–12). Series: American Landmarks. 2005, Oxford LB $32.95 (978-0-19-514118-4). A tour of 13 historic sites that played a significant role in African American history, with good illustrations and maps. (Rev: SLJ 8/05) [973]

10263 Hudson, Wade. *Powerful Words: More Than 200 Years of Extraordinary Writing by African Americans* (5–9). Illus. by Sean Qualls. 2004, Scholastic $19.95 (978-0-439-40969-8). Excerpts from the writings and speeches of both well-known and less-familiar African Americans are accompanied by notes on the context and the writer. (Rev: BL 2/15/04; SLJ 2/04) [081]

10264 Hurmence, Belinda, ed. *Slavery Time When I Was Chillun* (8–12). Illus. 1997, Putnam $13.99 (978-0-399-23194-0). A disturbing collection of 12 slave narratives that give firsthand accounts of brutality, family separation, and hard labor, as well as some of kindly masters and happy times. (Rev: BL 3/15/98) [975]

10265 Jacob, Iris. *My Sisters' Voices: Teenage Girls of Color Speak Out* (7–12). 2002, Holt paper $13.00 (978-0-8050-6821-4). Teen girls of color describe their feelings, aspirations, and disappointments in prose and poetry. (Rev: BL 3/1/02; SLJ 10/02; VOYA 12/02) [305.235]

10266 King, Wilma. *Toward the Promised Land: From Uncle Tom's Cabin to the Onset of the Civil War (1851–1861)* (7–10). Series: Milestones in Black American History. 1995, Chelsea paper $9.95 (978-0-7910-2691-5). This work examines the major trends and personalities in the struggle to end slavery before the Civil War, with material on Frederick Douglass, Sojourner Truth, Harriet Beecher Stowe, and John Brown. (Rev: BL 7/95; SLJ 10/95; VOYA 12/95) [973]

10267 Lester, Julius. *From Slave Ship to Freedom Road* (5–10). Illus. 1998, Dial $17.99 (978-0-8037-1893-7). This book combines art, history, and commentary to produce a graphically gripping history of slavery. (Rev: BL 2/15/98; HBG 9/98; SLJ 2/98*) [759.13]

10268 Lester, Julius. *To Be a Slave* (6–9). Illus. by Tom Feelings. 1968, Scholastic paper $4.50 (978-0-590-42460-8). A powerful account of what it means to be a slave drawn largely from primary documents. [326]

10269 McKissack, Patricia C., and Fredrick McKissack. *Black Hands, White Sails: The Story of African-American Whalers* (6–10). Illus. 1999, Scholastic paper $17.95 (978-0-590-48313-1). This account of African American involvement in the whaling industry from colonial times through the 19th century also touches on the abolitionist movement, the Underground Railroad, and the Civil War. (Rev: BCCB 11/99; BL 9/1/99; HB 11–12/99; HBG 4/00; VOYA 2/00) [639.2]

10270 Meltzer, Milton. *The Black Americans: A History in Their Own Words, 1619–1983* (7–10). 1984, Crowell paper $12.99 (978-0-06-446055-2). As told through letters, speeches, articles, and other original sources, this is a history of black people in America. [305.8]

10271 Newman, Shirlee P. *Slavery in the United States* (4–7). Series: Watts Library: History of Slavery. 2000, Watts LB $25.50 (978-0-531-11695-1). This account covers the shameful American record concerning slavery with coverage from the African slave trade through plantation life, the Underground Railroad, and abolitionists to the Civil War and emancipation. (Rev: BL 3/1/01) [973]

10272 Patrick, Diane. *The New York Public Library Amazing African American History: A Book of Answers for Kids* (5–9). Illus. 1998, Wiley paper $12.95 (978-0-471-19217-6). Using a question-and-answer format, this book traces the history of African Americans from slavery to the present day. (Rev: BL 2/15/98; SLJ 4/98) [973]

10273 Peltak, Jennifer. *The History of African-American Colleges and Universities* (7–12). Illus. Series: American Mosaic: African-American Contributions. 2003, Chelsea LB $30.00 (978-0-7910-7269-1). This volume looks at the history of black colleges and universities, enrollment trends, and the struggle for equality in education. (Rev: BL 10/15/03; HBG 4/04) [378.7]

10274 Rappaport, Doreen. *Free at Last! Stories and Songs of Emancipation* (4–8). Illus. by Shane W. Evans. 2004, Candlewick $19.99 (978-0-7636-1440-9). First-hand accounts form the basis of this portrait of the black experience from emancipation to the 1954 Supreme Court decision declaring school segregation illegal. (Rev: BL 2/15/04*; HB 5–6/04; SLJ 2/04) [973]

10275 Rappaport, Doreen. *No More! Stories and Songs of Slave Resistance* (4–7). Illus. by Shane W. Evans. 2002, Candlewick $17.99 (978-0-7636-0984-9). A collection of narratives, prose, poetry, and songs that describe the African slave experience and the various forms of rebellion that took place. (Rev: BCCB 4/02; BL 2/15/02; HB 3–4/02; HBG 10/02; SLJ 2/02*) [306.3]

10276 Reef, Catherine. *Africans in America: The Spread of People and Culture* (6–9). Series: Library of African American History. 1999, Facts on File $25.00 (978-0-8160-3772-8). The author traces the dispersion of African peoples and cultures in the New World as a result of the slave trade and their influence on the Americas. (Rev: BL 2/15/99; SLJ 6/99) [970.00496]

10277 Schomp, Virginia. *Marching toward Freedom* (6–10). Illus. Series: Drama of African-American History. 2008, Marshall Cavendish LB $23.95 (978-0-7614-2643-1). With lots of primary source material, this volume provides a good overview of the struggle for equal rights between the years 1929 and 1954, with profiles of key figures and stories about individuals. (Rev: BLO 6/17/08) [305.896]

10278 Sharp, Anne Wallace. *A Dream Deferred: The Jim Crow Era* (7–10). Illus. Series: Lucent Library of Black History. 2005, Gale LB $32.45 (978-1-59018-700-5). An overview of the impact of the Jim Crow laws that stretched from Reconstruction to the Supreme Court's decision in *Brown* v. *Board of Education* (1954). (Rev: BL 10/15/05) [323.1196]

10279 Sharp, Anne Wallace. *Separate but Equal: The Desegregation of America's Schools* (7–12). Series: Lucent Library of Black History. 2006, Gale LB $28.70 (978-1-59018-953-5). A thorough history of the education of African Americans, complete with interviews of those who experienced first hand the desegregation battles of the 1950s and 1960s. (Rev: SLJ 6/07) [379.2]

10280 Straub, Deborah G., ed. *African American Voices* (5–8). Illus. 1996, Gale $126.00 (978-0-8103-9497-1). This is a collection of excerpts from important speeches delivered by a vast array of African Americans, past and present. (Rev: SLJ 2/97) [973]

10281 Summers, Barbara, ed. *Open the Unusual Door: True Life Stories of Challenge, Adventure, and Success by Black Americans* (8–11). 2005, Houghton paper $7.99 (978-0-618-58531-1). Sixteen successful African Americans write about choices they made that changed the direction of their lives. (Rev: BL 1/1–15/06; SLJ 12/05) [920]

10282 Van Peebles, Mario, et al. *Panther: A Pictorial History of the Black Panthers and the Story Behind the Film* (8–12). 1995, Newmarket paper $16.95 (978-1-55704-227-9). The first part of this heavily illustrated book recounts the beginnings of the Black Panther Party and its eventual collapse; the second half describes the making of the movie about the party. (Rev: VOYA 2/96) [973]

10283 Weisbrot, Robert. *Marching Toward Freedom* (7–12). Series: Milestones in Black American History. 1994, Chelsea paper $8.95 (978-0-7910-2682-3). This history covers African American affairs from the founding of the Southern Christian Leadership Conference to the assassination of Malcolm X (1957–1965), with material on Martin Luther King, Jr., James Farmer, Elijah Muhammad, and Malcolm X, among others. (Rev: BL 11/15/94; SLJ 9/94; VOYA 10/94) [973]

10284 Woodson, Jacqueline, ed. *A Way Out of No Way: Writings About Growing Up Black in America* (8–12). Illus. 1996, Holt $15.95 (978-0-8050-4570-3). A fine collection of prose and poetry, fiction and nonfiction about growing up in America, from some of the best African American writers, among them James Baldwin, Paul Beatty, Jamaica Kincaid, and Langston Hughes. (Rev: BL 2/15/97; SLJ 7/97; VOYA 6/97) [808.898]

Asian Americans

10285 Coleman, Lori. *Vietnamese in America* (4–8). Series: In America. 2004, Lerner LB $27.93 (978-0-8225-3951-3). The reasons for Vietnamese migration to the United States and the life the newcomers find when they arrive are discussed in engaging narrative, with personal stories, notes on key figures, illustrations, and a timeline. Also use *Koreans in America* (2004). (Rev: BL 11/15/04; SLJ 3/05) [973]

10286 Daley, William. *The Chinese Americans* (5–8). Illus. 1995, Chelsea LB $21.95 (978-0-7910-3357-9); paper $9.95 (978-0-7910-3379-1). The background and culture of this group are explained, as well as its adjustment to life in America. (Rev: BL 1/1/88) [973.04951]

10287 Goldstein, Margaret J. *Japanese in America* (4–7). Series: In America. 2006, Lerner LB $27.93 (978-0-8225-3952-0). The author discusses the history of U.S.-Japan relations and the course of Japanese immigration to America from the 1800s to today, including the internments during World War

II; profiles of famous Japanese Americans are appended. (Rev: SLJ 5/06) [973.0495]

10288 Hamanaka, Sheila. *The Journey: Japanese Americans, Racism and Renewal* (5–9). Illus. by author. 1990, Orchard LB $20.99 (978-0-531-08449-6). With brief text, this book is a series of paintings from a large mural that describes the injustices suffered by Japanese Americans at the beginning of World War II. (Rev: BL 3/15/90; HB 5–6/90; SLJ 5/90; VOYA 6/90) [940.54]

10289 Harkrader, Lisa. *South Korea* (5–8). Illus. Series: Top Ten Countries of Recent Immigrants. 2004, Enslow LB $25.26 (978-0-7660-5181-2). Information on South Korea — culture, history, climate, and people — accompanies an explanation of the reasons for migration to the United States and discussion of the contributions of this community; supported by Web links. (Rev: SLJ 3/05) [304]

10290 Kitano, Harry. *The Japanese Americans*. 2nd ed. (5–8). Photos by Richard Hewett. Series: Land of Immigrants. 1995, Chelsea LB $19.95 (978-0-7910-3358-6); paper $9.95 (978-0-7910-3380-7). The story of Japanese Americans and their traditions and contributions to American life and culture. (Rev: BL 10/15/95; VOYA 2/96) [305]

10291 Nam, Vickie, ed. *Yell-Oh Girls! Emerging Voices Explore Culture, Identity, and Growing up Asian American* (8–12). Illus. 2001, HarperCollins paper $13.00 (978-0-06-095944-9). An anthology of fiction and poetry written by Asian American high school and college students, revealing their feelings about topics including heritage, stereotypes, adoption, and interracial dating. (Rev: BL 7/01; SLJ 10/01; VOYA 2/02) [305.235]

10292 Omoto, Susan. *Hmong Milestones in America: Citizens in a New World* (5–8). Illus. 2003, John Gordon Burke $27.00 (978-0-934272-57-5); paper $15.00 (978-0-934272-56-8). The author introduces the Hmong people's history and traditions and traces the steps of Hmong refugees who migrated to the United States, profiling five individuals who have found success in their new country. (Rev: BL 4/15/03) [973]

10293 Oppenheim, Joanne. *Dear Miss Breed: True Stories of the Japanese American Incarceration During World War II and a Librarian Who Made a Difference* (7–10). Illus. 2006, Scholastic $22.99 (978-0-439-56992-7). An affecting portrait of a World War II children's librarian and the incarcerated young Japanese Americans who benefited from her commitment to her profession. (Rev: BL 1/1–15/06*; SLJ 3/06; VOYA 2/06) [940.53]

10294 Perl, Lila. *To the Golden Mountain: The Story of the Chinese Who Built the First Transcontinental Railroad* (6–9). Series: Great Journeys. 2002, Marshall Cavendish LB $32.79 (978-0-7614-1324-0). The immigration of Chinese to build the transconti-

nental railroad and their treatment form the basis of this account that includes many firsthand sources. (Rev: BL 3/15/03; HBG 3/03; SLJ 2/03) [973]

10295 Ragaza, Angelo. *Lives of Notable Asian Americans: Business, Politics, Science* (6–10). Series: Asian American Experience. 1995, Chelsea LB $18.95 (978-0-7910-2189-7). Asian Americans who have contributed in the business, political, and scientific arenas. (Rev: BL 8/95; VOYA 12/95) [973]

10296 St. Pierre, Stephanie. *Teenage Refugees from Cambodia Speak Out* (7–12). 1995, Rosen LB $16.95 (978-0-8239-1848-5). Grim stories of the escape from the "killing fields" and powerful testimony to the reality of refugee life. (Rev: BL 5/15/95; SLJ 5/95) [973]

10297 She, Colleen. *Teenage Refugees from China Speak Out* (7–12). Series: In Their Own Voices. 1995, Rosen LB $27.95 (978-0-8239-1847-8). Interviews with native Chinese teenagers who are now living in the United States. (Rev: BL 6/1–15/95; SLJ 5/95) [305.23]

10298 Springstubb, Tricia. *The Vietnamese Americans* (6–12). Illus. Series: Immigrants in America. 2002, Gale $29.95 (978-1-56006-964-5). A look at how this ethnic group is faring in America, with stories of individual immigrants adding interest. (Rev: BL 4/1/02; SLJ 6/02) [305.895]

10299 Takaki, Ronald. *Ethnic Islands: The Emergence of Urban Chinese America* (6–10). Series: Asian American Experience. 1994, Chelsea LB $19.95 (978-0-7910-2180-4). First-person accounts of the Chinese American experience in the 20th century. (Rev: BL 9/15/94; SLJ 9/94) [973]

10300 Takaki, Ronald. *From Exiles to Immigrants: The Refugees from Southeast Asia* (6–10). Series: Asian American Experience. 1995, Chelsea LB $19.95 (978-0-7910-2185-9). Personal histories of Southeast Asian refugees in the United States. (Rev: BL 8/95; VOYA 12/95) [978]

10301 Takaki, Ronald. *From the Land of Morning Calm: The Koreans in America* (6–10). Series: Asian American Experience. 1994, Chelsea LB $19.95 (978-0-7910-2181-1). Oral histories and local documents challenge stereotypes that plague Korean Americans. (Rev: BL 9/1/94; SLJ 9/94; VOYA 12/94) [973]

10302 Takaki, Ronald. *In the Heart of Filipino America: Immigrants from the Pacific Isles* (6–10). Series: Asian American Experience. 1994, Chelsea LB $19.95 (978-0-7910-2187-3). A historic overview of Filipinos in the United States. (Rev: BL 12/15/94; VOYA 4/95) [973]

10303 Takaki, Ronald. *India in the West: South Asians in America* (6–10). Series: Asian American Experience. 1994, Chelsea LB $19.95 (978-0-7910-

2186-6). This overview of the Asian Indian experience in the United States describes how, when, and why South Asians came to this country and the problems they have confronted. (Rev: BL 12/15/94; SLJ 3/95) [970]

10304 Teitelbaum, Michael. *Chinese Immigrants* (5–8). Series: Immigration to the United States. 2004, Facts on File $35.00 (978-0-8160-5687-3). After an overview of the reasons underlying immigration in general, this illustrated volume looks at the circumstances of migrants from China, the group's history in the United States, and the contemporary situation, with sidebar features, a timeline, and a glossary. (Rev: SLJ 4/05)

10305 Wapner, Kenneth. *Teenage Refugees from Vietnam Speak Out* (7–12). Series: In Their Own Voices. 1995, Rosen LB $16.95 (978-0-8239-1842-3). Interviews with Vietnamese teenagers who are now living in the United States. (Rev: BL 6/1–15/95; SLJ 5/95) [305.23]

10306 Wu, Dana Ying-Hui, and Jeffrey Dao-Sheng Tung. *The Chinese-American Experience* (5–7). Illus. Series: Coming to America. 1993, Millbrook LB $22.40 (978-1-56294-271-7). The story of Chinese immigration to the United States, from exploitation, prejudice, and discrimination to gradual acceptance. (Rev: BL 6/1–15/93) [973]

10307 Zurlo, Tony. *The Japanese Americans* (6–12). Series: Immigrants in America. 2003, Gale LB $29.95 (978-1-59018-001-3). From Hawaii's sugar plantations to California's truck farms, this is the story of Japanese Americans and how they fought for full acceptance in America. (Rev: BL 11/15/03) [973]

Hispanic Americans

10308 Aliotta, Jerome J. *The Puerto Ricans* (5–8). Series: Land of Immigrants. 1995, Chelsea LB $21.95 (978-0-7910-3360-9). This account provides an extensive history of Puerto Ricans living in the United States, their struggles, traditions, and way of life. (Rev: BL 10/15/95) [305.868]

10309 Bandon, Alexandra. *Dominican Americans* (5–8). Illus. Series: Footsteps to America. 1995, New Discovery $22.00 (978-0-02-768152-9). A readable account of why many residents of the Dominican Republic left their country to come to the United States and the conditions they found. (Rev: SLJ 8/95) [973]

10310 Behnke, Alison. *Mexicans in America* (4–8). Series: In America. 2004, Lerner LB $27.93 (978-0-8225-3955-1). The reasons for Mexican migration to the United States and the life the newcomers find when they arrive are discussed in engaging narrative, with personal stories, notes on key figures, illustrations, and a timeline. (Rev: SLJ 3/05) [304.8]

10311 Catalano, Julie. *The Mexican Americans* (5–8). Illus. Series: Immigrant Experience. 1995, Chelsea LB $14.95 (978-0-7910-3359-3); paper $9.95 (978-0-7910-3381-4). This book traces the reasons for leaving Mexico, the immigrants' reception in the United States, and their contributions and achievements. (Rev: BL 11/15/95; SLJ 1/96) [973]

10312 Cerar, K. Melissa. *Teenage Refugees from Nicaragua Speak Out* (7–12). Series: In Their Own Voices. 1995, Rosen LB $27.95 (978-0-8239-1849-2). The horror of the contra war, after the corrupt rule of the Somoza family was ended by the Sandinistas, is recalled by Nicaraguan teens who fled their country, leaving their families, to seek refuge in the United States. (Rev: BL 6/1–15/95) [973]

10313 Cofer, Judith Ortiz, ed. *Riding Low on the Streets of Gold* (6–12). 2003, Arte Publico $14.95 (978-1-55885-380-5). Latino writers consider issues close to teen hearts in this collection of fiction, poetry, and memoirs. (Rev: BL 12/1/03; SLJ 6/04) [810]

10314 Cole, Melanie, et al. *Famous People of Hispanic Heritage* (4–7). Series: Contemporary American Success Stories. 1997, Mitchell Lane LB $21.95 (978-1-883845-44-5); paper $12.95 (978-1-883845-43-8). This useful series, now in nine volumes, profiles famous Hispanics, past and present, from around the world. (Rev: BL 3/15/98; HBG 3/98) [920]

10315 Doak, Robin. *Struggling to Become American: 1899–1940* (5–10). Series: Latino-American History. 2007, Chelsea House LB $35.00 (978-0-8160-6443-4). Doak looks at Latino immigration — especially from Puerto Rico, Cuba, and Mexico — and at the conditions of Hispanic laborers in the United States during World War I and the Great Depression; includes photographs, sidebars, political cartoons, maps, and so forth. (Rev: SLJ 7/07)

10316 Gay, Kathlyn. *Leaving Cuba: From Operation Pedro Pan to Elian* (6–12). Illus. 2000, Twenty-First Century LB $22.90 (978-0-7613-1466-0). The plight of young Elian Gonzalez brought attention to Cubans' efforts to escape their oppressive regime and the uncertain welcome they face in the United States. (Rev: BL 3/1/01; HBG 3/01; SLJ 1/01; VOYA 6/01) [362.87]

10317 Gernand, Renee. *The Cuban Americans* (5–8). Illus. 1995, Chelsea LB $21.95 (978-0-7910-3354-8); paper $9.95 (978-0-7910-3376-0). The contributions of Cuban Americans and reasons why they came to America. (Rev: BL 2/1/89) [973.0468729]

10318 Mendez, Adriana. *Cubans in America* (5–7). Illus. Series: In America. 1994, Lerner LB $19.93 (978-0-8225-1953-9). An account that describes why Cubans left their homeland, where they live in the United States, their lifestyles, and their contributions to society. (Rev: BL 8/94; SLJ 8/94) [973]

10319 Ochoa, George. *The New York Public Library Amazing Hispanic American History: A Book of Answers for Kids* (4–9). 1998, Wiley paper $12.95 (978-0-471-19204-6). Using a question-and-answer format, this work explores such topics as Hispanic American identity and history, cultural groups, accomplishments, and immigrant experiences. (Rev: BL 12/1/98; SLJ 11/98) [973]

10320 Perl, Lila. *North Across the Border: The Story of the Mexican Americans* (5–9). Series: Great Journeys. 2001, Benchmark LB $32.79 (978-0-7614-1226-7). The economic and social reasons for Mexican migration to the north through history are presented in text, quotations from primary sources, and many illustrations and maps. (Rev: BL 1/1–15/02; HBG 10/02; SLJ 3/02) [973.0468]

10321 Sonneborn, Liz. *The Cuban Americans* (6–12). Illus. Series: Immigrants in America. 2002, Gale $29.95 (978-1-56006-902-7). A look at how this ethnic group is faring in America, with stories of individual immigrants adding interest. (Rev: BL 4/1/02) [973]

10322 Taus-Bolstad, Stacy. *Puerto Ricans in America* (5–8). Series: In America. 2004, Lerner LB $27.93 (978-0-8225-3953-7). This overview of Puerto Rican migration to the United States looks at the motivations for moving and explores the lives of the new arrivals and the traditions they maintained. (Rev: BL 11/15/04) [304.8]

10323 Worth, Richard. *Mexican Immigrants* (5–8). Series: Immigration to the United States. 2004, Facts on File $35.00 (978-0-8160-5690-3). After an overview of the reasons underlying immigration in general, this illustrated volume looks at the circumstances of migrants from Mexico, the group's history in the United States, and the contemporary situation, with sidebar features, a timeline, and a glossary. Also use *Jewish Immigrants* and *Africans in America* (both 2004). (Rev: SLJ 4/05) [304.8]

Jewish Americans

10324 Finkelstein, Norman H. *Forged in Freedom: Shaping the Jewish-American Experience* (6–12). Illus. 2002, Jewish Publication Soc. $19.95 (978-0-8276-0748-4). Text and photographs present an overview of Jews' contributions to the United States, their influence on the culture, and the problems they have faced. (Rev: BL 8/02; HBG 3/03) [973.04]

10325 Horton, Casey. *The Jews* (4–8). Series: We Came to North America. 2000, Crabtree LB $25.27 (978-0-7787-0187-3); paper $8.95 (978-0-7787-0201-6). As well as discussing the reasons why Jews left Europe, this account describes the trip across the Atlantic, reception in America, and the many contributions to the United States. (Rev: SLJ 10/00) [973]

10326 Leder, Jane. *A Russian Jewish Family* (5–8). Series: Journey Between Two Worlds. 1996, Lerner LB $22.60 (978-0-8225-3401-3); paper $8.95 (978-0-8225-9744-5). This account compares the living conditions of a Jewish family in Russia and in their new American home. (Rev: BL 11/1/96; SLJ 11/96) [977.3]

10327 Lingen, Marissa. *The Jewish Americans* (4–7). Illus. Series: We Came to America. 2002, Mason Crest LB $19.95 (978-1-59084-109-9). Lingen traces the history of Jewish migration to the United States and provides a list of Jewish Americans of note. (Rev: SLJ 9/02) [973.049]

10328 Muggamin, Howard. *The Jewish Americans* (5–8). Series: Immigrant Experience. 1995, Chelsea LB $19.95 (978-0-7910-3365-4); paper $9.95 (978-0-7910-3387-6). An examination of Jewish Americans, their history of immigration and their reception in this country, and their achievements and contributions. (Rev: BL 11/15/95) [973]

10329 Rubin, Susan G. *L'Chaim! to Jewish Life in America! Celebrating from 1654 Until Today* (7–9). 2004, Abrams $24.95 (978-0-8109-5035-1). This beautifully illustrated volume chronicles the history of Jews in America with many quotations and personal stories. (Rev: BL 11/1/04; SLJ 1/05; VOYA 2/05) [973]

10330 Schleifer, Jay. *A Student's Guide to Jewish American Genealogy* (7–12). Series: American Family Tree. 1996, Oryx $36.95 (978-0-89774-977-0). An in-depth survey of Jewish history serves as a framework for realistic genealogical information, with plenty of valuable sources cited. (Rev: SLJ 1/97) [973]

Native Americans

10331 Adare, Sierra. *Mohawk* (4–8). Illus. 2003, Gareth Stevens LB $26.00 (978-0-8368-3665-3). An introduction to the history, culture, and current status of the Mohawk people, with photographs, maps, and interesting sidebar features that will be useful for reports. Also use *Apache* and *Nez Perce* (both 2003). (Rev: HBG 10/03; SLJ 9/03) [974.7004]

10332 Bial, Raymond. *The Mandan* (5–9). Series: Lifeways. 2002, Benchmark LB $34.21 (978-0-7614-1415-5). Two traditional stories, a recipe, and a language guide accompany information on the history, culture, beliefs, and key figures of the Mandan people. (Rev: HBG 3/03; LMC 8–9/03; SLJ 6/03) [978.004]

10333 Secakuku, Susan. *Meet Mindy: A Native Girl from the Southwest* (5–8). Photos by John Harrington. Series: My World: Young Native Americans Today. 2003, Beyond Words paper $15.95 (978-1-58270-091-5). A Hopi teen named Mindy talks about her life and heritage in this full-color photoessay. (Rev: BL 4/1/03; SLJ 3/03) [979.1004]

Other Ethnic Groups

10334 Brockman, Terra Castiglia. *A Student's Guide to Italian American Genealogy* (7–12). Series: American Family Tree. 1996, Oryx $35.00 (978-0-89774-973-2). This book, a guide to searching for Italian American ancestors, contains Web sites, computer programs, addresses, and other sources of information. (Rev: SLJ 10/96) [929]

10335 Burgan, Michael. *Italian Immigrants* (5–8). Series: Immigration to the United States. 2004, Facts on File $35.00 (978-0-8160-5681-1). After an overview of the reasons underlying immigration in general, this illustrated volume looks at the circumstances of migrants from Italy, the group's history in the United States, and the contemporary situation, with sidebar features, a timeline, and a glossary. (Rev: SLJ 4/05)

10336 Cavan, Seamus. *The Irish-American Experience* (5–7). Illus. Series: Coming to America. 1993, Millbrook LB $23.40 (978-1-56294-218-2). Beginning with the potato famine that forced millions of Irish to come to America, this is the story of the rise of Irish Americans to positions of prominence. (Rev: BCCB 4/93; BL 6/1–15/93) [973]

10337 Di Franco, J. Philip. *The Italian Americans* (5–8). Illus. 1995, Chelsea LB $14.95 (978-0-7910-3353-1); paper $9.95 (978-0-7910-3375-3). A heavily illustrated discussion of the culture that Italian immigrants left behind and their contributions to American life. (Rev: BL 1/1/88) [973.0451]

10338 Franck, Irene M. *The German-American Heritage* (7–12). Illus. 1988, Facts on File $21.95 (978-0-8160-1629-7). This book contains not only an account of the progress of Germans in this country but also a brief history of Germany. (Rev: BL 3/15/89) [973]

10339 Galicich, Anne. *The German Americans* (5–8). Illus. Series: Immigrant Experience. 1995, Chelsea LB $19.95 (978-0-7910-3362-3); paper $13.25 (978-0-7910-3384-5). This account traces the history of German Americans, from their reasons for leaving Germany and their initial reception in the United States to their present status. (Rev: BL 4/1/89) [973]

10340 Goldstein, Margaret J. *Irish in America* (5–8). Series: In America. 2004, Lerner LB $27.93 (978-0-8225-3950-6). This overview of Irish migration to the United States looks at the underlying reasons for the exodus and explores the lives of the new arrivals and the traditions they maintained. (Rev: BL 11/15/04) [973]

10341 Halliburton, Warren J. *The West Indian-American Experience* (7–10). 1994, Millbrook LB $23.90 (978-1-56294-340-0). Tells the story of a Jamaican family's emigration to the United States in the 1980s, the history of the Caribbean, and immigration to the United States. (Rev: BL 4/1/94; SLJ 7/94) [973]

10342 Hossell, Karen Price. *The Irish Americans* (6–12). Series: Immigrants in America. 2003, Gale LB $29.95 (978-1-56006-752-8). The story of the thousands of Irish people who migrated to America, where they faced discrimination before being assimilated into society and being accepted as true Americans. (Rev: BL 11/15/03) [973]

10343 Howard, Helen. *Living as a Refugee in America: Mohammed's Story* (6–9). Illus. Series: Children in Crisis. 2005, World Almanac $31.00 (978-0-8368-5959-1). This accessible story about Mohammed, an Afghan teenager who fled the Taliban with his family and eventually made his way to the United States, incorporates historical and cultural information plus discussion of such topics as discrimination. (Rev: BL 12/1/05*; SLJ 11/05) [973.086]

10344 Ingram, W. Scott. *Greek Immigrants* (5–8). Series: Immigration to the United States. 2004, Facts on File $35.00 (978-0-8160-5689-7). After an overview of the reasons underlying immigration in general, this illustrated volume looks at the circumstances of migrants from Greece, the group's history in the United States, and the contemporary situation, with sidebar features, a timeline, and a glossary. Also use *Japanese Immigrants* and *Polish Immigrants* (both 2004). (Rev: BL 4/1/04; HB 3–4/04; SLJ 4/05)

10345 Katz, William L. *Black Indians: A Hidden Heritage* (7–10). 1986, Macmillan $17.95 (978-0-689-31196-3). A history of the group that represented a mixture of the Indian and black races and its role in opening up the West. (Rev: BL 6/15/86; SLJ 8/86) [970]

10346 Kuropas, Myron B. *Ukrainians in America* (5–7). Illus. Series: In America. 1996, Lerner LB $19.93 (978-0-8225-1043-7). The story of Ukrainian immigrants to the United States, their cultural traditions, and their contributions to American life. (Rev: BL 3/15/96; SLJ 3/96) [973]

10347 Lock, Donna. *The Polish Americans* (5–8). Illus. Series: We Came to America. 2002, Mason Crest LB $19.95 (978-1-59084-112-9). A look at the customs and contributions of this ethnic group, including information on famous Polish Americans, with a bibliography, glossary, timeline, and resources for tracing ancestors. (Rev: BL 7/02) [305.891]

10348 McGill, Allyson. *The Swedish Americans* (5–8). Series: Immigrant Experience. 1997, Chelsea $19.95 (978-0-7910-4551-0); paper $9.95 (978-0-

7910-4552-7). Explains why Swedes have emigrated from their homeland, their reception in the United States, and their contributions to the nation. (Rev: BL 10/15/97) [322.4]

10349 Magocsi, Paul R. *The Russian Americans* (5–8). Illus. Series: Immigrant Experience. 1995, Chelsea LB $21.95 (978-0-7910-3367-8). Coverage includes reasons for leaving Russia, customs and traditions, contributions to their new nation, and famous Russian Americans. (Rev: BL 11/15/95; SLJ 1/96) [973]

10350 Naff, Alixa. *The Arab Americans* (6–10). Series: The Immigrant Experience. 1998, Chelsea $21.95 (978-0-7910-5051-4); paper $13.25 (978-0-7910-5053-8). After a brief description of Arab culture and homelands, this book describes the cycles of Arab immigration to this country, the reception Arabs received, their new identities and contributions, and famous Arab Americans such as Ralph Nader and Donna Shalala. (Rev: HBG 3/99; SLJ 1/99) [305.8]

10351 Paddock, Lisa, and Carl S. Rollyson. *A Student's Guide to Scandinavian American Genealogy* (7–12). Series: American Family Tree. 1996, Oryx $36.95 (978-0-89774-978-7). An introduction to the Scandinavian countries, people, and emigration to America, and information on how to research specific nationalities. (Rev: SLJ 10/96) [929]

10352 Paulson, Timothy J. *Irish Immigrants* (5–8). Series: Immigration to the United States. 2004, Facts on File $35.00 (978-0-8160-5682-8). After an overview of the reasons underlying immigration in general, this illustrated volume looks at the circumstances of migrants from Ireland, the group's history in the United States, and the contemporary situation, with sidebar features, a timeline, and a glossary. (Rev: SLJ 4/05)

10353 Sawyers, June S. *Famous Firsts of Scottish-Americans* (4–8). Illus. 1996, Pelican $13.95 (978-1-56554-122-1). Brief biographies of 30 Americans of Scottish descent, including Neil Armstrong, Alexander Calder, Herman Melville, and Patrick Henry. (Rev: BL 6/1–15/97) [920]

10354 Schouweiler, Thomas. *Germans in America* (5–7). Illus. Series: In America. 1994, Lerner LB $19.93 (978-0-8225-0245-6). The causes and results of German immigration to the United States are outlined, with good coverage of their contributions and important figures. (Rev: BL 1/15/95; SLJ 12/94) [973]

10355 Schur, Joan Brodsky. *The Arabs* (8–11). Illus. Series: Coming to America. 2005, Gale LB $34.95 (978-0-7377-2148-5). With profiles of several famous Arab Americans (including Ralph Nader and Naomi Shihab Nye), this title uses primary and secondary sources to present an overview of Arab

Americans, their reasons for migrating, their social mores, and their adaptation to their new country. (Rev: BL 3/15/05; SLJ 3/05) [973]

10356 Silverman, Robin L. *A Bosnian Family* (4–7). Illus. Series: Journey Between Two Worlds. 1997, Lerner LB $27.15 (978-0-8225-3404-4); paper $8.95 (978-0-8225-9754-4). The story of Velma Dusper, her homeland of Bosnia, and her journey with her family to freedom and a new home in North Dakota. (Rev: BL 6/1–15/97; SLJ 7/97) [304.8]

10357 Strazzabosco-Hayn, Gina. *Teenage Refugees from Iran Speak Out* (7–12). 1995, Rosen LB $27.95 (978-0-8239-1845-4). Iranian teens tell their grim stories as powerful testimony to the reality of refugee life. (Rev: BL 5/15/95; SLJ 5/95) [973]

10358 Tekavec, Valerie. *Teenage Refugees from Haiti Speak Out* (7–12). Series: In Their Own Voices. 1995, Rosen LB $16.95 (978-0-8239-1844-7). Interviews with native Haitian teenagers who are now living in the United States. (Rev: BL 6/1–15/95; SLJ 6/95) [305.23]

10359 Temple, Bob. *The Arab Americans* (5–8). Illus. Series: We Came to America. 2002, Mason Crest LB $19.95 (978-1-59084-102-0). Temple reviews the history of Arab immigration to North America, the group's customs and contributions, and famous Arab Americans, with the aid of photographs, a timeline, and glossary. (Rev: BL 7/02; SLJ 9/02) [305.892]

10360 Testa, Maria. *Something About America* (6–9). 2005, Candlewick $14.99 (978-0-7636-2528-3). In free verse, Testa recounts the poignant story of a young immigrant from Kosovo who was badly burned as she and her family fled their war-torn homeland. (Rev: BL 8/05; SLJ 9/05; VOYA 2/06) [811]

10361 Trumbauer, Lisa. *German Immigrants* (5–8). Series: Immigration to the United States. 2004, Facts on File $35.00 (978-0-8160-5683-5). After an overview of the reasons underlying immigration in general, this illustrated volume looks at the circumstances of migrants from Germany, the group's history in the United States, and the contemporary situation, with sidebar features, a timeline, and a glossary. Also use *Russian Immigrants* (2004). (Rev: SLJ 4/05)

10362 Ueda, Reed, and Sandra Stotsky, eds. *Irish-American Answer Book* (6–10). 1999, Chelsea LB $19.75 (978-0-7910-4795-8); paper $9.95 (978-0-7910-4796-5). Using a question-and-answer format, this book examines the history, culture, politics, and religion of Irish Americans from the 1800s to the present. (Rev: VOYA 2/99) [973]

10363 Watts, J. F. *The Irish Americans* (5–8). Series: Immigrant Experience. 1995, Chelsea paper $9.95

(978-0-7910-3388-3). A lively, informative account of why the Irish came to America, the conditions they found here, and how they have fared. (Rev: BL 10/15/95) [973]

10364 Zamenova, Tatyana. *Teenage Refugees from Russia Speak Out* (7–12). Series: In Their Own Voices. 1995, Rosen LB $27.95 (978-0-8239-1846-1). Teenage Russian refugees describe their lives under socialism, leaving Russia, and adjusting to life in North America. (Rev: BL 6/1–15/95) [973]

Forms of Dissent

10365 Williams, Mary E., ed. *Is It Unpatriotic to Criticize One's Country?* (7–9). Series: At Issue. 2005, Gale LB $29.95 (978-0-7377-2396-0); paper $21.20 (978-0-7377-2397-7). Previously published articles offer diverse views on whether criticism of one's country is unpatriotic. (Rev: SLJ 7/05) [323.6]

Social Concerns and Problems

General and Miscellaneous

10366 Able, Deborah. *Hate Groups*. Rev. ed. (7–9). Series: Issues in Focus. 2000, Enslow LB $26.60 (978-0-7660-1245-5). An in-depth look at hate groups in America, what motivates them, their targets, and ways to combat them, with details of recent incidents and court cases, and of the growing use of the Internet in this area. (Rev: HBG 3/01; SLJ 1/01) [305.8]

10367 Ancona, George. *Harvest* (4–7). Illus. 2001, Marshall Cavendish $15.95 (978-0-7614-5086-3). This volume examines the difficult lives and work of Mexican migrant workers and the crops they harvest, ending with a look at the contributions of labor leader Cesar Chavez. (Rev: BL 1/1–15/02; HBG 3/02; SLJ 4/02) [331.5]

10368 Andryszewski, Tricia. *The Militia Movement in America: Before and After Oklahoma City* (7–12). Illus. 1997, Millbrook LB $24.90 (978-0-7613-0119-6). This work traces the roots of the anti-government militia movement in the United States from the late 1800s to the present, with coverage of events in Ruby Ridge, Waco, Oklahoma City, and elsewhere. (Rev: BL 2/15/97; SLJ 3/97; VOYA 2/98) [320.4]

10369 Brimner, Larry. *A Migrant Family* (4–8). Illus. 1992, Lerner LB $23.95 (978-0-8225-2554-7). The daily life of 12-year-old Juan and his Mexican American family is captured in this photoessay. (Rev: BCCB 10/92; BL 9/15/92) [305.5]

10370 Cohen, Daniel. *Animal Rights: A Handbook for Young Adults* (6–9). 1993, Millbrook LB $24.90 (978-1-56294-219-9). Discusses the use of animals for medical experimentation, zoos, marine theme parks, rodeos, factory farming and hunting, puppy mills, and classroom dissection. (Rev: BL 7/93; VOYA 2/94) [179]

10371 D'Angelo, Laura. *Hate Crimes* (6–9). Illus. Series: Crime, Justice, and Punishment. 1997, Chelsea LB $30.00 (978-0-7910-4266-3). This book examines the nature and causes of hate crimes based on differences in race, ethnicity, religion, or sexual preference, and the individuals or groups responsible for them, with interesting case studies and psychological profiles. (Rev: BL 5/15/98; VOYA 4/00) [364.1]

10372 Desetta, Al, and Sybil Wolin, eds. *The Struggle to Be Strong: True Stories by Teens About Overcoming Tough Times* (6–12). Illus. 2000, Free Spirit paper $14.95 (978-1-57542-079-0). Teens talk about problems such as addicted and abusive parents, AIDS, drugs and alcohol, school, health, and so forth. (Rev: SLJ 8/00)

10373 Ennew, Judith. *Exploitation of Children* (6–10). Illus. Series: Global Issues. 1996, Raintree LB $19.98 (978-0-8172-4546-7). This book presents historical material, statistical data, case studies, and differing viewpoints on how children are exploited in many countries of the world. (Rev: BL 2/1/97; VOYA 6/97) [305.23]

10374 Gay, Kathlyn. *Militias: Armed and Dangerous* (7–12). Illus. Series: Issues in Focus. 1997, Enslow LB $26.60 (978-0-89490-902-3). A disturbing look at the militia movement in the U.S. and the attraction it holds for such malcontents as survivalists, neo-Nazis, white supremacists, Christian fanatics, and government haters. (Rev: BL 11/15/97; VOYA 2/98) [322.4]

10375 Gay, Kathlyn. *Neo-Nazis: A Growing Threat* (8–12). Illus. Series: In Focus. 1997, Enslow LB $20.95 (978-0-89490-901-6). After a discussion of eight recent neo-Nazi-related crimes, the author describes the philosophy and goals of this movement, current groups, and how to fight hate crimes. (Rev: BL 9/1/97; SLJ 10/97) [320.53]

10376 Gifford, Clive. *Violence on the Screen* (7–10). Illus. Series: Voices. 2006, Black Rabbit LB $21.95 (978-1-58340-985-5). Readers are presented with facts, statistics, and opinions about the possible effects of violence in movies and video games and on TV. (Rev: BL 12/15/06) [303.6]

10377 Ginn, Janel, ed. *Do Religious Groups in America Experience Discrimination?* (7–12). Illus. Series: At Issue. 2007, Gale LB $28.70 (978-0-7377-3399-0). Many interesting questions are addressed in the articles collected here, including whether feminists discriminate against Islamic women and whether the Episcopal Church discriminates against homosexuals. (Rev: BL 10/1/07) [305.609]

10378 Gold, Susan Dudley. *Gun Control* (8–12). Series: Open for Debate. 2003, Benchmark LB $37.07 (978-0-7614-1584-8). An evenhanded survey of the gun control controversy, discussing the Second Amendment, history of legislation, school shootings, and the activities of gun makers and dealers. (Rev: SLJ 3/04) [363.3]

10379 Gottfried, Ted. *Deniers of the Holocaust: Who They Are, What They Do, Why They Do It* (6–12). Illus. 2001, Twenty-First Century LB $29.90 (978-0-7613-1950-4). Gottfried provides ample evidence to dismiss the arguments of those who deny that the Holocaust took place and discusses the racism of white supremacists, the existence of Internet hate sites, and issues of free speech. (Rev: BL 9/1/01; HBG 3/02) [940.53]

10380 Gourley, Catherine. *Media Wizards: A Behind-the-Scenes Look at Media Manipulations* (5–9). 1999, Twenty-First Century LB $26.90 (978-0-7613-0967-3). An informative account of how the media can manipulate the truth. (Rev: HBG 3/00; SLJ 2/00; VOYA 4/00) [380.3]

10381 Griffin, Starla. *Girl, 13: A Global Snapshot of Generation e* (6–12). 2005, Hylas paper $22.95 (978-1-59258-112-2). Thirteen-year-olds around the world contributed to this volume, answering questions about their views of the world and writing essays about their lives and aspirations. (Rev: SLJ 2/06)

10382 Haddock, Patricia. *Teens and Gambling: Who Wins?* (7–12). Illus. Series: Issues in Focus. 1996, Enslow LB $20.95 (978-0-89490-719-7). The controversial subject of gambling is introduced — its lure, addiction, and problems, particularly as related to teenagers. (Rev: BL 8/96; SLJ 8/96; VOYA 10/96) [363.4]

10383 Haugen, David M., ed. *Animal Experimentation* (8–12). Series: At Issue. 1999, Greenhaven LB $26.20 (978-0-7377-0149-4). A collection of essays by experts that explore various viewpoints concern-

ing animal rights and experimentation on animals. (Rev: BL 11/15/99; SLJ 1/00) [179]

10384 Herumin, Wendy. *Child Labor Today: A Human Rights Issue* (7–12). Illus. Series: Issues in Focus Today. 2007, Enslow LB $23.95 (978-0-7660-2682-7). A look at the often-deplorable working conditions of children around the world, with many photographs and personal stories. (Rev: BL 11/15/07) [331.3]

10385 Hjelmeland, Andy. *Legalized Gambling: Solution or Illusion?* (8–12). Series: Pro/Con Issues. 1998, Lerner LB $30.35 (978-0-8225-2615-5). After a brief history of gambling since ancient times, this book discusses current legal forms of gambling, including lotteries and casinos, and the attendant topics of controversy. (Rev: HBG 3/99; SLJ 12/98) [795]

10386 Hoyt-Goldsmith, Diane. *Migrant Worker: A Boy from the Rio Grande Valley* (4–7). Illus. 1996, Holiday $15.95 (978-0-8234-1225-9). A photoessay about the grim living conditions endured by an 11-year-old Mexican American migrant worker. (Rev: BCCB 3/96; BL 3/1/96; SLJ 5/96) [331.5]

10387 Hyde, Margaret O. *Gambling: Winners and Losers* (6–10). 1995, Millbrook LB $23.40 (978-1-56294-532-9). A timely subject gets rather dry treatment in this book that tells of the history, types, and psychology of gambling, with quotations from many case studies. (Rev: BL 12/15/95; SLJ 3/96) [363.4]

10388 James, Barbara. *Animal Rights* (5–10). Series: Talking Points. 1999, Raintree LB $27.12 (978-0-8172-5317-2). Various aspects of the animal rights controversy are explored in an objective, straightforward manner. (Rev: BL 8/99) [179.3]

10389 Judson, Karen. *Animal Testing* (7–12). 2005, Benchmark LB $25.95 (978-0-7614-1882-5). Covers the history, science, ethics, and new laws relating to experimentation using animals, with sidebars, quotations, and color and black-and-white photographs. (Rev: SLJ 7/06)

10390 Kops, Deborah. *Racial Profiling* (6–9). Series: Open for Debate. 2006, Benchmark LB $27.95 (978-0-7614-2298-3). Kops gives a balanced overview of racial profiling, presenting various opinions for and against that will be useful for research. (Rev: SLJ 2/07)

10391 Kuhn, Betsy. *Prying Eyes: Privacy in the Twenty-first Century* (5–8). Illus. 2008, Lerner LB $38.60 (978-0-8225-7179-7). From video cameras that can track our every move to personal data stored on computers, this book looks at security/privacy issues and court cases related to them to provide an overview of the important issues in this arena. (Rev: BL 1/1–15/08; LMC 10/08; SLJ 5/08) [323.44]

10392 Landau, Elaine. *Land Mines: 100 Million Hidden Killers* (6–12). Series: Issues in Focus. 2000, Enslow LB $26.60 (978-0-7660-1240-0). This is an overview of where land mines are found, how they got there, and ways in which the danger they present can be overcome. (Rev: BL 9/15/00; HBG 3/01; VOYA 2/01) [363.3]

10393 Lang, Paul. *The English Language Debate: One Nation, One Language?* (7–12). Illus. 1995, Enslow LB $20.95 (978-0-89490-642-8). A well-documented account that explores such multicultural topics as the English-only movement, bilingual education, and other current political aspects of the teaching, status, and use of English in this country. (Rev: BL 6/1–15/95) [306.4]

10394 Levine, Herbert M. *Animal Rights* (7–12). Illus. Series: American Issues Debated. 1997, Raintree LB $31.40 (978-0-8172-4350-0). Should animals be banned from use in science? Should hunting be illegal? Should people be ashamed of wearing fur? These and other questions relating to animals are explored from different points of view. (Rev: BL 11/15/97; VOYA 2/98) [179]

10395 Levine, Herbert M. *Gun Control* (7–12). Illus. Series: American Issues Debated. 1997, Raintree LB $31.40 (978-0-8172-4351-7). The debate on the effectiveness of gun control in reducing crime is presented, along with questions concerning handgun bans, waiting periods, and penalties for illegal gun use. (Rev: BL 11/15/97) [363.3]

10396 MccGwire, Scarlett. *Surveillance: The Impact on our Lives* (7–9). Illus. Series: 21st Century Debates. 2001, Raintree LB $27.12 (978-0-7398-3172-4). An overview of the various ways in which our lives are monitored — by government, law enforcement authorities, companies, and so forth — and the benefits and dangers of such technologies as wire tapping and Web tracking. (Rev: BL 7/01; SLJ 7/01) [323.44]

10397 Menhard, Francha Roffe. *School Violence: Deadly Lessons* (8–12). Series: Teen Issues. 2000, Enslow LB $22.60 (978-0-7660-1358-2). Many acts of violence in schools are described, with material on their causes and possible prevention. (Rev: HBG 3/01; SLJ 9/00) [371.7]

10398 Milite, George A. *Gun Control* (8–12). Illus. Series: Compact Research. 2007, Reference Point LB $24.95 (978-1-60152-010-4). This compact volume provides lots of information for report writers, with illustrations, quotations from primary sources, lists of facts, statistical charts, and brief timelines. (Rev: SLJ 5/07) [363.3]

10399 Newman, Shirlee P. *Child Slavery in Modern Times* (4–7). Illus. Series: Watts Library: History of Slavery. 2000, Watts LB $25.50 (978-0-531-11696-8). From Europe to Asia and Africa, this book explores the deplorable lives of servitude forced on

child laborers and slaves, and how some have escaped. (Rev: BL 2/15/01; SLJ 3/01) [306.3]

10400 Ojeda, Auriana, ed. *Technology and Society* (6–12). Series: Opposing Viewpoints. 2002, Gale LB $36.20 (978-0-7377-0913-1); paper $24.95 (978-0-7377-0912-4). Technology's contributions to — and negative impact on — society are discussed here, with mention of Internet access, e-mail privacy, biotechnology, government regulation, the divide between rich and poor, and increasing social isolation. (Rev: BL 6/1–15/02; SLJ 6/02) [306.4]

10401 Owen, Marna. *Animal Rights: Yes or No?* (6–10). 1993, Lerner LB $30.35 (978-0-8225-2603-2). A discussion of the various positions on animal rights. (Rev: BL 1/15/94; SLJ 3/94) [179]

10402 Parker, David L., et al. *Stolen Dreams: Portraits of Working Children* (6–12). Illus. 1997, Lerner LB $19.93 (978-0-8225-2960-6). This compelling photoessay deals with child labor around the world, particularly in the Far East. (Rev: BL 11/1/97; HB 3–4/98; VOYA 2/98) [331.3]

10403 Patterson, Charles. *Animal Rights* (6–10). 1993, Enslow LB $20.95 (978-0-89490-468-4). A thorough examination of the topic, including a history of animal rights movements. (Rev: BL 10/15/93; SLJ 11/93; VOYA 2/94) [179]

10404 Pringle, Laurence. *The Animal Rights Controversy* (7–12). Illus. 1989, Harcourt $16.95 (978-0-15-203559-4). A book about the way animals are abused and misused that covers topics such as factory farming, experimentation, and zoos. (Rev: BL 1/15/90; SLJ 5/90; VOYA 4/90) [197]

10405 Roleff, Tamara L., ed. *Hate Crimes* (6–12). Series: Current Controversies. 2000, Greenhaven LB $36.20 (978-0-7377-0454-9); paper $24.95 (978-0-7377-0453-2). After describing what constitutes a hate crime, these essays focus on specific examples, laws, and the threat posed by groups that promote extreme, violent behaviors. (Rev: BL 2/15/01; SLJ 3/01) [364.1]

10406 Roleff, Tamara L. *Hate Groups* (7–12). Series: Opposing Viewpoints Digests. 2001, Greenhaven $27.45 (978-0-7377-0677-2). A concise and thought-provoking exploration of the problems of group hate and restrictions of free speech. (Rev: BL 1/1–15/02) [364.1]

10407 Roleff, Tamara L., ed. *The Rights of Animals* (6–12). Series: Current Controversies. 1999, Greenhaven LB $32.45 (978-0-7377-0069-5); paper $21.20 (978-0-7377-0068-8). This collection of provocative essays discusses such topics as cloning, animal organ transplants, hunting, trapping, and using animals in entertainment and experimentation. (Rev: BL 10/15/99) [179]

10408 Sherman, Aliza. *Working Together Against Violence Against Women* (6–10). Series: Library of

Social Activism. 1996, Rosen LB $27.95 (978-0-8239-2258-1). An examination of violence against women, including date rape, stranger rape, assault, and domestic violence, and of the actions being taken by both government and private agencies; advice on how teenagers can help themselves, a friend, and their communities is also offered. (Rev: SLJ 2/97; VOYA 6/97) [303.6]

10409 Stewart, Gail B. *Militias* (7–12). Illus. Series: Overview. 1997, Lucent LB $29.95 (978-1-56006-501-2). This book traces the historical development of the militia movement and discusses prominent contemporary militia groups, their purposes, the beliefs and attitudes of their members and leaders, their activities, and why they are flourishing. (Rev: BL 1/1–15/98; HBG 9/98) [322.4]

10410 Streissguth, Thomas. *Gun Control: The Pros and Cons* (6–9). Illus. Series: Hot Issues. 2001, Enslow LB $26.60 (978-0-7660-1673-6). A dispassionate look at both sides of the gun control debate, with a rundown of the status quo in each state and a glossary of gun-related terms. (Rev: BL 1/1–15/02; HBG 3/02) [344.73]

10411 Streissguth, Thomas. *Hatemongers and Demagogues* (6–9). 1995, Oliver LB $19.95 (978-1-881508-23-6). A survey of American leaders who have used hate and inflammatory language to incite violence, along with an examination of the conditions that led people to support these demagogues, from the individuals who provoked the Salem witch hunts to Louis Farrakhan. (Rev: BL 12/15/95; SLJ 2/96; VOYA 6/96) [305.8]

10412 Tipp, Stacey L. *Child Abuse: Detecting Bias* (5–7). Series: Opposing Viewpoints Juniors. 1991, Greenhaven LB $22.45 (978-0-89908-611-8). Four different issues involving child abuse (e.g., whether abusers should be sent to prison) are presented from various points of view. (Rev: BL 5/15/92; SLJ 3/92) [362.7]

10413 Torr, James D., ed. *Gambling* (7–12). Series: Opposing Viewpoints. 2002, Gale $36.20 (978-0-7377-0907-0); paper $24.95 (978-0-7377-0906-3). Essays examine the addictive nature of gambling, the benefits to the Native American tribes that run casinos, sports betting, state lotteries, Internet gambling, and so forth. (Rev: BL 4/15/02) [306.4]

10414 Torr, James D., ed. *Gun Violence* (6–12). Illus. Series: Opposing Viewpoints. 2001, Greenhaven LB $32.45 (978-0-7377-0713-7); paper $21.20 (978-0-7377-0712-0). Twenty-four essays present varied opinions on guns, gun ownership, and gun violence. (Rev: BL 12/1/01) [363.3]

10415 Wand, Kelly, ed. *The Animal Rights Movement* (8–12). Series: American Social Movements. 2002, Gale LB $25.96 (978-0-7377-1046-5). This collection of essays traces this movement from the advocates of animal welfare of the 18th century through the development of the concept of animal rights of the late-20th century. (Rev: BL 1/1–15/03; SLJ 2/03) [179]

10416 Williams, Mary E., ed. *The White Separatist Movement* (8–12). Series: American Social Movements. 2002, Gale LB $36.20 (978-0-7377-1054-0); paper $24.95 (978-0-7377-1053-3). This collection of essays, speeches, book excerpts, and personal observations looks at groups ranging from the Ku Klux Klan to neo-Nazi skinheads and discusses the reasons why people are attracted to such organizations. (Rev: BL 9/15/02) [305.8]

10417 Wiloch, Tom. *Everything You Need to Know About Protecting Yourself and Others from Abduction* (6–9). Illus. Series: Need to Know Library. 1998, Rosen LB $27.95 (978-0-8239-2553-7). This book describes the dangers of abduction and its frequency in America and provides safety tips for home, at school, while babysitting, jogging, and bicycling, and using the Internet. (Rev: SLJ 9/98) [364]

Environmental Issues

General and Miscellaneous

10418 Adair, Rick, ed. *Critical Perspectives on Politics and the Environment* (8–11). Series: Critical Anthologies on Environment and Climate. 2006, Rosen LB $31.95 (978-1-4042-0823-0). A compilation of 16 articles from *Scientific American* that focus on the tension between environmental and political issues, looking in turn at international treaties, domestic regulation, free trade, and current and future problems. (Rev: BL 11/1/06) [333.7]

10419 Andryszewski, Tricia. *The Environment and the Economy: Planting the Seeds for Tomorrow's Growth* (7–12). 1995, Millbrook LB $24.90 (978-1-56294-524-4). Traces the emergence of environment-versus-economy issues. (Rev: BL 12/1/95; SLJ 11/95) [363.7]

10420 Ballard, Carol. *The Search for Better Conservation* (4–7). Illus. Series: Science Quest. 2005, Gareth Stevens LB $26.00 (978-0-8368-4553-2). A look at how lack of conservation affects us, and what scientists are doing to tackle this problem. (Rev: BL 4/1/05)

10421 Ballesta, Laurent, and Pierre Descamp. *Planet Ocean: Voyage to the Heart of the Marine Realm* (8–12). Illus. 2007, National Geographic $40.00 (978-1-4262-0186-8). Full of eye-catching photographs, this ecology-focused volume visits various undersea environments to show just what we may lose to pollution, overfishing, and other threats. (Rev: BLO 11/19/07) [577.7]

10422 Begley, Ed. *Living Like Ed* (8–12). 2008, Clarkson Potter paper $18.00 (978-0-307-39643-3). Begley offers practical tips on adopting a greener way of living, categorizing the changes as "easy," "not-so-big," and "big" and looking separately at the home, transportation, recycling, energy, the garden and kitchen, clothing, and personal care. (Rev: BL 12/1/07) [333.72]

10423 Berne, Emma Carlson. *Global Warming and Climate Change* (8–12). Series: Compact Research. 2007, Reference Point LB $24.95 (978-1-60152-019-7). What are the consequences of global warming? What are the controversies surrounding global warming? These and other questions are discussed from various points of view, with facts, profiles, and illustrations. (Rev: SLJ 1/08)

10424 Bily, Cynthia A. *Global Warming* (8–12). 2006, Gale LB $34.95 (978-0-7377-2935-1); paper $23.70 (978-0-7377-2936-8). Pro and con essays provide diverse viewpoints on the threat of global warming, its causes and effects, and the measures to be taken to combat it. (Rev: SLJ 7/06)

10425 Blatt, Harvey. *America's Environmental Report Card: Are We Making the Grade?* (8–12). Illus. 2004, MIT $35.00 (978-0-262-02572-0). From global warming to water pollution, this volume looks at today's burning environmental issues and potential solutions. (Rev: BL 11/1/04) [363.7]

10426 Bowden, Rob. *Earth's Water Crisis* (7–12). Series: What If We Do Nothing? 2007, World Almanac LB $30.60 (978-0-8368-7754-0). Bowden underlines the importance of water in key areas of our lives, presents future scenarios, and asks readers what they would do. (Rev: LMC 11–12/07; SLJ 5/07) [333.91]

10427 Bowden, Rob. *Water Supply: Our Impact on the Planet* (5–8). Illus. Series: 21st Century Debates. 2003, Raintree LB $28.56 (978-0-7398-5506-5). A thought-provoking examination of the status of the world's water supply, predictions of a looming water crisis, and measures that could be taken to avert this. (Rev: BL 8/03; HBG 10/03) [363.6]

10428 Burnie, David. *Endangered Planet* (4–8). Illus. Series: Kingfisher Knowledge. 2004, Kingfisher $11.95 (978-0-7534-5776-4). This volume looks at how human requirements threaten the flora, fauna, and resources of our planet. (Rev: BL 9/1/04; SLJ 1/05) [333.95]

10429 Calhoun, Yael. *The Environment in the News* (8–12). Series: Science News Flash. 2007, Chelsea House LB $31.95 (978-0-7910-9253-8). Serious researchers will find this slim volume a useful starting place — it covers various viewpoints on many issues and provides graphs, illustrations, photographs, and resources for further information. (Rev: SLJ 8/07)

10430 Chandler, Gary, and Kevin Graham. *Environmental Causes* (5–10). Series: Celebrity Activists. 1997, Twenty-First Century LB $25.90 (978-0-8050-5232-9). This book discusses how entertainers including Robert Redford, Sting, and Chevy Chase and other celebrities such as Al Gore, Ted Turner, and Jerry Greenfield support environmental causes. (Rev: SLJ 1/98) [363.7]

10431 Cherry, Lynne. *How We Know What We Know about Our Changing Climate: Scientists and Kids Explore Global Warming* (4–7). Illus. by Gary Braasch. 2008, Dawn $17.95 (978-1-58469-103-7). Children are called to be "citizen scientists" as they learn about the scientific evidence for global warming and are armed with specific strategies to help turn things around. (Rev: BL 2/15/08; SLJ 6/08) [551.6]

10432 David, Laurie, and Cambria Gordon. *The Down-to-Earth Guide to Global Warming* (4–7). Illus. 2007, Scholastic paper $15.99 (978-0-439-02494-5). The authors balance alarming information on climate change and its impact with practical ways in which readers can reduce their carbon footprint and details of new technologies that may help. (Rev: BL 9/15/07; SLJ 11/07) [363.738]

10433 Dudley, William, ed. *Hurricane Katrina* (6–10). Series: At Issue. 2006, Gale LB $28.70 (978-0-7377-3551-2). An examination of the governmental, social, and natural forces that affected the victims of Hurricane Katrina and the city of New Orleans, this collection of articles will help students to see that there were many differing opinions on what action to take. (Rev: SLJ 9/06)

10434 Fridell, Ron. *Global Warming* (6–12). Illus. 2002, Watts LB $25.00 (978-0-531-11900-6). A detailed look at weather patterns of the past and how they may be used to predict future problems, with discussion of actions we can take to avoid disastrous global warming. (Rev: BL 10/15/02) [363.738]

10435 Gartner, Bob. *Working Together Against the Destruction of the Environment* (7–12). Series: Library of Social Activism. 1995, Rosen LB $16.95 (978-0-8239-1774-7). Describes efforts to protect the environment, such as recycling, emission laws, and sewage dump restrictions, and provides suggestions for how everyone can help. (Rev: BL 4/15/95) [363.7]

10436 Gore, Al, and Jane O'Connor. *An Inconvenient Truth* (6–12). Illus. 2007, Viking $23.00 (978-0-670-06271-3). The adult companion to the award-winning documentary, adapted for middle- and high-schoolers, will alarm readers and compel them to act. (Rev: BL 4/15/07; HB 5–6/07; SLJ 3/07*) [363.73874]

10437 Haddock, Patricia. *Environmental Time Bomb: Our Threatened Planet* (6–12). Series: Issues in Focus. 2000, Enslow LB $26.60 (978-0-7660-1229-5). Up-to-date information is given on current dangers to our environment. (Rev: BL 9/15/00; HBG 3/01; SLJ 12/00) [363.7]

10438 Ingram, W. Scott. *The Chernobyl Nuclear Disaster* (5–8). Series: Environmental Disasters. 2005, Facts on File $35.00 (978-0-8160-5755-9). Ingram assesses the continuing environmental fallout from the 1986 Chernobyl nuclear disaster. (Rev: SLJ 11/05) [333.79]

10439 Johnson, Rebecca L. *Investigating the Ozone Hole* (5–8). 1994, Lerner LB $28.75 (978-0-8225-1574-6). Using interviews, documents, and firsthand research, the author charts the development and possible consequences of an ozone hole above the Antarctic. (Rev: BL 3/1/94) [551.5]

10440 Juettner, Bonnie. *Energy* (5–8). Illus. Series: Our Environment. 2004, Gale LB $26.20 (978-0-7377-1821-8). Answers such questions as "How is energy managed?" and "Are we running out of energy?" in four chapters that feature many illustrations and large type. (Rev: SLJ 4/05) [333.79]

10441 Lishak, Antony. *Global Warming* (4–7). Illus. Series: What's That Got to Do with Me? 2007, Smart Apple Media LB $18.95 (978-1-59920-037-8). People from around the world who have been affected by climate change — and those who fear they may be — are interviewed to demonstrate various aspects of global warming. (Rev: BL 10/15/07; LMC 2/08) [363.738]

10442 Morris, Neil. *Global Warming* (7–12). Series: What If We Do Nothing? 2007, World Almanac LB $30.60 (978-0-8368-7755-7). Morris looks at how we measure climate change, the human and natural causes of these changes, and what we can do to prevent the situation from deteriorating further. (Rev: LMC 11–12/07; SLJ 5/07) [363.738]

10443 Nakaya, Andrea C., ed. *The Environment* (5–9). Series: Introducing Issues with Opposing Viewpoints. 2006, Gale LB $33.70 (978-0-7377-3459-1). This thought-provoking study examines the delicate balance between the preservation of our natural environment and the need for energy to fuel economic growth. (Rev: SLJ 8/06)

10444 Oxlade, Chris. *Global Warming* (5–7). Illus. Series: Our Planet in Peril. 2002, Capstone LB $22.60 (978-0-7368-1361-7). Attractive double-page spreads explore the concern about global warning, its causes, and options for the future. Also use *Nuclear Waste* (2003). (Rev: HBG 3/03; SLJ 4/03) [363.738]

10445 Parker, Janice, ed. *The Disappearing Forests* (5–8). Illus. Series: Understanding Global Issues. 2002, Smart Apple LB $19.95 (978-1-58340-168-2). A great deal of information about forest use, abuse, and conservation is packed into double-

paged spreads with color illustrations. (Rev: BL 10/15/02; HBG 3/03; SLJ 12/02) [634.9]

10446 Parks, Peggy. *Global Warming* (5–8). Illus. Series: Lucent Library of Science and Technology. 2004, Gale LB $29.95 (978-1-59018-319-9). Explores the controversies surrounding the theory of global warming and the potential consequences of the Earth's rising temperature. (Rev: BL 1/05)

10447 Parks, Peggy J. *Ecotourism* (5–8). Series: Our Environment. 2005, Gale LB $26.20 (978-0-7377-3048-7). All about how ecologically sensitive areas can be protected while being explored, with explanations of the advantages and disadvantages of this type of travel. (Rev: SLJ 5/06) [338.4]

10448 Parks, Peggy J. *Global Warming* (5–8). Illus. Series: Our Environment. 2004, Gale LB $26.20 (978-0-7377-1822-5). Answers such questions as "Caused by humans or caused by nature?" and "What can be done?" in four chapters that feature many illustrations and large type. (Rev: SLJ 4/05) [363.738]

10449 Parry, Ann. *Greenpeace* (5–8). Illus. Series: Humanitarian Organizations. 2005, Chelsea House LB $25.00 (978-0-7910-8815-9). Maps, timelines, factboxes, and color photographs add to this account of Greenpeace's history and mission. (Rev: SLJ 12/05)

10450 Peters, Celeste, ed. *The Energy Dilemma* (5–8). Illus. Series: Understanding Global Issues. 2002, Smart Apple LB $19.95 (978-1-58340-169-9). The information about energy sources, use, and conservation packed into these double-paged spreads with color illustrations will spark debate. (Rev: BL 10/15/02) [333.79]

10451 Petrikin, Jonathan S., ed. *Environmental Justice* (8–12). Series: At Issue. 1995, Greenhaven LB $19.95 (978-0-565-10264-7). A collection of essays exploring whether the wealthy and powerful are risking the health and living conditions of others while protecting their own resources. (Rev: BL 3/15/95) [363.7]

10452 Pringle, Laurence. *The Environmental Movement: From Its Roots to the Challenges of a New Century* (5–8). Illus. 2000, HarperCollins $16.95 (978-0-688-15626-8). This is a fine history of environmentalism in America, beginning with the conflicts between Native Americans and early settlers concerning natural resources and ending with current issues. (Rev: BL 4/1/00; HBG 10/00; SLJ 6/00) [363.7]

10453 Pringle, Laurence. *Global Warming: The Threat of Earth's Changing Climate* (4–8). Illus. 2001, North-South $16.95 (978-1-58717-009-6). A straightforward account that covers topics including the causes of global warming, the signs that it is occurring, and possible solutions. (Rev: BL 4/1/01; HBG 10/01; SLJ 6/01) [363.738]

10454 Reilly, Kathleen M. *Planet Earth: 25 Environmental Projects You Can Build Yourself* (4–7). Illus. Series: Projects You Can Build Yourself. 2008, Nomad $21.95 (978-1-934670-05-7); paper $14.95 (978-1-934670-04-0). A worm composting castle and a wind-powered bubble machine are just two of the projects in this book that teaches about the environment and important environmental issues. (Rev: BL 5/1/08) [507.8]

10455 Revkin, Andrew C. *The North Pole Was Here: Puzzles and Perils at the Top of the World* (6–9). 2006, Kingfisher $15.99 (978-0-7534-5993-5). Revkin, an environmental reporter for the *New York Times,* describes his journey to the North Pole with researchers and explores current thinking (in 2006) about the connection between the melting ice cap and global warming. (Rev: BL 5/1/06; SLJ 6/06*) [910]

10456 Robbins, Ocean, and Sol Solomon. *Choices for Our Future* (7–12). 1994, Book Publg. paper $9.95 (978-1-57067-002-2). The founders of Youth for Environmental Sanity believe that young people can convince other young people to adopt more ecologically responsible lifestyles. This book explains how we can all help. (Rev: BL 3/15/95) [363.7]

10457 Ryan, Bernard. *Protecting the Environment* (7–12). Series: Community Service for Teens. 1998, Ferguson LB $19.95 (978-0-89434-228-8). After a general introduction on volunteerism, the author describes how teens can become involved in existing conservation projects and begin their own. (Rev: BL 9/15/98; SLJ 2/99; VOYA 8/99) [363.7]

10458 Shaw, Jane. *Global Warming* (7–12). Illus. Series: Critical Thinking About Environmental Issues. 2002, Gale $33.70 (978-0-7377-1270-4). Readers will find a variety of opinions about the causes and severity of global warming. (Rev: BL 12/15/02) [363.738]

10459 Sheehan, Sean. *Greenpeace* (5–8). Series: World Watch. 2004, Raintree LB $18.99 (978-0-7398-6612-2). A thorough review of the sometimes controversial conservationist organization since its founding in 1970, with some graphic photographs. (Rev: BL 4/1/04; SLJ 3/04) [333.7]

10460 Solway, Andrew. *Biofuels* (5–8). Illus. Series: Energy for the Future and Global Warming. 2007, Gareth Stevens LB $26.60 (978-0-8368-8398-5); paper $9.95 (978-0-8368-8407-4). A brief introduction to the use of alternatives to fossil fuels — ethanol, biogas, and so forth — with an explanation of how these could benefit the environment. (Rev: BL 10/15/07) [662]

10461 Spilsbury, Louise, and Richard Spilsbury. *Water* (5–8). Series: Planet Under Pressure. 2006, Heinemann LB $31.43 (978-1-4034-8214-3). Discusses the demand for water, its sources, and what's being done to conserve it. (Rev: SLJ 3/07)

10462 Stefoff, Rebecca. *The American Environmental Movement* (7–10). 1995, Facts on File $25.00 (978-0-8160-3046-0). A study of efforts to preserve the environment from the 15th century to the present, with discussion of prominent figures and events in the movement. (Rev: BL 9/1/95; SLJ 9/95) [363.7]

10463 Suzuki, David, and Kathy Vanderlinden. *Eco-Fun* (5–8). Illus. 2001, Douglas & McIntyre paper $10.95 (978-1-55054-823-5). The activities in this collection reinforce some basic scientific concepts about air, water, earth, and fire, and encourage young readers to think about environmental issues and avoid pollution. (Rev: BL 6/1–15/01; SLJ 8/01) [577]

10464 Tanaka, Shelley. *Climate Change* (7–10). Series: Groundwood Guide. 2006, Groundwood $15.95 (978-0-88899-783-8). An introduction to the topic for the middle grades that presents possible solutions to the growing problem. (Rev: BL 12/1/06; SLJ 12/06) [363.738]

10465 Taudte, Jeca. *MySpace/OurPlanet: Change Is Possible* (8–11). Illus. 2008, HarperTeen paper $12.99 (978-0-06-156204-4). Chapters such as "Your Home, Your Planet" and "Your Free Time" are full of facts and advice on saving the environment, including many postings contributed by members of the OurPlanet online community. (Rev: BL 8/08; SLJ 8/08) [363.73874]

10466 VanCleave, Janice. *Janice VanCleave's Ecology for Every Kid* (4–7). Illus. 1996, Wiley paper $12.95 (978-0-471-10086-7). Clear instructions and many diagrams introduce a series of experiments that highlight environmental issues. (Rev: BL 3/1/96; SLJ 4/96) [574.5]

10467 Whitman, Sylvia. *This Land Is Your Land: The American Conservation Movement* (5–7). Illus. 1994, Lerner LB $30.35 (978-0-8225-1729-0). A history of the conservation movement from its beginnings in 1870 when there were efforts to save Yellowstone and ending with today's major problems such as oil spills and trash disposal. (Rev: BL 12/15/94; HB 3–4/94; SLJ 12/94) [363.7]

10468 Woods, Michael, and Mary B. Woods. *Environmental Disasters* (4–7). Illus. Series: Disasters Up Close. 2008, Lerner LB $27.93 (978-0-8225-6774-5). Love Canal, Bhopal, the *Exxon Valdez* — these are only three of the disasters covered in this well-illustrated account of disasters that could have been avoided. (Rev: BL 2/15/08; SLJ 8/08) [363.7]

10469 Woodward, John, and Eiki Eiki., eds. *Conserving the Environment* (7–12). Series: Current Controversies. 2006, Gale LB $34.95 (978-0-7377-2476-9); paper $23.70 (978-0-7377-2477-6). Including a review of relevant acts and discussion of various environmentally friendly options (renewable energy, organic farming, fuel-efficient vehicles), this volume explores the seriousness of the problem and what should be done at this point in time. (Rev: SLJ 2/07)

Pollution

10470 Bang, Molly. *Nobody Particular: One Woman's Fight to Save the Bays* (6–12). Illus. 2001, Holt $18.00 (978-0-8050-5396-8). Teens will connect to this appealingly presented account about Diane Wilson, who became an environmental activist working to restore the ecology of the bays around her Texas home. (Rev: BCCB 2/01; BL 2/1/01; HB 1–2/01; HBG 10/01; SLJ 1/01; VOYA 4/02) [363.738]

10471 Brown, Paul. *Global Pollution* (5–8). Illus. Series: Face the Facts. 2003, Raintree LB $28.56 (978-0-7398-6433-3). The effects of pollution on the environment are described in understandable terms, and practical responses from young people are suggested. (Rev: BL 11/15/03; HBG 10/03; SLJ 9/03) [303.73]

10472 Chapman, Matthew, and Rob Bowden. *Air Pollution* (5–8). Series: 21st Century Debates. 2002, Raintree LB $19.99 (978-0-7398-4874-6). The causes of air pollution, the present situation, and possible future solutions are presented in this well-illustrated book that presents various points of view and offers topics for debate. (Rev: BL 6/1–15/02; SLJ 4/06) [363.73]

10473 Collinson, Alan. *Pollution* (5–8). Series: Repairing the Damage. 1992, Macmillan LB $21.00 (978-0-02-722995-0). A historical overview of nuclear waste, river pollution, overpopulation, and other aspects of pollution. (Rev: BL 9/15/92) [363.73]

10474 Gifford, Clive. *Pollution* (4–7). Illus. Series: Planet Under Pressure. 2006, Heinemann LB $31.43 (978-1-4034-7742-2). An overview of the various types of pollution, their sources and impact, and possible future remedies. (Rev: SLJ 6/06)

10475 Hayley, James, ed. *Pollution* (8–12). Series: Current Controversies. 2002, Gale LB $36.20 (978-0-7377-1188-2). This book features in-depth essays by individuals — environmentalists, politicians, EPA representatives, and others — who present opposing views on the problem of pollution. (Rev: BL 12/15/02; SLJ 4/06) [363.73]

10476 Hoff, Mary, and Mary M. Rodgers. *Our Endangered Planet: Groundwater* (4–7). Illus. Series: Our Endangered Planet. 1991, Lerner LB $22.60 (978-0-8225-2500-4). A discussion of the supply, access, uses, and pollution of groundwater around the world. (Rev: BL 6/15/91; SLJ 5/91) [333.91]

10477 Leacock, Elspeth. *The Exxon Valdez Oil Spill* (5–8). Series: Environmental Disasters. 2005, Facts

on File $35.00 (978-0-8160-5754-2). A look at the environmental impact of the 1989 *Exxon Valdez* oil spill in Alaska's Prince William Sound. (Rev: SLJ 11/05) [363.7]

10478 Miller, Christina G., and Louise A. Berry. *Acid Rain: A Sourcebook for Young People* (6–8). Illus. 1986, Messner LB $12.95 (978-0-671-60177-5). An account that describes the origins of acid rain, its effects, and what can be done about it. (Rev: BL 2/15/87; SLJ 1/87) [363.7]

10479 Reed, Jennifer Bond. *Love Canal* (6–12). Series: Great Disasters: Reforms and Ramifications. 2002, Chelsea LB $30.00 (978-0-7910-6742-0). The story of the town that had to be evacuated in the 1970s when hazardous wastes leaked from a disposal site. (Rev: HBG 3/03; SLJ 12/02) [363.738]

10480 Riddle, John. *Bhopal* (6–10). Series: Great Disasters: Reforms and Ramifications. 2002, Chelsea LB $30.00 (978-0-7910-6741-3). The story of the leak of pesticide gas from a Union Carbide plant that killed more than 3,000 people in India in 1984. (Rev: HBG 3/03; SLJ 12/02; VOYA 12/02) [363.17]

10481 Roleff, Tamara L., ed. *Pollution: Disputed Land* (8–12). Series: Opposing Viewpoints. 1999, Greenhaven paper $21.20 (978-0-7377-0134-0). Some of the questions explored in this anthology of articles include Is pollution a serious problem? Do chemical pollutants present a health risk? and Is recycling an effective response? (Rev: BL 11/15/99) [363.73]

Recycling

10482 Dorion, Christiane. *Earth's Garbage Crisis* (7–12). Series: What If We Do Nothing? 2007, World Almanac LB $30.60 (978-0-8368-7753-3). Dorion discusses how and why we create so much garbage and the measures we need to take before this problem swamps us. (Rev: LMC 11–12/07; SLJ 5/07) [363.728]

10483 Hall, Eleanor J. *Recycling* (5–8). Illus. Series: Our Environment. 2004, Gale LB $26.20 (978-0-7377-1517-0). Answers such questions as "What is recycling?" and "What does the future hold?" in four chapters that feature many illustrations and large type. (Rev: SLJ 4/05) [363.72]

Population Issues

General and Miscellaneous

10484 Atkin, S. Beth. *Gunstories: Life-Changing Experiences with Guns* (7–10). Illus. 2006, Harper-Collins LB $17.89 (978-0-06-052660-3). In first-person accounts, teenagers write about their very varied experiences with guns. (Rev: BL 1/1–15/06; SLJ 1/06) [363.33]

10485 Bowden, Rob. *An Overcrowded World?* (5–8). Series: 21st Century Debates. 2002, Raintree LB $27.12 (978-0-7398-4872-2). Using a well-organized text, plus sidebars for additional facts and statements of opinion, this colorfully illustrated volume explores the current problems of overpopulation and the dire strain it causes on the earth's supplies. (Rev: BL 6/1–15/02) [304.6]

10486 Cox, Vic. *Guns, Violence, and Teens* (7–12). Illus. Series: Issues in Focus. 1997, Enslow LB $20.95 (978-0-89490-721-0). Topics covered in this book include the evolution of gun use in America, gun control, teenage violence, and the impact that guns have on teenagers. (Rev: BL 10/15/97; SLJ 1/98; VOYA 2/98) [363.4]

10487 Grapes, Bryan J., ed. *School Violence* (6–12). Series: Contemporary Issues Companion. 2000, Greenhaven LB $21.20 (978-0-7377-0331-3); paper $32.45 (978-0-7377-0332-0). Personal stories add to the urgency of the thought-provoking solutions suggested for school violence. (Rev: BL 10/15/00; SLJ 9/00) [371.7]

10488 Grapes, Bryan J., ed. *Violent Children* (8–12). Series: At Issue. 1999, Greenhaven LB $26.20 (978-0-7377-0159-3); paper $17.45 (978-0-7377-0158-6). In a series of articles that express many viewpoints, the problem of violent children at home and school is explored. (Rev: BL 11/15/99) [363.4]

10489 Hohm, Charles F., ed. *Population* (6–12). Series: Opposing Viewpoints. 2000, Greenhaven LB $32.45 (978-0-7377-0292-7); paper $21.20 (978-0-7377-0291-0). A collection of essays that explore problems with world population, its growth, and its possible control. (Rev: BL 9/15/00) [306]

10490 Mason, Paul. *Population* (4–7). Series: Planet Under Pressure. 2006, Heinemann LB $31.43 (978-1-4034-7741-5). The problems created by overpopulation are the focus of this book that also explores the underlying reasons and possible solutions. (Rev: SLJ 6/06)

10491 Proulx, Brenda, ed. *The Courage to Change: A Teen Survival Guide* (7–12). Illus. 2002, Second Story paper $16.95 (978-1-896764-41-2). A thought-provoking compilation of personal stories, poems, and photographs created by teens who participate in Canada's L.O.V.E. (Leave Out ViolencE) program. (Rev: BL 9/1/02; SLJ 7/02; VOYA 8/02) [364.4]

10492 Reef, Catherine. *Alone in the World: Orphans and Orphanages in America* (8–11). Illus. 2005, Clarion $18.00 (978-0-618-35670-6). A history of orphanages in America from the early years of the 18th century through their decline in the early 1900s. (Rev: BL 4/1/05; SLJ 6/05; VOYA 10/05) [362.73]

10493 Roberts, Anita. *Safe Teen: Powerful Alternatives to Violence* (7–12). 2001, Polestar paper $15.95 (978-1-896095-99-8). The author offers practical advice for teens looking for peaceful ways to solve potentially dangerous problems. (Rev: BL 12/15/01; SLJ 4/02; VOYA 2/02) [155.5]

10494 Warner, Rachel. *Refugees* (6–10). Illus. Series: Global Issues. 1996, Raintree LB $19.98 (978-0-8172-4547-4). After a brief history of the refugee problem, current case studies are used to explore this issue and how it is being confronted in today's world. (Rev: BL 3/15/97) [362.87]

10495 Winckler, Suzanne, and Mary M. Rodgers. *Our Endangered Planet: Population Growth* (4–7). Illus. Series: Our Endangered Planet. 1991, Lerner LB $27.15 (978-0-8225-2502-8). A discussion of the effects that rapid population growth has had on the environment. (Rev: BL 6/15/91; SLJ 5/91) [304.6]

Aging and Death

10496 Cozic, Charles P., ed. *An Aging Population* (8–12). Series: Opposing Viewpoints. 1996, Greenhaven LB $26.20 (978-1-56510-395-5). A collection of documents expressing various points of view on how the aged will affect America in the future, their entitlement programs, quality of life, health care, and society's acceptance of the elderly. (Rev: BL 7/96; SLJ 8/96; VOYA 10/96) [305.26]

10497 Gignoux, Jane Hughes. *Some Folk Say: Stories of Life, Death, and Beyond* (6–12). Illus. 1998, Foulketale $29.95 (978-0-9667168-0-1). A collection of 38 literary selections on various aspects of death and how people adjust to it, taken from world folklore and such writers as Shakespeare and Walt Whitman. (Rev: BL 2/15/99) [398.27]

Crime, Gangs, and Prisons

10498 Aaseng, Nathan. *Treacherous Traitors* (5–9). Series: Profiles. 1997, Oliver LB $19.95 (978-1-881508-38-0). This book profiles 12 Americans who were tried for treason, including Benedict Arnold, John Brown, Alger Hiss, Julius and Ethel Rosenberg, and Aldrich Ames. (Rev: SLJ 2/98) [355.3]

10499 Allman, Toney. *The Medical Examiner* (7–10). Illus. Series: Crime Scene Investigations. 2006, Gale LB $31.20 (978-1-59018-912-2). A look at the responsibilities, tools, methods, and training of a medical examiner. (Rev: SLJ 9/06)

10500 Barbour, Scott, ed. *Gangs* (8–12). Illus. Series: Introducing Issues with Opposing Viewpoints. 2005, Gale LB $33.70 (978-0-7377-3221-4). Diverse opinions are presented on topics including the reasons why young people join gangs and measures that can be taken to reduce the violence. (Rev: SLJ 1/06) [364.1]

10501 Bayer, Linda. *Drugs, Crime, and Criminal Justice* (7–10). Series: Crime, Justice, and Punishment. 2001, Chelsea LB $30.00 (978-0-7910-4262-5). This book, written by an analyst from the Office of National Drug Control Policy, looks at the relationship between drugs and crime and its impact on our judicial system. (Rev: BL 9/15/01; HBG 3/02) [364]

10502 Bender, David L. *Guns and Violence* (8–12). Series: Current Controversies. 1999, Greenhaven paper $21.20 (978-0-7377-0064-0). The pros and cons of gun control and measures to curb violence are among the topics discussed. [363.3]

10503 Beres, D. B. *Dusted and Busted! The Science of Fingerprinting* (4–8). Illus. Series: 24/7: Science Behind the Scenes: Forensic Files. 2007, Watts LB $25.00 (978-0-531-11822-1); paper $7.95 (978-0-531-15457-1). Introduces the scientific process of fingerprinting through easy-to-read text, illustrations, and real-life examples. (Rev: SLJ 7/07) [363.2]

10504 Black, Andy. *Organized Crime* (7–12). Series: Crime and Detection. 2003, Mason Crest LB $22.95 (978-1-59084-367-3). Organized crime in the United States and other countries including Russia and Britain is the main focus of this well-illustrated, large-format volume that will appeal to reluctant readers. Also use *Cyber Crime* and *Major Unsolved Crimes* (2003). (Rev: SLJ 10/03) [364.1]

10505 Blackwood, Gary L. *Gangsters* (4–7). Series: Bad Guys. 2001, Benchmark LB $28.50 (978-0-7614-1016-4). Al Capone is just one of the evildoers profiled in this volume that gives historical context for each "bad guy." Also use *Outlaws* and *Highwaymen* (both 2001). (Rev: HBG 3/02; SLJ 1/02) [364.106]

10506 Bosch, Carl. *Schools Under Siege: Guns, Gangs, and Hidden Dangers* (7–12). Illus. Series: Issues in Focus. 1997, Enslow LB $20.95 (978-0-89490-908-5). This work surveys teenage crime, its history and causes, the juvenile justice system, pertinent Supreme Court decisions, and types of school violence. (Rev: BL 8/97; SLJ 9/97) [363.1]

10507 Brownlie, Alison. *Crime and Punishment: Changing Attitudes, 1900–2000* (6–9). Illus. Series: Twentieth Century Issues. 1999, Raintree LB $28.54 (978-0-8172-5573-2). A compact, well-illustrated book that explores the concepts of crime and punishment with emphasis on today's organized crime and its international connections. (Rev: BL 3/15/00; HBG 9/00) [364]

10508 Butterfield, Moira. *Pirates and Smugglers* (5–7). Series: Kingfisher Knowledge. 2005, Kingfisher paper $12.95 (978-0-7534-5864-8). A broad historical survey of outlaws on the high seas, from early smugglers to today's dealers in drugs and exotic animals. (Rev: SLJ 12/05)

10509 Campbell, Andrea. *Forensic Science: Evidence, Clues, and Investigation* (6–12). Illus. Series: Crime, Justice, and Punishment. 2000, Chelsea House $30.00 (978-0-7910-4950-1). An overview of forensic crime investigation with reference to famous cases including the Boston Strangler and Tylenol tampering. (Rev: SLJ 12/99; VOYA 4/00) [363.25]

10510 Coleman, Janet Wyman. *Secrets, Lies, Gizmos, and Spies: A History of Spies and Espionage* (6–9). Illus. 2006, Abrams $24.95 (978-0-8109-5756-5). Readers learn all about the secrets of espionage, its history, famous spies and agencies, missions, and the weapons, tools, and gadgets used. (Rev: BL 10/1/06; LMC 2/07; SLJ 2/07) [327.12009]

10511 Coppin, Cheryl Branch. *Everything You Need to Know About Healing from Rape Trauma* (7–12). Series: Need to Know Library. 2000, Rosen $27.95 (978-0-8239-3122-4). Emphasizing that rape is about power not sex and that the victim is blameless, the author looks in particular at prevention and recovery. (Rev: SLJ 9/00) [362.883]

10512 Cothran, Helen, ed. *Sexual Violence* (8–12). Series: Opposing Viewpoints. 2003, Gale LB $36.20 (978-0-7377-1240-7). Twenty-five essays explore the reasons why people abuse others, the impact on the victims, the different forms of violence, and differing opinions on the extent of this phenomenon. (Rev: BL 6/1–15/03) [364.15]

10513 Dahl, Michael. *Computer Evidence* (4–8). Illus. Series: Forensic Crime Solvers. 2004, Capstone LB $23.93 (978-0-7368-2698-3). After a story that draws the readers in, Dahl looks at the use of computer evidence in tracking down and convicting criminals. Also use *Poison Evidence* (2004). (Rev: BL 5/1/04)

10514 Day, Nancy. *Violence in Schools: Learning in Fear* (7–12). Illus. Series: Issues in Focus. 1996, Enslow LB $20.95 (978-0-89490-734-0). Such forms of violence in schools as guns, sexual harassment, gay bashing, and gang fighting are discussed with material on their causes, effects, and the recent formation of student advocacy groups. (Rev: BL 6/1–15/96; SLJ 7/96) [371.5]

10515 De Angelis, Gina. *White-Collar Crime* (6–9). Illus. Series: Crime, Justice, and Punishment. 1999, Chelsea $30.00 (978-0-7910-4279-3). Such crimes as frauds, hoaxes, and computer hacking are described in this volume that shows that betraying the public trust is as much a crime as murder. (Rev: BL 12/15/99; HBG 4/00) [364.16]

10516 De Hahn, Tracee. *Crimes Against Children: Child Abuse and Neglect* (7–12). Series: Crime, Justice, and Punishment. 1999, Chelsea LB $30.00 (978-0-7910-4253-3). Laws concerning child abuse, the definition of child abuse, and protecting children against abuse are some of the topics covered in this volume. (Rev: HBG 4/00; SLJ 3/00) [362.76]

10517 Denega, Danielle. *Have You Seen This Face? The Work of Forensic Artists* (4–8). Illus. Series: 24/7: Science Behind the Scenes: Forensic Files. 2007, Watts LB $25.00 (978-0-531-11823-8); paper $7.95 (978-0-531-15458-8). Introduces the work of forensic artists through easy-to-read text, illustrations, and real-life examples. (Rev: SLJ 7/07) [363.2]

10518 Dudley, William, and Louise I. Gerdes, eds. *Gangs* (8–12). Series: Opposing Viewpoints. 2005, Gale LB $36.20 (978-0-7377-2234-5); paper $24.95 (978-0-7377-2235-2). A look at the causes of gang behavior and what can be done to combat the alarming increase in violence. (Rev: SLJ 8/05) [364.1]

10519 Egendorf, Laura K., ed. *Gangs* (6–12). Illus. Series: Opposing Viewpoints. 2000, Greenhaven LB $32.45 (978-0-7377-0510-2); paper $21.20 (978-0-7377-0509-6). Diverse viewpoints are offered on wide-ranging topics including gang behavior, racist tendencies, girl gangs, and the various laws and efforts to quell gang activities. (Rev: BL 3/1/01; SLJ 4/01) [364.1]

10520 Espejo, Roman, ed. *America's Prisons* (6–12). Series: Opposing Viewpoints. 2001, Gale paper $21.20 (978-0-7377-0787-8). Balanced essays examine the effectiveness of prisons and the treatment of prison inmates. (Rev: BL 4/1/02) [365]

10521 Farman, John. *The Short and Bloody History of Spies* (5–8). Illus. 2002, Lerner LB $19.93 (978-0-8225-0845-8); paper $5.95 (978-0-8225-0846-5). A witty and fascinating account of the intriguing lives of spies, with descriptions of spying techniques and gadgets. (Rev: BL 1/1–15/03; HBG 3/03) [327.12]

10522 Fodor, Margie Druss. *Megan's Law: Protection or Privacy?* (6–8). Illus. Series: Issues in Focus. 2001, Enslow LB $26.60 (978-0-7660-1586-9). A look at both sides of the difficult question of children's safety versus privacy for convicted sex offenders who have served their time. (Rev: BL 1/1–15/02; HBG 10/02; SLJ 3/02) [362.7]

10523 Fridell, Ron. *Forensic Science* (4–7). Series: Cool Science. 2006, Lerner LB $25.25 (978-0-8225-5935-1). The history of forensic science from 1910 to today is accompanied by information on the professionals involved (medical examiners, forensic entomologists) and the equipment used; effective photographs add to the appeal. (Rev: SLJ 4/07) [363.25]

10524 Fridell, Ron. *Spying: The Modern World of Espionage* (7–12). Illus. 2002, Millbrook LB $24.90 (978-0-7613-1662-6). What spies do, the technology they use, and the politics of espionage are all

covered in this concise volume. (Rev: BL 5/1/02; HBG 10/02; SLJ 4/02; VOYA 12/02) [327.1]

10525 Friedlander, Mark P., Jr., and Terry M. Phillips. *When Objects Talk: Solving a Crime with Science* (5–8). Illus. Series: Discovery! 2001, Lerner LB $27.93 (978-0-8225-0649-2). A fictional mystery serves to introduce criminal investigation techniques such as fingerprints and DNA. (Rev: HBG 3/02; SLJ 2/02; VOYA 2/02) [363.25]

10526 Gaines, Ann. *Prisons* (8–12). Series: Crime, Justice, and Punishment. 1998, Chelsea LB $30.00 (978-0-7910-4315-8). A thought-provoking look inside America's prisons, with background material on the history and philosophy of incarceration and an examination of issues in penology. (Rev: VOYA 4/99) [365]

10527 Gardner, Robert. *Crime Lab 101: Experimenting with Crime Detection* (6–9). 1992, Walker LB $14.85 (978-0-8027-8159-8). Details how law enforcement agencies use science and technology to solve crimes, with 25 crime lab activities and eight exercises. (Rev: BL 8/92; SLJ 10/92) [363.2]

10528 Gifford, Clive. *Spies* (5–9). Illus. Series: Kingfisher Knowledge. 2004, Kingfisher LB $11.95 (978-0-7534-5777-1). Stories of notable espionage achievements are included along with brisk facts, plenty of high-interest illustrations, a history of spying, and discussion of the future of this field. (Rev: BL 9/1/04; SLJ 5/05)

10529 Goldentyer, Debra. *Street Violence* (4–8). Series: Preteen Pressures. 1998, Raintree LB $25.69 (978-0-8172-5028-7). This book discusses types of street violence and how young people can protect themselves, as well as gang issues and alternatives to participation. (Rev: BL 5/15/98; HBG 10/98; SLJ 6/98) [364]

10530 Goodnough, David. *Stalking: A Hot Issue* (7–10). Series: Hot Issues. 2000, Enslow LB $27.93 (978-0-7660-1364-3). The motivations of stalkers, their strategies, how to deal with stalkers, and the legal actions that can be taken are all examined in this slim volume. (Rev: HBG 3/01; SLJ 12/00) [364.15]

10531 Graham, Ian. *Crime-Fighting* (5–8). Illus. Series: Science Spotlight. 1995, Raintree LB $24.26 (978-0-8114-3840-7). A discussion of scientific methods used in analyzing evidence at crime scenes, such as DNA testing. (Rev: SLJ 7/95) [364]

10532 Graham, Ian. *Fakes and Forgeries* (5–8). Illus. Series: Science Spotlight. 1995, Raintree LB $24.26 (978-0-8114-3843-8). Examines famous scandals in history involving such fakes as the Loch Ness monster, counterfeit money, and the forged Hitler diaries. (Rev: SLJ 7/95) [364]

10533 Grapes, Bryan J., ed. *Prisons* (8–12). Series: Current Controversies. 2000, Greenhaven LB $32.45 (978-0-7377-0147-0); paper $21.20 (978-0-7377-0146-3). This collection of sources explores facets of the penal system with material on the effectiveness of incarceration, the treatment of prisoners, privatization questions, and inmate labor. (Rev: BL 3/1/00) [365]

10534 Greenberg, Keith E. *Out of the Gang* (5–8). Illus. 1992, Lerner LB $19.93 (978-0-8225-2553-0). A realistic portrait of gang life, revealed by a man who escaped it and a boy who managed to stay out of it. (Rev: BCCB 6/92; BL 6/15/92; SLJ 9/92) [364.1]

10535 Guernsey, JoAnn B. *Youth Violence: An American Epidemic?* (7–10). Series: Frontline. 1996, Lerner LB $19.95 (978-0-8225-2627-8). Chapters in this book include discussions on violence at home and school, gangs and gang violence, and the influence of such factors as guns, drugs, alcohol, poverty, race, and discrimination. (Rev: SLJ 1/97; VOYA 2/97) [364.3]

10536 Hanrahan, Clare, ed. *America's Prisons* (7–12). Series: Opposing Viewpoints. 2006, Gale LB $34.95 (978-0-7377-3344-0); paper $23.70 (978-0-7377-3345-7). This thought-provoking title tackles the thorny issues surrounding America's penal system through a selection of pro and con essays. (Rev: SLJ 9/06)

10537 Harris, Elizabeth Snoke. *Crime Scene Science Fair Projects* (6–10). Illus. 2007, Sterling LB $19.95 (978-1-57990-765-5). After an introduction to forensic science and its application, Harris provides projects that teach about fingerprints, lie detection, and so forth. (Rev: SLJ 2/07)

10538 Hjelmeland, Andy. *Prisons: Inside the Big House* (4–8). Illus. Series: Pro/Con Issues. 1996, Lerner LB $30.35 (978-0-8225-2607-0). Opposing viewpoints are presented on the purposes of prisons, prison conditions, and alternate forms of rehabilitation. (Rev: BL 8/96; SLJ 9/96) [365]

10539 Innes, Brian. *Fingerprints and Impressions* (7–12). Illus. Series: Forensic Evidence. 2007, Sharpe Focus $39.95 (978-0-7656-8114-0). Readers learn about DNA fingerprinting and will gain an understanding of the work of forensic scientists. (Rev: LMC 2/08; SLJ 1/08)

10540 Innes, Brian. *Forensic Science* (8–12). 2003, Mason Crest LB $22.95 (978-1-59084-373-4). A well-illustrated exploration of historic and international crime investigations, with a look at evolving techniques and the importance of evidence in court cases. (Rev: SLJ 6/03) [363.25]

10541 Jackson, Donna M. *The Bone Detectives: How Forensic Anthropologists Solve Crimes and Uncover Mysteries of the Dead* (5–9). 1996, Little, Brown $17.95 (978-0-316-82935-9). A look at the

role of forensic anthropologists in solving crimes including murder. (Rev: BCCB 4/96; BL 4/1/96; HB 5–6/96; SLJ 5/96*; VOYA 8/96) [363.2]

10542 Johnson, Julie. *Why Do People Join Gangs?* (5–8). Series: Exploring Tough Issues. 2001, Raintree LB $25.69 (978-0-7398-3236-3). Johnson looks at gangs — who joins them and why, and how to get out of one — in the United States and abroad, and includes a chapter on dealing with bullies. Also use *Why Do People Fight Wars?* and *Why Are People Prejudiced?* (both 2002). (Rev: SLJ 11/01) [364.1]

10543 Johnson, Toni E. *Handcuff Blues: Helping Teens Stay Out of Trouble with the Law* (6–9). Illus. 1999, Goofy Foot paper $10.95 (978-1-885535-43-6). Twelve case histories about teens in trouble for drunk driving, vandalism, shoplifting, and drive-by shootings are given with background information, details of the crime, and finally the legal action taken and the outcome. (Rev: SLJ 8/99; VOYA 12/99) [364.3]

10544 Joyce, Jaime. *Bullet Proof! The Evidence That Guns Leave Behind* (5–10). Series: 24/7: Science Behind the Scenes. 2007, Watts LB $25.00 (978-0-531-11820-7); paper $7.95 (978-0-531-15455-7). Joyce uses three real cases to illustrate how ballistics experts can help to solve crimes; reluctant readers will enjoy this. (Rev: SLJ 8/07) [363.25]

10545 Kerrigan, Michael. *The History of Punishment* (7–12). Series: Crime and Detection. 2003, Mason Crest LB $22.95 (978-1-59084-386-4). A detailed and interesting overview of the kinds of punishments that have been imposed over the centuries on those who fail to adhere to a wide variety of laws and codes of conduct. (Rev: SLJ 12/03) [364.6]

10546 Klee, Sheila. *Working Together Against School Violence* (6–10). Series: Library of Political Assassinations. 1996, Rosen LB $16.95 (978-0-8239-2262-8). This guide introduces the increase in school violence and its causes in the context of violence in society, and shows students what they can do to reduce it in their schools. (Rev: SLJ 2/97) [371.5]

10547 Lewis, Brenda Ralph. *Hostage Rescue with the FBI* (6–10). Illus. Series: Rescue and Prevention: Defending Our Nation. 2003, Mason Crest LB $22.95 (978-1-59084-403-8). Famous hostage situations such as the *Achille Lauro* incident are mentioned in this well-illustrated survey of the process of rescuing hostages, negotiating with their takers, and the use of snipers. Also use *Police Crime Prevention* (2003). (Rev: SLJ 7/03) [364.15]

10548 Lock, Joan. *Famous Prisons* (7–12). Series: Crime and Detection. 2003, Mason Crest LB $22.95 (978-1-59084-380-2). Alcatraz, Sing Sing, San Quentin, and Dartmoor are among the prisons described, with historical and anecdotal information and accounts of famous inmates. (Rev: HBG 4/04; SLJ 12/03) [365]

10549 Margolis, Jeffrey A. *Teen Crime Wave: A Growing Problem* (7–12). Illus. Series: Issues in Focus. 1997, Enslow LB $26.60 (978-0-89490-910-8). The teenage crime phenomenon is examined, with material on frequency, causes, the juvenile justice system, Supreme Court decisions, and historical background. (Rev: BL 8/97; SLJ 9/97) [364.36]

10550 Marzilli, Alan. *Famous Crimes of the 20th Century* (8–12). Series: Crime, Justice, and Punishment. 2002, Chelsea LB $30.00 (978-0-7910-6788-8). The author looks at six well-known events — including the assassination of Martin Luther King Jr., the Watergate burglary, and the O. J. Simpson trial — and discusses the social importance of each. (Rev: SLJ 2/03)

10551 Nakaya, Andrea C., ed. *Juvenile Crime* (8–12). Series: Opposing Viewpoints. 2005, Gale LB $36.20 (978-0-7377-2945-0); paper $24.95 (978-0-7377-2946-7). A collection of diverse opinions on the causes of juvenile crime and on ways to prevent it, to punish or treat offenders, and to improve the juvenile justice system. (Rev: SLJ 1/06) [364.9]

10552 Newton, David E. *Teen Violence: Out of Control* (7–10). Illus. Series: Issues in Focus. 1995, Enslow LB $20.95 (978-0-89490-506-3). A well-researched account that covers all types of teen violence, the nature-nurture controversy, ways of preventing teen violence, and types of punishment currently being used. (Rev: BL 3/1/96; SLJ 6/96; VOYA 2/96) [364.3]

10553 Oliver, Marilyn Tower. *Gangs: Trouble in the Streets* (5–8). 1995, Enslow LB $20.95 (978-0-89490-492-9). Discusses the roots of gangs in the 19th century, aspects of modern gang life, and how members manage to quit gangs. (Rev: BL 8/95) [364.1]

10554 Oliver, Marilyn Tower. *Prisons: Today's Debate* (7–12). Series: Issues in Focus. 1997, Enslow LB $20.95 (978-0-89490-906-1). The debate concerning the effectiveness of America's prisons and their purposes is presented clearly, with all sides represented fairly. (Rev: BL 11/15/97; SLJ 12/97) [365]

10555 Orr, Tamra. *Violence in Our Schools: Halls of Hope, Halls of Fear* (6–12). 2003, Watts LB $30.50 (978-0-531-12268-6). Strategies for avoiding and defusing violence before it erupts are a focus of this volume that traces violent incidents back to the 1920s and looks at topics including bullying, gun control, homeschooling, and current school efforts in these areas. (Rev: BL 1/1–15/04; SLJ 12/03; VOYA 2/04) [371.7]

10556 Owen, David. *Police Lab: How Forensic Science Tracks Down and Convicts Criminals* (6–12).

Illus. 2002, Firefly $19.95 (978-1-55297-620-3); paper $9.95 (978-1-55297-619-7). The nitty-gritty of forensic science is covered here, with information about the investigations of some well-known crimes and criminals and attention-grabbing photographs, some of them grisly. (Rev: BL 12/15/02; HBG 3/03; SLJ 5/03) [363.25]

10557 Owens, Lois Smith, and Vivian Verdell Gordon. *Think About Prisons and the Criminal Justice System* (6–10). Series: Think. 1991, Walker LB $15.85 (978-0-8027-8121-5); paper $9.95 (978-0-8027-7370-8). Basic information on incarceration, crime and its consequences, the criminal justice system, and the basis for laws. (Rev: BL 6/1/92; SLJ 2/92) [364.973]

10558 Platt, Richard. *Forensics* (5–10). Illus. Series: Kingfisher Knowledge. 2005, Kingfisher paper $12.95 (978-0-7534-5862-4). This introduction to the use of the forensic sciences in crime investigation is presented in short blocks of text that will make it appealing to reluctant readers. (Rev: SLJ 11/05) [363.2]

10559 Powell, Phelan. *Major Unsolved Crimes* (6–9). Illus. Series: Crime, Justice, and Punishment. 1999, Chelsea $30.00 (978-0-7910-4277-9). Such crimes as the riddle of Jack the Ripper, the Zodiac killer, the Tylenol murders, and the Kennedy assassination are discussed in this fascinating volume. (Rev: BL 12/15/99; HBG 4/00) [364.15]

10560 Prokos, Anna. *Guilty by a Hair! Real-Life DNA Matches!* (4–8). Illus. Series: 24/7: Science Behind the Scenes: Forensic Files. 2007, Watts LB $25.00 (978-0-531-11821-4); paper $7.95 (978-0-531-18733-3). In clear, engaging prose with illustrations and real-life examples, this volume discusses the science behind DNA analysis used in crime investigations. (Rev: SLJ 7/07) [363.2]

10561 Prokos, Anna. *Killer Wallpaper: True Cases of Deadly Poisonings* (5–10). Series: 24/7: Science Behind the Scenes. 2007, Watts LB $25.00 (978-0-531-12061-3); paper $7.95 (978-0-531-15459-5). Prokos uses three real cases to illustrate the work of forensic toxicologists; reluctant readers will enjoy this. (Rev: SLJ 8/07) [363.2]

10562 Rabiger, Joanna. *Daily Prison Life* (7–12). Series: Crime and Detection. 2003, Mason Crest LB $22.90 (978-1-59084-384-0). Readers learn about the daily routine for prisoners in jails across America. (Rev: SLJ 12/03) [365]

10563 Rainis, Kenneth G. *Crime-Solving Science Projects: Forensic Science Experiments* (5–9). 2000, Enslow LB $26.60 (978-0-7660-1289-9). After defining forensic science, this book contains experiments and projects involving such areas as fingerprints, inks, writing samples, fibers, forgeries, and blood evidence. (Rev: HBG 10/01; SLJ 2/01) [363.2]

697

10564 Rainis, Kenneth G. *Fingerprints: Crime-Solving Science Experiments* (7–12). Illus. Series: Forensic Science Projects. 2006, Enslow LB $31.93 (978-0-7660-1960-7). Projects and experiments teach students about collecting evidence, taking notes, and reporting findings as well as the basics of fingerprinting; also use *Hair, Clothing, and Tire Track Evidence* (2006). (Rev: SLJ 7/07) [363.2]

10565 Rainis, Kenneth G. *Forgery: Crime-Solving Science Experiments* (4–8). Series: Forensic Science Projects. 2006, Enslow LB $31.93 (978-0-7660-1961-4). Rainis explores how forensic scientists identify forgeries, with 10 interesting case studies. (Rev: SLJ 5/07) [363.25]

10566 Roleff, Tamara L., ed. *Guns and Crime* (8–12). Series: At Issue. 1999, Greenhaven LB $26.20 (978-0-7377-0153-1). Both primary and secondary sources are included in this anthology that explores the relationship between guns and crime and the topic of gun control. (Rev: BL 12/15/99) [363.3]

10567 Roleff, Tamara L., ed. *Police Corruption* (6–12). Series: At Issue. 2003, Gale $29.95 (978-0-7377-1172-1); paper $21.20 (978-0-7377-1171-4). This is a thought-provoking exploration of the reasons why corruption can flourish within the law enforcement community. (Rev: BL 4/15/03) [353.4]

10568 Rollins, Barbara B., and Michael Dahl. *Ballistics* (4–7). Series: Edge Books, Forensic Crime Solvers. 2004, Capstone LB $23.93 (978-0-7368-2421-7). Report writers and reluctant readers will be attracted to this brief, concise discussion of the science of ballistics. (Rev: BL 5/1/04; SLJ 8/04) [363.25]

10569 Rollins, Barbara B., and Michael Dahl. *Blood Evidence* (4–8). Illus. Series: Forensic Crime Solvers. 2004, Capstone LB $23.93 (978-0-7368-2418-7). Reluctant readers will be attracted to the gruesome nature of the subject matter and the often lurid presentation of facts. (Rev: BL 5/1/04; SLJ 8/04) [363.25]

10570 Rollins, Barbara B., and Michael Dahl. *Cause of Death* (4–8). Illus. Series: Forensic Crime Solvers. 2004, Capstone LB $23.93 (978-0-7368-2420-0). This look at how crime scene technicians and medical examiners determine cause of death will draw in reluctant readers. (Rev: BL 5/1/04; SLJ 8/04) [614]

10571 Rollins, Barbara B., and Michael Dahl. *Fingerprint Evidence* (4–7). Series: Edge Books, Forensic Crime Solvers. 2004, Capstone LB $23.93 (978-0-7368-2419-4). After a story that draws the readers in, the authors describe the features of fingerprints and discusses their use in solving crimes. (Rev: BL 5/1/04; SLJ 8/04) [363.25]

10572 Ross, Stewart. *Spies and Traitors* (5–8). Series: Fact or Fiction? 1995, Millbrook LB $26.90 (978-1-56294-648-7). A history of the people who have placed themselves above their country in the dangerous game of espionage and betrayal. (Rev: BL 11/15/95; SLJ 3/96) [355.3]

10573 Salak, John. *Violent Crime: Is It out of Control?* (6–8). Series: Issues of Our Time. 1995, Twenty-First Century LB $22.90 (978-0-8050-4239-9). An honest presentation of why violent crimes are being committed more frequently and how young people are becoming increasingly involved in them. (Rev: BL 2/1/96; SLJ 2/96) [364.1]

10574 Schroeder, Andreas. *Scams!* (5–8). Series: True Stories from the Edge. 2004, Annick $18.95 (978-1-55037-853-5); paper $7.95 (978-1-55037-852-8). Ten stories reveal daring trickery, con jobs, and scams, including the 1938 radio broadcast of *War of the Worlds* that terrified millions of Americans and the baseless claim that a tribe of cavemen had been found living in a remote corner of the Philippines. (Rev: SLJ 8/04) [364.16]

10575 Schroeder, Andreas. *Thieves!* (5–10). Series: True Stories from the Edge. 2005, Annick $18.95 (978-1-55037-933-4); paper $8.95 (978-1-55037-932-7). Ten world-class crimes are described in compelling detail. (Rev: SLJ 3/06) [364]

10576 Silverstein, Herma. *Kids Who Kill* (7–10). Illus. 1997, Twenty-First Century LB $25.90 (978-0-8050-4369-3). This volume examines the reasons for the escalation in the number of juvenile killers, who they are, why they kill, the environmental factors involved, and how the court system deals with underage criminals. (Rev: BL 12/15/97; SLJ 1/98; VOYA 2/98) [364.14]

10577 Silverstein, Herma. *Threads of Evidence: Using Forensic Science to Solve Crimes* (7–12). 1996, Twenty-First Century LB $26.90 (978-0-8050-4370-9). A discussion of the new forensic technology now available to criminologists, such as the use of DNA, blood splatters, fibers, and shell casings, and the role this science has played in solving famous cases. (Rev: BL 12/1/96; SLJ 2/97; VOYA 6/97) [363.2]

10578 Solomon, Louis. *The Ma and Pa Murders and Other Perfect Crimes* (7–9). 1976, HarperCollins $12.95 (978-0-397-31577-2). This is an account of six unsolved crimes including the murders involving Lizzie Borden. [364]

10579 Steele, Philip. *Smuggling* (5–9). Series: Past and Present. 1993, Macmillan LB $20.00 (978-0-02-786884-5). A colorful history of smuggling through the ages. (Rev: BL 8/93) [364.1]

10580 Stewart, Gail B. *Gangs* (8–10). Illus. Series: The Other America. 1997, Lucent LB $27.45 (978-1-56006-340-7). Four gang members reveal in interviews why they joined, what gang life is like, and problems trying to leave gangs. (Rev: BL 5/15/97; SLJ 3/97; VOYA 4/98) [364.3]

10581 Streissguth, Thomas. *Hoaxers and Hustlers* (7–10). 1994, Oliver LB $19.95 (978-1-881508-13-7). Chronicles con artists and con games from the 1800s to the present, including pyramid schemes, the "Martian invasion" radio hoax, and Jim and Tammy Faye Bakker's real-estate scam. (Rev: BL 9/1/94; SLJ 7/94) [364.1]

10582 Thomas, Peggy. *Talking Bones: The Science of Forensic Anthropology* (6–9). Series: Science Sourcebooks. 1995, Facts on File $25.00 (978-0-8160-3114-6). This work provides an accessible introduction to the history and technology of forensic anthropology, with material on how forensic anthropologists are able to solve crimes through the analysis of human bones. (Rev: BL 10/15/95; SLJ 1/96; VOYA 4/96) [613]

10583 Townsend, John. *Breakouts and Blunders* (5–8). Series: True Crime. 2005, Raintree LB $31.43 (978-1-4109-1427-9). Attempted and successful escapes through history are the subject of this book in the True Crime series, which features a scrapbook format with engaging photographs and graphics. Also use *Fakes and Forgeries* and *Kidnappers and Assassins* (both 2005). (Rev: SLJ 6/06) [365.641]

10584 Trapani, Margi. *Working Together Against Gang Violence* (4–8). Series: The Library of Social Activism. 1996, Rosen LB $16.95 (978-0-8239-2260-4). After a general discussion on gang behavior, the author gives pointers to help young people cope with the threat of gangs and suggestions for working with others against gang violence. (Rev: SLJ 2/97) [302.3]

10585 Webber, Diane. *Do You Read Me? Famous Cases Solved by Handwriting Analysis!* (5–10). Series: 24/7: Science Behind the Scenes. 2007, Watts LB $25.00 (978-0-531-12066-8); paper $7.95 (978-0-531-15456-4). Webber uses three real cases to illustrate ways in which the study of handwriting can help to solve crimes; reluctant readers will enjoy this. (Rev: SLJ 8/07) [363.2]

10586 West, David. *Detective Work with Ballistics* (4–7). Illus. by Emanuele Boccanfuso. Series: Graphic Forensic Science. 2008, Rosen LB $21.95 (978-1-4042-1434-7). Graphic-novel-like depictions of actual cases in which ballistic evidence pointed to the culprit make this an interesting introduction to this forensic specialty. (Rev: BL 3/15/08) [363.25]

10587 Wiese, Jim. *Detective Science: 40 Crime-Solving, Case-Breaking, Crook-Catching Activities for Kids* (4–7). 1996, Wiley paper $12.95 (978-0-471-11980-7). Presents 40 experiments and activities that illustrate techniques in forensic science related to observing, collecting, and analyzing evidence. (Rev: BL 4/15/96; SLJ 6/96) [363.2]

10588 Wilker, Josh. *Classic Cons and Swindles* (6–9). Illus. Series: Crime, Justice, and Punishment. 1997, Chelsea LB $21.95 (978-0-7910-4251-9). This book explains such common con games and swindles as the pigeon drop and the bunco scam. (Rev: BL 9/1/97; VOYA 12/97) [364.163]

10589 Williams, Stanley, and Barbara C. Becnel. *Gangs and the Abuse of Power* (4–8). Series: Tookie Speaks Out Against Gang Violence. 1996, Rosen LB $18.75 (978-0-8239-2346-5). A former active gang member in Los Angeles tells what his life was like as a member and how to avoid his mistakes. Also use in this series *Gangs and Wanting to Belong* (1996). (Rev: SLJ 1/97) [302.3]

10590 Williams, Stanley, and Barbara C. Becnel. *Gangs and Weapons* (4–8). Series: Tookie Speaks Out Against Gang Violence. 1996, Rosen LB $18.75 (978-0-8239-2342-7). The use of weapons in gangs to gain and maintain power and how they are obtained are two of the topics covered in this cautionary account written by a former gang member who was seriously wounded in a shootout. Also use *Gangs and Your Friends* (1996). (Rev: SLJ 1/97) [302.3]

10591 Williams, Stanley, and Barbara C. Becnel. *Gangs and Your Neighborhood* (4–8). Series: Tookie Speaks Out Against Gang Violence. 1996, Rosen LB $18.75 (978-0-8239-2347-2). How gangs grow in neighborhoods and how they change them are two of the topics covered in this book about the dangers of gangs and how to avoid joining one. (Rev: SLJ 1/97) [302.3]

10592 Willis, Laurie, ed. *Hate Crimes* (7–12). Series: Social Issues Firsthand. 2007, Gale LB $28.70 (978-0-7377-2889-7). Hate crimes of various kinds are discussed in the articles and interview excerpts collected here. (Rev: BL 11/1/07) [364.15]

10593 Winchester, Elizabeth Siris. *The Right Bite: Dentists as Detectives* (4–8). Illus. Series: 24/7 Science Behind the Scenes: Forensic Files. 2007, Scholastic LB $26.00 (978-0-531-12062-0); paper $7.95 (978-0-531-18734-0). Conversational text focuses on the work of forensic dentists and offers multiple (sometimes gruesome) examples of cases in which their findings identified victims and perpetrators; factual inserts add interest and a final section discusses the equipment used. (Rev: BL 4/1/07; SLJ 6/07) [614]

10594 Woodford, Chris. *Criminal Investigation* (4–8). Illus. Series: Science Fact Files. 2001, Raintree LB $27.12 (978-0-7398-1016-3). A concise introduction to the forensic science with information on the newest equipment and techniques. (Rev: HBG 10/01; SLJ 1/02) [363.2]

10595 Wormser, Richard. *Juveniles in Trouble* (8–12). 1994, Messner $15.00 (978-0-671-86775-1). Extensive use of first-person narratives of troubled youths, with hard-hitting facts on important choices kids in trouble need to make. (Rev: BL 5/15/94; SLJ 6/94; VOYA 12/94) [364.3]

10596 Worth, Richard. *Children, Violence, and Murder* (7–10). Series: Crime, Justice, and Punishment. 2001, Chelsea LB $30.00 (978-0-7910-5154-2). Specific cases of young people who murder are presented, including Columbine High School, in this fascinating account that presents opposing views on the subject. (Rev: BL 6/1–15/01; HBG 10/01; SLJ 7/01) [364]

10597 Wright, Cynthia. *Everything You Need to Know About Dealing with Stalking* (7–12). Series: Need to Know Library. 2000, Rosen LB $27.95 (978-0-8239-2841-5). What to do if you're being stalked, as well as where to get help. (Rev: HBG 9/00; SLJ 3/00) [362.88]

10598 Wright, John D. *Fire and Explosives* (7–12). Series: Forensic Evidence. 2007, Sharpe Focus $39.95 (978-0-7656-8117-1). Readers learn about arson and explosives investigation and will gain an understanding of the work of forensic scientists. (Rev: LMC 2/08; SLJ 1/08)

10599 Yancey, Diane. *Murder* (7–10). Illus. Series: Inside the Crime Lab. 2006, Gale LB $32.45 (978-1-59018-619-0). Readers learn how clues found at a murder scene are analyzed and interpreted to reconstruct what happened; there are references to famous cases, and sidebar features and photographs add interest. (Rev: BL 4/1/06; SLJ 9/06) [363.25]

10600 Yeatts, Tabatha. *Forensics: Solving the Crime* (6–9). Illus. Series: Innovators. 2001, Oliver LB $21.95 (978-1-881508-75-5). An absorbing exploration of the development of forensics and the contributions of individual scientists, with clear explanations of some new technologies. (Rev: BCCB 2/02; HBG 10/02; SLJ 4/02) [363.25]

10601 Zeinert, Karen. *Victims of Teen Violence* (7–12). Illus. Series: Issues in Focus. 1996, Enslow LB $20.95 (978-0-89490-737-1). An exploration of teen violence that focuses on guns, gangs, sexual harassment, and gay bashing, and includes causes, consequences, victims, and solutions. (Rev: BL 6/1–15/96; SLJ 7/96; VOYA 8/96) [362.88]

10602 Ziff, John. *Espionage and Treason* (7–10). Series: Crime, Justice, and Punishment. 1999, Chelsea LB $30.00 (978-0-7910-4263-2). The Rosenbergs, Aldrich Ames, and Kim Philby are among the 20th-century spies covered in this survey of espionage and the motivations that drive traitors. (Rev: HBG 9/00; SLJ 4/00) [327.12]

Poverty, Homelessness, and Hunger

10603 Ayer, Eleanor. *Homeless Children* (5–8). Illus. Series: Overview. 1997, Lucent LB $29.95 (978-1-56006-177-9). The causes and consequences

of homelessness are explored, with a focus on children and the ways the problem is being handled. (Rev: BL 3/15/97) [362.7]

10604 Bowden, Rob. *Food Supply* (5–8). Series: 21st Century Debates. 2002, Raintree LB $27.12 (978-0-7398-4871-5). Trends and issues regarding the food supply, and possible solutions for shortages, are presented in this look at pros and cons. (Rev: BL 6/1–15/02) [338.19]

10605 De Koster, Katie, ed. *Poverty* (7–12). Series: Opposing Viewpoints. 1994, Greenhaven paper $16.20 (978-1-56510-065-7). Differing viewpoints are presented on such questions as what causes poverty and why women and minorities suffer from higher rates of poverty than white males. (Rev: BL 1/1/94) [362.5]

10606 Egendorf, Laura K., ed. *Poverty* (8–12). Series: Opposing Viewpoints. 1998, Greenhaven LB $32.45 (978-1-56510-947-6); paper $21.20 (978-1-56510-946-9). The seriousness of poverty today, its causes, and how it can be alleviated are covered in this collection of differing opinions on the subject. (Rev: BL 8/98) [362.5]

10607 Erlbach, Arlene. *Everything You Need to Know If Your Family Is on Welfare* (6–10). Series: Need to Know Library. 1997, Rosen LB $27.95 (978-0-8239-2433-2). This book explains the welfare system and details recipients' rights as well as offering tips on how to cope with being on welfare and the social stigma often associated with it. (Rev: SLJ 4/98) [362.5]

10608 Flood, Nancy Bohac. *Working Together Against World Hunger* (7–12). Series: Library of Social Activism. 1995, Rosen LB $27.95 (978-0-8239-1773-0). A rundown on world hunger, the conditions that cause it, and ways of becoming active in fighting it. (Rev: BL 4/15/95) [363.8]

10609 Fyson, Nance Lui. *Feeding the World* (6–8). Illus. 1985, Batsford $19.95 (978-0-7134-4264-9). An introduction to the world's increasing food problems, with material on staple crops and a discussion of food production and distribution. (Rev: BL 5/15/85) [338.19]

10610 Garlake, Teresa. *Poverty: Changing Attitudes, 1900–2000* (6–9). Series: 20th Century Issues. 1999, Raintree LB $28.54 (978-0-8172-5894-8). Garlake looks at the causes of poverty, events around the world that have contributed to poverty, attitudes toward this problem, and government efforts to contain it. (Rev: BL 11/15/00; HBG 9/00; SLJ 5/00) [362.5]

10611 Gottfried, Ted. *Homelessness: Whose Problem Is It?* (6–12). Series: Issue and Debate. 1999, Millbrook LB $25.90 (978-0-7613-0953-6). After reviewing the history of homelessness in the United States, opposing views are presented on the causes of homelessness today, the responsibility of government and the individual, and methods of countering it. (Rev: BL 4/1/99; SLJ 9/99) [305.569]

10612 Haugen, David M., and Matthew J. Box, eds. *Poverty* (8–11). Series: Social Issues Firsthand. 2005, Gale LB $29.95 (978-0-7377-2899-6). Wideranging essays present the plight of those living in poverty as well as the thoughts of those who are determined to do something about the problem. (Rev: BL 10/15/05) [362.5]

10613 Houle, Michelle E. *Lindsey Williams: Gardening for Impoverished Families* (4–7). Illus. Series: Young Heroes. 2007, Gale LB $27.45 (978-0-7377-3867-4). Young author Williams has won many awards for her agricultural activism; here she talks about ways to have good food without spending a fortune and about the importance and rewards of volunteering. (Rev: BL 2/15/08) [363.8]

10614 Johnson, Joan J. *Children of Welfare* (6–10). Illus. 1995, Twenty-First Century LB $23.40 (978-0-8050-2985-7). A look at the emergence of the welfare system, what it is today, and its impact on young people. (Rev: BL 6/1–15/97; SLJ 6/97) [362.71]

10615 Kowalski, Kathiann M. *Poverty in America: Causes and Issues* (6–12). Series: Issues in Focus. 2003, Enslow LB $20.95 (978-0-7660-1945-4). An exploration of unequal standards of living in America that looks at differences in levels of poverty and at homelessness, welfare, government efforts to alleviate the problem, and private-sector aid. (Rev: HBG 4/04; SLJ 11/03) [362.5]

10616 LeVert, Marianne. *The Welfare System* (7–12). 1995, Millbrook LB $25.90 (978-1-56294-455-1). A look at various issues that form the great welfare debate. (Rev: BL 4/15/95; SLJ 4/95) [361.6]

10617 Mason, Paul. *Poverty* (4–7). Illus. Series: Planet Under Pressure. 2006, Heinemann LB $31.43 (978-1-4034-7743-9). A clear presentation of how poverty affects people around the world, with charts, photographs, and profiles. (Rev: BL 4/1/06; SLJ 6/06) [362.5]

10618 Nichelason, Margery G. *Homeless or Hopeless?* (5–8). Illus. Series: Pro/Con Issues. 1994, Lerner LB $30.35 (978-0-8225-2606-3). After an explanation of the roots and causes of homelessness, clearly written statements debate who is responsible for homelessness and how it should be handled. (Rev: BL 6/1–15/94; SLJ 7/94) [362.5]

10619 Parker, Julie. *Everything You Need to Know About Living in a Shelter* (8–12). 1995, Rosen LB $27.95 (978-0-8239-1874-4). A straightforward account that describes life for teens living in shelters, with material on what they can do to control at least some aspects of their lives. (Rev: SLJ 12/95; VOYA 2/96) [362.5]

10620 Roleff, Tamara L., ed. *Inner-City Poverty* (8–12). Series: Contemporary Issues Companion. 2003, Gale LB $36.20 (978-0-7377-0841-7); paper $24.95 (978-0-7377-0840-0). This examination of theories about the causes of urban poverty, the resulting crime and drug use, the impact of the welfare system, and the potential for effective reform provides lots of material for students doing research. (Rev: LMC 4–5/03; SLJ 2/03) [362.5]

10621 Rozakis, Laurie. *Homelessness: Can We Solve the Problem?* (6–9). Series: Issues of Our Time. 1995, Twenty-First Century LB $22.90 (978-0-8050-3878-1). A well-rounded discussion that will encourage readers to form their own conclusions. (Rev: BL 7/95; SLJ 9/95) [362.5]

10622 Seymour-Jones, Carole. *Homelessness* (5–9). Series: Past and Present. 1993, Macmillan $20.00 (978-0-02-786882-1). A discussion of the causes of homelessness, the extent of the problem and who is affected, and ways to end it. (Rev: BL 8/93) [362.5]

10623 Stavsky, Lois, and I. E. Mozeson. *The Place I Call Home: Faces and Voices of Homeless Teens* (8–12). Illus. 1990, Shapolsky $14.95 (978-0-944007-81-5). A series of interviews with homeless teens reveals lives of violence, poverty, and drugs. (Rev: BL 11/15/90; SLJ 2/91) [362.7]

10624 Stearman, Kaye. *Homelessness* (5–10). Illus. Series: Talking Points. 1999, Raintree LB $27.12 (978-0-8172-5312-7). A worldwide view of homelessness, its causes — including eviction, natural disasters, and war — and international efforts to combat it. (Rev: BL 9/1/99; SLJ 8/99) [363.5]

10625 Stearman, Kaye. *Why Do People Live on the Streets?* (5–7). Series: Exploring Tough Issues. 2001, Raintree LB $25.69 (978-0-7398-3232-5). Among reasons given for homelessness are poverty and discrimination. (Rev: HBG 10/01; SLJ 7/01) [305.569]

10626 Worth, Richard. *Poverty* (5–8). Illus. Series: Overview. 1997, Lucent LB $29.95 (978-1-56006-192-2). A carefully researched title that gives a history of poverty in America, changing attitudes toward it, and current policies and practices. (Rev: BL 8/97; SLJ 9/97) [362.5]

Unemployment

10627 Alpern, Michele. *The Effects of Job Loss on the Family* (6–12). Illus. Series: Focus on Family Matters. 2002, Chelsea LB $25.00 (978-0-7910-6690-4). Personal teen experiences draw readers into this straightforward account of the financial and emotional upheavals caused by unemployment. (Rev: BL 10/15/02; HBG 3/03) [306.4]

Public Morals

10628 Berne, Emma Carlson. *Online Pornography* (8–12). Series: Opposing Viewpoints. 2007, Gale LB $36.20 (978-0-7377-3657-1); paper $23.70 (978-0-7377-3658-8). Is online pornography harmful to society? Is online pornography a form of free speech? Questions like these are discussed from different points of view. (Rev: SLJ 1/08)

10629 Burns, Kate, ed. *Censorship* (7–12). Series: History of Issues. 2006, Gale LB $34.95 (978-0-7377-2009-9). Primary documents help to illustrate the issues discussed in this pro and con review of censorship throughout American history. (Rev: SLJ 6/07)

10630 Cothran, Helen, ed. *Pornography* (8–12). Illus. Series: Opposing Viewpoints. 2001, Gale LB $36.20 (978-0-7377-0761-8); paper $24.95 (978-0-7377-0760-1). Debating teams will plenty of arguments to defend both sides of questions about the evils of pornography and whether it should be regulated and/or censored. (Rev: SLJ 12/01) [363.4]

10631 Day, Nancy. *Censorship or Freedom of Expression?* (7–12). Series: Pro/Con Issues. 2000, Lerner LB $25.26 (978-0-8225-2628-5). A look at censorship in areas including schools and the arts and entertainment, with discussion of age appropriateness and use of the Internet. (Rev: HBG 3/01; SLJ 1/01) [363.3]

10632 Dudley, William, ed. *Media Violence* (8–12). Series: Opposing Viewpoints. 1998, Greenhaven LB $32.45 (978-1-56510-945-2). This exploration of violence in television, motion pictures, song lyrics, and other media questions its extent, effects, and proposals to restrict it. (Rev: BL 8/89) [384]

10633 Gold, John C. *Board of Education v. Pico (1982)* (6–10). Illus. Series: Supreme Court Decisions. 1994, Twenty-First Century LB $25.90 (978-0-8050-3660-2). A thorough analysis of the Supreme Court case that began in a Long Island school and involved censoring library materials. (Rev: BL 11/15/94; SLJ 1/95) [344.73]

10634 MccGwire, Scarlett. *Censorship: Changing Attitudes 1900–2000* (6–9). Series: 20th Century Issues. 1999, Raintree LB $28.54 (978-0-8172-5574-9). McGwire looks at censorship at the beginning of the 20th century, global events around the world that contributed to censorship, the advent of movie rating systems, and the Internet. (Rev: HBG 9/00; SLJ 5/00) [363.3]

10635 Miller, J. Anthony. *Texas vs. Johnson: The Flag-Burning Case* (6–10). Illus. Series: Landmark Supreme Court Cases. 1997, Enslow LB $20.95 (978-0-89490-858-3). The limits of civil disobedience were the subject of this important Supreme Court case. (Rev: BL 7/97) [342.73]

10636 Ross, Val. *You Can't Read This: Forbidden Books, Lost Writing, Mistranslations and Codes* (7–10). 2006, Tundra $19.95 (978-0-88776-732-6). A survey of censorship of the written word throughout history. (Rev: BL 5/15/06) [028]

10637 Sherrow, Victoria. *Censorship in Schools* (6–9). Illus. Series: Issues in Focus. 1996, Enslow LB $20.95 (978-0-89490-728-9). After defining censorship, the author discusses when, how, and why it occurs in schools, with several citations of famous cases. (Rev: BL 1/1–15/97; SLJ 12/96; VOYA 4/97) [025.213]

10638 Steffens, Bradley. *Censorship* (7–10). Illus. 1996, Lucent LB $28.70 (978-1-56006-166-3). A historical survey that presents the conflict between freedom and censorship, beginning with the Ten Commandments and the Bill of Rights and ending with today's controversy over rock lyrics. (Rev: BL 2/15/96; SLJ 3/96) [363.3]

10639 Steins, Richard. *Censorship: How Does It Conflict with Freedom?* (5–9). Series: Issues of Our Time. 1995, Twenty-First Century LB $22.90 (978-0-8050-3879-8). A clearly written introduction to censorship, its history, and the various positions possible toward it. (Rev: BL 7/95; SLJ 9/95) [363.3]

10640 Wekesser, Carol, ed. *Pornography* (8–12). Series: Opposing Viewpoints. 1997, Greenhaven paper $21.20 (978-1-56510-517-1). What is pornography? Is it harmful? Should it be censored? Can it be controlled on the Internet? These are some of the questions explored in this collection of writings representing different points of view. (Rev: BL 12/15/96; SLJ 2/97) [363.7]

Sex Roles

10641 Chipman, Dawn, et al. *Cool Women: The Reference* (6–9). 1998, Girl Pr. paper $19.95 (978-0-9659754-0-7). This work spotlights an eclectic variety of heroines, past and present, real and fictional, from around the world, ranging from athletes and spies to Amazons and comic book queens, chosen for their uniqueness, strength, tenacity, contributions, and ability to blaze new trails for women. (Rev: VOYA 2/99) [305.4]

10642 Gourley, Catherine. *Flappers and the New American Woman: Perceptions of Women from 1918 through the 1920s* (7–12). Illus. Series: Images and Issues of Women in the Twentieth Century. 2007, Lerner LB $38.60 (978-0-8225-6060-9). An interesting chronological examination of the roles women played in this period and how they were portrayed in various media. (Rev: BL 1/1–15/08; LMC 2/08; SLJ 11/07) [305.40973]

10643 Hanmer, Trudy J. *The Gender Gap in Schools: Girls Losing Out* (7–12). Illus. Series: Issues in Focus. 1996, Enslow LB $20.95 (978-0-89490-718-0). Sex discrimination at the school level is introduced with an objective presentation of the many facets of this complex question. (Rev: BL 8/96; SLJ 6/96) [376]

10644 Levithan, David, and Billy Merrell, eds. *The Full Spectrum: A New Generation of Writing about Gay, Lesbian, Bisexual, Transgender, Questioning, and Other Identities* (8–11). 2006, Knopf LB $17.99 (978-0-375-93290-8); paper $9.95 (978-0-375-83290-1). Forty essays and other contributions by young people under age 23 reveal their own real-life experiences questioning or establishing their sexual identities. (Rev: BL 5/15/06; HB 7–8/06; SLJ 7/06) [306.76]

10645 Ross, Mandy. *The Changing Role of Women* (6–9). Series: 20th Century Perspectives. 2002, Heinemann LB $27.07 (978-1-58810-660-5). An exploration of the ways in which women's roles changed around the world during the 20th century. (Rev: SLJ 10/02) [305.42]

10646 Stearman, Kaye, and Nikki Van Der Gaag. *Gender Issues* (6–10). Illus. Series: Global Issues. 1996, Raintree LB $19.98 (978-0-8172-4545-0). Using historical background material, statistics, and case studies, the various issues involving gender roles and sex discrimination around the world are explored. (Rev: BL 3/15/97; VOYA 6/97) [305.3]

Social Action, Social Change, and Futurism

10647 Brownlie, Alison. *Charities — Do They Work?* (6–10). Series: Talking Points. 1999, Raintree LB $27.12 (978-0-8172-5319-6). In this brief account, the role of charities in American society is explored along with a discussion on their problems and accomplishments. (Rev: BL 12/15/99; HBG 9/00) [361]

10648 Coon, Nora E., ed. *It's Your Rite: Girls' Coming-of-Age Stories* (6–12). 2003, Beyond Words paper $9.95 (978-1-58270-074-8). Young authors from around the world describe practical and ceremonial milestones that mark their coming of age, and the associated worries and joys. (Rev: SLJ 10/03) [305.235]

10649 Fleming, Robert. *Rescuing a Neighborhood: The Bedford-Stuyvesant Volunteer Ambulance Corps* (4–8). Illus. 1995, Walker LB $16.85 (978-0-8027-8330-1). The story of how two determined, dedicated men organized emergency response services in their inner-city neighborhood. (Rev: BL 5/1/95; SLJ 9/95) [362]

10650 Gay, Kathlyn. *Volunteering: The Ultimate Teen Guide* (8–12). Series: It Happened to Me. 2004, Scarecrow $32.50 (978-0-8108-4922-8). This guide examines a wide range of volunteering opportunities for teenagers, from working with the elderly or the homeless to tutoring to building houses; real-life stories add interest. (Rev: SLJ 4/05; VOYA 4/05) [361.8]

10651 Halpin, Mikki. *It's Your World — If You Don't Like It, Change It: Activism for Teenagers* (7–12). 2004, Simon & Schuster paper $8.99 (978-0-689-87448-2). Covering activism on a wide range of topics — the environment, war, gay rights, women's rights, and so forth — this is a useful guide, providing practical ideas and sensible cautions. (Rev: BL 12/15/04; SLJ 12/04) [305.23]

10652 Hovanec, Erin M. *Get Involved! A Girl's Guide to Volunteering* (5–8). Series: Girls' Guides. 1999, Rosen LB $27.95 (978-0-8239-2985-6). Two case studies of successful volunteers are given in this account that explains where to volunteer, how to approach organizations, and how to determine one's interests. (Rev: HBG 10/00; SLJ 1/00; VOYA 2/00) [361]

10653 Karnes, Frances A., and Suzanne M. Bean. *Girls and Young Women Leading the Way: 20 True Stories About Leadership* (5–8). Illus. 1993, Free Spirit paper $12.95 (978-0-915793-52-5). Contains case histories of 20 girls who changed their communities by starting projects such as collecting food for the homeless or starting a recycling program. (Rev: SLJ 12/93) [307.1]

10654 Karnes, Frances A., and Kristen R. Stephens. *Empowered Girls: A Girl's Guide to Positive Activism, Volunteering, and Philanthropy* (6–12). 2005, Prufrock paper $14.95 (978-1-59363-163-5). A helpful, information-packed guide that will motivate young people to volunteer. (Rev: SLJ 2/06; VOYA 4/06) [361.8]

10655 Kronenwetter, Michael. *Protest!* (7–12). Illus. 1996, Twenty-First Century LB $23.40 (978-0-8050-4103-3). This book describes various forms of protest, from simple actions in everyday life to those aimed at changing social conditions in the U.S. and around the world, providing a historical, sociological, and psychological context. (Rev: BL 1/1–15/97; SLJ 1/97; VOYA 6/97) [303.48]

10656 Kurian, George Thomas, and Graham T. T. Molitor, eds. *The 21st Century* (8–12). 1999, Macmillan $130.00 (978-0-02-864977-1). This book makes predictions for future developments in such areas as abortion, artificial intelligence, crime, extinction, household appliances, sexual behavior, and utopias. (Rev: BL 4/1/99; SLJ 8/99) [133.3]

10657 Lesko, Wendy Schaetzel. *Youth: The 26% Solution* (7–12). 1998, Information U.S.A. paper $14.95 (978-1-878346-47-6). A community action handbook for teens prepared by Project 2000 that provides basic, workable advice, based on the premise that the 26 percent of the population of the United States under the age of 18 can make a difference. (Rev: BL 11/1/98; VOYA 12/98) [361.8]

10658 Lewis, Barbara A. *The Kid's Guide to Service Projects: Over 500 Service Ideas for Young People Who Want to Make a Difference* (4–7). 1995, Free Spirit paper $12.95 (978-0-915793-82-2). After an introduction on how to organize and conduct service projects, this book gives details on 500 ideas from running errands for seniors to working for voter registration. (Rev: SLJ 7/95) [307]

10659 Lewis, Barbara A. *The Kid's Guide to Social Action: How to Solve the Social Problems You Choose — and Turn Creative Thinking into Positive Action*. Rev. ed. (4–8). 1998, Free Spirit paper $18.95 (978-1-57542-038-7). An inspirational guide that shows how young people can make a difference by becoming involved in social action, such as instigating a cleanup of toxic waste, lobbying, or youth rights campaigns. (Rev: SLJ 1/99) [361.6]

10660 Marcovitz, Hal. *Teens and Volunteerism* (7–10). Series: The Gallup Youth Survey, Major Issues and Trends. 2005, Mason Crest LB $22.95 (978-1-59084-877-7). An attractive volume documenting Gallup findings on teens' attitudes toward various forms of volunteerism including community service, military service, and activism. (Rev: SLJ 1/06) [361.8]

10661 Meltzer, Milton. *Who Cares? Millions Do . . . A Book About Altruism* (7–10). 1994, Walker LB $16.85 (978-0-8027-8325-7). Stories of people who help their fellow beings, both individually and through organizations. (Rev: BL 11/15/94; VOYA 2/95) [171]

10662 Mintzer, Rich. *Helping Hands: How Families Can Reach Out to Their Community* (6–12). Series: Focus on Family Matters. 2002, Chelsea LB $25.00 (978-0-7910-6952-3). This is a basic introduction to volunteerism with tips on how teens can get involved in activities and projects that complement their interests and abilities. (Rev: BL 1/1–15/03) [361.8]

10663 Ryan, Bernard. *Caring for Animals* (7–12). 1998, Ferguson LB $19.95 (978-0-89434-227-1). After a general introduction to volunteerism, this book outlines ways that teens can help care for unwanted and abandoned animals in their neighborhood. (Rev: BL 9/15/98; SLJ 11/98; VOYA 8/99) [361.8]

10664 Ryan, Bernard. *Expanding Education and Literacy* (7–12). Series: Community Service for Teens. 1998, Ferguson LB $19.95 (978-0-89434-231-8). This book describes literacy and reading programs in the United States and how teens can participate in them. (Rev: BL 9/15/98; SLJ 11/98) [361.3]

10665 Ryan, Bernard. *Helping the Ill, Poor and the Elderly* (7–12). Series: Community Service for Teens. 1998, Ferguson LB $19.95 (978-0-89434-229-5). Outlines the many ways in which teens can help the less fortunate in their communities both informally and working through service agencies. (Rev: BL 9/15/98; SLJ 11/98) [361.8]

10666 Ryan, Bernard. *Promoting the Arts and Sciences* (7–12). Series: Community Service for Teens. 1998, Ferguson LB $19.95 (978-0-89434-234-9). This work tells how teens can become involved in local agencies that promote the arts and sciences and how their services can make a difference both to the community and to themselves. (Rev: BL 9/15/98; SLJ 2/99) [361.8]

10667 Ryan, Bernard, Jr. *Participating in Government: Opportunities to Volunteer* (7–12). Series: Community Service for Teens. 1998, Ferguson LB $19.95 (978-0-89434-230-1). An upbeat guide that advises teens about how they can volunteer in the areas of government and politics and become involved in their community. Also use *Promoting the Arts and Sciences: Opportunities to Volunteer* (1998). (Rev: SLJ 2/99) [302.14]

10668 Senker, Cath. *Poverty* (7–12). Illus. Series: What If We Do Nothing? 2007, Gareth Stevens LB $22.95 (978-0-8368-7757-1). Individuals can make a difference in fighting poverty, this title suggests, even as it lists discouraging statistics on the pervasiveness of poverty around the globe. (Rev: BL 4/1/07) [363]

10669 Shostak, Arthur B., ed. *Futuristics: Looking Ahead* (6–9). Illus. Series: Tackling Tomorrow Today. 2005, Chelsea House LB $35.00 (978-0-7910-8401-4). A collection of thought-provoking essays about the field of futuristics. (Rev: BL 4/1/05) [303.49]

Social Customs and Holidays

10670 Breuilly, Elizabeth, and Joanne O'Brien. *Festivals of the World: The Illustrated Guide to Celebrations, Customs, Events and Holidays* (6–12). Illus. 2002, Checkmark $29.95 (978-0-8160-4481-8). Festivals around the world are organized by religion, with maps, photographs, and interesting sidebar features. (Rev: SLJ 4/03) [394.2]

10671 Bruchac, Joseph. *Squanto's Journey: The Story of the First Thanksgiving* (4–8). Illus. by Greg Shed. 2000, Harcourt $17.00 (978-0-15-201817-7). A picture book for older readers about the Pilgrims, the first Thanksgiving, and the important role played by the Paluxet Indian Squanto in helping the colony survive. (Rev: BL 9/1/00; HBG 3/01; SLJ 11/00) [394.2]

10672 Gelber, Carol. *Love and Marriage Around the World* (5–7). 1998, Millbrook LB $23.90 (978-0-7613-0102-8). From courtship to the wedding, this book introduces marriage customs from around the world and among different ethnic groups. (Rev: BCCB 7–8/98; HBG 10/98; SLJ 6/98) [392]

10673 Graham-Barber, Lynda. *Mushy! The Complete Book of Valentine Words* (4–8). Illus. by Betsy Lewin. 1993, Avon paper $3.50 (978-0-380-71650-0). An explanation of the words, symbols, and customs concerning Valentine's Day. (Rev: BCCB 3/91; BL 2/15/91; SLJ 5/91) [394.2]

10674 Greene, Meg. *Rest in Peace: A History of American Cemeteries* (8–11). Illus. Series: People's History. 2008, Lerner LB $30.60 (978-0-8225-3414-3). American burial traditions are constantly evolving, and this volume looks at everything from early Native American practices to gigantic modern cemeteries, with mentions of ethnic communities and environmentally conscious options along the way. (Rev: BL 3/15/08; SLJ 6/08) [393.09]

10675 Harris, Zoe, and Suzanne Williams. *Pinatas and Smiling Skeletons* (4–8). Illus. 1998, Pacific View LB $19.95 (978-1-881896-19-7). This book introduces six festivals celebrated in Mexico: the Feast of the Virgin of Guadalupe, Christmas, Carnaval, Corpus Christi, Independence Day, and the Day of the Dead. (Rev: BL 3/15/99; HBG 3/99; SLJ 3/99) [394.26972]

10676 Karenga, Maulana. *Kwanzaa: A Celebration of Family, Community and Culture, Special Commemorative Edition* (6–12). Illus. 1997, Univ. of Sankore $24.95 (978-0-943412-21-4). This complete book on Kwanzaa explains its African and African American origins, devotes a chapter to each of its seven principles, suggests activities, and gives answers to the most frequently asked questions about this holiday. (Rev: SLJ 10/98) [394.2]

10677 Limburg, Peter R. *Weird! The Complete Book of Halloween Words* (4–7). Illus. by Betsy Lewin. 1989, Macmillan LB $13.95 (978-0-02-759050-0). This book defines 41 words and expressions, such as trick or treat, associated with Halloween. (Rev: BL 9/1/89; SLJ 9/89) [394]

10678 Lopez, Adriana, ed. *Fifteen Candles: 15 Tales of Taffeta, Hairspray, Drunk Uncles, and Other Quinceanera Stories* (8–12). 2007, HarperCollins paper $14.95 (978-0-06-124192-5). Fifteen contributions — some fiction, some nonfiction — describe varied quinceañera experiences. (Rev: BL 6/1–15/07; SLJ 10/07) [395.2]

10679 MacMillan, Dianne M. *Thanksgiving Day* (4–8). Series: Best Holiday Books. 1997, Enslow LB $23.93 (978-0-89490-822-4). In spite of a dull format, this book gives solid information about Thanksgiving, its history, common traditions, and modern observances. (Rev: SLJ 8/97) [394.2]

10680 Perl, Lila. *Piñatas and Paper Flowers: Holidays of the Americas in English and Spanish* (6–9). Illus. 1983, HarperCollins paper $7.95 (978-0-89919-155-3). The origins and customs of eight holidays celebrated in the Americas are outlined in a bilingual text. [394.2]

10681 Taylor, Charles A. *Juneteenth: A Celebration of Freedom* (5–8). Illus. by author. 2002, Open Hand $19.95 (978-0-940880-68-9). A well-organized account of this holiday, which celebrates emancipation, with a discussion of the history of slavery. (Rev: SLJ 11/02) [394.2]

10682 Wilkinson, Philip. *A Celebration of Customs and Rituals of the World* (5–8). Illus. 1996, Facts on File $44.00 (978-0-8160-3479-6). A discussion of customs and rituals connected with birth, death, marriage, and coming-of-age. (Rev: BL 4/1/96; VOYA 6/96) [394.2]

10683 Wilson, Sule Greg C. *Kwanzaa! Africa Lives in a New World Festival* (4–7). Series: The Library of African American Arts and Culture. 1999, Rosen LB $27.95 (978-0-8239-1857-7). This book begins with a history of slavery and the civil rights movement, then explains the origins and meaning of Kwanzaa. (Rev: SLJ 10/99) [641.59]

Terrorism

10684 Andryszewski, Tricia. *Terrorism in America* (6–10). Illus. Series: Headliners. 2002, Millbrook LB $25.90 (978-0-7613-2803-2). An overview of attacks against Americans both at home and abroad, with an interesting discussion of the difficulties of protecting civil rights while fighting terrorism. (Rev: BCCB 9/02; BL 8/02; HBG 3/03; SLJ 12/02) [363.3]

10685 Balkin, Karen F., ed. *The War on Terrorism* (7–12). Illus. Series: Opposing Viewpoints. 2004, Gale LB $36.20 (978-0-7377-2336-6); paper $24.95 (978-0-7377-2337-3). The 28 essays in this collection present both sides of the ongoing debate over the Bush administration's measures to combat terrorism. (Rev: SLJ 3/05) [973.9]

10686 Bingley, Richard. *Terrorism* (5–9). Series: Face the Facts. 2003, Raintree LB $28.56 (978-0-7398-6852-2). An examination of terrorism, its causes, and the efforts being made to combat it. (Rev: SLJ 4/04) [303.6]

10687 Campbell, Geoffrey. *A Vulnerable America* (7–12). Series: Library of Homeland Security. 2004, Gale LB $29.95 (978-1-59018-383-0). This book discusses national security, how the government dealt with terrorist attacks in the past, and how 9/11/01 changed intelligence activities. (Rev: BL 4/15/04; SLJ 5/04) [363.3]

10688 Cart, Michael, et al., eds. *911: The Book of Help* (8–12). Illus. 2002, Cricket $17.95 (978-0-8126-2659-9); paper $9.95 (978-0-8126-2676-6). A collection of essays, stories, and poems by well-known writers presented in sections titled "Healing," "Searching for History," "Asking Why? Why? Why?," and "Reacting and Recovering." (Rev: BL 7/02; HB 9–10/02; HBG 3/03; SLJ 9/02*) [818]

10689 Corona, Laurel. *Hunting Down the Terrorists: Declaring War and Policing Global Violations* (7–12). Series: Lucent Library of Homeland Security. 2004, Gale LB $29.95 (978-1-59018-382-3). This account describes international efforts to hunt down terrorists and the cooperative efforts that are emerging. (Rev: BL 5/15/04; SLJ 4/04) [364.1]

10690 Currie, Stephen. *Terrorists and Terrorist Groups* (6–12). Series: Lucent Terrorism Library. 2002, Gale LB $29.95 (978-1-59018-207-9). A thorough, well-researched survey of terrorist organizations that looks at their structures, beliefs, tactics, and key figures. (Rev: SLJ 11/02) [973.931]

10691 Fridell, Ron. *Terrorism: Political Violence at Home and Abroad* (6–9). Illus. Series: Issues in Focus. 2001, Enslow LB $26.60 (978-0-7660-1671-2). A balanced look at pre-September 2001 terrorism both at home and abroad, at the operations of terrorist networks, and at worldwide efforts to track and contain terrorists. (Rev: HBG 3/02; SLJ 3/02; VOYA 12/01) [303.6]

10692 Friedman, Lauri S., ed. *How Should the United States Treat Prisoners in the War on Terror?* (7–9). Series: At Issue. 2005, Gale LB $29.95 (978-0-7377-3113-2); paper $21.20 (978-0-7377-3114-9). Previously published articles examine questions surrounding the Geneva Convention and treatment of detainees in America's war on terror. (Rev: SLJ 7/05)

10693 Friedman, Lauri S. *Terrorist Attacks* (7–12). Series: Compact Research. 2007, Reference Point LB $24.95 (978-1-60152-022-7). Why do people commit terrorist attacks? How can terrorist attacks be prevented? These and other questions are discussed from various points of view, with facts, profiles, and illustrations. (Rev: SLJ 1/08)

10694 Gaines, Ann. *Terrorism* (7–12). Series: Crime, Justice, and Punishment. 1998, Chelsea LB $30.00 (978-0-7910-4596-1). Beginning with the bombing of Pan Am flight 103 over Lockerbie, Scotland, in 1988, this thorough account discusses terrorism around the world and the groups that are responsible. (Rev: BL 12/15/98; SLJ 3/99) [364.1]

10695 Goodman, Robin, and Andrea Henderson Fahnestock. *The Day Our World Changed: Children's Art of 9/11* (7–12). 2002, Abrams $19.95 (978-0-8109-3544-0). Children's words and art are the main focus of this handsome volume. (Rev: BL 9/15/02) [700]

10696 Gow, Mary. *Attack on America: The Day the Twin Towers Collapsed* (8–12). Illus. Series: American Disasters. 2002, Enslow LB $23.93 (978-0-7660-2118-1). This dramatic account of the events of September 11, 2001, includes many survivor and eyewitness accounts. (Rev: BL 9/1/02; HBG 3/03; SLJ 1/03) [973.931]

10697 Gupta, Dipak K. *Who Are the Terrorists?* (8–11). Series: Roots of Terrorism. 2006, Chelsea House $35.00 (978-0-7910-8306-2). This book describes more than 30 terrorist organizations deemed dangerous by the U.S.State Department, providing a balanced account with regard to Islam and looking at the activities of three Nobel Peace Prize winners who were once thought to be terrorists. (Rev: BL 7/06) [303.6]

10698 Hamilton, John. *Behind the Terror* (4–7). Series: War on Terrorism. 2002, ABDO LB $16.95 (978-1-57765-679-1). Using an accessible text and color photographs, this book reports on various international terrorist organizations, their leaders, and their tactics. (Rev: BL 5/15/02) [909.9]

10699 Hamilton, John. *Operation Enduring Freedom* (4–7). Series: War on Terrorism. 2002, ABDO LB $25.65 (978-1-57765-665-4). Using many color photographs and a matter-of-fact text, this book covers various aspects of the U.S. war against terrorism. (Rev: BL 5/15/02; HBG 10/02) [973.9]

10700 Hamilton, John. *Operation Noble Eagle* (4–7). Series: War on Terrorism. 2002, ABDO LB $25.65 (978-1-57765-664-7). A look at U.S. efforts to police and defend its borders as part of the war on terrorism. (Rev: BL 5/15/02; HBG 10/02) [973.9]

10701 Hampton, Wilborn. *September 11, 2001: Attack on New York City* (6–9). Illus. 2003, Candlewick $17.99 (978-0-7636-1949-7). Personal stories give depth to a description of the tragedy in New York City and speculation about the motivation of the perpetrators. (Rev: BL 7/03; HB 9–10/03; SLJ 7/03) [974.7]

10702 Haugen, David, and Susan Musser, eds. *Can the War on Terrorism Be Won?* (6–9). Series: At Issue: National Security. 2007, Gale LB $29.95 (978-0-7377-1973-4); paper $21.20 (978-0-7377-1974-1). A collection of articles and speeches that express diverse views on the conduct of the "War on Terror." (Rev: BL 1/1–15/08) [973.931]

10703 Kallen, Stuart A. *National Security* (7–12). Series: Compact Research. 2007, Reference Point LB $24.95 (978-1-60152-020-3). How serious a threat to national security is terrorism? How is the government protecting national security? These and other questions are discussed from various points of view, with facts, profiles, and illustrations. (Rev: SLJ 1/08)

10704 Katz, Samuel M. *Against All Odds: Counterterrorist Hostage Rescues* (6–12). Series: Terrorist

Dossiers. 2004, Lerner LB $26.60 (978-0-8225-1567-8). The notable hostage rescues by antiterrorist groups around the world covered here go back to the early 19th century. (Rev: SLJ 4/05; VOYA 6/05) [364.15]

10705 Katz, Samuel M. *At Any Cost: National Liberation Terrorism* (7–12). Series: Terrorist Dossiers. 2004, Lerner LB $26.60 (978-0-8225-0949-3). This is an excellent introduction to the terrorist groups active today whose cause is the liberation of their homelands. (Rev: BL 3/15/04; HBG 4/04; SLJ 3/04; VOYA 4/04) [363.2]

10706 Katz, Samuel M. *Jihad: Islamic Fundamentalist Terrorism* (7–12). Illus. Series: Terrorist Dossiers. 2003, Lerner LB $26.60 (978-0-8225-4031-1). A look at Middle East-based terrorist groups, their histories, and present-day activities. (Rev: BL 3/15/04; HBG 4/04; SLJ 5/04) [303.6]

10707 Katz, Samuel M. *Raging Within: Ideological Terrorism* (7–12). Series: Terrorist Dossiers. 2004, Lerner LB $26.60 (978-0-8225-4032-8). This book examines terrorists whose motivation is based on ideologies and religion. (Rev: BL 3/15/04; HBG 4/04; SLJ 5/04) [363.2]

10708 Lalley, Patrick. *9.11.01: Terrorists Attack the U.S* (4–7). Illus. 2002, Raintree LB $31.40 (978-0-7398-6021-2). A compact look at the terrorist attacks of September 11, 2001, their causes, the world of Islam, the history of the World Trade Center, and personal stories related to the attacks. (Rev: BL 4/1/02; HBG 10/02; SLJ 5/02; VOYA 8/02) [303.6250]

10709 Landau, Elaine. *Suicide Bombers: Foot Soldiers of the Terrorist Movement* (8–11). Illus. 2006, Lerner LB $31.93 (978-0-7613-3470-5). Examines suicide bombers, their motivation and reasoning, and how terrorist groups recruit and train them. (Rev: BL 11/1/06; LMC 3/07) [363.325]

10710 Louis, Nancy. *Heroes of the Day* (4–7). Series: War on Terrorism. 2002, ABDO LB $25.65 (978-1-57765-658-6). This account of September 11, 2001, describes through pictures and case studies the gallant feats of firefighters, police, and those who fought back on Flight 93. (Rev: BL 5/15/02; HBG 10/02; SLJ 6/02) [973.9]

10711 Louis, Nancy. *United We Stand* (4–7). Series: War on Terrorism. 2002, ABDO LB $25.65 (978-1-57765-660-9). In text and pictures, this account describes the support offered to the victims of the terrorist attacks of September 11, 2001, and their families. (Rev: BL 5/15/02; HBG 10/02) [909.9]

10712 Margulies, Phillip. *Al-Qaeda: Osama Bin Laden's Army of Terrorists* (5–7). Illus. Series: Inside the World's Most Infamous Terrorist Organizations. 2003, Rosen LB $27.95 (978-0-8239-3817-9). Al-Qaeda's history, missions, methods, and

structure are described, with a detailed profile of Osama Bin Laden. (Rev: BL 10/15/03) [973.93]

10713 Marquette, Scott. *America Under Attack* (4–7). Illus. Series: America at War. 2002, Rourke LB $20.95 (978-1-58952-386-9). This book for middle graders explains in simple terms the September 11, 2001 attacks and other acts of terrorism against the United States, as well as discussing resulting legislation and changing opinions in America. (Rev: BL 10/15/02) [973.931]

10714 Mason, Jeff, ed. *9-11: Emergency Relief* (7–12). Illus. 2002, Alternative Comics paper $14.95 (978-1-891867-12-5). In this moving collection, some of the world's best comic book artists and writers share with readers their personal reactions to the devastating terrorist attacks of September 11, 2001. (Rev: BL 2/15/02; SLJ 4/02; VOYA 4/02)

10715 Mitch, Frank. *Understanding September 11th: Answering Questions About the Attacks on America* (7–12). Illus. 2002, Viking $16.99 (978-0-670-03582-3). A thoughtful and thought-provoking, question-and-answer look at terrorism and the forces that can provoke such attacks, with information on Islam and the history of American involvement in the Middle East. (Rev: BL 9/1/02; HBG 3/03; SLJ 9/02; VOYA 12/02) [973.931]

10716 Pellowski, Michael J. *The Terrorist Trial of the 1993 Bombing of the World Trade Center: A Headline Court Case* (6–8). Series: Headline Court Cases. 2003, Enslow LB $26.60 (978-0-7660-2045-0). After a description of the bombing itself, Pellowski describes the search for the perpetrators, the trials of the accused, and the links between Islamic fundamentalism and continuing terrorist activities. (Rev: SLJ 11/03) [974.7]

10717 Roleff, Tamara L., ed. *America Under Attack: Primary Sources* (6–12). Illus. Series: Lucent Terrorism Library. 2002, Gale LB $29.95 (978-1-59018-216-1). Interviews, speeches, articles, and other items relating to the terrorist attacks of September 11, 2001, are collected in a volume that researchers will find useful. (Rev: BL 11/1/02; SLJ 9/02) [973.931]

10718 Rosaler, Maxine. *Hamas: Palestinian Terrorists* (5–7). Illus. Series: Inside the World's Most Infamous Terrorist Organizations. 2003, Rosen LB $27.95 (978-0-8239-3820-9). Hamas's history, missions, methods, and structure are described, with profiles of key figures. (Rev: BL 10/15/03) [950.940]

10719 Ruschmann, Paul. *The War on Terror* (7–10). Series: Point/Counterpoint. 2005, Chelsea House LB $32.95 (978-0-7910-8091-7). Offers opposing views on terrorism-related topics, including preemptive wars, the suspension of human rights, and anti-terror laws. (Rev: SLJ 9/05)

10720 Sherrow, Victoria. *The Oklahoma City Bombing: Terror in the Heartland* (4–8). Illus. Series: American Disasters. 1998, Enslow LB $23.93 (978-0-7660-1061-1). Using many first-person descriptions, this account of the Oklahoma City bombing ends with the sentencing of Timothy McVeigh and Terry Nichols. (Rev: BL 1/1–15/99; HBG 3/99; SLJ 3/99) [364.16]

10721 Sherrow, Victoria. *The World Trade Center Bombing: Terror in the Towers* (4–8). Illus. Series: American Disasters. 1998, Enslow LB $23.93 (978-0-7660-1056-7). An illustrated discussion of the events and individuals leading up to the 1993 World Trade Center bombing. (Rev: BL 1/1–15/99; HBG 3/99; SLJ 3/99; VOYA 4/99) [363.2]

10722 Shields, Charles J. *The 1993 World Trade Center Bombing* (6–8). Illus. 2001, Chelsea LB $30.00 (978-0-7910-5789-6). The author delves into the whys and hows of the first World Trade Center bombing and connects it to the attack of September 11, 2001. (Rev: BL 4/15/02; HBG 10/02; SLJ 8/02) [374.1]

10723 Stewart, Gail. *America Under Attack: September 11, 2001* (6–12). Series: Lucent Terrorism Library. 2002, Gale LB $29.95 (978-1-59018-208-6). Accounts of the terrorist attacks of September 11, 2001, include disturbing eyewitness testimonies. (Rev: BL 11/1/02; SLJ 9/02) [973.931]

10724 Stewart, Gail B. *Defending the Borders: The Role of Border and Immigration Control* (7–12). Series: Lucent Library of Homeland Security. 2004, Gale LB $29.95 (978-1-59018-376-2). This account presents the difficulties in fighting terrorism and other threats while keeping our borders open. (Rev: BL 5/15/04) [364.1]

10725 Streissguth, Thomas. *Combating the Global Terrorist Threat* (6–8). Illus. Series: American War Library: The War on Terrorism. 2004, Gale LB $29.95 (978-1-59018-327-4). An overview of efforts to combat terrorism in Afghanistan, Iraq, Pakistan, the Philippines, and Saudi Arabia. (Rev: BL 8/04) [973.93]

10726 Streissguth, Thomas. *International Terrorists* (6–10). Illus. Series: Profiles. 1993, Oliver LB $19.95 (978-1-881508-07-6). This book describes the causes of international terrorism, the responsible organizations, and famous incidents. (Rev: BL 10/15/93; SLJ 1/94; VOYA 2/94) [909.82]

10727 Taylor, Robert. *The History of Terrorism* (6–12). Illus. Series: Lucent Terrorism Library. 2002, Gale LB $29.95 (978-1-59018-206-2). A chronological look at the history of terrorism around the globe, with discussion of the reasons it has been so widespread and of terrorists' motivation. Also use *Terrorists and Terrorist Groups* (2002). (Rev: BL 11/1/02; SLJ 11/02) [303.6]

10728 Torr, James D. *Responding to Attack: Firefighters and Police* (7–12). Series: Lucent Library of Homeland Security. 2004, Gale LB $29.95 (978-1-59018-375-5). This account chronicles the part that the police and firefighters can play in counteracting a terrorist attack. (Rev: BL 5/15/04) [364.1]

10729 Uschan, Michael V. *The Beslan School Siege and Separatist Terrorism* (5–8). Illus. Series: Terrorism in Today's World. 2005, World Almanac LB $186.00 (978-0-8368-6555-4). The deadly 2004 attack on a Russian school by Chechen Muslim terrorists is only the first of several attacks described in this volume on independence movements that use violence. (Rev: BL 4/1/06) [947.5]

10730 Woolf, Alex. *Terrorism: The Impact on Our Lives* (6–10). Series: 21st Century Debates. 2003, Raintree LB $28.56 (978-0-7398-6034-2). From the terror of the French Revolution (when the word first appeared) to the activities of the IRA, Hamas, the PLO, the Tamil Tigers, Basque separatists (ETA), and al Qaeda, this is an overview of terrorism and how it affects us. (Rev: SLJ 6/04)

Urban and Rural Life

10731 De Angelis, Therese. *Blackout! Cities in Darkness* (4–8). Series: American Disasters. 2003, Enslow LB $23.93 (978-0-7660-2110-5). This book chronicles the events and people involved in some of the important blackouts that have crippled America's cities. (Rev: BL 11/15/03) [307.7]

10732 Hunter, David. *Teen Life among the Amish and Other Alternative Communities: Choosing a Lifestyle* (5–8). Series: Youth in Rural North America. 2007, Mason Crest LB $22.95 (978-1-4222-0017-9). Hunter introduces readers to the traditions and beliefs of Amish and other alternative communities found around the United States and Canada (including monasteries and kibbutzim), emphasizing how teens in these groupings cope with their different lifestyles; includes many photographs. (Rev: LMC 3/08; SLJ 2/08)

10733 Leuzzi, Linda. *Urban Life* (6–9). 1995, Chelsea LB $21.95 (978-0-7910-2841-4). A look at urban life in U.S. cities a century ago, from both a contemporary perspective and the viewpoint of someone living then. (Rev: BL 7/95; SLJ 9/95) [973]

Economics and Business

General and Miscellaneous

10734 Aaseng, Nathan. *Business Builders in Sweets and Treats* (5–8). Illus. Series: Business Builders. 2005, Oliver LB $24.95 (978-1-881508-84-7). This attractive title examines food companies that succeed through satisfying America's sweet tooth. (Rev: BL 12/1/05; HBG 4/06) [338.7]

10735 Frisch, Aaron. *The Story of Nike* (6–10). Series: Built for Success. 2003, Smart Apple Media LB $19.95 (978-1-58340-295-5). Traces Nike's development from a small importer to a major internationally recognized brand, with details of successes and setbacks, celebrity endorsements, and advertising campaigns. (Rev: SLJ 7/04) [338.7]

10736 Green, Meg. *The Young Zillionaire's Guide to Investments and Savings* (5–8). Series: Be a Zillionaire. 2000, Rosen LB $23.95 (978-0-8239-3261-0). A guide to the investment markets and methods of saving with good use of examples and case studies. (Rev: HBG 10/01; SLJ 3/01) [338.5]

10737 Harman, Hollis Page. *Money $ense for Kids!* 2nd ed. (4–7). Illus. 2004, Barron's paper $14.99 (978-0-7641-2894-3). Explains the basics of money and currency and of earning, saving, and investing, with exercises at the end of each chapter and a "Money Games" section. (Rev: SLJ 11/04) [332.024]

10738 Karnes, Frances A., and Suzanne M. Bean. *Girls and Young Women Entrepreneurs: True Stories About Starting and Running a Business Plus How You Can Do It Yourself* (6–10). Illus. 1997, Free Spirit paper $12.95 (978-1-57542-022-6). This inspirational book introduces dozens of young women ages 9 to 25 who have started business ventures, and provides advice and information for young females who would also like to become entrepreneurs. (Rev: SLJ 6/98) [338]

10739 Linecker, Adelia Cellini. *What Color Is Your Piggy Bank? Entrepreneurial Ideas for Self-Starting Kids* (6–8). 2004, Lobster paper $10.95 (978-1-894222-82-2). Suggestions for making money are presented in concise chapters on topics including brainstorming, creating a business plan, advertising, and opening a bank account; tip sheets are provided for common activities such as baby sitting and dog walking. (Rev: BL 6/1–15/04; SLJ 9/04) [650.1]

10740 Oleksy, Walter. *Business and Industry* (6–12). Illus. Series: Information Revolution. 1996, Facts on File $25.00 (978-0-8160-3075-0). This book describes how companies use Powerbook computers, supercomputers, modems, and videophones to distribute information, increase productivity, and make better business decisions. (Rev: BL 2/15/96; VOYA 6/96) [650]

10741 Richardson, Adele. *The Story of Disney* (6–10). Series: Built for Success. 2003, Smart Apple Media LB $19.95 (978-1-58340-291-7). Traces Disney's development into the major internationally recognized brand it is today, with a biography of Walt Disney, a timeline of important events, discussion of Disney's influence on our lives, and mention of criticism of Disney's liberties with history. (Rev: SLJ 7/04) [384.8]

10742 Seidman, David. *The Young Zillionaire's Guide to Supply and Demand* (5–7). Series: Be a Zillionaire. 2000, Rosen LB $26.50 (978-0-8239-3264-1). The basic principles of supply and demand are explained, with information on how they are influenced by producers and consumers and how they help create economic conditions. (Rev: SLJ 2/01) [330]

10743 Thomas, Keltie. *The Kids Guide to Money Cent$* (4–7). Illus. by Stephen MacEachern. 2004, Kids Can $14.95 (978-1-55337-389-6); paper $7.95 (978-1-55337-390-2). Readers follow three children — the Money Cent$ Gang — who join together to investigate the ins and outs of banking, credit, investment, and money making; quizzes and examples make the content clear and comic-strip scenes add appeal. (Rev: SLJ 7/04) [332.02]

10744 Wilson, Antoine. *The Young Zillionaire's Guide to Distributing Goods and Services* (5–7). Series: Be a Zillionaire. 2000, Rosen LB $26.50 (978-0-8239-3259-7). This book explains how goods and services are distributed, the importance of retailing and wholesaling, how transportation affects prices and availability, and how the Internet might change these conditions. (Rev: SLJ 2/01) [330]

Economic Systems and Institutions

General and Miscellaneous

10745 Aaseng, Nathan. *You Are the Corporate Executive* (7–10). Illus. Series: Great Decisions. 1997, Oliver LB $19.95 (978-1-881508-35-9). This book describes the work of a company's CEO and the nature and consequences of the decisions that CEOs have to make. (Rev: BL 6/1–15/97; SLJ 6/97) [658.4]

10746 Downing, David. *Capitalism* (5–8). Series: Political and Economic Systems. 2002, Heinemann LB $28.50 (978-1-4034-0315-5). In an attractive format, this book explains the capitalistic economic system, its history, key thinkers, and present status. (Rev: BL 1/1–15/03; HBG 3/03; SLJ 2/03) [330.12]

10747 Downing, David. *Communism* (5–8). Series: Political and Economic Systems. 2002, Heinemann LB $28.50 (978-1-4034-0316-2). The theoretical basis of communism is explained with material on its application, history, important thinkers and leaders, and different movements. (Rev: BL 1/1–15/03; HBG 3/03; SLJ 2/03) [335.43]

10748 O'Neill, Terry, and Karin L. Swisher, eds. *Economics in America* (7–10). Series: Opposing Viewpoints. 1992, Greenhaven paper $16.20 (978-0-89908-162-5). A look at the state of the U.S. economy, the budget deficit, taxation, the banking system, and the future of labor as of 1990. (Rev: BL 6/15/92) [338.973]

10749 Trahant, LeNora B. *The Success of the Navajo Arts and Crafts Enterprise* (7–10). Illus. Series: Success. 1996, Walker LB $16.85 (978-0-8027-8337-0). After a brief history of the Navajo Nation, the author describes how the arts and crafts of the Navajos have prospered under a manufacturing and marketing cooperative. (Rev: BL 5/15/96; SLJ 7/96) [381]

Stock Exchanges

10750 Bamford, Janet. *Street Wise: A Guide for Teen Investors* (8–12). 2000, Bloomberg paper $16.95 (978-1-57660-039-9). In clear prose, the author provides excellent material for the beginning stock trader or novice with bonds and mutual funds, with fine background material and sage conservative advice. (Rev: BL 10/1/00; SLJ 3/01) [332.6]

10751 Brennan, Kristine. *The Stock Market Crash of 1929* (8–12). Series: Great Disasters: Reforms and Ramifications. 2000, Chelsea LB $21.95 (978-0-7910-5268-6). This account of the crash and its causes and aftermath looks carefully at the economy of the time and discusses the changes of a similar crash happening today. (Rev: HBG 3/01; SLJ 12/00) [338.5]

10752 Caes, Charles J. *The Young Zillionaire's Guide to the Stock Market* (5–8). Series: Be a Zillionaire. 2000, Rosen LB $26.50 (978-0-8239-3265-8). Basic information on the inner workings of the stock market is presented with many examples from the corporate world. (Rev: HBG 10/01; SLJ 3/01) [332.6]

10753 McGowan, Eileen Nixon, and Nancy Lagow Dumas. *Stock Market Smart* (5–8). Illus. 2002, Millbrook LB $23.90 (978-0-7613-2113-2). An accessible question-and-answer presentation on the stock market and different types of investors, with illustrations, tips on saving, activities, a glossary, and list of resources. (Rev: BL 9/1/02; HBG 3/03; SLJ 10/02) [332.63]

Labor Unions and Labor Problems

10754 Bender, David, and Bruno Leone, eds. *Work* (7–12). Illus. Series: Opposing Viewpoints. 1995, Greenhaven paper $16.20 (978-1-56510-218-7). A collection of essays explores problems relating to workers and society such as the education of the workforce, government intervention, and inequality in the workplace. (Rev: BL 7/95; SLJ 8/95) [331]

10755 de Ruiz, Dana C., and Richard Larios. *La Causa: The Migrant Farmworkers' Story* (4–7). Illus. by Rudy Gutierrez. 1992, Raintree LB $30.40 (978-0-8114-7231-9). The story of the founding of the United Farm Workers highlights the work of Cesar Chavez and Dolores Huerta. (Rev: BL 6/1–15/93) [331]

10756 Laughlin, Rosemary. *The Pullman Strike of 1894*. Rev. ed. (7–12). 2006, Morgan Reynolds LB $26.95 (978-1-931798-89-1). A revised edition of this engrossing account of the bitter railroad strike, with good background material on the railroad industry, the planned city of Pullman, the depression of 1893, and the personalities involved, including Eugene Debs; additions include primary source excerpts and recommended Web sites. (Rev: SLJ 5/06)

10757 McKissack, Patricia C., and Fredrick McKissack. *A Long Hard Journey* (5–9). Illus. 1989, Walker LB $18.85 (978-0-8027-6885-8). A 150-year saga of the organization of porters into the first black American union, the Brotherhood of Sleeping Car Porters. (Rev: BL 9/15/89; SLJ 1/90; VOYA 12/89) [331]

10758 Stein, R. Conrad. *The Pullman Strike and the Labor Movement in American History* (6–10). Series: In American History. 2001, Enslow LB $26.60 (978-0-7660-1300-1). This account traces the history of the 1894 strike (one of America's longest) and the parts played by President Grover Cleveland, George Pullman, Eugene Debs, and social worker Jane Addams. (Rev: BL 8/01; HBG 10/01; SLJ 5/01) [331.892]

Money and Trade

10759 Holyoke, Nancy. *A Smart Girl's Guide to Money: How to Make It, Save It, and Spend It* (4–7). Illus. by Ali Douglass. Series: A Smart Girl's Guide. 2006, Pleasant paper $9.95 (978-1-59369-103-5). Shopping and investing are only two of the topics covered in this user-friendly guide. (Rev: BL 5/15/06; SLJ 5/06) [332.024]

10760 January, Brendan. *Globalize It!* (8–12). Illus. 2003, Millbrook LB $26.90 (978-0-7613-2417-1). The continuing advance of globalization and arguments for and against this phenomenon are thoughtfully examined in this accessible overview. (Rev: BL 1/1–15/04; SLJ 5/04) [337]

10761 Kummer, Patricia K. *Currency* (4–8). Series: Inventions That Shaped the World. 2004, Watts LB $30.50 (978-0-531-12341-6). After looking at the nature of currency, this title discusses modern forms and the role of currency in our lives. (Rev: SLJ 2/05) [332.4]

10762 Menhard, Francha Roffe. *Teen Consumer Smarts: Shop, Save, and Steer Clear of Scams* (7–12). Series: Teen Issues. 2002, Enslow LB $22.60 (978-0-7660-1667-5). A useful guide to money management that recommends regular saving and alerts readers to the dangers of credit cards

and fraudulent scams. (Rev: HBG 3/03; SLJ 1/03) [332.024]

10763 Resnick, Abraham. *Money* (6–8). Series: Overview. 1995, Lucent LB $29.95 (978-1-56006-165-6). A history of money from ancient times when barter was used to today, when the movement is toward a cashless society and the elimination of money. (Rev: BL 7/95) [332.4]

10764 *Sold! The Origins of Money and Trade* (5–8). Series: Buried Worlds. 1994, Runestone LB $28.75 (978-0-8225-3206-4). Explains the world origins of commerce and money, with coverage of how the earliest coins were made in the West and how other cultures developed unique forms of currency. (Rev: BL 9/15/94; SLJ 9/94) [737.4]

Marketing and Advertising

10765 Day, Nancy. *Advertising: Information or Manipulation?* (6–12). Series: Issues in Focus. 1999, Enslow LB $26.60 (978-0-7660-1106-9). In addition to presenting an introduction to advertising, its history, and its impact on U.S. society, this book questions many advertising practices, provides information on advertising methods and targeting, and offers tips on how to evaluate advertising critically. (Rev: BL 7/99) [659.1]

10766 Graydon, Shari. *Made You Look: How Advertising Works and Why You Should Know* (5–9). Illus. by Warren Clark. 2003, Annick $24.95 (978-1-55037-815-3); paper $14.95 (978-1-55037-814-6). The 8- to 14-year-old age group is an advertising target, and this title teaches readers to recognize the various techniques used and to assess products' value. (Rev: BL 12/1/03*; SLJ 12/03) [659.1]

10767 Mierau, Christina. *Accept No Substitutes! The History of American Advertising* (6–9). 2000, Lerner $26.60 (978-0-8225-1742-9). A social history of advertising in America starting with early handbills and progressing through catalogues and television to the Internet. (Rev: BCCB 6/00; BL 7/00; HBG 9/00; SLJ 9/00) [659.1]

10768 Petley, Julian. *Advertising* (7–10). Illus. Series: MediaWise. 2003, Smart Apple LB $28.50 (978-1-58340-255-9). A good introduction to the world of advertising, with discussion of creative and financial concerns. (Rev: BL 10/15/03; HBG 4/04; SLJ 11/03) [659.1]

Guidance and Personal Development

Education and Schools

10769 Armstrong, Thomas. *You're Smarter Than You Think: A Kid's Guide to Multiple Intelligences* (5–8). 2003, Free Spirit paper $15.95 (978-1-57542-113-1). Eight different intelligences are defined in understandable terms, with quizzes that help readers investigate their own strengths. (Rev: BL 4/15/03; SLJ 6/03; VOYA 6/03) [153.9]

10770 Banfield, Susan. *The Bakke Case: Quotas in College Admissions* (6–10). Series: Landmark Supreme Court Cases. 1998, Enslow LB $26.60 (978-0-89490-968-9). The court case that challenged quotas in higher education to correct racial inequality is chronicled in this dramatic account that gives good background information. (Rev: BL 2/15/98; SLJ 6/98) [378]

10771 Bluestein, Jane, and Eric D. Katz. *High School's Not Forever* (8–12). Illus. 2005, Health Communications paper $12.95 (978-0-7573-0256-5). High school students talk about their experiences in high school, covering a range of typical problems plus some of the joys of those years. (Rev: SLJ 1/06) [373.18]

10772 Cruz, Barbara C. *School Dress Codes: A Pro/Con Issue* (6–10). Series: Hot Pro/Con Issues. 2001, Enslow LB $27.93 (978-0-7660-1465-7). Cruz presents the case for and against dress codes from the students' and the adults' points of view. (Rev: HBG 3/02; SLJ 7/01) [371.8]

10773 Cruz, Barbara C. *Separate Sexes, Separate Schools* (7–10). Illus. Series: Hot Pro/Con Issues. 2000, Enslow LB $27.93 (978-0-7660-1366-7). This examination of the issues connected with same-sex schools is well organized and presents differing points of view on this complex topic. (Rev: BCCB 10/00; BL 2/1/01; HBG 3/01; SLJ 12/00; VOYA 6/01) [371.82]

10774 Davidson, Tish. *School Conflict* (4–8). Series: Life Balance. 2003, Watts LB $20.50 (978-0-531-12251-8); paper $6.95 (978-0-531-15571-4). This book examines the various conflicts, including violence, that exist in public education today and how these affect the lives and mental health of students. (Rev: BL 10/15/03; SLJ 3/04) [370]

10775 Farrell, Juliana, and Beth Mayall. *Middle School: The Real Deal* (5–7). Illus. 2001, HarperCollins paper $7.99 (978-0-380-81313-1). Advice on coping with school work, teachers, and social life is presented in an appealing format. (Rev: BL 6/1–15/01; VOYA 8/01) [373.18]

10776 Feldman, Ruth Tenzer. *Don't Whistle in School: The History of America's Public Schools* (6–10). Illus. 2001, Lerner LB $26.60 (978-0-8225-1745-0). A broad overview of American public education that includes everything from regional differences to education trends and landmark court rulings, with illustrations and photographs. (Rev: BL 11/1/01; HBG 3/02; SLJ 11/01; VOYA 4/02) [370]

10777 Greene, Rebecca. *The Teenagers' Guide to School Outside the Box* (8–12). Illus. 2000, Free Spirit paper $15.95 (978-1-57542-087-5). Many learning opportunities are available to teens, including travel, volunteer work, serving as an intern or apprentice, mentoring, and job shadowing. (Rev: BL 2/15/01; SLJ 3/01; VOYA 4/01) [373.2]

10778 Hurwitz, Sue. *High Performance Through Effective Scheduling* (8–12). Illus. Series: Learning-a-Living Library. 1996, Rosen LB $27.95 (978-0-8239-2204-8). This book discusses the basic skill of scheduling time and how it helps students at school, in extracurricular activities, and on the job. (Rev: BL 8/96; SLJ 12/96; VOYA 2/97) [640]

10779 Pendleton, Scott. *The Ultimate Guide to Student Contests, Grades 7–12* (6–12). Illus. 1997, Walker paper $15.95 (978-0-8027-7512-2). This is a guide to various academically oriented contests open to young adults, arranged by such subjects as mathematics and foreign languages. (Rev: BL 8/97) [373.18]

10780 Pickering, Marianne. *Lessons for Life: Education and Learning* (5–8). Series: Our Human Family. 1995, Blackbirch LB $27.45 (978-1-56711-127-9). A look at educational practices around the world that shows great similarities regardless of the culture. (Rev: SLJ 1/96) [370]

10781 Schneider, Meg. *Help! My Teacher Hates Me* (5–8). 1994, Workman paper $7.95 (978-1-56305-492-1). Helpful hints for developing a positive attitude in school. (Rev: BL 3/15/95) [371.8]

10782 Williams, Heidi. *Homeschooling* (7–10). Series: At Issue: Education. 2007, Gale LB $29.95 (978-0-7377-3685-4); paper $21.20 (978-0-7377-3686-1). The controversial practice of homeschooling is examined in 13 articles that look at both sides of such questions as academic worth and the possibility of government involvement. (Rev: BL 3/3/08) [370.04]

10783 Williams, Mary E., ed. *Education: Region Under Siege* (8–12). Series: Opposing Viewpoints. 1999, Greenhaven LB $32.45 (978-0-7377-0125-8). School choice, multicultural education, and educational reforms are three of the topics covered in this collection of different points of view on the subject of education. (Rev: BL 11/15/99) [370]

Development of Academic Skills

Study Skills

10784 Heiligman, Deborah. *The New York Public Library Kid's Guide to Research* (5–8). Illus. by David Cain. 1998, Scholastic paper $14.95 (978-0-590-30715-4). A fine introduction to research techniques including material on taking notes, using print and nonprint resources, conducting interviews and surveys, searching the Internet, and locating toll-free numbers. (Rev: HBG 3/99; SLJ 2/99) [808.023]

10785 Nathan, Amy. *Surviving Homework: Tips from Teens* (5–8). Illus. 1997, Millbrook LB $24.90 (978-1-56294-185-7). Using answers on questionnaires given to high school juniors and seniors, this book supplies many useful study tips and suggestions on how to organize one's time. (Rev: BL 6/1–15/97; SLJ 7/97) [372.12]

10786 Schumm, Jeanne Shay. *School Power: Strategies for Succeeding in School* (5–8). Illus. 1992, Free Spirit paper $15.95 (978-0-915793-42-6). Sen-sible suggestions for improving study skills: organization, note taking, improving reading, and writing reports. (Rev: BL 3/1/93) [371.3]

10787 Simpson, Carolyn. *High Performance Through Organizing Information* (8–12). Illus. Series: Learning-a-Living Library. 1996, Rosen LB $27.95 (978-0-8239-2207-9). This book discusses the importance of an organized work environment, whether in school, at home, or on the job, and how to create one using filing systems, to-do lists, data sources, and other strategies. (Rev: BL 8/96; SLJ 8/96; VOYA 2/97) [640]

Tests and Test Taking

10788 Kern, Roy, and Richard Smith. *The Grade Booster Guide for Kids* (7–9). 1987, Hilton Thomas paper $7.95 (978-0-944162-00-2). This book covers the proper strategies and techniques to use for successful test-taking. [371.3]

Writing and Speaking Skills

10789 Asher, Sandy. *Where Do You Get Your Ideas? Helping Young Writers Begin* (5–7). Illus. 1987, Walker LB $13.85 (978-0-8027-6691-5). Keeping a journal and other interesting ideas for would-be journalists. (Rev: BCCB 12/87; BL 9/15/87; SLJ 9/87) [808.02]

10790 Bauer, Marion Dane. *What's Your Story? A Young Person's Guide to Writing Fiction* (5–10). 1992, Clarion paper $7.95 (978-0-395-57780-6). An award-winning writer gives advice to young authors, including suggestions for planning, writing, and revising. (Rev: BL 4/15/92; SLJ 6/92*) [808.3]

10791 Bauer, Marion Dane. *A Writer's Story from Life to Fiction* (5–8). 1995, Clarion $14.95 (978-0-395-72094-3); paper $6.95 (978-0-395-75053-7). Readers and aspiring writers will enjoy this famous author's explanations of how she draws on her own experiences to develop her works. (Rev: BL 9/15/95; SLJ 10/95; VOYA 2/96) [813]

10792 Bentley, Nancy, and Donna Guthrie. *Writing Mysteries, Movies, Monster Stories, and More* (5–8). Illus. 2001, Millbrook LB $24.90 (978-0-7613-1452-3). This book gives solid information on all kinds of fictional writing, including novels, short stories, fantasy, science fiction, humor, and even movie scripts. (Rev: BL 3/15/01; HBG 10/01; SLJ 4/01; VOYA 8/01) [808]

10793 Betz, Adrienne, comp. *Scholastic Treasury of Quotations for Children* (4–8). 1998, Scholastic paper $16.95 (978-0-590-27146-2). From Socrates to Bill Clinton, this is a useful compendium of quotations arranged under 75 subjects. (Rev: SLJ 2/99) [080]

716

10794 Block, Francesca L., and Hillary Carlip. *Zine Scene: The Do-It-Yourself Guide to Zines* (8–12). Illus. 1998, Girl Pr. paper $14.95 (978-0-9659754-3-8). This is a step-by-step guide to producing one's own magazine, from getting started and writing to layout, production, and marketing. (Rev: VOYA 8/99) [808]

10795 Bodart, Joni Richards. *The World's Best Thin Books: What to Read When Your Book Report Is Due Tomorrow* (6–12). 2000, Scarecrow paper $16.95 (978-1-57886-007-4). For each of the books listed, the author provides background material, themes, characters, and possible book talk or book report ideas. (Rev: BL 1/1–15/00) [028.1]

10796 Cibula, Matt. *How to Be the Greatest Writer in the World* (4–8). Illus. by Brian Strassburg. 1999, Zino $11.95 (978-1-55933-276-7). A spiral-bound book that presents 88 interesting and engaging exercises to help youngsters who feel they have nothing to write about. (Rev: SLJ 2/00) [808]

10797 Craig, Steve. *Sports Writing: A Beginner's Guide* (6–12). Illus. 2002, Discover Writing paper $15.00 (978-0-9656574-9-5). A fine introduction to writing news and features about sports, to conducting good interviews, and to the training of journalists. (Rev: BL 9/1/02; VOYA 4/03) [070.449]

10798 Detz, Joan. *You Mean I Have to Stand Up and Say Something?* (7–12). 1986, Macmillan LB $13.95 (978-0-689-31221-2). An entertaining guide to effective speaking and overcoming the fear of facing an audience. (Rev: BCCB 2/87; BL 2/87; SLJ 3/87) [808.5]

10799 Dubrovin, Vivian. *Storytelling Adventures: Stories Kids Can Tell* (4–7). Illus. by Bobbi Shupe. 1997, Storycraft paper $14.95 (978-0-9638339-2-1). This book not only includes a selection of stories to tell but also suggests appropriate props to use, with directions on how to make them. (Rev: SLJ 5/97) [808.5]

10800 Dubrovin, Vivian. *Storytelling for the Fun of It* (4–8). Illus. by Bobbi Shupe. 1994, Storycraft paper $16.95 (978-0-9638339-0-7). This useful guide is divided into three parts that give general information, where and what kinds of stories to tell, and how to learn and perform them. (Rev: SLJ 4/94) [808.5]

10801 Estepa, Andrea, and Philip Kay, eds. *Starting with "I": Personal Essays by Teenagers* (7–12). 1997, Persea paper $13.95 (978-0-89255-228-3). This is a collection of 35 brief essays written by teenagers about their families, neighborhoods, race, and culture. (Rev: BL 9/15/97; SLJ 10/97; VOYA 10/97) [305.235]

10802 Fletcher, Ralph. *How to Write Your Life Story* (5–8). 2007, HarperCollins $15.99 (978-0-06-050770-1); paper $5.99 (978-0-06-050769-5). Writing exercises and examples will help readers to get started on autobiographies or memoirs. (Rev: BL 10/1/07; SLJ 11/07) [808]

10803 Fletcher, Ralph. *How Writers Work: Finding a Process That Works for You* (4–8). 2000, HarperTrophy paper $4.99 (978-0-380-79702-8). Using a conversational style, the author explains the process of writing with material on brainstorming, rough drafts, revising, proofreading, and publishing. (Rev: SLJ 12/00) [808]

10804 Fletcher, Ralph. *Poetry Matters: Writing a Poem from the Inside Out* (4–7). 2002, HarperTrophy paper $5.99 (978-0-380-79703-5). A how-to book for young poets, with ideas on how to make images and "music" with words. (Rev: BL 5/15/02; HBG 10/02; SLJ 2/02*) [808.1]

10805 Friedman, Lauri S., ed. *Racism* (7–12). Series: Writing the Critical Essay. 2006, Gale LB $26.20 (978-0-7377-3464-5). Essays on racism that originally appeared in an Opposing Viewpoints volume help students research, draft, and edit effective papers on this topic. (Rev: SLJ 9/06)

10806 Gaines, Ann Graham. *Don't Steal Copyrighted Stuff!* (5–10). Illus. 2008, Enslow LB $28.95 (978-0-7660-2861-6). Students who don't see the harm in cutting and pasting from the Internet will discover that plagiarism can ruin reputations and careers; the story of a writer who got caught brings this truth home, and there are plenty of practical tips on keeping one's work original. (Rev: BL 4/1/08; LMC 3/08) [808]

10807 Graham, Paula W. *Speaking of Journals: Children's Book Writers Talk About Their Diaries, Notebooks and Sketchbooks* (5–8). Illus. 1999, Boyds Mills paper $14.95 (978-1-56397-741-1). A book that discusses the how-tos and the rewards of keeping a personal journal, and features interviews with 27 writers including Jim Arnosky, Pam Conrad, and Jean George. (Rev: BL 3/1/99; SLJ 5/99; VOYA 2/00) [818]

10808 Guthrie, Donna, and Nancy Bentley. *The Young Journalist's Book: How to Write and Produce Your Own Newspaper* (4–7). Illus. 1998, Millbrook $24.40 (978-0-7613-0360-2). The authors explain what a journalist does and, in addition to explaining the parts of a newspaper, tells how to start one. (Rev: BL 3/1/99; HBG 3/99; SLJ 12/98) [070.1]

10809 Hambleton, Vicki, and Cathleen Greenwood. *So, You Wanna Be a Writer? How to Write, Get Published, and Maybe Even Make It Big!* (5–9). Illus. by Laura Eldridge and Corey Mistretta. Series: So, You Wanna Be. 2001, Beyond Words paper $8.95 (978-1-58270-043-4). Practical advice is offered in straightforward text with lots of examples, sample letters, interviews with published writers, details of writing contests, and lists of magazines that accept submissions from young writers. (Rev: SLJ 10/01; VOYA 2/02) [808]

10810 Hamilton, Fran Santoro. *Hands-On English* (4–8). Illus. 1998, Portico paper $9.95 (978-0-9664867-0-4). A user-friendly volume that takes a visual approach to illustrate sentence patterns, such as using icons to represent the eight parts of speech, with clear, interesting explanations. Also included are irregular verbs, using modifiers, spelling rules, punctuation and capitalization, homonyms, and how to make outlines. (Rev: SLJ 2/99; VOYA 4/99) [415]

10811 Hamilton, Martha, and Mitch Weiss. *Stories in My Pocket: Tales Kids Can Tell* (4–7). Illus. 1997, Fulcrum paper $15.95 (978-1-55591-957-3). This handbook of storytelling for young storytellers includes 30 tales to begin with. (Rev: BL 1/1–15/97) [372.6]

10812 Hamlett, Christina. *Screenwriting for Teens: The 100 Principles of Screenwriting Every Budding Writer Must Know* (8–12). 2006, Michael Wiese paper $18.95 (978-1-932907-18-6). Practical, friendly advice for screenwriting wannabes. (Rev: SLJ 2/07)

10813 Harmon, Charles, ed. *Using the Internet, Online Services, and CD-ROMs for Writing Research and Term Papers* (7–12). Illus. Series: NetGuide. 1996, Neal-Schuman paper $32.95 (978-1-55570-238-0). This book shows all of the steps in writing a report, from selecting and narrowing a topic to collecting information electronically to preparing the final copy. (Rev: BL 4/15/96; SLJ 6/97) [371.2]

10814 James, Elizabeth, and Carol Barkin. *How to Write a Term Paper* (7–12). 1980, Lothrop paper $3.95 (978-0-688-45025-0). A practical step-by-step approach to report writing that uses many examples. [808]

10815 James, Elizabeth, and Carol Barkin. *How to Write Super School Reports*. Rev. ed. (4–9). Series: A School Survival Guide Book. 1998, Lothrop $15.00 (978-0-688-16132-3). This research guide takes readers through the steps involved in writing a research paper with material on choosing a topic, finding facts, using a library, organizing notes, and putting the report together. (Rev: HBG 3/99; SLJ 2/99) [808.023]

10816 Janeczko, Paul B. *How to Write Poetry* (4–8). Series: Scholastic Guides. 1999, Scholastic paper $12.95 (978-0-590-10077-9). An enthusiastic, clearly written how-to manual that uses many examples from well-known poems. (Rev: BL 3/15/99; HBG 10/99; SLJ 7/99; VOYA 8/99) [808.1]

10817 Janeczko, Paul B., comp. *Poetry from A to Z: A Guide for Young Writers* (4–8). Illus. Series: Net-Guide. 1994, Simon & Schuster $16.95 (978-0-02-747672-9). This book of 72 poems, alphabetized by topic, gives examples to get young writers started,

and the 23 poets represented give advice on how to become a better poet. (Rev: BCCB 3/95; BL 12/15/94; VOYA 5/95) [808.1]

10818 Janeczko, Paul B., ed. *Seeing the Blue Between: Advice and Inspiration for Young Poets* (7–10). 2002, Candlewick $17.99 (978-0-7636-0881-1). More than 30 poets who write for young people give advice on writing, reading, and simply enjoying poetry, with selected poems and biographical information. (Rev: BL 3/15/02; HB 7–8/02; HBG 10/02; SLJ 5/02; VOYA 6/02) [811]

10819 Mlynowski, Sarah, and Farrin Jacobs. *See Jane Write: A Girl's Guide to Writing Chick Lit* (8–12). Illus. by Chuck Gonzalez. 2006, Quirk paper $14.95 (978-1-59474-115-9). Girls who love "chick lit" and who want to take advantage of its popularity will enjoy this practical and readable guide. (Rev: SLJ 9/06)

10820 Nobleman, Marc Tyler. *Extraordinary E-Mails, Letters, and Resumes* (5–8). Illus. by Kevin Pope. Series: F. W. Prep. 2005, Watts LB $31.00 (978-0-531-16759-5). Advice for students who want to write effective e-mails, letters, and resumés, with an explanation of the importance of communicating clearly. (Rev: SLJ 1/06) [808]

10821 Otfinoski, Steven. *Speaking Up, Speaking Out: A Kid's Guide to Making Speeches, Oral Reports, and Conversation* (5–8). Illus. 1996, Millbrook LB $24.90 (978-1-56294-345-5). All kinds of public-speaking situations are introduced, with suggestions on how to be a success at each. (Rev: BL 1/1–15/97; SLJ 1/97) [808.5]

10822 Rosen, Lucy. *High Performance Through Communicating Information* (8–12). Illus. Series: Learning-a-Living Library. 1996, Rosen LB $27.95 (978-0-8239-2201-7). Such communication skills as writing and speaking are discussed, with tips on how to improve them and apply them effectively. (Rev: BL 8/96; SLJ 3/97; VOYA 2/97) [153.6]

10823 Rosinsky, Natalie M. *Write Your Own Biography* (4–8). Series: Write Your Own. 2007, Compass Point LB $31.93 (978-0-7565-3366-3). A helpful guide to writing a biography with excerpts from published works and writing exercises. (Rev: SLJ 12/07) [808]

10824 Sullivan, Helen, and Linda Sernoff. *Research Reports: A Guide for Middle and High School Students* (6–10). 1996, Millbrook LB $24.90 (978-1-56294-694-4). A well-organized, concise book on writing reports that covers each step from selecting a topic to compiling the final bibliography. (Rev: SLJ 9/96) [372.6]

10825 Terban, Marvin. *Checking Your Grammar* (5–8). Series: Scholastic Guides. 1993, Scholastic paper $10.95 (978-0-590-49454-0). An attractive, witty guide to effective writing of all sorts of letters, book reports, essays, and reviews. (Rev: BL 10/1/93; SLJ 2/94) [428.2]

10826 Terban, Marvin. *Punctuation Power: Punctuation and How to Use It* (4–9). Illus. by Eric Brace. 2000, Scholastic paper $12.95 (978-0-590-38673-9). After a description of each punctuation mark and its uses, this account covers topics including bibliographies, quotations, play scripts, and sentences, and the kinds of punctuation they require. (Rev: SLJ 7/00) [410]

10827 Veljkovic, Peggy, and Arthur Schwartz, eds. *Writing from the Heart: Young People Share Their Wisdom* (5–9). 2001, Templeton Foundation paper $12.95 (978-1-890151-48-5). A collection of the best essays by young people that have been submitted to the Laws of Life program since it began in 1987. (Rev: SLJ 6/01) [170]

10828 Vinton, Ken. *Alphabet Antics: Hundreds of Activities to Challenge and Enrich Letter Learners of All Ages* (5–8). Illus. by author. 1996, Free Spirit paper $19.95 (978-0-915793-98-3). For each letter of the alphabet, there is a history, how it appears in different alphabets, important words that begin with that letter, a quotation from someone whose name starts with it, and a number of interesting related projects. (Rev: SLJ 1/97) [411]

10829 Waldo, Dixie. *Persuasive Speaking* (6–10). Illus. 2007, Rosen LB $19.95 (978-1-4042-1028-8). Tips for debaters will also be helpful to teams and individuals who speak in front of groups. (Rev: BL 4/1/07) [808.5]

10830 Wilber, Jessica. *Totally Private and Personal: Journaling Ideas for Girls and Young Women* (7–12). 1996, Free Spirit paper $9.95 (978-1-57542-005-9). The author, 14 years old when she wrote this book, offers advice for keeping a journal, including how, why, and what to put in it, with examples from her own journal. (Rev: VOYA 2/97) [808]

10831 Williams, Mary E. *Global Warming* (7–12). Illus. Series: Writing the Critical Essay. 2006, Gale LB $26.20 (978-0-7377-3210-8). Essays on global warming are presented along with questions to encourage students to evaluate their effectiveness; instructions for researching and editing a persuasive essay are included too. (Rev: SLJ 10/06)

10832 Wooldridge, Susan Goldsmith. *Poemcrazy: Freeing Your Life with Words* (6–12). 1996, Clarkson N. Potter paper $13.00 (978-0-609-80098-0). The author tries to show young people how to free their minds and spirits to write poetry and shares her own poetic experiences and inspirations as well as those of other poets. (Rev: VOYA 12/97) [811]

10833 Young, Sue. *Writing with Style* (5–8). Series: Scholastic Guides. 1997, Scholastic $12.95 (978-0-590-50977-0). A guide for the novice writer, with chapters on planning, presenting, and publishing one's work. (Rev: BL 3/1/97; SLJ 5/97) [372.6]

Academic Guidance

General and Miscellaneous

10834 Lieberman, Susan A. *The Real High School Handbook: How to Survive, Thrive, and Prepare for What's Next* (8–12). 1997, Houghton paper $13.00 (978-0-395-79760-0). A book of tips about prospering in high school and making it enjoyable, with material on topics including grade points, testing, course selection, and getting into a college. (Rev: BL 10/15/97) [373.18]

Colleges and Universities

10835 Funk, Gary. *A Balancing Act: Sports and Education* (5–8). Illus. Series: Sports Issues. 1995, Lerner LB $28.75 (978-0-8225-3301-6). A frank, thorough discussion of the many issues involved in sports and their place in educational institutions. (Rev: BL 1/1–15/96; SLJ 9/95) [796.04]

Scholarships and Financial Aid

10836 Karnes, Frances A., and Tracy L. Riley. *Competitions for Talented Kids: Win Scholarships, Big Prize Money, and Recognition* (7–10). 2005, Prufrock paper $17.95 (978-1-59363-156-7). More than 140 competitions covering a number of academic subjects, the performing arts, and leadership are listed alphabetically, with brief advice on entering these contests. (Rev: BL 12/1/05) [371.95]

10837 Minnis, Whitney. *How to Get an Athletic Scholarship: A Student-Athlete's Guide to Collegiate Athletics* (6–12). 1995, ASI paper $12.95 (978-0-9645153-0-7). Basic information on athletic scholarships and the recruitment process, plus tips on training and academic considerations. (Rev: BL 2/1/96) [796]

Careers and Occupational Guidance

General and Miscellaneous

10838 McGlothlin, Bruce. *High Performance Through Understanding Systems* (7–10). Series: Learning-a-Living Library. 1996, Rosen LB $27.95 (978-0-8239-2210-9). Aimed primarily at youths preparing to enter the world of work directly after graduation, this book explains systems ("any combination of elements that operate together and form a whole") in the family, at school, and at work, and tells how individuals can diagnose problems, predict outcomes, and improve the systems. (Rev: SLJ 3/97) [001.6]

10839 Reber, Deborah. *In Their Shoes: Extraordinary Women Describe Their Amazing Careers* (8–12). Illus. Series: The Real Deal. 2007, Simon & Schuster paper $12.99 (978-1-4169-2578-1). Girls will be inspired to pursue any career they want to after reading these accounts of women and the jobs they love, from sheriff to librarian, and their daily tasks. (Rev: BL 4/1/07; LMC 8–9/07; SLJ 5/07*) [331.4092]

10840 Strazzabosco, Jeanne M. *High Performance Through Dealing with Diversity* (8–12). Illus. Series: Learning-a-Living Library. 1996, Rosen LB $27.95 (978-0-8239-2202-4). Through applying attitudes of tolerance and positive feelings, this book prepares students to work with diverse populations in a multicultural workplace. (Rev: BL 8/96) [650.1]

Careers

General and Miscellaneous

10841 Alagna, Magdalena. *War Correspondents: Life Under Fire* (5–10). Series: Extreme Careers. 2003, Rosen LB $26.50 (978-0-8239-3798-1). The dangers of wartime assignments are emphasized in this volume that also stresses job requirements that include a good education and broad knowledge of world events. (Rev: BL 9/15/03; SLJ 11/03) [808]

10842 Bowman-Kruhm, Mary. *Careers in Child Care* (7–12). Series: Careers Library. 2000, Rosen LB $31.95 (978-0-8239-2891-0). A comprehensive, accessible overview of the types of jobs that are available for people who enjoy working with children, with practical guidance on finding employment. (Rev: HBG 10/01; SLJ 3/01)

10843 *Broadcasting*. 2nd ed. (7–12). Series: Careers in Focus. 2002, Ferguson LB $22.95 (978-0-89434-440-4). Careers in animation, lighting, reporting, editing, and weather forecasting are just a few of those covered in this concise introduction to the world of broadcasting and its educational requirements, employment outlook, and potential salaries. Also use *Fashion* (2002). (Rev: SLJ 7/01) [384.54]

10844 Burns, Monique. *Cool Careers Without College for People Who Love to Make Things Grow* (6–9). Series: Cool Careers Without College. 2004, Rosen LB $33.25 (978-0-8239-3789-9). Explores careers such as landscaper and soil conservationist that do not require college degrees, with application advice and information about activities on the job. (Rev: SLJ 10/04)

10845 Camelo, Wilson. *The U.S. Air Force and Military Careers* (7–10). Series: U.S. Armed Forces and Military Careers. 2006, Enslow LB $23.95 (978-0-7660-2524-0). Traces the history of the U.S. Air Force, its structure, its contributions to U.S. defense and major wars, recent operations, and the various career opportunities within the organization. (Rev: BL 10/15/06) [358.400973]

10846 Cefrey, Holly. *Archaeologists: Life Digging Up Artifacts* (5–10). Series: Extreme Careers. 2004, Rosen LB $26.50 (978-0-8239-3963-3). This is an introduction to the field of archeology, its problems, its opportunities, and its rewards. (Rev: BL 5/15/04) [930]

10847 Colbert, Judy. *Career Opportunities in the Travel Industry* (8–12). Series: Career Opportunities. 2004, Ferguson $49.50 (978-0-8160-4864-9). A quick overview of the wide number of opportunities in the travel industry, providing an outline of duties, salary ranges, employment outlook, required education and training, and so forth. (Rev: SLJ 7/04) [331.7]

10848 Coon, Nora E. *Teen Dream Jobs: How to Find the Job You Really Want Now!* (8–12). 2004, Beyond Words paper $9.95 (978-1-58270-093-9). Written by a teen, this is a reader-friendly guide that refers teens to online career-choice quizzes, gives advice on job-finding activities, and suggests possible careers and ways to enter them. (Rev: SLJ 6/04)

10849 Devantier, Alecia T., and Carol A. Turkington. *Extraordinary Jobs for Adventurers* (8–12). 2006, Ferguson $35 (978-0-8160-5852-5). Careers for the adventurous are found in fields including logging, vulcanology, and white-water rafting, according to this guide that gives worker profiles. Also use *Extraordinary Jobs for Creative People* and *Extraordinary Jobs in Agriculture and Nature* (both 2006). (Rev: SLJ 1/07)

10850 Duncan, Jane Caryl. *Careers in Veterinary Medicine* (8–12). Illus. 1994, Rosen LB $16.95 (978-0-8239-1678-8); paper $9.95 (978-0-8239-1719-8). A veterinarian gives an honest description of her profession and many practical tips. (Rev: BL 9/1/88; SLJ 10/88; VOYA 10/88) [636.089]

10851 *Food* (5–9). Series: Discovering Careers for Your Future. 2005, Ferguson $21.95 (978-0-8160-5848-8). Education and training, salaries, and outlook for the field are all covered here along with a description of the kinds of daily activities found in various positions. (Rev: SLJ 1/06)

10852 Frydenborg, Kay. *They Dreamed of Horses: Careers for Horse Lovers* (6–9). 1994, Walker LB $16.85 (978-0-8027-8284-7). Suggests career possibilities that involve working with horses, telling the stories of 13 women who love and work with them. (Rev: BL 7/94; SLJ 7/94; VOYA 8/94) [636.1]

10853 Giacobello, John. *Careers in the Fashion Industry* (7–12). Series: Exploring Careers. 1999, Rosen LB $18.95 (978-0-8239-2890-3). This book explains what it takes to get started in a variety of fashion-related careers, and includes tips on writing résumés, interviewing, and so forth. (Rev: SLJ 2/00) [746.9]

10854 Greenberger, Robert. *Cool Careers Without College for People Who Love to Drive* (8–12). Series: Cool Careers Without College. 2004, Rosen LB $33.25 (978-0-8239-3786-8). Benefits and disadvantages of this kind of work, education and

training, salary outlook, and a description of on-the-job activities are provided for a number of career choices, both working for others and as an entrepreneur. (Rev: SLJ 5/04)

10855 Haegele, Katie. *Nature Lovers* (7–12). Series: Cool Careers Without College. 2002, Rosen $33.25 (978-0-8239-3504-8). Jobs profiled here include Christmas tree farmer, ranch hand, fisherman, park ranger, and river guide, with accompanying information on training, pay, opportunities, and related occupations. (Rev: BL 5/15/02; SLJ 7/02) [331.7]

10856 Hayhurst, Chris. *Astronauts: Life Exploring Outer Space* (4–7). Series: Extreme Careers. 2001, Rosen LB $26.50 (978-0-8239-3364-8). A high-interest look at the extensive skills required to become an astronaut, with brief coverage of space exploration and profiles of astronauts. (Rev: SLJ 1/02) [629]

10857 Hayhurst, Chris. *Cool Careers Without College for Animal Lovers* (7–12). Illus. Series: Cool Careers Without College. 2002, Rosen LB $33.25 (978-0-8239-3500-0). Veterinary technician, groomer, and pet photographer are some of the options explored in this book that gives information on training and on-the-job activities. (Rev: BL 5/15/02; SLJ 7/02) [636]

10858 Hinton, Kerry. *Cool Careers Without College for People Who Love Food* (8–12). Series: Cool Careers Without College. 2004, Rosen LB $33.25 (978-0-8239-3787-5). Benefits and disadvantages of this kind of work, education and training, salary outlook, and a description of on-the-job activities are provided for a number of career choices, both working for others and as an entrepreneur. (Rev: SLJ 5/04)

10859 *History* (4–8). Illus. Series: Discovering Careers for Your Future. 2001, Ferguson LB $21.95 (978-0-89434-391-9). A useful introduction to the career opportunities in this field, with information on the skills required, potential earnings, and job outlook. (Rev: SLJ 11/01) [331.702]

10860 Hurwitz, Jane. *Choosing a Career in Animal Care* (4–8). Illus. Series: World of Work. 1996, Rosen LB $17.95 (978-0-8239-2268-0). Various careers in working with animals are described, along with the education required, desirable character traits, and ways to break into the field. (Rev: SLJ 8/97) [371.7]

10861 Jackson, Donna M. *ER Vets: Life in an Animal Emergency Room* (5–8). Illus. 2005, Houghton $17.00 (978-0-618-43663-7). With many photos, this is a behind-the-scenes look at life in a veterinary emergency clinic and the frustrations and joys to be found working there. (Rev: BL 11/1/05; SLJ 1/06*) [636.089]

10862 Jacobs, Shannon K. *Healers of the Wild: People Who Care for Injured and Orphaned Wildlife*

(4–7). Illus. 1998, Coyote Moon paper $19.95 (978-0-9661070-0-5). The process of helping orphaned, injured, or displaced wildlife is covered thoroughly under three operational headings: rescue, rehabilitation, and release. (Rev: BL 10/1/98) [339.946]

10863 Jaspersohn, William. *A Week in the Life of an Airline Pilot* (4–8). Illus. 1991, Little, Brown $14.95 (978-0-316-45822-1). A close-up look at the duties and lives of members of an airline crew. (Rev: BL 3/15/91; HB 5–6/91; SLJ 5/91) [629.132]

10864 Lee, Barbara. *Working with Animals* (4–8). Illus. Series: Exploring Careers. 1996, Lerner LB $23.93 (978-0-8225-1759-7). Profiles of 12 careers involving animals, such as veterinarian, animal shelter worker, or pet sitter. (Rev: BL 2/15/97) [591]

10865 Lytle, Elizabeth Stewart. *Careers in Cosmetology* (7–12). 1999, Rosen LB $26.50 (978-0-8239-2889-7). A survey of career options in the field of cosmetology, with descriptions of training and qualifications, profiles of cosmetologists, and general advice on job seeking. (Rev: SLJ 4/00) [646.7]

10866 McAlpine, Margaret. *Working in the Fashion Industry* (6–12). Series: My Future Career. 2005, Gareth Stevens LB $27.00 (978-0-8368-4774-1). Seven careers in the field of fashion are highlighted with plenty of good photographs, explanations of a typical day's activities, and "Good Points and Bad Points." (Rev: SLJ 1/06)

10867 McAlpine, Margaret. *Working in the Food Industry* (6–12). Series: My Future Career. 2005, Gareth Stevens LB $27.00 (978-0-8368-4776-5). Seven careers in the food industry are highlighted with plenty of good photographs, explanations of a typical day's activities, and "Good Points and Bad Points." (Rev: SLJ 1/06)

10868 McAlpine, Margaret. *Working with Animals* (6–10). Series: My Future Career. 2005, Gareth Stevens LB $27.00 (978-0-8368-4240-1). In addition to describing various jobs working with animals, McAlpine discusses the best personality type for each task and provides a detailed breakdown of a typical day. (Rev: SLJ 3/05) [636]

10869 McAlpine, Margaret. *Working with Children* (6–10). Series: My Future Career. 2005, Gareth Stevens LB $27.00 (978-0-8368-4241-8). In addition to describing various jobs working with children, McAlpine discusses the best personality type for each one and provides a detailed breakdown of a typical day. (Rev: SLJ 3/05) [362.7]

10870 Manley, Claudia B. *Secret Agents: Life as a Professional Spy* (4–7). Series: Extreme Careers. 2001, Rosen LB $26.50 (978-0-8239-3369-3). A high-interest look at the extensive skills required to become an intelligence agent and the kinds of intelligence that are gathered (strategic, tactical, counterintelligence), with material on the history of

espionage and on real-life and fictional spies. (Rev: SLJ 1/02) [327.12]

10871 Nelson, Corinna. *Working in the Environment* (6–8). Series: Exploring Careers. 1999, Lerner LB $23.93 (978-0-8225-1763-4). A recycling manager, a fisheries technician, and a nonprofit organization director are among the 12 people profiled in this title that describes the wide range of jobs related to the environment. (Rev: BL 7/99; SLJ 10/99) [363.7]

10872 Parks, Peggy J. *The News Media* (6–12). Illus. Series: Careers for the Twenty-First Century. 2002, Gale LB $27.45 (978-1-59018-205-5). A comprehensive look at careers in journalism, with historical information as well as descriptions of the day-to-day requirements and challenges and discussion of the benefits and drawbacks of the profession. (Rev: BL 10/15/02) [070.4]

10873 Pasternak, Ceel. *Cool Careers for Girls with Animals* (5–8). Series: Cool Careers for Girls. 1998, Impact $19.95 (978-1-57023-108-7); paper $12.95 (978-1-57023-105-6). Veterinarian, pet sitter, bird handler, animal trainer, and horse-farm owner are among the careers covered, supplemented by interviews with women who work in each field. (Rev: SLJ 4/99; VOYA 8/99) [371.7]

10874 Pasternak, Ceel, and Linda Thornburg. *Cool Careers for Girls in Air and Space* (6–12). Series: Cool Careers for Girls. 2001, Impact LB $12.95 (978-1-57023-147-6); paper $12.95 (978-1-57023-146-9). This account discusses various careers open to women in the aircraft and space industries with information on qualifications, working conditions, and compensation. (Rev: BL 4/15/01; SLJ 4/01) [629]

10875 Pasternak, Ceel, and Linda Thornburg. *Cool Careers for Girls in Food* (5–10). Series: Cool Careers for Girls. 2000, Impact $19.95 (978-1-57023-127-8); paper $12.95 (978-1-57023-120-9). The 11 women featured in this book are involved in various aspects of the food industry such as cheese making, baking, wine making, selling health food, and cooking for the military. (Rev: SLJ 2/00) [641]

10876 *Publishing* (5–9). Series: Discovering Careers for Your Future. 2005, Ferguson LB $21.95 (978-0-8160-5845-7). Education and training, salaries, and outlook for the field are all covered here along with a description of the kinds of daily activities found in various positions. (Rev: SLJ 1/06)

10877 Rauf, Don, and Monique Vescia. *Computer Game Designer* (6–9). Illus. Series: Virtual Apprentice. 2008, Ferguson LB $29.95 (978-0-8160-6754-1). Is it possible to make a living playing games? Yes, if you are a computer game designer. This book describes what game creators do and how they got where they are. (Rev: BL 4/1/08) [794.8]

10878 Reeves, Diane L. *Career Ideas for Kids Who Like Art* (5–9). Illus. Series: Career Ideas for Kids

Who Like. 1998, Facts on File $23.00 (978-0-8160-3681-3). An upbeat book that explores a variety of art-related careers, including many peripheral ones such as chef, animator, and photojournalist, with suggestions on how to test one's suitability for each area and reports from people working in the field. (Rev: SLJ 10/98; VOYA 8/98) [791]

10879 Reeves, Diane L. *Career Ideas for Kids Who Like Writing* (5–9). Illus. Series: Career Ideas for Kids Who Like. 1998, Facts on File $23.00 (978-0-8160-3685-1); paper $12.95 (978-0-8160-3691-2). A look at 15 careers related to writing, among them advertising copywriter, author, bookseller, editor, grant writer, journalist, librarian, literary agent, and publicist, with a self-test for each one and a profile of a person working in the field. (Rev: SLJ 3/99) [808]

10880 Reeves, Diane Lindsey. *Career Ideas for Kids Who Like Math* (4–8). Illus. by Nancy Bond. 2000, Facts on File $23.00 (978-0-8160-4095-7). Presents an amazing array of careers available for the mathematically inclined, arranged alphabetically with good solid information on each. (Rev: HBG 10/00; SLJ 9/00) [510]

10881 Reeves, Diane Lindsey. *Career Ideas for Kids Who Like Talking* (5–9). Illus. by Nancy Bond. Series: Career Ideas for Kids. 1998, Facts on File $23.00 (978-0-8160-3683-7); paper $12.95 (978-0-8160-3689-9). This is a guide to careers in communications, from hotel manager to publicist to broadcaster, with reports from people in the field, tests to check one's aptitude, and lists of resources. (Rev: SLJ 10/98) [331.7]

10882 Reeves, Diane Lindsey, and Gayle Bryan. *Career Ideas for Kids Who Like Money* (6–10). Illus. Series: Career Ideas. 2001, Facts on File $23.00 (978-0-8160-4319-4). An attractive introduction to careers such as business manager, e-merchant, entrepreneur, and investment banker, with personal profiles of individuals in the various fields and attractive cartoons. (Rev: BL 7/01; HBG 3/02; SLJ 8/01) [332]

10883 Reeves, Diane Lindsey, and Gayle Bryan. *Career Ideas for Kids Who Like Travel* (6–10). Series: Career Ideas for Kids. 2001, Checkmark $23.00 (978-0-8160-4325-5); paper $12.95 (978-0-8160-4326-2). A number of careers in the travel industry are presented with coverage of qualifications, training, rewards, and working conditions. (Rev: BL 3/15/02; HBG 10/02) [331.7]

10884 Reeves, Diane Lindsey, and Nancy Heubeck. *Career Ideas for Kids Who Like Adventure* (6–10). Illus. by Nancy Bond. Series: Career Ideas for Kids. 2001, Facts on File LB $23.00 (978-0-8160-4321-7). An attractive introduction to careers such as fire fighting, scuba diving, oil rig work, and piloting, with personal profiles of individuals in the various

fields and attractive cartoons. (Rev: BL 7/01; HBG 3/02; SLJ 8/01) [331.7]

10885 Reeves, Diane Lindsey, and Nancy Heubeck. *Career Ideas for Kids Who Like Animals and Nature* (6–10). Illus. by Nancy Bond. 2000, Facts on File $23.00 (978-0-8160-4097-1). Careers explored in this volume that includes practical advice plus profiles of workers in these jobs range from veterinarian and animal trainer to arborist and botanist. (Rev: HBG 9/00; SLJ 12/00) [570]

10886 Reeves, Diane Lindsey, and Gail Karlitz. *Career Ideas for Teens in Architecture and Construction* (8–12). Illus. Series: Career Ideas for Teens. 2005, Ferguson $40.00 (978-0-8160-5289-9). In addition to details of education requirements, salaries, and so forth, this attractive guide offers interview tips, advice from "real people," and questionnaires. (Rev: SLJ 2/06)

10887 Rosenberg, Aaron. *Cryptologists: Life Making and Breaking Codes* (5–10). Series: Extreme Careers. 2004, Rosen LB $26.50 (978-0-8239-3965-7). After some background material on the history of codes, this volume discusses career opportunities as a cryptologist. (Rev: BL 5/15/04; SLJ 5/90) [410]

10888 Schwager, Tina, and Michele Schuerger. *Cool Women, Hot Jobs — And How You Can Go for It, Too!* (7–12). Illus. 2002, Free Spirit paper $11.95 (978-1-57542-109-4). Profiles of women who work in a wide variety of jobs — from dolphin training and Egyptology to flying fighter planes and planning weddings — are accompanied by details of the job itself and suggestions for setting and achieving goals. (Rev: BL 6/1–15/02; SLJ 7/02; VOYA 8/02) [650.14]

10889 Seidman, David. *Careers in Journalism* (6–12). Illus. Series: Exploring Careers. 2000, Rosen LB $26.50 (978-0-8239-3298-6). Print journalism, broadcast journalism, writing, editing, and design are all covered in this introduction to a widely varied field. (Rev: BL 3/15/01; HBG 10/01; SLJ 2/01) [070.4]

10890 Talbert, Marc. *Holding the Reins: A Ride Through Cowgirl Life* (5–7). Photos by Barbara Van Cleve. 2003, HarperCollins $16.99 (978-0-06-029255-3). The demanding but exhilarating lives of modern-day cowgirls are shown here as the author follows four teens through the seasons. (Rev: BCCB 4/03; BL 1/1–15/03; HBG 10/03; SLJ 4/03) [978]

10891 Thompson, Lisa. *Creating Cuisine: Have You Got What It Takes to Be a Chef?* (5–8). Illus. Series: On the Job. 2008, Compass Point LB $19.95 (978-0-7565-3625-1). An inside look at professional kitchens and the training to become a restaurant cook. (Rev: BL 4/1/08) [641.5092]

10892 Turner, Chérie. *Adventure Tour Guides: Life on Extreme Outdoor Adventures* (5–10). Series: Extreme Careers. 2003, Rosen LB $26.50 (978-0-

8239-3793-6). A look at the profession of tour guiding on excursions such as white-water rafting and mountain climbing, with material on qualifications and future possibilities. (Rev: BL 9/15/03) [908]

10893 Vogt, Peter. *Career Opportunities in the Fashion Industry* (7–12). 2002, Facts on File $49.50 (978-0-8160-4616-4). More than 60 jobs in the fashion industry are described with details of daily activities, salary potential, necessary training, and future outlook. (Rev: SLJ 2/03) [746.9]

10894 Webster, Harriet. *Cool Careers Without College for People Who Love to Work with Children* (8–12). Series: Cool Careers Without College. 2004, Rosen LB $33.25 (978-0-8239-3792-9). Benefits and disadvantages of this kind of work, education and training, salary outlook, and a description of on-the-job activities are provided for a number of career choices, both working for others and as an entrepreneur. (Rev: SLJ 5/04)

10895 Weiss, Ann E. *The Glass Ceiling: A Look at Women in the Workforce* (8–12). 1999, Twenty-First Century LB $23.90 (978-0-7613-1365-6). After a brief history of women's place in the world of work, this book focuses on recent changes and new opportunities (and dangers) for women in the workforce. (Rev: BL 6/1–15/99; SLJ 9/99) [331.4]

10896 Whynott, Douglas. *A Country Practice: Scenes from the Veterinary Life* (7–10). 2004, Farrar $24.00 (978-0-86547-647-9). Covering all aspects of veterinary practice — including finances, staff, and bedside manner — this is an intriguing account of a year in the life of a veterinarian who treats both domestic pets and farm animals. (Rev: BL 11/1/04) [636.089]

10897 Willett, Edward. *Careers in Outer Space: New Business Opportunities* (4–9). Series: The Career Resource Library. 2002, Rosen LB $31.95 (978-0-8239-3358-7). An interesting look at opportunities in the fields of science, math, engineering, technology, communication, and, of course, aeronautics, with information on required skills and training and on the pros and cons of working in the public and private sectors. (Rev: SLJ 6/02) [629.4]

10898 Wilson, Wayne. *Careers in Publishing and Communications* (8–12). Series: Latinos at Work. 2001, Mitchell Lane LB $22.95 (978-1-58415-088-6). This career guide for Latinos explores job opportunities for authors, copy editors, disc jockeys, artists, and agents, and includes personal interviews with successful Hispanic Americans in these fields. (Rev: BL 10/15/01; HBG 3/02) [808]

10899 Zannos, Susan. *Careers in Science and Medicine* (8–12). Series: Latinos at Work. 2001, Mitchell Lane LB $22.95 (978-1-58415-084-8). Descriptions of careers in these fields are accompanied by information on salary and qualifications as well as profiles of Latino men and women who have found

success in a variety of career positions. (Rev: BL 10/15/01; HBG 3/02; SLJ 11/01) [502]

10900 Zannos, Susan. *Latino Entrepreneurs* (8–12). Series: Latinos at Work. 2001, Mitchell Lane LB $32.75 (978-1-58415-089-3). This book looks at the many possibilities for self-employment for Hispanics with personal interviews of successful Latinos in a variety of fields. (Rev: BL 3/15/02; HBG 10/02; SLJ 3/02) [650.1]

Arts, Entertainment, and Sports

10901 Aaseng, Nathan. *Wildshots: The World of the Wildlife Photographer* (5–8). Illus. 2001, Millbrook LB $29.90 (978-0-7613-1551-3). This account describes the work of a wildlife photographer and tells exciting stories about unusual encounters. (Rev: BL 3/1/01*; HBG 10/01; SLJ 3/01; VOYA 10/01) [778.9]

10902 Amara, Philip. *So, You Wanna Be a Comic Book Artist?* (5–8). Illus. by Pop Mhan. 2001, Beyond Words paper $9.95 (978-1-58270-058-8). A comprehensive, engaging look at the world of comic-book illustration, with tips on everything from buying supplies to submitting work to publishers. (Rev: BL 1/1–15/02; SLJ 4/02) [808]

10903 Apel, Melanie Ann. *Cool Careers Without College for Film and Television Buffs* (6–9). Series: Cool Careers Without College. 2002, Rosen LB $33.25 (978-0-8239-3501-7). A variety of options are presented for students interested in jobs in this sector, from actor and agent to grip, gaffer, makeup artist, animator, and puppeteer. (Rev: SLJ 7/02; VOYA 2/03) [331.7]

10904 *Art* (4–8). Illus. Series: Discovering Careers for Your Future. 2001, Ferguson LB $21.95 (978-0-89434-388-9). A useful introduction to career opportunities in art, with information on the skills required, potential earnings, and job outlook. (Rev: SLJ 11/01) [702.373]

10905 Croce, Nicholas. *Cool Careers without College for People Who Love Video Games* (6–12). Series: Cool Careers Without College. 2007, Rosen LB $33.25 (978-1-4042-0747-9). This is a well-organized book with detailed information about the careers available in the field of video games (writing, producing, marketing, for example). (Rev: SLJ 6/07)

10906 *Design.* 2nd ed. (7–12). Series: Careers in Focus. 2005, Ferguson $22.95 (978-0-8160-5865-5). Describes careers in the broad field of design — Including architects, fashion designers, exhibit designers, industrial designers, and toy and game designers. (Rev: SLJ 12/05)

10907 Flender, Nicole. *People Who Love Movement* (7–12). Series: Cool Careers Without College. 2002, Rosen $33.25 (978-0-8239-3505-5). Some of the non-college degree careers discussed are dancers, dance and yoga teachers, and fitness instructors in this book which also covers salaries, and job opportunities. (Rev: BL 5/15/02) [613.7]

10908 Hinton, Kerry. *Cool Careers Without College for Music Lovers* (7–12). Illus. Series: Cool Careers Without College. 2002, Rosen LB $30.60 (978-0-8239-3503-1). Music store clerk, promoter, and instrument repairman are some of the options explored in this book that gives information on training and on-the-job activities. (Rev: BL 5/15/02; SLJ 7/02) [780]

10909 Hofstetter, Adam B. *Cool Careers without College for People Who Love Sports* (6–12). Series: Cool Careers Without College. 2007, Rosen LB $33.25 (978-1-4042-0749-3). Scout, groundskeeper, official scorer, Zamboni driver — these are only a few of the sports careers detailed in this well-organized book. (Rev: SLJ 6/07) [796.023]

10910 Jay, Annie, and Luanne Feik. *Stars in Your Eyes . . . Feet on the Ground: A Practical Guide for Teenage Actors (and Their Parents!)* (7–12). Illus. 1999, Theatre Directories paper $16.95 (978-0-933919-42-6). A young actress gives practical advice on how to break into show business, including information on publicity photographs, auditions, managers, agents, publicity packages, résumés, and casting calls. (Rev: BL 6/1–15/99) [792.02]

10911 Johnson, Marlys H. *Careers in the Movies* (5–9). Series: Career Resource Library. 2001, Rosen LB $31.95 (978-0-8239-3186-6). Job descriptions and qualifications are clearly laid out in this guide for aspiring filmmakers that also discusses the history of the industry and the basic steps in film production. (Rev: SLJ 8/01) [791.43]

10912 Lantz, Francess. *Rock, Rap, and Rad: How to Be a Rock or Rap Star* (6–12). 1992, Avon paper $3.99 (978-0-380-76793-9). The author takes aspiring rock stars through the basic steps of choosing an instrument, finding other musicians and a place to play, lining up gigs, and on up to the top. (Rev: BL 7/93) [781.66]

10913 Lee, Barbara. *Working in Sports and Recreation* (5–9). Illus. Series: Exploring Careers. 1996, Lerner LB $23.93 (978-0-8225-1762-7). Twelve people involved in careers related to sports and recreation talk candidly about their professions. (Rev: BL 2/15/97) [796]

10914 Libal, Joyce, and Rae Simons. *Professional Athlete and Sports Official* (5–9). Series: Careers with Character. 2003, Mason Crest LB $22.95 (978-1-59084-321-5). The importance of character traits such as integrity, respect, fairness, and self-discipline when seeking careers in sports is emphasized here. (Rev: HBG 10/03; SLJ 4/03) [796]

10915 McAlpine, Margaret. *Working in Film and Television* (6–10). Series: My Future Career. 2005,

Gareth Stevens LB $27.00 (978-0-8368-4237-1). In addition to describing various jobs in the film and television world, McAlpine discusses the best personality type for each one and provides a detailed breakdown of a typical day. (Rev: SLJ 3/05) [791.43]

10916 McAlpine, Margaret. *Working in Music and Dance* (6–12). Series: My Future Career. 2005, Gareth Stevens LB $27.00 (978-0-8368-4777-2). Seven careers in the fields of music and dance are highlighted with plenty of good photographs, explanations of a typical day's activities, and "Good Points and Bad Points." (Rev: SLJ 1/06)

10917 McDaniels, Pellom. *So, You Want to Be a Pro?* (6–12). Illus. 1999, Addax $14.95 (978-1-886110-77-9). Atlanta Falcons player McDaniels offers encouragement to would-be professional athletes without encouraging unrealistic expectations. (Rev: BL 11/15/99; SLJ 3/00) [613.7]

10918 McLaglen, Mary, et al. *You Can Be a Woman Movie Maker* (4–8). Series: You Can Be a Woman. 2003, Cascade Pass $19.95 (978-1-880599-64-8); paper $14.95 (978-1-880599-63-1). Three women — a producer, an independent filmmaker, and an executive producer — talk about their jobs, how they got into the movie industry, and what a day on the job is like. Interviews and film clips are on an accompanying DVD. (Rev: SLJ 4/04) [791.43]

10919 Menard, Valerie. *Careers in Sports* (8–12). Series: Latinos at Work. 2001, Mitchell Lane LB $32.75 (978-1-58415-086-2). This book explores the career possibilities for Hispanic Americans in a variety of sports with several interesting case studies of Latinos who did well in them. (Rev: BL 3/15/02; HBG 10/02) [796]

10920 *Music* (6–12). 2004, Ferguson LB $22.95 (978-0-8160-5555-5). Describes careers in music, with information on qualifications, working conditions, salaries, opportunities, rewards, and methods of exploring and entering the field. (Rev: SLJ 1/05) [780]

10921 Nagle, Jeanne. *Careers in Coaching* (7–12). Series: Careers Library. 2000, Rosen LB $31.95 (978-0-8239-2966-5). This guide to how to become a successful coach covers all aspects of the job. (Rev: SLJ 7/00) [796]

10922 Nathan, Amy. *Meet the Musicians: From Prodigy (or Not) to Pro* (5–8). Illus. 2006, Holt $17.95 (978-0-8050-7743-8). Profiles of members of the New York Philharmonic give readers a good understanding of the different roles of various instruments and the careers of professional musicians. (Rev: BL 3/15/06; SLJ 5/06; VOYA 6/06) [750.92]

10923 Nathan, Amy. *The Young Musician's Survival Guide: Tips from Teens and Pros* (5–8). 2000, Oxford $21.99 (978-0-19-512611-2). A thorough study of how to break into the music world, with information on working with music teachers, conductors, and peers, and tips on practicing, choosing an instrument, and handling fears and frustrations. (Rev: BL 4/1/00; HBG 10/00; SLJ 6/00) [780]

10924 Parks, Peggy. *Music* (6–12). Series: Careers for the Twenty-First Century. 2002, Gale LB $27.45 (978-1-59018-223-9). This book provides a close look at six music-related careers — musician, composer, recording engineer, music therapist, music publicist, and music educator. (Rev: BL 10/15/02) [780]

10925 Parks, Peggy J. *Musician* (4–7). Illus. Series: Exploring Careers. 2004, Gale LB $26.20 (978-0-7377-2067-9). In addition to a description of the work that musicians (including DJs) do, there is a frank assessment of the opportunities available. (Rev: BL 3/15/04) [780]

10926 Parks, Peggy J. *Writer* (4–7). Illus. Series: Exploring Careers. 2004, Gale LB $26.20 (978-0-7377-2069-3). The ups and downs of a career in writing are frankly discussed in this slim guide. (Rev: BL 3/15/04) [808]

10927 Pasternak, Ceel, and Linda Thornburg. *Cool Careers for Girls in Sports* (5–10). Series: Cool Careers for Girls. 1999, Impact $19.95 (978-1-57023-107-0); paper $12.95 (978-1-57023-104-9). A golf pro, basketball player, ski instructor, sports broadcaster, trainer, sports psychologist, and athletic director are among the 10 women profiled in this overview of careers for women in sports. (Rev: SLJ 7/99; VOYA 8/99) [796]

10928 *Radio and Television* (5–9). Series: Discovering Careers for Your Future. 2005, Ferguson LB $21.95 (978-0-8160-5846-4). Education and training, salaries, and outlook for the field are all covered here along with a description of the kinds of daily activities found in various positions. (Rev: SLJ 1/06)

10929 Reeves, Diane L., and Peter Kent. *Career Ideas for Kids Who Like Sports* (5–9). Illus. Series: Career Ideas for Kids Who Like. 1998, Facts on File $23.00 (978-0-8160-3684-4); paper $12.95 (978-0-8160-3690-5). The 15 sports-related careers highlighted in this volume include coach, athlete, agent, sportscaster, and sports equipment manufacturer, with accompanying material on necessary skills, opportunities, duties, and a report from someone in the field. (Rev: SLJ 6/99) [796]

10930 Reeves, Diane Lindsey, and Gayle Bryan. *Career Ideas for Kids Who Like Music and Dance* (6–10). Series: Career Ideas for Kids. 2001, Checkmark $23.00 (978-0-8160-4323-1). This work presents a number of career opportunities in music and dance with material on training, qualifications, and working conditions. (Rev: BL 3/15/02; HBG 10/02) [790]

10931 Sommers, Michael A. *Wildlife Photographers: Life Through a Lens* (5–10). Series: Extreme Careers. 2003, Rosen LB $26.50 (978-0-8239-3638-0). A concise explanation of the work of wildlife photographers, the attributes needed, and the training and tenacity required to enter this field. (Rev: BL 9/15/03; SLJ 5/03) [771]

10932 Svitil, Torene. *So You Want to Work in Animation and Special Effects?* (6–9). Illus. Series: Careers in Film and Television. 2007, Enslow LB $23.95 (978-0-7660-2737-4). A look at how special effects and animation are rendered today in comparison with days past (1933's *King Kong* is used as an example) is followed by information on the training required for this field. (Rev: BL 4/1/07; SLJ 8/07) [778.5]

10933 Torres, John, and Susan Zannos. *Careers in the Music Industry* (8–12). Series: Latinos at Work. 2001, Mitchell Lane LB $32.75 (978-1-58415-085-5). Along with personal interviews with Hispanics who did well in the music world, there are descriptions of such related careers as singers, songwriters, managers, and agents. (Rev: BL 3/15/02; HBG 10/02) [780]

10934 Weigant, Chris. *Careers as a Disc Jockey* (8–12). Series: Careers. 1997, Rosen LB $16.95 (978-0-8239-2528-5). This informative book gives many practical tips on how to get started and be successful in radio, with material on making demo tapes, applying for jobs and internships, and working oneself up. There are interviews with eight DJs. Careers in management, sales, technical areas, talk shows, and others are included. (Rev: SLJ 12/97; VOYA 2/98) [384.54]

10935 Williamson, Walter. *Early Stages: The Professional Theater and the Young Actor* (6–9). 1986, Walker LB $12.85 (978-0-8027-6630-4). Through examining the careers of several young actors, tips are given on how to enter show business. (Rev: BL 7/86; SLJ 5/86) [792]

10936 Wilson, Wayne. *Careers in Entertainment* (8–12). Series: Latinos at Work. 2001, Mitchell Lane LB $32.75 (978-1-58415-083-1). With an emphasis on Hispanic American success stories, this book features careers in film, television, and theater. (Rev: BL 10/15/01; HBG 3/02) [791]

Business

10937 *Advertising and Marketing* (5–9). Series: Discovering Careers for Your Future. 2005, Ferguson $21.95 (978-0-8160-5847-1). Education and training, salaries, and outlook for the field are all covered here along with a description of the kinds of daily activities found in various positions. (Rev: SLJ 1/06)

10938 Giles, M. J. *Young Adult's Guide to a Business Career* (8–12). Illus. 2004, Business Bks. $14.95 (978-0-9723714-3-8). Full of useful tips, this guide describes more than 25 occupations in business and finance, giving details of benefits and drawbacks, salaries, educational requirements, and so forth. (Rev: SLJ 7/04) [331.7]

10939 Thomason-Carroll, Kristi L. *Young Adult's Guide to Business Communications* (8–12). Illus. 2004, Business Bks. $14.95 (978-0-9723714-4-5). Full of useful tips, this guide describes the basics required for a job in the business world, including telephone skills, the ability to communicate clearly by letter and e-mail, and proper behavior during meetings. (Rev: SLJ 7/04) [651.7]

Construction and Mechanical Trades

10940 Frew, Katherine. *Plumber* (5–8). Series: Great Jobs. 2004, Children's Pr. LB $24.50 (978-0-516-24088-6). This appealing, photo-filled title focuses on the plumbing trade, looking at job requirements, training, and tools, as well as providing a history of the plumbing business and a look at a typical day at work. (Rev: SLJ 7/04) [696]

10941 Overcamp, David. *Electrician* (5–8). Series: Great Jobs. 2004, Children's Pr. LB $24.50 (978-0-516-24086-2); paper $6.95 (978-0-516-25924-6). This appealing, photo-filled title focuses on the work of an electrician, looking at job requirements, training, and tools, as well as providing a history of the field and a look at a typical day at work. (Rev: SLJ 7/04) [621.3]

10942 Paige, Joy. *Cool Careers Without College for People Who Love to Build Things* (7–12). Series: Cool Careers Without College. 2002, Rosen LB $33.25 (978-0-8239-3506-2). Twenty careers in construction are outlined with useful information about salary, future prospects, and training. (Rev: BL 1/1–15/03; SLJ 7/02) [690]

10943 Pasternak, Ceel, and Linda Thornburg. *Cool Careers for Girls in Construction* (6–12). Illus. Series: Cool Careers for Girls. 2000, Impact $19.95 (978-1-57023-135-3); paper $12.95 (978-1-57023-131-5). From architect to ironworker, this book profiles a number of careers in construction for women, with material on salaries, working conditions, and qualifications needed. (Rev: BL 3/15/00; SLJ 7/00) [624]

10944 Weintraub, Aileen. *Auto Mechanic* (5–8). Series: Great Jobs. 2004, Children's Pr. LB $24.50 (978-0-516-24090-9). This appealing, photo-filled title focuses on the work of an auto mechanic, looking at job requirements, training, and tools, as well as providing a history of the trade and a look at a typical day at work. (Rev: SLJ 7/04) [629.28]

Education and Librarianship

10945 Reeves, Diane Lindsey, and Gail Karlitz. *Career Ideas for Teens in Education and Training* (8–12). Illus. Series: Career Ideas for Teens. 2005, Ferguson $40.00 (978-0-8160-5295-0). In addition to details of education requirements, salaries, and so forth, this attractive guide offers interview tips, advice from "real people," and questionnaires. (Rev: SLJ 2/06)

10946 Zannos, Susan. *Careers in Education* (8–12). Series: Latinos at Work. 2001, Mitchell Lane LB $22.95 (978-1-58415-081-7). Descriptions of careers in this field are accompanied by information on salary and qualifications as well as profiles of Latino men and women who have found success in a variety of career positions. (Rev: BL 10/15/01; HBG 3/02; SLJ 11/01; VOYA 6/02) [370]

Law, Police, and Other Society-Oriented Careers

10947 Bankston, John. *Careers in Community Service* (8–12). Series: Latinos at Work. 2001, Mitchell Lane LB $32.75 (978-1-58415-082-4). Aimed at Latino youths, this career guide features a multitude of jobs in non-profit agencies, including legal and medical fields, with accompanying stories of success. (Rev: BL 10/15/01; HBG 3/02; SLJ 1/02) [353.001]

10948 Binney, Greg A. *Careers in the Federal Emergency Management Agency's Search and Rescue Unit* (5–9). Illus. Series: Careers in Search and Rescue Operations. 2003, Rosen LB $26.50 (978-0-8239-3832-2). Starting with September 11, 2001, this volume explores the work of the teams that specialize in search and rescue after disasters such as tornadoes, hazardous materials spills, and building collapses, with material on the training required. (Rev: BL 10/15/03) [363.3]

10949 Cassedy, Patrice. *Law Enforcement* (6–12). Illus. Series: Careers for the Twenty-First Century. 2002, Gale LB $29.95 (978-1-56006-899-0). An attractive volume that covers the history of law enforcement and introduces the rewards and challenges of such professions as the police, federal agents, crime scene workers, and probation and correctional officers. (Rev: BL 10/15/02) [363.2]

10950 Croce, Nicholas. *Detectives: Life Investigating Crimes* (5–10). Series: Extreme Careers. 2003, Rosen LB $26.50 (978-0-8239-3796-7). As well as exploring the exciting side of detective work, this account explains the qualifications and training needed and the techniques that help do this job well. (Rev: BL 9/15/03) [340]

10951 Davis, Mary L. *Working in Law and Justice* (6–8). Series: Exploring Careers. 1999, Lerner LB

$28.75 (978-0-8225-1766-5). Twelve people are profiled representing various jobs and careers in law and related fields, among them a female deputy sheriff, a male law librarian, a bail bond agent, and a security firm owner. (Rev: BL 7/99; SLJ 10/99) [340]

10952 Fall, Mitchell. *Careers in Fire Departments' Search and Rescue Unit* (5–9). Series: Careers in Search and Rescue Operations. 2003, Rosen LB $26.50 (978-0-8239-3833-9). This account pays tribute to the heroism of fire departments' search and rescue operations particularly during the September 11, 2001 attacks and also gives a career guide to this occupation. (Rev: BL 10/15/03) [363]

10953 Fine, Jil. *Bomb Squad Specialist* (4–8). Series: Danger Is My Business. 2003, Children's Pr. LB $24.50 (978-0-516-24340-5). An illustrated glimpse of the perilous life of a bomb squad member in an age of terrorism, including information on how bombs work and how they are detected and disarmed. (Rev: SLJ 3/04) [363.2]

10954 Freedman, Jeri. *Careers in Emergency Medical Response Team's Search and Rescue Unit* (5–9). Illus. Series: Careers in Search and Rescue Operations. 2003, Rosen LB $26.50 (978-0-8239-3831-5). Starting with September 11, 2001, this volume explores the various roles played by emergency response teams, the use of equipment including helicopters and ambulances, and the training required. (Rev: BL 10/15/03) [616.0]

10955 Giacobello, John. *Bodyguards: Life Protecting Others* (5–10). Series: Extreme Careers. 2003, Rosen LB $26.50 (978-0-8239-3795-0). This book explores the duties and responsibilities of a bodyguard and includes information how to stay safe on the job and get ahead in this profession. (Rev: BL 9/15/03; SLJ 11/03) [340]

10956 Greene, Meg. *Careers in the National Guards' Search and Rescue Unit* (5–9). Series: Careers in Search and Rescue Operations. 2003, Rosen LB $26.50 (978-0-8239-3836-0). This account describes the vital role that citizen-soldiers play in the line of defense and tells of the their search and rescue activities during the terrorist attacks of September 11, 2001. (Rev: BL 10/15/03; SLJ 4/04) [335]

10957 Hopping, Lorraine Jean. *Investigating a Crime Scene* (7–10). Illus. Series: Crime Scene Science. 2007, World Almanac LB $22.95 (978-0-8368-7709-0). A matter-of-fact look at what it is like to examine crime scenes, this should appeal to teens interested in forensic work as a career and to those who just want more of what they see on TV. (Rev: BL 3/15/07) [614]

10958 Kiland, Taylor Baldwin. *The U.S. Navy and Military Careers* (5–8). Series: U.S. Armed Forces and Military Careers. 2006, Enslow LB $31.93 (978-0-7660-2523-3). Straightforward and informa-

tive, this title provides a history of the Navy, looks at its role in the nation's defense, and details various jobs within this branch of the armed forces. (Rev: SLJ 6/07)

10959 Murdico, Suzanne J. *Bomb Squad Experts: Life Defusing Explosive Devices* (5–10). Series: Extreme Careers. 2004, Rosen LB $26.50 (978-0-8239-3968-8). A look at the career opportunities in bomb squads, with material on training, salaries, and working conditions. (Rev: BL 5/15/04) [363]

10960 Oleksy, Walter. *Choosing a Career as a Firefighter* (6–9). Series: The World of Work. 2000, Rosen LB $25.25 (978-0-8239-3245-0). The details of a firefighter's life and of the training, duties, and educational and physical requirements of this and related careers will interest both browsers and report writers. (Rev: HBG 3/01; SLJ 3/01)

10961 Pasternak, Ceel, and Linda Thornburg. *Cool Careers for Girls in Law* (6–12). Series: Cool Careers for Girls. 2001, Impact LB $19.95 (978-1-57023-160-5); paper $12.95 (978-1-57023-157-5). Ten women who have succeeded in various areas of the legal profession are highlighted, with material on qualifications, salaries, and working conditions. (Rev: BL 4/15/01; SLJ 7/01) [340]

10962 Payment, Simone. *Frontline Marines: Fighting in the Marine Combat Arms Units* (5–8). Illus. Series: Extreme Careers. 2007, Rosen LB $26.50 (978-1-4042-0946-6). Students looking for exciting careers may want to look into the combat arms units of the U.S. Marines, suggests this book, which tells readers what these units do and explains the training involved. (Rev: BL 7/07) [359.9]

10963 Plum, Jennifer. *Careers in Police Departments' Search and Rescue Unit* (5–9). Series: Careers in Search and Rescue Operations. 2003, Rosen LB $26.50 (978-0-8239-3834-6). This account highlights the role of police officers in search and rescue operations particularly their acts of heroism during the attacks of September 11, 2001. (Rev: BL 10/15/03) [363]

10964 Roza, Greg. *Careers in the Coast Guard's Search and Rescue Unit* (5–9). Series: Careers in Search and Rescue Operations. 2003, Rosen LB $26.50 (978-0-8239-3835-3). This book covers the search and rescue operations involving the Coast Guard with particular emphasis on their vital role during the September 11, 2001, attacks. (Rev: BL 10/15/03; SLJ 4/04) [355]

10965 Stein, R. Conrad. *The U.S. Marine Corps and Military Careers* (5–8). Series: U.S. Armed Forces and Military Careers. 2006, Enslow LB $31.93 (978-0-7660-2521-9). This overview of careers in the U.S. Marine Corps discusses expectations, duties, and pay scales as well as the Marines' role in national defense. (Rev: SLJ 6/07)

10966 Wade, Linda R. *Careers in Law and Politics* (8–12). Series: Latinos at Work. 2001, Mitchell Lane LB $22.95 (978-1-58415-080-0). Along with interviews of successful Hispanic Americans in the fields of law and politics, this book describes such careers as lawyer, law professor, judge, police officer, and state representative. (Rev: BL 3/15/02; HBG 10/02; SLJ 3/02) [340]

10967 Wirths, Claudine G. *Choosing a Career in Law Enforcement* (6–10). Series: World of Work. 1996, Rosen LB $17.95 (978-0-8239-2274-1). Careers in law enforcement, such as police officer, security guard, and private investigator, are explored. (Rev: SLJ 3/97) [363]

Medicine and Health

10968 Asher, Dana. *Epidemiologists: Life Tracking Deadly Diseases* (5–10). Series: Extreme Careers. 2003, Rosen LB $26.50 (978-0-8239-3633-5). A concise explanation of the work of epidemiologists, the history of this discipline, and the training required to enter this field, with a case study. (Rev: BL 5/15/03; SLJ 5/03) [614.4]

10969 Field, Shelly. *Career Opportunities in Health Care.* 2nd ed. (7–12). 2002, Facts on File $49.50 (978-0-8160-4816-8). Information on 80 or so careers is organized in 16 categories, and includes a job profile, salary outlook, and details of necessary education and skills. (Rev: BL 11/1/02; SLJ 1/03) [610.69]

10970 *Health Care* (7–12). Series: What Can I Do Now? 2007, Ferguson $29.95 (978-0-8160-6031-3). Following a general introduction to the health care industry, this book describes jobs in the field, education and skill requirements, and salary ranges, and tells students what they can do now, emphasizing volunteer opportunities and internships. (Rev: SLJ 11/07) [610.69]

10971 Lee, Barbara. *Working in Health Care and Wellness* (4–8). Illus. Series: Exploring Careers. 1996, Lerner LB $23.93 (978-0-8225-1760-3). This book profiles 12 people who are in health care professions, and includes the pros and cons of each career. (Rev: BL 2/15/97) [610.69]

10972 Pasternak, Ceel, and Linda Thornburg. *Cool Careers for Girls in Health* (5–9). Series: Cool Careers for Girls. 1999, Impact $19.95 (978-1-57023-125-4); paper $12.95 (978-1-57023-118-6). This book describes health-related careers for girls — as doctors, nurses, dentists, personal trainers, medical technologists, physical therapists, and dietitians. (Rev: SLJ 10/99) [610]

10973 Reeves, Diane Lindsey, and Gail Karlitz. *Career Ideas for Teens in Health Science* (7–12). Illus. Series: Career Ideas for Teens. 2005, Ferguson $40.00 (978-0-8160-5290-5). In addition to details

of education requirements, salaries, and so forth, this attractive guide offers interview tips, advice from "real people," and questionnaires. (Rev: SLJ 2/06) [610.69]

Science and Engineering

10974 Burnett, Betty. *Math and Science Wizards* (7–12). Series: Cool Careers Without College. 2002, Rosen $33.25 (978-0-8239-3502-4). Jobs in medicine and science that do not require college degrees, such as chemical lab workers, miners, and doctors' helpers, are described with information on salaries, duties, training, and future outlooks. (Rev: BL 5/15/02; SLJ 7/02) [520]

10975 Hayhurst, Chris. *Arctic Scientists: Life Studying the Arctic* (5–10). Series: Extreme Careers. 2003, Rosen LB $26.50 (978-0-8239-3794-3). This guide to the life and work of Arctic scientists indicates exciting areas of research such as the plant and animal life and the effects of global warming. (Rev: BL 9/15/03; SLJ 11/03) [500]

10976 Hayhurst, Chris. *Volcanologists: Life Exploring Volcanoes* (5–10). Series: Extreme Careers. 2003, Rosen LB $26.50 (978-0-8239-3637-3). This career guide explains what is necessary to become a serious student of volcanoes and what to expect when one becomes a volcanologist. (Rev: BL 9/15/03) [551.2]

10977 Murdico, Suzanne J. *Forensic Scientists: Life Investigating Sudden Death* (5–12). Series: Extreme Careers. 2004, Rosen LB $26.50 (978-0-8239-3966-4). A look at this rapidly growing science and the career opportunities offered. (Rev: BL 5/15/04) [363.2]

10978 Pasternak, Ceel, and Linda Thornburg. *Cool Careers for Girls in Engineering* (5–8). Series: Cool Careers for Girls. 1999, Impact $19.95 (978-1-57023-126-1); paper $12.95 (978-1-57023-119-3). Examines engineering specializations — such as computer, biomedical, civil, and agricultural — and the opportunities for women in these fields. (Rev: SLJ 1/00) [620]

10979 Reeves, Diane Lindsey. *Career Ideas for Kids Who Like Science* (5–9). Illus. by Nancy Bond. Series: Career Ideas for Kids. 1998, Facts on File $23.00 (978-0-8160-3680-6); paper $12.95 (978-0-8060-3686-1). An upbeat, breezy introduction to 15 careers, providing aptitude tests and information on educational requirements, working conditions, activities, etc. (Rev: SLJ 9/98) [500]

10980 Swinburne, Stephen R. *The Woods Scientist* (4–8). Photos by Susan C. Morse. Illus. Series: Scientists in the Field. 2003, Houghton $16.00 (978-0-618-04602-7). Swinburne describes his fascinating expeditions in the company of a conservationist and ecologist in the woods of Vermont, and provides lots of information on risks to wildlife. (Rev: BCCB 3/03; BL 3/15/03; HBG 10/03; SLJ 4/03) [591.73]

Technical and Industrial Careers

10981 Apel, Melanie Ann. *Careers in Information Technology* (6–12). Illus. Series: Exploring Careers. 2000, Rosen LB $18.95 (978-0-8239-2892-7). Testimonials from working professionals add to this survey of opportunities in information technology that gives details on skills required and employment outlook. (Rev: BL 3/15/01; HBG 10/01; SLJ 2/01) [004]

10982 Bonnice, Sherry. *Computer Programmer* (8–12). Series: Careers with Character. 2003, Mason Crest LB $22.95 (978-1-59084-312-3). An explanation of the job requirements and opportunities of computer programmers is accompanied by discussion of the importance of integrity and ethical behavior. (Rev: LMC 4–5/03; SLJ 2/03) [005.1]

10983 Brown, Marty. *Webmaster* (4–8). Series: Coolcareers.com. 2000, Rosen LB $23.95 (978-0-8239-3111-8). This volume describes a Web page, types of networks, servers, browsers, and protocols and introduces some careers in Web-related areas. (Rev: SLJ 6/00) [004]

10984 Buell, Tonya. *Web Surfers* (7–12). Series: Cool Careers Without College. 2002, Rosen $30.60 (978-0-8239-3507-9). This book presents 12 careers for computer buffs with information about salaries, future prospects, and further research possibilities. (Rev: BL 5/15/02; SLJ 7/02; VOYA 2/03) [004.6]

10985 Cassedy, Patrice. *Computer Technology* (7–10). Series: Careers for the Twenty-First Century. 2004, Gale LB $29.95 (978-1-56006-896-9). Helpful information about work environment and job satisfaction accompanies the usual material on salary, career prospects, and so forth; the format has less appeal. (Rev: SLJ 11/04) [005]

10986 *Computer and Video Game Design* (7–12). Series: Careers in Focus. 2005, Ferguson $22.95 (978-0-8160-5850-1). Describes the tasks of artists and animators, game designers, packaging designers, technical support specialists, and video game testers. (Rev: SLJ 12/05)

10987 *Computers* (4–8). Illus. Series: Discovering Careers for Your Future. 2001, Ferguson LB $21.95 (978-0-89434-389-6). A useful introduction to the career opportunities in this field, with information on the skills required, potential earnings, and job outlook. (Rev: SLJ 11/01) [004.02373]

10988 *Computers.* 4th ed. (6–12). Series: Careers in Focus. 2004, Ferguson LB $22.95 (978-0-8160-5552-4). Describes careers in the computer field, with information on qualifications, working conditions, salaries, opportunities, rewards, and methods of exploring and entering the field; a helpful feature

is a list of acronyms and identification numbers used in government career indexes. (Rev: SLJ 1/05) [004]

10989 Fulton, Michael T. *Exploring Careers in Cyberspace* (7–12). Series: Careers. 1997, Rosen LB $31.95 (978-0-8239-2633-6). A worthwhile source of information on how to prepare oneself to work in cyberspace, the types of jobs available, and the way to make a solid impression. (Rev: BL 6/1–15/98; SLJ 7/98) [004.67802373]

10990 Garcia, Kimberly. *Careers in Technology* (8–12). Series: Latinos at Work. 2001, Mitchell Lane LB $32.75 (978-1-58415-087-9). An easy-to-read guide to careers in computer technology such as Web designers, programmers, and Internet marketing, with particular emphasis on Hispanic success stories in these fields. (Rev: BL 10/15/01; HBG 3/02; SLJ 1/02) [004.6]

10991 Gerardi, Dave, and Peter Suciu. *Careers in the Computer Game Industry* (6–12). Illus. Series: Careers in the New Economy. 2005, Rosen LB $31.95 (978-1-4042-0252-8). The authors review a wide array of job opportunities in the computer game industry, including designers, testers, graphic artists, animators, and programmers. (Rev: SLJ 10/05) [331.7]

10992 Henderson, Harry. *Career Opportunities in Computers and Cyberspace.* 2nd ed. (8–12). Series: Career Opportunities. 2004, Ferguson $49.50 (978-0-8160-5094-9). A quick overview of the wide number of opportunities in such fields as programming and software development, information systems management, and information science, providing an outline of duties, salary ranges, employment outlook, required education and training, and so forth. (Rev: SLJ 7/04) [004]

10993 Hovanec, Erin M. *Careers as a Content Provider for the Web* (5–8). Series: The Library of E-Commerce and Internet Careers. 2001, Rosen LB $26.50 (978-0-8239-3418-8). A basic guide to career opportunities in the high-tech sector, with personal stories, information on skills needed and how to get started, and lists of recommended resources, many of which are on the Web. Also use *E-Tailing: Careers Selling Over the Web* (2001). (Rev: SLJ 4/02) [004]

10994 McAlpine, Margaret. *Working with Computers* (6–10). Series: My Future Career. 2005, Gareth Stevens LB $27.00 (978-0-8368-4242-5). In addition to describing various jobs working with computers, McAlpine discusses the best personality type for each one and provides a detailed breakdown of a typical day. (Rev: SLJ 3/05) [004]

10995 McGinty, Alice B. *Software Designer* (4–8). Series: Coolcareers.com. 2000, Rosen LB $23.95 (978-0-8239-3149-1). This book explains what a software engineer does, the skills required, education needed, and future prospects. (Rev: SLJ 6/00) [004]

10996 Mazor, Barry. *Multimedia and New Media Developer* (4–8). Series: Coolcareers.com. 2000, Rosen LB $26.50 (978-0-8239-3102-6). This work explains the nature of multimedia careers, the training and skills necessary, and the job opportunities. (Rev: SLJ 6/00) [004]

10997 O'Donnell, Annie. *Computer Animator* (4–8). Series: Coolcareers.com. 2000, Rosen LB $23.95 (978-0-8239-3101-9). This book gives a brief history of animation and explains how it is used today, the specialized roles of animators, educational requirements, and the future of the industry. (Rev: SLJ 6/00) [004]

10998 Oleksy, Walter. *Video Game Designer* (4–8). Series: Coolcareers.com. 2000, Rosen LB $23.95 (978-0-8239-3117-0). This account explains how video games work and how they are designed, with material on the careers involved and the qualifications necessary. (Rev: SLJ 6/00) [794.8]

10999 Oleksy, Walter. *Web Page Designer* (4–8). Series: Coolcareers.com. 2000, Rosen LB $26.50 (978-0-8239-3112-5). This well-illustrated account, which features case studies of several teenagers, gives information on Web page construction, what a designer does, the training required, and the job outlook. (Rev: SLJ 6/00) [004]

11000 Pasternak, Ceel, and Linda Thornburg. *Cool Careers for Girls in Computers* (7–12). Illus. 1999, Impact paper $12.95 (978-1-57023-103-2). This

career book for girls features interviews with 10 women in computer-related fields, including a software engineer, sales executive, online specialist, technology trainer, and network administrator. (Rev: SLJ 4/00; VOYA 8/99) [004.6]

11001 Reeves, Diane Lindsey, and Peter Kent. *Career Ideas for Kids Who Like Computers* (5–9). Illus. by Nancy Bond. Series: Career Ideas for Kids. 1998, Facts on File $23.00 (978-0-8160-3682-0). An upbeat, breezy introduction to careers related to computers, providing aptitude tests and information on educational requirements, working conditions, activities, etc. (Rev: SLJ 6/99) [004]

11002 Sawyer, Sarah. *Career Building through Podcasting* (7–10). Illus. Series: Digital Career Building. 2007, Rosen LB $21.95 (978-1-4042-1944-1). Readers looking into tech careers will enjoy this exploration into how one can make a living podcasting. (Rev: BL 10/15/07; LMC 2/08) [070.5]

11003 Thornburg, Linda. *Cool Careers for Girls in Cybersecurity and National Safety* (8–11). Series: Cool Careers for Girls. 2004, Impact $21.95 (978-1-57023-209-1). This volume contains 10 case studies of women who have launched careers dealing with the protection of computer networks and the Internet as well as other high-tech areas. (Rev: BL 3/1/04; SLJ 10/04) [331.7]

11004 White, Katherine. *Oil Rig Workers: Life Drilling for Oil* (5–10). Series: Extreme Careers. 2003, Rosen LB $26.50 (978-0-8239-3797-4). A look at the lives of oil rig workers and day-to-day activities on a rig. (Rev: BL 9/15/03) [665.5]

Personal Finances

Money-Making Ideas

General and Miscellaneous

11005 Bernstein, Daryl. *Better Than a Lemonade Stand! Small Business Ideas for Kids* (5–8). Illus. 1992, Beyond Words paper $9.95 (978-0-941831-75-8). The author, a 15-year-old entrepreneur, provides ideas for starting 51 different small businesses and offers advice on start-up costs, billing, and customer relations. (Rev: BL 10/1/92; SLJ 1/93) [650.1]

11006 Byers, Patricia, et al. *The Kids Money Book: Great Money Making Ideas* (7–10). 1983, Liberty paper $4.95 (978-0-89709-041-4). A wide variety of jobs are introduced that can be part-time and money-producing. [658.1]

11007 Drew, Bonnie, and Noel Drew. *Fast Cash for Kids* (4–7). Illus. 1995, Career Pr. paper $13.99 (978-1-56414-154-5). The authors present a variety of possible ways to make money. (Rev: BL 6/15/87) [658.041]

11008 Kravetz, Stacy. *Girl Boss: Running the Show Like the Big Chicks* (7–10). Illus. 1999, Girl Pr. paper $19.95 (978-0-9659754-2-1). This book gives practical advice and tips for teenage girls who want to start a business of their own. (Rev: VOYA 8/99) [658.1]

11009 Otfinoski, Steven. *The Kid's Guide to Money: Earning It, Saving It, Spending It, Growing It, Sharing It* (4–8). Illus. 1996, Scholastic paper $4.95 (978-0-590-53853-4). This practical guide for kids on how to earn money and manage it responsibly includes budgeting, standard consumer advice, basic information about the stock market, credit cards, and sharing. (Rev: BL 4/1/96; SLJ 6/96; VOYA 6/96) [332.4]

Baby-sitting

11010 Barkin, Carol, and Elizabeth James. *The New Complete Babysitter's Handbook* (5–7). Illus. 1995, Clarion paper $7.95 (978-0-395-66558-9). A fine manual that covers such topics as first aid, ways to amuse children, and how to get jobs baby sitting. (Rev: BL 5/1/95; SLJ 6/95) [649.1]

11011 Weintraub, Aileen. *Everything You Need to Know About Being a Baby-Sitter: A Teen's Guide to Responsible Child Care* (5–8). 2000, Rosen LB $25.25 (978-0-8239-3085-2). This book covers all facets of baby-sitting from preparation, responsibilities, and safety precautions to employment opportunities. (Rev: SLJ 7/00) [649]

11012 Zakarin, Debra M. *The Ultimate Baby-Sitter's Handbook: So You Wanna Make Tons of Money?* (4–8). Illus. 1997, Price Stern Sloan paper $4.99 (978-0-8431-7936-1). A practical, easily read guide to baby-sitting and setting up a business. (Rev: BL 9/15/97; SLJ 12/97) [649]

Managing Money

11013 Bateman, Katherine R. *The Young Investor: Projects and Activities for Making Your Money Grow* (8–12). Illus. 2001, Chicago Review paper $13.95 (978-1-55652-396-0). The basics of investing are introduced in a straightforward, reassuring manner, with anecdotes about young investor "Billy Ray Fawns" to hold the reader's interest. (Rev: BL 12/15/01; SLJ 2/02) [332.6]

11014 Guthrie, Donna, and Jan Stiles. *Real World Math: Money, Credit, and Other Numbers in Your Life* (6–9). Illus. 1998, Millbrook $26.90 (978-0-7613-0251-3). A practical and entertaining guide that shows how math is used in everyday situations including shopping, managing money, buying a car, and using credit wisely. (Rev: BL 6/1–15/98; HBG 9/98; SLJ 6/98; VOYA 8/98) [332.024]

11015 Hurwitz, Jane. *High Performance Through Effective Budgeting* (8–12). Illus. Series: Learning-a-Living Library. 1996, Rosen LB $26.50 (978-0-8239-2203-1). Basic budgeting skills are presented for both personal and on-the-job application. (Rev: BL 8/96; SLJ 10/96; VOYA 2/97) [332.024]

11016 Nathan, Amy. *The Kids' Allowance Book* (4–7). Illus. 1998, Walker $15.95 (978-0-8027-8651-7). Children ages 9 to 14 present the pros and cons of allowances and money management. (Rev:

BCCB 6/98; BL 7/98; HBG 10/98; SLJ 10/98) [332.02]

11017 Rendon, Marion, and Rachel Kranz. *Straight Talk About Money* (7–12). Series: Straight Talk. 1992, Facts on File LB $27.45 (978-0-8160-2612-8). Provides a brief history and description of money and the U.S. economy, followed by suggestions young adults can use when earning and managing money. (Rev: BL 6/15/92) [332.4]

11018 Silver, Don. *The Generation Y Money Book: 99 Smart Ways to Handle Money* (7–12). 2000, Adams-Hall paper $15.95 (978-0-944708-64-4). Sound advice about money management, credit card use, planning for college, savings, and investment. (Rev: VOYA 6/01) [332.024]

734

Health and the Human Body

General and Miscellaneous

11019 Apel, Melanie Ann. *Coping with Stuttering* (6–10). Series: Coping. 2000, Rosen LB $31.95 (978-0-8239-2970-2). Practical advice for stutterers and for listeners is accompanied by information on celebrities who have conquered this problem. (Rev: SLJ 4/00) [616.85]

11020 Costello, Patricia. *Female Fitness Stars of TV and the Movies* (7–12). Series: Legends of Health and Fitness. 2000, Mitchell Lane LB $25.70 (978-1-58415-050-3). Cher, Goldie Hawn, and Demi Moore are among the actors profiled here as examples of professionals who put fitness high on their list of priorities. (Rev: SLJ 2/01)

11021 Debenedette, Valerie. *Caffeine* (7–10). Series: Drug Library. 1996, Enslow LB $26.60 (978-0-89490-741-8). A well-documented, well-organized look at caffeine, where it is found, its effects, and its abuse. (Rev: BL 9/15/96; SLJ 9/96) [615]

11022 Foley, Ronan. *World Health: The Impact on Our Lives* (5–8). Illus. Series: 21st Century Debates. 2003, Raintree LB $28.56 (978-0-7398-5507-2). A thorough and thought-provoking exploration of the health status of countries around the world and the reasons for the wide disparity between wealthy and poor nations. (Rev: BL 8/03; HBG 10/03; SLJ 7/03) [362.1]

11023 Gilbert, Richard J. *Caffeine: The Most Popular Stimulant* (8–12). Illus. 1986, Chelsea LB $19.95 (978-0-87754-756-3). Tea, coffee, and chocolate are covered in this account of what the author calls "the most popular drug in the world." (Rev: BL 7/86) [615]

11024 Gutman, Bill. *Harmful to Your Health* (5–8). Illus. Series: Focus on Safety. 1996, Twenty-First Century LB $24.90 (978-0-8050-4144-6). This vol-ume outlines the problems inherent in drugs, alcohol, AIDS, steroids, and sexual abuse, with material on how to be alert to their dangers. (Rev: BL 2/1/97; SLJ 2/97) [616.86]

11025 Hurley, Jennifer A., ed. *Addiction* (6–12). Illus. Series: Opposing Viewpoints. 1999, Greenhaven paper $13.96 (978-0-7377-0116-6). A collection of essays and opinions that explores various viewpoints on addiction including causes, treatments, and government intervention. (Rev: BL 3/15/00) [362.29]

11026 Iannucci, Lisa. *Birth Defects* (7–12). Illus. 2000, Enslow LB $26.60 (978-0-7660-1186-1). The stories of two babies with problems introduce this survey of birth defects and their causes, prevention, diagnosis, and treatment, along with discussion of the impact on the mothers. (Rev: HBG 9/00; SLJ 8/00) [616]

11027 Jukes, Mavis. *The Guy Book: An Owner's Manual* (6–12). Illus. 2002, Crown paper $12.95 (978-0-679-89028-7). Jukes takes an appealing, frank-talking approach to sex, health, and hygiene for young men, covering everything from dating and birth control to choosing clothes and slow dancing. (Rev: BL 1/1–15/02; HBG 10/02; SLJ 3/02; VOYA 6/02) [305.235]

11028 Jukes, Mavis, and Lilian Cheung. *Be Healthy! It's a Girl Thing: Food, Fitness, and Feeling Great* (5–8). Illus. by Debra Ziss. 2003, Crown LB $18.99 (978-0-679-99029-1); paper $12.95 (978-0-679-89029-4). The authors take a matter-of-fact, motivational approach to changes that arrive with puberty and the steps girls can take to be healthy and avoid weight gain and eating disorders. (Rev: BL 1/1–15/04; SLJ 12/03) [613]

11029 McCarthy-Tucker, Sherri. *Coping with Special-Needs Classmates* (5–8). 1993, Rosen LB $25.25 (978-0-8239-1598-9). First-person accounts describe physical, mental, and emotional problems faced by some young people. (Rev: SLJ 8/93) [616]

11030 Powell, Phelan. *Trailblazers of Physical Fitness* (7–12). Series: Legends of Health and Fitness. 2000, Mitchell Lane LB $25.70 (978-1-58415-024-4). Jack LaLanne and Richard Simmons are among the individuals profiled here as leading proponents of physical fitness. (Rev: SLJ 2/01)

11031 Rebman, Renee C. *Addictions and Risky Behaviors: Cutting, Bingeing, Snorting, and Other Dangers* (7–12). 2006, Enslow LB $31.93 (978-0-7660-2165-5). The many behaviors associated with addiction — alcohol, smoking, eating problems, drugs, inhalants, self-mutilation, Internet — are defined and the risks are clearly stated; resources include Web sites and related organizations. (Rev: SLJ 6/06)

11032 Sommers, Annie Leah. *Everything You Need to Know About Looking and Feeling Your Best: A Guide for Girls* (6–12). Series: Need to Know Library. 2000, Rosen LB $27.95 (978-0-8239-3079-1). This book aims to boost girls' self-images as well as their knowledge of health and hygiene. (Rev: HBG 9/00; SLJ 3/00) [613]

11033 Torr, James D., ed. *Health Care: Province Divided* (8–12). Series: Opposing Viewpoints. 1999, Greenhaven LB $32.45 (978-0-7377-0129-6); paper $13.96 (978-0-7377-0128-9). The problems of the healthcare system in the United States are presented from a variety of points of view including those of doctors and health policy experts. (Rev: BL 11/15/99; SLJ 2/00) [362.1]

11034 Winner, Cherie. *Circulating Life: Blood Transfusions from Ancient Superstition to Modern Medicine* (6–9). Illus. Series: Discovery! 2007, Lerner LB $29.27 (978-0-8225-6606-9). A fascinating look at the history of blood transfusion and the ways in which the safety and efficacy of this technique have improved as medical knowledge has increased and superstition has (generally) decreased. (Rev: BL 4/15/07; SLJ 6/07) [615]

Aging and Death

11035 Altman, Linda J. *Death: An Introduction to Medical-Ethical Dilemmas* (6–12). 2000, Enslow LB $26.60 (978-0-7660-1246-2). Physical, cultural, moral, and psychological issues relating to death are explored in this insightful, informative book. (Rev: BL 6/1–15/00; HBG 9/00; SLJ 8/00) [179.4]

11036 Cavan, Seamus. *Euthanasia: The Debate Over the Right to Die* (6–8). Series: Focus on Science and Society. 2000, Rosen LB $26.50 (978-0-8239-3215-3). This volume discusses ethical and legal considerations on both sides of the debate concerning euthanasia. (Rev: SLJ 1/01) [179.7]

11037 Colman, Penny. *Corpses, Coffins, and Crypts: A History of Burial* (7–12). Illus. 1997, Holt $19.95 (978-0-8050-5066-0). Customs associated with death and burial traditions in various cultures and times are covered in a text enlivened with many photographs. (Rev: BL 11/1/97; HBG 3/98; SLJ 12/97*) [393]

11038 Digiulio, Robert, and Rachel Kranz. *Straight Talk About Death and Dying* (7–12). Series: Straight Talk. 1995, Facts on File $27.45 (978-0-8160-3078-1). Among the topics covered in this book about death and dying are Kubler-Ross's five psychological stages experienced by the dying and various aspects of mourning. (Rev: BL 9/15/95; SLJ 12/95) [155.9]

11039 Gay, Kathlyn. *The Right to Die: Public Controversy, Private Matter* (7–12). Series: Issue and Debate. 1993, Millbrook LB $24.90 (978-1-56294-325-7). Discusses euthanasia and assisted suicide in depth — from Greek times to the present — and includes actual recent cases. (Rev: BL 10/1/93) [179]

11040 Giddens, Sandra, and Owen Giddens. *Coping with Grieving and Loss* (6–10). 2000, Rosen LB $25.25 (978-0-8239-2894-1). Practical advice about the process of grieving and funerals is accompanied by personal teen stories. (Rev: SLJ 4/00) [155.9]

11041 Gootman, Marilyn E. *When a Friend Dies: A Book for Teens About Grieving and Healing.* Rev. ed. (6–12). Ed. by Pamela Espeland. 2005, Free Spirit paper $9.95 (978-1-57542-170-4). An updated edition of a guide first published in 1994, this volume offers sound advice and reassurance for teenagers suffering the loss of a friend or peer, including quotes from bereaved teens. (Rev: SLJ 10/05) [155.9]

11042 Grollman, Earl A. *Straight Talk About Death for Teenagers: How to Cope with Losing Someone You Love* (7–12). 1993, Beacon paper $13.00 (978-0-8070-2501-7). Grollman validates the painful feelings teens experience following the death of a loved one, conveying a sense of the grief as well as the need to get on with life. (Rev: BL 4/1/93; SLJ 6/93; VOYA 8/93) [155.9]

11043 Hyde, Margaret O., and Lawrence E. Hyde. *Meeting Death* (5–8). 1989, Walker LB $15.85 (978-0-8027-6874-2). After a history of how various cultures regard death, the authors discuss this phenomenon, the concept of grieving, and how to face death. (Rev: BL 1/1/90; SLJ 11/89) [306.9]

11044 Knox, Jean. *Death and Dying* (8–12). Illus. Series: 21st Century Health and Wellness. 2000, Chelsea LB $24.95 (978-0-7910-5986-9). This comprehensive and detailed volume looks at the variety of rituals that accompany death, at the role of doctors and others in supporting the dying and their families, and at the possibility of an afterlife. (Rev: BL 11/15/00; HBG 10/01; SLJ 2/01) [155.9]

11045 Krementz, Jill. *How It Feels When a Parent Dies* (4–7). Illus. 1988, Knopf paper $15.00 (978-0-394-75854-1). Eighteen experiences of parental death are recounted.

11046 Latta, Sara. *Dealing with the Loss of a Loved One* (6–12). Series: Focus on Family Matters. 2002, Chelsea LB $25.00 (978-0-7910-6955-4). This work discusses the many facets of grief and explains how to deal with the behavioral, emotional, and physical changes that may occur after the death of a loved one. (Rev: BL 1/1–15/03; HBG 3/03) [128]

11047 Leone, Daniel, ed. *Physician-Assisted Suicide* (8–12). Series: At Issue. 1997, Greenhaven $26.20 (978-1-56510-019-0); paper $17.45 (978-1-56510-018-3). Authors represented in this anthology debate whether doctors should be allowed to help terminally ill patients end their lives rather than suffer prolonged pain. (Rev: BL 5/15/98; SLJ 5/98) [179.7]

11048 LeShan, Eda. *Learning to Say Good-bye: When a Parent Dies* (5–7). Illus. by Paul Giovanopoulos. 1976, Avon paper $8.00 (978-0-380-40105-5). A sympathetic explanation of the many reactions children have to death.

11049 Marzilli, Alan. *Physician-Assisted Suicide* (7–12). Series: Point/Counterpoint. 2003, Chelsea House LB $32.95 (978-0-7910-7485-5). The arguments for and against the right to choose how and when to die, whether medical advice should be necessary, and the implications of medical intervention are all discussed with reference to federal and state laws and court cases. (Rev: SLJ 4/04) [179]

11050 Myers, Edward. *When Will I Stop Hurting? Teens, Loss, and Grief* (7–12). Illus. by Kelly Adams. Series: It Happened to Me. 2004, Scarecrow $34.50 (978-0-8108-4921-1). Firsthand accounts from teens add to this discussion of the stages of grief and of warning signs that should be monitored. (Rev: SLJ 11/04) [155.9]

11051 Panno, Joseph. *Aging: Theories and Potential Therapies* (7–12). Illus. Series: The New Biology. 2004, Facts on File $35.00 (978-0-8160-4951-6). Panno examines various theories about the aging process, as well as methods to stave off the depredations of age. (Rev: SLJ 2/05)

11052 Rebman, Renee C. *Euthanasia and the "Right to Die": A Pro/Con Issue* (5–8). Illus. Series: Pro/Con Issues. 2002, Enslow LB $27.93 (978-0-7660-1816-7). An objective examination of both sides of the issue of euthanasia. (Rev: BL 9/1/02; HBG 3/03) [179.7]

11053 Schleifer, Jay. *Everything You Need to Know When Someone You Know Has Been Killed* (6–12).

Illus. Series: Need to Know Library. 1998, Rosen LB $27.95 (978-0-8239-2779-1). This book helps young people deal with sudden death, describes the grieving process, and gives advice concerning the painful issues associated with death. (Rev: BL 10/1/98) [155.9]

11054 Wagner, Heather Lehr. *Dealing with Terminal Illness in the Family* (6–12). Series: Focus on Family Matters. 2002, Chelsea $25.00 (978-0-7910-6692-8). This account explores the different emotions produced by the terminal illness of a loved one and how to cope with them. (Rev: BL 10/15/02; SLJ 10/02) [618]

11055 Wilson, Antoine. *You and a Death in Your Family* (5–8). Series: Family Matters. 2001, Rosen LB $26.50 (978-0-8239-3355-6). Wilson provides concise, readable advice on coping with the death of a relative or pet and stresses that youngsters should seek help when necessary. (Rev: SLJ 8/01) [155.9]

11056 Winters, Paul A., ed. *Death and Dying* (8–12). Series: Opposing Viewpoints. 1997, Greenhaven paper $21.20 (978-1-56510-670-3). Topics dealt with in this anthology of articles include the treatment of terminally ill patients, the right to die, how to cope with death, and whether death is the end of life. (Rev: BL 10/15/97; SLJ 2/98) [179]

11057 Wolfelt, Alan D. *Healing a Teen's Grieving Heart: 100 Practical Ideas* (6–12). 2001, Companion paper $11.95 (978-1-879651-24-1). Teens who have suffered a loss will find practical reassurance and comfort in the suggestions offered here. (Rev: SLJ 9/01; VOYA 8/01)

11058 Yount, Lisa. *Euthanasia* (6–12). Illus. Series: Overview. 2000, Lucent LB $29.95 (978-1-56006-697-2). Diverse opinions are presented in this book, allowing readers to formulate their own ideas about this issue. (Rev: BL 1/1–15/01) [179.7]

Alcohol, Drugs, and Smoking

11059 Alagna, Magdalena. *Everything You Need to Know About the Dangers of Binge Drinking* (6–10). Illus. Series: Need to Know Library. 2001, Rosen LB $27.95 (978-0-8239-3289-4). Warnings about the physical and psychological dangers of alcohol are interwoven with fictional examples. (Rev: BL 5/1/02) [362.292]

11060 Alvergue, Anne. *Ecstasy: The Danger of False Euphoria* (6–10). Illus. Series: Drug Abuse Prevention Library. 1997, Rosen LB $17.95 (978-0-8239-2506-3). A discussion of how the drug MDMA, known as ecstasy, affects the mind and body. (Rev: SLJ 5/98)

11061 Aretha, David. *Cocaine and Crack* (6–9). Illus. Series: Drugs. 2005, Enslow LB $25.26 (978-

0-7660-5276-5). Focuses on cocaine and its derivative, crack, examining how they are produced, their effects, and the dangers they pose to users. Also use *Ecstasy and Other Party Drugs* (2005). (Rev: SLJ 6/05) [362.29]

11062 Aretha, David. *On the Rocks: Teens and Alcohol* (6–8). 2006, Watts LB $30.50 (978-0-531-16792-2). Binge drinking and other forms of alcohol abuse are covered in this volume that also discusses the efficacy of various strategies to solve these problems. (Rev: SLJ 3/07) [613.81]

11063 Aretha, David. *Steroids and Other Performance-Enhancing Drugs* (6–9). Illus. Series: MyReportLinks.com. 2005, Enslow LB $25.26 (978-0-7660-5277-2). Explores the dangers of steroids and other performance-enhancing drugs, with password access to Web sites that are regularly monitored. (Rev: BL 6/1–15/05; SLJ 6/05) [362.29]

11064 Aue, Pamela Willwerth, ed. *Teen Drug Abuse* (8–12). Series: Opposing Viewpoints. 2006, Gale LB $34.95 (978-0-7377-3335-8). Cigarettes, alcohol, marijuana, inhalants, ritalin — they're all discussed in pro and con essays that will be particularly helpful for reports and debates. (Rev: SLJ 3/07) [362.2]

11065 Avraham, Regina. *The Downside of Drugs* (8–12). Illus. 1988, Chelsea LB $19.95 (978-1-55546-232-1). This account covers the effects of such drugs as nicotine, alcohol, narcotics, stimulants, and hallucinogens. (Rev: SLJ 6/88) [613.8]

11066 Avraham, Regina. *Substance Abuse* (8–12). 1988, Chelsea LB $19.95 (978-1-55546-219-2). This account describes how drugs affect behavior and how addiction is treated. (Rev: VOYA 4/89) [616.86]

11067 Banfield, Susan. *Inside Recovery: How the Twelve-Step Program Can Work for You* (7–10). Series: Drug Abuse Prevention Library. 1998, Rosen LB $27.95 (978-0-8239-2634-3). A look at the 12-steps to recovery and the many problems one can face going through this program, which has been a successful route for many addicts. (Rev: VOYA 2/99) [613.8]

11068 Barbour, Scott, ed. *Drug Legalization* (6–12). Series: Current Controversies. 2000, Greenhaven LB $21.20 (978-0-7377-0335-1); paper $32.45 (978-0-7377-0336-8). In this collection of essays, the drug legalization controversy is examined from various points of view. (Rev: BL 10/15/00) [364.1]

11069 Barter, James. *Hallucinogens* (8–12). Illus. Series: Drug Education Library. 2002, Gale LB $32.45 (978-1-56006-915-7). This absorbing and comprehensive book explains the effects of hallucinogens on the body, traces their use — in ancient rituals, in medical treatments, and as a recreational drug — and looks at the debates over their legaliza-

tion. Also in this series is *Marijuana*. (Rev: BL 6/1–15/02; SLJ 6/02) [362.29]

11070 Bayer, Linda. *Strange Visions: Hallucinogen-Related Disorders* (6–10). Illus. Series: Encyclopedia of Psychological Disorders. 2000, Chelsea $35.00 (978-0-7910-5315-7). Bayer explains how the abuse of certain drugs can produce hallucinations and possible permanent brain damage. (Rev: BL 11/1/00; HBG 9/00) [616.86]

11071 Beal, Eileen. *Ritalin: Its Use and Abuse* (7–10). Series: Drug Abuse Prevention Library. 1999, Rosen LB $17.95 (978-0-8239-2775-3). This book explores the drug Ritalin, widely used for attention deficit disorder, and presents the controversies surrounding it. (Rev: BL 5/15/99; VOYA 4/00) [616.85]

11072 Bellenir, Karen, ed. *Tobacco Information for Teens: Health Tips about the Hazards of Using Cigarettes, Smokeless Tobacco, and Other Nicotine Products* (7–12). Series: Teen Health. 2007, Omnigraphics $65.00 (978-0-7808-0976-5). Full of facts and statistics, this book covers types of tobacco, addiction, the impact on health, and ways to stop using the substance. (Rev: SLJ 9/07) [362.2]

11073 Berne, Emma Carlson. *Methamphetamine* (7–10). Illus. Series: Compact Research: Drugs. 2007, Reference Point LB $24.95 (978-1-60152-004-3). A look at the dangerous drug that is used in rural as well as urban areas in what some are calling an epidemic. Quotations from officials and former users will be useful to report writers. (Rev: BL 4/1/07; LMC 11/07; SLJ 5/07) [362.29]

11074 Biggers, Jeff. *Transgenerational Addiction* (6–9). Series: Drug Abuse Prevention Library. 1998, Rosen LB $27.95 (978-0-8239-2757-9); Hazelden paper $6.95 (978-1-56838-247-0). This book deals with entire families that battle addiction to drugs and alcohol, and how each member must deal with the challenge individually. (Rev: BL 5/15/98) [362.2913]

11075 Boyd, George A. *Drugs and Sex* (5–10). Illus. Series: Drug Abuse Prevention Library. 1994, Rosen LB $17.95 (978-0-8239-1538-5). A careful examination of the hazards of combining drugs and sex, including unsafe sex, pregnancy, AIDS, and other sexually transmitted diseases. (Rev: BL 6/1–15/94; SLJ 5/94) [613.9]

11076 Clayton, Lawrence. *Alcohol Drug Dangers* (4–7). Illus. Series: Drug Dangers. 1999, Enslow LB $27.93 (978-0-7660-1159-5). Using real-life case histories, this book describes the effects of alcohol on the body and mind. (Rev: BL 8/99; HBG 10/99) [362.292]

11077 Clayton, Lawrence. *Diet Pill Drug Dangers* (5–9). Series: Drug Dangers. 1999, Enslow LB $19.95 (978-0-7660-1158-8). With liberal use of case histories, this book explores the dangers of diet pill use, their effects on the human body, and prevention techniques. (Rev: HBG 10/99; SLJ 9/99) [362.29]

11078 Clayton, Lawrence. *Tranquilizers* (7–10). Illus. Series: Drug Library. 1997, Enslow LB $26.60 (978-0-89490-849-1). Information is presented about tranquilizers, their beneficial effects, and the potential consequences of abuse and addiction. (Rev: BL 3/15/97; SLJ 6/97) [615]

11079 Clayton, Lawrence. *Working Together Against Drug Addiction* (6–10). 1996, Rosen LB $27.95 (978-0-8239-2263-5). In addition to discussing drugs and addiction, this work takes an activist approach by providing ways for teens to locate drug and alcohol counselors and programs and ways they can become involved and make a difference. (Rev: SLJ 5/97) [362]

11080 Connelly, Elizabeth Russell. *Through a Glass Darkly: The Psychological Effects of Marijuana and Hashish* (8–12). Series: Encyclopedia of Psychological Disorders. 1999, Chelsea $39.00 (978-0-7910-4897-9). After an overview of the history of marijuana and hashish, this volume surveys their medicinal and recreational use, effects of interaction with other drugs, potential disorders from their use, the dangers of addiction, and treatments available. (Rev: VOYA 8/99) [362.29]

11081 Connolly, Sean. *Amphetamines* (7–9). Series: Just the Facts. 2000, Heinemann LB $24.22 (978-1-57572-254-2). An attractive look at the use and misuse of these drugs, with many illustrations. (Rev: BL 3/1/01; SLJ 2/01) [362.29]

11082 Connolly, Sean. *Cocaine* (7–9). Series: Just the Facts. 2000, Heinemann LB $24.22 (978-1-57572-255-9). This book introduces cocaine, its history, the culture surrounding it, its effects on the brain and body, and recovery issues. (Rev: BL 3/1/01; HBG 10/01; SLJ 2/01) [362.29]

11083 Connolly, Sean. *LSD* (7–9). Series: Just the Facts. 2000, Heinemann LB $24.22 (978-1-57572-258-0). This attractive book describes the history of LSD, and gives material on the emotional, mental, and physical problems with its use. (Rev: BL 3/1/01) [362.29]

11084 Connolly, Sean. *Steroids* (7–9). Series: Just the Facts. 2000, Heinemann LB $24.22 (978-1-57572-259-7). This attractively illustrated book introduces steroids, their use and abuse, and their effects on both the body and the brain. (Rev: BL 3/1/01; HBG 10/01; SLJ 2/01) [362.29]

11085 Connolly, Sean. *Tobacco* (7–9). Illus. Series: Just the Facts. 2000, Heinemann LB $24.22 (978-1-57572-260-3). The history of tobacco use is presented along with related health concerns, details of lawsuits against tobacco companies, and the sale of cigarettes to Third World countries. (Rev: BL 2/15/01; HBG 10/01) [362.29]

11086 Croft, Jennifer. *Drugs and the Legalization Debate* (6–10). Illus. Series: Drug Abuse Prevention Library. 1997, Rosen LB $17.95 (978-0-8239-2509-4). A well-balanced presentation of the pros and cons of legalizing drugs, along with a discussion of drug abuse and penalties and a brief look at how other countries deal with the issue. (Rev: SLJ 5/98) [362.29]

11087 Croft, Jennifer. *PCP: High Risk on the Streets* (7–10). Series: Drug Abuse Prevention Library. 1998, Rosen LB $27.95 (978-0-8239-2774-6). This book provides readers with important information about phencyclidine, or angel dust, the behavior it produces, and its dangers. (Rev: BL 11/15/98; SLJ 12/98) [362.29]

11088 Deeugenio, Deborah, and Debra Henn. *Diet Pills* (6–9). Illus. Series: Drugs, The Straight Facts. 2005, Chelsea House LB $30.00 (978-0-7910-8198-3). The authors explore the pitfalls of using drugs to lose weight. (Rev: SLJ 11/05)

11089 Dolmetsch, Paul, and Gail Mauricette, eds. *Teens Talk about Alcohol and Alcoholism* (6–9). 1986, Doubleday paper $15 (978-0-385-23084-1). Eighteen students from a junior high school in Bennington, Vermont, tell about the effects of alcohol on their lives. (Rev: BL 2/15/87) [362.2]

11090 Egendorf, Laura K. *Heroin* (8–10). Series: Compact Research. 2007, Reference Point LB $24.95 (978-1-60152-002-9). This compact volume provides lots of information for report writers, with illustrations, quotations from primary sources, lists of facts, statistical charts, and brief timelines. (Rev: SLJ 5/07) [363.29]

11091 Egendorf, Laura K. *Performance-Enhancing Drugs* (7–10). Illus. Series: Compact Research. 2007, Reference Point LB $24.95 (978-1-60152-003-6). A well-organized look at the drugs used to enhance sports performance and the dangers involved. (Rev: LMC 11–12/07; SLJ 9/07) [362.29]

11092 Elliot-Wright, Susan. *Heroin* (8–10). Series: Health Issues. 2004, Raintree LB $32.79 (978-0-7398-6894-2). This slim volume provides a concise history of heroin and examines the drug's effects on users and its impact on society. (Rev: SLJ 3/05) [363.29]

11093 Fitzhugh, Karla. *Steroids* (7–10). Illus. Series: Health Issues. 2003, Raintree LB $28.56 (978-0-7398-6426-5). An attractive, slim overview of steroids and how they affect the body. (Rev: SLJ 5/04) [362.29]

11094 Fooks, Louie. *The Drug Trade: The Impact on Our Lives* (6–10). Series: 21st Century Debates. 2003, Raintree LB $28.56 (978-0-7398-6033-5). Covers the types of illegal drugs being sold; the reasons why governments find it hard to control their growth/creation, distribution, and sale; the people who take these drugs; and the methods used to move them around the world. (Rev: SLJ 6/04) [362.2]

11095 Galas, Judith C. *Drugs and Sports* (5–8). Illus. Series: Overview. 1997, Lucent LB $29.95 (978-1-56006-185-4). A look at the kinds of illegal drugs taken by athletes, the reasons for their use, and the ways in which their use can be detected. (Rev: BL 3/15/97) [362.29]

11096 Glass, George. *Drugs and Fitting In* (6–9). Illus. Series: Drug Abuse Prevention Library. 1998, Rosen LB $27.95 (978-0-8239-2554-4). After a description of teen culture and its pressures to conform and be popular, this book presents alternatives and advice on how to remain drug-free. (Rev: BL 3/15/98; VOYA 6/98) [362.29]

11097 Glass, George. *Narcotics: Dangerous Painkillers* (6–9). Illus. Series: Drug Abuse Prevention Library. 1998, Rosen LB $17.95 (978-0-8239-2719-7). This book explains the dangers of abusing prescribed painkilling drugs and their street derivatives and discusses issues relating to addiction and treatment. (Rev: BL 5/15/98; SLJ 10/98) [616.8632]

11098 Goldish, Meish. *Dangers of Herbal Stimulants* (6–10). Illus. Series: Drug Abuse Prevention Library. 1997, Rosen LB $17.95 (978-0-8239-2555-1). Teens are enticed to use herbal substances to get high, lose weight, or solve other emotional and physical problems. This book describes the products available, their potential dangers, and the laws that regulate their use. (Rev: SLJ 5/98; VOYA 2/99) [362.29]

11099 Gottfried, Ted. *The Facts About Alcohol* (7–12). Series: Drugs. 2004, Benchmark LB $37.07 (978-0-7614-1805-4). A history of alcohol use plus discussion of its effects on the body and impact on society. (Rev: SLJ 3/05) [613.8]

11100 Gottfried, Ted. *Should Drugs Be Legalized?* (6–12). Illus. 2000, Twenty-First Century LB $23.90 (978-0-7613-1314-4). This work features a description of various kinds of drugs, their effects, their harmful aspects, and a discussion of the problems and benefits of legalizing their use. (Rev: BL 4/1/00; HBG 9/00; SLJ 7/00) [362.29]

11101 Grabish, Beatrice R. *Drugs and Your Brain* (6–10). Illus. Series: Drug Abuse Prevention Library. 1998, Rosen paper $6.95 (978-1-56838-214-2). This book describes how drugs affect the brain and the risks of permanent as well as short-term damage. (Rev: BL 4/15/98; SLJ 6/98) [616.86]

11102 Green, Carl R. *Nicotine and Tobacco* (4–8). Illus. Series: Drugs. 2005, Enslow LB $25.26 (978-0-7660-5283-3). Fictional scenarios are combined with information on the addictive qualities of nicotine and the dangers of smoking and other forms of tobacco use; Web links extend the text. (Rev: SLJ 11/05) [362.2]

11103 Grosshandler-Smith, Janet. *Working Together Against Drinking and Driving* (4–8). Series: The Library of Social Activism. 1996, Rosen LB $16.95 (978-0-8239-2259-8). With an emphasis on prevention, the author presents a general discussion on drinking and driving and its consequences, followed by pointers on how to avoid embarrassing situations, how to handle peer pressure about drinking. (Rev: SLJ 2/97) [613.8]

11104 Gwynne, Peter. *Who Uses Drugs?* (7–10). Illus. 1987, Chelsea LB $19.95 (978-1-55546-223-9). An overview of different kinds of drugs and who uses them. (Rev: BL 5/1/88) [362.2]

11105 Hanan, Jessica. *When Someone You Love Is Addicted* (5–9). Series: Drug Abuse Prevention Library. 1999, Rosen LB $27.95 (978-0-8239-2831-6). A short book that begins with teenage case histories and then discusses treatments and resources for young people with drug problems. (Rev: SLJ 7/99) [362.29]

11106 Haughton, Emma. *Alcohol* (7–10). Series: Talking Points. 1999, Raintree LB $27.12 (978-0-8172-5318-9). A candid look at the use and abuse of alcohol and its physical and emotional effects. (Rev: BL 8/99) [613.8]

11107 Heyes, Eileen. *Tobacco, USA: The Industry Behind the Smoke* (8–12). Illus. 1999, Twenty-First Century LB $24.90 (978-0-7613-0974-1). A concise study of the U.S. tobacco industry with material on its history, current farming techniques, government support and regulations, marketing ploys, and the industry's defensive battle against medical facts. (Rev: BL 12/15/99; HBG 4/00; SLJ 1/00) [338.2]

11108 Hodgson, Barbara. *In the Arms of Morpheus: The Tragic History of Morphine, Laudanum, and Patent Medicines* (6–12). Illus. 2001, Firefly $24.95 (978-1-55297-538-1). This thought-provoking survey of opium and its derivatives explores the drugs' history and the countless men and women — celebrated and unknown — who have used and abused them. (Rev: BL 11/15/01; VOYA 4/02) [362.29]

11109 Hyde, Margaret O. *Drug Wars* (7–12). 1990, Walker LB $12.85 (978-0-8027-6901-5). This account discusses the violence and despair that crack cocaine has brought to America and ways in which its production and distribution can be halted. (Rev: SLJ 6/90; VOYA 6/90) [616.86]

11110 Hyde, Margaret O. *Know About Drugs*. 4th ed. (5–8). 1995, Walker LB $15.85 (978-0-8027-8395-0). An introduction to drugs including marijuana, alcohol, PCP, inhalants, crack/cocaine, heroin, and nicotine. (Rev: BL 7/90; SLJ 3/96) [362.2]

11111 Hyde, Margaret O. *Know About Smoking*. Rev. ed. (5–8). Illus. 1995, Walker LB $14.85 (978-0-8027-8400-1). After a history of tobacco and nicotine, this book describes their effects on the body, addiction prevention, and the role of advertising in smoking. (Rev: BL 7/90; SLJ 9/95) [362.2]

11112 Hyde, Margaret O., and John F. Setaro. *Alcohol 101: An Overview for Teens* (5–10). 1999, Twenty-First Century LB $24.90 (978-0-7613-1274-1). Kinds of alcohol and their effects are described, with material on alcoholism and binge drinking. (Rev: HBG 3/00; SLJ 3/00; VOYA 12/00) [613.8]

11113 Hyde, Margaret O., and John F. Setaro. *Drugs 101: An Overview for Teens* (7–12). 2003, Twenty-First Century LB $25.90 (978-0-7613-2608-3). This well-researched and accessible introduction to the nature of addiction, illicit drugs, and the harmful results of their use features useful photographs, diagrams, and charts. (Rev: BL 5/15/03; HBG 10/03; SLJ 5/03; VOYA 10/03) [362.29]

11114 Hyde, Margaret O., and John K. Setaro. *Smoking 101: An Overview for Teens* (7–12). 2005, Twenty-First Century LB $26.60 (978-0-7613-2835-3). A nonjudgmental account of the physical effects of smoking, with information on tobacco advertising, the kinds of products marketed, and the industry both in the United States and around the world. (Rev: SLJ 1/06) [362.29]

11115 Jamiolkowski, Raymond M. *Drugs and Domestic Violence* (7–12). Series: Drug Abuse Prevention Library. 1996, Rosen LB $17.95 (978-0-8239-2062-4). Domestic violence increases when drugs are used in the home; this volume gives pointers to teens in these situations on how to stay safe. (Rev: SLJ 3/96) [362.2]

11116 Jeffrey, Laura S. *Marijuana = Busted* (6–9). Illus. Series: Busted! 2006, Enslow LB $23.95 (978-0-7660-2796-1). Scary stories of lives ruined, as well as facts about what marijuana does to the body and mind, will make readers think twice about using it. (Rev: BL 3/15/07) [613.8]

11117 Jones, Ralph. *Straight Talk: Answers to Questions Young People Ask About Alcohol* (7–9). 1989, TAB paper $4.95 (978-0-8306-9005-3). Fifty questions concerning alcohol and physical and psychological effects are answered in this short, straightforward book. (Rev: VOYA 12/89) [661]

11118 Kittleson, Mark J., ed. *The Truth About Alcohol* (8–12). Series: Truth About. 2004, Facts on File $35.00 (978-0-8160-5298-1). Discusses the effects and dangers of alcohol use, including binge drinking, alcoholism, unsafe sexual behavior, and impaired driving. (Rev: SLJ 4/05) [613.8]

11119 Klein, Wendy. *Drugs and Denial* (7–10). Series: Drug Abuse Prevention Library. 1998, Rosen LB $25.25 (978-0-8239-2773-9). This book describes the signs of addiction and the stages of adolescent drug use, helps teens to admit it if they have a drug problem, and provides tips for teens to help people they know who may be in denial. (Rev: BL 11/15/98) [362.29]

11120 Klosterman, Lorrie. *The Facts about Depressants* (7–12). Illus. Series: Drugs. 2005, Benchmark LB $25.95 (978-0-7614-1976-1). A helpful guide to depressants with some basic information about the various kinds on the market, their medical uses, how they are abused, and how they affect the body. (Rev: SLJ 5/06) [362.29]

11121 Knox, Jean McBee. *Drinking, Driving and Drugs* (7–10). Illus. 1988, Chelsea LB $19.95 (978-1-55546-231-4). An overview of this national problem with a focus on teenage offenders and victims. (Rev: BL 7/88; SLJ 9/88) [363.1]

11122 Kranz, Rachel. *Straight Talk About Smoking* (6–12). Series: Straight Talk. 1999, Facts on File LB $27.45 (978-0-8160-3976-0). This no-nonsense account explains why people start smoking, what smoking does to the body, the nature of addiction, and how to give up smoking. (Rev: BL 2/15/00; HBG 4/00; SLJ 3/00) [362.29]

11123 Laliberte, Michelle. *Marijuana* (6–9). Series: Drugs. 2005, Enslow LB $25.26 (978-0-7660-5281-9). Presents the hard facts about marijuana and its effects on the body, along with links to related online resources. (Rev: SLJ 10/05) [362.29]

11124 Landau, Elaine. *Hooked: Talking About Addiction* (5–10). Illus. 1995, Millbrook LB $22.90 (978-1-56294-469-8). This account defines addiction broadly — from use of alcohol and drugs to various forms of compulsive behavior — and gives suggestions for recovery. (Rev: BL 1/1–15/96; SLJ 1/96) [362.29]

11125 Landau, Elaine. *Meth: America's Drug Epidemic* (7–12). Illus. 2007, Twenty-First Century LB $30.60 (978-0-8225-6808-7). This cautionary book should scare readers away from methamphetamine by the photos alone and stories of users damaged by the drug serve as additional deterrents; the history of meth use, efforts to stop the current epidemic, and scientific details are also provided. (Rev: BL 10/15/07; SLJ 10/07) [362.29]

11126 Landau, Elaine. *Teenage Drinking* (7–12). Series: Issues in Focus. 1994, Enslow LB $20.95 (978-0-89490-575-9). An exploration of the causes and effects of teenage drinking and of prevention measures that have worked. (Rev: BL 11/15/94; SLJ 11/94; VOYA 12/94) [362.29]

11127 Lawler, Jennifer. *Drug Testing in Schools: A Pro/Con Issue* (5–8). Series: Hot Issues. 2000, Enslow LB $27.93 (978-0-7660-1367-4). The pros and cons of drug testing in schools are presented in an unbiased manner with sections on methods of drug testing, policies of various organizations, and the opinions of students, teachers, and parents. (Rev: HBG 3/01; SLJ 12/00) [362.29]

11128 Lawton, Sandra Augustyn, ed. *Drug Information for Teens: Health Tips about the Physical and Mental Effects of Substance Abuse.* 2nd ed. (7–12). Series: Teen Health. 2006, Omnigraphics $65 (978-0-7808-0862-1). Updating an earlier edition, this is a comprehensive, well-organized guide to substance abuse — drugs, chemicals, alcohol, and tobacco and including herbal supplements and caffeine and energy drinks — that covers treatment and drug testing as well as places to go to get help. (Rev: SLJ 12/06)

11129 Lee, Mary Price, and Richard S. Lee. *Drugs and Codependency* (6–10). Series: Drug Abuse Prevention Library. 1995, Rosen LB $17.95 (978-0-8239-2065-5). The vulnerability of teens who live in a household where drugs are abused is the focus of this volume. (Rev: BL 9/15/95; SLJ 10/95) [616.869]

11130 Lee, Mary Price, and Richard S. Lee. *Drugs and the Media* (5–10). Illus. Series: Drug Abuse Prevention Library. 1994, Rosen LB $17.95 (978-0-8239-1537-8). This book shows that the media often unintentionally glamorize drug use and describes how teens can evaluate the media's mixed messages. (Rev: BL 6/1–15/94; SLJ 5/94) [070.4]

11131 Lennard-Brown, Sarah. *Cocaine* (8–10). Series: Health Issues. 2004, Raintree LB $30.00 (978-0-7398-6893-5). A look at the history of cocaine as well as the drug's effects on users and its impact on society. (Rev: SLJ 3/05) [362.29]

11132 Lennard-Brown, Sarah. *Marijuana* (8–10). Series: Health Issues. 2004, Raintree LB $28.56 (978-0-7398-6896-6). Traces the history of marijuana and explores the drug's effects on users and on society. (Rev: SLJ 3/05) [362.29]

11133 Levert, Suzanne. *The Facts about LSD and Other Hallucinogens* (7–12). Illus. Series: Drugs. 2005, Benchmark LB $25.95 (978-0-7614-1974-7). A helpful guide to LSD and other hallucinogens, with some history and basic information about the various kinds on the market, their medical uses, how they are abused, and how they affect the body. (Rev: SLJ 5/06) [362.29]

11134 Levert, Suzanne. *The Facts About Steroids* (7–12). Illus. Series: Drugs. 2004, Benchmark LB $37.07 (978-0-7614-1808-5). Examines the effects of steroids on users, the health risks, and the laws governing steroid use. (Rev: SLJ 3/05) [362.29]

11135 Levine, Herbert M. *The Drug Problem* (7–12). Illus. Series: American Issues Debated. 1997, Raintree $31.40 (978-0-8172-4354-8). The pros and cons of issues relating to drugs are presented fairly, with discussion of the effectiveness of the war on drugs, the concept of decriminalizing drugs, and possible discrimination against minorities in our drug policies. (Rev: BL 11/15/97; VOYA 4/98) [362.2]

11136 Littell, Mary Ann. *Heroin Drug Dangers* (5–8). Series: Drug Dangers. 1999, Enslow LB $27.93 (978-0-7660-1156-4). A short, well-illustrat-

ed book that describes the physiological effects of heroin, the dangers of its use, and how to resist its temptations. (Rev: BL 9/15/99; HBG 3/00) [362.29]

11137 Littell, Mary Ann. *LSD* (6–9). Illus. Series: The Drug Library. 1996, Enslow LB $26.60 (978-0-89490-739-5). A history of the drug, details on how it is made, its different forms, and the physical and psychological effects of its use. (Rev: BL 12/1/96; SLJ 4/97) [362.29]

11138 Lookadoo, Justin. *The Dirt on Drugs: A Dateable Book* (6–10). Illus. Series: The Dirt. 2005, Revell paper $9.99 (978-0-8007-5919-3). A former Texas probation officer writes frankly about the dangers of drugs. (Rev: SLJ 7/05) [616.8]

11139 Lukas, Scott E. *Steroids* (7–10). Series: Drug Library. 1994, Enslow LB $26.60 (978-0-89490-471-4). An exploration of the physical, psychological, and legal consequences of using steroids. (Rev: BL 1/1/95; HBG 10/01; SLJ 1/95; VOYA 4/95) [362.29]

11140 McGuire, Paula. *Alcohol* (4–8). Illus. Series: Preteen Pressures. 1998, Raintree LB $25.69 (978-0-8172-5026-3). Topics discussed in this practical account include peer pressure to drink, the physical effects of alcohol, underage drinking, alcoholic parents, and ways to seek help. (Rev: BL 4/15/98; HBG 10/98) [362.29]

11141 McLaughlin, Miriam S., and Sandra P. Hazouri. *Addiction: The "High" That Brings You Down* (7–12). Series: Teen Issues. 1997, Enslow LB $20.95 (978-0-89490-915-3). This honest, accurate book lists causes of addiction, its characteristics, and the results of compulsive, uncontrolled behavior, with an emphasis on where teen addicts can find help and support at school and in the community. (Rev: SLJ 8/97; VOYA 10/97) [362.29]

11142 McMillan, Daniel. *Teen Smoking: Understanding the Risk* (6–12). Series: Issues in Focus. 1998, Enslow LB $20.95 (978-0-89490-722-7). An interesting, informative account that discusses nicotine addiction, secondhand smoke, health hazards, smoking prevention, and treatments for people who want to stop. (Rev: VOYA 8/98) [362.2]

11143 McMullin, Jordan, ed. *Marijuana* (6–9). Series: History of Drugs. 2005, Gale LB $36.20 (978-0-7377-1957-4). Excerpts from previously published materials — going back as far as the 16th century — chronicle the history of marijuana, focusing in particular on the controversy surrounding its use in Western society. (Rev: BL 4/1/05) [615]

11144 Masline, Shelagh Ryan. *Drug Abuse and Teens* (6–12). Illus. Series: Hot Issues. 2000, Enslow LB $27.93 (978-0-7660-1372-8). A clear, straightforward account that describes different drugs, ways they are abused, and how one can get help for drug problems. (Rev: BL 11/15/00; HBG 3/01) [362.29]

11145 Meer, Jeff. *Drugs and Sports* (7–12). Illus. 1987, Chelsea LB $19.95 (978-1-55546-226-0). An account that explains how various drugs affect an athlete's performance and how this abuse is being viewed by segments of the athletic world. (Rev: BL 11/1/87) [613]

11146 Menhard, Francha Roffe. *The Facts about Amphetamines* (7–12). Illus. Series: Drugs. 2005, Benchmark LB $25.95 (978-0-7614-1972-3). This guide gives a brief history of these drugs and basic information about the various kinds on the market, their medical uses, how they are abused, and how they affect the body. (Rev: SLJ 5/06) [362.29]

11147 Menhard, Francha Roffe. *The Facts About Inhalants* (7–12). Series: Drugs. 2004, Benchmark LB $37.07 (978-0-7614-1809-2). Explores the dangers associated with the use of inhalants. (Rev: SLJ 3/05) [362.29]

11148 Miller, Maryann. *Drugs and Date Rape* (6–10). Series: Drug Abuse Prevention Library. 1995, Rosen LB $17.95 (978-0-8239-2064-8). This book shows how drugs can break down important inhibitors, possibly leading to date rape, and how to avoid becoming a victim. (Rev: BL 9/15/95; SLJ 10/95) [362.88]

11149 Miller, Maryann. *Drugs and Gun Violence* (6–10). Series: Drug Abuse Prevention Library. 1995, Rosen LB $17.95 (978-0-8239-2060-0). This book explores the connection between violent crimes and drug use, with lessons that teens can use for survival. (Rev: BL 9/15/95; SLJ 10/95) [364.2]

11150 Miller, Maryann. *Drugs and Violent Crime* (6–10). Series: Drug Abuse Prevention Library. 1996, Rosen LB $27.95 (978-0-8239-2282-6). This book gives general information about drugs and their effects and explores the relationship between drug use and violent crime. (Rev: SLJ 3/97) [362.29]

11151 Monroe, Judy. *Antidepressants* (7–10). Series: Drug Library. 1997, Enslow LB $26.60 (978-0-89490-848-4). Current information is given about these frequently abused drugs, actual case studies are cited, and discussion questions are provided. (Rev: BL 5/15/97) [616.85]

11152 Monroe, Judy. *Inhalant Drug Dangers* (5–9). 1999, Enslow LB $27.93 (978-0-7660-1153-3). Using case histories — such as the story of Ian, who is addicted to inhaling fabric protector — this slim volume tells of the effects and dangers of inhalants. (Rev: BL 8/99; HBG 10/99; SLJ 9/99) [362.29]

11153 Monroe, Judy. *Nicotine* (7–10). Series: Drug Library. 1995, Enslow LB $26.60 (978-0-89490-505-6). A concise, easy-to-use look at nicotine, where it is found, its effects, and how to avoid its use. (Rev: BL 7/95; SLJ 9/95) [613.85]

11154 Monroe, Judy. *Steroid Drug Dangers* (5–8). Illus. Series: Drug Dangers. 1999, Enslow LB $27.93 (978-0-7660-1154-0). Case histories, facts, and statistics introduce the reader to steroid drugs and their legal and illegal uses, their effects and dangers, and the organizations that promote safe usage. (Rev: BL 9/15/99; HBG 3/00) [362.29]

11155 Murdico, Suzanne J. *Drug Abuse* (4–8). Series: Preteen Pressures. 1998, Raintree LB $25.69 (978-0-8172-5027-0). This work discusses drug abuse, with emphasis on healthy alternatives and solutions to typical drug-related problems faced by many young people. (Rev: BL 5/15/98; HBG 10/98) [362.2]

11156 Myers, Arthur. *Drugs and Emotions* (6–10). Series: Drug Abuse Prevention Library. 1996, Rosen LB $27.95 (978-0-8239-2283-3). This book explains how teens may be attracted to drugs as a way of dealing with feelings of sadness, pain, confusion, and frustration, and how they can become hooked on both legal and illegal drugs. Much of the discussion deals with how to recognize that a problem exists and where to get help. (Rev: SLJ 3/97) [362.29]

11157 Myers, Arthur. *Drugs and Peer Pressure* (6–10). Series: Drug Abuse Prevention Library. 1995, Rosen LB $17.95 (978-0-8239-2066-2). An exploration of peer pressure as a major reason why teens begin to use drugs, with suggestions for resisting it. (Rev: BL 9/15/95; SLJ 10/95) [362.29]

11158 Naff, Clay Farris. *Nicotine and Tobacco* (7–10). Illus. Series: Compact Research. 2007, Reference Point LB $24.95 (978-1-60152-006-7). A well-organized look at the use of nicotine and tobacco and the dangers involved. (Rev: LMC 11–12/07; SLJ 9/07) [613.85]

11159 Nakaya, Andrea C. *Marijuana* (8–10). Series: Compact Research. 2007, Reference Point LB $24.95 (978-1-60152-000-5). This compact volume provides lots of information for report writers, with illustrations, quotations from primary sources, lists of facts, statistical charts, and brief timelines. (Rev: SLJ 5/07) [362.29]

11160 Newman, Gerald, and Eleanor N. Layfield. *PCP* (7–10). Series: Drug Library. 1997, Enslow LB $26.60 (978-0-89490-852-1). Case studies, discussion questions, and chapter notes are highlights of this informative book on PCP, a frequently abused drug. (Rev: BL 12/15/97; HBG 3/98; SLJ 12/97) [362.2]

11161 Newton, David E. *Drug Testing: An Issue for School, Sports and Work* (6–12). Illus. Series: In Focus. 1999, Enslow LB $26.60 (978-0-89490-954-2). The question of civil rights vs. drug testing is explored in this volume that presents extreme positions and viewpoints in between. (Rev: BL 4/1/99; SLJ 4/99) [658.3]

11162 Nolan, Meghan, ed. *Let's Clear the Air: 10 Reasons Not to Start Smoking* (5–8). Illus. by Deanna Staffo. 2007, Lobster paper $14.95 (978-1-897073-66-7). In personal essays, young people reveal the reasons why they don't smoke — reasons ranging from the deaths of loved ones to the smell and the cost. (Rev: BL 1/1–15/08; LMC 2/08; SLJ 3/08) [613.85]

11163 Ojeda, Auriana, ed. *Smoking* (8–12). Series: Current Controversies. 2002, Gale LB $36.20 (978-0-7377-0857-8). A collection of writings that presents both sides of the debates on the controversial aspects of smoking — the provable health risks, the influence of advertising on young smokers, and so forth. (Rev: BL 7/02) [363.4]

11164 Olive, M. Foster. *Prescription Pain Relievers* (6–9). Illus. Series: Drugs, The Straight Facts. 2005, Chelsea House LB $30.00 (978-0-7910-8199-0). Describes how drugs work to relieve pain and the growing problems of abuse of such drugs. (Rev: SLJ 11/05) [613.8]

11165 Packard, Helen C. *Prozac: The Controversial Cure* (6–9). Illus. Series: Drug Abuse Prevention Library. 1998, Rosen LB $27.95 (978-0-8239-2551-3). This book explores the controversy around this antidepressant, called the miracle drug of the 1990s, and gives teens sound advice concerning its use and misuse. (Rev: BL 5/15/98; SLJ 10/98) [616.8527061]

11166 Packer, Alex J. *Highs! Over 150 Ways to Feel Really, REALLY Good . . . Without Alcohol or Other Drugs* (6–12). Illus. 2000, Free Spirit paper $15.95 (978-1-57542-074-5). Grouped into three areas (serenity, physical improvement, and creativity), the author describes 150 ways teenagers can feel good about themselves. (Rev: BL 11/1/00; SLJ 9/00) [158]

11167 Palenque, Stephanie Maher. *Crack and Cocaine=Busted!* (6–8). Series: Busted! 2005, Enslow LB $31.93 (978-0-7660-2169-3). A useful overview of cocaine and crack and the dangers these drugs pose to individual users and the community at large. (Rev: SLJ 9/05) [362.29]

11168 Richard, Pamela G. *Alcohol* (7–9). Series: Just the Facts. 2000, Heinemann LB $24.22 (978-1-57572-253-5). This account gives a history of alcohol use, how it affects the body and the brain, and treatments available for people who become addicted. (Rev: BL 3/1/01) [613.8]

11169 Robbins, Paul R. *Crack and Cocaine Drug Dangers* (5–9). Series: Drug Dangers. 1999, Enslow LB $27.93 (978-0-7660-1155-7). Charts, photographs, fact boxes, and a succinct text are used to discuss crack cocaine, its effects, and how to avoid its use. (Rev: BL 9/15/99; HBG 3/00) [362.29]

11170 Robbins, Paul R. *Designer Drugs* (7–12). Series: Drug Library. 1995, Enslow LB $26.60 (978-0-89490-488-2). An exploration of the growing problem of drugs made by "kitchen chemists." (Rev: BL 5/1/95; SLJ 5/95) [362.29]

11171 Robbins, Paul R. *Hallucinogens* (7–10). Illus. Series: Drug Library. 1996, Enslow LB $26.60 (978-0-89490-743-2). Drugs that cause auditory and visual hallucinations are described, along with their availability, dangerous effects, and current use. (Rev: BL 6/1–15/96; SLJ 7/96; VOYA 8/96) [362.29]

11172 Salak, John. *Drugs in Society: Are They Our Suicide Pill?* (6–9). Series: Issues of Our Time. 1993, Twenty-First Century LB $22.90 (978-0-8050-2572-9). Current opinions and treatments for drug addiction are discussed in this easily read book that examines how common drugs of all types are used and abused in our society. (Rev: BL 1/15/94; SLJ 2/94) [362.29]

11173 Sanders, Pete. *Smoking* (4–7). Illus. Series: What Do You Know About. 1996, Millbrook LB $23.90 (978-0-7613-0536-1). Covers the effects of smoking and ways in which youngsters can avoid getting hooked. (Rev: SLJ 3/97) [362.2]

11174 Sanders, Pete, and Steve Myers. *Drinking Alcohol* (4–8). Illus. Series: What Do You Know About. 1997, Millbrook LB $23.90 (978-0-7613-0573-6). An introduction to alcohol use and abuse, with material on how alcohol affects the body and behavior. (Rev: SLJ 10/97) [613.8]

11175 Santamaria, Peggy. *Drugs and Politics* (6–10). Series: Drug Abuse Prevention Library. 1994, Rosen LB $27.95 (978-0-8239-1703-7). A discussion of the influence of drugs on politics, such as in Colombia, where the government is involved with and intimidated by powerful drug interests. (Rev: BL 3/15/95; SLJ 3/95) [363.4]

11176 Schleichert, Elizabeth. *Marijuana* (7–10). Illus. Series: Drug Library. 1996, Enslow LB $26.60 (978-0-89490-740-1). This easy-to-read account discusses the history of marijuana use, its effects, availability, and controversies surrounding it, such as whether it should be made legal. (Rev: BL 6/1–15/96; SLJ 7/96; VOYA 8/96) [362.29]

11177 Schleifer, Jay. *Methamphetamine: Speed Kills* (5–9). Series: Drug Abuse Prevention Library. 1999, Rosen LB $25.25 (978-0-8239-2512-4). An introduction to this drug, its effects, the crime and violence associated with it, and agencies and organizations where help is available. (Rev: SLJ 7/99; VOYA 4/00) [362.29]

11178 Schnoll, Sidney. *Getting Help: Treatments for Drug Abuse* (7–12). Illus. 1986, Chelsea LB $19.95 (978-0-87754-775-4). This book concentrates on the many kinds of treatments available and the agencies involved in supplying this help. (Rev: BL 2/15/87) [362.2]

11179 Shannon, Joyce Brennfleck, ed. *Alcohol Information for Teens: Health Tips About Alcohol and Alcoholism* (7–12). Series: Teen Health. 2005, Omnigraphics $58.00 (978-0-7808-0741-9). Authoritative information about the effects of alcohol on the mind and body and the dangers of alcohol dependency. (Rev: SLJ 7/05) [613.8]

11180 Sheen, Barbara. *Teen Alcoholism* (7–12). Illus. Series: Teen Issues. 2004, Gale LB $29.95 (978-1-59018-501-8). This straightforward examination of teen alcoholism explores the individual and societal impact of the illness and offers a survey of possible treatment programs. (Rev: BL 7/04) [616.86]

11181 Sherry, Clifford J. *Drugs and Eating Disorders* (5–10). Illus. Series: Drug Abuse Prevention Library. 1994, Rosen LB $17.95 (978-0-8239-1540-8). Shows how diet pills and other weight-loss products can lead to drug abuse and, in some cases, addiction. (Rev: BL 6/1–15/94; SLJ 6/94) [616.85]

11182 Sherry, Clifford J. *Inhalants* (5–10). 1994, Rosen LB $17.95 (978-0-8239-1704-4). A look at inhalants, where they are found, and how they affect the body. (Rev: BL 2/15/95; SLJ 3/95) [362.29]

11183 Shuker, Nancy. *Everything You Need to Know About an Alcoholic Parent*. Rev. ed. (7–12). Illus. 1998, Rosen LB $27.95 (978-0-8239-2869-9). After a general discussion of alcoholism, Shuker explains how it changes human relationships and how young people can cope with it. (Rev: BL 1/15/90; VOYA 4/90) [362.29]

11184 Silverstein, Alvin, and Virginia Silverstein. *Alcoholism* (7–10). 1975, HarperCollins LB $12.89 (978-0-397-31648-9). Alcohol use and abuse are introduced, plus alcoholism and the problems it causes. [613.8]

11185 Simpson, Carolyn. *Methadone* (5–9). Series: Drug Abuse Prevention Library. 1997, Rosen LB $25.25 (978-0-8239-2286-4). The dangers of heroin are discussed, followed by an objective discussion of the pros and cons of methadone, the legal drug used to combat heroin addiction. (Rev: SLJ 11/97) [362.29]

11186 Somdahl, Gary L. *Marijuana Drug Dangers* (5–8). Series: Drug Dangers. 1999, Enslow LB $27.93 (978-0-7660-1214-1). After introducing marijuana and its effects, this account covers its misuse and abuse and ways to resist it. (Rev: BL 11/15/99; HBG 3/00) [362.29]

11187 Stewart, Gail B. *Teen Addicts* (7–12). Illus. Series: The Other America. 1999, Lucent LB $27.45 (978-1-56006-574-6). Four teenage drug addicts of different backgrounds share their stories. (Rev: BL 11/15/99; HBG 9/00) [362.29]

11188 Strazzabosco-Hayn, Gina. *Drugs and Sleeping Disorders* (7–12). Series: Drug Abuse Prevention Library. 1996, Rosen LB $27.95 (978-0-8239-2144-7). An exploration of sleep disorders and potential problems and dangers of using drugs for sleep. (Rev: SLJ 3/96) [362.2]

11189 Torr, James D., ed. *Drug Abuse* (8–12). Series: Opposing Viewpoints. 1999, Greenhaven paper $21.20 (978-0-7377-0050-3). This collection of articles and essays debates such topics as the extent of the nation's drug problem, the effectiveness of various programs, the value of government policies, and the legalization of selected drugs. (Rev: BL 4/15/99) [362.29]

11190 Torr, James D., ed. *Teens and Alcohol* (6–12). Series: Current Controversies. 2001, Gale LB $36.20 (978-0-7377-0859-2); paper $24.95 (978-0-7377-0858-5). A thought-provoking collection of essays on alcohol, drunk driving, health, the media, and the law that will be equally useful for report writers and the interested reader. (Rev: BL 5/1/02) [362.292]

11191 Trapani, Margi. *Inside a Support Group: Help for Teenage Children of Alcoholics* (6–9). Illus. Series: Drug Abuse Prevention Library. 1997, Rosen LB $27.95 (978-0-8239-2508-7). Teens with alcoholic parents get helpful information from this inside look at Alateen, an organization designed to help teens cope with a loved one's addiction to alcohol. (Rev: BL 12/15/97; SLJ 1/98) [362.292]

11192 Van Tuyl, Christine, ed. *Drunk Driving* (7–10). Illus. Series: Issues That Concern You. 2006, Gale $32.45 (978-0-7377-3239-9). Article excerpts present various points of view regarding legal drinking ages, blood-alcohol levels, the punishment of offenders, and so forth. (Rev: BL 10/15/06) [363.12]

11193 Wax, Wendy. *Say No and Know Why: Kids Learn About Drugs* (4–7). Illus. by Toby McAfee. 1992, Walker LB $13.85 (978-0-8027-8141-3). A serious look at drug problems as a 6th-grade class in the Bronx, New York, gets a visit from a local nurse and an assistant district attorney. (Rev: BL 1/15/93; SLJ 10/92) [362.29]

11194 Webb, Margot. *Drugs and Gangs* (7–12). Series: Drug Abuse Prevention Library. 1996, Rosen LB $17.95 (978-0-8239-2059-4). This book describes the connections between gangs and drugs, in both selling and using, and provides teens with tips on how to avoid these dangers. (Rev: SLJ 3/96; VOYA 6/96) [362.29]

11195 Weitzman, Elizabeth. *Let's Talk About Smoking* (4–8). Illus. Series: Let's Talk. 1996, Rosen LB $19.95 (978-0-8239-2307-6). This book explains why people smoke, its effects, and ways to avoid starting, with tips on how to give up. (Rev: BL 3/15/97; SLJ 1/97) [362.29]

11196 Wekesser, Carol, ed. *Chemical Dependency* (8–12). Illus. Series: Opposing Viewpoints. 1997, Greenhaven paper $21.20 (978-1-56510-551-5). Such topics as the magnitude of chemical dependency, its causes, treatments, and the possible reforming of drug laws are discussed in this collection of articles. (Rev: BL 7/97) [362.29]

11197 Wekesser, Carol, ed. *Smoking* (7–12). Series: Current Controversies. 1996, Greenhaven LB $32.45 (978-1-56510-534-8); paper $21.20 (978-1-56510-533-1). This collection of various opinions about smoking covers health risks, the amount of blame that tobacco companies should assume, measures to combat smoking, and the degree to which the government can interfere. (Rev: BL 12/15/96; SLJ 3/97) [362.29]

11198 Westcott, Patsy. *Why Do People Take Drugs?* (5–7). Series: Exploring Tough Issues. 2001, Raintree LB $25.69 (978-0-7398-3231-8). Drugs from caffeine to cocaine are explored, with discussion of society's attitudes toward drugs, legal issues, and the reasons some people are more tempted to abuse substances. (Rev: HBG 10/01; SLJ 7/01) [362.29]

11199 Wilkinson, Beth. *Drugs and Depression* (6–12). Illus. Series: Drug Abuse Prevention Library. 1994, Rosen LB $27.95 (978-0-8239-3004-3). Some young people turn to drugs to deal with their depression. This book shows the dangers in this approach and offers positive ways of handling depression and places to get assistance. (Rev: BL 6/1–15/94) [616.86]

11200 Woods, Geraldine. *Heroin* (7–10). Series: Drug Library. 1994, Enslow LB $26.60 (978-0-89490-473-8). A well-researched, clearly written, and carefully sourced book about heroin use and addiction. (Rev: BL 1/1/95; SLJ 1/95; VOYA 4/95) [362.29]

11201 Ziemer, Maryann. *Quaaludes* (7–10). Illus. Series: Drug Library. 1997, Enslow LB $26.60 (978-0-89490-847-7). The uses and effects of these frequently prescribed drugs are discussed, along with problems of misuse and addiction. (Rev: BL 3/15/97; SLJ 6/97) [613.8]

Bionics and Transplants

11202 Beecroft, Simon. *Super Humans: A Beginner's Guide to Bionics* (5–7). Illus. by Ian Thompson and Stephen Sweet. Series: Future Files. 1998, Millbrook LB $23.40 (978-0-7613-0621-4). This work explores such futuristic topics as cloning humans, gene manipulation, electronic body parts, and life extension. (Rev: HBG 10/98; SLJ 10/98) [617.9]

11203 Fullick, Ann. *Rebuilding the Body* (5–8). Illus. Series: Science at the Edge. 2002, Heinemann LB $27.86 (978-1-58810-700-8). An insightful volume about transplant procedures, including a section on how the organs of the body function and a

discussion about ethics. (Rev: BL 10/15/02; HBG 3/03; SLJ 4/03) [617.9]

11204 Kittredge, Mary. *Organ Transplants* (8–12). Series: 21st Century Health and Wellness. 1999, Chelsea House LB $24.95 (978-0-7910-5522-9). A history of progress in organ transplants is given, plus material on the ethical questions involved. (Rev: BL 4/15/00; HBG 9/00; SLJ 6/00) [617.9]

11205 McClellan, Marilyn. *Organ and Tissue Transplants: Medical Miracles and Challenges* (7–12). Series: Issues in Focus. 2003, Enslow LB $26.60 (978-0-7660-1943-0). The story of a critically injured teen draws readers into this discussion of transplants of organs and tissues and the ethical issues involved. (Rev: HBG 10/03; SLJ 5/03) [617.9]

11206 Murphy, Wendy. *Spare Parts: From Peg Legs to Gene Splices* (6–12). Illus. 2001, Twenty-First Century LB $23.90 (978-0-7613-1355-7). A history of medical advances that acknowledges the role of war in the development of increasingly advanced designs, with the moving story of one boy's anguish. (Rev: BCCB 3/01; BL 3/15/01; HBG 10/01) [617.9]

11207 Rosaler, Maxine. *Bionics* (5–9). Series: Science on the Edge. 2003, Gale LB $24.95 (978-1-56711-784-4). This account explores the science of fusing artificial parts with human parts to aid body functions and comments on the controversy surround this new science. (Rev: BL 10/15/03; SLJ 3/04) [174]

11208 Schwartz, Tina P. *Organ Transplants: A Survival Guide for the Entire Family: The Ultimate Teen Guide* (7–12). Illus. Series: It Happened to Me. 2005, Scarecrow $36.50 (978-0-8108-4924-2). A clear explanation, in question-and-answer format, of the complex problems relating to medical transplants, with discussion of the hazards and the emotional upheaval to be expected. (Rev: SLJ 10/05) [617.9]

Diseases and Illnesses

11209 Abramovitz, Melissa. *Lou Gehrig's Disease* (7–12). Illus. 2006, Gale LB $31.20 (978-1-59018-676-3). Sidebars, diagrams, and photographs help teens understand the causes, symptoms, and diagnosis of ALS, or Lou Gehrig's disease; potential future treatments are also discussed. (Rev: SLJ 7/06)

11210 Abrams, Liesa. *Chronic Fatigue Syndrome* (5–7). Illus. Series: Diseases and Disorders. 2003, Gale LB $32.45 (978-1-59018-039-6). The symptoms of and treatments for this mysterious condition and related medical problems are covered here, along with the research being undertaken. (Rev: SLJ 7/03) [616]

11211 Altman, Linda J. *Alzheimer's Disease* (7–9). Series: Diseases and Disorders. 2001, Lucent LB $32.45 (978-1-56006-695-8). In clear, concise prose, this account explains what Alzheimer's disease is, traces its causes, and gives current information on treatments. (Rev: BL 1/1–15/02) [616.8]

11212 Altman, Linda J. *Plague and Pestilence: A History of Infectious Disease* (6–12). Illus. Series: Issues in Focus. 1998, Enslow LB $26.60 (978-0-89490-957-3). A history of plagues and epidemics in world history, from the Black Death and leprosy to AIDS and spinal meningitis. (Rev: BL 3/1/99; HBG 3/99; SLJ 1/99) [614.4]

11213 Aronson, Virginia. *The Influenza Pandemic of 1918* (7–12). Illus. Series: Great Disasters: Reforms and Ramifications. 2000, Chelsea $30.00 (978-0-7910-5263-1). This detailed look at the deadly flu of 1918 serves as a reminder that modern travel makes such an event even more likely. (Rev: BL 10/15/00; HBG 3/01; SLJ 11/00; VOYA 2/01) [614.5]

11214 Balkin, Karen F., ed. *Food-Borne Illness* (7–12). Series: At Issue. 2004, Gale LB $29.95 (978-0-7377-1334-3); paper $21.20 (978-0-7377-1335-0). A collection of previously published articles that examine the dangers of food-borne illness and what can be done to protect consumers. (Rev: SLJ 4/05) [615.9]

11215 Barnard, Bryn. *Outbreak! Plagues That Changed History* (5–8). Illus. by author. 2005, Crown LB $19.99 (978-0-375-92986-1). Information on microbes and the study of microorganisms precedes details of specific epidemics. (Rev: SLJ 2/06) [614.4]

11216 Bellenir, Karen, ed. *Allergy Information for Teens: Health Tips About Allergic Reactions Such as Anaphylaxis, Respiratory Problems, and Rashes* (7–12). Illus. 2006, Omnigraphics $65 (978-0-7808-0799-0). Readers learn about allergy symptoms, tests, treatments, and management strategies with short Q&A sections, diagrams, and sidebars. (Rev: SLJ 7/06)

11217 Bellenir, Karen, ed. *Asthma Information for Teens: Health Tips About Managing Asthma and Related Concerns* (8–12). Illus. Series: Teen Health. 2005, Omnigraphics LB $65.00 (978-0-7808-0770-9). Information-packed but readable, this volume covers all aspects of asthma. (Rev: SLJ 9/05) [616.2]

11218 Benowitz, Steven I. *Cancer* (7–12). Series: Diseases and People. 1999, Enslow LB $26.60 (978-0-7660-1181-6). A discussion of the nature and treatment of various forms of cancer and of possible cures in the future. (Rev: BL 9/15/99; HBG 4/00) [616.994]

11219 Biskup, Michael D., and Karin L. Swisher, eds. *AIDS* (7–12). Series: Opposing Viewpoints. 1992, Greenhaven paper $16.20 (978-0-89908-165-6). The ethical questions surrounding AIDS are discussed, along with the effectiveness of testing and treatment, and the prevention of the disease's spread. (Rev: BL 11/15/92) [362.1]

11220 Bjorklund, Ruth. *Asthma* (4–7). Illus. Series: Health Alert. 2004, Benchmark LB $28.50 (978-0-7614-1803-0). In addition to describing the causes and treatment of asthma, this attractive title opens with a case history and also includes lists of famous people who suffer from the condition. (Rev: SLJ 5/05)

11221 Bjorklund, Ruth. *Food-Borne Illnesses* (4–7). Illus. Series: Health Alert. 2005, Marshall Cavendish LB $19.95 (978-0-7614-1917-4). This is a wide-ranging exploration of illnesses that can be caused by contaminated food — including those resulting from bacteria, poor hygiene, poor handling, and terrorism — and the treatments and preventions available. (Rev: SLJ 6/06) [615.9]

11222 Bowman-Kruhm, Mary. *Everything You Need to Know About Down Syndrome* (4–7). Series: Need to Know Library. 2000, Rosen LB $25.25 (978-0-8239-2949-8). Describes the causes, symptoms, and treatment of Down syndrome, and looks at the education and family life of individuals with this condition. (Rev: HBG 10/00; SLJ 3/00) [362.1]

11223 Brill, Marlene Targ. *Alzheimer's Disease* (4–7). Illus. Series: Health Alert. 2004, Benchmark LB $28.50 (978-0-7614-1799-6). In addition to describing the diagnosis and treatment of Alzheimer's disease, this attractive title opens with a case history and also includes lists of famous people who suffer from the condition. (Rev: SLJ 5/05) [362.19]

11224 Brill, Marlene Targ. *Tourette Syndrome* (6–12). Illus. Series: Twenty-First Century Medical Library. 2002, Millbrook LB $26.90 (978-0-7613-2101-9). This volume provides historical and medical information on the disorder named for neurologist Georges Gilles de la Tourette, presenting the stories of three teenagers who suffer from it. (Rev: BL 3/1/02; HBG 10/02; SLJ 4/02) [375]

11225 Bryan, Jenny. *Asthma* (5–10). Illus. Series: Just the Facts. 2004, Heinemann LB $27.07 (978-1-4034-4599-5). A well-organized explanation of asthma, illustrated with numerous color photographs and providing material on how air pollution and smoking are factors in causing or aggravating the disease. (Rev: SLJ 6/04) [616.2]

11226 Bryan, Jenny. *Diabetes* (5–10). Illus. Series: Just the Facts. 2004, Heinemann LB $27.07 (978-1-4034-4600-8). An illustrated overview of the disease, including causes and treatments and the effects of diet and cultural factors. (Rev: SLJ 6/04) [616.4]

11227 Bryan, Jenny. *Eating Disorders* (6–10). Series: Talking Points. 1999, Raintree LB $27.12 (978-0-8172-5321-9). Statistics and quotations from experts are used in this book that introduces various eating disorders, their causes, and treatments. (Rev: BL 12/15/99; HBG 9/00) [616.85]

11228 Bueche, Shelley. *The Ebola Virus* (4–7). Illus. Series: Parasites. 2003, Gale LB $24.95 (978-0-7377-1780-8). Although it's part of the Parasites series, this book focuses on the Ebola virus, which causes an infectious illness and is found widely in Central Africa. (Rev: BL 3/1/04; SLJ 6/04) [616.9]

11229 Burby, Liza N. *Bulimia Nervosa: The Secret Cycle of Bingeing and Purging* (6–10). Series: Teen Health Library of Eating Disorder Prevention. 1998, Rosen LB $27.95 (978-0-8239-2762-3). Bulimia is an eating disorder characterized by bingeing and purging. This book describes various eating disorders, then focuses on bulimia, its causes, physical and psychological effects, the roles of peer pressure, media images, family relationships, genetics, and treatment and recovery. (Rev: SLJ 1/99) [616.85]

11230 Burnfield, Alexander. *Multiple Sclerosis* (5–8). Series: Just the Facts. 2004, Heinemann LB $27.07 (978-1-4034-4602-2). An accessible explanation of multiple sclerosis, its symptoms, treatment, and the efforts being made to find new treatments and a cure. (Rev: SLJ 6/04) [616.8]

11231 Bush, Jenna. *Ana's Story: A Journey of Hope* (8–11). Illus. 2007, HarperCollins $18.99 (978-0-06-137908-6). Bush worked for UNICEF in Latin America and this story highlights the impact of HIV/AIDS in the area, recounting Ana's birth with the disease, the death of both her parents, the struggle to find an accepting home, her eventual success in finding love, and her hope for the future when she gives birth to a disease-free baby. (Rev: BL 8/07; HB 11–12/07; SLJ 10/07) [362] 🎖

11232 Byers, Ann. *Sexually Transmitted Diseases* (6–9). Illus. Series: Hot Issues. 1999, Enslow LB $27.93 (978-0-7660-1192-2). As well as a description of various sexually transmitted diseases, this work discusses transmission, symptoms, treatment, and risks. (Rev: BL 4/1/00; HBG 4/00) [616.95.]

11233 Carson, Mary Kay. *Epilepsy* (7–12). Series: Diseases and People. 1998, Enslow LB $26.60 (978-0-7660-1049-9). This book describes the causes of epilepsy, gives a history of society's attitude toward epileptics, and describes current treatments and drugs used to control it. (Rev: BL 7/98; SLJ 9/98; VOYA 2/99) [616.8]

11234 Cefrey, Holly. *Coping with Cancer* (6–12). Illus. Series: Coping. 2000, Rosen LB $26.50 (978-0-8239-2849-1). As well as discussing how cancer develops in various parts of the body, this book gives self-help advice for anyone who is diagnosed

with the disease. (Rev: BL 1/1–15/01; SLJ 12/00) [616.99]

11235 Cefrey, Holly. *Syphilis and Other Sexually Transmitted Diseases* (5–8). Illus. Series: Epidemics. 2001, Rosen LB $27.95 (978-0-8239-3488-1). Cefrey describes historic outbreaks and treatments, as well as the symptoms and cure, of syphilis and other sexually transmitted diseases. (Rev: BL 3/15/02) [616.95]

11236 Cefrey, Holly. *Yellow Fever* (5–8). Series: Epidemics. 2002, Rosen LB $27.95 (978-0-8239-3489-8). Yellow fever, spread by mosquitoes, was the cause of several epidemics in American cities during the 19th century before a cure was found by dedicated doctors who risked their lives. (Rev: BL 8/02) [616]

11237 Check, William A. *AIDS* (8–12). Illus. Series: Encyclopedia of Health. 1999, Chelsea LB $16.00 (978-0-7910-4885-6). This updated and revised edition gives a history of the AIDS epidemic, the latest information on breakthrough HIV treatment methods, and advice on how to avoid contracting the disease. (Rev: BL 8/98; SLJ 9/98) [616.9]

11238 Chiu, Christina. *Eating Disorder Survivors Tell Their Stories* (7–12). Series: Teen Health Library of Eating Disorder Prevention. 1998, Rosen LB $26.50 (978-0-8239-2767-8); Hazelden paper $6.95 (978-1-56838-259-3). In candid interviews, survivors of eating disorders share their experiences, treatments, and roads to recovery, and offer advice to other teens who might need help. (Rev: BL 3/1/99; SLJ 1/99; VOYA 4/99) [616.85]

11239 Clarke, Julie M., and Ann Kirby-Payne. *Understanding Weight and Depression* (7–10). Series: Teen Eating Disorder Prevention. 1999, Rosen LB $31.95 (978-0-8239-2994-8). This book discusses the psychological origins of eating disorders such as anorexia and bulimia and suggests ways to develop a healthy self-image. [616.8]

11240 Collier, James Lincoln. *Vaccines* (6–10). Series: Great Inventions. 2003, Benchmark LB $37.07 (978-0-7614-1539-8). As well as discussing the development and mechanism of vaccines themselves, this well-illustrated volume includes a survey of infectious diseases such as smallpox, cholera, diphtheria, influenza, and AIDS. (Rev: SLJ 3/04) [615]

11241 Curran, Christine Perdan. *Sexually Transmitted Diseases* (7–12). 1998, Enslow LB $26.60 (978-0-7660-1050-5). This work discusses various kinds of sexually transmitted diseases, including those that are bacterial, like syphilis, those that are viral, like HIV, and those that are neither, like scabies and pubic lice. (Rev: BL 12/15/98; VOYA 2/99) [616.95]

11242 Daugirdas, John T. *S.T.D. Sexually Transmitted Diseases, Including HIV/AIDS.* 3rd ed. (8–12). 1992, MedText $14.95 (978-0-9629279-1-1). This overview simplifies the language and prunes unnecessary medical terminology. (Rev: BL 10/1/92; SLJ 11/92) [616.951]

11243 Day, Nancy. *Killer Superbugs: The Story of Drug-Resistant Diseases* (6–9). Illus. Series: Issues in Focus. 2001, Enslow LB $26.60 (978-0-7660-1588-3). Day examines the factors that have led to the development of "superbugs," the role of antibiotics in the fight against disease, and the potential use of bacteria as weapons. (Rev: HBG 10/02; SLJ 1/02) [616]

11244 DiConsiglio, John. *When Birds Get Flu and Cows Go Mad!* (5–7). Illus. Series: 24/7 Science Behind the Scenes: Medical Files. 2007, Scholastic LB $26.00 (978-0-531-12069-9); paper $7.95 (978-0-531-17528-6). A lively discussion of bird flu, mad cow disease, E. coli bacteria, and other food-borne and headline-grabbing illnesses. (Rev: BL 12/1/07; LMC 3/08) [616.9]

11245 Dillon, Erin, ed. *Obesity* (7–12). Series: Issues That Concern You. 2006, Gale LB $32.45 (978-0-7377-2194-2). Colorful photographs underline the importance of this problem being discussed in this helpful volume that presents essays giving different points of view. (Rev: SLJ 2/07)

11246 Donnellan, William L. *The Miracle of Immunity* (5–8). Illus. Series: The Story of Science. 2002, Benchmark LB $29.93 (978-0-7614-1425-4). A history of mankind's discoveries about diseases and about the body's vulnerabilities and abilities to fend off infections, from the earliest times through AIDS. (Rev: HBG 3/03; LMC 4–5/03; SLJ 5/03) [616.07]

11247 Donnelly, Karen. *Coping with Lyme Disease* (6–12). Series: Coping. 2001, Rosen LB $31.95 (978-0-8239-3199-6). This introduction to the symptoms, diagnosis, treatment, and prevention of Lyme disease includes personal stories. (Rev: SLJ 7/01) [616.9]

11248 Donnelly, Karen. *Everything You Need to Know About Lyme Disease* (5–8). Illus. Series: Need to Know Library. 2000, Rosen LB $27.95 (978-0-8239-3216-0). This book explains how Lyme disease was discovered, how it is transmitted, its symptoms, and its treatments. (Rev: BL 12/1/00) [616.9]

11249 Donnelly, Karen. *Leprosy (Hansen's Disease)* (5–8). Series: Epidemics. 2002, Rosen LB $27.95 (978-0-8239-3498-0). This is the story of leprosy, the disease that created social outcasts of its victims, and of a man named Hansen who discovered an effective treatment. (Rev: BL 8/02) [616.9]

11250 Draper, Allison Stark. *Ebola* (5–8). Illus. Series: Epidemics. 2002, Rosen LB $27.95 (978-0-8239-3496-6). Discusses the Ebola virus in both scientific and human terms. Also use *Mad Cow Disease* (2002). (Rev: BL 8/02; SLJ 6/02) [616.9]

11251 Dudley, William, ed. *Epidemics* (8–12). Series: Opposing Viewpoints. 1998, Greenhaven LB $32.45 (978-1-56510-941-4). Topics covered in this anthology of different points of view include the threat of infectious diseases, the AIDS epidemic, vaccination programs, and the prevention of food-borne illnesses. (Rev: BL 11/15/98) [616.9]

11252 Edelson, Edward. *Allergies* (7–12). Illus. 1989, Chelsea LB $19.95 (978-0-7910-0055-7). Various types of allergies are described, including their effects and treatments that have been found to help sufferers. (Rev: BL 9/1/89; SLJ 12/89) [616.97]

11253 Edelson, Edward. *The Immune System* (6–12). Illus. Series: 21st Century Health and Wellness. 2000, Chelsea LB $36.00 (978-0-7910-5525-0). A revised edition of Edelson's presentation on the immune system and what happens when it fails to function. (Rev: BL 4/15/00; HBG 9/00; SLJ 6/00) [616.07]

11254 Eisenpreis, Bettijane. *Coping with Scoliosis* (7–10). Series: Coping. 1999, Rosen LB $31.95 (978-0-8239-2557-5). The author explores the physical and emotional issues involved in the diagnosis and treatment of scoliosis, curvature of the spine, using scientific explanations and firsthand accounts. (Rev: SLJ 5/99) [616]

11255 Elliot-Wright, Susan. *Epilepsy* (7–10). Illus. Series: Health Issues. 2003, Raintree LB $28.56 (978-0-7398-6423-4). An attractive, slim overview of epilepsy and how it affects the body and mind. (Rev: SLJ 5/04) [616.8]

11256 Ellis, Deborah. *Our Stories, Our Songs: African Children Talk About AIDS* (6–9). Illus. 2005, Fitzhenry & Whiteside $18.95 (978-1-55041-913-9). First-person accounts from children in Malawi and Zambia whose lives have been touched by AIDS paint a heartbreaking portrait of the devastation wrought by the disease in sub-Saharan Africa. (Rev: BL 10/1/05*; SLJ 11/05*) [362.1]

11257 Epstein, Rachel. *Eating Habits and Disorders* (7–12). Illus. 1990, Chelsea LB $19.95 (978-0-7910-0048-9). A little history on eating disorders is given, but the major focus of this book is on the kinds of eating disorders and their treatments. (Rev: BL 6/1/90; SLJ 8/90) [616.85]

11258 Erlanger, Ellen. *Eating Disorders: A Question and Answer Book About Anorexia Nervosa and Bulimia Nervosa* (6–8). Illus. 1988, Lerner LB $19.93 (978-0-8225-0038-4). Case studies are used to introduce the causes, symptoms, and treatment of these disorders. (Rev: BL 3/15/88; SLJ 4/88) [616.85]

11259 Favor, Lesli J. *Bacteria* (5–8). Illus. Series: Germs: The Library of Disease-Causing Organisms. 2004, Rosen LB $26.50 (978-0-8239-4491-0). An informative, illustrated discussion of bacteria, covering their discovery, how they survive, and the dangers they pose to humans. (Rev: SLJ 1/05) [616]

11260 Fine, Judylaine. *Afraid to Ask: A Book About Cancer* (7–12). 1986, Lothrop paper $6.95 (978-0-688-06196-8). In this straightforward account about the nature, causes, and treatment of cancer, the author tries to minimize the fear and emotion surrounding the topic. (Rev: BL 3/1/86; VOYA 8/86) [616.99]

11261 Flynn, Tom, and Karen Lound. *AIDS: Examining the Crisis* (7–12). 1995, Lerner LB $19.93 (978-0-8225-2625-4). An informative explanation in clear language about HIV and AIDS. (Rev: BL 5/1/95; SLJ 6/95) [362.1]

11262 Frankenberger, Elizabeth. *Food and Love: Dealing with Family Attitudes About Weight* (7–12). Series: Teen Health Library of Eating Disorder Prevention. 1998, Rosen LB $27.95 (978-0-8239-2760-9). This book explores the role the family plays in developing a healthy self-image and affecting a teenager's attitudes toward food. (Rev: VOYA 4/99) [616.85]

11263 Fredericks, Carrie, ed. *Autism* (7–10). Illus. Series: Perspectives on Diseases and Disorders. 2008, Gale LB $34.95 (978-0-7377-3869-8). Readers whose lives are affected by autism will be interested in this look at the disorder and its spectrum of symptoms; personal accounts by those with autism and parents of autistic children add to the presentation. (Rev: BL 4/1/08) [616.85]

11264 Friedlander, Mark P. *Outbreak: Disease Detectives at Work*. Rev. ed. (6–9). Illus. Series: Discovery! 2002, Lerner LB $27.93 (978-0-8225-0948-6). Friedlander presents an overview of past and present epidemics and of the efforts on the part of public health workers to control them and find cures, and adds a discussion of bioterrorism. (Rev: HBG 10/03; SLJ 3/03; VOYA 6/03) [614.4]

11265 Friedlander, Mark P., and Terry M. Phillips. *The Immune System: Your Body's Disease-Fighting Army* (6–10). 1997, Lerner LB $23.93 (978-0-8225-2858-6). Topics covered in this introduction to the immune system include the makeup of the immune system, how it reacts to invaders, vaccination, nutrition, allergies, disorders of the system, and medicines that help it. (Rev: BL 6/1–15/98) [616.079]

11266 Frissell, Susan, and Paula Harney. *Eating Disorders and Weight Control* (7–10). Illus. 1998, Enslow LB $26.60 (978-0-89490-919-1). This book covers anorexia, bulimia, binge eating disorders, and weight control issues with material on how to cope with them in a healthy, realistic manner. (Rev: BL 4/15/98; HBG 9/98; SLJ 3/98) [616.85]

11267 Gay, Kathlyn, and Sean McGarrahan. *Epilepsy: The Ultimate Teen Guide* (7–12). Illus. Series: Ultimate Teen Guide. 2003, Scarecrow LB $32.50 (978-0-8108-4339-4). This informative look at this

seizure disease and its impact on typical teen activities (sports, jobs, driving, and so forth) includes the personal experiences of coauthor McGarrahan, who was diagnosed with epilepsy at the age of 16. (Rev: BL 10/15/03; SLJ 10/03) [616]

11268 Gedatus, Gustav Mark. *Mononucleosis* (7–12). Series: Perspectives on Disease and Illness. 1999, Capstone LB $25.26 (978-0-7368-0283-3). An introduction to this disease, its transmission, and possible treatments. (Rev: SLJ 4/00) [616.9]

11269 Gillie, Oliver. *Cancer* (5–8). Series: Just the Facts. 2004, Heinemann LB $27.07 (978-1-4034-5144-6). Provides accessible explanations of cancer itself, plus the symptoms, diagnosis, and surgery, chemotherapy, and radiation involved in its treatment. (Rev: SLJ 2/05) [616.99]

11270 Gillie, Oliver. *Sickle Cell Disease* (5–8). Series: Just the Facts. 2004, Heinemann LB $27.07 (978-1-4034-4603-9). An examination of sickle cell anemia presented in an accessible style, with coverage of symptoms, treatment, and research. (Rev: SLJ 6/04) [616.1]

11271 Gilman, Laura Anne. *Coping with Cerebral Palsy* (5–9). Series: Coping. 2001, Rosen LB $31.95 (978-0-8239-3150-7). This is a self-help book that looks at ways to deal with school, work, and travel as well as coping with other people and their attitudes. (Rev: SLJ 2/02) [616.836]

11272 Gold, Susan Dudley. *Sickle Cell Disease* (4–7). Illus. Series: Health Watch. 2001, Enslow LB $23.93 (978-0-7660-1662-0). Readers are introduced to the symptoms and treatment of this disease through the true story of a young African American boy called Keone who received a successful stem-cell transplant. (Rev: HBG 3/02; SLJ 12/01) [616.1]

11273 Goldsmith, Connie. *Influenza: The Next Pandemic?* (6–9). Illus. 2006, Lerner $27.93 (978-0-7613-9457-0). Covers the history of the flu, past and present outbreaks, treatments, and new research being done to prevent the potentially deadly disease. (Rev: BL 9/1/06; SLJ 1/07) [614.5]

11274 Goldsmith, Connie. *Invisible Invaders: Dangerous Infectious Diseases* (7–10). Series: Discovery! 2006, Lerner LB $27.93 (978-0-8225-3416-7). This clearly written and well-illustrated book provides information on infectious diseases including SARS, Ebola, mad cow disease, and E.coli. (Rev: BL 5/1/06; SLJ 5/06) [362.196]

11275 Goldsmith, Connie. *Neurological Disorders* (6–10). Illus. Series: Amazing Brain. 2001, Blackbirch LB $24.95 (978-1-56711-422-5). Conditions such as Alzheimer's, autism, cerebral palsy, and schizophrenia are presented, with information on how the disease affects the brain and on the treatments available now. Also use *Addiction* (2001), which looks at the ways in which chemicals affect the brain and induce dependency. (Rev: BL 10/15/01; HBG 3/02; SLJ 9/01; VOYA 10/01) [616.8]

11276 Goldstein, Margaret J. *Everything You Need to Know About Multiple Sclerosis* (5–8). Series: Need to Know Library. 2001, Rosen LB $27.95 (978-0-8239-3292-4). An introduction to multiple sclerosis, its symptoms and treatment, and how it affects the nervous system, along with information on the importance of treating the emotional impact of this disease. (Rev: SLJ 5/01) [616]

11277 Goodfellow, Gregory. *Epilepsy* (7–9). Series: Diseases and Disorders. 2001, Lucent LB $32.45 (978-1-56006-701-6). The author describes the causes of epilepsy, how it is currently being treated, and how people live with this condition. (Rev: BL 1/1–15/02; SLJ 4/01) [616.8]

11278 Goodnough, David. *Eating Disorders: A Hot Issue* (5–8). Series: Hot Issues. 1999, Enslow LB $27.93 (978-0-7660-1336-0). This is a clear introduction to anorexia nervosa, bulimia, and binge eating with material and case studies on symptoms, causes, and consequences but little coverage of prevention and treatment. (Rev: HBG 3/00; SLJ 1/00) [618.92]

11279 Gordon, Sherri Mabry. *Peanut Butter, Milk, and Other Deadly Threats: What You Should Know About Food Allergies* (5–9). Series: Issues in Focus Today. 2006, Enslow LB $31.93 (978-0-7660-2529-5). This information-packed survey of food allergies identifies common culprit foods, explains the mechanics of allergic reactions, and also reports on medical research to find better treatments. (Rev: SLJ 11/06) [616.97]

11280 Grady, Denise. *Deadly Invaders: Virus Outbreaks around the World, from Marburg Fever to Avian Flu* (7–10). 2006, Kingfisher $16.95 (978-0-7534-5995-9). *New York Times* reporter Grady recalls her trip to Angola during the deadly outbreak of Marburg fever and describes the challenges faced in a community with few basic services; she also discusses other viral diseases including HIV and AIDS, West Nile, avian flu, SARS, and Hantavirus. (Rev: BL 10/1/06; LMC 4–5/07; SLJ 12/06*) [614.5]

11281 Gravelle, Karen, and Bertram A. John. *Teenagers Face to Face with Cancer* (7–12). 1986, Messner paper $5.95 (978-0-671-65975-2). From the accounts of 16 young people ages 13 to 21, one discovers what it is like to live with cancer. (Rev: BL 1/15/87; SLJ 2/87) [618.92]

11282 Greenberg, Alissa. *Asthma* (6–12). Illus. 2000, Watts $21.00 (978-0-531-11331-8). In this thorough presentation on asthma, readers will learn about the history, treatment, and management of this illness that often attacks people in their youth. (Rev: BL 2/15/01; SLJ 3/01) [616.2]

11283 Haney, Johannah. *Juvenile Diabetes* (4–7). Illus. Series: Health Alert. 2004, Benchmark LB $28.50 (978-0-7614-1798-9). In addition to describing the treatment and possible complications of juvenile diabetes, this attractive title opens with a case history and also includes lists of famous people who suffer from the condition. (Rev: SLJ 5/05)

11284 Harmon, Dan. *Anorexia Nervosa: Starving for Attention* (8–12). Series: Encyclopedia of Psychological Disorders. 1999, Chelsea $35.00 (978-0-7910-4901-3). Citing many case studies, some of prominent people, this work defines anorexia nervosa, discusses its causes and the physical consequences, and covers the treatments available. (Rev: VOYA 8/99) [616.85]

11285 Harmon, Dan. *Life out of Focus: Alzheimer's Disease and Related Disorders* (7–12). 1999, Chelsea $35.00 (978-0-7910-4896-2). This title demonstrates the devastating effect of Alzheimer's disease on sufferers and their caregivers, and provides biological and psychological explanations of the symptoms as well as solid data and analysis on research and various treatments. (Rev: BL 8/99) [616.8]

11286 Harris, Jacqueline. *Sickle Cell Disease* (6–10). 2001, Twenty-First Century LB $26.90 (978-0-7613-1459-2). After introducing three young victims of this disease, the author describes its symptoms and treatment and traces its history. (Rev: BL 9/15/01; HBG 3/02; SLJ 12/01) [616.1]

11287 Harris, Nancy, ed. *AIDS in Developing Countries* (6–12). Series: At Issue. 2004, Gale LB $29.95 (978-0-7377-1789-1). Through a series of essays that express different points of view, the AIDS situation in countries in Africa, Asia, and South America is explored. (Rev: BL 2/15/04) [616]

11288 Hawkins, Trisha. *Everything You Need to Know About Measles and Rubella* (4–8). Series: Need to Know Library. 2001, Rosen LB $27.95 (978-0-8239-3322-8). Simple text and photographs describe the diseases and methods of prevention and treatment, and discuss public-health issues. Also use *Everything You Need to Know About Chicken Pox and Shingles* (2001). (Rev: SLJ 8/01) [616.9]

11289 Hayhurst, Chris. *Cholera* (5–9). Series: Epidemics. 2001, Rosen LB $27.95 (978-0-8239-3345-7). In a readable style, Hayhurst discusses the history of cholera, formerly a deadly disease, and explains how its treatment was developed. Also use *Polio* and *Smallpox* (both 2001). (Rev: SLJ 7/01) [616.9]

11290 Hayhurst, Chris. *E. Coli* (4–7). Series: Epidemics. 2004, Rosen LB $27.95 (978-0-8239-4201-5). A look at the transmission, treatment, and prevention of this bacterium, with an emphasis on the importance of washing hands and food before eating. (Rev: SLJ 8/04) [616.9]

11291 Hicks, Terry Allan. *Allergies* (4–8). Illus. Series: Health Alert. 2005, Benchmark LB $19.95 (978-0-7614-1918-1). All about what allergies are, what brings them on, and how they are treated, with colorful sidebars and features that add to the text. (Rev: SLJ 5/06) [616.97]

11292 Hirschmann, Kris. *The Ebola Virus* (6–8). Illus. Series: Diseases and Disorders. 2006, Gale LB $31.20 (978-1-59018-672-5). Hirschmann gives an overview of the infectious disease discovered in 1976, for which no cure has yet been found. (Rev: SLJ 2/07)

11293 Hirschmann, Kris. *Salmonella* (4–7). Illus. Series: Parasites. 2003, Gale LB $24.95 (978-0-7377-1785-3). This fascinating examination of Salmonella bacteria, responsible for a wide variety of illnesses in the United States and elsewhere, is supplemented with numerous photos and microscopic views of the title bacteria. (Rev: BL 3/1/04) [615.4]

11294 Hoffmann, Gretchen. *Mononucleosis* (4–8). Illus. Series: Health Alert. 2005, Benchmark LB $19.95 (978-0-7614-1915-0). All about what "mono" is, its symptoms, and its treatment, with graphic features that add to the text. (Rev: SLJ 5/06) [616.9]

11295 Huegel, Kelly. *Young People and Chronic Illness: True Stories, Help, and Hope* (6–12). 1998, Free Spirit paper $14.95 (978-1-57542-041-7). After a series of case histories of young people suffering from such chronic illnesses as diabetes and asthma, this book discusses topics including getting support, coping with hospital stays, and planning for the future. (Rev: BL 11/15/98; SLJ 10/98; VOYA 2/99) [618.92]

11296 Hyde, Margaret O., and Elizabeth Forsyth. *AIDS: What Does It Mean to You?* Rev. ed. (6–10). 1995, Walker LB $15.85 (978-0-8027-8398-1). This book traces the process of infection and the progress of the disease in the body, along with material on its history, treatment, prevention, and worldwide statistics. (Rev: SLJ 3/96; VOYA 4/96) [616.97]

11297 Hyde, Margaret O., and Elizabeth Forsyth. *Diabetes* (4–7). Illus. 2003, Watts LB $26.00 (978-0-531-12209-9). Case studies of young people add to the easy-to-understand coverage of the disease, its different types, causes, symptoms, and popular methods of treatment. (Rev: SLJ 2/04) [616.4]

11298 Hyde, Margaret O., and Elizabeth Forsyth. *The Disease Book: A Kid's Guide* (5–8). Illus. 1997, Walker LB $17.85 (978-0-8027-8498-8). A simple, straightforward overview of the causes, symptoms, and treatments of more than 100 physical and mental diseases. (Rev: BL 9/15/97; HBG 3/98; SLJ 11/97) [616]

11299 Isle, Mick. *Everything You Need to Know About Food Poisoning* (4–8). Illus. Series: Need to Know Library. 2001, Rosen LB $27.95 (978-0-8239-3396-9). Safe ways to prepare food are the main focus of this book, which also describes the symptoms and treatment of food poisoning. (Rev: SLJ 10/01) [615.954]

11300 Johannsson, Phillip. *Heart Disease* (7–12). Series: Diseases and People. 1998, Enslow LB $20.95 (978-0-7660-1051-2). The causes and types of heart disease are described, along with an overview of current treatments and potential future advances. (Rev: BL 7/98) [616.1]

11301 Kittleson, Mark J., ed. *The Truth About Eating Disorders* (8–12). Series: Truth About. 2004, Facts on File $35.00 (978-0-8160-5300-1). Causes, diagnosis, and treatment are all covered in this user-friendly guide that looks at emotions along with physical symptoms and does not neglect adolescent males with eating problems. (Rev: SLJ 4/05) [[616.85]

11302 Kittredge, Mary. *The Common Cold* (7–12). Illus. Series: 21st Century Health and Wellness. 2000, Chelsea House LB $24.95 (978-0-7910-5985-2). An interesting history of cold cures introduces this overview of the causes, prevention, and treatment of this perennial nuisance. (Rev: BL 11/15/00; HBG 10/01; SLJ 3/01) [616.1]

11303 Kittredge, Mary. *Teens with AIDS Speak Out* (8–12). 1992, Messner paper $8.95 (978-0-671-74543-1). Combines facts and interviews on AIDS and its history, transmission, treatment, and prevention, as well as safer-sex practices and discrimination against people with AIDS. (Rev: BL 6/1/92; SLJ 7/92) [362.1]

11304 Kowalski, Kathiann M. *Attack of the Superbugs: The Crisis of Drug-Resistant Diseases* (7–12). Illus. 2005, Enslow LB $31.93 (978-0-7660-2400-7). With full-color photographs and diagrams, this book show how viruses and diseases become resistant to drug treatments and mutate, resulting in the return of diseases that were thought extinct. (Rev: SLJ 6/06)

11305 Lamb, Kirsten. *Cancer* (5–8). Series: Health Issues. 2002, Raintree LB $28.54 (978-0-7398-5219-4). An informative account that covers various kinds of cancer, giving real-life stories, and also deals with issues and choices facing teens today. (Rev: BL 12/15/02; HBG 3/03; SLJ 3/03) [616.99]

11306 Landau, Elaine. *Allergies* (4–7). Illus. Series: Understanding Illness. 1994, Twenty-First Century LB $24.90 (978-0-8050-2989-5). After a case history that explores allergies in personal terms, an objective presentation is given of their causes, effects, and treatment. (Rev: BL 12/15/94; SLJ 2/95) [616.97]

11307 Landau, Elaine. *Alzheimer's Disease: A Forgotten Life* (7–10). Illus. Series: Health and Human Disease. 2006, Scholastic LB $26.00 (978-0-531-16755-7). Symptoms, diagnosis, treatment, and prognosis are all covered here, plus a question-and-answer "ask the doctor" feature that adds pertinent information. (Rev: BL 12/1/05; SLJ 1/06) [616.8]

11308 Landau, Elaine. *Cancer* (4–7). Illus. Series: Understanding Illness. 1994, Twenty-First Century LB $24.90 (978-0-8050-2990-1). This book explains the many types of cancer, their causes, present-day treatments, and possible developments in the future. (Rev: BL 12/15/95; SLJ 2/95) [616.99]

11309 Landau, Elaine. *Epilepsy* (4–7). Illus. Series: Understanding Illness. 1994, Twenty-First Century LB $24.90 (978-0-8050-2991-8). Following the story of a youngster who has epilepsy, this account describes the disorder, its emotional and medical aspects, and treatments. (Rev: BL 12/15/94; SLJ 2/95) [616.8]

11310 Latta, Sara L. *Allergies* (6–10). Series: Diseases and People. 1998, Enslow LB $20.95 (978-0-7660-1048-2). Using a number of case studies, this book describes the nature of allergies, their symptoms, methods of detection, and treatments. (Rev: BL 7/98) [616.9]

11311 Latta, Sara L. *Food Poisoning and Foodborne Diseases* (7–12). Series: Diseases and People. 1999, Enslow LB $26.60 (978-0-7660-1183-0). Using case studies and questions and answers, this book describes the causes, effects, and treatments for food poisoning and related illnesses. (Rev: BL 9/15/99; HBG 4/00; SLJ 11/99) [615.9]

11312 Lawton, Sandra Augustyn, ed. *Eating Disorders Information for Teens: Health Tips About Anorexia, Bulimia, Binge Eating, and Other Eating Disorders* (7–12). Series: Teen Health. 2005, Omnigraphics $65.00 (978-0-7808-0783-9). This title explores all aspects of eating disorders as well as such related topics as body image, nutrition, self-esteem, and athleticism. (Rev: SLJ 12/05; VOYA 4/06)

11313 Lennard-Brown, Sarah. *Asthma* (5–8). Illus. Series: Health Issues. 2002, Raintree LB $28.54 (978-0-7398-5218-7). Color photographs and straightforward text explain the symptoms, diagnosis, and treatment of asthma. (Rev: BL 12/15/02; HBG 3/03) [616.2]

11314 Lennard-Brown, Sarah. *Autism* (5–8). Illus. Series: Health Issues. 2003, Raintree LB $28.56 (978-0-7398-6422-7). An in-depth introduction to autism, with attention to the difficulties people with autism face and what is being done to help them. (Rev: SLJ 5/04) [616.89]

11315 Leone, Daniel, ed. *Anorexia* (6–12). Series: At Issue. 2001, Greenhaven LB $26.20 (978-0-7377-0468-6); paper $17.45 (978-0-7377-0467-9). Revealing personal accounts provide different perspectives on coping with this condition. (Rev: BL 3/15/01) [616.85]

11316 LeVert, Marianne. *AIDS: A Handbook for the Future* (7–12). Illus. 1996, Millbrook LB $24.90 (978-1-56294-660-9). This book covers the basic facts about AIDS, its causes, prevention, present treatments, and current research. (Rev: BL 12/15/96; SLJ 11/96; VOYA 6/97) [616.97]

11317 Little, Marjorie. *Diabetes* (7–12). Series: Encyclopedia of Health. 1990, Chelsea LB $19.95 (978-0-7910-0061-8). A clear, organized account that covers the history of diabetes, its causes, and present-day treatments. (Rev: BL 3/15/91) [616.4]

11318 Lynette, Rachel. *Leprosy* (5–8). Illus. Series: Understanding Diseases and Disorders. 2005, Gale LB $26.20 (978-0-7377-3172-9). Straightforward text discusses the plight of leprosy patients around the world and through history; causes, treatments, and transmission are also discussed. (Rev: SLJ 6/06) [616.9]

11319 McGuire, Paula. *AIDS* (4–8). Series: Preteen Pressures. 1998, Raintree LB $25.69 (978-0-8172-5025-6). Straight facts and statistics are given on AIDS, including methods of prevention and stories of people with HIV/AIDS, such as Magic Johnson and the late Ryan White. (Rev: BL 5/15/98; HBG 10/98) [616,97]

11320 Majure, Janet. *AIDS* (7–10). 1998, Enslow LB $20.95 (978-0-7660-1182-3). This informative book describes AIDS, who gets it and how, symptoms, treatment, prevention, and prospects for the future, and touches on related social, economic, and legal issues. (Rev: VOYA 2/99) [616]

11321 Majure, Janet. *Breast Cancer* (7–12). Illus. 2000, Enslow LB $26.60 (978-0-7660-1312-4). A straightforward look at this disease's diagnosis and treatment, and at its social implications and its incidence around the world. (Rev: HBG 9/00; SLJ 10/00*) [616.99]

11322 Manning, Karen. *AIDS: Can This Epidemic Be Stopped?* (6–8). Series: Issues of Our Time. 1995, Twenty-First Century LB $22.90 (978-0-8050-4240-5). A frank, unbiased look at AIDS, its causes, effects on society, and perspectives for the future. (Rev: BL 2/1/96; SLJ 2/96; VOYA 4/96) [616.97]

11323 Margulies, Phillip. *Creutzfeldt-Jakob Disease* (4–7). Series: Epidemics. 2004, Rosen LB $27.95 (978-0-8239-4199-5). Examines the history and current state of knowledge about this rare disorder that affects the brain and is related to Mad Cow Disease. Also use *West Nile Virus* (2004). (Rev: SLJ 8/04) [616.8]

11324 Margulies, Phillip. *Down Syndrome* (6–8). Illus. Series: Genetic Diseases and Disorders . 2006, Rosen LB $26.50 (978-1-4042-0695-3). This guide to Down syndrome — covering the history of the disorder and our contemporary understanding — will be useful for researchers; it includes a chapter on daily living that touches on issues such as sex. (Rev: SLJ 2/07) [362.1]

11325 Margulies, Phillip. *Everything You Need to Know About Rheumatic Fever* (5–8). Series: The Need to Know Library. 2004, Rosen LB $27.95 (978-0-8239-4509-2). After a brief history of the disease and the discovery of its cause, this volume discusses symptoms, treatment, and the concern that the disease may become more prevalent as bacteria develop resistance to antibiotics. (Rev: SLJ 4/05)

11326 Marrin, Albert. *Dr. Jenner and the Speckled Monster: The Search for the Smallpox Vaccine* (4–8). Illus. 2002, Dutton $19.99 (978-0-525-46922-3). This highly readable and detailed account describes the impact of smallpox from the time of the Aztecs, major outbreaks over the years, the way the virus works, the work of Jenner in developing a vaccine, and the virus's potential as a weapon of mass destruction. (Rev: BL 11/15/02; HB 11–12/02; HBG 3/03; SLJ 1/03; VOYA 12/02) [614.5]

11327 Massari, Francesca. *Everything You Need to Know About Cancer* (5–9). Series: Need to Know Library. 2000, Rosen LB $27.95 (978-0-8239-3164-4). This book defines what cancer is and looks at its causes, prevention, symptoms, diagnosis, and treatment. (Rev: HBG 10/00; SLJ 8/00) [616.99]

11328 Medina, Loreta M., ed. *Bulimia* (6–12). Series: At Risk. 2003, Gale LB $29.95 (978-0-7377-1164-6). This book explores the symptoms and effects of bulimia and offers suggestions for intervention. (Rev: BL 1/1–15/03) [616.85]

11329 Miller, Debra A. *Pandemics* (8–12). Series: Hot Topics. 2006, Gale LB $31.20 (978-1-59018-965-8). A thoughtful exploration of infectious diseases and our ability to prevent and control outbreaks. (Rev: SLJ 4/07) [618.92]

11330 Miller, Martha J. *Kidney Disorders* (7–12). Series: Encyclopedia of Health. 1992, Chelsea LB $19.95 (978-0-7910-0066-3). This book explains the function of the kidneys, how they can malfunction, and treatments that are available, including transplants. (Rev: BL 12/1/92) [616.6]

11331 Moe, Barbara. *Coping with Eating Disorders* (7–10). 1999, Rosen $31.95 (978-0-8239-2974-0). Actual case histories are used to explain the characteristics of bulimia, anorexia, and compulsive-eating patterns. Practical coping suggestions are also offered. (Rev: BL 7/91; SLJ 11/91) [616.85]

11332 Moe, Barbara. *Coping with PMS* (7–12). Series: Coping. 1998, Rosen LB $25.25 (978-0-8239-2716-6). Supplemented by personal accounts, this book explains how PMS can be a manageable problem, with material on physiology, diet, lifestyle, attitude, and the relationship between nutrition and PMS control (recipes are included). (Rev: BL 5/15/98; SLJ 5/98) [618.172]

11333 Moe, Barbara. *Coping with Tourette Syndrome and Tic Disorders* (6–10). 2000, Rosen LB $26.50 (978-0-8239-2976-4). Solid information and many case studies are used in this examination of Tourette's syndrome, tic disorders, and related problems with material on how they affect moods, learning, activities, and sleep. (Rev: BL 7/00) [616.8]

11334 Moe, Barbara. *Everything You Need to Know About Migraines and Other Headaches* (7–12). Series: Need to Know Library. 2000, Rosen LB $27.95 (978-0-8239-3291-7). An accessible and thorough exploration of the symptoms, treatment, and prevention of migraines and other headaches. (Rev: HBG 10/01; SLJ 4/01) [616.8]

11335 Moe, Barbara. *Inside Eating Disorder Support Groups* (6–10). Series: Teen Health Library of Eating Disorder Prevention. 1998, Rosen LB $27.95 (978-0-8239-2769-2). After a general discussion of eating disorders and available treatments, this book explains the dynamics of support groups and how they can help teens recover from eating disorders and come to terms with their problems. (Rev: SLJ 1/99) [616.85]

11336 Moehn, Heather. *Everything You Need to Know When Someone You Know Has Leukemia* (5–10). Series: Need to Know Library. 2000, Rosen LB $27.95 (978-0-8239-3121-7). The basic facts about leukemia are covered with material on its various types and treatments, possible causes, and the emotional aspects of the illness. (Rev: SLJ 9/00) [616.99]

11337 Moehn, Heather. *Understanding Eating Disorder Support Groups* (7–12). Series: Teen Eating Disorder Prevention Library. 2000, Rosen LB $31.95 (978-0-8239-2992-4). Extensive information on the diagnosis, symptoms, and treatment of eating disorders precedes discussion of the types of support available; case studies appear throughout. (Rev: HBG 10/01; SLJ 2/01)

11338 Monroe, Judy. *Cystic Fibrosis* (5–9). Illus. Series: Perspectives on Disease and Illness. 2001, Capstone LB $25.26 (978-0-7368-1026-5). A straightforward account of the symptoms, diagnosis, and treatment of this disease, with discussion of the impact on the life of the patient and other family members. Also use *Breast Cancer* (2001). (Rev: HBG 3/02; SLJ 3/02) [616.3]

11339 Moragne, Wendy. *Allergies* (5–8). Series: Twenty-First Century Medical Library. 1999, Twenty-First Century LB $26.90 (978-0-7613-1359-5). After general material on allergies, their causes and treatment, this account describes specific allergies involving food, skin, rhinitis, drugs, and insects. (Rev: HBG 3/00; SLJ 3/00) [616.97]

11340 Morgan, Sally. *Germ Killers: Fighting Disease* (5–8). Series: Science at the Edge. 2002, Heinemann LB $27.86 (978-1-58810-699-5). Current advances in fighting disease are outlined with their current applications and future possibilities. (Rev: BL 10/15/02; HBG 3/03) [616]

11341 Mulcahy, Robert. *Diseases: Finding the Cure* (7–9). 1996, Oliver LB $21.95 (978-1-881508-28-1). After a general introduction on disease fighting, single chapters explore the breakthroughs of such scientists as Edward Jenner, Louis Pasteur, Alexander Fleming, and Jonas Salk, with a special afterword on AIDS. (Rev: SLJ 10/96) [616]

11342 Murphy, Wendy. *Asthma* (7–12). Series: Millbrook Medical Library. 1998, Millbrook LB $26.90 (978-0-7613-0364-0). Beginning with the causes of asthma, this book describes what happens during an attack, how the disease is controlled, and various avenues of medical treatment. (Rev: BL 1/1–15/99; HBG 3/99; SLJ 1/99) [616.2]

11343 Murphy, Wendy. *Orphan Diseases: New Hope for Rare Medical Conditions* (7–12). Illus. 2002, Millbrook LB $26.90 (978-0-7613-1919-1). Autism, cystic fibrosis, and dwarfism are among the conditions discussed, with information on origin, causes, treatment, and how patients cope with the condition. (Rev: BL 10/15/02; HBG 3/03) [362.1]

11344 Nakaya, Andrea C., ed. *Obesity* (8–12). Series: Opposing Viewpoints. 2005, Gale LB $36.20 (978-0-7377-3233-7). The causes of the soaring rates of obesity are discussed from various viewpoints, as well as who is responsible and what can be done to reduce this health problem. (Rev: SLJ 1/06) [616.3]

11345 Nash, Carol R. *AIDS: Choices for Life* (7–12). Illus. Series: Issues in Focus. 1997, Enslow LB $26.60 (978-0-89490-903-0). This book offers information about AIDS and protease inhibitors, drug cocktails, the AIDS virus, current and future medical concerns, and prevention tactics, plus a history of the disease. (Rev: BL 12/1/97; SLJ 12/97; VOYA 6/98) [616.97]

11346 Newton, David E., et al. *Sick! Diseases and Disorders, Injuries and Infections* (8–12). 1999, U.X.L $247.00 (978-0-7876-3922-8). Arranged alphabetically, this volume covers 140 illnesses, disorders, and injuries with material on symptoms, causes, diagnosis, prevention, and treatment. (Rev: BL 10/1/00) [616]

11347 Nye, Bill, and Kathleen W. Zoehfeld. *Bill Nye the Science Guy's Great Big Book of Tiny Germs* (4–7). Illus. by Bryn Barnard. 2005, Hyperion $16.99 (978-0-7868-0543-3). Solid information on bacteria and viruses is presented in an appealing and lively format. (Rev: BL 6/1–15/05; SLJ 7/05) [579]

11348 O'Brien, Eileen. *Starving to Win: Athletes and Eating Disorders* (6–12). Series: Teen Health Library of Eating Disorder Prevention. 1998, Rosen LB $26.50 (978-0-8239-2764-7). This book describes the pressures on athletes to gain or lose weight and

the temptation, particularly in track, gymnastics, ballet, and wrestling, to resort to dangerous crash diets, fasts, or drugs. The author stresses that health is more important than weight. (Rev: SLJ 2/99) [616.85]

11349 Orr, Tamra. *When the Mirror Lies: Anorexia, Bulimia, and Other Eating Disorders* (7–12). 2006, Watts LB $30.50 (978-0-531-16791-5); paper $17.95 (978-0-531-17977-2). Case studies help to draw readers into this friendly account of eating disorders and their impact. (Rev: SLJ 11/06) 🐝

11350 Ouriou, Katie. *Love Ya Like a Sister: A Story of Friendship* (8–12). Ed. by Julie Johnston. 1999, Tundra paper $7.95 (978-0-88776-454-7). After her death from leukemia when only 16 years old, Katie Ouriou's life and thoughts during her last months were reconstructed from journal entries and e-mail correspondence with her many friends. (Rev: SLJ 5/99; VOYA 6/99) [616.95]

11351 Panno, Joseph. *Cancer: The Role of Genes, Lifestyle and Environment* (7–12). Illus. Series: The New Biology. 2004, Facts on File $35.00 (978-0-8160-4950-9). In this title from the New Biology series, author Joseph Panno explores the role of genetics, lifestyle choices, and the environment in cancer. (Rev: SLJ 2/05; VOYA 8/04)

11352 Panno, Joseph. *Gene Therapy: Treating Disease by Repairing Genes* (7–12). Illus. Series: The New Biology. 2004, Facts on File $35.00 (978-0-8160-4948-6). The hot-button topic of gene therapy and its implications for the future treatment of diseases and physical injuries is explored here. (Rev: SLJ 2/05)

11353 Peters, Stephanie True. *The Battle Against Polio* (6–10). Illus. Series: Epidemic! 2004, Benchmark LB $29.93 (978-0-7614-1635-7). The history of polio, the toll it took on young lives, and the ultimately successful search for a vaccine are related in a compelling presentation. (Rev: BL 12/15/04; SLJ 2/05) [614.54]

11354 Pincus, Dion. *Everything You Need to Know About Cerebral Palsy* (4–7). Series: Need to Know Library. 2000, Rosen LB $27.95 (978-0-8239-2960-3). The causes and characteristics of cerebral palsy are discussed with material on the treatments and the daily life of those affected. (Rev: HBG 10/00; SLJ 3/00) [618.92]

11355 Pipher, Mary. *Hunger Pains: The Modern Woman's Tragic Quest for Thinness* (7–12). 1997, Ballantine paper $12.00 (978-0-345-41393-2). This book explains eating disorders, probes into their basic causes, and offers suggestions for help, with separate chapters on bulimia, anorexia, obesity, and diets. (Rev: VOYA 8/97) [616.95]

11356 Powers, Mary C. *Arthritis* (7–12). Series: Encyclopedia of Health. 1992, Chelsea LB $19.95 (978-0-7910-0057-1). Illustrated with black-and-white pictures, this book describes the causes of arthritis, therapies, and treatments. (Rev: BL 10/1/92) [616.7]

11357 Ramen, Fred. *Sleeping Sickness and Other Parasitic Tropical Diseases* (5–8). Series: Epidemics. 2002, Rosen LB $27.95 (978-0-8239-3499-7). After a history of parasitic diseases around the globe and the role played by bloodsucking killers like the tsetse fly, this account describes the treatments now available. (Rev: BL 8/02; SLJ 7/02) [616]

11358 Ray, Kurt. *Typhoid Fever* (5–8). Illus. Series: Epidemics. 2002, Rosen LB $27.95 (978-0-8239-3572-7). An introduction to the history and treatment of typhoid fever, including coverage of Typhoid Mary. (Rev: BL 3/15/02) [614.5]

11359 Ridgway, Tom. *Mad Cow Disease: Bovine Spongiform Encephalopathy* (6–8). Series: Epidemics. 2002, Rosen LB $27.95 (978-0-8239-3487-4). A fascinating account of how this disease affects its victims, how it spreads, and how scientists raced to discover more about it. (Rev: BL 8/02; SLJ 6/02) [616.8]

11360 Robbins, Paul R. *Anorexia and Bulimia* (7–12). Series: Diseases and People. 1998, Enslow LB $26.60 (978-0-7660-1047-5). The history of anorexia, bulimia, and binge eating is given, with material on symptoms, possible causes, prevention, and treatment. (Rev: BL 1/1–15/99; SLJ 1/99) [616.85]

11361 Rocha, Toni L. *Understanding Recovery from Eating Disorders* (6–10). Series: Teen Eating Disorder Prevention Library. 1999, Rosen $31.95 (978-0-8239-2884-2). This book offers first-person accounts of survivors of various types of eating disorders and also offers advice for teens who are in recovery programs. (Rev: BL 10/15/99; HBG 9/00; SLJ 7/00) [616.85]

11362 Roleff, Tamara L., ed. *AIDS* (7–12). Illus. Series: Opposing Viewpoints. 2003, Gale paper $24.95 (978-0-7377-1135-6). Articles address the spread of HIV and the current status of the epidemic, as well as treatment (including recommendations for pregnant women and infants), needle-exchange programs, and partner notification. (Rev: SLJ 11/03) [616.977]

11363 Romano, Amy. *Germ Warfare* (5–8). Illus. Series: Germs: The Library of Disease-Causing Organisms. 2004, Rosen LB $26.50 (978-0-8239-4493-4). An informative, illustrated overview of the history and current status of germ warfare, with discussion of what we can do to protect ourselves. (Rev: SLJ 1/05) [358]

11364 Rosaler, Maxine. *Botulism* (4–7). Series: Epidemics. 2004, Rosen LB $27.95 (978-0-8239-4197-1). A look at outbreaks of botulism and their causes and prevention. (Rev: SLJ 8/04) [614.5]

11365 Rosaler, Maxine. *Cystic Fibrosis* (6–8). Illus. Series: Genetic Diseases and Disorders . 2006, Rosen LB $26.50 (978-1-4042-0696-0). This guide to cystic fibrosis — covering history of our knowledge of the disorder and contemporary understanding — will be useful for researchers; (Rev: SLJ 2/07)

11366 Routh, Kristina. *Down Syndrome* (5–8). Series: Just the Facts. 2004, Heinemann LB $27.07 (978-1-4034-5145-3). An informative overview of this disease and its diagnosis and treatment, stressing the individuality of children with the syndrome. (Rev: SLJ 2/05) [362.1]

11367 Routh, Kristina. *Meningitis* (5–8). Illus. Series: Just the Facts. 2004, Heinemann LB $27.07 (978-1-4034-5146-0). The symptoms of meningitis are provided along with a thorough explanation of the disease and its diagnosis and treatment. (Rev: SLJ 2/05)

11368 Roy, Jennifer Rozines. *Depression* (4–7). Illus. Series: Health Alert. 2004, Benchmark LB $28.50 (978-0-7614-1800-9). In addition to describing the causes and treatment of depression, this attractive title opens with a case history and also includes lists of famous people who suffer from the condition. (Rev: SLJ 5/05)

11369 Sanders, Pete, and Steve Myers. *Anorexia and Bulimia* (4–8). Illus. by Mike Lacy and Liz Sawyer. Series: What Do You Know About. 1999, Millbrook LB $23.90 (978-0-7613-0914-7). Using an actual case study as a beginning, this book explores the causes, effects, and treatment of these eating disorders and covers the behavioral patterns of those afflicted. (Rev: HBG 10/99; SLJ 10/99) [618.92]

11370 Schwartz, Robert H., and Peter M. G. Deane. *Coping with Allergies* (4–7). Series: Coping. 1999, Rosen LB $31.95 (978-0-8239-2511-7). After a rundown of the types and causes of allergies, this account describes their physical and emotional impact and current treatments. (Rev: BL 2/15/00) [616.97]

11371 Senker, Cath. *World Health Organization* (5–8). Series: World Watch. 2004, Raintree LB $18.99 (978-0-7398-6614-6). The world's health problems and what is being done to combat them are the focus of this somber title, which looks at both the developing world and the wealthiest of nations. (Rev: BL 4/1/04; SLJ 3/04) [362.1]

11372 Sheen, Barbara. *Diabetes* (5–7). Illus. Series: Diseases and Disorders. 2003, Gale LB $32.45 (978-1-59018-244-4). The symptoms of and treatments for diabetes are covered here, with discussion of alternative treatments, how diabetics manage their disease, and the research being undertaken. (Rev: SLJ 7/03) [616.4]

11373 Shein, Lori. *AIDS* (5–8). Series: Overview. 1998, Lucent LB $29.95 (978-1-56006-193-9). A concise overview of the AIDS epidemic in the late 20th century, the attempts to treat and restrict the spread of the disease, and the controversies surrounding it. (Rev: BL 8/98) [616.99]

11374 Sherrow, Victoria. *Polio Epidemic: Crippling Virus Outbreak* (4–7). Series: American Disasters. 2001, Enslow LB $23.93 (978-0-7660-1555-5). In this readable account, Sherrow looks at the history of polio, its treatment, the epidemic in the United States that started in 1952, and the creation of the polio vaccine. (Rev: HBG 3/02; SLJ 3/02) [362.1]

11375 Silverstein, Alvin, et al. *AIDS: An All-About Guide for Young Adults* (6–12). Illus. Series: Issues in Focus. 1999, Enslow LB $20.95 (978-0-89490-716-6). In addition to discussing the history, diagnosis, treatment, and prevention of AIDS, the authors present interesting sidebar features and profiles of celebrities who have contracted the disease. (Rev: BL 11/15/99; HBG 4/00; SLJ 11/99) [616.97]

11376 Silverstein, Alvin, et al. *Asthma* (7–12). Illus. Series: Diseases and People. 1997, Enslow LB $20.95 (978-0-89490-712-8). This book discusses the nature, causes, and treatment of asthma and possible cures. (Rev: BL 2/15/97; SLJ 4/97; VOYA 6/97) [616.2]

11377 Silverstein, Alvin. *The Asthma Update* (5–8). 2006, Enslow LB $31.93 (978-0-7660-2482-3). A thorough look at asthma, its symptoms, history, treatments, and the research being done in hopes of finding a cure. (Rev: BL 12/1/06) [616.2]

11378 Silverstein, Alvin, et al. *Cancer: Conquering a Deadly Disease* (8–12). Series: Twenty-First Century Medical Library. 2005, Twenty-First Century LB $27.93 (978-0-7613-2833-9). Using case studies to introduce topics, this is a thorough exploration of new developments in the fight against cancer. (Rev: SLJ 3/06)

11379 Silverstein, Alvin, et al. *Chickenpox and Shingles* (6–10). Series: Diseases and People. 1998, Enslow LB $26.60 (978-0-89490-715-9). The nature and treatment of these two diseases are discussed, supplemented by case studies. (Rev: BL 7/98) [616]

11380 Silverstein, Alvin, et al. *Diabetes* (7–12). Illus. Series: Diseases and People. 1994, Enslow LB $26.60 (978-0-89490-464-6). An examination of the causes and treatment of diabetes, with material on how to detect it and sources of possible cures. (Rev: BL 10/15/94; SLJ 12/94; VOYA 12/94) [616.4]

11381 Silverstein, Alvin, et al. *The Flu and Pneumonia Update* (5–8). Illus. Series: Disease Update. 2006, Enslow LB $31.93 (978-0-7660-2480-9). Symptoms, treatment, history, and new research are all included in this discussion of flu and pneumonia. (Rev: BL 4/1/06; SLJ 9/06) [616.2]

11382 Silverstein, Alvin. *The Food Poisoning Update* (5–8). Illus. Series: Disease Update. 2007, Enslow LB $23.95 (978-0-7660-2748-0). A clear introduction to what causes food poisoning, how it affects the body, and how it can be avoided. (Rev: BL 12/1/07; SLJ 2/08) [615.9]

11383 Silverstein, Alvin, et al. *Hepatitis* (8–10). Series: Diseases and People. 1994, Enslow $26.60 (978-0-89490-467-7). The history of hepatitis is given along with material on treatment, prevention, and related ailments. [616.3]

11384 Silverstein, Alvin, et al. *Leukemia* (6–10). Illus. Series: Diseases and People. 2000, Enslow LB $26.60 (978-0-7660-1310-0). A look at the history, symptoms, diagnosis, treatment, social impact, and future of this disease. (Rev: HBG 10/01; SLJ 9/00) [616.99]

11385 Silverstein, Alvin, et al. *Lyme Disease* (4–7). Illus. 2000, Watts LB $25.50 (978-0-531-11751-4). This book introduces Lyme disease, its symptoms, history, the tick that carries it, prevention, and treatments. (Rev: BL 10/15/00) [616.9]

11386 Silverstein, Alvin, et al. *Mononucleosis* (7–10). Series: Diseases and People. 1994, Enslow LB $20.95 (978-0-89490-466-0). Examines this disease's history, causes, treatment, prevention, and societal response. (Rev: BL 1/15/95; HBG 10/01; SLJ 3/95) [616.9]

11387 Silverstein, Alvin, et al. *Parkinson's Disease* (7–10). Series: Diseases and People. 2001, Enslow LB $26.60 (978-0-7660-1593-7). Parkinson's disease is described, with information on its causes, symptoms. diagnosis, and treatment. (Rev: HBG 3/03) [616.8]

11388 Silverstein, Alvin, et al. *Rabies* (8–10). Series: Diseases and People. 1994, Enslow LB $26.60 (978-0-89490-465-3). Various aspects of rabies, including history, diagnosis, treatment, and prevention, are discussed in this account. (Rev: SLJ 7/94) [616.9]

11389 Silverstein, Alvin, et al. *Sickle Cell Anemia* (6–12). Illus. Series: Diseases and People. 1997, Enslow LB $26.60 (978-0-89490-711-1). A clear, concise description of the causes, effects, and treatment of this condition, with information on why it attacks African Americans in particular. (Rev: BL 2/15/97; SLJ 2/97; VOYA 6/97) [616.1]

11390 Silverstein, Alvin, and Virginia Silverstein. *Allergies* (7–10). Illus. 1977, HarperCollins $13.00 (978-0-397-31758-5). The types of allergies — such as hay fever and asthma — as well as their causes, effects, and treatments are discussed. [616.97]

11391 Silverstein, Alvin, and Virginia Silverstein. *The Breast Cancer Update* (5–9). Illus. Series: Disease Update. 2007, Enslow LB $31.93 (978-0-7660-2747-3). Symptoms, treatment, history, and new research are all included in this concise discussion of breast cancer. (Rev: SLJ 2/08)

11392 Silverstein, Alvin, and Virginia Silverstein. *Measles and Rubella* (6–12). Illus. Series: Diseases and People. 1997, Enslow LB $26.60 (978-0-89490-714-2). The authors examine the nature of measles and rubella, their treatment, and the possibility of a cure. (Rev: BL 3/1/98; SLJ 5/98) [616.9]

11393 Silverstein, Alvin, and Virginia Silverstein. *Runaway Sugar: All About Diabetes* (7–10). Illus. 1981, HarperCollins LB $12.89 (978-0-397-31929-9). Among other topics, this book discusses what causes diabetes and how it can be controlled. [616.4]

11394 Silverstein, Alvin, and Virginia Silverstein. *The STDs Update* (6–12). Series: Disease Update. 2006, Enslow LB $23.95 (978-0-7660-2484-7). A question-and-answer format and personal accounts of STD infections make this a useful resource. (Rev: SLJ 9/06)

11395 Silverstein, Alvin, and Virginia B. Silverstein. *Polio* (7–10). Series: Diseases and People. 2001, Enslow LB $26.60 (978-0-7660-1592-0). The symptoms, causes, prevention, and treatment of polio are discussed, with information on such well-known patients as Franklin D. Roosevelt. (Rev: HBG 3/02) [616.8]

11396 Simpson, Carolyn. *Coping with Sleep Disorders* (7–12). Series: Coping. 1995, Rosen LB $31.95 (978-0-8239-2068-6). This book discusses sleeping disorders from snoring to insomnia and offers a wide range of possible solutions. (Rev: SLJ 6/96; VOYA 8/96) [613.7]

11397 Simpson, Carolyn. *Everything You Need to Know About Asthma* (5–10). Illus. Series: Need to Know Library. 1998, Rosen LB $27.95 (978-0-8239-2567-4). Vital background information is given about the causes and effects, symptoms, and treatments of asthma. (Rev: SLJ 10/98) [616.2]

11398 Smart, Paul. *Everything You Need to Know About Mononucleosis* (5–9). Series: Need to Know Library. 1998, Rosen LB $27.95 (978-0-8239-2550-6). A straightforward presentation about the "kissing disease," which is often undiagnosed or mistaken for the flu and which requires long periods of rest for recovery. (Rev: SLJ 10/98) [616]

11399 Smith, Erica. *Anorexia Nervosa: When Food Is the Enemy* (6–10). Series: Teen Health Library of Eating Disorder Prevention. 1998, Rosen LB $27.95 (978-0-8239-2766-1). The author describes anorexia nervosa and its symptoms and treatment, and discusses what to do if you suspect someone is suffering from the eating disorder. Society's attitudes toward weight and body image and the role of peer pressure, media images, family relationships, and genetics are examined, along with how to deal with these influences. (Rev: SLJ 1/99) [616.85]

11400 Smith, Terry L. *Breast Cancer: Current and Emerging Trends in Detection and Treatment* (6–10). Illus. Series: Cancer and Modern Science. 2005, Rosen LB $29.25 (978-1-4042-0386-0). With photographs, diagrams, and sidebar features, this volume offers information on the diagnosis, treatment, and future issues of breast cancer, as well as ways to cope with the disease and survivor stories. (Rev: SLJ 5/06) [616.99]

11401 Snedden, Robert. *Fighting Infectious Diseases* (6–10). Illus. Series: Microlife. 2000, Heinemann LB $22.79 (978-1-57572-243-6). The body's immune system and other forms of defense against diseases are discussed in this well-illustrated account. (Rev: BL 9/15/00) [616.8]

11402 Sparks, Beatrice, ed. *It Happened to Nancy* (7–12). 1994, Avon paper $6.99 (978-0-380-77315-2). In diary format, this is the story of 14-year-old Nancy, who was raped by her boyfriend and infected with the HIV virus. (Rev: BL 6/1–15/94; SLJ 6/94; VOYA 10/94) [362.196]

11403 Spray, Michelle. *Growing Up with Scoliosis: A Young Girl's Story* (5–9). Illus. by author. 2002, Book Shelf paper $12.95 (978-0-9714160-3-1). An autobiographical account of the treatment of scoliosis and the emotional impact on the patient, with clear illustrations. (Rev: SLJ 12/02) [362.19673]

11404 Stanley, Debbie. *Understanding Anorexia Nervosa* (6–12). Series: Teen Eating Disorder Prevention Library. 1999, Rosen LB $31.95 (978-0-8239-2877-4). Why people get anorexia, how to get help for it, the dangers of this condition, and some of the myths surrounding it are all covered in this volume. (Rev: HBG 9/00; SLJ 2/00) [616.85]

11405 Stanley, Debbie. *Understanding Bulimia Nervosa* (6–10). Series: Teen Eating Disorder Prevention Library. 1999, Rosen $31.95 (978-0-8239-2878-1). A look at this eating disorder, in which a person binges and purges, with material on contributing factors and guidance to help recovery. (Rev: BL 10/15/99; HBG 9/00; SLJ 7/00) [616.85]

11406 Stewart, Gail B. *Sleep Disorders* (5–8). Illus. Series: Diseases and Disorders. 2002, Gale LB $32.45 (978-1-56006-909-6). Insomnia, narcolepsy, apnea, and night terrors are among the problems discussed here, with material on treatments, new research, and attitudes toward people who are always tired. (Rev: SLJ 3/03) [616.8498]

11407 Stewart, Gail B. *Teens with Cancer* (7–10). Photos by Carl Franzn. Series: The Other America. 2001, Gale LB $29.95 (978-1-56006-884-6). The first-person stories of four young people with life-threatening cancers reveal the hard realities such teens face. (Rev: SLJ 12/01)

11408 Stokes, Mark. *Colon Cancer: Current and Emerging Trends in Detection and Treatment* (6–10). Illus. Series: Cancer and Modern Science.

2005, Rosen LB $29.25 (978-1-4042-0387-7). With photographs, diagrams, and sidebar features, this volume offers information on the diagnosis, treatment, and future issues of colon cancer, as well as ways to cope with the disease and survivor stories. Also use *Prostate Cancer* (2005). (Rev: SLJ 5/06)

11409 Stone, Tanya L. *Medical Causes* (5–10). Series: Celebrity Activists. 1997, Twenty-First Century LB $25.90 (978-0-8050-5233-6). The contributions of such celebrity activists as Elizabeth Taylor, Elton John, Paul Newman, Jerry Lewis, and Linda Ellerbee to various medical causes are highlighted, with material on each of their causes. (Rev: SLJ 1/98) [616]

11410 Storad, Conrad J. *Inside AIDS: HIV Attacks the Immune System* (8–12). 1998, Lerner LB $27.93 (978-0-8225-2857-9). An unusual book about the HIV virus that tells about the cellular structure of the body, its immune system, and how the virus tricks the host cells into replicating it. (Rev: BL 12/15/98; HBG 3/99; SLJ 1/99) [616.97]

11411 Strada, Jennifer L. *Eating Disorders* (6–12). Illus. 2000, Lucent LB $29.95 (978-1-56006-659-0). Anorexia, bulimia, and binge eating are all described in this easy-to-read text, with discussion of causes, risk factors, treatment, and prevention. (Rev: BL 3/1/01; SLJ 4/01) [616.85]

11412 Susman, Edward. *Multiple Sclerosis* (4–7). Series: Diseases and People. 1999, Enslow LB $26.60 (978-0-7660-1185-4). A description of this debilitating disease that attacks the nervous system. (Rev: HBG 3/00; SLJ 2/00) [616]

11413 Veggeberg, Scott. *Lyme Disease* (7–12). 1998, Enslow LB $20.95 (978-0-7660-1052-9). An overview of the symptoms, diagnosis, treatment, and prevention of Lyme disease. (Rev: BL 7/98; HBG 10/98; SLJ 9/98) [616.7]

11414 Viegas, Jennifer. *Parasites* (5–8). Illus. Series: Germs: The Library of Disease-Causing Organisms. 2004, Rosen LB $26.50 (978-0-8239-4494-1). An informative, illustrated discussion of parasites, covering how they survive and the dangers they pose to humans. (Rev: SLJ 1/05) [574.5]

11415 Vogel, Carole G. *Breast Cancer: Questions and Answers for Young Women* (6–12). Illus. 2001, Twenty-First Century LB $25.90 (978-0-7613-1855-2). Teen readers will find clear answers to both emotional and physiological questions about breasts, breast development, and breast cancer. (Rev: HBG 10/01; SLJ 5/01; VOYA 8/01) [616.99]

11416 Vollstadt, Elizabeth Weiss. *Teen Eating Disorders* (7–12). Series: Teen Issues. 1999, Lucent LB $27.45 (978-1-56006-516-6). This book defines the various kinds of teenage eating disorders and, using many anecdotes, describes their causes, effects, treatment, and prevention. (Rev: BL 7/99; HBG 4/00; SLJ 8/99) [616.85]

11417 Wade, Mary Dodson. *ALS: Lou Gehrig's Disease* (6–12). Illus. Series: Diseases and People. 2001, Enslow LB $26.60 (978-0-7660-1594-4). The story of Lou Gehrig's illness introduces this incurable disease and its symptoms, treatment, and the research being conducted in search of a cure. (Rev: BL 1/1–15/02; HBG 10/02; SLJ 2/02) [616.8]

11418 Wainwright, Tabitha. *You and an Illness in Your Family* (5–8). Series: Family Matters. 2001, Rosen LB $26.50 (978-0-8239-3352-5). Concise, readable advice is accompanied by full-page photographs of young teens and the recommendation to seek help when necessary. (Rev: SLJ 8/01) [610]

11419 Walker, Pamela. *Everything You Need to Know About Body Dysmorphic Disorder: Dealing with a Distorted Body Image* (6–9). Series: Need to Know Library. 1999, Rosen LB $27.95 (978-0-8239-2954-2). Body dysmorphic disorder usually hits boys and girls in adolescence; symptoms, warning signs, ways of detection, and treatment are all covered here. (Rev: HBG 9/00; SLJ 8/00) [616.89]

11420 Walker, Pamela. *Understanding the Risk of Diet Drugs* (6–10). Series: Teen Eating Disorder Prevention Library. 2000, Rosen LB $25.25 (978-0-8239-2991-7). This book examines teen concerns about body image and overall appearance and provides information about eating disorders and weight-loss products. (Rev: BL 2/15/01; SLJ 1/01) [616.85]

11421 Ward, Brian. *Epidemic* (4–7). Illus. Series: Eyewitness Books. 2000, DK $15.99 (978-0-7894-6296-1). This book covers the nature of epidemics, their causes, how they are spread and contained, and gives examples from history. (Rev: BL 12/1/00; HBG 10/01) [614.4]

11422 Weeldreyer, Laura. *Body Blues: Weight and Depression* (6–12). Series: Teen Health Library of Eating Disorder Prevention. 1998, Rosen LB $27.95 (978-0-8239-2761-6). This book uses case studies of three teenagers who are trying to come to terms with food and their bodies to explore the relationship between weight and depression, and encourages teenagers to learn to accept their bodies rather than aspiring to some media ideal. (Rev: SLJ 2/99) [155.5]

11423 Weiss, Jonathan H. *Breathe Easy: Young People's Guide to Asthma* (4–7). Illus. 1994, Magination paper $9.95 (978-0-945354-62-8). An account that describes the causes of asthma, what happens during an attack, and how to manage this condition. (Rev: BL 2/15/95) [618.92]

11424 Whelan, Jo. *Diabetes* (5–8). Series: Health Issues. 2002, Raintree LB $28.54 (978-0-7398-5220-0). Case histories of youngsters with diabetes are used to explain the nature of this disease, the problems it produces, and the treatments available. (Rev: BL 12/15/02; HBG 3/03) [616.4]

11425 Willett, Edward. *Alzheimer's Disease* (6–12). Series: Diseases and People. 2002, Enslow LB $26.60 (978-0-7660-1596-8). As well as discussing the nature, treatment, and possible cures of Alzheimer's disease, this account uses many case studies, including that of President Reagan. (Rev: BL 8/02; HBG 10/02; SLJ 8/02) [616.8]

11426 Willett, Edward. *Hemophilia* (8–10). Series: Diseases and People. 2001, Enslow $26.60 (978-0-7660-1684-2). This account covers the history, symptoms, treatment, and prevention of hemophilia. (Rev: HBG 3/02; SLJ 12/01) [616.1]

11427 Williams, Mary E., ed. *Terminal Illness* (7–12). Series: Opposing Viewpoints. 2001, Greenhaven LB $32.45 (978-0-7377-0526-3); paper $21.20 (978-0-7377-0525-6). Euthanasia, the right to die, pain management, and the legalization of marijuana for the terminally ill are all discussed here, as are the choices of care available. (Rev: BL 5/1/01; SLJ 4/01) [362.1]

11428 Woolf, Alex. *Death and Disease* (5–8). Series: Medieval Realms. 2004, Gale LB $29.95 (978-1-59018-533-9). Black Death, leprosy, and other diseases are discussed, with their impact on society, and the practice of medicine in general is described. (Rev: BL 4/1/04; SLJ 3/05) [610]

11429 Yancey, Diane. *STDs: What You Don't Know Can Hurt You* (6–12). 2002, Millbrook LB $26.90 (978-0-7613-1957-3). The facts on common sexually transmitted diseases are combined with stories of teenagers with STDs, a section on prevention, and tests to help the reader determine his or her risk of becoming infected. (Rev: BL 4/1/02; HBG 10/02; SLJ 5/02) [616.95]

11430 Yancey, Diane. *Tuberculosis* (7–12). Series: Twenty-First Century Medical Library. 2001, Twenty-First Century LB $26.90 (978-0-7613-1624-4). Interesting illustrations and case studies draw the reader into this account of the historical and contemporary incidence of this disease. (Rev: HBG 10/01; SLJ 5/01) [616]

11431 Yount, Lisa. *Cancer* (5–8). Series: Overview. 1999, Lucent LB $29.95 (978-1-56006-363-6). This objective overview explains how cancer cells develop, types of cancer, causes, and past and present treatments, both traditional and alternative. (Rev: BL 9/15/99; HBG 3/00; SLJ 7/99) [616.994]

11432 Yount, Lisa. *Epidemics* (7–10). Illus. 1999, Lucent LB $29.95 (978-1-56006-441-1). An interesting overview of epidemics of the past, their causes, and the potential for future epidemics, including ones caused by biological weapons. (Rev: HBG 9/00; SLJ 4/00) [614.4]

Doctors, Hospitals, and Medicine

11433 Ballard, Carol. *From Cowpox to Antibiotics: Discovering Vaccines and Medicines* (6–9). Series: Chain Reactions. 2006, Heinemann LB $34.29 (978-1-4034-8839-8). Ballard discusses vaccines and medicines and their development over time. (Rev: SLJ 3/07) [615.372]

11434 Billitteri, Thomas J. *Alternative Medicine* (7–10). Series: Twenty-First Century Medical Library. 2001, Twenty-First Century LB $26.90 (978-0-7613-0965-9). This overview of alternative therapies such as hypnosis, acupuncture, and homeopathy balances success stories with solid information on the lack of rigorous scientific investigation and of FDA oversight. (Rev: HBG 3/02; SLJ 12/01; VOYA 4/02) [615.5]

11435 Cosner, Shaaron. *War Nurses* (6–9). Illus. 1988, Walker $17.85 (978-0-8027-6828-5). A history of the important role nurses have played tending the wounded from the Civil War through the Vietnam conflict. (Rev: BL 12/1/88; SLJ 12/88) [355.3]

11436 Davis, Sampson, et al. *We Beat the Street: How a Friendship Led to Success* (7–10). 2005, Dutton $16.99 (978-0-525-47407-4). Draper recounts the inspiring story of three young men who grew up in a tough neighborhood of Newark, New Jersey, escaped the mean streets of their childhood, and went on to become doctors. (Rev: BL 4/1/05; SLJ 5/05) [610]

11437 Dawson, Ian. *Renaissance Medicine* (6–9). Illus. Series: History of Medicine. 2005, Enchanted Lion LB $19.95 (978-1-59270-038-7). An informative, well-illustrated overview of medical developments in Europe from the mid-15th to mid-18th centuries. (Rev: BL 4/1/05; SLJ 11/05; VOYA 2/06) [610.9]

11438 de la Bédoyère, Guy. *The Discovery of Penicillin* (6–9). Illus. Series: Milestones in Modern Science. 2005, World Almanac LB $31.00 (978-0-8368-5852-5). Suitable for reports, this volume provides a good overview of the discovery of penicillin and its impact on public health. Also use *The First Polio Vaccine* (2005). (Rev: SLJ 1/06) [509]

11439 Dowswell, Paul. *Medicine* (5–8). Illus. Series: Great Inventions. 2001, Heinemann LB $25.64 (978-1-58810-213-3). A chronological look at new medical instruments and procedures over the ages, with diagrams and information on the inventors. (Rev: HBG 3/02; SLJ 2/02) [610]

11440 Edelson, Edward. *Sports Medicine* (8–12). Series: 21st Century Health and Wellness. 1999, Chelsea House $36.00 (978-0-7910-5521-2). This is a close look at sports medicine, its history, and its place in today's world. [617.1]

11441 Facklam, Margery, et al. *Modern Medicines: The Discovery and Development of Healing Drugs* (7–12). Series: Science and Technology in Focus. 2004, Facts on File $35.00 (978-0-8160-4706-2). This updated title traces the development of medications from ancient herbal remedies to today's powerful pharmaceuticals, discussing research and testing, the role of the FDA, and the economics of the pharmaceutical industry. (Rev: BL 8/04) [615]

11442 Farndon, John. *From Laughing Gas to Face Transplants: Discovering Transplant Surgery* (6–9). Series: Chain Reactions. 2006, Heinemann LB $34.29 (978-1-4034-8840-4). Farndon looks at transplant surgery from its inception to today's applications, with personal stories and quotations from specialists in the field. (Rev: SLJ 3/07)

11443 Fleischman, John. *Phineas Gage: A Gruesome But True Story About Brain Science* (7–10). Illus. 2002, Houghton $16.00 (978-0-618-05252-3). This riveting story of the amiable man whose personality changed when an iron rod shot through his brain presents lots of information on brain science and medical knowledge in the 19th century. (Rev: BL 3/1/02; HB 5–6/02; HBG 10/02; SLJ 3/02; VOYA 6/02) [362.1]

11444 Freedman, Jeri. *Stem Cell Research* (5–8). Illus. Series: America Debates. 2007, Rosen LB $21.95 (978-1-4042-1928-1). A technical and detailed examination of the issues surrounding stem cell research and the ethical questions that it provokes. (Rev: BL 12/1/07; LMC 2/08; SLJ 2/08) [616]

11445 Giddens, Sandra, and Owen Giddens. *Future Techniques in Surgery* (6–9). Illus. Series: Library of Future Medicine. 2003, Rosen LB $29.25 (978-0-8239-3667-0). A look at the new techniques and equipment that make less invasive procedures possible and reduce recovery time. (Rev: BL 10/15/03; LMC 10/03; SLJ 5/03) [617]

11446 Gilpin, Daniel. *Medicine* (6–9). Illus. Series: History of Invention. 2004, Facts on File $35.00 (978-0-8160-5442-8). A slim introductory overview of advances in medicine from prehistoric times to today, with maps, illustrations, and profiles of key figures. (Rev: SLJ 12/04) [610.9]

11447 Goldsmith, Connie. *Superbugs Strike Back: When Antibiotics Fail* (7–10). 2007, Lerner LB $29.27 (978-0-8225-6607-6). Discusses bacteria that have becoming resistant to antibiotics, how antibiotics work, their presence in the food chain, and what can be done to deal with the problem. (Rev: BL 6/1–15/07; SLJ 8/07) [615]

11448 Green, Jen. *Medicine* (4–7). Illus. Series: Routes of Science. 2004, Gale LB $23.70 (978-1-4103-0168-0). A look at the history of medicine and the scientific process, with profiles of key individu-

als and their discoveries, a chronology, and discussion of future advances. (Rev: SLJ 5/05)

11449 Ichord, Loretta Frances. *Toothworms and Spider Juice: An Illustrated History of Dentistry* (5–8). Illus. 2000, Millbrook LB $24.90 (978-0-7613-1465-3). A history of dentistry that reveals many of the barbaric treatments of the past and how superstition and ignorance gradually gave way to modern practices. (Rev: BCCB 2/00; BL 2/15/00; HBG 10/00; SLJ 2/00) [617.6]

11450 Jefferis, David. *Bio Tech: Frontiers of Medicine* (4–8). Illus. Series: Megatech. 2001, Crabtree paper $8.95 (978-0-7787-0061-6). An eye-catching look at future medical possibilities such as artificial body parts, enhanced use of robots, special foods, and so forth. (Rev: SLJ 6/02) [660.6]

11451 Judson, Karen. *Medical Ethics: Life and Death Issues* (7–10). 2001, Enslow LB $26.60 (978-0-7660-1585-2). After defining ethics, Judson presents a balanced overview of the potential positive and negative impacts of medical decisions, and discusses such topics as organ donation and the financial aspects of health care. (Rev: HBG 3/02; SLJ 9/01) [174]

11452 Kowalski, Kathiann M. *Alternative Medicine: Is It for You?* (7–9). Illus. Series: Issues in Focus. 1998, Enslow LB $26.60 (978-0-89490-955-9). After explaining the differences between traditional and alternative medicine, this book describes homeopathy, chiropractic medicine, medical practices from India and China, nutritional therapies, biofeedback, and healing based on prayer and meditation. (Rev: BL 10/1/98; SLJ 12/98) [615.5]

11453 Lawton, Sandra Augustyn, ed. *Complementary and Alternative Medicine Information for Teens: Health Tips about Non-Traditional and Non-Western Medical Practices* (7–12). Series: Teen Health. 2006, Omnigraphics LB $65.00 (978-0-7808-0966-6). The full subtitle of this book tells it all: Health Tips About Non-Traditional and Non-Western Medical Practices Including Information About Acupuncture, Chiropractic Medicine, Dietary and Herbal Supplements, Hypnosis, Massage Therapy, Prayer and Spirituality, Reflexology, Yoga, and More. (Rev: SLJ 5/07) [610]

11454 Levy, Debbie. *Medical Ethics* (6–12). Series: Overview. 2001, Lucent LB $29.95 (978-1-56006-547-0). Such topics as genetic engineering, experimental treatments, assisted suicide, and organ transplants are introduced and their relationship to medical ethics explored. (Rev: BL 9/15/01; SLJ 4/01) [174]

11455 Marcovitz, Hal. *Health Care* (7–12). Series: Gallup Major Trends and Events. 2007, Mason Crest LB $22.95 (978-1-59084-964-4). A useful, chronological survey of developments in health care over the last century, looking at such topics as polio,

AIDS, smoking, and obesity. (Rev: SLJ 10/07) [362.1]

11456 Miller, Brandon M. *Just What the Doctor Ordered: The History of American Medicine* (5–8). Series: People's History. 1997, Lerner LB $30.35 (978-0-8225-1737-5). A history of American medicine from early Indian ceremonies and remedies to today's use of laser surgery, placing medical developments in a historical context, such as the role disease played in the Revolutionary and Civil Wars. (Rev: SLJ 5/97*) [610.9]

11457 Moe, Barbara. *The Revolution in Medical Imaging* (6–9). Illus. Series: Library of Future Medicine. 2003, Rosen LB $29.25 (978-0-8239-3672-4). A look at breakthroughs such as CAT, PET, and MRI scans and the benefits they offer to both diagnostician and patient. (Rev: BL 10/15/03; SLJ 5/03) [61]

11458 Morley, David. *Healing Our World: Inside Doctors Without Borders* (7–10). Illus. 2007, Fitzhenry & Whiteside $18.95 (978-1-55041-565-0). An introduction to the organization that helps the sick around the world, with information on global health problems and what is being done to try to solve them. (Rev: BL 3/1/07; SLJ 5/07) [610]

11459 Murphy, Patricia J. *Everything You Need to Know About Staying in the Hospital* (5–8). Series: Need to Know Library. 2001, Rosen LB $27.95 (978-0-8239-3325-9). This volume explains the basic hospital process from admission to discharge and follows a patient through a typical day. (Rev: SLJ 5/01) [362.1]

11460 Murphy, Wendy, and Jack Murphy. *Nuclear Medicine* (7–12). Series: Encyclopedia of Health. 1993, Chelsea LB $19.95 (978-0-7910-0070-0). This work presents current information on the role played by nuclear research in health care, including radiation treatments. (Rev: BL 12/1/93) [616.07]

11461 Nardo, Don, ed. *Vaccines* (7–10). Illus. Series: Great Medical Discoveries. 2001, Gale LB $29.95 (978-1-56006-932-4). The history of inoculations (back to ancient China), the discoveries of scientists including Sabine and Salk, and current efforts to find new vaccines are all discussed here. (Rev: BL 3/1/02; SLJ 5/02) [615]

11462 Oleksy, Walter. *Science and Medicine* (6–12). Series: Information Revolution. 1995, Facts on File $25.00 (978-0-8160-3076-7). A summary of computer technology used in medicine and in science classrooms. (Rev: BL 11/15/95; SLJ 11/95) [502]

11463 Pascoe, Elaine, ed. *Crash: The Body in Crisis* (5–8). Illus. Series: Body Story. 2003, Gale LB $24.95 (978-1-4103-0062-1). Two people are badly hurt in a car crash — he is unconscious, she has a ruptured spleen — and readers accompany them to the emergency room and the operating room as they fight for their lives. (Rev: SLJ 4/04) [617.1]

11464 Rattenbury, Jeanne. *Understanding Alternative Medicine* (7–10). Illus. 1999, Watts LB $21.00 (978-0-531-11413-1). An attractive book that supplies information on topics including osteopathy, chiropractic treatments, homeopathy, acupuncture, herbal medicine, and mind–body therapy. (Rev: BL 6/1–15/99; SLJ 7/99) [615]

11465 Sherrow, Victoria. *Medical Imaging* (7–10). Illus. Series: Great Inventions. 2007, Marshall Cavendish LB $27.95 (978-0-7614-2231-0). From X-rays to ultrasound to MRI to the future, this is a review of medical imaging and its benefits. (Rev: SLJ 11/07) [616.07]

11466 Snedden, Robert. *Medical Ethics: Changing Attitudes 1900–2000* (4–7). 1999, Raintree LB $28.54 (978-0-8172-5893-1). Beginning with Hippocrates, this book gives a history of bioethics and follows with coverage of topics including reproductive rights, euthanasia, organ donation, psychiatry, eugenics, and cloning. (Rev: HBG 10/00; SLJ 5/00) [616]

11467 Stille, Darlene R. *Extraordinary Women of Medicine* (6–8). Illus. Series: Extraordinary People. 1997, Children's Pr. LB $40.00 (978-0-516-20307-2). A profile of 50 women who have reached prominence in medicine from the well-known, including the legendary Florence Nightingale, to many lesser-known, present-day achievers, spanning two centuries and organized according to groups or themes. (Rev: BL 10/1/97; HBG 3/98) [610]

11468 Townsend, John. *Bedpans, Blood and Bandages: A History of Hospitals* (6–9). Series: A Painful History of Medicine. 2005, Raintree LB $32.86 (978-1-4109-1334-0). The graphic illustrations in sometimes-unsettling history of hospitals from medieval times to the present will attract readers. Other volumes are *Pills, Powders and Potions: A History of Medication* and *Pox, Pus and Plague: A History of Disease and Infection* (both 2005). (Rev: SLJ 7/05) [610]

11469 Townsend, John. *Scalpels, Stitches and Scars: A History of Surgery* (4–7). Illus. Series: A Painful History of Medicine. 2005, Raintree LB $32.86 (978-1-4109-1332-6). Gory it may be but this title conveys accurate facts and the eye-catching illustrations will entice browsers. (Rev: BL 5/15/05; SLJ 7/05) [617]

11470 Van Steenwyk, Elizabeth. *Frontier Fever: The Silly, Superstitious — and Sometimes Sensible — Medicine of the Pioneers* (5–8). Illus. 1995, Walker LB $16.85 (978-0-8027-8403-2). A history of medicine in the United States from colonial times through the 19th century, including information on the training of caregivers. (Rev: BL 7/95; SLJ 12/95; VOYA 12/95) [610]

11471 Viegas, Jennifer. *Stem Cell Research* (6–10). Illus. Series: Library of Future Medicine. 2003,

Rosen LB $26.50 (978-0-8239-3669-4). A look at the composition of cells, the unique qualities of stem cells, and recent scientific discoveries about the use of embryonic stem cells and the growth of new human tissue, with discussion of possible future developments and the accompanying controversies. (Rev: SLJ 6/03) [616.02774]

11472 Waters, Sophie. *Seeing the Gynecologist* (6–12). Illus. Series: Girls' Health. 2007, Rosen LB $19.95 (978-1-4042-1948-9). Girls who don't know what to expect when visiting a gynecologist will be reassured by this straightforward book. (Rev: BL 10/15/07; LMC 2/08) [618.1]

11473 Winkler, Kathy. *Radiology* (4–8). Series: Inventors and Inventions. 1996, Benchmark LB $25.64 (978-0-7614-0075-2). This work outlines the history of radiology, provides short profiles of leaders in the field, and describes the effects of too many x-rays on tissue, how x-rays are made, their use in diagnosis and treatment, and other medical imaging such as ultrasound and MRIs. (Rev: BL 7/96; SLJ 9/96) [616.07]

11474 Woods, Michael, and Mary B. Woods. *The History of Medicine* (5–8). Series: Major Inventions Through History. 2005, Twenty-First Century LB $26.60 (978-0-8225-2336-9). An attractive look at medical developments through time and their impact on our lives. (Rev: SLJ 1/06) [610]

11475 Yount, Lisa. *Medical Technology* (6–12). Series: Milestones in Discovery and Invention. 1998, Facts on File $25.00 (978-0-8160-3568-7). An overview of medical inventors, including interesting accounts of the lives and work of such technologists as William Morton, Joseph Lister, Christian Barnard, and Norman Shumway. (Rev: BL 5/15/98; SLJ 6/98) [610.9]

Genetics

11476 Allan, Tony. *Understanding DNA: A Breakthrough in Medicine* (5–8). Illus. Series: Point of Impact. 2002, Heinemann LB $25.64 (978-1-58810-557-8). A history of genetics with profiles of the important scientists and discussion of future uses of this knowledge in cloning, medicine, and production of food. (Rev: SLJ 9/02) [572.8609]

11477 Beatty, Richard. *Genetics* (4–8). Illus. Series: Science Fact Files. 2001, Raintree LB $27.12 (978-0-7398-1015-6). Cells, chromosomes, genes, and genetic engineering are covered here, with profiles of key scientists. (Rev: HBG 10/01; SLJ 1/02) [660]

11478 Boon, Kevin Alexander. *The Human Genome Project: What Does Decoding DNA Mean for Us?* (8–12). Illus. Series: Issues in Focus. 2002, Enslow LB $26.60 (978-0-7660-1685-9). A discussion of

the benefits of and legal and ethical concerns about the Human Genome Project is preceded by information on genes and genetics. (Rev: HBG 3/03; SLJ 11/02) [599.93]

11479 Bornstein, Sandy. *What Makes You What You Are: A First Look at Genetics* (5–8). Illus. by Frank Cecala. 1989, Silver Burdett paper $6.95 (978-0-671-68650-5). This book affords a fine introduction to cell structure, dominant and recessive traits, and heredity. (Rev: SLJ 1/90) [573.2]

11480 Boskey, Elizabeth. *America Debates Genetic DNA Testing* (5–8). Series: America Debates. 2007, Rosen LB $29.25 (978-1-4042-1926-7). Presents facts and opinions on both sides of issues including prenatal and adult genetic testing. (Rev: LMC 2/08; SLJ 11/07) [362.196]

11481 Bryan, Jenny. *Genetic Engineering* (7–9). 1995, Thomson Learning LB $24.26 (978-1-56847-268-3). Recounts the advances of gene research, including a discussion of the ethical questions involved. (Rev: BL 8/95; SLJ 8/95) [575.1]

11482 Butterfield, Moira. *Genetics* (5–8). Illus. Series: 21st Century Science. 2003, Smart Apple LB $27.10 (978-1-58340-350-1). An accessible, large-format volume on genetics, cloning, and the use of genes in medicine and food engineering, with attractive full-color photographs. (Rev: BL 12/1/03) [576.5.]

11483 Cohen, Daniel. *Cloning* (7–10). 1998, Millbrook $22.90 (978-0-7613-0356-5). A balanced examination of the social and ethical concerns raised by the recent cloning of a sheep named Dolly, including the history and scientific background of this area of research and a discussion of genetic engineering. (Rev: SLJ 3/99) [575.1]

11484 Day, Trevor. *Genetics* (4–7). Illus. Series: Routes of Science. 2004, Gale LB $24.95 (978-1-4103-0301-1). A detailed examination of the development of genetics as a science, with profiles of key individuals and their discoveries, a chronology, and discussion of future advances. (Rev: SLJ 5/05)

11485 de la Bédoyère, Camilla. *The Discovery of DNA* (6–9). Illus. Series: Milestones in Modern Science. 2005, World Almanac LB $31.00 (978-0-8368-5851-8). Suitable for reports, this volume provides a good overview of the discovery of DNA. (Rev: SLJ 1/06) [574.87]

11486 DuPrau, Jeanne. *Cloning* (7–12). Illus. 1999, Lucent LB $29.95 (978-1-56006-583-8). This examination delves into the ethical issues involved in human cloning as well as cloning's use in plants and animals. (Rev: BL 11/15/99; HBG 9/00) [6606]

11487 Gallant, Roy A. *The Treasure of Inheritance* (5–8). Illus. Series: The Story of Science. 2002, Benchmark LB $29.93 (978-0-7614-1426-1). A history of mankind's discoveries about genetics and heredity, starting with the earliest efforts to improve crops and animals, with material on today's and future genetic engineering and the mapping of the human genome. (Rev: HBG 3/03; LMC 4–5/03; SLJ 5/03) [576.5]

11488 Gardner, Robert. *Health Science Projects About Heredity* (7–12). Illus. Series: Science Projects. 2001, Enslow LB $26.60 (978-0-7660-1438-1). Projects that include tracing an inherited trait and creating a family tree are accompanied by explanatory information and useful charts and diagrams. (Rev: HBG 3/02; SLJ 9/01) [576.5]

11489 George, Linda. *Gene Therapy* (5–9). Series: Science on the Edge. 2003, Gale LB $24.95 (978-1-56711-786-8). This book explain how genetic engineering can not only have applications in health and industry but also can arouse a great deal of controversy. (Rev: BL 10/15/03) [660]

11490 Hyde, Margaret O., and John F. Setaro. *Medicine's Brave New World: Bioengineering and the New Genetics* (7–12). Illus. 2001, Millbrook LB $29.90 (978-0-7613-1706-7). Cloning, stem cell research, and other breakthroughs in genetics are explored in this accessible book that also discusses the ethical issues faced by scientists in this field. (Rev: BL 12/15/01; HBG 10/02; SLJ 12/01; VOYA 2/02) [610]

11491 Jefferis, David. *Cloning: Frontiers of Genetic Engineering* (5–7). Series: Megatech. 1999, Crabtree LB $25.27 (978-0-7787-0048-7). This account discusses the history of genetic discoveries and theories, cell reproduction, and the present and possible future of genetic engineering with plants, animals, and humans. (Rev: SLJ 9/99) [174.957]

11492 Judson, Karen. *Genetic Engineering: Debating the Benefits and Concerns* (6–9). Illus. Series: Issues in Focus. 2001, Enslow LB $26.60 (978-0-7660-1587-6). An exploration of the pros and cons of genetic engineering, cloning, gene therapy, genetic testing, and the implications of genetic discrimination. (Rev: HBG 10/02; SLJ 12/01) [660.6]

11493 Kafka, Tina. *DNA on Trial* (6–12). Series: Overview. 2004, Gale LB $29.95 (978-1-59018-337-3). Stories of DNA's use in solving criminal cases are accompanied by discussion of the technology's potential flaws and of the process involved in DNA testing. (Rev: SLJ 3/05) [614]

11494 Morgan, Sally. *Body Doubles: Cloning Plants and Animals* (5–8). Illus. Series: Science at the Edge. 2002, Heinemann LB $27.86 (978-1-58810-698-8). A discussion of the scientific and ethical issues of cloning, with excellent diagrams. (Rev: BL 10/15/02; HBG 3/03) [660.6]

11495 Morgan, Sally. *From Mendel's Peas to Genetic Fingerprinting: Discovering Inheritance* (6–9). Illus. Series: Chain Reactions. 2006, Heinemann LB $34.29 (978-1-4034-8837-4). Morgan traces the

evolution of genetic science from Mendel's peas to today's genetic fingerprinting, ends with brief biographies of key individuals in the field. (Rev: SLJ 2/07)

11496 Morgan, Sally. *From Sea Urchins to Dolly the Sheep: Discovering Cloning* (6–9). Illus. Series: Chain Reactions. 2006, Heinemann LB $34.29 (978-1-4034-8838-1). Morgan traces developments in the field of cloning, from sea urchins in the 1890s to Dolly the sheep in 2003; ends with brief biographies of key individuals in the field. (Rev: SLJ 2/07)

11497 Nardo, Don. *Cloning* (5–9). Illus. Series: Science on the Edge. 2003, Gale $24.95 (978-1-56711-782-0). A concise overview of the techniques involved in cloning and the ways this science can be applied, with a balanced presentation of the pro and con arguments. (Rev: BL 10/15/03; SLJ 2/04) [660.6]

11498 Phelan, Glen. *Double Helix: The Quest to Uncover the Structure of DNA* (5–8). Series: Science Quest. 2006, National Geographic $17.95 (978-0-7922-5541-3). From Mendel's early experiments with pea plants through Crick and Watson's race to solve the mystery of DNA, this is an accessible and informative history that also looks at the wide range of social and scientific areas influenced by the discovery. (Rev: SLJ 4/07) [572.8]

11499 Seiple, Samantha, and Todd Seiple. *Mutants, Clones, and Killer Corn: Unlocking the Secrets of Biotechnology* (6–9). Illus. 2005, Lerner $29.27 (978-0-8225-4860-7). After explaining the basic concepts of genes, DNA, and cloning, the Seiples discuss advances in biotechnology, presenting both sides of controversial techniques. (Rev: BL 6/1–15/05; SLJ 7/05) [660.6]

11500 Silverstein, Alvin, et al. *DNA* (4–8). Series: Science Concepts. 2002, Millbrook LB $26.90 (978-0-7613-2257-3). This book examines the structure of DNA and clearly explains its components and functions and includes current topics such as the genome project, genetic engineering, gene therapy, and cloning. (Rev: BL 9/15/02; HBG 3/03; SLJ 11/02) [574.87]

11501 Snedden, Robert. *Cell Division and Genetics* (6–9). Illus. Series: Cells and Life. 2002, Heinemann LB $27.86 (978-1-58810-672-8). Cell structure and development, DNA, and patterns of inheritance are covered in this overview that uses diagrams and photographs to good effect in explaining complex topics. Also use *DNA and Genetic Engineering* (2002). (Rev: HBG 3/03; SLJ 1/03) [571.8]

11502 Tagliaferro, Linda. *Genetic Engineering: Progress or Peril?* (7–10). Illus. Series: Pro/Con Issues. 1997, Lerner LB $21.27 (978-0-8225-2620-9). This book presents the complex issues in the controversy over the manipulation of genes, such as the possibility of finding cures for hereditary diseases on the one hand, and on the other, the possibility of abusing it to create a made-to-order human race. (Rev: BL 9/1/97; SLJ 8/97) [575.1]

11503 Walker, Denise. *Inheritance and Evolution* (7–10). Series: Basic Biology. 2006, Smart Apple Media LB $23.95 (978-1-58340-989-3). This is a well-designed introduction to the basics of genetics, inheritance, natural selection, cloning, evolution, and extinction. (Rev: BL 10/15/06) [576]

11504 Wilcox, Frank H. *DNA: The Thread of Life* (7–10). Illus. 1988, Lerner LB $23.93 (978-0-8225-1584-5). The basic DNA structure and functions are explained. (Rev: SLJ 6/88) [574.87]

11505 Winters, Paul A. *Cloning* (8–12). Series: At Issue. 1997, Greenhaven LB $26.20 (978-1-56510-753-3); paper $17.45 (978-1-56510-752-6). The successful cloning of a sheep has ignited many ethical questions concerning its application to humans. This controversy is explored in this anthology of various points of view. (Rev: BL 5/15/98; SLJ 1/99; VOYA 8/98) [174.957]

11506 Yount, Lisa. *Biotechnology and Genetic Engineering*. Rev. ed. (8–12). Series: Library in a Book. 2004, Facts on File $45.00 (978-0-8160-5059-8). An overview of genetic engineering and biotechnology, with chapters on scientific achievements, ethical concerns, court battles, health issues, and scientific problems. (Rev: SLJ 2/05) [303.48]

11507 Yount, Lisa, ed. *Genetic Engineering* (6–12). Series: Current Controversies. 2002, Gale LB $32.45 (978-0-7377-1124-0); paper $21.20 (978-0-7377-1123-3). This anthology explores various aspects and attitudes toward this controversial subject, with a good representation of differing viewpoints from known authorities. (Rev: BL 8/02) [575.1]

Grooming, Personal Appearance, and Dress

11508 Altman, Douglas. *For Guys* (6–9). Illus. 1989, Rourke LB $19.93 (978-0-86625-284-3). This is a good grooming manual for boys that covers such topics as diet, exercise, clothes, and hygiene. (Rev: SLJ 6/89) [646.7]

11509 Brashich, Audrey D. *All Made Up: A Girl's Guide to Seeing Through Celebrity Hype . . . and Celebrating Real Beauty* (6–9). Illus. by Shawn Banner. 2006, Walker paper $9.95 (978-0-8027-7744-7). Written by a former model, this book discusses the marketing hype surrounding female celebrities and reassures readers that the stars' physical perfection is only an illusion. (Rev: BL 6/1–15/06; LMC 1–2/08*; SLJ 6/06) [305.235]

11510 Dawson, Mildred L. *Beauty Lab: How Science Is Changing the Way We Look* (5–10). 1997, Silver Moon $14.95 (978-1-881889-84-7). This work on health and hygiene contains chapters on skin, eyes, teeth, fitness, and hair. (Rev: SLJ 3/97) [613.7]

11511 Fitzhugh, Karla. *Body Image* (5–9). Series: Health Issues. 2004, Steck-Vaughn LB $32.79 (978-0-7398-6891-1). Body image and such related issues as cosmetic surgery, piercing, tattooing, eating disorders, and physical culture are examined in attractive text with informative charts and sidebars. (Rev: SLJ 11/05) [155.2]

11512 Gay, Kathlyn, and Christine Whittington. *Body Marks: Tattooing, Piercing, and Scarification* (6–12). Illus. 2002, Millbrook LB $29.90 (978-0-7613-2352-5); paper $14.95 (978-0-7613-1742-5). A look at the history of body modification around the world, with color photographs and discussion of current trends. (Rev: BL 12/1/02; HBG 3/03; SLJ 10/02) [391.6]

11513 Graydon, Shari. *In Your Face: The Culture of Beauty and You* (7–12). 2004, Annick paper $14.95 (978-1-55037-856-6). Graydon offers commonsense advice and reassurance to teenagers who may feel overwhelmed by the seemingly ubiquitous message that beauty is all-important. (Rev: BL 12/15/04; SLJ 3/05) [391.6/3]

11514 Hinds, Maurene J. *Focus on Body Image: How You Feel About How You Look* (6–9). Illus. Series: Teen Issues. 2002, Enslow LB $22.60 (978-0-7660-1915-7). A look at body image and self-esteem that discusses social pressures, eating disorders, the use of steroids, and a disorder known as muscle dysmorphia. (Rev: HBG 3/03; SLJ 1/03; VOYA 6/03) [306.4]

11515 Libal, Autumn. *Can I Change the Way I Look? A Teen's Guide to the Health Implications of Cosmetic Surgery, Makeovers, and Beyond* (7–12). Illus. Series: The Science of Health. 2005, Mason Crest LB $24.95 (978-1-59804-843-8). Libal clearly lays out the pitfalls of obsessing about body image, as well as the risks involved in piercing, tattooing, eating disorders, cosmetic surgery, and even common cosmetic products. (Rev: SLJ 7/05) [613.4]

11516 Mason, Linda. *Teen Makeup: Looks to Match Your Every Mood* (6–12). Illus. 2004, Watson-Guptill paper $16.95 (978-0-8230-2980-8). A photograph-filled how-to guide to the basics of skin care and makeup. (Rev: SLJ 11/04)

11517 Sommers, Michael A. *Everything You Need to Know About Looking and Feeling Your Best: A Guide for Guys* (6–9). Series: Need to Know Library. 1999, Rosen LB $27.95 (978-0-8239-3080-7). Good hygiene and grooming are not difficult or time-consuming, according to this book that also looks at the benefits of exercise and diet. (Rev: SLJ 8/00) [613]

11518 Tym, Kate. *Totally You! Every Girl's Guide to Looking Good* (6–8). Illus. by Gillian Martin. 1999, Element Books paper $4.95 (978-1-902618-44-9). Sleep, exercise, diet, makeup, aromatherapy, and other methods of pampering oneself are presented with practical, down-to-earth advice. (Rev: SLJ 4/00) [646.7]

11519 Warrick, Leanne. *Hair Trix for Cool Chix: The Real Girl's Guide to Great Hair* (6–12). Illus. by Debbie Boon. 2004, Watson-Guptill paper $9.95 (978-0-8230-2179-6). From quizzes and practical tips to step-by-step directions for different styles and accessories, this is a reader-friendly guide to hair care. (Rev: SLJ 7/04) [391.5]

11520 Weiss, Stefanie Iris. *Coping with the Beauty Myth: A Guide for Real Girls* (7–12). Series: Coping. 2002, Rosen LB $31.95 (978-0-8239-3757-8). Readers are urged to ignore unrealistic images presented in the media and to accept their own attributes and deficiencies as well as those of others. (Rev: SLJ 8/00) [155.5]

11521 Weiss, Stefanie Iris. *Everything You Need to Know About Mehndi, Temporary Tattoos, and Other Temporary Body Art* (8–12). Illus. Series: Need to Know Library. 2000, Rosen LB $25.25 (978-0-8239-3086-9). This account explores the cultural backgrounds associated with drawing on the body with henna, suggests methods of applying henna, and gives suggestions for patterns. (Rev: BL 7/00) [391.6]

The Human Body

General and Miscellaneous

11522 Allison, Linda. *Blood and Guts: A Working Guide to Your Own Little Insides* (5–8). 1976, Little, Brown paper $14.99 (978-0-316-03443-2). An off-putting title but a fine explanation of the functions of the human body.

11523 Brynie, Faith Hickman. *101 Questions About Your Immune System You Felt Defenseless to Answer . . . Until Now* (7–12). Illus. 2000, Twenty-First Century $27.90 (978-0-7613-1569-8). A question-and-answer format is used to explain the functioning and vulnerabilities of the immune system. (Rev: BL 6/1–15/00; HBG 9/00; SLJ 9/00; VOYA 4/01) [616.07]

11524 Brynie, Faith Hickman. *101 Questions About Your Skin* (7–12). Illus. by Sharon Lane Holm. Series: 101 Questions. 1999, Twenty-First Century LB $27.90 (978-0-7613-1259-8). This comprehensive, well-illustrated look at the composition, care, and diseases of the skin also includes information

on tattooing, the effects of the sun, and aging and will attract both report writers and browsers. (Rev: HBG 4/00; SLJ 11/99) [612.7]

11525 Calabresi, Linda. *Human Body* (4–7). Illus. Series: Insiders. 2008, Simon & Schuster $16.99 (978-1-4169-3861-3). Cross-sections, computer-aided graphics, and other visual wonders offer amazing views of the body in this large-format book that provides text information in snippets and sidebars. (Rev: BL 3/1/08; SLJ 5/08) [612]

11526 Ganeri, Anita. *Alive: The Living, Breathing Human Body Book* (5–7). Illus. 2007, DK $24.99 (978-0-7566-3211-3). Visual and audio effects accompany amazing graphics and text in this comprehensive and attention-grabbing pop-up anatomy book. (Rev: SLJ 3/08)

11527 Gardner, Robert. *Science Projects About the Human Body* (5–7). 1992, Enslow LB $26.60 (978-0-89490-443-1). Simple experiments and activities are used to illustrate various areas of the human body, such as the senses, bones, teeth, and hair. (Rev: SLJ 11/93) [612]

11528 Kim, Melissa L. *The Endocrine and Reproductive Systems* (5–10). Illus. Series: Human Body Library. 2003, Enslow LB $23.93 (978-0-7660-2020-7). Kim uses a conversational style to introduce detailed facts about these two body systems, with useful graphics and some practical advice. (Rev: BL 4/15/03; HBG 10/03) [612.4]

11529 McNally, Robert Aquinas, ed. *Skin Health Information for Teens: Health Tips About Dermatological Concerns and Skin Cancer Risks* (7–12). Illus. Series: Teen Health. 2003, Omnigraphics $58.00 (978-0-7808-0446-3). Detailed information is provided on health problems and risks including acne, cosmetics, tanning, tattoos, and piercing. (Rev: SLJ 1/04; VOYA 2/04) [616.5]

11530 Nilsson, Lennart. *Behold Man: A Photographic Journey of Discovery Inside the Body* (7–12). Illus. 1974, Little, Brown $29.95 (978-0-316-60751-3). An unusually illustrated book (many photographs represent magnifications of 45,000 times) on the body and its systems. [612]

11531 Parker, Steve. *Allergies* (5–8). Series: Just the Facts. 2004, Heinemann LB $27.07 (978-1-4034-4598-8). A comprehensive and accessible overview of allergies, their causes, symptoms, and treatment. (Rev: SLJ 6/04) [616.97]

11532 Parker, Steve. *Digestion and Reproduction* (6–9). Illus. Series: Understanding the Human Body. 2004, Gareth Stevens LB $26.00 (978-0-8368-4205-0). An attractive format is used to present solid information on the digestive and reproductive systems and the diseases that can affect them. Also use *Heart, Blood, and Lungs* (2004). (Rev: SLJ 4/05) [612]

11533 Parker, Steve. *Human Body: An Interactive Guide to the Inner Workings of the Body* (4–7). Illus. Series: Discoverology. 2008, Barron's $18.99 (978-0-7641-6083-7). Pop-ups, pullouts, gatefolds, cutaways, X-ray images, spinning wheels, and other visual elements make this guide to anatomy effective and interesting. (Rev: BL 6/1–15/08; SLJ 8/08) [612]

11534 Parker, Steve. *The Human Body Book* (6–9). Illus. 2007, DK $35.00 (978-0-7566-2856-9). Extraordinary pictures and illustrations provide great detail of the human body's systems and processes in this coffee-table-sized book that (along with clear, informative text) includes a CD containing many of the illustrations, charts, and diagrams. (Rev: SLJ 7/07) [612]

11535 Pascoe, Elaine, ed. *Out of Control: Brain Function and Immune Reactions* (5–8). Illus. Series: Body Story. 2003, Gale LB $24.95 (978-1-4103-0063-8). This fact-packed book looks first at a baby's brain function, before and after birth, and how its capabilities grow as he learns, then traces the reaction of a young woman's immune system as it copes with a severe allergic reaction to a wasp sting. (Rev: SLJ 4/04) [612.8]

11536 Rosen, Marvin. *Sleep and Dreaming* (6–12). Illus. Series: Gray Matter. 2005, Chelsea House LB $35.00 (978-0-7910-8639-1). Snoring, sleepwalking, and night terrors are among the topics covered in this survey of our sleep processes and our dreams; Freudian and Jungian theories are also addressed. (Rev: SLJ 3/06) [616]

11537 Sneddon, Pamela Shires. *Body Image: A Reality Check* (6–10). Series: Issues in Focus. 1999, Enslow LB $26.60 (978-0-89490-960-3). This book discusses body image and actions, often destructive, that people take to control it, including anorexia, bulimia, steroid use, cosmetic surgery, and body piercing. (Rev: BL 5/1/99; SLJ 7/99) [155.9]

11538 Trueit, Trudi Strain. *Dreams and Sleep* (4–8). Illus. Series: Life Balance. 2004, Watts LB $20.50 (978-0-531-12260-0). Discusses why we dream and what dreams mean and gives advice on getting a good night's sleep. (Rev: BL 10/15/03) [616.5]

11539 VanCleave, Janice. *The Human Body for Every Kid: Easy Activities That Make Learning Science Fun* (5–7). Illus. Series: Science for Every Kid. 1995, Wiley paper $12.95 (978-0-471-02408-8). The various systems in the human body are introduced and decribed, with many projects and experiments. (Rev: BL 4/15/95; SLJ 5/95) [612]

11540 Walker, Richard. *Body* (4–7). Illus. 2005, DK $19.99 (978-0-7566-1371-6). With a spiral binding, acetate overlays, and computer-generated 3-D images, this volume gives an in-depth view of the human body; there is an accompanying CD. (Rev: BL 12/1/05; SLJ 3/06) [611]

11541 Walker, Richard. *Human Body* (5–9). Illus. Series: DK/Google e.guides. 2005, DK $17.99 (978-0-7566-1009-8). This highly illustrated guide introduces readers to the human body and provides a link to a Web site that serves as a gateway to additional resources. (Rev: SLJ 8/05) [612]

11542 Walker, Richard. *Ouch! How Your Body Makes It Through a Very Bad Day* (5–8). Illus. 2007, DK $16.99 (978-0-7566-2536-8). Wonderfully gross, this day starts with some sneezes and progresses through a variety of events including urinating, sweating, vomiting, and being stung by a bee; the accompanying CD-ROM adds an inside view to these processes. (Rev: LMC 10/07; SLJ 7/07)

11543 Wiese, Jim. *Head to Toe Science: Over 40 Eye-Popping, Spine-Tingling, Heart-Pounding Activities That Teach Kids* (4–8). Illus. 2000, Wiley paper $12.95 (978-0-471-33203-9). A collection of experiments and projects that is arranged by body systems (e.g., nervous, digestive), accompanied by good instructions and scientific explanations. (Rev: BL 7/00; SLJ 7/00) [612]

Brain and Nervous System

11544 Andrews, Linda Wasmer. *Intelligence* (4–8). Series: Life Balance. 2003, Watts paper $6.95 (978-0-531-16608-6). This book explores the concept of intelligence, how it is measured, and how it affects daily life. (Rev: BL 10/15/03) [612]

11545 Barrett, Susan L. *It's All in Your Head: A Guide to Understanding Your Brain and Boosting Your Brain Power* (6–10). Illus. 1992, Free Spirit paper $10.95 (978-0-915793-45-7). Covers subjects as diverse as brain anatomy, intelligence, biofeedback, creativity, ESP, and brain scans. (Rev: BL 2/15/93) [153]

11546 Bayer, Linda. *Sleep Disorders* (6–12). Series: Encyclopedia of Psychological Disorders. 2000, Chelsea LB $35.00 (978-0-7910-5314-0). Insomnia, sleepwalking, and other sleep-related disorders are discussed. (Rev: BL 1/1–15/01; HBG 10/01; SLJ 2/01) [612.8]

11547 Berger, Melvin. *Exploring the Mind and Brain* (7–10). Illus. 1983, HarperCollins LB $12.89 (978-0-690-04252-8). A book about the functions — both normal and abnormal — of the brain. [612]

11548 Brynie, Faith Hickman. *101 Questions About Sleep and Dreams that Kept You Awake Nights . . . Until Now* (8–11). 2006, Lerner LB $27.93 (978-0-7613-2312-9). This is a sleep information handbook for teens, answering questions about dreaming, stages of sleep, the effect of sleep on the brain and body, and related topics. (Rev: BL 5/15/06) [612.8]

11549 Edelson, Edward. *Sleep* (7–10). Series: Encyclopedia of Health. 1991, Chelsea LB $19.95 (978-

0-7910-0092-2). This book discusses the uses of sleep, people's sleeping habits, and sleeping disorders. (Rev: BL 11/15/91) [612.8]

11550 Garfield, Patricia. *The Dream Book: A Young Person's Guide to Understanding Dreams* (5–8). 2002, Tundra paper $9.95 (978-0-88776-594-0). The author, a psychologist, explains the meanings of common (and uncommon) dreams and suggests how to use dreams to good effect. (Rev: BL 9/15/02; SLJ 9/02; VOYA 8/02) [154.6]

11551 Hayhurst, Chris. *The Brain and Spinal Cord: Learning How We Think, Feel, and Move* (5–9). Series: 3-D Library of the Human Body. 2002, Rosen LB $27.95 (978-0-8239-3528-4). Exceptional illustrations and a clear text are used to explain the composition of the brain with explanations of how it works and how emotions influence our thoughts. (Rev: BL 7/02; SLJ 7/02) [612.8]

11552 Innes, Brian. *Powers of the Mind* (4–7). Series: Unsolved Mysteries. 1999, Raintree LB $25.69 (978-0-8172-5488-9). A balanced account that explores the powers of the brain in such controversial areas as moving objects, planting thoughts, and predicting events. (Rev: BL 5/15/99; HBG 10/99) [612.8]

11553 Mcphee, Andrew T. *Sleep and Dreams* (7–12). Illus. 2001, Watts LB $26.00 (978-0-531-11735-4). Normal sleep patterns, sleep deprivation, and sleep disorders (sleep walking and sleep apnea) are discussed along with the nature and symbolism of dreams. (Rev: BL 6/1–15/01; SLJ 8/01) [616.8]

11554 Newquist, H. P. *The Great Brain Book: An Inside Look at the Inside of Your Head* (5–8). Illus. by Keith Kasnot. 2005, Scholastic $18.95 (978-0-439-45895-5). The structure of the brain, its inner workings, and the history of our knowledge of this organ are all discussed in detail; interesting anecdotes add to the presentation. (Rev: BL 6/1–15/05; SLJ 9/05) [612.8]

11555 Parker, Steve. *The Brain and Nervous System* (5–9). Illus. Series: Our Bodies. 2004, Raintree LB $28.56 (978-0-7398-6619-1). Details of the human body's brain and nervous system are accompanied by information on keeping them healthy. (Rev: BL 8/04)

11556 Parker, Steve. *Brain, Nerves, and Senses* (6–9). Illus. Series: Understanding the Human Body. 2004, Gareth Stevens LB $26.00 (978-0-8368-4204-3). An attractive format is used to present solid information on the brain and nervous system and the diseases that can affect them. (Rev: SLJ 4/05) [612.8]

11557 Policoff, Stephen P. *The Dreamer's Companion: A Beginner's Guide to Understanding Dreams and Using Them Creatively* (8–12). Illus. 1997, Chicago Review paper $12.95 (978-1-55652-280-2). This book covers mastering the art of lucid

dreaming, the causes of dreams, how to analyze them, and how to keep a dream journal. (Rev: BL 5/15/98; SLJ 6/98) [154.63]

11558 Routh, Kristina. *Epilepsy* (5–10). Illus. Series: Just the Facts. 2004, Heinemann LB $27.07 (978-1-4034-4601-5). An overview of epilepsy, with attention to its effect on individuals when it comes to driving, sports, education, and employment. (Rev: SLJ 6/04) [616.8]

11559 Saab, Carl Y. *The Spinal Cord* (6–12). Illus. Series: Gray Matter. 2005, Chelsea House LB $35.00 (978-0-7910-8511-0). Explores the importance of the spinal cord to the whole nervous system and discusses the impact of disorders and injuries. (Rev: SLJ 3/06)

11560 Silverstein, Alvin, et al. *The Nervous System* (5–8). Illus. Series: Human Body Systems. 1994, Twenty-First Century LB $28.90 (978-0-8050-2835-5). The human nervous system and how it functions and can malfunction are described, with information on the systems of other animals. (Rev: BL 3/15/95; SLJ 5/95) [612.8]

11561 Silverstein, Alvin, and Virginia Silverstein. *Sleep and Dreams* (7–9). 1974, HarperCollins LB $12.89 (978-0-397-31325-9). Research into sleep is reviewed along with a description of our sleep patterns, dreams, and what dreams mean. [154.6]

11562 Walker, Pam, and Elaine Wood. *The Brain and Nervous System* (8–12). Series: Understanding the Human Body. 2003, Gale LB $27.45 (978-1-59018-148-5). The roles of the nervous system and the brain in collecting information, processing it, and sending responses to the various parts of the body, are explained in this attractive introduction to this body system. (Rev: BL 3/15/03) [612]

Circulatory System

11563 Ballard, Carol. *The Heart and Circulatory System* (5–8). Illus. Series: The Human Body. 1997, Raintree LB $18.98 (978-0-8172-4800-0). Topics discussed in this nicely illustrated volume include how blood is made, how it is pumped through the body, and how the heart and circulation system work together. (Rev: BL 6/1–15/97; SLJ 8/97) [612.1]

11564 Brynie, Faith Hickman. *101 Questions About Blood and Circulation: With Answers Straight from the Heart* (6–10). Illus. by Sharon Lane Holm. Series: 101 Questions. 2001, Twenty-First Century LB $27.90 (978-0-7613-1455-4). A clear and comprehensive overview of the circulatory system, how it works, and the importance of proper diet and exercise. (Rev: HBG 10/01; SLJ 4/01) [612.1]

11565 Parker, Steve. *Heart, Lungs, and Blood* (5–9). Illus. Series: Our Bodies. 2004, Raintree LB $28.56 (978-0-7398-6621-4). Details of the human body's circulatory system are accompanied by information on keeping them healthy. (Rev: BL 8/04) [612.1]

11566 Parramon, Merce. *How Our Blood Circulates* (5–7). Illus. by Marcel Socias. Series: Invisible World. 1994, Chelsea LB $17.55 (978-0-7910-2127-9). Double-page spreads introduce the circulatory system and discuss such topics as blood cells, clotting, the heart and its functions, and the lymphatic system. (Rev: SLJ 8/94) [612]

11567 Romanek, Trudee. *Squirt! The Most Interesting Book You'll Ever Read About Blood* (4–7). Illus. by Rose Cowles. Series: Mysterious You. 2006, Kids Can $14.95 (978-1-55337-776-4); paper $7.95 (978-1-55337-777-1). This fascinating book with an engaging format discusses the human circulatory system, with information about other animals and their blood, too. (Rev: BL 5/15/06; HBG 10/06) [612.1]

11568 Silverstein, Alvin, and Virginia Silverstein. *Heart Disease* (8–12). 2006, Twenty-First Century LB $27.93 (978-0-7613-3420-0). This informative and easy-to-understand book explains the causes, treatment, and prevention of heart disease, using true stories as examples and incorporating medical information and photographs. (Rev: SLJ 8/06)

11569 Silverstein, Alvin, and Virginia Silverstein. *Heartbeats: Your Body, Your Heart* (7–10). Illus. 1983, HarperCollins LB $13.89 (978-0-397-32038-7). Following a description of the heart and how it works, there are sections on heart disease and research. [612]

11570 Viegas, Jennifer. *The Heart: Learning How Our Blood Circulates* (5–9). Illus. Series: 3-D Library of the Human Body. 2002, Rosen LB $27.95 (978-0-8239-3532-1). An introduction to the anatomy and function of the human heart and the circulatory system that includes illustrations, diagrams, a glossary, and other aids. (Rev: BL 7/02) [612.1]

Digestive and Excretory Systems

11571 Ballard, Carol. *The Stomach and Digestive System* (5–8). Illus. Series: The Human Body. 1997, Raintree LB $25.68 (978-0-8172-4801-7). Topics discussed in this nicely illustrated volume include the digestive organs, how they work together, how food is tasted, and where nutrients are stored. (Rev: BL 6/1–15/97; SLJ 8/97) [612.3]

11572 Brynie, Faith Hickman. *101 Questions About Food and Digestion That Have Been Eating at You . . . Until Now* (5–8). Illus. 2002, Millbrook LB $27.90 (978-0-7613-2309-9). A question-and-answer format succeeds in conveying lots of food for thought, with details on digestive functions, digestive disorders, food safety, fat cells, Mad Cow

disease, vitamins, and so forth. (Rev: BL 1/1–15/03; HBG 3/03; SLJ 3/03) [612.3]

11573 Monroe, Judy. *Coping with Ulcers, Heartburn, and Stress-Related Stomach Disorders* (7–12). Series: Coping. 2000, Rosen LB $31.95 (978-0-8239-2971-9). Fictional case histories convey lots of information about a variety of uncomfortable stomach conditions, stressing the importance of prevention and early treatment. (Rev: SLJ 6/00) [616.3]

11574 Parker, Steve. *Digestion* (5–9). Illus. Series: Our Bodies. 2004, Raintree LB $28.56 (978-0-7398-6620-7). Details of the human body's digestive system are accompanied by information on keeping them healthy. (Rev: BL 8/04) [612]

11575 Silverstein, Alvin, et al. *The Excretory System* (5–8). Illus. Series: Human Body Systems. 1994, Twenty-First Century LB $29.90 (978-0-8050-2834-8). A discussion on the human system of waste elimination. (Rev: BL 3/15/95; SLJ 3/95) [612.4]

11576 Simon, Seymour. *Guts: Our Digestive System* (5–8). Illus. 2005, HarperCollins LB $17.89 (978-0-06-054652-6). Photographs and straightforward yet fascinating text present the digestive system. (Rev: BL 3/1/05; SLJ 4/05) [612.3]

11577 Toriello, James. *The Stomach: Learning How We Digest* (5–9). Series: 3-D Library of the Human Body. 2002, Rosen LB $27.95 (978-0-8239-3536-9). Using outstanding diagrams and clear explanations, the digestive system is highlighted with material on each of its parts and their functions. (Rev: BL 7/02; SLJ 7/02) [612.3]

Musculoskeletal System

11578 Ballard, Carol. *The Skeleton and Muscular System* (5–8). Illus. Series: Human Body. 1997, Raintree $18.98 (978-0-8172-4805-5). This well-organized book introduces in text and pictures such topics as muscles and how they work, joint diseases, bones, and skeletal diseases. (Rev: SLJ 2/98) [612]

11579 Brynie, Faith Hickman. *101 Questions About Muscles: To Stretch Your Mind and Flex Your Brain* (7–12). Series: 101 Questions. 2007, Lerner LB $30.60 (978-0-8225-6380-8). Entertaining and interesting, this book uses a question-and-answer format to explore questions of interest to athletes, browsers, and researchers. (Rev: BL 12/1/07; SLJ 6/08) [612.7]

11580 Feinberg, Brian. *The Musculoskeletal System* (7–12). Series: Encyclopedia of Health. 1993, Chelsea LB $19.95 (978-0-7910-0028-1). An introduction to the muscles and bones in the human body and how they work together to form a single system. (Rev: BL 12/1/93) [612.7]

11581 Gold, Susan Dudley. *The Musculoskeletal System and the Skin* (5–10). Illus. Series: Human Body Library. 2003, Enslow LB $23.93 (978-0-7660-2023-8). Gold uses a conversational style to introduce detailed facts about the skeletal system, with useful graphics and some practical advice. (Rev: BL 4/15/03; HBG 10/03; SLJ 10/03) [612.7]

11582 Landau, Elaine. *Spinal Cord Injuries* (6–12). Illus. 2001, Enslow LB $26.60 (978-0-7660-1474-9). Stories of people who have suffered spinal cord injuries, including Gloria Estefan and Christopher Reeve, are interwoven with information on how spinal injuries affect the body and how patients cope. (Rev: BL 2/1/02; HBG 10/02) [617.4]

11583 Oleksy, Walter. *The Head and Neck: Learning How We Use Our Muscles* (5–9). Series: 3-D Library of the Human Body. 2002, Rosen LB $26.50 (978-0-8239-3531-4). The muscles of the head and neck and their roles in controlling the sense organs, chewing and swallowing, facial expressions, and conveying emotions are explained in this well-illustrated account. (Rev: BL 7/02) [612.7]

11584 Parker, Steve. *The Skeleton and Muscles* (5–9). Illus. Series: Our Bodies. 2004, Raintree LB $28.56 (978-0-7398-6622-1). Details of the human body's skeletal and muscular systems are accompanied by information on keeping them healthy. (Rev: BL 8/04) [612.7]

11585 Parker, Steve. *Skin, Muscles, and Bones* (6–9). Illus. Series: Understanding the Human Body. 2004, Gareth Stevens LB $26.00 (978-0-8368-4207-4). An attractive format is used to present solid information on the musculoskeletal system and the diseases and injuries that can affect it. (Rev: SLJ 4/05) [612.7]

11586 Sherman, Josepha. *The Upper Limbs: Learning How We Use Our Arms, Elbows, Forearms, and Hands* (5–9). Series: 3-D Library of the Human Body. 2002, Rosen LB $27.95 (978-0-8239-3537-6). The parts of the arm and hand are examined with illustrated material on how the muscles in these areas function and receive support from the skeletal structure. (Rev: BL 7/02) [612.7]

11587 Silverstein, Alvin, et al. *The Muscular System* (5–8). Illus. Series: Human Body Systems. 1994, Twenty-First Century $29.90 (978-0-8050-2836-2). Full-color diagrams, drawings, and photographs highlight this survey of the human muscular system. (Rev: BL 3/15/95; SLJ 5/95) [612.7]

11588 Viegas, Jennifer. *The Lower Limbs: Learning How We Use Our Thighs, Knees, Legs, and Feet* (5–9). Series: 3-D Library of the Human Body. 2002, Rosen LB $26.50 (978-0-8239-3533-8). The bones and muscles of the legs and feet and their functions are described in a clear text and excep-tional illustrations. (Rev: BL 7/02; SLJ 7/02) [612.7]

TEETH

11589 Lee, Jordan. *Coping with Braces and Other Orthodontic Work* (4–9). Series: Coping. 1998, Rosen LB $31.95 (978-0-8239-2721-0). A book about braces, their purposes, and the problems they can cause. (Rev: SLJ 11/98) [612.3]

11590 Siegel, Dorothy. *Dental Health* (7–12). Series: Encyclopedia of Health. 1994, Chelsea LB $19.95 (978-0-7910-0014-4). An explanation of what teeth are made of, their uses, diseases, and how to take care of them. (Rev: BL 1/1/94) [617.6]

11591 Silverstein, Alvin, and Virginia Silverstein. *So You're Getting Braces: A Guide to Orthodontics* (6–9). 1978, HarperCollins LB $12.89 (978-0-397-31786-8). The dental specialization of orthodontics is explained as well as why braces are often needed. [617.6]

Respiratory System

11592 Hayhurst, Chris. *The Lungs: Learning How We Breathe* (5–9). Series: 3-D Library of the Human Body. 2002, Rosen LB $27.95 (978-0-8239-3534-5). Amazing computer graphics are used to explain the composition of the lungs, how they work, and what keeps them healthy. (Rev: BL 7/02) [612.6]

11593 Parker, Steve. *The Lungs and Respiratory System* (5–8). Illus. Series: The Human Body. 1997, Raintree LB $18.98 (978-0-8172-4803-1). This nicely illustrated volume examines the organs used in breathing, tells how the respiratory system works, and explains what happens when it fails. (Rev: BL 6/1–15/97; SLJ 8/97) [612.2]

11594 Silverstein, Alvin, et al. *The Respiratory System* (5–8). Illus. Series: Human Body Systems. 1994, Twenty-First Century LB $29.90 (978-0-8050-2831-7). The purpose and process of breathing are discussed, with the text and illustrations focusing on the human respiratory system. (Rev: BL 3/15/95; SLJ 4/95) [612.2]

11595 Siy, Alexandra. *Sneeze!* (6–9). Illus. by Dennis Kunkel. 2007, Charlesbridge $16.95 (978-1-57091-653-3). Students will no longer need to be reminded to cover their sneezes after seeing the close-up photographs in this book; scientific information about germs, allergies, the flu, and the human body's immune system rounds out the book. (Rev: BL 7/07; HB 11–12/07; LMC 1/08; SLJ 9/07) [612.2]

Senses

11596 Cobb, Vicki. *How to Really Fool Yourself: Illusions for All Your Senses* (7–9). Illus. 1999, Wiley paper $12.95 (978-0-471-31592-6). A book about perception, how illusions are created, and how they are present in everyday life. [152.1]

11597 Martin, Paul D. *Messengers to the Brain: Our Fantastic Five Senses* (6–9). Illus. 1984, National Geographic LB $12.50 (978-0-87044-504-0). A well-illustrated introduction to the five senses and how they work. [612]

11598 Parker, Steve. *The Senses* (5–9). Illus. Series: Our Bodies. 2004, Raintree LB $28.56 (978-0-7398-6624-5). Details of the human senses are accompanied by information on keeping them healthy. (Rev: BL 8/04) [612]

11599 Sherman, Josepha. *The Ear: Learning How We Hear* (5–9). Series: 3-D Library of the Human Body. 2002, Rosen LB $26.50 (978-0-8239-3529-1). Using amazing illustrations and clear explanations, Sherman introduces the ear, its anatomy, uses, operation, and problems that can develop. (Rev: BL 7/02) [612.8]

11600 Silverstein, Alvin, et al. *Smelling and Tasting* (6–8). Illus. 2002, Millbrook LB $25.90 (978-0-7613-1667-1). Human and animal senses of smell and taste are covered in this well-organized and readable volume. Also use *Touching and Feeling* (2002). (Rev: BL 3/15/02; HBG 10/02; SLJ 8/02) [612.8]

11601 Silverstein, Alvin, and Virginia Silverstein. *Glasses and Contact Lenses: Your Guide to Eyes, Eyewear, and Eye Care* (6–9). Illus. 1989, HarperCollins LB $14.89 (978-0-397-32185-8). A description of how the eye functions, disorders connected with it, and how glasses can help. (Rev: BL 6/15/89; SLJ 6/89; VOYA 8/89) [617.7]

11602 Viegas, Jennifer. *The Eye: Learning How We See* (5–9). Illus. Series: 3-D Library of the Human Body. 2002, Rosen LB $27.95 (978-0-8239-3530-7). This volume on the anatomy and function of the human eye includes illustrations, diagrams, a glossary, and other aids. (Rev: BL 7/02) [612.8]

11603 Viegas, Jennifer. *The Mouth and Nose: Learning How We Taste and Smell* (5–9). Series: 3-D Library of the Human Body. 2002, Rosen LB $26.50 (978-0-8239-3535-2). The mouth and nose are featured in this heavily illustrated account that covers their composition, functions, and how they work together. (Rev: BL 7/02) [612]

Hygiene and Physical Fitness

11604 Ball, Jacqueline A. *Hygiene* (6–9). Illus. 1989, Rourke LB $19.93 (978-0-86625-285-0). This book is aimed at preteen and teenage girls and gives tips on care of nails, skin, hair, and so on. (Rev: SLJ 6/89) [613]

11605 Crump, Marguerite. *Don't Sweat It! Every Body's Answers to Questions You Don't Want to Ask: A Guide for Young People* (5–9). Illus. by Chris Sharp. 2002, Free Spirit paper $12.95 (978-1-57542-114-8). Crump tackles potentially embarrassing questions about personal hygiene. (Rev: SLJ 1/03; VOYA 2/03) [613.0433]

11606 Jenner, Bruce, and Bill Dobbins. *The Athletic Body: A Complete Fitness Guide for Teenagers — Sports, Strength, Health, Agility* (7–12). Illus. 1984, Simon & Schuster $17.95 (978-0-671-46549-0). A guide to physical fitness through sports, weight training, and good nutrition. [613.7]

11607 Johnson, Marlys. *Understanding Exercise Addiction* (7–12). Series: Teen Eating Disorder Prevention Library. 2000, Rosen LB $31.95 (978-0-8239-2990-0). This book offers teens the opportunity to assess whether attitudes toward exercise, eating, and the human body are normal. (Rev: SLJ 7/00) [616.86]

11608 Kaminker, Laura. *Exercise Addiction: When Fitness Becomes an Obsession* (6–10). Series: Teen Health Library of Eating Disorder Prevention. 1998, Rosen LB $27.95 (978-0-8239-2759-3). Some teens become addicted to exercise and exercise too much for the wrong reasons. This book defines the problem, risks, and causes, describes the symptoms, and tells where to get help and support if needed. (Rev: BL 3/1/89; SLJ 1/99) [613.7]

11609 Pascoe, Elaine, ed. *Spreading Menace: Salmonella Attack and the Hunger Craving* (5–8). Illus. Series: Body Story. 2003, Gale LB $24.95 (978-1-4103-0064-5). Two stories show how the body can react to food — Mike is infected with salmonella, and George's hunger is giving him a weight problem. (Rev: SLJ 4/04) [615.9]

11610 Savage, Jeff. *Fundamental Strength Training* (5–9). Photos by Jimmy Clarke. Series: Fundamental Sports. 1998, Lerner LB $26.40 (978-0-8225-3461-7). This beginner's manual discusses weight machines, training without weights, and various exercises for developing specific parts of the body. (Rev: HBG 10/99; SLJ 2/99) [613.7]

11611 Simon, Nissa. *Good Sports: Plain Talk About Health and Fitness for Teens* (7–10). Illus. 1990, HarperCollins LB $14.89 (978-0-690-04904-6). This book covers a variety of topics including nutrition, different kinds of exercise, and sports injuries. (Rev: BCCB 12/99; BL 9/15/90) [613]

11612 Stiefer, Sandy. *A Risky Prescription* (7–12). Illus. Series: Sports Issues. 1997, Lerner LB $28.75 (978-0-8225-3304-7). This book explores the relationship between sports and health, how some sports activities can lead to disabilities, and how performance-enhancing drugs can compromise or even ruin one's health. (Rev: BL 12/1/97; HBG 3/98; SLJ 3/98) [631.7]

11613 Vedral, Joyce L. *Toning for Teens: The 20-Minute Workout That Makes You Look Good and Feel Great!* (7–12). 2002, Warner paper $15.95 (978-0-446-67815-5). Three sets of dumbbells and a bench or step are the only items required for this daily workout; nutritional and fitness tips are included. (Rev: SLJ 8/02)

Mental Disorders and Emotional Problems

11614 Abeel, Samantha. *What Once Was White* (5–8). Illus. by Charles R. Murphy. 1993, Village $19.95 (978-0-941653-13-8). The author is a 13-year-old learning-disabled student who can't tell time but writes sensitive interpretations of a group of watercolor paintings. (Rev: SLJ 9/93*) [618.62]

11615 Adler, Joe Anne. *Stress: Just Chill Out!* (7–10). 1997, Enslow LB $26.60 (978-0-89490-918-4). This book identifies three types of stress frequently experienced by teenagers — life transition stress, enduring life stress, and chronic daily stress — with chapters on their causes and treatment. (Rev: SLJ 10/97) [152.4]

11616 Axelrod, Toby. *Working Together Against Teen Suicide* (6–10). Series: Library of Political Assassinations. 1996, Rosen LB $16.95 (978-0-8239-2261-1). The author examines the reasons for teenage suicide, suggests ways teens can cope with problems, and explains how telephone hotlines, community agencies, and institutions work to combat teen suicide and how teenagers can help. (Rev: SLJ 5/97) [394]

11617 Bayer, Linda. *Out of Control: Gambling and Other Impulse-Control Disorders* (6–12). Series: Encyclopedia of Psychological Disorders. 2000, Chelsea LB $35.00 (978-0-7910-5313-3). This account explores the nature, causes, and treatment of such types of compulsive behavior as gambling, kleptomania, pyromania, and hair pulling. (Rev: BL 1/1–15/01; HBG 3/01) [363.4]

11618 Bayer, Linda. *Personality Disorders* (6–12). Illus. Series: Encyclopedia of Psychological Disorders. 2000, Chelsea $35.00 (978-0-7910-5317-1). Ten types of personality disorders — including paranoid, schizoid, and antisocial — are defined and

discussed in this informative account. (Rev: BL 6/1–15/00; HBG 9/00; SLJ 9/00) [616.89]

11619 Bayer, Linda. *Uneasy Lives: Understanding Anxiety Disorders* (8–12). Series: Encyclopedia of Psychological Disorders. 2000, Chelsea House LB $39.00 (978-0-7910-5316-4). Anxiety disorders such as panic attacks, phobias, and obsessive-compulsive disorder are discussed. (Rev: HBG 9/00) [616.85]

11620 Beal, Eileen. *Everything You Need to Know About ADD ADHD* (6–8). Illus. Series: Need to Know Library. 1998, Rosen LB $27.95 (978-0-8239-2748-7). In six short chapters, the author describes attention deficit disorder and attention deficit hyperactivity disorder, their symptoms, the pros and cons of behavior modification and medications, and how teens can manage these disorders and use them to tap into special talents. (Rev: SLJ 9/98; VOYA 8/99) [371.9]

11621 Beckelman, Laurie. *Body Blues* (6–9). Illus. Series: Hot Line. 1994, Silver Burdett LB $17.95 (978-0-89680-842-3). This book is designed to help adolescents understand the changes that are occurring to their body and give reassurance through interviews with other teenagers experiencing the same changes. (Rev: BL 2/15/95) [155.5]

11622 Bellenir, Karen, ed. *Mental Health Information for Teens: Health Tips About Mental Wellness and Mental Illness*. 2nd ed. (6–12). Series: Teen Health. 2006, Omnigraphics $58 (978-0-7808-0863-8). A revised edition of this comprehensive and easy-to-use overview of topics relating to mental health — specific disorders, coping mechanisms, treatment, and so forth — with a new emphasis on self-injury and bullying. (Rev: SLJ 12/06)

11623 Bonnice, Sherry, and Carolyn Hoard. *Drug Therapy and Cognitive Disorders* (6–10). Illus. Series: Psychiatric Disorders: Drugs and Psychology for the Mind and Body. 2003, Mason Crest LB $24.95 (978-1-59084-562-2). Diagrams and charts reinforce the easily read text, which includes discussion of the nature of these disorders and how they are treated plus personal anecdotes from one of the authors. (Rev: SLJ 5/04)

11624 Borenstein, Gerri. *Therapy* (4–8). Illus. Series: Life Balance. 2003, Watts paper $6.95 (978-0-531-15585-1). This friendly, reassuring introduction explains what therapy consists of, the different kinds of professionals involved, and the ways in which privacy is maintained. (Rev: BL 10/15/03; SLJ 12/03) [616.89]

11625 Bowman-Kruhm, Mary, and Claudine G. Wirths. *Everything You Need to Know About Learning Disabilities* (6–12). Series: Need to Know Library. 1999, Rosen LB $27.95 (978-0-8239-2956-6). An introduction to learning disabilities and how people cope with them at school and in everyday life, with fictionalized case studies and information on getting help. (Rev: SLJ 1/00; VOYA 4/00) [616.85]

11626 Clarke, Alicia. *Coping with Self-Mutilation: A Helping Book for Teens Who Hurt Themselves* (7–10). Series: Coping. 1999, Rosen LB $26.50 (978-0-8239-2559-9). This volume defines various forms of self-mutilation, such as cutting and burning, examines the causes and the physiological and psychological effects, and discusses available treatments and self-help measures. (Rev: SLJ 5/99) [362.2]

11627 Cobain, Bev. *When Nothing Matters Anymore: A Survival Guide for Depressed Teens* (7–12). 1998, Free Spirit paper $13.95 (978-1-57542-036-3). The author, a psychiatric nurse who works with teens, discusses the types, causes, and warning signs of depression, the dangers of addictions and eating disorders, and the relationship between depression and suicide, and provides information on treatment options and suggestions for developing good mental and physical health. (Rev: SLJ 3/99; VOYA 2/99) [155]

11628 Corman, Catherine A., and Edward M. Hallowell. *Positively ADD: Real Success Stories to Inspire Your Dreams* (7–10). 2006, Walker $16.95 (978-0-8027-8988-4). Aimed at children with attention deficit disorder, this book includes profiles of successful adults who had ADD beginning in childhood. (Rev: BL 6/1–15/06; LMC 11–12/06; SLJ 9/06) [616.85]

11629 Crook, Marion. *Teenagers Talk About Suicide* (7–12). 1988, NC Pr. paper $12.95 (978-1-55021-013-2). Interviews with 30 Canadian teenagers who have tried suicide are reprinted. [362.2]

11630 Davis, Brangien. *What's Real, What's Ideal: Overcoming a Negative Body Image* (7–12). Series: Teen Health Library of Eating Disorder Prevention. 1998, Rosen LB $27.95 (978-0-8239-2771-5). Because teenager's bodies are changing so quickly, many become confused about an ideal figure. This book describes why teens develop negative body images and offers suggestions for overcoming self-defeating perceptions. (Rev: VOYA 4/99) [305.23]

11631 Demetriades, Helen A. *Bipolar Disorder, Depression, and Other Mood Disorders* (6–12). Series: Diseases and People. 2002, Enslow LB $26.60 (978-0-7660-1898-3). The causes and nature of unnatural mood swings and states of depression are examined and treatments that are currently available are discussed. (Rev: BL 12/15/02; HBG 3/03) [616.85]

11632 Dendy, Chris A. Zeigler, and Alex Zeigler. *A Bird's-Eye View of Life with ADD and ADHD: Advice from Young Survivors* (5–9). 2003, Cherish the Children paper $19.95 (978-0-9679911-3-9). A guide to ADD and ADHD, written by a dozen

teenagers with these disorders with the aim of helping others cope, with advice on succeeding in school, medication, driving, and so forth. (Rev: SLJ 4/04) [618.9]

11633 Dinner, Sherry H. *Nothing to Be Ashamed Of: Growing Up with Mental Illness in Your Family* (5–10). 1989, Lothrop LB $12.93 (978-0-688-08482-0). A psychologist gives good advice to those who live with a mentally ill person. (Rev: BL 6/1/89; SLJ 4/89; VOYA 8/89) [616.89]

11634 Donnelly, Karen. *Coping with Dyslexia* (6–9). Series: Coping. 2000, Rosen LB $31.95 (978-0-8239-2850-7). This volume offers short profiles of celebrities who have dyslexia as well as guidance on coping with this problem and choosing careers. (Rev: HBG 3/01; SLJ 12/00) [616.85]

11635 Fisher, Gary L., and Rhoda Woods Cummings. *The Survival Guide for Kids with LD (Learning Differences)* (5–8). Illus. 1990, Free Spirit paper $9.95 (978-0-915793-18-1). A book that explains various kinds of learning disabilities and how to cope with them. (Rev: BL 7/90; SLJ 6/90) [371.9]

11636 Fox, Annie, and Ruth Kirschner. *Too Stressed to Think? A Teen Guide to Staying Sane When Life Makes You Crazy* (7–12). Illus. 2005, Free Spirit paper $14.95 (978-1-57542-173-5). A handy review of stress, how to reduce it and how to prevent the external forces that cause it, with tips and various scenarios that illustrate relevant situations. (Rev: SLJ 6/06)

11637 Giacobello, John. *Everything You Need to Know About Anxiety and Panic Attacks* (5–9). Series: Need to Know Library. 2000, Rosen LB $27.95 (978-0-8239-3219-1). This book explains anxiety attacks' causes, symptoms, and treatments in a reassuring tone. (Rev: SLJ 1/01) [616]

11638 Giacobello, John. *Everything You Need to Know About the Dangers of Overachieving: A Guide for Relieving Pressure and Anxiety* (6–9). Series: Need to Know Library. 2000, Rosen $27.95 (978-0-8239-3107-1). Stress-reduction techniques are among the strategies here for limiting the disadvantages of a compelling desire to achieve. (Rev: SLJ 9/00) [155.9]

11639 Girod, Christina M. *Learning Disabilities* (7–9). Illus. Series: Diseases and Disorders. 2001, Lucent LB $27.45 (978-1-56006-844-0). This introduction to learning disabilities and their diagnosis and treatment is enhanced by the stories of adults, such as Cher, who have overcome this problem. Also use *Autism* (2001). (Rev: BL 10/15/01; SLJ 9/01) [371.9]

11640 Gold, Susan Dudley. *Attention Deficit Disorder* (4–8). Series: Health Watch. 2000, Enslow LB $23.93 (978-0-7660-1657-6). This account focuses on one boy from childhood to college and how he coped with attention deficit disorder. Several young people are profiled in the companion volume *Bipolar Disorder and Depression* (2000). (Rev: HBG 10/01; SLJ 2/01) [618.92]

11641 Gordon, James S. *Stress Management* (8–12). Illus. Series: 21st Century Health and Wellness. 2000, Chelsea LB $36.00 (978-0-7910-5987-6). This is a comprehensive and detailed examination of the causes of stress, the negative impact of stress, and ways to reduce stress. (Rev: BL 11/15/00; HBG 10/01; SLJ 2/01) [362]

11642 Grollman, Earl A., and Max Malikow. *Living When a Young Friend Commits Suicide: Or Even Starts Talking About It* (6–12). 1999, Beacon paper $12.00 (978-0-8070-2503-1). Using simple prose and a compassionate attitude, this book examines suicide from many standpoints and gives good advice on the grieving process. (Rev: BL 11/1/99; SLJ 1/00; VOYA 2/00) [368.28]

11643 Hall, David E. *Living with Learning Disabilities: A Guide for Students* (5–8). 1993, Lerner LB $19.93 (978-0-8225-0036-0). This book explains what learning disabilities are, what causes them, how they can be detected, and today's techniques for treatment. (Rev: BL 1/1/94; SLJ 4/94) [371.9]

11644 Harmon, Dan. *Schizophrenia: Losing Touch with Reality* (8–12). Series: Encyclopedia of Psychological Disorders. 2000, Chelsea House LB $35.00 (978-0-7910-4953-2). This author describes the mental condition known as schizophrenia, its symptoms, diagnosis, and treatments. (Rev: SLJ 1/00) [616.89]

11645 Hermes, Patricia. *A Time to Listen: Preventing Youth Suicide* (8–12). 1987, Harcourt $13.95 (978-0-15-288196-2). Through questions and answers plus many case studies, the author explores many aspects of suicidal behavior and its causes. (Rev: BL 4/1/88; SLJ 3/88; VOYA 6/88) [362.2]

11646 Hurley, Jennifer A., ed. *Mental Health* (7–12). Series: Current Controversies. 1999, Greenhaven LB $36.20 (978-1-56510-953-7). This anthology explores such questions as what constitutes good mental health, what treatments should be used for mentally ill patients, and how society and the legal system should respond to mentally ill people. (Rev: BL 7/99) [616.89]

11647 Hyde, Margaret O., and Elizabeth H. Forsyth. *Depression: What You Need to Know* (6–12). Illus. 2002, Watts $25.00 (978-0-531-11892-4). Information on celebrities and important figures who have experienced depression add to the details on the history, symptoms, and treatment of the condition. (Rev: BL 10/15/02; SLJ 12/02) [616.85]

11648 Hyde, Margaret O., and Elizabeth H. Forsyth. *Stress 101: An Overview for Teens* (7–10). Series: Teen Overviews. 2008, Lerner LB $26.60 (978-0-8225-6788-2). A thorough survey of the kinds of stress we suffer, their origins, their impact on our body, and ways to reduce and deal with stress. (Rev: BL 1/1–15/08; SLJ 4/08) [616.9]

11649 Hyman, Bruce M., and Cherry Pedroch. *Obsessive-Compulsive Disorder* (7–10). 2003, Millbrook LB $26.90 (978-0-7613-2758-5). Profiles of teens with OCD introduce a discussion of the condition that will aid understanding and will be useful for teens experiencing anxieties. (Rev: BL 12/15/03; HBG 4/04; SLJ 1/04; VOYA 2/04) [616.85]

11650 Irwin, Cait, et al. *Monochrome Days: A First-hand Account of One Teenager's Experience with Depression* (8–12). Illus. Series: Adolescent Mental Health Initiative. 2007, Oxford Univ. $30.00 (978-0-19-531004-7); paper $9.95 (978-0-19-531005-4). Irwin chronicles her own experience with depression — which began in 8th grade and included suicidal thoughts and inpatient treatment — and her co-authors add practical information about symptoms, treatment, and so forth. (Rev: SLJ 7/07) [616.85]

11651 Kahn, Ada P., and Ronald M. Doctor. *Phobias* (4–8). Series: Life Balance. 2003, Watts LB $20.50 (978-0-531-12256-3); paper $6.95 (978-0-531-15575-2). This book discusses the causes of phobias, the different types, how they affect people, and their treatment. (Rev: BL 10/15/03) [616.85]

11652 Kent, Deborah. *Snake Pits, Talking Cures, and Magic Bullets: A History of Mental Illness* (6–12). Illus. 2003, Millbrook LB $26.90 (978-0-7613-2704-2). The madhouses of old, shock treatments, psychotherapy, psychoanalysis, and today's effective drug therapies are among the topics discussed in this volume. (Rev: BL 5/1/03; HBG 4/04; SLJ 7/03) [616.89]

11653 Kittleson, Mark J., ed. *The Truth About Fear and Depression* (8–12). Series: Truth About. 2004, Facts on File $35.00 (978-0-8160-5301-8). Anxiety and depression are the main focus of this user-friendly volume that describes the causes of these problems, their treatment, individual experiences, and ways to get help. (Rev: SLJ 4/05) [616.85]

11654 Landau, Elaine. *Autism* (7–12). Illus. 2001, Watts $26.00 (978-0-531-11780-4). This straight-forward look at the history, symptoms, and treatment of autism includes personal stories. (Rev: BL 4/1/02; SLJ 12/01) [616.89]

11655 Landau, Elaine. *Schizophrenia* (4–8). Illus. Series: Life Balance. 2004, Watts LB $20.50 (978-0-531-12215-0); paper $6.95 (978-0-531-16614-7). An overview of the causes, symptoms, and treatment of this mental condition, with true stories of sufferers. (Rev: BL 10/15/03)

11656 Lauren, Jill. *Succeeding with LD: 20 True Stories About Real People with LD* (5–8). Illus. 1997, Free Spirit paper $14.95 (978-1-57542-012-7). Case studies of 20 people ages 10 to 61 who have overcome various learning difficulties. (Rev: BL 6/1–15/97; SLJ 7/97; VOYA 8/97) [371.92]

11657 Leder, Jane. *Dead Serious: A Book for Teenagers About Teenage Suicide* (7–12). 1987, Avon paper $3.50 (978-0-380-70661-7). This book deals specifically with the symptoms of a suicidal situation and how to cope with the after-effects of the suicide of a relative or friend. (Rev: SLJ 8/87; VOYA 6/87) [179]

11658 Lee, Mary Price, and Richard S. Lee. *Everything You Need to Know About Natural Disasters and Post-Traumatic Stress Disorder* (5–9). Series: Need to Know Library. 1996, Rosen LB $17.95 (978-0-8239-2053-2). This book explains how such disasters as hurricanes, floods, and earthquakes can cause post-traumatic stress disorder and how to get help and counseling. (Rev: SLJ 6/96; VOYA 8/96) [155.5]

11659 Leigh, Vanora. *Mental Illness* (5–10). Series: Talking Points. 1999, Raintree LB $27.12 (978-0-8172-5311-0). This book defines mental illness, gives examples, and discusses causes, treatments, and how to stay mentally healthy. (Rev: BL 8/99; SLJ 8/99) [362.2]

11660 Levine, Mel. *Keeping a Head in School: A Student's Book About Learning Abilities and Learning Disorders* (8–12). Illus. 1990, Educators Publg. paper $24.75 (978-0-8388-2069-8). This account deals with all sorts of learning disorders, how they affect the learning process, and how they can be treated. (Rev: BL 6/15/90) [371.9]

11661 Libal, Autumn. *Runaway Train: Youth with Emotional Disturbance* (7–12). Illus. Series: Youth with Special Needs. 2004, Mason Crest LB $24.95 (978-1-59084-732-9). The story of a disturbed high school student who resorts to cutting herself is combined with facts about the causes, symptoms, and treatment of severe emotional disturbance. (Rev: SLJ 12/04)

11662 Miller, Allen R. *Living with Depression* (6–12). Series: Teen's Guides. 2007, Facts on File LB $34.95 (978-0-8160-6345-1). This guide to recognizing and treating depression will help teenagers with the disease and those who know others who suffer with it. (Rev: BL 10/15/07) [618.92]

11663 Moe, Barbara. *Coping with Mental Illness* (7–10). Series: Coping. 2001, Rosen LB $31.95 (978-0-8239-3205-4). The diagnosis, symptoms, and treatment of major forms of mental illness are discussed, along with the types of professionals who can help. Also use *Schizophrenia* (2001). (Rev: SLJ 8/01) [616.89]

11664 Moehn, Heather. *Social Anxiety* (7–12). 2001, Rosen LB $31.95 (978-0-8239-3363-1). A strong fear of social situations often manifests itself during adolescence, and Moehn combines case studies and coping strategies with an overview of the condition

itself and a look at treatment alternatives. (Rev: BL 3/1/02; SLJ 5/02) [616.85]

11665 Monroe, Judy. *Phobias: Everything You Wanted to Know, But Were Afraid to Ask* (6–10). Series: Issues in Focus. 1996, Enslow LB $20.95 (978-0-89490-723-4). This book on phobias contains an "A to Z" list detailing each phobia as well as information on causes, treatments, and where to get help. (Rev: SLJ 6/96; VOYA 8/96) [616.85]

11666 Moragne, Wendy. *Depression* (7–12). Illus. Series: Medical Library. 2001, Twenty-First Century LB $24.90 (978-0-7613-1774-6). Signs, symptoms, diagnosis, and treatment of depression are introduced clearly and concisely with case histories of seven teenagers. (Rev: BL 5/15/01; HBG 10/01; SLJ 4/01; VOYA 10/01) [616.85]

11667 Paquette, Penny Hutchins, and Cheryl Gerson Tuttle. *Learning Disabilities: The Ultimate Teen Guide* (7–12). Series: It Happened to Me. 2003, Scarecrow LB $32.50 (978-0-8108-4261-8). Teens suffering from conditions including ADHD and dyslexia will find practical information on these disabilities, success stories, and advice on career and employment choices and strategies. (Rev: SLJ 10/03) [371.9]

11668 Partner, Daniel. *Disorders First Diagnosed in Childhood* (6–12). Series: Encyclopedia of Psychological Disorders. 2000, Chelsea LB $35.00 (978-0-7910-5312-6). This work discusses the symptoms, causes, and treatments for such disorders as autism and Tourette's syndrome. (Rev: BL 1/1–15/01; HBG 10/01; SLJ 2/01) [616.8]

11669 Pigache, Philippa. *ADHD* (4–8). Series: Just the Facts. 2004, Heinemann LB $27.07 (978-1-4034-5142-2). The symptoms, causes, and treatment of attention deficit hyperactivity disorder are described, with discussion of continuing research. (Rev: SLJ 5/05)

11670 Porterfield, Kay Marie. *Straight Talk About Learning Disabilities* (6–12). 1999, Facts on File $27.45 (978-0-8160-3865-7). Using three fictional case studies, the author discusses various kinds of learning disabilities, their symptoms, methods of diagnosis, and available treatments. (Rev: BL 2/15/00; HBG 4/00; SLJ 2/00; VOYA 4/00) [371.92]

11671 Powell, Mark. *Stress Relief: The Ultimate Teen Guide* (7–12). Illus. by Kelly Adams. Series: Ultimate Teen Guide. 2003, Scarecrow LB $32.50 (978-0-8108-4433-9). Typical causes of teen stress — relationships, homework, money, and so forth — are examined and practical suggestions for dealing with them are spelled out. (Rev: BL 10/15/03; SLJ 7/03; VOYA 4/03) [155.5]

11672 Quinn, Patricia O. *Adolescents and ADD: Gaining the Advantage* (6–12). Illus. 1996, Magination paper $12.95 (978-0-945354-70-3). As well as citing many case studies, this book on teens and attention deficit disorder provides useful background information plus tips on how to adjust to this condition and how to create a lifestyle that accommodates it. (Rev: BL 1/1–15/96; SLJ 3/96; VOYA 8/96) [371.94]

11673 Rashkin, Rachel. *Feeling Better: A Kid's Book About Therapy* (4–8). Illus. by Bonnie Adamson. 2005, Magination paper $9.95 (978-1-59147-238-4). Presented in journal format, this volume uses 12-year-old Maya's experiences with a therapist to offer useful insights into the process and its value. (Rev: SLJ 11/05) [618.92]

11674 Roleff, Tamara L., ed. *Suicide* (8–12). Series: Opposing Viewpoints. 1997, Greenhaven LB $32.45 (978-1-56510-665-9); paper $21.20 (978-1-56510-664-2). Twenty-four articles express various points of view concerning the ethical and legal aspects of suicide, with special attention to the causes of teen suicide and how it can be prevented. (Rev: BL 11/1/97; SLJ 1/98; VOYA 10/98) [362.28]

11675 Rosaler, Maxine. *Coping with Asperger Syndrome* (6–9). Series: Coping. 2004, Rosen LB $31.95 (978-0-8239-4482-8). This straightforward title provides valuable information on Asperger syndrome and its symptoms and treatment. (Rev: BL 3/1/05; SLJ 12/04) [616.89]

11676 Rosen, Marvin. *The Effects of Stress and Anxiety on the Family* (6–12). Series: Focus on Family Matters. 2002, Chelsea LB $25.00 (978-0-7910-6950-9). After describing situations that produce stress and anxiety in families, this account outlines effective coping strategies for healthy management of these emotions. (Rev: BL 1/1–15/03; HBG 3/03) [152.4]

11677 Rosen, Marvin. *Understanding Post-Traumatic Stress Disorder* (6–12). Series: Focus on Family Matters. 2003, Chelsea $25.00 (978-0-7910-6951-6). After a discussion of trauma and situations that cause it in teenagers, this book examines PTSD, its symptoms, and ways in which one can get help. (Rev: BL 10/15/02; SLJ 6/03) [616.89]

11678 Rosenberg, Marsha Sarah. *Coping When a Brother or Sister Is Autistic* (7–12). Series: Coping. 2001, Rosen LB $31.95 (978-0-8239-3194-1). Siblings of autistic children will find facts about the diagnosis and treatment of the disorder, as well as sympathetic, no-nonsense advice on dealing with the pressures of the situation. (Rev: SLJ 9/01) [618.92]

11679 Rosenberg, Marsha Sarah. *Everything You Need to Know When a Brother or Sister Is Autistic* (5–9). Series: Need to Know Library. 2000, Rosen LB $27.95 (978-0-8239-3123-1). Autism is defined and described, with material on its diagnosis and treatment plus coverage of how this condition can affect other members of the family. (Rev: SLJ 8/00) [616.8]

11680 Sanders, Pete, and Steve Myers. *Dyslexia* (4–8). Illus. by Mike Lacy and Liz Sawyer. Series: What Do You Know About. 1999, Millbrook LB $23.90 (978-0-7613-0915-4). Using a case study, this book explores one boy's problems with dyslexia, its causes, symptoms, and treatment. (Rev: HBG 10/99; SLJ 10/99) [617.7]

11681 Scowen, Kate. *My Kind of Sad: What It's Like to Be Young and Depressed* (7–12). Illus. by Jeff Szuc. 2006, Firefly $19.95 (978-1-55037-941-9); paper $10.95 (978-1-55037-940-2). Describes depression and how to tell between normal moods and feelings and what could be harmful; additional information on treatments and medications is included. (Rev: BL 9/15/06; SLJ 2/07) [616.85.5]

11682 Sebastian, Richard. *Compulsive Behavior* (7–12). Series: Encyclopedia of Health. 1993, Chelsea LB $19.95 (978-0-7910-0044-1). This book explores the origins of compulsive behavior, its consequences, and its treatment. (Rev: BL 1/1/93) [616.85]

11683 Sheen, Barbara. *Attention Deficit Disorder* (6–10). Series: Diseases and Disorders. 2001, Lucent LB $28.70 (978-1-56006-828-0). A comprehensive look at the history, causes, diagnosis, symptoms, and treatment of ADD, with quotations from individuals who suffer from the disorder. (Rev: SLJ 9/01) [616.85]

11684 Sherrow, Victoria. *Mental Illness* (6–9). Illus. Series: Overview. 1996, Lucent LB $29.95 (978-1-56006-168-7). After a general review of what constitutes mental illness, the author focuses on the history of society's treatment of the mentally ill, followed by a discussion of current controversies and approaches to therapy. (Rev: BL 3/1/96; SLJ 2/96; VOYA 8/96) [362.2]

11685 Shields, Charles. *Mental Illness and Its Effects on School and Work Environments* (6–10). Illus. Series: Encyclopedia of Psychological Disorders. 2000, Chelsea $35.00 (978-0-7910-5318-8). As well as giving a general introduction to the nature of mental illness, this work discusses how the mentally ill affect American society. (Rev: BL 11/1/00) [616.8]

11686 Silverstein, Alvin. *Depression* (6–10). Illus. Series: Diseases and People. 1997, Enslow LB $26.60 (978-0-89490-713-5). Topics covered in this appealing examination of depression include types, symptoms, and treatments. An extensive bibliography includes Internet sites. (Rev: BL 2/1/98; SLJ 4/98) [616.85]

11687 Silverstein, Alvin, and Virginia Silverstein. *Epilepsy* (7–10). Illus. 1975, HarperCollins $12.95 (978-0-397-31615-1). Sweeping aside all the untruths associated with this problem, the authors describe the cause and effect of seizures and their treatment. [616.8]

11688 Simpson, Carolyn, and Dwain Simpson. *Coping with Post-Traumatic Stress Disorder* (7–10). Series: Coping. 1997, Rosen LB $25.25 (978-0-8239-2080-8). Post-traumatic stress disorder (PTSD) affects people who have experienced natural disasters, rape, war, or other traumatic events. This book explains the causes and primary signs of PTSD and how it affects family and friends, as well as the victim, and provides useful information on treatment. (Rev: SLJ 10/97) [362]

11689 Sperekas, Nicole B. *SuicideWise: Taking Steps Against Teen Suicide* (8–12). Series: Teen Issues. 2000, Enslow LB $22.60 (978-0-7660-1360-5). The causes and prevention of teen suicide are covered, with advice on determining if a friend is in danger of attempting suicide. (Rev: HBG 9/00; VOYA 6/01) [362.28]

11690 Sprung, Barbara. *Stress* (4–8). Illus. Series: Preteen Pressures. 1998, Raintree LB $25.69 (978-0-8172-5033-1). A concise, practical account of the types and causes of stress in young people and how to manage it. (Rev: BL 4/15/98; HBG 10/98; SLJ 6/98) [155.4]

11691 Stewart, Gail B. *People with Mental Illness* (7–12). Series: The Other America. 2003, Gale LB $29.95 (978-1-59018-237-6). Personal stories of individuals with different conditions show how they cope with daily life and the impact on the families as well as the patients. (Rev: SLJ 6/03) [616.89]

11692 Stewart, Gail B. *Phobias* (7–9). Series: Diseases and Disorders. 2001, Lucent LB $32.45 (978-1-56006-726-9). The meaning of "phobia" is explained, with material on common phobias, what causes them, and how they can be treated. (Rev: BL 1/1–15/02; SLJ 10/01) [616.85]

11693 Williams, Julie. *Attention-Deficit / Hyperactivity Disorder* (6–12). Illus. Series: Diseases and People. 2001, Enslow LB $26.60 (978-0-7660-1598-2). Williams presents the symptoms, diagnosis, and treatment of ADHD, as well as its history, profiles of people who suffer from the condition, research that is being conducted, and the controversies that surround the condition. (Rev: BL 1/1–15/02; HBG 10/02; SLJ 2/02) [618.92]

11694 Williams, Julie. *Pyromania, Kleptomania, and Other Impulse-Control Disorders* (6–12). Series: Diseases and People. 2002, Enslow LB $26.60 (978-0-7660-1899-0). Various forms of abnormal mental obsessions are discussed with material on causes and treatments. (Rev: BL 12/15/02; HBG 3/03) [616.8]

11695 Wiltshire, Paula. *Dyslexia* (5–8). Illus. Series: Health Issues. 2002, Raintree LB $28.54 (978-0-7398-5221-7). Color photographs and straightforward text introduce dyslexia's symptoms and treatment and explain how it affects learning, with

tips on how to cope with the disability. (Rev: BL 12/15/02; HBG 3/03; SLJ 3/03) [616.85]

11696 Winkler, Kathleen. *Teens, Depression, and the Blues* (6–9). Series: Hot Issues. 2000, Enslow LB $27.93 (978-0-7660-1369-8). The stories of two teen girls suffering from depression introduce a discussion of causes, symptoms, treatment, and dangers of this condition. (Rev: BL 9/15/00; HBG 9/00; SLJ 8/00) [616.85]

11697 Wolff, Lisa. *Teen Depression* (6–12). Series: Overview: Teen Issues. 1998, Lucent LB $27.45 (978-1-56006-519-7). The complexities of teen depression and its causes, symptoms, and treatment are discussed. (Rev: BL 1/1–15/99) [616.85]

11698 Zeinert, Karen. *Suicide: Tragic Choice* (6–12). Illus. Series: Issues in Focus. 1999, Enslow LB $26.60 (978-0-7660-1105-2). All aspects of suicide are covered including history, demographic patterns, causes, the grief of survivors, cluster suicide, and assisted suicide. (Rev: BL 12/15/99; HBG 4/00; VOYA 4/00) [362.28]

11699 Zucker, Faye. *Depression* (4–8). Series: Life Balance. 2003, Watts LB $20.50 (978-0-531-12259-4); paper $6.95 (978-0-531-15578-3). This friendly, reassuring introduction explains the causes, diagnosis, and treatment of depression. (Rev: BL 10/15/03; SLJ 12/03) [616.85]

Nutrition and Diet

11700 Alters, Sandra. *Obesity* (7–12). Series: Introducing Issues with Opposing Viewpoints. 2006, Gale LB $32.45 (978-0-7377-3545-1). Fourteen articles look at the causes and nature of obesity and examine possible ways to deal with this epidemic; fact boxes, charts, photographs, and cartoon strips highlight key points. (Rev: SLJ 4/07) [616.3]

11701 Ballard, Carol. *Food for Feeling Healthy* (6–9). Illus. Series: Making Healthy Food Choices. 2006, Heinemann LB $32.86 (978-1-4034-8571-7). Using the new food pyramid, Ballard examines important factors in eating properly and discusses advertising, peer pressure, and food labels. (Rev: SLJ 4/07) [613.2]

11702 Bellenir, Karen, ed. *Diet Information for Teens: Health Tips About Diet and Nutrition, Including Facts About Nutrients, Dietary Guidelines, Breakfasts, School Lunches, Snacks, Party Food, Weight Control, Eating Disorders, and More* (7–12). 2001, Omnigraphics $48.00 (978-0-7808-0441-8). General nutrition information is amplified by topics of particular interest to teens, such as snacking, school lunches, and eating disorders. (Rev: SLJ 6/01; VOYA 8/01) [613.2]

11703 Bijlefeld, Marjolijn, and Sharon K. Zoumbaris. *Food and You: A Guide to Healthy Habits for Teens* (7–12). 2001, Greenwood $59.95 (978-0-313-31108-6). A comprehensive guide to healthy eating, weight, and exercise that provides lots of information for report writers. (Rev: SLJ 11/01; VOYA 2/02) [613.7]

11704 Drohan, Michele I. *Weight-Loss Programs: Weighing the Risks and Realities* (6–10). Illus. Series: Teen Health Library of Eating Disorder Prevention. 1998, Rosen LB $27.95 (978-0-8239-2770-8). This book explores weight-loss programs, sheds light on potential dangers, and discusses safe and sensible approaches to weight loss. (Rev: BL 3/1/99; SLJ 1/99) [616.85]

11705 Favor, Lesli J. *Weighing In: Nutrition and Weight Management* (8–11). Series: Food and Fitness. 2007, Marshall Cavendish LB $25.95 (978-0-7614-2555-7). Information on dieting, healthy weight, general and specialized nutrition, and eating disorders is provided in text, statistics, charts, sidebar features, and photographs. (Rev: BL 1/1–15/08; SLJ 6/08) [613.2]

11706 Fredericks, Carrie. *Obesity* (6–12). Illus. Series: Compact Research: Current Issues. 2008, Reference Point LB $24.95 (978-1-60152-040-1). Report writers and browsers will appreciate this well-organized examination of the causes, treatment, and prevention of obesity, full of facts, quotations, diagrams, and so forth. (Rev: BL 8/08) [616.3]

11707 Gay, Kathlyn. *Am I Fat? The Obesity Issue for Teens* (7–12). 2006, Enslow LB $31.93 (978-0-7660-2527-1). Obesity and the health issues associated with it are discussed, as well as strategies for living better and avoiding the wrong dieting decisions that many teens make. (Rev: SLJ 6/06)

11708 Ingram, Scott. *Want Fries with That? Obesity and the Supersizing of America* (8–11). Illus. 2005, Scholastic LB $26.00 (978-0-531-16756-4). Examines the relationship between America's burgeoning fast-food business and the country's obesity epidemic. (Rev: BL 11/15/05; SLJ 1/06) [362.196]

11709 Landau, Elaine. *A Healthy Diet* (4–7). Series: Watts Library. 2003, Watts LB $25.50 (978-0-531-12027-9). Landau explains the basics of good nutrition; the benefits of vitamins, minerals, and exercise; and the dangers of fad diets. (Rev: SLJ 9/03) [613.2]

11710 Lankford, Ron, ed. *Can Diets Be Harmful?* (7–12). Series: At Issue: Health. 2007, Gale LB $28.70 (978-0-7377-3397-6); paper $19.95 (978-0-7377-3398-3). Essays about nutrition and healthy weight tackle such issues as fad diets, eating disorders, and fast food, with some personal stories. (Rev: BL 1/1–15/08) [613.2]

11711 Loonin, Meryl. *Overweight America* (7–12). Series: Hot Topics. 2006, Gale LB $31.20 (978-1-59018-744-9). Covering the reasons why Americans are overweight, the way we eat and think about food. (Rev: SLJ 2/07)

11712 Moe, Barbara. *Understanding Negative Body Image* (6–10). Series: Teen Eating Disorder Prevention Library. 1999, Rosen $31.95 (978-0-8239-2865-1). Our culture stresses body weight and shape, and this book explores the many causes and harmful consequences of a negative body image. (Rev: BL 10/15/99; HBG 9/00; SLJ 1/00; VOYA 2/00) [613.4]

11713 Monroe, Judy. *Understanding Weight-Loss Programs* (6–10). Series: Teen Eating Disorder Prevention Library. 1999, Rosen LB $31.95 (978-0-8239-2866-8). This book discusses good and bad weight loss programs, how to evaluate them, and how to be on guard for bogus products. (Rev: BL 10/15/99; HBG 9/00; SLJ 1/00) [613.7]

11714 Morris, Neil. *Do You Know What's in Your Food?* (6–10). Series: Making Healthy Food Choices. 2006, Heinemann LB $32.86 (978-1-4034-8574-8). Morris challenges teens to look at the questionable components of the foods they eat — bacteria, fat, chemicals, additives, and so forth. Also use *Food for Sports* (2006),. (Rev: SLJ 2/07)

11715 Nardo, Don. *Vitamins and Minerals* (7–12). Series: Encyclopedia of Health. 1994, Chelsea LB $19.95 (978-0-7910-0032-8). A description of the vitamins and minerals needed by the human body and the importance of each. (Rev: BL 8/94; VOYA 6/94) [613.2]

11716 Pierson, Stephanie. *Vegetables Rock! A Complete Guide for Teenage Vegetarians* (7–12). 1999, Bantam paper $13.95 (978-0-553-37924-2). Animal rights and health issues are touched on in this book that describes philosophical and practical aspects of vegetarianism and provides a guide to good foods and balancing nutritional needs. (Rev: BL 3/1/99) [613.2]

11717 Schlosser, Eric, and Charles Wilson. *Chew on This: Everything You Don't Want to Know About Fast Food* (6–9). Illus. 2006, Houghton $16.00 (978-0-618-71031-7). An unsettling but informative discussion of fast food and its attractions. (Rev: BL 3/1/06*; SLJ 5/06) [394.1]

11718 Schwartz, Ellen. *I'm a Vegetarian: Amazing Facts and Ideas for Healthy Vegetarians* (5–8). Illus. by Farida Zaman. 2002, Tundra paper $9.95 (978-0-88776-588-9). The social aspects of being a vegetarian are handled here with humor and sensitivity. (Rev: BL 7/02; SLJ 9/02) [613.2]

11719 Serafin, Kim. *Everything You Need to Know About Being a Vegetarian* (5–8). Series: Need to Know Library. 1999, Rosen LB $27.95 (978-0-8239-2951-1). This book explains vegetarianism and its various varieties, the reasons why people become vegetarians, the nature of their diets, social problems involved, and names celebrities who are vegetarians. (Rev: SLJ 1/00; VOYA 4/00) [613.2]

11720 Tattersall, Clare. *Understanding Food and Your Family* (6–10). Series: Teen Eating Disorder Prevention Library. 1999, Rosen $31.95 (978-0-8239-2860-6). Using many facts and references to case studies, this book describes family dynamics and how eating patterns are developed within the family structure. (Rev: BL 10/15/99; HBG 9/00; SLJ 11/99; VOYA 2/00) [616.85]

11721 VanCleave, Janice. *Janice VanCleave's Food and Nutrition for Every Kid: Easy Activities That Make Learning Science Fun* (4–8). Illus. Series: Science for Every Kid. 1999, Wiley paper $12.95 (978-0-471-17665-7). Each of the 25 chapters in this book contains information about food, including food groups, the relationship between energy and food, how to read nutrition labels, and vitamins and minerals, plus dozens of easily performed projects that demonstrate these facts and concepts. (Rev: SLJ 8/99) [641.3]

11722 Weiss, Stefanie Iris. *Everything You Need to Know About Being a Vegan* (5–8). Series: Need to Know Library. 1999, Rosen LB $27.95 (978-0-8239-2958-0). This book discusses vegans, people who do not eat or use animal products (usually for religious reasons), their lifestyles, diets, and possible social problems. (Rev: SLJ 1/00; VOYA 4/00) [613.2]

11723 Williams, Kara. *Frequently Asked Questions about MyPyramid: Eating Right* (5–8). Illus. 2007, Rosen LB $20.95 (978-1-4042-1974-8). Introduces the 2005 version of the food pyramid as well as information on diet, nutrition, the human body, and exercise. (Rev: BL 6/1–15/07; LMC 10/07) [613.2]

11724 Zahensky, Barbara A. *Diet Fads* (4–8). Series: Danger Zone. Dieting and Eating Disorders. 2007, Rosen LB $27.95 (978-1-4042-1999-1). Fad and crash diets and the dangers of overeating and excessive weight loss are the focus of this practical guide. (Rev: LMC 10/07; SLJ 9/07) [613.2]

Physical Disabilities and Problems

11725 Cheney, Glenn. *Teens with Physical Disabilities: Real-Life Stories of Meeting the Challenges* (6–9). 1995, Enslow LB $20.95 (978-0-89490-625-1). Accounts of teens' daily lives as they struggle and triumph over the challenges imposed by disabilities. Includes short biographies and photographs. (Rev: BL 8/95; SLJ 8/95) [362.4]

11726 Costello, Elaine. *Signing: How to Speak with Your Hands* (7–9). Illus. 1995, Bantam paper $19.95 (978-0-553-37539-8). A simple explanation of and a guide to the use of sign language for the deaf. [001.56]

11727 Esherick, Joan. *Breaking Down Barriers: Youth with Physical Challenges* (6–9). Illus. Series: Youth with Special Needs. 2004, Mason Crest LB $24.95 (978-1-59084-737-4). Fiction and fact are interwoven in this presentation of five teens facing physical challenges — amputation, cerebral palsy, spina bifida, muscular dystrophy, and spinal cord injury. (Rev: SLJ 7/04) [362.4]

11728 Landau, Elaine. *Blindness* (4–7). Illus. Series: Understanding Illness. 1994, Twenty-First Century LB $24.90 (978-0-8050-2992-5). Both the emotional and scientific aspects of blindness are covered, with an excellent chapter on prevention. (Rev: BL 12/15/94; SLJ 2/95) [617.7]

11729 Landau, Elaine. *Deafness* (4–7). Illus. Series: Understanding Illness. 1994, Twenty-First Century LB $24.90 (978-0-8050-2993-2). Beginning with the story of a deaf child, this book explores the causes of deafness, the scientific and emotional factors involved, treatments, and problems in adjusting. (Rev: BL 12/15/94; SLJ 2/95) [617.8]

11730 Stewart, Gail B. *Teens with Disabilities* (8–12). Photos by Carl Franzén. Series: The Other America. 2000, Lucent LB $29.95 (978-1-56006-815-0). The personal — and positive — stories of four teens with physical disabilities show how people with these problems can be accommodated in family and social settings. (Rev: SLJ 3/01)

11731 Thornton, Denise. *Physical Disabilities: The Ultimate Teen Guide* (5–10). Series: It Happened to Me. 2007, Scarecrow $42.00 (978-0-8108-5300-3). In interviews, teens with disabilities describe how they cope at school, with technology and tools, getting around, sports, and so forth. (Rev: SLJ 10/07) [362.40835]

Reproduction and Child Care

11732 Almond, Lucinda, ed. *The Abortion Controversy* (8–12). Series: Current Controversies. 2007, Gale $23.70 (978-0-7377-3273-3). An updated collection of articles expressing many views on abortion and related issues including stem cell research and the rights of activists in general. (Rev: BL 12/1/07) [363.46]

11733 Alpern, Michele. *Teen Pregnancy* (6–12). Series: Focus on Family Matters. 2002, Chelsea $31.00 (978-0-7910-6695-9). This account explores various aspects of teen pregnancy, particularly the way in which it affects the entire family. (Rev: BL 10/15/02; HBG 3/03; SLJ 9/02) [618.2]

11734 Brynie, Faith Hickman. *101 Questions About Reproduction: Or How 1 + 1 = 3 or 4 or More . . . .* (6–10). Illus. by Sharon Lane Holm. 2005, Twenty-First Century LB $27.93 (978-0-7613-2311-2). Information on conception, pregnancy, childbirth, contraception (including a pill for males), abortion, reproductive disorders, and other issues of importance to teens is provided in a question-and-answer format with detailed black-and-white illustrations. (Rev: SLJ 1/06) [612]

11735 Byers, Ann. *Teens and Pregnancy: A Hot Issue* (6–12). Series: Hot Issues. 2000, Enslow LB $27.93 (978-0-7660-1365-0). Various aspects of teen pregnancy are discussed, from social factors that put teens at risk to the financial ramifications of single parenthood to ways in which teens can avoid pregnancy. (Rev: HBG 3/01; SLJ 1/01) [306.874]

11736 Coles, Robert. *The Youngest Parents* (8–12). Illus. 1997, Norton $27.50 (978-0-393-04082-1). The first two-thirds of this adult book consists of interviews by the author, a child psychiatrist, with teenagers who are or about to be parents, and the last part is a moving photoessay featuring many rural, underprivileged teen parents and their children. (Rev: BL 2/1/97; VOYA 6/98) [306.85]

11737 Day, Nancy. *Abortion: Debating the Issue* (8–12). Series: Issues in Focus. 1995, Enslow LB $20.95 (978-0-89490-645-9). A balanced presentation of the subject, with black-and-white photographs, glossary, and extensive notes. (Rev: BL 8/95; SLJ 12/95) [363.4]

11738 *Daycare and Diplomas: Teen Mothers Who Stayed in School* (7–12). Illus. 2001, Fairview paper $9.95 (978-1-57749-098-2). A group of young women who attend an unusual school that offers childcare relate the difficulties they have experienced in combining parenthood and education. (Rev: BL 5/15/01; VOYA 4/01) [306.874]

11739 Edelson, Paula. *Straight Talk About Teenage Pregnancy* (7–12). Series: Straight Talk. 1998, Facts on File $27.45 (978-0-8160-3717-9). A frank, nonjudgmental discussion on such topics as abstinence, safe sex, abortion, adoption, and teen parenting, to help young people make wise decisions and take responsibility for their actions. (Rev: BL 3/1/99; SLJ 2/99) [306.874]

11740 Fullick, Ann. *Test Tube Babies: In Vitro Fertilization* (5–8). Series: Science at the Edge. 2002, Heinemann LB $27.86 (978-1-58810-703-9). This attractive book balances hard science with thought-provoking discussion on this controversial topic. (Rev: BL 10/15/02; HBG 3/03; SLJ 4/03) [613.9]

11741 Gottfried, Ted. *Teen Fathers Today* (8–12). 2001, Twenty-First Century LB $24.90 (978-0-7613-1901-6). Real-life stories add immediacy to this practical guide to the challenges of becoming a father during the teen years. (Rev: HBG 3/02; SLJ 12/01; VOYA 2/02) [306.874]

11742 Gravelle, Karen, and Leslie Peterson. *Teenage Fathers* (7–12). 1992, Messner paper $5.95 (978-0-671-72851-9). Thirteen teenage boys describe their situations and feelings when they became fathers, with comments by the authors. (Rev: BL 10/15/92) [306.85]

11743 Heller, Tania. *Pregnant! What Can I Do? A Guide for Teenagers* (6–12). 2002, McFarland $29.95 (978-0-7864-1169-6). Valuable information about pregnancy, abortion, adoption, prenatal care, and parenting is provided in this thoughtful and reassuring volume. (Rev: SLJ 6/02; VOYA 6/02) [306.874/]

11744 Hughes, Tracy. *Everything You Need to Know About Teen Pregnancy* (7–12). Illus. Series: Need to Know Library. 1988, Rosen $24.50 (978-0-8239-0810-3). A simple, unbiased introduction to teen pregnancy and the options available. (Rev: SLJ 4/89) [612]

11745 Jakobson, Cathryn. *Think About Teenage Pregnancy* (7–12). Illus. 1993, Walker LB $15.85 (978-0-8027-8128-4); paper $9.95 (978-0-8027-7372-2). Problems of pregnant teenagers are addressed, with a look at possible options and the social issues involved. (Rev: SLJ 8/88; VOYA 10/88) [612]

11746 Keller, Kristin Thoennes. *Parenting an Infant* (8–12). Series: Skills for Teens Who Parent. 2000, Capstone LB $25.26 (978-0-7368-0702-9). Keller offers straightforward, accessible guidance to teens who are caring for very young children, with quotations from teen parents. Also use *Parenting a Toddler* (2000). (Rev: HBG 10/01; SLJ 7/01) [649]

11747 Lindsay, Jeanne W. *Pregnant? Adoption Is an Option: Making an Adoption Plan for a Child* (7–12). Illus. 1996, Morning Glory paper $11.95 (978-1-885356-08-6). Using quotations from many case studies, this book describes the steps in the adoption process and how to develop an adoption plan. (Rev: BL 12/1/96; SLJ 2/97; VOYA 4/97) [362.7]

11748 Lindsay, Jeanne W. *Teen Dads: Rights, Responsibilities and Joys* (7–12). Illus. 1993, Morning Glory $15.95 (978-0-930934-77-4); paper $9.95 (978-0-930934-78-1). Teenage fatherhood is explored with good quotations from case histories. (Rev: BL 10/15/93; SLJ 10/93; VOYA 2/94) [649.1]

11749 Lowenstein, Felicia. *The Abortion Battle: Looking at Both Sides* (7–12). Illus. Series: Issues in Focus. 1996, Enslow LB $20.95 (978-0-89490-724-1). After a presentation of the facts, the author analyzes arguments on both sides of the abortion controversy. Appended are a glossary, hotline numbers, and a reading list. (Rev: BL 7/96; SLJ 9/96; VOYA 8/96) [363.4]

11750 MacDonald, Fiona. *The First "Test-Tube Baby"* (6–12). Illus. Series: Days that Changed the World. 2004, World Almanac LB $31.00 (978-0-8368-5567-8); paper $11.95 (978-0-8368-5574-6). The science and ethics of in-vitro fertilization are explored in this overview of the 1978 birth of the world's first "test-tube baby." (Rev: BL 4/1/04; SLJ 7/04) [618.1]

11751 Moe, Barbara. *A Question of Timing: Successful Men Talk About Having Children* (6–12). Illus. Series: Teen Pregnancy Prevention Library. 1997, Rosen LB $23.95 (978-0-8239-2253-6). Men from a variety of backgrounds talk about why they waited to have children and how they feel about that choice. (Rev: BL 6/1–15/97; VOYA 10/97) [306.874]

11752 Orr, Tamra. *Test Tube Babies* (5–9). Series: Science on the Edge. 2003, Gale LB $24.95 (978-1-56711-788-2). This book discusses in vitro fertilization, and how it has helped many but also caused a great deal of controversy. (Rev: BL 10/15/03; SLJ 3/04) [612]

11753 Parker, Steve. *Reproduction* (5–9). Illus. Series: Our Bodies. 2004, Raintree LB $28.56 (978-0-7398-6623-8). Details of the human body's reproductive organs and how they function are accompanied by information on keeping them healthy. (Rev: BL 8/04) [612.6]

11754 Parker, Steve. *The Reproductive System* (5–8). Illus. Series: Human Body. 1997, Raintree LB $18.98 (978-0-8172-4806-2). A well-organized, straightforward account that covers male and female anatomy, genes, fertility problems, contraception, STDs, and human development from conception to adolescence. (Rev: SLJ 2/98) [613.9]

11755 Powers, Meghan, ed. *The Abortion Rights Movement* (8–11). Series: American Social Movements. 2006, Gale LB $36.20 (978-0-7377-1947-5). This collection of 18 articles, speeches, first-person accounts, and interviews lays out the case for abortion. (Rev: BL 2/15/06) [363.46]

11756 Rozakis, Laurie. *Teen Pregnancy: Why Are Kids Having Babies?* (5–8). Illus. Series: Issues of Our Time. 1993, Twenty-First Century LB $22.90 (978-0-8050-2569-9). A slim, easily read account that explains birth control and deplores the fact that teens do not have access to information about it. (Rev: SLJ 2/94) [612.6]

11757 Silverstein, Alvin, et al. *The Reproductive System* (5–8). Illus. Series: Human Body Systems. 1994, Twenty-First Century LB $16.95 (978-0-8050-2838-6). Reproduction in the plant and animal worlds is introduced, focusing on the human system and body parts. (Rev: BL 3/15/95) [612.6]

11758 Trapani, Margi. *Listen Up: Teenage Mothers Speak Out* (6–12). Illus. Series: Teen Pregnancy Prevention Library. 1997, Rosen LB $23.95 (978-0-8239-2254-3). Young women speak candidly about why they had children at an early age and the impact this has had on their lives. (Rev: BL 6/1–15/97; SLJ 6/97; VOYA 10/97) [306.874]

11759 Trapani, Margi. *Reality Check: Teenage Fathers Speak Out* (7–10). 1997, Rosen LB $23.95 (978-0-8239-2255-0). Case studies of teenage fathers who did not plan on becoming parents are discussed in this book that does not shun the hardships of being a teenage parent. (Rev: BL 6/1–15/97; SLJ 6/97; VOYA 10/97) [306.85]

11760 Wilks, Corinne Morgan, ed. *Dear Diary, I'm Pregnant: Teenagers Talk About Their Pregnancy* (7–12). Illus. 1997, Annick paper $9.95 (978-1-55037-440-7). Ten teenage girls talk about how they got pregnant, what they decided to do, and how the pregnancy has changed their lives. (Rev: BL 2/1/98; SLJ 8/97; VOYA 12/97) [306.874]

11761 Williams, Kara. *Fertility Technology: The Baby Debate* (6–8). Illus. Series: Focus on Science and Society. 2000, Rosen LB $26.50 (978-0-8239-3210-8). An interesting exploration of the types of fertility treatment available, the science behind them, and the controversies surrounding their use. (Rev: SLJ 1/01) [618.1]

Safety and First Aid

11762 Arnold, Caroline. *Coping with Natural Disasters* (7–10). Illus. 1988, Walker LB $14.85 (978-0-8027-6717-2). Natural disasters such as earthquakes, hurricanes, and blizzards are discussed, with information on how to react in these emergencies. (Rev: BCCB 6/88; BL 6/15/88; SLJ 6/88; VOYA 10/88) [904]

11763 Chaiet, Donna, and Francine Russell. *The Safe Zone: A Kid's Guide to Personal Safety* (4–7). Illus. 1998, Morrow paper $6.95 (978-0-688-16091-3). This book alerts youngsters to danger signs, gives advice on body language and self-esteem, and offers tips on how to avoid threatening situations. (Rev: BL 4/1/98; HBG 10/98) [613.6]

11764 Gutman, Bill. *Be Aware of Danger* (5–8). Illus. Series: Focus on Safety. 1996, Twenty-First Century LB $24.90 (978-0-8050-4142-2). Situations that could be dangerous to young people are highlighted and preventive measures outlined. (Rev: BL 2/1/97; SLJ 2/97) [613.6]

11765 Gutman, Bill. *Hazards at Home* (4–8). Series: Focus on Safety. 1996, Twenty-First Century LB $24.90 (978-0-8050-4141-5). A look at sources of potential accidents in the home with information on prevention and first-aid procedures. (Rev: SLJ 9/96) [363.1]

11766 Gutman, Bill. *Recreation Can Be Risky* (4–8). Series: Focus on Safety. 1996, Holt LB $24.90 (978-0-8050-4143-9). The author gives practical suggestions for enjoying such activities as baseball, biking, or hiking while also keeping safe through warm-up exercises, proper equipment, correct clothing, etc. (Rev: BL 7/96; SLJ 9/96; VOYA 10/96) [790]

11767 Orndorff, John C., and Suzanne Harper. *Terrorists, Tornados, and Tsunamis: How to Prepare for Life's Danger Zones* (7–12). Illus. 2007, Abrams $16.95 (978-0-8109-5767-1). A practical guide to preparing for all kinds of disasters, from storms to Internet predators. (Rev: BL 4/15/07; SLJ 5/07) [613.6]

11768 Roberts, Robin. *Sports Injuries: How to Stay Safe and Keep on Playing* (5–8). Series: Get in the Game! With Robin Roberts. 2001, Millbrook LB $23.90 (978-0-7613-2116-3). This general sports book that targets girls as a primary audience discusses safety in a variety of sports and how to cope with injuries. (Rev: BL 9/15/01; HBG 3/02; SLJ 1/02) [790]

11769 Wells, Donna K., and Bruce C. Morris. *Live Aware, Not in Fear: The 411 After 9-11 — A Book For Teens* (6–12). 2002, Health Communications paper $9.95 (978-0-7573-0013-4). The authors offer practical advice for teenagers who want to feel safe again, such as preparing escape routes and keeping a survival kit handy. (Rev: BL 5/15/02; VOYA 6/02) [363.3]

Sex Education and Sexual Identity

11770 Akagi, Cynthia G. *Dear Michael: Sexuality Education for Boys Ages 11–17* (6–10). Illus. 1996, Gylantic $12.95 (978-1-880197-16-5). Written by a mother to her adolescent son, these letters effectively explore male puberty, the male's role in conception, concerns about dating, and the problems involved in sexual relationships. (Rev: BL 1/1–15/97; VOYA 6/97) [613.9]

11771 Bailey, Jacqui. *Sex, Puberty and All That Stuff: A Guide to Growing Up* (5–10). Illus. by Jan McCafferty. 2004, Barron's paper $12.99 (978-0-7641-2992-6). In this comprehensive volume full of lighthearted illustrations, Bailey covers the wide range of changes that affect young people, emphasizing the individual's right to choose and the need to resist peer pressure. (Rev: SLJ 1/05) [613.9]

11772 Ball, Jacqueline A. *Puberty* (6–9). Illus. 1989, Rourke LB $19.93 (978-0-86625-283-6). This account aimed at young girls covers such topics as

maturation, social problems, and menstruation. (Rev: SLJ 6/89) [305.2]

11773 Brynie, Faith Hickman. *101 Questions About Sex and Sexuality: With Answers for the Curious, Cautious, and Confused* (6–12). Illus. Series: 101 Questions. 2003, Twenty-First Century LB $27.90 (978-0-7613-2310-5). Information on abstinence, contraception, sexually transmitted diseases, and other issues of importance to teens is provided in a question-and-answer format with detailed black-and-white illustrations. (Rev: HBG 10/03; SLJ 6/03; VOYA 4/04) [306.7]

11774 Bull, David. *Cool and Celibate? Sex or No Sex* (8–12). 1998, Element Books paper $4.95 (978-1-901881-17-2). The author argues against teens having sex until they are in stable married relationships. (Rev: SLJ 3/99) [362.29]

11775 Diamond, Shifra N. *Everything You Need to Know About Going to the Gynecologist* (7–12). Series: Need to Know Library. 1999, Rosen LB $27.95 (978-0-8239-2839-2). This book explains what a gynecologist does, when teenage girls should see one, and how to find one. There is helpful information on menstruation, breast self-examinations, treatments for common reproductive problems, contraception, myths, and what to expect from a pelvic examination. (Rev: SLJ 5/99; VOYA 8/99) [612]

11776 Dunbar, Robert E. *Homosexuality* (7–10). Series: Issues in Focus. 1995, Enslow LB $20.95 (978-0-89490-665-7). An objective introduction to homosexuality that contains some interesting first-person accounts. (Rev: BL 12/15/95; SLJ 6/96; VOYA 2/96) [305.9]

11777 Dunham, Kelli. *The Boy's Body Book: Everything You Need to Know for Growing Up YOU* (4–7). Illus. by Steven Björkman. 2007, Sterling paper $9.95 (978-1-933662-74-9). This is a straightforward review of the changes to expect during puberty; it also discusses stress, friendship, peer pressure, and family problems such as divorce. (Rev: LMC 2/08; SLJ 10/07) [612.6]

11778 Elliot-Wright, Susan. *Puberty* (7–10). Illus. Series: Health Issues. 2003, Raintree LB $28.56 (978-0-7398-6424-1). An attractive, slim overview of puberty and how it affects the body and mind. (Rev: SLJ 5/04) [612]

11779 Feinmann, Jane. *Everything a Girl Needs to Know About Her Periods* (5–9). Illus. 2003, Ronnie Sellers paper $14.95 (978-1-56906-555-6). This useful and reassuring guide to the female body changes of puberty focuses largely on the menstrual cycle. (Rev: BL 2/1/04) [618.083]

11780 Gowen, L. Kris. *Making Sexual Decisions: The Ultimate Teen Guide* (7–12). Illus. Series: It Happened to Me. 2003, Scarecrow $32.50 (978-0-8108-4647-0). Puberty, safe sex, birth control, and rape are among the topics raised in this volume, which stresses the value of being fully informed about one's options. (Rev: SLJ 11/03) [306.7]

11781 Gravelle, Karen, and Nick Castro. *What's Going on Down There? Answers to Questions Boys Find Hard to Ask* (5–10). Illus. by Robert Leighton. 1998, Walker paper $8.95 (978-0-8027-7540-5). Straightforward information for boys covers such topics as physical changes, sexual intercourse, peer pressure, and pregnancy and birth. (Rev: BL 11/1/98; HB 1–2/99; HBG 3/99; SLJ 12/98) [613]

11782 Hoch, Dean, and Nancy Hoch. *The Sex Education Dictionary for Today's Teens and Pre-Teens* (7–12). Illus. 1990, Landmark paper $12.95 (978-0-9624209-0-0). A dictionary of 350 words relating to sex, sexuality, and reproduction all given clear, concise definitions. (Rev: BL 8/90) [306.7]

11783 Huegel, Kelly. *GLBTQ: The Survival Guide for Queer and Questioning Teens* (7–12). Illus. 2003, Free Spirit paper $15.95 (978-1-57542-126-1). Quotations from teens are interspersed in the practical, common-sense advice for gay, lesbian, bisexual, transgendered, and questioning teens. (Rev: BL 10/1/03; SLJ 12/03; VOYA 12/03) [300.70]

11784 Hyde, Margaret O., and Elizabeth Forsyth. *Know About Gays and Lesbians* (7–12). 1994, Millbrook LB $23.40 (978-1-56294-298-4). This overview of homosexuality attacks stereotypes, surveys history, examines current controversies, reviews religious responses, and shows how pervasive homophobia still is. (Rev: BL 3/1/94; SLJ 4/94; VOYA 4/94) [305.9]

11785 Hyde, Margaret O., and Elizabeth H. Forsyth. *Safe Sex 101* (8–11). 2006, Lerner $26.60 (978-0-8225-3439-6). Straightforward and well-written, this book includes important information for teens on how to protect themselves from STDs and pregnancy, covering contraception as well as abstinence. (Rev: BL 5/1/06; SLJ 6/06) [613.9]

11786 Johnson, Eric W. *People, Love, Sex, and Families: Answers to Questions That Preteens Ask* (5–8). Illus. 1985, Walker LB $14.85 (978-0-8027-6605-2). Based on the results of a survey of 1,000 preteens, this book covers a broad range of topics, from sexual abuse to venereal disease to divorce and incest. (Rev: BL 3/15/86) [306.707]

11787 Jukes, Mavis. *Growing Up: It's a Girl Thing: Straight Talk About First Bras, First Periods and Your Changing Body* (4–8). Illus. 1998, Knopf paper $10.00 (978-0-679-89027-0). Essential information about the changes girls experience during puberty, with half the book devoted to what to expect and how to plan for their first period, presented in an easy, big-sister style. (Rev: BL 11/1/98; SLJ 11/98) [612]

11788 Jukes, Mavis. *It's a Girl Thing: How to Stay Healthy, Safe, and in Charge* (5–9). Illus. 1996,

Knopf paper $12.00 (978-0-679-87392-1). This guide to puberty for girls discusses such topics as menstruation, drinking and drugs, body changes, contraceptives, sexually transmitted diseases, and sexual abuse and harassment. (Rev: SLJ 6/96*) [612.6]

11789 Kemp, Kristen. *Healthy Sexuality* (5–10). Illus. Series: Life Balance. 2004, Watts LB $20.50 (978-0-531-12336-2); paper $6.95 (978-0-531-16689-5). Covering both boys and girls, this easy-to-understand volume looks at physical and emotional changes and provides practical tips on handling difficult decisions and confusing feelings. (Rev: BL 10/15/03; SLJ 4/05)

11790 Loulan, JoAnn, and Bonnie Worthen. *Period: A Girl's Guide to Menstruation with a Parent's Guide*. Rev. ed. (5–7). Illus. 2001, Book Peddlers paper $9.99 (978-0-916773-96-0). This practical guide to menstruation is arranged by such questions as "What do I do when I get my first period?" and "What kind of exercise can I do?" (Rev: BL 2/1/01; HBG 10/01) [612.6]

11791 Marcovitz, Hal. *Teens and Gay Issues* (7–10). Series: The Gallup Youth Survey, Major Issues and Trends. 2005, Mason Crest LB $22.95 (978-1-59084-873-9). An attractive volume documenting Gallup findings on gay teens' attitudes toward coming out, homophobia, the nature/nurture debate, and gay marriage and adoption. (Rev: SLJ 1/06) [305.9]

11792 Marcus, Eric. *What If Someone I Know Is Gay? Answers to Questions About What It Means to Be Gay and Lesbian* (7–12). 2007, Simon & Schuster paper $8.99 (978-1-4169-4970-1). This update of the title first published in 2001 uses new terminology and addresses questions that teenagers may have about their own sexuality as well as that of someone they know. (Rev: BL 10/1/07; SLJ 1/08) [306.766]

11793 Mosatche, Harriet S., and Karen Unger. *Too Old for This, Too Young for That! Your Survival Guide for the Middle-School Years* (5–8). Illus. 2000, Free Spirit paper $14.99 (978-1-57542-067-7). This guide to the early years of puberty contains material on self-esteem, family relationships, friendships, and activities; also included is a lengthy section on bodily changes and such events as the onset of menstruation, erections, and ejaculation. (Rev: BL 7/00; SLJ 9/00) [646.7]

11794 Movsessian, Shushann. *Puberty Girl* (4–7). Illus. 2005, Allen & Unwin paper $15.95 (978-1-74114-104-7). A frank and friendly guide covering such topics as body changes, conflict resolution, and personal boundaries, as well as the changes that puberty brings in the opposite sex. (Rev: BL 10/15/05; SLJ 10/05; VOYA 10/05) [612.6]

11795 O'Grady, Kathleen, and Paula Wansbrough, eds. *Sweet Secrets: Telling Stories of Menstruation* (6–10). 1997, Second Story paper $9.95 (978-0-

929005-33-1). Following an interesting review of attitudes and rituals relating to menstruation in various cultures throughout history, the main body of the book recounts 20 anecdotes about young teens and their first periods, interspersed with boxes providing information on topics including tampons, toxic shock syndrome, and breast examinations. (Rev: VOYA 6/98) [530.8]

11796 Pascoe, Elaine, ed. *Teen Dreams: The Journey Through Puberty* (5–8). Illus. Series: Body Story. 2003, Gale LB $24.95 (978-1-4103-0061-4). Puberty and the many changes it brings are the topic of this arresting and informative book, seen from the points of view of a teenage boy and girl. (Rev: SLJ 4/04) [612.6]

11797 Pfeifer, Kate Gruenwald. *Boy's Guide to Becoming a Teen* (4–7). Ed. by Amy B. Middleman. 2006, Jossey-Bass paper $12.95 (978-0-7879-8343-7). A guide to handling the physical, emotional, and social changes that accompany puberty in boys. (Rev: BL 5/15/06; SLJ 5/07) [613]

11798 Pfeifer, Kate Gruenwald. *Girl's Guide to Becoming a Teen* (4–7). Ed. by Amy B. Middleman. 2006, Jossey-Bass paper $12.95 (978-0-7879-8344-4). A guide to handling the physical, emotional, and social changes that accompany puberty in girls. (Rev: BL 5/15/06; SLJ 5/07) [613]

11799 Pogany, Susan Browning. *Sex Smart: 501 Reasons to Hold Off on Sex* (8–12). 1998, Fairview paper $14.95 (978-1-57749-043-2). The author uses quotations from teenagers, "Dear Abby," and other sources to explore emotional issues involved in making sexual choices and to argue for abstinence. (Rev: VOYA 4/99) [613.9]

11800 Price, Geoff. *Puberty Boy* (5–8). 2006, Allen & Unwin paper $15.95 (978-1-74114-563-2). A frank and friendly guide with an Australian accent that covers the important physical and emotional changes that accompany puberty. (Rev: BL 7/06; SLJ 9/06; VOYA 8/06) [612]

11801 Roleff, Tamara L., ed. *Sex Education* (7–12). Series: At Issue. 1999, Greenhaven LB $26.20 (978-0-7377-0009-1); paper $17.45 (978-0-7377-0008-4). A collection of essays and opinion on issues relating to teaching about sex, including contraception, sexual abstinence, safe sex, sexual identity, and families with gay parents. (Rev: BL 5/15/99) [613.9]

11802 Rooney, Frances, ed. *Hear Me Out: True Stories of Teens Confronting Homophobia* (8–12). 2005, Second Story paper $9.95 (978-1-896764-87-0). Young people who are volunteers in a Toronto organization called T.E.A.C.H. (Teens Educating and Confronting Homophobia) talk about prejudice they've experienced because of their sexual orientation. (Rev: BL 8/05; SLJ 5/05; VOYA 4/05) [306.76]

11803 Rue, Nancy N. *Everything You Need to Know About Getting Your Period* (6–9). Series: Need to Know Library. 1995, Rosen LB $27.95 (978-0-8239-1870-6). A straightforward discussion of the physiological changes that come with puberty. (Rev: BL 11/1/95; SLJ 1/96) [612.6]

11804 White, Joe. *Pure Excitement: A Radical Righteous Approach to Sex, Love, and Dating* (7–12). 1996, Focus on the Family paper $10.99 (978-1-56179-483-6). Taking a conservative approach, this book, written by a minister and using many conversations with teens, proposes that premarital sex is harmful to young adults. (Rev: VOYA 8/97) [613.9]

Sex Problems (Abuse, Harassment, etc.)

11805 Benedict, Helen. *Safe, Strong, and Streetwise* (8–12). 1987, Little, Brown paper $6.95 (978-0-87113-100-3). A rape crisis specialist discusses sexual assault, its prevention and treatment. (Rev: BL 1/1/87; SLJ 5/87; VOYA 2/87) [362.7]

11806 Chaiet, Donna. *Staying Safe at School* (7–12). Series: Get Prepared Library. 1995, Rosen LB $23.95 (978-0-8239-1864-5). How to stay alert and protect oneself while at school, plus tips for girls on avoiding violent crimes on or near school campuses. (Rev: BL 11/15/95; SLJ 2/96) [613.6]

11807 Chaiet, Donna. *Staying Safe at Work* (7–12). Series: Get Prepared Library. 1995, Rosen LB $23.95 (978-0-8239-1867-6). How to stay alert and protect oneself at work, with material for girls on how to create their own space and give clear messages to others. (Rev: BL 11/15/95; SLJ 2/96; VOYA 4/96) [613.6]

11808 Chaiet, Donna. *Staying Safe on Public Transportation* (7–12). Series: Get Prepared Library. 1995, Rosen LB $16.95 (978-0-8239-1866-9). This book for young women traveling alone on buses, trains, or subways stresses the importance of awareness, verbal and physical self-defense, having a plan, and listening to one's instincts. (Rev: BL 11/15/95; SLJ 2/96; VOYA 4/96) [363.1]

11809 Chaiet, Donna. *Staying Safe on the Streets* (7–12). Series: Get Prepared Library. 1995, Rosen LB $16.95 (978-0-8239-1865-2). Discusses situations young women should avoid outside the home and protection techniques. (Rev: SLJ 1/96) [613.6]

11810 Chaiet, Donna. *Staying Safe While Shopping* (7–12). Series: Get Prepared Library. 1995, Rosen LB $16.95 (978-0-8239-1869-0). This book tells girls how to stay alert and protect themselves while shopping. (Rev: BL 11/15/95; SLJ 1/96) [364]

11811 Chaiet, Donna. *Staying Safe While Traveling* (7–12). Series: Get Prepared Library. 1995, Rosen LB $23.95 (978-0-8239-1868-3). In this book for girls traveling alone, the importance of awareness, how to use verbal and physical self-defense, and listening to one's instincts are stressed and examples are given for handling specific situations. (Rev: BL 11/15/95; SLJ 2/96; VOYA 4/96) [363.1]

11812 Foltz, Linda Lee. *Kids Helping Kids: Break the Silence of Sexual Abuse* (4–9). 2003, Lighthouse Point $21.95 (978-0-9637966-8-4); paper $14.95 (978-0-9637966-9-1). Personal stories from young people and adults who suffered abuse as children illustrate the guilt and shame typically experienced and show how to get help. (Rev: SLJ 9/03) [362.7]

11813 Guernsey, JoAnn B. *Sexual Harassment: A Question of Power* (7–12). Series: Frontline. 1995, Lerner LB $19.95 (978-0-8225-2608-7). The issue of harassment in the workplace, school, and everyday life is discussed. Includes historical background and male perspectives. (Rev: BL 7/95; SLJ 8/95) [305.42]

11814 Hyde, Margaret O., and Elizabeth Forsyth. *The Sexual Abuse of Children and Adolescents* (7–12). Illus. 1997, Millbrook LB $22.40 (978-0-7613-0058-8). The causes and effects of sexual abuse of children and young adults are covered in this thorough account that also discusses such topics as the history of sexual abuse, Megan's Law, and possible treatments for sex offenders. (Rev: BL 2/15/97; SLJ 3/97; VOYA 8/97) [362.7]

11815 Landau, Elaine. *Sexual Harassment* (8–12). 1993, Walker LB $15.85 (978-0-8027-8266-3). Attempts to establish a sense of what constitutes inappropriate behavior, an issue still not agreed upon in the courts or in American society. (Rev: BL 6/1–15/93) [305.42]

11816 Lehman, Carolyn. *Strong at the Heart: How It Feels to Heal from Sexual Abuse* (8–11). 2005, Farrar $16.00 (978-0-374-37282-8). First-person accounts reveal the damage caused by sexual abuse and present strategies for healing. (Rev: BL 9/15/05; SLJ 11/05; VOYA 10/05) [362.76]

11817 McFarland, Rhoda. *Working Together Against Sexual Harassment* (7–12). Series: Library of Social Activism. 1996, Rosen LB $27.95 (978-0-8239-1775-4). Following a review of the history of sexual harassment (of females) and recent scandals, the book emphasizes how teens can combat sexual harassment by responding politically, from fighting for official policies against it at school to organizing chapters of NOW or other organizations. (Rev: SLJ 4/97; VOYA 6/97) [344.73]

11818 Mufson, Susan, and Rachel Kranz. *Straight Talk About Date Rape* (7–12). Series: Straight Talk.

1993, Facts on File $27.45 (978-0-8160-2863-4). Using examples and analogies, the authors define date rape, tell how it can be avoided, and give suggestions to help date-rape victims. (Rev: BL 9/1/93) [362.88]

11819 Munson, Lulie, and Karen Riskin. *In Their Own Words: A Sexual Abuse Workbook for Teenage Girls* (7–12). 1997, Child Welfare League of America paper $10.95 (978-0-87868-596-7). This manual (for use in therapy situations) helps girls who have been sexually abused work through their problems and plan for the future. (Rev: VOYA 10/97) [382.88]

11820 Nash, Carol R. *Sexual Harassment: What Teens Should Know* (7–12). Illus. Series: Issues in Focus. 1996, Enslow LB $20.95 (978-0-89490-735-7). After a general introduction to sexual harassment and its many forms, this account focuses on teens, the ways in which they encounter it, and techniques to fight it. (Rev: BL 7/96; SLJ 10/96; VOYA 8/96) [370.19]

11821 Reinert, Dale R. *Sexual Abuse and Incest* (7–12). Series: Teen Issues. 1997, Enslow LB $17.95 (978-0-89490-916-0). After a general explanation of what constitutes sexual abuse and incest, this work explains how to identify potential abusive situations and what to do about them. (Rev: BL 12/1/97; HBG 3/98; SLJ 12/97; VOYA 6/98) [362.76]

11822 Rosen, Marvin. *Dealing with the Effects of Rape and Incest* (6–12). Illus. 2002, Chelsea LB $25.00 (978-0-7910-6693-5). Teens' personal experiences of sexual abuse draw readers into this straightforward account of the upheavals caused by mistreatment and the various coping strategies recommended for young people. (Rev: BL 10/15/02; SLJ 10/02) [616.85]

11823 Shuker-Haines, Frances. *Everything You Need to Know About Date Rape* (7–12). Illus. 1995, Rosen LB $25.25 (978-0-8239-2882-8). The author explains how date rape occurs and what precautionary measures can be taken. (Rev: BL 1/15/90; VOYA 4/90) [362.88]

11824 White, Katherine. *Everything You Need to Know About Relationship Violence* (7–12). 2001, Rosen LB $27.95 (978-0-8239-3398-3). The author offers practical guidance on avoiding dating violence, recognizing risk factors, and assessing the health of a relationship. (Rev: SLJ 12/01) [306.73]

11825 Winkler, Kathleen. *Date Rape* (7–12). Illus. Series: Hot Issues. 1999, Enslow LB $27.93 (978-0-7660-1198-4). Personal stories and easily read data highlight this treatment of the date-rape problem. (Rev: BL 9/15/99; HBG 4/00; VOYA 4/01) [362.883]

Human Development and Behavior

General and Miscellaneous

11826 Barron, T. A. *The Hero's Trail: A Guide for Heroic Life* (4–7). Illus. 2002, Putnam $15.99 (978-0-399-23860-4). This collection of anecdotes about both real and fictional characters aims to define heroism, and explores how one can lead a heroic life. (Rev: BL 10/15/02; HBG 3/03; SLJ 12/02; VOYA 12/02) [170]

11827 Erlbach, Arlene. *Worth the Risk: True Stories About Risk Takers, Plus How You Can Be One, Too* (5–9). Illus. 1999, Free Spirit paper $12.95 (978-1-57542-051-6). These are 20 case studies of teenagers who took risks, from defying the dominant cliques in school to entering a burning house to save siblings. (Rev: BL 5/1/99; SLJ 8/99) [158]

11828 Fleischman, Paul, ed. *Cannibal in the Mirror* (5–10). Photos by John Whalen. 2000, Twenty-First Century LB $24.90 (978-0-7613-0968-0). This thought-provoking book takes 27 quotations that describe barbarous behavior of primitive societies and pairs each with a telling photograph of similar behavior in modern American society. (Rev: BL 4/15/00; HBG 10/00; SLJ 4/00) [150]

Psychology and Human Behavior

General and Miscellaneous

11829 Acker, Kerry. *Everything You Need to Know About the Goth Scene* (7–12). Illus. 2000, Rosen LB $27.95 (978-0-8239-3223-8). An informative and reliable guide to the origins, fashions, preferences, and behavior associated with the "Goth" movement. (Rev: BL 12/1/00; SLJ 3/01) [306]

11830 Allenbaugh, Kay. *Chocolate for a Teen's Dreams: Heartwarming Stories About Making Your Wishes Come True* (8–12). Series: Chocolate. 2003, Fireside paper $12.00 (978-0-7432-3703-1). A collection of stories by teens and older women about their dreams and desires, and how they came true. (Rev: SLJ 9/03) [305.235]

11831 Carlson, Dale B., and Hannah Carlson. *Where's Your Head? Teenage Psychology* (8–12). Illus. 1998, Bick paper $14.95 (978-1-884158-19-3). This book explores in readable format the basic elements of psychological thought concerning personality, influences on beliefs and behavior, the stages of adolescence, and mental illness. (Rev: VOYA 8/98) [150]

11832 Espeland, Pamela. *Knowing Me, Knowing You: The I-Sight Way to Understand Yourself and Others* (8–12). Illus. by Jeff Tolbert. 2001, Free Spirit paper $13.95 (978-1-57542-090-5). Combining psychological theories, self-testing, and interesting sidebar features, this is a look at the reasons why some people immediately appeal to us and others don't. (Rev: SLJ 1/02) [155.2]

11833 Gardner, Robert, and Barbara Gardner Conklin. *Health Science Projects About Psychology* (7–12). Illus. 2002, Enslow LB $26.60 (978-0-7660-1439-8). Interesting activities that illustrate psychological concepts are extended by suggestions for further investigation. (Rev: HBG 10/02; SLJ 7/02) [150]

11834 Hernández, Roger K. *Teens and Relationships* (7–10). Series: The Gallup Youth Survey, Major Issues and Trends. 2005, Mason Crest LB $22.95 (978-1-59084-875-3). An attractive volume documenting Gallup findings on teens' attitudes toward parents, divorce, blended families, friendship, and dating the opposite sex. (Rev: SLJ 1/06)

11835 Musgrave, Susan, ed. *Nerves Out Loud: Critical Moments in the Lives of Seven Teen Girls* (8–12). 2001, Annick $19.95 (978-1-55037-693-7); paper $9.95 (978-1-55037-692-0). Seven adult women look back at events and problems that absorbed them as teenagers. (Rev: BL 10/1/01; HBG 3/02; SLJ 10/01; VOYA 2/02) [305.235]

11836 O'Halloran, Barbara Collopy. *Creature Comforts: People and Their Security Objects* (6–12). Illus. by Betty Udesen. 2002, Houghton $17.00 (978-0-618-11864-9). First-person accounts, accompanied by photographs, explain why objects such as "blankies" prove invaluable to both children and adults. (Rev: BL 5/1/02; HBG 10/02; SLJ 3/02) [155.4]

11837 Ojeda, Auriana, ed. *Teens at Risk* (8–12). Illus. Series: Opposing Viewpoints. 2003, Gale paper $24.95 (978-0-7377-1916-1). Questions explored in this anthology involve the factors that put teens at risk, teenage sex and pregnancy, crime and violence, and substance abuse. (Rev: SLJ 11/03) [306]

11838 Rue, Nancy N. *Everything You Need to Know About Abusive Relationships.* Rev. ed. (7–12). Series: Need to Know Library. 1998, Rosen LB $25.25 (978-0-8239-2832-3). Advice on handling abusive behavior is accompanied by discussion of the kinds of abuse that occur. [362.7]

11839 Silverman, Robin L. *Reaching Your Goals* (4–8). Illus. Series: Life Balance. 2004, Watts LB $20.50 (978-0-531-12342-3); paper $6.95 (978-0-531-16691-8). Practical advice on building self-confidence, making smart decisions, and focusing on achievable goals. (Rev: BL 10/15/03)

Emotions and Emotional Behavior

11840 Alpern, Michele. *Overcoming Feelings of Hatred* (6–12). Series: Focus on Family Matters. 2003, Chelsea $25.00 (978-0-7910-6953-0). This work explores the social and psychological origins of hatred and show how teens can overcome these feelings, particularly toward other races and ethnicities. (Rev: BL 10/15/02; SLJ 6/03) [616]

Ethics and Moral Behavior

11841 Altman, Linda J. *Bioethics: Who Lives, Who Dies, and Who Decides* (7–12). Illus. Series: Issues in Focus Today. 2007, Enslow LB $23.95 (978-0-7660-2546-2). Both sides of moral issues in bioethics (such as cloning, abortion, and organ transplants) are presented fairly. (Rev: BL 3/15/07; SLJ 8/07) [174]

11842 Canfield, Jack, et al. *Chicken Soup for the Teenage Soul: 101 Stories of Life, Love and Learning* (7–12). 1997, Health Communications paper $14.95 (978-1-55874-463-9). An inspirational collection of writings, about one third by teenagers, that discuss the problems of growing up. (Rev: BL 10/1/97) [158.1]

11843 Canfield, Jack, and Mark V. Hansen. *Chicken Soup for the Teenage Soul II: 101 More Stories of Life, Love and Learning* (7–12). 1998, Health Communications $24.00 (978-1-55874-615-2); paper $14.95 (978-1-55874-616-9). A new collection of personal stories from teens that supply inspiration and guidance. (Rev: BL 11/1/98; HBG 3/99) [158.1]

11844 Egendorf, Laura K., and Jennifer A. Hurley, eds. *Teens at Risk* (8–12). Series: Opposing Viewpoints. 1998, Greenhaven LB $32.45 (978-1-56510-949-0); paper $21.20 (978-1-56510-948-3). Questions explored in this anthology involve the factors that put teens at risk, teenage crime and violence, prevention of teenage pregnancy, and the roles of government and the media in teenage difficulties. (Rev: BL 9/15/98) [306]

11845 Hurley, Jennifer A., ed. *American Values* (6–12). Series: Opposing Viewpoints. 2000, Greenhaven LB $32.45 (978-0-7377-0344-3); paper $21.20 (978-0-7377-0343-6). Conservative and liberal points of view are expressed in this collection of essays that discuss moral relativism, capitalism, religion, violence, pop culture, and character building. (Rev: BL 9/15/00; SLJ 10/00) [304.6]

11846 Kincher, Jonni. *The First Honest Book About Lies* (7–12). 1992, Free Spirit paper $14.95 (978-0-915793-43-3). Provides tools to extract "real" information from statistics, advertisements, and so forth, as well as techniques for arguing persuasively. (Rev: BL 3/1/93) [155.9]

11847 Margulies, Alice. *Compassion* (8–12). Illus. 1990, Rosen LB $19.95 (978-0-8239-1108-0). A discussion of the different kinds of compassion and how each helps both the individual and society. (Rev: SLJ 6/90) [152.4]

11848 Simpson, Carolyn. *High Performance Through Negotiation* (8–12). Series: Learning-a-Living Library. 1996, Rosen LB $26.50 (978-0-8239-2206-2). This book discusses negotiation skills and how students can resolve conflicts in a variety of situations. (Rev: BL 9/15/96; SLJ 10/96; VOYA 2/97) [158]

Etiquette and Manners

11849 Cabot, Meg. *Princess Lessons* (5–7). Illus. by Chesley McLaren. Series: Princess Diaries. 2003, HarperCollins $12.99 (978-0-06-052677-1). Princess Mia gives lighthearted tips and often quite practical tips on behaving like a real princess. (Rev: BL 5/15/03; HBG 10/03; VOYA 10/03) [646.7]

11850 Dougherty, Karla. *The Rules to Be Cool: Etiquette and Netiquette* (5–9). Series: Teen Issues.

2001, Enslow LB $22.60 (978-0-7660-1607-1). Respect and consideration for others are the key elements of Dougherty's rules of behavior, with an emphasis on politeness, kindness, and courtesy, on the Internet as well as at home and at school. (Rev: HBG 3/02; SLJ 10/01) [395]

11851 Holyoke, Nancy. *A Smart Girl's Guide to Manners* (4–7). Illus. by Cathi Mingus. 2005, Pleasant paper $9.95 (978-1-58485-983-3). A nice mix of good manners that ranges from introductions to cell phone etiquette to how and when to write real thank-you notes. (Rev: BL 11/1/05; SLJ 1/06; VOYA 12/05) [395]

11852 Hoving, Walter. *Tiffany's Table Manners for Teenagers* (7–12). Illus. 1989, Random $17.00 (978-0-394-82877-0). A practical guide to good table manners. (Rev: SLJ 6/89) [395]

11853 James, Elizabeth, and Carol Barkin. *Social Smarts: Manners for Today's Kids* (4–7). Illus. 1996, Clarion paper $7.95 (978-0-395-81312-6). Table manners and responsible, appropriate public behavior are two topics covered. (Rev: BL 9/1/96; SLJ 9/96) [395]

11854 Packer, Alex J. *How Rude! The Teenagers' Guide to Good Manners, Proper Behavior, and Not Grossing People Out* (6–12). Illus. 1997, Free Spirit paper $19.95 (978-1-57542-024-0). A candid, often humorous guide to good manners for teenagers that stresses common sense and covers situations ranging from inline skating to computer hacking. (Rev: BL 2/1/98; SLJ 2/98; VOYA 6/98) [395.1]

11855 Robert, Henry M. *Robert's Rules of Order* (8–12). 1993, Revell paper $5.99 (978-0-8007-8610-6). The most authoritative guide to running meetings. [060.4]

11856 Stewart, Marjabelle Young, and Ann Buchwald. *What to Do When and Why* (4–7). 1988, Luce $14.95 (978-0-88331-105-9). An easily read introduction to the basics of good manners and behavior.

Intelligence and Thinking

11857 Galbraith, Judy, and Jim Delisle. *The Gifted Kids' Survival Guide: A Teen Handbook.* Rev. ed. (7–12). Illus. 1996, Free Spirit paper $15.99 (978-1-57542-003-5). Topics covered in this very useful discussion of gifted children include definitions of giftedness, IQ testing, perfectionism, goal setting, college choices, peers, and suicide. (Rev: SLJ 2/97; VOYA 6/97) [371.95]

11858 Nikola-Lisa, W. *How We Are Smart* (4–7). Illus. by Scan Quails. 2006, Lee & Low $16.95 (978-1-58430-254-4). A picture book for older readers that looks at different kinds of intelligence, using double-page spreads about 12 famous people to illustrate these concepts. (Rev: BL 4/1/06; SLJ 6/06) [811]

11859 Wartik, Nancy, and La Vonne Carlson-Finnerty. *Memory and Learning* (7–12). Series: Encyclopedia of Health. 1993, Chelsea LB $19.95 (978-0-7910-0022-9). Explores two operations of the brain and explains how they function and sometimes malfunction. (Rev: BL 3/15/93; VOYA 8/93) [153.1]

Personal Guidance

11860 Allenbaugh, Kay. *Chocolate for a Teen's Soul: Life-Changing Stories for Young Women About Growing Wise and Growing Strong* (6–12). 2000, Simon & Schuster $12.00 (978-0-684-87081-6). Inspiring essays explore a wide array of issues, including first love, disabilities, beauty pageants, friendship, first jobs, and family relations. (Rev: VOYA 4/01) [152.4]

11861 Arredia, Joni. *Sex, Boys, and You: Be Your Own Best Girlfriend* (5–9). Illus. 1998, Perc Publg. paper $15.95 (978-0-9653203-2-0). A self-help book for younger teen girls with advice on how to accept oneself, when to say "no" to sex, how to assess one's strengths and weaknesses, and how to develop healthy relationships with boys. (Rev: SLJ 10/98) [305.23]

11862 Asgedom, Mawi. *The Code: The Five Secrets of Teen Success* (7–12). 2003, Little, Brown paper $9.99 (978-0-316-73689-3). Asgedom, a motivational speaker who was a refugee before coming to the United States and later attending Harvard, advises teens on strategies for success. (Rev: HBG 4/04; SLJ 11/03; VOYA 12/03)

11863 Bachel, Beverly K. *What Do You Really Want? How to Set a Goal and Go for It!* (6–12). Illus. 2001, Free Spirit paper $12.95 (978-1-57542-085-1). Bachel lays out ways to define and achieve goals, supported by quotations from teens who have tried them; reproducible forms are included. (Rev: BL 5/15/01; VOYA 8/01) [153.8]

11864 Benson, Peter L., and Judy Galbraith. *What Teens Need to Succeed: Proven, Practical Ways to Shape Your Own Future* (7–12). Illus. 1998, Free Spirit paper $15.95 (978-1-57542-027-1). Based on surveys from 350,000 U.S. teens, this book discusses positive "external assets" (families, peers, spiritual support systems, schools) and "internal assets" (honesty, motivation, decision-making skills, resistance skills) that contribute to a successful life. (Rev: SLJ 4/99; VOYA 8/99) [305.23]

11865 Blatt, Jessica. *The Teen Girl's Gotta-Have-It Guide to Boys: From Getting Them to Getting Over Them* (6–10). Illus. by Cynthia Frenette. 2007, Watson-Guptill paper $8.95 (978-0-8230-1725-6). Complete with self-quizzes, this is an entertaining, well-written guide for girls about dating and relationships. (Rev: SLJ 7/07)

11866 Blatt, Jessica. *The Teen Girl's Gotta-Have-It Guide to Embarrassing Moments: How to Survive Life's Cringe-Worthy Situations!* (6–10). Illus. by Cynthia Frenette. 2007, Watson-Guptill paper $8.95 (978-0-8230-1724-9). This is a lighthearted book that teaches girls how to overcome embarrassing situations with grace and humor. (Rev: SLJ 7/07)

11867 Bolden, Tonya, ed. *33 Things Every Girl Should Know: Stories, Songs, Poems and Smart Talk by 33 Extraordinary Women* (6–12). 1998, Crown paper $13.00 (978-0-517-70936-8). A collection of highly readable pieces by well-known and successful women on the difficult transition from childhood to adulthood. (Rev: BL 5/15/98; HBG 9/98; SLJ 5/98) [810.8092827]

11868 Bridgers, Jay. *Everything You Need to Know About Having an Addictive Personality* (7–12). Series: Need to Know Library. 1998, Rosen LB $27.95 (978-0-8239-2777-7). The author examines the social, psychological, and biochemical aspects of an "addictive personality," explains why some people are more susceptible to addiction than others, and offers sound advice on how teens can cope with addiction. (Rev: SLJ 1/99) [157]

11869 Brown, Bobbi, and Annemarie Iverson. *Bobbi Brown Teenage Beauty: Everything You Need to Look Pretty, Natural, Sexy and Awesome* (8–12). 2000, Cliff St. $25.00 (978-0-06-019636-3). As well as supplying beauty tips, this book stresses the importance of diet and exercise. (Rev: SLJ 12/00) [646.7]

11870 Camron, Roxanne. *60 Clues About Guys: A Guide to Feelings, Flirting, and Falling in Like* (6–10). Illus. by Ariane Elsammak. Series: 60 Clues About. 2002, Lunchbox paper $8.95 (978-0-9678285-5-8). For girls, this is a how-to manual for coping with relationships with the opposite sex, with a personal dating diary at the end. (Rev: SLJ 7/02)

11871 Canfield, Jack, et al., eds. *Chicken Soup for the Christian Teenage Soul: Stories of Faith, Love, Inspiration and Hope* (6–12). 2003, Health Communications paper $14.95 (978-0-7573-0095-0). Stories, poems, and cartoons of particular relevance to teens are grouped in thematic chapters. (Rev: BL 10/1/03) [242]

11872 Canfield, Jack, and Mark Victor Hansen, comps. *Chicken Soup for the Teenage Soul — The Real Deal: School: Cliques, Classes, Clubs and More* (7–12). Series: Chicken Soup for the Soul. 2005, Health Communications paper $14.95 (978-0-7573-0255-8). Written for teenagers by teenagers, this collection of essays addresses many problems that confront high school students today. (Rev: SLJ 11/05) [158]

11873 Carlson, Dale B., and Hannah Carlson. *Girls Are Equal Too: How to Survive — For Teenage Girls* (6–9). Illus. 1998, Bick paper $14.95 (978-1-884158-18-6). This work tells girls that it is okay to be smart, successful, a leader, and feel good. (Rev: VOYA 10/98) [305.23]

11874 Chopra, Deepak. *Fire in the Heart: A Spiritual Guide for Teens* (8–12). 2004, Simon & Schuster $14.95 (978-0-689-86216-8). In this book of spiritual advice for teens, the author uses the device of having a wise old man named Baba give self-help information. (Rev: BL 5/15/04; SLJ 8/04) [204]

11875 Chopra, Deepak. *Teens Ask Deepak: All the Right Questions* (7–10). 2006, Simon & Schuster $12.95 (978-0-689-86218-2). The popular spiritual guru turns his attention to teenage concerns — friendship, success, health, religion, and so forth. (Rev: BL 1/1–15/06; SLJ 1/06) [616]

11876 Choron, Sandra, and Harry Choron. *The Book of Lists for Teens* (7–12). 2002, Houghton paper $13.95 (978-0-618-17907-7). More than 300 lists cover a wide range of topics of interest to teens, such as music videos, sports, eating disorders, substance abuse, and bullying. (Rev: SLJ 1/03; VOYA 4/03) [031.02]

11877 Cohen-Posey, Kate. *How to Handle Bullies, Teasers and Other Meanies: A Book That Takes the Nuisance out of Name Calling and Other Nonsense* (4–7). 1995, Rainbow paper $8.95 (978-1-56825-029-8). A practical book that offers useful suggestions on how to handle bullies. (Rev: BCCB 12/95; BL 11/15/95) [646.7]

11878 Cordes, Helen. *Girl Power in the Classroom: A Book About Girls, Their Fears, and Their Future* (5–8). Illus. 2000, Lerner LB $30.35 (978-0-8225-2693-3). This book of personal guidance for girls describes how to conquer fears and cope with difficult situations at school. (Rev: BL 5/15/00; HBG 10/00; SLJ 5/00) [373.1822]

11879 Cordes, Helen. *Girl Power in the Mirror: A Book About Girls, Their Bodies, and Themselves* (5–8). Illus. 2000, Lerner LB $30.35 (978-0-8225-2691-9). This book for girls explains proper attitudes about appearance and gives coping strategies concerning pressures about one's looks. (Rev: BL 5/15/00; HBG 10/00; SLJ 5/00) [306.4]

11880 Corriveau, Danielle, ed. *Trail Mix: Stories of Youth Overcoming Adversity* (7–12). Illus. 2001, Corvo Communications $14.95 (978-0-9702366-0-9). Fourteen teens tell inspiring first-person stories about hard times and the value of spending time in an outdoor program. (Rev: BL 12/1/01; SLJ 1/02) [158.1]

11881 Covey, Sean. *The 6 Most Important Decisions You'll Ever Make: A Guide for Teens* (8–12). 2006, Fireside paper $15.95 (978-0-7432-6504-1). Advice on education, friendship, family, dating and sex, avoiding addiction, and nurturing healthy self-esteem is presented in lively text with lots of graphics, charts, cartoons, and so forth. (Rev: SLJ 2/07)

11882 Crist, James J. *What to Do When You're Scared and Worried: A Guide for Kids* (5–8). Illus. by Michael Chesworth. 2004, Free Spirit paper $9.99 (978-1-57542-153-7). Reassuring words and sound advice for young people troubled by such diverse issues as school exams, bullies, terrorism, nightmares, monsters, and the dark. (Rev: SLJ 7/04) [152.4]

11883 Daldry, Jeremy. *The Teenage Guy's Survival Guide: The Real Deal on Girls, Growing Up, and Other Guy Stuff* (6–9). 1999, Little, Brown paper $8.99 (978-0-316-17824-2). From pimples to pornography, this guide book for boys is humorous, frank, and truthful about such subjects as dating, masturbation, drugs, mood swings, and homosexuality. (Rev: BL 5/15/99; SLJ 7/99; VOYA 10/99) [305.235]

11884 Dee, Catherine, ed. *The Girls' Book of Wisdom: Empowering, Inspirational Quotes from Over 400 Fabulous Females* (5–8). Illus. by Lou M. Pollack. 1999, Little, Brown paper $8.95 (978-0-316-17956-0). A collection of quotations from more than 400 famous women grouped by such subjects as "Friends," "Happiness," and "Leadership." (Rev: SLJ 12/99; VOYA 4/00) [305.23]

11885 Dentemaro, Christine, and Rachel Kranz. *Straight Talk About Student Life* (6–10). Series: Straight Talk. 1993, Facts on File $27.45 (978-0-8160-2735-4). This book explores problems that students are likely to experience, including communication with teachers and other students, parental pressures, homework, and developing a healthy social life. (Rev: BL 9/1/93) [373.18]

11886 Desetta, Al. *The Courage to Be Yourself: True Stories by Teens About Cliques, Conflicts, and Overcoming Peer Pressure* (8–11). 2005, Free Spirit paper $13.99 (978-1-57542-185-8). Teens from a wide variety of backgrounds offer personal accounts of how they overcame adversities such as bullying, cliques, prejudice, and peer pressure. (Rev: BL 2/1/06; SLJ 6/06; VOYA 4/06) [305.235]

11887 Devillers, Julia. *GirlWise: How to Be Confident, Capable, Cool, and in Control* (8–12). 2002, Prima paper $12.95 (978-0-7615-6363-1). Topics covered in this accessible volume of advice from experts range from fashion and diet to car repair and doing laundry. (Rev: SLJ 12/02) [646.7]

11888 Drew, Naomi. *The Kids' Guide to Working Out Conflicts: How to Keep Cool, Stay Safe, and Get Along* (6–10). Illus. by Chris Sharp. 2004, Free Spirit paper $13.95 (978-1-57542-150-6). Misunderstandings, teasing, bullying, and sexual harassment are all discussed in this guide that includes scenarios and offers strategies for improving self-

control plus many quotations from middle school students. (Rev: SLJ 9/04) [303.6]

11889 Drill, Esther, et al. *Deal with It! A Whole New Approach to Your Body, Brain and Life as a Gurl* (8–12). Illus. 1999, Pocket paper $15.00 (978-0-671-04157-1). Much of the flavor of the popular Gurl.com site is duplicated in this eye-catching book full of frank information about sex, adolescent development and behavior, and succeeding in life. (Rev: BL 10/1/99) [305.235]

11890 Erlbach, Arlene. *The Middle School Survival Guide* (5–7). Illus. by Helen Flook. 2003, Walker $16.95 (978-0-8027-8852-8); paper $8.95 (978-0-8027-7657-0). The author offers tips on a wide variety of topics of interest to this age group (homework, drugs, sex, and so forth), interspersed with advice from students themselves. (Rev: BL 9/15/03; SLJ 9/03) [373.18]

11891 Espeland, Pamela. *Life Lists for Teens: Tips, Steps, Hints, and How-tos for Growing Up, Getting Along, Learning, and Having Fun* (8–12). 2003, Free Spirit paper $11.95 (978-1-57542-125-4). Lists of suggestions, tips, and resources cover all topics of interest to teens — health, school, homework, safety, bullying, pregnancy, abuse, and so forth. (Rev: LMC 11–12/03; SLJ 5/03; VOYA 6/03) [646.7]

11892 Ford, Amanda. *Be True to Yourself: A Daily Guide for Teenage Girls* (6–12). 2001, Conari paper $17.95 (978-1-57324-189-2). Drawing on her own experiences, Amanda Ford offers daily inspirational nuggets of wisdom for girls making the difficult passage to womanhood. (Rev: VOYA 6/01) [158.1]

11893 Fox, Annie. *Can You Relate? Real-World Advice for Teens on Guys, Girls, Growing Up, and Getting Along* (6–12). 2000, Free Spirit paper $15.95 (978-1-57542-066-0). This guidance book tells teens how to form relationships with family, peers, and girl or boy friends, with material on how to understand oneself. (Rev: BL 4/15/00; SLJ 7/00) [305.235]

11894 Goldstein, Mark A., and Myrna Chandler Goldstein. *Boys to Men: Staying Healthy Through the Teen Years* (7–12). 2000, Greenwood $59.95 (978-0-313-30966-3). This book is divided into three age groups between 12 and 21, and for each there are descriptions of changes that occur and how to adjust to them. (Rev: SLJ 6/01; VOYA 4/01) [613]

11895 Greenberg, Judith E. *A Girl's Guide to Growing Up: Making the Right Choices* (5–8). Illus. 2000, Watts LB $24.00 (978-0-531-11592-3). Lots of personal stories are quoted in this guidance book for preteen and teenage girls dealing with such subjects as school, risky behaviors, dating, sex, self-esteem, eating disorders, and cliques. (Rev: BL 2/15/01; SLJ 4/01; VOYA 6/01) [305.23]

11896 Harlan, Judith. *Girl Talk: Staying Strong, Feeling Good, Sticking Together* (6–10). Illus. 1977, Walker paper $8.95 (978-0-8027-7524-5). A breezy, lighthearted guide to approaching everyday problems faced by adolescent girls, with practical tips on how to solve them. (Rev: BL 12/1/97; VOYA 2/98) [305.23]

11897 Harris-Johnson, Debrah. *The African-American Teenagers' Guide to Personal Growth, Health, Safety, Sex and Survival: Living and Learning in the 21st Century* (6–12). 2000, Amber paper $19.95 (978-0-9655064-4-1). This guide for young African Americans growing up in America today covers such topics as family structure, friendships, sexual orientation, work, and spirituality. (Rev: BL 2/15/00; VOYA 6/02) [646.7]

11898 Hartman, Holly, ed. *Girlwonder: Every Girl's Guide to the Fantastic Feats, Cool Qualities, and Remarkable Abilities of Women and Girls* (4–8). Illus. 2003, Houghton paper $9.95 (978-0-618-31939-8). A browsable look at famous women and their accomplishments, interspersed with information and advice on topics ranging from romance to fashion. (Rev: SLJ 5/04) [305.235]

11899 Johnson, Kevin. *Does Anybody Know What Planet My Parents Are From?* (6–9). 1996, Bethany House paper $7.99 (978-1-55661-415-6). Using a religious framework and a breezy style, the author offers young teens advice on how to get along at home and at school. (Rev: BL 10/1/96; VOYA 2/97) [248.8]

11900 Johnston, Andrea. *Girls Speak Out: Finding Your True Self* (6–9). 1997, Scholastic paper $17.95 (978-0-590-89795-2). Based on a self-esteem and consciousness-raising workshop in which young women are encouraged to speak out and express their true feelings. (Rev: SLJ 2/97) [158]

11901 Johnston, Marianne. *Let's Talk About Being Shy* (4–8). Illus. Series: Let's Talk. 1996, Rosen LB $19.95 (978-0-8239-2304-5). The causes and possible cures of shyness are covered in this straightforward discussion. Also use *Let's Talk About Being Afraid* (1996). (Rev: BL 3/15/97) [155.4]

11902 Judson, Karen. *Resolving Conflicts: How to Get Along When You Don't Get Along* (6–12). Series: Issues in Focus Today. 2005, Enslow LB $31.93 (978-0-7660-2359-8). "Dealing with Difficult People" and "Turning Conflict into Collaboration" are two of the chapters in this thorough volume that also covers bullying and gives historical examples of effective conflict resolution. (Rev: SLJ 5/06) [303.6]

11903 Karnes, Frances A., and Suzanne M. Bean. *Girls and Young Women Inventing: Twenty True Stories About Inventors Plus How You Can Be One Yourself* (6–8). 1995, Free Spirit paper $12.95 (978-0-915793-89-1). The story of Jennifer Donabar and her invention of the electric clock is just one of the examples given in this survey of 20 young female inventors and their ingenuity, perseverance, imagination, and hard work. (Rev: BL 2/1/96; SLJ 12/95; VOYA 2/96) [920]

11904 Kaywell, Joan F., ed. *Dear Author: Letters of Hope* (8–11). 2007, Philomel $14.99 (978-0-399-23705-8). A collection of letters to YA authors from teens, many with serious problems. Readers with problems of their own will find reassurance and some good advice. (Rev: BCCB 6/07; BL 2/15/07; SLJ 5/07) [028.5]

11905 Keltner, Nancy, ed. *If You Print This, Please Don't Use My Name* (7–12). Illus. 1992, Terra Nova paper $8.95 (978-0-944176-03-0). Letters from a California advice column for teens on topics ranging from sexuality to school. (Rev: BL 1/1/92; SLJ 7/92) [305.23]

11906 King, Bart. *The Big Book of Girl Stuff* (4–8). Illus. by Jennifer Kalis. 2006, Gibbs Smith paper $19.99 (978-1-58685-819-3). A lighthearted, lightly organized guide to a great many topics of interest to growing girls, including why boys smell bad, etiquette, dieting, how to shop, and how to get a boy's attention. (Rev: SLJ 1/07) [646.7]

11907 Kirberger, Kimberly, ed. *No Body's Perfect: Stories by Teens About Body Image, Self-Acceptance, and the Search for Identity* (7–12). 2003, Scholastic paper $12.95 (978-0-439-42638-1). Mostly written by girls, these stories are intended to help teens grapple with problems of identity and image. (Rev: SLJ 6/03; VOYA 4/03)

11908 Kirberger, Kimberly. *On Relationships: A Book for Teenagers* (7–12). Series: Teen Love. 1999, Health Communications paper $14.95 (978-1-55874-734-0). Letters, stories, and poems tackle problems that arise in romantic relationships. (Rev: BL 10/15/99; SLJ 1/00) [306.7]

11909 Kirberger, Kimberly, and Colin Mortensen. *On Friendship: A Book for Teenagers* (6–10). Series: Teen Love. 2000, Health Communications paper $12.95 (978-1-55874-815-6). This comforting overview of the meaning of friendship features writings by teenagers. (Rev: BL 1/1–15/01; SLJ 4/01) [302.3]

11910 Kreiner, Anna. *Creating Your Own Support System* (7–10). Series: Need to Know Library. 1996, Rosen LB $27.95 (978-0-8239-2215-4). An easy-to-read account that teaches how to create a support system of friends, neighbors, relatives, clergy members, and teachers, if support is not available at home. (Rev: SLJ 1/97) [305.23]

11911 Landau, Elaine. *Interracial Dating and Marriage* (7–12). 1993, Messner LB $13.98 (978-0-671-75258-3). Narratives by 10 young adults and five adults relate experiences with and reactions to interracial relationships. (Rev: BL 11/1/93) [306.73]

11912 Lewis, Barbara A. *What Do You Stand For? A Kid's Guide to Building Character* (6–9). 1997, Free Spirit paper $19.95 (978-1-57542-029-5). This book explores the topic of character building through self-assessment, recommended readings, and activities that explore one's attitudes and reactions to real-life situations. (Rev: SLJ 1/00; VOYA 8/98) [305.23]

11913 Lindsay, Jeanne W. *Caring, Commitment and Change: How to Build a Relationship That Lasts* (7–12). Series: Teenage Couples. 1995, Morning Glory $15.95 (978-0-930934-92-7). A look at the personal issues involved in marriage. (Rev: BL 4/15/95; SLJ 3/95) [646.7]

11914 Lound, Karen. *Girl Power in the Family: A Book About Girls, Their Rights, and Their Voice* (5–10). Series: Girl Power. 2000, Lerner LB $30.35 (978-0-8225-2692-6). A book that explores the problems of growing up female today with material on gender roles, biases, and relationships. (Rev: HBG 10/00; SLJ 6/00) [303.6]

11915 McCune, Bunny, and Deb Traunstein. *Girls to Women: Sharing Our Stories* (7–10). Illus. 1998, Celestial Arts paper $14.95 (978-0-89087-881-1). Arranged under thematic chapters that deal with self-esteem, friendships, menstruation, sexuality, and mother–daughter relations, this collection of essays, stories, and poems explores various aspects of being young and female. (Rev: SLJ 4/99) [305.23]

11916 McIntyre, Tom. *The Behavior Survival Guide for Kids: How to Make Good Choices and Stay out of Trouble* (4–7). Illus. by Chris Sharp. 2003, Free Spirit paper $14.95 (978-1-57542-132-2). This accessible guide offers concrete suggestions for dealing with behavior disorders and improving relations with teachers, family members, and friends. (Rev: SLJ 1/04) [649]

11917 Moehn, Heather. *Everything You Need to Know About Cliques* (5–8). Series: Need to Know Library. 2001, Rosen LB $27.95 (978-0-8239-3326-6). Moehn uses first-person narratives to introduce such topics as making friends, peer pressure, bullies, insecurity, and popularity, with a look at how cliques continue after high school. (Rev: SLJ 12/01) [158.25]

11918 Morgenstern, Julie, and Jessi Morgenstern-Colon. *Organizing from the Inside Out for Teens: The Foolproof System for Organizing Your Room, Your Time, and Your Life* (7–12). Illus. 2002, Holt paper $15.00 (978-0-8050-6470-4). Strategies for managing the time, space, and responsibilities of typical teens are presented in this practical manual. (Rev: BL 1/1–15/03) [646.7]

11919 Morgenstern, Mindy. *The Real Rules for Girls* (8–12). Illus. 2000, Girl Pr. $14.95 (978-0-9659754-5-2). Advice on life, love, friends, and more is pre-

sented in an attractive, conversational way. (Rev: SLJ 3/00; VOYA 4/00)

11920 Musgrave, Susan, ed. *You Be Me: Friendship in the Lives of Teen Girls* (7–12). 2002, Annick $18.95 (978-1-55037-739-2); paper $7.95 (978-1-55037-738-5). Stories of girls' experiences show the sometimes difficult realities of teenage friendships. (Rev: BL 12/15/02; HBG 3/03; SLJ 1/03; VOYA 12/02) [305.235]

11921 Noel, Carol. *Get It? Got It? Good! A Guide for Teenagers* (7–12). Illus. 1996, Serious Business paper $7.95 (978-0-9649479-0-0). A teen self-help guide that discusses such topics as self-esteem, sex, health, relations with others, goals, and violence. (Rev: BL 6/1–15/96) [361.8]

11922 Nuwer, Hank. *High School Hazing: When Rites Become Wrongs* (8–12). Illus. 2000, Watts LB $24.00 (978-0-531-11682-1). After a discussion on the rationale behind hazing rituals, this account describes many that have resulted in unnecessary humiliation, physical harm, and even death. (Rev: BL 4/1/00) [373.18]

11923 Packard, Gwen K. *Coping When a Parent Goes Back to Work* (8–12). Series: Coping. 1995, Rosen LB $31.95 (978-0-8239-1698-6). Gives children whose parents return to work tips on adapting to the new situation. Includes real-life examples. (Rev: BL 7/95) [306.874]

11924 Parker, Julie. *High Performance Through Leadership* (8–12). Series: Learning-a-Living Library. 1996, Rosen LB $16.95 (978-0-8239-2205-5). This book discusses the ability to lead and teach others and shows students how they can take the initiative in problem solving and decision making. (Rev: BL 9/15/96; SLJ 12/96) [158]

11925 Paul, Anthea. *Girlosophy: A Soul Survivor Kit* (6–12). Series: Girlosophy. 2001, Allen & Unwin paper $16.95 (978-1-86508-432-9). This appealing guide aims to help teenage girls achieve their full potential by taking charge of their own destinies. (Rev: SLJ 11/01; VOYA 6/02)

11926 Peacock, Carol Antoinette. *Death and Dying* (4–8). Illus. Series: Life Balance. 2004, Watts LB $20.50 (978-0-531-12370-6); paper $6.95 (978-0-531-16728-1). A practical guide to dealing with death and dying, with advice on seeking help when necessary. (Rev: BL 10/15/03)

11927 Piquemal, Michel, and Melissa Daly. *When Life Stinks: How to Deal with Your Bad Moods, Blues, and Depression* (6–10). Illus. by Olivier Tossan. Series: Sunscreen. 2004, Abrams paper $9.95 (978-0-8109-4932-4). Sensible advice for adolescents suffering from normal anxieties and frustrations and for those who need to recognize that their problems are more deep-seated and professional help is necessary. (Rev: SLJ 4/05) [616.85]

11928 Rimm, Sylvia. *See Jane Win for Girls: A Smart Girl's Guide to Success* (5–9). Illus. 2003, Free Spirit paper $13.95 (978-1-57542-122-3). Rimm offers practical advice on social and academic achievement and general life skills, with quizzes, activities, and success stories. (Rev: LMC 10/03; SLJ 6/03) [305.235]

11929 Robinson, Sharon. *Jackie's Nine: Jackie Robinson's Values to Live By* (5–8). Illus. 2001, Scholastic paper $15.95 (978-0-439-23764-2). A collection of inspirational writings, selected by baseball legend Jackie Robinson's daughter and organized under headings including "Courage" and "Determination," that include material by and about such well-known individuals as Christopher Reeve and Oprah Winfrey. (Rev: BL 7/01; HBG 10/01; SLJ 6/01; VOYA 8/01) [158]

11930 Rutledge, Jill Zimmerman. *Dealing with the Stuff That Makes Life Tough: The 10 Things That Stress Girls Out and How to Cope with Them* (8–10). 2003, Contemporary paper $15.95 (978-0-07-142326-7). Body image, boys, homosexuality, smoking and drinking, divorce — these and other sources of stress are addressed with sensible advice and helpful anecdotes. (Rev: SLJ 1/04)

11931 Santamaria, Peggy. *High Performance Through Self-Management* (8–12). Series: Learning-a-Living Library. 1996, Rosen LB $26.50 (978-0-8239-2208-6). This volume shows students how to work with others and teaches them to identify, discuss, and resolve problems as a group. (Rev: BL 9/15/96; SLJ 8/96) [640]

11932 Schleifer, Jay. *The Dangers of Hazing* (7–12). Series: Need to Know Library. 1996, Rosen LB $25.25 (978-0-8239-2217-8). The phenomenon of hazing in high schools and colleges is discussed, with material on how to avoid it, its dangers, and how to report incidents. (Rev: SLJ 1/97) [305.23]

11933 Schneider, Meg. *Popularity Has Its Ups and Downs* (6–8). 1992, Messner paper $5.95 (978-0-671-72849-6). Common-sense information is presented about popularity and why it may not be what it seems, along with a discussion of self-confidence and friendship. (Rev: BL 11/15/92) [158]

11934 Schwager, Tina, and Michele Schuerger. *Gutsy Girls: Young Women Who Dare* (7–12). Illus. 1999, Free Spirit paper $15.95 (978-1-57542-059-2). The first part of this book profiles 25 "gutsy" individuals who have tackled a variety of challenges; the second part suggests ways to motivate yourself to achieve more. (Rev: SLJ 11/99; VOYA 2/00) [155.5]

11935 Schwager, Tina, and Michele Schuerger. *The Right Moves: A Girl's Guide to Getting Fit and Feeling Good* (6–12). 1998, Free Spirit paper $15.95 (978-1-57542-035-6). Topics including self-esteem, diet, and exercise are covered in this upbeat

guide for girls that promotes a positive, healthy lifestyle. (Rev: BL 1/1–15/99; SLJ 1/99*; VOYA 8/99) [613.7]

11936 Taylor, Julie. *The Girls' Guide to Friends* (7–12). 2002, Three Rivers paper $12.00 (978-0-609-80857-3). A lighthearted look at getting and keeping friends, with quizzes and other entertaining features. (Rev: BL 12/15/02) [158.2]

11937 Tym, Kate, and Penny Worms. *Coping with Your Emotions: A Guide to Taking Control of Your Life* (6–10). Illus. Series: Get Real. 2004, Raintree LB $29.93 (978-1-4109-0575-8). The magazine-style layout, case studies, quizzes, photos, and advice will draw teens to this discussion of issues including depression, peer pressure, love interests, schoolwork, and teacher conflicts. Also use *School Survival: A Guide to Taking Control of Your Life* (2004). (Rev: SLJ 3/05) [646]

11938 Wesson, Carolyn McLenahan. *Teen Troubles* (7–12). 1988, Walker $17.95 (978-0-8027-1011-6); paper $11.95 (978-0-8027-7310-4). A candid, sometimes humorous self-help book on teenage problems and how to face them. (Rev: VOYA 12/88) [155.5]

11939 Weston, Carol. *For Girls Only: Wise Words, Good Advice* (6–9). 2004, HarperCollins paper $8.99 (978-0-06-058318-7). An update of the earlier edition, adding quotations from contemporary celebrities to the mix that ranges from Aesop and Socrates to Oprah Winfrey and Madonna. (Rev: BL 11/1/04) [305.23]

11940 White, Lee, and Mary Ditson. *The Teenage Human Body Operator's Manual* (6–10). Illus. 1999, Northwest Media paper $9.95 (978-1-892194-01-5). Using an appealing layout and cartoon illustrations, this is an overview of teenagers' physical and psychological needs, touching on hygiene, nutrition, disease, pregnancy and birth control, and mental health. (Rev: SLJ 11/98) [305.23]

11941 Williams, Venus, and Serena Williams. *Venus and Serena: Serving from the Hip* (5–8). Illus. 2005, Houghton paper $14.00 (978-0-618-57653-1). The successful Williams sisters offer practical advice on self-respect, friendship, financial security, and other pertinent topics. (Rev: BL 5/15/05; SLJ 4/05) [796.342]

11942 Winkler, Kathleen. *Bullying: How to Deal with Taunting, Teasing, and Tormenting* (6–10). Series: Issues in Focus Today. 2005, Enslow $31.93 (978-0-7660-2355-0). Including a chapter on girls who bully, this is an accessible look at the problem that draws on discussions with both teens and professionals. (Rev: SLJ 12/05)

11943 Wirths, Claudine G., and Mary Bowman-Kruhm. *Coping with Confrontations and Encounters with the Police* (7–12). Series: Coping. 1997, Rosen LB $31.95 (978-0-8239-2431-8). This book gives teens essential and realistic information that will help them deal successfully with police encounters and minimize potential risks. (Rev: SLJ 4/98; VOYA 2/98) [364.3]

11944 Wolfelt, Alan D. *Healing Your Grieving Heart for Teens: 100 Practical Ideas* (6–12). 2001, Companion paper $11.95 (978-1-879651-23-4). The author, a teacher and grief counselor, offers 100 practical tips on accepting and dealing with grief and provides tasks that will help teens identify their needs. (Rev: BL 3/15/01; SLJ 9/01; VOYA 8/01)

11945 *Yikes! A Smart Girl's Guide to Surviving Tricky, Sticky, Icky Situations* (4–8). Illus. by Bonnie Timmons. Series: American Girl Library. 2002, Pleasant paper $8.95 (978-1-58485-530-9). Advice on everything from dealing with teachers and friends to coping with embarrassing situations and dangerous incidents. (Rev: SLJ 12/02) [305.23]

11946 Youngs, Bettie B., and Jennifer Leigh Youngs, eds. *More Taste Berries for Teens: A Second Collection of Inspirational Short Stories Encouragement on Life, Love, Friendship and Tough Issues* (6–12). Series: Taste Berries for Teens. 2000, Health Communications paper $12.95 (978-1-55874-813-2). Written almost exclusively by teens, the inspiring stories and essays in this collection touch on such varied issues of teen concern as love and relationships, family relations, friendship, deciding on a career, and getting into college. (Rev: VOYA 2/01)

11947 Zimmerman, Bill. *100 Things Guys Need to Know* (5–9). 2005, Free Spirit paper $13.95 (978-1-57542-167-4). Effective graphic design will draw teenage boys into this self-help guide that touches on a wide variety of topics, including body image, dating, school, friendship, and family. (Rev: SLJ 11/05) [305.235]

Social Groups

Family and Family Problems

11948 Alpern, Michele. *Let's Talk: Sharing Our Thoughts and Feelings During Times of Crisis* (6–12). Series: Focus on Family Matters. 2003, Chelsea $25.00 (978-0-7910-6954-7). This account examines reactions that accompany times of crisis, such as anxiety and depression, and shows how teens can share their feelings with parents and friends. (Rev: BL 10/15/02) [306.9]

11949 Armitage, Ronda. *Family Violence* (6–10). Series: Talking Points. 1999, Raintree LB $27.12 (978-0-7398-1371-3). This brief but balanced account explores family violence, its causes, types, and effects. (Rev: BL 12/15/99; HBG 9/00) [362.82]

11950 Bingham, Jane. *Why Do Families Break Up?* (4–8). Series: Exploring Tough Issues. 2004, Rain-

tree LB $29.93 (978-0-7398-6683-2). Every member of the family is considered in this comprehensive examination of divorce and how individuals of different ages cope. (Rev: SLJ 2/05) [306.8]

11951 Block, Joel D., and Susan S. Bartell. *Stepliving for Teens: Getting Along with Stepparents, Parents, and Siblings* (7–12). Series: Plugged In. 2001, Price Stern Sloan paper $4.99 (978-0-8431-7568-4). This helpful and practical guide to coping with new family members, written by two psychologists, includes advice on communicating effectively. (Rev: BCCB 7–8/01; SLJ 8/01) [306.8]

11952 Blue, Rose. *Staying Out of Trouble in a Troubled Family* (7–10). 1998, Twenty-First Century LB $24.90 (978-0-7613-0365-7). Using eight case studies, this book features family problems that will be familiar to teens, analyses by professionals, and avenues for help. (Rev: BL 2/1/99; HBG 3/99; SLJ 6/99) [362.7]

11953 Brondino, Jeanne, et al. *Raising Each Other* (7–12). Illus. 1988, Hunter House paper $8.95 (978-0-89793-044-4). This book, written and illustrated by a high school class, is about parent–teen relationships, problems, and solutions. (Rev: SLJ 1/89; VOYA 4/89) [306.1]

11954 Charlish, Anne. *Divorce* (5–10). Series: Talking Points. 1999, Raintree LB $27.12 (978-0-8172-5310-3). An overview of the causes of divorce, the legal aspects, and the difficult adjustments that must be made. (Rev: BL 8/99) [306.89]

11955 Cooper, Kay. *Where Did You Get Those Eyes? A Guide to Discovering Your Family History* (5–7). Illus. by Anthony Accardo. 1988, Walker LB $14.85 (978-0-8027-6803-2). A helpful guide for researching the family tree. (Rev: BCCB 11/88; BL 1/15/89; SLJ 2/89)

11956 Currie, Stephen. *Adoption* (5–8). Illus. Series: Overview. 1997, Lucent LB $29.95 (978-1-56006-183-0). A well-illustrated account of the history of adoption and present-day practices, procedures, and problems. (Rev: BL 5/15/97; SLJ 4/97) [362.7]

11957 Dudevszky, Szabinka. *Close-Up* (6–8). Trans. by Wanda Boeke. 1999, Front St. $15.95 (978-1-886910-40-9). The stories of 15 teens from the Netherlands who left their homes and lived in foster homes, reform schools, alone, or with friends. (Rev: HBG 4/00; SLJ 9/99; VOYA 12/99) [306]

11958 Flaming, Allen, and Kate Scowen, eds. *My Crazy Life: How I Survived My Family* (8–12). 2002, Annick paper $9.95 (978-1-55037-732-3). Ten teen narratives describe how each managed to deal with family problems such as abuse, addiction, AIDS, divorce, and homosexuality. (Rev: BL 9/1/02; HBG 10/02; SLJ 7/02) [306.87]

11959 Ford, Judy, and Amanda Ford. *Between Mother and Daughter: A Teenager and Her Mom Share* *the Secrets of a Strong Relationship* (6–12). 1999, Conari paper $14.95 (978-1-57324-164-9). Alternate chapters written by mother and daughter reveal the power of communication. (Rev: BL 8/99; VOYA 2/00) [306.874]

11960 Gardner, Richard. *The Boys and Girls Book About Stepfamilies* (6–9). 1985, Creative Therapeutics paper $6.50 (978-0-933812-13-0). Written from a youngster's view, this is a frank discussion of the problems that can exist in stepfamilies. [306.8]

11961 Gardner, Richard A. *Boys and Girls Book About Divorce* (5–8). Illus. 1992, Bantam paper $6.99 (978-0-553-27619-0). A self-help book written for adolescents trying to cope with parental marriage problems. [306.8]

11962 Gellman, Marc. *"Always Wear Clean Underwear!" and Other Ways Parents Say "I Love You"* (4–7). 1997, Morrow $14.95 (978-0-688-14492-0). Some kids think that the expressions featured in this book are parental nagging, but the message really is that parents care. (Rev: BL 10/1/97; HBG 3/98; SLJ 11/97) [306.874]

11963 Gerdes, Louise, ed. *Battered Women* (7–12). Series: Contemporary Issues Companion. 1998, Greenhaven LB $32.45 (978-1-56510-897-4). Personal narratives of battered women are used in this anthology that investigates patterns of domestic violence and examines legal and other measures that can be used to protect women. (Rev: BL 3/15/99) [362.82]

11964 Goldentyer, Debra. *Child Abuse* (4–8). Series: Preteen Pressures. 1998, Raintree LB $25.69 (978-0-8172-5032-4). This work describes the types, causes, and effects of child abuse and supplies material on how to change an abusive situation. (Rev: BL 5/15/98; HBG 10/98) [362.7]

11965 Goldentyer, Debra. *Divorce* (4–8). Series: Preteen Pressures. 1998, Raintree LB $25.69 (978-0-8172-5030-0). This work discusses the reasons for divorce, the legal aspects, the effect on children, remarriage, and relationships with new family members. (Rev: BL 5/15/98; HBG 10/98; SLJ 6/98) [306.8]

11966 Gravelle, Karen, and Susan Fischer. *Where Are My Birth Parents? A Guide for Teenage Adoptees* (7–12). 1993, Walker LB $15.85 (978-0-8027-8258-8). Includes firsthand experiences of young people who searched for their birth families with varied success. (Rev: BL 9/1/93; SLJ 7/93; VOYA 10/93) [362.7]

11967 Greenberg, Keith E. *Family Abuse: Why Do People Hurt Each Other?* (6–9). Illus. Series: Issues of Our Time. 1994, Twenty-First Century LB $22.90 (978-0-8050-3183-6). The causes and forms of family violence and abuse are traced, with coverage of their effects and how they can be prevented

or contained. (Rev: BL 6/1–15/94; SLJ 9/94) [362.82]

11968 Greenberg, Keith E. *Runaways* (6–10). 1995, Lerner LB $19.93 (978-0-8225-2557-8). Greenberg uses the personal approach, focusing on the lives of two runaways, to dispel the idea that runaways are "bad" kids. (Rev: BL 10/15/95; SLJ 12/95) [362.7]

11969 Greenberg, Keith E. *Zack's Story: Growing Up with Same-Sex Parents* (5–7). Illus. Series: Meeting the Challenge. 1996, Lerner LB $21.27 (978-0-8225-2581-3). A true account of 11-year-old Zack, who is growing up with his lesbian mother and her lover, whom he has grown to regard as a second mother. (Rev: BL 10/15/96; SLJ 3/97) [306]

11970 Harnack, Andrew. *Adoption* (7–12). Series: Opposing Viewpoints. 1995, Greenhaven paper $21.20 (978-1-56510-212-5). Presents various perspectives on the hot-button issues relating to adoption, with provocative articles from well-known advocates. (Rev: BL 10/15/95; VOYA 6/96) [362.7]

11971 Haugen, David M., and Matthew J. Box, eds. *Adoption* (8–12). Series: Social Issues Firsthand. 2005, Gale LB $29.95 (978-0-7377-2881-1). Personal accounts from adoptees, birth parents, and adoptive parents give moving perspectives on the process of adoption; gay parents, transracial adoptions, custody battles, and the search for adoptees and birth parents are all covered. (Rev: SLJ 2/06) [362.7]

11972 Hong, Maria. *Family Abuse: A National Epidemic* (8–12). Illus. Series: Issues in Focus. 1997, Enslow LB $20.95 (978-0-89490-720-3). This book takes a long, thorough look at this national epidemic that includes spousal and child abuse as well as children terrorizing a family and the abuse of elderly parents. (Rev: BL 12/1/97; SLJ 12/97; VOYA 6/98) [362.82]

11973 Hurley, Jennifer A., ed. *Child Abuse* (8–12). Series: Opposing Viewpoints. 1998, Greenhaven LB $32.45 (978-1-56510-935-3). Questions explored in this anthology of opinions include the causes of child abuse, false accusations, how the legal system should deal with child molesters, and how child abuse can be reduced. (Rev: BL 9/15/98) [362.7]

11974 Hyde, Margaret O. *Know About Abuse* (7–12). Series: Know About. 1992, Walker LB $14.85 (978-0-8027-8177-2). Provides facts on child abuse, reasons, symptoms, examples, and solutions, covering a wide range of abuse, from obvious to subtle. (Rev: BL 11/1/92; SLJ 9/92) [362.7]

11975 Isler, Claudia. *Caught in the Middle: A Teen Guide to Custody* (5–8). Series: The Divorce Resource. 2000, Rosen LB $27.95 (978-0-8239-3109-5). This book about divorce uses many actual case histories to explore such questions as what happens to the children when parents divorce and whether grandparents get visitation rights. (Rev: SLJ 6/00) [306.8]

11976 Kaminker, Laura. *Everything You Need to Know About Being Adopted* (7–12). Series: Need to Know Library. 1999, Rosen $27.95 (978-0-8239-2834-7). As well as the legal aspects of adoption, this account explores the problems young people may face when they are adopted. [362.7]

11977 Kinstlinger-Bruhn, Charlotte. *Everything You Need to Know About Breaking the Cycle of Domestic Violence* (6–10). Series: Need to Know Library. 1997, Rosen LB $25.25 (978-0-8239-2434-9). This book discusses physical, emotional, and sexual abuse, focusing on dating relationships and parental violence against children, and provides information on warning signs of an abusive relationship, how to seek help, and self-protection. (Rev: SLJ 4/98) [364.3]

11978 Koh, Frances M. *Adopted from Asia: How It Feels to Grow Up in America* (5–8). 1993, East-West $16.95 (978-0-9606090-6-2). The author has gathered stories, impressions, and opinions from 11 young people who were born in Korea and adopted by Caucasian Americans. (Rev: BL 2/15/94) [306.874]

11979 Krementz, Jill. *How It Feels to Be Adopted* (5–8). Illus. 1988, Knopf paper $15.00 (978-0-394-75853-4). Interviews with 19 young people, ages 8 to 16, on how it feels to be adopted. [362.7]

11980 Krementz, Jill. *How It Feels When Parents Divorce* (4–8). Illus. 1988, Knopf paper $15.00 (978-0-394-75855-8). Boys and girls, ages 8 to 16, share their experiences with divorced parents. [306.8]

11981 Krohn, Katherine. *Everything You Need to Know About Birth Order* (5–9). Series: Need to Know Library. 2000, Rosen LB $27.95 (978-0-8239-3228-3). An interesting book that looks at a number of theories about how birth order affects people. (Rev: SLJ 12/00) [306.85]

11982 Krohn, Katherine. *You and Your Parents' Divorce* (5–8). Series: Family Matters. 2001, Rosen LB $26.50 (978-0-8239-3354-9). Krohn writes about the practicalities and emotional problems of divorce in a style suitable for reluctant readers. (Rev: SLJ 8/01) [155.44]

11983 Lanchon, Anne. *All About Adoption* (6–9). Illus. by Monika Czarnecki. Series: Sunscreen. 2006, Abrams paper $9.95 (978-0-8109-9227-6). Lanchon offers commonsense advice and reassurance for teens who are adopted. (Rev: BL 4/1/06; SLJ 4/06) [649]

11984 La Valle, John. *Coping When a Parent Is in Jail* (8–12). Series: Coping. 1995, Rosen LB $18.95 (978-0-8239-1967-3). Discusses the effects on a child of having a parent in jail and tries to give an idea of what the parent's life in prison is like. (Rev: BL 7/95) [362.7]

11985 Leibowitz, Julie. *Finding Your Place: A Teen Guide to Life in a Blended Family* (5–8). 2000, Rosen LB $27.95 (978-0-8239-3114-9). This book explores possible problems and solutions for members of blended families. (Rev: SLJ 6/00) [645.7]

11986 Levine, Beth. *Divorce: Young People Caught in the Middle* (7–12). 1995, Enslow LB $20.95 (978-0-89490-633-6). A straightforward, commonsense manual for teens dealing with divorce. (Rev: BL 3/15/95; SLJ 6/95) [306.89]

11987 Libal, Joyce. *A House Between Homes: Youth in the Foster Care System* (6–9). Illus. Series: Youth with Special Needs. 2004, Mason Crest LB $24.95 (978-1-59084-740-4). Fiction and fact are interwoven in this presentation of two children in the foster care system, with information on the history of foster care and the current programs offered. (Rev: SLJ 7/04) [362.73]

11988 Lindsay, Jeanne W. *Coping with Reality: Dealing with Money, In-Laws, Babies and Other Details of Daily Life* (7–12). Series: Teenage Couples. 1995, Morning Glory $15.95 (978-0-930934-87-3); paper $9.95 (978-0-930934-86-6). Counsel on the day-to-day aspects of being a part of a couple. (Rev: BL 4/15/95; SLJ 3/95) [306.81]

11989 MacGregor, Cynthia. *The Divorce Helpbook for Kids* (4–7). 2001, Impact paper $13.95 (978-1-886230-39-2). In this candid, honest book, a divorced mother gives advice to children about how to survive their parent's divorce. (Rev: BL 2/1/02; SLJ 3/02) [306.89]

11990 MacGregor, Cynthia. *Jigsaw Puzzle Family: The Stepkids' Guide to Fitting It Together* (5–8). Series: Rebuilding Books. 2005, Impact paper $12.95 (978-1-886230-63-7). Offers reassuring, practical advice — with an emphasis on talking through problems and seeking solutions — for stepchildren who are having difficulty adjusting to life in a blended family. (Rev: BL 9/1/05; SLJ 10/05) [306.874]

11991 Meyer, Don, ed. *The Sibling Slam Book: What It's Really Like to Have a Brother or Sister with Special Needs* (7–12). 2005, Woodbine paper $15.95 (978-1-890627-52-2). Young people with special-needs siblings share their hopes, joys, fears, frustrations, and triumphs in this slam book. (Rev: SLJ 6/05)

11992 Mufson, Susan, and Rachel Kranz. *Straight Talk About Child Abuse* (7–12). Series: Straight Talk. 1991, Facts on File $27.45 (978-0-8160-2376-9). Beginning with a general discussion of child abuse, this book describes the common signs of physical, emotional, and sexual abuse, gives some case studies, and offers some solutions. (Rev: BL 4/1/91; SLJ 3/91) [362.7]

11993 Packer, Alex J. *Bringing Up Parents: The Teenager's Handbook* (8–12). Illus. 1993, Free Spirit paper $15.95 (978-0-915793-48-8). Discusses in detail the art of coping with parents: building trust, diffusing family power struggles, waging effective verbal battles, developing listening skills, and expressing feelings nonaggressively. (Rev: BL 5/1/93*; VOYA 8/93) [306.874]

11994 Rebman, Renee C. *Runaway Teens: A Hot Issue* (8–12). Series: Hot Issues. 2001, Enslow $27.93 (978-0-7660-1640-8). Why teens leave home is covered in this book, which also offers material on what happens to teens on the street and agencies that give them help. (Rev: HBG 10/01) [362.7]

11995 Rench, Janice E. *Family Violence: How to Recognize and Survive It* (6–8). 1992, Lerner LB $19.93 (978-0-8225-0047-6). This book speaks directly to children, with explanations of what constitutes different kinds of abuse, who is at fault, what motivates abusers, and what to do if violence occurs. (Rev: BL 11/1/92; SLJ 9/92) [362.82]

11996 Rosenberg, Maxine B. *Living with a Single Parent* (4–7). 1992, Macmillan $14.95 (978-0-02-777915-8). In interview format, this topic is presented through the opinions of youngsters from eight to 13. (Rev: BCCB 2/93; BL 11/15/92; SLJ 12/92) [306.85]

11997 Rue, Nancy N. *Coping with an Illiterate Parent* (7–12). Series: Coping. 1990, Rosen LB $31.95 (978-0-8239-1070-0). The causes, problems, and treatment of illiteracy as seen from a teenager's point of view. (Rev: BL 3/1/90; SLJ 10/90) [306]

11998 Ryan, Elizabeth A. *Straight Talk About Parents* (7–12). 1989, Facts on File $27.45 (978-0-8160-1526-9). A self-help manual to help teens sort out their feelings about parents. (Rev: BL 8/89; SLJ 9/89; VOYA 2/90) [306.8]

11999 Sanders, Pete, and Steve Myers. *Divorce and Separation* (4–8). Illus. Series: What Do You Know About. 1997, Millbrook LB $23.90 (978-0-7613-0574-3). An introduction to separation and divorce, with an emphasis on tips to help youngsters adjust and cope. (Rev: SLJ 10/97) [306.8]

12000 Shires-Sneddon, Pamela. *Brothers and Sisters: Born to Bicker?* (6–10). Series: Teen Issues. 1997, Enslow LB $26.60 (978-0-89490-914-6). This book explores a variety of sibling relationships, how social pressures affect them, and the damaging impact of drugs, alcohol, divorce, death, and abuse. (Rev: BL 4/15/97; VOYA 10/97) [306.875]

12001 Shultz, Margaret A. *Teens with Single Parents: Why Me?* (6–12). Series: Teen Issues. 1997, Enslow LB $26.60 (978-0-89490-913-9). Using interviews with teens as a focus, this book examines the problems of living with a single parent and

makes some suggestions for coping strategies. (Rev: BL 7/97; SLJ 10/97) [306.5]

12002 Simpson, Carolyn. *Everything You Need to Know About Living with a Grandparent or Other Relatives* (8–12). 1995, Rosen LB $27.95 (978-0-8239-1872-0). This book explores the various situations that may cause teenagers to move in with grandparents, how to adjust, ways to maintain privacy, and the emotions involved on both sides. (Rev: VOYA 2/96) [306]

12003 Smook, Rachel Gaillard. *Stepfamilies: How a New Family Works* (6–9). Illus. 2001, Enslow LB $22.60 (978-0-7660-1666-8). Teens relate their experiences in becoming part of a new family, and the author shows offers tips on adapting to new family situations. (Rev: BL 1/1–15/02; HBG 7/01) [306.874]

12004 Snow, Judith E. *How It Feels to Have a Gay or Lesbian Parent: A Book by Kids for Kids of All Ages* (5–8). 2004, Haworth $19.95 (978-1-56023-419-7); paper $12.95 (978-1-56023-420-3). Diverse reflections on what it means to have a gay or lesbian parent come from children, young adults, and adults (up to age 31). (Rev: BL 1/1–15/05; SLJ 10/04) [306.874]

12005 Swisher, Karin L., ed. *Single-Parent Families* (8–12). Series: At Issue. 1997, Greenhaven LB $26.20 (978-1-56510-544-7). An anthology that presents different viewpoints about the problems and rewards of being a single parent. (Rev: BL 1/1–15/97; SLJ 7/97) [306.85]

12006 Trueit, Trudi Strain. *Surviving Divorce* (7–10). Illus. Series: Scholastic Choices. 2006, Scholastic LB $22.50 (978-0-531-12368-3). Personal stories add to the facts and quizzes in this book and will reassure readers whose parents are divorcing. (Rev: BL 1/1–15/07) [306.89]

12007 Tym, Kate, and Penny Worms. *Coping with Families: A Guide to Taking Control of Your Life* (5–8). Series: Get Real. 2004, Raintree LB $28.56 (978-1-4109-0574-1). Expert advice and case studies are presented in an appealing format, plus a list of hotline numbers. Also use *Coping with Friends* (2004). (Rev: SLJ 5/05)

12008 Wagner, Heather Lehr. *The Blending of Foster and Adopted Children into the Family* (6–12). Series: Focus on Family Matters. 2002, Chelsea $25.00 (978-0-7910-6694-2). Various family structures and situations are described, with material on how to accept, nurture, and embrace these new family constructs. (Rev: BL 10/15/02; HBG 3/03; SLJ 12/02) [606.8]

12009 Wagner, Heather Lehr. *Understanding and Coping with Divorce* (6–12). Series: Focus on Family Matters. 2002, Chelsea $25.00 (978-0-7910-6691-1). The causes and effects of divorce are discussed, with emphasis on how teens can get through the difficult time when parents divorce. (Rev: BL 10/15/02; HBG 3/03; SLJ 12/02) [306.8]

12010 Weiss, Ann E. *Adoptions Today: Questions and Controversy* (7–12). Illus. 2001, Twenty-First Century LB $24.90 (978-0-7613-1914-6). This comprehensive and informative overview covers such topics as international adoptions, adoption by unconventional couples, open adoption, and privacy. (Rev: BL 12/15/01; HBG 3/02; VOYA 12/01) [362.73]

12011 Williams, Mary E., ed. *Adoption* (7–12). Series: Opposing Viewpoints. 2006, Gale LB $34.95 (978-0-7377-3301-3). Essays present both sides of various topics relating to adoption: gay adoptions, international adoptions, transracial adoptions, protection of identity, and so forth. (Rev: SLJ 11/06)

12012 Williams, Mary E., ed. *The Family* (8–12). Series: Opposing Viewpoints. 1997, Greenhaven paper $21.20 (978-1-56510-668-0). An anthology of articles presenting different points of view on the status of the family, divorce, work-related topics, adoption, and the changing values in society that affect the family structure. (Rev: BL 10/15/97; SLJ 12/97) [306.8]

12013 Wolfman, Ira. *Climbing Your Family Tree: Online and Off-Line Genealogy for Kids*. Rev. ed. (5–9). Illus. by Tim Robinson. 2002, Workman paper $13.95 (978-0-7611-2539-6). A wide-ranging look at genealogy and the ways of tracing family names through document research, interviews, and the World Wide Web. (Rev: SLJ 2/03; VOYA 10/03) [929]

Youth Groups

12014 Moore, David L. *Dark Sky, Dark Land: Stories of the Hmong Boy Scouts of Troop 100* (7–10). Illus. 1989, Tessera paper $14.95 (978-0-9623029-0-9). A collection of stories of hardship and bravery behind Boy Scout Troop 100 in Minneapolis composed of young refugees from war-torn Laos. (Rev: BL 9/15/90) [977.6]

Physical and Applied Sciences

General and Miscellaneous

12015 Aaseng, Nathan. *Yearbooks in Science: 1940–1949* (5–8). Illus. Series: Yearbooks in Science. 1995, Twenty-First Century LB $22.90 (978-0-8050-3434-9). An important decade in scientific discovery is chronicled, with emphasis on the impact of these advances on society. (Rev: BL 1/1–15/96; SLJ 5/96) [609]

12016 Aaseng, Nathan. *Yearbooks in Science: 1930–1939* (5–8). Illus. Series: Yearbooks in Science. 1995, Twenty-First Century LB $22.90 (978-0-8050-3433-2). An overview of the accomplishments in science in the 1930s arranged by such divisions as physics and chemistry. (Rev: BL 12/1/95; SLJ 1/96) [609]

12017 Arnold, Nick. *The Stunning Science of Everything: Science with the Squishy Bits Left In!* (4–8). Illus. by Tony De Saulles. 2006, Scholastic $10.99 (978-0-439-87777-0). This lighthearted look at science, brightly illustrated with cartoons, examines such diverse topics as the Big Bang theory, atoms, insects, humans, dinosaurs, and the universe. (Rev: HBG 4/07; LMC 3/07; SLJ 2/07; VOYA 2/07) [500]

12018 Beres, Samantha. *101 Things Every Kid Should Know About Science* (4–7). Illus. 1998, Lowell House paper $9.95 (978-1-56565-916-2). This information-packed book supplies basic scientific facts organized under headings such as chemistry, physics, biology, and geography. (Rev: BL 10/15/98; SLJ 12/98) [500]

12019 Carlson, Dale. *In and Out of Your Mind: Teen Science: Human Bites* (8–12). Illus. by Carol Nicklaus. 2002, Bick paper $14.95 (978-1-884158-27-8). Teens with a curious, contemplative nature will find food for thought in this look at the wonders of science, humankind, and the universe that touches on topics including evolution, environmental concerns, and medicine. (Rev: SLJ 9/02) [500]

12020 Crump, Donald J., ed. *On the Brink of Tomorrow: Frontiers of Science* (7–9). Illus. 1982, National Geographic $12.95 (978-0-87044-414-2). With many color illustrations, this account covers recent advances in such areas as physics, astronomy, and medicine. [500]

12021 Dolan, Graham. *The Greenwich Guide to Time and the Millennium* (4–7). Illus. by Jeff Edwards. 1999, Heinemann $16.95 (978-1-57572-802-5). Covers such subjects as time zones, calendars, centuries, and longitude. (Rev: SLJ 9/99) [529]

12022 Fradin, Dennis Brindell. *With a Little Luck: Surprising Stories of Amazing Discovery* (6–9). Illus. 2006, Dutton $17.99 (978-0-525-47196-7). Among the 11 serendipitous discoveries described here are Alexander Fleming's accidental invention of penicillin and Jocelyn Bell's discovery of pulsars. (Rev: BL 2/1/06*; SLJ 6/06) [509]

12023 Gutfreund, Geraldine M. *Yearbooks in Science: 1970–1979* (5–8). Illus. Series: Yearbooks in Science. 1995, Twenty-First Century LB $22.90 (978-0-8050-3437-0). A decade of new scientific concepts and inventions is discussed, with profiles of the scientists behind them. (Rev: BL 1/1–15/96; SLJ 5/96) [609]

12024 Hakim, Joy. *The Story of Science: Newton at the Center* (7–10). Illus. Series: Smithsonian's Story of Science. 2005, Smithsonian $24.95 (978-1-58834-161-7). In the second volume of the series, Hakim introduces readers to the discoveries of Copernicus, Galileo, Newton, and others. (Rev: BL 12/1/05; SLJ 12/05*; VOYA 2/05) [590]

12025 Hoyt, Beth Caldwell, and Erica Ritter. *The Ultimate Girls' Guide to Science: From Backyard Experiments to Winning the Nobel Prize!* (4–8). Illus. 2004, Beyond Words paper $9.95 (978-1-58270-092-2). Designed to pique girls' interest in the study of science, this attractive title offers brief profiles of famous female scientists as well as the major branches of science and also provides instructions for a number of scientific experiments. (Rev: SLJ 8/04) [500]

12026 Kramer, Stephen. *Hidden Worlds: Looking Through a Scientist's Microscope* (4–7). Illus. Series: Scientists in the Field. 2001, Houghton $16.00 (978-0-618-05546-3). Striking photographs, mostly taken with electron microscopes by scientist Dennis Kunkel, serve to illustrate this explanation of how scientists use microscopes in their work. (Rev: BL 8/01; HB 1–2/02; HBG 3/02; SLJ 9/01*) [570]

12027 McGowen, Tom. *The Beginnings of Science* (5–8). Illus. 1998, Twenty-First Century LB $26.90 (978-0-7613-3016-5). Beginning with primitive people and their use of magic, fire, counting, writing, and astronomy, this book traces the history of science up to the 16th century. (Rev: BL 12/1/98; HBG 3/99) [509]

12028 McGowen, Tom. *Yearbooks in Science: 1900–1919* (5–8). Illus. Series: Yearbooks in Science. 1995, Twenty-First Century LB $22.90 (978-0-8050-3431-8). An overview of human achievements in science and technology during the first 20 years of the 20th century, how they helped humanity, and the men and women involved. (Rev: BL 12/1/95; SLJ 1/96) [609]

12029 McGowen, Tom. *Yearbooks in Science: 1960–1969* (5–8). Illus. Series: Yearbooks in Science. 1996, Twenty-First Century LB $22.90 (978-0-8050-3436-3). Developments in the history of science and technology during the 1960s are covered in an exciting step-by-step approach. (Rev: BL 1/1–15/96; SLJ 5/96) [609]

12030 McGrayne, Sharon Bertsch. *Blue Genes and Polyester Plants: 365 More Surprising Scientific Facts, Breakthroughs and Discoveries* (8–12). 1997, Wiley paper $16.95 (978-0-471-14575-2). A compendium of strange and unusual facts from various branches of science. [500]

12031 Martin, Paul D. *Science: It's Changing Your World* (5–8). Illus. 1985, National Geographic LB $12.50 (978-0-87044-521-7). An overview of the science field today, crediting computers and lasers with the vast growth of scientific information. (Rev: BL 9/15/85; SLJ 10/85) [500]

12032 Masoff, Joy. *Oh, Yuck! The Encyclopedia of Everything Nasty* (4–8). Illus. by Terry Sirrell. 2001, Workman paper $14.95 (978-0-7611-0771-2). This unsavory, fact-filled look at smells, noises, creepy-crawlies, toilets, and other fascinating topics even includes some suitably gross experiments. (Rev: SLJ 5/01) [031.02]

12033 Newton, David E. *Yearbooks in Science: 1920–1929* (5–8). Illus. Series: Yearbooks in Sci-

ence. 1995, Twenty-First Century LB $22.90 (978-0-8050-3432-5). The history of scientific advances in the 1920s, with chapters on various fields that explain the breakthroughs, how they helped humanity, and the scientists involved. (Rev: BL 12/1/95; SLJ 1/96) [609]

12034 Schwartz, David M. *Q Is for Quark: A Science Alphabet Book* (4–9). Illus. by Kim Doner. 2001, Tricycle $15.95 (978-1-58246-021-5). An entertaining and informative alphabet book from atom to Zzzzzzzz that doesn't hesitate to tackle difficult topics. (Rev: HBG 3/02; SLJ 11/01) [500]

12035 Shields, Carol Diggory. *BrainJuice: Science, Fresh Squeezed!* (4–7). Illus. by Richard Thompson. 2003, Handprint $14.95 (978-1-59354-005-0). A humorous, rhyming look at grade-school science with appealing illustrations and useful mnemonic devices. (Rev: SLJ 3/04) [500]

12036 Silverstein, Herma. *Yearbooks in Science: 1990 and Beyond* (5–8). Illus. Series: Yearbooks in Science. 1995, Twenty-First Century LB $22.90 (978-0-8050-3439-4). The final volume in this series not only traces recent developments in science and technology but also presents the challenges of the future. (Rev: BL 1/1–15/96) [609]

12037 Spangenburg, Ray, and Diane Kit Moser. *The Birth of Science: Ancient Times to 1699*. Rev. ed. (6–10). Illus. Series: The History of Science. 2004, Facts on File $40.00 (978-0-8160-4851-9). A survey of the development of scientific knowledge from ancient times through the seventeenth century, with brief profiles of major scientists plus discussion of discoveries that didn't pan out. Also use *The Rise of Reason: 1700–1799, The Age of Synthesis: 1800–1895, Modern Science: 1896–1945*, and *Science Frontiers: 1946 to the Present* (all 2004). (Rev: SLJ 12/04) [509]

12038 Spangenburg, Raymond. *The History of Science from 1895 to 1945* (7–12). 1994, Facts on File $25.00 (978-0-8160-2742-2). Surveys scientific progress, discussing atomic energy, relativity, space exploration, genetics, and the achievements of various scientists spanning 100 years. (Rev: BL 9/1/94; VOYA 10/94) [509]

12039 Stein, Sara Bonnett. *The Science Book* (4–8). Illus. by author. 1980, Workman paper $9.95 (978-0-89480-120-4). A whole-earth approach to strange and fascinating science facts.

12040 Sullivan, Navin. *Time* (4–7). Series: Measure Up! . 2006, Marshall Cavendish LB $20.95 (978-0-7614-2321-8). This entertaining volume provides a history of the way humans have measured time, up to the present day and including the new rule for Daylight Saving Time. (Rev: LMC 8-9/07; SLJ 6/07) [529]

12041 Sussman, Art. *Dr. Art's Guide to Science: Connecting Atoms, Galaxies, and Everything in Between* (6–12). Illus. 2006, Jossey-Bass $22.95 (978-0-7879-8326-0). The author makes understanding science fun, using colorful illustrations, chapter overviews, activities, Web links to experiments, a "Glindex" (combining glossary and index), and "Stop & Think" pages. (Rev: SLJ 6/06)

12042 Swanson, Diane. *Nibbling on Einstein's Brain* (5–8). Illus. by Warren Clark. 2001, Firefly paper $14.95 (978-1-55037-686-9). Swanson looks at "bad" science and examines the difference between sound scientific theory and hype, teaching kids how to ask the right questions when analyzing advertis-ers' claims. (Rev: BL 2/15/02; HBG 3/02; SLJ 11/01) [507.2]

12043 Wollard, Kathy. *How Come?* (5–9). 1993, Workman paper $12.95 (978-1-56305-324-5). Provides answers to some common and not-so-common questions about ordinary things. (Rev: BL 5/1/94) [500]

12044 Wollard, Kathy. *How Come Planet Earth?* (4–7). Illus. by Debra Solomon. 1999, Workman paper $12.95 (978-0-7611-1239-6). This book contains 125 science questions asked by children involving subjects such as warts, dust, cholesterol, and volcanoes. (Rev: SLJ 5/00) [500]

Experiments and Projects

12045 Bardhan-Quallen, Sudipta. *Championship Science Fair Projects: 100 Sure-to-Win Experiments* (5–9). Illus. 2005, Sterling $19.95 (978-1-4027-1138-1). Clearly defined science projects (more than 100 at varying levels of difficulty) are accompanied by lists of materials, illustrations, and extension activities. (Rev: BL 8/05; SLJ 9/05; VOYA 8/05) [507]

12046 Bardhan-Quallen, Sudipta. *Last-Minute Science Fair Projects* (4–7). Illus. 2007, Sterling $19.95 (978-1-4027-1690-4). A guide to science experiments that can be done in a short amount of time using common household materials. (Rev: BL 5/15/07) [507.8]

12047 Bombaugh, Ruth J. *Science Fair Success*. Rev. ed. (8–12). 1999, Enslow LB $26.60 (978-0-7660-1163-2). This is a general guide to choosing, designing, and completing a successful science project. An appendix lists some prize winners. [507.8]

12048 Boring, Mel, and Leslie Dendy. *Guinea Pig Scientists: Bold Self-Experimenters in Science and Medicine* (5–9). Illus. by C. B. Mordan. 2005, Holt $19.95 (978-0-8050-7316-4). Scientists who served as their own guinea pigs — demonstrating their passion for science and often their foolhardiness — are the topic of this appealing volume. (Rev: BL 7/05*; SLJ 7/05*; VOYA 6/05) [616]

12049 Brown, Bob. *More Science for You: 112 Illustrated Experiments* (6–8). Illus. 1988, TAB paper $7.95 (978-0-8306-3125-4). A collection of simple experiments involving such topics as heat, sound, weight, and tricks. (Rev: VOYA 4/89) [507]

12050 Brown, Robert J. *333 Science Tricks and Experiments* (7–12). Illus. 1984, McGraw-Hill $15.95 (978-0-8306-0825-6). Basic scientific principles are demonstrated in experiments and projects. (Rev: BL 4/1/89) [507]

12051 Calhoun, Yael. *Plant and Animal Science Fair Projects Using Beetles, Weeds, Seeds, and More* (5–8). Illus. Series: Biology! Best Science Projects. 2005, Enslow LB $26.60 (978-0-7660-2368-0). Great ideas for biology-based science fair projects, with plenty of information for performing and presenting each activity correctly plus helpful charts and graphs. (Rev: SLJ 7/06) [570]

12052 Carrow, Robert. *Put a Fan in Your Hat! Inventions, Contraptions, and Gadgets Kids Can Build* (5–8). Illus. by Rick Brown. 1997, McGraw-Hill paper $14.95 (978-0-07-011658-0). Interesting projects include making a natural battery, building a motor, and creating a hat with a cooling fan. (Rev: BL 4/15/97; SLJ 5/97) [507]

12053 Cobb, Vicki. *The Secret Life of Hardware: A Science Experiment Book* (7–9). Illus. 1982, HarperCollins LB $13.89 (978-0-397-32000-4). A book of science activities and experiments that involve a hammer, saw, soaps, paints, and other commonly found items. [670]

12054 Dashefsky, H. Steven. *Zoology: 49 Science Fair Projects* (8–12). 1994, TAB paper $11.95 (978-0-07-015683-8). A step-by-step description of interesting science fair projects. (Rev: BL 1/15/95; SLJ 3/95) [591]

12055 Duensing, Edward. *Talking to Fireflies, Shrinking the Moon: Nature Activities for All Ages* (5–9). Illus. 1997, Fulcrum paper $15.95 (978-1-55591-310-6). More than 40 nature activities are included in this volume, including how to hypnotize a frog, weave a daisy chain, and whistle for woodchucks. (Rev: VOYA 10/97) [507]

12056 Fox, Tom. *Snowball Launchers, Giant-Pumpkin Growers, and Other Cool Contraptions* (5–8). Illus. by Joel Holland. 2006, Sterling paper $9.95 (978-0-8069-5515-5). A collection of 20 creative projects with clear instructions and explanations of scientific principles. (Rev: BL 1/1–15/07; SLJ 3/07)

12057 Gardner, Robert. *Kitchen Chemistry: Science Experiments to Do at Home* (4–8). Illus. 1989, Silver Burdett paper $4.95 (978-0-671-67576-9). These entertaining and instructive experiments can be performed in the kitchen with everyday equipment and supplies. [542]

12058 Gardner, Robert. *Science Fair Projects — Planning, Presenting, Succeeding* (8–12). Series: Science Projects. 1999, Enslow LB $26.60 (978-0-89490-949-8). A general work that gives good advice on choosing and executing a successful science project. [507.8]

12059 Gardner, Robert. *Science Projects About Kitchen Chemistry* (6–9). Series: Science Projects. 1999, Enslow LB $26.60 (978-0-89490-953-5). A book of clearly outlined experiments that range widely in difficulty and revolve around the kitchen and its contents. (Rev: SLJ 7/99) [507]

12060 Gardner, Robert. *Science Projects About Solids, Liquids, and Gases* (6–12). Series: Science Projects. 2000, Enslow LB $26.60 (978-0-7660-1168-7). The three states of matter are explored through a series of experiments and projects using material and objects found around the house. (Rev: BL 8/00; HBG 3/01; VOYA 2/01) [507]

12061 Gardner, Robert. *Science Projects About Sound* (6–12). Series: Science Projects. 2000, Enslow LB $26.60 (978-0-7660-1166-3). The experiments contained in the innovative project book explore the properties of sound and how it travels. (Rev: BL 8/00; HBG 3/01) [507]

12062 Gardner, Robert. *Science Projects About the Physics of Sports* (6–9). Illus. Series: Science Projects. 2000, Enslow LB $26.60 (978-0-7660-1167-0). Projects and experiments look at the scientific concepts involved in speed, force and motion, gravity, friction, and collisions. (Rev: HBG 9/00; SLJ 7/00) [530]

12063 Gardner, Robert. *Science Projects About the Science Behind Magic* (6–12). Series: Science Projects. 2000, Enslow LB $26.60 (978-0-7660-1164-9). Several science projects are outlined the explain the scientific principles behind some magic tricks. (Rev: BL 5/15/00; HBG 9/00; SLJ 7/00) [507]

12064 Haduch, Bill. *Science Fair Success Secrets: How to Win Prizes, Have Fun, and Think Like a Scientist* (5–8). Illus. by Philip Scheuer. 2002, Dutton paper $10.99 (978-0-525-46534-8). A handy and appealing introduction to how to conduct a science experiment, with examples of award-winning projects, a list of ideas, and metric conversion tables. (Rev: BL 12/1/02; SLJ 3/03) [507]

12065 Harris, Elizabeth Snoke. *First Place Science Fair Projects for Inquisitive Kids* (4–7). Illus. 2005,

Sterling LB $19.95 (978-1-57990-493-7). Project ideas in biology, chemistry, and physics mostly involve everyday materials and are presented in accessible text with an eight-week schedule and clear photographs. (Rev: SLJ 3/06) [507]

12066 Harris, Elizabeth Snoke. *Yikes! Wow! Yuck! Fun Experiments for Your First Science Fair* (4–7). Illus. by Nora Thompson. 2008, Sterling $12.95 (978-1-57990-930-7). The breezy, lighthearted tone of this book will appeal to young scientists looking for simple but interesting projects. (Rev: BL 4/15/08; SLJ 6/08) [507.8]

12067 Hauser, Jill F. *Gizmos and Gadgets: Creating Science Contraptions That Work (and Knowing Why)* (4–7). Illus. by Michael Kline. Series: Kids Can! 1999, Williamson paper $14.25 (978-1-885593-26-9). Outlines the construction of all sorts of gadgets from objects found in kitchen and garage closets and relates each to such scientific topics as motion, energy, balancing, and gravity. (Rev: SLJ 1/00) [745]

12068 Hussey, Lois J., and Catherine Pessino. *Collecting for the City Naturalist* (7–9). Illus. 1975, HarperCollins $12.95 (978-0-690-00317-8). Science activities that can be carried out in an urban environment, such as collecting spider webs, are outlined. [500.7]

12069 Iritz, Maxine Haren. *Blue-Ribbon Science Fair Projects* (7–12). 1991, McGraw-Hill paper $9.95 (978-0-07-157629-1). A variety of science fair projects for the novice are presented, with charts, graphs, photographs, and a chapter on choosing a topic. (Rev: BL 9/15/91) [507.8]

12070 Iritz, Maxine Haren. *Science Fair: Developing a Successful and Fun Project* (8–12). Illus. 1987, TAB $16.95 (978-0-8306-0936-9). A thorough step-by-step introduction to doing a science project. (Rev: BL 4/15/88) [507]

12071 Krieger, Melanie Jacobs. *How to Excel in Science Competitions*. Rev. ed. (6–10). Series: Science Fair Success. 1999, Enslow LB $26.60 (978-0-7660-1292-9). Students will find detailed guidance on choosing and conducting a science project, stories of winning projects, and profiles of successful students. (Rev: HBG 4/00; SLJ 4/00) [507.8]

12072 Lempke, Donald B., and Thomas K. Adamson. *Lessons in Science Safety with Max Axiom, Super Scientist* (5–8). Illus. by Tod Smith. Series: Graphic Science. 2006, Capstone LB $18.95 (978-0-7368-6834-1). This graphic-novel approach to teaching safe science procedures features an appealing adult. (Rev: BL 3/15/07) [507.8]

12073 Markle, Sandra. *Exploring Autumn: A Season of Science Activities, Puzzlers, and Games* (4–7). Illus. Series: Exploring Seasons. 1991, Avon paper $3.50 (978-0-380-71910-5). Science, history, myth, quizzes, and more combined in this book on seasonal activities in the classroom and home. (Rev: BL 1/1/91; SLJ 1/92) [574.5]

12074 Mercer, Bobby. *The Leaping, Sliding, Sprinting, Riding Science Book: 50 Super Sports Science Activities* (4–7). Illus. by Tom LaBaff. 2007, Sterling $14.95 (978-1-57990-785-3). Sports moves are used to illustrate scientific principles in this activity book with step-by-step instructions, discussions of the science, and lots of lively illustrations. (Rev: BL 5/1/07; SLJ 5/07) [796]

12075 Murphy, Pat. *Exploratopia* (4–7). Illus. 2006, Little, Brown $29.99 (978-0-316-61281-4). From San Francisco's Exploratorium, this is an interesting selection of facts, activities, and hands-on experiments that encourage students to learn about and explore the world around them. (Rev: BL 12/1/06; SLJ 1/07) [507.8]

12076 Newcomb, Rain, and Bobby Mercer. *Crash It! Smash It! Launch It!* (5–8). Illus. by Rain Newcomb. 2006, Sterling $14.95 (978-1-57990-795-2). More than 40 experiments provide great entertainment as well as scientific knowledge. (Rev: BL 11/1/06; SLJ 12/06) [507.8]

12077 Nye, Bill. *Bill Nye the Science Guy's Big Blast of Science* (5–8). Illus. 1993, Addison-Wesley paper $16.00 (978-0-201-60864-9). Matter, heat, light, electricity, magnetism, weather, and space are among the topics introduced in this quick and entertaining tour of the world of science. (Rev: BL 2/15/94) [507.8]

12078 Rainis, Kenneth. *Blood and DNA Evidence: Crime-Solving Science Experiments* (8–11). Illus. Series: Forensic Science Projects. 2006, Enslow LB $23.95 (978-0-7660-1958-4). Contains accounts of real-life crime cases and challenges the reader with step-by-step forensic science experiments to solve the case just as real detectives do. (Rev: BL 10/15/06; SLJ 5/07) [363.25]

12079 Richards, Roy. *101 Science Tricks: Fun Experiments with Everyday Materials* (4–8). Illus. by Alex Pang. 1992, Sterling $16.95 (978-0-8069-8388-2). Interesting, easy-to-do science and math activities emphasize the underlying principles. (Rev: BL 2/1/92; SLJ 1/92) [507.8]

12080 Rosner, Marc Alan. *Science Fair Success Using the Internet* (8–12). Series: Science Fair Success. 1999, Enslow LB $26.60 (978-0-7660-1172-4). As well as an explanation of how to use Internet resources, this book explains how the Internet can enhance science projects. [507.8]

12081 Rybolt, Thomas R., and Leah M. Rybolt. *Science Fair Success with Scents, Aromas, and Smells* (5–8). Series: Science Fair Success. 2002, Enslow LB $26.60 (978-0-7660-1625-5). Several science fair projects using the sense of smell are presented with clear instructions and easy-to-find materials. (Rev: BL 5/15/02; HBG 10/02; SLJ 11/02) [507]

12082 *Science Fairs: Ideas and Activities* (4–8). 1998, World Book $15.00 (978-0-7166-4498-9). Using many diagrams and logical step-by-step explanations, this work offers science projects in such areas as space, earth science, geology, botany, and machines. (Rev: SLJ 1/99) [507]

12083 Smith, Norman F. *How to Do Successful Science Projects.* Rev. ed. (5–8). Illus. 1990, Messner paper $5.95 (978-0-671-70686-9). This guide gives many fine tips and concentrates on the applications of the scientific method. (Rev: BL 7/90) [507.8]

12084 Sobey, Ed. *Wrapper Rockets and Trombone Straws: Science at Every Meal* (4–7). Illus. 1996, McGraw-Hill paper $14.95 (978-0-07-021745-4). Using simple items found in restaurants such as glasses, straws, and napkins, a number of simple tricks and experiments are introduced. (Rev: BL 3/1/97; SLJ 6/97) [500]

12085 Tocci, Salvatore. *Science Fair Success in the Hardware Store* (5–8). Series: Science Fair Success. 2000, Enslow LB $26.60 (978-0-7660-1287-5). A group of science fair projects that use materials and objects found in a hardware store, with clear explanations of the scientific principles behind each project. (Rev: BL 4/15/00; HBG 10/00) [507]

12086 Tocci, Salvatore. *Science Fair Success Using Supermarket Products* (5–8). Series: Science Fair Success. 2000, Enslow LB $26.60 (978-0-7660-1288-2). Using common items found in a supermarket, this work outlines a number of excellent science projects that demonstrate important scientific principles. (Rev: BL 4/15/00; HBG 10/00; SLJ 4/00) [507]

12087 Tocci, Salvatore. *Using Household Products* (5–8). Series: Science Fair Success. 2002, Enslow LB $26.60 (978-0-7660-1626-2). This useful volume outlines a number of science fair projects that can be done using materials found around the house. (Rev: BL 4/15/02; HBG 10/02) [509]

12088 UNESCO. *700 Science Experiments for Everyone* (5–8). Illus. 1964, Doubleday $19.95 (978-0-385-05275-7). An excellent collection of experiments, noted for its number of entries and breadth of coverage.

12089 VanCleave, Janice. *Janice VanCleave's A+ Projects in Chemistry: Winning Experiments for Science Fairs and Extra Credit* (6–10). 1993, Wiley paper $12.95 (978-0-471-58630-2). Thirty experiments that investigate such topics as calories, acids, and electrolytes, among others. (Rev: BL 12/1/95; SLJ 4/94) [930]

12090 VanCleave, Janice. *Janice VanCleave's Biology for Every Kid: 101 Easy Experiments That Really Work* (4–7). Illus. 1989, Wiley paper $12.95 (978-0-471-50381-1). This book outlines simple experiments that use readily available equipment and supplies. (Rev: BL 2/15/90) [574]

12091 VanCleave, Janice. *Janice VanCleave's Guide to More of the Best Science Fair Projects* (4–8). 2000, Wiley paper $14.95 (978-0-471-32627-4). After general information about the scientific method, research, and presentation, this book outlines about 50 projects in the areas of astronomy, biology, earth science, engineering, physical science, and mathematics. (Rev: SLJ 5/00) [509]

12092 VanCleave, Janice. *Janice VanCleave's 203 Icy, Freezing, Frosty, Cool and Wild Experiments* (4–7). 1999, Wiley paper $12.95 (978-0-471-25223-8). An excellent book filled with easily performed experiments in such areas as biology, chemistry, earth science, and physics. (Rev: SLJ 4/00) [507.8]

12093 Vecchione, Glen. *Blue Ribbon Science Fair Projects* (6–9). Illus. 2006, Sterling $19.95 (978-1-4027-1073-5). Ideas for projects in a wide range of subject areas are clearly presented, with background information, list of materials, hypothesis, steps to take, and so forth. (Rev: BL 2/1/06; SLJ 6/06) [507]

12094 Vecchione, Glen. *100 First Prize Make It Yourself Science Fair Projects* (4–8). Illus. 1998, Sterling $19.95 (978-0-8069-0703-1). The projects outlined in this good resource for project ideas range from the simple to complex and cover a wide range of branches of science. (Rev: SLJ 4/99) [507]

12095 Voth, Danna. *Kidsource: Science Fair Handbook* (5–8). Illus. 1998, Lowell House paper $9.95 (978-1-56565-514-0). This source provides excellent advice on selecting, preparing, and presenting science projects, with material on choosing workable topics, equipment needed, safety, measuring devices, and record keeping. (Rev: BL 2/15/99; SLJ 5/99) [507]

Astronomy and Space Science

General and Miscellaneous

12096 Banqueri, Eduardo. *The Night Sky* (6–10). Illus. Series: Field Guides. 2007, Enchanted Lion LB $16.95 (978-1-59270-066-0). An informative introduction to the night sky and how best to view it. (Rev: BL 5/15/07; LMC 11/07; SLJ 9/07) [523.80]

12097 Bortz, Fred. *Collision Course! Cosmic Impacts and Life on Earth* (4–7). Illus. 2001, Millbrook LB $25.90 (978-0-7613-1403-5). A straightforward discussion of an intriguing subject that includes material on past collisions and on detecting and perhaps deflecting future "near Earth objects." (Rev: BL 5/1/01; HBG 10/01; SLJ 5/01) [523.44]

12098 Campbell, Ann-Jeanette. *The New York Public Library: Amazing Space: A Book of Answers for Kids* (5–8). Illus. 1997, Wiley paper $12.95 (978-0-471-14498-4). This question-and-answer book introduces space exploration, the solar system, individual planets, galaxies, and related phenomena. (Rev: SLJ 7/97) [523]

12099 Cole, Michael D. *Hubble Space Telescope: Exploring the Universe* (4–7). Illus. Series: Countdown to Space. 1999, Enslow LB $23.93 (978-0-7660-1120-5). This close-up look at the Hubble space telescope covers its parts, uses, problems, and photographs that the telescope has sent back to earth. (Rev: BL 2/1/99; HBG 10/99) [522]

12100 Couper, Heather, and Nigel Henbest. *The History of Astronomy* (8–12). Illus. 2007, Firefly $59.95 (978-1-55407-325-2). From Stonehenge and other ancient monuments forward, this attractive volume documents man's interest in the skies and the scientific advances in studying them. (Rev: BL 12/1/07) [520]

12101 Dyer, Alan. *Space* (5–8). Illus. Series: Insiders. 2007, Simon & Schuster $16.99 (978-1-4169-3860-6). An introduction to the big bang, the solar system, stars and nebulas, galaxies, and so forth, with eye-catching illustrations. (Rev: LMC 10/07; SLJ 12/07) [520]

12102 Garlick, Mark A. *Astronomy: A Visual Guide* (8–12). Illus. 2004, Firefly $29.95 (978-1-55297-958-7). An excellent, photo-filled guide to observing and understanding the nighttime sky. (Rev: BL 10/15/04) [522]

12103 Hope, Terry. *Spacecam: Photographing the Final Frontier from Apollo to Hubble* (6–12). Illus. 2005, F & W $24.99 (978-0-7153-2164-5). Images captured from space — many never before published — offer fantastic views of Earth and beyond. (Rev: BL 12/15/05) [778.35]

12104 Jackson, Ellen. *The Mysterious Universe: Supernovae, Dark Energy, and Black Holes* (5–8). Illus. Series: Scientists in the Field. 2008, Houghton $18.00 (978-0-618-56325-8). Astronomer Alex Filippenko and his work at key observatories is the focus of this book that also describes such phenomena as supernovae and black holes in accessible text with informative diagrams and spectacular photographs. (Rev: BL 6/1–15/08; SLJ 6/08) [523.8]

12105 Jefferis, David. *Black Holes and Other Bizarre Space Objects* (5–8). Illus. Series: Science Frontiers. 2006, Crabtree LB $26.60 (978-0-7787-2856-6); paper $8.95 (978-0-7787-2870-2). Double-page spreads with color photographs and informative sidebars explore the life of stars, black holes, gamma-ray bursts, space telescopes, and so forth. (Rev: BL 4/1/06) [523.8]

12106 Macy, Sue. *Are We Alone? Scientists Search for Life in Space* (4–8). Illus. 2004, National Geographic $18.95 (978-0-7922-6567-2). Modern scientific efforts to find extraterrestrial life are discussed along with the popularity of flying saucers, crop circles, and other theories. (Rev: BL 10/1/04; SLJ 12/04*) [001.9]

12107 Maynard, Christopher. *The Young Scientist Book of Stars and Planets* (4–7). Illus. 1978, EDC LB $14.95 (978-0-88110-313-7); paper $6.95 (978-0-86020-094-9). Attractive illustrations and plentiful experiments and projects add to this book's appeal.

12108 Miller, Ron. *Extrasolar Planets* (7–12). Illus. Series: Worlds Beyond. 2002, Millbrook LB $25.90 (978-0-7613-2354-9). A handsome and accessible overview of the planets in our solar system and elsewhere in the universe that includes historical information, biographies of scientists, basic concepts, and many attention-grabbing illustrations. (Rev: BL 2/15/02; HBG 10/02; SLJ 3/02) [523]

12109 Mitchell, Mark G. *Seeing Stars: The McDonald Observatory and Its Astronomers* (6–10). 1997, Sunbelt Media $17.95 (978-1-57168-117-1). This is a history of the famous observatory operated by the University of Texas in Austin, with material on the equipment used and the day-to-day operation. (Rev: HBG 9/98; SLJ 5/98) [523]

12110 Moeschl, Richard. *Exploring the Sky: 100 Projects for Beginning Astronomers* (5–8). Illus. 1992, Chicago Review paper $16.95 (978-1-55652-160-7). Many ideas for experiments and observations in an information-packed book. (Rev: BL 5/1/89)

12111 Oleksy, Walter. *Mapping the Skies* (5–7). Series: Watts Library: Geography. 2002, Watts LB $25.50 (978-0-531-12031-6); paper $8.95 (978-0-531-16635-2). From the ancient Greeks and Romans through Galileo to astronomers today, this is a history of how the stars, planets, and space have been mapped. (Rev: BL 10/15/02) [520]

12112 Orr, Tamra. *The Telescope* (4–8). Series: Inventions That Shaped the World. 2004, Watts LB $30.50 (978-0-531-12344-7). Describes the invention of the telescope, the impact of the knowledge imparted, and future possibilities. (Rev: BL 4/1/04; SLJ 2/05) [522]

12113 Schorer, Lonnie Jones. *Kids to Space: A Space Traveler's Guide* (5–9). Illus. 2006, Apogee paper $29.95 (978-1-894959-42-1). Organized in almost 100 categories, this volume includes thousands of questions about space posed by children and answered by experts including NASA engineers, former astronauts, and astronomy professors. (Rev: SLJ 12/06) [500.5]

12114 Stott, Carole, and Clint Twist. *1001 Facts About Space* (7–12). Illus. Series: Backpack Books. 2002, DK paper $8.99 (978-0-7894-8450-5). A handy-sized overview full of illustrations that presents useful facts about the universe, galaxies, stars, solar system, and planets as well as pulsars, space

history, and stellar classification. (Rev: BL 3/15/02) [590]

12115 Taschek, Karen. *Death Stars, Weird Galaxies, and a Quasar-Spangled Universe: The Discoveries of the Very Large Array Telescope* (7–10). 2006, Univ. of New Mexico $17.95 (978-0-8263-3211-0). Compelling images of space captured from New Mexico's VLA (Very Large Array) telescope are combined with readable descriptions of recent discoveries in astronomy and an overview of the problems that still plague astronomers. (Rev: BL 5/1/06; SLJ 7/06) [522]

12116 Vogt, Gregory L. *Deep Space Astronomy* (5–8). Illus. 1999, Twenty-First Century LB $25.90 (978-0-7613-1369-4). This look beyond our own star system covers such topics as the development of space-based detectors, information-gathering techniques, and recent discoveries. (Rev: BL 1/1–15/00; HBG 3/00; SLJ 2/00) [520]

12117 Wills, Susan, and Steven Wills. *Astronomy: Looking at the Stars* (5–8). Illus. Series: Innovators. 2001, Oliver $21.95 (978-1-881508-76-2). A good starting point for research into astronomy, with profiles of individuals including Ptolemy, Copernicus, Galileo, and Newton. (Rev: HBG 10/02; SLJ 2/02) [520.922]

Astronautics and Space Exploration

12118 Angliss, Sarah. *Cosmic Journeys: A Beginner's Guide to Space and Time Travel* (5–7). Illus. by Alex Pang, et al. Series: Future Files. 1998, Millbrook LB $23.90 (978-0-7613-0620-7). This book explores such topics as traveling to other solar systems, time travel, black holes, and parallel universes. (Rev: HBG 10/98; SLJ 10/98) [629.4]

12119 Asimov, Isaac, and Frank White. *Think About Space: Where Have We Been and Where Are We Going?* (7–10). Illus. 1989, Walker LB $14.85 (978-0-8027-6766-0); paper $5.95 (978-0-8027-6767-7). A history of space exploration and a discussion of possible future developments. (Rev: BL 10/1/89; SLJ 11/89) [500.5]

12120 Barbree, Jay. *"Live from Cape Canaveral": Covering the Space Race, from Sputnik to Today* (8–12). 2007, Smithsonian $26.95 (978-0-06-123392-0). Journalist Barbree offers a behind-the-scenes look at the great events and personalities of space flight, from 1957 onward. (Rev: BL 9/1/07) [629.450973]

12121 Barter, James. *Space Stations* (5–8). Illus. Series: Lucent Library of Science and Technology. 2005, Gale LB $29.95 (978-1-59018-106-5). Explores the space stations that have been used for many years as medical laboratories and platforms for space study. (Rev: BL 1/05)

12122 Bredeson, Carmen. *The Challenger Disaster: Tragic Space Flight* (4–8). Series: American Disasters. 1999, Enslow LB $23.93 (978-0-7660-1222-6). An account of the 1986 tragedy. (Rev: BL 10/15/99; HBG 3/00) [629.5]

12123 Bredeson, Carmen. *John Glenn Returns to Orbit: Life on the Space Shuttle* (4–7). Series: Countdown to Space. 2000, Enslow LB $23.93 (978-0-7660-1304-9). This is the story of John Glenn, now a famous politician, his return to space, and the different conditions he encountered. (Rev: BL 8/00; HBG 10/00) [629.4]

12124 Bredeson, Carmen. *NASA Planetary Spacecraft: Galileo, Magellan, Pathfinder, and Voyager* (4–7). Series: Countdown to Space. 2000, Enslow LB $23.93 (978-0-7660-1303-2). This gives a good rundown on the NASA spacecraft used to explore planets, their individual missions, and their findings. (Rev: BL 9/15/00; HBG 10/01) [629.4]

12125 Briggs, Carole S. *Women in Space* (4–7). Series: A&E Biography. 1999, Lerner LB $27.93 (978-0-8225-4937-6). Includes profiles of astronauts including Sally Ride, Mae Jemison, Shannon Lucid, Eileen Collins, and two of their Russian counterparts. (Rev: SLJ 5/99) [629.45]

12126 Carlisle, Rodney P. *Exploring Space* (6–10). Series: Discovery and Exploration. 2004, Facts on File $40.00 (978-0-8160-5265-3). The motivations for exploring space are examined in clear, informative text plus photographs, illustrations, and excerpts from primary sources. (Rev: SLJ 12/04) [629.5]

12127 Clay, Rebecca. *Space Travel and Exploration* (4–8). Illus. Series: Secrets of Space. 1995, Twenty-First Century LB $23.90 (978-0-8050-4474-4). A history of modern space exploration, covering manned flights, space stations, space probes, and telescopes. (Rev: BL 7/97; SLJ 1/98) [629.5]

12128 Cole, Michael D. *Astronauts: Training for Space* (4–7). Illus. Series: Countdown to Space. 1999, Enslow LB $23.93 (978-0-7660-1116-8). Focusing mainly on Sally Ride, this account describes the rigorous training of NASA astronauts. (Rev: BL 2/1/99; HBG 10/99) [629.45]

12129 Cole, Michael D. *Galileo Spacecraft: Mission to Jupiter* (4–7). Series: Countdown to Space. 1999, Enslow LB $23.93 (978-0-7660-1119-9). *Galileo*'s journey to Jupiter is described with details of the preparations for the flight and its findings. Photographs, a glossary, and Web sites round out the coverage. (Rev: BL 2/15/99; HBG 10/99; SLJ 5/99) [629.45]

12130 Cole, Michael D. *Moon Base: First Colony on Space* (4–7). Series: Countdown to Space. 1999,

Enslow LB $23.93 (978-0-7660-1118-2). A futuristic look at what a space colony on the moon might look like and the problems involved in creating it. (Rev: BL 2/15/99; HBG 10/99; SLJ 5/99) [629.45]

12131 Cole, Michael D. *NASA Space Vehicles: Capsules, Shuttles, and Space Stations* (4–7). Series: Countdown to Space. 2000, Enslow LB $23.93 (978-0-7660-1308-7). Gives a rundown on these specialized vehicles plus a description of space stations and how they operate, with full-color photographs and clear, readable text. (Rev: BL 5/15/00; HBG 10/00; SLJ 12/00) [629.4]

12132 Cole, Michael D. *Space Emergency: Astronauts in Danger* (4–8). Illus. Series: Countdown to Space. 2000, Enslow LB $23.93 (978-0-7660-1307-0). An explosion on the command module of *Apollo 13* and a faulty landing bag on *Friendship 7* are two of the emergencies described in this book on crises in space exploration. (Rev: BL 2/1/00; HBG 10/00; SLJ 12/00) [629.45]

12133 Cole, Michael D. *Space Launch Disaster: When Liftoff Goes Wrong* (4–7). Series: Countdown to Space. 2000, Enslow LB $23.93 (978-0-7660-1309-4). This is a rundown of problems that can occur during the liftoff of space vehicles, with examples of actual disasters, many caught on camera. (Rev: BL 3/15/00; HBG 10/00; SLJ 8/00) [629]

12134 Collins, Martin. *After Sputnik: 50 Years of the Space Age* (8–12). Illus. 2007, Collins $35.00 (978-0-06-089781-9). With photographs accompanied by essays, this volume uses approximately 200 artifacts — John Glenn's space suit and a lunar rover, for example — to tell the story of the first 50 years of space exploration. (Rev: SLJ 7/07) [629.409]

12135 Dolan, Terrance. *Probing Deep Space* (6–9). Series: World Explorers. 1993, Chelsea LB $14.95 (978-0-7910-1326-7). A chronicle of how we have learned about outer space and the challenges that remain. (Rev: BL 10/1/93; VOYA 2/94) [520]

12136 Duggins, Pat. *Final Countdown: NASA and the End of the Space Shuttle Program* (8–12). 2007, Univ. Press of Florida $24.95 (978-0-8130-3146-0). Duggins tells the story of the space shuttle from initial inception to the planning of the final missions, with information on shuttle astronauts and on the two shuttle disasters. (Rev: BL 9/1/07) [629.45]

12137 Dyson, Marianne J. *Home on the Moon: Living on a Space Frontier* (5–8). Illus. 2003, National Geographic $18.95 (978-0-7922-7193-2). Dyson, a former NASA mission controller, discusses the resources available on the moon, explores the possibilities of building facilities there, and suggests activities. (Rev: BL 7/03; HBG 10/03; SLJ 9/03) [919.91]

12138 Dyson, Marianne J. *Space Station Science: Life in Free Fall* (4–7). Illus. 1999, Scholastic paper $16.95 (978-0-590-05889-6). Written by a former member of a NASA control team, this work explores living and working in space including details on a space station bathroom. (Rev: BL 11/15/99; HBG 10/00; SLJ 12/99) [629.45]

12139 English, June A., and Thomas D. Jones. *Mission: Earth: Voyage to the Home Planet* (4–7). Illus. 1996, Scholastic paper $16.95 (978-0-590-48571-5). The space program is introduced, with special coverage of the flights of the shuttle *Endeavor* in 1994 and its environmental studies. (Rev: BL 10/15/96; SLJ 10/96) [550]

12140 Fallen, Anne-Catherine. *USA from Space* (4–7). Illus. 1997, Firefly LB $19.95 (978-1-55209-159-3); paper $7.95 (978-1-55209-157-9). Excellent satellite pictures of parts of the earth are contained in this book, which also explains the value of satellite imagery in tracking pollution, population, and natural disasters. (Rev: BL 3/1/98; SLJ 12/97) [917.3]

12141 Farbman, Melinda, and Frye Gaillard. *Spacechimp: NASA's Ape in Space* (4–7). Series: Countdown to Space. 2000, Enslow LB $23.93 (978-0-7660-1478-7). The story of how animals in general have helped the space program and how one chimp's voyage into space contributed to progress. (Rev: BL 8/00; HBG 10/00) [629.4]

12142 Gaffney, Timothy R. *Secret Spy Satellites: America's Eyes in Space* (4–7). Series: Countdown to Space. 2000, Enslow LB $23.93 (978-0-7660-1402-2). With sharp illustrations and a strong narrative, this book describes U.S. spy satellites, their purposes, and findings. (Rev: BL 9/15/00; HBG 10/01) [629.4]

12143 Goldsmith, Mike. *Space* (4–7). Illus. Series: Kingfisher Voyages. 2005, Kingfisher $14.95 (978-0-7534-5910-2). An appealing overview of space exploration, with concise text, good photographs, and a foreword and comments by astronaut Sally Ride. (Rev: BL 10/15/05) [629.45]

12144 Harris, Alan, and Paul Weissman. *The Great Voyager Adventure: A Guided Tour Through the Solar System* (4–8). Illus. 1990, Simon & Schuster paper $16.95 (978-0-671-72538-9). Two scientists introduce the missions, paths, and discoveries of the Voyager spacecraft. (Rev: BL 2/1/91; SLJ 2/91) [523.4]

12145 Hasday, Judy L. *The Apollo 13 Mission* (6–9). Series: Overcoming Adversity. 2000, Chelsea LB $30.00 (978-0-7910-5310-2). This straightforward account of the difficulties encountered on this moon mission includes black-and-white photographs, a brief history of the space program, and the transcript of an interview with Apollo 13's flight director. (Rev: HBG 10/01; SLJ 1/01) [629.45]

12146 Holden, Henry M. *The Tragedy of the Space Shuttle Challenger* (4–8). Illus. Series: Space Flight Adventures and Disasters. 2004, Enslow LB $25.26

(978-0-7660-5165-2). An account of the ill-fated *Challenger* mission, backed up by a list of Web sites that provide additional information. (Rev: BL 10/1/04; SLJ 2/05) [629.5]

12147 Kennedy, Gregory. *The First Men in Space* (5–7). Illus. Series: World Explorers. 1991, Chelsea LB $21.95 (978-0-7910-1324-3). This book covers the early years and accomplishments of both Soviet and American space programs. (Rev: SLJ 8/91) [629.44]

12148 Kennedy, Gregory P. *Apollo to the Moon* (6–9). Series: World Explorers. 1992, Chelsea LB $32.00 (978-0-7910-1322-9). A chronicle of the Apollo moon landing expedition and descriptions of the astronauts involved. (Rev: BL 9/1/92; SLJ 7/92) [629.45]

12149 Kerrod, Robin. *Dawn of the Space Age* (5–7). Illus. Series: The History of Space Exploration. 2005, World Almanac LB $31.00 (978-0-8368-5705-4). A well-illustrated history of space exploration, from the ideas of Cyrano de Bergerac to the modern Mars probes. Also recommended in this series are *Space Probes*, *Space Shuttles*, and *Space Stations* (all 2004). (Rev: SLJ 3/05) [629.4]

12150 Kuhn, Betsy. *The Race for Space: The United States and the Soviet Union Compete for the New Frontier* (6–9). 2006, Lerner $29.27 (978-0-8225-5984-9). Follows the historical aspects of the space race between the United States and the former Soviet Union from the 1950's to the early 90's. (Rev: BL 8/06; SLJ 2/07) [629.45]

12151 Kupperberg, Paul. *Spy Satellites* (4–8). Illus. Series: Library of Satellites. 2003, Rosen LB $26.50 (978-0-8239-3854-4). The author discusses the history of U.S. spy satellites and how the country has used the information they have gleaned. (Rev: BL 5/15/03; SLJ 1/04) [327.1273]

12152 Lieurance, Suzanne. *The Space Shuttle Challenger Disaster in American History* (6–10). Series: In American History. 2001, Enslow LB $26.60 (978-0-7660-1419-0). The story of the tragic destruction of the *Challenger* space shuttle in January, 1986, that killed seven astronauts including teacher Christa McAuliffe. (Rev: BL 8/01; HBG 10/01; SLJ 9/01) [629]

12153 Markle, Sandra. *Pioneering Space* (5–8). 1992, Atheneum LB $14.95 (978-0-689-31748-4). A look at space travel and how people may succeed in living in space. (Rev: BL 9/1/92; SLJ 2/93) [629.4]

12154 Marsh, Carole. *Unidentified Flying Objects and Extraterrestrial Life* (5–8). Series: Secrets of Space. 1996, Twenty-First Century LB $25.90 (978-0-8050-4472-0). This book touches on a wide range of topics associated with UFOs, including a history of famous sightings, but the emphasis is on major SETI (Search for Extra Terrestrial Intelligence) projects undertaken to detect alien radio signals. The author concludes that there is no definitive proof of the existence of intelligent life outside Earth. (Rev: BL 12/1/96; SLJ 12/96) [001.9]

12155 Miller, Ron. *Satellites* (7–10). Illus. Series: Space Innovations. 2007, Lerner LB $31.93 (978-0-8225-7154-4). How do satellites get up there? Which country was the first to launch one? What do they do? Do they ever fall back to Earth? This well-designed book answers these questions and more, providing lots of relevant history. (Rev: BL 12/1/07) [629.44]

12156 Netzley, Patricia D. *Alien Abductions* (7–10). Series: Mystery Library. 2001, Lucent LB $27.45 (978-1-56006-767-2). This is a serious examination of claims concerning abductions by aliens with reference to cases that have been reported. (Rev: BL 9/15/01; SLJ 2/01) [001.9]

12157 Pogue, William R. *How Do You Go to the Bathroom in Space?* (7–12). 1991, Tor paper $7.99 (978-0-8125-1728-6). In a question-and-answer format, the author, who spent 84 days in space, discusses the practical aspects of space travel. (Rev: VOYA 12/85) [629.47]

12158 Ride, Sally, and Susan Okie. *To Space and Back* (8–12). Illus. 1986, Lothrop $21.99 (978-0-688-06159-3); paper $14.99 (978-0-688-09112-5). A photojourney that begins four hours before launch and ends after landing. (Rev: BL 11/86; SLJ 11/86; VOYA 12/86) [629]

12159 Sherman, Josepha. *Deep Space Observation Satellites* (4–8). Illus. Series: Library of Satellites. 2003, Rosen LB $26.50 (978-0-8239-3852-0). The author discusses the history of U.S. observation satellites and how the country has benefited from their discoveries. (Rev: BL 5/15/03) [522]

12160 Sullivan, George. *The Day We Walked on the Moon: A Photo History of Space Exploration* (5–8). Illus. 1990, Scholastic paper $4.95 (978-0-685-58532-0). The history of U.S. space exploration, showing the accomplishments of both the United States and the Soviet Union. (Rev: BL 9/1/90; SLJ 2/91) [629.4]

12161 Taylor, Robert. *Life Aboard the Space Shuttle* (6–10). Series: The Way People Live. 2002, Gale LB $29.95 (978-1-59018-154-6). How the astronauts live in a space shuttle and their daily chores are covered in this account that uses many primary and secondary quotations. (Rev: BL 7/02) [629.4]

12162 Thimmesh, Catherine. *Team Moon: How 400,000 People Landed Apollo 11 on the Moon* (5–10). 2006, Houghton $19.95 (978-0-618-50757-3). A breathless account of all the behind-the-scenes work that went into the Apollo space program, with plenty of photographs. Sibert Medal, 2007. (Rev: SLJ 6/06) [629.45]

12163 Vogt, Gregory L. *Apollo Moonwalks: The Amazing Lunar Missions* (4–7). Series: Countdown to Space. 2000, Enslow LB $23.93 (978-0-7660-1306-3). This account focuses on the moonwalks during the *Apollo 11* expedition and details what was found. (Rev: BL 8/00; HBG 10/00) [629.4]

12164 Vogt, Gregory L. *Disasters in Space Exploration* (5–8). Illus. 2001, Millbrook LB $25.90 (978-0-7613-1920-7). Accidents and failures that have marred the success rates of the American and Soviet space programs are covered in interesting detail with many photographs. (Rev: BL 10/1/01; HBG 3/02; SLJ 8/01*) [363.12]

12165 Vogt, Gregory L. *Disasters in Space Exploration*. Rev. ed. (5–8). 2003, Millbrook LB $25.90 (978-0-7613-2895-7). An illustrated survey of serious accidents that have befallen the U.S. and Soviet space programs, what caused them, and what was learned from them. This revised edition includes the *Columbia* space shuttle disaster of February 2003. (Rev: SLJ 3/04) [363.12]

12166 Vogt, Gregory L. *Spacewalks: The Ultimate Adventures in Orbit* (4–7). Series: Countdown to Space. 2000, Enslow LB $23.93 (978-0-7660-1305-6). This gives a history of spacewalks, tells who were the pioneers, and explains their purpose. (Rev: BL 8/00; HBG 10/00) [629.4]

12167 Voit, Mark. *Hubble Space Telescope: New Views of the Universe* (8–12). 2000, Abrams paper $19.95 (978-0-8109-2923-4). With an accompanying text, this book includes more than 100 photographs taken by the Hubble Space Telescope. (Rev: SLJ 4/01) [520]

12168 Wunsch, Susi Trautmann. *The Adventures of Sojourner: The Mission to Mars that Thrilled the World* (5–9). 1998, Mikaya LB $22.95 (978-0-9650493-5-1); paper $9.95 (978-0-9650493-6-8). This book describes the construction of the *Sojourner* rover and its performance on Mars after landing on July 4, 1997. (Rev: SLJ 2/99*) [629.5]

Comets, Meteors, and Asteroids

12169 Asimov, Isaac. *How Did We Find Out About Comets?* (5–7). Illus. 1975, Walker LB $10.85 (978-0-8027-6204-7). An introduction to comets and our knowledge and attitudes about them since ancient times. [523.6]

12170 Koppes, Steven N. *Killer Rocks from Outer Space: Asteroids, Comets, and Meteorites* (7–10). Illus. 2003, Lerner LB $27.93 (978-0-8225-2861-6). Koppes examines the science and history of planetary impacts by asteroids, comets, and meteorites and looks at steps being taken to protect the Earth from such impacts in the future. (Rev: BL 1/1–15/04; SLJ 3/04) [523.5]

12171 Miller, Ron. *Asteroids, Comets, and Meteors* (7–10). Illus. Series: Worlds Beyond. 2005, Twenty-First Century LB $27.93 (978-0-7613-2363-1). Using color photographs, vivid paintings, and helpful diagrams, this title introduces readers to asteroids, comets, and meteors. (Rev: SLJ 12/05)

Earth and the Moon

12172 Alessandrello, Anna. *The Earth: Origins and Evolution* (4–8). Illus. Series: Beginnings — Origins and Evolution. 1995, Raintree LB $24.26 (978-0-8114-3331-0). An oversize book with lavish illustrations that discusses the theories concerning the formation of the earth, its structure and composition, and ways in which it is changing. (Rev: BL 4/15/95; SLJ 6/95) [550]

12173 Caes, Charles J. *How Do We Know the Age of the Earth* (6–9). Illus. Series: Great Scientific Questions and the Scientists Who Answered Them. 2001, Rosen LB $26.50 (978-0-8239-3381-5). An absorbing account of efforts through the ages to establish the age of the our planet. (Rev: SLJ 12/01; VOYA 8/02) [551.7]

12174 Erickson, Jon. *Exploring Earth from Space* (8–12). Illus. 1989, TAB paper $15.95 (978-0-8306-3242-8). Beginning with the history of space exploration, this account also covers how we on Earth profit from the use of space. [500.5]

12175 Gallant, Roy A. *Earth's Place in Space* (5–8). Series: The Story of Science. 1999, Benchmark LB $28.50 (978-0-7614-0963-2). Using a chronological approach, this account traces our knowledge of the earth and its place in the solar system and space. (Rev: BL 2/15/00; HBG 3/00; SLJ 2/00) [525]

12176 Gallant, Roy A., and Christopher J. Schuberth. *Earth: The Making of a Planet* (7–10). Illus. 1998, Marshall Cavendish $14.95 (978-0-7614-5012-2). Beginning with the big bang, this book describes the creation of Earth, with material on landforms, seas, the moon, rocks and minerals, and the ocean floor, and speculates about Earth's future. (Rev: BL 7/98; HBG 9/98; SLJ 7/98) [550]

12177 Gardner, Robert. *Science Project Ideas About the Moon* (4–7). Illus. Series: Science Project Ideas. 1997, Enslow LB $25.26 (978-0-89490-844-6). After giving basic information about the moon, this book outlines projects involving ways of observing the moon and how to make models to show its movements. (Rev: BL 12/1/97; HBG 3/98) [523.3]

12178 Miller, Ron. *Earth and the Moon* (5–7). Illus. Series: Worlds Beyond. 2003, Twenty-First Century LB $25.90 (978-0-7613-2358-7). NASA photo-

graphs and computer-generated images are used throughout this account of the origin, composition, and evolution the Earth and its moon. (Rev: HBG 10/03; SLJ 8/03) [525]

12179 Patent, Dorothy Hinshaw. *Shaping the Earth* (4–7). Illus. 2000, Clarion $18.00 (978-0-395-85691-8). The evolution of the earth is traced in this compelling book that describes how the surface has changed and continues to change, with coverage of plate tectonics, ice ages, natural disasters, and descriptions of its natural wonders. (Rev: BL 3/15/00; HBG 10/00; SLJ 4/00) [550]

Stars

12180 Asimov, Isaac. *The Life and Death of Stars* (5–8). Illus. Series: Isaac Asimov's 21st Century Library of the Universe. 2005, Gareth Stevens LB $26.00 (978-0-8368-3967-8). A revised, well-illustrated edition of a previously published book, this discusses the birth of stars, profiles different types of stars, and looks at the future of our Sun. Also in this series: *Black Holes, Pulsars, and Quasars, The Milky Way and Other Galaxies, Our Planetary System,* and *Comets and Meteors* (all 2005). (Rev: BL 3/1/05; SLJ 8/05)

12181 Cobb, Allan. *How Do We Know How Stars Shine?* (6–9). Illus. Series: Great Scientific Questions and the Scientists Who Answered Them. 2001, Rosen LB $26.50 (978-0-8239-3380-8). Cobb traces man's growing knowledge of the stars from the ancient astronomers through recent discoveries, showing how each new fact builds upon the ones that came before. (Rev: BL 10/15/01; SLJ 12/01) [523.8]

12182 Croswell, Ken. *See the Stars* (4–8). Illus. 2000, Boyds Mills $16.95 (978-1-56397-757-2). Twelve constellations are introduced in double-page spreads, with material on where and when to look for them. (Rev: BL 11/1/00; HBG 3/01; SLJ 10/00) [523]

12183 Gallant, Roy A. *The Life Stories of Stars* (6–10). Series: Story of Science. 2000, Marshall Cavendish LB $29.93 (978-0-7614-1152-9). This is a colorful introduction to stars, how they are formed, and how they die. (Rev: BL 12/15/00; HBG 10/01; SLJ 2/01) [523.8]

12184 Gustafson, John. *Stars, Clusters and Galaxies* (5–8). Illus. Series: Young Stargazer's Guide to the Galaxy. 1993, Simon & Schuster LB $18.95 (978-0-671-72536-5); paper $6.95 (978-0-671-72537-2). Introduces stars, binary stars, star clusters, nebulae, and galaxies, and provides tips for viewing the night sky through binoculars and telescopes. (Rev: BL 7/93; SLJ 6/93; VOYA 10/93) [523.8]

12185 Kerrod, Robin. *The Star Guide: Learn How to Read the Night Sky Star by Star.* 2nd ed. (8–12). Illus. 2005, Wiley $29.95 (978-0-471-70617-5). This guide to identifying heavenly bodies is well organized for novices and includes a removable sky map. (Rev: BL 4/15/05) [523.8]

12186 Pearce, Q. L. *The Stargazer's Guide to the Galaxy* (4–8). Illus. by Mary Ann Fraser. 1991, Tor paper $6.99 (978-0-8125-9423-2). In this introduction to star gazing in the Northern Hemisphere, material covered includes a look at the night sky in each of the four seasons. (Rev: SLJ 12/91) [523]

12187 Rey, H. A. *Find the Constellations* (5–7). Illus. 1976, Houghton LB $20.00 (978-0-395-24509-5); paper $9.95 (978-0-395-24418-0). Through clear text and illustrations, the reader is helped to recognize stars and constellations in the northern United States. Also use *The Stars: A New Way to See Them* (1973).

12188 VanCleave, Janice. *Janice VanCleave's Constellations for Every Kid: Easy Activities That Make Learning Science Fun* (8–12). Illus. 1997, Wiley paper $12.95 (978-0-471-15979-7). An excellent guide to the heavens, with each chapter presenting a different constellation with concise facts, new concepts, simple activities, and solutions to problems. (Rev: BL 12/1/97; HBG 3/98; SLJ 10/97) [523.8]

Sun and the Solar System

12189 Aguilar, David A. *11 Planets: A New View of the Solar System* (5–8). Illus. 2008, National Geographic $16.95 (978-1-4263-0236-7). The author includes the eight planets and three dwarf planets in his calculation of the main celestial bodies in the solar system; attractive color paintings and photographs accompany the text. (Rev: BL 5/1/08; SLJ 9/08) [523]

12190 Bortolotti, Dan. *Exploring Saturn* (4–8). Illus. 2003, Firefly $19.95 (978-1-55297-766-8); paper $9.95 (978-1-55297-765-1). This highly visual volume with readable text presents facts about Saturn, explains how and when we acquired this knowledge, and looks at the Cassini-Huygens mission, scheduled to reach the planet in 2004. (Rev: BL 12/1/03; SLJ 5/04) [523.46]

12191 Feinstein, Stephen. *Saturn* (4–7). Illus. Series: Solar System. 2005, Enslow LB $25.26 (978-0-7660-5304-5). Useful for reports, this clearly written title includes links to Web sites for further research. (Rev: SLJ 12/05) [523.46]

12192 Gallant, Roy A. *When the Sun Dies* (6–10). 1998, Marshall Cavendish $14.95 (978-0-7614-5036-8). After discussing the history and structure of the solar system, the author gives a blow-by-blow account of our sun's last 9 billion years and his projections for its likely ending about a billion years from now. (Rev: SLJ 1/99; VOYA 6/99) [523.2]

12193 Gustafson, John. *Planets, Moons and Meteors: The Young Stargazer's Guide to the Galaxy* (4–8). Illus. 1992, Simon & Schuster LB $12.95 (978-0-671-72534-1); paper $6.95 (978-0-671-72535-8). This guidebook tells how and when to observe the solar system and provides basic information about the planets. (Rev: BL 11/1/92) [523]

12194 Miller, Ron. *Jupiter* (5–8). Series: Worlds Beyond. 2002, Millbrook LB $25.90 (978-0-7613-2356-3). An excellent oversize volume that explores the largest of the planets with amazing full-page color illustrations and a detailed text. Also use *Venus* (2002). (Rev: BL 8/02; HBG 3/03; SLJ 8/02) [523.4]

12195 Miller, Ron. *Mars* (7–10). Illus. Series: Worlds Beyond. 2005, Twenty-First Century LB $27.93 (978-0-7613-2362-4). Introduces readers to the planet Mars in a blend of easy-to-understand narrative and colorful space photos. (Rev: SLJ 12/05)

12196 Miller, Ron. *Mercury and Pluto* (5–8). Series: Worlds Beyond. 2003, Millbrook LB $25.90 (978-0-7613-2361-7). Information on these planets and their discoveries is presented clearly, with helpful illustrations. Also use *Saturn* (2003). (Rev: BL 11/15/03; SLJ 12/03) [523.4]

12197 Miller, Ron. *Saturn* (5–8). Series: Worlds Beyond. 2003, Millbrook LB $25.90 (978-0-7613-2360-0). A colorful volume that describes the discovery of the solar system and supplies details about the planet Saturn and its many rings. (Rev: BL 11/15/03; SLJ 12/03) [523.4]

12198 Miller, Ron. *The Sun* (5–8). Illus. Series: Worlds Beyond. 2002, Millbrook LB $25.90 (978-0-7613-2355-6). Miller explores the nature and structure of the sun and the importance of solar energy. (Rev: BL 4/1/02; HBG 10/02; SLJ 5/02) [523.7]

12199 Miller, Ron. *Uranus and Neptune* (5–7). Illus. Series: Worlds Beyond. 2003, Twenty-First Century LB $25.90 (978-0-7613-2357-0). NASA photographs and computer-generated images are used throughout this account of the discovery and exploration of these two planets and what we know about their origin, composition, and evolution. (Rev: HBG 10/03; SLJ 8/03) [523.47]

12200 O'Connell, Kim A. *Mercury* (4–7). Illus. Series: Solar System. 2005, Enslow LB $25.26 (978-0-7660-5209-3). A blend of easy-to-understand narrative, vivid color photographs, and links to related online resources introduce Mercury. Also use *Pluto* (2005). (Rev: SLJ 12/05) [523.4]

12201 Simon, Seymour. *Neptune* (4–8). Illus. 1991, Morrow $17.89 (978-0-688-09632-8). The voyage of *Voyager II* as it swept past Neptune provided scientists with more information on this planet than they had ever had. (Rev: BCCB 4/91; BL 2/15/91; HB 5–6/91; SLJ 4/91) [523.4]

12202 Spence, Pam. *Sun Observer's Guide* (7–12). Illus. 2004, Firefly paper $14.95 (978-1-55297-941-9). A useful guide to the sun and the equipment that ensures safe observation of it. (Rev: BL 11/1/04) [522]

Universe

12203 Asimov, Isaac. *The Birth of Our Universe* (5–8). Illus. Series: Isaac Asimov's 21st Century Library of the Universe. 2005, Gareth Stevens LB $26.00 (978-0-8368-3964-7). This is an update of a 1995 edition on the origins of the universe, with illustrations and photographs. (Rev: BL 3/1/05) [523.1]

12204 Fleisher, Paul. *The Big Bang* (5–8). Illus. Series: Great Ideas in Science. 2005, Twenty-First Century LB $27.93 (978-0-8225-2133-4). Students with a real interest in science will benefit most from this overview of theories about the creation of the universe, from creation myths onward. (Rev: BL 12/1/05; SLJ 12/05) [523.1]

12205 Miller, Ron. *Stars and Galaxies* (7–10). Illus. Series: Worlds Beyond. 2005, Twenty-First Century LB $27.93 (978-0-7613-3466-8). A comprehensive overview of the universe, discussing theories and facts about neighboring stars and distant galaxies alike, with wonderful NASA photos mixed with original art. (Rev: BL 12/1/05; SLJ 12/05) [523.8]

12206 Miotto, Enrico. *The Universe: Origins and Evolution* (5–8). Series: Beginnings. 1995, Raintree LB $24.26 (978-0-8114-3334-1). This basic outline of the history of the universe begins with the Big Bang theory and finishes with the "Big Crunch" that may end time. (Rev: BL 4/15/95) [523.1]

12207 Reed, George. *Eyes on the Universe* (6–10). Series: Story of Science. 2000, Marshall Cavendish LB $29.93 (978-0-7614-1154-3). A clear, attractively presented introduction to the universe and its components. (Rev: BL 12/15/00; HBG 10/01) [523]

12208 Ruiz, Andres L. *The Origin of the Universe* (4–9). Series: Sequences of Earth and Space. 1997, Sterling $12.95 (978-0-8069-9744-5). In simple, concise language, this work discusses various theories concerning the origin of the universe, including the Big Bang theory. (Rev: BL 12/15/97) [523]

12209 Villard, Ray, and Lynette Cook. *Infinite Worlds: An Illustrated Voyage to Planets Beyond Our Sun* (8–12). Illus. 2005, Univ. of California $39.95 (978-0-520-23710-0). Using known data, the author and illustrator speculate about the likely appearance of planets in other solar systems. (Rev: BL 6/1–15/05) [523.21]

Biological Sciences

General and Miscellaneous

12210 Bottone, Frank G., Jr. *The Science of Life: Projects and Principles for Beginning Biologists* (5–8). Illus. 2001, Chicago Review paper $14.95 (978-1-55652-382-3). Twenty-five projects introduce readers to the basics of biology and the rigors of scientific research. (Rev: SLJ 11/01) [570.78]

12211 Brooks, Bruce. *The Red Wasteland* (6–10). 1995, Holt $15.95 (978-0-8050-4495-9). A fine anthology of essays, stories, poems, and book excerpts by some of the best nature writers, who raise themes and questions about crucial issues relating to the environment. (Rev: BL 8/98; HBG 3/99; SLJ 6/98; VOYA 8/98) [808]

12212 Carson, Mary Kay. *Emi and the Rhino Scientist* (5–8). Illus. Series: Scientists in the Field. 2007, Houghton $18.00 (978-0-618-64639-5). Emi, a rhinoceros at the Cincinnati Zoo, gives birth in captivity (which is unusual for a rhino) thanks to the help of scientist Terri Roth in this exciting and informative account. (Rev: BL 12/1/07; HB 11–12/07; SLJ 11/07) [599.66]

12213 Castner, James L. *Layers of Life* (6–12). Illus. Series: Deep in the Amazon. 2001, Marshall Cavendish LB $28.50 (978-0-7614-1130-7). This volume explores the biodiversity found in each "layer" of the Amazonian rain forest, with color photographs. Also use *Partners and Rivals*, *River Life*, and *Surviving in the Rain Forest* (all 2001). (Rev: BL 12/15/01; HBG 3/02) [577.34]

12214 *DK Nature Encyclopedia* (5–8). 1998, DK paper $29.99 (978-0-7894-3411-1). A browsable reference book that covers topics including classification of living things, ecology, the origins and evolution of life, specific animal and plant groups, and the inner workings of plants and animals, all in a series of beautifully illustrated double-page spreads. (Rev: BL 12/1/98; SLJ 2/99) [574]

12215 Doris, Ellen. *Woods, Ponds, and Fields* (4–7). Illus. Series: Real Kids Real Science. 1994, Thames & Hudson $16.95 (978-0-500-19006-7). A book that gives background essays as well as step-by-step directions for nature study projects in all seasons. (Rev: BL 9/1/94) [508]

12216 Emory, Jerry. *Dirty, Rotten, Dead? A Worm's-eye View of Death, Decomposition . . . and Life* (5–8). Illus. 1996, Harcourt paper $15.00 (978-0-15-200695-2). Along with a number of experiments and ecological projects, this book discusses death and recycling in nature, including such topics as the parts of the human body that become waste (e.g. hair, nails, skin), digestion and human excretion, processing of sewage, water pollution, diseases of the immune system, and contemporary mortician practices. (Rev: SLJ 8/96) [628.4]

12217 Fullick, Ann. *Adaptation and Competition* (6–9). Illus. Series: Life Science in Depth. 2006, Heinemann LB $24.00 (978-1-4034-7518-3). Explores living organisms' ability to adapt to a wide array of climates and habitats and how these organisms compete with one another to survive. (Rev: BL 4/1/06) [587.4]

12218 Gallant, Roy A. *The Wonders of Biodiversity* (5–8). Illus. Series: The Story of Science. 2002, Benchmark $29.93 (978-0-7614-1427-8). Gallant discusses the importance of biodiversity, the plight of species that are affected by loss of habitat and other environmental factors, and species interdependence. (Rev: HBG 3/03; SLJ 2/03) [578]

12219 Johnson, Rebecca L. *Mighty Animal Cells* (5–7). Illus. by Jack Desrocher. Series: Microquests. 2007, Lerner LB $29.27 (978-0-8225-7137-7). Animal cell structure and cell division, followed by human cells, are discussed in chapters such as

"Meet the Organelles," "What Cells Do," and "Cells with Special Talents" in this reader-friendly but information-packed book with cartoon illustrations to spice up the text. (Rev: BL 10/15/07; HB 1–2/08*; SLJ 11/07) [571.6]

12220 Kelsey, Elin. *Strange New Species: Astonishing Discoveries of Life on Earth* (5–8). Illus. 2005, Maple Tree $24.95 (978-1-897066-31-7). A large-format, well-illustrated introduction to plant and animal classification and to newly discovered species. (Rev: BL 10/15/05; SLJ 2/06) [578]

12221 Panno, Joseph. *Animal Cloning: The Science of Nuclear Transfer* (7–12). Illus. Series: The New Biology. 2004, Facts on File $35.00 (978-0-8160-4947-9). A look at the controversial issue of animal cloning and its scientific implications. (Rev: SLJ 2/05)

12222 Panno, Joseph. *The Cell: Evolution of the First Organism* (7–12). Illus. Series: The New Biology. 2004, Facts on File $35.00 (978-0-8160-4946-2). Reviews theories about life's origin and examines such related topics as cell structure, cell cycle, genes, multi-cellular organisms, and neurons. (Rev: SLJ 2/05)

12223 Parker, Steve. *Survival and Change* (4–7). Series: Life Processes. 2001, Heinemann LB $21.36 (978-1-57572-340-2). Parker considers how organisms evolve and looks at how species behave under threat and the origin of new species in this concise book with diagrams, charts, and color photographs. (Rev: HBG 10/01; SLJ 7/01) [578.4]

12224 Quinlan, Susan E. *The Case of the Monkeys That Fell from the Trees: And Other Mysteries in Tropical Nature* (5–8). Illus. 2003, Boyds Mills $15.95 (978-1-56397-902-6). Quinlan introduces plant and animal mysteries in South and Central American tropical forests and shows how scientists approached solving them. (Rev: BL 3/1/03; HBG 10/03; SLJ 3/03; VOYA 10/03) [508.313]

12225 Raham, R. Gary. *Dinosaurs in the Garden: An Evolutionary Guide to Backyard Biology* (6–10). Illus. 1988, Plexus $22.95 (978-0-937548-10-3). The author uses common creatures to explain how they fit into the scheme of nature and overall patterns of evolution. (Rev: BL 12/1/88) [575]

12226 Silverstein, Alvin. *Adaptation* (6–9). Illus. Series: Science Concepts. 2007, Lerner LB $31.93 (978-0-8225-3434-1). This volume looks at evolution and adaptation and explores the factors involved. (Rev: BL 12/1/07; SLJ 4/08) [578.4]

12227 Silverstein, Alvin, et al. *Food Chains* (6–9). Series: Science Concepts. 1998, Twenty-First Century LB $26.90 (978-0-7613-3002-8). A clearly written account that explains the concept of food chains, with background information and many examples, and reviews the most current information. (Rev: HBG 3/99; SLJ 1/99) [574.5]

12228 Silverstein, Alvin, et al. *Symbiosis* (5–9). Series: Science Concepts. 1998, Twenty-First Century LB $26.90 (978-0-7613-3001-1). The concept of cooperation in nature for mutual benefit is explored, with explanations of various forms of symbiotic partnerships including the relationships humans have with animals, plants, fungi, and microorganisms. (Rev: HBG 3/99; SLJ 2/99) [574.5]

12229 Triefeldt, Laurie. *Plants and Animals* (4–8). Illus. Series: World of Wonder. 2007, Quill Driver $19.95 (978-1-884956-72-0). By the author of a nationally syndicated newspaper column called World of Wonder, this book, a companion to *People and Places*, covers a huge amount of material and will be helpful to report writers. (Rev: BL 4/1/08) [570]

12230 Turner, Pamela. *Life on Earth — and Beyond* (5–8). Illus. 2008, Charlesbridge $19.95 (978-1-58089-133-2); paper $11.95 (978-1-58089-134-9). Readers follow NASA astrobiologist Chris McKay as he searches for microbes in extreme environments on Earth — in hopes of determining if life can survive in extreme environments in space. (Rev: BL 2/1/08; SLJ 3/08) [571.0919]

12231 VanCleave, Janice. *Janice VanCleave's A+ Projects in Biology: Winning Experiments for Science Fairs and Extra Credit* (6–10). 1993, Wiley paper $12.95 (978-0-471-58628-9). Offers a variety of experiments in botany, zoology, and the human body. (Rev: BL 1/15/94; SLJ 11/93) [574]

12232 Walker, Pam, and Elaine Wood. *Ecosystem Science Fair Projects Using Worms, Leaves, Crickets, and Other Stuff* (6–12). Illus. Series: Biology! Best Science Projects. 2005, Enslow LB $26.60 (978-0-7660-2367-3). Biology science projects are clearly presented with background information necessary to full understanding of the underlying principles. (Rev: SLJ 7/05) [570]

12233 Wallace, Holly. *Classification* (4–7). Series: Life Processes. 2006, Heinemann LB $20.50 (978-1-4034-8845-9). A clear and colorful introduction to the classification of plants and animals. (Rev: BL 10/15/06) [570.1]

Botany

General and Miscellaneous

12234 Bonnet, Robert L., and G. Daniel Keen. *Botany: 49 Science Fair Projects* (6–10). Illus. 1989, TAB $16.95 (978-0-8306-9277-4). Well-explained projects involving such phenomena as photosynthesis, hydroponics, fungi, and germination. (Rev: BL 1/15/90; VOYA 2/90) [581]

12235 Greenaway, Theresa. *The Plant Kingdom* (5–8). Illus. 1999, Raintree LB $27.12 (978-0-8172-5886-3). Using diagrams, sidebars, and color photographs, this account introduces the basics of plant classification while also covering such topics as photosynthesis and plant reproduction. (Rev: BL 2/1/00) [580]

12236 Lincoff, Gary. *The Audubon Society Field Guide to North American Mushrooms* (7–12). Illus. 1981, Knopf $19.95 (978-0-394-51992-0). More than 700 species are introduced and pictured in color photographs. [589.2]

12237 Pascoe, Elaine. *Slime, Molds, and Fungus* (4–7). Series: Nature Close-Up. 1998, Blackbirch LB $23.70 (978-1-56711-182-8). Stunning photographs, good background information, and a number of interesting projects help introduce the world of fungi. (Rev: BL 9/15/98; HBG 3/99; SLJ 3/99) [589.2]

12238 Patent, Dorothy Hinshaw. *Plants on the Trail with Lewis and Clark.* (5–8). Photos by William Muñoz. 2003, Clarion $18.00 (978-0-618-06776-3). This introduction to the trees and plants seen by Lewis and Clark also discusses Lewis's training as a botanist and his contributions to the field. (Rev: BL 3/1/03; HBG 10/03; SLJ 5/03) [581.978]

12239 Silverstein, Alvin, et al. *Photosynthesis* (5–9). Series: Science Concepts. 1998, Twenty-First Century LB $26.90 (978-0-7613-3000-4). Photosynthesis is explained, with a history of the discoveries about the process and material on related issues including acid rain and the greenhouse effect. (Rev: HBG 3/99; SLJ 2/99) [581.1]

12240 Tesar, Jenny. *Fungi* (5–7). Illus. Series: Our Living World. 1994, Blackbirch LB $24.95 (978-1-56711-044-9). A volume that explains what a fungus is, how the various types reproduce and grow, their unique characteristics, and how they fit into food webs and chains. (Rev: BL 12/1/94) [589.2]

Foods, Farms, and Ranches

GENERAL AND MISCELLANEOUS

12241 Artley, Bob. *Once Upon a Farm* (4–9). Illus. by author. 2000, Pelican $21.95 (978-1-56554-753-7). Fine watercolors accompany a readable look at the seasons as experienced by the author while growing up on a farm in Iowa. (Rev: SLJ 12/00) [630]

12242 Bial, Raymond. *The Farms* (4–7). Photos by author. Illus. Series: Building America. 2001, Benchmark LB $27.07 (978-0-7614-1332-5). An interesting, beautifully illustrated look at the ways in which farms developed in America, with information on their structure and significance to the country as a whole. Also use *The Mills* (2001). (Rev: HBG 3/02; SLJ 2/02*) [630]

12243 *Bound for Glory: America in Color, 1939–43* (8–12). Illus. 2004, Abrams $35.00 (978-0-8109-4348-3). American farm life during the late 1930s and early 1940s is beautifully captured in these color photographs taken under the auspices of the Farm Security Administration, best known for earlier black-and-white collections. (Rev: BL 6/1–15/04) [779]

12244 Bowden, Rob. *Food and Farming* (5–8). Illus. Series: Sustainable World. 2004, Gale LB $26.20 (978-0-7377-1899-7). Bowden looks at conventional methods of farming and at the new focus on sustainable agriculture, providing lots of facts and statistics and highlighting choices we all can make that may improve the future. (Rev: BL 4/15/04; SLJ 10/04) [338]

12245 Busenberg, Bonnie. *Vanilla, Chocolate and Strawberry: The Story of Your Favorite Flavors* (6–9). Illus. Series: Discovery! 1994, Lerner LB $23.93 (978-0-8225-1573-9). With the generous use of maps, diagrams, and photographs, this is the breezy overview of three popular flavors, how they are produced, and how they are used. (Rev: BL 6/1–15/94) [664.5]

12246 Chandler, Gary, and Kevin Graham. *Natural Foods and Products* (4–8). Illus. Series: Making a Better World. 1996, Twenty-First Century LB $25.90 (978-0-8050-4623-6). This work discusses genetically engineered foods, safe eco-friendly methods of growing crops, and companies that engage in safe practices. (Rev: BL 12/15/96; SLJ 1/97) [333.76]

12247 Damerow, Gail. *Your Chickens: A Kid's Guide to Raising and Showing* (4–7). Illus. 1993, Storey paper $14.95 (978-0-88266-823-9). A straightforward, practical guide on raising prize-winning chickens that is both thorough and filled with information. (Rev: BL 5/15/94; SLJ 1/94) [636.5]

12248 Damerow, Gail. *Your Goats: A Kid's Guide to Raising and Showing* (4–7). Illus. 1993, Storey paper $14.95 (978-0-88266-825-3). This is a complete guide to raising, breeding, and showing goats, with many useful tips and helpful illustrations. (Rev: BL 5/15/94; SLJ 1/94) [636.3]

12249 Dunn-Georgiou, Elisha. *Everything You Need to Know About Organic Foods* (6–10). Illus. Series: Need to Know Library. 2002, Rosen LB $27.95 (978-0-8239-3551-2). An examination of the techniques that produce organic foods and the benefits of eating foods that are free of certain additives. (Rev: BL 5/1/02; SLJ 6/02) [641.3]

12250 Eagen, Rachel. *The Biography of Bananas* (4–7). Illus. Series: How Did That Get Here? 2005, Crabtree LB $26.60 (978-0-7787-2483-4). This richly illustrated title offers a wealth of information about the science and business of producing bananas. (Rev: BL 3/1/06) [634]

12251 Hayhurst, Chris. *Everything You Need to Know About Food Additives* (6–10). Illus. Series: Need to Know Library. 2002, Rosen LB $27.95 (978-0-8239-3548-2). An examination of the kinds of additives used in foods, their benefits and disadvantages, and the alternatives available to people seeking a healthier diet. (Rev: BL 5/1/02) [664]

12252 Hughes, Meredith S. *Flavor Foods: Spices and Herbs* (5–8). Series: Plants We Eat. 2000, Lerner LB $26.60 (978-0-8225-2835-7). This book explains how roots, leaves, flowers, seeds, fruit, and bark of some plants are transformed in the seasonings that flavor so many dishes. (Rev: BL 7/00; HBG 10/00) [633.8]

12253 Hughes, Meredith S. *Glorious Grasses: The Grains* (5–8). Series: Plants We Eat. 1999, Lerner LB $26.60 (978-0-8225-2831-9). A description of the history, cultivation, processing, and dietary importance of wheat, rice, corn, millet, barley, oats, and rye, plus recipes and activities. (Rev: BL 7/99; HBG 10/99; SLJ 8/99) [633.1]

12254 Hughes, Meredith S. *Tall and Tasty: Fruit Trees* (5–8). Series: Plants We Eat. 2000, Lerner LB $31.95 (978-0-8225-2837-1). This book explores the world of apples, peaches, mangoes, and other fruits that grow on trees and explains each one's life cycle, and how the fruit has migrated during its history. (Rev: BL 4/15/00; HBG 10/00) [641.3]

12255 Hughes, Meredith S. *Yes, We Have Bananas: Fruits from Shrubs and Vines* (5–8). Series: Plants We Eat. 1999, Lerner LB $26.60 (978-0-8225-2836-4). A fascinating introduction to bananas, pineapples, grapes, berries, and melons with material on how and where they grow, their cultivation and marketing, plus fun recipes and activities. (Rev: BL 11/15/99; HBG 3/00; SLJ 3/00) [641]

12256 Jango-Cohen, Judith. *The History of Food* (5–8). Series: Major Inventions Through History. 2005, Twenty-First Century LB $26.60 (978-0-8225-2484-7). Addresses inventions in the food industry such as canning, pasteurization, and genetically modified crops. (Rev: SLJ 2/06)

12257 Johnson, Sylvia A. *Apple Trees* (5–8). Illus. by Hiro Koike. 1983, Lerner LB $31.95 (978-0-8225-1479-4). The story of the apple tree and seed and fruit formation.

12258 Jones, Carol. *Cheese* (4–7). Illus. Series: From Farm to You. 2002, Chelsea $28.00 (978-0-7910-7005-5). This is an absorbing account of the techniques used in manufacturing cheese and the history of cheese, with an overview of the many varieties and a map of cheese eating around the world. Also use *Pasta and Noodles* (2002). (Rev: BL 11/1/02; HBG 3/03) [641.3]

12259 Lasky, Kathryn. *Sugaring Time* (4–7). Illus. 1998, Center for Applied Research paper $4.95 (978-0-87628-350-9). Through photographs and text, the process of maple sugar production in New England is described.

12260 Maestro, Betsy. *How Do Apples Grow?* (5–8). Illus. by Giulio Maestro. Series: Let's-Read-and-Find-Out. 1992, HarperCollins LB $16.89 (978-0-06-020056-5). The development of the apple from bud to fruit. (Rev: BL 12/15/91; HB 1–2/92; SLJ 2/92) [582]

12261 Meltzer, Milton. *Food* (4–8). Illus. 1998, Millbrook LB $24.90 (978-0-7613-0354-1). A fascinating history of food and how it affects our lives. (Rev: BL 1/1–15/99; HBG 3/99; SLJ 1/99) [641.3]

12262 Morgan, Sally. *Superfoods: Genetic Modification of Foods* (5–8). Series: Science at the Edge. 2002, Heinemann LB $27.86 (978-1-58810-702-2). A look at the history and genetic alteration of foods, with discussion of the controversy this has created. (Rev: BL 10/15/02; HBG 3/03; SLJ 4/03) [174.957]

12263 Morris, Neil. *Do You Know Where Your Food Comes From?* (4–7). Illus. 2006, Heinemann LB $32.86 (978-1-4034-8575-5). In this informative book students learn all about the global food market, where and how their food is produced, and how to make good food choices. (Rev: BL 12/1/06; SLJ 4/07) [363.8]

12264 Olney, Ross R. *The Farm Combine* (4–8). Illus. 1984, Walker LB $10.85 (978-0-8027-6568-0). The development of the reaper and thrasher is discussed, with information on today's combine harvester.

12265 Tesar, Jenny. *Food and Water: Threats, Shortages and Solutions* (5–9). Series: Our Fragile Planet. 1992, Facts on File LB $21.95 (978-0-8160-2495-7). A discussion of the world's water and food supplies, threats to them, and possible solutions. (Rev: BL 6/1/92) [333.91]

12266 Wardlaw, Lee. *Bubblemania* (4–8). 1997, Simon & Schuster paper $4.99 (978-0-689-81719-9). A thorough history of chewing gum, including descriptions of how gum is made, marketed, and distributed. (Rev: BL 10/1/97; SLJ 1/98) [641.3]

12267 Wardlaw, Lee. *We All Scream for Ice Cream: The Scoop on America's Favorite Dessert* (4–7). Illus. by Sandra Forrest. 2000, HarperTrophy paper $4.95 (978-0-380-80250-0). A history of this frozen dessert from ancient times to the present with a concentration on modern times and such variations as Eskimo pies and the Good Humor business. (Rev: SLJ 11/00) [637]

12268 Webber, Desiree Morrison. *Bone Head: Story of the Longhorn* (4–7). Illus. by Sandy Shropshire. 2003, Eakin $16.95 (978-1-57168-763-0). The longhorn's characteristics and the reasons for its early success but decline with the arrival of the railroad are explored in appealing text and archival photographs. (Rev: SLJ 2/04) [636.2]

VEGETABLES

12269 Hughes, Meredith S. *Cool as a Cucumber, Hot as a Pepper* (5–8). Series: Foods We Eat. 1999, Lerner LB $26.60 (978-0-8225-2832-6). This lively book on vegetables gives botanical information, details on growing and harvesting, the history of many of these plants, and a number of mouth-watering recipes. (Rev: BL 7/99; HBG 10/99; SLJ 8/99) [635]

12270 Hughes, Meredith S. *Spill the Beans and Pass the Peanuts: Legumes* (5–8). Series: Plants We Eat. 1999, Lerner LB $31.95 (978-0-8225-2834-0). Peas and beans are two of the legumes introduced in this book that explains, in an entertaining way, their origins, how they grow, their appearance, and nutritional value, plus giving the occasional recipe or activity. (Rev: BL 10/15/99; HBG 3/00; SLJ 12/99) [641.6]

12271 Hughes, Meredith S. *Stinky and Stringy* (5–8). Series: Plants We Eat. 1999, Lerner LB $31.95 (978-0-8225-2833-3). Stem and bulb vegetables onions and garlic are introduced with interesting historical information, details about their cultivation, harvesting and marketing, and a few tempting recipes. (Rev: BL 7/99; HBG 10/99; SLJ 8/99) [635]

12272 Hughes, Meredith S., and E. Thomas Hughes. *Buried Treasure: Roots and Tubers* (4–7). Series: Plants We Eat. 1998, Lerner LB $26.60 (978-0-8225-2830-2). Covering such vegetables as potatoes, sweet potatoes, carrots, turnips, beets, and radishes, this account describes the origin, history, cultivation, and importance of each. (Rev: HBG 3/99; SLJ 4/99) [635]

Forestry and Trees

12273 Cassie, Brian. *National Audubon Society First Field Guide: Trees* (4–8). 1999, Scholastic $17.95 (978-0-590-05472-0); paper $8.95 (978-0-590-05490-4). After a general, illustrated introduction to the characteristics and types of North American trees, this field guide then categorizes the trees according to the shape of their leaves. (Rev: BL 3/15/99; SLJ 7/99) [582.16]

12274 Gardner, Robert, and David Webster. *Science Project Ideas About Trees* (5–8). Illus. Series: Science Project Ideas. 1997, Enslow LB $25.26 (978-0-89490-846-0). The parts of trees and their functions are described, with activities involving leaves, seeds, flowers, roots, and twigs. (Rev: BL 12/1/97; HBG 3/98; SLJ 2/98) [582.16]

12275 Jorgensen, Lisa. *Grand Trees of America: Our State and Champion Trees* (4–7). Illus. 1992, Roberts paper $8.95 (978-1-879373-15-0). This book describes the official tree of each state and introduces the National Register of Big Trees. (Rev: BL 2/15/93) [582.16]

12276 Little, Elbert L. *The Audubon Society Field Guide to North American Trees: Eastern Region* (7–12). Illus. 1980, Knopf $19.95 (978-0-394-50760-6). This volume describes through text and pictures of leaves, needles, and so on, the trees found east of the Rocky Mountains. [582.16]

12277 Little, Elbert L. *The Audubon Society Field Guide to North American Trees: Western Region* (7–12). Illus. 1980, Knopf $19.95 (978-0-394-50761-3). Trees west of the Rockies are identified and pictured in photographs and drawings. [582.16]

12278 Pascoe, Elaine. *Leaves and Trees* (4–7). Series: Nature Close-Up. 2001, Blackbirch LB $23.70 (978-1-56711-474-4). Easy projects and a simple text are used to introduce the nature of trees and leaves and the living processes involved. (Rev: BL 9/15/01; HBG 3/02) [582.16]

12279 Petrides, George A. *A Field Guide to Trees and Shrubs* (7–12). Illus. 1973, Houghton paper $19.00 (978-0-395-35370-7). A total of 646 varieties found in northern United States and southern Canada are described and illustrated. [582.1]

12280 Whitman, Ann H., and Jane Friedman, eds. *Familiar Trees of North America: Eastern Region* (8–12). 1986, Knopf paper $9.00 (978-0-394-74851-1). As well as pictures and descriptions, this guide supplies historical information, habitats, and uses for 80 trees commonly found in the eastern parts of North America. [582.16]

12281 Whitman, Ann H., and Jane Friedman, eds. *Familiar Trees of North America: Western Region* (8–12). 1986, Knopf paper $9.00 (978-0-394-74852-8). This pocket guide covers 80 trees found commonly in the western United States. [582.16]

12282 Zim, Herbert S., and Alexander C. Martin. *Trees* (5–8). Illus. 1991, Western paper $21.27 (978-0-307-64056-7). A small, handy volume packed with information and color illustrations that help identify our most important trees. [582.16]

Plants and Flowers

12283 Busch, Phyllis B. *Wildflowers and the Stories Behind Their Names* (7–9). Illus. 1977, Macmillan $10.00 (978-0-684-14820-5). In this compact volume, 60 wildflowers are identified and pictured. [582.13]

12284 Dowden, Anne O. *From Flower to Fruit* (6–9). Illus. 1984, HarperCollins $14.95 (978-0-

690-04402-7). A description of seeds, how they are scattered, and how fruit is produced. [582]

12285 Garassino, Alessandro. *Plants: Origins and Evolution* (4–8). Illus. Series: Beginnings — Origins and Evolution. 1995, Raintree LB $24.26 (978-0-8114-3332-7). This treatment of plant evolution includes good factual data and discussion of several important concepts. (Rev: BL 4/15/95) [581.3]

12286 Gardner, Robert. *Science Projects About Plants* (5–8). Illus. Series: Science Projects. 1999, Enslow LB $26.60 (978-0-89490-952-8). This book contains a series of fascinating experiments and projects involving seeds, leaves, roots, stems, flowers, and whole plants. (Rev: BL 2/15/99; SLJ 5/99) [580]

12287 Hood, Susan, and National Audubon Society, eds. *Wildflowers* (5–8). Illus. 1998, Scholastic paper $17.95 (978-0-590-05464-5). Fifty common wildflowers are pictured and described, along with information on what equipment to use and what to look for to observe and study wildflowers (leaves, blooms, habitat, height, range). (Rev: BL 8/98; SLJ 8/98) [583]

12288 Johnson, Sylvia A. *Morning Glories* (4–7). Illus. 1985, Lerner LB $22.60 (978-0-8225-1462-6). Color photographs display the stages of this plant's development. (Rev: BCCB 3/86; BL 4/15/86; SLJ 4/86)

12289 Lerner, Carol. *Cactus* (4–7). Illus. 1992, Morrow LB $14.89 (978-0-688-09637-3). After explaining the parts of the cactus and how it can exist in near-waterless environments, this account describes different species. (Rev: BCCB 10/92; HB 1–2/93; SLJ 12/92) [635.7]

12290 Overbeck, Cynthia. *Carnivorous Plants* (4–8). Illus. by Kiyashi Shimizu. 1982, Lerner LB $31.95 (978-0-8225-1470-1). A survey of these plants and how they evolved. [581.5]

12291 Silverstein, Alvin, et al. *Plants* (7–10). Series: Kingdoms of Life. 1996, Twenty-First Century LB $25.90 (978-0-8050-3519-3). The classification system of plants is explained, from simple plants through ferns and on to flowering plants. (Rev: BL 6/1–15/96; SLJ 7/96) [581]

12292 Souza, D. M. *Freaky Flowers* (4–7). Series: Watts Library. 2002, Watts LB $25.50 (978-0-531-11981-5). Flowering plants are the main focus in this discussion of basic botany, the ways in which flowers attract pollinators, and the environmental dangers plants are facing. (Rev: SLJ 7/02) [582]

12293 Spellenberg, Richard. *Familiar Flowers of North America: Eastern Region* (8–12). 1986, Knopf paper $9.00 (978-0-394-74843-6). Photographs, diagrams, and descriptions are found in this guide to 80 wildflowers found in the eastern regions

of North America. Also use *Familiar Flowers of North America: Western Region*. [582.13]

12294 Winner, Cherie. *The Sunflower Family* (4–7). Illus. 1996, Carolrhoda LB $23.93 (978-1-57505-007-2); paper $7.95 (978-1-57505-029-4). Growth patterns, structures, and reproduction are topics covered in this account of the sunflower family, including thistles, daisies, and asters. (Rev: BL 10/1/96; SLJ 10/96) [583]

Seeds

12295 Burns, Diane L. *Berries, Nuts and Seeds* (4–7). Illus. by John F. McGee. 1996, NorthWord paper $7.95 (978-1-55971-573-7). Each page in this guide is devoted to a description of a single berry, nut, or seed. (Rev: BL 2/15/97) [582.13]

Zoology

General and Miscellaneous

12296 Aaseng, Nathan. *Nature's Poisonous Creatures* (5–9). Series: Scientific American Sourcebooks. 1997, Twenty-First Century LB $28.90 (978-0-8050-4690-8). After a general introduction to animal poisons, why they are produced, and their composition, this book devotes separate chapters to such venom-bearing vertebrates and invertebrates as sea wasps, blue-ringed octopi, African killer bees, and marine toads. (Rev: BL 2/1/98; SLJ 8/98) [591.6]

12297 Barrow, Lloyd H. *Science Fair Projects Investigating Earthworms* (5–8). Series: Science Fair Success. 2000, Enslow LB $26.60 (978-0-7660-1291-2). This book contains a fascinating number of experiments involving earthworms, with very explicit directions and explanations of the scientific principles behind each project. (Rev: BL 4/15/00; HBG 10/00) [595.1]

12298 Breidahl, Harry. *Extremophiles: Life in Extreme Environments* (6–8). Series: Life in Strange Places. 2001, Chelsea LB $28.00 (978-0-7910-6617-1). In addition to describing the organisms that thrive in environments such as Antarctica and deserts, this volume includes information on a working microbiologist and provides many photographs. (Rev: HBG 3/02; SLJ 1/02)

12299 Browning, Bel. *Animal Welfare* (5–8). Illus. Series: Face the Facts. 2003, Raintree LB $28.56 (978-0-7398-6430-2). Hot issues in animal protection such as whaling, intensive farming, and zoos are discussed, and practical responses from young people are suggested. (Rev: BL 11/15/03; HBG 10/03) [364.1]

12300 Cobb, Allan B. *Super Science Projects About Animals and Their Habitats* (4–8). Series: Psyched for Science. 2000, Rosen LB $26.50 (978-0-8239-3175-0). Six hand-on activities are introduced to help children observe animals and to study their adjustments to climate, habitat, and food. (Rev: SLJ 9/00) [591]

12301 Day, Nancy. *Animal Experimentation: Cruelty or Science?* Rev. ed. (7–9). Series: Issues in Focus. 2000, Enslow LB $26.60 (978-0-7660-1244-8). A balanced discussion of animal rights and of experiments that use animals, presenting alternatives to the practice. (Rev: HBG 3/01; SLJ 1/01) [179]

12302 Doris, Ellen. *Meet the Arthropods* (4–7). 1996, Thames & Hudson $16.95 (978-0-500-19010-4). Such arthropods as the horseshoe crab, potato beetle, and praying mantis are introduced with photographs and activities. (Rev: BL 10/15/96) [595.2]

12303 Ganeri, Anita. *Animals* (4–7). Series: Inside and Outside Guide. 2006, Heinemann LB $29.29 (978-1-4034-9084-1). This attractive guide provides in-depth introductions to 12 animals, with double-page spreads focusing on each animal's identifying characteristics and behaviors. (Rev: BL 10/15/06) [571.3]

12304 Halfmann, Janet. *Life in a Garden* (5–7). Photos by David Liebman. 2000, Creative LB $22.60 (978-1-58341-072-1). This book explores such life forms found in a garden as fungi, beetles, slugs, snails, and aphids. (Rev: SLJ 8/00) [635]

12305 Hiller, Ilo. *Introducing Mammals to Young Naturalists* (5–9). Illus. 1990, Texas A & M Univ. $9.00 (978-0-89096-427-9). An introduction to a number of mammals, from the common squirrel to the exotic armadillo. (Rev: BL 7/90) [599]

12306 Hodgkins, Fran. *Animals Among Us: Living with Suburban Wildlife* (5–8). Illus. 2000, Linnet LB $19.50 (978-0-208-02478-7). This book discusses the behavior and lifestyles of animals such as deer, coyotes, bears, skunks, and bats that live in suburbs, close to their original haunts. (Rev: BL 6/1–15/00; HB 7–8/00; HBG 10/00; SLJ 9/00; VOYA 12/00) [591.7]

12307 Johnson, Sylvia A. *Silkworms* (4–7). Illus. 1982, Lerner paper $5.95 (978-0-8225-9557-1). The life cycle of the silkworm, told in text and striking color pictures. [595.78]

12308 Kneidel, Sally. *Slugs, Bugs, and Salamanders: Discovering Animals in Your Garden* (5–7). Illus. by Anna-Maria L. Crum. 1997, Fulcrum paper $16.95 (978-1-55591-313-7). As well as introducing backyard insects and other small creatures, this account gives a number of tips on growing healthy flowers and vegetables. (Rev: SLJ 10/97) [595.7]

12309 Lauber, Patricia. *Fur, Feathers, and Flippers: How Animals Live Where They Do* (4–8). Illus. 1994, Scholastic paper $4.95 (978-0-590-45072-0). Using various habitats such as the grasslands of East Africa as examples, this photoessay describes how animals have adapted to their different environments. (Rev: BL 12/1/94*; SLJ 12/94) [591.5]

12310 Miles, Victoria. *Wild Science: Amazing Encounters Between Animals and the People Who Study Them* (5–8). Series: Scientists in the Field. 2004, Raincoast paper $18.95 (978-1-55192-618-6). This photo-filled volume introduces readers to scientists who study animals and describes memorable moments with animals in the wilderness. (Rev: BL 12/1/04; SLJ 12/04) [591.68]

12311 Noyes, Deborah. *One Kingdom: Our Lives with Animals* (7–10). Illus. 2006, Houghton $18.00 (978-0-618-49914-4). The bond between humans and animals is the topic of this thoughtful photoessay that looks in particular at zoos and conservation. (Rev: BL 10/15/06; HB 9–10/06; LMC 10/06; SLJ 11/06) [590]

12312 Palazzo, Tony. *The Biggest and the Littlest Animals* (4–7). Illus. by author. 1973, Lion LB $13.95 (978-0-87460-225-8). Many ways of comparing animals, including size and mobility, are explored.

12313 Pascoe, Elaine. *Snails and Slugs* (4–7). Series: Nature Close-Up. 1998, Blackbirch LB $23.70 (978-1-56711-181-1). Outstanding photographs, an interesting text, and several easy-to-do projects highlight this introduction to snails and slugs. (Rev: BL 9/15/98; HBG 3/99) [594.3]

12314 Whyman, Kate. *The Animal Kingdom* (5–8). Illus. 1999, Raintree LB $27.12 (978-0-8172-5885-6). A valuable account that introduces animal classification basics through text, sidebars, diagrams, and many eye-catching color photographs. (Rev: BL 2/1/00) [596]

12315 Woods, Geraldine. *Animal Experimentation and Testing: A Pro/Con Issue* (5–8). Series: Hot Issues. 1999, Enslow LB $27.93 (978-0-7660-1191-5). The controversial subject of using animals in experiments is discussed with a history of the problem, arguments for and against, and a summary of important actions taken by government and individual groups. (Rev: HBG 3/00; SLJ 3/00) [179.3]

Amphibians and Reptiles

GENERAL AND MISCELLANEOUS

12316 Behler, John. *National Audubon Society First Field Guide: Reptiles* (4–8). 1999, Scholastic $17.95 (978-0-590-05467-6); paper $11.95 (978-0-590-05487-4). This richly illustrated manual discusses common characteristics of North American reptiles, then presents individual species under four groups: crocodiles, turtles, lizards, and snakes. (Rev: BL 3/15/99; SLJ 7/99) [597.9]

12317 Crump, Marty. *Amphibians, Reptiles, and Their Conservation* (6–12). Illus. 2002, Linnet LB $25.00 (978-0-208-02511-1). After describing these animals and giving the pertinent scientific information, the author describes the challenges to their survival and what can be done to save them. (Rev: BL 12/1/02; HBG 3/03; SLJ 1/03; VOYA 6/03) [597.9]

12318 Dennard, Deborah. *Reptiles* (5–7). Illus. by Jennifer Owings Dewey. Series: Our Wild World. 2004, NorthWord $16.95 (978-1-55971-880-6). A compilation of four shorter books published by NorthWord in 2003, this volume examines the physical characteristics, natural habitat, diet, and behavior of alligators, crocodiles, lizards, snakes, and turtles. (Rev: SLJ 8/04) [597.9]

12319 Gibbons, Whit. *Their Blood Runs Cold: Adventures with Reptiles and Amphibians* (7–12). Illus. 1983, Univ. of Alabama paper $15.95 (978-0-8173-0133-0). An informal guide, geographically arranged, to snakes, crocodiles, turtles, salamanders, and toads. [597.6]

12320 King, F. Wayne, et al. *Discovery Channel Reptiles and Amphibians: An Explore Your World Handbook* (8–12). 2000, Discovery paper $14.95 (978-1-56331-839-9). Various reptiles and amphibians are identified in text and pictures, with material on defense mechanisms and habitats, as well as acquiring and caring for these creatures. [597.9]

12321 Wilkes, Sarah. *Amphibians* (5–9). Series: World Almanac Library of the Animal Kingdom. 2006, World Almanac LB $31.00 (978-0-8368-6208-9). This colorful guide identifies common species of amphibians and examines their physical characteristics, habitats, diets, behaviors, and life cycles. (Rev: SLJ 12/06) [597.5]

12322 Zabludoff, Marc. *The Reptile Class* (5–9). Illus. Series: Family Trees. 2005, Benchmark LB $32.79 (978-0-7614-1820-7). Habits, habitats, and other aspects of this varied class of animals; an engaging book with plenty of facts for report-writers. (Rev: SLJ 6/06) [597.9]

ALLIGATORS AND CROCODILES

12323 Fitzgerald, Patrick J. *Croc and Gator Attacks* (4–7). Series: Animal Attack! 2000, Children's paper $6.95 (978-0-516-23514-1). Aimed at the reluctant reader, this book tells true stories of attacks by crocodiles and alligators and gives information about these species and their differences. (Rev: SLJ 2/01) [597.98]

12324 Jango-Cohen, Judith. *Crocodiles* (5–8). Series: AnimalWays. 2000, Marshall Cavendish LB $31.36 (978-0-7614-1136-9). This book examines the habitat, range, classification, evolution, ana-

tomy, behavior, and endangered status of the crocodile. (Rev: BL 1/1–15/01; HBG 3/01) [597.98]

12325 Scherer, Glenn, and Marty Fletcher. *The American Crocodile: Help Save This Endangered Species!* (5–7). Illus. Series: Saving Endangered Species. 2007, Enslow $33.27 (978-1-59845-041-5). Report writers will welcome the information included in this volume and at the recommended Web links. (Rev: SLJ 11/07) [597.98]

12326 Snyder, Trish. *Alligator and Crocodile Rescue: Changing the Future for Endangered Wildlife* (4–8). Series: Firefly Animal Rescue. 2006, Firefly LB $19.95 (978-1-55297-920-4); paper $9.95 (978-1-55297-919-8). Examines the work being done to protect alligators and crocodiles in their natural habitats and also looks at the physical characteristics, diets, behaviors, and life cycles of these reptiles. (Rev: SLJ 12/06) [597.98]

FROGS AND TOADS

12327 Greenberg, Dan. *Frogs* (5–8). Series: AnimalWays. 2000, Marshall Cavendish LB $31.36 (978-0-7614-1138-3). As well as chapters devoted to the amazing variety of frogs, this book discusses their anatomy, habits, and survival skills. (Rev: BL 1/1–15/01; HBG 3/01) [597.8]

12328 Parsons, Harry. *The Nature of Frogs: Amphibians with Attitude* (6–12). Illus. 2001, Douglas & McIntyre $26.95 (978-1-55054-761-0). Readers will be drawn to the color photographs in this book and then intrigued by the informative text and mentions of these animals' portrayal in stories and legends. (Rev: BL 1/1–15/01; VOYA 6/01) [597.8]

12329 White, William. *All About the Frog* (4–8). Illus. Series: Sterling Color Nature. 1992, Sterling $14.95 (978-0-8069-8274-8). A brief history of the frog and a discussion of its anatomy, reproduction, food, adaptations, and likely future. (Rev: BL 7/92; SLJ 9/92) [597.8]

SNAKES AND LIZARDS

12330 Barth, Kelly L. *Snakes* (7–10). Series: Endangered Animals and Habitats. 2001, Lucent LB $27.45 (978-1-56006-696-5). This work focuses on the types of snakes that are threatened with extinction and the efforts employed to save them. (Rev: BL 3/15/01) [597.96]

12331 Behler, Deborah, and John Behler. *Snakes* (5–8). Series: AnimalWays. 2001, Marshall Cavendish LB $31.36 (978-0-7614-1265-6). Brilliant photographs highlight this fine introduction to snakes, their habitats, behavior, species, evolution, and anatomy. (Rev: BL 3/15/02; HBG 10/02) [597.96]

12332 Cherry, Jim. *Loco for Lizards* (7–12). Illus. 2000, Northland paper $7.95 (978-0-87358-763-1). This eclectic and entertaining overview of these reptiles provides basic scientific information plus a look at their important role in legends and contemporary culture. (Rev: SLJ 2/01) [597.95]

12333 Gaywood, Martin, and Ian Spellerberg. *Snakes* (6–12). Series: WorldLife Library. 1999, Voyageur paper $16.95 (978-0-89658-449-5). Facts about snakes and their ability to adapt to their environment are accompanied by discussion of their relationship with humans and eye-catching full-color photographs. (Rev: SLJ 4/00) [597.96]

12334 Greenaway, Theresa. *Snakes* (4–7). Series: The Secret World of . . . 2001, Raintree LB $18.98 (978-0-7368-3510-7). A look at the world of snakes with material on their structure, habitats, behavior, food, mating habits, and enemies. (Rev: BL 10/15/01) [597.96]

12335 Montgomery, Sy. *The Snake Scientist* (5–8). Series: Scientists in the Field. 1999, Houghton $16.00 (978-0-395-87169-0). This account captures the excitement of scientific discovery by focusing on a zoologist and young students who are studying the red-sided garter snake in Canada. (Rev: BCCB 4/99; BL 2/15/99; HB 7–8/99; HBG 9/99; SLJ 5/99) [597.96]

12336 Pipe, Jim. *The Giant Book of Snakes and Slithery Creatures* (4–8). Illus. 1998, Millbrook LB $27.90 (978-0-7613-0804-1). This richly illustrated, oversize volume contains details about snakes, lizards, and amphibians. (Rev: BL 8/98; HBG 9/98; SLJ 12/98) [597.9]

12337 Roever, J. M. *Snake Secrets* (6–9). 1979, Walker LB $11.85 (978-0-8027-6333-4). An indepth look at snakes, their behavior, and how people react to them. [597.96]

12338 Simon, Seymour. *Poisonous Snakes* (6–9). Illus. 1981, Macmillan $11.95 (978-0-590-07513-8). An explanation of venom and fangs is given and an introduction to the world's most famous poisonous snakes. [597.9]

TORTOISES AND TURTLES

12339 Hawxhurst, Joan C. *Turtles and Tortoises* (7–10). Series: Endangered Animals and Habitats. 2001, Lucent LB $28.70 (978-1-56006-731-3). An exploration of the turtles and tortoises that are threatened with extinction, why they are endangered, and methods being used to save them. (Rev: BL 3/15/01) [597.92]

12340 Hickman, Pamela. *Turtle Rescue: Changing the Future for Endangered Wildlife* (4–8). Series: Firefly Animal Rescue. 2006, Firefly $19.95 (978-1-55297-916-7); paper $9.95 (978-1-55297-915-0). Hickman provides a detailed but accessible overview of the dangers facing turtles around the world and what is being done to protect them. (Rev: SLJ 6/06) [597.92]

12341 Lockwood, Sophie. *Sea Turtles* (4–7). Illus. Series: World of Reptiles. 2006, Child's World LB $29.93 (978-1-59296-550-2). In addition to the kind of information needed for reports, Lockwood discusses conservation, how scientists track turtles, and the turtle's appearances in folklore and art. (Rev: BL 4/1/06) [597.92]

12342 Stefoff, Rebecca. *Turtles* (4–8). Illus. Series: AnimalWays. 2007, Marshall Cavendish LB $23.95 (978-0-7614-2539-7). Report writers will find plenty of valuable information about turtles' anatomy, habitat, evolution, and appearances in literature and legend as well as discussion of conservation efforts and many attractive photographs. (Rev: BL 2/8/08) [597.92]

Animal Behavior

GENERAL AND MISCELLANEOUS

12343 Crump, Donald J., ed. *How Animals Behave: A New Look at Wildlife* (5–8). Illus. 1984, National Geographic LB $12.50 (978-0-87044-505-7). A general, colorful introduction to why and how animals perform such functions as courting, living together, and caring for their young. [591.5]

12344 Crump, Donald J., ed. *Secrets of Animal Survival* (4–8). Illus. 1983, National Geographic LB $12.50 (978-0-87044-431-9). The survival tactics of animals in five geographical environments are discussed.

12345 Flegg, Jim. *Animal Movement* (4–7). Illus. by David Hosking. Series: Wild World. 1991, Millbrook LB $17.90 (978-1-878137-21-0). Various ways animals move and at what speeds are discussed in this well-illustrated book. (Rev: BL 1/1/91; SLJ 2/92) [591.18]

12346 Fredericks, Anthony D. *Animal Sharpshooters* (5–7). Illus. Series: Watts Library: Animals. 1999, Watts LB $25.50 (978-0-531-11700-2). This book focuses on the strange adaptations some animals have made to protect themselves and to find food. (Rev: BL 12/1/99; SLJ 12/99) [591.47]

12347 Gardner, Robert, and David Webster. *Science Project Ideas About Animal Behavior* (4–8). Illus. Series: Science Project Ideas. 1997, Enslow LB $25.26 (978-0-89490-842-2). A workmanlike compilation of projects involving animal behavior, such as the language of honeybees, with full background information and clear instructions. (Rev: BL 12/15/97; HBG 3/98; SLJ 2/98) [591]

12348 McGrath, Susan. *The Amazing Things Animals Do* (4–7). Illus. 1989, National Geographic $8.95 (978-0-87044-709-9). Unusual animal behavior is shown in such areas as communication, motion, raising young, and survival. (Rev: SLJ 2/90) [591.5]

12349 Settel, Joanne. *Exploding Ants: Amazing Facts About How Animals Adapt* (4–8). Illus. 1999, Simon & Schuster $16.00 (978-0-689-81739-7). Lurid details of animal life, such as predatory fireflies, regurgitating birds, and bloodsuckers, are presented in this attention-getting collection of biological facts. (Rev: BCCB 3/99; BL 4/15/99; HBG 10/99; SLJ 4/99) [591.5]

12350 Singer, Marilyn. *Venom* (5–8). Illus. 2007, Darby Creek $19.95 (978-1-58196-043-3). Poisonous animals and insects of the land, sea, and air are featured in this book, with plenty of strange facts and weird photographs. (Rev: BL 10/1/07; SLJ 11/07) [592.16]

COMMUNICATION

12351 Sayre, April Pulley. *Secrets of Sound: Studying the Calls and Songs of Whales, Elephants, and Birds* (4–7). Illus. 2002, Houghton $17.00 (978-0-618-01514-6). Fascinating profiles of scientists who study animal sounds serve to introduce readers to a number of scientific concepts. (Rev: BL 12/1/02; HB 9–10/02; HBG 3/03; SLJ 10/02) [559.159]

HOMES

12352 Bloom, Steve. *Untamed: Animals Around the World* (4–7). Illus. by Emmanuelle Zicot. 2005, Abrams $18.95 (978-0-8109-5956-9). Enthralling photographs of wild animals are accompanied by brief facts and an environmentalist message. (Rev: BL 12/1/05) [636]

12353 Robinson, W. Wright. *How Mammals Build Their Amazing Homes* (5–8). Illus. by Carlyn Iverson. Series: Animal Architects. 1999, Blackbirch LB $27.44 (978-1-56711-381-5). After defining what a mammal is, this account shows the homes of animals including beavers, chimpanzees, squirrels, prairie dogs, and moles, and describes how they are constructed. (Rev: HBG 3/00; SLJ 5/00) [591.56]

TRACKS

12354 Murie, Olaus J. *A Field Guide to Animal Tracks*. 2nd ed. (7–12). Illus. 1996, Houghton paper $8.95 (978-0-395-58297-8). This important volume in the Peterson Field Guide series first appeared in 1954 and now has become a classic in the area of identifying animal tracks and droppings. [591.5]

Animal Species

GENERAL AND MISCELLANEOUS

12355 Alden, Peter. *Peterson First Guide to Mammals of North America* (8–12). Illus. 1988, Houghton paper $5.95 (978-0-395-91181-5). An uncluttered basic guide to mammal identification with many

illustrations and useful background material. (Rev: BL 5/15/87) [599]

12356 Crump, Donald J., ed. *Amazing Animals of Australia* (6–9). Illus. 1984, National Geographic LB $12.50 (978-0-87044-520-0). A colorful introduction to such animals as the kangaroo and platypus. (Rev: BL 6/1/85) [591.9]

12357 Fenton, M. Brock. *Just Bats* (7–12). Illus. 1983, Univ. of Toronto paper $15.95 (978-0-8020-6464-6). An introduction to this frequently misunderstood and very useful flying rodent. [599.4]

12358 Grassy, John, and Chuck Keene. *National Audubon Society First Field Guide: Mammals* (4–8). Series: Audubon Society First Field Guide. 1998, Scholastic paper $17.95 (978-0-590-05471-3). An attractive guide to mammals, with maps showing habitats, a picture of each animal, and basic descriptive text. (Rev: SLJ 4/99) [599]

12359 Green, Jen, and David Burnie. *Mammal* (5–9). Illus. Series: DK/Google e.guides. 2005, DK $17.99 (978-0-7566-1139-2). This highly illustrated guide introduces readers to the evolution and diversity of mammals and provides a link to a Web site that serves as a gateway to additional resources. (Rev: SLJ 8/05) [599]

12360 Greenaway, Theresa. *The Secret Life of Bats* (4–7). Series: The Secret World of . . . 2002, Raintree LB $27.12 (978-0-7398-4982-8). An accessible, attractive volume that begins with little-known facts about bats and continues with information on their structure, habits, food, and habitats. (Rev: BL 8/02) [599.4]

12361 Hare, Tony. *Animal Fact-File: Head-to-Tail Profiles of More Than 90 Mammals* (4–8). 1999, Facts on File paper $18.95 (978-0-8160-4016-2). From aardvarks to wombats, this is an alphabetical guide to more than 90 mammals with details including classification, size, coloration, and habits. (Rev: SLJ 9/99; VOYA 6/00) [599]

12362 Jarrow, Gail, and Paul Sherman. *The Naked Mole-Rat Mystery: Scientific Sleuths at Work* (6–8). Illus. Series: Discovery! 1996, Lerner LB $28.75 (978-0-8225-2853-1). This is a thorough exploration of what we know, and how we found out about, the naked mole-rat, which is a mammal but has a reptilian body temperature and lives in colonies like social insects. (Rev: BL 9/1/96; SLJ 8/96) [599.32]

12363 Jarrow, Gail, and Paul Sherman. *Naked Mole-Rats* (4–7). Illus. Series: Nature Watch. 1996, Carolrhoda LB $28.75 (978-0-87614-995-9). An informative introduction to the naked mole-rat, a most unusual animal that seems to copy habits from a variety of other species. (Rev: SLJ 10/96) [599.32]

12364 Johnson, Sylvia A. *Bats* (4–7). Illus. 1985, Lerner paper $5.95 (978-0-8225-9500-7). Characteristics and behavior patterns of this flying mammal. (Rev: BCCB 3/86; BL 4/15/86; SLJ 2/86) [599.4]

12365 Marrin, Albert. *Saving the Buffalo* (5–7). 2006, Scholastic $18.99 (978-0-439-71854-7). This well-written, well-illustrated history traces the fortunes of the American bison from the days when huge herds covered the plains to near extinction at the end of the 19th century and then to an amazing recovery over the past century or so. (Rev: SLJ 12/06*) [599.64]

12366 Montgomery, Sy. *Quest for the Tree Kangaroo: An Expedition to the Cloud Forest of New Guinea* (5–8). Illus. by Nic Bishop. 2006, Houghton $18.00 (978-0-618-49641-9). Join researchers on a challenging expedition to the cloud forests of Papua New Guinea to learn more about the rare Matschie's tree kangaroo. Sibert Honor Book, 2007. (Rev: BL 12/1/06; SLJ 12/06*) [599.2]

12367 Murray, Peter. *Rhinos* (4–7). Series: The World of Mammals. 2005, Child's World LB $29.93 (978-1-59296-502-1). Arresting photographs and engaging text introduce the anatomy, behavior, habitat, and life cycle of the rhinoceros as well as the threats to the animal's survival in the wild. (Rev: SLJ 3/06) [599.72]

12368 North, Sterling. *Rascal: A Memoir of a Better Era* (7–12). Illus. 1963, Dutton $16.99 (978-0-525-18839-1). Remembrances of growing up in Wisconsin in 1918 and of the joys and problems of owning a pet raccoon. (Rev: BL 9/1/89) [599.74]

12369 Pringle, Laurence. *Strange Animals, New to Science* (4–7). Illus. 2002, Marshall Cavendish $16.95 (978-0-7614-5083-2). The results of scientists' efforts to discover new animal species are presented here, with color photographs and coverage of the reasons behind disappearing habitats. (Rev: BCCB 9/02; BL 7/02; HBG 10/02; SLJ 8/02) [591.68]

12370 Ross, Mark C., and David Reesor. *Predator: Life and Death in the African Bush* (7–12). Illus. 2007, Abrams $35.00 (978-0-8109-9301-3). Lions, cheetahs, hyenas, crocodiles, and leopards are shown in various activities in their native habitats, with accompanying text that discusses their daily lives, anatomy, behavior, and so forth. (Rev: BL 9/15/07) [599.7096]

12371 Ruff, Sue, and Don E. Wilson. *Bats* (5–8). Series: AnimalWays. 2000, Marshall Cavendish LB $31.36 (978-0-7614-1137-6). Some of the topics that are covered include anatomy, habits, range, classification, habitats, evolution, and survival skills. (Rev: BL 1/1–15/01; HBG 3/01) [599.4]

12372 Silverstein, Alvin, et al. *The Mustang* (4–8). Series: Endangered in America. 1997, Millbrook $24.90 (978-0-7613-0048-9). Examines the life cycle and behavior of the mustang, the reasons it has become endangered, and the measures being

taken to ensure its survival. (Rev: BL 3/15/97; SLJ 6/97) [636.1]

12373 Webber, Desiree Morrison. *The Buffalo Train Ride* (4–7). Illus. by Sandy Shropshire. 1999, Eakin $14.95 (978-1-57168-275-8). This is a history of the American buffalo, how it was hunted to near extinction, and the modern efforts to make sure it survives, with special attention to the work of William Hornaday. (Rev: HBG 3/00; SLJ 3/00) [591.52]

APE FAMILY

12374 Fleisher, Paul. *Gorillas* (5–8). Illus. Series: AnimalWays. 2000, Marshall Cavendish LB $28.50 (978-0-7614-1140-6). Color photographs and clear text introduce gorillas, their scientific classification, physical and behavioral characteristics, and relationship to humans. (Rev: BL 1/1–15/01; HBG 3/01) [599.884]

12375 Goodall, Jane. *The Chimpanzees I Love: Saving Their World and Ours* (5–8). Illus. 2001, Scholastic paper $18.95 (978-0-439-21310-3). Jane Goodall combines details of her own life researching chimpanzees with fact-filled descriptions of the animals' behavior and a cry for chimpanzee protection. (Rev: BL 12/1/01; HB 1–2/02; HBG 3/02; SLJ 9/01*) [599]

12376 Levine, Stuart P. *The Orangutan* (7–10). Series: Overview: Endangered Animals and Habitats. 1999, Lucent LB $18.96 (978-1-56006-560-9). This account introduces the orangutan and its habits with material on why it is endangered and efforts being made to save it. (Rev: BL 12/15/99) [599.8]

12377 Lewin, Ted, and Betsy Lewin. *Gorilla Walk* (4–8). 1999, Lothrop LB $17.89 (978-0-688-16510-9). A beautifully illustrated book about the Lewins' trip to Uganda to study mountain gorillas. (Rev: BL 8/99; HBG 4/00; SLJ 9/99) [599.8]

12378 Lockwood, Sophie. *Baboons* (4–7). Series: The World of Mammals. 2005, Child's World LB $29.93 (978-1-59296-497-0). Arresting photographs and engaging text introduce the anatomy, behavior, habitat, and life cycle of the baboon as well as the threats to the animal's survival in the wild. (Rev: SLJ 3/06) [599.8]

12379 Pimm, Nancy Roe. *The Heart of the Beast: Eight Great Gorilla Stories* (4–7). Illus. 2007, Darby Creek $18.95 (978-1-58196-054-9). True stories about famous gorillas provide information on their mental and physical development, behavior, and diet. (Rev: BL 6/1–15/07; SLJ 12/07) [599.884]

12380 Powzyk, Joyce. *In Search of Lemurs: My Days and Nights in a Madagascar Rain Forest* (4–7). Illus. 1998, National Geographic $17.95 (978-0-7922-7072-0). The author describes and illustrates her journey into the wilds of Madagascar and the many animals, plants, and birds she encountered, culminating in the elusive lemur. (Rev: BL 9/15/98; HBG 3/99; SLJ 10/98) [599.8]

12381 Stefoff, Rebecca. *Chimpanzees* (4–7). Illus. Series: AnimalWays. 2003, Benchmark LB $31.36 (978-0-7614-1579-4). A richly illustrated look at chimpanzees, from their physiology to their interaction with humans. (Rev: SLJ 3/04)

12382 Stefoff, Rebecca. *The Primate Order* (5–9). Illus. Series: Family Trees. 2005, Benchmark LB $32.79 (978-0-7614-1816-0). Habits, habitats, and human-like aspects of this order of animals; an engaging book with plenty of facts for report-writers. (Rev: SLJ 6/06) [599.8]

BEARS

12383 Calabro, Marian. *Operation Grizzly Bear* (5–8). Illus. 1989, Macmillan $13.95 (978-0-02-716241-7). An account by two naturalists on a 12-year study of silvertip bears in Yellowstone Park. (Rev: BL 3/15/90; VOYA 4/90) [599.74]

12384 Hunt, Joni Phelps. *A Band of Bears: The Rambling Life of a Lovable Loner* (5–8). Series: Jean-Michel Cousteau Presents. 2007, London Town paper $8.95 (978-0-9766134-5-9). With eye-catching photographs and stories of close encounters with these animals, this book looks at bears' characteristics, behavior, intelligence, and the threats to their survival. (Rev: SLJ 11/07) [599.78]

12385 Lockwood, Sophie. *Polar Bears* (5–8). Illus. Series: World of Mammals. 2005, Child's World LB $29.93 (978-1-59296-501-4). This slim but richly illustrated title looks at polar bears' physical characteristics, behavior, diet, relationship with the Inuit people, and the growing threats to their survival. (Rev: BL 10/15/05) [599.786]

12386 Milse, Thorsten. *Little Polar Bears* (7–12). Illus. 2006, Prestel $45.00 (978-3-7658-1586-7). As newly born polar bear cubs frolic and explore their surroundings in Hudson Bay, Manitoba, photographer Milse captures their every move amid a vast landscape, following the journey with their mother from birthing den to hunting grounds. (Rev: BL 11/15/06) [779.9599786]

12387 Montgomery, Sy. *Search for the Golden Moon Bear: Science and Adventure in the Asian Tropics* (5–9). 2004, Houghton $17.00 (978-0-618-35650-8). Nature writer Montgomery describes her search across war-torn Southeast Asia for the elusive golden moon bear. (Rev: BL 12/1/04; SLJ 12/04) [599.78]

12388 Preston-Mafham, Rod. *The Secret Life of Bears* (4–7). Series: The Secret World of . . . 2002, Raintree LB $27.12 (978-0-7398-4983-5). In this attractive volume readers learn why bears behave as they do, how they feed, communicate, and repro-

duce, and what dangers face their future. (Rev: BL 8/02) [599.74]

12389 Stefoff, Rebecca. *Bears* (5–8). Series: AnimalWays. 2001, Marshall Cavendish LB $31.36 (978-0-7614-1268-7). Various species of bears are introduced in text and color photographs with additional material on their location, anatomy, habits, and behavior. (Rev: BL 3/15/02; HBG 10/02) [599.74]

12390 Thomas, Keltie. *Bear Rescue: Changing the Future for Endangered Wildlife* (4–8). Series: Firefly Animal Rescue. 2006, Firefly LB $19.95 (978-1-55297-922-8); paper $9.95 (978-1-55297-921-1). Focuses on work that's being done on behalf of threatened bear species, including Indian sloth bears, Chinese black bears, and polar bears. (Rev: SLJ 12/06) [599.78]

12391 Turbak, Gary. *Grizzly Bears* (6–10). Series: World Life Library. 1997, Voyageur paper $14.95 (978-0-89658-334-4). High-quality photographs and concise, readable text are used to introduce the grizzly bear's life cycle, origin, habits, anatomy, and future. (Rev: SLJ 10/97) [599.74]

CATS (LIONS, TIGERS, ETC.)

12392 Aaseng, Nathan. *The Cheetah* (7–10). Series: Overview: Endangered Animals and Habitats. 2000, Lucent LB $27.45 (978-1-56006-680-4). After a description of the cheetah, its habits and environments, there is material on methods employed to save it. (Rev: BL 10/15/2000; HBG 3/01) [599.74]

12393 Aaseng, Nathan. *The Cougar* (7–10). Series: Endangered Animals and Habitats. 2001, Lucent LB $28.70 (978-1-56006-730-6). This book introduces this large American cat also known as a puma and explains why it is endangered and what efforts are being made to save it. (Rev: BL 3/15/01) [599.73]

12394 Adamson, Joy. *Born Free: A Lioness of Two Worlds* (7–12). 1987, Pantheon $11.95 (978-0-679-56141-5). First published in 1960, this is an account of a young lioness growing up in captivity in Kenya. [599.74]

12395 Becker, John E. *Wild Cats: Past and Present* (5–8). Illus. by Mark Hallett. 2008, Darby Creek $18.95 (978-1-58196-052-5). Lions, tigers, jaguars, and cheetahs are among the wild cats covered in this well-illustrated, large-format book that covers history, environmental threats, and conservation and will attract both researchers and browsers. (Rev: BL 3/15/08; SLJ 6/08) [599.75]

12396 Gamble, Cyndi. *Leopards: Natural History and Conservation* (7–10). Photos by Rodney Griffiths. Series: WorldLife Library. 2004, Voyageur paper $12.95 (978-0-89658-656-7). Introduces readers to the three leopard species of the world, their habitats, and the threats they face. (Rev: SLJ 4/05) [599.74]

12397 Levine, Stuart P. *The Tiger* (7–10). Series: Overview: Endangered Animals and Habitats. 1998, Lucent LB $28.70 (978-1-56006-465-7). This work describes the habits and habitats of the tiger and current efforts to protect it from extinction. (Rev: BL 10/15/98) [599.74]

12398 Lumpkin, Susan. *Small Cats* (5–8). Series: Great Creatures of the World. 1993, Facts on File $17.95 (978-0-8160-2848-1). A handsome over-sized volume about the smaller wild cats, with many photographs and charts. (Rev: BL 2/15/93) [599.74]

12399 Malaspina, Ann. *The Jaguar* (7–10). Series: Endangered Animals and Habitats. 2001, Lucent LB $29.95 (978-1-56006-813-6). An introduction to this large cat that is a native to Central and South America, the reasons why it is endangered, and the methods employed to save it. (Rev: BL 3/15/01) [599.74]

12400 Matignon, Karine Lou. *Tiger, Tiger* (8–12). Illus. 2004, Thames & Hudson $40.00 (978-0-500-51193-0). This informative, photo-filled volume uses *Two Brothers*, the film about two tiger siblings separated at birth, as the base for an exploration of tigers and the historic relationship between the big cats and humans. (Rev: BL 11/1/04) [599.7]

12401 Mills, Stephen. *Tiger* (8–12). Illus. 2004, Firefly paper $24.95 (978-1-55297-949-5). For report writers and general interest, this is an excellent introduction to tigers, their behavior, and the threats they face. (Rev: BL 11/1/04) [599.756]

12402 Schlaepfer, Gloria G. *Cheetahs* (5–8). Series: AnimalWays. 2001, Marshall Cavendish LB $31.36 (978-0-7614-1266-3). Cheetahs are introduced with material on anatomy, species identification, habitats, behavior, and endangered status. (Rev: BL 3/15/02; HBG 10/02) [599.7]

12403 Schneider, Jost. *Lynx* (4–7). Illus. 1994, Carolrhoda LB $28.75 (978-0-87614-844-0). The life cycle, habits, and behavior of the lynx are described. (Rev: BL 1/15/95; SLJ 3/95) [599.74]

12404 Seidensticker, John, and Susan Lumpkin. *Cats: Smithsonian Answer Book* (8–12). Illus. 2004, Smithsonian paper $24.95 (978-1-58834-126-6). From the characteristics of the common tabby to the exotic puma, researchers and browsers will find a wealth of information in this book, which is arranged in question-and-answer format and includes many color photographs. (Rev: BL 10/1/04) [599.75]

12405 Silverstein, Alvin, et al. *The Florida Panther* (4–7). Illus. Series: Endangered in America. 1997, Millbrook $24.90 (978-0-7613-0049-6). Explains why the Florida panther has become endangered, with material on its life cycle and behavior and the

efforts being made to save it. (Rev: BL 3/15/97; SLJ 6/97) [599.74]

12406 Sinha, Vivek R. *The Vanishing Tiger* (8–12). Illus. 2004, Trafalgar $29.95 (978-1-84065-441-7). A wonderful photographic record of an expedition to locate and photograph India's massive Bengal tiger. (Rev: BL 3/1/04) [599.7]

12407 Thompson, Sharon E. *Built for Speed: The Extraordinary, Enigmatic Cheetah* (5–8). Illus. 1998, Lerner LB $27.93 (978-0-8225-2854-8). The habits and lifestyle of this endangered animal are introduced with full-color illustrations. (Rev: BL 6/1–15/98; HBG 10/98) [599.75]

COYOTES, FOXES, AND WOLVES

12408 Brandenburg, Jim. *To the Top of the World: Adventures with Arctic Wolves* (5–7). Illus. 1993, Walker LB $17.85 (978-0-8027-8220-5). Amazing color photographs highlight this account of a photographer's experiences living near a pack of Arctic wolves. (Rev: BCCB 11/93; BL 1/1/94*; SLJ 12/93*) [599.74]

12409 Greenaway, Theresa. *Wolves, Wild Dogs, and Foxes* (4–7). Illus. Series: Secret World Of. 2001, Raintree LB $27.12 (978-0-7398-3507-4). Report writers will find information here about wolves, wild dogs, and foxes, including their diet, habitat, and behavior, with photographs and interesting facts. (Rev: BL 10/15/01; HBG 3/02; SLJ 1/02) [599.77]

12410 Johnson, Sylvia A., and Alice Aamodt. *Wolf Pack: Tracking Wolves in the Wild* (5–8). Illus. 1985, Lerner paper $27.93 (978-0-8225-9526-7). Fascinating details of the lives of these animals that travel in packs and share hunting, raising the young, and protection. (Rev: BCCB 12/85; BL 2/1/86; SLJ 1/86) [599.74442]

12411 McAllister, Ian. *The Last Wild Wolves: Ghosts of the Rain Forest* (7–12). Illus. 2007, Univ. of California $39.95 (978-0-520-25473-2). Beautiful photographs document the lives of wolves living on the Pacific Coast. (Rev: BL 12/15/07) [599.77309711]

12412 Murdico, Suzanne J. *Coyote Attacks* (4–7). 2000, Children's paper $6.95 (978-0-516-23513-4). As well as covering the causes of coyote attacks on animals and humans, this account gives basic information on coyotes, their habitat, survival techniques, behavior, and preferred food. (Rev: SLJ 3/01) [599.74]

12413 Silverstein, Alvin, et al. *The Red Wolf* (4–8). Illus. Series: Endangered Species. 1994, Millbrook LB $24.90 (978-1-56294-416-2). The story of the red wolf, once thought to have become extinct in the United States, and the recent efforts to reintroduce it in North Carolina. (Rev: BL 4/15/95) [333.95]

DEER FAMILY

12414 Cox, Daniel, and John Ozoga. *Whitetail Country* (8–12). Illus. 1988, Willow Creek Pr. $39.00 (978-0-932558-43-5). Wonderful photographs complement this account of the life and living habits of the deer. [599.73]

ELEPHANTS

12415 Groning, Karl, and Martin Saller. *Elephants: A Cultural and Natural History* (8–12). 1999, Konemann (978-3-8290-1752-7). Both the scientific and mythological aspects of elephants are covered, with material on behavior, anatomy, and habitats. (Rev: BL 6/1–15/99; SLJ 5/00) [599.67]

12416 Levine, Stuart P. *The Elephant* (7–10). Illus. Series: Overview: Endangered Animals and Habitats. 1997, Lucent LB $28.70 (978-1-56006-522-7). After a general introduction to the elephant and its characteristics, evolution, and habitats, the author describes how it has become endangered and current attempts at conservation. (Rev: BL 5/1/98; HBG 9/98) [599.67]

12417 Lewin, Ted, and Betsy Lewin. *Elephant Quest* (4–9). Illus. by authors. 2000, HarperCollins $15.95 (978-0-688-14111-0). This account of the flora and fauna of Botswana's Moremi Reserve also describes the author's search for elephants. (Rev: HB 1–2/01; HBG 3/01; SLJ 9/00) [599.67]

12418 Morgan, Jody. *Elephant Rescue: Changing the Future for Endangered Wildlife* (4–7). Illus. Series: Firefly Animal Rescue. 2005, Firefly $19.95 (978-1-55297-595-4); paper $9.95 (978-1-55297-594-7). This photo-filled book documents the many threats facing the world's remaining herds of African and Asian elephants, and discusses elephant physiology, behavior, and habitat. (Rev: BL 2/15/05; SLJ 5/05) [599.67]

12419 Overbeck, Cynthia. *Elephants* (4–7). Illus. 1981, Lerner LB $22.60 (978-0-8225-1452-7). Elephants and their life cycle and habitats are discussed in this well-illustrated volume. [599]

12420 Schlaepfer, Gloria G. *Elephants* (5–9). Illus. Series: AnimalWays. 2003, Marshall Cavendish $31.36 (978-0-7614-1390-5). In addition to material on physical characteristics, behavior, habitats, and threats, Schlaepfer touches on the animal's roles in history, mythology, religion, and literature. (Rev: BL 3/15/03; HBG 3/03) [599.67]

MARSUPIALS

12421 Collard, Sneed B. *Pocket Babies and Other Amazing Marsupials* (4–7). Illus. 2007, Darby Creek $18.95 (978-1-58196-046-4). A large-format introduction to marsupials around the world — including the opossum, kangaroo, koala, and wombat — and to the efforts being made to save the

many endangered marsupials. (Rev: BL 9/15/07; SLJ 10/07) [599.2]

12422 Malaspina, Ann. *The Koala* (7–10). Series: Endangered Animals and Habitats. 2002, Gale LB $28.70 (978-1-56006-876-1). That story of this animal that is threatened with extinction is told with material on methods currently employed to save it. (Rev: BL 5/15/02; SLJ 6/02) [599.2]

12423 Murray, Peter. *Kangaroos* (4–7). Series: The World of Mammals. 2005, Child's World LB $29.93 (978-1-59296-499-4). Arresting photographs and engaging text introduce the anatomy, behavior, habitat, and life cycle of the kangaroo as well as the threats to the animal's survival in the wild. (Rev: SLJ 3/06) [599.2]

12424 Penny, Malcolm. *The Secret Life of Kangaroos* (4–7). Series: The Secret World of . . . 2002, Raintree LB $27.12 (978-0-7398-4986-6). A visually interesting look at the world of the kangaroo with material on behavior, anatomy, reproduction, and how pollution and habitat destruction have affected these animals. (Rev: BL 8/02) [599.2]

PANDAS

12425 Jiguang, Xin, and Markus Kappeler. *The Giant Panda* (5–7). Trans. by Noel Simon. Illus. 1984, China Books paper $9.95 (978-0-8351-1388-5). China's giant panda is introduced in its natural habitat. (Rev: BL 12/15/86; HB 1–2/87; SLJ 12/86) [599]

12426 Presnall, Judith J. *The Giant Panda* (7–10). Illus. Series: Overview: Endangered Animals and Habitats. 1998, Lucent LB $22.45 (978-1-56006-463-3). A discussion of the giant panda's evolution, habitats, life span, and breeding habits, how it became endangered, and attempts to conserve this dwindling population. (Rev: BL 5/1/98) [599.789]

Birds

GENERAL AND MISCELLANEOUS

12427 Aziz, Laurel. *Hummingbirds: A Beginner's Guide* (5–8). Illus. 2002, Firefly LB $19.95 (978-1-55209-487-7); paper $9.95 (978-1-55209-374-0). This heavily illustrated book offers a great deal of information about hummingbirds, including their bills, metabolism, flight, nesting, and migration. (Rev: BL 6/1–15/02; HBG 10/02) [598.7]

12428 Bateman, Robert. *Bateman's Backyard Birds* (4–7). Illus. 2005, Barron's $14.99 (978-0-7641-5882-7). Wildlife artist Bateman introduces readers to numerous North American species of birds and the joys of birding in this beautifully illustrated guide. (Rev: BL 10/15/05) [598]

12429 Doris, Ellen. *Ornithology* (4–7). Illus. Series: Real Kids Real Science. 1994, Thames & Hudson

$16.95 (978-0-500-19008-1). An excellent manual on how to study birds in their natural habitats, with accompanying activities for all seasons. (Rev: BL 9/1/94) [598]

12430 Hoose, Phillip M. *The Race to Save the Lord God Bird* (5–8). 2004, Farrar $20.00 (978-0-374-36173-0). The sad tale of the ivory-billed woodpecker's decline is interwoven with discussion of the scientific and sociological implications. (Rev: BL 6/1–15/04; SLJ 9/04) [598.7]

12431 Julivert, Maria Angeles. *Birds* (6–9). Illus. Series: Field Guides. 2006, Enchanted Lion $16.95 (978-1-59270-058-5). This guide to bird watching provides information on different types of birds, their characteristics, behavior, and where they make their homes; its format as a naturalist's journal makes clear the joys of this activity. (Rev: BL 10/15/06; SLJ 1/07) [598]

12432 Kenyon, Linda. *Rainforest Bird Rescue: Changing the Future for Endangered Wildlife* (4–8). Series: Firefly Animal Rescue. 2006, Firefly LB $19.95 (978-1-55407-153-1); paper $9.95 (978-1-55407-152-4). This book discusses the threats to the tropical bird species that live in the world's rain forests, habitat that is rapidly disappearing, and profiles the men and women who are crusading to save them. (Rev: SLJ 12/06) [598.1734]

12433 Llamas, Andreu. *Birds Conquer the Sky* (4–8). Illus. by Miriam Ferrón and Miguel Ferrón. Series: Development of the Earth. 1996, Chelsea LB $17.55 (978-0-7910-3455-2). A science book that explains the evolution of birds from prehistoric land birds onward and defines their characteristics. (Rev: SLJ 7/96) [598]

12434 Martin, Gilles. *Birds* (5–8). Illus. 2005, Abrams $18.95 (978-0-8109-5878-4). An oversize book full of color photographs of birds, plus watercolor sketches and brief, quite advanced text that comments on various aspects of the birds. (Rev: BL 5/1/05; SLJ 5/05) [598.22]

12435 Parker, Edward. *Birds* (5–8). Photos by author. Series: Rain Forest. 2003, Raintree LB $27.12 (978-0-7398-5239-2). Birds that are found in rain forests are the topic of this overview that describes the dangers posed by humans through hunting, pollution, and agriculture. (Rev: HBG 3/03; SLJ 1/03) [598]

12436 Peterson, Roger Tory, and Virginia Marie Peterson. *A Field Guide to the Birds of Eastern and Central North America*. 5th ed. (8–12). 2002, Houghton $30.00 (978-0-395-74047-7). This book identifies birds found east of the Rockies with both verbal and pictorial descriptions. [598]

12437 Stokes, Donald, and Lillian Stokes. *The Bird Feeder Book: An Easy Guide to Attracting, Identifying, and Understanding Your Feeder Birds* (8–12). Illus. 1987, Little, Brown paper $12.95 (978-0-316-

81733-2). A manual that describes, with color photographs, 72 backyard birds, plus tips on how to attract and feed them. (Rev: BL 2/1/88) [598]

12438 Taylor, Kenny. *Puffins* (5–9). Series: World-Life Library. 1999, Voyageur paper $16.95 (978-0-89658-419-8). Outstanding photographs and conservation awareness are highlights of this introduction to puffins, their characteristics, habitats, and habits. (Rev: BL 8/99) [598.3]

12439 Weidensaul, Scott, and National Audubon Society, eds. *National Audubon Society First Field Guide: Birds* (4–8). Illus. 1998, Scholastic paper $17.95 (978-0-590-05446-1). After a general introduction to ornithology, this guide describes and pictures several species of birds, including markings, eating, mating and nesting habits, migration, and endangered status. (Rev: BL 8/98; SLJ 10/98) [598]

12440 Zim, Herbert S., and Ira N. Gabrielson. *Birds* (5–8). Illus. 1991, Western paper $21.27 (978-0-307-64053-6). A guide to the most commonly seen birds, with accompanying illustrations and basic materials. [598]

BEHAVIOR

12441 Elphick, Jonathan, ed. *Atlas of Bird Migration: Tracing the Great Journeys of the World's Birds* (8–12). Illus. 2007, Firefly $35.00 (978-1-55407-248-4). This handsome atlas presents the latest research into migration and the impact of climate change, with breeding/migration calendars, fact boxes on species, and much more for the bird watcher and researcher. (Rev: SLJ 6/07) [598.156]

12442 Johnson, Sylvia A. *Inside an Egg* (5–8). Illus. 1982, Lerner LB $31.95 (978-0-8225-1472-5); paper $5.95 (978-0-8225-9522-9). An excellently illustrated account tracing the growth of a chicken in an egg until it is hatched. [598]

12443 Leveille, Jean. *Birds in Love: The Secret Courting and Mating Rituals of Extraordinary Birds* (8–12). Illus. 2007, Voyageur $20.00 (978-0-7603-2807-1). Essays and photographs reveal a lot about the behavior of bird couples and bird families. (Rev: BL 12/15/07) [598.156]

12444 Read, Marie. *Secret Lives of Common Birds: Enjoying Bird Behavior Through the Seasons* (8–12). Illus. 2005, Houghton paper $14.95 (978-0-618-55872-8). Beautiful photographs and season-by-season discussion of bird behavior make this satisfying both for browsers and report writers. (Rev: BL 12/15/05) [598.15]

12445 Stokes, Donald. *A Guide to the Behavior of Common Birds* (7–12). Illus. 1979, Little, Brown $16.95 (978-0-316-81722-6). The first of three volumes, each of which describes the behavior of 25 different birds. Volume 2 is *A Guide to Bird Behav-*

ior: In the Wild and at Your Feeder (1985); volume 3 is *A Guide to Bird Behavior* (1989). [598]

EAGLES, HAWKS, AND OTHER BIRDS OF PREY

12446 Bailey, Jill. *Birds of Prey* (5–8). Illus. 1988, Facts on File $17.55 (978-0-8160-1655-6). In brief, lavishly illustrated chapters, various characteristics of birds of prey are explored and the most important types are described. (Rev: SLJ 1/89) [598]

12447 Bailey, Jill. *The Secret Life of Falcons* (4–7). Series: The Secret World of . . . 2002, Raintree LB $27.12 (978-0-7398-4985-9). This book describes the anatomy and habits of the falcon with material on how they feed, communicate, and reproduce. (Rev: BL 8/02) [598.9]

12448 Barghusen, Joan D. *The Bald Eagle* (7–10). Series: Overview: Endangered Animals and Habitats. 1998, Lucent LB $28.70 (978-1-56006-254-7). An introduction to the structure, habits, and habitats of the bald eagle and a description of the methods employed to save it. (Rev: BL 10/15/98) [598.9]

12449 Barth, Kelly L. *Birds of Prey* (7–10). Series: Overview: Endangered Animals and Habitats. 1999, Lucent LB $27.45 (978-1-56006-493-0). A well-illustrated account that introduces various birds of prey, explains why they are endangered, and describes methods used to save them. (Rev: BL 12/15/99; HBG 9/00) [598.9]

12450 Collard, Sneed B. *Birds of Prey: A Look at Daytime Raptors* (4–7). Illus. 1999, Watts LB $25.50 (978-0-531-20363-7). Eagles, hawks, ospreys, falcons, and vultures of North America are introduced with material on the appearance and habits of each. (Rev: BL 10/15/99; HBG 3/00) [598.9]

12451 Laubach, Christyna, et al. *Raptor! A Kid's Guide to Birds of Prey* (4–7). Illus. 2002, Storey paper $14.95 (978-1-58017-445-9). A large-format treasure trove of facts about raptors, with information on individual species, identification, habits, habitat, range maps, and so forth. (Rev: BL 12/1/02; HBG 3/03; SLJ 10/02) [598.9]

12452 Patent, Dorothy Hinshaw. *The Bald Eagle Returns* (4–8). Illus. 2000, Clarion $16.00 (978-0-395-91416-8). This book not only discusses the successful efforts to save the bald eagle but also gives material on its anatomy, habitats, mating, and behavior. (Rev: BCCB 1/01; BL 10/15/00; HBG 10/01; SLJ 11/00) [598.9]

12453 Snyder, Noel, and Helen Snyder. *Raptors of North America* (8–12). Illus. 2006, MBI $50.00 (978-0-7603-2582-7). Equally suitable for reference and browsing, this book contains a wealth of information about the more than 50 species of North

America's birds of prey. (Rev: BL 11/1/06) [598.9097]

OWLS

12454 Mowat, Farley. *Owls in the Family* (7–9). 1989, Tundra paper $6.99 (978-0-7710-6693-1). Two seemingly harmless owls turn a household upside down when they are adopted as pets. [598]

12455 Silverstein, Alvin, et al. *The Spotted Owl* (4–8). Illus. Series: Endangered Species. 1994, Millbrook LB $24.90 (978-1-56294-415-5). The story of the spotted owl, its endangered status, efforts to protect it, and the conflicts with the timber industry. (Rev: BL 4/15/95) [333.95]

PENGUINS

12456 Johnson, Sylvia A. *Penguins* (4–7). Illus. 1981, Lerner LB $22.60 (978-0-8225-1453-4). Handsome photographs enliven the text of this introduction to penguins and their habitats. [598]

12457 Lynch, Wayne. *Penguins!* (4–7). Illus. 1999, Firefly LB $19.95 (978-1-55209-421-1); paper $9.95 (978-1-55209-424-2). An appealing book that introduces penguins and their various species with coverage of their evolution, food, life cycle, habits, and habitats. (Rev: BCCB 12/99; BL 9/15/99; HBG 3/00) [598.47]

12458 Stefoff, Rebecca. *Penguins* (4–8). Illus. Series: AnimalWays. 2005, Benchmark LB $21.95 (978-0-7614-1743-9). Beautiful photographs enrich this well-organized volume that provides basic information on the penguin's characteristics, habits, and habitat. (Rev: SLJ 5/06) [598.4]

12459 Webb, Sophie. *My Season with Penguins: An Antarctic Journal* (4–8). Illus. by author. 2000, Houghton $15.00 (978-0-395-92291-0). Journal entries plus effective drawings show the joys and tribulations of a two-month stay in the Antarctic studying penguins and their behavior. (Rev: HB 11–12/00; HBG 3/01; SLJ 12/00) [598]

Environmental Protection and Endangered Species

12460 Barnes, Simon. *Planet Zoo* (4–7). Illus. 2001, Orion $29.95 (978-1-85881-488-9). An overview of 100 endangered species that conveys information in a conversational manner. (Rev: BL 8/01; SLJ 8/01) [578.68]

12461 Chandler, Gary, and Kevin Graham. *Guardians of Wildlife* (4–8). Illus. Series: Making a Better World. 1996, Twenty-First Century LB $25.90 (978-0-8050-4626-7). Solutions to overhunting, poaching, and overfishing are explored, as well as new wildlife management techniques. (Rev: BL 12/15/96; SLJ 4/97) [639.9]

12462 Cothran, Helen, ed. *Endangered Species* (8–12). Series: Opposing Viewpoints. 2000, Greenhaven paper $24.95 (978-0-7377-0505-8). Differing points of view are expressed concerning endangered species, with material on extinction, property rights, and international cooperation. [578.68]

12463 Feinstein, Stephen. *The Jaguar: Help Save This Endangered Species!* (4–7). Illus. Series: Saving Endangered Species. 2008, Enslow LB $24.95 (978-1-59845-065-1). Part of the MyReportLinks.com series, this introduction to jaguars and the threats they face features Web sites that report writers can access for more information. (Rev: BL 2/15/08) [599.75]

12464 Fletcher, Marty, and Glenn Scherer. *The Green Sea Turtle: Help Save This Endangered Species!* (5–7). Illus. Series: Saving Endangered Species. 2006, Enslow LB $33.27 (978-1-59845-033-0). A well-illustrated look at the plight of the endangered green sea turtle, with an overview of its physical characteristics, diet, habitat, and behavior. (Rev: SLJ 9/06) [597.92]

12465 Gardner, Robert. *Science Projects About the Environment and Ecology* (6–9). Series: Science Experiments. 1999, Enslow LB $26.60 (978-0-89490-951-1). This well-organized, clearly presented book offers a wide range of experiments involving conservation, ecology, and the environment, supplemented by charts, tables, and drawings. (Rev: SLJ 7/99) [363]

12466 Hoff, Mary, and Mary M. Rodgers. *Life on Land* (4–7). Illus. Series: Our Endangered Planet. 1992, Lerner LB $27.15 (978-0-8225-2507-3). This account covers such topics as the interdependence of all living things, pollution, and necessary food sources. (Rev: BL 1/15/93; SLJ 2/93) [333]

12467 Kendell, Patricia. *WWF* (5–8). Series: World Watch. 2004, Raintree LB $27.14 (978-0-7398-6615-3). Introduces the World Wildlife Fund's history, organization, and work on behalf of the endangered animals; sidebars provide key facts and relevant quotations. (Rev: BL 4/1/04; SLJ 6/04) [333.95]

12468 Lessem, Don. *Dinosaurs to Dodos: An Encyclopedia of Extinct Animals* (4–7). Illus. 1999, Scholastic paper $16.95 (978-0-590-31684-2). Moving through 12 time periods, this book describes each period and how geological changes caused the extinction of certain species and the creation of new ones. (Rev: BL 11/1/99; HBG 3/00; SLJ 11/99) [560]

12469 McClung, Robert M. *Last of the Wild: Vanished and Vanishing Giants of the Animal World* (8–12). Illus. 1997, Shoe String LB $27.50 (978-0-208-02452-7). Moving from continent to continent, this account gives historical and geographical background material on 60 animal species that have already disappeared or are currently in extreme danger of extinction. (Rev: BL 7/97; HBG 3/98; SLJ 11/97; VOYA 10/97) [591.51]

12470 McClung, Robert M. *Lost Wild America: The Story of Our Extinct and Vanishing Wildlife*. Rev. ed. (5–8). Illus. 1993, Shoe String LB $30.00 (978-0-208-02359-9). A history of American wildlife management from pioneer days to the present, with information on extinct and endangered species. (Rev: BL 1/1/94; SLJ 2/94*; VOYA 2/94) [591.5]

12471 Nirgiotis, Nicholas, and Theodore Nigiortis. *No More Dodos: How Zoos Help Endangered Wildlife* (5–8). Illus. 1996, Lerner LB $23.93 (978-0-8225-2856-2). An introduction to the many organizations that are trying to protect and preserve endangered wildlife worldwide. (Rev: BCCB 2/97; BL 2/15/97; SLJ 2/97) [639.9]

12472 Penny, Malcolm. *Endangered Species* (5–8). Series: 21st Century Debates. 2002, Raintree LB $27.12 (978-0-7398-4873-9). Topics covered in this well-illustrated book include a history of conservation, how species become endangered, methods for protection such as captive breeding, and saving habitats. (Rev: BL 6/1–15/02) [591]

12473 Salmansohn, Pete, and Stephen W. Kress. *Saving Birds: Heroes Around the World* (4–7). Illus. 2003, Tilbury House $16.95 (978-0-88448-237-6). Efforts to save endangered bird species are detailed in informative text and arresting, full-color photographs. (Rev: BL 3/15/03; HBG 10/03; SLJ 5/03) [333.95]

12474 Silverstein, Alvin, et al. *Saving Endangered Animals* (6–8). Series: Better Earth. 1993, Enslow LB $20.95 (978-0-89490-402-8). Practical information about saving threatened animal species and reintroducing them into their native environments. (Rev: BL 5/1/93; SLJ 5/93) [333.95]

12475 Simmons, Randy. *Endangered Species* (7–12). Illus. Series: Critical Thinking About Environmental Issues. 2002, Gale $33.70 (978-0-7377-1266-7). Readers will find a variety of opinions about the necessity of protecting endangered species. (Rev: BL 12/15/02; SLJ 6/03) [333.95]

12476 Thomas, Peggy. *Big Cat Conservation* (5–8). Illus. Series: Science of Saving Animals. 2000, Twenty-First Century LB $25.90 (978-0-7613-3231-2). This book focuses on seven species, including panthers, cheetahs, and tigers, and discusses wildlife conservation programs, challenges, and successes. (Rev: BL 6/1–15/00; HBG 10/00; SLJ 7/00) [333.95]

12477 Thomas, Peggy. *Bird Alert* (5–8). Series: The Science of Saving Animals. 2000, Twenty-First Century LB $25.90 (978-0-7613-1457-8). This book discusses conservation programs designed to save endangered bird species and tells how youngsters can get involved in saving birds. (Rev: BL 10/15/00; HBG 10/01; SLJ 12/00) [591.52]

12478 Thomas, Peggy. *Marine Mammal Preservation* (5–8). Series: The Science of Saving Animals. 2000, Twenty-First Century LB $25.90 (978-0-7613-1458-5). Focuses on endangered marine mammals and describes a wide range of conservation programs. (Rev: BL 10/15/00; HBG 10/01; SLJ 1/01) [574.92]

12479 Thomas, Peggy. *Reptile Rescue* (5–8). Illus. Series: Science of Saving Animals. 2000, Twenty-First Century LB $25.90 (978-0-7613-3232-9). A description of various conservation programs and how they operate in relation to several reptile species, including tortoises, crocodiles, and snakes. (Rev: BL 6/1–15/00; HBG 10/00; SLJ 7/00) [333.95]

Insects and Arachnids

GENERAL AND MISCELLANEOUS

12480 Berger, Melvin. *Killer Bugs* (4–8). Illus. 1990, Avon paper $3.50 (978-0-380-76036-7). This account explores the world of killer bees, fire ants, and other such bugs. (Rev: BL 12/15/90) [595.7]

12481 Burnie, David. *Insect* (5–9). Illus. Series: DK/Google e.guides. 2005, DK $17.99 (978-0-7566-1010-4). This highly illustrated guide introduces readers to the life cycle, behavior, diet, and habitat of insects and provides a link to a Web site that serves as a gateway to additional resources. (Rev: SLJ 8/05)

12482 *Discovery Channel Insects and Spiders: An Explore Your World Handbook* (8–12). 2000, Discovery paper $14.95 (978-1-56331-841-2). About 160 insects and spiders are identified in text and pictures, with material on their anatomy, behavior, evolution, and the possibility of keeping them as pets. [595.7]

12483 Fleisher, Paul. *Ants* (5–8). Series: Animal-Ways. 2001, Marshall Cavendish LB $31.36 (978-0-7614-1269-4). This introduction to ants and their habits and habitats also includes fine color images and material on species identification, anatomy, and classification. (Rev: BL 3/15/02; HBG 10/02) [595.79]

12484 Greenaway, Theresa. *Ants* (4–7). Series: The Secret World of . . . 2001, Raintree LB $18.98 (978-0-7368-3511-4). After presenting interesting and unusual facts about ants, this book examines their structure, homes, behavior, and enemies. (Rev: BL 10/15/01) [595.79]

12485 Jackson, Donna. *The Bug Scientists* (4–7). Illus. Series: Scientists in the Field. 2002, Houghton $16.00 (978-0-618-10868-8). In addition to describing a variety of professional jobs related to insects, this colorful volume presents excellent information

about insects and how they live. (Rev: BCCB 6/02; BL 4/1/02; HB 5–6/02; HBG 10/02; SLJ 4/02) [595.7]

12486 Johnson, Sylvia A. *Beetles* (4–7). Illus. 1982, Lerner LB $22.60 (978-0-8225-1476-3). Color photography highlights this account that concentrates on the scarab beetle.

12487 Johnson, Sylvia A. *Ladybugs* (5–8). Illus. by Yuko Sato. 1983, Lerner LB $22.60 (978-0-8225-1481-7). A description of the ladybug, its habits, behavior, and uses. [595.7]

12488 Milne, Lorus, and Margery Milne. *The Audubon Society Field Guide to North American Insects and Spiders* (7–12). Illus. 1980, Knopf $19.95 (978-0-394-50763-7). An extensive use of color photographs makes this a fine guide for identifying insects. [595.7]

12489 Pascoe, Elaine. *Ant Lions and Lacewings* (4–8). Photos by Dwight Kuhn. Series: Nature Close-Up. 2005, Gale LB $24.95 (978-1-4103-0310-3). Eye-catching close-ups illustrate information on these insects' life cycles and eating habits. Also use *Mantids and Their Relatives* (2005). (Rev: SLJ 6/05)

12490 Pascoe, Elaine. *Ants* (4–7). Series: Nature Close-Up. 1998, Blackbirch LB $23.70 (978-1-56711-183-5). Using outstanding photographs, this book introduces ants and a series of projects designed to teach more about these creatures. (Rev: BL 9/15/98; HBG 3/99; SLJ 3/99) [595.78]

12491 Pascoe, Elaine. *Crickets and Grasshoppers* (4–7). Series: Nature Close-Up. 1998, Blackbirch LB $23.70 (978-1-56711-176-7). Easy projects introduce youngsters to these insects in this book illustrated with color photographs. (Rev: BL 9/15/98; HBG 3/99) [595.7]

12492 Pascoe, Elaine. *Flies* (4–7). Series: Nature Close-Up. 2000, Blackbirch LB $27.44 (978-1-56711-149-1). This introduction to flies uses stunning photographs and text to describe their body parts, life cycle, and how to observe them; a few focused experiments are also included. (Rev: BL 4/15/00; HBG 3/01; SLJ 9/00) [595.7]

12493 Pipe, Jim. *The Giant Book of Bugs and Creepy Crawlies* (4–8). Illus. 1998, Millbrook LB $27.90 (978-0-7613-0716-7). Exotic and common insects and spiders are presented in this oversize book with eye-catching pictures and fascinating text. (Rev: BL 8/98) [595.7]

12494 Robinson, W. Wright. *How Insects Build Their Amazing Homes* (5–8). Illus. by Carlyn Iverson. Series: Animal Architects. 1999, Blackbirch LB $24.95 (978-1-56711-375-4). After defining what an insect is, this book shows how termites, wasps, ants, and bees construct their houses and nests. (Rev: HBG 3/00; SLJ 5/00) [595.7]

12495 Waldbauer, Gilbert. *Insights from Insects: What Bad Bugs Can Teach Us* (8–12). Illus. 2005, Prometheus paper $20.98 (978-1-59102-277-0). Friend or foe? Waldbauer profiles 20 insects that most humans consider pests and their roles in the natural world. (Rev: BL 3/15/05) [632]

12496 Wangberg, James K. *Do Bees Sneeze? And Other Questions Kids Ask About Insects* (7–10). Illus. 1997, Fulcrum paper $18.95 (978-1-55591-963-4). Full, interesting answers to more than 200 questions about insects on such subjects as physical characteristics, anatomical features, locomotion, behavior, habitat, and human health and safety. (Rev: BL 1/1–15/98; SLJ 4/98) [595.7]

12497 Wilkes, Sarah. *Insects* (5–9). Series: World Almanac Library of the Animal Kingdom. 2006, World Almanac LB $31.00 (978-0-8368-6211-9). A helpful introduction to members of the insect kingdom, this guide looks at physical characteristics that help to define this group as a whole, as well as specific species, habitats, diets, behaviors, and life cycles. (Rev: SLJ 12/06) [595.7]

12498 Wilsdon, Christina, and National Audubon Society, eds. *National Audubon Society First Field Guide: Insects* (4–8). Illus. 1998, Scholastic paper $17.95 (978-0-590-05447-8). Following a general introduction to entomology, specific insects are pictured and information is given on such topics as their eating, mating and social habits, physical structure, habitats, and identification markings. (Rev: BL 8/98; SLJ 10/98) [595]

12499 Zabludoff, Marc. *The Insect Class* (5–9). Illus. Series: Family Trees. 2005, Benchmark LB $29.93 (978-0-7614-1819-1). Habits, habitats, and other aspects of this varied class of animals; an engaging book with plenty of facts for report-writers. (Rev: SLJ 6/06) [595.7]

BUTTERFLIES, MOTHS, AND CATERPILLARS

12500 Preston-Mafham, Rod. *The Secret Life of Butterflies and Moths* (4–7). Series: The Secret World of . . . 2002, Raintree LB $27.12 (978-0-7398-4984-2). Beginning with little-known facts about butterflies and moths, this book explores their life cycles, behavior, mating habits, enemies, food, and habitats. (Rev: BL 8/02) [595.78]

12501 Pyle, Robert Michael. *The Audubon Society Field Guide to North American Butterflies* (7–12). Illus. 1981, Knopf $19.95 (978-0-394-51914-2). An introduction to more than 600 species of butterflies in about 1,000 color photographs and text. [595.7]

12502 Schappert, Phil. *The Last Monarch Butterfly: Conserving the Monarch Butterfly in a Brave New World* (8–12). Illus. 2004, Firefly paper $19.95 (978-1-55297-969-3). The fascinating story of the monarch butterfly and its incredible migrations is told with an emphasis on the threats it faces. (Rev: BL 12/15/04) [595.78]

12503 Schlaepfer, Gloria G. *Butterflies* (4–8). Illus. Series: AnimalWays. 2005, Benchmark LB $21.95 (978-0-7614-1745-3). Beautiful photographs of butterfly specimens enrich this well-organized volume that provides basic information on the butterfly's characteristics, habits, and habitat. (Rev: SLJ 5/06) [595.78]

12504 Stewart, Melissa. *Butterflies* (4–7). Illus. by Andrew Recher. Series: Our Wild World. 2007, NorthWord LB $10.95 (978-1-55971-966-7); paper $7.95 (978-1-55971-967-4). The behavior, physical characteristics and life cycles of butterflies are presented in great detail with many photographs. (Rev: SLJ 7/07) [595.78]

SPIDERS AND SCORPIONS

12505 Allman, Toney. *From Spider Webs to Man-Made Silk* (4–7). Illus. Series: Imitating Nature. 2005, Gale LB $24.95 (978-0-7377-3124-8). An introduction to scientists' attempts to replicate spider silk in the laboratory. (Rev: BL 10/15/05; LMC 3/06) [595.4]

12506 Dallinger, Jane. *Spiders* (4–7). Illus. 1981, Lerner LB $22.60 (978-0-8225-1456-5). Excellent color photographs complement the text.

12507 Greenaway, Theresa. *Spiders* (4–7). Series: The Secret World of . . . 2001, Raintree LB $18.98 (978-0-7368-3509-1). An information-crammed text and attractive illustrations introduce spiders, how and where they live, and their behavior. (Rev: BL 10/15/01) [595.4]

12508 Montgomery, Sy. *The Tarantula Scientist* (4–7). Photos by Nic Bishop. Series: Scientists in the Field. 2004, Houghton $18.00 (978-0-618-14799-1). This informative, photo-filled book chronicles the day-to-day field work of arachnologist Sam Marshall as he searches for tarantulas in the French Guianan rain forest. (Rev: BL 3/15/04; HB 7–8/04; SLJ 5/04) [595.4]

12509 Zabludoff, Marc. *Spiders* (4–8). Illus. Series: AnimalWays. 2005, Benchmark LB $21.95 (978-0-7614-1747-7). Beautiful photographs enrich this well-organized volume that provides basic information on the insect's characteristics, habits, and habitat. (Rev: SLJ 5/06) [595.4]

Marine and Freshwater Life

GENERAL AND MISCELLANEOUS

12510 Breidahl, Harry. *Diminutive Drifters: Microscopic Aquatic Life* (6–8). Illus. Series: Life in Strange Places. 2001, Chelsea LB $28.00 (978-0-7910-6618-8). In addition to describing phytoplankton and the environment in which these organisms thrive, this volume includes information on a working microbiologist and provides many photographs. (Rev: HBG 3/02; SLJ 1/02)

12511 Cerullo, Mary. *Sea Soup: Phytoplankton* (4–7). Illus. 1999, Tilbury House $16.95 (978-0-88448-208-6). An introduction to the microscopic world of tiny plants known as phytoplankton and their contributions to life on this planet. (Rev: BL 3/15/00; SLJ 5/00) [578.77]

12512 Cerullo, Mary. *Sea Soup: Zooplankton* (4–7). Illus. by Bill Curtsinger. 2001, Tilbury House $16.95 (978-0-88448-219-2). An inviting introduction to the world of tiny drifting animals known as zooplankton, with intriguing photographs. (Rev: BL 7/01; HBG 10/01; SLJ 8/01) [592.1776.]

12513 Collard, Sneed B., III. *On the Coral Reefs* (4–7). Illus. Series: Science Adventures. 2005, Marshall Cavendish LB $25.64 (978-0-7614-1953-2). In addition to a profile of a marine biologist who studies fish that eat parasites living on other fish, Collard presents information on scientific research methods and on global warming and other environmental threats. (Rev: BL 2/1/06; SLJ 5/06) [577.7]

12514 Halfmann, Janet. *Life in the Sea* (5–7). Series: LifeViews. 2000, Creative LB $22.60 (978-1-58341-074-5). All life in the sea is discussed with a focus on the tiniest — plankton, algae, sea spiders, coral, and worms. (Rev: SLJ 8/00) [591.92]

12515 Johnson, Jinny. *Simon and Schuster Children's Guide to Sea Creatures* (4–7). 1998, Simon & Schuster $19.95 (978-0-689-81534-8). This book contains broad coverage of the invertebrates, birds, mammals, and fish found in various parts of the oceans and their shores. (Rev: HBG 10/98; SLJ 5/98) [591]

12516 Meinkoth, Norman A. *The Audubon Society Field Guide to North American Seashore Creatures* (7–12). Illus. 1981, Knopf $19.95 (978-0-394-51993-7). This is a guide to such invertebrates as sponges, corals, urchins, and anemones. [592]

12517 Rehder, Harold A. *The Audubon Society Field Guide to North American Seashells* (7–12). Illus. 1981, Knopf $19.95 (978-0-394-51913-5). Seven hundred of the most common seashells from our coasts are pictured in color photographs and described in the text. [594]

12518 Treat, Rose. *The Seaweed Book: How to Find and Have Fun with Seaweed* (4–7). Illus. 1995, Star Bright paper $5.95 (978-1-887724-00-5). The identification, collection, and preservation of various kinds of seaweed. (Rev: BL 2/1/96) [589.45]

12519 Vogel, Carole G. *Ocean Wildlife* (5–9). Series: The Restless Sea. 2003, Watts LB $30.50 (978-0-531-12324-9); paper $12.95 (978-0-531-16681-9). A thorough examination of marine life, from algae to whales, with an emphasis on those

species facing extinction through pollution, overfishing, and other manmade threats. (Rev: SLJ 3/04) [591.77]

12520 Waller, Geoffrey. *SeaLife: A Complete Guide to the Marine Environment* (8–12). 1996, Smithsonian $55.00 (978-1-56098-633-1). A comprehensive reference to marine biology, including profiles of more than 600 species of marine animals, this guide is written in easy-to-understand language and includes numerous illustrations and maps. [591.7]

12521 Zabludoff, Marc. *The Protoctist Kingdom* (5–9). Series: Family Trees. 2005, Benchmark LB $32.79 (978-0-7614-1818-4). Habits, habitats, and other aspects of this newly classified kingdom of animals that includes algae; an engaging book with plenty of facts for report-writers. (Rev: SLJ 6/06) [579]

CORALS AND JELLYFISH

12522 Collard, Sneed B. *Lizard Island: Science and Scientists on Australia's Great Barrier Reef* (5–7). Illus. 2000, Watts LB $26.00 (978-0-531-11719-4). A lively and absorbing description of the work of scientists studying the forms of life on the Great Barrier Reef. (Rev: BL 2/1/01; SLJ 5/01; VOYA 12/01) [577.7]

12523 Johnson, Rebecca L. *The Great Barrier Reef: A Living Laboratory* (5–8). 1992, Lerner LB $28.75 (978-0-8225-1596-8). A look at the world's largest coral reef, off the coast of Australia. (Rev: BL 5/15/92; SLJ 7/92) [574.9943]

12524 Walker, Pam, and Elaine Wood. *The Coral Reef* (8–11). Illus. Series: Life in the Seas. 2005, Facts on File $35.00 (978-0-8160-5703-0). An excellent introduction to the world's coral reefs, looking at how they were formed, the creatures that thrive within them, and the threats they face. (Rev: BL 1/1–15/06) [5/8.77]

FISHES

12525 Eschmeyer, William N., and Earl S. Herald. *A Field Guide to Pacific Coast Fishes* (7–12). Illus. 1983, Houghton $20.00 (978-0-618-00212-2). In this volume in the Peterson Field Guide series, about 500 fish are described and illustrated. [597]

12526 Filisky, Michael. *Peterson First Guide to Fishes of North America* (7–12). Illus. 1989, Houghton paper $4.95 (978-0-393-91179-4). This is a concise version of the parent Peterson guide that gives basic material on common fish but with less detail. (Rev: BL 6/1/89) [597]

12527 Hirschmann, Kris. *Rays* (4–7). Illus. 2003, Gale LB $23.70 (978-0-7377-0988-9). Hirschmann presents basic information about the ray's anatomy, movement, feeding, defense, reproduction, and man's fascination with this fish. (Rev: BL 3/1/03) [597.3]

12528 Pascoe, Elaine. *Freshwater Fish* (4–8). Photos by Dwight Kuhn. Series: Nature Close-Up. 2005, Gale LB $24.95 (978-1-4103-0308-0). Eye-catching close-ups illustrate information on the life cycles and eating habits of freshwater fish. (Rev: SLJ 6/05)

12529 Schweid, Richard. *Consider the Eel* (8–12). Illus. 2002, Univ. of North Carolina $24.95 (978-0-8078-2693-5). A fascinating profile of the eel, with information on its history, life cycle, importance as a food product, and appearances in folklore, along with a selection of eel recipes. (Rev: BL 3/15/02) [597]

12530 Walker, Sally M. *Fossil Fish Found Alive: Discovering the Coelacanth* (5–8). Illus. 2002, Carolrhoda LB $17.95 (978-1-57505-536-7). An engaging look at the search for and study of coelacanths, a fish believed to be extinct until 1938. (Rev: BL 3/15/02; HB 1–2/03; HBG 3/03; SLJ 5/02*) [597.3]

12531 Wilkes, Sarah. *Fish* (5–9). Series: World Almanac Library of the Animal Kingdom. 2006, World Almanac LB $31.00 (978-0-8368-6210-2). This brightly illustrated guide to fish introduces specific species, physical characteristics, habitats, diets, behaviors, and life cycles. (Rev: SLJ 12/06) [597]

12532 Zim, Herbert S., and Hurst H. Shoemaker. *Fishes* (5–8). Illus. by James G. Irving. 1991, Western paper $21.27 (978-0-307-64059-8). This is a basic guide to both fresh and saltwater species.

SHARKS

12533 Capuzzo, Michael. *Close to Shore: The Terrifying Shark Attacks of 1916* (7–12). Illus. 2003, Crown $16.95 (978-0-375-82231-5). Photographs and newspaper clippings enhance this true story of a shark's brief and dangerous detour into a New Jersey creek in 1916. (Rev: BL 5/15/03; HBG 10/03; SLJ 4/03) [597.3]

12534 Carwardine, Mark. *Shark* (7–12). Illus. 2004, Firefly paper $24.95 (978-1-55297-948-8). Report writers and shark fans will find material of interest here. (Rev: BL 11/1/04) [597.3]

12535 Cerullo, Mary. *The Truth About Great White Sharks* (4–7). Illus. 2000, Chronicle $14.95 (978-0-8118-2467-5). A fascinating account with excellent underwater photographs that explores such topics about sharks as physical characteristics, behavior, feeding habits, and the difficulty of studying them. (Rev: BL 4/1/00; SLJ 7/00) [597.3]

12536 Dingerkus, Guido. *The Shark Watchers' Guide* (7–12). Illus. 1989, Messner paper $5.95 (978-0-671-68815-8). As well as materials on 30 different varieties of sharks, this book tells about shark anatomy, habits, and evolution and gives tips on how to handle a shark attack. (Rev: BL 11/15/85; SLJ 12/85) [597]

12537 Pope, Joyce. *1001 Facts About Sharks* (7–12). Series: Backpack Books. 2002, DK paper $8.99 (978-0-7894-8449-9). More than 550 illustrations and photographs are used to present basic facts about sharks, their anatomy, habits, and varieties. (Rev: BL 3/15/02) [597]

12538 Reader's Digest, eds. *Sharks: Silent Hunters of the Deep* (8–12). Illus. 1987, Reader's Digest $19.95 (978-0-86438-014-2). This handsomely illustrated account describes the ways of sharks, gives material on famous encounters, and identifies all 344 species. (Rev: BL 5/15/87; SLJ 1/88; VOYA 8/87) [597]

12539 Sieswerda, Paul L. *Sharks* (5–8). Series: AnimalWays. 2001, Marshall Cavendish LB $31.36 (978-0-7614-1267-0). Photographs, maps, and text introduce many species of sharks, their behavior, anatomy, and habitats. (Rev: BL 3/15/02; HBG 10/02) [597.31]

WHALES, DOLPHINS, AND OTHER SEA MAMMALS

12540 Chadwick, Douglas H. *The Grandest of Lives: Eye to Eye with Whales* (8–12). Illus. by author. 2006, Sierra Club $24.95 (978-1-57805-126-7). Chadwick followed scientists on their whale observations as he compiled this compelling overview of five species and their behavior, intelligence, and the threats they face. (Rev: BL 6/1–15/06) [599.5]

12541 Darling, Jim. *Gray Whales* (6–12). Series: World Life Library. 1999, Voyageur paper $16.95 (978-0-89658-447-1). Physiology, behavior, habitat, migration, and relations with humans are all discussed in this volume that contains lots of full-color photographs. (Rev: SLJ 4/00) [599.5]

12542 Greenaway, Theresa. *Whales* (4–7). Illus. Series: Secret World Of. 2001, Raintree LB $27.12 (978-0-7398-3508-1). A look at whales' diet, habitat, and behavior, with photographs and interesting facts. (Rev: BL 10/15/01; HBG 3/02) [599.5]

12543 Greenberg, Dan. *Whales* (5–9). Illus. Series: AnimalWays. 2003, Marshall Cavendish $31.36 (978-0-7614-1389-9). In addition to material on physical characteristics, behavior, habitats, and threats, Greenberg touches on the animal's roles in history, mythology, religion, and literature. (Rev: BL 3/15/03; HBG 3/03) [599.5]

12544 Hall, Howard. *A Charm of Dolphins: The Threatened Life of a Flippered Friend* (5–8). Series: Jean-Michel Cousteau Presents. 2007, London Town paper $8.95 (978-0-9766134-8-0). With eye-catching photographs and stories of close encounters with these animals, this book looks at dolphins' characteristics, behavior, intelligence, and the threats to their survival. (Rev: SLJ 11/07) [599.53]

12545 Hodgkins, Fran. *The Whale Scientists: Solving the Mystery of Whale Strandings* (5–8). Illus. Series: Scientists in the Field. 2007, Houghton $18.00 (978-0-618-55673-1). A look at scientists' efforts to understand why whales sometimes strand themselves on beaches, seemingly waiting for death; with accounts of efforts to rescue these huge mammals. (Rev: BL 12/1/07; HB 1–2/08; SLJ 12/07) [599.5]

12546 Kelsey, Elin. *Finding Out About Whales* (4–8). Illus. Series: Science Explorers. 1998, Owl $19.95 (978-1-895688-79-5); paper $9.95 (978-1-895688-80-1). This book discusses how information is gathered about whales and introduces five different species: blue, humpback, beluga, gray, and killer. (Rev: BL 3/1/99; SLJ 3/99) [595.5]

12547 Leon, Vicki. *A Pod of Killer Whales: The Mysterious Life of the Intelligent Orca* (5–8). Series: Jean-Michel Cousteau Presents. 2007, London Town paper $8.95 (978-0-9766134-7-3). With eye-catching photographs and stories of close encounters with these animals, this book looks at killer whales' characteristics, behavior, intelligence, and the threats to their survival. (Rev: SLJ 11/07) [599.53]

12548 Leon, Vicki. *A Raft of Sea Otters: The Playful Life of a Furry Survivor.* 2nd ed. (4–7). Illus. 2005, London Town paper $7.95 (978-0-9666490-4-8). This accessible introduction to the sea otter and its physical characteristics, behavior, diet, habitat, life cycle, and conservation threats is a picture-book-size revision of an earlier edition and contains excellent photographs. (Rev: BL 7/05) [599.7695]

12549 Lockwood, Sophie. *Whales* (4–7). Illus. Series: World of Mammals. 2008, Child's World LB $20.95 (978-1-59296-930-2). Well-suited to report writers, this surprisingly comprehensive title discusses whale behavior and physiology and includes information on conservation. (Rev: BLO 6/17/08; SLJ 6/08) [599.5]

12550 Nuzzolo, Deborah. *Bottlenose Dolphin Training and Interaction* (6–9). Illus. Series: SeaWorld Education. 2003, Sea World paper $7.99 (978-1-893698-03-1). An attractive introduction to this dolphin's habitat, physiology, and behavior, and to the ways in which they are trained at Sea World. (Rev: BL 6/1–15/03) [636.]

12551 Pascoe, Elaine, adapt. *Animal Intelligence: Why Is This Dolphin Smiling?* (5–8). 1997, Blackbirch $17.95 (978-1-56711-226-9). This book reports on the scientific research on communication between dolphins and humans, with reports on such projects as one by John Lilly to create, via computer, dolphin equivalents of human words. (Rev: HBG 3/98; SLJ 12/97) [599.5]

12552 Price-Groff, Claire. *The Manatee* (7–10). Series: Endangered Animals and Habitats. 1999, Lucent LB $27.45 (978-1-56006-445-9). This well-illustrated book describes this endangered sea mammal and tells about its habits, habitats, and appearance. (Rev: BL 9/15/99; HBG 4/00) [599.53]

12553 Read, Andrew. *Porpoises* (5–8). Illus. Series: WorldLife Library. 1999, Voyageur paper $16.95 (978-0-89658-420-4). With many color illustrations and large print, this book introduces porpoises, their characteristics, behavior, habitats, and how humans study them. (Rev: BL 8/99; VOYA 2/00) [599.53]

12554 Reiter, Chris. *The Blue Whale* (4–7). Series: Endangered and Threatened Animals. 2003, Enslow LB $25.26 (978-0-7660-5055-6). Standard information on the blue whale and its endangered status is accompanied by links to Web sites for further research. (Rev: HBG 10/03; SLJ 6/03) [599.5]

12555 Rinard, Judith E. *Amazing Animals of the Sea* (5–8). Illus. 1981, National Geographic LB $12.50 (978-0-87044-387-9). Whales, dolphins, sea otters, sea lions, seals, manatees, and other marine mammals are described.

12556 Silverstein, Alvin, et al. *The Manatee* (4–7). Illus. Series: Endangered in America. 1995, Millbrook LB $24.90 (978-1-56294-551-0). A profile of this sea creature, its lifestyle and habits, and how it became an endangered species. (Rev: BL 10/15/95; SLJ 1/96) [599.5]

12557 Simmonds, Mark. *Whales and Dolphins of the World* (8–12). Illus. 2005, MIT $29.95 (978-0-262-19519-5). This photo-filled volume introduces readers to the cetaceans — whales, dolphins, and porpoises — and to their relationship with humans. (Rev: BL 3/15/05) [599.5]

12558 Woog, Adam. *The Whale* (7–10). Series: Endangered Animals and Habitats. 1998, Lucent LB $27.45 (978-1-56006-460-2). A well-illustrated, fact-filled exploration of the different species of whales and the threats to their survival. (Rev: HBG 9/98) [599.5]

Microscopes, Microbiology, and Biotechnology

12559 Farrell, Jeanette. *Invisible Allies: Microbes That Shape Our Lives* (6–9). Illus. 2005, Farrar $17.00 (978-0-374-33608-0). The beneficial role of microbes (in food production, digestion, waste removal, and so forth) is the focus of this engaging title by the author of *Invisible Enemies* (1998). (Rev: BL 4/15/05*; SLJ 5/05; VOYA 8/05) [579]

12560 Latta, Sara L. *The Good, the Bad, the Slimy: The Secret Life of Microbes* (5–8). Photos by Dennis Kunkel. 2006, Enslow LB $31.93 (978-0-7660-1294-3). Bright photography and clear explanations will engage browsers and please report writers. (Rev: LMC 4-5/07; SLJ 8/07)

12561 Morgan, Sally. *From Microscopes to Stem Cell Research: Discovering Regenerative Medicine* (6–9). Illus. Series: Chain Reactions. 2006, Heinemann LB $34.29 (978-1-4034-8836-7). Morgan looks at ways in which the development of microscopes contributed to our knowledge of stem cells, ends with brief biographies of key individuals in the field. (Rev: SLJ 2/07)

12562 Rainis, Kenneth G. *Cell and Microbe Science Fair Projects Using Microscopes, Mold, and More* (6–12). Illus. Series: Biology! Best Science Projects. 2005, Enslow LB $26.60 (978-0-7660-2369-7). This introduction to the study of cells and microbes contains step-by-step instructions for a number of related experiments and projects. (Rev: SLJ 9/05) [578]

12563 Rainis, Kenneth G., and Bruce J. Russell. *Guide to Microlife* (7–12). Illus. 1996, Watts LB $36.00 (978-0-531-11266-3). A handbook to microscopic animals that describes habitats, the various groups of organisms, and projects. Each entry is accompanied by stunning photographs. (Rev: BL 2/15/97; SLJ 5/97) [576]

12564 Silverstein, Alvin, et al. *Cells* (4–8). Series: Science Concepts. 2002, Millbrook LB $26.90 (978-0-7613-2254-2). The functions and components of plant and animal cells are discussed along with such topics as cloning, cell fusion, and stem cell research. (Rev: BL 9/15/02; HBG 3/03) [574.87]

12565 Snedden, Robert. *The Benefits of Bacteria* (6–10). Illus. Series: Microlife. 2000, Heinemann LB $24.22 (978-1-57572-242-9). The beneficial functions of bacteria are discussed in this well-illustrated science book. (Rev: BL 9/15/00; SLJ 12/00) [576]

12566 Snedden, Robert. *Scientists and Discoveries* (6–10). Illus. Series: Microlife. 2000, Heinemann LB $22.79 (978-1-57572-244-3). This well-written account traces the development of the microscope and describes some of the discoveries that resulted such as vaccination, bacteriology, germ theory, antibiotics, and DNA. (Rev: BL 9/1/00) [579]

12567 Snedden, Robert. *A World of Microorganisms* (6–9). Series: Microlife. 2000, Heinemann LB $22.79 (978-1-57572-241-2). With clear explanations and many illustrations, this account discusses viruses, bacteria, protists, and fungi as well as the structure of cells and the chemistry of living organisms. (Rev: BL 9/1/00; SLJ 12/00) [579]

12568 Stefoff, Rebecca. *Microscopes and Telescopes* (7–10). Illus. Series: Great Inventions. 2007, Marshall Cavendish LB $27.95 (978-0-7614-2230-3). From early spectacles through the invention of refractors and reflectors to space telescopes and on into the future, this history of microscopes and tele-

scopes offers lots of hard scientific information. (Rev: SLJ 11/07) [502.8]

12569 Thomas, Peggy. *Bacteria and Viruses* (5–8). Illus. Series: Lucent Library of Science and Technology. 2005, Gale LB $29.95 (978-1-59018-438-7). Introduces the scientists who discovered bacteria and viruses and how we fight ones that harm us and attempt to use others to our benefit. (Rev: BL 1/05)

12570 Walker, Richard. *Microscopic Life* (4–8). Illus. Series: Kingfisher Knowledge. 2004, Kingfisher $11.95 (978-0-7534-5778-8). A well-illustrated look at the tiniest living things — bacteria, viruses, mites, fungi, and molds, for example — and how we study them and attempt to use them to our benefit. (Rev: BL 9/1/04; SLJ 1/05) [579]

Pets

GENERAL AND MISCELLANEOUS

12571 Albrecht, Kat. *The Lost Pet Chronicles: Adventures of a K-9 Cop Turned Pet Detective* (8–12). 2004, Bloomsbury $23.95 (978-1-58234-379-2). This is a memoir of a former police officer who has become a pet detective and a solver of such crimes as dognapping. (Rev: BL 3/1/04) [363.28]

12572 Gerstenfeld, Sheldon L. *The Bird Care Book: All You Need to Know to Keep Your Bird Healthy and Happy*. Rev. ed. (8–12). Illus. 1989, Addison-Wesley paper $17.00 (978-0-201-09559-3). A basic handbook on the choosing, care, and feeding of both pet and wild birds. (Rev: BL 9/15/89) [636.6]

12573 Hernandez-Divers, Sonia. *Geckos* (4–8). Illus. Series: Keeping Unusual Pets. 2003, Heinemann LB $25.64 (978-1-4034-0282-0). An appealing and informative introduction to geckos that provides much practical guidance on actually keeping one as a pet. Also use *Chinchillas, Ferrets, Snakes* (all 2002), and *Rats* (2003). (Rev: BL 3/15/03; HBG 10/03; SLJ 4/03) [639.3]

12574 Kent, Deborah. *Animal Helpers for the Disabled* (5–7). Illus. Series: Watts Library: Disability. 2003, Watts LB $25.50 (978-0-531-12017-0). Stories of animal accomplishments draw readers into this account, which covers the history of service animals, the kinds of animals used, and the training they undergo. (Rev: BL 10/15/03; LMC 11–12/03; SLJ 9/03) [636.08]

12575 Simon, Seymour. *Pets in a Jar: Collecting and Caring for Small Wild Animals* (7–10). Illus. 1975, Penguin paper $6.99 (978-0-14-049186-9). Valuable information is given on caring for such small pets as ants, crickets, crabs, and starfish. [639]

CATS

12576 Arnold, Caroline. *Cats: In from the Wild* (4–7). Photos by Richard Hewett. 1993, Carolrhoda

LB $19.93 (978-0-87614-692-7). Domestic and wild cats are highlighted with comparisons and contrasts. (Rev: BL 8/93) [636.8]

12577 Gerstenfeld, Sheldon L. *The Cat Care Book: All You Need to Know to Keep Your Cat Healthy and Happy.* Rev. ed. (8–12). Illus. 1989, Addison-Wesley paper $17.50 (978-0-201-09569-2). Tips on how to choose a cat and detailed information on taking care of cats as pets. (Rev: BL 9/15/89) [636.8]

12578 Mattern, Joanne. *The American Shorthair Cat* (4–7). Illus. Series: Learning About Cats. 2002, Capstone LB $23.93 (978-0-7368-1300-6). Beautiful photographs of frisky felines are accompanied by data about the physical characteristics and personality, with a glossary, bibliography, and lists of addresses and Web sites. Also use *The Manx Cat* (2002). (Rev: BL 12/1/02; HBG 3/03) [636.8]

12579 Morris, Desmond. *Catwatching* (8–12). 1987, Crown paper $8.95 (978-0-517-88053-1). Using a question-and-answer approach, the author explores many facets of cat behavior. (Rev: BL 4/1/87) [636.8]

12580 Singer, Marilyn. *Cats to the Rescue* (4–7). Illus. by Jean Cassels. 2006, Holt $16.95 (978-0-8050-7433-8). This collection of true cat stories focuses on feats ranging from catching tens of thousands of mice to detecting a gas leak. (Rev: BL 9/15/06; SLJ 11/06) [636.8]

12581 Stefoff, Rebecca. *Cats* (4–7). Series: AnimalWays. 2003, Benchmark LB $31.36 (978-0-7614-1577-0). A well-illustrated study of cats, their evolution, behavior, and human attitudes toward them. (Rev: SLJ 3/04) [636.8]

DOGS

12582 American Kennel Club. *The Complete Dog Book.* 19th ed. (7–12). Illus. 1998, Howell Book House $32.95 (978-0-87605-148-1). The standard manual for dog owners and guide to every AKC-recognized breed. (Rev: BL 6/15/85) [636.7]

12583 Bain, Terry. *You Are a Dog (Life Through the Eyes of Man's Best Friend)* (8–12). Illus. 2004, Harmony $16.00 (978-1-4000-5242-4). A humorous dog's-eye view of the world. (Rev: SLJ 1/05) [636.7]

12584 Benjamin, Carol Lea. *Dog Training for Kids.* Rev. ed. (5–8). Illus. 1988, Howell Book House $18.95 (978-0-87605-541-0). A simple guide to dog training that emphasizes the goal of having fun with a dog you are proud of. (Rev: SLJ 4/89) [636.7]

12585 Bolan, Sandra. *Caring for Your Mutt* (7–12). Illus. Series: Our Best Friend. 2008, Eldorado Ink LB $25.95 (978-1-932904-20-8). Readers who own mixed-breed (and no-breed) dogs will enjoy this book, which gives information on basic care and explains that mutts are sometimes puzzling and often pleasant surprises. (Rev: BL 4/1/08) [636.7]

12586 Fennell, Jan. *The Dog Listener: Learn How to Communicate with Your Dog for Willing Cooperation* (8–12). 2004, HarperResource paper $16.95 (978-0-06-008946-7). This comprehensive guide tells how one can peacefully coexist with one's dog and how successful training can be accomplished without violent behavior. (Rev: BL 1/1–15/04) [636.7]

12587 Fogle, Bruce, and Patricia Holden White. *New Complete Dog Training Manual* (8–12). 2002, DK $25.00 (978-0-7894-8398-0). This dog-training book shows how to create routines, implement commands, and break a dog's bad habits. [636.7]

12588 Gerstenfeld, Sheldon L. *The Dog Care Book: All You Need to Know to Keep Your Dog Healthy and Happy.* Rev. ed. (8–12). Illus. 1989, Addison-Wesley paper $17.00 (978-0-201-09667-5). Tips on selecting a dog plus extensive material on care and feeding. (Rev: BL 9/15/89) [636.7]

12589 Gorrell, Gena K. *Working Like a Dog: The Story of Working Dogs Through History* (4–8). Illus. 2003, Tundra $16.95 (978-0-88776-589-6). A comprehensive and very appealing look at dogs' services to man throughout history — as hunters and trackers, bomb sniffers, guide dogs, and companions, to name but a few. (Rev: BL 11/1/03; SLJ 12/03) [636.73]

12590 Grogan, John. *Marley: A Dog like No Other* (4–7). Illus. 2007, HarperCollins $16.99 (978-0-06-124033-1). An adaptation of Grogan's book for adults, *Marley & Me,* this story of a hopelessly out-of-control but lovable dog who dies too soon will touch young readers. (Rev: BL 7/07; SLJ 7/07) [636.752] 🦮

12591 Halls, Kelly Milner. *Wild Dogs: Past and Present* (4–7). Illus. 2005, Darby Creek $18.95 (978-1-58196-027-3). A wide-ranging introduction to dogs and their history, with attractive design, many photographs, and lots of factboxes about dogs both wild and domestic. (Rev: BL 12/1/05; SLJ 11/05) [599.77]

12592 Hampl, Patricia. *The Nature of Dogs* (7–12). Illus. by Mary Ludington. 2007, Simon & Schuster $35.00 (978-1-4165-4287-2). Beautiful photographs accompany well-written informative text about various breeds of dogs. (Rev: BL 9/15/07) [636.7]

12593 Maggitti, Phil. *Owning the Right Dog* (8–12). 1993, Tetra $29.95 (978-1-56465-110-5). Provides information on feeding, grooming, breeding, showing, and training, with color illustrations. (Rev: BL 11/1/93) [636.7]

12594 Mehus-Roe, Kristin. *Dogs for Kids! Everything You Need to Know about Dogs* (4–7). Illus. 2007, Bowtie paper $14.95 (978-1-931993-83-8).

From a history of dogs to information on breeds, anatomy, and behavior to advice on care and training — as the title says, this book is all you need. (Rev: BL 2/15/08; SLJ 6/07) [636.7]

12595 Murphy, Claire Rudolf, and Jane G. Haigh. *Gold Rush Dogs* (6–12). Illus. 2001, Alaska Northwest $16.95 (978-0-88240-534-6). Nine dogs that played important roles in the Yukon are profiled here with many sidebars that provide background historical detail. (Rev: BL 9/1/01; SLJ 9/01) [636.7]

12596 Page, Jake. *Dogs: A Natural History* (6–12). Illus. 2007, Smithsonian $24.95 (978-0-06-113259-9). Owner of six dogs, Page shares his extensive knowledge of doggy history, behavior, breeds, and relationship with humans. (Rev: BL 9/1/07) [636.7]

12597 Paulsen, Gary. *My Life in Dog Years* (5–10). Illus. 1998, Delacorte $15.95 (978-0-385-32570-7). The famous novelist tells about eight wonderful dogs that he has known and loved over the years. (Rev: BCCB 3/98; BL 1/1–15/98; SLJ 3/98; VOYA 4/98) [636.7]

12598 Presnall, Judith Janda. *Police Dogs* (4–7). Illus. Series: Animals with Jobs. 2002, Gale LB $23.70 (978-0-7377-0631-4). This well-illustrated account describes the various ways in which dogs are used to fight crime. (Rev: BL 4/1/02) [363.2]

12599 Rosenthal, Lisa. *A Dog's Best Friend: An Activity Book for Kids and Their Dogs* (4–7). Illus. by Bonnie Matthews. 1999, Chicago Review paper $12.95 (978-1-55652-362-5). This book that gives hints on how to choose a dog and care for a puppy offers 60 projects related to these subjects including crafts, recipes, and games. (Rev: SLJ 1/00) [636.7]

12600 Scalisi, Danny, and Libby Moses. *When Rover Just Won't Do: Over 2000 Suggestions for Naming Your Puppy* (8–12). 1993, Howell Book House $9.95 (978-0-87605-691-2). This collection of names for dogs includes more than 2,000 ideas, from Fajita to Rocky and Bullwinkle. (Rev: BL 11/1/93) [636.7]

12601 Silverstein, Alvin, et al. *Different Dogs* (4–7). Series: What a Pet! 2000, Twenty-First Century LB $23.90 (978-0-7613-1371-7). Several different breeds of dogs are introduced in pictures and text plus information on cost, food, housing, and training. (Rev: HBG 10/00; SLJ 5/00) [636.7]

FISHES

12602 Emmens, Cliff W. *A Step-by-Step Book About Tropical Fish* (8–12). Illus. 1988, TFH paper $5.95 (978-0-86622-471-0). A brief, brightly illustrated introduction to various types of tropical fish, their care, and housing. (Rev: BL 1/1/89) [639.34]

HORSES

12603 Budd, Jackie. *Seasons of the Horse: A Practical Guide to Year-Round Equine Care* (5–12). 2007, T.F.H. $29.95 (978-0-7938-0611-9). Well-organized and visually pleasing, this book provides a complete guide to caring for a horse, including nutrition and exercise. (Rev: SLJ 3/08)

12604 Budiansky, Stephen. *The World According to Horses: How They Run, See, and Think* (4–8). Illus. 2000, Holt $17.95 (978-0-8050-6054-6). This book explores horses' behavior — such as their sight and thinking powers — and goes on to explain how this knowledge was gained through observation and experiments. (Rev: BCCB 5/00; BL 3/1/00; HB 5–6/00; HBG 10/00; SLJ 7/00; VOYA 6/00) [636.1]

12605 Henry, Marguerite. *Album of Horses* (5–8). Illus. by Wesley Dennis. 1951, Macmillan paper $11.99 (978-0-689-71709-3). A beautifully illustrated guide to 20 breeds of horses.

12606 Hill, Cherry. *Horse Care for Kids* (4–8). Illus. 2002, Storey $23.95 (978-1-58017-476-3); paper $16.95 (978-1-58017-407-7). A very practical guide for young horse lovers and their parents using clear prose and topnotch illustrations to cover everything from selecting a horse and instructor to proper care and equine psychology. (Rev: BL 12/1/02; HBG 3/03; SLJ 1/03) [636.1]

12607 Jurmain, Suzanne. *Once upon a Horse: A History of Horses and How They Shaped Our History* (5–9). Illus. 1989, Lothrop $15.95 (978-0-688-05550-9). A history of the horse and how it has been domesticated and used by humans. (Rev: BL 12/15/89; SLJ 1/90; VOYA 4/90) [636.1]

12608 Kelley, Brent. *Horse Breeds of the World* (4–8). Series: Horse Library. 2001, Chelsea $25.00 (978-0-7910-6652-2). In addition to basic facts about nearly 40 types of horses around the world, this account looks briefly at the horse's evolutionary history and related species. (Rev: HBG 3/02; SLJ 3/02) [636.1]

12609 Meltzer, Milton. *Hold Your Horses! A Feedbag Full of Fact and Fable* (4–8). Illus. 1995, HarperCollins LB $16.89 (978-0-06-024478-1). The place of horses in history is explored in this account that looks at horses' role in art, war, sports, and work. (Rev: BCCB 12/95; BL 11/15/95; SLJ 12/95*) [636.1]

12610 Penny, Malcolm. *The Secret Life of Wild Horses* (4–7). Series: The Secret World of . . . 2002, Raintree LB $27.12 (978-0-7398-4987-3). A page of little-known facts about wild horses introduces this book that explores the horse's life, habits, mating, behavior, and threats to its future. (Rev: BL 8/02) [636.1]

12611 Presnall, Judith Janda. *Horse Therapists* (4–7). Illus. Series: Animals with Jobs. 2002, Gale

LB $23.70 (978-0-7377-0615-4). Numerous photographs show how horses are used in various therapeutic situations including exercise for people with physical and mental disabilities. (Rev: BL 4/1/02; SLJ 3/02) [636.1]

12612 Ransford, Sandy. *The Kingfisher Illustrated Horse and Pony Encyclopedia* (4–8). Photos by Bob Langrish. Illus. 2004, Kingfisher $24.95 (978-0-7534-5781-8). After describing the history and various breeds of horses, this comprehensive and highly illustrated volume explains how to care for horses and how to ride them well and safely. (Rev: BL 3/1/05; SLJ 1/05) [636.1]

12613 Richter, Judy. *Riding for Kids* (4–8). 2003, Storey Kids $23.95 (978-1-58017-511-1); paper $16.95 (978-1-58017-510-4). An introduction to horsemanship, from caring for horses and riding equipment to advice on safety, showing, and jumping. (Rev: BL 1/1–15/04; SLJ 3/04) [798.2]

12614 Stefoff, Rebecca. *Horses* (5–8). Illus. Series: AnimalWays. 2000, Marshall Cavendish LB $31.36 (978-0-7614-1139-0). A well-illustrated account that describes the physical and behavioral characteristics of horses, their place in the classification system, and their relationships with humans. (Rev: BL 1/1–15/01) [599.884]

12615 Stromberg, Tony. *Spirit Horses* (8–12). Illus. 2005, New World Library $40.00 (978-1-57731-499-8). A photographic celebration of horses in a large-format album, accompanied by quotes from diverse sources. (Rev: BL 11/1/05) [636.1]

12616 van der Linde, Laurel. *From Mustangs to Movie Stars: Five True Horse Legends of Our Time* (4–7). Illus. 1995, Millbrook LB $24.40 (978-1-56294-456-8). Biographies of five famous horses are recounted, from the racer Native Dancer to Cass Olé, who was the star of the film *The Black Stallion*. (Rev: BCCB 12/95; SLJ 12/95) [636.1]

Zoos, Aquariums, and Animal Care

12617 Balliet, Gay L. *Lions and Tigers and Mares . . . Oh My!* (8–12). 2004, RDR paper $17.95 (978-1-57143-105-9). In humorous, appealing text, the wife of a Pennsylvania veterinarian sheds new light on the day-to-day challenges facing a vet who treats large and exotic animals. (Rev: BL 9/15/04) [636.089]

12618 Brown, Bradford B. *While You're Here, Doc: Farmyard Adventures of a Maine Veterinarian* (8–12). 2006, Tilbury House paper $15.00 (978-0-88448-279-6). Entertaining stories about life as a veterinarian in rural Maine. (Rev: BL 3/15/06) [636.0]

12619 Rinard, Judith E. *Zoos Without Cages* (5–8). Illus. 1981, National Geographic LB $12.50 (978-0-87044-340-4). A description of the new zoos that strive to reproduce the natural habitat of the enclosed animals. [590.74]

Chemistry

General and Miscellaneous

12620 Angliss, Sarah. *Gold* (4–8). Series: The Elements. 1999, Marshall Cavendish LB $25.64 (978-0-7614-0887-1). Easy-to-follow diagrams, fact boxes, and color illustrations accompany an informative text that introduces gold, where it is mined and processed, its properties, value, and uses. (Rev: BL 2/15/00; HBG 10/00) [546]

12621 Baxter, Roberta. *Chemical Reaction* (4–8). Illus. Series: The Kidhaven Science Library. 2004, Gale LB $26.20 (978-0-7377-2072-3). Clear, concise text, supported by full-color photographs and diagrams, describes many types of reactions — oxidation and photosynthesis, for example — and discusses their uses. (Rev: SLJ 6/05)

12622 Beatty, Richard. *Copper* (4–8). Series: The Elements. 2000, Marshall Cavendish LB $25.64 (978-0-7614-0945-8). This book identifies the element copper, defines its properties and describes its uses in everyday life, especially in electrical cables. (Rev: BL 1/1–15/01; HBG 10/01; SLJ 2/01) [546]

12623 Beatty, Richard. *The Lanthanides* (4–8). Series: The Elements. 2007, Marshall Cavendish LB $19.95 (978-0-7614-2687-5). This detailed and thorough overview of the 15 metal elements in the Lanthanides provides fact boxes and clear explanations in a graphically pleasing format. (Rev: SLJ 3/08)

12624 Beatty, Richard. *Manganese* (5–8). Illus. Series: The Elements. 2004, Marshall Cavendish LB $25.64 (978-0-7614-1813-9). Easy-to-follow diagrams, fact boxes, and color illustrations accompany an informative text that introduces manganese and its properties, value, and uses. (Rev: BL 12/1/04)

12625 Beatty, Richard. *Phosphorus* (4–8). Series: The Elements. 2000, Marshall Cavendish LB $25.64 (978-0-7614-0946-5). This book describes this nonmetallic element, lists its properties, tells how it behaves, and discusses such uses as matches and fertilizers. (Rev: BL 1/1–15/01; HBG 10/01; SLJ 2/01) [546]

12626 Beatty, Richard. *Sulfur* (4–8). Series: The Elements. 2000, Marshall Cavendish LB $25.64 (978-0-7614-0948-9). Introduces this nonmetallic element, its characteristics, various compounds, and uses in everyday life, with color photographs, easy-to-follow diagrams, fact boxes, and a clear text. (Rev: BL 1/1–15/01; HBG 10/01; SLJ 2/01) [546]

12627 Blashfield, Jean F. *Calcium* (6–9). Series: Sparks of Life. 1998, Raintree LB $27.12 (978-0-8172-5040-9). From seashells to human bone structure, this volume explores the nature of calcium and its importance in the world. (Rev: BL 1/1–15/99) [546]

12628 Blashfield, Jean F. *Carbon* (6–9). Series: Sparks of Life. 1998, Raintree LB $27.12 (978-0-8172-5041-6). Carbon is a cornerstone of the elements. This book describes its uses and compounds, from the composition of proteins to the plant-based production of starches and sugars. (Rev: BL 1/1–15/99) [546]

12629 Blashfield, Jean F. *Hydrogen* (6–9). Series: Sparks of Life. 1998, Raintree LB $27.12 (978-0-8172-5038-6). This volume explores the many different forms and uses of hydrogen, from its role as a primary component of water to its role in the hydrocarbons used to fuel the modern world. (Rev: BL 1/1–15/99) [546]

12630 Blashfield, Jean F. *Nitrogen* (6–9). Series: Sparks of Life. 1998, Raintree LB $27.12 (978-0-8172-5039-3). The properties and value of nitrogen are explored, from its use in explosives to its role in fertilizers. (Rev: BL 1/1–15/99) [546]

12631 Blashfield, Jean F. *Oxygen* (6–9). Series: Sparks of Life. 1998, Raintree LB $27.12 (978-0-8172-5037-9). An introduction to oxygen, how it was discovered, its reaction with other elements to form compounds and mixtures, and its importance as the "breath of life." (Rev: BL 1/1–15/99) [546]

12632 Blashfield, Jean F. *Sodium* (6–9). Series: Sparks of Life. 1998, Raintree LB $27.12 (978-0-8172-5042-3). This volume describes the history of sodium, its importance as an element, and its role as an ingredient in table salt, soaps, detergents, explosives, preservatives, and other common and not-so-common items. (Rev: BL 1/1–15/99) [546]

12633 Brandolini, Anita. *Fizz, Bubble and Flash! Element Explorations and Atom Adventures for Hands-On Science Fun!* (4–7). Illus. by Michael Kline. Series: Kids Can! 2003, Williamson paper $14.25 (978-1-885593-83-2). A friendly narrative and cartoon-style drawing present activities that illustrate basic scientific concepts. (Rev: BL 1/1–15/04; SLJ 11/03) [546]

12634 Cobb, Allan. *Cadmium* (4–8). Series: The Elements. 2007, Marshall Cavendish LB $19.95 (978-0-7614-2686-8). This well-designed overview of cadmium is thorough and also includes a section on how the element relates to the health of human beings. (Rev: SLJ 3/08)

12635 Cobb, Vicki. *Chemically Active! Experiments You Can Do at Home* (6–9). Illus. 1985, Harper-Collins LB $14.89 (978-0-397-32080-6). A group of scientific experiments that demonstrate chemical principles and can be performed with common household items. (Rev: SLJ 8/85; VOYA 12/85) [507]

12636 Cooper, Chris. *Arsenic* (4–8). Illus. Series: The Elements. 2006, Benchmark LB $19.95 (978-0-7614-2203-7). A basic guide to arsenic's properties and uses (including as a poison and in industrial applications). (Rev: SLJ 5/07) [546]

12637 Farndon, John. *Aluminum* (4–8). Series: The Elements. 2000, Marshall Cavendish LB $25.64 (978-0-7614-0947-2). This silvery, metallic element is introduced, with material on its individual characteristics, how it behaves, and its many uses in everyday life. (Rev: BL 1/1–15/01; HBG 10/01) [546]

12638 Farndon, John. *Calcium* (5–8). 1999, Benchmark LB $25.64 (978-0-7614-0888-8). An attractive, readable book that explains calcium's atomic structure, where and how it occurs in nature, its reactions, compounds, and uses. (Rev: BL 2/15/00; HBG 10/00; SLJ 6/00) [540]

12639 Farndon, John. *Hydrogen* (5–8). Illus. Series: Elements. 1999, Marshall Cavendish LB $25.64 (978-0-7614-0886-4). As well as explaining hydrogen's place on the periodic table, this account traces the history of its discovery, its properties, reactive

combinations, and uses. (Rev: BL 2/15/00; HBG 10/00; SLJ 6/00) [546]

12640 Farndon, John. *Nitrogen* (5–8). Series: The Elements. 1998, Benchmark LB $25.64 (978-0-7614-0877-2). An informative science book that introduces nitrogen's properties, reactions, place in the periodic table, and importance in the human body and the environment, and environmental issues relating to nitrogen such as pollution from noxious gases and acid rain. (Rev: HBG 10/99; SLJ 2/99) [540]

12641 Farndon, John. *Oxygen* (5–8). Series: The Elements. 1998, Benchmark LB $25.64 (978-0-7614-0879-6). Oxygen, its properties, uses, and various chemical combinations are covered in this informative text that also discusses the ozone layer. (Rev: HBG 10/99; SLJ 2/99) [540]

12642 Gallant, Roy A. *The Ever-Changing Atom* (5–8). Series: The Story of Science. 1999, Benchmark LB $29.93 (978-0-7614-0961-8). Using a chronological approach, this book traces how and what we have found out about the atom and its structure. (Rev: BL 2/15/00; HBG 3/00; SLJ 2/00) [539]

12643 Gardner, Robert. *Chemistry Science Fair Projects Using Acids, Bases, Metals, Salts, and Inorganic Stuff* (7–10). Illus. Series: Chemistry! Best Science Projects. 2004, Enslow LB $26.60 (978-0-7660-2210-2). Experiments and projects that explore various aspects of inorganic chemistry are presented with background information and safety tips. (Rev: SLJ 2/05) [540]

12644 Gardner, Robert. *Chemistry Science Fair Projects Using French Fries, Gumdrops, Soap, and Other Organic Stuff* (7–12). Illus. Series: Chemistry! Best Science Projects. 2004, Enslow LB $26.60 (978-0-7660-2211-9). Progressively more complex experiments and projects explore various aspects of organic chemistry using everyday items. (Rev: SLJ 4/05) [540]

12645 Gardner, Robert. *Science Projects About Chemistry* (6–12). Series: Science Projects. 2001, Enslow LB $26.60 (978-0-89490-531-5). Gardner conveys the fun of learning in this book about the uses of chemistry and science projects involving chemistry. (Rev: BL 3/15/01; HBG 10/01; SLJ 2/95) [540]

12646 Goodstein, Madeline. *Plastics and Polymers Science Fair Projects: Using Hair Gel, Soda Bottles, and Slimy Stuff* (7–12). Illus. Series: Chemistry! Best Science Projects. 2004, Enslow LB $26.60 (978-0-7660-2123-5). Introduced by a discussion of the concept of polymers and a model of a hydrocarbon chain, subsequent projects build on this knowledge. (Rev: SLJ 7/04) [507]

12647 Goodstein, Madeline. *Water Science Fair Projects: Using Ice Cubes, Super Soakers, and*

Other Wet Stuff (7–12). Illus. Series: Chemistry! Best Science Projects. 2004, Enslow LB $26.60 (978-0-7660-2124-2). Projects that use everyday materials teach students about water and its properties. (Rev: SLJ 7/04)

12648 Gray, Leon. *Iodine* (5–8). Series: Elements (Group 7). 2004, Marshall Cavendish $25.64 (978-0-7614-1812-2). This introduction to iodine examines the importance of this substance to body chemistry, as well as how it was discovered, where it is found, and its physical characteristics. (Rev: BL 12/1/04) [546]

12649 Jackson, Tom. *Lithium* (4–8). Illus. Series: The Elements. 2006, Benchmark LB $19.95 (978-0-7614-2199-3). A basic guide to lithium's properties and uses in batteries and pharmaceuticals. (Rev: SLJ 5/07) [546]

12650 Lepora, Nathan. *Molybdenum* (4–8). Illus. Series: The Elements. 2006, Benchmark LB $19.95 (978-0-7614-2201-3). A basic guide to molybdenum's properties and uses (including its medical applications). (Rev: SLJ 5/07) [546]

12651 Mebane, Robert C., and Thomas R. Rybolt. *Adventures with Atoms and Molecules, Vol. 5: Chemistry Experiments for Young People* (7–10). 1995, Enslow LB $19.95 (978-0-89490-606-0). A basic user's guide to start young people thinking scientifically, with ideas for science fair projects. (Rev: BL 12/1/95) [540]

12652 Miller, Ron. *The Elements: What You Really Want to Know* (7–12). Illus. by author. 2005, Twenty-First Century LB $29.27 (978-0-7613-2794-3). After historical information and profiles of key scientists, Miller provides information on each element in order of atomic number. (Rev: SLJ 3/06) [540]

12653 O'Daly, Anne. *Sodium* (4–8). Series: The Elements. 2001, Marshall Cavendish LB $25.64 (978-0-7614-1271-7). Diagrams and full-color illustrations are used to introduce sodium and its characteristics and importance in everyday life. (Rev: BL 3/15/02; HBG 3/02) [546]

12654 Oxlade, Chris. *Acids and Bases*. Rev. ed. (6–8). Series: Chemicals in Action. 2007, Heinemann LB $31.43 (978-1-4329-0050-2). After explaining the nature of acids and bases, this attractively arranged volume looks at reactions that take place around us and provides a few experiments. Also use *Atoms, Elements and Compounds*, and *States of Matter* (all 2007). (Rev: SLJ 10/07) [546]

12655 Roza, Greg. *Calcium* (5–8). Illus. Series: Understanding the Elements of the Periodic Table. 2007, Rosen LB $26.50 (978-1-4042-1963-2). This reader-friendly volume contains a full overview of calcium, including basic information and interesting sidebar features such as the amount of calcium found in different foods. (Rev: SLJ 3/08)

12656 Saucerman, Linda. *Chlorine* (5–8). Illus. Series: Understanding the Elements of the Periodic Table. 2007, Rosen LB $26.50 (978-1-4042-1962-5). Little-known facts interspersed among basic details make this book about chlorine an interesting read. (Rev: SLJ 3/08)

12657 Sommers, Michael A. *Phosphorus* (5–8). Illus. 2007, Rosen LB $26.50 (978-1-4042-1960-1). An easy to understand overview of phosphorus, including attractive graphics and interesting, little known facts (includes charts, diagrams, illustrations, photos, reproductions, bibliography, further reading, glossary, index and Web sites). (Rev: SLJ 3/08)

12658 Sparrow, Giles. *Nickel* (5–8). Illus. Series: The Elements. 2004, Marshall Cavendish LB $25.64 (978-0-7614-1811-5). Easy-to-follow diagrams, fact boxes, and color illustrations accompany an informative text that introduces nickel and its properties, value, and uses. (Rev: BL 12/1/04)

12659 Stimola, Aubrey. *Sulfur* (5–8). Illus. 2007, Rosen LB $26.50 (978-1-4042-1961-8). This basic overview of sulfur is well-organized and easy to understand, and contains interesting facts such as the use of sulfur in medicine (includes charts, diagrams, illustrations, photos, reproductions, bibliography, further reading, glossary, index and Web sites). (Rev: SLJ 3/08)

12660 Stwertka, Albert. *The World of Atoms and Quarks* (7–12). Series: Scientific American Sourcebooks. 1995, Twenty-First Century LB $28.90 (978-0-8050-3533-9). Using profiles of important scientists, this work traces humankind's quest for an understanding of matter and its building blocks. (Rev: BL 12/1/95; SLJ 2/96) [539.7]

12661 Thomas, Jens. *Silicon* (4–8). Series: The Elements. 2001, Marshall Cavendish LB $25.64 (978-0-7614-1274-8). Thomas introduces this important element and its origins, discovery, and many uses. (Rev: BL 3/15/02; HBG 3/02) [546]

12662 Uttley, Colin. *Magnesium* (4–8). Series: The Elements. 1999, Marshall Cavendish LB $25.64 (978-0-7614-0889-5). This book explores magnesium, a silvery metallic element important in living organisms, and explains its place in the periodic table, as well as its forms, uses, and properties. (Rev: BL 2/15/00; HBG 10/00) [546]

12663 Watt, Susan. *Chlorine* (4–8). Series: The Elements. 2001, Marshall Cavendish LB $25.64 (978-0-7614-1272-4). Using diagrams, photographs, and a concise text, this book introduces this active, nonmetallic element with material on its composition, characteristics, and many uses — including as a disinfectant and in water purification. (Rev: BL 3/15/02; HBG 3/02) [546]

12664 Watt, Susan. *Cobalt* (4–8). Illus. Series: The Elements. 2006, Benchmark LB $19.95 (978-0-

7614-2200-6). A basic guide to cobalt's properties and uses. (Rev: SLJ 5/07) [546]

12665 Watt, Susan. *Lead* (4–8). Series: The Elements. 2001, Marshall Cavendish LB $25.64 (978-0-7614-1273-1). Explores the history, origins, discovery, characteristics, and uses of this heavy metallic element in everyday life. (Rev: BL 3/15/02; HBG 3/02) [546]

12666 Watt, Susan. *Mercury* (5–8). Illus. Series: The Elements. 2004, Marshall Cavendish LB $25.64 (978-0-7614-1814-6). Easy-to-follow diagrams, fact boxes, and color illustrations accompany an informative text that introduces mercury and its properties, value, and uses. (Rev: BL 12/1/04)

12667 Watt, Susan. *Silver* (4–8). Illus. Series: The Elements. 2002, Benchmark LB $25.64 (978-0-7614-1464-3). A concise introduction to this element, its history, where it is found and how it is mined, and its many uses. Also in this series is *Potassium* (2002). (Rev: HBG 3/03; LMC 4–5/03; SLJ 4/03) [546]

12668 Watt, Susan. *Zirconium* (4–8). Series: The Elements. 2007, Marshall Cavendish LB $19.95 (978-0-7614-2688-2). This volume covers all aspects of zirconium including its use in dating some rocks and minerals. (Rev: SLJ 3/08)

12669 West, Krista. *Bromine* (4–8). Series: The Elements. 2007, Marshall Cavendish LB $19.95 (978-0-7614-2685-1). The element bromine is covered in detail in this attractively designed volume. (Rev: SLJ 3/08)

Geology and Geography

Earth and Geology

12670 Blashfield, Jean F., and Richard P. Jacobs. *When Ice Threatened Living Things: The Pleistocene* (6–9). Illus. Series: Prehistoric North America. 2005, Heinemann LB $37.14 (978-1-4034-7662-3). Provides information on the geology of North America during the Pleistocene era, when much of the continent was covered in ice. Also use *When Land, Sea, and Life Began: The Precambrian, When Dinosaurs Ruled: The Mesozoic Era,* and *When Life Flourished in Ancient Seas: The Early Paleozoic Era* (all 2005). (Rev: SLJ 5/06)

12671 Calhoun, Yael. *Earth Science Fair Projects Using Rocks, Minerals, Magnets, Mud, and More* (5–8). Illus. Series: Earth Science! Best Science Projects. 2005, Enslow LB $26.60 (978-0-7660-2363-5). More than 20 geology-related projects are introduced with clear instructions and interesting background information. (Rev: BL 11/1/05) [550]

12672 Campbell, Ann-Jeanette, and Ronald Rood. *The New York Public Library Incredible Earth: A Book of Answers for Kids* (4–7). Illus. 1996, Wiley paper $14.95 (978-0-471-14497-7). Questions and answers involving science, collected from the reference department of the New York Public Library. (Rev: BL 9/15/96; SLJ 1/97) [550]

12673 Downs, Sandra. *Shaping the Earth: Erosion* (5–8). Series: Exploring Planet Earth. 2000, Twenty-First Century LB $24.90 (978-0-7613-1414-1). This book explores the force of erosion and how such phenomena as wind, waves, floods, rain, acid rain, freezing, and thawing can change the face of the land. (Rev: HBG 10/00; SLJ 7/00) [551]

12674 Gallant, Roy A. *Dance of the Continents* (5–8). Series: The Story of Science. 1999, Benchmark LB $29.93 (978-0-7614-0962-5). This book covers geological theory from the ancient Greeks to modern plate tectonics with material on earthquakes, volcanoes, geysers, and other phenomena. (Rev: BL 2/15/00; HBG 3/00; SLJ 3/00) [551]

12675 Gardner, Robert. *Planet Earth Science Fair Projects Using the Moon, Stars, Beach Balls, Frisbees, and Other Far-Out Stuff* (6–12). Illus. Series: Earth Science! Best Science Projects. 2005, Enslow LB $26.60 (978-0-7660-2362-8). Earth science projects are clearly presented with background information necessary to give full understanding of the underlying principles. (Rev: SLJ 7/05) [551]

12676 George, Linda. *Plate Tectonics* (4–9). Illus. 2003, Gale LB $23.70 (978-0-7377-1405-0). Concise information on the movement of continents, the formation of mountains, and volcanic and earthquake activity is presented with full-color photographs and diagrams. (Rev: SLJ 10/03) [551.1]

12677 Goodman, Billy. *Natural Wonders and Disasters* (4–7). Illus. Series: Planet Earth. 1991, Little, Brown $17.95 (978-0-316-32016-0). Full-color photographs help to explain the earth's natural wonders as well as such disasters as floods and typhoons. (Rev: BL 12/1/91; SLJ 1/92) [550]

12678 Hehner, Barbara Embury. *Blue Planet* (7–12). Series: Wide World. 1992, Harcourt $17.95 (978-0-15-200423-1). An examination of the interdependent systems that make up our planet, including plate tectonics, volcanoes, weather, satellites, and the ozone layer. (Rev: BL 11/15/92; SLJ 10/92) [508]

12679 Loeschnig, Louis V. *Simple Earth Science Experiments with Everyday Materials* (6–8). Illus. 1996, Sterling $14.95 (978-0-8069-0898-4). A well-organized book of activities and demonstrations that explore such subjects as soil, time, earthquakes, glaciers, gravity, and conservation. (Rev: BL 10/15/96) [550]

12680 O'Neill, Catherine. *Natural Wonders of North America* (7–12). Illus. 1984, National Geographic LB $12.50 (978-0-87044-519-4). Excellent color photographs complement the text and maps that describe such natural wonders as tundra regions, volcanoes, glaciers, and the Badlands of South Dakota. [557]

12681 Redfern, Martin. *The Kingfisher Young People's Book of Planet Earth* (4–8). 1999, Kingfisher $21.95 (978-0-7534-5180-9). A useful, enjoyable look at the earth's geology, atmosphere, and weather. (Rev: HBG 10/00; SLJ 2/00) [525]

12682 Silverstein, Alvin, et al. *Plate Tectonics* (5–8). Illus. Series: Science Concepts. 1998, Twenty-First Century LB $26.90 (978-0-7613-3225-1). An account that includes an introduction to the earth's crust and mantle, an explanation of plate tectonics theory, and information on the prediction of volcanic eruptions and earthquakes. (Rev: BL 2/1/99; HBG 10/99; SLJ 5/99) [555.1]

12683 VanCleave, Janice. *Janice VanCleave's A+ Projects in Earth Science: Winning Experiments for Science Fairs and Extra Credit* (5–10). Illus. 1999, Wiley paper $12.95 (978-0-471-17770-8). Thirty projects varying in complexity are included in this exploration of topography, minerals, atmospheric composition, the ocean floor, and erosion. (Rev: BL 12/1/98; SLJ 6/99) [550]

12684 Vogt, Gregory L. *Earth's Core and Mantle: Heavy Metal, Moving Rock* (6–9). Series: Earth's Spheres. 2007, Twenty-First Century LB $29.27 (978-0-7613-2837-7). Vogt explores the makeup of the universe, the creation of the Earth and its moon, and the planet's core and mantle. Also use *Lithosphere* (2007), which examines the crust, plate tectonics, volcanoes, and geysers. (Rev: SLJ 5/07) [551.1]

Earthquakes and Volcanoes

12685 Asimov, Isaac. *How Did We Find Out About Volcanoes?* (5–7). Illus. by David Wool. 1981, Avon paper $1.95 (978-0-380-59626-3). An overview of volcanoes, from Pompeii to Mount St. Helens. [550]

12686 Booth, Basil. *Earthquakes and Volcanoes* (5–8). Illus. Series: Repairing the Damage. 1992, Macmillan LB $13.95 (978-0-02-711735-6). A well-organized photoessay that explains the interrelationship between earthquakes and volcanoes. (Rev: BL 9/15/92; SLJ 10/92) [551.2]

12687 Burleigh, Robert, adapt. *Volcanoes: Journey to the Crater's Edge* (5–9). Photos by Philippe Bourseiller. Illus. by David Giraudon. 2003, Abrams $14.95 (978-0-8109-4590-6). Volcanoes, lava lakes, ash plumes, and other related phenomena are beautifully illustrated in this oversized photoessay. (Rev: BL 1/1–15/04; SLJ 12/03) [550]

12688 Christian, Spencer, and Antonia Felix. *Shake, Rattle and Roll: The World's Most Amazing Natural Forces* (6–10). Series: Spencer Christian's World of Wonders. 1997, Wiley paper $13.95 (978-0-471-15291-0). This book supplies good information and suitable projects involving earthquakes and volcanoes, with material on topics including plate tectonics, seismic waves, geysers, and hot springs. (Rev: SLJ 6/98) [551.2]

12689 Clarkson, Peter. *Volcanoes* (8–12). Series: World Life Library. 2000, Voyageur paper $16.95 (978-0-89658-502-7). Illustrated with color photographs and diagrams, this account gives general information about volcanoes and presents a tour of the world's most famous ones. [551.2]

12690 Harper, Kristine C. *The Mount St. Helens Volcanic Eruptions* (5–8). Series: Environmental Disasters. 2005, Facts on File $35.00 (978-0-8160-5757-3). The environment impact of Mount St. Helens' eruptions is examined in this title from the Environmental Disasters series. (Rev: SLJ 11/05)

12691 Lindop, Laurie. *Probing Volcanoes* (5–8). Illus. Series: Science on the Edge. 2003, Millbrook LB $26.90 (978-0-7613-2700-4). A lively introduction to the history of volcanoes and eruptions, the scientists who dare to study volcanoes, and techniques for collecting data and forecasting volcanic activity. (Rev: BL 12/1/03; SLJ 1/04) [551.21]

12692 Reed, Jennifer. *Earthquakes: Disaster and Survival, 2005* (4–7). Illus. Series: Disaster and Survival. 2005, Enslow LB $23.93 (978-0-7660-2381-9). Major earthquakes and their effects are detailed in text and personal accounts, with a chapter devoted to the December 2004 Asian tsunami. (Rev: BL 5/1/05; SLJ 10/05) [363.34]

12693 Rubin, Ken. *Volcanoes and Earthquakes* (4–7). Illus. Series: Insiders. 2007, Simon & Schuster $16.99 (978-1-4169-3862-0). Vivid illustrations accompany informative text, charts, and graphs introducing earthquakes and volcanoes and some of the important disasters that have taken place. (Rev: SLJ 10/07) [551.21]

12694 VanCleave, Janice. *Janice VanCleave's Volcanoes: Mind-Boggling Experiments You Can Turn into Science Fair Projects* (4–7). Illus. 1994, Wiley paper $10.95 (978-0-471-30811-9). Twenty experiments that explore the properties of erupting volcanoes using simple materials that can often be found around the house. (Rev: BL 7/94; SLJ 8/94) [551.2]

12695 Watson, Nancy. *Our Violent Earth* (4–8). Illus. 1982, National Geographic LB $12.50 (978-0-87044-388-6). A discussion of such phenomena as earthquakes, volcanoes, and floods. [363.3]

12696 Worth, Richard. *The San Francisco Earth-quake* (5–8). Illus. Series: Environmental Disasters. 2005, Facts on File $35.00 (978-0-8160-5756-6). Worth examines how the San Francisco earthquake of 1906 affected the region's environment. (Rev: SLJ 11/05) [363.34]

Icebergs and Glaciers

12697 Walker, Sally M. *Glaciers: Ice on the Move* (4–7). Illus. 1990, Carolrhoda LB $19.93 (978-0-87614-373-5). This book explains how glaciers are formed, where they are found, and how they move. (Rev: BCCB 9/90; BL 6/15/90; SLJ 8/90) [551.3]

Physical Geography

General and Miscellaneous

12698 Blaustein, Daniel. *The Everglades and the Gulf Coast* (4–7). 1999, Benchmark LB $28.50 (978-0-7614-0896-3). In addition to a tour of the wetlands of the southeastern United States, this book describes how the plants and animals there interact and how this changes human life. (Rev: HBG 10/00; SLJ 4/00) [574.5]

12699 Burnie, David. *Shrublands* (5–8). Series: Biomes Atlases. 2003, Raintree LB $31.42 (978-0-7398-5514-0). This comprehensive overview of shrublands describes the climate, flora and fauna, people, and future of these areas, and includes good maps. (Rev: SLJ 9/03) [577.3]

12700 Moore, Peter D. *Tundra* (6–10). Illus. by Richard Garratt. 2006, Chelsea House $39.50 (978-0-8160-5325-4). This interesting volume discusses not only the geography, geology, ecosystem, and biodiversity of tundras around the world but also history related to the tundra, uses of the tundra, and the future of the tundra in terms of climate change and conservation. (Rev: SLJ 12/06)

12701 Ricciuti, Edward R. *Chaparral* (5–7). Illus. Series: Biomes of the World. 1996, Benchmark LB $25.64 (978-0-7614-0137-7). An examination of the climate, vegetation, and life cycles of the chaparral, the biome situated between desert and grassland or forest and grassland, as in western North America from Oregon to Baja California. (Rev: SLJ 7/96) [574.5]

12702 Sauvain, Philip. *Rivers and Valleys* (4–7). Illus. Series: Geography Detectives. 1996, Carolrhoda LB $23.95 (978-0-87614-996-6). In two-page spreads, rivers and valleys are introduced, with material on geology, flood control, wildlife, and tourism. (Rev: SLJ 3/97) [551.48]

12703 Warhol, Tom. *Chaparral and Scrub* (5–8). Series: Earth's Biomes. 2006, Marshall Cavendish LB $32.79 (978-0-7614-2195-5). Report writers will appreciate this attractive introduction to the characteristics of this biome and its plants and animals; also use *Tundra* (2006). (Rev: LMC 8-9/07; SLJ 8/07) [577.3]

Deserts

12704 Allaby, Michael. *Deserts* (6–10). Illus. by Richard Garratt. Series: Biomes of the Earth. 2006, Chelsea House $39.50 (978-0-8160-5320-9). This interesting volume discusses not only the geography, geology, climates, and flora and fauna of deserts around the world but also history related to deserts, desert exploration, desert industries (oil, solar energy, minerals, and tourism), threats to deserts, and efforts to manage deserts. (Rev: LMC 1/07; SLJ 12/06)

12705 Patent, Dorothy Hinshaw. *Life in a Desert* (5–8). Series: Ecosystems in Action. 2003, Lerner LB $26.60 (978-0-8225-2140-2). This account explores the plant and animal life in deserts and how human intervention has changed this ecosystem. (Rev: BL 9/15/03; HBG 10/03) [574.5]

12706 Ruth, Maria Mudd. *The Deserts of the Southwest* (5–8). Series: Ecosystems of North America. 1998, Benchmark LB $28.50 (978-0-7614-0899-4). After an overview of the deserts of the Southwest and how they were formed, this book introduces desert plants and wildlife, how they interact, adaptations they have made to the desert environment, and the impact of human development. (Rev: HBG 10/99; SLJ 2/99) [591]

12707 Sayre, April Pulley. *Desert* (4–7). Illus. Series: Exploring Earth's Biomes. 1994, Twenty-First Century LB $25.90 (978-0-8050-2825-6). After a general introduction to deserts, a specific one is explored in brief chapters with excellent illustrations. (Rev: BL 1/1/95*; SLJ 1/95) [574.5]

12708 Warhol, Tom. *Desert* (5–8). Series: Earth's Biomes. 2006, Marshall Cavendish LB $32.79 (978-0-7614-2194-8). Report writers will appreciate this attractive introduction to the characteristics of this biome and its plants and animals. (Rev: SLJ 8/07) [577.54]

Forests and Rain Forests

12709 Chinery, Michael. *Poisoners and Pretenders* (5–8). Series: Secrets of the Rainforests. 2000, Crabtree LB $25.27 (978-0-7787-0219-1); paper $7.95 (978-0-7787-0229-0). After a brief description of a rain forest, this book looks at animals found there and their mimicry, camouflage, venom, natural selection, and adaptation to the environment.

Also use *Predators and Prey* (2000). (Rev: SLJ 2/01) [574.5]

12710 Goodman, Susan E. *Bats, Bugs, and Biodiversity: Adventures in the Amazonian Rain Forest* (4–8). Illus. 1995, Simon & Schuster $16.00 (978-0-689-31942-6). Some junior high students learn firsthand about the Amazon rain forest and its endangered ecology. (Rev: BL 12/1/97) [508]

12711 Jackson, Kay. *Rain Forests* (4–7). Illus. Series: Our Environment. 2007, Gale LB $23.70 (978-0-7377-3624-3). This well-illustrated volume explores why rain forests are important; what people, plants, and animals live there; why these areas are endangered; and what their future may hold. (Rev: BL 12/1/07) [577.34]

12712 Jackson, Tom. *Tropical Forests* (5–8). Series: Biomes Atlases. 2003, Raintree LB $31.42 (978-0-7398-5250-7). This comprehensive overview of tropical forests describes the climate, flora and fauna, people, and future of these areas, and includes good maps. (Rev: SLJ 9/03) [577.34]

12713 Johnson, Darv. *The Amazon Rainforest* (7–12). Series: Endangered Animals and Habitats. 1999, Lucent LB $27.45 (978-1-56006-369-8). After a description of the Amazon rain forest, this book chronicles how it is being destroyed and the efforts being made to save it. [577.3]

12714 Johnson, Linda Carlson. *Rain Forests: A Pro/Con Issue* (4–8). Series: Hot Issues. 1999, Enslow LB $21.95 (978-0-7660-1202-8). This book describes the rain forests of the world, how political and economic interests are destroying them, efforts to save them, and the pros and cons of conserving them. (Rev: HBG 10/00; SLJ 4/00) [574.5]

12715 Kallen, Stuart A. *Life in the Amazon Rain Forest* (6–10). Series: The Way People Live. 1999, Lucent LB $27.45 (978-1-56006-387-2). A description of the Amazon rain forest and of the Yanomami people who live there, their traditions, food, shelter, religion, encounters with Europeans, and the continuous threats to their existence. (Rev: HBG 4/00; SLJ 7/99) [574.5]

12716 Kaplan, Elizabeth. *Taiga* (5–7). Illus. Series: Biomes of the World. 1996, Benchmark LB $25.64 (978-0-7614-0135-3). This account discusses the climate, animal and plant life, soil, and seasonal changes in the taiga, the extensive forest in the Northern Hemisphere. (Rev: SLJ 7/96) [574.5]

12717 Lasky, Kathryn. *The Most Beautiful Roof in the World: Exploring the Rainforest Canopy* (5–8). 1997, Harcourt paper $9.00 (978-0-15-200897-0). The canopy of plants and animals found in the rain forest of Belize is explored by the author, a biologist, who also explains the methods scientists use to conduct research in this environment, sometimes under extremely difficult conditions. (Rev: BL 4/1/97; SLJ 4/97) [574.5]

12718 Lewington, Anna. *Atlas of the Rain Forests* (6–12). 1997, Raintree $22.98 (978-0-8172-4756-0). Enhanced by maps and photographs, this work contains information on the plant and animal life found in rain forests, the cultures of the people who live in them, and how these environments are changed by economic development. (Rev: BL 5/15/97; SLJ 8/97) [574.5]

12719 Lewington, Anna, and Edward Parker. *People of the Rain Forests* (4–7). Series: Wide World. 1998, Raintree $18.98 (978-0-8172-5061-4). As well as introducing rain forests, this book describes the people who live there, their tribal customs, their homes — including cities — and their everyday lives. (Rev: HBG 3/99; SLJ 1/99) [574.5]

12720 McLeish, Ewan. *Rain Forest Destruction* (7–12). Series: What If We Do Nothing? 2007, World Almanac LB $30.60 (978-0-8368-7758-8). McLeish looks at the causes and potentially catastrophic results of deforestation in the rain forests and discusses what we can do to stop the destruction. (Rev: LMC 11–12/07; SLJ 5/07) [578.734]

12721 MacMillan, Dianne M. *Life in a Deciduous Forest* (5–8). Series: Ecosystems in Action. 2003, Lerner LB $26.60 (978-0-8225-4684-9). This book explores the ecosystem, its flora and fauna, where trees shed their leaves in autumn. (Rev: BL 9/15/03; HBG 10/03) [574.5]

12722 Montgomery, Sy. *Encantado: Pink Dolphin of the Amazon* (5–8). Illus. by Diane Taylor-Snow. 2002, Houghton $18.00 (978-0-618-13103-7). The author describes the flora and fauna of the South American rain forest seen in her unsuccessful journey to locate the encantado, the elusive pink dolphin. (Rev: BL 4/1/02; HB 7–8/02; HBG 10/02; SLJ 5/02*) [599.53]

12723 Morrison, Marion. *The Amazon Rain Forest and Its People* (5–8). Series: People and Places. 1993, Thomson Learning LB $24.26 (978-1-56847-087-0). After a general history and a description of the region's plants, animals, and people, the author discusses the dangers developers pose to this rain forest. (Rev: BL 11/1/93) [333.75]

12724 Mutel, Cornelia F., and Mary M. Rodgers. *Our Endangered Planet: Tropical Rain Forests* (4–7). Illus. Series: Our Endangered Planet. 1991, Lerner LB $27.15 (978-0-8225-2503-5); paper $8.95 (978-0-8225-9629-5). Describes tropical rain forests and the environmental threats they face. (Rev: BL 6/15/91; SLJ 5/91) [333]

12725 Parker, Edward. *People* (5–8). Photos by author. Series: Rain Forest. 2003, Raintree LB $27.12 (978-0-7398-5242-2). An introduction to the various peoples of the rain forest. (Rev: HBG 3/03; SLJ 1/03) [304.2]

12726 Parker, Edward. *Rain Forest Mammals* (5–9). Illus. Series: Rain Forest. 2002, Raintree LB $27.12

(978-0-7398-5241-5). Mammals of the rain forest and the importance of preserving their habitat are introduced in close-up color photographs and a catchy layout, with a glossary, bibliography, and list of related organizations. Also use *Rain Forest Reptiles and Amphibians* (2002). (Rev: BL 12/1/02; HBG 3/03) [599]

12727 Rapp, Valerie. *Life in an Old Growth Forest* (5–8). Series: Ecosystems in Action. 2002, Lerner LB $26.60 (978-0-8225-2135-8). In pictures and text, this book introduces life in an established forest with material on the interdependence of organisms there, and how human intervention has changed this ecosystem. (Rev: BL 12/15/02; HBG 3/03; SLJ 2/03) [574.5]

12728 Sayre, April Pulley. *Taiga* (4–7). Illus. Series: Exploring Earth's Biomes. 1994, Twenty-First Century LB $25.90 (978-0-8050-2830-0). This book clearly describes the swampy, carnivorous forest and the wildlife found, for example, in northern Canada, where the tundra ends. (Rev: BL 1/15/95; SLJ 2/95) [574.5]

12729 Sayre, April Pulley. *Temperate Deciduous Forest* (4–7). Illus. Series: Exploring Earth's Biomes. 1994, Twenty-First Century LB $25.90 (978-0-8050-2828-7). Deciduous forests are introduced with material on their composition, uses, and the animal and other plant life found within their community. (Rev: BL 1/1/95*; SLJ 1/95) [574.5]

12730 Sayre, April Pulley. *Tropical Rain Forest* (4–7). Illus. Series: Exploring Earth's Biomes. 1994, Twenty-First Century LB $25.90 (978-0-8050-2826-3). The structure and contents of rain forests are explored with information on the plants, animals, and people that exist in this habitat. (Rev: BL 1/1/95; SLJ 1/95) [574.5]

12731 Welsbacher, Anne. *Life in a Rainforest* (5–8). Series: Ecosystems in Action. 2003, Lerner LB $26.60 (978-0-8225-4685-6). This illustrated account covers the plant and animal life in rain forests and explains how human intervention has changed, and often endangered, this ecosystem. (Rev: BL 9/15/03; HBG 10/03) [574.5]

Mountains

12732 Cumming, David. *Mountains* (5–8). Illus. Series: Habitats. 1995, Thomson Learning LB $24.26 (978-1-56847-388-8). Material covered includes the geology of mountains, their formation, and the life they support, and the effects of industry, tourism, and transportation. (Rev: BL 2/1/96) [551.4]

12733 Rotter, Charles. *Mountains* (5–8). Illus. Series: Images. 1994, Creative Editions LB $23.95 (978-0-88682-596-6). How mountains are formed is

discussed, with material on how they change and the life they support. (Rev: SLJ 12/94) [551.4]

12734 Stronach, Neil. *Mountains* (4–8). Series: Endangered People and Places. 1996, Lerner LB $22.60 (978-0-8225-2777-0). Geological aspects of mountains are covered, as well as the adjustments people make to live in mountainous regions. (Rev: SLJ 11/96) [333.73]

12735 Tocci, Salvatore. *Alpine Tundra: Life on the Tallest Mountain* (4–7). Series: Biomes and Habitats. 2005, Watts LB $25.50 (978-0-531-12365-2). Introduces the climate, flora, and fauna found high above sea level on the world's highest mountains. Also use *Arctic Tundra: Life at the North Pole* (2005). (Rev: SLJ 7/05) [577.5]

Ponds, Rivers, and Lakes

12736 Beck, Gregor Gilpin. *Watersheds: A Practical Handbook for Healthy Water* (7–12). Illus. 1999, Firefly $19.95 (978-1-55037-330-1). This account highlights the importance of water in our lives, with special attention to pollution, flooding, and other environmental problems. (Rev: BL 9/1/99) [333.73]

12737 Castaldo, Nancy. *River Wild: An Activity Guide to North American Rivers* (4–7). Illus. 2006, Chicago Review $14.95 (978-1-55652-585-8). From a general introduction to the water cycle and watersheds, this volume narrows in on specific rivers in North America and the flora and fauna found there, even offering profiles of riverkeepers. (Rev: BL 3/1/06; SLJ 6/06) [372.8991]

12738 Cumming, David. *Rivers and Lakes* (5–8). Series: Habitats. 1995, Thomson Learning LB $24.26 (978-1-56847-389-5). The plant and animal life that is supported by lakes and rivers is introduced, with accompanying information on geology and pollution. (Rev: BL 2/1/96) [551.48]

12739 Gilpin, Daniel. *The Snake River* (4–8). Illus. Series: Rivers of North America. 2003, Gareth Stevens LB $26.00 (978-0-8368-3761-2). Following the course of the Snake RIver in the Northwestern United States, with attention to the plant and animal life along it and its role in history. (Rev: SLJ 3/04)

12740 Gray, Leon. *The Missouri River* (4–8). Illus. Series: Rivers of North America. 2003, Gareth Stevens LB $26.00 (978-0-8368-3758-2). A trip along the Missouri, the longest river in the United States, from its source to its confluence with the Mississippi, with a look at the history that has been made on its banks. (Rev: SLJ 3/04)

12741 Harris, Tim. *The Mackenzie River* (4–8). Illus. Series: Rivers of North America. 2003, Gareth Stevens LB $26.00 (978-0-8368-3756-8). A visit to the Mackenzie River in Canada's Northwest Territories and the people, plants, and animals who have lived along it. (Rev: SLJ 3/04)

12742 Hawkes, Steve. *The Tennessee River* (4–8). Illus. Series: Rivers of North America. 2003, Gareth Stevens LB $26.00 (978-0-8368-3763-6). A trip along the length of the Tennessee River, with information on its history, natural attributes, and its effect on the people who live along its path. (Rev: SLJ 3/04)

12743 Hoff, Mary, and Mary M. Rodgers. *Our Endangered Planet: Rivers and Lakes* (4–7). Illus. Series: Our Endangered Planet. 1991, Lerner LB $22.60 (978-0-8225-2501-1). The causes and possible cures of water pollution are examined. (Rev: BL 6/15/91; SLJ 5/91) [363.73]

12744 Jackson, Tom. *The Arkansas River* (4–8). Illus. Series: Rivers of North America. 2003, Gareth Stevens LB $26.00 (978-0-8368-3752-0). Tracing the Arkansas River its entire length of nearly 1,500 miles, with coverage of the people who have lived along it over the centuries and its importance to them. (Rev: SLJ 3/04)

12745 Jackson, Tom. *The Ohio River* (4–8). Illus. Series: Rivers of North America. 2003, Gareth Stevens LB $26.00 (978-0-8368-3759-9). Following the Ohio River from Pittsburgh to its confluence with the Mississippi at Cairo, Illinois, with material on the people and places found along its banks. (Rev: SLJ 3/04)

12746 Rapp, Valerie. *Life in a River* (5–8). Illus. Series: Ecosystems in Action. 2002, Lerner LB $26.60 (978-0-8225-2136-5). The first title in a new series about ecosystems, this volume uses the example of the Columbia River to explain the concept and the interrelationship of rivers, animals, and humans. (Rev: BL 10/15/02; HBG 3/03; SLJ 1/03; VOYA 2/03) [577.6]

12747 Sayre, April Pulley. *Lake and Pond* (4–7). Illus. Series: Exploring Earth's Biomes. 1996, Twenty-First Century LB $25.90 (978-0-8050-4089-0). A colorful introduction to lake and pond habitats and the life forms found within them. (Rev: BL 6/1–15/96; SLJ 6/96) [574.05]

12748 Sayre, April Pulley. *River and Stream* (4–7). Illus. Series: Exploring Earth's Biomes. 1996, Twenty-First Century LB $25.90 (978-0-8050-4088-3). In a clearly written, informative style, this book presents material on rivers and streams, their ecology, and the various creatures and plants living in and around them. (Rev: BL 6/1–15/96; SLJ 6/96) [574.5]

12749 Stewart, Melissa. *Life in a Lake* (5–8). Series: Ecosystems in Action. 2002, Lerner LB $26.60 (978-0-8225-2138-9). The diversity and interdependence of life in a typical lake are introduced with material on how this ecosystem works and how man's interference has changed the balance of nature. (Rev: BL 12/15/02; HBG 3/03) [551.48]

12750 Walker, Sally M. *Life in an Estuary* (5–8). Series: Ecosystems in Action. 2002, Lerner LB $26.60 (978-0-8225-2137-2). A look at life at the tidal mouths of rivers and the diversity of life in these areas, its interdependence, the balance of nature, and how human interaction has changed this ecosystem. (Rev: BL 12/15/02; HBG 3/03; SLJ 2/03) [574]

Prairies and Grasslands

12751 Collard, Sneed B. *The Prairie Builders: Reconstructing America's Lost Grasslands* (5–8). Illus. 2005, Houghton $17.00 (978-0-618-39687-0). This wide-format look at a project to regenerate tallgrass prairie and populate it with native plants and animals includes excellent photographs. (Rev: BL 6/1–15/05; SLJ 8/05*) [635.9]

12752 Hoare, Ben. *Temperate Grasslands* (5–8). Series: Biomes Atlases. 2003, Raintree LB $31.42 (978-0-7398-5249-1). This comprehensive overview of grasslands describes the climate, flora and fauna, people, and future of these areas, and includes good maps. (Rev: SLJ 9/03) [577.4]

12753 Lynch, Wayne. *Prairie Grasslands* (6–9). Photos by author. Series: Our Wild World Ecosystems. 2006, NorthWord $16.95 (978-1-55971-946-9); paper $8.95 (978-1-55971-947-6). Grasslands, wetlands, badlands, and the connections between climate, soil, and plant and animal inhabitants are the focus of this well-illustrated title. (Rev: SLJ 1/07)

12754 Ormsby, Alison. *The Prairie* (5–8). Series: Ecosystems of North America. 1998, Benchmark LB $28.50 (978-0-7614-0897-0). A description of the prairie ecosystem and an examination of how the plants and animals in prairies affect one another and their environments. (Rev: HBG 10/99; SLJ 2/99) [551.4]

12755 Patent, Dorothy Hinshaw. *Life in a Grassland* (5–8). Series: Ecosystems in Action. 2002, Lerner LB $26.60 (978-0-8225-2139-6). Using excellent pictures and a clear text, this volume explores the flora and fauna of different kinds of grasslands, with material on conservation. (Rev: BL 12/15/02; HBG 3/03) [574.5]

12756 Rotter, Charles. *The Prairie* (5–8). Illus. Series: Images. 1994, Creative Editions LB $17.95 (978-0-88682-598-0). The nature of prairie grasslands is introduced, with material on the animals and plants found there. (Rev: SLJ 12/94) [574.5]

12757 Sayre, April Pulley. *Grassland* (4–7). Illus. Series: Exploring Earth's Biomes. 1994, Twenty-First Century LB $25.90 (978-0-8050-2827-0). A well-organized, clearly written account that explains what grasslands are and where they exist and the interaction of the creatures who live in this biome. (Rev: BL 1/15/95; SLJ 2/95) [574.5]

12758 Toupin, Laurie Peach. *Life in the Temperate Grasslands* (4–7). Series: Biomes and Habitats. 2005, Watts LB $25.50 (978-0-531-12385-0). Introduces the climatic conditions, plants, and wildlife of the world's temperate grasslands. Also use *Savannas: Life in the Tropical Grasslands* (2005). (Rev: SLJ 7/05) [577.4]

Rocks, Minerals, and Soil

12759 Chesterman, Charles W., and Kurt E. Lowe. *The Audubon Society Field Guide to North American Rocks and Minerals* (7–12). Illus. 1978, Knopf $19.95 (978-0-394-50269-4). A basic guide that includes color illustrations of nearly 800 rocks and minerals. [549]

12760 Downs, Sandra. *Earth's Hidden Treasures* (6–9). Series: Exploring Planet Earth. 1999, Twenty-First Century LB $24.90 (978-0-7613-1411-0). All about the planet's rocks and minerals and how they have been used by humans. (Rev: HBG 4/00; SLJ 2/00) [549]

12761 Eid, Alain. *1000 Photos of Minerals and Fossils* (5–9). Photos by Michel Viard. 2000, Barron's paper $24.95 (978-0-7641-5218-4). An oversized, nicely illustrated volume that introduces minerals in their natural and refined states with material on sites, fossils, and jewelry. (Rev: SLJ 10/00) [548]

12762 Farndon, John. *Rock and Mineral* (5–9). Illus. Series: DK/Google e.guides. 2005, DK $17.99 (978-0-7566-1140-8). This highly illustrated guide introduces readers to the basics of geology and provides a link to a Web site that serves as a gateway to additional resources. (Rev: SLJ 8/05) [552]

12763 Friend, Sandra. *Sinkholes* (4–7). Illus. 2002, Pineapple $18.95 (978-1-56164-258-8). This volume uncovers the geological and ecological causes of sinkholes, holes in the earth's surface that occur naturally, sometimes with devastating consequences. (Rev: BL 8/02; HBG 10/02) [551.44]

12764 Gallant, Roy A. *Rocks* (5–8). Series: Earth Sciences. 2000, Marshall Cavendish LB $25.64 (978-0-7614-1042-3). Illustrations and full-spread diagrams introduce rocks and minerals and their properties, forms, and uses. (Rev: BL 3/1/01; HBG 3/01; SLJ 3/01) [552.2]

12765 Kallen, Stuart A. *Gems* (4–7). Illus. Series: Wonders of the World. 2003, Gale LB $23.70 (978-0-7377-1028-1). The formation of precious stones,

their mining, and individual stones of note are all covered here. (Rev: BL 5/1/03) [553.8]

12766 Milne, Jean. *The Story of Diamonds* (5–8). 2000, Linnet LB $21.50 (978-0-208-02476-3). A book that explains where diamonds are found and how they are mined, evaluated, cut, polished, and used as jewels or in industry. (Rev: BL 2/1/00; HBG 10/00; SLJ 6/00; VOYA 4/01) [553.8]

12767 Pough, Frederick H. *A Field Guide to Rocks and Minerals.* 4th ed. (7–12). Illus. 1976, Houghton paper $20.00 (978-0-395-91096-2). This volume in the Peterson Field Guide series gives photographs and identifying information on 270 rocks and minerals. [549]

12768 Ricciuti, Edward R., and National Audubon Society, eds. *National Audubon Society First Field Guide: Rocks and Minerals* (5–8). Illus. 1998, Scholastic paper $17.95 (978-0-590-05463-8). A guide to equipment and techniques for observation and general information on geology, followed by an examination of 50 common rocks, their composition, texture, color, and environment. (Rev: BL 8/98; SLJ 8/98) [552]

12769 Staedter, Tracy. *Rocks and Minerals* (4–8). Series: Reader's Digest Pathfinders. 1999, Reader's Digest $16.99 (978-1-57584-290-5). An outstanding introduction to geology is organized in three sections — "Rocks," "Minerals," and "Collecting Rocks and Minerals" — with "discovery paths" featuring personal accounts, hands-on activities, vocabulary, and facts. (Rev: SLJ 11/99) [552]

12770 Trueit, Trudi Strain. *Rocks, Gems, and Minerals* (4–7). Series: Watts Library. 2003, Watts LB $25.50 (978-0-531-12195-5); paper $8.95 (978-0-531-16241-5). This attractive volume introduces readers to rocks, gems, and minerals and examines the natural forces that created them. (Rev: SLJ 1/04) [552]

12771 VanCleave, Janice. *Janice VanCleave's Rocks and Minerals: Mind-Boggling Experiments You Can Turn Into Science Fair Projects* (6–8). Series: Spectacular Science Projects. 1996, Wiley paper $10.95 (978-0-471-10269-4). In easy-to-follow steps, a series of experiments and projects are outlined that illustrate the properties and uses of a number of rocks and minerals. (Rev: BL 3/15/96; SLJ 3/96) [552]

12772 Winckler, Suzanne, and Mary M. Rodgers. *Soil* (4–7). Illus. Series: Our Endangered Planet. 1994, Lerner LB $27.15 (978-0-8225-2508-0). The depletion of our soil resources is the focus of this book, with emphasis on causes and possible solutions. (Rev: BL 5/15/94) [631.4]

Mathematics

General and Miscellaneous

12773 Caron, Lucille, and Philip M. St. Jacques. *Fractions and Decimals* (4–8). Illus. Series: Math Success. 2000, Enslow LB $22.60 (978-0-7660-1430-5). Many examples accompany explanations of how to add, subtract, multiply, and divide fractions and decimals. Also use *Addition and Subtraction* (2001). (Rev: HBG 3/01; SLJ 7/01) [513.2]

12774 Gardner, Robert. *Science Projects About Math* (8–12). Series: Science Projects. 1999, Enslow LB $26.60 (978-0-89490-950-4). Projects and experiments with mathematics are outlined, involving such subjects as light, time, distance, heights, and velocity. [507.8]

12775 Gardner, Robert. *Science Projects About Methods of Measuring* (6–12). Illus. Series: Science Projects. 2000, Enslow LB $26.60 (978-0-7660-1169-4). Different kinds of measurements are introduced, their relation to mass, area, volume, and temperature, and interesting suggestions for science projects in each category. (Rev: BL 4/1/00; HBG 9/00) [530.8]

12776 Haven, Kendall. *Marvels of Math: Fascinating Reads and Awesome Activities* (5–8). Illus. 1998, Teacher Ideas paper $23.50 (978-1-56308-585-7). This book chronicles 16 turning points in the history of mathematics, including the discovery of zero and the story of the first female to become a professor of mathematics. (Rev: VOYA 4/99) [510]

12777 Hershey, Robert L. *How to Think with Numbers* (7–9). Illus. 1987, Janson paper $7.95 (978-0-939765-14-0). Elementary mathematical concepts such as percentage and interest are explained through a series of puzzles and problems. [510]

12778 Kummer, Patricia K. *The Calendar* (5–8). Illus. Series: Inventions That Shaped the World.

2005, Watts LB $30.50 (978-0-531-12340-9). Traces the development of calendars from prehistoric times, with period and contemporary illustrations, lists of recommended resources, and a calendar. (Rev: BL 5/15/05) [529]

12779 Leech, Bonnie Coulter. *Mesopotamia: Creating and Solving Word Problems* (4–8). Series: Math for the Real World. 2007, Rosen LB $23.95 (978-1-4042-3357-7). Ancient number systems are among the mathematical concepts highlighted in this overview of the civilization of Mesopotamia that covers its people, buildings, writings, and calendars. (Rev: SLJ 2/07) [510]

12780 Long, Lynette. *Great Graphs and Sensational Statistics: Games and Activities That Make Math Easy and Fun* (4–7). Illus. 2004, Wiley paper $12.95 (978-0-471-21060-3). The games and activities in this large-format paperback will give new insights into the value of statistics and graphs and how the latter can be used to visually represent the former. (Rev: BL 5/1/04; SLJ 11/04) [372.7]

12781 Schwartz, David M. *G Is for Googol: A Math Alphabet Book* (6–10). Illus. 1998, Tricycle $15.95 (978-1-883672-58-4). A humorous romp through mathematical terms and concepts using an alphabetical approach and cartoon illustrations. (Rev: BL 10/15/98; HBG 3/99; SLJ 11/98) [510]

12782 Shea, Therese. *America's Electoral College: Choosing the President: Comparing and Analyzing Charts, Graphs, and Tables* (4–8). Series: Math for the Real World. 2007, Rosen LB $23.95 (978-1-4042-3358-4). Results of various elections, including the controversial 2000 polls, are used to demonstrate fundamental mathematical principles. (Rev: SLJ 2/07) [324.6097]

12783 Shea, Therese. *The Great Barrier Reef: Using Graphs and Charts to Solve Word Problems* (4–8). Series: Math for the Real World. 2007, Rosen LB

$23.95 (978-1-4042-3359-1). Charts and graphs are used to show the number of species found on the reef, the percentages of coral, the number of visitors, and so forth. (Rev: SLJ 2/07) [510]

12784 Shea, Therese. *The Transcontinental Railroad: Using Proportions to Solve Problems* (4–8). Series: Math for the Real World. 2007, Rosen LB $23.95 (978-1-4042-3361-4). The cost of laying the track, number of rails laid in a period, and other interesting aspects of construction of the railroad are considered using ratios, proportions, and other mathematical techniques. (Rev: SLJ 2/07) [513.24]

12785 Sullivan, Navin. *Area, Distance, and Volume* (4–7). Illus. Series: Measure Up. 2006, Marshall Cavendish LB $20.95 (978-0-7614-2323-2). Includes information on the history of measuring area, distance, and volume along with how to measure each and the devices used. (Rev: BL 2/15/07; SLJ 6/07) [598.47]

12786 Woods, Mary B., and Michael Woods. *Ancient Computing: From Counting to Calendars* (5–8). Series: Ancient Technologies. 2000, Runestone LB $25.26 (978-0-8225-2997-2). From the invention of the abacus and sundials to the creation of calculators and computers, this is a history of counting with material on the development of the calendar. (Rev: BL 9/15/00; HBG 3/01; SLJ 1/01) [510]

Mathematical Games and Puzzles

12787 Ball, Johnny. *Go Figure! A Totally Cool Book About Numbers* (4–7). Illus. 2005, DK $15.99 (978-0-7566-1374-7). A fascinating volume for math-minded youngsters and adults, introducing number-related games and puzzles as well as more sophisticated mathematical disciplines, such as chaos theory, fractals, and topology. (Rev: BL 10/15/05; SLJ 1/06) [510]

12788 Blum, Raymond. *Math Tricks, Puzzles and Games* (4–7). Illus. 1994, Sterling $14.95 (978-0-8069-0582-2). Kids who like math will particularly enjoy these tricks, mathematical games and puzzles, and calculator riddles. (Rev: BL 11/1/94) [793.7]

12789 Burns, Marilyn. *The I Hate Mathematics! Book* (5–8). Illus. by Martha Hairston. 1975, Little, Brown paper $14.99 (978-0-316-11741-8). A lively collection of puzzles and other mind stretchers that illustrate mathematical concepts.

12790 Burns, Marilyn. *Math for Smarty Pants: Or Who Says Mathematicians Have Little Pig Eyes* (6–9). Illus. 1982, Little, Brown paper $14.99 (978-0-316-11739-5). A series of games, puzzles, and tricks that use numbers. (Rev: BL 4/15/90) [513]

12791 Gardner, Martin. *Perplexing Puzzles and Tantalizing Teasers* (4–7). Illus. by Laszlo Kubinyi. 1988, Dover paper $7.95 (978-0-486-25637-5). An assortment of math problems, visual teasers, and tricky questions to challenge young, alert minds; perky drawings. [793.73]

12792 Salvadori, Mario, and Joseph P. Wright. *Math Games for Middle School: Challenges and Skill-Builders for Students at Every Level* (5–8). Illus. 1998, Chicago Review paper $14.95 (978-1-55652-288-8). After explaining the concepts involved in such mathematical areas as geometry, arithmetic, graphing, and linear equations, this work presents a series of puzzles for readers to solve. (Rev: BL 11/1/98) [510]

12793 Sharp, Richard M., and Seymour Metzner. *The Sneaky Square and 113 Other Math Activities for Kids* (4–8). Illus. 1990, TAB $15.95 (978-0-8306-8474-8); paper $8.95 (978-0-8306-3474-3). Readers are challenged to solve classic as well as new math and logic problems. (Rev: BL 1/1/91) [793.7]

12794 Vecchione, Glen. *Math Challenges: Puzzles, Tricks and Games* (6–10). Illus. 1997, Sterling $14.95 (978-0-8069-8114-7). A slim volume that contains a number of mathematical puzzles arranged by subject and followed by the solutions. (Rev: SLJ 10/97) [510]

Meteorology

General and Miscellaneous

12795 Allaby, Michael. *Fog, Smog and Poisoned Rain* (7–12). Illus. by Richard Garratt. Series: Dangerous Weather. 2003, Facts on File $40.00 (978-0-8160-4789-5). Natural sources of pollution such as volcanoes are included in this survey of dangerous weather phenomena. (Rev: SLJ 10/03) [363.739]

12796 Brezina, Corona. *Climate Change* (6–9). Illus. Series: In the News. 2007, Rosen LB $21.95 (978-1-4042-1913-7). Just what changes may be in store for the planet, what caused these changes, and what they mean for us. (Rev: BL 10/15/07) [363.738]

12797 Malone, Peter. *Close to the Wind: The Beaufort Scale* (4–8). Illus. by author. 2007, Putnam $16.99 (978-0-399-24399-8). An informative picture book that explains the history and use of the Beaufort scale that measures wind force at sea. (Rev: BL 6/1–15/07; LMC 11/07; SLJ 5/07) [551.51]

12798 Smith, Trevor. *Earth's Changing Climate* (5–8). Series: Understanding Global Issues. 2003, Smart Apple $19.95 (978-1-58340-358-7). Topics including global warming are discussed in this well-organized look at the world's climate, how it is gradually changing, and what can be done about it. (Rev: BL 11/15/03; SLJ 12/03) [551.6]

12799 Sullivan, Navin. *Temperature* (4–7). Series: Measure Up! . 2006, Marshall Cavendish LB $20.95 (978-0-7614-2322-5). This well-designed book about temperature includes at-home experiments and easy-to-follow charts. (Rev: LMC 8-9/07; SLJ 6/07)

Air

12800 Friend, Sandra. *Earth's Wild Winds* (5–8). Illus. Series: Exploring Planet Earth. 2002, Twenty-First Century LB $24.90 (978-0-7613-2673-1). Report writers will find good material in this attractively presented coverage of all kinds of winds that also looks at the ways in which humans have attempted to harness wind power. (Rev: HBG 3/03; SLJ 10/02) [551.518]

12801 Gallant, Roy A. *Atmosphere: Sea of Air* (4–8). Illus. Series: Earthworks. 2003, Marshall Cavendish $29.93 (978-0-7614-1366-0). An intriguing and well-presented look at how changes in the atmosphere affect us — from storms to beautiful rainbows and sunsets — and how we affect the atmosphere. (Rev: BL 3/15/03; HBG 3/03; SLJ 4/06) [551.51]

12802 Gardner, Robert. *Science Project Ideas About Air* (4–7). Series: Science Project Ideas. 1997, Enslow LB $25.26 (978-0-89490-838-5). The properties of air are explored in a series of experiments and projects with easy-to-follow directions. (Rev: BL 12/15/97; HBG 3/98; SLJ 4/98) [678.5]

12803 Gardner, Robert, and David Webster. *Experiments with Balloons* (4–7). Illus. Series: Getting Started in Science. 1995, Enslow LB $20.95 (978-0-89490-669-5). More than a dozen experiments explore balloons and the properties of air. (Rev: BL 12/1/95; SLJ 3/96) [507.8]

12804 Hoff, Mary, and Mary M. Rodgers. *Atmosphere* (4–7). Illus. Series: Our Endangered Planet. 1995, Lerner LB $27.15 (978-0-8225-2509-7). This account describes the atmosphere and current threats including the ozone layer problem. (Rev: BL 8/95; SLJ 12/95) [363.73]

12805 Yount, Lisa, and Mary M. Rodgers. *Our Endangered Planet: Air* (4–7). Illus. Series: Our Endangered Planet. 1995, Lerner LB $27.15 (978-0-8225-2510-3). The emphasis in this book is on how air pollution has become a major environmental issue and how everyone can take action to improve air quality. (Rev: BL 10/15/95) [363.73]

Storms

12806 Allaby, Michael. *Hurricanes* (7–12). Series: Dangerous Weather. 1997, Facts on File $35.00 (978-0-8160-3516-8). An exhaustive introduction to hurricanes covering such topics as conditions that can lead to them, why they are common in particular areas, historic hurricanes, their naming and tracking, and how global climate changes will affect them. (Rev: SLJ 4/98) [551.5]

12807 Allaby, Michael. *Tornadoes* (7–12). Series: Dangerous Weather. 1997, Facts on File $35.00 (978-0-8160-3517-5). This excellent book on tornadoes describes how they begin, their structure, travel patterns, interiors, historic tornadoes, and when and where tornadoes occur. (Rev: SLJ 4/98) [551.55]

12808 Bredeson, Carmen. *The Mighty Midwest Flood: Raging Rivers* (4–8). Series: American Disasters. 1999, Enslow LB $23.93 (978-0-7660-1221-9). This account describes the terrible midwestern flood of 1993 and gives background information on the Mississippi River complex and on the causes of floods. (Rev: BL 10/15/99; HBG 3/00) [363.4]

12809 Ceban, Bonnie J. *Tornadoes: Disaster and Survival* (4–7). Series: Deadly Disasters. 2005, Enslow LB $23.93 (978-0-7660-2383-3). Explores the science behind tornadoes and offers advice about how to prepare for and survive such natural disasters. (Rev: SLJ 10/05) [551.5]

12810 Cerveny, Randy. *Freaks of the Storm: From Flying Cows to Stealing Thunder* (8–12). Illus. 2006, Thunder's Mouth paper $16.95 (978-1-56025-801-8). Cerveny chronicles bizarre weather phenomena — from fish falling from the sky to chickens plucked bare by hurricane winds — and extremes of heat, cold, rainfall, and so forth. (Rev: BL 12/1/05) [551.5]

12811 De Hahn, Tracee. *The Blizzard of 1888* (7–12). Series: Great Disasters: Reforms and Ramifications. 2000, Chelsea $21.95 (978-0-7910-5787-2). Exciting illustrations and eyewitness accounts enhance this exploration of the impact of this famous blizzard and of the changes in infrastructure

and services that resulted from it. (Rev: BL 4/15/01; HBG 10/01; SLJ 6/01) [974.7]

12812 Gow, Mary. *Johnstown Flood: The Day the Dam Burst* (4–8). Series: American Disasters. 2003, Enslow LB $23.93 (978-0-7660-2109-9). The story of the terrible Pennsylvania flood of 1889 that resulted in more than 2,000 deaths. (Rev: BL 11/15/03; HBG 10/03) [973.8]

12813 Greenberg, Keith E. *Storm Chaser: Into the Eye of a Hurricane* (4–7). Series: Risky Business. 1997, Blackbirch LB $24.94 (978-1-56711-161-3). Tells about the people who track the paths of hurricanes and the dangers they often face. (Rev: BL 10/15/97; HBG 3/98; SLJ 12/97) [551.55]

12814 Harper, Kristine C. *Hurricane Andrew* (5–8). Series: Environmental Disasters. 2005, Facts on File $35.00 (978-0-8160-5759-7). The impact of 1992's Hurricane Andrew on Florida's wetlands is seen as a warning about the need to be more prepared. (Rev: SLJ 11/05) [551.5]

12815 Lindop, Laurie. *Chasing Tornadoes* (5–8). Illus. Series: Science on the Edge. 2003, Millbrook LB $26.90 (978-0-7613-2703-5). A lively introduction to tornadoes, the scientists who dare to study them, and techniques for collecting data and forecasting tornado activity. (Rev: BL 12/1/03; SLJ 1/04) [551.55]

12816 Miller, Debra A. *Hurricane Katrina: Devastation on the Gulf Coast* (6–8). Illus. Series: Overview. 2006, Gale LB $28.70 (978-1-59018-936-8). Miller faults the government for not responding quickly enough to the disaster, and offers quotations from eyewitnesses and survivors to back up her opinion. Also covered are the rebuilding efforts and the relocation of many storm victims. (Rev: SLJ 9/06) [363.34]

12817 Miller, Mara. *Hurricane Katrina Strikes the Gulf Coast* (5–8). Series: Deadly Disasters. 2006, Enslow LB $23.93 (978-0-7660-2803-6). The story of Hurricane Katrina and its disastrous impact on the Gulf Coast in 2005 is accompanied by personal stories plus information on other deadly storms. (Rev: BL 7/06; SLJ 9/06) [363.34]

12818 Nicolson, Cynthia Pratt. *Hurricane!* (4–8). Illus. Series: Disaster. 2002, Kids Can $14.95 (978-1-55074-906-9); paper $6.95 (978-1-55074-970-0). An accessible text and many photographs provide information on hurricane formation and intensity, on the preparations for major hurricanes, and on famous storms of the past. (Rev: HBG 3/03; SLJ 12/02) [551.552]

12819 Palser, Barb. *Hurricane Katrina: Aftermath of Disaster* (7–10). Series: Snapshots in History. 2006, Compass Point LB $31.93 (978-0-7565-2101-1). An interesting yet detailed look at how Katrina affected residents of New Orleans, and at the rescue and restoration efforts that followed the storm. (Rev: BL 12/1/06) [976]

12820 Sherrow, Victoria. *Hurricane Andrew: Nature's Rage* (4–8). Series: American Disasters. 1998, Enslow LB $23.93 (978-0-7660-1057-4). The story of the storm that caused millions of dollars of damage on the Atlantic Coast, told in dramatic text and pictures. (Rev: BL 1/1–15/99; HBG 3/99; VOYA 4/99) [551.5]

12821 Sherrow, Victoria. *Plains Outbreak Tornadoes: Killer Twisters* (4–8). Series: American Disasters. 1998, Enslow LB $23.93 (978-0-7660-1059-8). The causes and effects of the giant tornadoes that occur in the Midwest, with details of some of the most horrendous. (Rev: BL 1/1–15/99; HBG 3/99) [551.55]

12822 Simon, Seymour. *Tornadoes* (4–8). 1999, Morrow LB $16.89 (978-0-688-14647-4). Well-organized text discusses the weather conditions that give rise to tornadoes, how they form, where they are most likely to occur, and how scientists predict and track them, supplemented by large, riveting photographs showing meteorologists at work, a variety of tornadoes, and the devastation caused by major tornadoes. (Rev: BCCB 4/99; BL 5/99; HBG 9/99; SLJ 6/99) [551.55]

12823 Torres, John A. *Hurricane Katrina and the Devastation of New Orleans* (4–7). Series: Monumental Milestones. 2006, Mitchell Lane $29.95 (978-1-58415-473-0). An interview with a newlywed couple who lost everything in the storm draws readers into this account of the devastation. (Rev: BL 9/1/06) [363.34]

12824 Treaster, Joseph B. *Hurricane Force: In the Path of America's Deadliest Storms* (7–10). Illus. Series: New York Times Book. 2007, Kingfisher $16.95 (978-0-7534-3086-3). A reporter for the *New York Times* who witnessed firsthand the devastation wrought by Hurricane Katrina discusses that storm and hurricanes in general; with photographs and other visuals. (Rev: BL 3/1/07; SLJ 5/07) [551.55]

12825 Woods, Michael, and Mary B. Woods. *Tornadoes* (5–8). Illus. Series: Disasters Up Close. 2006, Lerner $27.93 (978-0-8225-4714-3). Eyewitness accounts add to this well-illustrated overview of tornadoes and the destruction they can cause. (Rev: BL 10/15/06) [551.55]

Water

12826 Allaby, Michael. *Floods* (8–10). Series: Dangerous Weather. 1998, Facts on File $35.00 (978-0-8160-3520-5). An overview of floods and flood-related topics such as land development and soil erosion, with graphic information and details of memorable floods of the past. [551.48]

12827 Gallant, Roy A. *Water* (5–8). Series: Earth Sciences. 2000, Marshall Cavendish LB $25.64 (978-0-7614-1040-9). This work introduces the importance of water on the earth, its three states, and the water cycle. (Rev: BL 3/1/01; HBG 3/01; SLJ 5/01) [551.57]

12828 Gallant, Roy A. *Water: Our Precious Resource* (4–8). Illus. Series: Earthworks. 2003, Marshall Cavendish $29.93 (978-0-7614-1365-3). A thought-provoking and well-presented overview of the sources of water; the ways in which we use, misuse, and recycle water; and efforts to preserve this vital natural resource. (Rev: BL 3/15/03; HBG 3/03; SLJ 2/03) [553.7]

12829 Morgan, Sally, and Adrian Morgan. *Water* (4–7). Illus. Series: Designs in Science. 1994, Facts on File $23.00 (978-0-8160-2982-2). The importance and uses of water are described, with information on water storage, filtering, and conservation, plus activities and experiments. (Rev: BL 7/94) [533.7]

Weather

12830 Allaby, Michael. *Droughts* (6–12). Illus. Series: Dangerous Weather. 1997, Facts on File $35.00 (978-0-8160-3519-9). Topics discussed in this comprehensive volume include how droughts are classified, droughts of the past, the Dust Bowl, irrigation, water storage, saving water, and jet streams and storm tracks. (Rev: BL 12/1/97) [551.55]

12831 Arnold, Caroline. *El Niño: Stormy Weather for People and Wildlife* (4–8). Illus. 1998, Clarion $16.00 (978-0-395-77602-5). A brief overview of El Niño, its causes and history, and how tracking and forecasting are used to make predictions. (Rev: BL 10/1/98; HBG 10/99; SLJ 12/98) [551.6]

12832 Banqueri, Eduardo. *Weather* (4–8). Illus. by Estudio Marcel Socías and Gabi Marfil. Series: Field Guides. 2006, Enchanted Lion $16.95 (978-1-59270-059-2). This information-packed guide explores a broad array of weather-related topics, including seasonal change, climatic zones, the science of meteorology, clouds, winds, storms, and the atmosphere. (Rev: SLJ 1/07) [551.5]

12833 Bredeson, Carmen. *El Niño and La Niña: Deadly Weather* (4–8). Series: American Disasters. 2002, Enslow LB $23.93 (978-0-7660-1551-7). A well-researched account of these two weather phenomena, their effects, and how they can be traced. (Rev: BL 6/1–15/02; HBG 10/02; SLJ 6/02) [551.6]

12834 Buckley, Bruce, et al. *Weather: A Visual Guide* (8–12). Illus. 2004, Firefly $39.95 (978-1-55297-957-0). Full of color photographs and clear graphics, this informative volume explores the forces that generate weather and the impact of weather extremes. (Rev: BL 10/15/04; SLJ 12/04; VOYA 4/05) [551.5]

12835 Burt, Christopher C. *Extreme Weather: A Guide and Record Book* (8–12). Illus. 2004, Norton paper $24.95 (978-0-393-32658-1). An overview of weather at its worst, this richly illustrated volume contains a wealth of meteorological data on extreme events, including heat, drought, cold, floods, thunderstorms, windstorms, tornadoes, and fog. (Rev: SLJ 2/05) [551.6]

12836 Carson, Mary Kay. *Weather Projects for Young Scientists* (4–7). 2007, Chicago Review paper $14.95 (978-1-55652-629-9). A detailed look at weather basics is intertwined with more than 40 projects, many appropriate for science fairs, and a few career profiles. (Rev: BL 12/1/06; SLJ 3/08) [551.5078]

12837 Cobb, Allan B. *Weather Observation Satellites* (5–9). Series: The Library of Satellites. 2003, Rosen LB $26.50 (978-0-8239-3856-8). This book shows how the development of satellites from the 1960s on has provided us with clear weather observations and accurate forecasts. (Rev: BL 11/15/03) [551.6]

12838 Dickinson, Terence. *Exploring the Sky by Day: The Equinox Guide to Weather and the Atmosphere* (7–10). Illus. 1988, Camden House paper $9.95 (978-0-920656-71-6). A book about weather that explores such subjects as types of clouds and kinds of precipitation. (Rev: BL 3/1/89; SLJ 1/89) [551.6]

12839 Gardner, Robert. *Science Project Ideas About Rain* (4–7). Series: Science Project Ideas. 1997, Enslow LB $25.26 (978-0-89490-843-9). Clear explanations and functional drawings and diagrams for a number of activities that study rain, its causes, and its effects. (Rev: BL 12/15/97; HBG 3/98; SLJ 1/98) [551.55]

12840 Gold, Susan Dudley. *Blame It on El Niño* (5–9). 1999, Raintree LB $28.54 (978-0-7398-1376-8). Covers El Niño, La Niña, how scientists predict and track them, and the effects of each globally. (Rev: HBG 3/00; SLJ 4/00) [551.6]

12841 Kahl, Jonathan D. *Weather Watch: Forecasting the Weather* (5–8). Series: How's the Weather? 1996, Lerner LB $21.27 (978-0-8225-2529-5). This work provides basic information on weather systems, maps, and forecasting tools, the history of weather forecasting and keeping weather records, and directions for making a weather station. (Rev: BL 6/1–15/96; SLJ 6/96) [551.6]

12842 Ramsey, Dan. *Weather Forecasting: A Young Meteorologist's Guide* (8–12). Illus. 1990, TAB $19.95 (978-0-8306-8338-3); paper $10.95 (978-0-8306-3338-8). A detailed and often technical examination of the techniques of weather forecasting with many tables, charts, and diagrams. (Rev: BL 10/15/90) [551.6]

12843 Rupp, Rebecca. *Weather! Watch How Weather Works* (4–8). Illus. 2003, Storey Kids paper $14.95 (978-1-58017-420-6). A well-illustrated and appealing introduction to the science of weather, with numerous experiments and projects. (Rev: SLJ 5/04) [551.6]

12844 Sayre, April Pulley. *El Niño and La Niña: Weather in the Headlines* (4–8). Illus. 2000, Twenty-First Century LB $25.90 (978-0-7613-1405-9). An exploration of this complex Pacific Ocean phenomenon that produces unusual weather conditions that affect the entire world. (Rev: BL 9/15/00; HBG 3/01) [551.6]

12845 Silverstein, Alvin, et al. *Weather and Climate* (4–7). Illus. Series: Science Concepts. 1998, Twenty-First Century LB $26.90 (978-0-7613-3223-7). This book introduces weather by explaining earth's atmosphere, rotation, and different climates with material on air and water movements, cloud formation, and recent climate changes. (Rev: BL 5/1/99; HBG 10/99) [551.5]

12846 Souza, D. M. *Northern Lights* (5–7). Illus. 1994, Carolrhoda LB $23.95 (978-0-87614-799-3); paper $7.95 (978-0-87614-629-3). A description of the northern lights and an explanation of what causes them. (Rev: BL 1/15/94) [538]

12847 Stein, Paul. *Forecasting the Climate of the Future* (5–7). Series: The Library of Future Weather and Climate. 2001, Rosen LB $29.25 (978-0-8239-3413-3). A fascinating, well-organized account that looks at long-range weather predictions and at the use and accuracy of computer models in forecasting future weather patterns, especially with regard to global warming. Also use *Storms of the Future* (2001), which looks at whether global warming might cause stronger storms. (Rev: SLJ 4/02) [551.5]

12848 Stein, Paul. *Ice Ages of the Future* (5–7). Series: The Library of Future Weather and Climate. 2001, Rosen LB $29.25 (978-0-8239-3415-7). A look at the possibility that the greenhouse effect and other factors could in fact cause a wave of colder rather than warmer air. (Rev: SLJ 11/01) [551.6]

12849 Stonehouse, Bernard. *Snow, Ice and Cold* (5–7). 1993, Macmillan LB $21.00 (978-0-02-788530-9). This work tells about how cultures and individuals have adjusted to severe cold climates. (Rev: SLJ 7/93) [551.6]

12850 Vogel, Carole G. *Weather Legends: Native American Lore and the Science of Weather* (4–8).

Illus. 2001, Millbrook LB $29.90 (978-0-7613-1900-9). Native American weather myths are paired with scientific information about actual weather phenomena. (Rev: BL 9/1/01; HBG 3/02; SLJ 10/01) [398.2]

12851 Vogt, Gregory L. *The Atmosphere: Planetary Heat Engine* (5–8). Illus. Series: Earth's Spheres. 2007, Lerner $29.27 (978-0-7613-2841-4). Examines a wide array of topics, including the composition of our air, weather and climate, and the use of satellites and other tools to study the atmosphere. (Rev: BL 4/1/07; SLJ 5/07) [551.5]

12852 Williams, Terry Tempest, and Ted Major. *The Secret Language of Snow* (4–8). Illus. by Jennifer Dewey. 1984, Pantheon $10.95 (978-0-394-96574-1). Different words for snow in the Eskimo language are used to explore this phenomenon.

12853 Wills, Susan, and Steven Wills. *Meteorology: Predicting the Weather* (5–7). Series: Innovators. 2004, Oliver LB $21.95 (978-1-881508-61-8). Introduces seven scientists who have made substantial contributions to the science of meteorology. (Rev: SLJ 7/04) [920]

Oceanography

General and Miscellaneous

12854 Burns, Loree Griffin. *Tracking Trash: Flotsam, Jetsam, and the Science of Ocean Motion* (7–10). Illus. Series: Scientists in the Field. 2007, Houghton $18.00 (978-0-618-58131-3). Trash in the ocean can help scientists study currents as well as posing a threat to animals and ecosystems, according to this attractive book. (Rev: BCCB 5/07; BL 4/1/07; HB 3–4/07; LMC 11/07; SLJ 3/07*) [551.46]

12855 Cobb, Allan B. *Super Science Projects About Oceans* (4–7). Series: Psyched for Science. 2000, Rosen LB $26.50 (978-0-8239-3174-3). Although the format is unattractive, this book contains six fine experiments that explore concepts involving the ocean. (Rev: SLJ 7/00) [551.46]

12856 Desonie, Dana. *Oceans: How We Use the Seas* (8–12). Illus. Series: Our Fragile Planet. 2007, Chelsea House LB $35.00 (978-0-8160-6216-4). An overview of oceanography with an emphasis on environmental protection and a no-frills format. (Rev: BL 10/15/07; SLJ 4/08) [551.46]

12857 Dinwiddie, Robert. *Ocean: The World's Last Wilderness Revealed* (7–12). Illus. 2006, DK $50.00 (978-0-7566-2205-3). With many eye-catching images and lots of information on the ocean environment (tides, waves, shallow seas, polar seas, and so forth) and the life found therein, this well-designed volume is useful both for browsers and researchers. (Rev: BL 11/15/06) [551.46]

12858 Dudley, William, ed. *Endangered Oceans* (8–12). Series: Opposing Viewpoints. 1999, Greenhaven LB $32.45 (978-0-7377-0063-3). This anthology of opinions about the spoiling of the oceans debates such topics as the seriousness of the problem, the effectiveness of present practices, interna-

tional policies, and how to save the whales. (Rev: BL 4/15/99; SLJ 8/99) [574.5]

12859 Hutchinson, Stephen, and Lawrence E. Hawkins. *Oceans: A Visual Guide* (8–12). Illus. 2005, Firefly $29.95 (978-1-55407-069-5). With dramatic photographs and highly readable text, oceanographers Hutchinson and Hawkins introduce readers to the oceans of the world and the qualities that clearly distinguish one from the other. (Rev: BL 10/15/05; VOYA 4/06) [551.46]

12860 McMillan, Beverly, and John A. Musick. *Oceans* (5–8). Illus. Series: Insiders. 2007, Simon & Schuster $16.99 (978-1-4169-3859-0). An introduction to Earth's oceans, marine life, ocean migrations, sea vents, coastal and polar seas, and so forth, with eye-catching illustrations. (Rev: LMC 10/07; SLJ 12/07) [551.46]

12861 Sayre, April Pulley. *Ocean* (4–7). Illus. Series: Exploring Earth's Biomes. 1996, Twenty-First Century LB $25.90 (978-0-8050-4084-5). An introduction to the nature and composition of oceans and the animal and plant life that they support. (Rev: BL 10/15/96; SLJ 1/97) [551.46]

12862 Sayre, April Pulley. *Seashore* (4–7). Illus. Series: Exploring Earth's Biomes. 1996, Twenty-First Century LB $25.90 (978-0-8050-4085-2). The composition of seashores and the life that they support are covered in this nicely illustrated account. (Rev: BL 10/15/96; SLJ 1/97) [574.5]

12863 VanCleave, Janice. *Janice VanCleave's Oceans for Every Kid: Easy Activities That Make Learning Science Fun* (5–7). Illus. Series: Science for Every Kid. 1996, Wiley paper $12.95 (978-0-471-12453-5). This book gives good background information about oceans plus a number of entertaining and instructive projects and activities. (Rev: BL 4/15/96; SLJ 5/96) [551.46]

12864 Vogel, Carole G. *Dangerous Crossings* (5–8). Illus. Series: The Restless Sea. 2003, Watts LB $30.50 (978-0-531-12325-6); paper $12.95 (978-0-531-16679-6). Ranging widely from tales of endurance at sea to pirates and problems created by global warming, this is an arresting account. (Rev: BL 1/1/04; SLJ 1/04) [910.4]

12865 Vogel, Carole G. *Human Impact* (5–9). Series: The Restless Sea. 2003, Watts LB $30.50 (978-0-531-12323-2). An examination of how mankind is endangering the sea and its creatures through activities including coastal development, global warming, and oil spills. (Rev: SLJ 3/04) [333.91]

12866 Vogel, Carole G. *Savage Waters* (5–8). Illus. Series: The Restless Sea. 2003, Watts LB $30.50 (978-0-531-12321-8); paper $12.95 (978-0-531-16682-6). An entertaining and attractive discussion of the origins of the world's oceans and seas and the forces that influence waves, tides, and tsunamis. Also use *Shifting Shores* (2003). (Rev: BL 1/1/04; SLJ 1/04) [551.46]

12867 Wroble, Lisa A. *The Oceans* (7–10). Series: Endangered Animals and Habitats. 1998, Lucent LB $27.45 (978-1-56006-464-0). A well-illustrated, fact-filled exploration of the oceans as habitats and the environmental dangers that threaten them. (Rev: HBG 9/98) [577.7]

12868 Young, Karen Romano. *Across the Wide Ocean: The Why, How, and Where of Navigation for Humans and Animals at Sea* (5–7). Illus. by author. 2007, HarperCollins $18.99 (978-0-06-009086-9). Before satellite global positioning technology, humans had to use many different methods to navigate at sea, and this book creatively explores many of these methods as well as those of sea creatures including turtles and whales. (Rev: SLJ 7/07) [623.89]

12869 Zim, Herbert S., and Lester Ingle. *Seashores* (5–8). Illus. 1991, Western $21.27 (978-0-307-64496-1). This is a guide to animals and plants found along the beaches.

Underwater Exploration and Sea Disasters

12870 Allen, Judy, et al. *Higher Ground* (5–8). Illus. 2006, Chrysalis paper $8.99 (978-1-84458-581-6). First-person accounts of survivors and rescue workers mixed with fictional treatments based on fact portray the impact on children of the deadly Indian Ocean tsunami of December 2004. (Rev: BCCB 5/06; BL 2/1/06; SLJ 3/06) [363.349]

12871 Gaines, Richard. *The Explorers of the Undersea World* (6–9). Illus. Series: World Explorers. 1993, Chelsea LB $19.95 (978-0-7910-1323-6). A fully illustrated history of underwater exploration, with particular emphasis on the life and work of Cousteau. (Rev: BL 12/15/93; SLJ 2/94) [561.46]

12872 Karwoski, Gail Langer. *Tsunami: The True Story of an April Fools' Day Disaster* (4–7). Illus. by John MacDonald. 2006, Darby Creek $17.95 (978-1-58196-044-0). Karwoski tells the story of a devastating 1946 tsunami, and expands the coverage to other destructive waves and their causes, effects, and the measures being taken to alert residents to their arrival. (Rev: SLJ 1/07) [363.34]

12873 Kusky, Timothy. *Tsunamis: Giant Waves from the Sea* (8–11). Illus. Series: Hazardous Earth. 2008, Facts on File $39.50 (978-0-8160-6464-9). Kusky explains the causes and behavior of these destructive waves, describes some particularly tragic occurrences, and looks at efforts to give people advance warning. (Rev: BL 4/1/08) [551.46]

12874 Lindop, Laurie. *Venturing the Deep Sea* (4–8). Series: Science on the Edge. 2005, Twenty-First Century LB $27.93 (978-0-7613-2701-1). A behind-the-scenes look at the technology employed by modern-day undersea explorers, with a clear explanation of the types of knowledge these researchers are seeking. (Rev: SLJ 8/06; VOYA 4/06) [551.46]

12875 Mallory, Kenneth. *Diving to a Deep-Sea Volcano* (4–7). Illus. 2006, Houghton $17.00 (978-0-618-33205-2). Take a dive with marine biologists as they explore deep-sea volcanoes and the creatures that live and thrive around them; scientific method, adventure, biography, and insight into a career are intertwined in this portrait of a marine biologist's work in an underwater habitat. (Rev: BL 12/1/06; SLJ 2/07) [551.2]

12876 Platt, Richard. *Shipwreck* (4–9). Series: Eyewitness Books. 1997, Knopf LB $20.99 (978-0-679-98569-3). An overview of the causes and consequences of the world's most famous maritime disasters. (Rev: BL 12/15/97) [387.2]

12877 Sloan, Frank. *Titanic*. Rev. ed. (5–8). 1998, Raintree $19.98 (978-0-8172-4091-2). This thorough account of the *Titanic* and its sinking covers the structure of the ship, why it sank, the inquiries that followed, the many attempts to find and explore the wreckage, and movies and plays inspired by it. (Rev: BL 9/1/98; HBG 9/99; SLJ 2/99) [910]

12878 Stewart, Gail B. *Catastrophe in Southern Asia: The Tsunami of 2004* (5–8). Series: Overview. 2005, Gale LB $29.95 (978-1-59018-831-6). An information-packed review of the tsunami itself, the human costs of the disaster, and the reconstruction efforts. (Rev: SLJ 12/05)

12879 *Sunk! Exploring Underwater Archaeology* (5–8). Series: Buried Worlds. 1994, Lerner LB $28.75 (978-0-8225-3205-7). Provides a general overview of how archaeologists interpret underwater discoveries to learn about aspects of ancient trade, commerce, and history. (Rev: BL 10/15/94; SLJ 9/94) [930.1]

12880 Torres, John A. *Disaster in the Indian Ocean: Tsunami 2004* (5–8). Illus. Series: Monumental Milestones: Great Events of Modern Times. 2005, Mitchell Lane LB $29.95 (978-1-58415-344-3). This slim volume, uneven in its coverage, nonetheless offers a chilling overview of the devastating Indian Ocean tsunami of December 2004 and includes a number of eyewitness accounts. (Rev: BL 10/15/05; SLJ 12/05) [909]

12881 Wade, Mary Dodson. *Tsunami: Monster Waves* (4–8). Series: American Disasters. 2002, Enslow LB $23.93 (978-0-7660-1786-3). This book explains in photographs and text how these giant sea swells are created, how they are tracked, and their effects. (Rev: BL 6/1–15/02; HBG 10/02; SLJ 10/02) [551.55]

12882 Whiting, Jim. *The Sinking of the Titanic* (6–9). 2006, Mitchell Lane LB $19.95 (978-1-58415-472-3). A brief, chronological account covering the building of the *Titanic* and its sister ships, the maiden voyage, the sinking, and the discovery of the wreck, with a review of current thinking on the cause of the accident. (Rev: SLJ 11/06)

Physics

General and Miscellaneous

12883 Barnett, Lincoln. *The Universe of Dr. Einstein* (8–12). 1980, Amereon $18.95 (978-0-8488-0146-5). A lucid explanation of Einstein's theory of relativity and how it has changed our ideas of the universe. [530.1]

12884 Bonnet, Bob, and Dan Keen. *Science Fair Projects: Physics* (4–7). Illus. 2000, Sterling $17.95 (978-0-8069-0707-9). This large-format book presents 47 projects demonstrating concepts in physics and using common materials as equipment. (Rev: BL 2/1/00; SLJ 4/00) [530]

12885 Bortz, Fred. *The Quark* (7–10). Illus. Series: The Library of Subatomic Particles. 2004, Rosen LB $27.95 (978-0-8239-4533-7). Suitable for reluctant readers, this is a clear explanation of the quark, featuring large text and many color illustrations. Also recommended in this series are *The Proton*, *The Photon*, and *The Electron* (all 2004). (Rev: SLJ 10/04)

12886 Bortz, Fred. *Techno Matters: The Materials Behind the Marvels* (7–12). Illus. 2001, Twenty-First Century LB $25.90 (978-0-7613-1469-1). The author, a physicist, uses plentiful illustrations and clear text to explain different types of matter (electro-matter, poly-matter, super-matter, and so forth) and the kinds of materials that have been produced over the years since the Stone Age. (Rev: BL 4/15/01; HBG 10/01; SLJ 10/01) [620.1]

12887 Durant, Penny R. *Bubblemania! Learn the Secrets to Creating Millions of Spectacular Bubbles!* (4–8). 1994, Avon paper $3.99 (978-0-380-77373-2). Through a series of easy experiments, surface tension, bubble formation, and the uses of bubbles are explained. (Rev: SLJ 7/94) [530]

12888 Evans, Neville. *The Science of Gravity* (5–8). Illus. Series: Science World. 2000, Raintree LB $25.69 (978-0-7398-1323-2). Explores the force of gravity and how it affects our lives, with additional material on air resistance, mass, and invisible forces. (Rev: BL 9/15/00; HBG 10/00) [531]

12889 Fleisher, Paul. *Liquids and Gases: Principles of Fluid Mechanics* (6–12). Illus. Series: Secrets of the Universe. 2001, Lerner LB $25.26 (978-0-8225-2988-0). Archimedes's principle, Pascal's law, and Bernoulli's principle are among the topics covered in this volume adapted from an adult title. (Rev: HBG 3/02; SLJ 12/01) [532]

12890 Fleisher, Paul. *Matter and Energy: Principles of Matter and Thermodynamics* (7–12). Illus. Series: Secrets of the Universe. 2001, Lerner LB $25.26 (978-0-8225-2986-6). The periodic tables and the basic principles of thermodynamics and matter are explained in conversational language with clear diagrams and simple experiments. (Rev: BL 8/01; HBG 3/02; SLJ 1/02) [530.11]

12891 Fleisher, Paul. *Relativity and Quantum Mechanics: Principles of Modern Physics* (6–9). Illus. Series: Secrets of the Universe. 2001, Lerner LB $25.26 (978-0-8225-2989-7). The basic principles of modern physics are presented in clear text with helpful graphics and explanations of terms and concepts. (Rev: HBG 3/02; SLJ 1/02) [530.11]

12892 Gardner, Robert. *Experiments with Bubbles* (4–7). Illus. Series: Getting Started in Science. 1995, Enslow LB $26.60 (978-0-89490-666-4). The properties of bubbles are explored in a series of experiments, each a little more complex than the last. (Rev: BL 12/1/95; SLJ 3/96) [530.4]

12893 Gardner, Robert. *Science Projects About Physics in the Home* (6–9). Series: Science Projects. 1999, Enslow LB $26.60 (978-0-89490-948-1). Ranging in difficulty from simple to complex, these projects about physics involving ideas from the living room, kitchen, playground, and bathroom are presented in a clear, straightforward way. (Rev: SLJ 5/99) [530]

12894 Gardner, Robert. *Science Projects About the Physics of Toys and Games* (6–12). Series: Science Projects. 2000, Enslow LB $26.60 (978-0-7660-1165-6). Ordinary toys and games are used to produce a series of projects that are challenging, educational, and fun. (Rev: BL 8/00; HBG 3/01; VOYA 2/01) [507]

12895 Gardner, Robert, and Eric Kemer. *Science Projects About Temperature and Heat* (6–12). Series: Science Projects. 2001, Enslow LB $26.60 (978-0-89490-534-6). Using clear instructions and detailed drawings, this book outlines a number of activities involving heat and how it is measured. (Rev: BL 3/15/01; HBG 10/01; SLJ 1/95) [536]

12896 Goldstein, Natalie. *How Do We Know the Nature of the Atom* (6–9). Illus. Series: Great Scientific Questions and the Scientists Who Answered Them. 2001, Rosen LB $26.50 (978-0-8239-3385-3). An absorbing account of efforts through the ages to reveal the secrets of the atom. (Rev: SLJ 12/01) [539.14]

12897 Goodstein, Madeline. *Fish Tank Physics Projects* (5–8). Series: Science Fair Success. 2002, Enslow LB $26.60 (978-0-7660-1624-8). Using a common fish tank and its contents, various aspects of laws of physics are presented in the form of science fair projects. (Rev: BL 5/15/02; HBG 10/02; SLJ 11/02) [621.9]

12898 Goodstein, Madeline. *Sports Science Projects: The Physics of Balls in Motion* (5–8). Illus. Series: Science Fair Success. 1999, Enslow LB $26.60 (978-0-7660-1174-8). This book contains 40 projects that use the properties of different sports balls to demonstrate principles of physics. (Rev: BL 2/15/00; HBG 10/00; SLJ 3/00) [530]

12899 Hakim, Joy. *Einstein Adds a New Dimension* (7–12). Illus. Series: Story of Science. 2007, Smithsonian $27.95 (978-1-58834-162-4). Not just about Einstein, this book also covers the giants upon whose shoulders Einstein stood and the many other factors in history and society that led to quantum theory; readable and compelling. (Rev: BL 12/1/07; SLJ 12/07) [509]

12900 Hammond, Richard. *Can You Feel the Force?* (5–8). Illus. 2006, DK $15.99 (978-0-7566-2033-2). Light, matter, friction, gravity, velocity — these and other basic physics principles are explained in a reader-friendly format that includes experiments, captions, sidebars, and other eye-catching elements. (Rev: SLJ 10/06) [530]

12901 Jerome, Kate Boehm. *Atomic Universe: The Quest to Discover Radioactivity* (5–8). Series: Science Quest. 2006, National Geographic $17.95 (978-0-7922-5543-7). An attractive and informative history of radioactivity, profiling key figures and placing the discovery and subsequent developments in scientific and social context. (Rev: SLJ 4/07) [539.7]

12902 Juettner, Bonnie. *Molecules* (4–8). Illus. 2004, Gale LB $26.20 (978-0-7377-2076-1). Clear, concise text, supported by full-color photographs and diagrams, describes the characteristics of atoms and molecules. (Rev: SLJ 6/05)

12903 McClafferty, Carla Killough. *The Head Bone's Connected to the Neck Bone: The Weird, Wacky, and Wonderful X-Ray* (6–9). Illus. 2001, Farrar $17.00 (978-0-374-32908-2). Unusual uses of x-rays — including industrial applications and art appraisal — are included in this entertaining book, along with a look at radiation's better-known function in medicine. (Rev: BL 11/1/01; HBG 3/02; SLJ 12/01; VOYA 2/02) [616.07]

12904 McGrath, Susan. *Fun with Physics* (5–9). Illus. 1986, National Geographic LB $12.50 (978-0-87044-581-1). An introduction to physics that uses everyday situations as examples and supplies a smattering of experiments. (Rev: SLJ 6/87) [530]

12905 Morgan, Sally, and Adrian Morgan. *Materials* (4–7). Illus. Series: Designs in Science. 1994, Facts on File $23.00 (978-0-8160-2985-3). Basic properties of matter and materials are explored in a series of experiments using everyday materials. (Rev: BL 7/94) [620.1]

12906 Parker, Barry. *The Mystery of Gravity* (5–8). Illus. Series: The Story of Science. 2002, Benchmark $29.93 (978-0-7614-1428-5). Parker traces our understanding of gravity from the early Greek philosophers through Einstein and Hubble, with discussion of the Big Bang theory and black holes. (Rev: HBG 3/03; SLJ 2/03) [531]

12907 Sonneborn, Liz. *Forces in Nature: Understanding Gravitational, Electrical, and Magnetic Force* (7–12). Illus. Series: Library of Physics. 2005, Rosen LB $26.50 (978-1-4042-0332-7). Explores a wide variety of forces, including gravitational, electrical, magnetic, and electromagnetic, using clear narrative with diagrams and photographs. (Rev: SLJ 12/05)

12908 Stille, Darlene R. *Physical Change: Reshaping Matter* (5–8). Illus. Series: Exploring Science. 2005, Compass Point LB $27.93 (978-0-7565-1257-6). An attractive format with plenty of graphics adds to the appeal of this brief discussion of the states of matter. (Rev: SLJ 7/06) [530]

12909 Stringer, John. *The Science of a Spring* (5–8). Illus. Series: Science World. 2000, Raintree LB $25.69 (978-0-7398-1322-5). Leaf and coil springs are introduced as well as the balance of forces in physics, the limits of springs, and their uses in such common objects as staplers. (Rev: BL 9/1/00; HBG 10/00; SLJ 8/00) [531]

12910 Sullivan, Navin. *Weight* (4–7). Illus. Series: Measure Up! . 2006, Marshall Cavendish LB $20.95 (978-0-7614-2324-9). Topics such as gravity and buoyancy are covered in this well-designed book about weight. (Rev: LMC 8-9/07; SLJ 6/07)

12911 Tiner, John Hudson. *Gravity* (4–7). Series: Understanding Science. 2002, Smart Apple $24.25 (978-1-58340-157-6). Through a number of simple projects, colorful illustrations, and a clear text, the fundamentals of gravity are explored. (Rev: BL 3/15/03; HBG 3/03) [531]

12912 Willett, Edward. *The Basics of Quantum Physics: Understanding the Photoelectric Effect and Line Spectra* (7–12). Illus. Series: Library of Physics. 2005, Rosen LB $26.50 (978-1-4042-0334-1). Examines the nature of light and the atom, key elements in the study of quantum physics, using clear narrative with diagrams and photographs. (Rev: SLJ 12/05)

Energy and Motion

General and Miscellaneous

12913 Asimov, Isaac. *How Did We Find Out About Solar Power?* (5–8). Illus. by David Wool. 1981, Walker LB $12.85 (978-0-8027-6423-2). An explanation of how man has benefited from solar power from the earliest time until today. [621.47]

12914 Ballard, Carol. *From Steam Engines to Nuclear Fusion* (6–9). Illus. Series: Chain Reactions. 2007, Heinemann LB $24.00 (978-1-4034-9554-9). The uses of energy, from the basic to the advanced, are covered, as well as the scientists who have contributed to this field and what the future advancements in energy theory may entail. (Rev: BL 4/1/07; SLJ 7/07) [621.042]

12915 Cruden, Gabriel. *Energy Alternatives* (5–8). Illus. Series: Lucent Library of Science and Technology. 2005, Gale LB $29.95 (978-1-59018-530-8). A look at the importance of finding alternatives to existing energy sources, covering such technologies as solar, wind, and geothermal power. (Rev: BL 1/05)

12916 Doherty, Paul, and Don Rathjen. *The Spinning Blackboard and Other Dynamic Experiments on Force and Motion* (4–8). Illus. Series: Exploratorium Science Snackbook. 1996, Wiley paper $13.95 (978-0-471-11514-4). The many activities in this well-organized, attractive book reveal important characteristics of force and motion. (Rev: BL 4/15/96; SLJ 6/96) [531]

12917 Egendorf, Laura K., ed. *Energy Alternatives* (5–9). Series: Introducing Issues with Opposing

Viewpoints. 2006, Gale LB $33.70 (978-0-7377-3458-4). Presents basic information about alternatives to fossil fuel-driven energy, along with diverse views on the feasibility and practicality of these alternative energy sources. (Rev: SLJ 8/06) [333.79]

12918 Gardner, Robert. *Bicycle Science Projects: Physics on Wheels* (6–9). Series: Science Fair Success. 2004, Enslow LB $26.60 (978-0-7660-1630-9). Gardner outlines 22 projects demonstrating physics principles, all of which use the common bicycle as their basic component. (Rev: BL 12/15/04; SLJ 2/05) [531/.6]

12919 Gardner, Robert. *Experiments with Motion* (5–8). Series: Getting Started in Science. 1995, Enslow LB $20.95 (978-0-89490-667-1). Projects using simple equipment illustrate the laws of motion and the ways in which motion differs in various situations. (Rev: BL 2/1/96; SLJ 2/96; VOYA 6/96) [531]

12920 Gardner, Robert. *Science Project Ideas About the Sun* (4–7). Series: Science Project Ideas. 1997, Enslow LB $25.26 (978-0-89490-845-3). The sun and solar energy are the subjects of this book that illustrates important concepts through a number of interesting projects and experiments. (Rev: BL 12/15/97; HBG 3/98; SLJ 1/98) [697.78]

12921 Gutnik, Martin J., and Natalie B. Gutnik. *Projects That Explore Energy* (5–8). Illus. Series: Investigate! 1994, Millbrook LB $21.40 (978-1-56294-334-9). A lucid, well-organized series of projects and experiments that explore power, force, and energy sources and resources. (Rev: BL 8/94; SLJ 6/94) [333.79]

12922 Jacobs, Linda. *Letting Off Steam: The Story of Geothermal Energy* (7–12). Illus. 1989, Carolrhoda LB $21.27 (978-0-87614-300-1). A lucid account that tells about the sources and the use of geothermal energy. (Rev: BL 9/15/89; SLJ 9/89) [333.8]

12923 Kallen, Stuart A. *World Energy Crisis* (8–12). Illus. Series: Compact Research. 2007, Reference Point LB $24.95 (978-1-60152-011-1). This compact volume provides lots of information for report writers, with illustrations, quotations from primary sources, lists of facts, statistical charts, and brief timelines. (Rev: SLJ 5/07) [333.79]

12924 Landau, Elaine. *The History of Energy* (5–8). Series: Major Inventions Through History. 2005, Twenty-First Century LB $26.60 (978-0-8225-3806-6). An attractive look at developments through time in the use of various forms of energy (fire, wind, water, coal, steam, oil and gasoline, electricity, and so forth) and their application in transportation and other sectors. (Rev: SLJ 1/06)

12925 Morgan, Sally. *Alternative Energy Sources* (7–10). Illus. Series: Science at the Edge. 2002, Heinemann LB $27.86 (978-1-4034-0322-3). A discussion of alternatives to fossil fuels and the respective advantages of wind, solar, geothermal, nuclear, and other sources of energy. (Rev: HBG 3/03; SLJ 1/03) [333.79]

12926 Morgan, Sally. *From Windmills to Hydrogen Fuel Cells: Discovering Alternative Energy* (6–9). Illus. Series: Chain Reactions. 2007, Heinemann LB $34.29 (978-1-4034-9555-6). Clear text and interesting graphics will draw readers into this overview of alternative energy sources, including solar, wind, and fuel cells. (Rev: SLJ 7/07)

12927 Nakaya, Andrea C. *Energy Alternatives* (8–12). Series: Compact Research. 2007, Reference Point LB $24.95 (978-1-60152-017-3). What alternative energy sources should be pursued? Can alternative energy be used for transportation? These and other questions are discussed from various points of view, with facts, profiles, and illustrations. (Rev: SLJ 1/08)

12928 Roberts, Jeremy. *How Do We Know the Laws of Motion?* (6–9). Illus. Series: Great Scientific Questions and the Scientists Who Answered Them. 2001, Rosen LB $26.50 (978-0-8239-3383-9). Roberts traces man's growing understanding of the laws of motion from the ancient Greeks through the discoveries of relativity and the "geometry of space." (Rev: BL 10/15/01) [531.1]

12929 Silverstein, Alvin, et al. *Energy* (4–7). Illus. Series: Science Concepts. 1998, Twenty-First Century LB $26.90 (978-0-7613-3222-0). Photographs, diagrams, and illustrations help to introduce six types of energy: electrical, magnetic, light, heat, sound, and nuclear. (Rev: BL 5/1/99; HBG 10/99) [621.042]

12930 Snedden, Robert. *Energy Alternatives* (6–10). Illus. Series: Essential Energy. 2001, Heinemann LB $24.22 (978-1-57572-441-6). Alternatives to fossil fuels are presented in brief but detailed spreads, with discussion of possible future energy solutions. (Rev: BL 1/1–15/02) [333.79]

12931 Stille, Darlene R. *Waves: Energy on the Move* (5–8). Illus. Series: Exploring Science. 2005, Compass Point LB $27.93 (978-0-7565-1259-0). An attractive format with plenty of graphics adds to the appeal of this brief discussion of waves in water, light, air, and other media. (Rev: SLJ 7/06) [531]

12932 Sullivan, Navin. *Speed* (4–7). Illus. Series: Measure Up! . 2006, Marshall Cavendish LB $20.95 (978-0-7614-2325-6). In addition to providing an overview of the science of speed, this volume includes high-quality graphics, information about historical versus modern methods, and at-home experiments. (Rev: LMC 8-9/07; SLJ 6/07)

12933 Viegas, Jennifer. *Kinetic and Potential Energy: Understanding Changes Within Physical Systems* (7–12). Illus. Series: Library of Physics. 2005, Rosen LB $26.50 (978-1-4042-0333-4). Examines the distinction between potential and kinetic energy,

as well as momentum, mechanical energy, and the laws of energy, using clear narrative with diagrams and photographs. (Rev: SLJ 12/05)

12934 Walker, Niki. *Generating Wind Power* (5–8). Illus. Series: Energy Revolution. 2007, Crabtree LB $25.20 (978-0-7787-2913-6); paper $8.95 (978-0-7787-2927-3). Wind is explored as an alternative energy source in this well-designed volume. Also use *Harnessing Power from the Sun* and *Biomass: Fueling Change* (both 2007). (Rev: SLJ 7/07)

12935 Woelfle, Gretchen. *The Wind at Work: An Activity Guide to Windmills* (4–8). 1997, Chicago Review paper $14.95 (978-1-55652-308-3). The history, types, and uses of windmills are covered, with many activities and a discussion of the future of wind power. (Rev: BL 9/1/97; SLJ 10/97*) [621.4]

12936 Woodford, Chris. *Energy* (4–7). Illus. Series: See for Yourself. 2007, DK $14.99 (978-0-7566-2561-0). This introductory guide to energy provides an easy-to-understand definition, offers examples of both kinetic and potential energy, identifies major energy sources, explains the processes through which energy is released, and discusses the problems inherent in energy usage. (Rev: BL 4/1/07) [333.79]

12937 Woodford, Chris. *Power and Energy* (6–9). Illus. Series: History of Invention. 2004, Facts on File $35.00 (978-0-8160-5440-4). A slim introductory overview of advances in power and energy from prehistoric times to today, with illustrations, and profiles of key figures. (Rev: SLJ 12/04)

Nuclear Energy

12938 Brennan, Kristine. *The Chernobyl Nuclear Disaster* (6–8). Series: Great Disasters. 2001, Chelsea LB $30.00 (978-0-7910-6322-4). The story of the world's worst nuclear disaster, which occurred in 1986, and the resulting reforms and changes. (Rev: BL 6/1–15/02; HBG 10/02) [621.48]

12939 Cole, Michael D. *Three Mile Island: Nuclear Disaster* (4–8). Series: American Disasters. 2002, Enslow LB $23.93 (978-0-7660-1556-2). An informative, well-researched account of the disaster that affected the development of nuclear power plants in this country. (Rev: BL 6/1–15/02; HBG 10/02; SLJ 6/02) [621.48]

12940 Daley, Michael J. *Nuclear Power: Promise or Peril?* (7–12). Illus. Series: Pro/Con Issues. 1997, Lerner LB $30.35 (978-0-8225-2611-7). This book examines conflicting opinions about nuclear power, the possibility of nuclear accidents, the demand for energy, and the problems involving storage of nuclear waste. (Rev: BL 11/1/97; SLJ 12/97) [333.792]

12941 DeAngelis, Therese. *Three Mile Island* (6–8). Series: Great Disasters. 2001, Chelsea LB $30.00 (978-0-7910-5785-8). This account describes the worst nuclear accident to occur in this country and the reforms and improvements it produced. (Rev: BL 6/1–15/02; HBG 10/02) [621.48]

12942 Higgins, Christopher. *Nuclear Submarine Disasters* (6–8). Series: Great Disasters. 2001, Chelsea LB $30.00 (978-0-7910-6329-3). After a general introduction to nuclear submarines, this account concentrates on the two American submarines that sank in the 1960s and the Russian submarine that sank in 2000. (Rev: BL 6/1–15/02; HBG 10/02; SLJ 6/02) [623.812]

12943 Kidd, J. S., and Renee A. Kidd. *Quarks and Sparks: The Story of Nuclear Power* (7–12). 1999, Facts on File $25.00 (978-0-8160-3587-8). A history of the development of nuclear power, with good coverage of the nuclear race during World War II and contemporary uses and problems. (Rev: BL 8/99; VOYA 10/99) [621.48]

12944 Lüsted, Marcia, and Greg Lusted. *A Nuclear Power Plant* (8–12). Illus. Series: Building History. 2005, Gale LB $32.45 (978-1-59018-392-2). Explores the history of nuclear power generation and considers the arguments for and against the construction of more nuclear power plants in the United States and elsewhere. (Rev: SLJ 6/05) [333.792]

12945 Snedden, Robert. *Nuclear Energy* (6–10). Illus. Series: Essential Energy. 2001, Heinemann LB $24.22 (978-1-57572-444-7). The process of producing nuclear power is presented in brief but detailed spreads, with discussion of the hazards. (Rev: BL 1/1–15/02) [333.79]

12946 Wilcox, Charlotte. *Powerhouse: Inside a Nuclear Power Plant* (4–8). Illus. 1996, Carolrhoda LB $27.15 (978-0-87614-945-4); paper $7.95 (978-0-87614-979-9). A history of nuclear energy is followed by a description of how a power plant operates and the dangers that are present. (Rev: BL 10/1/96; SLJ 9/96) [621.48]

Light, Color, and Laser Science

12947 Asimov, Isaac. *How Did We Find Out About Lasers?* (5–7). Illus. by Erika Kors. 1990, Walker LB $13.85 (978-0-8027-6936-7). A readable introduction to laser science by the veteran writer. (Rev: BL 8/90; SLJ 11/90) [621.36]

12948 Gardner, Robert. *Experiments with Light and Mirrors* (4–7). Illus. 1995, Enslow LB $20.95 (978-0-89490-668-8). Properties of light are explained and demonstrated using equipment such as mirrors and cardboard. (Rev: BL 2/1/96; SLJ 3/96) [535.2]

12949 Gardner, Robert. *Science Projects About Light* (4–8). Series: Science Projects. 1994, Enslow LB $26.60 (978-0-89490-529-2). This project book contains a wealth of demonstrations that explain the basic principles of light. (Rev: SLJ 1/95) [535]

12950 Kirkland, Kyle. *Light and Optics* (8–12). Illus. Series: Physics in Our World. 2007, Facts on File $35.00 (978-0-8160-6114-3). A good explanation of the physics of light is followed by a look at real-world examples and applications of light put to use. (Rev: BL 4/15/07) [535]

12951 Sitarski, Anita. *Cold Light: Creatures, Discoveries, and Inventions that Glow* (4–7). Illus. 2007, Boyds Mills $16.95 (978-1-59078-468-6). An interesting introduction to the phenomenon of luminescence — found in animals that glow but also in light-emitting diodes — this will appeal to report writers and browsers. (Rev: BL 12/1/07; LMC 1/08; SLJ 10/07) [535.35]

12952 Stille, Darlene R. *Manipulating Light: Reflection, Refraction, and Absorption* (5–8). Illus. Series: Exploring Science. 2005, Compass Point LB $27.93 (978-0-7565-1258-3). An attractive format with plenty of graphics adds to the appeal of this brief discussion of the nature of light. (Rev: SLJ 7/06) [535]

Magnetism and Electricity

12953 Bartholomew, Alan. *Electric Mischief* (4–7). Series: Kids Can Do It. 2002, Kids Can $12.95 (978-1-55074-923-6); paper $5.95 (978-1-55074-925-0). An activity book that outlines simple, safe experiments with electricity. (Rev: BL 3/15/03; HBG 3/03; SLJ 12/02) [537]

12954 Dreier, David. *Electrical Circuits: Harnessing Electricity* (5–7). Illus. Series: Exploring Science: Physical Science. 2007, Compass Point LB $19.95 (978-0-7565-3267-3). A user-friendly introduction to electricity and how we use it, with good graphics and interesting sidebar features. (Rev: BL 12/1/07; LMC 2/08) [537]

12955 Evans, Neville. *The Science of a Light Bulb* (5–8). Illus. Series: Science World. 2000, Raintree LB $25.69 (978-0-7398-1325-6). This work explains how Edison invented the light bulb, describes its parts, and tells how light is produced and how we see it. (Rev: BL 9/15/00; HBG 10/00) [535]

12956 Fleisher, Paul. *Waves: Principles of Light, Electricity, and Magnetism* (6–12). Illus. Series: Secrets of the Universe. 2001, Lerner LB $25.26 (978-0-8225-2987-3). Optics, electric current, and electromagnetism are among the topics covered in this volume adapted from an adult title. (Rev: HBG 3/02; SLJ 12/01) [539.2]

12957 Gardner, Robert. *Science Projects About Electricity and Magnets* (6–12). Series: Science Projects. 2001, Enslow LB $20.95 (978-0-89490-530-8). A number of interesting projects about electricity and magnets are presented in a clear text with careful drawings and safety tips. (Rev: BL 3/15/01; HBG 10/01; SLJ 1/95) [537]

12958 Tiner, John Hudson. *Magnetism* (4–7). Series: Understanding Science. 2002, Smart Apple LB $24.25 (978-1-58340-158-3). Using clear explanations, simple projects, and good illustrations, the concept of magnetism is introduced. (Rev: BL 3/15/03; HBG 3/03) [538.4]

12959 VanCleave, Janice. *Janice VanCleave's Electricity: Mind-Boggling Experiments You Can Turn into Science Fair Projects* (5–7). Illus. 1994, Wiley paper $10.95 (978-0-471-31010-5). As well as providing a discussion on the nature of electricity, this book offers 20 informative experiments that move from the very simple to the more complex. (Rev: BL 12/1/94; SLJ 11/94) [537]

12960 Woodford, Chris, and Martin Clowes. *Electricity* (4–7). Illus. 2004, Gale LB $23.70 (978-1-4103-0165-9). A detailed examination of the development of electricity, with profiles of key individuals and their discoveries, a chronology, and discussion of future advances. (Rev: SLJ 5/05)

Nuclear Physics

12961 Morgan, Sally. *From Greek Atoms to Quarks: Discovering Atoms* (6–9). Illus. Series: Chain Reactions. 2007, Heinemann LB $34.29 (978-1-4034-9551-8). With clear text and excellent graphics, this volume chronicles the history of humans' understanding of atoms and describes current subatomic research. (Rev: SLJ 7/07)

Sound

12962 Morgan, Sally, and Adrian Morgan. *Using Sound* (4–7). Illus. Series: Designs in Science. 1994, Facts on File $23.00 (978-0-8160-2981-5). The properties of sound and their relation to everyday life are covered in the text and a number of experiments using readily available materials. (Rev: BL 7/94) [534]

12963 Parker, Steve. *The Science of Sound: Projects and Experiments with Music and Sound Waves* (4–7). Illus. Series: Tabletop Scientist. 2005, Heinemann LB $29.29 (978-1-4034-7281-6). The 12 experiments and projects in this collection demonstrate the basic scientific principles of sound waves. (Rev: SLJ 12/05)

12964 Wright, Lynne. *The Science of Noise* (5–8). Illus. Series: Science World. 2000, Raintree LB $25.69 (978-0-7398-1324-9). This account describes how sound is produced, how it travels, how we hear it, and how it can be changed. (Rev: BL 9/1/00; HBG 10/00; SLJ 8/00) [534]

Technology and Engineering

General Works and Miscellaneous Industries

12965 Baker, Christopher W. *A New World of Simulators: Training with Technology* (5–8). Illus. 2001, Millbrook LB $23.90 (978-0-7613-1352-6). An introduction to the uses of simulators and their importance in training workers who operate complex technologies such as those found in airplanes, ships, and nuclear power plants. (Rev: BL 8/01; HBG 3/02; SLJ 8/01) [003]

12966 *CDs, Super Glue, and Salsa Series 2: How Everyday Products Are Made* (5–10). 1996, Gale LB $126.00 (978-0-7876-0870-5). This two-volume set tells how 30 everyday products are made, including air bags, bungee cords, contact lenses, ketchup, pencils, soda bottles, and umbrellas. (Rev: SLJ 8/97) [658.5]

12967 Cobb, Vicki. *Fireworks* (4–8). Photos by Michael Gold. Series: Where's the Science Here? 2005, Lerner LB $23.93 (978-0-7613-2771-4). A well-illustrated, engaging text covers the history and science of pyrotechnics; experiments require adult supervision. Also recommended in this series are *Junk Food* and *Sneakers* (both 2005). (Rev: SLJ 2/06)

12968 Colman, Penny. *Toilets, Bathtubs, Sinks, and Sewers: A History of the Bathroom* (5–8). 1994, Atheneum $16.00 (978-0-689-31894-8). A fascinating look at sanitation systems and inventions related to personal hygiene from ancient times to the present. (Rev: BCCB 2/95; BL 1/1/95; SLJ 3/95) [643]

12969 Crompton, Samuel Willard. *The Printing Press* (7–10). Series: Transforming Power of Technology. 2003, Chelsea House LB $30.00 (978-0-7910-7451-0). This interesting volume explores the impact of the invention of the printing press on liter-

acy and general social and economic conditions. (Rev: SLJ 6/04)

12970 Crump, Donald J., ed. *How Things Are Made* (6–9). Illus. 1981, National Geographic LB $12.50 (978-0-87044-339-8). An inquiry into how such objects as baseballs and light bulbs are made. [670]

12971 Crump, Donald J., ed. *How Things Work* (5–7). Illus. 1984, National Geographic LB $12.50 (978-0-87044-430-2). A handsome volume that explains the mechanics of a variety of objects from toasters to space shuttles. [600]

12972 Crump, Donald J., ed. *Small Inventions That Make a Big Difference* (6–9). Illus. 1984, National Geographic LB $12.50 (978-0-87044-503-3). A book on inventions and inventors that covers such common items as the zipper. [608]

12973 *Fantastic Feats and Failures* (4–8). Illus. by Jane Kurisu. 2004, Kids Can paper $9.95 (978-1-55337-634-7). Highs and lows of engineering (the Brooklyn Bridge in the first category, for example, and the Tacoma Narrows in the latter) are reviewed in this fascinating large-format book. (Rev: BL 9/15/04) [624.1]

12974 Goldberg, Jan. *Earth Imaging Satellites* (5–9). Series: The Library of Satellites. 2003, Rosen LB $26.50 (978-0-8239-3853-7). A survey of the various satellites and how their images of the earth's surface measure pollution, locate forest fires, find earthquake faults, and measure the size of polar caps. (Rev: BL 11/15/03) [629.46]

12975 Harrison, Ian. *The Book of Inventions* (8–12). Illus. 2004, National Geographic $30.00 (978-0-7922-8296-9). A photo-filled review of some eclectic and entertaining inventions, including sliced bread and the lava lamp. (Rev: BL 12/1/04) [609]

12976 Kassinger, Ruth G. *Iron and Steel: From Thor's Hammer to the Space Shuttle* (5–7). Illus.

Series: Material World. 2003, Millbrook LB $25.90 (978-0-7613-2111-8). The different ways in which humans have used and processed iron and steel through the ages is the focus of this book. (Rev: BL 5/15/03; HBG 10/03; SLJ 1/04) [669]

12977 Kerrod, Robin. *New Materials: Present Knowledge, Future Trends* (5–9). Illus. Series: 21st Century Science. 2003, Smart Apple Media LB $27.10 (978-1-58340-353-2). Numerous diagrams, photographs, and drawings help to explain the processing of raw materials and the need to conserve our limited resources. (Rev: SLJ 1/04) [620.11]

12978 Landau, Elaine. *The History of Everyday Life* (5–8). Series: Major Inventions Through History. 2005, Twenty-First Century LB $26.60 (978-0-8225-3808-0). Fireplaces, washing machines, and microwave ovens are among the inventions discussed here that have improved our everyday lives. (Rev: SLJ 2/06)

12979 Laxer, James. *Oil* (7–10). 2008, Groundwood $18.95 (978-0-88899-815-6); paper $10.00 (978-0-88899-816-3). An illuminating overview of the oil industry, with information on major oil companies, the industry's history, and its impact on the environment and politics. (Rev: BL 6/1–15/08) [333.8]

12980 Levy, Matthys, and Richard Panchyk. *Engineering the City* (6–12). Illus. 2000, Chicago Review $14.95 (978-1-55652-419-6). There are many curriculum connections in this book that includes information and activities relating to electricity, garbage, transportation, and other urban infrastructure issues. (Rev: BL 2/15/01) [624]

12981 Lockie, Mark. *Biometric Technology* (5–8). Series: Science at the Edge. 2002, Heinemann LB $27.86 (978-1-58810-701-5). Lockie explores the study of biometry and its applications in such areas as voice-speaker identification and facial recognition. (Rev: BL 10/15/02; HBG 3/03) [609]

12982 Macaulay, David, and Neil Ardley. *The New Way Things Work* (6–12). 1998, Houghton $35.00 (978-0-395-93847-8). With an emphasis on visual cutaways, this revision of a fascinating 1988 introduction to modern machines now includes more material on computers. (Rev: BL 12/1/98; HBG 9/99; SLJ 12/98) [600]

12983 *Machines and Inventions* (5–9). Series: Understanding Science and Nature. 1993, Time-Life Books $17.95 (978-0-8094-9704-1). Using a question-and-answer format, double-page spreads look at a variety of inventions including the box camera, printing press, and dynamite. (Rev: BL 1/15/94; SLJ 6/94) [621.8]

12984 Sandler, Martin W. *Inventors* (5–8). Series: Library of Congress Books. 1996, HarperCollins $24.95 (978-0-06-024923-6). Concentrating on the late 19th and 20th centuries, the book is divided into sections on inventors, transportation, communication, and entertainment. (Rev: SLJ 2/96) [608]

12985 Skurzynski, Gloria. *Almost the Real Things: Simulation in Your High Tech World* (5–8). 1991, Macmillan LB $16.95 (978-0-02-778072-7). Skurzynski explains how engineers and scientists simulate events from weightlessness to complex animation. (Rev: BCCB 10/91; BL 10/15/91; HB 11–12/91; SLJ 10/91) [620]

12986 Slavin, Bill. *Transformed: How Everyday Things Are Made* (4–7). Illus. 2005, Kids Can $24.95 (978-1-55337-179-3). A behind-the-scenes look at the manufacturing process for a wide array of everyday products. (Rev: BL 10/15/05; SLJ 1/06) [670]

12987 Smith, Elizabeth Simpson. *Paper* (4–8). Illus. 1984, Walker LB $10.85 (978-0-8027-6569-7). An exploration of the manufacture and use of paper.

12988 Sobey, Ed. *How to Enter and Win an Invention Contest* (6–12). Illus. 1999, Enslow LB $26.60 (978-0-7660-1173-1). A book that not only describes how to invent a new product but also tells how to enter it in a local or national competition. (Rev: BL 9/1/99) [607.973]

12989 Taylor, Barbara. *Be an Inventor* (5–9). Illus. 1987, Harcourt $11.95 (978-0-15-205950-7); paper $7.95 (978-0-15-205951-4). A discussion of the process of invention and some examples plus coverage of entries in a *Weekly Reader* invention contest. (Rev: BL 12/15/87; SLJ 3/88) [608]

12990 Thimmesh, Catherine. *Girls Think of Everything* (4–7). Illus. 2000, Houghton $16.00 (978-0-395-93744-0). A fresh, breezy account about women whose inventions include the windshield wiper, chocolate chip cookies, and Glo-paper. (Rev: BCCB 5/00; BL 3/15/00; HB 5–6/00; HBG 10/00; SLJ 4/00) [609.2]

12991 Vare, Ethlie Ann, and Greg Ptacek. *Women Inventors and Their Discoveries* (6–10). 1993, Oliver LB $19.95 (978-1-881508-06-9). A review of women who are known in the world of industry and technology for their unusual inventions. (Rev: BL 10/15/93; SLJ 1/94; VOYA 2/94) [609.2]

12992 Whiting, Jim. *James Watt and the Steam Engine* (5–8). Series: Uncharted, Unexplored, and Unexplained: Scientific Advancements of the 19th Century. 2006, Mitchell Lane LB $29.95 (978-1-58415-371-9). Brief biographical information about Watt is accompanied by a more detailed discussion of his invention and its importance. (Rev: SLJ 5/06) [621]

12993 Wilkinson, Philip, and Jacqueline Dineen. *Art and Technology Through the Ages* (5–8). Illus. Series: Ideas That Changed the World. 1995, Chelsea LB $14.95 (978-0-7910-2769-1). A survey of the evolution of art and communications, from cave paintings through advanced digital recording and computer graphics. (Rev: SLJ 11/95; VOYA 2/96) [501.4]

12994 Woodford, Chris. *Communication and Computers* (6–9). Illus. Series: History of Invention. 2004, Facts on File $35.00 (978-0-8160-5443-5). A slim introductory overview of advances in communications from prehistoric times to today, with maps, illustrations, and profiles of key figures. (Rev: SLJ 12/04)

12995 Woodford, Chris, et al. *Cool Stuff and How It Works* (8–12). Illus. 2005, DK $24.99 (978-0-7566-1465-2). The inner workings of products ranging from the digital camera to the microwave oven are explained in clear text with lots of bright, often high-tech illustrations. (Rev: BL 12/1/05) [600]

12996 Woodford, Chris, and Jon Woodcock. *Cool Stuff 2.0 and How It Works* (4–8). Illus. by Darren Awuah, et al. 2007, DK $24.99 (978-0-7566-3207-6). More than 100 new "cool" items are featured in this updated edition full of things that appeal to kids, such as robot cars and "silent flight" aircraft. (Rev: SLJ 3/08)

12997 Woods, Michael, and Mary B. Woods. *The History of Communication* (5–8). Series: Major Inventions Through History. 2005, Twenty-First Century LB $26.60 (978-0-8225-3807-3). An attractive look at developments through time in methods of communication — the printing press, telephone, radio, television, and the Internet — and the impact on our lives. (Rev: SLJ 1/06) [302.2]

Building and Construction

12998 Bial, Raymond. *The Houses* (4–8). Illus. Series: Building America. 2001, Marshall Cavendish LB $27.07 (978-0-7614-1335-6). A history of different types of housing in the United States that includes excellent photographs and drawings. (Rev: BL 3/1/02; HBG 3/02) [392.3]

12999 Boring, Mel. *Incredible Constructions: And the People Who Built Them* (4–7). Illus. 1985, Walker LB $13.85 (978-0-8027-6560-4). Hoover Dam, the Statue of Liberty, and other structures are featured in this history of engineering marvels. (Rev: BL 6/1/85; SLJ 8/86) [620]

13000 Caney, Steven. *Steven Caney's Ultimate Building Book* (4–8). Illus. by Lauren House. 2006, Running Pr. $29.95 (978-0-7624-0409-4). Starting with a history of construction and the basic techniques involved, Caney looks at the ways design and technology intersect and suggests a wide range of kid-tested building projects. (Rev: SLJ 1/07*) [624]

13001 Donovan, Sandy. *The Channel Tunnel* (4–7). Series: Great Building Feats. 2003, Lerner LB $27.93 (978-0-8225-4692-4). Using many black-and-white illustrations, diagrams, and maps, this is the exciting story of the underwater engineering marvel that links England and France. (Rev: BL 11/15/03; HBG 10/03; SLJ 11/03) [624.1]

13002 Dreyer, Francis. *Lighthouses* (4–7). Photos by Philip Plisson. 2005, Abrams $18.95 (978-0-8109-5958-3). A fascinating and strikingly beautiful overview of lighthouses — of the past and present — and of the courage and loneliness of the men and women who tend them. (Rev: BL 1/1–15/06) [387.1]

13003 DuTemple, Lesley A. *The Hoover Dam* (4–7). Series: Great Building Feats. 2003, Lerner LB $27.93 (978-0-8225-4691-7). This story traces the dam's construction from the planning stages through its technically difficult and dangerous construction and places this impressive structure in historical context. (Rev: BL 11/15/03; HBG 10/03; SLJ 11/03) [627]

13004 DuTemple, Lesley A. *The Panama Canal* (6–9). Series: Great Building Feats. 2002, Lerner LB $27.93 (978-0-8225-0079-7). An attractive and absorbing overview of this massive and challenging project. (Rev: HBG 10/03; LMC 2/03; SLJ 1/03*) [972.87]

13005 Gonzales, Doreen. *Seven Wonders of the Modern World* (4–7). Illus. Series: Seven Wonders of the World. 2005, Enslow LB $25.26 (978-0-7660-5292-5). Profiles seven marvels of modern construction, including the Panama Canal, Toronto's CN Tower, and the Empire State Building in New York City; the text is extended by constantly updated links to Web sites. (Rev: SLJ 11/05)

13006 Greene, Meg. *The Eiffel Tower* (5–8). Series: Building World Landmarks. 2004, Gale LB $24.95 (978-1-56711-315-0). The story of the construction of the Eiffel Tower, which when completed in 1899 was the tallest human-made structure in the world. (Rev: SLJ 7/04) [725]

13007 Kirkwood, Jon. *The Fantastic Cutaway Book of Giant Buildings* (4–7). Illus. 1997, Millbrook paper $9.95 (978-0-7613-0629-0). Using double-page spreads, outstanding graphics, and many fact boxes, this book features a wide variety of structures including the Statue of Liberty, the pyramids, the Colosseum, churches, operas houses, Grand Central Station, Munich's Olympic stadium, and skyscrapers. (Rev: BL 4/1/98; HBG 10/98) [720]

13008 Korres, Manolis. *The Stones of the Parthenon* (7–12). Trans. by D. Turner. Illus. 2001, Getty paper $14.95 (978-0-89236-607-1). The construction of the Parthenon is described in text and detailed drawings in this small-format book, which includes notes, a glossary, and a bibliography. (Rev: BL 2/1/01) [622]

13009 Macaulay, David. *Building Big* (7–12). Illus. 2000, Houghton $30.00 (978-0-395-96331-9). This companion book to a set of videos explains the problems posed by ambitious construction projects such as tunnels, bridges, dams, domes, and skyscrapers. (Rev: BL 12/15/00*; HB 1–2/01; HBG 3/01; SLJ 11/00; VOYA 4/01) [720]

13010 Macaulay, David. *Unbuilding* (5–8). Illus. by author. 1980, Houghton $19.00 (978-0-395-29457-4); paper $6.95 (978-0-395-45360-5). A book that explores the concept of tearing down the Empire State Building.

13011 Macaulay, David. *Underground* (5–10). Illus. by author. 1983, Houghton $19.00 (978-0-395-24739-6); paper $9.95 (978-0-395-34065-3). An exploration in text and detailed drawings of the intricate network of systems under city streets. [624]

13012 Mann, Elizabeth. *The Brooklyn Bridge* (4–7). Illus. Series: Wonders of the World. 1996, Mikaya $19.95 (978-0-9650493-0-6). The story of the building of the Brooklyn Bridge is told through the eyes of a family. (Rev: BL 2/1/97; SLJ 6/97*) [624]

13013 Mattern, Joanne. *The Chunnel* (5–8). Series: Building World Landmarks. 2004, Gale LB $24.95 (978-1-56711-301-3). The story of the long delays and eventual construction of the tunnel under the English Channel, linking England and France, with a focus on the new technology involved. (Rev: SLJ 7/04) [624.1]

13014 Owens, Thomas S. *Football Stadiums* (5–8). Illus. Series: Sports Palaces. 2001, Millbrook LB $25.90 (978-0-7613-1764-7). Rather than highlighting individual stadiums, this book covers general topics such as their design, replacement, funding, amenities, and history. (Rev: BL 4/1/01; HBG 10/01; SLJ 4/01) [796.332]

13015 Severance, John B. *Skyscrapers: How America Grew Up* (5–9). Illus. 2000, Holiday $18.95 (978-0-8234-1492-5). Beginning with an explanation of the architectural breakthroughs that made the building of skyscrapers possible, this account traces the construction of these buildings from 1851 to the end of the 20th century. (Rev: BL 6/1–15/00; HB 9–10/00; HBG 10/00; SLJ 7/00; VOYA 4/01) [720]

13016 Sullivan, George. *Built to Last: Building America's Amazing Bridges, Dams, Tunnels, and Skyscrapers* (5–8). Illus. 2005, Scholastic $18.99 (978-0-439-51737-9). Seventeen marvels of American engineering — including the Erie Canal, Hoover Dam, Brooklyn Bridge, and Boston's "Big Dig" — are presented in chronological chapters with good illustrations and fact boxes that add historical and technological context. (Rev: BL 12/1/05; SLJ 3/06*; VOYA 8/06) [624]

13017 Vogel, Jennifer. *A Library Story: Building a New Central Library* (4–7). 2006, Lerner $26.60 (978-0-8225-5916-0). The construction of the new central library in Minneapolis is the topic of this lively, well-illustrated book that looks at the reasons for the building, architectural and engineering concerns, and artistic choices that were made. (Rev: BL 8/06; SLJ 9/06) [727]

13018 Woods, Mary B., and Michael Woods. *Ancient Construction: From Tents to Towers* (5–8). Illus. Series: Ancient Technologies. 2000, Runestone LB $25.26 (978-0-8225-2998-9). From Stonehenge and the Colosseum to the Eiffel Tower and the Golden Gate Bridge, this is a history of building and construction. (Rev: BL 9/15/00; HBG 3/01; SLJ 1/01) [720]

13019 Yuan, Margaret Speaker. *The Royal Gorge Bridge* (5–8). Series: Building World Landmarks. 2004, Gale LB $24.95 (978-1-56711-352-5). Examines the engineering and construction challenges involved in the 1929 construction of Colorado's Royal Gorge Bridge. (Rev: SLJ 7/04) [624.2]

Clothing, Textiles, and Jewelry

13020 Bell, Alison. *Fearless Fashion* (6–10). Illus. 2005, Lobster paper $14.95 (978-1-894222-86-0). From preppy to punk to goth to boho, this volume analyzes seven hot fashion trends, looks at trends in history, and gives tips on developing one's own style. (Rev: SLJ 3/05) [391]

13021 Hoobler, Dorothy, and Thomas Hoobler. *Vanity Rules: A History of American Fashion and Beauty* (5–8). Illus. 2000, Twenty-First Century LB $28.90 (978-0-7613-1258-1). From the painted bodies of early Native Americans to today's body piercing, this is a history of the quest for personal beauty in America. (Rev: BL 4/1/00; HBG 10/00; SLJ 5/00) [391]

13022 Kyi, Tanya L. *The Blue Jean Book: The Story Behind the Seams* (6–9). Illus. 2005, Annick $24.95 (978-1-55037-917-4); paper $12.95 (978-1-55037-916-7). The colorful history of blue jeans — and their cultural and economic impact — is chronicled in this accessible volume. (Rev: BL 11/1/05; SLJ 1/06; VOYA 4/06) [391]

13023 Lawlor, Laurie. *Where Will This Shoe Take You? A Walk Through the History of Footwear* (5–8). Illus. 1996, Walker LB $18.85 (978-0-8027-8435-3). This is a history of footwear, from sandals worn by the ancients to the sneakers popular today. (Rev: BCCB 1/97; BL 11/15/96; SLJ 5/97; VOYA 6/97) [391]

13024 MacFarlane, Katherine. *The Jeweler's Art* (7–12). Series: Eye on Art. 2007, Gale LB $32.45

(978-1-59018-984-9). This book reviews the history of jewelry from ancient times through the Renaissance, Baroque and Rococo periods to the Victorians and Edwardians and contemporary styles and techniques. (Rev: LMC 2/08; SLJ 12/07) [739.27]

13025 Miller, Brandon M. *Dressed for the Occasion: What Americans Wore, 1620–1970* (5–8). 1999, Lerner LB $30.35 (978-0-8225-1738-2). A fascinating look at men's and women's fashions throughout history and how they reflect society's culture and values. (Rev: BCCB 5/99; BL 4/1/99; SLJ 9/99) [391]

13026 Ruby, Jennifer. *Underwear* (7–12). Series: Costumes in Context. 1996, Batsford $24.95 (978-0-7134-7663-7). This is a thoughtful, information-filled, illustrated history of underwear from 1066 through the 1990s. (Rev: SLJ 1/97) [646]

13027 Shaskan, Kathy. *How Underwear Got Under There: A Brief History* (5–8). Illus. by Regan Dunnick. 2007, Dutton $16.99 (978-0-525-47178-3). Shaskan takes a lighthearted look at the history of nether garments, looking at their various roles (protection, warmth, modesty, support, and so forth) and at changes in fashion and social attitudes; a lack of sources makes this most suitable for browsing. (Rev: BCCB 9/07; LMC 11-12/07; SLJ 8/07) [391.4]

13028 Smith, Elizabeth Simpson. *Cloth* (5–8). Illus. 1985, Walker LB $10.85 (978-0-8027-6577-2). The discovery of fiber and how cloth is made. (Rev: BL 8/85; SLJ 11/85) [677.02864]

13029 Tythacott, Louise. *Jewelry* (4–8). Illus. Series: Traditions Around the World. 1995, Thomson Learning LB $24.26 (978-1-56847-229-4). A history of jewelry, why it is worn, and the variety of materials and designs used. (Rev: SLJ 7/95) [739.27]

13030 Weaver, Janice. *From Head to Toe: Bound Feet, Bathing Suits, and Other Bizarre and Beautiful Things* (5–8). Illus. by Francis Blake. 2003, Tundra paper $16.95 (978-0-88776-654-1). History and culture are interwoven in this account of fashion fads over the years, mostly in the West. (Rev: SLJ 2/04) [391]

Computers, Automation, and the Internet

13031 Allman, Toney. *Internet Predators* (6–9). Illus. Series: Ripped from the Headlines. 2007, Erickson LB $23.95 (978-1-60217-000-1). Straightforward and practical advice about how to avoid the scary stuff that can happen to young people who surf the wrong sites and trust the wrong people on the Internet. (Rev: BL 4/1/07) [364.16]

13032 Baker, Christopher W. *Robots Among Us: The Challenges and Promises of Robotics* (5–8). Illus. Series: New Century Technology. 2002, Millbrook LB $23.90 (978-0-7613-1969-6). A lavishly illustrated account that describes the science of robotics, current developments, and what might be expected in the future. (Rev: BL 6/1–15/02; HBG 10/02; SLJ 9/02) [629.8]

13033 Baker, Christopher W. *Scientific Visualization: The New Eyes of Science* (5–8). Illus. Series: New Century Technology. 2000, Millbrook LB $23.90 (978-0-7613-1351-9). This book explores the ways in which computers enable scientists to study the universe and simulate events such as the creation of a black hole. (Rev: BL 4/1/00; HBG 3/01; SLJ 6/00) [507.2]

13034 Billings, Charlene W. *Supercomputers: Shaping the Future* (7–12). Series: Science Sourcebooks. 1995, Facts on File $25.00 (978-0-8160-3096-5). A history of the silicon revolution — focusing on the megamachines that are the most powerful computers in the world. (Rev: BL 10/15/95; SLJ 4/96; VOYA 4/96) [004.1]

13035 Billings, Charlene W., and Sean M. Grady. *Supercomputers: Charting the Future of Cybernetics*. Rev. ed. (8–12). Illus. Series: Science and Technology in Focus. 2004, Facts on File $35.00 (978-0-8160-4730-7). This revised and expanded edition covers the history of computing devices from ancient clay tablets onward and looks forward to the future potential of optical and quantum computers. (Rev: SLJ 6/04) [004.1]

13036 Bingham, Jane. *Internet Freedom: Where Is the Limit?* (5–8). Series: Behind the News. 2006, Heinemann LB $32.86 (978-1-4034-8833-6). Short news stories highlight the problems involved in the freedom we find on the Internet and chapters discuss how to evaluate the stories behind the news and the pros and cons of Internet regulation. (Rev: SLJ 4/07)

13037 Brooks, Sheldon. *Everything You Need to Know About Romance and the Internet: How to Stay Safe* (6–9). Series: Need to Know Library. 2001, Rosen LB $25.25 (978-0-8239-3399-0). Newcomers to the Internet will find solid, easily read advice on using chat rooms, email, and online dating services, with warnings about cyberstalkers and about meeting correspondents in person. (Rev: SLJ 9/01; VOYA 2/03) [025.04]

13038 Burns, Michael. *Digital Fantasy Painting: A Step-by-Step Guide to Creating Visionary Art on Your Computer* (7–12). Illus. 2002, Watson-Guptill paper $24.95 (978-0-8230-1574-0). Eye-catching illustrations make this an attractive volume for browsing as well as for use as a manual of graphic design. (Rev: SLJ 3/03; VOYA 2/03) [760]

13039 Chorlton, Windsor. *The Invention of the Silicon Chip: A Revolution in Daily Life* (5–8). Series: Point of Impact. 2002, Heinemann LB $25.64 (978-1-58810-554-7). Chorlton explores computers before and after the invention of the chip, introduces key players in the field, and discusses the impact of this new technology on society. (Rev: SLJ 9/02) [621.3815]

13040 Cothran, Helen, ed. *The Internet* (7–12). Illus. Series: Opposing Viewpoints. 2002, Gale LB $32.45 (978-0-7377-0780-9); paper $21.20 (978-0-7377-0779-3). Essays present conflicting opinions on such topics as the value of the Internet as an educational resource, privacy, and the social benefits/disadvantages of the technology. (Rev: SLJ 8/02) [303.48]

13041 de la Bédoyère, Guy. *The First Computers* (6–9). Illus. Series: Milestones in Modern Science. 2005, World Almanac LB $31.00 (978-0-8368-5854-9). Suitable for reports, this volume provides a good overview of the development of the first computers and the possibilities these offered. (Rev: SLJ 1/06) [004.6]

13042 Fritz, Sandy. *Robotics and Artificial Intelligence* (5–10). Illus. Series: Hot Science. 2003, Smart Apple LB $28.50 (978-1-58340-364-8). After describing robots' contributions in space, in the workplace, in danger spots, and in medicine, Fritz speculates on the future possibilities. (Rev: BL 12/1/03; HBG 4/04; SLJ 4/04) [629.8]

13043 German, Dave. *Dave Gorman's Googlewhack! Adventure* (8–12). Illus. 2004, Overlook $24.95 (978-1-58567-614-9). Gorman, a British stand-up comic, writes about his global quest to find googlewhacks — two-word Google search queries that yield a single, solitary hit — in the process of which he successfully put off writing a contracted novel. (Rev: BL 9/15/04) [910.4]

13044 Gordon, Sherri Mabry. *Downloading Copyrighted Stuff from the Internet: Stealing or Fair Use?* (7–10). Illus. Series: Issues in Focus Today. 2005, Enslow LB $31.93 (978-0-7660-2164-8). In concise, accessible text, Gordon defines fair use and copyright and examines issues involving downloading of text, music, games, and so forth. (Rev: BL 11/1/05; SLJ 11/05) [346.730]

13045 Graham, Ian. *The Internet: The Impact on Our Lives* (6–10). Illus. Series: 21st Century Debates. 2001, Raintree LB $27.12 (978-0-7398-3173-1). An absorbing and fact-filled overview of the influence of the Internet on politics and society, with material on issues such as censorship, e-business, and e-crime. (Rev: SLJ 11/01; VOYA 10/01) [303.48]

13046 Graham, Ian. *Internet Revolution* (7–10). Illus. Series: Science at the Edge. 2002, Heinemann LB $27.86 (978-1-4034-0325-4). The author traces the history of the Internet, looks at the ways we use it today, and discusses political and privacy issues. (Rev: HBG 3/03; SLJ 1/03) [004.67]

13047 Henderson, Harry. *The Internet* (6–9). Illus. Series: Overview. 1998, Lucent LB $29.95 (978-1-56006-215-8). A survey of the history of the Net, its uses, its impact on our way of life, and problems and controversies associated with it. (Rev: BL 9/1/98; SLJ 8/98) [004.678]

13048 Herumin, Wendy. *Censorship on the Internet: From Filters to Freedom of Speech* (5–12). Series: Issues in Focus. 2004, Enslow LB $26.60 (978-0-7660-1946-1). A look at the various ways we restrict the free exchange of information over the Internet and the pros and cons of doing so. (Rev: SLJ 4/04) [303.48]

13049 Jefferis, David. *Artificial Intelligence: Robotics and Machine Evolution* (5–7). Series: Megatech. 1999, Crabtree paper $8.95 (978-0-7787-0056-2). This is a survey of the variety of robotic devices in use at the end of the 20th century, some of the advances that are being made, and a glimpse into the future. (Rev: SLJ 9/99) [004]

13050 Jefferis, David. *Internet: Electronic Global Village* (4–8). Illus. Series: Megatech. 2001, Crabtree paper $8.95 (978-0-7787-0062-3). An eye-catching look at the development of the Internet and the World Wide Web and their uses in communication and commerce. (Rev: SLJ 6/02) [4.678]

13051 Jones, David. *Mighty Robots: Mechanical Marvels That Fascinate and Frighten* (5–8). Illus. 2006, Annick $24.95 (978-1-55037-929-7); paper $14.95 (978-1-55037-928-0). Artificial intelligence, mobility, and various robot roles are discussed in this look at the past, present, and future of robots. (Rev: BL 2/1/06) [629.8]

13052 Judson, Karen. *Computer Crime: Phreaks, Spies, and Salami Slicers* (6–10). Illus. Series: Issues in Focus. 2000, Enslow LB $26.60 (978-0-7660-1243-1). All kinds of cybercrimes are discussed including hacking, viruses, and computer fraud. (Rev: BL 3/15/00; HBG 9/00) [364.16]

13053 Knittel, John, and Michael Soto. *Everything You Need to Know About the Dangers of Computer Hacking* (5–8). Illus. 2000, Rosen LB $25.25 (978-0-8239-3034-0). This book points out the differences between a hacker and a cracker and, through this, discusses beneficial and harmful computer actions and how to avoid the latter. (Rev: BL 4/1/00; SLJ 5/00) [364.16]

13054 Lawler, Jennifer. *Cyberdanger and Internet Safety: A Hot Issue* (5–10). Series: Hot Issues. 2000, Enslow LB $27.93 (978-0-7660-1368-1). As well as introducing the Internet, this account explains how people abuse it with hidden identities, threatening or obscene material, loss of privacy, hacking, con tricks, pranks, and hoaxes. (Rev: HBG 3/01; SLJ 1/01; VOYA 4/01) [004.6]

13055 Lindsay, Dave. *Dave's Quick 'n' Easy Web Pages 2: A Guide to Creating Multi-page Web Sites* (6–10). Illus. by Sean Lindsay. 2004, Erin paper $11.95 (978-0-9690609-9-4). Readers with little prior knowledge will learn such techniques as creating frames and cascading style sheets as this straightforward title introduces concepts clearly with graphics and advice boxes. (Rev: SLJ 11/04) [005.7]

13056 Lindsay, Dave. *Dave's Quick 'n' Easy Web Pages: An Introductory Guide to Creating Web Sites*. 2nd ed. (5–9). Illus. by Sean Lindsay. 2001, Erin $11.95 (978-0-9690609-8-7). Young Dave, Webmaster of the popular Redwall site, gives good, basic information on HTML coding and Web page design. (Rev: SLJ 8/01) [005.7]

13057 McCormick, Anita Louise. *The Internet: Surfing the Issues* (5–10). Series: Issues in Focus. 1998, Enslow LB $26.60 (978-0-89490-956-6). A guide to the history, mechanics, and use of the Internet that also covers such topics as surfing, child pornography, hate groups, and censorship. (Rev: BL 10/1/98; SLJ 12/98) [004]

13058 MacDonald, Joan Vos. *Cybersafety: Surfing Safely Online* (5–7). Illus. Series: Teen Issues. 2001, Enslow LB $22.60 (978-0-7660-1580-7). Various dangers of venturing online are covered, from viruses and other problems that can infect your computer to activities such as hacking, cyberstalking, and copying software illegally. (Rev: HBG 3/02; SLJ 12/01) [004.6]

13059 Marshall, Elizabeth L. *A Student's Guide to the Internet*. Rev. ed. (6–9). 2001, Twenty-First Century LB $24.90 (978-0-7613-1661-9). This updated edition of a user-friendly guide to accessing the Internet for research and collaborative projects gives plenty of Web sites to explore. (Rev: HBG 10/02; SLJ 1/02; VOYA 2/02) [004.67]

13060 Menhard, Francha Roffe. *Internet Issues: Pirates, Censors, and Cybersquatters* (6–12). Illus. Series: Issues in Focus. 2001, Enslow LB $26.60 (978-0-7660-1687-3). Menhard's effective overview of problems concerning filtering, copyright, privacy, and piracy uses clear examples, many of which involve young people. (Rev: BL 2/1/02; HBG 10/02; SLJ 2/02) [384.3]

13061 Otfinoski, Steven. *Computers* (6–9). Illus. Series: Great Inventions. 2007, Marshall Cavendish LB $27.95 (978-0-7614-2597-7). This history of computers is told in accessible, interesting text with effective illustrations and details of key personalities. (Rev: BL 12/15/07) [004]

13062 Perry, Robert L. *Personal Computer Communications* (4–7). Illus. Series: Watts Library: Computer Science. 2000, Watts paper $8.95 (978-0-531-

16483-9). This work covers such topics as modems, networks, satellite and wireless technology, and the future of communications. (Rev: BL 10/15/00) [004.16]

13063 Rooney, Anne. *Computers: Faster, Smaller, and Smarter* (5–9). Illus. Series: The Cutting Edge. 2005, Heinemann LB $32.86 (978-1-4034-7426-1). Looks at the technology behind computers of the past, present, and future; a high-tech design completes the package. (Rev: SLJ 6/06) [004]

13064 Rothman, Kevin F. *Coping with Dangers on the Internet: Staying Safe On-Line* (7–12). Series: Coping. 2001, Rosen LB $31.95 (978-0-8239-3201-6). Readers will find practical advice on safe use of Web sites, e-mail, chat rooms, newsgroups, and so forth, with a useful list of acronyms and emoticons. (Rev: SLJ 8/01) [025.04]

13065 Selfridge, Benjamin, and Peter Selfridge. *A Kid's Guide to Creating Web Pages for Home and School* (5–10). Illus. 2004, Chicago Review paper $19.95 (978-1-56976-180-9). Simple instructions on creating Web pages using HTML are accompanied by helpful illustrations and sample finished pages. (Rev: SLJ 2/05) [005.7]

13066 Skurzynski, Gloria. *Robots: Your High-Tech World* (4–7). Illus. 1990, Macmillan LB $16.95 (978-0-02-782917-4). An overview of robotics and history and an explanation of how robots work. (Rev: BL 11/15/90; HB 1–2/91; SLJ 9/90) [629.8]

13067 Spangenburg, Ray, and Kit Moser. *Savvy Surfing on the Internet: Searching and Evaluating Web Sites* (5–8). Illus. Series: Issues in Focus. 2001, Enslow LB $26.60 (978-0-7660-1590-6). Readers are encouraged to view much of the information on the Internet with healthy suspicion and are given advice on efficient searching for and assessment of Web sites. (Rev: HBG 3/02; SLJ 12/01) [004.6]

13068 Thomas, Peggy. *Artificial Intelligence* (5–8). Illus. Series: Lucent Library of Science and Technology. 2005, Gale LB $29.95 (978-1-59018-437-0). An interesting overview of progress in efforts to create machines that can think like humans. (Rev: BL 1/05) [004]

13069 Thro, Ellen. *Robotics: The Marriage of Computers and Machines* (7–12). Series: Science Sourcebooks. 1993, Facts on File $25.00 (978-0-8160-2628-9). Presents this complicated subject in interesting, understandable terms, covering artificial intelligence and the use of robots underground, in factories, and in space exploration. (Rev: BL 7/93) [629.8]

13070 Trumbauer, Lisa. *Homework Help for Kids on the Net* (4–8). Series: Cool Sites. 2000, Millbrook LB $17.90 (978-0-7613-1655-8). This useful book lists and describes key sites covering general reference, math, language arts, history, geography, and science. (Rev: HBG 10/00; SLJ 7/00) [004]

13071 Weber, Sandra. *The Internet* (7–10). Series: Transforming Power of Technology. 2003, Chelsea House LB $30.00 (978-0-7910-7449-7). A look at the influence of the Internet on areas ranging from the economy to society to health care and at the implications for schools and libraries. (Rev: SLJ 6/04) [004.6]

13072 Weiss, Ann E. *Virtual Reality: A Door to Cyberspace* (7–12). Illus. 1996, Twenty-First Century LB $26.90 (978-0-8050-3722-7). This book describes the development of virtual reality and its accomplishments, applications, and uses, as well as the ethical issues surrounding its development. (Rev: BL 5/15/96*; SLJ 7/96; VOYA 10/96) [006]

13073 Williams, Brian. *Computers* (5–8). Illus. Series: Great Inventions. 2001, Heinemann LB $25.64 (978-1-58810-210-2). A chronological look at computers and their predecessors, from the abacus onward, with diagrams and information on the inventors. (Rev: HBG 3/02; SLJ 2/02) [004]

13074 Winters, Paul A. *Computers and Society* (7–12). Series: Current Controversies. 1997, Greenhaven LB $32.45 (978-1-56510-564-5). The articles in this anthology discuss the impact of computers on society and education, as well as problems involving privacy and censorship. (Rev: BL 7/97; SLJ 12/97) [303.48]

13075 Wolinsky, Art. *Communicating on the Internet* (4–8). Series: The Internet Library. 1999, Enslow LB $22.60 (978-0-7660-1260-8). This book on how to communicate safely and effectively on the Internet includes material on e-mail problems, computer etiquette, chat rooms, and newsgroups. (Rev: HBG 3/00; SLJ 3/00) [004]

13076 Wolinsky, Art. *Creating and Publishing Web Pages on the Internet* (4–8). Series: The Internet Library. 1999, Enslow LB $22.60 (978-0-7660-1262-2). Using many example Web pages, this book gives practical advice on how to create an interesting, well-organized, safe Web page with links to sites for further information. (Rev: HBG 10/00; SLJ 3/00) [004]

13077 Wolinsky, Art. *The History of the Internet and the World Wide Web* (5–9). Illus. Series: Internet Library. 1999, Enslow LB $22.60 (978-0-7660-1261-5). This volume explains how the Internet evolved during the Cold War and how it transfers and distributes information. (Rev: BL 12/15/99; HBG 3/00; SLJ 1/00; VOYA 2/00) [004.67]

13078 Wolinsky, Art. *Internet Power Research Using the Big6 Approach* (4–8). Illus. Series: The Internet Library. 2002, Enslow LB $22.60 (978-0-7660-2094-8). Readers accompany young researchers as they conduct searches using the Big6 method. (Rev: HBG 3/03; SLJ 12/02) [025.04]

13079 Wolinsky, Art. *Locating and Evaluating Information on the Internet* (5–9). Illus. 1999,

Enslow LB $22.60 (978-0-7660-1259-2). As well as directions on how to complete successful searches on the Internet, this work tells how to determine the usefulness and credibility of Web pages. (Rev: BL 12/15/99; HBG 3/00; SLJ 1/00; VOYA 2/00) [025.04]

13080 Wolinsky, Art. *Safe Surfing on the Internet* (4–8). Illus. 2003, Enslow LB $22.60 (978-0-7660-2030-6). Wolinksy presents information on safe use of the Internet and topics including proper use of language, copyright, privacy, and plagiarism. (Rev: HBG 10/03; LMC 8–9/03; SLJ 7/03) [004.67]

13081 Woodford, Chris. *Digital Technology* (4–7). Series: Science in Focus. 2006, Chelsea House LB $27.00 (978-0-7910-8861-6). A clear introduction to the world of digital technology, covering topics including smart cards, computer-aided design, mobile phones, and so forth in easy-to-understand language. (Rev: BL 10/15/06) [621.381]

13082 Wright, David. *Computers* (5–8). Series: Inventors and Inventions. 1995, Benchmark LB $25.64 (978-0-7614-0064-6). A look at the development of the computer, with brief profiles of important people in its history and an examination of the uses of computers in the world today. (Rev: SLJ 6/96) [004]

Electronics

13083 Bridgman, Roger. *Electronics* (4–8). Illus. Series: Eyewitness Science. 1993, DK LB $15.95 (978-1-56458-325-3). The field of electronics is introduced through full-color graphics, 3-D models, and detailed captions that explain important experiments, equipment, and concepts. (Rev: BL 11/15/93; SLJ 12/93) [621.38]

13084 Oxlade, Chris. *Electronics: MP3s, TVs, and DVDs* (5–9). Illus. Series: The Cutting Edge. 2005, Heinemann LB $32.86 (978-1-4034-7427-8). Looks at the technology behind popular electronic devices and at predictions about gadgets of the future; a high-tech design completes the package. (Rev: SLJ 6/06)

13085 Traister, John E., and Robert J. Traister. *Encyclopedic Dictionary of Electronic Terms* (7–12). Illus. 1984, Prentice Hall $18.95 (978-0-13-276981-5). All of the basic terms in electronics are explained, usually in fairly simple terms. [621.381]

Telecommunications

13086 Byers, Ann. *Communications Satellites* (5–9). Series: The Library of Satellites. 2003, Rosen LB

$26.50 (978-0-8239-3851-3). From the first important communications satellites launched in 1962, this account traces the growth of this technology and its possible future developments. (Rev: BL 11/15/03; SLJ 1/04) [001.51]

13087 Fisher, Trevor. *Communications* (7–9). Illus. 1985, Batsford $19.95 (978-0-7134-4631-9). This is a clear history of communication from the development of language to today's sophisticated telecommunications networks. (Rev: SLJ 2/86) [302.2]

13088 Gardner, Robert. *Communication* (6–9). Illus. Series: Yesterday's Science, Today's Technology. 1994, Twenty-First Century LB $25.90 (978-0-8050-2854-6). Today's electronic methods of communication are introduced with about 20 activities that would make good science fair projects. (Rev: BL 3/15/95) [303.48]

13089 Hegedus, Alannah, and Kaitlin Rainey. *Bleeps and Blips to Rocket Ships: Great Inventions in Communications* (5–9). Illus. by Bill Slavin. 2001, Tundra paper $17.95 (978-0-88776-452-3). This is a fact-packed and appealing look at the field of communications, with information on history and inventors and inventions as well as suggested activities. (Rev: SLJ 8/01) [609.71]

13090 McCormick, Anita Louise. *The Invention of the Telegraph and Telephone* (7–10). Series: In American History. 2004, Enslow LB $26.60 (978-0-7660-1841-9). The story behind these two great inventions and their impact on society are covered in this volume. (Rev: BL 3/15/04) [621]

13091 Maddison, Simon. *Telecoms: Present Knowledge, Future Trends* (5–9). Illus. Series: 21st Century Science. 2003, Smart Apple Media LB $27.10 (978-1-58340-352-5). Numerous diagrams, photographs, and drawings add to this overview of the history of telecommunications and the status of current technology. (Rev: SLJ 1/04) [384]

13092 Streissguth, Thomas. *Communications: Sending the Message* (5–8). Series: Innovators. 1997, Oliver LB $21.95 (978-1-881508-41-0). A compact, easy-to-understand history of communication from earliest times, through Gutenberg, Edison, and Marconi, to the present "information highway." (Rev: SLJ 2/98) [001.51]

13093 Winters, Paul A., ed. *The Information Revolution* (8–12). Series: Opposing Viewpoints. 1998, Greenhaven LB $32.45 (978-1-56510-801-1); paper $28.75 (978-1-56510-800-4). This anthology of essays explores issues raised by the advances in telecommunication technology via the telephone, television, and computer, and discusses the impact of these advances on society and education. (Rev: BL 6/1–15/98) [384]

Television, Motion Pictures, Radio, and Recording

13094 Abraham, Philip. *Television and Movies* (4–7). Illus. Series: American Pop Culture. 2004, Children's Pr. LB $24.50 (978-0-516-24074-9); paper $6.95 (978-0-516-25946-8). Traces the technological and cultural development of TV and movies in the United States. (Rev: SLJ 1/05)

13095 Hamilton, Jake. *Special Effects: In Film and Television* (4–8). Illus. 1998, DK $17.95 (978-0-7849-2813-4). This is an intriguing glimpse at special effects in film and television, using double-page spreads that each focus on a different aspect of production, such as storyboards, makeup, and stunts. (Rev: BCCB 9/98; BL 8/98; VOYA 10/98) [791.43]

13096 Oleksy, Walter. *Entertainment* (6–12). Series: Information Revolution. 1996, Facts on File $25.00 (978-0-8160-3077-4). An exploration of the revolutionary changes in the entertainment industry, including satellite TV broadcasting, digital widescreen TV, laser disc players, interactive CD-ROMs, and computer movies. (Rev: BL 2/15/96; SLJ 4/96; VOYA 10/96) [621]

13097 Petley, Julian. *The Media: The Impact on Our Lives* (6–10). Series: 21st Century Debates. 2001, Raintree LB $27.12 (978-0-7398-3175-5). An absorbing and fact-filled overview of the various forms of media — from newspapers, radio and TV, and film to commercial advertising — and their influence on politics and society. (Rev: SLJ 11/01) [302.23]

13098 Spilsbury, Richard. *Cartoons and Animation* (4–7). Illus. Series: Art off the Wall. 2006, Heinemann LB $23.00 (978-1-4034-8287-7). Surveys the history, techniques, and movie applications of cartooning and animation, and includes bold color illustrations of familiar characters and animators at work. (Rev: BL 1/1–15/07; SLJ 5/07) [741.5]

13099 Torr, James D., ed. *Violence in Film and Television* (6–12). Series: Examining Pop Culture. 2002, Gale $36.20 (978-0-7377-0865-3); paper $24.95 (978-0-7377-0864-6). This collection of essays examines the evolution of violence in television, movies, and video games. (Rev: BL 4/1/02; SLJ 3/02) [303.6]

Transportation

General and Miscellaneous

13100 Bial, Raymond. *The Canals* (4–8). Illus. Series: Building America. 2001, Marshall Cavendish LB $27.07 (978-0-7614-1336-3). This history of the

U.S. canal system and how it works includes excellent photographs and illustrations that help to explain the technical aspects of canals. (Rev: BL 3/1/02; HBG 3/02; SLJ 2/02*) [386]

13101 DuTemple, Lesley A. *New York Subways* (4–7). Illus. Series: Great Building Feats. 2003, Lerner LB $27.93 (978-0-8225-0378-1). DuTemple presents the history of the subway system with details of its difficult construction, continuing financial problems, and the damage caused in the destruction of the World Trade Center. (Rev: BL 1/1–15/03; HBG 10/03) [388.4]

13102 *Go! The Whole World of Transportation* (5–10). Illus. 2006, DK $26.99 (978-0-7566-2224-4). This wide-ranging, visually fascinating journey through the world of transportation touches on everything from buses and ferries to speedboats and fighter jets. (Rev: SLJ 2/07*) [388]

13103 Hamilton, John. *Transportation: A Pictorial History of the Past One Thousand Years* (4–7). Illus. Series: The Millennium. 2000, ABDO LB $25.65 (978-1-57765-361-5). A history of 1,000 years of transportation that includes animals, ships, trains, bicycles, motorcycles, cars, airplanes, and spacecraft. (Rev: BL 7/00; HBG 10/00; SLJ 10/00) [388.21]

13104 Herbst, Judith. *The History of Transportation* (5–8). Series: Major Inventions Through History. 2005, Twenty-First Century LB $26.60 (978-0-8225-2496-0). From the wheel to the airplane, technological innovations involving transport have had a profound impact on our lives as shown in this attractive, well-written volume. (Rev: SLJ 2/06) [973]

13105 Wilkinson, Philip, and Jacqueline Dineen. *Transportation* (5–8). Illus. 1995, Chelsea LB $21.95 (978-0-7910-2768-4). An informative, simple overview of inventions and changes that created the modern transportation systems of today. (Rev: VOYA 2/96) [629]

13106 Williams, Harriet. *Road and Rail Transportation* (6–9). Illus. Series: History of Invention. 2004, Facts on File $35.00 (978-0-8160-5437-4). A slim introductory overview of advances in transportation from prehistoric times to today, with maps, illustrations, and profiles of key figures. (Rev: SLJ 12/04) [629]

13107 Woodford, Chris. *Air and Space Travel* (6–9). Illus. Series: History of Invention. 2004, Facts on File $35.00 (978-0-8160-5436-7). A slim introductory overview of advances in aviation and space travel, with illustrations, and profiles of key figures. (Rev: SLJ 12/04)

13108 Woodford, Chris. *Ships and Submarines* (6–9). Illus. Series: History of Invention. 2004, Facts on File $35.00 (978-0-8160-5439-8). A slim introductory overview of advances in waterborne transport from prehistoric times to today, with maps, illustrations, and profiles of key figures. (Rev: SLJ 12/04)

Airplanes, Aeronautics, and Ballooning

13109 Berliner, Don. *Aviation: Reaching for the Sky* (5–8). Illus. Series: Innovators. 1997, Oliver LB $21.95 (978-1-881508-33-5). A thorough history of aviation, beginning with early hot-air balloons and dirigibles and continuing through the Wright Brothers and Sikorsky's helicopter to supersonic jets. (Rev: BL 5/1/97; SLJ 7/97) [629.133]

13110 Carson, Mary Kay. *The Wright Brothers for Kids: How They Invented the Airplane: 21 Activities Exploring the Science and History of Flight* (4–8). Illus. by Laura D'Argo. 2003, Chicago Review paper $14.95 (978-1-55652-477-6). After an account of the achievements of the Wrights and other early airplane enthusiasts, 21 activities allow readers to investigate some of the basic principles and to learn about equipment and means of communication. (Rev: SLJ 6/03) [629.13]

13111 Cole, Michael D. *TWA Flight 800: Explosion in Midair* (4–8). Series: American Disasters. 1999, Enslow LB $23.93 (978-0-7660-1217-2). A dramatic account of the air tragedy. (Rev: BL 1/1–15/99; HBG 10/99) [629.136]

13112 De Angelis, Gina. *The Hindenburg* (6–8). Series: Great Disasters: Reforms and Ramifications. 2000, Chelsea LB $30.00 (978-0-7910-5272-3). A description of the Hindenburg disaster precedes discussion of how this tragedy has influenced safety regulations. (Rev: HBG 3/01; SLJ 1/01) [363.12]

13113 Dick, Ron, and Dan Patterson. *Aviation Century: The Early Years* (8–12). Illus. 2003, Boston Mills $39.95 (978-1-55046-407-8). This volume rich in photographs, the first in a projected three-volume set, covers aviation to the 1930s. (Rev: BL 2/1/04) [629.13]

13114 Friedrich, Belinda. *The Explosion of TWA Flight 800* (8–10). Series: Great Disasters: Reforms and Ramifications. 2001, Chelsea LB $30.00 (978-0-7910-6325-5). An account of this tragedy over Long Island in 1996, detailing the recovery efforts, the investigation, and the many theories about the cause of the disaster. (Rev: HBG 10/02; SLJ 5/02) [363.12]

13115 Gaffney, Timothy R. *Air Safety: Preventing Future Disasters* (7–12). Illus. Series: Issues in Focus. 1999, Enslow LB $26.60 (978-0-7660-1108-3). Efforts being made to improve air safety are covered, with information on recent disasters, on why planes crash, and on how the causes of accidents are determined. (Rev: HBG 4/00; SLJ 2/00) [363.12]

13116 Gaffney, Timothy R. *Hurricane Hunters* (4–7). Series: Aircraft. 2001, Enslow LB $23.93

transport from prehistoric times to today, with maps, illustrations, and profiles of key figures. (Rev: SLJ 12/04)

(978-0-7660-1569-2). Information on the planes that investigate hurricanes is accompanied by quotations from the pilots and scientists who fly in them. (Rev: HBG 3/02; SLJ 2/02) [551.55]

13117 Hansen, Ole Steen. *Amazing Flights: The Golden Age* (4–7). Illus. Series: The Story of Flight. 2003, Crabtree LB $25.27 (978-0-7787-1202-2); paper $8.95 (978-0-7787-1218-3). Double-page spreads present text, feature sidebars, color photographs, and paintings on the people and events of flying after World War I — air races, barnstormers, Lindbergh, and more. (Rev: BL 10/15/03) [629.13]

13118 Hansen, Ole Steen. *Commercial Aviation* (4–7). Series: The Story of Flight. 2003, Crabtree $25.27 (978-0-7787-1205-3). The history and development of airlines and other forms of commercial aviation are discussed with coverage of present-day problems. (Rev: BL 10/15/03) [629.13]

13119 Hansen, Ole Steen. *Modern Military Aircraft* (4–7). Illus. Series: The Story of Flight. 2003, Crabtree LB $25.27 (978-0-7787-1204-6); paper $8.95 (978-0-7787-1220-6). A highly visual overview of military aircraft since World War II, with a spotter's guide. (Rev: BL 10/15/03) [623.]

13120 Hart, Philip S. *Flying Free: America's First Black Aviators* (5–9). 1992, Lerner LB $22.60 (978-0-8225-1598-2). The contributions of African Americans who succeeded against great odds to become aerial performers, combat pilots, and aviation instructors. (Rev: BL 10/15/92; SLJ 1/93) [629.13]

13121 Homan, Lynn M., and Thomas Reilly. *Women Who Fly* (5–8). Illus. by Rosalie M. Shepherd. 2004, Pelican $14.95 (978-1-58980-160-8). Women's efforts to establish a foothold in the male-dominated field of aviation are recounted in this book that is suitable for browsers. (Rev: BL 7/04; SLJ 9/04) [629.13]

13122 Masters, Nancy Robinson. *The Airplane* (4–8). Series: Inventions That Shaped the World. 2004, Watts LB $30.50 (978-0-531-12360-7). An interesting overview of the discovery and development of flight, with discussion of its impact on our lives today and in the future. (Rev: SLJ 2/05) [629.13]

13123 Maynard, Chris. *Aircraft* (5–8). Illus. Series: Need for Speed. 1999, Lerner LB $23.93 (978-0-8225-2485-4); paper $7.95 (978-0-8225-9855-8). Using double-page spreads, this work introduces high-speed aircraft. (Rev: BL 1/1–15/00; HBG 3/00; SLJ 2/00) [629.133]

13124 Millspaugh, Ben. *Aviation and Space Science Projects* (5–8). Illus. 1992, TAB paper $9.95 (978-0-8306-2156-9). The principles of flight are explored in 19 projects that vary in difficulty and complexity. (Rev: BL 1/15/92; SLJ 6/92) [629.1]

13125 Oxlade, Chris. *Airplanes: Uncovering Technology* (4–8). Illus. Series: Uncovering. 2006, Firefly $16.95 (978-1-55407-134-0). A well-illustrated survey of developments in air travel, with four overlay pages and a look at future possibilities. (Rev: SLJ 2/07) [629.133]

13126 Parker, Steve. *What's Inside Airplanes?* (4–8). Illus. Series: What's Inside? 1995, Bedrick LB $17.95 (978-0-87226-394-9). Elaborate illustrations show various types of airplanes and describe their parts, including pistons, propellers, fuel tanks, and landing gear. (Rev: SLJ 12/95) [629.133]

13127 Santella, Andrew. *Air Force One* (4–7). Illus. 2003, Millbrook LB $24.90 (978-0-7613-2617-5). An overview of the aircraft that have transported United States presidents, with an inside look at today's Air Force One. (Rev: BL 2/15/03; HBG 10/03; SLJ 8/03) [387.7]

13128 Sherrow, Victoria. *The Hindenburg Disaster: Doomed Airship* (4–8). Series: American Disasters. 2002, Enslow LB $23.93 (978-0-7660-1554-8). Excellent illustrations and a clear text are used to tell the story of the destruction of the mighty German dirigible. (Rev: BL 6/1–15/02; HBG 10/02; SLJ 6/02) [629.133]

Automobiles and Trucks

13129 Edmonston, Phil, and Maureen Sawa. *Car Smarts: Hot Tips for the Car Crazy* (7–10). Illus. by Gordon Sauve. 2003, Tundra paper $15.95 (978-0-88776-646-6). Attractive and lively, this is a large-format compendium of facts and advice about cars — their history, how they work, and their purchase and maintenance. (Rev: BL 4/1/04; SLJ 7/04; VOYA 10/04) [629.222]

13130 Italia, Bob. *Great Auto Makers and Their Cars* (6–10). Illus. Series: Profiles. 1993, Oliver LB $19.95 (978-1-881508-08-3). This is a history of automobiles with coverage of famous cars and biographies of famous engineers and automakers. (Rev: BL 10/15/93; SLJ 11/93) [629.2]

13131 Johnstone, Mike. *Monster Trucks* (5–8). Series: Need for Speed. 2002, Lerner LB $23.93 (978-0-8225-0388-0). In stunning action-filled text and pictures, this book highlights huge trucks that weigh thousands of pounds and stand more than 10 feet high. (Rev: BL 8/02; HBG 10/02; SLJ 7/02) [629.225]

13132 McKenna, A. T. *Corvette* (5–7). Series: Ultimate Car. 2000, ABDO LB $24.21 (978-1-57765-127-7). This introduction to this famous sports car includes material on its design, construction, and records it has broken. Similar material appears in companion books *Ferrari, Jaguar, Lamborghini, Mustang,* and *Porsche* (all 2000). (Rev: BL 3/1/01; HBG 10/01) [629]

13133 Mueller, Mike, and Bob Woods. *Corvette* (6–9). 2006, MBI paper $9.95 (978-0-7603-3231-3). A look at the corvette and its history with information on its evolvement over the years, showing up to the 2005 model. Color photographs included throughout. (Rev: BL 9/1/06)

13134 Nakaya, Andrea C., ed. *Cars in America* (7–12). Series: Opposing Viewpoints. 2006, Gale LB $34.95 (978-0-7377-3307-5); paper $23.70 (978-0-7377-3308-2). Opposing points of view are offered on everything from seatbelt laws to SUVs to urban sprawl. (Rev: SLJ 12/06)

13135 Raby, Philip. *Racing Cars* (5–8). Series: Need for Speed. 1999, Lerner LB $23.93 (978-0-8225-2487-8). Using an attention-getting format with plenty of color, action photographs, and sidebars, this book covers such topics as Le Mans, dragsters, the Camel T, dune buggies, and carting. (Rev: BL 1/1–15/00; HBG 3/00; SLJ 2/00) [623.8]

13136 Whitman, Sylvia. *Get Up and Go! The History of American Road Travel* (5–8). Illus. 1996, Lerner LB $30.35 (978-0-8225-1735-1). From primitive pathways to modern superhighways, this is a history of American roads and the vehicles that traveled them. (Rev: BL 10/15/96; SLJ 10/96; VOYA 2/97) [388.1]

Cycles

13137 Smedman, Lisa. *From Boneshakers to Choppers: The Rip-Roaring History of Motorcycles* (5–8). Illus. 2007, Annick $24.95 (978-1-55451-016-0); paper $14.95 (978-1-55451-015-3). Covering all types of motorcycles, as well as all types of riders, this well-illustrated book will be popular with fans of transportation, extreme sports, history, and American popular culture. (Rev: BL 11/15/07) [629.227]

Railroads

13138 Houghton, Gillian. *The Transcontinental Railroad: A Primary Source History of America's First Coast-to-Coast Railroad* (4–8). Series: Primary Sources in American History. 2003, Rosen LB $29.25 (978-0-8239-3684-7). Timelines and reproductions of period photographs and relevant items add to the narrative in this introduction to the planning and construction of the railroad in the mid-19th century. (Rev: SLJ 5/03) [385]

13139 Laughlin, Rosemary. *The Great Iron Link: The Building of the Central Pacific Railroad* (6–9). Illus. 1996, Morgan Reynolds LB $21.95 (978-1-883846-14-5). An interesting history of the Central Pacific Railroad that focuses on the five men who were responsible for its inception. (Rev: BL 10/15/96; SLJ 4/97) [385]

13140 Maynard, Chris. *High-Speed Trains* (5–8). Series: Need for Speed. 2002, Lerner LB $23.93 (978-0-8225-0387-3). This action-packed book looks at fast trains from around the world, propelled by steam, oil, magnets, and electricity. (Rev: BL 8/02; HBG 10/02) [625.1]

13141 Murphy, Jim. *Across America on an Emigrant Train* (6–12). 1993, Clarion $18.00 (978-0-395-63390-8). A cross-country train trip by Robert Louis Stevenson in 1879 is the backdrop for information on the history of railroads. (Rev: BCCB 1/94; BL 12/1/93*; SLJ 12/93*) [625.2]

13142 Streissguth, Thomas. *The Transcontinental Railroad* (6–8). Illus. Series: Building History. 1999, Lucent LB $28.70 (978-1-56006-564-7). Complete with a timeline, photographs, sidebars, and maps, this is a realistic account of the building of the transcontinental railroad. (Rev: BL 1/1–15/00; HBG 9/00) [385.]

13143 Weitzman, David. *A Subway for New York* (4–7). Illus. 2005, Farrar $17.00 (978-0-374-37284-2). The story behind the early-20th-century construction of New York City's first subway is presented in picture-book format. (Rev: BL 12/1/05; SLJ 2/06) [625.4]

13144 Weitzman, David. *Superpower: The Making of a Steam Locomotive* (6–9). Illus. 1987, Godine $35.00 (978-0-87923-671-7). A step-by-step guide to the parts of a locomotive and how they are assembled. (Rev: SLJ 1/88) [625.2]

13145 Wormser, Richard. *The Iron Horse: How Railroads Changed America* (6–9). 1993, Walker LB $19.85 (978-0-8027-8222-9). The economic and social impact of the railroad between 1830 and 1900, from the robber barons to the Gold Rush and massive influx of immigrants. (Rev: BL 12/15/93; SLJ 1/94; VOYA 4/94) [385]

13146 Yancey, Diane. *Camels for Uncle Sam* (4–7). Illus. 1995, Hendrick-Long $16.95 (978-0-937460-91-7). The story of the experiment that involved importing camels to the Southwest in the 1850s to help in railroad construction. (Rev: BL 9/15/95) [357]

13147 Zimmermann, Karl. *All Aboard! Passenger Trains Around the World* (4–7). Illus. 2006, Boyds Mills $19.95 (978-1-59078-325-2). Photo-filled double-page spreads show the excitement of travel by train and interweave history, geography, commerce, and technology. (Rev: BL 2/15/06; SLJ 6/06) [385]

13148 Zimmermann, Karl. *Steam Locomotives: Whistling, Chugging, Smoking Iron Horses of the Past* (4–8). Illus. 2004, Boyds Mills $19.95 (978-1-59078-165-4). Informative and photo-filled, this is an appealing history of steam engines. (Rev: BL 2/1/04; SLJ 7/04) [625.26]

Ships and Boats

13149 Bornhoft, Simon. *High Speed Boats* (5–8). Series: Need for Speed. 1999, Lerner LB $23.93 (978-0-8225-2488-5). Using a jazzy, attention-getting format with action photographs, sidebars with statistics and interesting facts, and different type sizes, this book covers present and future speedboats. (Rev: BL 1/1–15/00; HBG 3/00) [629.222]

13150 Butler, Daniel Allen. *Unsinkable: The Full Story of the RMS Titanic* (8–12). 1998, Stackpole Bks. $21.95 (978-0-8117-1814-1). First-person accounts add to the tension of this narrative. (Rev: BL 5/1/98) [910.4]

13151 Delgado, James P. *Wrecks of American Warships* (5–7). Series: Shipwrecks. 2000, Watts LB $25.50 (978-0-531-20376-7). This book describes how underwater archaeologists have discovered and explored such warships as the *Constitution, Philadelphia, Alabama,* and *Arizona.* (Rev: BL 10/15/00) [623.8]

13152 Kently, Eric. *The Story of the Titanic* (4–8). Illus. by Steve Noon. 2001, DK paper $17.99 (978-0-7894-7943-3). Details of life aboard ship, double-page spreads, cutaways and cross-sections, facts and trivia, and a well-designed layout are just a few of the features of this beautifully designed large-format book. (Rev: BL 12/15/01; HBG 3/02; SLJ 12/01) [363.1]

13153 Macaulay, David. *Ship* (5–8). 1993, Houghton $19.95 (978-0-395-52439-8). A fictional caravel is featured in this exploration of historical seagoing vessels and the work of underwater archaeologists. (Rev: BCCB 11/93; BL 10/15/93*; SLJ 11/93) [387.2]

13154 Mayell, Hillary. *Shipwrecks* (5–8). Illus. Series: Man-Made Disasters. 2004, Gale LB $29.95 (978-1-59018-058-7). Period photographs enhance the impact of stories of shipwrecks of all kinds — from fishing boats to luxury liners — during the 19th and 20th centuries. (Rev: SLJ 7/04) [910.4]

13155 Philbrick, Nathaniel. *Revenge of the Whale: The True Story of the Whaleship Essex* (6–10). Illus. 2002, Putnam $16.99 (978-0-399-23795-9). This abridged version of *In the Heart of the Sea* (Viking, 2000) relates for a younger audience the amazing story of the sperm whale that sank a ship in 1820 and the survival of a handful of crewmen. (Rev: BCCB 11/02; HB 1–2/03*; HBG 3/03; SLJ 9/02*) [910]

13156 Wilkinson, Philip. *Ships* (4–7). Illus. 2000, Kingfisher $16.95 (978-0-7534-5280-6). Straightforward text and handsome illustrations cover maritime history from the earliest sailing ships and discuss piracy, the slave trade, and superstitions about the sea. (Rev: BL 2/1/01; HBG 10/01; SLJ 1/01) [623.8]

13157 Zimmermann, Karl. *Steamboats: The Story of Lakers, Ferries, and Majestic Paddle-Wheelers* (4–7). Illus. 2007, Boyds Mills $19.95 (978-1-59078-434-1). Carefully researched by an aficionado, this detailed examination of the history, purpose, and engineering of steamboats contains biographical information and excellent archival and modern illustrations. (Rev: BL 1/1–15/07; SLJ 4/07) [623.82]

Weapons, Submarines, and the Armed Forces

13158 Aaseng, Nathan. *The Marine Corps in Action* (4–8). Series: U.S. Military Branches and Careers. 2001, Enslow LB $26.60 (978-0-7660-1637-8). An attractive introduction to all aspects of the Marine Corps that looks at the future of this military branch and the number of women and minorities included. (Rev: HBG 3/02; SLJ 4/02) [359.9]

13159 Benson, Michael. *The U.S. Marine Corps* (4–7). Illus. Series: U.S. Armed Forces. 2004, Lerner LB $26.60 (978-0-8225-1648-4). Introduces the history of the Marine Corps, followed by information on recruitment, training, and daily life. (Rev: BL 1/05; SLJ 3/05) [359.6]

13160 Byers, Ann. *America's Star Wars Program* (5–7). Series: The Library of Weapons of Mass Destruction. 2005, Rosen LB $27.95 (978-1-4042-0287-0). Photographs and text document the development of 20th-century missiles and America's controversial "Star Wars" strategy. (Rev: SLJ 11/05) [623]

13161 Cohen, Daniel. *The Manhattan Project* (7–12). 1999, Millbrook LB $24.90 (978-0-7613-0359-6). This account captures the spies, intrigue, politics, secrecy, and science that became part of the story of the first atomic bomb. (Rev: BL 7/99; SLJ 9/99) [355.8]

13162 Donovan, Sandy. *The U.S. Air Force* (4–7). Illus. Series: U.S. Armed Forces. 2004, Lerner LB $26.60 (978-0-8225-1436-7). Introduces the history of the Air Force, followed by information on recruitment, training, and daily life. Also use *U.S. Air Force Special Operations* (2004). (Rev: BL 1/05; SLJ 3/05) [358.4]

13163 Dudley, William, ed. *Biological Warfare* (8–12). Series: Opposing Viewpoints. 2003, Gale paper $24.95 (978-0-7377-1672-6). A collection of essays that explore the seriousness of the threat of biological warfare from terrorists using germs as weapons and how the United States and the world should respond. (Rev: BL 1/1–15/04; SLJ 5/04) [356]

13164 Egan, Tracie. *Weapons of Mass Destruction and North Korea* (5–7). Series: The Library of

Weapons of Mass Destruction. 2005, Rosen LB $27.95 (978-1-4042-0296-2). Explores what the West knows about North Korea's efforts to build stockpiles of biological, chemical, and — potentially — nuclear weapons. (Rev: SLJ 11/05) [623]

13165 Ermey, R. Lee. *Mail Call* (8–12). Illus. 2005, Hyperion paper $17.95 (978-1-4013-0779-0). History Channel personality offers facts and figures about military weaponry, modern warfare, and other military trivia. (Rev: BL 12/15/04) [355.009]

13166 Friedman, Lauri S. *Nuclear Weapons and Security* (8–12). Series: Compact Research. 2007, Reference Point LB $24.95 (978-1-60152-021-0). Is the United States likely to be attacked with nuclear weapons? Could the world survive a nuclear war? These and other questions are discussed from various points of view, with facts, profiles, and illustrations. (Rev: SLJ 1/08)

13167 Gay, Kathlyn. *Silent Death: The Threat of Biological and Chemical Warfare* (6–12). Illus. 2001, Twenty-First Century LB $24.90 (978-0-7613-1401-1). Gay presents a thorough and balanced assessment of the threat presented by biological and chemical weapons, compiled before the Iraq war. (Rev: BL 4/1/01; HBG 10/01; SLJ 4/01) [358]

13168 Gifford, Clive. *The Arms Trade* (6–9). Illus. Series: World Issues. 2004, Chrysalis LB $28.50 (978-1-59389-154-1). This thought-provoking title uses a question-and-answer format to examine the dimensions and ethics of the international arms trade. (Rev: BL 1/1–15/05)

13169 Gonen, Rivka. *Charge! Weapons and Warfare in Ancient Times* (5–8). Illus. 1993, Lerner LB $23.93 (978-0-8225-3201-9). A look at the development of weapons from sticks and stones to battering rams. (Rev: BCCB 12/93; BL 2/1/94; SLJ 2/94) [355.8]

13170 Grady, Sean M. *Explosives: Devices of Controlled Destruction* (6–10). Series: Encyclopedia of Discovery and Invention. 1995, Lucent LB $29.95 (978-1-56006-250-9). A history of explosives and their use in war and peace through the ages. (Rev: BL 4/15/95) [662]

13171 Gurstelle, William. *The Art of the Catapult: Build Greek Ballistae, Roman Onagers, English Trebuchets, and More Ancient Artillery* (5–12). Illus. 2004, Chicago Review paper $14.95 (978-1-55652-526-1). Information on history, physics, and military tactics, plus step-by-step instructions for the construction of 10 working catapults. (Rev: SLJ 11/04) [623.4]

13172 Hamilton, John. *Armed Forces* (4–7). Illus. Series: War on Terrorism. 2002, ABDO LB $25.65 (978-1-57765-674-6). An introduction to the U.S. military and the roles these services play in protecting the country, with color photographs, a glossary,

and list of Web sites. (Rev: BL 8/02; HBG 10/02) [355]

13173 Hamilton, John. *Weapons of War* (4–7). Illus. Series: War on Terrorism. 2002, ABDO LB $25.65 (978-1-57765-673-9). This account describes the weapons currently available to U.S. military personnel, including fighter planes, bombers, helicopters, bombs, missiles, and ships. (Rev: BL 5/1/02; HBG 10/02) [623.4]

13174 Hamilton, John. *Weapons of War: A Pictorial History of the Past One Thousand Years* (4–7). Illus. Series: The Millennium. 2000, ABDO LB $25.65 (978-1-57765-362-2). In a short space, this book traces 1,000 years of weapons including small weaponry, ships, firearms, military airplanes, tanks, missiles, and bombs. (Rev: BL 7/00; HBG 10/00; SLJ 10/00) [623.4]

13175 Hasan, Heather. *American Women of the Gulf War* (6–9). Illus. Series: American Women at War. 2004, Rosen LB $31.95 (978-0-8239-4447-7). Profiles women who participated in the Gulf War — as combatants, prisoners, and/or victims — and discusses the restrictions on their daily lives, providing social and historical context. (Rev: BL 10/15/04; SLJ 12/04) [956.704]

13176 Hasan, Tahara. *Anthrax Attacks Around the World* (4–8). Series: Terrorist Attacks. 2003, Rosen LB $27.95 (978-0-8239-3859-9). Examines the use of anthrax as a terrorist weapon and includes accounts of its use in Japan, the Soviet Union, and the United States. (Rev: SLJ 2/04) [303.6]

13177 Herbst, Judith. *The History of Weapons* (5–8). Series: Major Inventions Through History. 2005, Twenty-First Century LB $26.60 (978-0-8225-3805-9). An attractive look at the evolution of weapons from rocks and sticks to today's weapons of mass destruction. (Rev: SLJ 1/06) [623.4]

13178 Hibbert, Adam. *Chemical and Biological Warfare* (5–9). Series: Face the Facts. 2003, Raintree LB $28.56 (978-0-7398-6847-8). Part of a series on international issues, this volume examines the powers and dangers of chemical and biological weapons. (Rev: SLJ 4/04) [358]

13179 Kennedy, Robert C. *Life with the Navy Seals* (4–7). Series: On Duty. 2000, Children's LB $24.50 (978-0-516-23351-2). A look at this special branch of the U.S. Navy with material on its responsibilities, training, and career opportunities. (Rev: BL 3/1/01) [359]

13180 Landau, Elaine. *The New Nuclear Reality* (6–12). Illus. 2000, Twenty-First Century LB $22.90 (978-0-7613-1555-1). This account chronicles the post-war growth of countries that have nuclear arms including Russia, North Korea, Pakistan, and India. (Rev: BL 7/00; HBG 9/00; SLJ 9/00) [327.1]

13181 Lefkowitz, Arthur. *Bushnell's Submarine: The Best Kept Secret of the American Revolution* (7–10). Illus. 2006, Scholastic $16.99 (978-0-439-74352-5). The little-known story of the *Turtle,* America's first submarine, which was launched during the closing days of the American Revolution. (Rev: BL 2/15/06; SLJ 4/06) [973.3]

13182 Meltzer, Milton. *Weapons and Warfare: From the Stone Age to the Space Age* (5–9). Illus. 1996, HarperCollins LB $17.89 (978-0-06-024876-5). This work describes the evolution of weapons from clubs to the H-bomb, including how these weapons have been used and misused through the ages. (Rev: BCCB 2/97; BL 12/1/96; SLJ 1/97) [355.02]

13183 Myers, Walter Dean. *USS Constellation: Pride of the American Navy* (4–8). 2004, Holiday House $16.95 (978-0-8234-1816-9). Myers presents the colorful history of the *USS Constellation,* the last of America's all-sail fighting ships, in this volume with extensive illustrations and other materials. (Rev: BL 7/04; HB 7–8/04; SLJ 8/04) [359.8]

13184 Pelta, Kathy. *The U.S. Navy* (5–7). Illus. 1990, Lerner LB $23.93 (978-0-8225-1435-0). A look at the history and present status and activities of the U.S. Navy. (Rev: BL 12/1/90) [359]

13185 Regan, Paul, ed. *Weapon: A Visual History of Arms and Armor* (8–12). Illus. 2006, DK $40.00 (978-0-7566-2210-7). In the usual DK style, the history of handheld weapons is displayed with silhouetted images and captions, covering everything from the most primitive — such as a rock — to the automatic guns of today. (Rev: BL 11/1/06) [623.4]

13186 Richie, Jason. *Weapons: Designing the Tools of War* (5–10). Illus. 2000, Oliver LB $21.95 (978-1-881508-60-1). Using separate chapters for different categories of weapons — for example, submarines, battleships, and tanks — this is a history of the development of weaponry from 300 B.C. to today. (Rev: BL 5/1/00; HBG 10/00; SLJ 8/00) [623]

13187 Ripley, Tim. *Weapons Technology* (6–9). Illus. Series: History of Invention. 2004, Facts on File $35.00 (978-0-8160-5438-1). A slim introductory overview of advances in weapons from prehistoric times to today, with maps, illustrations, and profiles of key figures. (Rev: SLJ 12/04) [623.4]

13188 Sherrow, Victoria. *The Making of the Atom Bomb* (7–10). Series: World History. 2000, Lucent LB $27.45 (978-1-56006-585-2). A review of the development of the bomb, the decision to use the first one, and continuing work on these weapons. (Rev: BL 6/1–15/00; HBG 9/00; SLJ 9/00) [940.54]

13189 Speakman, Jay. *Weapons of War* (6–12). Series: American War Library: The Persian Gulf War. 2000, Lucent LB $19.96 (978-1-56006-640-8).

This heavily illustrated book covers the weapons that were used during the Persian Gulf War of 1991. (Rev: BL 3/1/01) [956.7]

13190 Streissguth, Thomas. *Nuclear Weapons: More Countries, More Threats* (6–12). Series: Issues in Focus. 2000, Enslow LB $26.60 (978-0-7660-1248-6). An overview of nuclear weapons, who controls the technology to produce them, and the efforts to control this threat to human survival. (Rev: BL 9/15/00; HBG 3/01) [355.02]

13191 Sullivan, Edward T. *The Ultimate Weapon: The Race to Develop the Atomic Bomb* (6–9). Illus. 2007, Holiday $24.95 (978-0-8234-1855-8). In addition to an overall account of the creation of the bomb, this book takes a behind-the-scenes look at activities at the three sites (Los Alamos; Oak Ridge, Tennessee; and Hanford, Washington) where the Manhattan Project came to fruition. (Rev: BCCB 9/07; BL 7/07; SLJ 8/07) [355.8]

13192 Torr, James D., ed. *Weapons of Mass Destruction* (7–10). Series: Opposing Viewpoints. 2004, Gale LB $36.20 (978-0-7377-2250-5); paper $24.95 (978-0-7377-2251-2). Terrorist attacks using nuclear or biological weapons, the threat from "rogue" nations, U.S. policies regarding its own weapons of mass destruction, and national defense are all discussed in essays introduced by focus questions. (Rev: SLJ 4/05) [355.02]

13193 Walker, Sally M. *Secrets of a Civil War Submarine: Solving the Mysteries of the H. L. Hunley* (7–10). Illus. 2005, Carolrhoda $18.95 (978-1-57505-830-6). Walker chronicles the story of the Confederate submarine *H. L. Hunley* from its design and construction through its successful attack on the *USS Housatonic* in 1864 to its discovery on the bottom of Charleston Harbor in 1995. Sibert Medal, 2006. (Rev: BL 4/15/05*; SLJ 5/05) [973.7]

13194 Warner, J. F. *The U.S. Marine Corps* (4–8). Illus. Series: Armed Services. 1991, Lerner LB $22.95 (978-0-8225-1432-9). From how to enlist to a discussion of the new technology, this is a well-organized introduction to the U.S. Marine Corps. (Rev: BL 2/1/92; SLJ 2/92) [359.6]

13195 Wolny, Philip. *Weapons Satellites* (5–9). Series: The Library of Satellites. 2003, Rosen LB $26.50 (978-0-8239-3855-1). This account explores the growing technology of weapon satellites that are capable of knocking out enemies' satellites, and launching attacks from outer space. (Rev: BL 11/15/03; SLJ 1/04) [629.46]

13196 Woods, Mary B., and Michael Woods. *Ancient Warfare: From Clubs to Catapults* (5–8). Series: Ancient Technologies. 2000, Runestone LB $25.26 (978-0-8225-2999-6). The weaponry of ancient civilizations including Greece and China. (Rev: BCCB 12/00; BL 9/15/00; HBG 3/01; SLJ 1/01) [623]

Recreation and Sports

Crafts, Hobbies, and Pastimes

General and Miscellaneous

13197 Albregts, Lisa, and Elizabeth Cape. *Best Friends: Tons of Crazy, Cool Things to Do with Your Girlfriends* (4–8). Illus. 1998, Chicago Review paper $12.95 (978-1-55652-326-7). Arranged by seasons, this activity book contains crafts, games, dances, snacks, and skits to amuse girls when they get together. (Rev: BL 3/1/99; SLJ 1/99) [796.083]

13198 Bell, Alison. *Let's Party!* (6–10). Illus. by Kun-Sung Chung. Series: What's Your Style? 2005, Lobster paper $14.95 (978-1-894222-99-0). Eight theme parties are suggested, complete with invitations, decorations, food, music, and so forth; particularly useful may be the tips on keeping parents at bay and dealing with crashers. (Rev: SLJ 3/06) [793.2]

13199 Birdseye, Tom. *A Kids' Guide to Building Forts* (5–8). Illus. by Bill Klein. 1993, Harbinger paper $11.95 (978-0-943173-69-6). A guide to the building of 19 kinds of forts, from the very simple to the more complex, some of which can be turned into clubhouses. (Rev: SLJ 9/93) [745.5]

13200 Boonyadhistarn, Thiranut. *Fingernail Art: Dazzling Fingers and Terrific Toes* (4–8). Illus. Series: Snap Books: Crafts. 2006, Capstone LB $25.26 (978-0-7368-6474-9). This colorful, well-thought-out guide offers interesting tips on decorating nail. (Rev: SLJ 2/07) [646.7]

13201 Boonyadhistarn, Thiranut. *Stamping Art: Imprint Your Designs* (4–8). Illus. Series: Snap Books: Crafts. 2006, Capstone LB $25.26 (978-0-7368-6477-0). Simple, step-by-step instructions guide readers through a variety of stamping projects that use accessible materials. (Rev: SLJ 2/07) [761]

13202 Brownrigg, Sheri. *Hearts and Crafts* (4–8). Illus. 1995, Tricycle paper $9.95 (978-1-883672-28-

7). Clear instructions show how to complete a variety of Valentine's Day projects, including making necklaces and candles. (Rev: BL 3/1/96; SLJ 3/96) [745.5]

13203 Check, Laura. *Create Your Own Candles: 30 Easy-to-Make Designs* (5–8). Illus. by Norma Jean Martin-Jourdenais. 2004, Williamson paper $8.95 (978-0-8249-8663-6). Safety is stressed in this guide to exciting (and complex) candle creations. (Rev: SLJ 11/04) [745.593]

13204 Cook, Nick. *Roller Coasters; or, I Had So Much Fun, I Almost Puked* (4–7). Illus. 1998, Carolrhoda LB $22.60 (978-1-57505-071-3). This intriguing book describes the excitement of a roller-coaster ride and discusses the history, types, construction, and safety features of various roller coasters. (Rev: BCCB 6/98; BL 4/15/98; HBG 10/98) [791]

13205 Dickins, Rosie. *Art Treasury: Pictures, Paintings, and Projects* (4–7). 2007, Usborne LB $19.99 (978-0-7945-1452-5). Each of the art projects in this exciting collection is inspired by an existing work of art. (Rev: BL 4/1/07) [709]

13206 Griffith, Saul, and Nick Dragotta. *Howtoons: The Possibilities Are Endless* (5–8). Illus. by Nick Dragotta. 2007, HarperCollins paper $15.99 (978-0-06-076158-5). A comic book and a project book in one, this will appeal to readers who are reluctant to pick up ordinary craft books; the "crafts" go beyond origami and include a marshmallow shooter, a tree swing, a rocket, and a flute. (Rev: BL 12/15/07; SLJ 5/08) [741.5]

13207 Hendry, Linda. *Making Gift Boxes* (4–8). Illus. by author. Series: Kids Can! 1999, Kids Can paper $5.95 (978-1-55074-503-0). The 14 boxes included in this fine craft book with clear instructions include a photo box, a garden box to grow seeds, a box for storing CDs, and a treasure box with false compartments. (Rev: SLJ 12/99) [745]

13208 Hennessy, Alena. *Alter This!* (8–12). Illus. 2007, Sterling $14.95 (978-1-57990-948-2). Books can be craft material! This unusual book encourages teens to use books to create art or practical objects — hardbacks can be purses or clocks, for example, or words can be cut out to create poetry or stories. (Rev: BL 12/15/07; SLJ 9/07) [745.593]

13209 Jennings, Lynette. *Have Fun with Your Room: 28 Cool Projects for Teens* (6–10). 2001, Simon & Schuster paper $12.00 (978-0-689-82585-9). The author offers a number of affordable ways to decorate bedrooms, with suggestions for walls, windows, headboards, bulletin boards, and so forth. (Rev: SLJ 11/01)

13210 Johnson, Ginger. *Make Your Own Christmas Ornaments* (6–9). Illus. by Norma Jean Martin-Jordenais. 2002, Williamson paper $8.95 (978-1-885593-79-5). A collection of 25 ornaments with clear instructions and photographs of finished products. (Rev: BL 12/15/02; SLJ 10/02) [745.5]

13211 Jovinelly, Joann, and Jason Netelkos. *The Crafts and Culture of a Medieval Monastery* (4–8). Illus. Series: Crafts of the Middle Ages. 2006, Rosen LB $29.25 (978-1-4042-0759-2). Crafts and history are interwoven in this interesting that looks at the history of monasteries, life within them, and the work that took place in scriptoria, gardens, and hospitals; crafts include prayer beads and a plague mask. Also use *The Crafts and Culture of a Medieval Town* (2006). (Rev: SLJ 4/07) [271.0094]

13212 Kerina, Jane. *African Crafts* (5–8). Illus. by Tom Feelings and Marylyn Katzman. 1970, Lion LB $13.95 (978-0-87460-084-1). Many projects arranged geographically by the region in Africa where they originated.

13213 McGraw, Sheila. *Gifts Kids Can Make* (4–8). Photos by Sheila McGraw and Joy von Tiedemann. 1994, Firefly paper $9.95 (978-1-895565-35-5). A craft book that gives directions for making 14 simple gifts, such as a cotton sock doll and a hobby horse, using easily obtainable materials. (Rev: SLJ 12/94) [745]

13214 MacLeod, Elizabeth. *Gifts to Make and Eat* (4–7). Illus. by June Bradford. Series: Kids Can Do It! 2001, Kids Can $12.95 (978-1-55074-956-4); paper $6.95 (978-1-55074-958-8). Kids learn through step-by-step instructions how to make an array of edible and craft gifts. (Rev: BL 11/1/01; HBG 3/02; SLJ 2/02) [641.5]

13215 Martin, Laura C. *Nature's Art Box: From T-Shirts to Twig Baskets, 65 Cool Projects for Crafty Kids to Make with Natural Materials You Can Find Anywhere* (4–8). Illus. by David Cain. 2003, Storey paper $16.95 (978-1-58017-490-9). These projects use natural materials such as twigs, moss, gourds, stones, shells, flowers, and leaves to make articles

including wreaths, necklaces, and a chess set. (Rev: HBG 10/03; SLJ 8/03*) [745.5]

13216 Merrill, Yvonne Y. *Hands-On Latin America: Art Activities for All Ages* (4–8). Illus. Series: Hands-On. 1998, Kits paper $20.00 (978-0-9643177-1-0). A collection of 30 interesting, affordable arts and crafts projects inspired by the ancient cultures of Latin America. (Rev: BL 9/1/98; SLJ 8/98) [980.07]

13217 Monaghan, Kathleen, and Hermon Joyner. *You Can Weave! Projects for Young Weavers* (4–7). Illus. 2001, Sterling $19.95 (978-0-87192-493-3). Step-by-step instructions and photographs guide young crafters through weaving projects of varying complexity. (Rev: BL 11/1/01) [746.41]

13218 Murillo, Kathy Cano. *The Crafty Diva's Lifestyle Makeover: Awesome Ideas to Spice Up Your Life!* (5–12). Illus. by Carrie Wheeler. 2005, Watson-Guptill paper $12.95 (978-0-8230-1008-0). The Crafty Diva is back with this collection of easy-to-follow instructions for 50 projects that cover everything from room makeovers to fashion accessories. (Rev: SLJ 9/05)

13219 Olson, Beverly, and Judy Lazzara. *Country Flower Drying* (8–12). 1988, Sterling paper $9.95 (978-0-8069-6746-2). A concise manual on raising and drying flowers plus tips on creating arrangements and other uses of dried flowers. [745.92]

13220 Powell, Michelle. *Mosaics* (4–7). Series: Step-by-Step. 2001, Heinemann LB $24.22 (978-1-57572-332-7). A number of fascinating projects creating mosaics are described with step-by-step instructions and many colorful illustrations. (Rev: BL 8/1/01; HBG 10/01; SLJ 10/01) [745]

13221 Powell, Michelle, and Judy Balchin. *Crafty Activities: Over 50 Fun and Easy Things to Make* (4–7). Illus. 2007, Search paper $19.95 (978-1-84448-250-4). Fifty crafts involving mosaics, printing, lettering, papier-mâché, card-making, and origami, attractively and clearly presented for the young crafter. (Rev: BL 12/15/07; SLJ 1/08) [745]

13222 Purdy, Susan. *Christmas Gifts for You to Make* (7–9). 1976, HarperCollins LB $12.89 (978-0-397-31695-3). Instructions on how to make a wide variety of gifts including puppets, note pads, and aprons. [745.5]

13223 Rhodes, Vicki. *Pumpkin Decorating* (4–8). 1997, Sterling $10.95 (978-0-8069-9574-8). Clear directions and full-color photographs demonstrate more than 80 designs for pumpkins. (Rev: SLJ 12/97) [745.5]

13224 Schwarz, Renee. *Funky Junk* (4–7). Series: Kids Can Do It! 2002, Kids Can $12.95 (978-1-55337-387-2); paper $5.95 (978-1-55337-388-9). Using easily found materials, this craft book supplies details on how to make unusual conversation pieces. (Rev: BL 3/15/03; HBG 10/03; SLJ 4/03) [745.5]

13225 Shannon, George W., and Pat Torlen. *The Stained Glass Home: Projects and Patterns* (8–12). 2007, Sterling $24.95 (978-1-895569-59-9). Two talented stained glass artists provide 23 projects, each one complete with patterns, directions, materials lists, and photographs, suitable for beginners as well as experienced crafters. (Rev: BL 12/15/06) [748.5]

13226 Simons, Robin. *Recyclopedia: Games, Science Equipment and Crafts from Recycled Materials* (5–8). Illus. by author. 1976, Houghton paper $13.95 (978-0-395-59641-8). Clear directions complemented by good illustrations characterize this book of interesting projects using waste materials.

13227 Taylor, Maureen. *Through the Eyes of Your Ancestors: A Step-by-Step Guide to Uncovering Your Family's History* (5–9). Illus. 1999, Houghton paper $8.95 (978-0-395-86982-6). Budding researchers learn how to investigate family history, from conducting interviews to visiting genealogical libraries. (Rev: BCCB 5/99; BL 3/1/99; HB 5–6/99; HBG 10/99; SLJ 5/99) [929.1]

13228 Taylor, Terry. *Altered Art: Techniques for Creating Altered Books, Boxes, Cards and More* (8–12). 2004, Lark $19.95 (978-1-57990-550-7). Terry Taylor provides a fascinating introduction into the world of altered art. (Rev: BL 12/15/04; SLJ 4/05)

13229 Temko, Florence. *Traditional Crafts from China* (5–7). Illus. Series: Culture Crafts. 2001, Lerner LB $23.93 (978-0-8225-2939-2). After a few words about crafts in general, this volume carefully outlines a number of projects relating to Chinese culture, including instructions for picture scrolls and tanagrams. (Rev: BL 2/15/01; HBG 10/01; SLJ 4/01) [745]

13230 Temko, Florence. *Traditional Crafts from the Caribbean* (5–7). Illus. Series: Culture Crafts. 2001, Lerner LB $23.93 (978-0-8225-2937-8). Step-by-step instructions with clear diagrams are given for a number of craft projects relating to Caribbean culture including yarn dolls, Puerto Rican masks, and metal cutouts. (Rev: BL 2/15/01; HBG 10/01; SLJ 4/01) [745]

13231 Torres, Laura. *Best Friends Forever! 199 Projects to Make and Share* (5–8). Illus. 2004, Workman paper $13.95 (978-0-7611-3274-5). Craft ideas that will appeal to young teens — bracelets, key chains, picture frames, and so forth — are clearly explained and organized into chapters such as "Cool Notes" and "Home and School." (Rev: SLJ 2/05) [745.5]

13232 Wagner, Lisa. *Cool Melt and Pour Soap* (4–7). Photos by Kelly Doudna. Illus. Series: Cool Crafts. 2005, ABDO LB $22.78 (978-1-59197-741-

4). Coloring, fragrance, and packaging are all covered in this guide to projects using soap. (Rev: SLJ 7/05)

13233 Weaver, Janice, and Frieda Wishinsky. *It's Your Room: A Decorating Guide for Real Kids* (6–10). Illus. by Claudia Dávila. 2006, Tundra paper $14.95 (978-0-88776-711-1). A step-by-step guide to room decoration, with tips on practical things like creating a budget and storage organization. (Rev: SLJ 6/06)

13234 White, Linda. *Haunting on a Halloween* (5–7). Illus. by Fran Lee. 2002, Gibbs Smith paper $9.95 (978-1-58685-112-5). Everything young party planners need to host a Halloween get-together, with instructions for crafts, food, decorations, and costumes. (Rev: BL 9/15/02) [745.594]

13235 Winters, Eleanor. *1-2-3 Calligraphy* (7–10). Illus. 2006, Sterling $14.95 (978-1-4027-1839-7). A companion to the author's *Calligraphy for Kids* (2004), this instructional book helps beginners gather the correct tools, learn different styles of calligraphy, and choose projects to practice their art. (Rev: BL 12/15/06; SLJ 1/07) [745.6]

American Historical Crafts

13236 Anderson, Maxine. *Great Civil War Projects You Can Build Yourself* (7–10). Illus. 2005, Nomad paper $16.95 (978-0-9749344-1-9). Craft projects explore various aspects of life on the Civil War battlefield and home front — making cornbread, a pinhole camera, a rag doll, and so forth. (Rev: BL 11/1/05; SLJ 11/05) [745.5]

13237 Beard, D. C. *The American Boys' Handy Book: What to Do and How to Do It* (5–7). Illus. 1983, Godine paper $12.95 (978-0-87923-449-2). A facsimile edition of a manual first published in 1882. [790.194]

13238 Greenwood, Barbara. *Pioneer Crafts* (4–8). Illus. 1997, Kids Can paper $6.95 (978-1-55074-359-3). This guide gives directions for 17 projects such as candle making, soap carving, and basket weaving. (Rev: BL 9/15/97; SLJ 9/97) [745.5]

13239 Merrill, Yvonne Y. *Hands-On Rocky Mountains: Art Activities About Anasazi, American Indians, Settlers, Trappers, and Cowboys* (4–8). Illus. 1996, Kits paper $16.95 (978-0-9643177-2-7). Historical groups from the Rocky Mountain region — early people, American Indians, trappers, settlers, and cowboys — are introduced and, for each, a series of craft projects is outlined. (Rev: BL 1/1–15/97; SLJ 4/97) [745.5]

13240 Tull, Mary, et al. *North America* (4–7). Series: Artisans Around the World. 1999, Raintree LB $27.12 (978-0-7398-0117-8). North American folk art is surveyed, from peoples including the Haida of western Canada, New Mexico's Pueblos, the Pennsylvanian German Americans, and African Americans. (Rev: BL 10/15/99; HBG 3/00) [970]

Clay Modeling and Ceramics

13241 Belcher, Judy. *Polymer Clay Creative Traditions: Techniques and Projects Inspired by the Fine and Decorative Arts* (8–12). Illus. 2006, Watson-Guptill paper $21.95 (978-0-8230-4065-0). Step-by-step instructions for more than 30 items that can be crafted from polymer clay. (Rev: BL 12/15/05) [745.57]

13242 Nicholson, Libby, and Yvonne Lau. *Creating with Fimo* (6–10). Illus. Series: Kids Can Crafts. 1999, Kids Can $12.95 (978-1-55074-310-4); paper $5.95 (978-1-55074-274-9). Using the nontoxic clay called Fimo (available in crafts stores) and the step-by-step instructions in this book, readers can complete 25 projects suitable for experienced crafters, such as making necklaces, earrings, and pins. (Rev: SLJ 5/99) [738]

13243 Rowe, Christine. *The Children's Book of Pottery* (4–7). Illus. 1989, Trafalgar $24.95 (978-0-7134-5995-1). A good British import about pottery making. (Rev: BL 12/1/89) [738.1]

13244 Scheunemann, Pam. *Cool Clay Projects* (4–7). Photos by Anders Hanson. Illus. Series: Cool Crafts. 2005, ABDO LB $22.78 (978-1-59197-740-7). Clear, step-by-step instructions for a number of clay projects are accompanied by full-color photos and tips about safety. (Rev: SLJ 7/05) [731.4]

Cooking

13245 Albyn, Carole Lisa, and Lois S. Webb. *The Multicultural Cookbook for Students* (6–9). 1993, Oryx paper $39.95 (978-0-89774-735-6). Provides 337 recipes from 122 countries, arranged geographically. (Rev: BL 2/15/94; SLJ 10/93) [641.59]

13246 Amari, Suad. *Cooking the Lebanese Way.* Rev. ed. (5–10). Series: Easy Menu Ethnic Cookbooks. 2003, Lerner LB $25.26 (978-0-8225-4116-5). Revised to include low-fat and vegetarian foods, this introduction to Lebanese cooking contains about 40 recipes, clearly explained and well-illustrated. (Rev: BL 9/15/02; HBG 3/03) [641.5]

13247 Andreev, Tania. *Food in Russia* (6–9). Illus. 1989, Rourke LB $26.60 (978-0-86625-343-7). Both an introduction to Russia and a survey of foods and typical recipes. (Rev: SLJ 12/89) [641.5]

13248 Bacon, Josephine. *Cooking the Israeli Way.* Rev. ed. (5–10). Series: Easy Menu Ethnic Cookbooks. 2002, Lerner LB $25.26 (978-0-8225-4112-7). After a general introduction to Israel, this book discusses cooking terms and ingredients, and then gives a series of tantalizing recipes with clear instructions. (Rev: BL 7/02; HBG 10/02) [641]

13249 Bayless, Rick, and Lanie Bayless. *Rick and Lanie's Excellent Kitchen Adventures* (7–12). Photos by Christopher Hirsheimer. 2004, Stewart, Tabori & Chang $29.95 (978-1-58479-331-1). A culinary tour of the world, sampling recipes from almost every continent. (Rev: SLJ 1/05) [641.5]

13250 Behnke, Alison, and Ehramjian Vartkes. *Cooking the Middle Eastern Way* (7–10). Illus. Series: Easy Ethnic Menu Cookbooks. 2005, Lerner LB $25.26 (978-0-8225-1238-7). An introduction to the basics of Middle East cooking plus a number of authentic recipes from the region. (Rev: BL 5/15/05) [641.5956]

13251 Bisignano, Alphonse. *Cooking the Italian Way.* Rev. ed. (5–10). Series: Easy Menu Ethnic Cookbooks. 2001, Lerner $25.26 (978-0-8225-4113-4); paper $7.95 (978-0-8225-4161-5). A revised edition that now includes vegetarian and low-fat recipes as well as an expanded introductory section on the country, the people, and the culture. (Rev: HBG 3/02; SLJ 9/01) [641]

13252 Carle, Megan, and Jill Carle. *Teens Cook: How to Cook What You Want to Eat* (7–12). 2004, Ten Speed paper $19.95 (978-1-58008-584-7). A witty and practical cookbook that introduces varied recipes used by teenage siblings Megan and Jill Carle. (Rev: SLJ 10/04; VOYA 12/04) [641]

13253 Chung, Okwha, and Judy Monroe. *Cooking the Korean Way.* Rev. ed. (5–10). Illus. Series: Easy Menu Ethnic Cookbooks. 2003, Lerner LB $25.26 (978-0-8225-4115-8). Tempting recipes and a brief look at where they come from. (Rev: BL 8/88; HBG 3/03; SLJ 9/88) [641.59519]

13254 Cornell, Kari. *Holiday Cooking Around the World.* Rev. ed. (5–10). Illus. Series: Easy Menu Ethnic Cookbooks. 2002, Lerner LB $25.26 (978-0-8225-4128-8); paper $7.95 (978-0-8225-4159-2). Beginning cooks will appreciate the clear instructions and varied options in this appealing book that includes cultural and social information. (Rev: BL 1/1–15/02; HBG 10/02; SLJ 5/02) [641.5]

13255 Coronado, Rosa. *Cooking the Mexican Way.* Rev. ed. (5–10). Series: Easy Menu Ethnic Cookbooks. 2002, Lerner LB $25.26 (978-0-8225-4117-2). Recipes organized by type of meal are preceded by a section that covers the geography, culture, and festivals and by information on equipment, ingredients, and eating customs. Other titles in this series include *Cooking the East African Way* and *Cooking* *the Spanish Way* (both 2001). (Rev: HBG 3/02; SLJ 2/02) [641]

13256 D'Amico, Joan, and Karen Eich Drummond. *The Science Chef Travels Around the World: Fun Food Experiments and Recipes for Kids* (4–8). Illus. 1996, Wiley paper $12.95 (978-0-471-11779-7). An entertaining combination of simple science experiments and international cooking, with recipes from 14 countries and activities that demonstrate scientific principles of various cooking and baking processes. (Rev: BL 2/1/96; SLJ 3/96) [641.5]

13257 Dosier, Susan. *Civil War Cooking: The Union* (6–10). 2000, Blue Earth Books $23.93 (978-0-7368-0351-9). Recipes accompany information on the foods eaten at the time, with full-color photographs and reproductions. (Rev: BL 8/00; HBG 9/00; SLJ 9/00) [641.5973]

13258 Dunnington, Rose. *Bake It Up! Desserts, Breads, Entire Meals and More* (6–12). Photos by Steven Mann. 2007, Sterling $9.95 (978-1-57990-778-5). Mouth-watering recipes are presented in an appealing and straightforward manner. Also use *Super Sandwiches: Wrap 'em, Stack 'em, Stuff 'em* (2007). (Rev: SLJ 2/07)

13259 Dunnington, Rose. *Big Snacks, Little Meals: After School, Dinnertime, Anytime* (6–9). 2006, Sterling $9.95 (978-1-57990-780-8). This spiral-bound cookbook is easy for teens to use and contains appealing recipes along with helpful photos to guide novice cooks. (Rev: BL 7/06; SLJ 8/06) [641.5]

13260 Dunnington, Rose. *The Greatest Cookies Ever: Dozens of Delicious, Chewy, Chunky, Fun and Foolproof Recipes* (4–8). Photos by Stewart O'Shields. 2005, Sterling $9.95 (978-1-57990-627-6). More than 70 recipes are included in this spiral-bound guide to cookie making, with useful information about measuring, substitutions, types of mixers, and safety. (Rev: BL 1/1–15/06; SLJ 2/06) [641.8]

13261 Erdosh, George. *The African-American Kitchen: Food for Body and Soul* (6–9). Illus. Series: Library of African-American Arts and Culture. 1999, Rosen LB $26.50 (978-0-8239-1850-8). A survey of dishes associated with African Americans, with recipes and cooking tips. (Rev: SLJ 8/99; VOYA 8/99) [641]

13262 Gaspari, Claudia. *Food in Italy* (6–9). Illus. 1989, Rourke LB $26.60 (978-0-86625-342-0). This account introduces Italy and its food and gives some recipes. (Rev: SLJ 12/89) [641.5]

13263 Gillies, Judi, and Jennifer Glossop. *The Jumbo Vegetarian Cookbook* (4–8). Illus. 2002, Kids Can paper $14.95 (978-1-55074-977-9). An introduction to the vegetarian lifestyle, including nutrition and recipes. (Rev: BCCB 7–8/02; BL 3/1/02; SLJ 7/02) [641.5]

13264 Gillies, Judi, and Jennifer Glossop. *The Kids Can Press Jumbo Cookbook* (5–8). Illus. 2000, Kids Can paper $14.95 (978-1-55074-621-1). After a few cooking tips, this book provides recipes that range from the simple (scrambled eggs) to the difficult (crepes and carrot cake). (Rev: BL 5/1/00; SLJ 6/00) [641.8]

13265 Gioffre, Rosalba. *The Young Chef's French Cookbook* (4–7). Series: I'm the Chef! 2001, Crabtree LB $25.27 (978-0-7787-0282-5); paper $8.95 (978-0-7787-0296-2). This oversize book uses double-page spreads to present 15 appetizing French recipes along with good background material, clear directions, and excellent illustrations. (Rev: BL 10/15/01) [641]

13266 Gioffre, Rosalba. *The Young Chef's Italian Cookbook* (4–7). Series: I'm the Chef! 2001, Crabtree LB $25.27 (978-0-7787-0279-5). Along with good background material, clear instructions are presented for 15 Italian dishes in this well-illustrated, oversize book. (Rev: BL 10/15/01; SLJ 11/01) [641]

13267 Gomez, Paolo. *Food in Mexico* (6–9). Illus. 1989, Rourke LB $26.60 (978-0-86625-341-3). As well as some typical recipes, this account introduces Mexico and its types of food. (Rev: SLJ 12/89) [641.5]

13268 Greenwald, Michelle. *The Magical Melting Pot: The All-Family Cookbook That Celebrates America's Diversity* (7–12). Illus. 2003, Cherry Pr. $29.95 (978-0-9717565-0-2). Chefs from ethnic restaurants around the country contribute favorite recipes and cultural explanations. (Rev: SLJ 11/03)

13269 Gunderson, Mary. *Pioneer Farm Cooking* (6–10). 2000, Blue Earth Books $23.93 (978-0-7368-0356-4). Recipes accompany information on the foods eaten at the time, with full-color photographs and reproductions. (Rev: HBG 9/00; SLJ 9/00) [394.1]

13270 Hargittai, Magdolna. *Cooking the Hungarian Way*. Rev. ed. (5–10). Series: Easy Menu Ethnic Cookbooks. 2002, Lerner LB $25.26 (978-0-8225-4132-5). After an introduction to Hungary and its cuisine, there are about 40 clearly presented recipes from appetizers through desserts. (Rev: BL 9/15/02; HBG 3/03) [641.5]

13271 Harrison, Supenn, and Judy Monroe. *Cooking the Thai Way*. Rev. ed. (5–10). Series: Easy Menu Ethnic Cookbooks. 2002, Lerner LB $25.26 (978-0-8225-4124-0); paper $7.95 (978-0-8225-0608-9). The country of Thailand is introduced followed by general information on its foods and several easy-to-follow recipes. (Rev: BL 9/15/02) [641.5]

13272 Hill, Barbara W. *Cooking the English Way*. Rev. ed. (5–10). Series: Easy Menu Ethnic Cookbooks. 2002, Lerner LB $25.26 (978-0-8225-4105-9). The land and people of England are briefly introduced followed by material on their favorite dishes and easy-to-follow recipes. (Rev: BL 9/15/02) [641.5]

13273 Ichord, Loretta Frances. *Double Cheeseburgers, Quiche, and Vegetarian Burritos: American Cooking from the 1920s through Today* (5–8). Illus. by Jan Davey Ellis. 2007, Lerner $25.26 (978-0-8225-5969-6). This title traces American cuisine from 1920 to the present, with chapters highlighting such trends as TV dinners, fast food, and the rise of organic foods; recipes round out a volume useful for both reports and browsing. (Rev: BL 1/1–15/07; SLJ 5/07) [394.1]

13274 Kaufman, Cheryl Davidson. *Cooking the Caribbean Way*. Rev. ed. (5–10). Illus. Series: Easy Menu Ethnic Cookbooks. 1988, Lerner LB $25.26 (978-0-8225-4103-5). A variety of dishes featuring the spices and fresh fruits that come from these islands. (Rev: BL 8/88; SLJ 9/88) [641.59729]

13275 Kaur, Sharon. *Food in India* (6–9). Illus. 1989, Rourke LB $26.60 (978-0-86625-339-0). This illustrated book gives recipes, and introduces the foods and dining customs of India. (Rev: SLJ 12/89) [641.5]

13276 Lagasse, Emeril. *Emeril's There's a Chef in My Family! Recipes to Get Everybody Cooking* (5–10). Photos by Quentin Bacon. Illus. by Charles Yuen. 2004, HarperCollins $22.99 (978-0-06-000439-2). Seventy-six recipes are presented with clear instructions that focus on the enjoyment of cooking. (Rev: SLJ 7/04) [641.5]

13277 Lagasse, Emeril. *Emeril's There's a Chef in My Soup: Recipes for the Kid in Everyone* (5–8). Illus. by Charles Yuen. 2002, HarperCollins $22.99 (978-0-688-17706-5). The famed TV chef presents a series of simple recipes for main dishes, pasta, desserts, breakfast and lunch items, and salads. (Rev: BL 5/1/02; HBG 10/02) [641.5]

13278 Lagasse, Emeril. *Emeril's There's a Chef in My World!* (5–8). Illus. 2006, HarperCollins $22.99 (978-0-06-073926-3). The famous chef adds to his successful series with a basic introduction to sandwiches, meals, snacks, and more from around the world, with sections on basic skills, safety, and equipment for beginners; cultural facts accompany each recipe. (Rev: BL 12/1/06; SLJ 2/07) [641.59]

13279 Lee, Frances. *The Young Chef's Chinese Cookbook* (4–7). Illus. Series: I'm the Chef! 2001, Crabtree LB $25.27 (978-0-7787-0280-1); paper $8.95 (978-0-7787-0294-8). Fifteen child-friendly recipes for Chinese dishes are presented with step-by-step directions and photographs. (Rev: BL 10/15/01; SLJ 11/01) [641.5951]

13280 Lewis, Sara. *Kids' Baking: 60 Delicious Recipes for Children to Make* (4–7). 2006, Sterling $12.95 (978-0-600-61561-3). Well-illustrated recipes for cakes, cookies, and breads are suitable

for children working with adult help. (Rev: BL 12/1/06) [641.8]

13281 Locricchio, Matthew. *The Cooking of China* (7–12). Series: Superchef. 2002, Marshall Cavendish LB $29.93 (978-0-7614-1214-4). After a general introduction to cooking principles, this book gives a region-by-region overview of the cuisine of China followed by a variety of authentic recipes. (Rev: BL 3/15/03; HBG 3/03; SLJ 2/03) [641]

13282 Locricchio, Matthew. *The Cooking of France* (7–12). Illus. Series: Superchef. 2002, Marshall Cavendish $29.93 (978-0-7614-1216-8). Recipes are accompanied by details on technique and equipment and by information about the country's traditions and festivals. Also use *The Cooking of Mexico* (2002). (Rev: BL 12/15/02; HBG 3/03; SLJ 2/03) [641.5944]

13283 Locricchio, Matthew. *The Cooking of Greece* (5–10). Photos by Jack McConnell. Illus. Series: Superchef. 2004, Benchmark LB $29.93 (978-0-7614-1729-3). Recipes follow an informative overview of regional cuisines in Greece and the ingredients commonly used. (Rev: SLJ 4/05)

13284 Locricchio, Matthew. *The Cooking of India* (4–8). Photos by Jack McConnell. Illus. Series: Superchef. 2004, Benchmark $29.93 (978-0-7614-1730-9). Clear instructions guide readers through the steps involved in making dishes from various areas of India; fresh ingredients are recommended and safety is emphasized. Also use *The Cooking of Thailand* (2004). (Rev: SLJ 2/05) [641.5954]

13285 Locricchio, Matthew. *The Cooking of Italy* (7–12). Series: Superchef. 2002, Marshall Cavendish LB $29.93 (978-0-7614-1215-1). The different regional cuisines of Italy are described and a number of traditional recipes clearly outlined and colorfully illustrated. (Rev: BL 3/15/03; HBG 3/03; SLJ 4/03) [641]

13286 Madavan, Vijay. *Cooking the Indian Way* (5–8). Illus. 1985, Lerner LB $19.93 (978-0-8225-0911-0). Cultural information is detailed plus both vegetarian and nonvegetarian recipes. (Rev: SLJ 9/85) [641.5954]

13287 Montgomery, Bertha Vining, and Constance Nabwire. *Cooking the West African Way*. Rev. ed. (5–10). Series: Easy Menu Ethnic Cookbooks. 2002, Lerner LB $25.26 (978-0-8225-4163-9). An appealing introduction to West African cuisine, with information on the land, people, and culture, and several low-fat and vegetarian recipes. (Rev: HBG 10/02; SLJ 5/02) [641.5966]

13288 Munsen, Sylvia. *Cooking the Norwegian Way*. Rev. ed. (5–10). Series: Easy Menu Ethnic Cookbooks. 2002, Lerner LB $25.26 (978-0-8225-4118-9). A revised edition of an earlier publication that gives information on the country and culture in addition to a selection of typical recipes. (Rev: BL 7/02; SLJ 9/02) [641.59]

13289 Nguyen, Chi, and Judy Monroe. *Cooking the Vietnamese Way* (5–10). Illus. Series: Easy Menu Ethnic Cookbooks. 1985, Lerner LB $25.26 (978-0-8225-4125-7). The authors introduce the land and people of Vietnam before giving recipes for regional dishes. (Rev: BL 9/15/85; SLJ 9/85) [641]

13290 Osseo-Asare, Fran. *A Good Soup Attracts Chairs: A First African Cookbook for American Kids* (5–9). 1993, Pelican $18.95 (978-0-88289-816-2). A basic cookbook for youngsters that explores African cooking past and present and gives more than 35 recipes. (Rev: BL 10/15/93; SLJ 8/93) [641.5966]

13291 Parnell, Helga. *Cooking the German Way.* Rev. ed. (5–10). Illus. Series: Easy Menu Ethnic Cookbooks. 1988, Lerner LB $25.26 (978-0-8225-4107-3). Includes such treats as Black Forest torte and apple cake. (Rev: BL 8/88) [641.5943]

13292 Parnell, Helga. *Cooking the South American Way.* Rev. ed. (5–10). Series: Easy Menu Ethnic Cookbooks. 2002, Lerner LB $25.26 (978-0-8225-4121-9). The continent of South America is introduced followed by about 40 clearly presented recipes from several different countries. (Rev: BL 9/15/02; HBG 3/03) [641.5]

13293 Paul, Anthea. *Girlosophy: Real Girls Eat* (8–12). 2006, Allen & Unwin paper $19.95 (978-1-74114-142-9). This colorful cookbook and healthy eating guide takes a holistic approach, giving suggestions on nurturing both the mind and body. (Rev: SLJ 6/06)

13294 Plotkin, Gregory, and Rita Plotkin. *Cooking the Russian Way.* Rev. ed. (5–10). Illus. Series: Easy Menu Ethnic Cookbooks. 2002, Lerner LB $25.26 (978-0-8225-4120-2). Included along with history and information are such recipes as Russian honey spice cake. (Rev: BL 10/15/86) [641.5947]

13295 Raab, Evelyn. *Clueless in the Kitchen: A Cookbook for Teens and Other Beginners* (8–12). Illus. 1998, Firefly paper $14.95 (978-1-55209-224-8). Cooking and kitchen basics are explained and recipes for good traditional dishes are given in this beginner's cookbook, with an emphasis on fresh ingredients and a section of suggested menus designed for particular guests or occasions. (Rev: BL 7/98; SLJ 9/98) [641.5]

13296 Ralph, Judy, and Ray Gompf. *The Peanut Butter Cookbook for Kids* (5–7). Illus. 1995, Hyperion paper $10.95 (978-0-7868-1028-4). An amazing collection of recipes involving peanut butter, including soups, snacks, and main dishes. (Rev: BL 10/1/95; SLJ 9/95) [641.6]

13297 Shaw, Maura D., and Synda Altschuler Byrne. *Foods from Mother Earth* (6–10). 1994, Shawan-

gunk Pr. paper $9.95 (978-1-885482-02-0). A vegetarian cookbook in which most of the recipes can be prepared in three or four easy steps. (Rev: BL 1/15/95; SLJ 2/95) [641.5]

13298 Sheen, Barbara. *Foods of Italy* (4–8). Series: A Taste of Culture. 2005, Gale LB $27.45 (978-0-7377-3034-0). Cultural and historical notes add to the simple, traditional recipes provided. Also use *Foods of Mexico* (2005). (Rev: SLJ 2/06) [641]

13299 Stern, Sam, and Susan Stern. *Cooking Up a Storm: The Teen Survival Cookbook* (6–9). 2006, Candlewick $16.99 (978-0-7636-2988-5). Filled with attractive photographs and clear recipes, this cookbook authored by a British teenage boy encourages young people to become independent in the kitchen. (Rev: BL 7/06) [641.5]

13300 Tan, Jennifer. *Food in China* (6–9). Illus. 1989, Rourke LB $21.27 (978-0-86625-338-3). Recipes are given plus general information on China, its food, and its people's eating habits. (Rev: SLJ 12/89) [641.5]

13301 Townsend, Sue, and Caroline Young. *Indonesia* (5–8). Illus. Series: A World of Recipes. 2003, Heinemann LB $27.07 (978-1-4034-0976-8). After a discussion of Indonesian food and ingredients, clear directions, with illustrations, are given for recipes that are graded by ease of preparation. Also use *Russia* and *Vietnam* (both 2003). (Rev: HBG 4/04; SLJ 9/03)

13302 Villios, Lynne W. *Cooking the Greek Way.* Rev. ed. (5–10). Illus. Series: Easy Menu Ethnic Cookbooks. 2003, Lerner LB $25.26 (978-0-8225-4131-8). The young cook is introduced to the cuisine of Greece, with a chapter covering utensils and ingredient needs and a glossary of basic cooking terms. Recipes are varied and easy to prepare. (Rev: BL 7/02; SLJ 9/02) [641]

13303 Waldee, Lynne Marie. *Cooking the French Way* (5–10). Illus. 2002, Lerner LB $25.26 (978-0-8225-4106-6). A nicely illustrated introduction to French recipes including breads and sauces. (Rev: HBG 3/02; SLJ 2/02) [641.5944]

13304 Walker, Barbara M. *The Little House Cookbook* (5–7). Illus. by Garth Williams. 1979, HarperCollins paper $9.99 (978-0-06-446090-3). Frontier food, such as green pumpkin pie from the Little House books, served up in tasty, easily used recipes.

13305 Warner, Margaret Brink, and Ruth Ann Hayward. *What's Cooking? Favorite Recipes from Around the World* (5–8). Illus. 1981, Little, Brown $16.95 (978-0-316-35252-9). A collection of recipes from more than 30 countries contibuted by American teenagers who also supply information on their ethnic origins. [641.5]

13306 Weston, Reiko. *Cooking the Japanese Way.* Rev. ed. (5–8). Illus. Series: Easy Menu Ethnic

Cookbooks. 2002, Lerner LB $25.26 (978-0-8225-4114-1). Directions for preparing traditional foods are given along with lists of terms, ingredients, and utensils. (Rev: HBG 3/02) [641.5952]

13307 Whitman, Sylvia. *What's Cooking? The History of American Food* (7–10). Illus. 2001, Lerner LB $22.60 (978-0-8225-1732-0). An absorbing account of how American nutrition and tastes have changed over the years, with discussion of methods of food preparation and preservation, the impact of outside forces such as transportation and war, the use of pesticides, and the advent of fast food. (Rev: BCCB 7–8/01; BL 8/01; HBG 10/01; SLJ 7/01; VOYA 8/01) [394.1]

13308 Wolke, Robert L. *What Einstein Told His Cook: Further Adventures in Kitchen Science, Vol. 2* (8–12). Illus. 2005, Norton $25.95 (978-0-393-05963-2). Frequently asked culinary questions are answered in this collection of essays on food and food preparation. (Rev: BL 3/15/05) [641.5]

13309 Yu, Ling. *Cooking the Chinese Way*. Rev. ed. (5–10). Illus. Series: Easy Menu Ethnic Cookbooks. 1982, Lerner LB $25.26 (978-0-8225-4104-2). From appetizers to desserts, with attractive illustrations. (Rev: HBG 3/02) [641.5]

13310 Zamojska-Hutchins, Danuta. *Cooking the Polish Way*. Rev. ed. (5–10). Illus. Series: Easy Menu Ethnic Cookbooks. 2002, Lerner LB $25.26 (978-0-8225-4119-6). Simple Polish recipes include traditional dishes such as pierogi. Glossary of terms, plus listing of utensils and ingredients used. (Rev: BL 7/02; HBG 10/02) [641.5]

13311 Zanzarella, Marianne. *The Good Housekeeping Illustrated Children's Cookbook* (5–8). Illus. 1997, Morrow $17.95 (978-0-688-13375-7). A visually appealing cookbook containing a number of excellent recipes, some of which require adult supervision. (Rev: BL 12/15/97; HBG 3/98; SLJ 1/98) [641.5]

Costume and Jewelry Making, Dress, and Fashion

13312 Aveline, Erick, and Joyce Chargueraud. *Temporary Tattoos* (6–12). Illus. 2001, Firefly LB $19.95 (978-1-55209-609-3); paper $9.95 (978-1-55209-601-7). A book of body art designs that provides plenty of practical tips and guidance on the use of cosmetics. (Rev: BL 11/15/01; HBG 3/02; SLJ 11/01; VOYA 4/02) [391.65]

13313 Baker, Diane. *Jazzy Jewelry: Power Beads, Crystals, Chokers, and Illusion and Tattoo Styles* (5–9). Illus. by Alexandra Michaels. 2001, Williamson paper $12.95 (978-1-885593-47-4). Jewelry projects for bead lovers include chokers, headbands,

and bobby pins, all presented with black-and-white line drawings and guidance on color choice, clasps and knots, and proper storage. (Rev: SLJ 7/01) [745.594]

13314 Baker, Diane. *Make Your Own Hairwear: Beaded Barrettes, Clips, Dangles and Headbands* (4–8). Illus. by Alexandra Michaels. 2001, Williamson paper $8.95 (978-1-885593-63-4). Easy instructions guide readers through the steps of making hair accessories using beads, shells, rhinestones, and other materials. (Rev: SLJ 4/02) [745.58]

13315 Baskett, Mickey. *Jazzy Jeans* (8–12). Illus. 2007, Sterling $24.95 (978-1-4027-3513-4). How to jazz up your jeans with appliqués, embroidery, painting, and so forth. (Rev: BL 1/1–15/07) [746.4]

13316 Boonyadhistarn, Thiranut. *Beading: Bracelets, Barrettes, and Beyond* (4–8). Illus. Series: Snap Books: Crafts. 2006, Capstone LB $25.26 (978-0-7368-6472-5). Simple, step-by-step instructions guide readers through a variety of fashion accessories that use accessible materials. (Rev: SLJ 2/07) [745.58]

13317 Campbell, Jean, ed. *The Art of Beaded Beads: Exploring Design, Color and Technique* (8–12). Illus. 2006, Sterling $24.95 (978-1-57990-825-6). Learn to make projects using beaded beads — beads made out of other seed beads using a variety of knots and stitches; detailed instructions are accompanied by color photographs. (Rev: BL 11/1/06) [745.58]

13318 Carnegy, Vicky. *Fashions of a Decade: The 1980s* (7–12). Series: Fashions of a Decade. 1990, Facts on File $25.00 (978-0-8160-2471-1). This elegantly illustrated volume traces styles and trends in fashion for this decade, linking them to social and political developments. There are volumes in this set for each decade from the 1920s to the 1990s. (Rev: BL 2/15/91; SLJ 5/91) [391]

13319 Cummings, Richard. *101 Costumes for All Ages, All Occasions* (5–9). Illus. 1987, Plays paper $12.95 (978-0-8238-0286-9). A variety of easily made costumes are described from Frankenstein and Captain Hook to Cleopatra and even a tube of toothpaste. (Rev: BL 1/1/88) [792.026]

13320 Di Salle, Rachel, and Ellen Warwick. *Junk Drawer Jewelry* (4–7). Photos by Ray Boudreau. Illus. by Jane Kurisu. Series: Kids Can Do It. 2006, Kids Can $12.95 (978-1-55337-965-2); paper $6.95 (978-1-55337-966-9). This innovative craft book offers step-by-step instructions for making jewelry using odds and ends found in the junk drawer at home. (Rev: SLJ 11/06) [745.5]

13321 Feldman, Elane. *Fashions of a Decade: The 1990s* (7–12). Series: Fashions of a Decade. 1992, Facts on File $25.00 (978-0-8160-2472-8). This is the last of the eight-volume set that traces fashion trends and styles decade by decade from the 1920s through the 1990s. (Rev: BL 12/15/92) [391]

13322 Gayle, Katie. *Snappy Jazzy Jewelry* (4–7). Illus. 1996, Sterling $14.95 (978-0-8069-3854-7). Making necklaces and earrings are two of the craft projects described, with many helpful photographs. (Rev: BL 5/15/96; SLJ 6/96) [745.594]

13323 Haab, Sherri. *Designer Style Handbags: Techniques and Projects for Unique, Fun, and Elegant Designs from Classic to Retro* (7–12). Photos by Dan Haab. 2005, Watson-Guptill paper $19.95 (978-0-8230-1288-6). Projects suitable for every skill level are accompanied by advice on choosing materials and include bags made from objects such as cigar boxes and candy tins as well as a variety of fabrics and yarns. (Rev: SLJ 1/06; VOYA 12/05) [646.4]

13324 Haab, Sherri, and Michelle Haab. *Dangles and Bangles: 25 Funky Accessories to Make and Wear* (6–9). Illus. 2005, Watson-Guptill paper $9.95 (978-0-8230-0064-7). Ideas for stylish accessories are accompanied by guidance on techniques and materials. (Rev: BL 7/05; SLJ 10/05; VOYA 10/05) [745.5]

13325 Hantman, Clea. *I Wanna Make My Own Clothes* (7–12). Illus. by Azadeh Houshyar. 2006, Simon & Schuster paper $9.99 (978-0-689-87462-8). Nearly 50 sewing projects are featured in this guide to making your own unique apparel, including black-and-white illustrations and ideas to spark creativity. (Rev: SLJ 6/06)

13326 Haxell, Kate. *Customizing Cool Clothes: From Dull to Divine in 30 Projects* (8–12). Illus. 2006, Interweave paper $21.95 (978-1-59668-015-9). With the help of photographs and easy-to-follow instructions, this guide shows you how to get creative and embellish your bland wardrobe. (Rev: BL 11/15/06) [746]

13327 Litherland, Janet, and Sue McAnally. *Broadway Costumes on a Budget: Big Time Ideas for Amateur Producers* (7–12). Illus. 1996, Meriwether paper $15.95 (978-1-56608-021-7). Information about period costumes is given in this helpful manual with instructions for making costumes for nearly 100 Broadway plays and musicals. (Rev: BL 12/1/96) [792.6]

13328 Newcomb, Rain. *Girls' World Book of Jewelry: 50 Cool Designs to Make* (5–8). Series: Kids Crafts. 2004, Lark Books paper $14.95 (978-1-57990-473-9). Up-to-date designs are accompanied by well-thought-out instructions and advice in this large-format volume. (Rev: BL 12/15/04; SLJ 4/05)

13329 Sadler, Judy Ann. *Beading: Bracelets, Earrings, Necklaces and More* (4–8). Illus. Series: Kids Can! 1998, Kids Can paper $6.95 (978-1-55074-338-8). Using photographs and simple instructions, directions are given for making a simple beading

loom and creating necklaces and bracelets. (Rev: BL 5/15/98) [745.594]

13330 Sadler, Judy Ann. *Hemp Jewelry* (4–7). Illus. Series: Kids Can Do It! 2005, Kids Can $12.95 (978-1-55337-774-0); paper $6.95 (978-1-55337-775-7). Sixteen projects for boys and girls using hemp, with drawings and photographs to illustrate the steps and the results. (Rev: BL 3/15/05; SLJ 5/05) [746.4]

13331 Scheunemann, Pam. *Cool Beaded Jewelry* (4–7). Photos by Anders Hanson. Illus. Series: Cool Crafts. 2005, ABDO LB $22.78 (978-1-59197-739-1). Step-by-step instructions and full-color photographs guide the user through beaded jewelry projects. (Rev: SLJ 7/05) [745]

13332 Sensier, Danielle. *Costumes* (5–7). Illus. Series: Traditions Around the World. 1994, Thomson Learning LB $24.26 (978-1-56847-227-0). The rituals and uses involved in costumes are introduced, as well as a general discussion of clothing in various regions and cultures. (Rev: BL 2/1/95; SLJ 3/95) [391]

13333 Warrick, Leanne. *Style Trix for Cool Chix: Your One-Stop Guide to Finding the Perfect Look* (7–10). Photos by Shona Wood. Illus. by Debbie Boon. 2005, Watson-Guptill paper $9.95 (978-0-8230-4940-0). A useful collection of tips on shopping, color coordination, closet organization, accessories, and finding clothes that fit. (Rev: SLJ 8/05; VOYA 8/05) [391]

Dolls and Other Toys

13334 Aronzo, Aranzi. *Cute Dolls* (6–10). Trans. by Rui Munakata. Illus. Series: Let's Make Cute Stuff. 2007, Vertical paper $14.95 (978-1-932234-78-7). A compact guide to making rag dolls that will appeal to manga fans. (Rev: BL 12/15/07) [745.59]

13335 McClary, Andrew. *Toys with Nine Lives: A Social History of American Toys* (6–12). Illus. 1997, Linnet LB $35.00 (978-0-208-02386-5). After a general history of toys and how they have changed in format and manufacture through the centuries, this account gives details on eight kinds of toys, including building blocks, dolls, and marbles. (Rev: BL 2/15/97; SLJ 1/98; VOYA 8/97) [790.1]

13336 Sadler, Judy Ann. *Beanbag Buddies and Other Stuffed Toys* (4–7). Illus. by June Bradford. Series: Kids Can! 1999, Kids Can paper $5.95 (978-1-55074-590-0). Using clear directions and many step-by-step illustrations, this book offers many ideas on how to create a variety of stuffed toys. (Rev: SLJ 10/99) [745]

Drawing and Painting

13337 Ames, Lee J. *Draw Fifty Cats* (4–7). Illus. 1986, Doubleday paper $8.95 (978-0-385-24640-8). Step-by-step ways of drawing different breeds and poses of cats. Also use *Draw Fifty Holiday Decorations* (1987). (Rev: BL 11/15/86) [743.69752]

13338 Balchin, Judy. *Creative Lettering* (4–7). Series: Step-by-Step. 2001, Heinemann LB $24.22 (978-1-57572-331-0). Using easy-to-find materials, this craft book gives clear directions for several fascinating lettering projects. (Rev: BL 8/1/01; HBG 10/01) [745.6]

13339 Balchin, Judy. *Decorative Painting* (4–7). Series: Step-by-Step. 2001, Heinemann LB $24.22 (978-1-57572-330-3). With easy-to-follow directions and illustrations that describe each step, this colorful book contains a number of simple projects that decorate with paints. (Rev: BL 8/1/01; HBG 10/01; SLJ 10/01) [745]

13340 Baron, Nancy. *Getting Started in Calligraphy* (5–8). 1979, Sterling paper $13.95 (978-0-8069-8840-5). This well-organized text shows how to draw letters with beauty and grace. [745.6]

13341 Bohl, Al. *Guide to Cartooning* (6–12). Illus. 1997, Pelican paper $14.95 (978-1-56554-177-1). Though actually a textbook, this work is a splendid guide to the history of cartooning as well as a practical guide to all the basics. (Rev: BL 9/15/97) [741.5]

13342 Butterfield, Moira. *Fun with Paint* (4–8). Illus. Series: Creative Crafts. 1994, Random paper $6.99 (978-0-679-83942-2). This simple introduction to painting covers various media and a number of creative projects, including making your own paints. (Rev: SLJ 3/94) [745]

13343 ComicsKey Staff. *How to Draw Kung Fu Comics* (4–8). 2004, ComicsOne paper $19.95 (978-1-58899-394-6). Cheung's instructions on creating architecture and perspective are particularly valuable. (Rev: BL 8/04) [741.5]

13344 DuBosque, Doug. *Draw! Grassland Animals: A Step-by-Step Guide* (4–7). Illus. by author. 1996, Peel paper $8.99 (978-0-939217-25-0). A step-by-step description of how to draw 31 animals from grasslands around the world. (Rev: SLJ 9/96) [741]

13345 DuBosque, Doug. *Draw Insects* (4–8). 1997, Peel paper $8.99 (978-0-939217-28-1). A carefully constructed drawing book that gives simple directions for drawing more than 80 insects, including millipedes, ticks, and spiders. (Rev: SLJ 6/98) [741.2]

13346 DuBosque, Doug. *Draw 3-D: A Step-by-Step Guide to Perspective Drawing* (4–9). Illus. by author. 1999, Peel paper $8.99 (978-0-939217-14-

4). Using easy-to-follow sketches, the author introduces the techniques of 3-D drawing, beginning with basic concepts involving depth and progressing to more difficult areas such as multiple vanishing points. (Rev: SLJ 5/99; VOYA 8/99) [741.2]

13347 DuBosque, Doug. *Learn to Draw Now!* (5–8). Illus. by author. Series: Learn to Draw. 1991, Peel paper $8.99 (978-0-939217-16-8). A simple, easily followed manual on how to draw that contains many interesting practice exercises. (Rev: SLJ 8/91) [743]

13348 Gordon, Louise. *How to Draw the Human Figure: An Anatomical Approach* (7–10). Illus. 1979, Penguin paper $18.00 (978-0-14-046477-1). This is both a short course on anatomy and a fine manual on how to draw the human body. [743]

13349 Gray, Peter. *Heroes and Villains* (5–8). Series: Kid's Guide to Drawing. 2006, Rosen LB $25.25 (978-1-4042-3330-0). Shows clearly how to draw manga heroes and villains and offers guidance on getting facial expressions just right. (Rev: BL 9/1/06; SLJ 9/06) [741.5]

13350 Hart, Christopher. *Christopher Hart's Cartoon Studio* (8–12). Illus. by author. 2003, Watson-Guptill paper $7.95 (978-0-8230-0624-3). Hart introduces cartoon techniques such as drawing the same characters consistently from different angles. Also use *Christopher Hart's Animation Studio* (2003). (Rev: SLJ 1/04) [741.5]

13351 Hart, Christopher. *Drawing on the Funny Side of the Brain* (7–12). Illus. 1998, Watson-Guptill paper $19.95 (978-0-8230-1381-4). This book describes how to create single and multipanel comic strips, with tips on joke writing, pacing, framing, color, and dialogue. (Rev: BL 7/98) [741.5]

13352 Hart, Christopher. *Kids Draw Anime* (4–8). Illus. 2002, Watson-Guptill paper $10.95 (978-0-8230-2690-6). Instructions on how to draw anime (Japanese cartoons) characters, with many colorful examples. (Rev: BL 2/1/03; SLJ 11/02) [741.5]

13353 Hart, Christopher. *Manga Mania: How to Draw Japanese Comics* (5–9). Illus. 2001, Watson-Guptill paper $19.95 (978-0-8230-3035-4). Hart looks at the techniques for drawing typical Japanese comic characters and animals, providing examples of published manga along with an introduction to the various genres of manga and an interview with a manga publisher. (Rev: BL 7/01; SLJ 7/01) [741.5]

13354 Hart, Christopher. *Manga Mania Chibi and Furry Characters: How to Draw the Adorable Mini-People and Cool Cat-Girls of Japanese Comics* (5–12). Illus. 2006, Watson-Guptill paper $19.95 (978-0-8230-2977-8). Fans of these super-cute manga characters will appreciate the step-by-step directions in this informative book. (Rev: SLJ 5/06) [741.5]

13355 Hart, Christopher. *Mecha Mania: How to Draw the Battling Robots, Cool Spaceships, and Military Vehicles of Japanese Comics* (4–8). Illus. 2002, Watson-Guptill paper $19.95 (978-0-8230-3056-9). Instructions on how to draw the high-tech, scary, fanciful machines and weapons that fill the pages of Japanese comic books. (Rev: BL 2/1/03; SLJ 4/03) [741.5]

13356 Hinds, Kathryn. *The City* (5–8). Illus. Series: Life in the Renaissance. 2003, Marshall Cavendish LB $29.93 (978-0-7614-1678-4). Using London, Paris, and Florence among the examples, this entry in a four-volume series explores most aspects of daily life within the walled cities of Western Europe during the 15th and 16th centuries. Also use *The Court* (2003). (Rev: BL 2/1/04; SLJ 4/04) [940.1]

13357 Hodge, Anthony. *Drawing* (4–8). Series: Mastering Art. 2004, Stargazer LB $.00 (978-1-932799-01-9). Along with basic information on materials, colors, and techniques, this slim volume looks at drawing the human body. Also use *Painting* (2004). (Rev: BL 11/1/04) [741.2]

13358 Janson, Klaus. *The DC Comics Guide to Pencilling Comics* (7–12). Illus. 2002, Watson-Guptill paper $19.95 (978-0-8230-1028-8). This practical guide for budding comics creators also contains lots of material for comics fans. (Rev: BL 5/1/02) [741.5]

13359 Lewis, Amanda. *Lettering: Make Your Own Cards, Signs, Gifts and More* (4–8). Illus. 1997, Kids Can paper $6.95 (978-1-55074-232-9). This book describes calligraphy and gothic lettering techniques, covering such topics as typefaces, displays, types of pens to purchase, how to determine pen size, and how to use pens, as well as explaining how to make letterhead stationery and newsletters on the computer. (Rev: BL 10/15/97; SLJ 1/98) [745.6]

13360 Mayne, Don. *Drawing Horses (That Look Real)* (4–8). Illus. by author. Series: Quick Starts for Kids! 2002, Williamson paper $8.95 (978-1-885593-74-0). Cartoonlike instructions take young artists step by step through using basic shapes to draw horses and to show movement and character. (Rev: SLJ 4/03) [743.6]

13361 Nagatomo, Haruno. *Draw Your Own Manga: Beyond the Basics* (7–12). Trans. from Japanese by Françoise White. Illus. by author. 2005, Kodansha paper $19.95 (978-4-7700-2304-9). Written and illustrated by Japanese manga artists, this is an entertaining yet professional guide to drawing in this style. (Rev: SLJ 9/05; VOYA 12/04) [741.5]

13362 Okum, David. *Manga Madness* (7–12). Illus. 2004, North Light paper $19.99 (978-1-58180-534-5). This is an excellent guide for would-be cartoonists and *manga* fans with step-by-step directions on how to produce your own art. (Rev: BL 3/15/04) [741.5]

13363 Peffer, Jessica. *DragonArt: How to Draw Fantastic Dragons and Fantasy Creatures* (5–12). Illus. by author. 2005, Impact paper $19.99 (978-1-58180-657-1). Beautiful creatures from the author's imagination fill the pages of this well-written book and will inspire young artists to develop their own fantasy style. (Rev: SLJ 5/06) [743]

13364 Pellowski, Michael M. *The Art of Making Comic Books* (4–8). Illus. 1995, Lerner LB $25.55 (978-0-8225-2304-8). A history of comic books, plus drawing techniques and advice on how to become a comic book artist. (Rev: BCCB 2/96; BL 1/1–15/96; SLJ 1/96) [741.5]

13365 Reinagle, Damon J. *Draw! Medieval Fantasies* (4–8). Illus. 1995, Peel paper $8.99 (978-0-939217-30-4). A how-to drawing book that gives simple instructions on creating such medieval subjects as dragons and castles. (Rev: BL 1/1–15/96; SLJ 3/96) [743]

13366 Reinagle, Damon J. *Draw Sports Figures* (4–8). Illus. 1997, Peel paper $8.99 (978-0-939217-32-8). In six chapters arranged by sport or sports category, the author gives easy-to-follow instructions on how to draw action figures. (Rev: SLJ 6/98) [742]

13367 Roche, Art. *Art for Kids: Comic Strips: Create Your Own Comic Strips from Start to Finish* (4–8). Illus. by author. 2007, Sterling LB $17.95 (978-1-57990-788-4). This is a practical guide to creating a comic strip, with tips on story ideas, design, creating characters, and writing jokes. (Rev: BCCB 5/07; LMC 8-9/07; SLJ 5/07) [741.5]

13368 Scott, Damian, and Kris Ex. *How to Draw Hip Hop* (7–12). 2006, Watson-Guptill paper $19.95 (978-0-8230-1446-0). This guide to drawing bright graffiti-style art with a manga flavor includes lots of back-and-forth between the authors, revealing a passion for hip-hop culture. (Rev: SLJ 7/06)

13369 Self, Caroline, and Susan Self. *Chinese Brush Painting: A Hands-on Introduction to the Traditional Art* (6–12). Illus. 2007, Tuttle $16.95 (978-0-8048-3877-1). An attractive introduction to Chinese calligraphy and brush painting, with history as well as step-by-step instructions. (Rev: BL 12/15/07) [751.4]

13370 Stephens, Jay. *Heroes!* (4–7). Illus. by author. 2007, Sterling $12.95 (978-1-57990-934-5). How to draw superheroes, masks, action moves, and so forth, with lots of great examples. (Rev: BL 12/1/07; SLJ 8/07) [741.5]

13371 Temple, Kathryn. *Drawing* (5–8). Illus. Series: Art for Kids. 2005, Sterling $17.95 (978-1-57990-587-3). A comprehensive and clearly written guide to equipment and techniques, with useful illustrations and practical exercises at the end of each section. (Rev: BL 5/1/05; SLJ 9/05) [741.2]

13372 Wallace, Mary. *I Can Make Art* (4–8). Series: I Can Make. 1997, Firefly paper $6.95 (978-1-895688-65-8). Art and crafts are combined in these 12 projects involving such techniques as watercolor, still life, chalk drawing, print making, and collage. (Rev: SLJ 12/97) [741.2]

13373 Wheeler, Annie. *Painting on a Canvas: Art Adventures for Kids* (5–8). Illus. by Debra Spina Dixon. 2006, Gibbs Smith $9.95 (978-1-58685-839-1). These projects are designed to get children's creative juices flowing and to introduce them to some of the techniques used by such world-famous artists as Matisse, Michelangelo, and Picasso. (Rev: SLJ 11/06) [701]

Gardening

13374 Klindienst, Patricia. *The Earth Knows My Name: Food, Culture, and Sustainability in the Gardens of Ethnic Americans* (8–12). Illus. 2006, Beacon $26.95 (978-0-8070-8562-2). A tour of 15 American gardens that represent the culture and ethnicity of their immigrant designers. (Rev: BL 4/1/06) [635.09]

13375 Winckler, Suzanne. *Planting the Seed: A Guide to Gardening* (6–10). Illus. 2002, Lerner LB $25.76 (978-0-8225-0081-0); paper $7.95 (978-0-8225-0471-9). This slim volume offers a wide range of gardening guidance, with material on organic gardening, the use of native plants, community gardens, and Native American traditions. (Rev: BL 5/1/02; HBG 10/02; SLJ 8/02) [635]

Magic Tricks and Optical Illusions

13376 Baker, James W. *Illusions Illustrated: A Professional Magic Show for Young Performers* (5–8). Illus. by Jeanette Swofford. 1994, Lerner paper $6.95 (978-0-8225-9512-0). Directions on how to put on a magic show with 10 different tricks.

13377 Churchill, E. Richard. *Optical Illusion Tricks and Toys* (6–10). Illus. 1989, Sterling $12.95 (978-0-8069-6868-1). A collection of more than 60 optical illusions and tricks that are both fun to perform and instructive in the principles of optics. (Rev: BL 7/89; SLJ 10/89) [152.1]

13378 Cobb, Vicki. *Magic . . . Naturally! Science Entertainments and Amusements* (7–9). Illus. 1976, HarperCollins $12.95 (978-0-397-31631-1). Thirty magic acts are described, each involving a scientific principle. [507]

13379 Colbert, David. *The Magical Worlds of Harry Potter: A Treasury of Myths, Legends, and Fasci-nating Facts* (5–9). Illus. 2001, Lumina $14.95 (978-0-9708442-0-0). Information on more than 50 topics in Harry's universe — such as alchemy, Grindylows, and Voldemort — arranged in alphabetical order. (Rev: SLJ 2/02) [823]

13380 Jones, Richard. *That's Magic! 40 Foolproof Tricks to Delight, Amaze and Entertain* (5–8). Illus. 2001, New Holland $19.95 (978-1-85974-668-4). Simple instructions and photographs teach the beginning magician a few tricks. (Rev: BL 1/1–15/02; SLJ 1/02) [793.8]

13381 Keable, Ian. *The Big Book of Magic Fun* (5–9). Photos by Steve Tanner. Illus. 2005, Barron's paper $14.99 (978-0-7641-3222-3). Step-by-step instructions, with photographs, are given for 40 tricks plus discussion of suitable props and a history of different kinds of magic and famous performers. (Rev: SLJ 3/06) [793.8]

13382 Mandelberg, Robert. *Mind-Reading Card Tricks* (6–9). Illus. by Ferruccio Sardella. 2004, Sterling paper $5.95 (978-1-4027-0948-7). Tricks that convince others that you are reading their minds are explained in detail, with difficulty ratings. (Rev: SLJ 3/05) [795.4]

13383 Tarr, Bill. *Now You See It, Now You Don't! Lessons in Sleight of Hand* (7–9). Illus. 1976, Random paper $19.95 (978-0-394-72202-3). More than 100 easy tricks to mystify one's friends. Each is graded by level of difficulty. [793.8]

13384 Wenzel, Angela. *Do You See What I See? The Art of Illusion* (5–8). Trans. from German by Rosie Jackson. 2001, Prestel $14.95 (978-3-7913-2488-3). Tricks with perspective and color, coded messages, and hidden images are all presented in this attractive volume that makes for excellent browsing. (Rev: HBG 3/02; SLJ 2/02) [152]

13385 *Wizardology: The Book of the Secrets of Merlin* (5–8). Illus. 2005, Candlewick $19.99 (978-0-7636-2895-6). This follow-up to *Dragonology* offers a variety of information for wannabe wizards. (Rev: BL 10/15/05)

13386 Zenon, Paul. *Simple Sleight-of-Hand: Card and Coin Tricks for the Beginning Magician* (4–7). Illus. 2007, Rosen LB $21.95 (978-1-4042-1070-7). Written by a practicing magician, this book walks the reader through 13 tricks that will astound and amaze; photographs provide additional explanation. (Rev: BL 11/15/07; SLJ 1/08) [793.8]

Masks and Mask Making

13387 Earl, Amanda, and Danielle Sensier. *Masks* (5–7). Illus. Series: Traditions Around the World. 1994, Thomson Learning LB $24.26 (978-1-56847-226-3). This multicultural introduction to masks discusses their origins and uses in religion, festivals, and the theater. (Rev: BL 2/1/95; SLJ 3/95) [391.43]

Paper Crafts

13388 Balchin, Judy. *Papier Mâché* (4–7). Illus. Series: Step-by-Step. 2000, Heinemann LB $24.22 (978-1-57572-328-0). Combines easy-to-follow projects with information on how papier-mâché has been used over the centuries, including applications in construction and furniture. (Rev: BL 10/15/00; HBG 10/01; SLJ 12/00) [745.54]

13389 Borja, Robert, and Corinne Borja. *Making Chinese Papercuts* (4–7). Illus. by authors. 1980, Whitman LB $15.99 (978-0-8075-4948-3). A clear explanation of an ancient art with many examples and photographs.

13390 Boursin, Didier. *Origami Paper Airplanes* (6–8). Illus. 2001, Firefly $19.95 (978-1-55209-626-0); paper $9.95 (978-1-55209-616-1). Paper airplane devotees will love the origami models offered here, which are categorized by difficulty of construction. Also use *Origami Paper Animals* (2001). (Rev: BCCB 12/01; BL 1/1–15/02; HBG 3/02; SLJ 12/01) [745.592]

13391 Grummer, Arnold E. *Paper by Kids* (5–7). Illus. 1990, Macmillan $12.95 (978-0-87518-191-2). A clear, well-organized guide to papermaking.

13392 Irvine, Joan. *How to Make Super Pop-Ups* (4–7). Illus. 1992, Morrow $14.00 (978-0-688-10690-4); paper $6.95 (978-0-688-11521-0). Lots of ideas and directions for making three-dimensional paper constructions with moving parts. (Rev: BL 1/15/93) [745]

13393 Kelly, Emery J. *Paper Airplanes: Models to Build and Fly* (4–8). Illus. 1997, Lerner LB $23.93 (978-0-8225-2401-4). This is a practical manual on making and flying paper airplanes, with good coverage of the principles of aerodynamics. (Rev: BL 12/1/97; HBG 3/98; SLJ 2/98) [745.592]

13394 Nguyen, Duy. *Monster Origami* (5–7). Illus. 2007, Sterling paper $9.95 (978-1-4027-4014-5). This how-to origami book provides easy-to-understand instructions on creating amazing paper monsters. (Rev: SLJ 3/08)

13395 Nguyen, Duy. *Origami Birds* (6–9). 2006, Sterling $19.95 (978-1-4027-1932-5). The folding techniques required to create 19 species of birds are presented in black-and-white instructions; color photographs of the finished products show how beautiful origami can be. (Rev: BL 1/1–15/07) [736.9]

13396 Powell, Michelle. *Printing* (4–7). Illus. Series: Step-by-Step. 2000, Heinemann LB $24.22 (978-1-57572-329-7). Various easy-to-follow printing projects are presented along with material on printing methods from ancient Egypt onward. (Rev: BL 10/15/00; HBG 10/01) [761]

13397 Schmidt, Norman. *Fabulous Paper Gliders* (6–12). 1998, Tamos Books $19.95 (978-1-895569-21-6). A history of glider development and the basic principles of aerodynamics are given along with patterns and step-by-step instructions for 16 gliders, all but one based on actual craft. (Rev: BL 5/15/98; SLJ 6/98) [745.592]

13398 Stevens, Clive. *Paperfolding* (4–7). Series: Step-by-Step. 2001, Heinemann LB $24.22 (978-1-57572-333-4). Easy-to-find materials are used in a number of exciting paper folding projects, each of which is described in clear, detailed directions with step-by-step illustrations. (Rev: BL 8/1/01; HBG 10/01; SLJ 10/01) [745.5]

13399 Watson, David. *Papermaking* (4–7). Series: Step-by-Step. 2000, Heinemann LB $24.22 (978-1-57572-327-3). This book shows how you can use old paper to make new paper and create a number of wonderful art objects following simple step-by-step directions. (Rev: BL 10/15/00; HBG 10/01) [745.5]

Photography, Video, and Film Making

13400 Bidner, Jenni. *The Kids' Guide to Digital Photography: How to Shoot, Save, Play with and Print Your Digital Photos* (7–10). Illus. 2004, Sterling $14.95 (978-1-57990-604-7). A user-friendly guide to digital photography and the transfer of the results to the Web and other applications. (Rev: BL 1/1–15/05; SLJ 5/05) [775]

13401 Czech, Kenneth P. *Snapshot: America Discovers the Camera* (6–9). Illus. 1996, Carolrhoda LB $30.35 (978-0-8225-1736-8). An account of the camera's long history in America and its influence on our culture. (Rev: BL 2/15/97; SLJ 12/96; VOYA 4/97) [770]

13402 Friedman, Debra. *Picture This: Fun Photography and Crafts* (4–7). Series: Kids Can Do It! 2003, Kids Can $12.95 (978-1-55337-046-8); paper $5.95 (978-1-55337-047-5). An easy-to-follow project book that combines photographs and crafts. (Rev: BL 3/15/03; HBG 10/03; SLJ 4/03) [770]

13403 Gaines, Thom. *Digital Photo Madness! 50 Weird and Wacky Things to Do with Your Digital Camera* (7–10). Illus. 2006, Sterling paper $9.95 (978-1-57990-624-5). The fun part of digital photography is altering the images, and this guide explains how, after first covering the basics. (Rev: BL 12/15/06; SLJ 8/06) [773]

13404 Morgan, Terri, and Shmuel Thaler. *Photography: Take Your Best Shot* (5–8). Illus. Series: Media Workshop. 1991, Lerner LB $21.27 (978-0-8225-2302-4). A comprehensive and well-put-together guide to photography that covers cameras, film, developing, composition, lighting, and special effects, as well as discussing career opportunities. (Rev: BL 10/1/91; SLJ 11/91) [771]

13405 Price, Susanna, and Tim Stephens. *Click! Fun with Photography* (4–8). 1997, Sterling $14.95 (978-0-8069-9541-0). A fine introduction to photography that covers both beginning and advanced subjects, including the operation of various cameras, exposure, lighting, different types of photography, and filters. (Rev: SLJ 8/97) [771]

13406 Shulman, Mark, and Hazlitt Korg. *Attack of the Killer Video Book: Tips and Tricks for Young Directors* (5–8). Illus. by Martha Newbigging. 2004, Annick $24.95 (978-1-55037-841-2); paper $12.95 (978-1-55037-840-5). Practical advice on all aspects of movie making will be helpful for aspiring directors. (Rev: BL 5/15/04; SLJ 6/04) [778.59]

13407 Varriale, Jim. *Take a Look Around: Photography Activities for Young People* (5–8). Illus. 1999, Millbrook LB $24.90 (978-0-7613-1265-9). Photographs taken by children in a summer camp photography class illustrate the importance of such elements as light and camera angles, framing, creating mood, and photographing action. (Rev: BL 3/15/00; HBG 3/00; SLJ 12/99; VOYA 2/00) [770]

Sewing and Other Needle Crafts

13408 Barnden, Betty. *Very Easy Crazy Patchwork* (7–12). Illus. 2007, Reader's Digest $24.95 (978-0-7621-0671-4); paper $19.95 (978-0-7621-0672-1). From a potholder to an evening purse or even a quilt, this book shows how to make attractive patchwork projects using hand techniques and sewing machines. (Rev: SLJ 5/07) [746.46]

13409 Brack, Heather, and Shannon Okey. *Felt Frenzy: 26 Projects for All Forms of Felting* (8–12). Illus. 2007, Interweave paper $21.95 (978-1-59668-009-8). For beginners and experts, this book contains projects creating purses, scarves, hats, and so forth through felting. (Rev: SLJ 7/07) [746]

13410 Bradberry, Sarah. *Kids Knit! Simple Steps to Nifty Projects* (4–8). Photos by Michael Hnatov. Illus. by Kim Coxey. 2004, Sterling $14.95 (978-0-8069-7733-1). Simple, clear instructions and illustrations add to the value of this book full of appealing projects. (Rev: BL 12/15/04; SLJ 2/05)

13411 Doherty, Elisabeth A. *Amigurumi! Super Happy Crochet Cute* (8–12). Illus. 2007, Sterling paper $14.95 (978-1-60059-017-7). Doherty provides patterns and clear instructions for 14 crocheted or knitted doll projects. (Rev: BL 9/15/07) [746.43]

13412 Eckman, Edie. *The Crochet Answer Book: Solutions to Every Problem You'll Ever Face, Answers to Every Question You'll Ever Ask* (7–12). Illus. 2005, Storey paper $12.95 (978-1-58017-598-2). For novice crocheters, this is a well-organized and comprehensive guide. (Rev: BL 12/15/05) [746.43]

13413 Hantman, Clea. *I Wanna Re-Do My Room* (7–12). Illus. by Azadeh Houshyar. 2006, Simon & Schuster paper $9.99 (978-0-689-87463-5). More than 50 projects are featured in this guide to room decoration, such as wall décor, box adornment, pillows, curtains, furniture, and storage ideas; illustrated with black-and-white photographs. (Rev: SLJ 6/06)

13414 Ivarsson, Anna-Stina Linden, et al. *Second-Time Cool: The Art of Chopping Up a Sweater* (7–10). Trans. by Maria Lundin. Illus. 2005, Annick $24.95 (978-1-55037-911-2); paper $12.95 (978-1-55037-910-5). Adventurous clothes recycling for the ambitious teen with too much old wool lying around. (Rev: BL 1/1–15/06; SLJ 1/06) [646.4]

13415 Kinsler, Gwen Blakley, and Jackie Young. *Crocheting* (4–7). Series: Kids Can Do It! 2003, Kids Can $12.95 (978-1-55337-176-2); paper $6.95 (978-1-55337-177-9). A simple introduction to crocheting with many easily followed diagrams and clear directions. (Rev: BL 3/15/03; HBG 10/03; SLJ 4/03) [745.5]

13416 Okey, Shannon. *Knitgrrl: Learn to Knit with 15 Fun and Funky Projects* (5–8). Photos by Shannon Fagan. Illus. 2005, Watson-Guptill paper $9.95 (978-0-8230-2618-0). Up-to-date designs are shown clearly and explained in detail. (Rev: BL 12/15/05*; SLJ 11/05; VOYA 12/05) [746.43]

13417 Okey, Shannon. *Knitgrrl 2: Learn to Knit with 16 All-New Patterns* (4–7). 2006, Watson-Guptill paper $9.99 (978-0-8230-2619-7). This sequel to *Knitgrrl* (2005) offers step-by-step instructions for 16 new projects, including bracelets, a sports bottle holder, and a cardigan. (Rev: BL 6/1–15/06; SLJ 6/06) [746]

13418 Percival, Kris. *Speed Knitting: 24 Quick and Easy Projects* (8–12). Illus. 2006, Chronicle paper $19.95 (978-0-8118-5245-6). Beginners will appreciate these simple projects that can be quickly accomplished. (Rev: BL 11/15/06) [746.32]

13419 Radcliffe, Margaret. *The Knitting Answer Book* (8–12). Illus. 2005, Storey paper $12.95 (978-1-58017-599-9). This well-organized volume introduces newcomers to knitting and also provides expert guidance for longtime knitters. (Rev: BL 12/15/05) [746.43]

13420 Ronci, Kelli. *Kids Crochet: Projects for Kids of All Ages* (4–8). Photos by John Gruen. Illus. by Lena Corwin. 2005, Stewart, Tabori & Chang $19.95 (978-1-58479-413-4). A poncho, a quilt, and a tool pouch are among the 15 crocheting projects presented, which are introduced by detailed coverage of techniques. (Rev: BL 5/15/04; SLJ 6/05) [745.5]

13421 Sadler, Judy Ann. *Corking* (4–8). Illus. Series: Kids Can! 1998, Kids Can paper $5.95 (978-1-55074-265-7). Provides directions for a handmade knitting device that is used to create knit tubes or corks popular in toys and headbands. (Rev: BL 5/15/98) [746.4]

13422 Sadler, Judy Ann. *Embroidery* (4–8). Illus. by June Bradford. Series: Kids Can Do It! 2004, Kids Can $12.95 (978-1-55337-616-3); paper $6.95 (978-1-55337-617-0). In addition to a thorough introduction to embroidery and various stitches, Sadler provides nine projects that progress in difficulty. (Rev: SLJ 8/04) [746.44]

13423 Sadler, Judy Ann, et al. *The Jumbo Book of Needlecrafts* (4–7). Illus. by Esperan a Melo, et al. 2005, Kids Can paper $16.95 (978-1-55337-793-1). After advice on getting started, step-by-step directions guide readers through a range of needlecraft projects. (Rev: SLJ 5/05)

13424 Sadler, Judy Ann. *Making Fleece Crafts* (4–7). Illus. by June Bradford. 2000, Kids Can $12.95 (978-1-55074-847-5); paper $6.95 (978-1-55074-739-3). Fifteen colorful and inviting projects using fleece including mittens, a scarf, and a jester's hat. (Rev: BL 9/15/00; SLJ 9/00) [745]

13425 Sadler, Judy Ann. *Quick Knits* (5–8). Illus. by Esperanca Melo. 2006, Kids Can $12.95 (978-1-55337-963-8); paper $6.95 (978-1-55337-964-5). Clear instructions, appealing projects, and suggestions for personalizing these are features of this introduction to knitting. (Rev: BL 1/1–15/07; SLJ 12/06) [746.43]

13426 Sadler, Judy Ann. *Simply Sewing* (4–8). Illus. by Jane Kurisu. Series: Kids Can Do It! 2004, Kids Can $12.95 (978-1-55337-659-0); paper $6.95 (978-1-55337-660-6). Detailed instructions for 12 projects — a makeup bag and a jeans skirt, for example — follow basic information on sewing by hand and by machine. (Rev: BL 12/15/04; SLJ 11/04)

13427 Storms, Biz. *All-American Quilts* (4–7). Illus. by June Bradford. Series: Kids Can Do It! 2003, Kids Can paper $6.95 (978-1-55337-539-5). Instructions are provided for making quilts with American themes — eagles, flags, and so forth. (Rev: BL 12/15/03; SLJ 1/04) [746.46]

13428 Storms, Biz. *Quilting* (4–7). Illus. by June Bradford. Series: Kids Can Do It! 2001, Kids Can $12.95 (978-1-55074-967-0); paper $5.95 (978-1-55074-805-5). Easy-to-follow, step-by-step instruc-

tions take kids through quilting projects of varying difficulty. (Rev: BL 11/1/01; HBG 3/02; SLJ 2/02) [746.46]

13429 Turner, Sharon. *Find Your Style and Knit It Too* (6–9). Illus. 2007, Wiley paper $14.99 (978-0-470-13987-5). Knitters can make fresh, fashionable projects using this book geared to middle- and high-schoolers that gives basic instructions. (Rev: BL 12/15/07) [746.43]

13430 Warwick, Ellen. *Injeanuity* (5–8). Illus. by Bernice Lum. 2006, Kids Can $12.95 (978-1-55337-681-1). Seventeen projects involving jeans and a sewing machine are shown with clear directions. (Rev: BL 6/1–15/06; SLJ 6/06) [746.9]

13431 Wenger, Jennifer, et al. *Teen Knitting Club: Chill Out and Knit Some Cool Stuff* (5–9). Illus. 2004, Artisan $17.95 (978-1-57965-244-9). Children who already know how to know will derive the most benefit from this collection of 35 appealing projects. (Rev: BL 12/15/04; SLJ 2/05)

13432 Werker, Kim. *Crochet Me: Designs to Fuel the Crochet Revolution* (8–12). Illus. 2007, Interweave paper $21.95 (978-1-59668-044-9). Not for beginners, this is a collection of crochet designs with information on designers and technical aspects. (Rev: BL 12/15/07) [746.43]

13433 Werker, Kim. *Get Hooked Again: Simple Steps to Crochet More Cool Stuff* (6–9). Illus. 2007, Watson-Guptill paper $11.95 (978-0-8230-5110-6). A second volume of crochet projects — a scarf, hat, choker, tote, and so forth — with clear explanations and helpful photographs. (Rev: BL 12/15/07; SLJ 2/08) [746.43]

13434 Willing, Karen Bates, and Julie Bates Dock. *Fabric Fun for Kids: Step-by-Step Projects for Children (and Their Grown-ups)* (4–9). 1997, Now & Then LB $17.95 (978-0-9641820-4-2); paper $12.95 (978-0-9641820-5-9). From simple sewing projects to more complex quilting work, this book gives good step-by-step instructions, provides a rundown on necessary sewing tools and materials, and discusses methods for putting designs on fabrics. (Rev: SLJ 4/98) [746.46]

13435 Wilson, Sule Greg C. *African American Quilting: The Warmth of Tradition* (4–7). Illus. Series: Library of African American Arts and Culture. 1999, Rosen LB $27.95 (978-0-8239-1854-6). This book traces African influences on textile patterns and techniques particularly as they have been applied to quilting by African Americans. (Rev: BL 2/15/00; SLJ 9/99) [746.46]

13436 Worrall, Jocelyn. *Simple Gifts to Stitch: 30 Elegant and Easy Projects* (8–12). Illus. 2007, Potter paper $19.95 (978-0-307-34756-5). Provides easy-to-follow patterns for scarves, bags, hats, aprons, pillows, and so forth. (Rev: SLJ 8/07) [746]

Stamp, Coin, and Other Types of Collecting

13437 Dyson, Cindy. *Rare and Interesting Stamps* (5–8). Series: Costume, Tradition, and Culture: Reflecting on the Past. 1998, Chelsea $19.75 (978-0-7910-5171-9). The stories behind 25 rare and unusual stamps start with Britain's first one-penny stamp, which bore a portrait of Queen Victoria. (Rev: BL 3/15/99; HBG 10/99) [769.56]

13438 Mackay, James. *The Guinness Book of Stamps, Facts and Feats* (7–12). Illus. 1989, Guinness $34.95 (978-0-85112-351-6). All sorts of curiosities about postage stamps such as the most valuable, the largest, and so on. (Rev: BL 4/15/89) [769.56]

13439 Owens, Thomas S. *Collecting Baseball Cards: 21st Century Edition*. Rev. ed. (4–8). 2001, Millbrook LB $26.90 (978-0-7613-1708-1). An entertaining introduction to collecting baseball cards, with information on the history of the industry, on how to determine the condition of cards, and how to use the Internet to buy and sell. (Rev: HBG 10/01; SLJ 7/01) [796]

13440 Owens, Thomas S. *Collecting Comic Books: A Young Person's Guide* (5–8). 1995, Millbrook LB $26.90 (978-1-56294-580-0). A beginner's guide to comic book collecting, with sections on kinds of collections, sources, and organizations. (Rev: BL 2/1/96; SLJ 1/96) [741.5]

13441 Owens, Thomas S. *Collecting Stock Car Racing Memorabilia* (4–8). Illus. 2001, Millbrook LB $26.90 (978-0-7613-1853-8). NASCAR fans in particular will appreciate this practical and detailed guide to collecting, which includes extensive lists of useful addresses. (Rev: BL 12/15/01; HBG 3/02; SLJ 11/01) [796.72]

13442 Pellant, Chris. *Collecting Gems and Minerals: Hold the Treasures of the Earth in the Palm of Your Hand* (5–8). Illus. 1998, Sterling $14.95 (978-0-8069-9760-5). After explaining how gems and minerals are formed, this book discusses necessary equipment for the hunter, where to look, how to identify specimens, and how to organize one's collection. (Rev: BL 6/1–15/98; SLJ 8/98) [553.8]

13443 *The Postal Service Guide to U.S. Stamps* (7–12). Illus. 1988, U.S. Postal Service $5.00 (978-0-9604756-8-1). A well-illustrated history of U.S. postage stamps. [769.56]

13444 *Scott Standard Postage Stamp Catalogue: Countries of the World* (7–12). 1997, Scott paper $35.00 (978-0-89487-231-0). This is the most comprehensive stamp catalog in print. Volume 1 deals with stamps from the English-speaking world; the other three volumes cover alphabetically the other countries of the world. [769.56]

Woodworking and Carpentry

13445 Schwarz, Renee. *Birdhouses* (4–7). Illus. Series: Kids Can Do It! 2005, Kids Can $12.95 (978-1-55337-549-4); paper $6.95 (978-1-55337-550-0). Nine different birdhouse projects for children to tackle, with illustrated instructions and photographs of the finished products. (Rev: BL 4/1/05; SLJ 5/05) [690]

13446 Walker, Lester. *Housebuilding for Children* (4–7). Illus. 1977, Overlook paper $16.95 (978-0-87951-332-0). The construction of six different kinds of houses, including a tree house, is clearly described in text and pictures.

Jokes, Puzzles, Riddles, and Word Games

13447 Becker, Helaine. *Funny Business: Clowning Around, Practical Jokes, Cool Comedy, Cartooning, and More* (5–8). Illus. by Claudia Dávila. 2005, Maple Tree $21.95 (978-1-897066-40-9); paper $9.95 (978-1-897066-41-6). Tips on body language, stand-up routines, clowning, and so forth are accompanied by discussion of various types of humor, a self-quiz, and recipes for delights including "Moose Droppings." (Rev: SLJ 1/06) [808.7]

13448 Rosenbloom, Joseph. *Biggest Riddle Book in the World* (6–9). Illus. 1977, Sterling paper $6.95 (978-0-8069-8884-9). Very clever riddles collected by a children's librarian. [808.7]

13449 Rosenbloom, Joseph. *Dr. Knock-Knock's Official Knock-Knock Dictionary* (6–9). Illus. 1977, Sterling paper $4.95 (978-0-8069-8936-5). This very humorous collection includes more than 500 knock-knock jokes. [808.7]

13450 Rosenbloom, Joseph. *The Gigantic Joke Book* (6–9). 1978, Sterling paper $6.95 (978-0-8069-7514-6). A large collection of jokes that span time from King Arthur to the space age. Also use *Funniest Joke Book Ever* (1986). [808.7]

13451 Schwartz, Alvin, comp. *Tomfoolery: Trickery and Foolery with Words* (6–9). Illus. 1973, HarperCollins $12.95 (978-0-397-31466-9). A collection of jokes and riddles from folklore and from children. [398]

13452 Schwartz, Alvin, comp. *Witcracks: Jokes and Jests from American Folklore* (6–9). Illus. 1973, HarperCollins LB $14.89 (978-0-397-31475-1). Tall tales, jokes, riddles, and humorous stories are included in this collection from our past. [398]

Mysteries, Curiosities, and Controversial Subjects

13453 Aaseng, Nathan. *The Bermuda Triangle* (7–10). Series: Mystery Library. 2001, Lucent LB $27.45 (978-1-56006-769-6). Using a variety of sources, this book explores the past and present of this controversial phenomenon. (Rev: BL 9/15/01) [001.9]

13454 Allen, Eugenie. *The Best Ever Kids' Book of Lists* (4–8). Illus. 1991, Avon paper $2.95 (978-0-380-76357-3). Brief lists of the biggest, smallest, strangest, ugliest, etc., with humorous drawings. (Rev: BL 12/15/91) [031.02]

13455 Allman, Toney. *Werewolves* (4–7). Series: Monsters. 2004, Gale LB $26.20 (978-0-7377-2620-6). An examination of the origins of the werewolf, with references to and illustrations from movie and TV appearances by these monsters. (Rev: SLJ 4/05) [398]

13456 Aslan, Madalyn. *What's Your Sign? A Cosmic Guide for Young Astrologers* (5–9). Illus. by Jennifer Kalis. 2002, Grosset $12.99 (978-0-448-42693-8). A lively, spiral-bound guide to the 12 signs of the zodiac and the personality traits they represent, with information on the underlying mythology and lists of famous people born under each sign. (Rev: SLJ 9/02) [133.5]

13457 Blackwood, Gary L. *Extraordinary Events and Oddball Occurrences* (4–7). Illus. Series: Secrets of the Unexplained. 1999, Marshall Cavendish LB $29.93 (978-0-7614-0748-5). A book that covers such unusual occurrences as strange things falling from the sky, teleportation, and unexplained appearances and disappearances. (Rev: BL 3/1/00; HBG 10/00) [001.9]

13458 Blackwood, Gary L. *Long-Ago Lives* (4–7). Illus. Series: Secrets of the Unexplained. 1999, Marshall Cavendish LB $19.95 (978-0-7614-0747-8). A look at the subject of reincarnation. (Rev: BL 3/1/00; HBG 10/00) [133.9]

13459 Campbell, Peter A. *Alien Encounters* (5–7). Illus. 2000, Millbrook LB $23.90 (978-0-7613-1402-8). An overview of eight supposed encounters between humans and aliens. (Rev: BL 7/00; HBG 10/00; SLJ 4/00) [001.9]

13460 Cohen, Daniel. *Prophets of Doom: The Millennium Edition* (6–8). 1999, Millbrook LB $24.90 (978-0-7613-1317-5). An updated edition of the 1992 volume on individuals and groups who have predicted the end of the world, with additions including David Koresh of the Heaven's Gate cult and Shoko Ashara, the cultist who released nerve gas into a Tokyo subway. (Rev: BL 5/15/99; SLJ 6/99) [133.3]

13461 Crisp, Tony. *Super Minds: People with Amazing Mind Power* (4–7). Illus. by Mary Kuper. 1999, Element Books paper $4.95 (978-1-901881-03-5). A survey of near-death experiences, feral children's case histories, and instances of strange mental powers. (Rev: SLJ 5/99) [001.9]

13462 Deem, James M. *How to Find a Ghost* (5–8). Illus. 1990, Avon paper $3.25 (978-0-380-70829-1). An attempt to explain how to have a supernatural experience. (Rev: BCCB 11/88; BL 11/1/88; SLJ 11/88) [133.1]

13463 Dugan, Ellen. *Elements of Witchcraft: Natural Magick for Teens* (8–12). 2003, Llewellyn paper $14.94 (978-1-73870-393-7). A practicing witch introduces teens to the basics of witchcraft, with tips on proper casting of spells and a discussion of ethical concerns. (Rev: BL 6/1–15/03) [133.4]

13464 Dumont-Le Cornec, Elisabeth. *Wonders of the World: Natural and Man-Made Majesties* (5–9). Illus. by Laureen Topalian. 2007, Abrams $24.95 (978-0-8109-9417-1). Seventy-one striking sites around the world, both natural and man-made and featured on the UNESCO World Heritage list, are shown in beautiful photographs. (Rev: BL 12/15/07) [031.02]

13465 Feldman, David. *Why Do Clocks Run Clockwise? And Other Imponderables: Mysteries of Everyday Life* (8–12). 1987, Harper & Row paper $12.95 (978-0-06-091515-5). Questions about everyday occurrences and objects, like "Why do nurses wear white?" are answered in this book of curiosities. [031.02]

13466 Feldman, David, and Kassie Schwan. *Do Elephants Jump? An Imponderables Book* (8–12). Illus. Series: Imponderables. 2004, HarperCollins $19.95 (978-0-06-053913-9). Why *do* elephants jump? Another intriguing — or unexpected — question is answered in this tenth installment in the attention-grabbing series. (Rev: BL 11/1/04) [031]

13467 Garden, Nancy. *Devils and Demons* (7–9). 1976, HarperCollins $11.95 (978-0-397-31666-3). An international survey of the weird demons in which various cultures and peoples believe. [133]

13468 Genge, N. E. *The Book of Shadows: The Unofficial Charmed Companion* (7–12). Illus. 2000, Three Rivers $14.00 (978-0-609-80652-4). A guide to some of the basic tenets of witchcraft that form the basis for *Charmed,* the popular TV series about teen witches. (Rev: SLJ 2/01; VOYA 6/01)

13469 Halls, Kelly Milner. *Tales of the Cryptids: Mysterious Creatures That May or May Not Exist* (4–7). Illus. by Rick Spears. 2006, Darby Creek $18.95 (978-1-58196-049-5). A fun, close-up look at cryptozoology, the study of legendary animals (that may or may not be real) such as the Loch Ness Monster and Bigfoot. (Rev: BL 11/15/06; SLJ 12/06) [001.944]

13470 Harvey, Michael. *The End of the World* (6–10). Series: Great Mysteries: Opposing Viewpoints. 1992, Greenhaven LB $22.45 (978-0-89908-096-3). A review of many of the dire predictions that foretold the end of the world. (Rev: BL 1/15/93) [001.9]

13471 Holt, David, and Bill Mooney, retel. *The Exploding Toilet: Modern Urban Legends* (7–12). Illus. by Kevin Pope. 2004, August House $16.95 (978-0-87483-754-4); paper $6.95 (978-0-87483-715-5). Amazing, often funny, shocking stories, many of which have appeared on the Internet. (Rev: SLJ 8/04) [398.2]

13472 Huang, Chungliang Al. *The Chinese Book of Animal Powers* (5–7). Illus. 1999, HarperCollins LB $16.89 (978-0-06-027729-1). The 12 animals of the Chinese zodiac are introduced in double-page spreads, and the characteristics and powers of each are outlined. (Rev: BCCB 12/99; BL 1/1–15/00; HBG 3/00) [133.5]

13473 Hubbard-Brown, Janet. *The Curse of the Hope Diamond* (4–7). Illus. 1991, Avon paper $2.99

(978-0-380-76222-4). A mystery style is used to introduce historical information about this jewel and the bad luck it seems to carry. (Rev: BL 12/15/91) [736.23]

13474 Innes, Brian. *The Bermuda Triangle* (4–7). Illus. Series: Unsolved Mysteries. 1999, Raintree LB $30.40 (978-0-8172-5485-8). The author explores many theories that have been proposed to explain disappearances off the southeast coast of the U.S. (Rev: BL 5/15/99; HBG 10/99) [001.94]

13475 Innes, Brian. *The Cosmic Joker* (4–7). Illus. Series: Unsolved Mysteries. 1999, Raintree LB $25.69 (978-0-8172-5487-2). This book introduces Charles Fort, the Cosmic Joker, and the many strange facts and coincidences he has uncovered. (Rev: BL 5/15/99; HBG 10/99; SLJ 9/99) [001.94]

13476 Innes, Brian. *Giant Humanlike Beasts* (4–7). Series: Unsolved Mysteries. 1999, Raintree LB $30.40 (978-0-8172-5484-1). This account explores stories about the Abominable Snowman, or yeti, and other sightings of primitive creatures, while questioning the possibility of living links with Neanderthals. (Rev: BL 5/15/99; HBG 10/99; SLJ 9/99) [001.9]

13477 Innes, Brian. *Millennium Prophecies* (5–8). Illus. 1999, Raintree LB $30.40 (978-0-8172-5486-5). All sorts of prophecies relating to the calendar and the millennium are explored in this attractive volume. (Rev: BL 5/15/99; HBG 10/99; SLJ 9/99; VOYA 10/99) [001.7]

13478 Innes, Brian. *Mysterious Healing* (5–8). Illus. Series: Unsolved Mysteries. 1999, Raintree LB $25.69 (978-0-8172-5489-6). Hands-on healing, acupuncture, iridology, and auras are some of the subjects discussed in this volume. (Rev: BL 5/15/99; HBG 10/99; SLJ 9/99; VOYA 10/99) [001.7]

13479 Johnson, Julie Tallard. *Teen Psychic: Exploring Your Intuitive Spiritual Powers* (8–12). 2003, Inner Traditions paper $14.95 (978-0-89281-094-9). An introduction to investigating and developing one's intuitive powers, with quizzes, exercises, mediations, and many personal stories from teens. (Rev: BL 1/1–15/04; VOYA 4/04) [131]

13480 Kallen, Stuart A. *Dreams* (4–8). Illus. Series: The Mystery Library. 2004, Gale LB $29.95 (978-1-59018-288-8). In this volume in the Mystery Library, Kallen examines topics including dream science, the interpretation of dreams, and telepathic dreaming. Also use *Ghosts, Possessions and Exorcisms,* and *Shamans* (all 2004). (Rev: BL 5/15/04) [154.6]

13481 Kallen, Stuart A. *Fortune-Telling* (4–8). Illus. Series: Mystery Library. 2004, Gale LB $29.95 (978-1-59018-289-5). This exploration of the history and mystery of fortune-telling separates fact from fiction. (Rev: BL 5/15/04) [133.3]

13482 Kallen, Stuart A. *Witches* (7–10). Illus. Series: Mystery Library. 2000, Lucent LB $29.95 (978-1-56006-688-0). A history of witchcraft precedes discussion of the beliefs and rituals of today's Wiccans. (Rev: BL 9/1/00; HBG 3/01; SLJ 9/00) [133.4]

13483 Kemp, Gillian. *Tea Leaves, Herbs, and Flowers: Fortune-Telling the Gypsy Way* (5–9). Illus. by Mary Kuper. Series: Elements of the Extraordinary. 1998, Element Books paper $5.95 (978-1-901881-92-9). A look at the art of reading tea leaves and the lore and language of flowers. (Rev: SLJ 1/99) [133.3]

13484 Krensky, Stephen. *Frankenstein* (4–7). Illus. Series: Monster Chronicles. 2006, Lerner LB $26.60 (978-0-8225-5923-8). A survey of the folklore and fiction featuring Frankenstein's monster, including excerpts from the famous Mary Shelley novel. Also use *Vampires* and *Werewolves* (both 2006). (Rev: SLJ 2/07) [823]

13485 McHargue, Georgess. *Meet the Werewolf* (6–9). 1976, HarperCollins $11.95 (978-0-397-31662-5). A factual account that explores the evidence concerning the existence of werewolves. Also use *Meet the Witches* (1984). [133.4]

13486 Miller, Raymond H. *Vampires* (4–7). Series: Monsters. 2004, Gale LB $26.20 (978-0-7377-2619-0). An examination of the origins of the vampire, with references to and illustrations from movie and TV appearances by these monsters. (Rev: SLJ 4/05) [398]

13487 Myers, Janet Nuzum. *Strange Stuff: True Stories of Odd Places and Things* (5–8). Illus. 1999, Linnet LB $19.50 (978-0-208-02405-3). A collection of curiosities — items about zombies, quicksand, scorpions, poisonous snakes, black holes, Bigfoot, mermaids, voodoo, the Bermuda Triangle, and feral children raised by wolves. (Rev: HBG 3/00; SLJ 7/99; VOYA 2/00) [001.9]

13488 Nardo, Don. *Atlantis* (5–8). Illus. Series: The Mystery Library. 2004, Gale LB $29.95 (978-1-59018-287-1). The author examines whether the ancient story of the lost continent of Atlantis — as described by Plato — could be true. (Rev: BL 5/15/04; SLJ 4/04) [001.94]

13489 Nardo, Don, and Bradley Steffens. *Medusa* (4–7). Series: Monsters. 2004, Gale LB $26.20 (978-0-7377-2617-6). Describes the mythological personage, telling the story of Perseus killing Medusa, and showing her role in paintings, sculptures, movie stills, and computer games. Also use *Cyclops* (2004). (Rev: SLJ 4/05) [398.2]

13490 Netzley, Patricia D. *ESP* (7–10). Series: Mystery Library. 2001, Lucent LB $29.95 (978-1-56006-770-2). A serious look at the phenomenon known as extrasensory perception, incorporating the latest research on the subject. (Rev: BL 9/15/01; SLJ 5/01) [133]

13491 Netzley, Patricia D. *Haunted Houses* (7–10). Illus. Series: Mystery Library. 2000, Lucent LB $29.95 (978-1-56006-685-9). A balanced account that examines specific cases of hauntings and discusses such topics as ghosts, poltergeists, seances, and mediums. (Rev: BL 9/1/00; HBG 3/01; SLJ 9/00; VOYA 4/01) [133.1]

13492 Netzley, Patricia D. *Unicorns* (6–10). Illus. Series: Mystery Library. 2000, Lucent LB $27.45 (978-1-56006-687-3). The unicorn's role in myth and legend is the focus of this interesting, well-illustrated volume. (Rev: SLJ 7/01) [398]

13493 O'Connell, Margaret F. *The Magic Cauldron: Witchcraft for Good and Evil* (7–9). 1976, Phillips $38.95 (978-0-87599-187-0). In this history of witchcraft, the reader learns that witches can be agents of both good and evil. [133]

13494 O'Neill, Catherine. *Amazing Mysteries of the World* (7–12). Illus. 1983, National Geographic LB $12.50 (978-0-87044-502-6). UFOs, Bigfoot, and Easter Island are only three of the many mysteries explored. [001.9]

13495 *Pick Me Up* (4–8). Illus. 2006, DK $29.99 (978-0-7566-2159-9). This attractive, child-friendly compilation of facts and figures offers information on a wide variety of topics, including nature, fashion, math, politics, popular culture, geography, music, movies, and technology. (Rev: SLJ 12/06) [900]

13496 Powell, Jillian. *Body Decoration* (4–8). Illus. Series: Traditions Around the World. 1995, Thomson Learning LB $24.26 (978-1-56847-276-8). An interesting book that explains the uses of body decoration in history and discusses tattooing, face painting, and body piercing. (Rev: SLJ 7/95) [617]

13497 Reid, Lori. *Hand Reading: Discover Your Future* (5–9). Illus. Series: Elements of the Extraordinary. 1998, Element Books paper $5.95 (978-1-901881-82-0). Palmistry is explained in detail, including the meaning of the shape of the hand and nails and of each line and curve, and how hand gestures can reveal clues to personalities. (Rev: SLJ 1/99) [133.6]

13498 *Ripley's Believe It or Not!* (4–7). Illus. 2004, Ripley $25.95 (978-1-893951-73-0). Packed with fascinating trivia and fun for browsing, this appealing volume focuses on weird and amazing facts. (Rev: SLJ 2/05) [031.02]

13499 Roberts, Nancy. *Southern Ghosts* (6–9). Illus. 1979, Sandlapper paper $7.95 (978-0-87844-075-7). Thirteen ghostly tales from the South are retold with photographs of their locales. [133]

13500 Roberts, Russell. *Vampires* (7–10). Series: Mystery Library. 2001, Lucent LB $27.45 (978-1-

56006-835-8). A research-oriented account that explores the origins of the legends and stories involving vampires. (Rev: BL 9/15/01) [001.9]

13501 Roleff, Tamara L., ed. *Black Magic and Witches* (5–8). Series: Fact or Fiction? 2003, Gale paper $18.70 (978-0-7377-1319-0). A good starting point for debate over witchcraft, with essays for and against witches, magic, and Harry Potter, and some history of persecution of witches. (Rev: SLJ 3/03) [133.43]

13502 Rosen, Michael J. *Balls! Round 2* (4–7). Illus. by John Margeson. Series: Balls! 2008, Darby Creek $18.95 (978-1-58196-066-2). This sequel to *Balls!* (2006) introduces even more balls — bocce, croquet, meatballs, even the Magic Eight ball — with all kinds of facts, puzzles, experiments, and fun. (Rev: BLO 6/17/08; SLJ 7/08) [796.3]

13503 Savage, Candace. *Wizards: An Amazing Journey Through the Last Great Age of Magic* (5–8). Illus. 2003, Greystone $17.95 (978-1-55054-943-0). An appealing, oversize book full of information on witchcraft and wizardry in the late 17th century, when science and sorcery were not far apart. (Rev: BL 6/1–15/03; VOYA 8/03) [133]

13504 Shaw, Maria. *Maria Shaw's Book of Love: Horoscopes, Palmistry, Numbers, Candles, Gemstones and Colors* (8–12). Illus. 2005, Llewellyn paper $14.95 (978-0-7387-0545-3). A lighthearted guide to unscientific methods of predicting the course of true love. (Rev: SLJ 2/05) [133.3]

13505 Shuker, Karl P. N. *Mysteries of Planet Earth: An Encyclopedia of the Inexplicable* (6–12). Illus. 1999, Carlton $22.95 (978-1-85868-802-2). A well-illustrated exploration of unusual — and mostly unexplained — phenomena including the Loch Ness monster, the Shroud of Turin, green polar bears, pea-soup fog, and the dodo bird. (Rev: VOYA 4/00) [001.94]

13506 Slade, Arthur. *Monsterology: Fabulous Lives of the Creepy, the Revolting, and the Undead* (5–8). Illus. by Derek Mah. 2005, Tundra paper $8.95 (978-0-88776-714-2). Dracula, Medusa, Dr. Jekyll/ Mr. Hyde, and Sasquatch are among the characters profiled in this entertaining volume, each with a list of loves and hates, favorite saying, and fashion rating. (Rev: SLJ 2/06; VOYA 2/06)

13507 Stein, Wendy. *Witches* (6–9). Series: Great Mysteries: Opposing Viewpoints. 1995, Greenhaven LB $17.96 (978-1-56510-240-8). A discussion of the real nature of witches. (Rev: BL 4/15/95; SLJ 3/95) [133.4]

13508 Van Praagh, James. *Looking Beyond: A Teen's Guide to the Spiritual World* (8–12). Illus. 2003, Simon & Schuster paper $12.00 (978-0-7432-2942-5). Psychic Van Praagh tells teens what his contacts with the spirit world have taught him about the meaning of life and what we can do to make the most of it. (Rev: BL 1/1–15/04) [133.9]

13509 Wand, Kelly, ed. *Ape-Men: Fact or Fiction?* (6–12). 2005, Gale LB $29.95 (978-0-7377-1892-8). This volume consists of ten essays about large, legendary apelike creatures (known variously as Bigfoot, Sasquatch, and Yeti) sighted from the Himalayas to North America; half of the essays refute their existence and the others conversely offer proof. (Rev: SLJ 6/06)

13510 Windham, Kathryn Tucker. *Jeffrey Introduces 13 More Southern Ghosts* (7–10). 1978, Univ. of Alabama paper $13.95 (978-0-8173-0381-5). A total of 13 ghosts tell their weird stories. [133]

13511 Winters, Paul A. *Paranormal Phenomena* (8–12). Illus. Series: Opposing Viewpoints. 1997, Greenhaven LB $26.20 (978-1-56510-558-4). This collection of articles explores such controversial topics as UFOs, life after death, and ESP. (Rev: BL 7/97; SLJ 9/97; VOYA 12/97) [133]

Sports and Games

General and Miscellaneous

13512 Aaseng, Nathan. *The Locker Room Mirror: How Sports Reflect Society* (7–10). 1993, Walker LB $15.85 (978-0-8027-8218-2). Aaseng argues that problems in professional sports today — cheating, drug abuse, violence, commercialization, discrimination — are reflections of society at large. (Rev: BL 6/1–15/93; SLJ 5/93) [306.4]

13513 Alexander, Kyle. *Pro Wrestling's Most Punishing Finishing Moves* (4–7). Series: Pro Wrestling Legends. 2000, Chelsea $25.00 (978-0-7910-5833-6). This book describes the most effective finishing moves in the sport of wrestling and fighters who use them. (Rev: BL 3/1/01; HBG 3/01) [796.8]

13514 Alexander, Kyle. *The Women of Pro Wrestling* (4–7). Illus. Series: Pro Wrestling Legends. 2000, Chelsea $25.00 (978-0-7910-5839-8); paper $25.00 (978-0-7910-5840-4). After introducing several famous women pro wrestlers, this account describes women's roles in this sport in and out of the ring. (Rev: BL 10/15/00; HBG 3/01) [796.812]

13515 Birkemoe, Karen. *Strike a Pose: The Planet Girl Guide to Yoga* (5–10). Illus. by Heather Collett. Series: Planet Girl. 2007, . This is a practical, easygoing guide to yoga poses, breathing, meditation, and uses in sports. (Rev: SLJ 8/07) [613.7]

13516 Bizley, Kirk. *Inline Skating* (4–7). Series: Radical Sports. 1999, Heinemann LB $24.22 (978-1-57572-942-8). As well as a history of inline skating, this book tells how to get started and gives information on equipment, techniques, terms, and safety. (Rev: SLJ 4/00) [796]

13517 Blumenthal, Karen. *Let Me Play: The Story of Title IX: The Law That Changed the Future of Girls in America* (6–10). Illus. 2005, Simon & Schuster $17.95 (978-0-689-85957-1). Personal anecdotes, political cartoons, and profiles of female athletes add to the story of the 1972 passage of Title IX, which bans sex discrimination in U.S. schools. (Rev: BL 7/05; SLJ 7/05*) [796]

13518 Ching, Jacqueline. *Adventure Racing* (7–10). Series: Ultra Sports. 2002, Rosen LB $26.50 (978-0-8239-3555-0). This is a fine introduction to this new, outdoor, multidiscipline sport that involves biking, paddling, and climbing plus survival skills and outdoor savvy. (Rev: BL 9/1/02) [796.5]

13519 Coleman, Lori. *Beginning Strength Training* (4–7). Photos by Jimmy Clarke. Series: Beginning Sports. 1998, Lerner LB $27.15 (978-0-8225-3511-9). This abridged version of *Jeff Savage's Fundamental Strength Training* is a beginner's book on body development. (Rev: HBG 10/99; SLJ 2/99) [796]

13520 Corbett, Doris, and John Cheffers, eds. *Unique Games and Sports Around the World: A Reference Guide* (4–9). Illus. 2001, Greenwood $85.00 (978-0-313-29778-6). More than 300 games and sports are organized by continent and then by country, with details of the number of players, equipment, rules, and so forth, and indications of whether this is a suitable game for the classroom or playground. (Rev: SLJ 8/01) [790.1]

13521 Crossingham, John. *Cheerleading in Action* (4–7). Series: Sports in Action. 2003, Crabtree LB $25.27 (978-0-7787-0333-4); paper $6.95 (978-0-7787-0353-2). This is a colorful, attractive introduction to cheerleading, the cheers, costumes, duties, and its importance in sports. (Rev: BL 11/15/03) [791]

13522 Crossingham, John. *In-Line Skating in Action* (4–7). Series: Sports in Action. 2002, Crabtree LB $25.27 (978-0-7787-0328-0); paper $6.95 (978-0-7737-0348-3). A fine introduction to this fast-growing sport with easy-to-follow descriptions of moves and techniques. (Rev: BL 1/1–15/03; SLJ 10/03) [796.9]

13523 Crossingham, John. *Lacrosse in Action* (4–7). Series: Sports in Action. 2002, Crabtree LB $25.27 (978-0-7787-0329-7); paper $6.95 (978-0-7737-0349-0). A clear, concise introduction to lacrosse that discusses techniques, equipment, rules, and safety precautions. (Rev: BL 1/1–15/03) [796.34]

13524 Crossingham, John. *Wrestling in Action* (4–7). Series: Sports in Action. 2003, Crabtree LB $25.27 (978-0-7787-0336-5); paper $6.95 (978-0-7787-0356-3). This introduction to wrestling describes basic moves, skills, and rules. (Rev: BL 11/15/03) [796.8]

13525 Dolan, Ellen M. *Susan Butcher and the Iditarod Trail* (5–7). Illus. 1993, Walker LB $15.85 (978-0-8027-8212-0). This book gives the history of the Iditarod sled dog race and tells the story of Susan Butcher, who first entered the race in 1978. (Rev: BL 4/1/93; SLJ 4/93) [798.8]

13526 Feinberg, Jeremy R. *Reading the Sports Page: A Guide to Understanding Sports Statistics* (7–10). 1992, Macmillan LB $21.00 (978-0-02-734420-2). Explains how to read baseball, basketball, football, hockey, and tennis statistics in newspaper sports pages. (Rev: BL 1/15/93; SLJ 1/93) [796]

13527 Gay, Kathlyn. *They Don't Wash Their Socks! Sports Superstitions* (6–9). Illus. 1990, Walker LB $14.85 (978-0-8027-6917-6). A compendium of myths and superstitions that helps explain some of the unusual behavior of players and coaches. (Rev: VOYA 8/90) [796]

13528 Gedatus, Gus. *In-Line Skating for Fitness* (4–7). Series: Nutrition and Fitness. 2001, Capstone LB $25.26 (978-0-7368-0707-4). Inline skating is introduced with an emphasis on fitness benefits and the necessity of a healthy diet. (Rev: BL 9/15/01; HBG 10/01) [796]

13529 Gryski, Camilla. *Cat's Cradle, Owl's Eyes: A Book of String Games* (4–7). Illus. by Tom Sankey. 1984, Morrow LB $15.93 (978-0-688-03940-0); paper $6.95 (978-0-688-03941-7). Explanations of 21 string figures, plus variations. [793.9]

13530 Gryski, Camilla. *Many Stars and More String Games* (4–8). Illus. by Tom Sankey. 1985, Morrow paper $7.95 (978-0-688-05792-3). Figures taken from a range of cultures to be mastered by agile fingers. (Rev: BL 12/15/85; SLJ 1/86) [793.9]

13531 Gryski, Camilla. *Super String Games* (6–8). Illus. 1988, Morrow paper $6.95 (978-0-688-07684-9). Directions for 26 string games from around the world are given in text and diagrams. (Rev: BL 3/1/88; SLJ 6/88) [793]

13532 Hall, Godfrey. *Games* (5–7). Illus. Series: Traditions Around the World. 1995, Thomson

Learning LB $24.26 (978-1-56847-345-1). An oversize book that covers, in text and large color pictures, various games played in different regions around the world. (Rev: BL 6/1–15/95; SLJ 9/95) [790.1]

13533 Hanmer, Trudy J. *The Hunting Debate* (6–9). Illus. Series: Issues in Focus. 1999, Enslow LB $26.60 (978-0-7660-1110-6). The author discusses various forms of hunting and the motives and methods behind each, with pro and con arguments by animal rights and gun control advocates. (Rev: BL 2/15/00; HBG 9/00; SLJ 6/00) [179.]

13534 Hastings, Penny. *Sports for Her: A Reference Guide for Teenage Girls* (7–12). Illus. 1999, Greenwood $57.95 (978-0-313-30551-1). The basics of many individual sports are covered, with tips on playing sports in general for the young female athlete. (Rev: SLJ 7/00; VOYA 6/00) [796]

13535 Hayhurst, Chris. *Wakeboarding! Throw a Tantrum* (4–8). Series: Extreme Sports. 2000, Rosen LB $26.50 (978-0-8239-3008-1). This new water sport is described with material on the equipment needed and the necessary safety precautions. (Rev: BL 6/1–15/00; SLJ 8/00) [797.1]

13536 Housewright, Ed. *Winning Track and Field for Girls* (7–12). 2003, Facts on File $35.00 (978-0-8160-5231-8). A history of women's track is followed by specific information on sprints, hurdles, cross-country, triathlon, and so forth, with details of record holders and quotations from famous athletes; final chapters cover mental and physical preparation. (Rev: SLJ 6/04; VOYA 6/04) [796.42]

13537 Howes, Chris. *Caving* (4–8). Series: Radical Sports. 2003, Heinemann LB $25.64 (978-1-58810-626-1). Technique, safety, gear, and other vital aspects are covered in this introduction to the sport. (Rev: BL 2/15/03; HBG 3/03) [796.52]

13538 Hu, Evaleen. *A Big Ticket: Sports and Commercialism* (4–7). Illus. 1998, Lerner LB $28.75 (978-0-8225-3305-4). This well-organized book explains the connections between sports and the media, including broadcast rights, endorsement contracts, pop culture, and the impact of television. (Rev: BL 7/98; HBG 10/98) [338.4]

13539 Hull, Mary. *The Composite Guide to Golf* (5–7). Series: Composite Guide. 1998, Chelsea LB $18.65 (978-0-7910-4726-2). An introduction to the game of golf and its history, along with highlights of the game's pioneers and current stars including Tiger Woods. (Rev: HBG 10/98; SLJ 9/98) [796.352]

13540 Hunter, Matt. *Pro Wrestling's Greatest Tag Teams* (4–7). Series: Pro Wrestling Legends. 2000, Chelsea $25.00 (978-0-7910-5835-0). This title covers such tag teams as the Road Warriors, the Midnight Express, the Nasty Boys, Public Enemy, and Harlem Heat. (Rev: BL 10/15/00; HBG 3/01) [796.8]

13541 Hunter, Matt. *Ric Flair: The Story of the Wrestler They Call "The Natural Boy"* (4–7). Series: Pro Wrestling Legends. 2000, Chelsea $25.00 (978-0-7910-5825-1). The story of the wrestler who has been at the top of his sport for most of the last three decades. (Rev: BL 10/15/00; HBG 3/01) [796.8]

13542 Judson, Karen. *Sports and Money: It's a Sell-out!* (7–12). Series: Issues in Focus. 1995, Enslow LB $20.95 (978-0-89490-622-0). A straightforward presentation that uses first-person accounts concerning the financial side of being in the sports business. (Rev: BL 11/15/95; SLJ 6/96) [796.0619]

13543 Kalman, Bobbie, and John Crossingham. *Extreme Sports* (4–8). Series: Extreme Sports No Limits! 2004, Crabtree LB $25.27 (978-0-7787-1673-0). All manner of extreme sports are covered in this overview. (Rev: BL 9/1/04)

13544 Kalman, Bobbie, and Sarah Dann. *Bowling in Action* (4–7). Series: Sports in Action. 2003, Crabtree LB $25.27 (978-0-7787-0335-8); paper $6.95 (978-0-7787-0355-6). This well-illustrated introduction to bowling includes material on equipment, techniques, rules, and bowling alleys. (Rev: BL 11/15/03) [794.6]

13545 Kaminker, Laura. *In-Line Skating! Get Aggressive* (5–8). Series: Extreme Sports. 1999, Rosen LB $26.50 (978-0-8239-3012-8). This book provides information for both beginning and advanced inline skaters and covers topics including equipment, history, techniques, and safety tips. (Rev: SLJ 4/00) [796]

13546 Kent, Deborah. *Athletes with Disabilities* (5–7). Illus. Series: Watts Library: Disabilities. 2003, Watts LB $25.50 (978-0-531-12019-4). Achievements of disabled athletes are accompanied by the history of such events as the Special Olympics and by information on new games, equipment, and techniques that widen horizons. (Rev: BL 10/15/03; SLJ 9/03) [371.9]

13547 Krause, Peter. *Fundamental Golf* (5–8). Photos by Andy King. Series: Fundamental Sports. 1995, Lerner LB $27.15 (978-0-8225-3454-9). A clear introduction to golf that covers history, equipment, swings, rules, and courses. (Rev: SLJ 9/95) [796.352]

13548 Lamovsky, Jesse, and Matthew Rosetti. *The Worst of Sports: Chumps, Cheats, and Chokers from the Games We Love* (8–12). Illus. 2007, Ballantine paper $13.95 (978-0-345-49891-5). Reluctant readers and sports fans will be drawn to this irreverent compilation of sorry facts about various sports. (Rev: BL 9/1/07; SLJ 12/07) [796.02]

13549 Luby, Thia. *Yoga for Teens: How to Improve Your Fitness, Confidence, Appearance, and Health — and Have Fun Doing It* (6–12). 2000, Clear Light $14.95 (978-1-57416-032-1). The benefits of yoga, particularly in the teen years, are presented with eye-catching photographs and clear instructions for achieving the poses. (Rev: SLJ 5/00) [613.7]

13550 Manley, Claudia B. *Competitive Volleyball for Girls* (4–7). Illus. Series: Sportsgirl. 2001, Rosen LB $26.50 (978-0-8239-3404-1). An introduction to the rules of volleyball, the training necessary, and the special opportunities for girls, with material on nutrition and the dangers of overtraining. (Rev: SLJ 3/02) [796.325]

13551 Margolis, Jeffrey A. *Violence in Sports* (6–12). Illus. 1999, Enslow LB $26.60 (978-0-89490-961-0). Using extensive documentation and numerous recent incidents, the author traces the decline in sportsmanship and the effect that violence is having on sports. (Rev: BL 9/1/99; HBG 4/00) [796]

13552 Mason, Paul. *Skiing* (4–8). Illus. 2003, Heinemann LB $25.64 (978-1-58810-628-5). Technique, safety, gear, and profiles of famous skiers are all covered in this introduction to the sport. (Rev: BL 2/15/03; HBG 3/03) [796.93]

13553 Miller, Thomas. *Taking Time Out: Recreation and Play* (5–8). Illus. Series: Our Human Family. 1995, Blackbirch LB $27.45 (978-1-56711-128-6). Divided into five broad geographic areas, this account describes how people enjoy themselves at play in various cultures. (Rev: SLJ 1/96) [794]

13554 Nicholson, Lois. *The Composite Guide to Lacrosse* (4–8). Series: The Composite Guide. 1998, Chelsea LB $18.65 (978-0-7910-4719-4). A fine guide to lacrosse, giving its history, how it is played today, and portraits of the game's greatest players. (Rev: HBG 3/99; SLJ 12/98) [796.34]

13555 Payan, Gregory. *Essential Snowmobiling for Teens* (5–9). Series: Outdoor Life. 2000, Children's paper $6.95 (978-0-516-23558-5). The invention of the snowmobile is covered plus material on license requirements, trail permits, equipment, clothing, safety, driving techniques, and maintenance. (Rev: SLJ 2/01) [796.94]

13556 Peters, Craig. *Chants, Cheers, and Jumps* (5–8). Illus. Series: Let's Go Team. 2003, Mason Crest $19.95 (978-1-59084-535-6). Readers will learn the difference between cheers and chants and how to do various jumps. Also use *Competitive Cheerleading* (2003). (Rev: BL 10/15/03; SLJ 9/03) [791.6]

13557 Peters, Craig. *Cheerleading Stars* (5–8). Series: Let's Go Team. 2003, Mason Crest LB $19.95 (978-1-59084-533-2). This book highlights the careers and accomplishments of a select group of star cheerleaders. (Rev: BL 10/15/03; HBG 4/04) [791]

13558 Peters, Craig. *Techniques of Dance for Cheerleading* (5–8). Series: Let's Go Team. 2003, Mason

Crest LB $19.95 (978-1-59084-531-8). The importance of stretching and safety measures are emphasized in this volume that discusses choreography and the similarities and differences between cheerleading and dancing. (Rev: SLJ 9/03) [791.6]

13559 Porter, David L. *Winning Weight Training for Girls: Fitness and Conditioning for Sports* (7–12). 2003, Facts on File $35.00 (978-0-8160-5185-4). The benefits of weight training for specific sports — basketball, softball, field hockey, and volleyball — are outlined following the basics of safe weight training. (Rev: SLJ 6/04) [613.7]

13560 Roberts, Jeremy. *Rock and Ice Climbing! Top the Tower* (4–8). Illus. Series: Extreme Sports. 2000, Rosen LB $26.50 (978-0-8239-3009-8). This book on climbing covers the dangers, different climbing styles, equipment, techniques, and venues, and profiles some young climbers. (Rev: BL 3/15/00; SLJ 8/00) [796.52]

13561 Roberts, Robin. *Sports for Life: How Athletes Have More Fun* (5–8). Illus. Series: Get in the Game! 2000, Millbrook LB $23.90 (978-0-7613-1407-3). This account, mainly for girls, explains how to enjoy sports through applying discipline, patience, cooperation, health, and the sheer fun of competition. (Rev: BL 1/1–15/01; HBG 3/01) [796]

13562 Roberts, Robin. *Which Sport Is Right for You?* (5–8). Series: Get in the Game! 2001, Millbrook LB $23.90 (978-0-7613-2117-0). Written with girls in mind, this short book explores how to choose a sport that is right for one's capabilities and interests. (Rev: BL 9/15/01; HBG 3/02; SLJ 1/02) [796]

13563 Rosen, Michael J. *Balls!* (4–7). 2006, Darby Creek $18.95 (978-1-58196-030-3). Balls used in all sorts of sports and their history, choice of shape, and method of construction are the topic of lighthearted discussion. (Rev: BL 6/1–15/06) [796.3]

13564 Ross, Dan. *Pro Wrestling's Greatest Wars* (4–7). Illus. Series: Pro Wrestling Legends. 2000, Chelsea $25.00 (978-0-7910-5837-4); paper $25.00 (978-0-7910-5838-1). Some of the great feuds in wrestling history, such as Harlem Heat vs. the Nasty Boys, are described in this fast read. (Rev: BL 10/15/00; HBG 3/01) [796.812]

13565 Ross, Dan. *The Story of the Wrestler They Call "The Rock"* (4–7). Series: Pro Wrestling Legends. 2000, Chelsea $25.00 (978-0-7910-5831-2). This is the story of the third-generation wrestler known as "The Rock." (Rev: BL 10/15/00; HBG 3/01) [796.8]

13566 Rowe, Julian. *Recreation* (4–7). Illus. Series: Science Encounters. 1997, Rigby paper $25.55 (978-1-57572-092-0). Shows how science is used in theme park rides, backpacking and camping equipment, computer games, television, scuba diving, and hang gliding. (Rev: SLJ 10/97) [796]

13567 Rowe, Julian. *Sports* (4–7). Illus. Series: Science Encounters. 1997, Rigby paper $25.55 (978-1-57572-089-0). Shows how science is used in such sports-related topics as the design of equipment, protective clothing, and sports medicine. (Rev: SLJ 10/97) [796]

13568 Ryan, Pat. *Rock Climbing* (4–7). Illus. Series: World of Sports. 2000, Smart Apple LB $16.95 (978-1-887068-57-4). In addition to covering the origins and evolution of rock climbing, this book discusses the basics of the sport, equipment, and star athletes. (Rev: BL 9/15/00) [796.52]

13569 Savage, Jeff. *A Sure Thing? Sports and Gambling* (7–12). Series: Sports Issues. 1996, Lerner LB $28.75 (978-0-8225-3303-0). After a brief history of gambling, this book looks at the many forms of gambling available today, from church bingo games to horse racing to Las Vegas casinos, with a focus on the connection between gambling and sports and emphasis on the dangers of gambling addiction. (Rev: BL 7/97; HBG 3/98; SLJ 11/97) [796]

13570 Savage, Jeff. *Top 10 Sports Bloopers and Who Made Them* (4–7). Illus. Series: Sports Top 10. 2000, Enslow LB $23.93 (978-0-7660-1271-4). This collection of 10 famous sports mistakes also gives good background information on the perpetrators and the causes of the errors. (Rev: BL 9/15/00; HBG 10/00; SLJ 10/00) [796]

13571 Scheppler, Bill. *The Ironman Triathlon* (7–10). Illus. 2002, Rosen LB $26.50 (978-0-8239-3556-7). Scheppler provides tips on training body and mind for the challenge of these races that combine running, swimming, and biking. (Rev: BL 9/1/02; VOYA 8/02) [796.42]

13572 Schwartz, Ellen. *I Love Yoga: A Guide for Kids and Teens* (5–12). Illus. by Ben Hodson. 2003, Tundra paper $9.95 (978-0-88776-598-8). Illustrated instructions for 18 basic poses are accompanied by breathing and relaxation exercises, discussion of the benefits of yoga, and a description of the different types of yoga practiced around the world. (Rev: SLJ 12/03; VOYA 10/03) [613.7]

13573 Shahan, Sherry. *Dashing Through the Snow: The Story of the Jr. Iditarod* (4–7). Illus. 1997, Millbrook $24.90 (978-0-7613-0208-7); paper $9.95 (978-0-7613-0143-1). All aspects of the 150-mile Junior Iditarod are touched upon in this account, including how these young mushers communicate with their dogs. (Rev: BL 3/1/97; SLJ 4/97) [798]

13574 Shannon, Joyce Brennfleck, ed. *Sports Injuries Information for Teens: Health Tips About Sports Injuries and Injury Prevention* (8–12). Series: Teen Health. 2003, Omnigraphics $58.00 (978-0-7808-0447-0). Basic information on sports injuries and treatment is provided in separate sections on such topics as emergency treatment, common injuries affecting teens, rehabilitation and physical therapy, injury prevention, and sports nutrition. (Rev: SLJ 7/04; VOYA 10/04) [617.1]

13575 Sheely, Robert, and Louis Bourgeois. *Sports Lab: How Science Has Changed Sports* (4–7). Illus. Series: Science Lab. 1994, Silver Moon $14.95 (978-1-881889-49-6). Traces the effect on sports of applying findings from such branches of science as aerodynamics, psychology, and medicine. (Rev: SLJ 9/94) [617.1]

13576 Silas, Elizabeth, and Diane Goodney. *Yoga* (4–8). Illus. Series: Life Balance. 2003, Watts LB $20.50 (978-0-531-12258-7); paper $6.95 (978-0-531-15577-6). Information on the spiritual and philosophical aspects of yoga follows chapters on basic yoga moves. (Rev: BL 10/15/03) [613.7]

13577 Skreslet, Laurie, and Elizabeth MacLeod. *To the Top of Everest* (5–9). Illus. 2001, Kids Can $16.95 (978-1-55074-721-8). Skreslet relates his lifelong ambition to climb Everest and his actual experiences doing so, with many facts about the mountain and the dangers involved and stunning photographs of his adventure. (Rev: BCCB 10/01; BL 9/15/01; HBG 3/02; SLJ 9/01*) [796.52]

13578 Smith, Graham. *Karting* (4–8). Series: Radical Sports. 2002, Heinemann LB $25.64 (978-1-58810-624-7). The sport of karting is introduced with discussion of equipment selection, basic skills, fitness and training, and safety. (Rev: BL 2/15/03; HBG 3/03) [796.7]

13579 Stark, Peter, and Steven M. Krauzer. *Winter Adventure: A Complete Guide to Winter Sports* (8–12). Series: Trailside Guide. 1995, Norton $17.95 (978-0-393-31400-7). This is a complete guide to winter sports including sledding, dogsledding, curling, ice skating, and cross-country skiing with additional material on organizations, safety tips, and information sources. [796.9]

13580 Steiner, Andy. *Girl Power on the Playing Field: A Book About Girls, Their Goals, and Their Struggles* (5–10). Series: Girl Power. 2000, Lerner LB $30.35 (978-0-8225-2690-2). This book explains women's roles in sports with good personal guidance for young girls on participation and goals. (Rev: HBG 10/00; SLJ 6/00) [796]

13581 Steiner, Andy. *A Sporting Chance: Sports and Gender* (4–8). Series: Sports Issues. 1995, Lerner LB $28.75 (978-0-8225-3300-9). An overview of the hurdles that female athletes have had to overcome and the persistent inequality between men and women in sports at all levels, from Little League to the pros. (Rev: BL 1/1–15/96; SLJ 1/96) [796]

13582 Sullivan, George. *Any Number Can Play: The Numbers Athletes Wear* (4–8). Illus. 2000, Millbrook LB $23.90 (978-0-7613-1557-5). A fascinating glimpse at players' devotion to their assigned numbers, along with information on retired and banned numbers and who uses the number 13. (Rev:

BL 12/15/00; HBG 3/01; SLJ 2/01; VOYA 2/01) [796]

13583 Sullivan, George. *Don't Step on the Foul Line: Sports Superstitions* (4–8). Illus. 2000, Millbrook LB $23.90 (978-0-7613-1558-2). This is an intriguing look at superstitions, customs, and traditions associated with many different sports. (Rev: BL 12/15/00; HBG 3/01; SLJ 2/01; VOYA 2/01) [796.357]

13584 Swissler, Becky. *Winning Lacrosse for Girls* (7–12). 2004, Facts on File $35.00 (978-0-8160-5183-0). A clear and detailed introduction to the game of lacrosse, covering its history as well as individual skills and team dynamics. (Rev: SLJ 5/04) [796.34]

13585 Takeda, Pete. *Climb! Your Guide to Bouldering, Sport Climbing, Trad Climbing, Ice Climbing, Alpinism, and More* (4–9). Illus. Series: Extreme Sports. 2002, National Geographic paper $8.95 (978-0-7922-6744-7). An attractive guide to climbing of all types — sport, wall, ice, alpine, and so forth — and to the equipment, techniques, and dangers. (Rev: SLJ 1/03) [796.5223]

13586 Tomlinson, Joe, and Ed Leigh. *Extreme Sports: In Search of the Ultimate Thrill* (8–12). 2004, Firefly $19.95 (978-1-55297-992-1). Explores the full spectrum of extreme sports — on land, in the air, and in or on the water. (Rev: SLJ 4/05; VOYA 10/05)

13587 Valliant, Doris. *Going to College* (5–8). Series: Let's Go Team. 2003, Mason Crest LB $19.95 (978-1-59084-541-7). This well-illustrated, breezy account describes the function of cheerleading in college sports activities. (Rev: BL 10/15/03; SLJ 1/04) [791]

13588 Valliant, Doris. *The History of Cheerleading* (5–8). Series: Let's Go Team. 2003, Mason Crest LB $19.95 (978-1-59084-534-9). Using many illustrations, this slim volume describes the history and function of cheerleading at various levels in this country. (Rev: BL 10/15/03; HBG 4/04; SLJ 1/04) [791]

13589 Weiss, Stefanie Iris. *Everything You Need to Know About Yoga: An Introduction for Teens* (7–12). Series: Need to Know Library. 1999, Rosen LB $25.25 (978-0-8239-2959-7). Yoga's ability to improve mental, spiritual, and physical health is the main focus of this volume. (Rev: SLJ 5/00) [613.7]

13590 Willard, Keith. *Ballooning* (4–7). Illus. Series: World of Sports. 2000, Smart Apple LB $16.95 (978-1-887068-51-2). This brief introduction to ballooning mentions star balloonists, different kinds of ballooning, the origins of this sport, and how one becomes proficient at it. (Rev: BL 9/15/00) [797.5]

13591 Willker, Joshua D. G. *Everything You Need to Know About the Dangers of Sports Gambling* (5–10). Illus. Series: Need to Know Library. 2000, Rosen LB $27.95 (978-0-8239-3229-0). This brief, well-written book surveys the world of gambling on sports, its legal and illegal aspects, and how it has ruined the careers of many fine athletes. (Rev: BL 1/1–15/01) [796]

13592 Wurdinger, Scott, and Leslie Rapparlie. *Ice Climbing* (5–9). Series: Adventure Sports. 2006, Creative Education LB $31.35 (978-1-58341-393-7). This well-designed guide to ice climbing familiarizes readers with the sport's history, equipment, competitions, and safety measures. (Rev: SLJ 12/06) [796.52]

13593 Young, Perry D. *Lesbians and Gays and Sports* (8–12). Series: Issues in Lesbian and Gay Life. 1995, Chelsea $24.95 (978-0-7910-2611-3); paper $12.95 (978-0-7910-2951-0). Looks at homosexuals in sports, with biographies of Kopay, Tilden, King, and Navratilova. (Rev: BL 6/1–15/95) [796]

Automobile Racing

13594 Benson, Michael. *Crashes and Collisions* (5–8). Series: Race Car Legends. 1997, Chelsea $25.00 (978-0-7910-4435-3). Multi-car pileups in car racing and the people who have survived them are the focus of this exciting volume. (Rev: HBG 3/98; SLJ 2/98) [629.228]

13595 Blackwood, Gary. *The Great Race: The Amazing Round-the-World Auto Race of 1908* (6–9). Illus. 2008, Abrams $19.95 (978-0-8109-9489-8). The epic race is described in detail with numerous photographs to help readers see what an undertaking it was for the six international teams that competed. (Rev: BL 4/15/08; SLJ 6/08) [796.72]

13596 Buckley, James. *NASCAR* (5–8). Illus. Series: Eyewitness Books. 2005, DK LB $19.99 (978-0-7566-1193-4). A visual pleasure for NASCAR fans, full of information about people, places, individual races, engineering advances, and so forth. (Rev: BL 9/1/05) [796.72]

13597 Caldwell, Dave. *Speed Show: How NASCAR Won the Heart of America* (5–8). 2006, Kingfisher $16.95 (978-0-7534-6011-5). The history of NASCAR, the basics of stock car racing, its famous drivers, its fans, and so forth are all described in this very readable book by a *New York Times* sports writer. (Rev: BL 11/15/06; SLJ 3/07) [796.720973]

13598 Eagen, Rachel. *NASCAR* (4–7). Series: Automania. 2006, Crabtree $26.60 (978-0-7787-3007-1). An excellent, photo-filled overview of NASCAR's history, rules, safety measures, cars, and leading drivers. (Rev: BL 9/1/06) [796.720973]

13599 Gifford, Clive. *Racing: The Ultimate Motorsports Encyclopedia* (6–12). Illus. 2006, Kingfisher $19.95 (978-0-7534-6040-5). Racing of all sorts — from motorbikes to stock cars, rally cars, and Formula One — is covered in this well-illustrated volume that also profiles 60 famous drivers. (Rev: SLJ 5/07) [796.72092]

13600 Johnstone, Mike. *NASCAR* (5–8). Series: Need for Speed. 2002, Lerner LB $23.93 (978-0-8225-0389-7). A look at the fast-growing sport of NASCAR auto racing, with detailed descriptions of the drivers, their cars, and the circuits. (Rev: BL 8/02; HBG 10/02; SLJ 7/02) [796.7]

13601 Kelley, K. C. *Hottest NASCAR Machines* (5–7). Series: Wild Wheels! 2007, Enslow LB $23.93 (978-0-7660-2869-2). Colorful photographs and helpful fact boxes highlight interesting information on cars used on the NASCAR circuit. Also use *Hottest Muscle Cars* and *Hottest Sports Cars* (both 2007). (Rev: SLJ 4/08)

13602 Parr, Danny. *Lowriders* (4–7). Illus. Series: Wild Rides! 2001, Capstone LB $23.93 (978-0-7368-0928-3). This volume on "lowrider" cars discusses the types of vehicles that are popular, the history of this trend, and the competitions that are held. (Rev: BL 10/15/01; HBG 3/02) [628.28]

13603 Pearce, Al. *Famous Tracks* (4–8). Series: Race Car Legends: Collector's Edition. 2005, Chelsea House LB $25.00 (978-0-7910-8692-6). Four well-known racetracks are the focus of this readable title full of photographs. (Rev: SLJ 5/06; VOYA 4/06) [796.72]

13604 Schaefer, A. R. *The Daytona 500* (4–7). Illus. Series: NASCAR Racing. 2004, Capstone LB $23.93 (978-0-7368-2423-1). This slim volume celebrates one of America's most famous automobile racing venues and some of the illustrious drivers who achieved fame there. (Rev: BL 4/1/04) [790.72]

Baseball

13605 Aretha, David. *Power in Pinstripes: The New York Yankees* (4–7). Illus. Series: Sensational Sports Teams. 2007, Enslow LB $24.95 (978-1-59845-044-6). Fans of this winning team will enjoy this book that includes the ball club's history, its top players, its World Series achievements, and lots of links to Web sites. (Rev: BL 7/07) [796.357]

13606 Aylesworth, Thomas G. *The Kids' World Almanac of Baseball* (4–8). Illus. 1996, World Almanac $8.95 (978-0-88687-787-3). An entertaining compendium of baseball facts. (Rev: BL 6/1/90) [796.357]

13607 Bissinger, Buzz. *Three Nights in August: Strategy, Heartbreak, and Joy Inside the Heart of a Manager* (8–12). 2005, Houghton $25.00 (978-0-618-40544-2). Bissinger dissects a three-game August 2003 series between baseball's St. Louis Cardinals and Chicago Cubs. (Rev: BL 3/1/05) [796.357]

13608 Collins, Ace, and John Hillman. *Blackball Superstars: Legendary Players of the Negro Baseball Leagues* (6–9). 1999, Avisson LB $19.95 (978-1-888105-38-4). This book profiles 12 stars of the Negro Baseball Leagues, including Satchel Paige and Josh Gibson, all of whom are now in the National Baseball Hall of Fame. (Rev: SLJ 8/99) [796.357]

13609 Forker, Dom. *Baseball Brain Teasers* (7–12). 1986, Sterling paper $6.95 (978-0-8069-6284-9). A baseball trivia book in which baseball situations are described and questions are asked about them. (Rev: SLJ 12/86) [796.357]

13610 Fuerst, Jeffrey B. *The Kids' Baseball Workout: A Fun Way to Get in Shape and Improve Your Game* (5–8). Illus. by Anne Canevari Green. 2002, Millbrook LB $24.90 (978-0-7613-2307-5). This book offers exercises, stretches, and skills that will help young baseball players improve their game. (Rev: BL 9/1/02; HBG 10/02; SLJ 7/02) [796.357]

13611 Galt, Margot F. *Up to the Plate: The All-American Girls Professional Baseball League* (6–9). Series: Sports Legacy. 1995, Lerner LB $31.95 (978-0-8225-3326-9). This history of the All-American Girls Professional Baseball League includes interviews with the players and their reactions to the movie *A League of Their Own*. (Rev: BL 7/95; SLJ 6/95) [796.357]

13612 Gardner, Robert, and Dennis Shortelle. *The Forgotten Players: The Story of Black Baseball in America* (5–8). Illus. 1993, Walker LB $13.85 (978-0-8027-8249-6). A discussion of the challenges that faced the players of the Negro Leagues. (Rev: BL 2/15/93; SLJ 4/93) [769.357]

13613 Gay, Douglas, and Kathlyn Gay. *The Not-So-Minor Leagues* (5–8). Illus. 1996, Millbrook LB $23.40 (978-1-56294-921-1). The history, importance, and present status of the minor leagues in baseball. (Rev: BL 5/15/96; SLJ 6/96) [796.357]

13614 Hample, Zack. *Watching Baseball Smarter: A Professional Fan's Guide for Beginners, Semi-Experts, and Deeply Serious Geeks* (8–12). 2007, Vintage paper $13.95 (978-0-307-28032-9). A guide to all aspects of baseball, from management to technique to trivia. (Rev: BL 2/1/07) [796.357]

13615 January, Brendan. *A Baseball All-Star* (6–8). Illus. Series: The Making of a Champion. 2004, Heinemann LB $29.93 (978-1-4034-5362-4). History, rules, training, and tactics are among the topics

discussed, along with information on key players. (Rev: SLJ 3/05) [796.357]

13616 Kellogg, David. *True Stories of Baseball's Hall of Famers* (4–8). Illus. 2000, Bluewood $8.95 (978-0-912517-41-4). Using a chronological approach, this book profiles 60 Hall of Famers and tells why each is there. (Rev: BL 10/15/00; VOYA 8/01) [796.357]

13617 Kisseloff, Jeff. *Who Is Baseball's Greatest Pitcher?* (5–7). Illus. 2003, Cricket $15.95 (978-0-8126-2685-8). The author presents profiles of 33 pitchers, with relevant statistics, and challenges the reader to choose the best and justify this decision. (Rev: BL 7/03; HBG 10/03; SLJ 5/03) [796.359]

13618 Krasner, Steven. *Play Ball like the Hall of Famers: Tips for Kids from 19 Baseball Greats* (6–9). Illus. by Keith Neely. 2005, Peachtree paper $14.95 (978-1-56145-339-9). Using a question-and-answer format, notable baseball players give advice on different topics — pitching, fielding, base-running, and so forth. (Rev: BL 5/1/05; SLJ 6/05) [796.357]

13619 Krasner, Steven. *Play Ball Like the Pros: Tips for Kids from 20 Big League Stars* (5–9). Illus. 2002, Peachtree paper $12.95 (978-1-56145-261-3). Each chapter features a professional player talking about the position he plays and giving tips to the young athlete. (Rev: BL 5/1/02; SLJ 6/02; VOYA 10/03) [796.357]

13620 Layden, Joe. *The Great American Baseball Strike* (5–8). Series: Headliners. 1995, Millbrook LB $25.90 (978-1-56294-930-3). A discussion of the issues that led to the 1995 baseball strike, with a review of the history of professional baseball and of the stormy relationship between the owners and players. (Rev: BL 11/15/95; SLJ 1/96) [796.357]

13621 McGuire, Mark, and Michael Sean Gormley. *The 100 Greatest Baseball Players of the 20th Century Ranked* (8–12). 2000, McFarland $30.00 (978-0-7864-0914-3). Using a variety of measuring techniques, the 100 greatest baseball players are ranked by importance. [796.357]

13622 Mackel, Kathy. *MadCat* (5–8). 2005, HarperCollins LB $16.89 (978-0-06-054870-4). Madelyn Catherine (aka MadCat), catcher on her local girls' fast-pitch softball team, is at the center of this story about sports, team play, and family involvement. (Rev: BL 2/15/05; SLJ 3/05)

13623 Mackin, Bob. *Record-Breaking Baseball Trivia* (5–8). 2000, Douglas & McIntyre $6.95 (978-1-55054-757-3). Questions, answers, and quizzes cover topics including baseball history, team play, World Series facts, and trivia from the plate and mound. (Rev: BL 9/15/00) [796.357]

13624 McKissack, Patricia C., and Fredrick McKissack. *Black Diamond: The Story of the Negro Base-*

ball Leagues (6–10). Illus. 1994, Scholastic paper $14.95 (978-0-590-45809-2). A history of African Americans in baseball and the Negro Baseball Leagues, until Jackie Robinson's entry into the major leagues. (Rev: BL 4/94; VOYA 10/94) [796.357]

13625 Nelson, Kadir. *We Are the Ship: The Story of Negro League Baseball* (5–8). Illus. by author. 2008, Hyperion $18.99 (978-0-7868-0832-8). Beautiful illustrations accompany a history of the league told by an anonymous but proud former player. (Rev: BL 2/1/08; SLJ 1/08) [796.357]

13626 Nitz, Kristin Wolden. *Softball* (5–9). Series: Play-by-Play. 2000, Lerner paper $23.93 (978-0-8225-9875-6). Good basic information about softball is given including history, rules, equipment, and positions. (Rev: SLJ 9/00) [796.357]

13627 Preller, James. *McGwire and Sosa: A Season to Remember* (4–7). Illus. 1998, Simon & Schuster paper $5.99 (978-0-689-82871-3). An oversize paperback that traces the baseball season that brought Sosa and McGwire to the nation's attention and made them sports heroes. (Rev: BL 1/1–15/99) [796.357]

13628 Skipper, John C. *Umpires: Classic Baseball Stories from the Men Who Made the Calls* (8–12). 1997, McFarland paper $29.95 (978-0-7864-0364-6). Great, memorable moments in the careers of 19 umpires. (Rev: VOYA 12/97) [796.323]

13629 Stewart, John. *The Baseball Clinic: Skills and Drills for Better Baseball: A Handbook for Players and Coaches* (6–10). 1999, Burford paper $12.95 (978-1-58080-073-0). Written by a major league scout, this book contains useful tips for young baseball players in the areas of pitching, fielding, hitting, base running, and catching. (Rev: SLJ 7/99) [796.357]

13630 Stewart, Mark. *Baseball: A History of the National Pastime* (7–10). Series: Watts History of Sports. 1998, Watts LB $34.50 (978-0-531-11455-1). A solid overview of the history of baseball, with good coverage of off-the-field aspects including labor-management conflicts and the influence of free agency. (Rev: HBG 9/98; SLJ 7/98) [796.357]

13631 Sullivan, George. *Baseball's Boneheads, Bad Boys, and Just Plain Crazy Guys* (5–8). Illus. by Anne Canevari Green. 2003, Millbrook LB $23.90 (978-0-7613-2321-1); paper $8.95 (978-0-7613-1928-3). An amusing collection of anecdotes that show the humor, superstitions, and general nuttiness of baseball players. (Rev: BL 7/03; HBG 10/03; SLJ 11/03) [790.357]

13632 Wong, Stephen. *Baseball Treasures* (4–7). Illus. by Susan Einstein. 2007, HarperCollins $16.99 (978-0-06-114464-6). An inside look at the Smithsonian Institution's collection of baseball memorabilia, revealing how much the equipment

has changed since the early days of the game. (Rev: BL 12/15/07) [796.3570]

13633 Young, Robert. *A Personal Tour of Camden Yards* (4–7). Series: How It Was. 1999, Lerner LB $30.35 (978-0-8225-3578-2). Designed to remind fans of famous old ballparks, this book visits Camden Yards, home of the Baltimore Orioles. The reader inspects the field, visits the old warehouse, and views the game from a skybox. (Rev: BL 6/1–15/99; HBG 10/99) [796.357]

Basketball

13634 Bird, Larry. *Bird on Basketball: How-to Strategies from the Great Celtics Champion*. Rev. ed. (8–12). Illus. 1988, Addison-Wesley paper $16.00 (978-0-201-14209-9). The basketball star associated with the Boston Celtics gives advice to young players on basics. [796.32]

13635 Glenn, Mike. *Lessons in Success from the NBA's Top Players* (5–7). Illus. 1998, Visions 3000 paper $14.95 (978-0-9649795-5-0). This noted sportsman tells about his career in the NBA while introducing each of the NBA teams and its strengths. (Rev: BL 7/98) [796.323]

13636 Grabowski, John F. *The Boston Celtics* (7–9). Series: Sports Greats. 2003, Gale LB $29.95 (978-1-56006-936-2). The story of the Boston basketball team, its history, accomplishments, and important individual players. (Rev: BL 3/15/03) [796.323]

13637 Grabowski, John F. *The Chicago Bulls* (7–9). Series: Sports Greats. 2002, Gale LB $29.95 (978-1-56006-937-9). After a chapter on the general history of this famous basketball team, there are individual chapters on famous team members past and present. (Rev: BL 9/1/02) [796.323]

13638 Ingram, Scott. *A Basketball All-Star* (6–8). Illus. Series: The Making of a Champion. 2004, Heinemann LB $29.93 (978-1-4034-5363-1). History, rules, training, and tactics are among the topics discussed, along with information on key players. (Rev: SLJ 3/05) [796.323]

13639 Joravsky, Ben. *Hoop Dreams: A True Story of Hardship and Triumph* (8–12). 1995, Turner paper $13.95 (978-0-06-097689-7). Based on the movie documentary, this book explores the dream on inner-city kids to play in the NBA. [796.323]

13640 Klein, Leigh, and Matt Masiero, eds. *My Favorite Moves: Shooting Like the Stars* (6–12). Series: Five Star Basketball. 2003, Wish paper $12.95 (978-1-930546-58-5). Best for readers already familiar with the game, this drill book includes advice from five professional women players. Also use *My Favorite Moves: Making the Big Plays* (2003). (Rev: SLJ 1/04) [796.323]

13641 Lace, William W. *The Houston Rockets Basketball Team* (5–8). Series: Sports Greats. 1997, Enslow LB $18.95 (978-0-89490-792-0). A profile of the Houston Rockets, with sketches of the key players. (Rev: BL 10/15/97; HBG 3/98) [796.323]

13642 Lannin, Joanne. *A History of Basketball for Girls and Women: From Bloomers to the Big Leagues* (5–9). Illus. Series: Sports Legacy. 2000, Lerner LB $26.63 (978-0-8225-3331-3); paper $9.95 (978-0-8225-9863-3). From the creation of basketball in 1891 to today, this account describes women's roles. (Rev: BL 1/1–15/01; HBG 3/01; SLJ 2/01; VOYA 4/01) [796.323]

13643 Lazenby, Roland. *The Show: The Inside Story of the Spectacular Los Angeles Lakers in the Words of Those Who Lived It* (8–12). Illus. 2006, McGraw-Hill $27.95 (978-0-07-143034-0). This excellent volume traces the NBA team's fortunes from its inauspicious beginnings in Minneapolis in the early 1950s through its most recent string of championships. (Rev: BL 11/15/05) [796.323]

13644 Lieberman-Cline, Nancy, and Robin Roberts. *Basketball for Women* (7–12). Illus. 1995, Human Kinetics paper $19.95 (978-0-87322-610-3). After a brief history of women's basketball, Lieberman-Cline, who has played in college, Olympics, and professional women's basketball, discusses the commitment required of a serious basketball player, how to formulate a plan for skill development, the recruitment process, and other concerns, and devotes seven chapters to more than 100 drill exercises. (Rev: VOYA 6/96) [796.323]

13645 Morris, Greggory. *Basketball Basics* (7–9). Illus. 1976, TreeHouse $6.95 (978-0-13-072256-0). A fine book for the beginner that explains basic moves, shots, and skills. [796.32]

13646 Owens, Thomas S. *Basketball Arenas* (5–8). Illus. Series: Sports Palaces. 2002, Millbrook LB $25.90 (978-0-7613-1766-1). Lots of basketball lore and history are included in a visit to the Boston Garden, Chicago Stadium, and the old Madison Square Garden. (Rev: BL 6/1–15/02; HBG 10/02) [796.323]

13647 Owens, Thomas S. *The Chicago Bulls Basketball Team* (5–8). Illus. Series: Sports Greats. 1997, Enslow LB $23.93 (978-0-89490-793-7). A history of the Chicago Bulls, with emphasis on the stars who have made the team famous. (Rev: BL 10/15/97; HBG 3/98) [796.323]

13648 Palmer, Chris. *Streetball: All the Ballers, Moves, Slams, and Shine* (8–12). Illus. 2004, Harper Resource paper $16.95 (978-0-06-072444-3). A celebration of urban playground basketball and the talented young people who enjoy it. (Rev: BL 11/15/04) [796.323]

13649 Pietrusza, David. *The Phoenix Suns Basketball Team* (5–8). Series: Sports Greats. 1997, Enslow LB $23.93 (978-0-89490-795-1). An introduction to the Phoenix Suns, their great games, and their star players. (Rev: BL 10/15/97; HBG 3/98) [796.323]

13650 Rogers, Glenn. *The San Antonio Spurs Basketball Team* (5–8). Series: Sports Greats. 1997, Enslow LB $23.93 (978-0-89490-797-5). Profiles of important players and stories behind important games are included in this introduction to the San Antonio Spurs. (Rev: BL 10/15/97; HBG 3/98) [796.323]

13651 Rutledge, Rachel. *The Best of the Best in Basketball* (4–7). Illus. Series: Women in Sports. 1998, Millbrook LB $24.90 (978-0-7613-1301-4). After a history of basketball, this account highlights women's role and covers today's most important female players. (Rev: BL 2/15/99; HBG 10/99; SLJ 3/99) [796.323]

13652 Steen, Sandra, and Susan Steen. *Take It to the Hoop: 100 Years of Women's Basketball* (6–8). Illus. 2003, Millbrook LB $25.90 (978-0-7613-2470-6). A comprehensive overview of women's basketball, from the first public game in the late 19th century. (Rev: BL 5/1/03; HBG 10/03; SLJ 9/03) [796.323]

13653 Stewart, Mark. *Basketball: A History of Hoops* (6–10). Series: Watts History of Sports. 1999, Watts LB $34.50 (978-0-531-11492-6). A chronological history of basketball that gives alternating treatment to college and pro games and includes how basketball has been influenced by off-the-court financial and social pressures. (Rev: HBG 9/99; SLJ 8/99) [796.323]

13654 Stewart, Mark. *The NBA Finals* (5–10). Series: Watts History of Sports. 2003, Watts LB $34.50 (978-0-531-11955-6). National Basketball Association finals over more than half a century are detailed year by year, with ample information on the teams and the players. (Rev: SLJ 3/04) [797]

13655 Thomas, Keltie. *How Basketball Works* (5–8). Illus. 2005, Maple Tree $16.95 (978-1-897066-18-8); paper $6.95 (978-1-897066-19-5). A lively overview of basketball's history, equipment, training, and skills, with interesting anecdotes and factoids. (Rev: BL 5/15/05) [796.323]

13656 Vancil, Mark. *NBA Basketball Offense Basics* (4–8). Illus. 1996, Sterling $16.95 (978-0-8069-4892-8). Action photographs and lively text demonstrate such techniques as dribbling, passing, and shooting. (Rev: BL 9/1/96) [796.332]

13657 Weatherspoon, Teresa, et al. *Teresa Weatherspoon's Basketball for Girls* (6–10). 1999, Wiley paper $15.95 (978-0-471-31784-5). This manual, by the famous basketball star and Olympic gold medalist, gives wonderful, practical information about playing the game and becoming a healthy, happy athlete. (Rev: BL 7/99; SLJ 8/99) [796.323]

13658 Wilker, Josh. *The Harlem Globetrotters* (5–10). Series: African-American Achievers. 1996, Chelsea LB $21.95 (978-0-7910-2585-7); paper $8.95 (978-0-7910-2586-4). This is a chronologically arranged history of the Harlem Globetrotters, the basketball team that has been entertaining crowds since 1927. (Rev: SLJ 3/97) [796.357]

Bicycling, Motorcycling, etc.

13659 Bach, Julie. *Bicycling* (4–7). Illus. Series: World of Sports. 2000, Smart Apple LB $16.95 (978-1-887068-53-6). A brief introduction to bicycling that gives material on the origins and evolution of the sport, equipment, and techniques, plus coverage of the sport's star athletes. (Rev: BL 9/15/00) [796.6]

13660 Bizley, Kirk. *Mountain Biking* (4–7). Series: Radical Sports. 1999, Heinemann LB $24.22 (978-1-57572-944-2). Color photographs and a simple text introduce mountain biking, its history, equipment, skills, and safety concerns. (Rev: SLJ 5/00) [796.6]

13661 Cole, Steve. *Kids' Easy Bike Care: Tune-Ups, Tools and Quick Fixes* (5–9). Illus. by Sarah Rakitin. Series: Quick Starts for Kids! 2003, Williamson paper $8.95 (978-1-885593-86-3). A detailed and accessible guide to the parts of a bicycle and their maintenance, bicycle safety, and preparing an emergency kit, with cartoon illustrations. (Rev: SLJ 12/03) [629.28]

13662 Cotter, Allison. *Cycling* (6–12). Illus. Series: History of Sports. 2002, Gale LB $29.95 (978-1-59018-071-6). From the invention of the bicycle to today's high-tech mountain and other specialist bikes, Cotter traces cycling's growth and looks at competitive and recreational aspects of the sport. (Rev: BL 9/1/02) [796.6]

13663 Crossingham, John. *Cycling in Action* (4–7). Illus. by Bonna Rouse. Series: Sports in Action. 2002, Crabtree LB $25.27 (978-0-7787-0118-7); paper $6.95 (978-0-7787-0124-8). Photographs and drawings illustrate important concepts in this introduction to the sport of cycling that covers equipment and technique. (Rev: BL 9/1/02) [796.4]

13664 Crowther, Nicky. *The Ultimate Mountain Bike Book: The Definitive Illustrated Guide to Bikes, Components, Techniques, Thrills and Trails.* Rev. ed. (7–12). 2002, Firefly paper $24.95 (978-1-55297-653-1). Beginning and advanced riders will all find material of interest in this revised practical guide full of appealing photographs. (Rev: SLJ 1/03; VOYA 12/02) [796.6]

13665 Deady, Kathleen W. *BMX Bikes* (4–7). Illus. Series: Wild Rides! 2001, Capstone LB $23.93 (978-0-7368-0925-2). Bicycle motocross fans will enjoy the color photographs and concise text that explains the equipment and skills needed for BMX (bicycle motocross) racing. (Rev: BL 10/15/01; HBG 3/02) [629.22]

13666 Dick, Scott. *BMX* (4–8). Series: Radical Sports. 2002, Heinemann LB $25.64 (978-1-58810-623-0). This introduction to bicycle motocross gives material on equipment, skills, training, and safety. (Rev: BL 2/15/03; HBG 3/03) [796.6]

13667 Freeman, Gary. *Motocross* (4–8). Series: Radical Sports. 2002, Heinemann LB $25.64 (978-1-58810-627-8). The sport of cross-country racing on motorcycles is introduced, with an emphasis on safety and skill development. (Rev: BL 2/15/03; HBG 3/03) [796.7]

13668 Haduch, Bill. *Go Fly a Bike! The Ultimate Book About Bicycle Fun, Freedom, and Science* (4–8). Illus. by Chris Murphy. 2004, Dutton $16.99 (978-0-525-47024-3). Packed with facts and cartoon illustrations, this comprehensive guide covers everything from the history of bicycling to practical tips for bike care and repair. (Rev: BL 2/1/04; SLJ 3/04) [796.6]

13669 Hayhurst, Chris. *Bicycle Stunt Riding!* (4–8). Series: Extreme Sports. 2000, Rosen LB $26.50 (978-0-8239-3011-1). In this book, readers will learn about stunts like the vert and mega spin as well as finding out about the bikes and the safety equipment needed to start this sport. (Rev: BL 6/1–15/00) [629]

13670 Hayhurst, Chris. *Mountain Biking: Get on the Trail* (4–8). Illus. Series: Extreme Sports. 2000, Rosen LB $26.50 (978-0-8239-3013-5). Stressing safety throughout, this book covers topics including the history of mountain biking, why mountain bikes are different than others, and riding techniques. (Rev: BL 3/15/00; SLJ 8/00) [796.6]

13671 King, Andy. *Fundamental Mountain Biking* (5–9). Series: Fundamental Sports. 1996, Lerner LB $27.15 (978-0-8225-3459-4). This introduction to mountain biking discusses its history, equipment, maneuvers, competitions, tricks, safety reminders, and repair tips. (Rev: SLJ 2/97) [796.64]

13672 Pavelka, Ed. *Bicycling Magazine's Basic Maintenance and Repair: Simple Techniques to Make Your Bike Ride Better and Last Longer* (8–12). 1999, Rodale paper $9.99 (978-1-57954-170-5). This book clearly explains how to maintain and repair a bicycle so it remains in tip-top condition. [629.28]

13673 Pinchuk, Amy. *The Best Book of Bikes* (4–7). Illus. 2003, Maple Tree paper $12.95 (978-1-894379-44-1). Diagrams, color photographs, and fascinating facts add to the appeal of the maintenance advice, racing strategies, and stunts provided. (Rev: BCCB 9/03; SLJ 9/03) [629.227]

13674 Raby, Philip, and Simon Nix. *Motorbikes* (5–8). Illus. Series: Need for Speed. 1999, Lerner LB $23.93 (978-0-8225-2486-1); paper $23.93 (978-0-8225-9854-1). A variety of motorbikes are introduced including dirt, motorcross, and land speed bikes. (Rev: BL 1/1–15/00; HBG 3/00; SLJ 2/00) [629.227]

13675 Sidwells, Chris. *Complete Bike Book* (8–12). Illus. 2005, DK paper $17.95 (978-0-7566-1427-0). History, technology, training, and maintenance are all covered in this volume for all levels of riders that also includes a stunning section of color photographs. (Rev: BL 9/1/05) [796.6]

13676 Turner, Chérie. *Marathon Cycling* (7–10). Series: Ultra Sports. 2002, Rosen LB $26.50 (978-0-8239-3553-6). Long-distance cycling competitions are described with material on tips and tricks, safety, gear, and racing events. (Rev: BL 9/1/02; SLJ 9/02) [796.6]

13677 Wurdinger, Scott, and Leslie Rapparlie. *Mountain Biking* (5–9). Series: Adventure Sports. 2006, Creative Education LB $31.35 (978-1-58341-396-8). Using many eye-catching photographs, this slim volume introduces the popular sport's history, equipment, competitions, and safety measures. (Rev: SLJ 12/06) [796.6]

Boxing and Wrestling

13678 Greenberg, Keith Elliot. *Pro Wrestling: From Carnivals to Cable TV* (6–12). Illus. 2000, Lerner LB $26.63 (978-0-8225-3332-0); paper $9.95 (978-0-8225-9864-0). With both historical and current information, this will please fans of professional wrestling and offer material for reports. (Rev: BL 2/15/01; HBG 3/01; SLJ 2/01; VOYA 2/01) [796.812]

13679 Jarman, Tom, and Reid Hanley. *Wrestling for Beginners* (7–12). Illus. 1983, Contemporary paper $15.95 (978-0-8092-5656-3). From a history of wrestling, this book moves on to skills, strategies, moves, and holds. [796.8]

13680 Lewin, Ted. *At Gleason's Gym* (4–7). Illus. by author. 2007, Roaring Brook $17.95 (978-1-59643-231-4). The history of the famous Gleason's Gym (where Muhammad Ali and Jake La Motta trained) is told as readers follow the progress of 9-year-old Sugar Boy Younan, already showing great promise as a boxer. (Rev: BL 9/1/07*; SLJ 10/07) [796.83]

Camping, Hiking, Backpacking, and Mountaineering

13681 Berger, Karen. *Hiking and Backpacking: A Complete Guide* (8–12). Series: Trailside Guide. 1995, Norton paper $18.95 (978-0-393-31334-5). A complete guide to outdoor hiking and backpacking with material on techniques, equipment, safety, camping, and related topics. [796.51]

13682 Brunelle, Lynn. *Camp Out! The Ultimate Kids' Guide* (5–12). Illus. by Brian Biggs and Elara Tanguy. 2007, Workman paper $11.95 (978-0-7611-4122-8). This volume is packed with information about camping out, covering equipment, planning, and skills, and offering games, activities, recipes, nature tips, and so forth. (Rev: SLJ 2/08)

13683 Drake, Jane, and Ann Love. *The Kids Campfire Book* (4–8). Illus. 1998, Kids Can paper $12.95 (978-1-55074-539-9). This manual describes how to select a location, build safe campfires, and later douse them, suggests fireside activities, including some science demonstrations, and offers safe cooking tips. (Rev: BL 3/15/98; HBG 9/98; SLJ 4/98) [796.54]

13684 Kalman, Bobbie, and John Crossingham. *Extreme Climbing* (4–8). Series: Extreme Sports No Limits! 2004, Crabtree LB $25.27 (978-0-7787-1671-6). Explores the full spectrum of climbing sports, looking at the specific challenges of each and offering readers valuable advice about equipment, climbing techniques, locations, and difficulty ratings, as well as profiles of notable climbers. (Rev: BL 9/1/04)

13685 McManus, Patrick F. *Kid Camping from Aaaaiii! to Zip* (5–7). Illus. by Roy Doty. 1979, Avon paper $3.99 (978-0-380-71311-0). A practical camping guide presented in an amusing way.

13686 Oxlade, Chris. *Rock Climbing* (4–8). Illus. Series: Extreme Sports. 2003, Lerner LB $22.60 (978-0-8225-1240-0). An appealing introduction to the history, equipment, techniques, safety concerns, and challenges of this sport. (Rev: BL 3/1/04; SLJ 5/04) [790.52]

13687 Venables, Stephen. *Voices from the Mountains: 40 True-Life Stories of Unforgettable Adventure, Drama, and Human Endurance* (8–12). Illus. 2006, Reader's Digest $26.95 (978-0-7621-0810-7). Eye-catching photographs add to these tales of mountain climbing, stories of determination and courage ranging from 1889 to 2005. (Rev: BL 2/1/07; SLJ 3/07) [796.552]

13688 Wurdinger, Scott, and Leslie Rapparlie. *Rock Climbing* (5–9). Series: Adventure Sports. 2006, Creative Education LB $31.35 (978-1-58341-394-4). Using many eye-catching photographs, this slim volume introduces to rock climbing and examines the sport's history, equipment, competitions, and safety measures. (Rev: SLJ 12/06) [796.5]

Chess, Checkers, and Other Board and Card Games

13689 Basman, Michael. *Chess for Kids* (4–8). Illus. 2001, DK paper $12.99 (978-0-7894-6540-5). A guide to the game of chess that includes everything from the basic moves and important strategies to information on the game's origins and the roles the game has played in arenas ranging from literature to history. (Rev: BL 7/01; HBG 10/01) [794.1]

13690 Kidder, Harvey. *The Kids' Book of Chess* (4–8). Illus. by Kimberly Bulcken. 1990, Workman paper $15.95 (978-0-89480-767-1). Using their origins in the Middle Ages as a focus, this book explains the role of each chess piece and the basics of the game. (Rev: SLJ 2/91) [794.1]

13691 Nottingham, Ted, and Bob Wade. *Winning Chess: Piece by Piece* (4–8). Illus. 1999, Sterling $17.95 (978-0-8069-9955-5). This book is for chess players who already know the basics and are ready to improve their techniques. (Rev: BL 11/15/99) [794.1]

13692 Sheinwold, Alfred. *101 Best Family Card Games* (5–12). Illus. 1993, Sterling paper $5.95 (978-0-8069-8635-7). A book filled with games enjoyed by many age groups. (Rev: BL 2/15/93) [795.4]

Fishing and Hunting

13693 Mason, Bill. *Sports Illustrated Fly Fishing: Learn from a Master.* Rev. ed. (8–12). 1994, Sports Illustrated paper $14.95 (978-1-56800-033-6). Equipment and techniques are emphasized in this illustrated introduction to fly fishing. [799.1]

13694 Schmidt, Gerald D. *Let's Go Fishing: A Book for Beginners* (4–7). Illus. by Brian W. Payne. 1990, Roberts Rinehart paper $11.95 (978-0-911797-84-8). This practical guide to freshwater fishing includes material on tackle and kinds of fish. (Rev: BL 3/1/91; SLJ 5/91) [799.1]

Football

13695 Anderson, Lars. *Carlisle vs. Army: Jim Thorpe, Dwight Eisenhower, Pop Warner, and the For-* gotten Story of Football's Greatest Battle (8–12). 2007, Random $24.95 (978-1-4000-6600-1). In 1912, the Carlisle Indian School football team, led by Jim Thorpe and coached by Pop Warner, played against the Army team, led by Dwight D. Eisenhower; the story of this exciting game is retold in historical context, with background on Thorpe's achievements, the rules of the Indian School, and other details. (Rev: BL 9/1/07) [796.332]

13696 Devaney, John. *Winners of the Heisman Trophy.* Rev. ed. (5–8). Illus. 1990, Walker LB $15.85 (978-0-8027-6907-7). A history of the award is given, with profiles of 15 past winners. (Rev: SLJ 6/90) [796.332]

13697 DiLorenzo, J. J. *The Miami Dolphins Football Team* (5–8). Series: Sports Greats. 1997, Enslow LB $23.93 (978-0-89490-796-8). A history of the Miami Dolphins that focuses on their brightest stars and best moments on the field. (Rev: BL 10/15/97; HBG 3/98) [796.48]

13698 Ingram, Scott. *A Football All-Pro* (6–8). Illus. Series: The Making of a Champion. 2004, Heinemann LB $29.93 (978-1-4034-5364-8). History, rules, training, and tactics are among the topics discussed, along with information on key players. (Rev: SLJ 3/05) [796.332]

13699 Lace, William W. *The Dallas Cowboys Football Team* (5–8). Illus. Series: Sports Greats. 1997, Enslow LB $23.93 (978-0-89490-791-3). Opening with the Dallas championship in 1973, this book traces the history of the team, with plenty of sports action. (Rev: BL 10/15/97; HBG 3/98) [796.48]

13700 McDonnell, Chris, ed. *The Football Game I'll Never Forget: 100 NFL Stars' Stories* (8–12). Illus. 2004, Firefly paper $24.95 (978-1-55297-850-4). One hundred football stars talk about the games they remember. (Rev: BL 9/1/04; VOYA 4/05) [796.332]

13701 Madden, John, and Bill Gutman. *John Madden's Heroes of Football: The Story of America's Game* (5–8). 2006, Dutton $18.99 (978-0-525-47698-6). The former NFL coach and popular football commentator chronicles the history of professional football, looking at how the game has changed over the years and profiling some of its best-known players and coaches. (Rev: BL 9/1/06; SLJ 2/07) [796.332092]

13702 Price, Christopher. *The Blueprint: How the New England Patriots Beat the System to Create the Last Great NFL Superpower* (8–12). Illus. 2007, St. Martin's $24.95 (978-0-312-36838-8). This is a compelling history of the Patriots with lots of behind-the-scenes information and interesting anecdotes. (Rev: BL 9/1/07) [796.332]

Gymnastics

13703 Kalman, Bobbie, and John Crossingham. *Gymnastics in Action* (4–7). Series: Sports in Action. 2002, Crabtree LB $25.27 (978-0-7787-0330-3); paper $6.95 (978-0-7737-0350-6). Various branches of gymnastics are introduced in text and pictures with coverage of techniques, equipment, and basic movements. (Rev: BL 1/1–15/03) [796.44]

Hockey

13704 Adelson, Bruce. *Hat Trick Trivia: Secrets, Statistics, and Little-Known Facts About Hockey* (4–7). Illus. 1998, Lerner LB $23.93 (978-0-8225-3315-3). History, statistics, and trivia are combined in this lively discussion of hockey and its players. (Rev: BL 1/1–15/99) [796.962]

13705 Connolly, Helen. *Field Hockey: Rules, Tips, Strategy, and Safety* (4–8). Series: Sports from Coast to Coast. 2005, Rosen LB $26.50 (978-1-4042-0182-8). This title puts the spotlight on field hockey, including a brief history of the sport as well as a look at its rules, equipment, training, and so forth. (Rev: SLJ 10/05)

13706 Foley, Mike. *Fundamental Hockey* (4–8). Series: Fundamental Sports. 1996, Lerner LB $27.15 (978-0-8225-3456-3). The basics of ice hockey are introduced, accompanied by a brief history of the sport and an explanation of what the various players do. (Rev: SLJ 3/96) [796.962]

13707 Jensen, Julie, adapt. *Beginning Hockey* (4–8). Photos by Andy King. Series: Beginning Sports. 1996, Lerner LB $22.60 (978-0-8225-3506-5). An introduction to hockey, its history, and the techniques and skills used by the players. (Rev: SLJ 3/96) [796.964]

13708 Kennedy, Mike. *Ice Hockey* (5–7). Series: Watts Library. 2003, Watts LB $25.50 (978-0-531-12273-0). This overview explores the history of the sport, its rules, and styles of play, and provides information on some of the key players. (Rev: SLJ 2/04) [796.962]

13709 McFarlane, Brian. *Real Stories from the Rink* (5–8). Illus. by Steve Nease. 2002, Tundra paper $14.95 (978-0-88776-604-6). Entertaining true stories give insight into ice hockey's history, rules, and players. (Rev: BL 2/15/03; SLJ 4/03) [796.962]

13710 McKinley, Michael, and Suzanne Levesque. *Ice Time: The Story of Hockey* (5–8). Illus. 2006, Tundra $18.95 (978-0-88776-762-3). This history of ice hockey focuses mainly on the development and current status of the game in Canada, also covering

international stars. (Rev: BL 12/1/06; SLJ 1/07) [796.962]

13711 Wilson, Stacy. *The Hockey Book for Girls* (4–7). Illus. 2000, Kids Can $12.95 (978-1-55074-860-4); paper $6.95 (978-1-55074-719-5). This book, by the former captain of Canada's women's Olympic hockey team, introduces ice hockey's rules, positions, strategies, and training and includes interviews with star players. (Rev: BL 3/1/01; HBG 3/01; SLJ 12/00) [796.962]

Horse Racing and Horsemanship

13712 Bolt, Betty. *Jumping* (4–8). Series: Horse Library. 2001, Chelsea $25.00 (978-0-7910-6657-7). Show jumping, eventing, and steeplechase riding are all covered in detail here. Also use *Western Riding*. (Rev: HBG 3/02; SLJ 3/02) [798.4]

13713 Davis, Caroline. *The Young Equestrian* (5–8). Illus. 2000, Firefly $29.95 (978-1-55209-495-2); paper $19.95 (978-1-55209-484-6). With a generous use of color photographs, this account devotes chapters to riding aids and techniques, choosing schools and proper equipment, buying and caring for a horse, and competitions. (Rev: BL 2/15/01; SLJ 2/01; VOYA 2/01) [798.2]

13714 Haas, Jessie. *Safe Horse, Safe Rider: A Young Rider's Guide to Responsible Horsekeeping* (4–7). Illus. 1994, Storey paper $16.95 (978-0-88266-700-3). This guide to horsemanship stresses safety and covers such topics as understanding horse behavior. (Rev: BL 1/1/95) [636.1]

13715 Kimball, Cheryl. *Horse Showing for Kids* (4–8). Illus. 2004, Storey paper $16.95 (978-1-58017-501-2). A comprehensive guide to showing horses, covering preparations for both horse and rider/handler, plus advice on safety, sportsmanship, and appropriate attire (for animals and humans). (Rev: SLJ 2/05) [798.2]

13716 Kirksmith, Tommie. *Ride Western Style: A Guide for Young Riders* (4–8). Illus. 1991, Howell Book House $16.95 (978-0-87605-895-4). Background information and step-by-step instructions for young people interested in learning to ride Western style. (Rev: BL 4/1/92; SLJ 7/92) [798.2]

13717 Mickle, Shelley Fraser. *Barbaro: America's Horse* (4–8). 2007, Simon & Schuster LB $16.89 (978-1-4169-4866-7); paper $8.99 (978-1-4169-4865-0). The tragic story of racehorse Barbaro is told in straightforward but moving text, with lots of details about horses, racing, and genetic choices, plus many photographs. (Rev: SLJ 7/07) [636.1]

13718 Tate, Nikki. *Behind the Scenes: The Racehorse* (5–8). Illus. 2008, Fitzhenry & Whiteside $22.95 (978-1-55455-018-0); paper $12.95 (978-1-

55455-032-6). Readers get an inside look at horse racing — breeding, training, jockeys and grooms, and so forth — and learn about both the glamor and the sometimes dangerous and harsh realities. (Rev: BL 2/1/08; SLJ 2/08) [798]

Ice Skating

13719 Wilkes, Debbi. *The Figure Skating Book: A Young Person's Guide to Figure Skating* (4–8). Illus. 2000, Firefly LB $19.95 (978-1-55209-444-0); paper $12.95 (978-1-55209-445-7). The author, an Olympic silver medalist, gives practical advice on figure skating from buying skates to simple and complicated skating techniques. (Rev: BL 7/00; SLJ 4/00) [796.9]

In-Line Skating

13720 Werner, Doug. *In-Line Skater's Start-Up: A Beginner's Guide to In-Line Skating and Roller Hockey* (6–12). 1995, Tracks paper $9.95 (978-1-884654-04-6). Using many black-and-white photographs, this book is both a guide to inline skating basics for beginners and an introduction to the growing sport of roller hockey. (Rev: BL 2/1/96) [796.2]

Martial Arts

13721 Atwood, Jane. *Capoeira: A Martial Art and a Cultural Tradition* (5–8). Series: The Library of African American Arts and Culture. 1999, Rosen LB $27.95 (978-0-8239-1859-1). Capoeira, a unique martial art developed by African slaves in Brazil, is described, along with its history and preparations for its debut in the 2004 Olympic games. (Rev: SLJ 8/99) [796.8]

13722 Konzak, Burt. *Samurai Spirit: Ancient Wisdom for Modern Life* (6–12). 2002, Tundra paper $8.95 (978-0-88776-611-4). Martial arts are the focus of this combination of traditional tales, historical and cultural information, and advice from the author, a teacher of martial arts. (Rev: SLJ 6/03) [813]

13723 Metil, Luana, and Jace Townsend. *The Story of Karate: From Buddhism to Bruce Lee* (6–9). 1995, Lerner LB $31.95 (978-0-8225-3325-2). A history of this martial art from its origins in the Far East to its present-day popularity. (Rev: BL 7/95) [796.8]

13724 Pawlett, Ray. *The Karate Handbook* (7–12). Illus. Series: Martial Arts. 2008, Rosen LB $29.95 (978-1-4042-1394-4). The basics about karate as well as its history and philosophy, accompanied by many helpful photographs. (Rev: BL 4/1/08) [796.815]

13725 Queen, J. Allen. *Learn Karate* (4–8). 1999, Sterling $17.95 (978-0-8069-8136-9). An excellent manual that covers the basics of karate — kicks, blocks, and stances — as well as stretches, meditation, safety, equipment, and sparring. (Rev: SLJ 5/99) [796.8]

13726 Rielly, Robin L. *Karate for Kids* (5–8). Illus. Series: The Martial Arts for Kids. 2004, Tuttle paper $13.95 (978-0-8048-3534-3). After an overview of the history of karate, this appealing volume with clear illustrations looks at the moves, rules and etiquette, uniform and belts, and so forth. (Rev: BL 9/1/04; SLJ 2/05) [796.815]

13727 Tegner, Bruce. *Bruce Tegner's Complete Book of Jujitsu* (7–12). Illus. 1978, Thor paper $14.00 (978-0-87407-027-9). A master in the martial arts introduces this ancient Japanese form of self-defense and gives basic information on stances and routines. [796.8]

13728 Tegner, Bruce. *Bruce Tegner's Complete Book of Self-Defense* (7–12). Illus. 1975, Thor paper $14.00 (978-0-87407-030-9). A basic primer on ways to defend oneself including hand blows and restraints. [796.8]

13729 Tegner, Bruce. *Karate: Beginner to Black Belt* (7–12). Illus. 1982, Thor paper $14.00 (978-0-87407-040-8). Techniques for both the novice and the experienced practitioner are explained in this account that stresses safety and fitness. [796.8]

13730 Tegner, Bruce, and Alice McGrath. *Self-Defense and Assault Prevention for Girls and Women* (7–12). Illus. 1977, Thor paper $10.00 (978-0-87407-026-2). Various defensive and offensive techniques are introduced in situations where they would be appropriate. [796.8]

Olympic Games

13731 Coffey, Wayne. *The Boys of Winter: The Untold Story of a Coach, a Dream, and the 1980 U.S. Olympic Hockey Team* (8–12). Illus. 2005, Crown $23.95 (978-1-4000-4765-9). In this inspiring look back at the 1980 Winter Olympics victory of the U.S. men's hockey team, sportswriter Coffey introduces readers to the players and coach who pulled off this miracle on ice. (Rev: BL 11/15/04; SLJ 5/05) [796.962]

13732 Fischer, David. *The Encyclopedia of the Summer Olympics* (4–8). Illus. Series: Watts Reference.

2003, Watts LB $37.00 (978-0-531-11886-3). Events from archery to wrestling are organized in alphabetical order, with historical information from the first games to the forthcoming 2004 games, profiles of athletes, lists of gold medal winners, information on rules and equipment, and fast facts. (Rev: SLJ 12/03) [796.4]

13733 Guttmann, Allen. *The Olympics, A History of the Modern Games*. 2nd ed. (8–12). Series: Illinois History of Sports. 2002, Univ. of Illinois $39.95 (978-0-252-02725-3); paper $16.95 (978-0-252-07046-4). This is an interesting history of the modern Olympics from Athens in 1896 to Seoul in 1988. with good coverage on social topics. [796.48]

13734 Kristy, Davida. *Coubertin's Olympics: How the Games Began* (5–8). 1995, Lerner LB $26.63 (978-0-8225-3327-6). How the Olympic games began and information about Baron Pierre de Coubertin, their founder. (Rev: BL 8/95; SLJ 11/95) [338.4]

13735 Macy, Sue. *Freeze Frame: A Photographic History of the Winter Olympics* (6–9). Illus. 2005, National Geographic $18.95 (978-0-7922-7887-0). A vivid overview of the Winter Games, looking at the various events and the challenges of these winter sports. (Rev: BL 12/15/05; SLJ 2/06) [796.98]

13736 Middleton, Haydn. *Modern Olympics* (4–8). Series: The Olympics. 2003, Heinemann LB $16.95 (978-1-4034-4677-0). A concise look at the modern games, with many illustrations, graphics, and sidebars, plus discussion of terrorism incidents, drug use, the choice of host cities, and the Paralympics. (Rev: SLJ 5/04) [796.48]

Running and Jogging

13737 Griffis, Molly Levite. *The Great American Bunion Derby* (5–10). 2003, Eakin $15.95 (978-1-57168-801-9); paper $9.95 (978-1-57168-810-1). The story of a poor part-Cherokee farm boy who joined a marathon run across the United States in the late 1920s and won the $25,000 top prize. (Rev: BL 1/1–15/04; SLJ 3/04) [796.42]

13738 Hayhurst, Chris. *Ultra Marathon Running* (7–10). Series: Ultra Sports. 2002, Rosen LB $26.50 (978-0-8239-3557-4). This work looks at different long running races, the athletes that engage in this sport, and the mind-boggling distances they run. (Rev: BL 9/1/02; SLJ 9/02) [796.4]

13739 Hughes, Morgan. *Track and Field: The Jumps: Instructional Guide to Track and Field* (4–8). Series: Compete Like a Champion. 2001, Rourke LB $27.93 (978-1-57103-290-4). This book includes material on the long jump, the triple jump, the high jump, and the pole vault, along with train-

ing tips. Also use in the same series *Track and Field: Middle and Long Distance Runs* and *Track and Field: The Sprints* (both 2001). (Rev: SLJ 3/01) [796.42]

13740 Manley, Claudia B. *Competitive Track and Field for Girls* (4–7). Illus. Series: Sportsgirl. 2001, Rosen LB $26.50 (978-0-8239-3408-9). An introduction to the rules of track and field competitions, the training necessary, and the special opportunities for girls, with material on nutrition and the dangers of overtraining. (Rev: SLJ 3/02) [796.42]

Sailing, Boating, and Canoeing

13741 Anderson, Scott. *Distant Fires* (8–12). Illus. 1990, Pfeifer-Hamilton paper $15.95 (978-0-938586-33-3). A journal of a 1,700-mile canoe trip from Minnesota to Canada's Hudson Bay. (Rev: BL 1/15/91; SLJ 4/91) [797.122]

13742 Heller, Peter. *Hell or High Water* (8–12). 2004, Rodale $24.95 (978-1-57954-872-8). Heller chronicles the 2002 conquest of Tibet's Tsangpo River by an elite kayaking team and discusses the attractions of this dangerous sport. (Rev: BL 9/15/04) [797.122]

13743 Revell, Phil. *Kayaking* (4–7). Series: Radical Sports. 1999, Heinemann LB $24.22 (978-1-57572-943-5). A history of kayaks and kayaking is followed by material on basic skills, equipment, safety concerns, and competitions. (Rev: SLJ 5/00) [797.1]

13744 Wurdinger, Scott, and Leslie Rapparlie. *Kayaking* (7–10). Illus. Series: Adventure Sports. 2006, Creative Education LB $21.95 (978-1-58341-397-5). Outlines the history of kayaking as well as the different types of boats, equipment used, the techniques and skills involved, competitions, and the dangers of the sport. (Rev: BL 10/15/06; SLJ 12/06) [797.122]

Skateboarding

13745 Andrejtschitsch, Jan, et al. *Action Skateboarding* (6–12). 1993, Sterling $16.95 (978-0-8069-8500-8). A handbook that provides a history of skateboarding, reviews equipment, and defines styles and terrains, with tips on tricks and maneuvers. (Rev: BL 6/1–15/93; SLJ 7/93) [795.2]

13746 Badillo, Steve, and Doug Werner. *Skateboarding: Book of Tricks* (7–12). 2003, Tracks paper $12.95 (978-1-884654-19-0). Basic and advanced moves are well illustrated in black-and-white photographs although Badillo is shown without protective gear. (Rev: SLJ 5/04) [796.2]

13747 Burke, L. M. *Skateboarding! Surf the Pavement* (5–8). Series: Extreme Sports. 1999, Rosen LB $26.50 (978-0-8239-3014-2). This book supplies information for beginning and advanced skateboarders with coverage of history, techniques, equipment, and safety considerations. (Rev: SLJ 4/00) [796]

13748 Crossingham, John. *Skateboarding in Action* (4–7). Series: Sports in Action. 2002, Crabtree LB $25.27 (978-0-7787-0117-0); paper $6.95 (978-0-7787-0123-1). A well-illustrated introduction to skateboarding with good material on equipment and injury prevention. (Rev: BL 9/1/02; SLJ 11/02) [795.2]

13749 Freimuth, Jeri. *Extreme Skateboarding Moves* (4–7). Illus. Series: Behind the Moves. 2001, Capstone LB $23.93 (978-0-7368-0783-8). Skateboard slang is just one appealing part of this account of proper equipment and technique, with safety tips and some tricks. (Rev: BL 6/1–15/01; HBG 10/01; SLJ 9/01) [796.22]

13750 Horsley, Andy. *Skateboarding* (4–7). Illus. Series: To the Limit. 2001, Raintree LB $25.69 (978-0-7398-3163-2). A brief history of skateboarding is included here along with material on equipment, moves, and some advice on turning pro. (Rev: BL 6/1–15/01) [796.22]

13751 Loizos, Constance. *Skateboard! Your Guide to Street, Vert, Downhill, and More* (4–9). Illus. Series: Extreme Sports. 2002, National Geographic paper $8.95 (978-0-7922-8229-7). An attractive guide to skateboarding equipment, technique, rules, etiquette, jargon, and safety. (Rev: SLJ 1/03) [796.22]

13752 Werner, Doug. *Skateboarder's Start-Up: A Beginner's Guide to Skateboarding* (4–8). 2000, Tracks paper $11.95 (978-1-884654-13-8). Using a question-and-answer format, this introduction to skateboarding covers such subjects as equipment, history, and basic skating and technical tricks. (Rev: SLJ 12/00) [795.2]

Skiing and Snowboarding

13753 Barr, Matt, and Chris Moran. *Snowboarding* (4–8). Illus. Series: Extreme Sports. 2003, Lerner LB $22.60 (978-0-8225-1242-4). An appealing introduction to the history, equipment, techniques, safety concerns, and stars of this increasingly popular sport. (Rev: BL 3/1/04; SLJ 5/04; VOYA 6/04) [790.9]

13754 Brown, Gillian C. P. *Snowboarding* (5–8). Illus. Series: X-treme Outdoors. 2003, Children's LB $24.50 (978-0-516-24322-1); paper $6.95 (978-0-516-24383-2). Equipment, technique, competition, and safety are covered here, as well as a history of this sport. (Rev: BL 4/15/03; SLJ 10/03) [796.9]

13755 Cazeneuve, Brian. *Cross-Country Skiing: A Complete Guide* (8–12). Series: Trailside Guide. 1995, Norton $18.95 (978-0-393-31335-2). An illustrated manual that covers equipment, techniques, clothing, safety and other topics relating to cross-country skiing. [796.93]

13756 Crossingham, John. *Snowboarding in Action* (4–7). Illus. by Bonna Rouse. Series: Sports in Action. 2002, Crabtree LB $25.27 (978-0-7787-0119-4); paper $6.95 (978-0-7787-0125-5). Aspiring snowboarders will find much of interest here, including basic techniques. (Rev: BL 9/1/02; SLJ 11/02) [796.9]

13757 Fraser, Andy. *Snowboarding* (4–7). Series: Radical Sports. 1999, Heinemann LB $24.22 (978-1-57572-946-6). This book covers the history of snowboarding, the equipment and clothing needed, techniques, terms, and how to get started. (Rev: SLJ 4/00) [796.9]

13758 Hayhurst, Chris. *Snowboarding! Shred the Powder* (5–8). Series: Extreme Sports. 1999, Rosen LB $26.50 (978-0-8239-3010-4). The book supplies both beginning and advanced information on this sport, including material on history, equipment, techniques, and safety considerations. (Rev: SLJ 4/00; VOYA 6/00) [796.9]

13759 Herran, Joe, and Ron Thomas. *Snowboarding* (5–8). Illus. Series: Action Sports. 2003, Chelsea LB $28.00 (978-0-7910-7003-1). Basic information on this sport's gear and performance is accompanied by biographical details about snowboarding champions. (Rev: BL 4/15/03; HBG 10/03) [796.9]

13760 Jensen, Julie, adapt. *Beginning Snowboarding* (4–8). Series: Beginning Sports. 1996, Lerner LB $27.15 (978-0-8225-3507-2). An introduction to snowboarding, with material on equipment, basic maneuvers, types of competition, and advanced stunts. (Rev: SLJ 3/96) [796.9]

13761 Kleh, Cindy. *Snowboarding Skills: The Back-to-Basics Essentials for All Levels* (7–12). Illus. 2002, Annick paper $16.95 (978-1-55297-626-5). Tips from an expert, with photographs and a glossary, make this a hip title for enthusiasts. (Rev: BL 12/15/02; SLJ 1/03) [796.9]

13762 Lurie, John. *Fundamental Snowboarding* (4–8). Series: Fundamental Sports. 1996, Lerner LB $27.15 (978-0-8225-3457-0). With eye-catching photographs, the equipment and principles of snowboarding are covered, with material on basic and advanced maneuvers, skills, and stunts. (Rev: SLJ 3/96) [796.9]

13763 Stiefer, Sandy. *Marathon Skiing* (7–10). Series: Ultra Sports. 2002, Rosen LB $26.50 (978-0-8239-3554-3). This work describes the sport of marathon skiing — cross-country skiing pushed to its limits. (Rev: BL 9/1/02) [796.95]

Soccer

13764 Blackall, Bernie. *Soccer* (4–8). Illus. by Vasja Koman. Series: Top Sport. 1999, Heinemann LB $21.36 (978-1-57572-840-7). This introduction to soccer covers history, equipment, rules, skills, and a few male and female stars. (Rev: SLJ 12/99) [796.334]

13765 Buxton, Ted. *Soccer Skills: For Young Players* (6–12). Illus. 2000, Firefly paper $14.95 (978-1-55209-329-0). A practical guide to training and technique that will be useful for beginners and advanced players. (Rev: SLJ 10/00; VOYA 12/00) [796.344]

13766 Coleman, Lori. *Soccer* (5–9). Series: Play-by-Play. 2000, Lerner paper $23.93 (978-0-8225-9876-3). A fine introduction to the rules, equipment, and tactics of soccer with historical coverage through 1999. (Rev: SLJ 9/00) [796.334]

13767 Gifford, Clive. *The Kingfisher Soccer Encyclopedia* (6–10). Illus. 2006, Kingfisher $19.95 (978-0-7534-5928-7). Covers all aspects of the sport, including basic rules, skills, legends, famous games, and winning teams. (Rev: SLJ 5/06) [796.334]

13768 Herbst, Dan. *Sports Illustrated Soccer: The Complete Player* (7–12). Illus. 1988, Sports Illustrated for Kids paper $9.95 (978-1-56800-038-1). Basic and advanced skills are explained plus a variety of game strategies. [796.334]

13769 Mackin, Bob. *Soccer the Winning Way: Play Like the Pros* (4–7). Illus. 2002, Douglas & McIntyre paper $10.95 (978-1-55054-825-9). A guide to mastering crucial soccer skills, with photographs and words of wisdom from the pros. (Rev: BL 5/15/02) [796]

13770 Owens, Thomas S., and Diana Star Helmer. *Soccer* (5–8). Series: Game Plan. 2000, Twenty-First Century LB $26.90 (978-0-7613-1400-4). This introduction to soccer covers the different positions, game strategy, and memorable games and players of the past. (Rev: HBG 10/00; SLJ 7/00) [796.334]

13771 Radnedge, Keir, and Mark Bushell. *The Treasures of the World Cup* (7–12). Illus. 2006, Trafalgar $50.00 (978-1-84442-321-7). A scrapbook-like collection of all kinds of goodies connected to the World Cup soccer competitions dating from 1930 to 2002. Stickers, letters, posters, tickets and other souvenirs will thrill soccer fans. (Rev: BL 8/06) [796.334668]

13772 Scott, Nina S. *The Thinking Kids Guide to Successful Soccer* (5–8). 1998, Millbrook LB $21.90 (978-0-7613-0324-4). An insider's look at strategies for kids playing soccer, including topics not frequently addressed such as dealing with inexperienced coaches, unfair calls from referees, not getting enough playing time, and pressures of competition. The author encourages kids to have a good time and not to worry about making mistakes. (Rev: BL 5/15/99; HBG 9/99; SLJ 4/99) [796.334]

13773 Sherman, Josepha. *Competitive Soccer for Girls* (4–7). Series: Sportsgirl. 2001, Rosen LB $26.50 (978-0-8239-3405-8). An introduction to the rules of soccer, the training necessary, and the special opportunities for girls, with material on nutrition and the dangers of overtraining. (Rev: SLJ 3/02) [796.334]

13774 Stewart, Mark. *Soccer: An Intimate History of the World's Most Popular Game* (7–10). Series: Watts History of Sports. 1998, Watts LB $34.50 (978-0-531-11456-8). With clear text and photographs, this book traces the history of soccer in the United States, with interesting material on memorable games, famous players, related off-the-field developments, and a discussion of why soccer is not as popular as other sports in the United States. (Rev: HBG 9/98; SLJ 7/98) [796.334]

13775 Stewart, Mark. *The World Cup* (5–10). Series: The Watts History of Sports. 2003, Watts LB $34.50 (978-0-531-11957-0). An overview of the international soccer championship that takes place every four years, this volume, which will be useful for reports, starts with the 1930 games and includes information on teams and players. (Rev: SLJ 3/04) [796.3]

13776 Woog, Dan. *The Ultimate Soccer Almanac* (6–12). Illus. 1998, Lowell House $12.95 (978-1-56565-951-3); paper $8.95 (978-1-56565-891-2). A review of the history of soccer, important players and teams, and rules of the game and how to play it. (Rev: BL 7/98) [796.334]

13777 Wukovits, John. *The Composite Guide to Soccer* (4–8). 1998, Chelsea LB $28.00 (978-0-7910-4718-7). A basic guide to the history, rules, positions, and playing techniques of this sport, with material on its European popularity. (Rev: HBG 3/99; SLJ 12/98; VOYA 6/99) [796.334]

Surfing, Water Skiing, and Other Water Sports

13778 Barker, Amanda. *Windsurfing* (4–7). Series: Radical Sports. 1999, Heinemann LB $24.22 (978-1-57572-948-0). After a history of windsurfing, this book describes equipment, safety tips, and basic skills. (Rev: SLJ 5/00) [797.2]

13779 Crossingham, John, and Niki Walker. *Swimming in Action* (4–7). Series: Sports in Action. 2002, Crabtree LB $25.27 (978-0-7787-0331-0); paper $6.95 (978-0-7737-0351-3). Color photographs and many diagrams are used with a clear text to describe swimming basics, with tips on various strokes and safety. (Rev: BL 1/1–15/03; SLJ 10/03) [977.2]

13780 Egan, Tracie. *Water Polo: Rules, Tips, Strategy, and Safety* (4–8). Series: Sports from Coast to Coast. 2005, Rosen LB $26.50 (978-1-4042-0186-6). Introduces readers to the sport of water polo, along with its rules, training, and equipment. (Rev: SLJ 10/05)

13781 Lourie, Peter. *First Dive to Shark Dive* (5–8). Illus. 2006, Boyds Mills $17.95 (978-1-59078-068-8). This attractive, interesting photoessay documents a 12-year-old girl's introduction to scuba diving among sharks. (Rev: BL 2/15/06; SLJ 6/06) [797.2]

13782 Manley, Claudia B. *Ultra Swimming* (7–10). Illus. Series: Ultra Sports. 2002, Rosen LB $26.50 (978-0-8239-3558-1). An introduction to the history of this demanding new sport that gives tips on improving performance, maintaining safety, and training both body and mind for the challenges. (Rev: BL 9/1/02) [797.2]

13783 Vander Hook, Sue. *Scuba Diving* (4–7). Illus. Series: World of Sports. 2000, Smart Apple LB $16.95 (978-1-887068-59-8). After a section on star scuba divers, this account describes the origins and evolution of the sport, its equipment, hazards, and techniques. (Rev: BL 9/15/00) [797.2]

13784 Werner, Doug. *Surfer's Start-Up: A Beginner's Guide to Surfing*. 2nd ed. (7–12). 1999, Tracks paper $11.95 (978-1-884654-12-1). A new edition of this standard instructional guide that covers basic instruction, surfing gear, safety, etiquette, and history. (Rev: SLJ 9/99) [797]

Tennis and Other Racquet Games

13785 Blackall, Bernie. *Tennis* (4–8). Illus. by Vasja Koman. Series: Top Sport. 1999, Heinemann $21.36 (978-1-57572-842-1). Double-page spreads present topics including the history of tennis, its equipment and rules, and important skills, plus a rundown on famous stars of the sport. (Rev: SLJ 12/99) [796.342]

13786 Crossingham, John. *Tennis in Action* (4–7). Series: Sports in Action. 2002, Crabtree LB $25.27 (978-0-7787-0116-3); paper $6.95 (978-0-7787-0122-4). A fine introduction to tennis told through a concise text with easy-to-follow descriptions and material on equipment, rules, and techniques. (Rev: BL 9/1/02; SLJ 11/02) [796.342]

13787 Kaiman, Bobbie, and Sarah Dann. *Badminton in Action* (4–7). Series: Sports in Action. 2003, Crabtree LB $25.27 (978-0-7787-0334-1); paper $6.95 (978-0-7787-0354-9). This basic introduction to badminton includes material on racquets, courts, rules, and strategies. (Rev: BL 11/15/03) [796.34]

13788 MacCurdy, Doug, and Shawn Tully. *Sports Illustrated Tennis: Strokes for Success! Rev. ed.* (8–12). 1994, Sports Illustrated paper $12.95 (978-1-56800-006-0). Using many illustrations, this volume covers topics like rules, equipment, techniques, and competitions. [796.342]

13789 Muskat, Carrie. *The Composite Guide to Tennis* (5–7). Series: Composite Guide. 1998, Chelsea LB $12.95 (978-0-7910-4728-6). Past and present tennis stars are mentioned along with a general introduction to the game. (Rev: HBG 10/98; SLJ 9/98) [796.342]

13790 Rutledge, Rachel. *The Best of the Best in Tennis* (4–7). Illus. 1998, Millbrook LB $24.90 (978-0-7613-1303-8). Using a lively text and many color photographs, this work gives a history of women in tennis and a rundown of today's most important female players. (Rev: BL 2/15/99; HBG 10/99; SLJ 3/99) [796.342]

13791 Sherrow, Victoria. *Tennis* (6–12). Series: History of Sports. 2003, Gale LB $29.95 (978-1-56006-959-1). The origins and evolution of the game are followed by information on recreational and competitive tennis and on outstanding players. (Rev: SLJ 9/03) [796.342]

Volleyball

13792 Giddens, Sandra, and Owen Giddens. *Volleyball: Rules, Tips, Strategy, and Safety* (4–8). Series: Sports from Coast to Coast. 2005, Rosen LB $26.50 (978-1-4042-0185-9). Introduces the sport of volleyball — including its rules, equipment, and strategies. (Rev: SLJ 10/05) [796.32]

13793 Sherrow, Victoria. *Volleyball* (6–12). Illus. Series: History of Sports. 2002, Gale LB $28.70 (978-1-56006-961-4). From the invention of volleyball as a second-class version of basketball to today's prominence around the world, Sherrow traces volleyball's growth and looks at competitive and recreational aspects of the sport. (Rev: BL 9/1/02) [796.325]

Author Index

Authors are arranged alphabetically by last name. Authors' and joint authors' names are followed by book titles — which are also arranged alphabetically — and the text entry number. Book titles may refer to those that appear as a main entry or as an internal entry mentioned in the text. Fiction titles are indicated by (F) following the entry number.

Aamodt, Alice. *Wolf Pack*, 12410
Aaron, Chester. *Lackawanna*, 1(F)
Out of Sight, Out of Mind, 2(F)
Aaseng, Nathan. *African-American Athletes*, 6778
American Dinosaur Hunters, 7546
Athletes, 6779
Barry Sanders, 6959
The Bermuda Triangle, 13453
Black Inventors, 6474
Business Builders in Broadcasting, 6475
Business Builders in Computers, 6476
Business Builders in Fast Food, 6477
Business Builders in Oil, 6478
Business Builders in Sweets and Treats, 10734
Carl Lewis, 7000
The Cheetah, 12392
Cherokee Nation v. Georgia, 8954
Construction, 6479
The Cougar, 12393
David Robinson, 6922
John Stockton, 6927
Jose Canseco, 6840
The Locker Room Mirror, 13512
The Marine Corps in Action, 13158
Michael Jordan, 6901
Nature's Poisonous Creatures, 12296
Navajo Code Talkers, 7929
The O. J. Simpson Trial, 9950
Paris, 7930
The Peace Seekers, 7046
Top 10 Basketball Scoring Small Forwards, 6780
Treacherous Traitors, 10498
True Champions, 6781
The White House, 9583
Wildshots, 10901
Yearbooks in Science: 1940–1949, 12015

Yearbooks in Science: 1930–1939, 12016
You Are the Corporate Executive, 10745
You Are the Explorer, 7531
You Are the General, 10059
You Are the General II, 7638
You Are the Juror, 9951
You Are the President, 9911
You Are the President II, 9912
You Are the Senator, 9928
You Are the Supreme Court Justice, 9952
Aaseng, Rolf E. *Augsburg Story Bible*, 9790
Abadzis, Nick. *Laika*, 2553(F)
Abbink, Emily. *Missions of the Monterey Bay Area*, 9645
Abbott, Hailey. *The Bridesmaid*, 789(F)
Abbott, Tony. *Firegirl*, 1132(F)
Kringle, 1820(F)
The Postcard, 3935(F)
Abdel-Fattah, Randa. *Does My Head Look Big in This?* 652(F)
Abe, Yoshitoshi. *New Feathers*, 2554(F)
Abeel, Samantha. *What Once Was White*, 11614
Abelove, Joan. *Go and Come Back*, 1768(F)
Able, Deborah. *Hate Groups*, 10366
Abouzeid, Chris. *Anatopsis*, 1821(F)
Abraham, Denise Gonzales. *Cecilia's Year*, 653(F), 654(F)
Surprising Cecilia, 654(F)
Abraham, Philip. *Television and Movies*, 13094
Abraham, Susan Gonzales. *Cecilia's Year*, 653(F), 654(F)
Surprising Cecilia, 654(F)
Abraham-Podietz, Eva. *Ten Thousand Children*, 7972
Abrahams, Peter. *Down the Rabbit Hole*, 3936(F)

Into the Dark, 3937
Up All Night, 4526(F)
Abrahams, Roger D., ed. *African Folktales*, 4827
Abramovitz, Melissa. *Lou Gehrig's Disease*, 11209
Abrams, Dennis. *Anthony Horowitz*, 5518
Hamid Karzai, 7119
Abrams, Judith Z. *The Secret World of Kabbalah*, 9735
Abrams, Liesa. *Chronic Fatigue Syndrome*, 11210
Acampora, Paul. *Defining Dulcie*, 3789(F)
Aciman, André. *Baby*, 790(F)
Acker, Kerry. *Everything You Need to Know About the Goth Scene*, 11829
Ackerman, Jane. *Louis Pasteur and the Founding of Microbiology*, 6729
Ackermann, Joan. *In the Space Left Behind*, 791(F)
Adair, Gene. *Alfred Hitchcock*, 5765
Adair, Rick, ed. *Critical Perspectives on Politics and the Environment*, 10418
Adams, Colleen. *Women's Suffrage*, 10070
Adams, Cynthia. *The Mysterious Case of Sir Arthur Conan Doyle*, 5485
Adams, Lenora. *Baby Girl*, 1254(F)
Adams, Richard. *Tales from Watership Down*, 1822(F)
Watership Down, 1823(F)
Adams, Sean. *Tim Duncan*, 6885
Adams, Simon. *Alexander*, 7144
World War II, 7931
Adams, W. Royce. *Me and Jay*, 3(F)
Adamson, Joy. *Born Free*, 12394
Adamson, Thomas K. *Lessons in Science Safety with Max Axiom, Super Scientist*, 12072

Cibula, Matt. *How to Be the Greatest Writer in the World*, 10796

Ciment, James. *Law and Order*, 9968

Cindrich, Lisa. *In the Shadow of the Pali*, 3328(F)

Cirrone, Dorian. *Prom Kings and Drama Queens*, 389(F)

Citra, Becky. *Never to Be Told*, 3630

Citrin, Michael. *The Fall of the Amazing Zalindas*, 130(F)

Clairday, Robynn. *Confessions of a Boyfriend Stealer*, 1322(F)

Clancy, Tom. *The Deadliest Game*, 4280(F)

Virtual Vandals, 4280(F)

Clare, Cassandra. *Toby Wheeler*, 4440(F)

Clare, John D. *Aztec Life*, 3016

Clare, John D., ed. *First World War*, 7907

The Voyages of Christopher Columbus, 5149

Clark, Ann Nolan. *Secret of the Andes*, 3017(F)

Clark, Catherine. *The Alison Rules*, 1323(F)

Frozen Rodeo, 390(F)

Clark, Charles. *Iran*, 8677

Islam, 9815

Life of a Nazi Soldier, 8466

Clark, Clara Gillow. *Hattie on Her Way*, 3329(F)

Hill Hawk Hattie, 3329(F)

Clark, Mary Higgins, ed. *The International Association of Crime Writers Presents Bad Behavior*, 3965(F)

Clarke, Alicia. *Coping with Self-Mutilation*, 11626

Clarke, Arthur C. *Childhood's End*, 4281(F)

Clarke, Judith. *Kalpana's Dream*, 2834(F)

Night Train, 1324(F)

One Whole and Perfect Day, 843(F)

Starry Nights, 3631(F)

Clarke, Julie M. *Understanding Weight and Depression*, 11239

Clarke, Nicole. *Spin City*, 1325

Clarkson, Peter. *Volcanoes*, 12689

Claro, Nicole. *Madonna*, 5797

Clay, Rebecca. *Space Travel and Exploration*, 12127

Claybourne, Anna. *The Renaissance*, 7842

The Usborne Book of Treasure Hunting, 7650

Claypool, Jane. *Saddam Hussein*, 7116

Clayton, Lawrence. *Alcohol Drug Dangers*, 11076

Diet Pill Drug Dangers, 11077

Tranquilizers, 11078

Working Together Against Drug Addiction, 11079

Cle, Troy. *The Marvelous Effect*, 1953(F)

Cleary, Beverly. *Dear Mr. Henshaw*, 246(F), 1326(F)

Fifteen, 4194(F)

The Luckiest Girl, 4195(F)

Sister of the Bride, 844(F)

Strider, 246(F)

Cleaver, Bill. *Dust of the Earth*, 846(F)

Ellen Grae, 1327(F)

Grover, 1328(F)

Hazel Rye, 1329(F)

Lady Ellen Grae, 1327(F)

Me Too, 1145(F)

Queen of Hearts, 847(F)

Cleaver, Vera. *Dust of the Earth*, 846(F)

Ellen Grae, 1327(F)

Grover, 1328(F)

Hazel Rye, 1329(F)

Lady Ellen Grae, 1327(F)

Me Too, 1145(F)

Queen of Hearts, 847(F)

Sweetly Sings the Donkey, 845(F)

Clee, Paul. *Before Hollywood*, 7496

Photography and the Making of the American West, 7421

Clement-Davies, David. *Fell*, 1954(F)

The Sight, 1954(F)

The Telling Pool, 1955(F)

Clements, Andrew. *The Report Card*, 391(F)

The School Story, 392(F)

Things Hoped For, 848(F)

Things Not Seen, 848(F), 4282(F)

A Week in the Woods, 393(F)

Clifford, Mary Louise. *The Land and People of Afghanistan*, 8353

Cline, Don. *Alias Billy the Kid, the Man Behind the Legend*, 6391

Cline, Eric H. *The Ancient Egyptian World*, 7738

Clinton, Catherine. *The Black Soldier*, 10241

Scholastic Encyclopedia of the Civil War, 9247

Clinton, Catherine, ed. *I, Too, Sing America*, 4733

A Poem of Her Own, 4734

Clinton, Cathryn. *A Stone in My Hand*, 1774(F)

Clippinger, Carol. *Open Court*, 4441(F)

Clive, A. Lawton. *Hiroshima*, 7957

Cloud Tapper, Suzanne. *The Abolition of Slavery*, 9185

Clowes, Martin. *Electricity*, 12960

Clugston, Chynna. *Queen Bee*, 2576(F)

Cobain, Bev. *When Nothing Matters Anymore*, 11627

Cobb, Allan. *Cadmium*, 12634

How Do We Know How Stars Shine? 12181

Cobb, Allan B. *Super Science Projects About Animals and Their Habitats*, 12300

Super Science Projects About Oceans, 12855

Weather Observation Satellites, 12837

Cobb, Katie. *Happenings*, 394(F)

Cobb, Vicki. *Chemically Active! Experiments You Can Do at Home*, 12635

Fireworks, 12967

How to Really Fool Yourself, 11596

Junk Food, 12967

Magic . . . Naturally! Science Entertainments and Amusements, 13378

The Secret Life of Hardware, 12053

Sneakers, 12967

Coburn, Ann. *Glint*, 3966(F)

Coburn, Broughton. *Triumph on Everest*, 7022

Cockcroft, James D. *Diego Rivera*, 5386

Latino Visions, 7422

Cocke, William. *A Historical Album of Virginia*, 9693

Coerr, Eleanor. *Mieko and the Fifth Treasure*, 3500(F)

Coetzee, Frans. *World War I*, 7908

Cofer, Judith Ortiz. *Call Me María*, 673(F)

An Island Like You, 674(F)

Cofer, Judith Ortiz, ed. *Riding Low on the Streets of Gold*, 10313

Coffey, Jan. *Tropical Kiss*, 4196(F)

Coffey, Wayne. *The Boys of Winter*, 13731

Katarina Witt, 6982

Cohen, Charles D. *The Seuss, the Whole Seuss, and Nothing but the Seuss*, 5501

Cohen, Daniel. *The Alaska Purchase*, 9383

Animal Rights, 10370

Cloning, 11483

Cults, 9846

The Impeachment of William Jefferson Clinton, 9914

Jesse Ventura, 7035

Joseph McCarthy, 6331

The Manhattan Project, 13161

Prophets of Doom, 13460

Southern Fried Rat and Other Gruesome Tales, 4920

Yellow Journalism, 5094

Cohen, Joel H. *R. L. Stine*, 5609

Cohen, Miriam. *Robert and Dawn Marie 4Ever*, 1330(F)

Cohen, Tish. *The Invisible Rules of the Zoe Lama*, 395(F)

Cohen-Posey, Kate. *How to Handle Bullies, Teasers and Other Meanies*, 11877

Cohn, Rachel. *Pop Princess*, 1331(F)

Gregor and the Marks of Secret,
1963(F)
Gregor the Overlander, 1964(F)
Collins, Yvonne. *The Black Sheep,*
853(F)
Introducing Vivien Leigh Reid,
400(F)
Introducing Vivien Leigh Reid:
Daughter of the Diva, 402(F)
The New and Improved Vivien
Leigh Reid, 401(F)
Now Starring Vivien Leigh Reid,
402(F)
Collinson, Alan. *Pollution,* 10473
Collison, Linda. *Star-Crossed,*
3018(F)
Collodi, Carlo. *The Adventures of*
Pinocchio, 1965(F), 4862(F)
Colman, Hila. *Rich and Famous Like*
My Mom, 854(F)
Colman, Penny. *Adventurous*
Women, 5115
Corpses, Coffins, and Crypts,
11037
Girls, 8891
Toilets, Bathtubs, Sinks, and
Sewers, 12968
Coman, Carolyn. *Many Stones,*
403(F)
What Jamie Saw, 855(F)
ComicsKey Staff. *How to Draw*
Kung Fu Comics, 13343
Comino, Sandra. *The Little Blue*
House, 3968(F)
Comora, Madeleine. *Taj Mahal,* 8307
Compestine, Ying Chang. *Revolution*
Is Not a Dinner Party, 2835(F)
Compston, Christine L. *Earl Warren,*
6376
Condit, Erin. *The Duvaliers,* 7266
Conford, Ellen. *The Alfred G.*
Graebner Memorial High
School Handbook of Rules and
Regulations, 3813(F)
Dear Lovey Hart, I Am Desperate,
3814(F)
Hail, Hail Camp Timberwood,
1337(F)
Seven Days to Be a Brand-New Me,
3815(F)
Why Me? 3816(F)
You Never Can Tell, 1338(F)
Conklin, Barbara Gardner. *Health*
Science Projects About
Psychology, 11833
Conley, Kate A. *Joseph Priestley and*
the Discovery of Oxygen, 6737
Conley, Kevin. *Benjamin Banneker,*
6550
Conlogue, Ray. *Shen and the*
Treasure Fleet, 2836(F)
Conlon-McKenna, Marita. *Fields of*
Home, 2896(F)
Under the Hawthorn Tree, 2896(F)
Wildflower Girl, 2896(F)
Conly, Jane L. *Crazy Lady!* 1339(F)

Racso and the Rats of NIMH,
1966(F)
Conly, Jane Leslie. *In the Night, on*
Lanvale Street, 3969(F)
Connelly, Elizabeth Russell. *Through*
a Glass Darkly, 11080
Connolly, Helen. *Field Hockey,*
13705
Connolly, James E. *Why the*
Possum's Tail Is Bare, 4902
Connolly, Sean. *Amphetamines,*
11081
Botticelli, 5288
Claude Monet, 5357
Cocaine, 11082
Gender Equality, 7651
LSD, 11083
Nelson Mandela, 7087
New Testament Miracles, 9796
The Right to Vote, 7651
Steroids, 11084
Tobacco, 11085
Connor, Leslie. *Waiting for Normal,*
856(F)
Conord, Bruce W. *John Lennon,*
5787
Conover, Sarah. *Beautiful Signs/Ayat*
Jamilah, 9816
Conover, Sarah, ed. *Kindness,* 4843
Conrad, Pam. *Our House,* 404(F)
Constable, Kate. *The Singer of All*
Songs, 1967(F)
The Tenth Power, 1968(F)
The Waterless Sea, 1969(F)
Conway, Lorie. *Forgotten Ellis*
Island, 9599
Cook, Lynette. *Infinite Worlds,*
12209
Cook, Nick. *Roller Coasters; or, I*
Had So Much Fun, I Almost
Puked, 13204
Cooley, Beth. *Shelter,* 857(F)
Cooley, Brian. *Make-a-Saurus,* 7554
Cooling, Wendy. *D Is for Dahl,* 5466
Coombs, Karen M. *Sarah on Her*
Own, 3091(F)
Coombs, Karen Mueller. *Jackie*
Robinson, 6865
Coombs, Kate. *The Runaway*
Princess, 4803
Coon, Nora E. *Teen Dream Jobs,*
10848
Coon, Nora E., ed. *It's Your Rite,*
10648
Cooney, Caroline B. *Both Sides of*
Time, 4197(F)
Diamonds in the Shadow, 1776(F)
Enter Three Witches, 2897(F)
The Face on the Milk Carton,
859(F)
Flash Fire, 36(F)
Flight No. 116 Is Down, 37(F)
A Friend at Midnight, 858(F)
Hit the Road, 405(F)
Night School, 3633(F)
Prisoner of Time, 1970(F)
Summer Nights, 1340(F)

Whatever Happened to Janie?
859(F)
Cooney, Miriam P. *Celebrating*
Women in Mathematics and
Science, 6490
Cooper, Chris. *Arsenic,* 12636
Cooper, Clare. *Ashar of Qarius,*
4285(F)
Cooper, Dan. *Enrico Fermi,* 6633
Cooper, Ilene. *Jack,* 6144
Up Close, 5861
Cooper, James Fenimore. *The*
Deerslayer, 333(F)
The Last of the Mohicans, 333(F)
The Pathfinder, 333(F)
The Pioneers, 333(F)
The Prairie, 333(F)
Cooper, Jason. *Árboles / Trees,* 8892
Aves / Birds, 8892
Banderas / Flags, 8892
Flores / Flowers, 8892
Cooper, John. *Rapid Ray,* 7001
Season of Rage, 8720
Cooper, Kay. *Where Did You Get*
Those Eyes? 11955
Why Do You Speak as You Do?
5059
Cooper, Michael. *Klondike Fever,*
8721
Cooper, Michael L. *Dust to Eat,* 9433
Fighting for Honor, 9466
Hero of the High Seas, 6308
Indian School, 8986
Jamestown 1607, 9087
Remembering Manzanar, 9467
Slave Spirituals and the Jubilee
Singers, 7471
Cooper, Robert. *Indonesia,* 8375
Cooper, Susan. *The Dark Is Rising,*
1973(F), 1974(F)
Don't Read This! 3693(F)
Green Boy, 1971(F)
Greenwitch, 1973(F), 1974(F)
The Grey King, 1973(F), 1974(F)
King of Shadows, 1972(F)
Over Sea, Under Stone, 1973(F),
1974(F)
Silver on the Tree, 1974(F)
Victory, 1975(F)
Cooperman, Stephanie H. *Chien-*
Shiung Wu, 6579
Copeland, Cynthia. *Elin's Island,*
3501(F)
Copeland, Mark. *The Bundle at*
Blackthorpe Heath, 3970(F)
Coppin, Cheryl Branch. *Everything*
You Need to Know About
Healing from Rape Trauma,
10511
Corbett, Doris, ed. *Unique Games*
and Sports Around the World,
13520
Corbett, Sue. *Free Baseball,* 4442(F)
Corbishley, Mike. *Ancient Rome,*
7811
First Civilizations, 7711

Harris, Elizabeth Snoke. *Crime Scene Science Fair Projects*, 10537
First Place Science Fair Projects for Inquisitive Kids, 12065
Yikes! Wow! Yuck! 12066
Harris, Geraldine. *Ancient Egypt*, 7743
Gods and Pharaohs from Egyptian Mythology, 4950
Harris, Jacqueline. *Sickle Cell Disease*, 11286
Harris, John. *Strong Stuff*, 4979
Harris, Laurie L., ed. *Biography Today*, 6504
Harris, Nancy, ed. *AIDS in Developing Countries*, 11287
Harris, Nathaniel. *Ancient Maya*, 7618
Democracy, 9856
The Great Depression, 9444
Hitler, 7205
Renaissance Art, 7383
The War in Former Yugoslavia, 8435
Harris, Robert. *Prince Across the Water*, 2922(F)
Harris, Robert J. *The Rogues*, 229(F)
Harris, Tim. *The Mackenzie River*, 12741
Harris, Zoe. *Pinatas and Smiling Skeletons*, 10675
Harris-Johnson, Debrah. *The African-American Teenagers' Guide to Personal Growth, Health, Safety, Sex and Survival*, 11897
Harrison, Cora. *The Famine Secret*, 2923(F)
Nauala and Her Secret Wolf, 2925(F)
The Secret of Drumshee Castle, 2924(F), 2925(F)
The Secret of the Seven Crosses, 2925(F)
Harrison, David L., ed. *Dude!* 4527(F)
Harrison, Ian. *The Book of Inventions*, 12975
Harrison, Mette Ivie. *The Monster in Me*, 939(F)
The Princess and the Hound, 2109(F)
Harrison, Michael. *It's My Life*, 78(F)
Harrison, Michael, comp. *The Oxford Treasury of Time Poems*, 4668
Harrison, Peter, ed. *African Nations and Leaders*, 8127
History of Southern Africa, 8207
Harrison, Supenn. *Cooking the Thai Way*, 13271
Harrison, Troon. *A Bushel of Light*, 3028(F)
Goodbye to Atlantis, 940(F)
Hart, Alison. *Fires of Jubilee*, 3215(F)
Gabriel's Horses, 3216(F), 3217(F)
Gabriel's Triumph, 3217(F)
Hart, Avery. *Ancient Greece!* 7781

Who Really Discovered America? 7663
Hart, Bruce. *Sooner or Later*, 4212(F)
Waiting Games, 4213(F)
Hart, Carole. *Sooner or Later*, 4212(F)
Waiting Games, 4213(F)
Hart, Christopher. *Christopher Hart's Animation Studio*, 13350
Christopher Hart's Cartoon Studio, 13350
Drawing on the Funny Side of the Brain, 13351
Kids Draw Anime, 13352
Manga Mania, 13353
Manga Mania Chibi and Furry Characters, 13354
Mecha Mania, 13355
Hart, Joyce. *Native Son*, 5653
Hart, Philip S. *Flying Free*, 13120
Up In the Air, 5147
Hartenian, Larry. *Benito Mussolini*, 7230
Hartinger, Brent. *Dreamquest*, 2110
Geography Club, 1442(F)
The Order of the Poison Oak, 1442(F)
Hartman, Holly, ed. *Girlwonder*, 11898
Hartman, Thomas. *How Do You Spell God?* 9751
Hartnett, Sonya. *The Silver Donkey*, 3477(F)
What the Birds See, 941(F)
Hartz, Paula. *Baha'i Faith*, 9753
Hartz, Paula R. *Taoism*, 9754
Harvey, Bonnie Carman. *Carry A. Nation*, 6446
Daniel Webster, 6379
Jane Addams, 5960
Harvey, Brett. *Farmers and Ranchers*, 9317
Harvey, Gill. *Orphan of the Sun*, 2754(F)
Harvey, Michael. *The End of the World*, 13470
Harvey-Fitzhenry, Alyxandra. *Waking*, 1443
Hasan, Heather. *American Women of the Gulf War*, 13175
Archimedes, 6548
Hasan, Tahara. *Anthrax Attacks Around the World*, 13176
Hasday, Judy. *James Earl Jones*, 5775
Madeleine Albright, 6243
Hasday, Judy L. *Albert Einstein*, 6617
The Apollo 13 Mission, 12145
Extraordinary People in the Movies, 5242
Extraordinary Women Athletes, 6792
The Tuskegee Airmen, 9471
Haskins, James. *Africa*, 8911
Jesse Jackson, 6002

Out of the Darkness, 10256
Haskins, Jim. *African American Entrepreneurs*, 6505
African American Military Heroes, 5900
African-American Religious Leaders, 5902
African Heroes, 7058
Bill Cosby, 5725
Black Dance in America, 7487
Bound for America, 7896
Conjure Times, 7524
The Day Fort Sumter Was Fired On, 9263
Donna Summer, 5852
Geography of Hope, 9397
The Harlem Renaissance, 9445
I Have a Dream, 6012
Louis Farrakhan and the Nation of Islam, 5987
Magic Johnson, 6900
One More River to Cross, 5901
Outward Dreams, 6506
Rosa Parks, 6027
Separate but Not Equal, 10113
Space Challenger, 5136
Spike Lee, 5785
Toni Morrison, 5558
Hassig, Susan M. *Iraq*, 8684
Panama, 8743
Hassinger, Peter W. *Shakespeare's Daughter*, 2926(F)
Hastings, Penny. *Sports for Her*, 13534
Hatch, Robert. *The Hero Project*, 5112
Hatch, William. *The Hero Project*, 5112
Hathaway, Jim. *Cameroon in Pictures*, 8241
Hathorn, Libby. *Thunderwith*, 942(F)
Hatt, Christine. *The American West*, 9318
Scientists and Their Discoveries, 6507
Slavery, 10257
World War I, 7918
Haugaard, Erik C. *The Revenge of the Forty-Seven Samurai*, 2842(F)
Under the Black Flag, 79(F)
Haugen, Brenda. *Alexander Hamilton*, 6295
Crazy Horse, 6269
Douglas MacArthur, 6327
Ethan Allen, 6245
Franklin Delano Roosevelt, 6202
Geronimo, 6286
Henry B. Gonzalez, 5993
Winston Churchill, 7171
Haugen, David, ed. *Can the War on Terrorism Be Won?* 10702
Haugen, David M., ed. *Adoption*, 11971
Animal Experimentation, 10383
China, 8288
Interracial Relationships, 10227
Poverty, 10612

971

Johnson, Eric W. *People, Love, Sex, and Families*, 11786

Johnson, Ginger. *Make Your Own Christmas Ornaments*, 13210

Johnson, Harriet McBryde. *Accidents of Nature*, 1190(F)

Johnson, Henry. *Travis and Freddy's Adventures in Vegas*, 4045(F)

Johnson, Jane. *The Shadow World*, 2185(F)

Johnson, Jinny. *Simon and Schuster Children's Guide to Sea Creatures*, 12515

Johnson, Joan J. *Children of Welfare*, 10614

Johnson, Julie. *Why Are People Prejudiced?* 10542

Why Do People Fight Wars? 10542

Why Do People Join Gangs? 10542

Johnson, Julie Tallard. *Teen Psychic*, 13479

Johnson, Kathleen Jeffrie. *Dumb Love*, 4216(F)

A Fast and Brutal Wing, 2186(F)

Johnson, Kevin. *Does Anybody Know What Planet My Parents Are From?* 11899

Johnson, Linda C. *Mother Teresa*, 7134

Johnson, Linda Carlson. *Rain Forests*, 12714

Johnson, Lissa Halls. *Fast Forward to Normal*, 1483(F)

Stuck in the Sky, 1483(F)

Johnson, Marlys. *Understanding Exercise Addiction*, 11607

Johnson, Marlys H. *Careers in the Movies*, 10911

Johnson, Maureen. *Devilish*, 3679(F)

Girl at Sea, 115(F)

Suite Scarlett, 490(F)

13 Little Blue Envelopes, 491(F)

Johnson, Nancy. *My Brother's Keeper*, 3221(F)

Johnson, Peter. *What Happened*, 969(F)

Johnson, Rebecca. *Ernest Shackleton*, 5217

Johnson, Rebecca L. *The Great Barrier Reef*, 12523

Investigating the Ozone Hole, 10439

Mighty Animal Cells, 12219

Johnson, Robert. *Shona*, 8225

Johnson, Rodney. *The Secret of Dead Man's Mine*, 4046(F)

Johnson, Scott. *Safe at Second*, 4471(F)

Johnson, Stephen T. *Alphabet City*, 5064

Johnson, Suzan. *Boss Tweed and Tammany Hall*, 6470

Johnson, Sylvia A. *Apple Trees*, 12257

Bats, 12364

Beetles, 12486

Inside an Egg, 12442

Ladybugs, 12487

Morning Glories, 12288

Penguins, 12456

Silkworms, 12307

Wolf Pack, 12410

Johnson, Terry. *Legal Rights*, 9902

Johnson, Toni E. *Handcuff Blues*, 10543

Johnson-Feelings, Dianne. *Presenting Laurence Yep*, 5027

Johnston, Andrea. *Girls Speak Out*, 11900

Johnston, Antony. *Point Blank*, 2612(F)

Stormbreaker, 2613(F)

Johnston, Ginny. *Giant Predators of the Ancient Seas*, 7557

Johnston, Lindsay Lee. *Soul Moon Soup*, 970(F)

Johnston, Marianne. *Let's Talk About Being Afraid*, 11901

Let's Talk About Being Shy, 11901

Johnston, Mark. *The Secret Agents Strike Back*, 4139(F)

Johnston, Robert D. *The Making of America*, 8917

Johnston, Tony. *The Ancestors Are Singing*, 4797

Any Small Goodness, 702(F)

Bone by Bone by Bone, 703(F)

Johnstone, Mike. *Monster Trucks*, 13131

NASCAR, 13600

Joinson, Carla. *Civil War Doctor*, 6761

Jones, Adrienne. *The Hawks of Chelney*, 267(F)

Jones, Carol. *Cheese*, 12258

Pasta and Noodles, 12258

Jones, Catherine. *Navajo Code Talkers*, 7996

Jones, Charlotte F. *Yukon Gold*, 8711

Jones, Charlotte Foltz. *Westward Ho! Explorers of the American West*, 5118

Jones, Claudia. *Riding Out the Storm*, 3680(F)

Jones, Constance. *The European Conquest of North America*, 9006

Jones, David. *Baboon*, 2187(F)

Mighty Robots, 13051

Jones, Diana Wynne. *Cart and Cwidder*, 2188(F)

The Crown of Dalemark, 2189(F)

Dark Lord of Derkholm, 2196(F)

The Game, 3681(F)

Hexwood, 4334(F)

House of Many Ways, 2190(F)

Howl's Moving Castle, 2191(F)

The Merlin Conspiracy, 2192(F)

The Pinhoe Egg, 2193(F)

The Time of the Ghost, 2194(F)

Unexpected Magic, 2195(F)

Year of the Griffin, 2196(F)

Jones, Frewin. *The Faerie Path*, 2197(F), 2198(F)

The Lost Queen, 2198(F)

The Sorcerer King, 2199(F)

Jones, Kimberly K. *Sand Dollar Summer*, 971(F)

Jones, Madeline. *Knights and Castles*, 7869

Jones, Marcia T. *Leprechauns Don't Play Basketball*, 1993(F)

Jones, Patrick. *Cheated*, 1484(F)

Things Change, 1485(F)

Jones, Ralph. *Straight Talk*, 11117

Jones, Richard. *That's Magic! 40 Foolproof Tricks to Delight, Amaze and Entertain*, 13380

Jones, Sarah. *Film*, 7498

Jones, Schuyler. *Pygmies of Central Africa*, 8162

Jones, Steven L. *The Red Tails*, 7997

Jones, Terry. *The Lady and the Squire*, 2942(F)

Jones, Thomas D. *Mission: Earth*, 12139

Jones, Traci L. *Standing against the Wind*, 704(F)

Jones, Veda Boyd. *Ewan McGregor*, 5796

George W. Bush, 6083

Government and Politics, 5906

Selena, 5841

Jones, Victoria Garrett. *Eleanor Roosevelt*, 6189

Marian Anderson, 5691

Jones-Brown, Delores D. *Race, Crime, and Punishment*, 10002

Jongman, Mariken. *Rits*, 972(F)

Jonsberg, Barry. *Am I Right or Am I Right?* 1486(F)

Dreamrider, 1191(F)

Joong-Ki, Park. *Shaman Warrior*, 2626(F)

Joosse, Barbara M. *Pieces of the Picture*, 973(F)

Joravsky, Ben. *Hoop Dreams*, 13639

Jordan, Anne Devereaux. *Slavery and Resistance*, 8918

Jordan, Denise M. *Julian Bond*, 5972

Walter Dean Myers, 5561

Jordan, Robert. *A Crown of Swords*, 2200(F)

Jordan, Rosa. *The Goatnappers*, 492(F)

Lost Goat Lane, 492(F)

Jordan, Sandra. *Andy Warhol, Prince of Pop*, 5405

Runaway Girl, 5289

Jordan, Sherryl. *The Hunting of the Last Dragon*, 2201(F)

Secret Sacrament, 2202(F), 2203(F)

Time of the Eagle, 2203(F)

Jorgensen, Christine T. *Death of a Dustbunny*, 4047(F)

Jorgensen, Lisa. *Grand Trees of America*, 12275

Jorgensen, Norman. *In Flanders Fields*, 3478(F)

Kendall, Martha E. *Failure Is Impossible*, 10120
Steve Wozniak, 6767
Susan B. Anthony, 5963
Kendell, Patricia. *WWF*, 12467
Kendra, Judith. *Tibetans*, 8365
Kennedy, Caroline, ed. *A Family of Poems*, 4677
Kennedy, Gregory. *The First Men in Space*, 12147
Kennedy, Gregory P. *Apollo to the Moon*, 12148
Kennedy, James. *The Order of Odd-Fish*, 2214(F)
Kennedy, John F. *Profiles in Courage*, 5911
Kennedy, Mike. *Ice Hockey*, 13708
Kennedy, Nick. *Kobe Bryant*, 6880
Kennedy, Robert C. *Life with the Navy Seals*, 13179
Kennen, Ally. *Beast*, 1497
Kennett, David. *Pharaoh*, 7750
Kenschaft, Lori. *Lydia Maria Child*, 5981
Kent, Deborah. *The American Revolution*, 9154
Animal Helpers for the Disabled, 12574
Athletes with Disabilities, 13546
Dorothy Day, 5982
In Colonial New England, 9104
In the Middle Colonies, 9104
In the Southern Colonies, 9104
Jimmy Carter, 6091
Mexico, 8770
Phillis Wheatley, 5636
Snake Pits, Talking Cures, and Magic Bullets, 11652
The Vietnam War, 9532
Kent, Jacqueline C. *Business Builders in Cosmetics*, 6512
Business Builders in Fashion, 6513
Kent, Peter. *Career Ideas for Kids Who Like Computers*, 11001
Career Ideas for Kids Who Like Sports, 10929
Kent, Zachary. *Charles Lindbergh and the Spirit of St. Louis*, 5182
The Civil War, 9271
Edgar Allan Poe, 5576
George Armstrong Custer, 6272
James Madison, 6171
Julius Caesar, 7162
The Mysterious Disappearance of Roanoke Colony in American History, 9105
The Persian Gulf War, 8097
William Seward, 6368
Kently, Eric. *The Story of the Titanic*, 13152
Kenyon, Karen Smith. *The Brontë Family*, 5438
Kenyon, Linda. *Rainforest Bird Rescue*, 12432
Keoke, Emory Dean. *Trade, Transportation, and Warfare*, 9012

Kephart, Beth. *House of Dance*, 978(F)
Undercover, 499(F)
Kepnes, Caroline. *Stephen Crane*, 5462
Kerby, Mona. *Robert E. Lee*, 6319
Kerina, Jane. *African Crafts*, 13212
Kerley, Barbara. *Walt Whitman*, 5643
Kern, Roy. *The Grade Booster Guide for Kids*, 10788
Kerr, Dan. *Candy on the Edge*, 1498(F)
Kerr, M. E. *Dinky Hocker Shoots Smack!* 1499(F)
Fell, 4053(F)
Fell Back, 4053(F)
Fell Down, 4053(F), 4054(F)
Gentlehands, 1500(F)
Someone Like Summer, 4219(F)
The Son of Someone Famous, 1501(F)
What I Really Think of You, 1502(F)
Kerr, P. B. *The Akhenatan Adventure*, 2215(F)
The Blue Djinn of Babylon, 2215(F)
Kerr, Rita. *Texas Footprints*, 3285(F)
Kerrigan, Michael. *The History of Punishment*, 10545
Kerrod, Robin. *Dawn of the Space Age*, 12149
New Materials, 12977
Space Probes, 12149
Space Shuttles, 12149
Space Stations, 12149
The Star Guide, 12185
Kesel, Barbara. *Meridian*, 2628(F)
Kessler, Liz. *Emily Windsnap and the Monster from the Deep*, 2216(F)
The Tail of Emily Windsnap, 2216(F), 2217(F)
Ketcham, Hank. *Hank Ketcham's Complete Dennis the Menace*, 5099
Ketchum, Liza. *Blue Coyote*, 1503(F)
Orphan Journey Home, 3166(F)
Where the Great Hawk Flies, 3103(F)
Key, Alexander. *The Forgotten Door*, 4336(F)
Key, Watt. *Alabama Moon*, 500(F)
Keyishian, Amy. *Stephen King*, 5532
Keyishian, Marjorie. *Stephen King*, 5532
Khalili, Nasser D. *Islamic Art and Culture*, 7386
Khanduri, Kamini. *Japanese Art and Culture*, 7411
Kheirabadi, Masoud. *Iran*, 8691
Kherdian, David. *The Revelations of Alvin Tolliver*, 501(F)
Kherdian, Jeron. *The Road from Home*, 7297
Kibuishi, Kazu. *The Stonekeeper*, 2629(F)
Kidd, J. S. *Quarks and Sparks*, 12943

Kidd, Renee A. *Quarks and Sparks*, 12943
Kidd, Ronald. *Monkey Town*, 3409(F)
Sammy Carducci's Guide to Women, 3837(F)
Kidder, Harvey. *The Kids' Book of Chess*, 13690
Kiesel, Stanley. *Skinny Malinky Leads the War for Kidness*, 4337(F)
The War Between the Pitiful Teachers and the Splendid Kids, 3838(F)
Kiland, Taylor Baldwin. *The U.S. Navy and Military Careers*, 10958
Kilbourne, Christina. *Dear Jo*, 1796(F)
Kilgallon, Conor. *India and Sri Lanka*, 8273
Kilgannon, Eily. *Folktales of the Yeats Country*, 4867
Killick, Jane. *Babylon 5*, 7511
Killien, Christi. *Artie's Brief*, 1504(F)
Killingray, David. *The Transatlantic Slave Trade*, 7897
Kilworth, Garry. *The Electric Kid*, 4338(F)
Kim, Melissa L. *The Endocrine and Reproductive Systems*, 11528
Kimball, Cheryl. *Horse Showing for Kids*, 13715
Kimball, Violet T. *Stories of Young Pioneers*, 9329
Kimmel, Elizabeth C. *The Ghost of the Stone Circle*, 2218(F)
Ice Story, 8861
Kimmel, Elizabeth Cody. *Dinosaur Bone War*, 6514
Ladies First, 5912
Lily B. on the Brink of Cool, 1505(F)
Lily B. on the Brink of Love, 1505(F)
Lily B. on the Brink of Paris, 502(F)
The Look-It-Up-Book of Explorers, 5119
Spin the Bottle, 1506(F)
Kimmel, Eric A. *The Witch's Face*, 4935
Wonders and Miracles, 9837
Kincher, Jonni. *The First Honest Book About Lies*, 11846
Kindermann, Barbara. *William Shakespeare's Romeo and Juliet*, 4621(F)
Kindl, Patrice. *Goose Chase*, 2219(F)
Lost in the Labyrinth, 4981(F)
Kindt, Matt. *2 Sisters*, 2630(F)
King, Andy. *Fundamental Mountain Biking*, 13671
King, Bart. *The Big Book of Girl Stuff*, 11906
King, Casey. *Oh, Freedom!* 10121

Mohr, Nicholasa. *El Bronx Remembered*, 727(F)
Felita, 728(F)
Going Home, 728(F)
Nilda, 729(F)
Moiles, Steven. *The Summer of My First Pediddle*, 1585(F)
Moiz, Azra. *Taiwan*, 8376
Molitor, Graham T. T., ed. *The 21st Century*, 10656
Molloy, Michael. *The House on Falling Star Hill*, 2322(F)
Peter Raven Under Fire, 2970(F)
The Time Witches, 2323(F)
The Witch Trade, 2323(F)
Molnar, Irma. *One-Time Dog Market at Buda and Other Hungarian Folktales*, 4872
Moloney, James. *Black Taxi*, 4080(F)
Trapped, 3698(F)
Molzahn, Arlene Bourgeois. *Top 10 American Women Sprinters*, 6801
Monaghan, Kathleen. *You Can Weave! Projects for Young Weavers*, 13217
Monaghan, Tom. *The Slave Trade*, 7898
Monroe, Judy. *Antidepressants*, 11151
Breast Cancer, 11338
Cooking the Korean Way, 13253
Cooking the Thai Way, 13271
Cooking the Vietnamese Way, 13289
Coping with Ulcers, Heartburn, and Stress-Related Stomach Disorders, 11573
Cystic Fibrosis, 11338
Inhalant Drug Dangers, 11152
Nicotine, 11153
The Nineteenth Amendment, 10144
Phobias, 11665
The Sacco and Vanzetti Controversial Murder Trial, 10008
Steroid Drug Dangers, 11154
The Susan B. Anthony Women's Voting Rights Trial, 10145
Understanding Weight-Loss Programs, 11713
Monroe, Kevin. *El Zombo Fantasma*, 2655(F)
Monseau, Virginia R. *Presenting Ouida Sebestyen*, 5589
Montejo, Victor, retel. *Popol Vuh*, 4896
Montes, Marisa. *A Circle of Time*, 3699(F)
Montgomery, Bertha Vining. *Cooking the West African Way*, 13287
Montgomery, Claire. *Hubert Invents the Wheel*, 3871(F)
Montgomery, L. M. *Anne of Avonlea*, 1034(F)
Anne of Green Gables, 1034(F)

Anne of Ingleside, 1034(F)
Anne of the Island, 1034(F)
Anne of Windy Poplars, 1034(F)
Anne's House of Dreams, 1034(F)
Christmas with Anne and Other Holiday Stories, 1035(F)
Emily Climbs, 1036(F)
Emily of New Moon, 1036(F)
Emily's Quest, 1036(F)
Montgomery, Monte. *Hubert Invents the Wheel*, 3871(F)
Montgomery, Sy. *Encantado*, 12722
Quest for the Tree Kangaroo, 12366
Search for the Golden Moon Bear, 12387
The Snake Scientist, 12335
The Tarantula Scientist, 12508
Monthei, Betty. *Looking for Normal*, 1037(F)
Montijo, Yolanda, ed. *Native Ways*, 9029
Moodley, Ermila. *Path to My African Eyes*, 730(F)
Mooney, Ben, ed. *You Never Did Learn to Knock*, 4565(F)
Mooney, Bill, retel. *The Exploding Toilet*, 13471
Mooney, Martin. *Brett Favre*, 6946
The Comanche Indians, 9032
Moore, David L. *Dark Sky, Dark Land*, 12014
Moore, Deborah. *Cityscapes*, 9635
Moore, Don. *Alex Raymond's Flash Gordon*, 2674(F)
Moore, Ishbel. *Daughter*, 1038(F)
Moore, Perry. *Hero*, 2324(F)
Moore, Peter. *Caught in the Act*, 1586(F)
Moore, Peter D. *Tundra*, 12700
Moore, Robin. *The Bread Sister of Sinking Creek*, 3298(F)
The Man with the Silver Oar, 3107(F)
Moore, Ruth Nulton. *Distant Thunder*, 3134(F)
Moore, Yvette. *Freedom Songs*, 731(F)
Moose, Katherine B. *Uniquely Delaware*, 9626
Uniquely Rhode Island, 9627
Mora, Pat. *My Own True Name*, 4763
Moragne, Wendy. *Allergies*, 11339
Depression, 11666
Morales, Leslie. *Esther Dyson*, 6606
Moran, Chris. *Snowboarding*, 13753
Moranville, Sharelle Byars. *A Higher Geometry*, 3459(F)
The Snows, 1587(F)
Morden, Simon. *The Lost Art*, 2325
Moredun, P. R. *The Dragon Conspiracy*, 2326(F)
Morey, Janet Nomura. *Famous Hispanic Americans*, 5932
Morey, Walt. *Angry Waters*, 147(F)
Death Walk, 148(F)
Gentle Ben, 276(F)

Kavik the Wolf Dog, 277(F)
Scrub Dog of Alaska, 277(F)
Year of the Black Pony, 278(F)
Morgan, Adrian. *Materials*, 12905
Using Sound, 12962
Water, 12829
Morgan, Clay. *The Boy Who Spoke Dog*, 279(F)
Morgan, David Lee. *LeBron James*, 6897
Morgan, Gwyneth. *Life in a Medieval Village*, 7878
Morgan, Jody. *Elephant Rescue*, 12418
Morgan, Julian. *Cleopatra*, 7762
Constantine, 7175
Morgan, Nicola. *Chicken Friend*, 1588(F)
The Highwayman's Footsteps, 2971(F)
Morgan, Nina. *Mother Teresa*, 7135
Morgan, Peggy. *Buddhism*, 9771
Morgan, Sally. *Alternative Energy Sources*, 12925
Body Doubles, 11494
From Greek Atoms to Quarks, 12961
From Mendel's Peas to Genetic Fingerprinting, 11495
From Microscopes to Stem Cell Research, 12561
From Sea Urchins to Dolly the Sheep, 11496
From Windmills to Hydrogen Fuel Cells, 12926
Germ Killers, 11340
Materials, 12905
Superfoods, 12262
Using Sound, 12962
Water, 12829
Morgan, Terri. *Chris Mullin*, 6913
Gabrielle Reece, 7031
Photography, 13404
Steve Young, 6966
Venus and Serena Williams, 6995
Morgane, Wendy. *New Jersey*, 9628
Morgenroth, Kate. *Echo*, 1212(F)
Morgenstern, Constance. *Waking Day*, 4689
Morgenstern, Julie. *Organizing from the Inside Out for Teens*, 11918
Morgenstern, Mindy. *The Real Rules for Girls*, 11919
Morgenstern-Colon, Jessi. *Organizing from the Inside Out for Teens*, 11918
Mori, Kyoko. *One Bird*, 1039(F)
Moriarty, Jaclyn. *The Murder of Bindy Mackenzie*, 550(F)
The Year of Secret Assignments, 1589(F)
Morin, Isobel V. *Impeaching the President*, 9918
Politics, American Style, 10046
Women Chosen for Public Office, 5933
Women of the U.S. Congress, 5934

Women Who Reformed Politics, 5935

Morley, David. *Healing Our World,* 11458

Morpurgo, Michael. *The Amazing Story of Adolphus Tips,* 3538(F)
Beowulf, 4873
Kensuke's Kingdom, 149(F)
Little Foxes, 2327(F)
The Mozart Question, 3539(F)
Private Peaceful, 3481(F)
War Horse, 3482(F)

Morpurgo, Michael, comp. *The Kingfisher Book of Great Boy Stories,* 4566(F)

Morpurgo, Michael, ed. *Ghostly Haunts,* 3700(F)

Morressy, John. *The Juggler,* 2792(F)

Morris, Bruce C. *Live Aware, Not in Fear,* 11769

Morris, Deborah. *Teens 911,* 150(F)

Morris, Desmond. *Catwatching,* 12579

Morris, Gerald. *The Ballad of Sir Dinadan,* 2793(F)
The Lioness and Her Knight, 2972(F)
Parsifal's Page, 2328(F)
The Princess, the Crone, and the Dung-Cart Knight, 2329(F)
The Quest of the Fair Unknown, 2973(F)
The Savage Damsel and the Dwarf, 2330(F)
The Squire, His Knight, and His Lady, 2794(F)
The Squire's Tale, 2795(F)

Morris, Greggory. *Basketball Basics,* 13645

Morris, Ian Macgregor. *Themistocles,* 7247

Morris, Jeffrey. *The FDR Way,* 6204
The Reagan Way, 9515

Morris, Juddi. *At Home with the Presidents,* 5936
The Harvey Girls, 9337
Tending the Fire, 5351

Morris, Neil. *Do You Know What's in Your Food?* 11714
Do You Know Where Your Food Comes From? 12263
Global Warming, 10442
The Life of Jesus, 9772
The Life of Moses, 9772

Morris, Taylor. *Class Favorite,* 551

Morris, Winifred. *Liar,* 1590(F)

Morris-Lipsman, Arlene. *Presidential Races,* 10057

Morrison, Grant. *Vimanarama,* 2656(F)

Morrison, John. *Cornel West,* 6472

Morrison, Lillian. *Way to Go!* 4690

Morrison, Marion. *The Amazon Rain Forest and Its People,* 12723
Brazil, 8832
Cuba, 8793

Ecuador, 8833
Guyana, 8834
Nicaragua, 8753

Morrison, Martha. *Judaism,* 9839

Morrison, Taylor. *Coast Mappers,* 9210

Morrison, Toni. *Remember,* 10146

Morrow, Robert. *Immigration,* 10206

Mortensen, Colin. *On Friendship,* 11909

Mortimer, Sean. *Hawk,* 7019

Morton, Joseph C. *The American Revolution,* 9161

Mosatche, Harriet S. *Too Old for This, Too Young for That! Your Survival Guide for the Middle-School Years,* 11793

Moser, Diane Kit. *The Age of Synthesis: 1800–1895,* 12037
Barbara McClintock, 6700
The Birth of Science, 12037
Modern Science: 1896–1945, 12037
The Rise of Reason: 1700–1799, 12037
Science Frontiers: 1946 to the Present, 12037

Moser, Kit. *The Crime of Genocide,* 9877
Savvy Surfing on the Internet, 13067

Moser, Laura. *Foreign Exposure,* 544(F)

Moses, Libby. *When Rover Just Won't Do,* 12600

Moses, Shelia P. *The Baptism,* 3460(F)
I, Dred Scott, 3173(F)
The Legend of Buddy Bush, 3461(F)

Mosher, Richard. *Zazoo,* 1804(F)

Moss, Marissa. *Vote 4 Amelia,* 552(F)

Moss, Nathaniel. *Ron Kovic,* 6442
W. E. B. Du Bois, 5985

Mouly, Francoise, ed. *Little Lit,* 4584(F)

Mountjoy, Shane. *Engel v. Vitale,* 10009

Mour, Stanley L. *American Jazz Musicians,* 5261

Mourlevat, Jean-Claude. *The Pull of the Ocean,* 1040(F)

Movsessian, Shushann. *Puberty Girl,* 11794

Mowat, Farley. *The Dog Who Wouldn't Be,* 280(F)
Lost in the Barrens, 151(F)
Owls in the Family, 12454

Mowll, Joshua. *Operation Red Jericho,* 152(F)
Operation Typhoon Shore, 153(F)

Mozeson, I. E. *The Place I Call Home,* 10623

Mudge, Jacqueline. *Kevin Nash,* 7028

Mueller, Mike. *Corvette,* 13133

Mufson, Susan. *Straight Talk About Child Abuse,* 11992
Straight Talk About Date Rape, 11818

Muggamin, Howard. *The Jewish Americans,* 10328

Mukerji, Dhan Gopal. *Gay-Neck,* 281(F)

Mulcahy, Robert. *Diseases,* 11341
Medical Technology, 6522

Mulford, Philippa Greene. *Making Room for Katherine,* 3872(F)

Mullin, Caryl Cude. *A Riddle of Roses,* 2331(F)

Mullin, Rita Thievon. *Thomas Jefferson,* 6129

Mullins, Tom, ed. *Running Lightly . . .,* 4764

Mulvihill, Margaret. *The Treasury of Saints and Martyrs,* 9803

Munan, Heidi. *Malaysia,* 8377

Mundis, Hester. *My Chimp Friday,* 4081(F)

Munduruku, Daniel. *Tales of the Amazon,* 4936

Munsen, Sylvia. *Cooking the Norwegian Way,* 13288

Munson, Lulie. *In Their Own Words,* 11819

Munson, Sammye. *Today's Tejano Heroes,* 5937

Murakami, Maki. *Kanpai!* 2657(F)

Murcia, Rebecca Thatcher. *Americo Paredes,* 5567
Dolores Huerta, 5999
E. B. White, 5641

Murdico, Suzanne J. *Bomb Squad Experts,* 10959
Coyote Attacks, 12412
Drug Abuse, 11155
Forensic Scientists, 10977
The Gulf War, 8102
Monica Seles, 6992

Murdoch, Patricia. *Exposure,* 1591(F)

Murdock, Catherine Gilbert. *Dairy Queen,* 553(F)
Diary Queen, 1592(F)
The Off Season, 1592(F)
Princess Ben, 2332

Murie, Olaus J. *A Field Guide to Animal Tracks,* 12354

Murillo, Kathy Cano. *The Crafty Diva's Lifestyle Makeover,* 13218

Murphy, Claire R. *Children of the Gold Rush,* 8730
Gold Rush Women, 5121

Murphy, Claire Rudolf. *Children of Alcatraz,* 9670
Daughters of the Desert, 9773
Free Radical, 1593(F)
Gold Rush Dogs, 12595

Murphy, Donald J., ed. *World War I,* 7919

Murphy, Jack. *Nuclear Medicine,* 11460

Murphy, Jim. *Across America on an Emigrant Train*, 13141
An American Plague, 9162
Desperate Journey, 3174(F)
Gone a-Whaling, 8713
The Great Fire, 9563
The Long Road to Gettysburg, 9276
Pick and Shovel Poet, 5471
The Real Benedict Arnold, 6251
A Young Patriot, 9163
Murphy, John. *Ali Khamenei*, 7120
Murphy, Nora. *A Hmong Family*, 10207
Murphy, Pat. *Exploratopia*, 12075
The Wild Girls, 554(F)
Murphy, Patricia J. *Everything You Need to Know About Staying in the Hospital*, 11459
Murphy, T. M. *The Secrets of Code Z*, 4082(F)
Murphy, Virginia R. *Across the Plains in the Donner Party*, 9338
Murphy, Wendy. *Asthma*, 11342
Nuclear Medicine, 11460
Orphan Diseases, 11343
Spare Parts, 11206
Murray, Aaron R. *Civil War Battles and Leaders*, 9277
Murray, Peter. *Kangaroos*, 12423
Rhinos, 12367
Murray, Stuart. *Vietnam War*, 9537
Murray, Susan. *Panic in Puerto Vallarta*, 4083(F)
Musgrave, Susan, ed. *Nerves Out Loud*, 11835
You Be Me, 11920
Musick, John A. *Oceans*, 12860
Muskat, Carrie. *The Composite Guide to Tennis*, 13789
Moises Alou, 6835
Sammy Sosa, 6873
Mussari, Mark. *Suzanne De Passe*, 6603
Musser, Susan, ed. *Can the War on Terrorism Be Won?* 10702
Mutel, Cornelia F. *Our Endangered Planet*, 12724
Mutén, Burleigh. *Grandfather Mountain*, 4816
Mutén, Burleigh, retel. *The Lady of Ten Thousand Names*, 4953
Muth, Jon. *Swamp Thing*, 2658(F)
Mwangi, Meja. *The Mzungu Boy*, 2822(F)
Myers, Anna. *Assassin*, 3229(F)
Hoggee, 3360(F)
Red-Dirt Jessie, 282(F)
Tulsa Burning, 3416(F)
Myers, Arthur. *Drugs and Emotions*, 11156
Drugs and Peer Pressure, 11157
Myers, Dennis. *Uniquely Nevada*, 9578
Myers, Edward. *Storyteller*, 2333(F)
Survival of the Fittest, 154(F)
When Will I Stop Hurting? 11050

Myers, Janet Nuzum. *Strange Stuff*, 13487
Myers, Steve. *Anorexia and Bulimia*, 11369
Divorce and Separation, 11999
Drinking Alcohol, 11174
Dyslexia, 11680
Myers, Walter Dean. *Angel to Angel*, 4765
At Her Majesty's Request, 7288
Autobiography of My Dead Brother, 732(F)
Blues Journey, 4691
The Dream Bearer, 733(F)
Fallen Angels, 3603(F)
Fast Sam, Cool Clyde, and Stuff, 734(F)
Game, 4486(F)
Harlem, 9629
The Harlem Hellfighters, 7920
Harlem Summer, 3417(F)
Hoops, 4487(F)
The Journal of Scott Pendleton Collins, 3540(F)
The Legend of Tarik, 2334(F)
Me, Mop, and the Moondance Kid, 4488(F)
145th Street, 735(F)
The Outside Shot, 4487(F)
Patrol, 3595(F)
Scorpions, 736(F)
Shooter, 1594(F)
Slam! 737(F)
Sunrise over Fallujah, 3603(F)
USS Constellation, 13183
Voices from Harlem, 4766
What They Found, 4567(F)
Won't Know Till I Get There, 1595(F)
The Young Landlords, 738(F)
Myracle, Lauren. *Eleven*, 555(F), 557(F)
The Fashion Disaster That Changed My Life, 556(F)
Rhymes with Witches, 3701(F)
Thirteen, 557(F)
ttyl, 1596(F)
Twelve, 557(F)

Na, An. *The Fold*, 739(F)
Wait for Me, 558(F)
Nabwire, Constance. *Cooking the West African Way*, 13287
Naden, Corinne J. *Barbara Jordan*, 6310
Chris Rock, 5833
Colin Powell, 6354
Dred Scott, 10010
Lenin, 7218
Monica Seles, 6991
People of Peace, 7053
Ronald McNair, 5185
Whoopi Goldberg, 5750
Naff, Alixa. *The Arab Americans*, 10350

Naff, Clay Farris. *Nicotine and Tobacco*, 11158
Naff, Clay Farris, ed. *Evolution*, 7597
Nagatomo, Haruno. *Draw Your Own Manga*, 13361
Nagle, Garrett. *South Africa*, 8213
Nagle, Jeanne. *Careers in Coaching*, 10921
Naidoo, Beverley. *No Turning Back*, 2823(F)
Out of Bounds, 4568(F)
Nakaya, Andrea C. *Energy Alternatives*, 12927
Marijuana, 11159
Nakaya, Andrea C., ed. *The Environment*, 10011
Nakaya, Andrea C., ed. *Cars in America*, 13134
Censorship, 10147
Civil Liberties, 10148
Civil Liberties and War, 10149
The Environment, 10443
Iraq, 8103
Juvenile Crime, 10551
Obesity, 11344
Nam, Vickie, ed. *Yell-Oh Girls!* 10291
Namioka, Lensey. *April and the Dragon Lady*, 740(F)
Yang the Third and Her Impossible Family, 741(F)
Nance, Andrew. *Daemon Hall*, 3702(F)
Nanji, Shenaaz. *Child of Dandelions*, 2824(F)
Napoli, Donna Jo. *Bound*, 4854(F)
Breath, 2974(F)
Fire in the Hills, 3541(F)
The Great God Pan, 2767(F)
Hush, 2796(F)
The King of Mulberry Street, 3361(F)
North, 155(F)
Sirena, 2768(F)
Stones in Water, 3541(F)
Nardo, Don. *The American Revolution*, 9164
Ancient Alexandria, 7763
Ancient Athens, 7788
Ancient Egypt, 7764
Ancient Greece, 7789
Artistry in Stone, 7343
Arts, Leisure, and Entertainment: Life of the Ancient Romans, 7826
Arts, Leisure, and Sport in Ancient Egypt, 7765
Atlantis, 13488
The Battle of Zama, 7822
Braving the New World, 1619–1784, 9113
Cleopatra, 7083
Cloning, 11497
Cyclops, 13489
Dinosaurs, 7578
Egyptian Mythology, 4954
Empires of Mesopotamia, 7766

Nicholson, Libby. *Creating with Fimo*, 13242

Nicholson, Lois. *Babe Ruth*, 6871
The Composite Guide to Lacrosse, 13554
Helen Keller, 6439
Michael Jackson, 5772
Oprah Winfrey, 5864

Nicholson, Lois P. *Dian Fossey*, 6640

Nicholson, Lorna Schultz. *Roughing*, 4489(F)
Too Many Men, 4490(F)

Nicholson, William. *Jango*, 2337(F)
Noman, 2336(F)
Seeker, 2337(F)

Nicieza, Fabian. *A Stake to the Heart*, 2660(F)

Nickerson, Sara. *How to Disappear Completely and Never Be Found*, 4085(F)

Nickles, Greg. *Germany*, 8475
Spanish Missions, 8919

Nicola, Christos. *The Secret of Priest's Grotto*, 8585

Nicolson, Cynthia Pratt. *Hurricane!* 12818

Nields, Nerissa. *Plastic Angel*, 561(F)

Nies, Judith. *Native American History*, 9033

Nigg, Joseph. *How to Raise and Keep a Dragon*, 2338(F)

Nigiortis, Theodore. *No More Dodos*, 12471

Nikola-Lisa, W. *How We Are Smart*, 11858

Nile, Richard. *Australian Aborigines*, 8413

Niles, Steve. *Gotham County Line*, 2661(F)

Nilsen, Alleen P. *Presenting M. E. Kerr*, 5531

Nilsen, Anna. *Art Auction Mystery*, 7366
The Great Art Scandal, 7367

Nilsson, Lennart. *Behold Man*, 11530

Nimmo, Jenny. *Charlie Bone and the Time Twister*, 2339(F)
Griffin's Castle, 2340(F)
Midnight for Charlie Bone, 2339(F)

Nimr, Sonia. *A Little Piece of Ground*, 1797(F)

Nirgiotis, Nicholas. *No More Dodos*, 12471

Nishi, Dennis. *The Inca Empire*, 8835

Nishi, Dennis, ed. *The Great Depression*, 9455

Nishiyama, Yuriko. *Harlem Beat*, 2662(F)

Nislick, June Levitt. *Zayda Was a Cowboy*, 743(F)

Nitz, Kristin Wolden. *Defending Irene*, 4491(F)
Softball, 13626

Nix, Garth. *Above the Veil*, 2341(F)

Across the Wall, 4569(F)
Drowned Wednesday, 2342(F)
Grim Tuesday, 2342(F)
Lady Friday, 2343(F)
Mister Monday, 2344(F)
One Beastly Beast, 2345(F)
Shade's Children, 4356(F)

Nix, Simon. *Motorbikes*, 13674

Nixon, Joan Lowery. *And Maggie Makes Three*, 1043(F)
A Candidate for Murder, 4086(F)
A Dangerous Promise, 3230(F)
The Dark and Deadly Pool, 4087(F)
The Ghosts of Now, 4088(F)
In the Face of Danger, 3299(F)
Land of Hope, 3362(F)
Maggie Forevermore, 1043(F)
Maggie, Too, 1043(F)
Murdered, My Sweet, 4089(F)
The Name of the Game Was Murder, 4090(F)
Nightmare, 4091(F)
The Other Side of Dark, 4092(F)
Shadowmaker, 4093(F)
The Weekend Was Murder! 4094(F)
Whispers from the Dead, 3705(F)

Njoku, Onwuka N. *Mbundu*, 8215

Nnoromele, Salome. *Somalia*, 8168

Nnoromele, Salome C. *Life Among the Ibo Women of Nigeria*, 8255

No, Yee-Jung. *Visitor*, 2663(F)

Nobleman, Marc Tyler.
Extraordinary E-Mails, Letters, and Resumes, 10820
The Sinking of the USS Indianapolis, 9476

Nodelman, Perry. *Out of Their Minds*, 2308(F)

Noel, Carol. *Get It? Got It? Good! A Guide for Teenagers*, 11921

Noël, Alyson. *Kiss and Blog*, 1606(F)
Saving Zoë, 562(F)

Noël, Michel. *Good for Nothing*, 3039(F)

Nofi, Albert A. *Spies in the Civil War*, 9278
The Underground Railroad and the Civil War, 9212

Nolan, Han. *A Summer of Kings*, 3463(F)
When We Were Saints, 563(F)

Nolan, Meghan, ed. *Let's Clear the Air*, 11162

Nolan, Paul T. *Folk Tale Plays Round the World*, 4606(F)

Nolan, Peggy. *The Spy Who Came in from the Sea*, 156(F)

Noll, Mark. *Protestants in America*, 9804

Noonan, Brandon. *Plenty Porter*, 3464(F)

Nordan, Robert. *The Secret Road*, 3135(F)

Nordin, Sofia. *In the Wild*, 157(F)

Norman, Rick. *Cross Body Block*, 4492(F)

Norman, Winifred Latimer. *Lewis Latimer*, 6692

Norris, Shana. *Something to Blog About*, 1607(F)

North, Sterling. *Rascal*, 12368

Northrup, Mary. *American Computer Pioneers*, 6523

Norton, Andre. *The Defiant Angels*, 4358(F)
House of Shadows, 3706(F)
Key Out of Time, 4357(F), 4358(F)
Time Traders II, 4358(F)

Norton, James R. *Haydn's World*, 5675

Nottingham, Ted. *Winning Chess*, 13691

November, Sharyn, ed. *Firebirds*, 4570(F)
Firebirds Rising, 4571(F)

Noyes, Alfred. *The Highwayman*, 4727

Noyes, Deborah. *Gothic!* 3707(F)
One Kingdom, 12311

Noyes, Deborah, ed. *The Restless Dead*, 3708(F)

Nuwer, Hank. *High School Hazing*, 11922

Nuzum, K. A. *A Small White Scar*, 1044(F)

Nuzzolo, Deborah. *Bottlenose Dolphin Training and Interaction*, 12550

Nwaezeigwe, Nwankwo T. *Ngoni*, 8169

Nwanunobi, C. O. *Malinke*, 8256
Soninke, 8257

Nye, Bill. *Bill Nye the Science Guy's Big Blast of Science*, 12077
Bill Nye the Science Guy's Great Big Book of Tiny Germs, 11347

Nye, Naomi S., ed. *The Space Between Our Footsteps*, 4799

Nye, Naomi Shihab. *Going Going*, 1807(F)
Honeybee, 4692

Nye, Robert. *Beowulf*, 4874

Nyoka, Gail. *Mella and the N'anga*, 2346(F)

Oates, Joyce Carol. *After the Wreck I Picked Myself Up, Spread My Wings, and Flew Away*, 1214(F)
Freaky Green Eyes, 1045(F)

Oatman, Eric. *Cowboys on the Western Trail*, 3300(F)

Oberman, Sheldon. *The Shaman's Nephew*, 8865
Solomon and the Ant, 4817

O'Brien, Eileen. *Starving to Win*, 11348

O'Brien, Joanne. *Festivals of the World*, 10670

Buddies, 3885(F)

The Graduation of Jake Moon, 1049(F)

Park, Linda Sue. *Archer's Quest*, 2359(F)

Keeping Score, 4493(F)

Project Mulberry, 750(F)

Seesaw Girl, 2855(F)

A Single Shard, 2856(F)

When My Name Was Keoko, 2857(F)

Park, Sang-Sun. *Ark Angels*, 2666(F)

Parker, Barry. *The Mystery of Gravity*, 12906

Parker, Cam. *A Horse in New York*, 288(F)

Parker, David L. *Stolen Dreams*, 10402

Parker, Edward. *Birds*, 12435

People, 12725

People of the Rain Forests, 12719

Peru, 8836

Rain Forest Mammals, 12726

Rain Forest Reptiles and Amphibians, 12726

Parker, Janice, ed. *The Disappearing Forests*, 10445

Parker, Julie. *Everything You Need to Know About Living in a Shelter*, 10619

High Performance Through Leadership, 11924

Parker, Marjorie Hodgson. *David and the Mighty Eighth*, 3546(F)

Parker, Robert B. *Edenville Owls*, 4494(F)

Parker, Steve. *Allergies*, 11531

The Brain and Nervous System, 11555

Brain, Nerves, and Senses, 11556

Digestion, 11574

Digestion and Reproduction, 11532

Heart, Blood, and Lungs, 11532

Heart, Lungs, and Blood, 11565

Human Body, 11533

The Human Body Book, 11534

The Lungs and Respiratory System, 11593

Reproduction, 11753

The Reproductive System, 11754

The Science of Sound, 12963

The Senses, 11598

The Skeleton and Muscles, 11584

Skin, Muscles, and Bones, 11585

Survival and Change, 12223

What's Inside Airplanes? 13126

Parker, Vic. *C. S. Lewis*, 5537

Pompeii AD 79, 8534

Parker-Rock, Michelle. *R. L. Stine*, 5610

Parkinson, Curtis. *Death in Kingsport*, 4097(F)

Domenic's War, 3547(F)

Storm-Blast, 162(F)

Parkinson, Siobhan. *Blue like Friday*, 1050(F)

Second Fiddle, 1610

Something Invisible, 570(F)

Parks, Deborah. *Nature's Machines*, 6690

Parks, Peggy. *Global Warming*, 10446

Music, 10924

Parks, Peggy J. *The Aswan High Dam*, 8643

Ecotourism, 10447

Global Warming, 10448

Musician, 10925

The News Media, 10872

Writer, 10926

Parks, Rosa. *Dear Mrs. Parks*, 10153

Rosa Parks, 6027

Parnell, Helga. *Cooking the German Way*, 13291

Cooking the South American Way, 13292

Parr, Danny. *Lowriders*, 13602

Parramon, Merce. *How Our Blood Circulates*, 11566

Parrilli, Mary Em. *The Cheyenne*, 9021

Parris, Ronald. *Hausa*, 8259

Rendille, 8173

Parry, Ann. *Greenpeace*, 10449

Parsons, Harry. *The Nature of Frogs*, 12328

Parsons, Tom. *Pierre Auguste Renoir*, 5383

Partner, Daniel. *Disorders First Diagnosed in Childhood*, 11668

The House of Representatives, 9939

Parton, Sarah. *Cleisthenes*, 7173

Partridge, Elizabeth. *Restless Spirit*, 5344

This Land Was Made for You and Me, 5671

Pasachoff, Naomi. *Alexander Graham Bell*, 6554

Ernest Rutherford, 6742

Linus Pauling, 6734

Niels Bohr, 6564

Pascal, Francine. *Fearless FBI*, 4098(F)

The Ruling Class, 1611(F)

Pascal, Janet B. *Arthur Conan Doyle*, 5486

Jacob Riis, 5583

Pascoe, Elaine. *Ant Lions and Lacewings*, 12489

Ants, 12490

Crickets and Grasshoppers, 12491

Flies, 12492

Freshwater Fish, 12528

History Around You, 9631

Leaves and Trees, 12278

Mantids and Their Relatives, 12489

Mexico and the United States, 8775

The Pacific Rim, 8276

Scholastic Kid's Almanac for the 21st Century, 7534

Slime, Molds, and Fungus, 12237

Snails and Slugs, 12313

Pascoe, Elaine, adapt. *Animal Intelligence*, 12551

Mysteries of the Rain Forest, 6736

Pascoe, Elaine, ed. *Crash*, 11463

Out of Control, 11535

The Pentagon, 7330

Spreading Menace, 11609

Teen Dreams, 11796

Pastan, Amy. *Martin Luther King, Jr.*, 6016

Presidents and First Ladies, 5876

Pasternak, Ceel. *Cool Careers for Girls in Air and Space*, 10874

Cool Careers for Girls in Computers, 11000

Cool Careers for Girls in Construction, 10943

Cool Careers for Girls in Engineering, 10978

Cool Careers for Girls in Food, 10875

Cool Careers for Girls in Health, 10972

Cool Careers for Girls in Law, 10961

Cool Careers for Girls in Sports, 10927

Cool Careers for Girls with Animals, 10873

Patchett, Kaye. *The Akashi Kaikyo Bridge*, 8340

Pateman, Robert. *Belgium*, 8538

Bolivia, 8837

Egypt, 8644

Kenya, 8174

Patent, Dorothy Hinshaw. *Animals on the Trail with Lewis and Clark*, 9067

The Bald Eagle Returns, 12452

The Buffalo and the Indians, 3074

Charles Darwin, 6598

In Search of Maiasaurs, 7579

The Incredible Story of China's Buried Warriors, 8297

Life in a Desert, 12705

Life in a Grassland, 12755

Lost City of Pompeii, 7830

Mystery of the Lascaux Cave, 7598

Plants on the Trail with Lewis and Clark., 12238

Secrets of the Ice Man, 7599

Shaping the Earth, 12179

Treasures of the Spanish Main, 8715

Paterra, Elizabeth. *Gary Paulsen*, 5572

Paterson, Katherine. *Bread and Roses, Too*, 3363(F)

Bridge to Terabithia, 571(F)

Come Sing, Jimmy Jo, 1051(F)

Jacob Have I Loved, 1052(F)

Jip, 3175(F)

The Master Puppeteer, 2858(F)

Of Nightingales That Weep, 2859(F)

Park's Quest, 1053(F)

Preacher's Boy, 3364(F)

Rebels of the Heavenly Kingdom, 2860(F)

Rampersad, Arnold, ed. *Poetry for Young People: Langston Hughes*, 4770

Ramsey, Dan. *Weather Forecasting*, 12842

Randall, Bernard. *Solon*, 7245

Randall, David. *Chandlefort*, 2393
Clovermead, 2393

Randall, Marta. *John F. Kennedy*, 6148

Randle, Kristen D. *Slumming*, 583(F)

Randolph, Ryan P. *Betsy Ross*, 6458
Paul Revere and the Minutemen of the American Revolution, 6455

Randolph, Sallie. *Richard M. Nixon, President*, 6177
Shaker Inventions, 9791
Shaker Villages, 9792
Woodrow Wilson, President, 6236

Random House, ed. *Muhammad Ali*, 6932

Rangaswamy, Padma. *Indian Americans*, 10211

Ransford, Sandy. *The Kingfisher Illustrated Horse and Pony Encyclopedia*, 12612

Ransome, Arthur. *Coot Club*, 178(F)
Peter Duck, 177(F)
Swallowdale, 177(F)
Swallows and Amazons, 177(F)
Winter Holiday, 178(F)

Rao, Sirish. *Sophocles' Oedipus the King*, 2769(F)

Raphael, Marie. *A Boy from Ireland*, 3367(F)
Streets of Gold, 3368(F)

Rapp, Valerie. *Life in a River*, 12746
Life in an Old Growth Forest, 12727

Rappaport, Doreen. *Free at Last! Stories and Songs of Emancipation*, 10274
In the Promised Land, 5941
No More! Stories and Songs of Slave Resistance, 10275
Nobody Gonna Turn Me 'Round, 10156

Rapparlie, Leslie. *Ice Climbing*, 13592
Kayaking, 13744
Mountain Biking, 13677
Rock Climbing, 13688

Rappoport, Ken. *Bobby Bonilla*, 6839
Eric Lindros, 6980
Grant Hill, 6894
Guts and Glory, 6804
Ladies First, 6805
Profiles in Sports Courage, 6806
Sheryl Swoopes, 6928
Tim Duncan, 6887
Wayne Gretzky, 6973

Rashkin, Rachel. *Feeling Better*, 11673

Raskin, Ellen. *The Westing Game*, 4109(F)

Raskin, Lawrie. *52 Days by Camel*, 8192

Rasmussen, R. Kent. *Farewell to Jim Crow*, 10157
Mark Twain for Kids, 5630

Rathjen, Don. *The Spinning Blackboard and Other Dynamic Experiments on Force and Motion*, 12916

Ratliff, Gerald L., ed. *Millennium Monologs*, 4607
Playing Contemporary Scenes, 4608

Rattenbury, Jeanne. *Understanding Alternative Medicine*, 11464

Rau, Christopher. *George Lucas*, 5791

Rau, Dana Meachen. *George Lucas*, 5791

Rau, Margaret. *The Mail Must Go Through*, 9343

Rauf, Don. *Computer Game Designer*, 10877

Rauth, Leslie. *Maryland*, 9711

Raven, Nicky. *Beowulf*, 4881

Rawcliffe, Michael. *Lenin*, 7219

Rawlings, Marjorie Kinnan. *The Yearling*, 292(F)

Rawlins, Carol B. *The Colorado River*, 8930
The Orinoco River, 8840

Ray, Delia. *Ghost Girl*, 3423(F)
Singing Hands, 3466(F)

Ray, Karen. *To Cross a Line*, 3553(F)

Ray, Kurt. *Typhoid Fever*, 11358

Rayban, Chloe. *Hollywood Bliss*, 584(F)
Hollywood Bliss: My Life Starring Mum, 584(F)

Rayburn, Tricia. *Maggie Bean Stays Afloat*, 1635(F)
The Melting of Maggie Bean, 585(F), 1635(F)

Raymond, Alex. *Alex Raymond's Flash Gordon*, 2674(F)

Read, Andrew. *Porpoises*, 12553

Read, Marie. *Secret Lives of Common Birds*, 12444

Read Magazine, ed. *Read into the Millennium*, 4370(F)

Reader, John. *Africa*, 8129

Reader's Digest, ed. *Sharks*, 12538

Reaver, Chap. *A Little Bit Dead*, 4110(F)

Reaves, Michael. *InterWorld*, 4303(F)

Reber, Deborah. *In Their Shoes*, 10839

Rebman, Renee C. *Addictions and Risky Behaviors*, 11031
Euthanasia and the "Right to Die," 11052
Life on Ellis Island, 9634
Runaway Teens, 11994
The Sistine Chapel, 7395

Redfern, Martin. *The Kingfisher Young People's Book of Planet Earth*, 12681

Redmond, Jim. *Uniquely North Dakota*, 9566

Reed, Don C. *The Kraken*, 1636(F)

Reed, Gary. *Mary Shelley's Frankenstein*, 2675(F)

Reed, George. *Eyes on the Universe*, 12207

Reed, Gregory J. *Dear Mrs. Parks*, 10153

Reed, Jennifer. *Earthquakes*, 12692
Elizabeth Bloomer, 7287
Leonardo da Vinci, 5320
Paula Danziger, 5474

Reed, Jennifer Bond. *Love Canal*, 10479
The Saudi Royal Family, 8698

Reeder, Carolyn. *Before the Creeks Ran Red*, 3234(F)
Captain Kate, 3235(F)

Reef, Catherine. *Africans in America*, 10276
Alone in the World, 10492
E. E. Cummings, 5465
George Gershwin, 5670
John Steinbeck, 5606
Paul Laurence Dunbar, 5488
Sigmund Freud, 6645
This Our Dark Country, 8261
Walt Whitman, 5645
William Grant Still, 5682

Rees, Celia. *Pirates!* 179(F)
Sorceress, 3075(F)
The Soul Taker, 3720(F)
Witch Child, 3075(F)

Rees, Douglas. *Vampire High*, 3721(F)

Rees, Elizabeth M. *The Wedding*, 2982(F)

Reesor, David. *Predator*, 12370

Reeve, Philip. *A Darkling Plain*, 2394(F)
Here Lies Arthur, 2799(F)
Infernal Devices, 4371(F)
Larklight, 4373(F)
Larklight, or, The Revenge of the White Spiders!, or, To Saturn's Rings and Back! 4372(F)
Mortal Engines, 4371(F)
Starcross, 4373(F)

Reeves, Diane L. *Career Ideas for Kids Who Like Art*, 10878
Career Ideas for Kids Who Like Sports, 10929
Career Ideas for Kids Who Like Writing, 10879

Reeves, Diane Lindsey. *Career Ideas for Kids Who Like Adventure*, 10884
Career Ideas for Kids Who Like Animals and Nature, 10885
Career Ideas for Kids Who Like Computers, 11001
Career Ideas for Kids Who Like Math, 10880
Career Ideas for Kids Who Like Money, 10882

Runholt, Susan. *The Mystery of the Third Lucretia*, 4121(F)

Runyon, Brent. *The Burn Journals*, 7312

Rupp, Rebecca. *Journey to the Blue Moon*, 3726(F)
Weather! 12843

Ruschmann, Paul. *The War on Terror*, 10719

Rushton, Rosie. *The Dashwood Sisters' Secrets of Love*, 2987(F)
Friends, Enemies, 594(F)

Russell, Barbara T. *The Taker's Stone*, 2411(F)

Russell, Bruce J. *Guide to Microlife*, 12563

Russell, Ching Yeung. *Child Bride*, 2864(F)
Lichee Tree, 2865(F)

Russell, Christopher. *Hunted*, 2801(F)

Russell, Colin A. *Michael Faraday*, 6631

Russell, Francine. *The Safe Zone*, 11763

Russell, Henry. *Germany*, 8477

Russell, P. Craig. *The Birthday of the Infanta*, 2681(F)
The Fairy Tales of Oscar Wilde, 2682(F)

Russo, Marisabina. *A Portrait of Pia*, 1070(F)

Rutberg, Becky. *Mary Lincoln's Dressmaker*, 6441

Ruth, Amy. *American Revolutionaries and Founders of the Nation*, 5931
Growing Up in the Great Depression, 9458
Herbert Hoover, 6120
Jane Austen, 5430
Louisa May Alcott, 5415
Queen Latifah, 5780

Ruth, Maria Mudd. *The Deserts of the Southwest*, 12706
The Mississippi River, 8931
The Pacific Coast, 9676

Rutledge, Jill Zimmerman. *Dealing with the Stuff That Makes Life Tough*, 11930

Rutledge, Rachel. *The Best of the Best in Basketball*, 13651
The Best of the Best in Figure Skating, 6808
The Best of the Best in Gymnastics, 6809
The Best of the Best in Soccer, 6810
The Best of the Best in Tennis, 13790
The Best of the Best in Track and Field, 6811
Marion Jones, 6998

Rutsala, David. *The Sea Route to Asia*, 7680

Ryan, Bernard. *Caring for Animals*, 10663

Condoleezza Rice, 6363
Expanding Education and Literacy, 10664
Helping the Ill, Poor and the Elderly, 10665
Promoting the Arts and Sciences, 10666
Protecting the Environment, 10457
Serving with Police, Fire, and EMS, 9948

Ryan, Bernard, Jr. *Participating in Government*, 10667
Promoting the Arts and Sciences: Opportunities to Volunteer, 10667

Ryan, Darlene. *Rules for Life*, 1071(F)
Saving Grace, 595(F)

Ryan, Elizabeth A. *Straight Talk About Parents*, 11998

Ryan, Mary C. *Frankie's Run*, 4239(F)
The Voice from the Mendelsohns' Maple, 1647(F)
Who Says I Can't? 3901(F)

Ryan, P. E. *Saints of Augustine*, 1648(F)

Ryan, Pam M. *Esperanza Rising*, 3425(F)

Ryan, Pam Muñoz. *Paint the Wind*, 1072(F)

Ryan, Pat. *Rock Climbing*, 13568

Rybolt, Leah M. *Science Fair Success with Scents, Aromas, and Smells*, 12081

Rybolt, Thomas R. *Adventures with Atoms and Molecules, Vol. 5*, 12651
Science Fair Success with Scents, Aromas, and Smells, 12081

Rydell, Robert W. *Fair America*, 8932

Rylant, Cynthia. *Boris*, 4772
God Went to Beauty School, 596(F)
The Heavenly Village, 2412(F)
Missing May, 1649(F)
Soda Jerk, 4773
Something Permanent, 4774

Saab, Carl Y. *The Spinal Cord*, 11559

Sabbeth, Alex. *Rubber-Band Banjos and a Java Jive Bass*, 7467

Sabbeth, Carol. *Monet and the Impressionists for Kids*, 7397

Sachar, Louis. *Holes*, 1650(F)
Sideways Arithmetic from Wayside School, 3902(F)
Small Steps, 1650(F)

Sachs, Marilyn. *Almost Fifteen*, 1651(F)
Baby Sister, 1073(F)
The Bears' House, 597(F)
Class Pictures, 1652(F)
Fourteen, 1653(F)
Just Like a Friend, 1074(F)

Sadler, Judy Ann. *Beading*, 13329
Beanbag Buddies and Other Stuffed Toys, 13336
Corking, 13421
Embroidery, 13422
Hemp Jewelry, 13330
The Jumbo Book of Needlecrafts, 13423
Making Fleece Crafts, 13424
Quick Knits, 13425
Simply Sewing, 13426

Saenagi, Ryo. *Psychic Power Nanaki*, 2683(F)

Saenz, Benjamin Alire. *He Forgot to Say Goodbye*, 1654

Saffer, Barbara. *The California Gold Rush*, 9348
Henry Hudson, 5175

Sage, Angie. *Book One*, 3727(F)
Flyte, 2413(F)
Magyk, 2413(F)
Physik, 2414(F)
Queste, 2415(F)
Septimus Heap, 3727(F)

Sahara, Mizu. *The Voices of a Distant Star*, 2684(F)

Saiko, Tatyana. *Russia*, 8577

St. Anthony, Jane. *Grace above All*, 1075(F)

St. Antoine, Sara, ed. *Stories from Where We Live*, 7681, 9712

St. George, Judith. *In the Line of Fire*, 8933
John and Abigail Adams, 6076

St. Jacques, Philip M. *Addition and Subtraction*, 12773
Fractions and Decimals, 12773

St. John, Lauren. *The White Giraffe*, 2416(F)

St. Pierre, Stephanie. *Teenage Refugees from Cambodia Speak Out*, 10296

Sakai, Stan. *Usagi Yojimbo*, 2685(F), 2686(F)

Sakura, Tsukuba. *Land of the Blindfolded*, 2687(F)

Salak, John. *Drugs in Society*, 11172
Violent Crime, 10573

Saldana, Rene. *The Whole Sky Full of Stars*, 1655(F)

Salinger, J. D. *The Catcher in the Rye*, 1656(F)

Salisbury, Cynthia. *Elizabeth Cady Stanton*, 6038
Phillis Wheatley, 5639

Salisbury, Graham. *Blue Skin of the Sea*, 4577(F)
House of the Red Fish, 3557(F)
Night of the Howling Dogs, 186(F)
Under the Blood-Red Sun, 3557(F)

Salisbury, Mark. *Planet of the Apes*, 7508

Salkeld, Audrey. *Mystery on Everest*, 5191

Sallah, Tijan M. *Wolof*, 8262

Saller, Martin. *Elephants*, 12415

Sallnow, John. *Russia*, 8577

Webb, Margot. *Drugs and Gangs*, 11194

Webb, Sophie. *My Season with Penguins*, 12459

Webber, Desiree Morrison. *Bone Head*, 12268
The Buffalo Train Ride, 12373

Webber, Diane. *Do You Read Me?* 10585

Weber, EdNah New Rider. *Rattlesnake Mesa*, 6471

Weber, Michael. *The American Revolution*, 9171
Causes and Consequences of the African-American Civil Rights Movements, 10174
Civil War and Reconstruction, 9292
Yorktown, 9172
The Young Republic, 9173

Weber, Sandra. *The Internet*, 13071

Webster, Christine. *Great Wall of China*, 7348

Webster, David. *Experiments with Balloons*, 12803
Science Project Ideas About Animal Behavior, 12347
Science Project Ideas About Trees, 12274

Webster, Harriet. *Cool Careers Without College for People Who Love to Work with Children*, 10894

Webster, M. L., retel. *On the Trail Made of Dawn*, 4915

Webster-Doyle, Terrence. *Breaking the Chains of the Ancient Warrior*, 4519(F)

Wedekind, Annie. *A Horse of Her Own*, 640(F)

Weeks, Marcus. *Mozart*, 5681

Weeks, Sarah. *My Guy*, 1118(F)

Weeldreyer, Laura. *Body Blues*, 11422

Weidensaul, Scott, ed. *National Audubon Society First Field Guide*, 12439

Weidhorn, Manfred. *Jackie Robinson*, 6868

Weidner, Daniel. *The Constitution*, 9908
Creating the Constitution, 9909

Weigant, Chris. *Careers as a Disc Jockey*, 10934

Weil, Ann. *Michael Dorris*, 5484

Wein, Elizabeth E. *A Coalition of Lions*, 2810(F)
The Lion Hunter, 2827(F)
The Sunbird, 2827(F), 2828(F)
The Winter Prince, 2810(F)

Wein, Len. *Secret of the Swamp Thing*, 2728

Weinberg, Karen. *Window of Time*, 2510(F)

Weinheimer, Beckie. *Converting Kate*, 1738(F)

Weinstein, Lauren. *Girl Stories*, 7321

Weintraub, Aileen. *Auto Mechanic*, 10944
Discovering Africa's Land, People, and Wildlife, 8133
Everything You Need to Know About Being a Baby-Sitter, 11011

Weir, Joan. *The Brideship*, 3051(F)
The Mysterious Visitor, 4172(F)

Weisberg, Barbara. *Susan B. Anthony*, 5965

Weisbrot, Robert. *Marching Toward Freedom*, 10283

Weisman, Joanne B. *Dwight D. Eisenhower*, 6106

Weiss, Ann E. *Adoptions Today*, 12010
The Glass Ceiling, 10895
Virtual Reality, 13072

Weiss, Helen S., ed. *Big City Cool*, 4587(F)
Dreams and Visions, 2511(F)

Weiss, Jonathan H. *Breathe Easy*, 11423

Weiss, M. Jerry, ed. *Big City Cool*, 4587(F)
Dreams and Visions, 2511(F)

Weiss, Mitch. *How and Why Stories*, 4810
Stories in My Pocket, 10811

Weiss, Stefanie Iris. *Coping with the Beauty Myth*, 11520
Everything You Need to Know About Being a Vegan, 11722
Everything You Need to Know About Mehndi, Temporary Tattoos, and Other Temporary Body Art, 11521
Everything You Need to Know About Yoga, 13589

Weissenberg, Fran. *The Streets Are Paved with Gold*, 1119(F)

Weissman, Paul. *The Great Voyager Adventure*, 12144

Weitzman, David. *A Subway for New York*, 13143
Superpower, 13144

Weitzman, Elizabeth. *Let's Talk About Smoking*, 11195

Wekesser, Carol. *Africa*, 8134

Wekesser, Carol, ed. *Chemical Dependency*, 11196
Pornography, 10640
Smoking, 11197

Welch, Catherine A. *Ida B. Wells-Barnett*, 6062
Margaret Bourke-White, 5292

Welch, R. C. *Scary Stories for Stormy Nights*, 3769(F)

Well, Ann. *Raul Julia*, 5776

Wells, Catherine. *Hillary Clinton*, 6266
John McCain, 6330

Wells, Don. *The Spice Trade*, 7688

Wells, Donald. *The Silk Road*, 7726

Wells, Donna. *America Comes of Age*, 9417

Wells, Donna K. *Live Aware, Not in Fear*, 11769

Wells, H. G. *First Men in the Moon*, 4404(F)
The Food of the Gods, 4404(F)
In the Days of the Comet, 4404(F)
The Invisible Man, 2729, 4405(F)
The Island of Doctor Moreau, 4404(F)
The Time Machine, 2730
Time Machine, 4406(F)
The War of the Worlds, 4407(F)

Wells, Rosemary. *Red Moon at Sharpsburg*, 3245(F)

Welsbacher, Anne. *Life in a Rainforest*, 12731

Welsh, T. K. *The Unresolved*, 3381(F)

Weltman, June. *Mystery of the Missing Candlestick*, 4173(F)

Welton, Jude. *Henri Matisse*, 5353

Welvaert, Scott R. *The Curse of the Wendigo*, 3770(F)

Wemmlinger, Raymond. *Booth's Daughter*, 3382(F)

Wenger, Jennifer. *Teen Knitting Club*, 13431

Wenzel, Angela. *Do You See What I See?* 13384
Rene Magritte, 7418

Wepman, Dennis. *Helen Keller*, 6440
Tamerlane, 7132

Werker, Kim. *Crochet Me*, 13432
Get Hooked Again, 13433

Werlin, Nancy. *Black Mirror*, 4174(F)
The Rules of Survival, 1120

Werner, Doug. *In-Line Skater's Start-Up*, 13720
Skateboarder's Start-Up, 13752
Skateboarding, 13746
Surfer's Start-Up, 13784

Wersba, Barbara. *Fat*, 1244(F)
Walter, 2512(F)
You'll Never Guess the End, 3926(F)

Werther, Scott P. *The Donner Party*, 9374

Wesson, Carolyn McLenahan. *Teen Troubles*, 11938

West, Alan. *José Martí*, 5549

West, David. *Detective Work with Ballistics*, 10586
Mesoamerican Myths, 2731

West, Krista. *Bromine*, 12669

Westall, Robert. *Ghost Abbey*, 3771(F)
Shades of Darkness, 3772(F)

Westcott, Patsy. *Why Do People Take Drugs?* 11198

Westen, Robin. *Oprah Winfrey*, 5866
Richard Wright, 5656

Westerfeld, Scott. *Blue Noon*, 3773
Extras, 4408(F)
Pretties, 4409(F), 4410(F)
The Secret Hour, 3774(F)
So Yesterday, 4175(F)

Whittenberg, Allison. *Life Is Fine*, 1741(F)

Whittington, Christine. *Body Marks*, 11512

Whyman, Kate. *The Animal Kingdom*, 12314

Whyman, Matt. *Icecore*, 4178(F)

Whynott, Douglas. *A Country Practice*, 10896

Whyte, Mariam. *Bangladesh*, 8330

Whytock, Cherry. *My Cup Runneth Over*, 3928(F)

My Scrumptious Scottish Dumplings, 3928(F)

Wibberley, Leonard. *The Mouse That Roared*, 3929(F)

Wieler, Diana. *RanVan*, 1742(F)

Wiener, Roberta. *Connecticut*, 9122

Delaware, 9122

Divided in Two, 9230

Life Goes On, 9231

Lost Cause, 9232

Maryland, 9122

On to Richmond, 9233

River to Victory, 9234

This Unhappy Country, 9235

Wiese, Jim. *Detective Science*, 10587

Head to Toe Science, 11543

Wiesner-Hanks, Merry E. *An Age of Voyages, 1350–1600*, 7689

Wignall, Paul. *Macbeth*, 5040

Wilber, Jessica. *Totally Private and Personal*, 10830

Wilbur, Frances. *The Dog with Golden Eyes*, 301(F)

Wilbur, Keith C. *Revolutionary Medicine, 1700–1800*, 8948

The Revolutionary Soldier, 1775–1783, 9175

Wilbur, Richard. *Opposites*, 5071

Wilburn, Deborah A. *Eddie Murphy*, 5809

Wilce, Ysabeau S. *Flora Segunda*, 2517(F)

Wilcox, Charlotte. *Mummies and Their Mysteries*, 7636

Mummies, Bones, and Body Parts, 7637

Powerhouse, 12946

Wilcox, Frank H. *DNA*, 11504

Wilcox, Jonathan. *Iceland*, 8610

Wild, Margaret. *Woolvs in the Sitee*, 3779(F)

Wilde, Oscar. *The Picture of Dorian Gray*, 330(F)

Wilder, Laura Ingalls. *By the Shores of Silver Lake*, 1125(F)

Farmer Boy, 1125(F)

The First Four Years, 1125(F)

Little House in the Big Woods, 1125(F)

Little House on the Prairie, 1125(F)

A Little House Traveler, 5648

Long Winter, 1125(F)

The Long Winter, 3315(F)

On the Banks of Plum Creek, 1125(F)

These Happy Golden Years, 1125(F)

West from Home, 9418

Wilds, Mary. *MumBet*, 5988

Raggin' the Blues, 5278

Wiley, Melissa. *On Tide Mill Lane*, 3194(F)

Wilhelm, Doug. *Falling*, 1743(F)

Wilker, Josh. *Classic Cons and Swindles*, 10588

The Harlem Globetrotters, 13658

Wilkerson, J. L. *From Slave to World-Class Horseman*, 7016

Sad-Face Clown, 5777

Story of Pride, Power and Uplift, 6702

Wilkes, Debbi. *The Figure Skating Book*, 13719

Wilkes, Sarah. *Amphibians*, 12321

Fish, 12531

Insects, 12497

Wilkinson, Beth. *Drugs and Depression*, 11199

Wilkinson, Brenda. *African American Women Writers*, 5279

Wilkinson, Philip. *Art and Technology Through the Ages*, 12993

Buddhism, 9787

A Celebration of Customs and Rituals of the World, 10682

The Early Inventions, 7606

Gandhi, 7110

The Industrial Revolution, 7902

The Kingfisher Student Atlas, 7545

The Magical East, 8278

The Mediterranean, 7727

Ships, 13156

Transportation, 13105

Wilks, Corinne Morgan, ed. *Dear Diary, I'm Pregnant*, 11760

Will, Emily Wade. *Haiti*, 8800

Willard, Keith. *Ballooning*, 13590

Willard, Nancy, ed. *Step Lightly*, 4714

Willett, Edward. *Alzheimer's Disease*, 11425

The Basics of Quantum Physics, 12912

Careers in Outer Space, 10897

Hemophilia, 11426

J. R. R. Tolkien, 5623

Jimi Hendrix, 5761

Orson Scott Card, 5446

Williams, Anthony. *The Battle of Iwo Jima*, 7987

Williams, Barbara. *World War II*, 8076

Williams, Brenda. *The Age of Discovery*, 7691

Williams, Brian. *The Age of Discovery*, 7691

Ancient America, 9054

Ancient Roman Women, 7836

Computers, 13073

The Modern World, 7690

The Story Behind John Steinbeck's Of Mice and Men, 5033

Tunnels, 2080(F)

Williams, Colleen Madonna Flood. *Yasir Arafat*, 7096

Williams, Dar. *Lights, Camera, Amalee*, 1817(F)

Williams, Earl P. *What You Should Know About the American Flag*, 5053

Williams, Harriet. *Road and Rail Transportation*, 13106

Williams, Heidi. *Homeschooling*, 10782

Williams, J. H. *Snow*, 2625(F)

Williams, Jeanne. *The Confederate Fiddle*, 3246(F)

Williams, Judith. *The Discovery and Mystery of a Dinosaur Named Jane*, 7585

Williams, Julie. *Attention-Deficit / Hyperactivity Disorder*, 11693

Pyromania, Kleptomania, and Other Impulse-Control Disorders, 11694

Williams, Kara. *Fertility Technology*, 11761

Frequently Asked Questions about MyPyramid, 11723

Williams, Laura E. *Behind the Bedroom Wall*, 3578(F)

The Spider's Web, 3008(F)

Williams, Lori Aurelia. *Shayla's Double Brown Baby Blues*, 1744(F)

When Kambia Elaine Flew in from Neptune, 1744(F), 1745(F)

Williams, Maiya. *The Golden Hour*, 2518(F), 2519(F)

The Hour of the Cobra, 2519(F)

The Hour of the Outlaw, 2520(F)

Williams, Marcia. *Chaucer's Canterbury Tales*, 2811(F)

Williams, Mark London. *Trail of Bones*, 2521(F)

Williams, Mary, ed. *Interracial America*, 10236

Williams, Mary E. *Global Warming*, 10831

Williams, Mary E., ed. *Adoption*, 12011

Civil Rights, 10175

Education, 10783

The Family, 12012

Is It Unpatriotic to Criticize One's Country? 10365

Terminal Illness, 11427

The White Separatist Movement, 10416

Williams, Michael. *The Genuine Half-Moon Kid*, 225(F)

Williams, Neva. *Patrick DesJarlait*, 5322

Williams, Rob. *Star Wars Rebellion*, 2732(F)

Coping with Confrontations and Encounters with the Police, 11943

Everything You Need to Know About Learning Disabilities, 11625

Wiseman, Eva. *Kanada,* 3581(F)

My Canary Yellow Star, 3582(F)

No One Must Know, 779(F)

Wishinsky, Frieda. *It's Your Room,* 13233

Queen of the Toilet Bowl, 780(F)

Wisler, G. Clifton. *All for Texas,* 3316(F)

Red Cap, 3247(F)

This New Land, 3117(F)

Wismer, Donald. *Starluck,* 4413(F)

Withers, Pam. *Camp Wild,* 227(F)

Skater Stuntboys, 4520(F)

Withington, William A. *Southeast Asia,* 8394

Withrow, Sarah. *What Gloria Wants,* 1749(F)

Wittlinger, Ellen. *Blind Faith,* 644(F)

Gracie's Girl, 645(F)

Hard Love, 1750(F)

Lombardo's Law, 4250(F)

Razzle, 646(F)

Sandpiper, 1751(F)

Zigzag, 1752(F)

Wittmann, Kelly. *The European Rediscovery of America,* 9076

Woelfle, Gretchen. *Jeannette Rankin,* 6361

The Wind at Work, 12935

Woff, Richard. *A Pocket Dictionary of Greek and Roman Gods and Goddesses,* 4991

Wojciechowska, Maia. *Shadow of a Bull,* 1753(F)

Wojtanik, Andrew. *Afghanistan to Zimbabwe,* 7692

Wolf, Allan. *Immersed in Verse,* 5088

New Found Land, 3317(F)

Wolf, Gita. *Sophocles' Oedipus the King,* 2769(F)

Wolf, Joan M. *Someone Named Eva,* 3583(F)

Wolf, Robert V. *Capital Punishment,* 10035

Wolfe, Art. *Africa,* 8135

Wolfe, Lois. *Students on Strike,* 10169

Wolfelt, Alan D. *Healing a Teen's Grieving Heart,* 11057

Healing Your Grieving Heart for Teens, 11944

Wolfert, Adrienne. *Making Tracks,* 3431(F)

Wolff, Lisa. *Teen Depression,* 11697

Wolff, Virginia E. *Bat 6,* 4521(F)

Make Lemonade, 1128(F)

Probably Still Nick Swansen, 1248(F)

Wolff, Virginia Euwer. *Make Lemonade,* 647(F)

True Believer, 647(F)

Wolfman, Ira. *Climbing Your Family Tree,* 12013

Wolfman, Marv. *The New Teen Titans Archives,* 2735(F)

Wolfson, Evelyn. *Growing Up Indian,* 9053

Inuit Mythology, 4916

King Arthur and His Knights in Mythology, 4890

Roman Mythology, 4992

Wolfson, Jill. *Home, and Other Big, Fat Lies,* 1754(F)

What I Call Life, 1755(F)

Wolin, Sybil, ed. *The Struggle to Be Strong,* 10372

Wolinsky, Art. *Communicating on the Internet,* 13075

Creating and Publishing Web Pages on the Internet, 13076

The History of the Internet and the World Wide Web, 13077

Internet Power Research Using the Big6 Approach, 13078

Locating and Evaluating Information on the Internet, 13079

Safe Surfing on the Internet, 13080

Wolke, Robert L. *What Einstein Told His Cook,* 13308

Wollard, Kathy. *How Come?* 12043

How Come Planet Earth? 12044

Wolny, Philip. *Weapons Satellites,* 13195

Wong, Janet S. *Behind the Wheel,* 4792

Wong, Joyce Lee. *Seeing Emily,* 1756(F)

Wong, Li Keng. *Good Fortune,* 7322

Wong, Stephen. *Baseball Treasures,* 13632

Wood, Angela. *Being a Jew,* 9843

Judaism, 9844

Wood, Beverley. *Dog Star,* 2526(F), 2527(F)

Jack's Knife, 2527(F)

Wood, Chris. *Dog Star,* 2526(F), 2527(F)

Jack's Knife, 2527(F)

Wood, Dan. *Jesse Jackson,* 6003

Wood, Elaine. *The Brain and Nervous System,* 11562

The Coral Reef, 12524

Ecosystem Science Fair Projects Using Worms, Leaves, Crickets, and Other Stuff, 12232

Wood, Marion. *Ancient America,* 9054

Wood, Maryrose. *My Life the Musical,* 648(F)

Sex Kittens and Horn Dawgs Fall in Love, 3930(F)

Wood, Richard. *Diana,* 7178

Wood, Tim. *The Renaissance,* 7893

Woodcock, Jon. *Cool Stuff 2.0 and How It Works,* 12996

Woodford, Chris. *Air and Space Travel,* 13107

Communication and Computers, 12994

Cool Stuff and How It Works, 12995

Cool Stuff 2.0 and How It Works, 12996

Criminal Investigation, 10594

Digital Technology, 13081

Electricity, 12960

Energy, 12936

Power and Energy, 12937

Ships and Submarines, 13108

Woodford, Susan. *The Parthenon,* 7800

Wooding, Chris. *Poison,* 2528(F)

Storm Thief, 4414(F)

Woodruff, Elvira. *Fearless,* 3009(F)

Orphan of Ellis Island, 2529(F)

The Ravenmaster's Secret, 3010(F)

Woodruff, Joan L. *The Shiloh Renewal,* 1249(F)

Woods, Bob. *Corvette,* 13133

Woods, Brenda. *Emako Blue,* 1818(F)

My Name Is Sally Little Song, 3196(F)

The Red Rose Box, 3475(F)

Woods, Geraldine. *Animal Experimentation and Testing,* 12315

Heroin, 11200

The Navajo, 9055

Science in Ancient Egypt, 7778

Woods, Mary. *Ancient Agriculture,* 7728

Ancient Machines from Wedges to Waterwheels, 7729

Woods, Mary B. *Ancient Communication,* 5054

Ancient Computing, 12786

Ancient Construction, 13018

Ancient Medicine, 7730

Ancient Transportation, 7731

Ancient Warfare, 13196

Environmental Disasters, 10468

The History of Communication, 12997

The History of Medicine, 11474

Tornadoes, 12825

Woods, Michael. *Ancient Agriculture,* 7728

Ancient Communication, 5054

Ancient Computing, 12786

Ancient Construction, 13018

Ancient Machines from Wedges to Waterwheels, 7729

Ancient Medicine, 7730

Ancient Transportation, 7731

Ancient Warfare, 13196

Environmental Disasters, 10468

The History of Communication, 12997

The History of Medicine, 11474

Tornadoes, 12825

Title Index

This index contains both main entry and internal titles cited in the entries. References are to entry numbers, not page numbers. All fiction titles are indicated by (F), following the entry number.

A Is for AARRGH! 3799(F)

A. Philip Randolph, 6030

A. Philip Randolph and the African-American Labor Movement, 6031

Aaron Burr: The Rise and Fall of an American Politician, 6262

Aaron Burr and the Young Nation, 6261

The Abacus Contest: Stories from Taiwan and China, 2880(F)

The Abduction, 119(F)

Abe Lincoln Grows Up, 6162

The Abernathy Boys, 105(F)

Abigail Adams, 6067, 6069

Abigail Adams: A Revolutionary Woman, 6066

Abigail Adams: First Lady and Patriot, 6068

Abner and Me, 2090(F)

The Abolition of Slavery: Fighting for a Free America, 9185

The Abolitionist Movement: Ending Slavery, 9206

Abolitionists and Slave Resistance: Breaking the Chains of Slavery, 8896

Aboriginal Art and Culture, 7407

Aboriginal Art of Australia: Exploring Cultural Traditions, 7408

The Aboriginal Peoples of Australia, 8402

Abortion: Debating the Issue, 11737

The Abortion Battle: Looking at Both Sides, 11749

The Abortion Controversy, 11732

The Abortion Rights Movement, 11755

Above the Veil, 2341(F)

The Abracadabra Kid: A Writer's Life, 5493

Abraham Joshua Heschel, 5998

Abraham Lincoln, 6154, 6161, 6164

Abraham Lincoln: Letters from a Slave Girl, 3233(F)

Abraham Lincoln: The Freedom President, 6163

Abraham Lincoln: The Writer, 6159

Abraham Lincoln: U.S. President, 6155

Abraham Lincoln for Kids: His Life and Times with 21 Activities, 6158

Abraham Lincoln's Gettysburg Address: Four Score and More . . ., 9257

Absolute Brightness, 521

Absolutely, Positively Not, 1526(F)

The Absolutely True Diary of a Part-Time Indian, 1257(F)

Abstract Expressionists, 5225

Accept No Substitutes! The History of American Advertising, 10767

An Acceptable Time, 2250(F)

Accidental Love, 1685

Accidents of Nature, 1190(F)

Acid Rain: A Sourcebook for Young People, 10478

Acids and Bases, 12654

The Acropolis, 7346

Across America: The Lewis and Clark Expedition, 9322

Across America on an Emigrant Train, 13141

Across the Grain, 1386(F)

Across the Great River, 694(F)

Across the Plains in the Donner Party, 9338

Across the Steel River, 201(F), 3045(F), 3046(F)

Across the Wall: A Tale of the Abhorsen and Other Stories, 4569(F)

Across the Wide and Lonesome Prairie: The Oregon Trail Diary of Hattie Campbell, 3270(F)

Across the Wide Ocean: The Why, How, and Where of Navigation for Humans and Animals at Sea, 12868

Acting Out, 4633

Action Skateboarding, 13745

An Actor on the Elizabethan Stage, 7520

The Actual Real Reality of Jennifer James, 3906(F)

Adam Canfield of the Slash, 642(F), 643(F)

Adam Canfield, Watch Your Back! 643(F)

Adam of the Road, 2786(F)

Adam Sandler, 5838

Adaptation, 12226

Adaptation and Competition, 12217

Addiction, 11025, 11275

Addiction: The "High" That Brings You Down, 11141

Addictions and Risky Behaviors: Cutting, Bingeing, Snorting, and Other Dangers, 11031

Addition and Subtraction, 12773

ADHD, 11669

Adolescent Rights: Are Young People Equal Under the Law? 10111

Adolescents and ADD: Gaining the Advantage, 11672

Adolf Hitler, 7203, 7207

Adolf Hitler and Nazi Germany, 7206

Adopted by Indians: A True Story, 9030

Adopted from Asia: How It Feels to Grow Up in America, 11978

Adoption, 11956, 11970, 11971, 12011

Adoptions Today: Questions and Controversy, 12010

The Adoration of Jenna Fox, 4362(F)

Adrift, 834(F)

Adventure Racing, 13518

Adventure Tour Guides: Life on Extreme Outdoor Adventures, 10892

Adventures in Oz, 2691(F)

The Adventures of Huckleberry Finn, 341(F)

The Adventures of Marco Polo, 5199

The Adventures of Midnight Son, 3302(F)

The Adventures of Pinocchio (Illus. by Roberta Innocenti), 1965(F), 4862(F)

Glasses and Contact Lenses: Your Guide to Eyes, Eyewear, and Eye Care, 11601

GLBTQ: The Survival Guide for Queer and Questioning Teens, 11783

Glint, 3966(F)

The Glitch in Sleep, 2140(F)

Global Pollution, 10471

Global Warming, 10424, 10434, 10441, 10442, 10444, 10446, 10448, 10458, 10831

Global Warming: The Threat of Earth's Changing Climate, 10453

Global Warming and Climate Change, 10423

Global Warning: Attack on the Pacific Rim! 146(F)

Globalize It! 10760

Gloria Estefan, 5743, 5744, 5745

Gloria Estefan: Singer and Entertainer, 5742

Gloria Steinem, 6040

Gloria Steinem: Feminist Extraordinaire, 6042

Gloria Steinem: The Women's Movement, 6041

Glorious Grasses: The Grains, 12253

A Glorious Past: Ancient Egypt, Ethiopia and Nubia, 7803

Glory Days and Other Stories, 1318(F)

A Glory of Unicorns, 1979(F)

The Glow Stone, 1156

Gnat Stokes and the Foggy Bottom Swamp Queen, 3682(F)

Go! 4193(F)

Go and Come Back, 1768(F)

Go Big or Go Home, 4328(F)

Go Figure! A Totally Cool Book About Numbers, 12787

Go Fly a Bike! The Ultimate Book About Bicycle Fun, Freedom, and Science, 13668

Go Saddle the Sea, 3938(F)

Go! The Whole World of Transportation, 13102

Goalkeeper in Charge, 4469(F)

The Goatnappers, 492(F)

The Goats, 1333(F)

Goblins in the Castle, 1980(F)

The God of Mischief, 2886(F)

God, the Universe, and Hot Fudge Sundaes, 1468(F)

God Went to Beauty School, 596(F)

God Within: Our Spiritual Future — As Told by Today's New Adults, 9780

Godless, 3825(F)

Gods and Goddesses of the Ancient Maya, 4946

Gods and Pharaohs from Egyptian Mythology, 4950

The Gods and Their Machines, 2279(F)

God's Mailbox: More Stories About Stories in the Bible, 9750

Gods of Manhattan, 2310(F)

Godzilla Takes the Bronx: The Inside Story of Hideki Matsui, 6860

Going Back Home: An Artist Returns to the South, 5408

Going for the Record, 1095(F)

Going Going, 1807(F)

Going Home, 728(F)

Going Nowhere Faster, 1276(F)

Going Postal, 3894(F)

Going to College, 13587

Going to the Getty: A Book About the Getty Center in Los Angeles, 9677

Going Where I'm Coming From: Memoirs of American Youth, 5259

Gold, 12620

The Gold Rush: A Primary Source History of the Search for Gold in California, 9339

Gold Rush Dogs, 12595

Gold Rush Fever: A Story of the Klondike, 1898, 8727

Gold Rush Women, 5121

Golden, 4805

The Golden Compass, 2388(F)

Golden Daffodils, 1171(F), 1172(F)

The Golden Dreams of Carlo Chuchio, 6(F)

Golden Girl and Other Stories, 1319(F)

The Golden Hour, 2518(F), 2519(F)

The Golden Rat, 2881(F)

Golden Tales: Myths, Legends, and Folktales from Latin America, 4932

Goldstone, 1528(F), 3034(F)

The Golem's Eye, 2461(F)

The Gollywhopper Games, 425(F)

Gone, 4309(F)

Gone a-Whaling: The Lure of the Sea and the Hunt for the Great Whale, 8713

Gone and Back, 3251(F)

Gone to Maui, 4244(F)

Goners: The Hunt Is On, 4381(F)

Good Brother, Bad Brother: The Story of Edwin Booth and John Wilkes Booth, 6255

Good-bye, Glamour Girl, 3563(F)

Good-bye Marianne: A Story of Growing Up in Nazi Germany, 3573(F)

Good-bye Pink Pig, 1824(F)

Good Enough, 788(F)

The Good Fight: How World War II Was Won, 7940

Good for Nothing, 3039(F)

Good Fortune: My Journey to Gold Mountain, 7322

Good Girl Work: Factories, Sweatshops, and How Women Changed Their Role in the American Workforce, 9393

The Good Housekeeping Illustrated Children's Cookbook, 13311

Good Masters! Sweet Ladies! 4628

Good Night, Mr. Tom, 3480(F)

A Good Soup Attracts Chairs: A First African Cookbook for American Kids, 13290

Good Sports: Plain Talk About Health and Fitness for Teens, 11611

The Good, the Bad, the Slimy: The Secret Life of Microbes, 12560

Good Wives, 331(F)

Good Women of a Well-Blessed Land: Women's Lives in Colonial America, 9110

Goodbye to Atlantis, 940(F)

Goodbye, Vietnam, 2877(F)

Goose Chase, 2219(F)

Goose Girl, 2102(F)

The Goose Girl, 2099(F), 2100(F)

The Gorgon's Gaze, 2077(F)

Gorilla Mountain: The Story of Wildlife Biologist Amy Vedder, 6756

Gorilla Walk, 12377

Gorillas, 12374

The Gorillas of Gill Park, 70(F), 1425(F)

The Gospel According to Larry, 615(F), 616(F)

Gossamer, 2267(F)

Got Geography! 4673

Gotham County Line: Batman, 2661(F)

Gothic Classics, 2671(F)

Gothic! Ten Original Dark Tales, 3707(F)

Gotta Get Some Bish Bash Bosh, 1258(F)

Gouverneur Morris: Creating a Nation, 6337

Government, 9103

Government and Politics, 5906, 9398

The Government of Mexico, 8779

Governments of the Western Hemisphere, 7659

Goy Crazy, 756(F)

Grab Hands and Run, 1815(F)

Grace above All, 1075(F)

Gracie's Girl, 645(F)

The Grade Booster Guide for Kids, 10788

The Graduation of Jake Moon, 1049(F)

Graffiti World: Street Art from Five Continents, 7361

Grail Quest: The Camelot Spell, 2918(F)

Grammar Snobs Are Great Big Meanies: A Guide to Language for Fun and Spite, 5058

Grand Canyon: Exploring a Natural Wonder, 9577

The Grand Jury, 9960

The Grand Tour, 2533(F)

The Grand Tour or the Purloined Coronation Regalia: Being a Revelation of Matters of High Confidentiality and Greatest Importance, Including Extracts from the Intimate Diary of a Noblewoman and the Sworn Testimony of a Lady of Quality, 2532(F)

Grand Trees of America: Our State and Champion Trees, 12275

The Grandest of Lives: Eye to Eye with Whales, 12540

Subject/Grade Level Index

All entries are listed by subject and then according to grade level suitability (see the key at the foot of pages for grade level designations). Subjects are arranged alphabetically and subject heads may be subdivided into nonfiction (e.g., "Africa") and fiction (e.g. "Africa — Fiction"). References to entries are by entry number, not page number.

Adoption
See also Foster care
IJ: 11956, 11978–79, 11983
JS: 11747, 11966, 11970–71, 11976, 12008, 12010–11

Adoption — Fiction
IJ: 113, 299, 742, 887, 938, 947, 953, 1012, 1528, 3299, 3392, 4488
JS: 576, 783, 811, 868, 956, 967, 975, 996, 1104, 1781, 4322

Adventure and adventurers — Fiction
IJ: 22

Adventure stories — Fiction
See also Mystery stories — Fiction; Sea stories — Fiction; Survival stories — Fiction
IJ: 1–3, 5–7, 10–11, 13–15, 17–19, 21, 24–25, 27, 30–31, 34, 38–39, 41, 43, 45–47, 50–51, 54–56, 58–59, 63, 66–67, 71–73, 76, 78–86, 88, 95–97, 102–7, 114, 116–18, 120–22, 126–27, 129, 131, 139, 146–47, 149, 154, 156–57, 159–60, 162, 164–66, 168, 170–71, 174–75, 177–78, 180, 182, 184–85, 187, 189, 191, 194, 196–99, 202–4, 210, 212, 215, 220, 222, 224, 226, 234, 236, 308, 329, 359, 363, 384, 388, 398, 443, 639, 754, 955, 992, 1092, 1198, 1333, 1430, 1837, 2042, 2123, 2158, 2160, 2166, 2187, 2348, 2375, 2472, 2501, 2604, 2612, 2701, 2704, 2721, 2770, 2803, 2812, 2836, 2884, 2892, 2909, 2942, 2945, 2956–57, 2969, 3020, 3024, 3046, 3049, 3057, 3081, 3090, 3095, 3116, 3125–26, 3131, 3146–47, 3158, 3162, 3165, 3187, 3190–91, 3225–26, 3235, 3249, 3252, 3275, 3280, 3289, 3302, 3307, 3330, 3371, 3397, 3502, 3571, 3750, 3912, 3915, 3944, 3995, 4010, 4040, 4045, 4082, 4100, 4132, 4158, 4170–71, 4184, 4287–88, 4290, 4422
J: 169 **JS:** 4, 8, 12, 26, 32, 36–37, 53, 60, 65, 68, 74, 77, 93–94, 98–100, 110–11, 115, 128, 132–37, 141, 148, 151–53, 158, 161, 167, 172, 181, 183, 190, 193, 195, 206–7, 213, 216–17, 219, 225, 227, 229–30, 303, 305–7, 325, 336, 341, 345, 458, 807, 1619, 1646, 1816, 2141, 2481, 2538, 2575, 2590, 2713, 2750, 2760, 2775, 2792, 2832, 2930, 2938, 2971, 3040, 3064, 3104, 3107, 3287, 3292, 4035–36, 4072, 4369

Adventurers and explorers — Biography
IJ: 5115, 5118–20, 5123, 5126–27, 5132, 5135, 5137–38, 5140–43, 5149–50, 5154–57, 5160–62, 5164, 5169, 5171, 5173–77, 5179, 5184, 5186–88, 5190, 5196–98, 5200–2, 5204–5, 5211–13, 5216, 6395, 7531, 7678, 7680, 7685, 7687, 8614, 8708, 8806, 8866, 9060, 9068, 9073, 9075–76, 9373 **JS:** 5151–53, 5158,

5163, 5170, 5172, 5178, 5189, 5199, 5217, 5219, 7656, 7661, 7699, 7892, 8838, 8857, 9061

***The Adventures of Huckleberry Finn* — Criticism**
IJ: 5032

Advertising
IJ: 10766–67, 12042 **JS:** 10765, 10768, 11846

Advertising — Biography
JS: 6687

Advertising — Careers
IJ: 10937

Advice columnists — Biography
IJ: 6443

Aeronautics

Aeronautics — Experiments and projects
IJ: 13124

Aeronautics — History
IJ: 13125

Affirmative action
See also Social action
IJ: 10128**JS:** 10229, 10236, 10770

Afghanistan
IJ: 8348–50, 8353, 8357, 8374, 10343 **JS:** 8355, 8360, 8378, 8386, 8391

Afghanistan — Biography
JS: 7119

Afghanistan — Fiction
IJ: 2839**JS:** 610

Africa
See also specific countries and regions, e.g., Ethiopia; West Africa
IJ: 8121, 8123–24, 8126, 8133, 8190, 8227, 8235, 8242, 8911, 11256
JS: 8125, 8127, 8134, 8207, 8212, 8221, 12370

Africa — Animals
IJ: 8199, 12417 **JS:** 8140, 12394

Africa — Anthropology
IJ: 8162

Africa — Art
IJ: 7404, 8120

Africa — Biography
IJ: 7058, 7288

Africa — Cookbooks
IJ: 13290**J:** 13287

Africa — Crafts
IJ: 8130, 13212

Africa — Exploration
IJ: 8136

Africa — Fiction
IJ: 116, 2187, 2334, 2346, 2820
JS: 1265, 1799, 2804, 2815, 2819, 2826–28, 4296

Africa — Folklore
IJ: 4828–30, 4832, 4834, 4837, 4922
JS: 4827, 4831, 4835, 4838

Africa — Geography
JS: 8129, 8135

Africa — History
IJ: 7715, 8120, 8132, 8149, 8236–37, 8239, 8246, 8248–49 **J:** 8131

Africa — Peoples
See also specific peoples, e.g., Zulu (African people)
IJ: 7715, 8138–39, 8141, 8166, 8173, 8179, 8182, 8186, 8224–25, 8228, 8233, 8256–57, 8259 **JS:** 8118–19, 8145, 8153, 8158, 8160, 8163, 8169, 8171–72, 8175–76, 8184–85, 8187–88, 8195, 8198, 8206, 8209, 8214–17, 8220, 8223, 8229–30, 8247, 8252–53, 8258, 8260, 8262

Africa — Poetry
IJ: 4800

Africa — Religion
JS: 9764

Africa, East

African Americans
See also Civil rights; Civil War (U.S.); Kwanzaa; Slavery; and names of individuals, e.g., Robinson, Jackie
IJ: 3143, 5940, 8911, 9416, 9717, 10010, 10071, 10137, 10238, 10240, 10243, 10249, 10263, 10275, 10323
J: 10239 **JS:** 5657, 6472, 7513, 8943, 10076–77, 10085, 10173, 10248, 10251, 10254, 10261, 10273, 10277, 10279

African Americans — Airplane pilots
JS: 9471

African Americans — Armed Forces
IJ: 5880, 7920, 8018, 8032, 9524, 10241 **JS:** 5900

African Americans — Art
IJ: 7420, 9435 **JS:** 5287, 7419, 9445

African Americans — Authors
IJ: 5265, 5267, 5279, 9435
JS: 4553, 5424, 5455, 5487, 5506, 5508, 5526, 5528, 5557, 5638, 5655, 9445, 10284

African Americans — Baseball
J: 6867

African Americans — Biography
See also specific fields, e.g., Boxing
IJ: 5136, 5146–48, 5173–74, 5185, 5275, 5278–79, 5345–46, 5395, 5408, 5421–23, 5488, 5524, 5617, 5636–37, 5639, 5651, 5676–77, 5682, 5686, 5690–91, 5693, 5707, 5719, 5725, 5729, 5737, 5751, 5753, 5759, 5764,

IJ = Upper Elementary/Lower Middle School; J = Middle School/Junior High; JS = Junior High/Senior High

IJ = Upper Elementary/Lower Middle School; J = Middle School/Junior High; JS = Junior High/Senior High

IJ = Upper Elementary/Lower Middle School; J = Middle School/Junior High; JS = Junior High/Senior High

IJ = Upper Elementary/Lower Middle School; J = Middle School/Junior High; JS = Junior High/Senior High

Archaeology
IJ: 7593, 7607–10, 7612–13, 7616, 7618–19, 7623, 7625, 7627, 7631–32, 7635, 7695–96, 7701, 7707, 7714, 7724, 7733, 7751, 7812, 8534, 8990 **JS:** 7614, 7628–29, 7634, 7640, 8715, 13193

Archaeology — Careers
J: 10846

Archaeology — Fiction
IJ: 1696, 1863

Archaeology — Underwater
IJ: 7630, 7722

Archimedes
IJ: 6547 **JS:** 6548

Architecture
See also Building and construction
IJ: 7328, 7330–31, 7333–34, 7338, 7342, 7347–48, 7371, 7424, 7433, 7761, 13005, 13007, 13464
JS: 7340, 13009

Architecture — Biography
IJ: 5350, 5410, 5412–13 **JS:** 5311, 5328, 5361, 5409, 5411

Architecture — Careers
JS: 10886

Architecture — History
IJ: 7329, 7825 **JS:** 7343, 7819

Arctic
See also Antarctic; North Pole; Polar regions
IJ: 8865–66, 8871, 8877 **JS:** 8873

Arctic — Animals
IJ: 8863

Arctic — Biography
IJ: 7308

Arctic — Careers
J: 10975

Arctic — Discovery and exploration
IJ: 5197

Arctic — Fiction
IJ: 104, 155, 209

Arctic — Plants
IJ: 8863

Argentina
IJ: 8802, 8814, 8821 **JS:** 8819

Argentina — Fiction
IJ: 3044 **JS:** 3052

Aristide, Jean-Bertrand — Fiction
JS: 3048

Aristotle
IJ: 7151

Arithmetic

Arizona
IJ: 9576, 9728

Arizona — Fiction
IJ: 1786

Arkansas
IJ: 9688

Arkansas River
IJ: 12744

Armed forces

Armed forces (U.S.)
See also specific branches, e.g., Air Force (U.S.)
IJ: 10060, 13158, 13172 **JS:** 10059, 13165

Armed forces (U.S.) — Biography
IJ: 6357 **JS:** 6355, 6358

Armed forces (U.S.) — Women
IJ: 8928, 9587, 10065 **JS:** 10063–64

Armenia
IJ: 8541, 8554

Armenia — History
IJ: 7297

Arms
IJ: 11586

Arms control
See Gun control
IJ: 9871

Armstrong, Lance
IJ: 7012 **JS:** 7013–15

Armstrong, Louis
IJ: 5693 **JS:** 5694

Armstrong, Neil
IJ: 5133–34

Army (U.S.)
JS: 10062, 13695

Army (U.S.) — Biography
IJ: 5913, 6325, 6327, 6359, 6367

Army (U.S.) — Fiction
IJ: 3282

Army (U.S.) — History
IJ: 8032

Army (U.S.) — Special Forces
IJ: 10061

Arnold, Benedict
IJ: 6247, 6249–50, 6252–53 **JS:** 6248, 6251

Arranged marriages — Fiction
JS: 2982

Arsenic
IJ: 12636

Arson — Fiction
JS: 1090

Art
See also Art appreciation; Drawing and painting; Museums; and as a subdivision under other subjects, e.g., Animals — Art; and names

of individuals, e.g., Van Gogh, Vincent
IJ: 7360, 7371, 7377, 7379, 7387, 7389–90, 7404, 7407, 7410–11, 7420, 7428–29, 7433–34, 7816, 7853, 9312 **J:** 4662, 9796 **JS:** 4557, 5055, 7327, 7354, 7362, 7403, 7419, 7422, 7432, 7436, 9620, 13024, 13038

Art — Biography
IJ: 5225, 5230, 5239, 5248, 5255, 5285, 5288, 5296, 5298–302, 5304–10, 5312, 5314, 5316–20, 5322, 5324, 5327, 5329–33, 5337–41, 5343, 5345–46, 5348, 5352–58, 5360, 5363–64, 5367, 5369, 5371–80, 5382–86, 5388, 5390–91, 5396, 5399, 5403–4, 5406–8, 7423, 7427 **J:** 5325 **JS:** 5247, 5286–87, 5289, 5297, 5303, 5315, 5334, 5336, 5359, 5362, 5366, 5368, 5370, 5381, 5387, 5389, 5398, 5400–1, 5405, 5501, 7838

Art — Careers
IJ: 10904

Art — Fiction
IJ: 509, 524, 1070, 1219, 1657, 2396, 2745, 2898, 3071, 3411, 4163 **JS:** 350, 988, 2787, 2900, 2928, 2982

Art — History
IJ: 5240–41, 7374, 7381–82, 7384, 7429, 7782, 7853, 8459, 12993 **JS:** 7359, 7363, 7375–76, 7383, 7391–92, 7394, 7401, 7413, 7838

Art — Poetry
JS: 4663

Art appreciation
IJ: 5307, 5391, 7355–58, 7366–67, 7369–70, 7372, 7388, 7412, 7414–18, 13205 **J:** 7368 **JS:** 7359, 7363, 7376, 7413

Arthritis
JS: 11356

Arthritis — Fiction
IJ: 1232

Arthropods
IJ: 12302

Arthur, Chester A.
IJ: 6078

Arthur, King
IJ: 4886, 4890, 7152 **JS:** 4877–78, 4891

Arthur, King — Fiction
IJ: 1973, 1990, 2330, 2542, 2571, 2918, 2972–73, 2990 **JS:** 2120, 2514, 2799, 2807, 2810, 2998

Arthurdale (WV)
IJ: 9449

Artificial intelligence
IJ: 13049, 13068

IJ = Upper Elementary/Lower Middle School; J = Middle School/Junior High; JS = Junior High/Senior High

IJ = Upper Elementary/Lower Middle School; J = Middle School/Junior High; JS = Junior High/Senior High

1450, 1547, 1558, 1589, 1997, 2235, 2301–2, 2843, 2853–54, 2870, 3684, 3691, 3848, 4067

Australia — Folklore
JS: 4858

Austria
IJ: 8478–79

Austria — Fiction
IJ: 293, 2940, 2953

Authors
JS: 5657

Authors — African American
IJ: 5025 JS: 5561

Authors — Asian American
IJ: 5249

Authors — Biography
IJ: 5223, 5226, 5228, 5231, 5246, 5255–56, 5260, 5265, 5267, 5270, 5279, 5377, 5415–18, 5420–21, 5423, 5425, 5427–28, 5430, 5432, 5434–37, 5442–45, 5447, 5449, 5452–53, 5456, 5458, 5461–62, 5464, 5466, 5469–70, 5472, 5474, 5477–79, 5484–85, 5489, 5491–92, 5494–95, 5503, 5505, 5512, 5515, 5518, 5524, 5529, 5537–38, 5541–44, 5546, 5549, 5555, 5562, 5564, 5566–72, 5574–76, 5578, 5580, 5582, 5586–87, 5590, 5593–98, 5600, 5602–5, 5607–13, 5616–19, 5622–26, 5628–30, 5632–33, 5635–37, 5639–41, 5646–48, 5651, 5659, 6018, 6062, 6345, 6347, 6444 J: 5227, 5273, 5588 JS: 5229, 5245, 5254, 5258–59, 5277, 5426, 5429, 5431, 5433, 5441, 5446, 5448, 5450–51, 5455, 5457, 5459–60, 5463, 5467–68, 5473, 5476, 5482–83, 5486–87, 5490, 5493, 5497, 5500–1, 5504, 5506–11, 5513–14, 5519–23, 5525–28, 5531–36, 5539–40, 5545, 5550–53, 5556–61, 5563, 5565, 5577, 5579, 5581, 5583, 5585, 5589, 5592, 5599, 5601, 5606, 5614–15, 5620–21, 5627, 5631, 5634, 5642, 5645, 5650, 5652–54, 5656, 5981, 13141

Authors — Careers
IJ: 5425

Authors — Criticism
JS: 5027

Authors — Fiction
IJ: 842, 1384, 3830 JS: 1036

Authors — Renaissance
IJ: 7853

Authors — Women
IJ: 5611 JS: 5015, 5232, 5448, 5451, 5473, 5526, 5557, 5589

Autism
IJ: 11314, 11679 JS: 11263, 11639, 11654, 11668, 11678

Autism — Fiction
IJ: 528

Automation
See Computers; Robots

Automobile accidents — Fiction
JS: 1216, 1487, 1557

Automobile racing
IJ: 13135, 13441, 13594, 13600–1, 13603–4 JS: 13599

Automobile racing — Biography
IJ: 6823–30

Automobile racing — Fiction
JS: 4417, 4457, 4464, 4466, 4478, 4517

Automobile racing — History
IJ: 13595

Automobile travel — Fiction
IJ: 405, 841 JS: 586, 3789

Automobiles
IJ: 13132, 13602 JS: 13129, 13134

Automobiles — Biography
IJ: 6557, 6638

Automobiles — History
IJ: 13136 JS: 13130

Automobiles — Maintenance and repair — Careers
IJ: 10944

Avalanches — Fiction
IJ: 3034

Avalon — Fiction
IJ: 2331

Avery, Oswald
IJ: 6549

Avi (author)
IJ: 5432, 5434 JS: 5433

Aviation
See also Airplanes
IJ: 13107, 13119

Aviation — Biography
JS: 6520

Aviation — Fiction
JS: 786

Aviation — History
IJ: 13109, 13117, 13121, 13125
JS: 6520

Azerbaijan
IJ: 8542 JS: 8574

Aztecs
See also Mexico — History
IJ: 3016, 7712, 7723, 8760, 8773, 8780 J: 8768 JS: 8763

Aztecs — Crafts
IJ: 8762, 8769

Aztecs — Fiction
JS: 3035

Aztecs — Folklore
IJ: 4826

Aztecs — Mythology
IJ: 2731, 4894, 4937

B

Babies — Fiction
IJ: 795 J: 1304

Baboons
IJ: 12378

Baboons — Fiction
IJ: 2187

Babylon 5 (television series)
JS: 7511

Babysitting
IJ: 11010–12

Babysitting — Fiction
IJ: 2525, 3831, 3858, 4114 JS: 677, 1086, 1549, 3658

Bach, Johann Sebastian
JS: 5660

Backpacking
JS: 13681

Bacon, Roger — Fiction
IJ: 2800

Bacteria
See also Germs
IJ: 11259, 11293, 11347, 12569
JS: 12565

Badgers — Fiction
IJ: 248, 2175

Badminton
IJ: 13787

Bagpipes — Fiction
IJ: 3993

Baha'i (religion)
JS: 4631, 9753

Bahrain
JS: 8688

Bailey, Anne
JS: 6383

Baker, Ella
JS: 5966

Baking
JS: 13258

Balanchine, George
IJ: 5696–97 JS: 5695

Balboa, Vasco Nunez de
IJ: 5135

Bald eagles
IJ: 12452 JS: 12448

Balkans
IJ: 8442 JS: 8435

Ball, Charles
IJ: 6384

IJ = Upper Elementary/Lower Middle School; J = Middle School/Junior High; JS = Junior High/Senior High

Beatles (musical group)
IJ: 5701, 5704 JS: 5702–3, 5787–88

Beaufort scale
IJ: 12797

Beauty
IJ: 11509JS: 11520

Beauty — Fiction
IJ: 974JS: 739

Beauty care
See also Grooming

Beauty contests — Fiction
JS: 3836

Beauty culture

Beckwourth, James
IJ: 6389

Bees — Fiction
JS: 2230

Beethoven, Ludwig Van
IJ: 5661–62

Beetles
IJ: 12486

Begin, Menachem
IJ: 7097

Beginning readers

Behavior
J: 11828JS: 11836

Behavior — Fiction
IJ: 1552

Behavioral problems
IJ: 11916

Beijing, China
IJ: 8279–80, 8296, 8298

Belarus
IJ: 8545

Belgium
IJ: 8536, 8538

Belize
IJ: 8746, 8757, 12717

Bell, Alexander Graham
IJ: 6552–55 JS: 6556

Bell, Cool Papa
IJ: 6836

Belleau Wood, Battle of
JS: 7922

Ben-Gurion, David
JS: 8656

Benin
IJ: 8228

Benin — Folklore
IJ: 4837

Benin (African kingdom)
IJ: 8245

Benjamin of Tudela — Fiction
IJ: 2803

Benz, Karl
IJ: 6557

Beowulf — **Adaptations**
IJ: 4882JS: 4873, 4881

Berlin, Germany
IJ: 8464JS: 7946

Berlin, Irving
IJ: 5663

Berlin Airlift
IJ: 8082

Berlin Wall
IJ: 8471JS: 8469

Berlioz, Hector
IJ: 5664

Bermuda Triangle
IJ: 13474JS: 13453

Berners-Lee, Tim
IJ: 6558–59

Bernstein, Leonard
IJ: 5665–66 JS: 5667

Bethune, Mary McLeod
IJ: 5970–71 JS: 5969

Bettis, Jerome
IJ: 6940

Bezos, Jeff
IJ: 6560–61

Bhatt, Ela
IJ: 7098

Bible — Biography
IJ: 9776

Bible — Women
IJ: 9807JS: 9773

Bible stories
IJ: 3172, 9743, 9750, 9763, 9790,
9797, 9801, 9807–8, 9810, 9812
J: 9786, 9796

Biculturalism
JS: 10230, 10233

Bicycle racing
JS: 13676

Bicycle racing — Biography
IJ: 7012JS: 7013–14

Bicycle stunt riding
IJ: 13669

Bicycles
See also Long-distance cycling;
Mountain bikes
IJ: 13659, 13659–60, 13663,
13665–66, 13668–70, 13673, 13677
JS: 13662, 13672, 13675

Bicycles — Biography
IJ: 7026, 7033 JS: 7015

Bicycles — Fiction
IJ: 4436

Bicycles — Repairs
IJ: 13661

Bielenberg, Christabel
IJ: 8051

Big bang theory
IJ: 12204, 12208

**Big Bend National Park —
Fiction**
IJ: 1449

Big cats
See individual species, e.g., Lions
IJ: 12395, 12398, 12476

Bilingual education
JS: 10393

Bill of Rights (U.S.)
See also Constitution (U.S.)
IJ: 9900, 9904 J: 9889 JS: 9890,
9897, 10023

Billy the Kid
IJ: 6390, 6392 JS: 6391

Billy the Kid — Fiction
IJ: 3310

Bin Laden, Osama
IJ: 7100–1 JS: 7099

Binge eating
JS: 11360

Bini (African people)
JS: 8230

Bioethics
IJ: 11207JS: 11841

Biofuels
IJ: 10460

Biography
See also under specific
occupations, e.g., Art —
Biography; specific sports, e.g.,
Baseball — Biography; and
cultural groups, e.g., Hispanic
Americans — Biography
IJ: 5874, 5903, 6504, 7061 JS: 5110

Biography — Collective
IJ: 5113, 5239, 5873, 5877, 5930,
6500, 6512, 7056, 7079 JS: 5111,
5114, 5233, 5277, 5944, 5957, 6475,
6482, 6492, 6520, 7074, 7647

Biological weapons
JS: 13163, 13163, 13167

Biology
See also Animals; Botany; and
individual animal species, e.g.,
Raccoons
IJ: 12214, 12217, 12229 JS: 12225

Biology — Adaptation
IJ: 12226

Biology — Biography
IJ: 6697

**Biology — Experiments and
projects**
IJ: 12090, 12210 JS: 12231–32

IJ = Upper Elementary/Lower Middle School; J = Middle School/Junior High; JS = Junior High/Senior High

IJ = Upper Elementary/Lower Middle School; J = Middle School/Junior High; JS = Junior High/Senior High

IJ = Upper Elementary/Lower Middle School; J = Middle School/Junior High; JS = Junior High/Senior High

IJ = Upper Elementary/Lower Middle School; J = Middle School/Junior High; JS = Junior High/Senior High

Bunche, Ralph
JS: 6260

Bunyan, Paul
JS: 4930

Burial customs
IJ: 7603 JS: 11037

Buried treasure
IJ: 7620, 7650, 9561, 9617

Buried treasure — Fiction
IJ: 17, 49, 57, 222–23, 226

Burke, Chris
IJ: 5712

Burma

Burma — Biography
IJ: 7131

Burma — Fiction
IJ: 3561

Burnett, Frances Hodgson
IJ: 5442

Burr, Aaron
IJ: 6261–62

Burroughs, Edgar Rice
IJ: 5443

Burroughs, John
IJ: 6571

Burton, Richard Francis
IJ: 5137

Bush, George H. W.
JS: 6080–82

Bush, George W.
IJ: 6083–84, 6086–89 JS: 6085, 9921

Bush, Laura Welch
IJ: 6090

Bush pilots — Alaska
IJ: 9668

Business

Business — Sports
IJ: 13538

Butcher, Susan
IJ: 7017

Butler, Jerry
IJ: 7420

Butterflies and moths
See also specific breeds, e.g.,
  Monarch butterflies
IJ: 12500, 12503–4 JS: 12501

Byars, Betsy
IJ: 5444–45

Byrd, Admiral Richard Evelyn
IJ: 5138

Byron, Lord

Byzantine Empire
IJ: 7876

C

Cabeza de Vaca, Alvar Nunez
IJ: 5139–40

Cable television
JS: 6755

Cabot, John
IJ: 5141

Cactus
IJ: 12289

Cadmium
IJ: 12634

Caesar, Augustus
IJ: 7157–58

Caesar, Julius
IJ: 7161–63, 7831 JS: 7159–60

Caffeine
JS: 11021, 11023

Cahokia Mounds (IL)
IJ: 8990

Cairo (Egypt)
IJ: 8640

Cajuns — Folklore
IJ: 4924

Calcium
IJ: 12627, 12638, 12655

Calculation (mathematics)
IJ: 12786

Caldecott, Randolph
IJ: 5295

Calder, Alexander
IJ: 5296

Calendars
See Time
IJ: 12778, 12786

California
IJ: 9646–47, 9672, 9675

California — Biography
IJ: 5215, 6374, 7265

California — Fiction
IJ: 29, 160, 697, 730, 1043, 3261–62, 3268, 3470 JS: 143, 558, 1541, 1735, 2036, 3292, 4195, 4583

California — History
IJ: 5213–14, 8919, 9060, 9645, 9650–51, 9654, 9657, 9663, 9667, 9669, 9683, 9685, 9687 JS: 7474, 9662

California Gold Rush

California Indians
IJ: 9029

California Trail
JS: 9314

Calligraphy
IJ: 13340, 13359 JS: 13235, 13369

Calusa Indians — Fiction
IJ: 34

Calvin, John
JS: 7164

Cambodia
IJ: 8382

Cambodia — Fiction
IJ: 2844–45

Cambodian Americans
IJ: 10199 JS: 10296

Cambodian Americans — Fiction
JS: 719, 1658

Camden Yards (Baltimore)
IJ: 13633

Camels — Fiction
IJ: 3282

Cameroon
IJ: 8241 JS: 8145, 8253

Campbell, Ben Nighthorse
IJ: 6263

Campfires
IJ: 13683

Camps and camping
IJ: 13683, 13685 J: 13682

Camps and camping — Fiction
IJ: 55, 114, 509, 1333, 1337, 1380, 3349, 3881, 3885, 4021 JS: 32, 227, 452, 1442, 1629, 1712, 4091

Canada
IJ: 7681, 8717–18, 8726, 8732, 8734–35, 8737 JS: 8714, 8725

Canada — Biography
IJ: 5555, 6793, 6981, 7001, 7032
JS: 6530, 7002

Canada — Fiction
IJ: 21, 41, 47, 165, 201, 447, 777, 779, 1022, 1092, 1139, 1256, 1463, 3013, 3015, 3019–21, 3023, 3029–30, 3042–43, 3045–47, 3049–50, 3857, 4172, 4537 J: 3032 JS: 60, 94, 151, 298, 406, 746, 1034, 1105, 1291, 1636, 2917, 3033, 3039, 3088, 3522, 3836, 4190

Canada — Geography
IJ: 7655

Canada — History
IJ: 8720, 8722, 8728, 8730
JS: 3177, 8719, 8729

Canada — Wildlife
JS: 12386

Canaletto
JS: 5297

Canals
IJ: 8749, 9143, 13100

Canals — Fiction
IJ: 3165

IJ = Upper Elementary/Lower Middle School; J = Middle School/Junior High; JS = Junior High/Senior High

IJ = Upper Elementary/Lower Middle School; J = Middle School/Junior High; JS = Junior High/Senior High

IJ = Upper Elementary/Lower Middle School; J = Middle School/Junior High; JS = Junior High/Senior High

IJ = Upper Elementary/Lower Middle School; J = Middle School/Junior High; JS = Junior High/Senior High

Chippewa Indians
IJ: 9013

Chippewa Indians — Fiction
JS: 1314

Chisholm Trail
JS: 9349

Chlorine
IJ: 12656, 12663

Cho, Margaret
JS: 5721

Chocolate
IJ: 12245

Choctaw Indians — Folklore
JS: 4912

Cholera
IJ: 11289

Chong, Gordon H.
JS: 5311

Chopin, Frederic
IJ: 5668

Choreography — Biography
IJ: 5235, 5697, 5754 JS: 5695

Christian life — Fiction
IJ: 366, 370, 1878 JS: 837, 1283, 1483

Christianity
IJ: 9803, 9805–6, 9809

Christianity — Biography
IJ: 7139 JS: 7164

Christianity — Fiction
JS: 1215, 1355, 2762

Christianity — History
JS: 9015

Christianity (U.S.) — Biography
JS: 5902

Christie, Agatha
IJ: 5456

Christmas
IJ: 9794

Christmas — Carols
See Christmas — Songs and carols

Christmas — Crafts
IJ: 13210 JS: 13222

Christmas — Fiction
IJ: 319, 335, 1035

Christmas — Greece
J: 9795

Christmas — Memoirs
IJ: 5475

Christmas — Poetry
IJ: 4730

Chronic fatigue syndrome
IJ: 11210

Chumash Indians
IJ: 8959

Church and state — U.S.

Church and state — United States
See also Freedom of religion
JS: 9958, 9989, 10004

Churches — History
IJ: 7862

Churchill, Sir Winston
IJ: 7169–72

Cid, El
IJ: 5144

Cinderella — Fiction
IJ: 2034

Circulatory system
See also Heart
IJ: 11532, 11563, 11565–67
JS: 11564

Circuses
JS: 7521

Circuses — Biography
IJ: 5777, 5870–71 JS: 5869

Circuses — Fiction
IJ: 3829, 3970 JS: 3000

Cisneros, Sandra
IJ: 5458 JS: 5457

Cities and city life
See also names of specific cities,
e.g., Boston (MA)
IJ: 7880, 10731, 10733 J: 13011
JS: 10620, 12068, 12980

Cities and city life — Fiction
JS: 620, 4587

Cities and city life — History
IJ: 8889, 13356

Citizenship (U.S.)
IJ: 10069

Civil disobedience
JS: 10635

Civil liberties
JS: 9902, 9966, 10109, 10692

Civil rights
See also names of civil rights
leaders, e.g., King, Martin Luther,
Jr.; and specific civil rights, e.g.,
Human rights; Women's rights
IJ: 5901, 6011, 6015, 6030, 8720,
9490, 9507, 9521, 10071, 10078,
10093, 10099–101, 10108, 10111,
10121–24, 10138, 10153, 10156,
10158, 10162, 10170–71, 10177,
10263 J: 10083, 10146 JS: 6331,
9492, 9495, 9516, 9910, 9955, 9959,
9964, 9976, 9983, 10021, 10024,
10076–77, 10080, 10085, 10089,
10091–92, 10094–96, 10098, 10102,
10110, 10113, 10117, 10125, 10129,
10131–32, 10134, 10136, 10139–40,
10143, 10148–49, 10154–55, 10159,
10161, 10173–76, 10178, 10180,
10237, 10283, 10638

Civil rights — Biography
IJ: 5898, 5963, 5972, 5985, 5993,
5998, 6003, 6006–7, 6013, 6017,
6024–25, 6028–29, 6032, 6044–45,
6048, 6061, 6469, 7047 J: 5995,
6016 JS: 5770, 5908, 5949,
5965–68, 5981, 5986, 5989–92, 6002,
6005, 6008–10, 6012, 6022–23,
6026–27, 6033–35, 6039, 6049, 6051,
6065, 6260, 6334

Civil rights — Documents
JS: 10090

Civil rights — Fiction
IJ: 3433, 3463, 3467 JS: 731, 3437,
3447

Civil rights — History
IJ: 10169 JS: 9488, 10082, 10106

Civil rights — Students

Civil rights — United States
JS: 10118

Civil War — Fiction
IJ: 3216

Civil War (U.S.)
See also names of specific battles,
e.g., Gettysburg, Battle of; and
names of individuals, e.g., Lee,
Robert E.
IJ: 6115, 6157, 6410, 8893, 9140,
9212, 9227, 9229–36, 9239–45, 9247,
9249–52, 9254, 9256–60, 9263, 9267,
9269–71, 9273–76, 9278, 9282–90,
9292, 10137 JS: 9237–38, 9246,
9248, 9253, 9261–62, 9268, 9272,
9277, 9293, 9328, 13193

Civil War (U.S.) — Biography
IJ: 5294, 5874, 5882, 5893–94, 6117,
6255, 6273, 6305, 6317, 6319, 6371,
6387 J: 6385 JS: 6116, 6274, 6304,
6318, 6320–21

Civil War (U.S.) — Cookbooks
IJ: 9255 JS: 13257

Civil War (U.S.) — Experiments and projects
IJ: 9265 JS: 13236

Civil War (U.S.) — Fiction
IJ: 1912, 3072, 3197–99, 3202–4,
3206, 3208–10, 3212, 3214–15,
3217–18, 3223–28, 3230–31,
3234–36, 3239–40, 3243–47
JS: 334, 3200–1, 3205, 3207, 3213,
3219, 3221–22, 3232, 3238, 3241–42

Civil War (U.S.) — Navies
IJ: 9279, 9290

Civil War (U.S.) — Poetry
IJ: 4756

Civil War (U.S.) — Prisons
IJ: 9280

Civil War (U.S.) — Songs
IJ: 7479

IJ = Upper Elementary/Lower Middle School; J = Middle School/Junior High; JS = Junior High/Senior High

Civil War (U.S.) — Women
IJ: 9281, 9294

Clairvoyance — Fiction
IJ: 3408

Clark, Eugenie
IJ: 6580

Clark, William
JS: 5178

Clay modeling
IJ: 13244 JS: 13241–42

Cleanliness
See Hygiene

Cleisthenes
JS: 7173

Clemenceau, Georges
JS: 7174

Clemente, Roberto
IJ: 6841–44

Cleopatra
IJ: 7085, 7762 JS: 7081–84

Cleopatra — Fiction
IJ: 2753, 2770

Clergy
IJ: 6014

Cleveland, Grover
JS: 6098

Climate
See also Weather
IJ: 12798, 12845

Climate change
IJ: 7649, 10441, 10460, 12796
JS: 10423, 10436

Clinton, Bill
IJ: 6099–101, 6103, 9491 JS: 6102,
9914

Clinton, Hillary Rodham
IJ: 6264–66

Cliques — Fiction
IJ: 1702, 2576 JS: 1302, 3701

Clocks and watches
See Time

Clones and cloning
IJ: 11202, 11482, 11491–92, 11494,
11496–97 JS: 11483, 11486, 11490,
11505, 12221

Clones and cloning — Fiction
IJ: 4321 JS: 4342

Clothing and dress
See also Costumes and costume
making; Fashion design; Shoes
IJ: 7658, 7698, 7888, 8273, 8493,
8936, 13027–28 JS: 13020, 13315,
13326, 13333, 13414

Clothing and dress — Crafts
IJ: 13430 JS: 13325

Clothing and dress — History
IJ: 8272, 13022, 13025 JS: 8881,
13026, 13318, 13321

Clowns
IJ: 5777 JS: 7529

Clowns — Fiction
JS: 1474

Clubs — Fiction
JS: 416

CNN (Cable Network News)
JS: 6755

Coaches (sports) — Careers
JS: 10921

Coal and coal mining — Fiction
IJ: 3332, 3434

Coal and coal mining — History
IJ: 9380

Coast Guard (U.S.) — Careers
IJ: 10964

Cobain, Kurt
JS: 5722

Cobalt
IJ: 12664

Coca industry — Fiction
IJ: 3025–26

Cocaine
See also Drugs and drug abuse
IJ: 11061, 11167, 11169 JS: 11082,
11109, 11131

Cochran, Jacqueline
IJ: 5145

Codes

Codes and ciphers
IJ: 9003

Codes and ciphers — Careers
J: 10887

Codes and ciphers — Fiction
IJ: 3495

Cody, Buffalo Bill
IJ: 5723

Cody, Buffalo Bill — Fiction
IJ: 3071, 3313

Coelacanths
IJ: 12530

Cold (disease)
JS: 11302

Cold War
IJ: 8110–11, 8113, 9486, 9519
JS: 8080, 8091, 8109, 9513–14

Cold War — Fiction
JS: 3450

Coleman, Bessie
IJ: 5146–48

Coleridge, Samuel Taylor
JS: 4719

Collections and collecting
IJ: 13439, 13441

**Colleges and universities —
Admissions**
JS: 10770

**Colleges and universities —
Fiction**
JS: 1200, 1572, 3671, 3958, 4224

Colombia
IJ: 8811, 8817

Colombia — History
JS: 8809

Colon cancer
JS: 11408

Colonial period (U.S.)
IJ: 6428, 8904, 9078–79, 9081,
9083–84, 9086–89, 9091–92, 9094,
9096–97, 9100–4, 9108, 9111–12,
9114, 9116–22, 9125, 9694, 10250
JS: 9106

**Colonial period (U.S.) —
Biography**
IJ: 5221, 5637, 6256, 6277, 6279,
6285, 6348, 6456, 6467 JS: 5988,
6282–83, 6351, 6380–81

**Colonial period (U.S.) —
Cookbooks**
IJ: 9092

Colonial period (U.S.) — Fiction
IJ: 2039, 3086, 3089, 3093–97,
3099–103, 3106, 3108, 3114, 3117
JS: 3091, 3104–5, 3111, 3119

**Colonial period (U.S.) —
History**
IJ: 9090, 9098–99, 9699, 9710
JS: 9105, 9123

**Colonial period (U.S.) —
Medicine**
IJ: 8948

**Colonial period (U.S.) —
Religion**
IJ: 9082

Colorado
IJ: 9572

Colorado — Fiction
IJ: 3264 JS: 1573, 1646

Colorado — History
IJ: 9582

Colorado River
IJ: 8930, 9373, 9577, 13003

Colors

Colosseum (Rome)
IJ: 7813, 7820

Coltrane, John
JS: 5724

Columbia (space shuttle)
IJ: 12165

IJ = Upper Elementary/Lower Middle School; J = Middle School/Junior High; JS = Junior High/Senior High

IJ = Upper Elementary/Lower Middle School; J = Middle School/Junior High; JS = Junior High/Senior High

IJ = Upper Elementary/Lower Middle School; J = Middle School/Junior High; JS = Junior High/Senior High

Country music — Biography
IJ: 5715, 5831 JS: 5710

Country music — History
IJ: 7454

Courage — Fiction
IJ: 3009

Courlander, Harold
JS: 5460

Courtroom trials
IJ: 9950, 9957, 9963, 9967, 9970, 9975, 9980, 9996, 9998, 10012–13, 10017, 10026, 10029–30 JS: 9951, 9953–54, 9959, 9962, 9972–73, 9976–77, 9979, 9983, 9989–90, 9993–95, 9999, 10001, 10003, 10008, 10019–21, 10024, 10034, 10092, 10097, 10633, 10635

Courts (U.S.)
IJ: 9950JS: 9960, 9965, 10000

Courts (U.S.) — History
IJ: 9968

Cousins — Fiction
IJ: 963, 1661 JS: 714, 1939

Coville, Bruce
IJ: 5461

Cowboys
IJ: 9311, 9347, 9353, 9430

Cowboys — African American
IJ: 9304

Cowboys — Biography
IJ: 5835–36

Cowboys — Fiction
IJ: 743, 1044, 1534, 3300, 3308, 3312 JS: 193, 4538

Cowboys — History
IJ: 8739

Cowgirls
IJ: 9352, 10890

Cows

Coyotes
IJ: 12412

Crack (drug)

Crack cocaine
IJ: 11061, 11167, 11169 JS: 11109

Crafts
See also specific crafts, e.g., Beads and beadwork
IJ: 7554, 7747, 7784, 7804, 7817, 8388, 8406, 8599, 8603, 8764, 8769, 12067, 13197, 13199, 13201–3, 13206–7, 13210–16, 13220–21, 13223–24, 13226, 13229–32, 13237–40, 13243, 13313–14, 13316, 13320, 13324, 13338–39, 13389, 13391–92, 13398, 13424, 13428 J: 13218 JS: 13208–9, 13222, 13225, 13228, 13241, 13317, 13323, 13326, 13408, 13411, 13413

Crafts — General
IJ: 13205

Crafts — Greece
IJ: 7779

Crafts — Historical
JS: 13236

Crafts — Rome
IJ: 7810

Crafts — Weaving
IJ: 13217

Crandall, Prudence
IJ: 6408

Crane, Stephen
IJ: 5462

Cranes — Poetry

Crazy Horse (Sioux chief)
IJ: 6267, 6269 JS: 6268

Creation — Mythology
IJ: 9761

Creationism
JS: 7604

Creative writing
J: 5081

Creative writing — Fiction
IJ: 505, 3923 JS: 3946

Creutzfeldt-Jakob disease
IJ: 11323

Crick, Francis
IJ: 6483

Crickets
IJ: 12491

Crime and criminals
IJ: 7644, 9315, 9511, 10031, 10371, 10498, 10505, 10507, 10515, 10522, 10525, 10531–32, 10538, 10543, 10553, 10559, 10573–74, 10579, 10582–83, 10588, 10594 J: 10575 JS: 9964, 10002, 10036, 10501, 10504, 10549–51, 10557, 10566–67, 10578, 10581, 10592, 10595–97, 11150, 13052

Crime and criminals — Biography
IJ: 6405, 6430, 6432

Crime and criminals — Fiction
IJ: 15, 145, 409, 1498, 1650, 1740, 1796, 2898, 2997, 3819, 4076, 4170 JS: 35, 396, 732, 835, 875, 1662, 1787, 4005, 4080

Crime and criminals — Juvenile
JS: 10000

Crime laboratories — Experiments and projects
IJ: 10527

Criminal justice
IJ: 10029, 10507, 10527 JS: 9965, 10000, 10002, 10023, 10036, 10557, 11493

Criminal justice — Fiction
JS: 3941

Criminals
See Crime and criminals

Criminals and crime — Fiction
JS: 4166

Croatian Americans — Fiction
IJ: 3399

Crocheting
IJ: 13415, 13420, 13433 JS: 13412, 13432

Cromwell, Oliver
JS: 7837, 8507

Cross-country skiing
JS: 13755, 13763

Crow, Joseph Medicine
IJ: 6270

Crow Indians — Biography
IJ: 6270

Crows — Fiction
IJ: 250

Cruise, Tom
IJ: 5727

Crusades
IJ: 7859JS: 7844, 7849

Crusades — Fiction
IJ: 1990, 2783–84 JS: 2789, 2805

Crutcher, Chris
IJ: 5464JS: 5463

Cryptograms

Cryptograms and cryptography
See Codes and ciphers
IJ: 7929

Cryptograms and cryptography — Careers
J: 10887

Cryptozoology
IJ: 13469

Cub Scouts
See Scouts and scouting

Cuba
IJ: 8789, 8793 JS: 7260, 8784, 8786, 8796–97

Cuba — Biography
IJ: 7261–63 JS: 5547–48, 5688, 7260, 7268–71

Cuba — Fiction
IJ: 59, 836 JS: 20, 3014

Cuba — Poetry
JS: 4796

Cuban Americans
See also Hispanic Americans

IJ = Upper Elementary/Lower Middle School; J = Middle School/Junior High; JS = Junior High/Senior High

IJ: 10317–18 **JS:** 10316, 10321

Cuban Americans — Biography
IJ: 5743–45

Cuban Americans — Fiction
IJ: 774, 4480 **JS:** 747, 4188

Cuban Missile Crisis
IJ: 9526 **JS:** 8081, 9500

Cubism
JS: 7396

Culpepper, Daunte
IJ: 6944

Cults
IJ: 9847–48, 9850–51, 13460
JS: 9845, 9849, 9852–54

Cults — Fiction
IJ: 459, 4181 **JS:** 407, 445, 635,
1411

Cults — History
JS: 9846

Cultural Revolution (China)
IJ: 5414 **JS:** 7296, 7324, 8292

Cultural Revolution (China) —
Fiction
IJ: 2835

Culture
IJ: 8772

Cummings, E. E.
JS: 5465

Cuna Indians — Art
IJ: 7435

Curie, Marie
IJ: 6584–85, 6587–89, 6591 **J:** 6592
JS: 6586, 6590

Curiosities
IJ: 7671, 12032, 13454, 13457,
13461, 13474–75, 13478, 13487
JS: 13465–66, 13470, 13479, 13494,
13505

Curses — Fiction
JS: 158

Curtis, Edward S.
JS: 5313

Custer, George Armstrong
IJ: 6271–72

Customs and rituals
IJ: 10682

Cycling
See also Bicycles

Cyprus
IJ: 8422

Cyrano de Bergerac — Fiction
JS: 2959

Cystic fibrosis
IJ: 11338, 11365

Czech Republic
IJ: 8430 **JS:** 8441, 8446

Czechoslovakia — Biography
JS: 5601, 7199

Czechoslovakia — Fiction
IJ: 1183

Czechoslovakia — History
IJ: 7943, 7999

D

D-Day (World War II)
IJ: 7968, 8047 **JS:** 9480

D-Day (World War II) —
Fiction
IJ: 3540

da Gama, Vasco
IJ: 5126–27, 5155–57, 8614

Dahl, Roald
IJ: 5466, 5469–70 **JS:** 5467

Dahl, Roald — Biography
JS: 5468

Dahomey
IJ: 8246

Dairying
IJ: 8246

Dakota Indians — Fiction
IJ: 3070, 3306

Dalai Lama
IJ: 7105 **JS:** 7104

Dali, Salvador
IJ: 5321

Dallas Cowboys (football team)
IJ: 13699

Dalton gang
IJ: 9315

Damadian, Raymond
IJ: 6593

Damon, Matt
IJ: 5728

Dams
IJ: 12999, 13003

Dance
See also specific types, e.g., Ballet,
Ballroom dancing
IJ: 7485, 7492 **JS:** 7482, 7487, 7489

Dance — Biography
IJ: 5235, 5686, 5736–37, 5754, 5764,
5803 **JS:** 5262

Dance — Careers
JS: 10907, 10916, 10930

Dance — Fiction
IJ: 1282, 2845 **JS:** 978, 1671, 1764

D'Angelo, Pascal
JS: 5471

Danish Americans — Biography
JS: 5583

Dante Alighieri
IJ: 5472

Danziger, Paula
IJ: 5474 **JS:** 5473

Darrow, Clarence
JS: 9990

Darwin, Charles
IJ: 6594–97, 6599–601 **JS:** 6598

Date rape
See also Rape
JS: 10408, 11148, 11818, 11823,
11825

Dating (social)
JS: 11834, 11865, 11870, 11913

Dating (social) — Fiction
IJ: 566, 707, 1461–62, 2555, 3837
JS: 495, 559, 621, 756, 1279, 1297,
1307, 1322, 1332, 1402, 1412, 1441,
1477, 1492, 1561, 1684, 1689, 1724,
1749, 3859, 3896, 4200

Dating (social) — Violence
See also Date rape
JS: 1231, 1234, 11824

Dave Matthews Band
JS: 7451

da Vinci, Leonardo
IJ: 5314, 5316–20, 7360 **JS:** 5315

da Vinci, Leonardo — Fiction
IJ: 2396

Davis, Jefferson
IJ: 6273 **JS:** 6274

Davis, Miles
IJ: 5729 **JS:** 5730

Davis, Terrell
IJ: 6945

Day, Dorothy
JS: 5982

Deaf
IJ: 11729 **JS:** 11726

Deaf — Biography
IJ: 6401, 6438

Deaf — Fiction
IJ: 299, 363, 1388, 3466, 3471

Dean, James
JS: 5731

Death
IJ: 1037, 9974, 11043, 11045, 11048,
11055, 11926, 12216 **JS:** 5008,
10497, 11035, 11037–40, 11042,
11044, 11046, 11053–54, 11056,
11350, 11427

Death — Biography
JS: 7320

Death — Customs
IJ: 7637

IJ = Upper Elementary/Lower Middle School; J = Middle School/Junior High; JS = Junior High/Senior High

Death — Fiction
IJ: 62, 175, 242, 253, 359, 371, 428, 469, 571, 590, 792, 862, 879, 892, 937, 945, 963, 973, 977, 1053, 1067, 1080, 1085, 1100, 1114, 1135, 1198, 1207, 1309, 1315, 1327–28, 1422, 1504, 1555, 1610, 1649, 2076, 3451, 3715, 4011, 4523, 4549 JS: 48, 403, 406, 413, 540, 562, 627, 644, 797, 802–3, 826, 888, 895, 954, 989, 1004, 1007, 1025, 1083, 1095, 1138, 1147, 1155, 1174, 1187–88, 1211–12, 1229, 1289, 1293, 1323, 1350–51, 1362, 1424, 1443, 1487, 1513, 1548, 1557, 1560, 1569, 1594, 1621, 1626, 1658, 1715, 1764, 2245, 2551, 3668, 3742, 4004, 4092, 4102, 4190, 4225, 4532

Death penalty
IJ: 9988, 10030–31, 10035
JS: 9971, 9978, 9981, 9985–86, 9992–93, 10027

Death Valley
IJ: 9313

de Aviles, Pedro Menendez
IJ: 9068

Decathlon — Biography
IJ: 7003

Declaration of Independence (U.S.)
IJ: 6337, 9135, 9147

Decomposition
IJ: 12216

de Coronado, Francisco Vasquez
IJ: 9075

Deer
JS: 12414

Deer — Fiction
IJ: 292–93 JS: 1621

Degas, Edgar
IJ: 7416

Degas, Edgar — Fiction
IJ: 2967

De la Hoya, Oscar
IJ: 6936

De la Renta, Oscar
IJ: 6602

de la Rocque, Marguerite — Fiction
JS: 69

Delaware (state)
IJ: 9626, 9639

Delaware (state) — History
IJ: 9099, 9122

Delaware Indians
IJ: 8961

Delhi, India
IJ: 8323

DeMallie, Howard R.
JS: 7289

Democracy
IJ: 7659, 9856 JS: 8630

Democratic Party — History
IJ: 9406, 10037

Demons — Fiction
JS: 3735

Deng Xiaoping

Denmark
IJ: 8597, 8601

Denmark — Biography
IJ: 5420

Denmark — Fiction
IJ: 3492, 3506, 3528, 3566, 3992

Denmark — Folklore
See also Scandinavia — Folklore

Denmark — History
JS: 8010

Dental care
See also Teeth
JS: 11590

Dentistry
IJ: 11591

Dentistry — History
IJ: 11449

dePaola, Tomie
IJ: 5475

De Passe, Suzanne
IJ: 6603

Deported aliens
JS: 10218

de Portola, Gaspar
IJ: 7265

Depression, Great
IJ: 8886, 8915, 8938, 9425, 9432, 9436, 9442, 9453, 9457–58, 9461 JS: 9426–27, 9439, 9443–44, 9451–52, 9454–56, 10260

Depression, Great — Fiction
IJ: 1, 234, 282, 1126, 1150, 2724, 3386, 3388–89, 3391–92, 3396, 3405, 3410–12, 3415, 3421, 3423, 3425, 3429–32, 3677 JS: 724, 3402, 3406, 3427, 3889

Depression, Great — Poetry
JS: 4774

Depression, Great —Fiction
IJ: 3414

Depression (mental state)
IJ: 11368, 11640, 11696, 11699 JS: 7318, 11199, 11239, 11422, 11627, 11631, 11647, 11650, 11653, 11662, 11666, 11681, 11686, 11697, 11927

Depression (mental state) — Fiction
IJ: 825, 1205, 1458 JS: 1016, 1155–56, 1176, 1201, 1247, 2870, 3600

Des Moines — Fiction
IJ: 3852

Desegregation
IJ: 10169 JS: 10279

Deserts
IJ: 12705–8 JS: 12704

Design

Design — Careers
JS: 10906

Designer drugs
See also Drugs and drug abuse
JS: 11170

DesJarlait, Patrick
IJ: 5322

de Soto, Hernando
IJ: 5159 JS: 5158

Detectives
IJ: 10587

Detectives — Biography
IJ: 6448–49

Detectives — Fiction
See Mystery stories — Fiction

Devers, Gail
JS: 6997

de Zavala, Lorenzo
IJ: 6275

Diabetes
IJ: 11283, 11297, 11372, 11424
J: 11226 JS: 11317, 11380, 11393

Diabetes — Fiction
IJ: 4489 JS: 1180

Diagnostic imaging
JS: 11465

Diamonds
IJ: 12766

Diana, Princess of Wales
IJ: 7176–78

Diaries
IJ: 2964, 5648, 7293, 9214, 10789, 10807 JS: 8568, 9523

Diaries — Fiction
IJ: 246, 385, 502, 552, 556, 801, 885, 926, 1106, 1150, 1160, 1612, 2753, 2820, 2851, 2921, 2947, 2954, 3022, 3056, 3079, 3149, 3250, 3268, 3288, 3339, 3345, 3371, 3599, 3839, 3895, 3899, 4893 J: 3032 JS: 587, 628, 1089, 1105, 1385, 1455, 1573, 1672, 1692, 3486, 3805, 3807–8, 3810, 3896–97

DiCaprio, Leonardo
IJ: 5732

IJ = Upper Elementary/Lower Middle School; J = Middle School/Junior High; JS = Junior High/Senior High

IJ = Upper Elementary/Lower Middle School; J = Middle School/Junior High; JS = Junior High/Senior High

Dominican Republic — Fiction
IJ: 799

Donkeys
IJ: 266

Donner Party
IJ: 9300, 9374 JS: 9332, 9338

Donner Party — Fiction
IJ: 3304

Dorris, Michael
IJ: 5484

Douglass, Frederick
JS: 5984

Dowd, Olympia
IJ: 5735

Down syndrome
IJ: 11222, 11324, 11366

Down syndrome — Biography
IJ: 5712J: 7299

Down syndrome — Fiction
IJ: 1044, 1139, 1644

Doyle, Sir Arthur Conan
IJ: 5485JS: 5486

Dr. Seuss
IJ: 5502, 5502

Dragons
IJ: 2422, 2539

Dragons — Fiction
IJ: 1982, 1999, 2006, 2008, 2072–73, 2087, 2097, 2117, 2454, 2549, 2618, 4803 J: 2011, 2338 JS: 1866, 1944, 2005, 2007, 2284, 2356, 2540, 4350

Drake, Sir Francis
IJ: 5160–62, 8501 JS: 5163

Drake, Sir Francis — Fiction
IJ: 2894

Drama
See also Plays
IJ: 7522

Drawing and painting
See also Art; Crafts
IJ: 7358, 13337, 13339, 13342–47, 13349, 13352–53, 13355, 13357, 13360, 13365–67, 13370–73
J: 13354, 13363 JS: 7351, 13341, 13348, 13358, 13361, 13368–69

Drawing and painting — Fiction
IJ: 3500

Dreams and dreaming
IJ: 11538, 11550, 13480 JS: 11536, 11553, 11557, 11561

Dreams and dreaming — Fiction
IJ: 2110, 2267, 2463 JS: 1191, 1471

Dred Scott Case
IJ: 9194, 9222, 10010 JS: 9200, 10006

Dred Scott Case — Fiction
JS: 3173

Dress

Dress codes
JS: 10772

Drew, Charles
JS: 6604

Drinker, Edward
IJ: 6514

Drinking and driving
IJ: 11103JS: 11121, 11192

Drinking and driving — Fiction
JS: 1155

Driving — Careers
JS: 10854

Drought
JS: 12830

Droughts — Fiction
IJ: 3407

Drug testing
IJ: 11127JS: 10022, 10160, 11161

Drugs

Drugs and drug abuse
See also specific drugs, e.g., Cocaine
IJ: 11061, 11063, 11074, 11077, 11096–97, 11105, 11110, 11116, 11127, 11136–37, 11152, 11154–55, 11164–65, 11167, 11169, 11172, 11177, 11185–86, 11193, 11198
J: 11075, 11130, 11181–82
JS: 9933, 10501, 11060, 11064–68, 11070–71, 11073, 11079, 11081–84, 11086–87, 11090–91, 11094, 11098, 11100–1, 11104, 11108–9, 11113, 11115, 11119–20, 11125–26, 11128–29, 11133, 11135, 11138–39, 11141, 11144–46, 11148–51, 11156–57, 11159–61, 11166, 11170–71, 11175, 11175–76, 11178, 11187–89, 11194, 11196, 11199–200, 11623

Drugs and drug abuse — Fiction
IJ: 1256JS: 91–92, 327, 672, 737, 776, 851, 921, 1146, 1195, 1209, 1365, 1372, 1639, 1648, 1743, 1793, 2929, 3590, 4450

Drugs and drug abuse — History
IJ: 11468

Drugs and drug abuse — Legalization
JS: 11068, 11086, 11100

Drugs and drug abuse — Sports
IJ: 11095JS: 11161

Drunk driving
See Drinking and driving

Du Bois, W. E. B.
IJ: 5985JS: 5986

Ducks and geese

Ducks and geese — Fiction
JS: 249

Dunbar, Paul Laurence
IJ: 5488JS: 5487

Duncan, Isadora
IJ: 5736

Duncan, Tim
IJ: 6885–89

Dunham, Katherine
IJ: 5737

Dunkerque, Battle of
JS: 249

Dust Bowl
IJ: 9433, 9438, 9453 JS: 9452, 9462

Dust Bowl — Fiction
IJ: 3421

Duvalier, François and Jean-Claude
IJ: 7266

Dvorak, Antonin
JS: 5669

Dylan, Bob
JS: 5738–39

Dysgraphia
IJ: 5432

Dyslexia
IJ: 11634–35, 11680, 11695

Dyslexia — Biography
IJ: 5727, 5752

Dyson, Esther
IJ: 6605–6

E

E. coli bacteria
IJ: 11290

Eagles
See also Bald eagles
IJ: 12452JS: 12448

Earhart, Amelia
IJ: 5164–67

Earle, Sylvia
IJ: 6607

Earnhardt, Dale, Jr.
IJ: 6824

Earp, Wyatt
IJ: 6409

Earring making
See Jewelry making

IJ = Upper Elementary/Lower Middle School; J = Middle School/Junior High; JS = Junior High/Senior High

IJ = Upper Elementary/Lower Middle School; J = Middle School/Junior High; JS = Junior High/Senior High

IJ = Upper Elementary/Lower Middle School; J = Middle School/Junior High; JS = Junior High/Senior High

England — Fiction
IJ: 5, 130, 175, 210, 243, 318–19, 567, 1011, 1259, 1334, 1740, 2023–24, 2042, 2220, 2442, 2777, 2785, 2800, 2884–85, 2902, 2904, 2908, 2915, 2924, 2937, 2952, 2961, 2979–80, 2984, 2987, 3007, 3009–10, 3192, 3717, 3921, 4006, 4111, 4161, 4295 **JS:** 4, 294, 311, 320, 326, 343, 564, 621, 693, 1421, 1634, 1822, 2772, 2776, 2808–9, 2905, 2920, 2948, 2962, 2966, 2992, 3000, 3002, 3845, 3896, 3906, 4080, 4112, 4162, 4208–9, 4298, 5018

England — Folklore
IJ: 4864, 4882, 4887, 4890
JS: 4871, 4873–74, 4876–78, 4881

England — History
IJ: 7152, 7183, 7288, 7863, 7865, 7868, 8482–83, 8497, 8500, 8513, 8515 **JS:** 7873, 8054, 8489, 8507, 8514, 8521

England — Poetry
IJ: 4720

English language — Etymology
JS: 5066

English-only movement
JS: 10393

Enlightenment, Age of
IJ: 7895

Entertainment industry
JS: 13096

Entertainment industry — Biography
IJ: 5723, 5757, 5846–47 **JS:** 5789

Entertainment industry — Careers
IJ: 10903 JS: 10910, 10936

Entomology
IJ: 12485 JS: 12495

Entrepreneurs
IJ: 11005

Entrepreneurs — Biography
JS: 6525

Entrepreneurs — Careers
JS: 10900

Entrepreneurs — Women
IJ: 5914 JS: 10738

Environment
See Ecology and environment

Environmental Protection Agency
IJ: 9934

Environmentalists — Biography

Epidemics
IJ: 11215, 11264, 11289, 11421
JS: 11213, 11251, 11329, 11432

Epidemiology — Careers
J: 10968

Epilepsy
IJ: 11309 J: 11558 JS: 11233, 11255, 11267, 11277, 11687

Epilepsy — Fiction
JS: 1238

Erie Canal
IJ: 3154, 9143, 9619, 9622

Erie Canal — Fiction
IJ: 3163, 3174

Eritrean Americans
IJ: 10185

Erosion
IJ: 12673

Escalante, Jaime
JS: 6412

Escapes
IJ: 7682

Eskimo

Eskimos

ESP
See Extrasensory perception (ESP)

Essays
IJ: 4547 JS: 5000, 5007, 10801

Estefan, Gloria
IJ: 5742–45

Estonia
IJ: 8555 JS: 8572, 8580

Estuaries
IJ: 12750

ETA (Spain)
IJ: 8611

Ethics and ethical behavior
See also Medical ethics; Morals
JS: 11845

Ethiopia
IJ: 8146, 8151, 8155 **J:** 8177
JS: 8160

Ethiopia — Fiction
IJ: 2817

Ethiopia — Folklore
IJ: 4829

Ethiopia — History
JS: 7803

Ethnic cleansing
See also Genocide
JS: 9867

Ethnic groups
See also Immigration (U.S.); and specific ethnic groups, e.g., Irish Americans
IJ: 9615, 10189, 10220 **JS:** 8920, 10221, 10229–30, 10235

Ethnic groups — Fiction
IJ: 683, 4563

Ethnic problems

Ethnography
IJ: 7673

Ethnology — Biography
IJ: 6667

Etiquette
IJ: 11849–50, 11850–51, 11853, 11856 **JS:** 11852, 11854

Etymology
IJ: 5057

Euclid
JS: 6629

Eurasia
JS: 8544

Europe
IJ: 7675, 8424

Europe — Fiction
JS: 491

European Community
JS: 8428

Euthanasia
See also Aging; Death; Elderly persons; Right to die
IJ: 11036, 11052 **JS:** 11039, 11056, 11058, 11427

Euthanasia — Fiction
JS: 1240

Evans, Walker
IJ: 5326

Everglades
IJ: 9705, 12698

Everglades — Fiction
IJ: 40, 66, 4129

Evers, Medgar
JS: 9516

Everyday life
See also Teenagers — Everyday life
IJ: 4534

Everyday life — Fiction
JS: 358

Everyday life — Israel
IJ: 8650

Everyday life — Jordan
IJ: 8690

Everyday life — Middle Ages
IJ: 7878

Evolution
See also Scopes Trial
IJ: 6594, 6694, 7558, 7589–90, 7592, 7595, 12223 **JS:** 7591, 7597, 7602, 7604, 11503, 12222, 12225

Evolution — Biography
IJ: 6595–97, 6599–600

Evolution — Fiction
IJ: 366

IJ = Upper Elementary/Lower Middle School; J = Middle School/Junior High; JS = Junior High/Senior High

F

IJ = Upper Elementary/Lower Middle School; J = Middle School/Junior High; JS = Junior High/Senior High

IJ = Upper Elementary/Lower Middle School; J = Middle School/Junior High; JS = Junior High/Senior High

IJ = Upper Elementary/Lower Middle School; J = Middle School/Junior High; JS = Junior High/Senior High

Folklore — Anthologies
IJ: 3670, 4801, 4809, 4811–13, 4815, 4819, 4823, 4826, 4832–33, 4841–43, 4845–46, 4848, 4856, 4865, 4867, 4872, 4887–88, 4902, 4907, 4922, 4928, 13451–52 J: 4810 JS: 4802, 4827, 4855, 4861, 4871, 4876, 4920, 4926

Folklore — Biography
JS: 5460

Folklore — Boys
IJ: 4824

Folklore — Celtic
JS: 4938

Folklore — England
IJ: 4882JS: 4873, 4881

Folklore — Great Britain
IJ: 4864

Folklore — India
IJ: 9760

Folklore — Jewish
IJ: 9761

Folklore — Latin America
IJ: 4932

Folklore — Mesopotamia
JS: 4944

Folklore — Plays
IJ: 4606

Folklore — United States
JS: 4637, 4930

Folklore — Women
IJ: 4839

Fon (African people)
IJ: 4837

Food
IJ: 11299, 11609, 11717, 11723, 12256, 12262, 12271, 13273
JS: 13308

Food — Additives
IJ: 11279JS: 12251

Food — Experiments and projects
IJ: 11721

Food — Fiction
IJ: 1851, 3928

Food — History
IJ: 10734, 12261 JS: 13307

Food — Women
J: 10875

Food and Drug Administration (U.S.)
JS: 9933

Food chain
IJ: 12227

Food industry
IJ: 12263

Food industry — Careers
IJ: 10851J: 10875 JS: 10858, 10867

Food poisoning
IJ: 11382JS: 11214, 11311

Food supply
IJ: 10604, 10609

Foods
IJ: 12246, 12253, 12265

Football
IJ: 13014, 13696–99 JS: 13695, 13702

Football — Biography
IJ: 6797, 6813–14, 6816, 6939–66, 13701

Football — Coaches
IJ: 6816

Football — Fiction
IJ: 553, 4000, 4463, 4470, 4475–76, 4515, 4523 JS: 711, 1592, 4435, 4443, 4446, 4450, 4455, 4492, 4510

Football — History
IJ: 13701

Forbidden City
IJ: 8296

Force (physics)
JS: 12907

Force (physics) — Experiments and projects
IJ: 12916

Ford, Henry
IJ: 6638

Forensic anthropology
IJ: 10582JS: 6641

Forensic sciences
IJ: 10503, 10513, 10517, 10523, 10525, 10541, 10560, 10565, 10568–71, 10582, 10586–87, 10593–94, 10600 J: 10544, 10558, 10561, 10585 JS: 10499, 10509, 10539–40, 10556, 10577, 10598–99, 10957, 12078

Forensic sciences — Biography
JS: 6641

Forensic sciences — Careers
J: 10977

Forensic sciences — Experiments and projects
IJ: 10563JS: 10537, 10564

Forensic sciences — Fiction
JS: 4119

Forests and forestry
See also Rain forests
IJ: 10445, 12716, 12721, 12727, 12729

Forests and forestry — Fiction
IJ: 1864

Forgery
IJ: 10565

Forgiveness — Fiction
JS: 3418

Forrest, Albert
IJ: 6970

Fort Sumter
JS: 9248

Fortifications
IJ: 7683

Forts
IJ: 13199

Forts — Civil War (U.S.)
IJ: 9244

Fortune, Amos
IJ: 6413

Fortune telling
IJ: 13481, 13483, 13497

Fortune telling — Fiction
IJ: 436

Fossey, Dian
IJ: 6639JS: 6640

Fossils
See also Paleontology
IJ: 7553, 7557, 7563–64, 7572
JS: 7582, 7588

Fossils — Fiction
IJ: 488

Foster care
IJ: 11987JS: 12008

Foster care — Biography
JS: 7311

Foster care — Fiction
IJ: 378, 899, 918, 927, 929, 938–39, 1022, 1054, 1080, 1360, 1396, 1464, 1665, 1754–55, 2509, 2837 JS: 535, 790, 890, 984, 1089, 1497, 4209

Fourth of July

Fox, Paula
IJ: 5495

Fox, Vicente
IJ: 7267

Foxes
IJ: 12409

Foxes — Fiction
IJ: 2327

Foxes — Folklore
IJ: 4934

Fractions
IJ: 12773

France
IJ: 8449–50, 8452–53, 8456
JS: 8457, 8460

France — Biography
IJ: 5304, 5306, 5360, 7210, 7231
JS: 7174, 7222, 7232

IJ = Upper Elementary/Lower Middle School; J = Middle School/Junior High; JS = Junior High/Senior High

France — Cookbooks
IJ: 13265J: 13303

France — Fiction
IJ: 121, 1804, 2800, 2893, 2912, 2941–42, 2951, 2954, 2967, 3479 J: 2615 JS: 244, 302–3, 820, 2780, 2959, 3511

France — History
See also specific topics, e.g., French Revolution
IJ: 7881, 8009, 8459, 8461 JS: 7233, 7900, 8448

France, Diane
JS: 6641

Francis of Assisi, Saint
IJ: 7186

Frank, Anne
IJ: 7188–89, 7191–93, 8069 JS: 7187, 7194–95, 7979

Frank, Anne — Diaries
JS: 7190

Frankenstein (Fictitious character)
IJ: 13484

Franklin, Benjamin
IJ: 6276–77, 6279–80, 6284–85 JS: 6278, 6281–83

Franklin, Benjamin — Fiction
IJ: 3843

Franklin, Rosalind
IJ: 6643JS: 6642

Franklin, Sir John
IJ: 8717

Fraunces, Phoebe
JS: 6414

Frederick the Great
JS: 8472

Freedom of religion
See also Schools — Prayer

Freedom of speech
IJ: 10123, 10639 JS: 9882, 9890, 10072, 10180, 10406

Freedom of the press
JS: 9890, 9994, 10096, 10180

Freedom of the press (U.S.)
JS: 10001

Freeman, Elizabeth
JS: 5988

Freeman, Morgan
JS: 5747

Fremont, John C.
IJ: 5169, 9316 JS: 9321

French, Daniel Chester
IJ: 9610

French and Indian War
IJ: 6226, 9084, 9109

French and Indian War — Biography
IJ: 6456

French and Indian War — Fiction
IJ: 3097, 3113 JS: 3088

French language
JS: 5062

French Revolution
IJ: 7674, 8458 JS: 7222, 8451

French Revolution — Fiction
IJ: 2893

Fresno (CA) — Fiction
JS: 1686

Freud, Sigmund
IJ: 6644JS: 6645

Friendship
JS: 11834, 11909, 11920, 11936

Friendship — Fiction
IJ: 123, 139, 163, 208, 220, 232, 255, 312, 346–47, 354, 356, 368, 378–79, 383–84, 397–98, 409, 412, 414–15, 419, 450, 454–55, 457, 460–61, 464, 469, 475, 477, 479–80, 487, 494, 504, 507–8, 510, 515, 522, 526, 542–43, 554–57, 566, 568, 570–71, 575, 594, 603, 605, 612, 617, 624, 626, 630, 637, 641, 645, 662, 671, 680, 685, 703–4, 750, 839, 870, 947, 997, 1011, 1050, 1064, 1075–76, 1131–32, 1141, 1227, 1267, 1271, 1287, 1329–30, 1335, 1339, 1348, 1354, 1358–59, 1378, 1391, 1396, 1422, 1425, 1432, 1436, 1461–62, 1506, 1516–18, 1521, 1528, 1554, 1588, 1610, 1622, 1624, 1665, 1683, 1687, 1690, 1697, 1739, 1758, 1763, 1798, 1834, 2131, 2555, 2935, 3042, 3046, 3148, 3165, 3206, 3220, 3253, 3306, 3333, 3378–79, 3388, 3394–95, 3433, 3442–43, 3462, 3468, 3509–10, 3525, 3528, 3803, 3815, 3885, 3909, 3920, 3931–32, 4149, 4157, 4223, 4440, 4471, 4494, 4512, 4514 JS: 267, 349, 352, 355, 367, 375, 386, 413, 421–22, 426, 431, 439, 458, 466, 474, 489, 506, 521, 525, 538, 548, 550, 561, 565, 600, 604, 608, 632, 646–47, 660, 670, 691, 695, 720, 802, 808, 995, 1146–48, 1152, 1169, 1177, 1188, 1199, 1218, 1220, 1242, 1252, 1262, 1264, 1283, 1296–97, 1302, 1313, 1322, 1340, 1351, 1366–69, 1371, 1393, 1401–2, 1408, 1412, 1424, 1434, 1442, 1448, 1457, 1469, 1473–74, 1478, 1490, 1511, 1524–25, 1529, 1532, 1535, 1545, 1570, 1572, 1576, 1578, 1581, 1596–97, 1606, 1629–30, 1648, 1652–55, 1670–71, 1673, 1698, 1715, 1722–23, 1729, 1733, 1749–50, 1765, 1818–19, 1998, 2692, 2829, 2934, 3436, 3450, 3534, 3542, 3597, 3679, 3817, 3847, 3886, 3956, 4192, 4443, 4464, 4499

Fritz, Jean
JS: 5496–97

Frogs and toads
IJ: 12327, 12329 JS: 12328

Frogs and toads — Fiction
IJ: 324

Frogs and toads — Folklore
IJ: 4850

Frontier life (U.S.)
IJ: 5909, 6404, 9016, 9041, 9296, 9298–300, 9302, 9304–6, 9310, 9313, 9315–20, 9329, 9335, 9337, 9341–42, 9346, 9350, 9352, 9357, 9360–61, 9364–65, 9374–75 J: 9308 JS: 9307, 9314, 9321, 9325, 9328, 9332–33, 9338, 9340, 9344–45, 9349, 9351, 9362, 9366, 9368–70, 9376, 9414

Frontier life (U.S.) — African Americans
IJ: 9327JS: 9326

Frontier life (U.S.) — Biography
IJ: 5812–14, 5884, 5951, 6298, 6395, 6398, 6424, 6429–30, 6432, 6449 JS: 5116, 6391, 6396–97, 9363

Frontier life (U.S.) — Cookbooks
JS: 13269

Frontier life (U.S.) — Crafts
IJ: 13238

Frontier life (U.S.) — Fiction
IJ: 1125, 3062–63, 3065, 3102, 3113, 3166, 3193, 3249, 3253, 3256, 3260–63, 3266–67, 3270–71, 3273, 3276–81, 3283, 3285, 3289–91, 3294, 3296–97, 3299, 3301–2, 3305–6, 3309, 3311–16 J: 3293 JS: 193, 333, 520, 3248, 3251, 3254, 3287, 3292, 3298

Frontier life (U.S.) — Poetry
JS: 4788

Frontier life (U.S.) — Women
IJ: 9297, 9336, 9359

Frost, Robert
IJ: 5499JS: 5498

Fruits
IJ: 12254–55, 12257

Fry, Varian
JS: 6415

Fugitives — Fiction
JS: 1593

Fulani (African people)
JS: 8247, 8253

Fulton, Robert
IJ: 6646–47

Fung, Inez
JS: 6648

IJ = Upper Elementary/Lower Middle School; J = Middle School/Junior High; JS = Junior High/Senior High

Fungi
See specific fungi, e.g., Mushrooms
IJ: 12237, 12240

Fur trade
JS: 8719

Furman *v.* Georgia
IJ: 10030**JS:** 9993

Future
IJ: 10669

Future — Fiction
JS: 2449, 3742, 4270

G

Gac-Artigas, Alejandro
IJ: 7290

Galan, Nely
IJ: 5872

Galapagos Islands
IJ: 8846**JS:** 8804, 8828

Galapagos Islands Biosphere Reserve
JS: 8828

Galaxies

Galileo
IJ: 6650–53 **JS:** 6649

Galileo (spacecraft)
IJ: 12129

Gambling
JS: 10382, 10385, 10387, 10413, 11617, 13569

Gambling — Fiction
JS: 465, 985, 1021, 1397

Gambling — Sports
J: 13591

Game reserves — Fiction
IJ: 2416

Games
See also Picture puzzles; Puzzles; Sports; and specific games, e.g., Chess
IJ: 12073, 13520, 13532, 13566–67
J: 13692

Games — Experiments and projects
JS: 12894

Gandhi, Indira
JS: 7106

Gandhi, Mahatma
IJ: 7107–8, 7110 **JS:** 7109

Ganges River
IJ: 8308, 8312, 8322

Gangs
IJ: 10529, 10534, 10542, 10553, 10584, 10589–91 **JS:** 10500, 10518–19, 10580, 11194

Gangs — Fiction
IJ: 50, 539, 1266 **JS:** 89–90, 478, 518, 736, 784, 1170, 1265, 1349, 1374, 1666, 1726, 1818

Gangsters — Biography
IJ: 5956, 6403

Gantos, Jack
JS: 5500

Garbage
JS: 10482

Gardens and gardening
IJ: 10613, 12304, 12304, 12308
JS: 13374–75

Gardens and gardening — Fiction
IJ: 683

Garfield, James A.
IJ: 6112–13

Garibaldi, Giuseppi
JS: 7196

Garner, Eleanor
JS: 7291

Garnett, Kevin
IJ: 6891–92

Garter snakes
IJ: 12335

Garvey, Marcus
JS: 5989–92

Gases
JS: 12889

Gates, Bill
IJ: 6655–59 **JS:** 6654

Gates, Henry Louis, Jr.
JS: 6416

Gauguin, Paul
IJ: 5327

Gay men

Gay men and lesbians
See also Lesbian mothers
IJ: 11969, 12004 **JS:** 4529, 4529, 10644, 11776, 11776, 11783–84, 11784, 11784, 11791–92, 11802

Gay men and lesbians — Biography
JS: 5451

Gay men and lesbians — Fiction
IJ: 1041, 1041, 1466, 1676, 1757
JS: 493, 521, 523, 588, 782, 782, 904, 904, 1290, 1404, 1414, 1442, 1457, 1503, 1510, 1526, 1553, 1572, 1630, 1648, 1667, 1704, 1715, 1719, 1727, 1750, 2324, 3436, 3569, 3569, 4445

Gay rights
JS: 10075, 10116, 10152

Gay rights — United States
JS: 10118

Gay youth
JS: 4529, 11776, 11802

Gay youth — Fiction
JS: 1414, 1503, 1704, 1727, 4445

Gaza Strip (Israel)
JS: 8667

Gbaya (African people)
JS: 8145

Geckos
IJ: 12573

Geeks — Fiction
JS: 533

Geese
See Ducks and geese

Gehrig, Lou
IJ: 6845

Gehry, Frank
JS: 5328

Geisel, Theodor
JS: 5501

Gems
IJ: 12765, 12770

Gems — Collecting
IJ: 13442

Gender roles
See also Sex roles
JS: 10646

Gene therapy

Genealogy
IJ: 11955, 12013, 13227 **JS:** 10334, 10351

Generals (U.S.) — Biography
JS: 5957

Genetic engineering
See also Clones and cloning
IJ: 11482, 11489, 11491 **JS:** 11352, 11481, 11483, 11490, 11502, 11506–7, 12221

Genetic engineering — Fiction
IJ: 4396**JS:** 4075

Genetic engineering — Foods
IJ: 12262

Genetic screening
IJ: 11480

Genetics
IJ: 11476–77, 11479, 11482, 11484, 11487, 11492, 11495, 11501, 12262
JS: 11351–52, 11478, 11481, 11483, 11486, 11488, 11502–4, 11506, 12221

IJ = Upper Elementary/Lower Middle School; J = Middle School/Junior High; JS = Junior High/Senior High

Genetics — Biography
IJ: 6699, 6709, 6711 JS: 6642, 6698, 6700

Genetics — Fiction
JS: 4073

Genghis Khan
IJ: 7111, 8271 JS: 7112–13

Genocide
See also Ethnic cleansing
J: 9873JS: 8161, 9863, 9866, 9877

Geography
IJ: 7545, 7660, 7677 J: 7692
JS: 7662

Geography — Experiments and projects
IJ: 7532

Geography — Poetry
IJ: 4673

Geology
See also Rocks and minerals
IJ: 7655, 12172, 12179, 12670, 12672–74, 12677, 12681, 12695, 12760, 12762, 12769, 13464
JS: 12678, 12680

Geology — Experiments and projects
IJ: 12671, 12679 J: 12683

Georgia (former Soviet Republic)
IJ: 8556JS: 8581

Georgia (state)
IJ: 9708, 9720

Georgia (state) — Fiction
IJ: 1306

Georgia Colony
IJ: 9699

Geothermal resources
JS: 12922

German Americans
IJ: 10339, 10354, 10361 JS: 10338

German Americans — Fiction
IJ: 3338

Germany
See also Holocaust
IJ: 8425, 8467–68, 8475, 8477, 8578
JS: 8469

Germany — Biography
IJ: 7206JS: 7202, 7207, 7229

Germany — Cookbooks
J: 13291

Germany — Fiction
IJ: 1192, 2791, 2798, 2935, 3008, 3549, 3578 JS: 1601, 2974, 3542, 3553

Germany — Folklore
IJ: 4865–66

Germany — History
IJ: 7203, 7970, 8015, 8051, 8067
JS: 7205, 7950, 7955, 7973, 7983–84, 7989, 8006, 8465–66, 8470, 8472–73, 10338

Germs
See also Bacteria

Geronimo
IJ: 6286–88

Geronimo — Fiction
JS: 3055

Gershwin, George
IJ: 5670

Getty, John Paul
JS: 6660

Getty Museum (Los Angeles)
IJ: 9677

Gettysburg, Battle of
IJ: 9236, 9269–70 JS: 9261, 9291

Gettysburg Address
IJ: 9257, 9276

Ghana
IJ: 8231–33, 8235, 8834

Ghana — Biography
IJ: 7323

Ghettos — World War II

Ghosts
See also Haunted houses
IJ: 57, 792, 1980, 2155, 3611, 3626, 3662, 3678, 3710, 3732, 3781, 13462, 13480, 13499 JS: 13491, 13510

Ghosts — Fiction
IJ: 1141, 1709, 2194, 2218, 2290, 3604, 3610, 3612, 3615–16, 3629, 3631, 3637, 3639, 3652, 3659, 3663–64, 3692, 3698, 3700, 3703–4, 3716–17, 3724–25, 3746, 3752, 3760, 3763–65, 3771, 3780, 3784, 3787, 3939–40, 4016, 4069, 4495, 4925
J: 3754 JS: 1004, 1454, 2079, 2395, 3623, 3625, 3630, 3638, 3654, 3667–69, 3688, 3693, 3706, 3751, 3753, 3759, 3783, 3786, 4589

Ghosts — Folklore
IJ: 3670, 4928–29 JS: 4918

Ghosts — Poetry
IJ: 4711

Ghosts — Short stories
IJ: 3675

Giacometti, Alberto
IJ: 5329

Giant pandas
IJ: 12425JS: 12426, 12426

Gibson, Althea
JS: 6990

Gibson, Josh
IJ: 6847JS: 6846

Gideon v. Wainwright
JS: 9976

Giff, Patricia Reilly
IJ: 5503

Gifted children
JS: 11857

Gilbreth family
JS: 5891

Gillespie, Dizzy
JS: 5748

Giovanni, Nikki
JS: 5504

Girl Scouts of America

Girls — Fiction
JS: 496, 1459–60

Girls — Grooming
IJ: 11518

Giuliani, Rudolph W.
IJ: 6289

Glacier National Park — Fiction
IJ: 4130

Glaciers and icebergs
IJ: 12697

Gladiators (Rome)
IJ: 7814JS: 7827

Glass making
JS: 7436

Glasses
IJ: 11601

Glenn, John
IJ: 6290–92, 12123

Glenn, Mike
IJ: 13635

Global warming
See also Ecology and environment
IJ: 8870, 10431–32, 10444, 10446, 10448, 10453, 10455, 12796, 12798, 12847 JS: 10423–24, 10434, 10442, 10458, 10464, 10831

Global warming — Fiction
JS: 1904

Globe Theatre (London)
IJ: 5591, 7349 JS: 5038

Globe Theatre (London) — Fiction
IJ: 2892

Globes
See Maps and globes

Goats
IJ: 12248

Goats — Fiction
IJ: 492

God — Fiction
IJ: 596

IJ = Upper Elementary/Lower Middle School; J = Middle School/Junior High; JS = Junior High/Senior High

IJ = Upper Elementary/Lower Middle School; J = Middle School/Junior High; JS = Junior High/Senior High

Great Lakes

Great Plains

Great Wall (China)
IJ: 7348, 8284, 8295

Great Zimbabwe
JS: 8156

Greece
IJ: 8522–24, 8526

Greece — Ancient

Greece — Architecture
JS: 7801

Greece — Art
IJ: 7387, 7390, 7782 JS: 7801

Greece — Biography
IJ: 7151, 7244 JS: 7145

Greece — Christmas
J: 9795

Greece — Cookbooks
J: 13283, 13302

Greece — Crafts
IJ: 7779, 7784

Greece — Fiction
IJ: 1785, 2392, 2889 JS: 2765,
2769, 4192

Greece — History
IJ: 7332–33, 7342, 7344, 7346, 7390,
7708, 7779–82, 7784–88, 7796, 7799
J: 7783 JS: 7173, 7245, 7247,
7789–95, 7797–98, 7800–1

Greece — Mythology
See also Mythology — Classical
IJ: 2392, 2489, 2693, 4969, 4977–80,
4982, 4985, 7787, 13489 JS: 4948,
4963–64, 4967–68, 4970–76

Greece — Mythology — Fiction
IJ: 2490, 3812, 3907–8 JS: 2058

Greek Americans
IJ: 10344

Greene, Nathanael
IJ: 6293

Greenhouse effect
IJ: 10453

Greenland — Fiction
IJ: 2227, 2452

Greenpeace
IJ: 9860, 10449, 10459

Gretzky, Wayne
IJ: 6973

Grey, Lady Jane — Fiction
IJ: 2984

Grief
JS: 11041, 11050, 11944

Grief — Biography
JS: 7320

Grief — Fiction
IJ: 862, 963, 977, 1080, 1364
JS: 48, 516, 840, 888, 954, 984,
1063, 1090, 1156, 1214, 1235, 1250,
1818

Grief — Poetry
IJ: 4666

Grimberg, Tina
JS: 7292

Grimke, Sarah and Angelina
IJ: 5994

Grimm brothers
IJ: 5505

Grinkov, Daria
IJ: 6971

Grizzly bears
IJ: 12383JS: 12391

Grizzly bears — Fiction
IJ: 240, 4130

Grooming
See also Cosmetics
IJ: 11508, 11517, 11604 J: 11510

Ground Zero (New York City)
IJ: 10708

Grove, Andrew
JS: 6670

Growing up
See also Adolescence; Coming of
age; Personal problems
JS: 11835

Growing up — Fiction
IJ: 208, 462, 612, 1278, 1425, 1584,
1688, 1699, 2850, 3470, 3874,
3876–77, 3881 JS: 161, 1284, 1310,
1435, 1480, 1587, 1752

Guam — Fiction
JS: 957

Guatemala
IJ: 8750JS: 8742, 8756

Guatemala — Biography
IJ: 7274, 8759 JS: 7273, 7275–76

Guatemala — Fiction
JS: 1773, 3038

Guevara, Che
JS: 7268–71

Guide dogs
IJ: 12574

Guide dogs — Fiction
JS: 536

Guilt — Fiction
JS: 560, 1424

Guitars
JS: 7464

Guitars — Biography
JS: 5758

Gulf Coast (U.S.)
JS: 9712

Gulf War

Gulf War (1991)
IJ: 6359, 8089, 8094, 8097, 8100,
8102, 10065, 13175 JS: 8104, 8115,
13189

Gulf War (1991) — Biography
IJ: 6367JS: 6355

Gun control
IJ: 9895, 10410 JS: 10378, 10395,
10398, 10484, 10486, 10566

Guns
IJ: 10590J: 10544 JS: 10414,
10484, 10502, 10566, 11149

Guns — Fiction
JS: 1560

Guns — Schools
JS: 10486

Gutenberg, Johann
IJ: 6671

Guthrie, Woody
JS: 5671–72

Guyana
IJ: 8823

Gymnastics
IJ: 13703

Gymnastics — Biography
IJ: 6789, 6809, 6967–68

Gynecology
JS: 11472, 11775

Gypsies
JS: 10234

Gypsies — Fiction
IJ: 2915, 3378

H

Hackers (computers)
IJ: 13053

Hackers (computers) — Fiction
JS: 638

Haida Indians
IJ: 8962

Haiku
IJ: 4651J: 4675

Hair — Crafts
IJ: 13314

Haiti
IJ: 8787, 8800 JS: 8799

Haiti — Biography
IJ: 7266

Haiti — Fiction
IJ: 3022JS: 1816, 3048

IJ = Upper Elementary/Lower Middle School; J = Middle School/Junior High; JS = Junior High/Senior High

IJ = Upper Elementary/Lower Middle School; J = Middle School/Junior High; JS = Junior High/Senior High

IJ = Upper Elementary/Lower Middle School; J = Middle School/Junior High; JS = Junior High/Senior High

IJ = Upper Elementary/Lower Middle School; J = Middle School/Junior High; JS = Junior High/Senior High

Hopi Indians
IJ: 10333

Hopkins, Lee Bennett
IJ: 5517

Hopper, Edward
IJ: 5331–33

Hornaday, William
IJ: 12373

Horner, Jack
IJ: 7579

Horowitz, Anthony
IJ: 5518

Horror stories

Horror stories — Fiction
IJ: 338, 2564, 2629, 3618–20, 3627, 3634, 3648, 3672–73, 3689, 3728–30, 3741, 3777, 3779, 3787, 4111, 4530 JS: 327, 1936, 2671, 2705, 3614, 3628, 3633, 3635, 3650, 3657–58, 3661, 3669, 3684–85, 3702, 3708, 3711–12, 3714, 3731, 3734–35, 3743, 3759, 3766, 3776, 3788, 4884

Horror stories — Folklore
JS: 4920

Horror stories — History and criticism
JS: 5012

Horse racing
IJ: 13717–18

Horse racing — Biography
IJ: 6799

Horse racing — Fiction
IJ: 234, 260, 3217

Horseback riding
IJ: 12612–13, 13712–13, 13716

Horseback riding — Biography
IJ: 7016

Horseback riding — Fiction
IJ: 263, 640 JS: 493

Horses
See also Barbaro (race horse)
IJ: 12372, 12604–14, 12616, 13713–15 J: 12603 JS: 12615

Horses — Art
JS: 7375

Horses — Careers
IJ: 10852

Horses — Fiction
IJ: 231–33, 235–36, 239, 242, 252, 258, 260–61, 263, 278, 288–89, 291, 295–97, 1072, 1534, 1879, 2749, 2933, 3216, 3340, 3482, 3752, 3844, 4539 JS: 93, 125, 286, 290, 294, 2761, 3076, 3287, 3383, 4023

Horses — Short stories
IJ: 234, 4572

Hospitals
IJ: 11459

Hospitals — Fiction
IJ: 384, 1185

Hospitals — History
IJ: 11468

Hostages
JS: 10547, 10704

Hot-air balloons

Hotels — Fiction
JS: 490

Houdini, Harry
IJ: 6425–27

Houdini, Harry — Fiction
IJ: 2645, 4063

House of Representatives (U.S.)
See also Congress (U.S.);
Government (U.S.)
JS: 9939

Houses
See also Building and construction
IJ: 12998, 13446

Houses — History
IJ: 7329

Houston, Sam
IJ: 6301–2

Houston, Whitney
IJ: 5767

Houston (TX) — Fiction
JS: 1745

Houston Rockets (basketball team)
IJ: 13641

Howard, Juwan
IJ: 6895–96

Howard, Ron
JS: 5768

Hubble, Edwin
IJ: 6678–80

Hubble space telescope
IJ: 12099 JS: 12167

Hübener, Helmuth — Fiction
JS: 3490

Hudson, Henry
IJ: 5175

Hudson, Henry — Fiction
IJ: 3084

Hudson River
IJ: 9643

Huerta, Dolores
IJ: 5999–6000

Hughes, Langston
JS: 5519–23

Hull House
IJ: 9559

Human-animal relationships
JS: 12311

Human body
See also specific parts and systems of the human body, e.g., Circulatory system
IJ: 11463, 11522, 11525–26, 11533–34, 11540–42 JS: 11530, 11537, 13348

Human body — Experiments and projects
IJ: 11527, 11539, 11543

Human development and behavior
JS: 11547, 11831

Human rights
See also Civil rights
IJ: 10107, 10130 J: 7938 JS: 5922, 10073, 10086, 10155, 10719

Human rights — Biography
IJ: 7047, 7241 JS: 7070, 7273, 7275–76

Human rights — Fiction
IJ: 2818

Humanitarians — Biography
IJ: 7133–34, 7136, 7251 JS: 7138, 7253

Hummingbirds
IJ: 12427

Humor and satire
See also Wit and humor
IJ: 13631 JS: 4996, 5007, 13043, 13548

Humorous poetry

Humorous stories — Fiction
IJ: 10, 57, 109, 288, 357, 374, 428, 442–43, 473, 476, 512, 551, 553, 613, 810, 864, 893, 913, 1002, 1337, 1391, 1507, 1521, 1650, 1693, 1832, 1856, 2060, 2251, 2456, 2597, 2718–19, 2721, 2741, 2777, 2904, 3027, 3264, 3364, 3489, 3660, 3717, 3790–96, 3798–99, 3802, 3811, 3813, 3815–16, 3818–20, 3822–23, 3826, 3828–35, 3837, 3839–40, 3843–44, 3849–55, 3857–58, 3860–61, 3865, 3867, 3870–72, 3874–82, 3884, 3887, 3890–93, 3895, 3899–900, 3902–4, 3907–9, 3912, 3914–21, 3923–25, 3928, 3931–32, 3944, 4071, 4177, 4343, 4380–81, 4475, 4523, 4807–8 JS: 341, 352, 506, 527, 577, 602, 628, 1370, 1467, 1489, 1512, 1598, 1713, 3789, 3797, 3800–1, 3804, 3807–8, 3810, 3817, 3824–25, 3827, 3836, 3838, 3841–42, 3845–48, 3856, 3859, 3862–64, 3869, 3873, 3886, 3888–89, 3894, 3896–98, 3901, 3905–6, 3910–11, 3922, 3926–27, 3929–30, 3933, 4207, 4231

Hundred Years War
IJ: 7209

IJ = Upper Elementary/Lower Middle School; J = Middle School/Junior High; JS = Junior High/Senior High

Hungarian Americans —
Fiction
IJ: 3438

Hungary
IJ: 7251, 8436

Hungary — Cookbooks
J: 13270

Hungary — Fiction
JS: 2993, 3499

Hungary — Folklore
IJ: 4872

Hunger
See also Poverty
JS: 10608

Hunger — Africa
IJ: 8126

Hunter, Clementine
JS: 5334

Hunters and hunting
IJ: 13533

Hunters and hunting — Fiction
IJ: 1731 JS: 1187

Huron Indians
IJ: 8963

Hurrican Katrina
JS: 10433

Hurricane Andrew
IJ: 12814, 12820

Hurricane Katrina
IJ: 12816–17, 12823 JS: 12819,
12824

Hurricane Katrina — Fiction
JS: 221

Hurricane Mitch — Fiction
IJ: 218

Hurricanes
IJ: 12813, 12818, 12820 JS: 12806

Hurricanes — Fiction
IJ: 62, 171, 411, 3158, 3343

Hurston, Zora Neale
IJ: 5524 JS: 5525–28

Hussein, Saddam
IJ: 7115, 7117 JS: 7116, 7118, 9540

Hutchinson, Anne
IJ: 6428

Hutu (African people)
IJ: 8182

Hydrogen
IJ: 12629, 12639

Hydrothermal vents
IJ: 12875

Hygiene
IJ: 11517, 11605 J: 11510
JS: 11032, 11940

Hyperactivity — Fiction
IJ: 1165, 1167

━━━━━━━━━━

I

I Know Why the Caged Bird
Sings — Criticism
JS: 5022

Ibo (African people)
JS: 8255

Ice — Poetry
IJ: 4793

Ice ages
IJ: 7599 JS: 7588

Ice climbing
IJ: 13560, 13592, 13684

Ice cream
IJ: 12267

Ice hockey
IJ: 13704, 13706–10 JS: 13731

Ice hockey — Biography
IJ: 6973, 6978–81 JS: 6977

Ice hockey — Fiction
IJ: 4426, 4428–30, 4453, 4459, 4489,
4508 JS: 4462

Ice hockey — Women
IJ: 13711

Ice skating
IJ: 13719

Ice skating — Biography
IJ: 6803, 6808, 6969, 6971–72,
6974–75, 6982–83 JS: 6976

Ice skating — Fiction
IJ: 4472 JS: 390, 499, 1617

Icebergs

Iceland
IJ: 8602, 8610

Idaho
IJ: 9579, 9665

Idaho — Fiction
IJ: 1542, 3860 JS: 867

Idar, Jovita
IJ: 6001

Identity (psychology) — Fiction
IJ: 1413 JS: 576, 739, 1005, 1420,
3959

Iditarod (Junior)
IJ: 13573

Iditarod Sled Dog Race (AK)
IJ: 7017, 13525

Iditarod Sled Dog Race (AK) —
Fiction
IJ: 159

Igbo (African people)
JS: 8258

Igloos
IJ: 8877

Iliad (mythology)
IJ: 4982, 4987

Illegal aliens
IJ: 10196 JS: 10192, 10203

Illegal aliens — Fiction
IJ: 1792 JS: 1620, 1771, 1777, 1815

Illinois
IJ: 9553, 9555–56

Illinois — History
IJ: 9223, 9551, 9570

Illiteracy
JS: 11997

Illiteracy — Fiction
IJ: 4432 JS: 418

Illness
See Diseases and illness
IJ: 11418

Illustrators
IJ: 7353

Illustrators — Biography
IJ: 5590

Imaginary animals — Fiction
IJ: 1843, 2166, 2169, 2251, 2273,
2633, 3830, 3843–44, 4057, 4299

Imaginary languages
JS: 7495

Immigration
IJ: 8728 JS: 10197, 10202, 10213,
10218

Immigration — Fiction
IJ: 671 JS: 1265, 2709, 3011, 3563

Immigration (Canada)
IJ: 8733

Immigration (Canada) —
Fiction
IJ: 415

Immigration (U.S.)
See also Ethnic groups
IJ: 5503, 7322, 8358, 8481, 8492,
8787, 8791, 8924, 9615, 9634, 9944,
10181, 10183, 10185, 10189,
10193–94, 10196, 10204, 10207,
10212, 10238, 10287, 10289, 10292,
10304, 10309, 10320, 10323, 10327,
10335, 10339, 10343–44, 10347–48,
10352, 10354, 10356, 10360–61
J: 10198 JS: 8159, 8327, 8659,
8742, 8766, 9599, 9864, 10182,
10186–88, 10190–92, 10195,
10200–1, 10203, 10205–6, 10211,
10214–16, 10231, 10298, 10300,
10307, 10321, 10341–42

IJ = Upper Elementary/Lower Middle School; J = Middle School/Junior High; JS = Junior High/Senior High

Immigration (U.S.) — Fiction
IJ: 351, 743, 774, 1792, 3147, 3182,
3321, 3332, 3338, 3342, 3359,
3361–62, 3367, 3374, 3393, 3401,
3438 JS: 77, 674, 694, 719, 1771,
3368, 3375, 3530, 4589

Immigration (U.S.) — History
IJ: 9408, 9596 J: 10315 JS: 10210,
10217

Immigration (U.S.) — Illegal
See also Illegal aliens

Immigration (U.S.) — Jews
IJ: 10325

Immigration and emigration
JS: 2917

**Immigration and emigration —
Fiction**
JS: 1811

Immune system
IJ: 11535 JS: 11253, 11265, 11401,
11523

Impeachment
JS: 9918

Imperialism
JS: 7684

Impressionism
IJ: 7382

Impressionism (art)
IJ: 4689, 5248, 7388, 7397–98

Improvisation (theater)
JS: 7519

In vitro fertilization
IJ: 11752

Inaugurations
JS: 9927

Incas
IJ: 7611, 8761, 8807–8, 8829, 8831,
8850 J: 8844 JS: 8835, 8845

Incas — Fiction
IJ: 3017

Incest
JS: 11821–22

Incest — Fiction
IJ: 1064

Indentured servants — Fiction
IJ: 3112, 3127, 3148

Independence Day (Mexico)

Independence Day (U.S.)

**Independence National
Historical Park**
IJ: 9642

India
IJ: 8312–15, 8317, 8319–20, 8322,
8324–25, 9765 JS: 8310, 8327

India — Art
IJ: 7407

India — Biography
IJ: 7098, 7108, 7110, 7133, 7135,
7137, 7305 JS: 7106, 7109, 7138

India — Cookbooks
IJ: 13275, 13284, 13286

India — Fiction
IJ: 281, 2851, 2871, 2875 JS: 665,
2832, 2867–68

India — Folklore
IJ: 4845 JS: 4847

India — History
IJ: 7107, 7717, 7719, 8273, 8316
JS: 8328

India — Religion
IJ: 9785

**Indian (Asian) Americans —
Fiction**
IJ: 986

**Indian (Asian) Americans —
Fiction**
IJ: 707 JS: 677

**Indian (Asian) Canadians —
Fiction**
IJ: 920

Indiana
IJ: 9554

Indiana — Fiction
IJ: 3387

**Indians of Central America —
Art**
IJ: 7435

**Indians of Central America —
Fiction**
JS: 1773

**Indians of Central America —
History**
IJ: 7670

Indians of North America
See also Native Americans and
specific groups, e.g., Cherokee
Indians
IJ: 9013, 9020, 9031, 9036, 9038,
9042

**Indians of North America —
Art**
IJ: 9018

**Indians of North America —
Biography**
IJ: 5996, 7011

**Indians of North America —
Fiction**
IJ: 66, 160, 752, 919, 1859, 3053–54,
3066, 3070, 3072, 3094, 3108, 3277
JS: 1773

**Indians of North America —
Folklore**
IJ: 4901–2, 4904–5, 4907

**Indians of North America —
History**
IJ: 9032, 9044, 9053

Indians of South America
JS: 8838

**Indians of South America —
Folklore**
IJ: 4933

Individualism — Fiction
JS: 1573

Indonesia
IJ: 8375, 8395, 12880

Indonesia — Cookbooks
IJ: 13301

Industrial design — Biography
IJ: 6681

Industrial Revolution
IJ: 7902, 9186, 9399 JS: 9393

**Industrial Revolution — United
States**
IJ: 8922

Industry — Biography
JS: 6572, 6660

Industry — History
IJ: 7902, 9399

Industry (U.S.) — History
IJ: 9385

Influenza
IJ: 11381

Influenza — Fiction
IJ: 3403

Influenza — History
IJ: 11273

Influenza epidemic (1918)
JS: 11213

Information handling
JS: 10787

Information Revolution
JS: 13093

Ingles, Mary Draper
IJ: 6429

Inhalants
IJ: 11152 J: 11182 JS: 11147

Injuries
JS: 11346

Inline skating
IJ: 13516, 13522, 13528, 13545
JS: 13720

Inouye, Daniel K.
JS: 6303

Insanity

Insects
See also names of specific insects,
e.g., Butterflies and moths

IJ = Upper Elementary/Lower Middle School; J = Middle School/Junior High; JS = Junior High/Senior High

IJ = Upper Elementary/Lower Middle School; J = Middle School/Junior High; JS = Junior High/Senior High

Iroquois Indians
JS: 9051

Iroquois Indians — History
IJ: 9050 **JS:** 9007

Irvin, Monte
IJ: 6849

Irving, Washington
IJ: 5529

Ishi
IJ: 8985

Islam
IJ: 7859, 9781, 9813, 9815–16
J: 10239 **JS:** 7327, 7386, 9817–22, 9824–27

Islam — Art
IJ: 7406 **JS:** 7386

Islam — Biography
IJ: 7126

Islam — Fiction
IJ: 2901

Islam — History
IJ: 9814 **JS:** 8326, 8391, 8552, 8559, 8574

Islam — Terrorism
JS: 10706

Islands
IJ: 9675

Islands — Fiction
IJ: 160, 222, 1230, 2903, 4414
JS: 68, 216, 1618, 1666

Israel
IJ: 8628, 8632, 8649–51, 8655, 8661, 8663, 8665 **JS:** 8660, 8667

Israel — Biography
IJ: 7097, 7123 **JS:** 7077, 7114, 7325

Israel — Cookbooks
J: 13248

Israel — Fiction
IJ: 1623, 1772, 1798 **JS:** 886, 2762

Israel — History
IJ: 8631, 8657, 8664 **JS:** 7114, 8637, 8656

Israel-U.S. relations
JS: 8652

Israeli-Arab relations
See also Arab-Israeli relations
IJ: 8653, 8669 **J:** 8668 **JS:** 8654

Israeli-Arab relations — Fiction
JS: 1819

Istanbul
IJ: 8421

Italian Americans
IJ: 10335, 10337 **JS:** 10334

Italian Americans — Biography
JS: 5471, 6633

Italian Americans — Fiction
IJ: 866, 3346, 3359, 3361, 3363, 3446

Italy
IJ: 8528–29, 8532, 8535

Italy — Biography
IJ: 5356, 5472, 6651, 7221, 7227
JS: 7196, 7226, 7230

Italy — Cookbooks
IJ: 13262, 13266, 13298 **J:** 13251
JS: 13285

Italy — Fiction
IJ: 354, 925, 1863, 2041, 2712, 2899, 3541, 4491 **JS:** 463, 1703, 2427, 2890, 2928

Italy — History
See also Roman Empire
IJ: 7360, 7885, 7891, 8534

Ive, Jonathan
IJ: 6681

Ivory Coast
IJ: 8238, 8264

Iwo Jima, Battle of
IJ: 7987

J

Jackson, Andrew
IJ: 5918, 6122–23, 9186, 9202
JS: 6124–25

Jackson, Bo
IJ: 6949–50

Jackson, Janet
IJ: 5769

Jackson, Jesse
IJ: 6003 **JS:** 6002

Jackson, Mahalia
JS: 5770

Jackson, Michael
IJ: 5771–72

Jackson, Samuel L.
IJ: 5773

Jackson, Shirley Ann
IJ: 6682

Jackson, Stonewall
IJ: 6305 **JS:** 6304

Jackson, William Henry
IJ: 5335

Jacobs, Harriet A.
IJ: 6004

Jacobsen, Ruth
JS: 7295

Jaguars
IJ: 12463 **JS:** 12399

Jamaica
IJ: 8790, 8795

Jamaica — Biography
IJ: 5799 **JS:** 5800

Jamaica — Fiction
IJ: 943 **JS:** 813

Jamaican Americans
JS: 10341

James, Jesse
IJ: 6430–32

James, LeBron
JS: 6897

James I, King of England
JS: 7208

Jamestown (VA)
IJ: 9087, 9108

Jamestown (VA) — Fiction
IJ: 3083, 3090, 3101 **JS:** 3087

Jamestown (VA) — History
IJ: 9085 **JS:** 9093

Jane Eyre **— Criticism**
JS: 5017

Janitors — Fiction
JS: 3789

Japan
IJ: 8333, 8335–36, 8340, 8344, 8346
JS: 8331, 8334, 8339, 8342–43, 8347

Japan — Art
IJ: 7409, 7411

Japan — Biography
IJ: 6874 **JS:** 6860

Japan — Cookbooks
IJ: 13306

Japan — Fiction
IJ: 485, 2640, 2710, 2848–49, 2858–59, 2861–62, 2869, 2878, 3500
JS: 2133, 2644, 2685–86, 2715, 2841–42, 2847

Japan — Folklore
IJ: 4846, 4853

Japan — History
IJ: 7716, 8272, 8332, 8341, 8345
JS: 8020, 8337

Japan — Mythology
IJ: 4947 **JS:** 4957

Japan — Religions
IJ: 9758

Japanese Americans
IJ: 9483, 10287–88, 10290, 10344
JS: 8078, 9463, 9469, 9482, 10307

Japanese Americans — Biography
IJ: 5819, 7303 **JS:** 5365, 6303

IJ = Upper Elementary/Lower Middle School; J = Middle School/Junior High; JS = Junior High/Senior High

IJ = Upper Elementary/Lower Middle School; J = Middle School/Junior High; JS = Junior High/Senior High

Journalism
IJ: 5083, 5092–93, 5104, 5107, 10789, 10808 JS: 5094–95, 5097, 7515

Journalism — Biography
IJ: 5243, 5582, 5858, 6393–94, 6739 JS: 5232, 5264, 5269, 6422, 6669, 6738

Journalism — Careers
J: 10841JS: 10872, 10889

Journalism — Fiction
IJ: 377, 448, 642–43, 4001 JS: 544, 1102, 1581, 4247

Journalism — Tabloid
JS: 5094–95

Journalism — Women
IJ: 5098JS: 6668

Journals
See also Diaries
IJ: 5086, 7290, 10807 J: 5325 JS: 10830

Journals — Fiction
IJ: 1029, 3309, 3319, 3380 JS: 2377

Joyner-Kersee, Jackie
JS: 6999

Judaism
See also Jews; Jews — History
IJ: 9735, 9783, 9830–33, 9836, 9839–40, 9842, 9844 JS: 9835, 9843

Judaism — Fiction
IJ: 3999

Judge, Oney — Fiction
JS: 3138

Judges
JS: 10007

Judicial system
IJ: 9997JS: 10007

Jujitsu
JS: 13727

Julia, Raul
IJ: 5776

Julius Caesar (play)
IJ: 4623

Juneteenth
IJ: 10681

Junior Iditarod

Junipero Serro, Father
IJ: 5214

Jupiter (planet)
IJ: 12129, 12194

Jury system
JS: 9951, 9960

Justice
JS: 9964

Justice — Fiction
IJ: 4055

Justice — Folklore
IJ: 4811

Juvenile delinquency
JS: 10595–96

Juvenile delinquency — Fiction
JS: 89–92, 951, 1535, 1700

K

Kahanamoku, Duke
IJ: 7025

Kahlo, Frida
IJ: 5337–41

Kahlo, Frida — Fiction
JS: 2119

Kahlo, Frida — Poetry
JS: 5336

Ka'iulani, Princess
IJ: 7143

Kalahari (Africa)
IJ: 8208

Kander, Lizzie
IJ: 6434

Kangaroos
IJ: 12423–24

Kansas
IJ: 9552

Kansas — Fiction
IJ: 245, 3244, 3815

Kansas — History
JS: 9226

Karan, Donna
IJ: 6688

Karate
See also Martial arts
IJ: 13723, 13725–26 JS: 13724, 13729

Karate — Fiction
IJ: 4512, 4519

Karts and karting
IJ: 13578

Karzai, Hamid
JS: 7119

Kayaks and kayaking
IJ: 9656, 13743 JS: 9652, 13742, 13744

Kazakhstan
IJ: 8562JS: 8548, 8552

Kehret, Peg
IJ: 5530

Keller, Helen
IJ: 6435, 6438 J: 6436 JS: 6437, 6439–40

Keller, Helen — Fiction
JS: 1210

Kelly, Emmett, Sr.
IJ: 5777

Kelly, Jim
IJ: 6951

Kennedy, Jacqueline
See Onassis, Jacqueline Kennedy

Kennedy, John F.
IJ: 5917, 6142–43, 6145–46, 6149, 9504, 9511 J: 6147 JS: 6144, 6148, 6150–52, 9517

Kennedy, John F., Jr.
IJ: 6153

Kennedy, Robert F.
IJ: 6314JS: 6313, 6315, 9493

Kennedy family
JS: 6141

Kent State University
IJ: 9533

Kentucky
IJ: 9689, 9698

Kentucky — Fiction
IJ: 816, 3441

Kenya
IJ: 8137–39, 8147, 8154, 8173–74, 8179–80, 8186 JS: 8143–44, 8153, 8158, 8160, 8163, 8184–85, 8187

Kenya — Biography
J: 7300JS: 5483, 8140

Kenya — Fiction
IJ: 2822

Kenya — Folklore
IJ: 4834

Kepler, Johannes
IJ: 6689

Kerr, M. E. — Criticism
JS: 5531

Kerry, John
JS: 6316

Key West (FL) — Fiction
IJ: 1363

Khamenei, Ali
JS: 7120

Kherdian, Jeron
IJ: 7297

Kidd, Jason
IJ: 6905–6

Kidnapping
IJ: 10417, 10583

Kidnapping — Fiction
IJ: 18, 78, 82, 119, 1312, 1361, 1430, 1976, 2798, 2830, 3364, 3951, 3966, 4100, 4108, 4114, 4155, 4177 JS: 140, 595, 859, 1626, 2282, 3938,

3955, 3987, 3989, 4012, 4019, 4042, 4073, 4386

Kidney diseases
JS: 11330

Kidney failure — Fiction
JS: 1204

Killer whales
IJ: 12547

Kim Il Sung
JS: 7121

Kim Jong II
JS: 7122

King, Coretta Scott
IJ: 6006–7 JS: 6008–9

King, Martin Luther, Jr.
IJ: 6011, 6013–15, 6017, 9507, 10124 J: 6016 JS: 6010, 6012, 9492, 10125

King, Stephen
JS: 5532–34

King Lear — **Adaptations**
JS: 2610

Kings and queens — Biography
IJ: 7056, 7068

Kings and queens — Fiction
IJ: 2598, 2813

Kipsigis (African people)
IJ: 8139

Kirby, Jack
IJ: 5342

Kissing — Fiction
JS: 4533

Kleckley, Elizabeth
JS: 6441

Klee, Paul
IJ: 5343

Klondike Gold Rush
IJ: 8711

Knights
See also Middle Ages
IJ: 7839, 7856, 7869, 7874

Knights — Fiction
IJ: 2793–95, 2973 JS: 2789, 3949

Knights — Folklore
IJ: 4815, 4879

Knitting
IJ: 13410, 13416–17, 13421, 13423, 13425, 13429, 13431 JS: 13418–19

Knitting — Fiction
IJ: 522, 4223 JS: 1532

Knossos (palace)
JS: 7628

Koalas
JS: 12422

Koehl, Mimi
JS: 6690

Kolbe, Saint Maximilian
IJ: 7214

Kolff, Willem
IJ: 6691

Kollek, Teddy
IJ: 7123

Kongo

Kongo (African people)
JS: 8172

Koran — Women
JS: 9773

Korea — Fiction
IJ: 2359, 2855–57 JS: 2833

Korean Americans
IJ: 10285, 10289, 11978 JS: 10301

Korean Americans — Fiction
IJ: 299, 709–10, 750, 763 JS: 558, 711, 739, 788, 2573

Korean War
IJ: 7905, 8088, 8112, 9541 JS: 8079, 8085, 8095, 9527, 9530

Korean War — Biography
JS: 7051

Korean War Veterans Memorial
IJ: 9590

Kosovo
IJ: 8429, 10360

Kossman, Nina
IJ: 7298

Kovic, Ron
JS: 6442

Ku Klux Klan
IJ: 10114

Ku Klux Klan — Fiction
IJ: 946, 3356, 3387, 3422 JS: 3404

Kurdish Americans
IJ: 10209

Kurdistan
JS: 8672

Kurds — Fiction
IJ: 8101 JS: 706

Kuwait
IJ: 8694 JS: 8688

Kwan, Michelle
IJ: 6975 JS: 6976

Kwanzaa
IJ: 10683 JS: 10676

Kyrgyzstan
JS: 8548, 8559

L

Labonte, Terry and Bobby
IJ: 6826

Labor movements
IJ: 8885 JS: 9379

Labor movements — Biography
JS: 5980, 6005, 6031

Labor problems
IJ: 5616, 9411 JS: 9390, 10758

Labor problems — Fiction
IJ: 3342 JS: 757

Labor unions
IJ: 10757 JS: 10754

Labor unions — Biography
IJ: 5979 JS: 5946

Labor unions — Fiction
IJ: 3363, 3434

Labor unions — History
IJ: 9411 JS: 10756, 10758

La Brea Tar Pits (CA)
IJ: 7583

Lacrosse
IJ: 13523, 13554 JS: 13584

Lacrosse — Fiction
IJ: 4431

LaDuke, Winona
IJ: 6018

Ladybugs
IJ: 12487

Lafayette, Marquis de
IJ: 7215–16

Lakes
IJ: 12738, 12747, 12749

Lakes (U.S.)
See Great Lakes

Lakota Indians — Fiction
IJ: 3061

Lambke, Bryan
J: 7299

Lancelot (knight)
IJ: 4886

Landers, Ann and Abigail Van Buren
IJ: 6443

Landmines
JS: 10392

Landmines — Fiction
IJ: 1802 JS: 1784

Lang, Lang
JS: 5778

Lange, Dorothea
JS: 5344

IJ = Upper Elementary/Lower Middle School; J = Middle School/Junior High; JS = Junior High/Senior High

IJ = Upper Elementary/Lower Middle School; J = Middle School/Junior High; JS = Junior High/Senior High

IJ = Upper Elementary/Lower Middle School; J = Middle School/Junior High; JS = Junior High/Senior High

Longboat, Tom
JS: 7002

Lopez, Jennifer
IJ: 5790

Lorenzo de Medici

Los Alamos (NM) — Fiction
IJ: 3449, 3525

Los Angeles — Ethnic groups
JS: 10221

Los Angeles — Fiction
IJ: 507, 702, 3442, 3475 JS: 36, 1541, 2655, 4019

Los Angeles Lakers (basketball team)
JS: 13643

Los Angeles riots
IJ: 10243

Loss
JS: 11046, 11057

Loss — Poetry
JS: 5008

Lou Gehrig's disease
JS: 11209, 11417

Lou Gehrig's disease — Fiction
IJ: 2874

Louis, Joe
IJ: 6938

Louis XIV, King of France
JS: 8448

Louisiana
IJ: 9704

Louisiana — Biography
JS: 6323

Louisiana — Fiction
IJ: 958, 4551

Louisiana — Folklore
IJ: 4924

Louisiana Purchase
IJ: 9136–37, 9188, 9354–55
JS: 9148

Love
See also Romance
JS: 5004, 11908

Love — Fiction
IJ: 3334, 3925, 4807 JS: 355, 1692, 2245, 2513, 2959

Love — Poetry
IJ: 4738–39 JS: 4660, 4684, 4789

Lovecraft, H. P.
IJ: 5542

Loving v. Virginia
JS: 9954

Lowry, Lois
IJ: 5543–44

LSD

LSD (drug)
IJ: 11137 JS: 11083, 11133

Luba (African people)
JS: 8176

Lucas, George
IJ: 5791–93

Lullabies
IJ: 7473

Luminescence
IJ: 12951

Lungs
See Respiratory system
IJ: 11592

Luo (African people)
IJ: 8138

Lusitania (ship)
IJ: 7921

Luxembourg
IJ: 8539

Lyme disease
IJ: 11248, 11385 JS: 11247, 11413

Lymphoma — Fiction
JS: 1188

Lynchings
JS: 8943

Lynx
IJ: 12403

Lyon, Maritcha Rémond
IJ: 6019

Lyon, Mary
IJ: 6020

M

Ma, Yo-Yo
IJ: 5794 JS: 5795

MacArthur, Douglas
IJ: 6324–27

Macbeth (play)
IJ: 4618 J: 4624

Macbeth (play) — Adaptations
IJ: 2578

Macbeth (play) — Criticism
IJ: 5040

Macbeth (play) — Fiction
JS: 2897

McCaffrey, Anne
JS: 5545

McCain, John
IJ: 6328, 6330 JS: 6329

McCarthy, Joseph
JS: 6331, 9494, 9501, 9522

McCarthyism
JS: 9513

McCarthyism — Fiction
JS: 1585

McClintock, Barbara
IJ: 6699, 6701 JS: 6698

Macdonald, Warren
JS: 7302

McGregor, Ewan
IJ: 5796

McGwire, Mark
IJ: 6855, 13627

Machiavelli, Niccolò
IJ: 7221

Machines and machinery
IJ: 12264 JS: 12982

Machines and machinery — History
IJ: 7729, 12983

Mackenzie River
IJ: 12741

McKinley, William
IJ: 6167

McNair, Ronald
IJ: 5185

Mad cow disease
IJ: 11359

Madagascar
IJ: 8196, 8211, 12380 JS: 8206

Madagascar — Animals
IJ: 12380

Maddux, Greg
IJ: 6856

Madison, Dolley
IJ: 6168–69

Madison, James
IJ: 6170–71 JS: 6172

Madison, James and Dolley
IJ: 6173

Madonna (singer)
JS: 5797–98

Mafia — Fiction
JS: 3454

Magazines
JS: 5090, 10794

Magee, John
IJ: 5546

Magellan, Ferdinand
IJ: 5127, 5186–88, 5190 JS: 5189

Magic and magicians
IJ: 4303, 13376, 13379–81, 13385
JS: 13378, 13383, 13463

Magic and magicians — Biography
IJ: 6426–27 JS: 5280

IJ = Upper Elementary/Lower Middle School; J = Middle School/Junior High; JS = Junior High/Senior High

Magic and magicians —
Experiments and projects
JS: 12063

Magic and magicians — Fiction
IJ: 1831, 1836, 1884, 1915, 2068,
2193, 2231–32, 2243, 2343, 2346,
2413, 2444, 2497, 2515, 3673, 3823
J: 2405 **JS:** 421, 1828–29, 1865,
1919, 1941, 1952, 1987, 2010, 2018,
2235, 2377, 2425, 2461, 2720, 2737,
3184, 3718

Magic and magicians —
Folklore
IJ: 4822

Magic tricks
IJ: 13386

Magical realism — Fiction
JS: 535

Magna Carta
JS: 8508

Magnesium
IJ: 12662

Magnetism
IJ: 12958**JS:** 12956

Magnetism — Experiments and
projects
JS: 12957

Magritte, Rene
IJ: 7418

Maine
IJ: 9605, 9611, 9636 **JS:** 12618

Maine — Fiction
IJ: 962, 971, 992, 1399, 3095, 3189,
3664 **JS:** 989, 3373

Makeup
See also Cosmetics

Malamutes — Fiction
IJ: 1107

Malawi
IJ: 8167**JS:** 8169

Malawi — Fiction
IJ: 2814

Malaysia
IJ: 8361, 8372–73, 8377, 8380

Malcolm X
IJ: 6021, 6024 **JS:** 6022–23, 6034,
9496

Mali
IJ: 8228**JS:** 8188, 8253

Mali — Fiction
IJ: 2813

Malinke (African people)
IJ: 8256

Mallory, George
IJ: 5191

Malone, Annie Turnbo
IJ: 6702

Malone, Karl
IJ: 6817

Malta
IJ: 8426

Mammals
See also specific mammals, e.g.,
Bears
IJ: 12305, 12358–59, 12361
JS: 12355

Mammals — Extinct
JS: 7588

Mammals — History
IJ: 7605

Mammals — Homes
IJ: 12353

Mammoths
IJ: 7547

Manatees
IJ: 12556**JS:** 12552

Manatees — Fiction
IJ: 3978, 4129

Mandan Indians — Fiction
JS: 3080

Mandan Indians — History
IJ: 8997

Mandela, Nelson
IJ: 7087–88 **JS:** 7089–90, 8194

Mandelbaum, Jack
J: 8070

Manganese
IJ: 12624

Manhattan Project
IJ: 13191**JS:** 13161

Manias
JS: 11694

Manitoba — Fiction
JS: 1746

Manjiro
IJ: 7303

Mankiller, Wilma
IJ: 6332

Manners
See Etiquette

Manning, Peyton
IJ: 6953–54

Manorialism
IJ: 7867,

Mantises,

Mantle, Mickey
IJ: 6857

Manufacturing
IJ: 12970, 12977, 12986 **J:** 12966

Manzano, Juan Francisco
JS: 5547

Maori (people) — Fiction
IJ: 2846**JS:** 755

Maori (people) — Folklore
JS: 4860

Maple sugar and syrup
IJ: 12259

Mapp *v.* Ohio
JS: 10020

Maps and globes
IJ: 4673, 7535–38, 7544, 9210
JS: 7539, 7543

Maps and globes — Biography
J: 6713

Maps and globes — History
IJ: 7540**JS:** 7541

Marathon (race)
JS: 13738

Marbury *v.* Madison
JS: 9973

Marching bands
IJ: 7441

Marie Antoinette
JS: 7222

Marijuana
See also Drugs and drug abuse
IJ: 11116, 11123, 11143, 11186
JS: 11069, 11080, 11132, 11159,
11176

Marin, Luis Munoz
IJ: 7272

Marine animals
See also Fish; Reptiles; and specific
animals, e.g., Sharks
IJ: 12514–15, 12519, 12555, 12865
JS: 12520

Marine biology
See also Marine life; Oceanography
IJ: 12513–14, 12519, 12860, 12875
JS: 10421, 12524, 12857

Marine biology — Biography
IJ: 6580, 6607

Marine Corps (U.S.)
IJ: 13159, 13194

Marine Corps (U.S.) — Careers
IJ: 10962, 10965

Marion, Francis
IJ: 6445

Marionettes
See Puppets and marionettes

Marketing — Careers
IJ: 10937

Markham, Beryl
JS: 5192

Marley, Bob
IJ: 5799**JS:** 5800

Marriage
See also Arranged marriages

IJ = Upper Elementary/Lower Middle School; J = Middle School/Junior High; JS = Junior High/Senior High

JS: 11913

Marriage — Fiction
IJ: 2864

Marriages

Mars (planet)
IJ: 12168**JS:** 12195

Marsh, Othniel Charles
IJ: 6514

Marshal, William
IJ: 7223

Marshall, Thurgood
IJ: 6335–36 **JS:** 6333–34

Marsupials
IJ: 12421

Martí, José J.
IJ: 5549**JS:** 5548

Martial arts
See also specific martial arts, e.g.,
Karate
IJ: 13721, 13723, 13725 **JS:** 13722,
13727–30

Martial arts — Biography
JS: 5782

Martial arts — Fiction
IJ: 1301, 2752, 2873, 4519
JS: 2573, 2646

Martians — Fiction
JS: 4407

Martin, Jesse
JS: 5193

Martin, Ricky
JS: 5801

Martinez, Maria
IJ: 5351

Martinez, Pedro
JS: 6858–59

Marx, Groucho
JS: 5802

Mary, Mother of Jesus
IJ: 9797

Mary, Queen of Scots
JS: 7224–25

Mary, Queen of Scots — Fiction
IJ: 2954**JS:** 2939

Maryland
IJ: 9703, 9711

Maryland — Fiction
IJ: 1112, 3206 **JS:** 1052

Maryland — History
IJ: 9122

Masada — Fiction
JS: 2758

Masai (African people)
IJ: 8166, 8186

**Masai (African people) —
Biography**
J: 7300

Masks and mask making
IJ: 7657, 13387

Mason-Dixon Line
IJ: 8893

Mass media
IJ: 5093, 5109, 7517, 10130, 13036
J: 11130 **JS:** 5105, 5105–6, 5108,
10048, 10632, 11844, 13096–97

Mass media — Violence
See also Violence
JS: 10632

Massachusetts
IJ: 9595, 9618

Massachusetts — Fiction
IJ: 3117, 3178, 3194, 3363
JS: 3167, 3179

Massachusetts — History
IJ: 9593**JS:** 7837

Mastodons

Materials
IJ: 12905, 12977

Mathematical puzzles

Mathematics
See also Mathematics — Puzzles;
Numbers; Puzzles; Statistics
IJ: 11014, 12773, 12779, 12782–84
JS: 12777, 12781

Mathematics — Biography
IJ: 6484, 6547, 6619, 6621–22
JS: 6490, 6508, 6548, 6623, 6629,
6649

Mathematics — Careers
IJ: 10880**JS:** 10974

**Mathematics — Experiments
and projects**
JS: 12774–75

Mathematics — Fiction
IJ: 526, 3902 **JS:** 3459

Mathematics — History
IJ: 6484, 12776

Mathematics — Puzzles
See also Puzzles
IJ: 12787–93 **JS:** 12777, 12794

Matisse, Henri
IJ: 5352–53

Matsui, Hideki
JS: 6860

Matter (physics)
IJ: 12905, 12908 **JS:** 12886, 12890

**Matter (physics) —
Experiments and projects**
JS: 12060

Mayan Indians
IJ: 7618, 7623, 7714, 8738, 8751,
8754

Mayan Indians — Biography
IJ: 7274

Mayan Indians — Fiction
IJ: 2501, 3024, 4893 **JS:** 1773,
3040, 4019

Mayan Indians — Folklore
IJ: 4896

Mayan Indians — Mythology
IJ: 2731, 4937, 4946

Mayer, Maria Goeppert
JS: 6703

Mayflower (ship)
IJ: 9058–59, 9077

Mayflower (ship) — Fiction
IJ: 3106, 3109

Mayflower Compact
IJ: 9077

Mayors — Biography
IJ: 6289

Mbundu (African people)
JS: 8215

Mbuti (African people)
JS: 8171

Mead, Margaret
IJ: 6704, 6706 **JS:** 6705

Measles
JS: 11392

Measures and measurement
IJ: 12785

**Measures and measurement —
Experiments and projects**
JS: 12775

Media — Violence

Media studies

Medical care

Medical ethics
See also Ethics and ethical behavior
IJ: 11466**JS:** 11451, 11454, 11481

Medical imaging
IJ: 11457

Medical technology
JS: 11475

Medici, Lorenzo de
IJ: 7227**JS:** 7226

Medicine
See also Diseases and illness;
Doctors
IJ: 11202, 11433, 11448, 11450,
11463, 11466, 12611 **J:** 11409
JS: 11206, 11452–53, 11458, 11460,
11465, 11471, 11475

IJ = Upper Elementary/Lower Middle School; J = Middle School/Junior High; JS = Junior High/Senior High

Medicine — Biography
IJ: 6491, 6495, 6522, 6691, 6718, 6745, 11467

Medicine — Careers
JS: 10899, 10974, 11436

Medicine — Computers
JS: 11462

Medicine — Fiction
IJ: 2894 JS: 2996

Medicine — History
IJ: 7730, 7874, 8948, 8976, 11428, 11437, 11439, 11446, 11456, 11468–70, 11474 JS: 8993, 11341, 11441, 11443

Medicine — Sports
JS: 11440

Medieval times
See Middle Ages

Mediterranean Sea
IJ: 7722

Mediterranean Sea — History
IJ: 7727

Medusa
IJ: 13489

Megan's Law
IJ: 10522

Mehndi
JS: 11521

Meitner, Lise
JS: 6707–8

Mekong River
IJ: 8270

Meltzer, Milton
JS: 5550

Melville, Herman
JS: 5551

Memoirs
IJ: 5402, 5475, 5843, 6270, 7018, 7274, 7293, 7313, 7322, 8002
J: 5325, 7299, 7315 JS: 5550, 5554, 7285–86, 7292, 7301–2, 7311, 7318, 7320–21, 7324–25, 7991, 8140, 11835, 12617–18

Memory
JS: 11859

Menchu, Rigoberta
IJ: 7274, 8759 JS: 7273, 7275–76

Mendel, Gregor
IJ: 6709, 6711 JS: 6710

Mendeleyev, Dmitri
IJ: 6712

Mendelssohn, Fanny
JS: 5679

Mengele, Josef
IJ: 7228 JS: 7229

Meningitis
IJ: 11367

Mennonites — Fiction
IJ: 1463 JS: 1292

Menominee Indians
IJ: 8965, 8996

Menstruation
See also Puberty
IJ: 11772, 11779, 11790, 11803
JS: 11795

Menstruation — Fiction
JS: 1162

Mental disorders
See Mental illness; and specific disorders, e.g., Compulsive behavior

Mental health
JS: 11622, 11646

Mental illness
See also Mental disorders; and specific disorders, e.g., Compulsive behavior
IJ: 11298, 11684 J: 11633, 11659
JS: 10036, 11618, 11623, 11626, 11631, 11644, 11646, 11652, 11663, 11682, 11685, 11685, 11691, 11694

Mental illness — Fiction
IJ: 994, 1160, 1183, 3042 JS: 381, 824, 988, 1003, 1152, 1154, 1174, 1177, 1179, 1189, 1213, 1225, 1245, 1586, 2186, 3110, 3989, 4077

Mental problems
See also Depression (mental state); Dyslexia; Epilepsy; Learning disabilities
IJ: 11029, 11635 JS: 11991

Mental problems — Biography
IJ: 6794

Mental problems — Fiction
IJ: 31, 958, 1139, 1142, 1208, 1226, 1228 JS: 1145, 1248

Mental retardation — Fiction
JS: 3355, 3666

Mercator, Gerardus
J: 6713

The Merchant of Venice — Adaptations
JS: 2611

Mercury (element)
IJ: 12666

Mercury (planet)
IJ: 12196, 12200

Merina (African people)
JS: 8206

Merlin — Fiction
IJ: 1869, 2542, 2544 JS: 1868

Mermaids and mermen — Fiction
IJ: 2023–24, 2131, 2216–17
JS: 2768

Mermaids and mermen — Folklore
JS: 4825

Mesa Verde National Park
IJ: 9056

Mesa Verde National Park — Fiction
IJ: 191

Mesopotamia
IJ: 7736, 7766, 7772–73, 12779

Mesopotamia — Folklore
JS: 4944

Mesopotamia — History
IJ: 7711, 7742, 7757 JS: 7769

Messiaen, Olivier
IJ: 5680

Metals — History
IJ: 12976

Meteorites — Fiction
IJ: 164

Meteorology
See also Weather
IJ: 12832, 12851, 12853 JS: 12171

Methadone
IJ: 11185

Methamphetamine (speed)
IJ: 11177 JS: 11073, 11125

Methamphetamine (speed) — Fiction
JS: 1793

Metric system
IJ: 12785

Mexia, Ynes
IJ: 6714

Mexican-American War
IJ: 9182–83, 9211

Mexican-American War — Biography
IJ: 7050

Mexican Americans
See also Hispanic Americans
IJ: 10310–11, 10323, 10369, 10386
JS: 10216

Mexican Americans — Biography
IJ: 5827, 5837, 5937, 6714
JS: 5457, 6341

Mexican Americans — Fiction
IJ: 675, 684, 697, 702, 765, 1020, 1198, 1688, 3316, 3425, 4058 J: 700
JS: 77, 655, 663, 667, 695, 1480–81, 1727, 4059, 4544, 4583

Mexican Americans — Folklore
IJ: 4917 JS: 4918

Mexican Americans — History
IJ: 10320

Mexicans — Fiction
IJ: 108

Mexico
IJ: 8765, 8767, 8770–71, 8774, 8776, 8779 JS: 8766, 8778

Mexico — Art
IJ: 8772 JS: 5387

Mexico — Biography
IJ: 5337, 5385, 5388, 7267, 7277–78, 7280 JS: 5368, 5389

Mexico — Cookbooks
IJ: 13267, 13298 J: 13255

Mexico — Crafts
IJ: 8764

Mexico — Fiction
IJ: 1065, 3036 JS: 65, 158, 586, 694, 3035, 3040–41, 4083

Mexico — Folklore
IJ: 4892, 4895, 4897, 4931 JS: 4935

Mexico — History
See also Aztecs
IJ: 3016, 7280, 7712, 8762, 8772–73, 8777, 8780, 9211, 10320 J: 8768
JS: 8781–82

Mexico — Holidays
IJ: 10675

Mexico — Poetry
IJ: 4797

Mexico-U.S. relations
JS: 8775

Miami Dolphins (football team)
IJ: 13697

Mice — Fiction
IJ: 2167, 2171, 3843

Michelangelo
IJ: 5354–56 JS: 7395

Michigan — Fiction
IJ: 3192, 3314 JS: 1484

Michigan — History
IJ: 9571

Microbiology
See Microscopes and microbiology

Microorganisms
IJ: 12298, 12560, 12567

Microscopes and microbiology
IJ: 12026, 12559, 12561, 12570
JS: 6729, 12562–63, 12566, 12566, 12568

Microscopes and microbiology — Biography
IJ: 6695, 6695 JS: 6732

Microscopes and microbiology — Experiments and projects
JS: 12562

Microsoft — Biography
IJ: 6655 JS: 6654

Middle Ages
See also Castles; Cathedrals; Feudalism
IJ: 7336–38, 7371, 7839, 7843, 7845, 7850–52, 7855–56, 7858–60, 7862, 7864, 7867, 7869–70, 7874, 7877–78, 7880–81, 7883–84, 7886–88, 7894, 8591, 11428, 13211, 13365
JS: 7335, 7345, 7840, 7844, 7846, 7854, 7857, 7871, 7879, 7889, 7892, 8514

Middle Ages — Biography
IJ: 7067, 7179, 7223 JS: 7167–68, 7180

Middle Ages — Cities
IJ: 7864

Middle Ages — Documents
JS: 7872

Middle Ages — Drama
IJ: 4628

Middle Ages — Fiction
IJ: 318, 1838, 2088, 2330, 2417–18, 2424, 2524, 2544, 2773, 2777–78, 2783–86, 2788, 2791, 2794–95, 2797–98, 2800–1, 2811–12, 2925, 2942, 2972, 3648 J: 2615 JS: 2772, 2775–76, 2779, 2781–82, 2789–90, 2792, 2796, 2802, 2804–6, 2808, 2974, 3002

Middle Ages — Folklore
IJ: 4879, 4885

Middle Ages — Towns
IJ: 7867

Middle Ages — Wars
JS: 7875

Middle East
See also specific countries, e.g., Israel
IJ: 8632, 8635–36 JS: 8629–30, 8634

Middle East — Biography
JS: 7077, 7094, 7116

Middle East — Crafts
IJ: 7802

Middle East — Fiction
IJ: 2963

Middle East — History
IJ: 7802, 8664

Middle East — Poetry
JS: 4799

Middle East — Women
JS: 8633

A Midsummer Night's Dream —
Adaptations
JS: 2560

A Midsummer Night's Dream —
Criticism
IJ: 5040 JS: 5041

Midwest (U.S.)
IJ: 9547, 9561

Midwest (U.S.) — Biography
IJ: 5885

Midwest (U.S.) — Fiction
IJ: 3394 JS: 344, 665, 846, 1619

Midwest (U.S.) — Floods
IJ: 12808

Midwest (U.S.) — History
IJ: 6423

Midwives — Fiction
JS: 2779

Migrant workers
IJ: 10367, 10369, 10386, 10755

Migrant workers — Fiction
IJ: 171, 697, 3036, 3420 J: 700
JS: 823, 1480–81

Migration
IJ: 7639

Mijikenda (African people)
JS: 8187

Military Academy (West Point)
See also Army (U.S.)
IJ: 9258

Military history
IJ: 8046 JS: 7647

Military history — Fiction
IJ: 3282

Military occupation — Fiction
JS: 4241

Military policy
JS: 10059

Militia movement (U.S.)
See also Neo-Nazis
JS: 10368, 10374, 10409

Militia movement (U.S.) — Fiction
JS: 144

Millay, Edna St. Vincent
JS: 5552

Miller, Arthur
JS: 5048, 5553

Miller, Norma
IJ: 5803

Miller, Reggie
IJ: 6909

Millman, Isaac
IJ: 7304

Mills
IJ: 7339, 12242

IJ = Upper Elementary/Lower Middle School; J = Middle School/Junior High; JS = Junior High/Senior High

IJ = Upper Elementary/Lower Middle School; J = Middle School/Junior High; JS = Junior High/Senior High

Morals, public

Moreno, Rita
IJ: 5807

Morgan, J. P.
JS: 6716

Morgan, Julia
JS: 5361

Mormons
IJ: 9358, 9551

Mormons — Fiction
JS: 583

Morocco
IJ: 8189, 8192

Morris, Gouvernor
IJ: 6337

Morrison, Jim
JS: 5808

Morrison, Toni
JS: 5556–59

Mosaics (crafts)
IJ: 13220

Mosaics (crafts) — History
IJ: 7695

Moscow
JS: 8549, 8560

Moses, Grandma
JS: 5362

Moses (Bible)
IJ: 9772

Mosques
JS: 7340

Moss, Randy
IJ: 6956–57

Mossi (African people)
JS: 8247, 8252

Motherhood

Mothers — Fiction
IJ: 572

Mothers and daughters
JS: 11959

Mothers and daughters — Fiction
IJ: 986

Mothers and daughters — Fiction
IJ: 464, 1046, 2874, 3408
JS: 400–2, 430, 644, 1005, 1016, 1056, 4565

Mothers and daughters — Poetry
JS: 4707

Mothers and sons — Fiction
JS: 1096

Moths
See Butterflies and moths

IJ: 12500

Motion (physics)
IJ: 12928 JS: 6721

Motion (physics) — Experiments and projects
IJ: 12916, 12919

Motion pictures
See also Animation (motion pictures)
IJ: 5324, 13094 JS: 2725, 7498, 7507–8, 7513, 10282, 10741, 13096, 13099

Motion pictures — Awards
JS: 7502

Motion pictures — Biography
IJ: 5242, 5716, 5786, 5791–93, 5804, 5848, 5850 J: 5783, 5834 JS: 5233, 5244, 5252, 5765, 5782, 5784–85, 5849, 5855

Motion pictures — Careers
IJ: 5425, 10911, 10918, 10932, 13406 JS: 7498, 7501, 7507, 10915

Motion pictures — Fiction
IJ: 1817 JS: 1469, 1513

Motion pictures — History
JS: 7496, 7500

Motion pictures — Scripts
JS: 7494, 10812

Motion pictures — Special effects
IJ: 13095 JS: 7501

Motocross
IJ: 13667

Motorbikes
IJ: 13674

Motorcycles
IJ: 13137, 13667 JS: 13599

Mount, William Sidney
IJ: 5363

Mount Everest
IJ: 7024, 13577

Mount Everest — Biography
IJ: 5191, 7022–23

Mount Rushmore National Park
IJ: 9560 JS: 9565

Mountain and rock climbing
IJ: 13560, 13568, 13577, 13585, 13684, 13686, 13688 JS: 13687

Mountain and rock climbing — Biography
IJ: 5191, 7021–24 JS: 7302

Mountain and rock climbing — Fiction
IJ: 211 JS: 195, 219

Mountain bikes
IJ: 13660, 13670–71, 13677
JS: 13664

Mountain bikes — Fiction
IJ: 4436

Mountain life — Fiction
JS: 1246

Mountain States (U.S.)

Mountaineering
See Mountain and rock climbing

Mountains
IJ: 12732–34

Mourning, Alonzo
IJ: 6912

Mouth
IJ: 11603

Moving — Fiction
IJ: 449–50, 607, 637, 730, 907–8, 1029, 1115, 1272, 1288, 1335, 1341, 1364, 1403, 1608, 1631, 1790, 1938, 2603 JS: 421, 438, 995, 1059, 1428, 1539, 1562, 1692, 1698, 1738, 1998, 3789

Mozart, Nannerl — Fiction
JS: 2965

Mozart, Wolfgang Amadeus
IJ: 5681

Mubarak, Hosni
JS: 7125

Mugabe, Robert
IJ: 7091

Muhammad
See Mohammed

Muir, John
JS: 6717

Mullin, Chris
IJ: 6913

Multiculturalism
JS: 10231, 10236, 10840

Multiculturalism — Fiction
JS: 686

Multimedia — Careers
IJ: 10996

Multiple intelligences
IJ: 10769

Multiple sclerosis
IJ: 11230, 11276, 11412

Multiple sclerosis — Fiction
JS: 1223

Mumbai
IJ: 8319

Mummies
IJ: 7603, 7615, 7617, 7621, 7624, 7633, 7636–37

Murals — History
IJ: 7352, 7378

Murder
JS: 10599

IJ = Upper Elementary/Lower Middle School; J = Middle School/Junior High; JS = Junior High/Senior High

Murder — Fiction
IJ: 609, 880, 2273, 2788, 2931, 3340, 3969, 4007 JS: 560, 1045, 1316, 1343, 1420, 1484, 2601, 3440, 3751, 3941, 3945, 4009, 4168

Murphy, Eddie
JS: 5809

Murray, Joseph E.
IJ: 6718

Murrow, Edward R.
JS: 9464

Muscles
IJ: 11578, 11583

Musculoskeletal system
IJ: 11584–88 J: 11581
JS: 11579–80, 11580

Museums
JS: 7363

Museums — Fiction
IJ: 118, 3626

Mushrooms
IJ: 12237 JS: 12236

Music
See also specific types of music, e.g., Rock music; specific instruments, e.g., Guitars
IJ: 5034, 5853, 7443–44

Music — African American
IJ: 7442

Music — Biography
IJ: 5224, 5251, 5253, 5266, 5275, 5278, 5663, 5665–66, 5676, 5682, 5693, 5704–7, 5714, 5794, 5826, 5839–40, 6447, 7317 JS: 5234, 5276, 5667, 5669, 5671–72, 5694, 5703, 5717, 5720, 5778, 5795

Music — Careers
IJ: 7437, 10922–23, 10925
JS: 10908, 10912, 10916, 10920, 10924, 10930, 10933

Music — Experiments and projects
IJ: 7467

Music — Fiction
IJ: 433, 484, 907, 1709, 1711, 1992, 2546, 3435 JS: 431, 483, 561, 589, 848, 1169, 1418, 1717, 4478

Music — History
IJ: 7438 JS: 7445

Music — Manuals
JS: 7439

Music — Poetry
JS: 4785

Music videos
IJ: 7437

Musical instruments
See also specific instruments, e.g., Guitars
IJ: 7465, 7467–68, 10922 JS: 7463

Musicals
See also Motion pictures — Musicals

Musicals — Fiction
JS: 648

Muslim Americans — Fiction
IJ: 726

Muslims
See also Islam

Muslims — Biography
JS: 6542

Muslims — Fiction
JS: 652, 693, 1783, 2642

Mussolini, Benito
JS: 7230

Mustangs (horses)
IJ: 12372

Mustangs (horses) — Fiction
IJ: 258

Mutes and mutism — Fiction
IJ: 1360, 3764, 4056

Myanmar (Burma)
IJ: 8395

Myers, Walter Dean
JS: 5560–61

Mystery stories
IJ: 2848

Mystery stories — Fiction
IJ: 9, 28–29, 49, 52, 70, 87, 112–13, 119, 130, 130, 138, 188, 201, 205, 220, 223, 296, 328, 414, 448, 508, 1884, 2127–29, 2231, 2442, 2527, 2668, 2763–64, 2849, 2881, 2885, 2945, 2957, 2980–81, 3031, 3099, 3264, 3286, 3329, 3397, 3426, 3470, 3611, 3629, 3644, 3683, 3695, 3709, 3725, 3732, 3748, 3756, 3765, 3798, 3832, 3913, 3935, 3939–40, 3942–44, 3947, 3952–53, 3957, 3961, 3967–69, 3971–72, 3974–75, 3978, 3980–81, 3983–84, 3990, 3992–94, 3997, 3999–4001, 4006, 4008, 4011, 4013, 4016, 4021, 4024–26, 4028–29, 4031–32, 4039–41, 4043–44, 4046, 4050–52, 4055–58, 4061–62, 4069, 4071, 4074, 4078–79, 4081–82, 4084–85, 4089–90, 4095, 4097, 4107, 4109, 4111, 4114–15, 4118, 4120, 4124–25, 4128–31, 4138–39, 4141–44, 4147–55, 4157, 4161, 4163–65, 4167, 4172–73, 4176, 4179–83, 4185, 4465, 4495, 4520, 5077, 7367 J: 3937 JS: 181, 311, 321–23, 339, 344–45, 452, 550, 565, 650, 1849, 2003, 2130, 2186, 2377, 2558, 2572, 2665, 2847, 2886, 2932, 3622, 3654, 3705, 3936, 3938, 3941, 3946, 3949–50, 3954, 3956, 3958, 3960, 3962, 3964–65, 3976, 3979, 3985–87, 3989, 3991, 3996, 3998, 4002–4, 4014–15, 4017–19, 4022–23, 4027, 4030, 4035–36, 4047–49,

4053–54, 4059–60, 4064, 4066–67, 4067–68, 4080, 4083, 4086–88, 4091–94, 4096, 4099, 4102–5, 4110, 4112–13, 4116–17, 4119, 4121–23, 4126–27, 4134–37, 4145–46, 4156, 4160, 4162, 4168–69, 4174–75, 4222, 4575

Mythology
See also Folklore; and as subdivision of specific countries, e.g., Greece — Mythology
IJ: 4940–43, 4947, 4951, 4953, 4955, 4961, 4966, 4978, 4993, 13489
JS: 4939, 4945, 4948, 4952, 4954, 4956, 4958, 4963

Mythology — Anthologies
IJ: 4950, 4980

Mythology — Aztecs
IJ: 2731

Mythology — Celts
JS: 4949

Mythology — Classical
IJ: 4987, 4991 JS: 2350, 4968, 4974, 4976

Mythology — Egypt
IJ: 4959

Mythology — Fiction
IJ: 2000 JS: 2765, 2767

Mythology — Greece
IJ: 2693, 4979, 4985–86 JS: 2003, 2350, 2768, 4964, 4967, 4981, 4988

Mythology — Greece — Fiction
IJ: 214, 2115, 2398–99, 2450, 2490, 3651

Mythology — Japan
JS: 4957

Mythology — Mayan Indians
IJ: 2731, 4946

Mythology — Native American
IJ: 4960

Mythology — Rome
IJ: 4984, 4992 JS: 4967, 4990

Mythology — Scandinavia
IJ: 4995 JS: 4994

N

Nader, Ralph
JS: 6338–40

Nagasaki, Japan
IJ: 7953 JS: 7985

Nail art
IJ: 13200

Naked mole rats
IJ: 12362–63

Namibia
IJ: 8199 JS: 8195, 8223

Nannies — Fiction
IJ: 374 JS: 353

Nantucket (MA) — Fiction
IJ: 3185

Napoleonic Wars
IJ: 8511

Napoleonic Wars — Fiction
IJ: 2970

Napster — Biography
IJ: 6630

Narcotics
IJ: 11097

NASA
JS: 12136

NASCAR
IJ: 6824, 6829, 13596–98, 13604

Nash, Kevin
IJ: 7028

Nast, Thomas
IJ: 5364

Natchez Trace
IJ: 9350

Natchez Trail — Fiction
IJ: 3249

Nation, Carry A.
IJ: 6446

Nation of Islam
J: 10239 JS: 10244

Nation of Islam — Biography
JS: 5987

National Association for the Advancement of Colored People (NAACP)
IJ: 10158

National debt
IJ: 9943

National Football League
JS: 13700

National Guard (U.S.) — Careers
IJ: 10956

National Institutes of Health (U.S.)
IJ: 9938

National Law Enforcement Officers Memorial (Washington, DC)
IJ: 9586

National parks (U.S.)
See also specific national parks, e.g., Yellowstone National Park

National parks (U.S.) — Fiction
IJ: 72

National security
JS: 10703

Native Americans
See also Inuit; and specific Indian tribes, e.g., Sioux Indians
IJ: 8955, 8957–58, 8962–63, 8965, 8967, 8969, 8984–85, 8996, 9000, 9002–4, 9021, 9023, 9028–30, 9034, 9046, 9048, 9052, 9055, 9069, 9302, 10332 J: 8986 JS: 8974, 8991, 9008, 9037, 9049, 13695

Native Americans — Art
IJ: 7428

Native Americans — Biography
IJ: 5211, 5330, 5351, 5484, 5889, 6263, 6267, 6269–70, 6286–88, 6332, 6353, 6370, 6375, 6407, 6451, 6459–60, 6471, 7009 JS: 5247, 5907, 6268, 6312, 6322, 6450, 6779, 7002, 7010, 9010

Native Americans — Burial grounds
JS: 7614

Native Americans — Childhood
IJ: 9034

Native Americans — Cookbooks
IJ: 9002

Native Americans — Crafts
JS: 5247

Native Americans — Fiction
IJ: 27–28, 34, 61, 126, 192, 546–47, 688, 722, 777, 1301, 1439, 1519, 3045–46, 3050, 3056–57, 3065, 3071, 3073, 3077–79, 3081–82, 3093, 3102–3, 3113, 3115, 3271, 3281, 3302, 3305, 3311, 3313, 3327, 3507, 3620, 4431, 8995 J: 770 JS: 93, 167, 333, 406, 715–16, 746, 1257, 1314, 3039, 3059–60, 3064, 3068–69, 3075–76, 3080, 3085, 3179, 3248, 3287, 3295, 4110, 4456, 4474

Native Americans — Folklore
IJ: 4900, 4903, 4910–11, 4915, 4917, 12850 JS: 4899, 4908–9, 4913–14, 4952

Native Americans — History
IJ: 3074, 7670, 8894, 8956, 8960, 8970, 8973, 8978–81, 8988, 8994, 8997–98, 9001, 9005, 9011, 9017, 9035, 9043, 9045, 9052, 9054, 9056–57, 9083, 9334 J: 7594 JS: 5313, 8712, 8983, 8992–93, 9006–7, 9009, 9012, 9019, 9022, 9024, 9033, 9040, 9051, 9065, 9309, 10345

Native Americans — Literature
IJ: 8998

Native Americans — Medicine
IJ: 8976

Native Americans — Music
IJ: 7438

Native Americans — Mythology
IJ: 4960

Native Americans — Religion
JS: 8977, 9015, 9767

Native Americans — Ships and boats
IJ: 8989

Native Americans — Treaties
IJ: 8999

Native Americans — Women
IJ: 9039 JS: 7425

Native Americans — World War II
IJ: 9003

Natural disasters
IJ: 12677, 12872 JS: 11762

Natural disasters — Fiction
JS: 4364

Natural history
See also Nature study
JS: 12068, 12857

Naturalists — Biography
IJ: 5618–19, 6571, 6663, 6667 JS: 6640, 6665–66, 6717

Nature
See also Biology; Natural history; Nature study
IJ: 7660, 9733, 12214 JS: 9620

Nature — Careers
JS: 10855

Nature — Fiction
IJ: 501

Nature study
IJ: 12215, 12305 JS: 9585, 12211

Nauvoo (IL)
IJ: 9551

Nava, Julian
JS: 6341

Navajo Arts and Crafts Enterprise (NACE)
JS: 10749

Navajo Indians
IJ: 8964, 8982, 9001, 9026, 9038, 9055 JS: 7996, 10749

Navajo Indians — Fiction
IJ: 752, 1947, 3053, 3072, 3495, 3507 JS: 93, 3067, 4018, 4156

Navajo Indians — History
IJ: 7929

Navels

Navigation
IJ: 12868

Navy (U.S.)
See also Armed forces (U.S.)

Navy (U.S.) — Biography
IJ: 6306, 6308 JS: 6307

IJ = Upper Elementary/Lower Middle School; J = Middle School/Junior High; JS = Junior High/Senior High

IJ = Upper Elementary/Lower Middle School; J = Middle School/Junior High; JS = Junior High/Senior High

IJ = Upper Elementary/Lower Middle School; J = Middle School/Junior High; JS = Junior High/Senior High

O

Nursing homes — Fiction
JS: 1088

Nutrition and diet
IJ: 11028, 11572, 11701, 11709,
11717, 11723–24, 12263, 13528
JS: 11606, 11611, 11703, 11705,
11714, 13293

**Nzingha (African queen) —
Fiction**
IJ: 2820

Oakland (CA)
IJ: 9653

Oakley, Annie
IJ: 5812–14

Oakley, Annie — Fiction
IJ: 3352

Obama, Barack
IJ: 6179–81

Obesity
IJ: 11088 JS: 11245, 11344, 11700,
11706–8, 11711

Obesity — Fiction
IJ: 477, 1499 JS: 1169, 1177, 1577,
1705, 2030

O'Brien, Dan
IJ: 7003

Observatories
JS: 12109

Obsessive-compulsive disorder
JS: 11649

**Obsessive-compulsive disorder
— Fiction**
JS: 1144, 1178

Occupational guidance
See also Vocational guidance

Occupations and work
IJ: 7480, 10953

**Occupations and work —
Fiction**
IJ: 357, 1624 JS: 1429, 4087

Oceanography
See also Marine biology; Marine
life; Underwater exploration
IJ: 12866, 12871, 12874 JS: 12854,
12856–57

Oceanography — Biography
IJ: 6527

**Oceanography — Experiments
and projects**
IJ: 12855

Oceans
See also Oceanography; Seashores;
and specific oceans, e.g., Atlantic
Ocean
IJ: 12515, 12519, 12860–61,
12864–65, 12868 JS: 12858–59,
12867

**Oceans — Experiments and
projects**
IJ: 12863

Oceans — Fiction
IJ: 197

Ochoa, Ellen
IJ: 5194–95

O'Connor, Sandra Day
IJ: 6344 JS: 6343

O'Donnell, Rosie
IJ: 5815–17

Odysseus
IJ: 4983

Odyssey (mythology)
IJ: 4987

Of Mice and Men **— Criticism**
IJ: 5033

Oglethorpe, James
IJ: 9699

Ohio
IJ: 9562, 9567

Ohio — Fiction
IJ: 934

Ohio River
IJ: 12745

Oil
IJ: 9726

Oil industry
IJ: 8092 JS: 12979

Oil industry — Biography
IJ: 6478, 6741

Oil industry — Careers
J: 11004

Oil spills
IJ: 9678

Ojibwa Indians
IJ: 8967, 9013, 9023 JS: 8987

Ojibwa Indians — Fiction
IJ: 3062–63 JS: 1314

O'Keeffe, Georgia
IJ: 5367 JS: 5366

O'Keeffe, Georgia — Fiction
IJ: 3411

Oklahoma
IJ: 9544, 9549

Oklahoma — Fiction
IJ: 282, 1115, 1439

Oklahoma — History
IJ: 9453

Oklahoma City
IJ: 10720

Oklahoma City bombing (1995)
IJ: 10720

Olajuwon, Hakeem
IJ: 6915

Olmos, Edward James
IJ: 5818

Olympic Games
IJ: 7000, 7006, 13732, 13736

Olympic Games — Biography
IJ: 6787, 6793, 6796, 6981, 7032

Olympic Games — History
IJ: 13734–35 JS: 13731, 13733

Oman
IJ: 8680

Omidyar, Pierre
IJ: 6726

O'Neal, Shaquille
IJ: 6916–17

Oneida Indians
IJ: 9028

Ontario
IJ: 8724

Ontario — Fiction
IJ: 228

Opera
JS: 7461

Opera — Biography
IJ: 5734

Opera — Plots
IJ: 7462

Operation Iraqi Freedom
IJ: 8087, 10065 JS: 8083, 8700,
8700, 9523, 9540

**Operation Iraqi Freedom —
Fiction**
JS: 3603

Oppenheimer, J. Robert
IJ: 6727 JS: 6728

Optical illusions
IJ: 13384 JS: 11596, 13377

Optics
IJ: 12947

**Oracle (computers) —
Biography**
IJ: 6627

Orangutans
JS: 12376

Orchestras
IJ: 7465–66, 10922

Oregon
IJ: 9666, 9680, 9686

IJ = Upper Elementary/Lower Middle School; J = Middle School/Junior High; JS = Junior High/Senior High

IJ = Upper Elementary/Lower Middle School; J = Middle School/Junior High; JS = Junior High/Senior High

IJ = Upper Elementary/Lower Middle School; J = Middle School/Junior High; JS = Junior High/Senior High

11939, 11941, 11983, 11990
JS: 9757, 9770, 10281, 10834, 11615, 11630, 11636, 11770, 11808, 11811, 11842–43, 11846, 11848, 11862–64, 11869, 11871–72, 11874–76, 11881, 11885, 11887, 11889, 11891, 11893, 11897, 11905, 11907, 11910–11, 11913, 11918, 11920–22, 11924, 11927, 11930–32, 11937–38, 11940, 11946

Personal guidance — African Americans
JS: 10281, 11897

Personal guidance — Boys
IJ: 11883, 11947 **JS:** 11027, 11894

Personal guidance — Fiction
JS: 1727

Personal guidance — Girls
IJ: 11851, 11861, 11873, 11878–79, 11895, 11900, 11906, 11928, 11945
J: 11914 **JS:** 11866–67, 11870, 11892, 11896, 11915, 11919, 11925, 11934–36

Personal guidance — Women
JS: 11860

Personal problems
IJ: 11917, 12007 **JS:** 11840, 11880

Personal problems — Fiction
IJ: 39, 62, 121, 228, 242, 289, 312, 412, 462, 570, 575, 613, 625, 710, 768, 825, 845, 852, 861, 884, 905, 919, 930, 973, 1030–31, 1049, 1085, 1114, 1135, 1137, 1165, 1167, 1182, 1185, 1207, 1255–56, 1266, 1268–69, 1275, 1278, 1280, 1282, 1288, 1295, 1306, 1308, 1315, 1326–28, 1330, 1333, 1337, 1339, 1341, 1346, 1353, 1375–77, 1392, 1394, 1398, 1403, 1406, 1410, 1415, 1419, 1422, 1427, 1431, 1436–37, 1439, 1447, 1449, 1451, 1458, 1464, 1475–76, 1493–96, 1504, 1509, 1518–20, 1522, 1528, 1531, 1536–37, 1542, 1555–56, 1565–66, 1582, 1613–15, 1645, 1647, 1651, 1657, 1661, 1675, 1678, 1683, 1688, 1694–96, 1709, 1716, 1718, 1721, 1731, 1747–48, 1753, 1757, 1761, 1766, 1780, 1824, 2244, 2778, 2823, 2895, 2935, 2988, 3017, 3030, 3156, 3212, 3258, 3268, 3351, 3387, 3425, 3431, 3475, 3565, 3740, 3814, 3878, 3880, 4085, 4422, 4426, 4535, 4563 **J:** 770, 1304 **JS:** 99, 183, 408, 587, 692, 699, 737, 781, 806, 835, 915, 951, 980, 1077, 1086, 1108, 1119, 1173, 1186, 1200, 1204, 1238, 1244, 1248–49, 1254, 1261, 1264, 1276, 1285, 1292–93, 1299–300, 1305, 1318–19, 1324, 1338, 1340, 1342–43, 1347, 1349–50, 1365, 1367, 1370, 1374, 1383, 1386–87, 1390, 1397, 1405, 1418, 1421, 1433, 1438, 1444, 1446, 1456, 1468, 1471, 1474, 1485–86, 1497, 1500–2, 1512, 1525, 1540–41, 1560, 1567–69, 1571, 1578,

1580, 1583, 1585, 1590, 1594, 1596, 1605, 1618–19, 1639, 1641–43, 1646, 1656, 1660, 1668, 1673, 1680, 1686, 1691, 1701, 1708, 1710, 1712–13, 1725, 1728, 1734, 1736, 1742, 1744–46, 1750, 1762, 1764, 1767, 1808, 1811, 1913, 1931, 1951, 2815, 2829, 3038, 3373, 3558, 3633, 3668, 3800, 3863, 3873, 3898, 3911, 4245, 4248, 4427, 4498–99, 4518

Personal problems — Poetry
IJ: 4743

Personality
JS: 11832

Personality disorders

Peru
IJ: 8813, 8818, 8831, 8836, 8839

Peru — Fiction
IJ: 154 **JS:** 1768

Peru — Folklore
IJ: 4934

Peruvian Indians — Fiction
JS: 1768

Peter the Great
IJ: 7235

Pets
See also specific pets, e.g., Dogs
IJ: 12580, 12591 **JS:** 12575

Pets — Detectives
JS: 12571

Petty family
IJ: 6828

Pharaohs — Fiction
IJ: 2751

Philadelphia (PA)
IJ: 9624, 9642

Philadelphia (PA) — Fiction
JS: 3120, 3128

Philadelphia (PA) — History
JS: 9162

Philanthropy — Biography
JS: 7076

Philip, King (Wampanoag chief)
IJ: 6353

Philippines
IJ: 8414, 8418

Philippines — Biography
JS: 7129

Philosophy — Biography
IJ: 7151, 7244

Phobias
IJ: 11651 **JS:** 11619, 11665, 11692

Phobias — Fiction
IJ: 1410 **JS:** 4548

Phoenix Suns (basketball team)
IJ: 13649

Phosphorus
IJ: 12625, 12657

Photography
IJ: 7373, 7421, 13402, 13404–5, 13407 **JS:** 5047, 7364–65, 7425, 8710, 10217, 12103, 13400, 13403

Photography — Biography
IJ: 5237, 5282, 5284, 5292, 5294, 5326, 5335 **JS:** 5271, 5283, 5290–91, 5293, 5313, 5344, 5583, 6608

Photography — Careers
IJ: 10901 **J:** 10931

Photography — Fiction
IJ: 1475, 3610

Photography — History
IJ: 7402, 7431, 13401 **JS:** 7399–400

Photojournalism
JS: 7365

Photojournalism — Biography
JS: 5392

Photojournalism — Fiction
JS: 348

Photosynthesis
IJ: 12239

Physical abnormalities — Fiction
IJ: 1556, 2509

Physical abuse
See also Child abuse
JS: 11963, 11977

Physical abuse — Fiction
JS: 1066, 1371, 1471

Physical disabilities
IJ: 11029, 11725, 11725, 11727–29
JS: 11730, 11991

Physical disabilities — Biography
IJ: 6794, 6833 **J:** 6436 **JS:** 6205, 6437, 6439–40, 6442

Physical disabilities — Fiction
IJ: 56, 146, 842, 1132, 1141, 1159, 1172, 1193, 1219, 1230, 1339, 2902, 3351, 3360, 3424, 4078, 4388
JS: 387, 1181, 1201, 1216, 1223, 1240, 1249, 1370, 1535, 1609, 1626, 3104, 4444

Physical disabilities — Sports
IJ: 6815

Physical fitness
See also Exercise
IJ: 11028, 11610 **JS:** 11020, 11030, 11606, 11613

Physical fitness — Careers
JS: 10907

Physical handicaps
See Physical disabilities, and specific handicaps, e.g., Deaf

---

IJ = Upper Elementary/Lower Middle School; J = Middle School/Junior High; JS = Junior High/Senior High

IJ = Upper Elementary/Lower Middle School; J = Middle School/Junior High; JS = Junior High/Senior High

IJ = Upper Elementary/Lower Middle School; J = Middle School/Junior High; JS = Junior High/Senior High

IJ = Upper Elementary/Lower Middle School; J = Middle School/Junior High; JS = Junior High/Senior High

IJ = Upper Elementary/Lower Middle School; J = Middle School/Junior High; JS = Junior High/Senior High

Rape — Fiction
IJ: 1348 JS: 708, 1153, 1261, 1263, 1670

Rasputin, Grigory
IJ: 7239

Rats
IJ: 12573

Rats — Fiction
IJ: 324, 1916, 1966, 1983, 2347

Ravens — Poetry
IJ: 4769

Rays
IJ: 12527

Reading — Fiction
IJ: 4551 JS: 4270

Reagan, Ronald
IJ: 5920, 6183–85, 9515 JS: 6186, 9508

Reality shows (TV) — Fiction
IJ: 817 JS: 498, 853, 1157, 4412

Ream, Vinnie — Fiction
JS: 3241

Recipes
See Cookbooks

Reconstruction (U.S.)
IJ: 9292, 9384–85, 9394, 9403, 9413, 9416 J: 9389 JS: 9238, 9395–96, 9407, 9419, 10259

Reconstruction (U.S.) — Fiction
IJ: 3344, 3352, 3358, 3370 JS: 3237

Reconstruction to World War I (U.S.)
See United States (1865–1914) — History

Recreation
IJ: 13197, 13553

Recreation — Careers
IJ: 10913

Recycling
See also Waste recycling
JS: 13414

Red Cross
IJ: 6388, 9858

Red Cross — Biography
J: 6385

Reece, Gabrielle
IJ: 7031

Reese, Della
IJ: 5828

Reeve, Christopher
IJ: 5830 JS: 5829

Reeves, Bass — Fiction
IJ: 3303

Reform Party (U.S.)
IJ: 10040

Reformation
IJ: 7882

Refugees
IJ: 9865, 9868, 9875, 10343, 10360
JS: 7982, 8742, 8766, 9864, 9867, 10184, 10215, 10300, 10494, 12014

Refugees — Fiction
IJ: 1782, 2844, 2877, 3574 JS: 610, 706, 1776, 1815–16

Refugees — Teenage
JS: 10296–97, 10305, 10312, 10357–58, 10364

Reggae music — Biography
JS: 5800

Reincarnation
IJ: 13458

Reincarnation — Fiction
IJ: 976, 3680 JS: 2513, 4066

Reiss, Johanna
JS: 7310

Relativity (physics)
IJ: 6618 JS: 12883

Religion
See also Prayers; and specific religions, e.g., Christianity
IJ: 7636, 7845, 7861, 7878, 9739, 9742–44, 9747, 9751–52, 9778, 9802
JS: 9736, 9741, 9745–46, 9748–49, 9759, 9766, 9768, 9771, 9775, 9779–80, 10377

Religion — Africa
JS: 9764

Religion — Biography
IJ: 6411, 7075, 7135 JS: 6417, 7164

Religion — Colonial period (U.S.)
IJ: 9082

Religion — Comparative
JS: 9741

Religion — Fiction
IJ: 892, 960, 1543, 3396, 4502
JS: 563, 1468, 1502, 1738, 3825, 4581

Religion — History
IJ: 6382, 6428, 7862, 9319 JS: 9740

Religion — Poetry
IJ: 4717 JS: 4708

Religion — Schools
IJ: 9975

Religion — United States
IJ: 8947 JS: 9740, 9878, 9897

Religious liberty
See Freedom of religion

Remarriage — Fiction
IJ: 1043

Rembert, Winfred
IJ: 5379

Rembrandt van Rijn
IJ: 5380 JS: 5381

Rembrandt van Rijn — Fiction
IJ: 2919 JS: 2900

Remington, Frederic
IJ: 5382

Renaissance
IJ: 7374, 7842, 7847, 7861, 7866, 7882, 7885, 7891, 7893, 13356
JS: 7542, 7838, 7890

Renaissance — Art
IJ: 7360 JS: 7383, 7392

Renaissance — Biography
IJ: 5314, 5316–19, 5355, 6651, 6653, 7221, 7227 JS: 5315, 7226

Renaissance — Fiction
IJ: 2943 JS: 2890, 2928, 2932

Renaissance — Science
IJ: 6582, 11437

Renaissance — Wars
JS: 7841

Rendille (African people)
IJ: 8173

Renoir, Pierre-Auguste
IJ: 5383–84

Report writing
IJ: 10786 JS: 10813, 10824

Reporters

Reproduction
See also Sex education
IJ: 11532, 11740, 11752–53
J: 11528 JS: 11734

Reproduction — Human
IJ: 11757, 11761

Reptiles
See also specific reptiles, e.g., Alligators and crocodiles
IJ: 12316, 12318, 12322, 12479, 12726 JS: 12317, 12319–20

Reptiles — Fiction
JS: 620

Republican Party
IJ: 9415, 10038 JS: 10045

Research
IJ: 12042

Research — Guides
IJ: 10784, 10815

Resistance Movement (World War II)
IJ: 8009 JS: 8052

Resistance movement (World War II) — Fiction
JS: 3511

Respiratory system
IJ: 11532, 11592–94

IJ = Upper Elementary/Lower Middle School; J = Middle School/Junior High; JS = Junior High/Senior High

IJ = Upper Elementary/Lower Middle School; J = Middle School/Junior High; JS = Junior High/Senior High

Rural youth
IJ: 10732

Russia
IJ: 7258, 7298, 8553, 8575–77, 8590, 10326 JS: 8549–50, 8564–65, 8573, 8588

Russia — Biography
IJ: 7237, 7239, 7258 JS: 7165, 7238

Russia — Cookbooks
IJ: 13247, 13301 J: 13294

Russia — Fiction
IJ: 2921, 2950, 2964, 3401 JS: 190, 2934, 3003, 3580, 3973

Russia — Folklore
IJ: 4875, 4880 JS: 4861

Russia — History
IJ: 8271, 8547 JS: 8582

Russia — Mythology
IJ: 4943

Russian Americans
IJ: 10349, 10361 JS: 10364

Russian Americans — Fiction
IJ: 3362JS: 657

Russian Revolution
IJ: 7674JS: 8588

Russian Revolution — Biography
JS: 7217–19

Russian Revolution — Fiction
IJ: 2964

Rustin, Bayard
IJ: 6032JS: 6033

Ruth, Babe
IJ: 6871

Ruth, Babe — Fiction
IJ: 2091

Rutherford, Ernest
JS: 6742

Rwanda
J: 8183JS: 8142, 8152, 8161, 8164

Ryan, Nolan
IJ: 6872

S

Sac and Fox Indians — History
IJ: 8978

Sacagawea
IJ: 5211

Sacagawea — Fiction
JS: 3255

Sacagewea — Fiction
IJ: 3301

Sacco and Vanzetti Case
JS: 10008

Sachar, Louis
IJ: 5587

Sadat, Anwar
IJ: 7130

Saddam Hussein

Safety
IJ: 11763–66 JS: 11762, 11767, 11769, 11808, 11811

Safety — Fiction
JS: 150

Safety education
IJ: 12072

Safety education — Women
JS: 11806–7, 11809–10

Sagan, Carl
IJ: 6743–44

Sailing and boating
See also Ships and boats
IJ: 5573

Sailing and boating — Biography
JS: 5193

Sailing and boating — Fiction
IJ: 170, 202 JS: 1350

St. Louis World's Fair, 1904
IJ: 9401

Saint Patrick — Fiction
IJ: 2910

Saints
IJ: 9789, 9803, 9811

Saints — Biography
IJ: 7073, 7186, 7214

Salem (MA) — History
IJ: 9102

Salem witch trials
IJ: 9080

Salk, Jonas
IJ: 6745–46

Samburu (African people)
JS: 8158

Same-sex marriage
JS: 10066

Samurai
IJ: 8338JS: 8337

Samurai — Fiction
IJ: 2859, 2861 JS: 12, 2133, 2841–42

San (African people)
JS: 8195

San Antonio (TX) — Fiction
IJ: 2089JS: 696

San Antonio Spurs (basketball team)
IJ: 13650

Sandburg, Carl
J: 5588

Sanders, Barry
IJ: 6959–60

Sandler, Adam
IJ: 5838

San Francisco (CA)
IJ: 9671, 9681

San Francisco (CA) — Fiction
IJ: 3626JS: 786

San Francisco (CA) — History
IJ: 9679, 9684

San Francisco earthquake
IJ: 9679, 12696 JS: 9655

San Francisco earthquake — Fiction
IJ: 3336

Sanitation — History
IJ: 12968

San Juan (Puerto Rico)
IJ: 8792

Santa Anna, Antonio Lopez de
IJ: 7278

Santa Claus
IJ: 9799

Santa Claus — Fiction
IJ: 2650

Santa Fe Trail
JS: 9351

Santa Fe Trail — Fiction
IJ: 3265–66, 3277

Santee Sioux Indians
IJ: 8979

Saratoga, Battle of
IJ: 9155

Sasquatch
JS: 13509

Satanism
JS: 9852

Satellites
IJ: 12974, 13086 JS: 12155

Satire

Saturn (planet)
IJ: 12190–91, 12197

Saudi Arabia
IJ: 8681, 8685, 8689 JS: 8674

Saudi Arabia — Biography
IJ: 8698

Savings (business)
IJ: 10736–37

IJ = Upper Elementary/Lower Middle School; J = Middle School/Junior High; JS = Junior High/Senior High

IJ = Upper Elementary/Lower Middle School; J = Middle School/Junior High; JS = Junior High/Senior High

September 11, 2001 — Fiction
IJ: 96, 471 JS: 1063

Sequoyah (Cherokee chief)
IJ: 6459–60

Serengeti Plain (Tanzania) — Fiction
IJ: 33

Serra, Junípero
IJ: 5213, 5215

Seti I
IJ: 7750

Settlement houses
IJ: 9377

Seuss, Dr.

Seventh-Day Adventists
IJ: 9847

Seward, William
JS: 6368

Sewing
See also Needlecrafts
IJ: 13423, 13426, 13430, 13434
JS: 13325, 13408, 13436

Sex — Fiction
JS: 1441, 1477, 1598, 1708, 1728, 1751, 3810, 4193, 4213

Sex education
See also Reproduction
IJ: 11754, 11757, 11786–88, 11793, 11803, 11883 J: 11075, 11781
JS: 11027, 11739, 11744, 11770, 11773–75, 11780, 11782, 11785, 11799, 11801, 11804, 11940

Sex education — Fiction
IJ: 599

Sex education — Girls
IJ: 11895

Sex offenders
IJ: 10522

Sex roles
See also Gender roles
IJ: 10641JS: 11802

Sex roles — Fiction
IJ: 362

Sexism
See also Sexual discrimination; Sexual harassment
JS: 10063, 11813, 11815

Sexual abuse
See also Child sexual abuse
IJ: 11786, 11812 JS: 11805, 11814, 11816, 11819, 11821–22

Sexual abuse — Children

Sexual abuse — Fiction
IJ: 410JS: 800, 882, 924, 1194, 1206, 1246, 1640

Sexual assault
See Date rape; Rape

Sexual discrimination
See also Sexism; Sexual harassment
JS: 10643, 10646

Sexual harassment
See also Sexism; Sexual discrimination
JS: 11813, 11815, 11817, 11820

Sexual orientation
JS: 10644

Sexual violence
See also Date rape; Rape
JS: 10512

Sexual violence — Fiction
JS: 1170

Sexually transmitted diseases
IJ: 11232JS: 11241–42, 11394, 11429

Shabazz, Betty
JS: 6034

Shackleton, Sir Ernest
IJ: 5216, 5218, 8858, 8861
JS: 5217, 5219

Shakers (religion)
IJ: 9791–93

Shakespeare, William
IJ: 4618, 5591, 5593–97, 7349
JS: 5038, 5044–45, 5592

Shakespeare, William — Adaptations
IJ: 5039J: 4625 JS: 4622

Shakespeare, William — Criticism
JS: 4626, 5041–43

Shakespeare, William — Fiction
IJ: 2891–92 JS: 463, 2926, 2955, 2966, 2978

Shakespeare, William — Plays
IJ: 4616–17, 4619–20, 4629

Shakespeare, William — Plays — Criticism
IJ: 5040

Shakespeare, William — Poetry
IJ: 4629

Shakur, Tupac — Fiction
IJ: 649

Shanghai, China
IJ: 8304

Sharks
IJ: 6580, 7551, 12535, 12539, 13781
JS: 12533–34, 12536–38

Sharks — Biography
IJ: 7018

Sharks — Fiction
JS: 241

Sharpton, Al
JS: 6369

Shawnee Indians — History
IJ: 9005

Shay's Rebellion
JS: 9152

Sheep — Fiction
IJ: 168JS: 2274

Shelley, Mary Wollstonecraft
IJ: 5598, 13484 JS: 5599

Shelters (homeless)
See also Homeless people; Poverty
JS: 10619

Shepard, Alan
IJ: 5220

Sherburne, Andrew
IJ: 6461

Sherlock Holmes — Fiction
JS: 321, 2558

Shetland Islands — Fiction
JS: 2153

Shingles (illness)
JS: 11379

Shinto (religion)
IJ: 9758

Ships and boats
See also Sailing and boating; and specific ships, e.g., *Titanic* (ship)
IJ: 8014, 9178, 13108, 13149, 13151, 13157

Ships and boats — Cookbooks
IJ: 9193

Ships and boats — Fiction
IJ: 17, 212, 3197 JS: 3530

Ships and boats — History
IJ: 7676, 9306, 13153, 13156, 13183

Ships and boats — Native Americans
IJ: 8989

Ships and boats— History
IJ: 13154

Shipwrecks
See also Sea disasters
IJ: 7631, 7722, 8989, 9306, 12864, 12876, 13151, 13153–54 JS: 13155

Shipwrecks — Fiction
IJ: 129, 308, 3037 JS: 216

Shoes
IJ: 13023

Shogun
IJ: 8341

Shona (African people)
IJ: 8225

Shoplifting — Fiction
JS: 580

Shopping — Fiction
JS: 1242

IJ = Upper Elementary/Lower Middle School; J = Middle School/Junior High; JS = Junior High/Senior High

IJ = Upper Elementary/Lower Middle School; J = Middle School/Junior High; JS = Junior High/Senior High

Slavery — Biography
IJ: 5994, 6004, 6050, 6058, 6384, 6447 JS: 5948, 5988, 6441

Slavery (U.S.)
IJ: 8911, 8918, 9140, 9190, 9223, 9227, 9266, 10010, 10137, 10249, 10271, 10275 JS: 8896, 8923, 8951–52, 9185, 9192, 9195, 9206, 9253, 10006, 10251

Slavery (U.S.) — Biography
IJ: 6046–47, 6055 JS: 5974, 6465

Slavery (U.S.) — Fiction
IJ: 712, 2521, 2818, 2820, 3021, 3135, 3142–45, 3151–52, 3155, 3159, 3161, 3164, 3168–72, 3185, 3188, 3196, 3198, 3211, 3217–18, 3226, 3233, 3345, 6413, 7708, 7742, 7896, 8246, 9085, 9179, 9194, 9196, 9205, 9212–13, 9222, 10250, 10252, 10257, 10268, 10276, 10399 J: 10267 JS: 179, 2247, 2796, 3014, 3138–39, 3153, 3173, 3176–77, 3183–84, 3186, 3237, 3377, 4767, 6051, 6056, 7897, 9113, 9189, 9200, 9215, 9217, 9225–26, 9907, 10074, 10086, 10126, 10141, 10151, 10167, 10179, 10254, 10264, 10266

Slavery (U.S.) — Folk songs
IJ: 7471, 7473

Slavery (U.S.) — History
IJ: 7666, 9184, 9203, 9273 JS: 9142, 9180

Sled dog racing
IJ: 13573

Sled dogs
See also Iditarod Sled Dog Race
IJ: 13525

Sled dogs — Fiction
IJ: 61, 159, 360, 1107 JS: 790

Sleep
IJ: 11538 JS: 11536, 11548–49, 11553, 11557, 11561

Sleep — Fiction
IJ: 2179

Sleep disorders
IJ: 11406 JS: 11396, 11546

Sleep disorders — Fiction
JS: 4133

Sleeping sickness
IJ: 11357

Sleepwalking
JS: 11546

Slovakia
IJ: 8563

Slovenia
IJ: 8439, 8589

Slugs
IJ: 12313

Slugs — Fiction
JS: 4305

Smallpox
IJ: 11326

Smell (sense)
IJ: 11600

Smell (sense) — Experiments and projects
IJ: 12081

Smith, Captain John
JS: 9093

Smith, Emmitt
IJ: 6961–62

Smith, John
IJ: 5221

Smith, Will
JS: 5844–45

Smoking
See also Nicotine; Tobacco industry
IJ: 11102, 11111, 11162, 11173, 11195 JS: 11072, 11085, 11114, 11122, 11142, 11153, 11158, 11163, 11197

Smoking — Fiction
JS: 1347

Smuggling
IJ: 10508, 10579

Smuggling — Fiction
IJ: 3529, 3921

Snails
IJ: 12313

Snake River
IJ: 12739

Snakes
See also individual species, e.g., Rattlesnakes
IJ: 12331, 12334–38, 12573 JS: 12330, 12333

Sneakers (shoes)
IJ: 12967

Sneezing
IJ: 11595

Snow
IJ: 12852

Snowboarding
IJ: 13753–54, 13756–60, 13762 JS: 13761

Snowboarding — Fiction
IJ: 4422, 4439 JS: 467

Snowmobiles
IJ: 13555

Soccer
IJ: 13764, 13766, 13769–70, 13772–73, 13777 J: 13775 JS: 13765, 13767–68, 13776

Soccer — Biography
IJ: 6810, 7030

Soccer — Fiction
IJ: 3923, 4460, 4465, 4469, 4483, 4491, 4514 JS: 466, 618, 1095, 1285, 1508, 2381, 4456

Soccer — History
JS: 13771, 13774

Social action
See also Activism; Affirmative action; Volunteerism
IJ: 10659, 11827 JS: 10608, 10657, 10661

Social action — Fiction
IJ: 1760

Social change — Biography
IJ: 5892, 6752

Social groups

Social problems
IJ: 10653 JS: 10381

Social work
IJ: 9377

Social work — Biography
IJ: 5958–60, 5962, 5983 JS: 5961, 5982

Society
JS: 10400

Socrates
IJ: 7244

Sodium
IJ: 12632, 12653

Softball
See Baseball
IJ: 13626

Softball — Fiction
IJ: 13622 JS: 589

Software

Software engineers — Careers
IJ: 10995

Soil ecology
IJ: 12772

Sojourner (Mars rover)
IJ: 12168

Solar energy
IJ: 12913

Solar energy — Experiments and projects
IJ: 12920

Solar system
See also Astronomy; Comets; Extraterrestrial life; Moon; Planets; Space exploration; Stars; Sun
IJ: 12098, 12189 JS: 12192, 12195

Soldiers — History
IJ: 9131

IJ = Upper Elementary/Lower Middle School; J = Middle School/Junior High; JS = Junior High/Senior High

IJ = Upper Elementary/Lower Middle School; J = Middle School/Junior High; JS = Junior High/Senior High

IJ = Upper Elementary/Lower Middle School; J = Middle School/Junior High; JS = Junior High/Senior High

IJ = Upper Elementary/Lower Middle School; J = Middle School/Junior High; JS = Junior High/Senior High

IJ = Upper Elementary/Lower Middle School; J = Middle School/Junior High; JS = Junior High/Senior High

IJ = Upper Elementary/Lower Middle School; J = Middle School/Junior High; JS = Junior High/Senior High

IJ = Upper Elementary/Lower Middle School; J = Middle School/Junior High; JS = Junior High/Senior High

IJ = Upper Elementary/Lower Middle School; J = Middle School/Junior High; JS = Junior High/Senior High

IJ: 13739–40 JS: 13536

Track and field — Biography
IJ: 6795, 6801, 6811, 6998, 7000, 7003–4, 7006, 7008, 7011, 7045
JS: 6997, 6999, 7005, 7007

Track and field — Fiction
IJ: 4497JS: 4474, 4477

Trade
JS: 10760

Trade Center

Trail of Tears
IJ: 9045

Trail of Tears — Fiction
IJ: 3056

Trains
See Railroads and trains
IJ: 13144

Tramps (U.S.)
JS: 8950

Tranquilizing drugs
JS: 11078, 11120

Transcontinental Railroad
IJ: 9331

Transcontinental Railroad — History
IJ: 12784

Transplants
JS: 11205

Transportation
See also specific types of transportation, e.g., Automobiles
IJ: 13104J: 13102

Transportation — History
IJ: 7731, 13103, 13105–6, 13136

Transvestism — Fiction
JS: 1136

Travel
IJ: 13147JS: 4998, 13043

Travel — Careers
JS: 10847, 10883

Travel — Fiction
IJ: 464, 1465 JS: 420, 491

Travels

Treason — Biography
IJ: 10498

Tree kangaroos
IJ: 12366

Trees
IJ: 8892, 12238, 12273, 12275, 12278, 12282 JS: 12276–77, 12279–80

Trees — Experiments and projects
IJ: 12274

Trees — Fiction
IJ: 3277

Trees — United States
JS: 12281

Trevino, Lee
IJ: 7034

Trials
See also Courts (U.S.)
IJ: 10108, 10716 JS: 9390, 9484, 10018, 10022, 10076, 10085, 10095–96, 10135, 10145, 10550

Trials — Fiction
JS: 3105

Triangle Shirtwaist Factory fire
IJ: 9409, 9411 JS: 9387

Triangle Shirtwaist Factory fire — Fiction
IJ: 3342

Triathlons
JS: 13571

Triathlons — Fiction
JS: 4445

Tricks
JS: 13377

Trinidad — Poetry
IJ: 4795

Trivia
IJ: 13498

Trivia — Biography
JS: 5925

Trojan War
IJ: 4982

Trojan War — Fiction
IJ: 4962

Trojan War (mythology)

Trompe l'oeil
IJ: 7355

Tropical fish
JS: 12602

Tropical forests
See Rain forests
IJ: 12712

Troy — History

Trucks and trucking
IJ: 13131

Truman, Harry S
IJ: 6218JS: 6217, 9517

Truth — Manipulation
IJ: 10380

Truth, Sojourner
IJ: 6046–48, 6050 JS: 6049

Tsunamis
IJ: 12692, 12870, 12872, 12878, 12880–81 JS: 12873

Tsunamis — Fiction
IJ: 2852JS: 176

Tuberculosis
JS: 11430

Tubman, Harriet
IJ: 6052–54, 9227 JS: 6051

Tubu (African people)
JS: 8118

Tundra

Tundras
IJ: 8875, 12735 JS: 12700

Tunisia — Fiction
IJ: 398

Tunnels
IJ: 7687, 13001

Turing, Alan
JS: 6754

Turkana (African people)
JS: 8160

Turkey
IJ: 7679, 8423, 8427, 8434, 8679, 8696, 10209

Turkey — Biography
JS: 7153

Turkey — Fiction
IJ: 2901

Turkey — Folklore
IJ: 4888

Turkmenistan
JS: 8548

Turner, Nat
IJ: 6055, 6057 JS: 6056

Turner, Ted
JS: 6755

Turtles and tortoises
IJ: 12340, 12342 JS: 12339

Turtles and tortoises — Fiction
IJ: 411

Tuskegee Airmen (World War II)
IJ: 7997, 8018 JS: 9471

Tuskegee Airmen (World War II) — Biography
IJ: 7282

Tutankhamen, King
IJ: 7092, 7751 JS: 7744

Tutsi (African people)
IJ: 8182

TWA Flight 800 (disaster)
IJ: 13111JS: 13114

Twain, Mark
IJ: 332, 5624–26, 5628–30
JS: 5627, 5631

Twain, Mark — Criticism
IJ: 5032

Twain, Shania
IJ: 5856

IJ = Upper Elementary/Lower Middle School; J = Middle School/Junior High; JS = Junior High/Senior High

IJ = Upper Elementary/Lower Middle School; J = Middle School/Junior High; JS = Junior High/Senior High

United States — History —
Plays
IJ: 4635

United States — History —
Songs
IJ: 7475

United States — Immigration
See Immigration (U.S.)

United States — Literary
history
IJ: 5025

United States — Pioneer life
See Frontier life (U.S.)

United States — Poetry
IJ: 4778J: 4748

United States — Politics
JS: 9912

United States — Postal Service

United States — Presidents
See Presidents (U.S.)

United States — Race relations
— Essays
JS: 10235

United States — Religion
IJ: 8947

United States — Revolutionary
War
See Revolutionary War (U.S.)

United States — States
IJ: 8953

United States — Wars
See also specific wars, e.g., World
War II

United States — Welfare

United States — Women
JS: 8912

United States (1763–1815)
IJ: 8937

United States (1776–1876) —
History
See also specific topics, e.g., Civil
War (U.S.)
IJ: 8973JS: 9156

United States (1789–1861) —
Fiction
IJ: 3149, 3156, 3288

United States (1789–1861) —
History
IJ: 7339, 8941, 9139, 9178, 9209,
9214, 9925 JS: 9217

United States (1789–1876) —
Fiction
IJ: 3178

United States (1789–1961) —
History
IJ: 9187

United States (1800–1860) —
History
JS: 9208

United States (1828–1860) —
History
IJ: 9186

United States (1865–1900) —
History
IJ: 9413

United States (1865–1914) —
History
IJ: 9371, 9405 JS: 9397

United States (1865–1950) —
Fiction
IJ: 758, 3320, 3323, 3346, 3370,
3385

United States (1865–1950) —
History
IJ: 8890, 8898, 8921, 8938–39, 9377,
9417, 9924

United States (1869–1914) —
History
IJ: 9392

United States (1900–1929) —
History
IJ: 9413

United States (1915–1945) —
History
JS: 9424

United States (1929–1949) —
History
IJ: 9413

United States (1948–1976) —
History
IJ: 9507

United States (1949–1969) —
History
IJ: 8111

United States (1951–) —
History
IJ: 9485–86

United States (1951–) —
History — Fiction
IJ: 3453

United States (1951–) — History
IJ: 9922

United States (1969–2004) —
History
IJ: 8111

United States (1980s) — History
IJ: 9498JS: 9497, 9508

United States (1990s) — History
IJ: 8899

United States (1910s) — History
IJ: 8902JS: 8944

United States (1920s) — History
IJ: 8902J: 9446 JS: 9459

United States (1930s) — History
J: 9434JS: 9428

United States (1940s) — History
J: 8945JS: 8881

United States (1950s) — Fiction
JS: 3440

United States (1950s) — History
IJ: 9499, 9519 JS: 8882, 9489,
9497, 9512

United States (1960s) — History
IJ: 8901JS: 9487, 9497, 9509

United States (1970s) — History
IJ: 8900JS: 9518

United States Army
See Army (U.S.)

United States Army — African
Americans
IJ: 10241

United States Coast Guard

United States-Israel relations
See Israel-U.S. relations

United States Marine Corps
See Marine Corps (U.S.)

United States-Mexico relations
See Mexico-U.S. relations

United States Navy
IJ: 13179, 13184

United States Navy — History
IJ: 13151

United States v. Nixon
JS: 9977

Universe
IJ: 12203–4, 12206, 12208
JS: 12205, 12207

Universities and colleges

Unser family
IJ: 6830

Uranus (planet)
IJ: 12199

Urban legends
JS: 13471

Uruguay
JS: 8827

USSR
See Soviet Union

Utah
IJ: 9574, 9581

Utah — Fiction
IJ: 72JS: 3597

Utopias
JS: 8940

Uzbekistan
IJ: 8587JS: 8548

IJ = Upper Elementary/Lower Middle School; J = Middle School/Junior High; JS = Junior High/Senior High

V

Vacations — Fiction
JS: 2262, 4192

Vaccines
IJ: 11433JS: 11240, 11304, 11353, 11461

Valdez (Alaska)
IJ: 9658

Valens, Ritchie
JS: 5857

Valentine's Day
IJ: 10673

Valentine's Day — Crafts
IJ: 13202

Vallejo, Mariano Guadalupe
IJ: 6374

Valley Forge encampment
IJ: 9127

Valleys
IJ: 12702

Vampires
IJ: 13484, 13486 JS: 13500

Vampires — Fiction
IJ: 2649, 2689, 3660, 3721, 3733, 3736–39, 3749–50, 3830 J: 2428
JS: 1180, 1845, 2085, 2181, 2300, 2660, 2705, 3661, 3685, 3696–97, 3731, 3866, 4030

Van Beek, Cato Bontjes
JS: 7249

Van Buren, Martin
IJ: 6219–20

Vancouver, Canada — Fiction
IJ: 3784

Vancouver (Canada)
IJ: 8723

Vandalism — Fiction
IJ: 1376

Van Gogh, Vincent
IJ: 5399JS: 5398, 5400–1

Vanilla
IJ: 12245

Vedder, Amy
IJ: 6756

Vegans
IJ: 11722

Vegetables
IJ: 12269, 12271–72

Vegetarian cooking
IJ: 13286JS: 13297

Vegetarianism
IJ: 11718–19, 13263 JS: 11716

Venezuela
IJ: 8840, 8847, 8849

Venezuela — Biography
JS: 7264

Venice — Fiction
IJ: 440

Venice — History
JS: 5683

Venice (Italy)
IJ: 8530

Ventura, Jesse
IJ: 7036–37, 9879 JS: 7035

Venus (planet)
IJ: 12194

Veracruz
IJ: 8774

Verbal abuse — Fiction
IJ: 1046

Vermont
IJ: 9607, 9633 JS: 9585

Vermont — Biography
IJ: 6246

Vermont — Fiction
IJ: 799, 2422, 3108, 3175, 3341, 3350, 3364, 3403, 3512 JS: 1061, 1501, 3788

Verne, Jules
IJ: 5632–33

Versailles, Palace of
JS: 8448

Vesey, Denmark
IJ: 6058

Veterinarians
JS: 12617

Veterinarians — Biography
JS: 12618

Veterinarians — Careers
IJ: 10860–61, 10864, 10873
JS: 10850, 10896

Veterinarians — Fiction
IJ: 3942

Veterinary medicine — Fiction
JS: 3383

Vice Presidents (U.S.) — Wives — Biographies
IJ: 6114

Victims' rights
JS: 10091

Victoria, Queen
JS: 7250, 8485

Victoria, Queen of England
IJ: 8483JS: 8518

Victoria, Queen of England — Fiction
IJ: 2947

Victorian Age
JS: 8518

Victorian Age — Fiction
IJ: 2366JS: 294, 2010

Victorian era — Fiction
JS: 2929

Victorian times — Fiction
IJ: 210

Video games — Careers
IJ: 10998JS: 10905, 10986, 10991

Video games — Fiction
IJ: 2696JS: 4075

Video recordings
IJ: 13406

Vietnam
IJ: 8114, 8362, 8371, 8389, 8392–93
JS: 8354, 8356, 9539

Vietnam — Cookbooks
IJ: 13301J: 13289

Vietnam — Fiction
IJ: 1804, 2850, 2877

Vietnam — Folklore
IJ: 4850, 4856

Vietnam Veterans Memorial
JS: 5349

Vietnam War
IJ: 8090, 9490, 9524, 9532, 9536–38, 9542 JS: 8084, 8093, 8096, 8105–6, 8117, 8356, 9525, 9528, 9531, 9534–35, 9539, 9984

Vietnam War — Biography
IJ: 6328JS: 6329, 6442

Vietnam War — Fiction
IJ: 1053, 1097, 1615, 3592, 3594–95, 3598–99, 3602 JS: 2840, 3590, 3593, 3596–97, 3600–1

Vietnam War — Protests
IJ: 9533JS: 9529

Vietnam War — Women
IJ: 9543

Vietnam War veterans — Fiction
JS: 3946

Vietnamese Americans
IJ: 10208, 10285 JS: 10298, 10305

Vietnamese Americans — Fiction
JS: 687

Vietnamese Americans — Memoirs
J: 7315

Vikings
IJ: 7720, 8591, 8603, 8605
JS: 8607–8

Vikings — Crafts
IJ: 8603

IJ = Upper Elementary/Lower Middle School; J = Middle School/Junior High; JS = Junior High/Senior High

IJ = Upper Elementary/Lower Middle School; J = Middle School/Junior High; JS = Junior High/Senior High

IJ = Upper Elementary/Lower Middle School; J = Middle School/Junior High; JS = Junior High/Senior High

IJ = Upper Elementary/Lower Middle School; J = Middle School/Junior High; JS = Junior High/Senior High

Wood, Michele
IJ: 5408

Wood block prints
IJ: 7409

Woodhull, Victoria
JS: 6063–65

Woods, Tiger
IJ: 7039–40 J: 7038 JS: 7041

Woodson, Carter G.
JS: 5650

Woodson, Jacqueline
IJ: 5651

Woodworking
IJ: 13446

Woolf, Virginia
JS: 5652

Word books
IJ: 5065, 5069, 5071, 10677

Word games and puzzles
See Games; Puzzles
IJ: 5065

Wordless books
IJ: 2718

Words
IJ: 5057, 5068

Words — Fiction
IJ: 3854

Wordsworth, William
JS: 4719

Workers and laboring classes
JS: 10754

Working animals
IJ: 12574

Working dogs
IJ: 12589

Working dogs — Fiction
IJ: 3594

Working mothers
JS: 11923

World Cup — History
JS: 13771

World Health Organization
IJ: 11371

World history
IJ: 7639, 7648, 7650, 7654, 7688, 7690–91, 7721 JS: 7641, 7665

World history — Controversies
JS: 7686

World Trade Center
See also September 11, 2001
IJ: 10708

World Trade Center bombing (1993)
IJ: 10716, 10721–22

World War II
IJ: 7962

World War I
IJ: 7905, 7907, 7909–13, 7915–18, 7920, 7923, 7926–28, 8886, 8890, 8916, 8939, 9420 JS: 7908, 7919, 7925, 8944, 9421–23

World War I — Battles
IJ: 7914, 7924 JS: 7922

World War I — Biography
IJ: 7166

World War I — Fiction
IJ: 201, 281, 1475, 2927, 3424, 3477–79, 3482 JS: 3476, 3481, 3483–86

World War I — Poetry
JS: 4648

World War II
See also specific topics, e.g., Holocaust
IJ: 3501, 6106, 6109, 7189, 7191, 7214, 7905, 7931–33, 7941, 7943–45, 7947–48, 7951–53, 7959–61, 7964, 7969–70, 7972, 7978, 7993, 7997, 7999, 8005, 8008–9, 8013–16, 8018–19, 8021–22, 8024, 8028–29, 8031–32, 8034, 8039, 8043, 8048, 8051, 8055–57, 8060–61, 8063, 8067–68, 8075–76, 8906, 8915, 8938, 9467, 9472, 9474–75, 9477–79, 9483 J: 7316, 8041–42, 8070, 8945 JS: 3554, 5397, 7903, 7930, 7936–37, 7939–40, 7942, 7946, 7955–56, 7963, 7965–66, 7971, 7974–77, 7979–80, 7983–86, 7988–89, 7992, 7995–96, 8000, 8003, 8006–7, 8010, 8025, 8027, 8035, 8038, 8040, 8045, 8049, 8054, 8058–59, 8064–66, 8071, 8077–78, 8116, 8466, 9463, 9466, 9468–71, 9473, 9480–82, 10260, 13188

World War II — Battles
JS: 8023, 8033

World War II — Biography
IJ: 5582, 5680, 5880, 6324, 6326–27, 7172, 7188, 7206, 7282 J: 7065 JS: 7204–5, 7207, 7229, 7243, 7249, 7289, 7291, 7294, 7310

World War II — Cryptography
IJ: 7929, 9003

World War II — Fiction
IJ: 156, 777, 994, 1616, 2889, 2975, 3398, 3472, 3487, 3489, 3491–93, 3495, 3497, 3500, 3503, 3505–7, 3509–10, 3512–15, 3518–19, 3521, 3524–25, 3527–29, 3531, 3538, 3540–41, 3546–47, 3549, 3555, 3557, 3560–61, 3564–66, 3570–72, 3574–79, 3583, 3587–88, 8595 JS: 244, 249, 689, 772, 1500, 1540, 2630, 2636, 2833, 2977, 3480, 3488, 3490, 3498–99, 3504, 3516–17, 3520, 3522, 3526, 3530, 3533–36, 3543–44,

3548, 3550–53, 3556, 3558, 3563, 3567–69, 3584, 4544

World War II — History
IJ: 7987, 8072, 9476

World War II — Japanese Americans
JS: 10293

World War II — Journalism
IJ: 5098

World War II — Nurses
IJ: 8004

World War II — Radio coverage
JS: 9464

World War II — Women
IJ: 5098, 8026, 8030

World War II Memorial
JS: 9465

World Wide Web
IJ: 6558, 10983, 13050, 13056, 13076, 13078–79 J: 13065 JS: 13055, 13064

World Wide Web — Careers
IJ: 10983, 10999

World Wide Web — Sites
IJ: 13070

World Wildlife Fund
IJ: 12467

World's Fairs — History
JS: 8932

World's Fairs — United States
JS: 8932

Worms
IJ: 12307

Worms — Experiments and projects
IJ: 12297

Worms — Fiction
IJ: 4299

Wozniak, Stephen
IJ: 6767–68

Wrestling
IJ: 13513, 13524, 13540, 13564–65 JS: 13678–79

Wrestling — Biography
IJ: 7028, 7036–37, 13541 JS: 7035

Wrestling — Fiction
IJ: 1110 JS: 1096, 2655

Wrestling — Women
IJ: 13514

Wright, Frank Lloyd
IJ: 5410, 5412–13 JS: 5409, 5411

Wright, Richard
JS: 5653–57

IJ = Upper Elementary/Lower Middle School; J = Middle School/Junior High; JS = Junior High/Senior High

Wright, Wilbur and Orville
IJ: 6503, 6769, 6771, 6773, 6775–77, 13110 JS: 6770, 6772, 6774

Wright, Wilbur and Orville — Fiction
IJ: 3325, 3339

Writers
See also Authors

Writing
IJ: 5054, 5082, 5086, 10789, 10791–92, 10796, 10803, 10809, 10825, 10827 J: 10790 JS: 4557, 5015, 5259, 10794, 10818, 10824, 10830

Writing — Careers
IJ: 10879, 10926 JS: 5079, 10797, 10898

Writing — Fiction
IJ: 392, 504, 554, 1326, 1505, 1718 JS: 679, 3922

Writing — Handbooks
IJ: 5077, 10810, 10833 J: 5081 JS: 5073

Writing — History
IJ: 5076 JS: 5080

Writing — Instruction
JS: 10805, 10819, 10831

Writing — Poetry
IJ: 10816 JS: 10832

Writing — Skills
IJ: 5084, 10802, 10820 JS: 5075, 5079, 10797, 10814

Writing — Study skills
JS: 10822

Writing skills
IJ: 10823 JS: 5087

Writings
IJ: 10807

Wyoming
IJ: 9573

Wyoming — Fiction
J: 3293

X

X-rays
IJ: 11457, 12903

Xhosa (African people)
JS: 8209

Xiaoping, Deng
IJ: 7140

Y

Yahoo! (computers) — Biography
IJ: 6531

Yana Indians — Fiction
JS: 4110

Yang, Jerry
IJ: 6531

Yangtze River
IJ: 8283, 8300

Yanomami (people)
JS: 12715

Yeats, William Butler
JS: 4719, 5658

Yeboah, Emmanuel Ofosu
IJ: 7323

Yellow fever
IJ: 11236 JS: 9162

Yellow fever — Fiction
JS: 3120, 3128

Yellowstone National Park
IJ: 12383

Yellowstone National Park — Fiction
IJ: 4131

Yeltsin, Boris
IJ: 7258

Yemen
IJ: 8686, 8706

Yep, Laurence — Criticism
JS: 5027

Yeti
IJ: 13476 JS: 13509

Yetis — Fiction
JS: 74

Yoga
IJ: 13576 J: 13515, 13572 JS: 13549, 13589

Yom Kippur — Fiction
IJ: 1493

Yorktown, Battle of
IJ: 9145, 9172

Yoruba (African People)
JS: 8229

Yorubaland (Africa)
IJ: 8249

Young, Steve
IJ: 6966

Young adult literature — Biography
JS: 5473, 5589

Young adult literature — Criticism
JS: 5023, 5531

Yu, Chun
JS: 7324

Yugoslavia
IJ: 8429

Yugoslavia — Biography
JS: 7248

Yukon — History
JS: 5121

Z

Zaharias, Babe Didrikson
IJ: 7045 JS: 7042–44

Zaire
JS: 8145, 8171–72, 8176

Zama, Battle of
JS: 7822

Zamora, Pedro
JS: 2734

Zedong, Mao
IJ: 7141, 8294 JS: 7142

Zenatti, Valérie
JS: 7325

Zenger, John Peter
JS: 10001

Zhang, Ange
IJ: 5414

Zimbabwe
IJ: 8193, 8218, 8225–26

Zimbabwe — Fiction
JS: 4296

Zimbabwe — History
IJ: 7091

Zindel, Paul
IJ: 5659

Zirconium
IJ: 12668

Zoology — Careers
JS: 10885

Zoos
IJ: 12619

Zulu (African people)
JS: 8214

Zuñi Indians — Folklore
IJ: 4905

Zuñi Indians — History
IJ: 8981

IJ = Upper Elementary/Lower Middle School; J = Middle School/Junior High; JS = Junior High/Senior High

About the Authors

CATHERINE BARR is the coauthor of other volumes in the Best Books series (*Best Books for Children* and *Best Books for High School Readers*) and of *Best New Media, Popular Series Fiction for K–6 Readers, Popular Series Fiction for Middle School and Teen Readers*, and *High/Low Handbook: Best Books and Web Sites for Reluctant Teen Readers, 4th Edition.*

JOHN T. GILLESPIE, renowned authority in children's literature, is the author of more than 30 books on collection development. In addition to the other volumes in the Best Books series (*Best Books for Children* and *Best Books for High School Readers*), he is also the author of *Teenplots, Classic Teenplots, The Newbery Companion: Booktalk and Related Materials for Newbery Medal and Honor Books, The Children's and Young Adult Literature Handbook: A Research and Reference Guide,* and *Historical Fiction for Young Readers (Grades 4–8): An Introduction.*